OFFICIAL
Major League
BASEBALL
FACT BOOK
2000 EDITION

OFFICIAL
Major League
BASEBALL
FACT BOOK
2000 EDITION

Brendan Roberts, Editor

Efrem Zimbalist III, President and CEO, Times Mirror Magazines; **James H. Nuckols**, President, The Sporting News; **Francis X. Farrell**, Senior Vice President, Publisher; **John D. Rawlings**, Senior Vice President, Editorial Director; **John Kastberg**, Vice President, General Manager; **Kathy Kinkeade**, Vice President, Operations; **Steve Meyerhoff**, Executive Editor; **Dale Bye and Bob Hille**, Managing Editors; **Joe Hoppel**, Senior Editor; **Craig Carter**, Statistical Editor; **Mark Bonavita and Sean Deveney**, Associate Editors; **David Walton**, Assistant Editor; **Marilyn Kasal**, Production Director; **Bob Parajon**, Prepress Director; **Michael Behrens**, Art Director, Special Projects; **Christen Webster**, Production Artist; **Joe Klaas, Dan Fitzgerald and Chris Paul**, Editorial Assistants.

A Times Mirror
Company

Historical statistics from *Total Baseball,* the official encyclopedia of Major League Baseball.

Statistical assistance provided by STATS, Inc., Skokie, Ill.

ISBN: 0-89204-630-9

10 9 8 7 6 5 4 3 2 1

Contents

INTRODUCTION

As we watched the New York Yankees jump for joy after winning their 25th World Series title in 1999, we were reminded again how timeless baseball is. Derek Jeter and Roger Clemens were just as excited as Babe Ruth and Lou Gehrig after the 1928 Yankees title. The fans in the stands in 1999 were merely the grandchildren or great-grandchildren of the same fans that piled into Yankee Stadium over 70 years earlier.

Oh, the game has changed plenty. The uniforms look different, and the players wear sliding shorts and batting gloves. The players are bigger, stronger, faster, more diverse and ... richer. The ballparks are more elaborate and the fields are maintained better. The fans are more stat-savvy and informed about both news on and off the field. More cities get to see major league baseball. The scores are slightly higher, and the pitchers appear a little greener.

But these are all only miniscule differences. No other sport has kept its flow and sense of history as baselll has. There's still the smell of hot dogs in the stands, the smudges of dirt on the uniforms, the inside fastballs, catchers flashing signs, towering home runs and diving catches. And really how much different is Craig Biggio than Eddie Collins, Rickey Henderson than Lou Brock or Pedro Martinez from Juan Marichal? Go to any sandlot baseball game, and you'll hear kids say they want to be the next Ken Griffey Jr. or Greg Maddux. Thirty-five years ago it was Willie Mays or Sandy Koufax.

Young or old, we all have a pleasant memory of a baseball moment. Maybe it's that first home run in Little League off the giant 6-foot righthander Billy Smith or a great offensive day against the older kids in the sandlot. Maybe it's the time you got to shake the meaty hand of Roger Maris, or when you just watched on TV as Mark McGwire broke Maris' home run record on September 8, 1999 in St. Louis. We all have some memory to ponder and smile about.

This wonderful game has evolved to the delight of fans everywhere—including Japan, Taiwan, Cuba and the Dominican Republic. Our players come from all walks of life and our fans are attending and watching on television in record numbers. A game that was created so long ago is every bit as strong today as it ever was. And these hungry baseball fans have a need to know. There are so many uncommon occurences, so much information to absorb and numbers to play with that baseball fans need a source to help them learn and keep up with the game.

That's where the fourth edition of the *Major League Baseball Fact Book* comes in. In its own organized way, the Fact Book presents baseball fans with the details, numbers and pictures of baseball's long and distinguished history. We offer an all-inclusive 512-page book that looks both to the season ahead and back at the seasons and players that have brought us to 2000.

There are images of the past: Mickey Mantle's 1956 Triple Crown season, Bucky Dent's unlikely homer in 1978, Pete Rose's all-time hits title. We offer a season-by-season review of each team and some of the great players that have played for them, including those players—like Nolan Ryan or Hank Aaron—who sit at the top of the statistical ladders. There are historic photos of everyone from Honus Wagner to Steve Garvey to Fred McGriff. For a baseball historian, this is a must-read.

We also offer an extended glimpse of the great 1999 season, including playoff stories and boxes, all the statistics a baseball fan could want, plenty of analysis and the spectacular photographs that *The Sporting News* is so well known for.

And finally, we'll prepare you for the 2000 season ahead and keep you informed throughout the season. We offer player information and projections, team directories, schedules, stadium diagrams, and ticket and broadcast information, as well as biographies of baseball's prominent faces and award winners.

This is your one-stop shop, all the information a baseball fan would need in one easy-to-carry book. And you'll find that by the end of the 2000 season, this handy book will be as well-used as an Ozzie Smith baseball glove.

—BRENDAN ROBERTS

2000 Preview

Seattle's Safeco Field opened for play July 15, 1999. The beautiful complex, built just south of the Kingdome, has a rectractable roof, below-field drainage hoses and a system of 11 scoreboards and displays.

INTRODUCTION

RICKEY TO CHASE THE BABE IN 2000

There's something to be said for longevity. And talent. Rickey Henderson has been blessed with both.

Of course, a high level of skill goes a long way toward ensuring a long career, and Henderson has been a force in the major leagues since arriving on the scene 21 years ago. Already the majors' all-time leader in stolen bases with 1,334, Henderson could conceivably move into the top spot in a second category in 2000 and vault into second place in another as well.

Coming off a 1999 season in which he drew 82 walks and scored 89 runs for the Mets, Henderson needs to coax 91 bases on balls this year to supplant Babe Ruth as the career leader. Heading into the new millennium, Henderson (1,972 walks) trails Ted Williams (2,019) and the Bambino (2,062). And he needs to score 72 runs—his total stands at 2,103—to move past Pete Rose, Hank Aaron and Ruth and into the No. 2 spot behind Ty Cobb (2,245 runs). Rose is fourth with 2,165 runs and Aaron and Ruth are tied for second at 2,174.

Henderson, 41, has more to look forward to in 2000. With 2,816 career hits, he figures to position himself for a place in the 3,000-hit club in 2001. He had 138 hits last season. And when he plays in his first game this year, the outfielder will became a rare four-decade player. He reached the majors in 1979, playing in 89 games for the A's.

Though there will be considerable focus on Henderson this season, the spotlight will beam elsewhere, too. And it figures to shine brightly on veteran warrior Cal Ripken, who, barring the unforeseen, will collect his 3,000th hit in April. Back miseries thwarted Ripken's bid to achieve the milestone in 1999, injuries limiting the Baltimore third baseman to 86 games and ending his season on September 21, a night on which he got No. 2,991.

Ripken saw enough action last season to reach another lofty plateau, slugging his 400th home run three weeks before being shut down for the year. Five players will strive for 400 this season, with two being locks, two having good chances and one facing long-shot odds. Ken Griffey Jr. begins the year at 398, and Fred McGriff enters the season with 390. Rafael Palmeiro, who hit a career-high 47 homers last year, has 361. Albert Belle, who had 37 in '99 but has reached 48 or more three times, has 358 career homers. The other contender,

Already the all-time steals leader, 41-year-old Rickey Henderson has the chance to become the all-time leader in runs and walks as well this season.

Harold Baines, stands at 373, but he hasn't hit as many as 27 home runs since 1984 (although he did finish with 25 last year).

Baines, like Henderson and Ripken, has shown amazing staying power. As a result, he has accumulated 1,583 RBIs in 20 seasons and needs only 70 in 2000 to climb from a tie for 27th on the all-time list to 18th. Along the way, he would pass such noted sluggers as Harmon Killebrew, Mike Schmidt, Ernie Banks and Tony Perez. Also, Baines is within 217 hits of 3,000, a figure that looks attainable in 2001 if the designated hitter, now 41, keeps a-going.

Rockies outfielder Larry Walker, a comparative youngster at 33, will attempt to accomplish something this season that only two other National Leaguers have done in the last half-century—win three consecutive batting crowns. Walker won the title with a .363 figure in 1998 and captured the championship with a .379 mark in '99. Stan Musial won three straight crowns for the Cardinals from 1950 through 1952, and the Padres' Tony Gwynn won three in a row to close out the 1980s and four straight beginning in 1994.

Pitchers will get their share of attention, too, in 2000. Randy Johnson, Roger Clemens, John Franco, John Wetteland and Rick Aguilera are among those with their eyes on a prize.

Johnson needs 307 strikeouts to become the 12th man in major league history to reach 3,000. The Arizona lefthander is coming off a 364-strikeout season. The Yankees' Clemens, who won 14 games last season, is three victories shy of 250 as he attempts to reach 300 by the end of his career. At age 37, the five-time Cy Young Award winner is beginning to fight the calendar in his quest for a career win total achieved by only 20 pitchers. Still, he figures to be on the brink of 300 by age 40—and quite possibly there.

For Mets reliever Franco, the task will be to inch closer to all-time saves leader Lee Smith. But Franco, the No. 2 man, will have to regain his old form if he's to threaten Smith's mark before calling it a career. Franco, who trails Smith 478-416, had injury problems and only 19 saves in '99—and he turns 40 in September.

The Rangers' Wetteland and the Cubs' Aguilera are approaching 300 saves, a total achieved by only 11 pitchers in big-league history. Wetteland, who at age 33 seems a good bet to mount a strong challenge to Smith's record, needs four saves to reach 300. Aguilera is 11 away from that plateau.

ALSO COMING TO A BALLPARK NEAR YOU

After hitting a record 70 home runs in 1998 and reaching 500 career homers in 1999, what's Mark McGwire to do in 2000? The answer: continue what seems to be an inexorable climb to the rarefied air of 600 home runs, a point scaled by only Hank Aaron, Babe Ruth and Willie Mays. McGwire, who has averaged 61 homers over the past four seasons, ranks 10th on the all-time list with 522. Even with an "off season" of, say, 52 homers, the Cardinals' Big Mac would sweep past Jimmie Foxx, Mickey Mantle, Mike Schmidt, Reggie Jackson and Harmon Killebrew and into fifth place. He then would be positioned to reach 600 around the All-Star break in 2001. ... The Yankees will gun for their fourth World Series crown in five years, a stretch of success unknown since the Yanks won five consecutive Series titles beginning in 1949. ... The Braves will gun for their ninth consecutive division championship and their fourth straight 100-victory season. ... The Mets' Jesse Orosco will join Henderson as a four-decade player. If righthander Mike Morgan hangs on, he'll be a member of the club, too. Morgan's big-league career goes back the furthest, to 1978. ... Having made post-season play faster than any major league team in history (their second year), the Diamondbacks have their sights set on winning two divisional championships in their first three seasons of existence. ... Familiar names in unfamiliar places: Juan Gonzalez (Detroit), Mike Hampton (New York Mets), Shawn Green (Los Angeles) and the duo of Vinny Castilla and Greg Vaughn (both Tampa Bay). ... The Giants, Astros and Tigers open new ballparks in 2000. The Giants leave 3Com (Candlestick) Park for Pacific Bell Park, the Astros go from the Astrodome to Enron Field and the Tigers move from historic Tiger Stadium to Comerica Park. The Brewers hoped to make the switch from County Stadium to Miller Park, but a construction accident at the new facility has delayed its opening until 2001.

—JOE HOPPEL

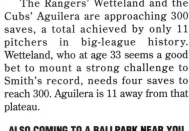

Commissioner Bud Selig

COMMISSIONER'S OFFICE

Address	245 Park Avenue, New York, NY 10167
Telephone	212-931-7800, 212-949-5654 (FAX)
Commissioner of Baseball	Allan H. (Bud) Selig
Chief operating officer, Major League Baseball	Paul Beeston
Executive vice president, baseball operations	Richard (Sandy) Alderson
Executive vice president, administration	Robert A. DuPuy
Senior vice president, domestic and international properties	Timothy Brosnan
Vice president, marketing	Kathleen Francis
Vice president, team services	Mark Gorris
Senior vice president and general manager, MLB productions	Stephen Hellmuth
Executive director, security/facility management	Kevin Hallinan
Executive director, public relations	Richard Levin
Executive director, human resources	Wendy L. Lewis
Executive director, baseball operations	William Murray
General counsel	Thomas J. Ostertag
Executive director, minor league operations	Jimmie Lee Solomon
Vice president, broadcasting and new media development	Leslie Sullivan
Chief financial officer	Jeffrey White

COO Paul Beeston

AMERICAN LEAGUE OFFICE

Address	350 Park Avenue, New York, NY 10022
Telephone	212-339-7600
Vice president	Carl R. Pohlad
Executive director of umpiring	Martin J. Springstead
Senior vice president	Phyllis Merhige
Director, waivers and player records	Brian Small
Coordinator, baseball information	Jason Carr
Administrator of umpires/travel	Tess Basta-Marino
Administrative assistants	Angelica Cintron, Carolyn Coen

LABOR RELATIONS COMMITTEE

Address	245 Park Avenue, New York, NY 10167
Telephone	212-931-7401, 212-949-5690 (FAX)
Executive V.P., labor and human resources	Robert D. Manfred Jr.
General labor counsel	Francis X. Coonelly
Associate counsels	Louis Melendez, John Westhoff
Attorney	Derek Jackson
Supervisor, salary and contract administration	John Ricco
Coordinator, salary and contract administration	Gillian Reckler

NATIONAL BASEBALL HALL OF FAME AND MUSEUM

Address	P.O. Box 590, Cooperstown, NY 13326
Telephone	607-547-7200, 607-547-2044 (FAX)
Chairman of Hall of Fame	Edward W. Stack
Vice president of business and administration	Frank Simio
Vice president and chief curator	William T. Spencer Jr.
Curator of collections	Peter P. Clark
Executive director of retail marketing	Barbara Shinn
Controller	Frances L. Althiser
Librarian	James L. Gates
Executive director of communications and education	Jeff Idelson
Executive director of communications and museum programs	John Ralph

NATIONAL ASSOCIATION OF PROFESSIONAL BASEBALL LEAGUES

Address	P.O. Box A, St. Petersburg, FL 33731
Telephone	727-822-6937, 727-821-5819 (FAX)
President	Mike Moore
Vice president/administration	Pat O'Conner
Executive director of development	Rob Dlugozima
General counsel	Ben Hayes
Director/licensing	Brian Earle
Director/media relations	Jim Ferguson
Director of baseball operations	Tim Brunswick
Director of marketing	Rod Meadows
Director of business/finance	Eric Krupa
Director of Professional Baseball Umpire Corporation	Mike Fitzpatrick
Director/Professional Baseball Employment Opportunities	Ann Perkins

HOWE SPORTSDATA INTERNATIONAL INC.

Address	Boston Fish Pier, West Building No. 1, Suite 302, Boston, MA 02210
Telephone	617-951-0070; 617-951-1379 (stats request); 617-737-9960 (FAX)
President	Jay Virshbo
Historical consultant	William Weiss

ELIAS SPORTS BUREAU

Address	500 Fifth Ave., New York, NY 10110
Telephone	212-869-1530, 212-354-0980 (FAX)
General manager	Seymour Siwoff

BASEBALL WRITERS' ASSOCIATION OF AMERICA

President	Charles Scroggins, Lowell (Mass.) Sun
Vice president	Ian MacDonald, Montreal Gazette
Secretary/treasurer	Jack O'Connell, Hartford Courant

NATIONAL LEAGUE OFFICE

Address	350 Park Avenue, New York, NY 10022
Telephone	212-339-7700
Senior vice president and secretary	Katy Feeney
Vice president, media relations and market dev.	Ricky Clemons
Executive director, player records	Nancy Crofts
Executive secretary	Rita Aughavin
Administrative assistant, umpires	Cathy Davis
Assistant, media relations and player records	Moises Rodriguez

MAJOR LEAGUE BASEBALL PLAYERS ASSOCIATION

Address	12 E. 49th St., 24th Floor, New York, NY 10017
Telephone	212-826-0808, 212-752-3649 (FAX)
Executive director and general counsel	Donald M. Fehr
Special assistants	Tony Bernazard, Steve Rogers
Associate general counsel	Eugene D. Orza
Assistant general counsel	Doyle R. Pryor, Michael Weiner
Counsel	Robert Leneghan
Director of licensing	Judy Heeter
Director of communications	Greg Bouris

MAJOR LEAGUE BASEBALL PLAYERS ALUMNI ASSOCIATION

Address	1631 Mesa Avenue, Suite C, Colorado Springs, Colo. 80906
Telephone	719-477-1870, 719-477-1875 (FAX)
President	Brooks Robinson
Vice presidents	Bob Boone, George Brett, Mike Hegan
	Chuck Hinton, Al Kaline, Carl Erskine
	Rusty Staub, Robin Yount
Secretary/treasurer	Fred Valentine

MAJOR LEAGUE SCOUTING BUREAU

Address	3500 Porsche Way, Suite 100, Ontario, CA 91764
Telephone	909-980-1881, 909-980-7794 (FAX)
Director	Frank Marcos

MAJOR LEAGUE UMPIRES ASSOCIATION

Address	1735 Market St., Suite 3420, Philadelphia, PA 19103
Telephone	215-979-3220, 215-979-3201 (FAX)
General counsel	Richard G. Phillips

BASEBALL ASSISTANCE TEAM INC.

Address	245 Park Avenue, New York, NY 10167
Telephone	212-931-7821
Chairman	Ralph Branca
President	Joe Garagiola
Vice presidents	Joe Black, Earl Wilson
Executive director	James J. Martin
Secretary/treasurer	Tom Ostertag

ASSOCIATION OF PROFESSIONAL BASEBALL PLAYERS OF AMERICA

Address	12062 Valley View, Suite 211, Garden Grove, CA 92645
Telephone	714-892-9900, 714-897-0233 (FAX)
President	John J. McHale
Vice presidents	Arthur Richman, Robert Kennedy
Secretary/treasurer	Dick Beverage

ANAHEIM ANGELS

AMERICAN LEAGUE WEST DIVISION

2000 SEASON

2000 Angels Schedule
Home games shaded. *—All-Star Game at Turner Field (Atlanta).

March
SUN	MON	TUE	WED	THU	FRI	SAT
26	27	28	29	30	31	

April
SUN	MON	TUE	WED	THU	FRI	SAT
						1
2	3 NYY	4 NYY	5 NYY	6	7 BOS	8 BOS
9 BOS	10 TOR	11 TOR	12 TOR	13	14 CWS	15 CWS
16 CWS	17 TOR	18 TOR	19 TOR	20 TOR	21 TB	22 TB
23 TB	24 DET	25 DET	26 DET	27 TB	28 TB	29 TB
30 TB						

May
SUN	MON	TUE	WED	THU	FRI	SAT
	1	2 BAL	3 BAL	4 BAL	5 SEA	6 SEA
7 SEA	8 OAK	9 OAK	10 OAK	11 TEX	12 TEX	13 TEX
14 TEX	15	16 BAL	17 BAL	18	19 KC	20 KC
21 KC	22	23 MIN	24 MIN	25 MIN	26 KC	27 KC
28 KC	29 CLE	30 CLE	31 CLE			

June
SUN	MON	TUE	WED	THU	FRI	SAT
				1	2 LA	3 LA
4 LA	5 SF	6 SF	7 SF	8	9 ARI	10 ARI
11 ARI	12	13 TB	14 TB	15 TB	16 BAL	17 BAL
18 BAL	19	20 KC	21 KC	22 KC	23 MIN	24 MIN
25 MIN	26 MIN	27 SEA	28 SEA	29 SEA	30 OAK	

July
SUN	MON	TUE	WED	THU	FRI	SAT
						1 OAK
2 OAK	3 SEA	4 SEA	5 SEA	6 SEA	7 COL	8 COL
9 COL	10	11	* 12	13 LA	14 LA	15 LA
16 SD	17 SD	18 SD	19 TEX	20 TEX	21 OAK	22 OAK
23 OAK	24 TEX	25 TEX	26 TEX	27 CWS	28 CWS	29 CWS
30 CWS	31 DET					

August
SUN	MON	TUE	WED	THU	FRI	SAT
		1 DET	2 DET	3	4 CLE	5 CLE
6 CLE	7 BOS	8 BOS	9 BOS	10	11 NYY	12 NYY
13 NYY	14	15 TOR	16 TOR	17 NYY	18 NYY	19 NYY
20 NYY	21 BOS	22 BOS	23 BOS	24	25 CLE	26 CLE
27 CLE	28 TOR	29 TOR	30 TOR	31		

September
SUN	MON	TUE	WED	THU	FRI	SAT
					1 CWS	2 CWS
3 CWS	4 DET	5 DET	6 DET	7 DET	8 BAL	9 BAL
10 BAL	11 BAL	12 TB	13 TB	14	15 MIN	16 MIN
17 MIN	18	19 KC	20 KC	21 KC	22 TEX	23 TEX
24 TEX	25 OAK	26 OAK	27 OAK	28 OAK	29 SEA	30 SEA

October
SUN	MON	TUE	WED	THU	FRI	SAT
1 SEA	2	3	4	5	6	7

FRONT-OFFICE DIRECTORY

Owner ....The Walt Disney Company
Chairman and chief executive officer, The Walt Disney Co. ....Michael Eisner
President ....Tony Tavares
Vice president and general manager ....Bill Stoneman
Vice president of finance/administration ....Andy Roundtree
Vice president, advertising sales and broadcasting ....Bob Wagner
Vice president, sales and marketing ....Ron Minegar
Vice president, communications ....Tim Mead
Vice president, ballpark operations ....Kevin Uhlich
Vice president, business and legal affairs ....Rick Schlesinger
Assistants general manager...Ken Forsch
Special assistant to the general manager ....Preston Gomez
Legal counsel/contract negotiations ....Mark Rosenthal
Director, scouting..Donny Rowland
Director, player development ....Darrell Miller
Manager, baseball operations..Tony Reagins
Equipment manager ....Ken Higdon
Visiting clubhouse manager..Brian Harkins
Senior video coordinator ....Diego Lopez
Manager, baseball information ....Larry Babcock
Manager, media services ....Nancy Mazmanian
Manager, publications ....Doug Ward
Manager, community relations ....To be announced
Media services/travel coordinator ....Tom Taylor
Director, ticket sales and customer service ....Lawrence Cohen
Director, marketing ....Lisa Manning
Manager, ticket operations...Sheila Brazelton

MINOR LEAGUE AFFILIATES

Class	Team	League	Manager
AAA	Edmonton	Pacific Coast	Carney Lansford
AA	Erie	Eastern	Garry Templeton
A	Boise	Northwest	Tom Kotchman
A	Cedar Rapids	Midwest	Mitch Seoane
A	Lake Elsinore	California	Mario Mendoza
Rookie	Butte	Pioneer	Joe Urso

BALLPARK INFORMATION

Ballpark (capacity, surface)
Edison International Field of Anaheim
(45,050, grass)
Address
2000 Gene Autry Way
Anaheim, CA 92806
Business phones
714-940-2000
Ticket information
714-634-2000
Ticket prices
$19 (field box)
$17.50 (terrace box, terrace disabled MVP)
$13 (lower view MVP)
$11 (lower view box)
$10 (upper value box, terrace disabled box)
$8 (terrace/club pavilion-adult)
$6 (left field pavilion-adult)
$5.50 (terrace/club pavilion-child)
$3 (left field pavilion-child)
Field dimensions (from home plate)
To left field at foul line, 330 feet
To center field, 404 feet
To right field at foul line, 330 feet
First game played
April 19, 1966 (White Sox 3, Angels 1)

ASSISTANCE STAFF

Medical director
Dr. Lewis Yocum

Team physician
Dr. Craig Milhouse

Head athletic trainer
Ned Bergert

Scouts

Don Archer	John Burden
Tom Burns	Todd Claus
Pete Coachman	David Crowson
Clay Daniel	Tom Davis
Jose Gomez	Steve Gruwell
Felipe Gutierrez	Kevin Ham
Rick Ingalls	Tim Kelly
Tom Kotchman	George Lauzerique
Jose Leiva	Guy Mader
Ron Marigny	Mario Mendoza
Tom Osowski	Paul Robinson
Rick Schroeder	Jack Uhey
Victor Villa	

Major league scouts

Jay Hankins	Jon Niederer
Rich Schlenker	Moose Stubing
Dale Sutherland	Gary Sutherland
John Van Ornum	

BROADCAST INFORMATION
Radio: KLAC-AM (570).
TV: KCAL-TV (Channel 9).
Cable TV: Fox Sports West.

SPRING TRAINING
Ballpark (city): Tempe Diablo Stadium (Tempe, Ariz.).
Ticket information: 602-254-3300, 800-326-0331.

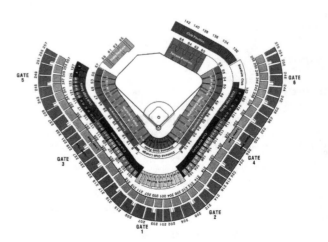

No.	PITCHERS	B/T	Ht./Wt.	Born	1999 clubs	Projection
18	Alvarez, Juan	L/L	6-0/175	8-9-73	Erie, Edmonton, Anaheim	If he has an outstanding spring, he could end up with the big club.
41	Belcher, Tim	R/R	6-3/235	10-19-61	Anaheim	The ace by default had surgery in November and is doubtful for opening day.
45	Cooper, Brian	R/R	6-1/185	8-19-74	Erie, Edmonton, Anaheim	Though not ready for the majors, he'll likely in the rotation out of necessity.
19	Dickson, Jason	L/R	6-0/195	3-30-73	DID NOT PLAY	If he doesn't make the rotation after missing '99, he'll be a long reliever.
27	Fyhrie, Mike	R/R	6-2/203	12-9-69	Edmonton, Anaheim	He was oh-fer in '99 decisions (0-4), and at 30 he has to make an impression.
21	Hasegawa, Shigetoshi	R/R	5-11/178	8-1-68	Anaheim	He's best in middle relief, but his inconsistency is a concern.
44	Hill, Ken	R/R	6-2/215	12-14-65	Anaheim	The No. 2 starter, his arthritic elbow makes it difficult to rely on him.
65	Holtz, Mike	L/L	5-9/188	10-10-72	Anaheim, Edmonton	One of the few lefties in the 'pen, he'll fill the void left by Magnante's departure.
43	Levine, Al	R/R	6-3/198	5-22-68	Anaheim	He's dependable and durable out of the 'pen; in fact, overuse should be a concern.
59	Nina, Elvin	R/R	6-0/185	11-25-75	Modesto, Midland, Erie	Acquired from the A's, he was 3-0 at Erie. Expect him to start at AAA.
36	Ortiz, Ramon	R/R	6-0/175	5-23-76	Erie, Edmonton, Anaheim	The top prospect in the organization, he'll get his baptism by fire in the rotation.
40	Percival, Troy	R/R	6-3/238	8-9-69	Anaheim	If he's recovered from offseason surgery, he's a top closer.
34	Petkovsek, Mark	R/R	6-0/198	11-18-65	Anaheim	He's solid as a righthanded setup man who can close if need be.
58	Pote, Lou	R/R	6-3/208	8-27-71	Edmonton, Anaheim	With a 2.15 ERA in 20 games in 1999, he has carved a nice middle-relief niche.
60	Schoeneweis, Scott	L/L	6-0/186	10-2-73	Anaheim, Edmonton	Once a rotation candidate, he appears slotted as a lefthanded middle reliever.
62	Shields, Scot	R/R	6-1/175	7-22-75	Lake Elsinore, Erie	He's got strikeout stuff, but he's probably at least a year or so away.
54	Turnbow, Derrick	R/R	6-3/180	1-25-78	Piedmont	He's a few years away but averages almost a strikeout an inning.
56	Washburn, Jarrod	L/L	6-1/198	8-13-74	Edmonton, Anaheim	The lefthander joins Ortiz and Cooper as youngsters ticketed for the rotation.
64	Wise, Matt	R/R	6-4/190	11-18-75	Erie	The rangy righthander likely will start the season at AAA.

No.	CATCHERS	B/T	Ht./Wt.	Born	1999 clubs	Projection
61	Dewey, Jason	R/R	6-1/190	4-18-77	Erie, Lake Elsinore	He hit .322 at Class A but struggled (.223) at AA and probably will start there.
8	Hemphill, Bret	B/R	6-2/200	12-17-71	Edmonton, Anaheim	He struggled offensively in a 12-game audition. Look for him to start at AAA.
63	Molina, Ben	R/R	5-11/207	7-20-74	Edmonton, Anaheim	Solid in August before an injury, he enters spring with a slight edge over Walbeck.
6	Walbeck, Matt	B/R	5-11/188	10-2-69	Anaheim	A switch-hitter with a decent arm, he needs to improve his offense.

No.	INFIELDERS	B/T	Ht./Wt.	Born	1999 clubs	Projection
37	Barnes, Larry	L/L	6-1/195	7-23-74	Erie	He's shown good power (20 HRs, 100 RBIs in '99), but is buried behind Vaughn.
9	DiSarcina, Gary	R/R	6-2/194	11-19-67	Lake Elsinore, Erie, Anaheim	He's the shortstop, but there is concern about his '99 struggles after an injury.
20	Durrington, Trent	R/R	5-10/188	8-27-75	Erie, Anaheim	The speedy second baseman will likely open in the majors out of necessity.
28	Glaus, Troy	R/R	6-5/229	8-3-76	Anaheim	He'll be more consistent with experience. He plays Gold Glove-caliber defense.
	Spiezio, Scott	R/R	6-2/222	9-21-72	Oakland, Vancouver	The A's were once very high on him, but injuries caused his production to fall off.
42	Vaughn, Mo	L/R	6-1/268	12-15-67	Anaheim	After limping through last year's disaster, he's primed for a monster season.

No.	OUTFIELDERS	B/T	Ht./Wt.	Born	1999 clubs	Projection
16	Anderson, Garret	L/L	6-3/220	6-30-72	Anaheim	A versatile outfielder, he can fill in solidly if Edmonds or Salmon is hurt.
10	Colangelo, Mike	R/R	6-1/185	10-22-76	Erie, Edmonton, Anaheim	He hit .362 at AAA. A big spring could get him a look.
55	DaVanon, Jeff	B/R	6-0/185	12-8-73	Midland, Edmonton, Anaheim	Though he hit .326 in his stint at AAA Edmonton, he could use more seasoning.
25	Edmonds, Jim	L/L	6-1/212	6-27-70	Lake Elsinore, Anaheim	If he can stay healthy, he's capable of Gold Glove defense and top-notch offense.
17	Erstad, Darin	L/L	6-2/212	6-4-74	Anaheim	His 1999 struggles have raised questions about whether he'll fulfill his potential.
22	Greene, Todd	R/R	5-10/208	5-8-71	Anaheim, Edmonton	The Angels may not find someplace to put him, but his bat should be somewhere.
48	Guzman, Elpidio	L/L	6-0/165	2-24-79	Cedar Rapids	Only 21, he'll need to add some power if he's going to progress to the majors.
35	Hutchins, Norm	R/R	5-11/198	11-20-75	Edmonton	He hit .250 at AAA and likely will start there to work on striking out less.
3	Palmeiro, Orlando	L/L	5-11/175	1-19-69	Anaheim	A decent lefthanded hitter (.278), he'll be pressed for at-bats if everyone's healthy.
15	Salmon, Tim	R/R	6-3/221	8-24-68	Anaheim, Lake Elsinore	Despite injury problems, he is a strong-armed cleanup hitter capable of 100 RBIs.

THE COACHING STAFF

Mike Scioscia: A respected major league veteran who is a product of the crosstown Dodgers organization, he becomes the 16th manager in franchise history, replacing Terry Collins, who resigned in September. Scioscia, 40, managed AAA Albuquerque to a 65-74 record in 1999 after having served as a Dodgers bench coach. He comes to the majors as somewhat of an unknown quantity and could be tested early given the Angels' well-chronicled clubhouse problems. His style would appear to be much more low-key than the intense Collins.

Bud Black: A major league pitcher for 15 seasons, he joins the team as pitching coach from the Indians' front office.

Alfredo Griffin: He'll be the first-base coach, a position he held with the Blue Jays in 1996 and '97.

Mickey Hatcher: He was Scioscia's hitting coach in Albuquerque in '99 and joins him in the same capacity with the Angels.

Joe Maddon: Entering his seventh season on the staff (he was interim manager after Terry Collins resigned), he'll continue as the bench coach.

Bobby Ramos: He's the bullpen coach after having managed a Devil Rays rookie-level team in '99.

Ron Roenicke: The AAA manager in the Giants organization in '99, he'll be the third-base coach.

THE TOP NEWCOMERS

Scott Spiezio: A solid fielder as the starting second baseman for Oakland, but he never took his offense to the next level. Now with Velarde back in Oakland, the Angels signed Spiezio to take over Velarde's still-vacant position.

THE TOP PROSPECTS

Doug Bridges: He's a few years away, but the righthander won 18, best in the minors, between two Class A stops.

Mike Colangelo: He has hit at every level and might be ready to step in should the team trade one of its four top outfielders.

Brian Cooper: He was 10-5 in AA and 2-1 in AAA before earning a call-up. Like Ramon Ortiz, he'll be learning on the job when he almost assuredly is handed a spot in the big-league rotation.

Seth Etherton: The top pick in 1998, he was 10-10 at AA Erie in '99 and struggled after being called up to AAA Edmonton (0-2, 5.48).

Ramon Ortiz: A combined 14-6 in the minors, he's apparently recovered from elbow problems. A taste of his potential: He set a team record with 12 strikeouts in his first AAA start and broke it with 13 in his second. Ortiz has a great arm, and the rest of the league will see it soon.

BALTIMORE ORIOLES

AMERICAN LEAGUE EAST DIVISION

2000 SEASON

2000 Orioles Schedule

Home games shaded. *—All-Star Game at Turner Field (Atlanta).

March

SUN	MON	TUE	WED	THU	FRI	SAT
26	27	28	29	30	31	

April

SUN	MON	TUE	WED	THU	FRI	SAT
						1
2	3 CLE	4	5 CLE	6 CLE	7 DET	8 DET
9 DET	10	11 KC	12 KC	13 KC	14 MIN	15 MIN
16 MIN	17 TB	18 TB	19 TB	20	21 OAK	22 OAK
23 OAK	24 CWS	25 CWS	26 CWS	27 CWS	28 TEX	29 TEX
30 TEX						

May

SUN	MON	TUE	WED	THU	FRI	SAT
	1	2 ANA	3 ANA	4	5 NYY	6 NYY
7 NYY	8 TOR	9 TOR	10 TOR	11 BOS	12 BOS	13 BOS
14 BOS	15	16 ANA	17 ANA	18 TEX	19 TEX	20 TEX
21 TEX	22	23 SEA	24 SEA	25 SEA	26 OAK	27 OAK
28 OAK	29 TB	30 TB	31 TB			

June

SUN	MON	TUE	WED	THU	FRI	SAT
				1 TB	2 MON	3 MON
4 MON	5 NYM	6 NYM	7 NYM	8	9 PHI	10 PHI
11 PHI	12	13 TEX	14 TEX	15 TEX	16 ANA	17 ANA
18 ANA	19 OAK	20 OAK	21 OAK	22 SEA	23 SEA	24 SEA
25 SEA	26	27 BOS	28 BOS	29 BOS	30 TOR	

July

SUN	MON	TUE	WED	THU	FRI	SAT
						1 TOR
2 TOR	3 TOR	4 NYY	5 NYY	6 NYY	7 PHI	8 PHI
9 PHI	10	11 *	12	13 ATL	14 ATL	15 ATL
16 FLA	17 FLA	18 FLA	19 BOS	20 BOS	21 TOR	22 TOR
23 TOR	24 NYY	25 NYY	26	27	28 CLE	29 CLE
30 CLE	31 MIN					

August

SUN	MON	TUE	WED	THU	FRI	SAT
		1 MIN	2 MIN	3	4 TB	5 TB
6 TB	7 DET	8 DET	9 DET	10 KC	11 KC	12 KC
13 KC	14 CWS	15 CWS	16 CWS	17 CWS	18 KC	19 KC
20 KC	21 KC	22	23 CWS	24 CWS	25 DET	26 DET
27 TB	28	29 DET	30 DET	31 DET		

September

SUN	MON	TUE	WED	THU	FRI	SAT
					1 CLE	2 CLE
3 CLE	4 MIN	5 MIN	6 MIN	7	8 ANA	9 ANA
10 ANA	11 ANA	12 TEX	13 TEX	14	15 SEA	16 SEA
17 SEA	18 OAK	19 OAK	20 OAK	21	22 BOS	23 BOS
24 BOS	25	26 TOR	27 TOR	28 TOR	29 NYY	30 NYY

October

SUN	MON	TUE	WED	THU	FRI	SAT
1 NYY	2	3	4	5	6	7

FRONT-OFFICE DIRECTORY

Chairman/chief executive officer ....Peter Angelos
Vice chairman, chief operating officer ....Joe Foss
Executive vice president ....John Angelos
Vice president/chief financial officer ....Robert Ames
Vice president, marketing and broadcasting ....Mike Lehr
Vice president, baseball operations ....Syd Thrift
Director, minor league operations ....Don Buford
Director of scouting..Tony DeMacio
Director, major and minor league instruction ....Tom Trebelhorn
Special assistants to the V.P., baseball operations ....Bruce Manno,
Bob Schaeffer
Assistant director, minor league operations.....................................Tripp Norton
Traveling secretary ....Philip Itzoe
Director, public relations ....Bill Stetka
Public relations assistant ....Kevin Behan
Director, ballpark operations ....Roger Hayden
Director, community relations ....Julie Wagner
Director, computer services ....James Kline
Director, ballpark entertainment ....To be announced
Director, publishing and advertising..................................Christina Palmisano
Director, fan and ticket services ....Donald Grove
Director, sales..Matthew Dryer

MINOR LEAGUE AFFILIATES

Class	Team	League	Manager
AAA	Rochester	International	Marv Foley
AA	Bowie	Eastern	Andy Etchebarren
A	Frederick	Carolina	Dave Machemer
A	Delmarva	South Atlantic	Joe Ferguson
Rookie	Bluefield	Appalachian	Duffy Dyer
Rookie	Gulf Coast Orioles	Gulf Coast	Jesus Alfaro

BROADCAST INFORMATION

Radio: WBAL-AM (1090).
TV: WJZ (Channel 13), WNUV (Channel 54), WFTY (Channel 50, Washington, D.C.).
Cable TV: Home Team Sports.

SPRING TRAINING

Ballpark (city): Fort Lauderdale Stadium (Fort Lauderdale, Fla.).
Ticket information: 954-523-3309, 305-358-5885, 561-776-9116.

ASSISTANCE STAFF

Head athletic trainer
Richard Bancells

Assistant athletic trainer
Brian Ebel

Strength and conditioning
Tim Bishop

Advance scout
Deacon Jones

Professional scouts
Danny Garcia   Curt Motton
Fred Uhlman Sr.

Nation cross-checker
Mike Ledna

Regional supervisors
Shawn Pender   Logan White

Full-time scouts
Dean Decillis, John Gillette, Troy Hoerner, Jim Howard, Ray Kraczyk, Gil Kubski, Jeff Morris, Lamar North, Deron Rombach, Harry Shelton, Ed Sprague, Marc Tramuta, Mike Tullier, Dominic Viola, Marc Ziegler

Director, Latin American scouting
Carlos Bernhardt

Caribbean & S. American supervisor
Jesus Halabi

International scouts
Ubaldo Heredia   Salvator Ramirez
Arturo Sanchez   Brett Ward

BALLPARK INFORMATION

Ballpark (capacity, surface)
Oriole Park at Camden Yards (48,876, grass)

Address
333 W. Camden St.
Baltimore, MD 21201

Business phone
410-685-9800

Ticket information
410-481-SEAT

Ticket prices
$35 (club box)
$30 (field box-sections 20-54)
$27 (field box-sections 14-18, 56-58)
$23 (terrace box-sections 19-53)
$22 (left field club, lower box)
$20 (terrace box-sections 1-17, 55-65)
$18 (left field lower box, upper box)
$16 (left field upper box; lower reserve sec. 19-53)
$13 (upper reserve; lower res. sec. 4, 7-17, 55-87)
$11 (left field upper reserve)
$9 (bleacher)
$7 (standing room)

Field dimensions (from home plate)
To left field at foul line, 333 feet
To center field, 400 feet
To right field at foul line, 318 feet

First game played
April 6, 1992 (Orioles 2, Indians 0)

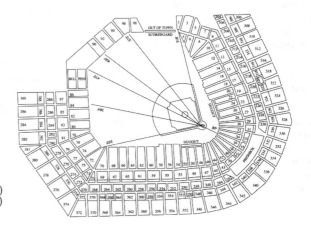

No.	PITCHERS	B/T	Ht./Wt.	Born	1999 clubs	Projection
	Aracena, Juan	R/R	6-0/190	12-17-76	Columbus, Kinston, Frederick	Came over from Cleveland in the 1999 Baines trade. A reliever with good control.
28	Dykhoff, Radhames	L/L	6-0/200	9-27-74	Rochester	Lefty reliever should stay at Rochester until disaster strikes in Baltimore.
19	Erickson, Scott	R/R	6-4/230	2-2-68	Baltimore	No. 2 starter is one of the most durable pitchers in the majors.
51	Falkenborg, Brian	R/R	6-6/195	1-18-78	Bowie, GC Orioles, Baltimore	Good young prospect must still prove injury troubles are behind him.
	Groom, Buddy	L/L	6-2/207	7-10-65	Oakland	This free-agent signee will fill the lefthanded setup role.
	Guzman, Juan	R/R	6-2/184	3-4-78	Delmarva	Young starter with big strikeout numbers in the minors.
	Hamilton, Jimmy	L/L	6-3/190	8-1-75	Akron, Buffalo, Rochester	Young strikeout pitcher should stay at Class AAA. At least for now.
41	Johnson, Jason	R/R	6-6/235	10-27-73	Rochester, Baltimore	After a promising season last year, team hopes he'll be a solid fifth starter.
	Maduro, Calvin	R/R	6-0/188	9-5-74	Rochester	Reacquired by the Orioles from Phillies for the '99 season. Still a minor leaguer.
	McElroy, Chuck	L/L	6-0/205	10-1-67	Colorado, New York N.L.	This veteran will be the first lefty out of bullpen and should be used often.
45	Molina, Gabe	R/R	5-11/207	5-3-75	Rochester, Baltimore	Closer/reliever was up and down last season and should continue that trend.
35	Mussina, Mike	R/R	6-2/183	12-8-68	Baltimore	One of the league's true aces; a Cy Young contender every year.
	Negrette, Richard	R/R	6-2/173	3-6-76	Akron, West Tenn	Acquired in December from the Cubs in a minor league trade, but not yet a factor.
43	Ponson, Sidney	R/R	6-1/225	11-2-76	Baltimore	With Aaron Sele's arrival, he's the fourth starter. May be on the brink of stardom.
32	Reyes, Al	R/R	6-1/208	4-10-71	Louisville, Milwaukee, Baltimore	Proved last season to be a valuable middle-relief/setup pitcher.
25	Riley, Matt	L/L	6-1/201	8-2-79	Frederick, Bowie, Baltimore	One of the team's top prospects, he could make the club out of spring training.
52	Ryan, B.J.	L/L	6-6/230	12-28-75	Chatt., Ind., Cin., Roch., Balt.	Team likes his potential and could use another lefty in the bullpen.
40	Timlin, Mike	R/R	6-4/210	3-10-66	Baltimore	Rebounded from a terrible slump last season to reclaim job as team's closer.
	Trombley, Mike	R/R	6-2/210	4-14-67	Minnesota	Signed in the offseason to be Timlin's setup man/occasional closer.

No.	CATCHERS	B/T	Ht./Wt.	Born	1999 clubs	Projection
21	Johnson, Charles	R/R	6-2/220	7-20-71	Baltimore	Still doesn't hit as well as team would like, but is one of the best behind the dish.
	Myers, Greg	L/R	6-2/225	4-14-66	San Diego, Rancho Cuca., Atl.	A solid veteran backup who won't play much.

No.	INFIELDERS	B/T	Ht./Wt.	Born	1999 clubs	Projection
14	Bordick, Mike	R/R	5-11/175	7-21-65	Baltimore	Improved his hitting last season and is one of league's most underrated fielders.
80	Casimiro, Carlos	R/R	5-11/170	11-8-76	Bowie	Second baseman has good tools but needs work before he can advance.
23	Clark, Will	L/L	6-1/200	3-13-64	Baltimore	When healthy, he's a slick fielder and good hitter, but he's not healthy often.
65	Coffie, Ivanon	L/R	6-1/182	5-16-77	Bowie, Frederick	Third baseman/shortstop has speed and power but commits a lot of errors.
18	Conine, Jeff	R/R	6-1/220	6-27-66	Baltimore	A very good first baseman/outfielder who figures to see plenty of action.
11	DeShields, Delino	L/R	6-1/175	1-15-69	Bowie, Balt., Delm., Frederick	Not much range for a second baseman, but a good bat. Health is a concern.
1	Garcia, Jesse	R/R	5-10/171	9-24-73	Baltimore, Rochester	Solid infielder who could make the club as a utilityman.
13	Hairston, Jerry Jr.	R/R	5-10/173	5-29-76	Rochester, Baltimore	This second baseman proved he belongs in the bigs last year; just needs a spot.
	Martinez, Eddy	R/R	6-2/173	10-23-77	Frederick	Shortstop stuck in the lower minor leagues because of the Orioles' shortstop depth.
10	Minor, Ryan	R/R	6-7/245	1-5-74	Rochester, Baltimore	Third baseman of the future whose biggest asset is his bat.
39	Pickering, Calvin	L/L	6-5/278	9-29-76	Rochester, Baltimore	Big-hitting first baseman could be called up if Clark gets hurt.
8	Ripken, Cal	R/R	6-4/220	8-24-60	Baltimore	He's coming off surgery but had one of his best offensive seasons last year.

No.	OUTFIELDERS	B/T	Ht./Wt.	Born	1999 clubs	Projection
6	Amaral, Rich	R/R	6-0/175	4-1-62	Baltimore	Veteran who can fill in at any outfield position when needed.
9	Anderson, Brady	L/L	6-1/202	1-18-64	Baltimore	May have lost a step but is still a decent fielder and above-average offensively.
88	Belle, Albert	R/R	6-2/210	8-25-66	Baltimore	Better than expected in right field, he's got one of the most powerful bats around.
33	Kingsale, Gene	B/R	6-3/194	8-20-76	Bowie, Rochester, Baltimore	Club would like to get young center fielder on roster, but there's no room for him.
	Matos, Luis	L/R	6-0/179	10-30-78	Frederick, Bowie	Top-flight defense and speed, but not much offense. He'll be back in the minors.
17	Surhoff, B.J.	L/R	6-1/200	8-4-64	Baltimore	Coming off career year, this left fielder is one of the league's most dependable.

No.	DESIGNATED HITTERS	B/T	Ht./Wt.	Born	1999 clubs	Projection
3	Baines, Harold	L/L	6-2/195	3-15-59	Baltimore, Cleveland	Like a fine wine, he just seems to get better with age.

THE COACHING STAFF

Mike Hargrove, manager: He was very successful in his eight seasons at the helm of the Indians, including five straight division titles, but never managed to get the team over the elusive World Series title. However, he may be the only manager suited to run this Baltimore team, as he knows how to deal with various personalities, not the least of which belongs to Albert Belle, a former Indian. With a veteran-laden team that has underachieved the past couple seasons, Hargrove should be eager to prove himself and get the most out of his players.

Terry Crowley: Known during his playing days as one of the game's most dangerous pinch hitters, Crowley has parlayed that skill into a successful career as a batting coach. He worked for the Orioles and Red Sox before spending eight years as hitting coach for Tom Kelly's Minnesota Twins, then came back for a second stint in Baltimore.

Sammy Ellis: Has coached in some capacity of five major league teams, the last one being the Red Sox in 1996. This ex-pitcher is Baltimore's new pitching coach. He has veteran talent—Mussina, Erickson and Sele. But he must bridge the gap and take young hurlers like Sidney Ponson to the next level. And, of course, he must improve the shaky bullpen.

Brian Graham: After starting the 1998 season as Cleveland's Class AAA Buffalo manager, Graham was a late-season fill-in for Charlie Manuel as the Indians' first base coach. He took over that job full time last season and came to Baltimore with Hargrove.

Elrod Hendricks: A former Orioles catcher, Hendricks begins his 23rd season as bullpen coach. He has a knack for working with young pitchers and catchers.

Eddie Murray: After completing a career that produced 504 home runs and 1,917 RBIs, Murray made his coaching debut two seasons ago in Baltimore. He has managing aspirations, but he's back for a third season in the dugout.

Jeff Newman: After eight straight seasons as Cleveland's third base coach, Newman comes to the O's as a bench coach. Before Cleveland, Newman coached and managed in the A's system for six years.

Sam Perlozzo: He will be working his 14th season as a major league third base coach, his fourth for the Orioles. He also has minor league managing experience.

THE TOP NEWCOMERS

Mike Trombley: After starting last season as a setup man in Minnesota, he became the closer when Rick Aguilera was traded and finished the season strong. He gives the team insurance in case Mike Timlin struggles in the closer role.

THE TOP PROSPECTS

Jerry Hairston Jr.: If not for Delino DeShields' large contract, Hairston would already be the starter at second base. Even if the team cannot unload DeShields, Hairston is likely to see a lot of playing time.

Ryan Minor: With Cal Ripken coming off the first injury-plagued season of his career, Minor could stick in the majors and see time in place of Ripken as well as spot duty at first base and DH.

Calvin Pickering: Injuries slowed him last season, and with Jeff Conine's presence, the team's first baseman of the future is likely to spend another year in the minors with occasional call-ups.

BOSTON RED SOX

AMERICAN LEAGUE EAST DIVISION

2000 SEASON

2000 Red Sox Schedule
Home games shaded. *—All-Star Game at Turner Field (Atlanta).

March
SUN	MON	TUE	WED	THU	FRI	SAT
26	27	28	29	30	31	

April
SUN	MON	TUE	WED	THU	FRI	SAT
						1
2	3 SEA	4 SEA	5 SEA	6	7 ANA	8 ANA
9 ANA	10	11 MIN	12 MIN	13 MIN	14 OAK	15 OAK
16 OAK	17 OAK	18 DET	19 DET	20 DET	21 CLE	22 CLE
23 CLE	24 TEX	25 TEX	26 TEX	27	28 CLE	29 CLE
30 CLE						

May
SUN	MON	TUE	WED	THU	FRI	SAT
	1 DET	2 DET	3 DET	4	5 TB	6 TB
7 TB	8 CWS	9 CWS	10 CWS	11 BAL	12 BAL	13 BAL
14 BAL	15 TOR	16 TOR	17 TOR	18	19 DET	20 DET
21 DET	22	23 TOR	24 TOR	25 TOR	26 NYY	27 NYY
28 NYY	29	30 KC	31 KC			

June
SUN	MON	TUE	WED	THU	FRI	SAT
				1 KC	2 PHI	3 PHI
4 PHI	5 FLA	6 FLA	7 FLA	8	9 ATL	10 ATL
11 ATL	12 NYY	13 NYY	14 NYY	15	16 TOR	17 TOR
18 TOR	19 NYY	20 NYY	21 NYY	22 NYY	23 TOR	24 TOR
25 TOR	26	27 BAL	28 BAL	29 BAL	30 CWS	

July
SUN	MON	TUE	WED	THU	FRI	SAT
						1 CWS
2 CWS	3 MIN	4 MIN	5 MIN	6 MIN	7 ATL	8 ATL
9 ATL	10	11 *	12	13 NYM	14 NYM	15 NYM
16 MON	17 MON	18 MON	19 BAL	20 BAL	21 CWS	22 CWS
23 CWS	24 MIN	25 MIN	26 MIN	27 OAK	28 OAK	29 OAK
30 OAK	31 SEA					

August
SUN	MON	TUE	WED	THU	FRI	SAT
		1 SEA	2 SEA	3	4 KC	5 KC
6 KC	7 ANA	8 ANA	9 ANA	10	11 TEX	12 TEX
13 TEX	14 TB	15 TB	16 TB	17 TB	18 TB	19 TB
20 TEX	21 ANA	22 ANA	23 ANA	24 KC	25 KC	26 KC
27 KC	28 TB	29 TB	30 TB	31		

September
SUN	MON	TUE	WED	THU	FRI	SAT
					1 SEA	2 SEA
3 SEA	4 SEA	5 OAK	6 OAK	7	8 NYY	9 NYY
10 NYY	11	12 CLE	13 CLE	14 CLE	15 DET	16 DET
17 DET	18	19 CLE	20 CLE	21 CLE	22 BAL	23 BAL
24 BAL	25	26 CWS	27 CWS	28 CWS	29 TB	30 TB

October
SUN	MON	TUE	WED	THU	FRI	SAT
1 TB	2	3	4	5	6	7

FRONT-OFFICE DIRECTORY

Chief executive officer ....John L. Harrington
Executive vice president and general manager ....Daniel F. Duquette
Executive vice president for administration ....John S. Buckley
Vice president and chief financial officer ....Robert C. Furbush
Vice president baseball operations ....Michael D. Port
Vice president broadcasting and technology ....James P. Healey
Vice president public affairs ....Richard L. Bresciani
Vice president sales and marketing ....Lawrence C. Cancro
Vice president stadium operations..Joseph F. McDermott
Vice president, assistant general manager and legal counsel ....Elaine W. Steward
Assistant general manager ....Edward P. Kenney
Director of communications and baseball information..........................Kevin J. Shea
Director of human resources and office management ....Michele Julian
Vice president, scouting ....W. Wayne Britton
Executive director of int'l baseball operations ....R. Ray Poitevint
Director of minor league operations ....Kent A. Qualls
Coordinator of Florida operations ....Ryan Richeal
Traveling secretary ....John F. McCormick
Special assistant for player development...John M. Pesky
Baseball administration coordinator ....Marci Blacker
Assistant scouting director ....Tom Moore
Technology manager ....Clay Rendon
Director of sales ....Michael Schetzel
Group sales manager ....Corey Bowdre
Telephone sales manager...Amy McCarthy
Property maintenance manager ....John Caron
600 Club and suites manager ....Dan Lyons
Food service manager ....Ed Pistorino
Premium seating sales manager ....Jeff Connors
Medical director ....Arthur M. Pappas M.D.
Baseball information coordinator ....Glenn Wilburn
Executive administrative assistant..Lorraine Leong
Controller ....Stanley H. Tran
Director of advertising and sponsorships ....Jeffrey E. Goldenberg
Director of facilities management ....Thomas L. Queenan Jr.
Director of ticket operations ....Joseph Helyar
Executive, public affairs...James "Lou" Gorman
Broadcasting manager ....James Shannahan

MINOR LEAGUE AFFILIATES

Class	Team	League	Manager
AAA	Pawtucket	International	Gary Jones
AA	Trenton	Eastern	Billy Gardner Jr.
A	Sarasota	Florida State	Ron Johnson
A	Augusta	South Atlantic	Mike Boulanger
A	Lowell	New York-Pennsylvania	Luis Aguayo
Rookie	Gulf Coast Red Sox	Gulf Coast	John Sanders

ASSISTANCE STAFF

Major League scout
Frank Malzone

Major League special assignment scout
G. Edwin Haas

Trainer
James W. Rowe Jr.

Strength and conditioning coordinator
Merle V. "B.J." Baker III

Instructors
Theodore S. Williams, Carl M. Yastrzemski

Scouts
Raymond Boone, Buzz Bowers, Kevin Burrell, Julian Camilo, Ben Cherington, Edwin Correa, Ray Crone Jr., George Digby, Johnny DiPuglia, Danny Doyle, William Enos, Ray Fagnant, Steve Flores, Mark Garcia, Robinson Garcia, Eddie Haas, Matt Haas, Ernie Jacobs, Jon Kodama, Wally Komatsubara, Chuck Koney, Kenneth Lee, Don Lehnardt, Frank Malzone, Luis Marin, Sebastien Martinez, Joe Mason, Jose Maza, Steve McAllister, Levy Ochoa, Ray Poitevint, Gary Rajsich, Carlos Ramirez, Eddie Robinson, Jim Robinson, Ed Roebuck, Edward Scott, Mathew Sczesny, Lee Sigman, Dick Sorkin, Jerry Stephenson, Joseph Stephenson, Lee Thomas, Fay Thompson, Michael Victoria, Charles Wagner, Jeffrey Zona

BROADCAST INFORMATION

Radio: WEEI-AM (680).
TV: WFXT (Fox 25).
Cable TV: New England Sports Network.

SPRING TRAINING

Ballpark (city): City of Palms Park (Fort Myers, Fla.).
Ticket information: 941-334-4700.

BALLPARK INFORMATION

Ballpark (capacity, surface)
Fenway Park (33,455, grass)
Address
4 Yawkey Way
Boston, MA 02215-3496
Business phone
617-267-9440
Ticket information
617-267-1700, 617-482-4769
Ticket prices
$45 (field box)
$40 (loge box and infield roof)
$28 (reserved grandstand)
$27 (right field boxes and right field roof)
$20 (outfield grandstand)
$16 (lower bleachers)
$14 (upper bleachers)
Field dimensions (from home plate)
To left field at foul line, 310 feet
To center field, 420 feet
To right field at foul line, 302 feet
First game played
April 20, 1912 (Red Sox 7, New York Highlanders 6)

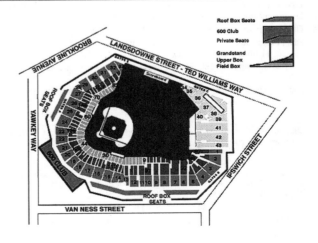

No.	PITCHERS	B/T	Ht./Wt.	Born	1999 clubs	Projection
47	Beck, Rod	R/R	6-1/235	8-3-68	Chicago N.L., Iowa, Boston	The Shooter will split time as a setup man and a spot closer if his arm is healthy.
61	Cho, Jin Ho	R/R	6-3/220	8-16-75	Pawtucket, Boston	Korean had a 5.72 ERA in seven starts in '99; will compete for a rotaion job.
37	Cormier, Rheal	L/L	5-10/187	4-23-67	Boston	This surprise find shut down lefty hitters (.198) in 1999 and remains in the 'pen.
13	Fassero, Jeff	L/L	6-1/195	1-5-63	Seattle, Texas	Reunion with Joe Kerrigan might be what this struggling lefty starter needs.
39	Florie, Bryce	R/R	5-11/192	5-21-70	Lakeland, Detroit, Boston	Former Tiger has an excellent slider and has good command of his pitches.
34	Garces, Richard	R/R	6-0/215	5-18-71	Pawtucket, Boston	His great control and effectiveness against both righties and lefties is key.
36	Gordon, Tom	R/R	5-9/190	11-18-67	Boston	Elbow injuries limited the closer to 21 games in '99 and may cost him all of 2000.
	Lee, Sang	L/L	6-1/190	3-11-71	Chunichi Dragons	Korean reliever spent the past two years in Japan and will provide bullpen depth.
32	Lowe, Derek	R/R	6-6/200	6-1-73	Boston	Promising sinkerballer has some of the best stuff in the game; will be the closer.
45	Martinez, Pedro J.	R/R	5-11/170	10-25-71	Boston	Cy Young winner put together one of the best seasons in baseball history.
48	Martinez, Ramon J.	R/R	6-4/184	3-22-68	Low., GC R.Sox, Sar., Paw., Bos.	Proved in the postseason that his shoulder is healthy and will be the No. 2 starter.
53	Ohka, Tomo	R/R	6-1/179	3-18-76	Trenton, Pawtucket, Boston	Had great success in the minors (15-0) but was roughed up in the majors.
	Pena, Juan	R/R	6-5/215	6-27-77	Paw., Bos., GC Red Sox, Sara.	Showed great promise in two starts last season and will get a shot at the rotation.
19	Rose, Brian	R/R	6-3/215	2-13-76	Pawtucket, Boston	Recovered well from 1998 elbow surgery. He is expected to be in the rotation.
17	Saberhagen, Bret	R/R	6-1/200	4-11-64	Boston, Trenton	Recurring shoulder problems may sideline the former Cy Young winner.
	Sekany, Jason	R/R	6-4/214	7-20-75	Trenton, Pawtucket	Will start the season at Class AAA after a good showing in Trenton (14-4 record).
49	Wakefield, Tim	R/R	6-2/210	8-2-66	Boston	He's a valuable asset because of his versatility, but a risk due to his lack of control.
46	Wasdin, John	R/R	6-2/195	8-5-72	Pawtucket, Boston, GC Red Sox	Bullpen righty must continue to improve his control and cut down on homers.
	Young, Tim	L/L	5-9/170	10-15-73	Trenton	Reliever might get a look at Pawtucket after a decent season in Trenton.

No.	CATCHERS	B/T	Ht./Wt.	Born	1999 clubs	Projection
10	Hatteberg, Scott	L/R	6-1/205	12-14-69	Bos., Paw., GC Red Sox, Sara.	Elbow troubles limited him to 30 games in '99; will serve as a backup.
56	Lomasney, Steve	R/R	6-0/195	8-29-77	Sarasota, Trenton, Boston	The team's top power prospect will start at Class AAA due to the catching depth.
33	Varitek, Jason	R/R	6-2/220	4-11-72	Boston	Game-calling and offense improve as he becomes one of the game's best catchers.

No.	INFIELDERS	B/T	Ht./Wt.	Born	1999 clubs	Projection
24	Alexander, Manny	R/R	5-10/180	3-20-71	Chicago N.L.	Will serve as a utility middle infielder for defensive purposes, but his bat is weak.
23	Daubach, Brian	L/R	6-1/201	2-11-72	Boston, Pawtucket	Breakthrough season eased the loss of Mo Vaughn; should be full-time DH.
3	Frye, Jeff	R/R	5-9/170	8-31-66	Boston, GC Red Sox, Pawtucket	Fundamentally sound at second base, but he has a history of injuries.
5	Garciaparra, Nomar	R/R	6-0/175	7-23-73	Boston	One of the game's great shortstops will be protected by better bats in the lineup.
30	Offerman, Jose	B/R	6-0/190	11-8-68	Boston	Second baseman is everything they expected offensively, but lacks glovework.
15	Sadler, Donnie	R/R	5-6/175	6-17-75	Boston, Pawtucket, GC Red Sox	The speediest Red Sox player will compete as a utility infielder.
24	Stanley, Mike	R/R	6-0/205	6-25-63	Boston	The former catcher gets the first base job by default and provides a veteran bat.
	Stenson, Dernell	L/L	6-1/232	6-17-78	Pawtucket, Gulf Coast Red Sox	Offensively-gifted prospect moved to first in the minors, but struggled defensively.
13	Valentin, John	R/R	6-0/185	2-18-67	Boston	Solid starting third baseman is coming off an offseason knee surgery.
38	Veras, Wilton	R/R	6-2/198	1-19-78	Trenton, Boston	This power prospect stepped in during Valentin's injury and hit .288.

No.	OUTFIELDERS	B/T	Ht./Wt.	Born	1999 clubs	Projection
	Allensworth, Jermaine	R/R	6-0/190	1-11-72	New York N.L., Norfolk	Bounced around the majors last year and will provide depth, speed and defense.
44	Coleman, Michael	R/R	5-11/215	8-16-75	Pawtucket, Boston	A fine combination of power, speed and athleticism, but won't crack the outfield.
3	Everett, Carl	B/R	6-0/190	6-3-71	Houston	Offseason acquisition will take over in center and provide a big bat in the middle.
20	Lewis, Darren	R/R	6-0/190	8-28-67	Boston	His defense is excellent; could platoon in right field if Nixon struggles.
7	Nixon, Trot	L/L	6-2/200	4-11-74	Boston	Heralded prospect arrived in 1999 with 15 homers and 52 RBIs; will start in right.
25	O'Leary, Troy	L/L	6-0/200	8-4-69	Boston	Starting left fielder has 30-homer, 100-RBI potential and plays solid defense.

THE COACHING STAFF

Jimy Williams, manager: Williams won the A.L. Manager of the Year Award after guiding the Red Sox to a 94-68 finish and their second consecutive wild card berth. Last season was the first time the team made consecutive postseason appearances since 1916 and the first time the Red Sox won a playoff series since 1986. The job he did is even more impressive considering the loss of Mo Vaughn, the lack of a bat to protect Nomar Garciaparra and the numerous injuries to the starting rotation. Williams is best known for his baseball knowledge, ability to keep players happy and the knack for getting the most from everyone on the roster. His resume includes coaching third base for the Braves for seven seasons and managing the Blue Jays from 1986-89.

Buddy Bailey: This will be his first season as the Red Sox's first base coach. He takes over for Dave Jauss, who held the position for three years. Bailey had been the team's minor league field co-ordinator and was a minor league manager for 14 seasons. Bailey also will serve as Boston's catching instructor.

John Cumberland: He begins his second season as the team's bullpen coach. Previously, he spent three season as Pawtucket's pitching coach and briefly filled that role with the Red Sox in 1995. He has worked as a minor league pitching coach or instructor since 1982 with several teams.

Joe Kerrigan: Back for his fourth season, Kerrigan is regarded as one of the best pitching coaches in the game and interviewed for the Indians' managing job in the offseason. Boston's 4.00 staff ERA was the best in the league in 1999. Kerrigan has 12 years of coaching experience and served as Montreal's pitching coach for five years before coming to Boston.

Wendell Kim: The team offered the third base coaching job to Ken Macha, who turned it down. That means Kim will return for his fourth season at third and as an infield instructor. He is widely known for his aggressive style and also has eight years of coaching experience in the San Francisco organization.

Jim Rice: The Red Sox legend has been with the organization for 28 years, and this is his fifth as Boston's hitting instructor. Previously, Rice was a roving minor league instructor for the team. Despite a lineup that included just one real threat, Rice's hitters had a decent .278 average in 1999.

THE TOP NEWCOMERS

Manny Alexander: The former Cub is solid defensively, had his best season at the plate in 1999 (.271) and can play shortstop, second base and third base. He should get most of his action spotting Offerman at second.

Jermaine Allensworth: Although it might seem like he has been around forever, Allensworth is only 27 and provides some depth in the outfield. Allensworth also has speed and is a better-than-average fielder.

Carl Everett: He provides a valuable bat and ends the Darren Lewis/Damon Buford platoon in center. The team will lose some defensive prowess in the outfield, but Everett's 25-homer, 100-RBI potential is a welcome addition to the middle of the lineup.

Jeff Fassero: The Red Sox are thrilled to have a lefty in the rotation, and they hope Joe Kerrigan can work his magic on the once-promising starter. Fassero was 56-43 with a 3.25 ERA with Kerrigan in Montreal and Seattle (1992-96), but he was 5-14 with a 7.20 ERA with the Mariners and Rangers in 1999.

THE TOP PROSPECTS

Michael Coleman: The Red Sox value his power (30 homers at Pawtucket), but the outfield depth could leave him on the outside looking in. He has a shot to make the team as a fifth outfielder and could see more action if Nixon and/or Lewis struggles at the plate.

Dernell Stenson: The Red Sox would love to plug this hitting prospect in at first base because of his bat (.270, 18 homers, 82 RBIs at Pawtucket), but his defense continues to hold him back.

Wilton Veras: There's no doubt he is the third baseman of the future, especially after the job he did during Valentin's injury last season. In addition to his great power potential, he is strong defensively and hustles. If Valentin is dealt, struggles at the plate or is injured, expect Veras to take over.

CHICAGO WHITE SOX

AMERICAN LEAGUE CENTRAL DIVISION

2000 SEASON

2000 White Sox Schedule

Home games shaded. *—All-Star Game at Turner Field (Atlanta).

March
SUN	MON	TUE	WED	THU	FRI	SAT
26	27	28	29	30	31	

April
SUN	MON	TUE	WED	THU	FRI	SAT
						1
2	3 TEX	4 TEX	5 TEX	6 TEX	7 OAK	8 OAK
9 OAK	10	11 TB	12 TB	13 TB	14 ANA	15 ANA
16 ANA	17 SEA	18 SEA	19 SEA	20	21 DET	22 DET
23 DET	24 BAL	25 BAL	26 BAL	27 BAL	28 DET	29 DET
30 DET						

May
SUN	MON	TUE	WED	THU	FRI	SAT
	1 TOR	2 TOR	3 TOR	4	5 KC	6 KC
7 KC	8 BOS	9 BOS	10 BOS	11	12 MIN	13 MIN
14 MIN	15	16 NYY	17 NYY	18	19 TOR	20 TOR
21 TOR	22 TOR	23 NYY	24 NYY	25 NYY	26 CLE	27 CLE
28 CLE	29 SEA	30 SEA	31 SEA			

June
SUN	MON	TUE	WED	THU	FRI	SAT
				1	2 HOU	3 HOU
4 HOU	5 CIN	6 CIN	7 CIN	8	9 CUB	10 CUB
11 CUB	12 CLE	13 CLE	14 CLE	15 NYY	16 NYY	17 NYY
18 NYY	19 CLE	20 CLE	21 CLE	22 CLE	23 NYY	24 NYY
25 NYY	26	27 MIN	28 MIN	29 MIN	30 BOS	

July
SUN	MON	TUE	WED	THU	FRI	SAT
						1 BOS
2 BOS	3 KC	4 KC	5 KC	6	7 CUB	8 CUB
9 CUB	10	11	* 12	13 STL	14 STL	15 STL
16 MIL	17 MIL	18 MIL	19 MIN	20 MIN	21 BOS	22 BOS
23 BOS	24 KC	25 KC	26 KC	27 ANA	28 ANA	29 ANA
30 ANA	31					

August
SUN	MON	TUE	WED	THU	FRI	SAT
		1 TEX	2 TEX	3	4 OAK	5 OAK
6 OAK	7	8 SEA	9 SEA	10 SEA	11 TB	12 TB
13 TB	14 BAL	15 BAL	16 BAL	17 BAL	18 TB	19 TB
20 TB	21 BAL	22	23 BAL	24 BAL	25 SEA	26 SEA
27 SEA	28 OAK	29 OAK	30 OAK	31		

September
SUN	MON	TUE	WED	THU	FRI	SAT
					1 ANA	2 ANA
3 ANA	4 TEX	5 TEX	6 TEX	7 TEX	8 CLE	9 CLE
10 CLE	11 DET	12 DET	13 DET	14	15 TOR	16 TOR
17 TOR	18 DET	19 DET	20 DET	21 MIN	22 MIN	23 MIN
24 MIN	25	26 BOS	27 BOS	28 BOS	29 KC	30 KC

October
SUN	MON	TUE	WED	THU	FRI	SAT
1 KC	2	3	4	5	6	7

FRONT-OFFICE DIRECTORY

Chairman..Jerry Reinsdorf
Vice chairman ....Eddie Einhorn
Executive vice president ....Howard Pizer
Senior vice president, major league operations ....Ron Schueler
Senior vice president, marketing and broadcasting ....Rob Gallas
Senior vice president, baseball ....Jack Gould
Vice president, administration and finance ....Tim Buzard
Vice president, stadium operations ....Terry Savarise
Vice president, free agent and major league scouting ....Larry Monroe
Vice president, player development...................Ken Williams
Director of baseball operations/assistant G.M. ....Dan Evans
Special assistants to Ron Schueler ....Ed Brinkman, Dave Yoakum
Special assignment...................................Mike Pazik
Director of scouting.................................Duane Shaffer
Director of minor league instruction ....Jim Snyder
Manager of team travel ....Ed Cassin
Assistant director, minor league/scouting administration ....Grace Guerrero Zwit
Assistant director, scouting and minor league operations ....Daniel Fabian
Director of broadcasting and marketing ....Bob Grim
Director of community relations ....Christine Makowski
Director of sales...................................Jim Muno
Director of ticket operations ....Bob DeVoy
Director of management information services ....Don Brown
Director of human resources ....Moira Foy
Controller ....Bill Waters
Director of public relations...........................Scott Reifert

MINOR LEAGUE AFFILIATES

Class	Team	League	Manager
AAA	Charlotte	International	Nick Leyva
AA	Birmingham	Southern	Nick Capra
A	Burlington	Midwest	To be announced
A	Winston-Salem	Carolina	Jerry Terrell
Rookie	Bristol	Appalachian	R.J. Reynolds
Rookie	Tucson	Arizona	Jerry Hairston

BROADCAST INFORMATION

Radio: ESPN-AM (1000).
TV: WGN-TV (Channel 9).
Cable TV: Fox Sports Chicago.

SPRING TRAINING

Ballpark (city): Tucson Electric Park (Tucson, Ariz.).
Ticket information: 888-683-3900.

ASSISTANCE STAFF

Trainers
Herm Schneider
Mark Anderson

Director of conditioning
Steve Odgers

Team physicians
Dr. James Boscardin, Dr. Hugo Cuadros,
Dr. Bernard Feldman, Dr. David Orth,
Dr. Scott Price, Dr. Lowell Scott Weil

Scouting national cross-checker
Doug Laumann

Scouting supervisors
Bob Fontaine, Ed Pebley, Ken Stauffer

Professional scouts
George Bradley | Gary Pellant

Full-time scouts
Joe Butler	Hernan Cortes
Alex Cosmidis	Nathan Durst
Roberto Espinoza	Denny Gonzalez
Larry Grefer	Warren Hughes
Miguel Ibarra	George Kachigian
John Kazanas	Jose Ortega
Paul Provas	Mark Salas
Michael Sgobba	John Tumminia

Part-time scouts
Darell Brown	Tommy Butler
Javier Ceteno	Curt Daniels
Mike Davenport	Mariano DeLeon
John Doldoorian	James Ellison
Matt Hattabaugh	Joe Ingalls
Jack Jolly	Robert Jones
Dario Lodigiani	Don Metzger
Glenn Murdock	Paul Murphy
Al Otto	Mike Paris
Jose Ponce	Wuarnner Rincones
Tony Rodriguez	Joe Rudi
Oswaldo Salazar	Alex Slattery
Keith Staab	Fermin Urbi

BALLPARK INFORMATION

Ballpark (capacity, surface)
Comiskey Park (44,321, grass)
Address
333 W. 35th St.
Chicago, IL 60616
Business phone
312-674-1000
Ticket information
312-674-1000
Ticket prices
$22 (lower deck box, club level)
$17 (lower deck reserved)
$15 (upper deck box)
$14 (bleacher reserved)
$10 (upper deck reserved)
Field dimensions (from home plate)
To left field at foul line, 347 feet
To center field, 400 feet
To right field at foul line, 347 feet
First game played
April 18, 1991 (Tigers 16, White Sox 0)

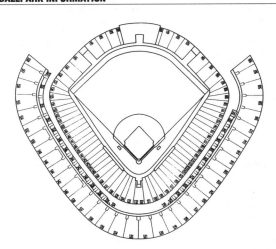

No.	PITCHERS	B/T	Ht./Wt.	Born	1999 clubs	Projection
37	Baldwin, James	R/R	6-3/235	7-15-71	Chicago A.L.	So far, he's been a disappointing talent but will still notch double digits in wins.
	Barcelo, Lorenzo	R/R	6-4/220	8-10-77	Ariz. White Sox, Burl., Birm.	Barcelo endured an arm injury in 1998 and will need more time in the minors.
57	Beirne, Kevin	L/R	6-4/210	1-1-74	Charlotte	Former Texas A&M football player has yet to cash in on potential, but still may.
44	Bradford, Chad	R/R	6-5/205	9-14-74	Charlotte, Chicago A.L.	Sidearm thrower has good control and closer potential. Will set up in 2000.
43	Castillo, Carlos	R/R	6-2/250	4-21-75	Charlotte, Chicago A.L.	Has the stuff to be a good swingman, but weight and ego hold him back.
51	Daneker, Pat	R/R	6-3/195	1-14-76	Charlotte, Chicago A.L., Birm.	Excellent control will get him to the big leagues eventually.
60	Davenport, Joe	R/R	6-5/225	3-24-76	Birm., Chicago A.L., Charlotte	Future is in short relief. Will pitch in the high minors and be called up as needed.
21	Eldred, Cal	R/R	6-4/237	11-24-67	Huntsville, Louisville, Milw.	A big disappointment the last few seasons, he'll try to win a spot in the rotation.
36	Eyre, Scott	L/L	6-1/200	5-30-72	Charlotte, Chicago A.L.	Former starter was brought along too quickly. Has to regain confidence.
29	Foulke, Keith	R/R	6-0/200	10-19-72	Chicago A.L.	Excellent slider has made him one of the A.L.'s best relievers.
46	Howry, Bob	L/R	6-5/220	8-4-73	Chicago A.L.	Hard slider and harder fastball have made him an ideal closer.
50	Lowe, Sean	R/R	6-2/205	3-29-71	Chicago A.L.	Appears to have worked out control problems. Will be a good long reliever.
62	Myette, Aaron	R/R	6-4/195	9-26-77	Birmingham, Chicago A.L.	Will get a chance to jump into the rotation from Class AA. Might not be ready.
40	Parque, Jim	L/L	5-11/165	2-8-76	Chicago A.L.	Lost nine straight decisions to end last year. Must avoid that dead-arm phase.
61	Pena, Jesus	L/L	6-0/170	3-8-75	Birmingham, Chicago A.L.	Could earn a bullpen slot with a strong spring, but will likely begin in the minors.
41	Simas, Bill	L/R	6-3/235	11-28-71	Chicago A.L.	Senior member of the staff has a tough fastball-slider combo.
33	Sirotka, Mike	L/L	6-1/200	5-13-71	Chicago A.L.	Will be the team's ace. Hard luck kept him from being a 15-game winner lin 1999.
47	Sturtze, Tanyon	R/R	6-5/205	10-12-70	Charlotte, Chicago A.L.	Ten-year minor league veteran earned a chance at the big leagues in 1999.
32	Wells, Kip	R/R	6-3/196	4-21-77	Win.-Salem, Birm., Chicago A.L.	Phenom has one of the team's best arms but has to hold up for an entire season.

No.	CATCHERS	B/T	Ht./Wt.	Born	1999 clubs	Projection
8	Fordyce, Brook	R/R	6-0/190	5-7-70	Chicago A.L.	Should hit about .250 in first opportunity to be a full-time starter.
10	Johnson, Mark	L/R	6-0/185	9-12-75	Chicago A.L.	Good backup. Makes up for lack of hitting ability by drawing walks.
15	Paul, Josh	R/R	6-1/185	5-19-75	Birmingham, Chicago A.L.	Pretty good athlete who will either be the third catcher or get work at Class AAA.

No.	INFIELDERS	B/T	Ht./Wt.	Born	1999 clubs	Projection
17	Caruso, Mike	L/R	6-0/172	5-27-77	Chicago A.L.	With Dellaero coming up, may have a limited time to prove himself.
21	Crede, Joe	R/R	6-3/195	4-26-78	Birmingham	With third base a void in the organization, Crede could be in Chicago by July.
34	Dellaero, Jason	B/R	6-2/195	12-17-76	Win.-Salem, Birm., Chicago A.L.	Could oust Caruso, but needs time to develop defense and patience at the plate.
5	Durham, Ray	B/R	5-8/180	11-30-71	Chicago A.L.	He's a top-notch leadoff hitter. Can hit .290 with 110 runs and 30 stolen bases.
14	Konerko, Paul	R/R	6-3/211	3-5-76	Chicago A.L.	Now that he's settled in Chicago, he will improve on last year's fine numbers.
39	Liefer, Jeff	L/R	6-3/195	8-17-74	Chicago A.L., Charlotte	Team wants his bat in the lineup, but has no spots. Might return to 3B.
31	Norton, Greg	B/R	6-1/205	7-6-72	Chicago A.L.	Struggled with the bat and the glove. Will keep the hot corner warm for Crede.
2	Valentin, Jose	B/R	5-10/173	10-12-69	Milwaukee, Louisville	He was obtained as a backup, but might be a starter very soon.
28	Wilson, Craig	R/R	6-0/185	9-3-70	Chicago A.L.	Can play seven positions and hits well enough to be an ideal utility man.

No.	OUTFIELDERS	B/T	Ht./Wt.	Born	1999 clubs	Projection
25	Abbott, Jeff	R/L	6-2/200	8-17-72	Chicago A.L., Charlotte	Has hit .340 in 423 minor league games, but there seems to be no room for him.
26	Christensen, McKay	L/L	5-11/180	8-14-75	Chicago A.L., Birm., Charlotte	Failed in last year's big-league tryout, but will get another shot.
45	Lee, Carlos	R/R	6-2/220	6-20-76	Charlotte, Chicago A.L.	Best hitter in the team's system should start and hit in the middle of the order.
30	Ordoñez, Magglio	R/R	6-0/200	1-28-74	Chicago A.L.	He has hit for average and power, and will hit cleanup and collect 100 RBIs.
27	Simmons, Brian	B/R	6-2/190	9-4-73	Chicago A.L., Charlotte	Another of the team's good young outfielders, but not good enough to start yet.
12	Singleton, Chris	L/L	6-2/195	8-15-72	Chicago A.L.	Will bat No. 2 in the lineup. Makes good contact and has power and speed.

No.	DESIGNATED HITTERS	B/T	Ht./Wt.	Born	1999 clubs	Projection
35	Thomas, Frank	R/R	6-5/270	5-27-68	Chicago A.L.	Had surgery on his foot, but that might not solve his drop in production.

THE COACHING STAFF

Jerry Manuel, manager: Manuel is a no-nonsense type, aggressive on the basepaths and quick with the hook on a struggling pitcher. He is slowly molding the team in his own image—he wants tough, young, aggressive players. He stood up to team icon Frank Thomas last season, showing he is in control. His team is still young and imexperienced, but Manuel has a core group to develop into a contender and the team seems confident that he can do it.

Nardi Contreras: This will be the second full season for Contreras as the White Sox pitching coach. He was reunited with White Sox manager Jerry Manuel in May of 1998. He had served as a pitching coach with Manuel in the Expos organization in 1990 and 1991.

Wallace Johnson: Beginning his third season as the White Sox third base coach, Wallace is noted for his aggressive style while directing Sox baserunners. He also is responsible for supervising White Sox outfielders.

Von Joshua: Joshua enters his second full season as the team's hitting coach and has been in the organization since 1993. He worked with several of the club's young hitters while in the minor leagues, including Jeff Abbott, Greg Norton and Magglio Ordoñez.

Art Kusnyer: Intelligent baseball man is in his fourth season as the White Sox bullpen coach. He held the same position from 1980-87 under three White Sox managers.

Bryan Little: This will be Little's third full season as the team's first base coach. He served five seasons (1993-97) as a roving instructor in the White Sox minor league system and managed for three seasons in the Padres system.

Joe Nossek: Few minds in the game are as acute as that of Nossek, who has been the bench coach for 10 years, serving with four managers. A master at the little things, like aligning the defense and stealing signs. He has 30 years of baseball experience as a player, minor-league manager and major-league coach.

THE TOP NEWCOMERS

Cal Eldred: He showed a lot of promise early in his career and has the will to win his starts. But arm injuries and D.L. time have cut his starts and his fastball down a notch or two. Hopes to simply get a second chance to win 16 games again.

Jose Valentin: Can play shortstop and third base and will backup at both of those positions unless there's ineffectiveness or injuries. The little guy has power but strikes out a lot.

THE TOP PROSPECTS

Joe Crede: He could be the third baseman for a long time at Comiskey even though he struggled a bit last season. He'll begin the season in the minors, but he'll be back by the All-Star break.

Jason Dellaero: First-round pick in 1997 got off to a slow start in 1998 and did the same in 1999. But he improved after getting promoted to Class AA Birmingham last year. If he works on striking out less, he could be the team's shortstop by the end of the season.

Carlos Lee: Probably the team's best prospect. He hit well early in the season but tailed off in September. Still, he finished at .293 and the team expects him to be a run-producer in his first full major league season.

Aaron Myette: Was 12-7 with a 3.66 ERA and 135 strikeouts in 164.2 innings at Class AA Birmingham. He'll have a shot at the No. 5 spot in the rotation.

Kip Wells: Made only one bad start in seven outings last year. He has the ability to be the team's best starter, but he's only 22, so there is some question as to whether he can handle such a role.

CLEVELAND INDIANS

AMERICAN LEAGUE CENTRAL DIVISION

2000 SEASON

2000 Indians Schedule
Home games shaded. *—All-Star Game at Turner Field (Atlanta).

March
SUN	MON	TUE	WED	THU	FRI	SAT
26	27	28	29	30	31	

April
SUN	MON	TUE	WED	THU	FRI	SAT
						1
2	3 BAL	4	5 BAL	6 BAL	7 TB	8 TB
9 TB	10 OAK	11 OAK	12 OAK	13	14 TEX	15 TEX
16 TEX	17	18 OAK	19 OAK	20 OAK	21 BOS	22 BOS
23 BOS	24 SEA	25 SEA	26 SEA	27	28 BOS	29 BOS
30 BOS						

May
SUN	MON	TUE	WED	THU	FRI	SAT
	1 NYY	2 NYY	3 NYY	4 TOR	5 TOR	6 TOR
7 TOR	8 MIN	9 MIN	10 MIN	11 KC	12 KC	13 KC
14 KC	15	16 DET	17 DET	18 DET	19 NYY	20 NYY
21 NYY	22	23 DET	24 DET	25 DET	26 CWS	27 CWS
28 CWS	29 ANA	30 ANA	31 ANA			

June
SUN	MON	TUE	WED	THU	FRI	SAT
				1	2 STL	3 STL
4 STL	5 MIL	6 MIL	7 MIL	8	9 CIN	10 CIN
11 CIN	12 CWS	13 CWS	14 CWS	15	16 DET	17 DET
18 DET	19 CWS	20 CWS	21 CWS	22 CWS	23 DET	24 DET
25 DET	26 DET	27 KC	28 KC	29 KC	30 MIN	

July
SUN	MON	TUE	WED	THU	FRI	SAT
						1 MIN
2 MIN	3	4 TOR	5 TOR	6 TOR	7 CIN	8 CIN
9 CIN	10	11 *	12	13 PIT	14 PIT	15 PIT
16 HOU	17 HOU	18 HOU	19 KC	20 KC	21 MIN	22 MIN
23 MIN	24	25 TOR	26 TOR	27	28 BAL	29 BAL
30 BAL	31					

August
SUN	MON	TUE	WED	THU	FRI	SAT
		1 TB	2 TB	3 TB	4 ANA	5 ANA
6 ANA	7 TEX	8 TEX	9 TEX	10	11 SEA	12 SEA
13 SEA	14 OAK	15 OAK	16 OAK	17	18 SEA	19 SEA
20 SEA	21	22 OAK	23 OAK	24 OAK	25 ANA	26 ANA
27 ANA	28 TEX	29 TEX	30 TEX	31 TEX		

September
SUN	MON	TUE	WED	THU	FRI	SAT
					1 BAL	2 BAL
3 BAL	4 TB	5 TB	6 TB	7 TB	8 CWS	9 CWS
10 CWS	11	12 BOS	13 BOS	14 BOS	15 NYY	16 NYY
17 NYY	18 NYY	19 BOS	20 BOS	21 BOS	22 KC	23 KC
24 KC	25 MIN	26 MIN	27 MIN	28 MIN	29 TOR	30 TOR

October
SUN	MON	TUE	WED	THU	FRI	SAT
1 TOR	2	3	4	5	6	7

FRONT-OFFICE DIRECTORY

Owner/CEO/chairman of the board ....Richard E. Jacobs
Executive vice president, general manager...John Hart
Executive vice president, business ....Dennis Lehman
Vice president of baseball operations/assistant general manager.................Mark Shapiro
Director, player development ....Neal Huntington
Director, scouting ....John Mirabelli
Vice president, public relations ....Bob DiBiasio
Vice president, marketing and communications...Jeff Overton
Vice president, finance ....Ken Stefanov
Director, media relations...Bart Swain
Manager, media relations, administrations & credentials ....Susie Giuliano
Coordinator, media relations ....Curtis Danburg
Director of team travel ....Mike Seghi
Special assistant to general manager for major league scouting.................Tom Giordano

MINOR LEAGUE AFFILIATES

Class	Team	League	Manager
AAA	Buffalo	International	Joel Skinner
AA	Akron	Eastern	Eric Wedge
A	Kinston	Carolina	Brad Komminsk
A	Columbus	South Atlantic	Ricky Gutierrez
A	Mahoning Valley	New York-Pennsylvania	Ted Kubiak
Rookie	Burlington	Appalachian	Dave Turgeon

BROADCAST INFORMATION
Radio: WTAM (1100 AM).
TV: WUAB-TV (Channel 43).
Cable TV: Fox Sports Ohio.

SPRING TRAINING
Ballpark (city): Chain O'Lakes (Winter Haven, Fla.).
Ticket information: 941-293-3900.

ASSISTANCE STAFF

Head trainer
Paul Spicuzza

Assistant trainer
Jim Warfield

Clubhouse manager
Ted Walsh

Visiting clubhouse
Cy Buynak

Groundskeeper
Brandon Koehnke

Nat. cross-checker, West Coast supervisor
Jesse Flores

Nat. cross-checker, East Coast supervisor
Jerry Jordan

Midwest supervisor
Bob Mayer

Full-time scouts
Steve Abney	Scott Anderson
Doug Baker	Keith Boeck
Jim Bretz	Paul Cogan
Henry Cruz	Dan Durst
Jim Gabella	Rene Gayo
Mark Germann	Chris Jefts
Tim Kissner	Chad McDonald
Dave Miller	Chuck Ricci
Bill Schudlich	

BALLPARK INFORMATION

Ballpark (capacity, surface)
Jacobs Field (43,863, grass)
Address
2401 Ontario St.
Cleveland, OH 44115
Business phone
216-420-4200
Ticket information
216-241-8888
Ticket prices
$35 (field box)
$32 (club seating)
$24 (lower box & view box)
$19 (lower reserved, upper box & mezzanine)
$16 (bleachers)
$12 (upper reserved)
$7 (reserved general admission)
$6 (Standing room only)
Field dimensions (from home plate)
To left field at foul line, 325 feet
To center field, 405 feet
To right field at foul line, 325 feet
First game played
April 4, 1994 (Indians 4, Mariners 3, 11 innings)

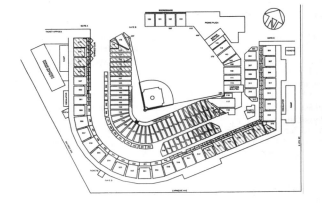

2000 PREVIEW

No.	PITCHERS	B/T	Ht./Wt.	Born	1999 clubs	Projection
	Baez, Danys	R/R	6-4/225	9-10-77	Played in Cuba	This big righthander signed in November—he's an outstanding talent from Cuba.
64	Brammer, J.D.	R/R	6-4/235	1-30-75	Akron	This 1996 draft pick will stay in the minors at least another year.
50	Brower, Jim	R/R	6-2/205	12-29-72	Buffalo, Cleveland	He opened eyes in a September call-up and should make the team in long relief.
34	Burba, Dave	R/R	6-4/240	7-7-66	Cleveland	A workhorse who can give his manager innings and victories.
40	Colon, Bartolo	R/R	6-0/225	5-24-75	Cleveland	Durable fireballer could become the team's ace with continued maturity.
56	DePaula, Sean	R/R	6-4/215	11-7-73	Kinston, Akron, Buffalo, Cle.	Came out of nowhere to be one of the team's few effective playoff relievers .
31	Finley, Chuck	L/L	6-6/226	11-26-62	Anaheim	Long sought-after free agent was signed for one reason: He's a Yankees killer.
	Kamieniecki, Scott	R/R	6-0/200	4-19-64	Bowie, Frederick, Balt., Roch.	He's been battling injuries. When healthy, he's an effective reliever/spot starter.
20	Karsay, Steve	R/R	6-3/205	3-24-72	Cleveland	A fireballer who can come in in long relief or be a spot starter.
36	Martin, Tom	L/L	6-1/200	5-21-70	Akron, Cleveland, Buffalo	He could work in relief, but must prove injury problems are behind him.
71	Martinez, Willie	R/R	6-2/185	1-4-78	Akron, Buffalo	The best pitching prospect in Cleveland's system, he should stay in Class AAA.
41	Nagy, Charles	R/R	6-3/200	5-5-67	Cleveland	He allows hits and has a high ERA, but will still rack up wins with his determination.
39	Reed, Steve	R/R	6-2/212	3-11-66	Cleveland	Struggled with injuries last season. Allows a lot of hits, but is a solid setup man.
73	Rincon, Ricardo	L/L	5-10/187	4-13-70	Cleveland, Akron	He had a sore elbow last season, limiting his effectiveness. He's deadly vs. lefties.
54	Riske, Dave	R/R	6-2/175	10-23-76	Akron, Buffalo, Cleveland	A reliever with a good arsenal, he could earn a spot in the bullpen this spring.
53	Shuey, Paul	R/R	6-3/215	9-16-70	Cleveland, Buffalo	Inconsistent, injury-prone setup man with an outside shot at becoming the closer.
	Speier, Justin	R/R	6-4/205	11-6-73	Richmond, Atlanta	The son of Chris Speier has talent, but has struggled to earn a role in the bullpen.
	Vargas, Martin	R/R	6-0/155	2-22-78	Columbus, Kinston	Being groomed for bullpen work after being a starter his first few years in the minors.
27	Wright, Jaret	R/R	6-2/230	12-29-75	Cleveland, Buffalo, Akron	Team had hoped he'd become an ace. Now it hopes he can win a starting spot.

No.	CATCHERS	B/T	Ht./Wt.	Born	1999 clubs	Projection
15	Alomar, Sandy	R/R	6-5/215	6-18-66	Cleveland, Akron, Buffalo	Solid veteran backstop trying to make it through a full season without injuries.
2	Diaz, Einar	R/R	5-10/165	12-28-72	Cleveland	A good young backup who figures to see plenty of action.

No.	INFIELDERS	B/T	Ht./Wt.	Born	1999 clubs	Projection
12	Alomar, Roberto	B/R	6-0/185	2-5-68	Cleveland	Second baseman regained standing as one of the league's best all-around players.
66	Branyan, Russell	L/R	6-3/195	12-19-75	Buffalo, Cleveland	He puts up big power numbers but strikes out too much. Will start at Class AAA.
6	Cabrera, Jolbert	R/R	6-0/177	12-8-72	Cleveland, Buffalo	After nine years in the minors, he could win a utility job.
17	Fryman, Travis	R/R	6-1/195	3-25-69	Cleveland, Akron, Buffalo	Third baseman isn't spectacular in any category, but is solid in all.
72	McDonald, John	R/R	5-11/175	9-24-74	Akron, Buffalo, Cleveland	Good enough to play shortstop in the majors, but will settle for a backup role.
68	Peoples, Danny	R/R	6-1/225	1-20-75	Akron	This first baseman has great power and strikes out a lot—just like Thome.
44	Sexson, Richie	R/R	6-7/206	12-29-74	Cleveland	Backup first baseman/outfielder seeks a permanent spot to display his great power.
25	Thome, Jim	L/R	6-4/220	8-27-70	Cleveland	Decent fielder and one of the league's best-hitting first basemen.
13	Vizquel, Omar	B/R	5-9/175	4-24-67	Cleveland	Improved plate production to go with superb defense at shortstop.
35	Wilson, Enrique	B/R	5-11/160	7-27-75	Cleveland	The team's top utilityman will hit for a good average and steal some bases.

No.	OUTFIELDERS	B/T	Ht./Wt.	Born	1999 clubs	Projection
51	Cruz, Jacob	L/L	6-0/179	1-28-73	Cleveland, Buffalo	A smart hitter who could start in center field while Kenny Lofton recovers.
23	Justice, David	L/L	6-3/200	4-14-66	Cleveland	A solid offensive player who will see time in left field and at DH.
7	Lofton, Kenny	L/L	6-0/180	5-31-67	Cleveland	Still a solid leadoff hitter and great in center but must return from shoulder surgery.
62	Morgan, Scott	R/R	6-7/230	7-19-73	Akron, Buffalo	He has good power numbers but probably will get another season at Class AAA.
61	Ramirez, Alex	R/R	5-11/176	10-3-74	Buffalo, Cleveland	A backup who could see more action if Lofton is on the D.L. for long.
24	Ramirez, Manny	R/R	6-0/205	5-30-72	Cleveland	He is the most feared cleanup hitter in baseball and is protected well in the lineup.
52	Roberts, Dave	L/L	5-10/175	5-31-72	Buffalo, Cleveland	He has excellent speed and could start and lead off while Lofton heals.

THE COACHING STAFF

Charlie Manuel, manager: Manuel is in his first year as manager after spending six seasons as the Indians' hitting coach. Under his instruction, the 1999 Indians scored a franchise-record and major league-best 1,009 runs, becoming the first team since the 1950 Red Sox to eclipse 1,000 runs. From 1990-93, Manuel managed the Indians' Class AAA affiliates at Colorado Springs and Charlotte. In 1992, he was named the Pacific Coast League Manager of the Year. Prior to joining the Indians he was with the Twins organization for six years.

Luis Isaac: He has been a player, coach, manager and scout in the Indians' organization since 1965. He returns for his seventh season as bullpen coach.

Clarence Jones: Jones is in his second season, his first as a hitting coach, on Cleveland's major league coaching staff after being named outfield coach last season. He had a lot of success as the hitting coach for the Braves for much of the '90s.

Grady Little: He is in his first season as the team's bench coach and will also instruct the club's catchers. He spent the previous three seasons as bench coach in Boston.

Dick Pole: After spending last season with the Angels and guiding them to the fifth-best ERA in the A.L., Pole will be in his first season as the Indians' pitching coach. He hopes to have similar success with the pleasant mix of young and old Cleveland starters.

Jim Riggleman: Riggleman managed the Cubs for five seasons from 1995-99 and compiled a record of 374-419. He comes to the Indians as a bench coach and has aspirations of becoming a manager again.

Ted Uhlaender: Uhlaender is in his first season as the team's baserunning and outfield coach after spending the last two seasons with the Giants as a special assistant in player personnel.

Dan Williams: Williams is in his fifth full season on the major league coaching staff. His duties include catching starting and relief pitchers in the bullpen, throwing batting practice and hitting fungoes.

THE TOP NEWCOMERS

Chuck Finley: Finley is near the end of his career, but he finally gives the Tribe a lefthanded ace who consistently beats the playoff-nemesis Yankees. The Indians gave the 37-year-old a lot of money and he shouldn't disappoint. He is durable, tough in the big games and still has nasty stuff.

Scott Kamieniecki: When healthy, he's a spot starter and innings-eater out of the bullpen. Doesn't have outstanding stuff but throws smart pitches.

THE TOP PROSPECTS

Russell Branyan: A power-hitting third baseman who, if he cuts down on his strikeouts, could push Travis Fryman. He is the Indians' third baseman of the not-too-distant future.

Alex Ramirez: A serious power threat who will be a backup in the outfield, and could even start in center if Kenny Lofton starts the season on the D.L.

Enrique Wilson: He is a very good defensive player and even showed some life in his bat, but, stuck behind Roberto Alomar and Omar Vizquel, all Wilson can do is settle for a utility job. He's a potential .300 hitter if given a shot to play everyday and would start on most teams.

DETROIT TIGERS
AMERICAN LEAGUE CENTRAL DIVISION

2000 SEASON

2000 Tigers Schedule
Home games shaded. *—All-Star Game at Turner Field (Atlanta).

March
SUN	MON	TUE	WED	THU	FRI	SAT
26	27	28	29	30	31	

April
SUN	MON	TUE	WED	THU	FRI	SAT
						1
2	3 OAK	4 OAK	5 OAK	6	7 BAL	8 BAL
9 BAL	10	11 SEA	12 SEA	13 SEA	14 TB	15 TB
16 TB	17	18 BOS	19 BOS	20 BOS	21 CWS	22 CWS
23 CWS	24 ANA	25 ANA	26 ANA	27	28 CWS	29 CWS
30 CWS						

May
SUN	MON	TUE	WED	THU	FRI	SAT
	1 BOS	2 BOS	3 BOS	4 MIN	5 MIN	6 MIN
7 MIN	8 KC	9 KC	10 KC	11	12 NYY	13 NYY
14 NYY	15	16 CLE	17 CLE	18 CLE	19 BOS	20 BOS
21 BOS	22	23 CLE	24 CLE	25 CLE	26 TOR	27 TOR
28 TOR	29 TEX	30 TEX	31 TEX			

June
SUN	MON	TUE	WED	THU	FRI	SAT
				1	2 CUB	3 CUB
4 CUB	5 PIT	6 PIT	7 PIT	8	9 STL	10 STL
11 STL	12 TOR	13 TOR	14 TOR	15	16 CLE	17 CLE
18 CLE	19	20 TOR	21 TOR	22 TOR	23 CLE	24 CLE
25 CLE	26 CLE	27 NYY	28 NYY	29 NYY	30 KC	

July
SUN	MON	TUE	WED	THU	FRI	SAT
						1 KC
2 KC	3 TB	4 TB	5 TB	6	7 MIL	8 MIL
9 MIL	10	11 *	12	13 HOU	14 HOU	15 HOU
16 CIN	17 CIN	18 CIN	19 NYY	20 NYY	21 KC	22 KC
23 KC	24 TB	25 TB	26 TB	27 TEX	28 TEX	29 TEX
30 TEX	31 ANA					

August
SUN	MON	TUE	WED	THU	FRI	SAT
		1 ANA	2 ANA	3	4 MIN	5 MIN
6 MIN	7 BAL	8 BAL	9 BAL	10 BAL	11 OAK	12 OAK
13 OAK	14 SEA	15 SEA	16 SEA	17	18 MIN	19 MIN
20 OAK	21 SEA	22 SEA	23 SEA	24 SEA	25 MIN	26 MIN
27 MIN	28	29 BAL	30 BAL	31 BAL		

September
SUN	MON	TUE	WED	THU	FRI	SAT
					1 TEX	2 TEX
3 TEX	4 ANA	5 ANA	6 ANA	7 ANA	8 TOR	9 TOR
10 TOR	11 CWS	12 CWS	13 CWS	14	15 BOS	16 BOS
17 BOS	18 CWS	19 CWS	20 CWS	21	22 NYY	23 NYY
24 NYY	25 NYY	26 KC	27 KC	28 KC	29 MIN	30 MIN

October
SUN	MON	TUE	WED	THU	FRI	SAT
1 MIN	2	3	4	5	6	7

FRONT-OFFICE DIRECTORY
Owner ....Michael Illitch
President, chief executive officer ....John McHale Jr.
Vice president, baseball operations/general manager ....Randy Smith
Vice president, business operations ....David H. Glazier
Assistant general manager ....Steve Lubratich
Assistants to baseball operations ....Ricky Bennett, Hiroshi Yoshimura
Assistant baseball operations, foreign affairs ....Ramon Pena
Special assistants to the general manager ....Al Hargesheimer, Randy Johnson
Director of scouting ....Greg Smith
Latin American liason ....Luis Mayoral
Director minor league operations ....Dave Miller
Traveling secretary ....Bill Brown
Director of public relations ....Tyler Barnes
Assistant director of public relations ....David Matheson
Manager, community relations ....Celia Bobrowsky
Coordinator, community relations ....Fred Feliciano
Coordinator, public relations ....Giovanni Loria
Coordinator, public relations ....Melanie Waters
Coordinator, community relations ....Masico Brown
Marketing manager ....Ellen Hill
Director of park operations ....Tom Folk
Special assistant to the president ....Gary Vitto
Director of corporate sales ....Dan Sinagoga
Director of finance ....Jennifer Marosso
Director of ticket services ....Ken Marchetti
Director of ticket sales ....Barry Gibson
Director of merchandise ....Kayla French

MINOR LEAGUE AFFILIATES
Class	Team	League	Manager
AAA	Toledo	International	Dave Anderson
AA	Jacksonville	Southern	Gene Roof
A	Lakeland	Florida State	Skeeter Barnes
A	West Michigan	Midwest	Bruce Fields
A	Oneonta	To be announced	Kevin Bradshaw
Rookie	Gulf Coast Tigers	Gulf Coast	Gary Green

BROADCAST INFORMATION
Radio: WJR-AM (760).
TV: WKBD (Channel 50).
Cable TV: Fox Sports Detroit.

SPRING TRAINING
Ballpark (city): Marchant Stadium (Lakeland, Fla.).
Ticket information: 941-603-6278 or 941-603-6279.

ASSISTANCE STAFF
Medical director/head trainer
Russ Miller

Assistant trainer
Steve Carter

Strength and conditioning coach
Denny Taft

Manager, home clubhouse
Jim Schmakel

Assistant manager, visiting clubhouse
John Nelson

Team physicians
David J. Collon M.D., Terry Lock M.D.
Louis Saco M.D., Michael Workings M.D.

Scouts
Scott Bream	Bill Buck
Jerome Cochran	Tim Grieve
Rob Guzik	Jack Hays
Mike Herbert	Joe Hodges
Lou Laslo	Dennis Lieberthal
Jeff Malinoff	Mark Monahan
Pat Murtaugh	Steve Nichols
Jim Olander	Frank Paine
Derrick Ross	Mike Stafford
Steve Taylor	Clyde Weir
Jeff Wetherby	Rob Wilfong
Ellis Williams	Steve Williams
Gary York	Harold Zonder

BALLPARK INFORMATION
Ballpark (capacity, surface)
Comerica Park (40,000)
Address
2100 Woodward
Detroit, MI 48201
Business phone
313-962-4000
Ticket information
313-471-BALL
Ticket prices
$30 and $25 (box seats)
$20, $15, $14 and $12 (reserved seats)
$8 (Fan stands)
Field dimensions (from home plate)
To left field at foul line, 345 feet
To center field, 420 feet
To right field at foul line, 330 feet
First game played
Scheduled for April 11, 2000 vs. Mariners

No.	PITCHERS	B/T	Ht./Wt.	Born	1999 clubs	Projection
14	Anderson, Matt	R/R	6-4/200	8-17-76	Detroit, Toledo	The flame thrower will win a middle relief job if he eliminates control problems.
20	Blair, Willie	R/R	6-1/185	12-18-65	Detroit	After a tough '99 season, the former 16-game winner is best suited for long relief.
45	Borkowski, Dave	R/R	6-1/200	2-7-77	Toledo, Detroit	After being promoted last season, he'll compete for the No. 5 spot in the rotation.
26	Brocail, Doug	L/R	6-5/235	5-16-67	Detroit	He has become the team's most reliable reliever and will protect late-inning leads.
50	Greisinger, Seth	R/R	6-3/200	7-29-75	Lakeland, Toledo	After missing last season because of elbow surgery, he has at the rotation.
	Heams, Shane	R/R	6-1/175	9-29-75	West Michigan	Converted outfielder has strikeout ability (101 in 68 innings in Class A) in 1999.
35	Hiljus, Erik	R/R	6-5/230	12-25-72	Lakeland, Jacks., Toledo, Det.	Has nasty stuff. Struck out 111 batters in 89 1/3 total innings in 1999.
	Johnson, Mark	R/R	6-3/226	5-2-75	Norwich, GC Yankees, Tampa	He was 9-3 for the Yankees' Class AA squad and will fight for a rotation spot.
59	Jones, Todd	L/R	6-3/230	4-24-68	Detroit	Doesn't have dominating stuff, but the closer consistently records 30 saves a year.
	Keller, Kris	R/R	6-2/225	3-1-78	West Michigan	Had a lot of success as the setup man/closer in the Midwest League in 1999.
41	Kida, Masao	R/R	6-2/210	9-12-68	Detroit, Toledo	The Japanese hurler still has a lot to learn in the States after success in Japan.
30	Mlicki, Dave	R/R	6-4/205	6-8-68	Los Angeles, Detroit	The team's ace finished strong last season (14-13) and should carry that over.
38	Moehler, Brian	R/R	6-3/235	12-31-71	Detroit	The No. 2 starter doesn't have great stuff but is a true inning-eater and winner.
49	Nitkowski, C.J.	L/L	6-3/205	3-9-73	Detroit	After converting to a starter in '99, he should be the team's No. 4 starter this year.
	Patterson, Danny	R/R	6-0/225	2-17-71	Texas, Oklahoma	This reliever came over in the Gonzalez trade and can be used in many facets.
	Roberts, Willis	R/R	6-3/175	6-19-75	Toledo, Detroit	Struggled with his control last season but can be used as a starter or reliever.
44	Runyan, Sean	L/L	6-3/210	6-21-74	Detroit, Toledo	Injuries plagued the reliever in '99. The Tigers are banking on him this season.
	Santos, Victor	R/R	6-3/175	10-2-76	Jacksonville	Led the Southern League in games started and strikeouts and is a legit prospect.
	Tatis, Ramon	L/L	6-3/205	2-5-73	Durham	Has great stuff but little control. Will be in the minors until he finds it.
	Villafuerte, Brandon	5-11/165	12-17-75	Portland, Jacksonville	This former 66th-round pick can either start games or relieve.
36	Weaver, Jeff	/	6-5/200	8-22-76	Detroit, Jacksonville	Tigers think he'll recover from his late-season struggles and secure a rotation spot.

No.	CATCHERS	B/T	Ht./Wt.	Born	1999 clubs	Projection
12	Ausmus, Brad	R/R	5-11/195	4-14-69	Detroit	The All-Star has a great arm, handles the staff well and is the perfect No. 2 hitter.
	Cardona, Javier	/	6-1/185	9-15-75	Jacksonville	Hit .309 with 26 homers and 92 RBIs in Class AA. Promotion to Toledo to come.
31	Fick, Robert	L/R	6-1/189	3-15-74	GC Tigers, W.Mich., Toledo,Det.	A shoulder injury hampers him, but his offense could get him some time at DH.
	Munson, Eric	L/R	6-3/220	10-3-77	Lakeland, West Michigan	The third pick overall in the 1999 draft is the team's future star, but not this year.
	Zaun, Gregg	B/R	5-10/190	4-14-71	Texas	The switch-hitting catcher was acquired in the Gonzalez trade for depth purposes.

No.	INFIELDERS	B/T	Ht./Wt.	Born	1999 clubs	Projection
25	Alvarez, Gabe	R/R	6-1/205	3-6-74	Toledo, Detroit	Because of his weak defense at third, he is a candidate to DH.
17	Clark, Tony	B/R	6-7/245	6-15-72	Detroit, Toledo	The first baseman's breakout year finally should arrive with Gonzalez behind him.
8	Cruz, Deivi	R/R	6-0/184	11-6-75	Detroit	Already strong defensively, a move down in the lineup should him offensively.
9	Easley, Damion	R/R	5-11/185	11-11-69	Detroit	Like Cruz, expect his numbers to improve as the offensive workload is taken away.
7	Palmer, Dean	R/R	6-1/210	12-27-68	Detroit	Quietly had another huge year. His numbers will improve with Gonzalez there.
	Santana, Pedro	R/R	5-11/160	9-21-76	Jacksonville	The speedy infielder needs to cut down his errors in the minors.
	Sasser, Rob	R/R	6-3/205	3-9-75	Tulsa, Jacksonville	The third baseman committed 35 errors last season and has to improve that.

No.	OUTFIELDERS	B/T	Ht./Wt.	Born	1999 clubs	Projection
34	Encarnacion, Juan	R/R	6-3/187	3-8-76	Detroit	The developing star assumes the center field job with Kapler gone.
24	Garcia, Karim	L/L	6-0/172	10-29-75	Detroit	Saw time in right field last season but failed to impress. Still has a great swing.
19	Gonzalez, Juan	R/R	6-3/220	10-16-69	Texas	Two-time MVP will handle right field and provide a big bat to the lineup.
4	Higginson, Bobby	L/R	5-11/195	8-18-70	Detroit	If he stays healthy/productive, he will play left field and bat third.
21	Jefferies, Gregg	B/R	5-10/185	8-1-67	Detroit, Toledo	Hit the D.L. three times last season and is relegated to a utility role this year.
29	Polonia, Luis	L/L	5-8/150	10-27-64	Toledo, Detroit	Tigers' leadoff man is best suited for left field but will handle the DH duties.
	Wakeland, Chris	L/L	6-0/185	6-15-74	Jacks., GC Tigers, Lakeland	He's been a consistent .300 hitter in the minors but won't get a chance in the bigs.

THE COACHING STAFF

Phil Garner, manager: Garner takes over for Larry Parrish as the manager of the upstart Tigers. He seemed to do very well in Milwaukee for what he had to work with. The team had to go in another direction, and he wasn't the man to do it. But he should be a positive force in Detroit. He's an outstanding tactician and motivator who churns the most out of his roster, especially from veteran players. He'll have to keep the veteran offense at top-notch level while slowly getting his rotation and shaky bullpen to battle for victories.

Bill Madlock: He'll take over as the team's new hitting coach. He certainly knows hitting well, he was a four-time N.L. batting champion and three-time N.L. All-Star during his 14-plus seasons from 1973-87. He has spent the past two seasons as a hitting coach in the minor leagues, most recently for Class AAA Buffalo in the Indians' organization.

Doug Mansolino: He's a veteran major and minor league coach and a former minor league manager who served as Garner's third base coach in 1998 and 1999. Prior to joining the Brewers organization, he managed Class A Capital City in the Mets chain after spending eight seasons with the White Sox, including five on the major league staff.

Bob Melvin: The former catcher has baseball savvy and strategy. He'll be the bench coach for the Tigers, a position he held with Garner and the Brewers last season. The prior two seasons, he was the Brewers' special assignment and professional scout.

Lance Parrish: The former Tiger catcher is a holdover from Larry Parrish's staff and will handle the third base coaching duties for his second season. Parrish, a fan favorite in Detroit for 10 big-league seasons, also relates very well with his players.

Juan Samuel : The former jack-of-all-trades major league joined Larry Parrish's staff last season as the first base coach with the additional job of instructing baserunners. He had 396 career steals and has a lot of tricks of the trade to share to the young players.

Dan Warthen: He began last season as the pitching coach for the Tigers' Class AAA Toledo squad, but was named to replace Rick Adair as the club's major league pitching coach on July 9. The Tigers are the third club for whom Warthen has served as major league pitching coach, also filling the capacity for the Padres and Mariners.

THE TOP NEWCOMERS

Juan Gonzalez: This was a risky acquisition considering Gonzalez is a free agent after this season, but he provides another big bat and run production. Plus he will put fans in the seats, all big needs for the Tigers as they open the beautiful Comerica Park. Just imagine the 4-5-6 potential of Gonzalez, Clark and Palmer. A.L. pitcher should shudder.

Danny Patterson: Very versatile out of the bullpen and was a key part of Texas' outstanding bullpen last season. He should carry over the team's success to Detroit.

Gregg Zaun: He's not spectacular offensively. He's not spectacular defensively. But he's adequate at both and the ideal backup catcher. His switch-hitting abilities have made him a popular backup for many teams the past few years.

THE TOP PROSPECTS

Shane Heams: Still learning how to become a pitcher after making the move from the outfield in 1996. So far getting by on his great arm.

Eric Munson The third pick overall in the 1999 draft didn't disappointment in his half-season in the minors. He clouted 14 homers and showed a lot of maturity in Class A. The Tigers likely will keep him in Class AA this year though he skills may be big-league ready.

KANSAS CITY ROYALS

AMERICAN LEAGUE CENTRAL DIVISION

2000 SEASON

2000 Royals Schedule

Home games shaded. *=All-Star Game at Turner Field (Atlanta).

March

SUN	MON	TUE	WED	THU	FRI	SAT
26	27	28	29	30	31	

April

SUN	MON	TUE	WED	THU	FRI	SAT
						1
2	3 TOR	4 TOR	5 TOR	6 TOR	7 MIN	8 MIN
9 MIN	10 MIN	11 BAL	12 BAL	13 BAL	14 NYY	15 NYY
16 NYY	17	18 MIN	19 MIN	20 MIN	21 SEA	22 SEA
23 SEA	24	25 TB	26 TB	27	28 SEA	29 SEA
30 SEA						

May

SUN	MON	TUE	WED	THU	FRI	SAT
	1 OAK	2 OAK	3 OAK	4	5 CWS	6 CWS
7 CWS	8 DET	9 DET	10 DET	11 CLE	12 CLE	13 CLE
14 CLE	15 OAK	16 OAK	17 OAK	18	19 ANA	20 ANA
21 ANA	22	23 TEX	24 TEX	25 TEX	26 ANA	27 ANA
28 ANA	29	30 BOS	31 BOS			

June

SUN	MON	TUE	WED	THU	FRI	SAT
				1 BOS	2 PIT	3 PIT
4 PIT	5 STL	6 STL	7 STL	8	9 PIT	10 PIT
11 PIT	12 SEA	13 SEA	14 SEA	15	16 OAK	17 OAK
18 OAK	19	20 ANA	21 ANA	22 ANA	23 OAK	24 OAK
25 OAK	26	27 CLE	28 CLE	29 CLE	30 DET	

July

SUN	MON	TUE	WED	THU	FRI	SAT
						1 DET
2 DET	3 CWS	4 CWS	5 CWS	6	7 HOU	8 HOU
9 HOU	10	11 *	12	13 MIL	14 MIL	15 MIL
16 CUB	17 CUB	18 CUB	19 CLE	20 CLE	21 DET	22 DET
23 DET	24 CWS	25 CWS	26 CWS	27 TB	28 TB	29 TB
30 TB	31					

August

SUN	MON	TUE	WED	THU	FRI	SAT
		1 NYY	2 NYY	3 NYY	4 BOS	5 BOS
6 BOS	7 TOR	8 TOR	9 TOR	10 TOR	11 BAL	12 BAL
13 BAL	14	15 MIN	16 MIN	17 MIN	18 BAL	19 BAL
20 BAL	21 BAL	22 TOR	23 TOR	24 BOS	25 BOS	26 BOS
27 BOS	28	29 MIN	30 MIN	31 TB		

September

SUN	MON	TUE	WED	THU	FRI	SAT
					1 TB	2 TB
3 TB	4 NYY	5 NYY	6 NYY	7 NYY	8 TEX	9 TEX
10 TEX	11 SEA	12 SEA	13 SEA	14 TEX	15 TEX	16 TEX
17 TEX	18	19 ANA	20 ANA	21 ANA	22 CLE	23 CLE
24 CLE	25	26 DET	27 DET	28 DET	29 CWS	30 CWS

October

SUN	MON	TUE	WED	THU	FRI	SAT
1 CWS	2	3	4	5	6	7

FRONT-OFFICE DIRECTORY

Board of directors ....David Glass, Richard Green, Mike Herman, Jolia I. Kauffman, Janice Kreamer, Joseph McGuff, Louis Smith
Chairman of the board and chief executive officer...David Glass
President ....Mike Herman
Executive vice president and general manager ....Herk Robinson
Senior vice president, business operations/administration ....Art Chaudry
Vice president and assistant general manager baseball operations ....Allard Baird
Vice president, baseball operations ....George Brett
Vice president, marketing and communications ....Mike Levy
Vice president, finance and information systems ....Dale Rohr
General counsel and assistant secretary ....Jay Newcom
Senior director, minor league operations..Bob Hegman
Senior director, scouting ....Terry Wetzel
Assistant general manager, baseball administration ....Muzzy Jackson
Senior special assistant to the general manager ....Art Stewart
Director, team travel ....Dave Witty
Minor league operations coordinator ....Shaun McGinn
Scouting operations coordinator ....Jin Wong
Senior director, operations and administration..Jay Hinrichs
Director, event ops and revenue development ....Chris Richardson
Director, stadium operations ....Rodney Lewallen
Director, ticket operations ....Christine Burgeson
Director, group sales ....Michele Kammerer
Director, Royal Lancer program ....Larry Sherrard
Director, season ticket services ....Joe Grigoli
Senior director/controller ....John Luther
Director, payroll and benefit accounting ....Tom Pfannenstiel
Director, information systems ....Jim Edwards
Director, marketing...Tonya Mangels
Publications/internet coordinator ....Chad Rader
Senior director, communications ....Jim Lachimia
Director, media relations ....Steve Fink
Manager, community relations and special markets ....Shani Tate
Media relations coordinator ....Chris Stathos
Director, corporate sponsorships ....Kevin Battle

MINOR LEAGUE AFFILIATES

Class	Team	League	Manager
AAA	Omaha	Pacific Coast	John Mizerock
AA	Wichita	Texas	Keith Bodie
A	Wilmington	Carolina	Jeff Garber
A	Charleston (WV)	South Atlantic	Joe Szekely
A	Spokane	Northwest	Tom Poquette
Rookie	Gulf Coast Royals	Gulf Coast	Ron Karkovice

BALLPARK INFORMATION

Ballpark (capacity, surface)
Kauffman Stadium (40,529, grass)

Address
P.O. Box 419969
Kansas City, MO 64141-6969

Business phone
816-921-8000

Ticket information
816-921-8000

Ticket prices
$17 (club box)
$15 (field box)
$13 (plaza reserved)
$12 (view upper box)
$11 (view upper reserved)
$7 (general admission)
$5.50 (Royal nights)

Field dimensions (from home plate)
To left field at foul line, 330 feet
To center field, 400 feet
To right field at foul line, 330 feet

First game played
April 10, 1973 (Royals 12, Rangers 1)

ASSISTANCE STAFF

Team physician
Dr. Steve Joyce

Athletic trainer
Nick Swartz

Assistant athletic trainer
Lee Kuntz

Strength and conditioning coordinator
Tim Maxey

Equipment manager
Mike Burkhalter

Visiting clubhouse manager
Chuck Hawke

Major League scout
Gail Henley

Advance scout
Ron Clark

Special assignment scout
John Wathan

National cross-checkers
Pat Jones, Jeff McKay, Earl Winn

Latin American scouting coordinator
Albert Gonzalez

Territorial scouts
Frank Baez, Bob Bishop, Jason Bryans, Albert Gonzalez, Dave Herrera, Keith Hughes, Phil Huttman, Gary Johnson, Cliff Pastornicky, Bill Price, Johnny Ramos, Sean Rooney, Chet Sergo, Greg Smith, Craig Struss, Gerald Turner, Junior Vizcaino, Mark Willoughby, Dennis Woody

BROADCAST INFORMATION

Radio: KMBZ-AM (980).
TV: KMBC (Channel 9), KCWB (Channel 29).
Cable TV: Fox Sports Midwest.

SPRING TRAINING

Ballpark (city): Baseball City Stadium (Davenport, Fla.).
Ticket information: 941-424-2500.

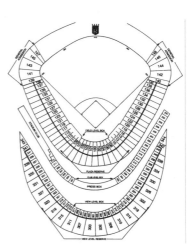

2000 PREVIEW

No.	PITCHERS	B/T	Ht./Wt.	Born	1999 clubs	Projection
	Bottalico, Ricky	L/R	6-1/217	8-26-69	St. Louis	After a so-so year as St. Louis' closer, Ricky will play the same role across the state.
58	Byrdak, Tim	L/L	5-11/180	10-31-73	Omaha, Kansas City	He probably will be in the bullpen but is far from a finished product.
53	Carter, Lance	R/R	6-1/190	12-18-74	Wichita, Kansas City	He picked up 13 saves with a 0.78 ERA in 44 appearances in Wichita.
	D'Amico, Jeff	R/R	6-3/200	11-9-74	Midland, Vancouver, Omaha	The former infielder most likely will find himself back in the minors.
49	Fussell, Chris	R/R	6-2/200	5-19-76	Omaha, Kansas City	He did a little of everything last year and might make the rotation in 2000.
	Green, Tyler	R/R	6-5/205	2-18-70	Scranton/Wilkes-Barre	The former Phillie has had trouble staying healthy but should make the team.
	Lamber, Justin	R/L	6-0/210	5-22-76	Wilmington	A strikeout pitcher who needs to learn better control. He'll go to Wichita to do so.
	Lundquist, David	R/R	6-2/200	6-4-73	Chicago A.L., Charlotte	He had arm surgery a few years ago but is a hard thrower and may stick in the 'pen.
45	Moreno, Orber	R/R	6-2/190	4-27-77	Omaha, Kansas City, GC Royals	Longtime minor leaguer finally went to Kansas City last year, but got hurt in June.
57	Murray, Dan	R/R	6-1/195	11-21-73	Norfolk, New York N.L., K.C.	The Royals acquired him from the Mets in September to provide rotation depth.
	Rakers, Jason	R/R	6-2/200	6-29-73	Buffalo, Cleveland	Despite struggling in 1999 in the Cleveland organization, K.C. still likes his talent.
54	Reichert, Dan	R/R	6-3/175	7-12-76	Omaha, Kansas City	Though he may struggle, the first-rounder has a chance to win a rotation spot.
30	Rigby, Brad	R/R	6-6/215	5-14-73	Oak., Vancouver, Kansas City	He struggled with K.C. last year but will be a part of the revamped bullpen.
50	Rosado, Jose	L/L	6-0/185	11-9-74	Kansas City	It's not his fault he's a Royal—he still is one of the league's top lefties.
46	Santiago, Jose	R/R	6-3/215	11-5-74	K.C., GC Royals, Wich., Omaha	He had the team's best ERA last season and could get a shot at the closer's role.
	Spradlin, Jerry	B/R	6-7/245	6-14-67	Cleveland, San Francisco	A hard thrower who hasn't established himself; has the inside track to be the closer.
41	Stein, Blake	R/R	6-7/240	8-3-73	Vancouver, Oak., Kansas City	He was impressive as a starter for the Royals and will return to the rotation.
37	Suppan, Jeff	R/R	6-2/210	1-2-75	Kansas City	He is expected to continue improving after finally having a breakthrough season.
55	Suzuki, Mac	R/R	6-3/205	5-31-75	Seattle, Kansas City	Once considered a prospect, he'll find himself a spot starter and middle reliever.
	Walker, Jamie	L/L	6-2/190	7-1-71	Omaha, Gulf Coast Royals	Injuries limited him to just six starts in 1999 and he'll need to work back to KC.
34	Wallace, Derek	R/R	6-3/215	9-1-71	Norfolk, Kansas City	Has had plenty of arm troubles but will get a chance to earn a job as a setup man.
47	Witasick, Jay	R/R	6-4/235	8-28-72	Kansas City	He is a part of the starting rotation and might be the team's top strikeout pitcher.

No.	CATCHERS	B/T	Ht./Wt.	Born	1999 clubs	Projection
13	Fasano, Sal	R/R	6-2/230	8-10-71	Omaha, Kansas City	He's a solid defensive player who hasn't been able to hit much in the majors.
	Johnson, Brian	R/R	6-2/210	1-8-68	Cincinnati, Indianapolis	He isn't much better than Fasano, but has played on a couple of winners.

No.	INFIELDERS	B/T	Ht./Wt.	Born	1999 clubs	Projection
3	Febles, Carlos	R/R	5-11/185	5-24-76	Kansas City	Injuries derailed last season, but Febles is an exciting all-around player.
7	Giambi, Jeremy	L/L	6-0/200	9-30-74	Kansas City, Omaha	One of the team's top hitting prospects, but needs to stay healthy.
32	Holbert, Ray	R/R	6-0/185	9-25-70	Omaha, GC Royals, Kansas City	He has good speed and could be a solid utilityman.
19	Randa, Joe	R/R	5-11/190	12-18-69	Kansas City	Usually a solid player, but probably won't repeat last year's success.
	Reboulet, Jeff	R/R	6-0/175	4-30-64	Baltimore	He does a lot of things well and could be a valuable bench player.
1	Sanchez, Rey	R/R	5-9/175	10-5-67	Kansas City	The center of the team's surprisingly strong infield, he was a good re-signing.
29	Sweeney, Mike	R/R	6-2/215	7-22-73	Kansas City	He struggles with the glove at first base but, man, did he hit the ball last season.

No.	OUTFIELDERS	B/T	Ht./Wt.	Born	1999 clubs	Projection
36	Beltran, Carlos	B/R	6-1/190	4-24-77	Kansas City	There's a lot of pressure on the five-tool talent as the key to the team's offense.
27	Brown, Dee	L/R	6-0/215	3-27-78	Wilmington, Wichita, K.C.	One of the team's top prospects, he won't get much time unless there are injuries.
18	Damon, Johnny	L/L	6-2/190	11-5-73	Kansas City	Though not a superstar, Damon has emerged as a productive all-around player.
	Dunwoody, Todd	L/L	6-1/195	4-11-75	Florida, Calgary	Looking for a shot with a new ballclub after struggling with Florida.
24	Dye, Jermaine	R/R	6-5/220	1-28-74	Kansas City	He finally stayed healthy and, surprise, started to fulfill his high potential.
38	Pose, Scott	L/R	5-11/190	2-11-67	Kansas City	A solid reserve outfielder, he offers good speed and a decent lefthanded bat.
52	Quinn, Mark	R/R	6-1/195	5-21-74	Omaha, Kansas City	Outstanding last year in his September callup, he'll need an injury to stay up.
	Tomlinson, Goef	L/L	6-1/190	8-19-76	Wichita	Speedy outfielder may have trouble finding room in a crowded outfield.

THE COACHING STAFF

Tony Muser, manager: The low-key Muser dragged the Royals out of the A.L. Central cellar in his first full season as manager in 1998, but ended just a half game from it last season and set the franchise's lowest winning percentage. Still there were signs of life from the sucessful expansion franchise. The Royals offense produced well. They put a lot of runs on the board, especially early in the season, which is a promising sign for a young team such as this. Muser was knocked for his use of the Kansas City relievers, which continually lost leads from the starters or put the game out of reach. He's got a young staff and his use of an inferior pitching staff will again be tested.

Tom Burgmeier: A lefthander who spent five of his 17 big-league seasons with the Royals, Burgmeier begins his third season as Muser's bullpen coach—not exactly the team you want to have that title with. Still, he has some new pitchers to work with and improve.

Rich Dauer: The former Baltimore infielder survived the transition from Boone to Muser and returns another season as third base coach. Dauser has worked seven years in the Royals' system.

Lamar Johnson: He replaced Tom Poquette as hitting coach last season after working the same position for Milwaukee. He got good results. The team hit .282 in 1999 after hitting just .263 a year ago. And the players who did the clouting are still there and will improve.

Jamie Quirk: Another Boone-regim holdover, Quirk will again be Muser's righthand man. Before joining Boone's staff in 1996, Quirk served two years as bullpen coach.

Brent Strom: He begins his first season as the Royals pitching, replacing Mark Wiley in December. Spent the 1998 and 1999 seasons in the Montreal Expos organization, 1997 with the San Diego Padres and the previous seven seasons with the Houstons Astros organization. He has been around, but this is his first year as a major league pitching coach.

Frank White: The distinguished Royal star returns to his job as first base coach after joining Muser's staff after the 1997 All-Star break. White, one of the most popular players in team history, is a Kansas City native.

THE TOP NEWCOMERS

Ricky Bottalico: Philadelphia knew he was losing his stuff when they traded him to St. Louis last season. He didn't impress over there. But he's the closer in K.C. come hell or high water.

Tyler Green: Picked him off the Philadelphia scrap heap in the offseason. The former first-round pick has had trouble staying healthy for much of his career. When healthy, his mean breaking stuff has made him effective. The Royals hope there's still magic in his surgically-repaired arm.

Brian Johnson: Since Mike Sweeney has moved to first base to maximize his offense, this gritty veteran will take over the catching duties. Relatively light-hitting but is a smart player and receives a good game.

Jeff Reboulet: He hopes to be used more often than he was in Baltimore. Known as simply a versatile utility player who hits lefties much better than righties.

Jerry Spradlin: The embattled reliever has intimidating stuff but has had hardly been imitidating to hitters. The Royals have given him the closer's role to lose.

THE TOP PROSPECTS

Jeremy Giambi: A little more than a prospect by now, but Jason's little brother didn't display the pop in his bat he is capable of. Injuries may have been the cause of that. Look for the intense player to ease into his role and improve, just like his Jason did in Oakland.

Mark Quinn: Is this guy for real? In only his rookie minor league season in 1995 has this 25-year-old hit under .300. Last year, he hit a Pacific Coast League-leading .360 with 25 homers and 84 RBIs in just 107 games before joining the Royals in September with similar success. Though he plays in a packed outfield, look for the Royals to find a way to get him more at-bats as long as he keeps getting hits.

MINNESOTA TWINS

AMERICAN LEAGUE CENTRAL DIVISION

2000 SEASON

2000 Twins Schedule
Home games shaded. *—All-Star Game at Turner Field (Atlanta).

March
SUN	MON	TUE	WED	THU	FRI	SAT
26	27	28	29	30	31	

April
SUN	MON	TUE	WED	THU	FRI	SAT
						1
2	3 TB	4 TB	5 TB	6 TB	7 KC	8 KC
9 KC	10 KC	11 BOS	12 BOS	13 BOS	14 BAL	15 BAL
16 BAL	17	18 KC	19 KC	20 KC	21 TEX	22 TEX
23 TEX	24 NYY	25 NYY	26 NYY	27	28 OAK	29 OAK
30 OAK						

May
SUN	MON	TUE	WED	THU	FRI	SAT
	1	2 SEA	3 SEA	4 SEA	5 DET	6 DET
7 DET	8 CLE	9 CLE	10 CLE	11	12 CWS	13 CWS
14 CWS	15 SEA	16 SEA	17 SEA	18 OAK	19 OAK	20 OAK
21 OAK	22	23 ANA	24 ANA	25 ANA	26 TEX	27 TEX
28 TEX	29	30 TOR	31 TOR			

June
SUN	MON	TUE	WED	THU	FRI	SAT
				1 TOR	2 CIN	3 CIN
4 CIN	5 HOU	6 HOU	7 HOU	8	9 MIL	10 MIL
11 MIL	12 OAK	13 OAK	14 OAK	15 SEA	16 SEA	17 SEA
18 SEA	19	20 TEX	21 TEX	22 TEX	23 ANA	24 ANA
25 ANA	26 ANA	27 CWS	28 CWS	29 CWS	30 CLE	

July
SUN	MON	TUE	WED	THU	FRI	SAT
						1 CLE
2 CLE	3 BOS	4 BOS	5 BOS	6 BOS	7 PIT	8 PIT
9 PIT	10	11 *	12	13 CUB	14 CUB	15 CUB
16 STL	17 STL	18 STL	19 CWS	20 CWS	21 CLE	22 CLE
23 CLE	24 BOS	25 BOS	26 BOS	27 NYY	28 NYY	29 NYY
30 NYY	31 BAL					

August
SUN	MON	TUE	WED	THU	FRI	SAT
		1 BAL	2 BAL	3	4 DET	5 DET
6 DET	7 TB	8 TB	9 TB	10 TB	11 TOR	12 TOR
13 TOR	14	15 KC	16 KC	17 KC	18 TOR	19 TOR
20 TOR	21	22 TB	23 TB	24	25 DET	26 DET
27 DET	28	29 KC	30 KC	31		

September
SUN	MON	TUE	WED	THU	FRI	SAT
					1 NYY	2 NYY
3 NYY	4 BAL	5 BAL	6 BAL	7	8 SEA	9 SEA
10 SEA	11	12 OAK	13 OAK	14	15 ANA	16 ANA
17 ANA	18 TEX	19 TEX	20 TEX	21 CWS	22 CWS	23 CWS
24 CWS	25 CLE	26 CLE	27 CLE	28 CLE	29 DET	30 DET

October
SUN	MON	TUE	WED	THU	FRI	SAT
1 DET	2	3	4	5	6	7

FRONT-OFFICE DIRECTORY
Owner ....Carl R. Pohlad
President..............Jerry Bell
Chairman of executive committee ....Howard Fox
Directors ....Carl R. Pohlad, Eloise Pohlad, James O. Pohlad, Robert C. Pohlad, William M. Pohlad, T. Geron (Jerry) Bell, Kirby Puckett, Chris Clouser
Vice president, general manager..............Terry Ryan
Vice president, assistant general manager ....Bill Smith
Assistant general manager ....Wayne Krivsky
Executive vice president, baseball..............Kirby Puckett
Vice president, operations ....Matt Hoy
Director of minor leagues ....Jim Rantz
Director of scouting ....Mike Radcliff
Director of baseball operations ....Rob Antony
Traveling secretary..............Remzi Kiratli
Manager, media relations..............Sean Harlin

MINOR LEAGUE AFFILIATES
Class	Team	League	Manager
AAA	Salt Lake	Pacific Coast	Phil Roof
AA	New Britain	Eastern	John Russell
A	Fort Myers	Florida State	Jose Marzan
A	Quad City	Midwest	Stan Cliburn
Rookie	Elizabethton	Appalachian	Jeff Carter
Rookie	Gulf Coast Twins	Gulf Coast	Al Newman

BROADCAST INFORMATION
Radio: WCCO-AM (830).
TV: KMSP-TV (Channel 9).
Cable TV: Midwest SportsChannel.

SPRING TRAINING
Ballpark (city): Lee County Sports Complex (Fort Myers, Fla.).
Ticket information: 800-33-TWINS.

ASSISTANCE STAFF
Team physicians
Dr. Dan Buss
Dr. Tom Jetzer
Dr. VeeJay Eyunni
Dr. John Steubs

Scouts
Vern Followell (Pro Scouting Supervisor)
Deron Johnson (West Supervisor)
Earl Frishman (East Supervisor)
Mike Ruth (Midwest Supervisor)

Kevin Bootay	Ellsworth Brown
Larry Corrigan	Cal Ermer
Marty Esposito	Bill Harford
John Leavitt	Joel Lepel
Bill Lohr	Lee MacPhail
Joe McIlvaine	Bill Mele
Gregg Miller	Bill Milos
Tim O'Neil	Hector Otero
Mark Quimuyog	Ricky Taylor
Brad Weitzel	John Wilson

International scouts
David Kim
Jose Leon
Howard Norsetter
Yoshi Okamoto
Johnny Sierra

BALLPARK INFORMATION

Ballpark (capacity, surface)
Hubert H. Humphrey Metrodome (48,678, artificial)
Address
34 Kirby Puckett Place
Minneapolis, MN 55415
Business phone
612-375-1366
Ticket information
1-800-33-TWINS
Ticket prices
$19 (VIP level, lower deck club level)
$17 (lower deck club)
$14 (lower deck reserved)
$12 (upper deck club level)
$9 (g.a., lower left field)
$4 (g.a., upper deck)
Field dimensions (from home plate)
To left field at foul line, 343 feet
To center field, 408 feet
To right field at foul line, 327 feet
First game played
April 6, 1982 (Mariners 11, Twins 7)

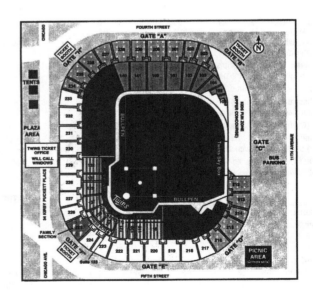

No.	PITCHERS	B/T	Ht./Wt.	Born	1999 clubs	Projection
38	Bergman, Sean	R/R	6-4/225	4-11-70	Houston, New Orleans, Atlanta	Will have a chance to make the rotation, but long relief is more likely.
58	Carrasco, Hector	R/R	6-2/220	10-22-69	Ft. Myers, Salt Lake, Minnesota	Shoulder surgery did not fix setup man's control problems.
59	Cressend, Jack	R/R	6-1/190	5-13-75	Trenton, New Britain	Smart pitcher who gets the most out of his talent. Will likely start at Class AAA.
18	Guardado, Eddie	R/L	6-0/194	10-2-70	Minnesota, New Britain	Rubber-armed reliever will be a setup and long-relief man.
32	Hawkins, LaTroy	R/R	6-5/204	12-21-72	Minnesota	The perennial prospect, he has made 98 career starts and has a 6.16 ERA.
51	Kinney, Matt	R/R	6-4/200	12-16-76	New Britain, Gulf Coast Twins	Started horribly, had elbow surgery and will make a clean start in 2000.
40	Kusiewicz, Mike	R/L	6-2/190	11-1-76	Arizona Rockies	Showed promise in 1998, but injuries slowed him last season.
19	Lincoln, Mike	R/R	6-2/211	4-10-75	Minnesota, Salt Lake	Control pitcher with good minor league numbers, but not yet ready for the bigs.
53	Mays, Joe	B/R	6-1/185	12-10-75	Minnesota	Took over No. 3 rotation spot midway through 1999 and will likely keep it in 2000.
20	Miller, Travis	R/L	6-3/209	11-2-72	Salt Lake, Minnesota	Will be team's top lefty setup man after a 2.72 ERA in 52 appearances in 1999.
21	Milton, Eric	L/L	6-3/220	8-4-75	Minnesota	Had an erratic 1999, including a no-hitter, but will be more consistent this season.
49	Perkins, Dan	R/R	6-2/193	3-15-75	Minnesota, Salt Lake	He's a good reliever but has an outside shot of being the team's No. 5 starter.
22	Radke, Brad	R/R	6-2/188	10-27-72	Minnesota	Could consistently win 15-20 games a year with his four good pitches.
52	Randall, Scott	R/R	6-3/190	10-29-75	Colorado Springs, Carolina	Durable prospect will spend a season adjusting to Class AAA.
55	Redman, Mark	L/L	6-5/220	1-5-74	Salt Lake, Minnesota	Sometimes leaves pitches up—doom in the Metrodome. He's a rotation hopeful.
33	Romero, J.C.	B/L	5-11/195	6-4-76	New Britain, Salt Lake, Minn.	Pitched well in the minors as a lefthanded setup man.
54	Ryan, Jason	B/R	6-3/195	1-23-76	W. Tenn., N.B., Salt Lake, Minn.	Will be a big league starter at some point, but not this season.
23	Sampson, Benj	L/L	6-2/210	4-27-75	Minnesota, Salt Lake	Doesn't appear to have the talent to pitch in the big leagues.
57	Santana, Johan	L/L	6-0/155	3-13-79	Michigan	Struggled at Class A, walking too many batters. He's a long shot.
37	Stentz, Brent	R/R	6-5/225	7-24-75	Salt Lake, New Britain	Closer of the future will work on his control in Class AAA for one more season.
46	Wells, Bob	R/R	6-0/200	11-1-66	Minnesota	Was a godsend for the team in 1999—a reliable, veteran middle reliever.

No.	CATCHERS	B/T	Ht./Wt.	Born	1999 clubs	Projection
39	Moeller, Chad	R/R	6-3/207	2-18-75	New Britain	Not a high-ranking prospect, but might stick if the team carries three catchers.
9	Pierzynski, A.J.	L/R	6-3/220	12-30-76	Salt Lake, Minnesota	Good defensive catcher who needs a lot of work at the plate.
17	Valentin, Javier	B/R	5-10/192	9-19-75	Minnesota	Will be the starter, but has to adjust to the rigors of the job.

No.	INFIELDERS	B/T	Ht./Wt.	Born	1999 clubs	Projection
8	Coomer, Ron	R/R	5-11/206	11-18-66	Minnesota	Will play first and DH and hit cleanup as he continues to be solid.
2	Davidson, Cleatus	B/R	5-10/170	11-1-76	New Britain, Minnesota	Capable of 40 steals, but likely incapable of hitting much higher than .250.
15	Guzman, Cristian	B/R	6-0/188	3-21-78	Minnesota	Despite 1999 struggles, he's one of the team's top prospects.
7	Hocking, Denny	B/R	5-10/183	4-2-70	Minnesota	Steady bench player who does everything but pitch and catch.
47	Koskie, Corey	L/R	6-3/217	6-28-73	Minnesota	After platooning in 1999, will be a solo act at third. Hit .316 vs. righthanders.
25	Mientkiewicz, Doug	L/R	6-2/193	6-19-74	Minnesota	Will get another chance to platoon at first base, but does not have enough power.
27	Ortiz, David	L/L	6-4/237	11-18-75	Salt Lake, Minnesota	Recovered from wrist surgery and hit 30 home runs at Class AAA. Might play DH.
1	Rivas, Luis	R/R	5-10/175	8-30-79	New Britain	Good speed and above-average power for a shortstop.
26	Valdez, Mario	L/R	6-2/190	11-19-74	Charlotte	Power-hitting infielder may someday have a place with the Twins.
12	Walker, Todd	L/R	6-0/181	5-25-73	Minnesota	Will bat in the leadoff spot, play second base and likely hit around .275.

No.	OUTFIELDERS	B/T	Ht./Wt.	Born	1999 clubs	Projection
31	Allen, Chad	R/R	6-1/195	2-6-75	Minnesota	Allen hit .294 before the All-Star break, but .254 after. Will start in left field.
30	Buchanan, Brian	R/R	6-4/230	7-21-73	Salt Lake	Has power, but won't make it in the majors until he cuts down on strikeouts.
16	Cummings, Midre	L/R	6-0/195	10-14-71	New Britain, Salt Lake, Minn.	Might get time as a pinch hitter or emergency outfielder.
48	Hunter, Torii	R/R	6-2/205	7-18-75	Minnesota	Could get a shot at an outfield job after strong second half (.295) in 1999.
11	Jones, Jacque	L/L	5-10/176	4-25-75	Salt Lake, Minnesota	Hit .289 to earn the starting job in center—and he'll keep it if he can hit lefties.
50	Lawton, Matt	L/R	5-10/186	11-3-71	Minnesota, Ft. Myers, GC Twins	Subject to slumps, but he walks a lot, so he's never a liability. Will bat third.

THE COACHING STAFF

Tom Kelly, manager: The team he has to work with does not fit Kelly's style. Kelly, in his 14th year with the Twins and the longest-serving manager, would rather play for big innings, but he just does not have the hitters to do it. He has calmly accepted his fate, though, and seems comfortable managing in Minnesota no matter what kind of roster he has been given.

Ron Gardenhire: Gardenhire, 43, was a good minor-league manager from 1988-1990, before moving to the big-league level as a base coach. This will be his second season as the third base coach, and he could be a managerial candidate.

Paul Molitor: The team emphasizes that Molitor will not be a bench coach—Kelly hates that position. The career .306 hitter will help out with baserunning and getting hitters into the right mind-frame for their at-bats.

Rick Stelmaszek: Stelmaszek joined the Twins organization as a minor league manager in 1978 and has been with the team in some capacity ever since. He has been the bullpen coach since 1980 and served in the 1988 and 1992 All-Star games.

Dick Such: Such works well with veteran pitchers, but there are few veterans here to work with. Young pitchers who seem to have talent have struggled when they have gotten to the big leagues. There are some talented pitchers on the staff Such will work to develop.

Scott Ullger: Ullger is in his second season as batting coach. They went from 734 runs in 1998 to 686 last year. Ullger does not have much to work with, but it might not be a good sign that the team brought in Molitor to "help" him.

Jerry White: White is entering his second season as the Twins first base coach. An aggressive runner in his 11 years as a major league player, White is also aggressive as a coach.

THE TOP NEWCOMERS

Sean Bergman: After winning a surprising 12 games as a fifth starter in 1998, it was back to normalcy for Bergman in 1999. He struggled as a starter in Houston (4-6, 5.36) before going to Atlanta as a reliever. The Twins will use him as a long reliever, which should mean a lot of work given the youth on the pitching staff.

THE TOP PROSPECTS

Christian Guzman: Guzman spent all of last season in Minnesota. He should do it again this year, but he has to improve in all facets of the game. He has to be a more consistent fielder. He has to show more range and he has to be more disciplined at the plate. Last season, he had 22 walks and 90 strikeouts. He also stole just nine bases in 16 attempts.

Jacque Jones: He made a smooth transition from the minor leagues to the major leagues last season, posting similar numbers. He hit .289 in 95 games and, like most hitters his age, still struggles with too many strikeouts. As he corrects that problem, his average should climb to around .300 or higher.

Corey Koskie: After platooning last season, Koskie should be the full-time third baseman this year. He hit .310 last season, best on the team, and has the power to hit 20 home runs. If he can hit lefthanders, he could develop into an All-Star.

Mike Lincoln: Lincoln is a control pitcher, keeping his pitches around the plate. It worked in Class AA, but against big-league hitters, he allowed 102 hits in 76.1 innings and went 3-10 with a 6.84 ERA. Lincoln will get a fresh start this season in Class AAA and try to work back into the majors.

Luis Rivas: He's been a professional since he was 16, so he has already developed ahead of schedule. He is beginning to display more patience at the plate. Rivas has gap power and good speed. His fielding may not be well-suited for shortstop, though.

NEW YORK YANKEES

AMERICAN LEAGUE EAST DIVISION

2000 SEASON

2000 Yankees Schedule
Home games shaded.   *—All-Star Game at Turner Field (Atlanta).

March
SUN	MON	TUE	WED	THU	FRI	SAT
26	27	28	29	30	31	

April
SUN	MON	TUE	WED	THU	FRI	SAT
						1
2	3 ANA	4 ANA	5 ANA	6	7 SEA	8 SEA
9 SEA	10	11 TEX	12 TEX	13 TEX	14 KC	15 KC
16 KC	17 TEX	18 TEX	19 TEX	20	21 TOR	22 TOR
23 TOR	24 MIN	25 MIN	26 MIN	27	28 TOR	29 TOR
30 TOR						

May
SUN	MON	TUE	WED	THU	FRI	SAT
	1 CLE	2 CLE	3 CLE	4	5 BAL	6 BAL
7 BAL	8 TB	9 TB	10 TB	11	12 DET	13 DET
14 DET	15	16 CWS	17 CWS	18	19 CLE	20 CLE
21 CLE	22	23 CHI	24 CHI	25 CHI	26 BOS	27 BOS
28 BOS	29 OAK	30 OAK	31 OAK			

June
SUN	MON	TUE	WED	THU	FRI	SAT
				1	2 ATL	3 ATL
4 ATL	5 MON	6 MON	7 MON	8	9 NYM	10 NYM
11 NYM	12 BOS	13 BOS	14 BOS	15 CWS	16 CWS	17 CWS
18 CWS	19 BOS	20 BOS	21 BOS	22 BOS	23 CHI	24 CHI
25 CHI	26	27 DET	28 DET	29 DET	30 TB	

July
SUN	MON	TUE	WED	THU	FRI	SAT
						1 TB
2 TB	3	4 BAL	5 BAL	6 BAL	7 NYM	8 NYM
9 NYM	10	11 *	12	13 FLA	14 FLA	15 FLA
16 PHI	17 PHI	18 PHI	19 DET	20 DET	21 TB	22 TB
23 TB	24 BAL	25 BAL	26 BAL	27 MIN	28 MIN	29 MIN
30 MIN	31					

August
SUN	MON	TUE	WED	THU	FRI	SAT
		1 KC	2 KC	3 KC	4 SEA	5 SEA
6 SEA	7 OAK	8 OAK	9 OAK	10 ANA	11 ANA	12 ANA
13 ANA	14 TEX	15 TEX	16 TEX	17 ANA	18 ANA	19 ANA
20 ANA	21	22 TEX	23 TEX	24 TEX	25 OAK	26 OAK
27 OAK	28 SEA	29 SEA	30 SEA	31		

September
SUN	MON	TUE	WED	THU	FRI	SAT
					1 MIN	2 MIN
3 MIN	4 KC	5 KC	6 KC	7 KC	8 BOS	9 BOS
10 BOS	11	12 TOR	13 TOR	14 TOR	15 CLE	16 CLE
17 CLE	18 CLE	19 TOR	20 TOR	21 TOR	22 DET	23 DET
24 DET	25 DET	26 TB	27 TB	28 TB	29 BAL	30 BAL

October
SUN	MON	TUE	WED	THU	FRI	SAT
1 BAL	2	3	4	5	6	7

FRONT-OFFICE DIRECTORY

Principal owner ....George M. Steinbrenner III
General partners ....Harold Z. Steinbrenner, Stephen W. Swindal
President ....Randy Levine
Executive vice president, general counsel ....Lonn Trost
Vice president, ticket operations ....Frank Swaine
Vice president, business development ....Joseph M. Perello
Vice president, chief financial officer ....Marty Greenspun
Controller ....Robert Brown
Special advisory group ....Clyde King, Dick Williams
Vice president, general manager ....Brian Cashman
Vice president, baseball operations ....Mark Newman
Vice president, scouting ....Lin Garrett
Vice president, international and pro scouting................Gordon Blakeley
Vice president, player personnel ....Billy Connors
Vice president, business development..........................Sonny Hight
Director of player development ....Rob Thomson
Director of player personnel ....Damon Oppenheimer
Director of baseball operations............................Dan Matheson
Director of major league scouting............................Gene Michael
Assistant general manager ....Kim Ng
Major League administrator ....Tom May
Traveling secretary ....David Szen
Director of customer service ....Joel White
Director of office administration and services ....Harvey C. Winston
Manager, stadium operations ....Kirk Randazzo
Assistant, stadium operations ....Bob Pelegrino
Stadium superintendent ....Bob Wilkinson
Director, video and broadcast operations....................Doyal Martin
Assistant director, video and broadcast operations ....Joe Pullia
Executive director of ticket operations ....Jeff Kline
Senior ticket director ....Ken Skrypek
Director of media relations and publicity ....Rick Cerrone
Director, publications and multimedia ....Dan Cahalane
Assistant director of media relations and publicity..........Jason Zillo
Senior advisor ....Arthur Richman
Director of marketing..Deborah A. Tymon
Director of community relations/special asst. to G. M. Steinbrenner ....Brian Smith
Special assistant ....Joe Pepitone

MINOR LEAGUE AFFILIATES

Class	Team	League	Manager
AAA	Columbus	International	Trey Hillman
AA	Norwich	Eastern	Dan Radison
A	Tampa	Florida State	Tom Nieto
A	Greensboro	South Atlantic	Stan Hough
A	Staten Island	New York-Pennsylvania	Joe Arnold
Rookie	Gulf Coast Yankees	Gulf Coast	Derek Shelton

BALLPARK INFORMATION

Ballpark (capacity, surface)
Yankee Stadium (57,546, grass)
Address
Yankee Stadium
E. 161 St. and River Ave., Bronx, NY 10451
Business phone
718-293-4300
Ticket information
212-307-1212, 718-293-6013
Ticket prices
$35 (main-infield)
$32 (loge-infield)
$30 (main & loge-outfield, main reserved-infield)
$26 (main reserved-outfield)
$15 (tier)
$8 (bleachers)
Field dimensions (from home plate)
To left field at foul line, 318 feet
To center field, 408 feet
To right field at foul line, 314 feet
First game played
April 18, 1923 (Yankees 4, Red Sox 1)

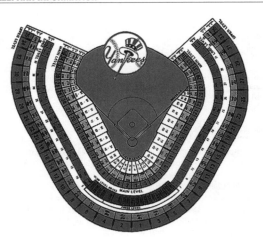

ASSISTANCE STAFF

Team physician
Dr. Stuart Hershon
Head trainer
Gene Monahan
Assistant trainer
Steve Donohue
Strength and conditioning coach
Jeff Mangold
Stadium superintendent
Bob Wilkinson
Head groundskeeper
Dan Cunningham
Regional cross-checkers
Joe Arnold, Tim Kelly, Greg Orr
Pro scouts
Joe Caro, Bill Emslie, Mick Kelleher, Bob Miske, Mike Naples
Scouts
Mike Baker, Mark Batchko, Steve Boros, Bobby DeJardin, Dick Groch, Steve Lemke, Abe Martinez, Bob Miske, Scott Pleis, Cesar Presbott, Gus Quattlebaum Joe Robison, Phil Rossi, Steve Swail, Leon Wurth, Bill Young
Coordinator of the Pacific Rim
John Cox
Coordinator of Latin American scouting
Carlos Rios
Foreign scouts
Manuel Duran, Ricardo Finol, Karl Heron, Ricardo Heron, Rudy Jabalera, Victor Mata, Jim Patterson, Jose Quintero, Edgar Rodriguez, Arquimedes Rojas, Freddy Tiburcio
Special assignment scouts
Stump Merrill, Ket Barber

BROADCAST INFORMATION
Radio: WABC (770-AM).
TV: WNYW-TV (Channel 5).
Cable TV: Madison Square Garden Network.

SPRING TRAINING
Ballpark (city): Legends Field (Tampa, Fla.).
Ticket information: 813-879-2244, 813-287-8844.

No.	PITCHERS	B/T	Ht./Wt.	Born	1999 clubs	Projection
59	Bradley, Ryan	R/R	6-4/226	10-26-75	Columbus	Bradley has established himself as a prospect, but is unlikely to stick in long relief.
41	Buddie, Mike	R/R	6-3/210	12-12-70	Columbus, New York A.L.	He was excellent at Class AAA last year but needs a strong spring.
22	Clemens, Roger	R/R	6-4/230	8-4-62	New York A.L.	The five-time Cy Young winner needs a strong season to rescue his reputation.
36	Cone, David	L/R	6-1/190	1-2-63	New York A.L.	Cone may have some of the best stuff in the majors, but injury is always a worry.
64	De Los Santos, Luis	R/R	6-2/187	11-1-77	Columbus, Gulf Coast Yankees	There seems to be no room on the staff for this young starting pitcher.
67	Einertson, Darrell	R/R	6-2/190	9-4-72	GC Yankees, Tampa, Norwich	He's a minor league reliever who missed the first half of 1999 with injuries.
58	Erdos, Todd	R/R	6-1/190	11-21-73	Columbus, New York A.L.	Talented pitcher who has not spot on this deep staff.
	Ford, Ben	R/R	6-7/200	8-15-75	Columbus	Big Ben has good stuff, but little luck controlling it thus far.
38	Grimsley, Jason	R/R	6-3/180	8-7-67	New York A.L.	Won seven games as one of the top setup men and will again be in the bullpen.
26	Hernandez, Orlando	R/R	6-2/190	10-11-65	New York A.L.	No matter his age (still in question), he's one of the majors' top starters.
57	Juden, Jeff	B/R	6-8/265	1-19-71	Columbus, New York A.L.	He's a journeyman starter who is looking to make the club in some capacity.
55	Mendoza, Ramiro	R/R	6-2/155	6-15-72	New York A.L.	An aspiring starter, Mendoza was dominant as a setup man in the playoffs.
43	Nelson, Jeff	R/R	6-8/225	11-17-66	N.York A.L., GC Yankees, Tampa	The batters know he's going to throw a slider, but they still can't hit it.
46	Pettitte, Andy	L/L	6-5/225	6-15-72	Tampa, New York A.L.	He almost pitched his way out of town but regrouped and had a great second half.
42	Rivera, Mariano	R/R	6-2/170	11-29-69	New York A.L.	With all the bats he broke last season, it's rumored he's in the wood-bat business.
29	Stanton, Mike	L/L	6-1/215	6-2-67	New York A.L.	Slipped a little in recent years, but is still one of the league's best lefty specialists.
62	Tessmer, Jay	R/R	6-3/190	12-26-71	Columbus, New York A.L.	Though successful as a closer in Class AAA, he's struggled in big-league chances.
27	Watson, Allen	L/L	6-1/212	11-18-70	N.Y.-N.L., Sea., Colum., N.Y.-A.L.	He's made the rounds recently and finally found a home in the Yankees' bullpen.
	Westbrook, Jake	R/R	6-3/200	9-29-77	Harrisburg	Westbrook, traded to the team for Hideki Irabu, is not close to the majors.
52	Yarnall, Ed	L/L	6-3/234	12-4-75	Columbus, New York A.L.	Yarnall takes over the fifth spot in the rotation and should be better than Irabu.

No.	CATCHERS	B/T	Ht./Wt.	Born	1999 clubs	Projection
13	Leyritz, Jim	R/R	5-11/220	12-27-63	S.D., R.Cuca.., L.V., N.Y.-A.L.	He'll get time as the righthanded DH and will back up at first base and catcher.
20	Posada, Jorge	B/R	6-2/205	8-17-71	New York A.L.	Now that Girardi's gone, the team's catcher of the future finally will start.

No.	INFIELDERS	B/T	Ht./Wt.	Born	1999 clubs	Projection
35	Bellinger, Clay	R/R	6-3/195	11-18-68	New York A.L., Columbus	He's not much at the plate, but his versatility in the field will give him opportunities.
18	Brosius, Scott	R/R	6-1/202	8-15-66	New York A.L., Tampa	One of the majors' top glovemen, his offense should rebound in 2000.
2	Jeter, Derek	R/R	6-3/195	6-26-74	New York A.L.	His numbers aren't as gaudy as A-Rod's or Nomar's, but he may be better than both.
59	Jimenez, D'Angelo	R/R	6-0/160	12-21-77	Columbus, New York A.L.	A shortstop by trade, he also can play second and third and is solid at the plate.
11	Knoblauch, Chuck	R/R	5-9/170	7-7-68	New York A.L.	He had throwing yips last season, but is still one of the majors' top leadoff hitters.
24	Martinez, Tino	L/R	6-2/210	12-7-67	New York A.L.	Count on him for good defense and 25 homers and 100 RBIs every season.
58	Soriano, Alfonso	R/R	6-1/160	1-7-78	Norw., GC Yanks, Colu., N.Y.-A.L.	Considered the team's top prospect, Soriano may have to wait for a big-league job.

No.	OUTFIELDERS	B/T	Ht./Wt.	Born	1999 clubs	Projection
	Jones, Terry	B/R	5-10/165	2-15-71	Ottawa, Montreal	A good glove and great speed, but this journeyman has a light bat.
17	Ledee, Ricky	L/L	6-1/160	11-22-73	New York A.L., Columbus	Solid after an early slump and could be one of the game's most pleasant surprises.
84	McDonald, Donzell	B/R	5-11/165	2-20-75	Norwich	His forte is his speed; might be able to earn a late promotion as a pinch runner.
21	O'Neill, Paul	L/L	6-4/215	2-25-63	New York A.L.	After seven years as one of the A.L.'s most dependable, this may be his last year.
47	Spencer, Shane	R/R	5-11/210	2-20-72	New York A.L., Columbus	He was Mr. September in 1998 and will again be part of the left field platoon.
39	Strawberry, Darryl	L/L	6-6/215	3-12-62	Columbus, New York A.L.	He'll be the team's primary DH and is still one if the game's most feared hitters.
51	Williams, Bernie	B/R	6-2/205	9-13-68	New York A.L.	Don't just look at his numbers—you've got to see him play to understand his value.

THE COACHING STAFF

Joe Torre, manager: Four incredible New York seasons have wiped away the mediocrity of previous managerial stops and stamped Torre as one of the great bosses in the storied history of baseball's premier franchise. The 1998 and '99 chemistry that helped the Yankees win back-to-back World Series championships was a tribute to Torre's ability to forge strong relationships with those above him (George Steinbrenner) and those below (the players). His squad battled adversity, including his own bout with prostate cancer, on and off the field and he kept the squad together through it. Torre manages with an upfront, treat-everybody-the-same approach that generates locker-room respect and chemistry.

Chris Chambliss: Torre loves him. He is best remembered in New York circles for his ALCS-winning home run in 1976 against the Royals. But he is quickly becoming known as a solid hitting coach. He's entering his four season on the job with New York, following his three years in the same job for Torre in St. Louis. His best lesson: patience at the plate.

Tony Cloninger: The veteran Cloninger begins his eighth season as New York's bullpen coach, his 14th in the Yankees system.

Lee Mazzilli: The former lefty outfielder/first baseman replaces Jose Cardenal as the first base coach for his first season.

Willie Randolph: His name has been brought up as a future managerial candidate. The 13-year second baseman enters his seventh season as the team's third base coach and has a pretty staff and organization to teach him how to be a great manager.

Mel Stottlemyre: Undoubtedly one of the top pitching coaches in the league. Granted, he's got a good staff to work with, but he has kept them focused and on top of their game—especially when it counted—much like the way he was as a pitcher.

Don Zimmer: Torre's bench coach, guru and righthand man took over for Torre in 1999 during Torre's absence. The ex-manager admitted the experience wore him down and claims he wouldn't manage again in the majors even if offered. That fits the Yankees just fine.

THE TOP NEWCOMERS

Terry Jones: Acquired from Los Angeles in a January trade for a player to be named later. The 29-year-old outfielder will provide outfield depth, especially in center field. He's got good speed. He covers a lot of ground in the outfield and can steal bases.

THE TOP PROSPECTS

Drew Henson: The University of Michigan quarterback has great talent but obviously battles other obligations.

Nick Johnson: Should something happen to Tino Martinez, the Yankees may not lose too much if this guy stepped in and performed the way he's capable of. The 21-year-old has amazing patience at the plate, has good power and is a smart baserunner.

Alfonso Soriano: Signed from Japan a year ago, this young infielder can do it all. He can hit for power, steal bases and displays a flashy, albeit inconsistent, glove. His first season for the Yankees was met with mixed results. At times, he looked overmatched, others he showed he could hit for average and power. The Yankees have the luxury of being able to bring him along slowly . . . and that's what they'll do.

OAKLAND ATHLETICS

AMERICAN LEAGUE WEST DIVISION

2000 SEASON

2000 Athletics Schedule

Home games shaded. *—All-Star Game at Turner Field (Atlanta).

March
SUN	MON	TUE	WED	THU	FRI	SAT
26	27	28	29	30	31	

April
SUN	MON	TUE	WED	THU	FRI	SAT
						1
2	3 DET	4 DET	5 DET	6	7 CWS	8 CWS
9 CWS	10 CLE	11 CLE	12 CLE	13	14 BOS	15 BOS
16 BOS	17 BOS	18 CLE	19 CLE	20 CLE	21 BAL	22 BAL
23 BAL	24 TOR	25 TOR	26 TOR	27	28 MIN	29 MIN
30 MIN						

May
SUN	MON	TUE	WED	THU	FRI	SAT
	1 KC	2 KC	3 KC	4	5 TEX	6 TEX
7 TEX	8 ANA	9 ANA	10 ANA	11 SEA	12 SEA	13 SEA
14 SEA	15 KC	16 KC	17 KC	18 MIN	19 MIN	20 MIN
21 MIN	22	23 TB	24 TB	25 TB	26 BAL	27 BAL
28 BAL	29 NYY	30 NYY	31 NYY			

June
SUN	MON	TUE	WED	THU	FRI	SAT
				1	2 SF	3 SF
4 SF	5 SD	6 SD	7 SD	8	9 LA	10 LA
11 LA	12 MIN	13 MIN	14 MIN	15	16 KC	17 KC
18 KC	19 BAL	20 BAL	21 BAL	22	23 KC	24 KC
25 KC	26	27 TEX	28 TEX	29 TEX	30 ANA	

July
SUN	MON	TUE	WED	THU	FRI	SAT
						1 ANA
2 ANA	3 TEX	4 TEX	5 TEX	6	7 ARI	8 ARI
9 ARI	10	11	* 12	13 SF	14 SF	15 SF
16 COL	17 COL	18 COL	19 SEA	20 SEA	21 ANA	22 ANA
23 ANA	24 SEA	25 SEA	26 SEA	27 BOS	28 BOS	29 BOS
30 BOS	31 TOR					

August
SUN	MON	TUE	WED	THU	FRI	SAT
		1 TOR	2 TOR	3	4 CWS	5 CWS
6 CWS	7	8 NYY	9 NYY	10 NYY	11 DET	12 DET
13 DET	14 CLE	15 CLE	16 CLE	17	18 DET	19 DET
20 DET	21 DET	22 CLE	23 CLE	24 CLE	25 NYY	26 NYY
27 NYY	28 CWS	29 CWS	30 CWS	31		

September
SUN	MON	TUE	WED	THU	FRI	SAT
					1 TOR	2 TOR
3 TOR	4 TOR	5 BOS	6 BOS	7	8 TB	9 TB
10 TB	11 TB	12 MIN	13 MIN	14	15 TB	16 TB
17 TB	18 BAL	19 BAL	20 BAL	21 SEA	22 SEA	23 SEA
24 SEA	25 ANA	26 ANA	27 ANA	28 ANA	29 TEX	30 TEX

October
SUN	MON	TUE	WED	THU	FRI	SAT
1 TEX	2	3	4	5	6	7

FRONT-OFFICE DIRECTORY

Owners ....Stephen C. Schott, Ken Hofmann
President ....Michael P. Crowley
General manager ....Billy Beane
Assistant general manager ....Paul DePodesta
Special assistant to the general manager ....Bill Rigney
Director of player development ....Keith Lieppman
Director of player personnel...J.P Ricciardi
Director of scouting ....Grady Fuson
Director of minor league operations ....Ted Polakowski
Director of baseball administration ....Pam Pitts
Traveling secretary ....Mickey Morabito
Scouting and player development assistant............................Danny McCormack
Baseball operations assistant ....Dave Forst
Senior director of broadcasting and communications ....Ken Pries
Director of public relations ....Jim Young
Baseball information manager ....Mike Selleck
Broadcasting manager ....Robert Buan
Senior director of stadium operations ....David Rinetti
Senior director of sales and marketing ....David Alioto
Director of corporate sales..Franklin Lowe
Director of promotions and special events ....Susan Weiglein
Director of ticket sales ....Dennis Murphy
Director of business services ....David Lozow
Executive assistant ....Carolyn Jones
Executive assistant, baseball operations ....Betty Shinoda

MINOR LEAGUE AFFILIATES

Class	Team	League	Manager
AAA	Vancouver	Pacific Coast	Bob Geren
AA	Midland	Texas	Tony DeFrancesco
A	Modesto	California	Greg Sparks
A	Visalia	California	Juan Navarette
A	Vancouver	Northwest	Dave Joppie
Rookie	Scotttsdale A's	Arizona	John Kuehl

BROADCAST INFORMATION

Radio: KABL-AM (960).
TV: KICU-TV (Channel 36).
Cable TV: Fox Sports Bay Area.

SPRING TRAINING

Ballpark (city): Phoenix Stadium (Phoenix, Ariz.).
Ticket information: 602-392-0074.

BALLPARK INFORMATION

Ballpark (capacity, surface)
Network Associates Coliseum (43,662, grass)
Address
Oakland Athletics
7677 Oakport St., Suite 200
Oakland, CA 94621
Business phone
510-638-4900
Ticket information
510-638-4627
Ticket prices
$24 (plaza club)
$22 (MVP infield)
$16 (field level-infield)
$15 (field level, plaza-infield)
$14 (plaza)
$5 (upper reserved)
$4 (bleachers)
Field dimensions (from home plate)
To left field at foul line, 330 feet
To center field, 400 feet
To right field at foul line, 330 feet
First game played
April 17, 1968 (Orioles 4, Athletics 1)

ASSISTANCE STAFF

Team physician
Dr. Allan Pont

Team orthopedist
Dr. Jerrald Goldman

Trainers
Larry Davis
Steven Sayles

Equipment manager
Steve Vucinich

Visiting clubhouse manager
Mike Thalblum

Special assignment scout
Dick Bogard

National cross-checkers
Ron Hopkins   Chris Pittaro

Major League advance scout
Bob Johnson

Supervisor of international scouting
Eric Kubota

Scouts
Steve Bowden	Tom Clark
Ruben Escalera	Kelly Heath
Tim Holt	John Kuehl
Rick Magnante	Gary McGraw
Billy Owens	John Poloni
Jim Pransky	Will Shock
Rich Sparks	Ron Vaughn

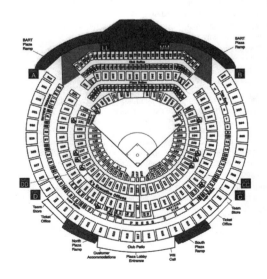

No.	PITCHERS	B/T	Ht./Wt.	Born	1999 clubs	Projection
19	Appier, Kevin	R/R	6-2/200	12-6-67	Kansas City, Oakland	The No. 1 starter, his inconsistency and long-ball problems are concerns.
40	Dubose, Eric	L/L	6-3/215	5-15-76	Midland	A big lefthander with a low-90s fastball, he's a long shot to get a look this spring.
49	Enochs, Chris	R/R	6-3/225	10-11-75	Midland, Visalia	He struggled after shoulder problems; expect him to start at AA.
62	Gregg, Kevin	R/R	6-5/203	6-20-78	Visalia, Midland, Vancouver	Good enough to earn two promotions, but he needs at least a year at AAA.
32	Harville, Chad	R/R	5-9/180	9-16-76	Midland, Vancouver, Oakland	A smallish hard thrower who may be the closer of the future.
31	Heredia, Gil	R/R	6-1/221	10-26-65	Oakland	An innings-eater (200-plus) who has to cut down on homers allowed (22).
15	Hudson, Tim	R/R	6-0/160	7-14-75	Midland, Vancouver, Oakland	This slender righthander, 11-2 last year, is a star in the making.
45	Isringhausen, Jason	R/R	6-3/210	9-7-72	Norfolk, New York N.L., Oakland	His 2.13 ERA in 20 games with the A's gets him the closer's job.
24	Jones, Doug	R/R	6-2/224	6-24-57	Oakland	At 42, he offers veteran leadership, a killer changeup and the ability to close.
58	Kubinski, Tim	L/L	6-4/205	1-20-72	Vancouver, Oakland	Another of a lefty-loaded staff who has a shot at making the team.
59	Laxton, Brett	L/R	6-2/210	10-5-73	Vancouver, Oakland	He led AAA Vancouver with 13 wins and will get a look because he's lefthanded.
52	Magnante, Mike	L/L	6-1/185	6-17-65	Anaheim	A lefthanded specialist, he'll be an upgrade over departed Buddy Groom.
17	Mahay, Ron	L/L	6-2/190	6-28-71	Oakland, Vancouver	He was terrific in September and should push for a rotation spot.
33	Mathews, T.J.	R/R	6-1/214	1-19-70	Oakland, Vancouver	Coming off arm surgery, he's a key setup man.
51	Miller, Justin	R/R	6-2/195	8-27-77	Salem	Acquired from the Rockies in the Jimmy Haynes deal, he's at least a year away.
39	Olivares, Omar	R/R	6-0/205	7-6-67	Anaheim, Oakland	Seems to be one of those rare pitchers who has gotten better in his 30s.
30	Prieto, Ariel	R/R	6-2/247	10-22-69	DID NOT PLAY	Coming off Tommy John surgery in '98, he's a long shot to make the rotation.
	Service, Scott	R/R	6-6/230	2-26-67	Kansas City	A durable big man, he can soak up long-relief innings if need be.
54	Vasquez, Leo	L/L	6-4/193	7-1-73	Binghamton, Midland, Van.	A big lefty with strikeout stuff, he'll likely spend the year at AAA.
61	Vizcaino, Luis	R/R	5-11/169	6-1-77	Midland, Vancouver, Oakland	His numbers aren't overwhelming, but he's progressing. Likely ticketed for AAA.

No.	CATCHERS	B/T	Ht./Wt.	Born	1999 clubs	Projection
7	Ardoin, Danny	R/R	6-0/218	7-8-74	Vancouver	The top defensive catcher in the system, he could push for a major league job.
55	Hernandez, Ramon	R/R	6-0/227	5-20-76	Vancouver, Oakland	An offensive threat, he was better than expected defensively.
23	Hinch, A.J.	R/R	6-1/207	5-15-74	Oakland, Vancouver	He hasn't proved he can hit in the majors and his throwing is a concern.

No.	INFIELDERS	B/T	Ht./Wt.	Born	1999 clubs	Projection
3	Chavez, Eric	L/R	6-0/204	12-7-77	Oakland	Hampered by a foot injury in '99, he'll only get better with experience.
50	Espada, Josue	R/R	5-10/175	8-30-75	Midland, Vancouver	A big spring could earn him a long look as the backup middle infielder.
16	Giambi, Jason	L/R	6-3/235	1-8-71	Oakland	Another big year (.315, 33 HRs, 123 RBIs) proves he's legit.
11	Menechino, Frank	R/R	5-9/175	1-7-71	Vancouver, Oakland	A slick-fielding third baseman, he also hit over .300 at AAA.
60	Ortiz, Jose	R/R	5-9/177	6-13-77	Vancouver	Made the move from 2B to SS, which leaves him behind Tejada and Espada.
36	Piatt, Adam	R/R	6-2/195	2-8-76	Midland, Vancouver	The Texas League triple crown winner, he'll still likely start the season at AAA.
9	Saenz, Olmedo	R/R	6-0/185	10-8-70	Oakland, Vancouver	A pleasant surprise as 3B fill-in last season; he'll now back up at third and first.
4	Tejada, Miguel	R/R	5-9/188	5-25-76	Oakland	Still plenty of upside, offensively and defensively, as he gets more experience.
13	Velandia, Jorge	R/R	5-9/185	1-12-75	Oakland	A defensive specialist, he's the front-runner to be the backup middle infielder.
8	Velarde, Randy	R/R	6-0/200	11-24-62	Anaheim, Oakland	Even if he doesn't duplicate 1999's career year, he's a dependable No. 2 hitter.

No.	OUTFIELDERS	B/T	Ht./Wt.	Born	1999 clubs	Projection
22	Becker, Rich	L/L	5-10/193	2-1-72	Milwaukee, Oakland	He came over after Tony Phillips broke his leg and was re-signed in December.
28	Christenson, Ryan	R/R	6-0/191	3-28-74	Oakland, Vancouver	He's adequate defensively with good range but needs to step up at the plate.
23	Encarnacion, Mario	R/R	6-2/205	9-24-77	Midland, Vancouver	This might be the year, at age 22, he pushes for some major league time.
14	Grieve, Ben	L/R	6-4/230	5-4-76	Oakland	His weak throwing arm means he needs to produce better at the plate.
37	Long, Terrence	L/L	6-1/190	2-29-76	Norfolk, New York N.L., Van.	He's the center fielder of the future but still needs seasoning.
44	Porter, Bo	R/R	6-2/195	7-5-72	Iowa, Chicago N.L.	A Rule 5 pickup who has yet to prove he can he hit major league pitching.
12	Stairs, Matt	L/R	5-9/217	2-27-68	Oakland	If he stays healthy, he gives the team lefthanded pop.

No.	DESIGNATED HITTERS	B/T	Ht./Wt.	Born	1999 clubs	Projection
5	Jaha, John	R/R	6-1/217	5-27-66	Oakland	A big power threat who can also play some 1B when Giambi needs a rest.

THE COACHING STAFF

Art Howe, manager: Howe's low-key personality is perfect for this A's team, a surprising contender in 1999 with an 87-75 record. He's a standout teacher and terrific motivator of young players. However, last season's success (a 13-game swing from 1998) will breed expectations, particularly in the relatively weak A.L. West. His 304-344 record in Oakland may be deceptive in that until only recently has he had much talent to work with.

Thad Bosley: He returns as the team's hitting coach for his second season.

Brad Fischer: This is his 22nd year in the A's organization, his fourth as the bullpen coach.

Ken Macha: Macha enters his second season as Howe's bench coach; if last year's success is an indicator, they make a good pairing. But already Macha's name is being mentioned when there are major league managerial openings.

Rick Peterson: He enters his third season as the pitching coach, overseeing the development of some very talented young arms.

Mike Quade: After 13 years as minor league manager, he steps up to the big leagues as first base coach after leading Vancouver to the AAA World Series title.

Ron Washington: He'll be in his fourth season as the A's third-base coach and has the responsibility of continuing to develop Oakland's young, but talented infield.

THE TOP NEWCOMERS

Bo Porter: He's a Rule 5 draftee from the Cubs last December. Porter is a speedy young outfielder and former University of Iowa football player, but hasn't proved he's ready to handle big-league pitching.

Scott Service: He led the Royals in appearances for the second consecutive season with 68 in 1999. He will likely get as many or more as an Athletic.

THE TOP PROSPECTS

Brett Laxton: He was the biggest winner (13) on a Vancouver staff loaded with talent.

Mark Mulder: A non-roster invitee to spring training, the second pick in the 1998 draft has made a quick rise through the organization with a nasty, moving fastball in the low-90-mph range.

Adam Piatt: The first Texas League triple crown winner (.345, 39 homers, 135 RBIs) since 1927, he has emerged as a legitimate power threat. But he's a third baseman, and second-year player Eric Chavez appears to be firmly entrenched there.

Barry Zito: A talented lefthander and the team's first-round pick in 1999, he had only one loss in three levels (AAA, AA and A) last season.

SEATTLE MARINERS
AMERICAN LEAGUE WEST DIVISION

2000 SEASON

2000 Mariners Schedule
Home games shaded. *—All-Star Game at Turner Field (Atlanta).

March
SUN	MON	TUE	WED	THU	FRI	SAT
26	27	28	29	30	31	

April
SUN	MON	TUE	WED	THU	FRI	SAT
						1
2	3 BOS	4 BOS	5 BOS	6	7 NYY	8 NYY
9 NYY	10	11 DET	12 DET	13 DET	14 TOR	15 TOR
16 TOR	17 CWS	18 CWS	19 CWS	20	21 KC	22 KC
23 KC	24 CLE	25 CLE	26 CLE	27	28 KC	29 KC
30 KC						

May
SUN	MON	TUE	WED	THU	FRI	SAT
	1 MIN	2 MIN	3 MIN	4	5 ANA	6 ANA
7 ANA	8 TEX	9 TEX	10 TEX	11 OAK	12 OAK	13 OAK
14 OAK	15 MIN	16 MIN	17 MIN	18	19 TB	20 TB
21 TB	22	23 BAL	24 BAL	25 BAL	26 TB	27 TB
28 TB	29 CWS	30 CWS	31 CWS			

June
SUN	MON	TUE	WED	THU	FRI	SAT
				1	2 SD	3 SD
4 SD	5 COL	6 COL	7 COL	8	9 SF	10 SF
11 SF	12 KC	13 KC	14 KC	15	16 MIN	17 MIN
18 MIN	19 TB	20 TB	21 BAL	22 BAL	23 BAL	24 BAL
25 BAL	26	27 ANA	28 ANA	29 ANA	30 TEX	

July
SUN	MON	TUE	WED	THU	FRI	SAT
						1 TEX
2 TEX	3 ANA	4 ANA	5 ANA	6 ANA	7 LA	8 LA
9 LA	10	11	* 12	13 SD	14 SD	15 SD
16 ARI	17 ARI	18 ARI	19 OAK	20 OAK	21 TEX	22 TEX
23 TEX	24 OAK	25 OAK	26 TOR	27 TOR	28 TOR	29 TOR
30 TOR	31 BOS					

August
SUN	MON	TUE	WED	THU	FRI	SAT
		1 BOS	2 BOS	3	4 NYY	5 NYY
6 NYY	7 NYY	8 CWS	9 CWS	10 CWS	11 CLE	12 CLE
13 CLE	14 DET	15 DET	16 DET	17	18 CLE	19 CLE
20 CLE	21	22 DET	23 DET	24 DET	25 CWS	26 CWS
27 CWS	28 NYY	29 NYY	30 NYY	31		

September
SUN	MON	TUE	WED	THU	FRI	SAT
					1 BOS	2 BOS
3 BOS	4 BOS	5 TOR	6 TOR	7 TOR	8 MIN	9 MIN
10 MIN	11 KC	12 KC	13 KC	14	15 BAL	16 BAL
17 BAL	18 TB	19 TB	20 TB	21 OAK	22 OAK	23 OAK
24 OAK	25	26 TEX	27 TEX	28 TEX	29 ANA	30 ANA

October
SUN	MON	TUE	WED	THU	FRI	SAT
1 ANA	2	3	4	5	6	7

FRONT-OFFICE DIRECTORY

Chairman and chief executive officer ....Howard Lincoln
Board of directors ....Howard Lincoln, chairman; John Ellis, chairman emeritus; Minoru Arakawa; Chris Larson; John McCaw; Frank Shrontz; Craig Watjen
President and chief operating officer ....Chuck Armstrong
Executive vice president, baseball operations ....Pat Gillick
Executive vice president, business operations ....Bob Aylward
Executive vice president, finance and ballpark ops. ....Kevin Mather
Vice president, baseball administration ....Lee Pelekoudas
Vice president, scouting and player development ....Roger Jongewaard
Vice president, communications ....Randy Adamack
Vice president, ballpark operations ....Neil Campbell
Vice president, ballpark planning and development.......................................John Palmer
Controller ....Tim Kornegay
Director, Pacific Rim scouting ....Jim Colborn
Director, player development ....Benny Looper
Director, professional scouting ....Ken Compton
Director, scouting ....Frank Mattox
Director, team travel ....Ron Spellecy
Director, baseball information ....Tim Hevly
Director, broadcasting and communications ....Dave Aust
Director, public information ....Rebecca Hale
Special assignment ....Woody Woodward
Coordinator of baseball technical information ....Mike Kuharich
Coordinator of minor league instruction ....Mike Goff
Home clubhouse manager..Scott Gilbert
Visiting clubhouse manager ....Henry Genzale

MINOR LEAGUE AFFILIATES

Class	Team	League	Manager
AAA	Tacoma	Pacific Coast	Dave Myers
AA	Orlando	Southern	Dan Rohn
A	Lancaster	California	Mark Parent
A	Wisconsin	Midwest	Gary Thurman
A	Everett	Northwest	Terry Pollreisz
Rookie	Peoria Mariners	Arizona	Omer Munoz Jr.

BROADCAST INFORMATION
Radio: KIRO-AM (710).
TV: KIRO-TV (Channel 7).
Cable TV: Fox Sports Northwest.

SPRING TRAINING
Ballpark: Peoria Stadium (Peoria, Ariz.).
Ticket information: 602-784-4444.

ASSISTANCE STAFF
Medical director
Dr. Larry Pedegana
Trainers
Rick Griffin, Tom Newberg, Ken Roll
Team physicians
Dr. Mitchel Storey
Team dentist
Dr. Robert Hughes
Video coordinator
Carl Hamilton
Strength and conditioning coach
Allen Wirtala
Head groundskeeper
Steve Peeler
Assistant groundskeeper
Eddie Busque
Advance scout
Stan Williams
National cross-checker
Steve Jongewaard
Major league scouts
Brandy Davis, Bob Harrison, Bill Kearns, Steve Pope
Scouting supervisors
Curtis Dishman, Ken Madeja, John McMichen, Carroll Sembera.
Scouts
Dave Alexander, Maximo Alvarez, Brian Ballentine, Jeff Brisson, Mark Brown, Jon Bunnell, Rodney Davis, Ramon de los Santos, Murray Gage-Cole, Pete Garcia, Phil Geisler, Ron Hafner, Des Hamilton, Larry Harper, Ted Heid, Jae Lee, Stan Lewis, Mark Lummus, Wilmer Mardera, Juan Marquez, John Martin, Luis Martinez, Mauro Mazzotti, Tom McNamara, Julio Molina, Omer Munoz Sr., Myron Pines, Phil Pote, Steve Rath, Eric Robinson, Jesus Salazar, Raul Santana, Alex Smith, Jim Stewart, Harry Stricklett, Derek Valenzuela, Kyle Van Hook, Ray Vince, Curtis Wallace, Karel Williams, Selwyn Young

BALLPARK INFORMATION

Ballpark (capacity, surface)
Safeco Field (47,116, grass)
Address
1st Ave. S. & Atlantic
Seattle, WA 98104
Business phone
206-346-4001
Ticket information
206-346-4001
Ticket prices
$37 (terrace club infield)
$32 (lower box)
$29 (terrace club outfield)
$27 (field)
$18 (view box, lower outfield reserved)
$14 (view reserved)
$9 (left field bleachers)
$5 (center field bleachers)
Field dimensions (from home plate)
To left field at foul line, 331 feet
To center field, 405 feet
To right field at foul line, 326 feet
First game played
July 15, 1999 (Padres 3, Mariners 2)

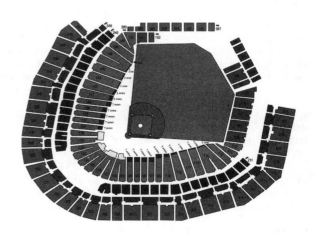

No.	PITCHERS	B/T	Ht./Wt.	Born	1999 clubs	Projection
45	Abbott, Paul	R/R	6-3/195	9-15-67	Tacoma, Seattle	He went 6-2 with twice as many strikeouts as walks. He's a valuable fifth starter.
26	Cloude, Ken	R/R	6-1/180	1-9-75	Tacoma, Seattle	He throws hard, but must learn to change speeds to get back into the rotation.
43	Davey, Tom	R/R	6-7/230	9-11-73	Toronto, Syracuse, Seattle	A lanky righthander, he's expected to be a reliable middle reliever.
23	Franklin, Ryan	R/R	6-3/185	3-5-73	Tacoma, Seattle	He struggled with control last September. Barring a big spring, he'll start at AAA.
61	Fuentes, Brian	L/L	6-4/220	8-9-75	New Haven	He'll likely start the season at AAA, where he needs to work on his control.
34	Garcia, Freddy	R/R	6-4/235	10-6-76	Seattle	He was durable (200-plus innings) and successful (17-8) as a breakout rookie.
54	Halama, John	L/L	6-5/200	2-22-72	Seattle	He changes speeds and locates well, making him a younger version of Moyer.
32	Hinchliffe, Brett	R/R	6-5/190	7-21-74	Seattle, Tacoma	He was underwhelming (0-4, 8.80 ERA) in 1999, casting a doubt on his future.
	Hodges, Kevin	R/R	6-4/200	6-24-73	Jackson, New Orleans, Tacoma	He gave up more than a hit an inning at AAA, where he's ticketed to play.
	Mears, Chris	R/R	6-4/180	1-20-78	Wisconsin, Lancaster	He struggled (3-6) on a bad Class A team, but showed some strikeout potential.
55	Meche, Gil	R/R	6-3/180	9-8-78	New Haven, Tacoma, Seattle	At 8-4, he was a surprise as a rookie. He'll get a shot at a rotation spot.
49	Mesa, Jose	R/R	6-3/225	5-22-66	Seattle	He had 33 saves, but allows too many baserunners. His closer's job is tenuous.
34	Montane, Ivan	R/R	6-2/195	6-3-73	Wisconsin, New Haven	He averaged more than a strikeout an inning at AA and is the closer of the future.
50	Moyer, Jamie	L/L	6-0/170	11-18-62	Seattle	The veteran and ace of the staff, he lives off a great changeup.
30	Paniagua, Jose	R/R	6-2/185	8-20-73	Seattle	He thrives as a righthanded setup man who can close occasionally.
23	Ramsay, Robert	L/L	6-5/220	12-3-73	Pawtucket, Seattle, Tacoma	By going 4-1 with a 1.08 ERA at AAA, he's earned a long look this spring.
53	Rhodes, Arthur	L/L	6-2/205	10-24-69	Baltimore	Rhodes will open as a setup man unless Mesa falters.
33	Rodriguez, Frankie	R/R	6-0/210	12-11-72	Salt Lake, Seattle	He'll get a shot at the rotation, but has to cut the number of hits he allows.
	Sasaki, Kazuhiro	R/R	6-4/208	2-22-68	Yokohama BayStars	A star in Japan but unproven in the U.S., he's ticketed for righthanded setup.
	Sele, Aaron	R/R	6-5/215	6-25-70	Texas	No. 3 starter is tied for the second-most major league wins the past two seasons.
53	Sinclair, Steve	L/L	6-2/190	8-2-71	Syracuse, Toronto, Sea., Tac.	A disappointment after coming over from the Jays, he needs a big spring.
48	Spencer, Sean	L/L	5-11/185	5-29-75	Tacoma, Seattle	After a strikeout-an-inning showing at AAA, he's aiming for a bullpen slot.
67	Stark, Dennis	R/R	6-2/210	10-27-74	New Haven, Seattle	His five-game audition was a disaster (9.95 ERA). He'll likely start in Tacoma.
31	Williams, Todd	R/R	6-3/210	2-13-71	Indianapolis, Tacoma, Seattle	He was impressive enough in September to get a look.
46	Zimmerman, Jordan	R/L	6-0/200	4-28-75	New Haven, Sea., Tac., Everett	His ERA (1.08) didn't match his record (1-4) at AA. Look for him at AAA.

No.	CATCHERS	B/T	Ht./Wt.	Born	1999 clubs	Projection
17	Lampkin, Tom	L/R	5-11/195	3-4-64	Seattle	A lefthanded hitter, he's proved to be the perfect backup to Wilson.
6	Wilson, Dan	R/R	6-3/202	3-25-69	Seattle	He's a solid everyday catcher, but the team would like to see more offense.

No.	INFIELDERS	B/T	Ht./Wt.	Born	1999 clubs	Projection
25	Bell, David	R/R	5-10/175	9-14-72	Seattle	Solid at 2B after Guillen got hurt, he'll begin spring as the starter.
8	Guillen, Carlos	B/R	6-1/180	9-30-75	Seattle	Coming off a season-ending knee injury, this potential star makes the shift to 3B.
	McLemore, Mark	B/R	5-11/207	10-4-64	Texas	His knees are a concern, but he's a valuable clubhouse presence and can play LF.
5	Olerud, John	L/L	6-5/220	8-5-68	New York N.L.	He's back home after proving with the Mets that he's among the best.
3	Rodriguez, Alex	R/R	6-3/195	7-27-75	Seattle	The best five-tool shortstop today, but will pending free agency be a distraction?

No.	OUTFIELDERS	B/T	Ht./Wt.	Born	1999 clubs	Projection
	Alexander, Chad	R/R	6-1/195	5-22-74	Jackson, New Orleans	A Rule 5 pick from the Astros, he hit .369 in the Arizona Fall League.
19	Buhner, Jay	R/R	6-3/215	8-13-64	Seattle	He's battled injuries the last few years but is still a devastating hitter.
1	Gipson, Charles	R/R	6-2/180	12-16-72	Sea., Tac., New Haven, Everett	He has a good glove and terrific arm, but has to have a big spring.
24	Griffey Jr., Ken	L/L	6-3/205	11-21-69	Seattle	Despite a tumultuous offseason, he's still a superstar who anchors any lineup.
22	Hunter, Brian	R/R	6-3/180	3-5-71	Detroit, Seattle	He led the league with 44 SBs, but needs to be more of a consistent hitter.
5	Ibanez, Raul	L/R	6-2/200	6-2-72	Seattle, Tacoma	It'll be tough to find a spot for him on the big club.
	Javier, Stan	B/R	6-0/202	1-9-64	San Francisco, Houston	He's a perfect fourth outfielder who provides veteran stability.
47	Mabry, John	L/R	6-4/195	10-17-70	Seattle	His versatility and lefthanded bat should help him in a crowded outfield picture.
12	Monahan, Shane	L/R	6-0/195	8-12-74	Tacoma, Seattle	Like Ibanez, he looks like an odd man out, which means back to AAA.

No.	DESIGNATED HITTERS	B/T	Ht./Wt.	Born	1999 clubs	Projection
11	Martinez, Edgar	R/R	5-11/200	1-2-63	Seattle	When it comes to hitting, there are few better.

THE COACHING STAFF

Lou Piniella, manager: For a while last season, it looked like Piniella (1,019-949 in 13 major league seasons) wouldn't reach this, his eighth season as the Mariners' manager. But he's back and G.M. Pat Gillick has begun to rework Seattle's roster so that his fiery manager appears to have a shot at breaking the Rangers' two-year hold on the A.L. West title. He ranks as the winningest manager in franchise history with 540.

Larry Bowa: He joins the staff as third base and infield coach after three years as the Angels' third base coach.

John McLaren: He enters his fifth season with Piniella, his third as bench coach. He has been coaching at the major league level for 14 seasons.

John Moses: An advance scout in '99, he returns to the staff as first base and outfield coach.

Gerald Perry: He comes to the team as hitting coach after three seasons as a minor league hitting instructor with the Red Sox.

Bryan Price: The Mariners' minor-league pitching coordinator for three seasons, he replaces Stan Willimas as the major league pitching coach.

Matt Sinatro: A former major league catcher, Sinatro is entering his sixth season as bullpen coach.

THE TOP NEWCOMERS

Carlos Guillen: Because his rookie season ended before it really started (he suffered a knee injury in the fifth game), he's still considered a newcomer. He goes to camp coming off surgery on both knees, a caveat when considering his previous "can't-miss" tag.

Stan Javier: He's as dependable a defensive outfielder as they come. And he doesn't have such a bad bat either. The Mariners may use him often, whether it's to spell an injured Mariner (like Buhner), platoon in leftfield or enter as a pinch-hitter or defensive replacement.

Mark McLemore: At 35, his most productive years are behind him, but he's a terrific presence in the clubhouse and will afford Piniella the flexibility of being able to play him at second base and the outfield.

John Olerud: He makes a trip home as a 31-year-old seemingly in the prime of his career. His steady bat and dependable were a big part of the Mets' plans last year, and they'll be truly sorry they let him get away this offseason.

Arthur Rhodes: A lefty in the bullpen is always nice to have. Though he struggled a bit with the Orioles last season, he is very versatile in relief. He can throw long relief, act as a lefthanded specialist, pitch regularly and even close games. The Mariners gave the 30-year-old hurler plenty of money to fill at least one of those roles consistently.

Aaron Sele: After an offseason rift in which he nearly signed a three-year deal with Baltimore, Sele heads to Seattle and should enjoy the more spacious surroundings of Safeco Field. Better yet, he get to battle with his ex-Rangers mates for the division title. He's won 37 games the last two seasons with the Rangers, but won't have Texas' run support this season.

THE TOP PROSPECTS

Ryan Anderson: Hmm, 6-10 and lefthanded? "The Little Unit" skipped A ball, starting his pro career at AA New Haven in '99, where, although he went 9-13 he also led the Eastern League in strikeouts with 162 in 134 innings. He'll likely get some time at AAA to work on his control.

TAMPA BAY DEVIL RAYS

AMERICAN LEAGUE EAST DIVISION

2000 SEASON

2000 Devil Rays Schedule

Home games shaded. *—All-Star Game at Turner Field (Atlanta).

March

SUN	MON	TUE	WED	THU	FRI	SAT
26	27	28	29	30	31	

April

SUN	MON	TUE	WED	THU	FRI	SAT
						1
2 MIN	3 MIN	4 MIN	5 MIN	6 MIN	7 CLE	8 CLE
9 CLE	10	11 CWS	12 CWS	13 CWS	14 DET	15 DET
16 DET	17 BAL	18 BAL	19 BAL	20	21 ANA	22 ANA
23 ANA	24	25 KC	26 KC	27 ANA	28 ANA	29 ANA
30 ANA						

May

SUN	MON	TUE	WED	THU	FRI	SAT
	1	2 TEX	3 TEX	4 TEX	5 BOS	6 BOS
7 BOS	8 NYY	9 NYY	10 NYY	11	12 TOR	13 TOR
14 TOR	15 TEX	16 TEX	17 TEX	18	19 SEA	20 SEA
21 SEA	22	23 OAK	24 OAK	25 OAK	26 SEA	27 SEA
28 SEA	29 BAL	30 BAL	31 BAL			

June

SUN	MON	TUE	WED	THU	FRI	SAT
				1 BAL	2 NYM	3 NYM
4 NYM	5 PHI	6 PHI	7 PHI	8	9 FLA	10 FLA
11 FLA	12	13 ANA	14 ANA	15 ANA	16 TEX	17 TEX
18 TEX	19 SEA	20 SEA	21 SEA	22	23 TEX	24 TEX
25 TEX	26	27 TOR	28 TOR	29 TOR	30 NYY	

July

SUN	MON	TUE	WED	THU	FRI	SAT
						1 NYY
2 NYY	3 DET	4 DET	5 DET	6	7 FLA	8 FLA
9 FLA	10	11	* 12	13 MON	14 MON	15 MON
16 ATL	17 ATL	18 ATL	19 TOR	20 TOR	21 NYY	22 NYY
23 NYY	24 DET	25 DET	26 DET	27 KC	28 KC	29 KC
30 KC	31					

August

SUN	MON	TUE	WED	THU	FRI	SAT
		1 CLE	2 CLE	3 CLE	4 BAL	5 BAL
6 BAL	7 MIN	8 MIN	9 MIN	10 MIN	11 CWS	12 CWS
13 CWS	14 BOS	15 BOS	16 BOS	17	18 CWS	19 CWS
20 CWS	21 CWS	22 MIN	23 MIN	24	25 BAL	26 BAL
27 BAL	28 BOS	29 BOS	30 BOS	31 KC		

September

SUN	MON	TUE	WED	THU	FRI	SAT
					1 KC	2 KC
3 KC	4 CLE	5 CLE	6 CLE	7 CLE	8 OAK	9 OAK
10 OAK	11 OAK	12 ANA	13 ANA	14	15 OAK	16 OAK
17 OAK	18 SEA	19 SEA	20 SEA	21	22 TOR	23 TOR
24 TOR	25 TOR	26 NYY	27 NYY	28 NYY	29 BOS	30 BOS

October

SUN	MON	TUE	WED	THU	FRI	SAT
1 BOS	2	3	4	5	6	7

FRONT-OFFICE DIRECTORY

Managing general partner/CEO ....Vincent J. Naimoli
Senior vice president, baseball operations/general manager ....Chuck LaMar
Senior vice president, administration and general counsel ....John P. Higgins
Vice president of sales and marketing ....John Browne
Vice president of public relations ....Rick Vaughn
Vice president of operations & facilities ....Rick Nafe
Assistant general manager/baseball operations ....Bart Braun
Assistant general manager/administration ....Scott Proefrock
Special assistants to the general manager ....Eddie Bane, Wade Boggs, Bill Livesey
Director of scouting ....Dan Jennings
Special advisor for baseball operations ....Frank Howard
Director of minor league operations ....Tom Foley
Assistant to player development ....Mitch Lukevics
Traveling secretary ....Jeffrey Ziegler
Travel consultant..Dirk Smith
Controller ....Patrick Smith
Director of human resources ....Louise "Jeep" Weber
Director of business administration ....Bill Wiener, Jr.
Senior director of corporate sales & broadcasting....................................Larry McCabe
Manager of broadcast operations ....Joe Ciaravino
Director of corporate sales ....Tom Whaley
Manager of sponsorship coordination ....Tammy Atmore, Kelly Davis
Manager of promotions & special events....................................Christopher Dean
Director of ticket operations..Robert Bennett
Assistant director of ticket operations..Ken Mallory
Director of ticket sales ....Carola Ross
Assistant to V.P., public relations ....Carmen Molina
Director of publications..Matt Lorenz
Media relations manager ....Chris Costello
Assistant media relations manager ....Greg Landy
Manager of community relations ....Liz-Beth Lauck
Director of event productions & entertainment....................................John Franzone
Video producer..Jason Rundle
Video coordinator..Chris Fernandez

MINOR LEAGUE AFFILIATES

Class	Team	League	Manager
AAA	Durham	International	Bill Evers
AA	Orlando	Southern	To be announced
A	St. Petersburg	Florida State	Mike Ramsey
A	Charleston (W.Va.)	South Atlantic	Charlie Montoyo
Rookie	Hudson Valley	New York-Pennsylvania	To be announced
Rookie	Princeton	Appalachian	Edwin Rodriguez

BALLPARK INFORMATION

Ballpark (capacity, surface)
Tropicana Field (43,819, artificial)
Address
One Tropicana Drive, St. Petersburg, FL 33607
Business phone
727-825-3137
Ticket information
727-825-3250
Ticket prices
$160 (home plate box), $65 (field box)
$35 (lower club box), $30 (diamond club box & reserved)
$22 (lower box), $20 (lower reserved, terrace box)
$17 (upper box), $14 (terrace reserved, outfield)
$10 (the beach, upper reserved), $8 (upper general admission)
Field dimensions (from home plate)
To left field at foul line, 315 feet
To center field, 404 feet
To right field at foul line, 320 feet
First game played
March 31, 1998 (Tigers 11, Devil Rays 6)

ASSISTANCE STAFF

Head trainer
Jamie Reed
Assistant head trainer
Ken Crenshaw
Strength and conditioning coordinator
Kevin Harmon
Medical team physician
Dr. Michael Reilly
Orthopaedic team physician
Dr. Koco Eaton
Head groundskeeper
Mike Williams
Clubhouse operations-home
Carlos Ledezma
Clubhouse operations-visitor
Guy Gallagher
Major League scouts
Jerry Gardner, Bart Johnson, Matt Keough, Al LaMacchia, Don Lindeberg, Don Williams
Crosscheckers
Jack Gillis, R.J. Harrison, Stan Meek
Area scouts
Fernando Arango, Jonathan Bonifay, Todd Brown, Skip Bundy, Matt Dodd, Kevin Elfering, Steve Foster, Doug Gassaway, Matt Kinzer, Paul Kirsch, Edwin Rodriguez, Charles Scott, Mac Seibert, Craig F. Weissmann, Doug Witt
Part-time scouts
Jorge Calvo Lara Sr., Jorge Calvo Jr., Philip Elhage, Benny Latino, Daniel McConnon, Adrian T. Meagher, Jose Perez, Juan Pringle, Junior Ramirez, Gustavo Rodriguez, Freddy Torres, Mel Zitter

BROADCAST INFORMATION

Radio: WFLA-AM (970).
TV: MORE-TV (Channel 32); WTSP (Channel 10).
Cable TV: SportsChannel Florida.

SPRING TRAINING

Ballpark (city): Al Lang Stadium (St. Petersburg, Fla.).
Ticket information: 727-825-3250.

2000 PREVIEW

No.	PITCHERS	B/T	Ht./Wt.	Born	1999 clubs	Projection
40	Alvarez, Wilson	L/L	6-1/235	3-24-70	Tampa Bay	Lefthanded ace's injuries have kept him from returning to 1997 form.
47	Duvall, Mike	R/L	6-0/185	10-11-74	Tampa Bay, Durham	Hard-throwing lefty relief specialist who could start in Class AAA.
	Guzman, Juan	R/R	5-11/195	10-28-66	Baltimore, Cincinnati	The hard-throwing righthander was a great signing for Tampa Bay this offseason.
39	Hernandez, Roberto	R/R	6-4/235	11-11-64	Tampa Bay	How important is he? Of the Devil Rays' 69 victories, he had 43 saves and two wins.
27	Lidle, Cory	R/R	5-11/180	3-22-72	St. Petersburg, Durham, T.B.	Injured in 1999, but hasn't been a factor for the five organizations he's played for.
32	Lopez, Albie	R/R	6-2/185	8-18-71	Tampa Bay, St. Petersburg	Pitched great in the '99 second half and will split time with Mecir as the setup man.
45	Mecir, Jim	B/R	6-1/195	5-16-70	Tampa Bay	Trying to bounce back from an elbow fracture, he will split time as the setup man.
63	Morris, Jim	L/L	6-3/215	1-19-64	Orlando, Durham, Tampa Bay	The great story of 1999 (former high-school teacher), he'll still has to prove himself.
	Ogea, Chad	L/R	6-2/220	11-9-70	Philadelphia	The Devil Rays hope he regains the magic he displayed for Cleveland years ago.
	Reitsma, Chris	R/R	6-5/214	12-31-77	Sarasota	He's a ways away. Despite good build and stuff, he has struggled in the minors.
56	Rekar, Bryan	R/R	6-3/210	6-3-72	Durham, Tampa Bay	Struggled as a starter before hitting the D.L. in July for the remainder of the season.
24	Rupe, Ryan	R/R	6-5/230	3-31-75	Orlando, Tampa Bay	The Rays hope he'll pitch like a veteran, despite his age.
31	Saunders, Tony	L/L	6-2/205	4-29-74	Tampa Bay, Durham	He'll be in camp with the Devil Rays but won't be pitching anytime soon.
62	Sparks, Jeff	R/R	6-3/220	4-4-72	Nashville, Durham, Tampa Bay	Coming over in the Jose Guillen trade last year, he's a big-time strikeout pitcher.
46	Trachsel, Steve	R/R	6-4/205	10-31-70	Chicago N.L.	Despite leading the N.L. in losses last year, he was still durable and dependable.
34	Wheeler, Dan	R/R	6-3/222	12-10-77	Orlando, Durham, Tampa Bay	At 22, he'll step into the rotation on a full-time basis.
51	White, Rick	R/R	6-4/215	12-23-68	Tampa Bay	He pitched well in '99—solid relief and a lot of innings. He'll do the same in 2000.
43	Yan, Esteban	R/R	6-4/230	6-22-74	Tampa Bay, St. Petersburg	Might struggle early as he makes the transition from middle reliever to starter.

No.	CATCHERS	B/T	Ht./Wt.	Born	1999 clubs	Projection
8	Difelice, Mike	R/R	6-2/205	5-28-69	Tampa Bay	A gritty backup whose offense is undervalued.
6	Flaherty, John	R/R	6-1/200	10-21-67	Tampa Bay	Had a breakout year in 1999, displaying his good bat and great arm.

No.	INFIELDERS	B/T	Ht./Wt.	Born	1999 clubs	Projection
13	Cairo, Miguel	R/R	6-1/160	5-4-74	Tampa Bay, Orlando, St. Pete.	Has mental lapses on defense but will provide plenty of exciting offense.
20	Castilla, Vinny	R/R	6-1/205	7-4-67	Colorado	Tropicana Field isn't much different than Coors Field. Expect 35-plus homers again.
71	Cox, Steve	L/L	6-4/222	10-31-74	Durham, Tampa Bay	The first base-loaded team doesn't have room for this '99 International League MVP.
26	Graffanino, Tony	R/R	6-1/195	6-6-72	Durham, Tampa Bay	Versatile infielder who is Cairo's backup at second base.
15	Lamb, David	B/R	6-2/165	6-6-75	Tampa Bay, Durham	Switch-hitting middle infielder will begin the season as a backup.
29	McGriff, Fred	L/L	6-3/215	10-31-63	Tampa Bay	Remember the washed-up talk he got in 1998? No sir—another huge year in '99.
	Rolls, Damian	R/R	6-2/205	9-15-77	Vero Beach	A future Devil Rays third baseman, but not close to being a present one.
9	Smith, Robert	R/R	6-3/190	5-10-74	Tampa Bay, Durham	A four-position utilityman who still won't get a shot at third with Castilla there.
19	Stocker, Kevin	B/R	6-1/175	2-13-70	Tampa Bay, St. Petersburg	A knee injury slowed and eventually ended his '99 season, but he'll be recovered.

No.	OUTFIELDERS	B/T	Ht./Wt.	Born	1999 clubs	Projection
33	Canseco, Jose	R/R	6-4/240	7-2-64	Tampa Bay	The Bash Brother is back in top form. If healthy, he'll hit DH and devastate the A.L.
11	Guillen, Jose	R/R	5-11/195	5-17-76	Pittsburgh, Nash., Durham, T.B.	The sky's the limit for this guy, but he needs patience at the plate.
14	Martinez, Dave	L/L	5-10/175	9-26-64	Tampa Bay	Will compete for time with Guillen in right field. He's been a steady performer.
3	McCracken, Quinton	B/R	5-7/173	3-16-70	Tampa Bay	Needs his reconstructed knee to be 100 percent or he's not the same great player.
1	Sanchez, Alex	L/L	5-10/180	8-26-76	Orlando, Durham	Has outstanding speed but hasn't found a way to harness it defensively.
21	Trammell, Bubba	R/R	6-2/220	11-6-71	Durham, Tampa Bay	Has moments of brilliance and a flare for a clutch hit . . . still the fourth outfielder.
23	Vaughn, Greg	R/R	6-0/202	7-3-65	Cincinnati	Had another huge year RBI year in Cincinnati and joins a powerful lineup.
	Wilcox, Luke	L/R	6-4/225	11-15-73	Orlando, Durham	A .328 average in 39 games late last season has him heading on the right track.
	Williams, Gerald	R/R	6-2/187	8-10-66	Atlanta	Proved his value late in Atlanta's regular season and the playoffs.
2	Winn, Randy	B/R	6-2/175	6-9-74	Tampa Bay, Durham	The speedster will start at Class AAA to work on his leadoff skills and throwing.

THE COACHING STAFF

Larry Rothschild, manager: The only goal for the second-year Devil Rays last season was an improvement from 1998 and some excitement to go with it. It was definitely achieved as the team won six more games in arguably the best division in baseball—the A.L. East. The Devil Rays' philosophy has changed. They want to win, or at least improve greatly, this year. They have signed several top free agents and figure to have a powerful lineup. But the former pitching coach for the 1997 Marlins' championship squad will have quite a task with this makeshift pitching staff.

Jose Cardenal: He certainly brings success with him. Cardenal has coached for the mighty Yankees for his last seven seasons, earning three titles along the way. The 18-year major leaguer should bring some the Yankees' and Joe Torre's winning attitude with him. He'll be the first base and outfielders coach with the Devil Rays.

Orlando Gomez: Served as the bullpen coach for his first year in 1999. Had served as an assistant in Texas in 1991 and 1992.

Billy Hatcher: The 12-year big leaguer returns for his third season as first base coach after spending the previous two seasons coaching in the Devil Rays' minor league system. He's got some good young basestealers to keep his eye on.

Leon Roberts: Roberts is in his second year as the Devil Rays' hitting coach. Certainly, his debut season was quite a success. After hitting just .261 with 111 homers in 1998, the Devil Rays recorded a .274 mark with 145 homers in 1999. Those numbers, at least the homer total, will skyrocket this season.

Bill Russell: Russell joins the major league staff for his first year. The former Dodger manager managed Tampa Bay's Class AA team in Orlando in 1999, taking them to the Southern League title.

Rick Williams: He brings his 19 years of professional coaching experience to his role as the pitching coach. He must turn some of the young pitchers on Tampa Bay's staff into viable starters.

THE TOP NEWCOMERS

Vinny Castilla: What can you say about a player who has hit an average of 39.8 homers and 118 RBIs over the last four seasons? He's a bad fielder? Not so, he's a vast improvement over the platoon at third base the last few years.

Juan Guzman: When healthy, he has dominant stuff. He has the potential to fire a one-hitter on any given day but get shelled his next start. He'll need guidance to be successful again.

Chad Ogea: Injuries and simple lack of success have put him into the doghouses of both Cleveland and Philadelphia the past two seasons. The Devil Rays are counting on him to be healthy and productive again.

Steve Trachsel: There's something to be said for durability in today's game, and Trachsel has it. In his nine-year minor and major league career, he has spent just 15 days on a disabled list.

Greg Vaughn: The unfortunate thing is: either he or Jose Canseco's defensive skills are stuck in the outfield. The fortunate thing is: that allows both of their bats to get into the lineup. Vaughn is only the capper in a lineup that features four straight 35-plus homer candidates in McGriff, Canseco, Castilla and he.

Gerald Williams: He clobbers lefties, has decent power and speed, plays smart in the outfield and has a good arm. So what doesn't this guy have? Right now, a starting spot. He'll have to battle McCracken for center field in a deep outfield. Either way, he'll get his at-bats and see plenty of action.

THE TOP PROSPECTS

Steve Cox: This kid put up incredible numbers last season in Durham of the Class AAA International League. He hit .341 with 49 doubles, 25 homers and 127 RBIs in 134 games. But the path is blocked for this first baseman. We'll have to see him in a future year.

Dan Wheeler: The Devil Rays would love to work him along slowly, but they just don't have that luxury. He'll have to take his lumps in the starting rotation this season.

TEXAS RANGERS
AMERICAN LEAGUE WEST DIVISION

2000 SEASON

2000 Rangers Schedule
Home games shaded. *—All-Star Game at Turner Field (Atlanta).

March
SUN	MON	TUE	WED	THU	FRI	SAT
26	27	28	29	30	31	

April
SUN	MON	TUE	WED	THU	FRI	SAT
						1
2	3 CWS	4 CWS	5 CWS	6 CWS	7 TOR	8 TOR
9 TOR	10	11 NYY	12 NYY	13 NYY	14 CLE	15 CLE
16 CLE	17 NYY	18 NYY	19 NYY	20	21 MIN	22 MIN
23 MIN	24 BOS	25 BOS	26 BOS	27	28 BAL	29 BAL
30 BAL						

May
SUN	MON	TUE	WED	THU	FRI	SAT
	1	2 TB	3 TB	4 TB	5 OAK	6 OAK
7 OAK	8 SEA	9 SEA	10 SEA	11 ANA	12 ANA	13 ANA
14 ANA	15 TB	16 TB	17 TB	18 BAL	19 BAL	20 BAL
21 BAL	22	23 KC	24 KC	25 KC	26 MIN	27 MIN
28 MIN	29 DET	30 DET	31 DET			

June
SUN	MON	TUE	WED	THU	FRI	SAT
				1	2 ARI	3 ARI
4 ARI	5 LA	6 LA	7 LA	8	9 COL	10 COL
11 COL	12	13 BAL	14 BAL	15 BAL	16 TB	17 TB
18 TB	19	20 MIN	21 MIN	22 MIN	23 TB	24 TB
25 TB	26	27 OAK	28 OAK	29 OAK	30 SEA	

July
SUN	MON	TUE	WED	THU	FRI	SAT
						1 SEA
2 SEA	3 OAK	4 OAK	5 OAK	6 SD	7 SD	8 SD
9 SD	10	11 *	12	13 ARI	14 ARI	15 ARI
16 SF	17 SF	18 SF	19 ANA	20 ANA	21 SEA	22 SEA
23 SEA	24 ANA	25 ANA	26 ANA	27 DET	28 DET	29 DET
30 DET	31					

August
SUN	MON	TUE	WED	THU	FRI	SAT
		1 CWS	2 CWS	3 TOR	4 TOR	5 TOR
6 TOR	7	8 CLE	9 CLE	10 CLE	11 BOS	12 BOS
13 BOS	14 NYY	15 NYY	16 NYY	17 BOS	18 BOS	19 BOS
20 BOS	21	22 NYY	23 NYY	24 NYY	25 TOR	26 TOR
27 TOR	28 CLE	29 CLE	30 CLE	31 CLE		

September
SUN	MON	TUE	WED	THU	FRI	SAT
					1 DET	2 DET
3 DET	4 CWS	5 CWS	6 CWS	7 CWS	8 KC	9 KC
10 KC	11	12 BAL	13 BAL	14 KC	15 KC	16 KC
17 KC	18 MIN	19 MIN	20 MIN	21	22 ANA	23 ANA
24 ANA	25	26 SEA	27 SEA	28 SEA	29 OAK	30 OAK

October
SUN	MON	TUE	WED	THU	FRI	SAT
1 OAK	2	3	4	5	6	7

FRONT-OFFICE DIRECTORY
Chairman of the board ....Thomas O. Hicks
President ....James R. Lites
Executive vice president, general manager ....Doug Melvin
Executive vice president, finance and operations ....John F. McMichael
Executive vice president, broadcasting and sales ....Bill Strong
Executive vice president, marketing and communications ....Jeff Cogen
Senior vice president, communications ....John Blake
Vice president, community development/relations ....Norm Lyons
Vice president, finance ....Chip Sawicki
Vice president, facilities and construction ....Billy Ray Johnson
Vice president, diversified operations ....Rick McLaughlin
Vice president, information technology ....Steve McNeill
Vice president, business operations ....Geoff Moore
Vice president, event operations ....Tim Murphy
Vice president, merchandising ....Steve Shills
Vice president, corporate sales ....Charlie Seraphin
Director, Legends of the Game museum ....Tom Smith
Director, human resources ....Terry Turner
Corporate counsel ....Lance Lankford
Assistant vice president, ticket sales ....Brian Byrnes
Assistant vice president, corporate services ....Jill Cogen
Assistant vice president, ticket operations ....Augie Manfredo
Assistant vice president, marketing ....Christy Martinez
Assistant vice president, advertising sales...................................David Peart
Controller ....Kellie Fischer
Assistant general manager ....Dan O'Brien
Director, Major League administration ....Judy Johns
Director, scouting ....Chuck McMichael
Director, player development ....Reid Nichols
Assistant director, player development ....John Lombardo
Assistant director, professional and international scouting ....Monty Clegg
Assistant to director of player development ....Debbie Bent
Director of travel ....Chris Lyngos
Director, media relations...Kurt Daniels
Director, community relations ....Taunee Paur Taylor
Director, community development ....Rhonda Houston
Assistant director, communications ....Dana Wilcox
Assistant director, media relations...Brad Horn
Senior director, events ....Lee Gleiser
Senior director, entertainment ....Chuck Morgan
Senior director, graphic design ....Rainer Uhlir

MINOR LEAGUE AFFILIATES
Class	Team	League	Manager
AAA	Oklahoma	Pacific Coast	DeMarlo Hale
AA	Tulsa	Texas	Bobby Jones
A	Charlotte	Florida State	Jim Byrd
A	Savannah	South Atlantic	Paul Carey
Rookie	Pulaski	Appalachian	Bruce Crabbe
Rookie	Gulf Coast Rangers	Gulf Coast	Darryl Kennedy

BALLPARK INFORMATION
Ballpark (capacity, surface)
The Ballpark in Arlington (49,166, grass)
Address
1000 Ballpark Way, Arlington, TX 76011
Business phone
817-273-5222
Ticket information
817-273-5100
Ticket prices
$37.50 (lower box), $35 (club box),
$30 (club reserved), $25 (corner box),
$20 (terrace club box),
$17.50 (left field reserved; lower home run porch),
$14 (upper box), $12 (upper home run porch),
$10 (upper reserved; bleachers),
$6 (grandstand reserved), $5 (grandstand)
Field dimensions (from home plate)
To left field at foul line, 334 feet
To center field, 400 feet
To right field at foul line, 325 feet
First game played
April 11, 1994 (Brewers 4, Rangers 3)

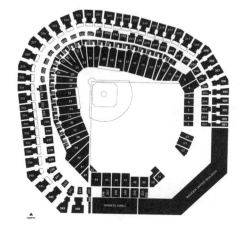

ASSISTANCE STAFF
Director, medical services
Dr. John Conway

Head trainer
Danny Wheat

Visiting clubhouse manager
Joe Macko

Equipment & home clubhouse manager
Zack Minasian

National cross-checkers
Tim Hallgren	David Klipstein
Jeff Taylor	

Latin coordinator
Manny Batista

Scouts
Dave Birecki	Carl Cassell
Jim Cuthbert	Mike Daughtry
Jay Eddings	Kip Fagg
Jim Fairey	Tim Fortugno
Mark Giegler	Joel Grampietro
Mike Grouse	Todd Guggiana
Doug Harris	Zackary Hoyrst
Ray Jackson	Jim Lentine
Dennis Meeks	Sammy Melendez
Gary Neibauer	Mike Paustian
Javier Rodriguez	Randy Taylor
Ron Toenjes	Greg Whitworth
Jeff Wren	

BROADCAST INFORMATION
Radio: KRLD-AM (1080); KESS (1270), Spanish.
TV: KXAS-TV (Channel 5); KXTX-TV (Channel 39).
Cable TV: Fox Sports Net.

SPRING TRAINING
Ballpark (city): Charlotte County Stadium (Port Charlotte, Fla.).
Ticket information: 941-625-9500.

No.	PITCHERS	B/T	Ht./Wt.	Born	1999 clubs	Projection
53	Benoit, Joaquin	R/R	6-3/205	7-26-79	Charlotte	Control was a problem, but he showed potential that he needs to polish.
54	Clark, Mark	R/R	6-5/235	5-12-68	Texas, Savannah, Charlotte	He goes to camp with a rotation spot, but he needs to have a good spring.
33	Cordero, Francisco	R/R	6-2/200	8-11-77	Jacksonville, Detroit	Labeled one of the keys to the Juan Gonzalez trade, he's the closer of the future.
23	Crabtree, Tim	R/R	6-4/220	10-13-69	Texas	He appeared in a team-high 68 games and likely will be a bullpen mainstay again.
46	Davis, Doug	R/L	6-3/190	9-21-75	Tulsa, Oklahoma, Texas	His 153 strikeouts and 2.72 ERA at AA/AAA were the organization's best in 1999.
47	Elder, David	R/R	6-0/180	9-23-75	Charlotte, Tulsa	He struggled to throw strikes at AA; a good spring could lift him to AAA.
38	Glynn, Ryan	R/R	6-3/195	11-1-74	Oklahoma, Texas	Unimpressive in three 1999 stops in the majors, but he's got good stuff.
32	Helling, Rick	R/R	6-3/220	12-15-70	Texas	A 20-game winner in '98, he needs to recapture the deception.
50	Johnson, Jonathan	R/R	6-0/180	7-16-74	Okla., GC Rangers, Tulsa, Texas	His most impressive work was at Oklahoma (8-4). He'll likely start there again.
52	Kolb, Danny	R/R	6-4/215	3-29-75	Tulsa, Oklahoma, Texas	He earned a look by posting decent numbers (2-1, 4.80 ERA) after his call-up.
36	Lee, Corey	B/L	6-2/185	12-26-74	Tulsa, Oklahoma, Texas	He got shelled in his only major league outing, but has talent.
28	Loaiza, Esteban	R/R	6-3/210	12-31-71	Texas, Oklahoma	Likely the No. 3 starter, he stuck with the hard stuff and had a great second half.
39	Moreno, Juan	L/L	6-1/205	2-28-75	Tulsa	Trying to earn a spot in the bullpen after tallying a 2.30 ERA in AA.
51	Munoz, Mike	L/L	6-2/198	7-12-65	Texas	A lefthanded specialist, he offers bullpen flexibility.
	Oliver, Darren	R/L	6-2/210	10-6-70	St. Louis	Gets his second tour of duty with the Rangers after a good season with the Cards.
40	Perisho, Matt	L/L	6-0/205	6-8-75	Oklahoma, Texas	He could push for a rotation spot if he can throw strikes.
37	Kenny Rogers	L-L	6-1/205	11-10-64	Oakland, New York N.L.	He was 10-4 last year and the team hopes he can be a rotation mainstay.
49	Sikorski, Brian	R/R	6-1/190	7-27-74	New Orleans	He was 7-10 with Houston's AAA affiliate, but at 25 he showed strikeout stuff.
45	Smith, Chuck	R/R	6-1/185	10-21-69	Oklahoma	He's probably past "prospect age," and his 5-4 record at AAA has him unnoticed.
22	Thompson, Justin	L/L	6-4/215	3-8-73	Detroit	He's got No. 1 stuff when healthy, a fastball in the 90s and a great changeup.
43	Venafro, Mike	L/L	5-10/180	8-2-73	Oklahoma, Texas	He was solid as a lefthanded setup man, a job he'll hold again this season.
35	Wetteland, John	R/R	6-2/215	8-21-66	Texas	Though not as dominating as he once was, his 43 saves were second in the A.L.
59	Zimmerman, Jeff	R/R	6-1/200	8-9-72	Oklahoma, Texas	He emerged as one of the best setup men in the A.L., going 9-3 with a 2.39 ERA.

No.	CATCHERS	B/T	Ht./Wt.	Born	1999 clubs	Projection
37	Haselman, Bill	R/R	6-3/223	5-25-66	Detroit	Back as the game's version of the Maytag repairman: Pudge's backup.
2	King, Cesar	R/R	6-0/215	2-28-78	Tulsa	Once considered a comer, he struggled at AA (.227 in 95 games).
7	Rodriguez, Ivan	R/R	5-9/205	11-30-71	Texas	One of the best ever, the 1999 A.L. MVP proved his offense isn't a fluke.

No.	INFIELDERS	B/T	Ht./Wt.	Born	1999 clubs	Projection
10	Alicea, Luis	B/R	5-9/176	7-29-65	Texas	Better as a utilityman, he'll platoon at second.
27	Catalanotto, Frank	L/R	6-0/195	4-27-74	Detroit	Acquired in the Gonzalez trade, he's the other half of the 2B platoon.
11	Clayton, Royce	R/R	6-0/183	1-2-70	Texas, Oklahoma	He finally has solidified what has been the organization's black-hole position.
44	Dransfeldt, Kelly	R/R	6-2/195	4-16-75	Oklahoma, Texas	Once projected as the future second baseman, his status has fallen.
53	Grabowski, Jason	L/R	6-3/200	5-24-76	Charlotte, Tulsa	He opened eyes by hitting .313 with a .407 OBP in the Florida State League.
14	Lamb, Mike	L/R	6-1/185	8-9-75	Tulsa, Oklahoma	A terror at AA, his arrival in the majors was accelerated by Todd Zeile's departure.
25	Palmeiro, Rafael	L/L	6-0/190	9-24-64	Texas	He'll be back at first, where he can earn his Gold Glove. He'll hit either way.
4	Sheldon, Scott	R/R	6-3/215	11-20-68	Oklahoma, Texas	He put up good numbers at AAA and hopes to make the team as an extra infielder.
9	Stevens, Lee	L/L	6-4/235	7-10-67	Texas	Expected to be the lefthanded DH, he filled in terrifically at first base in 1999.

No.	OUTFIELDERS	B/T	Ht./Wt.	Born	1999 clubs	Projection
3	Curtis, Chad	R/R	5-10/185	11-6-68	New York A.L.	He's expected to be the fourth outfielder, in case Mateo or Kapler falter.
29	Greer, Rusty	L/R	6-0/195	1-21-69	Texas	Suddenly the outfield veteran, his gritty presence is good for the younger lineup.
18	Kapler, Gabe	R/R	6-2/208	8-31-75	Detroit, Toledo	This former minor league player of the year will replace Gonzalez in right.
38	Mateo, Ruben	R/R	6-0/185	2-10-78	Texas, Oklahoma	A five-tool potential star who'll start in center. But can he stay healthy?
16	Simms, Mike	R/R	6-4/230	1-12-67	Charlotte, Oklahoma, Texas	The righthanded half of the DH platoon, he's coming off an Achilles' tendon injury.

THE COACHING STAFF

Johnny Oates, manager: He and his staff remain intact for their sixth season in Texas, a sign of the loyalty he commands and the stability he has brought. The byproduct: another A.L. West title for a team that had struggled mightily before his arrival. Oates' quiet, businesslike approach played well with a veteran team, but this year's Rangers squad is much younger. No matter their age, however, players like his calm, professional demeanor, and he's one of the game's hardest-working managers.

Dick Bosman: He receives high marks as a pitching coach and gets credit for the outstanding work of one of the game's top middle-relief corps.

Bucky Dent: The dugout coach, he also works with the infield, which means he'll be working to make Mike Lamb a major-leaguer.

Larry Hardy: A former pitcher and minor league manager, he enters his sixth season as the Rangers' bullpen coach

Rudy Jaromillo: He's underrated as a hitting coach, but the Rangers' numbers are a tribute to his work.

Ed Napoleon: He brings 30 years of coaching experience to his job as first base coach.

Jerry Narron: He has managerial experience in the minors, and enters his sixth year as Texas' third base coach.

THE TOP NEWCOMERS

Frank Catalanotto: He'll platoon at second base with Luis Alicea. The Rangers don't know what kind of return they will get from him. He showed moments of stardom with Detroit. Either way, they should get the reliable glove that Luis Alicea can't give them.

Gabe Kapler: He comes from the Tigers in the Gonzalez trade. A former minor league player of the year, he'll be under some pressure to help replace the former MVP.

Darren Oliver: Quietly had a good season with the Cardinals; he had only nine wins but the shaky Cardinals bullpen lost him many more. Didn't live up the Rangers' expectations early in his career but will get a spot in the rotation for redemption.

Kenny Rogers: Kenny struggled in the playoffs for the Mets, but had an overall solid season with the Mets and A's. As he has gotten older, he's also gotten smarter, making up for a lack of pitch speed with location and deception. He has given up on the strikeouts and is content with the groundouts, something the Rangers hope they see a lot of in The Ballpark.

Justin Thompson: The lefthander, coming off shoulder surgery, is the present-day key to the Gonzalez deal. If he's healthy, then the deal looks good; if not, then it could be a long year. Thompson has great stuff, a hard fastball and a deceptive, moving changeup. If healthy, could be the top lefthander in the A.L.

THE TOP PROSPECTS

Francisco Cordero: The third key component of the Gonzalez trade, he has at age 22 the potential to be a great closer, the future replacement for John Wetteland.

Mike Lamb: When free agent Todd Zeile bolted for the Mets, Lamb's major league timetable was moved up. He hit .324 at AA Tulsa and led Rangers minor-leaguers in runs, hits and doubles. Only 24, he could've used a year at AAA.

Ruben Mateo: He wore out the Pacific Coast League (.336, 18 HRs and 62 RBIs) before being called up to the majors, where an ongoing problem reared its head: He got injured, breaking a wrist and missing the rest of the regular season. If he can stay healthy, he has the potential to make Rangers fans forget Gonzalez.

Jason Romano: He hit .312 at Class A Charlotte. More to the point, he's got speed that the organization has been lacking: He had 34 stolen bases and an organization-best 14 triples.

TORONTO BLUE JAYS

AMERICAN LEAGUE EAST DIVISION

2000 SEASON

2000 Blue Jays Schedule

Home games shaded. *—All-Star Game at Turner Field (Atlanta).

March

SUN	MON	TUE	WED	THU	FRI	SAT
26	27	28	29	30	31	

April

SUN	MON	TUE	WED	THU	FRI	SAT
						1
2	3 KC	4 KC	5 KC	6 KC	7 TEX	8 TEX
9 TEX	10 ANA	11 ANA	12 ANA	13	14 SEA	15 SEA
16 SEA	17 ANA	18 ANA	19 ANA	20 ANA	21 NYY	22 NYY
23 NYY	24 OAK	25 OAK	26 OAK	27	28 NYY	29 NYY
30 NYY						

May

SUN	MON	TUE	WED	THU	FRI	SAT
	1 CWS	2 CWS	3 CWS	4 CLE	5 CLE	6 CLE
7 CLE	8 BAL	9 BAL	10 BAL	11	12 TB	13 TB
14 TB	15 BOS	16 BOS	17 BOS	18	19 CWS	20 CWS
21 CWS	22 CWS	23 BOS	24 BOS	25 BOS	26 DET	27 DET
28 DET	29	30 MIN	31 MIN			

June

SUN	MON	TUE	WED	THU	FRI	SAT
				1 MIN	2 FLA	3 FLA
4 FLA	5 ATL	6 ATL	7 ATL	8	9 MON	10 MON
11 MON	12 DET	13 DET	14 DET	15	16 BOS	17 BOS
18 BOS	19	20 DET	21 DET	22 DET	23 BOS	24 BOS
25 BOS	26	27 TB	28 TB	29 TB	30 BAL	

July

SUN	MON	TUE	WED	THU	FRI	SAT
						1 BAL
2 BAL	3 BAL	4 CLE	5 CLE	6 CLE	7 MON	8 MON
9 MON	10	11 *	12	13 PHI	14 PHI	15 PHI
16 NYM	17 NYM	18 NYM	19 TB	20 TB	21 BAL	22 BAL
23 BAL	24	25 CLE	26 CLE	27 SEA	28 SEA	29 SEA
30 SEA	31 OAK					

August

SUN	MON	TUE	WED	THU	FRI	SAT
		1 OAK	2 OAK	3 TEX	4 TEX	5 TEX
6 TEX	7 KC	8 KC	9 KC	10 KC	11 MIN	12 MIN
13 MIN	14	15 ANA	16 ANA	17	18 MIN	19 MIN
20 MIN	21	22 KC	23 KC	24	25 TEX	26 TEX
27 TEX	28 ANA	29 ANA	30 ANA	31		

September

SUN	MON	TUE	WED	THU	FRI	SAT
					1 OAK	2 OAK
3 OAK	4	5 SEA	6 SEA	7 DET	8 DET	9 DET
10 DET	11	12 NYY	13 NYY	14 NYY	15 CWS	16 CWS
17 CWS	18	19 NYY	20 NYY	21 TB	22 TB	23 TB
24 TB	25 TB	26 BAL	27 BAL	28 BAL	29 CLE	30 CLE

October

SUN	MON	TUE	WED	THU	FRI	SAT
1 CLE	2	3	4	5	6	7

FRONT-OFFICE DIRECTORY

President, baseball operations ....Gord Ash
Vice president, sales and marketing ....Terry Zuk
Vice president, finance and operations ....Stu Hutcheson
Vice president, baseball ....Bob Mattick
Vice president, baseball operations ....Tim McCleary
Assistant general manager and director of player personnel........................Dave Stewart
Special assistants to president and G.M. ....Wayne Morgan, Mel Queen, Al Widmar
Vice president, media relations ....Howard Starkman
Vice president, finance and administration ....Susan Brioux
Director, scouting ....Tim Wilken
Assistant director, scouting ....Chris Buckley
Director, player development ....Jim Hoff
Director, Canadian scouting ....Bill Byckowski
Director, minor leagues ....Bob Nelson
Director, Florida operations ....Ken Carson
Director, operations ....Mario Coutinho
Director, marketing ....Peter Cosentino
Director, corporate partnerships ....Mark Lemmon
Box office manager ....Randy Low
General manager, TBJ merchandising...Michael Andrejak
Manager, team travel ....John Brioux

MINOR LEAGUE AFFILIATES

Class	Team	League	Manager
AAA	Syracuse	International	Pat Kelly
AA	Tennessee	Southern	Rocket Wheeler
A	Dunedin	Florida State	Marty Pevey
A	Hagerstown	South Atlantic	Rolando Pino
A	St. Catharines	New York-Penn.	Eddie Rodriguez
Rookie	Medicine Hat	Pioneer	Paul Elliott

BROADCAST INFORMATION

Radio: CHUM (1050).
TV: CBC-TV.
Cable TV: The Sports Network, CTV SportsNet.

SPRING TRAINING

Ballpark (city): Dunedin Stadium at Grant Field (Dunedin, Fla.).
Ticket information: 800-707-8269; 727-733-0429.

ASSISTANCE STAFF

Trainers
George Poulis   Scott Shannon

Strength and conditioning coordinator
Jeff Krushell

Team physicians
Dr. Allan Gross   Dr. Steve Mirabello
Dr. Ron Taylor

Advance scout
Sal Butera

Scouts
Charles Aliano	Tony Arias
Andy Beene	David Blume
Chris Bourjos	Bus Campbell
Rick Cerrone	Jeff Cornell
Ellis Dungan	Joe Ford
Tom Hinkle	Tim Huff
Jim Hughes	Duane Larson
Ted Lekas	Mike Mangan
Ben McLure	Marty Miller
Bill Moore	Ty Nichols
Andy Pienovi	Denerius Pittman
Jorge Rivera	Marteese Robinson
Joe Siers	Mark Snipp
Ron Tostenson	

BALLPARK INFORMATION

Ballpark (capacity, surface)
SkyDome (45,100, artificial)
Address
One Blue Jays Way
Suite 3200
Toronto, Ontario M5V 1J1
Business phone
416-341-1000
Ticket information
416-341-1234
Ticket prices
$42 (premium dugout level)
$39 (field level-infield)
$33.50 (field level-bases)
$30.75 (field level-baselines; Skyclub outfield)
$23 (100 level-outfield; Skydeck-infield;
   SkyClub bleachers)
$16 (Skydeck-bases)
$7 (Skydeck-baselines)
Field dimensions (from home plate)
To left field at foul line, 330 feet
To center field, 400 feet
To right field at foul line, 330 feet
First game played
June 5, 1989 (Brewers 5, Blue Jays 3)

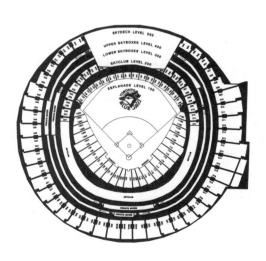

No.	PITCHERS	B/T	Ht./Wt.	Born	1999 clubs	Projection
34	Andrews, Clayton	R/L	6-0/180	5-15-78	Knoxville, Syracuse	More time in the minors awaits this lefty. He struggled in Class AAA in '99.
49	Bale, John	L/L	6-4/205	5-22-74	Knoxville, Syracuse, Toronto	Unless a spot opens up in the rotation, Bale will start the season in the bullpen.
36	Borbon, Pedro	L/L	6-1/205	11-15-67	Los Angeles	Will compete with Lance Painter as the lefthanded setup man for Billy Koch.
26	Carpenter, Chris	R/R	6-6/225	4-27-75	Toronto, St. Catharines	Elbow surgery shut him down after 24 starts in '99, but his rotation slot is secure.
53	Coco, Pasqual	R/R	6-1/185	9-24-77	Hagerstown, Dunedin	Starter shined in Class A and will pick up where he left off in Class AA.
45	DeWitt, Matt	R/R	6-3/210	9-4-77	Arkansas	DeWitt won nine games at the Class AA level in '99 but is considered a project.
45	Escobar, Kelvim	R/R	6-1/195	4-11-76	Toronto	Hard thrower who has a spot in the rotation despite an inconsistent finish in '99.
66	Estrella, Leo	R/R	6-1/185	2-20-75	Dunedin	After a 14-7 record in Class A, this starter could move up to Knoxville this season.
52	Frascatore, John	R/R	6-1/223	2-4-70	Arizona, Toronto	Impressed the team with eight relief wins in '99 and will be in the bullpen again.
51	Glover, Gary	R/R	6-5/205	12-3-76	Knoxville, Syracuse, Toronto	After an 8-2 season with Knoxville, the starter will make the jump to Syracuse.
32	Halladay, Roy	R/R	6-6/225	5-14-77	Toronto	This flame-thrower will join the rotation in 2000, not split time like last season.
50	Hamilton, Joey	R/R	6-4/230	9-9-70	Toronto, Syracuse	The Jays expect a full rebound from the shoulder surgery that shortened 1999.
44	Koch, Billy	R/R	6-3/205	12-14-74	Syracuse, Toronto	He had surprising success as a rookie (31 saves in 35 chances), and he's just 25.
13	Munro, Peter	R/R	6-2/210	6-14-75	Toronto, Syracuse	He is a long-relief candidate, but he will have competition from Bale and others.
40	Painter, Lance	L/L	6-1/200	7-21-67	St. Louis, Arkansas	Offseason acquisition provides a valuable lefthanded arm out of the bullpen.
48	Quantrill, Paul	L/L	6-1/190	11-3-68	Dunedin, Syracuse, Toronto	The veteran hurler will be the top righthanded arm out of the bullpen before Koch.
39	Rodriguez, Nerio	R/R	6-1/205	3-22-73	Syracuse, Toronto	Versatile enough to fill a role as a starter or reliever if he catches on with Jays.
46	Sneed, John	L/R	6-6/250	6-30-76	Dunedin, Knoxville	Last year's Minor League Pitcher of the Year. will begin at Class AA Knoxville.
33	Wells, David	L/L	6-4/235	5-20-63	Toronto	Barring a trade, the crafty veteran will remain in the rotation.

No.	CATCHERS	B/T	Ht./Wt.	Born	1999 clubs	Projection
30	Castillo, Alberto	R/R	6-0/185	2-10-70	St. Louis	Backup had a career offensive year, but some question his ability to handle a staff.
9	Fletcher, Darrin	L/R	6-2/205	10-3-66	Toronto, Syracuse	Won the starting job in 1999 and had his best year at the plate.
17	Phelps, Josh	R/R	6-3/220	5-12-78	Dunedin	Strong-armed backstop will take the next step after a promising year at Class A.

No.	INFIELDERS	B/T	Ht./Wt.	Born	1999 clubs	Projection
7	Batista, Tony	R/R	6-0/185	12-9-73	Arizona, Toronto	The shortstop might find himself at third base given Alex Gonzalez's return.
28	Blake, Casey	R/R	6-2/200	8-23-73	Syracuse, Toronto, St. Cath.	Heavy-hitting prospect will get a chance to win the third base job outright.
16	Bush, Homer	R/R	5-10/180	11-12-72	Toronto, Dunedin	He's solid at second and can steal bases, but he needs to cut down his strikeouts.
25	Delgado, Carlos	L/R	6-3/225	6-25-72	Toronto	First baseman has excellent power and run-producing ability, and he's in his prime.
8	Gonzalez, Alex	R/R	6-0/200	4-8-73	Toronto	Shoulder surgery wiped out most of his 1999 season but he is expected back.
4	Grebeck, Craig	R/R	5-7/155	12-29-64	Toronto, Syracuse	The valuable utilityman and disciplined hitter will back up Bush at second base.
6	Lawrence, Joe	R/R	6-2/200	2-13-77	Knoxville	His season at Knoxville ended early with an ankle injury; figures to be there again.
19	Segui, David	B/L	6-1/202	7-19-66	Seattle, Toronto	He will bat fifth in the order and handle the DH duties, despite a good glove.
12	Witt, Kevin	L/R	6-4/210	1-5-76	Syracuse, Toronto	He has shown power and can play several positions, but is still waiting for a chance.
31	Woodward, Chris	R/R	6-0/173	6-27-76	Syracuse, Toronto	The shortstop doesn't figure to be in the plans unless a trade opens up a spot.

No.	OUTFIELDERS	B/T	Ht./Wt.	Born	1999 clubs	Projection
23	Cruz Jr., Jose	B/R	6-0/200	4-19-74	Toronto, Syracuse	Still considered the starter in center, although his bat hasn't been as projected.
43	Mondesi, Raul	R/R	5-11/215	3-12-71	Los Angeles	Five-tool right fielder will bat third and might improve his numbers at SkyDome.
27	Sanders, Anthony	R/R	6-2/205	3-2-74	Syracuse, Toronto	Showed improvement at Class AAA Syracuse and will remain there to improve.
24	Stewart, Shannon	R/R	6-1/205	2-25-74	Toronto	His offensive production fell in the second half but he gets on base and steals.
16	Thompson, Andy	R/R	6-3/215	10-8-75	Knoxville, Syracuse	Will remain at Syracuse, where he drove in 42 runs in 62 games last season.
10	Wells, Vernon	R/R	6-1/210	12-8-78	Dunedin, Knox., Syracuse, Tor.	He went from Class A to the majors and will get a shot at the center field job.

THE COACHING STAFF

Jim Fregosi, manager: After taking over the team late in spring training last season, he led the Blue Jays to a third-place finish. For a brief time in the second half, the Jays competed for the wild card. Fregosi has a reputation as a players' manager and is a veteran of the game. This season, Fregosi has expressed a desire to move away from the home run and concentrate more on patience at the plate and moving runners over. Fregosi has past managerial experience with the Angels, White Sox and Phillies and also has managed in the minors with the Cardinals. In 1993, he guided the Phillies to the World Series against the Blue Jays.

Terry Bevington: The third base coach was the only member of last year's coaching staff to survive. He managed at Class AAA Syracuse prior to last year, has managed more than 1,000 minor league games and also managed the Chicago White Sox from 1995-97.

Lee Elia: The former Cubs (1982-83) and Phillies (1987-88) manager takes over the bench coach role in Toronto. Elia also has been Philadelphia's director of minor league instruction and has nine seasons of managerial experience in the minors. On the major league level, he also has been a third base coach, a bench coach, a dugout coach and a hitting instructor.

Cito Gaston: Looks who's back. Gaston managed the Blue Jays from 1989-97, when he was fired by current GM Gord Ash. He is Toronto's all-time winningest manager and won two World Series with the Jays. Gaston served as the team's batting coach from 1982-89 and returns to that same role under Fregosi. The drawback? He has a reputation for being impatient with younger hitters.

Bobby Knoop: Fregosi's double-play partner in the 1960s and close friend takes over the first-base coaching job. Knoop was the Angels' first base coach from 1979-96.

Roly de Armas: The Blue Jays' new bullpen coach spent last season with the Diamondbacks as a minor league catching coordinator and manager of their Arizona League team. He has 17 years of managerial experience in the minors (mostly with the Phillies), and his most recent major league coaching position was as the White Sox's bullpen coach in 1996.

Rick Langford: After serving as the pitching coach at Class AAA Syracuse last season, he takes over that same role with the Blue Jays. This will be Langford's fifth season with the organization in a coaching capacity, and he knows many of the Jays' young pitchers very well after working with them in lower levels.

THE TOP NEWCOMERS

Pedro Borbon: The situational lefty will help fill the bullpen void left by the departure of Graeme Lloyd. After missing most of 1997 and '98 with elbow injuries, he was 4-3 with a 4.09 ERA with Los Angeles last season.

Alberto Castillo: Castillo was one of the biggest surprises for the Cardinals last season and actually took over the starting job toward the end of the season. However, he fell out of favor with the Cards' coaching staff after some concentration problems and questionable handling of the staff. He is solid defensively and has a good arm.

Raul Mondesi: The former Dodger should make it easier to forget about Shawn Green. Jays GM Gord Ash thinks Mondesi has 40-40 potential, and he is correct. Mondesi should see plenty of good pitches batting in front of Delgado, and his number should improve at SkyDome and in the A.L. Also a plus are Mondesi's fiery character and all-out style of play.

Lance Painter: He provides some versatility to the staff. In 1999 with St. Louis, Painter started four games and relieved 52 others. He is a valuable lefthanded option out of the bullpen.

THE TOP PROSPECTS

Casey Blake: Because the third-base situation is unsettled, Blake has a chance to make some noise. His glove is solid, but his offense needs some fine-tuning. Because of his attempt to hit for more power, Blake's average dipped. Still, he connected for 22 homers at Class AAA Syracuse.

John Sneed: He is still at least a year away, but the Jays like what they have seen so far. At Dunedin, he struck out 143 batters in 125 innings, then fanned 28 in 28 innings at Knoxville. The bad news is that his walks also rose at the Class AA level.

Vernon Wells: He is the center fielder of the future, and the future appears to be the 2001 season. At stints at the Class A, AA and AAA levels last season, Wells hit 18 homers and drove in 81 runs. However, the Blue Jays don't want to rush him along and have him fall into the same trap Cruz did, so Wells likely will begin the year at Syracuse.

ARIZONA DIAMONDBACKS
NATIONAL LEAGUE WEST DIVISION

2000 SEASON

2000 Diamondbacks Schedule
Home games shaded. *—All-Star Game at Turner Field (Atlanta).

March
SUN	MON	TUE	WED	THU	FRI	SAT
26	27	28	29	30	31	

April
SUN	MON	TUE	WED	THU	FRI	SAT
						1
2	3	4 PHI	5 PHI	6 PHI	7 PIT	8 PIT
9 PIT	10 SD	11 SD	12 SD	13 SD	14 SF	15 SF
16 SF	17 COL	18 COL	19 COL	20 COL	21 SF	22 SF
23 SF	24	25 PHI	26 PHI	27 PHI	28 CUB	29 CUB
30 CUB						

May
SUN	MON	TUE	WED	THU	FRI	SAT
	1	2 MIL	3 MIL	4 MIL	5 SD	6 SD
7 SD	8 LA	9 LA	10 LA	11	12 SD	13 SD
14 SD	15	16 MON	17 MON	18 MON	19 NYM	20 NYM
21 NYM	22	23 PIT	24 PIT	25 PIT	26 MIL	27 MIL
28 MIL	29 STL	30 STL	31 STL			

June
SUN	MON	TUE	WED	THU	FRI	SAT
				1 STL	2 TEX	3 TEX
4 TEX	5 CUB	6 CUB	7 CUB	8	9 ANA	10 ANA
11 ANA	12 LA	13 LA	14 LA	15 LA	16 COL	17 COL
18 COL	19 SD	20 SD	21 SD	22	23 COL	24 COL
25 COL	26 HOU	27 HOU	28 HOU	29 HOU	30 CIN	

July
SUN	MON	TUE	WED	THU	FRI	SAT
						1 CIN
2 CIN	3 CIN	4 HOU	5 HOU	6 HOU	7 OAK	8 OAK
9 OAK	10	11 *	12	13 TEX	14 TEX	15 TEX
16 SEA	17 SEA	18 SEA	19 STL	20 STL	21 CIN	22 CIN
23 CIN	24	25 STL	26 STL	27 STL	28 FLA	29 FLA
30 FLA	31					

August
SUN	MON	TUE	WED	THU	FRI	SAT
		1 ATL	2 ATL	3 ATL	4 NYM	5 NYM
6 NYM	7 MON	8 MON	9 MON	10	11 PIT	12 PIT
13 PIT	14 PHI	15 PHI	16 PHI	17	18 CUB	19 CUB
20 CUB	21 MIL	22 MIL	23 MIL	24	25 NYM	26 NYM
27 NYM	28 MON	29 MON	30 MON	31		

September
SUN	MON	TUE	WED	THU	FRI	SAT
					1 FLA	2 FLA
3 FLA	4	5 ATL	6 ATL	7 ATL	8 FLA	9 FLA
10 FLA	11 LA	12 LA	13 LA	14	15 ATL	16 ATL
17 ATL	18 LA	19 LA	20 LA	21 SF	22 SF	23 SF
24 SF	25	26 COL	27 COL	28 COL	29 SF	30 SF

October
SUN	MON	TUE	WED	THU	FRI	SAT
1 SF	2	3	4	5	6	

FRONT-OFFICE DIRECTORY

Managing general partner .... Jerry Colangelo
President .... Richard Dozer
Vice president and general manager .... Joe Garagiola Jr.
Senior executive vice president, baseball operations .... Roland Hemond
Senior vice president, sales and marketing .... Scott Brubaker
Vice president, finance .... Thomas Harris
Vice president, tickets and special services .... Dianne Aquilar
Vice president, sales .... Blake Edwards
Vice president, community affairs .... Mark Fernandez
Senior assistant to the general manager .... Mel Didier
Assistant to the general manager .... Bryan Lambe
Director of Hispanic marketing .... Richard Saenz
Director of Tucson operations .... Rich Tomey
Director of public relations .... Mike Swanson
Director of ballpark services .... Russ Amaral
Director of suite services .... Diney Mahoney
Director of team travel .... Roger Riley
Director of minor league operations .... Tommy Jones
Director of Pacific Rim operations .... Jim Marshall
Director of scouting .... Mike Rizzo
Assistant director of scouting .... Bob Miller

MINOR LEAGUE AFFILIATES

Class	Team	League	Manager
AAA	Tucson	Pacific Coast	Tom Spencer
AAA	El Paso	Texas	Don Wakamatsu
A	High Desert	California	Scott Coolbaugh
A	South Bend	Midwest	Dave Jorn
Rookie	Missoula	Pioneer	Chip Hale
Rookie	Tucson	Arizona	Roly de Armas

BROADCAST INFORMATION
Radio: KTAR-AM (620).
TV: KTVK (Channel 3)
Cable TV: Fox Sports Net Arizona.

SPRING TRAINING
Ballpark (city): Tuscon Electric Park (Tucson, Ariz.).
Ticket information: 800-638-4253, 520-434-1111.

ASSISTANCE STAFF

Trainer
Paul Lessard

Assistant trainer
Dave Edwards

Club physician
Dr. David Zeman

National scouting supervisor
Kendall Carter
Scouting coordinators
Derek Bryant, Junior Noboa
Professional scouts
Bill Earnhart, Mike Piatnik

Special assistants to general manager
Shooty Babitt, Ron Hassey, Bryan Lambe

Advance scout
Dick Scott

Regional scouting supervisors
Ed Durkin, Kris Kline, Steve Springer

Area scouting supervisors
Ray Blanco, Ray Corbett, Jason Goligoski, Brian Guinn, Scott Jaster, James Keller, Chris Knabenshue, Hal Kurtzman, Greg Lonigro, Howard McCullough, Louie Medina, Matt Merullo, Carlos Porte, Phillip Rizzo, Mike Valarezo, Brad Vaughn, Luke Wrenn

Scouts
Pablo Abreu, Juan Aguirre, Ossie Alvarez, Pete Carmona, John Cole, Luis Delgado, Leo Figueroa, Jose Martin, Tony Levato, Jonathan Leyba, David May, Rafael Mena, Jose Diaz Perez, Juan Salabarria, Joel Serna, Mark Smelko, Bob Sullivan, Jorge Urribari, Roberto Verdugo, John Wadsworth, Doyle Wilson, John Wright

BALLPARK INFORMATION

Ballpark (capacity, surface)
Bank One Ballpark (49,033)
Address
401 East Jefferson
Phoenix, AZ 85004
Business phone
602-462-6500
Ticket information
602-514-8400
Ticket prices
$10 to $22.50 (lower level)
$1 to $15.50 (upper level)
$35 to $55 (lower level premium seats)
$27 and $33 (Inifiniti Diamond level)
Field dimensions (from home plate)
To left field at foul line, 330 feet
To center field, 407 feet
To right field at foul line, 334 feet
First game played
March 31, 1998 (Rockies 9, Diamondbacks 2)

No.	PITCHERS	B/T	Ht./Wt.	Born	1999 clubs	Projection
34	Anderson, Brian	B/L	6-1/190	4-26-72	Arizona, Tucson	He had a strong August and September, which will warrant a spot in the rotation.
	Bierbroldt, Nick	L/L	6-5/190	5-16-78	El Paso, Tucson	Arizona's first-round pick in 1996 has struggled in the minors, but he's young.
	Brohawn, Troy	L/L	6-1/190	1-14-73	Tucson	Pitched just 13-plus innings due to an injury in 1999 that could slow him this year.
41	Chouinard, Bobby	R/R	6-1/190	5-1-72	Tucson, Arizona	Offseason trouble with the law has at least the start of his season in jeopardy.
	Clontz, Brad	R/R	6-1/203	4-25-71	Nashville, Pittsburgh	The Diamondbacks acquired him for long relief due to his durability.
37	Daal, Omar	L/L	6-3/185	3-1-72	Arizona	Had a career-best 16 wins and is a solid No. 3 in the rotation.
	Figueroa, Nelson	B/R	6-1/155	5-18-74	Tucson, AZL Diamondbacks	Though he spent time on the D.L., he had a lot of success in Tucson.
46	Holmes, Darren	R/R	6-0/202	4-25-66	Arizona, AZL D-backs, Tucson	Another strong arm in a veteran-filled bullpen.
51	Johnson, Randy	R/L	6-10/230	9-10-63	Arizona	Think he enjoyed his first full season in the N.L.? The rest of the league sure didn't.
49	Kim, Byung-Hyun	R/R	5-11/176	1-21-79	El Paso, Tucs., Ariz., AL D-backs	Worked his way through the minors and left anguished hitters in his wake in '99.
31	Mantei, Matt	R/R	6-1/190	7-7-73	Florida, Arizona	The savior of the bullpen last season, finishing with 22 saves the second half.
	Norris, Ben	B/L	6-3/185	12-6-77	High Desert, El Paso	Young lefty starting pitcher is at least a year away.
19	Plesac, Dan	L/L	6-5/217	2-4-62	Toronto, Arizona	Now a situational lefty who throws strikes.
	Randolph, Steve	L/L	6-3/185	5-1-74	El Paso, Tucson, AZL D-backs	His control problems led to a 2-9 overall record last season.
27	Reynoso, Armando	R/R	6-0/204	5-1-66	Arizona	A good No. 4 or No. 5 starter. He stepped in and won 10 games last season.
36	Springer, Russ	R/R	6-4/220	11-7-68	Richmond, Atlanta	The Braves loved this guy, even in the playoffs. He strengthens the bullpen.
32	Stottlemyre, Todd	L/R	6-3/200	5-20-65	Arizona, AZL Diamondbacks	His shoulder could give out at any time. Showalter will minimize his innings.
22	Swindell, Greg	R/L	6-3/230	1-2-65	Arizona	He's the primary lefty in the bullpen and will act as the lefthanded setup man.

No.	CATCHERS	B/T	Ht./Wt.	Born	1999 clubs	Projection
48	Barajas, Rod	R/R	6-2/220	9-5-75	El Paso, Arizona	He has great defensive skills and a good bat, but needs some work in the minors.
26	Miller, Damian	R/R	6-2/190	10-13-69	Arizona	Replacing Stinnett last season, he proved to be a solid catcher and a good hitter.
35	Stinnett, Kelly	R/R	5-11/195	2-4-70	Arizona	Suffered a deep thigh bruise and split time with Miller. Will do the same this year.

No.	INFIELDERS	B/T	Ht./Wt.	Born	1999 clubs	Projection
33	Bell, Jay	R/R	6-0/182	12-11-65	Arizona	A second baseman hitting 38 homers and driving in 112 runs? What an asset.
44	Durazo, Erubiel	L/L	6-3/225	1-23-74	El Paso, Tucson, Arizona	He's hit everywhere, including the majors. That'll continue for the first baseman.
28	Colbrunn, Greg	R/R	6-0/205	7-26-69	Arizona	Primarily a pinch hitter who'll start against lefthanders.
6	Fox, Andy	L/R	6-4/205	1-12-71	Arizona	The lanky Fox is a solid backup with a good lefthanded bat.
2	Frias, Hanley	B/R	6-0/165	12-5-73	Arizona, Tucson	A versatile switch-hitter with no place in the talented middle infield.
29	Harris, Lenny	L/R	5-10/220	10-28-64	Colorado, Arizona	His 115 pinch hits tops all active players. This utilityman is valuable to Airzona.
7	Klassen, Danny	R/R	6-0/175	9-22-75	Tucson, AZL D-backs, Arizona	Can play second base or shortstop but likely will do it in the minors.
	Ordaz, Luis	R/R	5-11/170	8-12-75	St. Louis, Memphis	Believed to be an everyday shortstop. The Diamondbacks acquired him for depth.
	Spivey, Junior	R/R	6-0/185	1-28-75	El Paso	Slick infielder who spent much of last season on El Paso's and Arizona's DLs.
9	Williams, Matt	R/R	6-2/210	11-28-65	Arizona	The Diamondbacks expected a lot from him—he's more than provided.
5	Womack, Tony	L/R	5-9/159	9-25-69	Tucson, Arizona	He'll start everyday at shortstop. But he hasn't played there primarily since 1995.

No.	OUTFIELDERS	B/T	Ht./Wt.	Born	1999 clubs	Projection
63	Conti, Jason	L/R	5-11/180	1-27-75	Tucson	Speedy outfielder will only crack the talented outfield if there are injuries.
25	Dellucci, David	L/L	5-10/180	10-31-73	Arizona	Hitting .394 when his season was cut short. He'll get at-bats even if he doesn't start.
12	Finley, Steve	L/L	6-2/180	3-12-65	Arizona	Had a resurgence of sorts last year and the production will continue.
23	Gilkey, Bernard	R/R	6-0/200	9-24-66	Arizona	Started off the season with a bang, but fizzled. Now he's the fifth outfielder.
20	Gonzalez, Luis	L/R	6-2/190	9-2-67	Arizona	Had a .268 career average before career-best .336 mark in '99. Will that continue?
16	Lee, Travis	L/L	6-3/210	5-26-75	Arizona	Spent the offseason learning to play right field and will likely start there.

THE COACHING STAFF

Buck Showalter, manager: Showalter deserves much of the credit for the team's amazing turnaround last season (35 more wins). He displays little emotion during games, which fits with his no-frills team. This veteran ballclub needs his direction and there are few managers who are as on top of every detail as Showalter is. He is professional, he is smart . . . he is a true fit for Arizona.

Brian Butterfield: Like Showalter, Butterfield has been working with the organization since 1996 as an infield instructor, minor league manager and scout. Butterfield, who coached first base for the Yankees in 1994 and '95, handles third base duties for the Diamondbacks. Most of his career was spent as a player, manager and coach in the Yankees' system.

Mark Connor: As a longtime Yankees' coach, Connor served under managers Yogi Berra, Billy Martin, Lou Piniella, Bucky Dent, Stump Merrill and Showalter. Connor, the Diamondbacks' first pitching coach, has done a wonderful job with the staff. Though he has a good group of pitchers, courtesy of Jerry Colangelo, he has taken them to higher levels. Omar Daal, Matt Mantei, even Randy Johnson, have taken their careers to the next plateau.

Dwayne Murphy: The six-time Gold Glove-winning center fielder for the Athletics coaches first base and outfielders. He has his work cut out for him, working with the repositioned Travis Lee in right field.

Jim Presley: He begins his third season as a big-league hitting instructor after handling that job for two seasons in Arizona's minor league system. His veteran ballclub showed tremendous power last year (216 homers), much like Presley did at times as a player with the Mariners, Braves and Padres.

Glenn Sherlock: Another former Yankees employee, Sherlock handles the bullpen and catchers. He has coached and managed at the minor league level and spent the 1996 and '97 seasons as catching coordinator in the Arizona system.

Carlos Tosca: This 16-year minor league manager brings experience to the dugout as Showalter's bench coach. Before joining Arizona, Tosca managed Florida's Class AAA Charlotte team. He works well with young players and fits right in with Showalter's no-nonsense approach.

THE TOP NEWCOMERS

Brad Clontz: The side-arming righthander was acquired in December to provide bullpen depth and eat up innings in long relief.

Luis Ordaz: The Cardinals, for a brief point in time, were very high on this guy as a shortstop. His three-year trial with the big club proved his bat was too weak and his glove was suspect. The Diamondbacks acquired him for infield depth in case Womack can't cut it at short.

Russ Springer: The second part of the bullpen-strengthening offseason and should be welcomed as a potential righthanded setup man. The Braves used him in many different situations.

THE TOP PROSPECTS

Rod Barajas: In his four years of minor league ball, this catcher has shown surprising power with the bat and a great arm. But his 14 errors both last year in Class AA El Paso and Class A High Desert indicates he needs defensive work.

Byung-Hyun Kim: In 80-plus innings last year on the Diamondbacks and three minor league clubs, Kim struck out 105 batters. He has incredible stuff but needs a little refinement and adjustment before he'll see the rotation.

ATLANTA BRAVES

NATIONAL LEAGUE EAST DIVISION

2000 SEASON

2000 Braves Schedule

Home games shaded. *—All-Star Game at Turner Field (Atlanta).

March

SUN	MON	TUE	WED	THU	FRI	SAT
26	27	28	29	30	31	

April

SUN	MON	TUE	WED	THU	FRI	SAT
						1
2	3 COL	4 COL	5 COL	6	7 SF	8 SF
9 SF	10 CUB	11	12 CUB	13 CUB	14 MIL	15 MIL
16 MIL	17	18 PHI	19 PHI	20 PHI	21 PIT	22 PIT
23 PIT	24	25 LA	26 LA	27 LA	28 SD	29 SD
30 SD						

May

SUN	MON	TUE	WED	THU	FRI	SAT
	1 LA	2 LA	3 LA	4	5 PHI	6 PHI
7 PHI	8 FLA	9 FLA	10 FLA	11 FLA	12 PHI	13 PHI
14 PHI	15	16 SF	17 SF	18 SD	19 SD	20 SD
21 SD	22	23 MIL	24 MIL	25 MIL	26 HOU	27 HOU
28 HOU	29 CUB	30 CUB	31 CUB			

June

SUN	MON	TUE	WED	THU	FRI	SAT
				1	2 NYY	3 NYY
4 NYY	5 TOR	6 TOR	7 TOR	8	9 BOS	10 BOS
11 BOS	12 PIT	13 PIT	14 PIT	15 PIT	16 PHI	17 PHI
18 PHI	19 CUB	20 CUB	21 CUB	22 CUB	23 MIL	24 MIL
25 MIL	26 MON	27 MON	28	29 NYM	30 NYM	

July

SUN	MON	TUE	WED	THU	FRI	SAT
						1 NYM
2 NYM	3 MON	4 MON	5 MON	6 MON	7 BOS	8 BOS
9 BOS	10	11 *	12	13 BAL	14 BAL	15 BAL
16 TB	17 TB	18 TB	19 FLA	20 FLA	21 NYM	22 NYM
23 NYM	24	25 FLA	26 FLA	27 FLA	28 HOU	29 HOU
30 HOU	31					

August

SUN	MON	TUE	WED	THU	FRI	SAT
		1 ARI	2 ARI	3 ARI	4 STL	5 STL
6 STL	7 CIN	8 CIN	9 CIN	10	11 LA	12 LA
13 LA	14 SD	15 SD	16 SD	17	18 SF	19 SF
20 SF	21 COL	22 COL	23 COL	24 STL	25 STL	26 STL
27 STL	28 CIN	29 CIN	30 CIN	31 CIN		

September

SUN	MON	TUE	WED	THU	FRI	SAT
					1 HOU	2 HOU
3 HOU	4	5 ARI	6 ARI	7 ARI	8 MON	9 MON
10 MON	11	12 FLA	13 FLA	14 FLA	15 ARI	16 ARI
17 ARI	18 NYM	19 NYM	20 NYM	21	22 MON	23 MON
24 MON	25 MON	26 NYM	27 NYM	28 NYM	29 COL	30 COL

October

SUN	MON	TUE	WED	THU	FRI	SAT
1 COL	2	3	4	5	6	7

FRONT-OFFICE DIRECTORY

Owner	R.E. Turner III
Chairman of the board of directors	William C. Bartholomay
President	Stanley H. Kasten
Executive vice president and general manager	John Schuerholz
Senior vice president and assistant to the president	Henry L. Aaron
Senior vice president, administration	Bob Wolfe
Vice president, assistant general manager	Frank Wren
Vice president, director of marketing and broadcasting	Wayne Long
Vice president	Lee Douglas
Vice president of development	Janet Marie Smith
Vice president of human resources	Michelle Thomas
Special assistants to general manager	Bill Lajoie, Brian Murphy
Special assistant to general manager/player development	Jose Martinez
Special assistant, scouting and player development	Guy Hansen
Director of team travel and equipment manager	Bill Acree
Director of player development	Dick Balderson
Director of scouting	Roy Clark
Assistant director of scouting and player development	Dayton Moore
Senior director of promotions and civic affairs	Miles McRea
Vice president/controller	Chip Moore
Director of ticket sales	Paul Adams
Director of minor league business operations	Bruce Baldwin
Director of stadium operations and security	Larry Bowman
Director of Braves foundation	Danny Goodwin
Field director	Ed Mangan
Director of ticket operations	Ed Newman
Team counsel	David Payne
Director of community relations	Cara Maglione
Director of special events	David Lee
Director of audio video operations	Jennifer Berger
Director of corporate sales	Jim Allen
Director of public relations	Jim Schultz
Media relations manager	Glen Serra
Public relations assistants	Steve Copses, Robert Gahagan, Kim Zieglar

MINOR LEAGUE AFFILIATES

Class	Team	League	Manager
AAA	Richmond	International	Randy Ingle
AA	Greenville	Southern	Paul Runge
A	Myrtle Beach	Carolina	Brian Snitker
A	Macon	South Atlantic	Jeff Treadway
A	Jamestown	New York-Penn	Jim Saul
Rookie	Danville	Appalachian	J.J. Cannon
Rookie	Gulf Coast Braves	Gulf Coast	Rick Albert

BROADCAST INFORMATION

Radio: WSB-AM (750).
TV: TBS-TV (Channel 17).
Cable TV: SportsSouth.

SPRING TRAINING

Ballpark (city): Disney Wide World Sports Baseball Stadium (Kissimmee, Fla.).
Ticket information: 407-839-3900; 407-939-1418.

ASSISTANCE STAFF

Trainer
Dave Pursley

Club physician
Dr. David T. Watson

Associate physicians
Dr. William Barber, Dr. John Cantwell
Dr. Norman Elliott

Major league scouts
Dick Balderson, Scott Nethery, Bobby Wine

National supervisors
Tony LaCava

Regional supervisors
Harold Cronin, Paul Faulk, John Flannery, Bob Wadsworth

Area supervisors
Mike Baker, Dan Bates, Tyrone Brooks, Stu Cann, Rob English, Ralph Garr, Rod Gilbreath, John Hagemann, J. Harrison, Kurt Kemp, Brian Kohlscheen, Jim Martz, Marco Paddy, Donnie Popllin, J.J. Picollo, John Ramey, John Stewart

Scouts
Nez Balelo, Jim Buchert, Joe Caputo, Todd Cook, Edgar Fernandez, Jose Figueroa, Pedro Flores, Bill Froberg, Ruben Garcia, Luis Herrera, Bob Isabelle, Rafael Josela, James Kane, Dewayne Kitts, Seong Yeol Kwak, Al Kubski, Duk Jung Lee, Jose Leon, Robert Lucas, William Marcot, Giorgio Moretti, Jose Mota, Dario Paulino, Ernie Pedersen, Elvis Pineda, Ubaldo Salinas, Olivio Sanasota, Charlie Smith, Miguel Teren, Ted Thornton, Marv Throneberry, Carlos Torres, Rip Tutor, Gary Wilson, Murray Zuk

International supervisors
Felix Francisco, Gil Garrido, Andres Lopez, Julian Perez, Rolando Petit, Fernando Villescusa

Eastern Rim coordinator
Phil Dale

Latin American coordinator
Rene Francisco

BALLPARK INFORMATION

Ballpark (capacity, surface)
Turner Field (50,062, grass)
Address
P.O. Box 4064, Atlanta, GA 30302
Business phone
404-522-7630
Ticket information
404-249-6400 or 800-326-4000
Ticket prices
$35 (dugout level)
$29 (club level)
$25 (field level, terrace level)
$17 (field pavilion, terrace pavilion)
$12 (upper level)
$5 (upper pavilion)
$1 (skyline)
Field dimensions (from home plate)
To left field at foul line, 335 feet
To center field, 401 feet
To right field at foul line, 330 feet
First game played
April 4, 1997 (Braves 5, Cubs 4)

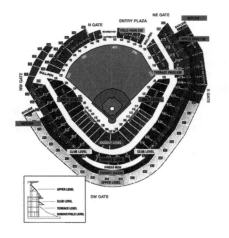

No.	PITCHERS	B/T	Ht./Wt.	Born	1999 clubs	Projection
74	Abreu, Winston	R/R	6-2/155	4-5-77	Macon, Myrtle Beach	Righthander pitched well enough in 1999 to move up the organizational ladder.
48	Chen, Bruce	B/L	6-1/180	6-19-77	Richmond, Atlanta	Didn't pitch well enough to warrant being fifth starter; will have to impress early.
51	Cortes, David	R/R	5-11/195	10-15-73	Richmond, Atlanta	Spent much of '99 season as the closer in Richmond, but not ready for the bigs.
50	Ebert, Derrin	R/L	6-3/200	8-21-76	Atlanta, Richmond	Was 8-7 as starter at Richmond last year, but still no roster spot for this lefty.
47	Glavine, Tom	L/L	6-0/185	3-25-66	Atlanta	Had a bit of an off year, but still won 14 games.
46	Ligtenberg, Kerry	R/R	6-2/215	5-11-71	DID NOT PLAY	Coming off elbow surgery, the Braves will ease him back into the closing role.
31	Maddux, Greg	R/R	6-0/185	4-14-66	Atlanta	Won 19 games despite having an ERA over 3.00 for the first time since 1990.
68	Marquis, Jason	L/R	6-1/185	8-21-78	Myrtle Beach, Greenville	Had an ERA under 1.00 at Myrtle Beach which prompted the promotion to AA.
30	McGlinchy, Kevin	R/R	6-5/220	6-28-77	Atlanta	He's a mainstay in the Braves bullpen and should continue to improve.
36	Medina, Rafael	R/R	6-3/200	2-15-75	Calgary, Florida	Pitched out of the bullpen full time in 1999, will get more seasoning in Richmond.
34	Millwood, Kevin	R/R	6-4/220	12-24-74	Atlanta	At 25, finished third in Cy Young voting behind Johnson and Hampton.
61	Moss, Damian	R/L	6-0/187	11-24-76	Macon, Greenville	Had yet another injury-plagued year, might get back on track this year.
45	Mulholland, Terry	R/L	6-3/220	3-9-63	Chicago N.L., Atlanta	After trade from Cubs, became an effective starter/reliever for the Braves.
43	Perez, Odalis	L/L	6-0/150	6-7-78	Atlanta	Didn't fare too well as fifth starter; ended on the disabled list with elbow troubles.
37	Remlinger, Mike	L/L	6-1/210	3-23-66	Atlanta	Jack-of-all-trades lefty out of the bullpen for the Braves.
72	Rivera, Luis	R/R	6-3/163	6-21-78	Myrtle Beach	Will likely get promoted after holding batters to a .191 average in Myrtle Beach.
49	Rocker, John	R/L	6-4/225	10-17-74	Atlanta	Established himself as dominant closer after Ligtenberg's injury forced there.
40	Seanez, Rudy	R/R	5-10/190	10-20-68	Atlanta	Another bullpen specialist who won six games for the Braves.
29	Smoltz, John	R/R	6-3/220	5-15-67	Atlanta, Greenville	Elbow problems forced him to change arm angle and he didn't miss a beat.
56	Stull, Everett	R/R	6-3/200	8-24-71	Richmond, Atlanta	Was 8-8 with Richmond and will likely get more starts there in 2000.
70	Villegas, Ismael	R/R	6-1/188	8-12-76	Richmond	Young righthander might get chance to pitch out of the Braves bullpen in 2000.

No.	CATCHERS	B/T	Ht./Wt.	Born	1999 clubs	Projection
8	Lopez, Javy	R/R	6-3/200	11-5-70	Atlanta	Was having another great year until a knee injury sidelined him for the season.
11	Matos, Pascual	R/R	6-2/160	12-23-74	Richmond, Atlanta	With Lopez and Perez solidified, he will be back in Richmond.
12	Perez, Eddie	R/R	6-1/185	5-4-68	Atlanta	Played well in Lopez's absence in the regular season and came on strong in the playoffs.

No.	INFIELDERS	B/T	Ht./Wt.	Born	1999 clubs	Projection
14	Galarraga, Andres	R/R	6-3/235	6-18-61	DID NOT PLAY	Might take a while for him to regain form after cancer treatment last season.
20	Garcia, Freddy	R/R	6-2/224	8-1-72	Pittsburgh, Nashville, Atlanta	Will probably be a role player off the bench and used in the infield and outfield.
13	Guillen, Ozzie	L/R	5-11/165	1-20-64	Atlanta	Should spell Weiss at shortstop a couple days a week.
28	Helms, Wes	R/R	6-4/230	5-12-76	Gulf Coast Braves, Greenville	Will likely end up in Richmond to show how well he handles the bat.
10	Jones, Chipper	B/R	6-4/210	4-24-72	Atlanta	Shouldn't have a hard time duplicating MVP numbers from last year.
22	Joyner, Wally	L/L	6-2/200	6-16-62	San Diego, Las Vegas	Will be around to back up Galarraga at first base and provide a veteran lefty bat.
7	Lockhart, Keith	L/R	5-10/170	11-10-64	Atlanta	Another good bat off the bench and can provide good defense on the infield.
15	Simon, Randall	L/L	6-0/180	5-26-75	Atlanta, Richmond	Might end up back in minors this year with Galarraga and Joyner on the team.
4	Veras, Quilvio	B/R	5-10/183	4-3-71	San Diego	The Braves are hoping he'll be the leadoff man they've been searching for.
22	Weiss, Walt	B/R	6-0/168	11-28-63	Atlanta	After solid postseason, he might have won back the starting shortstop job.

No.	OUTFIELDERS	B/T	Ht./Wt.	Born	1999 clubs	Projection
57	Brignac, Junior	R/R	6-3/175	2-15-78	Macon, Myrtle Beach	Shortstop who was converted to outfielder this year. Should be back in minors.
25	Jones, Andruw	R/R	6-1/210	4-23-77	Atlanta	Should show more improvement at the plate; needs to cut down on strikeouts.
33	Jordan, Brian	R/R	6-1/206	3-29-67	Atlanta	Had career-high average and RBI marks and will only improve in a better lineup.
26	Lombard, George	L/R	6-0/202	9-14-75	Richmond, Atlanta	The prospect should start in Richmond and possibly get a call-up to the big club.
16	Sanders, Reggie	R/R	6-1/185	12-1-67	San Diego	This outfielder gives the Braves yet another 20-homer, 30-steal threat.

THE COACHING STAFF

Bobby Cox, manager: Despite a lot of injuries to starters in 1999, Cox managed this team to 103 victories, the most in the majors. The only problem was losing four straight to the Yankees in the World Series. No one can argue with 900 regular season wins and eight consecutive NLCS appearances in the '90s.

Pat Corrales: Former major league manager with Cleveland and Philadelphia had a very successful first year as dugout coach. Used many years of experience to help this club through a season of ups and downs.

Bobby Dews: In 24th year as a member of the Braves organization had good results as a bullpen coach, the emergence of John Rocker made everyone forget about Kerry Ligtenberg. Let's not forget the work he did with Mike Remlinger, Kevin McGlinchy and Rudy Seanez.

Glen Hubbard: Former Braves player made his way to a successful first season as first base coach.

Leo Mazzone: Has been a part of the Braves organization since 1979 and has developed one more name to add to the list of Maddux, Glavine and Smoltz: Kevin Millwood.

Merv Rettenmund: Ex-major league outfielder who is joining the Braves coaching staff to replace Don Baylor, who was hired as Cubs manager.

THE TOP NEWCOMERS

Wally Joyner: A first basemen, he will be available to play if Galarraga isn't fully back into game shape right away. When he's not playing first, he can provide a lefthanded bat off the bench.

Reggie Sanders: Had his best season since 1995. Will only bolster the Braves line up by adding speed, power and slick fielding in the outfield.

Quilvio Veras: Switch-hitting second basemen gives Braves a new dimension at the plate, a leadoff hitter, and he can play second base as well as Bret Boone does.

THE TOP PROSPECTS

Wes Helms: Blocked in the organization by Chipper Jones, he should see lots of action in the minors this year.

George Lombard: Injuries kept him from showing what he can do at Class AAA Richmond. He should be ready for a comeback after last year. If he hits like he did in 1998, he'll fit in well with the big club.

Luis Rivera: Winless in 13 starts at Myrtle Beach in 1999, but his stuff was still there. He should go back to his winning ways if healthy this year. He still struck out 81 batters in only 66 2/3 innings for the Class A club.

CHICAGO CUBS

NATIONAL LEAGUE CENTRAL DIVISION

2000 SEASON

2000 Cubs Schedule

Home games shaded. *—All-Star Game at Turner Field (Atlanta).
† Game played in Tokyo.

March
SUN	MON	TUE	WED	THU	FRI	SAT
26	27	28	29 † NYM	30 † NYM	31	

April
SUN	MON	TUE	WED	THU	FRI	SAT
						1
2	3 STL	4	5 STL	6 STL	7 CIN	8 CIN
9 CIN	10 ATL	11	12 ATL	13 ATL	14 FLA	15 FLA
16 FLA	17 FLA	18 MON	19 MON	20 MON	21 NYM	22 NYM
23 NYM	24	25 HOU	26 HOU	27 HOU	28 ARIZ	29 ARIZ
30 ARIZ						

May
SUN	MON	TUE	WED	THU	FRI	SAT
	1	2 HOU	3 HOU	4 HOU	5 PIT	6 PIT
7 PIT	8 MIL	9 MIL	10 MIL	11 MIL	12 MON	13 MON
14 MON	15	16 LA	17 LA	18 LA	19 CIN	20 CIN
21 CIN	22	23 COL	24 COL	25 COL	26 SF	27 SF
28 SF	29 ATL	30 ATL	31 ATL			

June
SUN	MON	TUE	WED	THU	FRI	SAT
				1	2 DET	3 DET
4 DET	5 ARIZ	6 ARIZ	7 ARIZ	8	9 CWS	10 CWS
11 CWS	12	13 NYM	14 NYM	15	16 MON	17 MON
18 MON	19	20 ATL	21 ATL	22 ATL	23 FLA	24 FLA
25 FLA	26	27 PIT	28 PIT	29 PIT	30 MIL	

July
SUN	MON	TUE	WED	THU	FRI	SAT
						1 MIL
2 MIL	3 PIT	4 PIT	5 PIT	6	7 CWS	8 CWS
9 CWS	10	11 *	12	13 MIN	14 MIN	15 MIN
16 KC	17 KC	18 KC	19 PHI	20 PHI	21 MIL	22 MIL
23 MIL	24	25 PHI	26 PHI	27 PHI	28 SF	29 SF
30 SF	31 COL					

August
SUN	MON	TUE	WED	THU	FRI	SAT
		1 COL	2 COL	3 SD	4 SD	5 SD
6 SD	7 LA	8 LA	9 LA	10	11 CIN	12 CIN
13 CIN	14 STL	15 STL	16 STL	17	18 ARIZ	19 ARIZ
20 ARIZ	21 HOU	22 HOU	23 HOU	24	25 LA	26 LA
27 LA	28 SD	29 SD	30 SD	31 SD		

September
SUN	MON	TUE	WED	THU	FRI	SAT
					1 SF	2 SF
3 SF	4 COL	5 COL	6 COL	7	8 HOU	9 HOU
10 HOU	11 CIN	12 CIN	13 CIN	14 STL	15 STL	16 STL
17 STL	18 MIL	19 MIL	20 MIL	21	22 STL	23 STL
24 STL	25 PHI	26 PHI	27 PHI	28 PHI	29 PIT	30 PIT

October
SUN	MON	TUE	WED	THU	FRI	SAT
1 PIT	2	3	4	5	6	7

FRONT-OFFICE DIRECTORY

Board of directors ....Dennis FitzSimons, Andrew B. MacPhail, Andrew McKenna
President and chief executive officer ....Andrew B. MacPhail
Vice president/general manager ....Ed Lynch
Director, player development and scouting ....Jim Hendry
Director, baseball operations ....Scott Nelson
Special assistants to the general manager ....Keith Champion, Larry Himes, Ken Kravec
Major league advance scout ....Terry Collins
Traveling secretary ....Jimmy Bank
Executive vice president, business operations..................Mark McGuire
Manager, information systems ....Carl Rice
PC systems specialist ....Kyle Hoker
Senior legal counsel/corporate secretary ....Crane Kenney
Controller ....Jodi Norman
Director, human resources ....Jenifer Surma
Vice president, marketing and broadcasting ....John McDonough
Director, promotions and advertising ....Jay Blunk
Director, publications ....Lena McDonagh
Manager, publications ....Jay Rand
Director, stadium operations ....Paul Rathje
Manager, event operations/security ....Mike Hill
Head groundskeeper ....Roger Baird
Director, ticket operations...Frank Maloney
Director, media relations ....Sharon Pannozzo
Manager, media information ....Chuck Wasserstrom
Media relations assistant................................Benjamin de la Fuente

MINOR LEAGUE AFFILIATES

Class	Team	League	Manager
AAA	Iowa	International	Dave Trembley
AA	West Tenn	Southern	Dave Bialas
A	Daytona	Florida State	Richie Zisk
A	Lansing	Midwest	Steve McFarland
A	Eugene	Northwest	Danny Sheaffer
Rookie	Mesa Cubs	Arizona	Carmelo Martinez

BROADCAST INFORMATION

Radio: WGN-AM (720).
TV: WGN-TV (Channel 9); WCIU-TV (Channel 26).
Cable TV: Fox Sports Net Chicago.

SPRING TRAINING

Ballpark (city): HoHoKam Park (Mesa, Ariz.).
Ticket information: 800-638-4253.

ASSISTANCE STAFF

Team physician
Michael Schafer, M.D.

Head athletic trainer
David Tumbas

Assistant athletic trainer
Steve Melendez

Strength and conditioning coordinator
Mark Wilbert

Home clubhouse manager, emeritus
Yosh Kawano

Home clubhouse manager
Tom Hellman

Visiting clubhouse manager
Dana Noeltner

Coordinator of scouting
John Stockstill

Pacific Rim coordinator
Leon Lee

Regional scouting supervisors
Joe Housey, Brad Kelley, Larry Maxie

Coordinator, Latin American operations
Oneri Fleita

Scouts
Mark Adair, Billy Blitzer, Tom Bourque, Jim Crawford, Steve Fuller, Al Geddes, John Gracio, Gene Handley, Bill Harford, Steve Hinton, Sam Hughes, Spider Jorgensen, Buzzy Keller, Scott May, Brian Milner, Hector Ortega, Fred Peterson, Ted Powers, Marc Russo, Jose Serra, Mark Servais, Tom Shafer, Mike Soper, Billy Swoope, Jose Trujillo, Glen Van Proyen

BALLPARK INFORMATION

Ballpark (capacity, surface)
Wrigley Field (39,056, grass)

Address
1060 W. Addison St., Chicago, IL 60613-4397

Business phone
773-404-2827

Ticket information
773-404-2827

Ticket prices
$25 (club box, field box)
$20 (terrace box, upper deck box, family section)
$16 (terrace reserved)
$15 (bleachers)
$10 (adult upper deck reserved)
$6 (under 14 upper deck reserved)

Field dimensions (from home plate)
To left field at foul line, 355 feet
To center field, 400 feet
To right field at foul line, 353 feet

First game played
April 20, 1916 (Cubs 7, Reds 6)

No.	PITCHERS	B/T	Ht./Wt.	Born	1999 clubs	Projection
38	Aguilera, Rick	R/R	6-5/210	12-31-61	Minnesota, Chicago N.L.	Aguilera pressed after being acquired in '99 but is expected to return to form.
53	Bowie, Micah	L/L	6-4/210	11-10-74	Richmond, Atlanta, Chicago N.L.	If Kerry Wood isn't ready for opening day, Bowie might crack the rotation.
	Downs, Scott	L/L	6-2/190	3-17-76	N.Br., Ft. Myers, Dayt., W. Tenn	Downs sizzled in the Class AA Southern League (8-1 record, 1.35 ERA).
44	Farnsworth, Kyle	B/R	6-4/215	4-14-76	Iowa, Chicago N.L.	Dominant at times as a rookie last season. Needs to refine his breaking pitches.
	Gissell, Chris	R/R	6-5/200	1-4-78	West Tenn	A 3-8 record and 5.99 ERA in Class AA were somewhat disappointing.
54	Gonzalez, Jeremi	R/R	6-2/215	1-8-75	Daytona, West Tenn, Iowa	He underwent "Tommy John surgery" last season. His future is unclear.
30	Guthrie, Mark	R/L	6-4/215	9-22-65	Boston, Pawtucket, Chicago N.L.	He altered his mechanics to get better command of the strike zone.
49	Heredia, Felix	L/L	6-0/180	6-18-76	Chicago N.L.	He led the Cubs with 69 appearances last season but remains inconsistent.
52	Karchner, Matt	R/R	6-4/220	6-28-67	Chicago N.L., Iowa	With Terry Adams gone to the Dodgers, Karchner will be righthanded setup man.
56	King, Ray	L/L	6-1/230	1-15-74	Iowa, Chicago N.L.	Made 10 relief appearances in '99 but never retired the first batter he faced.
32	Lieber, Jon	L/R	6-3/225	4-2-70	Chicago N.L.	He ranked among the N.L.'s top 10 in strikeouts and fewest walks per nine IP.
55	Lorraine, Andrew	L/L	6-3/200	8-11-72	Iowa, Chicago N.L.	He made his Cubs debut with a shutout but never got into a groove thereafter.
33	McNichol, Brian	L/L	6-5/225	5-20-74	Iowa, Chicago N.L.	He was ineffective in four late-season appearances after a strong AAA year.
	Meyers, Mike	R/R	6-2/210	10-18-77	Daytona, West Tenn	Excelled in Class A (10-3, 1.93 ERA) and Class AA (4-0, 1.09).
59	Myers, Rodney	R/R	6-1/215	6-26-69	Iowa, Chicago N.L.	Worked 46 times out of the Cubs' bullpen and again will contend for a job.
50	Norton, Phil	B/L	6-1/190	2-1-76	West Tenn, Iowa	He pitched well in Class AA last season but found the going tough in Class AAA.
	Quevedo, Ruben	R/R	6-1/230	1-5-79	Richmond, Iowa	Former Braves farmhand is a strong prospect. At 20, he won nine games in AAA.
41	Rain, Steve	R/R	6-6/260	6-2-75	West Tenn, Chicago N.L., Iowa	Rain, who pitched well in the minors, has an intimidating presence.
36	Tapani, Kevin	R/R	6-1/190	2-18-64	Chicago N.L.	A 19-game winner in '98, he had an injury-marred '99. Can he rebound at age 36?
	Valdes, Ismael	R/R	6-3/215	8-21-73	Los Angeles	Only 26, he is projected as a valuable addition and innings eater.
	Williams, Brian	R/R	6-2/225	2-15-69	Houston	This decent middle reliever will have to adjust from the deep Houston bullpen.
34	Wood, Kerry	R/R	6-5/230	6-16-77	DID NOT PLAY	Whatever the Cubs get from this 1998 rookie sensation will be a plus.
	Young, Danny	R/L	6-4/210	11-3-71	West Tenn	He put up some good numbers while pitching primarily in relief in Class AA.

No.	CATCHERS	B/T	Ht./Wt.	Born	1999 clubs	Projection
22	Cline, Pat	R/R	6-4/230	10-9-74	Iowa	He batted only .228 in Class AAA but the Cubs still think he can make it.
	Girardi, Joe	R/R	5-11/200	10-14-64	New York A.L.	His leadership, game-calling and handling of pitchers are major assets.
19	Molina, Jose	R/R	6-1/215	6-3-75	West Tenn, Iowa, Chicago N.L.	Made it to the majors in '99 but is overmatched at the plate.
16	Reed, Jeff	L/R	6-2/200	11-12-62	Colorado, Chicago N.L.	A steady operative and a lefthanded bat, he figures to start a couple times a week.

No.	INFIELDERS	B/T	Ht./Wt.	Born	1999 clubs	Projection
7	Andrews, Shane	R/R	6-1/220	8-28-71	Montreal, Ottawa, Chicago N.L.	He showed some thump with the Cubs, due in part to batting coach Jeff Pentland.
17	Grace, Mark	L/L	6-2/200	6-28-64	Chicago N.L.	A lifetime .310 hitter who shows no signs of slowing down.
	Gutierrez, Ricky	R/R	6-1/175	5-23-70	Houston, Jackson, New Orleans	Dependable at shortstop, the former Astro could be adequate offensively.
18	Liniak, Cole	R/R	6-1/190	8-23-76	Pawtucket, Chicago N.L.	He could contend for a reserve job at third or second base.
20	Meyers, Chad	R/R	6-0/190	8-8-75	West Tenn, Iowa, Chicago N.L.	His hopes of starting at second base ended when the Cubs obtained Eric Young.
11	Nieves, Jose	R/R	6-1/180	6-16-75	Iowa, Chicago N.L.	Like Meyers, Nieves seemed a possibility to start—until Gutierrez was obtained.
	Young, Eric	R/R	5-8/175	5-18-67	Los Angeles, San Bernardino	The former Dodger gives the Cubs a leadoff hitter. He stole 51 bases in '99.
	Zuleta, Julio	R/R	6-6/230	3-28-75	West Tenn	First baseman Zuleta is an emerging power threat (21 homers, 97 RBIs in AA).

No.	OUTFIELDERS	B/T	Ht./Wt.	Born	1999 clubs	Projection
28	Brown, Roosevelt	L/R	5-11/195	8-3-75	West Tenn, Chicago N.L., Iowa	He has good power potential but needs to work on the rest of his game.
	Buford, Damon	R/R	5-10/180	6-12-70	Boston	His great range should be a boon to the outfield. He also has some pop in his bat.
8	Hill, Glenallen	R/R	6-3/230	3-22-65	Chicago N.L.	A superb role player, Hill hit .300 with 20 homers in 253 at-bats.
40	Rodriguez, Henry	L/L	6-2/225	11-8-67	Chicago N.L.	Hampered by injuries, he nonetheless hit 31 homers in '98 and 26 in '99.
21	Sosa, Sammy	R/R	6-0/220	11-12-68	Chicago N.L.	After hitting 129 homers in two seasons, what's there to do?

THE COACHING STAFF

Don Baylor, manager: The first manager in Rockies history, he guided Colorado for six seasons. Baylor led the Rockies into the playoffs in the Colorado franchise's third year of existence (1995), winning N.L. Manager of the Year honors. He had three consecutive winning seasons for the fledgling team. Last year, he served as hitting coach for the pennant-winning Braves. A stickler for details, Baylor is a disciplinarian who has surrounded himself with a teaching-oriented staff. A hard-nosed player who spent 19 years in the majors, he is accustomed to winning (having played in seven League Championship Series and three World Series). He abhors the Cubs' "lovable losers" reputation and vows to turn things around on the North Side.

Oscar Acosta: The Cubs' new pitching coach, he is in his first coaching job in the majors. Manager of the Cubs' Class A Lansing affiliate last season, he spent the previous three years as pitching coach for the Yankees' Class AAA Columbus farm team.

Sandy Alomar Sr.: A former coach for the Padres (1986-90) and onetime winter-league manager, he takes over as the Cubs' bullpen coach. The father of major leaguers Sandy Jr. and Roberto, he had a 15-year career as a big-league infielder.

Gene Glynn: Glynn will coach at third base for the Cubs. The former Rockies and Expos coach also is in charge of infield defense. He managed the first professional team the Colorado organization ever fielded, at Bend in the Northwest League in 1992.

Rene Lachemann: When the N.L. expanded in 1993, Lachemann was manager of the new Florida team and Baylor was manager of the new Colorado club. Now, Lachemann will serve as Baylor's bench coach. He comes to Chicago from St. Louis, where he served three years as the third base coach. Before guiding the Marlins for three-plus seasons, he managed the Mariners and the Brewers.

Jeff Pentland: He continues as the Cubs' hitting coach, a position he assumed in July 1997. Pentland formerly served as the Mets' minor league hitting coordinator and as a college coach.

Billy Williams: He begins his 14th season as a Cubs coach, this time as first base coach and outfield instructor. Williams, a Hall of Fame player for the Cubs, is in his third coaching stint with the club. He also has been a coach for the A's.

THE TOP NEWCOMERS

Joe Girardi: Back with the organization that drafted him, Girardi figures to hit better than the .239 average he posted for the Yankees last year. More playing time would seem to ensure that. No matter. Girardi is back in a Cubs uniform because of what he'll provide behind the plate and the leadership he'll lend after playing for three World Series title teams in four years.

Ismael Valdes: Still young, he has been an effective major league pitcher—as his 3.38 career ERA attests. Valdes still needs to get over some mental and physical humps, but he possibly could help the Cubs make a major turnaround in the N.L. Central.

Brian Williams: After not playing in the bigs in 1998, he performed quite well in the middle relief role for Houston last year. The Cubs need him, and expect a lot from him, this year.

Eric Young: Not as steady at second base as the departed Mickey Morandini, Young nonetheless has better range—and his all-around offensive game is superior. As the leadoff hitter, he is a key component to a Cubs offense that can't rely on Sammy Sosa alone.

THE TOP PROSPECTS

Scott Downs: Always in need of strong arms—and coveting lefthanded pitching—Chicago has to be encouraged by Downs' performance in 1999. Including a stint in the low minors, he was 13-2 with Cubs affiliates and had an ERA under 1.50.

Mike Meyers: Only 22, the Canadian is showing exceptional promise for a 26th-round draft choice. He struck out 173 batters in 140 1/3 minor league innings last season.

Ruben Quevedo: The righthander has to watch his weight. He has three quality pitches and a smooth delivery—so smooth that his fastball can be deceptive.

CINCINNATI REDS

NATIONAL LEAGUE CENTRAL DIVISION

2000 SEASON

2000 Reds Schedule

Home games shaded. *—All-Star Game at Turner Field (Atlanta).

March

SUN	MON	TUE	WED	THU	FRI	SAT
26	27	28	29	30	31	

April

SUN	MON	TUE	WED	THU	FRI	SAT
						1
2	3 MIL	4	5 MIL	6 MIL	7 CUB	8 CUB
9 CUB	10 COL	11 COL	12 COL	13	14 LA	15 LA
16 LA	17	18 SF	19 SF	20 SF	21 LA	22 LA
23 LA	24	25 NYM	26 NYM	27 NYM	28 PIT	29 PIT
30 PIT						

May

SUN	MON	TUE	WED	THU	FRI	SAT
	1 PIT	2 PHI	3 PHI	4 PHI	5 STL	6 STL
7 STL	8	9 SD	10 SD	11 SD	12 HOU	13 HOU
14 HOU	15 HOU	16 PIT	17 PIT	18 PIT	19 CUB	20 CUB
21 CUB	22 LA	23 LA	24 LA	25	26 FLA	27 FLA
28 FLA	29	30 MON	31 MON			

June

SUN	MON	TUE	WED	THU	FRI	SAT
				1 MON	2 MIN	3 MIN
4 MIN	5 CWS	6 CWS	7 CWS	8	9 CLE	10 CLE
11 CLE	12 SF	13 SF	14 SF	15	16 SD	17 SD
18 SD	19	20 COL	21 COL	22 COL	23 SD	24 SD
25 SD	26 STL	27 STL	28 STL	29 STL	30 ARI	

July

SUN	MON	TUE	WED	THU	FRI	SAT
						1 ARI
2 ARI	3 ARI	4 STL	5 STL	6 STL	7 CLE	8 CLE
9 CLE	10	11	* 12	13 COL	14 COL	15 COL
16 DET	17 DET	18 DET	19 HOU	20 HOU	21 ARI	22 ARI
23 ARI	24 HOU	25 HOU	26 HOU	27	28 MON	29 MON
30 MON	31 NYM					

August

SUN	MON	TUE	WED	THU	FRI	SAT
		1 NYM	2 NYM	3	4 FLA	5 FLA
6 FLA	7 ATL	8 ATL	9 ATL	10	11 CUB	12 CUB
13 CUB	14 MIL	15 MIL	16 MIL	17	18 PIT	19 PIT
20 PIT	21 PHI	22 PHI	23 PHI	24 PHI	25 FLA	26 FLA
27 FLA	28 ATL	29 ATL	30 ATL	31 ATL		

September

SUN	MON	TUE	WED	THU	FRI	SAT
					1 MON	2 MON
3 MON	4 NYM	5 NYM	6 NYM	7	8 PIT	9 PIT
10 PIT	11 CUB	12 CUB	13 CUB	14 MIL	15 MIL	16 MIL
17 MIL	18 SF	19 SF	20 SF	21	22 HOU	23 HOU
24 HOU	25	26 MIL	27 MIL	28 MIL	29 STL	30 STL

October

SUN	MON	TUE	WED	THU	FRI	SAT
1 STL	2	3	4	5	6	7

FRONT-OFFICE DIRECTORY

Chief executive officer ....Carl H. Lindner
Chief operating officer ....John Allen
General manager ....Jim Bowden
Assistant general manager......................................Darrell "Doc" Rodgers
Senior director of player development/scouting ....Leland Maddox
Special assistant to the general manager/advance scout ....Gene Bennett
Special assistants to the general manager......................Bob Boone, Larry Barton, Jr.,
Johnny Bench, Al Goldis
Director of baseball administration ....Brad Kullman
Major league scout/national cross-checker ....Kasey McKeon
Executive assistant to the general manager ....Lois Schneider
Senior advisor, player development ....Sheldon "Chief" Bender
Administrative assistant, player development ....Lois Hudson
Director of scouting ....De Jon Watson
Senior advisor, scouting...Bob Zuk
Director of scouting administration..Wilma Mann
Traveling secretary ....Gary Wahoff
Director media relations ....Rob Butcher
Public relations assistant..Larry Herms
Controller ....Anthony Ward
Director, stadium operations ....Jody Pettyjohn
Director, ticket department ....John O'Brien
Director, season/group sales ....Pat McCaffrey
Director of communications ....Mike Ringering
Assistant director of communications ....Ralph Mitchell
Director of new stadium development ....Jenny Gardner
Marketing consultant ....Cal Levy
Legal counsel ....Robert C. Martin
Director, group sales ....Brad Blettner
Assistant director, media relations ....Michael Vassallo
Executive assistant to chief operating officer ....Joyce Pfarr
Business and broadcast administrator...Ginny Kamp

MINOR LEAGUE AFFILIATES

Class	Team	League	Manager
AAA	Indianapolis	International	Dave Miley
AA	Chattanooga	Southern	Michael Rojas
A	Clinton	Midwest	Jay Sorg
A	Dayton	Midwest	Freddie Benavides
Rookie	Billings	Pioneer	Russ Nixon
Rookie	Gulf Coast Reds	Gulf Coast	Luis Quinones

BROADCAST INFORMATION

Radio: WLW-AM (700).
Cable TV: Fox Sports Ohio.

SPRING TRAINING

Ballpark (city): Ed Smith Stadium
(Sarasota, Fla.).
Ticket information: 941-954-4101.

BALLPARK INFORMATION

Ballpark (capacity, surface)
Cinergy Field (52,953, artificial)
Address
100 Cinergy Field
Cincinnati, OH 45202
Business phone
513-421-4510
Ticket information
513-421-7337, 1-800-829-5353
Ticket prices
$21, $18 (blue level box seats)
$16, $14 (green level box seats)
$13 (yellow level box seats)
$12 (red level box seats)
$11 (green level reserved seats)
$8 (red level reserved seats)
$5 ("top six" reserved seats)
Field dimensions (from home plate)
To left field at foul line, 330 feet
To center field, 404 feet
To right field at foul line, 330 feet
First game played
June 30, 1970 (Braves 8, Reds 2)

ASSISTANCE STAFF

Head trainer
Greg Lynn

Assistant trainer
Mark Mann

Conditioning coordinator
Lance Sewell

Field superintendent
Jeff Guilkey

Senior clubhouse & equipment manager
Bernie Stowe

Reds clubhouse & equipment manager
Rick Stowe

Visiting clubhouse & equipment manager
Mark Stowe

Cross-checkers

Johnny Almaraz	Alvin Rittman
Ross Sapp	Bill Scherrer

Scouting supervisors

Terry Abott	Butch Baccala
Howard Bowens	John Brickley
Mark Corey	Robert Filotei
Jerry Flowers	Jimmy Gonzales
David Jennings	Robert Koontz
Craig Kornfeld	Steve Kring
Brian Mejia	Cotton Nye
Tom Severtson	Perry Smith
Brian Wilson	Greg Zunino

Scouts

Amador Arias	John Bellino
Fred Blair	Kevin Carcamo
Felix Delgado	Jim Grief
Don Gust	Frank Henderson
Don Hill	Thomas Herrera
Juan Linares	Anthony Lowe
Victor Mateo	Denny Nagel
Rafael Nava	Everett Renteria
Glenn Serviente	Marlon Styles
Lee Toole	Ruben Vargas

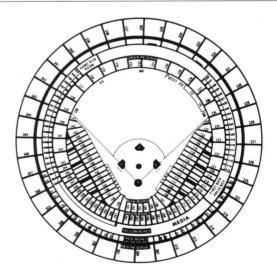

No.	PITCHERS	B/T	Ht./Wt.	Born	1999 clubs	Projection
50	Bell, Rob	R/R	6-5/226	1-17-77	Chattanooga, Gulf Coast Reds	The team's top pitching prospect, but he's a year away from the majors.
60	Burnside, Adrian	R/L	6-3/168	3-15-77	San Bernardino	A Rule 5 draftee from the Dodgers, he'll relieve and spot start.
72	Flury, Patrick	R/R	6-1/220	3-14-73	Chattanooga, Indianapolis	Needs to prove he can get it done at the Class AAA level.
59	Gaillard, Eddie	R/R	6-2/195	8-13-70	Durham, Tampa Bay	He has had arm troubles in the past and pitched only eight games last season.
32	Graves, Danny	R/R	5-11/185	8-7-73	Cincinnati	A workhorse out of the bullpen capable of pitching in more than 70 games.
38	Harnisch, Pete	R/R	6-0/228	9-23-66	Cincinnati	He led the team in starts but his shoulder is a question mark.
63	Dessens, Elmer	R/R	6-0/187	1-13-72	Yomiuri Giants	He will try win bullpen job after year in Japan.
67	Murray, Heath	L/L	6-4/215	4-19-73	Las Vegas, San Diego	He would have to make a huge impression to make the major league staff.
15	Neagle, Denny	L/L	6-3/225	9-13-68	Indianapolis, Cincinnati	Now that he's healthy, he could become the team's No. 1 pitcher.
58	Parris, Steve	R/R	6-0/195	12-17-67	Indianapolis, Cincinnati	He should be solidified in the rotation after solid '99.
49	Reyes, Dennys	L/L	6-3/246	4-19-77	Cincinnati	Lefthanded setup man is tough to hit from both sides of the plate.
46	Riedling, John	R/R	5-11/190	8-29-75	Chattanooga, Indianapolis	If he makes the major league team, it'll be as a reliever.
56	Sullivan, Scott	R/R	6-3/210	3-13-71	Cincinnati	Bullpen workhorse has led N.L. relievers in innings the last two seasons.
40	Tomko, Brett	R/R	6-4/216	4-7-73	Cincinnati, Indianapolis	He is the closest thing the Reds have to a power pitcher.
41	Villone, Ron	L/L	6-3/237	1-16-70	Indianapolis, Cincinnati	He should be in the rotation, but could move back to the bullpen.
36	White, Gabe	L/L	6-2/200	11-20-71	Cincinnati	Hard-throwing lefty struck out 61 batters in 61 innings last year.
48	Williamson, Scott	R/R	6-0/185	2-17-76	Cincinnati	A little overused last season, he is very effective in one-inning stints.
51	Winchester, Scott	R/R	6-2/210	4-20-73	Rockford	This reliever should start the season at Class AA or AAA.

No.	CATCHERS	B/T	Ht./Wt.	Born	1999 clubs	Projection
26	LaRue, Jason	R/R	5-11/200	3-19-74	Indianapolis, Cincinnati	Backup this season but might have future as a starter.
10	Taubensee, Eddie	L/R	6-3/230	10-31-68	Cincinnati	He has the potential to hit for a high average and has power to the gaps.

No.	INFIELDERS	B/T	Ht./Wt.	Born	1999 clubs	Projection
17	Boone, Aaron	R/R	6-2/200	3-9-73	Cincinnati, Indianapolis	He has good pop and could up his home run and RBI totals.
21	Casey, Sean	L/R	6-4/226	7-2-74	Cincinnati	An N.L. batting title is in his future, as early as this season.
69	Cromer, D.T.	L/L	6-2/190	3-19-71	Indianapolis	He had 107 RBIs in Class AAA, but is a bench player in the majors.
6	Dawkins, Travis	R/R	6-1/180	5-12-79	Rock., Chattanooga, Cincinnati	Shortstop with good speed and defense should start at Class AAA.
11	Larkin, Barry	R/R	6-0/185	4-28-64	Cincinnati	His power numbers are sagging, but he's still a great offensive player.
75	Larson, Brandon	R/R	6-0/210	5-24-76	Rockford, Chattanooga	He has good power but needs to prove he can stay healthy.
28	Lewis, Mark	R/R	6-1/195	11-30-69	Cincinnati	Utility infielder can fill in at any infield position.
23	Morris, Hal	L/L	6-2/195	4-9-65	Cincinnati	Backup to Casey hit .405 with runners in scoring position in '99.
3	Reese, Pokey	R/R	5-11/180	6-10-73	Cincinnati	Gold Glove second baseman has a nice blend of offensive skills.
23	Stynes, Chris	R/R	5-10/185	1-19-73	Cincinnati	As a pinch hitter, he batted .364 last season.
68	Wright, Ron	R/R	6-1/230	1-21-76	Altoona	He has to prove in minors he has overcome lingering back problems.

No.	OUTFIELDERS	B/T	Ht./Wt.	Born	1999 clubs	Projection
46	Bartee, Kimera	R/R	6-0/200	7-21-72	Toledo, Detroit	Outstanding fielder with speed will likely be at Indianapolis.
9	Bichette, Dante	R/R	6-3/238	11-18-63	Colorado	He gets the chance to prove he can hit outside of Coors.
44	Cameron, Mike	R/R	6-2/190	1-8-73	Cincinnati	Center fielder with speed and power will hit leadoff.
66	Clark, Brady	R/R	6-2/195	4-18-73	Chattanooga	Despite good numbers thus far, he is not a big prospect given the outfield depth.
73	Frank, Mike	L/L	6-2/195	1-14-75	Indianapolis	No room for him right now in the Reds' deep outfield, but a good bench player.
24	Ochoa, Alex	R/R	6-0/195	3-29-72	Milwaukee	Solid fourth outfielder will mostly start against lefties.
34	Tucker, Michael	L/R	6-2/185	6-25-71	Cincinnati	Fourth outfielder still has adjustments to make at the plate.
25	Young, Dmitri	B/R	6-2/235	10-11-73	Cincinnati	A hot second half got him off the bench and starting in right field.

THE COACHING STAFF

Jack McKeon, manager: McKeon's 50th season in professional baseball was a memorable one as he guided the Reds to a 96-67 record—his highest victory total in 11 seasons as a big-league manager. Under McKeon, the Reds tied the Mets for the N.L. wild card but lost a one-game playoff. McKeon's grandfatherly approach has played well in his 2-plus seasons as Cincinnati's manager. McKeon was hired by the Reds in January of 1993 as senior advisor of player personnel and replaced Ray Knight as Cincinnati's manager on July 25, 1997. He had previously managed the Royals, Athletics and Padres.

Dave Collins: This will be Collins' second season as the team's first base coach. He was a player for the Reds from 1978-81 and 1987-89.

Harry Dunlop: This will be his third season as the team's third base coach. He was a bench coach for Cincinnati from 1979-82.

Ken Griffey Sr.: Griffey, who starred on the Big Red Machine teams in the 1970s, is in his fourth season on the Reds staff and his second as a bench coach.

Don Gullett: Gullet coached in the Reds system for three years before joining the big-league staff in 1993 as a bullpen coach. Two months later he was promoted to his current position of pitching coach.

Tom Hume: The former Reds pitcher is in his fifth season on Cincinnati's coaching staff.

Dennis Menke: This is Menske's second season as hitting coach. He formerly served as a minor league manager with the Astros and Phillies.

Ron Oester: This is Oester's 24th season in the Reds organization. The former Reds second baseman will be coaching first base for his second season.

THE TOP NEWCOMERS

Kimera Bartee: A speedy outfielder acquired from the Tigers in a trade for a player to be named later and cash in December. Bartee can cover a lot of range in the outfield and on the basepaths but his bat has been suspect in the major leagues. Figures to be little more than a fourth outfielder and/or defensive replacement.

Dante Bichette: Acquired from the Rockies for outfielder Jeffrey Hammonds and pitcher Stan Belinda, Bichette will have to fill the offensive void left by the departure of free agent Greg Vaughn. Bichette has proved both durable and consistent in his Colorado years. But he'll have to prove his age (36) and departure from Coors Field aren't factors.

Alex Ochoa: The journeyman still has the tools—a good arm and a sometimes powerful bat. But is now labeled as a bad fielder who specializes in hitting lefties.

THE TOP PROSPECTS

Rob Bell: Bell was an important part of the trade that brought Denny Neagle over from Atlanta. Bell has had some elbow problems but throws in the mid-90s and could be in the majors by 2001.

Travis Dawkins: Dawkins will eventually replace Barry Larkin at shortstop. Dawkins has Gold-Glove caliber defensive skills and great offensive potential.

Brandon Larson: Larson has the ability to hit the ball out of the stadium to all fields. He needs to prove he can stay healthy for a full season at Class AA before he joins the big club.

Jason LaRue: LaRue got an early callup last season when backup catcher Brian Johnson was injured. He's made big strides defensively in the past few years and has a line-drive swing. He could platoon with Taubensee at some point this season.

COLORADO ROCKIES

NATIONAL LEAGUE WEST DIVISION

2000 SEASON

2000 Rockies Schedule

Home games shaded. *—All-Star Game at Turner Field (Atlanta).

March

SUN	MON	TUE	WED	THU	FRI	SAT
26	27	28	29	30	30	

April

SUN	MON	TUE	WED	THU	FRI	SAT
						1
2	3 ATL	4 ATL	5 ATL	6	7 FLA	8 FLA
9 FLA	10 CIN	11 CIN	12 CIN	13 STL	14 STL	15 STL
16 STL	17 ARI	18 ARI	19 ARI	20 ARI	21 STL	22 STL
23 STL	24 STL	25 MON	26 MON	27	28 NYM	29 NYM
30 NYM						

May

SUN	MON	TUE	WED	THU	FRI	SAT
	1 MON	2 MON	3 MON	4	5 SF	6 SF
7 SF	8 HOU	9 HOU	10 HOU	11	12 SF	13 SF
14 SF	15	16 NYM	17 NYM	18 NYM	19 PHI	20 PHI
21 PHI	22	23 CUB	24 CUB	25 CUB	26 PIT	27 PIT
28 PIT	29 HOU	30 HOU	31 HOU			

June

SUN	MON	TUE	WED	THU	FRI	SAT
				1	2 MIL	3 MIL
4 MIL	5 SEA	6 SEA	7 SEA	8	9 TEX	10 TEX
11 TEX	12	13 HOU	14 HOU	15 HOU	16 ARI	17 ARI
18 ARI	19	20 CIN	21 CIN	22 CIN	23 ARI	24 ARI
25 ARI	26 SF	27 SF	28 SF	29 SD	30 SD	

July

SUN	MON	TUE	WED	THU	FRI	SAT
						1 SD
2 SD	3 SD	4 SF	5 SF	6 SF	7 ANA	8 ANA
9 ANA	10	11	* 12	13 CIN	14 CIN	15 CIN
16 OAK	17 OAK	18 OAK	19 LA	20 LA	21 SD	22 SD
23 SD	24 LA	25 LA	26 LA	27 LA	28 MIL	29 MIL
30 MIL	31 CUB					

August

SUN	MON	TUE	WED	THU	FRI	SAT
		1 CUB	2 CUB	3	4 PHI	5 PHI
6 PHI	7 PIT	8 PIT	9	10	11 MON	12 MON
13 MON	14 MON	15 NYM	16 NYM	17 NYM	18 FLA	19 FLA
20 FLA	21 ATL	22 ATL	23 ATL	24	25 PIT	26 PIT
27 PIT	28 PHI	29 PHI	30 PHI	31		

September

SUN	MON	TUE	WED	THU	FRI	SAT
					1 MIL	2 MIL
3 MIL	4 CUB	5 CUB	6 CUB	7	8 LA	9 LA
10 LA	11 SD	12 SD	13 SD	14 LA	15 LA	16 LA
17 LA	18	19 SD	20 SD	21 SD	22 FLA	23 FLA
24 FLA	25	26 ARI	27 ARI	28 ARI	29 ATL	30 ATL

October

SUN	MON	TUE	WED	THU	FRI	SAT
1 ATL	2	3	4	5	6	

FRONT-OFFICE DIRECTORY

Chairman, president and corporate executive officer................Jerry McMorris
Vice chairmen................................Charles Monfort, Richard Monfort
Executive vice president, business operations ....Keli McGregor
Executive vice president, general manager..............................Dan O'Dowd
Senior vice president, chief financial officer...............................Hal Roth
Senior vice president, corporate counsel ....Clark Weaver
Vice president, finance...Michael Kent
Vice president, sales and marketing ....Greg Feasel
Vice president, ticket operations and sales...................Sue Ann McClaren
Senior director, public relations and communications ....Jay Alves
Senior director, Coors Field operations ....Kevin Kahn
Senior director, personnel and administration ....Liz Stecklein
Senior director, corporate sales ....Marcy English Glasser
Director, player development..Paul Egins
Director of scouting ....Bill Schmidt
Director, baseball administration ....Tony Siegle
Director, broadcasting...Eric Brummond
Director, community affairs ....Roger Kinney
Director, information systems ....Mary Burns
Director, merchandising ....Jim Kellogg
Director, promotions and special events ....Alan Bossart
Director, team travel..Brandy Lay
Director, ticket sales..Jill Roberts
Director, ticket services & spring training business operations ....Chuck Javernick

MINOR LEAGUE AFFILIATES

Class	Team	League	Manager
AAA	Colorado Springs	Pacific Coast	Chris Cron
AA	Carolina	Southern	Ron Gideon
A	Salem	Carolina	Alan Cockrell
A	Asheville	South Atlantic	Joe Mikulik
A	Portland	Northwest	Billy White
Rookie	Rockies	Arizona	P.J. Carey

BROADCAST INFORMATION

Radio: KOA-AM (850), KCUV-AM (1150).
TV: KWGN-TV (Channel 2).
Cable TV: Fox Sports Rocky Mountain.

SPRING TRAINING

Ballpark (city): Hi Corbett Field (Tucson, Ariz.).
Ticket information: 1-800-388-ROCK.

ASSISTANCE STAFF

Head groundskeeper
Mark Razum

Coordinator of instruction
Rick Mathews

National cross-checkers
Bill Gayton   Dave Holliday

Regional cross-checkers
Jay Darnell   Robyn Lynch
Danny Montgomery

Major League scouts
Pat Daugherty   Jim Fregosi Jr.
Dave Garcia   Will George
Milt May   Mark Wiley

Professional scouts
Joe McDonald   Art Pontarelli
Steve Schryver

Scouts
John Cedarburg   Ty Coslow
Dar Cox   Mike Ericson
Abe Flores   Mike Garlatti
Bert Holt   Greg Hopkins
Bill Hughes   Damon Iannelli
Eric Johnson   Bill Mackenzie
Jay Matthews   Lance Nichols
Sean O'Connor   Brooks Roybal
Ed Santa   Nick Venuto
Tom Wheeler

International scouts
Phil Allen, Dario Arias, Francisco Cartava, Cristobal A. Giron, Tim Ireland, Alexander Marquez, Oscar Martinez, Brian McRobie, Atanacio Mendez, Jorge Moreno, Ramon Pena, Jorge Posada, Jesus Rizales, Reed Spencer, Ron Steele

BALLPARK INFORMATION

Ballpark (capacity, surface)
Coors Field (50,381, grass)
Address
2001 Blake St., Denver, CO 80205-2000
Business phone
303-292-0200
Ticket information
800-388-7625
Ticket prices
$32 (club level, infield)
$30 (club level, outfield)
$27 (infield box)
$21.50 (outfield box)
$16/13 (lower reserved, infield/outfield)
$12 (upper reserved infield, RF box)
$11 (lower reserved corner)
$10 (RF mezzanine)
$9 (upper reserved, outfield; lower pavilion)
$8 (lower pavilion)
$7 (upper reserved corner)
$6/5 (lower/upper RF reserved)
$4/1 (rockpile)
Field dimensions (from home plate)
To left field at foul line, 347 feet
To center field, 415 feet
To right field at foul line, 350
First game played
April 26, 1995 (Rockies 11, Mets 9, 14 innings)

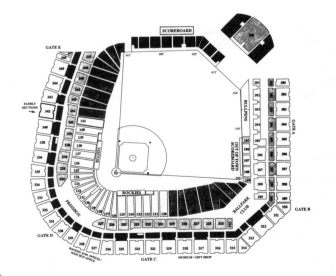

No.	PITCHERS	B/T	Ht./Wt.	Born	1999 clubs	Projection
30	Arrojo, Rolando	R/R	6-4/220	7-18-68	Tampa Bay, St. Petersburg	His extensive repertoire and good command will be big assets at Coors Field.
34	Astacio, Pedro	R/R	6-2/208	11-28-69	Colorado	A staff ace where pitchers fear to tread, this fierce competitor has to come up big.
38	Aybar, Manny	R/R	6-2/208	11-28-69	St. Louis	Aybar needs consistency, but he figures to make a bid for a starting job.
37	Belinda, Stan	R/R	6-3/215	8-6-66	Indianapolis, Cincinnati	His three-quarters delivery will offer a different look coming out of the bullpen.
43	Beltran, Rigo	L/L	5-11/185	11-13-69	Norf., N.York N.L., C.Spr., Colo.	He was hammered after the All-Star break last season but could rebound.
41	Bohanon, Brian	L/L	6-2/240	8-1-68	Colorado	The lefthander got off to a 6-1 start but now must fight for a place in the rotation.
	Croushore, Rick	R/R	6-4/210	8-7-70	Memphis, St. Louis	A power pitcher and a bulldog type, he was effective for St. Louis in the first half.
44	DeJean, Mike	R/R	6-2/212	9-28-70	Colorado, Colorado Springs	Bouncing back from 1999 (8.41 ERA, 83 hits in 61 innings) will take some doing.
45	Dipoto, Jerry	R/R	6-2/205	5-24-68	Colorado	Exceptional as a setup man, he returns to the closer role.
49	Jimenez, Jose	R/R	6-3/190	7-7-73	St. Louis, Memphis	As a rookie, he was very good (a no-hitter) and very bad (demoted to minors).
	Karl, Scott	L/L	6-2/209	8-9-71	Milwaukee	He was 11-11 for a struggling Brewers team but yielded 246 hits in 197 2/3 IP.
	Lee, David	R/R	6-1/202	3-12-73	Carolina, Colo., Colo. Springs	The reliever was effective on three levels in '99—including the majors.
	Myers, Mike	L/L	6-4/214	6-26-69	Milwaukee	This situational reliever is a rarity—a side-wheeling lefthander.
51	Shoemaker, Steve	L/L	6-1/214	2-3-73	Colorado Springs	His 6.00 ERA at Colorado Springs isn't too encouraging but he has still has talent.
	Tavarez, Julian	L/R	6-2/190	5-22-73	San Fran., Fresno, San Jose	Remember when he was 10-2 for the Indians? Maybe not—it was 1995.
52	Thomson, John	R/R	6-3/187	10-1-73	Colorado, Colo. Springs, Salem	Thomson was 1-10 with an 8.04 ERA in '99 (and had a 9.45 ERA Class AAA).
21	Yoshii, Masato	R/R	6-2/210	4-20-65	New York N.L.	His deceiving, dipping pitches are a fit for Coors Field.

No.	CATCHERS	B/T	Ht./Wt.	Born	1999 clubs	Projection
	Mayne, Brent	L/R	6-1/192	4-19-68	San Francisco	He figures to do much of the catching until Ben Petrick is ready.
7	Petrick, Ben	R/R	6-0/199	4-7-77	Carolina, Colo. Springs, Colo.	Rockies' catcher of the future is very athletic and can hit but needs polish.

No.	INFIELDERS	B/T	Ht./Wt.	Born	1999 clubs	Projection
	Butler, Brent	R/R	6-0/180	2-11-78	Arkansas	With Neifi Perez blocking his way, Butler will be converted into a second baseman.
26	Cirillo, Jeff	R/R	6-1/195	9-23-69	Milwaukee	Excellent glove man should thrive offensively at Coors Field. Likely to hit cleanup.
17	Helton, Todd	L/L	6-2/206	8-20-73	Colorado	An emerging all-around star, the disciplined Helton will continue to improve.
3	Lansing, Mike	R/R	6-0/195	4-3-68	Colorado	He must rebound from an injury-plagued year and hit well behind Tom Goodwin.
	Ledesma, Aaron	R/R	6-2/210	6-3-71	St. Pete., Durham, Tampa Bay	Handyman swings a pretty good bat (.300 average in 714 career at-bats).
5	Perez, Neifi	B/R	6-0/175	6-2-75	Colorado	Strong defender has good power for a middle infielder and is durable.
29	Shumpert, Terry	R/R	6-2/195	8-16-66	Colorado Springs, Colorado	If Lansing falters, Shumpert (.347 average, 10 homers) will step right in.
	Sosa, Juan	R/R	6-1/175	8-19-75	Carolina, Colo. Springs, Colo.	Perez's presence doesn't bode well for Sosa's future with the Rockies.

No.	OUTFIELDERS	B/T	Ht./Wt.	Born	1999 clubs	Projection
	Bragg, Darren	L/R	5-9/180	9-7-69	St. Louis	His skills are perfect for Coors Field—good speed in the outfield and an alley hitter.
11	Echevarria, Angel	R/R	6-3/226	5-25-71	Colorado	He impressed in his first real opportunity, hitting .293 with 11 homers in 191 ABs.
24	Gibson, Derrick	R/R	6-2/244	2-5-75	Colorado Springs, Colorado	Former highly regarded prospect has now spent seven seasons in the minors.
	Goodwin, Tom	L/L	6-1/175	7-27-68	Texas, Charlotte	He provides a much-needed leadoff hitter and basestealing threat.
	Hammonds, Jeffrey	R/R	6-0/195	3-5-71	Cincinnati	Replacing Dante Bichette will be tough, despite coming off a career year.
28	Latham, Chris	B/R	6-0/198	5-26-73	Minnesota, Salt Lake	Four straight years at Class AAA Salt Lake indicate he's probably reserve material.
19	Clemente, Edgard	R/R	5-11/188	12-15-75	Colorado Springs, Colorado	He struggles against righthanded pitchers but has a great arm, like uncle Roberto.
33	Walker, Larry	L/R	6-3/237	12-1-66	Colorado	This hitting machine shoots for his third consecutive N.L. batting title.

THE COACHING STAFF

Buddy Bell, manager: He will benefit from a three-year stint (1996 through 1998) as manager of the Tigers. Though Tiger Stadium was a hitter-friendly ballpark, Bell will have to deal with something above and beyond at Coors Field—big comebacks, frequent lead changes, high scores, bloated ERAs and scarred psyches. Plus, he will have to mesh holdovers and newcomers on one of the most made-over clubs in recent history. His ability to have a calming effect and show sternness at the same time should help immensely—as will his energy and enthusiasm. The fact Detroit made a 26-game turnaround in the standings from '96 to '97 demonstrated he could step right in and have impact.

Rich Donnelly: He was a mainstay under Jim Leyland, having served with the former Colorado manager through 11 seasons in Pittsburgh, two in Florida and one in Denver. He's the third base coach.

Toby Harrah: A 17-season major league player, Harrah will be Bell's bench coach. He also will make great use of his longtime experience as a third baseman and shortstop in his role as infield instructor.

Clint Hurdle: He is one of only two holdovers from Leyland's 1999 Rockies staff. Colorado's hitting coach, he has to preach patience to hitters who often go up hacking in a ballpark where offensive fireworks are the norm.

Fred Kendall: He's the new bullpen coach and catching instructor. A catcher for 12 seasons in the majors, he's the father of Pirates catcher Jason Kendall.

Marcel Lachemann: He is considered one of the game's top pitching coaches. A former manager of the Angels, he also spent 11 seasons as pitching coach for that club. He was the first pitching coach in Florida Marlins history. Lachemann has 32 years of professional baseball experience.

Dallas Williams: He will coach at first base and be an outfield and baserunning instructor. A longtime minor league outfielder who played only 20 games in the majors, he also should provide lessons in stick-to-itiveness.

THE TOP NEWCOMERS

Rolando Arrojo: He won 14 games for the first-year Devil Rays in 1998. He's adept at changing speeds and should bounce back from an off season. His stuff on the mound seem to be a fit for Coors Field, but that tag has been labeled before with little return.

Darren Bragg: The Rockies were pleased with this January signing and should find a lot of playing time for his lefthanded bat and good wheels in the outfield.

Jeff Cirillo: A steady, line-drive hitter who uses all fields, he should hit 25 homers and drive in 100 runs (both would be career highs) and erase any misgivings about Vinny Castilla's departure. He's also a fiery ballplayer who could inspire the younger players.

Tom Goodwin: He's the bona fide center fielder Colorado has never had. Stole 39 bases for Texas last season and has a career high of 66. Has great range in the outfield and will take away a lot of hits in the massive outfield space.

Scott Karl: He has won 44 games in the past four seasons for a Milwaukee team that wasn't exactly a juggernaut.

Masato Yoshii: Another part of the Rockies' plan to fit the pitching staff to Coors Field. Thus, Bobby M. Jones and Lariel Gonzalez high Coors Field numbers were traded for his deceptional off-speed pitches and lateral-moving fastball.

THE TOP PROSPECTS

David Lee: He showed he could pitch at the major league level and might make a major bullpen contribution in 2000.

Ben Petrick: With additional work on his receiving and throwing, Petrick should be ready. He hit 19 homers in 84 games in Class AAA.

FLORIDA MARLINS

NATIONAL LEAGUE EAST DIVISION

2000 SEASON

2000 Marlins Schedule
Home games shaded. *—All-Star Game at Turner Field (Atlanta).

March
SUN	MON	TUE	WED	THU	FRI	SAT
26	27	28	29	30	31	

April
SUN	MON	TUE	WED	THU	FRI	SAT
						1
2	3 SF	4 SF	5 SF	6 SF	7 COL	8 COL
9 COL	10 MIL	11	12 MIL	13 MIL	14 CUB	15 CUB
16 CUB	17 CUB	18 PIT	19 PIT	20 PIT	21 PHI	22 PHI
23 PHI	24 PHI	25 SF	26 SF	27	28 LA	29 LA
30 LA						

May
SUN	MON	TUE	WED	THU	FRI	SAT
	1 SD	2 SD	3 SD	4	5 NYM	6 NYM
7 NYM	8 ATL	9 ATL	10 ATL	11 ATL	12 NYM	13 NYM
14 NYM	15	16 SD	17 SD	18 SD	19 LA	20 LA
21 LA	22	23 STL	24 STL	25 STL	26 CIN	27 CIN
28 CIN	29 PIT	30 PIT	31 PIT			

June
SUN	MON	TUE	WED	THU	FRI	SAT
				1	2 TOR	3 TOR
4 TOR	5 BOS	6 BOS	7 BOS	8	9 TB	10 TB
11 TB	12 PHI	13 PHI	14 PHI	15	16 PIT	17 PIT
18 PIT	19 MIL	20 MIL	21 MIL	22 MIL	23 CUB	24 CUB
25 CUB	26 NYM	27 NYM	28 NYM	29	30 MON	

July
SUN	MON	TUE	WED	THU	FRI	SAT
						1 MON
2 MON	3 NYM	4 NYM	5 NYM	6	7 TB	8 TB
9 TB	10	11	*12	13 NYY	14 NYY	15 NYY
16 BAL	17 BAL	18 BAL	19 ATL	20 ATL	21 MON	22 MON
23 MON	24	25 ATL	26 ATL	27 ATL	28 ARI	29 ARI
30 ARI	31 HOU					

August
SUN	MON	TUE	WED	THU	FRI	SAT
		1 HOU	2 HOU	3 HOU	4 CIN	5 CIN
6 CIN	7 STL	8 STL	9 STL	10	11 SD	12 SD
13 SD	14 LA	15 LA	16 LA	17	18 COL	19 COL
20 COL	21 SF	22 SF	23 SF	24	25 COL	26 COL
27 CIN	28 STL	29 STL	30 STL	31		

September
SUN	MON	TUE	WED	THU	FRI	SAT
					1 ARI	2 ARI
3 ARI	4 HOU	5 HOU	6 HOU	7 HOU	8 ARI	9 ARI
10 ARI	11	12 ATL	13 ATL	14 ATL	15 PHI	16 PHI
17 PHI	18 MON	19 MON	20 MON	21 MON	22 COL	23 COL
24 COL	25	26 MON	27 MON	28 MON	29 PHI	30 PHI

October
SUN	MON	TUE	WED	THU	FRI	SAT
1 PHI	2	3	4	5	6	7

FRONT-OFFICE DIRECTORY

Chairman ....John W. Henry
Vice chairman ....David Ginsberg
Executive vice president and general manager...................David Dombrowski
Executive vice president and chief financial officer ....Jonathan D. Mariner
Senior vice president of sales, communications and marketing ....Julio G. Rebull
Vice president, communications and broadcasting...............Ron Colangelo
Vice president, sales ....Lou DePaoli
Assistant general manager ....Dave Littlefield
Director of scouting, including Latin American operations...................Al Avila
Director of major league administration ....Dan Lunetta
Special assistants to the general manager ....Andre Dawson, Orrin Freeman
Tony Perez, Scott Reid
Director, field operations ....Rob Leary
Director of team travel ....Bill Beck
Video coordinator ....Cullen McRae
Manager, scouting information ....Cheryl Evans
Manager, minor league administration ....Kim-Lee Carkeek Luchs
Manager, player development ....Mike Parkinson
Manager, baseball information systems..David Kuan
Director, media relations ....Eric M. Carrington
Assistant director, media relations ....Julio C. Sarmiento
Coordinator, media relations ....Jonathan Jensen
Manager, broadcasting ....Sandra van Meek
Manager, community affairs ....Israel Negron
Director of creative servies and in-game entertainment ....Leslie Riguero
Manager, publications and creative services ....Renee Torguson
Director of marketing ....John Pierce
Marketing manager ....Liz Capra
Director, marketing partnerships ....Jim Frevola
Director, season and group sales ....Pat McNamara
Director, finance/controller ....Susan Jaison
Director, information technology ....Ken Strand
Director, administration ....Mike Whittle
Director, legal affairs..Lucinda Treat
Director, public affairs..Susan Budd
Vice president, ticket operations ....Bill Galante

MINOR LEAGUE AFFILIATES

Class	Team	League	Manager
AAA	Calgary	Pacific Coast	Lynn Jones
AA	Portland	Eastern	Rick Renteria
A	Brevard County	Florida State	Dave Huppert
A	Kane County	Midwest	Russ Morman
A	Utica	New York-Pennsylvania	Jon Deeble
Rookie	Gulf Coast Marlins	Gulf Coast	Kevin Boles

BALLPARK INFORMATION

Ballpark (capacity, surface)
Pro Player Stadium (42,530, grass)
Address
2267 N.W. 199th St., Miami, FL 33056
Business phone
305-626-7400
Ticket information
305-350-5050
Ticket prices
$28 (club level section A), $21 (infield box)
$20 (club level section B)
$15 (club level section C)
$12.50 (terrace box, mezzanine box)
$10 (club level-senior citizens)
$9 (outfield reserved, adult)
$7 (mezzanine reserved, adult)
$4 (outfield reserved, children 12 and under)
$2 (mezzanine)
Field dimensions (from home plate)
To left field at foul line, 330 feet
To center field, 434 feet
To right field at foul line, 345 feet
First game played
April 5, 1993 (Marlins 6, Dodgers 3)

SISTANCE STAFF

Team physician
Dr. Dan Kanell

Head athletic trainer
Larry Starr

Strength and conditioning director
Rick Slate

Equipment manager
Mike Wallace

Visiting clubhouse manager
Matt Rosenthal

National cross-checkers
David Chedd, Murray Cook, Mike Russell, Tim Schmidt, Bill Singer

Scouts
John Booker, Dick Egan, Manny Estrada, Kelvin Bowles, Lou Fitzgerald, Charlie Silvers, Ty Brown, John Castleberry, John Deeble, Brad Del Barba, Louis Eljaua, David Finley, Bob Laurie, Steve Minor, Steve Mondile, Jax Robertson, Cucho Rodriguez, Jimmy Rough, Dennis Sheehan, Keith Snider, Stan Zielinski

Director, Dominican Republic operations
Jesus Alou

Latin America scouts
Holbert Cabrera, Pedro Cintron, Miguel Angel Garcia, Pablo Lantigua, Cucho Rodriguez, Cesar Santiago, Hubert Silva, Ramon Webster

BROADCAST INFORMATION
Radio: WQAM (560 AM); WQBA-AM (1140 AM, Spanish language).
TV: WAMI-TV (Channel 69).
Cable TV: SportsChannel Florida.

SPRING TRAINING
Ballpark (city): Space Coast Stadium (Melbourne, Fla.).
Ticket information: 321-633-9200.

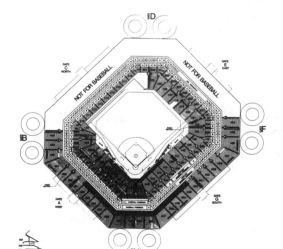

No.	PITCHERS	B/T	Ht./Wt.	Born	1999 clubs	Projection
57	Alfonseca, Antonio	R/R	6-5/235	4-16-72	Florida	Hard thrower filled in nicely as the closer after Mantei's departure last season.
56	Almanza, Armando	L/L	6-3/205	10-26-72	Calgary, Portland, Florida	He's the top lefthanded setup man in the bullpen, but has shoulder problems.
59	Almonte, Hector	R/R	6-2/190	10-17-75	Portland, Florida	Will continue to develop in low-pressure situations until he matures.
61	Beckett, Josh	R/R	6-4/190	5-15-80	DID NOT PLAY	Second pick overall in the 1999 draft. That's right, 1999. He's headed to the minors.
43	Burnett, A.J.	R/R	6-5/205	1-3-77	Portland, Florida	Pitched well enough in limited time in 1999 to earn the No. 4 spot in the rotation.
47	Camp, Jared	R/R	6-2/195	5-4-75	Kinston, Akron, Buffalo	This youngster is still trying to learn control.
38	Cornelius, Reid	R/R	6-0/200	6-2-70	Calgary, Florida	This journeyman pitched well enough for the Marlins in '99 to earn a roster spot.
40	Darensbourg, Vic	L/L	5-10/165	11-13-70	Florida, Calgary	The ultimate situational lefty. He pitched 34-plus innings in 56 appearances in '99.
46	Dempster, Ryan	R/R	6-1/201	5-3-77	Calgary, Florida	He's young but very talented. He has a potential for big strikeout numbers.
20	Edmondson, Brian	R/R	6-2/175	1-29-73	Florida	Fighting for a job as a setup man, but might end up in Class AAA.
32	Fernandez, Alex	R/R	6-1/225	8-13-69	Florida	The Marlins will slowly raise his pitch count limit in his starts—very good news.
54	Fontenot, Joe	R/R	6-2/185	3-20-77	Calgary	He's been out since May due to an arm injury and has something to prove.
53	Lara, Nelson	R/R	6-4/185	7-15-78	Kane County	Picked up 10 saves in Class A ball but had more walks than strikeouts.
41	Looper, Braden	R/R	6-5/225	10-28-74	Florida	Youngster with a great arm who'll see time only in low-pressure situations.
33	Miceli, Dan	R/R	6-0/216	9-9-70	San Diego	Acquired in the offseason to give the Marlins some experience in the bullpen.
36	Nunez, Vladimir	R/R	6-4/224	3-15-75	Tucson, Arizona, Florida	This young righthander appears to be locked into the starting rotation.
21	Sanchez, Jesus	L/L	5-10/155	10-11-74	Florida, Calgary	Despite good stuff, he struggled in 1999 and will work out problems in Class AAA.
58	Tejera, Michael	L/L	5-9/175	10-18-76	Portland, Calgary, Florida	This Cuban defector is a prospect as a starting pitcher, displaying a nasty curve.

No.	CATCHERS	B/T	Ht./Wt.	Born	1999 clubs	Projection
6	Castro, Ramon	R/R	6-3/225	3-1-76	Calgary, Florida	The first Puerto Rican ever drafted in the first round will start for the Marlins.
52	Redmond, Mike	R/R	6-1/185	5-5-71	Florida	He's hit better than .300 his first two years and is loved by the pitching staff.

No.	INFIELDERS	B/T	Ht./Wt.	Born	1999 clubs	Projection
10	Berg, David	R/R	5-11/185	9-3-70	Florida	He's a solid backup at second base, shortstop and third base.
1	Castillo, Luis	B/R	5-11/175	9-12-75	Florida	Quietly one of the league's top leadoff hitters and will be for years to come.
45	Garcia, Amaury	R/R	5-10/160	5-20-75	Calgary, Florida	The second baseman has a good bat and runs well, but gets caught stealing too much.
11	Gonzalez, Alex	R/R	6-0/170	2-15-77	Florida	The Marlins' only All-Star is prone to slumps with the bat, but his glove is sound.
25	Lee, Derrek	R/R	6-5/225	9-6-75	Florida, Calgary	He gets his third chance to keep the starting job at first base.
19	Lowell, Mike	R/R	6-4/205	2-24-74	Calgary, Florida	His time was limited in '99 due to cancer but he'll start at third base and hit for power.
15	Millar, Kevin	R/R	6-0/185	9-24-71	Calgary, Florida	A true utilityman with the ability to start, but not place to.
3	Ozuna, Pablo	R/R	6-0/160	8-25-78	Portland	He's an incredible hitter but Gonzalez's glove keeps him from shortstop.
26	Rolison, Nate	L/R	6-5/240	3-27-77	Portland	Drafted in 1995 to hit for power and play first, but has developed slowly.

No.	OUTFIELDERS	B/T	Ht./Wt.	Born	1999 clubs	Projection
23	Bautista, Danny	R/R	5-11/170	5-24-72	Calgary, Florida	Longtime backup provides rare power off the bench.
37	Brown, Brant	L/L	6-3/220	6-22-71	Pittsburgh	Just waiting to gain back a starting spot after a mediocre year in Pittsburgh.
30	Floyd, Cliff	L/R	6-4/240	12-5-72	Florida, Calgary	He's the anchor of the lineup, but is coming off an injury-plagued 1999 season.
7	Kotsay, Mark	L/L	6-0/190	12-2-75	Florida	He's got Gold Glove-caliber defense in right field, but his bat needs improvement.
14	Ramirez, Julio	R/R	5-11/170	8-10-77	Portland, Florida	He's their top prospect and may be promoted soon. Needs more plate discipline.
44	Wilson, Preston	R/R	6-2/193	7-19-74	Florida	The runner-up for the Rookie of the Year has upscale potential but needs maturity.

THE COACHING STAFF

John Boles, manager: Boles has familiarity with the Marlins' system as he has spent time as the team's player development director prior to be rehired to manage the club last season. That experience makes him the best man to head this organization-provided squad. Through trades and drafts, the Marlins will have to provide a steady flow of raw talent from within and build for the future. He filled his staff with a group of Florida minor league instructors and managers—the coaches who have nursed the organization's prospects through their formative professional years. Look for Boles to be patient and understanding, qualities that will be needed if the Marlins hope to regain championship status.

Joe Breeden: He has spent seven years in the Marlins' system, five as the organization's roving catching instructor and two as the big-league bullpen coach. Breeden also will bring three years of managerial experience in the Royals' system to his new job as bench coach.

Rich Dubee: He's the only holdover from Jim Leyland's 1998 staff and a six-year member of the Marlins' organization. Dubee returns for a third season as pitching coach after three years as the organization's pitching coordinator. He's got quite a young staff to work with and needs to be them up emotionally.

Fredi Gonzalez: Third base duties will fall into the capable hands of Gonzalez, an eight-year minor league manager and seven-year member of the Marlins' organization.

Rusty Kuntz: He returns for his second year as the Marlins' first base coach, a position he held from 1989-92 with the Mariners and in 1995 and '96 with the Marlins. Kuntz also has serves as the organization's baserunning and outfield instructor.

Jack Maloof: This former minor league manager and hitting instructor will spend his eighth Marlins season as their big-league hitting coach.

Tony Taylor: A former minor league manager and big-league coach for the Phillies, his former major league team. Taylor, a six-year minor league instructor for the Marlins, will coach infielders.

THE TOP NEWCOMERS

Brant Brown: The Pirates expected a lot of him last season. But he hit .232 and eventually found himself on the bench often. Now he's not in the limelight with pressure to a big-time star as some have expected. He also is without a starting spot. But look for him to still get at least 350 at-bats.

Dan Miceli: Florida's bullpen was very young and inexperienced last season and it became a big frustration for the organization's fans and coaching staff. Miceli will certainly help that. Not only does he have tough pitches to deal with, he's got a "bulldog" attitude which should rub off to the passive Marlins pitching staff.

Vladimir Nunez: The hard-throwing Cuban defector came over in December as the player to be named later in the Matt Mantei trade. He just had no place on the talented Arizona pitching staff, but there's plenty of room for him in Florida. In fact, Florida intends for him to be the No. 3 or No. 4 starter.

THE TOP PROSPECTS

Brad Penny: He wowed the Arizona Fall League with his high-90s fastball and might have a shot at the starting rotation. For now, he'll start in Class AA and continue working on his control.

Pablo Ozuna: Well, his average slipped to .281 in 1999 after two seasons over .300 in the minor leagues. His bat is sound though he could fill out a bit. However, Gonzalez's superior defense, at least at this point, will keep him from the bigs this year.

Julio Ramirez: He has the best tools in the system and is Florida's center fielder of the future. He can steal bases, plays well on defense and is believed to be the second coming of Cesar Cedeno. His only flaw is he doesn't make good contact. He'll continue to work on that this season with a possibility for a late promotion.

HOUSTON ASTROS

NATIONAL LEAGUE CENTRAL DIVISION

2000 SEASON

2000 Astros Schedule

Home games shaded. *—All-Star Game at Turner Field (Atlanta).

March

SUN	MON	TUE	WED	THU	FRI	SAT
26	27	28	29	30	31	

April

SUN	MON	TUE	WED	THU	FRI	SAT
						1
2	3 PIT	4	5 PIT	6 PIT	7 PHI	8 PHI
9 PHI	10 STL	11 STL	12 STL	13	14 SD	15 SD
16 SD	17 LA	18 LA	19 LA	20	21 SD	22 SD
23 SD	24	25 CUB	26 CUB	27 CUB	28 MIL	29 MIL
30 MIL						

May

SUN	MON	TUE	WED	THU	FRI	SAT
	1 MIL	2 CUB	3 CUB	4 CUB	5 LA	6 LA
7 LA	8 COL	9 COL	10 COL	11	12 CIN	13 CIN
14 CIN	15 CIN	16 MIL	17 MIL	18 MIL	19 MON	20 MON
21 MON	22	23 PHI	24 PHI	25 PHI	26 ATL	27 ATL
28 ATL	29 COL	30 COL	31 COL			

June

SUN	MON	TUE	WED	THU	FRI	SAT
				1	2 CWS	3 CWS
4 CWS	5 MIN	6 MIN	7 MIN	8	9 SD	10 SD
11 SD	12	13 COL	14 COL	15 COL	16 SF	17 SF
18 SF	19	20 LA	21 LA	22 LA	23 SF	24 SF
25 SF	26 ARIZ	27 ARIZ	28 ARIZ	29 ARIZ	30 STL	

July

SUN	MON	TUE	WED	THU	FRI	SAT
						1 STL
2 STL	3	4 ARIZ	5 ARIZ	6 ARIZ	7 KC	8 KC
9 KC	10	11 *	12	13 DET	14 DET	15 DET
16 CLE	17 CLE	18 CLE	19 CIN	20 CIN	21 STL	22 STL
23 STL	24 CIN	25 CIN	26 CIN	27	28 ATL	29 ATL
30 ATL	31 FLA					

August

SUN	MON	TUE	WED	THU	FRI	SAT
		1 FLA	2 FLA	3 FLA	4 MON	5 MON
6 MON	7 NYM	8 NYM	9 NYM	10 NYM	11 PHI	12 PHI
13 PHI	14 PIT	15 PIT	16 PIT	17	18 MIL	19 MIL
20 MIL	21 CUB	22 CUB	23 CUB	24	25 MON	26 MON
27 MON	28 NYM	29 NYM	30 NYM	31		

September

SUN	MON	TUE	WED	THU	FRI	SAT
					1 ATL	2 ATL
3 ATL	4 FLA	5 FLA	6 FLA	7 FLA	8 CUB	9 CUB
10 CUB	11 SF	12 SF	13 SF	14 PIT	15 PIT	16 PIT
17 PIT	18	19 STL	20 STL	21 STL	22 CIN	23 CIN
24 CIN	25	26 PIT	27 PIT	28 PIT	29 MIL	30 MIL

October

SUN	MON	TUE	WED	THU	FRI	SAT
1 MIL	2	3	4	5	6	7

FRONT-OFFICE DIRECTORY

Chairman and chief executive officer ....Drayton McLane Jr.
President...Tal Smith
Senior vice president, business operations ....Bob McClaren
Senior vice president, sales and marketing ....Pam Gardner
General manager ....Gerry Hunsicker
Assistant general manager...Tim Purpura
Special assistant to the G.M. for international scouting ....Andros Reiner
Director of scouting ....David Lakey
Director of baseball administration ....Barry Waters
Vice president, finance ....Robert McBurnett
Vice president, sales and broadcasting...Jamie Hildreth
Vice president, ticket sales and services ....John Sorrentino
Vice president, community development ....Marian Harper
Vice president, market development..Rosi Hernandez
Vice president, communications ....Rob Matwick
Director of media relations ....Warren Miller
Assistant director of media relations ....Alyson Footer
Communications manager ....Todd Fedewa

MINOR LEAGUE AFFILIATES

Class	Team	League	Manager
AAA	New Orleans	Pacific Coast	Tony Pena
AA	Round Rock	Texas	Jackie Moore
A	Kissimmee	Florida State	Manny Acta
A	Michigan	Midwest	Al Pedrique
A	Auburn	New York-Pennsylvania	To be announced
Rookie	Martinsville	Appalachian	Brad Wellman

BROADCAST INFORMATION

Radio: KTRH-AM (740); KXYZ-AM (1320, Spanish language).
TV: KNWS-TV (Channel 51).
Cable TV: Fox Sports Southwest.

SPRING TRAINING

Ballpark (city): Osceola County Stadium (Kissimmee, Fla.).
Ticket information: 407-839-3900.

ASSISTANCE STAFF

Professional scouts
Leo Labossiere, Kimball Crossley, Joe Pittman, Tom Romenesko, Scipio Spinks,

Major league scouts
Stan Benjamin, Walt Matthews, Tom Mooney, Fred Nelson, Bob Skinner, Paul Weaver, Tom Wiedenbauer

Full-time scouts

Bob Blair	Joe Bogar
Ralph Bratton	Chuck Carlson
Gerry Craft	Doug Deutsch
James Farrar	David Henderson
Dan Huston	Marc Johnson
Brian Keegan	Bill Kelso
Bob King	Mike Maggart
Jerry Marik	Tom McCormack
Mel Nelson	Joe Robinson
Tad Slowik	Frankie Thon
Tim Tolman	Danny Watkins
Gene Wellman	

Foreign scouts

Ricardo Aponte	Jesus Aristimuno
Sergio A. Beltre	Rafael Cariel
Alexis Corro	Arnold Elles
Mario Gonzalez	Julio Linares
Rodney Linares	Omar Lopez
Carlos Maldonado	Ramon Morales
Oscar Padron	Guillermo Ramirez
Rafael Ramirez	Wolfgang Ramos
Anibal Reluz	Adriano Rodriguez
Dr. Lester Storey	Pablo Torrealba
Calixto Vargas	Mark Van Zanten

BALLPARK INFORMATION

Ballpark (capacity, surface)
Enron Field (42,000, grass)

Address
P.O. Box 288
Houston, TX 77001-0288

Business phone
713-799-9500

Ticket information
713-799-9567 or 800-ASTROS-2

Ticket prices
$29 (dugout)
$28 (club)
$25 (field level)
$24 (club)
$17 (Crawford box)
$15 (bullpen box)
$12 (mezzanine, terrace deck)
$10 (upper deck)
$5-$1 (outfield deck)

Field dimensions (from home plate)
To left field at foul line, 315 feet
To center field, 435 feet
To right field at foul line, 326 feet

First game played
Scheduled for April 7, 2000 vs. Phillies

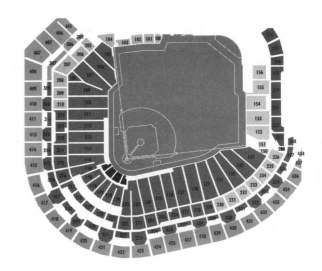

No.	PITCHERS	B/T	Ht./Wt.	Born	1999 clubs	Projection
51	Cabrera, Jose	R/R	6-0/180	3-24-72	New Orleans, Houston	If he can stay healthy, he'll be a plus in the bullpen.
29	Dotel, Octavio	R/R	6-0/175	11-25-75	Norfolk, New York N.L.	Acquired from the Mets, he should be the No. 4 starter.
50	Elarton, Scott	R/R	6-7/240	2-23-76	Houston	He is expected to be in the rotation, despite coming off shoulder surgery.
60	Franklin, Wayne	L/L	6-2/195	3-9-74	Kissimmee, Jackson	After 20 saves at Class AA, he will begin season at New Orleans.
54	Green, Jason	R/R	6-1/205	6-5-75	Jackson	Hard-throwing righthander has future as middle reliever.
19	Henry, Doug	R/R	6-4/205	12-10-63	Houston, New Orleans, Jackson	If healthy, he should be an effective setup man.
44	Holt, Chris	R/R	6-4/205	9-18-71	Houston	His 5-13 record was misleading; he had the second-worst run support in the N.L.
55	Ireland, Eric	R/R	6-1/170	3-11-77	Kissimmee, Jackson	He could be in Houston's rotation by 2001.
42	Lima, Jose	R/R	6-2/205	9-30-72	Houston	He is expected to fill the void left by Mike Hampton's departure.
59	McKnight, Tony	R/R	6-5/205	6-29-77	Jackson	He has overcome elbow and shoulder problems and should start at New Orleans.
46	Miller, Trever	R/L	6-4/195	5-29-73	Houston	He is tough on lefthanders but needs to show improvement to stay in the bullpen.
52	Miller, Wade	R/R	6-2/185	9-13-76	New Orleans, Houston	With a strong spring, he could make the team as a long reliever.
44	Powell, Brian	R/R	6-2/205	10-10-73	New Orleans	Reliever will have to prove himself at Class AAA before getting promoted.
39	Powell, Jay	R/R	6-4/225	1-9-72	Houston	To be more effective, he needs to get better control of his sinkerball.
37	Reynolds, Shane	R/R	6-3/210	3-26-68	Houston	He is the workhorse of the rotation and can improve upon his 16 wins from '99.
56	Robertson, Jeromie	L/L	6-1/190	3-30-77	Jackson	He made big strides as a starter last season and should start at New Orleans.
66	Rodriguez, Wilfredo	L/L	6-3/180	3-20-79	Kissimmee	He's on track to be in the Astros' rotation in 2002.
13	Wagner, Billy	L/L	5-11/180	7-25-71	Houston	After developing a slider last season, he has become a dominant closer in the N.L.

No.	CATCHERS	B/T	Ht./Wt.	Born	1999 clubs	Projection
6	Bako, Paul	L/R	6-2/205	6-20-72	New Orleans, Houston	The team likely won't carry three catchers, so he could be left out.
20	Eusebio, Tony	R/R	6-2/210	4-27-67	Houston	He'll see a reduction in playing time with the addition of Meluskey.
21	Meluskey, Mitch	B/R	6-0/185	9-18-73	Houston	Switch-hitter is back after shoulder surgery and should be solid offensively.

No.	INFIELDERS	B/T	Ht./Wt.	Born	1999 clubs	Projection
5	Bagwell, Jeff	R/R	6-0/195	5-27-68	Houston	He is almost guaranteed to hit at least 30 homers and drive in 100 runs.
7	Biggio, Craig	R/R	5-11/180	12-14-65	Houston	He is among the best in baseball at getting on base and scoring runs.
27	Bogar, Tim	R/R	6-2/198	10-28-66	Houston	With Ricky Gutierrez gone, he'll see a lot more playing time.
11	Caminiti, Ken	B/R	6-0/200	4-21-63	Houston, New Orleans	When healthy, he's still a productive hitter in the middle of the lineup.
	Everett, Adam	R/R	6-0/156	2-2-77	Trenton	Shortstop of the future could be in the majors this season.
4	Hernandez, Carlos	R/R	5-9/175	12-12-75	New Orleans, Houston	Backup at second base won't see much action if he doesn't hit better.
9	Johnson, Russ	R/R	5-10/180	2-22-73	New Orleans, Houston	He can play second, shortstop and third but isn't an everyday player.
68	Lugo, Julio	R/R	6-1/165	11-16-75	Jackson	He will compete with Everett for the shortstop job in 2001.
62	McNeal, Aaron	R/R	6-3/230	4-28-78	Michigan	Power-hitting first baseman will be at Class AA this season.
28	Spiers, Bill	L/R	6-2/190	6-5-66	Houston	His versatility and good bat make him the team's most valuable bench player.
64	Truby, Chris	R/R	6-2/190	12-9-73	Jackson	Third baseman with blossoming power will start in New Orleans.
31	Ward, Daryle	L/L	6-2/230	6-27-75	New Orleans, Houston	The big lefthandeder is the team's fourth outfielder and should get plenty of ABs.

No.	OUTFIELDERS	B/T	Ht./Wt.	Born	1999 clubs	Projection
18	Alou, Moises	R/R	6-3/195	7-3-66	DID NOT PLAY	He's the starter again in left field and will continue his All-Star production.
29	Barker, Glen	R/R	5-10/180	5-10-71	Houston	Speedy reserve won't get much playing time in crowded outfield.
22	Berkman, Lance	B/L	6-1/205	2-10-76	New Orleans, Houston	He'll likely start the season at New Orelans so he can get more playing time.
19	Cedeno, Roger	B/R	6-1/205	8-16-74	New York N.L.	Speedy switch-hitter will play center field and hit in the No. 2 spot.
15	Hidalgo, Richard	R/R	6-3/190	7-2-75	Houston	Back after knee surgery, he has a nice package of power and defense.
23	Mieske, Matt	R/R	6-0/194	2-13-68	Seattle, Houston	Reserve outfielder crushes lefthanded pitching but struggles against righties.

THE COACHING STAFF

Larry Dierker, manager: When Dierker stepped out of the broadcast booth and into the fire amid snickers and disbelief after the 1996 season, he brought relief and a welcome attitude change to an Astros clubhouse that had been intimidated by predecessor Terry Collins' in-your-face style. Three consecutive division titles and 283 victories later, the snickers have turned to praise and Dierker is being hailed as one of the top managers in the game. Dierker isn't the most conventional manager—he leaves his starting pitchers in the game longer than most managers and he likes to play the hunch. Dierker's next goal is to get Houston past the first round of the playoffs, something he was unable to accomplish the last three years.

Jose Cruz: One of the most popular and successful players to wear a Houston uniform, Cruz returns for a fourth season in the role of first base coach. He still holds Astros records in numerous career offensive categories.

Mike Cubbage: He will continue to direct traffic at third base after spending six seasons with the Mets in the same capacity. Cubbage is a 26-year veteran of baseball.

Matt Galante: Galante managed the Astros for part of last season while Larry Dierker recovered from brain surgery. This will be his third season as a bench coach after spending 1997 as a special assistant to general manager Gerry Hunsicker.

Tom McCraw: A veteran of 25 years as a coach and instructor, McCraw works with the Astros hitters. Like Cubbage, McCraw came over from New York where he worked five years as the Mets hitting coach, with much success.

Vern Ruhle: He's a veteran of the college coaching ranks and pitched for the Astros from 1978-84. This is Ruhle's fourth season as the pitching coach.

John Tamargo: Tamargo is in his second season as bullpen coach. He has 13 years of managing experience in the Mets and Astros systems.

THE TOP NEWCOMERS

Roger Cedeno: Cedeno came over from the Mets in the trade for Mike Hampton. Cedeno will start in center field and should be the team's top base-stealing threat. He'll get plenty of run-scoring opportunities in the stacked Houston lineup and has something to prove: his great 1999 season was not fluke.

Octavio Dotel: Dotel also came over from the Mets in the Hampton deal. This will be his first full season as a starter. He has a good fastball but needs to develop better control.

THE TOP PROSPECTS

Lance Berkman: Berkman has made a successful switch from first base to the outfield. He makes good contact and has lots of power. He will start at Class AAA New Orleans but could be one of the first players called up.

Mitch Meluskey: Meluskey missed most of last season because of shoulder surgery but is expected to split the catching duties with Tony Eusebio. Meluskey needs to improve defensively, but he should be a plus on offense. He makes contact and has good power to the gaps.

Wade Miller: If Miller doesn't make the team as a long reliever out of spring training, he's a candidate to be the first pitcher called up if there's an injury. He has good control of four pitches and will eventually be a part of the starting rotation.

LOS ANGELES DODGERS

NATIONAL LEAGUE WEST DIVISION

2000 SEASON

2000 Dodgers Schedule

Home games shaded. *—All-Star Game at Turner Field (Atlanta).

March

SUN	MON	TUE	WED	THU	FRI	SAT
26	27	28	29	30	31	

April

SUN	MON	TUE	WED	THU	FRI	SAT
						1
2	3 MON	4 MON	5 MON	6 MON	7 NYM	8 NYM
9 NYM	10	11 SF	12 SF	13 SF	14 CIN	15 CIN
16 CIN	17 HOU	18 HOU	19 HOU	20	21 CIN	22 CIN
23 CIN	24	25 ATL	26 ATL	27 ATL	28 FLA	29 FLA
30 FLA						

May

SUN	MON	TUE	WED	THU	FRI	SAT
	1 ATL	2 ATL	3 ATL	4	5 HOU	6 HOU
7 HOU	8 ARI	9 ARI	10 ARI	11	12 STL	13 STL
14 STL	15	16 CUB	17 CUB	18 CUB	19 FLA	20 FLA
21 FLA	22 CIN	23 CIN	24 CIN	25	26 PHI	27 PHI
28 PHI	29 NYM	30 NYM	31 NYM			

June

SUN	MON	TUE	WED	THU	FRI	SAT
				1	2 ANA	3 ANA
4 ANA	5 TEX	6 TEX	7 TEX	8	9 OAK	10 OAK
11 OAK	12 ARI	13 ARI	14 ARI	15 ARI	16 STL	17 STL
18 STL	19	20 HOU	21 HOU	22 HOU	23 STL	24 STL
25 STL	26 SD	27 SD	28 SD	29 SD	30 SF	

July

SUN	MON	TUE	WED	THU	FRI	SAT
						1 SF
2 SF	3	4 SD	5 SD	6 SD	7 SEA	8 SEA
9 SEA	10	11	* 12	13 ANA	14 ANA	15 ANA
16 PIT	17 PIT	18 PIT	19 COL	20 COL	21 SF	22 SF
23 SF	24 COL	25 COL	26 COL	27 COL	28 PHI	29 PHI
30 PHI	31 PIT					

August

SUN	MON	TUE	WED	THU	FRI	SAT
		1 PIT	2 PIT	3	4 MIL	5 MIL
6 MIL	7 CUB	8 CUB	9 CUB	10	11 ATL	12 ATL
13 ATL	14 FLA	15 FLA	16 FLA	17	18 NYM	19 NYM
20 NYM	21 MON	22 MON	23 MON	24 MON	25 CUB	26 CUB
27 CUB	28 MIL	29 MIL	30 MIL	31 MIL		

September

SUN	MON	TUE	WED	THU	FRI	SAT
					1 PHI	2 PHI
3 PHI	4 PIT	5 PIT	6 PIT	7	8 COL	9 COL
10 COL	11 ARI	12 ARI	13 ARI	14 COL	15 COL	16 COL
17 COL	18 ARI	19 ARI	20 ARI	21	22 SD	23 SD
24 SD	25	26 SF	27 SF	28 SF	29 SD	30 SD

October

SUN	MON	TUE	WED	THU	FRI	SAT
1 SD	2	3	4	5	6	7

FRONT-OFFICE DIRECTORY

President and CEO ....Bob Graziano
Board of directors ....Chase Carey, Peter Chernin, Peter O'Malley,
Bob Graziano, Sam Fernandez
Executive vice president and general manager ....Kevin Malone
Executive vice president and CMO ....Kris Rone
Senior vice president, communications..Derrick Hall
Senior vice president ....Tommy Lasorda
Vice president, communications ....Tommy Hawkins
Traveling secretary ....Bill DeLury
Assistant secretary and general counsel..................................Santiago Fernandez
Managing director, Dodgertown ....Craig Callan
Assistant general manager ....Bill Geivett
Director of player development ....Jerry Weinstein
Director of finance and CFO ....Christine Hurley
Director of management information services ....Mike Mularky
Director of ticket marketing ....Bob Wymbs
Director of media relations ....To be announced
Assistant director of media relations..Shaun Rachau
Director of broadcasting and new media....................................Brent Shyer
Director of community relations ....Don Newcombe
Director of public affairs ....Monique Brandon
Director of stadium operations ....Doug Duennes
Director of ticket operations ....Billy Hunter
Director of human resources and administration ....Gina Galasso
Special assistants to the general manager, scouting.........................Ed Creech

MINOR LEAGUE AFFILIATES

Class	Team	League	Manager
AAA	Albuquerque	Pacific Coast	Tom Gamboa
AA	San Antonio	Texas	Rick Burleson
A	San Bernardino	California	Dino Ebel
A	Vero Beach	Florida State	John Shoemaker
A	Yakima	Northwest	Butch Hughes
Rookie	Great Falls	Pioneer	Juan Bustabad

BROADCAST INFORMATION

Radio: XTRA (1150); KWKW-AM (1330, Spanish language).
TV: KTLA-TV (Channel 5); Fox Sports.
Cable TV: Fox Sports Net 2.

SPRING TRAINING

Ballpark (city): Holman Stadium (Vero Beach, Fla.).
Ticket information: 561-569-6858.

ASSISTANCE STAFF

Head trainer
Stan Johnston

Assistant trainer
Matt Wilson

Physical therapist
Pat Screnar

Strength and conditioning
Todd Clausen

Club physicians
Dr. Herndon Harding   Dr. Frank Jobe
Dr. Michael F. Mellman

Special assistant to general manager
Jeff Schugel

Assistant director of scouting
Matt Slater

Senior scouting advisor
Don Welke

Pro scouts
Phil Favia, Dan Freed, Carl Loewenstine, Marty Maier, Terry Reynolds, Ron Rizzi, Mark Weidemaier

Full-time scouts
John Barr, Gib Bodet, Mike Brito, Ray Brown, Doug Carpenter, Jim Chapman, Bob Darwin, Joe Ferrone, Scott Groot, Mike Hankins, Hanke Jones, Lon Joyce, John Kosciak, Marty Lamb, Jimmy Lester, Mike Leuzinger, Bump Merriweather, Camilo Pascual, Bill Pleis, Willie Powell, Scott Sharp, Mark Sheehy, Chris Smith, Bob Szymkowski, Tom Thomas, Mitch Webster

BALLPARK INFORMATION

Ballpark (capacity, surface)
Dodger Stadium (56,000, grass)
Address
1000 Elysian Park Ave.
Los Angeles, CA 90012
Business phone
323-224-1500
Ticket information
323-224-1448
Ticket prices
$17 (field box)
$15 (inner reserve)
$13 (loge box)
$10 (outer reserve)
$6 (top deck, left & right pavilion)
Field dimensions (from home plate)
To left field at foul line, 330 feet
To center field, 395 feet
To right field at foul line, 330 feet
First game played
April 10, 1962 (Reds 6, Dodgers 3)

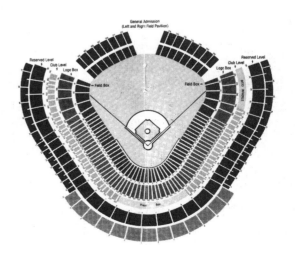

No.	PITCHERS	B/T	Ht./Wt.	Born	1999 clubs	Projection
	Adams, Terry	R/R	6-3/205	3-6-73	West Tenn, Chicago N.L.	Coming over from Chicago, he helps solidify a deep Dodgers bullpen.
52	Arnold, Jamie	R/R	6-2/188	3-24-74	Albuquerque, Los Angeles	Long reliever logged a 7.45 ERA after the All-Star break last season.
27	Brown, Kevin	R/R	6-4/200	3-14-65	Los Angeles	Still one of the league's top hurlers; would have won 20 games on most teams.
37	Dreifort, Darren	R/R	6-2/211	5-3-72	Los Angeles	A decent starter, he has resisted team's attempts to move him back to the 'pen.
46	Gagne, Eric	R/R	6-2/195	1-7-76	San Antonio, Los Angeles	Recovering nicely after surgery in 1997—12-4, 2.63 ERA in Class AA last season.
	Garcia, Apostol	R/R	6-0/155	8-3-76	Jacksonville, San Antonio	He's recovering from an injury and has not pitched above Class AA.
49	Herges, Matt	L/R	6-0/200	4-1-70	Albuquerque, Los Angeles	After seven seasons in the minors, reliever pitched well after August call-up.
	Hershiser, Orel	R/R	6-3/195	9-16-58	New York N.L.	The Bulldog is still a reliable No. 4 starter, capable of chewing up innings.
60	Judd, Mike	R/R	6-1/217	6-30-75	Albuquerque, Los Angeles	Hard thrower should get a shot to make the team, either as a starter or reliever.
65	Masaoka, Onan	R/L	6-0/180	10-27-77	Los Angeles	Lefty with a live fastball; started strong in '99, but tailed off in second half.
75	Mills, Alan	R/R	6-1/195	10-18-66	Los Angeles	Great four-seam fastball makes him one of the team's most consistent relievers.
	Naulty, Dan	R/R	6-6/224	1-6-70	New York A.L., Columbus	Reliever allowed a .225 opponents average last year; adds bullpen depth.
	Olson, Gregg	R/R	6-4/210	10-11-66	Arizona	Proved he wasn't a closer anymore last year but was a great situational reliever.
13	Osuna, Antonio	R/R	5-11/206	4-12-73	San Bernardino, Los Angeles	He is the team's future closer, but elbow surgery may keep him out all of 2000.
61	Park, Chan Ho	R/R	6-2/204	6-30-73	Los Angeles	Regained old form at season's end, going 7-1 after a 6-10 start.
33	Perez, Carlos	L/L	6-3/210	1-14-71	Los Angeles, Albuquerque	Mechanical problems sent him on a puzzling nosedive (2-10).
	Ricketts, Chad	R/R	6-5/225	2-12-75	West Tenn	Five-year minor leaguer came over in an offseason trade from the Cubs.
41	Shaw, Jeff	R/R	6-2/200	7-7-66	Los Angeles	With 34 saves, this late bloomer is still one of the league's best closers.
54	Williams, Jeff	R/L	6-0/185	6-6-72	Albuquerque, Los Angeles	Went 2-0 with a 4.04 ERA in three starts after a September call-up.

No.	CATCHERS	B/T	Ht./Wt.	Born	1999 clubs	Projection
9	Hundley, Todd	B/R	5-11/199	5-27-69	Los Angeles	Hasn't fully recovered from 1997 elbow surgery. Gave up switch hitting in 1999.
16	LoDuca, Paul	R/R	5-10/185	4-12-72	Los Angeles, Albuquerque	Good defense and hard work will keep him in the majors as a backup.
63	Pena, Angel	R/R	5-10/228	2-16-75	Albuquerque, Los Angeles	Quick feet, a good arm and a powerful bat make him the team's best backstop.

No.	INFIELDERS	B/T	Ht./Wt.	Born	1999 clubs	Projection
29	Beltre, Adrian	R/R	5-11/170	4-7-78	Los Angeles	After underage signing flap, should be ready to improve on last year's numbers.
66	Bocachica, Hiram	R/R	5-11/165	3-4-76	San Antonio	Has the speed, glove and a good enough bat to be a big-league shortstop.
17	Castro, Juan	R/R	5-10/187	6-20-72	Albuquerque, Los Angeles	Slap hitter plays well enough defense to earn a backup spot.
3	Cora, Alex	L/R	6-0/180	10-18-75	Albuquerque, Los Angeles	Joey Cora's brother is a better fielder, but not as good a hitter.
8	Grudzielanek, Mark	R/R	6-1/185	6-30-70	Los Angeles, San Bernardino	He's short on defense, but he's a free swinger who hit .326 last season.
25	Hansen, Dave	L/R	6-0/195	11-24-68	Los Angeles	Hit .252 in 100 games, but playing time will likely decline as Beltre takes over.
23	Karros, Eric	R/R	6-4/226	11-4-67	Los Angeles	Still gets overlooked, even after best offensive season of his career.
	Orie, Kevin	R/R	6-4/215	9-1-72	Florida, Calgary	Good defense, but has yet to fulfill offensive promise.
5	Vizcaino, Jose	B/R	6-1/180	3-26-68	Los Angeles	Not a flashy offensive or defensive player, but more reliable than Grudzielanek.

No.	OUTFIELDERS	B/T	Ht./Wt.	Born	1999 clubs	Projection
57	Gibbs, Kevin	B/R	6-2/185	4-3-74	Albuquerque	Shoulder surgery limited him to 21 at-bats last season.
15	Green, Shawn	L/L	6-4/200	11-10-72	Toronto	Finally gives the team a lefthanded power hitter for the middle of the lineup.
28	Hollandsworth, Todd	L/L	6-2/215	4-20-73	San Bernardino, Los Angeles	Abundant time on the D.L.the last three years has stunted his development.
47	Hubbard, Trenidad	R/R	5-9/185	5-11-66	Albuquerque, Los Angeles	Has made a career off of being a fifth outfielder and a reliable pinch hitter.
	Santangelo, F.P.	B/R	5-10/190	10-24-67	San Francisco	The ultimate utilityman. Plays every position, switch hits and is durable.
10	Sheffield, Gary	R/R	5-11/205	11-18-68	Los Angeles	His big bat is the key to the lineup—hit .301 with 34 home runs and 101 RBIs.
22	White, Devon	B/R	6-2/190	12-29-62	Los Angeles	Should be healthy again after offseason shoulder surgery.

THE COACHING STAFF

Davey Johnson, manager: Last season was the worst in Johnson's 13-year career. He has a history of winning, having taken the Mets, the Reds and the Orioles to the playoffs, but he also has a history of being difficult to get along with. Last year was beyond his control, though, as many of the team's problems were from malcontent players fighting among themselves. In fact, Johnson often seemed listless last season, as though the situation had deteriorated beyond his understanding. But many of the team's least congenial players—Raul Mondesi, Eric Young and Ismael Valdes—have been sent elsewhere. Johnson now has a talented and happy bunch to work with, and should improve dramatically over last season.

Rick Dempsey: This will be Dempsey's 34th year in professional baseball, and his second as the Dodgers' third base coach. He had previously spent four years as a Class AAA manager and may eventually be a major league managerial candidate.

Rick Down: Has been a major league hitting instructor for six years now, with a reputation for increasing team power. Joined the Dodgers before last season. Under Down, team went from 159 home runs to 187 and average went from .252 to .266.

Glenn Hoffman: Hoffman is a mild mannered coach with a thorough knowledge of the game. Went 47-41 in a brief stint as interim Dodger manager in 1998. This marks his third season as a coach with the Dodgers.

Manny Mota: He begins his 43rd season in baseball and 31st with the Dodgers, including 11 as a player. He will continue in his role as a floating coach for the Dodgers.

Claude Osteen: Osteen replaced Charlie Hough as the Dodger pitching coach on May 26 of last season after starting the season as the pitching coach at Class AAA Albuquerque. Has had stints as a pitching coach with the Phillies, Cardinals and Rangers.

John Shelby: Shelby is entering his third season as the Dodgers' first-base coach after spending five years as a manager in the minors. He was part of the Dodgers' 1988 World Championship team, and also part of the Orioles' 1983 champions.

Jim Tracy: Joined the Dodgers last year after working with Felipe Alou for four years as the Expos' bench coach. Spent seven years as a minor league manager, going 501-486 with affiliates for the Reds, Cubs and Expos.

THE TOP NEWCOMERS

Terry Adams: In a bullpen that is already stocked with good arms, Adams will be one of the team's top relievers. He is reliable, durable and keeps the ball low, inducing a lot of groundballs.

Shawn Green: Blossomed into one of the game's best power hitters with 77 home runs and 223 RBIs over the last two seasons. In the last 10 years, the Dodgers have seriously lacked the kind of lefthanded power that Green possesses.

Orel Hershiser: Provides not only a solid pitcher for the fourth or fifth spot in the rotation but the kind of clubhouse leadership the team has lacked ... since the last time he was with the Dodgers.

Dan Naulty: An underrated reliever who did not quite fit in with the Yankees, Naulty is a versatile thrower who can go short stints or can work in long relief.

Gregg Olson: He failed miserably as the closer of the Diamondbacks in the first half of last season. But he thrived in other roles in the bullpen. Will do the same for the Dodgers.

F.P. Santangelo: Don't undermine this guy's value to a club, especially the banged-up Dodgers. His versatility is necessary and his skills and ability to switch-hit should get him in the lineup often.

THE TOP PROSPECTS

Onan Masaoka: Masaoka made the Dodger roster out of spring training as a lefthanded setup man despite making just 21 relief appearances in four years in the minors. But he kept his spot in the majors all season and made 54 appearances, going 2-4, with a 4.32 ERA.

Angel Pena: Pena is expected to be the Dodgers' catcher of the future, and with Todd Hundley's struggles, he should be the catcher of the present. His problem is food. He is generously listed at 228, but Pena is closer to 250. He hit .208 in 120 at-bats for the Dodgers last year and must stay in shape to win a job.

MILWAUKEE BREWERS

NATIONAL LEAGUE CENTRAL DIVISION

2000 SEASON

2000 Brewers Schedule

Home games shaded. *—All-Star Game at Turner Field (Atlanta).

March

SUN	MON	TUE	WED	THU	FRI	SAT
26	27	28	29	30	31	

April

SUN	MON	TUE	WED	THU	FRI	SAT
						1
2	3 CIN	4	5 CIN	6 CIN	7 STL	8 STL
9 STL	10 FLA	11	12 FLA	13 FLA	14 ATL	15 ATL
16 ATL	17	18 NYM	19 NYM	20 NYM	21 MON	22 MON
23 MON	24	25 STL	26 STL	27 STL	28 HOU	29 HOU
30 HOU						

May

SUN	MON	TUE	WED	THU	FRI	SAT
	1 HOU	2 ARI	3 ARI	4 ARI	5 MON	6 MON
7 MON	8 CUB	9 CUB	10 CUB	11 CUB	12 PIT	13 PIT
14 PIT	15	16 HOU	17 HOU	18 HOU	19 SF	20 SF
21 SF	22	23 ATL	24 ATL	25 ATL	26 ARI	27 ARI
28 ARI	29 SD	30 SD	31 SD			

June

SUN	MON	TUE	WED	THU	FRI	SAT
				1	2 COL	3 COL
4 COL	5 CLE	6 CLE	7 CLE	8	9 MIN	10 MIN
11 MIN	12 MON	13 MON	14 MON	15	16 NYM	17 NYM
18 NYM	19 FLA	20 FLA	21 FLA	22 FLA	23 ATL	24 ATL
25 ATL	26	27 PHI	28 PHI	29 PHI	30 CUB	

July

SUN	MON	TUE	WED	THU	FRI	SAT
						1 CUB
2 CUB	3 PHI	4 PHI	5 PHI	6 PHI	7 DET	8 DET
9 DET	10	11	* 12	13 KC	14 KC	15 KC
16 CWS	17 CWS	18 CWS	19 PIT	20 PIT	21 CUB	22 CUB
23 CUB	24	25 PIT	26 PIT	27 PIT	28 COL	29 COL
30 COL	31 SF					

August

SUN	MON	TUE	WED	THU	FRI	SAT
		1 SF	2 SF	3	4 LA	5 LA
6 LA	7 SF	8 SF	9 SF	10	11 STL	12 STL
13 STL	14 CIN	15 CIN	16 CIN	17	18 HOU	19 HOU
20 HOU	21 ARI	22 ARI	23 ARI	24	25 SD	26 SD
27 SD	28 LA	29 LA	30 LA	31		

September

SUN	MON	TUE	WED	THU	FRI	SAT
					1 COL	2 COL
3 COL	4 SD	5 SD	6 SD	7	8 STL	9 STL
10 STL	11 NYM	12 NYM	13 NYM	14 CIN	15 CIN	16 CIN
17 CIN	18 CUB	19 CUB	20 CUB	21 PIT	22 PIT	23 PIT
24 PIT	25	26 CIN	27 CIN	28 CIN	29 HOU	30 HOU

October

SUN	MON	TUE	WED	THU	FRI	SAT
1 HOU	2	3	4	5	6	7

FRONT-OFFICE DIRECTORY

President and chief executive officer ....Wendy Selig-Prieb
Senior vice president and general manager ....Dean Taylor
Vice president and general counsel ....Tom Gausden
Assistant general counsel ....Eugene "Pepi" Randolph
Special assistant to the president ....Sal Bando
Vice president, new ballpark development ....Michael Bucek
Vice president, stadium operations ....Scott Jenkins
Vice president, corporate affairs ....Laurel Prieb
Vice president, finance ....Paul Baniel
Vice president, ticket sales ....Bob Voight
Vice president, player personnel ....David Wilder
Director, community relations ....Michael Downs
Director, event services ....Steve Ethier
Director, grounds ....Gary Vanden Berg
Director, media relations ....Jon Greenberg
Director, player development ....Greg Riddoch
Director, Brewers Gold Club & Baseball for Wisconsin ....Mike Harlan
Director, publications...Mario Ziino
Director, ticket operations ....John Barnes
Director, scouting ....Jack Zdurienick
Director, clubhouse operations ....Tony Migliaccio
Traveling secretary ....Dan Larrea

MINOR LEAGUE AFFILIATES

Class	Team	League	Manager
AAA	Louisville	International	Steve Smith
AA	Huntsville	Southern	Carlos Lezcano
A	Stockton	California	Barry Moss
A	Beloit	Midwest	Don Money
Rookie	Helena	Pioneer	Dan Norman
Rookie	Ogden	Pioneer	Ed Sedar

BROADCAST INFORMATION

Radio: WTMJ-AM (620).
TV: WCGV-TV (Channel 24).
Cable TV: Midwest Sports Channel.

SPRING TRAINING

Ballpark (city): Maryvale Baseball Park (Phoenix, Ariz.).
Ticket information: 602-245-5500.

ASSISTANCE STAFF

Trainers
John Adam   Roger Caplinger

Strength and conditioning coach
Phil Falco

Team physicians
Dr. Richard Franklin, Dr. Angelo Mattalino

Southwest supervisor/cross-checker
Ric Wilson

Midwest supervisor/cross-checker
Tom Allison

International supervisor/cross-checker
Epy Guerrero

East Coast supervisor/cross-checker
Bobby Heck

Professional scouts
Carl Blando   Alan Regier
Daranka Shaheed   Elanis Westbrooks

Major League scouts
Russ Bove   Ken Califano
Larry Haney   Al Monchak
Chuck Tanner   Dick Wiencek

Scouts
Larry Aaron, Fred Beane, Jeff Brookens, Kevin Christman, Steve Connelly, Felix Delgado, Mike Farrell, Dick Foster, Mike Gibbons, Manolo Hernandez, Elvio Jimenez, Brian Johnson, Tim Johnson, Harvey Kuenn Jr., John Logan, Demie Mainieri, Alex Morales, Douglas Reynolds, Corey Rodriguez, Bruce Seid, Jonathan Story, Tom Tanous, John Viney, Red Whitsett, Walter Youse

BALLPARK INFORMATION

Ballpark (capacity, surface)
County Stadium (53,192, grass)
Address
County Stadium
P.O. Box 3099
Milwaukee, WI 53201-3099
Business phone
414-933-4114
Ticket information
414-933-9000, 800-933-7890
Ticket prices
$28 (diamond box)
$20 (lower box)
$16 (lower grandstand)
$14 (upper box)
$8 (upper grandstand)
$7 (general admission)
$5 (bleachers)
Field dimensions (from home plate)
To left field at foul line, 315 feet
To center field, 402 feet
To right field at foul line, 315 feet
First game played
April 7, 1970 (Angels 12, Brewers 0)

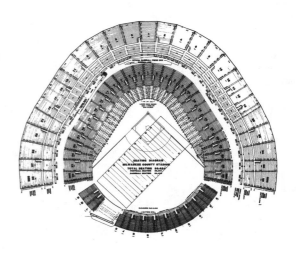

No.	PITCHERS	B/T	Ht./Wt.	Born	1999 clubs	Projection
53	Acevedo, Juan	R/R	6-2/220	5-5-70	St. Louis	He'll be used as a starter but has experience as a closer and middle reliever.
47	Bere, Jason	R/R	6-4/189	5-26-71	Cincinnati, Ind., Louisville, Milw.	His velocity is down, but he'll compete for a spot in the rotation.
32	Coppinger, Rocky	R/R	6-5/240	3-19-74	Baltimore, Milwaukee	Hard thrower might get a chance to start but is likely a setup man.
13	D'Amico, Jeff	R/R	6-7/250	12-27-75	Beloit, Hunts., Louisville, Milw.	He's missed two years with shoulder problems but could be the No. 4 starter.
28	De Los Santos, Valerio	L/L	6-2/180	10-6-75	Milwaukee	He was once considered a potential closer but will be used as a lefty specialist.
48	Estrada, Horacio	L/L	6-0/160	10-19-75	Louisville, Milwaukee	If he has a strong spring, he could make the club as a starter.
40	Fox, Chad	R/R	6-3/190	9-3-70	Milwaukee	He is coming off a second elbow surgery and will try to prove he's healthy.
51	Haynes, Jimmy	R/R	6-4/203	9-5-72	Oakland	He is expected to be the No. 5 starter.
39	Leskanic, Curtis	R/R	6-0/186	4-2-68	Colorado	This intense middle reliever's numbers should improve outside of Coors.
38	Navarro, Jaime	R/R	6-4/250	3-27-68	Chicago A.L.	Back to where his career was fairly productive.
26	Peterson, Kyle	R/R	6-3/215	4-9-76	Louisville, Milwaukee	If he works out control problems, he'll be an effective No. 4 starter.
46	Pulsipher, Bill	L/L	6-3/200	10-9-73	Milwaukee, Louisville	He has struggled with injuries and control and has something to prove as a starter.
52	Roque, Rafael	L/L	6-4/189	10-27-73	Milwaukee, Louisville	If he isn't the No. 5 starter, he'll be used a long reliever.
59	Snyder, John	R/R	6-3/200	8-16-74	Chicago A.L., Charlotte	Gives up too many homers and lost last six decisions. Will battle for rotation spot.
49	Weathers, Dave	R/R	6-3/230	9-25-69	Milwaukee	He could get a couple of spot starts but is primarily a long reliever.
27	Wickman, Bob	R/R	6-1/227	2-6-69	Milwaukee	Closer has a sharp slider and sinker that should produce 30 saves.
41	Williams, Matt	B/L	6-0/175	4-12-71	Norwich, Columbus	He was picked up in the Rule 5 draft from the Yankees and will be in the bullpen.
37	Woodard, Steve	L/R	6-4/217	5-15-75	Milwaukee	One of the teams' most dependable starters, he could win 12-15 games.
38	Wright, Jamey	R/R	6-5/221	12-24-74	Colorado, Colorado Springs	Improvements to mechanics could help him reach double-digits in wins.

No.	CATCHERS	B/T	Ht./Wt.	Born	1999 clubs	Projection
25	Banks, Brian	B/R	6-3/208	9-28-70	Milwaukee, Louisville	He can also play first and outfield and might make the club as utility player.
12	Blanco, Henry	R/R	5-11/190	8-29-71	Colorado Springs, Colorado	He is regarded as one of the better receivers in the N.L.
50	Cancel, Robinson	R/R	6-0/195	5-4-76	Huntsville, Louisville, Milw.	He's shown improvement but needs another season in the minors.
31	Hughes, Bobby	R/R	6-4/229	4-10-71	Milwaukee	He struggled last season but will compete for backup spot.
	Houston, Tyler	L/R	6-1/210	1-17-71	Chicago N.L., Cleveland	This lefty-hitting catcher has good offensive punch but not much defense.

No.	INFIELDERS	B/T	Ht./Wt.	Born	1999 clubs	Projection
22	Barker, Kevin	R/R	6-3/205	7-26-75	Louisville, Milwaukee	Solid-hitting rookie will see most of the time at first.
10	Belliard, Ron	R/R	5-8/180	7-4-76	Louisville, Milwaukee	He'll start at second, could hit .300 and should have more steals.
7	Berry, Sean	R/R	5-11/200	3-22-66	Milwaukee	He is no longer a regular, but could get starts at first base against lefties.
16	Collier, Lou	R/R	5-10/182	8-21-73	Milwaukee, Louisville	Speedy backup can play shortstop, third base, second base or the outfield.
18	Hernandez, Jose	R/R	6-1/180	7-14-69	Chicago N.L., Atlanta	New third baseman could hit 25 home runs but must cut down on strikeouts.
8	Loretta, Mark	R/R	6-0/190	8-14-71	Milwaukee	He'll get a chance to play everyday at shortstop because of his defense.
57	Perez, Santiago	B/R	6-2/150	12-30-75	Louisville	He'll start out at Louisville and await any injuries to starters.

No.	OUTFIELDERS	B/T	Ht./Wt.	Born	1999 clubs	Projection
20	Burnitz, Jeromy	L/R	6-0/205	4-15-69	Milwaukee	He'll start in right field, hit cleanup and could hit 40 homers for the first time.
61	Green, Chad	B/R	5-10/180	6-28-75	Huntsville	Center fielder of the future will play at Louisville this season.
9	Grissom, Marquis	R/R	5-11/188	4-17-67	Milwaukee	Center fielder provides good defense and still has very good speed.
5	Jenkins, Geoff	L/R	6-1/204	7-21-74	Milwaukee	He will be a 100-RBI guy some year very soon. Maybe this year.
33	Mouton, Lyle	R/R	6-4/230	5-13-69	Rochester, Louisville, Milw.	He has some power and will compete for a backup job.
33	Sweeney, Mark	L/L	6-1/195	10-26-69	Cincinnati, Indianapolis	Lefty pinch-hitting specialist can be a backup in the outfield or at first base.

THE COACHING STAFF

Davey Lopes, manager: Lopes got his first opportunity to manage in the majors when he was named the 12th manager in Brewers history on November 4, 1999. He has the tough task of leading a team with a low payroll to its first winning season since 1992. Lopes will try to instill the aggressiveness and energy level he displayed in 16 seasons as a player to a young team that has had lot of personnel changes. Lopes had spent the previous five seasons as the first base coach for the Padres. He had also been a first base coach for the Orioles (1992-94) and the Rangers (1988-91). He managed in the Arizona Fall League following the 1993 and 1998 seasons.

Gary Allenson: Allenson joins the team as the first base coach after managing Milwaukee's Class AAA team the last two seasons. He has also managed at the minor league level for the Astros, Red Sox, Rangers and Yankees.

Bob Apodaca: Apodaca will be Lopes' pitching coach and try to get the most out of a pitching staff that has several new faces. Before coming to Milwaukee, Apodaca had served 28 seasons in the Mets' organization.

Rod Carew: Carew, the team's new hitting coach, knows what he's talking about when it comes to hitting and teaching. In 19 seasons as a player, he hit .300 or better 15 times. He spent the last eight seasons as a hitting instructor for the Angels with much success. He takes the same harsh work ethic to coaching hitters as he to himself as a hitter.

Bill Castro: The only holdover from former manager Phil Garner's staff, Castro begins his ninth season as the Brewers bullpen coach, his 13th in the Milwaukee organization.

Jerry Royster: Royster is in his first season as the team's bench coach and will also be the Brewers spring training camp coordinator. He has previously managed in the minors for the Padres and Dodgers and was a player in the majors for 16 seasons (1973-88).

Chris Speier: The team's new third base coach has coached or managed in the pros since 1990 after ending a 19-year playing career in the majors. The previous two seasons, he managed the Diamondbacks' Class AAA team.

THE TOP NEWCOMERS:

Juan Acevedo: Last year with St. Louis, Acevedo was used as a starter, middle reliever and closer and wasn't effective in any of those roles. The Brewers have made it clear they want him to be a starter but he doesn't have the arm to throw more than 160 innings.

Henry Blanco: With Dave Nilsson gone, the Brewers decided they needed a catcher with good defensive tools. So they acquired Blanco from Colorado in a multiplayer deal. Blanco doesn't provide much offense, so he may be removed for pinch hitters in critical at-bats.

Jose Hernandez: Hernandez can play all four infield positions and the outfield, but the Brewers plan to use him as the starting third baseman. He provides solid defense and decent offensive numbers.

Curtis Leskanic: Leskanic, who came over in a trade Colorado, should be a key part of the Brewers' bullpen. He his durable and has the ability to pitch often. Last season for Colorado, he pitched more than one inning in 32 of his relief appearances.

Jaime Navarro: He's been shelled everywhere he's gone the last few years. But if nothing else, he's been durable. The Brewers' injury-plagued rotation needs him to eat innings.

John Snyder: Showed a lot of promise last season with the White Sox but struggled late in the season. The plus side: he's only 25.

Jamey Wright: Wright comes over to the Brewers with some confidence. He is throwing his changeup again for strikes was 4-2 with a 4.41 ERA in the final two months of last season for the Rockies. His ERA will drop outside of Coors Field, and he could be an effective part of Milwaukee's rotation.

THE TOP PROSPECTS

Kevin Barker: Barker was called up last season because Sean Berry was struggling at first base. This season, Barker should see the majority of the playing time, although Berry will get most of the starts against lefthanders. Barker has a nice stroke but not a lot of power.

Chad Green: Milwaukee fans likely won't see Green patrolling center field until September or opening day of 2001. He has good speed and defensive skills. If he becomes more selective at the

MONTREAL EXPOS

NATIONAL LEAGUE EAST DIVISION

2000 SEASON

2000 Expos Schedule
Home games shaded. *—All-Star Game at Turner Field (Atlanta).

March
SUN	MON	TUE	WED	THU	FRI	SAT
26	27	28	29	30	31	

April
SUN	MON	TUE	WED	THU	FRI	SAT
						1
2	3 LA	4 LA	5 LA	6 LA	7 SD	8 SD
9 SD	10	11 PIT	12 PIT	13 PIT	14 PHI	15 PHI
16 PHI	17 PHI	18 CUB	19 CUB	20 CUB	21 MIL	22 MIL
23 MIL	24	25 COL	26 COL	27	28 SF	29 SF
30 SF						

May
SUN	MON	TUE	WED	THU	FRI	SAT
	1 COL	2 COL	3 COL	4	5 MIL	6 MIL
7 MIL	8	9 PHI	10 PHI	11 PHI	12 CUB	13 CUB
14 CUB	15	16 ARI	17 ARI	18 ARI	19 HOU	20 HOU
21 HOU	22	23 SF	24 SF	25 SF	26 SD	27 SD
28 SD	29	30 CIN	31 CIN			

June
SUN	MON	TUE	WED	THU	FRI	SAT
				1 CIN	2 BAL	3 BAL
4 BAL	5 NYY	6 NYY	7 NYY	8	9 TOR	10 TOR
11 TOR	12 MIL	13 MIL	14 MIL	15	16 CUB	17 CUB
18 CUB	19 PIT	20 PIT	21 PIT	22 PIT	23 PHI	24 PHI
25 PHI	26	27 ATL	28 ATL	29	30 FLA	

July
SUN	MON	TUE	WED	THU	FRI	SAT
						1 FLA
2 FLA	3 ATL	4 ATL	5 ATL	6 ATL	7 TOR	8 TOR
9 TOR	10	11 *	12	13 TB	14 TB	15 TB
16 BOS	17 BOS	18 BOS	19 NYM	20 NYM	21 FLA	22 FLA
23 FLA	24	25 NYM	26 NYM	27 NYM	28 CIN	29 CIN
30 CIN	31 STL					

August
SUN	MON	TUE	WED	THU	FRI	SAT
		1 STL	2 STL	3	4 HOU	5 HOU
6 HOU	7 ARI	8 ARI	9 ARI	10	11 COL	12 COL
13 COL	14 COL	15 SF	16 SF	17 SF	18 SD	19 SD
20 SD	21 LA	22 LA	23 LA	24 LA	25 HOU	26 HOU
27 HOU	28 ARI	29 ARI	30 ARI	31		

September
SUN	MON	TUE	WED	THU	FRI	SAT
					1 CIN	2 CIN
3 CIN	4 STL	5 STL	6 STL	7 STL	8 ATL	9 ATL
10 ATL	11	12 PHI	13 PHI	14 NYM	15 NYM	16 NYM
17 NYM	18 FLA	19 FLA	20 FLA	21 ATL	22 ATL	23 ATL
24 ATL	25 ATL	26 FLA	27 FLA	28 FLA	29 NYM	30 NYM

October
SUN	MON	TUE	WED	THU	FRI	SAT
1 NYM	2	3	4	5	6	7

FRONT-OFFICE DIRECTORY
Chairman, chief operating officer and managing general partner ....Jeffrey H. Loria
Executive vice president ....David P. Samson
Vice president and general manager ....Jim Beattie
Vice president/director of international operations ....Fred Ferreira
Assistant general manager ....Larry Beinfest
Assistant to the general manager ....Mike Berger
Director, scouting ....Jim Fleming
Director, player development...Don Reynolds
Assistant director, scouting ....Gregg Leonard
Assistant director, player development...Adam Wogan
Coordinator, team travel ....Sean Cunningham
Vice president, finance and treasurer ....Michel Bussiere
Vice president, stadium operations...Claude Delorme
Director, media relations ....P.J. Loyello
Director, media services ....Monique Giroux
Directors, advertising sales....................Luigi Carola, John D. Terlizzi, Danielle La Roche
Director, promotions and special events ....Gina Hackl
Director, administration, sales and marketing................................Stephany Peschlow
General manager, Jupiter Stadium limited ....Rob Rabenecker
Director, stadium operations...Denis Pare
Director, management information systems ....Yves Poulin
Director, season ticket sales...Gilles Leonard
Director, business development...Real Sureau
Director, downtown ballpark ticket office ....Chantal Dalpe
Director, Olympic Stadium ticket office ....Hubert Richard

MINOR LEAGUE AFFILIATES
Class	Team	League	Manager
AAA	Ottawa	International	Jeff Cox
AA	Harrisburg	Eastern	Doug Sisson
A	Jupiter	Florida State	Luis Dorante
A	Cape Fear	South Atlantic	Bill Masse
A	Vermont	New York-Pennsylvania	Tim Leiper
Rookie	Gulf Coast Expos	Gulf Coast	Steve Phillips

ASSISTANCE STAFF
Team orthopedist
Dr. Larry Coughlin

Team physician
Dr. Michael Thomassin

Minor league field coordinator
Rich Sweet

Minor league pitching coordinator
Wayne Rosenthal

Minor league hitting coordinator
Jim Bowie

Minor league infield/baserunning coord.
Craig Shipley

Assistant director, International scouting
Randy Kierce

Major League scouts
Mike Berger   Bob Cluck

Scouts
Alex Agostino	Matt Anderson
Mark Baca	Carlos Berroa
Dennis Cardoza	Robby Corsaro
Dave Dangler	Marc DelPiano
Scott Engler	Scott Goldby
John Hughes	Joe Jordan
Mark Leavit	Dave Malpass
Darryl Monroe	Bob Oldis
Steve Payne	Scott Stanley
Len Strelitz	Tommy Thompson

BROADCAST INFORMATION
Radio/TV/Cable TV: To be announced.

SPRING TRAINING
Ballpark (city): Roger Dean Stadium (Jupiter, Fla.).
Ticket information: 561-775-1818.

BALLPARK INFORMATION

Ballpark (capacity, surface)
Olympic Stadium (46,500, artificial)
Address
P.O. Box 500, Station M
Montreal, Que. H1V 3P2
Business phone
514-253-3434
Ticket information
800-GO-EXPOS
Ticket prices
$36 (VIP box seats)
$26 (box seats)
$16 (terrace)
$8 (general admission)
Field dimensions (from home plate)
To left field at foul line, 325 feet
To center field, 404 feet
To right field at foul line, 325 feet
First game played
April 15, 1977 (Phillies 7, Expos 2)

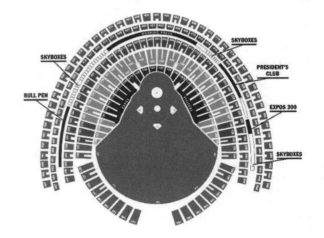

No.	PITCHERS	B/T	Ht./Wt.	Born	1999 clubs	Projection
51	Armas Jr., Tony	R/R	6-4/205	4-29-78	Harrisburg, Montreal	He's one of the better pitching prospects and could work his way into the rotation.
48	Batista, Miguel	R/R	6-2/195	2-19-71	Ottawa, Montreal	Though he began last season as a starter, he is reliever or spot starter this year.
	Billingsley, Brent	L/L	6-2/200	4-19-75	Calgary, Florida	This hard-throwing lefty and former Marlins prospect has struggled in the minors.
	Blank, Matt	L/L	6-2/195	4-5-76	Jupiter, Harrisburg	He's pitching well, but his below-average fastball might keep him from the bigs.
30	Hermanson, Dustin	R/R	6-2/200	12-21-72	Montreal	The team's ace had a down year in 1999 but is expected to bounce back in 2000.
14	Irabu, Hideki	R/R	6-4/240	5-5-69	New York A.L.	He had some fine starts for the Yankees and could thrive in a pressure-free situation.
47	Johnson, Mike	L/R	6-2/170	10-3-75	Ottawa, Montreal	He figures to be little more than a spot starter.
44	Kline, Steve	B/L	6-1/215	8-22-72	Montreal	He's coming off a strong season and could get more time as a late-inning reliever.
28	Lilly, Ted	L/L	6-0/185	1-4-76	Ottawa, Montreal	Has good command of at least three pitches and might join the rotation soon.
27	Lloyd, Graeme	L/L	6-7/234	4-9-67	Toronto	This sought-after middle reliever decided to stay north of the border.
	McLeary, Marty	R/R	6-5/212	10-26-74	Sarasota, Augusta	He's a Rule 5 draftee who hasn't pitched above the Class A level.
29	Moore, Trey	L/L	6-0/190	10-2-72	DID NOT PLAY	Will have a lot to prove after missing 1999 rehabbing from shoulder surgery.
40	Mota, Guillermo	R/R	6-4/205	7-25-73	Ottawa, Montreal	This former shortstop taken in 1996 from the Mets can throw in the high-90s.
45	Pavano, Carl	R/R	6-5/230	1-8-76	Montreal, Ottawa	No longer considered a potential No. 1 starter, he's still a solid part of the rotation.
49	Powell, Jeremy	R/R	6-5/230	6-18-76	Ottawa, Montreal	Crafty hurler with good control and a lot of minor league success.
56	Smart, J.D.	R/R	6-2/180	11-12-73	Montreal, Ottawa	Should spend most of his time this year with Montreal in the bullpen.
51	Strickland, Scott	R/R	5-11/180	4-26-76	Jupiter, Harris., Ottawa, Mont.	Worked his way from Class A to the pros in '99 with impressive stats along the way.
32	Telford, Anthony	R/R	6-0/195	3-6-66	Montreal	He has been the team's most durable reliever in the past three seasons.
35	Thurman, Mike	R/R	6-5/210	7-22-73	Montreal	Though not a power pitcher, he's coming off an excellent season is on the rise.
41	Urbina, Ugueth	R/R	6-0/205	2-15-74	Montreal	He shrugged off a bad start and somehow managed to lead the league in saves.
23	Vazquez, Javier	R/R	6-2/195	7-25-76	Montreal, Ottawa	Just 23, he had a respectable season in '99 and will continue to improve in 2000.

No.	CATCHERS	B/T	Ht./Wt.	Born	1999 clubs	Projection
13	Henley, Bob	R/R	6-2/205	1-30-73	Gulf Coast Expos	He probably will be the team's backup if he manages to stay healthy.
63	Schneider, Brian	L/R	6-1/200	11-26-76	Harrisburg	This catcher has an above-average arm but below-average bat.
16	Widger, Chris	R/R	6-2/215	5-21-71	Montreal	Though he's a decent hitter with some power, Widger is injury-prone.

No.	INFIELDERS	B/T	Ht./Wt.	Born	1999 clubs	Projection
5	Barrett, Michael	R/R	6-2/200	10-22-76	Montreal, Ottawa	He should excel at the plate now that he's the team's primary third baseman.
50	Blum, Geoff	B/R	6-3/195	4-26-73	Ottawa, Montreal	He got time as a starter at shortstop last year, but is better suited in a utility role.
18	Cabrera, Orlando	R/R	5-10/175	11-2-74	Montreal	The team still thinks he'll be an above-average shortstop with good offensive skills.
53	Coquillette, Trace	R/R	5-11/185	6-4-74	Ottawa, Montreal	This versatile infielder is a potential .300 hitter if he finds a spot.
	De La Rosa, Tomas	R/R	5-10/165	1-28-78	Harrisburg	This 21-year-old shortstop is a year or two from the bigs.
20	Fullmer, Brad	L/R	6-0/215	1-17-75	Montreal, Ottawa	He's a suspect fielder and his offense has progressed slowly, but he'll start at first.
4	Guerrero, Wilton	B/R	6-0/175	10-24-74	Montreal	The club might give him time in the outfield in hopes he earns more playing time.
12	Mordecai, Mike	R/R	5-10/185	12-13-67	Montreal	Better suited as a solid utilityman, he likely will start at second base.
	Nunnari, Talmadge	L/L	6-1/200	4-9-75	Jupiter, Harrisburg	Has hit over .290 at each stop since being drafted in the ninth round in 1997.
33	Seguignol, Fernando	B/R	6-5/230	1-19-75	Ottawa, Montreal	He has good power potential and might get a chance to start at first base.
3	Vidro, Jose	B/R	5-11/190	8-27-74	Montreal	A hidden gem, he needs to work on his fielding but emerged as an excellent hitter.

No.	OUTFIELDERS	B/T	Ht./Wt.	Born	1999 clubs	Projection
33	Bergeron, Peter	L/R	6-0/185	11-9-77	Harrisburg, Ottawa, Montreal	He is a year away from full-time duty, but the team likes his leadoff potential.
	Bradley, Milton	B/R	6-0/180	4-15-78	Harrisburg	He is the favorite to open the season as the team's leadoff hitter.
27	Guerrero, Vladimir	R/R	6-3/205	2-9-76	Montreal	With another stellar season, Guerrero might find himself as an MVP candidate.
40	Martinez, Manny	R/R	6-0/180	10-3-70	Montreal	He has good defensive skills and will be a late-inning replacement and pinch runner.
22	White, Rondell	R/R	6-0/210	2-23-72	Montreal	He can be an excellent player when he's healthy, but he's rarely healthy.

THE COACHING STAFF

Felipe Alou, manager: His seven-year .505 winning percentage under difficult circumstances in cost-conscious Montreal is an incredible tribute to his ability to motivate players and work with what's he got. Alou's hands-on approach and patience have been tested by Montreal's notoriety for developing young players to stardom, then shipping them away for more prospects. Alou is generally thought of as one of the best managers in the game. And other teams know it; they have tried to hire him away from the struggling franchise, but Alou's loyalty and patience with the organization has been inspiring.

Brad Arnsberg: The former pitcher for six major league organizations will serve as bullpen coach for his first season with the Montreal Expos organization. He was the pitching coach for Class AAA Oklahoma in the Texas Rangers' organization last season and for other clubs within the Rangers' organization the three years prior to that.

Pierre Arsenault: The former batting-practice pitcher is entering his ninth season with the Expos. Arsenault is a valuable link to the French-Canadian population of Montreal.

Bobby Cuellar: He is entering his sixth season as a major league pitching coach, and may have one of the tougher pitching coach jobs in the business. He has young, inexperienced pitchers who pitch in one of the tougher divisions in baseball.

Pete Mackanin: He was The Sporting News' 1995 Minor League Manager of the Year at Class AAA Ottawa. He will handle the third base coaching duties for the fourth season under Alou.

Luis Pujols: He has handled the first base coaching duties for seven Montreal seasons and has worked in the organization since 1987.

Pat Roessler: He served as the minor league hitting coordinator for the Pittsburgh Pirates the last two seasons after serving in the same capacity withing Montreal's organization from 1995-97. He has been instructing swingers since 1988 and will replace Tommy Harper as the hitting coach.

THE TOP NEWCOMERS

Brent Billingsley: He's a hard-throwing lefty, always good to have. But he has really struggled to get people out in his major and minor league career and was let go by the Marlins, a bad omen.

Hideki Irabu: Montreal's goals was to spend some money and pick up some ringers this offseason. Here's a good start. Irabu will join the ethnically diverse squad and enjoy the calm, relaxed atmosphere of Montreal much more than the tense, high-pressured world of being a Yankee. After learning the National League hitters a bit, he'll flourish in Montreal.

Graeme Lloyd: This big lefthander is one of the best lefties in baseball out of the bullpen. He can throw long and often, and he's murder on lefties. He'll join this third team in as many seasons.

THE TOP PROSPECTS

Tony Armas Jr.: The Expos hope he will make them forget about trading away Pedro Martinez to get him. He won't this year, but may someday. Despite being just 21, he is intelligent beyond his years and has a decent fastball, a good curve and a deceiving changeup. Just needs one more year of seasoning but might be with the club again after the All-Star break.

Milton Bradley: The speedy outfielder will make the jump from Class AA to Montreal this season, and he has the tools to do it successfully. Has the potential to be a .300 hitter and 30-steal player.

Scott Strickland: In 99 2/3 innings for four different clubs, including Montreal, this 23-year-old reliever recorded a 2.89 ERA with 126 strikeouts. Not too shabby. Those numbers should get him a shot at the shaky Montreal bullpen this season.

NEW YORK METS

NATIONAL LEAGUE EAST DIVISION

2000 SEASON

2000 Mets Schedule

Home games shaded. *—All-Star Game at Turner Field (Atlanta).
† Game played in Tokyo.

March

SUN	MON	TUE	WED	THU	FRI	SAT
26	27	28	29 CUB	30 † CUB	31	

April

SUN	MON	TUE	WED	THU	FRI	SAT
						1
2	3 SD	4	5 SD	6 SD	7 LA	8 LA
9 LA	10 PHI	11	12 PHI	13 PHI	14 PIT	15 PIT
16 PIT	17	18 MIL	19 MIL	20 MIL	21 CUB	22 CUB
23 CUB	24	25 CIN	26 CIN	27 CIN	28 COL	29 COL
30 COL						

May

SUN	MON	TUE	WED	THU	FRI	SAT
	1 SF	2 SF	3 SF	4 SF	5 FLA	6 FLA
7 FLA	8	9 PIT	10 PIT	11 PIT	12 FLA	13 FLA
14 FLA	15	16 COL	17 COL	18 COL	19 ARI	20 ARI
21 ARI	22 SD	23 SD	24 SD	25	26 STL	27 STL
28 STL	29 LA	30 LA	31 LA			

June

SUN	MON	TUE	WED	THU	FRI	SAT
				1	2 TB	3 TB
4 TB	5 BAL	6 BAL	7 BAL	8	9 NYY	10 NYY
11 NYY	12	13 CUB	14 CUB	15	16 MIL	17 MIL
18 MIL	19	20 PHI	21 PHI	22 PHI	23 PIT	24 PIT
25 PIT	26 FLA	27 FLA	28 FLA	29 ATL	30 ATL

July

SUN	MON	TUE	WED	THU	FRI	SAT
						1 ATL
2 ATL	3 FLA	4 FLA	5 FLA	6	7 NYY	8 NYY
9 NYY	10	11 *	12	13 BOS	14 BOS	15 BOS
16 TOR	17 TOR	18 TOR	19 MON	20 MON	21 ATL	22 ATL
23 ATL	24	25 MON	26 MON	27 MON	28 STL	29 STL
30 STL	31 CIN					

August

SUN	MON	TUE	WED	THU	FRI	SAT
		1 CIN	2 CIN	3	4 ARI	5 ARI
6 ARI	7 HOU	8 HOU	9 HOU	10 HOU	11 SF	12 SF
13 SF	14 COL	15 COL	16 COL	17 COL	18 LA	19 LA
20 LA	21 SD	22 SD	23 SD	24	25 ARI	26 ARI
27 ARI	28 HOU	29 HOU	30 HOU	31		

September

SUN	MON	TUE	WED	THU	FRI	SAT
					1 STL	2 STL
3 STL	4 CIN	5 CIN	6 CIN	7	8 PHI	9 PHI
10 PHI	11 MIL	12 MIL	13 MIL	14 MON	15 MON	16 MON
17 MON	18 ATL	19 ATL	20 ATL	21 PHI	22 PHI	23 PHI
24 PHI	25	26 ATL	27 ATL	28 MON	29 MON	30 MON

October

SUN	MON	TUE	WED	THU	FRI	SAT
1 MON	2	3	4	5	6	7

FRONT-OFFICE DIRECTORY

Chairman of the board ....Nelson Doubleday
President and chief executive officer ....Fred Wilpon
Directors..Nelson Doubleday, Fred Wilpon, Saul B. Katz,
Steve Phillips, Marvin B. Tepper
Special advisor to the board of directors.................................Richard Cummins
Senior vice president and general manager ....Steve Phillips
Senior assistant general manager/international scouting director ....Omar Minaya
Assistant general manager/player personnel ....Jim Duquette
Assistant general manager/amateur scouting...............................Gary Larocque
Assistant general manager/professional scouting ....Carmen Fusco
Special assistants to the G.M. ....Larry Doughty, Darrell Johnson, Harry Minor
Assistant directors of amateur scouting......................Jack Bowen, Fred Wright
Assistant director of player personnel ....Kevin Morgan
Senior vice president and treasurer ....Harold W. O'Shaughnessy
Senior vice president of business and legal affairs ....David Howard
Vice president, marketing ....Mark Bingham
Vice president, purchasing and special projects........................Bob Mandt
Vice president, ticket sales and services ....Bill Ianniciello
Senior vice president and consultant ....J. Frank Cashen
Director of marketing...Kit Geis
Director of marketing production..Tim Gunkel
Director of human resources ....To be announced
General counsel ....David Cohen
Director, administrative and data processing ....Russ Richardson
Director, community outreach ....Jill Knee
Director of corporate sales...Paul Danforth
Controller ....Lennie Labita
Director of media relations ....Jay Horwitz
Director, ticket operations ....Dan DeMato
Manager, customer relations...Joann Galardy
Director of staidum operations ....Kevin McCarthy

MINOR LEAGUE AFFILIATES

Class	Team	League	Manager
AAA	Norfolk	International	John Gibbons
AA	Binghamton	Eastern	Doug Davis
A	St. Lucie	Florida State	Dave Engle
A	Capital City	South Atlantic	John Stephenson
A	Pittsfield	New York-Pennsylvania	Tony Tijerina
Rookie	Kingsport	Appalachian	Edgar Alfonzo

ASSISTANCE STAFF

Club physician
Dr. David Altchek

Club psychologist/Employee Assistance Program
Dr. Allan Lans

Team trainers
Fred Hina   Scott Lawrenson

Special assignment scouts
Buddy Kerr   Darrell Johnson

Professional scouts
Bruce Benedict, Erwin Bryant, Howard Johnson, Roland Johnson, Bill Latham, Mike Toomey, Tim Teufel

Regional scouting supervisors
Paul Fryer   Gene Kerns
Terry Tripp

Scouting supervisors
Kevin Blankenship	Quincy Boyd
Larry Chase	Joe DelliCarri
Kevin Frady	Chuck Hensley Jr.
Dave Lottsfeldt	Fred Mazuca
Marlin McPhail	Randy Milligan
Bob Minor	Greg Morhardt
Joe Morlan	Joe Nigro
Jim Reeves	Junior Roman
Bob Rossi	Joe Salermo
Greg Tubbs	

BROADCAST INFORMATION

Radio: WFAN-AM (660).
TV: WPIX (Channel 11).
Cable TV: Fox Sports New York.

SPRING TRAINING

Ballpark (city): Thomas J. White Stadium (Port St. Lucie, Fla.).
Ticket information: 561-871-2115.

BALLPARK INFORMATION

Ballpark (capacity, surface)
Shea Stadium (56,521, grass)
Address
123-01 Roosevelt Ave.
Flushing, NY 11368
Business phone
718-507-METS
Ticket information
718-507-TIXX
Ticket prices
$57 (Metropolitan Club gold)
$54 (Metropolitan Club)
$37 (inner field box, inner loge box)
$33 (middle field box)
$30 (outer field box, outer loge box, mezzanine box, upper box)
$26 (loge reserved)
$21 (mezzanine reserved, upper box)
$12 (upper reserved, back rows loge and mezzanine)
Field dimensions (from home plate)
To left field at foul line, 338 feet
To center field, 410 feet
To right field at foul line, 338 feet
First game played
April 17, 1964 (Pirates 4, Mets 3)

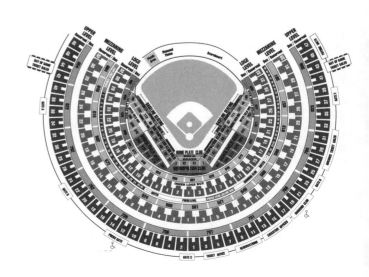

No.	PITCHERS	B/T	Ht./Wt.	Born	1999 clubs	Projection
49	Benitez, Armando	R/R	6-4/229	11-3-72	New York N.L.	May take over closer role from John Franco after last's year performance.
	Cammack, Eric	R/R	6-1/180	8-14-75	Binghamton, Norfolk	Had 100 strikeouts and 19 saves in just over 65 innings of minor league ball.
27	Cook, Dennis	L/L	6-3/190	10-4-62	New York N.L.	Had 10 wins out of bullpen as a set-up man and lefthanded specialist.
45	Franco, John	L/L	5-10/185	9-17-60	New York N.L., Binghamton	He and Benitez should provide a formidable lefty-righty punch to close games.
	Gonzalez, Dicky	R/R	5-11/170	10-21-78	St. Lucie, Norfolk	After winning 14 games at St. Lucie, he should start with Norfolk.
38	Gonzalez, Lariel	R/R	6-4/228	5-25-76	Colorado Springs, Carolina	The reliever wasn't overpowering in Class AA and was rocked in Class AAA.
10	Hampton, Mike	R/L	5-10/180	9-9-72	Houston	Could prove to be the one player the Mets need to unseat the Braves.
28	Jones, Bobby J.	R/R	6-4/225	2-10-70	New York N.L., Bing., Norfolk	Still a solid starter for the Mets this year if healthy.
36	Jones, Bobby M.	R/L	6-0/178	4-11-72	Colorado, Colorado Springs	The lefty still throws hard, but will have to shake his low Coors Field confidence.
22	Leiter, Al	L/L	6-3/220	10-23-65	New York N.L.	Not having to be the No. 1 starter with Hampton around should help him.
23	Mahomes, Pat	R/R	6-4/212	8-9-70	Norfolk, New York N.L.	After signing with Mets from Japan, he was a perfect 8-0 out of the bullpen.
	Mann, Jim	R/R	6-3/225	11-17-74	Knoxville, Syracuse	Might see some action out of the bullpen this year with Dotel gone.
	Orosco, Jesse	R/L	6-2/205	4-21-57	Baltimore	Back with the Mets again, he may take some heat off of Cook versus lefties.
35	Reed, Rick	R/R	6-1/195	8-16-65	New York N.L., Norfolk, Bing.	He will be moved down to the No. 3 slot and not have to pitch as many innings.
	Roberts, Grant	R/R	6-3/205	9-13-77	Binghamton, Norfolk	Should see more starts at Norfolk after being a combined 9-7 last year.
48	Rusch, Glendon	L/L	6-1/200	11-7-74	Oma., GC Royals, K.C., N.Y.-N.L.	Might be the odd lefthander out with the steady Cook and Orosco back in the fold.
99	Wendell, Turk	L/R	6-2/205	5-19-67	New York N.L.	Made 80 games appearances in 1999 and should see the same workload in 2000.
32	Wilson, Paul	R/R	6-5/235	3-28-73	DID NOT PLAY	Injury-prone hurler might be able to pitch if his shoulder holds up. That's a big if.

No.	CATCHERS	B/T	Ht./Wt.	Born	1999 clubs	Projection
31	Piazza, Mike	R/R	6-3/215	9-4-68	New York N.L.	All-Star should be eager for season after lackluster performance in the playoffs.
7	Pratt, Todd	R/R	6-3/230	2-9-67	New York N.L.	Should provide veteran leadership and will to win as backup catcher.
3	Wilson, Vance	R/R	5-11/190	3-17-73	Norfolk, New York N.L.	Will be back at Norfolk after an injury-plagued 1999 season.

No.	INFIELDERS	B/T	Ht./Wt.	Born	1999 clubs	Projection
13	Alfonzo, Edgardo	R/R	5-11/187	11-8-73	New York N.L.	Established career highs in home runs, RBIs and runs scored last season.
15	Franco, Matt	L/R	6-1/210	8-19-69	New York N.L.	One of the top lefthanded pinch-hitters in baseball.
11	Halter, Shane	R/R	6-0/180	11-8-69	Norfolk, New York N.L.	A true utility player who can play all positions and should do so for the Mets.
33	Kinkade, Mike	R/R	6-1/210	5-6-73	New York N.L., Norfolk	Must hit like he did in Norfolk (.308) in order for him to stay with the Mets.
17	Lopez, Luis	B/R	5-11/166	9-4-70	New York N.L.	Provides switch-hitting bat off the bench and decent infield defense off the bench.
10	Ordonez, Rey	R/R	5-9/159	11-11-72	New York N.L.	A potent middle combo with Alfonzo. He also had a career-high batting average.
30	Toca, Jorge	R/R	6-3/220	1-7-75	Bing., Norfolk, New York N.L.	This prospect displayed last season his sound defense and above-average bat.
4	Ventura, Robin	L/R	6-1/198	7-14-67	New York N.L.	Provided Mets with exactly what they needed, a good hitter behind Piazza.
	Zeile, Todd	R/R	6-1/200	9-9-65	Texas	Will play his first season at first base. But the Mets signed him for his bat.

No.	OUTFIELDERS	B/T	Ht./Wt.	Born	1999 clubs	Projection
50	Agbayani, Benny	R/R	5-11/225	12-28-71	Norfolk, New York N.L.	Will be a reliable part-time or fill-in outfielder as he showed last year.
14	Bell, Derek	R/R	6-2/215	12-11-68	Houston	Glad to be out of Houston, and should return to form in devastating Mets lineup.
	Escobar, Alex	R/R	6-1/180	9-6-78	Gulf Coast Mets, St. Lucie	Injured for the majority of 1999. Should be back in the minors for 2000.
18	Hamilton, Darryl	L/R	6-1/192	12-3-64	Colorado, New York N.L.	Showed he can hit away from Coors Field. Will again start in center field.
24	Henderson, Rickey	R/L	5-10/190	12-25-58	New York N.L.	Still one of the best leadoff hitters in the game, he should be splitting time in left.
	LeBron, Juan	R/R	6-6/205	6-7-77	DID NOT PLAY	We haven't seen what he could do yet, and we likely won't this year either.
6	Mora, Melvin	R/R	5-10/180	2-2-72	Norfolk, New York N.L.	Solid defense and spectular 1999 postseason will likely keep him with the Mets.
22	Nunnally, Jon	L/R	5-10/190	11-9-71	Pawtucket, Boston	Journeyman outfielder will be ready in case of outfield injuries.
44	Payton, Jay	R/R	5-10/185	11-22-72	St. Lucie, Norf., New York N.L.	Part-time player used primarily as a pinch-hitter/runner.

THE COACHING STAFF

Bobby Valentine, manager: Love him or hate him, he does one thing well and that's win ballgames. He can get the most out of his players. In his four years as a manager, he has a .550 winning percentage. The Mets had 97 regular-season wins under his guidance and should duplicate that this year.

Al Jackson: Re-joined the Mets as a minor league pitching coordinator in 1991 and became the bullpen/assistant coach midway through the 1999 season. Helped turn the bullpen around and develop Benitez and Mahomes into huge bullpen factors.

Tom Robson: As batting coach, the one project he has for this team is finding a replacement in the lineup for John Olerud.

Cookie Rojas: Has three years under his belt as the Mets third base coach and infield coach. Who can argue with the infield he had last year, possibly one of the best, defensively, of all-time. A challenge for this season will be getting Todd Zeile acquainted with his new surroundings at first base.

John Stearns: Former Met catcher/infielder returns home to bolster the coaching staff.

Dave Wallace: Joined the Mets as pitching coach on June 6, 1999. He was the pitching coach for the Dodgers from 1995-97, so he and Piazza should have a good understanding of how to deal with a pitching staff. Twice during his tenure with the Dodgers, the staff posted the second-best ERA in the National League, behind only the Braves.

Mookie Wilson: After ten years as the Mets center fielder, who better to teach the young outfielders the nooks and crannies at Shea Stadium. And as first base coach, the former basestealer helps the Mets immensely.

THE TOP NEWCOMERS

Derek Bell: A change of scenery should help get his career back in order. He fell out of favor with Houston management and fans last year and his production fell off with it. He's still got great power and a great arm, along with a little speed.

Mike Hampton: Lefthanded pitcher may be the player the Mets need to get past the Braves. He was 22-4 with Houston in 1999. He's durable, deceptive, a good fielder and a good hitter. In other words, he's got that Braves starter mentality.

Bobby M. Jones: Figures to be the No. 5 starter and/or long reliever for the Mets. He throws hard, which means a lot more in Shea Stadium than in Coors Field.

Todd Zeile: While he won't make you forget John Olerud's defense, he will help the Mets lineup by providing another power-hitting righthanded bat. Should pick up a lot of RBIs with all the baserunners on for his at-bats.

THE TOP PROSPECTS

Alex Escobar: Was injured almost all of last year, so he will be in the minors to start the season. But don't be surprised if you hear about him soon. He batted .310 with 27 home runs and 91 RBIs in just 112 games with Class A Capital City in 1998.

Paul Wilson: Still has yet to make a big-league start since 1996, and another year on the disabled list last year didn't help. Maybe this year he'll get a chance to display the talent that made him the first pick overall in the 1994 draft.

Vance Wilson: Injuries limited him to 15 games total in 1999. With a full season at Class AAA Norfolk, he should be able to supplant Todd Pratt as the backup catcher by next year.

PHILADELPHIA PHILLIES

NATIONAL LEAGUE EAST DIVISION

2000 SEASON

2000 Phillies Schedule
Home games shaded. *—All-Star Game at Turner Field (Atlanta).

March
SUN	MON	TUE	WED	THU	FRI	SAT
26	27	28	29	30	31	

April
SUN	MON	TUE	WED	THU	FRI	SAT
						1
2	3	4 ARI	5 ARI	6 ARI	7 HOU	8 HOU
9 HOU	10 NYM	11	12 NYM	13 NYM	14 MON	15 MON
16 MON	17	18 ATL	19 ATL	20 ATL	21 FLA	22 FLA
23 FLA	24 FLA	25 ARI	26 ARI	27 STL	28 STL	29 STL
30 STL						

May
SUN	MON	TUE	WED	THU	FRI	SAT
	1	2 CIN	3 CIN	4 CIN	5 ATL	6 ATL
7 ATL	8	9 MON	10 MON	11 MON	12 ATL	13 ATL
14 ATL	15	16 STL	17 STL	18 COL	19 COL	20 COL
21 COL	22	23 HOU	24 HOU	25 HOU	26 LA	27 LA
28 LA	29 SF	30 SF	31 SF			

June
SUN	MON	TUE	WED	THU	FRI	SAT
				1	2 BOS	3 BOS
4 BOS	5 TB	6 TB	7 TB	8	9 BAL	10 BAL
11 BAL	12 FLA	13 FLA	14	15	16 ATL	17 ATL
18 ATL	19 ATL	20 NYM	21 NYM	22 NYM	23 MON	24 MON
25 MON	26	27 MIL	28 MIL	29 MIL	30 PIT	

July
SUN	MON	TUE	WED	THU	FRI	SAT
						1 PIT
2 PIT	3 MIL	4 MIL	5 MIL	6 MIL	7 BAL	8 BAL
9 BAL	10	11	* 12	13 TOR	14 TOR	15 TOR
16 NYY	17 NYY	18 NYY	19 CUB	20 CUB	21 CUB	22 PIT
23 PIT	24	25 CUB	26 CUB	27 CUB	28 SD	29 SD
30 LA	31 SD					

August
SUN	MON	TUE	WED	THU	FRI	SAT
		1 SD	2 SD	3	4 COL	5 COL
6 COL	7 SD	8 SD	9 SD	10 HOU	11 HOU	12 HOU
13 HOU	14 ARI	15 ARI	16 ARI	17	18 STL	19 STL
20 STL	21 CIN	22 CIN	23 CIN	24 CIN	25 SF	26 SF
27 SF	28 COL	29 COL	30 COL	31		

September
SUN	MON	TUE	WED	THU	FRI	SAT
					1 LA	2 LA
3 LA	4 SF	5 SF	6 SF	7	8 NYM	9 NYM
10 NYM	11	12 MON	13 MON	14	15 FLA	16 FLA
17 FLA	18 PIT	19 PIT	20 PIT	21 NYM	22 NYM	23 NYM
24 NYM	25 CUB	26 CUB	27 CUB	28 CUB	29 FLA	30 FLA

October
SUN	MON	TUE	WED	THU	FRI	SAT
1 FLA	2	3	4	5	6	7

FRONT-OFFICE DIRECTORY
Managing general partner, president, CEO..........David Montgomery
Chairman, general partner ....Bill Giles
Partners ....Claire S. Betz, Tri-Play Associates (Alexander K. Buck, J. Mahlon Buck Jr., William C. Buck), Double Play, Inc. (John Middleton, chairman), Fitz Eugene Dixon Jr.
Secretary and general counsel ....Bill Webb
Senior vice president, finance and planning ....Jerry Clothier
Special assistant to the president..........Sharon Swainson
Director, business development ....Joe Giles
Vice president and general manager ....Ed Wade
Assistant general manager ....Ruben Amaro Jr.
Controller..........John Fusco
Director, scouting ....Mike Arbuckle
Senior advisors to general manager ....Dallas Green, Paul Owens
Director, minor league field operations/instruction ....Gary Ruby
Director, minor league operations ....Steve Noworyta
Executive assistant to the general manager..........Susan Ingersoll
Traveling secretary..........Eddie Ferenz
Vice president, public relations ....Larry Shenk
Manager, publicity ....Leigh Tobin
Manager, media relations..........Gene Dias
Vice president, advertising sales ....Dave Buck
Director, information systems ....Brian Lamoreaux
Vice president, ticket operations ....Richard Deats
Director, ticket department ....Dan Goroff
Director, sales ....John Weber
Director, broadcasting and video services ....Rory McNeil
Director, stadium operations ....Mike DiMuzio

MINOR LEAGUE AFFILIATES
Class	Team	League	Manager
AAA	Scranton/Wilkes-Barre	International	Marc Bombard
AA	Reading	Eastern	Gary Varsho
A	Clearwater	Florida State	Ken Oberkfell
A	Piedmont	South Atlantic	Greg Legg
A	Batavia	New York-Pennsylvania	Frank Klebe
Rookie	Gulf Coast Phillies	Gulf Coast	Ramon Aviles

BROADCAST INFORMATION
Radio: WPHT Talk Radio 1210.
TV: UPN (Channel 57).
Cable TV: Comcast Sportsnet.

SPRING TRAINING
Ballpark (city): Jack Russell Stadium (Clearwater, Fla.).
Ticket information: 215-463-1000, 727-442-8496.

ASSISTANCE STAFF
Club physician
Dr. Michael Ciccotti

Club trainers
Jeff Cooper   Mark Andersen

Mgr., equipment and home clubhouse
Frank Coppenbarger

Manager, visiting clubhouse
Kevin Steinhour

National supervisor
Marti Wolever

Director, Florida operations
John Timberlake

Director, Latin American operations
Sal Artiaga

Director, Major League scouts
Gordon Lakey

Major League scout
Jimmy Stewart

Advance scout, Major Leagues
Hank King

Special assignment scouts
Jim Fregosi Jr.   Dean Jongewaard

Coordinator, professional coverage
Dick Lawlor

Regular scouts
Sal Agostinelli, Emil Belich, Jim Fregosi Jr., Steve Gillispie, Bill Harper, Ken Hultzapple, Marlon James, Jerry Lafferty, Matt Lundin, Miguel Machado, Lloyd Merritt, Venice Murray, Dave Owen, Arthur Parrack, Scott Ramsay, Mitch Sokol, Doug Takaragawa, Roy Tanner

BALLPARK INFORMATION
Ballpark (capacity, surface)
Veterans Stadium (62,411, artificial)
Address
P.O. Box 7575
Philadelphia, PA 19101
Business phone
215-463-6000
Ticket information
215-463-1000
Ticket prices
$22.50 (field box)
$19 (sections 258-201)
$19 (terrace box)
$17 (loge box)
$13 (reserved, 600 level)
$7 (reserved, 700 level, adult gen. admission)
$5 (children's general admission)
Field dimensions (from home plate)
To left field at foul line, 330 feet
To center field, 408 feet
To right field at foul line, 330 feet
First game played
April 10, 1971 (Phillies 4, Expos 1)

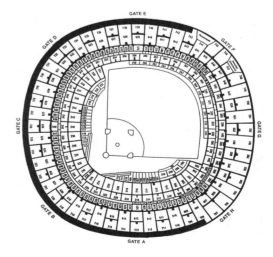

No.	PITCHERS	B/T	Ht./Wt.	Born	1999 clubs	Projection
30	Aldred, Scott	L/L	6-4/220	6-12-68	Tampa Bay, Philadelphia	The Phillies have room for him as a situational lefty. He filled the role well in '99.
43	Ashby, Andy	R/R	6-1/202	7-11-67	San Diego	Traded for him in the offseason to be the staff ace in Schilling's absence.
46	Barrios, Manuel	R/R	6-0/185	9-21-74	Indianapolis	Can work as a starter and reliever but figures to be little more than a role player.
45	Brantley, Jeff	R/R	5-10/197	9-5-63	Philadelphia	His '99 season was cut short by surgery. Jackson's signing relegates his role.
62	Brester, Jason	L/L	6-3/190	12-7-76	Carolina, Reading	This lefthander will be back at Class AA to start the season.
55	Brock, Chris	R/R	6-0/185	2-5-70	San Francisco	If Schilling is out, Brock could start in the Phillies rotation. Otherwise it's long relief.
49	Brownson, Mark	L/R	6-2/185	6-17-75	Colorado Springs, Colorado	His stuff indicates he might be able to shake off his inflated Coors Field ERA.
34	Byrd, Paul	R/R	6-1/184	12-3-70	Philadelphia	Emerged as a potential 20-game winner last season but struggled against lefties.
72	Coggin, Dave	R/R	6-4/205	10-30-76	Reading	Made only nine starts last season due to injuries. Will start back at Reading.
61	Gomes, Wayne	R/R	6-2/227	1-15-73	Philadelphia	He and Brantley are slated as setup men in a surprisingly tough bullpen.
42	Jackson, Mike	R/R	6-2/225	12-22-64	Cleveland	He's the closer but has battled elbow, shoulder and knee injuries.
78	Nickle, Doug	R/R	6-4/210	10-2-74	Clearwater	He picked up 28 saves in Class A with 60 appearances. His durability is a plus.
31	Person, Robert	R/R	6-0/194	10-6-69	Dunedin, Toronto, Philadelphia	Outside of Schilling, he has the best arm on the staff, including three "out" pitches.
35	Politte, Cliff	R/R	5-11/185	2-27-74	Reading, Philadelphia	Despite another winning minor league year, he won't make it into the rotation.
44	Reyes, Carlos	B/R	6-0/190	4-4-69	San Diego	A valuable middle reliever, as the Padres have found.
38	Schilling, Curt	R/R	6-4/231	11-14-66	Philadelphia	Expected out until July after shoulder surgery. But it may be earlier with Schilling.
52	Schrenk, Steve	R/R	6-3/215	11-20-68	Scranton/Wilkes-Barre, Phila.	He's a long reliever and/or a spot starter at best.
37	Shumaker, Anthony	L/L	6-5/219	5-14-73	Reading, Scranton/W.B., Phila.	This lefty might find his way into the rotation with Schilling out.
47	Telemaco, Amaury	R/R	6-3/222	1-19-74	Tucson, Arizona, Philadelphia	Versatile pitcher. Can throw one or seven innings on any given night.
54	Wolf, Randy	L/L	6-0/194	8-22-76	Scranton/Wilkes-Barre, Phila.	Showed signs of brilliance in 1999 but needs to avoid big innings.

No.	CATCHERS	B/T	Ht./Wt.	Born	1999 clubs	Projection
14	Bennett, Gary	R/R	6-0/208	4-17-72	Philadelphia	A good offensive player off the bench. Will battle with Prince for the backup job.
24	Lieberthal, Mike	R/R	6-0/190	1-18-72	Philadelphia	He's durable, can hit, is good defensively and has a great attitude. What can't he do?
12	Prince, Tom	R/R	5-11/206	8-13-64	GC Phils, Clear., Scr./W.B., Phila.	Veteran catcher known for good defense but a light stick.

No.	INFIELDERS	B/T	Ht./Wt.	Born	1999 clubs	Projection
16	Anderson, Marlon	L/R	5-11/198	1-6-74	Philadelphia	First season as a starter was an adventure, especially defensively. But he's talented.
26	Arias, Alex	R/R	6-3/202	11-20-67	Philadelphia	Should be a backup once again at shortstop if Relaford is healthy.
2	Brogna, Rico	L/L	6-2/203	4-18-70	Philadelphia	Quietly drove in 206 runs the past two years and played Gold Glove-caliber defense.
67	Duncan, Carlos	R/R	6-1/185	6-30-77	Piedmont	Speedy middle infielder appears headed for Class AA.
23	Jordan, Kevin	R/R	6-1/201	10-9-69	Philadelphia	Versatile infielder provides a good bat off the bench but lacks speed.
19	Martinez, Felix	B/R	6-0/180	5-18-74	Wichita, Omaha, Kansas City	The Royals were once very high on this speedy, switch-hitting middle infielder.
8	Relaford, Desi	B/R	5-9/174	9-16-73	Philadelphia, Clearwater	Played in only 65 games last season and struggled offensively and defensively.
17	Rolen, Scott	R/R	6-4/226	4-4-75	Philadelphia	Spent offseason strengthening his lower back and should return to top-notch form.
68	Rollins, Jimmy	B/R	5-8/154	11-27-78	Reading, Scranton/W.B.	This 21-year-old shortstop prospect is just waiting to oust Relaford or Arias.

No.	OUTFIELDERS	B/T	Ht./Wt.	Born	1999 clubs	Projection
53	Abreu, Bobby	L/R	6-0/197	3-11-74	Philadelphia	Emerged as the talented high-average hitter the team had hoped for.
33	Burrell, Pat	R/R	6-4/225	10-10-76	Reading, Scranton/W.B.	First pick overall in the 1998 draft spent the fall learning to play the outfield.
25	Ducey, Rob	L/R	6-2/183	5-24-65	Philadelphia	A capable veteran backup in the outfield who showed surprising power in 1999.
5	Gant, Ron	R/R	6-0/196	3-2-65	Philadelphia	It's make-or-break for Gant; he's getting pushed by young Pat Burrell in left field.
6	Glanville, Doug	R/R	6-2/172	8-25-70	Philadelphia	Consistent .300 hitter and 30-stolen base performer: the ideal leadoff hitter.
29	Magee, Wendell	R/R	6-0/220	8-3-72	Scranton/Wilkes-Barre, Phila.	Still trying to shake the "can't hit in the majors" label.
11	Sefcik, Kevin	R/R	5-10/182	2-10-71	Philadelphia	A converted infielder who can play any outfield position and has baserunning savvy.
63	Taylor, Reggie	L/R	6-1/178	1-12-77	Reading	Speedy outfielder doesn't have a place this year in the bigs.

THE COACHING STAFF

Terry Francona, manager: He was dealt a few big blows losing Schilling and Rolen last season. The team faltered thereafter but there were enough bright spots (Glanville, Byrd, Abreu) to indicate that Francona can develop his young players and get everything out of them. He's got all the tools to rebuild this team but may not wait too long to replace the dead wait, players like Ron Gant and even Desi Relaford, with bona fide stars like Pat Burrell or Jimmy Rollins. He knows how to motivate those young players and is slowly building his roster to his strengths.

Galen Cisco: This longtime minor and major league pitching coach provides a steadying influence for his mix of young and old players. He has plenty of talent to work with in Ashby, Person, Schilling, Wolf and a good bullpen. But can these stars avoid injuries?

Chuck Cottier: He's one of three former big-league managers on a staff that provides strong support for Francona. Cottier offers advice as Francona's righthand man in the dugout.

Ramon Henderson: This 10-year member of the Phillies organization joined Philadelphia in 1998 as the bullpen coach. He had been working as a coach in the minor leagues prior to that.

Hal McRae: The former Royals star begins his fourth season as Phillies hitting coach after serving the Reds in the same capacity in 1995 and '96. McRae, who studied under former batting guru Charlie Lau, managed the Royals for three-plus seasons (1991-94). He has some great young hitters to work with.

Brad Mills: Francona's former college teammate managed four seasons in the Rockies' system. He handles first base coaching duties.

John Vukovich: This two-time interim major league manager directs traffic as the third base coach. This is his fourth season with the duty.

THE TOP NEWCOMERS

Andy Ashby: He has 31 wins over the last two seasons and should help the rest of the staff as an innings-eater and consistent starter. Ashby took a while to come into his own after mediocre seasons with the Phillies and Rockies earlier in his career. But the righthander has developed a nasty sinker and is throwing in the low-90s with great location. No worries here.

Chris Brock: Appears headed to long relief despite starting all of his 19 games last season with San Francisco. May be pressed into duty if the aged starting rotation suffers more injuries.

Mark Brownson: Typical Coors Field story so far . . . shelled and injured. Hoping to make a splash with the Phillies.

Mike Jackson: The 35-year-old reliever tied with Paul Assenmacher for the most games pitched in the '90s, and his body is starting to show it. When healthy, he's a hard thrower with a tough attitude—perfect for a closer.

Felix Martinez: Has proven he can steal bases and play several positions. But his defensive skills and attitude have been shaky, forcing his dismissal from the Royals organization. May surprise with a second chance.

THE TOP PROSPECTS

Pat Burrell: The 1998 first overall pick has been blasting his way through the minors, leaving bruised baseballs and shellshocked pitchers in his wake. He's indicated he's ready for the majors but has to make a transition from first base to the outfield. He spent time in the Arizona Fall League learning to do so. Certainly the Phillies would rather replace Ron Gant than Rico Brogna.

Doug Nickle: This Class A closer has shown durability, incredible stuff and a tough demeanor as a closer. Given the age of the key relievers in the Phillies bullpen, Nickle is being slowly groomed for the future.

Jimmy Rollins: The Phillies are very high on this young shortstop. He needs to improve his defense and mature a year or two before he's ready to handle major league action.

Anthony Shumaker: This lefthander may be forced into the rotation given Schilling's injury. But he may not be ready for it. He hasn't proved he can win consistently in the minors.

PITTSBURGH PIRATES

NATIONAL LEAGUE CENTRAL DIVISION

2000 SEASON

2000 Pirates Schedule

Home games shaded. *—All-Star Game at Turner Field (Atlanta).

March

SUN	MON	TUE	WED	THU	FRI	SAT
26	27	28	29	30	31	

April

SUN	MON	TUE	WED	THU	FRI	SAT
						1
2	3 HOU	4	5 HOU	6 HOU	7 ARI	8 ARI
9 ARI	10	11 MON	12 MON	13 MON	14 NYM	15 NYM
16 NYM	17	18 FLA	19 FLA	20 FLA	21 ATL	22 ATL
23 ATL	24	25 SD	26 SD	27 SD	28 CIN	29 CIN
30 CIN						

May

SUN	MON	TUE	WED	THU	FRI	SAT
	1 CIN	2 STL	3 STL	4 STL	5 CUB	6 CUB
7 CUB	8	9 NYM	10 NYM	11 NYM	12 MIL	13 MIL
14 MIL	15	16 CIN	17 CIN	18 CIN	19 STL	20 STL
21 STL	22	23 ARI	24 ARI	25 ARI	26 COL	27 COL
28 COL	29 FLA	30 FLA	31 FLA			

June

SUN	MON	TUE	WED	THU	FRI	SAT
				1	2 KC	3 KC
4 KC	5 DET	6 DET	7 DET	8	9 KC	10 KC
11 KC	12 ATL	13 ATL	14 ATL	15 ATL	16 FLA	17 FLA
18 FLA	19 MON	20 MON	21 MON	22 MON	23 NYM	24 NYM
25 NYM	26	27 CUB	28 CUB	29 CUB	30 PHI	

July

SUN	MON	TUE	WED	THU	FRI	SAT
						1 PHI
2 PHI	3 CUB	4 CUB	5 CUB	6	7 MIN	8 MIN
9 MIN	10	11	* 12	13 CLE	14 CLE	15 CLE
16 LA	17 LA	18 LA	19 MIL	20 MIL	21 PHI	22 PHI
23 PHI	24	25 MIL	26 MIL	27 MIL	28 SD	29 SD
30 SD	31 LA					

August

SUN	MON	TUE	WED	THU	FRI	SAT
		1 LA	2 LA	3 SF	4 SF	5 SF
6 SF	7 COL	8 COL	9 COL	10	11 ARI	12 ARI
13 ARI	14 HOU	15 HOU	16 HOU	17	18 CIN	19 CIN
20 CIN	21 STL	22 STL	23 STL	24	25 COL	26 COL
27 COL	28 SF	29 SF	30 SF	31 SF		

September

SUN	MON	TUE	WED	THU	FRI	SAT
					1 SD	2 SD
3 SD	4 LA	5 LA	6 LA	7	8 CIN	9 CIN
10 CIN	11 STL	12 STL	13 STL	14 HOU	15 HOU	16 HOU
17 HOU	18 PHI	19 PHI	20 PHI	21 MIL	22 MIL	23 MIL
24 MIL	25	26 HOU	27 HOU	28 HOU	29 CUB	30 CUB

October

SUN	MON	TUE	WED	THU	FRI	SAT
1 CUB	2	3	4	5	6	7

FRONT-OFFICE DIRECTORY

General partner ....Kevin S. McClatchy
Board of directors ....William B. Allen, Donald Beaver, Frank Brenner, Chip Ganassi, Kevin S. McClatchy, Mayor Tom Murphy, G. Ogden Nutting, William E. Springer
Chief operating officer ....Dick Freeman
Senior vice president and general manager................................Cam Bonifay
Assistant general manager/baseball operations ....John Sirignano
Assistant general manager/player personnel ....Roy Smith
Senior advisor/player personnel ....Lenny Yochim
Special assistants to the G.M. ....Chet Montgomery, Ken Parker, Willie Stargell
Vice president, finance and administration ....Jim Plake
Vice president, broadcasting and marketing ....Vic Gregovits
Vice president, communications and new ballpark development ......Steven N. Greenberg
Vice president, operations ....Dennis DaPra
Vice president, special events.......................................Nellie Briles
Controller ....David Bowman
Director of finance ....Patti Mistick
Traveling secretary ....Greg Johnson
Director of corporate sales and broadcasting.........................Mark Ferraco
Director of Florida baseball operations ....Mike Kennedy
Director of community services and sales................................Al Gordon
Director of corporate relations ....Nellie Briles
Director of human resources ....Sarah Tarosky
Director of information systems ....Terry Zeigler
Director of marketing communications.................................Mike Gordon
Director of in-game entertainment ....Eric Wolff
Director of media relations ....Jim Trdinich
Director of merchandising ....Joe Billetdeaux
Director of player development...................................Paul Tinnell
Director of community and player relations ....Kathy Guy
Director of promotions and advertising ....Rick Orienza
Director of sales ....Jim Alexander

MINOR LEAGUE AFFILIATES

Class	Team	League	Manager
AAA	Nashville	Pacific Coast	Trent Jewett
AA	Altoona	Eastern	Marty Brown
A	Lynchburg	Carolina	Tracy Woodson
A	Hickory	South Atlantic	Jay Loviglio
A	Williamsport	New York-Pennsylvania	Curtis Wilkerson
Rookie	Gulf Coast Pirates	Gulf Coast	Woody Huyke

BALLPARK INFORMATION

Ballpark (capacity, surface)
Three Rivers Stadium (47,972, artificial)
Address
600 Stadium Circle
Pittsburgh, PA 15212
Business phone
412-323-5000
Ticket information
800-BUY-BUCS
Ticket prices
$20 (field box-infield)
$19 (field box-outfield)
$18 (club box-infield)
$17 (club box-outfield)
$13 (terrace box; family box)
$10 (reserved seats)
$3 (g.a., children 14 and under)
Field dimensions (from home plate)
To left field at foul line, 335 feet
To center field, 400 feet
To right field at foul line, 335 feet
First game played
July 16, 1970 (Reds 3, Pirates 2)

ASSISTANCE STAFF

Club physician
Dr. Joseph Coroso

Team orthopedist
Dr. Jack Failla

Head trainer
Kent Biggerstaff

Equipment manager
Roger Wilson

Director of scouting
Mickey White

Scouting coordinators
Tom Barnard   Dana Brown
Mark McKnight

Special assignment scout
Jim Guinn

Latin America coordinators
Pablo Cruz (advisor)   Jose Luna

Scouting supervisors

Jason Angel	Russell Bowen
Grant Brittain	Dan Durst
Duane Gustavson	James House
Mike Kendall	Jose Luna
Greg McClain	Jon Mercurio
Jack Powell	Everett Russell
Delvy Santiago	Rob Sidwell
Charlie Sullivan	Mike Williams
Ted Williams	

BROADCAST INFORMATION

Radio: KDKA-AM (1020).
Cable TV: Fox Sports Pittsburgh.

SPRING TRAINING

Ballpark (city): McKechnie Field
(Bradenton, Fla.).
Ticket information: 941-748-4610.

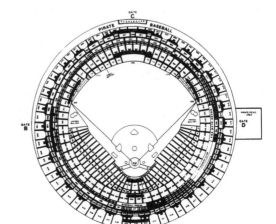

No.	PITCHERS	B/T	Ht./Wt.	Born	1999 clubs	Projection
55	Anderson, Jimmy	L/L	6-1/207	1-22-76	Nashville, Pittsburgh	He may have a future as a starter but for now is a middle reliever.
69	Arroyo, Bronson	R/R	6-5/180	2-24-77	Altoona, Nashville	He will spend this season at Nashville but could be No. 3 starter in 2001.
34	Benson, Kris	R/R	6-4/188	11-7-74	Pittsburgh	He should continue to improve in his second big-league season.
60	Boyd, Jason	R/R	6-3/173	2-23-73	Tucson, Nashville, Pittsburgh	He's the "player to be named" in the Womack trade. He'll be a setup man.
41	Christiansen, Jason	R/L	6-5/241	9-21-69	Pittsburgh, Altoona, Nashville	If he's healthy, he should be the No. 1 lefthander in the bullpen.
67	Cordova, Francisco	R/R	6-1/197	4-26-72	Pittsburgh, Nashville, Altoona	He has had a drop velocity and is no longer the No. 1 starter.
64	Garcia, Mike	R/R	6-2/220	5-11-68	Mex. City R.Devils, Nash. Pitt.	He has spent 11 years in the minors and will have a tough time making the club.
51	Loiselle, Rich	R/R	6-5/253	1-12-72	Pittsburgh	Former closer won't be ready to pitch at the start of the season.
58	O'Connor, Brian	L/L	6-2/190	1-4-77	Altoona	He should get a full season as a starter at Nashville.
53	Pena, Alex	R/R	6-2/205	9-9-77	Hickory, Altoona	Reliever still has to work on his stuff at Class AA Altoona.
31	Peters, Chris	L/L	6-1/170	1-28-72	Pittsburgh, Nashville	If his shoulder is healthy, he will compete for a spot in the rotation.
48	Ritchie, Todd	R/R	6-3/222	11-7-71	Nashville, Pittsburgh	If he can win 15 games again, it would be a major boost to the team.
47	Sauerbeck, Scott	R/L	6-3/197	11-9-71	Pittsburgh	He needs to establish consistency and prove last year wasn't a fluke.
22	Schmidt, Jason	R/R	6-5/213	1-29-73	Pittsburgh	If Schmidt cuts down his walks and home runs, he can improve on his 13 wins.
46	Schourek, Pete	L/L	6-5/220	5-10-69	Pittsburgh	He should get a chance to start because of his guaranteed contract.
56	Silva, Jose	R/R	6-5/235	12-19-73	Nashville, Pittsburgh	Potential closer is out until May after arm surgery.
39	Wallace, Jeff	L/L	6-2/238	4-12-76	Nashville, Pittsburgh	If he can control his wildness, he'll win a bullpen job.
35	Wilkins, Marc	R/R	5-11/212	10-21-70	Altoona, Nashville, Pittsburgh	He will compete for a righthanded spot in the bullpen.
43	Williams, Mike	R/R	6-2/204	7-29-68	Pittsburgh	He struggled in the second half but will get another chance.

No.	CATCHERS	B/T	Ht./Wt.	Born	1999 clubs	Projection
7	Haad, Yamid	R/R	6-2/204	9-2-77	Lynchburg, Altoona, Pittsburgh	With Jason Kendall back, he probably will be back in Nashville.
18	Kendall, Jason	R/R	6-0/195	6-26-74	Pittsburgh	If he returns to form, he's one the league's top catchers.
15	Osik, Keith	R/R	6-0/192	10-22-68	Pittsburgh, Nashville	He's a strong backup on defense but doesn't hit well.

No.	INFIELDERS	B/T	Ht./Wt.	Born	1999 clubs	Projection
10	Nunez, Abraham	B/R	5-11/185	3-16-76	Pittsburgh, Nashville	He has a chance to be the backup at shortstop.
6	Benjamin, Mike	R/R	6-0/172	11-22-65	Pittsburgh	With Meares back, he'll see less time at shortstop. But he's a good utility player.
12	Cordero, Wil	R/R	6-2/200	10-3-71	Cleveland, Akron	He could see a lot of time at third base but will also play the outfield.
25	Cruz, Ivan	L/L	6-2/219	5-3-68	Nashville, Pittsburgh, Altoona	Looks to get a job as a lefthanded hitter off the bench.
2	Meares, Pat	R/R	6-0/187	9-6-68	Pittsburgh, Nashville	Injuries limited him to 21 games in '99, but he's back as the regular shortstop.
30	Morris, Warren	L/R	5-11/179	1-11-74	Pittsburgh	Good contact hitter is coming off a strong rookie season at second.
16	Ramirez, Aramis	R/R	6-1/219	6-25-78	Nashville, Pittsburgh	Power-hitting prospect will get a chance to start at third base.
29	Young, Kevin	R/R	6-3/222	6-16-69	Pittsburgh	Young is a good power threat but could also steal 25 bases.

No.	OUTFIELDERS	B/T	Ht./Wt.	Born	1999 clubs	Projection
37	Aven, Bruce	R/R	5-9/180	3-4-72	Florida	He'll be used as a backup outfielder and used mostly in left field.
13	Brown, Adrian	B/R	6-0/185	2-7-74	Pittsburgh, Nashville	He's a valuable backup because he can play all three outfield positions well.
19	Brown, Emil	R/R	6-2/193	12-29-74	Nashville, Pittsburgh	He probably needs another year at Class AAA before he's ready for the majors.
24	Giles, Brian	L/L	5-10/200	1-20-71	Pittsburgh	He's the team's top offensive player and could hit 40 homers and drive in 120 runs.
3	Hermansen, Chad	R/R	6-2/185	9-10-77	Nashville, Pittsburgh	He should now be ready for the majors and will likely start in right field.
52	Hernandez, Alex	L/L	6-4/186	5-28-77	Altoona	He will play at Nashville this season.
28	Martin, Al	L/L	6-2/214	11-24-67	Pittsburgh	He bounced back last year and will hit leadoff and play left field.

THE COACHING STAFF

Gene Lamont, manager: Lamont became the caretaker of Pittsburgh's reconstruction program when Jim Leyland left for Florida. Lamont, who managed the White Sox for three-plus seasons from 1992-95, was the perfect choice for this low-budget operation. He's patient, maintains a realistic perspective and has a sharp eye for talent and evaluation. Lamont is quiet, but forceful. He reminds many Pittsburgh old-timers of longtime Pirates manager Danny Murtaugh.

Joe Jones: Jones begins his fourth season as Lamont's first base coach after 18 years in the Reds' organization. Jones, a former minor league manager and instructor, served one season as Kansas City's first base coach and part of another as its bench coach.

Jack Lind: After seven seasons as the Pirates' minor league coordinator of instruction, Lind returned to field duty under Lamont and has done a nice job directing traffic as the third base coach. Lind has managerial experience in the Angels' and Reds' organizations.

Lloyd McClendon: The Pirates young hitters enjoy working with McClendon, who is beginning his fourth season as hitting instructor. McClendon, an eight-year major leaguer who spent his final seasons (1990-94) with the Pirates, joined Lamont's staff after serving the organization as its minor league hitting instructor in 1996.

Rick Renick: He brings experience and success to the dugout as Lamont's bench coach. Renick spent five seasons managing at the Class AAA level after serving as the third base and hitting coach for the 1987 World Series-champion Twins.

Pete Vuckovich: The former A.L. Cy Young winner stepped out of the Pirates' front office to become one of the most respected pitching coaches in the game and the caretaker of a young staff. Vuckovich, who served as an assistant G.M. and director of player personnel in 1996, is equal parts instructor, coach and father figure for an experienced group.

Spin Williams: The only holdover from Leyland's staff, Williams begins his seventh season as the team's bullpen coach and the 19th in the organization.

THE TOP NEWCOMERS

Wil Cordero: Cordero will see time in the outfield but could also play a lot at third base depending on how rookie Aramis Ramirez performs. Cordero isn't great defensively, but he posts good offensive numbers.

THE TOP PROSPECTS

Bronson Arroyo: Arroyo will be pitching at Nashville this season but could get a September callup. He was hit hard in three starts at Class AAA last season but should do better this year. He can throw four pitches—a fastball, curveball, slider and a changeup—for strikes and could be in the middle of the Pirates' rotation next season.

Chad Hermansen: Hermansen was the team's No. 1 pick in the 1995 draft and had a September call-up last season. He has good power but needs to cut down on his strikeouts. He can play center field, but will mostly play in right field.

ST. LOUIS CARDINALS

NATIONAL LEAGUE CENTRAL DIVISION

2000 SEASON

2000 Cardinals Schedule

Home games shaded. *—All-Star Game at Turner Field (Atlanta).

March

SUN	MON	TUE	WED	THU	FRI	SAT
26	27	28	29	30	31	

April

SUN	MON	TUE	WED	THU	FRI	SAT
						1
2	3 CUB	4	5 CUB	6 CUB	7 MIL	8 MIL
9 MIL	10 HOU	11 HOU	12 HOU	13 HOU	14 COL	15 COL
16 COL	17	18 SD	19 SD	20 COL	21 COL	22 COL
23 COL	24 COL	25 MIL	26 MIL	27 MIL	28 PHI	29 PHI
30 PHI						

May

SUN	MON	TUE	WED	THU	FRI	SAT
	1	2 PIT	3 PIT	4 PIT	5 CIN	6 CIN
7 CIN	8 SF	9 SF	10 SF	11	12 LA	13 LA
14 LA	15	16 PHI	17 PHI	18 PHI	19 PIT	20 PIT
21 PIT	22	23 FLA	24 FLA	25 FLA	26 NYM	27 NYM
28 NYM	29 ARI	30 ARI	31 ARI			

June

SUN	MON	TUE	WED	THU	FRI	SAT
				1 ARI	2 CLE	3 CLE
4 CLE	5 KC	6 KC	7 KC	8	9 DET	10 DET
11 DET	12 SD	13 SD	14 SD	15	16 LA	17 LA
18 LA	19	20 SF	21 SF	22 SF	23 LA	24 LA
25 LA	26 CIN	27 CIN	28 CIN	29 CIN	30 HOU	

July

SUN	MON	TUE	WED	THU	FRI	SAT
						1 HOU
2 HOU	3	4 CIN	5 CIN	6 CIN	7 SF	8 SF
9 SF	10	11 *	12 CWS	13 CWS	14 CWS	15 CWS
16 MIN	17 MIN	18 MIN	19 ARI	20 ARI	21 HOU	22 HOU
23 HOU	24	25 ARI	26 ARI	27 ARI	28 NYM	29 NYM
30 NYM	31 MON					

August

SUN	MON	TUE	WED	THU	FRI	SAT
		1 MON	2 MON	3	4 ATL	5 ATL
6 ATL	7 FLA	8 FLA	9 FLA	10	11 MIL	12 MIL
13 MIL	14 CUB	15 CUB	16 CUB	17	18 PHI	19 PHI
20 PHI	21 PIT	22 PIT	23 PIT	24 ATL	25 ATL	26 ATL
27 ATL	28 FLA	29 FLA	30 FLA	31		

September

SUN	MON	TUE	WED	THU	FRI	SAT
					1 NYM	2 NYM
3 NYM	4 MON	5 MON	6 MON	7 MON	8 MIL	9 MIL
10 MIL	11 PIT	12 PIT	13 PIT	14 CUB	15 CUB	16 CUB
17 CUB	18	19 HOU	20 HOU	21 HOU	22 CUB	23 CUB
24 CUB	25	26 SD	27 SD	28 SD	29 CIN	30 CIN

October

SUN	MON	TUE	WED	THU	FRI	SAT
1 CIN	2	3	4	5	6	7

FRONT-OFFICE DIRECTORY

Chairman of the board/general partner ....William O. DeWitt Jr.
Chairman ....Frederick O. Hanser
Secretary-treasurer ....Andrew N. Baur
President ....Mark C. Lamping
Vice president, general manager ....Walt Jocketty
Administrative assistant to the president ....Julie Laningham
Senior executive assistant to vice president, G.M. ....Judy Carpenter-Barada
Vice president, player personnel ....Jerry Walker
Special assistant to the general manager ....Bob Gebhard
Senior vice president, sales and marketing ....Dan Farrell
Vice president, controller ....Brad Wood
Vice president, community relations ....Marty Hendin
Vice president, business development ....Bill DeWitt III
Vice president, stadium operations ....Joe Abernathy
Vice president, ticket operations ....Josie Arnold
Vice president, sales ....Kevin Wade
Director, group sales ....Joe Strohm
Manager, ticket sales ....Mark Murray
Director, corporate sales/marketing...Thane Van Breuseqen
Group director, community outreach/Cardinals Care ....Tim Hanser
Director, target marketing ....Ted Savage
Director, media relations ....Brian Bartow
Manager, media relations and publications...Steve Zesch
Assistant to director, media relations...Brad Hainje
Traveling secretary ....C.J. Cherre
Director, player development ....Mike Jorgensen
Director, player procurement ....Jeff Scott
Director, scouting operations ....John Mozeliak
Director, minor league operations..Scott Smulczenski
Manager, baseball information/player development ....John Vuch

MINOR LEAGUE AFFILIATES

Class	Team	League	Manager
AAA	Memphis	Pacific Coast	Gaylen Pitts
AA	Arkansas	Texas	Chris Maloney
A	Prince William	Carolina	Joe Cunningham
A	Peoria	Midwest	Tom Lawless
A	New Jersey	New York-Pennsylvania	Jeff Shireman
Rookie	Johnson City	Appalachian	To be announced

ASSISTANCE STAFF

Major league trainer
Barry Weinberg

Assistant major league trainer
Brad Henderson

Medical/rehabilitation coordinator
Mark O'Neal

Equipment manager
Buddy Bates

Assistant equipment manager
Rip Rowan

Special assignment scouts
Bing Devine	Marty Keough
Jim Leyland	Fred McAlister
Joe Sparks (advance scout)	
Mike Squires	

National cross-checker
Mike Roberts

Regional cross-checkers
Tim Conroy	Clark Crist

Scouts
Randy Benson	Jorge Brito
Roberto Diaz	Chuck Fick
Ben Galante	Steve Grilli
Manny Guerra	Dave Karaff
Scott Melvin	Scott Nichols
Jay North	Dan Ontiveros
Joe Rigoli	Tommy Shields
Roger Smith	Steve Turco
Dane Walker	

BROADCAST INFORMATION

Radio: KMOX-AM (1120).
TV: KPLR-TV (Channel 11).
Cable TV: Fox Sports Midwest.

SPRING TRAINING

Ballpark (city): Roger Dean Stadium (Jupiter, Fla.).
Ticket information: 561-966-3309.

BALLPARK INFORMATION

Ballpark (capacity, surface)
Busch Stadium (49,738, grass)
Address
250 Stadium Plaza
St. Louis, MO 63102
Business phone
314-421-3060
Ticket information
314-421-2400
Ticket prices
$30 (field boxes-infield)
$28 (loge boxes-infield)
$25 (field boxes-outfield)
$24 (loge boxes-outfield)
$20(terrace boxes-infield, loge reserved-infield)
$18 (loge reserved-outfield, terrace boxes-outfield)
$15 (terrace reserved-adults)
$8 (bleachers)
$7 (terrace reserved-children, upper terrace res.-adults)
$3 (upper terrace reserved-children)
Field dimensions (from home plate)
To left field at foul line, 330 feet
To center field, 402 feet
To right field at foul line, 330 feet
First game played
May 12, 1966 (Cardinals 4, Braves 3)

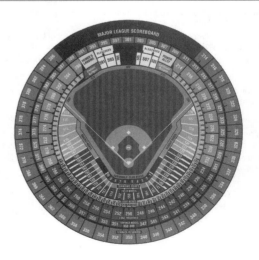

No.	PITCHERS	B/T	Ht./Wt.	Born	1999 clubs	Projection
77	Ambrose, John	R/R	6-5/180	11-1-74	Arkansas	Will start at Class AAA Memphis but could reach the majors as reliever.
30	Ankiel, Rick	L/L	6-1/210	7-19-79	Arkansas, Memphis, St. Louis	The Cardinals will be careful not overwork baseball's top lefthanded prospect.
41	Benes, Alan	R/R	6-5/235	1-21-72	Ark., Potomac, Mem., St. Louis	After missing nearly two seasons, he hopes to make 15-20 starts.
	Benes, Andy	R/R	6-6/245	8-20-67	Arizona	Was very productive in his Cardinal years (1996 and '97) and will be again.
37	Bottenfield, Kent	R/R	6-3/240	11-14-68	St. Louis	Last year's staff ace doesn't have the arm or stuff to go more than seven innings.
66	Brunette, Justin	L/L	6-2/200	10-7-75	Peoria, Arkansas	A lefthanded specialist who'll be at Memphis.
63	Hackman, Luther	R/R	6-4/195	10-10-74	Carolina, Colo. Springs, Colo.	With a good spring, could make the club as a reliever.
62	Heiserman, Rick	R/R	6-7/225	2-22-73	Memphis, St. Louis	Closer at Memphis will probably start the season in minors, but may get a call-up.
40	Hentgen, Pat	R/R	6-2/195	11-13-68	Toronto	Has struggled since winning Cy Young in '96 but throws lots of innings.
65	Hutchinson, Chad	R/R	6-5/230	2-21-77	Arkansas, Memphis	Hard-throwing righthander only needs better control to reach majors.
57	Kile, Darryl	R/R	6-5/212	12-2-68	Colorado	A change in altitude could make curveball pitcher a winner again.
70	Matthews, Mike	L/L	6-2/175	10-24-73	Buffalo, Akron, Trenton, Ark.	This lefty will probably begin the season at Memphis.
32	Mohler, Mike	R/L	6-2/208	7-26-68	St. Louis, Memphis	Lefthanded specialist had a 2.60 ERA after the 1999 All-Star break.
35	Morris, Matt	R/R	6-5/210	8-9-74	DID NOT PLAY	He could return from elbow surgery around the All-Star break.
36	Radinsky, Scott	L/L	6-3/215	3-3-68	St. Louis	Tough lefthander out of the bullpen if healthy again after elbow surgery.
58	Slocumb, Heathcliff	R/R	6-3/220	6-7-66	Baltimore, Memphis, St. Louis	Could appear in more than 70 games as a setup man.
50	Spoljaric, Paul	R/L	6-3/210	9-24-70	Philadelphia, Toronto	His ERA has been over 6.25 the last two seasons, but is another lefty in the 'pen.
55	Stephenson, Garrett	R/R	6-5/208	1-2-72	Memphis, Arkansas, St. Louis	Best bet his role will be as a spot starter and long reliever.
43	Thompson, Mark	R/R	6-2/212	4-7-71	Indianapolis, Mem., St. Louis	With a strong spring, he has a chance to be the team's No. 5 starter.
46	Veres, Dave	R/R	6-2/220	10-19-66	Colorado	New closer was 20-for-21 in save opportunities on the road for Rockies.

No.	CATCHERS	B/T	Ht./Wt.	Born	1999 clubs	Projection
26	Marrero, Eli	R/R	6-1/180	11-17-73	St. Louis	Nothing wrong with his defense but has to begin to produce on offense.
22	Matheny, Mike	R/R	6-3/205	9-22-70	Toronto	Backup does a good job of handling a pitching staff.

No.	INFIELDERS	B/T	Ht./Wt.	Born	1999 clubs	Projection
61	Haas, Chris	L/R	6-1/205	10-15-76	Memphis	Has generated good power in the minors but needs to hit for a higher average.
8	Kennedy, Adam	L/R	6-2/180	1-10-76	Memphis, St. Louis	With addition of Vina, will see a lot of playing time in the outfield.
47	McEwing, Joe	R/R	5-11/170	10-19-72	St. Louis	Tailed off after a hot first half but is a versatile bench player.
25	McGwire, Mark	R/R	6-5/250	10-1-63	St. Louis	Will try to hit at least 50 home runs for fourth consecutive season.
21	Paquette, Craig	R/R	6-0/190	3-28-69	Norfolk, St. Louis	Had 37 RBIs in 48 games for the Cards. Will play at second and in the outfield.
27	Polanco, Placido	R/R	5-10/168	10-10-75	St. Louis, Memphis	Can play second base or shortstop and hit .280 as a reserve.
3	Renteria, Edgar	R/R	6-1/180	8-7-75	St. Louis	Team's top basestealing threat will hit No. 2.
68	Richard, Chris	L/L	6-2/185	6-7-74	Arkansas, Memphis	Power-hitting first baseman will be at Memphis this season.
28	Sutton, Larry	L/L	6-0/185	5-14-70	Kansas City, GC Royals, Omaha	Reserve outfielder has failed to produce offensively in the majors.
23	Tatis, Fernando	R/R	5-10/175	1-1-75	St. Louis	Don't be surprised if he becomes the first Cardinal to join the 30-30 club.
1	Vina, Fernando	L/R	5-9/170	4-16-69	Milwaukee, Beloit	Gives team a leadoff hitter who can play Gold Glove-caliber defense at second.
64	Woolf, Jason	B/R	6-1/170	6-6-77	Arkansas	Will be at Memphis. Good speed and power to the gaps.

No.	OUTFIELDERS	B/T	Ht./Wt.	Born	1999 clubs	Projection
24	Davis, Eric	R/R	6-3/185	5-29-62	St. Louis	He has a history of making good comebacks. He'll need one after shoulder surgery.
7	Drew, J.D.	L/R	6-1/195	11-20-75	St. Louis, Memphis	Despite a rough rookie campaign, he still has 30-30 potential.
22	Howard, Thomas	B/R	6-2/205	12-11-64	Memphis, St. Louis	His bat makes him one of the team's top reserves.
16	Lankford, Ray	L/L	5-11/200	6-5-67	St. Louis	He should post better numbers after playing last season on bad knees.
15	Powell, Dante	R/R	6-2/185	8-25-73	Arizona, Tucson	He hasn't been able to duplicate good minor league production to the majors.
76	Saturria, Luis	R/R	6-2/165	7-21-76	Arkansas	His offense slumped last season and he needs more time in the minors.

THE COACHING STAFF

Tony La Russa, manager: La Russa, who is entering his fifth season as St. Louis' manager and 21st season overall, leads all active managers with 1,639 victories. Despite a successful career that has included five division title with three different teams, La Russa has something to prove this season. He hasn't taken St. Louis to the postseason since '96 and the club is 231-254 the last three years. La Russa is still considered a good strategist, but he hasn't been able to overcome injuries to his team. La Russ hopes the offseason upgrades to the pitching staff will prevent him from having to move over his relievers to the rotation.

Mark DeJohn: DeJohn has been in the Cardinals organization since 1986 and has been on the major league coaching staff since 1996. He has managed minor league teams for the Tigers, Royals and Cardinals.

Dave Duncan: The Duncan-La Russa relationship goes back to 1983 with the White Sox. When La Russa went to Oakland, Duncan went with him and helped mold the A's pitching staff into one of the A.L.'s best. Duncan has history of resurrecting pitchers' careers and he'll get the chance to do so again this season.

Mike Easler: This is Easler's second season as hitting coach, and he'll have the tough task of cutting down on the team's 1,202 strikeouts.

Marty Mason: Mason is the team's new bullpen coach. He's been in the organization 14 seasons, the last three as pitching coach at Class AAA.

Dave McKay: This is McKay's 14th season as a coach on Tony La Russa's staff. He has been La Russa's first base coach since 1989.

Jose Oquendo: Oquendo, who played for the Cardinals in the 1980s, is in his second season on the major league staff.

THE TOP NEWCOMERS

Andy Benes: The final piece of the starting pitching puzzle that St. Louis general manager Walt Jocketty has put together for this season. Benes was dependable and productive in his two Cardinal seasons, and he enjoyed playing in St. Louis. In 1998, he was the ace of the Diamondbacks staff. By the close of the '99 season, he was their No. 4, though his stuff hadn't diminished.

Pat Hentgen: At the very least, Hentgen should eat up a lot of innings. However, the Cards think he could be a 15-game winner again and even emerge as the staff ace. He still has the stuff, a low-90s fastball with a nasty curveball.

Darryl Kile: Kile's curveball should be much more effective away from Colorado and he could return to the form that made him a 19-game winner in 1997.

Dave Veres: Veres has been a full-time closer for only one season but his split-finger fastball should serve him well in St. Louis.

Fernando Vina: The Cardinals haven't had a second baseman with Vina's defensive ability since the 1980s. He also fills St. Louis' hole at the top of the order.

THE TOP PROSPECTS

Rick Ankiel: Ankiel is expected to be a big part of the pitching rotation. He has the ability to blow away batters with his fastball, fool batters with a slow curve or jam righthanded hitters with a hard slider. He is still learning command of the strike zone.

Chad Hutchison: Hutchison throws a mid-90s fastball and an above-average slider. He'll start the season at Class AAA Memphis and should be in the 2001 rotation.

Adam Kennedy: Kennedy has hit well at every level he's played but he may not have the defense to play second. He will likely fill in at several different positions this year, most notably second base and the outfield.

SAN DIEGO PADRES

NATIONAL LEAGUE WEST DIVISION

2000 SEASON

2000 Padres Schedule

Home games shaded. *—All-Star Game at Turner Field (Atlanta).

March

SUN	MON	TUE	WED	THU	FRI	SAT
26	27	28	29	30	31	

April

SUN	MON	TUE	WED	THU	FRI	SAT
						1
2	3 NYM	4	5 NYM	6 NYM	7 MON	8 MON
9 MON	10 ARI	11 ARI	12 ARI	13 HOU	14 HOU	15 HOU
16 HOU	17	18 STL	19 STL	20 STL	21 HOU	22 HOU
23 HOU	24	25 PIT	26 PIT	27 PIT	28 ATL	29 ATL
30 ATL						

May

SUN	MON	TUE	WED	THU	FRI	SAT
	1 FLA	2 FLA	3 FLA	4	5 ARI	6 ARI
7 ARI	8	9 CIN	10 CIN	11 CIN	12 ARI	13 ARI
14 ARI	15	16 FLA	17 FLA	18 FLA	19 ATL	20 ATL
21 ATL	22 NYM	23 NYM	24 NYM	25	26 MON	27 MON
28 MON	29 MIL	30 MIL	31 MIL			

June

SUN	MON	TUE	WED	THU	FRI	SAT
				1	2 SEA	3 SEA
4 SEA	5 OAK	6 OAK	7 OAK	8	9 HOU	10 HOU
11 HOU	12 STL	13 STL	14 STL	15	16 CIN	17 CIN
18 CIN	19 ARI	20 ARI	21 ARI	22	23 CIN	24 CIN
25 CIN	26 LA	27 LA	28 LA	29 LA	30 COL	

July

SUN	MON	TUE	WED	THU	FRI	SAT
						1 COL
2 COL	3 COL	4 LA	5 LA	6 LA	7 TEX	8 TEX
9 TEX	10	11	* 12	13 SEA	14 SEA	15 SEA
16 ANA	17 ANA	18 ANA	19 SF	20 SF	21 COL	22 COL
23 COL	24 SF	25 SF	26 SF	27	28 PIT	29 PIT
30 PIT	31 PHI					

August

SUN	MON	TUE	WED	THU	FRI	SAT
		1 PHI	2 PHI	3 CUB	4 CUB	5 CUB
6 CUB	7 PHI	8 PHI	9 PHI	10 FLA	11 FLA	12 FLA
13 FLA	14 ATL	15 ATL	16 ATL	17	18 MON	19 MON
20 MON	21 NYM	22 NYM	23 NYM	24	25 MIL	26 MIL
27 MIL	28 CUB	29 CUB	30 CUB	31 CUB		

September

SUN	MON	TUE	WED	THU	FRI	SAT
					1 PIT	2 PIT
3 PIT	4 MIL	5 MIL	6 MIL	7 SF	8 SF	9 SF
10 SF	11 COL	12 COL	13 COL	14	15 SF	16 SF
17 SF	18	19 COL	20 COL	21 COL	22 LA	23 LA
24 LA	25	26 STL	27 STL	28 STL	29 LA	30 LA

October

SUN	MON	TUE	WED	THU	FRI	SAT
1 LA	2	3	4	5	6	7

FRONT-OFFICE DIRECTORY

Chairman ....John Moores
President and chief executive officer ....Larry Lucchino
Executive vice president/chief operating officer ....Jack McGrory
Senior vice president, public affairs............................Charles Steinberg
Senior vice president, baseball operations and general manager ....Kevin Towers
Vice president, corporate development ....Michael Dee
Vice president, special counsel ....Bob Vizas
Vice president, finance...Bob Wells
Vice president, community relations ....Michele Anderson
Vice president, Hispanic and multicultural marketing ....Enrique Morones
Assistant general manager ....Fred Uhlman Jr.
Director, merchandising..Michael Babida
Controller ....Steve Fitch
Director, administrative services ....Lucy Freeman
Director, ticket operations and services ....Dave Gilmore
Director, stadium operations.......................................Mark Guglielmo
Director, player development..Tye Waller
Director, minor league operations ....Priscilla Oppenheimer
Director/team travel ....Brian Prilaman
Director, public relations ....Glenn Geffner
Director, fan services..Tim Katzman
Director, scouting ....Brad Sloan

MINOR LEAGUE AFFILIATES

Class	Team	League	Manager
AAA	Las Vegas	Pacific Coast	Duane Espy
AA	Mobile	Southern	Mike Basso
A	Rancho Cucamonga	California	Tom Le Vasseur
A	Fort Wayne	Midwest	Craig Colbert
Rookie	Idaho Falls	Pioneer	Don Werner
Rookie	Peoria Padres	Arizona	Howard Bushong

BROADCAST INFORMATION

Radio: KOGO-AM (600), KURS-AM (1040, Spanish).
TV: KUSI (Channel 9).
Cable TV: Channel 4 Padres.

SPRING TRAINING

Ballpark (city): Peoria Stadium (Peoria, Ariz.).
Ticket information: 623-878-4337, 800-409-1511.

ASSISTANCE STAFF

Trainer
Todd Hutcheson

Assistant trainer
Jim Daniel

Strength and conditioning coach
Sam Gannelli

Club physicians

Cliff Colwell	Jan Fronek
Paul Hirshman	Blaine Phillips

Major League scouts

Ken Bracey	Ray Crone Sr.
Moose Johnson	

Advance scout
Jeff Gardner

International scouting supervisor
Bill Clark

Professional scouts

Chas Bolton	Rich Hacker
Ben McLure	Gary Roenicke
Van Smith	

Full-time scouts

Miguel Blanco	Joe Bochy
Rich Bordi	Bob Buob
Julio Coronado	Bob Cummings
Takeo Daigo	Lane Decker
Jimmy Dreyer	Leroy Dreyer
Ronquito Garcia	Robert Gutierrez
Chris Gwynn	Andy Hancock
Timothy Harkness	Mike Keenan
William Killian	Steve Leavitt
Don Lyle	Jose Martinez
Tim McWilliam	Juan Melo
Darryl Milne	Rene Mons
Gary Nickels	Chuck Pierce
Jack Pierce	Gene Thompson
Mark Wasinger	Jim Woodward

BALLPARK INFORMATION

Ballpark (capacity, surface)
Qualcomm Stadium (56,133, grass)
Address
P.O. Box 2000
San Diego, CA 92112-2000
Business phone
619-881-6500
Ticket information
888-723-7379
Ticket prices
$18 (club level, field level, IF)
$16 (plaza level/IF)
$14 (plaza level, loge level)
$11 (press level)
$8 (grandstand)
$7 (view level/IF)
$6 (view level)
$5 (RF & LF bleachers, view level)
Field dimensions (from home plate)
To left field at foul line, 327 feet
To center field, 405 feet
To right field at foul line, 330 feet
First game played
April 8, 1969 (Padres 2, Astros 1)

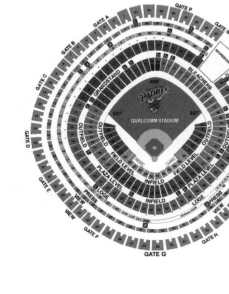

No.	PITCHERS	B/T	Ht./Wt.	Born	1999 clubs	Projection
40	Almanzar, Carlos	R/R	6-2/200	11-6-73	Las Vegas, San Diego	He'll get looks as a starter due to his hard fastball but will be back in the bullpen.
37	Boehringer, Brian	B/R	6-2/190	1-8-70	San Diego	Offseason shoulder surgery won't likely keep him out of the starting rotation.
58	Carlyle, Buddy	L/R	6-3/175	12-21-77	Las Vegas, San Diego	This lefty will need a break to get into the rotation, otherwise it's back to Las Vegas.
31	Clement, Matt	R/R	6-3/195	8-12-74	San Diego	Learned a lot his debut season, now he's ready to be a 15-game winner.
39	Cunnane, Will	R/R	6-2/175	4-24-74	Las Vegas, San Diego	Should be back in the bullpen and shuffled again between the bigs and Las Vegas.
43	Guzman, Domingo	R/R	6-0/210	4-5-75	Mobile, San Diego	This kid throws hard, but it's straight as an arrow. Will go back to the minors.
41	Hitchcock, Sterling	L/L	6-1/192	4-29-71	San Diego	Padres may be looking to deal him. If not, he's their ace.
51	Hoffman, Trevor	R/R	6-0/205	10-13-67	San Diego	Still one of the top relievers in the game, but doesn't get many save opportunities.
46	Loewer, Carlton	R/R	6-6/211	9-24-73	Phila., GC Phillies, Clearwater	Suffered a broken leg in January and is expected to be out until July.
60	Lopez, Rodrigo	R/R	6-1/180	12-14-75	Mobile	Will start back in Mobile and continue working his way up the minor league chain.
34	Meadows, Brian	R/R	6-4/200	11-21-75	Florida	This finesse righthander should be in the rotation with a chance to improve.
27	Montgomery, Steve	R/R	6-4/200	12-25-70	Scranton/W.B., Philadelphia	Opponents hit just .203 against him after the All-Star break.
48	Myers, Randy	L/L	6-1/210	9-19-62	DID NOT PLAY	He has to prove his shoulder is recovered from surgery; he needs his velocity.
	Serafini, Daniel	R/L	6-3/210	1-25-74	Chicago N.L., Iowa	Was shelled with the Cubs before being demoted back to Class AAA.
64	Serrano, Wascar	R/R	6-2/178	6-2-78	Mobile, Rancho Cucamonga	Will start out in Class AA and is at least a year away.
36	Wall, Donne	R/R	6-1/205	7-11-67	San Diego	Has been a good fit in the Padres' bullpen. Surprisingly tough on lefties.
50	Whisenant, Matt	R/L	6-3/215	6-8-71	Kansas City, San Diego	A true power lefty, Whisenant must improve his control problems.
18	Williams, Woody	R/R	6-0/195	8-19-66	San Diego	He finished last season strong and should be a 15-game winner.

No.	CATCHERS	B/T	Ht./Wt.	Born	1999 clubs	Projection
13	Davis, Ben	B/R	6-4/215	3-10-77	Las Vegas, San Diego	Scouts loved this kid's build and talent. Has a great arm and is a switch hitter.
7	Gonzalez, Wikie	R/R	5-11/203	5-17-74	Mobile, Las Vegas, San Diego	A long-term project, easily behind Davis and Hernandez.
9	Hernandez, Carlos	R/R	5-11/215	5-24-67	DID NOT PLAY	Despite missing all of last season with an Achilles' injury, he's the starter.

No.	INFIELDERS	B/T	Ht./Wt.	Born	1999 clubs	Projection
24	Boone, Bret	R/R	5-10/180	4-6-69	Atlanta	Returns home to Southern California and should provide stability at second base.
10	Gomez, Chris	R/R	6-1/195	6-16-71	San Diego, Las Vegas	A consistent defensive player, but with limited offensive capabilities.
2	Jackson, Damian	R/R	5-11/185	8-6-73	San Diego	His blazing speed should get him into the lineup, but where? His OBP is too low.
18	Klesko, Ryan	L/L	6-3/220	6-12-71	Atlanta	Klesko hasn'tcompletely lived up to his potential but a change of scenery might help.
12	Magadan, Dave	L/R	6-4/215	9-30-62	San Diego	The veteran infielder figures to be a backup but will be used as a pinch-hitter often.
23	Nevin, Phil	R/R	6-2/231	1-19-71	Las Vegas, San Diego	Will hit cleanup and play third base again for the Padres.
14	Newhan, David	L/R	5-10/180	9-7-73	Las Vegas, San Diego	Can play all infield positions and hits lefthanded. That'll keep him in the bigs.

No.	OUTFIELDERS	B/T	Ht./Wt.	Born	1999 clubs	Projection
26	Darr, Mike	L/R	6-3/205	3-21-76	Las Vegas, San Diego	This muscular lefty should start the season in Class AAA.
25	Dehaan, Kory	L/R	6-2/187	7-16-76	Lynchburg, Altoona	May be awhile before this 23-year-old is a contributor but he's in the plans.
19	Gwynn, Tony	L/L	5-11/220	5-9-60	San Diego	Injuries have slowed him, and will continue to, but he's still a hitting machine.
21	Matthews Jr., Gary	B/R	6-3/200	8-25-74	Las Vegas, San Diego	He has been decimated by injuries in the minors, but he's still a prospect.
8	Owens, Eric	R/R	6-0/198	2-3-71	San Diego	He got a lot of at-bats (466) last season just filling in for injured regulars.
28	Rivera, Ruben	R/R	6-3/200	11-14-73	San Diego	His .195 average last season was a disappointment, but he's still only 26.
53	Tucci, Peter	R/R	6-2/205	10-8-75	Mobile	He came over in the Woody Williams trade. He won't be a factor quite yet.
29	Vander Wal, John	L/L	6-2/197	4-29-66	San Diego	One of the best lefty pinch hitters around. Unfortunately, that means he doesn't start.

THE COACHING STAFF

Bruce Bochy, manager: He's had some poor Padres teams to work with but he always make them competitive. He did a wonderful job with the talented 1998 club that went to the World Series and even worked through injuries, new personnel and lack of talent to put an overachieving club on the field last season. A 14-game win streak last season had the baseball world stunned. He is a mainstay here and deserves to be.

Greg Booker: After five years as a pitching coach within the Indians organization, Booker is begining his third season as bullpen coach for the Padres. He's got some good arms to work with, but they're young.

Tim Flannery: The former Padres infielder begins his fifth season as the third base coach under Bochy. Flannery previously worked three seasons as a minor league manager.

Ben Ogilvie: Ogilvie was hired in the offseason to replace Merv Rettenmund, who is now in Atlanta, as hitting coach. The knock on Rettenmund was that his hitters were too passive, the former Brewer, Tiger and Red Sox outfielder should be able to improve that with these young hitters.

Rob Picciolo: He's beginning his 15th year in the Padres organization, his seventh as the team's bench coach. Picciolo, a former big-league infielder, also has been the team's first base coach.

Dave Smith: The Padres' pitching coach had a quite a tough task last season: following Dave Stewart and taking over a suspect pitching staff. Stewart had certainly left his mark on the pitching staff, bringing a certain amount of toughness and attitude to a formerly passive squad. But those players' careers who have turned around due to his guidance are slowly leaving, like Ashby and Hamilton. Smith will have to pass the attitude on to his new personnel.

Alan Trammell: Trammell takes over as first base coach in his first season with the Padres. The former Tiger shortstop originally from Southern California stole 212 bases in his career, and the smart player has plenty to pass on.

THE TOP NEWCOMERS

Bret Boone: At 30, Boone is in his prime. He's a Gold Glove second baseman, a durable player, a .280-plus hitter and a probable 20-homer, 90-RBI guy. A little more speed, and he'd still be a Brave.

Ryan Klesko: His defense is suspect at best at first base, but a chance to play everyday without the threat of being overtaken should help Klesko. His inability to hit lefthanders may have been caused by the fact that he has been kept from facing them for much of his career. The sky's the limit for this lefthander, and he still has 40-homer, 110-RBI potential.

Carlton Loewer: An injury-plagued career was just made worse when he fell from a deer blind while hunting in Louisiana in January. He suffered a broken leg and is projected to be sidelined until July. Not good news for the Padres, who counted on him to fire 200-plus innings and win in double figures.

Brian Meadows: Acquired in an offseason trade with Florida, Meadows has clearly inferior stuff but a winning attitude. He allowed a lot of hits in his two years as a starter with Florida and doesn't strike out a lot of hitters. Yet he found a way to stay in games and his .440 winning percentage is not nearly as bad as the team's .364 percentage the last two years.

Steve Montgomery: Montgomery showed real promise for the Phillies last season. He should be the setup man for the Padres.

THE TOP PROSPECTS

Adam Eaton: Not on the 40-man roster yet, but a key cog in the Andy Ashby trade with Philadelphia. The Padres management have labeled him as a potential ace with incredible stuff. He'll start the year in the minors, but might be with the staff sometime after the All-Star break.

Wikie Gonzalez: He's stuck behind Carlos Hernandez and the heralded Ben Davis at catcher, but this youngster's maturity and defensive skills keep him in consideration. He has a very quick release and has baserunners thinking twice about trying to steal. His bat still needs to come around.

Gary Mathews Jr.: He's actually been a prospect for the last few years, but injuries have kept him from showing off his talent. And he's got plenty of it. He's a switch-hitter with decent speed and good glovework. Still, he'll start in the minors and probably won't be a star this year.

SAN FRANCISCO GIANTS

NATIONAL LEAGUE WEST DIVISION

2000 SEASON

2000 Giants Schedule

Home games shaded. *—All-Star Game at Turner Field (Atlanta).

March

SUN	MON	TUE	WED	THU	FRI	SAT
26	27	28	29	30	31	

April

SUN	MON	TUE	WED	THU	FRI	SAT
						1
2	3 FLA	4 FLA	5 FLA	6 FLA	7 ATL	8 ATL
9 ATL	10	11 LA	12 LA	13 LA	14 ARI	15 ARI
16 ARI	17	18 CIN	19 CIN	20 CIN	21 ARI	22 ARI
23 ARI	24	25 FLA	26 FLA	27	28 MON	29 MON
30 MON						

May

SUN	MON	TUE	WED	THU	FRI	SAT
	1 NYM	2 NYM	3 NYM	4 NYM	5 COL	6 COL
7 COL	8 STL	9 STL	10 STL	11	12 COL	13 COL
14 COL	15	16 ATL	17 ATL	18 ATL	19 MIL	20 MIL
21 MIL	22	23 MON	24 MON	25 MON	26 CUB	27 CUB
28 CUB	29 PHI	30 PHI	31 PHI			

June

SUN	MON	TUE	WED	THU	FRI	SAT
				1	2 OAK	3 OAK
4 OAK	5 ANA	6 ANA	7 ANA	8	9 SEA	10 SEA
11 SEA	12 CIN	13 CIN	14 CIN	15	16 HOU	17 HOU
18 HOU	19	20 STL	21 STL	22 STL	23 HOU	24 HOU
25 HOU	26 COL	27 COL	28 COL	29 COL	30 LA	

July

SUN	MON	TUE	WED	THU	FRI	SAT
						1 LA
2 LA	3	4 COL	5 COL	6 COL	7 STL	8 STL
9 STL	10	11	* 12	13 OAK	14 OAK	15 OAK
16 TEX	17 TEX	18 TEX	19 SD	20 SD	21 LA	22 LA
23 LA	24 SD	25 SD	26 SD	27	28 CUB	29 CUB
30 CUB	31 MIL					

August

SUN	MON	TUE	WED	THU	FRI	SAT
		1 MIL	2 MIL	3 PIT	4 PIT	5 PIT
6 PIT	7 MIL	8 MIL	9 MIL	10	11 NYM	12 NYM
13 NYM	14 NYM	15 MON	16 MON	17 MON	18 ATL	19 ATL
20 ATL	21 FLA	22 FLA	23 FLA	24	25 PHI	26 PHI
27 PHI	28 PIT	29 PIT	30 PIT	31 PIT		

September

SUN	MON	TUE	WED	THU	FRI	SAT
					1 CUB	2 CUB
3 CUB	4 PHI	5 PHI	6 PHI	7 SD	8 SD	9 SD
10 SD	11 HOU	12 HOU	13 HOU	14	15 SD	16 SD
17 SD	18 CIN	19 CIN	20 CIN	21 ARI	22 ARI	23 ARI
24 LA	25	26 LA	27 LA	28 ARI	29 ARI	30 ARI

October

SUN	MON	TUE	WED	THU	FRI	SAT
1 ARI	2	3	4	5	6	7

FRONT-OFFICE DIRECTORY

President and managing general partner ....Peter A. Magowan
Executive vice president/chief operating officer.........................Larry Baer
Senior vice president and general manager ....Brian Sabean
Special assistant to the general manager ....Ron Perranoski
Vice president and assistant general manager...........................Ned Colletti
Vice president of player personnel ....Dick Tidrow
Director of player development ....Jack Hiatt
Coordinator of International operations ....Rick Ragazzo
Senior vice president and chief financial officer ....John Yee
Senior vice president, ballpark operations/security....................Jorge Costa
Vice president, communications ....Bob Rose
Senior vice president, corporate marketing ....Mario Alioto
Senior vice president, consumer marketing...........................Tom McDonald
General manager, retail...Connie Kullberg
Director of ballpark operations..Gene Telucci
Vice president, ticket services ....Russ Stanley
Director of travel ....Reggie Younger Jr.
Senior vice president and general counsel ....Jack Bair
Media relations manager...Jim Moorehead

MINOR LEAGUE AFFILIATES

Class	Team	League	Manager
AAA	Fresno	Pacific Coast	Shane Turner
AA	Shreveport	Texas	Bill Hayes
A	San Jose	California	Keith Comstock
A	Bakersfield	California	Lenn Sakata
Rookie	Salem-Keizer	Northwest	Fred Stanley
Rookie	Giants	Arizona	To be announced

BROADCAST INFORMATION

Radio: KNBR-AM (680).
TV: KTVU-TV (Channel 2).
Cable TV: Fox Sports Net.

SPRING TRAINING

Ballpark (city): Scottsdale Stadium (Scottsdale, Ariz.).
Ticket information: 602-990-7972, 602-784-4444.

ASSISTANCE STAFF

National cross-checker
Randy Waddill

Eastern cross-checker
Paul Turco

Western cross-checker
Doug Mapson

Major league advance scout
Pat Dobson

Major league scout
Cal Emery

Special assignment scouts
Joe DiCarlo   Stan Saleski
Bob Hartsfield

Scouts
Mateo Alou, Steve Arnieri, Jose Cassino, Dick Cole, Joe DiCarlo, Pat Dobson, Charlie Gonzales, Tom Korenek, Doug Mapson, Alan Marr, Doug McMillan, Bobby Myrick, Matt Nerland, Bo Osborne, Luis Pena, Carlos Ramirez, Stan Saleski, Bienvenido Sanchez, John Shafer, Joe Strain, Todd Thomas, Alex Torres, Glenn Tufts, Paul Turco, Ciro Villalobos, Randy Waddill, Darren Wittcke, Tom Zimmer

BALLPARK INFORMATION

Ballpark (capacity, surface)
Pacific Bell Park (To be announced)

Address
24 Willie Mays Plaza
San Francisco, CA 94107

Business phone
415-972-2000

Ticket information
To be announced

Ticket prices
$23 (lower box)
$18 (view box)
$18 (arcade)
$15 (view reserved)
$10 (bleachers)

Field dimensions (from home plate)
To left field at foul line, 335 feet
To center field, 400 feet
To right field at foul line, 328 feet

First game played
Scheduled for April 11, 2000 vs. Los Angeles

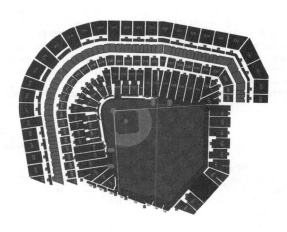

No.	PITCHERS	B/T	Ht./Wt.	Born	1999 clubs	Projection
37	Del Toro, Miguel	R/R	6-1/180	6-22-72	San Francisco, Fresno	Strong September gives him a shot at the big-league roster.
56	Embree, Alan	L/L	6-2/190	1-23-70	San Francisco	Hard thrower is one of the top lefthanded setup men around.
55	Estes, Shawn	L/L	6-2/192	2-18-73	San Francisco	If he can get his command back, he's a top-notch pitcher. That's a big "if" though.
26	Gardner, Mark	R/R	6-1/220	3-1-62	San Francisco, San Jose	Age may have caught up to him. Started badly and finished in the bullpen.
61	Hernandez, Livan	R/R	6-2/225	2-20-75	Florida, San Francisco	With a full season in San Francisco, he should win 11-13 games.
49	Johnstone, John	R/R	6-3/210	11-25-68	San Francisco	Will appear in 70 games as team's top righthanded setup man.
	Maurer, David	R/L	6-2/205	2-23-75	Mobile	Owns a 3.08 ERA in 127 minor league appearances, but needs time at Class AAA.
36	Nathan, Rob	R/R	6-4/195	11-22-74	Shreveport, San Fran., Fresno	After impressive debut season, he will get a chance to be a full-time starter.
31	Nen, Robb	R/R	6-5/215	11-28-69	San Francisco	He'll be ready for 2000 after elbow surgery, but will lose his job if not consistent.
48	Ortiz, Russ	R/R	6-1/210	6-5-74	San Francisco	Won 18 games in his first full season. Needs to cut down his walks.
	Ray, Ken	R/R	6-2/200	11-27-74	Wichita, Omaha, Kansas City	Has saved some games in the minors the last few years but his ERA was high.
47	Rodriguez, Felix	R/R	6-1/190	12-5-72	San Francisco	Has a live arm, but does not have the mental makeup to be a closer or starter.
46	Rueter, Kirk	L/L	6-3/205	12-1-70	San Francisco	Has won 31 games the last two seasons despite high ERAs. His luck could run out.

No.	CATCHERS	B/T	Ht./Wt.	Born	1999 clubs	Projection
5	Estalella, Bobby	R/R	6-1/205	8-23-74	Clearwater, Scran./W.B., Phila.	Acquired from the Phillies to fill spot until Chiaramonte is ready to take over.
33	Mirabelli, Doug	R/R	6-1/218	10-18-70	Fresno, San Francisco	A good hitter, Mirabelli could give Estalella a run for playing time behind the plate.
51	Torrealba, Yorvit	R/R	5-11/180	7-19-78	Shreveport, Fresno, San Jose	Decent hitter will get a look only if the team carries three catchers.

No.	INFIELDERS	B/T	Ht./Wt.	Born	1999 clubs	Projection
35	Aurilia, Rich	R/R	6-1/185	9-2-71	San Francisco	Quietly hit 22 home runs last year and has the ability to do it again.
18	Canizaro, Jay	R/R	5-9/178	7-4-73	Fresno, San Francisco	Hit well in September. Could be Kent's backup, but will have to have a good spring.
52	Castro, Nelson	R/R	5-10/190	6-4-76	Lake Elsinore	Outstanding speed (53 SB last year) but has not played above Class A.
57	Crespo, Felipe	B/R	5-11/200	3-5-73	Fresno	Switch-hitter will probably play in the minors and be called up as needed.
62	Delgado, Wilson	B/R	5-11/160	7-15-75	Fresno, San Francisco	Shortstop of the future could back up Aurilia, but needs time starting.
53	Feliz, Pedro	R/R	6-1/195	4-27-77	Shreveport	Solid infielder with power, but expect him to spend another year in the minors.
21	Kent, Jeff	R/R	6-1/205	3-7-68	San Francisco	Consistently slowed by injuries, but the second baseman hits for average and power.
34	Martinez, Ramon E.	R/R	6-1/187	10-10-72	San Francisco, Fresno	Struggled early as Kent's backup, but improved enough to get another chance.
22	Minor, Damon	L/L	6-7/230	1-9-75	Shreveport	Distant power prospect had a good year, but still needs some polish.
32	Mueller, Bill	B/R	5-10/180	3-17-71	San Francisco, Fresno	Will be the Giants No. 2 hitter, and will hit .290-.300 as usual.
6	Snow, J.T.	L/L	6-2/205	2-26-68	San Francisco	Should be healthy and have good numbers again—.280, 25 home runs, 90 RBIs.

No.	OUTFIELDERS	B/T	Ht./Wt.	Born	1999 clubs	Projection
7	Benard, Marvin	L/L	5-9/185	1-20-70	San Francisco	Did well in first full season as a leadoff hitter, but should cut down strikeouts.
25	Bonds, Barry	L/L	6-2/210	7-24-64	San Francisco	Season ended with October knee surgery; will be healthy and productive in 2000.
23	Burks, Ellis	R/R	6-2/205	9-11-64	San Francisco	Despite offseason surgery on both knees, expect a 30-homer season from Burks.
8	Murray, Calvin	R/R	5-11/190	7-30-71	Fresno, San Francisco	Strong all-around prospect will be the fifth outfielder. Hits for power and average.
1	Rios, Armando	L/L	5-9/185	9-13-71	Fresno, San Francisco	Impressive hitter will be an asset if any injuries occur. Hit .327 last year in 150 ABs.

THE COACHING STAFF

Dusty Baker, manager: Players like to play for Baker, who, now in his eighth season, has a reputation for getting the most out of his players. His methods are often unorthodox but his teams always seem to be in contention against more talented and higher-priced clubs. He likes to have a reliable bullpen and is quick to go to it if a starter looks shaky. Baker's relief corps is consistently among the best, and the Giants get a lot of come-from-behind wins because of it. He also demands that his hitters be disciplined, and usually puts out a lineup heavy on walks—another way to get the most out of limited talent.

Gene Clines: Clines joined Baker's staff as hitting and outfield coach for the 1997 season and under his tutelage, the Giants have ranked in the top four in the N.L. in runs scored each of his first four seasons. He has served as a major league coach for 13 years.

Sonny Jackson: Jackson returned to the third base coaching box last year after spending 1998 as a bench coach while recovering from knee surgery. Prior to joining the Giants in 1996, he spent the previous 19 years as a manager, coach, instructor and scout within the Braves' organization.

Juan Lopez: This will be Lopez's 11th campaign in the Giants' organization and his third year on the major league level. He was elevated to full-time coach status, last season serving as bullpen coach as well as handling the catching corps.

Dave Righetti: Righetti, one of the great relievers of the 1980s, finished his career in San Francisco with two seasons in 1991-92. He replaces Ron Perranoski, another former reliever, as the pitching coach. He'll do his best with this veteran staff.

Robby Thompson: He's a former Giants All-Star who will join Baker's staff for his first season. He'll coach first base.

Ron Wotus: Enters his second season as the Giants' bench coach and his 11th year in the Giants organization, including seven as a manager in the farm system (1991-97). Wotus was twice won Manager of the Year awards while posting a 554-412 (.574) overall record in the minors.

THE TOP NEWCOMERS

Bobby Estalella: He strikes out a lot, but Estalella, locked behind Mike Lieberthal in Philadelphia, has power potential and can really turn on those fastballs. He is a decent defensive catcher, possessing a good arm but slow feet.

Ken Ray: Hopes to get another chance for redemption after pitching for Kansas City's horrendous bullpen last season.

THE TOP PROSPECTS

Giuseppe Chiarmonte: He may get limited big-league action this year, but Chiarmonte won't likely be the Giants' catcher until 2001. Chiarmonte has a good head for catching and has worked with most of the team's young pitchers. He also has power, but needs time to work on reducing strikeouts and improving his footwork.

Scott Linebrink: He struggled last season while recovering from shoulder surgery, going 1-8 with a 6.44 ERA. But if he rebounds early this season, he might get a chance to crack the Giants' rotation by the end of the season.

Joe Nathan: The team has a spot reserved in the rotation for Nathan after an impressive debut. He allowed just two earned runs in his first two starts. He finished 7-3 with a 4.09 ERA as a starter and the team is hoping he can win 10 games this year.

Armando Rios: He's getting into his prime years, but Rios is still stuck behind the Giants' big-name outfielders. Still, he's a good hitter and works well as the team's fourth outfielder. He hit .327 with seven homers and 19 RBIs in his limited time, mostly as a pinch hitter, last season.

1999 IMPORTANT DATES

January 4-14—Period in which a player may make submission to arbitration.

January 8—The last day for former clubs to re-sign players who refused arbitration.

January 18—Office of the Commissioner and MLBPA will exchange salary arbitration filing figures.

January 20-21—Office of the Commissioner and MLBPA will schedule arbitration hearing dates.

January 31-February 18—Salary arbitration hearings held.

February 18—The first date in which injured players, pitchers and catchers may be invited to attend spring training workouts.

February 23—The first date all other players may be invited to attend spring training workouts.

March 1—The mandatory date players are required to report for first spring training workout.

March 2—The first date to renew contracts. The 10-day renewal period ends on March 11.

March 9—The first date clubs may ask waivers on draft-excluded players acquired after August 15, 1999, or players chosen in the 1999 Rule 5 draft. Special waivers are required for all outright assignments to the National Association from September 1, 1999, through May 2, 2000.

March 14—The first date that draft-excluded/selected players may be assigned to a National Association club.

March 15—Unconditional release waivers requested today until 2 p.m. (EDT) March 29 will owe 45 days termination pay.

March 16—The first date that draft-excluded/selected players may be assigned to a National Association club.

March 18—The last day to assign an injured player to a National Association club until the close of the championship season provided that: the player has less than three years of Major League service; the assignment would not be the player's second career outright since 3-19-90; the player had no Major League service prior to the season; the player was not selected by the assignor Major League team in the immediately preceding Rule 5 draft.

March 29—The last date to request unconditional release waivers by 2 p.m. (EDT) without incurring full-season salary.

April 3—The official opening of the 2000 championship season. All clubs are required to cut down to 25 players by midnight, April 2, and transmit rosters to the league office by noon on April 3.

May 1—The earliest date former clubs may re-sign free agents who refused arbitration and were unsigned after July 31.

May 2—Waivers secured on or after November 11 expire at 5 p.m. (EDT).

May 3—The new waiver period begins. Waivers secured on or after this date are good through 5 p.m. (ET) July 31.

May 15—The earliest date clubs may re-sign players whom they unconditionally released after midnight August 31, 1999.

May 29—The start of the amateur free agent closed period regarding the summer draft—12:01 a.m.

June 5-7—The summer free-agent draft.

July 11—The All-Star Game at Atlanta's Turner Field.

July 31—Waivers secured on or after May 3, 2000, expire at 5 p.m. (EDT). Players may be traded between Major League clubs until midnight without any waivers in effect.

August 1—New waiver period begins. Beginning this date and ending on the day following the close of the championship season, players may be assigned between Major League clubs only after Major League waivers have been secured during the current waiver period.

August 15—The last date to bring players up for "full trial" to avoid draft-excluded status.

August 31—Any player released after midnight may not be re-signed to a Major League contract by the club that released him until May 15 of the following season.

Post-season rosters are established at midnight. To be eligible, a player must be a bona fide member of a qualifying team on August 31 and must remain a bona fide member until the end of the season.

September 1—The active player limit is increased from 25 to 40. After this date, outright assignments to the National Association can be made only with special waivers in effect.

October 1—Players on optional assignment must be recalled.

October 1—The official closing of the 1999 season.

October 2—Starting on this date, players may be traded between Major League clubs without waivers in effect.

October 9—The last date to request waivers on draft-excluded players until 25 days prior to the opening of the next season.

October 10—The beginning of the closed period for Major League waiver requests. Special waivers may still be requested on players that are not draft excluded for the next Rule 5 draft.

November 10—Waivers secured on or after August 1, 2000, expire at 5 p.m. (ET).

November 11—The new waiver period begins. Major League waiver requests can be withdrawn by a club on a player only once in each waiver period; subsequent Major League waiver requests in that period are irrevocable.

Waivers (exclusive of special waivers) secured on this day and after shall be in effect until the 30th day of the following championship season.

November (TBA)—Dates for filing Rookie, A, AA, AAA and Major League reserve lists will be announced as soon as the dates are determined.

December 20—The last date to tender contracts.

NOTE: The dates will be used unless notified differently.

RULES AND INFORMATION

SUSPENDED GAMES

A game may be suspended and completed at a future date for any of the following reasons:

1. A legally imposed curfew

2. The game is still tied at 1 a.m., local time. No inning may begin after 1 a.m., though an inning already in progress may be completed.

3. Any other mechanical difficulties that make continuing play overly difficult or dangerous.

4. Darkness falls and law prevents the use of lights.

5. Weather conditions make playing overly difficult or dangerous.

DISABLED LISTS

15-day: The player must remain off the active roster for a minimum of 15 calendar days, starting on the day following the player's last game.

60-day: Same rules apply, however, this may only be used when the team's 40-man roster is full. Any player placed on the 60-day disabled list after August 1 may not play for the remainder of the season, including any postseason games.

MAJOR LEAGUE SERVICE

A player gets service time:

1. For every day spent on an active roster, a Major League disabled list or a suspended list.

2. The day he physically reports to the team upon being called up from the minor leagues.

3. For however long it takes him, within reason, to report to his new team following a trade.

4. Up to and including the day he is sent down to the minors.

5. Up to and including the day he was notified of his unconditional release.

6. At the rate of 172 days per season, even though the regular season spans 183 days.

QUALIFICATIONS FOR INDIVIDUAL CHAMPIONSHIPS

Batting championship: It is awarded to the player with the highest batting average and at least 502 plate appearances. A player who falls short of the required 502 plate appearances can still win the title if the difference between his plate appearance total and 502 can be added as hitless at-bats and he still has the highest average.

Pitching championship: Awarded to the pitcher with the lowest ERA and at least 162 innings pitched.

Fielding championship: Awarded to each position player with the highest fielding average. Pitchers need a minimum of 162 innings, catchers 82 games and all other positions 108 games.

Night games: Night games are defined as any game beginning at or after 5 p.m. local time.

Streaks: A consecutive-game hitting streak will continue if the player fails to get a hit, but his at-bats result in a combination of any of the following: a walk, being hit by a pitch, defensive interference or a sacrifice bunt. The streak is terminated if the player's at-bats result only in a sacrifice fly.

A consecutive-games played streak is extended by a half inning of defensive play or a single at-bat, but pinch running will not extend the streak. The player's streak also continues if he is ejected from the game before he can satisfy any of the above requirements.

HOW TO COMPUTE:

Batting average: Divide at-bats into hits.

ERA: Multiply earned runs by 9 and divide the total by innings pitched.

Slugging percentage: Divide total bases by total times at bat (not including walks, hit by pitcher, sacrifices or interference).

On-base percentage: Divide the on-base total (hits, walks and hit by pitcher) by total plate appearances (at-bats, walks, hit by pitcher, sacrifices).

Fielding average: Add putouts and assists, divide the sum by total chances (putouts, assists, and errors).

Winning percentage: Divide the number of games won by the total games played.

Magic number: Determine the number of games yet to be played and add one. Then subtract the number of games the second-place team trails the first-place team in the loss column.

1999 Review

Whatta team! The Yankees dominated the century—winning 25 World Series titles—and closed it as champions, ousting N.L. powerhouse Atlanta in four games.

INTRODUCTION

So how can you possibly follow the magical 1998 season—the home run record chase, a team that won 125 games, a near-mystical perfect game at Yankee Stadium ... ?

The 1999 season actually fared pretty well as a follow-up act—offensive firepower, overpowering starting pitchers, statistical plateaus by our hitting heroes and other things that makes baseball so great. There were pennant races, a playoff game to settle a wild-card postseason spot, surprise contenders (Oakland and Cincinnati) playoff and a near-mystical perfect game at Yankee Stadium.

The heroics came from a pleasant mix of veterans and up-and-coming stars. Among the performances from veterans: Mark McGwire's 65 home runs (and 63 from Sammy Sosa); Cal Ripken's six-hit game in Atlanta on June 13; Jose Canseco's early home run barrage; David Cone's perfect game; Randy Johnson's 364 strikeouts; Tony Gwynn's and Wade Boggs' 3,000th hits; Rafael Palmeiro's 47-homer season; Rickey Henderson's 37 stolen bases at age 40, and Harold Baines' .312 average, 25 home runs and 103 RBIs, also at 40.

But the game's young heroes did their part to make '99 a memorable season: Nomar Garciaparra's .357 average; Rey Ordonez's 100-game (and counting) errorless streak at shortstop; Alex Rodriguez's 42 home runs in just 129 games; Pedro Martinez's 23 wins and 313 strikeouts; Jose Lima and Mike Hampton's 20-win seasons; Fernando Tatis' two-grand slam inning on April 23 in Los Angeles; Edgardo Alfonzo's 6-hit, three-homer game in Houston on August 30, and Manny Ramirez's 165 RBIs.

3,000 HITS—AND MORE

To start the season, San Diego's Tony Gwynn, Tampa Bay's Wade Boggs and Baltimore's Cal Ripken Jr. all were within reach of 3,000 hits. Only 21 players in baseball's history had reached that lofty plateau, and never had three players done it in a season. Gwynn needed 72, Boggs 78 and Ripken 122.

With seasons as we have come to expect from those three players, the 3,000-hit mark certainly would be surpassed easily.

But it wasn't.

Gwynn, 39, suffered a calf injury May 21 and landed on the disabled list 25 hits short of the 3,000 mark. He missed 19 games, only pinch-hit in many more after that and played just 111 games in the season.

Boggs, 41, split time with Bobby Smith at third base for the Devil Rays early in the season, then suffered a strained hamstring May 5 and joined the disabled list. He suffered a knee injury later in the season, requiring surgery and played in just 90 games.

Ironman Ripken Jr., 39, was hampered with back problems much of the season. The same man who played in every game for more than 16 seasons only played 86 in 1999. Though he hit .340 and reached another plateau—his 400th homer on September 2—he fell nine hits shy of 3,000.

But the other two made it. Gwynn was the first, a single to right-center field off Dan Smith in the first inning August 6 at Olympic Stadium in Montreal. The celebration included a modest wave to the audience and a kiss from Tony's mother. And in typical Tony Gwynn fashion, No. 3,000 was only the first of four hits that night. Only two players had reached the mark in fewer games—Ty Cobb and Nap Lajoie.

Boggs reached the mark with a bang one night later at Tropicana Field in Tampa. He became the first player to reach No. 3,000 with a homer, lining a 2-2 pitch from Chris Haney over the right field wall in the sixth inning.

His trip around the basepaths was accompanied by fireworks and an uncharacteristic display of excitement from Boggs. As he reached second base, he pointed to the sky in honor of his deceased mother; then he got on his knees and kissed home plate. He was joined on the field by his father, wife and son for the festivities.

Gwynn will continue to add to his total this season, and Ripken should reach the mark early in the season. But Boggs announced his retirement November 11 and finished with 3,010 hits, 21st on the all-time list.

Tony Gwynn kept piling up the hits in 1999. He's now 18th on the all-time list.

NEW YORK, NEW YORK

There is little doubt that the Yankees were the franchise of the 20th century. The team captured its 25th World Series title with a four-game sweep of the N.L. powerhouse Atlanta Braves. Behind the Yankees, the next highest championship total by a franchise is nine by the Athletics and Cardinals.

While the defending champion Yankees were heavy favorites on paper, they spent much of the season dealing with adversity both on and off the field. Manager Joe Torre was diagnosed with prostate cancer on March 10, just two days after the death of Yankees great Joe DiMaggio, and missed the first 36 games of the season. Veteran slugger Darryl Strawberry was arrested April 14 in Tampa and subsequently suspended, not playing with the Yankees until September. Roger Clemens was acquired for Yankees favorite David Wells among others during spring training, but Clemens fought injuries and ineffectiveness for much of the year. Three players—Scott Brosius, Luis Sojo and Paul O'Neill—lost their fathers during the season. Charles O'Neill died before Game 4 of the World Series, but his son played that night and brought home the title.

If there is such a thing as an "exhausting" title, it was this one. Playing under scrutiny only the Yankees could face, they faced adversity, and they dealt with it professionally and humbly.

Yankees fan or not, it was hard not to like this team. They didn't hit a lot of homers in a season that may be characterized by the long ball. They didn't have 300-strikeout pitchers or a 20-game winner. They didn't whoop and holler after good or bad plays. They didn't bash each other in the press or squabble about contracts. They just won—a total 109 times in 1999—because they played baseball unselfishly and fundamentally sound.

THE HOME RUNS

Mark McGwire and Sammy Sosa again stole our hearts and eyes for every at-bat as the two put on another home run duel throughout the season.

Not having to deal with the scrutiny of breaking a decades-old single-season record as during the 1998 season, the two calmly went about their business of hitting big flies. Sosa led the chase most of the season, but McGwire again finished on top with 65. Sosa had 63. The follow-up performances certainly showed the 1998 season was no fluke. These two sluggers now own the top four homer seasons in history.

OTHER NEWS

It was a year in which offense dominated much of baseball, but no team came close to Cleveland's massive numbers. The Indians scored 1,009 runs (6.2 per game), shattering the team record of 952. ... Jose Canseco joined Cal Ripken Jr. in the 400-homer club in 1999. McGwire passed 500 with his 43rd homer of the season. ... Ivan Rodriguez brought home the A.L. MVP Award with his offensive and defensive prowess, edging Boston's Martinez, who was the A.L. leader with his 23 wins, 313 strikeouts and 2.07 ERA. The spectacular year brought him his second Cy Young Award. ... Arizona's Johnson, the N.L. Cy Young winner, had the third highest strikeout total of all-time, fanning 364. ... The opening of Safeco Field in Seattle on July 15 was welcomed by Seattle pitchers. The beautiful, spacious facility allowed Mariners pitchers to record a 4.36 ERA in the second half after tallying a 6.00 ERA in the first half with home games in the Kingdome. ... There were two other no-hitters, in addition to Cone's perfect game. Cone set down 27 straight Montreal Expos at Yankee Stadium on July 18, the first no-hitter pitched in interleague play. Less heralded Jose Jimenez of the Cardinals and Eric Milton of the Twins also threw no-hitters. Jimenez's came June 25th in Phoenix, beating Johnson and the division-winning Diamondbacks. Milton accomplished his feat September 11 in Minnesota. He entered the game with a 6-11 record; he left it with a no-hit gem over Anaheim. ... Tampa Bay's Jim Morris was a former high school teacher/coach who rose to major league play as a 35-year-old rookie pitcher. ... Finally, baseball lost some of its legends in 1999: Pee Wee Reese, DiMaggio, Early Wynn, Cal Ripken Sr., Joe Adcock and Catfish Hunter.

—BRENDAN ROBERTS

FINAL STANDINGS, LEADERS, AWARDS

AMERICAN LEAGUE STANDINGS

FINAL

EAST DIVISION

Team	N.Y.	Bos	Tor.	Bal.	T.B.	Cle.	Chi.	Det.	K.C.	Min.	Tex.	Oak.	Sea.	Ana.	Atl.	N.Y.	Phi.	Mon.	Fla.	W	L	Pct.	GB
New York	—	4	10	9	8	7	7	7	4	6	8	6	9	4	1-2	3-3	1-2	2-1	2-1	98	64	.605	
Boston	8	—	9	7	4	8	7	7	8	6	4	4	7	9	2-4	1-2	1-2	0-3	2-1	94	68	.580	4.0
Toronto	2	3	—	11	8	7	4	10	7	6	4	2	2	9	3-0	0-3	1-2	4-2	1-2	84	78	.519	14.0
Baltimore	4	5	1	—	5	1	7	5	6	8	6	5	5	9	3-0	1-2	3-3	3-0	1-2	78	84	.481	20.0
Tampa Bay	4	9	5	7	—	4	4	5	8	5	4	1	4	5	0-3	1-2	1-2	1-2	1-5	69	93	.426	29.0

CENTRAL DIVISION

Team	Cle.	Chi.	Det.	K.C.	Min.	N.Y.	Bos.	Tor.	Bal.	T.B.	Tex.	Oak.	Sea.	Ana.	Hou.	Cin.	Pit.	St.L.	Mil.	Chi.	W	L	Pct.	GB
Cleveland	—	9	8	7	9	3	4	5	9	5	3	10	7	9	1-2	4-2	....	1-2	2-1		97	65	.599	
Chicago	3	—	7	6	8	5	6	3	6	5	3	4	5		1-2	....	2-1	1-2	4-2		75	86	.466	21.5
Detroit	5	5	—	7	6	5	5	2	5	4	5	4	3	5	0-3	2-1	2-1	3-3	1-2		69	92	.429	27.5
Kansas City	5	6	4	—	5	5	2	3	4	2	4	6	7	5	0-3	0-3	1-2	2-1	1-2	2-1	64	97	.398	32.5
Minnesota	3	3	6	8	—	4	4	4	1	5	0	7	4	4	1-2	2-1	2-1	2-1	2-0	1-2	63	97	.394	33.0

WEST DIVISION

Team	Tex.	Oak.	Sea.	Ana.	N.Y.	Bos.	Tor.	Bal.	T.B.	Cle.	Chi.	Det.	K.C.	Min.	Ari.	S.F.	L.A.	S.D.	Col.	W	L	PCT	GB
Texas	—	7	8	6	4	5	6	6	7	5	5	6	8	12	3-3	3-0	2-1	1-2	1-2	95	67	.586	—
Oakland	5	—	6	4	4	6	8	7	9	2	7	6	6	5	2-1	3-3	3-0	1-2	3-0	87	75	.537	8.0
Seattle	5	6	—	6	1	3	7	5	8	3	5	5	6	8	2-1	1-2	0-3	2-4	2-1	79	83	.488	16.0
Anaheim	6	8	6	—	6	1	3	3	7	1	5	5	7	6	1-2	1-2	2-4	0-3	2-1	70	92	.432	25.0

Tie game—Minnesota at Chicago A.L., October 3 (6½ innings).
Note: Read across for wins, down for losses.
Clinching dates: New York (East)—September 30, second game; Cleveland (Central)—September 8; Texas (West)—September 26; Boston (wild card)—September 30.

HOME

Team	Oak.	Tex.	Bos.	N.Y.	Cle.	Sea.	Bal.	Tor.	Chi.	Det.	Ana.	K.C.	T.B.	Min.	N.L.	W	L	Pct.
Oakland	..	4	4	2	1	4	4	2	4	2	3	5	5	4	8	52	29	.642
Texas	5	..	3	2	4	4	3	1	3	4	3	4	2	6	6	51	30	.630
Boston	2	4	..	4	3	4	2	4	4	5	6	3	1	3	4	49	32	.605
New York	2	4	2	..	4	5	4	5	4	5	2	1	3	2	5	48	33	.593
Cleveland	5	1	1	1	..	4	6	1	4	4	4	4	4	4	4	47	34	.580
Seattle	4	2	1	0	1	..	5	4	4	4	3	2	4	5	4	43	38	.531
Baltimore	3	3	1	1	1	4	..	1	4	2	4	4	3	5	5	41	40	.506
Toronto	0	1	1	1	2	0	6	..	1	5	6	3	5	3	6	40	41	.494
Chicago	3	4	3	3	1	2	1	1	..	3	3	2	4	4	4	38	42	.475
Detroit	2	3	4	4	3	1	3	1	2	..	3	5	1	2	4	38	43	.469
Anaheim	5	3	1	2	1	3	1	3	4	4	..	3	4	3	2	37	44	.457
Kansas City	5	3	1	3	3	3	2	2	2	3	2	..	1	1	2	33	47	.413
Tampa Bay	0	0	4	1	2	2	4	3	2	3	3	5	..	2	2	33	48	.407
Minnesota	3	0	3	2	1	3	0	3	2	2	1	3	1	..	5	31	50	.383
N.L. clubs	5	5	7	5	4	6	3	6	4	5	5	5	7	3	..	..	..	..
Lost	46	37	36	31	31	45	44	37	44	49	48	50	45	47	..	581	551	.513

ROAD

Team	Cle.	N.Y.	Bos.	Tex.	Tor.	Bal.	Chi.	Sea.	T.B.	Oak.	Ana.	Min.	Det.	K.C.	N.L.	W	L	Pct.
Cleveland	..	2	3	2	4	3	5	3	1	5	5	5	4	3	5	50	31	.617
New York	3	..	2	4	5	5	3	4	5	4	2	4	2	3	4	50	31	.617
Boston	5	4	..	0	5	5	3	3	2	3	2	3	2	5	2	45	36	.556
Texas	3	2	2	..	5	3	2	4	6	2	3	6	1	1	4	44	37	.543
Toronto	5	1	2	3	..	5	3	2	3	2	3	3	5	4	3	44	37	.543
Baltimore	0	3	3	0	0	..	3	1	2	5	3	2	6			37	44	.457
Chicago	2	2	2	1	5	2	..	2	2	0	4	4	4	5	2	37	44	.457
Seattle	2	1	2	3	3	0	4	..	4	2	3	3	3	3	3	36	45	.444
Tampa Bay	2	3	5	4	2	3	2	2	..	1	2	3	2	3	2	36	45	.444
Oakland	1	2	2	1	6	3	3	2	4	..	1	1	4	1	4	35	46	.432
Anaheim	0	4	0	3	0	2	1	3	3	3	..	3	3	4	4	33	48	.407
Minnesota	2	2	1	0	1	1	1	1	4	2	3	..	4	5	5	32	47	.405
Detroit	2	1	1	2	1	2	3	2	3	2	2	4	..	2	4	31	49	.388
Kansas City	2	2	1	1	1	2	4	4	1	1	3	4	1	..	4	31	50	.383
N.L. clubs	5	4	5	3	3	4	5	5	7	1	7	4	5	7	..	..	..	..
Lost	34	33	32	30	41	40	42	38	48	29	44	50	43	47	..	541	590	.478

MONTHLY

Through April 30

East Team	W	L	GB
New York	14	7	—
Toronto	13	11	2.5
Tampa Bay	12	12	3.5
Boston	11	11	3.5
Baltimore	6	16	8.5

Central Team	W	L	GB
Cleveland	16	6	—
Chicago	11	9	4.0
Detroit	11	12	5.5
Kansas City	9	11	6.0
Minnesota	9	14	7.5

West Team	W	L	GB
Texas	13	10	—
Anaheim	11	12	2.0
Seattle	11	12	2.0
Oakland	10	14	3.5

Through May 31

East Team	W	L	GB
Boston	31	19	—
New York	29	20	1.5
Toronto	24	28	8.0
Tampa Bay	23	28	8.5
Baltimore	19	31	12.0

Central Team	W	L	GB
Cleveland	33	16	—
Kansas City	23	26	10.0
Chicago	22	25	10.0
Detroit	21	30	13.0
Minnesota	18	32	15.5

West Team	W	L	GB
Texas	30	20	—
Oakland	27	24	3.5
Seattle	26	24	4.0
Anaheim	24	27	6.5

Through June 30

East Team	W	L	GB
New York	46	29	—
Boston	45	32	2.0
Toronto	39	41	9.5
Tampa Bay	33	44	14.0
Baltimore	32	44	14.5

Central Team	W	L	GB
Cleveland	50	26	—
Chicago	37	38	12.5
Detroit	33	45	18.0
Kansas City	32	44	18.0
Minnesota	29	47	21.0

West Team	W	L	GB
Texas	45	33	—
Seattle	39	38	5.5
Oakland	37	40	7.5
Anaheim	35	42	9.5

Through July 31

East Team	W	L	GB
New York	62	40	—
Toronto	58	48	6.0
Boston	56	47	6.5
Baltimore	46	57	16.5
Tampa Bay	43	61	20.0

Central Team	W	L	GB
Cleveland	63	40	—
Chicago	48	54	14.5
Minnesota	44	58	18.5
Kansas City	43	60	20.0
Detroit	42	62	21.5

West Team	W	L	GB
Texas	61	42	—
Oakland	53	50	8.0
Seattle	50	53	11.0
Anaheim	43	59	17.5

Through August 31

East Team	W	L	GB
New York	81	50	—
Boston	74	58	7.5
Toronto	70	64	12.5
Tampa Bay	59	73	22.5
Baltimore	58	73	23.0

Central Team	W	L	GB
Cleveland	81	50	—
Chicago	62	71	20.0
Minnesota	56	74	24.5
Detroit	53	78	28.0
Kansas City	51	81	30.5

West Team	W	L	GB
Texas	79	54	—
Oakland	72	60	6.5
Seattle	66	66	12.5
Anaheim	51	80	27.0

Through October 3 (Final)

East Team	W	L	GB
New York	98	64	—
Boston	94	68	4.0
Toronto	84	78	14.0
Baltimore	78	84	20.0
Tampa Bay	69	93	29.0

Central Team	W	L	GB
Cleveland	97	65	—
Chicago	75	86	21.5
Detroit	69	92	27.5
Kansas City	64	97	32.5
Minnesota	63	97	33.0

West Team	W	L	GB
Texas	95	67	—
Oakland	87	75	8.0
Seattle	79	83	16.0
Anaheim	70	92	25.0

NATIONAL LEAGUE STANDINGS

FINAL

EAST DIVISION

Team	Atl.	N.Y.	Phi.	Mon.	Fla.	Hou.	Cin.	Pit.	St.L.	Mil.	Chi.	Ari.	S.F.	L.A.	S.D.	Col.	N.Y.	Bos.	Tor.	Bal.	T.B.	W	L	PCT	GB
Atlanta	—	9	8	9	9	6	8	6	8	5	2	5	4	5	5	5	2-1	4-2	0-3	0-3	3-0	103	59	.636	—
New York	3	—	6	8	10	5	5	7	5	5	6	2	7	4	7	5	3-3	2-1	2-1	2-1	2-1	97	66	.595	6.5
Philadelphia	5	6	—	6	11	1	3	3	4	7	1	3	4	4	5	3	1-2	3-0	2-4	0-3	2-1	77	85	.475	26.0
Montreal	4	5	6	—	4	2	3	3	5	4	5	1	4	7	3	4	1-2	1-2	2-1	2-1	5-1	68	94	.420	35.0
Florida	4	3	2	8	—	2	1	3	3	5	3	1	4	7	3	4	1-2	1-2	2-1	2-1	5-1	64	98	.395	39.0

CENTRAL DIVISION

Team	Hou.	Cin.	Pit.	St.L.	Mil.	Chi.	Atl.	N.Y.	Phi.	Mon.	Fla.	Ari.	S.F.	L.A.	S.D.	Col.	Cle.	Chi.	Det.	K.C.	Min.	W	L	PCT	GB
Houston	—	4	5	5	8	9	1	4	6	7	7	4	5	6	8	6	2-1	2-1	3-0	3-0	2-1	97	65	.599	—
Cincinnati	9	—	7	8	6	8	1	5	6	4	6	8	4	6	3	7	2-4	....	1-2	3-0	1-2	96	67	.589	1.5
Pittsburgh	7	6	—	7	4	6	3	2	4	6	4	4	3	6	7	5	2-1	1-2	1-2	2-1	1-2	78	83	.484	18.5
St. Louis	7	4	5	—	6	6	1	2	5	4	4	4	3	6	7	5	....	2-1	3-3	1-2	1-2	75	86	.466	21.5
Milwaukee	5	6	8	7	—	6	2	2	5	5	4	4	2	3	3	3	2-1	2-1	2-1	0-2	2-1	74	87	.460	22.5
Chicago	3	5	7	5	6	—	5	3	2	6	2	2	6	4	6	4	1-2	2-4	....	1-2	2-1	67	95	.414	30.0

WEST DIVISION

Team	Ari.	S.F.	L.A.	S.D.	Col.	Atl.	N.Y.	Phi.	Mon.	Fla.	Hou.	Cin.	Pit.	St.L.	Mil.	Chi.	Tex.	Oak.	Sea.	Ana.	W	L	PCT	GB
Arizona	—	9	7	11	6	4	7	8	6	8	5	1	5	4	5	7	3-3	1-2	1-2	2-1	100	62	.617	—
San Fran.	3	—	5	7	9	5	2	6	5	5	6	5	5	7	6	7	0-3	3-3	2-1	1-2	86	76	.531	14.0
Los Angeles	6	8	—	3	5	4	6	4	5	2	3	3	3	3	6	7	1-2	0-3	3-0	4-2	77	85	.475	23.0
San Diego	2	5	9	—	9	4	2	3	6	1	3	6	2	5	3	3	2-1	2-1	4-2	3-0	74	88	.457	26.0
Colorado	7	4	8	4	—	4	4	5	6	5	2	2	4	6	5	5	2-1	0-3	1-2	1-2	72	90	.444	28.0

Note: Read across for wins, down for losses.
Clinching dates: Atlanta (East)—September 26, second game; Houston (Central)—October 3; Arizona (West)—September 24; New York (wild card)—October 4.

HOME

Team	Atl.	Ari.	Hou.	N.Y.	S.F.	S.D.	Pit.	Cin.	Phi.	Col.	St.L.	L.A.	Fla.	Mon.	Chi.	Mil.	A.L.	W	L	Pct.
Atlanta	..	3	3	5	2	3	5	6	4	2	5	1	5	4	1	2	5	56	25	.691
Arizona	1	..	2	4	4	6	2	0	6	3	2	5	4	4	4	5	3	52	29	.642
Houston	1	3	..	1	2	6	4	1	2	3	3	4	2	4	4	5	5	50	32	.610
New York	2	0	3	..	5	5	5	0	4	2	2	1	5	3	2	7	4	49	32	.605
San Francisco	4	1	3	1	..	4	2	1	4	6	1	5	2	2	2	3	6	49	32	.605
San Diego	4	1	1	1	1	..	4	2	1	6	1	5	4	2	3	5	0	46	35	.568
Pittsburgh	2	1	5	1	3	1	..	3	2	3	4	2	4	5	0	3	1	45	36	.556
Cincinnati	1	5	4	2	2	2	4	..	2	1	4	5	1	4	2	3	3	45	37	.549
Philadelphia	2	1	0	4	2	2	2	2	..	0	4	4	2	3	4	1	5	41	40	.506
Colorado	3	4	1	3	3	3	0	0	3	..	4	4	1	2	1	5	2	39	42	.481
St. Louis	0	2	4	1	1	1	2	1	3	2	..	2	2	1	4	2	6	38	42	.475
Los Angeles	2	4	1	1	3	1	2	1	1	4	2	..	5	1	3	1	5	37	44	.457
Florida	2	0	0	2	3	1	2	1	1	4	2	3	..	5	1	3	3	35	45	.438
Montreal	2	1	0	1	3	3	2	2	1	4	0	2	1	..	2	3	6	35	46	.432
Chicago	2	0	1	3	1	5	5	2	3	2	1	1	1	2	..	3	4	34	47	.420
Milwaukee	1	2	3	0	0	3	2	3	4	2	3	1	1	1	3	..	0	32	48	.400
A.L. clubs	5	5	2	4	6	1	6	3	4	3	4	3	7	3	2	3	..	683	612	.527
Lost	34	33	33	34	44	53	47	30	45	48	44	41	53	48	48	39	..			

ROAD

Team	Cin.	Ari.	Hou.	N.Y.	Atl.	Mil.	L.A.	St.L.	S.F.	Phi.	Pit.	Chi.	Col.	Mon.	Fla.	S.D.	A.L.	W	L	Pct.
Cincinnati	..	3	5	3	0	3	3	3	2	4	3	5	3	2	2	4	6	51	30	.630
Arizona	1	..	3	3	3	4	2	2	5	2	3	3	2	3	5	4	4	48	33	.593
Houston	3	1	..	2	3	0	2	2	3	4	1	5	3	3	2	5	4	47	33	.588
New York	5	2	2	..	1	3	3	3	2	2	2	3	3	5	5	2	4	48	34	.585
Atlanta	2	2	3	4	..	3	4	3	2	4	1	1	3	5	4	2	4	47	34	.580
Milwaukee	3	2	2	2	1	..	1	4	4	1	6	3	1	4	0	1	2	42	39	.519
Los Angeles	2	2	2	3	2	5	..	1	3	4	3	3	4	0	1	2	5	40	41	.494
St. Louis	1	2	3	1	1	4	2	..	2	2	2	2	3	2	2	3	4	37	44	.457
San Francisco	4	2	1	1	3	3	3	2	..	0	1	3	3	3	0	3	6	37	44	.457
Philadelphia	1	0	1	2	3	2	1	3	0	..	1	2	4	5	2	2	6	36	45	.444
Pittsburgh	3	1	2	1	1	4	2	2	1	1	..	3	2	2	1	3	4	33	47	.413
Chicago	3	2	2	3	2	3	3	0	1	2	2	..	1	5	1	2	3	33	48	.407
Colorado	2	3	1	1	1	1	4	4	1	4	2	3	..	2	1	2	4	33	48	.407
Montreal	1	2	2	4	2	2	1	1	1	1	1	2	0	..	3	2	6	33	48	.407
Florida	0	1	2	1	2	2	4	1	2	1	2	1	3	1	..	2	5	29	53	.354
San Diego	1	1	0	1	2	0	2	4	1	2	2	1	3	1	2	..	6	28	53	.346
A.L. clubs	5	3	1	2	4	4	3	2	2	6	4	4	3	4	4	3	..	622	674	.480
Lost	37	29	32	32	25	48	44	42	32	40	36	47	42	46	45	35	..			

MONTHLY

Through April 30

East

Team	W	L	GB
Atlanta	15	7	—
New York	14	9	1.5
Philadelphia	11	11	4.0
Montreal	7	14	7.5
Florida	6	17	9.5

Central

Team	W	L	GB
Houston	13	9	—
St. Louis	12	9	0.5
Chicago	10	10	2.0
Cincinnati	9	12	3.5
Pittsburgh	9	12	3.5
Milwaukee	9	13	4.0

West

Team	W	L	GB
San Fran.	16	8	—
Los Angeles	13	10	2.5
Arizona	13	11	3.0
Colorado	9	10	4.5
San Diego	9	13	6.0

Through May 31

East

Team	W	L	GB
Atlanta	31	20	—
New York	27	24	4.0
Philadelphia	25	24	5.0
Montreal	18	30	11.5
Florida	16	35	15.0

Central

Team	W	L	GB
Houston	29	20	—
Chicago	27	20	1.0
Cincinnati	25	22	3.0
Pittsburgh	26	24	3.5
St. Louis	25	24	4.0
Milwaukee	23	27	6.5

West

Team	W	L	GB
Arizona	31	21	—
San Fran.	27	24	3.5
Los Angeles	26	24	4.0
Colorado	21	27	8.0
San Diego	19	30	10.5

Through June 30

East

Team	W	L	GB
Atlanta	44	31	—
New York	44	34	3.0
Philadelphia	40	36	6.0
Montreal	30	44	15.0
Florida	27	51	20.0

Central

Team	W	L	GB
Cincinnati	43	31	—
Houston	44	32	—
Pittsburgh	39	37	5.0
Chicago	37	37	6.0
St. Louis	37	40	7.5
Milwaukee	35	41	9.0

West

Team	W	L	GB
Arizona	43	35	—
San Fran.	43	35	2.5
San Diego	37	38	4.5
Colorado	34	40	7.0
Los Angeles	34	41	7.5

Through July 31

East

Team	W	L	GB
Atlanta	63	43	—
New York	62	43	0.5
Philadelphia	57	47	5.0
Florida	41	64	21.5
Montreal	38	62	22.0

Central

Team	W	L	GB
Houston	64	41	—
Cincinnati	59	43	3.5
St. Louis	52	52	11.5
Pittsburgh	50	53	13.0
Milwaukee	49	53	13.5
Chicago	48	53	14.0

West

Team	W	L	GB
Arizona	59	46	—
San Fran.	56	48	2.5
San Diego	54	50	4.5
Colorado	46	58	12.5
Los Angeles	45	59	13.5

Through August 31

East

Team	W	L	GB
Atlanta	84	50	—
New York	80	53	3.5
Philadelphia	67	64	15.5
Montreal	56	76	27.0
Florida	53	79	30.0

Central

Team	W	L	GB
Houston	79	55	—
Cincinnati	76	55	1.5
Pittsburgh	66	67	12.5
St. Louis	64	69	14.5
Milwaukee	57	74	20.5
Chicago	54	77	23.5

West

Team	W	L	GB
Arizona	79	54	—
San Fran.	71	61	7.5
Los Angeles	62	70	16.5
San Diego	61	72	18.0
Colorado	60	74	19.5

Through October 4 (Final)

East

Team	W	L	GB
Atlanta	103	59	—
New York	97	66	6.5
Philadelphia	77	85	26.0
Montreal	68	94	35.0
Florida	64	98	39.0

Central

Team	W	L	GB
Houston	97	65	—
Cincinnati	96	67	1.5
Pittsburgh	78	83	18.5
St. Louis	75	86	21.5
Milwaukee	74	87	22.5
Chicago	67	95	30.0

West

Team	W	L	GB
Arizona	100	62	—
San Fran.	86	76	14.0
Los Angeles	77	85	23.0
San Diego	74	88	26.0
Colorado	72	90	28.0

SHUTOUTS

Team	Bos.	Cle.	N.Y.	Bal.	Tex.	Oak.	Tor.	Min.	K.C.	T.B.	Sea.	Ana.	Det.	Chi.	N.L.	W	L	Pct.
Boston	—	0	1	3	0	0	3	0	1	0	1	1	1	1	0	12	5	.706
Cleveland	0	—	0	0	1	0	0	0	0	1	1	1	0	1	1	6	3	.667
New York	0	0	—	0	1	1	0	1	0	1	2	0	3	0	1	10	6	.625
Baltimore	1	0	1	—	0	0	1	4	0	0	0	1	1	1	1	11	8	.579
Texas	1	1	1	0	—	0	1	0	0	0	2	1	1	0	0	9	7	.563
Oakland	0	0	0	1	1	—	0	0	0	0	0	0	1	2	2	5	4	.556
Toronto	0	1	0	1	0	1	—	1	1	0	0	1	1	0	1	9	8	.529
Minnesota	0	0	0	0	0	1	1	—	0	0	0	2	2	1	1	8	10	.444
Kansas City	0	0	1	1	0	0	0	0	—	0	0	1	0	0	0	3	4	.429
Tampa Bay	0	0	0	2	0	0	1	0	0	—	0	1	1	0	0	5	7	.417
Seattle	0	0	0	0	1	0	0	2	0	1	—	1	0	0	0	6	9	.400
Anaheim	1	0	2	0	2	0	0	0	1	1	0	—	0	0	0	7	11	.389
Detroit	1	0	0	0	1	0	0	1	0	0	1	1	—	1	0	6	12	.333
Chicago	1	0	0	0	0	0	0	1	0	0	0	0	1	—	0	3	7	.300
N.L. Clubs	0	1	0	0	0	1	1	0	1	2	2	0	0	0	—	—	—	—
Lost	5	3	6	8	7	4	8	10	4	7	9	11	12	7	—	100	101	.498

A.L. shutouts vs. N.L. clubs (7): Baltimore vs. Atlanta; Cleveland vs. Pittsburgh; Minnesota vs. Chicago N.L.; New York A.L. vs. Montreal; Oakland vs. San Diego and Arizona; Toronto vs. Montreal.

RECORD VS. DIVISIONS

Team	vs. A.L. East W	L	Pct.	vs. A.L. Central W	L	Pct.	vs. A.L. West W	L	Pct.	vs. N.L. W	L	Pct.	Total W	L	Pct.
New York	31	18	.633	31	22	.585	27	15	.643	9	9	.500	98	64	.605
Cleveland	26	27	.491	33	16	.673	29	13	.690	9	9	.500	97	65	.599
Texas	29	26	.527	35	17	.673	21	16	.568	10	8	.556	95	67	.586
Boston	28	21	.571	36	20	.643	24	15	.615	6	12	.333	94	68	.580
Oakland	34	18	.654	26	30	.464	15	21	.417	12	6	.667	87	75	.537
Toronto	24	25	.490	34	20	.630	17	24	.415	9	9	.500	84	78	.519
Seattle	24	27	.471	31	25	.554	17	20	.459	7	11	.389	79	83	.488
Baltimore	15	34	.306	27	22	.551	25	21	.543	11	7	.611	78	84	.481
Chicago	25	29	.463	24	23	.511	17	25	.405	9	9	.500	75	86	.466
Anaheim	20	36	.357	24	28	.462	20	16	.556	6	12	.333	70	92	.432
Detroit	21	34	.382	23	25	.479	17	23	.425	8	10	.444	69	92	.429
Tampa Bay	25	25	.500	26	22	.542	14	32	.304	4	14	.222	69	93	.426
Kansas City	16	33	.327	20	28	.417	22	24	.478	6	12	.333	64	97	.398
Minnesota	18	31	.367	20	28	.417	15	31	.326	10	7	.588	63	97	.394
Totals	336	384	.467	390	326	.545	280	296	.486	116	135	.462	1122	1141	.496

ONE-RUN DECISIONS

	W	L	Pct.
New York	22	12	.647
Texas	24	16	.600
Toronto	26	18	.591
Cleveland	26	19	.578
Tampa Bay	27	20	.574
Oakland	22	19	.537
Chicago	20	19	.513
Boston	21	20	.512
Anaheim	23	25	.479
Seattle	20	23	.465
Detroit	19	22	.463
Minnesota	19	26	.422
Baltimore	16	26	.381
Kansas City	11	32	.256
Totals	296	297	.499

DOUBLEHEADERS

	Won	Lost	Split
Anaheim	1	0	0
Seattle	1	0	0
Boston	0	0	1
Chicago	2	2	2
New York	0	0	1
Oakland	0	0	1
Texas	1	1	0
Baltimore	0	1	1
Kansas City	0	2	1
Tampa Bay	0	1	0
Cleveland	0	0	0
Detroit	0	0	0
Minnesota	0	0	0
Toronto	0	0	0
Totals	5	7	7

DAY GAMES

	W	L	Pct.
Boston	36	22	.621
New York	33	24	.579
Oakland	32	26	.552
Cleveland	27	22	.551
Seattle	22	21	.512
Toronto	26	26	.500
Tampa Bay	21	22	.488
Texas	17	18	.486
Baltimore	23	25	.479
Chicago	25	28	.472
Detroit	22	25	.468
Minnesota	19	24	.442
Anaheim	12	19	.387
Kansas City	14	32	.304
Totals	329	334	.496

NIGHT GAMES

	W	L	Pct.
Cleveland	70	43	.619
New York	65	40	.619
Texas	78	49	.614
Boston	58	46	.558
Oakland	55	49	.529
Toronto	58	52	.527
Baltimore	55	59	.482
Seattle	57	62	.479
Chicago	50	58	.463
Anaheim	58	73	.443
Kansas City	50	65	.435
Detroit	47	67	.412
Tampa Bay	48	71	.403
Minnesota	44	73	.376
Totals	793	807	.496

EXTRA-INNING GAMES

	W	L	Pct.
New York	7	2	.778
Texas	6	2	.750
Toronto	6	3	.667
Baltimore	8	6	.571
Minnesota	6	5	.545
Boston	4	4	.500
Cleveland	7	7	.500
Detroit	5	5	.500
Seattle	5	6	.455
Chicago	6	9	.400
Anaheim	4	8	.333
Kansas City	5	10	.333
Tampa Bay	3	6	.333
Oakland	3	7	.300
Totals	75	80	.484

ON GRASS

	W	L	Pct.
Cleveland	82	56	.594
Boston	83	57	.593
New York	83	58	.589
Toronto	33	26	.559
Texas	74	64	.536
Oakland	75	67	.528
Baltimore	70	71	.496
Seattle	49	59	.454
Tampa Bay	29	35	.453
Chicago	62	80	.437
Anaheim	62	81	.434
Detroit	57	76	.429
Minnesota	27	39	.409
Kansas City	55	83	.399
Totals	841	852	.497

ON TURF

	W	L	Pct.
Texas	21	3	.875
New York	15	6	.714
Chicago	13	6	.684
Cleveland	15	9	.625
Oakland	12	8	.600
Seattle	30	24	.556
Boston	11	11	.500
Toronto	51	52	.495
Detroit	12	16	.429
Anaheim	8	11	.421
Tampa Bay	40	58	.408
Kansas City	9	14	.391
Minnesota	36	58	.383
Baltimore	8	13	.381
Totals	281	289	.493

vs. LEFTHANDERS

	W	L	Pct.
Texas	20	10	.667
Cleveland	28	15	.651
Chicago	16	11	.593
New York	19	14	.576
Oakland	23	17	.575
Detroit	15	14	.517
Boston	18	17	.514
Anaheim	19	19	.500
Kansas City	15	17	.469
Toronto	13	15	.464
Baltimore	12	15	.444
Seattle	13	22	.371
Minnesota	13	24	.351
Tampa Bay	8	23	.258
Totals	232	233	.499

vs. RIGHTHANDERS

	W	L	Pct.
New York	79	50	.612
Boston	76	51	.598
Cleveland	69	50	.580
Texas	75	57	.568
Toronto	71	63	.530
Oakland	64	58	.525
Seattle	66	61	.520
Baltimore	66	69	.489
Tampa Bay	61	70	.466
Chicago	59	75	.440
Anaheim	51	73	.411
Detroit	54	78	.409
Minnesota	50	73	.407
Kansas City	49	80	.380
Totals	890	908	.495

SHUTOUTS

Team	Cin.	Hou.	Ari.	Atl.	S.F.	N.Y.	L.A.	Chi.	Phi.	Mil.	St.L.	Fla.	Col.	S.D.	Mon.	Pit.	A.L.	W	L	Pct.
Cincinnati...........	—	2	1	0	0	1	0	0	0	1	2	0	0	2	0	2	0	11	3	.786
Houston.............	0	—	1	0	0	0	0	2	0	0	2	0	0	0	1	1	1	8	5	.615
Arizona.............	0	0	—	0	0	0	1	1	2	1	0	1	0	2	0	0	1	9	6	.600
Atlanta	1	0	1	—	0	3	0	0	1	0	1	1	0	0	1	0	0	9	6	.600
San Fran.	0	0	0	0	—	0	0	0	0	0	0	2	0	0	0	1	0	3	2	.600
New York	1	1	0	0	2	—	0	0	0	0	0	1	0	0	1	1	0	7	5	.583
Los Angeles	0	0	0	0	0	0	—	2	0	0	0	1	1	0	1	0	1	6	6	.500
Chicago	0	1	0	1	0	1	1	—	0	0	0	0	0	1	0	1	0	6	7	.462
Philadelphia	1	0	0	0	0	0	0	1	—	0	0	0	0	1	0	1	0	6	7	.462
Milwaukee	0	0	0	0	0	0	0	0	2	—	0	1	0	0	1	0	1	5	6	.455
St. Louis	0	0	2	0	0	0	0	0	0	0	—	0	0	0	1	0	0	3	4	.429
Florida	0	0	0	2	0	0	0	0	1	0	0	—	0	0	1	0	1	5	7	.417
Colorado	0	0	0	0	0	0	0	0	0	2	0	0	—	0	0	0	0	2	3	.400
San Diego	0	0	0	2	0	0	1	1	0	0	0	0	1	—	0	1	0	6	10	.375
Montreal............	0	0	0	0	0	0	1	0	0	0	0	0	0	1	—	0	2	4	8	.333
Pittsburgh	0	1	0	0	0	0	0	0	0	1	0	0	1	0	0	—	0	3	7	.300
A.L. clubs	0	0	1	1	0	0	0	1	0	0	0	0	0	1	2	1	—			
Lost	3	5	6	6	2	5	6	7	7	6	4	7	3	10	8	7	—	93	92	.503

N.L. shutouts vs. A.L. clubs (8): Arizona vs. Seattle; Florida vs. Tampa Bay; Houston vs. Cleveland; Los Angeles vs. Seattle; Milwaukee vs. Kansas City; Montreal vs. Tampa Bay and Toronto; San Francisco vs. Oakland.

RECORD VS. DIVISIONS

Team	vs. N.L. East			vs. N.L. Central			vs. N.L. West			vs. A.L.			Total		
	W	L	Pct.	W	L	Pct.	W	L	Pct.	W	L	Pct.	W	L	Pct.
Arizona...............	33	12	.733	27	24	.529	33	18	.647	7	8	.467	100	62	.617
Atlanta	35	16	.686	35	13	.729	24	21	.533	9	9	.500	103	59	.636
Chicago	18	23	.439	28	34	.452	15	29	.341	6	9	.400	67	95	.414
Cincinnati...........	22	20	.524	38	25	.603	29	14	.674	7	8	.467	96	67	.589
Colorado	24	21	.533	21	32	.396	23	29	.442	4	8	.333	72	90	.444
Florida	17	34	.333	17	31	.354	19	26	.422	11	7	.611	64	98	.395
Houston	25	16	.610	31	31	.500	29	15	.659	12	3	.800	97	65	.599
Los Angeles	21	23	.477	26	26	.500	22	29	.431	8	7	.533	77	85	.475
Milwaukee	18	23	.439	32	30	.516	16	28	.364	8	6	.571	74	87	.460
Montreal.............	19	31	.380	22	28	.440	19	25	.432	8	10	.444	68	94	.420
New York	27	23	.540	33	18	.647	25	19	.568	12	6	.667	97	66	.595
Philadelphia	28	22	.560	22	28	.440	16	28	.364	11	7	.611	77	85	.475
Pittsburgh	19	22	.463	30	32	.484	22	21	.512	7	8	.467	78	83	.484
San Diego	18	26	.409	20	33	.377	25	25	.500	11	4	.733	74	88	.457
San Francisco	23	21	.523	32	21	.604	24	26	.480	7	8	.467	86	76	.531
St. Louis	16	25	.390	27	34	.443	25	19	.568	7	8	.467	75	86	.466
Totals	363	358	.503	441	440	.501	366	372	.496	135	116	.538	1305	1286	.504

ONE-RUN DECISIONS

	W	L	Pct.
New York	27	19	.587
Atlanta	29	21	.580
Philadelphia	25	19	.568
Houston	22	18	.550
San Francisco ..	27	23	.540
San Diego	28	25	.528
Chicago	26	24	.520
Colorado	24	23	.511
Arizona.........	24	24	.500
St. Louis	26	27	.491
Pittsburgh	20	22	.476
Cincinnati	21	24	.467
Milwaukee	22	27	.449
Los Angeles	21	27	.438
Florida	19	25	.432
Montreal	16	28	.364
Totals	377	376	.501

DOUBLEHEADERS

	Won	Lost	Split
San Francisco	1	0	0
Florida	2	0	1
Cincinnati........	1	0	1
New York	1	0	1
St. Louis	1	0	2
Atlanta	0	0	1
Chicago	0	1	2
Milwaukee	0	0	2
Houston	0	0	2
Philadelphia	0	0	1
Pittsburgh	0	0	2
Montreal	0	1	0
San Diego	0	1	0
Arizona..........	0	0	0
Colorado	0	0	0
Los Angeles	0	0	0
Totals	6	4	15

DAY GAMES

	W	L	Pct.
Arizona............	25	14	.641
Atlanta	29	17	.630
Cincinnati	34	24	.586
New York	32	23	.582
Houston	26	19	.578
Milwaukee	30	25	.545
Los Angeles	25	21	.543
San Francisco	40	34	.541
Pittsburgh	24	22	.522
Philadelphia	25	25	.500
Chicago	41	50	.451
St. Louis	23	28	.451
Colorado	29	38	.433
San Diego	23	31	.426
Florida	15	29	.341
Montreal.........	14	30	.318
Totals	435	430	.503

NIGHT GAMES

	W	L	Pct.
Atlanta	74	42	.638
Arizona...........	75	48	.610
Houston	71	46	.607
New York	65	43	.602
Cincinnati........	62	43	.590
San Francisco	46	42	.523
St. Louis	52	58	.473
San Diego	51	57	.472
Pittsburgh	54	61	.470
Philadelphia	52	60	.464
Montreal.........	54	64	.458
Colorado	43	52	.453
Los Angeles	52	64	.448
Florida	49	69	.415
Milwaukee	44	62	.415
Chicago	26	45	.366
Totals	870	856	.504

EXTRA-INNING GAMES

	W	L	Pct.
Atlanta	17	5	.773
Cincinnati	9	4	.692
Pittsburgh....	9	4	.692
Houston	8	5	.615
Florida	6	4	.600
New York ...	6	5	.545
St. Louis	9	8	.529
Arizona	11	10	.524
San Diego ...	6	6	.500
San Fran. ...	7	7	.500
Milwaukee ..	8	9	.471
Chicago	5	6	.455
Colorado	4	6	.400
Philadelphia	4	9	.308
Los Angeles	4	12	.250
Montreal	3	11	.214
Totals	116	111	.511

ON GRASS

	W	L	Pct.
Atlanta	88	48	.647
Cincinnati	36	20	.643
Arizona	89	51	.636
Houston	34	23	.596
New York	79	56	.585
San Fran.	71	63	.530
San Diego....	68	72	.486
St. Louis	64	70	.478
Los Angeles	63	72	.467
Colorado......	63	77	.450
Milwaukee ...	58	75	.436
Philadelphia	27	35	.435
Chicago	58	76	.433
Pittsburgh ...	24	34	.414
Montreal......	23	34	.404
Florida	52	80	.394
Totals	897	886	.503

ON TURF

	W	L	Pct.
New York	18	10	.643
Houston	63	42	.600
Atlanta	15	11	.577
Milwaukee ..	16	12	.571
Cincinnati ...	60	47	.561
San Fran. ...	15	13	.536
Pittsburgh....	54	49	.524
Los Angeles	14	13	.519
Arizona	11	11	.500
Philadelphia	50	50	.500
Montreal......	45	60	.429
Colorado	9	13	.409
St. Louis	11	16	.407
Florida	12	18	.400
Chicago	9	19	.321
San Diego ...	6	16	.273
Totals	408	400	.505

vs. LEFTHANDERS

	W	L	Pct.
Arizona	32	16	.667
Atlanta	29	15	.659
Houston	27	16	.628
Cincinnati ...	27	17	.614
New York	22	18	.550
Chicago	25	22	.532
Los Angeles	24	25	.490
Philadelphia	19	22	.463
Florida	18	21	.462
Montreal......	18	21	.462
Colorado	23	28	.451
Milwaukee ...	21	27	.438
San Fran. ...	18	28	.391
St. Louis	17	29	.370
Pittsburgh....	17	30	.362
San Diego ...	15	32	.319
Totals	352	367	.490

vs. RIGHTHANDERS

	W	L	Pct.
Atlanta	74	44	.627
New York	75	48	.610
Arizona	68	46	.596
Houston	70	49	.588
San Fran.	68	48	.586
Cincinnati	69	50	.580
Pittsburgh....	61	53	.535
San Diego ...	59	56	.513
St. Louis	58	57	.504
Philadelphia	58	63	.479
Los Angeles	53	60	.469
Milwaukee ..	53	60	.469
Colorado	49	62	.441
Montreal......	50	73	.407
Florida	46	77	.374
Chicago	42	73	.365
Totals	953	919	.509

TOP 15 QUALIFIERS FOR BATTING CHAMPIONSHIP
(502 or more plate appearances)

Batter	Team	BA	G	PA	AB	R	H	TB	2B	3B	HR	RBI	SH	SF	HBP	BB	IBB	SO	SB	CS	GIDP	SLG	OBP
Garciaparra, Nomar	Bos.	.357	135	595	532	103	190	321	42	4	27	104	0	4	8	51	7	39	14	3	11	.603	.418
Jeter, Derek	N.Y.	.349	158	739	627	134	219	346	37	9	24	102	3	6	12	91	5	116	19	8	12	.552	.438
Williams, Bernie	N.Y.	.342	158	697	591	116	202	317	28	6	25	115	0	5	1	100	17	95	9	10	11	.536	.435
Martinez, Edgar	Sea.	.337	142	608	502	86	169	278	35	1	24	86	0	3	6	97	6	99	7	2	12	.554	.447
Ramirez, Manny	Cle.	.333	147	640	522	131	174	346	34	3	44	165	0	9	13	96	9	131	2	4	12	.663	.442
Vizquel, Omar	Cle.	.333	144	664	574	112	191	250	36	4	5	66	17	7	1	65	0	50	42	9	8	.436	.397
Rodriguez, Ivan	Tex.	.332	144	630	600	116	199	335	29	1	35	113	0	5	4	24	2	64	25	12	31	.558	.356
Fernandez, Tony	Tor.	.328	142	576	485	73	159	218	41	0	6	75	0	4	10	77	11	62	6	7	10	.449	.427
Gonzalez, Juan	Tex.	.326	144	629	562	114	183	338	36	1	39	128	0	12	4	51	7	105	3	3	10	.601	.378
Palmeiro, Rafael	Tex.	.324	158	674	565	96	183	356	30	1	47	148	0	9	3	97	14	69	2	4	13	.630	.420
Alomar, Roberto	Cle.	.323	159	694	563	138	182	300	40	3	24	120	12	13	7	99	3	96	37	6	13	.533	.422
Sweeney, Mike	K.C.	.322	150	643	575	101	185	299	44	2	22	102	0	4	10	54	0	48	6	1	21	.520	.387
Bush, Homer	Tor.	.320	128	523	485	69	155	204	26	4	5	55	8	3	6	21	0	82	32	8	9	.421	.353
Velarde, Randy	Ana.-Oak.	.317	156	711	631	105	200	287	25	7	16	76	4	0	6	70	2	98	24	8	19	.455	.390
Giambi, Jason	Oak.	.315	158	695	575	115	181	318	36	1	33	123	0	8	7	105	6	106	1	1	11	.553	.422

TOP 15 QUALIFIERS FOR EARNED-RUN AVERAGE CHAMPIONSHIP
(162 or more innings pitched)

Pitcher	Team	W	L	WP	ERA	G	GS	CG	SHO	GF	SV	IP	H	BFP	R	ER	HR	SH	SF	HBP	BB	IBB	SO	WP	BK
Martinez, Pedro	Bos.	23	4	.852	2.07	31	29	5	1	1	0	213.1	160	835	56	49	9	3	6	9	37	1	313	6	0
Cone, David	N.Y.	12	9	.571	3.44	31	31	1	1	0	0	193.1	164	827	84	74	21	5	6	11	90	2	177	7	1
Mussina, Mike	Bal.	18	7	.720	3.50	31	31	4	0	0	0	203.1	207	842	88	79	16	9	7	1	52	0	172	2	0
Radke, Brad	Min.	12	14	.462	3.75	33	33	4	0	0	0	218.2	239	910	97	91	28	5	5	1	44	0	121	4	0
Rosado, Jose	K.C.	10	14	.417	3.85	33	33	5	0	0	0	208.0	197	882	103	89	24	8	4	5	72	1	141	4	0
Moyer, Jamie	Sea.	14	8	.636	3.87	32	32	4	0	0	0	228.0	235	945	108	98	23	6	2	9	48	1	137	3	0
Colon, Bartolo	Cle.	18	5	.783	3.95	32	32	1	1	0	0	205.0	185	858	97	90	24	5	4	7	76	5	161	4	0
Sirotka, Mike	Chi.	11	13	.458	4.00	32	32	3	1	0	0	209.0	236	909	108	93	24	5	9	3	57	2	125	4	0
Garcia, Freddy	Sea.	17	8	.680	4.07	33	33	2	1	0	0	201.1	205	888	96	91	18	3	6	10	90	4	170	12	3
Hernandez, Orlando	N.Y.	17	9	.654	4.12	33	33	2	1	0	0	214.1	187	910	108	98	24	3	11	8	87	2	157	4	0
Olivares, Omar	Ana.-Oak.	15	11	.577	4.16	32	32	4	0	0	0	205.2	217	885	105	95	19	3	7	9	81	0	85	6	0
Halama, John	Sea.	11	10	.524	4.22	38	24	1	1	7	0	179.0	193	763	88	84	20	5	9	7	56	3	105	4	0
Burba, Dave	Cle.	15	9	.625	4.25	34	34	1	0	0	0	220.0	211	940	113	104	30	2	3	8	96	3	174	13	0
Mays, Joe	Min.	6	11	.353	4.37	49	20	2	1	8	0	171.0	179	746	92	83	24	7	6	2	67	2	115	6	0
Finley, Chuck	Ana.	12	11	.522	4.43	33	33	1	0	0	0	213.1	197	913	117	105	23	7	3	8	94	2	200	15	0

BATTING LEADERS

Games
- 162 B.J. Surhoff, Bal.
- 161 Albert Belle, Bal.
- 160 Mike Bordick, Bal.
- 160 Ken Griffey Jr., Sea.
- 159 Roberto Alomar, Cle.
- 159 Miguel Tejada, Oak.
- 159 Tino Martinez, N.Y.

At-bats
- 673 B.J. Surhoff, Bal.
- 663 Carlos Beltran, K.C.
- 631 Mike Bordick, Bal.
- 631 Randy Velarde, Ana.-Oak.
- 628 Joe Randa, K.C.

Runs scored
- 138 Roberto Alomar, Cle.
- 134 Derek Jeter, N.Y.
- 134 Shawn Green, Tor.
- 131 Manny Ramirez, Cle.
- 123 Ken Griffey Jr., Sea.

Hits
- 219 Derek Jeter, N.Y.
- 207 B.J. Surhoff, Bal.
- 202 Bernie Williams, N.Y.
- 200 Randy Velarde, Ana.-Oak.
- 199 Ivan Rodriguez, Tex.

RBIs
- 165 Manny Ramirez, Cle.
- 148 Rafael Palmeiro, Tex.
- 134 Ken Griffey Jr., Sea.
- 134 Carlos Delgado, Tor.
- 128 Juan Gonzalez, Tex.

Total bases
- 361 Shawn Green, Tor.
- 356 Rafael Palmeiro, Tex.
- 349 Ken Griffey Jr., Sea.
- 346 Manny Ramirez, Cle.
- 346 Derek Jeter, N.Y.

Doubles
- 45 Shawn Green, Tor.
- 44 Jermaine Dye, K.C.
- 44 Mike Sweeney, K.C.
- 42 Nomar Garciaparra, Bos.
- 41 Todd Zeile, Tex.
- 41 Rusty Greer, Tex.
- 41 Tony Fernandez, Tor.

Triples
- 11 Jose Offerman, Bos.
- 9 Johnny Damon, K.C.
- 9 Derek Jeter, N.Y.
- 9 Carlos Febles, K.C.
- 8 Jermaine Dye, K.C.
- 8 Joe Randa, K.C.
- 8 Ray Durham, Chi.
- 8 Luis Polonia, Det.

Home runs
- 48 Ken Griffey Jr., Sea.
- 47 Rafael Palmeiro, Tex.
- 44 Manny Ramirez, Cle.
- 44 Carlos Delgado, Tor.
- 42 Shawn Green, Tor.
- 42 Alex Rodriguez, Sea.

Walks
- 127 Jim Thome, Cle.
- 105 Jason Giambi, Oak.
- 101 Albert Belle, Bal.
- 101 John Jaha, Oak.
- 100 Bernie Williams, N.Y.

On-base percentage
- .447 Edgar Martinez, Sea.
- .442 Manny Ramirez, Cle.
- .438 Derek Jeter, N.Y.
- .435 Bernie Williams, N.Y.
- .427 Tony Fernandez, Tor.

Slugging percentage
- .663 Manny Ramirez, Cle.
- .630 Rafael Palmeiro, Tex.
- .603 Nomar Garciaparra, Bos.

- .601 Juan Gonzalez, Tex.
- .588 Shawn Green, Tor.

Stolen bases
- 44 Brian L. Hunter, Det.-Sea.
- 42 Omar Vizquel, Cle.
- 39 Tom Goodwin, Tex.
- 37 Roberto Alomar, Cle.
- 37 Shannon Stewart, Tor.

Caught stealing
- 14 Shannon Stewart, Tor.
- 14 Mike Caruso, Chi.
- 12 Juan Encarnacion, Det.
- 12 Ivan Rodriguez, Tex.
- 12 Jose Offerman, Bos.

Sacrifice bunts
- 17 Omar Vizquel, Cle.
- 14 Darren Lewis, Bos.
- 14 Deivi Cruz, Det.
- 12 Roberto Alomar, Cle.
- 12 Carlos Febles, K.C.

Sacrifice flies
- 13 Roberto Alomar, Cle.
- 12 Juan Gonzalez, Tex.
- 10 Mike Bordick, Bal.
- 10 John Flaherty, T.B.
- 10 Paul O'Neill, N.Y.
- 10 Carlos Beltran, K.C.

Strikeouts
- 171 Jim Thome, Cle.
- 153 Dean Palmer, Det.
- 143 Troy Glaus, Ana.
- 141 Carlos Delgado, Tor.
- 135 Jose Canseco, T.B.

Intentional walks
- 17 Ken Griffey Jr., Sea.
- 17 Bernie Williams, N.Y.
- 15 Albert Belle, Bal.
- 14 Rafael Palmeiro, Tex.
- 13 Jim Thome, Cle.
- 13 Frank Thomas, Chi.

PITCHING LEADERS

Wins
- 23 Pedro Martinez, Bos.
- 18 Bartolo Colon, Cle
- 18 Mike Mussina, Bal.
- 18 Aaron Sele, Tex.
- 17 Freddy Garcia, Sea.
- 17 Orlando Hernandez, N.Y.
- 17 Charles Nagy, Cle.
- 17 David Wells, Tor.

Losses
- 16 Brian Moehler, Det.
- 15 Jim Parque, Chi.
- 15 Bobby Witt, T.B.
- 14 Kevin Appier, K.C.-Oak.
- 14 Jeff Fassero, Sea.-Tex.
- 14 LaTroy Hawkins, Min.
- 14 Brad Radke, Min.
- 14 Jose Rosado, K.C.

Games
- 76 Buddy Groom, Oak.
- 76 Bob Wells, Min.
- 75 Mike Trombley, Min.
- 74 Graeme Lloyd, Tor.
- 74 Derek Lowe, Bos.

Games started
- 35 Rick Helling, Tex.
- 34 Kevin Appier, K.C.-Oak.
- 34 Dave Burba, Cle.
- 34 Scott Erickson, Bal.
- 34 Pat Hentgen, Tor.
- 34 Eric Milton, Min.
- 34 David Wells, Tor.

Games finished
- 66 Roberto Hernandez, T.B.
- 65 Mike Jackson, Cle.
- 63 Mariano Rivera, N.Y.
- 62 Todd Jones, Det.
- 60 Jose Mesa, Sea.

Complete games
- 7 David Wells, Tor.
- 6 Scott Erickson, Bal.
- 6 Sidney Ponson, Bal.

Shutouts
- 5 Pedro Martinez, Bos.
- 5 Eric Milton, Min.
- 5 Jose Rosado, K.C.

Innings pitched
- 231.2 David Wells, Tor.
- 230.1 Scott Erickson, Bal.
- 228.0 Jaime Moyer, Sea.
- 220.0 Dave Burba, Cle.
- 219.1 Rick Helling, Tex.

Shutouts
- 3 Scott Erickson, Bal.
- 2 Eric Milton, Min.
- 2 Brian Moehler, Det.
- 2 Aaron Sele, Tex.
- 2 Bobby Witt, T.B.

Hits allowed
- 246 David Wells, Tor.
- 244 Scott Erickson, Bal.
- 244 Aaron Sele, Tex.
- 239 Brad Radke, Min.
- 238 LaTroy Hawkins, Min.
- 238 Charles Nagy, Cle.

Home runs allowed
- 41 Rick Helling, Tex.
- 35 Jeff Fassero, Sea.-Tex.
- 35 Sidney Ponson, Bal.
- 34 James Baldwin, Chi.
- 32 Pat Hentgen, Tor.
- 32 David Wells, Tor.

Runs allowed
- 136 LaTroy Hawkins, Min.
- 135 Jeff Fassero, Sea.-Tex.
- 132 David Wells, Tor.
- 131 Kevin Appier, K.C.-Oak.
- 130 Bobby Witt, T.B.

Earned runs allowed
- 129 LaTroy Hawkins, Min.
- 125 Jeff Fassero, Sea.-Tex.
- 124 David Wells, Tor.
- 123 Scott Erickson, Bal.
- 120 Kevin Appier, K.C.-Oak.

Batting average yielded
- .205 Pedro Martinez, Bos.
- .229 David Cone, N.Y.
- .233 Orlando Hernandez, N.Y.
- .242 Bartolo Colon, Cle.
- .243 Eric Milton, Min.

Walks
- 99 Scott Erickson, Bal.
- 96 Dave Burba, Cle.
- 96 Bobby Witt, T.B.
- 94 Chuck Finley, Ana.
- 90 Roger Clemens, N.Y.
- 90 David Cone, N.Y.
- 90 Freddy Garcia, Sea.

Strikeouts
- 313 Pedro Martinez, Bos.
- 200 Chuck Finley, Ana.
- 186 Aaron Sele, Tex.
- 177 David Cone, N.Y.
- 174 Dave Burba, Cle.

Hit batsmen
- 17 Jeff Weaver, Det.
- 14 Rolando Arrojo, T.B.
- 12 Dave Mlicki, Det.
- 12 Ryan Rupe, T.B.
- 12 Aaron Sele, Tex.

Wild pitches
- 15 Chuck Finley, Ana.
- 13 Dave Burba, Cle.
- 13 Tom Candiotti, Oak.-Cle.
- 12 Freddy Garcia, Sea.
- 11 James Baldwin, Chi.
- 11 John Snyder, Chi.
- 11 Makoto Suzuki, Sea.-K.C.

Saves
- 45 Mariano Rivera, N.Y.
- 43 Roberto Hernandez, T.B.
- 43 John Wetteland, Tex.
- 39 Mike Jackson, Cle.
- 33 Jose Mesa, Sea.

1999 REVIEW

TOP 15 QUALIFIERS FOR BATTING CHAMPIONSHIP
(502 or more plate appearances)

Batter	Team	BA	G	PA	AB	R	H	TB	2B	3B	HR	RBI	SH	SF	HBP	BB	IBB	SO	SB	CS	GIDP	SLG	OBP
Walker, Larry	Col.	.379	127	513	438	108	166	311	26	4	37	115	0	6	12	57	8	52	11	4	12	.710	.458
Gonzalez, Luis	Ari.	.336	153	693	614	112	206	337	45	4	26	111	1	5	7	66	6	63	9	5	13	.549	.403
Abreu, Bobby	Phi.	.335	152	662	546	118	183	300	35	11	20	93	0	4	3	109	8	113	27	9	13	.549	.446
Casey, Sean	Cin.	.332	151	669	594	103	197	320	42	3	25	99	0	5	9	61	13	88	0	2	15	.539	.399
Cirillo, Jeff	Mil.	.326	157	697	607	98	198	280	35	1	15	88	3	7	5	75	4	83	7	4	15	.461	.401
Grudzielanek, Mark	L.A.	.326	123	534	488	72	159	213	23	5	7	46	2	3	10	31	1	65	6	6	13	.436	.376
Everett, Carl	Hou.	.325	123	535	464	86	151	265	33	4	25	108	2	8	11	50	5	82	27	7	9	.571	.398
Glanville, Doug	Phi.	.325	150	692	628	101	204	287	38	6	11	73	5	6	6	68	0	77	7	6	14	.457	.376
Helton, Todd	Col.	.320	159	656	578	114	185	339	39	5	35	113	0	4	6	68	6	77	7	6	14	.587	.395
Jones, Chipper	Atl.	.319	157	701	567	116	181	359	41	1	45	110	0	6	2	126	18	94	25	3	20	.633	.441
Guerrero, Vladimir	Mon.	.316	160	674	610	102	193	366	37	5	42	131	0	2	7	55	14	62	14	7	18	.600	.378
Henderson, Rickey	N.Y.	.315	121	526	438	89	138	204	30	1	12	42	1	3	2	82	1	82	37	14	4	.466	.423
Hamilton, Darryl	Col.-N.Y.*	.315	146	568	505	82	159	213	19	4	9	45	3	1	2	57	0	39	6	8	9	.422	.386
Giles, Brian	Pit.	.315	141	627	521	109	164	320	33	3	39	115	0	8	3	95	7	80	6	2	14	.614	.418
Cedeno, Roger	N.Y.	.313	155	525	453	90	142	185	23	4	4	36	7	2	3	60	3	100	66	17	5	.408	.396

TOP 15 QUALIFIERS FOR EARNED-RUN AVERAGE CHAMPIONSHIP
(162 or more innings pitched)

Pitcher	Team	W	L	WP	ERA	G	GS	CG	SHO	GF	SV	IP	H	BFP	R	ER	HR	SH	SF	HBP	BB	IBB	SO	WP	BK
Johnson, Randy	Ari.	17	9	.654	2.48	35	35	12	2	0	0	271.2	207	1079	86	75	30	4	3	9	70	3	364	4	2
Millwood, Kevin	Atl.	18	7	.720	2.68	33	33	2	0	0	0	228.0	168	906	80	68	24	9	3	4	59	2	205	5	0
Hampton, Mike	Hou.	22	4	.846	2.90	34	34	3	2	0	0	239.0	206	979	86	77	12	10	9	5	101	2	177	9	0
Brown, Kevin	L.A.	18	9	.667	3.00	35	35	5	1	0	0	252.1	210	1018	99	84	19	7	1	7	59	1	221	4	1
Smoltz, John	Atl.	11	8	.579	3.19	29	29	1	1	0	0	186.1	168	746	70	66	14	10	5	4	40	2	156	2	0
Ritchie, Todd	Pit.	15	9	.625	3.49	28	26	2	0	0	0	172.2	169	716	79	67	17	3	2	4	54	3	107	7	0
Schilling, Curt	Phi.	15	6	.714	3.54	24	24	8	1	0	0	180.1	159	735	74	71	25	11	5	3	37	8	136	1	0
Maddux, Greg	Atl.	19	9	.679	3.57	33	33	4	0	0	0	219.1	258	940	103	87	16	15	5	4	44	2	187	8	0
Lima, Jose	Hou.	21	10	.677	3.58	35	35	3	0	0	0	246.1	256	1024	108	98	30	5	7	2	44	2	187	8	0
Daal, Omar	Ari.	16	9	.640	3.65	32	32	2	1	0	0	214.2	188	895	92	87	21	4	7	7	79	3	148	3	2
Harnisch, Pete	Cin.	16	10	.615	3.68	33	33	2	2	0	0	198.1	190	833	86	81	25	10	6	5	57	2	120	3	0
Ashby, Andy	S.D.	14	10	.583	3.80	31	31	4	3	0	0	206.0	204	862	95	87	26	10	1	7	54	4	132	6	0
Ortiz, Russ	S.F.	18	9	.667	3.81	33	33	3	0	0	0	207.2	189	922	109	88	24	11	6	6	125	5	164	13	0
Reynolds, Shane	Hou.	16	14	.533	3.85	35	35	4	2	0	0	231.2	250	963	108	99	23	11	5	1	37	0	197	4	0
Bottenfield, Kent	St.L	18	7	.720	3.97	31	31	0	0	0	0	190.1	197	843	91	84	21	11	9	5	89	5	124	1	0

BATTING LEADERS

Games
162 Jeff Bagwell, Hou.
162 Andruw Jones, Atl.
162 John Olerud, N.Y.
162 Sammy Sosa, Chi.
161 Mark Grace, Chi.
161 Barry Larkin, Cin.
161 J.T. Snow, S.F.
161 Robin Ventura, N.Y.

At-bats
690 Neifi Perez, Col.
639 Craig Biggio, Hou.
628 Edgardo Alfonzo, N.Y.
628 Doug Glanville, Phi.
627 Matt Williams, Ari.

Runs scored
143 Jeff Bagwell, Hou.
132 Jay Bell, Ari.
123 Craig Biggio, Hou.
123 Edgardo Alfonzo, N.Y.
118 Bobby Abreu, Phi.
118 Mark McGwire, St.L.

Hits
206 Luis Gonzalez, Ari.
204 Doug Glanville, Phi.
198 Jeff Cirillo, Mil.
197 Sean Casey, Cin.
193 Neifi Perez, Col.
193 Vladimir Guerrero, Mon.

RBIs
147 Mark McGwire, St.L.
142 Matt Williams, Ari.
141 Sammy Sosa, Chi.
133 Dante Bichette, Col.
131 Vladimir Guerrero, Mon.

Total bases
397 Sammy Sosa, Chi.
366 Vladimir Guerrero, Mon.
363 Mark McGwire, St.L.
359 Chipper Jones, Atl.
339 Todd Helton, Col.

Doubles
56 Craig Biggio, Hou.
45 Luis Gonzalez, Ari.
45 Jose Vidro, Mon.
44 Mark Grace, Chi.
43 Geoff Jenkins, Mil.

Triples
11 Bobby Abreu, Phi.
11 Neifi Perez, Col.
10 Steve Finley, Ari.
10 Tony Womack, Ari.
9 Mike Cameron, Cin.
9 Mark Kotsay, Fla.

Home runs
65 Mark McGwire, St.L.
63 Sammy Sosa, Chi.
45 Greg Vaughn, Cin.
45 Chipper Jones, Atl.
42 Vladimir Guerrero, Mon.
42 Jeff Bagwell, Hou.

Walks
149 Jeff Bagwell, Hou.
133 Mark McGwire, St.L.
126 Chipper Jones, Atl.
125 John Olerud, N.Y.
109 Bobby Abreu, Phi.

On-base percentage
.458 Larry Walker, Col.
.454 Jeff Bagwell, Hou.
.446 Bobby Abreu, Phi.
.441 Chipper Jones, Atl.
.427 John Olerud, N.Y.

Slugging percentage
.710 Larry Walker, Col.
.697 Mark McGwire, St.L.
.635 Sammy Sosa, Chi.
.633 Chipper Jones, Atl.
.614 Brian S. Giles, Pit.

Stolen bases
72 Tony Womack, Ari.
66 Roger Cedeno, N.Y.
51 Eric Young, L.A.
50 Luis Castillo, Fla.
38 Mike Cameron, Cin.
38 Pokey Reese, Cin.

Caught stealing
22 Eric Young, L.A.
17 Roger Cedeno, N.Y.
17 Luis Castillo, Fla.
14 Quilvio Veras, S.D.
14 Rickey Henderson, N.Y.
14 Craig Biggio, Hou.
14 Marvin Benard, S.F.

Sacrifice bunts
17 Shane Reynolds, Hou.
13 Abraham Nunez, Pit.
13 Greg Maddux, Atl.
13 Jose Lima, Hou.
13 Kevin Brown, L.A.

Sacrifice flies
10 Dante Bichette, Col.
10 Mark Grace, Chi.
9 Jay Bell, Ari.
9 Mark Kotsay, Fla.
9 Edgardo Alfonzo, N.Y.
9 Brian Jordan, Atl.
9 Gary Sheffield, L.A.

Strikeouts
171 Sammy Sosa, Chi.
156 Preston Wilson, Fla.
145 Mike Cameron, Cin.
145 Jose Hernandez, Chi.-Atl.
143 Ruben Rivera, S.D.

Intentional walks
21 Mark McGwire, St.L.
18 Chipper Jones, Atl.
16 Jeff Bagwell, Hou.
14 Vladimir Guerrero, Mon.
13 Sean Casey, Cin.

PITCHING LEADERS

Wins
22 Mike Hampton, Hou.
21 Jose Lima, Hou.
19 Greg Maddux, Atl.
18 Kent Bottenfield, St.L.
18 Kevin Brown, L.A.
18 Kevin Millwood, Atl.
18 Russ Ortiz, S.F.

Losses
18 Steve Trachsel, Chi.
16 Dennis Springer, Fla.
15 Brian Meadows, Fla.
14 Shane Reynolds, Hou.
14 Sterling Hitchcock, S.D.
14 Kris Benson, Pit.
14 Dustin Hermanson, Mon.
14 Ismael Valdes, L.A.
14 Jose Jimenez, St.L.

Games
82 Steve Kline, Mon.
80 Turk Wendell, N.Y.
79 Scott Sullivan, Cin.
79 Anthony Telford, Mon.
77 Armando Benitez, N.Y.

Games started
35 Shane Reynolds, Hou.
35 Tom Glavine, Atl.
35 Jose Lima, Hou.
35 Kevin Brown, L.A.
35 Randy Johnson, Ari.

Games finished
64 Robb Nen, S.F.
63 Dave Veres, Col.
63 Bob Wickman, Mil.
62 Ugueth Urbina, Mon.
61 John Rocker, Atl.

Complete games
12 Randy Johnson, Ari.
8 Curt Schilling, Phi.
7 Pedro Astacio, Col.
5 Kevin Brown, L.A.
4 Shane Reynolds, Hou.
4 Steve Trachsel, Chi.
4 Greg Maddux, Atl.
4 Andy Ashby, S.D.

Innings pitched
271.2 Randy Johnson, Ari.
252.1 Kevin Brown, L.A.
246.1 Jose Lima, Hou.
239.0 Mike Hampton, Hou.
234.0 Tom Glavine, Atl.

Shutouts
3 Andy Ashby, S.D.
2 Randy Johnson, Ari.
2 Mike Hampton, Hou.
2 Shane Reynolds, Hou.
2 Pete Harnisch, Cin.
2 Dennis Springer, Fla.
2 Jose Jimenez, St.L.

Hits allowed
259 Tom Glavine, Atl.
258 Pedro Astacio, Col.
258 Greg Maddux, Atl.
256 Jose Lima, Hou.
250 Shane Reynolds, Hou.

Home runs allowed
38 Pedro Astacio, Col.
36 Chad Ogea, Phi.
34 Andy Benes, Ari.
34 Paul Byrd, Phi.
33 Darryl Kile, Col.
33 Woody Williams, S.D.

Runs allowed
150 Darryl Kile, Col.
146 Brian Bohanon, Col.
140 Pedro Astacio, Col.
133 Steve Trachsel, Chi.
121 Dennis Springer, Fla.
121 Scott Karl, Mil.
121 Shawn Estes, S.F.

Earned runs allowed
140 Darryl Kile, Col.
136 Brian Bohanon, Col.
130 Pedro Astacio, Col.
127 Steve Trachsel, Chi.
113 Chan Ho Park, L.A.

Batting average yielded
.202 Kevin Millwood, Atl.
.208 Randy Johnson, Ari.
.222 Kevin Brown, L.A.
.236 Omar Daal, Ari.
.237 Curt Schilling, Phi.

Walks
125 Russ Ortiz, S.F.
112 Shawn Estes, S.F.
109 Darryl Kile, Col.
101 Mike Hampton, Hou.
100 Chan Ho Park, L.A.

Strikeouts
364 Randy Johnson, Ari.
221 Kevin Brown, L.A.
210 Pedro Astacio, Col.
205 Kevin Millwood, Atl.
197 Shane Reynolds, Hou.

Hit batsmen
17 Paul Byrd, Phi.
14 Chan Ho Park, L.A.
14 Brian Bohanon, Col.
11 Pedro Astacio, Col.
11 Darren Oliver, Col.
11 Jose Jimenez, St.L.
11 Orel Hershiser, N.Y.

Wild pitches
15 Sterling Hitchcock, S.D.
15 Shawn Estes, S.F.
13 Russ Ortiz, S.F.
13 Darryl Kile, Col.
13 Scott Williamson, Cin.

Saves
41 Ugueth Urbina, Mon.
40 Trevor Hoffman, S.D.
39 Billy Wagner, Hou.
38 John Rocker, Atl.
37 Robb Nen, S.F.
37 Bob Wickman, Mil.

AMERICAN LEAGUE MVP

Player, Team	1	2	3	4	5	6	7	8	9	10	Pts.
Ivan Rodriguez, Texas	7	6	7	-	5	2	1	-	-	-	252
Pedro Martinez, Boston	8	6	4	1	2	2	3	-	-	-	239
Roberto Alomar, Cleveland	4	7	6	4	4	-	1	1	-	-	226
Manny Ramirez, Cleveland	4	4	5	9	1	5	-	-	-	-	226
Rafael Palmeiro, Texas	4	1	2	4	8	4	3	1	-	1	193
Derek Jeter, New York	1	2	2	9	3	7	2	1	1	-	177
Nomar Garciaparra, Boston	-	2	2	-	5	5	10	2	1	-	137
Jason Giambi, Oakland	-	-	-	1	-	1	2	6	3	5	49
Shawn Green, Toronto	-	-	-	-	-	1	-	4	10	7	44
Ken Griffey Jr., Seattle	-	-	-	-	-	-	2	6	6	4	42
Bernie Williams, New York	-	-	-	-	-	1	1	2	2	2	21
Carlos Delgado, Toronto	-	-	-	-	-	-	2	1	1	3	16
Juan Gonzalez, Texas	-	-	-	-	-	-	1	1	1	1	10
Mariano Rivera, New York	-	-	-	-	-	-	-	2	1	1	9
Alex Rodriguez, Seattle	-	-	-	-	-	-	-	-	1	2	4
Omar Vizquel, Cleveland	-	-	-	-	-	-	-	1	-	-	3
Matt Stairs, Oakland	-	-	-	-	-	-	-	-	1	-	2
John Jaha, Oakland	-	-	-	-	-	-	-	-	-	1	1
B.J. Surhoff, Baltimore	-	-	-	-	-	-	-	-	-	1	1

14 points awarded for a first-place vote, 9 for a second, 8 for a third, 7 for a fourth, etc.

NATIONAL LEAGUE MVP

Player, Team	1	2	3	4	5	6	7	8	9	10	Pts.
Chipper Jones, Atlanta	29	2	1	-	-	-	-	-	-	-	432
Jeff Bagwell, Houston	1	20	6	4	1	-	-	-	-	-	276
Matt Williams, Arizona	2	7	21	-	1	-	1	-	-	-	269
Greg Vaughn, Cincinnati	-	1	2	7	2	3	3	2	1	-	121
Mark McGwire, St. Louis	-	1	1	3	1	3	6	5	7	3	115
Robin Ventura, New York	-	1	-	4	5	7	2	1	-	-	113
Mike Piazza, New York	-	-	-	5	7	2	3	1	3	1	109
Edgardo Alfonzo, New York	-	-	1	6	4	2	-	1	-	1	88
Sammy Sosa, Chicago	-	-	-	-	3	5	2	6	5	8	87
Larry Walker, Colorado	-	-	-	-	-	1	4	-	5	4	35
Vladimir Guerrero, Montreal	-	-	-	1	-	-	2	4	1	5	34
Craig Biggio, Houston	-	-	-	1	2	1	1	-	2	-	32
Jay Bell, Arizona	-	-	-	-	1	2	2	1	2	-	31
Sean Casey, Cincinnati	-	-	-	-	1	2	1	-	-	3	23
Randy Johnson, Arizona	-	-	-	-	2	1	-	1	-	1	21
Billy Wagner, Houston	-	-	-	-	1	-	2	1	-	2	19
Carl Everett, Houston	-	-	-	-	-	-	-	4	1	1	15
Luis Gonzalez, Arizona	-	-	-	-	-	-	1	1	2	1	12
Brian Jordan, Atlanta	-	-	-	-	1	1	-	-	-	-	11
Brian Giles, Pittsburgh	-	-	-	-	-	2	-	-	-	1	11
Mike Hampton, Houston	-	-	-	-	-	-	1	2	-	-	10
Barry Larkin, Cincinnati	-	-	-	1	-	-	-	-	-	-	7
Bobby Abreu, Philadelphia	-	-	-	-	-	-	1	-	1	-	6
Barry Bonds, San Francisco	-	-	-	-	-	-	-	1	-	-	3
Matt Mantei, Florida-Arizona	-	-	-	-	-	-	-	1	-	-	3
Jeff Kent, San Francisco	-	-	-	-	-	-	-	-	1	-	2
Kevin Millwood, Atlanta	-	-	-	-	-	-	-	-	1	-	2
Trevor Hoffman, San Diego	-	-	-	-	-	-	-	-	-	1	1

14 points awarded for a first-place vote, 9 for a second, 8 for a third, 7 for a fourth, etc.

A.L. CY YOUNG

Player, Team	1	2	3	Pts.
Pedro Martinez, Boston	28	-	-	140
Mike Mussina, Baltimore	-	16	6	54
Mariano Rivera, New York	-	6	9	27
Bartolo Colon, Cleveland	-	3	5	14
Aaron Sele, Texas	-	-	4	4
David Cone, New York	-	1	-	3
Jamie Moyer, Seattle	-	1	-	3
John Wetteland, Texas	-	1	-	3
Freddy Garcia, Seattle	-	-	2	2
Keith Foulke, Chicago	-	-	1	1
Roberto Hernandez, Tampa Bay	-	-	1	1

5 points awarded for a first-place vote, 3 for a second, 1 for a third.

A.L. ROOKIE OF THE YEAR

Player, Team	1	2	3	Pts.
Carlos Beltran, Kansas City	26	1	-	133
Freddy Garcia, Seattle	1	12	4	45
Jeff Zimmerman, Texas	-	6	9	27
Brian Daubach, Boston	1	3	2	16
Tim Hudson, Oakland	-	3	4	13
Chris Singleton, Chicago	-	2	3	9
Carlos Lee, Chicago	-	1	1	4
Billy Koch, Toronto	-	-	4	4
Trot Nixon, Boston	-	-	1	1

5 points awarded for a first-place vote, 3 for a second, 1 for a third.

A.L. MANAGER OF THE YEAR

Manager, Team	1	2	3	Pts.
Jimy Williams, Boston	20	5	-	115
Art Howe, Oakland	5	19	3	85
Joe Torre, New York	-	4	9	21
Johnny Oates, Texas	1	-	13	18
Mike Hargrove, Cleveland	2	-	3	13

5 points awarded for a first-place vote, 3 for a second, 1 for a third.

Ivan Rodriguez's offensive and defensive skills earned him the 1999 A.L. MVP.

Pedro Martinez earned his second Cy Young Award in 1999 with a 23-4 record, 313 strikeouts and a 2.07 ERA.

N.L. CY YOUNG

Player, Team	1	2	3	Pts.
Randy Johnson, Arizona	20	11	1	134
Mike Hampton, Houston	11	17	4	110
Kevin Millwood, Atlanta	1	4	19	36
Jose Lima, Houston	-	-	3	3
Billy Wagner, Houston	-	-	3	3
Kevin Brown, Los Angeles	-	-	1	1
Trevor Hoffman, San Diego	-	-	1	1

5 points awarded for a first-place vote, 3 for a second, 1 for a third.

N.L. ROOKIE OF THE YEAR

Player, Team	1	2	3	Pts.
Scott Williamson, Cincinnati	17	9	6	118
Preston Wilson, Florida	9	11	10	88
Warren Morris, Pittsburgh	6	10	9	69
Kris Benson, Pittsburgh	-	1	2	5
Alex Gonzalez, Florida	-	1	1	4
Joe McEwing, St. Louis	-	-	3	3
Kevin McGlinchy, Atlanta	-	-	1	1

5 points awarded for a first-place vote, 3 for a second, 1 for a third.

N.L. MANAGER OF THE YEAR

Manager, Team	1	2	3	Pts.
Jack McKeon, Cincinnati	17	9	3	115
Bobby Cox, Atlanta	10	14	6	98
Larry Dierker, Houston	4	6	10	48
Buck Showalter, Arizona	1	1	9	17
Bobby Valentine, New York	-	2	4	10

5 points awarded for a first-place vote, 3 for a second, 1 for a third.

GOLD GLOVE WINNERS

First basemen	PO	A	E	Pct.
A.L.: Rafael Palmeiro, Rangers 261	13	1		.996
N.L.: J.T. Snow, Giants 1221	122	6		.996

Second basemen				
A.L.: Roberto Alomar, Indians 270	466	6		.992
N.L.: Pokey Reese, Reds 325	409	7		.991

Shortstops				
A.L.: Omar Vizquel, Indians 221	396	15		.976
N.L.: Rey Ordonez, Mets 220	416	4		.994

Third basemen				
A.L.: Scott Brosius, Yankees 87	239	13		.962
N.L.: Robin Ventura, Mets...............123	320	9		.980

Outfielders				
A.L.: Ken Griffey Jr., Mariners 387	10	9		.978
A.L.: Bernie Williams, Yankees 381	9	5		.987
A.L.: Shawn Green, Blue Jays 340	5	1		.997
N.L.: Andruw Jones, Braves 492	13	10		.981
N.L.: Larry Walker, Rockies 204	13	4		.982
N.L.: Steve Finley, Diamondbacks 397	5	2		.995

Catchers				
A.L.: Ivan Rodriguez, Rangers..........850	83	7		.993
N.L.: Mike Lieberthal, Phillies 881	62	3		.997

Pitchers				
A.L.: Mike Mussina, Orioles 14	46	1		.984
N.L.: Greg Maddux, Braves 29	58	4		.956

Note: Voting by Major League players and managers is conducted by THE SPORTING NEWS.

SILVER SLUGGERS

First basemen	Avg.	H	HR	RBI
A.L.: Carlos Delgado, Blue Jays	.272	156	44	134
N.L.: Jeff Bagwell, Astros	.304	171	42	126

Second basemen				
A.L.: Roberto Alomar, Indians........	.323	182	24	120
N.L.: Edgardo Alfonzo, Mets..........	.304	191	27	108

Shortstops				
A.L.: Alex Rodriguez, Mariners	.285	143	42	111
N.L.: Barry Larkin, Reds	.293	171	12	75

Third basemen				
A.L.: Dean Palmer, Tigers	.263	147	38	100
N.L.: Chipper Jones, Braves	.319	181	45	110

Outfielders				
A.L.: Ken Griffey Jr., Mariners........	.285	173	48	134
A.L.: Manny Ramirez, Indians........	.333	174	44	165
A.L.: Shawn Green, Blue Jays	.309	190	42	123
N.L.: Sammy Sosa, Cubs	.288	180	63	141
N.L.: Larry Walker, Rockies	.379	166	37	115
N.L.: Vladimir Guerrero, Expos......	.316	193	42	131

Catchers				
A.L.: Ivan Rodriguez, Rangers	.332	199	35	113
N.L.: Mike Piazza, Mets**............	.303	162	40	124

Pitcher				
N.L.: Mike Hampton, Astros	.311	23	0	10

Designated hitter				
A.L.: Rafael Palmeiro, Rangers......	.324	183	47	148

Note: Voting by Major League players and managers is conducted by THE SPORTING NEWS.

PLAYERS OF THE WEEK

April 4-11   Position
A.L.: Chili Davis, Yankees ....designated hitter
N.L.: Raul Mondesi, Dodgers...........................outfield

April 12-18
A.L.: Tim Salmon, Angels ....outfield
N.L.: Jay Bell, Diamondbacks ....second base

April 19-25
A.L.: Jose Canseco, Devil Rays.............designated hitter
N.L.: Matt Williams, Diamondbacks.........................third base

Ken Griffey Jr. can do much more than wield the bat. He won his 10th straight Gold Glove Award in 1999, the longest streak for an active player.

April 26-May 2
A.L.: Shannon Stewart, Blue Jays ....outfield
N.L.: Larry Walker, Rockies ....outfield

May 3-9
A.L.: Fred McGriff, Devil Rays.......................first base
N.L.: Brian Giles, Pirates ....outfield

May 10-16
A.L.: Mo Vaughn, Angels ....first base
N.L.: Carl Everett, Astros ....outfield

May 17-23
A.L.: Jermaine Dye, Royals ....outfield
N.L.: Dante Bichette, Rockies ....outfield
     Mike Lieberthal, Phillies ....catcher

May 24-30
A.L.: Greg Norton, White Sox ....third base
N.L.: Randy Johnson ....pitcher

May 31-June 6
A.L.: Frank Thomas, White Sox...........DH/first base
     Troy Glaus, Angels ....third base
N.L.: Steve Finley, Diamondbacks ....outfield

June 7-13
A.L.: Joe Randa, Royals.............................third base
N.L.: Matt Williams, Diamondbacks.........................third base

June 14-20
A.L.: Tony Fernandez, Blue Jays ....third base
     Pedro Martinez, Red Sox.......................pitcher
N.L.: Todd Helton, Rockies ....first base

June 21-27
A.L.: Tino Martinez, Yankees.....................first base
N.L.: Jose Jimenez, Cardinals......................pitcher

June 28-July 4
A.L.: Mike Sweeney, Royals.........................catcher
N.L.: Reggie Sanders, Padres ....outfield

July 5-11
A.L.: Manny Ramirez, Indians ....outfield
N.L.: Mike Piazza, Mets ....catcher

July 12-18
A.L.: David Cone, Yankees ....pitcher
N.L.: Kevin Young, Pirates ....first base

July 19-25
A.L.: Todd Zeile, Rangers...........................third base
N.L.: Octavio Dotel, Mets ....pitcher

July 26-August 1
A.L.: Roberto Alomar, Indians ....second base
N.L.: Robin Ventura, Mets ....third base

August 2-8
A.L.: Wade Boggs, Devil Rays ....third base
     Miguel Tejada, Athletics ....shortstop

N.L.: Tony Gwynn, Padres ....outfield
     Mark McGwire, Cardinals ....first base

August 9-15
A.L.: Brian Daubach, Red Sox.....................first base
N.L.: Dante Bichette, Rockies ....outfield
     Vladimir Guerrero, Expos........................outfield

August 16-22
A.L.: Rafael Palmeiro, Rangers ....DH/first base
N.L.: Randy Johnson, Diamondbacks..........................pitcher

August 23-29
A.L.: Carlos Lee, White Sox ....outfield
N.L.: J.T. Snow, Giants ....first base

August 30-September 5
A.L.: Edgar Martinez, Mariners ....designated hitter
N.L.: Brian Giles, Pirates ....outfield

September 6-12
A.L.: Eric Milton, Twins................................pitcher
N.L.: Aaron Boone, Reds ....third base

September 13-19
A.L.: Nomar Garciaparra, Red Sox ....shortstop
N.L.: Jeff Cirillo, Brewers ....third base

September 20-26
A.L.: Albert Belle, Orioles ....outfield
N.L.: Eric Karros, Dodgers ....first base

September 27-October 4
A.L.: Homer Bush, Blue Jays ....second base
N.L.: Vladimir Guerrero, Expos ....outfield

PLAYERS OF THE MONTH

April	Avg.	R	HR	RBI
A.L.: Manny Ramirez, Indians........	.337	19	7	30
N.L.: Matt Williams, D-backs	.357	18	8	25

May				
A.L.: Nomar Garciaparra, Red Sox	.355	26	10	33
N.L.: Sammy Sosa, Cubs	.321	26	13	27

June				
A.L.: Rafael Palmeiro, Rangers......	.369	14	6	30
N.L.: Jeromy Burnitz, Brewers	.317	23	12	31

July				
A.L.: Joe Randa, Royals	.442	21	6	19
N.L.: Mark McGwire, Cardinals......	.295	21	16	30

August				
A.L.: Rafael Palmeiro, Rangers......	.318	25	15	39
Ivan Rodriguez, Rangers......	.349	29	12	28
N.L.: Vladimir Guerrero, Expos......	.355	26	12	29

September				
A.L.: Albert Belle, Orioles	.381	24	8	30
N.L.: Greg Vaughn, Reds	.287	28	14	33

PITCHERS OF THE MONTH

April	W	L	Pct.	ERA
A.L.: Pedro Martinez, Red Sox 4	1		.800	2.21
N.L.: John Smoltz, Braves 4	0		1.000	1.51

May				
A.L.: Pedro Martinez, Red Sox 6	0		1.000	1.84
N.L.: Curt Schilling, Phillies...............5	1		.833	2.42

June				
A.L.: Pedro Martinez, Red Sox 4	1		.800	2.25
N.L.: Al Leiter, Mets 5	0		1.000	2.62

July				
A.L.: Hideki Irabu, Yankees 4	0		1.000	2.64
N.L.: Randy Johnson, D-backs 2	3		.400	1.13

August				
A.L.: Mariano Rivera, Yankees............1	0		1.000	0.00
N.L.: Greg Maddux, Braves 6	0		1.000	3.69

September				
A.L.: Pedro Martinez, Red Sox 4	0		1.000	0.88
N.L.: Denny Neagle, Reds 5	0		1.000	2.00

BATTERS

BATTING AVERAGE
(minimum 3,000 at-bats)
1. Tony Gwynn ...344
2. Mike Piazza ...329
3. Edgar Martinez ...322
4. Frank Thomas ...320
5. Paul Molitor ...313
   Larry Walker ...313
7. Kirby Puckett ...312
8. Mark Grace ...310
   Kenny Lofton ...310
10. Roberto Alomar ...308
11. Manny Ramirez ...307
    Hal Morris ...307
13. Julio Franco ...304
    Wade Boggs ...304
    Jeff Bagwell ...304
    Bernie Williams ...304
17. Dante Bichette ...303
    Barry Larkin ...303
19. Barry Bonds ...302
    Will Clark ...302
    Ken Griffey Jr. ...302

GAMES
1. Rafael Palmeiro ...1,526
2. Craig Biggio ...1,515
3. Mark Grace ...1,491
4. Jay Bell ...1,487
5. Cal Ripken ...1,475
6. Fred McGriff ...1,472
7. Steve Finley ...1,457
8. Todd Zeile ...1,445
9. Barry Bonds ...1,434
10. Roberto Alomar ...1,421
11. Paul O'Neill ...1,420
12. Marquis Grissom ...1,409
13. Ken Griffey Jr. ...1,408
14. Robin Ventura ...1,399
15. John Olerud ...1,390

AT-BATS
1. Rafael Palmeiro ...5,848
2. Craig Biggio ...5,823
3. Cal Ripken ...5,710
4. Mark Grace ...5,650
5. Jay Bell ...5,619
6. Steve Finley ...5,571
7. Marquis Grissom ...5,529
8. Roberto Alomar ...5,443
9. Fred McGriff ...5,399
10. Ken Griffey Jr. ...5,377
11. Todd Zeile ...5,262
12. Dante Bichette ...5,231
13. Matt Williams ...5,179
14. Travis Fryman ...5,176
15. Paul O'Neill ...5,155

RUNS
1. Barry Bonds ...1,091
2. Craig Biggio ...1,042
3. Ken Griffey Jr. ...1,002
4. Frank Thomas ...968
5. Rafael Palmeiro ...965
6. Roberto Alomar ...951
7. Chuck Knoblauch ...950
8. Tony Phillips ...946
9. Rickey Henderson ...932
10. Jeff Bagwell ...921
11. Jay Bell ...890
12. Larry Walker ...882
13. Albert Belle ...881
14. Steve Finley ...870
15. Edgar Martinez ...854

HITS
1. Mark Grace ...1,754
2. Rafael Palmeiro ...1,747
3. Craig Biggio ...1,728
4. Tony Gwynn ...1,713
5. Roberto Alomar ...1,678
6. Ken Griffey Jr. ...1,622
7. Cal Ripken ...1,589
8. Dante Bichette ...1,584
9. Fred McGriff ...1,573
10. Paul Molitor ...1,568
11. Frank Thomas ...1,564
12. Chuck Knoblauch ...1,533
13. Steve Finley ...1,532
14. Marquis Grissom ...1,531
15. Jay Bell ...1,529

DOUBLES
1. Mark Grace ...364
2. Craig Biggio ...362
3. Edgar Martinez ...358
4. Albert Belle ...344
5. Rafael Palmeiro ...343
6. Dante Bichette ...330
   Tony Gwynn ...330
8. Paul O'Neill ...328
9. John Olerud ...322
10. Roberto Alomar ...321
11. Thomas, Frank ...317
12. Jeff Bagwell ...314
    Larry Walker ...314
14. Jay Bell ...309
15. Cal Ripken ...305

TRIPLES
1. Lance Johnson ...113
2. Steve Finley ...83
3. Delino DeShields ...63
4. Jose Offerman ...62
5. Kenny Lofton ...60
6. Chuck Knoblauch ...59
7. Brady Anderson ...58
   Brian McRae ...58
9. Brett Butler ...57
10. Jay Bell ...55
11. Paul Molitor ...54
12. Roberto Alomar ...51
    Barry Larkin ...51
14. Mickey Morandini ...50
15. Tony Fernandez ...48

HOME RUNS
1. Mark McGwire ...405
2. Ken Griffey Jr. ...382
3. Barry Bonds ...361
4. Albert Belle ...351
5. Juan Gonzalez ...339
6. Sammy Sosa ...332
7. Rafael Palmeiro ...328
8. Jose Canseco ...303
9. Frank Thomas ...301
10. Fred McGriff ...300
    Matt Williams ...300
12. Cecil Fielder ...288
13. Greg Vaughn ...287
14. Jeff Bagwell ...263
    Mo Vaughn ...263
16. Larry Walker ...262
17. Jay Buhner ...260
18. Andres Galarraga ...255
19. Joe Carter ...245

RUNS BATTED IN
1. Albert Belle ...1,099
2. Ken Griffey Jr. ...1,091
3. Barry Bonds ...1,076
4. Juan Gonzalez ...1,068
   Rafael Palmeiro ...1,068
6. Frank Thomas ...1,040
7. Dante Bichette ...979
8. Fred McGriff ...975
9. Jeff Bagwell ...961
10. Matt Williams ...960
11. Mark McGwire ...956
12. Sammy Sosa ...928
13. Cecil Fielder ...924
14. Paul O'Neill ...923
15. Joe Carter ...914

WALKS
1. Barry Bonds ...1,146
2. Frank Thomas ...1,076
3. Tony Phillips ...977
4. Rickey Henderson ...976
5. Mark McGwire ...951
6. Jeff Bagwell ...885
7. Edgar Martinez ...854
8. John Olerud ...820
9. Fred McGriff ...787
10. Mickey Tettleton ...740
11. Robin Ventura ...734
12. Craig Biggio ...730
13. Brady Anderson ...724
14. Gary Sheffield ...723
15. Chili Davis ...716

STRIKEOUTS
1. Sammy Sosa ...1,322
2. Jose Canseco ...1,205
3. Cecil Fielder ...1,172
4. Jay Buhner ...1,145
5. Ray Lankford ...1,141
6. Greg Vaughn ...1,137
7. Travis Fryman ...1,113
8. Jay Bell ...1,095
9. Fred McGriff ...1,085
10. Dean Palmer ...1,082
11. Mo Vaughn ...1,081
12. Andres Galarraga ...1,080
13. Devon White ...1,042
14. Mark McGwire ...1,040
15. Tony Phillips ...1,009

STOLEN BASES
1. Otis Nixon ...478
2. Rickey Henderson ...463
3. Kenny Lofton ...433
4. Delino DeShields ...393
5. Marquis Grissom ...381
6. Barry Bonds ...343
7. Chuck Knoblauch ...335
8. Craig Biggio ...319
9. Roberto Alomar ...311
10. Lance Johnson ...297
11. Eric Young ...292
12. Vince Coleman ...280
13. Barry Larkin ...266
14. Brady Anderson ...257
15. Tom Goodwin ...252

PITCHERS

EARNED RUN AVERAGE
(minimum 1,000 innings pitched)
1. Greg Maddux ...2.58
2. Jose Rijo ...2.74
3. Pedro J. Martinez ...2.83
4. Roger Clemens ...3.02
5. Randy Johnson ...3.14
6. Tom Glavine ...3.21
   David Cone ...3.21
8. Kevin Brown ...3.25
9. Curt Schilling ...3.31
10. John Smoltz ...3.32
11. Dennis Martinez ...3.37
12. Ismael Valdes ...3.38
13. Bret Saberhagen ...3.43
14. Ramon J. Martinez ...3.45
15. Kevin Appier ...3.47
16. Mike Mussina ...3.50
    Mike Hampton ...3.50
18. Bill Swift ...3.53
19. Zane Smith ...3.55
20. Jimmy Key ...3.62

WINS
1. Greg Maddux ...176
2. Tom Glavine ...164
3. Roger Clemens ...152
4. Randy Johnson ...150
5. Kevin Brown ...143
   John Smoltz ...143
7. David Cone ...141
8. Mike Mussina ...136
9. Chuck Finley ...135
10. Scott Erickson ...130
11. David Wells ...127

LOSSES
1. Andy Benes ...116
2. Tim Belcher ...115
3. Bobby Witt ...113
4. Jaime Navarro ...112
5. Tom Candiotti ...110
6. Scott Erickson ...108
   Chuck Finley ...108
8. John Burkett ...101
   Mike Morgan ...101
10. Terry Mulholland ...100
11. Kevin Brown ...98
    Todd Stottlemyre ...98
13. Kevin Tapani ...97
14. Jim Abbott ...96
15. Doug Drabek ...95
    Darryl Kile ...95
    John Smoltz ...95
18. Kevin Appier ...90
19. Roger Clemens ...89
    Bob Tewksbury ...89

GAMES
1. Paul Assenmacher ...644
   Mike Jackson ...644
3. Doug Jones ...618
4. Dan Plesac ...612
5. Jesse Orosco ...594
6. Mike Stanton ...591
7. Jeff Montgomery ...578
8. Eric Plunk ...557
9. Rick Aguilera ...553
10. Scott Radinsky ...552
11. Chuck McElroy ...551
12. Randy Myers ...543
13. Rod Beck ...540
14. Dennis Eckersley ...530
15. Mel Rojas ...525
    John Wetteland ...525

GAMES STARTED
1. Greg Maddux ...331
2. Tom Glavine ...327
3. Chuck Finley ...316
4. John Smoltz ...315
5. Andy Benes ...314
   Kevin Brown ...314
7. John Burkett ...308
8. Scott Erickson ...306
9. Roger Clemens ...305
10. Tim Belcher ...302
11. Randy Johnson ...290
    Kevin Tapani ...290
13. David Cone ...287
14. Jaime Navarro ...285
15. Todd Stottlemyre ...283

COMPLETE GAMES
1. Greg Maddux ...75
2. Randy Johnson ...65
3. Jack McDowell ...61
4. Kevin Brown ...58
5. Roger Clemens ...57
   Curt Schilling ...57
7. Scott Erickson ...47
8. Chuck Finley ...46
9. John Smoltz ...42
10. Doug Drabek ...41
    Terry Mulholland ...41
12. David Cone ...40
13. Mike Mussina ...39
14. Tom Glavine ...38
15. Dennis Martinez ...36
    David Wells ...36

SHUTOUTS
1. Randy Johnson ...25
2. Roger Clemens ...24
3. Greg Maddux ...23
4. Ramon J. Martinez ...18
5. Kevin Brown ...16
   David Cone ...16
   Scott Erickson ...16
8. Doug Drabek ...14
   Tom Glavine ...14
   Dennis Martinez ...14
   Mike Mussina ...14
   John Smoltz ...14
13. Chuck Finley ...13
    Jack McDowell ...13
    Curt Schilling ...13

SAVES
1. John Wetteland ...295
2. Dennis Eckersley ...293
3. Randy Myers ...291
4. Jeff Montgomery ...285
5. Rick Aguilera ...282
6. John Franco ...268
7. Rod Beck ...260
8. Lee Smith ...244
9. Roberto Hernandez ...234
10. Trevor Hoffman ...228
11. Doug Jones ...223
12. Gregg Olson ...190
13. Tom Henke ...189
14. Robb Nen ...185
15. Mike Henneman ...156

INNINGS PITCHED
1. Greg Maddux ...2,394.2
2. Tom Glavine ...2,228.0
3. Kevin Brown ...2,211.1
4. Roger Clemens ...2,178.2
5. Chuck Finley ...2,144.0
6. John Smoltz ...2,143.1
7. Andy Benes ...2,069.1
8. Randy Johnson ...2,064.1
9. David Cone ...2,018.0
10. Scott Erickson ...2,014.2
11. Tim Belcher ...1,959.1
12. John Burkett ...1,935.0
13. Jaime Navarro ...1,913.1
14. David Wells ...1,897.0
15. Kevin Appier ...1,868.2

WALKS
1. Randy Johnson ...910
2. Chuck Finley ...888
3. Bobby Witt ...846
4. David Cone ...774
5. Darryl Kile ...767
6. Tom Glavine ...764
7. Roger Clemens ...731
8. Tom Gordon ...714
9. Wilson Alvarez ...706
10. Tim Belcher ...700
11. Andy Benes ...698
12. Scott Erickson ...697
13. Ken Hill ...683
    Todd Stottlemyre ...683
15. John Smoltz ...669

STRIKEOUTS
1. Randy Johnson ...2,538
2. Roger Clemens ...2,101
3. David Cone ...1,928
4. John Smoltz ...1,893
5. Chuck Finley ...1,784
6. Greg Maddux ...1,764
7. Andy Benes ...1,655
8. Kevin Brown ...1,581
9. Curt Schilling ...1,561
10. Pedro J. Martinez ...1,534
11. Kevin Appier ...1,494
12. Tom Glavine ...1,465
13. Todd Stottlemyre ...1,369
14. Mike Mussina ...1,325
15. Bobby Witt ...1,270
16. Tom Gordon ...1,260
17. Darryl Kile ...1,247
18. David Wells ...1,244
19. Juan Guzman ...1,240
20. John Burkett ...1,233

ANAHEIM ANGELS

Date	Opp.	Res.	Score	(inn.*)	Hits	Opp. hits	Winning pitcher	Losing pitcher	Save	Record	Pos.	GB
4-6	Cle.	W	6-5		11	10	Holtz	Karsay	Percival	1-0	1st	...
4-7	Cle.	L	1-9		4	13	Burba	Hill		1-1	2nd	0.5
4-8	Cle.	L	1-9		4	13	Colon	Sparks		1-2	T2nd	1.0
4-9	At Tex.	W	8-4		12	10	Finley	Burkett		2-2	T1st	...
4-10	At Tex.	W	10-0		19	3	Olivares	Helling		3-2	1st	+1.0
4-11	At Tex.	L	3-6		6	12	Sele	Belcher	Wetteland	3-3	T1st	...
4-12	At Tex.	W	13-5		20	7	Magnante	Clark		4-3	T1st	...
4-13	At Oak.	L	2-3		9	7	Oquist	Sparks	Taylor	4-4	T1st	...
4-14	At Oak.	L	5-6		9	7	Mathews	Finley	Taylor	4-5	T2nd	1.0
4-15	At Oak.	W	12-1		18	5	Olivares	Heredia		5-5	2nd	1.0
4-16	Sea.	W	9-5		14	5	Belcher	Moyer		6-5	T1st	...
4-17	Sea.	L	3-4	(10)	8	7	Paniagua	Percival	Mesa	6-6	T1st	...
4-18	Sea.	L	5-8		10	10	Cloude	Sparks	Mesa	6-7	T2nd	1.0
4-20	At Tor.	L	1-5		8	7	Escobar	Finley		6-8	T2nd	1.0
4-21	At Tor.	L	2-3		8	10	Carpenter	Olivares	Person	6-9	T2nd	1.0
4-22	At Tor.	L	7-8		8	13	Davey	Petkovsek	Lloyd	6-10	4th	2.0
4-23	At K.C.	W	4-2		6	4	Hasegawa	Montgomery	Percival	7-10	4th	2.0
4-24	At K.C.	L	3-4		6	8	Santiago	Hasegawa		7-11	4th	3.0
4-26	Tor.	W	4-3	(11)	10	8	Percival	Rodriguez		8-11	T3rd	3.0
4-27	Tor.	L	1-10		5	13	Hentgen	Olivares		8-12	T3rd	3.0
4-28	Tor.	W	12-10		14	15	Petkovsek	Lloyd	Percival	9-12	T2nd	3.0
4-29	Tor.	W	17-1		15	4	Hill	Halladay		10-12	T2nd	2.0
4-30	Chi.	W	3-1		5	5	Petkovsek	Navarro	Percival	11-12	T2nd	2.0
5-1	Chi.	L	5-8		13	14	Lundquist	Percival	Howry	11-13	T2nd	2.0
5-2	Chi.	W	6-3		11	5	Olivares	Parque		12-13	T2nd	2.0
5-3	Chi.	L	1-8		4	12	Snyder	Belcher		12-14	T2nd	2.0
5-4	At Det.	L	1-3		8	9	Brocail	Holtz	Jones	12-15	4th	2.5
5-5	At Det.	W	4-1		6	3	Sparks	Weaver	Percival	13-15	4th	2.5
5-6	At Det.	L	2-4		7	10	Florie	Finley	Jones	13-16	4th	2.5
5-7	At Bos.	L	0-6		6	10	Martinez	Olivares		13-17	4th	2.5
5-8	At Bos.	L	1-6		4	12	Pena	Belcher	Lowe	13-18	4th	3.5
5-9	At Bos.	L	2-4		10	10	Portugal	Hill	Wakefield	13-19	4th	4.5
5-11	At N.Y.	W	9-7		14	8	Petkovsek	Mendoza	Percival	14-19	4th	4.0
5-12	At N.Y.	W	1-0		6	3	Finley	Cone	Percival	15-19	T3rd	3.5
5-13	At N.Y.	W	2-0		9	6	Olivares	Irabu	Percival	16-19	3rd	3.5
5-14	T.B.	W	8-3		10	5	Belcher	Witt		17-19	3rd	3.5
5-15	T.B.	L	1-3		3	7	Saunders	Hill	Hernandez	17-20	3rd	4.5
5-16	T.B.	L	4-7		10	13	Alvarez	Sparks		17-21	3rd	4.5
5-18	At Bal.	L	3-5		7	8	Mussina	Finley	Timlin	17-22	4th	4.0
5-19	At Bal.	W	5-4		8	11	Levine	Timlin	Percival	18-22	4th	4.0
5-20	At Bal.	W	6-4		9	9	Belcher	Johnson	Percival	19-22	4th	3.5
5-21	At T.B.	L	9-10		14	12	White	Magnante	Hernandez	19-23	4th	3.5
5-22	At T.B.	W	8-6		16	9	Petkovsek	Newman	Percival	20-23	4th	3.5
5-23	At T.B.	W	4-0	(10)	4	3	Finley	Hernandez		21-23	T3rd	2.5
5-25	Bal.	W	4-1		6	6	Olivares	Erickson	Percival	22-23	T2nd	3.0
5-26	Bal.	L	2-3		4	4	Ponson	Belcher	Rhodes	22-24	4th	4.0
5-27	Bal.	L	3-6		7	12	Guzman	Hill	Timlin	22-25	4th	4.5
5-28	K.C.	L	4-11		10	12	Appier	Finley		22-26	4th	5.5
5-29	K.C.	W	4-3		7	6	Sparks	Fussell	Percival	23-26	4th	5.5
5-30	K.C.	W	4-3		7	6	Olivares	Rosado	Percival	24-26	4th	5.5
5-31	Min.	L	2-3		10	8	Hawkins	Hasegawa	Trombley	24-27	4th	6.5
6-1	Min.	W	5-1		7	5	Hill	Lincoln		25-27	4th	6.5
6-2	Min.	W	2-1		9	5	Finley	Radke	Percival	26-27	4th	6.5
6-4	At L.A.	L	4-5		10	11	Brown	Olivares	Shaw	26-28	4th	7.5
6-5	At L.A.	L	4-7		7	12	Masaoka	Belcher	Shaw	26-29	4th	7.5
6-6	At L.A.	W	7-5		11	9	Hill	Perez	Percival	27-29	4th	6.5
6-7	At S.F.	L	2-5		7	5	Ortiz	Finley	Nen	27-30	4th	7.5
6-8	At S.F.	L	2-6		5	12	Estes	Sparks		27-31	4th	8.5
6-9	At S.F.	W	2-1		7	4	Belcher	Brock	Percival	28-31	4th	7.5
6-11	Ari.	L	2-12		8	18	Reynoso	Hill		28-32	4th	8.5
6-12	Ari.	W	4-3		10	6	Petkovsek	Benes	Percival	29-32	4th	7.5
6-13	Ari.	L	1-3	(13)	9	9	Nunez	Petkovsek	Olson	29-33	4th	7.5
6-15	At Tor.	L	2-13		6	18	Wells	Belcher		29-34	4th	7.0
6-16	At Tor.	L	2-3		6	8	Lloyd	Schoeneweis	Koch	29-35	4th	8.0
6-17	At Tor.	L	0-3		8	5	Escobar	Hill	Koch	29-36	4th	9.0
6-18	At N.Y.	L	1-4		5	8	Pettitte	Finley	Rivera	29-37	4th	10.0
6-19	At N.Y.	L	2-6		3	11	Irabu	Olivares	Mendoza	29-38	4th	10.0
6-20	At N.Y.	W	4-2		8	7	Belcher	Cone	Percival	30-38	4th	9.0
6-22	At Sea.	W	4-2		8	6	Petkovsek	Garcia	Percival	31-38	4th	7.5
6-23	At Sea.	L	3-8		10	10	Halama	Hill	Rodriguez	31-39	4th	8.5
6-24	At Sea.	W	12-7		16	9	Schoeneweis	Mesa	Petkovsek	32-39	4th	8.5
6-25	Oak.	W	4-3		8	9	Percival	Jones		33-39	4th	8.5
6-26	Oak.	W	5-4		10	7	Magnante	Rigby	Percival	34-39	4th	7.5
6-27	Oak.	W	4-3		12	7	Sparks	Rogers	Percival	35-39	4th	6.5
6-28	Tex.	L	1-9		7	9	Morgan	Finley		35-40	4th	7.5
6-29	Tex.	L	0-5		1	13	Burkett	Olivares		35-41	4th	8.5
6-30	Tex.	L	4-18		10	20	Glynn	Hill		35-42	4th	9.5

HIGHLIGHTS

High point: The Angels, despite losing outfielders Tim Salmon and Jim Edmonds and pitcher Tim Belcher to injury, won six of eight games against the A's, Mariners and Rockies just before the All-Star break, trimming their 9½-game deficit in the A.L. West race to 6½.

Low point: Interim manager Joe Maddon gave almost all of his starters the day off on September 11, and the Angels were no-hit by Minnesota's Eric Milton, who entered the game with a 6-11 record.

Turning point: After beating the Dodgers in their first game after the All-Star break, the Angels lost 11 straight, falling 16 games behind division-leading Texas. While the bats cooled, tensions heated up in the clubhouse. The on-field collapse and off-field turmoil led to the resignations of manager Terry Collins (in early September) and general manager Bill Bavasi (the last weekend of the season).

Most valuable player: The Angels' most consistent and productive player was second baseman Randy Velarde, who in 95 games hit .306 with nine homers, 48 RBIs and 13 stolen bases and also played superb defense. He was traded to the A's on July 29.

Most valuable pitcher: Lefthander Chuck Finley rebounded from a horrendous slump to go 7-1 with a 2.16 ERA in his last 11 starts. The veteran finished with a 12-11 record and 4.43 ERA and struck out 200 batters for the third time in four years.

Most improved player: After a sizzling start, third baseman Troy Glaus struggled for a month and there were rumblings he might be banished to Class AAA. But he regained a more consistent stroke and finished with 29 homers and 79 RBIs.

Most pleasant surprise: Pitcher Omar Olivares, who again had to win a rotation spot in spring training. He developed a nice cut fastball to go with his sinker and went 8-9 with a 4.05 ERA before being sent to Oakland with Velarde.

Key injuries: Shortstop Gary DiSarcina (broken forearm) and Edmonds (torn cartilage in his shoulder) suffered spring-training injuries that sidelined them for 12 weeks and four months, respectively. Mo Vaughn incurred a severe sprain of his left ankle on opening night, an injury that hampered him all season, and Salmon sprained his left wrist in early May and was out for 2½ months.

Notable: Struggling with a sprained ankle, Vaughn hit .281 with a team-high 33 homers and 108 RBIs. ... Salmon, despite his lengthy absence, knocked in 69 runs in 98 games. ... The Angels had the fifth-best team ERA (4.79) and tied for the third-best fielding percentage (.983) in the A.L.

—MIKE DiGIOVANNA

MISCELLANEOUS

RECORDS

1999 regular-season record: 70-92 (4th in A.L. West); 37-44 at home; 33-48 on road; 20-36 vs. A.L. East; 24-28 vs. A.L. Central; 20-16 vs. A.L. West; 6-12 vs. N.L. West; 19-19 vs. lefthanded starters; 51-73 vs. righthanded starters; 62-81 on grass; 8-11 on turf; 17-28 in daytime; 53-64 at night; 23-25 in one-run games; 4-8 in extra-inning games; 1-0-0 in doubleheaders.

Team record past five years: 387-405 (.489, ranks 8th in league in that span).

TEAM LEADERS

Batting average: Garret Anderson (.303).
At-bats: Garret Anderson (620).
Runs: Garret Anderson (88).
Hits: Garret Anderson (188).
Total Bases: Garret Anderson (291).
Doubles: Garret Anderson (36).
Triples: Darin Erstad (5).
Home runs: Mo Vaughn (33).
Runs batted in: Mo Vaughn (108).
Stolen bases: Darin Erstad, Randy Velarde (13).
Slugging percentage: Mo Vaughn (.508).
On-base percentage: Mo Vaughn (.358).
Wins: Chuck Finley (12).
Earned-run average: Chuck Finley (4.43).
Complete games: Omar Olivares (3).
Shutouts: None.
Saves: Troy Percival (31).
Innings pitched: Chuck Finley (213.1).
Strikeouts: Chuck Finley (200).

Date	Opp.	Res.	Score	(inn.*)	Hits	Opp. hits	Winning pitcher	Losing pitcher	Save	Record	Pos.	GB
7-2	At Oak.	W	10-6		14	10	Petkovsek	Harville		36-42	4th	9.5
7-3	At Oak.	L	7-9		13	12	Heredia	Finley	Taylor	36-43	4th	9.5
7-4	At Oak.	W	5-2		12	5	Olivares	Oquist		37-43	4th	8.5
7-5	Sea.	L	0-10		3	14	Fassero	Hasegawa		37-44	4th	8.5
7-6	Sea.	W	8-2		9	7	Petkovsek	Rodriguez		38-44	4th	7.5
7-7	Sea.	W	10-3		16	13	Sparks	Moyer		39-44	4th	7.5
7-9	At Col.	W	9-6		15	12	Finley	Kile	Percival	40-44	4th	7.5
7-10	At Col.	W	9-3		13	6	Olivares	Astacio		41-44	4th	6.5
7-11	At Col.	L	2-8		5	11	Dipoto	Fyhrie		41-45	4th	6.5
7-15	L.A.	W	7-6	(10)	10	12	Petkovsek	Mills		42-45	3rd	6.5
7-16	L.A.	L	1-3		5	5	Valdes	Olivares	Shaw	42-46	3rd	7.5
7-17	L.A.	L	3-13		7	14	Park	Sparks		42-47	4th	7.5
7-18	S.D.	L	3-6		10	14	Boehringer	Fyhrie	Hoffman	42-48	4th	8.5
7-19	S.D.	L	1-4	(10)	9	8	Miceli	Hasegawa	Hoffman	42-49	4th	9.5
7-20	S.D.	L	1-2		6	5	Ashby	Petkovsek	Hoffman	42-50	4th	10.5
7-21	At Tex.	L	5-9		10	13	Sele	Olivares	Zimmerman	42-51	4th	11.5
7-22	At Tex.	L	7-9		15	10	Burkett	Sparks	Zimmerman	42-52	4th	12.5
7-23	At Bal.	L	0-1		6	7	Guzman	McDowell	Timlin	42-53	4th	13.5
7-24	At Bal.	L	4-8		6	17	Johnson	Hill		42-54	4th	14.5
7-25	At Bal.	L	7-8	(11)	6	11	Kamieniecki	Holtz		42-55	4th	15.5
7-26	At T.B.	L	0-7		4	11	Witt	Olivares		42-56	4th	16.0
7-27	At T.B.	W	10-5		12	13	Magnante	Callaway		43-56	4th	16.0
7-28	At T.B.	L	1-4		6	11	Rupe	McDowell	Hernandez	43-57	4th	16.0
7-30	Min.	L	1-3		7	9	Radke	Hill		43-58	4th	17.5
7-31	Min.	L	0-8		3	11	Milton	Finley		43-59	4th	17.5
8-1	Min.	W	2-1		7	2	Sparks	Mays	Percival	44-59	4th	17.5
8-2	K.C.	L	4-12		11	17	Rosado	McDowell		44-60	4th	18.5
8-3	K.C.	L	0-7		5	10	Suppan	Fyhrie		44-61	4th	19.5
8-4	K.C.	W	4-3		10	6	Hill	Witasick	Percival	45-61	4th	19.5
8-5	Bos.	W	8-0		14	4	Finley	Rose		46-61	4th	19.0
8-6	Bos.	L	1-5		8	10	Saberhagen	Sparks		46-62	4th	19.0
8-7	Bos.	L	3-14		8	19	Rapp	Belcher		46-63	4th	20.0
8-8	Bos.	L	3-9		6	13	Martinez	McDowell		46-64	4th	20.0
8-9	Cle.	L	0-4		7	9	Colon	Hill		46-65	4th	20.0
8-10	Cle.	L	1-2	(10)	4	7	Rincon	Petkovsek	Jackson	46-66	4th	21.0
8-11	Cle.	L	3-4		10	10	Burba	Sparks	Jackson	46-67	4th	22.0
8-13	At Det.	L	7-8	(10)	10	9	Jones	Hasegawa		46-68	4th	21.0
8-14	At Det.	W	7-4		12	10	Magnante	Moehler	Percival	47-68	4th	20.0
8-15	At Det.	W	10-2		14	7	Finley	Thompson		48-68	4th	20.0
8-16	At Chi.	L	1-6		6	10	Sirotka	Washburn		48-69	4th	21.0
8-17	At Chi.	L	3-4	(12)	12	7	Howry	Holtz		48-70	4th	22.0
8-18	At Chi.	L	3-4		6	6	Baldwin	Magnante	Howry	48-71	4th	23.0
8-19	At Chi.	W	9-2		14	6	Ortiz	Parque		49-71	4th	22.0
8-20	Det.	W	5-1		7	5	Finley	Moehler		50-71	4th	22.0
8-21	Det.	L	0-5		4	9	Weaver	Washburn		50-72	4th	23.0
8-22	Det.	L	3-12		8	17	Mlicki	Sparks		50-73	4th	24.0
8-23	Det.	W	6-5		9	11	Percival	Brocail		51-73	4th	23.0
8-24	Tor.	L	1-5		6	10	Hentgen	Ortiz	Koch	51-74	4th	23.0
8-25	Tor.	L	2-7		6	9	Hamilton	Finley		51-75	4th	24.0
8-27	At Bos.	L	3-4		6	5	Garces	Percival	Lowe	51-76	4th	25.0
8-28	At Bos.	L	6-7		10	8	Lowe	Pote		51-77	4th	26.0
8-29	At Bos.	L	4-7		11	10	Rapp	Belcher	Lowe	51-78	4th	27.0
8-30	At Cle.	L	5-7		7	7	Colon	Levine	Jackson	51-79	4th	27.0
8-31	At Cle.	L	12-14		14	19	Poole	Percival	Shuey	51-80	4th	27.0
9-1	At Cle.	L	1-8		8	12	Burba	Washburn		51-81	4th	28.0
9-2	At Cle.	L	5-6		11	10	Nagy	Sparks	Jackson	51-82	4th	28.0
9-3	N.Y.	W	8-2		15	10	Belcher	Pettitte		52-82	4th	28.0
9-4	N.Y.	L	6-9		6	10	Watson	Alvarez	Rivera	52-83	4th	28.0
9-5	N.Y.	L	3-8		6	13	Yarnall	Fyhrie		52-84	4th	28.5
9-6	N.Y.	W	5-3		6	5	Washburn	Clemens	Percival	53-84	4th	29.0
9-7	Chi.	W	14-1		12	4	Cooper	Sirotka		54-84	4th	29.0
9-8	Chi.	W	6-5	(10)	10	7	Percival	Simas		55-84	4th	29.0
9-10	At Min.	W	4-2		13	4	Finley	Radke	Percival	56-84	4th	28.0
9-11	At Min.	L	0-7		0	10	Milton	Ortiz		56-85	4th	28.0
9-12	At Min.	W	6-3		9	5	Washburn	Mays		57-85	4th	27.0
9-13	At Min.	W	6-5		10	10	Magnante	Hawkins	Hasegawa	58-85	4th	27.0
9-14†	At K.C.	W	8-6		12	15	Pote	Morman	Hasegawa	59-85		
9-14‡	At K.C.	W	6-5		9	5	Hasegawa	Byrdak	Percival	60-85	4th	26.5
9-15	At K.C.	W	1-0		7	3	Finley	Carter	Percival	61-85	4th	26.5
9-16	At K.C.	L	1-7		6	12	Suppan	Ortiz		61-86	4th	27.0
9-17	Bal.	L	2-4		6	12	Erickson	Washburn	Timlin	61-87	4th	27.0
9-18	Bal.	L	3-6		8	5	Ponson	Cooper	Timlin	61-88	4th	28.0
9-19	Bal.	L	4-5		9	11	Molina	Percival	Timlin	61-89	4th	28.0
9-20	T.B.	W	10-5		11	13	Finley	Alvarez		62-89	4th	27.5
9-21	T.B.	W	7-5		9	7	Ortiz	Eiland	Percival	63-89	4th	26.5
9-22	T.B.	W	8-5		11	11	Washburn	Wheeler		64-89	4th	25.5
9-24	At Sea.	L	3-4	(10)	5	8	Mesa	Percival		64-90	4th	26.5
9-25	At Sea.	W	7-3		6	4	Finley	Moyer		65-90	4th	26.5
9-26	At Sea.	L	2-3		6	8	Davey	Hasegawa		65-91	4th	27.5
9-28	Oak.	L	3-9		4	14	Hudson	Washburn	Mahay	65-92	4th	29.0
9-29	Oak.	W	7-4		12	4	Hasegawa	Mathews	Pote	66-92	4th	28.0
9-30	Oak.	W	5-4		10	13	Petkovsek	Isringhausen	Pote	67-92	4th	28.0
10-1	Tex.	W	7-6		9	8	Holtz	Morgan		68-92	4th	27.0
10-2	Tex.	W	15-3		14	9	Hasegawa	Helling		69-92	4th	26.0
10-3	Tex.	W	1-0		3	5	Washburn	Morgan	Pote	70-92	4th	25.0

Monthly records: April (11-12), May (13-15), June (11-15), July (8-17), August (8-21), September (16-12), October (3-0).
*Innings, if other than nine. † First game of a doubleheader. ‡ Second game of a doubleheader.

MEMORABLE GAMES

June 24 at Seattle

Trailing 7-3 to the Seattle Mariners after seven innings, the Angels exploded for six runs in the top of the eighth and three in the top of the ninth. Mo Vaughn blasted a three-run homer in the eighth and another three-run shot in the ninth to lead a 12-7 victory in the Kingdome.

Anaheim	AB	R	H	RBI	Seattle	AB	R	H	RBI
Erstad, 1b	3	4	1	1	B.Hunter, lf-cf	3	1	0	1
Velarde, 2b	6	3	5	4	A.Rodrgz, ss	5	2	3	3
M.Vaughn, dh	6	2	5	6	Griffey Jr., cf	4	0	0	0
T.Greene, rf	5	0	0	0	Ibanez, rf	1	0	0	0
Sheets, ss	1	0	0	0	E.Martinez, dh	4	0	0	1
G.Anderson, cf	4	0	1	1	Huskey, 1b	3	0	0	0
Glaus, 3b	4	0	1	0	Mabry, 1b-3b	1	0	1	0
R.Williams, lf	3	0	1	0	D.Bell, 2b	3	0	0	0
O.Palmro, ph-lf	2	1	1	0	D.Wilson, c	3	1	1	0
Walbeck, c	4	1	0	0	R.Davis, 3b	3	1	1	0
DiSarcina, ss	3	0	0	0	Segui, ph-1b	1	0	1	0
Luke, ph-rf	1	1	1	0	Gipson, rf-cf	3	2	2	1
					Lmpkin, ph-lf	1	0	0	0
Totals	**42**	**12**	**16**	**12**	**Totals**	**35**	**7**	**9**	**6**

Anaheim.....................................0 0 2 0 1 00 6 3— 12
Seattle ....2 3 0 2 0 00 0 0— 7

E—Seattle 1. DP—Anaheim 1. LOB—Anaheim 10, Seattle 5. 2B—Erstad (13), M.Vaughn (6), R.Davis (9). HR—Velarde (7), M.Vaughn 2 (16), A.Rodriguez (12). SB—A.Rodriguez (6), Gipson (1). SF—G.Anderson, B.Hunter.

Anaheim	IP	H	R	ER	BB	SO
C.Finley	4	6	7	6	3	4
Hasegawa	2.1	1	0	0	0	1
Schoeneweis (W, 1-1)	0.2	1	0	0	0	1
Petkovsek (S, 1)	2	1	0	0	0	0

Seattle	IP	H	R	ER	BB	SO
Fassero	6	6	3	3	3	2
Paniagua	1.1	3	3	3	2	2
Mesa (BS 2; L 0-3)	0.1	3	3	3	1	0
Cloude	1	3	2	2	0	0
Watson	0.1	1	1	1	0	0

WP—C.Finley, Paniagua. PB—Walbeck. U—HP, DiMuro. 1B, Everitt. 2B, Roe. 3B, Hirschbeck. T—3:26. A—26,431.

August 31 at Cleveland

It appeared the Angels would end a six-game losing streak when they took a 12-4 lead over Cleveland into the top of the eighth inning. But the Indians scored 10 runs on nine hits in the bottom of the eighth, five off Mark Petkovsek and four off Troy Percival, including a game-winning three-run homer by Richie Sexson, for a 14-12 victory. Percival also hit David Justice with a pitch, sparking a bench-clearing brawl.

Anaheim	AB	R	H	RBI	Cleveland	AB	R	H	RBI
O.Palmeiro, lf	6	2	3	2	D.Roberts, cf	5	0	1	0
Durrington, 2b	3	1	1	0	Vizquel, ss-rf	5	2	1	1
T.Greene, ph	1	0	0	0	Alomar, 2b	5	2	3	2
G.Anderson, cf	4	1	2	2	M.Ramirez, rf	3	0	1	2
M.Vaughn, dh	5	1	2	2	A.Ramirez, ph	1	1	1	0
Salmon, rf	2	2	1	2	Baines, ph	1	0	1	2
Erstad, 1b	4	1	1	0	Baerga, pr-3b	0	1	0	0
Glaus, 3b	4	3	2	4	Thome, dh-1b	4	4	3	1
B.Molina, c	2	1	1	0	Sexson, 1b-lf	5	2	4	5
Huson, ph	1	0	0	0	Justice, lf	3	1	1	1
DiSarcina, ss	3	0	0	0	Nagy, pr	0	0	0	0
Edmonds, ph	1	0	1	0	Shuey, p	0	0	0	0
					E.Wlsn, 3b-ss	5	1	2	0
					Ei.Diaz, c	4	0	1	0
Totals	**36**	**12**	**14**	**12**	**Totals**	**41**	**14**	**19**	**14**

Anaheim......................................1 0 0 2 0 2 2 5 0— 12
Cleveland ....0 1 2 0 0 1 0 (10) x— 14

E—DiSarcina (13), Durrington (2). DP—Anaheim 2, Cleveland 1. LOB—Anaheim 8, Cleveland 6. 2B—O.Palmeiro (12), M.Vaughn (14), Alomar (36), Thome (23), Ei.Diaz (17). HR—Salmon (11), Glaus 2 (24), Thome (26), Sexson (25). SB—Alomar (31), Sexson (3). CS—B.Molina (1), D.Roberts (3). S—Durrington, Erstad, DiSarcina.

Anaheim	IP	H	R	ER	BB	SO
C.Finley	7	10	4	1	1	6
Petkovsek	0	5	5	5	0	0
Hasegawa	0.2	1	1	1	0	0
Percival (BS 6; L 3-	0	3	4	4	1	0
Pote	0.1	0	0	0	0	0

Cleveland	IP	H	R	ER	BB	SO
Gooden	5	5	3	3	2	2
S.Reed	1	2	2	2	1	1
Assenmacher	1	2	2	2	0	0
DePaula	0.1	1	4	4	3	0
Poole (W, 1-0)	0.2	2	1	1	1	0
Shuey (S, 5)	1	2	0	0	0	2

HBP—B.Molina by Gooden, Justice by Percival. WP—Percival. U—HP, Cooper. 1B, Cederstrom. 2B, Barrett. 3B, McClelland. T—3:49. A—43,284.

1999 REVIEW

INDIVIDUAL STATISTICS

BATTING

Name	G	TPA	AB	R	H	TB	2B	3B	HR	RBI	Avg.	Obp.	Slg.	SH	SF	HP	BB	IBB	SO	SB	CS	GDP	vs RHP AB	vs RHP Avg.	vs RHP HR	vs RHP RBI	vs LHP AB	vs LHP Avg.	vs LHP HR	vs LHP RBI
Anderson, Garret	157	660	620	88	188	291	36	2	21	80	.303	.336	.469	0	6	0	34	8	81	3	4	15	459	.312	18	57	161	.280	3	23
Erstad, Darin	142	638	585	84	148	219	22	5	13	53	.253	.308	.374	2	3	1	47	3	101	13	7	16	428	.245	8	34	157	.274	5	19
Glaus, Troy	154	631	551	85	132	248	29	0	29	79	.240	.331	.450	0	3	6	71	1	143	5	1	9	435	.246	24	62	116	.216	5	17
Vaughn, Mo	139	592	524	63	147	266	20	0	33	108	.281	.358	.508	0	3	11	54	7	127	0	0	11	372	.258	22	60	152	.336	11	48
Velarde, Randy	95	425	376	57	115	165	15	4	9	48	.306	.383	.439	2	0	4	43	1	56	13	4	8	284	.292	6	36	92	.348	3	12
Salmon, Tim	98	422	353	60	94	173	24	2	17	69	.266	.372	.490	0	6	0	63	2	82	4	1	7	280	.257	15	54	73	.301	2	15
Greene, Todd	97	338	321	36	78	140	20	0	14	42	.243	.275	.436	0	2	3	12	0	63	1	4	8	226	.239	12	26	95	.253	2	16
Palmeiro, Orlando	109	372	317	46	88	105	12	1	1	23	.278	.364	.331	6	3	6	39	1	30	5	5	4	282	.287	1	21	35	.200	0	2
Walbeck, Matt	107	321	288	26	69	88	8	1	3	22	.240	.308	.306	3	1	3	26	1	46	2	3	12	224	.232	3	17	64	.266	0	5
DiSarcina, Gary	81	298	271	32	62	74	7	1	1	29	.229	.273	.273	9	1	2	15	0	32	2	2	8	211	.237	1	24	60	.200	0	5
Sheets, Andy	87	269	244	22	48	67	10	0	3	29	.197	.236	.275	6	5	0	14	0	59	1	2	6	174	.190	1	22	70	.214	2	7
Huson, Jeff	97	245	225	21	59	68	7	1	0	18	.262	.307	.302	1	3	0	16	0	27	10	1	9	214	.266	0	18	11	.182	0	0
Edmonds, Jim	55	233	204	34	51	87	17	2	5	23	.250	.339	.426	0	1	0	28	0	45	5	4	3	141	.277	5	18	63	.190	0	5
Durrington, Trent	43	136	122	14	22	24	2	0	0	2	.180	.237	.197	5	0	0	9	0	28	4	3	1	83	.157	0	0	39	.231	0	2
Molina, Ben	31	109	101	8	26	34	5	0	1	10	.257	.312	.337	0	0	2	6	0	6	0	1	5	82	.256	0	5	19	.263	1	5
Decker, Steve	28	79	63	5	15	21	6	0	0	5	.238	.372	.333	1	1	1	13	0	9	0	0	4	35	.314	0	3	28	.143	0	2
Williams, Reggie	30	71	63	8	14	22	1	2	1	6	.222	.286	.349	1	1	1	5	0	21	2	1	3	31	.194	1	2	32	.250	0	4
O'Brien, Charlie	27	67	62	3	6	9	0	0	1	4	.097	.136	.145	1	1	2	1	0	12	0	0	1	47	.043	0	0	15	.267	1	4
Unroe, Tim	27	59	54	5	13	18	2	0	1	6	.241	.305	.333	0	0	1	4	0	16	0	0	0	22	.136	0	0	32	.313	1	6
Pritchett, Chris	20	49	45	3	7	11	1	0	1	2	.156	.188	.244	1	1	0	2	0	9	1	1	0	41	.171	1	2	4	.000	0	0
Luke, Matt	18	32	30	4	9	18	0	0	3	6	.300	.344	.600	0	0	0	2	0	10	0	0	2	21	.381	2	5	9	.111	1	1
Hemphill, Bret	12	27	21	3	3	3	0	0	0	2	.143	.269	.143	1	1	0	4	0	4	0	0	1	13	.154	0	0	8	.125	0	2
DaVanon, Jeff	7	22	20	4	4	9	0	1	1	4	.200	.273	.450	0	0	0	2	0	7	0	1	0	14	.286	1	4	6	.000	0	0
Silvestri, Dave	3	11	11	0	1	2	1	0	0	1	.091	.091	.182	0	0	0	0	0	1	0	0	1	5	.200	0	1	6	.000	0	0
Olivares, Omar	20	7	6	0	2	3	1	0	0	0	.333	.333	.500	1	0	0	0	0	1	0	0	0	6	.333	0	0	0	.000	0	0
Belcher, Tim	24	5	5	0	1	2	1	0	0	0	.200	.200	.400	0	0	0	0	0	2	0	0	0	5	.200	0	0	0	.000	0	0
Finley, Chuck	33	5	4	0	0	0	0	0	0	0	.000	.000	.000	1	0	0	0	0	3	0	0	0	3	.000	0	0	1	.000	0	0
Sparks, Steve	29	3	3	0	1	2	1	0	0	2	.333	.333	.667	0	0	0	0	0	1	0	0	0	0	.000	0	0	3	.333	0	2
Hill, Ken	26	3	3	0	0	0	0	0	0	0	.000	.000	.000	0	0	0	0	0	0	0	0	1	0	.000	0	0	3	.000	0	0
Colangelo, Mike	1	3	2	0	1	1	0	0	0	0	.500	.667	.500	0	0	0	1	0	0	0	0	0	0	.000	0	0	2	.500	0	0
Magnante, Mike	53	0	0	0	0	0	0	0	0	0	.000	.000	.000	0	0	0	0	0	0	0	0	0	0	.000	0	0	0	.000	0	0
Petkovsek, Mark	64	0	0	0	0	0	0	0	0	0	.000	.000	.000	0	0	0	0	0	0	0	0	0	0	.000	0	0	0	.000	0	0
Percival, Troy	60	0	0	0	0	0	0	0	0	0	.000	.000	.000	0	0	0	0	0	0	0	0	0	0	.000	0	0	0	.000	0	0
Levine, Al	50	0	0	0	0	0	0	0	0	0	.000	.000	.000	0	0	0	0	0	0	0	0	0	0	.000	0	0	0	.000	0	0
Fyhrie, Mike	16	0	0	0	0	0	0	0	0	0	.000	.000	.000	0	0	0	0	0	0	0	0	0	0	.000	0	0	0	.000	0	0
Hasegawa, Shigetoshi	64	0	0	0	0	0	0	0	0	0	.000	.000	.000	0	0	0	0	0	0	0	0	0	0	.000	0	0	0	.000	0	0
Washburn, Jarrod	16	0	0	0	0	0	0	0	0	0	.000	.000	.000	0	0	0	0	0	0	0	0	0	0	.000	0	0	0	.000	0	0
Schoeneweis, Scott	31	0	0	0	0	0	0	0	0	0	.000	.000	.000	0	0	0	0	0	0	0	0	0	0	.000	0	0	0	.000	0	0

Players with more than one A.L. team

Name	G	TPA	AB	R	H	TB	2B	3B	HR	RBI	Avg.	Obp.	Slg.	SH	SF	HP	BB	IBB	SO	SB	CS	GDP	vs RHP AB	vs RHP Avg.	vs RHP HR	vs RHP RBI	vs LHP AB	vs LHP Avg.	vs LHP HR	vs LHP RBI
Olivares, Oak.	12	0	0	0	0	0	0	0	0	0	.000	.000	.000	0	0	0	0	0	0	0	0	0	6	.333	0	0	0	.000	0	0
Olivares, Ana.-Oak.	32	7	6	0	2	3	1	0	0	0	.333	.333	.500	1	0	0	0	0	1	0	0	0	6	.333	0	0	0	.000	0	0
Velarde, Oak.	61	286	255	48	85	122	10	3	7	28	.333	.401	.478	2	0	2	27	1	42	11	4	11	284	.292	6	36	92	.348	3	12
Velarde, Ana.-Oak.	156	711	631	105	200	287	25	7	16	76	.317	.390	.455	4	0	6	70	2	98	24	8	19	490	.308	12	56	141	.348	4	20

PITCHING

Name	W	L	Pct.	ERA	IP	H	R	ER	HR	SH	SF	HB	BB	IBB	SO	G	GS	CG	ShO	GF	Sv	vs. RH AB	vs. RH Avg.	vs. RH HR	vs. RH RBI	vs. LH AB	vs. LH Avg.	vs. LH HR	vs. LH RBI
Finley, Chuck	12	11	.522	4.43	213.1	197	117	105	23	7	3	8	94	2	200	33	33	1	0	0	0	643	.249	20	83	158	.234	3	16
Sparks, Steve	5	11	.313	5.42	147.2	165	101	89	21	2	8	9	82	0	73	28	26	0	0	1	0	307	.270	12	51	280	.293	9	38
Belcher, Tim	6	8	.429	6.73	132.1	168	104	99	27	6	9	5	46	0	52	24	24	0	0	0	0	258	.318	14	44	276	.312	13	49
Olivares, Omar	8	9	.471	4.05	131.0	135	62	59	11	3	5	6	49	0	49	20	20	3	0	0	0	243	.300	3	24	252	.246	8	32
Hill, Ken	4	11	.267	4.77	128.1	129	72	68	14	3	8	4	76	1	76	26	22	0	0	2	0	232	.302	7	29	246	.240	7	32
Levine, Al	1	1	.500	3.39	85.0	76	40	32	13	2	7	3	29	2	37	50	1	0	0	12	0	188	.255	8	30	120	.233	5	14
Petkovsek, Mark	10	4	.714	3.47	83.0	85	37	32	6	5	5	2	21	2	43	64	0	0	0	18	1	192	.286	5	39	124	.242	1	12
Hasegawa, Shigetoshi	4	6	.400	4.91	77.0	80	45	42	14	3	4	2	34	2	44	64	1	0	0	26	2	177	.277	11	33	113	.274	3	13
Magnante, Mike	5	2	.714	3.38	69.1	68	30	26	2	0	7	3	29	4	44	53	0	0	0	13	0	154	.292	1	23	106	.217	1	14
Washburn, Jarrod	4	5	.444	5.25	61.2	61	36	36	6	1	2	1	26	0	39	16	10	0	0	3	0	183	.273	5	23	51	.216	1	5
Percival, Troy	4	6	.400	3.79	57.0	38	24	24	9	0	1	3	22	0	58	60	0	0	0	50	31	92	.152	4	9	112	.214	5	25
Fyhrie, Mike	0	4	.000	5.05	51.2	61	32	29	8	0	1	0	21	1	26	16	7	0	0	5	0	127	.307	4	19	86	.256	4	15
Ortiz, Ramon	2	3	.400	6.52	48.1	50	35	35	7	0	2	2	25	0	44	9	9	0	0	0	0	90	.233	1	5	99	.293	6	27
Schoeneweis, Scott	1	1	.500	5.49	39.1	47	27	24	4	0	1	0	14	1	22	31	0	0	0	6	0	96	.313	3	16	64	.266	1	11
Pote, Lou	1	1	.500	2.15	29.1	23	9	7	1	1	0	0	12	1	20	20	0	0	0	10	3	67	.239	1	5	38	.184	0	4
Cooper, Brian	1	1	.500	4.88	27.2	23	15	15	3	0	1	4	18	0	15	5	5	0	0	0	0	51	.196	0	4	50	.260	3	10
Holtz, Mike	2	3	.400	8.06	22.1	26	20	20	3	1	0	2	15	1	17	28	0	0	0	9	0	50	.340	2	12	38	.237	1	4
McDowell, Jack	0	4	.000	8.05	19.0	31	17	17	4	1	1	2	5	0	12	4	4	0	0	0	0	39	.359	2	7	45	.378	2	7
Mintz, Steve	0	0	.000	3.60	5.0	8	2	2	1	0	0	0	2	0	2	3	0	0	0	2	0	12	.500	1	1	9	.222	0	1
Alvarez, Juan	0	1	.000	3.00	3.0	1	1	1	0	1	0	0	4	0	4	8	0	0	0	1	0	3	.000	0	0	6	.167	0	1

PITCHERS WITH MORE THAN ONE A.L. TEAM

Name	W	L	Pct.	ERA	IP	H	R	ER	HR	SH	SF	HB	BB	IBB	SO	G	GS	CG	ShO	GF	Sv	vs. RH AB	vs. RH Avg.	vs. RH HR	vs. RH RBI	vs. LH AB	vs. LH Avg.	vs. LH HR	vs. LH RBI
Olivares, Oak.	7	2	.778	4.34	74.2	82	43	36	8	0	2	3	32	0	36	12	12	1	0	0	0	243	.300	3	24	252	.246	8	32
Olivares, Ana.-Oak.	15	11	.577	4.16	205.2	217	105	95	19	3	7	9	81	0	85	32	32	4	0	7	0	393	.290	7	45	392	.263	12	53

DESIGNATED HITTERS

Name	AB	Avg.	HR	RBI
Vaughn, Mo	260	.292	21	64
Greene, Todd	161	.236	7	25
Edmonds, Jim	36	.250	0	3
Palmeiro, Orlando	33	.303	0	2
Salmon, Tim	24	.042	1	5
Anderson, Garret	16	.500	0	1
Pritchett, Chris	12	.167	0	0
Huson, Jeff	11	.273	0	4
Unroe, Tim	9	.222	0	1
Erstad, Darin	8	.000	0	0
Decker, Steve	7	.143	0	0
Williams, Reggie	4	.250	0	1
Glaus, Troy	4	.000	0	0
DaVanon, Jeff	3	.000	0	0
Walbeck, Matt	2	.500	0	0
Sparks, Steve	0	-	0	0
Durrington, Trent	0	-	0	0

FIELDING

FIRST BASEMEN

Player	Pct.	G	PO	A	E	TC	DP
Erstad, Darin	.999	78	669	41	1	711	59
Vaughn, Mo	.995	72	584	35	3	622	62
Pritchett, Chris	.990	15	96	8	1	105	8
Huson, Jeff	1.000	8	25	1	0	26	3
Decker, Steve	1.000	6	30	4	0	34	2
Luke, Matt	1.000	4	20	4	0	24	5
Edmonds, Jim	1.000	2	19	1	0	20	2

SECOND BASEMEN

Player	Pct.	G	PO	A	E	TC	DP
Velarde, Randy	.986	95	191	307	7	505	61
Durrington, Trent	.966	41	73	98	6	177	19
Huson, Jeff	.993	41	53	92	1	146	20
Sheets, Andy	.929	7	6	7	1	14	0
Silvestri, Dave	1.000	1	0	3	0	3	0
Unroe, Tim	-	1	0	0	0	0	0

THIRD BASEMEN

Player	Pct.	G	PO	A	E	TC	DP
Glaus, Troy	.954	153	114	277	19	410	25
Huson, Jeff	.971	9	11	22	1	34	4
Unroe, Tim	1.000	3	1	2	0	3	0
Sheets, Andy	.500	1	0	1	1	2	0

SHORTSTOPS

Player	Pct.	G	PO	A	E	TC	DP
DiSarcina, Gary	.963	81	138	249	15	402	62
Sheets, Andy	.966	76	107	174	10	291	37
Huson, Jeff	.939	22	14	32	3	49	7
Silvestri, Dave	.833	1	2	3	1	6	0

OUTFIELDERS

Player	Pct.	G	PO	A	E	TC	DP
Anderson, Garret	.993	153	406	7	3	416	1
Palmeiro, Orlando	.994	92	154	6	1	161	0
Salmon, Tim	.981	89	204	7	4	215	1
Erstad, Darin	1.000	69	185	7	0	192	1
Edmonds, Jim	.992	42	119	4	1	124	1
Greene, Todd	.974	30	36	1	1	38	0
Williams, Reggie	.974	24	34	3	1	38	3
Unroe, Tim	1.000	12	13	1	0	14	0
Luke, Matt	1.000	6	8	0	0	8	0
DaVanon, Jeff	1.000	5	5	0	0	5	0
Huson, Jeff	1.000	2	1	0	0	1	0
Colangelo, Mike	1.000	1	1	1	0	2	1
Silvestri, Dave	1.000	1	1	0	0	1	0

CATCHERS

Player	Pct.	G	PO	A	E	TC	DP	PB
Walbeck, Matt	.989	97	407	46	5	458	9	6
Molina, Ben	.991	30	192	19	2	213	2	3
O'Brien, Charlie	.993	27	140	11	1	152	2	0
Decker, Steve	.987	17	73	4	1	78	0	5
Greene, Todd	.984	12	55	7	1	63	0	5
Hemphill, Bret	.955	12	36	6	2	44	1	1

PITCHERS

Player	Pct.	G	PO	A	E	TC	DP
Petkovsek, Mark	.955	64	5	16	1	22	1
Hasegawa, Shigetoshi	1.000	64	5	14	0	19	1
Percival, Troy	1.000	60	3	1	0	4	0
Magnante, Mike	1.000	53	3	13	0	16	3
Levine, Al	.895	50	5	12	2	19	3
Finley, Chuck	.921	33	7	28	3	38	1
Schoeneweis, Scott	1.000	31	1	10	0	11	1
Sparks, Steve	.933	28	7	35	3	45	4
Holtz, Mike	1.000	28	2	5	0	7	0
Hill, Ken	1.000	26	6	25	0	31	3
Belcher, Tim	.929	24	11	15	2	28	1
Olivares, Omar	.941	20	6	26	2	34	2
Pote, Lou	1.000	20	0	5	0	5	1
Washburn, Jarrod	1.000	16	2	5	0	7	3
Fyhrie, Mike	1.000	16	2	3	0	5	0
Ortiz, Ramon	1.000	9	4	6	0	10	0
Alvarez, Juan	1.000	8	0	2	0	2	0
Cooper, Brian	1.000	5	2	5	0	7	2
McDowell, Jack	1.000	4	0	6	0	6	0
Mintz, Steve	-	3	0	0	0	0	0

Pitcher	Bal. W-L	Bos. W-L	Chi. W-L	Cle. W-L	Det. W-L	K.C. W-L	Min. W-L	N.Y. W-L	Oak. W-L	Sea. W-L	T.B. W-L	Tex. W-L	Tor. W-L	N.L. W-L	Total W-L
Alvarez, Juan	0-0	0-0	0-0	0-0	0-0	0-0	0-0	0-1	0-0	0-0	0-0	0-0	0-0	0-0	0-1
Belcher, Tim	1-1	0-3	0-0	0-0	0-0	0-0	0-0	2-0	0-0	1-0	1-0	0-1	0-1	1-1	6-8
Cooper, Brian	0-1	0-0	1-0	0-0	0-0	0-0	0-0	0-0	0-0	0-0	0-0	0-0	0-0	0-0	1-1
Finley, Chuck	0-1	1-0	0-0	0-0	2-1	1-1	2-1	1-1	0-2	1-0	2-0	1-1	0-2	1-1	12-11
Fyhrie, Mike	0-0	0-0	0-0	0-0	0-0	0-0	0-1	0-0	0-0	0-0	0-0	0-0	0-0	0-2	0-4
Hasegawa, Shigetoshi	0-0	0-0	0-0	0-0	0-0	2-1	0-1	0-0	1-0	0-2	0-0	1-0	0-0	0-1	4-6
Hill, Ken	0-2	0-1	0-0	0-2	0-0	1-0	1-1	0-0	0-1	0-1	0-1	1-1	1-1	0-0	4-11
Holtz, Mike	0-1	0-0	0-1	1-0	0-0	0-0	0-0	0-0	0-0	0-0	0-0	0-0	0-0	0-0	1-2
Levine, Al	1-0	0-0	0-0	0-1	0-0	0-0	0-0	0-0	0-0	0-0	0-0	0-0	0-0	0-0	1-1
Magnante, Mike	0-0	0-0	0-0	0-0	1-0	0-0	0-0	0-0	0-0	0-0	0-1	1-0	0-0	0-0	5-2
McDowell, Jack	0-1	0-0	0-1	0-0	0-0	0-1	0-0	0-0	0-0	0-0	0-0	0-0	0-0	0-0	0-4
Mintz, Steve	0-0	0-0	0-0	0-0	0-0	0-0	0-0	0-0	0-0	0-0	0-0	0-0	0-0	0-0	0-0
Olivares, Omar	1-0	0-1	1-0	0-0	0-1	0-1	0-0	1-1	2-0	0-1	0-0	1-2	0-2	1-2	8-9
Ortiz, Ramon	0-0	0-0	1-0	0-0	0-0	0-1	0-0	0-0	0-0	1-0	0-0	0-0	0-0	0-0	2-3
Percival, Troy	0-1	0-1	1-1	0-1	1-0	0-0	0-0	0-0	0-2	0-0	0-0	0-0	0-0	0-0	4-6
Petkovsek, Mark	0-0	0-1	1-0	0-0	0-0	0-0	0-0	1-0	2-0	1-0	0-0	0-0	1-1	2-2	10-4
Pote, Lou	0-0	0-1	0-0	0-0	1-0	0-0	0-0	0-0	0-0	0-0	0-0	0-0	0-0	0-0	1-1
Schoeneweis, Scott	0-0	0-0	0-0	0-0	0-0	0-0	0-1	0-0	0-0	0-0	0-0	0-1	0-0	0-0	1-1
Sparks, Steve	0-1	0-1	0-3	1-1	1-0	1-0	0-1	0-0	1-1	0-1	1-1	0-1	0-1	0-2	5-11
Washburn, Jarrod	0-1	0-0	0-1	0-1	0-1	0-0	1-0	1-0	0-1	0-0	1-0	1-0	0-0	0-0	4-5
Totals	3-9	1-9	5-5	1-9	5-5	7-5	6-4	6-4	8-4	6-6	7-5	6-6	3-9	6-12	70-92

INTERLEAGUE: Petkovsek 1-0, Hill 1-0, Olivares 0-2, Belcher 0-1, Sparks 0-1 vs. Dodgers; Fyhrie 0-1, Petkovsek 0-1, Hasegawa 0-1 vs. Padres; Belcher 1-0, Finley 0-1, Sparks 0-1 vs. Giants; Finley 1-0, Olivares 1-0, Fyhrie 0-1 vs. Rockies; Petkovsek 1-1, Hill 0-1 vs. Diamondbacks. Total: 6-12.

MISCELLANEOUS

HOME RUNS BY PARK

At Anaheim (74): Vaughn 16, Glaus 12, Anderson 10, Salmon 7, Greene 7, Erstad 7, Velarde 4, Edmonds 3, Sheets 3, DiSarcina 1, Walbeck 1, Unroe 1, Pritchett 1, DaVanon 1.
At Baltimore (6): Velarde 3, Greene 2, O'Brien 1.
At Boston (0):
At Chicago (AL) (5): Vaughn 3, Molina 1, Glaus 1.
At Cleveland (8): Salmon 2, Anderson 2, Glaus 2, Vaughn 1, Edmonds 1.
At Colorado (6): Glaus 3, Anderson 2, Williams 1.
At Detroit (11): Salmon 2, Anderson 2, Greene 2, Glaus 2, Vaughn 1, Walbeck 1, Erstad 1.
At Kansas City (8): Salmon 3, Vaughn 1, Edmonds 1, Luke 1, Erstad 1, Glaus 1.
At Los Angeles (4): Glaus 2, Walbeck 1, Erstad 1.
At Minnesota (4): Vaughn 3, Glaus 1.
At New York (AL) (6): Vaughn 2, Anderson 1, Greene 1, Luke 1, Glaus 1.
At Oakland (4): Salmon 2, Greene 1, Glaus 1.
At San Francisco (0):
At Seattle (2): Vaughn 1, Erstad 1.
At Tampa Bay (2): Vaughn 1, Anderson 1.
At Texas (8): Glaus 3, Vaughn 1, Salmon 1, Anderson 1, Palmeiro 1, Greene 1.
At Toronto (5): Anderson 2, Velarde 1, Vaughn 1, Erstad 1.

LOW-HIT GAMES

No-hitters: None.
One-hitters: None.
Two-hitters: None.

10-STRIKEOUT GAMES

Chuck Finley 2, **Total:** 2.

FOUR OR MORE HITS IN ONE GAME

Randy Velarde 4 (including one five-hit game), Garret Anderson 4, Mo Vaughn 3 (including one five-hit game), Tim Salmon 2, Jim Edmonds 2, Darin Erstad 1, Troy Glaus 1, **Total:** 17.

MULTI-HOMER GAMES

Tim Salmon 3, Mo Vaughn 2, Troy Glaus 2, Garret Anderson 1, **Total:** 8.

GRAND SLAMS

4-15: Tim Salmon (off Oakland's Kevin Jarvis).
4-16: Todd Greene (off Seattle's Jamie Moyer).
4-29: Andy Sheets (off Toronto's Roy Halladay).
5-14: Mo Vaughn (off Tampa Bay's Bobby Witt).
6-5: Matt Walbeck (off Los Angeles's Chan Ho Park).

PINCH HITTERS

(Minimum 5 at-bats)

Name	AB	Avg.	HR	RBI
Huson, Jeff	27	.259	0	3
Walbeck, Matt	16	.250	0	0
Palmeiro, Orlando	12	.333	0	0
Greene, Todd	11	.273	1	4
Sheets, Andy	7	.143	0	0
Luke, Matt	7	.143	1	2
Williams, Reggie	5	.200	0	1
Unroe, Tim	5	.000	0	0

DEBUTS

4-7: Scott Schoeneweis, P.
6-13: Mike Colangelo, LF.
6-28: Bret Hemphill, C.
8-6: Trent Durrington, 2B.
8-11: Lou Pote, P.
8-19: Ramon Ortiz, P.
9-1: Juan Alvarez, P.
9-7: Brian Cooper, P.
9-7: Jeff DaVanon, RF.

GAMES BY POSITION

Catcher: Matt Walbeck 97, Ben Molina 30, Charlie O'Brien 27, Steve Decker 17, Todd Greene 12, Bret Hemphill 12.
First base: Darin Erstad 78, Mo Vaughn 72, Chris Pritchett 15, Jeff Huson 8, Steve Decker 6, Matt Luke 4, Jim Edmonds 2.
Second base: Randy Velarde 95, Jeff Huson 41, Trent Durrington 41, Andy Sheets 7, Dave Silvestri 1, Tim Unroe 1.
Third base: Troy Glaus 153, Jeff Huson 9, Tim Unroe 3, Andy Sheets 1.
Shortstop: Gary DiSarcina 81, Andy Sheets 76, Jeff Huson 22, Dave Silvestri 1.
Outfield: Garret Anderson 153, Orlando Palmeiro 92, Tim Salmon 89, Darin Erstad 69, Jim Edmonds 42, Todd Greene 30, Reggie Williams 24, Tim Unroe 12, Matt Luke 6, Jeff DaVanon 5, Jeff Huson 2, Dave Silvestri 1, Mike Colangelo 1.
Designated hitter: Mo Vaughn 67, Todd Greene 44, Orlando Palmeiro 10, Jim Edmonds 9, Tim Unroe 8, Jeff Huson 7, Tim Salmon 7, Chris Pritchett 5, Garret Anderson 4, Steve Decker 3, Reggie Williams 3, Darin Erstad 2, Jeff DaVanon 2, Matt Walbeck 1, Steve Sparks 1, Troy Glaus 1, Trent Durrington 1.

STREAKS

Wins: 5 (September 11-15).
Losses: 11 (July 16-26).
Consecutive games with at least one hit: 17, Garret Anderson (August 30-September 17).
Wins by pitcher: 4, Chuck Finley (September 10-25).

ATTENDANCE

Home: 2,252,330.
Road: 2,216,258.
Highest (home): 43,911 (July 15 vs. Los Angeles).
Highest (road): 55,626 (June 20 vs. New York).
Lowest (home): 16,165 (September 20 vs. Tampa Bay).
Lowest (road): 5,377 (April 13 vs. Oakland).

BALTIMORE ORIOLES

DAY BY DAY

Date	Opp.	Res.	Score	(inn.*)	Hits	Opp. hits	Winning pitcher	Losing pitcher	Save	Record	Pos.	GB
4-5	T.B.	W	10-7		13	12	Mussina	Alvarez	Timlin	1-0	T1st	...
4-7	T.B.	L	5-8		13	14	Saunders	Guzman	Hernandez	1-1	T3rd	1.0
4-8	T.B.	L	3-6		9	10	Witt	Erickson		1-2	T4th	2.0
4-9	Tor.	L	4-7		6	8	Escobar	Ponson		1-3	5th	3.0
4-10	Tor.	W	1-0		6	6	Mussina	Carpenter	Timlin	2-3	T3rd	3.0
4-11	Tor.	L	5-9		8	10	Halladay	Orosco		2-4	5th	3.0
4-13	At N.Y.	L	3-6		10	7	Nelson	Rhodes		2-5	5th	4.0
4-14	At N.Y.	L	7-14		9	17	Cone	Erickson		2-6	5th	5.0
4-15	At N.Y.	W	9-7		18	10	Rhodes	Rivera	Timlin	3-6	5th	4.0
4-16	At Tor.	L	6-7		12	10	Lloyd	Bones	Person	3-7	5th	4.0
4-17	At Tor.	L	4-7		7	10	Wells	Linton	Lloyd	3-8	5th	4.5
4-18	At Tor.	L	0-6		3	7	Halladay	Guzman		3-9	5th	5.5
4-20	At T.B.	L	3-5		6	12	Santana	Erickson	Hernandez	3-10	5th	6.5
4-21	At T.B.	L	8-14		11	17	Rekar	Mussina		3-11	5th	7.5
4-22	At T.B.	L	0-1		1	4	Saunders	Ponson	Hernandez	3-12	5th	8.5
4-23	Oak.	W	7-4		8	9	Fetters	Haynes		4-12	5th	7.5
4-24	Oak.	L	0-3		4	6	Oquist	Erickson	Taylor	4-13	5th	7.5
4-25	Oak.	L	10-11		9	10	Rigby	Timlin	Taylor	4-14	5th	8.5
4-27	K.C.	W	8-4		12	10	Mussina	Appier	Timlin	5-14	5th	8.5
4-28	K.C.	L	2-8		5	10	Rosado	Guzman		5-15	5th	8.5
4-29	K.C.	L	5-15		7	15	Suppan	Erickson	Santiago	5-16	5th	9.5
4-30	Min.	W	7-1		8	4	Ponson	Hawkins		6-16	5th	8.5
5-1	Min.	L	2-7		8	11	Radke	Coppinger		6-17	5th	9.5
5-2	Min.	W	6-0		9	6	Mussina	Milton		7-17	5th	9.5
5-4	Chi.	W	9-5	(10)	10	9	Timlin	Lundquist		8-17	5th	8.0
5-5	Chi.	W	8-0		7	6	Guzman	Navarro		9-17	5th	8.0
5-6	Chi.	W	4-2		5	8	Ponson	Baldwin	Timlin	10-17	5th	8.0
5-7	At Det.	W	9-4		12	10	Mussina	Thompson		11-17	5th	8.0
5-8	At Det.	L	6-7		8	5	Blair	Kamieniecki	Jones	11-18	5th	8.0
5-9	At Det.	W	5-0		7	5	Erickson	Mlicki		12-18	5th	8.0
5-10	At Cle.	L	4-6		7	8	Burba	Guzman	Jackson	12-19	5th	8.5
5-11	At Cle.	L	6-11		11	12	Colon	Ponson		12-20	5th	8.5
5-12	At Cle.	L	5-6		9	10	Assenmacher	Timlin	Shuey	12-21	5th	8.5
5-13	At Tex.	L	7-15		13	13	Morgan	Kamieniecki		12-22	5th	8.5
5-14	At Tex.	L	6-7		15	11	Crabtree	Rhodes	Wetteland	12-23	5th	8.5
5-15	At Tex.	L	1-8		7	14	Helling	Johns		12-24	5th	8.5
5-16	At Tex.	W	16-5		24	11	Ponson	Sele		13-24	5th	8.5
5-18	Ana.	W	5-3		8	7	Mussina	Finley	Timlin	14-24	5th	8.0
5-19	Ana.	L	4-5		11	8	Levine	Timlin	Percival	14-25	5th	9.0
5-20	Ana.	L	4-6		9	9	Belcher	Johnson	Percival	14-26	5th	9.0
5-21	Tex.	W	3-2		7	6	Ponson	Helling		15-26	5th	9.0
5-22	Tex.	L	7-8		14	7	Crabtree	Timlin	Wetteland	15-27	5th	10.0
5-23	Tex.	W	15-6		15	14	Mussina	Morgan		16-27	5th	10.0
5-25	At Ana.	L	1-4		6	6	Olivares	Erickson	Percival	16-28	5th	11.0
5-26	At Ana.	W	3-2		4	4	Ponson	Belcher	Rhodes	17-28	5th	10.0
5-27	At Ana.	W	6-3		12	7	Guzman	Hill	Timlin	18-28	5th	9.0
5-28	At Oak.	L	1-2		4	6	Candiotti	Mussina	Taylor	18-29	5th	10.0
5-29	At Oak.	W	7-5		13	10	Johns	Mathews	Rhodes	19-29	5th	10.0
5-30	At Oak.	L	5-11		10	16	Rigby	Erickson		19-30	5th	11.0
5-31	At Sea.	L	6-10		12	13	Moyer	Ponson	Mesa	19-31	5th	12.0
6-1	At Sea.	W	14-11		14	14	Johns	Garcia		20-31	5th	12.0
6-2	At Sea.	L	2-4		12	6	Paniagua	Mussina	Mesa	20-32	5th	12.0
6-4	Phi.	L	5-9		9	18	Ogea	Erickson		20-33	5th	13.0
6-5	Phi.	W	7-6	(10)	12	7	Timlin	Montgomery		21-33	5th	12.0
6-6	Phi.	L	7-11		14	19	Bennett	Bones		21-34	5th	12.0
6-8†	At Fla.	L	1-2		6	6	Edmondson	Timlin		21-35		
6-8‡	At Fla.	L	3-5		11	11	Alfonseca	Kamieniecki	Mantei	21-36	5th	12.0
6-9	At Fla.	W	4-2		12	5	Erickson	Springer	Rhodes	22-36	5th	11.5
6-11	At Atl.	W	6-2		12	5	Ponson	Maddux		23-36	5th	11.5
6-12	At Atl.	W	5-0		13	6	Guzman	Millwood		24-36	5th	11.5
6-13	At Atl.	W	22-1		25	6	Mussina	Smoltz		25-36	4th	10.5
6-14	K.C.	W	7-1		12	9	Erickson	Appier		26-36	4th	10.5
6-15	K.C.	W	6-5	(10)	13	11	Timlin	Service		27-36	4th	10.5
6-16	K.C.	W	2-1		7	9	Ponson	Rosado		28-36	4th	9.5
6-17	At Chi.	L	3-9		12	11	Sirotka	Guzman	Foulke	28-37	4th	9.5
6-18	At Chi.	W	3-2		8	7	Mussina	Navarro		29-37	4th	9.5
6-19	At Chi.	W	11-9	(11)	12	17	Rhodes	Foulke	Kamieniecki	30-37	4th	9.5
6-20	At Chi.	W	8-4		12	10	Johnson	Baldwin	Timlin	31-37	4th	8.5
6-22	Bos.	W	5-3		7	9	Rhodes	Guthrie	Timlin	32-37	4th	8.5
6-23	Bos.	L	0-5		8	9	Saberhagen	Guzman		32-38	4th	9.5
6-24	Bos.	L	1-2		7	7	Portugal	Mussina	Wakefield	32-39	4th	10.5
6-25	N.Y.	L	8-9		13	16	Naulty	Timlin	Rivera	32-40	4th	11.5
6-26	N.Y.	L	4-7		8	11	Cone	Johnson	Rivera	32-41	4th	12.5
6-27	N.Y.	L	2-6		7	12	Hernandez	Ponson		32-42	4th	13.5
6-29	At Tor.	L	5-6	(10)	12	10	Frascatore	Rhodes		32-43	4th	14.5
6-30	At Tor.	L	9-10	(10)	16	12	Frascatore	Orosco		32-44	5th	14.5

Date	Opp.	Res.	Score	(inn.*)	Hits	Opp. hits	Winning pitcher	Losing pitcher	Save	Record	Pos.	GB
7-1	At Tor.	L	6-8		9	10	Frascatore	Timlin	Koch	32-45	5th	15.5
7-2	At N.Y.	L	1-2		8	7	Cone	Johnson	Rivera	32-46	5th	16.5
7-3	At N.Y.	L	5-6		6	9	Grimsley	Rhodes		32-47	5th	17.5
7-4	At N.Y.	W	7-3		9	9	Guzman	Mendoza	Kamieniecki	33-47	5th	16.5
7-5	At N.Y.	W	9-1		13	7	Mussina	Pettitte		34-47	5th	15.5
7-6	Tor.	L	3-4	(10)	8	7	Lloyd	Timlin	Koch	34-48	5th	16.5
7-7	Tor.	L	6-7		13	6	Spoljaric	Molina	Koch	34-49	5th	16.5
7-8	Tor.	L	6-11		14	15	Escobar	Ponson		34-50	5th	17.5
7-9	At Phi.	L	2-4		8	5	Schilling	Guzman		34-51	5th	17.5
7-10	At Phi.	W	8-4		13	6	Mussina	Byrd		35-51	5th	16.5
7-11	At Phi.	W	6-2		12	6	Erickson	Ogea		36-51	5th	16.5
7-15	Mon.	W	8-2		9	11	Ponson	Thurman		37-51	5th	15.5
7-16	Mon.	W	9-4		17	9	Mussina	Smith		38-51	5th	14.5
7-17	Mon.	W	2-1		4	6	Erickson	Hermanson		39-51	5th	14.5
7-18	N.Y. (NL)	L	6-8		12	12	Yoshii	Guzman	Benitez	39-52	5th	15.5
7-19	N.Y. (NL)	L	1-4		4	9	Dotel	Johnson	Benitez	39-53	5th	15.5
7-20	N.Y. (NL)	W	4-1		9	6	Ponson	Leiter		40-53	5th	15.5
7-21	At Bos.	W	6-1		11	6	Mussina	Saberhagen		41-53	4th	15.5
7-22	At Bos.	W	5-2		12	8	Erickson	Cho	Timlin	42-53	4th	15.5
7-23	Ana.	W	1-0		7	6	Guzman	McDowell	Timlin	43-53	4th	15.5
7-24	Ana.	W	8-4		17	6	Johnson	Hill		44-53	4th	15.5
7-25	Ana.	W	8-7	(11)	11	6	Kamieniecki	Holtz		45-53	4th	15.5
7-27	Tex.	L	6-8		11	14	Sele	Mussina	Wetteland	45-54	4th	16.5
7-28	Tex.	W	8-6		13	8	Erickson	Burkett	Timlin	46-54	4th	15.5
7-29	Tex.	L	1-3		3	6	Morgan	Guzman	Wetteland	46-55	4th	15.5
7-30	At Sea.	L	4-7		7	7	Meche	Johnson	Mesa	46-56	4th	16.5
7-31	At Sea.	L	2-5		8	9	Moyer	Ponson	Mesa	46-57	4th	16.5
8-1	At Sea.	L	1-3		8	3	Abbott	Mussina	Mesa	46-58	4th	16.5
8-2	At Oak.	L	1-7		4	9	Appier	Erickson		46-59	4th	17.5
8-3	At Oak.	L	2-12		9	12	Hudson	Bones		46-60	4th	17.5
8-4	At Oak.	W	9-5		14	8	Johnson	Haynes		47-60	4th	17.5
8-5	Det.	W	6-3		11	9	Ponson	Weaver	Timlin	48-60	4th	17.5
8-6	Det.	L	3-4		7	11	Mlicki	Mussina	Jones	48-61	4th	18.5
8-7	Det.	W	5-4		9	7	Erickson	Borkowski	Timlin	49-61	4th	18.5
8-8	Det.	L	2-5	(11)	10	8	Brocail	Kamieniecki	Jones	49-62	4th	19.5
8-9	At T.B.	L	9-10		12	15	Rupe	Johnson	Hernandez	49-63	4th	20.5
8-10	At T.B.	W	17-1		20	6	Ponson	Eiland		50-63	4th	19.5
8-11	At T.B.	W	4-2		13	10	Mussina	Arrojo	Timlin	51-63	4th	19.5
8-13	At Cle.	L	3-6		9	8	Rincon	Erickson	Jackson	51-64	4th	20.5
8-14	At Cle.	L	1-7		4	6	Karsay	Johnson		51-65	4th	20.5
8-15	At Cle.	L	1-5		5	13	Colon	Ponson		51-66	4th	20.5
8-17	Min.	W	8-3		13	10	Mussina	Mays		52-66	4th	21.0
8-18	Min.	W	2-0		5	5	Erickson	Hawkins		53-66	4th	20.0
8-19	Min.	W	9-3		11	5	Johnson	Perkins		54-66	4th	19.0
8-21†	Chi.	L	3-4		7	14	Simas	Reyes	Howry	54-67		
8-21‡	Chi.	L	5-8	(10)	14	13	Howry	Johns	Foulke	54-68	4th	20.0
8-22	Chi.	W	9-4		16	7	Johns	Navarro		55-68	4th	20.0
8-23	At K.C.	W	4-2		10	8	Erickson	Reichert	Timlin	56-68	4th	20.0
8-24	At K.C.	W	5-3	(10)	10	7	Kamieniecki	Wallace	Timlin	57-68	4th	20.0
8-25	At K.C.	L	6-8		11	14	Suppan	Linton	Montgomery	57-69	4th	20.0
8-26	At K.C.	L	0-6		4	11	Witasick	Ponson		57-70	4th	20.5
8-27	At Det.	L	4-5		5	11	Weaver	Reyes	Jones	57-71	4th	21.5
8-28	At Det.	L	3-4		10	7	Mlicki	Erickson	Jones	57-72	4th	22.5
8-29	At Det.	W	11-4		13	7	Johnson	Nitkowski		58-72	4th	22.5
8-31	T.B.	L	0-3		3	11	Rupe	Ponson	Hernandez	58-73	5th	23.0
9-1	T.B.	W	3-1		5	5	Johns	Wheeler	Timlin	59-73	4th	22.0
9-2	T.B.	W	11-6		13	14	Erickson	Arrojo		60-73	4th	22.0
9-3	Cle.	L	6-7		10	9	Assenmacher	Reyes	Jackson	60-74	4th	22.0
9-4	Cle.	W	3-1		9	6	Linton	Colon	Timlin	61-74	4th	22.0
9-5	Cle.	L	7-15		11	12	Brower	Ponson		61-75	4th	23.0
9-6	Cle.	L	6-7		9	8	Burba	Johns	Jackson	61-76	4th	23.0
9-7	At Min.	W	5-0		10	3	Erickson	Mays		62-76	4th	22.0
9-8	At Min.	W	10-0		14	6	Johnson	Hawkins		63-76	4th	22.0
9-9	At Min.	W	6-5		12	7	Reyes	Miller	Timlin	64-76	4th	21.5
9-10	Sea.	W	5-4	(12)	9	9	Reyes	Ramsay		65-76	4th	20.5
9-11	Sea.	W	4-2		12	4	Johns	Garcia	Timlin	66-76	4th	19.5
9-12	Sea.	W	4-1		9	5	Erickson	Halama		67-76	4th	18.5
9-13	Sea.	W	5-4	(10)	9	11	Ryan	Mesa		68-76	4th	17.5
9-14	Oak.	W	13-6		16	11	Mussina	Oquist		69-76	4th	17.5
9-17	At Ana.	W	4-2		12	6	Erickson	Washburn	Timlin	70-76	4th	18.5
9-18	At Ana.	W	6-3		5	8	Ponson	Cooper	Timlin	71-76	4th	17.5
9-19	At Ana.	W	5-4		11	9	Molina	Percival	Timlin	72-76	4th	17.5
9-21	At Tex.	W	4-2		7	6	Johnson	Loaiza	Timlin	73-76	4th	17.5
9-22	At Tex.	W	7-4		9	10	Erickson	Helling	Timlin	74-76	4th	17.5
9-23†	Oak.	L	6-9		8	15	Mathews	Molina	Isringhausen	74-77		
9-23‡	Oak.	W	12-4		12	8	Johns	Olivares		75-77	4th	18.0
9-24	At Bos.	W	1-0		8	6	Mussina	Saberhagen	Timlin	76-77	4th	18.0
9-25	At Bos.	L	1-4		4	6	Martinez	Linton	Garces	76-78	4th	18.0
9-26	At Bos.	W	8-5		5	8	Johnson	Wakefield	Orosco	77-78	4th	17.0
9-27	At Bos.	L	3-5		8	8	Martinez	Erickson	Lowe	77-79	4th	17.0
9-28	N.Y.	L	5-9		10	10	Mendoza	Ponson		77-80	4th	18.0
9-30†	N.Y.	W	5-0		5	8	Mussina	Clemens		78-80		
9-30‡	N.Y.	L	5-12		12	17	Hernandez	Corsi		78-81	4th	18.0
10-1	Bos.	L	2-6		8	12	Ohka	Linton		78-82	4th	19.0
10-2	Bos.	L	0-8		3	12	Martinez	Johns		78-83	4th	20.0
10-3	Bos.	L	0-1	(10)	6	5	Rose	Timlin	Wakefield	78-84	4th	20.0

Monthly records: April (6-16), May (13-15), June (13-13), July (14-13), August (12-16), September (20-8), October (0-3).
*Innings, if other than nine. † First game of a doubleheader. ‡ Second game of a doubleheader.

MEMORABLE GAMES

June 13 at Atlanta

Third baseman Cal Ripken turned in the best offensive performance of his storied career with six hits in six at-bats. He homered twice and drove in six runs to lead the Orioles to a stunning 22-1 victory over the eventual National League-champion Braves. Righthander Mike Mussina, often the victim of sketchy offensive support, had nothing to complain about as the Orioles ran up one of the biggest single-game run totals in club history.

Baltimore	AB	R	H	RBI	Atlanta	AB	R	H	RBI
B.Anderson, cf	6	0	1	2	O.Guillen, ss	3	0	0	0
Bordick, ss	4	1	1	0	McGlinchy, p	0	0	0	0
Reboulet, ss	3	0	0	0	Lockhart, 3b	1	0	0	0
Surhoff, lf	3	2	2	1	B.Boone, 2b	2	0	0	0
Amaral, lf	3	1	2	0	C.Jones, 3b	3	0	1	0
Belle, rf	6	3	3	1	R.Springer, p	0	0	0	0
W.Clark, 1b	4	4	4	5	Remlinger, p	0	0	0	0
Conine, 1b	1	1	0	0	O.Nixon, ph	1	0	0	0
Ripken Jr., 3b	6	5	6	6	Seanez, p	0	0	0	0
DeShields, 2b	5	2	2	1	B.Jordan, rf	2	1	1	0
C.Johnson, c	3	2	1	3	G.Williams, rf	2	0	1	0
Figga, c	1	0	0	0	J.Lopez, c	2	0	1	0
Mussina, p	5	1	2	3	E.Perez, c	2	0	0	0
Coppinger, p	1	0	1	0	Klesko, lf	3	0	2	1
					A.Jones, cf	4	0	0	0
					Simon, 1b	4	0	0	0
					Smoltz, p	0	0	0	0
					Speier, p	1	0	0	0
					DeRsa, ph-ss	2	0	0	0
Totals	**51**	**22**	**25**	**22**	**Totals**	**32**	**1**	**6**	**1**

Baltimore ....502 423 402— 22
Atlanta ....000 100 000— 1

LOB—Baltimore 8, Atlanta 7. 2B—Surhoff (16), Belle (4), W.Clark 3 (8), Ripken Jr. (12), Mussina (1), C.Jones (15), J.Lopez (14), G.Williams (7). HR—W.Clark (5), Ripken Jr. 2 (7), C.Johnson (12). SF—Klesko.

Baltimore	IP	H	R	ER	BB	SO
Mussina (W, 8-3)	7	5	1	1	1	4
Coppinger	2	1	0	0	1	1

Atlanta	IP	H	R	ER	BB	SO
Smoltz (L, 7-2)	2.1	7	7	7	2	2
Speier	2.2	7	6	6	1	2
McGlinchy	1	3	3	3	0	0
R.Springer	1	3	4	4	3	2
Remlinger	1	1	0	0	0	0
Seanez	1	4	2	2	0	2

U—HP, Cuzzi. 1B, Nauert. 2B, Gorman. 3B, Crawford. T—3:03. A—45,738.

September 2 at Baltimore

Future Hall of Famer Cal Ripken launched his historic 400th career home run off Tampa Bay pitcher Rolando Arrojo in an 11-6 victory over the Devil Rays. The milestone home run was supposed to be the first of two historic moments for Ripken, who was in range for his 3,000th hit, but renewed back soreness forced him to undergo surgery later in the month – still nine hits short of 3,000.

Tampa Bay	AB	R	H	RBI	Baltimore	AB	R	H	RBI
Cairo, 2b	5	1	2	0	DeShields, 2b	3	0	0	0
D.Martinez, cf	5	0	3	2	Reboulet, 2b	2	0	0	0
Canseco, dh	5	1	2	0	Bordick, ss	4	2	1	0
McGriff, 1b	3	1	1	1	Surhoff, dh	5	2	3	2
Flaherty, c	5	1	2	1	Belle, rf	4	2	2	2
Sorrento, lf	5	0	1	1	May, lf	3	1	1	1
J.Guillen, rf	3	0	0	0	Amaral, pr-lf	0	0	0	0
Perry, 3b	3	1	1	1	Conine, 1b	5	1	3	3
Ledesma, ss	4	1	2	0	Ripken Jr., 3b	4	1	1	3
					Minor, 3b	1	0	0	0
					Kingsale, cf	4	1	1	0
					C.Johnson, c	3	1	1	0
					Figga, c	0	0	0	0
Totals	**38**	**6**	**14**	**6**	**Totals**	**38**	**11**	**13**	**11**

Tampa Bay ....002 002 002— 6
Baltimore ....025 003 10x— 11

E—Sorrento (5), Cairo (8). DP—Baltimore 2. LOB—Tampa Bay 9, Baltimore 9. 2B—Bordick (26), Belle (23), Conine 2 (27). HR—Ripken Jr. (16). SB—Cairo (18). SF—Perry.

Tampa Bay	IP	H	R	ER	BB	SO
Arrojo (L, 4-10)	2.2	7	7	7	1	3
Ri.White	3.1	6	3	0	1	2
Newman	1	0	1	1	2	1
Duvall	1	0	0	0	1	0

Baltimore	IP	H	R	ER	BB	SO
Erickson (W, 11-11)	6.1	10	4	4	2	2
B.Ryan	1.2	0	0	0	0	2
Fetters	1	4	2	2	0	0

HBP—J.Guillen by Erickson, Bordick by Newman. U—HP, Reynolds. 1B, Marty Foster. 2B, Morrison. 3B, Miller. T—2:59. A—39,172.

BATTING

Name	G	TPA	AB	R	H	TB	2B	3B	HR	RBI	Avg.	Obp.	Slg.	SH	SF	HP	BB	IBB	SO	SB	CS	GDP	vs RHP AB	vs RHP Avg.	vs RHP HR	vs RHP RBI	vs LHP AB	vs LHP Avg.	vs LHP HR	vs LHP RBI
Surhoff, B.J.	162	727	673	104	207	331	38	1	28	107	.308	.347	.492	1	8	2	43	1	78	5	1	15	514	.302	21	71	159	.327	7	36
Bordick, Mike	160	708	631	93	175	254	35	7	10	77	.277	.334	.403	8	10	5	54	1	102	14	4	25	524	.252	7	54	107	.402	3	23
Belle, Albert	161	722	610	108	181	330	36	1	37	117	.297	.400	.541	0	4	7	101	15	82	17	3	19	512	.283	26	90	98	.367	11	27
Anderson, Brady	150	692	564	109	159	269	28	5	24	81	.282	.404	.477	1	7	24	96	7	105	36	7	6	471	.291	20	61	93	.237	4	20
Conine, Jeff	139	485	444	54	129	201	31	1	13	75	.291	.335	.453	1	7	3	30	0	40	0	3	12	351	.293	8	60	93	.280	5	15
Johnson, Charles	135	492	426	58	107	176	19	1	16	54	.251	.340	.413	4	3	4	55	2	107	0	0	13	364	.234	13	45	62	.355	3	9
Baines, Harold	107	390	345	57	111	201	16	1	24	81	.322	.395	.583	0	2	0	43	3	38	1	2	14	297	.323	21	66	48	.313	3	15
Ripken Jr., Cal	86	354	332	51	113	194	27	0	18	57	.340	.368	.584	3	3	3	13	3	31	0	1	14	283	.343	16	52	49	.327	2	5
DeShields, Delino	96	374	330	46	87	120	11	2	6	34	.264	.339	.364	5	1	1	37	0	52	11	8	5	289	.277	5	31	41	.171	1	3
Clark, Will	77	294	251	40	76	121	15	0	10	29	.303	.395	.482	0	3	2	38	2	42	2	2	5	199	.332	10	26	52	.192	0	3
Hairston Jr., Jerry	50	193	175	26	47	73	12	1	4	17	.269	.323	.417	4	0	3	11	0	24	9	4	2	148	.257	3	14	27	.333	1	3
Reboulet, Jeff	99	192	154	25	25	29	4	0	0	4	.162	.317	.188	3	0	2	33	0	29	1	0	1	103	.126	0	2	51	.235	0	2
Amaral, Rich	91	156	137	21	38	48	8	1	0	11	.277	.348	.350	1	2	1	15	0	20	9	6	1	64	.203	0	7	73	.342	0	4
Minor, Ryan	46	133	124	13	24	40	7	0	3	10	.194	.241	.323	0	1	0	8	0	43	1	0	1	109	.193	2	9	15	.200	1	1
Figga, Mike	41	91	86	12	19	26	4	0	1	5	.221	.236	.302	2	1	0	2	0	27	0	2	1	75	.227	1	5	11	.182	0	0
Kingsale, Gene	28	95	85	9	21	23	2	0	0	7	.247	.301	.271	2	1	2	5	0	13	1	3	3	73	.247	0	7	12	.250	0	0
Otanez, Willis	29	89	80	7	17	26	3	0	2	11	.213	.273	.325	1	1	1	6	0	16	0	0	3	57	.211	2	10	23	.217	0	1
May, Derrick	26	54	49	5	13	25	0	0	4	12	.265	.315	.510	0	1	0	4	0	6	0	0	2	49	.265	4	12	0	.000	0	0
Pickering, Calvin	23	51	40	4	5	9	1	0	1	5	.125	.314	.225	0	0	0	11	0	16	0	0	1	40	.125	1	5	0	.000	0	0
Webster, Lenny	16	45	36	1	6	7	1	0	0	3	.167	.333	.194	0	0	1	8	0	5	0	0	1	21	.143	0	1	15	.200	0	2
Garcia, Jesse	17	34	29	6	6	12	0	0	2	2	.207	.258	.414	3	0	0	2	0	3	0	0	1	26	.231	2	2	3	.000	0	0
Mussina, Mike	31	11	11	1	3	4	1	0	0	4	.273	.273	.364	0	0	0	0	0	1	0	0	0	11	.273	0	4	0	.000	0	0
Guzman, Juan	21	6	6	0	1	1	0	0	0	1	.167	.167	.167	0	0	0	0	0	4	0	0	0	6	.167	0	1	0	.000	0	0
Davis, Tommy	5	6	6	0	1	1	0	0	0	0	.167	.167	.167	0	0	0	0	0	2	0	0	1	6	.167	0	0	0	.000	0	0
Erickson, Scott	34	7	6	0	0	0	0	0	0	0	.000	.000	.000	1	0	0	0	0	2	0	0	0	6	.000	0	0	0	.000	0	0
Ponson, Sidney	32	4	3	0	0	0	0	0	0	0	.000	.000	.000	1	0	0	0	0	0	0	0	0	3	.000	0	0	0	.000	0	0
Johnson, Jason	22	2	2	0	0	0	0	0	0	0	.000	.000	.000	0	0	0	0	0	1	0	0	0	2	.000	0	0	0	.000	0	0
Coppinger, Rocky	11	1	1	0	1	1	0	0	0	0	1.000	1.000	1.000	0	0	0	0	0	0	0	0	0	1	1.000	0	0	0	.000	0	0
Johns, Doug	32	1	1	0	0	0	0	0	0	0	.000	.000	.000	0	0	0	0	0	1	0	0	0	1	.000	0	0	0	.000	0	0
Orosco, Jesse	65	0	0	0	0	0	0	0	0	0	.000	.000	.000	0	0	0	0	0	0	0	0	0	0	.000	0	0	0	.000	0	0
Timlin, Mike	62	0	0	0	0	0	0	0	0	0	.000	.000	.000	0	0	0	0	0	0	0	0	0	0	.000	0	0	0	.000	0	0
Kamieniecki, Scott	43	0	0	0	0	0	0	0	0	0	.000	.000	.000	0	0	0	0	0	0	0	0	0	0	.000	0	0	0	.000	0	0
Bones, Ricky	31	0	0	1	0	0	0	0	0	0	.000	.000	.000	0	0	0	0	0	0	0	0	0	0	.000	0	0	0	.000	0	0
Rhodes, Arthur	43	0	0	0	0	0	0	0	0	0	.000	.000	.000	0	0	0	0	0	0	0	0	0	0	.000	0	0	0	.000	0	0
Molina, Gabe	20	0	0	0	0	0	0	0	0	0	.000	.000	.000	0	0	0	0	0	0	0	0	0	0	.000	0	0	0	.000	0	0

Players with more than one A.L. team

Name	G	TPA	AB	R	H	TB	2B	3B	HR	RBI	Avg.	Obp.	Slg.	SH	SF	HP	BB	IBB	SO	SB	CS	GDP	vs RHP AB	vs RHP Avg.	vs RHP HR	vs RHP RBI	vs LHP AB	vs LHP Avg.	vs LHP HR	vs LHP RBI
Baines, Cle.	28	96	85	5	23	28	2	0	1	22	.271	.354	.329	0	0	0	11	0	10	0	0	2	297	.323	21	66	48	.313	3	15
Baines, Bal.-Cle.	135	486	430	62	134	229	18	1	25	103	.312	.387	.533	0	2	0	54	3	48	1	2	16	377	.313	22	86	53	.302	3	17
Figga, N.Y.	2	0	0	0	0	0	0	0	0	0	.000	.000	.000	0	0	0	0	0	0	0	0	0	75	.227	1	5	11	.182	0	0
Figga, N.Y.-Bal.	43	91	86	12	19	26	4	0	1	5	.221	.236	.302	2	1	0	2	0	27	0	2	1	75	.227	1	5	11	.182	0	0
Otanez, Tor.	42	137	127	21	32	55	8	0	5	13	.252	.307	.433	0	0	1	9	0	30	0	0	3	57	.211	2	10	23	.217	0	1
Otanez, Bal.-Tor.	71	226	207	28	49	81	11	0	7	24	.237	.293	.391	1	1	2	15	0	46	0	0	6	155	.206	7	18	52	.327	0	6
Webster, Bos.	6	17	14	0	0	0	0	0	0	1	.000	.176	.000	0	0	1	2	0	2	0	0	0	21	.143	0	1	15	.200	0	2
Webster, Bal.-Bos	22	62	50	1	6	7	1	0	0	4	.120	.290	.140	0	0	2	10	0	7	0	0	1	29	.103	0	1	21	.143	0	3

PITCHING

Name	W	L	Pct.	ERA	IP	H	R	ER	HR	SH	SF	HB	BB	IBB	SO	G	GS	CG	ShO	GF	Sv	vs. RH AB	vs. RH Avg.	vs. RH HR	vs. RH RBI	vs. LH AB	vs. LH Avg.	vs. LH HR	vs. LH RBI
Erickson, Scott	15	12	.556	4.81	230.1	244	127	123	27	7	6	11	99	4	106	34	34	6	3	0	0	432	.289	13	57	440	.270	14	62
Ponson, Sidney	12	12	.500	4.71	210.0	227	118	110	35	4	7	1	80	2	112	32	32	6	0	0	0	412	.274	17	67	393	.290	18	42
Mussina, Mike	18	7	.720	3.50	203.1	207	88	79	16	9	7	1	52	0	172	31	31	4	0	0	0	408	.267	9	39	365	.268	7	36
Guzman, Juan	5	9	.357	4.18	122.2	124	63	57	18	4	3	3	65	3	95	21	21	1	1	0	0	229	.284	12	24	239	.247	6	35
Johnson, Jason	8	7	.533	5.46	115.1	120	74	70	16	2	4	3	55	0	71	22	21	0	0	0	0	235	.289	8	30	215	.242	8	33
Johns, Doug	6	4	.600	4.47	86.2	81	45	43	9	1	7	8	25	2	50	32	5	0	0	2	0	240	.288	7	32	87	.138	2	14
Timlin, Mike	3	9	.250	3.57	63.0	51	30	25	9	1	1	5	23	3	50	62	0	0	0	52	27	123	.244	5	18	108	.194	4	17
Linton, Doug	1	4	.200	5.95	59.0	69	41	39	14	4	0	2	25	1	31	14	8	0	0	0	0	114	.325	6	20	119	.269	8	20
Kamieniecki, Scott	2	4	.333	4.95	56.1	52	32	31	4	4	3	4	29	2	39	43	3	0	0	18	2	110	.236	1	14	98	.265	3	15
Rhodes, Arthur	3	4	.429	5.43	53.0	43	37	32	9	2	2	0	45	6	59	43	0	0	0	11	3	127	.228	8	23	68	.206	1	9
Bones, Ricky	0	3	.000	5.98	43.2	59	29	29	7	2	1	2	19	0	26	30	2	0	0	7	0	97	.299	4	15	86	.349	3	16
Orosco, Jesse	0	2	.000	5.34	32.0	28	21	19	5	2	3	2	20	3	35	65	0	0	0	12	1	54	.204	2	11	63	.270	3	15
Fetters, Mike	1	0	1.000	5.81	31.0	35	23	20	5	1	0	2	22	2	22	27	0	0	0	10	0	72	.264	2	16	54	.296	3	10
Reyes, Al	2	3	.400	4.85	29.2	23	16	16	4	3	2	3	16	2	28	27	0	0	0	6	0	66	.227	3	10	36	.222	1	10
Molina, Gabe	1	2	.333	6.65	23.0	22	19	17	4	0	0	0	16	1	14	20	0	0	0	7	0	53	.226	3	14	33	.303	1	3
Coppinger, Rocky	0	1	.000	8.31	21.2	25	21	20	8	0	1	0	19	0	17	11	2	0	0	7	0	47	.340	6	14	38	.237	2	5
Ryan, B.J.	1	0	1.000	2.95	18.1	9	6	6	0	0	1	0	12	1	28	13	0	0	0	3	0	34	.118	0	2	26	.192	0	6
Corsi, Jim	0	1	.000	2.70	13.1	15	4	4	2	1	0	0	1	0	8	13	0	0	0	3	0	24	.208	0	0	27	.370	2	4
Riley, Matt	0	0	.000	7.36	11.0	17	9	9	4	0	1	0	13	0	6	3	3	0	0	0	0	39	.385	3	7	6	.333	1	2
Slocumb, Heathcliff	0	0	.000	12.46	8.2	15	12	12	2	0	0	2	9	2	12	10	0	0	0	7	0	21	.381	2	7	17	.412	0	4
Falkenborg, Brian	0	0	.000	0.00	3.0	2	0	0	0	0	0	0	2	0	1	2	0	0	0	0	0	5	.200	0	0	5	.200	0	0

PITCHERS WITH MORE THAN ONE A.L. TEAM

Name	W	L	Pct.	ERA	IP	H	R	ER	HR	SH	SF	HB	BB	IBB	SO	G	GS	CG	ShO	GF	Sv	vs. RH AB	vs. RH Avg.	vs. RH HR	vs. RH RBI	vs. LH AB	vs. LH Avg.	vs. LH HR	vs. LH RBI
Corsi, Bos.	1	2	.333	5.25	24.0	25	15	14	4	3	1	2	19	3	14	23	0	0	0	5	0	24	.208	0	0	27	.370	2	4
Corsi, Bos.-Bal.	1	3	.250	4.34	37.1	40	19	18	6	4	1	2	20	3	22	36	0	0	0	1	0	80	.238	3	10	59	.356	3	11

DESIGNATED HITTERS

Name	AB	Avg.	HR	RBI	Name	AB	Avg.	HR	RBI	Name	AB	Avg.	HR	RBI
Baines, Harold	336	.327	24	76	May, Derrick	28	.214	1	2	Webster, Lenny	3	.333	0	1
Surhoff, B.J.	56	.357	0	6	Amaral, Rich	27	.296	0	5	Kingsale, Gene	2	.000	0	0
Conine, Jeff	40	.250	0	7	Pickering, Calvin	14	.071	0	1	Garcia, Jesse	0	-	0	0
Anderson, Brady	34	.235	3	9	Clark, Will	12	.000	0	1					
Belle, Albert	29	.414	0	6	Otanez, Willis	6	.333	0	1					

INDIVIDUAL STATISTICS

FIELDING

FIRST BASEMEN

Player	Pct.	G	PO	A	E	TC	DP
Conine, Jeff	.993	99	831	52	6	889	108
Clark, Will	.995	63	575	42	3	620	54
Pickering, Calvin	.960	8	46	2	2	50	8
Otanez, Willis	1.000	5	6	0	0	6	0
Amaral, Rich	1.000	2	4	2	0	6	1
Minor, Ryan	.917	1	10	1	1	12	1
Davis, Tommy	1.000	1	2	0	0	2	0

SECOND BASEMEN

Player	Pct.	G	PO	A	E	TC	DP
DeShields, Delino	.977	93	178	249	10	437	54
Hairston Jr., Jerry	1.000	50	115	154	0	269	47
Reboulet, Jeff	.993	36	54	83	1	138	21
Garcia, Jesse	1.000	6	7	8	0	15	3
Amaral, Rich	-	2	0	0	0	0	0

THIRD BASEMEN

Player	Pct.	G	PO	A	E	TC	DP
Ripken Jr., Cal	.932	85	36	142	13	191	11
Reboulet, Jeff	.987	56	19	56	1	76	4
Minor, Ryan	.963	45	26	79	4	109	8
Otanez, Willis	.917	22	16	28	4	48	2
Conine, Jeff	.000	4	0	0	1	1	0
Surhoff, B.J.	1.000	2	1	5	0	6	0
Garcia, Jesse	1.000	2	0	1	0	1	0
Amaral, Rich	-	1	0	0	0	0	0

SHORTSTOPS

Player	Pct.	G	PO	A	E	TC	DP
Bordick, Mike	.989	159	277	511	9	797	132
Reboulet, Jeff	1.000	10	6	13	0	19	0
Garcia, Jesse	1.000	7	9	13	0	22	5

OUTFIELDERS

Player	Pct.	G	PO	A	E	TC	DP
Belle, Albert	.985	154	252	17	4	273	2
Surhoff, B.J.	1.000	148	282	16	0	298	5
Anderson, Brady	.997	136	308	3	1	312	1
Amaral, Rich	1.000	50	66	0	0	66	0
Kingsale, Gene	.980	24	48	1	1	50	0
Conine, Jeff	1.000	13	17	1	0	18	0
May, Derrick	1.000	5	7	1	0	8	1

CATCHERS

Player	Pct.	G	PO	A	E	TC	DP	PB
Johnson, Charles	.994	135	770	66	5	841	14	3
Figga, Mike	.973	41	168	12	5	185	1	2
Webster, Lenny	.986	12	67	6	1	74	2	0
Davis, Tommy	.909	4	9	1	1	11	0	0

PITCHERS

Player	Pct.	G	PO	A	E	TC	DP
Orosco, Jesse	.875	65	2	5	1	8	0
Timlin, Mike	.813	62	5	8	3	16	1
Kamieniecki, Scott	1.000	43	5	16	0	21	1
Rhodes, Arthur	1.000	43	0	6	0	6	0
Erickson, Scott	.971	34	24	42	2	68	5
Ponson, Sidney	.950	32	12	26	2	40	6
Johns, Doug	1.000	32	10	11	0	21	0
Mussina, Mike	.984	31	14	46	1	61	3
Bones, Ricky	1.000	30	2	2	0	4	0
Fetters, Mike	.667	27	2	4	3	9	0
Reyes, Al	1.000	27	0	5	0	5	1
Johnson, Jason	.882	22	4	11	2	17	1
Guzman, Juan	.895	21	2	15	2	19	5
Molina, Gabe	1.000	20	1	2	0	3	0
Linton, Doug	1.000	14	5	8	0	13	0
Corsi, Jim	1.000	13	1	5	0	6	0
Ryan, B.J.	1.000	13	0	1	0	1	0
Coppinger, Rocky	1.000	11	3	1	0	4	0
Slocumb, Heathcliff	-	10	0	0	0	0	0
Riley, Matt	1.000	3	0	2	0	2	0
Falkenborg, Brian	1.000	2	1	0	0	1	0

PITCHING AGAINST EACH CLUB

Pitcher	Ana. W-L	Bos. W-L	Chi. W-L	Cle. W-L	Det. W-L	K.C. W-L	Min. W-L	N.Y. W-L	Oak. W-L	Sea. W-L	T.B. W-L	Tex. W-L	Tor. W-L	N.L. W-L	Total W-L
Bones, Ricky	0-0	0-0	0-0	0-0	0-0	0-0	0-0	0-0	0-1	0-0	0-0	0-0	0-0	0-1	0-3
Coppinger, Rocky	0-0	0-0	0-0	0-0	0-0	0-0	0-1	0-0	0-0	0-0	0-0	0-0	0-0	0-0	0-1
Corsi, Jim	0-0	0-0	0-0	0-0	0-0	0-0	0-0	0-1	0-0	0-0	0-0	0-0	0-0	0-0	0-1
Erickson, Scott	1-1	1-1	0-0	0-1	2-1	2-1	2-0	0-1	0-3	1-0	1-2	2-0	0-0	3-1	15-12
Falkenborg, Brian	0-0	0-0	0-0	0-0	0-0	0-0	0-0	0-0	0-0	0-0	0-0	0-0	0-0	0-0	0-0
Fetters, Mike	0-0	0-0	0-0	0-0	0-0	0-0	0-0	1-0	0-0	0-0	0-0	0-0	0-0	0-0	1-0
Guzman, Juan	2-0	0-1	1-1	0-1	0-0	0-1	0-0	1-0	0-0	0-1	0-1	0-1	0-1	1-2	5-9
Johns, Doug	0-0	1-1	1-1	0-1	0-0	0-1	0-0	0-0	2-0	1-0	0-1	0-0	0-0	0-0	6-4
Johnson, Jason	1-1	1-0	1-0	0-1	1-0	0-0	2-0	0-2	1-0	0-1	0-1	1-0	0-0	0-1	8-7
Kamieniecki, Scott	1-0	0-0	0-0	0-0	0-2	1-0	0-0	0-0	0-0	0-0	0-0	0-0	0-1	0-1	2-4
Linton, Doug	0-0	0-2	0-0	1-0	0-0	0-0	0-0	0-0	0-0	0-0	0-0	0-1	0-0	0-0	1-3
Molina, Gabe	1-0	0-0	0-0	0-0	0-0	0-0	0-0	0-0	0-1	0-0	0-0	0-0	0-1	0-0	1-2
Mussina, Mike	1-0	2-1	1-0	0-0	1-1	0-0	2-0	2-0	1-1	0-2	2-1	1-1	1-0	3-0	18-7
Orosco, Jesse	0-0	0-0	0-0	0-0	0-0	0-0	0-0	0-0	0-0	0-0	0-0	0-0	0-0	0-0	0-0
Ponson, Sidney	2-0	0-0	1-0	0-3	1-0	1-1	1-0	0-2	0-0	0-2	1-0	1-1	0-0	3-0	12-12
Reyes, Al	0-0	0-0	0-1	0-1	0-1	0-0	0-0	1-0	0-0	0-0	0-0	0-0	0-0	0-0	2-3
Rhodes, Arthur	0-0	1-0	0-0	0-0	0-0	0-0	1-2	0-0	0-0	0-0	0-0	0-1	0-0	0-0	3-4
Riley, Matt	0-0	0-0	0-0	0-0	0-0	0-0	0-0	0-0	0-0	0-0	0-0	0-0	0-0	0-1	0-1
Ryan, B.J.	0-0	0-0	0-0	0-0	0-0	0-0	0-0	1-0	0-0	0-0	0-0	0-0	0-0	0-0	1-0
Slocumb, Heathcliff	0-0	0-0	0-0	0-0	0-0	0-0	0-0	0-0	0-0	0-0	0-0	0-0	0-0	0-0	0-0
Timlin, Mike	0-1	0-0	0-0	0-1	0-0	1-0	0-0	0-0	0-1	0-0	0-0	0-1	0-2	1-1	3-9
Totals	9-3	5-7	7-3	1-9	5-5	6-4	8-1	4-9	5-7	5-5	5-7	6-6	1-11	11-7	78-84

INTERLEAGUE: Ponson 1-0, Guzman 1-0, Mussina 1-0 vs. Braves; Ponson 1-0, Mussina 1-0, Erickson 1-0 vs. Expos; Ponson 1-0, Guzman 0-1, Johnson 0-1 vs. Mets; Erickson 1-1, Timlin 1-0, Mussina 1-0, Bones 0-1, Guzman 0-1 vs. Phillies; Erickson 1-0, Timlin 0-1, Kamieniecki 0-1 vs. Marlins. Total: 11-7.

MISCELLANEOUS

HOME RUNS BY PARK

At Anaheim (7): Baines 2, Surhoff 1, Anderson 1, Belle 1, Bordick 1, May 1.
At Atlanta (8): Ripken Jr. 2, Clark 2, Surhoff 1, Anderson 1, Bordick 1, Johnson 1.
At Baltimore (98): Belle 19, Baines 12, Ripken Jr. 12, Anderson 10, Surhoff 9, Johnson 8, Conine 7, Clark 5, DeShields 4, Bordick 3, Minor 3, May 2, Otanez 1, Pickering 1, Hairston Jr. 1, Garcia 1.
At Boston (2): Belle 2.
At Chicago (AL) (11): Surhoff 3, Baines 2, Belle 2, Ripken Jr. 1, Clark 1, Anderson 1, Bordick 1.
At Cleveland (4): Conine 3, Surhoff 1.
At Detroit (12): Johnson 4, Baines 1, Surhoff 1, Anderson 1, Belle 1, DeShields 1, Bordick 1, May 1, Conine 1.
At Florida (3): Surhoff 2, Conine 1.
At Kansas City (4): Anderson 2, Belle 1, Figga 1.
At Minnesota (6): Anderson 3, Surhoff 1, Belle 1, Hairston Jr. 1.
At New York (AL) (9): Belle 3, Baines 2, Surhoff 2, Ripken Jr. 1, Clark 1.
At Oakland (8): Baines 2, Surhoff 2, Bordick 2, Anderson 1, Belle 1.
At Philadelphia (2): Clark 1, Hairston Jr. 1.
At Seattle (0):
At Tampa Bay (5): Surhoff 2, Baines 1, Belle 1, Otanez 1.
At Texas (13): Belle 4, Johnson 3, Anderson 2, Baines 1, Ripken Jr. 1, DeShields 1, Garcia 1.
At Toronto (9): Surhoff 3, Baines 1, Anderson 1, Belle 1, Bordick 1, Conine 1, Hairston Jr. 1.

LOW-HIT GAMES

No-hitters: None.
One-hitters: None.
Two-hitters: None.

10-STRIKEOUT GAMES

Mike Mussina 4, **Total:** 4.

FOUR OR MORE HITS IN ONE GAME

Albert Belle 4, B.J. Surhoff 3(including one five-hit game), Mike Bordick 3, Jeff Conine 3, Jerry Hairston Jr. 3, Cal Ripken Jr. 2(including one six-hit game), Charles Johnson 2, Harold Baines 1, Will Clark 1, **Total: 22.**

MULTI-HOMER GAMES

Albert Belle 4, Brady Anderson 3, Cal Ripken Jr. 2, Charles Johnson 2, Harold Baines 1, B.J. Surhoff 1, Jeff Conine 1, **Total: 14.**

GRAND SLAMS

5-4: Harold Baines (off Chicago's David Lundquist).
5-27: Brady Anderson (off Anaheim's Mike Magnante).
7-4: B.J. Surhoff (off New York's Ramiro Mendoza).

PINCH HITTERS

(Minimum 5 at-bats)

Name	AB	Avg.	HR	RBI
Conine, Jeff	25	.360	2	8
Amaral, Rich	21	.286	0	1
May, Derrick	13	.308	1	5
Baines, Harold	12	.250	0	6
Clark, Will	11	.455	0	0
Pickering, Calvin	9	.111	0	0
DeShields, Delino	7	.143	0	2
Anderson, Brady	6	.167	0	1

DEBUTS

4-5: Jesse Garcia, 2B.
5-1: Gabe Molina, P.
5-14: Tommy Davis, C.
9-9: Matt Riley, P.
10-1: Brian Falkenborg, P.

GAMES BY POSITION

Catcher: Charles Johnson 135, Mike Figga 41, Lenny Webster 12, Tommy Davis 4.
First base: Jeff Conine 99, Will Clark 63, Calvin Pickering 8, Willis Otanez 5, Rich Amaral 2, Ryan Minor 1, Tommy Davis 1.
Second base: Delino DeShields 93, Jerry Hairston Jr. 50, Jeff Reboulet 36, Jesse Garcia 6, Rich Amaral 2.
Third base: Cal Ripken Jr. 85, Jeff Reboulet 56, Ryan Minor 45, Willis Otanez 22, Jeff Conine 4, B.J. Surhoff 2, Jesse Garcia 2, Rich Amaral 1.
Shortstop: Mike Bordick 159, Jeff Reboulet 10, Jesse Garcia 7.
Outfield: Albert Belle 154, B.J. Surhoff 148, Brady Anderson 136, Rich Amaral 50, Gene Kingsale 24, Jeff Conine 13, Derrick May 5.
Designated hitter: Harold Baines 96, Jeff Conine 19, Rich Amaral 18, B.J. Surhoff 13, Brady Anderson 10, Derrick May 9, Albert Belle 7, Calvin Pickering 7, Will Clark 3, Willis Otanez 3, Lenny Webster 2, Gene Kingsale 2, Jesse Garcia 1.

STREAKS

Wins: 13 (September 5-22).
Losses: 10 (June 23-July 3).
Consecutive games with at least one hit: 21, B.J. Surhoff (May 29-June 20).
Wins by pitcher: 5, Scott Erickson (September 2-22).

ATTENDANCE

Home: 3,344,707.
Road: 2,212,672.
Highest (home): 48,544 (July 24 vs. Anaheim).
Highest (road): 47,923 (June 12 vs. Atlanta).
Lowest (home): 34,347 (April 29 vs. Kansas City).
Lowest (road): 7,443 (May 28 vs. Oakland).

BOSTON RED SOX

DAY BY DAY

Date	Opp.	Res.	Score	(inn.*)	Hits	Opp. hits	Winning pitcher	Losing pitcher	Save	Record	Pos.	GB
4-5	At K.C.	W	5-3		13	6	Martinez	Appier	Gordon	1-0	T1st	...
4-7	At K.C.	W	6-0		13	4	Saberhagen	Rosado		2-0	1st	+0.5
4-8	At K.C.	W	4-1		10	4	Wakefield	Suppan	Gordon	3-0	1st	+1.0
4-9	At T.B.	W	4-1		11	4	Portugal	Arrojo		4-0	1st	+1.0
4-10	At T.B.	W	5-3		6	7	Martinez	Santana	Gordon	5-0	1st	+1.0
4-11	At T.B.	L	4-5		8	7	Aldred	Lowe	Hernandez	5-1	T1st	...
4-13	Chi.	W	6-0		7	7	Saberhagen	Parque		6-1	1st	...
4-15	Chi.	L	0-4		6	8	Snyder	Martinez		6-2	2nd	0.5
4-16	T.B.	L	2-6		7	13	Rekar	Wakefield		6-3	2nd	0.5
4-17	T.B.	W	8-5		11	9	Portugal	Saunders		7-3	1st	...
4-18	T.B.	L	1-5		5	7	Witt	Rapp		7-4	2nd	1.0
4-19	T.B.	L	1-4		6	9	Arrojo	Saberhagen	Hernandez	7-5	T2nd	1.5
4-20	At Det.	W	1-0		3	3	Martinez	Weaver	Lowe	8-5	T2nd	1.5
4-21	At Det.	L	2-9		8	15	Moehler	Wakefield		8-6	3rd	2.5
4-22	At Det.	L	0-1		2	3	Thompson	Portugal	Jones	8-7	4th	3.5
4-23	Cle.	L	6-7		7	9	Karsay	Corsi	Jackson	8-8	4th	3.5
4-24	Cle.	W	9-4		13	12	Harikkala	DeLucia		9-8	4th	2.5
4-25	Cle.	W	3-2		12	7	Martinez	Shuey		10-8	3rd	2.5
4-26	At Min.	L	2-6		10	9	Radke	Wakefield	Trombley	10-9	4th	3.0
4-27	At Min.	L	5-6		11	9	Guardado	Corsi	Aguilera	10-10	4th	4.0
4-28	At Min.	W	9-4		11	13	Rapp	Lincoln		11-10	3rd	3.0
4-30	At Oak.	L	9-13		12	10	Mathews	Lowe		11-11	T3rd	3.5
5-1	At Oak.	W	7-2		15	6	Martinez	Heredia		12-11	3rd	3.5
5-2	At Oak.	L	5-7		12	9	Jones	Harikkala	Taylor	12-12	T3rd	4.5
5-3	At Oak.	L	11-12	(10)	13	11	Mathews	Gross		12-13	4th	4.5
5-5	Tex.	L	3-8		8	12	Helling	Rapp		12-14	4th	5.0
5-6	Tex.	W	3-2		10	10	Cormier	Sele	Wakefield	13-14	4th	5.0
5-7	Ana.	W	6-0		10	6	Martinez	Olivares		14-14	4th	5.0
5-8	Ana.	W	6-1		12	4	Pena	Belcher	Lowe	15-14	3rd	4.0
5-9	Ana.	W	4-2		10	10	Portugal	Hill	Wakefield	16-14	2nd	4.0
5-10	Sea.	W	12-4		10	9	Wasdin	Hinchliffe		17-14	2nd	3.5
5-11	Sea.	L	5-8		10	14	Moyer	Wakefield		17-15	2nd	3.5
5-12	Sea.	W	9-2		11	6	Martinez	Suzuki		18-15	2nd	2.5
5-14	At Tor.	W	5-0		11	6	Pena	Wells		19-15	2nd	1.0
5-15	At Tor.	W	6-5		14	10	Wasdin	Plesac	Gordon	20-15	T1st	...
5-16	At Tor.	L	6-9		12	11	Lloyd	Gross		20-16	2nd	1.0
5-17	At Tor.	W	8-7		13	13	Wasdin	Lloyd		21-16	2nd	0.5
5-18	N.Y.	W	6-3		10	13	Martinez	Cone	Gordon	22-16	1st	+0.5
5-19	N.Y.	W	6-0		15	8	Rose	Irabu		23-16	1st	+1.5
5-20	N.Y.	L	1-3		3	5	Hernandez	Portugal	Rivera	23-17	1st	+0.5
5-21	Tor.	W	5-2		5	4	Rapp	Escobar		24-17	1st	+1.0
5-22	Tor.	W	6-4		14	6	Wakefield	Carpenter	Gordon	25-17	1st	+1.5
5-23	Tor.	W	10-8		13	15	Martinez	Hentgen	Gordon	26-17	1st	+1.5
5-25	At N.Y.	W	5-2		10	6	Rose	Irabu	Gordon	27-17	1st	+2.5
5-26	At N.Y.	L	3-8		8	11	Hernandez	Portugal	Rivera	27-18	1st	+1.5
5-27	At N.Y.	L	1-4		2	9	Clemens	Rapp	Rivera	27-19	1st	+0.5
5-28	At Cle.	W	12-5		18	9	Wakefield	Wright	Lowe	28-19	1st	+0.5
5-29	At Cle.	W	4-2		8	5	Martinez	Colon	Gordon	29-19	1st	+0.5
5-30	At Cle.	W	4-2		9	3	Rose	Gooden	Gordon	30-19	1st	+0.5
5-31	Det.	W	8-7		12	12	Wasdin	Anderson	Gordon	31-19	1st	+1.5
6-1	Det.	W	5-4		9	12	Wasdin	Brocail	Lowe	32-19	1st	+1.5
6-2	Det.	L	2-4		6	7	Thompson	Wakefield	Jones	32-20	1st	+1.5
6-4	Atl.	W	5-1		9	3	Martinez	Glavine		33-20	1st	+1.5
6-5	Atl.	L	5-6		11	9	Maddux	Gordon	Rocker	33-21	1st	+0.5
6-6	Atl.	L	2-3	(10)	3	6	Seanez	Portugal	Rocker	33-22	1st	+0.5
6-7	At Mon.	L	2-8		6	13	Pavano	Saberhagen		33-23	1st	+0.5
6-8	At Mon.	L	1-5		4	9	Smith	Wakefield		33-24	1st	+0.5
6-9	At Mon.	L	1-13		5	14	Thurman	Martinez		33-25	2nd	0.5
6-11	At N.Y. (NL)	W	3-2	(12)	11	8	Corsi	Franco	Wasdin	34-25	2nd	0.5
6-12	At N.Y. (NL)	L	2-4		7	8	Leiter	Rapp	Franco	34-26	2nd	1.5
6-13	At N.Y. (NL)	L	4-5		8	11	Hershiser	Portugal	Wendell	34-27	2nd	1.5
6-14	Min.	W	4-3		11	7	Wasdin	Trombley		35-27	2nd	1.5
6-15	Min.	W	4-2		12	6	Martinez	Milton	Wakefield	36-27	2nd	1.5
6-16	Min.	W	5-1		7	8	Rose	Perkins	Guthrie	37-27	2nd	0.5
6-17	Min.	L	7-8		12	11	Hawkins	Rapp	Trombley	37-28	2nd	1.5
6-18	Tex.	L	1-4		3	8	Morgan	Portugal	Zimmerman	37-29	2nd	1.5
6-19	Tex.	W	7-4		15	6	Cho	Clark	Wakefield	38-29	2nd	1.5
6-20	Tex.	W	5-2		12	8	Martinez	Glynn	Wakefield	39-29	2nd	0.5
6-21	Tex.	W	5-4		10	9	Wasdin	Helling	Wakefield	40-29	2nd	...
6-22	At Bal.	L	3-5		9	7	Rhodes	Guthrie	Timlin	40-30	2nd	1.0
6-23	At Bal.	W	5-0		9	8	Saberhagen	Guzman		41-30	2nd	1.0
6-24	At Bal.	W	2-1		7	7	Portugal	Mussina	Wakefield	42-30	2nd	1.0
6-25	Chi.	W	6-1		13	7	Cho	Snyder	Guthrie	43-30	2nd	1.0
6-26	Chi.	W	17-1		14	3	Martinez	Baldwin	Wasdin	44-30	2nd	1.0
6-27	Chi.	L	6-7		9	8	Simas	Wakefield	Howry	44-31	2nd	2.0
6-28	Chi.	W	14-1		21	8	Saberhagen	Sirotka		45-31	2nd	1.5
6-30	T.B.	L	10-11	(10)	12	14	Hernandez	Wasdin		45-32	2nd	2.0

HIGHLIGHTS

High point: With Pedro Martinez pitching six hitless innings, the Red Sox completed a Division Series comeback with a 12-8 victory over the Indians in Game 5. After losing the first two games, the Red Sox showed their resiliency and season-long ability to overachieve by winning three in a row (one game by a 23-7 score).

Low point: Boston went quickly in the ALCS, winning only one game against the Yankees (hammering Roger Clemens and getting great pitching from Martinez).

Turning point: The Red Sox were in a tight wild-card race when they began a 12-game, two-week, four-city trip in early September. They went 9-3 against the Mariners, A's, Yankees and Indians, sealing a postseason spot.

Most valuable player: Nomar Garciaparra, who won the A.L. batting title with a .357 average. The shortstop had 42 doubles, 27 homers, 104 RBIs and 14 SBs.

Most valuable pitcher: Martinez, who posted one of the most dominant seasons in decades. He went 23-4 with a 2.07 ERA and had 313 strikeouts and only 37 walks in 213.1 innings. Martinez pitched a 17-strikeout, one-hit game against the Yankees and had a 16-strikeout, three-hit performance against the Braves.

Most improved player: Jason Varitek established himself as one of the game's top young catchers, a take-charge player who hit .269 with 20 homers and 76 RBIs. His most eye-popping number: 39 doubles.

Most pleasant surprise: Rookie Brian Daubach. He wasn't expected to make the team after signing a minor-league contract, and even after earning a roster spot in spring training, he was demoted in April. But he returned to fill a void in the middle of the lineup, finishing with a .294 average, 21 homers and 73 RBIs in 381 at-bats.

Key injuries: Closer Tom Gordon, who had 46 saves in 1998, missed a large portion of the season because of an elbow injury. Bret Saberhagen was limited to 22 starts because of three stints on the D.L. Third baseman John Valentin was beaned in June and went on the D.L., and he missed three weeks in September with tendinitis in his left knee. Catcher Scott Hatteberg was out three months with an elbow injury, and second baseman Jeff Frye was sidelined 2.5 months with a knee strain. The team also lost rookie pitcher Juan Pena, who missed the final four months with tendinitis in his right shoulder after going 2-0 with a 0.69 ERA in two May starts.

Notable: The Red Sox made back-to-back postseason appearances for the first time since 1915-1916. ... Pedro Martinez became the second pitcher in major league history (Randy Johnson is the other) to record 300 or more strikeouts in each league.

—PAUL DOYLE

MISCELLANEOUS

RECORDS

1999 regular-season record: 94-68 (2nd in A.L. East); 49-32 at home; 45-36 on road; 28-21 vs. A.L. East; 36-20 vs. A.L. Central; 24-15 vs. A.L. West; 6-12 vs. N.L. East; 18-17 vs. lefthanded starters; 76-51 vs. righthanded starters; 83-57 on grass; 11-11 on turf; 38-22 in daytime; 56-46 at night; 21-20 in one-run games; 4-4 in extra-inning games; 0-0-1 in double-headers.

Team record past five years: 435-357 (.549, ranks 3rd in league in that span).

TEAM LEADERS

Batting average: Nomar Garciaparra (.357).
At-bats: Troy O'Leary (596).
Runs: Jose Offerman (107).
Hits: Nomar Garciaparra (190).
Total Bases: Nomar Garciaparra (321).
Doubles: Nomar Garciaparra (42).
Triples: Jose Offerman (11).
Home runs: Troy O'Leary (28).
Runs batted in: Nomar Garciaparra (104).
Stolen bases: Jose Offerman (18).
Slugging percentage: Nomar Garciaparra (.603).
On-base percentage: Nomar Garciaparra (.418).
Wins: Pedro Martinez (23).
Earned-run average: Pedro Martinez (2.07).
Complete games: Pedro Martinez (5).
Shutouts: Pedro Martinez (1).
Saves: Derek Lowe, Tim Wakefield (15).
Innings pitched: Pedro Martinez (213.1).
Strikeouts: Pedro Martinez (313).

Date	Opp.	Res.	Score	(inn.*)	Hits	Opp. hits	Winning pitcher	Losing pitcher	Save	Record	Pos.	GB
7-1	T.B.	L	3-12		7	16	Alvarez	Cho		45-33	2nd	3.0
7-2	At Chi.	W	6-1		10	7	Martinez	Parque		46-33	2nd	3.0
7-3	At Chi.	L	2-11		9	16	Sirotka	Rose		46-34	2nd	4.0
7-4	At Chi.	W	5-2		10	6	Saberhagen	Navarro	Wakefield	47-34	2nd	3.0
7-5	At T.B.	W	4-2		9	9	Portugal	Rekar	Wakefield	48-34	2nd	2.0
7-6	At T.B.	L	4-6		9	7	Lopez	Wasdin	Hernandez	48-35	2nd	3.0
7-7	At T.B.	L	2-3		7	7	Eiland	Martinez	Hernandez	48-36	2nd	3.0
7-8	At T.B.	L	2-3		9	8	Witt	Rose	Hernandez	48-37	2nd	4.0
7-9	At Atl.	W	5-4		5	8	Saberhagen	Chen	Wakefield	49-37	2nd	3.0
7-10	At Atl.	L	1-2	(11)	6	10	Seanez	Wasdin		49-38	2nd	3.0
7-11	At Atl.	L	1-8		6	8	Maddux	Cho		49-39	2nd	4.0
7-15	Phi.	W	6-4		12	9	Rose	Byrd	Wakefield	50-39	2nd	3.0
7-16	Phi.	L	4-5		8	10	Person	Saberhagen	Gomes	50-40	2nd	3.0
7-17	Phi.	L	3-11		7	18	Wolf	Portugal		50-41	2nd	4.0
7-18	Fla.	W	11-9		12	14	Lowe	Nunez	Wakefield	51-41	2nd	4.0
7-19	Fla.	L	7-10		15	16	Meadows	Ohka	Alfonseca	51-42	2nd	4.0
7-20	Fla.	W	7-1		12	5	Rose	Hernandez		52-42	2nd	4.0
7-21	Bal.	L	1-6		6	11	Mussina	Saberhagen		52-43	2nd	5.0
7-22	Bal.	L	2-5		8	12	Erickson	Cho	Timlin	52-44	T2nd	6.0
7-23	At Det.	L	5-14		8	15	Moehler	Ohka		52-45	3rd	7.0
7-24	At Det.	W	11-4		13	10	Portugal	Weaver	Lowe	53-45	2nd	7.0
7-25	At Det.	L	1-9		6	10	Mlicki	Rose		53-46	3rd	8.0
7-27	At Tor.	W	11-9		18	14	Guthrie	Halladay	Wakefield	54-46	3rd	8.0
7-28	At Tor.	W	8-0		11	2	Rapp	Hamilton		55-46	2nd	7.0
7-30	N.Y.	L	3-13		7	16	Irabu	Portugal		55-47	3rd	7.5
7-31	N.Y.	W	6-5		12	15	Lowe	Mendoza		56-47	3rd	6.5
8-1	N.Y.	W	5-4		9	9	Saberhagen	Hernandez	Wakefield	57-47	3rd	5.5
8-2	Cle.	L	5-7		10	8	Karsay	Garces	Jackson	57-48	3rd	6.5
8-3	Cle.	L	4-5		7	6	Shuey	Wakefield	Jackson	57-49	3rd	6.5
8-4	Cle.	W	7-2		10	10	Portugal	Colon		58-49	3rd	6.5
8-5	At Ana.	L	0-8		4	14	Finley	Rose		58-50	3rd	7.5
8-6	At Ana.	W	5-1		10	8	Saberhagen	Sparks		59-50	3rd	7.5
8-7	At Ana.	W	14-3		19	8	Rapp	Belcher		60-50	2nd	7.5
8-8	At Ana.	W	9-3		13	6	Martinez	McDowell		61-50	2nd	7.5
8-9	At K.C.	L	2-5		4	9	Suppan	Portugal		61-51	3rd	8.5
8-10	At K.C.	W	9-6	(10)	16	13	Wakefield	Whisenant	Garces	62-51	3rd	7.5
8-11	At K.C.	W	9-3		12	5	Saberhagen	Rosado		63-51	3rd	7.5
8-13	Sea.	W	11-6		10	8	Lowe	Fassero		64-51	2nd	7.5
8-14	Sea.	W	13-2		19	8	Martinez	Halama		65-51	2nd	6.5
8-15	Sea.	L	3-4		6	8	Meche	Portugal	Mesa	65-52	2nd	6.5
8-16	Oak.	W	6-5		11	7	Lowe	Jones		66-52	2nd	6.5
8-17	Oak.	L	1-12		10	17	Heredia	Saberhagen		66-53	2nd	7.5
8-18	Oak.	W	7-4		13	3	Garces	Appier	Lowe	67-53	2nd	6.5
8-19	Oak.	L	2-6		4	12	Hudson	Martinez	Mathews	67-54	2nd	6.5
8-20	At Tex.	L	3-4		6	10	Loaiza	Portugal	Wetteland	67-55	2nd	7.5
8-21	At Tex.	L	2-9		9	12	Helling	Rose		67-56	2nd	7.5
8-22	At Tex.	L	0-6		8	10	Sele	Wakefield		67-57	2nd	8.5
8-23	At Min.	W	4-1		10	10	Rapp	Hawkins	Lowe	68-57	2nd	8.5
8-24	At Min.	W	7-1		11	5	Martinez	Ryan		69-57	2nd	8.5
8-25	At Min.	L	3-6		5	8	Radke	Portugal		69-58	2nd	8.5
8-27	Ana.	W	4-3		5	6	Garces	Percival	Lowe	70-58	2nd	8.5
8-28	Ana.	W	7-6		8	10	Lowe	Pote		71-58	2nd	8.5
8-29	Ana.	W	7-4		10	11	Rapp	Belcher	Lowe	72-58	2nd	8.5
8-30	K.C.	W	9-1		14	5	Martinez	Suppan		73-58	2nd	8.5
8-31	K.C.	W	6-3		11	4	Garces	Witasick	Lowe	74-58	2nd	7.5
9-1	K.C.	W	4-3		6	3	Mercker	Rosado	Beck	75-58	2nd	6.5
9-2	K.C.	L	2-4		7	9	Suzuki	Martinez	Fussell	75-59	2nd	7.5
9-3	At Sea.	L	1-2		3	9	Moyer	Lowe		75-60	2nd	7.5
9-4	At Sea.	W	4-0		6	3	Martinez	Abbott		76-60	2nd	7.5
9-5	At Sea.	W	9-7		13	12	Garces	Paniagua	Lowe	77-60	2nd	7.5
9-6	At Sea.	W	3-2		10	5	Florie	Halama	Lowe	78-60	2nd	6.5
9-7	At Oak.	W	5-3		10	6	Wakefield	Heredia	Lowe	79-60	2nd	5.5
9-8	At Oak.	L	2-6		5	8	Appier	Rapp		79-61	2nd	6.5
9-10	At N.Y.	W	3-1		12	1	Martinez	Pettitte		80-61	2nd	5.5
9-11	At N.Y.	W	11-10		10	12	Garces	Irabu	Beck	81-61	2nd	4.5
9-12	At N.Y.	W	4-1		7	5	Cormier	Clemens	Beck	82-61	2nd	3.5
9-13	At Cle.	L	7-11		10	12	Nagy	Wakefield	Shuey	82-62	2nd	3.5
9-14	At Cle.	W	12-3		16	4	Lowe	Gooden		83-62	2nd	3.5
9-15	At Cle.	W	6-4	(13)	10	12	Wasdin	Brower		84-62	2nd	3.5
9-17	Det.	W	14-3		16	8	Florie	Blair		85-62	2nd	4.0
9-18	Det.	W	9-1		13	7	Saberhagen	Weaver		86-62	2nd	3.0
9-19	Det.	W	7-3		11	5	Wakefield	Mlicki	Lowe	87-62	2nd	3.0
9-21	Tor.	W	3-0		11	3	Martinez	Hentgen		88-62	2nd	3.0
9-22	Tor.	L	9-14		10	22	Escobar	Rapp		88-63	2nd	4.0
9-23	Tor.	L	5-7		12	11	Wells	Beck	Koch	88-64	2nd	5.0
9-24	Bal.	L	0-1		6	8	Mussina	Saberhagen	Timlin	88-65	2nd	6.0
9-25	Bal.	W	4-1		6	4	Martinez	Linton	Garces	89-65	2nd	5.0
9-26	Bal.	L	5-8		8	5	Johnson	Wakefield	Orosco	89-66	2nd	5.0
9-27	Bal.	W	5-3		8	8	Martinez	Erickson	Lowe	90-66	2nd	4.0
9-29†	At Chi.	W	6-2		10	10	Mercker	Parque		91-66		
9-29‡	At Chi.	L	2-4		7	6	Foulke	Gordon	Howry	91-67	2nd	4.5
9-30	At Chi.	L	2-5		8	9	Lowe	Rose	Howry	91-68	2nd	5.0
10-1	At Bal.	W	6-2		12	8	Ohka	Linton		92-68	2nd	5.0
10-2	At Bal.	W	8-0		12	3	Martinez	Johns		93-68	2nd	5.0
10-3	At Bal.	W	1-0	(10)	5	6	Rose	Timlin	Wakefield	94-68	2nd	4.0

Monthly records: April (11-11), May (20-8), June (14-13), July (11-15), August (18-11), September (17-10), October (3-0).
*Innings, if other than nine. † First game of a doubleheader. ‡ Second game of a doubleheader.

MEMORABLE GAMES

August 16 at Boston

In a season marked by comeback victories, this was the best and most important. The 6-5 victory over the Athletics ended with a bases-loaded, three-run double by rookie Brian Daubach, who hit a 3-and-2 changeup off Tim Worrell. Trailing 5-2, the Red Sox scored one run in the seventh and entered the ninth trailing by two runs. But with two out, Daubach's drive cleared the bases for the victory.

Oakland	AB	R	H	RBI	Boston	AB	R	H	RBI
Christenson, cf	4	2	1	0	Offerman, 2b	5	1	3	1
Velarde, 2b	4	0	2	1	Joh.Valntn, 3b	5	0	1	1
Ja.Giambi, 1b	3	0	0	0	Daubach, 1b	4	1	1	3
Saenz, 1b	1	0	0	0	Garcipprra, ss	3	0	0	0
Jaha, dh	4	0	1	1	O'Leary, lf	4	0	0	0
Stairs, rf	4	0	0	0	Jefferson, dh	3	0	2	1
Grieve, lf	4	0	1	0	Stanley, ph-dh	1	0	0	0
J.McDnld, pr-lf	0	0	0	0	Varitek, c	4	0	1	0
Tejada, ss	2	1	0	0	D.Lewis, pr	0	1	0	0
Chavez, 3b	4	1	1	0	Sadler, cf	3	1	1	0
Hinch, c	4	1	1	3	Huskey, ph	1	0	1	0
					T.Nixon, rf	4	1	1	0
Totals	**34**	**5**	**7**	**5**	**Totals**	**37**	**6**	**11**	**6**

Oakland .... 0 0 4   0 0 0 1 0 0— 5
Boston .... 0 0 0   1 1 0 1 0 3— 6

E—Chavez (9), Sadler (5). DP—Oakland 1. LOB—Oakland 5, Boston 7. 2B—Daubach (29). HR—Hinch (6). SB—Christenson (6), Hinch (6).

Oakland	IP	H	R	ER	BB	SO
Olivares	6.1	7	3	2	1	1
McMichael (H, 2)	1	0	0	0	0	1
Groom (H, 22)	0.1	0	0	0	0	0
D.Jones (L, 3-5)	1	3	3	3	0	1
Worrell (BS 4)	0	1	0	0	0	0

Boston	IP	H	R	ER	BB	SO
Rose	2.1	4	4	4	2	2
Guthrie	3.1	0	0	0	1	4
Garces	2.1	3	1	1	0	3
D.Lowe (W, 4-2)	1	0	0	0	0	2

HBP—Garciaparra by Olivares. PB—Hinch. U—HP, Evans. 1B, DiMuro. 2B, Miller. 3B, Meriwether. T—3:13. A—30,957.

September 10 at New York

Pedro Martinez had one of the great pitching performances of his generation, striking out 17 while allowing one hit in a 3-1 victory over the eventual-champion Yankees at Yankee Stadium. Martinez allowed a homer to Chili Davis in the second before pitching seven perfect innings. His 120-pitch outing ended with five consecutive strikeouts and eight of the last nine Yankee hitters went down on strikeouts. The 17 strikeouts were the most ever against the Yankees.

Boston	AB	R	H	RBI	NY Yankees	AB	R	H	RBI
Offerman, 2b	4	0	2	1	Knoblauch, 2b	3	0	0	0
D.Lewis, rf	4	0	0	0	Jeter, ss	3	0	0	0
Garciaparra, ss	3	1	0	0	O'Neill, rf	3	0	0	0
Stanley, 1b	5	1	4	2	B.Williams, cf	3	0	0	0
Huskey, dh	5	0	0	0	T.Martinez, 1b	3	0	0	0
O'Leary, lf	4	0	3	0	C.Davis, dh	3	1	1	1
Buford, cf	4	0	0	0	Ledee, lf	3	0	0	0
Varitek, c	4	0	1	0	Brosius, 3b	3	0	0	0
W.Veras, 3b	4	1	2	0	Girardi, c	3	0	0	0
					Strawbrry, ph	1	0	0	0
Totals	**37**	**3**	**12**	**3**	**Totals**	**27**	**1**	**1**	**1**

Boston .... 0 0 0   0 0 2 0 0 1— 3
NY Yankees .... 0 1 0   0 0 0 0 0 0— 1

DP—Boston 0, NY Yankees 2. LOB—Boston 12, NY Yankees 0. 2B—Stanley (21), O'Leary (32), W.Veras (2). 3B—W.Veras (1). HR—Stanley (17), C.Davis (18). CS—Knoblauch (8). S—D.Lewis.

Boston	IP	H	R	ER	BB	SO
P.Martinez (W, 21-4)	9	1	1	1	0	17

NY Yankees	IP	H	R	ER	BB	SO
Pettitte (L, 12-11)	6	8	2	2	3	2
Nelson	1.1	0	0	0	0	0
Stanton	0.2	3	1	1	0	1
Grimsley	1	1	0	0	1	1

HBP—Knoblauch by P.Martinez. U—HP, Reynolds. 1B, Roe. 2B, J.Hirschbeck. 3B, Merrill. T—2:53. A—55,239.

1999 REVIEW

INDIVIDUAL STATISTICS

BATTING

Name	G	TPA	AB	R	H	TB	2B	3B	HR	RBI	Avg.	Obp.	Slg.	SH	SF	HP	BB	IBB	SO	SB	CS	GDP	vs RHP AB	vs RHP Avg.	vs RHP HR	vs RHP RBI	vs LHP AB	vs LHP Avg.	vs LHP HR	vs LHP RBI
O'Leary, Troy	157	661	596	84	167	295	36	4	28	103	.280	.343	.495	0	5	4	56	5	91	1	2	21	440	.257	24	72	156	.346	4	31
Offerman, Jose	149	693	586	107	172	255	37	11	8	69	.294	.391	.435	2	7	2	96	5	79	18	12	11	448	.301	5	51	138	.268	3	18
Garciaparra, Nomar	135	595	532	103	190	321	42	4	27	104	.357	.418	.603	0	4	8	51	7	39	14	3	11	422	.346	18	72	110	.400	9	32
Varitek, Jason	144	544	483	70	130	233	39	2	20	76	.269	.330	.482	5	8	2	46	2	85	1	2	13	380	.266	17	57	103	.282	3	19
Lewis, Darren	135	538	470	63	113	145	14	6	2	40	.240	.311	.309	14	4	5	45	0	52	16	10	5	330	.245	1	26	140	.229	1	14
Valentin, John	113	503	450	58	114	179	27	1	12	70	.253	.315	.398	1	8	4	40	2	68	0	1	11	356	.247	12	66	94	.277	0	4
Stanley, Mike	136	512	427	59	120	199	22	0	19	72	.281	.393	.466	0	4	11	70	3	94	0	0	8	301	.272	11	50	126	.302	8	22
Daubach, Brian	110	420	381	61	112	214	33	3	21	73	.294	.360	.562	0	0	3	36	0	92	0	1	5	337	.297	20	64	44	.273	1	9
Nixon, Trot	124	447	381	67	103	180	22	5	15	52	.270	.357	.472	2	8	3	53	1	75	3	1	7	338	.290	14	50	43	.116	1	2
Buford, Damon	91	324	297	39	72	109	15	2	6	38	.242	.294	.367	1	3	2	21	0	74	9	2	5	187	.241	5	23	110	.245	1	15
Jefferson, Reggie	83	225	206	21	57	87	13	1	5	17	.277	.338	.422	0	0	2	17	0	54	0	0	9	195	.282	4	16	11	.182	1	1
Merloni, Lou	43	140	126	18	32	42	7	0	1	13	.254	.307	.333	3	1	2	8	0	16	0	0	6	77	.299	0	6	49	.184	1	7
Huskey, Butch	45	131	124	18	33	60	6	0	7	28	.266	.305	.484	0	0	0	7	1	20	0	0	6	74	.270	4	16	50	.260	3	12
Veras, Wilton	36	127	118	14	34	47	5	1	2	13	.288	.323	.398	0	2	2	5	0	14	0	2	5	76	.303	1	10	42	.262	1	3
Frye, Jeff	41	131	114	14	32	38	3	0	1	12	.281	.362	.333	1	1	1	14	1	11	2	2	2	81	.284	1	10	33	.273	0	2
Sadler, Donnie	49	115	107	18	30	37	5	1	0	4	.280	.313	.346	3	0	0	5	0	20	2	1	1	78	.321	0	4	29	.172	0	0
Hatteberg, Scott	30	100	80	12	22	30	5	0	1	11	.275	.410	.375	0	1	1	18	0	14	0	0	2	65	.277	1	9	15	.267	0	2
Gubanich, Creighton	18	52	47	4	13	20	2	1	1	11	.277	.346	.426	0	0	2	3	0	13	0	0	3	23	.261	1	6	24	.292	0	5
Nunnally, Jon	10	14	14	4	4	5	1	0	0	1	.286	.286	.357	0	0	0	0	0	6	0	0	0	14	.286	0	1	0	.000	0	0
Webster, Lenny	6	17	14	0	0	0	0	0	0	1	.000	.176	.000	0	0	1	2	0	2	0	0	0	8	.000	0	0	6	.000	0	1
Coleman, Michael	2	6	5	1	1	1	0	0	0	0	.200	.333	.200	0	0	0	1	0	0	0	0	0	1	.000	0	0	4	.250	0	0
Saberhagen, Bret	22	5	4	0	0	0	0	0	0	0	.000	.200	.000	0	0	0	1	0	2	0	0	0	2	.000	0	0	2	.000	0	0
Portugal, Mark	31	4	3	0	0	0	0	0	0	0	.000	.000	.000	1	0	0	0	0	0	0	0	0	2	.000	0	0	1	.000	0	0
Wakefield, Tim	49	3	3	0	0	0	0	0	0	0	.000	.000	.000	0	0	0	0	0	3	0	0	0	3	.000	0	0	0	.000	0	0
Martinez, Pedro	31	2	2	0	0	0	0	0	0	0	.000	.000	.000	0	0	0	0	0	1	0	0	0	2	.000	0	0	0	.000	0	0
Rapp, Pat	37	2	2	0	0	0	0	0	0	0	.000	.000	.000	0	0	0	0	0	1	0	0	0	0	.000	0	0	2	.000	0	0
Fonville, Chad	3	4	2	1	0	0	0	0	0	0	.000	.500	.000	0	0	0	2	0	0	1	0	0	0	.000	0	0	2	.000	0	0
Rose, Brian	22	3	2	0	0	0	0	0	0	0	.000	.000	.000	1	0	0	0	0	0	0	0	0	2	.000	0	0	0	.000	0	0
Lomasney, Steve	1	2	2	0	0	0	0	0	0	0	.000	.000	.000	0	0	0	0	0	2	0	0	0	1	.000	0	0	1	.000	0	0
Cho, Jin Ho	9	1	1	0	0	0	0	0	0	0	.000	.000	.000	0	0	0	0	0	0	0	0	0	1	.000	0	0	0	.000	0	0
Corsi, Jim	23	0	0	0	0	0	0	0	0	0	.000	.000	.000	0	0	0	0	0	0	0	0	0	0	.000	0	0	0	.000	0	0
Gordon, Tom	21	0	0	0	0	0	0	0	0	0	.000	.000	.000	0	0	0	0	0	0	0	0	0	0	.000	0	0	0	.000	0	0
Guthrie, Mark	46	0	0	0	0	0	0	0	0	0	.000	.000	.000	0	0	0	0	0	0	0	0	0	0	.000	0	0	0	.000	0	0
Garces, Rich	30	0	0	0	0	0	0	0	0	0	.000	.000	.000	0	0	0	0	0	0	0	0	0	0	.000	0	0	0	.000	0	0
Beck, Rod	12	0	0	0	0	0	0	0	0	0	.000	.000	.000	0	0	0	0	0	0	0	0	0	0	.000	0	0	0	.000	0	0
Cormier, Rheal	60	0	0	0	0	0	0	0	0	0	.000	.000	.000	0	0	0	0	0	0	0	0	0	0	.000	0	0	0	.000	0	0
Wasdin, John	45	0	0	0	0	0	0	0	0	0	.000	.000	.000	0	0	0	0	0	0	0	0	0	0	.000	0	0	0	.000	0	0
Lowe, Derek	74	0	0	0	0	0	0	0	0	0	.000	.000	.000	0	0	0	0	0	0	0	0	0	0	.000	0	0	0	.000	0	0
Bullinger, Kirk	4	0	0	0	0	0	0	0	0	0	.000	.000	.000	0	0	0	0	0	0	0	0	0	0	.000	0	0	0	.000	0	0
Ohka, Tomokazu	8	0	0	0	0	0	0	0	0	0	.000	.000	.000	0	0	0	0	0	0	0	0	0	0	.000	0	0	0	.000	0	0
Florie, Bryce	14	0	0	0	0	0	0	0	0	0	.000	.000	.000	0	0	0	0	0	0	0	0	0	0	.000	0	0	0	.000	0	0

Players with more than one A.L. team

Name	G	TPA	AB	R	H	TB	2B	3B	HR	RBI	Avg.	Obp.	Slg.	SH	SF	HP	BB	IBB	SO	SB	CS	GDP	vs RHP AB	vs RHP Avg.	vs RHP HR	vs RHP RBI	vs LHP AB	vs LHP Avg.	vs LHP HR	vs LHP RBI
Florie, Det.	27	1	1	0	0	0	0	0	0	0	.000	.000	.000	0	0	0	0	0	1	0	0	0	0	.000	0	0	0	.000	0	0
Florie, Det.-Bos.	41	1	1	0	0	0	0	0	0	0	.000	.000	.000	0	0	0	0	0	1	0	0	0	1	.000	0	0	0	.000	0	0
Huskey, Sea.	74	292	262	44	76	130	9	0	15	49	.290	.353	.496	0	3	0	27	0	45	3	1	3	74	.270	4	16	50	.260	3	12
Huskey, Sea.-Bos.	119	423	386	62	109	190	15	0	22	77	.282	.338	.492	0	3	0	34	1	65	3	1	9	276	.264	13	48	110	.327	9	29
Webster, Bal.	16	45	36	1	6	7	1	0	0	3	.167	.333	.194	0	0	1	8	0	5	0	0	1	8	.000	0	0	6	.000	0	1
Webster, Bal.-Bos.	22	62	50	1	6	7	1	0	0	4	.120	.290	.140	0	0	2	10	0	7	0	0	1	29	.103	0	1	21	.143	0	3

PITCHING

Name	W	L	Pct.	ERA	IP	H	R	ER	HR	SH	SF	HB	BB	IBB	SO	G	GS	CG	ShO	GF	Sv	vs. RH AB	vs. RH Avg.	vs. RH HR	vs. RH RBI	vs. LH AB	vs. LH Avg.	vs. LH HR	vs. LH RBI
Martinez, Pedro	23	4	.852	2.07	213.1	160	56	49	9	3	6	9	37	1	313	31	29	5	1	1	0	366	.186	5	24	414	.222	4	27
Portugal, Mark	7	12	.368	5.51	150.1	179	100	92	28	3	6	4	41	1	79	31	27	1	0	1	0	320	.303	17	49	293	.280	11	41
Rapp, Pat	6	7	.462	4.12	146.1	147	78	67	13	3	0	7	69	1	90	37	26	0	0	3	0	270	.263	7	29	289	.263	6	33
Wakefield, Tim	6	11	.353	5.08	140.0	146	93	79	19	1	8	5	72	2	104	49	17	0	0	28	15	319	.254	12	46	229	.284	7	33
Saberhagen, Bret	10	6	.625	2.95	119.0	122	43	39	11	4	2	2	11	0	81	22	22	0	0	0	0	251	.255	8	25	210	.276	3	15
Lowe, Derek	6	3	.667	2.63	109.1	84	35	32	7	1	2	4	25	1	80	74	0	0	0	32	15	223	.188	3	21	181	.232	4	22
Rose, Brian	7	6	.538	4.87	98.0	112	59	53	19	2	0	2	29	2	51	22	18	0	0	1	0	209	.335	13	44	191	.220	6	13
Wasdin, John	8	3	.727	4.12	74.1	66	38	34	14	2	2	0	18	0	57	45	0	0	0	17	2	159	.233	9	30	121	.240	5	17
Cormier, Rheal	2	0	1.000	3.69	63.1	61	34	26	4	1	3	5	18	2	39	60	0	0	0	7	0	152	.276	3	13	96	.198	1	18
Guthrie, Mark	1	1	.500	5.83	46.1	50	32	30	9	0	3	2	20	3	36	46	0	0	0	15	2	113	.239	7	25	69	.333	2	13
Garces, Rich	5	1	.833	1.55	40.2	25	9	7	1	0	0	0	18	1	33	30	0	0	0	4	2	80	.150	1	5	66	.197	0	2
Cho, Jin Ho	2	3	.400	5.72	39.1	45	26	25	7	1	3	2	8	0	16	9	7	0	0	1	0	80	.325	6	20	77	.247	1	6
Florie, Bryce	2	0	1.000	4.80	30.0	33	19	16	2	0	1	1	15	3	25	14	2	0	0	4	0	61	.213	0	6	56	.357	2	13
Mercker, Kent	2	0	1.000	3.51	25.2	23	12	10	0	0	1	1	13	0	17	5	5	0	0	0	0	75	.213	0	7	23	.304	0	2
Corsi, Jim	1	2	.333	5.25	24.0	25	15	14	4	3	1	2	19	3	14	23	0	0	0	5	0	56	.250	3	10	32	.344	1	7
Martinez, Ramon	2	1	.667	3.05	20.2	14	8	7	2	0	1	2	8	0	15	4	4	0	0	0	0	40	.200	1	4	33	.182	1	3
Gordon, Tom	0	2	.000	5.60	17.2	17	11	11	2	0	0	1	12	2	24	21	0	0	0	15	11	39	.205	2	6	30	.300	0	6
Beck, Rod	0	1	.000	1.93	14.0	9	3	3	0	0	0	1	5	0	12	12	0	0	0	8	3	23	.261	0	2	26	.115	0	1
Pena, Juan	2	0	1.000	0.69	13.0	9	1	1	0	0	0	0	3	0	15	2	2	0	0	0	0	20	.200	0	0	26	.192	0	1
Harikkala, Tim	1	1	.500	6.23	13.0	15	9	9	0	2	0	1	6	1	7	7	0	0	0	2	0	23	.217	0	6	26	.385	0	4
Ohka, Tomokazu	1	2	.333	6.23	13.0	21	12	9	2	0	1	0	6	0	8	8	2	0	0	3	0	30	.400	0	8	28	.321	1	5
Gross, Kip	0	2	.000	7.82	12.2	15	11	11	3	1	1	3	8	2	9	11	1	0	0	7	0	21	.381	0	1	29	.241	3	10
Wolcott, Bob	0	0	.000	8.10	6.2	8	6	6	1	0	1	1	3	0	2	4	0	0	0	1	0	11	.455	1	4	13	.231	0	2
Santana, Marino	0	0	.000	15.75	4.0	8	7	7	3	0	1	0	3	0	4	3	0	0	0	1	0	10	.400	1	5	8	.500	2	3
Bullinger, Kirk	0	0	.000	4.50	2.0	2	1	1	0	0	0	0	2	0	0	4	0	0	0	0	0	6	.333	0	0	1	.000	0	0

PITCHERS WITH MORE THAN ONE A.L. TEAM

Name	W	L	Pct.	ERA	IP	H	R	ER	HR	SH	SF	HB	BB	IBB	SO	G	GS	CG	ShO	GF	Sv	vs. RH AB	vs. RH Avg.	vs. RH HR	vs. RH RBI	vs. LH AB	vs. LH Avg.	vs. LH HR	vs. LH RBI
Corsi, Bal.	0	1	.000	2.70	13.1	15	4	4	2	1	0	0	1	0	8	13	0	0	0	3	0	56	.250	3	10	32	.344	1	7
Corsi, Bos.-Bal.	1	3	.250	4.34	37.1	40	19	18	6	4	1	2	20	3	22	36	0	0	0	1	0	80	.238	3	10	59	.356	3	11
Florie, Det.	2	1	.667	4.56	51.1	61	31	26	6	3	1	1	20	2	40	27	3	0	0	6	0	61	.213	0	6	56	.357	2	13
Florie, Det.-Bos.	4	1	.800	4.65	81.1	94	50	42	8	3	2	2	35	5	65	41	5	0	0	2	0	175	.223	1	16	151	.364	7	32

DESIGNATED HITTERS

Name	AB	Avg.	HR	RBI
Jefferson, Reggie	184	.272	4	15
Daubach, Brian	149	.329	8	32
Huskey, Butch	103	.233	6	21
Offerman, Jose	69	.246	0	5
Stanley, Mike	52	.288	2	9
Hatteberg, Scott	21	.381	0	3
Gubanich, Creighton	9	.444	0	3
Nunnally, Jon	6	.333	0	0
Valentin, John	5	.200	0	0
Frye, Jeff	5	.000	0	0
Buford, Damon	4	.000	0	0
Varitek, Jason	3	.333	0	0
Merloni, Lou	1	.000	0	1
Sadler, Donnie	0	-	0	0
Lewis, Darren	0	-	0	0

INDIVIDUAL STATISTICS

FIELDING

FIRST BASEMEN

Player	Pct.	G	PO	A	E	TC	DP
Stanley, Mike	.988	111	830	60	11	901	71
Daubach, Brian	.983	61	418	35	8	461	35
Offerman, Jose	1.000	8	48	3	0	51	7
Jefferson, Reggie	1.000	2	8	1	0	9	0
Merloni, Lou	.909	1	9	1	1	11	0

SECOND BASEMEN

Player	Pct.	G	PO	A	E	TC	DP
Offerman, Jose	.975	128	237	318	14	569	70
Frye, Jeff	.980	26	41	56	2	99	9
Sadler, Donnie	.935	10	7	22	2	31	4
Merloni, Lou	.949	8	17	20	2	39	4
Fonville, Chad	.900	2	6	3	1	10	1

THIRD BASEMEN

Player	Pct.	G	PO	A	E	TC	DP
Valentin, John	.954	111	84	208	14	306	16
Veras, Wilton	.929	35	23	56	6	85	7
Merloni, Lou	.885	9	6	17	3	26	1
Sadler, Donnie	.813	9	7	6	3	16	0
Frye, Jeff	.882	7	5	10	2	17	0
Huskey, Butch	1.000	2	1	1	0	2	0
Gubanich, Creighton	1.000	1	1	3	0	4	0
Daubach, Brian	-	1	0	0	0	0	0

SHORTSTOPS

Player	Pct.	G	PO	A	E	TC	DP
Garciaparra, Nomar	.972	134	232	357	17	606	72
Merloni, Lou	.956	24	36	50	4	90	12
Sadler, Donnie	.930	14	18	22	3	43	5
Frye, Jeff	1.000	2	6	5	0	11	1

OUTFIELDERS

Player	Pct.	G	PO	A	E	TC	DP
O'Leary, Troy	.993	157	296	9	2	307	3
Lewis, Darren	.994	130	309	4	2	315	2
Nixon, Trot	.968	121	209	3	7	219	1
Buford, Damon	.985	84	189	6	3	198	2
Sadler, Donnie	.941	8	14	2	1	17	1
Huskey, Butch	1.000	4	4	1	0	5	0
Daubach, Brian	1.000	2	2	0	0	2	0
Coleman, Michael	-	2	0	0	0	0	0
Nunnally, Jon	-	2	0	0	0	0	0
Merloni, Lou	-	1	0	0	0	0	0

CATCHERS

Player	Pct.	G	PO	A	E	TC	DP	PB
Varitek, Jason	.990	140	972	66	11	1049	8	3
Hatteberg, Scott	.993	23	128	14	1	143	1	2
Gubanich, Creighton	.979	14	39	8	1	48	1	3
Webster, Lenny	1.000	6	25	3	0	28	1	1
Steve Lomasney	1.000	1	7	2	0	9	0	0

PITCHERS

Player	Pct.	G	PO	A	E	TC	DP
Lowe, Derek	1.000	74	8	14	0	22	1
Cormier, Rheal	.889	60	1	7	1	9	1
Wakefield, Tim	.950	49	7	12	1	20	1
Guthrie, Mark	1.000	46	1	6	0	7	0
Wasdin, John	.889	45	3	5	1	9	0
Rapp, Pat	1.000	37	7	15	0	22	2
Portugal, Mark	1.000	31	9	22	0	31	1
Martinez, Pedro	.966	31	13	15	1	29	0
Garces, Rich	1.000	30	5	6	0	11	0
Corsi, Jim	1.000	23	2	3	0	5	0
Rose, Brian	.960	22	6	18	1	25	2
Saberhagen, Bret	1.000	22	5	18	0	23	0
Gordon, Tom	1.000	21	0	1	0	1	0
Florie, Bryce	1.000	14	1	7	0	8	1
Beck, Rod	1.000	12	1	2	0	3	0
Gross, Kip	1.000	11	0	1	0	1	0
Cho, Jin Ho	1.000	9	1	5	0	6	1
Ohka, Tomokazu	1.000	8	0	3	0	3	0
Harikkala, Tim	1.000	7	0	2	0	2	0
Mercker, Kent	.900	5	1	8	1	10	0
Bullinger, Kirk	1.000	4	1	2	0	3	1
Martinez, Ramon	1.000	4	1	2	0	3	1
Wolcott, Bob	-	4	0	0	0	0	0
Santana, Marino	1.000	3	0	1	0	1	0
Pena, Juan	1.000	2	3	1	0	4	0

PITCHING AGAINST EACH CLUB

Pitcher	Ana. W-L	Bal. W-L	Chi. W-L	Cle. W-L	Det. W-L	K.C. W-L	Min. W-L	N.Y. W-L	Oak. W-L	Sea. W-L	T.B. W-L	Tex. W-L	Tor. W-L	N.L. W-L	Total W-L
Beck, Rod	0-0	0-0	0-0	0-0	0-0	0-0	0-0	0-0	0-0	0-0	0-0	0-0	0-1	0-0	0-1
Bullinger, Kirk	0-0	0-0	0-0	0-0	0-0	0-0	0-0	0-0	0-0	0-0	0-0	0-0	0-0	0-0	0-0
Cho, Jin Ho	0-0	0-1	1-0	0-0	0-0	0-0	0-0	0-0	0-0	0-1	1-0	0-0	0-0	0-1	2-3
Cormier, Rheal	0-0	0-0	0-0	0-0	0-0	0-0	0-0	1-0	0-0	0-0	0-0	1-0	0-0	0-0	2-0
Corsi, Jim	0-0	0-0	0-0	0-1	0-0	0-0	0-1	0-0	0-0	0-0	0-0	0-0	0-0	1-0	1-2
Florie, Bryce	0-0	0-0	0-0	0-0	1-0	0-0	0-0	0-0	0-0	1-0	0-0	0-0	0-0	0-0	2-0
Garces, Rich	1-0	0-0	0-0	0-1	0-0	1-0	0-0	1-0	0-0	1-0	0-0	1-0	0-0	0-0	5-1
Gordon, Tom	0-0	0-0	0-1	0-0	0-0	0-0	0-0	0-0	0-0	0-0	0-0	0-0	0-0	0-1	0-2
Gross, Kip	0-0	0-1	0-0	0-0	0-0	0-0	0-0	0-0	0-1	0-0	0-0	0-0	0-0	0-0	0-2
Guthrie, Mark	0-0	0-1	0-0	0-0	0-0	0-0	0-0	0-0	0-0	0-0	0-0	0-0	1-0	0-0	1-1
Harikkala, Tim	0-0	0-0	1-0	0-0	0-0	0-0	0-0	0-0	0-0	0-1	0-0	0-0	0-0	0-0	1-1
Lowe, Derek	1-0	0-0	1-0	1-0	0-0	0-1	1-0	0-1	0-0	0-1	1-0	0-0	0-0	1-0	6-3
Martinez, Pedro	2-0	1-0	2-1	2-0	1-0	2-0	2-0	2-0	2-0	3-1	1-1	0-0	2-0	1-1	23-4
Martinez, Ramon	0-0	2-0	0-0	0-0	0-0	0-0	0-0	0-0	0-0	0-0	0-0	0-0	0-1	0-0	2-1
Mercker, Kent	0-0	0-1	1-0	0-0	0-0	0-0	0-1	0-0	0-0	0-0	0-0	0-0	0-0	0-0	1-2
Ohka, Tomokazu	0-0	0-0	0-0	0-0	0-0	0-0	0-0	0-0	0-0	0-0	0-0	0-0	0-0	0-1	0-1
Pena, Juan	1-0	0-0	0-0	0-0	0-0	0-0	0-0	1-0	0-0	0-0	0-0	0-0	0-0	0-0	2-0
Portugal, Mark	1-0	0-0	1-0	1-1	0-1	0-1	0-1	0-3	0-0	3-0	0-2	1-0	0-0	0-3	7-12
Rapp, Pat	2-0	0-0	0-0	0-0	0-0	0-0	2-1	0-1	0-1	0-0	0-1	0-1	2-1	0-1	6-7
Rose, Brian	0-1	1-0	0-2	1-0	0-1	0-0	1-0	2-0	0-0	0-1	0-1	0-0	0-0	2-0	7-6
Saberhagen, Bret	1-0	1-1	3-0	0-1	1-0	2-0	1-0	0-0	0-0	0-0	0-1	0-0	0-1	1-2	10-6
Santana, Marino	0-0	0-0	0-0	0-0	0-0	0-0	0-0	0-0	0-0	0-0	0-0	0-0	0-0	0-0	0-0
Wakefield, Tim	0-0	0-1	0-1	1-2	1-2	2-0	0-1	0-0	0-1	0-1	1-0	0-1	1-0	0-1	6-11
Wasdin, John	0-0	1-0	0-0	0-0	1-0	0-0	0-0	1-0	0-1	1-1	1-0	2-0	1-0	0-1	8-3
Wolcott, Bob	0-0	0-0	0-0	0-0	0-0	0-0	0-0	0-0	0-0	0-0	0-0	0-0	0-0	0-0	0-0
Totals	9-1	7-5	7-5	8-4	7-5	8-2	6-4	8-4	4-6	7-3	4-9	4-5	9-3	6-12	94-68

INTERLEAGUE: Martinez 1-0, Saberhagen 1-0, Gordon 0-1, Portugal 0-1, Wasdin 0-1, Cho 0-1 vs. Braves; Saberhagen 0-1, Wakefield 0-1, Martinez 0-1 vs. Expos; Corsi 1-0, Rapp 0-1, Portugal 0-1 vs. Mets; Rose 1-0, Saberhagen 0-1, Portugal 0-1 vs. Phillies; Lowe 1-0, Rose 1-0, Ohka 0-1 vs. Marlins. Total: 6-12.

HOME RUNS BY PARK

At Anaheim (6): Daubach 3, O'Leary 2, Stanley 1.
At Atlanta (4): Stanley 2, Buford 1, Veras 1.
At Baltimore (10): O'Leary 2, Varitek 2, Stanley 1, Offerman 1, Jefferson 1, Valentin 1, Buford 1, Merloni 1.
At Boston (80): Garciaparra 14, O'Leary 13, Varitek 12, Daubach 11, Stanley 8, Offerman 5, Valentin 5, Buford 3, Nixon 3, Huskey 2, Lewis 2, Jefferson 1, Frye 1, Hatteberg 1.
At Chicago (AL) (2): O'Leary 1, Garciaparra 1.
At Cleveland (13): Garciaparra 4, Nixon 3, Varitek 2, Stanley 1, Offerman 1, O'Leary 1, Daubach 1.
At Detroit (9): Nixon 3, O'Leary 2, Garciaparra 2, Offerman 1, Daubach 1.
At Kansas City (9): Valentin 2, O'Leary 2, Nixon 2, Stanley 1, Huskey 1, Daubach 1.
At Minnesota (8): Nixon 3, Jefferson 2, Lewis 1, Buford 1, O'Leary 1.
At Montreal (1): Daubach 1.
At New York (AL) (9): Garciaparra 3, Stanley 2, O'Leary 1, Huskey 1, Nixon 1, Daubach 1.
At New York (NL) (2): O'Leary 1, Daubach 1.
At Oakland (4): Valentin 2, O'Leary 1, Gubanich 1.
At Seattle (6): Garciaparra 3, Varitek 3.
At Tampa Bay (5): Stanley 2, Valentin 1, O'Leary 1, Veras 1.
At Texas (1): Huskey 1.
At Toronto (7): Huskey 2, Stanley 1, Jefferson 1, Valentin 1, Varitek 1, Daubach 1.

LOW-HIT GAMES

No-hitters: None.
One-hitters: Pedro Martinez, September 10 vs. New York, W 3-1.
Two-hitters: None.

10-STRIKEOUT GAMES

Pedro Martinez 19, **Total:** 19.

FOUR OR MORE HITS IN ONE GAME

Jose Offerman 5, Nomar Garciaparra 5, Mike Stanley 1, Jeff Frye 1, John Valentin 1, Troy O'Leary 1, Trot Nixon 1, Jason Varitek 1, Brian Daubach 1 (including one five-hit game), **Total:** 17.

MULTI-HOMER GAMES

Nomar Garciaparra 5, Jason Varitek 2, Jose Offerman 1, Butch Huskey 1, Trot Nixon 1, **Total:** 10.

GRAND SLAMS

5-3: Creighton Gubanich (off Oakland's Jimmy Haynes).
5-10: Nomar Garciaparra (off Seattle's Brett Hinchliffe).
5-10: Nomar Garciaparra (off Seattle's Eric Weaver).
5-22: John Valentin (off Toronto's Chris Carpenter).
6-28: Jose Offerman (off Chicago's Bryan Ward).
7-28: Butch Huskey (off Toronto's Joey Hamilton).
10-2: Damon Buford (off Baltimore's Gabe Molina).

PINCH HITTERS

(Minimum 5 at-bats)

Name	AB	Avg.	HR	RBI
Jefferson, Reggie	27	.296	1	2
Stanley, Mike	14	.214	1	6
Huskey, Butch	13	.385	1	5
Daubach, Brian	10	.100	0	0
Buford, Damon	8	.500	0	2
Varitek, Jason	8	.375	1	2

DEBUTS

4-16: Creighton Gubanich, C.
5-8: Juan Pena, P.
7-1: Wilton Veras, 3B.
7-19: Tomokazu Ohka, P.
10-3: Steve Lomasney, C.

GAMES BY POSITION

Catcher: Jason Varitek 140, Scott Hatteberg 23, Creighton Gubanich 14, Lenny Webster 6, Steve Lomasney 1.
First base: Mike Stanley 111, Brian Daubach 61, Jose Offerman 8, Reggie Jefferson 2, Lou Merloni 1.
Second base: Jose Offerman 128, Jeff Frye 26, Donnie Sadler 10, Lou Merloni 8, Chad Fonville 2.
Third base: John Valentin 111, Wilton Veras 35, Donnie Sadler 9, Lou Merloni 9, Jeff Frye 7, Butch Huskey 2, Brian Daubach 1, Creighton Gubanich 1.
Shortstop: Nomar Garciaparra 134, Lou Merloni 24, Donnie Sadler 14, Jeff Frye 2.
Outfield: Troy O'Leary 157, Darren Lewis 130, Trot Nixon 121, Damon Buford 84, Donnie Sadler 8, Butch Huskey 4, Jon Nunnally 2, Michael Coleman 2, Brian Daubach 2, Lou Merloni 1.
Designated hitter: Reggie Jefferson 58, Brian Daubach 43, Butch Huskey 37, Mike Stanley 20, Jose Offerman 17, Scott Hatteberg 6, Damon Buford 5, Donnie Sadler 4, Jon Nunnally 3, Lou Merloni 3, Darren Lewis 3, Jeff Frye 2, Jason Varitek 2, Creighton Gubanich 2, John Valentin 1.

STREAKS

Wins: 6 (August 27-September 1, September 13-21).
Losses: 5 (June 5-9).
Consecutive games with at least one hit: 17, Nomar Garciaparra (June 13-July 2).
Wins by pitcher: 9, Pedro Martinez (April 20-June 4).

ATTENDANCE

Home: 2,446,328.
Road: 2,413,271.
Highest (home): 33,777 (July 30 vs. New York).
Highest (road): 56,028 (September 12 vs. New York).
Lowest (home): 18,809 (April 16 vs. Tampa Bay).
Lowest (road): 7,003 (June 7 vs. Montreal).

CHICAGO WHITE SOX

DAY BY DAY

Date	Opp.	Res.	Score	(inn.*)	Hits	Opp. hits	Winning pitcher	Losing pitcher	Save	Record	Pos.	GB
4-5	At Sea.	W	8-2		12	6	Baldwin	Fassero		1-0	T1st	...
4-6	At Sea.	W	11-3		15	6	Parque	Moyer		2-0	T1st	+0.5
4-7	At Sea.	L	3-7		10	10	Garcia	Snyder	Mesa	2-1	1st	+0.5
4-9	K.C.	L	5-10		9	13	Barber	Sirotka		2-2	T2nd	1.0
4-10	K.C.	L	4-9		7	15	Pittsley	Navarro	Service	2-3	T2nd	2.0
4-11	K.C.	L	1-3		5	8	Appier	Baldwin	Montgomery	2-4	T3rd	3.0
4-13	At Bos.	L	0-6		7	7	Saberhagen	Parque		2-5	4th	4.0
4-15	At Bos.	W	4-0		8	6	Snyder	Martinez		3-5	T3rd	4.0
4-16	At K.C.	L	2-7		9	8	Appier	Sirotka		3-6	4th	4.5
4-17	At K.C.	W	6-5		11	7	Lowe	Montgomery	Howry	4-6	T3rd	4.0
4-18	At K.C.	W	7-5		12	11	Baldwin	Barber	Howry	5-6	2nd	4.0
4-20	Sea.	W	3-1		8	5	Parque	Fassero	Howry	6-6	T2nd	4.0
4-21	Sea.	W	2-1		5	6	Snyder	Paniagua	Howry	7-6	2nd	4.0
4-23	Det.	W	5-0		9	5	Sirotka	Blair		8-6	2nd	3.5
4-24	Det.	W	3-1		4	6	Navarro	Mlicki	Howry	9-6	2nd	2.5
4-25	Det.	L	4-9		6	12	Weaver	Baldwin		9-7	2nd	2.5
4-28†	T.B.	W	10-7		14	8	Parque	Rekar	Howry	10-7		
4-28‡	T.B.	W	9-1		10	9	Snyder	Saunders		11-7	2nd	3.0
4-29	T.B.	L	1-4		4	9	Alvarez	Sirotka	Hernandez	11-8	2nd	4.0
4-30	At Ana.	L	1-3		5	5	Petkovsek	Navarro	Percival	11-9	2nd	4.0
5-1	At Ana.	W	8-5		14	13	Lundquist	Percival	Howry	12-9	2nd	4.0
5-2	At Ana.	L	3-6		5	11	Olivares	Parque		12-10	2nd	4.0
5-3	At Ana.	W	8-1		12	4	Snyder	Belcher		13-10	2nd	4.0
5-4	At Bal.	L	5-9	(10)	9	10	Timlin	Lundquist		13-11	2nd	4.5
5-5	At Bal.	L	0-8		6	7	Guzman	Navarro		13-12	2nd	4.5
5-6	At Bal.	L	2-4		8	5	Ponson	Baldwin	Timlin	13-13	2nd	5.5
5-7	Oak.	W	7-1		10	7	Parque	Candiotti		14-13	2nd	5.5
5-8	Oak.	W	5-3		11	8	Snyder	Haynes	Howry	15-13	2nd	4.5
5-9	Oak.	L	0-3		4	8	Oquist	Sirotka	Jones	15-14	2nd	5.5
5-10	Tex.	W	5-2		12	6	Navarro	Helling		16-14	2nd	5.5
5-11	Tex.	L	5-11		12	15	Zimmerman	Howry		16-15	2nd	6.5
5-14	At N.Y.	W	8-2		9	6	Parque	Hernandez	Simas	17-15	2nd	7.0
5-15	At N.Y.	W	12-4		17	13	Snyder	Mendoza		18-15	2nd	7.0
5-16	At N.Y.	L	1-2		8	8	Pettitte	Sirotka	Rivera	18-16	2nd	7.0
5-17	Cle.	L	9-13		12	17	Colon	Navarro		18-17	2nd	8.0
5-18	Cle.	L	0-13		2	13	Gooden	Baldwin		18-18	3rd	9.0
5-19	Cle.	L	7-13		9	18	Nagy	Parque		18-19	3rd	10.0
5-22†	N.Y.	L	2-10		7	13	Clemens	Snyder		18-20		
5-22‡	N.Y.	W	2-1		6	2	Sirotka	Pettitte	Simas	19-20	3rd	9.0
5-23	N.Y.	L	7-8	(10)	12	9	Rivera	Simas		19-21	3rd	10.0
5-24	At Cle.	W	10-3		15	10	Lowe	Gooden		20-21	3rd	9.0
5-25	At Cle.	L	1-3		6	8	Nagy	Parque	Jackson	20-22	3rd	10.0
5-26	At Cle.	L	2-6		8	11	Burba	Sirotka	Shuey	20-23	3rd	11.0
5-27	At Det.	L	5-10		9	14	Weaver	Snyder		20-24	3rd	11.5
5-28	At Det.	W	9-1		15	7	Navarro	Thompson		21-24	3rd	10.5
5-29	At Det.	W	7-1		13	5	Baldwin	Moehler		22-24	3rd	9.5
5-30	At Det.	L	2-3		9	11	Mlicki	Parque	Jones	22-25	3rd	9.5
6-1	At Tor.	W	6-2		13	7	Sirotka	Escobar		23-25	2nd	9.0
6-2	At Tor.	L	7-9		15	15	Carpenter	Snyder	Koch	23-26	2nd	10.0
6-3	At Tor.	W	10-3		16	7	Navarro	Hentgen		24-26	2nd	9.5
6-4	Pit.	L	3-6	(11)	10	9	Wilkins	Simas		24-27	2nd	9.5
6-5	Pit.	W	6-5		15	8	Parque	Benson	Foulke	25-27	2nd	9.5
6-6	Pit.	W	4-3		8	8	Sirotka	Silva	Howry	26-27	2nd	9.5
6-7	Hou.	L	2-8		8	17	Lima	Snyder		26-28	2nd	10.0
6-8	Hou.	W	4-3		7	9	Navarro	Reynolds	Howry	27-28	2nd	9.0
6-9	Hou.	L	4-13		9	17	Hampton	Baldwin		27-29	2nd	10.0
6-11	At Chi. (NL)	W	5-3	(6)	11	5	Parque	Lieber		28-29	3rd	9.5
6-12	At Chi. (NL)	W	8-2		18	8	Sirotka	Trachsel		29-29	2nd	9.5
6-13	At Chi. (NL)	W	6-4		12	7	Simas	Aguilera	Foulke	30-29	2nd	9.5
6-14	T.B.	W	9-7		9	11	Snyder	Alvarez	Howry	31-29	2nd	9.0
6-15	T.B.	L	2-3		12	6	Rupe	Baldwin	Hernandez	31-30	2nd	10.0
6-16	T.B.	W	3-2	(11)	8	8	Lowe	Charlton		32-30	2nd	10.0
6-17	Bal.	W	9-3		11	12	Sirotka	Guzman	Foulke	33-30	2nd	10.0
6-18	Bal.	L	2-3		7	8	Mussina	Navarro		33-31	2nd	10.0
6-19	Bal.	L	9-11	(11)	17	12	Rhodes	Foulke	Kamieniecki	33-32	2nd	11.0
6-20	Bal.	L	4-8		10	12	Johnson	Baldwin	Timlin	33-33	2nd	12.0
6-22	Min.	W	6-1		12	8	Parque	Hawkins		34-33	2nd	11.5
6-23	Min.	L	10-12		16	19	Sampson	Sirotka	Trombley	34-34	2nd	12.5
6-24	Min.	W	5-3		13	14	Navarro	Radke	Howry	35-34	2nd	11.5
6-25	At Bos.	L	1-6		7	13	Cho	Snyder	Guthrie	35-35	2nd	11.5
6-26	At Bos.	L	1-17		3	14	Martinez	Baldwin	Wasdin	35-36	2nd	11.5
6-27	At Bos.	W	7-6		8	9	Simas	Wakefield	Howry	36-36	2nd	11.5
6-28	At Bos.	L	1-14		8	21	Saberhagen	Sirotka		36-37	2nd	12.5
6-29	At K.C.	L	4-7		10	11	Appier	Navarro	Service	36-38	2nd	13.5
6-30	At K.C.	W	10-9	(10)	16	14	Howry	Service		37-38	2nd	12.5

HIGHLIGHTS

High point: On June 13, Mike Caruso hit a rare home run—and it was well-timed. His two-run drive off Rick Aguilera snapped a 4-4 tie in the eighth inning and lifted the White Sox to a three-game sweep of the Cubs at Wrigley Field.

Low point: On August 8, Frank Thomas made a costly error at first base at Oakland and the A's went on to complete a four-game sweep. An angry Thomas said, "I bleeping booted it. That's why I'm a DH. I'm not a first baseman." After showing excellent leadership in the first half of the season, Thomas unraveled after the All-Star break.

Turning point: In their first game of the second half of the season, at St. Louis, the White Sox lost, 3-2, in 13 innings. Ahead 2-1, the Sox thought they were victims of a bad call in the ninth on what appeared to be a game-ending double play. The tying run scored on the play. The defeat set the tone for a 33-43 record after the break for a Sox team that went 42-43 in the first half.

Most valuable player: In just his second full season in the majors, Magglio Ordonez established himself as an elite player. The right fielder batted .301 and led the team in home runs (30) and RBIs (117).

Most valuable pitcher: Keith Foulke had a dominant season, posting a team-low 2.22 ERA and limiting hitters to a .188 average. A setup man who also saw work as a closer, he used a nasty changeup to great effect in striking out 123 batters in 105.1 innings.

Most improved player: Young Paul Konerko was a minor league star but a major league bust until coming to the White Sox. As the 1999 season progressed, the first baseman/DH got into a groove and finished with 24 home runs and 81 RBIs.

Most pleasant surprise: Center fielder Chris Singleton, who was given a shot to start in mid-May. He went on to bat .300, hit 17 homers, drive in 72 runs and play solid defense.

Key injuries: Thomas didn't play after September 6 and underwent surgery to remove a bone spur from his right ankle. John Snyder, who was sensational early in the season (6-1 with a 2.00 ERA), tailed off badly and wound up having elbow surgery in September.

Notable: The White Sox finished second in the A.L. Central for the fourth consecutive year. ... Thomas, limited to a 135-game season, failed to hit 20 homers or drive in 100 runs for the first time in his career. He had 15 homers and 77 RBIs. ... Ray Durham became the first player in Sox history to score 100 runs and steal 30 bases in three consecutive seasons.

—SCOT GREGOR

MISCELLANEOUS

RECORDS

1999 regular-season record: 75-86 (2nd in A.L. Central); 38-42 at home; 37-44 on road; 25-29 vs. A.L. East; 24-23 vs. A.L. Central; 17-25 vs. A.L. West; 9-9 vs. N.L. Central; 16-11 vs. lefthanded starters; 59-75 vs. righthanded starters; 62-80 on grass; 13-6 on turf; 24-29 in daytime; 51-57 at night; 20-19 in one-run games; 6-9 in extra-inning games; 3-2-2 in double-headers.

Team record past five years: 388-402 (.491, ranks 7th in league in that span).

TEAM LEADERS

Batting average: Frank Thomas (.305).
At-bats: Magglio Ordonez (624).
Runs: Ray Durham (109).
Hits: Magglio Ordonez (188).
Total bases: Magglio Ordonez (318).
Doubles: Frank Thomas (36).
Triples: Ray Durham (8).
Home runs: Magglio Ordonez (30).
Runs batted in: Magglio Ordonez (117).
Stolen bases: Ray Durham (34).
Slugging percentage: Paul Konerko (.511).
On-base percentage: Frank Thomas (.414).
Wins: James Baldwin (12).
Earned-run average: Mike Sirotka (4.00).
Complete games: Mike Sirotka (3).
Shutouts: Mike Sirotka (2).
Saves: Bob Howry (28).
Innings pitched: Mike Sirotka (209.0).
Strikeouts: Mike Sirotka (125).

Date	Opp.	Res.	Score	(inn.*)	Hits	Opp. hits	Winning pitcher	Losing pitcher	Save	Record	Pos.	GB
7-1	At K.C.	W	6-2		8	7	Baldwin	Pisciotta		38-38	2nd	12.5
7-2	Bos.	L	1-6		7	10	Martinez	Parque		38-39	2nd	12.5
7-3	Bos.	W	11-2		16	9	Sirotka	Rose		39-39	2nd	13.0
7-4	Bos.	L	2-5		6	10	Saberhagen	Navarro	Wakefield	39-40	2nd	13.0
7-6	K.C.	L	7-8	(10)	16	14	Whisenant	Foulke		39-41	2nd	14.0
7-7	K.C.	W	7-1		10	10	Parque	Suzuki		40-41	2nd	13.0
7-8	K.C.	W	6-5		10	10	Foulke	Byrdak		41-41	2nd	13.0
7-9	Chi. (NL)	W	3-2		9	9	Howry	Adams		42-41	2nd	12.0
7-10	Chi. (NL)	L	2-10		8	12	Lieber	Navarro		42-42	2nd	13.0
7-11	Chi. (NL)	L	3-6		6	7	Trachsel	Baldwin	Adams	42-43	2nd	13.0
7-15	At StL.	L	2-3	(13)	8	10	Croushore	Rizzo		42-44	2nd	14.0
7-16	At StL.	W	9-8		15	11	Navarro	Acevedo	Howry	43-44	2nd	13.0
7-17	At StL.	L	6-8		8	9	Stephenson	Ward	Bottalico	43-45	2nd	13.0
7-18	At Mil.	L	4-5		9	13	Plunk	Rizzo		43-46	2nd	13.0
7-19	At Mil.	W	10-8	(12)	18	11	Simas	Coppinger	Foulke	44-46	2nd	12.0
7-20	At Mil.	L	4-5		9	10	Plunk	Lowe	Wickman	44-47	2nd	13.0
7-21	At Min.	W	6-3	(10)	13	11	Simas	Carrasco	Howry	45-47	2nd	12.0
7-22	At Min.	L	0-3		5	11	Mays	Baldwin	Trombley	45-48	2nd	12.0
7-23	Tor.	L	1-2		7	8	Hamilton	Parque	Koch	45-49	2nd	12.0
7-24	Tor.	W	6-5		6	9	Eyre	Escobar	Howry	46-49	2nd	11.0
7-25	Tor.	L	3-11		5	17	Carpenter	Sirotka		46-50	2nd	11.0
7-26	Tor.	L	3-4	(11)	13	9	Frascatore	Howry	Koch	46-51	2nd	12.0
7-27	N.Y.	L	3-5		10	10	Hernandez	Baldwin	Rivera	46-52	2nd	13.0
7-28	N.Y.	W	11-3		19	11	Castillo	Pettitte		47-52	2nd	13.0
7-29	N.Y.	W	5-1		9	5	Snyder	Cone	Foulke	48-52	2nd	12.5
7-30	At Cle.	L	2-10		6	17	Colon	Sirotka		48-53	2nd	13.5
7-31	At Cle.	L	10-13		18	13	Shuey	Castillo	Jackson	48-54	2nd	14.5
8-1	At Cle.	W	6-3		11	6	Baldwin	Nagy	Howry	49-54	2nd	13.5
8-2	At Det.	W	6-2		11	7	Wells	Moehler		50-54	2nd	13.5
8-3	At Det.	W	9-6		15	9	Snyder	Thompson	Howry	51-54	2nd	13.5
8-5	At Oak.	L	6-7	(11)	11	11	Mathews	Eyre		51-55	2nd	13.5
8-6	At Oak.	L	1-9		5	15	Heredia	Navarro		51-56	2nd	13.5
8-7	At Oak.	L	1-11		6	14	Appier	Parque		51-57	2nd	14.5
8-8	At Oak.	L	5-7		11	9	Jones	Foulke		51-58	2nd	14.5
8-9	At Sea.	L	4-6		6	7	Meche	Snyder	Mesa	51-59	2nd	15.5
8-10	At Sea.	L	3-4		8	9	Moyer	Howry		51-60	2nd	16.5
8-11	At Sea.	L	2-11		6	10	Abbott	Navarro		51-61	2nd	17.5
8-13†	Tex.	W	4-2		11	6	Wells	Burkett	Howry	52-61		
8-13‡	Tex.	W	7-4		9	14	Baldwin	Glynn		53-61	2nd	17.0
8-14	Tex.	W	8-7		16	11	Howry	Zimmerman		54-61	2nd	17.0
8-15	Tex.	L	0-10		6	16	Loaiza	Snyder		54-62	2nd	18.0
8-16	Ana.	W	6-1		10	6	Sirotka	Washburn		55-62	2nd	17.0
8-17	Ana.	W	4-3	(12)	7	12	Howry	Holtz		56-62	2nd	16.0
8-18	Ana.	W	4-3		6	6	Baldwin	Magnante	Howry	57-62	2nd	15.0
8-19	Ana.	L	2-9		6	14	Ortiz	Parque		57-63	2nd	16.0
8-21†	At Bal.	W	4-3		14	7	Simas	Reyes	Howry	58-63		
8-21‡	At Bal.	W	8-5	(10)	13	14	Howry	Johns	Foulke	59-63	2nd	16.0
8-22	At Bal.	L	4-9		7	16	Johns	Navarro		59-64	2nd	17.0
8-23	At T.B.	W	10-2		13	8	Baldwin	Witt		60-64	2nd	16.0
8-24	At T.B.	L	5-6		5	11	Alvarez	Parque	Hernandez	60-65	2nd	16.0
8-25	At T.B.	W	6-1		12	7	Foulke	Rupe		61-65	2nd	16.0
8-26	At T.B.	L	7-9		14	13	White	Snyder	Hernandez	61-66	2nd	16.5
8-27	Oak.	L	6-9		13	10	Olivares	Sirotka	Isringhausen	61-67	2nd	17.5
8-28	Oak.	L	5-7		7	10	Heredia	Navarro	Jones	61-68	2nd	18.5
8-29	Oak.	W	7-2		10	10	Baldwin	Appier	Foulke	62-68	2nd	17.5
8-30†	Sea.	L	2-5		9	12	Garcia	Parque	Mesa	62-69		
8-30‡	Sea.	L	6-14		11	15	Cloude	Castillo	Rodriguez	62-70	2nd	19.0
8-31	Sea.	L	4-11		9	15	Halama	Snyder		62-71	2nd	20.0
9-1	Sea.	L	2-3		8	10	Meche	Sirotka	Mesa	62-72	2nd	21.0
9-3	At Tex.	L	4-10		10	15	Burkett	Baldwin		62-73	2nd	22.5
9-4	At Tex.	W	12-3		15	11	Castillo	Loaiza		63-73	2nd	21.5
9-6†	At Tex.	L	6-8		10	9	Helling	Parque	Wetteland	63-74		
9-6‡	At Tex.	L	3-6		12	8	Fassero	Snyder	Wetteland	63-75	2nd	23.5
9-7	At Ana.	L	1-14		4	12	Cooper	Sirotka		63-76	2nd	23.5
9-8	At Ana.	L	5-6	(10)	7	10	Percival	Simas		63-77	2nd	23.5
9-10	Cle.	L	6-14		5	14	Colon	Wells		63-78	2nd	24.5
9-11	Cle.	L	3-4		7	10	Burba	Parque	Jackson	63-79	2nd	25.5
9-12	Cle.	W	4-3		12	11	Sirotka	Wright	Howry	64-79	2nd	24.5
9-13	Det.	L	2-3		4	9	Mlicki	Snyder	Jones	64-80	2nd	25.5
9-14	Det.	L	0-7		4	11	Nitkowski	Myette		64-81	2nd	25.5
9-15	Det.	W	3-1		10	3	Baldwin	Moehler	Foulke	65-81	2nd	24.5
9-17	At Tor.	W	7-3		14	8	Wells	Escobar		66-81	2nd	23.0
9-18	At Tor.	W	7-4		13	10	Navarro	Quantrill	Howry	67-81	2nd	23.0
9-19	At Tor.	W	3-2		5	6	Sirotka	Halladay	Howry	68-81	2nd	22.0
9-21	At N.Y.	L	1-3		6	10	Pettitte	Baldwin	Rivera	68-82	2nd	22.5
9-22	At N.Y.	L	4-5		9	9	Rivera	Navarro		68-83	2nd	23.5
9-23	At N.Y.	L	2-5		7	12	Clemens	Parque	Rivera	68-84	2nd	23.5
9-24	At Min.	L	2-6		2	7	Mays	Myette		68-85	2nd	24.5
9-25	At Min.	W	13-4		18	6	Sirotka	Hawkins		69-85	2nd	24.5
9-26	At Min.	W	3-0		12	6	Baldwin	Ryan	Howry	70-85	2nd	24.5
9-27	At Min.	W	3-1		5	5	Simas	Wells	Foulke	71-85	2nd	24.0
9-29†	Bos.	L	2-6		10	10	Mercker	Parque		71-86		
9-29‡	Bos.	W	4-2		6	7	Foulke	Gordon	Howry	72-86	2nd	24.0
9-30	Bos.	W	5-2		9	8	Lowe	Rose	Howry	73-86	2nd	24.0
10-1	Min.	W	9-8		13	12	Baldwin	Ryan	Howry	74-86	2nd	23.0
10-2	Min.	W	6-1		11	8	Wells	Perkins		75-86	2nd	22.0
10-3	Min.	T	1-1	(7)	4	6				75-86	2nd	21.5

Monthly records: April (11-9), May (11-16), June (15-13), July (11-16), August (14-17), September (11-15), October (2-0).
*Innings, if other than nine. † First game of a doubleheader. ‡ Second game of a doubleheader.

MEMORABLE GAMES

June 13 at Chicago

Mike Caruso's two-run homer off Rick Aguilera snapped a 4-4 tie in the eighth inning and lifted the White Sox to a 6-4 win over their cross-town rivals. The victory also gave the Sox a three-game sweep over the Cubs at Wrigley Field and the young team's confidence rose to a season-high level.

White Sox	AB	R	H	RBI	Chi Cubs	AB	R	H	RBI
Durham, 2b	4	2	4	1	C.Goodwin, cf	4	0	1	0
Caruso, ss	4	1	1	2	Blauser, ph	1	0	0	0
Thomas, 1b	4	1	1	0	Morandini, 2b	4	0	1	0
M.Ordonez, rf	4	1	2	1	Aguilera, p	0	0	0	0
C.Lee, lf	4	0	2	1	R.Myers, p	0	0	0	0
Foulke, p	1	0	0	0	G.Hill, ph	1	0	0	0
Singleton, cf	3	0	1	0	S.Sosa, rf	4	1	2	0
D.Jcksn, ph-cf	2	0	0	0	Ma.Grace, 1b	3	2	1	1
Norton, 3b	4	0	1	1	H.Rodrgz, lf	2	0	0	0
Fordyce, c	3	1	0	0	Houston, c	3	0	0	0
Navarro, p	0	0	0	0	Gaetti, 3b	3	1	1	3
B.Ward, p	0	0	0	0	J.Hernndz, ss	4	0	0	0
Konerko, ph	1	0	0	0	Tapani, p	1	0	0	0
S.Lowe, p	0	0	0	0	Mulholland, p	1	0	0	0
Simas, p	0	0	0	0	S.Sanders, p	0	0	0	0
Liefer, ph-lf	1	0	0	0	F.Heredia, p	0	0	0	0
Alxnder, ph-2b	2	0	1	0					
Totals	**35**	**6**	**12**	**6**	**Totals**	**33**	**4**	**7**	**4**

Chi White Sox ....001 100 220— 6
Chi Cubs ....020 101 000— 4

E—Ma.Grace (5). DP—Chicago Cubs 2. LOB—Chicago White Sox 9, Chicago Cubs 7. 2B—Durham (14), Alexander (4). 3B—Durham (5). HR—Caruso (1), Ma.Grace (8), Gaetti (6). S—Caruso, Navarro. SF—Gaetti.

Chi White Sox	IP	H	R	ER	BB	SO
Navarro	3	2	2	2	1	5
B.Ward	2	1	1	1	1	0
S.Lowe	1	1	1	1	2	0
Simas (W, 1-2)	1	2	0	0	0	1
Foulke (S, 2)	2	1	0	0	0	1

Chi Cubs	IP	H	R	ER	BB	SO
Tapani	4	5	2	2	1	1
Mulholland	2.1	3	2	2	3	0
S.Sanders (BS 3)	0	2	0	0	0	0
F.Heredia	0.2	0	0	0	0	0
Aguilera (L, 3-2)	1	2	2	2	0	0
R.Myers	1	0	0	0	0	2

HBP—Thomas by Tapani. WP—S.Lowe, Tapani, Mulholland. U—HP,Winters. 1B, Carlson. 2B, Davidson. 3B, Montague. T—2:52. A—38,017.

July 6 at Chicago

Though the White Sox didn't win, center fielder Chris Singleton had a monster game (5-for-6, 4 RBI) and became the first Sox player to hit for the cycle since Carlton Fisk (May 16, 1984). Singleton also became the first A.L. rookie to hit for the cycle since Texas' Oddibe McDowell (July 23, 1985).

Kansas City	AB	R	H	RBI	White Sox	AB	R	H	RBI
C.Beltran, cf	6	0	1	1	Durham, 2b	3	3	0	0
Randa, 3b	6	2	3	2	Singleton, cf	6	3	5	4
Damon, lf	3	1	1	1	Thomas, 1b	5	0	2	2
Mi.Sweeney, 1b	5	0	1	0	D.Jackson, pr	0	0	0	0
Dye, rf	5	1	1	1	L.Rodrgz, ss	0	0	0	0
Je.Giambi, dh	4	2	1	0	M.Ordonez, rf	5	0	2	0
Kreuter, c	4	0	1	0	C.Lee, lf	5	0	2	1
Febles, 2b	5	2	3	0	Konerko, dh	5	0	2	0
R.Sanchez, ss	5	0	2	3	Norton, 3b-1b	5	0	0	0
					Fordyce, c	5	0	2	0
					Caruso, ss	3	1	1	0
					Liefer, ph	1	0	0	0
					C.Wilsn, ss-3b	0	0	0	0
Totals	**43**	**8**	**14**	**8**	**Totals**	**43**	**7**	**16**	**7**

Kansas City ....022 002 100 1— 8
Chi White Sox ....000 220 102 0— 7

E—Febles (9), C.Beltran (9). DP—Kansas City 1, Chicago White Sox 1. LOB—Kansas City 9, Chicago White Sox 10. 2B—Randa (16), Mi.Sweeney (22), Febles (19), Singleton (18), M.Ordonez (17). 3B—R.Sanchez (4), Singleton (5). HR—Randa 2 (9), Damon (8), Dye (17), Singleton (6). SB—Caruso (7). CS—Caruso (8). S—C.Wilson.

Kansas City	IP	H	R	ER	BB	SO
Suppan	7	10	5	5	1	2
J.Montgomery (BS 5)	1.2	5	2	2	1	2
Whisenant (W, 4-3)	1.1	1	0	0	0	1

Chi White Sox	IP	H	R	ER	BB	SO
Baldwin	6	8	6	6	3	4
S.Lowe	2	2	1	1	1	1
Simas	1	1	0	0	0	1
Foulke (L, 0-2)	1	3	1	1	0	0

HBP—Durham by Suppan. WP—Baldwin. U—HP,Meriwether. 1B, Evans. 2B, McCoy. 3B, Barrett. T—3:14. A—11,251.

1999 REVIEW

BATTING

Name	G	TPA	AB	R	H	TB	2B	3B	HR	RBI	Avg.	Obp.	Slg.	SH	SF	HP	BB	IBB	SO	SB	CS	GDP	vs RHP AB	Avg.	HR	RBI	vs LHP AV	Avg.	HR	RBI
Ordonez, Magglio	157	677	624	100	188	318	34	3	30	117	.301	.349	.510	0	5	1	47	4	64	13	6	24	521	.298	27	102	103	.320	3	15
Durham, Ray	153	694	612	109	181	266	30	8	13	60	.296	.373	.435	3	2	4	73	1	105	34	11	9	476	.294	10	47	136	.301	3	13
Caruso, Mike	136	564	529	60	132	157	11	4	2	35	.250	.280	.297	11	1	3	20	0	36	12	14	6	420	.245	2	29	109	.266	0	6
Konerko, Paul	142	564	513	71	151	262	31	4	24	81	.294	.352	.511	1	3	2	45	0	68	1	0	19	397	.287	19	58	116	.319	5	23
Singleton, Chris	133	530	496	72	149	243	31	6	17	72	.300	.328	.490	4	6	1	22	1	45	20	5	10	420	.281	14	57	76	.408	3	15
Lee, Carlos	127	518	492	66	148	228	31	2	16	84	.293	.312	.463	1	7	4	13	0	72	4	2	11	399	.291	13	75	93	.301	3	9
Thomas, Frank	135	590	486	74	148	229	36	0	15	77	.305	.414	.471	0	8	9	87	13	66	3	3	15	411	.314	12	70	75	.253	3	7
Norton, Greg	132	510	436	62	111	185	26	0	16	50	.255	.358	.424	1	2	2	69	3	93	4	4	11	362	.265	16	47	74	.203	0	3
Fordyce, Brook	105	362	333	36	99	153	25	1	9	49	.238	.301	.459	3	2	3	21	0	48	2	0	5	240	.283	5	31	93	.333	4	18
Wilson, Craig	98	282	252	28	60	82	8	1	4	26	.238	.301	.325	6	1	0	23	0	22	1	1	5	182	.220	3	21	70	.286	1	5
Johnson, Mark L.	73	248	207	27	47	70	11	0	4	16	.227	.344	.338	1	2	2	36	0	58	3	1	2	171	.222	3	14	36	.250	1	2
Jackson, Darrin	73	155	149	22	41	64	9	1	4	16	.275	.288	.430	2	1	0	3	0	20	4	1	4	72	.194	0	1	77	.351	4	15
Simmons, Brian	54	135	126	14	29	50	3	3	4	17	.230	.281	.397	0	0	0	9	0	30	4	0	3	101	.248	4	15	25	.160	0	2
Liefer, Jeff	45	122	113	8	28	37	7	1	0	14	.248	.295	.327	0	1	0	8	0	28	2	0	3	105	.257	0	12	8	.125	0	2
Rodriguez, Liu	39	111	93	8	22	31	2	2	1	12	.237	.343	.333	3	0	3	12	0	11	0	0	5	71	.225	1	11	22	.273	0	1
Abbott, Jeff	17	64	57	5	9	15	0	0	2	6	.158	.222	.263	1	0	1	5	0	12	1	1	4	37	.081	1	2	20	.300	1	4
Christensen, McKay	28	60	53	10	12	16	1	0	1	6	.226	.271	.302	1	2	0	4	0	7	2	1	1	48	.250	1	5	5	.000	0	1
Dellaero, Jason	11	35	33	1	3	3	0	0	0	2	.091	.114	.091	0	1	0	1	0	13	0	0	0	27	.074	0	1	6	.167	0	1
Paul, Josh	6	18	18	2	4	5	1	0	0	1	.222	.222	.278	0	0	0	0	0	4	0	0	0	16	.250	0	1	2	.000	0	0
Sirotka, Mike	32	8	8	1	2	2	0	0	0	0	.250	.250	.250	0	0	0	0	0	3	0	0	1	6	.333	0	0	2	.000	0	0
Parque, Jim	31	6	5	0	2	2	0	0	0	0	.400	.400	.400	1	0	0	0	0	1	0	0	0	2	.500	0	0	3	.333	0	0
Navarro, Jaime	32	4	3	0	0	0	0	0	0	0	.000	.000	.000	1	0	0	0	0	1	0	0	0	3	.000	0	0	0	.000	0	0
Baldwin, James	35	2	2	1	1	3	0	1	0	1	.500	.500	1.500	0	0	0	0	0	1	0	0	0	2	.500	0	1	0	.000	0	0
Foulke, Keith	67	2	2	0	0	0	0	0	0	0	.000	.000	.000	0	0	0	0	0	1	0	0	0	2	.000	0	0	0	.000	0	0
Daneker, Pat	3	2	2	0	0	0	0	0	0	0	.000	.000	.000	0	0	0	0	0	1	0	0	0	2	.000	0	0	0	.000	0	0
Simas, Bill	70	0	0	0	0	0	0	0	0	0	.000	.000	.000	0	0	0	0	0	0	0	0	0	0	.000	0	0	0	.000	0	0
Eyre, Scott	21	0	0	0	0	0	0	0	0	0	.000	.000	.000	0	0	0	0	0	0	0	0	0	0	.000	0	0	0	.000	0	0
Lowe, Sean	64	0	0	0	0	0	0	0	0	0	.000	.000	.000	0	0	0	0	0	0	0	0	0	0	.000	0	0	0	.000	0	0
Rizzo, Todd	3	0	0	0	0	0	0	0	0	0	.000	.000	.000	0	0	0	0	0	0	0	0	0	0	.000	0	0	0	.000	0	0
Howry, Bob	69	0	0	0	0	0	0	0	0	0	.000	.000	.000	0	0	0	0	0	0	0	0	0	0	.000	0	0	0	.000	0	0
Ward, Bryan	40	1	0	0	0	0	0	0	0	0	.000	1.000	.000	0	0	0	1	0	0	0	0	0	0	.000	0	0	0	.000	0	0
Davenport, Joe	3	0	0	0	0	0	0	0	0	0	.000	.000	.000	0	0	0	0	0	0	0	0	0	0	.000	0	0	0	.000	0	0

PITCHING

Name	W	L	Pct.	ERA	IP	H	R	ER	HR	SH	SF	HB	BB	IBB	SO	G	GS	CG	ShO	GF	Sv	vs. RH AB	Avg.	HR	RBI	vs. LH AB	Avg.	HR	RBI
Sirotka, Mike	11	13	.458	4.00	209.0	236	108	93	24	5	9	3	57	2	125	32	32	3	1	0	0	647	.287	17	76	188	.266	7	27
Baldwin, James	12	13	.480	5.10	199.1	219	119	113	34	4	7	7	81	1	123	35	33	1	0	1	0	368	.285	18	50	419	.272	16	55
Parque, Jim	9	15	.375	5.13	173.2	210	111	99	23	5	8	10	79	2	111	31	30	1	0	0	0	545	.292	18	75	157	.325	5	24
Navarro, Jaime	8	13	.381	6.09	159.2	206	126	108	29	3	4	11	71	1	74	32	27	0	0	1	0	332	.265	12	50	327	.361	17	58
Snyder, John	9	12	.429	6.68	129.1	167	103	96	27	3	7	6	49	0	67	25	25	1	0	0	0	271	.325	14	49	186	.297	13	46
Foulke, Keith	3	3	.500	2.22	105.1	72	28	26	11	3	0	3	21	4	123	67	0	0	0	31	9	198	.192	5	14	186	.183	6	15
Lowe, Sean	4	1	.800	3.67	95.2	90	39	39	10	3	9	4	46	1	62	64	0	0	0	13	0	210	.262	5	32	134	.261	5	19
Simas, Bill	6	3	.667	3.75	72.0	73	36	30	6	4	4	6	32	6	41	70	0	0	0	21	2	154	.266	5	35	124	.258	1	18
Howry, Bob	5	3	.625	3.59	67.2	58	34	27	8	3	1	3	38	3	80	69	0	0	0	54	28	120	.233	5	10	133	.226	3	19
Castillo, Carlos	2	2	.500	5.71	41.0	45	26	26	10	0	0	0	14	1	23	18	2	0	0	6	0	87	.230	4	8	77	.325	6	16
Ward, Bryan	0	1	.000	7.55	39.1	63	36	33	10	0	1	0	11	1	35	40	0	0	0	8	0	102	.382	4	20	69	.348	6	15
Wells, Kip	4	1	.800	4.04	35.2	33	17	16	2	0	2	3	15	0	29	7	7	0	0	0	0	43	.209	1	3	90	.267	1	12
Eyre, Scott	1	1	.500	7.56	25.0	38	22	21	6	0	1	1	15	2	17	21	0	0	0	8	0	69	.377	6	18	43	.279	0	6
Lundquist, David	1	1	.500	8.59	22.0	28	21	21	3	2	2	1	12	0	18	17	0	0	0	7	0	50	.320	1	8	39	.308	2	10
Pena, Jesus	0	0	.000	5.31	20.1	21	15	12	3	1	0	1	23	5	20	26	0	0	0	1	0	38	.289	2	11	43	.233	1	6
Myette, Aaron	0	2	.000	6.32	15.2	17	11	11	2	0	0	2	14	1	11	4	3	0	0	0	0	31	.161	0	3	33	.364	2	7
Daneker, Pat	0	0	.000	4.20	15.0	14	8	7	1	2	1	0	6	0	5	3	2	0	0	1	0	31	.258	0	5	24	.250	1	3
Sturtze, Tanyon	0	0	.000	0.00	6.0	4	0	0	0	0	0	0	2	0	2	1	1	0	0	0	0	2	.500	0	0	18	.167	0	0
Bradford, Chad	0	0	.000	19.64	3.2	9	8	8	1	0	0	0	5	0	3	0	0	0	0	0	0	11	.364	0	2	8	.625	1	5
Davenport, Joe	0	0	.000	0.00	1.2	1	0	0	0	0	0	0	2	0	0	3	0	0	0	2	0	3	.000	0	0	2	.500	0	0
Rizzo, Todd	0	2	.000	6.75	1.1	4	2	1	0	1	0	0	3	1	2	3	0	0	0	2	0	4	.250	0	1	4	.750	0	0

DESIGNATED HITTERS

Name	AB	Avg.	HR	RBI	Name	AB	Avg.	HR	RBI	Name	AB	Avg.	HR	RBI
Thomas, Frank	295	.281	7	45	Ordonez, Magglio	5	.400	0	0	Singleton, Chris	0	-	0	0
Konerko, Paul	167	.311	9	30	Simmons, Brian	4	.500	0	1	Rodriguez, Liu	0	-	0	0
Lee, Carlos	63	.190	2	11	Norton, Greg	4	.250	0	1	Wilson, Craig	0	-	0	0
Durham, Ray	17	.235	0	1	Jackson, Darrin	2	.000	0	0	Caruso, Mike	0	-	0	0
Liefer, Jeff	15	.333	0	4	Johnson, Mark L.	1	.000	0	0					

INDIVIDUAL STATISTICS

FIELDING

FIRST BASEMEN

Player	Pct.	G	PO	A	E	TC	DP
Konerko, Paul	.995	92	740	58	4	802	72
Thomas, Frank	.990	49	385	18	4	407	40
Norton, Greg	.972	26	67	3	2	72	9
Liefer, Jeff	1.000	15	96	11	0	107	11
Lee, Carlos	.966	5	24	4	1	29	3
Wilson, Craig	1.000	1	4	0	0	4	0

SECOND BASEMEN

Player	Pct.	G	PO	A	E	TC	DP
Durham, Ray	.974	148	305	412	19	736	100
Rodriguez, Liu	.985	22	25	41	1	67	6
Wilson, Craig	.938	7	6	9	1	16	1

THIRD BASEMEN

Player	Pct.	G	PO	A	E	TC	DP
Norton, Greg	.922	120	93	201	25	319	17
Wilson, Craig	.969	72	47	108	5	160	10
Konerko, Paul	-	1	0	0	0	0	0
Rodriguez, Liu	-	1	0	0	0	0	0

SHORTSTOPS

Player	Pct.	G	PO	A	E	TC	DP
Caruso, Mike	.957	132	183	348	24	555	86
Wilson, Craig	.985	22	29	38	1	68	8
Rodriguez, Liu	.958	14	20	26	2	48	6
Dellaero, Jason	.917	11	16	28	4	48	5

OUTFIELDERS

Player	Pct.	G	PO	A	E	TC	DP
Ordonez, Magglio	.991	153	331	12	3	346	4
Singleton, Chris	.990	127	376	9	4	389	3
Lee, Carlos	.981	105	201	3	4	208	0
Jackson, Darrin	.972	64	103	2	3	108	0
Simmons, Brian	.976	46	79	2	2	83	1
Christensen, McKay	.943	27	50	0	3	53	0
Liefer, Jeff	1.000	17	28	1	0	29	1
Abbott, Jeff	.962	17	25	0	1	26	0

CATCHERS

Player	Pct.	G	PO	A	E	TC	DP	PB
Fordyce, Brook	.987	103	561	30	8	599	5	4
Johnson, Mark L.	.993	72	413	33	3	449	6	10
Paul, Josh	1.000	6	40	2	0	42	0	0

PITCHERS

Player	Pct.	G	PO	A	E	TC	DP
Simas, Bill	1.000	70	7	6	0	13	1
Howry, Bob	1.000	69	2	3	0	5	0
Foulke, Keith	.947	67	5	13	1	19	0
Lowe, Sean	1.000	64	5	14	0	19	1
Ward, Bryan	1.000	40	0	6	0	6	0
Baldwin, James	.943	35	12	21	2	35	0
Sirotka, Mike	.879	32	5	24	4	33	0
Navarro, Jaime	.923	32	9	15	2	26	2
Parque, Jim	.964	31	6	21	1	28	1
Pena, Jesus	1.000	26	0	5	0	5	0
Snyder, John	1.000	25	10	16	0	26	1
Eyre, Scott	1.000	21	0	1	0	1	0
Castillo, Carlos	1.000	18	1	5	0	6	0
Lundquist, David	1.000	17	1	2	0	3	0
Wells, Kip	.778	7	4	3	2	9	0
Myette, Aaron	1.000	4	0	1	0	1	0
Bradford, Chad	1.000	3	1	3	0	4	0
Daneker, Pat	1.000	3	0	3	0	3	0
Davenport, Joe	1.000	3	0	1	0	1	0
Rizzo, Todd	-	3	0	0	0	0	0
Sturtze, Tanyon	1.000	1	0	1	0	1	1

PITCHING AGAINST EACH CLUB

Pitcher	Ana. W-L	Bal. W-L	Bos. W-L	Cle. W-L	Det. W-L	K.C. W-L	Min. W-L	N.Y. W-L	Oak. W-L	Sea. W-L	T.B. W-L	Tex. W-L	Tor. W-L	N.L. W-L	Total W-L
Baldwin, James	1-0	0-2	0-1	1-1	2-1	2-1	2-1	0-2	1-0	1-0	1-1	1-1	0-0	0-2	12-13
Bradford, Chad	0-0	0-0	0-0	0-0	0-0	0-0	0-0	0-0	0-0	0-0	0-0	0-0	0-0	0-0	0-0
Castillo, Carlos	0-0	0-0	0-0	0-1	0-0	0-0	0-0	1-0	0-0	0-1	0-0	1-0	0-0	0-0	2-2
Daneker, Pat	0-0	0-0	0-0	0-0	0-0	0-0	0-0	0-0	0-0	0-0	0-0	0-0	0-0	0-0	0-0
Davenport, Joe	0-0	0-0	0-0	0-0	0-0	0-0	0-0	0-0	0-0	0-0	0-0	0-0	0-0	0-0	0-0
Eyre, Scott	0-0	0-0	0-0	0-0	0-0	0-0	0-0	0-0	0-1	0-0	0-0	0-0	1-0	0-0	1-1
Foulke, Keith	0-1	1-0	0-0	0-0	0-0	1-1	0-0	0-0	0-1	0-0	0-0	1-0	0-0	0-0	3-3
Howry, Bob	1-0	1-0	0-0	0-0	0-0	1-0	0-0	0-0	0-1	0-0	1-1	0-1	0-0	1-0	5-3
Lowe, Sean	0-0	0-0	1-0	1-0	0-0	1-0	0-0	0-0	0-0	0-0	0-0	0-0	1-0	0-1	4-1
Lundquist, David	1-0	0-1	0-0	0-0	0-0	0-0	0-0	0-0	0-0	0-0	0-0	0-0	0-0	0-0	1-1
Myette, Aaron	0-0	0-0	0-0	0-0	0-1	0-0	0-1	0-0	0-0	0-0	0-0	0-0	0-0	0-0	0-2
Navarro, Jaime	0-1	0-3	0-1	2-0	0-2	1-0	0-1	0-2	0-1	1-0	1-0	1-0	0-1	2-1	8-13
Parque, Jim	0-2	0-0	0-3	0-3	0-1	1-0	1-1	1-1	0-1	2-1	1-1	0-1	1-0	2-0	9-15
Pena, Jesus	0-0	0-0	0-0	0-0	0-0	0-0	0-0	0-0	0-0	0-0	0-0	0-0	0-0	0-0	0-0
Rizzo, Todd	0-0	0-0	0-0	0-0	0-0	0-0	0-0	0-0	0-0	0-0	0-0	0-0	0-0	0-2	0-2
Simas, Bill	0-1	1-0	1-0	0-0	0-0	0-0	2-0	0-0	0-1	0-0	0-0	0-0	0-0	2-1	6-3
Sirotka, Mike	1-1	1-0	1-1	1-2	1-0	0-2	1-1	1-1	0-2	0-1	0-1	0-0	2-1	2-0	11-13
Snyder, John	1-0	0-1	1-1	0-1	1-2	0-0	1-0	2-1	1-0	1-3	1-1	0-1	0-0	0-1	9-12
Sturtze, Tanyon	0-0	0-0	0-0	0-0	0-0	0-0	0-0	0-0	0-0	0-0	0-0	0-0	0-0	0-0	0-0
Ward, Bryan	0-0	0-0	0-0	0-0	0-0	0-0	0-0	0-0	0-0	0-0	0-0	0-0	0-0	0-1	0-1
Wells, Kip	0-0	0-0	1-0	0-0	1-0	1-0	0-0	1-0	0-0	0-0	0-0	0-0	0-1	0-0	4-1
Totals	5-5	3-7	5-7	3-9	7-5	6-6	8-3	5-7	3-7	4-8	6-4	5-5	6-4	9-9	75-86

INTERLEAGUE: Simas 1-0, Rizzo 0-1, Lowe 0-1 vs. Brewers; Parque 1-0, Sirotka 1-0, Howry 1-0, Simas 1-0, Navarro 0-1, Baldwin 0-1 vs. Cubs; Navarro 1-0, Snyder 0-1, Baldwin 0-1 vs. Astros; Parque 1-0, Sirotka 1-0, Simas 0-1 vs. Pirates; Navarro 1-0, Ward 0-1, Rizzo 0-1 vs. Cardinals. Total: 9-9.

MISCELLANEOUS

HOME RUNS BY PARK

At Anaheim (7): Singleton 2, Durham 1, Fordyce 1, Norton 1, Abbott 1, Ordonez 1.

At Baltimore (3): Konerko 2, Durham 1.

At Boston (7): Ordonez 2, Wilson 2, Thomas 1, Norton 1, Singleton 1.

At Chicago (AL) (77): Ordonez 16, Konerko 16, Lee 10, Thomas 9, Durham 7, Fordyce 5, Norton 5, Singleton 5, Johnson 2, Jackson 1, Christensen 1.

At Chicago (NL) (4): Thomas 1, Norton 1, Caruso 1, Johnson 1.

At Cleveland (4): Fordyce 1, Ordonez 1, Johnson 1, Simmons 1.

At Detroit (11): Norton 5, Thomas 1, Durham 1, Fordyce 1, Konerko 1, Wilson 1, Singleton 1.

At Kansas City (5): Ordonez 3, Thomas 1, Rodriguez 1.

At Milwaukee (5): Durham 1, Ordonez 1, Konerko 1, Lee 1, Singleton 1.

At Minnesota (6): Konerko 2, Singleton 2, Ordonez 1, Simmons 1.

At New York (AL) (6): Singleton 3, Norton 1, Caruso 1, Lee 1.

At Oakland (4): Thomas 1, Norton 1, Ordonez 1, Konerko 1.

At Seattle (3): Thomas 1, Norton 1, Lee 1.

At St. Louis (4): Ordonez 2, Durham 1, Singleton 1.

At Tampa Bay (3): Jackson 1, Fordyce 1, Lee 1.

At Texas (3): Wilson 1, Lee 1, Singleton 1.

At Toronto (5): Ordonez 2, Simmons 2, Lee 1.

LOW-HIT GAMES

No-hitters: None.
One-hitters: None.
Two-hitters: None.

10-STRIKEOUT GAMES

Total: 0.

FOUR OR MORE HITS IN ONE GAME

Chris Singleton 5 (including two five-hit games), Ray Durham 4, Brook Fordyce 3, Frank Thomas 2, Magglio Ordonez 2, Darrin Jackson 1, Paul Konerko 1, **Total:** 18.

MULTI-HOMER GAMES

Greg Norton 3, Magglio Ordonez 2, Ray Durham 1, Paul Konerko 1, Craig Wilson 1, Chris Singleton 1, **Total:** 9.

GRAND SLAMS

4-28: Magglio Ordonez (off Tampa Bay's Tony Saunders).
5-17: Carlos Lee (off Cleveland's Bartolo Colon).
6-17: Paul Konerko (off Baltimore's Jesse Orosco).
7-17: Magglio Ordonez (off St. Louis's Kent Bottenfield).
10-1: Carlos Lee (off Minnesota's Jason Ryan).

PINCH HITTERS

(Minimum 5 at-bats)

Name	AB	Avg.	HR	RBI
Jackson, Darrin	12	.250	0	2
Fordyce, Brook	10	.300	0	2
Konerko, Paul	9	.333	0	2
Liefer, Jeff	9	.222	0	3
Norton, Greg	6	.000	0	0
Simmons, Brian	5	.400	0	1

DEBUTS

4-6: McKay Christensen, CF.
4-6: David Lundquist, P.
4-7: Jeff Liefer, 1B.
4-10: Chris Singleton, PH.
5-7: Carlos Lee, LF.
6-9: Liu Rodriguez, SS.
7-2: Pat Daneker, P.
7-20: Joe Davenport, P.
8-2: Kip Wells, P.
8-7: Jesus Pena, P.
9-7: Jason Dellaero, SS.
9-7: Josh Paul, C.
9-7: Aaron Myette, P.

GAMES BY POSITION

Catcher: Brook Fordyce 103, Mark L. Johnson 72, Josh Paul 6.

First base: Paul Konerko 92, Frank Thomas 49, Greg Norton 26, Jeff Liefer 15, Carlos Lee 5, Craig Wilson 1.

Second base: Ray Durham 148, Liu Rodriguez 22, Craig Wilson 7.

Third base: Greg Norton 120, Craig Wilson 72, Paul Konerko 1, Liu Rodriguez 1.

Shortstop: Mike Caruso 132, Craig Wilson 22, Liu Rodriguez 14, Jason Dellaero 11.

Outfield: Magglio Ordonez 153, Chris Singleton 127, Carlos Lee 105, Darrin Jackson 64, Brian Simmons 46, McKay Christensen 27, Jeff Abbott 17, Jeff Liefer 17.

Designated hitter: Frank Thomas 82, Paul Konerko 46, Carlos Lee 16, Jeff Liefer 7, Ray Durham 4, Darrin Jackson 3, Brian Simmons 3, Magglio Ordonez 2, Mike Caruso 2, Chris Singleton 2, Liu Rodriguez 2, Greg Norton 1, Craig Wilson 1, Mark L. Johnson 1.

STREAKS

Wins: 6 (April 16-24).
Losses: 7 (August 5-11).
Consecutive games with at least one hit: 21, Frank Thomas (May 24-June 15).
Wins by pitcher: 6, John Snyder (April 15-May 15).

ATTENDANCE

Home: 1,338,851.
Road: 2,276,887.
Highest (home): 44,153 (July 9 vs. Chicago).
Highest (road): 51,656 (April 5 vs. Seattle).
Lowest (home): 8,980 (April 20 vs. Seattle).
Lowest (road): 9,022 (September 27 vs. Minnesota).

CLEVELAND INDIANS

DAY BY DAY

Date	Opp.	Res.	Score	(inn.*)	Hits	Opp. hits	Winning pitcher	Losing pitcher	Save	Record	Pos.	GB
4-6	At Ana.	L	5-6		10	11	Holtz	Karsay	Percival	0-1	T4th	1.5
4-7	At Ana.	W	9-1		13	4	Burba	Hill		1-1	T2nd	0.5
4-8	At Ana.	W	9-1		13	4	Colon	Sparks		2-1	T1st	...
4-9	At Min.	W	14-5		20	8	Nagy	Hawkins		3-1	1st	+1.0
4-10	At Min.	W	12-7		16	11	Karsay	Lincoln		4-1	1st	+2.0
4-11	At Min.	W	9-8		17	9	Wright	Radke	Jackson	5-1	1st	+2.0
4-12	K.C.	W	5-2	(10)	11	8	Shuey	Santiago		6-1	1st	+3.0
4-14	K.C.	W	11-4		14	10	Colon	Suppan		7-1	1st	+4.0
4-17†	Min.	W	5-1		10	5	Nagy	Radke		8-1		
4-17‡	Min.	L	8-13	(11)	12	16	Aguilera	Jackson		8-2	1st	+3.5
4-18	Min.	W	3-2		8	9	Shuey	Wells	Jackson	9-2	1st	+4.0
4-20	Oak.	W	5-1		9	3	Colon	Rogers		10-2	1st	+4.0
4-21	Oak.	W	5-4		14	8	Reed	Taylor		11-2	1st	+4.0
4-22	Oak.	L	1-4		3	8	Candiotti	Nagy	Taylor	11-3	1st	+3.5
4-23	At Bos.	W	7-6		9	7	Karsay	Corsi	Jackson	12-3	1st	+3.5
4-24	At Bos.	L	4-9		12	13	Harikkala	DeLucia		12-4	1st	+2.5
4-25	At Bos.	L	2-3		7	12	Martinez	Shuey		12-5	1st	+2.5
4-26	At Oak.	W	5-4	(10)	9	10	Karsay	Taylor	Jackson	13-5	1st	+3.0
4-27	At Oak.	W	8-5		12	11	Nagy	Candiotti	Jackson	14-5	1st	+3.5
4-28	At Oak.	W	4-1		6	6	Wright	Haynes	Jackson	15-5	1st	+3.0
4-29	At Oak.	W	8-3		9	4	Burba	Oquist		16-5	1st	+4.0
4-30	At Tex.	L	5-7		11	13	Helling	Colon	Wetteland	16-6	1st	+4.0
5-1	At Tex.	W	5-3		8	9	Gooden	Sele	Jackson	17-6	1st	+4.0
5-2	At Tex.	L	6-8		8	11	Clark	Nagy	Wetteland	17-7	1st	+4.0
5-3	At Tex.	W	10-4		16	6	Wright	Morgan		18-7	1st	+4.0
5-5	Sea.	L	5-6		10	10	Fassero	Burba	Mesa	18-8	1st	+4.5
5-6	Sea.	W	8-4		8	7	Colon	Weaver		19-8	1st	+5.5
5-7	T.B.	W	20-11		21	13	Wagner	Mecir		20-8	1st	+5.5
5-8	T.B.	L	6-7		12	14	Rekar	Nagy	Hernandez	20-9	1st	+4.5
5-9	T.B.	W	5-4		6	11	Wright	Alvarez	Jackson	21-9	1st	+5.5
5-10	Bal.	W	6-4		8	7	Burba	Guzman	Jackson	22-9	1st	+5.5
5-11	Bal.	W	11-6		12	11	Colon	Ponson		23-9	1st	+6.5
5-12	Bal.	W	6-5		10	9	Assenmacher	Timlin	Shuey	24-9	1st	+7.0
5-14	At Det.	W	4-2		6	8	Karsay	Brocail	Shuey	25-9	1st	+7.0
5-15	At Det.	W	12-7		12	10	Burba	Mlicki		26-9	1st	+7.0
5-16	At Det.	L	3-9		7	10	Weaver	Wright	Kida	26-10	1st	+7.0
5-17	At Chi.	W	13-9		17	12	Colon	Navarro		27-10	1st	+8.0
5-18	At Chi.	W	13-0		13	2	Gooden	Baldwin		28-10	1st	+8.5
5-19	At Chi.	W	13-7		18	9	Nagy	Parque		29-10	1st	+8.5
5-21	Det.	L	6-9		10	11	Nitkowski	Shuey	Jones	29-11	1st	+8.0
5-22	Det.	L	2-6		7	10	Weaver	Wright		29-12	1st	+8.0
5-23	Det.	W	7-4		10	8	Shuey	Jones		30-12	1st	+8.0
5-24	Chi.	L	3-10		10	15	Lowe	Gooden		30-13	1st	+7.5
5-25	Chi.	W	3-1		8	6	Nagy	Parque	Jackson	31-13	1st	+8.5
5-26	Chi.	W	6-2		11	8	Burba	Sirotka	Shuey	32-13	1st	+9.5
5-28	Bos.	L	5-12		9	18	Wakefield	Wright	Lowe	32-14	1st	+9.0
5-29	Bos.	L	2-4		5	8	Martinez	Colon	Gordon	32-15	1st	+9.0
5-30	Bos.	L	2-4		3	9	Rose	Gooden	Gordon	32-16	1st	+9.0
5-31	At N.Y.	W	7-1		7	7	Nagy	Hernandez		33-16	1st	+10.0
6-1	At N.Y.	L	5-11		9	13	Clemens	Burba		33-17	1st	+9.0
6-2	At N.Y.	W	10-7		15	9	Karsay	Pettitte	Jackson	34-17	1st	+10.0
6-4	Chi. (NL)	L	4-5		8	8	Aguilera	Jackson	Adams	34-18	1st	+9.5
6-5	Chi. (NL)	W	8-7	(11)	16	11	Jackson	Sanders		35-18	1st	+9.5
6-6	Chi. (NL)	W	4-2		8	8	Nagy	Trachsel	Shuey	36-18	1st	+9.5
6-8	Mil.	L	1-2	(10)	13	10	Roque	Assenmacher	Wickman	36-19	1st	+9.0
6-9	Mil.	W	6-5	(10)	9	9	Jackson	Roque		37-19	1st	+10.0
6-10	Mil.	L	9-15		14	14	Nomo	Colon		37-20	1st	+9.5
6-11	At Cin.	W	8-6		7	13	Shuey	Williamson	Jackson	38-20	1st	+9.5
6-12	At Cin.	W	4-3		9	5	Nagy	Harnisch	Jackson	39-20	1st	+9.5
6-13	At Cin.	W	7-3		9	10	Burba	Avery	Karsay	40-20	1st	+9.5
6-15	Oak.	W	8-3		12	8	Wright	Haynes		41-20	1st	+10.0
6-16	Oak.	W	9-8		10	9	Karsay	Taylor		42-20	1st	+10.0
6-17	Oak.	W	10-6		18	9	Shuey	Worrell		43-20	1st	+10.0
6-18	Sea.	L	4-9		11	10	Halama	Nagy		43-21	1st	+10.0
6-19	Sea.	W	10-6		10	12	Burba	Watson	Jackson	44-21	1st	+11.0
6-20	Sea.	W	13-5		14	11	Wright	Rodriguez		45-21	1st	+12.0
6-21	Sea.	W	4-3	(12)	12	10	Karsay	Mesa		46-21	1st	+12.5
6-22	At Tor.	L	3-4		8	6	Escobar	Gooden	Koch	46-22	1st	+11.5
6-23	At Tor.	W	9-6		12	10	Nagy	Quantrill		47-22	1st	+12.5
6-24	At Tor.	L	0-3		3	5	Halladay	Burba	Koch	47-23	1st	+11.5
6-25	At K.C.	L	2-8		6	12	Suppan	Wright		47-24	1st	+11.5
6-26	At K.C.	L	7-11		6	8	Montgomery	Rincon		47-25	1st	+11.5
6-27	At K.C.	W	6-5		9	13	Reed	Byrdak	Jackson	48-25	1st	+11.5
6-28	At K.C.	W	6-1		12	7	Nagy	Witasick		49-25	1st	+12.5
6-29	Min.	W	5-4		9	7	Reed	Trombley		50-25	1st	+13.5
6-30	Min.	L	3-5		5	9	Milton	Wright	Trombley	50-26	1st	+12.5

HIGHLIGHTS

High point: The Indians rolled to their fifth consecutive A.L. Central title against overmatched divisional opposition. The championship continued the most successful run in franchise history.

Low point: Losing a best-of-five division series after seemingly having it won. The collapse cost Mike Hargrove his job, even though he was only eight wins short of becoming the winningest manager in team history.

Turning point: One victory away from sweeping the division series, the Indians tied the Red Sox 3-3 in the top of seventh of Game 3 but yielded six runs to Boston in its half of the inning. The Red Sox won, 9-3, and then erupted for 23-7 and 12-8 victories.

Most valuable player: Manny Ramirez led the majors with 165 RBIs, but this honor goes to second baseman Roberto Alomar. Signed as a free agent in the offseason, Alomar was the A.L.'s best all-around player. He batted .323 with 138 runs, 24 homers, 120 RBIs and 37 stolen bases. He made only six errors.

Most valuable pitcher: Righthander Bartolo Colon, who took steps toward becoming a long-sought No. 1 pitcher. He went 18-5 with a 3.95 ERA. Colon was dominant in the second half, going 11-2 with a 2.60 ERA. At age 24, he's on the verge of becoming one of the league's top starters.

Most improved player: Richie Sexson. Despite playing in only 134 games, he finished third on the team in home runs (31) and RBIs (116).

Most pleasant surprise: Steve Karsay, who made the team as the last man on the pitching staff. Pitching mostly in a setup role, he was 10-2 with a 2.97 ERA.

Key injuries: The Indians were able to field their projected opening-day lineup only four times all season. Sandy Alomar Jr. tore a knee ligament in May and missed four months. Travis Fryman tore a knee ligament in July and missed two months. Wil Cordero broke his wrist in June and missed three months. Kenny Lofton pulled a hamstring in July and missed six weeks. Jacob Cruz tore a ligament in his thumb in August and missed the rest of the season.

Notable: The Indians scored a club-record 1,009 runs in the regular season. ... Ramirez became the first major leaguer to top the 160-RBI mark since Jimmie Foxx drove in 175 runs in 1938. ... The Indians went a combined 10-22 against New York, Boston and Texas, the A.L.'s other playoff teams. ... The Indians hit 12 grand slams, tying a major league record.

—STEVE HERRICK

MISCELLANEOUS

RECORDS

1999 regular-season record: 97-65 (1st in A.L. Central); 47-34 at home; 50-31 on road; 26-27 vs. A.L. East; 33-16 vs. A.L. Central; 29-13 vs. A.L. West; 9-9 vs. N.L. Central; 28-15 vs. lefthanded starters; 69-50 vs. righthanded starters; 82-56 on grass; 15-9 on turf; 28-22 in daytime; 69-43 at night; 26-19 in one-run games; 7-7 in extra-inning games; 1-0-1 in doubleheaders.

Team record past five years: 471-319 (.596, ranks 2nd in league in that span).

TEAM LEADERS

Batting average: Manny Ramirez (.333).
At-bats: Omar Vizquel (574).
Runs: Roberto Alomar (138).
Hits: Omar Vizquel (191).
Total bases: Manny Ramirez (346).
Doubles: Roberto Alomar (40).
Triples: Richie Sexson (7).
Home runs: Manny Ramirez (44).
Runs batted in: Manny Ramirez (165).
Stolen bases: Omar Vizquel (42).
Slugging percentage: Manny Ramirez (.663).
On-base percentage: Manny Ramirez (.442).
Wins: Bartolo Colon (18).
Earned-run average: Bartolo Colon (3.95).
Complete games: Dave Burba, Bartolo Colon, Charles Nagy (1).
Shutouts: Bartolo Colon (1).
Saves: Mike Jackson (39).
Innings pitched: Dave Burba (220.0).
Strikeouts: Dave Burba (174).

Date	Opp.	Res.	Score	(inn.*)	Hits	Opp. hits	Winning pitcher	Losing pitcher	Save	Record	Pos.	GB
7-1	Min.	W	7-5		9	12	Colon	Carrasco	Jackson	51-26	1st	+12.5
7-2	K.C.	L	7-9	(10)	8	12	Whisenant	Shuey		51-27	1st	+12.5
7-3†	K.C.	W	9-8		11	10	Candiotti	Pisciotta	Jackson	52-27		
7-3‡	K.C.	W	9-5		10	10	Langston	Wengert	Jackson	53-27	1st	+13.0
7-4	K.C.	L	9-10		12	13	Appier	Burba	Byrdak	53-28	1st	+13.0
7-6	At Min.	W	3-1		8	6	Wright	Milton	Jackson	54-28	1st	+14.0
7-7	At Min.	L	3-4		8	6	Trombley	Reed		54-29	1st	+13.0
7-8	At Min.	W	9-2		16	10	Nagy	Lincoln		55-29	1st	+13.0
7-9	Cin.	L	2-3		4	5	Avery	Burba	Williamson	55-30	1st	+12.0
7-10	Cin.	W	11-10		15	10	Jackson	Williamson		56-30	1st	+13.0
7-11	Cin.	L	4-9		9	14	Graves	Shuey		56-31	1st	+13.0
7-15	At Pit.	W	2-0		7	3	Colon	Schmidt	Jackson	57-31	1st	+14.0
7-16	At Pit.	L	3-11		12	13	Cordova	Burba		57-32	1st	+13.0
7-17	At Pit.	L	10-13		16	16	Benson	Nagy	Williams	57-33	1st	+13.0
7-18	At Hou.	L	0-2		4	4	Hampton	Wright		57-34	1st	+13.0
7-19	At Hou.	L	2-3	(11)	6	4	Cabrera	Candiotti		57-35	1st	+12.0
7-20	At Hou.	W	7-1		12	6	Colon	Reynolds		58-35	1st	+13.0
7-21	Tor.	L	3-4		8	6	Frascatore	Jackson	Koch	58-36	1st	+12.0
7-22	Tor.	L	3-4		10	7	Wells	Nagy	Koch	58-37	1st	+12.0
7-23	At N.Y.	L	8-9	(10)	10	13	Grimsley	Jackson		58-38	1st	+12.0
7-24	At N.Y.	L	1-21		9	21	Irabu	Langston		58-39	1st	+11.0
7-25	At N.Y.	L	1-2		6	6	Mendoza	Rincon		58-40	1st	+11.0
7-26	Det.	W	6-3		12	10	Burba	Thompson	Jackson	59-40	1st	+12.0
7-27	Det.	W	14-5		19	9	Nagy	Borkowski		60-40	1st	+13.0
7-28	Det.	W	7-2		11	5	Gooden	Moehler		61-40	1st	+13.0
7-30	Chi.	W	10-2		17	6	Colon	Sirotka		62-40	1st	+13.5
7-31	Chi.	W	13-10		13	18	Shuey	Castillo	Jackson	63-40	1st	+14.5
8-1	Chi.	L	3-6		6	11	Baldwin	Nagy	Howry	63-41	1st	+13.5
8-2	At Bos.	W	7-5		8	10	Karsay	Garces	Jackson	64-41	1st	+13.5
8-3	At Bos.	W	5-4		6	7	Shuey	Wakefield	Jackson	65-41	1st	+13.5
8-4	At Bos.	L	2-7		10	10	Portugal	Colon		65-42	1st	+13.0
8-6	At T.B.	L	2-4		7	7	Yan	Burba	Hernandez	65-43	1st	+13.5
8-7	At T.B.	W	15-10		19	14	Nagy	Witt		66-43	1st	+14.5
8-8	At T.B.	L	3-5		6	11	Alvarez	Wright	Hernandez	66-44	1st	+14.5
8-9	At Ana.	W	4-0		9	7	Colon	Hill		67-44	1st	+15.5
8-10	At Ana.	W	2-1	(10)	7	4	Rincon	Petkovsek	Jackson	68-44	1st	+16.5
8-11	At Ana.	W	4-3		10	10	Burba	Sparks	Jackson	69-44	1st	+17.5
8-13	Bal.	W	6-3		8	9	Rincon	Erickson	Jackson	70-44	1st	+17.0
8-14	Bal.	W	7-1		6	4	Karsay	Johnson		71-44	1st	+17.0
8-15	Bal.	W	5-1		13	5	Colon	Ponson		72-44	1st	+18.0
8-16	Tex.	L	5-13		10	16	Munoz	Rincon		72-45	1st	+17.0
8-17	Tex.	L	4-15		9	19	Sele	Langston		72-46	1st	+16.0
8-18	Tex.	L	1-6		7	9	Burkett	Nagy		72-47	1st	+15.0
8-19	Tex.	W	8-0		11	7	Karsay	Morgan		73-47	1st	+16.0
8-20	At Sea.	W	7-4		8	9	Colon	Halama	Jackson	74-47	1st	+16.5
8-21	At Sea.	W	6-0		9	6	Burba	Meche		75-47	1st	+16.0
8-22	At Sea.	W	7-4	(10)	11	7	Riske	Mesa	Jackson	76-47	1st	+17.0
8-23	At Sea.	L	1-4		5	6	Abbott	Nagy	Mesa	76-48	1st	+16.0
8-24	At Oak.	L	10-11		8	12	Mathews	Shuey		76-49	1st	+16.0
8-25	At Oak.	W	12-4		15	6	Colon	Oquist		77-49	1st	+16.0
8-27	T.B.	W	2-1		9	6	Burba	Arrojo	Jackson	78-49	1st	+17.5
8-28	T.B.	W	3-0		7	4	Nagy	Witt	Jackson	79-49	1st	+18.5
8-29	T.B.	L	4-6		10	11	Alvarez	Haney	Hernandez	79-50	1st	+17.5
8-30	Ana.	W	7-5		7	7	Colon	Levine	Jackson	80-50	1st	+19.0
8-31	Ana.	W	14-12		19	14	Poole	Percival	Shuey	81-50	1st	+20.0
9-1	Ana.	W	8-1		12	8	Burba	Washburn		82-50	1st	+21.0
9-2	Ana.	W	6-5		10	11	Nagy	Sparks	Jackson	83-50	1st	+21.5
9-3	At Bal.	W	7-6		9	10	Assenmacher	Reyes	Jackson	84-50	1st	+22.5
9-4	At Bal.	L	1-3		6	9	Linton	Colon	Timlin	84-51	1st	+21.5
9-5	At Bal.	W	15-7		12	11	Brower	Ponson		85-51	1st	+22.0
9-6	At Bal.	W	7-6		8	9	Burba	Johns	Jackson	86-51	1st	+23.5
9-7	At Tex.	L	3-4		6	10	Sele	Reed	Wetteland	86-52	1st	+23.5
9-8	At Tex.	L	0-3		8	7	Burkett	Haney	Wetteland	86-53	1st	+23.5
9-10	At Chi.	W	14-6		14	5	Colon	Wells		87-53	1st	+24.5
9-11	At Chi.	W	4-3		10	7	Burba	Parque	Jackson	88-53	1st	+25.5
9-12	At Chi.	L	3-4		11	12	Sirotka	Wright	Howry	88-54	1st	+24.5
9-13	Bos.	W	11-7		12	10	Nagy	Wakefield	Shuey	89-54	1st	+25.5
9-14	Bos.	L	3-12		4	16	Lowe	Gooden		89-55	1st	+25.5
9-15	Bos.	L	4-6	(13)	12	10	Wasdin	Brower		89-56	1st	+24.5
9-16	N.Y.	L	5-9		10	12	Irabu	Burba		89-57	1st	+24.0
9-17	N.Y.	L	4-9		5	9	Clemens	Wright		89-58	1st	+23.0
9-18	N.Y.	W	5-4		8	12	Nagy	Hernandez	Jackson	90-58	1st	+23.0
9-19	N.Y.	L	7-11		9	18	Watson	Martin		90-59	1st	+22.0
9-20	At Det.	L	3-4	(10)	9	9	Jones	Riske		90-60	1st	+21.5
9-21	At Det.	W	6-1		8	4	Burba	Borkowski		91-60	1st	+22.5
9-22	At Det.	W	9-1		16	2	Wright	Moehler		92-60	1st	+23.5
9-23	At Det.	L	5-7		6	11	Blair	Nagy	Jones	92-61	1st	+23.5
9-24	At Tor.	W	18-4		15	9	Brower	Munro		93-61	1st	+24.5
9-25	At Tor.	W	9-6		13	9	Colon	Spoljaric	Jackson	94-61	1st	+24.5
9-26	At Tor.	W	11-7		14	9	Shuey	Koch		95-61	1st	+24.5
9-28	At K.C.	W	2-1		8	3	Brower	Witasick	Jackson	96-61	1st	+24.5
9-29	At K.C.	L	2-5		4	9	Rosado	Nagy		96-62	1st	+24.0
9-30	Tor.	W	9-2		8	9	Colon	Spoljaric		97-62	1st	+24.0
10-1	Tor.	L	6-8		11	12	Quantrill	Karsay	Koch	97-63	1st	+23.0
10-2	Tor.	L	3-7		8	14	Hentgen	Wright	Koch	97-64	1st	+22.0
10-3	Tor.	L	2-9		10	9	Wells	Burba		97-65	1st	+21.5

Monthly records: April (16-6), May (17-10), June (17-10), July (13-14), August (18-10), September (16-12), October (0-3).
*Innings, if other than nine. † First game of a doubleheader. ‡ Second game of a doubleheader.

MEMORABLE GAMES

May 7 at Cleveland

How does a team go from being eight runs down in the sixth inning to winning by nine runs? The Indians did it in their 20-11 win over Tampa Bay. Cleveland trailed 10-2, but scored four in the sixth and seven in both the seventh and eighth. The Indians pounded out 16 hits in the final three innings.

Tampa Bay	AB	R	H	RBI	Cleveland	AB	R	H	RBI
McCracken, cf	6	1	1	0	Lofton, cf	4	2	1	0
D.Martinez, rf	4	2	1	0	E.Wilson, ss	5	2	3	1
Perry, 3b	5	3	3	2	Alomar, 2b	5	2	3	5
McGriff, 1b	3	3	2	3	M.Ramirez, rf	4	3	3	2
Flaherty, c	5	1	2	1	Fryman, 3b	6	2	2	3
Sorrento, lf	5	0	2	3	W.Cordero, dh	6	3	3	2
Clyburn, dh	4	0	1	0	Justice, lf	4	4	4	5
Lamb, 2b	5	0	0	0	Alomar Jr., c	6	2	2	1
Stocker, ss	5	1	1	0	Sexson, 1b	4	0	0	0
Totals	**42**	**11**	**13**	**9**	**Totals**	**44**	**20**	**21**	**19**

Tampa Bay ....0 1 3 5 0 1 1 0 0— 11
Cleveland ....0 0 1 1 0 4 7 7 x— 20

E—Flaherty (1), Lamb 2 (2), M.Ramirez 2 (2), E.Wilson (3). DP—Tampa Bay 1. LOB—Tampa Bay 10, Cleveland 9. 2B—D.Martinez (7), Perry (1), McGriff (7), Flaherty (6), Sorrento (4), E.Wilson (4), Alomar Jr. (8). 3B—Alomar (2). HR—McGriff (11), Alomar (5), Fryman (6), W.Cordero (3), Justice 2 (5). SB—McCracken (6), Stocker (6). CS—Alomar (1). Reached, catcher's interference—Lofton by Flaherty.

Tampa Bay	IP	H	R	ER	BB	SO
B.Witt	5.1	9	6	6	2	3
Ri.White	1	4	4	4	1	1
Aldred	0	0	1	1	0	0
Mecir (BS 2; L 0-1)	0.2	2	2	1	2	1
Gaillard	0.2	5	7	0	2	1
Rekar	0.1	1	0	0	0	1

Cleveland	IP	H	R	ER	BB	SO
Gooden	3.2	8	7	4	1	5
P.Wagner (W, 1-0)	3.1	5	4	2	2	0
S.Reed (H, 6)	1	0	0	0	0	0
DeLucia	1	0	0	0	1	1

HBP—Perry by P.Wagner, Clyburn by P.Wagner, Justice by Aldred. WP—Gooden. U—HP, Clark. 1B, Young. 2B, Tschida. 3B, Reed. T—4:00. A—40,601.

August 31 at Cleveland

Trailing Anaheim 12-4 in the eighth inning, the Indians exploded for 10 runs and stunned the Angels, 14-12. Eight of the runs came with two outs. Richie Sexson's three-run homer off closer Troy Percival put the Indians ahead for good. Percival then hit the next batter, David Justice, in the ribs with a fastball that started a brawl and led to the ejection of both players. The Indians became the first team in history to rally from an eight-run deficit three times in one season.

Anaheim	AB	R	H	RBI	Cleveland	AB	R	H	RBI
O.Palmeiro, lf	6	2	3	2	D.Roberts, cf	5	0	1	0
Durrington, 2b	3	1	1	0	Vizquel, ss-rf	5	2	1	1
T.Greene, ph	1	0	0	0	Alomar, 2b	5	2	3	2
G.Anderson, cf	4	1	2	2	M.Ramirez, rf	3	0	1	2
M.Vaughn, dh	5	1	2	2	A.Ramirez, ph	1	1	1	0
Salmon, rf	2	2	1	2	Baines, ph	1	0	1	2
Erstad, 1b	4	1	1	0	Baerga, pr-3b	0	1	0	0
Glaus, 3b	4	3	2	4	Thome, dh-1b	4	4	3	1
B.Molina, c	2	1	1	0	Sexson, 1b-lf	5	2	4	5
Huson, ph	1	0	0	0	Justice, lf	3	1	1	1
DiSarcina, ss	3	0	0	0	Nagy, pr	0	0	0	0
Edmonds, ph	1	0	1	0	Shuey, p	0	0	0	0
					E.Wlsn, 3b-ss	5	1	2	0
					Ei.Diaz, c	4	0	1	0
Totals	**36**	**12**	**14**	**12**	**Totals**	**41**	**14**	**19**	**14**

Anaheim..1 0 0 2 0 2 2 5 0— 12
Cleveland ....0 1 2 0 0 1 0 (10) x— 14

E—DiSarcina (13), Durrington (2). DP—Anaheim 2, Cleveland 1. LOB—Anaheim 8, Cleveland 6. 2B—O.Palmeiro (12), M.Vaughn (14), Alomar (36), Thome (23), Ei.Diaz (17). HR—Salmon (11), Glaus 2 (24), Thome (26), Sexson (25). SB—Alomar (31), Sexson (3). CS—B.Molina (1), D.Roberts (3). S—Durrington, Erstad, DiSarcina.

Anaheim	IP	H	R	ER	BB	SO
C.Finley	7	10	4	1	1	6
Petkovsek	0	5	5	5	0	0
Hasegawa	0.2	1	1	1	0	0
Percival (BS 6; L 3-4)	0	3	4	4	1	0
Pote	0.1	0	0	0	0	0

Cleveland	IP	H	R	ER	BB	SO
Gooden	5	5	3	3	2	2
S.Reed	1	2	2	2	1	1
Assenmacher	1	2	2	2	0	0
DePaula	0.1	1	4	4	3	0
Poole (W, 1-0)	0.2	2	1	1	1	0
Shuey (S, 5)	1	2	0	0	0	2

HBP—B.Molina by Gooden, Justice by Percival. WP—Percival. U—HP, Cooper. 1B-Cederstrom. 2B, Barrett. 3B, McClelland. T—3:49. A—43,284.

INDIVIDUAL STATISTICS

BATTING

Name	G	TPA	AB	R	H	TB	2B	3B	HR	RBI	Avg.	Obp.	Slg.	SH	SF	HP	BB	IBB	SO	SB	CS	GDP	vs RHP AB	vs RHP Avg.	vs RHP HR	vs RHP RBI	vs LHP AB	vs LHP Avg.	vs LHP HR	vs LHP RBI
Vizquel, Omar	144	664	574	112	191	250	36	4	5	66	.333	.397	.436	17	7	1	65	0	50	42	9	8	427	.333	4	51	147	.333	1	15
Alomar, Roberto	159	694	563	138	182	300	40	3	24	120	.323	.422	.533	12	13	7	99	3	96	37	6	13	418	.318	18	99	145	.338	6	21
Ramirez, Manny	147	640	522	131	174	346	34	3	44	165	.333	.442	.663	0	9	13	96	9	131	2	4	12	407	.319	36	127	115	.383	8	38
Thome, Jim	146	629	494	101	137	267	27	2	33	108	.277	.426	.540	0	4	4	127	13	171	0	0	6	360	.292	27	79	134	.239	6	29
Sexson, Richie	134	525	479	72	122	246	17	7	31	116	.255	.305	.514	0	8	4	34	0	117	3	3	19	342	.246	20	81	137	.277	11	35
Lofton, Kenny	120	561	465	110	140	201	28	6	7	39	.301	.405	.432	5	5	6	79	2	84	25	6	6	349	.327	7	34	116	.224	0	5
Justice, David	133	530	429	75	123	204	18	0	21	88	.287	.413	.476	0	5	2	94	11	90	1	3	14	328	.299	16	69	101	.248	5	19
Diaz, Einar	119	427	392	43	110	142	21	1	3	32	.281	.328	.362	6	1	5	23	0	41	11	4	10	298	.302	1	25	94	.213	2	7
Wilson, Enrique	113	368	332	41	87	117	22	1	2	24	.262	.310	.352	4	6	1	25	1	41	5	4	12	222	.266	1	19	110	.255	1	5
Fryman, Travis	85	350	322	45	82	132	16	2	10	48	.255	.309	.410	0	2	1	25	1	57	2	1	13	256	.250	8	35	66	.273	2	13
Cordero, Wil	54	217	194	35	58	97	15	0	8	32	.299	.364	.500	0	2	6	15	0	37	2	0	7	139	.317	6	26	55	.255	2	6
Roberts, David	41	156	143	26	34	44	4	0	2	12	.238	.281	.308	3	1	0	9	0	16	11	3	0	107	.243	2	11	36	.222	0	1
Alomar Jr., Sandy	37	144	137	19	42	73	13	0	6	25	.307	.322	.533	1	2	0	4	0	23	0	1	1	103	.291	4	18	34	.353	2	7
Ramirez, Alex	48	102	97	11	29	46	6	1	3	18	.299	.327	.474	1	0	1	3	0	26	1	1	1	48	.313	1	8	49	.286	2	10
Cruz, Jacob	32	96	88	14	29	45	5	1	3	17	.330	.368	.511	1	1	1	5	0	13	0	2	4	75	.280	2	12	13	.615	1	5
Baines, Harold	28	96	85	5	23	28	2	0	1	22	.271	.354	.329	0	0	0	11	0	10	0	0	2	80	.275	1	20	5	.200	0	2
Baerga, Carlos	22	63	57	4	13	16	0	0	1	5	.228	.274	.281	1	1	0	4	1	10	1	1	3	40	.250	1	4	17	.176	0	1
Branyan, Russ	11	42	38	4	8	13	2	0	1	6	.211	.286	.342	0	0	1	3	0	19	0	0	0	33	.242	1	6	5	.000	0	0
Cabrera, Jolbert	30	39	37	6	7	8	1	0	0	0	.189	.231	.216	0	0	1	1	0	8	3	0	1	13	.154	0	0	24	.208	0	0
Houston, Tyler	13	30	27	2	4	8	1	0	1	3	.148	.233	.296	0	0	0	3	0	11	0	0	0	24	.125	1	3	3	.333	0	0
Levis, Jesse	10	29	26	0	4	4	0	0	0	3	.154	.214	.154	1	0	1	1	0	6	0	0	1	23	.130	0	2	3	.333	0	1
Manto, Jeff	12	37	25	5	5	8	0	0	1	2	.200	.444	.320	1	0	0	11	0	11	0	0	0	20	.200	1	2	5	.200	0	0
Whiten, Mark	8	28	25	2	4	8	1	0	1	4	.160	.250	.320	0	0	0	3	0	4	0	0	1	17	.176	1	4	8	.125	0	0
McDonald, John	18	21	21	2	7	7	0	0	0	0	.333	.333	.333	0	0	0	0	0	3	0	1	2	14	.357	0	0	7	.286	0	0
Turner, Chris	12	22	21	3	4	4	0	0	0	0	.190	.227	.190	0	0	0	1	0	8	1	0	0	11	.273	0	0	10	.100	0	0
Borders, Pat	6	20	20	2	6	8	0	1	0	3	.300	.300	.400	0	0	0	0	0	3	0	1	0	15	.200	0	0	5	.600	0	3
Colon, Bartolo	32	8	7	0	1	1	0	0	0	0	.143	.143	.143	1	0	0	0	0	5	0	0	0	5	.200	0	0	2	.000	0	0
Nagy, Charles	34	6	6	0	0	0	0	0	0	0	.000	.000	.000	0	0	0	0	0	5	0	0	0	4	.000	0	0	2	.000	0	0
Burba, Dave	34	4	3	0	1	1	0	0	0	0	.333	.500	.333	0	0	0	1	0	0	0	0	0	2	.500	0	0	1	.000	0	0
Gooden, Dwight	26	3	2	1	1	4	0	0	1	2	.500	.667	2.000	0	0	0	1	0	1	0	0	0	2	.500	1	2	0	.000	0	0
Langston, Mark	25	2	2	0	1	1	0	0	0	0	.500	.500	.500	0	0	0	0	0	1	0	0	0	2	.500	0	0	0	.000	0	0
Wright, Jaret	26	1	1	0	0	0	0	0	0	0	.000	.000	.000	0	0	0	0	0	1	0	0	0	0	.000	0	0	1	.000	0	0
Candiotti, Tom	7	0	0	0	0	0	0	0	0	0	.000	.000	.000	0	0	0	0	0	0	0	0	0	0	.000	0	0	0	.000	0	0
Assenmacher, Paul	55	0	0	0	0	0	0	0	0	0	.000	.000	.000	0	0	0	0	0	0	0	0	0	0	.000	0	0	0	.000	0	0
Jackson, Mike	72	0	0	0	0	0	0	0	0	0	.000	.000	.000	0	0	0	0	0	0	0	0	0	0	.000	0	0	0	.000	0	0
Reed, Steve	63	0	0	0	0	0	0	0	0	0	.000	.000	.000	0	0	0	0	0	0	0	0	0	0	.000	0	0	0	.000	0	0
Karsay, Steve	50	0	0	0	0	0	0	0	0	0	.000	.000	.000	0	0	0	0	0	0	0	0	0	0	.000	0	0	0	.000	0	0
Shuey, Paul	72	0	0	0	0	0	0	0	0	0	.000	.000	.000	0	0	0	0	0	0	0	0	0	0	.000	0	0	0	.000	0	0
Rincon, Ricky	59	0	0	0	0	0	0	0	0	0	.000	.000	.000	0	0	0	0	0	0	0	0	0	0	.000	0	0	0	.000	0	0

Players with more than one A.L. team

Name	G	TPA	AB	R	H	TB	2B	3B	HR	RBI	Avg.	Obp.	Slg.	SH	SF	HP	BB	IBB	SO	SB	CS	GDP	vs RHP AB	vs RHP Avg.	vs RHP HR	vs RHP RBI	vs LHP AB	vs LHP Avg.	vs LHP HR	vs LHP RBI
Baines, Bal.	107	390	345	57	111	201	16	1	24	81	.322	.395	.583	0	2	0	43	3	38	1	2	14	80	.275	1	20	5	.200	0	2
Baines, Bal.-Cle.	135	486	430	62	134	229	18	1	25	103	.312	.387	.533	0	2	0	54	3	48	1	2	16	377	.313	22	86	53	.302	3	17
Borders, Tor.	6	15	14	1	3	6	0	0	1	3	.214	.267	.429	0	0	0	1	0	2	0	0	0	15	.200	0	0	5	.600	0	3
Borders, Cle.-Tor.	12	35	34	3	9	14	0	1	1	6	.265	.286	.412	0	0	0	1	0	5	0	1	0	15	.200	0	0	19	.316	1	6
Manto, N.Y.	6	10	8	0	1	1	0	0	0	0	.125	.300	.125	0	0	0	2	0	4	0	0	0	20	.200	1	2	5	.200	0	0
Manto, Cle.-N.Y.	18	47	33	5	6	9	0	0	1	2	.182	.413	.273	1	0	0	13	0	15	0	0	0	23	.217	1	2	10	.100	0	0

PITCHING

Name	W	L	Pct.	ERA	IP	H	R	ER	HR	SH	SF	HB	BB	IBB	SO	G	GS	CG	ShO	GF	Sv	vs. RH AB	vs. RH Avg.	vs. RH HR	vs. RH RBI	vs. LH AB	vs. LH Avg.	vs. LH HR	vs. LH RBI
Burba, Dave	15	9	.625	4.25	220.0	211	113	104	30	2	3	8	96	3	174	34	34	1	0	0	0	452	.279	17	67	379	.224	13	36
Colon, Bartolo	18	5	.783	3.95	205.0	185	97	90	24	5	4	7	76	5	161	32	32	1	1	0	0	398	.229	10	39	368	.255	14	46
Nagy, Charles	17	11	.607	4.95	202.0	238	120	111	26	5	4	6	59	4	126	33	32	1	0	0	0	411	.263	15	50	402	.323	11	61
Wright, Jaret	8	10	.444	6.06	133.2	144	99	90	18	3	3	7	77	1	91	26	26	0	0	0	0	264	.261	8	37	255	.294	10	44
Gooden, Dwight	3	4	.429	6.26	115.0	127	90	80	18	1	4	9	67	3	88	26	22	0	0	0	0	238	.277	8	42	213	.286	10	32
Shuey, Paul	8	5	.615	3.53	81.2	68	37	32	8	4	1	1	40	7	103	72	0	0	0	28	6	166	.223	5	22	139	.223	3	20
Karsay, Steve	10	2	.833	2.97	78.2	71	29	26	6	2	3	2	30	3	68	50	3	0	0	13	1	153	.281	4	23	134	.209	2	11
Jackson, Mike	3	4	.429	4.06	68.2	60	32	31	11	2	2	2	26	1	55	72	0	0	0	65	39	129	.225	9	27	130	.238	2	6
Reed, Steve	3	2	.600	4.23	61.2	69	33	29	10	4	5	3	20	5	44	63	0	0	0	15	0	155	.297	3	29	87	.264	7	19
Langston, Mark	1	2	.333	5.25	61.2	69	40	36	9	3	2	0	29	6	43	25	5	0	0	2	0	169	.302	5	26	71	.254	4	16
Rincon, Ricky	2	3	.400	4.43	44.2	41	22	22	6	2	1	1	24	5	30	59	0	0	0	14	0	92	.261	3	9	73	.233	3	11
Haney, Chris	0	2	.000	4.69	40.1	43	22	21	3	0	0	3	16	0	22	13	4	0	0	1	0	121	.264	1	13	38	.289	2	10
Assenmacher, Paul	2	1	.667	8.18	33.0	50	32	30	6	1	2	1	17	5	29	55	0	0	0	8	0	78	.449	3	21	66	.227	3	11
Brower, Jim	3	1	.750	4.56	25.2	27	13	13	8	1	1	1	10	1	18	9	2	0	0	1	0	58	.259	4	7	42	.286	4	7
Candiotti, Tom	1	1	.500	11.05	14.2	19	18	18	3	2	0	1	7	0	11	7	2	0	0	1	0	39	.282	1	9	23	.348	2	8
Riske, David	1	1	.500	8.36	14.0	20	15	13	2	1	1	0	6	0	16	12	0	0	0	3	0	41	.341	2	10	19	.316	0	5
De Paula, Sean	0	0	.000	4.63	11.2	8	6	6	0	2	0	0	3	0	18	11	0	0	0	4	0	21	.238	0	0	19	.158	0	4
DeLucia, Rich	0	1	.000	6.75	9.1	13	7	7	4	0	0	0	9	2	7	6	0	0	0	2	0	21	.238	2	4	20	.400	2	5
Martin, Tom	0	1	.000	8.68	9.1	13	9	9	2	0	1	0	3	1	8	6	0	0	0	0	0	26	.346	2	7	14	.286	0	2
Stevens, Dave	0	0	.000	10.00	9.0	10	10	10	1	0	1	0	8	1	6	5	0	0	0	0	0	18	.278	0	4	17	.294	1	4
Wagner, Paul	1	0	1.000	4.15	4.1	5	4	2	0	0	0	2	3	0	0	3	0	0	0	1	0	6	.167	0	0	13	.308	0	4
Spradlin, Jerry	0	0	.000	18.00	3.0	6	6	6	1	0	0	0	3	0	2	4	0	0	0	1	0	9	.333	0	0	6	.500	1	6
Rakers, Jason	0	0	.000	4.50	2.0	2	1	1	1	0	0	0	1	0	0	1	0	0	0	0	0	3	.333	0	0	5	.200	1	1
Poole, Jim	1	0	1.000	18.00	1.0	2	2	2	0	0	1	0	3	1	0	3	0	0	0	0	0	0	.000	0	0	3	.667	0	4
Tam, Jeff	0	0	.000	81.00	0.1	2	3	3	0	1	0	0	1	1	0	1	0	0	0	0	0	1	1.000	0	0	1	1.000	0	0

PITCHERS WITH MORE THAN ONE A.L. TEAM

Name	W	L	Pct.	ERA	IP	H	R	ER	HR	SH	SF	HB	BB	IBB	SO	G	GS	CG	ShO	GF	Sv	vs. RH AB	vs. RH Avg.	vs. RH HR	vs. RH RBI	vs. LH AB	vs. LH Avg.	vs. LH HR	vs. LH RBI
Candiotti, Oak.	3	5	.375	6.35	56.2	67	46	40	11	0	4	2	23	0	30	11	11	0	0	0	0	39	.282	1	9	23	.348	2	8
Candiotti, Oak.-Cle.	4	6	.400	7.32	71.1	86	64	58	14	2	4	3	30	0	41	18	13	0	0	4	0	164	.341	10	38	123	.244	4	17

DESIGNATED HITTERS

Name	AB	Avg.	HR	RBI	Name	AB	Avg.	HR	RBI	Name	AB	Avg.	HR	RBI
Justice, David	121	.240	7	25	Ramirez, Alex	50	.260	1	6	Cruz, Jacob	3	.333	0	0
Thome, Jim	114	.298	9	30	Branyan, Russ	12	.333	0	3	Lofton, Kenny	2	.000	0	0
Sexson, Richie	88	.205	3	17	Alomar Jr., Sandy	5	.400	0	1	Baerga, Carlos	2	.000	0	0
Baines, Harold	82	.268	1	20	Alomar, Roberto	4	.250	0	0	Wilson, Enrique	1	.000	0	0
Cordero, Wil	79	.291	3	12	Ramirez, Manny	3	1.000	0	0	Cabrera, Jolbert	0	-	0	0

INDIVIDUAL STATISTICS

FIELDING

FIRST BASEMEN
Player	Pct.	G	PO	A	E	TC	DP
Thome, Jim	.994	111	930	83	6	1019	93
Sexson, Richie	.988	61	517	51	7	575	48
Manto, Jeff	1.000	1	5	0	0	5	0

SECOND BASEMEN
Player	Pct.	G	PO	A	E	TC	DP
Alomar, Roberto	.992	156	270	466	6	742	102
Wilson, Enrique	1.000	21	16	19	0	35	2
McDonald, John	1.000	7	7	11	0	18	4
Baerga, Carlos	1.000	6	5	9	0	14	3
Cabrera, Jolbert	1.000	6	4	4	0	8	1

THIRD BASEMEN
Player	Pct.	G	PO	A	E	TC	DP
Fryman, Travis	.969	85	41	146	6	193	12
Wilson, Enrique	.965	61	24	86	4	114	2
Baerga, Carlos	.964	15	8	19	1	28	1
Manto, Jeff	1.000	10	7	16	0	23	2
Houston, Tyler	1.000	10	3	11	0	14	1
Branyan, Russ	.960	8	6	18	1	25	0
Borders, Pat	-	1	0	0	0	0	0

SHORTSTOPS
Player	Pct.	G	PO	A	E	TC	DP
Vizquel, Omar	.976	143	221	396	15	632	88
Wilson, Enrique	.960	35	37	58	4	99	21
McDonald, John	.917	6	1	10	1	12	1

OUTFIELDERS
Player	Pct.	G	PO	A	E	TC	DP
Ramirez, Manny	.975	145	267	7	7	281	2
Lofton, Kenny	.989	119	255	11	3	269	3
Justice, David	.977	93	161	7	4	172	3
Sexson, Richie	1.000	49	66	3	0	69	0
Roberts, David	1.000	39	87	0	0	87	0
Cordero, Wil	.981	29	51	0	1	52	0
Ramirez, Alex	.920	29	22	1	2	25	0
Cruz, Jacob	1.000	24	48	0	0	48	0
Cabrera, Jolbert	.957	16	22	0	1	23	0
Whiten, Mark	1.000	7	11	1	0	12	0
Vizquel, Omar	-	1	0	0	0	0	0

CATCHERS
Player	Pct.	G	PO	A	E	TC	DP	PB
Diaz, Einar	.988	119	751	81	10	842	8	5
Alomar Jr., Sandy	.974	35	257	10	7	274	2	1
Turner, Chris	.964	12	50	3	2	55	0	0
Levis, Jesse	1.000	9	53	3	0	56	0	0
Borders, Pat	.943	5	32	1	2	35	0	2
Houston, Tyler	1.000	1	4	0	0	4	0	0

PITCHERS
Player	Pct.	G	PO	A	E	TC	DP
Jackson, Mike	.947	72	2	16	1	19	1
Shuey, Paul	1.000	72	3	10	0	13	1
Reed, Steve	.933	63	4	10	1	15	0
Rincon, Ricky	1.000	59	1	10	0	11	1
Assenmacher, Paul	1.000	55	1	4	0	5	1
Karsay, Steve	.857	50	8	10	3	21	1
Burba, Dave	.980	34	20	29	1	50	4
Nagy, Charles	.982	33	21	33	1	55	3
Colon, Bartolo	.962	32	20	31	2	53	4
Wright, Jaret	.903	26	13	15	3	31	0
Gooden, Dwight	1.000	26	5	16	0	21	1
Langston, Mark	.882	25	7	8	2	17	1
Haney, Chris	.875	13	4	3	1	8	1
Riske, David	.750	12	1	2	1	4	0
De Paula, Sean	1.000	11	0	2	0	2	0
Brower, Jim	1.000	9	1	2	0	3	0
Candiotti, Tom	1.000	7	0	5	0	5	0
DeLucia, Rich	-	6	0	0	0	0	0
Martin, Tom	-	6	0	0	0	0	0
Stevens, Dave	1.000	5	0	1	0	1	0
Spradlin, Jerry	-	4	0	0	0	0	0
Wagner, Paul	1.000	3	1	0	0	1	0
Poole, Jim	-	3	0	0	0	0	0
Tam, Jeff	1.000	1	0	1	0	1	0
Rakers, Jason	-	1	0	0	0	0	0

PITCHING AGAINST EACH CLUB

Pitcher	Ana. W-L	Bal. W-L	Bos. W-L	Chi. W-L	Det. W-L	K.C. W-L	Min. W-L	N.Y. W-L	Oak. W-L	Sea. W-L	T.B. W-L	Tex. W-L	Tor. W-L	N.L. W-L	Total W-L
Assenmacher, Paul	0-0	2-0	0-0	0-0	0-0	0-0	0-0	0-0	0-0	0-0	0-0	0-0	0-0	0-1	2-1
Brower, Jim	0-0	1-0	0-1	0-0	0-0	1-0	0-0	0-0	0-0	0-0	0-0	0-0	1-0	0-0	3-1
Burba, Dave	3-0	2-0	0-0	2-0	3-0	0-1	0-0	0-2	1-0	2-1	1-1	0-0	0-2	1-2	15-9
Candiotti, Tom	0-0	0-0	0-0	0-0	0-0	1-0	0-0	0-0	0-0	0-0	0-0	0-0	0-0	0-1	1-1
Colon, Bartolo	3-0	2-1	0-2	3-0	0-0	1-0	1-0	0-0	2-0	2-0	0-0	0-1	2-0	2-1	18-5
De Paula, Sean	0-0	0-0	0-0	0-0	0-0	0-0	0-0	0-0	0-0	0-0	0-0	0-0	0-0	0-0	0-0
DeLucia, Rich	0-0	0-0	0-1	0-0	0-0	0-0	0-0	0-0	0-0	0-0	0-0	0-0	0-0	0-0	0-1
Gooden, Dwight	0-0	0-0	0-2	1-0	0-0	0-0	0-0	0-0	0-0	0-0	1-0	0-1	1-1	0-0	3-4
Haney, Chris	0-0	0-0	0-0	1-0	0-0	0-0	0-0	0-1	0-0	0-0	1-0	0-1	0-1	1-1	3-4
Jackson, Mike	0-0	0-0	0-1	0-0	0-0	0-0	0-0	0-1	0-0	0-0	0-1	0-0	0-0	3-1	3-4
Karsay, Steve	0-1	1-0	2-0	1-0	1-0	0-0	1-0	0-0	1-0	1-0	1-0	0-0	1-0	0-1	10-2
Langston, Mark	0-0	0-0	0-0	0-0	1-0	0-0	0-0	0-1	0-0	0-0	0-0	0-1	0-0	0-0	1-2
Martin, Tom	0-0	0-0	0-0	0-0	0-0	0-0	0-0	0-0	0-0	0-0	0-0	0-0	0-0	0-0	0-0
Nagy, Charles	1-0	0-0	1-0	2-1	1-1	1-1	3-0	2-0	1-0	0-2	2-1	0-2	1-1	2-1	17-11
Poole, Jim	1-0	0-0	0-0	0-0	0-0	0-0	0-0	0-0	0-0	0-0	0-0	0-0	0-0	0-0	1-0
Rakers, Jason	0-0	0-0	0-0	0-0	0-0	0-0	0-0	0-0	0-0	0-0	0-0	0-0	0-0	0-0	0-0
Reed, Steve	0-0	0-0	0-0	0-0	0-0	1-0	1-1	0-0	0-0	0-0	1-1	0-0	0-0	0-0	3-2
Rincon, Ricky	1-0	1-0	0-0	0-0	0-1	0-0	0-0	0-1	0-0	0-0	0-0	0-0	0-1	0-0	2-3
Riske, David	0-0	0-0	0-0	0-0	0-0	0-0	0-0	0-0	0-0	0-0	0-0	0-0	0-0	0-0	0-0
Shuey, Paul	0-0	0-0	1-1	1-1	1-1	1-1	0-0	0-0	1-0	0-0	1-0	0-0	1-0	1-1	8-5
Spradlin, Jerry	0-0	0-0	0-0	0-0	0-0	0-0	0-0	0-0	0-0	0-0	0-0	0-0	0-0	0-0	0-0
Stevens, Dave	0-0	0-0	0-0	0-0	0-0	0-0	0-0	0-0	0-0	0-0	0-0	0-0	0-0	0-0	0-0
Tam, Jeff	0-0	0-0	0-0	0-0	0-0	0-0	0-0	0-0	0-0	0-0	0-0	0-0	0-0	0-0	0-0
Wagner, Paul	0-0	0-0	0-0	0-0	0-0	0-0	0-0	0-0	0-0	1-0	0-0	0-0	0-0	0-0	1-0
Wright, Jaret	0-0	0-0	0-1	0-1	1-2	0-0	2-1	2-1	0-1	0-0	2-0	0-1	1-1	0-1	8-10
Totals	9-1	9-1	4-8	9-3	8-5	7-5	9-3	3-7	10-2	7-3	5-4	3-7	5-7	9-9	97-65

INTERLEAGUE: Jackson 1-0, Assenmacher 0-1, Colon 0-1 vs. Brewers; Jackson 1-1, Nagy 1-0 vs. Cubs; Shuey 1-1, Burba 1-1, Jackson 1-0, Nagy 1-0 vs. Reds; Colon 1-0, Wright 0-1, Candiotti 0-1 vs. Astros; Colon 1-0, Burba 0-1, Nagy 0-1 vs. Pirates. Total: 9-9.

MISCELLANEOUS

HOME RUNS BY PARK
At Anaheim (5): Alomar 2, Ramirez 2, Vizquel 1.
At Baltimore (5): Ramirez 2, Alomar 1, Thome 1, Ramirez 1.
At Boston (8): Thome 3, Justice 1, Fryman 1, Lofton 1, Cordero 1, Sexson 1.
At Chicago (AL) (10): Justice 3, Sexson 3, Lofton 2, Ramirez 2.
At Cincinnati (6): Ramirez 2, Gooden 1, Alomar 1, Lofton 1, Sexson 1.
At Cleveland (110): Ramirez 21, Thome 19, Sexson 18, Alomar 12, Justice 11, Fryman 6, Alomar Jr. 4, Vizquel 3, Cordero 3, Cruz 3, Diaz 2, Ramirez 2, Baines 1, Baerga 1, Manto 1, Lofton 1, Wilson 1, Roberts 1.
At Detroit (8): Alomar 2, Thome 2, Justice 1, Fryman 1, Cordero 1, Ramirez 1.
At Houston (2): Alomar 1, Ramirez 1.
At Kansas City (4): Justice 1, Whiten 1, Sexson 1, Wilson 1.
At Minnesota (6): Thome 2, Ramirez 2, Cordero 1, Sexson 1.
At New York (AL) (7): Alomar 1, Fryman 1, Thome 1, Cordero 1, Ramirez 1, Sexson 1, Branyan 1.
At Oakland (12): Ramirez 5, Thome 3, Justice 2, Vizquel 1, Fryman 1.
At Pittsburgh (2): Justice 1, Thome 1.
At Seattle (5): Sexson 2, Alomar 1, Ramirez 1, Diaz 1.
At Tampa Bay (3): Alomar 1, Thome 1, Ramirez 1.
At Texas (8): Alomar 2, Lofton 2, Sexson 2, Alomar Jr. 1, Ramirez 1.
At Toronto (8): Ramirez 2, Alomar Jr. 1, Justice 1, Cordero 1, Houston 1, Sexson 1, Roberts 1.

LOW-HIT GAMES
No-hitters: None.
One-hitters: None.
Two-hitters: None.

10-STRIKEOUT GAMES
Dave Burba 3, **Total:** 3.

FOUR OR MORE HITS IN ONE GAME
Omar Vizquel 2, Kenny Lofton 2, Manny Ramirez 2, Roberto Alomar 1, David Justice 1, Jim Thome 1, Einar Diaz 1, Richie Sexson 1, **Total:** 11.

MULTI-HOMER GAMES
Manny Ramirez 4, Roberto Alomar 2, Richie Sexson 2, David Justice 1, Travis Fryman 1, Jim Thome 1, **Total:** 11.

GRAND SLAMS
5-7: Roberto Alomar (off Tampa Bay's Eddie Gaillard).
5-15: David Justice (off Detroit's Dave Mlicki).
5-18: Manny Ramirez (off Chicago's James Baldwin).
5-19: Richie Sexson (off Chicago's Bryan Ward).
5-23: Omar Vizquel (off Detroit's Todd Jones).
5-31: Jim Thome (off New York's Orlando Hernandez).
7-23: Roberto Alomar (off New York's David Cone).
8-14: Jim Thome (off Baltimore's Jason Johnson).
8-24: Jim Thome (off Oakland's Tim Hudson).
9-10: David Justice (off Chicago's Carlos Castillo).
9-24: Manny Ramirez (off Toronto's Mike Romano).
9-24: David Roberts (off Toronto's John Hudek).

PINCH HITTERS
Name	AB	Avg.	HR	RBI
(Minimum 5 at-bats)				
Wilson, Enrique	16	.313	0	1
Sexson, Richie	10	.100	0	3
Ramirez, Alex	8	.375	0	1
Cabrera, Jolbert	7	.143	0	0
Cruz, Jacob	7	.000	0	0
Justice, David	5	.400	1	2
McDonald, John	5	.400	0	0

DEBUTS
7-4: John McDonald, PH.
8-7: David Roberts, CF.
8-14: David Riske, P.
8-31: Sean De Paula, P.
9-5: Jim Brower, P.

GAMES BY POSITION
Catcher: Einar Diaz 119, Sandy Alomar Jr. 35, Chris Turner 12, Jesse Levis 9, Pat Borders 5, Tyler Houston 1.
First base: Jim Thome 111, Richie Sexson 61, Jeff Manto 1.
Second base: Roberto Alomar 156, Enrique Wilson 21, John McDonald 7, Carlos Baerga 6, Jolbert Cabrera 6.
Third base: Travis Fryman 85, Enrique Wilson 61, Carlos Baerga 15, Jeff Manto 10, Tyler Houston 10, Russ Branyan 8, Pat Borders 1.
Shortstop: Omar Vizquel 143, Enrique Wilson 35, John McDonald 6.
Outfield: Manny Ramirez 145, Kenny Lofton 119, David Justice 93, Richie Sexson 49, David Roberts 39, Wil Cordero 29, Alex Ramirez 29, Jacob Cruz 24, Jolbert Cabrera 16, Mark Whiten 7, Omar Vizquel 1.
Designated hitter: David Justice 34, Jim Thome 34, Harold Baines 25, Richie Sexson 24, Wil Cordero 23, Alex Ramirez 14, Jolbert Cabrera 5, Russ Branyan 4, Roberto Alomar 2, Manny Ramirez 2, Jacob Cruz 2, Sandy Alomar Jr. 1, Carlos Baerga 1, Kenny Lofton 1, Enrique Wilson 1.

STREAKS
Wins: 8 (October 1-April 17).
Losses: 5 (July 21-25).
Consecutive games with at least one hit: 13, Roberto Alomar (August 22-September 4), David Justice (June 10-23).
Wins by pitcher: 5, Charles Nagy (May 19-June 12), Dave Burba (August 21-September 11), Bartolo Colon (August 9-30).

ATTENDANCE
Home: 3,384,788.
Road: 2,455,211.
Highest (home): 43,399 (September 1 vs. Anaheim).
Highest (road): 54,944 (July 25 vs. New York).
Lowest (Home): 40,587 (May 11 vs. Baltimore).
Lowest (road): 7,161 (April 27 vs. Oakland).

DETROIT TIGERS

1999 REVIEW

DAY BY DAY

Date	Opp.	Res.	Score	(inn.*)	Hits	Opp. hits	Winning pitcher	Losing pitcher	Save	Record	Pos.	GB
4-5	At Tex.	W	11-5		13	5	Moehler	Helling		1-0	T1st	...
4-6	At Tex.	L	0-6		7	12	Sele	Thompson		1-1	3rd	1.0
4-7	At Tex.	L	7-10		12	18	Morgan	Blair	Wetteland	1-2	4th	1.0
4-9	At N.Y.	L	3-12	(7)	3	9	Cone	Graterol		1-3	T4th	2.0
4-10	At N.Y.	L	0-5		3	10	Clemens	Moehler		1-4	5th	3.0
4-11	At N.Y.	L	2-11		5	9	Hernandez	Thompson		1-5	5th	4.0
4-12	Min.	L	0-1	(12)	3	6	Aguilera	Runyan		1-6	5th	5.0
4-14	Min.	W	7-1		13	3	Weaver	Hawkins		2-6	5th	5.0
4-15	Min.	L	6-8		11	10	Wells	Moehler	Aguilera	2-7	5th	5.5
4-16	N.Y.	W	8-1		5	7	Thompson	Hernandez		3-7	5th	5.0
4-17	N.Y.	W	3-1		10	6	Anderson	Nelson	Jones	4-7	5th	4.5
4-18	N.Y.	W	5-1		9	6	Mlicki	Mendoza		5-7	T3rd	4.5
4-20	Bos.	L	0-1		3	5	Martinez	Weaver	Lowe	5-8	4th	5.5
4-21	Bos.	W	9-2		15	8	Moehler	Wakefield		6-8	4th	5.5
4-22	Bos.	W	1-0		3	2	Thompson	Portugal	Jones	7-8	3rd	4.5
4-23	At Chi.	L	0-5		5	9	Sirotka	Blair		7-9	3rd	5.5
4-24	At Chi.	L	1-3		6	4	Navarro	Mlicki	Howry	7-10	3rd	5.5
4-25	At Chi.	W	9-4		12	6	Weaver	Baldwin		8-10	3rd	4.5
4-26	At Sea.	W	7-0		15	7	Moehler	Moyer		9-10	3rd	4.5
4-27	At Sea.	W	5-1		10	9	Thompson	Hinchliffe		10-10	3rd	4.5
4-28	At Sea.	L	6-8		8	10	Garcia	Blair		10-11	3rd	5.5
4-29	At Sea.	L	6-22		15	19	Cloude	Nitkowski		10-12	3rd	6.5
4-30	At T.B.	W	7-5		12	7	Weaver	Arrojo	Jones	11-12	3rd	5.5
5-1	At T.B.	L	3-4		4	7	Witt	Moehler	Hernandez	11-13	3rd	6.5
5-2	At T.B.	W	8-2		12	10	Thompson	Santana		12-13	3rd	5.5
5-3	At T.B.	L	6-14		12	12	Yan	Blair		12-14	3rd	6.5
5-4	Ana.	W	3-1		9	8	Brocail	Holtz	Jones	13-14	3rd	6.0
5-5	Ana.	L	1-4		3	6	Sparks	Weaver	Percival	13-15	3rd	6.0
5-6	Ana.	W	4-2		10	7	Florie	Finley	Jones	14-15	3rd	6.0
5-7	Bal.	L	4-9		10	12	Mussina	Thompson		14-16	3rd	7.0
5-8	Bal.	W	7-6		5	8	Blair	Kamieniecki	Jones	15-16	3rd	6.0
5-9	Bal.	L	0-5		5	7	Erickson	Mlicki		15-17	4th	7.0
5-11	Oak.	L	2-6		6	10	Rigby	Weaver		15-18	4th	8.5
5-12	Oak.	L	1-2		4	4	Heredia	Thompson	Taylor	15-19	4th	9.5
5-14	Cle.	L	2-4		8	6	Karsay	Brocail	Shuey	15-20	4th	10.5
5-15	Cle.	L	7-12		10	12	Burba	Mlicki		15-21	4th	11.5
5-16	Cle.	W	9-3		10	7	Weaver	Wright	Kida	16-21	4th	10.5
5-18	At Tor.	L	5-7		9	8	Hentgen	Thompson	Koch	16-22	4th	12.0
5-19	At Tor.	W	7-3		11	6	Moehler	Wells		17-22	4th	12.0
5-20	At Tor.	L	0-7		7	14	Halladay	Mlicki		17-23	4th	12.5
5-21	At Cle.	W	9-6		11	10	Nitkowski	Shuey	Jones	18-23	4th	11.5
5-22	At Cle.	W	6-2		10	7	Weaver	Wright		19-23	4th	10.5
5-23	At Cle.	L	4-7		8	10	Shuey	Jones		19-24	4th	11.5
5-24	Tor.	L	6-12		10	8	Wells	Moehler		19-25	4th	11.5
5-25	Tor.	L	3-5		11	8	Halladay	Mlicki	Koch	19-26	4th	12.5
5-26	Tor.	L	5-9		7	12	Escobar	Blair	Lloyd	19-27	4th	13.5
5-27	Chi.	W	10-5		14	9	Weaver	Snyder		20-27	4th	13.0
5-28	Chi.	L	1-9		7	15	Navarro	Thompson		20-28	4th	13.0
5-29	Chi.	L	1-7		5	13	Baldwin	Moehler		20-29	4th	13.0
5-30	Chi.	W	3-2		11	9	Mlicki	Parque	Jones	21-29	4th	12.0
5-31	At Bos.	L	7-8		12	12	Wasdin	Anderson	Gordon	21-30	4th	13.0
6-1	At Bos.	L	4-5		12	9	Wasdin	Brocail	Lowe	21-31	4th	13.0
6-2	At Bos.	W	4-2		7	6	Thompson	Wakefield	Jones	22-31	4th	13.0
6-4	StL.	W	4-1		7	4	Moehler	Jimenez	Jones	23-31	4th	12.0
6-5	StL.	L	2-7		5	15	Bottenfield	Blair	Bottalico	23-32	4th	13.0
6-6	StL.	L	4-8		9	14	Croushore	Nitkowski	Aybar	23-33	4th	14.0
6-7	Pit.	W	9-4		10	8	Brunson	Schmidt		24-33	3rd	13.5
6-8	Pit.	W	11-4		15	7	Cruz	Ritchie		25-33	3rd	12.5
6-9	Pit.	L	3-15		10	17	Cordova	Moehler		25-34	4th	13.5
6-11	At StL.	W	8-2		7	10	Mlicki	Bottenfield		26-34	4th	13.0
6-12	At StL.	L	7-8	(14)	8	17	Radinsky	Blair		26-35	4th	14.0
6-13	At StL.	W	3-1	(10)	11	9	Jones	Bottalico	Brocail	27-35	3rd	14.0
6-14	Sea.	W	8-7		10	13	Kida	Cloude		28-35	3rd	13.5
6-15	Sea.	L	4-5		9	6	Rodriguez	Moehler	Mesa	28-36	3rd	14.5
6-16	Sea.	L	1-7		9	13	Moyer	Mlicki		28-37	3rd	15.5
6-17	Sea.	L	3-4		7	7	Garcia	Jones	Mesa	28-38	3rd	16.5
6-18	Oak.	W	8-3		10	3	Thompson	Oquist		29-38	3rd	15.5
6-19	Oak.	L	1-13		11	16	Hudson	Cruz		29-39	3rd	16.5
6-20	Oak.	L	5-6		6	8	Haynes	Moehler	Taylor	29-40	3rd	17.5
6-21	Oak.	W	13-11		12	13	Brocail	Rigby	Jones	30-40	3rd	17.5
6-22	At K.C.	L	2-4		8	9	Rosado	Florie	Service	30-41	3rd	17.5
6-23	At K.C.	L	1-10		5	15	Witasick	Thompson		30-42	4th	18.5
6-24	At K.C.	W	6-4		9	13	Cruz	Mathews	Jones	31-42	3rd	17.5
6-25	Min.	W	2-0		6	6	Moehler	Milton		32-42	3rd	16.5
6-26	Min.	L	0-1		5	6	Mays	Mlicki	Trombley	32-43	4th	16.5
6-27	Min.	L	7-12		11	17	Hawkins	Weaver		32-44	4th	17.5
6-29	At N.Y.	L	0-3		8	6	Clemens	Thompson		32-45	4th	19.0
6-30	At N.Y.	W	8-2		11	12	Moehler	Pettitte		33-45	3rd	18.0

HIGHLIGHTS

High point: The Tigers closed their 88-season run at Tiger Stadium with an 8-2 victory over the Royals on September 27. Rookie Rob Fick hit a game-clinching grand slam off the right field roof. In an emotional postgame ceremony, players from past teams ran to their old positions in uniform.

Low point: The team fell to 49-77 with a season-defining 3-2 loss in Seattle on August 25. Kimera Bartee hit an inning-opening triple in that game, but he was tagged out on a one-hopper to third baseman Russ Davis, who then threw to first for a double play.

Turning point: The club had rallied to a 15-16 mark after a 1-6 start, but a 5-0 defeat to the Orioles on May 9 began a five-game losing streak. The Tigers' slump reached 15 losses in 21 games, and they permanently fell out of contention.

Most valuable player: Catcher Brad Ausmus, the team's only All-Star Game participant, had a solid year offensively and defensively after being reacquired from Houston. He hit .275 and was one of the club's better contact hitters, even batting leadoff occasionally. Defensively, Ausmus kept opposing runners in check and drew raves from pitchers for the rapport he developed with them.

Most valuable pitcher: Righthander Dave Mlicki paid dividends after being obtained from Los Angeles, compiling a staff-high 14 victories that included wins in eight consecutive starts. He posted a 2.88 ERA during the streak and provided a much-needed anchor for a thin rotation.

Most improved player: Shortstop Deivi Cruz. Aided by a weight-transfer tip by coach Alan Trammell, Cruz emerged from the doldrums and finished at .284 with 13 homers and 58 RBIs—all career highs. Three weeks into May, Cruz was hitting .223 with no homers and three RBIs.

Most pleasant surprise: Veteran outfielder Luis Polonia, who had played the previous two years in the Mexican League. Recalled from Class AAA Toledo in late May, he provided a spark at leadoff. Polonia hit in the .400 range for several weeks and finished at .324 with a career-high 10 homers in 87 games.

Key injuries: Higginson missed a month with a toe injury. Righthander Seth Greisinger, perhaps the team's future ace, missed the entire season after surgery on his elbow. Lefthanded reliever Sean Runyan, who pitched in a club-record-tying 88 games in 1998, developed a shoulder injury and made only 12 appearances. Lefthander Justin Thompson made his last start on August 15 before going on the D.L. with shoulder and neck injuries.

Notable: The Tigers experienced their sixth consecutive losing season. ... Third baseman Dean Palmer, signed as a free agent in November 1998, put up strong numbers (38 homers, 100 RBIs). ... The club went the entire decade without a Gold Glove winner.

—REID CREAGER

MISCELLANEOUS

RECORDS

1999 regular-season record: 69-92 (3rd in A.L. Central); 38-43 at home; 31-49 on road; 21-34 vs. A.L. East; 23-25 vs. A.L. Central; 17-23 vs. A.L. West; 8-10 vs. N.L. Central; 15-14 vs. lefthanded starters; 54-78 vs. righthanded starters; 57-76 on grass; 12-16 on turf; 26-30 in daytime; 43-62 at night; 19-22 in one-run games; 5-5 in extra-inning games.

Team record past five years: 326-465 (.412, ranks 13th in league in that span).

TEAM LEADERS

Batting average: Deivi Cruz (.284).
At-bats: Dean Palmer (560).
Runs: Dean Palmer (92).
Hits: Tony Clark (150).
Total bases: Dean Palmer (290).
Doubles: Deivi Cruz (35).
Triples: Luis Polonia (8).
Home runs: Dean Palmer (38).
Runs batted in: Dean Palmer (100).
Stolen bases: Juan Encarnacion (33).
Slugging percentage: Dean Palmer (.518).
On-base percentage: Brad Ausmus (.365).
Wins: Dave Mlicki (14).
Earned-run average: Dave Mlicki (4.60).
Complete games: Dave Mlicki, Brian Moehler (2).
Shutouts: Brian Moehler (2).
Saves: Todd Jones (30).
Innings pitched: Brian Moehler (196.1).
Strikeouts: Dave Mlicki (119).

Date	Opp.	Res.	Score	(inn.*)	Hits	Opp. hits	Winning pitcher	Losing pitcher	Save	Record	Pos.	GB
7-1	At N.Y.	L	0-6		3	11	Irabu	Mlicki		33-46	3rd	19.0
7-2	At Min.	L	4-11		7	13	Hawkins	Weaver		33-47	4th	19.0
7-3	At Min.	L	2-7		5	13	Lincoln	Cruz		33-48	4th	20.5
7-4	At Min.	W	15-5		19	8	Thompson	Perkins		34-48	4th	19.5
7-6	N.Y.	L	8-9	(10)	9	17	Rivera	Jones	Mendoza	34-49	4th	20.5
7-7	N.Y.	W	6-4		12	10	Mlicki	Cone	Brocail	35-49	4th	19.5
7-8	N.Y.	L	2-3		8	9	Hernandez	Nitkowski	Rivera	35-50	4th	20.5
7-9	Mil.	L	1-4		6	9	Woodard	Cruz	Wickman	35-51	4th	20.5
7-10	Mil.	W	9-3		14	6	Thompson	Abbott		36-51	3rd	20.5
7-11	Mil.	L	2-3		9	6	Nomo	Moehler	Wickman	36-52	3rd	20.5
7-15	At Hou.	L	6-8		12	9	Miller	Blair	Wagner	36-53	3rd	21.5
7-16	At Hou.	L	1-2		4	8	Cabrera	Brocail		36-54	4th	21.5
7-17	At Hou.	L	2-3	(10)	9	10	Wagner	Jones		36-55	4th	21.5
7-18	At Cin.	W	9-8	(10)	9	11	Brocail	Graves	Jones	37-55	4th	20.5
7-19	At Cin.	W	7-6		11	10	Nitkowski	Sullivan	Jones	38-55	4th	19.5
7-20	At Cin.	L	2-5		7	8	Parris	Mlicki	Graves	38-56	4th	20.5
7-21	K.C.	W	10-5		12	11	Thompson	Appier		39-56	3rd	19.5
7-22	K.C.	W	9-8		8	15	Florie	Rosado	Jones	40-56	3rd	18.5
7-23	Bos.	W	14-5		15	8	Moehler	Ohka		41-56	3rd	17.5
7-24	Bos.	L	4-11		10	13	Portugal	Weaver	Lowe	41-57	3rd	17.5
7-25	Bos.	W	9-1		10	6	Mlicki	Rose		42-57	3rd	16.5
7-26	At Cle.	L	3-6		10	12	Burba	Thompson	Jackson	42-58	3rd	17.5
7-27	At Cle.	L	5-14		9	19	Nagy	Borkowski		42-59	T3rd	18.5
7-28	At Cle.	L	2-7		5	11	Gooden	Moehler		42-60	5th	19.5
7-30	At Tor.	L	2-8		6	10	Escobar	Weaver		42-61	5th	20.5
7-31	At Tor.	L	6-7		15	12	Halladay	Mlicki	Koch	42-62	5th	21.5
8-1	At Tor.	L	5-8		9	10	Hentgen	Borkowski	Koch	42-63	5th	21.5
8-2	Chi.	L	2-6		7	11	Wells	Moehler		42-64	5th	22.5
8-3	Chi.	L	6-9		9	15	Snyder	Thompson	Howry	42-65	5th	23.5
8-5	At Bal.	L	3-6		9	11	Ponson	Weaver	Timlin	42-66	5th	23.5
8-6	At Bal.	W	4-3		11	7	Mlicki	Mussina	Jones	43-66	5th	22.5
8-7	At Bal.	L	4-5		7	9	Erickson	Borkowski	Timlin	43-67	5th	23.5
8-8	At Bal.	W	5-2	(11)	8	10	Brocail	Kamieniecki	Jones	44-67	5th	22.5
8-10	At Tex.	L	3-4	(12)	11	8	Patterson	Cruz		44-68	5th	24.0
8-11	At Tex.	L	2-8		6	12	Helling	Blair		44-69	5th	25.0
8-12	At Tex.	W	3-1		8	5	Mlicki	Sele	Jones	45-69	5th	24.5
8-13	Ana.	W	8-7	(10)	9	10	Jones	Hasegawa		46-69	5th	24.5
8-14	Ana.	L	4-7		10	12	Magnante	Moehler	Percival	46-70	5th	25.5
8-15	Ana.	L	2-10		7	14	Finley	Thompson		46-71	5th	26.5
8-16	T.B.	L	1-9		8	13	Arrojo	Weaver		46-72	5th	26.5
8-17	T.B.	W	3-1		8	6	Mlicki	Witt	Jones	47-72	5th	25.5
8-18	T.B.	L	0-4		1	9	Alvarez	Borkowski	Lopez	47-73	5th	25.5
8-20	At Ana.	L	1-5		5	7	Finley	Moehler		47-74	5th	27.0
8-21	At Ana.	W	5-0		9	4	Weaver	Washburn		48-74	5th	27.0
8-22	At Ana.	W	12-3		17	8	Mlicki	Sparks		49-74	T4th	27.0
8-23	At Ana.	L	5-6		11	9	Percival	Brocail		49-75	T4th	27.0
8-24	At Sea.	L	0-5		6	7	Garcia	Blair		49-76	T4th	27.0
8-25	At Sea.	L	2-3		9	7	Halama	Moehler	Mesa	49-77	5th	28.0
8-27	Bal.	W	5-4		11	5	Weaver	Reyes	Jones	50-77	5th	28.0
8-28	Bal.	W	4-3		7	10	Mlicki	Erickson	Jones	51-77	4th	28.0
8-29	Bal.	L	4-11		7	13	Johnson	Nitkowski		51-78	4th	28.0
8-30	Tex.	W	1-0		10	3	Moehler	Loaiza		52-78	4th	28.0
8-31	Tex.	W	14-6		16	11	Cordero	Kolb		53-78	4th	28.0
9-1	Tex.	L	7-14		12	15	Helling	Weaver	Wetteland	53-79	4th	29.0
9-2	Tex.	W	8-7		15	13	Mlicki	Zimmerman	Jones	54-79	4th	29.0
9-3	At Oak.	L	4-7		9	9	Appier	Cruz	Isringhausen	54-80	4th	30.0
9-4	At Oak.	L	1-2		4	9	Hudson	Cordero		54-81	4th	30.0
9-5	At Oak.	W	5-4		10	8	Blair	Haynes	Jones	55-81	4th	30.0
9-6	At Oak.	W	9-7		13	13	Borkowski	Olivares	Jones	56-81	4th	30.0
9-8	At T.B.	W	5-1		10	7	Mlicki	Witt		57-81	4th	28.5
9-9	At T.B.	L	3-5		13	8	Arrojo	Nitkowski	Hernandez	57-82	4th	29.0
9-10	Tor.	W	7-6		12	12	Jones	Frascatore		58-82	T3rd	29.0
9-11	Tor.	L	5-9		11	11	Spoljaric	Cordero		58-83	4th	30.0
9-12	Tor.	L	3-5		8	10	Escobar	Weaver	Koch	58-84	4th	30.0
9-13	At Chi.	W	3-2		9	4	Mlicki	Snyder	Jones	59-84	T3rd	30.0
9-14	At Chi.	W	7-0		11	4	Nitkowski	Myette		60-84	3rd	29.0
9-15	At Chi.	L	1-3		3	10	Baldwin	Moehler	Foulke	60-85	3rd	29.0
9-17	At Bos.	L	3-14		8	16	Florie	Blair		60-86	3rd	28.5
9-18	At Bos.	L	1-9		7	13	Saberhagen	Weaver		60-87	3rd	29.5
9-19	At Bos.	L	3-7		5	11	Wakefield	Mlicki	Lowe	60-88	T3rd	29.5
9-20	Cle.	W	4-3	(10)	9	9	Jones	Riske		61-88	T3rd	28.5
9-21	Cle.	L	1-6		4	8	Burba	Borkowski		61-89	T3rd	29.5
9-22	Cle.	L	1-9		2	16	Wright	Moehler		61-90	4th	30.5
9-23	Cle.	W	7-5		11	6	Blair	Nagy	Jones	62-90	4th	29.5
9-24	K.C.	L	3-7		7	9	Rosado	Mlicki		62-91	4th	30.5
9-25	K.C.	W	11-3		10	8	Nitkowski	Suzuki		63-91	4th	30.5
9-26	K.C.	W	6-1		8	4	Borkowski	Stein		64-91	3rd	30.5
9-27	K.C.	W	8-2		11	11	Moehler	Suppan		65-91	3rd	30.0
9-28	At Min.	W	7-4		9	9	Anderson	Trombley	Jones	66-91	3rd	30.0
9-29	At Min.	W	6-3		7	9	Mlicki	Mays	Jones	67-91	3rd	29.0
9-30	At Min.	W	6-5		14	8	Cordero	Wells	Jones	68-91	3rd	29.0
10-1	At K.C.	L	5-9		14	9	Suzuki	Borkowski		68-92	3rd	29.0
10-2	At K.C.	W	4-3		10	8	Weaver	Suppan	Jones	69-92	3rd	28.0

Monthly records: April (11-12), May (10-18), June (12-15), July (9-17), August (11-16), September (15-13), October (1-1).
*Innings, if other than nine. † First game of a doubleheader. ‡ Second game of a doubleheader.

MEMORABLE GAMES

April 5 at Texas

Juan Encarnacion hit the first pitch of the Tigers' season for a home run, and Brian Moehler took a no-hitter into the seventh inning in an 11-5 rout of the A.L. West champions. Bobby Higginson and Damion Easley added three-run homers. Moehler allowed his first hit when Juan Gonzalez lined a single to center with one out in the seventh. The Tigers lost their next six games, including a 1-0, 12-inning defeat in their home opener, and never were above .500 again.

Detroit	AB	R	H	RBI	Texas	AB	R	H	RBI
Encarnacion, lf	5	2	2	2	T.Goodwin, cf	4	0	0	0
Jefferies, dh	3	0	1	1	Alicea, 2b	3	1	0	0
K.Garcia, ph-dh	1	0	0	0	Greer, lf	3	1	0	1
Easley, 2b	5	1	2	3	J.Gonzalez, rf	3	0	2	2
T.Clark, 1b	5	1	2	0	R.Palmro, dh	3	0	1	1
Palmer, 3b	4	1	2	0	I.Rodriguez, c	4	0	0	0
Higginson, rf	4	1	1	3	L.Stevens, 1b	4	1	1	1
Kapler, rf	1	0	0	0	Zeile, 3b	3	1	0	0
D.Cruz, ss	4	1	2	0	Clayton, ss	3	1	0	0
L.Garcia, ss	1	0	0	0					
Ausmus, c	3	2	1	0					
B.Hunter, cf	2	2	0	0					
Totals	38	11	13	9	Totals	31	5	5	5

Detroit .... 1 0 0   7 0 3 0 0 0— 11
Texas .... 0 0 0   0 0 0 1 3 1— 5

E—Zeile (1), L.Stevens (1), Clayton (1). DP—Detroit 1, Texas 2. LOB—Detroit 5, Texas 4. 2B—D.Cruz (1), R.Palmeiro (1). HR—Encarnacion (1), Easley (1), Higginson (1), L.Stevens (1). CS—Encarnacion (1), Jefferies (1).

Detroit	IP	H	R	ER	BB	SO
Moehler (W, 1-0)	7	2	1	1	2	6
Kida	0.2	2	3	3	2	0
Nitkowski	0.1	0	0	0	0	0
Brocail	1	1	1	1	0	2

Texas	IP	H	R	ER	BB	SO
Helling (L, 0-1)	3	7	7	5	2	0
Loaiza	2	4	3	1	2	2
Morgan	3	2	0	0	0	3
Munoz	1	0	0	0	0	0

HBP—Ausmus by Helling, B.Hunter by Helling, Greer by Moehler. PB—Ausmus. U—HP, McKean. 1B, Kaiser. 2B, Joyce. 3B, Craft. T—2:56. A—46,650.

September 27 at Detroit

Rookie Robert Fick hit a game-clinching grand slam off the right field roof in the eighth inning, and the Tigers closed their 88-year run at the corner of Michigan and Trumbull with an 8-2 victory over the Kansas City Royals. Fick's hit was the last one at the venerable ballpark. It was the team's 6,783rd regular-season game at The Corner, starting with a 6-4 win over Cleveland on April 10, 1912.

Kansas City	AB	R	H	RBI	Detroit	AB	R	H	RBI
Febles, 2b	4	0	1	0	Polonia, lf	3	1	2	1
Pose, ph	1	0	0	0	Jefferies, ph	1	0	0	0
R.Sanchez, ss	5	0	2	0	Bartee, cf	1	0	0	0
C.Beltran, cf	4	1	3	0	Ausmus, c	3	0	1	0
Dye, rf	3	0	1	0	T.Clark, 1b	4	0	0	0
Mi.Sweeney, 1b	4	0	1	0	Palmer, 3b	3	1	2	0
Randa, 3b	4	0	1	1	Easley, 2b	3	2	3	0
Quinn, lf	3	1	1	1	K.Garcia, rf-lf	3	2	1	2
Je.Giambi, dh	4	0	0	0	Kapler, cf-rf	3	1	1	0
Kreuter, c	4	0	1	0	Fick, dh	2	1	1	5
					D.Cruz, ss	4	0	0	0
Totals	36	2	11	2	Totals	30	8	11	8

Kansas City .... 0 1 1   0 0 0 0 0 0— 2
Detroit .... 1 1 0   0 0 2 0 4 x— 8

E—Dye (5). DP—Kansas City 2, Detroit 2. LOB—Kansas City 10, Detroit 5. 2B—C.Beltran (27), Palmer (24), Easley (30). HR—Quinn (6), Polonia (8), K.Garcia (13), Fick (3). SB—Kapler (11). CS—Palmer (3). S—Easley. SF—Fick.

Kansas City	IP	H	R	ER	BB	SO
Suppan (L, 10-11)	5.1	8	4	4	3	1
Morman	1.2	0	0	0	1	0
J.Montgomery	1	3	4	4	1	0

Detroit	IP	H	R	ER	BB	SO
Moehler (W, 10-16)	6	9	2	2	2	5
F.Cordero (H, 6)	0.1	2	0	0	1	1
Brocail (H, 20)	1.2	0	0	0	0	2
To.Jones	1	0	0	0	0	2

U—HP, Roe. 1B, Reed. 2B, Merrill. 3B, Reynolds. T—2:58. A—43,356.

BATTING

Name	G	TPA	AB	R	H	TB	2B	3B	HR	RBI	Avg.	Obp.	Slg.	SH	SF	HP	BB	IBB	SO	SB	CS	GDP	vs RHP AB	Avg.	HR	RBI	vs LHP AB	Avg.	HR	RBI
Palmer, Dean	150	631	560	92	147	290	25	2	38	100	.263	.339	.518	0	4	10	57	3	153	3	3	12	460	.235	28	76	100	.390	10	24
Easley, Damion	151	627	549	83	146	238	30	1	20	65	.266	.346	.434	2	6	19	51	2	124	11	3	15	463	.261	16	56	86	.291	4	9
Clark, Tony	143	609	536	74	150	272	29	0	31	99	.280	.361	.507	0	3	6	64	7	133	2	1	14	429	.284	24	80	107	.262	7	19
Cruz, Deivi	155	553	518	64	147	221	35	0	13	58	.284	.302	.427	14	5	4	12	0	57	1	4	10	425	.282	12	48	93	.290	1	10
Encarnacion, Juan	132	538	509	62	130	229	30	6	19	74	.255	.287	.450	4	2	9	14	1	113	33	12	12	414	.254	14	56	95	.263	5	18
Ausmus, Brad	127	527	458	62	126	190	25	6	9	54	.275	.365	.415	3	1	14	51	0	71	12	9	11	386	.277	9	46	72	.264	0	8
Kapler, Gabe	130	468	416	60	102	186	22	4	18	49	.245	.315	.447	4	4	2	42	0	74	11	5	7	341	.238	14	38	75	.280	4	11
Higginson, Bob	107	445	377	51	90	144	18	0	12	46	.239	.351	.382	0	2	2	64	2	66	4	6	2	294	.231	10	36	83	.265	2	10
Polonia, Luis	87	355	333	46	108	175	21	8	10	32	.324	.357	.526	2	2	2	16	0	32	17	9	2	310	.332	9	29	23	.217	1	3
Garcia, Karim	96	310	288	38	69	127	10	3	14	32	.240	.288	.441	0	1	0	20	1	67	2	4	2	250	.232	13	27	38	.289	1	5
Catalanotto, Frank	100	315	286	41	79	131	19	0	11	35	.276	.327	.458	0	5	9	15	1	49	3	4	5	260	.277	11	34	26	.269	0	1
Jefferies, Gregg	70	225	205	22	41	67	8	0	6	18	.200	.258	.327	0	3	4	13	1	11	3	4	9	158	.215	5	15	47	.149	1	3
Haselman, Bill	48	153	143	13	39	59	8	0	4	14	.273	.320	.413	0	0	0	10	1	26	2	0	4	104	.260	3	10	39	.308	1	4
Bartee, Kimera	41	89	77	11	15	22	1	3	0	3	.195	.279	.286	3	0	0	9	0	20	3	3	2	45	.178	0	2	32	.219	0	1
Hunter, Brian L.	18	62	55	8	13	17	2	1	0	0	.236	.311	.309	1	0	1	5	0	11	0	3	0	43	.233	0	0	12	.250	0	0
Alvarez, Gabe	22	56	53	5	11	20	3	0	2	4	.208	.250	.377	0	0	0	3	0	9	0	0	0	38	.211	2	4	15	.200	0	0
Wood, Jason	27	47	44	5	7	11	1	0	1	8	.159	.196	.250	1	0	0	2	0	13	0	0	0	20	.150	1	6	24	.167	0	2
Fick, Robert	15	49	41	6	9	18	0	0	3	10	.220	.327	.439	0	1	0	7	0	6	1	0	1	37	.189	3	10	4	.500	0	0
Garcia, Luis	8	9	9	0	1	2	1	0	0	0	.111	.111	.222	0	0	0	0	0	2	0	0	0	7	.143	0	0	2	.000	0	0
Thompson, Justin	24	5	5	0	0	0	0	0	0	0	.000	.000	.000	0	0	0	0	0	2	0	0	0	2	.000	0	0	3	.000	0	0
Weaver, Jeff	31	5	4	2	2	3	1	0	0	0	.500	.500	.750	1	0	0	0	0	1	0	0	0	4	.500	0	0	0	.000	0	0
Macias, Jose	5	4	4	2	1	4	0	0	1	2	.250	.250	1.000	0	0	0	0	0	1	0	0	0	4	.250	1	2	0	.000	0	0
Mlicki, Dave	31	6	4	0	0	0	0	0	0	0	.000	.333	.000	0	0	0	2	0	3	0	0	0	4	.000	0	0	0	.000	0	0
Borkowski, Dave	17	3	3	0	0	0	0	0	0	1	.000	.000	.000	0	0	0	0	0	2	0	0	0	3	.000	0	1	0	.000	0	0
Blair, Willie	39	1	1	0	0	0	0	0	0	0	.000	.000	.000	0	0	0	0	0	0	0	0	0	1	.000	0	0	0	.000	0	0
Florie, Bryce	27	1	1	0	0	0	0	0	0	0	.000	.000	.000	0	0	0	0	0	1	0	0	0	1	.000	0	0	0	.000	0	0
Nitkowski, C.J.	69	1	1	0	0	0	0	0	0	0	.000	.000	.000	0	0	0	0	0	1	0	0	0	1	.000	0	0	0	.000	0	0
Moehler, Brian	32	2	1	0	0	0	0	0	0	0	.000	.500	.000	0	0	0	0	0	1	0	0	0	0	.000	0	0	1	.000	0	0
Brocail, Doug	70	0	0	0	0	0	0	0	0	0	.000	.000	.000	0	0	0	0	0	0	0	0	0	0	.000	0	0	0	.000	0	0
Jones, Todd	65	0	0	0	0	0	0	0	0	0	.000	.000	.000	0	0	0	0	0	0	0	0	0	0	.000	0	0	0	.000	0	0
Cruz, Nelson	29	0	0	0	0	0	0	0	0	0	.000	.000	.000	0	0	0	0	0	0	0	0	0	0	.000	0	0	0	.000	0	0
Kida, Masao	49	0	0	0	0	0	0	0	0	0	.000	.000	.000	0	0	0	0	0	0	0	0	0	0	.000	0	0	0	.000	0	0

Players with more than one A.L. team

Name	G	TPA	AB	R	H	TB	2B	3B	HR	RBI	Avg.	Obp.	Slg.	SH	SF	HP	BB	IBB	SO	SB	CS	GDP	vs RHP AB	Avg.	HR	RBI	vs LHP AB	Avg.	HR	RBI
Florie, Bos.	14	0	0	0	0	0	0	0	0	0	.000	.000	.000	0	0	0	0	0	0	0	0	0	1	.000	0	0	0	.000	0	0
Florie, Det.-Bos.	41	1	1	0	0	0	0	0	0	0	.000	.000	.000	0	0	0	0	0	1	0	0	0	1	.000	0	0	0	.000	0	0
Hunter, Sea.	121	527	484	71	112	145	11	5	4	34	.231	.277	.300	3	7	1	32	0	80	44	5	8	43	.233	0	0	12	.250	0	0
Hunter, Det.-Sea.	139	589	539	79	125	162	13	6	4	34	.232	.280	.301	4	7	2	37	0	91	44	8	8	437	.243	4	33	102	.186	0	1

PITCHING

Name	W	L	Pct.	ERA	IP	H	R	ER	HR	SH	SF	HB	BB	IBB	SO	G	GS	CG	ShO	GF	Sv	vs. RH AB	Avg.	HR	RBI	vs. LH AB	Avg.	HR	RBI
Moehler, Brian	10	16	.385	5.04	196.1	229	116	110	22	8	5	7	59	5	106	32	32	2	2	0	0	388	.291	7	41	392	.296	15	58
Mlicki, Dave	14	12	.538	4.60	191.2	209	108	98	24	3	8	12	70	1	119	31	31	2	0	0	0	415	.280	11	47	342	.272	13	50
Weaver, Jeff	9	12	.429	5.55	163.2	176	104	101	27	5	5	17	56	2	114	30	29	0	0	1	0	276	.236	7	26	358	.310	20	71
Thompson, Justin	9	11	.450	5.11	142.2	152	85	81	24	1	7	4	59	1	83	24	24	0	0	0	0	443	.275	20	56	112	.268	4	21
Blair, Willie	3	11	.214	6.85	134.0	169	107	102	29	3	4	4	44	0	82	39	16	0	0	8	0	274	.292	16	47	275	.324	13	44
Brocail, Doug	4	4	.500	2.52	82.0	60	23	23	7	4	2	4	25	1	78	70	0	0	0	22	2	150	.200	2	16	141	.213	5	14
Nitkowski, C.J.	4	5	.444	4.30	81.2	63	44	39	11	1	4	3	45	3	66	68	7	0	0	7	0	191	.215	6	20	105	.210	5	19
Borkowski, Dave	2	6	.250	6.10	76.2	86	58	52	10	1	2	4	40	0	50	17	12	0	0	2	0	162	.265	7	26	142	.303	3	26
Cruz, Nelson	2	5	.286	5.67	66.2	74	44	42	11	2	4	3	23	1	46	29	6	0	0	10	0	136	.265	2	25	127	.299	9	20
Jones, Todd	4	4	.500	3.80	66.1	64	30	28	7	3	1	1	35	1	64	65	0	0	0	62	30	117	.222	3	14	130	.292	4	17
Kida, Masao	1	0	1.000	6.26	64.2	73	48	45	6	1	4	4	30	1	50	49	0	0	0	21	1	142	.296	3	24	111	.279	3	21
Florie, Bryce	2	1	.667	4.56	51.1	61	31	26	6	3	1	1	20	2	40	27	3	0	0	6	0	114	.228	1	10	95	.368	5	19
Anderson, Matt	2	1	.667	5.68	38.0	33	27	24	8	0	2	1	35	1	32	37	0	0	0	9	0	86	.233	1	14	56	.232	7	19
Cordero, Francisco	2	2	.500	3.32	19.0	19	7	7	2	2	4	0	18	2	19	20	0	0	0	4	0	37	.405	1	8	30	.133	1	4
Brunson, Will	1	0	1.000	6.00	12.0	18	9	8	3	1	2	0	6	1	9	17	0	0	0	1	0	25	.400	3	8	24	.333	0	7
Runyan, Sean	0	1	.000	3.38	10.2	9	4	4	2	1	2	1	3	1	6	12	0	0	0	2	0	21	.238	1	8	17	.235	1	3
Hiljus, Erik	0	0	.000	5.19	8.2	7	5	5	2	0	1	0	5	0	1	6	0	0	0	0	0	18	.222	0	4	11	.273	2	4
Rojas, Mel	0	0	.000	22.74	6.1	12	16	16	3	0	1	3	4	0	6	5	0	0	0	2	0	17	.412	1	8	14	.357	2	10
Graterol, Beiker	0	1	.000	15.75	4.0	7	7	7	3	0	0	0	4	1	2	1	1	0	0	0	0	11	.091	0	2	5	.600	2	5
Lira, Felipe	0	0	.000	10.80	3.1	7	5	4	2	0	0	0	3	0	4	5	0	0	0	0	0	7	.429	1	3	11	.364	1	3
Roberts, Willis	0	0	.000	13.50	1.1	3	4	2	0	0	1	0	1	0	0	1	0	0	0	0	0	1	1.000	0	0	5	.400	0	4

PITCHERS WITH MORE THAN ONE A.L. TEAM

Name	W	L	Pct.	ERA	IP	H	R	ER	HR	SH	SF	HB	BB	IBB	SO	G	GS	CG	ShO	GF	Sv	vs. RH AB	Avg.	HR	RBI	vs. LH AB	Avg.	HR	RBI
Florie, Bos.	2	0	1.000	4.80	30.0	33	19	16	2	0	1	1	15	3	25	14	2	0	0	4	0	114	.228	1	10	95	.368	5	19
Florie, Det.-Bos.	4	1	.800	4.65	81.1	94	50	42	8	3	2	2	35	5	65	41	5	0	0	2	0	175	.223	1	16	151	.364	7	32

DESIGNATED HITTERS

Name	AB	Avg.	HR	RBI	Name	AB	Avg.	HR	RBI	Name	AB	Avg.	HR	RBI
Polonia, Luis	172	.337	6	20	Alvarez, Gabe	33	.152	1	2	Wood, Jason	3	.000	0	0
Jefferies, Gregg	171	.199	4	15	Fick, Robert	29	.172	3	9	Kapler, Gabe	1	.000	0	0
Higginson, Bob	67	.239	3	5	Catalanotto, Frank	28	.179	1	2	Nitkowski, C.J.	0	-	0	0
Clark, Tony	41	.293	2	7	Haselman, Bill	17	.294	1	3	Bartee, Kimera	0	-	0	0
Palmer, Dean	33	.303	0	5	Garcia, Karim	8	.250	0	0					

1999 REVIEW

INDIVIDUAL STATISTICS

FIELDING

FIRST BASEMEN

Player	Pct.	G	PO	A	E	TC	DP
Clark, Tony	.992	132	1126	85	10	1221	111
Catalanotto, Frank	1.000	32	219	11	0	230	29
Wood, Jason	.972	5	35	0	1	36	3
Jefferies, Gregg	1.000	3	19	4	0	23	1

SECOND BASEMEN

Player	Pct.	G	PO	A	E	TC	DP
Easley, Damion	.989	147	302	421	8	731	111
Catalanotto, Frank	.966	32	24	61	3	88	7
Jefferies, Gregg	1.000	2	0	1	0	1	0
Macias, Jose	1.000	1	1	6	0	7	0
Wood, Jason	1.000	1	0	1	0	1	0
Garcia, Luis	-	1	0	0	0	0	0

THIRD BASEMEN

Player	Pct.	G	PO	A	E	TC	DP
Palmer, Dean	.945	141	89	240	19	348	24
Catalanotto, Frank	.946	21	9	26	2	37	4
Wood, Jason	.909	9	5	5	1	11	0
Alvarez, Gabe	1.000	2	0	1	0	1	0

SHORTSTOPS

Player	Pct.	G	PO	A	E	TC	DP
Cruz, Deivi	.983	155	230	453	12	695	106
Easley, Damion	1.000	19	16	24	0	40	5
Wood, Jason	.818	9	2	7	2	11	1
Garcia, Luis	1.000	7	3	2	0	5	0

OUTFIELDERS

Player	Pct.	G	PO	A	E	TC	DP
Encarnacion, Juan	.968	131	264	10	9	283	2
Kapler, Gabe	.981	128	302	4	6	312	2
Higginson, Bob	.983	88	175	2	3	180	0
Garcia, Karim	.958	81	152	7	7	166	1
Polonia, Luis	.986	40	68	4	1	73	0
Bartee, Kimera	.985	38	67	0	1	68	0
Hunter, Brian L.	1.000	18	49	1	0	50	0
Alvarez, Gabe	1.000	5	3	0	0	3	0
Jefferies, Gregg	1.000	2	2	0	0	2	0

CATCHERS

Player	Pct.	G	PO	A	E	TC	DP	PB
Ausmus, Brad	.998	127	754	56	2	812	5	7
Haselman, Bill	.996	39	231	13	1	245	0	4
Fick, Robert	1.000	4	24	1	0	25	0	1

PITCHERS

Player	Pct.	G	PO	A	E	TC	DP
Brocail, Doug	1.000	70	11	6	0	17	1
Nitkowski, C.J.	.880	68	5	17	3	25	0
Jones, Todd	.875	65	2	5	1	8	0
Kida, Masao	1.000	49	2	7	0	9	0
Blair, Willie	1.000	39	6	15	0	21	0
Anderson, Matt	1.000	37	0	1	0	1	0
Moehler, Brian	1.000	32	18	31	0	49	2
Mlicki, Dave	.917	31	14	19	3	36	2
Weaver, Jeff	1.000	30	9	18	0	27	3
Cruz, Nelson	.926	29	8	17	2	27	0
Florie, Bryce	.667	27	1	5	3	9	0
Thompson, Justin	.941	24	5	11	1	17	1
Cordero, Francisco	1.000	20	2	5	0	7	1
Borkowski, Dave	.810	17	7	10	4	21	1
Brunson, Will	1.000	17	0	3	0	3	1
Runyan, Sean	1.000	12	1	3	0	4	0
Hiljus, Erik	1.000	6	0	1	0	1	0
Rojas, Mel	1.000	5	0	1	0	1	0
Lira, Felipe	1.000	2	1	0	0	1	0
Roberts, Willis	.500	1	0	1	1	2	0
Graterol, Beiker	1.000	1	0	1	0	1	0

PITCHING AGAINST EACH CLUB

Pitcher	Ana. W-L	Bal. W-L	Bos. W-L	Chi. W-L	Cle. W-L	K.C. W-L	Min. W-L	N.Y. W-L	Oak. W-L	Sea. W-L	T.B. W-L	Tex. W-L	Tor. W-L	N.L. W-L	Total W-L
Anderson, Matt	0-0	0-0	0-1	0-0	0-0	0-0	1-0	1-0	0-0	0-0	0-0	0-0	0-0	0-0	2-1
Blair, Willie	0-0	1-0	0-1	1-0	0-0	0-0	0-0	0-0	1-0	0-2	0-1	0-2	0-1	0-3	3-11
Borkowski, Dave	0-0	0-1	0-0	0-0	0-2	1-1	0-0	0-0	0-0	0-0	0-1	0-0	0-0	0-0	2-6
Brocail, Doug	1-1	1-0	0-1	0-0	0-1	0-0	0-0	0-0	1-0	0-0	0-0	0-0	0-0	1-1	4-4
Brunson, Will	0-0	0-0	0-0	0-0	0-0	0-0	0-0	0-0	0-0	0-0	0-0	0-0	0-0	1-0	1-0
Cordero, Francisco	0-0	0-0	0-0	0-0	0-0	0-0	1-0	0-0	0-1	0-0	0-0	1-0	0-1	0-0	2-2
Cruz, Nelson	0-0	0-0	0-0	0-0	0-0	1-0	0-1	0-0	0-2	0-0	0-0	0-1	0-0	1-1	2-5
Florie, Bryce	1-0	0-0	0-0	0-0	0-0	0-0	1-0	0-0	0-0	0-0	0-0	0-0	0-0	0-0	2-1
Graterol, Beiker	0-0	0-0	0-0	0-0	0-0	0-0	0-0	0-0	0-1	0-0	0-0	0-0	0-0	0-0	0-1
Hiljus, Erik	0-0	0-0	0-0	0-0	0-0	0-0	0-0	0-0	0-0	0-0	0-0	0-0	0-0	0-0	0-0
Jones, Todd	1-0	0-0	0-0	0-0	1-1	0-0	0-0	0-0	0-1	0-0	0-0	0-0	1-0	1-1	4-4
Kida, Masao	0-0	0-0	0-0	0-0	0-0	0-0	0-0	0-0	0-0	1-0	0-0	0-0	0-0	0-0	1-0
Lira, Felipe	0-0	0-0	0-0	0-0	0-0	0-0	0-0	0-0	0-0	0-0	0-0	0-0	0-0	0-0	0-0
Mlicki, Dave	1-0	2-1	1-1	2-1	0-1	0-1	1-1	2-1	0-1	2-0	2-0	2-0	0-3	1-1	14-12
Moehler, Brian	0-2	2-0	2-0	0-3	0-2	1-0	1-1	1-1	1-2	0-1	1-1	0-1	1-1	1-2	10-16
Nitkowski, C.J.	0-0	0-1	0-0	1-0	1-0	1-0	0-0	0-0	0-1	0-0	0-0	0-0	0-0	1-1	4-5
Roberts, Willis	0-0	0-0	0-0	0-0	0-0	0-0	0-0	0-0	0-0	0-0	0-0	0-0	0-0	0-0	0-0
Rojas, Mel	0-0	0-0	0-0	0-0	0-0	0-0	0-0	0-0	0-0	0-0	0-0	0-0	0-0	0-0	0-0
Runyan, Sean	0-0	0-0	0-0	0-0	0-0	0-0	0-0	0-0	0-0	0-0	0-0	0-0	0-0	0-0	0-0
Thompson, Justin	0-1	0-1	2-0	0-2	0-1	1-1	1-0	1-2	1-1	1-0	1-0	0-1	0-1	1-0	9-11
Weaver, Jeff	1-1	1-1	0-3	2-0	2-0	1-0	1-2	0-0	0-1	0-0	1-1	0-1	0-2	0-0	9-12
Totals	5-5	5-5	5-7	5-7	5-7	7-4	6-6	5-7	4-6	3-7	4-5	5-5	2-10	8-10	69-92

INTERLEAGUE: Thompson 1-0, Cruz 0-1, Moehler 0-1 vs. Brewers; Brocail 1-0, Nitkowski 0-1, Mlicki 0-1 vs. Reds; Blair 0-1, Brocail 0-1, Jones 0-1 vs. Astros; Brunson 1-0, Cruz 1-0, Moehler 0-1 vs. Pirates; Moehler 1-0, Jones 1-0, Mlicki 1-0, Blair 0-2, Nitkowski 0-1 vs. Cardinals. Total: 8-10.

MISCELLANEOUS

HOME RUNS BY PARK

At Anaheim (3): Easley 1, Garcia 1, Encarnacion 1.
At Baltimore (5): Encarnacion 2, Palmer 1, Cruz 1, Catalanotto 1.
At Boston (8): Palmer 2, Encarnacion 2, Ausmus 1, Higginson 1, Fick 1, Kapler 1.
At Chicago (AL) (5): Garcia 2, Palmer 1, Fick 1, Kapler 1.
At Cincinnati (7): Clark 3, Easley 2, Palmer 1, Encarnacion 1.
At Cleveland (6): Catalanotto 2, Palmer 1, Garcia 1, Clark 1, Cruz 1.
At Detroit (118): Palmer 24, Easley 12, Clark 12, Kapler 12, Cruz 9, Polonia 8, Higginson 8, Encarnacion 6, Catalanotto 6, Jefferies 5, Ausmus 5, Garcia 4, Haselman 2, Alvarez 2, Wood 1, Fick 1, Macias 1.
At Houston (2): Palmer 1, Clark 1.
At Kansas City (7): Clark 3, Kapler 2, Polonia 1, Encarnacion 1.
At Minnesota (9): Palmer 2, Polonia 1, Haselman 1, Garcia 1, Clark 1, Encarnacion 1, Catalanotto 1, Kapler 1.
At New York (AL) (3): Haselman 1, Higginson 1, Clark 1.
At Oakland (4): Clark 2, Palmer 1, Garcia 1.
At Seattle (1): Clark 1.
At St. Louis (7): Palmer 2, Clark 2, Cruz 1, Encarnacion 1, Catalanotto 1.
At Tampa Bay (7): Jefferies 1, Palmer 1, Easley 1, Garcia 1, Clark 1, Cruz 1, Kapler 1.
At Texas (8): Easley 2, Clark 2, Encarnacion 2, Ausmus 1, Higginson 1.
At Toronto (6): Palmer 1, Ausmus 1, Higginson 1, Garcia 1, Clark 1, Encarnacion 1.

LOW-HIT GAMES

No-hitters: None.
One-hitters: None.
Two-hitters: None.

10-STRIKEOUT GAMES

C.J. Nitkowski 1, Justin Thompson 1, **Total:** 2.

FOUR OR MORE HITS IN ONE GAME

Luis Polonia 4 (including one five-hit game), Karim Garcia 2, Frank Catalanotto 2, Damion Easley 1, Brad Ausmus 1, Juan Encarnacion 1, **Total:** 11.

MULTI-HOMER GAMES

Tony Clark 3, Bob Higginson 2, Dean Palmer 1, Damion Easley 1, Karim Garcia 1, Deivi Cruz 1, Juan Encarnacion 1, Frank Catalanotto 1, Gabe Kapler 1, **Total:** 12.

GRAND SLAMS

6-11: Juan Encarnacion (off St. Louis's Manny Aybar).
6-20: Dean Palmer (off Oakland's T.J. Mathews).
9-27: Robert Fick (off Kansas City's Jeff Montgomery).

PINCH HITTERS

(Minimum 5 at-bats)

Name	AB	Avg.	HR	RBI
Catalanotto, Frank	24	.292	1	6
Jefferies, Gregg	19	.158	0	0
Garcia, Karim	14	.071	0	0
Alvarez, Gabe	8	.250	0	0
Polonia, Luis	6	.333	0	1
Haselman, Bill	6	.167	0	0

DEBUTS

4-5: Masao Kida, P.
4-5: Luis Garcia, SS.
4-9: Beiker Graterol, P.
4-14: Jeff Weaver, P.
5-12: Jose Macias, 2B.
7-2: Willis Roberts, P.
7-17: Dave Borkowski, P.
8-2: Francisco Cordero, P.
9-10: Erik Hiljus, P.

GAMES BY POSITION

Catcher: Brad Ausmus 127, Bill Haselman 39, Robert Fick 4.
First base: Tony Clark 132, Frank Catalanotto 32, Jason Wood 5, Gregg Jefferies 3.
Second base: Damion Easley 147, Frank Catalanotto 32, Gregg Jefferies 2, Jason Wood 1, Luis Garcia 1, Jose Macias 1.
Third base: Dean Palmer 141, Frank Catalanotto 21, Jason Wood 9, Gabe Alvarez 2.
Shortstop: Deivi Cruz 155, Damion Easley 19, Jason Wood 9, Luis Garcia 7.
Outfield: Juan Encarnacion 131, Gabe Kapler 128, Bob Higginson 88, Karim Garcia 81, Luis Polonia 40, Kimera Bartee 38, Brian L. Hunter 18, Gabe Alvarez 5, Gregg Jefferies 2.
Designated hitter: Gregg Jefferies 45, Luis Polonia 43, Bob Higginson 17, Gabe Alvarez 12, Tony Clark 11, Dean Palmer 9, Bill Haselman 9, Frank Catalanotto 9, Robert Fick 8, Karim Garcia 7, Gabe Kapler 2, C.J. Nitkowski 1, Kimera Bartee 1, Jason Wood 1.

STREAKS

Wins: 6 (September 25-30).
Losses: 9 (July 26-August 5).
Consecutive games with at least one hit: 19, Tony Clark (July 10-August 1).
Wins by pitcher: 8, Dave Mlicki (August 6-September 13).

ATTENDANCE

Home: 2,026,441.
Road: 2,163,323.
Highest (home): 47,449 (April 12 vs. Minnesota).
Highest (road): 56,583 (April 9 vs. New York).
Lowest (home): 11,818 (April 15 vs. Minnesota).
Lowest (road): 9,837 (April 23 vs. Chicago).

1999 REVIEW

DAY BY DAY

Date	Opp.	Res.	Score	(inn.*)	Hits	Opp. hits	Winning pitcher	Losing pitcher	Save	Record	Pos.	GB
4-5	Bos.	L	3-5		6	13	Martinez	Appier	Gordon	0-1	5th	1.0
4-7	Bos.	L	0-6		4	13	Saberhagen	Rosado		0-2	5th	1.5
4-8	Bos.	L	1-4		4	10	Wakefield	Suppan	Gordon	0-3	5th	2.0
4-9	At Chi.	W	10-5		13	9	Barber	Sirotka		1-3	T4th	2.0
4-10	At Chi.	W	9-4		15	7	Pittsley	Navarro	Service	2-3	T2nd	2.0
4-11	At Chi.	W	3-1		8	5	Appier	Baldwin	Montgomery	3-3	2nd	2.0
4-12	At Cle.	L	2-5	(10)	8	11	Shuey	Santiago		3-4	T2nd	3.0
4-14	At Cle.	L	4-11		10	14	Colon	Suppan		3-5	T2nd	4.0
4-16	Chi.	W	7-2		8	9	Appier	Sirotka		4-5	T2nd	3.5
4-17	Chi.	L	5-6		7	11	Lowe	Montgomery	Howry	4-6	T3rd	4.0
4-18	Chi.	L	5-7		11	12	Baldwin	Barber	Howry	4-7	5th	5.0
4-19	Min.	L	4-6		8	11	Hawkins	Suppan	Aguilera	4-8	5th	5.5
4-20	Min.	L	7-8	(13)	12	14	Aguilera	Witasick		4-9	5th	6.5
4-21	Min.	W	3-2	(10)	9	7	Mathews	Guardado		5-9	5th	6.5
4-23	Ana.	L	2-4		4	6	Hasegawa	Montgomery	Percival	5-10	5th	7.0
4-24	Ana.	W	4-3		8	6	Santiago	Hasegawa		6-10	5th	6.0
4-27	At Bal.	L	4-8		10	12	Mussina	Appier	Timlin	6-11	5th	7.0
4-28	At Bal.	W	8-2		10	5	Rosado	Guzman		7-11	5th	7.0
4-29	At Bal.	W	15-5		15	7	Suppan	Erickson	Santiago	8-11	4th	7.0
4-30	N.Y.	W	13-6		15	12	Morman	Pettitte		9-11	4th	6.0
5-1	N.Y.	L	4-8		7	13	Cone	Pittsley		9-12	4th	7.0
5-2	N.Y.	L	8-9		14	14	Grimsley	Santiago	Rivera	9-13	4th	7.0
5-3	N.Y.	W	9-3		8	7	Service	Hernandez		10-13	4th	7.0
5-4	At T.B.	W	5-3		7	11	Mathews	Hernandez	Montgomery	11-13	4th	6.5
5-5	At T.B.	L	7-10		9	17	White	Witasick	Hernandez	11-14	4th	6.5
5-6	At T.B.	L	4-5		11	8	Aldred	Morman	Hernandez	11-15	4th	7.5
5-7	At Min.	W	5-1		9	7	Appier	Milton		12-15	4th	7.5
5-8	At Min.	W	6-2		11	5	Rosado	Perkins	Santiago	13-15	4th	6.5
5-9	At Min.	W	7-2		9	9	Suppan	Lincoln		14-15	3rd	6.5
5-10	At Min.	W	8-4		14	8	Witasick	Hawkins		15-15	3rd	6.5
5-11	Tor.	L	2-8		10	14	Escobar	Pittsley		15-16	3rd	7.5
5-12	Tor.	W	7-1		11	3	Appier	Carpenter		16-16	3rd	7.5
5-13	Tor.	L	2-8		10	13	Hentgen	Rosado		16-17	3rd	8.0
5-14	At Sea.	W	12-7		19	10	Service	Fassero		17-17	3rd	8.0
5-15	At Sea.	W	11-10		17	8	Santiago	Paniagua	Montgomery	18-17	3rd	8.0
5-16	At Sea.	L	1-5		9	9	Moyer	Fussell		18-18	3rd	8.0
5-18	Oak.	W	13-3		17	6	Appier	Heredia		19-18	2nd	8.5
5-19	Oak.	W	14-3		13	6	Rosado	Candiotti	Mathews	20-18	2nd	8.5
5-20	Oak.	W	7-1		9	5	Suppan	Oquist		21-18	2nd	8.0
5-21	Sea.	L	2-5		11	12	Moyer	Witasick		21-19	2nd	8.0
5-22	Sea.	L	4-7		11	12	Carmona	Fussell	Mesa	21-20	2nd	8.0
5-23	Sea.	W	5-4		11	9	Whisenant	Paniagua	Montgomery	22-20	2nd	8.0
5-25	At Oak.	L	3-5		5	7	Oquist	Rosado	Jones	22-21	2nd	8.5
5-26	At Oak.	L	1-3		5	5	Haynes	Suppan	Taylor	22-22	2nd	9.5
5-27	At Oak.	L	1-6		6	8	Rogers	Witasick		22-23	2nd	10.0
5-28	At Ana.	W	11-4		12	10	Appier	Finley		23-23	2nd	9.0
5-29	At Ana.	L	3-4		6	7	Sparks	Fussell	Percival	23-24	2nd	9.0
5-30	At Ana.	L	3-4		6	7	Olivares	Rosado	Percival	23-25	2nd	9.0
5-31	At Tex.	L	3-4	(10)	9	7	Crabtree	Santiago		23-26	2nd	10.0
6-1	At Tex.	L	1-3		3	6	Zimmerman	Whisenant	Wetteland	23-27	3rd	10.0
6-2	At Tex.	L	4-7		10	6	Sele	Appier	Wetteland	23-28	3rd	11.0
6-5†	Cin.	L	4-9		9	13	Parris	Rosado		23-29		
6-5‡	Cin.	L	4-7	(10)	7	13	Williamson	Montgomery		23-30	3rd	12.0
6-6	Cin.	L	3-14		9	22	Sullivan	Witasick		23-31	3rd	13.0
6-7	StL.	L	5-7		7	12	Slocumb	Appier	Bottalico	23-32	4th	13.5
6-8	StL.	W	11-10		15	14	Service	Oliver	Montgomery	24-32	4th	12.5
6-9	StL.	W	17-13		19	18	Whisenant	Radinsky		25-32	3rd	12.5
6-11	At Pit.	W	10-3		9	8	Rosado	Benson		26-32	3rd	12.0
6-12	At Pit.	L	8-9		13	17	Christiansen	Whisenant		26-33	3rd	13.0
6-13	At Pit.	L	4-8		9	8	Schmidt	Whisenant	Williams	26-34	4th	14.0
6-14	At Bal.	L	1-7		9	12	Erickson	Appier		26-35	4th	14.5
6-15	At Bal.	L	5-6	(10)	11	13	Timlin	Service		26-36	4th	15.5
6-16	At Bal.	L	1-2		9	7	Ponson	Rosado		26-37	4th	16.5
6-18	At Tor.	W	6-5		10	12	Witasick	Hentgen	Whisenant	27-37	4th	16.0
6-19	At Tor.	L	0-7		3	10	Halladay	Appier		27-38	4th	17.0
6-20	At Tor.	L	1-2		4	5	Wells	Service		27-39	4th	18.0
6-21	At Tor.	L	4-11		12	13	Hamilton	Fussell		27-40	4th	19.0
6-22	Det.	W	4-2		9	8	Rosado	Florie	Service	28-40	4th	18.0
6-23	Det.	W	10-1		15	5	Witasick	Thompson		29-40	3rd	18.0
6-24	Det.	L	4-6		13	9	Cruz	Mathews	Jones	29-41	4th	18.0
6-25	Cle.	W	8-2		12	6	Suppan	Wright		30-41	4th	17.0
6-26	Cle.	W	11-7		8	6	Montgomery	Rincon		31-41	3rd	16.0
6-27	Cle.	L	5-6		13	9	Reed	Byrdak	Jackson	31-42	3rd	17.0
6-28	Cle.	L	1-6		7	12	Nagy	Witasick		31-43	4th	18.0
6-29	Chi.	W	7-4		11	10	Appier	Navarro	Service	32-43	3rd	18.0
6-30	Chi.	L	9-10	(10)	14	16	Howry	Service		32-44	4th	18.0

HIGHLIGHTS

High point: Jeff Suppan completed a May sweep of Oakland at home with a complete-game 7-1 triumph. With the three victories, Kansas City was 21-18 and in second place in the A.L. Central.

Low point: The Royals went from 22-20 on May 23 to 23-32 on June 7. The 1-12 stretch included a nine-game losing streak. They never recovered. In a loss at Texas, the Rangers' Lee Stevens hit a game-tying, three-run home run with two out in the ninth, fore-shadowing Kansas City's chronic bullpen troubles.

Turning point: Jeff King's retirement on May 24. The Royals were two games over .500 on that date before embarking on a 1-8 road swing. A solid infield experienced a drop-off, with Kansas City quickly finding out that Mike Sweeney and Jeremy Giambi were below-average first basemen. And King's power was missed.

Most valuable player: Jermaine Dye stayed healthy and blossomed into a top defensive right fielder and a legitimate power threat with 27 homers and 119 RBIs. Center fielder Carlos Beltran was a force, too, winning A.L. Rookie of the Year honors.

Most valuable pitcher: Lefthander Jose Rosado established himself as the staff ace following Kevin Appier's departure. He owned the A.L.'s fifth-best ERA (3.85) and won 10 games for the first time.

Most improved player: Sweeney put together an impressive season after nearly being traded and changing positions (moving from catcher to first). He hit 44 doubles, had 102 RBIs and batted .322.

Most pleasant surprise: Shortstop Rey Sanchez arrived with question marks, but he combined with rookie Carlos Febles for a potent double-play combination and hit .294.

Key injuries: King's back ailment was one factor in his retirement. Second baseman Febles was slowed at times by shoulder injuries, and a dislocated finger put him on the D.L. for three weeks. Closer Jeff Montgomery missed nearly a month with hip tendinitis. Rookie pitcher Dan Reichert missed two months' worth of starts because of a cracked bone in his elbow. Left fielder Johnny Damon's rib-cage injury late in the year halted his team record of consecutive games played at 305.

Notable: Beltran became the first major league rookie in 24 years to reach 100 RBIs and 100 runs. ... Sweeney tied an American League record with at least one RBI in 13 consecutive games. He also had a 25-game hitting streak. ... Dye ranked in the A.L.'s top 10 in doubles, triples, RBIs and extra-base hits and tied for the lead with 17 outfield assists. ... Kansas City's .398 winning percentage was the worst in club history.

—LUCIANA CHAVEZ

MISCELLANEOUS

RECORDS

1999 regular-season record: 64-97 (4th in A.L. Central); 33-47 at home; 31-50 on road; 16-33 vs. A.L. East; 20-28 vs. A.L. Central; 22-24 vs. A.L. West; 6-12 vs. N.L. Central; 15-17 vs. lefthanded starters; 49-80 vs. righthanded starters; 55-83 on grass; 9-14 on turf; 14-35 in daytime; 50-62 at night; 11-32 in one-run games; 5-10 in extra-inning games; 0-3-1 in double-headers.

Team record past five years: 348-440 (.442, ranks 11th in league in that span).

TEAM LEADERS

Batting average: Mike Sweeney (.322).
At-bats: Carlos Beltran (663).
Runs: Carlos Beltran (112).
Hits: Joe Randa (197).
Total bases: Jermaine Dye (320).
Doubles: Jermaine Dye, Mike Sweeney (44).
Triples: Johnny Damon, Carlos Febles (9).
Home runs: Jermaine Dye (27).
Runs batted in: Jermaine Dye (119).
Stolen bases: Johnny Damon (36).
Slugging percentage: Jermaine Dye (.526).
On-base percentage: Mike Sweeney (.387).
Wins: Jose Rosado, Jeff Suppan (10).
Earned-run average: Jose Rosado (3.85).
Complete games: Jose Rosado (5).
Shutouts: Jeff Suppan, Jay Witasick (1).
Saves: Jeff Montgomery (12).
Innings pitched: Jeff Suppan (208.2).
Strikeouts: Jose Rosado (141).

Date	Opp.	Res.	Score	(inn.*)	Hits	Opp. hits	Winning pitcher	Losing pitcher	Save	Record	Pos.	GB
7-1	Chi.	L	2-6		7	8	Baldwin	Pisciotta		32-45	4th	19.0
7-2	At Cle.	W	9-7	(10)	12	8	Whisenant	Shuey		33-45	3rd	18.0
7-3†	At Cle.	L	8-9		10	11	Candiotti	Pisciotta	Jackson	33-46		
7-3‡	At Cle.	L	5-9		10	10	Langston	Wengert	Jackson	33-47	3rd	20.0
7-4	At Cle.	W	10-9		13	12	Appier	Burba	Byrdak	34-47	3rd	19.0
7-6	At Chi.	W	8-7	(10)	14	16	Whisenant	Foulke		35-47	3rd	19.0
7-7	At Chi.	L	1-7		10	10	Parque	Suzuki		35-48	3rd	19.0
7-8	At Chi.	L	5-6		10	10	Foulke	Byrdak		35-49	3rd	20.0
7-9	Hou.	L	5-6		12	9	Cabrera	Montgomery	Holt	35-50	3rd	20.0
7-10	Hou.	L	2-3		10	10	Hampton	Appier	Wagner	35-51	4th	21.0
7-11	Hou.	L	3-7		9	8	Lima	Suppan	Powell	35-52	4th	21.0
7-16†	At Mil.	L	0-2		4	9	Woodard	Appier	Wickman	35-53		
7-16‡	At Mil.	W	12-10		15	13	Ray	Pittsley	Service	36-53	3rd	21.0
7-17	At Mil.	L	3-11		7	17	Nomo	Rosado		36-54	3rd	21.0
7-18	At Chi. (NL)	W	5-4		8	11	Suppan	Tapani	Service	37-54	3rd	20.0
7-19	At Chi. (NL)	W	10-2		13	6	Witasick	Trachsel		38-54	3rd	19.0
7-20	At Chi. (NL)	L	7-8		14	15	Sanders	Barber	Adams	38-55	3rd	20.0
7-21	At Det.	L	5-10		11	12	Thompson	Appier		38-56	4th	20.0
7-22	At Det.	L	8-9		15	8	Florie	Rosado	Jones	38-57	5th	20.0
7-23	Oak.	W	12-7		15	10	Morman	Haynes	Barber	39-57	5th	19.0
7-24	Oak.	L	2-12		11	9	Oquist	Witasick		39-58	5th	19.0
7-25	Oak.	W	13-11	(10)	19	10	Service	Harville		40-58	5th	18.0
7-27	Sea.	W	9-7		15	15	Appier	Fassero	Service	41-58	T3rd	18.5
7-28	Sea.	W	5-3		9	8	Rosado	Garcia	Service	42-58	T3rd	18.5
7-29	Sea.	L	4-8		8	15	Halama	Suppan		42-59	4th	19.0
7-30	At Tex.	L	2-9		9	14	Loaiza	Witasick		42-60	4th	20.0
7-31	At Tex.	W	12-8		19	13	Reichert	Munoz	Service	43-60	4th	20.0
8-1	At Tex.	L	5-12		10	16	Sele	Barber		43-61	4th	20.0
8-2	At Ana.	W	12-4		17	11	Rosado	McDowell		44-61	4th	20.0
8-3	At Ana.	W	7-0		10	5	Suppan	Fyhrie		45-61	3rd	20.0
8-4	At Ana.	L	3-4		6	10	Hill	Witasick	Percival	45-62	3rd	20.0
8-6	Min.	L	8-9		14	17	Miller	Service	Trombley	45-63	4th	20.0
8-7	Min.	L	5-6		9	8	Wells	Rigby	Trombley	45-64	4th	21.0
8-8	Min.	L	3-7		7	11	Hawkins	Rigby	Carrasco	45-65	4th	21.0
8-9	Bos.	W	5-2		9	4	Suppan	Portugal		46-65	4th	21.0
8-10	Bos.	L	6-9	(10)	13	16	Wakefield	Whisenant	Garces	46-66	4th	22.0
8-11	Bos.	L	3-9		5	12	Saberhagen	Rosado		46-67	4th	23.0
8-12	T.B.	L	6-7		11	12	Witt	Reichert	Hernandez	46-68	4th	23.5
8-13	T.B.	W	2-1		10	6	Service	Yan		47-68	4th	23.5
8-14	T.B.	L	4-11		9	13	Rupe	Suppan		47-69	4th	24.5
8-15	T.B.	L	3-5		5	14	Eiland	Suzuki	Hernandez	47-70	4th	25.5
8-17	At N.Y.	L	2-5		7	7	Hernandez	Rosado	Rivera	47-71	4th	25.0
8-18	At N.Y.	W	3-0		8	6	Reichert	Pettitte	Montgomery	48-71	4th	24.0
8-19	At N.Y.	W	4-1	(11)	6	5	Rigby	Grimsley	Montgomery	49-71	4th	24.0
8-20	At T.B.	L	4-5		8	8	Hernandez	Service		49-72	4th	25.0
8-21	At T.B.	L	2-8		8	10	Eiland	Witasick		49-73	4th	26.0
8-22	At T.B.	L	1-2		6	3	Arrojo	Rosado		49-74	T4th	27.0
8-23	Bal.	L	2-4		8	10	Erickson	Reichert	Timlin	49-75	T4th	27.0
8-24	Bal.	L	3-5	(10)	7	10	Kamieniecki	Wallace	Timlin	49-76	T4th	27.0
8-25	Bal.	W	8-6		14	11	Suppan	Linton	Montgomery	50-76	4th	27.0
8-26	Bal.	W	6-0		11	4	Witasick	Ponson		51-76	4th	26.5
8-27	At Min.	L	1-4		7	10	Milton	Rosado	Trombley	51-77	4th	27.5
8-28	At Min.	L	3-4	(10)	6	10	Wells	Morman		51-78	5th	28.5
8-29	At Min.	L	2-6		8	7	Hawkins	Stein	Wells	51-79	5th	28.5
8-30	At Bos.	L	1-9		5	14	Martinez	Suppan		51-80	5th	29.5
8-31	At Bos.	L	3-6		4	11	Garces	Witasick	Lowe	51-81	5th	30.5
9-1	At Bos.	L	3-4		3	6	Mercker	Rosado	Beck	51-82	5th	31.5
9-2	At Bos.	W	4-2		9	7	Suzuki	Martinez	Fussell	52-82	5th	31.5
9-3	Tor.	L	4-5		14	9	Quantrill	Morman	Koch	52-83	5th	32.5
9-4	Tor.	L	3-6		4	13	Hentgen	Suppan	Frascatore	52-84	5th	32.5
9-5	Tor.	W	6-3		11	9	Witasick	Escobar	Fussell	53-84	5th	32.5
9-7	N.Y.	W	6-3		10	13	Rosado	Cone	Montgomery	54-84	5th	32.0
9-8	N.Y.	L	5-9		15	11	Hernandez	Rusch	Rivera	54-85	5th	32.0
9-10	Tex.	W	7-3		12	11	Stein	Loaiza	Montgomery	55-85	5th	32.0
9-11	Tex.	W	9-6		13	14	Suppan	Helling	Montgomery	56-85	5th	32.0
9-12	Tex.	W	6-3		9	9	Witasick	Sele	Morman	57-85	5th	31.0
9-13	Tex.	L	4-8	(10)	9	11	Wetteland	Santiago		57-86	5th	32.0
9-14†	Ana.	L	6-8		15	12	Pote	Morman	Hasegawa	57-87		
9-14‡	Ana.	L	5-6		5	9	Hasegawa	Byrdak	Percival	57-88	5th	32.5
9-15	Ana.	L	0-1		3	7	Finley	Carter	Percival	57-89	5th	32.5
9-16	Ana.	W	7-1		12	6	Suppan	Ortiz		58-89	5th	31.5
9-17	At Oak.	W	9-3		15	7	Witasick	Hudson		59-89	5th	30.5
9-18	At Oak.	L	4-8		8	13	Olivares	Rosado	Isringhausen	59-90	5th	31.5
9-19	At Oak.	L	3-12		6	12	Heredia	Fussell		59-91	5th	31.5
9-20	At Sea.	W	10-9		15	9	Santiago	Hinchliffe	Montgomery	60-91	5th	30.5
9-21	At Sea.	L	3-13		13	15	Garcia	Suppan	Rodriguez	60-92	5th	31.5
9-22	At Sea.	W	12-6		14	13	Witasick	Halama		61-92	5th	31.5
9-24	At Det.	W	7-3		9	7	Rosado	Mlicki		62-92	5th	31.0
9-25	At Det.	L	3-11		8	10	Nitkowski	Suzuki		62-93	5th	32.0
9-26	At Det.	L	1-6		4	8	Borkowski	Stein		62-94	5th	33.0
9-27	At Det.	L	2-8		11	11	Moehler	Suppan		62-95	5th	33.5
9-28	Cle.	L	1-2		3	8	Brower	Witasick	Jackson	62-96	5th	34.5
9-29	Cle.	W	5-2		9	4	Rosado	Nagy		63-96	5th	33.5
10-1	Det.	W	9-5		9	14	Suzuki	Borkowski		64-96	4th	33.0
10-2	Det.	L	3-4		8	10	Weaver	Suppan	Jones	64-97	4th	33.0

Monthly records: April (9-11), May (14-15), June (9-18), July (11-16), August (8-21), September (12-15), October (1-1).
*Innings, if other than nine. † First game of a doubleheader. ‡ Second game of a doubleheader.

MEMORABLE GAMES

May 4 at Tampa Bay

This one signaled the arrival of center fielder Carlos Beltran, the 1999 A.L. Rookie of the Year. Trailing 3-1, Beltran had already made a great defensive play before batting in the ninth with the bases loaded. He hung in during a tough at-bat, fouling off several pitches, then laced a bases-clearing triple on a two-strike pitch to give the Royals the lead en route to a 5-3 victory.

Kansas City	AB	R	H	RBI	Tampa Bay	AB	R	H	RBI
C.Beltran, cf	4	1	1	3	McCrckn, cf-lf	3	1	1	0
Randa, 3b	3	0	0	0	D.Martinez, rf	4	0	1	0
Damon, lf	5	0	2	1	Canseco, dh	3	1	2	1
Mi.Sweeney, dh	4	1	1	0	McGriff, 1b	4	1	2	2
Dye, rf	4	1	1	0	Flaherty, c	4	0	2	0
Leius, 1b	2	0	0	0	Boggs, 3b	3	0	0	0
Pose, ph	0	1	0	0	Lamb, 2b	1	0	0	0
Kreuter, c	0	0	0	0	Sorrento, lf	3	0	1	0
Spehr, c	3	0	1	0	Winn, cf	1	0	0	0
Sutton, ph-1b	0	0	0	1	B.Smth, 2b-3b	4	0	1	0
Febles, 2b	3	0	0	0	Stocker, ss	3	0	1	0
R.Sanchez, ss	3	1	1	0					
Totals	**31**	**5**	**7**	**5**	**Totals**	**33**	**3**	**11**	**3**

Kansas City ....0 0 0   0 0 0   0 0 5 —5
Tampa Bay ....1 0 0   1 0 0   0 1 0 —3

E—B.Smith (5). DP—Kansas City 3. LOB—Kansas City 8, Tampa Bay 5. 2B—McGriff (5). 3B—C.Beltran (1). HR—McGriff (7). SB—Stocker (5). CS—Randa (1), Damon (1), R.Sanchez (3), B.Smith (2). SF—Sutton.

Kansas City	IP	H	R	ER	BB	SO
Suppan	7	10	2	2	1	3
Te.Mathews (W, 2-0)	1	1	1	1	1	0
J.Montgomery (S, 2)	1	0	0	0	0	1

Tampa Bay	IP	H	R	ER	BB	SO
W.Alvarez	7	3	0	0	3	7
Mecir (H, 6)	0.2	0	0	0	1	1
Ro.Hernndez (BS 1; L 0-2	1	3	5	5	3	0
Aldred	0	1	0	0	0	0
Gaillard	0.1	0	0	0	0	0

HBP—C.Beltran by Mecir. U—HP, Welke. 1B, Garcia. 2B, Reilly. 3B, Johnson. T—3:08. A—15,470.

June 26 at Kansas City

The Royals often couldn't beat teams they should have, but they cranked it up against the best teams on occasion. Kansas City trailed 7-1 in this one before scoring 10 runs in the eighth. Jermaine Dye and Chad Kreuter each had two hits in the inning and drove in five of the 10 runs. It allowed Kansas City to kick off a tough, four-game series against the dominant A.L. Central team with two victories.

Cleveland	AB	R	H	RBI	Kansas City	AB	R	H	RBI
Lofton, cf	4	1	2	0	C.Beltran, cf	5	1	2	1
Vizquel, ss	4	1	0	0	Febles, 2b	3	1	0	1
Alomar, 2b	2	0	1	2	Damon, lf	3	2	1	2
E.Wilson, 2b	2	0	0	0	Mi.Swney, 1b	4	1	1	1
Justice, rf	1	2	0	0	Dye, rf	4	2	2	2
Sexson, 1b	3	1	1	1	Je.Giambi, dh	3	1	0	0
Thome, dh	3	1	1	1	Kreuter, c	4	1	2	3
Fryman, 3b	4	0	0	0	Leius, 3b	3	1	0	0
Whiten, lf	3	1	1	3	R.Sanchez, ss	2	0	0	0
Ei.Diaz, c	4	0	0	0	J.Hansen, ss	0	1	0	0
Totals	**30**	**7**	**6**	**7**	**Totals**	**31**	**11**	**8**	**10**

Cleveland ....0 3 4   0 0 0   0 0 0 —7
Kansas City ....0 0 0   0 0 0 1 (10) x— 11

DP—Cleveland 1, Kansas City 2. LOB—Cleveland 5, Kansas City 2. 2B—Lofton (14), Alomar (18), Dye (16), Kreuter (13). 3B—Sexson (2). HR—Whiten (1), Damon (7). SB—Lofton (23).

Cleveland	IP	H	R	ER	BB	SO
Colon	7.1	4	4	4	1	5
Shuey	0	1	3	3	2	0
Rincon (L, 0-1)	0	0	1	1	1	0
Karsay (BS, 1)	0.2	3	3	3	2	0

Kansas City	IP	H	R	ER	BB	SO
Fussell	2	2	6	6	5	2
Suzuki	3	3	1	1	1	1
Pisciotta	2	1	0	0	2	0
J.Montgomery (W, 1-3	1	0	0	0	0	1
Service	1	0	0	0	0	0

HBP—Alomar by Suzuki. WP—Shuey. U—HP, Shulock. 1B, Scott. 2B, Diaz. 3B, Cousins. T—3:13. A—29,358.

INDIVIDUAL STATISTICS

BATTING

Name	G	TPA	AB	R	H	TB	2B	3B	HR	RBI	Avg.	Obp.	Slg.	SH	SF	HP	BB	IBB	SO	SB	CS	GDP	vs RHP AB	Avg.	HR	RBI	vs LHP AB	Avg.	HR	RBI
Beltran, Carlos	156	723	663	112	194	301	27	7	22	108	.293	.337	.454	0	10	4	46	2	123	27	8	17	531	.298	15	89	132	.273	7	19
Randa, Joe	156	689	628	92	197	297	36	8	16	84	.314	.363	.473	1	7	3	50	4	80	5	4	15	527	.306	15	74	101	.356	1	10
Dye, Jermaine	158	673	608	96	179	320	44	8	27	119	.294	.354	.526	0	6	1	58	4	119	2	3	17	507	.300	22	101	101	.267	5	18
Damon, Johnny	145	660	583	101	179	278	39	9	14	77	.307	.379	.477	3	4	3	67	5	50	36	6	13	443	.300	13	57	140	.329	1	20
Sweeney, Mike	150	643	575	101	185	299	44	2	22	102	.322	.387	.520	0	4	10	54	0	48	6	1	21	475	.316	18	84	100	.350	4	18
Sanchez, Rey	134	518	479	66	141	177	18	6	2	56	.294	.329	.370	10	3	4	22	2	48	11	5	14	384	.286	2	48	95	.326	0	8
Febles, Carlos	123	524	453	71	116	186	22	9	10	53	.256	.336	.411	12	3	9	47	0	91	20	4	16	356	.250	8	41	97	.278	2	12
Kreuter, Chad	107	368	324	31	73	103	15	0	5	35	.225	.309	.318	2	2	6	34	1	65	0	0	16	281	.217	3	30	43	.279	2	5
Giambi, Jeremy	90	336	288	34	82	106	13	1	3	34	.285	.373	.368	1	4	3	40	5	67	0	0	7	240	.283	3	28	48	.292	0	6
Spehr, Tim	60	187	155	26	32	66	7	0	9	26	.206	.324	.426	2	2	6	22	0	47	1	0	2	107	.234	7	21	48	.146	2	5
Pose, Scott	86	160	137	27	39	42	3	0	0	12	.285	.377	.307	1	1	0	21	1	22	6	2	3	124	.266	0	11	13	.462	0	1
Sutton, Larry	43	118	102	14	23	35	6	0	2	15	.225	.308	.343	1	2	0	13	0	17	1	0	4	95	.232	1	11	7	.143	1	4
Holbert, Ray	34	115	100	14	28	31	3	0	0	5	.280	.330	.310	6	1	0	8	0	20	7	4	4	83	.289	0	5	17	.235	0	0
Hansen, Jed	49	94	79	16	16	26	1	0	3	5	.203	.289	.329	4	1	0	10	0	32	0	1	0	61	.197	3	4	18	.222	0	1
Leius, Scott	37	82	74	8	15	19	1	0	1	10	.203	.244	.257	0	3	1	4	0	8	1	0	1	41	.195	0	5	33	.212	1	5
King, Jeff	21	91	72	14	17	28	2	0	3	11	.236	.385	.389	0	1	3	15	1	10	2	0	1	59	.237	2	8	13	.231	1	3
Scarsone, Steve	46	79	68	2	14	19	5	0	0	6	.206	.295	.279	1	1	0	9	0	24	1	0	0	51	.255	0	6	17	.059	0	0
Quinn, Mark	17	65	60	11	20	44	4	1	6	18	.333	.385	.733	0	0	1	4	0	11	1	0	1	51	.333	5	17	9	.333	1	1
Fasano, Sal	23	75	60	11	14	31	2	0	5	16	.233	.373	.517	0	1	7	7	0	17	0	1	1	52	.212	4	14	8	.375	1	2
Vitiello, Joe	13	45	41	4	6	10	1	0	1	4	.146	.222	.244	0	0	2	2	0	9	0	0	2	27	.185	1	4	14	.071	0	0
Brown, Dermal	12	27	25	1	2	2	0	0	0	0	.080	.148	.080	0	0	0	2	0	7	0	0	0	25	.080	0	0	0	.000	0	0
Lopez, Mendy	7	21	20	2	8	10	0	1	0	3	.400	.429	.500	0	0	1	0	0	5	0	0	0	18	.333	0	1	2	1.000	0	2
Martinez, Felix	6	7	7	1	1	1	0	0	0	0	.143	.143	.143	0	0	0	0	0	0	0	0	1	6	.167	0	0	1	.000	0	0
Suppan, Jeff	32	5	5	0	1	1	0	0	0	1	.200	.200	.200	0	0	0	0	0	0	0	0	0	5	.200	0	1	0	.000	0	0
Rosado, Jose	33	5	5	0	0	0	0	0	0	0	.000	.000	.000	0	0	0	0	0	4	0	0	0	4	.000	0	0	1	.000	0	0
Witasick, Jay	32	5	5	0	0	0	0	0	0	0	.000	.000	.000	0	0	0	0	0	4	0	0	0	5	.000	0	0	0	.000	0	0
Reichert, Dan	8	4	3	0	1	1	0	0	0	0	.333	.333	.333	1	0	0	0	0	2	0	0	0	1	1.000	0	0	2	.000	0	0
Byrdak, Tim	33	2	2	1	1	2	1	0	0	0	.500	.500	1.000	0	0	0	0	0	0	0	0	0	1	1.000	0	0	1	.000	0	0
Appier, Kevin	22	2	2	0	0	0	0	0	0	0	.000	.000	.000	0	0	0	0	0	1	0	0	0	2	.000	0	0	0	.000	0	0
Mathews, Terry	24	1	1	0	0	0	0	0	0	0	.000	.000	.000	0	0	0	0	0	1	0	0	0	1	.000	0	0	0	.000	0	0
Montgomery, Jeff	49	0	0	0	0	0	0	0	0	0	.000	.000	.000	0	0	0	0	0	0	0	0	0	0	.000	0	0	0	.000	0	0
Service, Scott	68	0	0	0	0	0	0	0	0	0	.000	.000	.000	0	0	0	0	0	0	0	0	0	0	.000	0	0	0	.000	0	0
Barber, Brian	8	1	0	0	0	0	0	0	0	0	.000	.000	.000	1	0	0	0	0	0	0	0	0	0	.000	0	0	0	.000	0	0
Suzuki, Makoto	22	0	0	0	0	0	0	0	0	0	.000	.000	.000	0	0	0	0	0	0	0	0	0	0	.000	0	0	0	.000	0	0
Morman, Alvin	49	0	0	0	0	0	0	0	0	0	.000	.000	.000	0	0	0	0	0	0	0	0	0	0	.000	0	0	0	.000	0	0
Whisenant, Matt	48	0	0	0	0	0	0	0	0	0	.000	.000	.000	0	0	0	0	0	0	0	0	0	0	.000	0	0	0	.000	0	0
Santiago, Jose	34	0	0	0	0	0	0	0	0	0	.000	.000	.000	0	0	0	0	0	0	0	0	0	0	.000	0	0	0	.000	0	0
Ray, Ken	13	0	0	0	0	0	0	0	0	0	.000	.000	.000	0	0	0	0	0	0	0	0	0	0	.000	0	0	0	.000	0	0

Players with more than one A.L. team

Name	G	TPA	AB	R	H	TB	2B	3B	HR	RBI	Avg.	Obp.	Slg.	SH	SF	HP	BB	IBB	SO	SB	CS	GDP	vs RHP AB	Avg.	HR	RBI	vs LHP AB	Avg.	HR	RBI
Appier, Oak.	12	0	0	0	0	0	0	0	0	0	.000	.000	.000	0	0	0	0	0	0	0	0	0	2	.000	0	0	0	.000	0	0
Appier, K.C.-Oak.	34	2	2	0	0	0	0	0	0	0	.000	.000	.000	0	0	0	0	0	1	0	0	0	2	.000	0	0	0	.000	0	0
Suzuki, Sea.	16	0	0	0	0	0	0	0	0	0	.000	.000	.000	0	0	0	0	0	0	0	0	0	0	.000	0	0	0	.000	0	0
Suzuki, Sea.-K.C.	38	0	0	0	0	0	0	0	0	0	.000	.000	.000	0	0	0	0	0	0	0	0	0	0	.000	0	0	0	.000	0	0

PITCHING

Name	W	L	Pct.	ERA	IP	H	R	ER	HR	SH	SF	HB	BB	IBB	SO	G	GS	CG	ShO	GF	Sv	vs. RH AB	Avg.	HR	RBI	vs. LH AB	Avg.	HR	RBI
Suppan, Jeff	10	12	.455	4.53	208.2	222	113	105	28	7	5	3	62	4	103	32	32	4	1	0	0	408	.289	11	59	402	.259	17	42
Rosado, Jose	10	14	.417	3.85	208.0	197	103	89	24	8	4	5	72	1	141	33	33	5	0	0	0	644	.250	18	68	149	.242	6	21
Witasick, Jay	9	12	.429	5.57	158.1	191	108	98	23	4	8	8	83	1	102	32	28	1	1	2	0	322	.286	12	47	307	.322	11	45
Appier, Kevin	9	9	.500	4.87	140.1	153	81	76	18	5	3	6	51	3	78	22	22	1	0	0	0	272	.239	11	35	276	.319	7	33
Service, Scott	5	5	.500	6.09	75.1	87	51	51	13	4	7	3	42	8	68	68	0	0	0	29	8	178	.264	6	37	118	.339	7	25
Stein, Blake	1	2	.333	4.09	70.1	59	33	32	10	2	1	7	41	1	43	12	11	0	0	0	0	129	.209	4	15	128	.250	6	17
Suzuki, Makoto	2	3	.400	5.16	68.0	77	45	39	9	2	0	3	30	1	36	22	9	0	0	3	0	134	.291	4	19	134	.284	5	22
Fussell, Chris	0	5	.000	7.39	56.0	72	51	46	9	1	4	5	36	3	37	17	8	0	0	3	2	124	.339	5	21	95	.316	4	21
Morman, Alvin	2	4	.333	4.05	53.1	66	27	24	6	0	4	4	23	0	31	49	0	0	0	2	1	123	.317	4	19	92	.293	2	10
Montgomery, Jeff	1	4	.200	6.84	51.1	72	40	39	7	2	2	2	21	3	27	49	0	0	0	36	12	115	.313	5	26	95	.379	2	20
Santiago, Jose	3	4	.429	3.42	47.1	46	23	18	7	1	3	2	14	2	15	34	0	0	0	15	2	102	.284	5	24	81	.210	2	8
Whisenant, Matt	4	4	.500	6.35	39.2	40	28	28	4	1	0	7	26	1	27	48	0	0	0	21	1	93	.280	2	14	57	.246	2	12
Mathews, Terry	2	1	.667	4.38	39.0	44	21	19	4	0	4	2	17	1	19	24	1	0	0	7	1	90	.300	3	16	62	.274	1	10
Reichert, Dan	2	2	.500	9.08	36.2	48	38	37	2	1	1	2	32	1	20	8	8	0	0	0	0	74	.311	0	9	73	.342	2	19
Byrdak, Tim	0	3	.000	7.66	24.2	32	24	21	5	3	0	1	20	2	17	33	0	0	0	5	1	52	.404	2	13	52	.212	3	13
Wengert, Don	0	1	.000	9.25	24.1	41	26	25	6	0	2	0	5	0	10	11	1	0	0	2	0	52	.308	3	14	57	.439	3	14
Pittsley, Jim	1	2	.333	6.94	23.1	33	22	18	2	0	1	1	15	0	7	5	5	0	0	0	0	44	.318	1	6	54	.352	1	9
Rigby, Brad	1	2	.333	7.17	21.1	33	20	17	6	1	2	2	5	0	10	20	0	0	0	6	0	47	.340	5	13	47	.362	1	11
Barber, Brian	1	3	.250	9.64	18.2	31	20	20	6	1	1	2	10	2	7	8	3	0	0	1	1	41	.415	5	18	40	.350	1	4
Ray, Ken	1	0	1.000	8.74	11.1	23	12	11	2	0	0	1	6	0	0	13	0	0	0	4	0	37	.486	1	9	13	.385	1	3
Wallace, Derek	0	1	.000	3.24	8.1	7	4	3	2	1	1	0	5	0	5	8	0	0	0	4	0	18	.222	2	4	9	.333	0	1
Murray, Dan	0	0	.000	6.48	8.1	9	8	6	4	0	0	1	4	0	8	4	0	0	0	0	0	22	.273	4	8	12	.250	0	0
Pisciotta, Marc	0	2	.000	8.64	8.1	9	8	8	1	0	0	0	10	0	3	8	0	0	0	3	0	20	.250	0	3	12	.333	1	1
Moreno, Orber	0	0	.000	5.63	8.0	4	5	5	1	0	0	0	6	0	7	7	0	0	0	3	0	19	.158	1	3	9	.111	0	0
Carter, Lance	0	1	.000	5.06	5.1	3	3	3	2	0	0	0	3	0	3	6	0	0	0	3	0	13	.154	1	2	5	.200	1	1
Rusch, Glendon	0	1	.000	15.75	4.0	7	7	7	1	0	0	1	3	0	4	3	0	0	0	1	0	12	.417	1	5	7	.286	0	1
Durbin, Chad	0	0	.000	0.00	2.1	1	0	0	0	0	0	0	1	0	3	1	0	0	0	0	0	4	.000	0	0	4	.250	0	0

PITCHERS WITH MORE THAN ONE A.L. TEAM

Name	W	L	Pct.	ERA	IP	H	R	ER	HR	SH	SF	HB	BB	IBB	SO	G	GS	CG	ShO	GF	Sv	vs. RH AB	Avg.	HR	RBI	vs. LH AB	Avg.	HR	RBI
Appier, Oak.	7	5	.583	5.77	68.2	77	50	44	9	2	2	1	33	1	53	12	12	0	0	0	0	272	.239	11	35	276	.319	7	33
Appier, K.C.-Oak.	16	14	.533	5.17	209.0	230	131	120	27	7	5	7	84	4	131	34	34	1	0	5	0	412	.262	16	65	411	.297	11	48
Rigby, Oak.	3	4	.429	4.33	62.1	69	31	30	5	1	3	5	26	7	26	29	0	0	0	5	0	47	.340	5	13	47	.362	1	11
Rigby, Oak.-K.C.	4	6	.400	5.06	83.2	102	51	47	11	2	5	7	31	7	36	49	0	0	0	5	0	174	.259	6	30	163	.350	5	32
Stein, Oak.	0	0	.000	16.88	2.2	6	5	5	1	0	0	0	6	0	4	1	1	0	0	0	0	129	.209	4	15	128	.250	6	17
Stein, Oak.-K.C.	1	2	.333	4.56	73.0	65	38	37	11	2	1	7	47	1	47	13	12	0	0	1	0	137	.226	5	18	133	.256	6	18
Suzuki, Sea.	0	2	.000	9.43	42.0	47	47	44	7	0	3	4	34	2	32	16	4	0	0	3	0	134	.291	4	19	134	.284	5	22
Suzuki, Sea.-K.C.	2	5	.286	6.79	110.0	124	92	83	16	2	3	7	64	3	68	38	13	0	0	3	0	212	.288	9	43	222	.284	7	38

DESIGNATED HITTERS

Name	AB	Avg.	HR	RBI
Sweeney, Mike	273	.333	13	53
Giambi, Jeremy	173	.283	1	22
Pose, Scott	50	.280	0	6
Leius, Scott	23	.087	1	4
Damon, Johnny	15	.267	1	4
Sutton, Larry	13	.231	0	2
Brown, Dermal	7	.143	0	0
Vitiello, Joe	6	.167	0	0
Quinn, Mark	4	.750	2	4
Beltran, Carlos	4	.500	0	2
Dye, Jermaine	4	.000	0	0
Scarsone, Steve	2	.000	0	0
Kreuter, Chad	2	.000	0	0
King, Jeff	1	1.000	0	0
Hansen, Jed	0	-	0	0

INDIVIDUAL STATISTICS

FIELDING

FIRST BASEMEN

Player	Pct.	G	PO	A	E	TC	DP
Sweeney, Mike	.981	74	584	41	12	637	76
Sutton, Larry	.987	30	215	13	3	231	19
Giambi, Jeremy	.991	26	208	8	2	218	22
King, Jeff	.990	20	188	15	2	205	21
Leius, Scott	.971	13	61	6	2	69	13
Scarsone, Steve	1.000	12	69	9	0	78	8
Vitiello, Joe	1.000	10	65	7	0	72	11
Hansen, Jed	-	1	0	0	0	0	0

SECOND BASEMEN

Player	Pct.	G	PO	A	E	TC	DP
Febles, Carlos	.979	122	272	375	14	661	101
Hansen, Jed	.989	21	44	44	1	89	18
Holbert, Ray	.978	11	14	30	1	45	4
Scarsone, Steve	.938	9	17	13	2	32	3
Lopez, Mendy	1.000	6	11	16	0	27	5
Martinez, Felix	1.000	1	1	2	0	3	1
Leius, Scott	-	1	0	0	0	0	0

THIRD BASEMEN

Player	Pct.	G	PO	A	E	TC	DP
Randa, Joe	.952	156	119	314	22	455	28
Leius, Scott	1.000	10	7	14	0	21	3
Hansen, Jed	1.000	4	2	1	0	3	0
Scarsone, Steve	-	3	0	0	0	0	0
Holbert, Ray	-	1	0	0	0	0	0

SHORTSTOPS

Player	Pct.	G	PO	A	E	TC	DP
Sanchez, Rey	.982	134	242	452	13	707	111
Holbert, Ray	.987	22	31	46	1	78	16
Scarsone, Steve	.977	16	15	27	1	43	7
Hansen, Jed	1.000	10	11	22	0	33	3
Leius, Scott	-	2	0	0	0	0	0
Martinez, Felix	-	2	0	0	0	0	0
Lopez, Mendy	-	1	0	0	0	0	0

OUTFIELDERS

Player	Pct.	G	PO	A	E	TC	DP
Dye, Jermaine	.984	157	362	17	6	385	6
Beltran, Carlos	.972	154	395	16	12	423	2
Damon, Johnny	.987	140	301	8	4	313	0
Pose, Scott	.970	25	29	3	1	33	1
Quinn, Mark	.964	15	25	2	1	28	0
Giambi, Jeremy	1.000	5	5	0	0	5	0
Brown, Dermal	.929	3	12	1	1	14	0
Hansen, Jed	-	2	0	0	0	0	0
Sutton, Larry	-	1	0	0	0	0	0

CATCHERS

Player	Pct.	G	PO	A	E	TC	DP	PB
Kreuter, Chad	.994	101	460	44	3	507	8	6
Spehr, Tim	.990	59	274	11	3	288	4	3
Fasano, Sal	1.000	23	143	8	0	151	0	1
Sweeney, Mike	1.000	4	4	2	0	6	0	0

PITCHERS

Player	Pct.	G	PO	A	E	TC	DP
Service, Scott	.833	68	2	3	1	6	0
Morman, Alvin	.933	49	4	10	1	15	1
Montgomery, Jeff	1.000	49	3	9	0	12	2
Whisenant, Matt	.875	48	2	5	1	8	0
Santiago, Jose	1.000	34	4	4	0	8	0
Rosado, Jose	.944	33	7	27	2	36	1
Byrdak, Tim	1.000	33	2	6	0	8	1
Suppan, Jeff	.977	32	16	27	1	44	0
Witasick, Jay	.889	32	4	12	2	18	0
Mathews, Terry	1.000	24	4	4	0	8	0
Appier, Kevin	.958	22	10	13	1	24	2
Suzuki, Makoto	.917	22	5	6	1	12	0
Rigby, Brad	.500	20	1	1	2	4	0
Fussell, Chris	.727	17	2	6	3	11	3
Ray, Ken	1.000	13	1	3	0	4	2
Stein, Blake	1.000	12	2	4	0	6	0
Wengert, Don	1.000	11	0	3	0	3	0
Reichert, Dan	1.000	8	3	3	0	6	1
Barber, Brian	1.000	8	1	3	0	4	0
Pisciotta, Marc	.667	8	0	2	1	3	0
Wallace, Derek	.500	8	0	1	1	2	0
Moreno, Orber	1.000	7	1	1	0	2	0
Carter, Lance	1.000	6	0	1	0	1	0
Pittsley, Jim	.857	5	0	6	1	7	0
Murray, Dan	1.000	4	2	0	0	2	0
Rusch, Glendon	-	3	0	0	0	0	0
Durbin, Chad	-	1	0	0	0	0	0

PITCHING AGAINST EACH CLUB

Pitcher	Ana. W-L	Bal. W-L	Bos. W-L	Chi. W-L	Cle. W-L	Det. W-L	Min. W-L	N.Y. W-L	Oak. W-L	Sea. W-L	T.B. W-L	Tex. W-L	Tor. W-L	N.L. W-L	Total W-L
Appier, Kevin	1-0	0-2	0-1	3-0	1-0	0-1	1-0	0-0	1-0	1-0	0-0	0-1	1-1	0-3	9-9
Barber, Brian	0-0	0-0	0-0	1-1	0-0	0-0	0-0	0-0	0-0	0-0	0-0	0-1	0-0	0-1	1-3
Byrdak, Tim	0-1	0-0	0-1	0-1	0-0	0-0	0-0	0-0	0-0	0-0	0-0	0-0	0-0	0-0	0-3
Carter, Lance	0-1	0-0	0-0	0-0	0-0	0-0	0-0	0-0	0-0	0-0	0-0	0-0	0-0	0-0	0-1
Durbin, Chad	0-0	0-0	0-0	0-0	0-0	0-0	0-0	0-0	0-0	0-0	0-0	0-0	0-0	0-0	0-0
Fussell, Chris	0-1	0-0	0-0	0-0	0-0	0-0	0-0	0-0	0-1	0-2	0-0	0-1	0-0	0-0	0-5
Mathews, Terry	0-0	0-0	0-0	0-0	0-0	0-1	1-0	1-0	0-0	0-0	0-0	0-0	0-0	0-0	2-1
Montgomery, Jeff	0-1	0-0	0-0	0-1	1-0	0-0	0-0	0-0	0-0	0-0	0-0	0-0	0-0	0-2	1-4
Moreno, Orber	0-0	0-0	0-0	0-0	0-0	0-0	0-0	0-0	0-0	0-0	0-0	0-0	0-0	0-0	0-0
Morman, Alvin	0-1	0-0	0-0	0-0	0-0	0-1	1-0	1-0	0-1	0-0	0-0	0-1	0-0	0-0	2-4
Murray, Dan	0-0	0-0	0-0	0-0	0-0	0-0	0-1	0-1	0-0	0-0	0-0	0-0	0-0	0-0	0-2
Pisciotta, Marc	0-0	0-0	0-0	0-1	0-1	0-0	0-0	0-0	0-0	0-0	0-0	0-0	0-0	0-0	0-2
Pittsley, Jim	0-0	0-0	0-1	1-0	0-0	0-0	0-0	0-1	0-0	0-0	0-0	0-0	0-0	0-0	1-2
Ray, Ken	0-0	0-0	0-0	0-0	0-0	0-0	0-0	0-0	0-0	0-0	0-0	0-0	0-0	1-0	1-0
Reichert, Dan	0-1	0-0	0-0	0-0	0-0	0-0	0-0	0-0	1-0	0-1	0-0	1-0	0-0	0-0	2-2
Rigby, Brad	0-0	0-0	0-2	0-0	0-0	0-0	0-0	0-0	1-0	0-0	0-0	0-0	0-0	0-0	1-2
Rosado, Jose	1-1	1-1	0-3	0-0	1-0	2-1	1-1	1-1	1-2	1-1	0-0	0-1	0-0	1-2	10-14
Rusch, Glendon	0-0	0-0	0-0	0-0	0-0	0-0	0-0	0-0	0-0	0-0	0-0	0-0	0-0	0-0	0-0
Santiago, Jose	1-0	0-0	0-0	0-0	0-1	0-0	0-1	0-0	2-0	0-2	0-0	0-0	0-0	0-0	3-4
Service, Scott	0-0	0-1	0-0	0-1	0-1	0-0	1-0	1-0	1-1	1-1	0-0	0-0	0-0	1-0	5-5
Stein, Blake	0-0	0-0	0-1	0-0	0-0	0-1	0-0	0-0	0-0	0-0	0-0	1-0	0-0	0-0	1-2
Suppan, Jeff	2-0	2-0	1-2	0-0	0-1	0-2	1-1	0-0	1-1	0-2	1-1	1-0	0-1	1-1	10-12
Suzuki, Makoto	0-0	1-0	0-0	0-0	0-0	0-0	0-1	0-0	0-1	0-0	0-1	0-0	1-0	0-0	2-3
Wallace, Derek	0-0	0-1	0-0	0-0	0-0	0-0	0-0	0-0	0-0	0-0	0-0	0-0	0-0	0-0	0-1
Wengert, Don	0-0	0-0	0-0	0-0	0-0	0-0	0-0	0-0	0-0	0-1	0-0	0-0	0-0	0-0	0-1
Whisenant, Matt	0-0	0-0	0-1	1-0	1-0	0-0	0-0	0-0	0-0	1-0	0-0	0-1	0-0	1-2	4-4
Witasick, Jay	0-1	1-0	0-1	1-0	1-0	1-0	0-2	0-2	0-1	1-1	0-2	1-1	2-0	1-1	9-12
Totals	5-7	4-6	2-8	6-6	5-7	4-7	5-8	5-4	6-6	6-5	2-8	4-6	3-7	6-12	64-97

INTERLEAGUE: Ray 1-0, Appier 0-1, Rosado 0-1 vs. Brewers; Suppan 1-0, Witasick 1-0, Barber 0-1 vs. Cubs; Rosado 0-1, Montgomery 0-1, Witasick 0-1 vs. Reds; Montgomery 0-1, Appier 0-1, Suppan 0-1 vs. Astros; Rosado 1-0, Whisenant 0-2 vs. Pirates; Whisenant 1-0, Service 1-0, Appier 0-1 vs. Cardinals. Total: 6-12.

MISCELLANEOUS

HOME RUNS BY PARK

At Anaheim (7): Dye 3, Spehr 1, Randa 1, Febles 1, Beltran 1.
At Baltimore (4): Spehr 1, Damon 1, Febles 1, Beltran 1.
At Boston (1): Fasano 1.
At Chicago (AL) (12): Randa 3, Sweeney 2, Beltran 2, King 1, Leius 1, Sanchez 1, Damon 1, Dye 1.
At Chicago (NL) (5): Randa 2, Spehr 1, Damon 1, Beltran 1.
At Cleveland (8): Dye 6, Sweeney 1, Febles 1.
At Detroit (5): Sweeney 2, Damon 1, Febles 1, Quinn 1.
At Kansas City (74): Dye 15, Beltran 12, Sweeney 10, Randa 7, Damon 5, Febles 5, Spehr 4, Hansen 3, Kreuter 2, King 2, Fasano 2, Sutton 2, Giambi 2, Quinn 2, Sanchez 1.
At Milwaukee (4): Spehr 1, Damon 1, Sweeney 1, Dye 1.
At Minnesota (3): Damon 2, Beltran 1.
At New York (AL) (0):
At Oakland (3): Sweeney 1, Fasano 1, Quinn 1.
At Pittsburgh (3): Randa 2, Beltran 1.
At Seattle (7): Quinn 2, Spehr 1, Vitiello 1, Fasano 1, Dye 1, Beltran 1.
At Tampa Bay (4): Sweeney 2, Kreuter 1, Damon 1.
At Texas (4): Sweeney 2, Kreuter 1, Beltran 1.
At Toronto (2): Randa 1, Giambi 1.

LOW-HIT GAMES

No-hitters: None.
One-hitters: None.
Two-hitters: None.

10-STRIKEOUT GAMES

Jay Witasick 1, **Total:** 1.

FOUR OR MORE HITS IN ONE GAME

Joe Randa 5 (including two five-hit games), Carlos Beltran 5, Jermaine Dye 3, Mike Sweeney 2, Carlos Febles 2, Chad Kreuter 1, Rey Sanchez 1, Ray Holbert 1, Johnny Damon 1, Jeremy Giambi 1, **Total:** 22.

MULTI-HOMER GAMES

Jermaine Dye 4, Joe Randa 3, Mike Sweeney 3, Mark Quinn 2, Sal Fasano 1, Carlos Beltran 1, **Total:** 14.

GRAND SLAMS

5-1: Larry Sutton (off New York's Tony Fossas).
5-14: Mike Sweeney (off Seattle's Jeff Fassero).

PINCH HITTERS

(Minimum 5 at-bats)

Name	AB	Avg.	HR	RBI
Pose, Scott	39	.179	0	4
Giambi, Jeremy	10	.200	0	1
Leius, Scott	9	.111	0	3
Sutton, Larry	8	.250	0	1
Kreuter, Chad	7	.000	0	1
Scarsone, Steve	6	.167	0	0
Brown, Dermal	5	.000	0	0

DEBUTS

5-25: Orber Moreno, P.
7-10: Ken Ray, P.
7-16: Dan Reichert, P.
9-14: Mark Quinn, DH.
9-15: Lance Carter, P.
9-26: Chad Durbin, P.

GAMES BY POSITION

Catcher: Chad Kreuter 101, Tim Spehr 59, Sal Fasano 23, Mike Sweeney 4.
First base: Mike Sweeney 74, Larry Sutton 30, Jeremy Giambi 26, Jeff King 20, Scott Leius 13, Steve Scarsone 12, Joe Vitiello 10, Jed Hansen 1.
Second base: Carlos Febles 122, Jed Hansen 21, Ray Holbert 11, Steve Scarsone 9, Mendy Lopez 6, Scott Leius 1, Felix Martinez 1.
Third base: Joe Randa 156, Scott Leius 10, Jed Hansen 4, Steve Scarsone 3, Ray Holbert 1.
Shortstop: Rey Sanchez 134, Ray Holbert 22, Steve Scarsone 16, Jed Hansen 10, Scott Leius 2, Felix Martinez 2, Mendy Lopez 1.
Outfield: Jermaine Dye 157, Carlos Beltran 154, Johnny Damon 140, Scott Pose 25, Mark Quinn 15, Jeremy Giambi 5, Dermal Brown 3, Jed Hansen 2, Larry Sutton 1.
Designated hitter: Mike Sweeney 71, Jeremy Giambi 48, Scott Pose 18, Scott Leius 6, Larry Sutton 5, Johnny Damon 4, Jed Hansen 3, Steve Scarsone 2, Joe Vitiello 2, Dermal Brown 2, Carlos Beltran 2, Chad Kreuter 1, Jeff King 1, Jermaine Dye 1, Mark Quinn 1.

STREAKS

Wins: 4 (May 5-10).
Losses: 9 (May 29-June 7).
Consecutive games with at least one hit: 25, Mike Sweeney (July 18-August 13).
Wins by pitcher: 4, Jay Witasick (September 5-22).

ATTENDANCE

Home: 1,501,293.
Road: 2,177,728.
Highest (home): 40,257 (April 5 vs. Boston).
Highest (road): 46,549 (July 31 vs. Texas).
Lowest (home): 10,781 (September 15 vs. Anaheim).
Lowest (road): 6,839 (May 25 vs. Oakland).

Minnesota Twins

DAY BY DAY

Date	Opp.	Res.	Score	(inn.*)	Hits	Opp. hits	Winning pitcher	Losing pitcher	Save	Record	Pos.	GB
4-6	Tor.	W	6-1		15	10	Radke	Hentgen		1-0	2nd	0.5
4-7	Tor.	L	3-9		7	15	Wells	Lincoln	Halladay	1-1	T2nd	0.5
4-8	Tor.	W	11-9		15	13	Trombley	Hamilton	Aguilera	2-1	T1st	...
4-9	Cle.	L	5-14		8	20	Nagy	Hawkins		2-2	T2nd	1.0
4-10	Cle.	L	7-12		11	16	Karsay	Lincoln		2-3	T2nd	2.0
4-11	Cle.	L	8-9		9	17	Wright	Radke	Jackson	2-4	T3rd	3.0
4-12	At Det.	W	1-0	(12)	6	3	Aguilera	Runyan		3-4	T2nd	3.0
4-14	At Det.	L	1-7		3	13	Weaver	Hawkins		3-5	T2nd	4.0
4-15	At Det.	W	8-6		10	11	Wells	Moehler	Aguilera	4-5	2nd	3.5
4-17†	At Cle.	L	1-5		5	10	Nagy	Radke		4-6		
4-17‡	At Cle.	W	13-8	(11)	16	12	Aguilera	Jackson		5-6	2nd	3.5
4-18	At Cle.	L	2-3		9	8	Shuey	Wells	Jackson	5-7	T3rd	4.5
4-19	At K.C.	W	6-4		11	8	Hawkins	Suppan	Aguilera	6-7	2nd	4.0
4-20	At K.C.	W	8-7	(13)	14	12	Aguilera	Witasick		7-7	T2nd	4.0
4-21	At K.C.	L	2-3	(10)	7	9	Mathews	Guardado		7-8	3rd	5.0
4-22	Tex.	L	4-6		10	6	Sele	Milton	Wetteland	7-9	4th	5.0
4-23	Tex.	L	2-4		6	12	Clark	Lincoln	Wetteland	7-10	4th	6.0
4-24	Tex.	L	2-7		9	10	Morgan	Hawkins		7-11	4th	6.0
4-25	Tex.	L	5-9		10	11	Helling	Perkins		7-12	5th	6.0
4-26	Bos.	W	6-2		9	10	Radke	Wakefield	Trombley	8-12	4th	6.0
4-27	Bos.	W	6-5		9	11	Guardado	Corsi	Aguilera	9-12	4th	6.0
4-28	Bos.	L	4-9		13	11	Rapp	Lincoln		9-13	4th	7.0
4-30	At Bal.	L	1-7		4	8	Ponson	Hawkins		9-14	5th	7.5
5-1	At Bal.	W	7-2		11	8	Radke	Coppinger		10-14	5th	7.5
5-2	At Bal.	L	0-6		6	9	Mussina	Milton		10-15	5th	7.5
5-4	N.Y.	W	8-5		17	7	Lincoln	Mendoza	Aguilera	11-15	5th	7.5
5-5	N.Y.	L	3-5		5	11	Pettitte	Hawkins	Rivera	11-16	5th	7.5
5-6	N.Y.	L	3-4	(10)	7	14	Grimsley	Aguilera	Rivera	11-17	5th	8.5
5-7	K.C.	L	1-5		7	9	Appier	Milton		11-18	5th	9.5
5-8	K.C.	L	2-6		5	11	Rosado	Perkins	Santiago	11-19	5th	9.5
5-9	K.C.	L	2-7		9	9	Suppan	Lincoln		11-20	5th	10.5
5-10	K.C.	L	4-8		8	14	Witasick	Hawkins		11-21	5th	11.5
5-11	At T.B.	W	2-1		5	6	Radke	Rupe	Aguilera	12-21	5th	11.5
5-12	At T.B.	W	9-4		14	8	Milton	Arrojo	Trombley	13-21	5th	11.5
5-14	At Oak.	L	5-7		11	10	Worrell	Lincoln	Taylor	13-22	5th	12.5
5-15	At Oak.	L	5-6		10	8	Mathews	Guardado		13-23	5th	13.5
5-16	At Oak.	L	2-4		5	5	Haynes	Radke	Taylor	13-24	5th	13.5
5-17	At Sea.	L	5-15		9	16	Halama	Milton		13-25	5th	14.5
5-18	At Sea.	L	1-10		8	13	Garcia	Perkins		13-26	5th	15.5
5-19	At Sea.	L	0-7		5	11	Fassero	Lincoln		13-27	5th	16.5
5-21	Oak.	W	2-1	(15)	14	8	Miller	Jones		14-27	5th	15.5
5-22	Oak.	W	2-1	(10)	5	5	Wells	Rigby		15-27	5th	14.5
5-23	Oak.	W	8-3		15	7	Milton	Heredia		16-27	5th	14.5
5-24	Sea.	W	10-5		12	12	Perkins	Fassero		17-27	5th	13.5
5-25	Sea.	L	5-15		10	17	Halama	Rath		17-28	5th	14.5
5-26	Sea.	L	3-11		7	12	Moyer	Hawkins		17-29	5th	15.5
5-28	At Tex.	L	4-6		9	10	Sele	Radke	Wetteland	17-30	5th	15.5
5-29	At Tex.	L	3-4	(10)	12	11	Wetteland	Trombley		17-31	5th	15.5
5-30	At Tex.	L	2-3		6	9	Zimmerman	Mays	Wetteland	17-32	5th	15.5
5-31	At Ana.	W	3-2		8	10	Hawkins	Hasegawa	Trombley	18-32	5th	15.5
6-1	At Ana.	L	1-5		5	7	Hill	Lincoln		18-33	5th	15.5
6-2	At Ana.	L	1-2		5	9	Finley	Radke	Percival	18-34	5th	16.5
6-4	Hou.	L	6-7		6	14	Hampton	Trombley	Wagner	18-35	5th	16.5
6-5	Hou.	L	5-6		11	9	Elarton	Mays	Wagner	18-36	5th	17.5
6-6	Hou.	W	13-6		21	12	Sampson	Bergman		19-36	5th	17.5
6-7	Cin.	W	8-6		14	9	Lincoln	Avery	Trombley	20-36	5th	17.0
6-8	Cin.	W	5-2		12	5	Radke	Villone	Trombley	21-36	5th	16.0
6-9	Cin.	L	1-3		8	6	Tomko	Milton	Graves	21-37	5th	17.0
6-11	At Mil.	W	9-7		16	13	Wells	Weathers	Trombley	22-37	5th	16.5
6-12	At Mil.	W	8-6		15	15	Sampson	Eldred	Trombley	23-37	5th	16.5
6-14	At Bos.	L	3-4		7	11	Wasdin	Trombley		23-38	5th	17.5
6-15	At Bos.	L	2-4		6	12	Martinez	Milton	Wakefield	23-39	5th	18.5
6-16	At Bos.	L	1-5		8	7	Rose	Perkins	Guthrie	23-40	5th	19.5
6-17	At Bos.	W	8-7		11	12	Hawkins	Rapp	Trombley	24-40	5th	19.5
6-18	T.B.	W	8-5		12	10	Wells	Aldred	Trombley	25-40	5th	18.5
6-19	T.B.	L	3-4		10	10	Rekar	Radke	Hernandez	25-41	5th	19.5
6-20	T.B.	L	5-6	(11)	9	12	Newman	Trombley		25-42	5th	20.5
6-21	T.B.	L	2-3		5	9	Rupe	Radlosky	Hernandez	25-43	5th	21.5
6-22	At Chi.	L	1-6		8	12	Parque	Hawkins		25-44	5th	21.5
6-23	At Chi.	W	12-10		19	16	Sampson	Sirotka	Trombley	26-44	5th	21.5
6-24	At Chi.	L	3-5		14	13	Navarro	Radke	Howry	26-45	5th	21.5
6-25	At Det.	L	0-2		6	6	Moehler	Milton		26-46	5th	21.5
6-26	At Det.	W	1-0		6	5	Mays	Mlicki	Trombley	27-46	5th	20.5
6-27	At Det.	W	12-7		17	11	Hawkins	Weaver		28-46	5th	20.5
6-29	At Cle.	L	4-5		7	9	Reed	Trombley		28-47	5th	22.0
6-30	At Cle.	W	5-3		9	5	Milton	Wright	Trombley	29-47	5th	21.0

HIGHLIGHTS

High point: Second-year pitcher Eric Milton threw a no-hitter against Anaheim on September 11. He struck out 13 batters in the game played at the Metrodome.

Low point: In its last game before the All-Star break, Minnesota lost to the Pirates, 10-2. Righthander Todd Ritchie, a former No. 1 draft pick of the Twins, was the winner in that July 11 game, which added insult to injury for a franchise with a long history of failing to develop pitchers.

Turning point: The fourth game of the year—really. The Twins had taken two of three from the Blue Jays to open the season, looking competitive in the process, and they had some optimism entering a series with Cleveland. The Twins got their comeuppance—and a shot of reality—in the first game against the Indians, falling 14-5 (and then losing 12-7 and 9-8).

Most valuable player: Designated hitter/outfielder Marty Cordova is the choice. He hit .285 with 14 home runs and 70 RBIs.

Most valuable pitcher: Brad Radke somehow went 12-14 with a 3.75 ERA, which would have allowed him to win 20 games with a good team.

Most improved player: Milton progressed from a pitcher who couldn't make it through the fifth inning to one who finished second on the team in innings pitched (206.1). He led Minnesota in complete games (five) and shutouts (two).

Most pleasant surprise: Shortstop Cristian Guzman was a raw rookie with supposedly no chance of hitting major league pitching. He proved to be one of the Twins' toughest players and one of the league's most promising fielders. And by season's end, there were indications he could hit big-league pitching (he batted .291 in July and .284 in August).

Key injuries: Right fielder Matt Lawton got beaned in early June, suffering a fracture of his right eye socket, and he never fully recovered. The injury killed what was projected to be his breakthrough season.

Notable: The Twins finally found some semblance of decent starting pitching. Radke is a legitimate ace, Milton is progressing rapidly at age 24, Joe Mays had a stretch of brilliance during the middle of the season and, strangely, Hawkins, who has a nice array of pitches but fails to get results, could still make it.

—JIM SOUHAN

MISCELLANEOUS

RECORDS

1999 regular-season record: 63-97 (5th in A.L. Central); 31-50 at home; 32-47 on road; 18-31 vs. A.L. East; 20-28 vs. A.L. Central; 15-31 vs. A.L. West; 10-7 vs. N.L. Central; 13-24 vs. lefthanded starters; 50-73 vs. righthanded starters; 27-39 on grass; 36-58 on turf; 21-25 in daytime; 42-72 at night; 19-26 in one-run games; 6-5 in extra-inning games; 0-0-1 in doubleheaders.

Team record past five years: 335-455 (.424, ranks 12th in league in that span).

TEAM LEADERS

Batting average: Todd Walker (.279).
At-bats: Todd Walker (531).
Runs: Chad Allen (69).
Hits: Todd Walker (148).
Total bases: Todd Walker (211).
Doubles: Todd Walker (37).
Triples: Terry Steinbach, Todd Walker (4).
Home runs: Ron Coomer (16).
Runs batted in: Marty Cordova (70).
Stolen bases: Matt Lawton (26).
Slugging percentage: Todd Walker (.397).
On-base percentage: Todd Walker (.343).
Wins: Brad Radke (12).
Earned-run average: Brad Radke (3.75).
Complete games: Eric Milton (5).
Shutouts: Eric Milton (2).
Saves: Mike Trombley (24).
Innings pitched: Brad Radke (218.2).
Strikeouts: Eric Milton (163).

Date	Opp.	Res.	Score	(inn.*)	Hits	Opp. hits	Winning pitcher	Losing pitcher	Save	Record	Pos.	GB
7-1	At Cle.	L	5-7		12	9	Colon	Carrasco	Jackson	29-48	5th	22.0
7-2	Det.	W	11-4		13	7	Hawkins	Weaver		30-48	5th	21.0
7-3	Det.	W	7-2		13	5	Lincoln	Cruz		31-48	5th	21.5
7-4	Det.	L	5-15		8	19	Thompson	Perkins		31-49	5th	21.5
7-6	Cle.	L	1-3		6	8	Wright	Milton	Jackson	31-50	5th	22.5
7-7	Cle.	W	4-3		6	8	Trombley	Reed		32-50	5th	21.5
7-8	Cle.	L	2-9		10	16	Nagy	Lincoln		32-51	5th	22.5
7-9	Pit.	W	5-4		9	8	Radke	Silva	Trombley	33-51	5th	21.5
7-10	Pit.	W	5-4		10	12	Guardado	Williams		34-51	5th	21.5
7-11	Pit.	L	2-10		5	17	Ritchie	Mays		34-52	5th	21.5
7-15	At Chi. (NL)	L	3-9		9	17	Sanders	Radke	Adams	34-53	5th	22.5
7-16	At Chi. (NL)	L	10-11		15	16	Adams	Trombley		34-54	5th	22.5
7-17	At Chi. (NL)	W	8-0		14	3	Mays	Mulholland		35-54	5th	21.5
7-18	At StL.	W	5-2		7	9	Hawkins	Oliver		36-54	5th	20.5
7-19	At StL.	L	4-8		9	14	Mercker	Lincoln	Bottalico	36-55	5th	20.5
7-20	At StL.	W	4-2		7	7	Radke	Luebbers	Trombley	37-55	5th	20.5
7-21	Chi.	L	3-6	(10)	11	13	Simas	Carrasco	Howry	37-56	5th	20.5
7-22	Chi.	W	3-0		11	5	Mays	Baldwin	Trombley	38-56	4th	19.5
7-23	Sea.	W	5-4		13	7	Carrasco	Paniagua		39-56	4th	18.5
7-24	Sea.	W	10-3		12	6	Wells	Meche		40-56	4th	17.5
7-25	Sea.	L	3-4		7	9	Moyer	Radke	Mesa	40-57	4th	17.5
7-26	Oak.	L	7-14		12	16	Groom	Sampson		40-58	T4th	18.5
7-27	Oak.	W	3-2		6	5	Mays	Taylor	Guardado	41-58	T3rd	18.5
7-28	Oak.	W	5-3		9	8	Hawkins	Haynes	Trombley	42-58	T3rd	18.5
7-30	At Ana.	W	3-1		9	7	Radke	Hill		43-58	3rd	18.5
7-31	At Ana.	W	8-0		11	3	Milton	Finley		44-58	3rd	18.5
8-1	At Ana.	L	1-2		2	7	Sparks	Mays	Percival	44-59	3rd	18.5
8-2	At Tex.	L	4-5		9	8	Zimmerman	Guardado	Wetteland	44-60	3rd	19.5
8-3	At Tex.	L	5-9		14	13	Morgan	Sampson		44-61	4th	20.5
8-4	At Tex.	L	1-3		4	10	Loaiza	Radke	Wetteland	44-62	4th	20.5
8-6	At K.C.	W	9-8		17	14	Miller	Service	Trombley	45-62	3rd	19.5
8-7	At K.C.	W	6-5		8	9	Wells	Rigby	Trombley	46-62	3rd	19.5
8-8	At K.C.	W	7-3		11	7	Hawkins	Rigby	Carrasco	47-62	3rd	18.5
8-10	Tor.	L	6-10		11	15	Escobar	Radke		47-63	3rd	20.0
8-11	Tor.	L	3-6		7	12	Carpenter	Milton		47-64	3rd	21.0
8-12	Tor.	W	3-0		6	5	Mays	Hentgen	Trombley	48-64	3rd	20.5
8-13	At N.Y.	L	2-14		6	22	Pettitte	Hawkins		48-65	3rd	21.5
8-14	At N.Y.	W	6-3		8	9	Wells	Cone	Trombley	49-65	3rd	21.5
8-15	At N.Y.	W	5-3		10	12	Radke	Irabu	Trombley	50-65	3rd	21.5
8-16	At N.Y.	L	0-2		4	3	Clemens	Milton	Rivera	50-66	3rd	21.5
8-17	At Bal.	L	3-8		10	13	Mussina	Mays		50-67	3rd	21.5
8-18	At Bal.	L	0-2		5	5	Erickson	Hawkins		50-68	3rd	21.5
8-19	At Bal.	L	3-9		5	11	Johnson	Perkins		50-69	3rd	22.5
8-20	N.Y.	L	3-9		9	9	Irabu	Radke	Nelson	50-70	3rd	23.5
8-21	N.Y.	W	6-1		13	7	Milton	Clemens	Guardado	51-70	3rd	23.5
8-22	N.Y.	L	3-5		4	13	Hernandez	Mays	Rivera	51-71	3rd	24.5
8-23	Bos.	L	1-4		10	10	Rapp	Hawkins	Lowe	51-72	3rd	24.5
8-24	Bos.	L	1-7		5	11	Martinez	Ryan		51-73	3rd	24.5
8-25	Bos.	W	6-3		8	5	Radke	Portugal		52-73	3rd	24.5
8-27	K.C.	W	4-1		10	7	Milton	Rosado	Trombley	53-73	3rd	24.5
8-28	K.C.	W	4-3	(10)	10	6	Wells	Morman		54-73	3rd	24.5
8-29	K.C.	W	6-2		7	8	Hawkins	Stein	Wells	55-73	3rd	23.5
8-30	At Tor.	L	1-2		5	2	Hentgen	Ryan	Koch	55-74	3rd	24.5
8-31	At Tor.	W	14-3		20	9	Radke	Hamilton		56-74	3rd	24.5
9-1	At Tor.	L	0-4		5	5	Escobar	Milton		56-75	3rd	25.5
9-2	At Tor.	L	1-6		4	11	Wells	Mays		56-76	3rd	26.5
9-3	At T.B.	L	2-4		11	8	Charlton	Guardado	Hernandez	56-77	3rd	27.5
9-4	At T.B.	L	3-11		10	18	Lopez	Miller		56-78	3rd	27.5
9-5	At T.B.	W	4-1		10	5	Radke	Rupe		57-78	3rd	27.5
9-6	At T.B.	W	13-7		16	11	Carrasco	White		58-78	3rd	27.5
9-7	Bal.	L	0-5		3	10	Erickson	Mays		58-79	3rd	27.5
9-8	Bal.	L	0-10		6	14	Johnson	Hawkins		58-80	3rd	27.5
9-9	Bal.	L	5-6		7	12	Reyes	Miller	Timlin	58-81	3rd	28.0
9-10	Ana.	L	2-4		4	13	Finley	Radke	Percival	58-82	T3rd	29.0
9-11	Ana.	W	7-0		10	0	Milton	Ortiz		59-82	3rd	29.0
9-12	Ana.	L	3-6		5	9	Washburn	Mays		59-83	3rd	29.0
9-13	Ana.	L	5-6		10	10	Magnante	Hawkins	Hasegawa	59-84	T3rd	30.0
9-14	Tex.	L	4-5		10	10	Kolb	Guardado	Wetteland	59-85	4th	30.0
9-15	Tex.	L	3-8		9	12	Loaiza	Radke		59-86	4th	30.0
9-17	At Sea.	L	3-4		6	7	Abbott	Trombley		59-87	4th	29.5
9-18	At Sea.	L	0-5		2	11	Meche	Mays		59-88	4th	30.5
9-19	At Sea.	W	2-1		6	5	Hawkins	Moyer	Trombley	60-88	T3rd	29.5
9-20	At Oak.	W	4-0		11	7	Ryan	Appier		61-88	T3rd	28.5
9-21	At Oak.	L	3-5		7	9	Mahay	Carrasco	Isringhausen	61-89	T3rd	29.5
9-22	At Oak.	W	5-4		7	8	Redman	Worrell	Trombley	62-89	3rd	29.5
9-24	Chi.	W	6-2		7	2	Mays	Myette		63-89	3rd	29.0
9-25	Chi.	L	4-13		6	18	Sirotka	Hawkins		63-90	3rd	30.0
9-26	Chi.	L	0-3		6	12	Baldwin	Ryan	Howry	63-91	4th	31.0
9-27	Chi.	L	1-3		5	5	Simas	Wells	Foulke	63-92	4th	31.5
9-28	Det.	L	4-7		9	9	Anderson	Trombley	Jones	63-93	4th	32.5
9-29	Det.	L	3-6		9	7	Mlicki	Mays	Jones	63-94	4th	32.5
9-30	Det.	L	5-6		8	14	Cordero	Wells	Jones	63-95	4th	33.5
10-1	At Chi.	L	8-9		12	13	Baldwin	Ryan	Howry	63-96	5th	33.5
10-2	At Chi.	L	1-6		8	11	Wells	Perkins		63-97	5th	33.5
10-3	At Chi.	T	1-1	(7)	6	4				63-97	5th	33.0

Monthly records: April (9-14), May (9-18), June (11-15), July (15-11), August (12-16), September (7-21), October (0-2).
*Innings, if other than nine. † First game of a doubleheader. ‡ Second game of a doubleheader.

MEMORABLE GAMES

April 8 at Minneapolis

The Twins rallied for an 11-9 victory over the Blue Jays to win the first homestand of the season. The win puts the Twins at 2-1, the only time the team would be over .500 all season. In this game, the Minnesota heroes were the young players who are supposed to be the team's future.

Toronto	AB	R	H	RBI	Minnesota	AB	R	H	RBI
Stewart, lf	5	1	2	0	T.Hunter, cf	5	0	2	0
Grebeck, 2b	4	1	3	2	Hockng, ss-2b	5	0	0	0
Sh.Green, rf	5	1	1	2	T.Walker, 2b	4	2	2	0
Hollins, dh	4	1	2	0	C.Guzman, ss	0	0	0	0
C.Delgado, 1b	4	1	1	0	M.Cordva, dh	4	1	4	2
T.Fernndez, 3b	5	0	0	0	Lawton, rf	5	1	1	0
J.Cruz, cf	3	2	1	1	Allen, lf	4	2	1	0
A.Gonzalez, ss	4	2	3	2	Mientkwicz, 1b	3	3	1	1
Matheny, c	3	0	0	0	Steinbach, c	3	2	1	1
W.Greene, ph	0	0	0	0	Koskie, 3b	4	1	3	5
Berroa, ph	1	0	0	0	Coomer, 3b	0	0	0	0
Fletcher, c	1	0	0	0					
Totals	39	9	13	7	Totals	38	11	15	9

```
Toronto .................001  502 100— 9
Minnesota ...............142  310 00x— 11
```

E—A.Gonzalez (1), Koskie (2), Allen (1). DP—Toronto 2, Minnesota 1. LOB—Toronto 9, Minnesota 9. 2B—Grebeck 2 (2), A.Gonzalez (1), M.Cordova (2), Lawton (3), Mientkiewicz (3), Koskie (1). HR—Sh.Green (1), J.Cruz (1). SB—T.Walker (1).

Toronto	IP	H	R	ER	BB	SO
J.Hamilton (L, 0-1)	2.1	9	7	7	3	1
Ludwick	1	3	3	3	2	0
Munro	2.2	3	1	0	0	3
Plesac	1	0	0	0	1	0
Lloyd	1	0	0	0	0	0

Minnesota	IP	H	R	ER	BB	SO
Milton	3.2	8	6	4	1	1
Trombley (W, 1-0)	1.1	1	0	0	1	1
Mays	1	2	3	3	4	1
Guardado (H, 1)	2	1	0	0	0	3
Aguilera (S, 1)	1	1	0	0	0	0

U—HP, Merrill. 1B, Hirschbeck. 2B, Phillips. 3B, Roe. T—3:17. A—9,431.

September 11 at Minneapolis

The highlight of the Twins' 1999 season came as Eric Milton, one year after being rushed to the majors because of the Twins' dearth of pitching, gave notice that he might indeed be something special. The lefthander struck out 13 Angels in this no-hit gem and wound up leading the team in starts, complete games, shutouts and strikeouts.

Anaheim	AB	R	H	RBI	Minnesota	AB	R	H	RBI
DaVanon, rf	3	0	0	0	J.Jones, cf	4	1	1	0
O.Palmeiro, cf	2	0	0	0	Hocking, ss	4	1	2	3
T.Greene, lf	3	0	0	0	Lawton, rf	3	1	1	0
Glaus, 3b	3	0	0	0	Steinbach, c	4	1	2	1
Decker, dh	3	0	0	0	T.Walker, dh	3	0	0	0
Luke, 1b	3	0	0	0	Koskie, 3b	4	1	2	1
Hemphill, c	3	0	0	0	T.Hunter, cf	4	1	1	0
Durrington, 2b	3	0	0	0	Mientkiewicz, 1b	3	1	1	0
Sheets, ss	3	0	0	0	Davidson, 2b	3	0	0	1
Totals	26	0	0	0	Totals	32	7	10	6

```
Anaheim....................000  000 000— 0
Minnesota .................130  020 01x— 7
```

E—Hemphill (1). DP—Anaheim 1. LOB—Anaheim 1, Minnesota 4. 2B—Steinbach (15), Koskie (17), Mientkiewicz (21). 3B—J.Jones (2), Steinbach (4). HR—Hocking (7). SB—Lawton (24). CS—DaVanon (1), Hocking (6).

Anaheim	IP	H	R	ER	BB	SO
Ra.Ortiz (L, 1-2)	4.1	7	6	6	1	3
Levine	1.2	0	0	0	0	0
Holtz	1	1	0	0	0	1
Mintz	1	2	1	1	1	1

Minnesota	IP	H	R	ER	BB	SO
Milton (W, 7-11)	9	0	0	0	2	13

HBP—Lawton by Ra.Ortiz. WP—Holtz. BALKS—Ra.Ortiz. U—HP, Tim Welke. 1B, Tschida. 2B, Craft. 3B, Joyce. T—2:28. A—11,222.

BATTING

Name	G	TPA	AB	R	H	TB	2B	3B	HR	RBI	Avg.	Obp.	Slg.	SH	SF	HP	BB	IBB	SO	SB	CS	GDP	vs RHP				vs LHP			
																							AB	Avg.	HR	RBI	AB	Avg.	HR	RBI
Walker, Todd	143	586	531	62	148	211	37	4	6	46	.279	.343	.397	0	2	1	52	5	83	18	10	15	430	.302	5	36	101	.178	1	10
Allen, Chad	137	523	481	69	133	190	21	3	10	46	.277	.330	.395	1	2	2	37	1	89	14	7	10	365	.268	7	37	116	.302	3	9
Coomer, Ron	127	501	467	53	123	198	25	1	16	65	.263	.307	.424	0	3	1	30	1	96	2	1	16	352	.259	11	50	115	.278	5	15
Cordova, Marty	124	488	425	62	121	197	28	3	14	70	.285	.365	.464	0	6	9	48	2	96	13	4	22	323	.310	12	59	102	.206	2	11
Guzman, Cristian	131	456	420	47	95	116	12	3	1	26	.226	.267	.276	7	4	3	22	0	90	9	7	5	305	.200	0	18	115	.296	1	8
Lawton, Matt	118	476	406	58	105	144	18	0	7	54	.259	.353	.355	0	7	6	57	1	54	11	7	11	306	.248	5	39	100	.290	2	15
Hocking, Denny	136	421	386	47	103	146	18	2	7	41	.267	.307	.378	4	6	3	22	1	54	11	7	10	258	.279	4	27	128	.242	3	14
Hunter, Torii	135	422	384	52	98	146	17	2	9	35	.255	.309	.380	1	5	6	26	1	72	10	6	9	272	.239	7	23	112	.295	2	12
Koskie, Corey	117	392	342	42	106	160	21	0	11	58	.310	.387	.468	2	3	5	40	4	72	4	4	6	297	.316	11	53	45	.267	0	5
Steinbach, Terry	101	380	338	35	96	132	16	4	4	42	.284	.358	.391	0	2	2	38	1	54	2	2	10	283	.290	4	35	55	.255	0	7
Mientkiewicz, Doug	118	379	327	34	75	108	21	3	2	32	.229	.324	.330	3	2	4	43	3	51	1	1	13	288	.226	2	24	39	.256	0	8
Jones, Jacque	95	347	322	54	93	148	24	2	9	44	.289	.329	.460	1	3	4	17	1	63	3	4	7	286	.297	8	36	36	.222	1	8
Gates, Brent	110	346	306	40	78	104	13	2	3	38	.255	.332	.340	1	5	1	34	1	56	1	3	11	191	.241	1	15	115	.278	2	23
Valentin, Javier	78	247	218	22	54	83	12	1	5	28	.248	.313	.381	1	5	1	22	0	39	0	0	2	155	.219	4	20	63	.317	1	8
Cummings, Midre	16	42	38	1	10	13	0	0	1	9	.263	.310	.342	0	1	0	3	0	7	2	0	0	28	.250	1	7	10	.300	0	2
Pierzynski, A.J.	9	24	22	3	6	8	2	0	0	3	.273	.333	.364	0	0	1	1	0	4	0	0	0	18	.333	0	3	4	.000	0	0
Davidson, Cleatus	12	24	22	3	3	3	0	0	0	3	.136	.136	.136	2	0	0	0	0	4	2	0	2	17	.118	0	3	5	.200	0	0
Latham, Chris	14	24	22	1	2	2	0	0	0	3	.091	.083	.091	0	2	0	0	0	13	0	0	0	19	.105	0	3	3	.000	0	0
Ortiz, David	10	25	20	1	0	0	0	0	0	0	.000	.200	.000	0	0	0	5	0	12	0	0	2	18	.000	0	0	2	.000	0	0
Radke, Brad	33	5	5	0	0	0	0	0	0	0	.000	.000	.000	0	0	0	0	0	2	0	0	0	3	.000	0	0	2	.000	0	0
Sampson, Benj	30	3	3	0	0	0	0	0	0	0	.000	.000	.000	0	0	0	0	0	2	0	0	0	2	.000	0	0	1	.000	0	0
Mays, Joe	49	5	3	0	0	0	0	0	0	0	.000	.400	.000	0	0	0	2	0	1	0	0	0	2	.000	0	0	1	.000	0	0
Perkins, Dan	29	2	2	0	1	1	0	0	0	0	.500	.500	.500	0	0	0	0	0	0	0	0	0	0	.000	0	0	2	.500	0	0
Hawkins, LaTroy	33	2	2	0	0	0	0	0	0	0	.000	.000	.000	0	0	0	0	0	1	0	0	0	2	.000	0	0	0	.000	0	0
Milton, Eric	34	3	2	0	0	0	0	0	0	0	.000	.333	.000	0	0	0	1	0	1	0	0	0	2	.000	0	0	0	.000	0	0
Lincoln, Mike	18	1	1	0	0	0	0	0	0	0	.000	.000	.000	0	0	0	0	0	0	0	0	0	0	.000	0	0	1	.000	0	0
Trombley, Mike	75	0	0	0	0	0	0	0	0	0	.000	.000	.000	0	0	0	0	0	0	0	0	0	0	.000	0	0	0	.000	0	0
Guardado, Eddie	63	0	0	0	0	0	0	0	0	0	.000	.000	.000	0	0	0	0	0	0	0	0	0	0	.000	0	0	0	.000	0	0
Carrasco, Hector	40	0	0	0	0	0	0	0	0	0	.000	.000	.000	0	0	0	0	0	0	0	0	0	0	.000	0	0	0	.000	0	0
Wells, Bob	76	0	0	0	0	0	0	0	0	0	.000	.000	.000	0	0	0	0	0	0	0	0	0	0	.000	0	0	0	.000	0	0
Miller, Travis	52	0	0	0	0	0	0	0	0	0	.000	.000	.000	0	0	0	0	0	0	0	0	0	0	.000	0	0	0	.000	0	0
Romero, J.C.	5	0	0	0	0	0	0	0	0	0	.000	.000	.000	0	0	0	0	0	0	0	0	0	0	.000	0	0	0	.000	0	0

PITCHING

Name	W	L	Pct.	ERA	IP	H	R	ER	HR	SH	SF	HB	BB	IBB	SO	G	GS	CG	ShO	GF	Sv	vs RH				vs LH			
																						AB	Avg.	HR	RBI	AB	Avg.	HR	RBI
Radke, Brad	12	14	.462	3.75	218.2	239	97	91	28	5	5	1	44	0	121	33	33	4	0	0	0	399	.278	14	41	456	.281	14	53
Milton, Eric	7	11	.389	4.49	206.1	190	111	103	28	3	6	3	63	2	163	34	34	5	2	0	0	629	.240	21	78	154	.253	7	19
Hawkins, LaTroy	10	14	.417	6.66	174.1	238	136	129	29	1	5	1	60	2	103	33	33	1	0	0	0	394	.335	11	52	342	.310	18	63
Mays, Joe	6	11	.353	4.37	171.0	179	92	83	24	7	6	2	67	2	115	49	20	2	1	8	0	342	.284	9	46	322	.255	15	43
Wells, Bob	8	3	.727	3.81	87.1	79	41	37	8	5	3	5	28	4	44	76	0	0	0	18	1	202	.243	5	34	121	.248	3	15
Trombley, Mike	2	8	.200	4.33	87.1	93	42	42	15	2	3	2	28	2	82	75	0	0	0	56	24	193	.296	11	39	146	.240	4	13
Perkins, Dan	1	7	.125	6.54	86.2	117	69	63	14	2	4	5	43	0	44	29	12	0	0	0	0	193	.363	7	37	166	.283	7	29
Lincoln, Mike	3	10	.231	6.84	76.1	102	59	58	11	2	6	1	26	0	27	18	15	0	0	0	0	156	.282	5	25	162	.358	6	26
Sampson, Benj	3	2	.600	8.11	71.0	107	65	64	17	1	5	0	34	3	56	30	4	0	0	2	0	208	.361	13	44	97	.330	4	17
Miller, Travis	2	2	.500	2.72	49.2	55	19	15	3	2	2	0	16	3	40	52	0	0	0	12	0	111	.288	2	9	83	.277	1	7
Carrasco, Hector	2	3	.400	4.96	49.0	48	29	27	3	0	1	1	18	0	35	39	0	0	0	10	1	120	.242	1	18	64	.297	2	10
Guardado, Eddie	2	5	.286	4.50	48.0	37	24	24	6	2	1	2	25	4	50	63	0	0	0	13	2	93	.258	4	19	74	.176	2	9
Ryan, Jason	1	4	.200	4.87	40.2	46	23	22	9	0	1	3	17	0	15	8	8	1	0	0	0	86	.256	7	13	75	.320	2	7
Aguilera, Rick	3	1	.750	1.27	21.1	10	3	3	2	0	0	0	2	0	13	17	0	0	0	16	6	46	.109	0	1	28	.179	2	3
Redman, Mark	1	0	1.000	8.53	12.2	17	13	12	3	0	0	1	7	0	11	5	1	0	0	0	0	44	.273	3	11	13	.385	0	2
Romero, J.C.	0	0	.000	3.72	9.2	13	4	4	0	0	0	0	0	0	4	5	0	0	0	3	0	26	.385	0	3	13	.231	0	1
Radlosky, Rob	0	1	.000	12.46	8.2	15	12	12	7	0	0	1	4	0	3	7	0	0	0	2	0	28	.429	6	11	12	.250	1	4
Rath, Gary	0	1	.000	11.57	4.2	6	6	6	1	0	0	0	5	0	1	5	1	0	0	1	0	15	.333	1	3	5	.200	0	0

DESIGNATED HITTERS

Name	AB	Avg.	HR	RBI	Name	AB	Avg.	HR	RBI	Name	AB	Avg.	HR	RBI
Cordova, Marty	320	.272	9	48	Lawton, Matt	21	.238	0	2	Steinbach, Terry	1	.000	0	0
Walker, Todd	121	.256	1	9	Cummings, Midre	19	.316	0	4	Allen, Chad	1	.000	0	0
Koskie, Corey	45	.267	3	10	Ortiz, David	15	.000	0	0	Davidson, Cleatus	0	-	0	0
Coomer, Ron	25	.240	1	6	Gates, Brent	4	.250	0	3					

FIELDING

FIRST BASEMEN

Player	Pct.	G	PO	A	E	TC	DP
Mientkiewicz, Doug	.997	110	882	50	3	935	75
Coomer, Ron	.996	71	518	47	2	567	57
Gates, Brent	1.000	5	27	0	0	27	2
Hocking, Denny	1.000	2	7	0	0	7	0
Ortiz, David	1.000	1	7	0	0	7	1

SECOND BASEMEN

Player	Pct.	G	PO	A	E	TC	DP
Walker, Todd	.984	103	168	270	7	445	54
Hocking, Denny	.994	56	77	85	1	163	22
Gates, Brent	1.000	47	44	95	0	139	19
Davidson, Cleatus	.973	6	13	23	1	37	7

THIRD BASEMEN

Player	Pct.	G	PO	A	E	TC	DP
Koskie, Corey.............	.962	79	33	143	7	183	8
Gates, Brent	.972	61	27	79	3	109	10
Coomer, Ron	.969	57	24	101	4	129	9
Hocking, Denny	1.000	6	1	5	0	6	1

SHORTSTOPS

Player	Pct.	G	PO	A	E	TC	DP
Guzman, Cristian	.959	131	196	363	24	583	82
Hocking, Denny	.987	61	62	95	2	159	22
Davidson, Cleatus	1.000	4	5	5	0	10	1
Gates, Brent	-	1	0	0	0	0	0

OUTFIELDERS

Player	Pct.	G	PO	A	E	TC	DP
Allen, Chad................	.975	133	267	9	7	283	3
Hunter, Torii	.997	130	284	7	1	292	3
Lawton, Matt	.982	109	213	3	4	220	0
Jones, Jacque	.980	93	231	9	5	245	2
Hocking, Denny	1.000	38	46	5	0	51	0
Cordova, Marty	.927	29	38	0	3	41	0
Koskie, Corey.............	.962	25	25	0	1	26	0
Latham, Chris	1.000	14	13	0	0	13	0
Cummings, Midre	1.000	5	5	0	0	5	0
Coomer, Ron	-	1	0	0	0	0	0

CATCHERS

Player	Pct.	G	PO	A	E	TC	DP	PB
Steinbach, Terry	.991	96	539	30	5	574	5	5
Valentin, Javier	.998	76	387	27	1	415	4	6
Pierzynski, A.J.	1.000	9	35	2	0	37	1	1

PITCHERS

Player	Pct.	G	PO	A	E	TC	DP
Wells, Bob	.923	76	3	9	1	13	0
Trombley, Mike	1.000	75	8	9	0	17	0
Guardado, Eddie	.900	63	0	9	1	10	1
Miller, Travis	1.000	52	3	8	0	11	0
Mays, Joe	.976	49	17	23	1	41	2
Carrasco, Hector	.833	39	5	0	1	6	0
Milton, Eric	.889	34	8	16	3	27	1
Radke, Brad	1.000	33	21	36	0	57	5
Hawkins, LaTroy	.962	33	7	18	1	26	3
Sampson, Benj	1.000	30	3	4	0	7	0
Perkins, Dan	.938	29	7	8	1	16	0
Lincoln, Mike	1.000	18	5	12	0	17	0
Aguilera, Rick	1.000	17	2	1	0	3	0
Ryan, Jason	1.000	8	3	4	0	7	1
Radlosky, Rob	.667	7	1	1	1	3	0
Romero, J.C.	.667	5	1	1	1	3	1
Redman, Mark	1.000	5	2	0	0	2	0
Rath, Gary	1.000	5	0	1	0	1	0

Pitcher	Ana. W-L	Bal. W-L	Bos. W-L	Chi. W-L	Cle. W-L	Det. W-L	K.C. W-L	N.Y. W-L	Oak. W-L	Sea. W-L	T.B. W-L	Tex. W-L	Tor. W-L	N.L. W-L	Total W-L
Aguilera, Rick	0-0	0-0	0-0	0-0	1-0	1-0	1-0	0-1	0-0	0-0	0-0	0-0	0-0	0-0	3-1
Carrasco, Hector	0-0	0-0	0-0	0-1	0-1	0-0	0-0	0-0	0-1	1-0	1-0	0-0	0-0	0-0	2-3
Guardado, Eddie	0-0	0-0	1-0	0-0	0-0	0-0	0-1	0-0	0-1	0-0	0-1	0-2	0-0	1-0	2-5
Hawkins, LaTroy	1-1	0-3	1-1	0-2	0-1	2-1	3-1	0-2	1-0	1-1	0-0	0-0	0-0	1-0	10-14
Lincoln, Mike	0-1	0-0	0-1	0-0	0-2	1-0	0-1	1-0	0-1	0-0	0-0	0-0	0-1	1-1	3-10
Mays, Joe	0-2	0-2	0-1	2-0	0-0	1-1	0-0	0-1	0-1	0-1	0-0	0-1	1-1	1-2	6-11
Miller, Travis	0-0	0-1	0-0	0-0	0-0	0-0	1-0	0-0	1-0	0-0	0-1	0-0	0-0	0-0	2-2
Milton, Eric	2-0	0-1	0-1	0-0	1-1	0-1	1-1	1-1	1-0	0-1	1-0	0-0	0-2	0-1	7-11
Perkins, Dan	0-0	0-1	0-1	0-1	0-1	0-0	0-0	0-0	0-1	1-0	0-0	0-1	0-0	0-0	1-7
Radke, Brad	1-2	1-0	2-0	0-1	0-2	0-0	0-0	1-1	0-1	0-1	2-1	0-3	2-1	3-1	12-14
Radlosky, Rob	0-0	0-0	0-0	0-0	0-0	0-0	0-0	0-0	0-0	0-0	0-0	0-0	0-0	0-0	0-1
Rath, Gary	0-0	0-0	0-0	0-0	0-0	0-0	0-0	0-0	0-0	0-1	0-0	0-0	0-0	0-0	0-1
Redman, Mark	0-0	0-0	0-0	0-0	0-0	0-0	0-0	1-0	0-0	0-0	0-0	0-0	0-0	0-0	1-0
Romero, J.C.	0-0	0-0	0-0	0-0	0-0	0-0	0-0	0-0	0-0	0-0	0-0	0-0	0-0	0-0	0-0
Ryan, Jason	0-0	0-0	0-1	0-2	0-0	0-0	0-0	0-0	1-0	0-0	0-0	0-0	0-1	0-0	1-4
Sampson, Benj	0-0	0-0	0-0	0-0	0-0	0-0	0-0	0-1	0-0	0-0	0-0	0-0	0-0	2-0	3-2
Trombley, Mike	0-0	0-0	0-1	0-0	1-1	0-1	0-0	0-0	0-0	0-0	0-1	0-0	1-0	0-2	2-8
Wells, Bob	0-0	0-0	0-0	0-1	0-1	1-1	2-0	1-0	1-0	1-0	0-0	0-0	1-0	0-0	8-3
Totals	4-6	1-8	4-6	3-8	3-9	6-6	8-5	4-6	7-5	4-8	5-5	0-12	4-6	10-7	63-97

INTERLEAGUE: Wells 1-0, Sampson 1-0 vs. Brewers; Mays 1-0, Radke 0-1, Trombley 0-1 vs. Cubs; Lincoln 1-0, Radke 1-0, Milton 0-1 vs. Reds; Sampson 1-0, Trombley 0-1, Mays 0-1 vs. Astros; Radke 1-0, Guardado 1-0, Mays 0-1 vs. Pirates; Hawkins 1-0, Radke 1-0, Lincoln 0-1 vs. Cardinals. Total: 10-7.

HOME RUNS BY PARK

At Anaheim (2): Hunter 1, Koskie 1.
At Baltimore (3): Coomer 2, Hocking 1.
At Boston (2): Hunter 1, Allen 1.
At Chicago (AL) (4): Coomer 1, Cordova 1, Lawton 1, Jones 1.
At Chicago (NL) (4): Hocking 1, Coomer 1, Hunter 1, Allen 1.
At Cleveland (8): Steinbach 1, Hocking 1, Coomer 1, Lawton 1, Hunter 1, Valentin 1, Koskie 1, Allen 1.
At Detroit (7): Koskie 2, Gates 1, Coomer 1, Walker 1, Hunter 1, Allen 1.
At Kansas City (7): Cordova 2, Allen 2, Coomer 1, Lawton 1, Hunter 1.
At Milwaukee (2): Cordova 1, Koskie 1.
At Minnesota (47): Cordova 9, Coomer 6, Jones 5, Walker 4, Koskie 4, Allen 4, Steinbach 3, Gates 2, Hocking 2, Lawton 2, Hunter 2, Valentin 2, Cummings 1, Guzman 1.
At New York (AL) (2): Valentin 1, Mientkiewicz 1.
At Oakland (3): Coomer 2, Lawton 1.
At Seattle (0):
At St. Louis (2): Hocking 1, Jones 1.
At Tampa Bay (6): Koskie 2, Walker 1, Hunter 1, Mientkiewicz 1, Jones 1.
At Texas (2): Hocking 1, Valentin 1.
At Toronto (3): Coomer 1, Cordova 1, Jones 1.

LOW-HIT GAMES

No-hitters: Eric Milton, September 11 vs. Anaheim, W 7-0.
One-hitters: None.
Two-hitters: Jason Ryan, August 30 vs. Toronto, L 2-1.

10-STRIKEOUT GAMES

Eric Milton 3, **Total:** 3.

FOUR OR MORE HITS IN ONE GAME

Denny Hocking 2 (including one five-hit game), Matt Lawton 2, Ron Coomer 1, Marty Cordova 1, Todd Walker 1, Corey Koskie 1, Doug Mientkiewicz 1, Chad Allen 1, **Total:** 10.

MULTI-HOMER GAMES

Ron Coomer 2, Corey Koskie 1, **Total:** 3.

GRAND SLAMS

4-17: Matt Lawton (off Cleveland's Jerry Spradlin).
4-26: Torii Hunter (off Boston's Tim Wakefield).
6-4: Denny Hocking (off Houston's Mike Hampton).
7-24: Corey Koskie (off Seattle's Frank Rodriguez).

PINCH HITTERS

(Minimum 5 at-bats)

Name	AB	Avg.	HR	RBI
Gates, Brent..................	25	.200	0	4
Hocking, Denny.............	23	.130	0	2
Cordova, Marty	14	.357	0	3
Mientkiewicz, Doug	11	.182	0	0
Koskie, Corey	10	.600	0	1

Name	AB	Avg.	HR	RBI
Coomer, Ron	8	.500	0	3
Hunter, Torii.....................	8	.000	0	0
Lawton, Matt	6	.333	1	7
Cummings, Midre	6	.167	1	4
Walker, Todd	5	.400	0	1

DEBUTS

4-6: Chad Allen, LF.
4-6: Cristian Guzman, SS.
4-7: Dan Perkins, P.
4-7: Mike Lincoln, P.
4-7: Joe Mays, P.
5-25: Rob Radlosky, P.
5-30: Cleatus Davidson, PR.
6-9: Jacque Jones, RF.
7-24: Mark Redman, P.
8-24: Jason Ryan, P.
9-15: J.C. Romero, P.

GAMES BY POSITION

Catcher: Terry Steinbach 96, Javier Valentin 76, A.J. Pierzynski 9.
First base: Doug Mientkiewicz 110, Ron Coomer 71, Brent Gates 5, Denny Hocking 2, David Ortiz 1.
Second base: Todd Walker 103, Denny Hocking 56, Brent Gates 47, Cleatus Davidson 6.
Third base: Corey Koskie 79, Brent Gates 61, Ron Coomer 57, Denny Hocking 6.
Shortstop: Cristian Guzman 131, Denny Hocking 61, Cleatus Davidson 4, Brent Gates 1.
Outfield: Chad Allen 133, Torii Hunter 130, Matt Lawton 109, Jacque Jones 93, Denny Hocking 38, Marty Cordova 29, Corey Koskie 25, Chris Latham 14, Midre Cummings 6, Ron Coomer 1.
Designated hitter: Marty Cordova 85, Todd Walker 34, Corey Koskie 12, Ron Coomer 7, Matt Lawton 6, Midre Cummings 5, David Ortiz 5, Chad Allen 2, Terry Steinbach 1, Brent Gates 1, Cleatus Davidson 1.

STREAKS

Wins: 4 (May 21-24, July 27-31, August 25-29).
Losses: 9 (September 25-October 3).
Consecutive games with at least one hit: 11, Cristian Guzman (July 11-25).
Wins by pitcher: 3, Brad Radke (August 25-September 5), Joe Mays (July 17-27).

ATTENDANCE

Home: 1,202,829.
Road: 2,217,425.
Highest (home): 45,601 (April 6 vs. Toronto).
Highest (road): 56,180 (August 15 vs. New York).
Lowest (Home): 8,716 (September 13 vs. Anaheim).
Lowest (road): 6,498 (September 21 vs. Oakland).

NEW YORK YANKEES

1999 REVIEW

DAY BY DAY

Date	Opp.	Res.	Score	(inn.*)	Hits	Opp. hits	Winning pitcher	Losing pitcher	Save	Record	Pos.	GB
4-5	At Oak.	L	3-5		5	7	Mathews	Stanton		0-1	T4th	1.0
4-6	At Oak.	W	7-4		12	5	Hernandez	Candiotti	Rivera	1-1	3rd	0.5
4-7	At Oak.	W	4-0		8	5	Mendoza	Haynes		2-1	2nd	0.5
4-9	Det.	W	12-3	(7)	9	3	Cone	Graterol		3-1	2nd	1.0
4-10	Det.	W	5-0		10	3	Clemens	Moehler		4-1	2nd	1.0
4-11	Det.	W	11-2		9	5	Hernandez	Thompson		5-1	T1st	...
4-13	Bal.	W	6-3		7	10	Nelson	Rhodes		6-1	T1st	...
4-14	Bal.	W	14-7		17	9	Cone	Erickson		7-1	1st	+0.5
4-15	Bal.	L	7-9		10	18	Rhodes	Rivera	Timlin	7-2	1st	+0.5
4-16	At Det.	L	1-8		7	5	Thompson	Hernandez		7-3	1st	+0.5
4-17	At Det.	L	1-3		6	10	Anderson	Nelson	Jones	7-4	3rd	0.5
4-18	At Det.	L	1-5		6	9	Mlicki	Mendoza		7-5	3rd	1.5
4-20	Tex.	W	4-0		13	4	Cone	Burkett		8-5	T2nd	1.5
4-21	Tex.	W	4-2		6	5	Clemens	Helling	Rivera	9-5	2nd	1.5
4-23	Tor.	W	6-4		9	10	Hernandez	Wells	Rivera	10-5	2nd	1.0
4-24	Tor.	W	7-4		9	9	Mendoza	Plesac	Rivera	11-5	T1st	...
4-25	Tor.	W	4-3	(11)	9	5	Grimsley	Person		12-5	1st	+1.0
4-27	At Tex.	W	7-6		14	7	Stanton	Wetteland	Rivera	13-5	1st	+1.5
4-28	At Tex.	L	6-8		10	12	Munoz	Stanton	Wetteland	13-6	1st	+1.5
4-29	At Tex.	W	5-3		6	9	Mendoza	Morgan	Rivera	14-6	1st	+2.5
4-30	At K.C.	L	6-13		12	15	Morman	Pettitte		14-7	1st	+2.5
5-1	At K.C.	W	8-4		13	7	Cone	Pittsley		15-7	1st	+2.5
5-2	At K.C.	W	9-8		14	14	Grimsley	Santiago	Rivera	16-7	1st	+3.5
5-3	At K.C.	L	3-9		7	8	Service	Hernandez		16-8	1st	+2.5
5-4	At Min.	L	5-8		7	17	Lincoln	Mendoza	Aguilera	16-9	1st	+2.5
5-5	At Min.	W	5-3		11	5	Pettitte	Hawkins	Rivera	17-9	1st	+3.5
5-6	At Min.	W	4-3	(10)	14	7	Grimsley	Aguilera	Rivera	18-9	1st	+3.5
5-7	Sea.	W	10-1		10	5	Irabu	Suzuki		19-9	1st	+4.5
5-8	Sea.	L	5-14		8	19	Garcia	Hernandez		19-10	1st	+3.5
5-9	Sea.	W	6-1		9	3	Grimsley	Fassero		20-10	1st	+4.0
5-11	Ana.	L	7-9		8	14	Petkovsek	Mendoza	Percival	20-11	1st	+3.5
5-12	Ana.	L	0-1		3	6	Finley	Cone	Percival	20-12	1st	+2.5
5-13	Ana.	L	0-2		6	9	Olivares	Irabu	Percival	20-13	1st	+2.0
5-14	Chi.	L	2-8		6	9	Parque	Hernandez	Simas	20-14	1st	+1.0
5-15	Chi.	L	4-12		13	17	Snyder	Mendoza		20-15	T1st	...
5-16	Chi.	W	2-1		8	8	Pettitte	Sirotka	Rivera	21-15	1st	+1.0
5-18	At Bos.	L	3-6		13	10	Martinez	Cone	Gordon	21-16	2nd	0.5
5-19	At Bos.	L	0-6		8	15	Rose	Irabu		21-17	2nd	1.5
5-20	At Bos.	W	3-1		5	3	Hernandez	Portugal	Rivera	22-17	2nd	0.5
5-22†	At Chi.	W	10-2		13	7	Clemens	Snyder		23-17		
5-22‡	At Chi.	L	1-2		2	6	Sirotka	Pettitte	Simas	23-18	2nd	1.5
5-23	At Chi.	W	8-7	(10)	9	12	Rivera	Simas		24-18	2nd	1.5
5-25	Bos.	L	2-5		6	10	Rose	Irabu	Gordon	24-19	2nd	2.5
5-26	Bos.	W	8-3		11	8	Hernandez	Portugal	Rivera	25-19	2nd	1.5
5-27	Bos.	W	4-1		9	2	Clemens	Rapp	Rivera	26-19	2nd	0.5
5-28	At Tor.	W	10-6		16	9	Pettitte	Carpenter		27-19	2nd	0.5
5-29	At Tor.	W	8-3		12	7	Cone	Hentgen		28-19	2nd	0.5
5-30	At Tor.	W	8-3		9	8	Irabu	Wells		29-19	2nd	0.5
5-31	Cle.	L	1-7		7	7	Nagy	Hernandez		29-20	2nd	1.5
6-1	Cle.	W	11-5		13	9	Clemens	Burba		30-20	2nd	1.5
6-2	Cle.	L	7-10		9	15	Karsay	Pettitte	Jackson	30-21	2nd	1.5
6-4	N.Y. (NL)	W	4-3		5	7	Grimsley	Reed	Rivera	31-21	2nd	1.5
6-5	N.Y. (NL)	W	6-3		11	9	Hernandez	Yoshii	Rivera	32-21	2nd	0.5
6-6	N.Y. (NL)	L	2-7		6	8	Leiter	Clemens		32-22	2nd	0.5
6-7	At Phi.	L	5-6		7	9	Byrd	Pettitte		32-23	2nd	0.5
6-8	At Phi.	L	5-11		8	11	Perez	Grimsley		32-24	2nd	0.5
6-9	At Phi.	W	11-5		13	9	Cone	Ogea		33-24	1st	+0.5
6-11	At Fla.	W	8-4		11	6	Hernandez	Meadows	Rivera	34-24	1st	+0.5
6-12	At Fla.	W	5-4		6	9	Clemens	Hernandez	Rivera	35-24	1st	+1.5
6-13	At Fla.	L	2-8		5	13	Fernandez	Pettitte		35-25	1st	+1.5
6-14	Tex.	W	8-2		14	8	Irabu	Clark		36-25	1st	+1.5
6-15	Tex.	W	6-2		6	4	Cone	Glynn		37-25	1st	+1.5
6-16	Tex.	L	0-3		4	5	Helling	Hernandez	Wetteland	37-26	1st	+0.5
6-17	Tex.	L	2-4		7	10	Sele	Clemens	Wetteland	37-27	1st	+0.5
6-18	Ana.	W	4-1		8	5	Pettitte	Finley	Rivera	38-27	1st	+1.5
6-19	Ana.	W	6-2		11	3	Irabu	Olivares	Mendoza	39-27	1st	+1.5
6-20	Ana.	L	2-4		7	8	Belcher	Cone	Percival	39-28	1st	+0.5
6-22	At T.B.	W	7-0		12	3	Hernandez	Witt		40-28	1st	+1.0
6-23	At T.B.	W	12-4		19	11	Clemens	Eiland		41-28	1st	+1.0
6-24	At T.B.	W	7-3		13	7	Pettitte	Rekar	Mendoza	42-28	1st	+1.0
6-25	At Bal.	W	9-8		16	13	Naulty	Timlin	Rivera	43-28	1st	+1.0
6-26	At Bal.	W	7-4		11	8	Cone	Johnson	Rivera	44-28	1st	+1.0
6-27	At Bal.	W	6-2		12	7	Hernandez	Ponson		45-28	1st	+2.0
6-29	Det.	W	3-0		6	8	Clemens	Thompson		46-28	1st	+2.0
6-30	Det.	L	2-8		12	11	Moehler	Pettitte		46-29	1st	+2.0

HIGHLIGHTS

High point: What else? The last out of the millennium, Keith Lockhart's pop fly to Chad Curtis in left field on October 27. With that, the Yankees swept the Braves and won their 25th World Series title and third in four years.

Low point: The spring. In March, news of Torre's cancer diagnosis stunned the club. Then, in April, the team was shaken by Darryl Strawberry's arrest in Florida on charges of cocaine possession and solicitation (he pleaded no contest to both).

Turning point: Stuck in a four-game losing streak and down 6-1 in the eighth inning of a September 14 game in Toronto, the Yankees rallied to win. Bernie Williams hit an eighth-inning, game-tying grand slam against Billy Koch, and Paul O'Neill homered with the bases loaded in the ninth for the victory. The win rejuvenated the Yankees and helped them stave off Boston in the A.L. East.

Most valuable player: Derek Jeter. The always-improving Jeter, 25, set career highs in many offensive categories and improved his defense as well. While most teammates slumped in the first half of the season, the shortstop reached base safely in the club's first 53 games.

Most valuable pitcher: Mariano Rivera. Once the Yankees took a lead into the ninth, they were virtually certain of victory. The closer converted 45 of 49 save opportunities.

Most improved player: Andy Pettitte, who flashed some of his 1996 and 1997 form. Once the July 31 trading deadline passed, the lefthander seemed at ease and went 5-1 with a 1.76 ERA in six August starts. And he was 2-0 in postseason play.

Most pleasant surprise: Jason Grimsley. A non-roster invitee to spring training, Grimsley helped bridge the gap from the starters to Rivera and finished 7-2 with a 3.60 ERA. He was particularly effective in May (1.21 ERA in 13 games) and September (0.96 in seven games).

Key injuries: Really, the most significant absence was that of Torre. After being diagnosed with prostate cancer in March and then undergoing surgery, he missed the last three weeks of spring training and the first 36 games of the season. The Yankees were fortunate that they lost only one player—reliever Jeff Nelson—for an extended time because of injury. Nelson had two stints on the D.L. and underwent arthroscopic surgery on his elbow in June.

Notable: David Cone pitched a perfect game against the Expos on July 18. ... Bernie Williams, in the first season of his seven-year, $87.5 million contract, put up career highs in batting average (.342), hits (202), runs (116), RBIs (115), walks (100) and games (158).
—KEN DAVIDOFF

MISCELLANEOUS

RECORDS

1999 regular-season record: 98-64 (1st in A.L. East); 48-33 at home; 50-31 on road; 31-18 vs. A.L. East; 31-22 vs. A.L. Central; 27-15 vs. A.L. West; 9-9 vs. N.L. East; 19-14 vs. lefthanded starters; 79-50 vs. righthanded starters; 83-58 on grass; 15-6 on turf; 34-24 in daytime; 64-40 at night; 22-12 in one-run games; 7-2 in extra-inning games; 0-0-2 in doubleheaders.
Team record past five years: 479-313 (.605, ranks 1st in league in that span).

TEAM LEADERS

Batting average: Derek Jeter (.349).
At-bats: Derek Jeter (627).
Runs: Derek Jeter (134).
Hits: Derek Jeter (219).
Total bases: Derek Jeter (346).
Doubles: Paul O'Neill (39).
Triples: Derek Jeter (9).
Home runs: Tino Martinez (28).
Runs batted in: Bernie Williams (115).
Stolen bases: Chuck Knoblauch (28).
Slugging percentage: Derek Jeter (.552).
On-base percentage: Derek Jeter (.438).
Wins: Orlando Hernandez (17).
Earned-run average: David Cone (3.44).
Complete games: Orlando Hernandez, Hideki Irabu (2).
Shutouts: Roger Clemens, David Cone, Orlando Hernandez, Hideki Irabu (1).
Saves: Mariano Rivera (45).
Innings pitched: Orlando Hernandez (214.1).
Strikeouts: David Cone (177).

Date	Opp.	Res.	Score	(inn.*)	Hits	Opp. hits	Winning pitcher	Losing pitcher	Save	Record	Pos.	GB
7-1	Det.	W	6-0		11	3	Irabu	Mlicki		47-29	1st	+3.0
7-2	Bal.	W	2-1		7	8	Cone	Johnson	Rivera	48-29	1st	+3.0
7-3	Bal.	W	6-5		9	6	Grimsley	Rhodes		49-29	1st	+4.0
7-4	Bal.	L	3-7		9	9	Guzman	Mendoza	Kamieniecki	49-30	1st	+3.0
7-5	Bal.	L	1-9		7	13	Mussina	Pettitte		49-31	1st	+2.0
7-6	At Det.	W	9-8	(10)	17	9	Rivera	Jones	Mendoza	50-31	1st	+3.0
7-7	At Det.	W	4-6		10	12	Mlicki	Cone	Brocail	50-32	1st	+3.0
7-8	At Det.	W	3-2		9	8	Hernandez	Nitkowski	Rivera	51-32	1st	+4.0
7-9	At N.Y. (NL)	L	2-5		5	12	Leiter	Clemens	Benitez	51-33	1st	+3.0
7-10	At N.Y. (NL)	W	8-9		11	9	Mahomes	Rivera		51-34	1st	+3.0
7-11	At N.Y. (NL)	W	6-3		13	8	Irabu	Hershiser	Rivera	52-34	1st	+4.0
7-15	Atl.	L	2-6		7	10	Glavine	Clemens		52-35	1st	+3.0
7-16	Atl.	L	7-10		14	12	Springer	Rivera	Rocker	52-36	1st	+3.0
7-17	Atl.	W	11-4		13	12	Pettitte	Perez	Grimsley	53-36	1st	+4.0
7-18	Mon.	W	6-0		8	0	Cone	Vazquez		54-36	1st	+4.0
7-19	Mon.	L	4-6		10	12	Kline	Mendoza	Urbina	54-37	1st	+4.0
7-20	Mon.	W	7-4		9	9	Clemens	Thurman	Rivera	55-37	1st	+4.0
7-21	T.B.	W	4-3		8	7	Hernandez	Witt	Rivera	56-37	1st	+5.0
7-22	T.B.	W	5-4		12	9	Pettitte	Rekar	Rivera	57-37	1st	+6.0
7-23	Cle.	W	9-8	(10)	13	10	Grimsley	Jackson		58-37	1st	+6.0
7-24	Cle.	W	21-1		21	9	Irabu	Langston		59-37	1st	+7.0
7-25	Cle.	W	2-1		6	6	Mendoza	Rincon		60-37	1st	+7.0
7-27	At Chi.	W	5-3		10	10	Hernandez	Baldwin	Rivera	61-37	1st	+7.5
7-28	At Chi.	L	3-11		11	19	Castillo	Pettitte		61-38	1st	+7.0
7-29	At Chi.	L	1-5		5	9	Snyder	Cone	Foulke	61-39	1st	+6.5
7-30	At Bos.	W	13-3		16	7	Irabu	Portugal		62-39	1st	+7.0
7-31	At Bos.	L	5-6		15	12	Lowe	Mendoza		62-40	1st	+6.0
8-1	At Bos.	L	4-5		9	9	Saberhagen	Hernandez	Wakefield	62-41	1st	+5.0
8-2	Tor.	W	3-1		7	7	Pettitte	Wells	Rivera	63-41	1st	+6.0
8-3	Tor.	L	1-3		5	11	Hamilton	Cone	Koch	63-42	1st	+5.0
8-4	Tor.	W	8-3		8	9	Irabu	Escobar		64-42	1st	+6.0
8-5	At Sea.	W	7-4		12	6	Clemens	Moyer	Rivera	65-42	1st	+6.5
8-6	At Sea.	W	11-8		15	13	Watson	Fassero	Rivera	66-42	1st	+6.5
8-7	At Sea.	W	1-0		3	4	Pettitte	Garcia	Rivera	67-42	1st	+7.5
8-8	At Sea.	W	9-3		11	6	Cone	Halama		68-42	1st	+7.5
8-9	At Oak.	W	12-8		9	13	Mendoza	Haynes		69-42	1st	+7.5
8-10	At Oak.	L	1-6		9	10	Olivares	Clemens	Jones	69-43	1st	+6.5
8-11	At Oak.	W	5-3		8	6	Watson	Jones	Rivera	70-43	1st	+6.5
8-13	Min.	W	14-2		22	6	Pettitte	Hawkins		71-43	1st	+7.5
8-14	Min.	L	3-6		9	8	Wells	Cone	Trombley	71-44	1st	+6.5
8-15	Min.	L	3-5		12	10	Radke	Irabu	Trombley	71-45	1st	+6.5
8-16	Min.	W	2-0		3	4	Clemens	Milton	Rivera	72-45	1st	+6.5
8-17	K.C.	W	5-2		7	7	Hernandez	Rosado	Rivera	73-45	1st	+7.5
8-18	K.C.	L	0-3		6	8	Reichert	Pettitte	Montgomery	73-46	1st	+6.5
8-19	K.C.	L	1-4	(11)	5	6	Rigby	Grimsley	Montgomery	73-47	1st	+6.5
8-20	At Min.	W	9-3		9	9	Irabu	Radke	Nelson	74-47	1st	+7.5
8-21	At Min.	L	1-6		7	13	Milton	Clemens	Guardado	74-48	1st	+7.5
8-22	At Min.	W	5-3		13	4	Hernandez	Mays	Rivera	75-48	1st	+8.5
8-23	At Tex.	W	21-3		23	10	Pettitte	Burkett		76-48	1st	+8.5
8-24	At Tex.	W	10-7	(11)	11	14	Mendoza	Lee	Rivera	77-48	1st	+8.5
8-25	At Tex.	L	3-7		8	12	Loaiza	Irabu		77-49	1st	+8.5
8-27	Sea.	W	8-0		12	5	Clemens	Meche		78-49	1st	+8.5
8-28	Sea.	W	2-1		8	4	Rivera	Paniagua		79-49	1st	+8.5
8-29	Sea.	W	11-5		12	10	Pettitte	Abbott	Rivera	80-49	1st	+8.5
8-30	Oak.	W	7-4		8	10	Nelson	Mathews	Rivera	81-49	1st	+8.5
8-31	Oak.	L	2-3	(11)	8	10	Jones	Mendoza	Isringhausen	81-50	1st	+7.5
9-1	Oak.	L	1-7		6	10	Olivares	Clemens		81-51	1st	+6.5
9-2	Oak.	W	9-3		14	8	Hernandez	Heredia		82-51	1st	+7.5
9-3	At Ana.	L	2-8		10	15	Belcher	Pettitte		82-52	1st	+7.5
9-4	At Ana.	W	9-6		10	6	Watson	Alvarez	Rivera	83-52	1st	+7.5
9-5	At Ana.	W	8-3		13	6	Yarnall	Fyhrie		84-52	1st	+7.5
9-6	At Ana.	L	3-5		5	6	Washburn	Clemens	Percival	84-53	1st	+6.5
9-7	At K.C.	L	3-6		13	10	Rosado	Cone	Montgomery	84-54	1st	+5.5
9-8	At K.C.	W	9-5		11	15	Hernandez	Rusch	Rivera	85-54	1st	+6.5
9-10	Bos.	L	1-3		1	12	Martinez	Pettitte		85-55	1st	+5.5
9-11	Bos.	L	10-11		12	10	Garces	Irabu	Beck	85-56	1st	+4.5
9-12	Bos.	L	1-4		5	7	Cormier	Clemens	Beck	85-57	1st	+3.5
9-13	At Tor.	L	1-2		4	5	Wells	Hernandez		85-58	1st	+3.5
9-14	At Tor.	W	10-6		9	11	Mendoza	Koch		86-58	1st	+3.5
9-15	At Tor.	W	6-4		7	8	Pettitte	Hentgen	Rivera	87-58	1st	+3.5
9-16	At Cle.	W	9-5		12	10	Irabu	Burba		88-58	1st	+4.0
9-17	At Cle.	W	9-4		9	5	Clemens	Wright		89-58	1st	+3.0
9-18	At Cle.	L	4-5		12	8	Nagy	Hernandez	Jackson	89-59	1st	+3.0
9-19	At Cle.	W	11-7		18	9	Watson	Martin		90-59	1st	+3.0
9-21	Chi.	W	3-1		10	6	Pettitte	Baldwin	Rivera	91-59	1st	+3.0
9-22	Chi.	W	5-4		9	9	Rivera	Navarro		92-59	1st	+4.0
9-23	Chi.	W	5-2		12	7	Clemens	Parque	Rivera	93-59	1st	+5.0
9-24	T.B.	W	4-3	(11)	9	7	Stanton	Charlton		94-59	1st	+6.0
9-25	T.B.	L	1-2		5	11	Arrojo	Cone	Hernandez	94-60	1st	+5.0
9-26	T.B.	L	5-6		11	15	Lidle	Mendoza	Hernandez	94-61	1st	+5.0
9-27	T.B.	L	6-10		9	11	Duvall	Irabu	Sparks	94-62	1st	+4.0
9-28	At Bal.	W	9-5		10	10	Mendoza	Ponson		95-62	1st	+4.5
9-30†	At Bal.	L	0-5		8	5	Mussina	Clemens		95-63		
9-30‡	At Bal.	W	12-5		17	12	Hernandez	Corsi		96-63	1st	+5.0
10-1	At T.B.	W	11-7		14	9	Mendoza	Arrojo	Rivera	97-63	1st	+5.0
10-2	At T.B.	W	3-2		9	6	Cone	Alvarez	Rivera	98-63	1st	+5.0
10-3	At T.B.	L	2-6		6	6	Gaillard	Juden	Hernandez	98-64	1st	+4.0

Monthly records: April (14-7), May (15-13), June (17-9), July (16-11), August (19-10), September (15-13), October (2-1).
*Innings, if other than nine. † First game of a doubleheader. ‡ Second game of a doubleheader.

MEMORABLE GAMES

June 1 at New York

Roger Clemens joins Carl Hubbell (24), Elroy Face (22) and Rube Marquard (20) as the only pitchers in major league history to win 20 consecutive decisions. Clemens' 20th straight victory extended his A.L. record as well. Though he was shaky against a devastating lineup, Clemens' Yankee mates would hammer Dave Burba to earn Clemens the victory. The 36-year-old righthander would lose his next start, against the Mets, five days later.

Cleveland	AB	R	H	RBI		NY Yankees	AB	R	H	RBI
Lofton, cf	3	2	1	0		Knoblauch, 2b	4	2	2	1
Vizquel, ss	4	0	1	0		Jeter, ss	3	2	2	3
Alomar, 2b	3	0	2	1		O'Neill, rf	5	2	3	2
M.Ramirez, rf	5	0	0	1		B.Williams, cf	3	2	3	2
Thome, 1b	4	0	0	0		T.Martinez, 1b	4	0	1	0
W.Cordero, dh	3	2	2	1		C.Davis, dh	4	0	2	1
Justice, lf	3	0	0	0		Tarasco, lf	2	0	0	0
Fryman, 3b	4	1	2	2		Curtis, ph-lf	1	0	0	0
Ei.Diaz, c	4	0	1	0		Posada, c	1	1	0	1
						Brosius, 3b	4	1	1	0
Totals	33	5	9	5		Totals	31	11	13	10

Cleveland ....101 100 020 —5
NY Yankees ....201 201 23x —11

DP—Cleveland 2. LOB—Cleveland 8, NY Yankees 6. 2B—Knoblauch (10), Jeter (14), O'Neill (10). HR—W.Cordero (5), Fryman (8), Knoblauch (4), O'Neill (5), B.Williams (7). CS—Fryman (1), Jeter (4). S—Vizquel, Alomar. SF—B.Williams, Posada.

Cleveland	IP	H	R	ER	BB	SO
Burba (L, 5-2)	4	7	5	5	5	2
D.Stevens	2	2	1	1	1	1
Assenmacher	0	2	2	2	1	0
S.Reed	1.2	2	3	3	0	1
Rincon	0.1	0	0	0	0	0

NY Yankees	IP	H	R	ER	BB	SO
Clemens (W, 5-0)	6.2	7	3	3	2	4
Grimsley (H, 3)	1.1	1	2	2	1	0
M.Rivera	1	1	0	0	0	0

HBP—Lofton by Clemens, W.Cordero by Grimsley, Jeter by S.Reed. WP—Burba, Grimsley 2. U—HP, Young. 1B, Tschida. 2B, Reed. 3B, Clark. T—3:18. A—32,759.

July 18 at New York

On a day when the Yankees celebrated their history, they added a wonderful chapter to it. Don Larsen threw out the first pitch to Yogi Berra on Yogi Berra Day, and then David Cone and Joe Girardi went out and duplicated what Larsen and Berra did on October 8, 1956. Cone needed just 88 pitches and survived a third-inning rain delay to become the 14th modern-day pitcher to toss a perfect game.

Montreal	AB	R	H	RBI		NY Yankees	AB	R	H	RBI
W.Guerrero, dh	3	0	0	0		Knoblauch, 2b	2	1	1	0
Te.Jones, cf	2	0	0	0		Jeter, ss	4	1	1	2
J.Mouton, cf	1	0	0	0		O'Neill, rf	4	1	1	0
Ro.White, lf	3	0	0	0		B.Williams, cf	4	0	1	1
V.Guerrero, rf	3	0	0	0		T.Martinez, 1b	4	0	1	0
Vidro, 2b	3	0	0	0		C.Davis, dh	3	1	1	0
Fullmer, 1b	3	0	0	0		Ledee, lf	4	1	1	2
Widger, c	3	0	0	0		Brosius, 3b	2	1	0	0
Andrews, 3b	2	0	0	0		Girardi, c	3	0	1	1
McGuire, ph	1	0	0	0						
O.Cabrera, ss	3	0	0	0						
Totals	27	0	0	0		Totals	30	6	8	6

Montreal ....000 000 000 —0
NY Yankees ....050 000 01x —6

DP—Montreal 1. LOB—Montreal 0, NY Yankees 4. 2B—O'Neill (20), Girardi (9). HR—Jeter (16), Ledee (3).

Montreal	IP	H	R	ER	BB	SO
Vazquez (L, 2-5)	7	7	6	6	2	3
Ayala	1	1	0	0	0	0

NY Yankees	IP	H	R	ER	BB	SO
Cone (W, 10-4)	9	0	0	0	0	10

HBP—Knoblauch by Vazquez, Brosius by Vazquez. U—HP, Barrett. 1B, McCoy. 2B, Evans. 3B, Meriwether. T—2:16. A—41,930.

—117—

INDIVIDUAL STATISTICS

BATTING

Name	G	TPA	AB	R	H	TB	2B	3B	HR	RBI	Avg.	Obp.	Slg.	SH	SF	HP	BB	IBB	SO	SB	CS	GDP	vs RHP AB	Avg.	HR	RBI	vs LHP AB	Avg.	HR	RBI
Jeter, Derek	158	739	627	134	219	346	37	9	24	102	.349	.438	.552	3	6	12	91	5	116	19	8	12	503	.366	19	84	124	.282	5	18
Knoblauch, Chuck	150	715	603	120	176	274	36	4	18	68	.292	.393	.454	3	5	21	83	0	57	28	9	7	489	.297	14	51	114	.272	4	17
O'Neill, Paul	153	675	597	70	170	274	39	4	19	110	.285	.353	.459	0	10	2	66	1	89	11	9	24	439	.319	16	84	158	.190	3	26
Williams, Bernie	158	697	591	116	202	317	28	6	25	115	.342	.435	.536	0	5	1	100	17	95	9	10	11	426	.359	20	93	165	.297	5	22
Martinez, Tino	159	665	589	95	155	270	27	2	28	105	.263	.341	.458	0	4	3	69	7	86	3	4	14	409	.264	21	74	180	.261	7	31
Davis, Chili	146	554	476	59	128	212	25	1	19	78	.269	.366	.445	0	3	2	73	7	100	4	1	12	365	.263	7	48	108	.194	10	23
Brosius, Scott	133	529	473	64	117	196	26	1	17	71	.247	.307	.414	2	9	6	39	2	74	9	3	13	280	.225	8	39	99	.303	4	18
Posada, Jorge	112	437	379	50	93	152	19	2	12	57	.245	.341	.401	0	2	3	53	2	91	1	0	9	211	.275	7	36	39	.282	2	4
Ledee, Ricky	88	280	250	45	69	119	13	5	9	40	.276	.346	.476	0	2	0	28	5	73	4	3	2	160	.256	7	36	49	.184	0	4
Girardi, Joe	65	229	209	23	50	74	16	1	2	27	.239	.271	.354	8	2	0	10	0	26	3	1	16	122	.197	3	12	83	.184	0	4
Spencer, Shane	71	226	205	25	48	80	8	0	8	20	.234	.301	.390	0	1	2	18	0	51	0	4	1	121	.240	4	18	74	.297	1	6
Curtis, Chad	96	245	195	37	51	72	6	0	5	24	.262	.398	.369	1	3	3	43	0	35	8	4	4	104	.231	1	12	23	.348	1	4
Sojo, Luis	49	133	127	20	32	44	6	0	2	16	.252	.275	.346	2	0	0	4	0	17	0	0	3	33	.152	0	1	33	.303	1	4
Leyritz, Jim	31	79	66	8	15	21	4	1	0	5	.227	.354	.318	0	0	0	13	1	17	0	0	0	43	.302	2	5	6	.500	1	1
Strawberry, Darryl	24	66	49	10	16	30	5	0	3	6	.327	.500	.612	0	0	0	17	0	16	2	0	0	34	.147	0	1	11	.364	1	1
Bellinger, Clay	32	46	45	12	9	14	2	0	1	2	.200	.217	.311	0	0	0	1	0	10	1	0	1	29	.172	0	3	2	.000	0	0
Tarasco, Tony	14	35	31	5	5	7	2	0	0	3	.161	.229	.226	0	1	0	3	0	5	1	0	1	16	.313	0	3	4	.750	0	1
Jimenez, D'Angelo	7	23	20	3	8	10	2	0	0	4	.400	.478	.500	0	0	0	3	0	4	0	0	0	3	.333	0	0	5	.000	0	0
Manto, Jeff	6	10	8	0	1	1	0	0	0	0	.125	.300	.125	0	0	0	2	0	4	0	0	0	4	.000	0	0	4	.250	1	1
Soriano, Alfonso	9	8	8	2	1	4	0	0	1	1	.125	.125	.500	0	0	0	0	0	3	0	1	0	5	.200	0	0	0	.000	0	0
Pettitte, Andy	31	6	5	0	1	1	0	0	0	0	.200	.333	.200	0	0	0	1	0	2	0	0	0	3	.000	0	0	1	.000	0	0
Clemens, Roger	30	5	4	0	0	0	0	0	0	0	.000	.000	.000	1	0	0	0	0	3	0	0	0	4	.000	0	0	0	.000	0	0
Irabu, Hideki	32	7	4	0	0	0	0	0	0	0	.000	.000	.000	2	0	0	1	0	3	0	0	0	4	.000	0	0	0	.000	0	0
Cone, David	31	3	3	1	1	2	1	0	0	1	.333	.333	.667	0	0	0	0	0	1	0	0	0	3	.333	0	1	0	.000	0	0
Hernandez, Orlando	33	3	3	1	1	1	0	0	0	0	.333	.333	.333	0	0	0	0	0	0	0	0	0	2	.000	0	0	1	1.000	0	0
Stanton, Mike	73	1	1	0	0	0	0	0	0	0	.000	.000	.000	0	0	0	0	0	1	0	0	0	1	.000	0	0	0	.000	0	0
Grimsley, Jason	55	0	0	0	0	0	0	0	0	0	.000	.000	.000	0	0	0	0	0	0	0	0	0	0	.000	0	0	0	.000	0	0
Rivera, Mariano	66	0	0	0	0	0	0	0	0	0	.000	.000	.000	0	0	0	0	0	0	0	0	0	0	.000	0	0	0	.000	0	0
Naulty, Dan	33	0	0	0	0	0	0	0	0	0	.000	.000	.000	0	0	0	0	0	0	0	0	0	0	.000	0	0	0	.000	0	0
Mendoza, Ramiro	53	0	0	0	0	0	0	0	0	0	.000	.000	.000	0	0	0	0	0	0	0	0	0	0	.000	0	0	0	.000	0	0
Erdos, Todd	4	0	0	0	0	0	0	0	0	0	.000	.000	.000	0	0	0	0	0	0	0	0	0	0	.000	0	0	0	.000	0	0
Figga, Mike	2	0	0	0	0	0	0	0	0	0	.000	.000	.000	0	0	0	0	0	0	0	0	0	0	.000	0	0	0	.000	0	0

Players with more than one A.L. team

Name	G	TPA	AB	R	H	TB	2B	3B	HR	RBI	Avg.	Obp.	Slg.	SH	SF	HP	BB	IBB	SO	SB	CS	GDP	vs RHP AB	Avg.	HR	RBI	vs LHP AB	Avg.	HR	RBI
Figga, Bal.	41	91	86	12	19	26	4	0	1	5	.221	.236	.302	2	1	0	2	0	27	0	2	1	0	.000	0	0	0	.000	0	0
Figga, N.Y.-Bal.	43	91	86	12	19	26	4	0	1	5	.221	.236	.302	2	1	0	2	0	27	0	2	1	75	.227	1	5	11	.182	0	0
Manto, Cle.	12	37	25	5	5	8	0	0	1	2	.200	.444	.320	1	0	0	11	0	11	0	0	0	3	.333	0	0	5	.000	0	0
Manto, Cle.-N.Y.	18	47	33	5	6	9	0	0	1	2	.182	.413	.273	1	0	0	13	0	15	0	0	0	23	.217	1	2	10	.100	0	0

PITCHING

Name	W	L	Pct.	ERA	IP	H	R	ER	HR	SH	SF	HB	BB	IBB	SO	G	GS	CG	ShO	GF	Sv	vs. RH AB	Avg.	HR	RBI	vs. LH AB	Avg.	HR	RBI
Hernandez, Orlando	17	9	.654	4.12	214.1	187	108	98	24	3	11	8	87	2	157	33	33	2	1	0	0	369	.187	9	29	432	.273	15	63
Cone, David	12	9	.571	3.44	193.1	164	84	74	21	5	6	11	90	1	177	31	31	1	1	0	0	355	.214	6	34	360	.244	15	46
Pettitte, Andy	14	11	.560	4.70	191.2	216	105	100	20	6	6	3	89	3	121	31	31	0	0	0	0	598	.293	12	62	149	.275	8	29
Clemens, Roger	14	10	.583	4.60	187.2	185	101	96	20	10	5	9	90	0	163	30	30	1	1	0	0	343	.259	14	52	365	.263	6	38
Irabu, Hideki	11	7	.611	4.84	169.1	180	98	91	26	2	4	6	46	0	133	32	27	2	1	2	0	312	.244	10	41	363	.287	16	49
Mendoza, Ramiro	9	9	.500	4.29	123.2	141	68	59	13	6	4	3	27	3	80	53	6	0	0	15	3	265	.283	3	26	231	.286	10	37
Grimsley, Jason	7	2	.778	3.60	75.0	66	39	30	7	3	3	4	40	5	49	55	0	0	0	25	1	172	.273	5	30	114	.167	2	11
Rivera, Mariano	4	3	.571	1.83	69.0	43	15	14	2	0	2	3	18	3	52	66	0	0	0	63	45	105	.219	1	9	140	.143	1	5
Stanton, Mike	2	2	.500	4.33	62.1	71	30	30	5	4	2	1	18	4	59	73	1	0	0	10	0	156	.308	3	18	90	.256	2	15
Naulty, Dan	1	0	1.000	4.38	49.1	40	24	24	8	1	1	4	22	0	25	33	0	0	0	20	0	74	.257	2	4	53	.208	1	3
Watson, Allen	4	0	1.000	2.10	34.1	30	8	8	3	0	0	0	10	0	30	21	0	0	0	6	0	76	.250	1	14	34	.235	1	5
Nelson, Jeff	2	1	.667	4.15	30.1	27	14	14	2	2	2	3	22	2	35	39	0	0	0	8	0	46	.283	1	7	21	.190	0	1
Yarnall, Ed	1	0	1.000	3.71	17.0	17	8	7	1	0	0	0	10	0	13	5	2	0	0	2	0	17	.294	2	5	9	.000	0	0
Erdos, Todd	0	0	.000	3.86	7.0	5	4	3	2	0	1	0	4	0	4	4	0	0	0	1	0	21	.381	0	6	15	.533	1	6
Tessmer, Jay	0	0	.000	14.85	6.2	16	11	11	1	0	1	0	4	2	3	6	0	0	0	4	0	15	.133	0	3	10	.300	1	5
Juden, Jeff	0	1	.000	1.59	5.2	5	9	1	1	0	0	1	3	0	9	2	1	0	0	0	0	7	.429	1	1	2	.000	0	0
Buddie, Mike	0	0	.000	4.50	2.0	3	1	1	1	0	0	0	1	2	0	2	0	0	0	0	0	7	.429	0	1	2	.000	0	0
Fossas, Tony	0	0	.000	36.00	1.0	6	4	4	1	0	0	0	1	0	5	0	0	0	0	0	0	4	.750	0	1	5	.600	1	6

PITCHERS WITH MORE THAN ONE A.L. TEAM

Name	W	L	Pct.	ERA	IP	H	R	ER	HR	SH	SF	HB	BB	IBB	SO	G	GS	CG	ShO	GF	Sv	vs. RH AB	Avg.	HR	RBI	vs. LH AB	Avg.	HR	RBI
Watson, Sea.	0	1	.000	12.00	3.0	6	9	4	5	0	1	0	3	0	2	3	0	0	0	2	0	74	.257	2	4	53	.208	1	3
Watson, Sea.-N.Y.	4	1	.800	2.89	37.1	36	17	12	8	0	1	0	13	0	32	24	0	0	0	1	0	80	.275	4	8	62	.226	4	9

DESIGNATED HITTERS

Name	AB	Avg.	HR	RBI	Name	AB	Avg.	HR	RBI	Name	AB	Avg.	HR	RBI
Davis, Chili	463	.270	19	73	Curtis, Chad	4	.500	0	1	Brosius, Scott	1	.000	0	0
Strawberry, Darryl	42	.310	3	5	Soriano, Alfonso	3	.333	1	1	Tarasco, Tony	0	-	0	0
Leyritz, Jim	29	.241	0	1	Posada, Jorge	3	.000	0	0	Sojo, Luis	0	-	0	0
Spencer, Shane	9	.333	0	2	Ledee, Ricky	1	1.000	0	1					
Williams, Bernie	5	.400	0	0	Bellinger, Clay	1	.000	0	0					

INDIVIDUAL STATISTICS

FIELDING

FIRST BASEMEN

Player	Pct.	G	PO	A	E	TC	DP
Martinez, Tino	.995	158	1297	106	7	1410	110
Leyritz, Jim	.986	9	60	8	1	69	6
Bellinger, Clay	1.000	8	7	1	0	8	1
Sojo, Luis	1.000	4	8	0	0	8	0
Manto, Jeff	1.000	3	14	1	0	15	1
Posada, Jorge	1.000	1	4	1	0	5	1

SECOND BASEMEN

Player	Pct.	G	PO	A	E	TC	DP
Knoblauch, Chuck	.963	150	254	425	26	705	67
Sojo, Luis	.986	16	30	40	1	71	12
Jimenez, D'Angelo	1.000	1	1	1	0	2	0
Bellinger, Clay	-	1	0	0	0	0	0

THIRD BASEMEN

Player	Pct.	G	PO	A	E	TC	DP
Brosius, Scott	.962	132	87	239	13	339	20
Sojo, Luis	.974	20	15	23	1	39	3
Bellinger, Clay	1.000	16	12	16	0	28	1
Jimenez, D'Angelo	1.000	6	2	8	0	10	2
Leyritz, Jim	.800	1	2	2	1	5	0
Manto, Jeff	-	1	0	0	0	0	0

SHORTSTOPS

Player	Pct.	G	PO	A	E	TC	DP
Jeter, Derek	.978	158	230	391	14	635	87
Sojo, Luis	1.000	6	12	9	0	21	2
Bellinger, Clay	1.000	1	2	1	0	3	0
Soriano, Alfonso	.500	1	0	1	1	2	1

OUTFIELDERS

Player	Pct.	G	PO	A	E	TC	DP
Williams, Bernie	.987	155	381	9	5	395	3
O'Neill, Paul	.974	151	291	10	8	309	3
Curtis, Chad	.990	81	98	2	1	101	0
Ledee, Ricky	.942	77	143	3	9	155	0
Spencer, Shane	1.000	64	108	5	0	113	3
Tarasco, Tony	1.000	12	11	0	0	11	0
Bellinger, Clay	1.000	2	2	0	0	2	0

CATCHERS

Player	Pct.	G	PO	A	E	TC	DP	PB
Posada, Jorge	.993	109	705	46	5	756	7	17
Girardi, Joe	.984	65	452	34	8	494	5	1
Figga, Mike	1.000	2	3	0	0	3	0	0
Leyritz, Jim	-	1	0	0	0	0	0	0

PITCHERS

Player	Pct.	G	PO	A	E	TC	DP
Stanton, Mike	.889	73	2	6	1	9	0
Rivera, Mariano	1.000	66	12	10	0	22	2
Grimsley, Jason	1.000	55	8	13	0	21	0
Mendoza, Ramiro	.971	53	11	23	1	35	1
Nelson, Jeff	.889	39	3	5	1	9	2
Hernandez, Orlando	.955	33	17	25	2	44	3
Naulty, Dan	1.000	33	2	9	0	11	0
Irabu, Hideki	1.000	32	2	13	0	15	0
Pettitte, Andy	.956	31	5	38	2	45	3
Cone, David	.950	31	7	12	1	20	1
Clemens, Roger	.979	30	16	30	1	47	2
Watson, Allen	.833	21	1	4	1	6	0
Tessmer, Jay	1.000	6	0	1	0	1	0
Yarnall, Ed	1.000	5	1	4	0	5	0
Fossas, Tony	-	5	0	0	0	0	0
Erdos, Todd	1.000	4	0	1	0	1	0
Juden, Jeff	1.000	2	0	1	0	1	0
Buddie, Mike	1.000	2	1	0	0	1	0

PITCHING AGAINST EACH CLUB

Pitcher	Ana. W-L	Bal. W-L	Bos. W-L	Chi. W-L	Cle. W-L	Det. W-L	K.C. W-L	Min. W-L	Oak. W-L	Sea. W-L	T.B. W-L	Tex. W-L	Tor. W-L	N.L. W-L	Total W-L
Buddie, Mike	0-0	0-0	0-0	0-0	0-0	0-0	0-0	0-0	0-0	0-0	0-0	0-0	0-0	0-0	0-0
Clemens, Roger	0-1	0-1	1-1	2-0	2-0	2-0	0-0	1-0	0-2	2-0	1-1	1-1	0-0	2-3	14-10
Cone, David	0-2	3-0	0-1	0-1	0-0	1-1	1-1	0-1	0-0	1-1	1-1	2-0	1-1	2-1	12-9
Erdos, Todd	0-0	0-0	0-0	0-0	0-0	0-0	0-0	0-0	0-0	0-0	0-0	0-0	0-0	0-0	0-0
Fossas, Tony	0-0	0-0	0-0	0-0	0-0	0-0	0-0	0-0	0-0	0-0	0-0	0-0	0-0	0-0	0-0
Grimsley, Jason	0-0	1-0	0-0	0-0	1-0	0-0	0-0	1-1	1-0	0-0	1-0	0-0	1-0	1-1	7-2
Hernandez, Orlando	0-0	2-0	2-1	1-1	0-2	2-1	2-1	1-0	0-0	0-1	2-0	0-1	1-1	2-0	17-9
Irabu, Hideki	1-1	0-0	1-3	0-0	2-0	1-0	0-0	1-1	0-0	1-0	1-1	2-0	1-0	1-0	11-7
Juden, Jeff	0-0	0-0	0-0	0-0	0-0	0-0	0-0	0-0	0-0	0-1	0-0	0-0	0-0	0-0	0-1
Mendoza, Ramiro	0-1	1-1	0-1	0-1	0-0	0-0	0-0	0-1	2-1	0-0	0-1	1-1	2-0	0-1	9-9
Naulty, Dan	0-0	1-0	0-0	0-0	0-0	0-0	0-0	0-0	0-0	0-0	0-0	0-0	0-0	0-0	1-0
Nelson, Jeff	0-0	1-0	0-0	0-0	0-0	0-0	0-0	0-0	0-0	0-0	1-1	0-0	0-0	0-0	2-1
Pettitte, Andy	1-1	0-1	0-1	2-2	0-1	0-1	0-2	2-0	0-0	2-0	2-0	1-0	3-0	1-2	14-11
Rivera, Mariano	0-0	0-1	0-1	2-0	1-0	0-0	0-0	0-0	0-0	1-0	0-0	0-0	0-0	0-2	4-3
Stanton, Mike	0-0	0-0	0-0	0-0	0-0	0-0	0-0	0-1	0-0	1-0	1-1	0-0	0-0	0-0	2-2
Tessmer, Jay	0-0	0-0	0-0	0-0	0-0	0-0	0-0	0-0	0-0	0-0	0-0	0-0	0-0	0-0	0-0
Watson, Allen	1-0	0-0	0-0	0-0	1-0	0-0	0-0	1-0	0-0	0-0	1-0	0-0	0-0	0-0	4-0
Yarnall, Ed	1-0	0-0	0-0	0-0	0-0	0-0	0-0	0-0	0-0	0-0	0-0	0-0	0-0	0-0	1-0
Totals	4-6	9-4	4-8	7-5	7-3	7-5	4-5	6-4	9-1	8-4	8-4	10-2		9-9	98-64

INTERLEAGUE: Pettitte 1-0, Clemens 0-1, Rivera 0-1 vs. Braves; Cone 1-0, Clemens 1-0, Mendoza 0-1 vs. Expos; Grimsley 1-0, Hernandez 1-0, Irabu 1-0, Clemens 0-2, Rivera 0-1 vs. Mets; Cone 1-0, Pettitte 0-1, Grimsley 0-1 vs. Phillies; Hernandez 1-0, Clemens 1-0, Pettitte 0-1 vs. Marlins. Total: 9-9.

MISCELLANEOUS

HOME RUNS BY PARK

At Anaheim (7): Martinez 2, Davis 1, Strawberry 1, Jeter 1, Posada 1, Spencer 1.
At Baltimore (10): Spencer 3, Martinez 2, Williams 2, Brosius 2, Sojo 1.
At Boston (6): Knoblauch 2, O'Neill 1, Williams 1, Jeter 1, Posada 1.
At Chicago (AL) (6): Martinez 1, Williams 1, Brosius 1, Curtis 1, Jeter 1, Posada 1.
At Cleveland (6): O'Neill 3, Jeter 2, Ledee 1.
At Detroit (4): Davis 1, Martinez 1, Brosius 1, Jeter 1.
At Florida (4): O'Neill 1, Williams 1, Brosius 1, Posada 1.
At Kansas City (3): Martinez 1, Williams 1, Brosius 1.
At Minnesota (8): Davis 2, Williams 2, Brosius 2, Posada 1, Ledee 1.
At New York (AL) (84): Jeter 15, Davis 12, Knoblauch 11, Williams 11, O'Neill 9, Martinez 7, Brosius 4, Posada 4, Ledee 4, Spencer 2, Strawberry 1, Girardi 1, Sojo 1, Soriano 1, Bellinger 1.
At New York (NL) (7): O'Neill 2, Posada 2, Ledee 2, Knoblauch 1.
At Oakland (9): Williams 2, Curtis 2, Jeter 2, Davis 1, Knoblauch 1, Ledee 1.
At Philadelphia (3): Martinez 2, Jeter 1.
At Seattle (8): Martinez 2, Brosius 2, O'Neill 1, Knoblauch 1, Williams 1, Curtis 1.
At Tampa Bay (10): Martinez 3, Davis 2, Strawberry 1, Girardi 1, Williams 1, Brosius 1, Spencer 1.
At Texas (12): Martinez 6, Knoblauch 2, O'Neill 1, Brosius 1, Curtis 1, Posada 1.
At Toronto (6): Williams 2, O'Neill 1, Martinez 1, Brosius 1, Spencer 1.

LOW-HIT GAMES

No-hitters: David Cone, July 18 vs. Montreal, W 6-0.
One-hitters: None.
Two-hitters: None.

10-STRIKEOUT GAMES

David Cone 3, Roger Clemens 1, Andy Pettitte 1, Hideki Irabu 1, Orlando Hernandez 1, **Total:** 7.

FOUR OR MORE HITS IN ONE GAME

Bernie Williams 7, Chuck Knoblauch 4 (including two five-hit games), Tino Martinez 3, Chili Davis 2 (including one five-hit game), Jorge Posada 2, Joe Girardi 1, Scott Brosius 1, Derek Jeter 1, D'Angelo Jimenez 1, **Total:** 22.

MULTI-HOMER GAMES

Tino Martinez 3, Bernie Williams 3, Paul O'Neill 2, Scott Brosius 1, Jorge Posada 1, **Total:** 10.

GRAND SLAMS

4-9: Chili Davis (off Detroit's Beiker Graterol).
5-26: Tino Martinez (off Boston's John Wasdin).
8-9: Bernie Williams (off Oakland's Mike Oquist).
8-13: Chuck Knoblauch (off Minnesota's Benj Sampson).
8-20: Ricky Ledee (off Minnesota's Brad Radke).
9-14: Bernie Williams (off Toronto's Billy Koch).
9-14: Paul O'Neill (off Toronto's Paul Spoljaric).

PINCH HITTERS

(Minimum 5 at-bats)

Name	AB	Avg.	HR	RBI
Davis, Chili	16	.250	0	5
Curtis, Chad	14	.357	0	4
Posada, Jorge	11	.182	0	0
Strawberry, Darryl	8	.375	0	1
Leyritz, Jim	8	.250	0	1
Ledee, Ricky	7	.286	0	4
Spencer, Shane	7	.286	1	1

DEBUTS

4-9: Clay Bellinger, PH.
7-15: Ed Yarnall, P.
9-14: Alfonso Soriano, DH.
9-15: D'Angelo Jimenez, 3B.

GAMES BY POSITION

Catcher: Jorge Posada 109, Joe Girardi 65, Mike Figga 2, Jim Leyritz 1.
First base: Tino Martinez 158, Jim Leyritz 9, Clay Bellinger 8, Luis Sojo 4, Jeff Manto 3, Jorge Posada 1.
Second base: Chuck Knoblauch 150, Luis Sojo 16, Clay Bellinger 1, D'Angelo Jimenez 1.
Third base: Scott Brosius 132, Luis Sojo 20, Clay Bellinger 16, D'Angelo Jimenez 6, Jeff Manto 1, Jim Leyritz 1.
Shortstop: Derek Jeter 158, Luis Sojo 6, Alfonso Soriano 1, Clay Bellinger 1.
Outfield: Bernie Williams 155, Paul O'Neill 151, Chad Curtis 81, Ricky Ledee 77, Shane Spencer 64, Tony Tarasco 12, Clay Bellinger 2.
Designated hitter: Chili Davis 132, Darryl Strawberry 17, Jim Leyritz 14, Chad Curtis 14, Alfonso Soriano 6, Ricky Ledee 5, Clay Bellinger 4, Shane Spencer 3, Luis Sojo 2, Bernie Williams 2, Scott Brosius 1, Tony Tarasco 1, Jorge Posada 1.

STREAKS

Wins: 7 (October 3-April 14, June 20-29, July 20-27).
Losses: 5 (May 11-15).
Consecutive games with at least one hit: 17, Bernie Williams (June 18-July 6).
Wins by pitcher: 3, Roger Clemens (May 22-June 1), David Cone (April 9-20), Andy Pettitte (August 2-13), Hideki Irabu (July 24-August 4).

ATTENDANCE

Home: 3,292,629.
Road: 2,652,405.
Highest (home): 56,583 (April 9 vs. Detroit).
Highest (road): 53,869 (July 11 vs. New York).
Lowest (home): 23,404 (July 19 vs. Montreal).
Lowest (road): 14,207 (September 7 vs. Kansas City).

OAKLAND ATHLETICS

DAY BY DAY

Date	Opp.	Res.	Score	(inn.*)	Hits	Opp. hits	Winning pitcher	Losing pitcher	Save	Record	Pos.	GB
4-5	N.Y.	W	5-3		7	5	Mathews	Stanton		1-0	1st	+0.5
4-6	N.Y.	L	4-7		5	12	Hernandez	Candiotti	Rivera	1-1	T2nd	0.5
4-7	N.Y.	L	0-4		5	8	Mendoza	Haynes		1-2	T3rd	1.0
4-9	At Sea.	L	1-6		3	10	Henry	Rogers		1-3	4th	1.0
4-10	At Sea.	W	11-4		17	9	Heredia	Fassero		2-3	T2nd	1.0
4-11	At Sea.	L	8-11		12	18	Moyer	Candiotti		2-4	4th	1.0
4-12	At Sea.	L	3-6		9	12	Garcia	Haynes	Mesa	2-5	4th	2.0
4-13	Ana.	W	3-2		7	9	Oquist	Sparks	Taylor	3-5	4th	1.0
4-14	Ana.	W	6-5		7	9	Mathews	Finley	Taylor	4-5	T2nd	1.0
4-15	Ana.	L	1-12		5	18	Olivares	Heredia		4-6	T3rd	2.0
4-16	Tex.	W	8-2		17	3	Candiotti	Sele		5-6	3rd	1.0
4-17	Tex.	W	11-3		13	6	Haynes	Clark		6-6	T1st	...
4-18	Tex.	L	2-6		7	15	Morgan	Oquist		6-7	T2nd	1.0
4-20	At Cle.	L	1-5		3	9	Colon	Rogers		6-8	T2nd	1.0
4-21	At Cle.	L	4-5		8	14	Reed	Taylor		6-9	T2nd	1.0
4-22	At Cle.	W	4-1		8	3	Candiotti	Nagy	Taylor	7-9	2nd	1.0
4-23	At Bal.	L	4-7		9	8	Fetters	Haynes		7-10	T2nd	2.0
4-24	At Bal.	W	3-0		6	4	Oquist	Erickson	Taylor	8-10	2nd	2.0
4-25	At Bal.	W	11-10		10	9	Rigby	Timlin	Taylor	9-10	2nd	2.0
4-26	Cle.	L	4-5	(10)	10	9	Karsay	Taylor	Jackson	9-11	2nd	2.5
4-27	Cle.	L	5-8		11	12	Nagy	Candiotti	Jackson	9-12	2nd	2.5
4-28	Cle.	L	1-4		6	6	Wright	Haynes	Jackson	9-13	4th	3.5
4-29	Cle.	L	3-8		4	9	Burba	Oquist		9-14	4th	3.5
4-30	Bos.	W	13-9		10	12	Mathews	Lowe		10-14	4th	3.5
5-1	Bos.	L	2-7		6	15	Martinez	Heredia		10-15	4th	3.5
5-2	Bos.	W	7-5		9	12	Jones	Harikkala	Taylor	11-15	4th	3.5
5-3	Bos.	W	12-11	(10)	11	13	Mathews	Gross		12-15	4th	2.5
5-4	At Tor.	W	13-4		13	11	Oquist	Halladay	Jones	13-15	2nd	2.0
5-5	At Tor.	W	8-2		15	5	Rogers	Escobar		14-15	2nd	2.0
5-6	At Tor.	W	3-2		6	10	Heredia	Carpenter	Taylor	15-15	2nd	1.0
5-7	At Chi.	L	1-7		7	10	Parque	Candiotti		15-16	2nd	1.0
5-8	At Chi.	L	3-5		8	11	Snyder	Haynes	Howry	15-17	2nd	2.0
5-9	At Chi.	W	3-0		8	4	Oquist	Sirotka	Jones	16-17	2nd	2.0
5-11	At Det.	W	6-2		10	6	Rigby	Weaver		17-17	2nd	1.5
5-12	At Det.	W	2-1		4	4	Heredia	Thompson	Taylor	18-17	2nd	1.0
5-14	Min.	W	7-5		10	11	Worrell	Lincoln	Taylor	19-17	2nd	1.5
5-15	Min.	W	6-5		8	10	Mathews	Guardado		20-17	2nd	1.5
5-16	Min.	W	4-2		5	5	Haynes	Radke	Taylor	21-17	2nd	0.5
5-18	At K.C.	L	3-13		6	17	Appier	Heredia		21-18	T1st	...
5-19	At K.C.	L	3-14		6	13	Rosado	Candiotti	Mathews	21-19	2nd	1.0
5-20	At K.C.	L	1-7		5	9	Suppan	Oquist		21-20	2nd	1.5
5-21	At Min.	L	1-2	(15)	8	14	Miller	Jones		21-21	2nd	1.5
5-22	At Min.	L	1-2	(10)	5	5	Wells	Rigby		21-22	3rd	2.5
5-23	At Min.	L	3-8		7	15	Milton	Heredia		21-23	T3rd	2.5
5-25	K.C.	W	5-3		7	5	Oquist	Rosado	Jones	22-23	T2nd	3.0
5-26	K.C.	W	3-1		5	5	Haynes	Suppan	Taylor	23-23	T2nd	3.0
5-27	K.C.	W	6-1		8	6	Rogers	Witasick		24-23	2nd	2.5
5-28	Bal.	W	2-1		6	4	Candiotti	Mussina	Taylor	25-23	2nd	2.5
5-29	Bal.	L	5-7		10	13	Johns	Mathews	Rhodes	25-24	3rd	3.5
5-30	Bal.	W	11-5		16	10	Rigby	Erickson		26-24	2nd	3.5
5-31	T.B.	W	10-7		7	11	Groom	Yan		27-24	2nd	3.5
6-1	T.B.	W	5-2		3	10	Rogers	Eiland	Taylor	28-24	2nd	3.5
6-2	T.B.	L	6-7		8	11	Yan	Mathews	Hernandez	28-25	2nd	4.5
6-4	At S.F.	L	3-4	(15)	9	9	Spradlin	Taylor		28-26	2nd	4.5
6-5	At S.F.	L	0-8		8	10	Rueter	Oquist		28-27	2nd	5.5
6-6	At S.F.	W	7-6		8	12	Groom	Johnstone	Taylor	29-27	2nd	4.5
6-8	At S.D.	L	3-5		8	11	Wall	Groom	Hoffman	29-28	3rd	6.0
6-9	At S.D.	W	3-0		8	4	Haynes	Clement	Taylor	30-28	T2nd	5.0
6-10	At S.D.	L	1-2		4	7	Hitchcock	Heredia	Hoffman	30-29	3rd	5.5
6-11	L.A.	W	12-6		16	9	Oquist	Perez	Mathews	31-29	3rd	5.5
6-12	L.A.	W	4-3		8	12	Rogers	Valdes	Taylor	32-29	2nd	4.5
6-13	L.A.	W	9-3		8	10	Hudson	Dreifort		33-29	2nd	3.5
6-15	At Cle.	L	3-8		8	12	Wright	Haynes		33-30	2nd	3.0
6-16	At Cle.	L	8-9		9	10	Karsay	Taylor		33-31	T2nd	4.0
6-17	At Cle.	L	6-10		9	18	Shuey	Worrell		33-32	3rd	5.0
6-18	At Det.	L	3-8		3	10	Thompson	Oquist		33-33	3rd	6.0
6-19	At Det.	W	13-1		16	11	Hudson	Cruz		34-33	3rd	5.0
6-20	At Det.	W	6-5		8	6	Haynes	Moehler	Taylor	35-33	T2nd	4.0
6-21	At Det.	L	11-13		13	12	Brocail	Rigby	Jones	35-34	T2nd	4.0
6-22	At Tex.	W	5-3		11	11	Mathews	Wetteland	Taylor	36-34	2nd	3.0
6-23	At Tex.	L	6-7		7	13	Morgan	Oquist	Wetteland	36-35	2nd	4.0
6-24	At Tex.	L	2-5		7	6	Burkett	Hudson	Wetteland	36-36	2nd	5.0
6-25	At Ana.	L	3-4		9	8	Percival	Jones		36-37	T2nd	6.0
6-26	At Ana.	L	4-5		7	10	Magnante	Rigby	Percival	36-38	3rd	6.0
6-27	At Ana.	L	3-4		7	12	Sparks	Rogers	Percival	36-39	3rd	6.0
6-29	Sea.	L	1-2	(12)	9	7	Paniagua	Mathews	Mesa	36-40	3rd	7.5
6-30	Sea.	W	14-5		14	12	Hudson	Fassero		37-40	3rd	7.5

HIGHLIGHTS

High point: The A's seized sole possession of the wild-card lead on August 22 when Randy Velarde delivered a two-out bloop single in the ninth inning against Toronto. The 4-3 victory moved the club 12 games over .500—exactly its standing at season's end.

Low point: Oakland, trailing the A.L. West-leading Rangers by 5½ games and down 4½ games to the Red Sox in the wild-card race, went to Texas for a three-game series in late September, just one day after playing a makeup doubleheader in Baltimore. The A's were swept by the Rangers—and outscored, 32-11. Texas clinched the division crown in the series finale.

Turning point: The A's vaulted into postseason contention after acquiring second baseman Randy Velarde and pitchers Omar Olivares, Kevin Appier and Jason Isringhausen in trading-deadline deals. Beginning July 30, Oakland won nine of 10 games.

Most valuable player: First baseman Jason Giambi, who had career highs in batting average (.315), home runs (33) and RBIs (123), one shy of the Oakland record, held by Jose Canseco. Also, he improved vastly in the field and played a key leadership role.

Most valuable pitcher: Tim Hudson jumped from Class AA to Class AAA to the big leagues by June. After going 7-0 in the minors, he compiled an 11-2 record and a 3.23 ERA for the A's. Hudson really opened eyes by winning against Randy Johnson and Pedro Martinez.

Most improved player: Gil Heredia, who emerged as Oakland's steadiest starter. He won a career-high 13 games and led the A.L. in fewest walks per nine innings pitched (1.5).

Most pleasant surprise: DH John Jaha made an amazing comeback at age 33 by hitting 35 home runs and driving in 111 runs. He was Oakland's lone representative at the All-Star Game.

Key injuries: Sparkplug utility player Tony Phillips, a vocal leader, was sidelined for the final seven weeks of the season when he broke his left leg at Toronto on August 15. Another valuable veteran, outfielder Tim Raines, was diagnosed with lupus and didn't play after July 18. Rookie third baseman Eric Chavez missed a month with a heel injury, and T.J. Mathews, the team's top setup man, spent time on the D.L. with a sore elbow—an ailment that bothered him much of the season and required surgery.

Notable: The A's notched their first winning season since 1992 . ... The club's 13-game improvement from 1998 was the largest gain among A.L. clubs. ... Oakland's 4.69 ERA was third-best in the league. ... The A's drew 770 walks, the fifth-highest total in major league history. ... Isringhausen went 8-for-8 in save opportunities down the stretch.

—SUSAN SLUSSER

MISCELLANEOUS

RECORDS

1999 regular-season record: 87-75 (2nd in A.L. West); 52-29 at home; 35-46 on road; 34-18 vs. A.L. East; 26-30 vs. A.L. Central; 15-21 vs. A.L. West; 12-6 vs. N.L. West; 23-17 vs. lefthanded starters; 64-58 vs. righthanded starters; 75-67 on grass; 12-8 on turf; 33-27 in daytime; 54-48 at night; 22-19 in one-run games; 3-7 in extra-inning games; 0-0-1 in doubleheaders.

Team record past five years: 371-421 (.468, ranks 10th in league in that span).

TEAM LEADERS

Batting average: Jason Giambi (.315).
At-bats: Miguel Tejada (593).
Runs: Jason Giambi (115).
Hits: Jason Giambi (181).
Total bases: Jason Giambi (318).
Doubles: Jason Giambi (36).
Triples: Tony Phillips, Miguel Tejada (4).
Home runs: Matt Stairs (38).
Runs batted in: Jason Giambi (123).
Stolen bases: Tony Phillips, Randy Velarde (11).
Slugging percentage: John Jaha (.556).
On-base percentage: Jason Giambi (.422).
Wins: Gil Heredia (13).
Earned-run average: Gil Heredia (4.81).
Complete games: Kenny Rogers (3).
Shutouts: None.
Saves: Billy Taylor (26).
Innings pitched: Gil Heredia (200.1).
Strikeouts: Tim Hudson (132).

Date	Opp.	Res.	Score	(inn.*)	Hits	Opp. hits	Winning pitcher	Losing pitcher	Save	Record	Pos.	GB
7-1	Sea.	W	5-4		10	7	Taylor	Paniagua		38-40	3rd	7.0
7-2	Ana.	L	6-10		10	14	Petkovsek	Harville		38-41	3rd	8.0
7-3	Ana.	W	9-7		12	13	Heredia	Finley	Taylor	39-41	3rd	7.0
7-4	Ana.	L	2-5		5	12	Olivares	Oquist		39-42	3rd	7.0
7-5	Tex.	W	4-2		12	6	Hudson	Burkett	Taylor	40-42	3rd	6.0
7-6	Tex.	W	4-0		5	4	Haynes	Glynn		41-42	3rd	5.0
7-7	Tex.	L	4-7		7	10	Zimmerman	Rigby	Wetteland	41-43	3rd	6.0
7-9	At Ari.	W	5-2		8	12	Heredia	Benes	Taylor	42-43	T2nd	6.0
7-10	At Ari.	W	2-0		3	3	Hudson	Johnson	Taylor	43-43	2nd	5.0
7-11	At Ari.	L	4-7		6	7	Daal	Haynes	Mantei	43-44	2nd	5.0
7-15	S.F	W	11-9		12	10	Jones	Nen		44-44	2nd	5.0
7-16	S.F	W	4-2		5	5	Heredia	Ortiz	Taylor	45-44	2nd	5.0
7-17	S.F	L	2-7		6	10	Rueter	Groom		45-45	2nd	5.0
7-18	Col.	W	3-2		5	5	Haynes	Jones	Taylor	46-45	2nd	5.0
7-19	Col.	W	10-5		12	10	Worrell	Ramirez	Jones	47-45	2nd	5.0
7-20	Col.	W	4-3		5	6	Rogers	Kile	Taylor	48-45	2nd	5.0
7-21	At Sea.	W	13-3		15	7	Heredia	Fassero		49-45	2nd	5.0
7-22	At Sea.	L	4-5	(10)	4	10	Abbott	Jones		49-46	2nd	6.0
7-23	At K.C.	L	7-12		10	15	Morman	Haynes	Barber	49-47	2nd	7.0
7-24	At K.C.	W	12-2		9	11	Oquist	Witasick		50-47	2nd	7.0
7-25	At K.C.	L	11-13	(10)	10	19	Service	Harville		50-48	2nd	8.0
7-26	At Min.	W	14-7		16	12	Groom	Sampson		51-48	2nd	7.5
7-27	At Min.	L	2-3		5	6	Mays	Taylor	Guardado	51-49	2nd	8.5
7-28	At Min.	L	3-5		8	9	Hawkins	Haynes	Trombley	51-50	2nd	8.5
7-30	T.B.	W	4-1		8	5	Oquist	Eiland	Taylor	52-50	2nd	9.0
7-31	T.B.	W	5-1		5	7	Olivares	Arrojo	Jones	53-50	2nd	8.0
8-1	T.B.	W	10-6		12	12	Heredia	Witt	Mathews	54-50	2nd	8.0
8-2	Bal.	W	7-1		9	4	Appier	Erickson		55-50	2nd	8.0
8-3	Bal.	W	12-2		12	9	Hudson	Bones		56-50	2nd	8.0
8-4	Bal.	L	5-9		8	14	Johnson	Haynes		56-51	2nd	9.0
8-5	Chi.	W	7-6	(11)	11	11	Mathews	Eyre		57-51	2nd	8.5
8-6	Chi.	W	9-1		15	5	Heredia	Navarro		58-51	2nd	7.5
8-7	Chi.	W	11-1		14	6	Appier	Parque		59-51	2nd	7.5
8-8	Chi.	W	7-5		9	11	Jones	Foulke		60-51	2nd	6.5
8-9	N.Y.	L	8-12		13	9	Mendoza	Haynes		60-52	2nd	6.5
8-10	N.Y.	W	6-1		10	9	Olivares	Clemens	Jones	61-52	2nd	6.5
8-11	N.Y.	L	3-5		6	8	Watson	Jones	Rivera	61-53	2nd	7.5
8-13	At Tor.	W	9-8		12	8	Appier	Halladay	Jones	62-53	2nd	5.5
8-14	At Tor.	W	13-5		14	11	Hudson	Hamilton		63-53	2nd	4.5
8-15	At Tor.	W	9-5		15	10	Oquist	Escobar		64-53	2nd	4.5
8-16	At Bos.	L	5-6		7	11	Lowe	Jones		64-54	2nd	5.5
8-17	At Bos.	W	12-1		17	10	Heredia	Saberhagen		65-54	2nd	5.5
8-18	At Bos.	L	4-7		3	13	Garces	Appier	Lowe	65-55	2nd	6.5
8-19	At Bos.	W	6-2		12	4	Hudson	Martinez	Mathews	66-55	2nd	5.5
8-20	Tor.	L	0-11		4	13	Hamilton	Oquist		66-56	2nd	6.5
8-21	Tor.	W	8-4		9	8	Olivares	Carpenter		67-56	2nd	6.5
8-22	Tor.	W	4-3		8	12	Jones	Koch		68-56	2nd	6.5
8-23	Tor.	L	4-9		11	14	Wells	Appier		68-57	2nd	6.5
8-24	Cle.	W	11-10		12	8	Mathews	Shuey		69-57	2nd	5.5
8-25	Cle.	L	4-12		6	15	Colon	Oquist		69-58	2nd	6.5
8-27	At Chi.	W	9-6		10	13	Olivares	Sirotka	Isringhausen	70-58	2nd	6.5
8-28	At Chi.	W	7-5		10	7	Heredia	Navarro	Jones	71-58	2nd	6.5
8-29	At Chi.	L	2-7		10	10	Baldwin	Appier	Foulke	71-59	2nd	7.5
8-30	At N.Y.	L	4-7		10	8	Nelson	Mathews	Rivera	71-60	2nd	7.5
8-31	At N.Y.	W	3-2	(11)	10	8	Jones	Mendoza	Isringhausen	72-60	2nd	6.5
9-1	At N.Y.	W	7-1		10	6	Olivares	Clemens		73-60	2nd	6.5
9-2	At N.Y.	L	3-9		8	14	Hernandez	Heredia		73-61	2nd	6.5
9-3	Det.	W	7-4		9	9	Appier	Cruz	Isringhausen	74-61	2nd	6.5
9-4	Det.	W	2-1		9	4	Hudson	Cordero		75-61	2nd	5.5
9-5	Det.	L	4-5		8	10	Blair	Haynes	Jones	75-62	2nd	6.0
9-6	Det.	L	7-9		13	13	Borkowski	Olivares	Jones	75-63	2nd	7.5
9-7	Bos.	L	3-5		6	10	Wakefield	Heredia	Lowe	75-64	2nd	8.5
9-8	Bos.	W	6-2		8	5	Appier	Rapp		76-64	2nd	8.5
9-10	At T.B.	W	7-2		14	8	Hudson	Alvarez		77-64	2nd	7.5
9-11	At T.B.	W	5-4		6	8	Olivares	Rupe	Jones	78-64	2nd	6.5
9-12	At T.B.	W	4-3		6	6	Heredia	Wheeler	Isringhausen	79-64	2nd	5.5
9-13	At T.B.	W	8-3		13	7	Appier	Witt		80-64	2nd	5.5
9-14	At Bal.	L	6-13		11	16	Mussina	Oquist		80-65	2nd	6.5
9-17	K.C.	L	3-9		7	15	Witasick	Hudson		80-66	2nd	7.0
9-18	K.C.	W	8-4		13	8	Olivares	Rosado	Isringhausen	81-66	2nd	7.0
9-19	K.C.	W	12-3		12	6	Heredia	Fussell		82-66	2nd	6.0
9-20	Min.	L	0-4		7	11	Ryan	Appier		82-67	2nd	6.5
9-21	Min.	W	5-3		9	7	Mahay	Carrasco	Isringhausen	83-67	2nd	5.5
9-22	Min.	L	4-5		8	7	Redman	Worrell	Trombley	83-68	2nd	5.5
9-23†	At Bal.	W	9-6		15	8	Mathews	Molina	Isringhausen	84-68		
9-23‡	At Bal.	L	4-12		8	12	Johns	Olivares		84-69	2nd	5.5
9-24	At Tex.	L	4-12		8	18	Sele	Heredia		84-70	2nd	6.5
9-25	At Tex.	L	4-10		6	9	Burkett	Appier		84-71	2nd	7.5
9-26	At Tex.	L	3-10		7	12	Loaiza	Jarvis		84-72	2nd	8.5
9-28	At Ana.	W	9-3		14	4	Hudson	Washburn	Mahay	85-72	2nd	9.0
9-29	At Ana.	L	4-7		4	12	Hasegawa	Mathews	Pote	85-73	2nd	9.0
9-30	At Ana.	L	4-5		13	10	Petkovsek	Isringhausen	Pote	85-74	2nd	10.0
10-1	Sea.	W	5-1		7	4	Appier	Ramsay	Jones	86-74	2nd	9.0
10-2	Sea.	L	2-10		8	12	Garcia	Laxton		86-75	2nd	9.0
10-3	Sea.	W	3-1		11	4	Mahay	Halama	Isringhausen	87-75	2nd	8.0

Monthly records: April (10-14), May (17-10), June (10-16), July (16-10), August (19-10), September (13-14), October (2-1).
*Innings, if other than nine. † First game of a doubleheader. ‡ Second game of a doubleheader.

MEMORABLE GAMES

August 19 at Boston

A day after recently-acquired ace Kevin Appier had surrendered seven runs in a loss to the Red Sox, rookie Tim Hudson went eight-plus innings and gave up one earned run in a matchup against Pedro Martinez, the AL's dominant pitcher. Hudson improved his record to 8-1 and the victory put the A's just a game behind Boston in the wild-card race. Miguel Tejada hit his 16th homer of the season, three more than he'd hit the previous year as a rookie.

Oakland	AB	R	H	RBI	Boston	AB	R	H	RBI
Becker, cf-lf	4	0	1	1	Offerman, 2b	4	0	0	0
Velarde, 2b	5	0	0	0	Joh.Valntn, 3b	4	0	0	0
Ja.Giambi, dh	5	2	3	1	Daubach, 1b	3	0	0	0
Stairs, rf	4	1	1	0	Garcprra, ss	4	0	1	0
Spiezio, 1b	4	0	1	0	O'Leary, lf	4	0	0	0
Grieve, lf	3	0	1	0	Jefferson, dh	3	1	1	1
Jaha, ph	1	0	1	2	Huskey, ph	1	0	0	0
Christnsn, pr-cf	0	0	0	0	Varitek, c	4	0	1	0
Tejada, ss	4	1	2	2	D.Lewis, cf	2	1	0	0
Chavez, 3b	4	1	1	0	T.Nixon, rf	2	0	1	1
Hinch, c	4	1	1	0					
Totals	**38**	**6**	**12**	**6**	**Totals**	**31**	**2**	**4**	**2**

Oakland ....000 111 021 —6
Boston ....000 020 000 —2

E—Tejada (14), Offerman (11). LOB—Oakland 6, Boston 5. 2B—Ja.Giambi (28), Chavez (20). 3B—T.Nixon (5). HR—Tejada (16), Jefferson (5). CS—Christenson (5). S—Becker, D.Lewis.

Oakland	IP	H	R	ER	BB	SO
Hudson (W, 8-1)	8	4	2	1	2	7
Groom (H, 23)	0.1	0	0	0	0	0
T..Mathews (S, 3)	0.2	0	0	0	0	1

Boston	IP	H	R	ER	BB	SO
P.Martinez (L, 17-4)	7	7	3	3	0	11
Cormier	0.1	2	2	2	0	1
Florie	0.2	1	0	0	0	1
Guthrie	1	2	1	1	0	0

WP—Hudson, Florie. U—HP, Meriwether. 1B, Evans. 2B, DiMuro. 3B, Miller. T—2:51. A—33,393.

August 24 at Oakland

The A's had lost nine of the 10 games they'd played against the Indians in 1999, and Cleveland jumped out to a five-run lead in the first inning behind a Jim Thome grand slam off Tim Hudson. The A's responded with a five-run third that included a grand slam by DH John Jaha, the team's key offseason pickup. The Indians continued to jump on top, but the A's kept coming back. Finally, midseason acquisition Randy Velarde tied it with a homer in the bottom of the eighth and Jaha banged his second homer of the game and 30th of the season with two out, and T.J. Mathews pitched a perfect ninth for the save.

Cleveland	AB	R	H	RBI	Oakland	AB	R	H	RBI
D.Roberts, cf	4	1	0	0	Becker, cf-lf	4	1	0	0
Vizquel, ss	2	2	1	0	Velarde, 2b	5	3	3	2
Alomar, 2b	5	2	3	1	Ja.Giambi, 1b	4	2	1	0
M.Ramirez, rf	4	2	1	1	Jaha, dh	4	3	3	5
Justice, lf	2	2	1	1	Stairs, rf	5	0	1	1
Sexson, 1b	5	0	1	2	Christenson, cf	0	0	0	0
Thome, dh	3	1	1	4	Grieve, lf	3	0	1	0
Baerga, 3b	5	0	0	0	McDnald, ph-cf	1	0	0	0
Levis, c	4	0	0	0	Tejada, ss	3	0	1	1
					Spiezio, 3b	3	1	1	1
					Hinch, c	3	1	1	1
Totals	**34**	**10**	**8**	**9**	**Totals**	**35**	**11**	**12**	**11**

Cleveland ....500 001 310—10
Oakland ....005 100 32x—11

E—Tejada (17). DP—Oakland 1. LOB—Cleveland 7, Oakland 6. 2B—Vizquel (26), M.Ramirez (23), Justice (17), Sexson (14), Grieve (17), Tejada (28). HR—Thome (24), Velarde 2 (3), Jaha 2 (30), Spiezio (6), Hinch (7). SB—D.Roberts (5), Alomar (29), Velarde (7). SF—Tejada.

Cleveland	IP	H	R	ER	BB	SO
Karsay	3	4	5	5	1	0
Rakers	2	2	1	1	1	0
Riske	1	3	3	3	1	0
Rincon (H, 10)	0.1	1	0	0	0	0
Shuey (BS 6; L 7-5)	1.2	2	2	2	1	2

Oakland	IP	H	R	ER	BB	SO
Hudson	6.1	6	9	8	6	6
McMichael	1	1	1	1	3	0
Mathews (W, 8-3)	1.2	1	0	0	0	2

HBP—M.Ramirez by Hudson, Ja.Giambi by Karsay. U—HP, Kosc. 1B, Morrison. 2B, Hickox. 3B, Miller. T—3:22. A—17,417.

INDIVIDUAL STATISTICS

1999 REVIEW

BATTING

Name	G	TPA	AB	R	H	TB	2B	3B	HR	RBI	Avg.	Obp.	Slg.	SH	SF	HP	BB	IBB	SO	SB	CS	GDP	vs RHP AB	vs RHP Avg.	vs RHP HR	vs RHP RBI	vs LHP AB	vs LHP Avg.	vs LHP HR	vs LHP RBI
Tejada, Miguel	159	674	593	93	149	253	33	4	21	84	.251	.325	.427	9	5	10	57	3	94	8	7	11	453	.245	17	64	140	.271	4	20
Giambi, Jason	158	695	575	115	181	318	36	1	33	123	.315	.422	.553	0	8	7	105	6	106	1	1	11	394	.330	25	86	181	.282	8	37
Stairs, Matt	146	623	531	94	137	283	26	3	38	102	.258	.366	.533	0	1	2	89	6	124	2	7	8	366	.268	30	76	165	.236	8	26
Grieve, Ben	148	558	486	80	129	234	21	0	28	86	.265	.358	.481	0	1	8	63	2	108	4	0	17	377	.297	25	73	109	.156	3	13
Jaha, John	142	570	457	93	126	254	23	0	35	111	.276	.414	.556	0	3	9	101	2	129	2	0	14	328	.259	24	82	129	.318	11	29
Phillips, Tony	106	484	406	76	99	176	24	4	15	49	.244	.362	.433	0	2	5	71	3	94	11	3	7	314	.258	15	46	92	.196	0	3
Chavez, Eric	115	402	356	47	88	152	21	2	13	50	.247	.333	.427	0	0	0	46	4	56	1	1	7	307	.257	13	47	49	.184	0	3
Christenson, Ryan	106	319	268	41	56	82	12	1	4	24	.209	.305	.306	8	4	1	38	0	58	7	5	6	175	.160	1	8	93	.301	3	16
Velarde, Randy	61	286	255	48	85	122	10	3	7	28	.333	.401	.478	2	0	2	27	1	42	11	4	11	206	.330	6	20	49	.347	1	8
Saenz, Olmedo	97	296	255	41	70	121	18	0	11	41	.275	.363	.475	0	3	15	22	1	47	1	1	6	144	.257	8	25	111	.297	3	16
Spiezio, Scott	89	283	247	31	60	108	24	0	8	33	.243	.324	.437	1	3	2	29	3	36	0	0	5	177	.249	7	26	70	.229	1	7
Macfarlane, Mike	81	246	226	24	55	84	17	0	4	31	.243	.282	.372	1	5	1	13	0	52	0	0	7	179	.223	3	24	47	.319	1	7
Hinch, A.J.	76	228	205	26	44	71	4	1	7	24	.215	.260	.346	9	1	2	11	0	41	6	2	4	156	.212	6	21	49	.224	1	3
McDonald, Jason	100	220	187	26	39	52	2	1	3	8	.209	.310	.278	4	1	3	25	0	48	6	3	2	133	.203	2	4	54	.222	1	4
Hernandez, Ramon	40	158	136	13	38	54	7	0	3	21	.279	.363	.397	1	2	1	18	0	11	1	0	5	94	.245	0	9	42	.357	3	12
Raines, Tim	58	164	135	20	29	46	5	0	4	17	.215	.337	.341	1	2	0	26	1	17	4	1	5	71	.197	1	6	64	.234	3	11
Becker, Rich	40	153	125	21	33	39	3	0	1	10	.264	.395	.312	1	0	2	25	0	43	3	2	3	117	.265	1	8	8	.250	0	2
Velandia, Jorge	63	51	48	4	9	10	1	0	0	2	.188	.235	.208	0	0	1	2	0	13	2	0	0	34	.235	0	2	14	.071	0	0
Menechino, Frank	9	9	9	0	2	2	0	0	0	0	.222	.222	.222	0	0	0	0	0	4	0	0	0	8	.125	0	0	1	1.000	0	0
Heredia, Gil	33	8	6	0	0	0	0	0	0	0	.000	.143	.000	1	0	0	1	0	1	0	0	0	4	.000	0	0	2	.000	0	0
Hudson, Tim	24	5	4	0	1	1	0	0	0	0	.250	.400	.250	0	0	0	1	0	2	0	0	0	1	.000	0	0	3	.333	0	0
Haynes, Jimmy	30	5	4	0	0	0	0	0	0	0	.000	.000	.000	1	0	0	0	0	1	0	0	0	2	.000	0	0	2	.000	0	0
Rogers, Kenny	19	3	3	0	0	0	0	0	0	1	.000	.000	.000	0	0	0	0	0	1	0	0	0	3	.000	0	1	0	.000	0	0
Oquist, Mike	28	2	2	0	0	0	0	0	0	0	.000	.000	.000	0	0	0	0	0	1	0	0	0	0	.000	0	0	2	.000	0	0
Jones, Doug	70	0	0	0	0	0	0	0	0	0	.000	.000	.000	0	0	0	0	0	0	0	0	0	0	.000	0	0	0	.000	0	0
Groom, Buddy	76	0	0	0	0	0	0	0	0	0	.000	.000	.000	0	0	0	0	0	0	0	0	0	0	.000	0	0	0	.000	0	0
Worrell, Tim	53	0	0	0	0	0	0	0	0	0	.000	.000	.000	0	0	0	0	0	0	0	0	0	0	.000	0	0	0	.000	0	0
Taylor, Billy	43	0	0	0	0	0	0	0	0	0	.000	.000	.000	0	0	0	0	0	0	0	0	0	0	.000	0	0	0	.000	0	0
Mathews, T.J.	50	0	0	0	0	0	0	0	0	0	.000	.000	.000	0	0	0	0	0	0	0	0	0	0	.000	0	0	0	.000	0	0
Rigby, Brad	29	0	0	0	0	0	0	0	0	0	.000	.000	.000	0	0	0	0	0	0	0	0	0	0	.000	0	0	0	.000	0	0
Harville, Chad	15	0	0	0	0	0	0	0	0	0	.000	.000	.000	0	0	0	0	0	0	0	0	0	0	.000	0	0	0	.000	0	0
Appier, Kevin	12	0	0	0	0	0	0	0	0	0	.000	.000	.000	0	0	0	0	0	0	0	0	0	0	.000	0	0	0	.000	0	0
Olivares, Omar	12	0	0	0	0	0	0	0	0	0	.000	.000	.000	0	0	0	0	0	0	0	0	0	0	.000	0	0	0	.000	0	0

Players with more than one A.L. team

Name	G	TPA	AB	R	H	TB	2B	3B	HR	RBI	Avg.	Obp.	Slg.	SH	SF	HP	BB	IBB	SO	SB	CS	GDP	vs RHP AB	vs RHP Avg.	vs RHP HR	vs RHP RBI	vs LHP AB	vs LHP Avg.	vs LHP HR	vs LHP RBI
Appier, K.C.	22	2	2	0	0	0	0	0	0	0	.000	.000	.000	0	0	0	0	0	1	0	0	0	0	.000	0	0	0	.000	0	0
Appier, K.C.-Oak.	34	2	2	0	0	0	0	0	0	0	.000	.000	.000	0	0	0	0	0	1	0	0	0	2	.000	0	0	0	.000	0	0
Olivares, Ana.	20	7	6	0	2	3	1	0	0	0	.333	.333	.500	1	0	0	0	0	1	0	0	0	0	.000	0	0	0	.000	0	0
Olivares, Ana.-Oak.	32	7	6	0	2	3	1	0	0	0	.333	.333	.500	1	0	0	0	0	1	0	0	0	6	.333	0	0	0	.000	0	0
Velarde, Ana.	95	425	376	57	115	165	15	4	9	48	.306	.383	.439	2	0	4	43	1	56	13	4	8	206	.330	6	20	49	.347	1	8
Velarde, Ana.-Oak.	156	711	631	105	200	287	25	7	16	76	.317	.390	.455	4	0	6	70	2	98	24	8	19	490	.308	12	56	141	.348	4	20

PITCHING

Name	W	L	Pct.	ERA	IP	H	R	ER	HR	SH	SF	HB	BB	IBB	SO	G	GS	CG	ShO	GF	Sv	vs. RH AB	vs. RH Avg.	vs. RH HR	vs. RH RBI	vs. LH AB	vs. LH Avg.	vs. LH HR	vs. LH RBI
Heredia, Gil	13	8	.619	4.81	200.1	228	119	107	22	3	0	8	34	4	117	33	33	1	0	0	0	398	.279	15	57	409	.286	7	43
Haynes, Jimmy	7	12	.368	6.34	142.0	158	112	100	21	4	5	2	80	3	93	30	25	0	0	2	0	254	.280	15	52	307	.283	6	44
Oquist, Mike	9	10	.474	5.37	140.2	158	86	84	18	3	1	2	64	5	89	28	24	0	0	1	0	274	.292	10	30	285	.274	8	43
Hudson, Tim	11	2	.846	3.23	136.1	121	56	49	8	1	2	4	62	2	132	21	21	1	0	0	0	246	.240	4	24	265	.234	4	22
Rogers, Kenny	5	3	.625	4.30	119.1	135	66	57	8	4	6	9	41	0	68	19	19	3	0	0	0	364	.283	6	42	104	.308	2	12
Jones, Doug	5	5	.500	3.55	104.0	106	43	41	10	3	3	3	24	3	63	70	0	0	0	35	10	193	.280	5	25	204	.255	5	28
Olivares, Omar	7	2	.778	4.34	74.2	82	43	36	8	0	2	3	32	0	36	12	12	1	0	0	0	150	.273	4	21	140	.293	4	21
Worrell, Tim	2	2	.500	4.15	69.1	69	38	32	6	1	1	3	34	1	62	53	0	0	0	17	0	140	.229	4	17	130	.285	2	31
Appier, Kevin	7	5	.583	5.77	68.2	77	50	44	9	2	2	1	33	1	53	12	12	0	0	0	0	140	.307	5	30	135	.252	4	15
Rigby, Brad	3	4	.429	4.33	62.1	69	31	30	5	1	3	5	26	7	26	29	0	0	0	5	0	127	.228	1	17	116	.345	4	21
Mathews, T.J.	9	5	.643	3.81	59.0	46	28	25	9	5	1	2	20	4	42	50	0	0	0	15	3	119	.202	4	17	95	.232	5	18
Candiotti, Tom	3	5	.375	6.35	56.2	67	46	40	11	0	4	2	23	0	30	11	11	0	0	0	0	125	.360	9	29	100	.220	2	9
Groom, Buddy	3	2	.600	5.09	46.0	48	29	26	1	2	0	1	18	5	32	76	0	0	0	6	0	73	.315	1	10	102	.245	0	17
Taylor, Billy	1	5	.167	3.98	43.0	48	23	19	3	4	2	2	14	3	38	43	0	0	0	38	26	81	.222	2	12	86	.349	1	13
Isringhausen, Jason	0	1	.000	2.13	25.1	21	6	6	2	0	0	1	12	2	20	20	0	0	0	18	8	50	.280	2	7	44	.159	0	2
Mahay, Ron	2	0	1.000	1.86	19.1	8	4	4	2	0	0	0	3	0	15	6	1	0	0	2	1	44	.114	1	1	21	.143	1	2
McMichael, Greg	0	0	.000	5.40	15.0	15	9	9	3	1	1	2	12	2	3	17	0	0	0	4	0	34	.324	3	10	19	.211	0	0
Harville, Chad	0	2	.000	6.91	14.1	18	11	11	2	0	1	0	10	1	15	15	0	0	0	8	0	33	.333	1	4	25	.280	1	3
Jarvis, Kevin	0	1	.000	11.57	14.0	28	19	18	6	0	1	1	6	0	11	4	1	0	0	0	0	36	.472	4	15	31	.355	2	6
Kubinski, Tim	0	0	.000	5.84	12.1	14	8	8	3	0	1	1	5	1	7	14	0	0	0	4	0	30	.300	2	7	20	.250	1	4
Laxton, Brett	0	1	.000	7.45	9.2	12	12	8	1	0	3	2	7	1	9	3	2	0	0	0	0	24	.333	1	6	14	.286	0	1
Vizcaino, Luis	0	0	.000	5.40	3.1	3	2	2	1	0	0	0	3	0	2	1	0	0	0	1	0	6	.167	0	0	7	.286	1	2
Stein, Blake	0	0	.000	16.88	2.2	6	5	5	1	0	0	0	6	0	4	1	1	0	0	0	0	8	.500	1	3	5	.400	0	1

PITCHERS WITH MORE THAN ONE A.L. TEAM

Name	W	L	Pct.	ERA	IP	H	R	ER	HR	SH	SF	HB	BB	IBB	SO	G	GS	CG	ShO	GF	Sv	vs. RH AB	vs. RH Avg.	vs. RH HR	vs. RH RBI	vs. LH AB	vs. LH Avg.	vs. LH HR	vs. LH RBI
Appier, K.C.	9	9	.500	4.87	140.1	153	81	76	18	5	3	6	51	3	78	22	22	1	0	0	0	140	.307	5	30	135	.252	4	15
Appier, K.C.-Oak.	16	14	.533	5.17	209.0	230	131	120	27	7	5	7	84	4	131	34	34	1	0	5	0	412	.262	16	65	411	.297	11	48
Candiotti, Cle.	1	1	.500	11.05	14.2	19	18	18	3	2	0	1	7	0	11	7	2	0	0	1	0	125	.360	9	29	100	.220	2	9
Candiotti, Oak.-Cle.	4	6	.400	7.32	71.1	86	64	58	14	2	4	3	30	0	41	18	13	0	0	4	0	164	.341	10	38	123	.244	4	17
Olivares, Ana.	8	9	.471	4.05	131.0	135	62	59	11	3	5	6	49	0	49	20	20	3	0	0	0	150	.273	4	21	140	.293	4	21
Olivares, Ana.-Oak.	15	11	.577	4.16	205.2	217	105	95	19	3	7	9	81	0	85	32	32	4	0	7	0	393	.290	7	45	392	.263	12	53
Rigby, K.C.	1	2	.333	7.17	21.1	33	20	17	6	1	2	2	5	0	10	20	0	0	0	6	0	127	.228	1	17	116	.345	4	21
Rigby, Oak.-K.C.	4	6	.400	5.06	83.2	102	51	47	11	2	5	7	31	7	36	49	0	0	0	5	0	174	.259	6	30	163	.350	5	32
Stein, K.C.	1	2	.333	4.09	70.1	59	33	32	10	2	1	7	41	1	43	12	11	0	0	0	0	8	.500	1	3	5	.400	0	1
Stein, Oak.-K.C.	1	2	.333	4.56	73.0	65	38	37	11	2	1	7	47	1	47	13	12	0	0	1	0	137	.226	5	18	133	.256	6	18

DESIGNATED HITTERS

Name	AB	Avg.	HR	RBI
Jaha, John	431	.285	35	105
Giambi, Jason	57	.351	4	14
Saenz, Olmedo	21	.190	1	3
Stairs, Matt	16	.125	0	0
Grieve, Ben	12	.083	0	0
Raines, Tim	9	.222	0	2
Spiezio, Scott	8	.125	0	1
Phillips, Tony	4	.000	0	0
Chavez, Eric	2	.500	0	0
Macfarlane, Mike	1	.000	0	0
McDonald, Jason	1	.000	0	0
Velandia, Jorge	0	-	0	0
Hudson, Tim	0	-	0	0
Becker, Rich	0	-	0	0
Christenson, Ryan	0	-	0	0
Menechino, Frank	0	-	0	0

FIELDING

FIRST BASEMEN

Player	Pct.	G	PO	A	E	TC	DP
Giambi, Jason	.995	142	1251	45	7	1303	128
Saenz, Olmedo	.994	28	153	12	1	166	11
Spiezio, Scott	1.000	10	51	1	0	52	6
Jaha, John	1.000	8	42	4	0	46	3
Stairs, Matt	1.000	1	2	0	0	2	0

SECOND BASEMEN

Player	Pct.	G	PO	A	E	TC	DP
Phillips, Tony	.974	66	96	164	7	267	41
Velarde, Randy	.977	61	107	186	7	300	43
Velandia, Jorge	.989	52	36	57	1	94	13
Spiezio, Scott	.984	42	57	127	3	187	25
McDonald, Jason	1.000	1	1	0	0	1	0

THIRD BASEMEN

Player	Pct.	G	PO	A	E	TC	DP
Chavez, Eric	.961	105	69	155	9	233	13
Saenz, Olmedo	.938	56	27	79	7	113	12
Spiezio, Scott	.927	31	16	35	4	55	1
Velandia, Jorge	1.000	2	1	1	0	2	0
Phillips, Tony	-	2	0	0	0	0	0
Menechino, Frank	1.000	1	1	1	0	2	0
Giambi, Jason	-	1	0	0	0	0	0

SHORTSTOPS

Player	Pct.	G	PO	A	E	TC	DP
Tejada, Miguel	.973	159	292	471	21	784	110
Velandia, Jorge	.938	8	9	21	2	32	4
Menechino, Frank	1.000	5	3	6	0	9	2
Chavez, Eric	-	2	0	0	0	0	0
Phillips, Tony	-	1	0	0	0	0	0

OUTFIELDERS

Player	Pct.	G	PO	A	E	TC	DP
Stairs, Matt	.981	139	245	13	5	263	1
Grieve, Ben	.988	137	232	6	3	241	2
Christenson, Ryan	.969	104	213	3	7	223	1
McDonald, Jason	.993	89	149	3	1	153	1
Phillips, Tony	.937	62	85	4	6	95	1
Becker, Rich	.986	39	66	4	1	71	1
Raines, Tim	1.000	38	61	0	0	61	0

CATCHERS

Player	Pct.	G	PO	A	E	TC	DP	PB
Macfarlane, Mike	.997	79	351	43	1	395	8	6
Hinch, A.J.	.987	73	368	26	5	399	4	10
Hernandez, Ramon	.980	40	274	19	6	299	5	2

PITCHERS

Player	Pct.	G	PO	A	E	TC	DP
Groom, Buddy	1.000	76	1	13	0	14	1
Jones, Doug	.895	70	5	12	2	19	2
Worrell, Tim	1.000	53	1	3	0	4	0
Mathews, T.J.	1.000	50	6	7	0	13	0
Taylor, Billy	1.000	43	1	5	0	6	0
Heredia, Gil	.975	33	10	29	1	40	2
Haynes, Jimmy	.800	30	1	19	5	25	1
Rigby, Brad	.714	29	1	4	2	7	1
Oquist, Mike	.947	28	1	17	1	19	3
Hudson, Tim	.970	21	10	22	1	33	3
Isringhausen, Jason	1.000	20	1	4	0	5	0
Rogers, Kenny	.942	19	6	43	3	52	2
McMichael, Greg	1.000	17	0	1	0	1	0
Harville, Chad	-	15	0	0	0	0	0
Kubinski, Tim	1.000	14	0	4	0	4	0
Olivares, Omar	.950	12	7	12	1	20	2
Appier, Kevin	1.000	12	3	8	0	11	0
Candiotti, Tom	.889	11	1	7	1	9	1
Mahay, Ron	1.000	6	0	2	0	2	0
Jarvis, Kevin	1.000	4	2	1	0	3	0
Laxton, Brett	.500	3	0	1	1	2	0
Stein, Blake	-	1	0	0	0	0	0
Vizcaino, Luis	-	1	0	0	0	0	0

Pitcher	Ana. W-L	Bal. W-L	Bos. W-L	Chi. W-L	Cle. W-L	Det. W-L	K.C. W-L	Min. W-L	N.Y. W-L	Sea. W-L	T.B. W-L	Tex. W-L	Tor. W-L	N.L. W-L	Total W-L
Appier, Kevin	0-0	1-0	1-1	1-1	0-0	1-0	0-0	0-1	0-0	1-0	1-0	0-1	1-1	0-0	7-5
Candiotti, Tom	0-0	0-0	0-0	0-1	1-1	0-0	0-1	0-0	0-1	0-1	0-0	1-0	0-0	0-0	3-5
Groom, Buddy	0-0	0-0	0-0	0-0	0-0	0-0	0-1	1-0	0-0	0-0	1-0	0-0	0-0	1-2	3-2
Harville, Chad	0-1	0-0	0-0	0-0	0-0	0-0	0-0	0-0	0-0	0-0	0-0	0-0	0-0	0-0	0-2
Haynes, Jimmy	0-0	0-2	0-0	0-1	0-2	1-1	1-1	1-1	0-2	0-1	0-0	2-0	0-0	2-1	7-12
Heredia, Gil	1-1	0-0	1-2	2-0	0-0	1-0	1-1	0-1	2-0	2-0	0-1	1-0	2-1	1-0	13-8
Hudson, Tim	1-0	1-0	1-0	0-0	0-0	2-0	0-0	0-1	1-0	1-1	1-1	1-0	2-0	1-0	11-2
Isringhausen, Jason	0-1	0-0	0-0	0-0	0-0	0-0	0-0	0-0	0-0	0-0	0-0	0-0	0-0	0-0	0-1
Jarvis, Kevin	0-0	0-0	0-0	0-0	0-0	0-0	0-0	0-0	0-0	0-1	0-0	0-0	0-0	0-0	0-1
Jones, Doug	0-1	0-0	1-1	1-0	0-0	0-0	1-1	0-1	0-1	0-0	0-0	0-0	1-0	1-0	5-5
Kubinski, Tim	0-0	0-0	0-0	0-0	0-0	0-0	0-1	0-0	0-0	0-0	0-0	0-0	0-0	0-0	0-1
Laxton, Brett	0-0	0-0	0-0	0-0	0-0	0-0	0-0	0-0	0-0	0-0	0-0	0-0	0-0	0-0	0-0
Mahay, Ron	0-0	0-0	0-0	0-0	0-0	0-0	0-0	1-0	0-0	0-0	0-0	0-0	0-0	0-0	1-0
Mathews, T.J.	1-1	1-1	2-0	1-0	1-0	0-0	0-0	0-0	1-1	0-0	0-1	1-0	0-0	1-0	9-5
McMichael, Greg	0-0	0-0	0-0	0-0	0-0	0-0	0-0	0-0	0-0	0-0	0-0	0-0	0-0	0-0	0-0
Olivares, Omar	0-0	0-1	0-0	1-0	0-0	0-1	1-0	0-0	2-0	0-0	2-0	0-0	1-0	0-0	7-2
Oquist, Mike	1-1	1-1	0-0	1-0	0-2	0-1	2-1	0-0	0-0	1-0	0-2	2-1	0-1	1-1	9-10
Rigby, Brad	0-1	2-0	0-0	0-0	0-0	0-0	1-1	0-0	0-1	0-0	0-0	0-0	0-0	0-0	3-4
Rogers, Kenny	0-1	0-0	0-0	0-1	1-0	0-1	0-1	1-0	0-0	0-0	0-0	1-0	2-0	0-0	5-3
Stein, Blake	0-0	0-0	0-0	0-0	0-0	0-0	0-0	0-0	0-0	0-0	0-0	0-0	0-0	0-0	0-0
Taylor, Billy	0-0	0-0	0-0	0-0	0-3	0-0	0-0	0-0	1-0	0-0	0-0	0-0	0-0	0-1	1-5
Vizcaino, Luis	0-0	0-0	0-0	0-0	0-0	0-0	0-0	0-0	0-0	0-0	0-0	0-0	0-0	0-0	0-0
Worrell, Tim	0-0	0-0	0-0	0-0	0-1	0-0	0-0	1-1	0-0	0-0	0-0	0-0	0-0	1-0	2-2
Totals	4-8	7-5	6-4	7-3	2-10	6-4	6-6	5-7	4-6	6-6	9-1	5-7	8-2	12-6	87-75

INTERLEAGUE: Oquist 1-0, Rogers 1-0, Hudson 1-0 vs. Dodgers; Haynes 1-0, Groom 0-1, Heredia 0-1 vs. Padres; Groom 1-1, Heredia 1-0, Jones 1-0, Taylor 0-1, Oquist 0-1 vs. Giants; Haynes 1-0, Worrell 1-0, Rogers 1-0 vs. Rockies; Heredia 1-0, Hudson 1-0, Haynes 0-1 vs. Diamondbacks. Total: 12-6.

HOME RUNS BY PARK

At Anaheim (8): Giambi 3, Grieve 2, Stairs 1, Jaha 1, McDonald 1.
At Arizona (5): Raines 1, Stairs 1, McDonald 1, Grieve 1, Hernandez 1.
At Baltimore (14): Stairs 5, Phillips 2, Macfarlane 1, Velarde 1, Jaha 1, Giambi 1, Spiezio 1, Tejada 1, Grieve 1.
At Boston (5): Tejada 2, Spiezio 1, Grieve 1, Hinch 1.
At Chicago (AL) (6): Phillips 1, Stairs 1, Jaha 1, Saenz 1, Tejada 1, Grieve 1.
At Cleveland (6): Phillips 2, Grieve 2, Spiezio 1, Chavez 1.
At Detroit (14): Jaha 5, Giambi 3, Grieve 2, Raines 1, Stairs 1, Tejada 1, Chavez 1.
At Kansas City (10): Stairs 3, Giambi 3, Jaha 2, Tejada 1, Christenson 1.
At Minnesota (6): Stairs 3, Macfarlane 1, Jaha 1, Spiezio 1.
At New York (AL) (4): Stairs 1, Saenz 1, Spiezio 1, Tejada 1.
At Oakland (112): Jaha 18, Giambi 17, Stairs 15, Grieve 13, Tejada 12, Saenz 8, Chavez 8, Phillips 5, Velarde 4, Spiezio 3, Hinch 3, Raines 2, Christenson 2, Becker 1, Hernandez 1.
At San Diego (1): Phillips 1.
At San Francisco (4): Phillips 1, Macfarlane 1, Stairs 1, Giambi 1.
At Seattle (4): Jaha 2, Chavez 1, Hernandez 1.
At Tampa Bay (6): Giambi 3, Velandia 1, Stairs 1, Saenz 1.
At Texas (8): Grieve 3, Jaha 2, Macfarlane 1, Stairs 1, Chavez 1.
At Toronto (15): Stairs 3, Giambi 2, Tejada 2, Grieve 2, Hinch 2, Phillips 1, Velarde 1, McDonald 1, Chavez 1.

LOW-HIT GAMES

No-hitters: None.
One-hitters: None.
Two-hitters: None.

10-STRIKEOUT GAMES

Tim Hudson 2, **Total:** 2.

FOUR OR MORE HITS IN ONE GAME

Jason Giambi 3, Tony Phillips 1, Mike Macfarlane 1, Randy Velarde 1, John Jaha 1, Ramon Hernandez 1, **Total:** 8.

MULTI-HOMER GAMES

John Jaha 5, Jason Giambi 4, Randy Velarde 1, Matt Stairs 1, Miguel Tejada 1, Ben Grieve 1, **Total:** 13.

GRAND SLAMS

4-25: Jason Giambi (off Baltimore's Ricky Bones).
4-30: Matt Stairs (off Boston's Kip Gross).
7-21: Eric Chavez (off Seattle's Ken Cloude).
7-23: Jason Giambi (off Kansas City's Makoto Suzuki).
7-25: John Jaha (off Kansas City's Brian Barber).
8-13: Matt Stairs (off Toronto's Paul Spoljaric).
8-14: A.J. Hinch (off Toronto's Joey Hamilton).
8-24: John Jaha (off Cleveland's Steve Karsay).

PINCH HITTERS

(Minimum 5 at-bats)

Name	AB	Avg.	HR	RBI
Saenz, Olmedo	20	.200	0	2
Raines, Tim	18	.333	0	3
Chavez, Eric	13	.462	0	6
Jaha, John	11	.091	0	4
Spiezio, Scott	10	.100	0	0
Grieve, Ben	8	.375	0	3
McDonald, Jason	8	.125	0	0
Macfarlane, Mike	6	.333	0	1
Becker, Rich	5	.400	0	1

DEBUTS

6-8: Tim Hudson, P.
6-21: Brett Laxton, P.
6-23: Chad Harville, P.
6-29: Ramon Hernandez, C.
7-23: Luis Vizcaino, P.
9-6: Frank Menechino, SS.

GAMES BY POSITION

Catcher: Mike Macfarlane 79, A.J. Hinch 73, Ramon Hernandez 40.
First base: Jason Giambi 142, Olmedo Saenz 28, Scott Spiezio 10, John Jaha 8, Matt Stairs 1.
Second base: Tony Phillips 66, Randy Velarde 61, Jorge Velandia 52, Scott Spiezio 42, Jason McDonald 1.
Third base: Eric Chavez 105, Olmedo Saenz 56, Scott Spiezio 31, Tony Phillips 2, Jorge Velandia 2, Jason Giambi 1, Frank Menechino 1.
Shortstop: Miguel Tejada 159, Jorge Velandia 8, Frank Menechino 5, Eric Chavez 2, Tony Phillips 1.
Outfield: Matt Stairs 139, Ben Grieve 137, Ryan Christenson 104, Jason McDonald 89, Tony Phillips 62, Rich Becker 39, Tim Raines 38.
Designated hitter: John Jaha 121, Jason Giambi 15, Olmedo Saenz 8, Scott Spiezio 6, Matt Stairs 5, Jason McDonald 5, Ben Grieve 4, Tim Raines 3, Eric Chavez 3, Frank Menechino 3, Tim Hudson 2, Tony Phillips 1, Mike Macfarlane 1, Rich Becker 1, Jorge Velandia 1, Ryan Christenson 1.

STREAKS

Wins: 6 (May 7-16).
Losses: 6 (May 18-23, June 23-29).
Consecutive games with at least one hit: 18, Jason Giambi (July 23-August 10).
Wins by pitcher: 4, Gil Heredia (July 3-21).

ATTENDANCE

Home: 1,434,610.
Road: 2,248,055.
Highest (home): 51,263 (July 17 vs. San Francisco).
Highest (road): 46,178 (September 25 vs. Texas).
Lowest (home): 5,377 (April 13 vs. Anaheim).
Lowest (road): 11,181 (May 7 vs. Chicago).

1999 REVIEW

SEATTLE MARINERS

1999 REVIEW

DAY BY DAY

Date	Opp.	Res.	Score	(inn.*)	Hits	Opp. hits	Winning pitcher	Losing pitcher	Save	Record	Pos.	GB
4-5	Chi.	L	2-8		8	12	Baldwin	Fassero		0-1	T3rd	0.5
4-6	Chi.	L	3-11		6	15	Parque	Moyer		0-2	4th	1.5
4-7	Chi.	W	7-3		10	10	Garcia	Snyder	Mesa	1-2	T3rd	1.0
4-9	Oak.	W	6-1		10	3	Henry	Rogers		2-2	T1st	...
4-10	Oak.	L	4-11		9	17	Heredia	Fassero		2-3	T2nd	1.0
4-11	Oak.	W	11-8		18	12	Moyer	Candiotti		3-3	T1st	...
4-12	Oak.	W	6-3		12	9	Garcia	Haynes	Mesa	4-3	T1st	...
4-13	Tex.	L	6-15		10	19	Morgan	Cloude		4-4	T1st	...
4-14	Tex.	L	6-9		11	17	Zimmerman	Paniagua	Wetteland	4-5	T2nd	1.0
4-15	Tex.	L	3-4	(10)	5	9	Crabtree	Halama	Wetteland	4-6	T3rd	2.0
4-16	At Ana.	L	5-9		5	14	Belcher	Moyer		4-7	4th	2.0
4-17	At Ana.	W	4-3	(10)	7	8	Paniagua	Percival	Mesa	5-7	4th	1.0
4-18	At Ana.	W	8-5		10	10	Cloude	Sparks	Mesa	6-7	T2nd	1.0
4-20	At Chi.	L	1-3		5	8	Parque	Fassero	Howry	6-8	T2nd	1.0
4-21	At Chi.	L	1-2		6	5	Snyder	Paniagua	Howry	6-9	T2nd	1.0
4-23	At T.B.	L	4-5		7	11	White	Halama	Hernandez	6-10	4th	2.5
4-24	At T.B.	W	9-4		12	8	Henry	Arrojo		7-10	3rd	2.5
4-25	At T.B.	W	6-4		12	6	Paniagua	Hernandez	Mesa	8-10	3rd	2.5
4-26	Det.	L	0-7		7	15	Moehler	Moyer		8-11	T3rd	3.0
4-27	Det.	L	1-5		9	10	Thompson	Hinchliffe		8-12	T3rd	3.0
4-28	Det.	W	8-6		10	8	Garcia	Blair		9-12	T2nd	3.0
4-29	Det.	W	22-6		19	15	Cloude	Nitkowski		10-12	T2nd	2.0
4-30	Tor.	W	11-9		10	12	Halama	Person	Mesa	11-12	T2nd	2.0
5-1	Tor.	L	3-9		11	13	Carpenter	Moyer	Davey	11-13	T2nd	2.0
5-2	Tor.	W	3-2		7	8	Cloude	Plesac		12-13	T2nd	2.0
5-3	Tor.	L	10-16		13	17	Wells	Garcia		12-14	T2nd	2.0
5-5	At Cle.	W	6-5		10	10	Fassero	Burba	Mesa	13-14	3rd	2.0
5-6	At Cle.	L	4-8		7	8	Colon	Weaver		13-15	3rd	2.0
5-7	At N.Y.	L	1-10		5	10	Irabu	Suzuki		13-16	3rd	2.0
5-8	At N.Y.	W	14-5		19	8	Garcia	Hernandez		14-16	3rd	2.0
5-9	At N.Y.	L	1-6		3	9	Grimsley	Fassero		14-17	3rd	3.0
5-10	At Bos.	L	4-12		9	10	Wasdin	Hinchliffe		14-18	3rd	3.0
5-11	At Bos.	W	8-5		14	10	Moyer	Wakefield		15-18	3rd	3.0
5-12	At Bos.	L	2-9		6	11	Martinez	Suzuki		15-19	T3rd	3.5
5-14	K.C.	L	7-12		10	19	Service	Fassero		15-20	4th	5.0
5-15	K.C.	L	10-11		8	17	Santiago	Paniagua	Montgomery	15-21	4th	6.0
5-16	K.C.	W	5-1		9	9	Moyer	Fussell		16-21	4th	5.0
5-17	Min.	W	15-5		16	9	Halama	Milton		17-21	T3rd	4.0
5-18	Min.	W	10-1		13	8	Garcia	Perkins		18-21	3rd	3.0
5-19	Min.	W	7-0		11	5	Fassero	Lincoln		19-21	3rd	3.0
5-21	At K.C.	W	5-2		12	11	Moyer	Witasick		20-21	3rd	2.0
5-22	At K.C.	W	7-4		12	11	Carmona	Fussell	Mesa	21-21	2nd	2.0
5-23	At K.C.	L	4-5		9	11	Whisenant	Paniagua	Montgomery	21-22	2nd	2.0
5-24	At Min.	L	5-10		12	12	Perkins	Fassero		21-23	T2nd	3.0
5-25	At Min.	W	15-5		17	10	Halama	Rath		22-23	T2nd	3.0
5-26	At Min.	W	11-3		12	7	Moyer	Hawkins		23-23	T2nd	3.0
5-28	T.B.	W	6-1		11	5	Garcia	Alvarez		24-23	3rd	3.0
5-29	T.B.	W	11-5		12	10	Fassero	Rupe		25-23	2nd	3.0
5-30	T.B.	L	7-15		15	17	Rekar	Cloude		25-24	3rd	4.0
5-31	Bal.	W	10-6		13	12	Moyer	Ponson	Mesa	26-24	3rd	4.0
6-1	Bal.	L	11-14		14	14	Johns	Garcia		26-25	3rd	5.0
6-2	Bal.	W	4-2		6	12	Paniagua	Mussina	Mesa	27-25	3rd	5.0
6-4	At S.D.	L	2-3		7	6	Wall	Paniagua	Hoffman	27-26	3rd	5.0
6-5	At S.D.	L	2-3	(10)	9	7	Reyes	Mesa		27-27	3rd	6.0
6-6	At S.D.	W	4-1		7	4	Garcia	Ashby	Paniagua	28-27	3rd	5.0
6-7	At Col.	W	4-2		8	9	Halama	Jones	Mesa	29-27	T2nd	5.0
6-8	At Col.	W	10-5		15	10	Rodriguez	Brownson	Cloude	30-27	2nd	5.0
6-9	At Col.	L	11-16		12	12	Bohanon	Fassero		30-28	T2nd	5.0
6-11	S.F	W	7-3		10	9	Moyer	Gardner	Mesa	31-28	2nd	5.0
6-12	S.F	L	11-15		15	22	Rueter	Garcia		31-29	3rd	5.0
6-13	S.F	L	4-8		7	13	Tavarez	Paniagua		31-30	3rd	5.0
6-14	At Det.	L	7-8		13	10	Kida	Cloude		31-31	3rd	5.0
6-15	At Det.	W	5-4		6	9	Rodriguez	Moehler	Mesa	32-31	3rd	4.0
6-16	At Det.	W	7-1		13	9	Moyer	Mlicki		33-31	T2nd	4.0
6-17	At Det.	W	4-3		7	7	Garcia	Jones	Mesa	34-31	2nd	4.0
6-18	At Cle.	W	9-4		10	11	Halama	Nagy		35-31	2nd	4.0
6-19	At Cle.	L	6-10		12	10	Burba	Watson	Jackson	35-32	2nd	4.0
6-20	At Cle.	L	5-13		11	14	Wright	Rodriguez		35-33	T2nd	4.0
6-21	At Cle.	L	3-4	(12)	10	12	Karsay	Mesa		35-34	T2nd	4.0
6-22	Ana.	L	2-4		6	8	Petkovsek	Garcia	Percival	35-35	3rd	4.0
6-23	Ana.	W	8-3		10	10	Halama	Hill	Rodriguez	36-35	T2nd	4.0
6-24	Ana.	L	7-12		9	16	Schoeneweis	Mesa	Petkovsek	36-36	T2nd	6.0
6-25	Tex.	L	4-14		6	18	Glynn	Rodriguez		36-37	T2nd	6.0
6-26	Tex.	W	5-4		8	12	Paniagua	Venafro	Mesa	37-37	2nd	5.0
6-27	Tex.	W	5-2		10	6	Garcia	Sele	Mesa	38-37	2nd	4.0
6-29	At Oak.	W	2-1	(12)	7	9	Paniagua	Mathews	Mesa	39-37	2nd	4.5
6-30	At Oak.	L	5-14		12	14	Hudson	Fassero		39-38	2nd	5.5

HIGHLIGHTS

High point: The final Mariners game in Kingdome history was the feel-good moment of the year, with a crowd of 56,530 attracted to festivities featuring the best players in franchise history. Fittingly, Ken Griffey Jr. hit a three-run home run in the June 27 game, leading the Mariners to a 5-2 victory over Texas.

Low point: The first home series in September, when the Mariners—trying to creep back into the wild-card race—played host to Boston for four games. Seattle won the first game, but Pedro Martinez shut down the Mariners the next day and the Red Sox took the next two games as well. By September 13, Seattle had lost seven of nine games and dropped out of postseason contention.

Turning point: On July 5, the Mariners won their third consecutive game, improving to 42-40, and were within four games of first-place Texas in the A.L. West. On July 6, Seattle began a seven-game losing streak that dropped the club eight games back—and the Mariners weren't two games above .500 again until September.

Most valuable player: Ken Griffey Jr. had another outstanding year. He won his 10th Gold Glove and was an All-Star Game selection for the 10th time. In 160 games, he hit 48 home runs and drove in 134 runs.

Most valuable pitcher: Veteran Jamie Moyer was a coach between starts, but no one had a more consistent season than rookie Freddy Garcia. He led the team with 17 victories and never lost consecutive decisions.

Most improved player: After a tough 1998 season in which his 34 errors led the majors, third baseman Russ Davis played 124 games and committed just 12 errors. Offensively, he slumped to .245 but hit a career-best 21 homers.

Most pleasant surprise: David Bell left spring training as a reserve infielder. Five games later, the Mariners lost injured second baseman Carlos Guillen for the season. Bell stepped in and contributed career highs in homers (21) and RBIs (78).

Key injuries: Veterans Butch Henry and Mark Leiter were acquired in the offseason to solidify a young pitching staff, but both went down early and combined for only 26.1 innings all season. Shortstop Alex Rodriguez missed 5 1/2 weeks because of knee surgery, outfielder Jay Buhner was limited to 87 games because of a myriad of injuries and Guillen went down with a torn ACL. Also, Davis broke a foot and John Mabry suffered a kneecap fracture.

Notable: The Mariners moved into Safeco Field on July 15 and wound up going 23-19 in their new ballpark. They were 20-19 at the Kingdome in 1999. ... Despite playing in only 129 games, Rodriguez hit 42 homers and knocked in 111 runs. ... Edgar Martinez batted .337, marking the fifth time in eight seasons he had hit at least .325.

—LARRY LaRUE

MISCELLANEOUS

RECORDS

1999 regular-season record: 79-83 (3rd in A.L. West); 43-38 at home; 36-45 on road; 24-27 vs. A.L. East; 31-25 vs. A.L. Central; 17-20 vs. A.L. West; 7-11 vs. N.L. West; 13-22 vs. lefthanded starters; 66-61 vs. righthanded starters; 49-59 on grass; 30-24 on turf; 24-23 in daytime; 55-60 at night; 20-23 in one-run games; 5-6 in extra-inning games; 1-0-0 in doubleheaders.

Team record past five years: 409-382 (.517, ranks 6th in league in that span).

TEAM LEADERS

Batting average: Edgar Martinez (.337).
At-bats: Ken Griffey Jr. (606).
Runs: Ken Griffey Jr. (123).
Hits: Ken Griffey Jr. (173).
Total bases: Ken Griffey Jr. (349).
Doubles: Edgar Martinez (35).
Triples: Brian L. Hunter (7).
Home runs: Ken Griffey Jr. (48).
Runs batted in: Ken Griffey Jr. (134).
Stolen bases: Brian L. Hunter (44).
Slugging percentage: Alex Rodriguez (.586).
On-base percentage: Edgar Martinez (.447).
Wins: Freddy Garcia (17).
Earned-run average: Jamie Moyer (3.87).
Complete games: Jamie Moyer (4).
Shutouts: Freddy Garcia, John Halama (1).
Saves: Jose Mesa (33).
Innings pitched: Jamie Moyer (228.0).
Strikeouts: Freddy Garcia (170).

Date	Opp.	Res.	Score	(inn.*)	Hits	Opp. hits	Winning pitcher	Losing pitcher	Save	Record	Pos.	GB
7-1	At Oak.	L	4-5		7	10	Taylor	Paniagua		39-39	2nd	6.0
7-2	At Tex.	L	6-7		14	10	Wetteland	Cloude		39-40	2nd	7.0
7-3	At Tex.	W	13-12		15	15	Paniagua	Crabtree	Mesa	40-40	2nd	6.0
7-4	At Tex.	W	6-0		12	6	Halama	Morgan		41-40	2nd	5.0
7-5	At Ana.	W	10-0		14	3	Fassero	Hasegawa		42-40	2nd	4.0
7-6	At Ana.	L	2-8		7	9	Petkovsek	Rodriguez		42-41	2nd	4.0
7-7	At Ana.	L	3-10		13	16	Sparks	Moyer		42-42	2nd	5.0
7-9	At L.A.	L	0-5		7	11	Valdes	Garcia		42-43	T2nd	6.0
7-10	At L.A.	L	1-2		3	6	Shaw	Paniagua		42-44	3rd	6.0
7-11	At L.A.	L	3-14		6	15	Dreifort	Fassero	Masaoka	42-45	3rd	6.0
7-15	S.D.	L	2-3		8	7	Cunnane	Mesa	Miceli	42-46	4th	7.0
7-16	S.D.	L	1-2		9	8	Hitchcock	Fassero	Hoffman	42-47	4th	8.0
7-17	S.D.	W	9-1		11	5	Garcia	Williams		43-47	3rd	7.0
7-18	Ari.	W	8-7	(10)	10	11	Mesa	Kim		44-47	3rd	7.0
7-19	Ari.	W	7-5		11	8	Meche	Anderson		45-47	3rd	7.0
7-20	Ari.	L	0-6		8	15	Johnson	Marte		45-48	3rd	8.0
7-21	Oak.	L	3-13		7	15	Heredia	Fassero		45-49	3rd	9.0
7-22	Oak.	W	5-4	(10)	10	4	Abbott	Jones		46-49	3rd	9.0
7-23	At Min.	L	4-5		7	13	Carrasco	Paniagua		46-50	3rd	10.0
7-24	At Min.	L	3-10		6	12	Wells	Meche		46-51	3rd	11.0
7-25	At Min.	W	4-3		9	7	Moyer	Radke	Mesa	47-51	3rd	11.0
7-27	At K.C.	L	7-9		15	15	Appier	Fassero	Service	47-52	3rd	12.0
7-28	At K.C.	L	3-5		8	9	Rosado	Garcia	Service	47-53	3rd	12.0
7-29	At K.C.	W	8-4		15	8	Halama	Suppan		48-53	3rd	12.0
7-30	Bal.	W	7-4		7	7	Meche	Johnson	Mesa	49-53	3rd	12.0
7-31	Bal.	W	5-2		9	8	Moyer	Ponson	Mesa	50-53	3rd	11.0
8-1	Bal.	W	3-1		3	8	Abbott	Mussina	Mesa	51-53	3rd	11.0
8-2	T.B.	W	4-0		8	6	Garcia	Callaway	Paniagua	52-53	3rd	11.0
8-3	T.B.	W	5-2		10	9	Halama	Rupe	Mesa	53-53	3rd	11.0
8-4	T.B.	L	1-7		5	15	Eiland	Meche		53-54	3rd	12.0
8-5	N.Y.	L	4-7		6	12	Clemens	Moyer	Rivera	53-55	3rd	12.5
8-6	N.Y.	L	8-11		13	15	Watson	Fassero	Rivera	53-56	3rd	12.5
8-7	N.Y.	L	0-1		4	3	Pettitte	Garcia	Rivera	53-57	3rd	13.5
8-8	N.Y.	L	3-9		6	11	Cone	Halama		53-58	3rd	13.5
8-9	Chi.	W	6-4		7	6	Meche	Snyder	Mesa	54-58	3rd	12.5
8-10	Chi.	W	4-3		9	8	Moyer	Howry		55-58	3rd	12.5
8-11	Chi.	W	11-2		10	6	Abbott	Navarro		56-58	3rd	12.5
8-13	At Bos.	L	6-11		8	10	Lowe	Fassero		56-59	3rd	11.5
8-14	At Bos.	L	2-13		8	19	Martinez	Halama		56-60	3rd	11.5
8-15	At Bos.	W	4-3		8	6	Meche	Portugal	Mesa	57-60	3rd	11.5
8-16	At Tor.	W	7-5		11	10	Moyer	Carpenter	Mesa	58-60	3rd	11.5
8-17	At Tor.	W	8-5		12	7	Abbott	Hentgen	Mesa	59-60	3rd	11.5
8-18	At Tor.	W	5-1		10	6	Garcia	Wells	Paniagua	60-60	3rd	11.5
8-20	Cle.	L	4-7		9	8	Colon	Halama	Jackson	60-61	3rd	12.0
8-21	Cle.	L	0-6		6	9	Burba	Meche		60-62	3rd	13.0
8-22	Cle.	L	4-7	(10)	7	11	Riske	Mesa	Jackson	60-63	3rd	14.0
8-23	Cle.	W	4-1		6	5	Abbott	Nagy	Mesa	61-63	3rd	13.0
8-24	Det.	W	5-0		7	6	Garcia	Blair		62-63	3rd	12.0
8-25	Det.	W	3-2		7	9	Halama	Moehler	Mesa	63-63	3rd	12.0
8-27	At N.Y.	L	0-8		5	12	Clemens	Meche		63-64	3rd	13.0
8-28	At N.Y.	L	1-2		4	8	Rivera	Paniagua		63-65	3rd	14.0
8-29	At N.Y.	L	5-11		10	12	Pettitte	Abbott	Rivera	63-66	3rd	15.0
8-30†	At Chi.	W	5-2		12	9	Garcia	Parque	Mesa	64-66		
8-30‡	At Chi.	W	14-6		15	11	Cloude	Castillo	Rodriguez	65-66	3rd	13.5
8-31	At Chi.	W	11-4		15	9	Halama	Snyder		66-66	3rd	12.5
9-1	At Chi.	W	3-2		10	8	Meche	Sirotka	Mesa	67-66	3rd	12.5
9-3	Bos.	W	2-1		9	3	Moyer	Lowe		68-66	3rd	12.0
9-4	Bos.	L	0-4		3	6	Martinez	Abbott		68-67	3rd	12.0
9-5	Bos.	L	7-9		12	13	Garces	Paniagua	Lowe	68-68	3rd	12.5
9-6	Bos.	L	2-3		5	10	Florie	Halama	Lowe	68-69	3rd	14.0
9-7	Tor.	W	7-4		9	7	Meche	Wells	Mesa	69-69	3rd	14.0
9-8	Tor.	W	4-3		7	9	Mesa	Koch		70-69	3rd	14.0
9-10	At Bal.	L	4-5	(12)	9	9	Reyes	Ramsay		70-70	3rd	14.0
9-11	At Bal.	L	2-4		4	12	Johns	Garcia	Timlin	70-71	3rd	14.0
9-12	At Bal.	L	1-4		5	9	Erickson	Halama		70-72	3rd	14.0
9-13	At Bal.	L	4-5	(10)	11	9	Ryan	Mesa		70-73	3rd	15.0
9-14	At T.B.	W	5-1		7	7	Moyer	Arrojo		71-73	3rd	15.0
9-15	At T.B.	L	4-8		10	13	Lopez	Rodriguez		71-74	3rd	16.0
9-16	At T.B.	W	5-3		6	5	Garcia	Yan	Mesa	72-74	3rd	15.5
9-17	Min.	W	4-3		7	6	Abbott	Trombley		73-74	3rd	14.5
9-18	Min.	W	5-0		11	2	Meche	Mays		74-74	3rd	14.5
9-19	Min.	L	1-2		5	6	Hawkins	Moyer	Trombley	74-75	3rd	14.5
9-20	K.C.	L	9-10		9	15	Santiago	Hinchliffe	Montgomery	74-76	3rd	15.0
9-21	K.C.	W	13-3		15	13	Garcia	Suppan	Rodriguez	75-76	3rd	14.0
9-22	K.C.	L	6-12		13	14	Witasick	Halama		75-77	3rd	14.0
9-24	Ana.	W	4-3	(10)	8	5	Mesa	Percival		76-77	3rd	14.0
9-25	Ana.	L	3-7		4	6	Finley	Moyer		76-78	3rd	15.0
9-26	Ana.	W	3-2		8	6	Davey	Hasegawa		77-78	3rd	15.0
9-27	At Tex.	L	2-3		7	10	Crabtree	Sinclair	Wetteland	77-79	3rd	16.0
9-28	At Tex.	L	0-10		5	15	Morgan	Halama		77-80	3rd	16.0
9-29	At Tex.	W	7-3		13	9	Meche	Sele		78-80	3rd	16.0
9-30	At Tex.	L	0-7		4	8	Burkett	Hinchliffe		78-81	3rd	17.0
10-1	At Oak.	L	1-5		4	7	Appier	Ramsay	Jones	78-82	3rd	17.0
10-2	At Oak.	W	10-2		12	8	Garcia	Laxton		79-82	3rd	16.0
10-3	At Oak.	L	1-3		4	11	Mahay	Halama	Isringhausen	79-83	3rd	16.0

Monthly records: April (11-12), May (15-12), June (13-14), July (11-15), August (16-13), September (12-15), October (1-2).
*Innings, if other than nine. † First game of a doubleheader. ‡ Second game of a doubleheader.

MEMORABLE GAMES

June 27 at Seattle

In front of the 40th sellout crowd in franchise history, the Mariners closed the Kingdome with a 5-2 victory over Texas. The best player in franchise history, Ken Griffey Jr., slammed a three-run home run in the first inning.

Texas	AB	R	H	RBI	Seattle	AB	R	H	RBI
T.Goodwin, cf	4	1	1	0	B.Hunter, lf	5	1	3	0
McLemore, 2b	3	0	0	0	A.Rodrgz, ss	4	2	1	0
Greer, lf	4	1	2	2	Griffey Jr., cf	3	1	1	3
J.Gonzalez, rf	4	0	0	0	E.Martinez, dh	4	0	1	1
R.Palmeiro, dh	2	0	0	0	Segui, 1b	3	0	0	0
Zeile, 3b	4	0	3	0	Huskey, rf	4	0	0	0
L.Stevens, 1b	3	0	0	0	Gipson, lf	0	0	0	0
Zaun, c	4	0	0	0	Mabry, 3b	4	0	1	0
Clayton, ss	3	0	0	0	D.Bell, 2b	4	1	2	0
Shave, ss	0	0	0	0	D.Wilson, c	4	0	1	0
Alicea, ph	0	0	0	0					
Totals	31	2	6	2	Totals	35	5	10	4

Texas ....200 000 000—2
Seattle ....301 100 00x—5

E—Clayton (11), Shave (4), Zaun (3), Mabry (7). DP—Seattle 3. LOB—Texas 10, Seattle 10. 2B—Zeile (20), E.Martinez (15), Mabry (7). 3B—B.Hunter (3). HR—Greer (7), Griffey Jr. (27). SB—B.Hunter (21), Griffey Jr. 2 (14), D.Wilson (2).

Texas	IP	H	R	ER	BB	SO
Sele (L, 7-6)	7	8	5	4	4	5
Patterson	0.2	2	0	0	0	1
Venafro	0.1	0	0	0	0	1

Seattle	IP	H	R	ER	BB	SO
F.Garcia (W, 9-4)	5	5	2	2	6	3
F.Rodriguez (H, 2)	3	1	0	0	0	2
Mesa (S, 16)	1	0	0	0	2	0

U—HP, O'Nora. 1B, Joyce. 2B, Cooper. 3B, McKean. T—3:02. A—56,530.

July 15 at Seattle

In Safeco Field's inaugural game on July 15, Seattle took a 2-1 lead into the ninth inning. But, Jose Mesa relieved Jamie Moyer and gave up two runs—walking four Padres in the process—in the 3-2 loss. Unlike most games in the cozy Kingdome, there were no home runs hit in this game.

San Diego	AB	R	H	RBI	Seattle	AB	R	H	RBI
Q.Veras, 2b	4	1	2	1	D.Bell, 2b	4	1	3	1
Owens, lf	3	0	1	1	Segui, 1b	4	0	1	1
R.Sanders, rf	5	0	0	0	Griffey Jr., cf	3	0	1	0
Nevin, dh-c	4	0	2	1	A.Rodrgz, ss	4	0	0	0
Joyner, 1b	3	0	1	0	E.Martinez, dh	4	0	1	0
R.Rivera, cf	3	1	0	0	Buhner, rf	4	0	0	0
G.Arias, 3b	3	0	0	0	Huskey, lf	4	0	0	0
Vander Wal, ph	0	1	0	0	R.Davis, 3b	3	0	1	0
Miceli, p	0	0	0	0	D.Wilson, c	3	1	1	0
B.Davis, c	3	0	1	0					
Giovnola, ph-ss	0	0	0	0					
D.Jackson, ss	3	0	0	0					
Magadn, ph-3b	1	0	0	0					
Totals	32	3	7	3	Totals	33	2	8	2

San Diego ....001 000 002—3
Seattle ....000 000 020—2

DP—San Diego 1. LOB—San Diego 9, Seattle 5. 2B—D.Bell 3 (18), Segui (21), Griffey Jr. (15), D.Wilson (12). SB—R.Rivera (7). CS—R.Davis (2). S—Owens. SF—Owens.

San Diego	IP	H	R	ER	BB	SO
Ashby	7.2	7	2	2	0	8
H.Murray	0	1	0	0	1	0
Cunnane (W, 2-0)	0.1	0	0	0	0	0
Miceli (S, 2)	1	0	0	0	0	1

Seattle	IP	H	R	ER	BB	SO
Moyer	8	7	1	1	1	9
Mesa (BS 3; L, 0-4)	0.1	0	2	2	4	1
P.Abbott	0.2	0	0	0	0	0

U—HP, Joyce. 1B, Garcia. 2B, Reilly. 3B, O'Nora. T—3:10. A—44,607.

INDIVIDUAL STATISTICS

BATTING

Name	G	TPA	AB	R	H	TB	2B	3B	HR	RBI	Avg.	Obp.	Slg.	SH	SF	HP	BB	IBB	SO	SB	CS	GDP	vs RHP AB	vs RHP Avg.	vs RHP HR	vs RHP RBI	vs LHP AB	vs LHP Avg.	vs LHP HR	vs LHP RBI
Griffey Jr., Ken	160	706	606	123	173	349	26	3	48	134	.285	.384	.576	0	2	7	91	17	108	24	7	8	436	.307	40	107	170	.229	8	27
Bell, David	157	667	597	92	160	258	31	2	21	78	.268	.331	.432	3	7	2	58	0	90	7	4	7	479	.280	18	63	118	.220	3	15
Martinez, Edgar	142	608	502	86	169	278	35	1	24	86	.337	.447	.554	0	3	6	97	6	99	7	2	12	393	.331	14	62	109	.358	10	24
Rodriguez, Alex	129	572	502	110	143	294	25	0	42	111	.285	.357	.586	1	8	5	56	2	109	21	7	12	390	.287	35	94	112	.277	7	17
Hunter, Brian L.	121	527	484	71	112	145	11	5	4	34	.231	.277	.300	3	7	1	32	0	80	44	5	8	394	.244	4	33	90	.178	0	1
Davis, Russ	124	478	432	55	106	188	17	1	21	59	.245	.304	.435	7	2	5	32	1	111	3	3	13	328	.229	13	41	104	.298	8	18
Wilson, Dan	123	457	414	46	110	158	23	2	7	38	.266	.315	.382	10	2	2	29	4	83	5	0	10	312	.269	6	31	102	.255	1	7
Segui, David	90	382	345	43	101	156	22	3	9	39	.293	.352	.452	1	3	1	32	4	43	1	2	9	283	.307	8	36	62	.226	1	3
Buhner, Jay	87	343	266	37	59	112	11	0	14	38	.222	.388	.421	0	3	5	69	0	100	0	0	6	202	.208	6	22	64	.266	8	16
Huskey, Butch	74	292	262	44	76	130	9	0	15	49	.290	.353	.496	0	3	0	27	0	45	3	1	3	202	.262	9	32	60	.383	6	17
Mabry, John	87	285	262	34	64	105	14	0	9	33	.244	.297	.401	2	1	0	20	1	60	2	1	6	234	.244	9	31	28	.250	0	2
Ibanez, Raul	87	227	209	23	54	88	7	0	9	27	.258	.313	.421	0	1	0	17	1	32	5	1	4	188	.261	8	25	21	.238	1	2
Lampkin, Tom	76	227	206	29	60	102	11	2	9	34	.291	.345	.495	1	2	5	13	1	32	1	3	2	179	.291	9	30	27	.296	0	4
Bournigal, Rafael	55	108	95	16	26	37	5	0	2	14	.274	.317	.389	4	2	0	7	0	6	0	0	5	78	.256	1	9	17	.353	1	5
Gipson, Charles	55	89	80	16	18	27	5	2	0	9	.225	.287	.338	2	0	1	6	0	13	3	4	2	55	.200	0	8	25	.280	0	1
Jackson, Ryan	32	77	68	4	16	19	3	0	0	10	.235	.299	.279	0	2	1	6	0	19	3	3	3	59	.220	0	8	9	.333	0	2
Blowers, Mike	19	50	46	2	11	18	1	0	2	7	.239	.300	.391	0	0	0	4	0	12	0	0	2	20	.250	1	4	26	.231	1	3
Timmons, Ozzie	26	48	44	4	5	10	2	0	1	3	.114	.188	.227	0	0	0	4	0	12	0	1	0	15	.133	1	2	29	.103	0	1
Cedeno, Domingo	21	48	42	4	9	17	2	0	2	8	.214	.313	.405	0	0	1	5	0	9	1	1	1	35	.171	2	7	7	.429	0	1
Mieske, Matt	24	43	41	11	15	27	0	0	4	7	.366	.395	.659	0	0	0	2	1	9	0	0	0	17	.294	1	1	24	.417	3	6
Guillen, Carlos	5	21	19	2	3	6	0	0	1	3	.158	.200	.316	1	0	0	1	0	6	0	0	1	12	.167	1	2	7	.143	0	1
Monahan, Shane	16	15	15	3	2	2	0	0	0	0	.133	.133	.133	0	0	0	0	0	6	0	0	0	14	.071	0	0	1	1.000	0	0
Guevara, Giomar	10	12	12	2	3	5	2	0	0	2	.250	.250	.417	0	0	0	0	0	2	0	0	0	12	.250	0	2	0	.000	0	0
Fassero, Jeff	30	7	7	0	0	0	0	0	0	0	.000	.000	.000	0	0	0	0	0	5	0	0	0	3	.000	0	0	4	.000	0	0
Halama, John	38	6	5	1	1	2	1	0	0	0	.200	.333	.400	0	0	0	1	0	2	0	0	0	3	.000	0	0	2	.500	0	0
Garcia, Freddy	34	6	4	0	1	1	0	0	0	1	.250	.250	.250	2	0	0	0	0	1	0	0	0	3	.333	0	1	1	.000	0	0
Rodriguez, Frank	30	3	3	1	1	1	0	0	0	1	.333	.333	.333	0	0	0	0	0	0	0	0	0	2	.500	0	1	1	.000	0	0
Moyer, Jamie	32	4	2	0	1	1	0	0	0	0	.500	.667	.500	1	0	0	1	0	1	0	0	0	2	.500	0	0	0	.000	0	0
Cloude, Ken	31	2	2	0	0	0	0	0	0	0	.000	.000	.000	0	0	0	0	0	0	0	0	0	2	.000	0	0	0	.000	0	0
Mesa, Jose	68	0	0	0	0	0	0	0	0	0	.000	.000	.000	0	0	0	0	0	0	0	0	0	0	.000	0	0	0	.000	0	0
Abbott, Paul	25	0	0	0	0	0	0	0	0	0	.000	.000	.000	0	0	0	0	0	0	0	0	0	0	.000	0	0	0	.000	0	0
Carmona, Rafael	9	0	0	0	0	0	0	0	0	0	.000	.000	.000	0	0	0	0	0	0	0	0	0	0	.000	0	0	0	.000	0	0
Suzuki, Makoto	16	0	0	0	0	0	0	0	0	0	.000	.000	.000	0	0	0	0	0	0	0	0	0	0	.000	0	0	0	.000	0	0
Paniagua, Jose	59	0	0	0	0	0	0	0	0	0	.000	.000	.000	0	0	0	0	0	0	0	0	0	0	.000	0	0	0	.000	0	0
Sinclair, Steve	18	0	0	0	0	0	0	0	0	0	.000	.000	.000	0	0	0	0	0	0	0	0	0	0	.000	0	0	0	.000	0	0
Zimmerman, Jordan	12	0	0	0	0	0	0	0	0	0	.000	.000	.000	0	0	0	0	0	0	0	0	0	0	.000	0	0	0	.000	0	0
Scheffer, Aaron	4	0	0	0	0	0	0	0	0	0	.000	.000	.000	0	0	0	0	0	0	0	0	0	0	.000	0	0	0	.000	0	0
Marte, Damaso	5	0	0	0	0	0	0	0	0	0	.000	.000	.000	0	0	0	0	0	0	0	0	0	0	.000	0	0	0	.000	0	0
Meche, Gil	16	0	0	0	0	0	0	0	0	0	.000	.000	.000	0	0	0	0	0	0	0	0	0	0	.000	0	0	0	.000	0	0
Stark, Dennis	5	0	0	0	0	0	0	0	0	0	.000	.000	.000	0	0	0	0	0	0	0	0	0	0	.000	0	0	0	.000	0	0

PLAYERS WITH MORE THAN ONE A.L. TEAM

Name	G	TPA	AB	R	H	TB	2B	3B	HR	RBI	Avg.	Obp.	Slg.	SH	SF	HP	BB	IBB	SO	SB	CS	GDP	vs RHP AB	vs RHP Avg.	vs RHP HR	vs RHP RBI	vs LHP AB	vs LHP Avg.	vs LHP HR	vs LHP RBI
Fassero, Sea.-Tex.	37	7	7	0	0	0	0	0	0	0	.000	.000	.000	0	0	0	0	0	5	0	0	0	3	.000	0	0	4	.000	0	0
Hunter, Det.-Sea.	139	589	539	79	125	162	13	6	4	34	.232	.280	.301	4	7	2	37	0	91	44	8	8	437	.243	4	33	102	.186	0	1
Huskey, Sea.-Bos.	119	423	386	62	109	190	15	0	22	77	.282	.338	.492	0	3	0	34	1	65	3	1	9	276	.264	13	48	110	.327	9	29
Segui, Sea.-Tor.	121	486	440	57	131	206	27	3	14	52	.298	.355	.468	1	4	1	40	4	60	1	2	10	370	.303	13	48	70	.271	1	4
Suzuki, Sea.-K.C.	38	0	0	0	0	0	0	0	0	0	.000	.000	.000	0	0	0	0	0	0	0	0	0	0	.000	0	0	0	.000	0	0

PITCHING

Name	W	L	Pct.	ERA	IP	H	R	ER	HR	SH	SF	HB	BB	IBB	SO	G	GS	CG	ShO	GF	Sv	vs RH AB	vs RH Avg.	vs RH HR	vs RH RBI	vs LH AB	vs LH Avg.	vs LH HR	vs LH RBI
Moyer, Jamie	14	8	.636	3.87	228.0	235	108	98	23	6	2	9	48	1	137	32	32	4	0	0	0	666	.278	16	68	214	.234	7	25
Garcia, Freddy	17	8	.680	4.07	201.1	205	96	91	18	3	6	10	90	4	170	33	33	2	1	0	0	355	.273	6	40	424	.255	12	42
Halama, John	11	10	.524	4.22	179.0	193	88	84	20	5	9	7	56	3	105	38	24	1	1	7	0	510	.280	15	57	175	.286	5	23
Fassero, Jeff	4	14	.222	7.38	139.0	188	123	114	34	1	6	4	73	3	101	30	24	0	0	1	0	458	.341	31	96	127	.252	3	20
Meche, Gil	8	4	.667	4.73	85.2	73	48	45	9	5	3	2	57	1	47	16	15	0	0	0	0	129	.233	4	22	179	.240	5	15
Paniagua, Jose	6	11	.353	4.06	77.2	75	37	35	5	4	3	7	52	4	74	59	0	0	0	16	3	157	.255	2	21	127	.276	3	25
Rodriguez, Frank	2	4	.333	5.65	73.1	94	47	46	11	0	1	4	30	2	47	28	5	0	0	10	3	153	.307	4	24	146	.322	7	28
Abbott, Paul	6	2	.750	3.10	72.2	50	31	25	9	3	4	0	32	3	68	25	7	0	0	8	0	121	.231	6	18	138	.159	3	18
Cloude, Ken	4	4	.500	7.96	72.1	106	67	64	10	1	4	5	46	5	35	31	6	0	0	8	1	171	.333	6	32	135	.363	4	36
Mesa, Jose	3	6	.333	4.98	68.2	84	42	38	11	2	4	4	40	4	42	68	0	0	0	60	33	118	.271	3	14	157	.331	8	31
Suzuki, Makoto	0	2	.000	9.43	42.0	47	47	44	7	0	3	4	34	2	32	16	4	0	0	3	0	78	.282	5	24	88	.284	2	16
Hinchliffe, Brett	0	4	.000	8.80	30.2	41	31	30	10	1	0	4	21	0	14	11	4	0	0	2	0	70	.329	6	16	57	.316	4	11
Henry, Butch	2	0	1.000	5.04	25.0	30	15	14	1	0	1	2	10	0	15	7	4	0	0	0	0	69	.333	1	8	30	.233	0	1
Davey, Tom	1	0	1.000	4.71	21.0	22	13	11	0	0	0	4	14	1	17	16	0	0	0	5	0	50	.220	0	2	32	.344	0	3
Ramsay, Robert	0	2	.000	6.38	18.1	23	13	13	3	0	1	0	9	1	11	6	3	0	0	1	0	49	.367	3	12	22	.227	0	2
Sinclair, Steve	0	1	.000	3.95	13.2	15	8	6	1	0	0	1	10	2	15	18	0	0	0	5	0	35	.314	1	6	21	.190	0	2
Franklin, Ryan	0	0	.000	4.76	11.1	10	6	6	2	0	0	1	8	1	6	6	0	0	0	2	0	19	.316	2	5	23	.174	0	1
Carmona, Rafael	1	0	1.000	7.94	11.1	18	11	10	3	2	2	0	9	1	0	9	0	0	0	3	0	21	.476	3	8	23	.348	0	2
Bunch, Mel	0	0	.000	11.70	10.0	20	13	13	3	0	1	0	7	0	4	5	1	0	0	4	0	27	.444	2	10	20	.400	1	5
Williams, Todd	0	0	.000	4.66	9.2	11	5	5	1	1	0	1	7	0	7	13	0	0	0	7	0	28	.250	0	3	10	.400	1	4
Weaver, Eric	0	1	.000	10.61	9.1	14	12	11	2	0	0	0	8	1	14	8	0	0	0	2	0	32	.313	2	11	12	.333	0	3
Marte, Damaso	0	1	.000	9.35	8.2	16	9	9	3	0	0	0	6	0	3	5	0	0	0	2	0	23	.348	3	7	18	.444	0	3
Zimmerman, Jordan	0	0	.000	7.88	8.0	14	8	7	0	0	0	1	4	0	3	12	0	0	0	2	0	17	.294	0	2	19	.474	0	9
Stark, Dennis	0	0	.000	9.95	6.1	10	8	7	0	0	0	0	4	0	4	5	0	0	0	2	0	14	.286	0	0	13	.462	0	3
Scheffer, Aaron	0	0	.000	1.93	4.2	6	5	1	0	0	3	1	3	0	4	4	0	0	0	3	0	8	.375	0	1	9	.333	0	4
Watson, Allen	0	1	.000	12.00	3.0	6	9	4	5	0	1	0	3	0	2	3	0	0	0	2	0	6	.500	2	4	9	.333	3	6
Spencer, Sean	0	0	.000	21.60	1.2	5	4	4	0	0	0	0	3	0	2	2	0	0	0	0	0	6	.667	0	2	3	.333	0	0
Leiter, Mark	0	0	.000	6.75	1.1	2	1	1	0	0	0	0	0	0	1	2	0	0	0	0	0	5	.400	0	2	1	.000	0	0

PITCHERS WITH MORE THAN ONE A.L. TEAM

Name	W	L	Pct.	ERA	IP	H	R	ER	HR	SH	SF	HB	BB	IBB	SO	G	GS	CG	ShO	GF	Sv	vs RH AB	vs RH Avg.	vs RH HR	vs RH RBI	vs LH AB	vs LH Avg.	vs LH HR	vs LH RBI
Davey, Tor.-Sea.	2	1	.667	4.71	65.0	62	41	34	5	1	2	7	40	1	59	45	0	0	0	2	1	147	.238	4	24	101	.267	1	13
Fassero, Sea.-Tex.	5	14	.263	7.20	156.1	208	135	125	35	2	7	4	83	3	114	37	27	0	0	7	0	515	.330	32	102	140	.271	3	26
Sinclair, Tor.-Sea.	0	1	.000	6.52	19.1	22	16	14	5	0	0	2	14	2	18	21	0	0	0	0	0	48	.313	4	10	31	.226	1	4
Suzuki, Sea.-K.C.	2	5	.286	6.79	110.0	124	92	83	16	2	3	7	64	3	68	38	13	0	0	3	0	212	.288	9	43	222	.284	7	38
Watson, Sea.-N.Y.	4	1	.800	2.89	37.1	36	17	12	8	0	1	0	13	0	32	24	0	0	0	1	0	80	.275	4	8	62	.226	4	9

DESIGNATED HITTERS

Name	AB	Avg.	HR	RBI	Name	AB	Avg.	HR	RBI	Name	AB	Avg.	HR	RBI
Martinez, Edgar	483	.333	21	82	Lampkin, Tom	6	.333	0	1	Ibanez, Raul	1	.000	0	0
Griffey Jr., Ken	24	.292	1	4	Mabry, John	4	.000	0	1	Monahan, Shane	1	.000	0	0
Huskey, Butch	23	.217	3	6	Mieske, Matt	3	.000	0	0	Gipson, Charles	0	-	0	0
Timmons, Ozzie	9	.222	0	1	Blowers, Mike	2	.000	0	0	Bournigal, Rafael	0	-	0	0

INDIVIDUAL STATISTICS

FIELDING

FIRST BASEMEN

Player	Pct.	G	PO	A	E	TC	DP
Segui, David	.996	90	700	61	3	764	86
Jackson, Ryan	.989	29	167	11	2	180	19
Ibanez, Raul	.987	21	147	7	2	156	18
Mabry, John	.992	20	120	10	1	131	11
Blowers, Mike	1.000	14	72	6	0	78	14
Huskey, Butch	.988	10	76	3	1	80	10
Martinez, Edgar	1.000	5	29	2	0	31	2
Wilson, Dan	1.000	5	10	2	0	12	1
Bell, David	1.000	4	15	1	0	16	2
Buhner, Jay	1.000	1	9	0	0	9	1
Timmons, Ozzie	1.000	1	1	0	0	1	0

SECOND BASEMEN

Player	Pct.	G	PO	A	E	TC	DP
Bell, David	.978	154	313	426	17	756	118
Bournigal, Rafael	.983	17	26	33	1	60	10
Gipson, Charles	1.000	3	1	1	0	2	1
Guillen, Carlos	1.000	2	6	6	0	12	5
Cedeno, Domingo	1.000	1	1	2	0	3	0

THIRD BASEMEN

Player	Pct.	G	PO	A	E	TC	DP
Davis, Russ	.959	124	71	207	12	290	17
Mabry, John	.873	24	21	34	8	63	1
Gipson, Charles	.983	17	13	45	1	59	4
Bournigal, Rafael	.900	8	5	4	1	10	0
Blowers, Mike	.875	4	2	5	1	8	1
Cedeno, Domingo	-	1	0	0	0	0	0
Huskey, Butch	-	1	0	0	0	0	0

SHORTSTOPS

Player	Pct.	G	PO	A	E	TC	DP
Rodriguez, Alex	.977	129	213	382	14	609	104
Bournigal, Rafael	.987	28	28	47	1	76	13
Cedeno, Domingo	.941	20	17	47	4	68	11
Guevara, Giomar	.870	9	6	14	3	23	2
Guillen, Carlos	.938	3	6	9	1	16	1
Gipson, Charles	.750	3	2	1	1	4	0
Davis, Russ	-	2	0	0	0	0	0
Bell, David	1.000	1	1	0	0	1	0

OUTFIELDERS

Player	Pct.	G	PO	A	E	TC	DP
Griffey Jr., Ken	.978	158	387	10	9	406	5
Hunter, Brian L.	.985	121	252	14	4	270	3
Buhner, Jay	.993	85	127	7	1	135	2
Ibanez, Raul	.988	57	83	1	1	85	0
Huskey, Butch	1.000	53	101	1	0	102	0
Mabry, John	.989	43	80	6	1	87	1
Gipson, Charles	.960	28	19	5	1	25	0
Mieske, Matt	1.000	20	25	1	0	26	0
Timmons, Ozzie	1.000	17	12	0	0	12	0
Monahan, Shane	1.000	9	7	0	0	7	0
Lampkin, Tom	-	2	0	0	0	0	0
Bournigal, Rafael	-	1	0	0	0	0	0
Jackson, Ryan	-	1	0	0	0	0	0

CATCHERS

Player	Pct.	G	PO	A	E	TC	DP	PB
Wilson, Dan	.995	121	743	46	4	793	7	3
Lampkin, Tom	.985	56	292	27	5	324	5	5
Ibanez, Raul	1.000	1	4	0	0	4	0	0

PITCHERS

Player	Pct.	G	PO	A	E	TC	DP
Mesa, Jose	.947	68	11	7	1	19	2
Paniagua, Jose	.923	59	7	5	1	13	0
Halama, John	.951	38	7	32	2	41	5
Garcia, Freddy	.953	33	13	28	2	43	1
Moyer, Jamie	.969	32	15	47	2	64	9
Cloude, Ken	1.000	31	3	9	0	12	0
Fassero, Jeff	1.000	30	4	27	0	31	2
Rodriguez, Frank	.950	28	6	13	1	20	2
Abbott, Paul	1.000	25	7	8	0	15	1
Sinclair, Steve	1.000	18	0	1	0	1	0
Meche, Gil	1.000	16	10	8	0	18	0
Suzuki, Makoto	1.000	16	1	5	0	6	0
Davey, Tom	1.000	16	0	3	0	3	0
Williams, Todd	1.000	13	0	1	0	1	0
Zimmerman, Jordan	1.000	12	0	1	0	1	0
Hinchliffe, Brett	.875	11	5	2	1	8	0
Carmona, Rafael	.500	9	1	0	1	2	0
Weaver, Eric	.500	8	0	1	1	2	0
Henry, Butch	1.000	7	0	2	0	2	0
Franklin, Ryan	1.000	6	1	1	0	2	1
Ramsay, Robert	1.000	6	0	1	0	1	0
Bunch, Mel	1.000	5	0	2	0	2	0
Marte, Damaso	1.000	5	0	1	0	1	0
Stark, Dennis	-	5	0	0	0	0	0
Scheffer, Aaron	.000	4	0	0	1	1	0
Watson, Allen	1.000	3	0	1	0	1	0
Leiter, Mark	-	2	0	0	0	0	0
Spencer, Sean	-	2	0	0	0	0	0
Jackson, Ryan	-	1	0	0	0	0	0

PITCHING AGAINST EACH CLUB

Pitcher	Ana. W-L	Bal. W-L	Bos. W-L	Chi. W-L	Cle. W-L	Det. W-L	K.C. W-L	Min. W-L	N.Y. W-L	Oak. W-L	T.B. W-L	Tex. W-L	Tor. W-L	N.L. W-L	Total W-L
Abbott, Paul	0-0	1-0	0-1	1-0	1-0	0-0	0-0	1-0	0-1	1-0	0-0	0-0	1-0	0-0	6-2
Bunch, Mel	0-0	0-0	0-0	0-0	0-0	0-0	0-0	0-0	0-0	0-0	0-0	0-0	0-0	0-0	0-0
Carmona, Rafael	0-0	0-0	0-0	0-0	0-0	0-0	1-0	0-0	0-0	0-0	0-0	0-0	0-0	0-0	1-0
Cloude, Ken	1-0	0-0	0-0	1-0	0-0	1-1	0-0	0-0	0-0	0-0	0-1	0-2	1-0	0-0	4-4
Davey, Tom	1-0	0-0	0-0	0-0	0-0	0-0	0-0	0-0	0-0	0-0	0-0	0-0	0-0	0-0	1-0
Fassero, Jeff	1-0	0-0	0-1	0-2	1-0	0-0	0-2	1-1	0-2	0-3	1-0	0-0	0-0	0-3	4-14
Franklin, Ryan	0-0	0-0	0-0	0-0	0-0	0-0	0-0	0-0	0-0	0-0	0-0	0-0	0-0	0-0	0-0
Garcia, Freddy	0-1	0-2	0-0	2-0	0-0	3-0	1-1	1-0	1-1	2-0	3-0	1-0	1-1	2-2	17-8
Halama, John	1-0	0-1	0-2	1-0	1-1	1-0	1-1	2-0	0-1	0-1	1-1	1-2	1-0	1-0	11-10
Henry, Butch	0-0	0-0	0-0	0-0	0-0	0-0	0-0	0-0	0-0	1-0	1-0	0-0	0-0	0-0	2-0
Hinchliffe, Brett	0-0	0-0	0-1	0-0	0-0	0-1	0-1	0-0	0-0	0-0	0-0	0-1	0-0	0-0	0-4
Leiter, Mark	0-0	0-0	0-0	0-0	0-0	0-0	0-0	0-0	0-0	0-0	0-0	0-0	0-0	0-0	0-0
Marte, Damaso	0-0	0-0	0-0	0-0	0-0	0-0	0-0	0-0	0-0	0-0	0-0	0-0	0-0	0-1	0-1
Meche, Gil	0-0	1-0	1-0	2-0	0-1	0-0	0-0	1-1	0-1	0-0	0-1	1-0	1-0	1-0	8-4
Mesa, Jose	1-1	0-1	0-0	0-0	0-2	0-0	0-0	0-0	0-0	0-0	0-0	0-0	1-0	1-2	3-6
Moyer, Jamie	0-3	2-0	2-0	1-1	0-0	1-1	2-0	2-1	0-1	1-0	1-0	0-0	1-1	1-0	14-8
Paniagua, Jose	1-0	1-0	0-1	0-1	0-0	0-0	0-2	0-1	0-1	1-1	1-0	2-1	0-0	0-3	6-11
Ramsay, Robert	0-0	0-1	0-0	0-0	0-0	0-0	0-0	0-0	0-0	0-1	0-0	0-0	0-0	0-0	0-2
Rodriguez, Frank	0-1	0-0	0-0	0-0	0-1	1-0	0-0	0-0	0-0	0-0	0-1	0-1	0-0	1-0	2-4
Scheffer, Aaron	0-0	0-0	0-0	0-0	0-0	0-0	0-0	0-0	0-0	0-0	0-0	0-0	0-0	0-0	0-0
Sinclair, Steve	0-0	0-0	0-0	0-0	0-0	0-0	0-0	0-0	0-0	0-0	0-0	0-1	0-0	0-0	0-1
Spencer, Sean	0-0	0-0	0-0	0-0	0-0	0-0	0-0	0-0	0-0	0-0	0-0	0-0	0-0	0-0	0-0
Stark, Dennis	0-0	0-0	0-0	0-0	0-0	0-0	0-0	0-0	0-0	0-0	0-0	0-0	0-0	0-0	0-0
Suzuki, Makoto	0-0	0-0	0-1	0-0	0-0	0-0	0-0	0-0	0-1	0-0	0-0	0-0	0-0	0-0	0-2
Watson, Allen	0-0	0-0	0-0	0-0	0-1	0-0	0-0	0-0	0-0	0-0	0-0	0-0	0-0	0-0	0-1
Weaver, Eric	0-0	0-0	0-0	0-0	0-1	0-0	0-0	0-0	0-0	0-0	0-0	0-0	0-0	0-0	0-1
Williams, Todd	0-0	0-0	0-0	0-0	0-0	0-0	0-0	0-0	0-0	0-0	0-0	0-0	0-0	0-0	0-0
Zimmerman, Jordan	0-0	0-0	0-0	0-0	0-0	0-0	0-0	0-0	0-0	0-0	0-0	0-0	0-0	0-0	0-0
Totals	6-6	5-5	3-7	8-4	3-7	7-3	5-7	8-4	1-9	6-6	8-4	5-8	7-2	7-11	79-83

INTERLEAGUE: Garcia 0-1, Paniagua 0-1, Fassero 0-1 vs. Dodgers; Garcia 2-0, Mesa 0-2, Fassero 0-1, Paniagua 0-1 vs. Padres; Moyer 1-0, Paniagua 0-1, Garcia 0-1 vs. Giants; Halama 1-0, Rodriguez 1-0, Fassero 0-1 vs. Rockies; Mesa 1-0, Meche 1-0, Marte 0-1 vs. Diamondbacks. Total: 7-11.

MISCELLANEOUS

HOME RUNS BY PARK

At Anaheim (17): Rodriguez 4, Martinez 2, Griffey Jr. 2, Huskey 2, Mabry 2, Davis 2, Buhner 1, Segui 1, Cedeno 1.
At Baltimore (6): Bell 2, Martinez 1, Blowers 1, Davis 1, Rodriguez 1.
At Boston (8): Rodriguez 3, Bell 2, Buhner 1, Lampkin 1, Huskey 1.
At Chicago (AL) (8): Martinez 3, Rodriguez 2, Buhner 1, Lampkin 1, Ibanez 1.
At Cleveland (9): Griffey Jr. 3, Huskey 2, Wilson 1, Mabry 1, Davis 1, Bell 1.
At Colorado (8): Griffey Jr. 3, Huskey 2, Segui 1, Rodriguez 1, Bell 1.
At Detroit (4): Griffey Jr. 1, Wilson 1, Hunter 1, Rodriguez 1.
At Kansas City (9): Davis 2, Buhner 1, Martinez 1, Griffey Jr. 1, Hunter 1, Rodriguez 1, Bell 1, Ibanez 1.
At Los Angeles (2): Griffey Jr. 1, Segui 1.
At Minnesota (14): Griffey Jr. 5, Rodriguez 3, Martinez 1, Mieske 1, Huskey 1, Hunter 1, Davis 1, Timmons 1.
At New York (AL) (6): Buhner 1, Lampkin 1, Griffey Jr. 1, Davis 1, Bell 1, Ibanez 1.
At Oakland (3): Rodriguez 1, Bell 1, Ibanez 1.
At San Diego (3): Martinez 1, Lampkin 1, Rodriguez 1.
At Seattle (47): Griffey Jr. 14, Rodriguez 13, Lampkin 4, Buhner 3, Martinez 3, Ibanez 3, Davis 2, Bell 2, Blowers 1, Wilson 1, Mabry 1.
At Tampa Bay (13): Buhner 3, Griffey Jr. 3, Segui 2, Wilson 1, Mabry 1, Rodriguez 1, Bell 1, Ibanez 1.
At Texas (7): Rodriguez 2, Martinez 1, Wilson 1, Hunter 1, Davis 1, Ibanez 1.
At Toronto (5): Martinez 2, Buhner 1, Griffey Jr. 1, Rodriguez 1.

LOW-HIT GAMES

No-hitters: None.
One-hitters: None.
Two-hitters: None.

10-STRIKEOUT GAMES

Freddy Garcia 4, Paul Abbott 1, Jeff Fassero 1, **Total:** 6.

FOUR OR MORE HITS IN ONE GAME

Ken Griffey Jr. 2, Jay Buhner 1, Edgar Martinez 1, Butch Huskey 1, John Mabry 1 (including one five-hit game), Alex Rodriguez 1, **Total:** 7.

MULTI-HOMER GAMES

Alex Rodriguez 6, Edgar Martinez 4, Ken Griffey Jr. 4, Russ Davis 2, Butch Huskey 1, John Mabry 1, **Total:** 18.

GRAND SLAMS

4-29: Ken Griffey Jr. (off Detroit's Mel Rojas).
4-30: Ken Griffey Jr. (off Toronto's Graeme Lloyd).
5-17: Butch Huskey (off Minnesota's Joe Mays).
5-26: Edgar Martinez (off Minnesota's LaTroy Hawkins).
7-17: Raul Ibanez (off San Diego's Carlos Reyes).
7-19: Alex Rodriguez (off Arizona's Vicente Padilla).
7-30: Alex Rodriguez (off Baltimore's Arthur Rhodes).
8-9: Jay Buhner (off Chicago's John Snyder).
8-30: Edgar Martinez (off Chicago's Bill Simas).
9-16: Alex Rodriguez (off Tampa Bay's Esteban Yan).

PINCH HITTERS

(Minimum 5 at-bats)

Name	AB	Avg.	HR	RBI
Lampkin, Tom	23	.130	0	4
Ibanez, Raul	22	.182	0	2
Timmons, Ozzie	8	.000	0	0
Mabry, John	6	.167	0	0
Wilson, Dan	6	.167	0	1

DEBUTS

4-5: Brett Hinchliffe, P.
4-7: Freddy Garcia, P.
5-6: Sean Spencer, P.
5-15: Ryan Franklin, P.
5-17: Jordan Zimmerman, P.
6-13: Aaron Scheffer, P.
6-30: Damaso Marte, P.
7-6: Gil Meche, P.
8-27: Robert Ramsay, P.
9-15: Dennis Stark, P.

GAMES BY POSITION

Catcher: Dan Wilson 121, Tom Lampkin 56, Raul Ibanez 1.
First base: David Segui 90, Ryan Jackson 29, Raul Ibanez 21, John Mabry 20, Mike Blowers 14, Butch Huskey 10, Edgar Martinez 5, Dan Wilson 5, David Bell 4, Jay Buhner 1, Ozzie Timmons 1.
Second base: David Bell 154, Rafael Bournigal 17, Charles Gipson 3, Carlos Guillen 2, Domingo Cedeno 1.
Third base: Russ Davis 124, John Mabry 24, Charles Gipson 17, Rafael Bournigal 8, Mike Blowers 4, Domingo Cedeno 1, Butch Huskey 1.
Shortstop: Alex Rodriguez 129, Rafael Bournigal 28, Domingo Cedeno 20, Giomar Guevara 9, Charles Gipson 3, Carlos Guillen 3, Russ Davis 2, David Bell 1.
Outfield: Ken Griffey Jr. 158, Brian L. Hunter 121, Jay Buhner 85, Raul Ibanez 57, Butch Huskey 53, John Mabry 43, Charles Gipson 28, Matt Mieske 20, Ozzie Timmons 17, Shane Monahan 9, Tom Lampkin 2, Rafael Bournigal 1, Ryan Jackson 1.
Designated hitter: Edgar Martinez 134, Butch Huskey 7, Ken Griffey Jr. 6, Ozzie Timmons 5, Charles Gipson 4, Shane Monahan 3, Tom Lampkin 2, Mike Blowers 1, Rafael Bournigal 1, Matt Mieske 1, John Mabry 1, Raul Ibanez 1.

STREAKS

Wins: 6 (May 16-22, July 27-August 3).
Losses: 7 (July 6-16).
Consecutive games with at least one hit: 16, Ken Griffey Jr. (May 10-28).
Wins by pitcher: 5, Jamie Moyer (May 11-31).

ATTENDANCE

Home: 2,915,908.
Road: 2,447,119.
Highest (home): 56,530 (June 27 vs. Texas).
Highest (road): 54,787 (August 28 vs. New York).
Lowest (home): 19,617 (April 27 vs. Detroit).
Lowest (road): 8,980 (April 20 vs. Chicago).

TAMPA BAY DEVIL RAYS

1999 REVIEW

DAY BY DAY

Date	Opp.	Res.	Score	(inn.*)	Hits	Opp. hits	Winning pitcher	Losing pitcher	Save	Record	Pos.	GB
4-5	At Bal.	L	7-10		12	13	Mussina	Alvarez	Timlin	0-1	5th	1.0
4-7	At Bal.	W	8-5		14	13	Saunders	Guzman	Hernandez	1-1	T3rd	1.0
4-8	At Bal.	W	6-3		10	9	Witt	Erickson		2-1	T2nd	1.0
4-9	Bos.	L	1-4		4	11	Portugal	Arrojo		2-2	T3rd	2.0
4-10	Bos.	L	3-5		7	6	Martinez	Santana	Gordon	2-3	T3rd	3.0
4-11	Bos.	W	5-4		7	8	Aldred	Lowe	Hernandez	3-3	T3rd	2.0
4-12	At Tor.	L	1-7		6	12	Wells	Saunders		3-4	4th	2.5
4-13	At Tor.	W	8-5		15	11	White	Hamilton	Hernandez	4-4	T3rd	2.5
4-14	At Tor.	L	6-7	(11)	12	12	Lloyd	Lopez		4-5	4th	3.5
4-15	At Tor.	L	1-11		2	11	Carpenter	Santana		4-6	4th	3.5
4-16	At Bos.	W	6-2		13	7	Rekar	Wakefield		5-6	4th	2.5
4-17	At Bos.	L	5-8		9	11	Portugal	Saunders		5-7	4th	3.0
4-18	At Bos.	W	5-1		7	5	Witt	Rapp		6-7	4th	3.0
4-19	At Bos.	W	4-1		9	6	Arrojo	Saberhagen	Hernandez	7-7	4th	2.5
4-20	Bal.	W	5-3		12	6	Santana	Erickson	Hernandez	8-7	4th	2.5
4-21	Bal.	W	14-8		17	11	Rekar	Mussina		9-7	4th	2.5
4-22	Bal.	W	1-0		4	1	Saunders	Ponson		10-7	3rd	2.5
4-23	Sea.	W	5-4		11	7	White	Halama	Hernandez	11-7	3rd	1.5
4-24	Sea.	L	4-9		8	12	Henry	Arrojo		11-8	3rd	1.5
4-25	Sea.	L	4-6		6	12	Paniagua	Hernandez	Mesa	11-9	4th	2.5
4-28†	At Chi.	L	7-10		8	14	Parque	Rekar	Howry	11-10		
4-28‡	At Chi.	L	1-9		9	10	Snyder	Saunders		11-11	4th	3.5
4-29	At Chi.	W	4-1		9	4	Alvarez	Sirotka	Hernandez	12-11	4th	3.5
4-30	Det.	L	5-7		7	12	Weaver	Arrojo	Jones	12-12	T3rd	3.5
5-1	Det.	W	4-3		7	4	Witt	Moehler	Hernandez	13-12	4th	3.5
5-2	Det.	L	2-8		10	12	Thompson	Santana		13-13	T3rd	4.5
5-3	Det.	W	14-6		12	12	Yan	Blair		14-13	3rd	3.5
5-4	K.C.	L	3-5		11	7	Mathews	Hernandez	Montgomery	14-14	3rd	3.5
5-5	K.C.	W	10-7		17	9	White	Witasick	Hernandez	15-14	T2nd	3.5
5-6	K.C.	W	5-4		8	11	Aldred	Morman	Hernandez	16-14	2nd	3.5
5-7	At Cle.	L	11-20		13	21	Wagner	Mecir		16-15	T2nd	4.5
5-8	At Cle.	W	7-6		14	12	Rekar	Nagy	Hernandez	17-15	2nd	3.5
5-9	At Cle.	L	4-5		11	6	Wright	Alvarez	Jackson	17-16	3rd	4.5
5-11	Min.	L	1-2		6	5	Radke	Rupe	Aguilera	17-17	T3rd	4.5
5-12	Min.	L	4-9		8	14	Milton	Arrojo	Trombley	17-18	T3rd	4.5
5-14	At Ana.	L	3-8		5	10	Belcher	Witt		17-19	4th	4.0
5-15	At Ana.	W	3-1		7	3	Saunders	Hill	Hernandez	18-19	3rd	3.0
5-16	At Ana.	W	7-4		13	10	Alvarez	Sparks		19-19	3rd	3.0
5-17	At Tex.	W	13-3		15	6	Rupe	Burkett		20-19	3rd	2.5
5-18	At Tex.	W	5-4		10	14	Arrojo	Morgan	Hernandez	21-19	3rd	2.0
5-19	At Tex.	L	6-7		11	9	Zimmerman	Aldred	Wetteland	21-20	3rd	3.0
5-21	Ana.	W	10-9		12	14	White	Magnante	Hernandez	22-20	3rd	2.5
5-22	Ana.	L	6-8		9	16	Petkovsek	Newman	Percival	22-21	3rd	3.5
5-23	Ana.	L	0-4	(10)	3	4	Finley	Hernandez		22-22	3rd	4.5
5-24	Tex.	L	3-12		10	16	Clark	Arrojo		22-23	3rd	5.0
5-25	Tex.	L	2-7		9	11	Venafro	Witt		22-24	4th	6.0
5-26	Tex.	L	6-8		11	12	Helling	Santana	Wetteland	22-25	4th	6.0
5-28	At Sea.	L	1-6		5	11	Garcia	Alvarez		22-26	4th	6.5
5-29	At Sea.	L	5-11		10	12	Fassero	Rupe		22-27	4th	7.5
5-30	At Sea.	W	15-7		17	15	Rekar	Cloude		23-27	4th	7.5
5-31	At Oak.	L	7-10		11	7	Groom	Yan		23-28	4th	8.5
6-1	At Oak.	L	2-5		10	3	Rogers	Eiland	Taylor	23-29	4th	9.5
6-2	At Oak.	W	7-6		11	8	Yan	Mathews	Hernandez	24-29	4th	8.5
6-4	Fla.	L	0-10		7	11	Springer	Rupe		24-30	4th	9.5
6-5	Fla.	L	7-9		9	14	Meadows	Duvall	Mantei	24-31	4th	9.5
6-6	Fla.	L	6-11		9	17	Alfonseca	Yan		24-32	4th	9.5
6-7	At Atl.	L	5-9		13	10	Smoltz	Eiland	Rocker	24-33	4th	9.5
6-8	At Atl.	L	2-11		8	16	Perez	Alvarez		24-34	4th	9.5
6-9	At Atl.	L	3-4	(12)	10	13	McGlinchy	White		24-35	4th	10.0
6-11	At Mon.	L	4-5		9	9	Batista	Witt	Urbina	24-36	4th	11.0
6-12	At Mon.	W	5-3		14	9	Callaway	Hermanson	Hernandez	25-36	4th	11.0
6-13	At Mon.	L	0-4		3	8	Pavano	Rekar		25-37	5th	11.0
6-14	At Chi.	L	7-9		11	9	Snyder	Alvarez	Howry	25-38	5th	12.0
6-15	At Chi.	W	3-2		6	12	Rupe	Baldwin	Hernandez	26-38	5th	12.0
6-16	At Chi.	L	2-3	(11)	8	8	Lowe	Charlton		26-39	5th	12.0
6-18	At Min.	L	5-8		10	12	Wells	Aldred	Trombley	26-40	5th	12.5
6-19	At Min.	W	4-3		10	10	Rekar	Radke	Hernandez	27-40	5th	12.5
6-20	At Min.	W	6-5	(11)	12	9	Newman	Trombley		28-40	5th	11.5
6-21	At Min.	W	3-2		9	5	Rupe	Radlosky	Hernandez	29-40	5th	11.0
6-22	N.Y.	L	0-7		3	12	Hernandez	Witt		29-41	5th	12.0
6-23	N.Y.	L	4-12		11	19	Clemens	Eiland		29-42	5th	13.0
6-24	N.Y.	L	3-7		7	13	Pettitte	Rekar	Mendoza	29-43	5th	14.0
6-25	Tor.	W	11-4		14	6	Alvarez	Wells		30-43	5th	14.0
6-26	Tor.	W	5-2		9	12	Rupe	Hamilton	Hernandez	31-43	5th	14.0
6-27	Tor.	W	8-0		10	3	Witt	Escobar		32-43	5th	14.0
6-28	Tor.	L	2-3	(10)	8	10	Carpenter	Eiland	Koch	32-44	5th	14.5
6-30	At Bos.	W	11-10	(10)	14	12	Hernandez	Wasdin		33-44	4th	14.0

HIGHLIGHTS

High point: At a juncture when all was lost and most teams were scratching off the days until October, the Devil Rays went into Yankee Stadium on the next-to-last weekend of the season and took three of four, stalling the Yankees' division-clinching celebration. It marked their first-ever wins at the Stadium.

Low point: Trying to fight through a stretch of injuries, the Rays returned from the West Coast on June 4 and were shut out, 10-0, by the Marlins and former teammate Dennis Springer. The defeat touched off a seven-game losing streak, dropping Tampa Bay 12 games below .500.

Turning point: The Rays were cruising along at 22-20 when injuries ravaged their lineup, stalled their momentum and crushed their spirit. The result was a season-wrecking 2-16 stretch.

Most valuable player: In the final year of his contract, Fred McGriff played like his old self. He led the team in batting (.310), hits (164), doubles (30), total bases (292) and RBIs (104). The payoff: a new two-year deal.

Most valuable pitcher: Closer Roberto Hernandez, who recorded a career-high 43 saves (in 47 opportunities). Hernandez also won two games, giving him a hand in 45 of the Rays' 69 victories.

Most improved player: Catcher John Flaherty rebounded from a horrendous season with one of his best, raising his average 71 points to .278. He also had career highs in homers (14) and RBIs (71).

Most pleasant surprise: The Rays figured they would see Ryan Rupe pitch at some point in 1999—they just didn't know it would be so soon. A year out of Texas A&M, Rupe joined the rotation in early May from Class AA Orlando and compiled an 8-9 record.

Key injuries: Tampa Bay made an astonishing 22 D.L. moves, and five of the injured players underwent season-ending surgeries. Outfielder Quinton McCracken (torn ACL) and pitcher Tony Saunders (broken left arm) suffered brutal on-field injuries two days apart in late May. And DH Jose Canseco missed six weeks after undergoing back surgery.

Notable: Boggs got his 3,000th hit on August 7 against Cleveland and reached the milestone in unprecedented fashion—with a home run. ... Canseco was having a big season—31 homers in 82 games—before being sidelined. He hit only three homers in 31 games after his return. ... Jim Morris, 35, made an amazing transformation from high school coach to major league pitcher after an impressive tryout. In five relief appearances, he held hitters to a .167 average. ... No Rays pitcher posted a double-figure victory total.

—MARC TOPKIN

MISCELLANEOUS

RECORDS

1999 regular-season record: 69-93 (5th in A.L. East); 33-48 at home; 36-45 on road; 25-25 vs. A.L. East; 26-22 vs. A.L. Central; 14-32 vs. A.L. West; 4-14 vs. N.L. East; 8-23 vs. lefthanded starters; 61-70 vs. righthanded starters; 29-35 on grass; 40-58 on turf; 23-22 in daytime; 46-71 at night; 27-20 in one-run games; 3-6 in extra-inning games; 0-1-0 in doubleheaders.

Team record past five years: 132-192 in two years (.407, ranks 14th in league in that span).

TEAM LEADERS

Batting average: Fred McGriff (.310).
At-bats: Fred McGriff (529).
Runs: Dave Martinez (79).
Hits: Fred McGriff (164).
Total bases: Fred McGriff (292).
Doubles: Fred McGriff (30).
Triples: Miguel Cairo, Dave Martinez (5).
Home runs: Jose Canseco (34).
Runs batted in: Fred McGriff (104).
Stolen bases: Miguel Cairo (22).
Slugging percentage: Jose Canseco (.563).
On-base percentage: Fred McGriff (.405).
Wins: Wilson Alvarez (9).
Earned-run average: Rick White (4.08).
Complete games: Bobby Witt (3).
Shutouts: Bobby Witt (2).
Saves: Roberto Hernandez (43).
Innings pitched: Bobby Witt (180.1).
Strikeouts: Wilson Alvarez (128).

Date	Opp.	Res.	Score	(inn.*)	Hits	Opp. hits	Winning pitcher	Losing pitcher	Save	Record	Pos.	GB
7-1	At Bos.	W	12-3		16	7	Alvarez	Cho		34-44	4th	14.0
7-2	At Tor.	W	8-7		11	14	Aldred	Escobar	Hernandez	35-44	4th	14.0
7-3	At Tor.	L	0-5		3	13	Carpenter	Witt		35-45	4th	15.0
7-4	At Tor.	L	3-6		11	10	Hentgen	White	Koch	35-46	4th	15.0
7-5	Bos.	L	2-4		9	9	Portugal	Rekar	Wakefield	35-47	4th	15.0
7-6	Bos.	W	6-4		7	9	Lopez	Wasdin	Hernandez	36-47	4th	15.0
7-7	Bos.	W	3-2		7	7	Eiland	Martinez	Hernandez	37-47	4th	14.0
7-8	Bos.	W	3-2		8	9	Witt	Rose	Hernandez	38-47	4th	14.0
7-9	At Fla.	L	4-11		11	12	Hernandez	Rupe		38-48	4th	14.0
7-10	At Fla.	W	9-8		14	15	Rekar	Springer	Hernandez	39-48	4th	13.0
7-11	At Fla.	L	2-3		6	5	Fernandez	Alvarez	Alfonseca	39-49	4th	14.0
7-15	N.Y. (NL)	L	7-8	(10)	13	8	Benitez	Charlton		39-50	4th	14.0
7-16	N.Y. (NL)	L	7-9		11	15	Reed	Eiland	Cook	39-51	4th	14.0
7-17	N.Y. (NL)	W	3-2		8	8	Alvarez	Hershiser	Hernandez	40-51	4th	14.0
7-18	Phi.	L	2-3		4	7	Schilling	Lopez		40-52	4th	15.0
7-19	Phi.	L	3-16		7	22	Ogea	Rekar		40-53	4th	15.0
7-20	Phi.	W	5-4	(13)	12	10	Charlton	Schrenk		41-53	4th	15.0
7-21	At N.Y.	L	3-4		7	8	Hernandez	Witt	Rivera	41-54	5th	16.0
7-22	At N.Y.	L	4-5		9	12	Pettitte	Rekar	Rivera	41-55	5th	17.0
7-23	Tex.	L	8-11		17	13	Kolb	Rupe		41-56	5th	18.0
7-24	Tex.	L	3-5		5	11	Loaiza	Newman	Wetteland	41-57	5th	19.0
7-25	Tex.	L	3-4		7	8	Helling	Arrojo	Wetteland	41-58	5th	20.0
7-26	Ana.	W	7-0		11	4	Witt	Olivares		42-58	5th	19.5
7-27	Ana.	L	5-10		13	12	Magnante	Callaway		42-59	5th	20.5
7-28	Ana.	W	4-1		11	6	Rupe	McDowell	Hernandez	43-59	5th	19.5
7-30	At Oak.	L	1-4		5	8	Oquist	Eiland	Taylor	43-60	5th	20.0
7-31	At Oak.	L	1-5		7	5	Olivares	Arrojo	Jones	43-61	5th	20.0
8-1	At Oak.	L	6-10		12	12	Heredia	Witt	Mathews	43-62	5th	20.0
8-2	At Sea.	L	0-4		6	8	Garcia	Callaway	Paniagua	43-63	5th	21.0
8-3	At Sea.	L	2-5		9	10	Halama	Rupe	Mesa	43-64	5th	21.0
8-4	At Sea.	W	7-1		15	5	Eiland	Meche		44-64	5th	21.0
8-6	Cle.	W	4-2		7	7	Yan	Burba	Hernandez	45-64	5th	21.5
8-7	Cle.	L	10-15		14	19	Nagy	Witt		45-65	5th	22.5
8-8	Cle.	W	5-3		11	6	Alvarez	Wright	Hernandez	46-65	5th	22.5
8-9	Bal.	W	10-9		15	12	Rupe	Johnson	Hernandez	47-65	5th	22.5
8-10	Bal.	L	1-17		6	20	Ponson	Eiland		47-66	5th	22.5
8-11	Bal.	L	2-4		10	13	Mussina	Arrojo	Timlin	47-67	5th	23.5
8-12	At K.C.	W	7-6		12	11	Witt	Reichert	Hernandez	48-67	5th	23.0
8-13	At K.C.	L	1-2		6	10	Service	Yan		48-68	5th	24.0
8-14	At K.C.	W	11-4		13	9	Rupe	Suppan		49-68	5th	23.0
8-15	At K.C.	W	5-3		14	5	Eiland	Suzuki	Hernandez	50-68	5th	22.0
8-16	At Det.	W	9-1		13	8	Arrojo	Weaver		51-68	5th	22.0
8-17	At Det.	L	1-3		6	8	Mlicki	Witt	Jones	51-69	5th	23.0
8-18	At Det.	W	4-0		8	1	Alvarez	Borkowski	Lopez	52-69	5th	22.0
8-20	K.C.	W	5-4		8	8	Hernandez	Service		53-69	5th	21.5
8-21	K.C.	W	8-2		10	8	Eiland	Witasick		54-69	5th	20.5
8-22	K.C.	W	2-1		3	6	Arrojo	Rosado		55-69	5th	20.5
8-23	Chi.	L	2-10		8	13	Baldwin	Witt		55-70	5th	21.5
8-24	Chi.	W	6-5		11	5	Alvarez	Parque	Hernandez	56-70	5th	21.5
8-25	Chi.	L	1-6		7	12	Foulke	Rupe		56-71	5th	21.5
8-26	Chi.	W	9-7		13	14	White	Snyder	Hernandez	57-71	5th	21.0
8-27	At Cle.	L	1-2		6	9	Burba	Arrojo	Jackson	57-72	5th	22.0
8-28	At Cle.	L	0-3		4	7	Nagy	Witt	Jackson	57-73	5th	23.0
8-29	At Cle.	W	6-4		11	10	Alvarez	Haney	Hernandez	58-73	5th	23.0
8-31	At Bal.	W	3-0		11	3	Rupe	Ponson	Hernandez	59-73	4th	22.5
9-1	At Bal.	L	1-3		5	5	Johns	Wheeler	Timlin	59-74	5th	22.5
9-2	At Bal.	L	6-11		14	13	Erickson	Arrojo		59-75	5th	23.5
9-3	Min.	W	4-2		8	11	Charlton	Guardado	Hernandez	60-75	5th	22.5
9-4	Min.	W	11-3		18	10	Lopez	Miller		61-75	5th	22.5
9-5	Min.	L	1-4		5	10	Radke	Rupe		61-76	5th	23.5
9-6	Min.	L	7-13		11	16	Carrasco	White		61-77	5th	23.5
9-8	Det.	L	1-5		7	10	Mlicki	Witt		61-78	5th	24.0
9-9	Det.	W	5-3		8	13	Arrojo	Nitkowski	Hernandez	62-78	5th	23.5
9-10	Oak.	L	2-7		8	14	Hudson	Alvarez		62-79	5th	23.5
9-11	Oak.	L	4-5		8	6	Olivares	Rupe	Jones	62-80	5th	23.5
9-12	Oak.	L	3-4		6	6	Heredia	Wheeler	Isringhausen	62-81	5th	23.5
9-13	Oak.	L	3-8		7	13	Appier	Witt		62-82	5th	23.5
9-14	Sea.	L	1-5		7	7	Moyer	Arrojo		62-83	5th	24.5
9-15	Sea.	W	8-4		13	10	Lopez	Rodriguez		63-83	5th	24.5
9-16	Sea.	L	3-5		5	6	Garcia	Yan	Mesa	63-84	5th	25.5
9-17	At Tex.	W	7-5		13	16	Newman	Helling	Hernandez	64-84	5th	25.5
9-18	At Tex.	L	1-6		6	9	Sele	Witt		64-85	5th	25.5
9-19	At Tex.	W	15-2		15	7	Arrojo	Burkett		65-85	5th	25.5
9-20	At Ana.	L	5-10		13	11	Finley	Alvarez		65-86	5th	26.0
9-21	At Ana.	L	5-7		7	9	Ortiz	Eiland	Percival	65-87	5th	27.0
9-22	At Ana.	L	5-8		11	11	Washburn	Wheeler		65-88	5th	28.0
9-24	At N.Y.	L	3-4	(11)	7	9	Stanton	Charlton		65-89	5th	29.5
9-25	At N.Y.	W	2-1		11	5	Arrojo	Cone	Hernandez	66-89	5th	28.5
9-26	At N.Y.	W	6-5		15	11	Lidle	Mendoza	Hernandez	67-89	5th	27.5
9-27	At N.Y.	W	10-6		11	9	Duvall	Irabu	Sparks	68-89	5th	26.5
9-28	Tor.	L	2-8		5	13	Wells	Wheeler		68-90	5th	27.5
9-29	Tor.	L	2-6		9	14	Escobar	Witt		68-91	5th	28.0
10-1	N.Y.	L	7-11		9	14	Mendoza	Arrojo	Rivera	68-92	5th	29.0
10-2	N.Y.	L	2-3		6	9	Cone	Alvarez	Rivera	68-93	5th	30.0
10-3	N.Y.	W	6-2		6	6	Gaillard	Juden	Hernandez	69-93	5th	29.0

Monthly records: April (12-12), May (11-16), June (10-16), July (10-17), August (16-12), September (9-18), October (1-2).
*Innings, if other than nine. † First game of a doubleheader. ‡ Second game of a doubleheader.

MEMORABLE GAMES

May 7 at Cleveland

All you have to know is the Rays led by eight and lost by nine. Tampa Bay rolled to a 10-2 lead in the sixth inning and seemed headed for an easy victory. But the Indians roared back with 18 runs over the final three innings, fueled by a grand slam and two three-run homers, and they ended up with the easy 20-11 win.

Tampa Bay	AB	R	H	RBI	Cleveland	AB	R	H	RBI
McCracken, cf	6	1	1	0	Lofton, cf	4	2	1	0
D.Martinez, rf	4	2	1	0	E.Wilson, ss	5	2	3	1
Perry, 3b	5	3	3	2	Alomar, 2b	5	2	3	5
McGriff, 1b	3	3	2	3	M.Ramirez, rf	4	3	3	2
Flaherty, c	5	1	2	1	Fryman, 3b	6	2	2	3
Sorrento, lf	5	0	2	3	W.Cordro, dh	6	3	3	2
Clyburn, dh	4	0	1	0	Justice, lf	4	4	4	5
Lamb, 2b	5	0	0	0	Alomar Jr., c	6	2	2	1
Stocker, ss	5	1	1	0	Sexson, 1b	4	0	0	0
Totals	**42**	**11**	**13**	**9**	**Totals**	**44**	**20**	**21**	**19**

Tampa Bay	0 1 3	5 0 1	1 0 0—11
Cleveland	0 0 1	1 0 4	7 7 x—20

E—Flaherty (1), Lamb 2 (2), M.Ramirez 2 (2), E.Wilson (3). DP—Tampa Bay 1. LOB—Tampa Bay 10, Cleveland 9. 2B—D.Martinez (7), Perry (1), McGriff (7), Flaherty (6), Sorrento (4), E.Wilson (4), Alomar Jr. (8). 3B—Alomar (2). HR—McGriff (11), Alomar (5), Fryman (6), W.Cordero (3), Justice 2 (5). SB—McCracken (6), Stocker (6). CS—Alomar (1). Reached, catcher's interference—Lofton by Flaherty.

Tampa Bay	IP	H	R	ER	BB	SO
B.Witt	5.1	9	6	6	2	3
Ri.White	1	4	4	4	1	1
Aldred	0	0	1	1	0	0
Mecir (BS 2; L 0-1)	0.2	2	2	1	2	1
Gaillard	0.2	5	7	0	2	1
Rekar	0.1	1	0	0	0	1

Cleveland	IP	H	R	ER	BB	SO
Gooden	3.2	8	7	4	1	5
P.Wagner (W, 1-0)	3.1	5	4	2	2	0
S.Reed (H, 6)	1	0	0	0	0	0
DeLucia	1	0	0	0	1	1

HBP—Perry by P.Wagner, Clyburn by P.Wagner, Justice by Aldred. WP—Gooden. U—HP, Clark. 1B, Young. 2B, Tschida. 3B, Reed. T—4:00. A—40,601.

August 7 at Tampa Bay

After an 0-fer the night before, Wade Boggs calmly strides to the plate before an electric Tropicana Field crowd of 39,512 and rips career hits Nos. 2,998, 2,999 and—in dramatic fashion—3,000. The historic hit is quite a blast—no other player joined the 3,000-hit club with a home run. Boggs celebrated the occasion with a memorable run around the bases.

Cleveland	AB	R	H	RBI	Tampa Bay	AB	R	H	RBI
D.Roberts, cf	5	3	3	0	Lowery, cf	3	2	1	1
Vizquel, ss	5	3	2	1	Boggs, 3b	4	2	3	4
Alomar, 2b	4	3	2	0	Graffanino, 2b	5	0	1	0
M.Ramirez, rf	3	4	3	5	McGriff, dh	5	0	1	3
A.Ramirez, rf	0	0	0	0	Trammell, lf	4	2	2	0
Thome, 1b	5	2	4	4	Sorrento, 1b	4	0	1	1
Justice, dh	5	0	2	2	Flaherty, c	5	1	2	1
Sexson, lf	6	0	2	2	D.Martinez, rf	5	1	1	0
Branyan, 3b	4	0	0	0	Ledesma, ss	4	2	2	0
E.Wilson, 3b	1	0	0	0					
Ei.Diaz, c	5	0	1	0					
Totals	**43**	**15**	**19**	**14**	**Totals**	**39**	**10**	**14**	**10**

Cleveland	3 0 3	4 1 0	2 0 2—15
Tampa Bay	0 0 4	2 1 2	1 0 0—10

E—Ri.White (2), Rekar (1). DP—Tampa Bay 1. LOB—Cleveland 10, Tampa Bay 7. 2B—D.Roberts (1), Vizquel (20), Alomar 2 (30), M.Ramirez (19), Thome (20), McGriff (26), Trammell 2 (12), Ledesma (10). HR—M.Ramirez (28), Thome (21), Boggs (2). SB—D.Roberts (1). S—Alomar. SF—Lowery.

Cleveland	IP	H	R	ER	BB	SO
Nagy (W, 13-7)	5	9	7	7	3	3
Haney	1	2	2	2	0	0
Shuey	1.1	3	1	1	1	2
Rincon (H, 9)	0.1	0	0	0	0	0
Karsay (H, 8)	0.1	0	0	0	0	0
M.Jackson	1	0	0	0	0	0

Tampa Bay	IP	H	R	ER	BB	SO
B.Witt (L, 6-8)	2	6	6	6	2	1
Rekar	1.1	5	4	4	2	2
Ri.White	2.2	3	3	3	2	2
Yan	0.1	0	0	0	0	0
Duvall	2.1	5	2	2	1	0
A.Lopez	0.1	0	0	0	0	1

HBP—M.Ramirez by Yan. WP—Nagy. U—HP, Diaz. 1B, Garcia. 2B, Reilly. 3B, O'Nora. T—3:44. A—39,512.

1999 REVIEW

1999 REVIEW

BATTING

Name	G	TPA	AB	R	H	TB	2B	3B	HR	RBI	Avg.	Obp.	Slg.	SH	SF	HP	BB	IBB	SO	SB	CS	GDP	vs RHP				vs LHP			
																							AB	Avg.	HR	RBI	AB	Avg.	HR	RBI
McGriff, Fred	144	620	529	75	164	292	30	1	32	104	.310	.405	.552	0	4	1	86	11	107	1	0	12	381	.339	24	79	148	.236	8	25
Martinez, Dave	143	594	514	79	146	199	25	5	6	66	.284	.361	.387	10	5	5	60	3	76	13	6	6	426	.293	5	52	88	.239	1	14
Cairo, Miguel	120	508	465	61	137	171	15	5	3	36	.295	.335	.368	7	5	7	24	0	46	22	7	13	379	.274	3	31	86	.384	0	5
Flaherty, John	117	482	446	53	124	185	19	0	14	71	.278	.310	.415	1	10	6	19	0	64	0	2	14	366	.301	13	67	80	.175	1	4
Canseco, Jose	113	502	430	75	120	242	18	1	34	95	.279	.369	.563	0	7	7	58	3	135	3	0	14	341	.276	26	69	89	.292	8	26
Winn, Randy	79	324	303	44	81	111	16	4	2	24	.267	.307	.366	1	2	1	17	0	63	9	9	3	223	.278	1	22	80	.238	1	2
Ledesma, Aaron	93	312	294	32	78	93	15	0	0	30	.265	.305	.316	1	0	3	14	1	35	1	1	14	229	.266	0	23	65	.262	0	7
Sorrento, Paul	99	348	294	40	69	118	14	1	11	42	.235	.351	.401	0	1	4	49	1	101	1	1	4	256	.227	9	37	38	.289	2	5
Boggs, Wade	90	334	292	40	88	110	14	1	2	29	.301	.377	.377	0	4	0	38	2	23	1	0	14	245	.306	1	24	47	.277	1	5
Trammell, Bubba	82	328	283	49	82	143	19	0	14	39	.290	.384	.505	0	1	1	43	1	37	0	2	7	217	.309	10	30	66	.227	4	9
Stocker, Kevin	79	286	254	39	76	94	11	2	1	27	.299	.369	.370	4	0	4	24	0	41	9	7	4	193	.316	1	22	61	.246	0	5
Perry, Herbert	66	239	209	29	53	83	10	1	6	32	.254	.331	.397	0	4	10	16	1	42	0	0	13	147	.259	5	29	62	.242	1	3
Smith, Bobby	68	219	199	18	36	51	4	1	3	19	.181	.244	.256	2	1	1	16	0	64	4	4	8	157	.185	3	17	42	.167	0	2
Lowery, Terrell	66	206	185	25	48	71	15	1	2	17	.259	.330	.384	0	1	1	19	0	53	0	2	1	133	.271	1	14	52	.231	1	3
DiFelice, Mike	51	191	179	21	55	84	11	0	6	27	.307	.346	.469	0	1	3	8	0	23	0	0	1	130	.315	4	18	49	.286	2	9
Guillen, Jose	47	186	168	24	41	57	10	0	2	13	.244	.312	.339	0	1	7	10	1	36	0	0	9	125	.240	2	10	43	.256	0	3
McCracken, Quinton	40	165	148	20	37	48	6	1	1	18	.250	.317	.324	1	1	1	14	0	23	6	5	7	113	.248	1	16	35	.257	0	2
Graffanino, Tony	39	142	130	20	41	64	9	4	2	19	.315	.364	.492	2	0	1	9	0	22	3	2	1	100	.300	2	14	30	.367	0	5
Lamb, David	55	134	124	18	28	38	5	1	1	13	.226	.284	.306	0	0	0	10	0	18	0	1	4	100	.240	1	8	24	.167	0	5
Clyburn, Danny	28	89	81	8	16	29	4	0	3	5	.198	.270	.358	0	0	1	7	0	21	0	0	5	47	.170	2	4	34	.235	1	1
Butler, Rich	7	22	20	2	3	4	1	0	0	0	.150	.227	.200	0	0	0	2	0	4	0	0	0	16	.188	0	0	4	.000	0	0
Cox, Steve	6	19	19	0	4	5	1	0	0	0	.211	.211	.263	0	0	0	0	0	2	0	0	2	15	.200	0	0	4	.250	0	0
Rekar, Bryan	27	5	5	0	1	1	0	0	0	0	.200	.200	.200	0	0	0	0	0	2	0	0	0	4	.250	0	0	1	.000	0	0
Rupe, Ryan	24	4	4	0	0	0	0	0	0	0	.000	.000	.000	0	0	0	0	0	1	0	0	1	2	.000	0	0	2	.000	0	0
Callaway, Mickey	6	3	3	0	2	2	0	0	0	1	.667	.667	.667	0	0	0	0	0	0	0	0	0	3	.667	0	1	0	.000	0	0
Alvarez, Wilson	28	3	3	0	0	0	0	0	0	0	.000	.000	.000	0	0	0	0	0	1	0	0	0	2	.000	0	0	1	.000	0	0
Witt, Bobby	32	2	2	0	0	0	0	0	0	0	.000	.000	.000	0	0	0	0	0	1	0	0	0	2	.000	0	0	0	.000	0	0
Santana, Julio	22	1	1	0	1	1	0	0	0	1	1.000	1.000	1.000	0	0	0	0	0	0	0	0	0	1	1.000	0	1	0	.000	0	0
Franco, Julio	1	1	1	0	0	0	0	0	0	0	.000	.000	.000	0	0	0	0	0	1	0	0	0	1	.000	0	0	0	.000	0	0
Eiland, Dave	21	2	1	0	0	0	0	0	0	0	.000	.000	.000	1	0	0	0	0	0	0	0	0	1	.000	0	0	0	.000	0	0
Charlton, Norm	42	0	0	0	0	0	0	0	0	0	.000	.000	.000	0	0	0	0	0	0	0	0	0	0	.000	0	0	0	.000	0	0
Aldred, Scott	37	0	0	0	0	0	0	0	0	0	.000	.000	.000	0	0	0	0	0	0	0	0	0	0	.000	0	0	0	.000	0	0
Hernandez, Roberto	72	0	0	0	0	0	0	0	0	0	.000	.000	.000	0	0	0	0	0	0	0	0	0	0	.000	0	0	0	.000	0	0
Lopez, Albie	51	0	0	0	0	0	0	0	0	0	.000	.000	.000	0	0	0	0	0	0	0	0	0	0	.000	0	0	0	.000	0	0
White, Rick	63	0	0	0	0	0	0	0	0	0	.000	.000	.000	0	0	0	0	0	0	0	0	0	0	.000	0	0	0	.000	0	0
Yan, Esteban	50	0	0	0	0	0	0	0	0	0	.000	.000	.000	0	0	0	0	0	0	0	0	0	0	.000	0	0	0	.000	0	0
Duvall, Mike	40	1	0	0	0	0	0	0	0	0	.000	1.000	.000	0	0	0	1	0	0	0	0	0	0	.000	0	0	0	.000	0	0

PITCHING

Name	W	L	Pct.	ERA	IP	H	R	ER	HR	SH	SF	HB	BB	IBB	SO	G	GS	CG	ShO	GF	Sv	vs. RH				vs. LH			
																						AB	Avg.	HR	RBI	AB	Avg.	HR	RBI
Witt, Bobby	7	15	.318	5.84	180.1	213	130	117	23	7	8	3	96	1	123	32	32	3	2	0	0	338	.317	11	54	363	.292	12	56
Alvarez, Wilson	9	9	.500	4.22	160.0	159	92	75	22	3	3	6	79	1	128	28	28	1	0	0	0	495	.257	15	57	116	.276	7	21
Rupe, Ryan	8	9	.471	4.55	142.1	136	81	72	17	1	7	12	57	2	97	24	24	0	0	0	0	292	.247	9	34	245	.261	8	38
Arrojo, Rolando	7	12	.368	5.18	140.2	162	84	81	23	5	3	14	60	2	107	24	24	2	0	0	0	246	.272	7	27	302	.315	16	50
White, Rick	5	3	.625	4.08	108.0	132	56	49	8	2	5	1	38	5	81	63	1	0	0	11	0	246	.301	4	40	188	.309	4	29
Rekar, Bryan	6	6	.500	5.80	94.2	121	68	61	14	3	2	5	41	2	55	27	12	0	0	2	0	200	.305	10	34	186	.323	4	24
Eiland, Dave	4	8	.333	5.60	80.1	98	59	50	8	2	4	3	27	1	53	21	15	0	0	0	0	179	.307	5	33	154	.279	3	17
Hernandez, Roberto	2	3	.400	3.07	73.1	68	27	25	1	2	3	4	33	1	69	72	0	0	0	66	43	137	.248	1	13	141	.241	0	16
Lopez, Albie	3	2	.600	4.64	64.0	66	40	33	8	1	4	1	24	2	37	51	0	0	0	14	1	150	.267	6	24	101	.257	2	14
Yan, Esteban	3	4	.429	5.90	61.0	77	41	40	8	6	3	9	32	4	46	50	1	0	0	15	0	120	.342	4	21	116	.310	4	18
Santana, Julio	1	4	.200	7.32	55.1	66	49	45	10	1	1	7	32	0	34	22	5	0	0	7	0	118	.331	6	26	102	.265	4	17
Charlton, Norm	2	3	.400	4.44	50.2	49	29	25	4	2	3	1	36	0	45	42	0	0	0	9	0	130	.238	3	20	61	.295	1	18
Saunders, Tony	3	3	.500	6.43	42.0	53	39	30	6	1	2	4	29	0	30	9	9	0	0	0	0	125	.328	5	22	43	.279	1	8
Duvall, Mike	1	1	.500	4.05	40.0	46	21	18	5	1	1	2	27	1	40	40	0	0	0	7	0	86	.267	1	12	71	.324	4	25
Wheeler, Daniel	0	4	.000	5.87	30.2	35	20	20	7	1	0	0	13	1	32	6	6	0	0	0	0	59	.271	1	3	63	.302	6	15
Aldred, Scott	3	2	.600	5.18	24.1	26	15	14	1	2	1	2	14	0	22	37	0	0	0	9	0	54	.296	1	8	41	.244	0	11
Mecir, Jim	0	1	.000	2.61	20.2	15	7	6	0	0	2	1	14	0	15	17	0	0	0	3	0	45	.200	0	3	28	.214	0	5
Callaway, Mickey	1	2	.333	7.45	19.1	30	20	16	2	0	1	0	14	1	11	5	4	0	0	0	0	51	.294	1	10	33	.455	1	3
Newman, Alan	2	2	.500	6.89	15.2	22	12	12	2	0	0	1	9	0	20	18	0	0	0	5	0	28	.321	1	3	38	.342	1	12
Sparks, Jeff	0	0	.000	5.40	10.0	6	6	6	1	1	0	1	12	1	17	8	0	0	0	2	1	21	.238	1	4	14	.071	0	2
Gaillard, Eddie	1	0	1.000	2.08	8.2	12	9	2	1	1	0	0	4	0	7	8	0	0	0	1	0	24	.292	0	4	13	.385	1	4
Lidle, Cory	1	0	1.000	7.20	5.0	8	4	4	0	0	0	0	2	0	4	5	1	0	0	1	0	18	.278	0	1	4	.750	0	3
Morris, Jim	0	0	.000	5.79	4.2	3	3	3	1	0	0	1	2	0	3	5	0	0	0	3	0	14	.214	1	3	4	.000	0	0
Boggs, Wade	0	0	.000	6.75	1.1	3	1	1	0	0	0	0	0	1	1	1	0	0	0	0	0	6	.500	0	1	1	.000	0	0

DESIGNATED HITTERS

Name	AB	Avg.	HR	RBI	Name	AB	Avg.	HR	RBI	Name	AB	Avg.	HR	RBI
Canseco, Jose	406	.271	32	91	Trammell, Bubba	16	.313	2	4	Lamb, David	1	.000	0	0
McGriff, Fred	70	.229	3	9	Clyburn, Danny	12	.333	0	0	Lowery, Terrell	0	-	0	0
Sorrento, Paul	28	.143	1	2	Ledesma, Aaron	4	.250	0	0	Callaway, Mickey	0	-	0	0
Boggs, Wade	25	.200	0	1	Flaherty, John	3	.333	0	0	Graffanino, Tony	0	-	0	0
Perry, Herbert	21	.238	1	2	Cairo, Miguel	2	.000	0	0					

INDIVIDUAL STATISTICS

FIELDING

FIRST BASEMEN

Player	Pct.	G	PO	A	E	TC	DP
McGriff, Fred	.989	125	1037	88	13	1138	132
Sorrento, Paul	.995	27	203	9	1	213	19
Perry, Herbert	1.000	14	77	4	0	81	13
Ledesma, Aaron	1.000	4	27	6	0	33	4
Boggs, Wade	1.000	4	32	0	0	32	3
Cox, Steve	1.000	4	19	1	0	20	5
Franco, Julio	1.000	1	2	0	0	2	0

SECOND BASEMEN

Player	Pct.	G	PO	A	E	TC	DP
Cairo, Miguel	.986	117	251	377	9	637	102
Graffanino, Tony	.990	17	38	65	1	104	14
Ledesma, Aaron	.990	17	43	56	1	100	18
Lamb, David	.949	15	12	25	2	39	6
Smith, Bobby	.964	13	22	32	2	56	7

THIRD BASEMEN

Player	Pct.	G	PO	A	E	TC	DP
Boggs, Wade	.942	74	45	100	9	154	14
Smith, Bobby	.933	59	26	100	9	135	13
Perry, Herbert	.955	42	32	75	5	112	11
Ledesma, Aaron	.907	26	11	28	4	43	1
Graffanino, Tony	-	1	0	0	0	0	0

SHORTSTOPS

Player	Pct.	G	PO	A	E	TC	DP
Stocker, Kevin	.957	76	137	216	16	369	55
Ledesma, Aaron	.978	50	83	135	5	223	37
Lamb, David	.945	35	46	75	7	128	28
Graffanino, Tony	.951	17	28	49	4	81	14

OUTFIELDERS

Player	Pct.	G	PO	A	E	TC	DP
Martinez, Dave	.985	140	253	8	4	265	1
Winn, Randy	.995	77	180	4	1	185	0
Trammell, Bubba	.993	74	142	2	1	145	1
Lowery, Terrell	.971	60	97	4	3	104	1
Sorrento, Paul	.957	57	87	2	4	93	1
Guillen, Jose	.966	47	80	5	3	88	0
McCracken, Quinton	.988	40	80	1	1	82	0
Clyburn, Danny	1.000	24	39	3	0	42	1
Butler, Rich	1.000	6	8	0	0	8	0
Canseco, Jose	1.000	6	7	1	0	8	0
Perry, Herbert	1.000	6	4	0	0	4	0
Cox, Steve	1.000	2	1	0	0	1	0

CATCHERS

Player	Pct.	G	PO	A	E	TC	DP	PB
Flaherty, John	.993	115	726	87	6	819	12	4
DiFelice, Mike	.987	51	344	28	5	377	5	8

PITCHERS

Player	Pct.	G	PO	A	E	TC	DP
Hernandez, Roberto	.933	72	4	10	1	15	1
White, Rick	.917	63	6	16	2	24	1
Lopez, Albie	.909	51	3	7	1	11	1
Yan, Esteban	1.000	50	8	9	0	17	2
Charlton, Norm	.889	42	2	6	1	9	0
Duvall, Mike	.900	40	5	4	1	10	2
Aldred, Scott	1.000	37	0	2	0	2	0
Witt, Bobby	.929	32	12	27	3	42	4
Alvarez, Wilson	.897	28	2	24	3	29	1
Rekar, Bryan	.950	27	6	13	1	20	2
Rupe, Ryan	.850	24	5	12	3	20	5
Santana, Julio	.889	22	3	5	1	9	1
Eiland, Dave	1.000	21	5	15	0	20	1
Newman, Alan	.500	18	0	1	1	2	0
Mecir, Jim	1.000	17	1	4	0	5	0
Saunders, Tony	.900	9	4	5	1	10	0
Gaillard, Eddie	1.000	8	0	3	0	3	0
Sparks, Jeff	-	8	0	0	0	0	0
Wheeler, Daniel	1.000	6	1	2	0	3	0
Callaway, Mickey	1.000	5	0	4	0	4	0
Lidle, Cory	1.000	5	0	2	0	2	0
Morris, Jim	-	5	0	0	0	0	0
Boggs, Wade	-	1	0	0	0	0	0

PITCHING AGAINST EACH CLUB

Pitcher	Ana. W-L	Bal. W-L	Bos. W-L	Chi. W-L	Cle. W-L	Det. W-L	K.C. W-L	Min. W-L	N.Y. W-L	Oak. W-L	Sea. W-L	Tex. W-L	Tor. W-L	N.L. W-L	Total W-L
Aldred, Scott	0-0	0-0	1-0	0-0	0-0	0-0	1-0	0-1	0-0	0-0	0-0	0-1	1-0	0-0	3-2
Alvarez, Wilson	1-1	0-1	1-0	2-1	2-1	1-0	0-0	0-0	0-0	0-1	0-1	0-0	1-0	1-2	9-9
Arrojo, Rolando	0-0	0-2	1-1	0-0	0-1	2-1	1-0	0-1	1-1	0-1	0-2	2-2	0-0	0-0	7-12
Boggs, Wade	0-0	0-0	0-0	0-0	0-0	0-0	0-0	0-0	0-0	0-0	0-0	0-0	0-0	0-0	0-0
Callaway, Mickey	0-1	0-0	0-0	0-0	0-0	0-0	0-0	0-0	0-0	0-1	0-0	0-0	0-0	1-0	1-2
Charlton, Norm	0-0	0-0	0-0	0-1	0-0	0-0	1-0	0-1	0-0	0-0	0-0	0-0	0-0	1-1	2-3
Duvall, Mike	0-0	0-0	0-0	0-0	0-0	0-0	0-0	1-0	0-0	0-0	0-0	0-0	0-0	0-1	1-1
Eiland, Dave	0-1	0-1	1-0	0-0	0-0	0-0	2-0	0-0	0-1	0-2	1-0	0-0	0-1	0-2	4-8
Gaillard, Eddie	0-0	0-0	0-0	0-0	0-0	0-0	0-0	1-0	0-0	0-0	0-0	0-0	0-0	0-0	1-0
Hernandez, Roberto	0-1	0-0	1-0	0-0	0-0	0-0	1-1	0-0	0-0	0-0	0-0	0-0	0-0	0-0	2-3
Lidle, Cory	0-0	0-0	0-0	0-0	0-0	0-0	0-0	1-0	0-0	0-0	0-0	0-0	0-0	0-0	1-0
Lopez, Albie	0-0	0-0	1-0	0-0	0-0	0-0	0-0	0-0	0-0	0-0	0-0	0-1	0-0	1-1	3-2
Mecir, Jim	0-0	0-0	0-0	0-0	0-0	0-0	0-0	0-0	0-0	0-1	0-0	0-0	0-0	0-0	0-1
Morris, Jim	0-0	0-0	0-0	0-0	0-0	0-0	0-0	0-0	0-0	0-0	0-0	0-0	0-0	0-0	0-0
Newman, Alan	0-1	0-0	0-0	0-0	0-0	0-0	1-0	0-0	0-0	0-0	1-0	0-0	0-0	0-0	2-1
Rekar, Bryan	0-0	1-0	1-1	0-1	1-0	0-0	0-0	0-0	0-0	0-0	1-0	0-0	0-0	1-2	6-6
Rupe, Ryan	1-0	2-0	0-0	1-1	0-0	0-0	1-0	1-2	0-0	0-1	0-2	1-1	1-0	0-2	8-9
Santana, Julio	0-1	0-0	1-0	0-0	0-0	0-0	0-1	0-0	0-0	0-0	0-1	0-0	0-0	0-0	1-4
Saunders, Tony	1-0	2-0	0-1	0-1	0-1	0-0	0-0	0-0	0-0	0-0	0-0	0-0	0-0	0-0	3-3
Sparks, Jeff	0-0	0-0	0-0	0-0	0-0	0-0	0-0	0-0	0-0	0-0	0-0	0-0	0-0	0-0	0-0
Wheeler, Daniel	0-1	0-1	0-0	0-0	0-0	0-0	0-0	0-0	0-1	0-0	0-0	0-1	0-0	0-0	0-4
White, Rick	1-0	0-0	0-0	1-0	0-0	0-0	1-0	0-1	0-0	0-0	1-0	0-0	1-1	0-1	5-3
Witt, Bobby	1-1	1-0	2-0	0-1	0-0	0-2	1-2	1-0	0-0	0-2	0-2	0-0	0-2	1-2	7-15
Yan, Esteban	0-0	0-0	0-0	0-0	1-0	1-0	0-1	0-0	0-0	1-1	0-1	0-1	0-0	0-0	3-4
Totals	5-7	7-5	9-4	4-6	4-5	5-4	8-2	5-5	4-8	1-9	4-8	4-8	5-8	4-14	69-93

INTERLEAGUE: Eiland 0-1, White 0-1, Alvarez 0-1 vs. Braves; Callaway 1-0, Witt 0-1, Rekar 0-1 vs. Expos; Alvarez 1-0, Charlton 0-1, Eiland 0-1 vs. Mets; Charlton 1-0, Lopez 0-1, Rekar 0-1 vs. Phillies; Rekar 0-1, Rupe 0-2, Duvall 0-1, Yan 0-1, Alvarez 0-1 vs. Marlins. Total: 4-14.

MISCELLANEOUS

HOME RUNS BY PARK

At Anaheim (3): Canseco 1, Martinez 1, Flaherty 1.
At Atlanta (2): McGriff 1, Canseco 1.
At Baltimore (3): Canseco 1, Martinez 1, Flaherty 1.
At Boston (11): Canseco 3, Boggs 1, Martinez 1, Sorrento 1, Flaherty 1, Cairo 1, Trammell 1, Clyburn 1, Smith 1.
At Chicago (AL) (7): Canseco 3, McGriff 2, Smith 1, Lamb 1.
At Cleveland (5): McGriff 2, Canseco 1, Sorrento 1, Clyburn 1.
At Detroit (2): McGriff 1, Lowery 1.
At Florida (2): Flaherty 1, Trammell 1.
At Kansas City (5): Trammell 2, Sorrento 1, Flaherty 1, Graffanino 1.
At Minnesota (1): Canseco 1.
At Montreal (1): Canseco 1.
At New York (AL) (4): McGriff 2, Trammell 2.
At Oakland (3): Canseco 1, Graffanino 1, Lowery 1.
At Seattle (2): McGriff 1, DiFelice 1.
At Tampa Bay (66): McGriff 18, Canseco 12, Sorrento 6, Trammell 6, Perry 5, DiFelice 5, Flaherty 3, Martinez 2, Winn 2, Boggs 1, Stocker 1, McCracken 1, Cairo 1, Guillen 1, Clyburn 1, Smith 1.
At Texas (15): Flaherty 5, Canseco 4, McGriff 3, Sorrento 1, Trammell 1, Guillen 1.
At Toronto (7): Canseco 4, McGriff 1, Martinez 1, Trammell 1.

LOW-HIT GAMES

No-hitters: None.
One-hitters: None.
Two-hitters: None.

10-STRIKEOUT GAMES

Wilson Alvarez 1, Daniel Wheeler 1, **Total:** 2.

FOUR OR MORE HITS IN ONE GAME

Fred McGriff 3, Jose Canseco 2, Dave Martinez 1, Paul Sorrento 1, Kevin Stocker 1, Herbert Perry 1, Aaron Ledesma 1, Miguel Cairo 1, Mike DiFelice 1, Randy Winn 1, **Total:** 13.

MULTI-HOMER GAMES

Fred McGriff 2, Jose Canseco 2, John Flaherty 2, Herbert Perry 1, **Total:** 7.

GRAND SLAMS

8-18: Terrell Lowery (off Detroit's Dave Borkowski).
10-3: Randy Winn (off New York's Jeff Juden).

PINCH HITTERS

(Minimum 5 at-bats)

Name	AB	Avg.	HR	RBI
Sorrento, Paul	10	.100	0	0
Boggs, Wade	6	.000	0	0
Lamb, David	6	.000	0	0
Perry, Herbert	5	.400	0	0

DEBUTS

4-12: David Lamb, SS.
5-5: Ryan Rupe, P.
5-14: Alan Newman, P.
6-12: Mickey Callaway, P.
9-1: Daniel Wheeler, P.
9-12: Jeff Sparks, P.
9-18: Jim Morris, P.
9-19: Steve Cox, PH.

GAMES BY POSITION

Catcher: John Flaherty 115, Mike DiFelice 51.
First base: Fred McGriff 125, Paul Sorrento 27, Herbert Perry 14, Wade Boggs 4, Aaron Ledesma 4, Steve Cox 4, Julio Franco 1.
Second base: Miguel Cairo 117, Aaron Ledesma 17, Tony Graffanino 17, David Lamb 15, Bobby Smith 13.
Third base: Wade Boggs 74, Bobby Smith 59, Herbert Perry 42, Aaron Ledesma 26, Tony Graffanino 1.
Shortstop: Kevin Stocker 76, Aaron Ledesma 50, David Lamb 35, Tony Graffanino 17.
Outfield: Dave Martinez 140, Randy Winn 77, Bubba Trammell 74, Terrell Lowery 60, Paul Sorrento 57, Jose Guillen 47, Quinton McCracken 40, Danny Clyburn 24, Jose Canseco 6, Herbert Perry 6, Rich Butler 6, Steve Cox 2.
Designated hitter: Jose Canseco 106, Fred McGriff 18, Paul Sorrento 9, Wade Boggs 7, Bubba Trammell 6, Herbert Perry 5, Danny Clyburn 4, David Lamb 3, Miguel Cairo 2, John Flaherty 1, Aaron Ledesma 1, Tony Graffanino 1, Terrell Lowery 1, Mickey Callaway 1.

STREAKS

Wins: 6 (April 17-23).
Losses: 7 (May 22-29, June 4-11).
Consecutive games with at least one hit: 13, Dave Martinez (May 26-June 9), John Flaherty (August 7-27).
Wins by pitcher: 3, Wilson Alvarez (August 18-29), Ryan Rupe (June 15-26).

ATTENDANCE

Home: 1,749,567.
Road: 2,207,319.
Highest (home): 40,756 (October 2 vs. New York).
Highest (road): 50,403 (September 25 vs. New York).
Lowest (home): 14,887 (September 8 vs. Detroit).
Lowest (road): 7,067 (June 11 vs. Montreal).

DAY BY DAY

Date	Opp.	Res.	Score	(inn.*)	Hits	Opp. hits	Winning pitcher	Losing pitcher	Save	Record	Pos.	GB
4-5	Det.	L	5-11		5	13	Moehler	Helling		0-1	T3rd	0.5
4-6	Det.	W	6-0		12	7	Sele	Thompson		1-1	T2nd	0.5
4-7	Det.	W	10-7		18	12	Morgan	Blair	Wetteland	2-1	1st	+0.5
4-9	Ana.	L	4-8		10	12	Finley	Burkett		2-2	T1st	...
4-10	Ana.	L	0-10		3	19	Olivares	Helling		2-3	T2nd	1.0
4-11	Ana.	W	6-3		12	6	Sele	Belcher	Wetteland	3-3	T1st	...
4-12	Ana.	L	5-13		7	20	Magnante	Clark		3-4	3rd	1.0
4-13	At Sea.	W	15-6		19	10	Morgan	Cloude		4-4	T1st	...
4-14	At Sea.	W	9-6		17	11	Zimmerman	Paniagua	Wetteland	5-4	1st	+1.0
4-15	At Sea.	W	4-3	(10)	9	5	Crabtree	Halama	Wetteland	6-4	1st	+1.0
4-16	At Oak.	L	2-8		3	17	Candiotti	Sele		6-5	T1st	...
4-17	At Oak.	L	3-11		6	13	Haynes	Clark		6-6	T1st	...
4-18	At Oak.	W	6-2		15	7	Morgan	Oquist		7-6	1st	+1.0
4-20	At N.Y.	L	0-4		4	13	Cone	Burkett		7-7	1st	+1.0
4-21	At N.Y.	L	2-4		5	6	Clemens	Helling	Rivera	7-8	1st	+1.0
4-22	At Min.	W	6-4		6	10	Sele	Milton	Wetteland	8-8	1st	+1.0
4-23	At Min.	W	4-2		12	6	Clark	Lincoln	Wetteland	9-8	1st	+2.0
4-24	At Min.	W	7-2		10	9	Morgan	Hawkins		10-8	1st	+2.0
4-25	At Min.	W	9-5		11	10	Helling	Perkins		11-8	1st	+2.0
4-27	N.Y.	L	6-7		7	14	Stanton	Wetteland	Rivera	11-9	1st	+2.5
4-28	N.Y.	W	8-6		12	10	Munoz	Stanton	Wetteland	12-9	1st	+3.0
4-29	N.Y.	L	3-5		9	6	Mendoza	Morgan	Rivera	12-10	1st	+2.0
4-30	Cle.	W	7-5		13	11	Helling	Colon	Wetteland	13-10	1st	+2.0
5-1	Cle.	L	3-5		9	8	Gooden	Sele	Jackson	13-11	1st	+2.0
5-2	Cle.	W	8-6		11	8	Clark	Nagy	Wetteland	14-11	1st	+2.0
5-3	Cle.	L	4-10		6	16	Wright	Morgan		14-12	1st	+2.0
5-5	At Bos.	W	8-3		12	8	Helling	Rapp		15-12	1st	+2.0
5-6	At Bos.	L	2-3		10	10	Cormier	Sele	Wakefield	15-13	1st	+1.0
5-7	At Tor.	L	6-9		7	17	Hentgen	Clark	Koch	15-14	1st	+1.0
5-8	At Tor.	W	4-3		7	7	Morgan	Wells	Wetteland	16-14	1st	+2.0
5-9	At Tor.	W	11-6		20	8	Patterson	Munro		17-14	1st	+2.0
5-10	At Chi.	L	2-5		6	12	Navarro	Helling		17-15	1st	+1.5
5-11	At Chi.	W	11-5		15	12	Zimmerman	Howry		18-15	1st	+1.5
5-13	Bal.	W	15-7		13	13	Morgan	Kamieniecki		19-15	1st	+1.5
5-14	Bal.	W	7-6		11	15	Crabtree	Rhodes	Wetteland	20-15	1st	+1.5
5-15	Bal.	W	8-1		14	7	Helling	Johns		21-15	1st	+1.5
5-16	Bal.	L	5-16		11	24	Ponson	Sele		21-16	1st	+0.5
5-17	T.B.	L	3-13		6	15	Rupe	Burkett		21-17	T1st	...
5-18	T.B.	L	4-5		14	10	Arrojo	Morgan	Hernandez	21-18	T1st	...
5-19	T.B.	W	7-6		9	11	Zimmerman	Aldred	Wetteland	22-18	1st	+1.0
5-21	At Bal.	L	2-3		6	7	Ponson	Helling		22-19	1st	+1.5
5-22	At Bal.	W	8-7		7	14	Crabtree	Timlin	Wetteland	23-19	1st	+2.0
5-23	At Bal.	L	6-15		14	15	Mussina	Morgan		23-20	1st	+2.0
5-24	At T.B.	W	12-3		16	10	Clark	Arrojo		24-20	1st	+3.0
5-25	At T.B.	W	7-2		11	9	Venafro	Witt		25-20	1st	+3.0
5-26	At T.B.	W	8-6		12	11	Helling	Santana	Wetteland	26-20	1st	+3.0
5-28	Min.	W	6-4		10	9	Sele	Radke	Wetteland	27-20	1st	+2.5
5-29	Min.	W	4-3	(10)	11	12	Wetteland	Trombley		28-20	1st	+3.0
5-30	Min.	W	3-2		9	6	Zimmerman	Mays	Wetteland	29-20	1st	+3.5
5-31	K.C.	W	4-3	(10)	7	9	Crabtree	Santiago		30-20	1st	+3.5
6-1	K.C.	W	3-1		6	3	Zimmerman	Whisenant	Wetteland	31-20	1st	+3.5
6-2	K.C.	W	7-4		6	10	Sele	Appier	Wetteland	32-20	1st	+4.5
6-4	At Ari.	L	3-11		4	12	Johnson	Clark		32-21	1st	+4.5
6-5	At Ari.	W	9-8		9	7	Venafro	Holmes	Wetteland	33-21	1st	+5.5
6-6	At Ari.	L	2-4		7	6	Benes	Helling	Olson	33-22	1st	+4.5
6-7	At L.A.	W	3-2		10	6	Sele	Valdes	Wetteland	34-22	1st	+5.0
6-8	At L.A.	W	7-6	(13)	16	11	Zimmerman	Mills	Munoz	35-22	1st	+5.0
6-9	At L.A.	L	2-7		5	11	Brown	Clark		35-23	1st	+4.0
6-11	Col.	W	3-2		8	6	Zimmerman	McElroy	Wetteland	36-23	1st	+5.0
6-12	Col.	L	7-8		13	13	Astacio	Sele	Veres	36-24	1st	+4.5
6-13	Col.	L	2-4		7	8	Jones	Morgan	Veres	36-25	1st	+3.5
6-14	At N.Y.	L	2-8		8	14	Irabu	Clark		36-26	1st	+3.0
6-15	At N.Y.	L	2-6		4	6	Cone	Glynn		36-27	1st	+3.0
6-16	At N.Y.	W	3-0		5	4	Helling	Hernandez	Wetteland	37-27	1st	+4.0
6-17	At N.Y.	W	4-2		10	7	Sele	Clemens	Wetteland	38-27	1st	+4.0
6-18	At Bos.	W	4-1		8	3	Morgan	Portugal	Zimmerman	39-27	1st	+4.0
6-19	At Bos.	L	4-7		6	15	Cho	Clark	Wakefield	39-28	1st	+4.0
6-20	At Bos.	L	2-5		8	12	Martinez	Glynn	Wakefield	39-29	1st	+4.0
6-21	At Bos.	L	4-5		9	10	Wasdin	Helling	Wakefield	39-30	1st	+4.0
6-22	Oak.	L	3-5		11	11	Mathews	Wetteland	Taylor	39-31	1st	+3.0
6-23	Oak.	W	7-6		13	7	Morgan	Oquist	Wetteland	40-31	1st	+4.0
6-24	Oak.	W	5-2		6	7	Burkett	Hudson	Wetteland	41-31	1st	+5.0
6-25	At Sea.	W	14-4		18	6	Glynn	Rodriguez		42-31	1st	+6.0
6-26	At Sea.	L	4-5		12	8	Paniagua	Venafro	Mesa	42-32	1st	+4.0
6-27	At Sea.	L	2-5		6	10	Garcia	Sele	Mesa	42-33	1st	+4.0
6-28	At Ana.	W	9-1		9	7	Morgan	Finley		43-33	1st	+4.5
6-29	At Ana.	W	5-0		13	1	Burkett	Olivares		44-33	1st	+4.5
6-30	At Ana.	W	18-4		20	10	Glynn	Hill		45-33	1st	+5.5

HIGHLIGHTS

High point: September 30, when the Rangers set a franchise record with their 95th victory, a 7-0 win over Seattle that came in Texas' regular-season home finale. Four days earlier, the Rangers had clinched their third A.L. West title in four seasons.

Low point: October 9, when the Rangers went quietly in Game 3 of the Division Series against New York. With the 3-0 victory, the Yankees swept the Rangers out of the playoffs for the second consecutive season. In each series, the Rangers scored only one run.

Turning point: With two on and one out in the first inning of Game 1 of the Division Series, cleanup hitter Juan Gonzalez was overmatched against Yankees righthander Orlando Hernandez and struck out. The Rangers didn't score in that inning or in the game, and lost 8-0.

Most valuable player: Yes, catcher Ivan Rodriguez won the league MVP honor, but Rafael Palmeiro is the choice here. Palmeiro hit .324 with 47 home runs and 148 RBIs and was the Rangers' top clutch hitter. He hit .358 with runners in scoring position and .500 with the bases loaded. Rodriguez had one of the best offensive seasons by a catcher in major league history, batting .332 with 35 home runs, 113 RBIs and 116 runs scored. He also threw out a major league-record 54.2 percent of runners trying to steal.

Most valuable pitcher: With a shaky rotation in place, Texas added rookie righthander Jeff Zimmerman from the minors eight days into the season to strengthen the bullpen. Zimmerman won his first nine decisions and had a sub-2.00 ERA for most of the year.

Most improved player: By mid-May, Esteban Loaiza was sidelined with a broken hand and all but written out of the Rangers' long-term plans. But the righthander stood out upon his return, going 9-4 with a 3.72 ERA after the All-Star break, and now looms large in Texas' future.

Most pleasant surprise: Zimmerman, who went from being "just another body" to one of the top setup men in the majors.

Key injuries: Palmeiro was limited to 28 games at first base because of two offseason arthroscopic knee surgeries. Mike Simms, one of Palmeiro's backups, underwent heel surgery and had exactly two at-bats. Rookie center fielder Ruben Mateo broke a bone in his right wrist on August 4 and didn't return.

Notable: Juan Gonzalez had another big season (.326 average, 39 homers and 128 RBIs), but fell out of favor because of a questionable attitude. ... The Rangers had four 100-RBI men—Palmeiro, Gonzalez, Rodriguez and left fielder Rusty Greer. Third basemen Todd Zeile wound up with 98. ... Aaron Sele, a 19-game winner in 1998, won 18 times in '99. ... John Wetteland's 43 saves moved him within four of 300 for his career.

—EVAN GRANT

MISCELLANEOUS

RECORDS

1999 regular-season record: 95-67 (1st in A.L. West); 51-30 at home; 44-37 on road; 29-26 vs. A.L. East; 35-17 vs. A.L. Central; 21-16 vs. A.L. West; 10-8 vs. N.L. West; 20-10 vs. lefthanded starters; 75-57 vs. righthanded starters; 74-64 on grass; 21-3 on turf; 17-18 in daytime; 78-49 at night; 24-16 in one-run games; 6-2 in extra-inning games; 1-1-0 in doubleheaders.

Team record past five years: 424-368 (.535, ranks 4th in league in that span).

TEAM LEADERS

Batting average: Ivan Rodriguez (.332).
At-bats: Ivan Rodriguez (600).
Runs: Ivan Rodriguez (116).
Hits: Ivan Rodriguez (199).
Total bases: Rafael Palmeiro (356).
Doubles: Rusty Greer, Todd Zeile (41).
Triples: Mark McLemore (7).
Home runs: Rafael Palmeiro (47).
Runs batted in: Rafael Palmeiro (148).
Stolen bases: Tom Goodwin (39).
Slugging percentage: Rafael Palmeiro (.630).
On-base percentage: Rafael Palmeiro (.420).
Wins: Aaron Sele (18).
Earned-run average: Aaron Sele (4.79).
Complete games: Rick Helling (3).
Shutouts: Aaron Sele (2).
Saves: John Wetteland (43).
Innings pitched: Rick Helling (219.1).
Strikeouts: Aaron Sele (186).

Date	Opp.	Res.	Score	(inn.*)	Hits	Opp. hits	Winning pitcher	Losing pitcher	Save	Record	Pos.	GB
7-2	Sea.	W	7-6		10	14	Wetteland	Cloude		46-33	1st	+7.0
7-3	Sea.	L	12-13		15	15	Paniagua	Crabtree	Mesa	46-34	1st	+6.0
7-4	Sea.	L	0-6		6	12	Halama	Morgan		46-35	1st	+5.0
7-5	At Oak.	L	2-4		6	12	Hudson	Burkett	Taylor	46-36	1st	+4.0
7-6	At Oak.	L	0-4		4	5	Haynes	Glynn		46-37	1st	+4.0
7-7	At Oak.	W	7-4		10	7	Zimmerman	Rigby	Wetteland	47-37	1st	+5.0
7-9	At S.D.	W	7-2		8	9	Sele	Williams		48-37	1st	+6.0
7-10	At S.D.	L	4-5		9	8	Wall	Wetteland		48-38	1st	+5.0
7-11	At S.D.	L	2-6		4	11	Miceli	Loaiza		48-39	1st	+5.0
7-15	Ari.	W	3-2		7	5	Venafro	Mantei		49-39	1st	+5.0
7-16	Ari.	W	9-8		14	10	Wetteland	Chouinard		50-39	1st	+5.0
7-17	Ari.	L	6-8	(10)	11	13	Plesac	Wetteland	Mantei	50-40	1st	+5.0
7-18	S.F	W	5-4		7	9	Morgan	Gardner	Wetteland	51-40	1st	+5.0
7-19	S.F	W	14-7		17	10	Loaiza	Brock		52-40	1st	+5.0
7-20	S.F	W	6-3		10	7	Helling	Estes		53-40	1st	+5.0
7-21	Ana.	W	9-5		13	10	Sele	Olivares	Zimmerman	54-40	1st	+5.0
7-22	Ana.	W	9-7		10	15	Burkett	Sparks	Zimmerman	55-40	1st	+6.0
7-23	At T.B.	W	11-8		13	17	Kolb	Rupe		56-40	1st	+7.0
7-24	At T.B.	W	5-3		11	5	Loaiza	Newman	Wetteland	57-40	1st	+7.0
7-25	At T.B.	W	4-3		8	7	Helling	Arrojo	Wetteland	58-40	1st	+8.0
7-27	At Bal.	W	8-6		14	11	Sele	Mussina	Wetteland	59-40	1st	+8.5
7-28	At Bal.	L	6-8		8	13	Erickson	Burkett	Timlin	59-41	1st	+8.5
7-29	At Bal.	W	3-1		6	3	Morgan	Guzman	Wetteland	60-41	1st	+9.0
7-30	K.C.	W	9-2		14	9	Loaiza	Witasick		61-41	1st	+9.0
7-31	K.C.	L	8-12		13	19	Reichert	Munoz	Service	61-42	1st	+8.0
8-1	K.C.	W	12-5		16	10	Sele	Barber		62-42	1st	+8.0
8-2	Min.	W	5-4		8	9	Zimmerman	Guardado	Wetteland	63-42	1st	+8.0
8-3	Min.	W	9-5		13	14	Morgan	Sampson		64-42	1st	+8.0
8-4	Min.	W	3-1		10	4	Loaiza	Radke	Wetteland	65-42	1st	+9.0
8-6	Tor.	L	4-5		11	10	Carpenter	Zimmerman	Koch	65-43	1st	+7.5
8-7	Tor.	W	6-0		13	6	Sele	Hentgen		66-43	1st	+7.5
8-8	Tor.	L	7-8		11	11	Frascatore	Venafro	Koch	66-44	1st	+6.5
8-9	Tor.	L	4-19		7	25	Hamilton	Morgan		66-45	1st	+6.5
8-10	Det.	W	4-3	(12)	8	11	Patterson	Cruz		67-45	1st	+6.5
8-11	Det.	W	8-2		12	6	Helling	Blair		68-45	1st	+7.5
8-12	Det.	L	1-3		5	8	Mlicki	Sele	Jones	68-46	1st	+7.0
8-13†	At Chi.	L	2-4		6	11	Wells	Burkett	Howry	68-47		
8-13‡	At Chi.	L	4-7		14	9	Baldwin	Glynn		68-48	1st	+5.5
8-14	At Chi.	L	7-8		11	16	Howry	Zimmerman		68-49	1st	+4.5
8-15	At Cle.	W	10-0		16	6	Loaiza	Snyder		69-49	1st	+4.5
8-16	At Cle.	W	13-5		16	10	Munoz	Rincon		70-49	1st	+5.5
8-17	At Cle.	W	15-4		19	9	Sele	Langston		71-49	1st	+5.5
8-18	At Cle.	W	6-1		9	7	Burkett	Nagy		72-49	1st	+6.5
8-19	At Cle.	L	0-8		7	11	Karsay	Morgan		72-50	1st	+5.5
8-20	Bos.	W	4-3		10	6	Loaiza	Portugal	Wetteland	73-50	1st	+6.5
8-21	Bos.	W	9-2		12	9	Helling	Rose		74-50	1st	+6.5
8-22	Bos.	W	6-0		10	8	Sele	Wakefield		75-50	1st	+6.5
8-23	N.Y.	L	3-21		10	23	Pettitte	Burkett		75-51	1st	+6.5
8-24	N.Y.	L	7-10	(11)	14	11	Mendoza	Lee	Rivera	75-52	1st	+5.5
8-25	N.Y.	W	7-3		12	8	Loaiza	Irabu		76-52	1st	+6.5
8-27	At Tor.	W	8-2		14	6	Helling	Carpenter		77-52	1st	+6.5
8-28	At Tor.	W	9-7		14	14	Sele	Wells	Wetteland	78-52	1st	+6.5
8-29	At Tor.	W	4-2		11	9	Burkett	Halladay	Wetteland	79-52	1st	+7.5
8-30	At Det.	L	0-1		3	10	Moehler	Loaiza		79-53	1st	+7.5
8-31	At Det.	L	6-14		11	16	Cordero	Kolb		79-54	1st	+6.5
9-1	At Det.	W	14-7		15	12	Helling	Weaver	Wetteland	80-54	1st	+6.5
9-2	At Det.	L	7-8		13	15	Mlicki	Zimmerman	Jones	80-55	1st	+6.5
9-3	Chi.	W	10-4		15	10	Burkett	Baldwin		81-55	1st	+6.5
9-4	Chi.	L	3-12		11	15	Castillo	Loaiza		81-56	1st	+5.5
9-6†	Chi.	W	8-6		9	10	Helling	Parque	Wetteland	82-56		
9-6‡	Chi.	W	6-3		8	12	Fassero	Snyder	Wetteland	83-56	1st	+7.5
9-7	Cle.	W	4-3		10	6	Sele	Reed	Wetteland	84-56	1st	+8.5
9-8	Cle.	W	3-0		7	8	Burkett	Haney	Wetteland	85-56	1st	+8.5
9-10	At K.C.	L	3-7		11	12	Stein	Loaiza	Montgomery	85-57	1st	+7.5
9-11	At K.C.	L	6-9		14	13	Suppan	Helling	Montgomery	85-58	1st	+6.5
9-12	At K.C.	L	3-6		9	9	Witasick	Sele	Morman	85-59	1st	+5.5
9-13	At K.C.	W	8-4	(10)	11	9	Wetteland	Santiago		86-59	1st	+5.5
9-14	At Min.	W	5-4		10	10	Kolb	Guardado	Wetteland	87-59	1st	+6.5
9-15	At Min.	W	8-3		12	9	Loaiza	Radke		88-59	1st	+7.0
9-17	T.B.	L	5-7		16	13	Newman	Helling	Hernandez	88-60	1st	+7.0
9-18	T.B.	W	6-1		9	6	Sele	Witt		89-60	1st	+7.0
9-19	T.B.	L	2-15		7	15	Arrojo	Burkett		89-61	1st	+6.0
9-21	Bal.	L	2-4		6	7	Johnson	Loaiza	Timlin	89-62	1st	+5.5
9-22	Bal.	L	4-7		10	9	Erickson	Helling	Timlin	89-63	1st	+5.5
9-24	Oak.	W	12-4		18	8	Sele	Heredia		90-63	1st	+6.5
9-25	Oak.	W	10-4		9	6	Burkett	Appier		91-63	1st	+7.5
9-26	Oak.	W	10-3		12	7	Loaiza	Jarvis		92-63	1st	+8.5
9-27	Sea.	W	3-2		10	7	Crabtree	Sinclair	Wetteland	93-63	1st	+9.0
9-28	Sea.	W	10-0		15	5	Morgan	Halama		94-63	1st	+9.0
9-29	Sea.	L	3-7		9	13	Meche	Sele		94-64	1st	+9.0
9-30	Sea.	W	7-0		8	4	Burkett	Hinchliffe		95-64	1st	+10.0
10-1	At Ana.	L	6-7		8	9	Holtz	Morgan		95-65	1st	+9.0
10-2	At Ana.	L	3-15		9	14	Hasegawa	Helling		95-66	1st	+9.0
10-3	At Ana.	L	0-1		5	3	Washburn	Morgan	Pote	95-67	1st	+8.0

Monthly records: April (13-10), May (17-10), June (15-13), July (16-9), August (18-12), September (16-10), October (0-3).
*Innings, if other than nine. † First game of a doubleheader. ‡ Second game of a doubleheader.

MEMORABLE GAMES

May 31 at Texas
In the midst of what would become a season-long, nine-game winning streak that gives them solid control of the A.L. West, the Rangers rally for their third consecutive one-run victory. Down 3-0 at the start of the ninth, Lee Stevens hit a two-out, three-run homer to tie the game. The Rangers won it in the 10th on a Juan Gonzalez single.

Kansas City	AB	R	H	RBI	Texas	AB	R	H	RBI
C.Beltran, cf	5	0	1	0	T.Goodwin, cf	5	1	2	0
Sutton, 1b	5	1	1	0	McLemore, 2b	3	0	0	0
Damon, lf	3	1	2	0	Greer, lf	4	0	0	0
Mi.Sweeney, dh	4	0	1	1	J.Gonzlez, rf	5	0	1	1
Dye, rf	4	0	0	0	R.Palmro, dh	3	0	0	0
Kreuter, c	4	1	1	1	I.Rodriguez, c	4	1	1	0
Randa, 3b	5	0	2	0	Zeile, 3b	4	1	1	0
Scarsone, 2b	3	0	1	0	L.Stevens, 1b	3	1	1	3
R.Sanchez, ss	4	0	0	0	Shave, ss	3	0	1	0
Totals	37	3	9	2	Totals	34	4	7	4

Texas ....002 001 000 0—3
Anaheim ....000 000 0031 —4

DP—Texas 2. LOB—Kansas City 10, Texas 8. 2B—Sutton (6), Rodriguez (10). HR—Kreuter (3), L.Stevens (10). S—McLemore.

Kansas City	IP	H	R	ER	BB	SO
Suppan	7.2	3	0	0	2	6
Whisenant (H, 4)	0.1	0	0	0	1	0
J.Montgomery (BS 3)	1	2	3	3	1	2
J.Santiago (L, 2-3)	0.1	2	1	1	1	0

Texas	IP	H	R	ER	BB	SO
Glynn	6	6	3	3	5	5
Venafro	0.1	1	0	0	0	0
Patterson	1.2	1	0	0	1	1
Munoz	0.2	1	0	0	0	0
Crabtree (W, 4-0)	1.1	0	0	0	0	1

WP—Suppan, Whisenant, Glynn 2. U—HP, Cousins. 1B, Shulock. 2B, Scott. 3B, Brinkman. T—3:05. A—28,965.

June 30 at Anaheim
Texas displays true dominance of the A.L. West with an 18-4 thrashing of Anaheim for a three-game sweep. In 1998, the pesky Angels hung with the Rangers in the standings most of the year and wouldn't go away. This year, there would be no such thing.

Texas	AB	R	H	RBI	Anaheim	AB	R	H	RBI
McLemore, 2b	6	2	2	2	Erstad, lf-1b	3	0	1	0
I.Rodriguez, c	2	2	1	0	Sheets, ph-3b	2	0	0	0
Zaun, pr-c	2	1	0	0	O.Palmro, rf-lf	4	1	1	0
Greer, lf	6	3	3	0	M.Vaughn, 1b	2	0	0	0
J.Gonzalez, rf	4	2	2	1	R.Williams, rf	3	2	2	1
Sc.Green, ph-cf	2	0	1	0	Velarde, 2b	3	1	1	1
R.Palmeiro, dh	4	2	4	4	G.Andrson, cf	4	0	1	1
Alicea, ph-dh	2	1	1	0	T.Greene, dh	4	0	0	0
Zeile, 3b	4	3	4	4	Huson, 3b-1b	4	0	1	0
L.Stevens, 1b	3	1	0	2	Walbeck, c	3	0	0	0
R.Kelly, cf-rf	4	1	1	2	Hemphill, c	2	0	2	1
Clayton, ss	5	0	1	2	DiSarcina, ss	4	0	1	0
Shave, ss	1	0	0	0					
Totals	45	18	20	17	Totals	36	4	10	4

Texas ....302 611 302—18
Anaheim ....000 002 020—4

E—Huson (2), Sheets (10). DP—Texas 1, Anaheim 1. LOB—Texas 12, Anaheim 8. 2B—R.Palmeiro (17), Zeile 2 (22), R.Kelly (8), Velarde (10). 3B—R.Williams 2 (2). HR—McLemore (3). SB—McLemore (7), I.Rodriguez (16). SF—McLemore, Zeile, L.Stevens.

Texas	IP	H	R	ER	BB	SO
Glynn (W, 2-2)	6	4	2	2	3	5
Patterson	1	2	0	0	0	0
Venafro	1	4	2	2	0	1
Kolb	1	0	0	0	0	1

Anaheim	IP	H	R	ER	BB	SO
K.Hill (L, 3-8)	3.1	8	8	8	4	3
Schoeneweis	1.2	6	4	3	1	0
Holtz	2	4	4	4	2	0
Magnante	1	1	0	0	0	0
Hasegawa	1	2	0	0	1	0

HBP—R.Kelly by Hasegawa. U—HP, Reilly. 1B, Ford. 2B, Johnson. 3B, Garcia. T—3:15. A—23,450.

−133−

1999 REVIEW

BATTING

Name	G	TPA	AB	R	H	TB	2B	3B	HR	RBI	Avg.	Obp.	Slg.	SH	SF	HP	BB	IBB	SO	SB	CS	GDP	vs RHP AB	Avg	HR	RBI	vs LHP AB	Avg	HR	RBI
Rodriguez, Ivan	144	630	600	116	199	335	29	1	35	113	.332	.356	.558	0	5	1	24	2	64	25	12	31	486	.333	29	93	114	.325	6	20
Zeile, Todd	156	656	588	80	172	287	41	1	24	98	.293	.354	.488	1	7	4	56	3	94	1	2	20	471	.293	21	76	117	.291	3	22
McLemore, Mark	144	664	566	105	155	207	20	7	6	45	.274	.363	.366	9	6	0	83	2	79	16	8	8	462	.299	5	41	104	.163	1	4
Palmeiro, Rafael	158	674	565	96	183	356	30	1	47	148	.324	.420	.630	0	9	3	97	14	69	2	4	13	419	.341	36	108	146	.274	11	40
Gonzalez, Juan	144	629	562	114	183	338	36	1	39	128	.326	.378	.601	0	12	4	51	7	105	3	3	10	448	.321	30	105	114	.342	9	23
Greer, Rusty	147	662	556	107	167	274	41	3	20	101	.300	.405	.493	0	5	5	96	2	67	2	2	17	432	.306	17	77	124	.282	3	24
Stevens, Lee	146	576	517	76	146	251	31	1	24	81	.282	.344	.485	0	7	0	52	10	132	2	3	19	415	.277	20	58	102	.304	4	23
Clayton, Royce	133	520	465	69	134	207	21	5	14	52	.288	.346	.445	3	4	3	39	1	100	8	6	6	367	.283	9	29	98	.306	5	23
Goodwin, Tom	109	455	405	63	105	138	12	6	3	33	.259	.324	.341	7	3	0	40	0	61	39	11	7	344	.259	3	29	61	.262	0	4
Kelly, Roberto	87	319	290	41	87	130	17	1	8	37	.300	.355	.448	0	2	5	21	0	57	6	1	5	195	.272	6	23	95	.358	2	14
Alicea, Luis	68	196	164	33	33	52	10	0	3	17	.201	.316	.317	3	1	0	28	0	32	2	1	4	102	.147	2	12	62	.290	1	5
Mateo, Ruben	32	127	122	16	29	55	9	1	5	18	.238	.268	.451	0	0	1	4	0	28	3	0	2	102	.216	4	14	20	.350	1	4
Zaun, Gregg	43	106	93	12	23	30	2	1	1	12	.247	.314	.323	1	2	0	10	0	7	1	0	2	74	.257	1	12	19	.211	0	0
Shave, Jon	43	83	73	10	21	25	4	0	0	9	.288	.350	.342	3	0	2	5	0	17	1	0	0	47	.255	0	3	26	.346	0	6
Dransfeldt, Kelly	16	57	53	3	10	14	1	0	1	5	.189	.232	.264	1	0	0	3	0	12	0	0	2	46	.174	1	5	7	.286	0	0
Green, Scarborough	18	14	13	4	4	4	0	0	0	0	.308	.357	.308	0	0	0	1	0	2	0	1	0	6	.333	0	0	7	.286	0	0
Morgan, Mike	34	4	4	0	1	1	0	0	0	0	.250	.250	.250	0	0	0	0	0	2	0	0	0	4	.250	0	0	0	.000	0	0
Sele, Aaron	33	6	4	0	0	0	0	0	0	0	.000	.200	.000	1	0	0	1	0	2	0	0	0	4	.000	0	0	0	.000	0	0
Simms, Mike	4	2	2	0	1	1	0	0	0	0	.500	.500	.500	0	0	0	0	0	1	0	0	0	2	.500	0	0	0	.000	0	0
Burkett, John	30	2	2	0	0	0	0	0	0	0	.000	.000	.000	0	0	0	0	0	2	0	0	0	2	.000	0	0	0	.000	0	0
Clark, Mark	15	2	2	0	0	0	0	0	0	0	.000	.000	.000	0	0	0	0	0	2	0	0	0	1	.000	0	0	1	.000	0	0
Helling, Rick	35	2	2	0	0	0	0	0	0	0	.000	.000	.000	0	0	0	0	0	2	0	0	0	2	.000	0	0	0	.000	0	0
Patterson, Danny	53	1	1	0	0	0	0	0	0	0	.000	.000	.000	0	0	0	0	0	0	0	0	0	1	.000	0	0	0	.000	0	0
Sheldon, Scott	2	1	1	0	0	0	0	0	0	0	.000	.000	.000	0	0	0	0	0	0	0	0	0	1	.000	0	0	0	.000	0	0
Glynn, Ryan	13	1	1	0	0	0	0	0	0	0	.000	.000	.000	0	0	0	0	0	0	0	0	1	1	.000	0	0	0	.000	0	0
Wetteland, John	62	0	0	0	0	0	0	0	0	0	.000	.000	.000	0	0	0	0	0	0	0	0	0	0	.000	0	0	0	.000	0	0
Munoz, Mike	56	0	0	0	0	0	0	0	0	0	.000	.000	.000	0	0	0	0	0	0	0	0	0	0	.000	0	0	0	.000	0	0
Loaiza, Esteban	30	0	0	0	0	0	0	0	0	0	.000	.000	.000	0	0	0	0	0	0	0	0	0	0	.000	0	0	0	.000	0	0
Crabtree, Tim	68	0	0	0	0	0	0	0	0	0	.000	.000	.000	0	0	0	0	0	0	0	0	0	0	.000	0	0	0	.000	0	0
Zimmerman, Jeff	65	0	0	0	0	0	0	0	0	0	.000	.000	.000	0	0	0	0	0	0	0	0	0	0	.000	0	0	0	.000	0	0
Venafro, Mike	65	0	0	0	0	0	0	0	0	0	.000	.000	.000	0	0	0	0	0	0	0	0	0	0	.000	0	0	0	.000	0	0
Kolb, Danny	16	0	0	0	0	0	0	0	0	0	.000	.000	.000	0	0	0	0	0	0	0	0	0	0	.000	0	0	0	.000	0	0
Fassero, Jeff	7	0	0	0	0	0	0	0	0	0	.000	.000	.000	0	0	0	0	0	0	0	0	0	0	.000	0	0	0	.000	0	0

Players with more than one A.L. team

Name	G	TPA	AB	R	H	TB	2B	3B	HR	RBI	Avg.	Obp.	Slg.	SH	SF	HP	BB	IBB	SO	SB	CS	GDP	vs RHP AB	Avg	HR	RBI	vs LHP AB	Avg	HR	RBI
Fassero, Sea.	30	7	7	0	0	0	0	0	0	0	.000	.000	.000	0	0	0	0	0	5	0	0	0	0	.000	0	0	0	.000	0	0
Fassero, Sea.-Tex.	37	7	7	0	0	0	0	0	0	0	.000	.000	.000	0	0	0	0	0	5	0	0	0	3	.000	0	0	4	.000	0	0

PITCHING

Name	W	L	Pct.	ERA	IP	H	R	ER	HR	SH	SF	HB	BB	IBB	SO	G	GS	CG	ShO	GF	Sv	vs RH AB	Avg	HR	RBI	vs LH AB	Avg	HR	RBI
Helling, Rick	13	11	.542	4.84	219.1	228	127	118	41	5	10	6	85	5	131	35	35	3	0	0	0	436	.282	21	62	401	.262	20	50
Sele, Aaron	18	9	.667	4.79	205.0	244	115	109	21	1	3	12	70	3	186	33	33	2	2	0	0	435	.299	10	48	399	.286	11	56
Burkett, John	9	8	.529	5.62	147.1	184	95	92	18	5	3	3	46	1	96	30	25	0	0	1	0	292	.336	11	55	307	.280	7	31
Morgan, Mike	13	10	.565	6.24	140.0	184	108	97	25	3	5	7	48	2	61	34	25	1	0	1	0	295	.329	11	49	274	.318	14	47
Loaiza, Esteban	9	5	.643	4.56	120.1	128	65	61	10	7	4	0	40	2	77	30	15	0	0	4	0	252	.290	9	32	214	.257	1	25
Zimmerman, Jeff	9	3	.750	2.36	87.2	50	24	23	9	3	6	2	23	1	67	65	0	0	0	14	3	156	.173	3	19	146	.158	6	13
Clark, Mark	3	7	.300	8.60	74.1	103	73	71	17	1	4	1	34	1	44	15	15	0	0	0	0	154	.331	4	26	159	.327	13	37
Venafro, Mike	3	2	.600	3.29	68.1	63	29	25	4	5	2	3	22	0	37	65	0	0	0	11	0	137	.299	3	26	114	.193	1	14
Wetteland, John	4	4	.500	3.68	66.0	67	30	27	9	1	5	0	19	1	60	62	0	0	0	59	43	120	.258	5	14	136	.265	4	16
Crabtree, Tim	5	1	.833	3.46	65.0	71	26	25	4	1	1	1	18	1	54	68	0	0	0	21	0	156	.314	3	27	98	.224	1	10
Patterson, Danny	2	0	1.000	5.67	60.1	77	38	38	5	0	2	1	19	3	43	53	0	0	0	18	0	167	.281	5	26	86	.349	0	18
Glynn, Ryan	2	4	.333	7.24	54.2	71	46	44	10	0	1	1	35	0	39	13	10	0	0	2	0	110	.291	4	21	115	.339	6	20
Munoz, Mike	2	1	.667	3.93	52.2	52	24	23	5	1	3	1	18	2	27	56	0	0	0	11	1	98	.235	2	8	100	.290	3	17
Kolb, Danny	2	1	.667	4.65	31.0	33	18	16	2	0	0	1	15	0	15	16	0	0	0	6	0	73	.260	2	7	50	.280	0	4
Fassero, Jeff	1	0	1.000	5.71	17.1	20	12	11	1	1	1	0	10	0	13	7	3	0	0	1	0	57	.246	1	6	13	.462	0	6
Perisho, Matt	0	0	.000	2.61	10.1	8	3	3	0	0	0	0	2	1	17	4	1	0	0	3	0	27	.148	0	3	11	.364	0	0
Gunderson, Eric	0	0	.000	7.20	10.0	20	8	8	1	0	1	0	2	0	6	11	0	0	0	3	0	25	.440	0	5	23	.391	1	6
Johnson, Jonathan	0	0	.000	15.00	3.0	9	5	5	0	0	1	1	2	0	3	1	0	0	0	0	0	10	.400	0	5	7	.714	0	2
Davis, Doug	0	0	.000	33.75	2.2	12	10	10	3	0	0	0	3	0	3	2	0	0	0	0	0	10	.800	2	7	10	.400	1	5
Lee, Corey	0	0	.000	27.00	1.0	2	3	3	1	0	0	0	1	0	1	1	0	0	0	1	0	2	.000	0	0	3	.667	1	3

PITCHERS WITH MORE THAN ONE A.L. TEAM

Name	W	L	Pct.	ERA	IP	H	R	ER	HR	SH	SF	HB	BB	IBB	SO	G	GS	CG	ShO	GF	Sv	vs RH AB	Avg	HR	RBI	vs LH AB	Avg	HR	RBI
Fassero, Sea.	4	14	.222	7.38	139.0	188	123	114	34	1	6	4	73	3	101	30	24	0	0	1	0	57	.246	1	6	13	.462	0	6
Fassero, Sea.-Tex.	5	14	.263	7.20	156.1	208	135	125	35	2	7	4	83	3	114	37	27	0	0	7	0	515	.330	32	102	140	.271	3	26

DESIGNATED HITTERS

Name	AB	Avg.	HR	RBI	Name	AB	Avg.	HR	RBI	Name	AB	Avg.	HR	RBI
Palmeiro, Rafael	458	.321	37	115	Zeile, Todd	3	.333	1	2	McLemore, Mark	0	-	0	0
Gonzalez, Juan	56	.393	3	16	Simms, Mike	2	.500	0	0	Greer, Rusty	0	-	0	0
Stevens, Lee	32	.250	2	5	Shave, Jon	1	1.000	0	0	Mateo, Ruben	0	-	0	0
Alicea, Luis	9	.222	0	0	Green, Scarborough	0	-	0	0					
Rodriguez, Ivan	4	.000	0	0	Zaun, Gregg	0	-	0	0					

INDIVIDUAL STATISTICS
FIELDING

FIRST BASEMEN
Player	Pct.	G	PO	A	E	TC	DP
Stevens, Lee	.994	133	1228	60	8	1296	128
Palmeiro, Rafael	.996	28	261	13	1	275	23
Shave, Jon	1.000	9	43	1	0	44	7
Simms, Mike	1.000	1	0	1	0	1	0
Zeile, Todd	1.000	1	1	0	0	1	0

SECOND BASEMEN
Player	Pct.	G	PO	A	E	TC	DP
McLemore, Mark	.983	135	261	433	12	706	93
Alicea, Luis	.980	37	60	87	3	150	19
Shave, Jon	1.000	1	1	1	0	2	1

THIRD BASEMEN
Player	Pct.	G	PO	A	E	TC	DP
Zeile, Todd	.941	155	104	294	25	423	23
Alicea, Luis	.905	10	6	13	2	21	3
Shave, Jon	.889	6	2	6	1	9	1
Sheldon, Scott	1.000	2	2	3	0	5	0

SHORTSTOPS
Player	Pct.	G	PO	A	E	TC	DP
Clayton, Royce	.961	133	204	406	25	635	91
Shave, Jon	.953	24	26	55	4	85	14
Dransfeldt, Kelly	.966	16	31	54	3	88	13

OUTFIELDERS
Player	Pct.	G	PO	A	E	TC	DP
Greer, Rusty	.983	145	286	3	5	294	1
Gonzalez, Juan	.983	131	223	7	4	234	3
Goodwin, Tom	.989	107	258	4	3	265	0
Kelly, Roberto	.981	85	155	4	3	162	2
Mateo, Ruben	1.000	31	62	3	0	65	0
McLemore, Mark	1.000	11	15	0	0	15	0
Green, Scarborough	1.000	9	6	0	0	6	0
Alicea, Luis	-	1	0	0	0	0	0
Simms, Mike	-	1	0	0	0	0	0

CATCHERS
Player	Pct.	G	PO	A	E	TC	DP	PB
Rodriguez, Ivan	.993	141	850	83	7	940	13	1
Zaun, Gregg	.984	37	165	15	3	183	0	1

PITCHERS
Player	Pct.	G	PO	A	E	TC	DP
Crabtree, Tim	1.000	68	6	4	0	10	0
Venafro, Mike	1.000	65	2	18	0	20	0
Zimmerman, Jeff	1.000	65	3	7	0	10	0
Wetteland, John	.875	62	2	5	1	8	0
Munoz, Mike	.923	56	3	9	1	13	2
Patterson, Danny	1.000	53	3	6	0	9	1
Helling, Rick	.903	35	4	24	3	31	2
Morgan, Mike	.943	34	7	26	2	35	3
Sele, Aaron	.950	33	8	30	2	40	2
Burkett, John	1.000	30	7	18	0	25	2
Loaiza, Esteban	1.000	30	8	17	0	25	0
Kolb, Danny	1.000	16	1	7	0	8	0
Clark, Mark	.875	15	3	4	1	8	1
Glynn, Ryan	1.000	13	2	3	0	5	0
Gunderson, Eric	1.000	11	0	1	0	1	0
Fassero, Jeff	1.000	7	0	2	0	2	0
Perisho, Matt	1.000	4	0	2	0	2	0
Davis, Doug	1.000	2	0	1	0	1	0
Johnson, Jonathan	-	1	0	0	0	0	0
Lee, Corey	-	1	0	0	0	0	0

PITCHING AGAINST EACH CLUB

Pitcher	Ana. W-L	Bal. W-L	Bos. W-L	Chi. W-L	Cle. W-L	Det. W-L	K.C. W-L	Min. W-L	N.Y. W-L	Oak. W-L	Sea. W-L	T.B. W-L	Tor. W-L	N.L. W-L	Total W-L
Burkett, John	2-1	0-1	0-0	1-1	2-0	0-0	0-0	0-0	0-2	2-1	1-0	0-2	1-0	0-0	9-8
Clark, Mark	0-1	0-0	0-1	0-0	1-0	0-0	0-0	0-1	0-1	0-1	1-0	1-0	0-1	0-2	3-7
Crabtree, Tim	0-0	2-0	0-0	0-0	0-0	0-0	1-0	0-0	0-0	0-0	2-1	0-0	0-0	0-0	5-1
Davis, Doug	0-0	0-0	0-0	0-0	0-0	0-0	0-0	0-0	0-0	0-0	0-0	0-0	0-0	0-0	0-0
Fassero, Jeff	0-0	0-0	0-0	1-0	0-0	0-0	0-0	0-0	0-0	0-0	0-0	0-0	0-0	0-0	1-0
Glynn, Ryan	1-0	0-0	0-1	0-0	0-0	0-0	0-0	0-0	0-1	0-1	0-0	0-0	0-0	0-0	2-4
Gunderson, Eric	0-0	0-0	0-0	0-0	0-0	0-0	0-0	0-0	0-0	0-0	0-0	0-0	0-0	0-0	0-0
Helling, Rick	0-2	1-2	2-1	1-1	1-0	2-1	0-1	1-0	1-1	0-0	0-0	2-1	1-0	1-1	13-11
Johnson, Jonathan	0-0	0-0	0-0	0-0	0-0	0-0	0-0	0-0	0-0	0-0	0-0	0-0	0-0	0-0	0-0
Kolb, Danny	0-0	0-0	0-0	0-0	0-0	0-1	0-0	1-0	0-0	0-0	1-0	0-0	0-0	0-0	2-1
Lee, Corey	0-0	0-0	0-0	0-0	0-0	0-0	0-0	0-0	0-1	0-0	0-0	0-0	0-0	0-0	0-1
Loaiza, Esteban	0-0	0-0	1-0	1-1	0-0	0-1	1-1	2-0	1-0	1-0	0-0	0-0	0-0	1-1	9-5
Morgan, Mike	1-2	2-1	1-0	0-0	0-2	1-0	0-0	0-0	2-1	2-0	0-1	0-1	1-1	1-1	13-10
Munoz, Mike	0-0	0-0	0-0	0-0	1-0	0-0	0-0	0-0	0-1	0-0	0-0	0-0	0-0	0-0	2-1
Patterson, Danny	0-0	0-0	0-0	0-0	0-0	1-0	0-0	0-0	0-0	0-0	0-0	0-0	0-0	0-0	2-0
Perisho, Matt	0-0	0-0	0-0	0-0	0-0	0-0	0-0	0-0	0-0	0-0	0-0	0-0	0-0	0-0	0-0
Sele, Aaron	2-0	1-1	1-1	0-0	2-1	1-1	2-1	1-0	1-1	0-2	1-0	2-0	2-1	2-1	18-9
Venafro, Mike	0-0	0-0	0-0	0-0	0-0	0-0	0-0	0-0	0-0	0-1	1-0	0-0	0-1	2-0	3-2
Wetteland, John	0-0	0-0	0-0	0-0	0-0	0-0	0-0	1-0	1-0	0-1	1-0	0-0	0-0	1-2	4-4
Zimmerman, Jeff	0-0	0-0	0-0	1-1	0-0	0-1	0-0	2-0	0-0	0-0	1-0	1-0	0-1	2-0	9-3
Totals	6-6	6-6	5-4	5-4	5-5	7-3	5-5	6-4	12-0	4-8	7-5	8-5	8-4	6-4	10-8 95-67

INTERLEAGUE: Sele 1-0, Zimmerman 1-0, Clark 0-1 vs. Dodgers; Sele 1-0, Wetteland 0-1, Loaiza 0-1 vs. Padres; Morgan 1-0, Loaiza 1-0, Helling 1-0 vs. Giants; Zimmerman 1-0, Sele 0-1, Morgan 0-1 vs. Rockies; Venafro 2-0, Wetteland 1-1, Clark 0-1, Helling 0-1 vs. Diamondbacks. Total: 10-8.

MISCELLANEOUS

HOME RUNS BY PARK

At Anaheim (8): Gonzalez 2, Clayton 2, McLemore 1, Palmeiro 1, Rodriguez 1, Goodwin 1.

At Arizona (5): Palmeiro 2, Gonzalez 2, Clayton 1.

At Baltimore (12): Palmeiro 2, Gonzalez 2, Rodriguez 2, McLemore 1, Kelly 1, Alicea 1, Zeile 1, Clayton 1, Mateo 1.

At Boston (5): Rodriguez 2, Zeile 1, Gonzalez 1, Stevens 1.

At Chicago (AL) (13): Greer 5, Gonzalez 2, Stevens 2, Rodriguez 2, Palmeiro 1, Zeile 1.

At Cleveland (10): Palmeiro 3, Rodriguez 2, Clayton 2, McLemore 1, Alicea 1, Gonzalez 1.

At Detroit (10): Gonzalez 2, Greer 2, Palmeiro 1, Alicea 1, Zeile 1, Rodriguez 1, Clayton 1, Zaun 1.

At Kansas City (3): Palmeiro 1, Gonzalez 1, Rodriguez 1.

At Los Angeles (1): Gonzalez 1.

At Minnesota (13): Palmeiro 3, Stevens 3, Kelly 2, Zeile 2, Rodriguez 2, Gonzalez 1.

At New York (AL) (4): Gonzalez 2, Zeile 1, Stevens 1.

At Oakland (5): Stevens 2, Palmeiro 1, Zeile 1, Rodriguez 1.

At San Diego (7): Palmeiro 2, Mateo 2, Gonzalez 1, Rodriguez 1, Clayton 1.

At Tampa Bay (12): Rodriguez 3, Zeile 2, Gonzalez 2, Stevens 2, Palmeiro 1, Kelly 1, Greer 1.

At Texas (103): Palmeiro 28, Gonzalez 14, Zeile 13, Rodriguez 12, Stevens 10, Greer 10, Clayton 6, Kelly 4, McLemore 2, Mateo 2, Goodwin 1, Dransfeldt 1.

At Toronto (10): Gonzalez 3, McLemore 1, Palmeiro 1, Zeile 1, Stevens 1, Rodriguez 1, Goodwin 1, Greer 1.

LOW-HIT GAMES

No-hitters: None.
One-hitters: None.
Two-hitters: None.

10-STRIKEOUT GAMES

Aaron Sele 3, Rick Helling 2, Matt Perisho 1, **Total:** 6.

FOUR OR MORE HITS IN ONE GAME

Ivan Rodriguez 6 (including one five-hit game), Todd Zeile 4, Rafael Palmeiro 3, Juan Gonzalez 2, Mark McLemore 1, Lee Stevens 1, Tom Goodwin 1, Rusty Greer 1, Ruben Mateo 1, **Total:** 20.

MULTI-HOMER GAMES

Juan Gonzalez 5, Ivan Rodriguez 5, Rafael Palmeiro 3, Rusty Greer 2, Roberto Kelly 1, Lee Stevens 1, **Total:** 17.

GRAND SLAMS

4-13: Ivan Rodriguez (off Seattle's Makoto Suzuki).
5-11: Rusty Greer (off Chicago's Bryan Ward).
5-13: Roberto Kelly (off Baltimore's Scott Kamieniecki).
6-5: Rafael Palmeiro (off Arizona's Darren Holmes).
7-22: Rafael Palmeiro (off Anaheim's Steve Sparks).
9-6: Todd Zeile (off Chicago's Jim Parque).
9-25: Todd Zeile (off Oakland's Kevin Appier).
9-26: Rafael Palmeiro (off Oakland's Tim Kubinski).

PINCH HITTERS
(Minimum 5 at-bats)
Name	AB	Avg.	HR	RBI
Alicea, Luis	14	.143	0	0
Kelly, Roberto	7	.143	0	1
Zaun, Gregg	5	.400	0	1
Stevens, Lee	5	.200	0	1

DEBUTS

4-13: Jeff Zimmerman, P.
4-24: Mike Venafro, P.
5-1: Kelly Dransfeldt, SS.
5-16: Ryan Glynn, P.
6-4: Danny Kolb, P.
6-12: Ruben Mateo, CF.
8-9: Doug Davis, P.
8-24: Corey Lee, P.

GAMES BY POSITION

Catcher: Ivan Rodriguez 141, Gregg Zaun 37.
First base: Lee Stevens 133, Rafael Palmeiro 28, Jon Shave 9, Todd Zeile 1, Mike Simms 1.
Second base: Mark McLemore 135, Luis Alicea 37, Jon Shave 1.
Third base: Todd Zeile 155, Luis Alicea 10, Jon Shave 6, Scott Sheldon 2.
Shortstop: Royce Clayton 133, Jon Shave 24, Kelly Dransfeldt 16.
Outfield: Rusty Greer 145, Juan Gonzalez 131, Tom Goodwin 107, Roberto Kelly 85, Ruben Mateo 31, Mark McLemore 11, Scarborough Green 9, Luis Alicea 1, Mike Simms 1.
Designated hitter: Rafael Palmeiro 128, Juan Gonzalez 14, Lee Stevens 8, Luis Alicea 7, Scarborough Green 4, Jon Shave 3, Mike Simms 2, Gregg Zaun 2, Mark McLemore 1, Todd Zeile 1, Ivan Rodriguez 1, Rusty Greer 1, Ruben Mateo 1.

STREAKS

Wins: 9 (May 23-June 2, July 18-27).
Losses: 4 (October 1-April 5, June 12-15, June 19-22, July 3-6, August 12-14).
Consecutive games with at least one hit: 20, Ivan Rodriguez (May 8-June 1).
Wins by pitcher: 4, Aaron Sele (July 21-August 7), Rick Helling (August 21-September 6), Esteban Loaiza (July 19-August 4).

ATTENDANCE

Home: 2,774,514.
Road: 2,080,223.
Highest (home): 47,204 (July 4 vs. Seattle).
Highest (road): 56,530 (June 27 vs. Seattle).
Lowest (home): 23,175 (April 11 vs. Anaheim).
Lowest (road): 7,490 (July 5 vs. Oakland).

1999 REVIEW

DAY BY DAY

Date	Opp.	Res.	Score	(inn.*)	Hits	Opp. hits	Winning pitcher	Losing pitcher	Save	Record	Pos.	GB
4-6	At Min.	L	1-6		10	15	Radke	Hentgen		0-1	T4th	1.0
4-7	At Min.	W	9-3		15	7	Wells	Lincoln	Halladay	1-1	T3rd	1.0
4-8	At Min.	L	9-11		13	15	Trombley	Hamilton	Aguilera	1-2	T4th	2.0
4-9	At Bal.	W	7-4		8	6	Escobar	Ponson		2-2	T3rd	2.0
4-10	At Bal.	L	0-1		6	6	Mussina	Carpenter	Timlin	2-3	T3rd	3.0
4-11	At Bal.	W	9-5		10	8	Halladay	Orosco		3-3	T3rd	2.0
4-12	T.B.	W	7-1		12	6	Wells	Saunders		4-3	3rd	1.5
4-13	T.B.	L	5-8		11	15	White	Hamilton	Hernandez	4-4	T3rd	2.5
4-14	T.B.	W	7-6	(11)	12	12	Lloyd	Lopez		5-4	3rd	2.5
4-15	T.B.	W	11-1		11	2	Carpenter	Santana		6-4	3rd	1.5
4-16	Bal.	W	7-6		10	12	Lloyd	Bones	Person	7-4	3rd	0.5
4-17	Bal.	W	7-4		10	7	Wells	Linton	Lloyd	8-4	2nd	...
4-18	Bal.	W	6-0		7	3	Halladay	Guzman		9-4	1st	+1.0
4-20	Ana.	W	5-1		7	8	Escobar	Finley		10-4	1st	+1.5
4-21	Ana.	W	3-2		10	8	Carpenter	Olivares	Person	11-4	1st	+1.5
4-22	Ana.	W	8-7		13	8	Davey	Petkovsek	Lloyd	12-4	1st	+2.0
4-23	At N.Y.	L	4-6		10	9	Hernandez	Wells	Rivera	12-5	1st	+1.0
4-24	At N.Y.	L	4-7		9	9	Mendoza	Plesac	Rivera	12-6	2nd	...
4-25	At N.Y.	L	3-4	(11)	5	9	Grimsley	Person		12-7	2nd	1.0
4-26	At Ana.	L	3-4	(11)	8	10	Percival	Rodriguez		12-8	2nd	1.5
4-27	At Ana.	W	10-1		13	5	Hentgen	Olivares		13-8	2nd	1.5
4-28	At Ana.	L	10-12		15	14	Petkovsek	Lloyd	Percival	13-9	2nd	1.5
4-29	At Ana.	L	1-17		4	15	Hill	Halladay		13-10	2nd	2.5
4-30	At Sea.	L	9-11		12	10	Halama	Person	Mesa	13-11	2nd	2.5
5-1	At Sea.	W	9-3		13	11	Carpenter	Moyer	Davey	14-11	2nd	2.5
5-2	At Sea.	L	2-3		8	7	Cloude	Plesac		14-12	2nd	3.5
5-3	At Sea.	W	16-10		17	13	Wells	Garcia		15-12	2nd	2.5
5-4	Oak.	L	4-13		11	13	Oquist	Halladay	Jones	15-13	2nd	2.5
5-5	Oak.	L	2-8		5	15	Rogers	Escobar		15-14	T2nd	3.5
5-6	Oak.	L	2-3		10	6	Heredia	Carpenter	Taylor	15-15	3rd	4.5
5-7	Tex.	W	9-6		17	7	Hentgen	Clark	Koch	16-15	T2nd	4.5
5-8	Tex.	L	3-4		7	7	Morgan	Wells	Wetteland	16-16	4th	4.5
5-9	Tex.	L	6-11		8	20	Patterson	Munro		16-17	4th	5.5
5-11	At K.C.	W	8-2		14	10	Escobar	Pittsley		17-17	T3rd	4.5
5-12	At K.C.	L	1-7		3	11	Appier	Carpenter		17-18	T3rd	4.5
5-13	At K.C.	W	8-2		13	10	Hentgen	Rosado		18-18	3rd	3.5
5-14	Bos.	L	0-5		6	11	Pena	Wells		18-19	3rd	3.5
5-15	Bos.	L	5-6		10	14	Wasdin	Plesac	Gordon	18-20	4th	3.5
5-16	Bos.	W	9-6		11	12	Lloyd	Gross		19-20	4th	3.5
5-17	Bos.	L	7-8		13	13	Wasdin	Lloyd		19-21	4th	4.0
5-18	Det.	W	7-5		8	9	Hentgen	Thompson	Koch	20-21	4th	3.5
5-19	Det.	L	3-7		6	11	Moehler	Wells		20-22	4th	4.5
5-20	Det.	W	7-0		14	7	Halladay	Mlicki		21-22	4th	3.5
5-21	At Bos.	L	2-5		4	5	Rapp	Escobar		21-23	4th	4.5
5-22	At Bos.	L	4-6		6	14	Wakefield	Carpenter	Gordon	21-24	4th	5.5
5-23	At Bos.	L	8-10		15	13	Martinez	Hentgen	Gordon	21-25	4th	6.5
5-24	At Det.	W	12-6		8	10	Wells	Moehler		22-25	4th	6.0
5-25	At Det.	W	5-3		8	11	Halladay	Mlicki	Koch	23-25	3rd	6.0
5-26	At Det.	W	9-5		12	7	Escobar	Blair	Lloyd	24-25	3rd	5.0
5-28	N.Y.	L	6-10		9	16	Pettitte	Carpenter		24-26	3rd	5.5
5-29	N.Y.	L	3-8		7	12	Cone	Hentgen		24-27	3rd	6.5
5-30	N.Y.	L	3-8		8	9	Irabu	Wells		24-28	3rd	7.5
6-1	Chi.	L	2-6		7	13	Sirotka	Escobar		24-29	3rd	9.0
6-2	Chi.	W	9-7		15	15	Carpenter	Snyder	Koch	25-29	3rd	8.0
6-3	Chi.	L	3-10		7	16	Navarro	Hentgen		25-30	3rd	8.5
6-4	Mon.	W	6-2		9	6	Wells	Ayala		26-30	3rd	8.5
6-5	Mon.	L	0-5		3	6	Batista	Hamilton		26-31	3rd	8.5
6-6	Mon.	W	9-2		13	8	Escobar	Hermanson		27-31	3rd	7.5
6-7	At N.Y. (NL)	L	2-8		8	14	Hershiser	Halladay		27-32	3rd	7.5
6-8	At N.Y. (NL)	L	3-11		4	14	Isringhausen	Hentgen		27-33	3rd	7.5
6-9	At N.Y. (NL)	L	3-4	(14)	15	11	Mahomes	Davey		27-34	3rd	8.0
6-11	At Phi.	L	4-8		9	9	Wolf	Hamilton		27-35	3rd	9.0
6-12	At Phi.	L	2-7		6	9	Byrd	Escobar		27-36	3rd	10.0
6-13	At Phi.	W	7-2		13	4	Hentgen	Schilling		28-36	3rd	9.0
6-15	Ana.	W	13-2		18	6	Wells	Belcher		29-36	3rd	9.5
6-16	Ana.	W	3-2		8	6	Lloyd	Schoeneweis	Koch	30-36	3rd	8.5
6-17	Ana.	W	3-0		5	8	Escobar	Hill	Koch	31-36	3rd	7.5
6-18	K.C.	L	5-6		12	10	Witasick	Hentgen	Whisenant	31-37	3rd	8.5
6-19	K.C.	W	7-0		10	3	Halladay	Appier		32-37	3rd	8.5
6-20	K.C.	W	2-1		5	4	Wells	Service		33-37	3rd	7.5
6-21	K.C.	W	11-4		13	12	Hamilton	Fussell		34-37	3rd	7.0
6-22	Cle.	W	4-3		6	8	Escobar	Gooden	Koch	35-37	3rd	7.0
6-23	Cle.	L	6-9		10	12	Nagy	Quantrill		35-38	3rd	8.0
6-24	Cle.	W	3-0		5	3	Halladay	Burba	Koch	36-38	3rd	8.0
6-25	At T.B.	L	4-11		6	14	Alvarez	Wells		36-39	3rd	9.0
6-26	At T.B.	L	2-5		12	9	Rupe	Hamilton	Hernandez	36-40	3rd	10.0
6-27	At T.B.	L	0-8		3	10	Witt	Escobar		36-41	3rd	11.0
6-28	At T.B.	W	3-2		10	8	Carpenter	Eiland	Koch	37-41	3rd	10.5
6-29	Bal.	W	6-5	(10)	10	12	Frascatore	Rhodes		38-41	3rd	10.5
6-30	Bal.	W	10-9	(10)	12	16	Frascatore	Orosco		39-41	3rd	9.5

HIGHLIGHTS

High point: With first baseman Carlos Delgado hitting his eighth homer in six games, the Blue Jays improved their record to 65-51 on August 11 with a victory over the Twins. They held a one-game lead on Boston in the wild-card race.

Low point: The Blue Jays lost all six games of a mid-August homestand against Oakland and Seattle, then got swept by Texas in late August for a nine-game losing streak at SkyDome. In between, assistant G.M. Dave Stewart questioned the players' intensity.

Turning point: When Toronto lost 10 of 13 games in a stretch ending September 21, shattering the club's wild-card hopes.

Most valuable player: Outfielder Shawn Green, followed closely by shortstop Tony Batista. Green followed his first 30-30 season by establishing career highs in batting average, runs, home runs and RBIs. Batista, obtained from Arizona in June, was a revelation. In 98 games, he had 26 homers and 79 RBIs.

Most valuable pitcher: Billy Koch, who had been a starter at Class AAA Syracuse before being called up in May. Soon designated as the Jays' closer, he converted 31 of 35 save opportunities in his rookie season.

Most improved player: Coming off a solid 1998 season, catcher Darrin Fletcher bumped up his numbers with a .291 average, 18 homers and 80 RBIs.

Most pleasant surprise: After coming over from the Yankees in the Roger Clemens trade, Homer Bush asked not to be compared with former Jays standout second baseman Roberto Alomar. Bush gave a good imitation, though, batting .320 and stealing 32 bases.

Key injuries: Shortstop Alex Gonzalez suffered a shoulder tear and didn't play after May 16. Bush was sidelined for a month with a ligament tear in a finger. Fletcher was out nearly a month after being struck in the eye by a ball that ricocheted off a batting cage. Setup man Paul Quantrill, recovering from a broken leg incurred in a snowmobiling accident, missed the first 10 weeks. Hamilton was shut down for the season after an August 31 start against Minnesota. Starter Chris Carpenter was out most of June with elbow inflammation and underwent surgery in September. Middle reliever Bill Risley missed the entire season because of back problems.

Notable: Green established a franchise record with a 28-game hitting streak. ... David Wells led the A.L. in complete games with seven and topped all of the league's lefthanders in victories with 17. ... Delgado tied George Bell's club record of 134 RBIs despite missing the last 10 games because of injury. ... Delgado (44) and Green (42) combined for 86 homers.
—TOM MALONEY

MISCELLANEOUS

RECORDS

1999 regular-season record: 84-78 (3rd in A.L. East); 40-41 at home; 44-37 on road; 24-25 vs. A.L. East; 34-20 vs. A.L. Central; 17-24 vs. A.L. West; 9-9 vs. N.L. East; 13-15 vs. lefthanded starters; 71-63 vs. righthanded starters; 33-26 on grass; 51-52 on turf; 27-26 in daytime; 57-52 at night; 26-18 in one-run games; 6-3 in extra-inning games; 0-0-0 in doubleheaders.

Team record past five years: 378-414 (.477, ranks 9th in league in that span).

TEAM LEADERS

Batting average: Tony Fernandez (.328).
At-bats: Shawn Green (614).
Runs: Shawn Green (134).
Hits: Shawn Green (190).
Total bases: Shawn Green (361).
Doubles: Shawn Green (45).
Triples: Homer Bush (4).
Home runs: Carlos Delgado (44).
Runs batted in: Carlos Delgado (134).
Stolen bases: Shannon Stewart (37).
Slugging percentage: Shawn Green (.588).
On-base percentage: Tony Fernandez (.427).
Wins: David Wells (17).
Earned-run average: Pat Hentgen (4.79).
Complete games: David Wells (7).
Shutouts: Chris Carpenter, Roy Halladay, David Wells (1).
Saves: Billy Koch (31).
Innings pitched: David Wells (231.2).
Strikeouts: David Wells (169).

Date	Opp.	Res.	Score	(inn.*)	Hits	Opp. hits	Winning pitcher	Losing pitcher	Save	Record	Pos.	GB
7-1	Bal.	W	8-6		10	9	Frascatore	Timlin	Koch	40-41	3rd	9.5
7-2	T.B.	L	7-8		14	11	Aldred	Escobar	Hernandez	40-42	3rd	10.5
7-3	T.B.	W	5-0		13	3	Carpenter	Witt		41-42	3rd	10.5
7-4	T.B.	W	6-3		10	11	Hentgen	White	Koch	42-42	3rd	9.5
7-6	At Bal.	W	4-3	(10)	7	8	Lloyd	Timlin	Koch	43-42	3rd	9.0
7-7	At Bal.	W	7-6		6	13	Spoljaric	Molina	Koch	44-42	3rd	8.0
7-8	At Bal.	W	11-6		15	14	Escobar	Ponson		45-42	3rd	8.0
7-9	At Mon.	L	3-4		9	16	Urbina	Lloyd		45-43	3rd	8.0
7-10	At Mon.	W	7-6		9	11	Quantrill	Telford	Koch	46-43	3rd	7.0
7-11	At Mon.	W	1-0		4	2	Wells	Pavano		47-43	3rd	7.0
7-15	Fla.	L	6-8		11	11	Looper	Koch	Alfonseca	47-44	3rd	7.0
7-16	Fla.	L	2-4		11	10	Springer	Hentgen	Alfonseca	47-45	3rd	7.0
7-17	Fla.	W	6-1		10	6	Wells	Edmondson		48-45	3rd	7.0
7-18	Atl.	W	3-2		10	6	Hamilton	Millwood	Koch	49-45	3rd	7.0
7-19	Atl.	W	8-7	(10)	9	10	Frascatore	Hudek		50-45	3rd	6.0
7-20	Atl.	W	11-6		15	13	Halladay	Glavine		51-45	3rd	6.0
7-21	At Cle.	W	4-3		6	8	Frascatore	Jackson	Koch	52-45	3rd	6.0
7-22	At Cle.	W	4-3		7	10	Wells	Nagy	Koch	53-45	T2nd	6.0
7-23	At Chi.	W	2-1		8	7	Hamilton	Parque	Koch	54-45	2nd	6.0
7-24	At Chi.	L	5-6		9	6	Eyre	Escobar	Howry	54-46	3rd	7.0
7-25	At Chi.	W	11-3		17	5	Carpenter	Sirotka		55-46	2nd	6.0
7-26	At Chi.	W	4-3	(11)	9	13	Frascatore	Howry	Koch	56-46	2nd	6.5
7-27	Bos.	L	9-11		14	18	Guthrie	Halladay	Wakefield	56-47	2nd	7.5
7-28	Bos.	L	0-8		2	11	Rapp	Hamilton		56-48	2nd	7.5
7-30	Det.	W	8-2		10	6	Escobar	Weaver		57-48	2nd	7.0
7-31	Det.	W	7-6		12	15	Halladay	Mlicki	Koch	58-48	2nd	6.0
8-1	Det.	W	8-5		10	9	Hentgen	Borkowski	Koch	59-48	2nd	5.0
8-2	At N.Y.	L	1-3		7	7	Pettitte	Wells	Rivera	59-49	2nd	6.0
8-3	At N.Y.	W	3-1		11	5	Hamilton	Cone	Koch	60-49	2nd	5.0
8-4	At N.Y.	L	3-8		9	8	Irabu	Escobar		60-50	2nd	6.0
8-6	At Tex.	W	5-4		10	11	Carpenter	Zimmerman	Koch	61-50	2nd	6.5
8-7	At Tex.	L	0-6		6	13	Sele	Hentgen		61-51	3rd	7.5
8-8	At Tex.	W	8-7		11	11	Frascatore	Venafro	Koch	62-51	3rd	7.5
8-9	At Tex.	W	19-4		25	7	Hamilton	Morgan		63-51	3rd	7.5
8-10	At Min.	W	10-6		15	11	Escobar	Radke		64-51	2nd	6.5
8-11	At Min.	W	6-3		12	7	Carpenter	Milton		65-51	2nd	6.5
8-12	At Min.	L	0-3		5	6	Mays	Hentgen	Trombley	65-52	2nd	7.0
8-13	Oak.	L	8-9		8	12	Appier	Halladay	Jones	65-53	3rd	8.0
8-14	Oak.	L	5-13		11	14	Hudson	Hamilton		65-54	3rd	8.0
8-15	Oak.	L	5-9		10	15	Oquist	Escobar		65-55	3rd	8.0
8-16	Sea.	L	5-7		10	11	Moyer	Carpenter	Mesa	65-56	3rd	9.0
8-17	Sea.	L	5-8		7	12	Abbott	Hentgen	Mesa	65-57	3rd	10.0
8-18	Sea.	L	1-5		6	10	Garcia	Wells	Paniagua	65-58	3rd	10.0
8-20	At Oak.	W	11-0		13	4	Hamilton	Oquist		66-58	3rd	9.5
8-21	At Oak.	L	4-8		8	9	Olivares	Carpenter		66-59	3rd	9.5
8-22	At Oak.	L	3-4		12	8	Jones	Koch		66-60	3rd	10.5
8-23	At Oak.	W	9-4		14	11	Wells	Appier		67-60	3rd	10.5
8-24	At Ana.	W	5-1		10	6	Hentgen	Ortiz	Koch	68-60	3rd	10.5
8-25	At Ana.	W	7-2		9	6	Hamilton	Finley		69-60	3rd	9.5
8-27	Tex.	L	2-8		6	14	Helling	Carpenter		69-61	3rd	10.5
8-28	Tex.	L	7-9		14	14	Sele	Wells	Wetteland	69-62	3rd	11.5
8-29	Tex.	L	2-4		9	11	Burkett	Halladay	Wetteland	69-63	3rd	12.5
8-30	Min.	W	2-1		2	5	Hentgen	Ryan	Koch	70-63	3rd	12.5
8-31	Min.	L	3-14		9	20	Radke	Hamilton		70-64	3rd	12.5
9-1	Min.	W	4-0		5	5	Escobar	Milton		71-64	3rd	11.5
9-2	Min.	W	6-1		11	4	Wells	Mays		72-64	3rd	11.5
9-3	At K.C.	W	5-4		9	14	Quantrill	Morman	Koch	73-64	3rd	10.5
9-4	At K.C.	W	6-3		13	4	Hentgen	Suppan	Frascatore	74-64	3rd	10.5
9-5	At K.C.	L	3-6		9	11	Witasick	Escobar	Fussell	74-65	3rd	11.5
9-7	At Sea.	L	4-7		7	9	Meche	Wells	Mesa	74-66	3rd	11.0
9-8	At Sea.	L	3-4		9	7	Mesa	Koch		74-67	3rd	12.0
9-10	At Det.	L	6-7		12	12	Jones	Frascatore		74-68	3rd	12.0
9-11	At Det.	W	9-5		11	11	Spoljaric	Cordero		75-68	3rd	11.0
9-12	At Det.	W	5-3		10	8	Escobar	Weaver	Koch	76-68	3rd	10.0
9-13	N.Y.	W	2-1		5	4	Wells	Hernandez		77-68	3rd	9.0
9-14	N.Y.	L	6-10		11	9	Mendoza	Koch		77-69	3rd	10.0
9-15	N.Y.	L	4-6		8	5	Pettitte	Hentgen	Rivera	77-70	3rd	11.0
9-17	Chi.	L	3-7		8	14	Wells	Escobar		77-71	3rd	12.5
9-18	Chi.	L	4-7		10	13	Navarro	Quantrill	Howry	77-72	3rd	12.5
9-19	Chi.	L	2-3		6	5	Sirotka	Halladay	Howry	77-73	3rd	13.5
9-21	At Bos.	L	0-3		3	11	Martinez	Hentgen		77-74	3rd	14.5
9-22	At Bos.	W	14-9		22	10	Escobar	Rapp		78-74	3rd	14.5
9-23	At Bos.	W	7-5		11	12	Wells	Beck	Koch	79-74	3rd	14.5
9-24	Cle.	L	4-18		9	15	Brower	Munro		79-75	3rd	15.5
9-25	Cle.	L	6-9		9	13	Colon	Spoljaric	Jackson	79-76	3rd	15.5
9-26	Cle.	L	7-11		9	14	Shuey	Koch		79-77	3rd	15.5
9-28	At T.B.	W	8-2		13	5	Wells	Wheeler		80-77	3rd	15.0
9-29	At T.B.	W	6-2		14	9	Escobar	Witt		81-77	3rd	14.5
9-30	At Cle.	L	2-9		9	8	Colon	Spoljaric		81-78	3rd	15.0
10-1	At Cle.	W	8-6		12	11	Quantrill	Karsay	Koch	82-78	3rd	15.0
10-2	At Cle.	W	7-3		14	8	Hentgen	Wright	Koch	83-78	3rd	15.0
10-3	At Cle.	W	9-2		9	10	Wells	Burba		84-78	3rd	14.0

Monthly records: April (13-11), May (11-17), June (15-13), July (19-7), August (12-16), September (11-14), October (3-0).
*Innings, if other than nine. † First game of a doubleheader. ‡ Second game of a doubleheader.

MEMORABLE GAMES

August 9 at Texas

The Jays set a team record with 25 hits, including Carlos Delgado's 13th career homer against Texas, the most by any Rangers' opponent. Winning for the third time in a four-game series at The Ballpark, the Jays got four hits from Shawn Green (four RBIs), Homer Bush and sub Jacob Brumfield.

Toronto	AB	R	H	RBI	Texas	AB	R	H	RBI
Stewart, lf	5	4	2	2	McLmore, 2b	5	0	1	0
T.Batista, ss	5	3	3	3	I.Rodriguez, c	3	1	1	1
Wodwrd, ph-ss	1	1	1	0	Zaun, ph-c	0	0	0	1
Sh.Green, rf	5	3	3	4	R.Palmro, dh	4	2	2	1
C.Delgado, 1b	5	2	3	4	J.Gonzalez, rf	4	0	0	0
Fletcher, c	6	0	1	2	Zeile, 3b	2	0	0	0
W.Greene, dh	6	0	1	1	Alicea, 3b	1	0	0	0
Brumfield, cf	6	1	4	0	L.Stevens, 1b	4	0	0	0
Otanez, 3b	6	3	3	0	R.Kelly, lf	4	1	2	0
Bush, 2b	6	2	4	3	T.Goodwin, cf	3	0	1	0
					Shave, ss	3	0	1	0
Totals	51	19	25	19	Totals	33	4	7	4

Toronto			.302	014	630	—	19
Texas			.201	000	100	—	4

E—Bush (12), Zeile (20). DP—Texas 2. LOB—Toronto 8, Texas 6. 2B—Stewart (22), T.Batista (10), Sh.Green (32), C.Delgado (30), Fletcher (19), Otanez (6). 3B—R.Palmeiro (1). HR—T.Batista (16), Sh.Green (33), C.Delgado (31), Bush (2), I.Rodriguez (23), R.Palmeiro (28). CS—R.Kelly (1). SF—Zaun.

Toronto	IP	H	R	ER	BB	SO
J.Hamilton (W, 5-6)	5	5	3	3	2	4
Quantrill	2	2	1	1	0	0
Spoljaric	2	0	0	0	0	1

Texas	IP	H	R	ER	BB	SO
Morgan (L, 12-7)	5	9	6	4	1	3
Patterson	0.1	3	3	3	0	0
D.Davis	2.1	11	10	10	0	2
Venafro	1.1	2	0	0	1	0

HBP—Stewart by Morgan, Shave by Spoljaric. U—HP, McClelland. 1B, Cederstrom. 2B, Eddings. 3B, Katzenmeier. T—3:04. A—23,235.

September 14 at Toronto

New York had lost four straight, including a 2-1 decision the night before to former Yankee David Wells The Jays carried a four-run lead into the eighth inning, but Bernie Williams tied the game with a grand slam off closer Billy Koch and Paul O'Neill won it in the ninth with another slam off Paul Spoljaric. Toronto would fall out of the playoff race by losing six straight to the Yankees (2), White Sox (3) and Red Sox (1).

NY Yankees	AB	R	H	RBI	Toronto	AB	R	H	RBI
Knoblauch, 2b	4	2	1	0	Bush, 2b	4	0	0	0
Jeter, ss	3	2	1	1	Segui, dh	5	2	2	0
O'Neill, rf	5	2	1	4	Sh.Green, rf	4	2	2	2
B.Williams, cf	5	1	2	4	C.Delgado, 1b	5	1	1	0
Strawberry, dh	4	0	1	0	T.Fernndz, 3b	5	1	2	1
Soriano, pr-dh	1	0	0	0	Fletcher, c	4	1	2	3
T.Martinez, 1b	3	0	0	0	T.Batista, ss	4	0	1	0
Posada, c	4	1	2	0	Brumfield, lf	4	0	0	0
Ledee, lf	4	1	1	0	V.Wells, cf	3	0	1	0
Sojo, 3b	2	0	0	1	W.Greene, ph	1	0	0	0
C.Davis, ph	1	0	0	0	J.Cruz, cf	0	0	0	0
Bellinger, 3b	1	1	0	0					
Totals	37	10	9	10	Totals	39	6	11	6

NY Yankees			.001	000	054	—	10
Toronto			.002	002	200	—	6

E—O'Neill (7), Cone (1), T.Fernandez (16), Fletcher (2). DP—NY Yankees 1, Toronto 1. LOB—NY Yankees 4, Toronto 8. 2B—B.Williams (23), Strawberry (3), Ledee (12), Segui (25). HR—O'Neill (16), B.Williams (23), Sh.Green (39), Fletcher (17). CS—Bush (6).

NY Yankees	IP	H	R	ER	BB	SO
Cone	6	6	4	4	2	10
Watson	0.2	4	2	2	0	1
Mendoza (W, 7-8)	1.1	0	0	0	0	2
M.Rivera	1	1	0	0	0	2

Toronto	IP	H	R	ER	BB	SO
Halladay	7.2	5	4	2	2	6
Lloyd	0	0	1	0	0	0
Koch (BS 4; L 0-4)	0.2	3	4	3	2	1
Spoljaric	0.2	1	1	1	0	0

WP—Cone. PB—Fletcher. U—HP, Diaz. 1B, McKean. 2B, McKean. 3B, Meriwether. T—3:13. A—29,140.

-137-

BATTING

Name	G	TPA	AB	R	H	TB	2B	3B	HR	RBI	Avg.	Obp.	Slg.	SH	SF	HP	BB	IBB	SO	SB	CS	GDP	vs RHP AB	vs RHP Avg.	vs RHP HR	vs RHP RBI	vs LHP AB	vs LHP Avg.	vs LHP HR	vs LHP RBI
Green, Shawn	153	696	614	134	190	361	45	0	42	123	.309	.384	.588	0	5	11	66	4	117	20	7	13	450	.320	34	84	164	.280	8	39
Stewart, Shannon	145	682	608	102	185	250	28	2	11	67	.304	.371	.411	3	4	8	59	0	83	37	14	12	505	.291	10	55	103	.369	1	12
Delgado, Carlos	152	681	573	113	156	327	39	0	44	134	.272	.377	.571	0	7	15	86	7	141	1	1	11	421	.259	32	101	152	.309	12	33
Fernandez, Tony	142	576	485	73	159	218	41	0	6	75	.328	.427	.449	0	4	10	77	11	62	6	7	10	342	.330	5	53	143	.322	1	22
Bush, Homer	128	523	485	69	155	204	26	4	5	55	.320	.353	.421	8	3	6	21	0	82	32	8	9	409	.311	4	43	76	.368	1	12
Fletcher, Darrin	115	448	412	48	120	200	26	0	18	80	.291	.339	.485	0	4	6	26	0	47	0	0	16	333	.306	11	54	79	.228	7	26
Batista, Tony	98	409	375	61	107	212	25	1	26	79	.285	.328	.565	3	5	4	22	1	79	2	0	11	314	.296	23	68	61	.230	3	11
Cruz, Jose	106	414	349	63	84	151	19	3	14	45	.241	.358	.433	1	0	0	64	5	91	14	4	6	269	.230	12	35	80	.275	2	10
Greene, Willie	81	248	226	22	46	89	7	0	12	41	.204	.266	.394	0	2	0	20	0	56	0	0	4	206	.209	12	40	20	.150	0	1
Brumfield, Jacob	62	195	170	25	40	60	8	3	2	19	.235	.307	.353	3	3	0	19	0	39	1	2	2	128	.203	1	12	42	.333	1	7
Matheny, Mike	57	179	163	16	35	50	6	0	3	17	.215	.271	.307	2	1	1	12	0	37	0	0	3	108	.241	1	9	55	.164	2	8
Gonzalez, Alex	38	173	154	22	45	64	13	0	2	12	.292	.370	.416	0	0	3	16	0	23	4	2	4	113	.301	1	9	41	.268	1	3
Otanez, Willis	42	137	127	21	32	55	8	0	5	13	.252	.307	.433	0	0	1	9	0	30	0	0	3	98	.204	5	8	29	.414	0	5
Kelly, Pat	37	130	116	17	31	56	7	0	6	20	.267	.318	.483	1	3	0	10	0	23	0	1	1	92	.250	6	14	24	.333	0	6
Grebeck, Craig	34	135	113	18	41	48	7	0	0	10	.363	.443	.425	3	1	2	15	0	13	0	0	2	84	.381	0	6	29	.310	0	4
Hollins, Dave	27	104	99	12	22	33	5	0	2	6	.222	.260	.333	0	0	0	5	0	22	0	0	2	79	.215	2	6	20	.250	0	0
Segui, David	31	104	95	14	30	50	5	0	5	13	.316	.365	.526	0	1	0	8	0	17	0	0	1	87	.287	5	12	8	.625	0	1
Wells, Vernon	24	92	88	8	23	31	5	0	1	8	.261	.293	.352	0	0	0	4	0	18	1	1	6	71	.225	1	7	17	.412	0	1
McRae, Brian	31	101	82	11	16	30	3	1	3	11	.195	.340	.366	1	0	2	16	1	22	0	1	2	53	.132	2	4	29	.310	1	7
Berroa, Geronimo	22	73	62	11	12	18	3	0	1	6	.194	.315	.290	0	0	2	9	0	15	0	0	5	43	.163	0	2	19	.263	1	4
Blake, Casey	14	41	39	6	10	15	2	0	1	1	.256	.293	.385	0	0	0	2	0	7	0	0	1	35	.286	1	1	4	.000	0	0
Witt, Kevin	15	37	34	3	7	11	1	0	1	5	.206	.250	.324	1	0	0	2	0	9	0	0	0	28	.179	1	3	6	.333	0	2
Lennon, Patrick	9	32	29	3	6	11	2	0	1	6	.207	.281	.379	0	0	1	2	0	12	0	0	0	24	.208	1	5	5	.200	0	1
Martin, Norberto	9	33	27	3	6	8	2	0	0	0	.222	.364	.296	0	0	2	4	0	4	0	0	2	24	.250	0	0	3	.000	0	0
Dalesandro, Mark	16	29	27	3	5	5	0	0	0	1	.185	.207	.185	0	1	1	0	0	2	1	0	1	22	.227	0	0	5	.000	0	1
Woodward, Chris	14	29	26	1	6	7	1	0	0	2	.231	.276	.269	0	1	0	2	0	6	0	0	1	17	.294	0	2	9	.111	0	0
Borders, Pat	6	15	14	1	3	6	0	0	1	3	.214	.267	.429	0	0	0	1	0	2	0	0	0	0	.000	0	0	14	.214	1	3
Brown, Kevin L.	2	9	9	1	4	6	2	0	0	1	.444	.444	.667	0	0	0	0	0	3	0	0	0	7	.571	0	0	2	.000	0	1
Goodwin, Curtis	2	8	8	0	0	0	0	0	0	0	.000	.000	.000	0	0	0	0	0	3	0	0	0	6	.000	0	0	2	.000	0	0
Sanders, Anthony	3	7	7	1	2	3	1	0	0	2	.286	.286	.429	0	0	0	0	0	2	0	0	1	0	.000	0	0	7	.286	0	2
Butler, Rob	8	8	7	1	1	1	0	0	0	1	.143	.250	.143	0	0	1	0	0	0	0	0	0	7	.143	0	1	0	.000	0	0
Hentgen, Pat	34	6	6	0	1	1	0	0	0	0	.167	.167	.167	0	0	0	0	0	4	0	0	0	6	.167	0	0	0	.000	0	0
Wells, David	34	7	6	0	0	0	0	0	0	0	.000	.000	.000	1	0	0	0	0	0	0	0	0	4	.000	0	0	2	.000	0	0
Hamilton, Joey	22	2	2	0	0	0	0	0	0	0	.000	.000	.000	0	0	0	0	0	1	0	0	0	0	.000	0	0	2	.000	0	0
Halladay, Roy	36	3	2	0	0	0	0	0	0	0	.000	.000	.000	1	0	0	0	0	2	0	0	0	2	.000	0	0	0	.000	0	0
Carpenter, Chris	24	2	1	0	0	0	0	0	0	0	.000	.500	.000	0	0	0	1	0	1	0	0	0	1	.000	0	0	0	.000	0	0
Escobar, Kelvim	33	1	1	0	0	0	0	0	0	0	.000	.000	.000	0	0	0	0	0	1	0	0	0	1	.000	0	0	0	.000	0	0
Koch, Billy	56	1	1	0	0	0	0	0	0	0	.000	.000	.000	0	0	0	0	0	1	0	0	0	1	.000	0	0	0	.000	0	0
Plesac, Dan	30	0	0	0	0	0	0	0	0	0	.000	.000	.000	0	0	0	0	0	0	0	0	0	0	.000	0	0	0	.000	0	0
Quantrill, Paul	41	0	0	0	0	0	0	0	0	0	.000	.000	.000	0	0	0	0	0	0	0	0	0	0	.000	0	0	0	.000	0	0
Lloyd, Graeme	74	0	0	0	0	0	0	0	0	0	.000	.000	.000	0	0	0	0	0	0	0	0	0	0	.000	0	0	0	.000	0	0
Spoljaric, Paul	37	0	0	0	0	0	0	0	0	0	.000	.000	.000	0	0	0	0	0	0	0	0	0	0	.000	0	0	0	.000	0	0
Frascatore, John	33	0	0	0	0	0	0	0	0	0	.000	.000	.000	0	0	0	0	0	0	0	0	0	0	.000	0	0	0	.000	0	0
Davey, Tom	29	0	0	0	0	0	0	0	0	0	.000	.000	.000	0	0	0	0	0	0	0	0	0	0	.000	0	0	0	.000	0	0

Players with more than one A.L. team

Name	G	TPA	AB	R	H	TB	2B	3B	HR	RBI	Avg.	Obp.	Slg.	SH	SF	HP	BB	IBB	SO	SB	CS	GDP	vs RHP AB	vs RHP Avg.	vs RHP HR	vs RHP RBI	vs LHP AB	vs LHP Avg.	vs LHP HR	vs LHP RBI
Borders, Cle.	6	20	20	2	6	8	0	1	0	3	.300	.300	.400	0	0	0	0	0	3	0	1	0	0	.000	0	0	14	.214	1	3
Borders, Cle.-Tor.	12	35	34	3	9	14	0	1	1	6	.265	.286	.412	0	0	0	1	0	5	0	1	0	15	.200	0	0	19	.316	1	6
Otanez, Bal.	29	89	80	7	17	26	3	0	2	11	.213	.273	.325	1	1	1	6	0	16	0	0	3	98	.204	5	8	29	.414	0	5
Otanez, Bal.-Tor.	71	226	207	28	49	81	11	0	7	24	.237	.293	.391	1	1	2	15	0	46	0	0	6	155	.206	7	18	52	.327	0	6
Segui, Sea.	90	382	345	43	101	156	22	3	9	39	.293	.352	.452	1	3	1	32	4	43	1	2	9	87	.287	5	12	8	.625	0	1
Segui, Sea.-Tor.	121	486	440	57	131	206	27	3	14	52	.298	.355	.468	1	4	1	40	4	60	1	2	10	370	.303	13	48	70	.271	1	4

PITCHING

Name	W	L	Pct.	ERA	IP	H	R	ER	HR	SH	SF	HB	BB	IBB	SO	G	GS	CG	ShO	GF	Sv	vs. RH AB	vs. RH Avg.	vs. RH HR	vs. RH RBI	vs. LH AB	vs. LH Avg.	vs. LH HR	vs. LH RBI
Wells, David	17	10	.630	4.82	231.2	246	132	124	32	6	6	6	62	2	169	34	34	7	1	0	0	751	.266	26	90	156	.295	6	30
Hentgen, Pat	11	12	.478	4.79	199.0	225	115	106	32	3	11	3	65	1	118	34	34	1	0	0	0	392	.265	14	46	395	.306	18	60
Escobar, Kelvim	14	11	.560	5.69	174.0	203	118	110	19	2	8	10	81	2	129	33	30	1	0	2	0	346	.306	9	44	348	.279	10	54
Carpenter, Chris	9	8	.529	4.38	150.0	177	81	73	16	4	6	3	48	1	106	24	24	4	1	0	0	324	.290	5	36	278	.299	11	33
Halladay, Roy	8	7	.533	3.92	149.1	156	76	65	19	3	4	4	79	1	82	36	18	1	1	2	1	282	.266	12	44	296	.274	7	33
Hamilton, Joey	7	8	.467	6.52	98.0	118	73	71	13	0	2	3	39	0	56	22	18	0	0	1	0	189	.243	8	33	207	.348	5	32
Lloyd, Graeme	5	3	.625	3.63	72.0	68	36	29	11	1	1	4	23	4	47	74	0	0	0	25	3	164	.238	5	19	108	.269	6	17
Koch, Billy	0	5	.000	3.39	63.2	55	26	24	5	4	1	3	30	5	57	56	0	0	0	48	31	119	.261	2	13	115	.209	3	12
Spoljaric, Paul	2	2	.500	4.65	62.0	62	41	32	9	5	3	2	32	2	63	37	2	0	0	7	0	163	.233	4	24	77	.312	5	20
Munro, Peter	0	2	.000	6.02	55.1	70	38	37	6	1	4	2	23	0	38	31	2	0	0	9	0	112	.366	6	23	108	.269	0	16
Quantrill, Paul	3	2	.600	3.33	48.2	53	19	18	5	1	2	4	17	1	28	41	0	0	0	13	0	119	.294	2	19	69	.261	3	9
Davey, Tom	1	1	.500	4.70	44.0	40	28	23	5	1	2	3	26	0	42	29	0	0	0	10	1	97	.247	4	22	69	.232	1	10
Frascatore, John	7	1	.875	3.41	37.0	42	16	14	5	5	2	1	9	4	22	33	0	0	0	14	1	86	.279	4	17	58	.310	1	9
Plesac, Dan	0	3	.000	8.34	22.2	28	21	21	4	3	1	0	9	1	26	30	0	0	0	5	0	47	.404	4	16	44	.205	0	4
Person, Robert	0	2	.000	9.82	11.0	9	12	12	1	0	2	4	15	1	12	11	0	0	0	7	2	22	.273	1	8	17	.176	0	2
Sinclair, Steve	0	0	.000	12.71	5.2	7	8	8	4	0	0	1	4	0	3	3	0	0	0	1	0	13	.308	3	4	10	.300	1	2
Romano, Mike	0	0	.000	11.81	5.1	8	8	7	1	0	1	0	5	0	3	3	0	0	0	1	0	11	.364	1	5	11	.364	0	4
Hudek, John	0	0	.000	12.27	3.2	8	5	5	1	0	1	0	1	0	2	3	0	0	0	1	0	10	.600	0	2	7	.286	1	5
Rodriguez, Nerio	0	1	.000	13.50	2.0	2	3	3	2	0	0	0	2	0	2	2	0	0	0	1	0	3	.000	0	0	5	.400	2	3
Bale, John	0	0	.000	13.50	2.0	2	3	3	1	0	0	0	2	0	4	1	0	0	0	0	0	6	.333	1	3	2	.000	0	0
Glover, Gary	0	0	.000	0.00	1.0	0	0	0	0	0	0	0	1	0	0	1	0	0	0	1	0	1	.000	0	0	1	.000	0	0
Ludwick, Eric	0	0	.000	27.00	1.0	3	3	3	0	0	0	0	2	0	0	1	0	0	0	0	0	3	.667	0	1	3	.333	0	0

PITCHERS WITH MORE THAN ONE A.L. TEAM

Name	W	L	Pct.	ERA	IP	H	R	ER	HR	SH	SF	HB	BB	IBB	SO	G	GS	CG	ShO	GF	Sv	vs. RH AB	vs. RH Avg.	vs. RH HR	vs. RH RBI	vs. LH AB	vs. LH Avg.	vs. LH HR	vs. LH RBI
Davey, Sea.	1	0	1.000	4.71	21.0	22	13	11	0	0	0	4	14	1	17	16	0	0	0	5	0	97	.247	4	22	69	.232	1	10
Davey, Tor.-Sea.	2	1	.667	4.71	65.0	62	41	34	5	1	2	7	40	1	59	45	0	0	0	2	1	147	.238	4	24	101	.267	1	13
Sinclair, Sea.	0	1	.000	3.95	13.2	15	8	6	1	0	0	1	10	2	15	18	0	0	0	5	0	13	.308	3	4	10	.300	1	2
Sinclair, Tor.-Sea.	0	1	.000	6.52	19.1	22	16	14	5	0	0	2	14	2	18	21	0	0	0	0	0	48	.313	4	10	31	.226	1	4

DESIGNATED HITTERS

Name	AB	Avg.	HR	RBI
Greene, Willie	184	.212	9	33
Hollins, Dave	95	.211	2	6
Segui, David	84	.310	5	12
Berroa, Geronimo	53	.226	1	4
Grebeck, Craig	36	.417	0	1
McRae, Brian	32	.219	1	7
Witt, Kevin	30	.200	1	3
Fernandez, Tony	24	.250	0	2
Delgado, Carlos	19	.421	4	5
Dalesandro, Mark	13	.154	0	1
Borders, Pat	9	.333	1	2
Stewart, Shannon	8	.250	0	1
Otanez, Willis	6	.333	0	0
Kelly, Pat	5	.200	0	1
Sanders, Anthony	4	.500	0	2
Gonzalez, Alex	4	.000	0	0
Brumfield, Jacob	3	.000	0	0
Butler, Rob	1	1.000	0	1

INDIVIDUAL STATISTICS

FIELDING

FIRST BASEMEN

Player	Pct.	G	PO	A	E	TC	DP
Delgado, Carlos	.990	147	1306	84	14	1404	134
Otanez, Willis	1.000	13	89	7	0	96	11
Segui, David	.955	4	19	2	1	22	3

SECOND BASEMEN

Player	Pct.	G	PO	A	E	TC	DP
Bush, Homer	.984	109	220	350	9	579	81
Kelly, Pat	.962	35	60	92	6	158	17
Grebeck, Craig	.959	17	32	39	3	74	7
Martin, Norberto	.974	8	9	29	1	39	8
Fernandez, Tony	1.000	1	0	2	0	2	0

THIRD BASEMEN

Player	Pct.	G	PO	A	E	TC	DP
Fernandez, Tony	.939	132	65	212	18	295	21
Otanez, Willis	.953	24	16	25	2	43	6
Blake, Casey	1.000	14	12	23	0	35	4
Greene, Willie	.917	7	4	7	1	12	0
Woodward, Chris	1.000	2	0	3	0	3	0
Dalesandro, Mark	1.000	2	0	1	0	1	0
Grebeck, Craig	1.000	2	1	0	0	1	0

SHORTSTOPS

Player	Pct.	G	PO	A	E	TC	DP
Batista, Tony	.975	98	165	308	12	485	72
Gonzalez, Alex	.980	37	69	132	4	205	34
Bush, Homer	.920	18	26	54	7	87	5
Woodward, Chris	.939	10	8	23	2	33	2
Grebeck, Craig	.882	4	9	6	2	17	3
Martin, Norberto	-	1	0	0	0	0	0

OUTFIELDERS

Player	Pct.	G	PO	A	E	TC	DP
Green, Shawn	.997	152	340	5	1	346	1
Stewart, Shannon	.981	142	257	4	5	266	1
Cruz, Jose	.990	106	277	8	3	288	2
Brumfield, Jacob	.978	53	126	5	3	134	0
Wells, Vernon	1.000	24	50	4	0	54	1
McRae, Brian	1.000	13	28	1	0	29	1
Lennon, Patrick	1.000	8	23	1	0	24	1
Greene, Willie	1.000	3	3	0	0	3	0
Goodwin, Curtis	1.000	2	7	1	0	8	0
Berroa, Geronimo	1.000	2	4	0	0	4	0
Butler, Rob	1.000	2	1	0	0	1	0
Sanders, Anthony	1.000	1	1	0	0	1	0

CATCHERS

Player	Pct.	G	PO	A	E	TC	DP	PB
Fletcher, Darrin	.997	113	638	42	2	682	4	10
Matheny, Mike	.995	57	346	33	2	381	8	2
Dalesandro, Mark	1.000	8	22	2	0	24	2	1
Borders, Pat	1.000	3	7	2	0	9	0	0
Brown, Kevin L.	1.000	2	10	1	0	11	0	0

PITCHERS

Player	Pct.	G	PO	A	E	TC	DP
Lloyd, Graeme	1.000	74	1	4	0	5	0
Koch, Billy	1.000	56	3	12	0	15	0
Quantrill, Paul	1.000	41	2	9	0	11	1
Spoljaric, Paul	.889	37	0	8	1	9	0
Halladay, Roy	1.000	36	8	16	0	24	3
Hentgen, Pat	.925	34	15	22	3	40	4
Wells, David	1.000	34	7	30	0	37	2
Escobar, Kelvim	.944	33	6	11	1	18	1
Frascatore, John	1.000	33	2	6	0	8	0
Munro, Peter	1.000	31	3	8	0	11	0
Plesac, Dan	1.000	30	0	2	0	2	0
Davey, Tom	.778	29	4	3	2	9	1
Carpenter, Chris	.962	24	10	15	1	26	3
Hamilton, Joey	1.000	22	4	10	0	14	0
Person, Robert	-	11	0	0	0	0	0
Romano, Mike	1.000	3	1	0	0	1	0
Hudek, John	-	3	0	0	0	0	0
Sinclair, Steve	-	3	0	0	0	0	0
Rodriguez, Nerio	-	2	0	0	0	0	0
Ludwick, Eric	1.000	1	1	0	0	1	0
Bale, John	-	1	0	0	0	0	0
Glover, Gary	-	1	0	0	0	0	0

PITCHING AGAINST EACH CLUB

Pitcher	Ana. W-L	Bal. W-L	Bos. W-L	Chi. W-L	Cle. W-L	Det. W-L	K.C. W-L	Min. W-L	N.Y. W-L	Oak. W-L	Sea. W-L	T.B. W-L	Tex. W-L	N.L. W-L	Total W-L
Bale, John	0-0	0-0	0-0	0-0	0-0	0-0	0-0	0-0	0-0	0-0	0-0	0-0	0-0	0-0	0-0
Carpenter, Chris	1-0	0-1	0-1	2-0	0-0	0-0	1-0	0-0	0-1	0-2	1-1	3-0	1-1	0-0	9-8
Davey, Tom	1-0	0-0	0-0	0-0	0-0	0-0	0-0	0-0	0-0	0-0	0-0	0-0	0-0	0-1	1-1
Escobar, Kelvim	2-0	2-0	1-1	0-3	1-0	3-0	1-1	2-0	0-1	0-2	0-0	1-2	0-0	1-1	14-11
Frascatore, John	0-0	3-0	0-0	1-0	1-0	0-1	0-0	0-0	0-0	0-0	0-0	1-0	0-0	1-0	7-1
Glover, Gary	0-0	0-0	0-0	0-0	0-0	0-0	0-0	0-0	0-0	0-0	0-0	0-0	0-0	0-0	0-0
Halladay, Roy	0-1	2-0	0-1	1-0	1-0	3-0	1-0	0-0	0-2	0-0	0-0	0-1	0-0	1-1	8-7
Hamilton, Joey	1-0	0-1	0-1	1-0	0-0	0-0	1-0	0-2	1-0	1-1	0-2	1-0	0-0	1-2	7-8
Hentgen, Pat	2-0	0-1	0-2	0-1	1-0	2-0	2-1	1-2	0-2	0-0	0-1	1-0	1-1	1-2	11-12
Hudek, John	0-0	0-0	0-0	0-0	0-0	0-0	0-0	0-0	0-0	0-0	0-0	0-0	0-0	0-0	0-0
Koch, Billy	0-0	0-0	0-0	0-0	0-1	0-0	0-0	0-1	0-1	0-1	0-0	0-0	0-0	0-1	0-5
Lloyd, Graeme	1-1	2-0	1-1	0-0	0-0	0-0	0-0	1-0	0-0	0-0	0-0	1-0	0-0	0-1	5-3
Ludwick, Eric	0-0	0-0	0-1	0-0	0-0	0-0	0-1	0-0	0-0	0-0	0-0	0-0	0-0	0-0	0-2
Munro, Peter	0-0	0-0	0-0	0-1	0-0	0-0	0-0	0-0	0-1	0-0	0-0	0-0	0-0	0-0	0-2
Person, Robert	0-0	0-0	0-1	0-0	0-0	0-0	0-0	0-0	0-1	0-0	0-0	0-0	0-0	0-0	0-2
Plesac, Dan	0-0	0-0	0-1	0-1	0-0	0-0	0-1	0-0	0-0	0-0	0-0	0-0	0-0	0-0	0-3
Quantrill, Paul	0-0	0-0	0-0	0-1	0-1	0-0	1-0	0-0	0-0	0-0	0-0	0-0	1-0	1-0	3-2
Rodriguez, Nerio	0-1	0-0	0-0	0-0	0-0	0-0	0-0	0-0	0-0	0-0	0-0	0-0	0-0	0-0	0-1
Romano, Mike	0-0	0-0	0-0	0-0	0-0	0-0	0-0	0-0	0-0	0-0	0-0	0-0	0-0	0-0	0-0
Sinclair, Steve	0-0	0-0	0-0	0-0	0-0	0-0	0-0	0-0	0-0	0-0	0-0	0-0	0-0	0-0	0-0
Spoljaric, Paul	0-0	1-0	0-0	0-0	0-0	1-0	0-2	0-0	0-0	0-0	0-0	0-0	0-0	0-0	2-2
Wells, David	1-0	1-0	1-1	0-0	2-0	1-1	1-0	2-0	1-3	0-1	1-2	2-1	0-2	3-0	17-10
Totals	9-3	11-1	3-9	4-6	7-5	10-2	7-3	6-4	2-10	2-8	2-7	8-5	4-6	9-9	84-78

INTERLEAGUE: Hamilton 1-0, Frascatore 1-0, Halladay 1-0 vs. Braves; Wells 2-0, Escobar 1-0, Quantrill 1-0, Hamilton 0-1, Lloyd 0-1 vs. Expos; Halladay 0-1, Davey 0-1, Hentgen 0-1 vs. Mets; Hentgen 1-0, Hamilton 0-1, Escobar 0-1 vs. Phillies; Wells 1-0, Koch 0-1, Hentgen 0-1 vs. Marlins. Total: 9-9.

MISCELLANEOUS

HOME RUNS BY PARK

At Anaheim (10): Green 3, Delgado 2, Kelly 1, Brumfield 1, Gonzalez 1, Stewart 1, Witt 1.
At Baltimore (11): Batista 3, Stewart 2, Otanez 2, Fletcher 1, Greene 1, Delgado 1, Green 1.
At Boston (1): Green 1.
At Chicago (AL) (4): Batista 2, Green 1, Matheny 1.
At Cleveland (11): Green 2, Batista 2, Otanez 2, Segui 1, Greene 1, Delgado 1, Cruz 1, Blake 1.
At Detroit (11): Delgado 3, Fletcher 2, Green 2, Lennon 1, Hollins 1, Segui 1, Batista 1.
At Kansas City (7): Green 3, Segui 1, Greene 1, Delgado 1, Bush 1.
At Minnesota (13): Delgado 5, Stewart 2, Fernandez 1, Green 1, Batista 1, Bush 1, Cruz 1.
At Montreal (4): Delgado 1, Green 1, Stewart 1.
At New York (AL) (3): Segui 1, Green 1, Batista 1.
At New York (NL) (4): Cruz 2, Fletcher 1, Brumfield 1.
At Oakland (5): Batista 2, Fletcher 1, McRae 1, Greene 1.
At Philadelphia (3): Fletcher 1.
At Seattle (4): Delgado 2, Green 1, Batista 1.
At Tampa Bay (5): Batista 2, McRae 1, Green 1, Stewart 1.
At Texas (10): Delgado 5, Green 2, Fletcher 1, Batista 1, Bush 1.
At Toronto (96): Green 20, Delgado 17, Fletcher 10, Batista 9, Greene 8, Cruz 8, Fernandez 5, Kelly 5, Stewart 4, Bush 2, Borders 1, Hollins 1, Segui 1, McRae 1, Gonzalez 1, Matheny 1, Otanez 1, Wells 1.

LOW-HIT GAMES

No-hitters: None.
One-hitters: None.
Two-hitters: Chris Carpenter, April 15 vs. Tampa Bay, W 11-1. David Wells, July 11 vs. Montreal, W 1-0.

10-STRIKEOUT GAMES

Total: 0.

FOUR OR MORE HITS IN ONE GAME

Tony Fernandez 5 (including one five-hit game), Shannon Stewart 3, Craig Grebeck 2, Carlos Delgado 2, Shawn Green 2, Jacob Brumfield 1, Willie Greene 1, Alex Gonzalez 1, Homer Bush 1, Vernon Wells 1, **Total: 19.**

MULTI-HOMER GAMES

Carlos Delgado 6, Shawn Green 3, Darrin Fletcher 2, Pat Kelly 2, Tony Batista 1, Willis Otanez 1, **Total: 15.**

GRAND SLAMS

7-19: Shawn Green (off Atlanta's Bruce Chen).
7-20: Darrin Fletcher (off Atlanta's Mike Remlinger).
10-3: Tony Batista (off Cleveland's Mike Jackson).

PINCH HITTERS

(Minimum 5 at-bats)

Name	AB	Avg.	HR	RBI
Greene, Willie	20	.300	3	6
McRae, Brian	10	.200	0	2
Witt, Kevin	8	.125	0	2
Brumfield, Jacob	7	.143	1	2
Grebeck, Craig	5	.000	0	0

DEBUTS

4-6: Tom Davey, P.
4-6: Peter Munro, P.
4-26: Anthony Sanders, DH.
5-5: Billy Koch, P.
6-7: Chris Woodward, SS.
8-14: Casey Blake, 3B.
8-30: Vernon Wells, CF.
9-5: Mike Romano, P.
9-30: Gary Glover, P.
9-30: John Bale, P.

GAMES BY POSITION

Catcher: Darrin Fletcher 113, Mike Matheny 57, Mark Dalesandro 8, Pat Borders 3, Kevin L. Brown 2.
First base: Carlos Delgado 147, Willis Otanez 13, David Segui 4.
Second base: Homer Bush 109, Pat Kelly 35, Craig Grebeck 17, Norberto Martin 8, Tony Fernandez 1.
Third base: Tony Fernandez 132, Willis Otanez 24, Casey Blake 14, Willie Greene 7, Craig Grebeck 2, Mark Dalesandro 2, Chris Woodward 2.
Shortstop: Tony Batista 98, Alex Gonzalez 37, Homer Bush 18, Chris Woodward 10, Craig Grebeck 4, Norberto Martin 1.
Outfield: Shawn Green 152, Shannon Stewart 142, Jose Cruz 106, Jacob Brumfield 53, Vernon Wells 24, Brian McRae 13, Patrick Lennon 8, Willie Greene 3, Geronimo Berroa 2, Rob Butler 2, Curtis Goodwin 2, Anthony Sanders 1.
Designated hitter: Willie Greene 51, David Segui 25, Dave Hollins 23, Geronimo Berroa 17, Brian McRae 15, Kevin Witt 11, Craig Grebeck 10, Tony Fernandez 6, Jacob Brumfield 6, Carlos Delgado 5, Mark Dalesandro 5, Pat Borders 3, Rob Butler 3, Pat Kelly 2, Shannon Stewart 2, Willis Otanez 2, Anthony Sanders 2, Alex Gonzalez 1.

STREAKS

Wins: 8 (April 14-22).
Losses: 7 (August 12-18).
Consecutive games with at least one hit: 28, Shawn Green (June 29-July 31).
Wins by pitcher: 3, David Wells (April 7-17), David Wells (July 11-22), Pat Hentgen (May 7-18), Pat Hentgen (August 24-September 4), John Frascatore (June 29-July 1), Chris Carpenter (June 2-July 3).

ATTENDANCE

Home: 2,163,473.
Road: 2,186,897.
Highest (home): 40,175 (May 29 vs. New York).
Highest (road): 52,833 (August 4 vs. New York).
Lowest (home): 20,258 (May 4 vs. Oakland).
Lowest (road): 9,220 (April 7 vs. Minnesota).

ARIZONA DIAMONDBACKS

DAY BY DAY

Date	Opp.	Res.	Score	(inn.*)	Hits	Opp. hits	Winning pitcher	Losing pitcher	Save	Record	Pos.	GB
4-5	At L.A.	L	6-8	(11)	12	13	Shaw	Frascatore		0-1	T4th	1.0
4-6	At L.A.	L	2-3	(10)	5	10	Mills	Anderson		0-2	5th	1.0
4-7	At L.A.	L	4-6		7	12	Valdes	Benes	Shaw	0-3	5th	3.0
4-9	At Atl.	L	2-3	(10)	6	8	Rocker	Frascatore		0-4	5th	4.5
4-10	At Atl.	W	8-3		16	6	Johnson	Glavine		1-4	5th	3.5
4-11	At Atl.	L	2-3		7	5	McGlinchy	Olson		1-5	5th	4.5
4-12	L.A.	W	12-6		10	11	Benes	Park		2-5	T4th	4.0
4-13	L.A.	W	7-6	(16)	21	11	Chouinard	Mlicki		3-5	4th	3.0
4-14	L.A.	W	6-2		11	4	Daal	Perez		4-5	4th	2.0
4-15	L.A.	L	1-8		2	8	Dreifort	Johnson		4-6	4th	3.0
4-16	S.F	W	10-4		14	8	Stottlemyre	Gardner	Anderson	5-6	4th	2.0
4-17	S.F	L	5-8		10	9	Rueter	Benes		5-7	5th	3.0
4-18	S.F	W	12-3		11	6	Reynoso	Ortiz		6-7	4th	2.0
4-19	Phi.	W	3-2		8	4	Daal	Perez	Swindell	7-7	T2nd	2.0
4-20	Phi.	W	8-1		10	7	Johnson	Spoljaric		8-7	T2nd	1.0
4-21	Phi.	W	4-2		8	7	Stottlemyre	Schilling	Olson	9-7	2nd	1.0
4-23	At S.D.	W	10-6		11	10	Benes	Hitchcock		10-7	2nd	0.5
4-24	At S.D.	L	2-7		7	11	Williams	Daal		10-8	2nd	1.5
4-25	At S.D.	W	5-3	(11)	12	5	Swindell	Miceli	Olson	11-8	2nd	1.5
4-26	At Hou.	L	2-5		7	6	Lima	Stottlemyre	Wagner	11-9	2nd	2.0
4-27	At Hou.	L	0-11		6	14	Reynolds	Reynoso		11-10	2nd	3.0
4-28	At Hou.	W	10-6		14	7	Holmes	Wagner		12-10	2nd	3.0
4-29	At Hou.	L	2-5		4	12	Hampton	Daal	Wagner	12-11	3rd	4.0
4-30	At Mil.	W	3-2		10	7	Holmes	Myers	Olson	13-11	3rd	3.0
5-1	At Mil.	W	5-3		10	8	Stottlemyre	Abbott	Olson	14-11	3rd	2.0
5-2	At Mil.	L	5-6		8	13	Weathers	Olson	Wickman	14-12	3rd	2.0
5-3	At Cin.	L	3-4		8	9	Williamson	Holmes		14-13	3rd	2.0
5-4	At Cin.	L	4-6		9	7	Reyes	Daal	Graves	14-14	3rd	3.0
5-5	At Cin.	W	5-1		8	4	Johnson	Avery		15-14	3rd	2.0
5-7	N.Y.	W	14-7		15	12	Stottlemyre	Hershiser		16-14	3rd	2.0
5-8	N.Y.	L	2-4		6	11	Yoshii	Benes	Benitez	16-15	3rd	3.0
5-9	N.Y.	W	11-6		13	16	Daal	Reed		17-15	3rd	2.0
5-10	Mon.	W	7-6		11	13	Olson	Ayala		18-15	3rd	2.0
5-11	Mon.	W	4-3	(10)	7	9	Olson	Mota		19-15	2nd	1.0
5-12	Mon.	W	8-6		10	10	Telemaco	Smart		20-15	2nd	1.0
5-14	Col.	L	1-4		6	9	Bohanon	Benes		20-16	3rd	1.0
5-15	Col.	W	9-2		16	3	Johnson	Kile		21-16	T1st	...
5-16	Col.	L	1-5		7	6	Astacio	Daal		21-17	2nd	1.0
5-17	At S.F	W	12-1		13	4	Frascatore	Estes		22-17	T1st	...
5-18	At S.F	W	7-3		11	11	Reynoso	Brock		23-17	1st	+1.0
5-19	At S.F	L	3-8		6	9	Rueter	Benes		23-18	T1st	...
5-20	At Col.	L	4-8		7	10	Kile	Johnson		23-19	2nd	0.5
5-21	At Col.	L	7-8	(11)	16	14	Leskanic	Frascatore		23-20	2nd	1.5
5-22	At Col.	W	8-3		14	11	Daal	Jones		24-20	2nd	1.5
5-23	At Col.	L	6-7		11	11	McElroy	Olson		24-21	2nd	1.5
5-24	S.D.	W	6-5		13	13	Benes	Ashby	Olson	25-21	2nd	1.0
5-25	S.D.	W	4-0		6	6	Johnson	Hitchcock		26-21	2nd	1.0
5-26	S.D.	W	3-2	(11)	8	8	Olson	Miceli		27-21	2nd	1.0
5-28	At N.Y.	W	2-1		6	6	Daal	Reed	Olson	28-21	1st	+0.5
5-29	At N.Y.	W	8-7		13	11	Reynoso	Beltran	Kim	29-21	1st	+1.5
5-30	At N.Y.	W	10-1		15	6	Johnson	Yoshii		30-21	1st	+2.5
5-31	At Mon.	W	8-5	(10)	16	10	Holmes	Kline	Olson	31-21	1st	+3.5
6-1	At Mon.	L	8-10		14	12	Mota	Frascatore	Urbina	31-22	1st	+2.5
6-2	At Mon.	W	15-2		20	5	Daal	Vazquez		32-22	1st	+3.5
6-4	Tex.	W	11-3		12	4	Johnson	Clark		33-22	1st	+3.0
6-5	Tex.	L	8-9		7	9	Venafro	Holmes	Wetteland	33-23	1st	+2.0
6-6	Tex.	W	4-2		6	7	Benes	Helling	Olson	34-23	1st	+3.0
6-7	Chi.	L	6-7		12	13	Adams	Holmes		34-24	1st	+2.0
6-8	Chi.	L	3-5		6	5	Aguilera	Olson	Adams	34-25	1st	+1.0
6-9	Chi.	W	8-7		18	12	Johnson	Mulholland	Nunez	35-25	1st	+2.0
6-11	At Ana.	W	12-2		18	8	Reynoso	Hill		36-25	1st	+3.0
6-12	At Ana.	L	3-4		6	10	Petkovsek	Benes	Percival	36-26	1st	+2.0
6-13	At Ana.	W	3-1	(13)	9	9	Nunez	Petkovsek	Olson	37-26	1st	+2.0
6-14	Fla.	W	2-0		8	4	Johnson	Dempster	Olson	38-26	1st	+3.0
6-15	Fla.	W	4-3		8	12	Anderson	Springer	Olson	39-26	1st	+4.0
6-16	Fla.	W	12-6		17	12	Reynoso	Meadows		40-26	1st	+4.0
6-18	Atl.	L	0-6		6	12	Smoltz	Benes		40-27	1st	+2.5
6-19	Atl.	W	7-3		10	7	Daal	Perez		41-27	1st	+2.5
6-20	Atl.	L	4-10		10	12	Glavine	Johnson		41-28	1st	+1.5
6-21	Cin.	L	4-7	(10)	9	15	White	Nunez	Graves	41-29	1st	+1.5
6-22	Cin.	L	7-8		13	12	Reyes	Vosberg	Graves	41-30	1st	+1.5
6-23	Cin.	L	7-9		8	17	Avery	Benes	Williamson	41-31	1st	+1.5
6-24	StL.	W	8-7		11	14	Nunez	Bottalico		42-31	1st	+2.0
6-25	StL.	L	0-1		0	5	Jimenez	Johnson		42-32	1st	+2.0
6-26	StL.	L	1-2	(10)	7	5	Aybar	Nunez		42-33	1st	+2.0
6-27	StL.	W	3-2	(10)	8	7	Nunez	Bottalico		43-33	1st	+2.0
6-29	At Cin.	L	4-5		5	7	Graves	Padilla		43-34	1st	+1.0
6-30	At Cin.	L	0-2		1	7	Villone	Johnson	Williamson	43-35	T1st	...

HIGHLIGHTS

High point: Clinching its first division title on September 24 in San Francisco was easily the pinnacle of a remarkable season for the second-year franchise, which made a 35-game turnaround in the standings.

Low point: Just one week into the season, the Diamondbacks suffered their third ninth-inning blown save, in a 3-2 loss at Atlanta on April 11. Gregg Olson, who had 30 saves in 1998, was pitching his way out of the closer role. And the D-backs were 1-5.

Turning point: July 11, the day Matt Mantei recorded his first save for the Diamondbacks after arriving in a trade from Florida. The club had lost 15 of its previous 22 games after improving to 40-26 on June 16. With Mantei on hand, Arizona had the final piece to its 1999 puzzle.

Most valuable player: After experiencing a '98 season that bordered on embarrassing, third baseman Matt Williams rebounded with a vengeance by hitting 35 home runs and driving in a career-high 142 runs.

Most valuable pitcher: Free-agent signee Randy Johnson proved he still ranked among the game's great pitchers. He led the league in complete games (12), ERA (2.48), strikeouts (364) and innings pitched (271.2) en route to winning the Cy Young Award.

Most improved player: Left fielder Luis Gonzalez, who at age 32 led the N.L. in hits with 206 and batted a career-high .336. Gonzalez had a 30-game hitting streak, topped 100 RBIs for the first time and displayed extra-base power with 45 doubles and 26 homers.

Most pleasant surprise: First baseman Erubiel Durazo, who made a stunning climb up the ladder. After hitting .403 in 64 games in Class AA and then .407 in 30 games in Class AAA, the former Mexican Leaguer was promoted to the D-backs—and kept on hitting. Durazo contributed 11 homers, 30 RBIs and a .329 average in 52 games.

Key injuries: Starter Todd Stottlemyre, off to a 4-1 start, was diagnosed with a partial tear of his rotator cuff on May 17. Rejecting surgery, he began three months of intense rehabilitation and returned three weeks into August. He wound up notching Arizona's only postseason victory (against the Mets in the division series).

Notable: The Diamondbacks reached the playoffs quicker than any expansion team in history, surpassing the Rockies' feat of qualifying in their third season. Their division title came six years faster than the previous expansion record (the Mets and Royals won crowns in their eighth seasons). ... Arizona had four players reach 100 RBIs (Williams, Bell, Gonzalez and Steve Finley) and four score 100 runs (Bell, Gonzalez, Finley and Tony Womack).

—PEDRO GOMEZ

MISCELLANEOUS

RECORDS

1999 regular-season record: 100-62 (1st in N.L. West); 52-29 at home; 48-33 on road; 33-12 vs. N.L. East; 27-24 vs. N.L. Central; 33-18 vs. N.L. West; 7-8 vs. A.L. West; 32-16 vs. lefthanded starters; 68-46 vs. righthanded starters; 89-51 on grass; 11-11 on turf; 26-14 in daytime; 74-48 at night; 24-24 in one-run games; 11-10 in extra-inning games; 0-0-0 in doubleheaders.

Team record past five years: 165-159 in two years (.509, ranks 7th in league in that span).

TEAM LEADERS

Batting average: Luis Gonzalez (.336).
At-bats: Matt Williams (627).
Runs: Jay Bell (132).
Hits: Luis Gonzalez (206).
Total bases: Luis Gonzalez (337).
Doubles: Luis Gonzalez (45).
Triples: Tony Womack, Steve Finley (10).
Home runs: Jay Bell (38).
Runs batted in: Matt Williams (142).
Stolen bases: Tony Womack (72).
Slugging percentage: Jay Bell (.557).
On-base percentage: Luis Gonzalez (.403).
Wins: Randy Johnson (17).
Earned-run average: Randy Johnson (2.48).
Complete games: Randy Johnson (12).
Shutouts: Randy Johnson (2).
Saves: Matt Mantei (22).
Innings pitched: Randy Johnson (271.2).
Strikeouts: Randy Johnson (364).

Date	Opp.	Res.	Score	(inn.*)	Hits	Opp. hits	Winning pitcher	Losing pitcher	Save	Record	Pos.	GB
7-1	At Cin.	L	1-2	(10)	7	7	Williamson	Plesac		43-36	2nd	1.0
7-2	At StL.	W	9-5		15	9	Anderson	Oliver		44-36	2nd	1.0
7-3	At StL.	L	1-2	(10)	4	5	Painter	Kim		44-37	2nd	2.0
7-4	At StL.	W	17-5		19	13	Benes	Croushore		45-37	2nd	1.0
7-5	At StL.	L	0-1		2	4	Jimenez	Johnson		45-38	2nd	2.0
7-6	Hou.	L	1-3		5	7	Lima	Daal	Wagner	45-39	2nd	3.0
7-7	Hou.	W	13-7		14	11	Chouinard	Miller		46-39	2nd	2.0
7-8	Hou.	W	8-7	(11)	15	13	Olson	Williams		47-39	2nd	1.5
7-9	Oak.	L	2-5		12	8	Heredia	Benes	Taylor	47-40	2nd	2.5
7-10	Oak.	L	0-2		3	3	Hudson	Johnson	Taylor	47-41	2nd	3.5
7-11	Oak.	W	7-4		7	6	Daal	Haynes	Mantei	48-41	2nd	2.5
7-15	At Tex.	L	2-3		5	7	Venafro	Mantei		48-42	2nd	2.5
7-16	At Tex.	L	8-9		10	14	Wetteland	Chouinard		48-43	2nd	2.5
7-17	At Tex.	W	8-6	(10)	13	11	Plesac	Wetteland	Mantei	49-43	2nd	2.5
7-18	At Sea.	L	7-8	(10)	11	10	Mesa	Kim		49-44	2nd	2.5
7-19	At Sea.	L	5-7		8	11	Meche	Anderson		49-45	2nd	2.5
7-20	At Sea.	W	6-0		15	8	Johnson	Marte		50-45	2nd	1.5
7-21	At Hou.	W	7-4		10	8	Chouinard	Powell	Mantei	51-45	2nd	1.5
7-22	At Hou.	W	2-1		7	7	Benes	Lima	Mantei	52-45	2nd	0.5
7-23	L.A.	W	10-1		11	2	Daal	Perez		53-45	2nd	0.5
7-24	L.A.	W	3-0		7	6	Anderson	Dreifort	Mantei	54-45	1st	+0.5
7-25	L.A.	L	1-2		3	8	Brown	Johnson	Shaw	54-46	1st	+0.5
7-26	At S.D.	W	2-0		7	6	Reynoso	Hitchcock	Mantei	55-46	1st	+0.5
7-27	At S.D.	W	4-3		10	7	Olson	Reyes	Mantei	56-46	1st	+0.5
7-28	At S.D.	W	7-4		10	6	Daal	Boehringer	Plesac	57-46	1st	+1.5
7-30	At L.A.	W	6-5		9	11	Chouinard	Shaw	Mantei	58-46	1st	+2.5
7-31	At L.A.	W	4-2		9	6	Johnson	Valdes		59-46	1st	+2.5
8-1	At L.A.	L	2-4		9	11	Masaoka	Benes	Shaw	59-47	1st	+2.5
8-2	S.F	W	16-6		14	16	Reynoso	Rueter		60-47	1st	+3.5
8-3	S.F	L	1-3		3	6	Hernandez	Daal	Nen	60-48	1st	+2.5
8-4	S.F	W	8-4		10	8	Anderson	Nathan		61-48	1st	+3.5
8-6	At Phi.	L	2-4	(11)	6	8	Gomes	Chouinard		61-49	1st	+3.5
8-7	At Phi.	W	8-2		9	7	Benes	Schilling		62-49	1st	+4.5
8-8	At Phi.	W	7-4		13	10	Reynoso	Ogea	Mantei	63-49	1st	+4.5
8-9	At Chi.	W	10-7		15	8	Daal	Sanders		64-49	1st	+5.5
8-10	At Chi.	W	3-1		5	9	Swindell	Lieber	Olson	65-49	1st	+6.5
8-11	At Chi.	W	7-5	(11)	15	9	Plesac	Rain	Olson	66-49	1st	+7.5
8-13	Mil.	L	1-3		4	7	Nomo	Benes	Wickman	66-50	1st	+6.5
8-14	Mil.	L	2-4		10	6	Karl	Reynoso	Wickman	66-51	1st	+6.5
8-15	Mil.	W	4-0		7	7	Daal	Pulsipher		67-51	1st	+7.5
8-16	Chi.	W	10-3		14	7	Johnson	Lieber		68-51	1st	+7.5
8-17	Chi.	W	4-0		7	3	Anderson	Lorraine		69-51	1st	+8.5
8-18	Chi.	W	3-1		10	5	Benes	Tapani	Mantei	70-51	1st	+8.5
8-20	At Pit.	L	4-5		5	11	Ritchie	Stottlemyre	Williams	70-52	1st	+7.5
8-21	At Pit.	W	4-2		9	6	Johnson	Anderson		71-52	1st	+7.5
8-22	At Pit.	W	7-5		10	7	Daal	Schmidt	Mantei	72-52	1st	+7.5
8-23	At Pit.	W	2-1		8	7	Reynoso	Cordova	Mantei	73-52	1st	+8.0
8-24	At Fla.	W	5-4		6	4	Benes	Almanza	Mantei	74-52	1st	+8.0
8-25	At Fla.	W	7-2		8	7	Stottlemyre	Nunez		75-52	1st	+7.5
8-26	At Fla.	W	12-2		11	8	Johnson	Meadows		76-52	1st	+8.5
8-27	N.Y.	L	3-6		8	11	Dotel	Daal	Benitez	76-53	1st	+8.5
8-28	N.Y.	W	5-3		8	6	Reynoso	Cook	Mantei	77-53	1st	+8.5
8-29	N.Y.	W	8-4		12	10	Anderson	Leiter	Olson	78-53	1st	+8.5
8-30	Mon.	W	5-4		9	8	Chouinard	Batista	Mantei	79-53	1st	+8.5
8-31	Mon.	L	1-2		6	6	Thurman	Johnson	Urbina	79-54	1st	+7.5
9-1	Mon.	L	1-8		7	11	Hermanson	Daal		79-55	1st	+6.5
9-3	At Atl.	L	3-7		8	9	Millwood	Reynoso		79-56	1st	+5.0
9-4	At Atl.	W	5-4		10	5	Benes	Smoltz	Mantei	80-56	1st	+5.0
9-5	At Atl.	W	7-5		10	7	Olson	Rocker	Mantei	81-56	1st	+6.0
9-7	At Mil.	W	11-9		12	13	Holmes	Dale	Mantei	82-56	1st	+6.5
9-8	At Mil.	W	9-1		14	7	Daal	Nomo		83-56	1st	+7.5
9-9	At Mil.	L	8-9		11	14	Karl	Reynoso	Wickman	83-57	1st	+7.0
9-10	Phi.	W	3-1		7	6	Johnson	Person		84-57	1st	+8.0
9-11	Phi.	W	4-0		12	6	Benes	Wolf		85-57	1st	+8.0
9-12	Phi.	W	5-0		11	7	Stottlemyre	Grace		86-57	1st	+8.0
9-13	Pit.	W	5-1		8	10	Daal	Schmidt	Chouinard	87-57	1st	+8.5
9-14	Pit.	W	2-1		3	4	Swindell	Wilkins	Mantei	88-57	1st	+8.5
9-15	Pit.	L	1-5		7	7	Benson	Reynoso		88-58	1st	+7.5
9-17	Fla.	L	6-10		7	16	Burnett	Benes		88-59	1st	+6.0
9-18	Fla.	W	8-6	(10)	11	15	Swindell	Almonte		89-59	1st	+7.0
9-19	Fla.	W	8-7		15	11	Olson	Looper		90-59	1st	+8.0
9-20	At Col.	L	7-12		12	15	Wright	Daal		90-60	1st	+8.0
9-21	At Col.	W	7-6		11	8	Olson	Ramirez	Mantei	91-60	1st	+9.0
9-22	At Col.	W	11-3		11	7	Benes	Hackman		92-60	1st	+9.0
9-24	At S.F	W	11-3		17	5	Johnson	Estes		93-60	1st	+10.5
9-25	At S.F	W	7-3		14	8	Olson	Nen		94-60	1st	+11.5
9-26	At S.F	W	7-1		14	6	Daal	Rueter		95-60	1st	+12.5
9-27	Col.	W	10-3		10	9	Anderson	Bohanon		96-60	1st	+13.0
9-28	Col.	W	9-3		15	6	Benes	Hackman		97-60	1st	+14.0
9-29	Col.	L	1-4		8	8	Astacio	Reynoso		97-61	1st	+13.0
9-30	S.D.	W	5-3		11	6	Johnson	Hitchcock	Mantei	98-61	1st	+14.0
10-1	S.D.	L	1-6		6	12	Williams	Stottlemyre		98-62	1st	+13.0
10-2	S.D.	W	7-5		7	7	Kim	Whisenant	Mantei	99-62	1st	+13.0
10-3	S.D.	W	10-3		11	7	Anderson	Murray		100-62	1st	+14.0

Monthly records: April (13-11), May (18-10), June (12-14), July (16-11), August (20-8), September (19-7), October (2-1).
*Innings, if other than nine. † First game of a doubleheader. ‡ Second game of a doubleheader.

MEMORABLE GAMES

April 13 at Phoenix

After blowing a 4-1 lead, the two teams went scoreless for seven innings before the Dodgers tallied three in the top of the 16th. But with two runners on, a badly hobbled Kelly Stinnett delivered a pinch-hit, game-tying three-run blast into the seats. A few batters later, the Diamondbacks would win the game and then seven of the next nine games during its first homestand.

Los Angeles	AB	R	H	RBI	Arizona	AB	R	H	RBI
E.Young, 2b	8	1	2	0	Womck, rf-2b	7	0	2	1
D.White, cf	7	0	0	0	J.Bell, 2b	6	2	4	2
Sheffield, lf	7	1	2	2	Powell, pr-rf	2	0	1	1
Mondesi, rf	6	1	1	0	T.Lee, 1b	6	0	1	0
Hundley, c	6	0	1	0	M.Willms, 3b	8	0	3	0
Brumfield, pr	0	1	0	0	L.Gonzlz, lf	5	1	1	0
LoDuca, c	0	0	0	0	S.Finley, cf	8	1	2	0
Karros, 1b	6	0	1	0	A.Fox, ss	4	0	2	0
Grudzlnek, ss	5	1	2	0	Holmes, p	0	0	0	0
Mlicki, p	0	0	0	0	Dellucci, ph	0	0	0	0
Borbon, p	0	0	0	0	Olson, p	0	0	0	0
Beltre, 3b	4	1	1	1	Gilkey, ph	1	0	0	0
Valdes, p	2	0	0	0	Swindell, p	0	0	0	0
Masaoka, p	0	0	0	0	Colbrunn, ph	1	0	0	0
J.Vizcaino, ph	1	0	0	0	Chouinard, p	0	0	0	0
Mills, p	0	0	0	0	Stinnett, ph	1	1	1	2
D.Hansen, ph	1	0	1	1	D.Miller, c	8	1	2	0
Shaw, p	0	0	0	0	Reynoso, p	2	0	1	1
Cromer, ss	3	0	0	1	B.Andrson, p	0	0	0	0
					T.Batista, ss	4	1	1	0
Totals	**56**	**6**	**11**	**5**	**Totals**	**63**	**7**	**21**	**7**

Los Angeles	000	001	012	000	000	2—	6
Arizona	000	112	000	000	000	3—	7

E—Mondesi (1), M.Williams (1), Chouinard (1). DP—Los Angeles 1, Arizona 1. LOB—Los Angeles 10, Arizona 21. 2B—E.Young (4), Hundley (2), Beltre (3), M.Williams (4), D.Miller (3), D.Powell (1). 3B—D.Hansen (1). HR—Sheffield (2), J.Bell 2 (4), Stinnett (1). SB—E.Young (6), Womack (2), J.Bell (1), L.Gonzalez (2), A.Fox (1). S—Hundley, Mlicki 2, J.Bell, Reynoso. SF—Womack.

Los Angeles	IP	H	R	ER	BB	SO
Valdes	5.2	9	4	4	3	3
Masaoka	1.1	0	0	0	1	2
Mills	1	1	0	0	2	1
Shaw	2	1	0	0	1	1
Mlicki (L, 0-1)	5.1	8	3	3	1	1
Borbon	0	2	0	0	0	0

Arizona	IP	H	R	ER	BB	SO
Reynoso	7	5	1	1	1	4
B.Anderson (H, 1)	0.2	2	1	1	0	0
Holmes (BS 1)	1.1	3	2	2	0	0
Olson	2	0	0	0	0	1
Swindell	2	0	0	0	0	2
Chouinard (W, 1-0)	3	1	2	0	3	1

HBP—Karros by Reynoso. PB—D.Miller. U—HP, DeMuth. 1B, Reliford. 2B, Kellogg. 3B, Holbrook. T—5:14. A—31,197.

July 24 at Arizona

Facing their fiercest rivals and arguably the division favorite, Diamondbacks starter Brian Anderson equalized a somewhat potent Dodgers lineup, pitching eight scoreless innings. Closer Matt Mantei, making just his sixth appearance since being acquired in a trade, struck out three in the ninth for the 3-0 victory. Arizona moved into first place and remained there the rest of the season.

Los Angeles	AB	R	H	RBI	Arizona	AB	R	H	RBI
Grudzlnk, ss	4	0	2	0	Womack, 2b	3	0	1	0
J.Vizcaino, 2b	4	0	0	0	A.Fox, ss	3	0	0	0
Sheffield, lf	4	0	1	0	L.Gonzalez, lf	4	0	1	0
Karros, 1b	3	0	1	0	M.Willms, 3b	4	1	1	0
D.White, cf	4	0	1	0	S.Finley, cf	3	1	1	2
Mondesi, rf	4	0	0	0	T.Lee, 1b	3	0	0	0
Beltre, 3b	4	0	1	0	Gilkey, rf	3	1	1	1
Hundley, c	3	0	0	0	Stinnett, c	3	0	1	0
Dreifort, p	2	0	0	0	B.Anderson, p	3	0	1	0
Borbon, p	0	0	0	0	Mantei, p	0	0	0	0
Hubbard, ph	1	0	0	0					
Mills, p	0	0	0	0					
Totals	**33**	**0**	**6**	**0**	**Totals**	**29**	**3**	**7**	**3**

Los Angeles	000	000	000—	0
Arizona	000	300	00x—	3

DP—Los Angeles 1. LOB—Los Angeles 7, Arizona 7. 2B—Grudzielanek (9), Beltre (18), L.Gonzalez (27). 3B—B.Anderson (1). HR—S.Finley (19), Gilkey (6). SB—Womack (40). CS—S.Finley (2).

Los Angeles	IP	H	R	ER	BB	SO
Dreifort (L, 8-9)	6	6	3	3	3	6
Borbon	1	0	0	0	0	0
Mills	1	1	0	0	1	1

Arizona	IP	H	R	ER	BB	SO
B.Anderson (W, 3-2)	8	5	0	0	0	8
Mantei (S, 5)	1	1	0	0	1	3

HBP—Womack by Dreifort. U—HP, Bonin. 1B, Rapuano. 2B, Pulli. 3B, C.Williams. T—2:30. A—47,824.

BATTING

Name	G	TPA	AB	R	H	TB	2B	3B	HR	RBI	Avg.	Obp.	Slg.	SH	SF	HP	BB	IBB	SO	SB	CS	GDP	vs RHP AB	Avg.	HR	RBI	vs LHP AB	Avg.	HR	RBI
Williams, Matt	154	678	627	98	190	336	37	2	35	142	.303	.344	.536	0	8	2	41	9	93	2	0	17	450	.291	23	97	177	.333	12	45
Gonzalez, Luis	153	693	614	112	206	337	45	4	26	111	.336	.403	.549	1	5	7	66	6	63	9	5	13	449	.339	23	79	165	.327	3	32
Womack, Tony	144	684	614	111	170	227	25	10	4	41	.277	.332	.370	9	7	2	52	0	68	72	13	4	445	.272	2	23	169	.290	2	18
Finley, Steve	156	663	590	100	156	310	32	10	34	103	.264	.336	.525	2	5	3	63	7	94	8	4	4	401	.267	24	65	189	.259	10	38
Bell, Jay	151	688	589	132	170	328	32	6	38	112	.289	.374	.557	4	9	4	82	2	132	7	4	9	421	.268	26	74	168	.339	12	38
Lee, Travis	120	436	375	57	89	136	16	2	9	50	.237	.337	.363	0	3	0	58	4	50	17	3	10	273	.245	6	32	102	.216	3	18
Miller, Damian	86	320	296	35	80	132	19	0	11	47	.270	.316	.446	0	3	2	19	3	78	0	0	6	193	.244	6	30	103	.320	5	17
Stinnett, Kelly	88	317	284	36	66	121	13	0	14	38	.232	.302	.426	2	2	5	24	2	83	2	1	4	218	.211	11	28	66	.303	3	10
Fox, Andy	99	320	274	34	70	104	12	2	6	33	.255	.351	.380	1	3	9	33	10	61	4	1	4	228	.276	6	28	46	.152	0	5
Gilkey, Bernard	94	241	204	28	60	102	16	1	8	39	.294	.379	.500	1	5	2	29	2	42	2	2	7	100	.250	4	13	104	.337	4	26
Durazo, Erubiel	52	185	155	31	51	92	4	2	11	30	.329	.422	.594	0	3	1	26	1	43	1	1	1	137	.343	8	23	18	.222	3	7
Frias, Hanley	69	180	150	27	41	51	3	2	1	16	.273	.391	.340	1	0	0	29	2	18	4	3	2	102	.294	1	15	48	.229	0	1
Batista, Tony	44	164	144	16	37	57	5	0	5	21	.257	.335	.396	0	2	2	16	3	17	2	0	1	95	.211	2	12	49	.347	3	9
Colbrunn, Greg	67	153	135	20	44	70	5	3	5	24	.326	.392	.519	0	2	4	12	0	23	1	1	3	38	.237	0	5	97	.361	5	19
Dellucci, David	63	123	109	27	43	55	7	1	1	15	.394	.463	.505	0	0	3	11	0	24	2	0	3	93	.419	1	13	16	.250	0	2
Johnson, Randy	35	104	97	1	12	16	4	0	0	6	.124	.124	.165	7	0	0	0	0	46	0	0	1	59	.119	0	3	38	.132	0	3
Daal, Omar	32	77	69	8	16	18	2	0	0	4	.232	.254	.261	6	0	0	2	0	10	0	0	2	46	.152	0	2	23	.391	0	2
Benes, Andy	33	73	58	6	9	12	0	0	1	5	.155	.222	.207	10	0	1	4	0	17	0	0	1	40	.175	1	5	18	.111	0	0
Reynoso, Armando	31	58	49	3	8	10	2	0	0	2	.163	.180	.204	8	0	0	1	0	26	0	0	0	36	.167	0	1	13	.154	0	1
Anderson, Brian	32	42	38	4	5	10	0	1	1	2	.132	.171	.263	1	1	0	2	0	10	1	0	1	28	.143	1	1	10	.100	0	1
Stottlemyre, Todd	17	40	32	0	4	5	1	0	0	0	.125	.243	.156	3	0	0	5	0	12	0	0	0	28	.107	0	0	4	.250	0	0
Harris, Lenny	19	30	29	2	11	15	1	0	1	7	.379	.367	.517	0	1	0	0	0	1	1	0	0	25	.360	0	5	4	.500	1	2
Ryan, Rob	20	30	29	4	7	14	1	0	2	5	.241	.267	.483	0	0	0	1	0	8	0	0	0	27	.222	2	5	2	.500	0	0
Powell, Dante	22	28	25	4	4	7	3	0	0	1	.160	.222	.280	1	0	0	2	0	6	2	1	0	7	.286	0	0	18	.111	0	1
Ward, Turner	10	26	23	6	8	15	1	0	2	7	.348	.385	.652	0	1	0	2	0	6	0	0	0	13	.385	2	4	10	.300	0	3
Barajas, Rod	5	18	16	3	4	8	1	0	1	3	.250	.294	.500	1	0	0	1	0	1	0	0	0	13	.154	0	1	3	.667	1	2
Young, Ernie	6	15	11	1	2	2	0	0	0	0	.182	.400	.182	0	0	1	3	0	2	0	0	0	1	.000	0	0	10	.200	0	0
Diaz, Edwin	4	8	5	2	2	4	2	0	0	1	.400	.625	.800	0	0	0	3	1	1	0	0	0	0	.000	0	0	5	.400	0	1
Swindell, Greg	63	6	4	0	0	0	0	0	0	0	.000	.000	.000	2	0	0	0	0	1	0	0	1	4	.000	0	0	0	.000	0	0
Chouinard, Bobby	32	4	3	0	0	0	0	0	0	0	.000	.000	.000	1	0	0	0	0	3	0	0	0	2	.000	0	0	1	.000	0	0
Nunez, Vladimir	27	3	3	0	0	0	0	0	0	0	.000	.000	.000	0	0	0	0	0	1	0	0	0	1	.000	0	0	2	.000	0	0
Holmes, Darren	44	2	2	0	0	0	0	0	0	0	.000	.000	.000	0	0	0	0	0	2	0	0	0	2	.000	0	0	0	.000	0	0
Sabel, Erik	7	2	2	0	0	0	0	0	0	0	.000	.000	.000	0	0	0	0	0	2	0	0	0	2	.000	0	0	0	.000	0	0
Klassen, Danny	1	1	1	0	1	1	0	0	0	0	1.000	1.000	1.000	0	0	0	0	0	0	0	0	0	0	.000	0	0	1	1.000	0	0
Plesac, Dan	34	1	1	0	0	0	0	0	0	0	.000	.000	.000	0	0	0	0	0	1	0	0	0	0	.000	0	0	1	.000	0	0
Kim, Byung-Hyun	25	1	1	0	0	0	0	0	0	0	.000	.000	.000	0	0	0	0	0	0	0	0	0	1	.000	0	0	0	.000	0	0
Vosberg, Ed	4	0	0	0	0	0	0	0	0	0	.000	.000	.000	0	0	0	0	0	0	0	0	0	0	.000	0	0	0	.000	0	0
Olson, Gregg	61	1	0	0	0	0	0	0	0	0	.000	1.000	.000	0	0	0	1	0	0	0	0	0	0	.000	0	0	0	.000	0	0
Frascatore, John	26	0	0	0	0	0	0	0	0	0	.000	.000	.000	0	0	0	0	0	0	0	0	0	0	.000	0	0	0	.000	0	0
Mantei, Matt	30	0	0	0	0	0	0	0	0	0	.000	.000	.000	0	0	0	0	0	0	0	0	0	0	.000	0	0	0	.000	0	0
Telemaco, Amaury	5	0	0	0	0	0	0	0	0	0	.000	.000	.000	0	0	0	0	0	0	0	0	0	0	.000	0	0	0	.000	0	0
Carlson, Dan	2	0	0	0	0	0	0	0	0	0	.000	.000	.000	0	0	0	0	0	0	0	0	0	0	.000	0	0	0	.000	0	0
Padilla, Vicente	5	0	0	0	0	0	0	0	0	0	.000	.000	.000	0	0	0	0	0	0	0	0	0	0	.000	0	0	0	.000	0	0

Players with more than one N.L. team

Name	G	TPA	AB	R	H	TB	2B	3B	HR	RBI	Avg.	Obp.	Slg.	SH	SF	HP	BB	IBB	SO	SB	CS	GDP	vs RHP AB	Avg.	HR	RBI	vs LHP AB	Avg.	HR	RBI
Harris, Col.	91	164	158	15	47	59	12	0	0	13	.297	.323	.373	0	0	0	6	0	6	1	1	7	25	.360	0	5	4	.500	1	2
Harris, Col.-Ari.	110	194	187	17	58	74	13	0	1	20	.310	.330	.396	0	1	0	6	0	7	2	1	7	170	.300	0	18	17	.412	1	2
Mantei, Fla.	35	1	1	0	0	0	0	0	0	0	.000	.000	.000	0	0	0	0	0	1	0	0	0	0	.000	0	0	0	.000	0	0
Mantei, Fla.-Ari.	65	1	1	0	0	0	0	0	0	0	.000	.000	.000	0	0	0	0	0	1	0	0	0	1	.000	0	0	0	.000	0	0
Nunez, Fla.	17	27	25	0	4	4	0	0	0	2	.160	.160	.160	2	0	0	0	0	5	0	0	0	1	.000	0	0	2	.000	0	0
Nunez, Ari.-Fla.	44	30	28	0	4	4	0	0	0	2	.143	.143	.143	2	0	0	0	0	6	0	0	0	24	.167	0	2	4	.000	0	0
Telemaco, Phi.	44	0	0	0	0	0	0	0	0	0	.000	.000	.000	0	0	0	0	0	0	0	0	0	0	.000	0	0	0	.000	0	0
Telemaco, Ari.-Phi.	49	0	0	0	0	0	0	0	0	0	.000	.000	.000	0	0	0	0	0	0	0	0	0	0	.000	0	0	0	.000	0	0
Vosberg, S.D.	15	0	0	0	0	0	0	0	0	0	.000	.000	.000	0	0	0	0	0	0	0	0	0	0	.000	0	0	0	.000	0	0
Vosberg, S.D.-Ari.	19	0	0	0	0	0	0	0	0	0	.000	.000	.000	0	0	0	0	0	0	0	0	0	0	.000	0	0	0	.000	0	0
Ward, Pit.	49	109	91	2	19	21	2	0	0	8	.209	.311	.231	3	1	1	13	0	9	2	2	2	13	.385	2	4	10	.300	0	3
Ward, Pit.-Ari.	59	135	114	8	27	36	3	0	2	15	.237	.326	.316	3	2	1	15	0	15	2	2	2	71	.254	2	6	43	.209	0	9

PITCHING

Name	W	L	Pct.	ERA	IP	H	R	ER	HR	SH	SF	HB	BB	IBB	SO	G	GS	CG	ShO	GF	Sv	vs. RH AB	Avg.	HR	RBI	vs. LH AB	Avg.	HR	RBI
Johnson, Randy	17	9	.654	2.48	271.2	207	86	75	30	4	3	9	70	3	364	35	35	12	2	0	0	906	.219	30	74	87	.103	0	3
Daal, Omar	16	9	.640	3.65	214.2	188	92	87	21	4	7	7	79	3	148	32	32	2	1	0	0	656	.242	19	74	142	.204	2	10
Benes, Andy	13	12	.520	4.81	198.1	216	117	106	34	6	3	4	82	3	141	33	32	0	0	0	0	425	.273	20	56	366	.273	14	52
Reynoso, Armando	10	6	.625	4.37	167.0	178	90	81	20	6	6	6	67	7	79	31	27	0	0	1	0	322	.289	9	44	323	.263	11	37
Anderson, Brian	8	2	.800	4.57	130.0	144	69	66	18	4	0	1	28	3	75	31	19	2	1	4	1	408	.275	17	51	108	.296	1	4
Stottlemyre, Todd	6	3	.667	4.09	101.1	106	51	46	12	3	1	6	40	1	74	17	17	0	0	0	0	226	.235	6	26	170	.312	6	22
Swindell, Greg	4	0	1.000	2.51	64.2	54	19	18	8	4	0	1	21	1	51	63	0	0	0	15	1	142	.239	7	18	93	.215	1	5
Olson, Gregg	9	4	.692	3.71	60.2	54	28	25	9	1	2	2	25	2	45	61	0	0	0	36	14	137	.197	6	23	90	.300	3	13
Holmes, Darren	4	3	.571	3.70	48.2	50	21	20	3	2	0	1	25	8	35	44	0	0	0	9	0	125	.264	1	14	66	.258	2	11
Chouinard, Bobby	5	2	.714	2.68	40.1	31	16	12	3	4	4	0	12	2	23	32	0	0	0	9	1	99	.232	2	13	42	.190	1	5
Nunez, Vladimir	3	2	.600	2.91	34.0	29	15	11	2	2	3	1	20	5	28	27	0	0	0	11	1	84	.214	1	8	36	.306	1	4
Frascatore, John	1	4	.200	4.09	33.0	31	16	15	6	1	1	1	12	4	15	26	0	0	0	10	0	77	.312	4	16	44	.159	2	4
Mantei, Matt	0	1	.000	2.79	29.0	20	10	9	1	1	0	3	19	0	49	30	0	0	0	28	22	53	.245	1	6	51	.137	0	4
Kim, Byung-Hyun	1	2	.333	4.61	27.1	20	15	14	2	1	0	5	20	2	31	25	0	0	0	10	1	61	.180	1	9	34	.265	1	6
Plesac, Dan	2	1	.667	3.32	21.2	22	9	8	3	1	0	0	8	1	27	34	0	0	0	6	1	31	.355	2	9	54	.204	1	5
Sabel, Erik	0	0	.000	6.52	9.2	12	7	7	1	0	0	2	6	2	6	7	0	0	0	1	0	26	.269	0	3	14	.357	1	1
Telemaco, Amaury	1	0	1.000	7.50	6.0	7	5	5	2	1	0	0	6	1	2	5	0	0	0	3	0	13	.154	1	3	8	.625	1	3
Carlson, Dan	0	0	.000	9.00	4.0	5	4	4	0	0	0	0	0	0	3	2	0	0	0	1	0	13	.154	0	1	5	.600	0	1
Vosberg, Ed	0	1	.000	3.38	2.2	6	1	1	0	0	0	0	0	0	2	4	0	0	0	0	0	7	.286	0	0	6	.667	0	1
Padilla, Vicente	0	1	.000	16.88	2.2	7	5	5	1	1	0	0	3	0	0	5	0	0	0	2	0	11	.455	1	6	4	.500	0	2

PITCHERS WITH MORE THAN ONE N.L. TEAM

Name	W	L	Pct.	ERA	IP	H	R	ER	HR	SH	SF	HB	BB	IBB	SO	G	GS	CG	ShO	GF	Sv	vs. RH AB	Avg.	HR	RBI	vs. LH AB	Avg.	HR	RBI
Mantei, Fla.	1	2	.333	2.72	36.1	24	11	11	4	0	1	2	25	1	50	35	0	0	0	32	10	53	.245	1	6	51	.137	0	4
Mantei, Fla.-Ari.	1	3	.250	2.76	65.1	44	21	20	5	1	1	5	44	1	99	65	0	0	0	1	32	120	.217	1	8	113	.159	4	13
Nunez, Fla.	4	8	.333	4.58	74.2	66	48	38	9	5	3	3	34	1	58	17	12	0	0	1	0	84	.214	1	8	36	.306	1	4
Nunez, Ari.-Fla.	7	10	.412	4.06	108.2	95	63	49	11	7	6	4	54	6	86	44	12	0	0	6	1	239	.226	5	26	153	.268	6	21
Telemaco, Phi.	3	0	1.000	5.55	47.0	45	29	29	8	3	1	2	20	3	41	44	0	0	0	7	0	13	.154	1	3	8	.625	1	3
Telemaco, Ari.-Phi.	4	0	1.000	5.77	53.0	52	34	34	10	4	1	2	26	4	43	49	0	0	0	1	0	132	.235	7	24	69	.304	3	13
Vosberg, S.D.	0	0	.000	9.72	8.1	16	11	9	1	2	2	2	3	0	6	15	0	0	0	3	0	7	.286	0	0	6	.667	0	1
Vosberg, S.D.-Ari.	0	1	.000	8.18	11.0	22	12	10	1	2	2	2	3	0	8	19	0	0	0	2	0	25	.400	0	5	26	.462	1	8

INDIVIDUAL STATISTICS

FIELDING

FIRST BASEMEN

Player	Pct.	G	PO	A	E	TC	DP
Lee, Travis	.997	114	802	62	3	867	65
Durazo, Erubiel	1.000	44	324	20	0	344	25
Colbrunn, Greg	.996	39	203	19	1	223	21

SECOND BASEMEN

Player	Pct.	G	PO	A	E	TC	DP
Bell, Jay	.968	148	320	340	22	682	86
Womack, Tony	.971	19	30	36	2	68	6
Frias, Hanley	1.000	8	4	6	0	10	2
Diaz, Edwin	1.000	2	0	3	0	3	0

THIRD BASEMEN

Player	Pct.	G	PO	A	E	TC	DP
Williams, Matt	.977	153	123	299	10	432	30
Fox, Andy	.909	12	5	15	2	22	2
Harris, Lenny	1.000	5	3	5	0	8	2
Colbrunn, Greg	-	2	0	0	0	0	0

SHORTSTOPS

Player	Pct.	G	PO	A	E	TC	DP
Fox, Andy	.958	82	95	181	12	288	33
Frias, Hanley	.965	53	42	95	5	142	16
Batista, Tony	.979	43	60	130	4	194	27
Womack, Tony	.982	19	16	40	1	57	5
Diaz, Edwin	1.000	2	4	2	0	6	0
Bell, Jay	-	1	0	0	0	0	0

OUTFIELDERS

Player	Pct.	G	PO	A	E	TC	DP
Finley, Steve	.995	155	397	5	2	404	0
Gonzalez, Luis	.983	148	271	10	5	286	1
Womack, Tony	.992	123	247	9	2	258	2
Gilkey, Bernard	.969	53	90	3	3	96	0
Dellucci, David	1.000	31	37	1	0	38	0
Powell, Dante	.929	15	13	0	1	14	0
Ward, Turner	1.000	5	11	0	0	11	0
Ryan, Rob	1.000	5	7	0	0	7	0
Young, Ernie	1.000	4	10	1	0	11	1
Harris, Lenny	1.000	2	3	0	0	3	0
Lee, Travis	1.000	2	3	0	0	3	0

CATCHERS

Player	Pct.	G	PO	A	E	TC	DP	PB
Miller, Damian	.991	86	622	61	6	689	9	11
Stinnett, Kelly	.990	86	549	37	6	592	7	5
Barajas, Rod	1.000	5	30	1	0	31	0	1

PITCHERS

Player	Pct.	G	PO	A	E	TC	DP
Swindell, Greg	1.000	63	3	10	0	13	2
Olson, Gregg	1.000	61	4	9	0	13	0
Holmes, Darren	.917	44	6	5	1	12	1
Johnson, Randy	.865	35	4	28	5	37	2
Plesac, Dan	1.000	34	1	4	0	5	0
Benes, Andy	.933	33	13	15	2	30	1
Daal, Omar	.959	32	13	34	2	49	2
Chouinard, Bobby	.889	32	2	6	1	9	1
Anderson, Brian	.958	31	10	36	2	48	1
Reynoso, Armando	.930	31	12	28	3	43	4
Mantei, Matt	1.000	30	1	4	0	5	0
Nunez, Vladimir	1.000	27	1	6	0	7	0
Frascatore, John	1.000	26	1	2	0	3	0
Kim, Byung-Hyun	1.000	25	2	7	0	9	0
Stottlemyre, Todd	.952	17	8	12	1	21	1
Sabel, Erik	1.000	7	0	2	0	2	1
Telemaco, Amaury	1.000	5	0	1	0	1	0
Padilla, Vicente	-	5	0	0	0	0	0
Vosberg, Ed	-	4	0	0	0	0	0
Carlson, Dan	-	2	0	0	0	0	0

PITCHING AGAINST EACH CLUB

Pitcher	Atl. W-L	Chi. W-L	Cin. W-L	Col. W-L	Fla. W-L	Hou. W-L	L.A. W-L	Mil. W-L	Mon. W-L	N.Y. W-L	Phi. W-L	Pit. W-L	S.D. W-L	S.F. W-L	StL. W-L	A.L. W-L	Total W-L
Anderson, B.	0-0	1-0	0-0	1-0	0-0	0-0	1-1	0-0	0-0	1-0	0-0	0-0	1-0	1-0	1-0	0-1	8-2
Benes, Andy	1-1	1-0	0-0	2-1	1-1	1-0	1-2	0-1	0-0	0-1	2-0	0-0	2-0	0-2	1-0	1-2	13-12
Carlson, D.	0-0	0-0	0-0	0-0	0-0	0-0	0-0	0-0	0-0	0-0	0-0	0-0	0-0	0-0	0-0	0-0	0-0
Chouinard, B.	0-0	0-0	0-0	0-0	0-0	2-0	2-0	0-0	0-0	1-0	0-0	0-1	0-0	0-0	0-0	0-1	5-2
Daal, Omar	1-0	0-0	0-1	1-2	0-0	0-2	2-0	1-1	2-1	1-0	2-0	1-1	1-1	0-0	1-0	1-0	16-9
Frascatore, J.	0-1	0-0	0-0	0-1	0-0	0-1	0-0	0-0	0-1	0-0	0-0	1-0	0-0	0-0	0-0	0-0	1-4
Holmes, D.	0-0	0-1	0-0	0-0	0-0	1-0	0-0	2-0	1-0	0-0	0-0	0-0	0-0	0-0	0-0	0-1	4-3
Johnson, Ra.	1-1	2-0	1-1	1-1	2-0	0-0	1-2	0-0	0-1	1-0	2-0	0-0	2-0	1-0	0-2	2-1	17-9
Kim, B.	0-0	0-0	0-0	0-0	0-0	0-0	0-0	0-0	0-0	0-0	0-0	1-0	0-0	0-1	0-0	0-1	1-2
Mantei, M.	0-0	0-0	0-0	0-0	0-0	0-0	0-0	0-0	0-0	0-0	0-0	0-0	0-0	0-0	0-0	0-1	0-1
Nunez, V.	0-0	0-0	0-1	0-0	0-0	0-0	0-0	0-0	0-0	0-0	0-0	0-0	0-0	0-0	2-1	1-0	3-2
Olson, G.	1-1	0-1	0-0	1-1	1-0	1-0	0-0	0-1	2-0	0-0	0-0	2-0	0-0	0-0	1-0	0-0	9-4
Padilla, V.	0-0	0-0	0-1	0-0	0-0	0-0	0-0	0-0	0-0	0-0	0-0	0-0	0-0	0-0	0-0	0-0	0-1
Plesac, D.	0-0	1-0	0-0	0-0	0-0	0-0	0-0	0-0	0-0	0-0	0-0	0-0	0-0	0-0	0-0	1-0	2-1
Reynoso, A.	0-1	0-0	0-0	0-1	1-0	0-1	0-1	0-2	1-0	2-0	1-1	1-0	3-0	0-0	0-0	1-0	10-6
Sabel, E.	0-0	0-0	0-0	0-0	0-0	0-0	0-0	0-0	0-0	0-0	0-0	0-0	0-0	0-0	0-0	0-0	0-0
Stottlemyre, T.	0-0	1-0	0-0	0-0	0-1	0-0	1-0	0-0	1-0	0-0	0-0	0-1	1-0	0-0	1-0	0-0	6-3
Swindell, G.	0-0	1-0	0-0	0-0	0-0	0-0	0-0	0-0	1-0	0-0	0-0	1-0	1-0	0-0	0-0	0-0	4-0
Telemaco, A.	0-0	0-0	0-0	0-0	0-0	0-0	0-0	0-0	0-0	0-0	0-0	0-0	0-0	0-0	0-0	0-0	0-0
Vosberg, Ed	0-0	0-0	0-1	0-0	0-0	0-0	0-0	0-0	0-0	0-0	0-0	0-0	0-0	0-0	0-0	0-0	0-1
Totals	4-5	7-2	1-8	6-7	8-1	5-4	7-6	5-4	6-3	7-2	8-1	5-2	11-2	9-3	4-4	7-8	100-62

INTERLEAGUE: Daal 1-0, Benes 0-1, Johnson 0-1 vs. Athletics; Johnson 1-0, Kim 0-1, Anderson 0-1 vs. Mariners; Johnson 1-0, Benes 1-0, Plesac 1-0, Holmes 0-1, Mantei 0-1, Chouinard 0-1 vs. Rangers; Reynoso 1-0, Nunez 1-0, Benes 0-1 vs. Angels. Total: 7-8.

MISCELLANEOUS

HOME RUNS BY PARK

At Anaheim (6): Bell 2, Williams 1, Finley 1, Stinnett 1, Fox 1.
At Arizona (101): Bell 21, Williams 17, Finley 17, Gonzalez 10, Lee 7, Gilkey 4, Fox 4, Durazo 4, Stinnett 3, Miller 3, Ward 2, Colbrunn 2, Harris 1, Anderson 1, Womack 1, Batista 1, Frias 1, Ryan 1, Barajas 1.
At Atlanta (8): Gonzalez 2, Durazo 2, Williams 1, Gilkey 1, Batista 1, Lee 1.
At Chicago (NL) (2): Williams 1, Finley 1.
At Cincinnati (4): Bell 1, Williams 1, Womack 1, Miller 1.
At Colorado (11): Bell 2, Williams 2, Stinnett 2, Miller 2, Finley 1, Gonzalez 1, Batista 1.
At Florida (4): Durazo 2, Bell 1, Miller 1.
At Houston (3): Williams 1, Benes 1, Womack 1.
At Los Angeles (10): Gonzalez 4, Williams 2, Gilkey 2, Bell 1, Finley 1.
At Milwaukee (14): Finley 5, Williams 3, Bell 2, Miller 2, Gonzalez 1, Durazo 1.
At Montreal (6): Finley 2, Williams 1, Gonzalez 1, Colbrunn 1, Stinnett 1.
At New York (NL) (4): Finley 2, Bell 1, Batista 1.
At Philadelphia (6): Bell 1, Williams 1, Gonzalez 1, Colbrunn 1, Miller 1, Durazo 1.
At Pittsburgh (7): Gonzalez 3, Bell 1, Williams 1, Durazo 1, Ryan 1.
At San Diego (8): Bell 2, Williams 2, Finley 2, Stinnett 2.
At San Francisco (10): Stinnett 2, Williams 1, Finley 1, Gonzalez 1, Colbrunn 1, Womack 1, Batista 1, Miller 1, Lee 1.
At Seattle (4): Stinnett 2, Gilkey 1, Gonzalez 1.
At St. Louis (3): Gonzalez 1, Fox 1, Dellucci 1.
At Texas (5): Bell 3, Finley 1, Stinnett 1.

LOW-HIT GAMES

No-hitters: None.
One-hitters: None.
Two-hitters: None.

10-STRIKEOUT GAMES

Randy Johnson 23, Andy Benes 2, Omar Daal 1, **Total:** 26.

FOUR OR MORE HITS IN ONE GAME

Steve Finley 4, Jay Bell 3, Luis Gonzalez 3, Tony Womack 3, Matt Williams 1, Lenny Harris 1, Tony Batista 1 (including one five-hit game), David Dellucci 1, Travis Lee 1 (including one five-hit game), **Total:** 18.

MULTI-HOMER GAMES

Steve Finley 7, Jay Bell 3, Matt Williams 2, Luis Gonzalez 2, Bernard Gilkey 1, Kelly Stinnett 1, Damian Miller 1, Travis Lee 1, Erubiel Durazo 1, **Total:** 19.

GRAND SLAMS

4-12: Travis Lee (off Los Angeles's Chan Ho Park).
4-23: Matt Williams (off San Diego's Brian Boehringer).
5-10: Steve Finley (off Montreal's Javier Vazquez).
5-18: Travis Lee (off San Francisco's Rich Rodriguez).
7-11: Jay Bell (off Oakland's Jimmy Haynes).

7-21: Tony Womack (off Houston's Billy Wagner).
8-26: Damian Miller (off Florida's Brent Billingsley).
9-7: Matt Williams (off Milwaukee's Eric Plunk).

PINCH HITTERS

(Minimum 5 at-bats)

Name	AB	Avg.	HR	RBI
Gilkey, Bernard	39	.333	1	9
Dellucci, David	36	.278	0	6
Colbrunn, Greg	24	.375	1	8
Ryan, Rob	15	.200	0	2
Harris, Lenny	12	.500	0	4
Lee, Travis	9	.222	0	1
Durazo, Erubiel	8	.375	1	4
Frias, Hanley	7	.429	0	1
Fox, Andy	7	.143	0	1
Ward, Turner	6	.500	1	2

DEBUTS

5-29: Byung-Hyun Kim, P.
6-29: Vicente Padilla, P.
7-9: Erik Sabel, P.
7-26: Erubiel Durazo, PH.
8-20: Rob Ryan, PH.
9-25: Rod Barajas, C.

GAMES BY POSITION

Catcher: Kelly Stinnett 86, Damian Miller 86, Rod Barajas 5.
First base: Travis Lee 114, Erubiel Durazo 44, Greg Colbrunn 39.
Second base: Jay Bell 148, Tony Womack 19, Hanley Frias 8, Edwin Diaz 2.
Third base: Matt Williams 153, Andy Fox 12, Lenny Harris 5, Greg Colbrunn 2.
Shortstop: Andy Fox 82, Hanley Frias 53, Tony Batista 43, Tony Womack 19, Edwin Diaz 2, Jay Bell 1.
Outfield: Steve Finley 155, Luis Gonzalez 148, Tony Womack 123, Bernard Gilkey 53, David Dellucci 31, Dante Powell 15, Turner Ward 5, Rob Ryan 5, Ernie Young 4, Lenny Harris 2, Travis Lee 2.
Designated hitter: Luis Gonzalez 4, Jay Bell 2, Greg Colbrunn 2, Steve Finley 1, David Dellucci 1.

STREAKS

Wins: 7 (May 24-31, September 20-28).
Losses: 4 (April 5-9, June 20-23).
Consecutive games with at least one hit: 30, Luis Gonzalez (April 11-May 18).
Wins by pitcher: 5, Randy Johnson (May 25-June 14).

ATTENDANCE

Home: 3,017,489.
Road: 2,446,492.
Highest (home): 48,053 (June 26 vs. St. Louis).
Highest (road): 61,674 (April 24 vs. San Diego).
Lowest (home): 28,103 (May 11 vs. Montreal).
Lowest (road): 5,048 (May 31 vs. Montreal).

1999 REVIEW

DAY BY DAY

Date	Opp.	Res.	Score	(inn.*)	Hits	Opp. hits	Winning pitcher	Losing pitcher	Save	Record	Pos.	GB
4-5	Phi.	L	4-7		8	8	Schilling	Glavine	Brantley	1-0	T1st	...
4-6	Phi.	W	11-3		17	13	Maddux	Ogea	Ebert	1-1	T1st	...
4-7	Phi.	W	4-0		7	5	Smoltz	Loewer		2-1	T1st	...
4-8	Phi.	L	3-6		4	7	Byrd	Millwood	Brantley	2-2	T2nd	1.0
4-9	Ari.	W	3-2	(10)	8	6	Rocker	Frascatore		3-2	T1st	...
4-10	Ari.	L	3-8		6	16	Johnson	Glavine		3-3	T2nd	1.0
4-11	Ari.	W	3-2		5	7	McGlinchy	Olson		4-3	T2nd	1.0
4-12	At Phi.	W	8-6		9	10	Cather	Ryan	Seanez	5-3	2nd	1.0
4-14	At Phi.	W	10-4		12	9	Millwood	Byrd		6-3	2nd	1.0
4-17	At Col.	L	4-5		8	10	McElroy	Rocker		6-4	2nd	1.0
4-18	At Col.	W	20-5		24	10	Maddux	Astacio		7-4	T1st	...
4-19	At L.A.	W	11-3		18	8	Smoltz	Perez		8-4	1st	+0.5
4-20	At L.A.	L	4-5		4	10	Dreifort	Millwood	Shaw	8-5	2nd	0.5
4-21	At L.A.	W	11-4	(12)	13	7	Remlinger	Kubenka		9-5	1st	+0.5
4-23	At Fla.	L	1-9		9	14	Hernandez	Glavine		9-6	2nd	1.0
4-24	At Fla.	W	8-7		13	12	Maddux	Edmondson	Rocker	10-6	T1st	...
4-25	At Fla.	W	5-1		9	6	Smoltz	Meadows		11-6	1st	+1.0
4-26	At Fla.	W	5-3		9	5	Seanez	Alfonseca		12-6	1st	+1.5
4-27	Pit.	L	3-5		7	10	Schmidt	Perez	Williams	12-7	1st	+1.0
4-28	Pit.	W	5-4		9	8	Glavine	Christiansen		13-7	1st	+1.5
4-29	Pit.	W	8-1		10	11	Maddux	Silva		14-7	1st	+1.5
4-30	Cin.	W	3-0		6	1	Smoltz	Avery		15-7	1st	+1.5
5-1	Cin.	W	5-1		10	3	Millwood	Harnisch		16-7	1st	+1.5
5-2	Cin.	W	3-2		8	6	Perez	Neagle	Rocker	17-7	1st	+1.5
5-3	StL.	W	4-2		8	10	Remlinger	Jimenez	Rocker	18-7	1st	+1.5
5-4	StL.	L	1-9		4	16	Aybar	Maddux		18-8	1st	+1.5
5-5	StL.	W	12-3		16	7	Smoltz	Bottenfield		19-8	1st	+2.5
5-7	At S.D.	L	3-4		4	9	Boehringer	Rocker	Hoffman	19-9	1st	+2.5
5-8	At S.D.	W	11-1		14	8	Glavine	Ashby		20-9	1st	+2.5
5-9	At S.D.	L	0-5		5	12	Hitchcock	Maddux		20-10	1st	+2.5
5-10	At S.F	L	1-4		4	7	Ortiz	Smoltz	Nen	20-11	1st	+2.5
5-11	At S.F	W	9-8	(12)	10	9	Rocker	Rodriguez		21-11	1st	+3.0
5-12	At S.F	L	1-5		7	12	Brock	Millwood		21-12	1st	+2.0
5-14	At Chi.	L	0-9		7	10	Lieber	Glavine		21-13	1st	+1.5
5-15	At Chi.	L	1-5		6	15	Trachsel	Maddux		21-14	1st	+0.5
5-16	At Chi.	W	8-5		11	8	McGlinchy	Myers	Rocker	22-14	1st	+1.5
5-17	Pit.	W	2-1		7	5	Millwood	Ritchie	Rocker	23-14	1st	+2.0
5-18	Pit.	W	12-4		16	12	Perez	Schmidt		24-14	1st	+3.0
5-19	Pit.	W	7-3		6	6	Glavine	Cordova		25-14	1st	+4.0
5-20	Chi.	L	5-6	(12)	10	10	Serafini	McGlinchy		25-15	1st	+2.5
5-21	Chi.	L	4-8		8	9	Adams	McGlinchy		25-16	1st	+1.5
5-22	Chi.	W	4-2		7	7	Millwood	Tapani	Rocker	26-16	1st	+2.5
5-23	Chi.	L	1-5		5	6	Mulholland	Perez		26-17	1st	+1.5
5-24	At Mil.	L	7-10		13	13	Woodard	Glavine		26-18	1st	+1.5
5-25	At Mil.	W	5-2		12	8	Seanez	Wickman	Rocker	27-18	1st	+1.5
5-26	At Mil.	W	3-2	(10)	11	6	Seanez	Weathers	Rocker	28-18	1st	+1.5
5-27	At Mil.	W	8-7		11	13	Millwood	Karl	Seanez	29-18	1st	+2.0
5-28	L.A.	W	4-2		8	6	Perez	Dreifort	Rocker	30-18	1st	+3.0
5-29	L.A.	L	1-2		5	7	Perez	Glavine	Shaw	30-19	1st	+3.0
5-30	L.A.	L	4-5	(11)	8	9	Borbon	Remlinger	Shaw	30-20	1st	+3.0
5-31	Col.	W	3-1		8	8	Millwood	Astacio	Rocker	31-20	1st	+4.0
6-1	Col.	W	7-2		6	6	Smoltz	Jones		32-20	1st	+5.0
6-2	Col.	L	2-3	(11)	9	5	Dipoto	Springer		32-21	1st	+5.0
6-4	At Bos.	L	1-5		3	9	Martinez	Glavine		32-22	1st	+4.5
6-5	At Bos.	W	6-5		9	11	Maddux	Gordon	Rocker	33-22	1st	+5.5
6-6	At Bos.	W	3-2	(10)	6	3	Seanez	Portugal	Rocker	34-22	1st	+5.5
6-7	T.B.	W	9-5		10	13	Smoltz	Eiland	Rocker	35-22	1st	+5.5
6-8	T.B.	W	11-2		16	8	Perez	Alvarez		36-22	1st	+5.5
6-9	T.B.	W	4-3	(12)	13	10	McGlinchy	White		37-22	1st	+6.0
6-11	Bal.	L	2-6		5	12	Ponson	Maddux		37-23	1st	+5.5
6-12	Bal.	L	0-5		6	13	Guzman	Millwood		37-24	1st	+4.5
6-13	Bal.	L	1-22		6	25	Mussina	Smoltz		37-25	1st	+4.5
6-14	At Hou.	L	4-10		10	13	Hampton	Perez	Miller	37-26	1st	+4.0
6-15	At Hou.	W	4-3		7	6	Glavine	Elarton	Rocker	38-26	1st	+4.0
6-16	At Hou.	W	3-1		14	3	Maddux	Bergman	Rocker	39-26	1st	+4.0
6-17	At Hou.	W	8-5		13	6	Millwood	Lima	Seanez	40-26	1st	+4.0
6-18	At Ari.	W	6-0		12	6	Smoltz	Benes		41-26	1st	+4.0
6-19	At Ari.	L	3-7		7	10	Daal	Perez		41-27	1st	+4.0
6-20	At Ari.	W	10-4		12	10	Glavine	Johnson		42-27	1st	+4.0
6-22	Mon.	L	1-2		9	8	Thurman	Maddux	Urbina	42-28	1st	+3.0
6-23	Mon.	W	7-3		13	7	Millwood	Batista		43-28	1st	+3.0
6-24	Mon.	W	3-2	(11)	13	7	McGlinchy	Mota		44-28	1st	+3.0
6-25	N.Y.	L	2-10		8	13	Reed	Perez		44-29	1st	+2.0
6-26	N.Y.	W	7-2		7	7	Glavine	Dotel		45-29	1st	+3.0
6-27	N.Y.	W	1-0		4	3	Maddux	Yoshii	Rocker	46-29	1st	+4.0
6-28	At Mon.	W	13-5		16	11	Millwood	Batista		47-29	1st	+4.0
6-29	At Mon.	L	5-6		10	10	Urbina	Rocker		47-30	1st	+3.0
6-30	At Mon.	L	5-7		8	10	Kline	McGlinchy	Urbina	47-31	1st	+3.0

HIGHLIGHTS

High point: The Braves won an unprecedented eighth consecutive division title. They also captured their fifth N.L. pennant in the 1990s and became the first team in nearly three decades to post three straight 100-win seasons. All this despite losing three key players—Andres Galarraga, Kerry Ligtenberg and Javy Lopez.

Low point: August 4, when the Pirates beat the Braves and dropped Atlanta two games behind the Mets in the N.L. East. After building a six-game lead in June, the Braves saw their lead erode during July (when they went 16-12).

Turning point: The Braves swept the Mets in a three-game series in Atlanta September 21-23 to boost their division lead to four games. They then swept three in Montreal to clinch the N.L. East crown before arriving in New York for a rematch with the Mets.

Most valuable player: Chipper Jones, who hit a career-best 45 home runs and reached 100 RBIs for the fourth year in a row. His homer total set an N.L. record for a switch hitter. He batted .319 and drew 126 walks—both career highs.

Most valuable pitcher: John Rocker had little experience as a closer when the role was thrust on him by Ligtenberg's season-ending injury in spring training. He responded with 38 saves, one shy of Mark Wohlers' club record, and struck out 104 batters in 72.1 innings.

Most improved player: Left fielder Gerald Williams, who was inserted into the lineup as the leadoff hitter in early August and ignited the club. He wound up with a career-high 17 homers and drove in 68 runs. The Braves went 39-14 once Williams was installed in the leadoff spot.

Most pleasant surprise: Kevin Millwood demonstrated his 17-win season of 1998 was no fluke. He won 18 games, lowered his ERA from 4.08 to 2.68 and led the majors' starting pitchers by holding opponents to a .202 average.

Key injuries: Galarraga missed the season after being diagnosed with lymphoma in spring training. Ligtenberg was lost after tearing an elbow ligament. Lopez went down with a knee injury in July and didn't return. Lefthander Odalis Perez tore a ligament in his elbow in July and was sidelined the rest of the season. Reliever Rudy Seanez didn't pitch after August 20 because of a stress fracture in his elbow. And John Smoltz, troubled by a sore elbow, had two stints on the disabled list.

Notable: Chipper's 87 extra-base hits set a club record. ... Free-agent acquisition Brian Jordan proved valuable, hitting 23 homers with 115 RBIs. ... Greg Maddux's ERA jumped from 2.22 to 3.57, but he still won 19 games. ... Atlanta scored a franchise-record 840 runs.

—BILL ZACK

MISCELLANEOUS

RECORDS

1999 regular-season record: 103-59 (1st in N.L. East); 56-25 at home; 47-34 on road; 35-16 vs. N.L. East; 35-13 vs. N.L. Central; 24-21 vs. N.L. West; 9-9 vs. A.L. East; 29-15 vs. lefthanded starters; 74-44 vs. righthanded starters; 88-48 on grass; 15-11 on turf; 29-17 in daytime; 74-42 at night; 29-21 in one-run games; 17-5 in extra-inning games; 0-0-1 in double-headers.

Team record past five years: 496-296 (.626, ranks 1st in league in that span).

TEAM LEADERS

Batting average: Chipper Jones (.319).
At-bats: Bret Boone (608).
Runs: Chipper Jones (116).
Hits: Chipper Jones (181).
Total bases: Chipper Jones (359).
Doubles: Chipper Jones (41).
Triples: Andruw Jones (5).
Home runs: Chipper Jones (45).
Runs batted in: Brian Jordan (115).
Stolen bases: Otis Nixon (26).
Slugging percentage: Chipper Jones (.633).
On-base percentage: Chipper Jones (.441).
Wins: Greg Maddux (19).
Earned-run average: Kevin Millwood (2.68).
Complete games: Greg Maddux (4).
Shutouts: John Smoltz (1).
Saves: John Rocker (38).
Innings pitched: Tom Glavine (234.0).
Strikeouts: Kevin Millwood (205).

Date	Opp.	Res.	Score	(inn.*)	Hits	Opp. hits	Winning pitcher	Losing pitcher	Save	Record	Pos.	GB
7-1	At Mon.	W	4-1		12	7	Glavine	Smith		48-31	1st	+3.0
7-2	At N.Y.	W	16-0		15	3	Maddux	Yoshii		49-31	1st	+4.0
7-3	At N.Y.	W	3-0		7	3	Millwood	Leiter	Rocker	50-31	1st	+5.0
7-4	At N.Y.	L	6-7		8	11	Cook	Smoltz	Benitez	50-32	1st	+4.0
7-5	Fla.	W	6-5		11	8	McGlinchy	Alfonseca		51-32	1st	+4.0
7-6	Fla.	L	2-5		4	17	Fernandez	Glavine	Mantei	51-33	1st	+3.0
7-7	Fla.	W	7-3		8	6	Maddux	Dempster		52-33	1st	+4.0
7-8	Fla.	W	5-2		8	7	Millwood	Meadows		53-33	1st	+5.0
7-9	Bos.	L	4-5		8	5	Saberhagen	Chen	Wakefield	53-34	1st	+4.0
7-10	Bos.	W	2-1	(11)	10	6	Seanez	Wasdin		54-34	1st	+4.0
7-11	Bos.	W	8-1		8	6	Maddux	Cho		55-34	1st	+5.0
7-15	At N.Y. (AL)	W	6-2		10	7	Glavine	Clemens		56-34	1st	+5.0
7-16	At N.Y. (AL)	W	10-7		12	14	Springer	Rivera	Rocker	57-34	1st	+5.0
7-17	At N.Y. (AL)	L	4-11		12	13	Pettitte	Perez	Grimsley	57-35	1st	+5.0
7-18	At Tor.	L	2-3		6	10	Hamilton	Millwood	Koch	57-36	1st	+4.0
7-19	At Tor.	L	7-8	(10)	10	9	Frascatore	Hudek		57-37	1st	+3.0
7-20	At Tor.	L	6-11		13	15	Halladay	Glavine		57-38	1st	+3.0
7-21	At Fla.	L	0-2		7	9	Springer	Maddux		57-39	1st	+2.0
7-22	At Fla.	W	6-3		11	6	McGlinchy	Fernandez	Rocker	58-39	1st	+2.0
7-23†	At Phi.	L	5-6		9	7	Telemaco	Seanez	Gomes	58-40		
7-23‡	At Phi.	W	3-1		7	5	Chen	Shumaker	Rocker	59-40	1st	+1.5
7-24	At Phi.	L	3-4		6	11	Montgomery	Bowie	Gomes	59-41	1st	+0.5
7-25	At Phi.	W	5-4	(10)	12	8	Rocker	Montgomery		60-41	1st	+0.5
7-26	Mil.	W	6-1		8	6	Maddux	Karl		61-41	1st	+0.5
7-27	Mil.	W	10-2		14	6	Millwood	Nomo		62-41	1st	+1.5
7-28	Mil.	L	4-10		9	13	Pulsipher	Chen		62-42	1st	+0.5
7-30	Phi.	L	2-9		5	12	Byrd	Smoltz		62-43	2nd	0.5
7-31	Phi.	W	8-6		12	11	Glavine	Person	Rocker	63-43	1st	+0.5
8-1	Phi.	W	12-4		10	8	Maddux	Wolf		64-43	1st	+0.5
8-3	At Pit.	L	1-7		4	7	Benson	Millwood		64-44	2nd	1.0
8-4	At Pit.	L	2-3		5	5	Ritchie	Smoltz	Williams	64-45	2nd	2.0
8-5	At Pit.	W	6-3		9	7	Remlinger	Hansell	Rocker	65-45	2nd	1.5
8-6	S.F	W	7-3		10	11	Maddux	Estes		66-45	2nd	1.5
8-7	S.F	W	15-4		16	11	Mulholland	Ortiz		67-45	2nd	0.5
8-8	S.F	L	2-5		8	8	Rueter	Millwood	Nen	67-46	2nd	0.5
8-9	Hou.	W	5-3		10	14	Seanez	Henry	Rocker	68-46	1st	+0.5
8-10	Hou.	W	6-4		8	8	Glavine	Reynolds	Rocker	69-46	1st	+0.5
8-11	Hou.	W	8-5		10	11	Maddux	Lima	Rocker	70-46	1st	+0.5
8-13	At L.A.	W	7-3		12	5	Millwood	Dreifort		71-46	1st	+1.0
8-14	At L.A.	L	1-8		5	14	Brown	Smoltz		71-47	T1st	...
8-15	At L.A.	W	5-4	(11)	10	12	Remlinger	Arnold	Rocker	72-47	T1st	...
8-16	At Col.	W	14-6		17	17	Maddux	Jones		73-47	T1st	...
8-17	At Col.	L	2-3		10	8	Lee	Mulholland	Veres	73-48	T1st	...
8-18	At Col.	L	1-4		8	3	Veres	Rocker		73-49	2nd	1.0
8-19	At Col.	W	9-7	(14)	13	11	Chen	Lee	Mulholland	74-49	2nd	0.5
8-20	S.D.	W	4-3	(11)	7	6	Remlinger	Reyes		75-49	2nd	...
8-21	S.D.	W	6-2		10	8	Maddux	Ashby		76-49	2nd	...
8-22	S.D.	W	3-2		9	6	Rocker	Miceli		77-49	1st	+0.5
8-23	Cin.	W	6-2		6	4	Millwood	Tomko	Springer	78-49	1st	+0.5
8-24	Cin.	W	6-4		10	5	Smoltz	Harnisch	Rocker	79-49	1st	+1.5
8-25	Cin.	W	5-2		7	8	Glavine	Neagle	Rocker	80-49	1st	+1.5
8-27	At StL.	W	2-1		8	8	Springer	Acevedo	Rocker	81-49	1st	+1.5
8-28	At StL.	W	3-0	(13)	7	4	Remlinger	Painter	Rocker	82-49	1st	+2.5
8-29	At StL.	W	4-3	(12)	.9	8	McGlinchy	Acevedo		83-49	1st	+3.5
8-30	At Cin.	L	3-11		6	12	Neagle	Glavine		83-50	1st	+2.5
8-31	At Cin.	W	8-2		11	9	Maddux	Guzman		84-50	1st	+3.5
9-1	At Cin.	W	8-7		11	13	Mulholland	Villone	Rocker	85-50	1st	+3.5
9-3	Ari.	W	7-3		9	8	Millwood	Reynoso		86-50	1st	+4.5
9-4	Ari.	L	4-5		5	10	Benes	Smoltz	Mantei	86-51	1st	+3.5
9-5	Ari.	L	5-7		7	10	Olson	Rocker	Mantei	86-52	1st	+2.5
9-6	StL.	W	4-1		9	3	Maddux	Stephenson		87-52	1st	+2.5
9-7	StL.	W	3-2		9	6	Remlinger	Oliver		88-52	1st	+3.5
9-8	StL.	W	5-4		7	9	Millwood	Ankiel	Rocker	89-52	1st	+3.5
9-10	At S.F	W	4-2		10	8	Remlinger	Ortiz	Rocker	90-52	1st	+4.0
9-11	At S.F	L	2-3		7	8	Rueter	Glavine	Nen	90-53	1st	+3.0
9-12	At S.F	L	4-8		9	13	Nathan	Maddux		90-54	1st	+2.0
9-13	At S.D.	L	0-3		4	11	Williams	Mulholland	Hoffman	90-55	1st	+1.0
9-14	At S.D.	W	11-4		14	7	Millwood	Carlyle		91-55	1st	+2.0
9-15	At S.D.	L	1-4		4	9	Clement	Smoltz	Hoffman	91-56	1st	+1.0
9-17	Mon.	W	6-5	(10)	5	12	Remlinger	Kline		92-56	1st	+2.0
9-18	Mon.	L	3-4		11	8	Hermanson	Maddux	Urbina	92-57	1st	+1.0
9-19	Mon.	W	5-1		7	7	Millwood	Lilly		93-57	1st	+1.0
9-21	N.Y.	W	2-1		8	6	Remlinger	Cook	Rocker	94-57	1st	+2.0
9-22	N.Y.	W	5-2		6	8	Glavine	Hershiser	Rocker	95-57	1st	+3.0
9-23	N.Y.	W	6-3		13	7	Maddux	Leiter	Rocker	96-57	1st	+4.0
9-24	At Mon.	W	4-3	(10)	9	4	Bergman	Mota	Remlinger	97-57	1st	+5.0
9-25	At Mon.	W	5-3		9	10	Mulholland	Vazquez	Rocker	98-57	1st	+6.0
9-26	At Mon.	W	10-0		13	6	Smoltz	Powell		99-57	1st	+7.0
9-28	At N.Y.	W	9-3		13	9	Glavine	Hershiser		100-57	1st	+8.0
9-29	At N.Y.	L	2-9		5	13	Leiter	Maddux		100-58	1st	+7.0
9-30	At N.Y.	W	4-3	(11)	8	6	Mulholland	Dotel		101-58	1st	+8.0
10-1	Fla.	W	4-1		8	6	Smoltz	Meadows	Rocker	102-58	1st	+8.0
10-2	Fla.	L	0-1	(10)	7	2	Looper	Ebert	Alfonseca	102-59	1st	+7.0
10-3	Fla.	W	18-0		21	5	Glavine	Springer		103-59	1st	+7.0

Monthly records: April (15-7), May (16-13), June (16-11), July (16-12), August (21-7), September (17-8), October (2-1).
*Innings, if other than nine. † First game of a doubleheader. ‡ Second game of a doubleheader.

MEMORABLE GAMES

July 16 at New York

Andruw Jones hit a three-run homer off Yankees closer Mariano Rivera with two outs in the ninth inning to cap a four-run rally and give the Braves a 10-7 win. Ryan Klesko had singled home Otis Nixon to tie the game before Jones took Rivera deep, the Braves' fifth homer of the game.

Atlanta	AB	R	H	RBI	NY Yankees	AB	R	H	RBI
Weiss, ss	5	0	0	0	Knoblauch, 2b	4	1	1	0
B.Boone, 2b	5	0	0	0	Jeter, ss	4	2	3	2
C.Jones, 3b	2	2	1	1	O'Neill, rf	5	0	1	0
O.Nixon, pr	0	1	0	0	B.Williams, cf	5	1	2	1
Lockhart, 3b	0	0	0	0	T.Martinez, 1b	4	0	0	2
B.Jordan, rf	4	2	2	1	C.Davis, dh	4	1	1	0
Klesko, lf	5	2	4	4	Ledee, lf	4	1	3	0
G.Willms, pr-lf	0	1	0	0	Posada, c	4	1	1	0
J.Lopez, dh	5	0	1	0	Brosius, 3b	4	0	2	2
A.Jones, cf	4	2	3	4					
Simon, 1b	5	0	0	0					
E.Perez, c	3	0	1	0					
Totals	**38**	**10**	**12**	**10**	**Totals**	**38**	**7**	**14**	**7**

Atlanta	011	130	004—10
NY Yankees	200	301	100— 7

DP—Atlanta 2, NY Yankees 1. LOB—Atlanta 7, NY Yankees 8. 2B—B.Jordan (19), B.Williams (15). 3B—B.Williams (2). HR—C.Jones (22), Klesko 2 (15), A.Jones 2 (18), Jeter (15). SB—Knoblauch (16), Ledee (1), Brosius (5). SF—T.Martinez.

Atlanta	IP	H	R	ER	BB	SO
G.Maddux	3.1	9	5	5	2	1
Remlinger	3.1	4	2	2	1	1
McGlinchy	0.1	0	0	0	0	0
R.Springer (W, 1-1)	1	1	0	0	0	1
Rocker (S, 18)	1	0	0	0	0	1

NY Yankees	IP	H	R	ER	BB	SO
O.Hernandez	4.2	8	6	6	3	3
Mendoza	3.1	1	0	0	1	2
M.Rivera (BS 4; L 2-3)	1	3	4	4	1	0

HBP—E.Perez by O.Hernandez. WP—Mendoza. U—HP, Evans. 1B, Meriwether. 2B, Barrett. 3B, McCoy. T—3:04. A—50,469.

September 23 at Atlanta

Chipper Jones hit his fourth home run of the series, a three-run shot off Al Leiter in the sixth inning, to erase a one-run deficit. John Rocker closed out the game with his third straight save as the Braves completed a three-game sweep of the Mets and upped their division lead to four games.

NY Mets	AB	R	H	RBI	Atlanta	AB	R	H	RBI
Henderson, lf	2	1	1	0	G.Willms, lf	5	2	2	0
Agbayani, lf	2	0	0	0	B.Boone, 2b	3	2	2	0
Alfonzo, 2b	5	0	1	0	C.Jones, 3b	2	1	1	3
Olerud, 1b	4	0	0	1	A.Jones, cf	4	1	3	1
Piazza, c	4	1	1	1	B.Jordan, rf	4	0	2	0
Ventura, 3b	4	1	1	0	B.Hunter, 1b	4	0	1	0
D.Hamilton, cf	4	0	1	0	J.Herndez, ss	3	0	1	0
R.Cedeno, rf	3	0	1	0	Weiss, ss	1	0	1	0
Dunston, ph	1	0	0	0	E.Perez, c	3	0	0	0
R.Ordonez, ss	3	0	1	1	G.Maddux, p	3	0	0	0
A.Leiter, p	2	0	0	0	Remlinger, p	0	0	0	0
Mahomes, p	0	0	0	0	Klesko, ph	0	0	0	0
M.Franco, ph	1	0	0	0	O.Nixon, pr	0	0	0	0
Wendell, p	0	0	0	0	Rocker, p	0	0	0	0
Taylor, p	0	0	0	0					
Mora, ph	0	0	0	0					
Totals	**35**	**3**	**7**	**3**	**Totals**	**32**	**6**	**13**	**4**

NY Mets	110	001 000—	3
Atlanta	100	040 10x—	6

E—Olerud (9), Wendell (2), B.Boone (12), C.Jones (15). DP—NY Mets 2, LOB—NY Mets 8, Atlanta 8. 2B—Henderson (28), Alfonzo (40), G.Williams (23), B.Boone (37), A.Jones (31), Weiss (13). HR—Piazza (38), C.Jones (45). SB—G.Williams (19), O.Nixon (23). CS—B.Boone (9), A.Jones (11), B.Jordan (7). SH—B.Boone, E.Perez.

NY Mets	IP	H	R	ER	BB	SO
A.Leiter (L, 11-12)	5	11	5	4	2	5
Mahomes	1	0	0	0	0	2
Wendell	1	1	1	0	1	0
Taylor	1	1	0	0	1	0

Atlanta	IP	H	R	ER	BB	SO
G.Maddux (W, 19-8)	7	7	3	2	1	6
Remlinger (H, 21)	1	0	0	0	0	1
Rocker (S, 36)	1	0	0	0	2	1

WP—Rocker. U—HP, Gibson. 1B, Rapuano. 2B, Kellogg. 3B, C.Williams. T—2:46. A—49,228.

BATTING

Name	G	TPA	AB	R	H	TB	2B	3B	HR	RBI	Avg.	Obp.	Slg.	SH	SF	HP	BB	IBB	SO	SB	CS	GDP	vs RHP AB	vs RHP Avg.	vs RHP HR	vs RHP RBI	vs LHP AB	vs LHP Avg.	vs LHP HR	vs LHP RBI
Boone, Bret	152	671	608	102	153	253	38	1	20	63	.252	.310	.416	9	2	5	47	0	112	14	9	11	444	.241	15	48	164	.280	5	15
Jones, Andruw	162	679	592	97	163	286	35	5	26	84	.275	.365	.483	0	2	9	76	11	103	24	12	12	451	.277	20	64	141	.270	6	20
Jordan, Brian	153	645	576	100	163	268	28	4	23	115	.283	.346	.465	0	9	9	51	2	81	13	8	9	452	.270	17	83	124	.331	6	32
Jones, Chipper	157	701	567	116	181	359	41	1	45	110	.319	.441	.633	0	6	2	126	18	94	25	3	20	425	.308	30	75	142	.352	15	35
Williams, Gerald	143	467	422	76	116	193	24	1	17	68	.275	.335	.457	4	2	6	33	1	67	19	11	8	240	.267	8	36	182	.286	9	32
Klesko, Ryan	133	466	404	55	120	215	28	2	21	80	.297	.376	.532	0	7	2	53	8	69	5	2	6	355	.324	20	73	49	.102	1	7
Perez, Eddie	104	339	309	30	77	115	17	0	7	30	.249	.299	.372	4	3	6	17	4	40	0	1	9	208	.240	6	24	101	.267	1	6
Weiss, Walt	110	327	279	38	63	90	13	4	2	29	.226	.315	.323	6	4	3	35	1	48	7	3	1	204	.235	0	22	75	.200	2	7
Lopez, Javy	65	269	246	34	78	131	18	1	11	45	.317	.375	.533	0	0	3	20	2	41	0	3	6	193	.311	6	32	53	.340	5	13
Guillen, Ozzie	92	255	232	21	56	75	16	0	1	20	.241	.284	.323	5	3	0	15	2	17	4	2	6	182	.231	1	16	50	.280	0	4
Simon, Randall	90	237	218	26	69	100	16	0	5	25	.317	.367	.459	0	1	1	17	6	25	2	2	10	200	.325	4	21	18	.222	1	4
Hunter, Brian	114	223	181	28	45	77	12	1	6	30	.249	.367	.425	5	2	4	31	1	40	0	1	6	57	.158	2	8	124	.290	4	22
Hernandez, Jose	48	180	166	22	42	62	8	0	4	19	.253	.302	.373	1	1	0	12	3	44	4	1	5	107	.196	3	9	59	.356	1	10
Lockhart, Keith	108	184	161	20	42	50	3	1	1	21	.261	.337	.311	0	3	1	19	0	21	3	1	2	149	.275	1	19	12	.083	0	2
Nixon, Otis	84	176	151	31	31	35	2	1	0	8	.205	.309	.232	1	1	0	23	1	15	26	7	1	124	.194	0	6	27	.259	0	2
Millwood, Kevin	33	86	78	4	12	17	2	0	1	6	.154	.175	.218	6	0	0	2	0	29	0	0	2	55	.182	1	6	23	.087	0	0
Myers, Greg	34	86	72	10	16	24	2	0	2	9	.222	.337	.333	0	1	0	13	2	16	0	0	1	61	.213	2	7	11	.273	0	2
Glavine, Tom	36	77	65	3	9	10	1	0	0	4	.138	.200	.154	7	0	0	5	0	17	0	0	0	46	.174	0	4	19	.053	0	0
Maddux, Greg	33	79	64	7	11	20	1	1	2	7	.172	.197	.313	13	0	1	1	0	18	0	0	0	45	.222	2	6	19	.053	0	1
Smoltz, John	29	72	62	11	17	24	4	0	1	7	.274	.338	.387	4	0	1	5	0	28	0	0	0	50	.220	1	5	12	.500	0	2
Perez, Odalis	18	34	30	1	4	4	0	0	0	3	.133	.133	.133	4	0	0	0	0	10	0	0	0	19	.158	0	1	11	.091	0	2
Battle, Howard	15	19	17	2	6	9	0	0	1	5	.353	.421	.529	0	0	0	2	0	3	0	0	1	6	.167	0	0	11	.455	1	5
Mulholland, Terry	16	20	16	2	2	2	0	0	0	0	.125	.222	.125	2	0	0	2	0	4	0	0	1	10	.000	0	0	6	.333	0	0
Chen, Bruce	16	12	11	0	0	0	0	0	0	0	.000	.000	.000	1	0	0	0	0	6	0	0	0	6	.000	0	0	5	.000	0	0
Matos, Pascual	6	8	8	0	1	1	0	0	0	2	.125	.125	.125	0	0	0	0	0	1	0	0	1	5	.200	0	2	3	.000	0	0
Fabregas, Jorge	6	8	8	0	0	0	0	0	0	0	.000	.000	.000	0	0	0	0	0	0	0	0	2	7	.000	0	0	1	.000	0	0
DeRosa, Mark	7	8	8	0	0	0	0	0	0	0	.000	.000	.000	0	0	0	0	0	2	0	0	0	6	.000	0	0	2	.000	0	0
Lombard, George	6	7	6	1	2	2	0	0	0	0	.333	.429	.333	0	0	0	1	0	2	2	0	0	3	.333	0	0	3	.333	0	0
Speier, Justin	19	3	3	0	1	1	0	0	0	0	.333	.333	.333	0	0	0	0	0	2	0	0	0	1	.000	0	0	2	.500	0	0
Garcia, Freddy	2	3	2	1	1	4	0	0	1	1	.500	.667	2.000	0	0	0	1	0	1	0	0	0	0	.000	0	0	2	.500	1	1
Remlinger, Mike	73	4	2	1	0	0	0	0	0	0	.000	.000	.000	2	0	0	0	0	2	0	0	0	2	.000	0	0	0	.000	0	0
McGlinchy, Kevin	64	2	2	0	0	0	0	0	0	0	.000	.000	.000	0	0	0	0	0	1	0	0	0	2	.000	0	0	0	.000	0	0
Seanez, Rudy	56	2	1	1	0	0	0	0	0	0	.000	.500	.000	0	0	0	1	0	1	0	0	0	1	.000	0	0	0	.000	0	0
Hudek, John	15	1	1	0	0	0	0	0	0	0	.000	.000	.000	0	0	0	0	0	1	0	0	0	0	.000	0	0	1	.000	0	0
Ebert, Derrin	5	1	1	0	0	0	0	0	0	0	.000	.000	.000	0	0	0	0	0	1	0	0	0	0	.000	0	0	1	.000	0	0
Wohlers, Mark	2	0	0	0	0	0	0	0	0	0	.000	.000	.000	0	0	0	0	0	0	0	0	0	0	.000	0	0	0	.000	0	0
Springer, Russ	49	0	0	0	0	0	0	0	0	0	.000	.000	.000	0	0	0	0	0	0	0	0	0	0	.000	0	0	0	.000	0	0
Bergman, Sean	6	0	0	0	0	0	0	0	0	0	.000	.000	.000	0	0	0	0	0	0	0	0	0	0	.000	0	0	0	.000	0	0
Stull, Everett	1	0	0	0	0	0	0	0	0	0	.000	.000	.000	0	0	0	0	0	0	0	0	0	0	.000	0	0	0	.000	0	0
Cather, Mike	4	0	0	0	0	0	0	0	0	0	.000	.000	.000	0	0	0	0	0	0	0	0	0	0	.000	0	0	0	.000	0	0
Rocker, John	74	0	0	0	0	0	0	0	0	0	.000	.000	.000	0	0	0	0	0	0	0	0	0	0	.000	0	0	0	.000	0	0
Winkelsas, Joe	1	0	0	0	0	0	0	0	0	0	.000	.000	.000	0	0	0	0	0	0	0	0	0	0	.000	0	0	0	.000	0	0
Bowie, Micah	3	0	0	0	0	0	0	0	0	0	.000	.000	.000	0	0	0	0	0	0	0	0	0	0	.000	0	0	0	.000	0	0
Cortes, David	4	0	0	0	0	0	0	0	0	0	.000	.000	.000	0	0	0	0	0	0	0	0	0	0	.000	0	0	0	.000	0	0

Players with more than one N.L. team

Name	G	TPA	AB	R	H	TB	2B	3B	HR	RBI	Avg.	Obp.	Slg.	SH	SF	HP	BB	IBB	SO	SB	CS	GDP	vs RHP AB	vs RHP Avg.	vs RHP HR	vs RHP RBI	vs LHP AB	vs LHP Avg.	vs LHP HR	vs LHP RBI
Bergman, Hou.	19	29	28	4	3	9	0	0	2	2	.107	.107	.321	1	0	0	0	0	12	0	0	0	0	.000	0	0	0	.000	0	0
Bergman, Hou.-Atl.	25	29	28	4	3	9	0	0	2	2	.107	.107	.321	1	0	0	0	0	12	0	0	0	20	.100	1	1	8	.125	1	1
Bowie, Chi.	11	15	14	0	3	3	0	0	0	3	.214	.267	.214	0	1	0	1	0	3	0	0	0	0	.000	0	0	0	.000	0	0
Bowie, Atl.-Chi.	14	15	14	0	3	3	0	0	0	3	.214	.267	.214	0	1	0	1	0	3	0	0	0	9	.333	0	2	5	.000	0	1
Fabregas, Fla.	82	260	223	20	46	69	10	2	3	21	.206	.289	.309	4	5	2	26	6	27	0	0	7	7	.000	0	0	1	.000	0	0
Fabregas, Fla.-Atl.	88	268	231	20	46	69	10	2	3	21	.199	.280	.299	4	5	2	26	6	27	0	0	9	211	.190	3	17	20	.300	0	4
Garcia, Pit.	55	135	130	16	30	53	5	0	6	23	.231	.252	.408	0	1	0	4	0	41	0	0	3	0	.000	0	0	2	.500	1	1
Garcia, Pit.-Atl.	57	138	132	17	31	57	5	0	7	24	.235	.261	.432	0	1	0	5	0	42	0	0	3	46	.174	1	8	86	.267	6	16
Hernandez, Chi.	99	388	342	57	93	154	12	2	15	43	.272	.357	.450	1	0	5	40	3	101	7	2	5	107	.196	3	9	59	.356	1	10
Hernandez, Chi.-Atl.	147	568	508	79	135	216	20	2	19	62	.266	.339	.425	2	1	5	52	6	145	11	3	10	340	.253	11	38	168	.292	8	24
Hudek, Cin.	2	0	0	0	0	0	0	0	0	0	.000	.000	.000	0	0	0	0	0	0	0	0	0	0	.000	0	0	1	.000	0	0
Hudek, Cin.-Atl.	17	1	1	0	0	0	0	0	0	0	.000	.000	.000	0	0	0	0	0	1	0	0	0	0	.000	0	0	1	.000	0	0
Mulholland, Chi.	26	35	32	0	3	3	0	0	0	3	.094	.094	.094	3	0	0	0	0	17	0	0	0	10	.000	0	0	6	.333	0	0
Mulholland, Chi.-Atl.	42	55	48	2	5	5	0	0	0	3	.104	.140	.104	5	0	0	2	0	21	0	0	1	30	.067	0	3	18	.167	0	0
Myers, S.D.	50	141	128	9	37	50	4	0	3	15	.289	.355	.391	0	0	0	13	2	14	0	0	5	61	.213	2	7	11	.273	0	2
Myers, S.D.-Atl.	84	227	200	19	53	74	6	0	5	24	.265	.348	.370	0	1	0	26	4	30	0	0	6	171	.269	5	21	29	.241	0	3

PITCHING

Name	W	L	Pct.	ERA	IP	H	R	ER	HR	SH	SF	HB	BB	IBB	SO	G	GS	CG	ShO	GF	Sv	vs. RH AB	vs. RH Avg.	vs. RH HR	vs. RH RBI	vs. LH AB	vs. LH Avg.	vs. LH HR	vs. LH RBI
Glavine, Tom	14	11	.560	4.12	234.0	259	115	107	18	22	10	4	83	14	138	35	35	2	0	0	0	702	.292	16	87	202	.267	2	21
Millwood, Kevin	18	7	.720	2.68	228.0	168	80	68	24	9	3	4	59	2	205	33	33	2	0	0	0	418	.175	9	33	413	.230	15	41
Maddux, Greg	19	9	.679	3.57	219.1	258	103	87	16	15	5	4	37	8	136	33	33	4	0	0	0	469	.288	8	46	410	.300	8	51
Smoltz, John	11	8	.579	3.19	186.1	168	70	66	14	10	5	4	40	2	156	29	29	1	1	0	0	376	.229	7	34	311	.264	7	32
Perez, Odalis	4	6	.400	6.00	93.0	100	65	62	12	3	4	1	53	2	82	18	17	0	0	0	0	312	.266	9	40	51	.333	3	11
Remlinger, Mike	10	1	.909	2.37	83.2	66	24	22	9	2	1	1	35	5	81	73	0	0	0	14	1	224	.219	6	11	83	.205	3	10
Rocker, John	4	5	.444	2.49	72.1	47	24	20	5	2	0	1	37	4	104	74	0	0	0	61	38	204	.191	3	21	57	.140	2	11
McGlinchy, Kevin	7	3	.700	2.82	70.1	66	25	22	6	4	4	1	30	7	67	64	0	0	0	21	0	163	.270	3	21	96	.229	3	9
Mulholland, Terry	4	2	.667	2.98	60.1	64	24	20	5	3	1	0	13	2	39	16	8	0	0	3	1	196	.291	4	15	38	.184	1	5
Seanez, Rudy	6	1	.857	3.35	53.2	47	21	20	3	0	2	1	21	1	41	56	0	0	0	13	3	113	.230	0	11	88	.239	3	9
Chen, Bruce	2	2	.500	5.47	51.0	38	32	31	11	1	1	2	27	3	45	16	7	0	0	3	0	138	.203	8	19	45	.222	3	9
Springer, Russ	2	1	.667	3.42	47.1	31	20	18	5	0	2	2	22	2	49	49	0	0	0	8	1	103	.204	2	13	65	.154	3	10
Speier, Justin	0	0	.000	5.65	28.2	28	18	18	8	0	1	0	13	1	22	19	0	0	0	8	0	62	.226	5	11	51	.275	3	11
Hudek, John	0	1	.000	6.48	16.2	21	14	12	1	0	1	1	11	0	18	15	0	0	0	12	0	41	.341	1	10	30	.233	0	4
Ebert, Derrin	0	1	.000	5.63	8.0	9	5	5	2	0	0	0	5	1	4	5	0	0	0	3	1	18	.333	0	2	12	.250	2	3
Bergman, Sean	1	0	1.000	2.84	6.1	5	2	2	0	1	0	0	3	0	6	6	0	0	0	1	0	16	.250	0	1	7	.143	0	0
Bowie, Micah	0	1	.000	13.50	4.0	8	6	6	1	0	0	0	4	0	2	3	0	0	0	2	0	14	.357	0	0	5	.600	1	6
Cortes, David	0	0	.000	4.91	3.2	3	3	2	0	0	0	0	4	0	2	4	0	0	0	4	0	11	.182	0	3	3	.333	0	0
Cather, Mike	1	0	1.000	10.13	2.2	5	3	3	2	0	0	0	1	0	0	4	0	0	0	0	0	6	.500	2	3	6	.333	0	1
Stull, Everett	0	0	.000	13.50	0.2	2	3	1	0	0	1	0	2	0	0	1	0	0	0	0	0	0	.000	0	0	4	.500	0	3
Wohlers, Mark	0	0	.000	27.00	0.2	1	2	2	0	1	0	0	6	0	0	2	0	0	0	0	0	2	.000	0	0	1	1.000	0	1
Winkelsas, Joe	0	0	.000	54.00	0.1	4	2	2	0	1	0	0	1	1	0	1	0	0	0	0	0	3	1.000	0	2	1	1.000	0	0

PITCHERS WITH MORE THAN ONE N.L. TEAM

Name	W	L	Pct.	ERA	IP	H	R	ER	HR	SH	SF	HB	BB	IBB	SO	G	GS	CG	ShO	GF	Sv	vs. RH AB	vs. RH Avg.	vs. RH HR	vs. RH RBI	vs. LH AB	vs. LH Avg.	vs. LH HR	vs. LH RBI
Bergman, Hou.	4	6	.400	5.36	99.0	130	60	59	9	3	4	3	26	1	38	19	16	2	1	1	0	16	.250	0	1	7	.143	0	0
Bergman, Hou.-Atl.	5	6	.455	5.21	105.1	135	62	61	9	4	4	3	29	1	44	25	16	2	1	4	0	216	.343	4	31	199	.307	5	27
Bowie, Chi.	2	6	.250	9.96	47.0	73	54	52	8	3	3	2	30	2	39	11	11	0	0	0	0	14	.357	0	0	5	.600	1	6
Bowie, Atl.-Chi.	2	7	.222	10.24	51.0	81	60	58	9	3	3	2	34	2	41	14	11	0	0	3	0	190	.347	8	44	33	.455	1	13
Hudek, Cin.	0	1	.000	27.00	1.0	4	3	3	1	0	0	0	3	0	0	2	0	0	0	0	0	41	.341	1	10	30	.233	0	4
Hudek, Cin.-Atl.	0	2	.000	7.64	17.2	25	17	15	2	0	1	1	14	0	18	17	0	0	0	1	0	44	.386	2	14	33	.242	0	4
Mulholland, Chi.	6	6	.500	5.15	110.0	137	71	63	16	6	3	1	32	4	44	26	16	0	0	4	0	196	.291	4	15	38	.184	1	5
Mulholland, Chi.-Atl.	10	8	.556	4.39	170.1	201	95	83	21	9	4	1	45	6	83	42	24	0	0	4	1	532	.299	17	58	145	.290	4	21

INDIVIDUAL STATISTICS

FIELDING

FIRST BASEMEN

Player	Pct.	G	PO	A	E	TC	DP
Hunter, Brian	.99	101	425	36	4	465	37
Klesko, Ryan	.989	75	493	30	6	529	37
Simon, Randall	.994	70	462	27	3	492	38
Perez, Eddie	1.000	2	4	0	0	4	0
Fabregas, Jorge	1.000	1	0	1	0	1	0
Hernandez, Jose	1.000	1	1	0	0	1	0

SECOND BASEMEN

Player	Pct.	G	PO	A	E	TC	DP
Boone, Bret	.982	151	270	424	13	707	78
Lockhart, Keith	1.000	25	26	58	0	84	11
Guillen, Ozzie	1.000	1	1	0	0	1	0

THIRD BASEMEN

Player	Pct.	G	PO	A	E	TC	DP
Jones, Chipper	.950	156	88	238	17	343	10
Lockhart, Keith	.875	10	1	6	1	8	1
Guillen, Ozzie	1.000	6	3	9	0	12	1
Battle, Howard	1.000	6	2	4	0	6	0

SHORTSTOPS

Player	Pct.	G	PO	A	E	TC	DP
Weiss, Walt	.963	102	108	203	12	323	41
Guillen, Ozzie	.965	53	54	137	7	198	29
Hernandez, Jose	.964	45	48	114	6	168	24
DeRosa, Mark	1.000	2	2	2	0	4	0
Jones, Chipper	1.000	1	0	1	0	1	0

OUTFIELDERS

Player	Pct.	G	PO	A	E	TC	DP
Jones, Andruw	.981	162	492	13	10	515	1
Jordan, Brian	.990	150	295	9	3	307	3
Williams, Gerald	.985	139	188	9	3	200	2
Klesko, Ryan	1.000	53	61	2	0	63	0
Nixon, Otis	.981	52	52	0	1	53	0
Hunter, Brian	1.000	8	10	0	0	10	0
Lombard, George	1.000	4	4	0	0	4	0
Hernandez, Jose	1.000	1	5	0	0	5	0
Garcia, Freddy	-	1	0	0	0	0	0

CATCHERS

Player	Pct.	G	PO	A	E	TC	DP	PB
Perez, Eddie	.993	98	616	48	5	669	7	4
Lopez, Javy	.991	60	413	29	4	446	3	6
Myers, Greg	.994	31	166	12	1	179	2	0
Matos, Pascual	1.000	5	13	1	0	14	0	0
Fabregas, Jorge	1.000	4	21	0	0	21	0	0

PITCHERS

Player	Pct.	G	PO	A	E	TC	DP
Rocker, John	1.000	74	1	10	0	11	0
Remlinger, Mike	.933	73	4	10	1	15	1
McGlinchy, Kevin	.833	64	4	6	2	12	0
Seanez, Rudy	1.000	56	4	5	0	9	0
Springer, Russ	1.000	49	1	4	0	5	0
Glavine, Tom	.986	35	12	59	1	72	6
Maddux, Greg	.956	33	29	58	4	91	3
Millwood, Kevin	.943	33	13	20	2	35	0
Smoltz, John	.975	29	9	30	1	40	3
Speier, Justin	1.000	19	5	2	0	7	0
Perez, Odalis	1.000	18	4	17	0	21	1
Mulholland, Terry	.938	16	2	13	1	16	0
Chen, Bruce	.750	16	0	3	1	4	0
Hudek, John	1.000	15	1	2	0	3	0
Bergman, Sean	1.000	6	0	2	0	2	0
Ebert, Derrin	1.000	5	0	2	0	2	0
Cortes, David	.500	4	0	1	1	2	0
Cather, Mike	1.000	4	0	1	0	1	0
Bowie, Micah		3	0	0	0	0	0
Wohlers, Mark	.000	2	0	0	1	1	0
Stull, Everett	-	1	0	0	0	0	0
Winkelsas, Joe	-	1	0	0	0	0	0

PITCHING AGAINST EACH CLUB

Pitcher	Ari. W-L	Chi. W-L	Cin. W-L	Col. W-L	Fla. W-L	Hou. W-L	L.A. W-L	Mil. W-L	Mon. W-L	N.Y. W-L	Phi. W-L	Pit. W-L	S.D. W-L	S.F. W-L	StL. W-L	A.L. W-L	Total W-L
Bergman, S.	0-0	0-0	0-0	0-0	0-0	0-0	0-0	0-0	1-0	0-0	0-0	0-0	0-0	0-0	0-0	0-0	1-0
Bowie, M.	0-0	0-0	0-0	0-0	0-0	0-0	0-0	0-0	0-0	0-0	0-1	0-0	0-0	0-0	0-0	0-0	0-1
Cather, M.	0-0	0-0	0-0	0-0	0-0	0-0	0-0	0-0	0-0	1-0	0-0	0-0	0-0	0-0	0-0	0-0	1-0
Chen, B.	0-0	0-0	0-0	1-0	0-0	0-0	0-0	0-1	0-0	1-0	0-0	0-0	0-0	0-0	0-0	0-1	2-2
Cortes, D.	0-0	0-0	0-0	0-0	0-0	0-0	0-0	0-0	0-0	0-0	0-0	0-0	0-0	0-0	0-0	0-0	0-0
Ebert, D.	0-0	0-0	0-0	0-0	0-1	0-0	0-0	0-0	0-0	0-0	0-0	0-0	0-0	0-0	0-0	0-0	0-1
Glavine, T.	1-1	0-1	1-1	0-1	1-2	2-0	0-1	0-1	1-0	3-0	1-1	2-0	1-0	0-1	0-0	1-2	14-11
Hudek, J.	0-0	0-0	0-0	0-0	0-0	0-0	0-0	0-0	0-0	0-0	0-0	0-0	0-0	0-0	0-0	0-1	0-1
Maddux, G.	0-0	0-1	1-0	2-0	2-1	2-0	0-0	0-0	0-2	3-1	2-0	1-0	1-1	1-1	1-1	2-1	19-9
McGlinchy, K.	1-0	1-2	0-0	2-0	0-0	0-0	0-0	0-0	1-1	0-0	0-0	0-0	0-0	0-0	1-0	1-0	7-3
Millwood, K.	1-0	1-0	2-0	1-0	1-0	1-0	1-1	2-0	3-0	1-0	1-1	0-0	1-0	0-2	1-0	0-2	18-7
Mulholland, T.	0-0	1-0	0-1	0-0	0-0	1-0	0-0	0-0	1-0	0-0	0-0	0-1	0-1	0-0	0-0	0-0	4-2
Perez, O.	0-1	1-0	0-0	0-0	0-1	1-0	0-0	0-0	0-1	0-0	1-1	0-0	0-0	0-0	0-0	1-1	4-6
Remlinger, M.	0-0	0-0	0-0	0-0	0-0	0-0	2-1	0-0	1-0	0-1	1-0	0-0	1-0	0-0	0-0	0-0	10-1
Rocker, J.	1-1	0-0	0-0	0-2	0-0	0-0	0-0	0-0	1-0	0-1	0-0	1-0	1-1	0-0	0-0	0-0	4-5
Seanez, R.	0-0	0-0	0-0	0-0	1-0	0-0	0-0	2-0	0-0	0-1	0-0	0-0	0-0	0-0	1-0	2-0	6-1
Smoltz, J.	1-1	0-0	2-0	1-0	1-0	0-0	0-1	1-0	0-1	0-1	1-1	0-1	0-1	1-0	1-1	1-1	11-8
Speier, J.	0-0	0-0	0-0	0-0	0-0	0-0	0-0	0-0	0-0	0-0	0-0	0-0	0-0	0-0	0-0	0-0	0-0
Springer, R.	0-0	0-0	0-0	0-1	0-0	0-0	0-0	0-0	0-1	0-0	0-0	0-0	0-0	0-0	0-0	2-1	2-1
Stull, E.	0-0	0-0	0-0	0-0	0-0	0-0	0-0	0-0	0-0	0-0	0-0	0-0	0-0	0-0	0-0	0-0	0-0
Winkelsas, J.	0-0	0-0	0-0	0-0	0-0	0-0	0-0	0-0	0-0	0-0	0-0	0-0	0-0	0-0	0-0	0-0	0-0
Wohlers, M.	0-0	0-0	0-0	0-0	0-0	0-0	0-0	0-0	0-0	0-0	0-0	0-0	0-0	0-0	0-0	0-0	0-0
Totals	5-4	2-5	8-1	5-4	9-4	6-1	5-4	5-2	9-4	9-3	8-5	6-3	5-4	4-5	8-1	9-9	103-59

INTERLEAGUE: Maddux 0-1, Millwood 0-1, Smoltz 0-1 vs. Orioles; Maddux 2-0, Seanez 2-0, Glavine 0-1, Chen 0-1 vs. Red Sox; Glavine 1-0, Springer 1-0, Perez 0-1 vs. Yankees; Millwood 0-1, Hudek 0-1, Glavine 0-1 vs. Blue Jays; Smoltz 1-0, McGlinchy 1-0, Perez 1-0 vs. Devil Rays. Total: 9-9.

MISCELLANEOUS

HOME RUNS BY PARK

At Arizona (6): Lopez 3, Williams 2, Jones 1.
At Atlanta (86): Jones 25, Klesko 12, Jordan 11, Jones 10, Boone 9, Williams 7, Maddux 2, Hunter 2, Simon 2, Myers 1, Smoltz 1, Hernandez 1, Lopez 1, Garcia 1, Battle 1.
At Boston (2): Jordan 1, Klesko 1.
At Chicago (NL) (5): Boone 2, Jordan 1, Jones 1, Jones 1.
At Cincinnati (6): Weiss 1, Hunter 1, Boone 1, Jones 1, Perez 1, Jones 1.
At Colorado (13): Hunter 2, Hernandez 2, Jordan 2, Jones 2, Perez 2, Williams 1, Jones 1, Simon 1.
At Florida (5): Jordan 2, Jones 2, Boone 1.
At Houston (4): Lopez 2, Jones 2.
At Los Angeles (10): Jones 4, Jordan 2, Lopez 2, Boone 1, Jones 1.
At Milwaukee (8): Jones 3, Weiss 1, Hunter 1, Klesko 1, Lopez 1, Lockhart 1.
At Montreal (7): Williams 2, Perez 2, Jones 2, Guillen 1.
At New York (AL) (7): Klesko 2, Jones 2, Jordan 1, Williams 1, Jones 1.
At New York (NL) (12): Jones 3, Jordan 2, Boone 2, Williams 2, Klesko 1, Perez 1, Simon 1.
At Philadelphia (12): Boone 2, Klesko 2, Lopez 2, Jones 2, Jones 2, Williams 1, Simon 1.
At Pittsburgh (1): Myers 1.
At San Diego (4): Hernandez 1, Klesko 1, Perez 1, Millwood 1.
At San Francisco (7): Boone 2, Jordan 1, Klesko 1, Williams 1, Jones 1, Jones 1.
At St. Louis (1): Jones 1.
At Toronto (1): Jones 1.

LOW-HIT GAMES

No-hitters: None.
One-hitters: John Smoltz, April 30 vs. Cincinnati, W 3-0.
Two-hitters: None.

10-STRIKEOUT GAMES

Kevin Millwood 4, Greg Maddux 1, John Smoltz 1, **Total:** 6.

FOUR OR MORE HITS IN ONE GAME

Ryan Klesko 2, Javy Lopez 2, Eddie Perez 2 (including one five-hit game), Ozzie Guillen 1, Bret Boone 1, Gerald Williams 1, Chipper Jones 1, Andruw Jones 1 (including one five-hit game), Randall Simon 1, **Total:** 12.

MULTI-HOMER GAMES

Chipper Jones 6, Bret Boone 2, Ryan Klesko 2, Javy Lopez 2, Andruw Jones 2, Brian Jordan 1, Gerald Williams 1, Eddie Perez 1, **Total:** 17.

GRAND SLAMS

5-19: Brian Jordan (off Pittsburgh's Francisco Cordova).
8-1: Gerald Williams (off Philadelphia's Randy Wolf).

PINCH HITTERS

(Minimum 5 at-bats)

Name	AB	Avg.	HR	RBI
Lockhart, Keith	61	.246	1	12
Guillen, Ozzie	31	.226	0	3
Hunter, Brian	23	.261	0	3
Williams, Gerald	22	.227	1	3
Simon, Randall	19	.105	0	2
Nixon, Otis	15	.133	0	0
Battle, Howard	8	.375	0	2
Klesko, Ryan	8	.250	0	3
Perez, Eddie	6	.000	0	0
DeRosa, Mark	6	.000	0	0
Weiss, Walt	5	.400	0	0
Lopez, Javy	5	.200	1	2
Myers, Greg	5	.000	0	0

DEBUTS

4-5: Kevin McGlinchy, P.
4-6: Derrin Ebert, P.
4-10: Joe Winkelsas, P.
5-11: Pascual Matos, PH.
7-24: Micah Bowie, P.
8-30: David Cortes, P.

GAMES BY POSITION

Catcher: Eddie Perez 98, Javy Lopez 60, Greg Myers 31, Pascual Matos 5, Jorge Fabregas 4.
First base: Brian Hunter 101, Ryan Klesko 75, Randall Simon 70, Eddie Perez 2, Jose Hernandez 1, Jorge Fabregas 1.
Second base: Bret Boone 151, Keith Lockhart 25, Ozzie Guillen 1.
Third base: Chipper Jones 156, Keith Lockhart 10, Ozzie Guillen 6, Howard Battle 6.
Shortstop: Walt Weiss 102, Ozzie Guillen 53, Jose Hernandez 45, Mark DeRosa 2, Chipper Jones 1.
Outfield: Andruw Jones 162, Brian Jordan 150, Gerald Williams 139, Ryan Klesko 53, Otis Nixon 52, Brian Hunter 8, George Lombard 4, Jose Hernandez 1, Freddy Garcia 1.
Designated hitter: Javy Lopez 4, Keith Lockhart 4, Ryan Klesko 1.

STREAKS

Wins: 10 (August 17-29).
Losses: 5 (July 17-21).
Consecutive games with at least one hit: 14, Bret Boone (April 27-May 11), Andruw Jones (August 13-27).
Wins by pitcher: 8, Greg Maddux (July 26-September 6).

ATTENDANCE

Home: 3,284,901.
Road: 2,482,171.
Highest (home): 50,203 (July 31 vs. Philadelphia).
Highest (road): 55,785 (July 17 vs. New York).
Lowest (home): 26,990 (April 27 vs. Pittsburgh).
Lowest (road): 7,069 (June 29 vs. Montreal).

DAY BY DAY

Date	Opp.	Res.	Score	(inn.*)	Hits	Opp. hits	Winning pitcher	Losing pitcher	Save	Record	Pos.	GB
4-6	At Hou.	W	2-4		8	8	Reynolds	Trachsel	Wagner	0-1	T4th	1.0
4-7	At Hou.	W	9-2		12	5	Tapani	Hampton		1-1	T1st	...
4-8	At Hou.	W	2-1		6	6	Lieber	Lima	Beck	2-1	T1st	...
4-9	At Pit.	L	1-2		4	2	Benson	Sanders	Williams	2-2	T1st	...
4-10	At Pit.	L	3-9		5	9	Sauerbeck	Woodall		2-3	T3rd	1.0
4-11	At Pit.	L	6-9		13	12	Schmidt	Trachsel		2-4	T4th	2.0
4-12	Cin.	L	2-7		6	13	Avery	Tapani		2-5	6th	2.5
4-14	Cin.	W	5-4		6	9	Lieber	Harnisch	Beck	3-5	T4th	2.0
4-16	At Mil.	W	9-4		13	8	Heredia	Pulsipher		4-5	T3rd	2.0
4-17	At Mil.	L	4-5		9	8	Myers	Beck		4-6	T5th	3.0
4-18	At Mil.	W	6-5	(10)	13	11	Beck	de los Santos	Serafini	5-6	4th	2.0
4-20	Hou.	L	4-10		9	16	Lima	Lieber	Elarton	5-7	4th	3.5
4-21	Hou.	L	3-10		10	13	Reynolds	Sanders		5-8	T5th	3.5
4-23	N.Y.	L	5-6		8	13	Cook	Beck	Franco	5-9	6th	4.5
4-24	N.Y.	W	2-0		5	8	Mulholland	Watson	Beck	6-9	5th	3.5
4-25	N.Y.	W	8-4		8	11	Myers	Hershiser		7-9	5th	3.5
4-27	At Fla.	L	0-8		6	14	Edmondson	Sanders		7-10	5th	4.5
4-28	At Fla.	W	6-1		16	3	Trachsel	Hernandez		8-10	5th	3.5
4-29	At Fla.	W	5-2		12	10	Farnsworth	Sanchez	Beck	9-10	3rd	2.5
4-30	S.D.	W	6-5		9	10	Mulholland	Spencer	Beck	10-10	3rd	2.0
5-1	S.D.	W	2-1		7	3	Tapani	Clement	Heredia	11-10	3rd	2.0
5-2	S.D.	W	3-2		12	6	Myers	Rivera	Beck	12-10	3rd	2.0
5-3	Col.	L	1-6		6	12	Bohanon	Trachsel		12-11	3rd	2.0
5-4	Col.	W	13-12		14	17	Beck	Dipoto		13-11	3rd	2.0
5-5	Col.	L	6-13		10	18	Astacio	Mulholland		13-12	3rd	3.0
5-7	At Cin.	L	2-3		6	13	Graves	Beck		13-13	T3rd	4.0
5-8	At Cin.	W	7-4		11	11	Lieber	Neagle	Beck	14-13	3rd	3.0
5-9	At Cin.	L	5-8		7	13	Williamson	Adams	Graves	14-14	4th	3.0
5-10	At L.A.	L	3-4		12	7	Valdes	Trachsel	Shaw	14-15	4th	4.0
5-11	At L.A.	W	10-5		11	9	Farnsworth	Perez		15-15	T3rd	4.0
5-12	At L.A.	L	2-3		5	8	Arnold	Beck		15-16	4th	5.0
5-14	Atl.	W	9-0		10	7	Lieber	Glavine		16-16	T2nd	5.0
5-15	Atl.	W	5-1		15	6	Trachsel	Maddux		17-16	2nd	5.0
5-16	Atl.	L	5-8		8	11	McGlinchy	Myers	Rocker	17-17	4th	5.0
5-17	At Fla.	W	8-1		12	4	Tapani	Dempster		18-17	3rd	4.5
5-18	At Fla.	W	4-1	(11)	10	3	Heredia	Springer	Sanders	19-17	3rd	4.5
5-19	At Fla.	W	8-7		12	11	Myers	Mantei	Adams	20-17	2nd	3.5
5-20	At Atl.	W	6-5	(12)	10	10	Serafini	McGlinchy		21-17	2nd	3.5
5-21	At Atl.	W	8-4		9	8	Adams	McGlinchy		22-17	2nd	2.5
5-22	At Atl.	L	2-4		7	7	Millwood	Tapani	Rocker	22-18	2nd	2.5
5-23	At Atl.	W	5-1		6	5	Mulholland	Perez		23-18	2nd	2.5
5-24	Fla.	L	5-7		9	12	Mantei	Aguilera		23-19	T2nd	3.5
5-25	Fla.	L	3-6		8	8	Meadows	Trachsel		23-20	T3rd	4.5
5-26	Fla.	W	6-4		11	7	Aguilera	Looper		24-20	2nd	4.5
5-28	StL.	W	6-3		14	7	Tapani	Painter	Aguilera	25-20	2nd	3.0
5-29	StL.	W	4-3		8	9	Heredia	Bottalico		26-20	2nd	2.0
5-30	StL.	W	7-4		12	10	Lieber	Jimenez		27-20	2nd	1.0
6-1	S.D.	L	0-1	(6)	3	4	Ashby	Trachsel		27-21	2nd	2.0
6-2	S.D.	W	9-8		14	11	Sanders	Hoffman		28-21	2nd	2.0
6-3	S.D.	W	7-2		7	10	Tapani	Clement		29-21	2nd	1.0
6-4	At Cle.	W	5-4		8	8	Aguilera	Jackson	Adams	30-21	2nd	1.0
6-5	At Cle.	L	7-8	(11)	11	16	Jackson	Sanders		30-22	2nd	2.0
6-6	At Cle.	L	2-4		8	8	Nagy	Trachsel	Shuey	30-23	3rd	2.0
6-7	At Ari.	W	7-6		13	12	Adams	Holmes		31-23	2nd	1.0
6-8	At Ari.	W	5-3		5	6	Aguilera	Olson	Adams	32-23	2nd	1.0
6-9	At Ari.	L	7-8		12	18	Johnson	Mulholland	Nunez	32-24	2nd	2.0
6-11	Chi. (AL)	L	3-5	(6)	5	11	Parque	Lieber		32-25	2nd	3.0
6-12	Chi. (AL)	L	2-8		8	18	Sirotka	Trachsel		32-26	2nd	4.0
6-13	Chi. (AL)	L	4-6		7	12	Simas	Aguilera	Foulke	32-27	2nd	4.5
6-14	At Mil.	L	1-5		9	11	Woodard	Farnsworth		32-28	3rd	5.5
6-15	At Mil.	W	7-4		9	10	Lieber	Abbott	Adams	33-28	2nd	4.5
6-16	At Mil.	L	4-11		6	12	Nomo	Trachsel		33-29	2nd	4.5
6-17	At S.F	L	2-3		4	10	Nen	Serafini		33-30	4th	4.5
6-18	At S.F	L	5-8		8	10	Ortiz	Tapani	Nen	33-31	4th	5.5
6-19	At S.F	L	5-11		6	9	Estes	Farnsworth		33-32	4th	6.5
6-20	At S.F	L	6-7		11	9	Embree	Aguilera		33-33	4th	7.5
6-22	At Col.	W	13-12		14	15	Sanders	DeJean	Aguilera	34-33	3rd	7.0
6-23	At Col.	L	1-10		7	19	Astacio	Mulholland		34-34	4th	7.0
6-24	At Col.	W	12-10		15	18	Tapani	Jones		35-34	3rd	6.0
6-25	Phi.	L	2-3		3	6	Ogea	Lieber	Gomes	35-35	4th	6.0
6-26	Phi.	L	2-6		8	11	Person	Trachsel		35-36	5th	6.0
6-27	Phi.	W	13-7		15	11	Mulholland	Grace		36-36	4th	5.0
6-29	Mil.	L	6-17		9	21	Woodard	Tapani		36-37	4th	6.0
6-30	Mil.	W	5-4		7	10	Karchner	Weathers	Aguilera	37-37	4th	6.0
7-1	Mil.	L	12-19		11	21	Myers	Trachsel		37-38	4th	7.0
7-2	At Phi.	L	1-14		6	17	Wolf	Mulholland		37-39	4th	7.0
7-3	At Phi.	L	8-21		11	21	Byrd	Farnsworth		37-40	6th	8.0

HIGHLIGHTS

High point: The Cubs finished a 9-3 run on June 8 when they won at Arizona. The victory gave Chicago a 32-23 record and put the Cubs one game out of first place in the N.L. Central. At that point, Chicago's starting pitching was among the league's best.

Low point: The Cubs tumbled 30 games below .500 at 56-86 when they lost at Houston on September 11. It took a monumental collapse—63 defeats in 87 games.

Turning point: Four days in June. First, down 8-1 to the Diamondbacks' Randy Johnson, the Cubs closed within 8-7 before Lance Johnson was picked off first base to end the June 9 game. Then the club came home and was swept in three games by the White Sox.

Most valuable player: In a dismal season, right fielder Sammy Sosa was a shining light as he won at Arizona with 63 home runs and 141 RBIs. Though he finished second to the Cardinals' Mark McGwire in the homer race, Sosa became the first man to hit 60 homers in consecutive seasons when he connected off Milwaukee's Jason Bere on September 18.

Most valuable pitcher: Righthander Jon Lieber was the only Cubs pitcher to win 10 games. Lieber started the season 8-3 but didn't capture his ninth victory until September 25 (a drought of 2 1/2 months). He set career highs in strikeouts (186) and innings pitched (203.1).

Most improved player: Kyle Farnsworth came up late in April and won his first two decisions before suffering through massive growing pains (he twice was sent back to Class AAA Iowa). But the righthander finished up well, winning three of his last five decisions.

Most pleasant surprise: Veteran left fielder Glenallen Hill hit an even .300 with 20 home runs and 55 RBIs as a part-timer. Plus, he was positive in the clubhouse.

Key injuries: Kerry Wood, the 1998 rookie sensation, missed the entire season because of major surgery after blowing out his right elbow in spring training. Righthander Jeremi Gonzalez suffered a setback in his recovery from '98 elbow surgery and, like Wood, underwent "Tommy John surgery." Overall, the Cubs placed 13 players on the D.L. in '99.

Notable: After winning the wild card in '98, the Cubs hoped to post their first back-to-back winning seasons since 1971-1972—but failed miserably. ... The team ERA of 5.27 was the worst in club history, as were the number of homers allowed (221) and runs given up (920). ... Mark Grace led the majors in hits (1,754) and doubles (364) in the 1990s. Third baseman Gary Gaetti became the 40th player in big-league history to play in 2,500 games.

—BRUCE MILES

MISCELLANEOUS

RECORDS

1999 regular-season record: 67-95 (6th in N.L. Central); 34-47 at home; 33-48 on road; 18-23 vs. N.L. East; 28-34 vs. N.L. Central; 15-29 vs. N.L. West; 6-9 vs. A.L. Central; 25-22 vs. lefthanded starters; 42-73 vs. righthanded starters; 58-76 on grass; 9-19 on turf; 41-49 in daytime; 26-46 at night; 26-24 in one-run games; 5-6 in extra-inning games; 0-1-2 in doubleheaders.

Team record past five years: 374-419 (.472, ranks 11th in league in that span).

TEAM LEADERS

Batting average: Mark Grace (.309).
At-bats: Sammy Sosa (625).
Runs: Sammy Sosa (114).
Hits: Mark Grace (183).
Total bases: Sammy Sosa (397).
Doubles: Mark Grace (44).
Triples: Lance Johnson (6).
Home runs: Sammy Sosa (63).
Runs batted in: Sammy Sosa (141).
Stolen bases: Lance Johnson (13).
Slugging percentage: Sammy Sosa (.635).
On-base percentage: Mark Grace (.390).
Wins: Jon Lieber (10).
Earned-run average: Jon Lieber (4.07).
Complete games: Steve Trachsel (4).
Shutouts: Kyle Farnsworth, Jon Lieber, Andrew Lorraine (1).
Saves: Terry Adams (13).
Innings pitched: Steve Trachsel (205.2).
Strikeouts: Jon Lieber (186).

1999 REVIEW

Date	Opp.	Res.	Score	(inn.*)	Hits	Opp. hits	Winning pitcher	Losing pitcher	Save	Record	Pos.	GB
7-4	At Phi.	L	2-6		7	12	Schilling	Tapani		37-41	6th	8.0
7-5	At Pit.	W	5-2		9	11	Lieber	Schmidt	Aguilera	38-41	6th	8.0
7-6	At Pit.	L	1-6		9	8	Ritchie	Trachsel		38-42	6th	8.0
7-7	At Pit.	L	1-4		5	8	Cordova	Mulholland		38-43	6th	8.0
7-8	At Pit.	W	9-4		11	5	Serafini	Benson	Sanders	39-43	6th	8.0
7-9	At Chi. (AL)	L	2-3		9	9	Howry	Adams		39-44	6th	9.0
7-10	At Chi. (AL)	W	10-2		12	8	Lieber	Navarro		40-44	6th	8.0
7-11	At Chi. (AL)	W	6-3		7	6	Trachsel	Baldwin	Adams	41-44	6th	8.0
7-15	Min.	W	9-3		17	9	Sanders	Radke	Adams	42-44	T4th	8.0
7-16	Min.	W	11-10		16	15	Adams	Trombley		43-44	T3rd	8.0
7-17	Min.	L	0-8		3	14	Mays	Mulholland		43-45	6th	9.0
7-18	K.C.	L	4-5		11	8	Suppan	Tapani	Service	43-46	6th	10.0
7-19	K.C.	L	2-10		6	13	Witasick	Trachsel		43-47	6th	11.0
7-20	K.C.	W	8-7		15	14	Sanders	Barber	Adams	44-47	6th	10.0
7-21	Pit.	W	2-1		9	6	Aguilera	Christiansen		45-47	T4th	9.0
7-22	Pit.	W	5-3		10	8	Mulholland	Benson	Adams	46-47	4th	8.0
7-23	At N.Y.	L	4-5		7	9	Cook	Tapani	Benitez	46-48	5th	9.5
7-24	At N.Y.	L	1-2		6	5	Dotel	Trachsel	Benitez	46-49	T5th	10.5
7-25	At N.Y.	L	1-5		8	5	Leiter	Serafini		46-50	6th	11.5
7-26	At Mon.	L	1-6		9	9	Smith	Lieber		46-51	6th	12.5
7-27	At Mon.	W	4-2		8	10	Mulholland	Hermanson	Adams	47-51	5th	13.0
7-28	At Mon.	L	2-8		3	10	Vazquez	Tapani		47-52	6th	13.5
7-30	N.Y.	L	9-10		13	14	Mahomes	Farnsworth	Benitez	47-53	6th	14.0
7-31	N.Y.	W	17-10		14	18	Serafini	Isringhausen		48-53	6th	14.0
8-1	N.Y.	L	4-5	(13)	10	10	Mahomes	Sanders		48-54	6th	14.0
8-2	Mon.	L	1-5		6	7	Hermanson	Tapani	Urbina	48-55	6th	14.5
8-3	Mon.	L	4-9		12	13	Vazquez	Bowie		48-56	6th	15.5
8-4	Mon.	W	5-1		7	5	Trachsel	Powell		49-56	5th	14.5
8-5	Mon.	L	2-5		10	10	Thurman	Lieber	Urbina	49-57	T5th	15.5
8-6†	Hou.	L	1-6		8	10	Lima	Farnsworth	Powell	49-58		
8-6‡	Hou.	W	6-0		9	3	Lorraine	Bergman		50-58	5th	15.5
8-7	Hou.	L	4-10		5	14	Elarton	Tapani		50-59	6th	16.5
8-8	Hou.	L	2-6		7	14	Hampton	Bowie		50-60	6th	17.5
8-9	Ari.	L	7-10		8	15	Daal	Sanders		50-61	6th	17.5
8-10	Ari.	L	1-3		9	5	Swindell	Lieber	Olson	50-62	6th	17.5
8-11	Ari.	L	5-7	(11)	9	15	Plesac	Rain	Olson	50-63	6th	17.5
8-13	At StL.	L	1-7		8	7	Bottenfield	Farnsworth		50-64	6th	17.5
8-14	At StL.	W	9-7		10	10	Adams	Slocumb		51-64	6th	17.5
8-15	At StL.	L	5-6		9	13	Bottalico	Adams		51-65	6th	17.5
8-16	At Ari.	L	3-10		7	14	Johnson	Lieber		51-66	6th	18.5
8-17	At Ari.	L	0-4		3	7	Anderson	Lorraine		51-67	6th	19.5
8-18	At Ari.	L	1-3		5	10	Benes	Tapani	Mantei	51-68	6th	20.5
8-20	Col.	L	3-11		7	14	Astacio	Farnsworth		51-69	6th	21.0
8-21	Col.	W	8-6		10	12	Bowie	Thomson	Adams	52-69	6th	21.0
8-22	Col.	L	2-3		6	5	Wright	Trachsel	Veres	52-70	6th	21.5
8-24	S.F	L	4-12		9	18	Estes	Lorraine		52-71	6th	22.0
8-25†	S.F	L	5-11		7	14	Ortiz	Tapani		52-72		
8-25‡	S.F	L	5-6		10	9	Rueter	Lieber	Nen	52-73	6th	22.5
8-26	S.F	W	11-10		16	11	Adams	Nen		53-73	6th	22.0
8-27	At L.A.	L	0-9		7	13	Valdes	Trachsel		53-74	6th	22.5
8-28	At L.A.	L	3-4		8	7	Park	Lorraine	Shaw	53-75	6th	22.5
8-29	At L.A.	W	6-0		9	2	Farnsworth	Dreifort		54-75	6th	22.5
8-30	At S.D.	L	4-8		11	10	Wall	Heredia		54-76	6th	22.5
8-31	At S.D.	L	3-7		5	9	Ashby	Bowie		54-77	6th	23.5
9-1	At S.D.	W	1-0		2	4	Trachsel	Hitchcock	Adams	55-77	6th	22.5
9-3	L.A.	L	6-8		12	9	Park	Sanders	Shaw	55-78	6th	23.5
9-4	L.A.	L	0-6		2	11	Brown	Farnsworth		55-79	6th	24.5
9-5	L.A.	L	1-4		7	6	Dreifort	Lieber	Shaw	55-80	6th	25.5
9-6	Cin.	L	3-6		7	7	Guzman	Bowie	Graves	55-81	6th	26.5
9-7†	Cin.	W	2-1		5	4	Trachsel	Villone	Adams	56-81		
9-7‡	Cin.	L	3-10		10	16	Tomko	McNichol		56-82	6th	27.0
9-8	Cin.	L	4-6		9	9	Parris	Lorraine	Graves	56-83	6th	28.0
9-9	Cin.	L	3-5		9	14	Sullivan	Farnsworth	Graves	56-84	6th	29.0
9-10	At Hou.	L	4-6	(13)	9	12	Wagner	Ayala		56-85	6th	30.0
9-11	At Hou.	L	3-5		7	7	Lima	Bowie	Wagner	56-86	6th	31.0
9-12	At Hou.	L	1-7		6	12	Holt	Trachsel		56-87	6th	32.0
9-14	At Cin.	W	4-3		6	9	Farnsworth	Harnisch	Adams	57-87	6th	32.5
9-15	At Cin.	L	4-5		12	10	Neagle	Lieber	Graves	57-88	6th	32.5
9-16	At Cin.	W	7-6		9	8	Adams	Graves	Aguilera	58-88	6th	32.0
9-17	Mil.	W	6-5	(10)	7	11	Aguilera	Peterson		59-88	6th	31.0
9-18	Mil.	L	4-7	(14)	10	9	Peterson	Guthrie		59-89	6th	31.0
9-19	Mil.	W	8-7	(10)	12	10	Aguilera	Ramirez		60-89	6th	31.0
9-20	StL.	L	2-7		8	9	Thompson	Lieber		60-90	6th	31.0
9-21	StL.	L	2-7		3	8	Bottenfield	Lorraine		60-91	6th	32.0
9-22	StL.	W	5-3		8	7	Trachsel	Stephenson	Aguilera	61-91	6th	31.0
9-23	Pit.	W	8-5		13	7	Bowie	Peters	Aguilera	62-91	6th	30.5
9-24	Pit.	W	9-0		14	5	Farnsworth	Schmidt		63-91	6th	30.5
9-25	Pit.	W	3-1		5	3	Lieber	Cordova		64-91	6th	29.5
9-26	Pit.	L	4-8	(11)	8	15	Sauerbeck	Guthrie		64-92	6th	29.5
9-28	At Phi.	W	8-2		10	9	Trachsel	Wolf		65-92	6th	29.5
9-29	At Phi.	L	0-5		4	12	Brewer	Bowie		65-93	6th	29.5
9-30	At Phi.	L	1-2		3	7	Person	McNichol	Montgomery	65-94	6th	30.0
10-1	At StL.	W	3-2		7	7	Lieber	Thompson		66-94	6th	29.0
10-2	At StL.	W	6-3		10	6	Lorraine	Stephenson	Aguilera	67-94	6th	29.0
10-3	At StL.	L	5-9	(5)	6	10	Luebbers	Trachsel	Ankiel	67-95	6th	30.0

Monthly records: April (10-10), May (17-10), June (10-17), July (11-16), August (6-24), September (11-17), October (2-1).
*Innings, if other than nine. † First game of a doubleheader. ‡ Second game of a doubleheader.

MEMORABLE GAMES

June 9 at Arizona

The Cubs started the day just one game out of first place. After falling behind 8-1 to the Diamondbacks, the Cubs rallied with six runs in the eighth. But with two outs in the ninth, pinch-runner Lance Johnson was picked off first base. It was the beginning of the end for Chicago, they finished last in the Central.

Chi Cubs	AB	R	H	RBI	Arizona	AB	R	H	RBI
Blauser, 3b	3	0	0	0	Womack, rf	5	1	2	1
Serafini, p	0	0	0	0	J.Bell, 2b	5	2	2	2
R.Brown, ph	1	0	0	0	Gilkey, lf	4	1	2	0
S.Sanders, p	0	0	0	0	Kim, p	0	0	0	0
F.Heredia, p	0	0	0	0	V.Nunez, p	0	0	0	0
Alxndr, 2b-ss-3b	5	1	3	1	M.Wllms, 3b	5	1	1	2
S.Sosa, cf	5	1	1	1	T.Lee, 1b	5	2	5	0
G.Hill, rf	5	1	3	1	D.Miller, c	5	0	3	1
Gaetti, 1b	2	0	0	0	S.Finley, cf	5	0	1	1
Morndni, ph-2b	3	1	1	1	T.Batista, ss	2	1	2	0
H.Rodrgz, lf	3	1	0	0	Ra.Johnson, p	2	0	0	0
L.Johnson, pr	0	0	0	0	Dellucci, lf	0	0	0	0
B.Sntgo, c-1b-c	4	1	3	1					
J.Hrndz, ss-1b	1	0	0	0					
Ma.Grce, ph-1b	1	0	0	0					
Mulholland, p	1	0	0	0					
R.Myers, p	1	0	0	0					
Hston, ph-c-3b	2	1	1	1					
Totals	**37**	**7**	**12**	**6**	**Totals**	**38**	**8**	**18**	**7**

Chi Cubs ....100 000 060— 7
Arizona.......................................013 211 00x— 8

E—Gaetti (7), D.Miller (2). DP—Chi. Cubs 2, Arizona 1. LOB—Chi Cubs 8, Arizona 11. 2B—G.Hill 2 (4), Houston (4), Womack (5), J.Bell (11), T.Lee (8), D.Miller (12). 3B—Morandini (3), T.Lee (1). HR—S.Sosa (21), J.Bell (18), M.Williams (17). SB—Alexander (1), G.Hill (1), Womack (28), T.Lee (12). CS—L.Johnson (3). SH—Ra.Johnson 2.

Chi Cubs	IP	H	R	ER	BB	SO
Mulholland (L, 3-2)	3	10	6	6	2	0
R.Myers	3	7	2	2	1	3
Serafini	1	0	0	0	0	0
S.Sanders	0.2	1	0	0	0	1
F.Heredia	0.1	0	0	0	0	0

Arizona	IP	H	R	ER	BB	SO
Ra.Johnson (W, 8-2)	7	10	6	6	3	14
Kim (H, 1)	1	2	1	0	0	2
V.Nunez (S, 1)	1	0	0	0	1	0

HBP—Blauser by Ra.Johnson. PB—D.Miller. U—HP, Winters. 1B, Davidson. 2B, Montague. 3B, Kulpa. T—2:56. A—46,033.

September 18 at Chicago

Sammy Sosa became the first man in major league history to hit at least 60 home runs in back-to-back seasons when he connected off the Brewers' Jason Bere in the sixth inning of a 7-4 loss that took 14 innings to complete.

Milwaukee	AB	R	H	RBI	Chi Cubs	AB	R	H	RBI
Grissom, cf	7	1	1	0	R.Brown, cf	5	1	2	0
Loretta, 1b	5	0	1	0	F.Heredia, p	0	0	0	0
Cirillo, 3b	6	0	0	0	Ayala, p	0	0	0	0
Burnitz, rf	6	1	1	2	Alexander, ph	1	0	0	0
Belliard, 2b	6	1	1	1	Aguilera, p	0	0	0	0
Ochoa, lf	4	2	1	0	Liniak, 3b	1	0	0	0
Jos.Valntn, ss	5	2	1	0	Meyers, 2b	2	0	1	0
Cancel, c	3	0	1	2	Morndni, ph-2b	3	0	0	0
Jenkins, ph	1	0	0	0	Ma.Grace, 1b	5	2	1	0
Wickman, p	0	0	0	0	S.Sosa, rf	6	1	2	1
Weathers, p	0	0	0	0	H.Rodrgz, lf	6	0	1	0
L.Mouton, ph	1	0	0	0	S.Sanders, p	0	0	0	0
Peterson, p	1	0	0	0	Andrews, 3b	5	0	1	2
Bere, p	2	0	1	0	Guthrie, p	0	0	0	0
Plunk, p	0	0	0	0	Porter, lf	1	0	0	0
K.Barker, ph	1	0	0	0	Nieves, ss	4	0	1	0
Roque, p	0	0	0	0	G.Hill, ph	0	0	0	0
H.Ramirez, p	0	0	0	0	Blauser, ss	2	0	0	0
M.Myers, p	0	0	0	0	J.Molina, c	2	0	0	0
Coppinger, p	0	0	0	0	L.Jnson, ph-cf	1	0	0	1
C.Greene, c	0	0	0	0	Bowie, p	2	0	1	0
Banks, ph-c	3	0	1	2	Gaetti, ph	1	0	0	0
					R.Myers, p	0	0	0	0
					J.Reed, ph-c	3	0	0	0
Totals	**51**	**7**	**9**	**7**	**Totals**	**50**	**4**	**10**	**4**

Milwaukee ....100 200 001 000 03— 7
Chi Cubs ....100 001 101 000 00— 4

E—Cancel (2), Nieves (14). DP—Milwaukee 2. LOB—Milwaukee 6, Chi Cubs 17. 2B—Grissom (24), Ochoa (16), Cancel (2), Nieves (7). 3B—Banks (1). HR—Burnitz (32), Belliard (7), Sosa (60). SB—Ochoa (5).

Milwaukee	IP	H	R	ER	BB	SO
Bere	5.2	5	2	2	4	5
Plunk (H, 14)	0.1	0	0	0	0	0
Roque (H, 6)	0.2	0	1	1	1	1
H.Ramirez	0	0	0	0	1	0
M.Myers	0	0	0	0	1	0
Coppinger (BS 2)	1.1	2	0	0	1	0
Wickman (BS 8)	1	1	1	1	3	2
Weathers	2	1	0	0	0	2
Peterson (W, 2-6)	3	1	0	0	2	2

Chi Cubs	IP	H	R	ER	BB	SO
Bowie	6	5	3	3	2	5
R.Myers	2	0	0	0	0	2
F.Heredia	0	1	1	1	0	0
Ayala	2	0	0	0	1	4
Aguilera	1	0	0	0	0	1
Guthrie (L, 0-1)	2.1	1	1	1	0	2
S.Sanders	0.2	2	2	2	1	1

WP—Bowie, Ayala. U—HP, Gibson. 1B, Rapuano. 2B, Lamphugh. 3B, C.Williams. T—4:44. A—39,304.

INDIVIDUAL STATISTICS

BATTING

Name	G	TPA	AB	R	H	TB	2B	3B	HR	RBI	Avg.	Obp.	Slg.	SH	SF	HP	BB	IBB	SO	SB	CS	GDP	vs RHP AB	vs RHP Avg.	vs RHP HR	vs RHP RBI	vs LHP AB	vs LHP Avg.	vs LHP HR	vs LHP RBI
Sosa, Sammy	162	712	625	114	180	397	24	2	63	141	.288	.367	.635	0	6	3	78	8	171	7	8	17	462	.279	45	104	163	.313	18	37
Grace, Mark	161	688	593	107	183	285	44	5	16	91	.309	.390	.481	0	10	2	83	4	44	3	4	14	394	.310	12	57	199	.307	4	34
Morandini, Mickey	144	521	456	60	110	150	18	5	4	37	.241	.319	.329	7	4	6	48	2	61	6	6	10	359	.265	4	35	97	.155	0	2
Rodriguez, Henry	130	504	447	72	136	243	29	0	26	87	.304	.381	.544	0	1	0	56	6	113	2	4	9	308	.334	18	69	139	.237	8	18
Santiago, Benito	109	386	350	28	87	132	18	3	7	36	.249	.313	.377	0	2	2	32	6	71	1	1	12	218	.248	2	15	132	.250	5	21
Hernandez, Jose	99	388	342	57	93	154	12	2	15	43	.272	.357	.450	1	0	5	40	3	101	7	2	5	233	.279	8	29	109	.257	7	14
Johnson, Lance	95	377	335	46	87	113	11	6	1	21	.260	.332	.337	4	1	0	37	0	20	13	3	6	266	.278	1	19	69	.188	0	2
Gaetti, Gary	113	308	280	22	57	95	9	1	9	46	.204	.260	.339	0	5	2	21	0	51	0	1	5	162	.191	6	32	118	.220	3	14
Hill, Glenallen	99	278	253	43	76	147	9	1	20	55	.300	.353	.581	0	3	0	22	1	61	5	1	7	147	.259	16	39	106	.358	4	16
Houston, Tyler	100	279	249	26	58	96	9	1	9	27	.233	.309	.386	1	1	0	28	4	67	1	1	7	223	.238	8	25	26	.192	1	2
Blauser, Jeff	104	238	200	41	48	84	5	2	9	26	.240	.347	.420	2	2	8	26	0	52	2	2	0	106	.217	5	17	94	.266	4	9
Nieves, Jose	54	199	181	16	45	62	9	1	2	18	.249	.291	.343	3	3	4	8	0	25	0	2	5	136	.228	1	14	45	.311	1	4
Alexander, Manny	90	189	177	17	48	63	11	2	0	15	.271	.309	.356	1	1	0	10	0	38	4	0	1	84	.250	0	5	93	.290	0	10
Goodwin, Curtis	89	175	157	15	38	46	6	1	0	9	.242	.298	.293	4	1	0	13	1	38	2	4	7	132	.250	0	7	25	.200	0	2
Reed, Jeff	57	181	150	18	39	57	11	2	1	17	.260	.381	.380	0	1	2	28	0	34	1	1	4	128	.281	0	13	22	.136	1	4
Meyers, Chad	43	156	142	17	33	42	9	0	0	4	.232	.292	.296	2	0	3	9	1	27	4	2	5	100	.270	0	4	42	.143	0	0
Andrews, Shane	19	76	67	13	17	36	4	0	5	14	.254	.329	.537	0	1	1	7	1	21	0	1	0	53	.189	4	11	14	.500	1	3
Brown, Roosevelt	33	70	64	6	14	25	6	1	1	10	.219	.239	.391	3	1	0	2	0	14	1	0	2	62	.226	1	10	2	.000	0	0
Trachsel, Steve	34	71	63	4	7	8	1	0	0	0	.111	.125	.127	7	0	0	1	0	25	1	0	0	50	.140	0	0	13	.000	0	0
Lieber, Jon	31	71	58	8	7	8	1	0	0	2	.121	.188	.138	7	1	0	5	0	23	0	0	1	36	.111	0	2	22	.136	0	0
Tapani, Kevin	23	47	39	1	2	3	1	0	0	3	.051	.119	.077	5	0	0	3	0	21	0	0	0	31	.065	0	3	8	.000	0	0
Farnsworth, Kyle	27	44	35	3	3	3	0	0	0	2	.086	.158	.086	6	0	1	2	0	10	0	0	0	25	.120	0	2	10	.000	0	0
Mulholland, Terry	26	35	32	0	3	3	0	0	0	3	.094	.094	.094	3	0	0	0	0	17	0	0	0	20	.100	0	3	12	.083	0	0
Martinez, Sandy	17	30	30	1	5	8	0	0	1	1	.167	.167	.267	0	0	0	0	0	11	0	0	0	25	.160	1	1	5	.200	0	0
Liniak, Cole	12	30	29	3	7	9	2	0	0	2	.241	.267	.310	0	0	0	1	0	4	0	1	2	27	.222	0	2	2	.500	0	0
Porter, Bo	24	29	26	2	5	6	1	0	0	0	.192	.250	.231	1	0	0	2	0	13	0	0	1	11	.273	0	0	15	.133	0	0
Molina, Jose	10	21	19	3	5	6	1	0	0	1	.263	.333	.316	0	0	0	2	1	4	0	0	0	14	.286	0	0	5	.200	0	1
Sanders, Scott	67	20	18	0	5	7	2	0	0	1	.278	.278	.389	2	0	0	0	0	6	0	0	0	13	.231	0	1	5	.400	0	0
Lorraine, Andrew	12	20	15	1	2	3	1	0	0	0	.133	.188	.200	4	0	0	1	0	9	0	0	0	9	.111	0	0	6	.167	0	0
Bowie, Micah	11	15	14	0	3	3	0	0	0	3	.214	.267	.214	0	0	0	1	0	3	0	0	0	9	.333	0	2	5	.000	0	1
Serafini, Dan	42	16	12	1	1	1	0	0	0	0	.083	.267	.083	1	0	0	3	0	7	0	0	0	9	.111	0	0	3	.000	0	0
Myers, Rodney	46	7	7	2	3	4	1	0	0	1	.429	.429	.571	0	0	0	0	0	2	0	0	0	5	.400	0	1	2	.500	0	0
Jennings, Robin	5	5	5	0	1	1	0	0	0	0	.200	.200	.200	0	0	0	0	0	2	0	0	0	4	.250	0	0	1	.000	0	0
Heredia, Felix	69	4	4	0	2	2	0	0	0	1	.500	.500	.500	0	0	0	0	0	0	0	0	0	2	.500	0	0	2	.500	0	1
Woodall, Brad	6	4	2	0	1	1	0	0	0	0	.500	.750	.500	0	0	0	2	0	0	0	0	0	1	1.000	0	0	1	.000	0	0
Adams, Terry	52	2	2	0	0	0	0	0	0	0	.000	.000	.000	0	0	0	0	0	2	0	0	0	1	.000	0	0	1	.000	0	0
McNichol, Brian	4	3	2	0	0	0	0	0	0	0	.000	.000	.000	1	0	0	0	0	1	0	0	0	2	.000	0	0	0	.000	0	0
Aguilera, Rick	44	1	1	0	0	0	0	0	0	0	.000	.000	.000	0	0	0	0	0	0	0	0	0	1	.000	0	0	0	.000	0	0
King, Ray	10	1	1	0	0	0	0	0	0	0	.000	.000	.000	0	0	0	0	0	1	0	0	0	0	.000	0	0	1	.000	0	0
Guthrie, Mark	11	0	0	0	0	0	0	0	0	0	.000	.000	.000	0	0	0	0	0	0	0	0	0	0	.000	0	0	0	.000	0	0
Beck, Rod	31	0	0	0	0	0	0	0	0	0	.000	.000	.000	0	0	0	0	0	0	0	0	0	0	.000	0	0	0	.000	0	0
Ayala, Bobby	13	0	0	0	0	0	0	0	0	0	.000	.000	.000	0	0	0	0	0	0	0	0	0	0	.000	0	0	0	.000	0	0
Miller, Kurt	4	0	0	0	0	0	0	0	0	0	.000	.000	.000	0	0	0	0	0	0	0	0	0	0	.000	0	0	0	.000	0	0
Karchner, Matt	16	0	0	0	0	0	0	0	0	0	.000	.000	.000	0	0	0	0	0	0	0	0	0	0	.000	0	0	0	.000	0	0
Creek, Doug	3	0	0	0	0	0	0	0	0	0	.000	.000	.000	0	0	0	0	0	0	0	0	0	0	.000	0	0	0	.000	0	0
Barker, Richie	5	0	0	0	0	0	0	0	0	0	.000	.000	.000	0	0	0	0	0	0	0	0	0	0	.000	0	0	0	.000	0	0
Rain, Steve	16	0	0	0	0	0	0	0	0	0	.000	.000	.000	0	0	0	0	0	0	0	0	0	0	.000	0	0	0	.000	0	0

Players with more than one N.L. team

Name	G	TPA	AB	R	H	TB	2B	3B	HR	RBI	Avg.	Obp.	Slg.	SH	SF	HP	BB	IBB	SO	SB	CS	GDP	vs RHP AB	vs RHP Avg.	vs RHP HR	vs RHP RBI	vs LHP AB	vs LHP Avg.	vs LHP HR	vs LHP RBI
Andrews, Mon.	98	328	281	28	51	92	8	0	11	37	.181	.287	.327	0	4	0	43	2	88	1	0	10	53	.189	4	11	14	.500	1	3
Andrews, Mon.-Chi.	117	404	348	41	68	128	12	0	16	51	.195	.295	.368	0	5	1	50	3	109	1	1	10	257	.183	12	42	91	.231	4	9
Ayala, Mon.	53	1	1	0	0	0	0	0	0	0	.000	.000	.000	0	0	0	0	0	0	0	0	0	0	.000	0	0	0	.000	0	0
Ayala, Mon.-Chi.	66	1	1	0	0	0	0	0	0	0	.000	.000	.000	0	0	0	0	0	0	0	0	0	1	.000	0	0	0	.000	0	0
Bowie, Atl.	3	0	0	0	0	0	0	0	0	0	.000	.000	.000	0	0	0	0	0	0	0	0	0	9	.333	0	2	5	.000	0	1
Bowie, Atl.-Chi.	14	15	14	0	3	3	0	0	0	3	.214	.267	.214	0	0	0	1	0	3	0	0	0	9	.333	0	2	5	.000	0	1
Hernandez, Atl.	48	180	166	22	42	62	8	0	4	19	.253	.302	.373	1	1	0	12	3	44	4	1	5	233	.279	8	29	109	.257	7	14
Hernandez, Chi.-Atl.	147	568	508	79	135	216	20	2	19	62	.266	.339	.425	2	1	5	52	6	145	11	3	10	340	.253	11	38	168	.292	8	24
Mulholland, Atl.	16	20	16	2	2	2	0	0	0	0	.125	.222	.125	2	0	0	2	0	4	0	0	1	20	.100	0	3	12	.083	0	0
Mulholland, Chi.-Atl.	42	55	48	2	5	5	0	0	0	3	.104	.140	.104	5	0	0	2	0	21	0	0	1	30	.067	0	3	18	.167	0	0
Reed, Col.	46	125	106	11	27	38	5	0	2	11	.255	.360	.358	0	1	1	17	1	24	0	1	3	128	.281	0	13	22	.136	1	4
Reed, Col.-Chi.	103	306	256	29	66	95	16	2	3	28	.258	.373	.371	0	2	3	45	1	58	1	2	7	219	.274	2	21	37	.162	1	7

PITCHING

Name	W	L	Pct.	ERA	IP	H	R	ER	HR	SH	SF	HB	BB	IBB	SO	G	GS	CG	ShO	GF	Sv	vs. RH AB	vs. RH Avg.	vs. RH HR	vs. RH RBI	vs. LH AB	vs. LH Avg.	vs. LH HR	vs. LH RBI
Trachsel, Steve	8	18	.308	5.56	205.2	226	133	127	32	6	14	3	64	4	149	34	34	4	0	0	0	452	.277	16	63	355	.285	16	53
Lieber, Jon	10	11	.476	4.07	203.1	226	107	92	28	7	11	1	46	6	186	31	31	3	1	0	0	450	.236	10	40	360	.333	18	55
Tapani, Kevin	6	12	.333	4.83	136.0	151	81	73	12	8	7	4	33	2	73	23	23	1	0	0	0	304	.293	5	46	235	.264	7	31
Farnsworth, Kyle	5	9	.357	5.05	130.0	140	80	73	28	6	2	3	52	1	70	27	21	1	1	1	0	302	.268	18	44	214	.276	10	33
Mulholland, Terry	6	6	.500	5.15	110.0	137	71	63	16	6	3	1	32	4	44	26	16	0	0	4	0	336	.304	13	43	107	.327	3	16
Sanders, Scott	4	7	.364	5.52	104.1	112	69	64	19	8	3	0	53	8	89	67	6	0	0	16	2	268	.265	12	47	137	.299	7	19
Adams, Terry	6	3	.667	4.02	65.0	60	33	29	9	1	3	0	28	2	57	52	0	0	0	38	13	143	.287	6	26	102	.186	3	10
Myers, Rodney	3	1	.750	4.38	63.2	71	34	31	10	4	2	1	25	2	41	46	0	0	0	5	0	160	.269	10	31	86	.326	0	9
Serafini, Dan	3	2	.600	6.93	62.1	86	51	48	9	8	3	1	32	3	17	42	4	0	0	8	1	173	.358	5	33	85	.282	4	16
Lorraine, Andrew	2	5	.286	5.55	61.2	71	42	38	9	6	2	0	22	3	40	11	11	2	1	0	0	206	.296	9	33	36	.278	0	3
Heredia, Felix	3	1	.750	4.85	52.0	56	35	28	7	1	4	1	25	2	50	69	0	0	0	15	1	113	.292	4	22	93	.247	3	19
Bowie, Micah	2	6	.250	9.96	47.0	73	54	52	8	3	3	2	30	2	39	11	11	0	0	0	0	176	.347	8	44	28	.429	0	7
Aguilera, Rick	6	3	.667	3.69	46.1	44	22	19	6	4	2	2	10	1	32	44	0	0	0	25	8	105	.200	4	16	68	.338	2	10
Beck, Rod	2	4	.333	7.80	30.0	41	26	26	5	2	2	0	13	3	13	31	0	0	0	19	7	73	.301	4	17	51	.373	1	8
Karchner, Matt	1	0	1.000	2.50	18.0	16	5	5	3	1	0	2	9	0	9	16	0	0	0	2	0	43	.256	2	5	25	.200	1	2
Ayala, Bobby	0	1	.000	2.81	16.0	11	7	5	4	1	0	2	5	1	15	13	0	0	0	4	0	44	.205	3	6	13	.154	1	2
Woodall, Brad	0	1	.000	5.63	16.0	17	12	10	5	0	1	1	6	0	7	6	3	0	0	3	0	45	.267	4	7	18	.278	1	2
Rain, Steve	0	1	.000	9.20	14.2	28	17	15	1	3	1	1	7	0	12	16	0	0	0	5	0	41	.415	0	13	26	.423	1	7
Guthrie, Mark	0	2	.000	3.65	12.1	7	6	5	1	2	0	0	4	2	9	11	0	0	0	0	0	30	.167	1	4	11	.182	0	0
King, Ray	0	0	.000	5.91	10.2	11	8	7	2	1	0	1	10	0	5	10	0	0	0	0	0	25	.280	2	7	13	.308	0	2
McNichol, Brian	0	2	.000	6.75	10.2	15	8	8	4	0	1	1	7	0	12	4	2	0	0	1	0	38	.368	4	7	7	.143	0	1
Creek, Doug	0	0	.000	10.50	6.0	6	7	7	1	0	1	0	8	1	6	3	0	0	0	2	0	16	.313	0	2	7	.143	1	4
Barker, Richie	0	0	.000	7.20	5.0	6	4	4	0	0	1	0	4	1	3	5	0	0	0	1	0	12	.250	0	2	8	.375	0	2
Miller, Kurt	0	0	.000	18.00	3.0	6	6	6	1	1	0	0	3	0	1	4	0	0	0	1	0	9	.333	1	5	4	.750	0	1
Gaetti, Gary	0	0	.000	18.00	1.0	2	2	2	1	0	0	0	1	0	1	1	0	0	0	1	0	3	.333	0	1	2	.500	1	1

PITCHERS WITH MORE THAN ONE N.L. TEAM

Name	W	L	Pct.	ERA	IP	H	R	ER	HR	SH	SF	HB	BB	IBB	SO	G	GS	CG	ShO	GF	Sv	vs. RH AB	vs. RH Avg.	vs. RH HR	vs. RH RBI	vs. LH AB	vs. LH Avg.	vs. LH HR	vs. LH RBI
Ayala, Mon.	1	6	.143	3.68	66.0	60	36	27	6	4	3	4	34	1	64	53	0	0	0	17	0	44	.205	3	6	13	.154	1	2
Ayala, Mon.-Chi.	1	7	.125	3.51	82.0	71	43	32	10	5	3	6	39	2	79	66	0	0	0	3	0	181	.215	7	31	131	.244	3	24
Bowie, Atl.	0	1	.000	13.50	4.0	8	6	6	1	0	0	0	4	0	2	3	0	0	0	2	0	176	.347	8	44	28	.429	0	7
Bowie, Atl.-Chi.	2	7	.222	10.24	51.0	81	60	58	9	3	3	2	34	2	41	14	11	0	0	3	0	190	.347	8	44	33	.455	1	13
Mulholland, Atl.	4	2	.667	2.98	60.1	64	24	20	5	3	1	0	13	2	39	16	8	0	0	3	1	336	.304	13	43	107	.327	3	16
Mulholland, Chi.-Atl.	10	8	.556	4.39	170.1	201	95	83	21	9	4	1	45	6	83	42	24	0	0	4	1	532	.299	17	58	145	.290	4	21

INDIVIDUAL STATISTICS

FIELDING

FIRST BASEMEN

Player	Pct.	G	PO	A	E	TC	DP
Grace, Mark	.994	160	1335	93	8	1436	115
Gaetti, Gary	.957	8	39	6	2	47	6
Houston, Tyler	1.000	2	1	0	0	1	0
Hernandez, Jose	1.000	1	2	0	0	2	0
Santiago, Benito	1.000	1	2	0	0	2	0
Andrews, Shane	-	1	0	0	0	0	0

SECOND BASEMEN

Player	Pct.	G	PO	A	E	TC	DP
Morandini, Mickey	.991	132	239	319	5	563	72
Meyers, Chad	.983	32	49	69	2	120	13
Blauser, Jeff	.961	25	41	32	3	76	9
Alexander, Manny	.927	17	21	17	3	41	4

THIRD BASEMEN

Player	Pct.	G	PO	A	E	TC	DP
Gaetti, Gary	.962	81	35	140	7	182	8
Houston, Tyler	.901	63	35	83	13	131	7
Alexander, Manny	.893	22	8	17	3	28	0
Andrews, Shane	.955	19	8	34	2	44	6
Blauser, Jeff	.897	18	7	19	3	29	0
Liniak, Cole	1.000	10	8	8	0	16	1
Reed, Jeff	-	1	0	0	0	0	0

SHORTSTOPS

Player	Pct.	G	PO	A	E	TC	DP
Hernandez, Jose	.971	92	114	249	11	374	51
Nieves, Jose	.935	52	67	162	16	245	29
Alexander, Manny	.988	30	27	54	1	82	9
Blauser, Jeff	.985	22	21	43	1	65	7
Gaetti, Gary	1.000	1	0	1	0	1	0

OUTFIELDERS

Player	Pct.	G	PO	A	E	TC	DP
Sosa, Sammy	.978	162	399	8	9	416	3
Rodriguez, Henry	.974	122	222	7	6	235	1
Johnson, Lance	.988	91	235	6	3	244	1
Goodwin, Curtis	.983	76	115	3	2	120	2
Hill, Glenallen	.955	62	81	3	4	88	0
Porter, Bo	.941	21	16	0	1	17	0
Hernandez, Jose	1.000	20	24	0	0	24	0
Brown, Roosevelt	.955	18	20	1	1	22	0
Meyers, Chad	1.000	14	27	0	0	27	0
Alexander, Manny	-	2	0	0	0	0	0
Blauser, Jeff	1.000	1	1	0	0	1	0
Houston, Tyler	-	1	0	0	0	0	0

CATCHERS

Player	Pct.	G	PO	A	E	TC	DP	PB
Santiago, Benito	.990	107	560	43	6	609	8	10
Reed, Jeff	.987	49	282	17	4	303	3	2
Houston, Tyler	.952	18	73	6	4	83	1	1
Martinez, Sandy	.959	12	45	2	2	49	0	0
Molina, Jose	1.000	10	44	5	0	49	1	1

PITCHERS

Player	Pct.	G	PO	A	E	TC	DP
Heredia, Felix	1.000	69	1	4	0	5	0
Sanders, Scott	.850	67	5	12	3	20	2
Adams, Terry	.933	52	8	6	1	15	0
Myers, Rodney	.857	46	2	4	1	7	0
Aguilera, Rick	1.000	44	4	6	0	10	1
Serafini, Dan	1.000	42	3	5	0	8	0
Trachsel, Steve	1.000	34	18	20	0	38	3
Lieber, Jon	.946	31	18	17	2	37	1
Beck, Rod	1.000	31	4	4	0	8	0
Farnsworth, Kyle	.846	27	9	13	4	26	1
Mulholland, Terry	.852	26	6	17	4	27	1
Tapani, Kevin	1.000	23	2	18	0	20	0
Rain, Steve	1.000	16	3	3	0	6	0
Karchner, Matt	1.000	16	1	1	0	2	0
Ayala, Bobby	1.000	13	1	2	0	3	0
Lorraine, Andrew	.909	11	2	8	1	11	0
Bowie, Micah	.857	11	0	6	1	7	0
Guthrie, Mark	1.000	11	0	1	0	1	0
King, Ray	1.000	10	0	1	0	1	0
Woodall, Brad	1.000	6	1	2	0	3	1
Barker, Richie	1.000	5	1	0	0	1	0
McNichol, Brian	-	4	0	0	0	0	0
Miller, Kurt	-	4	0	0	0	0	0
Creek, Doug	-	3	0	0	0	0	0
Gaetti, Gary	-	1	0	0	0	0	0

PITCHING AGAINST EACH CLUB

Pitcher	Ari. W-L	Atl. W-L	Cin. W-L	Col. W-L	Fla. W-L	Hou. W-L	L.A. W-L	Mil. W-L	Mon. W-L	N.Y. W-L	Phi. W-L	Pit. W-L	S.D. W-L	S.F. W-L	StL. W-L	A.L. W-L	Total W-L
Adams, T.	1-0	1-0	1-1	0-0	0-0	0-0	0-0	0-0	0-0	0-0	0-0	0-0	0-0	1-0	1-1	1-1	6-3
Aguilera, R.	1-0	0-0	0-0	0-0	1-1	0-0	0-0	2-0	0-0	0-0	0-0	1-0	0-0	0-1	0-0	1-1	6-3
Ayala, B.	0-0	0-0	0-0	0-0	0-0	0-1	0-0	0-0	0-0	0-0	0-0	0-0	0-0	0-0	0-0	0-0	0-1
Barker, R.	0-0	0-0	0-0	0-0	0-0	0-0	0-0	0-0	0-0	0-0	0-0	0-0	0-0	0-0	0-0	0-0	0-0
Beck, Rod	0-0	0-0	0-1	1-0	0-0	0-0	0-1	1-1	0-0	0-1	0-0	0-0	0-0	0-0	0-0	0-0	2-4
Bowie, M.	0-0	0-0	0-1	1-0	0-0	0-2	0-0	0-0	0-1	0-0	0-1	1-0	0-1	0-0	0-0	0-0	2-6
Creek, D.	0-0	0-0	0-0	0-0	0-0	0-0	0-0	0-0	0-0	0-0	0-0	0-0	0-0	0-0	0-0	0-0	0-0
Farnsworth, K.	0-0	0-0	1-1	0-1	1-0	0-1	2-1	0-1	0-0	0-1	0-1	1-0	0-0	0-1	0-1	0-0	5-9
Gaetti, Gary	0-0	0-0	0-0	0-0	0-0	0-0	0-0	0-0	0-0	0-0	0-0	0-0	0-0	0-0	0-0	0-0	0-0
Guthrie, M.	0-0	0-0	0-0	0-0	0-0	0-0	0-0	0-1	0-0	0-0	0-0	0-1	0-0	0-0	0-0	0-0	0-2
Heredia, F.	0-0	0-0	0-0	0-0	1-0	0-0	0-0	1-0	0-0	0-0	0-0	0-0	0-1	0-0	1-0	0-0	3-1
Karchner, M.	0-0	0-0	0-0	0-0	0-0	0-0	0-0	1-0	0-0	0-0	0-0	0-0	0-0	0-0	0-0	0-0	1-0
King, Ray	0-0	0-0	0-0	0-0	0-0	0-0	0-0	0-0	0-0	0-0	0-0	0-0	0-0	0-0	0-0	0-0	0-0
Lieber, Jon	0-2	1-0	2-1	0-0	0-0	1-1	0-1	1-0	0-2	0-0	0-1	2-0	0-0	0-1	2-1	1-1	10-11
Lorraine, A.	0-1	0-0	0-1	0-0	0-0	1-0	0-1	0-0	0-0	0-0	0-0	0-0	0-0	0-1	1-1	0-0	2-5
McNichol, B.	0-0	0-0	0-1	0-0	0-0	0-0	0-0	0-0	0-0	0-0	0-1	0-0	0-0	0-0	0-0	0-0	0-2
Miller, Kurt	0-0	0-0	0-0	0-0	0-0	0-0	0-0	0-0	0-0	0-0	0-0	0-0	0-0	0-0	0-0	0-0	0-0
Mulholland, T.	0-1	1-0	0-0	0-2	0-0	0-0	0-0	0-0	1-0	1-0	1-1	1-1	1-0	0-0	0-0	0-1	6-6
Myers, R.	0-0	0-1	0-0	0-0	1-0	0-0	0-0	0-0	0-0	1-0	0-0	0-0	1-0	0-0	0-0	0-0	3-1
Rain, S.	0-1	0-0	0-0	0-0	0-0	0-0	0-0	0-0	0-0	0-0	0-0	0-0	0-0	0-0	0-0	0-0	0-1
Sanders, S.	0-1	0-0	0-0	1-0	0-1	0-1	0-1	0-0	0-0	0-1	0-0	0-1	1-0	0-0	0-0	2-1	4-7
Serafini, D.	0-0	1-0	0-0	0-0	0-0	0-0	0-0	0-0	0-0	1-1	0-0	1-0	0-0	0-1	0-0	0-0	3-2
Tapani, K.	0-1	0-1	0-1	1-0	1-0	1-1	0-0	0-1	0-2	0-1	0-1	0-0	2-0	0-2	1-0	0-1	6-12
Trachsel, S.	0-0	1-0	1-0	0-2	1-1	0-2	0-2	0-2	1-0	0-1	1-1	0-2	1-1	0-0	1-1	1-3	8-18
Woodall, B.	0-0	0-0	0-0	0-0	0-0	0-0	0-0	0-0	0-0	0-0	0-0	0-1	0-0	0-0	0-0	0-0	0-1
Totals	2-7	5-2	5-8	4-5	6-3	3-9	2-7	6-6	2-5	3-6	2-7	7-6	6-3	1-7	7-5	6-9	67-95

INTERLEAGUE: Lieber 1-1, Trachsel 1-1, Aguilera 0-1, Adams 0-1 vs. White Sox; Aguilera 1-0, Sanders 0-1, Trachsel 0-1 vs. Indians; Sanders 1-0, Tapani 0-1, Trachsel 0-1 vs. Royals; Sanders 1-0, Adams 1-0, Mulholland 0-1 vs. Twins. Total: 6-9.

MISCELLANEOUS

HOME RUNS BY PARK

At Arizona (6): Sosa 3, Rodriguez 2, Houston 1.
At Atlanta (8): Sosa 2, Rodriguez 2, Gaetti 1, Blauser 1, Grace 1, Hernandez 1.
At Chicago (AL) (4): Hill 2, Hernandez 1, Houston 1.
At Chicago (NL) (98): Sosa 33, Rodriguez 14, Hill 11, Grace 8, Blauser 7, Gaetti 6, Hernandez 5, Andrews 4, Morandini 3, Santiago 2, Houston 2, Nieves 2, Johnson 1.
At Cincinnati (8): Santiago 2, Rodriguez 2, Hill 1, Sosa 1, Hernandez 1, Andrews 1.
At Cleveland (2): Gaetti 1, Hill 1.
At Colorado (8): Sosa 3, Hernandez 2, Blauser 1, Grace 1, Rodriguez 1.
At Florida (6): Sosa 3, Rodriguez 2, Grace 1.
At Houston (4): Hill 1, Grace 1, Hernandez 1, Rodriguez 1.
At Los Angeles (6): Sosa 2, Houston 2, Grace 1, Hernandez 1.
At Milwaukee (10): Santiago 2, Sosa 2, Gaetti 1, Hill 1, Grace 1, Morandini 1, Hernandez 1, Houston 1.
At Montreal (2): Hill 1, Sosa 1.
At New York (NL) (2): Sosa 2.
At Philadelphia (7): Sosa 3, Hill 1, Grace 1, Hernandez 1, Martinez 1.
At Pittsburgh (6): Santiago 1, Hill 1, Sosa 1, Hernandez 1, Rodriguez 1, Houston 1.
At San Diego (2): Sosa 2.
At San Francisco (4): Grace 1, Sosa 1, Rodriguez 1, Houston 1.
At St. Louis (6): Sosa 4, Reed 1, Brown 1.

LOW-HIT GAMES

No-hitters: None.
One-hitters: None.
Two-hitters: Kyle Farnsworth, August 29 vs. Los Angeles, W 6-0.

10-STRIKEOUT GAMES

Jon Lieber 2, **Total:** 2.

FOUR OR MORE HITS IN ONE GAME

Glenallen Hill 2 (including one five-hit game), Sammy Sosa 2, Lance Johnson 1, Mark Grace 1, Mickey Morandini 1, **Total:** 7.

MULTI-HOMER GAMES

Sammy Sosa 6, Glenallen Hill 2, Henry Rodriguez 2, Benito Santiago 1, Mickey Morandini 1, **Total:** 12.

GRAND SLAMS

5-4: Mark Grace (off Colorado's Darryl Kile).
5-21: Gary Gaetti (off Atlanta's Bruce Chen).
7-31: Gary Gaetti (off New York's Octavio Dotel).

PINCH HITTERS

(Minimum 5 at-bats)

Name	AB	Avg.	HR	RBI
Blauser, Jeff	44	.250	3	7
Alexander, Manny	41	.293	0	2
Hill, Glenallen	34	.235	4	8
Gaetti, Gary	27	.111	0	1
Houston, Tyler	26	.077	1	3
Morandini, Mickey	19	.158	0	2
Goodwin, Curtis	15	.133	0	1
Brown, Roosevelt	13	.077	0	1
Reed, Jeff	10	.300	0	1
Johnson, Lance	6	.333	0	0
Santiago, Benito	6	.167	0	0
Martinez, Sandy	6	.167	0	0
Porter, Bo	6	.167	0	0
Rodriguez, Henry	5	.400	0	2
Jennings, Robin	5	.200	0	0

DEBUTS

4-25: Richie Barker, P.
4-29: Kyle Farnsworth, P.
5-9: Bo Porter, PH.
5-18: Roosevelt Brown, PH.
5-21: Ray King, P.
7-17: Steve Rain, P.
8-6: Chad Meyers, CF.
9-3: Cole Liniak, 3B.
9-6: Jose Molina, C.
9-7: Brian McNichol, P.

GAMES BY POSITION

Catcher: Benito Santiago 107, Jeff Reed 49, Tyler Houston 18, Sandy Martinez 12, Jose Molina 10.
First base: Mark Grace 160, Gary Gaetti 8, Tyler Houston 2, Benito Santiago 1, Jose Hernandez 1, Shane Andrews 1.
Second base: Mickey Morandini 132, Chad Meyers 32, Jeff Blauser 25, Manny Alexander 17.
Third base: Gary Gaetti 81, Tyler Houston 63, Manny Alexander 22, Shane Andrews 19, Jeff Blauser 18, Cole Liniak 10, Jeff Reed 1.
Shortstop: Jose Hernandez 92, Jose Nieves 52, Manny Alexander 30, Jeff Blauser 22, Gary Gaetti 1.
Outfield: Sammy Sosa 162, Henry Rodriguez 122, Lance Johnson 91, Curtis Goodwin 76, Glenallen Hill 62, Bo Porter 21, Jose Hernandez 20, Roosevelt Brown 18, Chad Meyers 14, Manny Alexander 2, Jeff Blauser 1, Tyler Houston 1.
Designated hitter: Glenallen Hill 4, Henry Rodriguez 2.

STREAKS

Wins: 5 (April 27-May 2,May 16-21).
Losses: 6 (August 7-13,September 7-12).
Consecutive games with at least one hit: 18, Sammy Sosa (May 26-June 15).
Wins by pitcher: 2, Terry Mulholland (April 24-30), Kevin Tapani (May 28-June 3), Steve Trachsel (September 1-7), Steve Trachsel (September 22-28), Jon Lieber (April 8-14), Jon Lieber (May 8-14), Jon Lieber (July 5-10).

ATTENDANCE

Home: 2,813,800.
Road: 2,800,559.
Highest (home): 40,553 (June 25 vs. Philadelphia).
Highest (road): 58,086 (July 3 vs. Philadelphia).
Lowest (Home): 17,999 (April 21 vs. Houston).
Lowest (road): 9,608 (July 28 vs. Montreal).

CINCINNATI REDS

DAY BY DAY

Date	Opp.	Res.	Score	(inn.*)	Hits	Opp. hits	Winning pitcher	Losing pitcher	Save	Record	Pos.	GB
4-5	S.F	L	8-11		12	15	Embree	Hudek	Nen	0-1	T4th	1.0
4-6	S.F	L	6-7		11	11	Tavarez	Graves	Nen	0-2	T4th	1.5
4-7	S.F	L	3-8		6	7	Ortiz	Avery		0-3	6th	1.5
4-9	At StL.	W	3-0		5	6	Harnisch	Oliver		1-3	T5th	1.0
4-10	At StL.	L	2-4		7	6	Acevedo	Williamson		1-4	6th	2.0
4-11	At StL.	W	4-2		6	10	Bere	Osborne	Graves	2-4	T4th	2.0
4-12	At Chi.	W	7-2		13	6	Avery	Tapani		3-4	4th	1.5
4-14	At Chi.	L	4-5		9	6	Lieber	Harnisch	Beck	3-5	T4th	2.0
4-16	Pit.	W	6-5		9	9	Graves	Christiansen		4-5	T3rd	2.0
4-17	Pit.	L	6-7	(10)	9	11	Christiansen	White		4-6	T5th	3.0
4-18	Pit.	L	2-4		7	8	Loiselle	Graves	Williams	4-7	6th	3.0
4-20	N.Y.	L	2-3		8	8	Cook	Harnisch	Franco	4-8	6th	4.5
4-21	N.Y.	W	7-4		7	3	Sullivan	Yoshii	Graves	5-8	T5th	3.5
4-22	N.Y.	L	1-4		6	7	Leiter	Tomko	Franco	5-9	6th	4.0
4-23	Hou.	W	7-5		10	11	Sullivan	Holt	Graves	6-9	5th	4.0
4-24	Hou.	L	3-4		5	6	Elarton	Graves	Wagner	6-10	6th	4.0
4-25	Hou.	W	7-6		10	8	Harnisch	Henry	Williamson	7-10	6th	4.0
4-27	At Phi.	L	0-1	(10)	5	7	Brantley	White		7-11	6th	5.0
4-28	At Phi.	W	12-8		13	13	Williamson	Brantley		8-11	6th	4.0
4-29	At Phi.	W	7-3		13	8	Bere	Loewer		9-11	T4th	3.0
4-30	At Atl.	L	0-3		1	6	Smoltz	Avery		9-12	T4th	3.5
5-1	At Atl.	L	1-5		3	10	Millwood	Harnisch		9-13	5th	4.5
5-2	At Atl.	L	3-5		6	8	Perez	Neagle	Rocker	9-14	6th	5.5
5-3	Ari.	W	4-3		9	8	Williamson	Holmes		10-14	6th	4.5
5-4	Ari.	W	6-4		7	9	Reyes	Daal	Graves	11-14	6th	4.5
5-5	Ari.	L	1-5		4	8	Johnson	Avery		11-15	6th	5.5
5-7	Chi.	W	3-2		13	6	Graves	Beck		12-15	6th	5.5
5-8	Chi.	L	4-7		11	11	Lieber	Neagle	Beck	12-16	6th	5.5
5-9	Chi.	W	8-5		13	7	Williamson	Adams	Graves	13-16	6th	5.5
5-11	Mil.	W	9-1		12	4	Avery	Eldred		14-16	5th	5.0
5-12	Mil.	L	7-8		12	15	Karl	Harnisch	Wickman	14-17	6th	6.0
5-14	S.D.	L	3-7		9	8	Ashby	Neagle	Hoffman	14-18	6th	7.0
5-15	S.D.	W	6-2		4	8	Parris	Hitchcock	Williamson	15-18	6th	7.0
5-16	S.D.	W	3-0		6	4	Tomko	Williams	Williamson	16-18	5th	6.0
5-17	At Col.	W	7-2		10	6	Harnisch	Jones		17-18	5th	5.5
5-18	At Col.	W	5-3		10	6	Graves	Leskanic	Williamson	18-18	T4th	5.5
5-19	At Col.	W	24-12		28	15	Parris	Dipoto	Villone	19-18	4th	4.5
5-21	At S.D.	L	4-5		10	10	Williams	Tomko	Hoffman	19-19	4th	5.0
5-22	At S.D.	W	3-0		9	3	Harnisch	Murray		20-19	4th	4.0
5-23	At S.D.	W	6-2		7	2	Avery	Clement	Williamson	21-19	4th	4.0
5-25	L.A.	W	3-2		5	7	Parris	Brown	Graves	22-19	2nd	4.5
5-26	L.A.	L	3-9		7	10	Park	Tomko		22-20	3rd	5.5
5-27	L.A.	L	3-4		7	8	Valdes	Harnisch	Shaw	22-21	4th	5.5
5-28	At Fla.	L	1-8		9	8	Dempster	Avery		22-22	4th	5.5
5-29	At Fla.	W	8-1		17	7	Bere	Fernandez		23-22	3rd	4.5
5-30	At Fla.	W	6-4		12	10	Graves	Edmondson		24-22	3rd	3.5
5-31	At N.Y.	W	5-3		8	6	Villone	Leiter	Williamson	25-22	3rd	3.0
6-1	At N.Y.	W	4-0		10	7	Harnisch	Hershiser		26-22	3rd	3.0
6-2	At N.Y.	W	8-7		11	8	Williamson	Franco	Sullivan	27-22	3rd	3.0
6-5†	At K.C.	W	9-4		13	9	Parris	Rosado		28-22		
6-5‡	At K.C.	W	7-4	(10)	13	7	Williamson	Montgomery		29-22	3rd	2.5
6-6	At K.C.	W	14-3		22	9	Sullivan	Witasick		30-22	2nd	1.5
6-7	At Min.	L	6-8		9	14	Lincoln	Avery	Trombley	30-23	2nd	2.5
6-8	At Min.	L	2-5		5	12	Radke	Villone	Trombley	30-24	3rd	2.5
6-9	At Min.	W	3-1		6	8	Tomko	Milton	Graves	31-24	3rd	2.5
6-11	Cle.	L	6-8		13	7	Shuey	Williamson	Jackson	31-25	3rd	3.5
6-12	Cle.	L	3-4		5	9	Nagy	Harnisch	Jackson	31-26	3rd	4.5
6-13	Cle.	L	3-7		10	9	Burba	Avery	Karsay	31-27	3rd	5.0
6-14	N.Y.	W	8-4		10	5	Williamson	McMichael		32-27	2nd	5.0
6-15	N.Y.	L	3-11		9	12	Reed	Tomko		32-28	3rd	5.0
6-16	N.Y.	L	2-5		8	10	Yoshii	Parris	Franco	32-29	T3rd	5.0
6-17	Mil.	W	2-0		8	4	Harnisch	Karl	Williamson	33-29	2nd	4.0
6-18	Mil.	W	7-1		11	3	Avery	Roque		34-29	2nd	4.0
6-19	Mil.	L	1-10		4	12	Woodard	Villone		34-30	2nd	5.0
6-20	Mil.	L	4-7		9	10	Weathers	Reyes	Wickman	34-31	2nd	6.0
6-21	At Ari.	W	7-4	(10)	15	9	White	Nunez	Graves	35-31	2nd	5.0
6-22	At Ari.	W	8-7		12	13	Reyes	Vosberg	Graves	36-31	2nd	4.0
6-23	At Ari.	W	9-7		17	8	Avery	Benes	Williamson	37-31	2nd	4.0
6-24	At Hou.	W	3-0		5	1	Villone	Hampton	Graves	38-31	2nd	3.0
6-25	At Hou.	W	10-7		12	10	Tomko	Holt	Williamson	39-31	2nd	2.0
6-26	At Hou.	W	8-1		11	2	Parris	Bergman		40-31	2nd	1.0
6-27	At Hou.	W	5-2		12	5	Harnisch	Lima		41-31	T1st	...
6-29	Ari.	W	5-4		7	5	Graves	Padilla		42-31	T1st	...
6-30	Ari.	W	2-0		7	1	Villone	Johnson	Williamson	43-31	T1st	...
7-1	Ari.	W	2-1	(10)	7	7	Williamson	Plesac		44-31	1st	+1.0
7-2	Hou.	L	5-7		11	15	Powell	Belinda	Wagner	44-32	T1st	...
7-3	Hou.	W	10-0		13	5	Harnisch	Elarton	Reyes	45-32	1st	+1.0
7-4	Hou.	L	3-5		12	8	Reynolds	Avery	Wagner	45-33	T1st	...
7-5	Hou.	W	5-2		11	6	Villone	Holt	Graves	46-33	1st	+1.0

Date	Opp.	Res.	Score	(inn.*)	Hits	Opp. hits	Winning pitcher	Losing pitcher	Save	Record	Pos.	GB
7-6	At StL.	L	5-6		9	10	Bottenfield	Tomko	Bottalico	46-34	T1st	...
7-7	At StL.	L	1-2		9	7	Croushore	Williamson		46-35	T1st	...
7-8	At StL.	W	8-5		11	10	Harnisch	Mercker	Graves	47-35	1st	+1.0
7-9	At Cle.	W	3-2		5	4	Avery	Burba	Williamson	48-35	1st	+1.0
7-10	At Cle.	L	10-11		10	15	Jackson	Williamson		48-36	T1st	...
7-11	At Cle.	W	9-4		14	9	Graves	Shuey		49-36	T1st	...
7-15	Col.	W	10-7		12	12	Parris	Kile	Graves	50-36	T1st	...
7-16	Col.	L	2-6		4	11	Astacio	Villone	Veres	50-37	2nd	1.0
7-17	Col.	W	3-2		3	8	Williamson	Dipoto		51-37	2nd	1.0
7-18	Det.	L	8-9	(10)	11	9	Brocail	Graves	Jones	51-38	2nd	2.0
7-19	Det.	L	6-7		10	11	Nitkowski	Sullivan	Jones	51-39	2nd	3.0
7-20	Det.	W	5-2		8	7	Parris	Mlicki	Graves	52-39	2nd	2.0
7-21	StL.	W	1-0		3	1	Villone	Jimenez	Williamson	53-39	2nd	1.0
7-22	StL.	L	5-6		8	5	Painter	Graves	Bottalico	53-40	2nd	1.0
7-23	At S.F	L	5-6		9	7	Spradlin	Sullivan	Nen	53-41	2nd	2.5
7-24	At S.F	W	7-6		6	8	Williamson	Nen	Graves	54-41	2nd	2.5
7-25	At S.F	W	2-1	(14)	5	4	Belinda	Nen		55-41	2nd	2.5
7-26	At L.A.	W	5-3	(10)	13	8	Belinda	Shaw		56-41	2nd	2.5
7-27	At L.A.	W	5-3	(10)	15	10	Graves	Mills	Williamson	57-41	2nd	2.5
7-28	At L.A.	L	1-9		7	13	Checo	Reyes	Arnold	57-42	2nd	3.5
7-29	At L.A.	W	7-5		14	9	Harnisch	Dreifort	Williamson	58-42	2nd	2.5
7-30	S.F	W	7-4		10	9	Neagle	Gardner	Williamson	59-42	2nd	2.5
7-31	S.F	L	1-11		8	15	Estes	Villone		59-43	2nd	3.5
8-1	S.F	W	9-1		12	6	Tomko	Ortiz		60-43	2nd	2.5
8-3	Col.	W	2-1		8	6	Williamson	DeJean		61-43	2nd	2.5
8-4	Col.	W	6-3		12	7	Neagle	Kile	Graves	62-43	2nd	1.5
8-5	Col.	L	1-2		4	10	Astacio	Guzman		62-44	2nd	2.5
8-6	At Mil.	W	9-2		15	4	Villone	Woodard	Sullivan	63-44	2nd	2.0
8-7	At Mil.	L	4-6		9	11	Weathers	Graves	Wickman	63-45	2nd	3.0
8-8	At Mil.	W	8-2		11	7	Harnisch	Nomo	Belinda	64-45	2nd	3.0
8-9	At Pit.	W	4-2		7	2	Neagle	Ritchie	Williamson	65-45	2nd	2.0
8-10	At Pit.	W	6-1		13	6	Guzman	Schourek		66-45	2nd	1.0
8-11	At Pit.	L	4-5		9	9	Williams	Williamson		66-46	2nd	1.0
8-13	Phi.	W	5-4		11	13	Williamson	Schrenk		67-46	T1st	...
8-14	Phi.	W	4-1		14	4	Harnisch	Ogea	Graves	68-46	T1st	...
8-15	Phi.	L	3-9		7	10	Person	Neagle		68-47	T1st	...
8-16	Pit.	W	9-2		10	5	Guzman	Schourek		69-47	T1st	...
8-17	Pit.	W	7-4	(12)	7	8	Graves	Williams		70-47	T1st	...
8-18	Pit.	L	6-12		11	13	Cordova	Tomko		70-48	2nd	1.0
8-19	Pit.	W	1-0		7	1	Harnisch	Benson	Williamson	71-48	T1st	...
8-20	Mon.	L	3-5		8	9	Batista	Sullivan	Urbina	71-49	2nd	1.0
8-21	Mon.	W	9-3		11	8	Guzman	Thurman		72-49	2nd	1.0
8-22	Mon.	W	4-3	(11)	12	11	Sullivan	Urbina		73-49	2nd	0.5
8-23	At Atl.	L	2-6		4	6	Millwood	Tomko	Springer	73-50	2nd	0.5
8-24	At Atl.	L	4-6		5	10	Smoltz	Harnisch	Rocker	73-51	2nd	1.5
8-25	At Atl.	L	2-5		8	7	Glavine	Neagle	Rocker	73-52	2nd	1.5
8-26	At Mon.	W	10-4		14	8	Guzman	Thurman	Williamson	74-52	2nd	1.0
8-27	At Mon.	W	4-1		10	4	Villone	Hermanson	Graves	75-52	2nd	0.5
8-28	At Mon.	L	6-8		9	11	Kline	Williamson		75-53	2nd	0.5
8-29	At Mon.	L	6-8		10	8	Mota	Harnisch	Urbina	75-54	2nd	1.5
8-30	Atl.	W	11-3		12	6	Neagle	Glavine		76-54	2nd	0.5
8-31	Atl.	L	2-8		9	11	Maddux	Guzman		76-55	2nd	1.5
9-1	Atl.	L	7-8		13	11	Mulholland	Villone	Rocker	76-56	2nd	1.5
9-3	At Phi.	L	2-10		6	12	Schilling	Parris		76-57	2nd	2.5
9-4	At Phi.	W	22-3		19	11	Harnisch	Byrd	Belinda	77-57	2nd	2.5
9-5	At Phi.	W	9-7		13	7	Neagle	Person	Sullivan	78-57	2nd	2.5
9-6	At Chi.	W	6-3		7	7	Guzman	Bowie	Graves	79-57	2nd	2.5
9-7†	At Chi.	L	1-2		4	5	Trachsel	Villone	Adams	79-58		
9-7‡	At Chi.	W	10-3		16	10	Tomko	McNichol		80-58	2nd	3.0
9-8	At Chi.	W	6-4		9	9	Parris	Lorraine	Graves	81-58	2nd	3.0
9-9	At Chi.	W	5-3		14	9	Sullivan	Farnsworth	Graves	82-58	2nd	3.0
9-10	Fla.	W	4-2		5	7	Neagle	Springer	Graves	83-58	2nd	3.0
9-11	Fla.	W	12-4		9	9	Guzman	Nunez		84-58	2nd	3.0
9-12	Fla.	W	11-5		13	9	Villone	Burnett		85-58	2nd	3.0
9-13	Fla.	W	7-4		8	10	Parris	Sanchez	Graves	86-58	2nd	3.0
9-14	Chi.	L	3-4		9	6	Farnsworth	Harnisch	Adams	86-59	2nd	4.0
9-15	Chi.	W	5-4		10	12	Neagle	Lieber	Graves	87-59	2nd	3.0
9-16	Chi.	L	6-7		8	9	Adams	Graves	Aguilera	87-60	2nd	3.5
9-17	At Pit.	L	1-3		7	4	Ritchie	Villone	Sauerbeck	87-61	2nd	3.5
9-18	At Pit.	W	3-0		7	6	Parris	Peters		88-61	2nd	2.5
9-19	At Pit.	L	5-8		9	8	Schmidt	Harnisch	Clontz	88-62	2nd	3.5
9-20	At S.D.	W	12-1		15	3	Neagle	Carlyle		89-62	2nd	2.5
9-21	At S.D.	L	2-6		7	9	Clement	Williamson		89-63	2nd	3.5
9-22	At S.D.	W	4-3		8	9	Villone	Ashby	Graves	90-63	2nd	2.5
9-24	StL.	W	5-4		10	7	Parris	Croushore	Graves	91-63	2nd	2.5
9-25	StL.	W	6-1		9	4	Neagle	Jimenez	Graves	92-63	2nd	1.5
9-26	StL.	W	7-5	(12)	10	9	Williamson	Mohler		93-63	2nd	0.5
9-27	StL.	W	9-7		14	8	Belinda	Croushore	Reyes	94-63	T1st	...
9-28	At Hou.	W	4-1		8	4	Harnisch	Lima	Williamson	95-63	1st	+1.0
9-29	At Hou.	L	1-4		7	7	Hampton	Parris	Wagner	95-64	T1st	...
10-1	At Mil.	L	3-4	(10)	5	10	Coppinger	Sullivan		95-65	T1st	...
10-2	At Mil.	L	6-10		12	14	Peterson	Guzman		95-66	2nd	1.0
10-3	At Mil.	W	7-1		12	6	Harnisch	Eldred	Villone	96-66	2nd	1.0
10-4	N.Y.	L	0-5		2	9	Leiter	Parris		96-67	2nd	1.5

Monthly records: April (9-12), May (16-10), June (18-9), July (16-12), August (17-12), September (19-9), October (1-3).
*Innings, if other than nine. † First game of a doubleheader. ‡ Second game of a doubleheader.

MEMORABLE GAMES

July 21 at Cincinnati

No single performance clinched the N.L. Rookie of the Year Award for Scott Williamson, but this one certainly furthered his candidacy. Williamson inherited a runner on first base with nobody out in the ninth inning and struck out the three most dangerous Cardinals—Ray Lankford, Mark McGwire and Fernando Tatis—to seal the victory. Ron Villone, whose switch from the bullpen helped solidify the starting rotation, dominated St. Louis.

St. Louis	AB	R	H	RBI	Cincinnati	AB	R	H	RBI
Drew, cf	3	0	1	0	Reese, 2b	4	1	2	1
McEwing, lf	2	0	0	0	D.Young, rf	3	0	1	0
Lankford, ph	1	0	0	0	Tucker, rf	0	0	0	0
McGwire, 1b	4	0	0	0	Casey, 1b	2	0	0	0
Tatis, 3b	4	0	0	0	G.Vaughn, lf	3	0	0	0
Renteria, ss	3	0	0	0	Larkin, ss	2	0	0	0
Bragg, rf	3	0	0	0	A.Boone, 3b	3	0	0	0
A.Castillo, c	1	0	0	0	Cameron, cf	3	0	0	0
Dunston, ph	1	0	0	0	LaRue, c	3	0	0	0
Aybar, p	0	0	0	0	Villone, p	3	0	0	0
D.Howard, 2b	3	0	0	0	Williamson, p	0	0	0	0
J.Jimenez, p	2	0	0	0					
T.Howard, ph	1	0	0	0					
Marrero, c	0	0	0	0					
Totals	**28**	**0**	**1**	**0**	**Totals**	**26**	**1**	**3**	**1**

St. Louis .... 000 000 000 —0
Cincinnati .... 000 100 00x —1

E—Cameron (5). DP—St. Louis 1. LOB—St. Louis 4, Cincinnati 3. 2B—Drew (11). HR—Reese (6). SB—D.Young (2).

St. Louis	IP	H	R	ER	BB	SO
J.Jimenez (L, 5-10)	7	3	1	1	2	2
Aybar	1	0	0	0	0	2

Cincinnati	IP	H	R	ER	BB	SO
Villone (W, 5-3)	8	1	0	0	2	5
Williamson (S, 12)	1	0	0	0	0	3

HBP—McEwing by Villone. U—HP, Froemming. 1B, Wegner. 2B, M.Hirschbeck. 3B, Bell. T—2:17. A—33,958.

August 17 at Cincinnati

Manager Jack McKeon called this the defining moment of the Reds' wondrous season, and it's difficult to argue with him. Chris Stynes, the team's "25th man" as its least-used player, won the game with a two-out, pinch-hit homer off Mike Williams. The Reds' bullpen, which was statistically the NL's best, limited Pittsburgh to two singles in the final six innings.

Pittsburgh	AB	R	H	RBI	Cincinnati	AB	R	H	RBI
A.Martin, lf	5	0	0	0	Cameron, cf	4	1	0	0
A.Brown, rf	4	0	0	0	Tucker, rf	3	1	0	0
Giles, cf	4	0	1	0	Williamson, p	0	0	0	0
K.Young, 1b	5	1	1	0	D.Yng, ph-1b	1	1	0	0
Sprague, 3b	4	2	1	1	Casey, 1b	5	1	1	1
W.Morris, 2b	5	1	2	0	Graves, p	0	0	0	0
J.Oliver, c	5	0	1	1	Stynes, ph	1	1	1	3
Benjamin, ss	5	0	2	2	G.Vaughn, lf	5	0	1	1
Schmidt, p	2	0	0	0	Larkin, ss	2	1	1	1
Clontz, p	0	0	0	0	Taubensee, c	5	0	0	0
Sauerbeck, p	0	0	0	0	A.Boone, 3b	2	0	0	0
Wehner, ph	1	0	0	0	G.White, p	0	0	0	0
M.Wilkins, p	0	0	0	0	Hammnds, rf	2	0	0	0
B.Brown, ph	1	0	0	0	Reese, 2b	5	0	1	1
Silva, p	0	0	0	0	Villone, p	2	0	1	0
Sveum, ph	1	0	0	0	H.Morris, ph	0	0	0	0
M.Williams, p	0	0	0	0	M.Lewis, 3b	3	1	1	0
Totals	**42**	**4**	**8**	**4**	**Totals**	**40**	**7**	**7**	**7**

Pittsburgh .... 020 002 000 000—4
Cincinnati .... 201 001 000 003—7

E—Villone (2). DP—Pittsburgh 1, Cincinnati 2. LOB—Pittsburgh 5, Cincinnati 6. 2B—W.Morris (18), Benjamin (15), Casey (32), G.Vaughn (12), M.Lewis (14). 3B—Larkin (3). HR—Stynes (2). SB—Benjamin (7), Cameron (31), Larkin 2 (21), A.Boone (11). CS—Reese (6).

Pittsburgh	IP	H	R	ER	BB	SO
Schmidt	5.1	4	4	4	3	4
Clontz (BS 1)	0.1	1	0	0	0	0
Sauerbeck	0.1	0	0	0	0	0
M.Wilkins	2	0	0	0	1	3
Silva	3	0	0	0	1	3
M.Williams (L, 2-3)	0.2	2	3	3	1	1

Cincinnati	IP	H	R	ER	BB	SO
Villone	6	6	4	4	2	4
G.White	1	1	0	0	0	1
Williamson	3	1	0	0	0	4
Graves (W, 8-6)	2	0	0	0	0	1

HBP—Sprague by Villone, Cameron by Schmidt, A.Boone by Schmidt. U—HP, Nelson. 1B, Hu.Wendelstedt. 2B, M.Hirschbeck. 3B, Emmel. T—3:50. A—19,118.

BATTING

Name	G	TPA	AB	R	H	TB	2B	3B	HR	RBI	Avg.	Obp.	Slg.	SH	SF	HP	BB	IBB	SO	SB	CS	GDP	vs RHP AB	Avg.	HR	RBI	vs LHP AB	Avg.	HR	RBI
Casey, Sean	151	669	594	103	197	320	42	3	25	99	.332	.399	.539	0	5	9	61	13	88	0	2	15	424	.356	17	70	170	.271	8	29
Reese, Pokey	149	636	585	85	167	244	37	5	10	52	.285	.330	.417	5	5	6	35	3	81	38	7	9	439	.282	7	39	146	.295	3	13
Larkin, Barry	161	687	583	108	171	245	30	4	12	75	.293	.390	.420	5	4	2	93	5	57	30	8	12	436	.305	7	56	147	.259	5	19
Vaughn, Greg	153	643	550	104	135	294	20	2	45	118	.245	.347	.535	0	5	3	85	3	137	15	2	9	409	.240	34	86	141	.262	11	32
Cameron, Mike	146	636	542	93	139	254	34	9	21	66	.256	.357	.469	5	3	6	80	2	145	38	12	4	422	.246	14	51	120	.292	7	15
Boone, Aaron	139	521	472	56	132	210	26	5	14	72	.280	.330	.445	5	5	8	30	2	79	17	6	6	367	.297	12	64	105	.219	2	8
Taubensee, Eddie	126	461	424	58	132	221	22	2	21	87	.311	.354	.521	1	5	1	30	1	67	0	2	12	364	.308	19	76	60	.333	2	11
Young, Dmitri	127	409	373	63	112	188	30	2	14	56	.300	.352	.504	0	4	2	30	1	71	3	1	11	264	.314	11	43	109	.266	3	13
Tucker, Michael	133	340	296	55	75	126	8	5	11	44	.253	.338	.426	0	4	3	37	3	81	11	4	5	257	.268	9	37	39	.154	2	7
Hammonds, Jeffrey	123	293	262	43	73	137	13	0	17	41	.279	.347	.523	2	1	1	27	0	64	3	6	4	122	.254	9	24	140	.300	8	17
Lewis, Mark	88	184	173	18	44	78	16	0	6	28	.254	.280	.451	2	2	0	7	1	24	0	0	8	118	.246	5	22	55	.273	1	6
Johnson, Brian	45	127	117	12	27	49	7	0	5	18	.231	.286	.419	1	0	0	9	0	31	0	0	2	57	.193	2	8	60	.267	3	10
Stynes, Chris	73	129	113	18	27	34	1	0	2	14	.239	.310	.301	3	1	0	12	1	13	5	2	2	89	.225	2	12	24	.292	0	2
Morris, Hal	80	112	102	10	29	38	9	0	0	16	.284	.348	.373	0	0	0	10	0	21	0	0	1	81	.284	0	13	21	.286	0	3
LaRue, Jason	36	103	90	12	19	35	7	0	3	10	.211	.311	.389	0	0	2	11	1	32	4	1	4	53	.245	1	5	37	.162	2	5
Harnisch, Pete	33	75	66	6	10	17	4	0	1	5	.152	.164	.258	8	0	0	1	0	20	0	0	1	56	.161	0	3	10	.100	1	2
Tomko, Brett	33	58	47	3	10	12	2	0	0	2	.213	.260	.255	8	0	0	3	0	17	0	0	0	35	.200	0	1	12	.250	0	1
Villone, Ron	29	49	43	0	3	3	0	0	0	0	.070	.091	.070	5	0	0	1	0	10	0	0	0	33	.091	0	0	10	.000	0	0
Parris, Steve	22	43	38	1	6	6	0	0	0	4	.158	.158	.158	5	0	0	0	0	11	0	0	0	23	.217	0	3	15	.067	0	1
Neagle, Denny	20	43	37	1	6	7	1	0	0	2	.162	.184	.189	5	0	0	1	0	9	0	0	0	28	.179	0	1	9	.111	0	1
Sweeney, Mark	37	35	31	6	11	20	3	0	2	7	.355	.429	.645	0	1	0	4	1	9	0	0	2	31	.355	2	7	0	.000	0	0
Guzman, Juan	12	30	26	1	3	3	0	0	0	2	.115	.148	.115	3	0	0	1	0	10	0	0	0	21	.048	0	1	5	.400	0	1
Avery, Steve	19	28	26	1	2	2	0	0	0	1	.077	.077	.077	2	0	0	0	0	11	0	0	0	19	.105	0	1	7	.000	0	0
Sullivan, Scott	79	15	15	1	0	0	0	0	0	0	.000	.000	.000	0	0	0	0	0	11	0	0	0	14	.000	0	0	1	.000	0	0
Bere, Jason	12	17	14	2	4	4	0	0	0	1	.286	.333	.286	2	0	1	0	0	7	0	0	0	9	.222	0	0	5	.400	0	1
Dawkins, Travis	7	8	7	1	1	1	0	0	0	0	.143	.250	.143	0	0	1	0	0	4	0	0	0	4	.250	0	0	3	.000	0	0
Williamson, Scott	62	11	7	0	0	0	0	0	0	0	.000	.125	.000	3	0	0	1	0	6	0	0	0	6	.000	0	0	1	.000	0	0
Graves, Danny	75	5	5	0	0	0	0	0	0	0	.000	.000	.000	0	0	0	0	0	2	0	0	0	5	.000	0	0	0	.000	0	0
Belinda, Stan	29	4	4	0	1	1	0	0	0	0	.250	.250	.250	0	0	0	0	0	1	0	0	0	3	.333	0	0	1	.000	0	0
Reyes, Dennys	65	4	4	0	0	0	0	0	0	0	.000	.000	.000	0	0	0	0	0	3	0	0	0	4	.000	0	0	0	.000	0	0
Greene, Rick	1	2	2	0	0	0	0	0	0	0	.000	.000	.000	0	0	0	0	0	2	0	0	0	2	.000	0	0	0	.000	0	0
Robinson, Kerry	9	1	1	4	0	0	0	0	0	0	.000	.000	.000	0	0	0	0	0	1	0	1	0	1	.000	0	0	0	.000	0	0
Hudek, John	2	0	0	0	0	0	0	0	0	0	.000	.000	.000	0	0	0	0	0	0	0	0	0	0	.000	0	0	0	.000	0	0
White, Gabe	50	0	0	0	0	0	0	0	0	0	.000	.000	.000	0	0	0	0	0	0	0	0	0	0	.000	0	0	0	.000	0	0
Ryan, B.J.	1	0	0	0	0	0	0	0	0	0	.000	.000	.000	0	0	0	0	0	0	0	0	0	0	.000	0	0	0	.000	0	0

Players with more than one N.L. team

Name	G	TPA	AB	R	H	TB	2B	3B	HR	RBI	Avg.	Obp.	Slg.	SH	SF	HP	BB	IBB	SO	SB	CS	GDP	vs RHP AB	Avg.	HR	RBI	vs LHP AB	Avg.	HR	RBI
Bere, Mil.	5	10	8	1	3	3	0	0	0	0	.375	.500	.375	0	0	0	2	0	2	0	0	0	9	.222	0	0	5	.400	0	1
Bere, Cin.-Mil.	17	27	22	3	7	7	0	0	0	1	.318	.400	.318	2	0	1	2	0	9	0	0	0	14	.286	0	0	8	.375	0	1
Hudek, Atl.	15	1	1	0	0	0	0	0	0	0	.000	.000	.000	0	0	0	0	0	1	0	0	0	0	.000	0	0	0	.000	0	0
Hudek, Cin.-Atl.	17	1	1	0	0	0	0	0	0	0	.000	.000	.000	0	0	0	0	0	1	0	0	0	0	.000	0	0	1	.000	0	0

PITCHING

Name	W	L	Pct.	ERA	IP	H	R	ER	HR	SH	SF	HB	BB	IBB	SO	G	GS	CG	ShO	GF	Sv	vs. RH AB	Avg.	HR	RBI	vs. LH AB	Avg.	HR	RBI
Harnisch, Pete	16	10	.615	3.68	198.1	190	86	81	25	10	6	5	57	2	120	33	33	2	2	0	0	418	.249	11	42	336	.256	14	39
Tomko, Brett	5	7	.417	4.92	172.0	175	103	94	31	9	5	4	60	10	132	33	26	1	0	1	0	346	.275	19	58	320	.250	12	35
Villone, Ron	9	7	.563	4.23	142.2	114	70	67	8	9	3	5	73	2	97	29	22	0	0	2	2	433	.212	6	47	87	.253	2	13
Parris, Steve	11	4	.733	3.50	128.2	124	59	50	16	7	3	6	52	4	86	22	21	2	1	0	0	268	.228	10	29	209	.301	6	23
Sullivan, Scott	5	4	.556	3.01	113.2	88	41	38	10	4	4	8	47	4	78	79	0	0	0	16	3	253	.202	7	27	153	.242	3	15
Neagle, Denny	9	5	.643	4.27	111.2	95	54	53	23	3	5	4	40	3	76	20	19	0	0	0	0	334	.237	19	40	81	.198	4	10
Graves, Danny	8	7	.533	3.08	111.0	90	42	38	10	5	2	2	49	4	69	75	0	0	0	56	27	223	.233	6	28	173	.220	4	16
Avery, Steve	6	7	.462	5.16	96.0	75	62	55	11	3	6	1	78	0	51	19	19	0	0	0	0	262	.225	9	32	76	.211	2	17
Williamson, Scott	12	7	.632	2.41	93.1	54	29	25	8	5	2	1	43	6	107	62	0	0	0	40	19	169	.172	3	17	146	.171	5	12
Guzman, Juan	6	3	.667	3.03	77.1	70	33	26	10	3	1	1	21	3	60	12	12	1	0	0	0	162	.204	8	18	132	.280	2	11
Reyes, Dennys	2	2	.500	3.79	61.2	53	30	26	5	4	3	3	39	1	72	65	1	0	0	12	2	133	.226	3	19	95	.242	2	14
White, Gabe	1	2	.333	4.43	61.0	68	31	30	13	2	1	2	14	1	61	50	0	0	0	18	0	168	.244	11	27	74	.365	2	14
Bere, Jason	3	0	1.000	6.85	43.1	56	37	33	6	5	1	2	40	3	28	12	10	0	0	0	0	85	.353	5	14	87	.299	1	16
Belinda, Stan	3	1	.750	5.27	42.2	42	26	25	11	2	1	1	18	3	40	29	0	0	0	12	2	97	.258	6	10	66	.258	5	17
Greene, Rick	0	0	.000	4.76	5.2	7	4	3	2	0	0	0	1	0	3	1	0	0	0	0	0	13	.154	0	0	11	.455	2	5
Ryan, B.J.	0	0	.000	4.50	2.0	4	1	1	0	0	0	0	1	0	1	1	0	0	0	0	0	8	.500	0	1	0	.000	0	0
Hudek, John	0	0	.000	27.00	1.0	4	3	3	1	0	0	0	3	0	2	2	0	0	0	0	0	3	1.000	1	4	3	.333	0	0

PITCHERS WITH MORE THAN ONE N.L. TEAM

Name	W	L	Pct.	ERA	IP	H	R	ER	HR	SH	SF	HB	BB	IBB	SO	G	GS	CG	ShO	GF	Sv	vs. RH AB	Avg.	HR	RBI	vs. LH AB	Avg.	HR	RBI
Bere, Mil.	2	0	1.000	4.63	23.1	23	15	12	3	1	1	0	10	0	19	5	4	0	0	0	0	85	.353	5	14	87	.299	1	16
Bere, Cin.-Mil.	5	0	1.000	6.08	66.2	79	52	45	9	6	2	2	50	3	47	17	14	0	0	2	0	131	.336	8	24	131	.267	1	17
Hudek, Atl.	0	1	.000	6.48	16.2	21	14	12	1	0	1	1	11	0	18	15	0	0	0	12	0	3	1.000	1	4	3	.333	0	0
Hudek, Cin.-Atl.	0	2	.000	7.64	17.2	25	17	15	2	0	1	1	14	0	18	17	0	0	0	1	0	44	.386	2	14	33	.242	0	4

1999 REVIEW

INDIVIDUAL STATISTICS

FIELDING

FIRST BASEMEN
Player	Pct.	G	PO	A	E	TC	DP
Casey, Sean	.995	148	1189	55	6	1250	109
Morris, Hal	.991	25	107	6	1	114	10
Young, Dmitri	1.000	9	56	1	0	57	5
Sweeney, Mark	1.000	1	2	0	0	2	1

SECOND BASEMEN
Player	Pct.	G	PO	A	E	TC	DP
Reese, Pokey	.991	146	325	409	7	741	91
Stynes, Chris	.956	43	48	60	5	113	11
Lewis, Mark	.500	2	0	1	1	2	0

THIRD BASEMEN
Player	Pct.	G	PO	A	E	TC	DP
Boone, Aaron	.958	136	86	253	15	354	17
Lewis, Mark	.938	52	21	54	5	80	7
Stynes, Chris	.929	8	2	11	1	14	0

SHORTSTOPS
Player	Pct.	G	PO	A	E	TC	DP
Larkin, Barry	.978	161	220	401	14	635	77
Reese, Pokey	1.000	16	15	16	0	31	4
Dawkins, Travis	1.000	7	2	4	0	6	1
Boone, Aaron	1.000	6	1	5	0	6	2

OUTFIELDERS
Player	Pct.	G	PO	A	E	TC	DP
Cameron, Mike	.979	146	372	7	8	387	3
Vaughn, Greg	.986	144	264	8	4	276	2
Tucker, Michael	.990	114	182	8	2	192	0
Hammonds, Jeffrey	1.000	106	157	5	0	162	2
Young, Dmitri	.976	91	160	4	4	168	0
Morris, Hal	1.000	4	3	0	0	3	0
Stynes, Chris	-	4	0	0	0	0	0
Robinson, Kerry	-	2	0	0	0	0	0
Sweeney, Mark	1.000	1	1	0	0	1	0

CATCHERS
Player	Pct.	G	PO	A	E	TC	DP	PB
Taubensee, Eddie	.989	124	733	48	9	790	8	5
Johnson, Brian	.995	39	201	11	1	213	2	4
LaRue, Jason	.990	35	179	15	2	196	0	2

PITCHERS
Player	Pct.	G	PO	A	E	TC	DP
Sullivan, Scott	.842	79	6	10	3	19	0
Graves, Danny	1.000	75	7	21	0	28	3
Reyes, Dennys	.833	65	0	5	1	6	0
Williamson, Scott	.900	62	2	7	1	10	1
White, Gabe	1.000	50	1	2	0	3	0
Tomko, Brett	.938	33	10	20	2	32	2
Harnisch, Pete	.893	33	7	18	3	28	1
Villone, Ron	.854	29	7	28	6	41	1
Belinda, Stan	1.000	29	0	5	0	5	0
Parris, Steve	.962	22	8	17	1	26	6
Neagle, Denny	1.000	20	2	5	0	7	1
Avery, Steve	.952	19	4	16	1	21	0
Guzman, Juan	.929	12	5	8	1	14	1
Bere, Jason	.889	12	1	7	1	9	1
Hudek, John	-	2	0	0	0	0	0
Greene, Rick	-	1	0	0	0	0	0
Ryan, B.J.	-	1	0	0	0	0	0

PITCHING AGAINST EACH CLUB

Pitcher	Ari. W-L	Atl. W-L	Chi. W-L	Col. W-L	Fla. W-L	Hou. W-L	L.A. W-L	Mil. W-L	Mon. W-L	N.Y. W-L	Phi. W-L	Pit. W-L	S.D. W-L	S.F. W-L	StL. W-L	A.L. W-L	Total W-L
Avery, S.	1-1	0-1	0-0	0-0	0-1	0-0	1-0	2-0	0-0	0-0	0-0	0-0	1-0	0-1	0-0	1-2	6-7
Belinda, S.	0-0	0-0	0-0	0-0	0-0	0-1	1-0	0-0	0-0	0-0	0-0	0-0	0-0	0-0	0-0	0-0	3-1
Bere, J.	0-0	0-0	0-0	0-0	1-0	0-0	0-0	0-0	0-0	0-0	1-0	0-0	0-0	0-0	1-0	0-0	3-1
Graves, D.	1-0	0-0	1-1	1-0	1-0	0-1	1-0	0-1	0-0	0-0	0-0	2-1	0-0	0-1	0-1	1-1	8-7
Greene, R.	0-0	0-0	0-0	0-0	0-0	0-0	0-0	0-0	0-0	0-0	0-0	0-0	0-0	0-0	0-0	0-0	0-0
Guzman, J.	0-0	0-1	1-0	0-0	1-0	0-0	0-0	0-1	2-0	0-0	0-0	0-0	0-0	0-0	0-0	0-0	6-3
Harnisch, P.	0-0	0-2	0-2	1-0	0-0	4-0	1-1	3-1	0-1	1-1	2-0	1-1	1-0	0-0	2-0	0-1	16-10
Hudek, J.	0-0	0-0	0-0	0-0	0-0	0-0	0-0	0-0	0-0	0-0	0-0	0-0	0-1	0-0	0-0	0-0	0-1
Neagle, D.	0-0	1-2	1-1	1-0	1-0	0-0	0-0	0-0	0-0	0-0	1-1	1-0	1-1	1-0	1-0	0-0	9-5
Parris, S.	0-0	0-0	1-0	2-0	1-1	1-0	0-0	0-0	0-2	0-1	1-0	1-0	0-0	1-0	2-0	0-0	11-4
Reyes, D.	2-0	0-0	0-0	0-0	0-0	0-1	0-1	0-0	0-0	0-0	0-0	0-0	0-0	0-0	0-0	0-0	2-2
Ryan, B.J.	0-0	0-0	0-0	0-0	0-0	0-0	0-0	0-0	0-0	0-0	0-0	0-0	0-0	0-0	0-0	0-0	0-0
Sullivan, S.	0-0	0-0	0-0	0-0	0-0	1-0	0-0	0-0	0-1	1-1	0-0	0-0	0-1	0-0	0-0	1-1	5-4
Tomko, B.	0-0	0-1	1-0	0-0	0-0	1-0	0-1	0-0	0-0	0-2	0-0	0-1	1-1	1-0	0-0	1-0	5-7
Villone, R.	1-0	0-1	0-1	0-1	1-0	2-0	0-1	0-0	1-1	1-0	0-0	1-0	0-1	1-0	1-0	0-1	9-7
White, G.	1-0	0-0	0-0	0-0	0-0	0-0	0-1	1-0	0-0	0-0	0-0	0-1	0-1	0-0	0-0	0-0	1-2
Williamson, S.	2-0	0-0	1-0	2-0	0-0	0-0	0-0	0-0	0-1	2-0	2-0	0-1	0-1	0-0	1-2	1-2	12-7
Totals	8-1	1-8	8-5	7-2	6-1	9-4	4-3	6-6	4-3	5-5	6-3	7-6	6-3	4-5	8-4	7-8	96-67

INTERLEAGUE: Avery 1-1, Graves 1-0, Williamson 0-2, Harnisch 0-1 vs. Indians; Parris 1-0, Sullivan 0-1, Graves 0-1 vs. Tigers; Parris 1-0, Sullivan 1-0, Williamson 1-0 vs. Royals; Tomko 1-0, Avery 0-1, Villone 0-1 vs. Twins. Total: 7-8.

MISCELLANEOUS

HOME RUNS BY PARK
At Arizona (5): Larkin 1, Vaughn 1, Taubensee 1, Hammonds 1, Casey 1.
At Atlanta (3): Tucker 1, Cameron 1, Boone 1.
At Chicago (NL) (14): Vaughn 5, Cameron 3, Boone 3, Larkin 1, Taubensee 1, Young 1.
At Cincinnati (97): Vaughn 20, Cameron 12, Casey 11, Young 9, Taubensee 8, Larkin 7, Boone 7, Hammonds 5, Tucker 5, Reese 5, Johnson 3, Lewis 2, Stynes 1, Sweeney 1, LaRue 1.
At Cleveland (3): Vaughn 1, Taubensee 1, Cameron 1.
At Colorado (9): Hammonds 3, Casey 3, Vaughn 1, Lewis 1, Johnson 1.
At Florida (1): Hammonds 1.
At Houston (5): Tucker 2, Casey 2, Taubensee 1.
At Kansas City (7): Vaughn 2, Hammonds 2, Casey 2, Larkin 1.
At Los Angeles (3): Taubensee 1, Young 1, Casey 1.
At Milwaukee (12): Vaughn 4, Taubensee 2, Cameron 2, Tucker 1, Stynes 1, Young 1, Boone 1.
At Minnesota (3): Taubensee 1, Reese 1, Boone 1.
At Montreal (2): Hammonds 1, Tucker 1.
At New York (NL) (3): Vaughn 2, Reese 1.
At Philadelphia (17): Taubensee 4, Hammonds 3, Vaughn 2, Young 2, Lewis 1, Johnson 1, Sweeney 1, Reese 1, Boone 1, Casey 1.
At Pittsburgh (6): Larkin 1, Vaughn 1, Hammonds 1, Cameron 1, Casey 1, LaRue 1.
At San Diego (6): Vaughn 2, Harnisch 1, Taubensee 1, Lewis 1, Casey 1.
At San Francisco (5): Vaughn 1, Lewis 1, Tucker 1, Reese 1, LaRue 1.
At St. Louis (8): Vaughn 3, Casey 2, Larkin 1, Cameron 1, Reese 1.

LOW-HIT GAMES
No-hitters: None.
One-hitters: None.
Two-hitters: None.

10-STRIKEOUT GAMES
Pete Harnisch 1, Brett Tomko 1, **Total:** 2.

FOUR OR MORE HITS IN ONE GAME
Sean Casey 4 (including one five-hit game), Eddie Taubensee 2, Pokey Reese 2 (including one five-hit game), Barry Larkin 1, Hal Morris 1, Mark Lewis 1, Jeffrey Hammonds 1, Aaron Boone 1, **Total:** 13.

MULTI-HOMER GAMES
Jeffrey Hammonds 3, Greg Vaughn 2, Mike Cameron 2, Sean Casey 2, Eddie Taubensee 1, Aaron Boone 1, **Total:** 11.

GRAND SLAMS
8-21: Aaron Boone (off Montreal's Mike Thurman).
8-21: Eddie Taubensee (off Montreal's Bobby Ayala).

PINCH HITTERS
(Minimum 5 at-bats)

Name	AB	Avg.	HR	RBI
Morris, Hal	45	.222	0	6
Sweeney, Mark	31	.355	2	7
Young, Dmitri	29	.345	1	8
Lewis, Mark	29	.172	0	3
Tucker, Michael	22	.318	1	3
Hammonds, Jeffrey	19	.158	1	4
Johnson, Brian	12	.167	0	1
Stynes, Chris	11	.364	1	3
Taubensee, Eddie	7	.286	0	2

DEBUTS
4-5: Scott Williamson, P.
6-15: Jason LaRue, C.
6-19: Rick Greene, P.
7-28: B.J. Ryan, P.
9-3: Travis Dawkins, SS.

GAMES BY POSITION
Catcher: Eddie Taubensee 124, Brian Johnson 39, Jason LaRue 35.
First base: Sean Casey 148, Hal Morris 25, Dmitri Young 9, Mark Sweeney 1.
Second base: Pokey Reese 146, Chris Stynes 43, Mark Lewis 2.
Third base: Aaron Boone 136, Mark Lewis 52, Chris Stynes 8.
Shortstop: Barry Larkin 161, Pokey Reese 16, Travis Dawkins 7, Aaron Boone 6.
Outfield: Mike Cameron 146, Greg Vaughn 144, Michael Tucker 114, Jeffrey Hammonds 106, Dmitri Young 91, Hal Morris 4, Chris Stynes 4, Kerry Robinson 2, Mark Sweeney 1.
Designated hitter: Greg Vaughn 6, Hal Morris 1, Dmitri Young 1, Sean Casey 1.

STREAKS
Wins: 10 (June 19-July 1).
Losses: 3 (April 17-20, April 30-May 2, May 26-28, June 11-13, August 23-25, August 31-September 3, September 29-October 2).
Consecutive games with at least one hit: 16, Barry Larkin (June 20-July 6), Eddie Taubensee (May 22-June 13).
Wins by pitcher: 6, Denny Neagle (August 30-September 25).

ATTENDANCE
Home: 2,061,222.
Road: 2,243,007.
Highest (home): 55,112 (April 5 vs. San Francisco).
Highest (road): 55,992 (October 3 vs. Milwaukee).
Lowest (home): 13,943 (May 3 vs. Arizona).
Lowest (road): 6,796 (August 26 vs. Montreal).

COLORADO ROCKIES

DAY BY DAY

Date	Opp.	Res.	Score	(inn.*)	Hits	Opp. hits	Winning pitcher	Losing pitcher	Save	Record	Pos.	GB
4-4	At S.D.§	W	8-2		18	6	Kile	Ashby		1-0	1st	+0.5
4-6	At S.D.	L	3-4		9	9	Hitchcock	Astacio	Hoffman	1-1	T3rd	1.0
4-7	At S.D.	L	1-2		8	8	Rivera	Jones		1-2	4th	2.0
4-8	At L.A.	W	4-2		5	5	Bohanon	Perez	Veres	2-2	T3rd	2.0
4-9	At L.A.	L	6-9		9	17	Dreifort	Thomson	Shaw	2-3	T3rd	3.0
4-10	At L.A.	L	0-2		3	5	Brown	Kile	Shaw	2-4	4th	3.0
4-12	S.D.	L	5-8	(11)	10	13	Wall	Veres	Reyes	2-5	T4th	4.0
4-15	S.D.	W	6-4		10	4	Bohanon	Clement	Veres	3-5	5th	3.0
4-17	Atl.	W	5-4		10	8	McElroy	Rocker		4-5	4th	2.5
4-18	Atl.	L	5-20		10	24	Maddux	Astacio		4-6	5th	2.5
4-19	Mon.	W	11-10		11	20	Veres	Urbina		5-6	5th	2.5
4-22	At S.F	W	8-5		13	9	Bohanon	Rueter	Veres	6-6	T3rd	1.5
4-23	At S.F.	L	2-7		6	10	Ortiz	Kile		6-7	4th	2.5
4-24	At S.F.	L	4-8		4	11	Estes	Astacio		6-8	5th	3.5
4-25	At S.F.	L	6-7		9	10	Embree	DeJean	Nen	6-9	5th	4.5
4-27	At StL.	L	5-7		10	8	Oliver	Thomson	Radinsky	6-10	5th	5.5
4-28	At StL.	W	9-7		11	14	Bohanon	Jimenez	Veres	7-10	5th	5.5
4-29	At StL.	W	6-2		11	8	Kile	Mercker		8-10	4th	5.5
4-30	At Pit.	W	7-2		8	8	Astacio	Schourek		9-10	4th	4.5
5-1	At Pit.	L	3-9		8	9	Ritchie	Wright		9-11	4th	4.5
5-2	At Pit.	L	5-8		8	12	Schmidt	Thomson	Williams	9-12	4th	4.5
5-3	At Chi.	W	6-1		12	6	Bohanon	Trachsel		10-12	4th	3.5
5-4	At Chi.	W	12-13		17	14	Beck	Dipoto		10-13	4th	4.5
5-5	At Chi.	W	13-6		18	10	Astacio	Mulholland		11-13	4th	3.5
5-7	Phi.	L	1-8		7	14	Schilling	Thomson		11-14	4th	4.5
5-8	Phi.	L	2-7		9	12	Bennett	Bohanon		11-15	4th	5.5
5-9	Phi.	L	8-10		12	17	Ryan	Veres	Gomes	11-16	4th	5.5
5-10	N.Y.	W	10-3		12	7	Astacio	Leiter		12-16	4th	5.5
5-11	N.Y.	W	8-5		12	11	Jones	Jones		13-16	4th	4.5
5-12	N.Y.	L	5-10		10	15	Reed	Thomson		13-17	4th	5.5
5-14	At Ari.	W	4-1		9	6	Bohanon	Benes		14-17	4th	4.5
5-15	At Ari.	L	2-9		3	16	Johnson	Kile		14-18	4th	4.5
5-16	At Ari.	W	5-1		6	7	Astacio	Daal		15-18	4th	4.5
5-17	Cin.	L	2-7		6	10	Harnisch	Jones		15-19	4th	4.5
5-18	Cin.	L	3-5		6	10	Graves	Leskanic	Williamson	15-20	4th	5.5
5-19	Cin.	L	12-24		15	28	Parris	Dipoto	Villone	15-21	5th	5.5
5-20	Ari.	W	8-4		10	7	Kile	Johnson		16-21	4th	5.0
5-21	Ari.	W	8-7	(11)	14	16	Leskanic	Frascatore		17-21	4th	5.0
5-22	Ari.	L	3-8		11	14	Daal	Jones		17-22	4th	6.0
5-23	Ari.	W	7-6		11	11	McElroy	Olson		18-22	4th	5.0
5-24	At Hou.	L	2-5		9	8	Reynolds	Bohanon		18-23	4th	5.5
5-25	At Hou.	L	1-2	(12)	5	9	Elarton	DeJean		18-24	4th	6.5
5-26	At Hou.	L	2-3		7	9	Powell	Astacio		18-25	4th	7.5
5-27	At Hou.	W	4-3		7	4	Dipoto	Miller	Veres	19-25	4th	6.5
5-28	At Phi.	W	5-3		7	12	Leskanic	Byrd	Veres	20-25	4th	6.0
5-29	At Phi.	L	0-2		4	4	Schilling	Bohanon		20-26	4th	7.0
5-30	At Phi.	W	1-0		7	5	Kile	Poole	Veres	21-26	4th	7.0
5-31	At Atl.	L	1-3		8	8	Millwood	Astacio	Rocker	21-27	4th	8.0
6-1	At Atl.	L	2-7		6	6	Smoltz	Jones		21-28	4th	8.0
6-2	At Atl.	W	3-2	(11)	5	9	Dipoto	Springer		22-28	4th	8.0
6-4	Mil.	W	9-8	(10)	17	17	Veres	Wickman		23-28	4th	8.0
6-5	Mil.	W	12-11		13	14	DeJean	Plunk	Dipoto	24-28	4th	7.0
6-6	Mil.	W	10-5		14	9	Astacio	Karl		25-28	4th	7.0
6-7	Sea.	L	2-4		9	8	Halama	Jones	Mesa	25-29	4th	7.0
6-8	Sea.	L	5-10		10	15	Rodriguez	Brownson	Cloude	25-30	4th	7.0
6-9	Sea.	W	16-11		12	12	Bohanon	Fassero		26-30	4th	7.0
6-11	At Tex.	L	2-3		6	8	Zimmerman	McElroy	Wetteland	26-31	4th	8.0
6-12	At Tex.	W	8-7		13	13	Astacio	Sele	Veres	27-31	4th	7.0
6-13	At Tex.	W	4-2		8	7	Jones	Morgan	Veres	28-31	4th	7.0
6-14	S.F	W	5-4		7	8	Leskanic	Johnstone	Veres	29-31	3rd	7.0
6-15	S.F	W	15-6		16	15	Bohanon	Brock		30-31	3rd	7.0
6-16	S.F	L	2-15		6	19	Gardner	Kile		30-32	3rd	8.0
6-18	Fla.	W	11-10		18	13	McElroy	Mantei		31-32	3rd	7.0
6-19	Fla.	W	10-2		15	7	Jones	Fernandez		32-32	3rd	7.0
6-20	Fla.	W	8-7		11	15	Bohanon	Dempster	Veres	33-32	3rd	6.0
6-22	Chi.	L	12-13		15	14	Sanders	DeJean	Aguilera	33-33	3rd	5.5
6-23	Chi.	W	10-1		19	7	Astacio	Mulholland		34-33	3rd	4.5
6-24	Chi.	L	10-12		18	15	Tapani	Jones		34-34	3rd	5.5
6-25	At S.D.	L	1-10		7	10	Boehringer	Bohanon		34-35	3rd	5.5
6-26	At S.D.	L	6-13		10	9	Clement	Brownson		34-36	3rd	5.5
6-27	At S.D.	L	3-5		7	8	Hitchcock	Kile	Hoffman	34-37	3rd	6.5
6-28	At S.D.	L	7-8		14	10	Williams	Astacio	Hoffman	34-38	4th	7.0
6-29	At S.F.	L	1-10		6	13	Rueter	Jones		34-39	4th	7.0
6-30	At S.F.	L	1-4		7	8	Ortiz	Bohanon	Nen	34-40	4th	7.0
7-1	At S.F.	L	1-7		6	9	Estes	Kile		34-41	4th	8.0
7-2	S.D.	L	3-15		8	19	Hitchcock	Astacio		34-42	4th	9.0
7-3†	S.D.	W	12-10		17	13	Ramirez	Williams	Veres	35-42		
7-3‡	S.D.	W	8-6		15	9	Jones	Murray	Veres	36-42	4th	8.5
7-4	S.D.	L	0-11		6	17	Ashby	Bohanon		36-43	4th	8.5

HIGHLIGHTS

High point: On June 23, the Rockies beat the Cubs, 10-1, for their eighth win in 10 games. The victory improved Colorado's record to 34-33—only the second time the team had been over .500 since winning on opening day—and pulled it within 4½ games of first place.

Low point: The Rockies lost 18 of their final 30 games to finish last in the N.L. West for the first time in their seven-year existence, and their .444 winning percentage was the second-lowest in club history.

Turning point: The Rockies dropped a 12-10 game to the Cubs on June 24, beginning a nine-game losing streak that dropped them nine games from the top. During the streak (which included all seven games of a trip to San Diego and San Francisco), the Rockies were outscored 84-33.

Most valuable player: Larry Walker, who hit .379 with 37 home runs and 115 RBIs. Besides winning his second straight N.L. batting title, Walker also led the N.L. in slugging percentage (.710) and on-base percentage (.458). He became the first major leaguer to lead his league in those three categories since the Royals' George Brett did it in the A.L. in 1980 and the first National Leaguer to accomplish the feat since the Cardinals' Stan Musial in 1948.

Most valuable pitcher: Pedro Astacio, who tied the franchise record for victories (17) and set Rockies marks for complete games (seven), strikeouts (210) and innings pitched (232). He went 7-2 in his final 12 starts and pitched at least seven innings in 12 of his 15 outings after the All-Star break.

Most improved player: After spending the first two months of the season in Class AAA, veteran handyman Terry Shumpert hit .347 with 26 doubles and 10 homers in 92 games. He was 14-for-14 in steal attempts.

Most pleasant surprise: Dave Veres, who before the 1999 season never had been a full-time closer and had only 15 career saves. He set a Rockies record with 31 saves and pitched in a career-high 73 games.

Key injuries: Second baseman Mike Lansing didn't play after May 20 and underwent back surgery. Walker had only 438 at-bats, missing time because of assorted injuries. Versatile Kurt Abbott was sidelined a month overall with a mild concussion and a groin strain. And catcher Kirt Manwaring missed all of May with a broken finger.

Notable: Walker hit an astonishing .461 at home. ... Rockies pitchers set an N.L. record by allowing 737 walks and also yielded 1,028 runs. No N.L. team had permitted 1,000 since the Phillies gave up a major league-record 1,199 in 1930. ... Todd Helton hit for the cycle on June 19 against Florida. ... Colorado scored in every inning of its May 5 game against the Cubs, winning 13-6 at Wrigley Field. No team had achieved that feat in 35 years.

—JACK ETKIN

MISCELLANEOUS

RECORDS

1999 regular-season record: 72-90 (5th in N.L. West); 39-42 at home; 33-48 on road; 24-21 vs. N.L. East; 21-32 vs. N.L. Central; 23-29 vs. West; 4-8 vs. A.L. West; 23-28 vs. lefthanded starters; 49-62 vs. righthanded starters; 63-77 on grass; 9-13 on turf; 30-38 in daytime; 42-52 at night; 24-23 in one-run games; 4-6 in extra-inning games; 4-1-0 in doubleheaders.

Team record past five years: 392-400 (.495, ranks 9th in league in that span).

TEAM LEADERS

Batting average: Larry Walker (.379).
At-bats: Neifi Perez (690).
Runs: Todd Helton (114).
Hits: Neifi Perez (193).
Total bases: Todd Helton (339).
Doubles: Todd Helton (39).
Triples: Neifi Perez (11).
Home runs: Larry Walker (37).
Runs batted in: Dante Bichette (133).
Stolen bases: Terry Shumpert (14).
Slugging percentage: Larry Walker (.710).
On-base percentage: Larry Walker (.458).
Wins: Pedro Astacio (17).
Earned-run average: Pedro Astacio (5.04).
Complete games: Pedro Astacio (7).
Shutouts: Brian Bohanon (1).
Saves: Dave Veres (31).
Innings pitched: Pedro Astacio (232.0).
Strikeouts: Pedro Astacio (210).

Date	Opp.	Res.	Score	(inn.*)	Hits	Opp. hits	Winning pitcher	Losing pitcher	Save	Record	Pos.	GB
7-5	L.A.	W	8-4		14	11	Kile	Brown		37-43	4th	8.5
7-6	L.A.	W	5-2		10	6	Astacio	Dreifort		38-43	4th	8.5
7-7	L.A.	W	7-5		14	11	DeJean	Arnold	Veres	39-43	4th	7.5
7-8	L.A.	L	8-11		12	12	Park	Bohanon	Shaw	39-44	4th	8.0
7-9	Ana.	L	6-9		12	15	Finley	Kile	Percival	39-45	4th	9.0
7-10	Ana.	L	3-9		6	13	Olivares	Astacio		39-46	4th	10.0
7-11	Ana.	W	8-2		11	5	Dipoto	Fyhrie		40-46	4th	9.0
7-15	At Cin.	L	7-10		12	12	Parris	Kile	Graves	40-47	4th	9.0
7-16	At Cin.	W	6-2		11	4	Astacio	Villone	Veres	41-47	4th	8.0
7-17	At Cin.	L	2-3		8	3	Williamson	Dipoto		41-48	T4th	9.0
7-18	At Oak.	L	2-3		5	5	Haynes	Jones	Taylor	41-49	T4th	9.0
7-19	At Oak.	L	5-10		10	12	Worrell	Ramirez	Jones	41-50	5th	9.0
7-20	At Oak.	L	3-4		6	5	Rogers	Kile	Taylor	41-51	5th	9.0
7-21	At L.A.	W	5-4		13	8	Astacio	Valdes	Veres	42-51	5th	9.0
7-22†	At L.A.	W	4-1		8	3	Jones	Park	Veres	43-51		
7-22‡	At L.A.	W	12-11		13	15	Lee	Masaoka	Veres	44-51	4th	7.5
7-23	StL.	L	4-6		12	11	Oliver	Ramirez	Slocumb	44-52	4th	8.5
7-24	StL.	L	2-10		11	15	Mercker	Kile		44-53	4th	9.0
7-25	StL.	L	4-6		9	8	Luebbers	Astacio	Aybar	44-54	T4th	9.0
7-26	Hou.	L	5-8		10	17	Williams	Veres	Wagner	44-55	T4th	10.0
7-27	Hou.	L	3-6		10	12	Lima	Bohanon	Wagner	44-56	T4th	11.0
7-28	Hou.	L	8-16		18	21	Hampton	Ramirez		44-57	5th	12.0
7-29	Hou.	W	4-2		11	9	Kile	Holt	Veres	45-57	4th	11.5
7-30	At StL.	W	5-4		9	7	Astacio	Aybar	Veres	46-57	4th	11.5
7-31	At StL.	L	5-6		11	10	Painter	Leskanic	Bottalico	46-58	4th	12.5
8-1	At StL.	W	5-4		13	10	Bohanon	Jimenez	Veres	47-58	4th	11.5
8-3	At Cin.	L	1-2		6	8	Williamson	DeJean		47-59	4th	12.0
8-4	At Cin.	L	3-6		7	12	Neagle	Kile	Graves	47-60	T4th	13.0
8-5	At Cin.	W	2-1		10	4	Astacio	Guzman		48-60	4th	12.5
8-6	At Fla.	L	1-9		3	13	Fernandez	Jones		48-61	4th	12.5
8-7	At Fla.	L	1-4		7	7	Meadows	Bohanon	Alfonseca	48-62	T4th	13.5
8-8	At Fla.	L	1-2		4	4	Dempster	Wright	Alfonseca	48-63	5th	14.5
8-9	At Mil.	L	6-7		9	11	Wickman	Veres		48-64	5th	15.5
8-10	At Mil.	L	1-2	(10)	6	3	Coppinger	Veres		48-65	5th	16.5
8-11	At Mil.	W	8-5		14	10	Jones	Woodard		49-65	5th	16.5
8-13†	Mon.	L	13-14	(10)	15	14	Urbina	Dipoto	Telford	49-66		
8-13‡	Mon.	L	6-8		11	13	Vazquez	Bohanon	Urbina	49-67	5th	17.0
8-14	Mon.	W	11-8		18	11	Kile	Powell	Veres	50-67	5th	16.0
8-15†	Mon.	W	8-2		9	7	Thomson	Thurman	Ramirez	51-67		
8-15‡	Mon.	W	12-4		14	12	Astacio	Bennett		52-67	5th	15.5
8-16	Atl.	L	6-14		17	17	Maddux	Jones		52-68	5th	16.5
8-17	Atl.	W	3-2		8	10	Lee	Mulholland	Veres	53-68	5th	16.5
8-18	Atl.	W	4-1		3	8	Veres	Rocker		54-68	5th	16.5
8-19	Atl.	L	7-9	(14)	11	13	Chen	Lee	Mulholland	54-69	5th	17.0
8-20	At Chi.	W	11-3		14	7	Astacio	Farnsworth		55-69	5th	16.0
8-21	At Chi.	L	6-8		12	10	Bowie	Thomson	Adams	55-70	5th	17.0
8-22	At Chi.	W	3-2		5	6	Wright	Trachsel	Veres	56-70	4th	17.0
8-24	At Pit.	W	3-2		8	7	Leskanic	Williams	Veres	57-70	4th	17.5
8-25	At Pit.	L	3-9		7	14	Peters	Kile		57-71	4th	18.5
8-26	At Pit.	L	4-8		8	15	Anderson	Astacio		57-72	5th	19.5
8-28†	Phi.	W	11-6		15	9	Lee	Aldred		58-72		
8-28‡	Phi.	W	4-0		11	4	Bohanon	Grahe		59-72	4th	18.5
8-29	Phi.	W	6-5		14	9	Kile	Byrd	Veres	60-72	4th	18.5
8-30	Pit.	L	8-11		16	16	Peters	Ramirez	Williams	60-73	5th	19.5
8-31	Pit.	L	8-9	(10)	18	14	Williams	Lee	Silva	60-74	5th	19.5
9-1	Pit.	L	8-9		12	12	Sauerbeck	Veres	Clontz	60-75	5th	19.5
9-3	At N.Y.	W	5-2	(10)	8	10	Leskanic	Wendell	Veres	61-75	5th	18.5
9-4	At N.Y.	L	2-4		11	5	Leiter	Bohanon	Benitez	61-76	5th	19.5
9-5	At N.Y.	L	2-6		9	9	Yoshii	Kile		61-77	5th	20.5
9-6	At Mon.	W	5-3		10	9	Astacio	Thurman	Veres	62-77	5th	20.0
9-7	At Mon.	L	1-4		6	5	Hermanson	Thomson	Urbina	62-78	5th	21.0
9-8	At Mon.	W	5-1		7	6	Wright	Smith		63-78	5th	21.0
9-10	Mil.	W	15-3		14	9	Bohanon	Pulsipher		64-78	5th	20.5
9-11	Mil.	W	7-6		12	8	Dipoto	Coppinger	Veres	65-78	T4th	20.5
9-12	Mil.	L	9-12		13	16	Plunk	Veres	Wickman	65-79	5th	21.5
9-13	N.Y.	L	5-6		13	9	Wendell	Veres	Benitez	65-80	5th	22.5
9-14	N.Y.	W	7-2		10	7	Wright	Dotel		66-80	5th	22.5
9-15	N.Y.	L	5-10		11	13	Wendell	Dipoto	Benitez	66-81	5th	22.5
9-17	L.A.	W	18-10		20	11	Hackman	Checo		67-81	5th	21.5
9-18	L.A.	L	4-5		10	9	Park	Astacio	Shaw	67-82	5th	22.5
9-19	L.A.	L	2-5	(8)	7	8	Brown	Thomson	Borbon	67-83	5th	23.5
9-20	Ari.	W	12-7		15	12	Wright	Daal		68-83	5th	22.5
9-21	Ari.	L	6-7		8	11	Olson	Ramirez	Mantei	68-84	5th	23.5
9-22	Ari.	L	3-11		7	11	Benes	Hackman		68-85	5th	24.5
9-24	At Fla.	W	5-3		8	9	Astacio	Edmondson	Veres	69-85	5th	24.5
9-25	At Fla.	L	2-8		6	13	Dempster	Thomson		69-86	5th	25.5
9-26	At Fla.	W	8-6		8	12	Leskanic	Medina	Veres	70-86	5th	25.5
9-27	At Ari.	L	3-10		9	10	Anderson	Bohanon		70-87	5th	26.5
9-28	At Ari.	L	3-9		6	15	Benes	Hackman		70-88	5th	27.5
9-29	At Ari.	W	4-1		8	8	Astacio	Reynoso		71-88	5th	26.5
10-1	S.F.	L	4-9		7	11	Ortiz	Thomson		71-89	5th	27.0
10-2	S.F.	L	7-16		13	18	Rueter	Wright		71-90	5th	28.0
10-3	S.F.	W	9-8		11	12	Veres	Embree		72-90	5th	28.0

Monthly records: April (9-10), May (12-17), June (13-13), July (12-18), August (14-16), September (11-14), October (1-2).
*Innings, if other than nine. † First game of a doubleheader. ‡ Second game of a doubleheader. §At Monterrey, Mex.

MEMORABLE GAMES

April 28 at St. Louis

A strained right rib cage forced Larry Walker to begin the season on the disabled list and miss the first seven games. He was muddling along with a .235 average, no homers and five RBI in eight games before finding his timing on a damp night and tying club records with three home runs and eight RBI. Walker hit a three-run home run in the first and another in the second, singled in the fifth and hit a two-run homer in the seventh with a heavy rain falling.

Colorado	AB	R	H	RBI	St. Louis	AB	R	H	RBI
D.Hamilton, cf	4	2	1	0	Bragg, cf	4	1	2	0
Lansing, 2b	5	3	3	1	Renteria, ss	2	1	0	1
L.Walker, rf	5	3	4	8	McGwire, 1b	4	2	2	1
Bichette, lf	5	0	2	0	E.Davis, rf	5	1	4	2
Veres, p	0	0	0	0	Tatis, 3b	5	0	1	1
Castilla, 3b	4	0	0	0	Dunston, lf	4	0	1	1
Helton, 1b	3	0	0	0	Busby, p	0	0	0	0
N.Perez, ss	4	0	0	0	Marrero, ph	1	0	0	0
J.Reed, c	3	1	1	0	A.Castillo, c	4	0	1	0
Bohanon, p	2	0	0	0	McEwing, 2b	4	1	2	1
Dipoto, p	0	0	0	0	J.Jimenez, p	0	0	0	0
Watkins, lf	0	0	0	0	D.Oliver, p	0	0	0	0
					Mohler, p	1	0	0	0
					Painter, p	0	0	0	0
					Lankford, ph	1	1	1	0
					Radinsky, p	0	0	0	0
					McGee, lf	1	0	0	0
Totals	35	9	11	9	Totals	36	7	14	7

Colorado	3 4 0	0 0 0	2 0 0	—9
St. Louis	3 1 1	0 0 1	0 0 1	—7

E—Bichette (3). DP—Colorado 1. LOB—Colorado 5, St. Louis 8. 2B—McGwire (4), Lankford (2). HR—L.Walker 3 (3). SB—E.Davis (2). CS—L.Walker (1), Tatis (2). S—Bohanon, D.Oliver. SF—Renteria.

Colorado	IP	H	R	ER	BB	SO
Bohanon (W, 4-0)	5	9	5	5	2	1
Dipoto (H, 3)	3	2	1	1	1	3
Veres (S, 4)	1	3	1	1	0	1

St. Louis	IP	H	R	ER	BB	SO
J.Jimenez (L, 2-1)	2	6	7	7	1	0
Mohler	2.2	2	0	0	1	1
Painter	1.1	0	0	0	0	2
Radinsky	1	2	2	2	0	0
Busby	2	1	0	0	3	1

HBP—McGwire by Bohanon. U—HP, Kellogg. 1B, Holbrook. 2B, DeMuth. 3B, Reliford. T—3:11. A—34,545.

August 28 at Denver

Brian Bohanon completed a sweep of a day-night doubleheader by pitching a four-hitter for the first shutout of his career and winning the fastest nine-inning game at Coors Field—2 hours, 7 minutes. All four hits were singles as Bohanon allowed just two runners to reach second base and joined Mark Thompson (Aug. 6, 1996) and Roger Bailey (May 4, 1997) as the only Rockies pitchers to throw a shutout at Coors Field.

Philadelphia	AB	R	H	RBI	Colorado	AB	R	H	RBI
Sefcik, cf	4	0	1	0	N.Perez, ss	4	1	1	0
Gant, lf	4	0	0	0	Helton, 1b	4	1	1	2
Abreu, rf	4	0	2	0	L.Walker, rf	4	1	4	0
K.Jordan, 3b	3	0	1	0	Bichette, lf	4	0	1	1
Brogna, 1b	3	0	0	0	Castilla, 3b	4	0	1	0
Lieberthal, c	3	0	0	0	L.Harris, 2b	3	0	1	0
A.Arias, ss	2	0	0	0	Shmprt, ph-2b	1	0	0	0
Doster, 2b	3	0	0	0	Barry, cf	3	0	1	0
Grahe, p	1	0	0	0	Blanco, c	3	0	0	0
D.Cedeno, ph	1	0	0	0	Bohanon, p	3	1	1	0
Brewer, p	0	0	0	0					
Totals	28	0	4	0	Totals	33	4	11	3

Philadelphia	0 0 0	0 0 0	0 0 0—	0
Colorado	0 0 3	0 0 0	0 1 x—	4

DP—Philadelphia 2, Colorado 2. LOB—Philadelphia 5, Colorado 5. 2B—N.Perez (25), Helton (30), L.Walker (20), L.Harris (10), Barry (12). 3B—L.Walker (4). CS—Sefcik (3).

Philadelphia	IP	H	R	ER	BB	SO
Grahe (L, 0-1)	7	9	3	3	0	0
Brewer	1	2	1	1	0	0

Colorado	IP	H	R	ER	BB	SO
Bohanon (W, 11-10)	9	4	0	0	4	10

U—HP, Randazzo. 1B, C.Williams. 2B, Rapuano. 3B, Emmel. T—2:07. A—47,217.

INDIVIDUAL STATISTICS

1999 REVIEW

BATTING

Name	G	TPA	AB	R	H	TB	2B	3B	HR	RBI	Avg.	Obp.	Slg.	SH	SF	HP	BB	IBB	SO	SB	CS	GDP	vs RHP AB	vs RHP Avg.	vs RHP HR	vs RHP RBI	vs LHP AB	vs LHP Avg.	vs LHP HR	vs LHP RBI
Perez, Neifi	157	732	690	108	193	278	27	11	12	70	.280	.307	.403	9	4	1	28	0	54	13	5	4	481	.301	6	48	209	.230	6	22
Castilla, Vinny	158	674	615	83	169	294	24	1	33	102	.275	.331	.478	0	5	1	53	7	75	2	3	15	446	.294	25	83	169	.225	8	19
Bichette, Dante	151	659	593	104	177	321	38	2	34	133	.298	.354	.541	0	10	2	54	3	84	6	6	15	427	.293	26	100	166	.313	8	33
Helton, Todd	159	657	578	114	185	339	39	5	35	113	.320	.395	.587	0	4	6	68	6	77	7	6	14	415	.349	31	85	163	.245	4	28
Walker, Larry	127	513	438	108	166	311	26	4	37	115	.379	.458	.710	0	6	12	57	8	52	11	4	12	296	.395	28	78	142	.345	9	37
Hamilton, Darryl	91	379	337	63	102	131	11	3	4	24	.303	.374	.389	2	1	1	38	0	21	4	5	7	229	.301	2	18	108	.306	2	6
Abbott, Kurt	96	305	286	41	78	123	17	2	8	41	.273	.310	.430	2	1	0	16	0	69	3	2	4	194	.273	6	29	92	.272	2	12
Blanco, Henry	88	303	263	30	61	97	12	3	6	28	.232	.320	.369	3	2	1	34	1	38	1	1	4	164	.238	3	15	99	.222	3	13
Shumpert, Terry	92	304	262	58	91	153	26	3	10	37	.347	.413	.584	4	5	2	31	2	41	14	0	2	176	.324	7	29	86	.395	3	8
Echevarria, Angel	102	211	191	28	56	96	7	0	11	35	.293	.360	.503	0	0	3	17	0	34	1	3	11	93	.301	4	16	98	.286	7	19
Barry, Jeff	74	192	168	19	45	76	16	0	5	26	.268	.344	.452	0	3	2	19	1	29	0	4	4	128	.250	3	14	40	.325	2	12
Clemente, Edgard	57	171	162	24	41	79	10	2	8	25	.253	.282	.488	1	1	0	7	0	46	0	0	4	110	.218	5	18	52	.327	3	7
Harris, Lenny	91	164	158	15	47	59	12	0	0	13	.297	.323	.373	0	0	0	6	0	6	1	1	7	145	.290	0	13	13	.385	0	0
Lansing, Mike	35	155	145	24	45	66	9	0	4	15	.310	.344	.455	1	1	1	7	0	22	2	0	3	92	.293	3	10	53	.340	1	5
Manwaring, Kirt	48	155	137	17	41	56	7	1	2	14	.299	.374	.409	0	1	5	12	1	23	0	0	4	99	.293	1	7	38	.316	1	7
Reed, Jeff	46	125	106	11	27	38	5	0	2	11	.255	.360	.358	0	1	1	17	1	24	0	1	3	91	.264	2	8	15	.200	0	3
Astacio, Pedro	37	94	86	5	20	24	2	1	0	7	.233	.241	.279	7	0	0	1	0	24	0	0	0	52	.212	0	5	34	.265	0	2
Bohanon, Brian	34	81	71	6	14	19	2	0	1	7	.197	.250	.268	5	0	0	5	0	20	0	0	2	53	.189	0	6	18	.222	1	1
Petrick, Ben	19	72	62	13	20	35	3	0	4	12	.323	.417	.565	0	0	0	10	0	13	1	0	1	50	.320	4	12	12	.333	0	0
Sexton, Chris	35	70	59	9	14	19	0	1	1	7	.237	.357	.322	0	0	0	11	1	10	4	2	2	25	.120	0	1	34	.324	1	6
Kile, Darryl	32	64	52	3	7	7	0	0	0	4	.135	.196	.135	8	0	0	4	0	20	0	0	3	32	.219	0	3	20	.000	0	1
Phillips, J.R.	25	40	39	5	9	19	4	0	2	4	.231	.250	.487	0	0	1	0	0	13	0	0	0	38	.237	2	4	1	.000	0	0
Wright, Jamey	16	35	32	0	4	5	1	0	0	2	.125	.125	.156	3	0	0	0	0	13	0	0	0	27	.111	0	2	5	.200	0	0
Gibson, Derrick	10	29	28	2	5	12	1	0	2	6	.179	.207	.429	0	0	1	0	0	7	0	0	2	20	.100	1	3	8	.375	1	3
Jones, Bobby M.	30	34	27	3	4	5	1	0	0	4	.148	.200	.185	4	1	0	2	0	7	0	0	0	19	.158	0	2	8	.125	0	2
McRae, Brian	7	27	23	1	6	11	2	0	1	1	.261	.370	.478	0	0	2	2	0	7	0	0	0	22	.273	1	1	1	.000	0	0
Watkins, Pat	16	22	19	2	1	1	0	0	0	0	.053	.143	.053	1	0	0	2	0	5	0	0	1	12	.083	0	0	7	.000	0	0
Thomson, John	14	20	18	1	3	4	1	0	0	1	.167	.250	.222	0	0	0	2	0	7	0	0	0	15	.200	0	1	3	.000	0	0
Petersen, Chris	7	15	13	1	2	2	0	0	0	2	.154	.267	.154	0	0	0	2	0	3	0	0	0	3	.000	0	0	10	.200	0	2
Sosa, Juan	11	11	9	3	2	2	0	0	0	0	.222	.364	.222	0	0	0	2	0	2	0	0	0	6	.333	0	0	3	.000	0	0
Brownson, Mark	7	11	9	1	1	1	0	0	0	0	.111	.111	.111	2	0	0	0	0	2	0	0	0	5	.000	0	0	4	.250	0	0
Ramirez, Roberto	32	9	7	1	1	1	0	0	0	0	.143	.250	.143	1	0	1	0	0	0	0	0	0	4	.000	0	0	3	.333	0	0
Cangelosi, John	7	6	6	0	1	2	1	0	0	0	.167	.167	.333	0	0	0	0	0	4	0	0	0	5	.200	0	0	1	.000	0	0
Lee, David	36	5	5	1	1	1	0	0	0	0	.200	.200	.200	0	0	0	0	0	2	0	0	0	2	.500	0	0	3	.000	0	0
Hackman, Luther	5	5	5	1	1	1	0	0	0	0	.200	.200	.200	0	0	0	0	0	3	0	0	0	5	.200	0	0	0	.000	0	0
Dipoto, Jerry	63	6	5	0	0	0	0	0	0	0	.000	.167	.000	0	0	0	1	0	2	0	0	1	3	.000	0	0	2	.000	0	0
Leskanic, Curt	63	4	4	1	2	5	0	0	1	3	.500	.500	1.250	0	0	0	0	0	2	0	0	0	4	.500	1	3	0	.000	0	0
Kelly, Mike	2	2	2	0	1	2	1	0	0	1	.500	.500	1.000	0	0	0	0	0	0	0	0	0	2	.500	0	1	0	.000	0	0
Beltran, Rigo	12	2	2	0	1	1	0	0	0	0	.500	.500	.500	0	0	0	0	0	0	0	0	0	1	1.000	0	0	1	.000	0	0
DeJean, Mike	57	2	2	0	0	0	0	0	0	0	.000	.000	.000	0	0	0	0	0	1	0	0	0	2	.000	0	0	0	.000	0	0
McElroy, Chuck	41	2	1	0	0	0	0	0	0	0	.000	.000	.000	1	0	0	0	0	0	0	0	0	1	.000	0	0	0	.000	0	0
Wainhouse, Dave	19	1	1	0	0	0	0	0	0	0	.000	.000	.000	0	0	0	0	0	1	0	0	0	1	.000	0	0	0	.000	0	0
Veres, Dave	73	1	1	0	0	0	0	0	0	0	.000	.000	.000	0	0	0	0	0	0	0	0	0	1	.000	0	0	0	.000	0	0
Porzio, Mike	16	0	0	0	0	0	0	0	0	0	.000	.000	.000	0	0	0	0	0	0	0	0	0	0	.000	0	0	0	.000	0	0

Players with more than one N.L. team

Name	G	TPA	AB	R	H	TB	2B	3B	HR	RBI	Avg.	Obp.	Slg.	SH	SF	HP	BB	IBB	SO	SB	CS	GDP	vs RHP AB	vs RHP Avg.	vs RHP HR	vs RHP RBI	vs LHP AB	vs LHP Avg.	vs LHP HR	vs LHP RBI
Beltran, N.Y.	21	1	1	0	0	0	0	0	0	0	.000	.000	.000	0	0	0	0	0	0	0	0	1	1	1.000	0	0	1	.000	0	0
Beltran, N.Y.-Col.	33	3	3	0	1	1	0	0	0	0	.333	.333	.333	0	0	0	0	0	0	0	0	1	1	1.000	0	0	2	.000	0	0
Hamilton, N.Y.	55	189	168	19	57	82	8	1	5	21	.339	.410	.488	1	0	1	19	0	18	2	3	2	229	.301	2	18	108	.306	2	6
Hamilton, Col.-N.Y.	146	568	505	82	159	213	19	4	9	45	.315	.386	.422	3	1	2	57	0	39	6	8	9	358	.327	7	36	147	.286	2	9
Harris, Ari.	19	30	29	2	11	15	1	0	1	7	.379	.367	.517	0	1	0	0	0	1	1	0	0	145	.290	0	13	13	.385	0	0
Harris, Col.-Ari.	110	194	187	17	58	74	13	0	1	20	.310	.330	.396	0	1	0	6	0	7	2	1	7	170	.300	0	18	17	.412	1	2
McElroy, N.Y.	15	0	0	0	0	0	0	0	0	0	.000	.000	.000	0	0	0	0	0	0	0	0	0	1	.000	0	0	0	.000	0	0
McElroy, Col.-N.Y.	56	2	1	0	0	0	0	0	0	0	.000	.000	.000	1	0	0	0	0	0	0	0	0	1	.000	0	0	0	.000	0	0
McRae, N.Y.	96	344	298	35	66	104	12	1	8	36	.221	.320	.349	0	2	5	39	1	57	2	6	6	22	.273	1	1	1	.000	0	0
McRae, N.Y.-Col.	103	371	321	36	72	115	14	1	9	37	.224	.323	.358	0	2	7	41	1	64	2	6	6	259	.224	9	35	62	.226	0	2
Reed, Chi.	57	181	150	18	39	57	11	2	1	17	.260	.381	.380	0	1	2	28	0	34	1	1	4	91	.264	2	8	15	.200	0	3
Reed, Col.-Chi.	103	306	256	29	66	95	16	2	3	28	.258	.373	.371	0	2	3	45	1	58	1	2	7	219	.274	2	21	37	.162	1	7

PITCHING

Name	W	L	Pct.	ERA	IP	H	R	ER	HR	SH	SF	HB	BB	IBB	SO	G	GS	CG	ShO	GF	Sv	vs. RH AB	vs. RH Avg.	vs. RH HR	vs. RH RBI	vs. LH AB	vs. LH Avg.	vs. LH HR	vs. LH RBI
Astacio, Pedro	17	11	.607	5.04	232.0	258	140	130	38	6	10	11	75	6	210	34	34	7	0	0	0	497	.268	25	74	409	.306	13	54
Bohanon, Brian	12	12	.500	6.20	197.1	236	146	136	30	18	3	14	92	1	120	33	33	3	1	0	0	628	.301	23	112	147	.320	7	23
Kile, Darryl	8	13	.381	6.61	190.2	225	150	140	33	9	9	6	109	5	116	32	32	1	0	0	0	395	.281	17	55	359	.318	16	79
Jones, Bobby M.	6	10	.375	6.33	112.1	132	91	79	24	7	4	6	77	0	74	30	20	0	0	1	0	362	.304	18	70	90	.244	6	14
Wright, Jamey	4	3	.571	4.87	94.1	110	52	51	10	3	4	4	54	3	49	16	16	0	0	0	0	205	.293	7	29	152	.329	3	20
Dipoto, Jerry	4	5	.444	4.26	86.2	91	44	41	10	1	5	3	44	4	69	63	0	0	0	18	1	178	.275	8	23	148	.284	2	18
Leskanic, Curt	6	2	.750	5.08	85.0	87	54	48	7	5	3	5	49	4	77	63	0	0	0	5	0	210	.257	4	32	110	.300	3	25
Veres, Dave	4	8	.333	5.14	77.0	88	46	44	14	5	2	2	37	7	71	73	0	0	0	63	31	175	.263	8	27	128	.328	6	19
Thomson, John	1	10	.091	8.04	62.2	85	62	56	11	4	2	1	36	1	34	14	13	1	0	1	0	147	.361	5	41	115	.278	6	14
DeJean, Mike	2	4	.333	8.41	61.0	83	61	57	13	3	3	2	32	8	31	56	0	0	0	17	0	155	.310	9	29	93	.376	4	25
Lee, David	3	2	.600	3.67	49.0	43	21	20	4	3	2	4	29	1	38	36	0	0	0	11	0	128	.242	4	16	46	.261	0	4
McElroy, Chuck	3	1	.750	6.20	40.2	48	29	28	9	0	2	0	28	3	37	41	0	0	0	12	0	103	.311	5	23	59	.271	4	13
Ramirez, Roberto	1	5	.167	8.26	40.1	68	42	37	8	2	0	0	22	2	32	32	4	0	0	6	1	123	.350	5	28	62	.403	3	12
Brownson, Mark	0	2	.000	7.89	29.2	42	26	26	8	4	0	1	8	0	21	7	7	0	0	0	0	54	.241	4	7	72	.403	4	14
Wainhouse, Dave	0	0	.000	6.91	28.2	37	22	22	6	0	3	0	16	0	18	19	0	0	0	11	0	62	.355	4	17	50	.300	2	12
Hackman, Luther	1	2	.333	10.69	16.0	26	19	19	5	2	0	0	12	0	10	5	3	0	0	0	0	28	.393	1	7	42	.357	4	11
Porzio, Mike	0	0	.000	8.59	14.2	21	14	14	5	1	0	0	10	0	10	16	0	0	0	3	0	42	.333	4	11	22	.318	1	2
Beltran, Rigo	0	0	.000	7.36	11.0	20	9	9	2	1	0	1	7	1	15	12	0	0	0	2	0	24	.375	1	6	28	.393	1	5

PITCHERS WITH MORE THAN ONE N.L. TEAM

Name	W	L	Pct.	ERA	IP	H	R	ER	HR	SH	SF	HB	BB	IBB	SO	G	GS	CG	ShO	GF	Sv	vs. RH AB	vs. RH Avg.	vs. RH HR	vs. RH RBI	vs. LH AB	vs. LH Avg.	vs. LH HR	vs. LH RBI
Beltran, N.Y.	1	1	.500	3.48	31.0	30	15	12	5	2	0	0	12	2	35	21	0	0	0	10	0	24	.375	1	6	28	.393	1	5
Beltran, N.Y.-Col.	1	1	.500	4.50	42.0	50	24	21	7	3	0	1	19	3	50	33	0	0	0	0	0	99	.253	5	18	73	.342	2	10
McElroy, N.Y.	0	0	.000	3.38	13.1	12	5	5	0	1	1	1	8	1	7	15	0	0	0	7	0	103	.311	5	23	59	.271	4	13
McElroy, Col.-N.Y.	3	1	.750	5.50	54.0	60	34	33	9	1	3	1	36	4	44	56	0	0	0	3	0	131	.298	5	30	79	.266	4	20

INDIVIDUAL STATISTICS

FIELDING

FIRST BASEMEN

Player	Pct.	G	PO	A	E	TC	DP
Helton, Todd	.993	156	1243	103	9	1355	152
Echevarria, Angel	1.000	10	58	4	0	62	6
Abbott, Kurt	1.000	8	57	3	0	60	6
Phillips, J.R.	1.000	4	3	0	0	3	1

SECOND BASEMEN

Player	Pct.	G	PO	A	E	TC	DP
Abbott, Kurt	.989	66	124	145	3	272	34
Shumpert, Terry	.988	54	102	151	3	256	35
Lansing, Mike	.990	35	91	98	2	191	40
Harris, Lenny	.924	24	46	51	8	105	19
Sexton, Chris	.949	10	19	18	2	39	3
Petersen, Chris	.955	6	9	12	1	22	5

THIRD BASEMEN

Player	Pct.	G	PO	A	E	TC	DP
Castilla, Vinny	.954	157	96	298	19	413	32
Shumpert, Terry	.947	14	6	12	1	19	3
Harris, Lenny	1.000	2	2	0	0	2	0

SHORTSTOPS

Player	Pct.	G	PO	A	E	TC	DP
Perez, Neifi	.981	157	260	481	14	755	124
Sexton, Chris	1.000	6	3	7	0	10	1
Abbott, Kurt	.857	3	3	3	1	7	2
Sosa, Juan	.875	2	4	3	1	8	1
Shumpert, Terry	1.000	2	1	2	0	3	1
Petersen, Chris	1.000	1	3	4	0	7	1

OUTFIELDERS

Player	Pct.	G	PO	A	E	TC	DP
Bichette, Dante	.951	144	238	17	13	268	3
Walker, Larry	.982	114	204	13	4	221	3
Hamilton, Darryl	1.000	82	205	1	0	206	0
Barry, Jeff	1.000	56	90	4	0	94	0
Clemente, Edgard	.972	49	101	2	3	106	1
Echevarria, Angel	.985	49	64	3	1	68	1
Shumpert, Terry	.952	19	20	0	1	21	0
Harris, Lenny	.933	14	12	2	1	15	1
Sexton, Chris	1.000	13	12	1	0	13	0
Gibson, Derrick	.944	10	15	2	1	18	1
Watkins, Pat	1.000	10	10	0	0	10	0
Phillips, J.R.	.933	7	11	3	1	15	2
McRae, Brian	1.000	7	14	0	0	14	0
Sosa, Juan	1.000	6	2	0	0	2	0
Abbott, Kurt	1.000	4	4	0	0	4	0
Cangelosi, John	1.000	1	1	0	0	1	0
Blanco, Henry	-	1	0	0	0	0	0
Kelly, Mike	-	1	0	0	0	0	0

CATCHERS

Player	Pct.	G	PO	A	E	TC	DP	PB
Blanco, Henry	.992	86	562	58	5	625	12	5
Manwaring, Kirt	.981	44	243	21	5	269	4	1
Reed, Jeff	.983	36	160	15	3	178	1	0
Petrick, Ben	.982	19	100	7	2	109	1	3

PITCHERS

Player	Pct.	G	PO	A	E	TC	DP
Veres, Dave	1.000	73	7	5	0	12	0
Leskanic, Curt	.864	63	6	13	3	22	1
Dipoto, Jerry	.938	63	4	11	1	16	0
DeJean, Mike	1.000	56	4	11	0	15	2
McElroy, Chuck	1.000	41	1	8	0	9	1
Lee, David	1.000	36	3	7	0	10	0
Astacio, Pedro	.911	34	16	25	4	45	3
Bohanon, Brian	.973	33	7	29	1	37	2
Kile, Darryl	.971	32	10	24	1	35	2
Ramirez, Roberto	1.000	32	2	5	0	7	1
Jones, Bobby M.	.875	30	4	10	2	16	0
Wainhouse, Dave	1.000	19	3	4	0	7	1
Wright, Jamey	.964	16	9	18	1	28	2
Porzio, Mike	1.000	16	0	3	0	3	0
Thomson, John	1.000	14	9	10	0	19	1
Beltran, Rigo	1.000	12	1	1	0	2	0
Brownson, Mark	.857	7	1	5	1	7	0
Hackman, Luther	1.000	5	2	4	0	6	0
Harris, Lenny	-	0	0	0	0	0	0

PITCHING AGAINST EACH CLUB

Pitcher	Ari. W-L	Atl. W-L	Chi. W-L	Cin. W-L	Fla. W-L	Hou. W-L	L.A. W-L	Mil. W-L	Mon. W-L	N.Y. W-L	Phi. W-L	Pit. W-L	S.D. W-L	S.F. W-L	StL. W-L	A.L. W-L	Total W-L
Astacio, P.	2-0	0-2	3-0	2-0	1-0	0-1	2-1	1-0	2-0	1-0	0-0	1-0	0-3	0-1	1-1	1-1	17-11
Beltran, R.	0-0	0-0	0-0	0-0	0-0	0-0	0-0	0-0	0-0	0-0	0-0	0-0	0-0	0-0	0-0	0-0	0-0
Bohanon, B.	1-1	0-0	1-0	0-0	1-1	0-2	1-1	1-0	0-1	0-1	1-2	0-0	1-2	2-1	2-0	1-0	12-12
Brownson, M.	0-0	0-0	0-0	0-0	0-0	0-0	0-0	0-0	0-0	0-0	0-0	0-0	0-1	0-0	0-0	0-1	0-2
DeJean, M.	0-0	0-0	0-1	0-1	0-0	0-1	1-0	1-0	0-0	0-1	0-0	0-0	0-0	0-0	0-0	0-0	2-4
Dipoto, J.	0-0	1-0	0-1	0-2	0-0	1-0	0-0	0-0	0-1	0-0	0-0	0-0	0-0	0-0	1-0	1-0	4-5
Hackman, L.	0-2	0-0	0-0	0-0	0-0	0-0	0-0	0-0	0-0	0-0	0-0	0-0	0-0	0-0	0-0	0-0	1-2
Harris, L.	0-0	0-0	0-0	0-0	0-0	0-0	0-0	0-0	0-0	0-0	0-0	0-0	0-0	0-0	0-0	0-0	0-0
Jones, Bob M.	0-1	0-2	0-1	0-1	1-1	0-0	1-0	0-0	1-0	0-0	0-0	1-1	0-1	0-1	0-0	1-2	6-10
Kile, D.	1-1	1-0	0-0	0-2	1-0	1-1	1-1	0-0	1-0	0-1	2-0	1-1	1-1	0-3	1-1	0-2	8-13
Lee, D.	0-0	1-1	0-0	0-0	0-0	0-0	0-0	0-0	0-0	0-0	0-0	0-0	0-0	0-0	0-0	0-0	3-2
Leskanic, C.	1-0	1-0	0-0	0-0	0-0	0-0	0-0	1-0	1-0	0-1	0-0	1-0	0-0	1-0	0-1	0-0	6-2
McElroy, C.	1-0	1-0	0-0	0-0	0-0	0-0	0-0	0-0	0-0	0-0	0-0	0-0	0-0	0-0	0-1	0-1	3-1
Porzio, M.	0-1	0-0	0-0	0-0	0-0	0-0	0-1	0-0	0-0	0-0	0-0	0-0	0-0	0-0	0-0	0-0	0-0
Ramirez, R.	0-1	0-0	0-0	0-0	0-0	0-1	0-0	0-0	0-0	0-0	0-0	1-0	0-0	0-0	0-1	0-1	1-5
Thomson, J.	0-0	0-0	0-1	0-0	0-0	0-0	0-2	0-0	1-1	0-1	0-0	0-1	0-0	0-1	0-0	0-1	1-10
Veres, D.	0-0	1-0	0-0	0-0	0-0	0-0	0-0	1-3	1-0	0-0	0-1	0-1	1-0	0-0	0-0	0-0	4-8
Wainhouse, D.	0-0	0-0	0-0	0-0	0-0	0-0	0-0	0-0	0-0	0-0	0-0	0-0	0-0	0-0	0-0	0-0	0-0
Wright, J.	1-0	0-0	0-1	0-0	0-0	0-0	0-0	0-0	0-0	0-0	0-0	0-0	0-0	0-0	0-0	0-0	0-3
Totals	7-6	4-5	5-4	2-7	5-4	2-6	8-5	6-3	6-3	4-5	5-4	2-7	4-9	4-9	4-5	4-8	72-90

INTERLEAGUE: Jones 0-1, Ramirez 0-1, Kile 0-1 vs. Athletics; Bohanon 1-0, Jones 0-1, Brownson 0-1 vs. Mariners; Astacio 1-0, Jones 1-0, McElroy 0-1 vs. Rangers; Dipoto 1-0, Kile 0-1, Astacio 0-1 vs. Angels. Total: 4-8.

MISCELLANEOUS

HOME RUNS BY PARK

At Arizona (5): Bichette 2, Castilla 2, Perez 1.

At Atlanta (3): Reed 1, Castilla 1, Helton 1.

At Chicago (NL) (6): Bichette 1, Walker 1, Castilla 1, Echevarria 1, Perez 1, Sexton 1.

At Cincinnati (5): Manwaring 1, Walker 1, Hamilton 1, Echevarria 1, Perez 1.

At Colorado (144): Walker 26, Helton 23, Bichette 20, Castilla 20, Shumpert 8, Perez 8, Clemente 7, Abbott 6, Echevarria 5, Barry 4, Petrick 4, Blanco 3, Hamilton 2, Lansing 2, Gibson 2, Manwaring 1, Bohanon 1, Leskanic 1, Phillips 1.

At Florida (4): Helton 2, McRae 1, Phillips 1.

At Houston (0):

At Los Angeles (8): Blanco 2, Helton 2, Bichette 1, Castilla 1, Abbott 1, Barry 1.

At Milwaukee (2): Echevarria 1, Clemente 1.

At Montreal (4): Helton 2, Bichette 1, Walker 1.

At New York (NL) (1): Castilla 1.

At Oakland (3): Bichette 1, Walker 1, Blanco 1.

At Philadelphia (3): Reed 1, Castilla 1, Helton 1.

At Pittsburgh (8): Walker 3, Castilla 2, Shumpert 1, Echevarria 1, Helton 1.

At San Diego (7): Bichette 3, Castilla 2, Walker 1, Perez 1.

At San Francisco (8): Bichette 2, Lansing 2, Hamilton 1, Castilla 1, Echevarria 1, Helton 1.

At St. Louis (9): Walker 3, Helton 2, Bichette 1, Shumpert 1, Castilla 1, Echevarria 1.

At Texas (2): Bichette 1, Abbott 1.

LOW-HIT GAMES

No-hitters: None.
One-hitters: None.
Two-hitters: None.

10-STRIKEOUT GAMES

Pedro Astacio 5, Brian Bohanon 1, **Total:** 6.

FOUR OR MORE HITS IN ONE GAME

Dante Bichette 6, Larry Walker 4, Neifi Perez 4, Darryl Hamilton 2, Vinny Castilla 2, Todd Helton 2, Kirt Manwaring 1, Mike Lansing 1, Kurt Abbott 1, Angel Echevarria 1, **Total:** 24.

MULTI-HOMER GAMES

Todd Helton 6, Dante Bichette 4, Larry Walker 4, Vinny Castilla 3, Terry Shumpert 1, Angel Echevarria 1, Henry Blanco 1, Edgard Clemente 1, Derrick Gibson 1, Ben Petrick 1, **Total:** 23.

GRAND SLAMS

7-3: Neifi Perez (off San Diego's Heath Murray).
9-17: Dante Bichette (off Los Angeles's Robinson Checo).

PINCH HITTERS

(Minimum 5 at-bats)

Name	AB	Avg.	HR	RBI
Harris, Lenny	56	.357	0	8
Echevarria, Angel	47	.319	4	14
Barry, Jeff	19	.211	1	2
Shumpert, Terry	16	.313	0	1
Phillips, J.R.	16	.250	2	3
Reed, Jeff	15	.267	0	2
Walker, Larry	14	.286	1	5
Abbott, Kurt	13	.308	1	4
Hamilton, Darryl	9	.000	0	0
Sexton, Chris	8	.375	0	0
Helton, Todd	6	.333	0	3
Clemente, Edgard	6	.167	0	1
Cangelosi, John	6	.167	0	0
Watkins, Pat	6	.000	0	0

DEBUTS

5-3: Chris Sexton, LF.
5-22: David Lee, P.
5-25: Chris Petersen, SS.
7-9: Mike Porzio, P.
9-1: Luther Hackman, P.
9-1: Ben Petrick, C.
9-10: Juan Sosa, PH.

GAMES BY POSITION

Catcher: Henry Blanco 86, Kirt Manwaring 44, Jeff Reed 36, Ben Petrick 19.

First base: Todd Helton 156, Angel Echevarria 10, Kurt Abbott 8, J.R. Phillips 4.

Second base: Kurt Abbott 66, Terry Shumpert 54, Mike Lansing 35, Lenny Harris 24, Chris Sexton 10, Chris Petersen 6.

Third base: Vinny Castilla 157, Terry Shumpert 14, Lenny Harris 2.

Shortstop: Neifi Perez 157, Chris Sexton 6, Kurt Abbott 3, Terry Shumpert 2, Juan Sosa 2, Chris Petersen 1.

Outfield: Dante Bichette 144, Larry Walker 114, Darryl Hamilton 82, Jeff Barry 56, Angel Echevarria 49, Edgard Clemente 49, Terry Shumpert 19, Lenny Harris 14, Chris Sexton 13, Pat Watkins 10, Derrick Gibson 10, Brian McRae 7, J.R. Phillips 7, Juan Sosa 6, Kurt Abbott 4, John Cangelosi 1, Mike Kelly 1, Henry Blanco 1.

Designated hitter: Dante Bichette 2, Lenny Harris 2, Jeff Reed 1, Kirt Manwaring 1, Larry Walker 1.

STREAKS

Wins: 4 (May 31-June 6, June 11-15).
Losses: 9 (June 24-July 2).
Consecutive games with at least one hit: 20, Larry Walker (April 25-May 19).
Wins by pitcher: 5, Brian Bohanon (April 8-May 3).

ATTENDANCE

Home: 3,316,152.
Road: 2,239,250.
Highest (home): 48,876 (June 24 vs. Chicago).
Highest (road): 61,247 (April 6 vs. San Diego).
Lowest (home): 36,483 (August 15 vs. Montreal).
Lowest (road): 5,517 (September 7 vs. Montreal).

FLORIDA MARLINS

1999 REVIEW

DAY BY DAY

Date	Opp.	Res.	Score	(inn.*)	Hits	Opp. hits	Winning pitcher	Losing pitcher	Save	Record	Pos.	GB
4-4	N.Y.	W	6-2		12	9	Fernandez	Leiter		1-0	T1st	...
4-6	N.Y.	L	3-12		8	13	Reed	Hernandez	Watson	1-1	T1st	...
4-7	N.Y.	L	0-6		6	13	Jones	Sanchez		1-2	T4th	1.0
4-9	Phi.	W	7-4		9	5	Meadows	Spoljaric		2-2	4th	0.5
4-10	Phi.	L	2-5		6	8	Schilling	Springer	Brantley	2-3	5th	1.5
4-11	Phi.	L	1-2		5	6	Ogea	Fernandez	Brantley	2-4	5th	2.5
4-12	At N.Y.	L	1-8		5	9	Jones	Hernandez		2-5	5th	3.5
4-14	At N.Y.	L	1-4		5	3	Hershiser	Sanchez	Franco	2-6	5th	4.5
4-15	At N.Y.	W	11-4		18	9	Meadows	Yoshii		3-6	5th	3.5
4-16	At Phi.	L	3-17		7	16	Schilling	Springer		3-7	5th	3.5
4-17	At Phi.	L	1-2		7	7	Gomes	Alfonseca		3-8	5th	4.5
4-18	At Phi.	L	2-7		8	14	Loewer	Ojala		3-9	5th	4.5
4-19	At S.F	L	4-5		7	5	Johnstone	Alfonseca	Nen	3-10	5th	5.5
4-20	At S.F	W	7-2		11	7	Meadows	Brock	Edmondson	4-10	5th	5.0
4-21	At S.F	L	0-4		5	5	Nathan	Springer		4-11	5th	5.5
4-23	Atl.	W	9-1		14	9	Hernandez	Glavine		5-11	5th	5.5
4-24	Atl.	L	7-8		12	13	Maddux	Edmondson	Rocker	5-12	5th	5.5
4-25	Atl.	L	1-5		6	9	Smoltz	Meadows		5-13	5th	6.5
4-26	Atl.	L	3-5		5	9	Seanez	Alfonseca		5-14	5th	7.5
4-27	Chi.	W	8-0		14	6	Edmondson	Sanders		6-14	5th	6.5
4-28	Chi.	L	1-6		3	16	Trachsel	Hernandez		6-15	5th	7.5
4-29	Chi.	L	2-5		10	12	Farnsworth	Sanchez	Beck	6-16	5th	8.5
4-30	Hou.	L	1-8		9	9	Bergman	Meadows		6-17	5th	9.5
5-1	Hou.	L	4-6		11	10	Lima	Springer	Wagner	6-18	5th	10.5
5-2	Hou.	L	2-3		9	13	Reynolds	Fernandez	Wagner	6-19	5th	11.5
5-3	Mil.	L	4-6	(13)	11	12	Wickman	Corbin		6-20	5th	12.5
5-4	Mil.	L	1-8		7	10	Eldred	Sanchez		6-21	5th	12.5
5-5	Mil.	L	0-2		8	7	Karl	Meadows	Wickman	6-22	5th	13.5
5-7	At L.A.	W	6-3		8	9	Springer	Dreifort	Mantei	7-22	5th	12.5
5-8	At L.A.	L	1-8		3	14	Brown	Hernandez		7-23	5th	13.5
5-9	At L.A.	W	6-4		7	6	Edmondson	Borbon	Mantei	8-23	5th	12.5
5-10	At S.D.	L	5-7		8	12	Miceli	Alfonseca	Hoffman	8-24	5th	12.5
5-11	At S.D.	W	5-4		15	10	Dempster	Spencer	Mantei	9-24	5th	12.5
5-12	At S.D.	L	7-8		15	10	Wall	Edmondson	Hoffman	9-25	5th	12.5
5-14	At Mil.	W	14-6		14	8	Sanchez	Roque	Mantei	10-25	5th	11.5
5-15	At Mil.	L	2-7		4	11	Woodard	Meadows		10-26	5th	11.5
5-16	At Mil.	W	3-2		9	14	Hernandez	Nomo	Mantei	11-26	4th	11.5
5-17	Chi.	L	1-8		4	12	Tapani	Dempster		11-27	5th	12.5
5-18	Chi.	L	1-4	(11)	3	10	Heredia	Springer	Sanders	11-28	5th	13.5
5-19	Chi.	L	7-8		11	12	Myers	Mantei	Adams	11-29	5th	14.5
5-20	Pit.	W	4-3	(14)	12	12	Alfonseca	Williams		12-29	5th	13.5
5-21	Pit.	W	8-1		10	4	Hernandez	Schourek		13-29	4th	12.5
5-22	Pit.	L	4-11		8	14	Ritchie	Springer		13-30	5th	13.5
5-23	Pit.	L	5-6		11	10	Wallace	Darensbourg	Williams	13-31	5th	13.5
5-24	At Chi.	W	7-5		12	9	Mantei	Aguilera		14-31	4th	12.5
5-25	At Chi.	W	6-3		8	8	Meadows	Trachsel		15-31	4th	12.5
5-26	At Chi.	L	4-6		7	11	Aguilera	Looper		15-32	5th	13.5
5-28	Cin.	W	8-1		8	9	Dempster	Avery		16-32	5th	14.0
5-29	Cin.	L	1-8		7	17	Bere	Fernandez		16-33	5th	14.0
5-30	Cin.	L	4-6		10	12	Graves	Edmondson		16-34	5th	14.0
5-31	StL.	L	2-5		10	11	Bottenfield	Meadows	Bottalico	16-35	5th	15.0
6-1	StL.	L	4-8		8	11	Acevedo	Hernandez		16-36	5th	16.0
6-2	StL.	W	10-2		14	8	Dempster	Painter		17-36	5th	15.0
6-3	StL.	W	4-2		5	8	Looper	Oliver	Mantei	18-36	5th	14.5
6-4	At T.B.	W	10-0		11	7	Springer	Rupe		19-36	5th	13.5
6-5	At T.B.	W	9-7		14	9	Meadows	Duvall	Mantei	20-36	4th	13.5
6-6	At T.B.	W	11-6		17	9	Alfonseca	Yan		21-36	5th	13.5
6-8†	Bal.	W	2-1		6	6	Edmondson	Timlin		22-36		
6-8‡	Bal.	W	5-3		11	11	Alfonseca	Kamieniecki	Mantei	23-36	5th	13.5
6-9	Bal.	L	2-4		5	12	Erickson	Springer	Rhodes	23-37	5th	14.5
6-11	N.Y. (AL)	L	4-8		6	11	Hernandez	Meadows	Rivera	23-38	5th	14.5
6-12	N.Y. (AL)	L	4-5		9	6	Clemens	Hernandez	Rivera	23-39	5th	14.5
6-13	N.Y. (AL)	W	8-2		13	5	Fernandez	Pettitte		24-39	5th	13.5
6-14	At Ari.	L	0-2		4	8	Johnson	Dempster	Olson	24-40	5th	13.5
6-15	At Ari.	L	3-4		12	8	Anderson	Springer	Olson	24-41	5th	14.5
6-16	At Ari.	L	6-12		12	17	Reynoso	Meadows		24-42	5th	15.5
6-18	At Col.	L	10-11		13	18	McElroy	Mantei		24-43	5th	17.0
6-19	At Col.	L	2-10		7	15	Jones	Fernandez		24-44	5th	17.0
6-20	At Col.	L	7-8		15	11	Bohanon	Dempster	Veres	24-45	5th	18.0
6-22	At N.Y.	L	2-8		4	14	McMichael	Springer	Benitez	24-46	5th	18.0
6-23	At N.Y.	L	3-6		7	8	Leiter	Meadows	Franco	24-47	5th	19.0
6-24	At N.Y.	L	2-3		9	8	Cook	Hernandez	Franco	24-48	5th	20.0
6-25	At Mon.	L	3-4		5	12	Pavano	Fernandez	Urbina	24-49	5th	20.0
6-26	At Mon.	W	9-3		12	8	Dempster	Smith		25-49	5th	20.0
6-27	At Mon.	W	4-3		6	8	Springer	Thurman	Mantei	26-49	5th	20.0
6-28	N.Y.	L	4-10		11	14	Leiter	Meadows		26-50	5th	21.0
6-29	N.Y.	L	1-5		5	9	Hershiser	Hernandez		26-51	5th	21.0
6-30	N.Y.	W	4-3	(10)	9	8	Alfonseca	Benitez		27-51	5th	20.0

HIGHLIGHTS

High point: It didn't get a lot better than opening day, when Alex Fernandez, making his first start since undergoing rotator-cuff surgery in October 1997, pitched five strong innings and defeated the Mets, 6-2.

Low point: On May 5, Florida lost to Milwaukee, 2-0, completing a 2-11 homestand (the Marlins scored only 26 runs in those 11 defeats) that dropped the team's overall record to 6-22.

Turning point: The Marlins won seven consecutive games August 6-13, sweeping home series' against the Rockies and Giants and winning a trip opener at San Diego. Coming on the heels of a 14-13 July that was Florida's first winning month since August 1997, the streak built some confidence in a young team that badly needed it.

Most valuable player: Second baseman Luis Castillo, who finally emerged as one of the National League's best leadoff hitters in the second half of the season. Castillo ended up with a .302 batting average and 50 stolen bases despite missing the final 23 games with a shoulder injury.

Most valuable pitcher: Fernandez made only 24 starts and worked just 141 innings, but gave the club a chance to win virtually every time he took the ball—and the righthander provided expert guidance for the Marlins' young pitchers, too. His record: 7-8, with a 3.38 ERA.

Most improved player: Antonio Alfonseca, who took over the closer's role July 9 after Matt Mantei was traded to Arizona. From that point on, the hard-throwing righthander was 21-for-23 in save opportunities.

Most pleasant surprise: Righthander A.J. Burnett put up poor numbers (6-12 record, 5.52 ERA) at Class AA Portland, but Florida played a hunch and brought up its best pitching prospect in mid-August. Burnett made seven starts, going 4-2 with a 3.48 ERA.

Key injuries: Cliff Floyd injured his knee in spring training and then went down with an ankle injury at midseason. Expected to be a threat in the middle of the order, Floyd played in only 69 games. The still-recuperating Fernandez missed sizable chunks of time, as was expected. Armando Almanza was sidelined for the final month with a shoulder injury, depriving the team of its top lefthanded reliever.

Notable: Florida did something no other major league club did in 1999—it pounded Red Sox ace Pedro Martinez. Five days after Martinez's scintillating performance in the All-Star Game, the Marlins hammered him for 12 hits and seven earned runs in 3.2 innings. ... Center fielder Preston Wilson led all major league rookies with 26 home runs. ... Brian Meadows was the only double-figure winner on the pitching staff with 11 victories. ... The Marlins lost a total of 206 games in 1998 and 1999.

—DAN GRAZIANO

MISCELLANEOUS

RECORDS

1999 regular-season record: 64-98 (5th in N.L. East); 35-45 at home; 29-53 on road; 17-34 vs. N.L. East; 17-31 vs. N.L. Central; 19-26 vs. N.L. West; 11-7 vs. A.L. East; 18-21 vs. lefthanded starters; 46-77 vs. righthanded starters; 53-80 on grass; 11-18 on turf; 17-30 in daytime; 47-68 at night; 19-25 in one-run games; 6-4 in extra-inning games; 2-0-1 in doubleheaders.

Team record past five years: 357-434 (.451, ranks 15th in league in that span).

TEAM LEADERS

Batting average: Luis Castillo (.302).
At-bats: Alex Gonzalez (560).
Runs: Alex Gonzalez (81).
Hits: Alex Gonzalez (155).
Total bases: Preston Wilson (242).
Doubles: Alex Gonzalez (28).
Triples: Mark Kotsay (9).
Home runs: Preston Wilson (26).
Runs batted in: Preston Wilson (71).
Stolen bases: Luis Castillo (50).
Slugging percentage: Preston Wilson (.502).
On-base percentage: Luis Castillo (.384).
Wins: Brian Meadows (11).
Earned-run average: Dennis Springer (4.86).
Complete games: Dennis Springer (3).
Shutouts: Dennis Springer (2).
Saves: Antonio Alfonseca (21).
Innings pitched: Dennis Springer (196.1).
Strikeouts: Ryan Dempster (126).

Date	Opp.	Res.	Score	(inn.*)	Hits	Opp. hits	Winning pitcher	Losing pitcher	Save	Record	Pos.	GB
7-1	N.Y.	L	8-12		13	12	Dotel	Dempster		27-52	5th	21.0
7-3	Mon.	W	6-1		9	7	Meadows	Batista		28-52	5th	21.5
7-4	Mon.	W	5-1		8	8	Hernandez	Powell		29-52	5th	20.5
7-5	At Atl.	L	5-6		8	11	McGlinchy	Alfonseca		29-53	5th	21.5
7-6	At Atl.	W	5-2		17	4	Fernandez	Glavine	Mantei	30-53	5th	20.5
7-7	At Atl.	L	3-7		6	8	Maddux	Dempster		30-54	5th	21.5
7-8	At Atl.	L	2-5		7	8	Millwood	Meadows		30-55	5th	22.5
7-9	T.B.	W	11-4		12	11	Hernandez	Rupe		31-55	5th	21.5
7-10	T.B.	L	8-9		15	14	Rekar	Springer	Hernandez	31-56	5th	22.5
7-11	T.B.	W	3-2		5	6	Fernandez	Alvarez	Alfonseca	32-56	5th	22.5
7-15	At Tor.	W	8-6		11	11	Looper	Koch	Alfonseca	33-56	5th	22.5
7-16	At Tor.	W	4-2		10	11	Springer	Hentgen	Alfonseca	34-56	5th	22.5
7-17	At Tor.	L	1-6		6	10	Wells	Edmondson		34-57	5th	22.5
7-18	At Bos.	L	9-11		14	12	Lowe	Nunez	Wakefield	34-58	5th	22.5
7-19	At Bos.	W	10-7		16	15	Meadows	Ohka	Alfonseca	35-58	5th	21.5
7-20	At Bos.	L	1-7		5	12	Rose	Hernandez		35-59	5th	21.5
7-21	Atl.	W	2-0		9	7	Springer	Maddux		36-59	4th	20.5
7-22	Atl.	L	3-6		6	11	McGlinchy	Fernandez	Rocker	36-60	4th	21.5
7-23	Mil.	W	5-4		13	8	Nunez	Wickman		37-60	4th	21.0
7-24	Mil.	W	4-1		9	6	Meadows	Peterson	Alfonseca	38-60	4th	20.0
7-25	Mil.	W	4-3		10	8	Sanchez	Weathers	Alfonseca	39-60	4th	20.0
7-26	At Phi.	L	1-9		7	15	Person	Nunez		39-61	4th	21.0
7-27	At Phi.	W	6-2		12	7	Fernandez	Wolf	Alfonseca	40-61	4th	21.0
7-28	At Phi.	L	4-9		8	13	Schrenk	Dempster		40-62	4th	21.0
7-29	At Phi.	L	1-12		6	13	Ogea	Meadows		40-63	4th	21.5
7-30	At Pit.	W	8-7		14	11	Edmondson	Hansell	Alfonseca	41-63	4th	21.0
7-31	At Pit.	L	2-4		8	5	Schmidt	Edmondson	Williams	41-64	4th	21.5
8-1	At Pit.	L	1-2		5	10	Cordova	Fernandez		41-65	4th	22.5
8-3	Phi.	L	5-6		9	12	Telemaco	Edmondson	Gomes	41-66	5th	23.5
8-4	Phi.	L	1-4		10	9	Byrd	Springer	Schrenk	41-67	5th	24.5
8-5	Phi.	L	3-9		10	12	Person	Nunez		41-68	5th	25.0
8-6	Col.	W	9-1		13	3	Fernandez	Jones		42-68	5th	25.0
8-7	Col.	W	4-1		7	7	Meadows	Bohanon	Alfonseca	43-68	5th	24.0
8-8	Col.	W	2-1		4	4	Dempster	Wright	Alfonseca	44-68	5th	23.0
8-9	S.F	W	5-4		12	12	Sanchez	Johnstone		45-68	5th	22.5
8-10	S.F	W	8-7	(12)	13	13	Edmondson	Rodriguez		46-68	5th	22.5
8-11	S.F	W	6-5	(10)	12	9	Sanchez	Nen		47-68	5th	22.5
8-13	At S.D.	W	4-3		13	10	Meadows	Boehringer	Alfonseca	48-68	5th	22.5
8-14	At S.D.	L	4-6		9	10	Clement	Sanchez	Hoffman	48-69	5th	22.5
8-15	At S.D.	L	6-7		10	15	Ashby	Springer	Hoffman	48-70	5th	23.5
8-16	At L.A.	W	7-5		8	11	Nunez	Park		49-70	4th	23.5
8-17	At L.A.	W	6-1		11	7	Burnett	Judd	Springer	50-70	4th	22.5
8-18	At L.A.	L	0-7		7	11	Dreifort	Meadows		50-71	4th	23.5
8-20	Hou.	L	4-6	(16)	15	7	Miller	Sanchez	Wagner	50-72	5th	24.0
8-21	Hou.	L	4-5		8	8	Henry	Edmondson	Wagner	50-73	5th	25.0
8-24	Ari.	L	4-5		4	6	Benes	Almanza	Mantei	50-74	5th	27.0
8-25	Ari.	L	2-7		7	8	Stottlemyre	Nunez		50-75	5th	28.0
8-26	Ari.	L	2-12		8	11	Johnson	Meadows		50-76	5th	28.5
8-27†	At Hou.	L	2-3		9	8	Lima	Springer	Wagner	50-77		
8-27‡	At Hou.	W	3-1		11	7	Dempster	Holt	Alfonseca	51-77	5th	29.0
8-28	At Hou.	W	5-2		10	7	Burnett	Elarton	Alfonseca	52-77	5th	29.0
8-29	At Hou.	L	4-10		10	14	Hampton	Fernandez		52-78	5th	30.0
8-30	At StL.	W	4-2		13	5	Nunez	Bottenfield	Alfonseca	53-78	5th	29.0
8-31	At StL.	L	1-8		5	12	Luebbers	Meadows		53-79	5th	30.0
9-1	At StL.	L	3-9		9	10	Stephenson	Dempster		53-80	5th	31.0
9-3	S.D.	L	3-6		8	9	Williams	Burnett	Hoffman	53-81	5th	32.0
9-4	S.D.	W	6-4		6	3	Fernandez	Carlyle	Alfonseca	54-81	5th	31.0
9-5	S.D.	L	2-5		6	9	Clement	Nunez	Hoffman	54-82	5th	31.0
9-6	L.A.	W	8-6		15	10	Meadows	Valdes	Alfonseca	55-82	5th	31.0
9-7	L.A.	W	2-1		6	7	Sanchez	Herges	Alfonseca	56-82	5th	31.0
9-8	L.A.	W	5-4	(13)	12	13	Medina	Masaoka		57-82	5th	31.0
9-10	At Cin.	L	2-4		7	5	Neagle	Springer	Graves	57-83	5th	32.0
9-11	At Cin.	L	4-12		9	9	Guzman	Nunez		57-84	5th	32.0
9-12	At Cin.	L	5-11		9	13	Villone	Burnett		57-85	5th	32.0
9-13	At Cin.	L	4-7		10	8	Parris	Sanchez	Graves	57-86	5th	32.0
9-14	At S.F	L	0-3		4	8	Estes	Dempster		57-87	5th	33.0
9-15	At S.F	L	3-4		5	9	Ortiz	Springer	Nen	57-88	5th	33.0
9-16	At S.F	L	5-6		9	9	Patrick	Nunez	Nen	57-89	5th	33.5
9-17	At Ari.	W	10-6		16	7	Burnett	Benes		58-89	5th	33.5
9-18	At Ari.	L	6-8	(10)	15	11	Swindell	Almonte		58-90	5th	33.5
9-19	At Ari.	L	7-8		11	15	Olson	Looper		58-91	5th	34.5
9-21†	Mon.	W	5-3		8	11	Springer	Telford	Alfonseca	59-91		
9-21‡	Mon.	W	4-0		8	7	Cornelius	Powell		60-91	5th	34.0
9-22	Mon.	L	3-5		7	7	Batista	Nunez	Urbina	60-92	5th	35.0
9-23	Mon.	W	2-1		4	9	Burnett	Hermanson	Alfonseca	61-92	5th	35.0
9-24	Col.	L	3-5		9	8	Astacio	Edmondson	Veres	61-93	5th	36.0
9-25	Col.	W	8-2		13	6	Dempster	Thomson		62-93	5th	36.0
9-26	Col.	L	6-8		12	8	Leskanic	Medina	Veres	62-94	5th	37.0
9-27	At Mon.	L	4-8		8	7	Telford	Almonte		62-95	5th	37.5
9-28	At Mon.	W	5-3		11	8	Nunez	Hermanson	Alfonseca	63-95	5th	37.5
9-29	At Mon.	L	3-5		6	8	Kline	Looper	Urbina	63-96	5th	37.5
10-1	At Atl.	L	1-4		6	8	Smoltz	Meadows	Rocker	63-97	5th	39.0
10-2	At Atl.	W	1-0	(10)	2	7	Looper	Ebert	Alfonseca	64-97	5th	38.0
10-3	At Atl.	L	0-18		5	21	Glavine	Springer		64-98	5th	39.0

Monthly records: April (6-17), May (10-18), June (11-16), July (14-13), August (12-15), September (10-17), October (1-2).
*Innings, if other than nine. † First game of a doubleheader. ‡ Second game of a doubleheader.

MEMORABLE GAMES

August 6 at Florida

Alex Fernandez, limited all season to 100 pitches per start as he attempted his comeback from rotator cuff surgery, pitched a brilliant and emotional 98-pitch complete game. The hurler also hit an eighth-inning home run to cap the Marlins' 9-1 victory.

Colorado	AB	R	H	RBI	Florida	AB	R	H	RBI
N.Perez, ss	4	0	0	0	L.Castillo, 2b	5	2	3	2
Helton, 1b	4	0	0	0	Berg, ss	4	1	1	0
L.Walker, rf	3	0	0	0	Aven, lf	5	1	2	4
Barry, rf	0	0	0	0	Millar, 1b	4	0	2	0
Bichette, lf	3	0	0	0	P.Wilson, cf	3	1	0	0
Veres, p	0	0	0	0	Kotsay, rf	0	0	0	0
Castilla, 3b	3	0	0	0	Bautsta, rf-cf	4	0	1	0
McRae, cf	3	1	1	1	Lowell, 3b	4	2	2	2
L.Harris, 2b	3	0	1	0	Redmond, c	4	1	1	0
Manwaring, c	3	0	1	0	A.Fernandz, p	4	1	1	1
B.Jones, p	1	0	0	0					
D.Lee, p	0	0	0	0					
Sexton, ph	1	0	0	0					
DeJean, p	0	0	0	0					
Shumpert, lf	0	0	0	0					
Echevarria, ph	1	0	0	0					
Totals	**29**	**1**	**3**	**1**	**Totals**	**37**	**9**	**13**	**9**

Colorado ....000 010 000 —1
Florida ....100 500 21x —9

DP—Florida 1. LOB—Colorado 1, Florida 7. 2B—L.Castillo (17), Berg (9), Lowell (8). HR—McRae (1), Aven (8), Lowell (5), A.Fernandez (2). SB—L.Castillo 2 (32), P.Wilson (4), Bautista (1).

Colorado	IP	H	R	ER	BB	SO
B.Jones (L, 5-9)	3.2	8	6	6	3	3
D.Lee	1.1	1	0	0	0	1
DeJean	2	2	2	2	0	1
Veres	1	2	1	1	0	1

Florida	IP	H	R	ER	BB	SO
A.Fernandez (W, 6-7)	9	3	1	1	0	2

WP—B.Jones. U—HP, M.Hirschbeck. 1B, Bell. 2B, Wegner. 3B, Nelson. T—2:26. A—14,032.

September 8 at Florida

In a game that perfectly summed up the Marlins' home season—one which featured 16 different rain delays and three postponements—the Dodgers and Marlins waited through three hours and 14 minutes of rain delays and played 13 innings. The Marlins finally won 5-4 in the bottom of the 13th, but a game that was scheduled to start at 4:05 p.m. ended at 11:28 p.m.

Los Angeles	AB	R	H	RBI	Florida	AB	R	H	RBI
E.Young, 2b	2	0	0	0	L.Castillo, 2b	2	1	0	0
Judd, p	0	0	0	0	A.Gonzlz, ss	3	0	2	1
Hundley, c	2	0	1	0	Medina, p	0	0	0	0
Cora, ss	4	0	1	0	Berg, ss-2b	4	2	0	0
Cromer, ph-ss	2	0	0	0	Floyd, lf	3	0	1	1
Mills, p	0	0	0	0	H.Almonte, p	0	0	0	0
Masaoka, p	0	0	0	0	Aven, ph	1	0	0	0
Mondesi, rf	5	0	0	0	Looper, p	0	0	0	0
Karros, 1b	6	0	1	0	Lowell, ph	1	0	0	0
D.White, cf	6	0	1	0	J.Sanchez, p	0	0	0	0
Hollndswrth, lf	4	2	3	0	Edmndsn, p	0	0	0	0
Beltre, 3b	5	2	3	0	Millar, ph	1	0	0	0
LoDuca, c	3	0	1	2	Alfonseca, p	0	0	0	0
D.Hansen, ph	0	0	0	1	Clapinski, ss	1	0	1	0
Shaw, p	0	0	0	0	P.Wilson, cf	5	1	3	1
M.Maddux, p	0	0	0	0	Orie, 3b	5	0	0	0
Grudzilnek, ph	1	0	0	0	Kotsay, rf	6	0	3	2
J.Castro, ss	0	0	0	0	D.Lee, 1b	5	0	1	0
Park, p	1	0	1	0	Redmond, c	2	0	0	0
Counsell, ph	1	0	1	0	Bautista, ph	1	0	0	0
Arnold, p	0	0	0	0	R.Castro, c	1	0	0	0
J.Vizcno, ph-2b	3	0	0	1	Tejera, p	0	0	0	0
					Roskos, ph	1	0	0	0
					Cornelius, p	1	0	0	0
					Dunwoody, lf	4	1	1	0
Totals	**45**	**4**	**13**	**4**	**Totals**	**47**	**5**	**12**	**5**

Los Angeles....................020 000 001 001 0— 4
Florida ....110 000 001 001 1— 5

E—Hollandsworth (2), Masaoka (1). DP—Los Angeles 1, Florida 2. LOB—Los Angeles 7, Florida 18. 2B—Beltre 2 (25), Kotsay (18). HR—P.Wilson (23). SB—L.Castillo (50), P.Wilson (7), A.Gonzalez (3). CS—E.Young (16), D.White (5), Hollandsworth (1). SH—E.Young, Kotsay. SF—D.Hansen.

Los Angeles	IP	H	R	ER	BB	SO
Park	4	3	2	2	5	2
Arnold	2	0	0	0	1	0
Judd	2	1	0	0	0	4
Shaw (BS 5)	1	2	1	0	0	1
M.Maddux	2	2	0	0	1	0
Mills (BS 4)	0.1	2	1	1	2	0
Masaoka (L, 2-4)	1	2	1	1	2	3

Florida	IP	H	R	ER	BB	SO
Tejera	2	5	2	2	2	1
Cornelius	3	1	0	0	1	2
H.Almonte	2	2	0	0	0	2
Looper	2	2	1	1	0	1
J.Sanchez	0.1	0	0	0	0	1
Edmondson	1.2	0	0	0	0	3
Alfonseca	1	2	1	1	0	1
Medina (W, 1-0)	1	1	0	0	0	0

HBP—P.Wilson by Arnold. WP—Park. U—HP, M.Hirschbeck. 1B, Fletcher. 2B, Froemming. 3B, Jeff.Nelson. T—4:19. A—9,615.

BATTING

Name	G	TPA	AB	R	H	TB	2B	3B	HR	RBI	Avg.	Obp.	Slg.	SH	SF	HP	BB	IBB	SO	SB	CS	GDP	vs RHP AB	vs RHP Avg.	vs RHP HR	vs RHP RBI	vs LHP AB	vs LHP Avg.	vs LHP HR	vs LHP RBI
Gonzalez, Alex	136	591	560	81	155	241	28	8	14	59	.277	.308	.430	1	3	12	15	0	113	3	5	13	446	.283	11	46	114	.254	3	13
Kotsay, Mark	148	535	495	57	134	199	23	9	8	50	.271	.306	.402	2	9	0	29	5	50	7	6	11	414	.271	7	39	81	.272	1	11
Castillo, Luis	128	563	487	76	147	178	23	4	0	28	.302	.384	.366	6	3	0	67	0	85	50	17	3	387	.300	0	20	100	.310	0	8
Wilson, Preston	149	543	482	67	135	242	21	4	26	71	.280	.350	.502	0	6	9	46	3	156	11	4	15	359	.279	17	48	123	.285	9	23
Aven, Bruce	137	440	381	57	110	169	19	2	12	70	.289	.370	.444	0	6	9	44	1	82	3	0	6	276	.293	8	51	105	.276	4	19
Millar, Kevin	105	407	351	48	100	152	17	4	9	67	.285	.362	.433	1	8	7	40	2	64	1	0	7	258	.283	6	48	93	.290	3	19
Lowell, Mike	97	344	308	32	78	129	15	0	12	47	.253	.317	.419	0	5	5	26	1	69	0	0	8	236	.254	6	33	72	.250	6	14
Berg, Dave	109	336	304	42	87	116	18	1	3	25	.286	.348	.382	3	0	2	27	0	59	2	2	7	221	.303	3	22	83	.241	0	3
Floyd, Cliff	69	285	251	37	76	130	19	1	11	49	.303	.379	.518	0	2	2	30	5	47	5	6	8	192	.302	7	40	59	.305	4	9
Redmond, Mike	84	278	242	22	73	85	9	0	1	27	.302	.381	.351	5	0	5	26	2	34	0	0	8	150	.300	0	16	92	.304	1	11
Orie, Kevin	77	267	240	26	61	95	16	0	6	29	.254	.322	.396	0	2	3	22	1	43	1	0	8	183	.251	5	26	57	.263	1	3
Fabregas, Jorge	82	260	223	20	46	69	10	2	3	21	.206	.289	.309	4	5	2	26	6	27	0	0	7	204	.196	3	17	19	.316	0	4
Lee, Derrek	70	236	218	21	45	71	9	1	5	20	.206	.263	.326	0	1	0	17	1	70	2	1	3	171	.199	4	15	47	.234	1	5
Bautista, Danny	70	211	205	32	59	86	10	1	5	24	.288	.303	.420	0	1	1	4	0	30	3	0	5	140	.293	4	18	65	.277	1	6
Dunwoody, Todd	64	200	186	20	41	59	6	3	2	20	.220	.270	.317	0	1	1	12	0	41	3	4	1	159	.220	2	16	27	.222	0	4
Hyers, Tim	58	96	81	8	18	30	4	1	2	12	.222	.333	.370	0	1	0	14	0	11	0	0	1	65	.185	2	11	16	.375	0	1
Castro, Ramon	24	78	67	4	12	22	4	0	2	4	.179	.282	.328	0	1	0	10	3	14	0	0	1	55	.182	2	4	12	.167	0	0
Counsell, Craig	37	73	66	4	10	11	1	0	0	2	.152	.211	.167	2	0	0	5	0	10	0	0	1	57	.158	0	2	9	.111	0	0
Clapinski, Chris	36	66	56	6	13	18	1	2	0	2	.232	.348	.321	0	0	1	9	0	12	1	0	1	38	.211	0	1	18	.278	0	1
Meadows, Brian	31	59	50	6	7	10	3	0	0	1	.140	.173	.200	7	0	0	2	0	21	0	0	0	38	.132	0	1	12	.167	0	0
Springer, Dennis	38	54	50	2	6	7	1	0	0	2	.120	.118	.140	3	1	0	0	0	17	0	0	0	42	.143	0	2	8	.000	0	0
Dempster, Ryan	26	51	49	5	5	6	1	0	0	2	.102	.120	.122	1	0	0	1	0	22	0	0	1	35	.086	0	2	14	.143	0	0
Hernandez, Livan	20	47	45	5	13	21	2	0	2	7	.289	.283	.467	1	1	0	0	0	5	0	0	2	37	.270	1	4	8	.375	1	3
Fernandez, Alex	25	46	43	3	10	20	1	0	3	7	.233	.233	.465	3	0	0	0	0	5	0	0	1	21	.286	3	4	22	.182	0	3
Nunez, Vladimir	17	27	25	0	4	4	0	0	0	2	.160	.160	.160	2	0	0	0	0	5	0	0	0	23	.174	0	2	2	.000	0	0
Garcia, Amaury	10	27	24	6	6	14	0	1	2	2	.250	.333	.583	0	0	0	3	0	11	0	0	0	10	.200	0	0	14	.286	2	2
Ramirez, Julio	15	22	21	3	3	4	1	0	0	2	.143	.182	.190	0	0	0	1	0	6	0	1	0	9	.222	0	2	12	.083	0	0
Burnett, A.J.	7	17	17	1	2	2	0	0	0	0	.118	.118	.118	0	0	0	0	0	10	0	0	0	13	.154	0	0	4	.000	0	0
Roskos, John	13	13	12	0	2	4	2	0	0	1	.167	.231	.333	0	0	0	1	0	7	0	0	0	8	.000	0	0	4	.500	0	1
Sanchez, Jesus	60	15	12	0	1	1	0	0	0	0	.083	.154	.083	2	0	0	1	0	5	0	0	0	9	.111	0	0	3	.000	0	0
Edmondson, Brian	68	11	11	0	4	6	2	0	0	2	.364	.364	.545	0	0	0	0	0	4	0	0	0	9	.222	0	0	2	1.000	0	2
Cornelius, Reid	5	6	5	0	1	1	0	0	0	0	.200	.200	.200	1	0	0	0	0	2	0	0	0	5	.200	0	0	0	.000	0	0
Garcia, Guillermo	4	4	4	0	1	1	0	0	0	0	.250	.250	.250	0	0	0	0	0	2	0	0	0	2	.000	0	0	2	.500	0	0
Almanza, Armando	14	3	3	0	0	0	0	0	0	0	.000	.000	.000	0	0	0	0	0	2	0	0	1	2	.000	0	0	1	.000	0	0
Alfonseca, Antonio	73	2	2	0	0	0	0	0	0	0	.000	.000	.000	0	0	0	0	0	2	0	0	0	1	.000	0	0	1	.000	0	0
Corbin, Archie	17	1	1	0	0	0	0	0	0	0	.000	.000	.000	0	0	0	0	0	1	0	0	0	1	.000	0	0	0	.000	0	0
Mantei, Matt	35	1	1	0	0	0	0	0	0	0	.000	.000	.000	0	0	0	0	0	1	0	0	0	1	.000	0	0	0	.000	0	0
Ojala, Kirt	8	0	0	0	0	0	0	0	0	0	.000	.000	.000	0	0	0	0	0	0	0	0	0	0	.000	0	0	0	.000	0	0
Medina, Rafael	20	0	0	0	0	0	0	0	0	0	.000	.000	.000	0	0	0	0	0	0	0	0	0	0	.000	0	0	0	.000	0	0
Looper, Braden	72	1	0	0	0	0	0	0	0	0	.000	.000	.000	0	0	0	0	0	0	0	0	0	0	.000	0	0	0	.000	0	0
Darensbourg, Vic	56	1	0	0	0	0	0	0	0	0	.000	1.000	.000	0	0	0	1	0	0	0	0	0	0	.000	0	0	0	.000	0	0
Billingsley, Brent	8	0	0	0	0	0	0	0	0	0	.000	.000	.000	0	0	0	0	0	0	0	0	0	0	.000	0	0	0	.000	0	0
Almonte, Hector	15	0	0	0	0	0	0	0	0	0	.000	.000	.000	0	0	0	0	0	0	0	0	0	0	.000	0	0	0	.000	0	0
Tejera, Michael	3	0	0	0	0	0	0	0	0	0	.000	.000	.000	0	0	0	0	0	0	0	0	0	0	.000	0	0	0	.000	0	0

Players with more than one N.L. team

Name	G	TPA	AB	R	H	TB	2B	3B	HR	RBI	Avg.	Obp.	Slg.	SH	SF	HP	BB	IBB	SO	SB	CS	GDP	vs RHP AB	vs RHP Avg.	vs RHP HR	vs RHP RBI	vs LHP AB	vs LHP Avg.	vs LHP HR	vs LHP RBI
Counsell, L.A.	50	122	108	20	28	34	6	0	0	9	.259	.311	.315	3	2	0	9	0	14	1	0	1	57	.158	0	2	9	.111	0	0
Counsell, Fla.-L.A.	87	195	174	24	38	45	7	0	0	11	.218	.274	.259	5	2	0	14	0	24	1	0	2	150	.213	0	7	24	.250	0	4
Fabregas, Atl.	6	8	8	0	0	0	0	0	0	0	.000	.000	.000	0	0	0	0	0	0	0	0	2	204	.196	3	17	19	.316	0	4
Fabregas, Fla.-Atl.	88	268	231	20	46	69	10	2	3	21	.199	.280	.299	4	5	2	26	6	27	0	0	9	211	.190	3	17	20	.300	0	4
Hernandez, S.F.	11	26	18	1	4	4	0	0	0	1	.222	.300	.222	6	0	1	1	0	5	0	0	0	37	.270	1	4	8	.375	1	3
Hernandez, Fla.-S.F.	31	73	63	6	17	25	2	0	2	8	.270	.288	.397	7	1	1	1	0	10	0	0	2	47	.234	1	5	16	.375	1	3
Mantei, Ari.	30	0	0	0	0	0	0	0	0	0	.000	.000	.000	0	0	0	0	0	0	0	0	0	1	.000	0	0	0	.000	0	0
Mantei, Fla.-Ari.	65	1	1	0	0	0	0	0	0	0	.000	.000	.000	0	0	0	0	0	1	0	0	0	1	.000	0	0	0	.000	0	0
Nunez, Ari.	27	3	3	0	0	0	0	0	0	0	.000	.000	.000	0	0	0	0	0	1	0	0	0	23	.174	0	2	2	.000	0	0
Nunez, Ari.-Fla.	44	30	28	0	4	4	0	0	0	2	.143	.143	.143	2	0	0	0	0	6	0	0	0	24	.167	0	2	4	.000	0	0

PITCHING

Name	W	L	Pct.	ERA	IP	H	R	ER	HR	SH	SF	HB	BB	IBB	SO	G	GS	CG	ShO	GF	Sv	vs. RH AB	vs. RH Avg.	vs. RH HR	vs. RH RBI	vs. LH AB	vs. LH Avg.	vs. LH HR	vs. LH RBI
Springer, Dennis	6	16	.273	4.86	196.1	231	121	106	23	12	10	7	64	3	83	38	29	3	2	3	1	445	.285	11	63	317	.328	12	55
Meadows, Brian	11	15	.423	5.60	178.1	214	117	111	31	16	8	5	57	5	72	31	31	0	0	0	0	358	.291	13	43	351	.313	18	57
Dempster, Ryan	7	8	.467	4.71	147.0	146	77	77	21	3	6	6	93	2	126	25	25	0	0	0	0	296	.243	9	31	262	.282	12	33
Fernandez, Alex	7	8	.467	3.38	141.0	135	60	53	10	3	6	4	41	1	91	24	24	1	0	0	0	253	.225	3	23	283	.276	7	35
Hernandez, Livan	5	9	.357	4.76	136.0	161	78	72	17	3	4	2	55	3	97	20	20	2	0	0	0	279	.290	8	34	269	.297	9	35
Edmondson, Brian	5	8	.385	5.84	94.0	106	65	61	11	6	7	6	44	5	58	68	0	0	0	14	1	211	.261	8	31	154	.331	3	26
Looper, Braden	3	3	.500	3.80	83.0	96	43	35	7	5	5	1	31	6	50	72	0	0	0	22	0	191	.257	3	33	137	.343	4	25
Alfonseca, Antonio	4	5	.444	3.24	77.2	79	28	28	4	3	1	4	29	6	46	73	0	0	0	49	21	162	.278	3	18	126	.270	1	11
Sanchez, Jesus	5	7	.417	6.01	76.1	84	53	51	16	2	7	4	60	11	62	59	10	0	0	8	0	199	.307	13	48	90	.256	3	17
Nunez, Vladimir	4	8	.333	4.58	74.2	66	48	38	9	5	3	3	34	1	58	17	12	0	0	1	0	155	.232	4	18	117	.256	5	17
Burnett, A.J.	4	2	.667	3.48	41.1	37	23	16	3	1	3	0	25	2	33	7	7	0	0	0	0	86	.221	1	13	67	.269	2	6
Mantei, Matt	1	2	.333	2.72	36.1	24	11	11	4	0	1	2	25	1	50	35	0	0	0	32	10	67	.194	0	2	62	.177	4	9
Darensbourg, Vic	0	1	.000	8.83	34.2	50	36	34	3	5	2	5	21	1	16	56	0	0	0	5	0	75	.413	1	24	72	.264	2	20
Medina, Rafael	1	1	.500	5.79	23.1	20	15	15	3	1	0	1	20	2	16	20	0	0	0	4	0	50	.260	1	7	38	.184	2	8
Corbin, Archie	0	1	.000	7.29	21.0	25	20	17	2	1	1	1	15	0	30	17	0	0	0	4	0	48	.271	1	8	38	.316	1	6
Cornelius, Reid	1	0	1.000	3.26	19.1	16	7	7	0	1	0	0	5	1	12	5	2	0	0	0	0	39	.282	0	5	31	.161	0	3
Almanza, Armando	0	1	.000	1.72	15.2	8	4	3	1	1	1	1	9	1	20	14	0	0	0	2	0	36	.194	1	3	16	.063	0	1
Almonte, Hector	0	2	.000	4.20	15.0	20	7	7	1	1	1	0	6	2	8	15	0	0	0	6	0	37	.270	0	3	22	.455	1	5
Ojala, Kirt	0	1	.000	14.34	10.2	21	17	17	1	0	2	0	6	0	5	8	1	0	0	2	0	36	.417	0	11	12	.500	1	7
Billingsley, Brent	0	0	.000	16.43	7.2	11	14	14	3	0	1	2	10	0	3	8	0	0	0	3	0	17	.412	2	9	12	.333	1	4
Tejera, Michael	0	0	.000	11.37	6.1	10	8	8	1	0	0	0	5	0	7	3	1	0	0	1	0	16	.438	1	6	10	.300	0	0

PITCHERS WITH MORE THAN ONE N.L. TEAM

Name	W	L	Pct.	ERA	IP	H	R	ER	HR	SH	SF	HB	BB	IBB	SO	G	GS	CG	ShO	GF	Sv	vs. RH AB	vs. RH Avg.	vs. RH HR	vs. RH RBI	vs. LH AB	vs. LH Avg.	vs. LH HR	vs. LH RBI
Hernandez, S.F.	3	3	.500	4.38	63.2	66	32	31	6	4	2	0	21	2	47	10	10	0	0	0	0	279	.290	8	34	269	.297	9	35
Hernandez, Fla.-S.F.	8	12	.400	4.64	199.2	227	110	103	23	7	6	2	76	5	144	30	30	2	0	6	0	411	.280	11	52	384	.292	12	44
Mantei, Ari.	0	1	.000	2.79	29.0	20	10	9	1	1	0	3	19	0	49	30	0	0	0	28	22	67	.194	0	2	62	.177	4	9
Mantei, Fla.-Ari.	1	3	.250	2.76	65.1	44	21	20	5	1	1	5	44	1	99	65	0	0	0	1	32	120	.217	1	8	113	.159	4	13
Nunez, Ari.	3	2	.600	2.91	34.0	29	15	11	2	2	3	1	20	5	28	27	0	0	0	11	1	155	.232	4	18	117	.256	5	17
Nunez, Ari.-Fla.	7	10	.412	4.06	108.2	95	63	49	11	7	6	4	54	6	86	44	12	0	0	6	1	239	.226	5	26	153	.268	6	21

INDIVIDUAL STATISTICS

FIELDING

FIRST BASEMEN

Player	Pct.	G	PO	A	E	TC	DP
Millar, Kevin	.995	94	719	53	4	776	80
Lee, Derrek	.994	66	463	47	3	513	44
Kotsay, Mark	1.000	19	104	8	0	112	9
Hyers, Tim	1.000	14	71	3	0	74	6
Orie, Kevin	1.000	1	1	0	0	1	1

SECOND BASEMEN

Player	Pct.	G	PO	A	E	TC	DP
Castillo, Luis	.976	126	257	343	15	615	75
Berg, Dave	1.000	29	51	80	0	131	16
Counsell, Craig	.980	12	20	29	1	50	4
Garcia, Amaury	.932	8	15	26	3	44	5
Clapinski, Chris	1.000	2	0	2	0	2	0

THIRD BASEMEN

Player	Pct.	G	PO	A	E	TC	DP
Lowell, Mike	.981	83	59	143	4	206	12
Orie, Kevin	.961	64	51	120	7	178	8
Berg, Dave	.911	19	13	28	4	45	3
Clapinski, Chris	.882	9	6	9	2	17	1
Millar, Kevin	1.000	1	0	2	0	2	0

SHORTSTOPS

Player	Pct.	G	PO	A	E	TC	DP
Gonzalez, Alex	.955	135	237	339	27	603	85
Berg, Dave	.969	37	39	87	4	130	12
Clapinski, Chris	.955	6	9	12	1	22	4

OUTFIELDERS

Player	Pct.	G	PO	A	E	TC	DP
Wilson, Preston	.973	136	320	10	9	339	1
Kotsay, Mark	.981	129	245	19	5	269	5
Aven, Bruce	.984	102	181	4	3	188	1
Floyd, Cliff	.952	62	115	4	6	125	0
Bautista, Danny	.979	60	140	3	3	146	0
Dunwoody, Todd	.981	55	102	3	2	107	0
Hyers, Tim	1.000	15	15	0	0	15	0
Ramirez, Julio	.950	11	19	0	1	20	0
Clapinski, Chris	1.000	3	2	0	0	2	0
Berg, Dave	-	3	0	0	0	0	0
Millar, Kevin	1.000	1	1	0	0	1	0

CATCHERS

Player	Pct.	G	PO	A	E	TC	DP	PB
Redmond, Mike	.992	82	444	45	4	493	5	3
Fabregas, Jorge	.989	78	404	52	5	461	2	4
Castro, Ramon	.992	24	105	17	1	123	1	3
Garcia, Guillermo	1.000	3	5	0	0	5	0	
Roskos, John	1.000	1	5	0	0	5	0	

PITCHERS

Player	Pct.	G	PO	A	E	TC	DP
Alfonseca, Antonio	1.000	73	5	14	0	19	2
Looper, Braden	1.000	72	3	8	0	11	0
Edmondson, Brian	1.000	68	6	15	0	21	1
Sanchez, Jesus	1.000	59	7	8	0	15	1
Darensbourg, Vic	1.000	56	1	4	0	5	0
Springer, Dennis	.913	38	12	30	4	46	5
Mantei, Matt	.833	35	2	3	1	6	0
Meadows, Brian	.943	31	12	21	2	35	1
Dempster, Ryan	.962	25	10	15	1	26	4
Fernandez, Alex	.971	24	7	27	1	35	3
Hernandez, Livan	.971	20	12	21	1	34	1
Medina, Rafael	1.000	20	1	1	0	2	0
Nunez, Vladimir	.905	17	6	13	2	21	1
Corbin, Archie	1.000	17	0	1	0	1	0
Almonte, Hector	1.000	15	1	3	0	4	1
Almanza, Armando	1.000	14	0	2	0	2	1
Billingsley, Brent	1.000	8	1	0	0	1	1
Ojala, Kirt	-	8	0	0	0	0	0
Burnett, A.J.	.875	7	2	5	1	8	0
Cornelius, Reid	1.000	5	0	5	0	5	0
Tejera, Michael	1.000	3	1	3	0	4	2

PITCHING AGAINST EACH CLUB

Pitcher	Ari. W-L	Atl. W-L	Chi. W-L	Cin. W-L	Col. W-L	Hou. W-L	L.A. W-L	Mil. W-L	Mon. W-L	N.Y. W-L	Phi. W-L	Pit. W-L	S.D. W-L	S.F. W-L	StL. W-L	A.L. W-L	Total W-L
Alfonseca, A.	0-0	0-2	0-0	0-0	0-0	0-0	0-0	0-0	1-0	0-0	0-1	1-0	0-1	0-1	0-0	2-0	4-5
Almanza, A.	0-1	0-0	0-0	0-0	0-0	0-0	0-0	0-0	0-0	0-0	0-0	0-0	0-0	0-0	0-0	0-0	0-1
Almonte, H.	0-1	0-0	0-0	0-0	0-0	0-0	0-0	0-0	0-0	0-0	0-0	0-0	0-0	0-0	0-0	0-0	0-2
Billingsley, B.	0-0	0-0	0-0	0-0	0-0	0-0	0-0	0-0	0-0	0-0	0-0	0-0	0-0	0-0	0-0	0-0	0-0
Burnett, A.J.	1-0	0-0	0-0	0-0	0-0	1-0	0-0	0-0	1-0	0-0	0-0	0-0	0-0	0-0	0-0	0-0	4-2
Corbin, A.	0-0	0-0	0-0	0-0	0-0	0-0	0-1	0-0	0-0	0-0	0-0	0-1	0-0	0-0	0-0	0-0	0-1
Cornelius, R.	0-0	0-0	0-0	0-0	0-0	0-0	0-0	0-0	1-0	0-0	0-0	0-0	0-0	0-0	0-0	0-0	1-0
Darensbrg, V.	0-0	0-0	0-0	0-0	0-0	0-0	0-0	0-0	0-0	0-0	0-0	0-1	0-0	0-0	0-0	0-0	0-1
Dempster, R.	0-1	0-1	0-1	1-0	2-1	1-0	0-0	0-0	1-0	0-1	0-0	1-0	0-1	0-1	1-1	0-0	7-8
Edmondson, B.	0-0	0-1	1-0	0-1	0-0	0-1	0-0	0-0	0-0	0-1	1-1	0-1	1-0	0-0	1-1	1-1	5-8
Fernandez, A.	1-1	0-1	0-0	1-0	0-1	0-2	0-0	0-0	1-0	1-1	1-0	0-0	0-0	1-0	0-1	2-0	7-8
Hernandez, L.	0-0	0-1	0-1	0-1	0-0	0-0	0-1	1-0	1-0	0-4	0-1	0-1	1-0	0-0	1-2	1-1	5-9
Looper, B.	0-1	1-0	0-0	0-0	0-0	0-0	1-0	0-0	0-1	0-0	0-0	0-0	0-0	0-0	0-0	1-0	3-3
Mantei, M.	0-0	0-0	0-0	0-0	0-0	0-0	0-0	0-0	0-0	0-0	0-0	0-0	0-0	0-0	0-0	0-0	1-1
Meadows, B.	0-2	0-3	1-0	0-0	1-0	0-1	1-1	1-2	1-0	1-2	1-1	0-0	1-0	1-0	0-2	2-1	11-15
Medina, R.	0-0	0-0	0-0	0-0	0-0	0-0	0-0	0-0	0-1	0-0	0-0	0-0	0-0	0-0	0-0	0-0	1-1
Nunez, V.	0-1	0-0	0-0	0-1	0-0	0-1	1-0	1-1	0-0	0-2	0-1	0-1	1-0	1-0	0-1	0-0	4-8
Ojala, Kirt	0-0	0-0	0-0	0-0	0-0	0-0	0-0	0-1	0-0	0-0	0-1	0-1	0-0	0-0	0-0	0-0	0-1
Sanchez, J.	0-0	0-1	0-1	0-1	0-0	1-0	2-1	0-0	0-2	0-1	0-0	0-0	2-0	0-0	0-0	0-0	5-7
Springer, D.	0-1	1-1	0-1	0-1	0-0	0-2	0-0	2-0	0-1	0-3	0-1	0-1	0-1	0-2	0-2	2-2	6-16
Tejera, M.	0-0	0-0	0-0	0-0	0-0	0-0	0-0	0-0	0-0	0-0	0-0	0-0	0-0	0-0	0-0	0-0	0-0
Totals	1-8	4-9	3-6	1-6	4-5	2-7	7-2	5-4	8-4	3-10	2-11	3-4	3-6	4-5	3-4	11-7	64-98

INTERLEAGUE: Edmondson 1-0, Alfonseca 1-0, Springer 0-1 vs. Orioles; Meadows 1-0, Nunez 0-1, Hernandez 0-1 vs. Red Sox; Fernandez 1-0, Meadows 0-1, Hernandez 0-1 vs. Yankees; Looper 1-0, Springer 1-0, Edmondson 0-1 vs. Blue Jays; Springer 1-1, Meadows 1-0, Hernandez 1-0, Alfonseca 1-0, Fernandez 1-0 vs. Devil Rays. Total: 11-7.

MISCELLANEOUS

HOME RUNS BY PARK

At Arizona (8): Lowell 3, Floyd 2, Wilson 2, Orie 1.

At Atlanta (5): Bautista 1, Floyd 1, Millar 1, Wilson 1, Lowell 1.

At Boston (1): Wilson 1.

At Chicago (NL) (8): Wilson 3, Fabregas 1, Kotsay 1, Berg 1, Millar 1, Gonzalez 1.

At Cincinnati (6): Wilson 2, Lee 1, Berg 1, Gonzalez 1, Garcia 1.

At Colorado (4): Orie 1, Kotsay 1, Wilson 1, Gonzalez 1.

At Florida (48): Wilson 8, Gonzalez 7, Lowell 7, Kotsay 5, Floyd 4, Fernandez 3, Aven 3, Millar 3, Bautista 2, Hernandez 2, Fabregas 1, Orie 1, Dunwoody 1, Berg 1.

At Houston (0):

At Los Angeles (7): Aven 2, Wilson 2, Floyd 1, Dunwoody 1, Millar 1.

At Milwaukee (6): Orie 2, Floyd 1, Kotsay 1, Aven 1, Wilson 1.

At Montreal (6): Gonzalez 2, Bautista 1, Lee 1, Aven 1, Garcia 1.

At New York (NL) (3): Orie 1, Aven 1, Wilson 1.

At Philadelphia (3): Lee 1, Millar 1, Wilson 1.

At Pittsburgh (1): Wilson 1.

At San Diego (7): Aven 2, Gonzalez 2, Floyd 1, Fabregas 1, Lee 1.

At San Francisco (6): Floyd 1, Lee 1, Millar 1, Wilson 1, Redmond 1, Castro 1.

At St. Louis (2): Bautista 1, Castro 1.

At Tampa Bay (5): Hyers 2, Aven 2, Wilson 1.

At Toronto (2): Millar 1, Lowell 1.

LOW-HIT GAMES

No-hitters: None.
One-hitters: None.
Two-hitters: None.

10-STRIKEOUT GAMES

Ryan Dempster 1, **Total:** 1.

FOUR OR MORE HITS IN ONE GAME

Dave Berg 4, Preston Wilson 3, Luis Castillo 2, Derrek Lee 2, Bruce Aven 2, Alex Gonzalez 2, Danny Bautista 1, Tim Hyers 1, Todd Dunwoody 1, Mike Redmond 1, **Total:** 19.

MULTI-HOMER GAMES

Tim Hyers 1, Bruce Aven 1, Preston Wilson 1, Mike Lowell 1, **Total:** 4.

GRAND SLAMS

5-7: Bruce Aven (off Los Angeles's Alan Mills).
6-6: Bruce Aven (off Tampa Bay's Julio Santana).
8-9: Mike Lowell (off San Francisco's John Johnstone).
8-16: Preston Wilson (off Los Angeles's Mike Maddux).
9-6: Mark Kotsay (off Los Angeles's Ismael Valdes).

PINCH HITTERS

(Minimum 5 at-bats)

Name	AB	Avg.	HR	RBI
Aven, Bruce	26	.269	2	10
Hyers, Tim	26	.192	0	1
Counsell, Craig	24	.083	0	1
Berg, Dave	23	.174	0	0
Lowell, Mike	15	.133	1	3
Kotsay, Mark	13	.538	1	1
Wilson, Preston	13	.385	3	4
Clapinski, Chris	13	.231	0	1
Roskos, John	11	.182	0	1
Orie, Kevin	11	.091	0	1
Bautista, Danny	10	.400	1	3
Dunwoody, Todd	8	.250	0	1
Millar, Kevin	8	.000	0	0
Fabregas, Jorge	7	.143	0	0
Floyd, Cliff	5	.000	0	0

DEBUTS

5-20: Brent Billingsley, P.
7-5: Amaury Garcia, PH.
7-17: Chris Clapinski, PH.
7-26: Hector Almonte, P.
7-29: Armando Almanza, P.
8-17: A.J. Burnett, P.
8-27: Ramon Castro, C.
9-8: Michael Tejera, P.
9-10: Julio Ramirez, PR.

GAMES BY POSITION

Catcher: Mike Redmond 82, Jorge Fabregas 78, Ramon Castro 24, Guillermo Garcia 3, John Roskos 1.

First base: Kevin Millar 94, Derrek Lee 66, Mark Kotsay 19, Tim Hyers 14, Kevin Orie 1.

Second base: Luis Castillo 126, Dave Berg 29, Craig Counsell 12, Amaury Garcia 8, Chris Clapinski 2.

Third base: Mike Lowell 83, Kevin Orie 64, Dave Berg 19, Chris Clapinski 9, Kevin Millar 1.

Shortstop: Alex Gonzalez 135, Dave Berg 37, Chris Clapinski 6.

Outfield: Preston Wilson 136, Mark Kotsay 129, Bruce Aven 102, Cliff Floyd 62, Danny Bautista 60, Todd Dunwoody 55, Tim Hyers 15, Julio Ramirez 11, Chris Clapinski 3, Dave Berg 3, Kevin Millar 1.

Designated hitter: Bruce Aven 6, Cliff Floyd 3, Tim Hyers 1, Chris Clapinski 1.

STREAKS

Wins: 7 (June 2-8, August 6-13).
Losses: 10 (June 14-25).
Consecutive games with at least one hit: 22, Luis Castillo (August 9-September 3).
Wins by pitcher: 3, Brian Meadows (April 9-20).

ATTENDANCE

Home: 1,369,420.
Road: 2,154,782.
Highest (home): 42,110 (June 12 vs. New York).
Highest (road): 61,355 (August 14 vs. San Diego).
Lowest (home): 8,468 (September 21 vs. Montreal).
Lowest (road): 5,156 (September 27 vs. Montreal).

HOUSTON ASTROS

DAY BY DAY

Date	Opp.	Res.	Score	(inn.*)	Hits	Opp. hits	Winning pitcher	Losing pitcher	Save	Record	Pos.	GB
4-6	Chi.	W	4-2		8	8	Reynolds	Trachsel	Wagner	1-0	T1st	...
4-7	Chi.	L	2-9		5	12	Tapani	Hampton		1-1	T1st	...
4-8	Chi.	L	1-2		6	6	Lieber	Lima	Beck	1-2	T3rd	1.0
4-9	Mil.	W	3-2		7	5	Elarton	Wickman	Wagner	2-2	T1st	...
4-10	Mil.	L	2-8		7	13	Pulsipher	Holt	Weathers	2-3	T3rd	1.0
4-11	Mil.	W	5-2		13	8	Reynolds	Roque	Wagner	3-3	T2nd	1.0
4-13	At S.F	W	7-3		12	6	Hampton	Ortiz	Powell	4-3	T1st	...
4-14	At S.F	W	6-3		14	8	Lima	Estes	Wagner	5-3	T1st	...
4-15	At S.F	L	2-5		6	9	Brock	Bergman	Nen	5-4	2nd	0.5
4-16	StL.	L	3-5		11	9	Oliver	Reynolds	Bottalico	5-5	2nd	1.5
4-17	StL.	L	5-8		11	10	Jimenez	Holt		5-6	T3rd	2.5
4-18	StL.	W	8-4		16	9	Powell	Painter		6-6	3rd	1.5
4-20	At Chi.	W	10-4		16	9	Lima	Lieber	Elarton	7-6	3rd	2.0
4-21	At Chi.	W	10-3		13	10	Reynolds	Sanders		8-6	T2nd	1.0
4-23	At Cin.	L	5-7		11	10	Sullivan	Holt	Graves	8-7	T2nd	2.0
4-24	At Cin.	W	4-3		6	5	Elarton	Graves	Wagner	9-7	2nd	1.0
4-25	At Cin.	L	6-7		8	10	Harnisch	Henry	Williamson	9-8	2nd	2.0
4-26	Ari.	W	5-2		6	7	Lima	Stottlemyre	Wagner	10-8	2nd	1.5
4-27	Ari.	W	11-0		14	6	Reynolds	Reynoso		11-8	2nd	1.5
4-28	Ari.	L	6-10		7	14	Holmes	Wagner		11-9	2nd	1.5
4-29	Ari.	W	5-2		12	4	Hampton	Daal	Wagner	12-9	2nd	0.5
4-30	At Fla.	W	8-1		9	9	Bergman	Meadows		13-9	1st	+0.5
5-1	At Fla.	W	6-4		10	11	Lima	Springer	Wagner	14-9	1st	+0.5
5-2	At Fla.	W	3-2		13	9	Reynolds	Fernandez	Wagner	15-9	1st	+0.5
5-3	At N.Y.	L	3-5		6	9	Reed	Holt	Franco	15-10	1st	+0.5
5-4	At N.Y.	W	6-1		13	3	Hampton	Leiter		16-10	1st	+0.5
5-5	At N.Y.	W	5-4		8	11	Powell	Benitez	Wagner	17-10	1st	+1.5
5-7	Mon.	W	5-2		8	9	Lima	Batista		18-10	1st	+2.0
5-8	Mon.	L	5-6		9	12	Hermanson	Reynolds	Urbina	18-11	1st	+2.0
5-9	Mon.	L	2-4		9	13	Pavano	Holt	Urbina	18-12	1st	+2.0
5-10	Pit.	W	6-0		13	5	Hampton	Schourek		19-12	1st	+2.0
5-11	Pit.	W	19-8		18	14	Bergman	Ritchie		20-12	1st	+3.0
5-12	Pit.	W	6-2		10	8	Lima	Schmidt		21-12	T1st	+4.0
5-14	S.F	W	7-4		14	7	Reynolds	Rueter	Wagner	22-12	T1st	+5.0
5-15	S.F	W	10-5		12	9	Hampton	Gardner		23-12	1st	+5.0
5-16	S.F	L	4-5	(11)	9	10	Nen	Elarton	Nathan	23-13	1st	+4.0
5-18	At L.A.	W	11-3		12	9	Lima	Perez		24-13	1st	+4.0
5-19	At L.A.	L	2-5		5	8	Brown	Reynolds		24-14	1st	+3.5
5-20	At L.A.	W	4-3	(10)	6	9	Wagner	Shaw		25-14	1st	+3.5
5-21	At S.F	L	3-4		7	12	Johnstone	Powell	Nen	25-15	1st	+2.5
5-22	At S.F	L	1-3		4	7	Ortiz	Holt	Nen	25-16	1st	+2.5
5-23	At S.F	W	4-1		5	4	Lima	Nathan	Wagner	26-16	1st	+2.5
5-24	Col.	W	5-2		8	9	Reynolds	Bohanon		27-16	1st	+3.5
5-25	Col.	W	2-1	(12)	9	5	Elarton	DeJean		28-16	1st	+4.5
5-26	Col.	W	3-2		9	7	Powell	Astacio		29-16	1st	+4.5
5-27	Col.	L	3-4		4	7	Dipoto	Miller	Veres	29-17	1st	+4.0
5-28	At Pit.	L	5-6		6	9	Ritchie	Lima	Williams	29-18	1st	+3.0
5-29	At Pit.	L	1-5		5	8	Cordova	Reynolds		29-19	1st	+2.0
5-30	At Pit.	L	3-7		4	11	Benson	Hampton		29-20	1st	+1.0
6-1	At Mil.	W	3-0	(8)	5	6	Bergman	Karl		30-20	1st	+2.0
6-2	At Mil.	W	9-1		9	4	Lima	Eldred		31-20	1st	+2.0
6-3	At Mil.	L	1-4		7	10	Woodard	Reynolds	Wickman	31-21	1st	+1.0
6-4	At Min.	W	7-6		14	6	Hampton	Trombley	Wagner	32-21	1st	+1.0
6-5	At Min.	W	6-5		9	11	Elarton	Mays	Wagner	33-21	1st	+2.0
6-6	At Min.	L	6-13		12	21	Sampson	Bergman		33-22	1st	+1.5
6-7	At Chi. (AL)	W	8-2		17	8	Lima	Snyder		34-22	1st	+2.0
6-8	At Chi. (AL)	L	3-4		9	7	Navarro	Reynolds	Howry	34-23	1st	+1.0
6-9	At Chi. (AL)	W	13-4		17	9	Hampton	Baldwin		35-23	1st	+2.0
6-11	S.D.	W	2-1		5	4	Bergman	Williams	Wagner	36-23	1st	+3.0
6-12	S.D.	W	3-2		7	7	Lima	Wall	Wagner	37-23	1st	+4.0
6-13	S.D.	W	4-3		9	8	Reynolds	Murray	Wagner	38-23	1st	+4.5
6-14	Atl.	W	10-4		13	10	Hampton	Perez	Miller	39-23	1st	+5.0
6-15	Atl.	L	3-4		6	7	Glavine	Elarton	Rocker	39-24	1st	+4.5
6-16	Atl.	L	1-3		3	14	Maddux	Bergman	Rocker	39-25	1st	+4.5
6-17	Atl.	L	5-8		6	13	Millwood	Lima	Seanez	39-26	1st	+4.0
6-18	Mon.	W	6-6			6	Reynolds	Hermanson		40-26	1st	+4.0
6-19	Mon.	W	5-2		10	8	Hampton	Pavano	Wagner	41-26	1st	+5.0
6-20	Mon.	W	11-3		9	11	Holt	Smith		42-26	1st	+6.0
6-21	At StL.	L	3-5		5	10	Bottenfield	Bergman	Bottalico	42-27	1st	+5.0
6-22	At StL.	L	3-4	(14)	11	13	Mohler	McCurry		42-28	1st	+4.0
6-23	At StL.	W	8-4		12	14	Reynolds	Acevedo		43-28	1st	+4.0
6-24	Cin.	L	0-3		1	5	Villone	Hampton	Graves	43-29	1st	+3.0
6-25	Cin.	L	7-10		10	12	Tomko	Holt	Williamson	43-30	1st	+2.0
6-26	Cin.	L	1-8		2	11	Parris	Bergman		43-31	1st	+1.0
6-27	Cin.	L	2-5		5	12	Harnisch	Lima		43-32	T1st	...
6-29	StL.	W	5-4		7	8	Elarton	Aybar	Wagner	44-32	T1st	...
6-30	StL.	W	11-3		13	8	Hampton	Jimenez		45-32	T1st	...

HIGHLIGHTS

High point: Entering the final two days of the season tied with Cincinnati for first place in the N.L. Central, the Astros turned to their two 20-game winners, Jose Lima and Mike Hampton. The staff standouts beat the Dodgers, 3-0 and 9-4, while the Reds split two games in Milwaukee. The Sunday division clincher—in which Hampton ran his record to 22-4—was the final regular-season game in Astrodome history.

Low point: The darkest day was June 13 when manager Larry Dierker suffered a grand mal seizure in the dugout during a game against San Diego. He underwent brain surgery two days later and missed 27 games (Houston was 13-14 during his absence).

Turning point: When the Astros asserted themselves and won a club-record 12 consecutive games from September 3-14. Hampton won three times in that stretch.

Most valuable player: First baseman Jeff Bagwell, who hit .304 with 42 homers, 126 RBIs and 30 stolen bases. It was the second 30-30 season of Bagwell's career.

Most valuable pitcher: Lefthander Hampton, who shed his label of inconsistency in a compelling manner. He fashioned a 2.90 ERA and worked at least seven innings in 28 of his 34 starts. The Astros were 29-5 when Hampton took the mound.

Most improved player: Closer Billy Wagner actually got better in 1999, adding a slider to his repertoire and becoming virtually unhittable. He held opponents to a .135 average, averaged 14.9 strikeouts per nine innings, saved a career-high 39 games and posted a 1.57 ERA.

Most pleasant surprise: Injuries having ravaged the Astros' outfield, converted first baseman Daryle Ward became the everyday left fielder down the stretch and acquitted himself well. In 150 at-bats, he hit .273 with eight homers and 30 RBIs.

Key injuries: Left fielder Moises Alou, who hit 38 homers and drove in 124 runs in 1998, missed the entire season after undergoing surgery for a knee injury incurred in pre-camp workouts. Third baseman Ken Caminiti was sidelined 79 games because of a torn muscle in his right calf. Shortstop Ricky Gutierrez spent two stints on the disabled list because of broken bones in his hands, and outfielder Richard Hidalgo had his season shortened because of knee surgery.

Notable: Houston's 97 victories marked the second-highest total in franchise history. ... Hampton and Wagner established club records for wins and saves, respectively. ... Center fielder Carl Everett had a breakthrough season. He finished tied for seventh in the N.L. batting race with a .325 mark, hit 25 homers, knocked in 108 runs and stole 27 bases. ... The '99 season was the Astros' 35th and last at the Astrodome. They will move to Enron Field in 2000.

—CARLTON THOMPSON

MISCELLANEOUS

RECORDS

1999 regular-season record: 97-65 (1st in N.L. Central); 50-32 at home; 47-33 on road; 25-16 vs. N.L. East; 31-31 vs. N.L. Central; 29-15 vs. N.L. West; 12-3 vs. A.L. Central; 27-16 vs. lefthanded starters; 70-49 vs. righthanded starters; 34-23 on grass; 63-42 on turf; 27-19 in daytime; 70-46 at night; 22-18 in one-run games; 8-5 in extra-inning games; 0-0-2 in double-headers.

Team record past five years: 441-351 (.557, ranks 2nd in league in that span).

TEAM LEADERS

Batting average: Carl Everett (.325).
At-bats: Craig Biggio (639).
Runs: Jeff Bagwell (143).
Hits: Craig Biggio (188).
Total bases: Jeff Bagwell (332).
Doubles: Craig Biggio (56).
Triples: Ricky Gutierrez, Bill Spiers (5).
Home runs: Jeff Bagwell (42).
Runs batted in: Jeff Bagwell (126).
Stolen bases: Jeff Bagwell (30).
Slugging percentage: Jeff Bagwell (.591).
On-base percentage: Jeff Bagwell (.454).
Wins: Mike Hampton (22).
Earned-run average: Mike Hampton (2.90).
Complete games: Shane Reynolds (4).
Shutouts: Mike Hampton, Shane Reynolds (2).
Saves: Billy Wagner (39).
Innings pitched: Jose Lima (246.1).
Strikeouts: Shane Reynolds (197).

Date	Opp.	Res.	Score	(inn.*)	Hits	Opp. hits	Winning pitcher	Losing pitcher	Save	Record	Pos.	GB
7-1	StL.	L	4-10		10	12	Bottenfield	Holt		45-33	2nd	1.0
7-2	At Cin.	W	7-5		15	11	Powell	Belinda	Wagner	46-33	T1st	...
7-3	At Cin.	L	0-10		5	13	Harnisch	Elarton	Reyes	46-34	2nd	1.0
7-4	At Cin.	W	5-3		8	12	Reynolds	Avery	Wagner	47-34	T1st	...
7-5	At Cin.	L	2-5		6	11	Villone	Holt	Graves	47-35	2nd	1.0
7-6	At Ari.	W	3-1		7	5	Lima	Daal	Wagner	48-35	T1st	...
7-7	At Ari.	L	7-13		11	14	Chouinard	Miller		48-36	T1st	...
7-8	At Ari.	L	7-8	(11)	13	15	Olson	Williams		48-37	2nd	1.0
7-9	At K.C.	W	6-5		9	12	Cabrera	Montgomery	Holt	49-37	2nd	1.0
7-10	At K.C.	W	3-2		10	10	Hampton	Appier	Wagner	50-37	T1st	...
7-11	At K.C.	W	7-3		8	9	Lima	Suppan	Powell	51-37	T1st	...
7-15	Det.	W	8-6		9	12	Miller	Blair	Wagner	52-37	T1st	...
7-16	Det.	W	2-1		8	4	Cabrera	Brocail		53-37	1st	+1.0
7-17	Det.	W	3-2	(10)	10	9	Wagner	Jones		54-37	1st	+1.0
7-18	Cle.	W	2-0		4	4	Hampton	Wright		55-37	1st	+2.0
7-19	Cle.	W	3-2	(11)	4	6	Cabrera	Candiotti		56-37	1st	+3.0
7-20	Cle.	L	1-7		6	12	Colon	Reynolds		56-38	1st	+2.0
7-21	Ari.	L	4-7		8	10	Chouinard	Powell	Mantei	56-39	1st	+1.0
7-22	Ari.	L	1-2		7	7	Benes	Lima	Mantei	56-40	1st	+1.0
7-23	S.D.	W	7-4		7	8	Hampton	Wall		57-40	1st	+2.5
7-24	S.D.	W	5-2		10	8	Holt	Clement	Wagner	58-40	1st	+2.5
7-25	S.D.	W	5-2		11	8	Reynolds	Ashby		59-40	1st	+2.5
7-26	At Col.	W	8-5		17	10	Williams	Veres	Wagner	60-40	1st	+2.5
7-27	At Col.	W	6-3		12	10	Lima	Bohanon	Wagner	61-40	1st	+2.5
7-28	At Col.	W	16-8		21	18	Hampton	Ramirez		62-40	1st	+3.5
7-29	At Col.	L	2-4		9	11	Kile	Holt	Veres	62-41	1st	+2.5
7-30	At S.D.	W	5-1		8	6	Reynolds	Clement		63-41	1st	+2.5
7-31	At S.D.	W	8-5		10	7	Henry	Miceli		64-41	1st	+3.5
8-1	At S.D.	L	3-10		6	15	Hitchcock	Lima		64-42	1st	+2.5
8-3	L.A.	W	7-2		10	6	Hampton	Dreifort		65-42	1st	+2.5
8-4	L.A.	L	1-2		4	4	Brown	Holt		65-43	1st	+1.5
8-5	L.A.	W	7-0		11	5	Reynolds	Valdes		66-43	1st	+2.5
8-6†	At Chi.	W	6-1		10	8	Lima	Farnsworth	Powell	67-43		
8-6‡	At Chi.	L	0-6		3	9	Lorraine	Bergman		67-44	1st	+2.0
8-7	At Chi.	W	10-4		14	5	Elarton	Tapani		68-44	1st	+3.0
8-8	At Chi.	W	6-2		14	7	Hampton	Bowie		69-44	1st	+3.0
8-9	At Atl.	L	3-5		14	10	Seanez	Henry	Rocker	69-45	1st	+2.0
8-10	At Atl.	L	4-6		8	8	Glavine	Reynolds	Rocker	69-46	1st	+1.0
8-11	At Atl.	L	5-8		11	10	Maddux	Lima	Rocker	69-47	1st	+1.0
8-13	Pit.	L	5-6	(13)	11	8	Clontz	Miller	Williams	69-48	T1st	...
8-14	Pit.	W	7-1		6	6	Holt	Benson		70-48	T1st	...
8-15	Pit.	L	0-2		7	5	Ritchie	Reynolds	Williams	70-49	T1st	...
8-16	Mil.	W	2-0		8	2	Lima	Peterson	Wagner	71-49	T1st	...
8-17	Mil.	W	8-6		9	11	Elarton	Eldred	Wagner	72-49	T1st	...
8-18	Mil.	W	6-4		9	8	Williams	Plunk	Wagner	73-49	1st	+1.0
8-19	Mil.	L	5-6		10	17	Coppinger	Powell	Wickman	73-50	2nd	...
8-20	At Fla.	W	6-4	(16)	7	15	Miller	Sanchez	Wagner	74-50	1st	+1.0
8-21	At Fla.	W	5-4		8	8	Henry	Edmondson	Wagner	75-50	1st	+1.0
8-23	At N.Y.	L	2-3		10	8	Benitez	Powell		75-51	1st	+0.5
8-24	At N.Y.	W	5-1	(10)	8	5	Wagner	Cook		76-51	1st	+1.5
8-25	At N.Y.	L	0-4		7	12	Rogers	Reynolds	Cook	76-52	1st	+1.5
8-27†	Fla.	W	3-2		8	9	Lima	Springer	Wagner	77-52		
8-27‡	Fla.	L	1-3		7	11	Dempster	Holt	Alfonseca	77-53	1st	+0.5
8-28	Fla.	L	2-5		7	10	Burnett	Elarton	Alfonseca	77-54	1st	+0.5
8-29	Fla.	W	10-4		14	10	Hampton	Fernandez		78-54	1st	+1.5
8-30	N.Y.	L	1-17		5	21	Yoshii	Reynolds		78-55	1st	+0.5
8-31	N.Y.	W	6-2		7	7	Lima	Wendell		79-55	1st	+1.5
9-1	N.Y.	L	5-9		7	18	Dotel	Holt		79-56	1st	+1.5
9-3	At Mon.	W	8-1		11	7	Hampton	Smith		80-56	1st	+2.5
9-4	At Mon.	W	5-2	(10)	6	8	Cabrera	Urbina		81-56	1st	+2.5
9-5	At Mon.	W	6-2		12	9	Elarton	Telford		82-56	1st	+2.5
9-6	At Phi.	W	6-5		6	12	Lima	Wolf	Wagner	83-56	1st	+2.5
9-7	At Phi.	W	8-6		12	10	Powell	Gomes	Henry	84-56	1st	+3.0
9-8	At Phi.	W	10-2		12	8	Hampton	Schilling		85-56	1st	+3.0
9-9	At Phi.	W	3-1		9	4	Reynolds	Montgomery	Wagner	86-56	1st	+3.0
9-10	Chi.	W	6-4	(13)	12	9	Wagner	Ayala		87-56	1st	+3.0
9-11	Chi.	W	5-3		7	7	Lima	Bowie	Wagner	88-56	1st	+3.0
9-12	Chi.	W	7-1		12	6	Holt	Trachsel		89-56	1st	+3.0
9-13	Phi.	W	13-2		10	6	Hampton	Grahe		90-56	1st	+3.0
9-14	Phi.	W	12-2		16	8	Reynolds	Byrd		91-56	1st	+4.0
9-15	Phi.	L	6-8	(10)	12	14	Gomes	Henry	Brewer	91-57	1st	+3.0
9-17	At StL.	L	8-11		8	18	Stephenson	Lima	Bottalico	91-58	1st	+3.5
9-18	At StL.	L	6-13		11	13	Oliver	Hampton		91-59	1st	+2.5
9-19	At StL.	W	4-3		10	7	Holt	Croushore	Wagner	92-59	1st	+3.5
9-20	At Pit.	L	5-11		9	14	Schourek	Reynolds		92-60	1st	+2.5
9-21	At Pit.	W	6-3		8	10	Elarton	Benson	Henry	93-60	1st	+3.5
9-22	At Pit.	L	2-3		6	5	Ritchie	Lima		93-61	1st	+2.5
9-24	At Mil.	W	9-4		7	8	Miller	Plunk	Powell	94-61	1st	+2.5
9-25	At Mil.	L	2-3		10	9	Karl	Reynolds	Wickman	94-62	1st	+1.5
9-26	At Mil.	L	3-11		9	16	Peterson	Elarton		94-63	1st	+0.5
9-28	Cin.	L	1-4		4	8	Harnisch	Lima	Williamson	94-64	2nd	1.0
9-29	Cin.	W	4-1		7	7	Hampton	Parris	Wagner	95-64	T1st	...
10-1	L.A.	L	1-5		7	9	Gagne	Reynolds		95-65	T1st	...
10-2	L.A.	W	3-0		6	9	Lima	Park	Wagner	96-65	1st	+1.0
10-3	L.A.	W	9-4		8	7	Hampton	Checo		97-65	1st	+1.0

Monthly records: April (13-9), May (16-11), June (16-12), July (19-9), August (15-14), September (16-9), October (2-1).
*Innings, if other than nine. † First game of a doubleheader. ‡ Second game of a doubleheader.

MEMORABLE GAMES

June 9 at Chicago

First baseman Jeff Bagwell hit home runs in three consecutive at-bats in a six-RBI performance against the White Sox. It was Bagwell's second three-homer game of the season—he also did it at Wrigley Field on April 21—and the third of his career. He joined Johnny Mize (1938) and Ralph Kiner (1947) as the only players to have two three-homer games in the same city and in the same season.

Houston	AB	R	H	RBI	Chi White Sox	AB	R	H	RBI
Biggio, 2b	2	2	1	1	Durham, 2b	4	0	0	0
Ru.Jhnsn, ph-2b	1	1	1	0	L.Rodrigz, ss	4	1	0	0
Spiers, 3b	6	2	2	0	Thomas, 1b	4	0	1	0
Bagwell, 1b	6	3	3	6	M.Ordonz, rf	3	1	1	0
D.Bell, rf	6	2	4	1	C.Lee, lf	3	0	1	1
Everett, cf	4	1	2	3	D.Jackson, cf	4	1	1	0
Hidalgo, lf	4	0	0	0	Konerko, dh	4	1	1	2
D.Ward, dh	4	0	2	1	C.Wilson, 3b	4	0	2	0
Eusebio, c	5	1	0	0	Fordyce, c	4	0	2	0
Bogar, ss	5	1	2	1					
Totals	**43**	**13**	**17**	**13**	**Totals**	**34**	**4**	**9**	**3**

Houston ....2 0 2 0 0 4 1 2 2— 13
Chi White Sox ....0 0 0 1 0 1 0 2 0— 4

E—Eusebio (1), Thomas (2), L.Rodriguez (1). LOB—Houston 10, Chi.White Sox 7. 2B—Bogar (11), Ru.Johnson (4). HR—Bagwell 3 (20), Everett (5), Bogar (1), Konerko (5). SB—M.Ordonez (7). S—Everett. SF—Biggio, C.Lee. SB—M.Ordonez (7).

Houston	IP	H	R	ER	BB	SO
Hampton (W, 7-2)	6.2	7	2	1	3	6
Elarton	1.1	2	2	2	0	1
B.Wagner	1	0	0	0	0	3

Chi White Sox	IP	H	R	ER	BB	SO
Baldwin (L, 3-5)	5.1	9	7	7	4	1
S.Lowe	0.2	2	1	1	0	0
B.Ward	1	1	1	0	0	2
Simas	1	3	2	2	1	1
Foulke	1	2	2	2	0	3

WP—Elarton. U—HP, Craft. 1B, McKean. 2B, Joyce. 3B, O'Nora. T—3:06. A—12,138.

September 10 at Houston

Center fielder Carl Everett, who had been on the disabled list because of a strained right groin, returned to the lineup in dramatic fashion, smashing two home runs, including the game-winner in a 13-inning victory over the Cubs. Everett's homers came from opposite sides of the plate, and the first came on the first pitch he saw after sitting out 20 games.

Chi Cubs	AB	R	H	RBI	Houston	AB	R	H	RBI
R.Brown, cf-lf	5	1	2	1	Biggio, 2b	5	0	2	1
Meyers, 2b	3	0	1	0	D.Bell, rf	6	0	0	0
Adams, p	0	0	0	0	Bagwell, 1b	6	1	1	0
Gaetti, 3b	2	0	0	0	Evrtt, cf-lf-cf	6	2	2	3
Ma.Grace, 1b	4	0	0	1	Caminiti, 3b	3	0	0	0
S.Sosa, rf	6	0	0	0	G.Barker, pr-cf	0	1	0	0
H.Rodrigz, lf	4	0	0	0	R.Thmpsn, ph-lf	1	0	0	0
L.Johnson, cf	1	0	0	0	D.Ward, lf	4	0	3	0
J.Reed, c	3	1	1	0	C.Hernndz, pr	0	1	0	0
Porter, pr	0	0	0	0	Ru.Johnsn, 3b	1	0	0	0
J.Molina, c	0	0	0	0	Bako, c	4	0	0	0
Liniak, 3b	3	1	2	1	Gutierrez, ss	5	1	4	1
Aguilera, p	0	0	0	0	Elarton, p	1	0	0	0
G.Hill, ph	1	0	0	0	Berkman, ph	1	0	0	0
Guthrie, p	0	0	0	0	Tre.Miller, p	0	0	0	0
Ayala, p	0	0	0	0	B.Williams, p	0	0	0	0
Nieves, ss	5	1	2	1	Spiers, ph	1	0	0	0
Lieber, p	3	0	1	0	Ja.Powell, p	0	0	0	0
Morandni, 2b	1	0	0	0	Mieske, ph	1	0	0	0
					D.Henry, p	0	0	0	0
					J.Cabrera, p	0	0	0	0
					Eusebio, ph	1	0	0	0
					B.Wagner, p	0	0	0	0
Totals	**41**	**4**	**9**	**4**	**Totals**	**46**	**6**	**12**	**5**

Chi Cubs ....0 3 0 0 1 0 0 0 0 0 0 0 0—4
Houston.......................................0 1 0 0 0 0 0 1 2 0 0 0 2—6

DP—Chi.Cubs 2, Houston 2. LOB—Chi Cubs 6, Houston 7. 2B—R.Brown (1), Liniak (2), Nieves (5), Biggio (53). 3B—Gutierrez (5). HR—Everett 2 (23). SB—Gutierrez (2), G.Barker (15), C.Hernandez (3). CS—Liniak (1). S—R.Brown, Meyers. SF—Ma.Grace.

Chi Cubs	IP	H	R	ER	BB	SO
Lieber	8	7	2	2	0	9
Adams (BS 3)	0.1	2	2	2	2	1
Aguilera	1.2	0	0	0	0	0
Guthrie	1.1	1	0	0	0	0
Ayala (L, 0-1)	0.2	2	2	2	1	1

Houston	IP	H	R	ER	BB	SO
Elarton	5	6	4	4	3	3
Tre.Miller	2.1	3	0	0	0	1
B.Williams	0.2	0	0	0	0	1
Ja.Powell	1	0	0	0	0	1
D.Henry	2	0	0	0	2	1
J.Cabrera	1	0	0	0	0	0
B.Wagner (W, 4-1)	1	0	0	0	0	1

WP—Adams, Elarton. PB—Bako. U—HP, Rieker. 1B, Davis. 2B, Wegner. 3B, Emmel. T—3:45. A—48,879.

1999 REVIEW

BATTING

Name	G	TPA	AB	R	H	TB	2B	3B	HR	RBI	Avg.	Obp.	Slg.	SH	SF	HP	BB	IBB	SO	SB	CS	GDP	vs RHP AB	vs RHP Avg.	vs RHP HR	vs RHP RBI	vs LHP AB	vs LHP Avg.	vs LHP HR	vs LHP RBI
Biggio, Craig	160	749	639	123	188	292	56	0	16	73	.294	.386	.457	5	6	11	88	9	107	28	14	5	489	.290	12	55	150	.307	4	18
Bagwell, Jeff	162	729	562	143	171	332	35	0	42	126	.304	.454	.591	0	7	11	149	16	127	30	11	18	432	.289	33	100	130	.354	9	26
Bell, Derek	128	568	509	61	120	178	22	0	12	66	.236	.306	.350	0	5	4	50	1	129	18	6	20	387	.214	7	43	122	.303	5	23
Everett, Carl	123	535	464	86	151	265	33	3	25	108	.325	.398	.571	2	8	11	50	5	94	27	7	5	347	.326	21	88	117	.325	4	20
Spiers, Bill	127	444	393	56	113	153	18	5	4	39	.288	.363	.389	3	1	0	47	2	45	10	5	10	353	.278	4	29	40	.375	0	10
Hidalgo, Richard	108	449	383	49	87	161	25	2	15	56	.227	.328	.420	0	5	4	56	2	73	8	5	5	206	.238	11	39	177	.215	4	17
Eusebio, Tony	103	363	323	31	88	115	15	0	4	33	.272	.353	.356	0	0	0	40	4	67	0	0	9	208	.250	2	19	115	.313	2	14
Bogar, Tim	106	354	309	44	74	106	16	2	4	31	.239	.328	.343	0	3	4	38	5	52	3	5	10	205	.268	3	24	104	.183	1	7
Caminiti, Ken	78	329	273	45	78	130	11	1	13	56	.286	.386	.476	0	7	3	46	3	58	6	2	7	205	.268	12	49	68	.338	1	7
Gutierrez, Ricky	85	311	268	33	70	90	7	5	1	25	.261	.354	.336	3	1	2	37	4	45	2	5	9	202	.223	1	17	66	.379	0	8
Bako, Paul	73	247	215	16	55	77	14	1	2	17	.256	.332	.358	3	3	0	26	3	57	1	1	4	197	.264	2	16	18	.167	0	1
Johnson, Russ	83	183	156	24	44	69	10	0	5	23	.282	.358	.442	4	3	0	20	0	31	2	3	3	96	.281	3	12	60	.283	2	11
Ward, Daryle	64	161	150	11	41	71	6	0	8	30	.273	.311	.473	0	2	0	9	0	31	0	0	3	92	.250	5	19	58	.328	3	11
Mieske, Matt	54	118	109	13	31	51	5	0	5	22	.284	.316	.468	1	2	0	6	1	22	0	0	4	80	.250	4	15	29	.379	1	7
Berkman, Lance	34	106	93	10	22	36	2	0	4	15	.237	.321	.387	0	1	0	12	0	21	5	1	2	58	.241	3	14	35	.229	1	1
Lima, Jose	36	91	75	4	6	6	0	0	0	0	.080	.115	.080	13	0	0	3	0	24	0	0	3	54	.074	0	3	21	.095	0	7
Hampton, Mike	34	88	74	10	23	32	3	3	0	10	.311	.373	.432	5	1	1	7	0	18	0	0	2	50	.280	0	8	24	.375	0	2
Barker, Glen	81	90	73	23	21	26	2	0	1	11	.288	.384	.356	4	1	1	11	0	19	17	6	0	50	.280	1	9	23	.304	0	2
Reynolds, Shane	35	86	66	4	11	16	2	0	1	14	.167	.188	.242	17	1	0	2	0	27	0	0	1	49	.163	1	12	17	.176	0	2
Javier, Stan	20	75	64	12	21	27	4	1	0	4	.328	.405	.422	1	1	0	9	0	8	3	1	2	46	.348	0	3	18	.278	0	1
Diaz, Alex	30	53	50	3	11	16	2	0	1	7	.220	.264	.320	0	0	0	3	0	13	2	2	0	32	.219	1	6	18	.222	0	1
Holt, Chris	32	55	45	3	3	3	0	0	0	2	.067	.125	.067	7	0	0	3	0	14	0	0	1	32	.063	0	2	13	.077	0	0
Howell, Jack	37	41	33	2	7	12	2	0	1	1	.212	.316	.364	0	0	0	8	0	9	0	0	1	27	.185	1	2	6	.333	0	1
Meluskey, Mitch	10	38	33	4	7	11	1	0	1	3	.212	.316	.333	0	0	0	5	1	6	1	0	1	21	.190	0	2	12	.250	0	1
Knorr, Randy	13	31	30	2	5	6	1	0	0	0	.167	.194	.200	0	0	0	1	0	8	0	0	0	12	.000	0	0	18	.278	0	0
Bergman, Sean	19	29	28	4	3	9	0	0	2	2	.107	.107	.321	1	0	0	0	0	12	0	0	0	20	.100	1	1	8	.125	1	1
Elarton, Scott	43	33	26	1	5	5	0	0	0	1	.192	.192	.192	7	0	0	0	0	10	0	0	0	20	.250	0	1	6	.000	0	0
Thompson, Ryan	12	22	20	2	4	8	1	0	1	5	.200	.273	.400	0	0	0	2	0	7	0	0	1	11	.182	1	3	9	.222	0	2
Hernandez, Carlos E.	16	15	14	4	2	2	0	0	0	0	.143	.143	.143	1	0	0	0	0	3	1	0	0	12	.167	0	0	2	.000	0	0
Williams, Brian	50	3	3	0	1	1	0	0	0	1	.333	.333	.333	0	0	0	0	0	0	0	0	0	2	.000	0	0	1	1.000	0	1
Miller, Trever	47	5	3	0	0	0	0	0	0	0	.000	.000	.000	2	0	0	0	0	1	0	0	0	3	.000	0	0	0	.000	0	0
Henry, Doug	35	1	1	0	0	0	0	0	0	0	.000	.000	.000	0	0	0	0	0	1	0	0	0	1	.000	0	0	0	.000	0	0
Miller, Wade	5	1	1	0	0	0	0	0	0	0	.000	.000	.000	0	0	0	0	0	1	0	0	0	0	.000	0	0	1	.000	0	0
Slusarski, Joe	3	0	0	0	0	0	0	0	0	0	.000	.000	.000	0	0	0	0	0	0	0	0	0	0	.000	0	0	0	.000	0	0
McCurry, Jeff	5	0	0	0	0	0	0	0	0	0	.000	.000	.000	0	0	0	0	0	0	0	0	0	0	.000	0	0	0	.000	0	0
Powell, Jay	67	0	0	0	0	0	0	0	0	0	.000	.000	.000	0	0	0	0	0	0	0	0	0	0	.000	0	0	0	.000	0	0
Wagner, Billy	66	0	0	0	0	0	0	0	0	0	.000	.000	.000	0	0	0	0	0	0	0	0	0	0	.000	0	0	0	.000	0	0
Cabrera, Jose	26	0	0	0	0	0	0	0	0	0	.000	.000	.000	0	0	0	0	0	0	0	0	0	0	.000	0	0	0	.000	0	0

Players with more than one N.L. team

Name	G	TPA	AB	R	H	TB	2B	3B	HR	RBI	Avg.	Obp.	Slg.	SH	SF	HP	BB	IBB	SO	SB	CS	GDP	vs RHP AB	vs RHP Avg.	vs RHP HR	vs RHP RBI	vs LHP AB	vs LHP Avg.	vs LHP HR	vs LHP RBI
Bergman, Atl.	6	0	0	0	0	0	0	0	0	0	.000	.000	.000	0	0	0	0	0	0	0	0	0	20	.100	1	1	8	.125	1	1
Bergman, Hou.-Atl.	25	29	28	4	3	9	0	0	2	2	.107	.107	.321	1	0	0	0	0	12	0	0	0	20	.100	1	1	8	.125	1	1
Javier, S.F.	112	371	333	49	92	118	15	1	3	30	.276	.335	.354	7	1	1	29	4	55	13	6	4								
Javier, S.F.-Hou.	132	446	397	61	113	145	19	2	3	34	.285	.347	.365	8	2	1	38	4	63	16	7	6	288	.271	0	23	109	.321	3	11

PITCHING

Name	W	L	Pct.	ERA	IP	H	R	ER	HR	SH	SF	HB	BB	IBB	SO	G	GS	CG	ShO	GF	Sv	vs RH AB	vs RH Avg.	vs RH HR	vs RH RBI	vs LH AB	vs LH Avg.	vs LH HR	vs LH RBI
Lima, Jose	21	10	.677	3.58	246.1	256	108	98	30	5	7	2	44	2	187	35	35	3	0	0	0	545	.248	16	54	421	.287	14	48
Hampton, Mike	22	4	.846	2.90	239.0	206	86	77	12	10	9	5	101	2	177	34	34	3	2	0	0	713	.259	10	66	141	.149	2	9
Reynolds, Shane	16	14	.533	3.85	231.2	250	108	99	23	11	5	1	37	0	197	35	35	4	2	0	0	491	.269	13	57	418	.282	10	39
Holt, Chris	5	13	.278	4.66	164.0	193	92	85	12	9	8	8	57	1	115	32	26	0	0	2	1	329	.298	8	44	309	.307	4	31
Elarton, Scott	9	5	.643	3.48	124.0	111	55	48	8	7	4	4	43	0	121	42	15	0	0	8	1	251	.227	4	33	215	.251	4	27
Bergman, Sean	4	6	.400	5.36	99.0	130	60	59	9	3	4	3	26	1	38	19	16	2	1	1	0	200	.350	4	30	192	.313	5	27
Powell, Jay	5	4	.556	4.32	75.0	82	38	36	3	5	2	0	40	4	77	67	0	0	0	26	4	166	.265	1	10	125	.304	2	15
Wagner, Billy	4	1	.800	1.57	74.2	35	14	13	5	2	1	1	23	1	124	66	0	0	0	55	39	211	.128	4	10	48	.167	1	5
Williams, Brian	2	1	.667	4.41	67.1	69	35	33	4	5	4	5	35	2	53	50	0	0	0	15	0	143	.231	3	19	111	.324	1	14
Miller, Trever	3	2	.600	5.07	49.2	58	29	28	6	2	2	5	29	1	37	47	0	0	0	11	1	118	.339	3	14	76	.237	3	11
Henry, Doug	2	3	.400	4.65	40.2	45	24	21	8	1	0	3	24	0	36	35	0	0	0	17	2	87	.253	5	10	73	.315	3	4
Cabrera, Jose	4	0	1.000	2.15	29.1	21	7	7	3	0	3	0	9	2	28	26	0	0	0	11	0	58	.241	1	4	49	.143	2	3
Miller, Wade	0	1	.000	9.58	10.1	17	11	11	4	0	0	0	5	0	8	5	1	0	0	2	0	25	.440	2	7	22	.273	2	4
McCurry, Jeff	0	1	.000	15.75	4.0	11	8	7	1	0	0	0	2	0	3	5	0	0	0	1	0	13	.538	1	4	10	.400	0	1
Slusarski, Joe	0	0	.000	0.00	3.2	1	0	0	0	0	0	0	0	0	3	3	0	0	0	1	0	8	.125	0	0	4	.000	0	0

PITCHERS WITH MORE THAN ONE N.L. TEAM

Name	W	L	Pct.	ERA	IP	H	R	ER	HR	SH	SF	HB	BB	IBB	SO	G	GS	CG	ShO	GF	Sv	vs RH AB	vs RH Avg.	vs RH HR	vs RH RBI	vs LH AB	vs LH Avg.	vs LH HR	vs LH RBI
Bergman, Atl.	1	0	1.000	2.84	6.1	5	2	2	0	1	0	0	3	0	6	6	0	0	0	1	0	16	.188	0	1	7	.286	0	0
Bergman, Hou.-Atl.	5	6	.455	5.21	105.1	135	62	61	9	4	4	3	29	1	44	25	16	2	1	4	0	216	.343	4	31	199	.307	5	27

INDIVIDUAL STATISTICS

FIELDING

FIRST BASEMEN

Player	Pct.	G	PO	A	E	TC	DP
Bagwell, Jeff	.994	161	1336	107	8	1451	141
Ward, Daryle	1.000	10	36	2	0	38	6
Howell, Jack	1.000	5	9	2	0	11	4
Spiers, Bill	1.000	1	3	0	0	3	0
Berkman, Lance	1.000	1	1	0	0	1	1

SECOND BASEMEN

Player	Pct.	G	PO	A	E	TC	DP
Biggio, Craig	.985	155	359	430	12	801	117
Johnson, Russ	.960	15	16	32	2	50	6
Hernandez, Carlos E.	1.000	7	5	11	0	16	3
Spiers, Bill	1.000	4	5	10	0	15	0
Bogar, Tim	1.000	1	1	2	0	3	1

THIRD BASEMEN

Player	Pct.	G	PO	A	E	TC	DP
Caminiti, Ken	.932	75	52	139	14	205	17
Spiers, Bill	.958	71	40	143	8	191	11
Johnson, Russ	.944	36	16	52	4	72	8
Bogar, Tim	1.000	12	6	20	0	26	0
Howell, Jack	1.000	3	1	3	0	4	0
Gutierrez, Ricky	1.000	1	0	1	0	1	0
Lima, Jose	-	1	0	0	0	0	0

SHORTSTOPS

Player	Pct.	G	PO	A	E	TC	DP
Bogar, Tim	.977	90	123	255	9	387	65
Gutierrez, Ricky	.971	80	102	202	9	313	37
Spiers, Bill	1.000	13	22	23	0	45	7
Johnson, Russ	.833	2	1	4	1	6	1
Hernandez, Carlos E.	.667	2	2	0	1	3	0

OUTFIELDERS

Player	Pct.	G	PO	A	E	TC	DP
Bell, Derek	.985	126	192	4	3	199	1
Everett, Carl	.978	121	256	11	6	273	4
Hidalgo, Richard	.991	108	214	15	2	231	3
Barker, Glen	.981	57	50	2	1	53	1
Mieske, Matt	1.000	36	54	1	0	55	0
Spiers, Bill	.976	31	40	0	1	41	0
Ward, Daryle	.944	31	33	1	2	36	0
Berkman, Lance	.955	27	42	0	2	44	0
Javier, Stan	1.000	18	31	1	0	32	0
Thompson, Ryan	.800	10	3	1	1	5	1
Diaz, Alex	.900	8	8	1	1	10	0
Biggio, Craig	1.000	6	6	1	0	7	0
Elarton, Scott	-	1	0	0	0	0	0

CATCHERS

Player	Pct.	G	PO	A	E	TC	DP	PB
Eusebio, Tony	.994	98	652	37	4	693	3	4
Bako, Paul	.988	71	461	35	6	502	10	4
Knorr, Randy	1.000	11	54	3	0	57	0	1
Meluskey, Mitch	1.000	10	62	6	0	68	1	0

PITCHERS

Player	Pct.	G	PO	A	E	TC	DP
Powell, Jay	.800	67	1	7	2	10	0
Wagner, Billy	1.000	66	2	5	0	7	1
Williams, Brian	1.000	50	4	11	0	15	1
Miller, Trever	1.000	47	3	7	0	10	0
Elarton, Scott	1.000	42	4	8	0	12	0
Reynolds, Shane	1.000	35	18	41	0	59	3
Lima, Jose	.951	35	18	21	2	41	1
Henry, Doug	.889	35	2	6	1	9	0
Hampton, Mike	.946	34	12	41	3	56	4
Holt, Chris	.968	32	14	16	1	31	2
Cabrera, Jose	1.000	26	0	2	0	2	0
Bergman, Sean	1.000	19	4	8	0	12	1
Miller, Wade	1.000	5	0	2	0	2	0
McCurry, Jeff	-	5	0	0	0	0	0
Slusarski, Joe	-	3	0	0	0	0	0

PITCHING AGAINST EACH CLUB

Pitcher	Ari. W-L	Atl. W-L	Chi. W-L	Cin. W-L	Col. W-L	Fla. W-L	L.A. W-L	Mil. W-L	Mon. W-L	N.Y. W-L	Phi. W-L	Pit. W-L	S.D. W-L	S.F. W-L	StL. W-L	A.L. W-L	Total W-L
Bergman, S.	0-0	0-1	0-1	0-1	0-0	1-0	0-0	1-0	0-0	0-0	0-0	0-0	1-0	0-1	0-1	0-1	4-6
Cabrera, J.	0-0	0-0	0-0	0-0	0-0	0-0	0-0	0-0	1-0	0-0	0-0	0-0	0-0	0-0	0-0	3-0	4-0
Elarton, S.	0-0	0-1	1-0	1-1	0-0	1-0	0-0	2-1	0-0	0-0	0-0	0-0	0-1	1-0	1-0	0-1	9-5
Hampton, M.	1-0	1-0	1-1	1-1	1-0	1-0	2-0	0-0	2-0	1-0	2-0	1-1	1-0	2-0	1-1	4-0	22-4
Henry, D.	0-0	0-1	0-0	0-1	0-0	0-0	0-0	0-0	0-0	0-1	0-0	0-0	0-0	0-0	0-0	0-0	2-3
Holt, C.	0-0	0-0	1-0	0-3	0-0	0-1	0-1	0-1	1-1	0-2	0-1	0-0	0-0	0-0	1-2	0-0	5-13
Lima, J.	2-1	0-2	3-1	0-2	1-0	2-0	2-0	2-0	1-0	1-0	1-0	1-2	1-1	2-0	0-1	2-0	21-10
McCurry, J.	0-0	0-0	0-0	0-0	0-0	0-0	0-0	0-0	0-0	0-0	0-0	0-0	0-0	0-1	0-0	0-0	0-1
Miller, T.	0-0	0-0	0-0	0-0	1-0	0-0	0-0	0-0	0-0	0-0	0-0	0-0	0-0	0-0	0-0	1-0	3-2
Miller, W.	0-1	0-0	0-0	0-0	0-0	0-0	0-0	0-0	0-0	0-0	0-0	0-0	0-0	0-0	0-0	0-0	0-1
Powell, Jay	0-0	0-0	0-0	1-0	1-0	0-0	0-0	0-1	0-0	1-1	1-0	0-0	0-0	1-0	0-0	0-0	5-4
Reynolds, S.	1-0	0-1	2-0	1-0	0-1	1-0	1-2	1-2	1-1	0-2	2-0	0-3	3-0	1-0	1-1	0-2	16-14
Slusarski, J.	0-0	0-0	0-0	0-0	0-0	0-0	0-0	0-0	0-0	0-0	0-0	0-0	0-0	0-0	0-0	0-0	0-0
Wagner, B.	0-1	0-0	0-0	0-0	0-0	0-0	1-0	0-0	0-0	1-0	0-0	0-0	0-0	0-0	0-0	0-0	4-1
Williams, Br.	0-1	1-0	0-0	0-0	1-0	0-0	0-0	1-0	0-0	0-0	0-0	0-0	0-0	0-0	0-0	0-0	2-1
Totals	4-5	1-6	9-3	4-9	6-2	7-2	6-3	8-5	7-2	4-5	6-1	5-7	8-1	5-4	5-7	12-3	97-65

INTERLEAGUE: Lima 1-0, Hampton 1-0, Reynolds 0-1 vs. White Sox; Hampton 1-0, Cabrera 1-0, Reynolds 0-1 vs. Indians; Miller 1-0, Wagner 1-0, Cabrera 1-0 vs. Tigers; Cabrera 1-0, Hampton 1-0, Lima 1-0 vs. Royals; Hampton 1-0, Elarton 1-0, Bergman 0-1 vs. Twins. Total: 12-3.

MISCELLANEOUS

HOME RUNS BY PARK

At Arizona (4): Biggio 2, Bagwell 1, Hidalgo 1.
At Atlanta (1): Bagwell 1.
At Chicago (AL) (6): Bagwell 3, Everett 2, Bogar 1.
At Chicago (NL) (8): Bagwell 3, Everett 3, Hidalgo 1, Meluskey 1.
At Cincinnati (9): Bagwell 2, Bell 2, Everett 2, Caminiti 1, Mieske 1, Hidalgo 1.
At Colorado (6): Mieske 2, Biggio 1, Bagwell 1, Johnson 1, Ward 1.
At Florida (11): Bagwell 3, Caminiti 2, Everett 2, Spiers 1, Bell 1, Hidalgo 1, Barker 1.
At Houston (65): Bagwell 12, Everett 11, Biggio 10, Bell 5, Hidalgo 5, Caminiti 4, Eusebio 2, Bogar 2, Johnson 2, Bako 2, Ward 2, Barker 2, Spiers 1, Reynolds 1, Diaz 1, Gutierrez 1, Mieske 1, Bergman 1.
At Kansas City (2): Howell 1, Bagwell 1.
At Los Angeles (5): Bagwell 3, Eusebio 1, Everett 1.
At Milwaukee (5): Caminiti 1, Spiers 1, Bagwell 1, Everett 1, Hidalgo 1.
At Minnesota (5): Bagwell 2, Hidalgo 2, Johnson 1.
At Montreal (4): Caminiti 2, Bell 1, Ward 1.
At New York (NL) (7): Bagwell 2, Everett 2, Bell 1, Mieske 1, Hidalgo 1.
At Philadelphia (7): Ward 2, Caminiti 1, Biggio 1, Bagwell 1, Thompson 1, Johnson 1.
At Pittsburgh (1): Hidalgo 1.
At San Diego (7): Bagwell 2, Ward 2, Berkman 2, Bogar 1.
At San Francisco (8): Bagwell 2, Caminiti 1, Biggio 1, Spiers 1, Bell 1, Bergman 1, Hidalgo 1.
At St. Louis (7): Bagwell 2, Caminiti 1, Biggio 1, Bell 1, Eusebio 1, Everett 1.

LOW-HIT GAMES

No-hitters: None.
One-hitters: None.
Two-hitters: None.

10-STRIKEOUT GAMES

Shane Reynolds 3, Jose Lima 3, Scott Elarton 1, **Total:** 7.

FOUR OR MORE HITS IN ONE GAME

Carl Everett 5, Craig Biggio 4, Derek Bell 3, Ricky Gutierrez 3, Matt Mieske 1, Russ Johnson 1, Paul Bako 1, **Total:** 18.

MULTI-HOMER GAMES

Jeff Bagwell 4, Carl Everett 4, Ken Caminiti 2, Matt Mieske 1, Lance Berkman 1, **Total:** 12.

GRAND SLAMS

6-13: Derek Bell (off San Diego's Heath Murray).
6-20: Carl Everett (off Montreal's Ugueth Urbina).
7-23: Matt Mieske (off San Diego's Donne Wall).
7-28: Jeff Bagwell (off Colorado's Mike Porzio).
8-31: Ken Caminiti (off New York's Turk Wendell).

PINCH HITTERS

(Minimum 5 at-bats)

Name	AB	Avg.	HR	RBI
Johnson, Russ	35	.343	1	6
Ward, Daryle	25	.320	2	4
Spiers, Bill	23	.348	0	7
Diaz, Alex	21	.190	1	3
Howell, Jack	20	.250	0	0
Mieske, Matt	17	.235	0	5
Barker, Glen	12	.083	0	0
Eusebio, Tony	12	.083	0	0
Berkman, Lance	9	.000	0	0
Thompson, Ryan	5	.200	1	1
Hernandez, Carlos E.	5	.000	0	0

DEBUTS

4-7: Glen Barker, PH.
5-26: Carlos E. Hernandez, PR.
7-7: Wade Miller, P.
7-16: Lance Berkman, PH.

GAMES BY POSITION

Catcher: Tony Eusebio 98, Paul Bako 71, Randy Knorr 11, Mitch Meluskey 10.
First base: Jeff Bagwell 161, Daryle Ward 10, Jack Howell 5, Bill Spiers 1, Lance Berkman 1.
Second base: Craig Biggio 155, Russ Johnson 15, Carlos E. Hernandez 7, Bill Spiers 4, Tim Bogar 1.
Third base: Ken Caminiti 75, Bill Spiers 71, Russ Johnson 36, Tim Bogar 12, Jack Howell 3, Ricky Gutierrez 1, Jose Lima 1.
Shortstop: Tim Bogar 90, Ricky Gutierrez 80, Bill Spiers 13, Russ Johnson 2, Carlos E. Hernandez 2.
Outfield: Derek Bell 126, Carl Everett 121, Richard Hidalgo 108, Glen Barker 57, Matt Mieske 36, Bill Spiers 31, Daryle Ward 31, Lance Berkman 27, Stan Javier 18, Ryan Thompson 10, Alex Diaz 8, Craig Biggio 6, Scott Elarton 1.
Designated hitter: Daryle Ward 3, Jack Howell 2, Craig Biggio 2, Jeff Bagwell 2, Carl Everett 2, Glen Barker 1.

STREAKS

Wins: 12 (September 1-14).
Losses: 4 (May 27-30, June 24-27, August 9-13).
Consecutive games with at least one hit: 14, Ken Caminiti (April 27-May 14), Jeff Bagwell (April 24-May 8).
Wins by pitcher: 8, Jose Lima (April 14-May 23).

ATTENDANCE

Home: 2,706,020.
Road: 2,056,627.
Highest (home): 54,037 (September 28 vs. Cincinnati).
Highest (road): 60,516 (July 31 vs. San Diego).
Lowest (home): 17,064 (May 10 vs. Pittsburgh).
Lowest (road): 8,302 (September 5 vs. Montreal).

LOS ANGELES DODGERS

DAY BY DAY

Date	Opp.	Res.	Score	(inn.*)	Hits	Opp. hits	Winning pitcher	Losing pitcher	Save	Record	Pos.	GB
4-5	Ari.	W	8-6	(11)	13	12	Shaw	Frascatore		1-0	T1st	...
4-6	Ari.	W	3-2	(10)	10	5	Mills	Anderson		2-0	T1st	...
4-7	Ari.	W	6-4		12	7	Valdes	Benes	Shaw	3-0	T1st	...
4-8	Col.	L	2-4		5	5	Bohanon	Perez	Veres	3-1	2nd	1.0
4-9	Col.	W	9-6		17	9	Dreifort	Thomson	Shaw	4-1	2nd	1.0
4-10	Col.	W	2-0		5	3	Brown	Kile	Shaw	5-1	T1st	...
4-12	At Ari.	L	6-12		11	10	Benes	Park		5-2	2nd	1.0
4-13	At Ari.	L	6-7	(16)	11	21	Chouinard	Mlicki		5-3	2nd	1.0
4-14	At Ari.	L	2-6		4	11	Daal	Perez		5-4	2nd	1.0
4-15	At Ari.	W	8-1		8	2	Dreifort	Johnson		6-4	2nd	1.0
4-16	At S.D.	L	0-3		5	11	Ashby	Brown		6-5	2nd	1.0
4-17	At S.D.	W	7-3		8	9	Park	Reyes		7-5	2nd	1.0
4-18	At S.D.	L	3-4		8	8	Miceli	Masaoka	Hoffman	7-6	2nd	1.0
4-19	Atl.	L	3-11		8	18	Smoltz	Perez		7-7	T2nd	2.0
4-20	Atl.	W	5-4		10	4	Dreifort	Millwood	Shaw	8-7	T2nd	1.0
4-21	Atl.	L	4-11	(12)	7	13	Remlinger	Kubenka		8-8	3rd	2.0
4-23	StL.	L	5-12		11	11	Jimenez	Park		8-9	3rd	2.5
4-24	StL.	W	6-1		8	6	Valdes	Osborne		9-9	3rd	2.5
4-25	StL.	L	4-6		8	9	Bottenfield	Dreifort	Acevedo	9-10	3rd	3.5
4-27	At Mil.	W	3-2		7	6	Brown	Roque	Shaw	10-10	3rd	3.5
4-28	At Mil.	W	3-2		10	11	Park	Woodard	Shaw	11-10	2nd	3.5
4-29	At Mil.	W	10-4		13	8	Valdes	Eldred		12-10	2nd	3.5
4-30	At Phi.	W	4-3		8	9	Perez	Byrd	Shaw	13-10	2nd	2.5
5-1	At Phi.	W	12-6		12	13	Dreifort	Spoljaric		14-10	2nd	1.5
5-2	At Phi.	L	3-12		8	13	Schilling	Brown		14-11	2nd	1.5
5-3	At Mon.	W	7-0		13	7	Park	Hermanson		15-11	2nd	0.5
5-4	At Mon.	L	1-2		4	7	Pavano	Valdes	Urbina	15-12	2nd	1.5
5-5	At Mon.	W	8-2		13	4	Arnold	Vazquez		16-12	2nd	0.5
5-7	Fla.	L	3-6		9	8	Springer	Dreifort	Mantei	16-13	2nd	1.5
5-8	Fla.	W	8-1		14	3	Brown	Hernandez		17-13	2nd	1.5
5-9	Fla.	L	4-6		6	7	Edmondson	Borbon	Mantei	17-14	2nd	1.5
5-10	Chi.	W	4-3		7	12	Valdes	Trachsel	Shaw	18-14	2nd	1.5
5-11	Chi.	L	5-10		9	11	Farnsworth	Perez		18-15	3rd	1.5
5-12	Chi.	W	3-2		8	5	Arnold	Beck		19-15	3rd	1.5
5-14	At StL.	W	7-3		10	8	Brown	Jimenez		20-15	2nd	0.5
5-15	At StL.	L	5-8		12	12	Bottenfield	Park		20-16	3rd	0.5
5-16	At StL.	L	4-5		9	8	Bottalico	Shaw		20-17	3rd	1.5
5-18	Hou.	L	3-11		9	12	Lima	Perez		20-18	3rd	2.0
5-19	Hou.	W	5-2		8	5	Brown	Reynolds		21-18	3rd	1.0
5-20	Hou.	L	3-4	(10)	9	6	Wagner	Shaw		21-19	3rd	1.5
5-21	StL.	L	6-10		7	10	Acevedo	Valdes	Aybar	21-20	3rd	2.5
5-22	StL.	W	10-7		14	12	Dreifort	Sodowsky	Shaw	22-20	3rd	2.5
5-23	StL.	L	3-8		11	14	Oliver	Perez		22-21	3rd	2.5
5-25	At Cin.	L	2-3		7	5	Parris	Brown	Graves	22-22	3rd	3.5
5-26	At Cin.	W	9-3		10	7	Park	Tomko		23-22	3rd	3.5
5-27	At Cin.	W	4-3		8	7	Valdes	Harnisch	Shaw	24-22	3rd	2.5
5-28	At Atl.	L	2-4		6	8	Perez	Dreifort	Rocker	24-23	3rd	3.0
5-29	At Atl.	W	2-1		7	5	Perez	Glavine	Shaw	25-23	3rd	3.0
5-30	At Atl.	W	5-4	(11)	9	8	Borbon	Remlinger	Shaw	26-23	3rd	3.0
5-31	At Pit.	L	4-5		9	7	Wilkins	Arnold	Williams	26-24	3rd	4.0
6-1	At Pit.	L	2-4		7	8	Schmidt	Valdes	Williams	26-25	3rd	4.0
6-2	At Pit.	L	4-8		8	11	Ritchie	Dreifort		26-26	3rd	5.0
6-4	Ana.	W	5-4		11	10	Brown	Olivares	Shaw	27-26	3rd	5.0
6-5	Ana.	W	7-4		12	7	Masaoka	Belcher	Shaw	28-26	3rd	4.0
6-6	Ana.	L	5-7		9	11	Hill	Perez	Percival	28-27	3rd	5.0
6-7	Tex.	L	2-3		6	10	Sele	Valdes	Wetteland	28-28	3rd	5.0
6-8	Tex.	L	6-7	(13)	11	16	Zimmerman	Mills	Munoz	28-29	3rd	5.0
6-9	Tex.	W	7-2		11	5	Brown	Clark		29-29	3rd	5.0
6-11	At Oak.	L	6-12		9	16	Oquist	Perez	Mathews	29-30	3rd	6.0
6-12	At Oak.	L	3-4		12	8	Rogers	Valdes	Taylor	29-31	3rd	6.0
6-13	At Oak.	L	3-9		10	8	Hudson	Dreifort		29-32	3rd	7.0
6-15	Pit.	L	1-11		7	14	Ritchie	Brown		29-33	4th	8.5
6-16	Pit.	W	6-5		12	11	Borbon	Clontz	Shaw	30-33	4th	8.5
6-17	Pit.	L	3-8		5	14	Benson	Park		30-34	4th	9.0
6-18	Phi.	L	1-2		4	6	Schilling	Valdes	Gomes	30-35	4th	9.0
6-19	Phi.	W	8-1		13	7	Dreifort	Person		31-35	4th	9.0
6-20	Phi.	W	3-2		6	5	Brown	Ogea	Shaw	32-35	4th	8.0
6-22	S.D.	L	1-4		7	7	Hitchcock	Park	Hoffman	32-36	4th	7.5
6-23	S.D.	L	2-6		5	7	Williams	Valdes	Hoffman	32-37	4th	7.5
6-24	S.D.	L	1-2		5	6	Ashby	Dreifort	Miceli	32-38	4th	8.5
6-25	At S.F.	W	4-2		9	6	Brown	Estes	Shaw	33-38	4th	7.5
6-26	At S.F.	W	7-6		15	11	Mills	Nen	Shaw	34-38	4th	6.5
6-27	At S.F.	L	7-8		12	14	Gardner	Park	Nen	34-39	5th	7.5
6-29	At S.D.	L	3-4	(12)	5	13	Wall	Maddux		34-40	5th	7.5
6-30	At S.D.	L	2-11		8	14	Boehringer	Brown		34-41	5th	7.5
7-1	At S.D.	L	3-6		5	10	Clement	Dreifort	Hoffman	34-42	5th	8.5
7-2	S.F.	L	3-6		9	8	Brock	Perez	Nen	34-43	5th	9.5
7-3	S.F.	L	1-9		4	12	Gardner	Park		34-44	5th	10.5
7-4	S.F.	W	7-1		11	5	Valdes	Rueter		35-44	5th	9.5

1999 REVIEW

HIGHLIGHTS

High point: The Dodgers won five of their first six games. Raul Mondesi was powering the club with his bat, and the pitching staff appeared to be as good as advertised—maybe better.

Low point: When Mondesi blasted manager Davey Johnson and GM Kevin Malone in an expletive-filled tirade on August 11 at Montreal. The right fielder said Johnson and Malone treated him unfairly, and he demanded to be traded. The comments rocked the organization.

Turning point: After the 5-1 start, the Dodgers went 3-7 against the Diamondbacks, Padres and Braves. Their many deficiencies were exposed during that span, including catcher Todd Hundley's ineffectiveness against baserunners. Bothered by late-1997 surgery on his right elbow, Hundley threw out only 18 percent of basestealers.

Most valuable player: Outfielder Gary Sheffield. He made a successful switch from right field to left and had an outstanding offensive season, batting .301 with 34 home runs and 101 RBIs. He became the second player in Dodgers history to bat at least .300 with 30 homers, 100 RBIs, 100 runs and 100 walks (the other: Duke Snider, who did it for Brooklyn in 1955).

Most valuable pitcher: Righthander Kevin Brown. The Dodgers got their money's worth after making Brown the game's highest-paid player with a seven-year, $105 million contract. Brown went 18-9 with a 3.00 ERA, and he struck out 221 batters (walking only 59) in 252.1 innings.

Most improved player: Third baseman Adrian Beltre. Predictably, he had struggled the year before after being rushed to the big leagues from Class AA. But Beltre didn't disappoint after Dodgers officials committed to him as the everyday third baseman—he batted .275 with 15 homers, 27 doubles and 67 RBIs.

Most pleasant surprise: Rookie righthander Eric Gagne had a 2.10 ERA in five starts after being promoted from Class AA (where he was 12-4 and named the organization's minor league pitcher of the year).

Key injuries: Outfielder Todd Hollandsworth missed three weeks because of a strained right hamstring. Pitcher Robinson Checo was sidelined two months due to a strained right groin. Second baseman Eric Young was out a month due to various leg injuries.

Notable: First baseman Eric Karros established career highs in batting (.304), hits (176), RBIs (112) and doubles (40). He also matched his career best in homers with 34. ... Mark Grudzielanek finished the season with a team-high .326 average, the highest mark for a shortstop in franchise history. ... Manager Johnson used 109 lineups.

—JASON REID

MISCELLANEOUS

RECORDS

1999 regular-season record: 77-85 (3rd in N.L. West); 37-44 at home; 40-41 on road; 21-23 vs. N.L. East; 26-26 vs. N.L. Central; 22-29 vs. N.L. West; 8-7 vs. A.L. West; 24-25 vs. lefthanded starters; 53-60 vs. righthanded starters; 63-72 on grass; 14-13 on turf; 25-21 in daytime; 52-64 at night; 21-27 in one-run games; 4-12 in extra-inning games; 0-1-0 in doubleheaders.

Team record past five years: 416-376 (.525, ranks 3rd in league in that span).

TEAM LEADERS

Batting average: Mark Grudzielanek (.326).
At-bats: Raul Mondesi (601).
Runs: Gary Sheffield (103).
Hits: Eric Karros (176).
Total bases: Eric Karros (318).
Doubles: Eric Karros (40).
Triples: Adrian Beltre, Mark Grudzielanek, Raul Mondesi (5).
Home runs: Eric Karros, Gary Sheffield (34).
Runs batted in: Eric Karros (112).
Stolen bases: Eric Young (51).
Slugging percentage: Eric Karros (.550).
On-base percentage: Gary Sheffield (.407).
Wins: Kevin Brown (18).
Earned-run average: Kevin Brown (3.00).
Complete games: Kevin Brown (5).
Shutouts: Kevin Brown, Darren Dreifort, Ismael Valdes (1).
Saves: Jeff Shaw (34).
Innings pitched: Kevin Brown (252.1).
Strikeouts: Kevin Brown (221).

Date	Opp.	Res.	Score	(inn.*)	Hits	Opp. hits	Winning pitcher	Losing pitcher	Save	Record	Pos.	GB
7-5	At Col.	L	4-8		11	14	Kile	Brown		35-45	5th	10.5
7-6	At Col.	L	2-5		6	10	Astacio	Dreifort		35-46	5th	11.5
7-7	At Col.	L	5-7		11	14	DeJean	Arnold	Veres	35-47	5th	11.5
7-8	At Col.	W	11-8		12	12	Park	Bohanon	Shaw	36-47	5th	11.0
7-9	Sea.	W	5-0		11	7	Valdes	Garcia		37-47	5th	11.0
7-10	Sea.	W	2-1		6	3	Shaw	Paniagua		38-47	5th	11.0
7-11	Sea.	W	14-3		15	6	Dreifort	Fassero	Masaoka	39-47	5th	10.0
7-15	At Ana.	L	6-7	(10)	12	10	Petkovsek	Mills		39-48	5th	10.0
7-16	At Ana.	W	3-1		5	5	Valdes	Olivares	Shaw	40-48	5th	9.0
7-17	At Ana.	W	13-3		14	7	Park	Sparks		41-48	T4th	9.0
7-18	At Pit.	L	5-6	(10)	14	11	Sauerbeck	Mills		41-49	T4th	9.0
7-19	At Pit.	W	12-7		14	6	Dreifort	Silva		42-49	4th	8.0
7-20	At Pit.	W	8-4		13	7	Brown	Clontz		43-49	4th	7.0
7-21	Col.	L	4-5		8	13	Astacio	Valdes	Veres	43-50	4th	8.0
7-22†	Col.	L	1-4		3	8	Jones	Park	Veres	43-51		
7-22‡	Col.	L	11-12		15	13	Lee	Masaoka	Veres	43-52	5th	8.5
7-23	At Ari.	L	1-10		2	11	Daal	Perez		43-53	5th	9.5
7-24	At Ari.	L	0-3		6	7	Anderson	Dreifort	Mantei	43-54	5th	10.0
7-25	At Ari.	W	2-1		8	3	Brown	Johnson	Shaw	44-54	T4th	9.0
7-26	Cin.	L	3-5	(10)	8	13	Belinda	Shaw		44-55	T4th	10.0
7-27	Cin.	L	3-5	(10)	10	15	Graves	Mills	Williamson	44-56	T4th	11.0
7-28	Cin.	W	9-1		13	7	Checo	Reyes	Arnold	45-56	4th	11.0
7-29	Cin.	L	5-7		9	14	Harnisch	Dreifort	Williamson	45-57	T4th	11.5
7-30	Ari.	L	5-6		11	9	Chouinard	Shaw	Mantei	45-58	5th	12.5
7-31	Ari.	L	2-4		6	9	Johnson	Valdes		45-59	5th	13.5
8-1	Ari.	W	4-2		11	9	Masaoka	Benes	Shaw	46-59	5th	12.5
8-3	At Hou.	L	2-7		6	10	Hampton	Dreifort		46-60	5th	13.0
8-4	At Hou.	W	2-1		4	4	Brown	Holt		47-60	T4th	13.0
8-5	At Hou.	L	0-7		5	11	Reynolds	Valdes		47-61	5th	13.5
8-6	At N.Y.	L	1-2		5	4	Dotel	Park	Benitez	47-62	5th	13.5
8-7	At N.Y.	W	7-6		13	11	Borbon	Taylor	Shaw	48-62	T4th	13.5
8-8	At N.Y.	W	14-3		14	7	Dreifort	Reed		49-62	4th	13.5
8-9	At N.Y.	W	9-2		13	6	Brown	Hershiser		50-62	4th	13.5
8-10	At Mon.	L	4-6		7	8	Thurman	Valdes	Urbina	50-63	4th	14.5
8-11	At Mon.	W	9-7		11	15	Maddux	Ayala	Shaw	51-63	4th	14.5
8-12	At Mon.	W	10-5		11	10	Judd	Hermanson		52-63	T3rd	14.0
8-13	Atl.	L	3-7		5	12	Millwood	Dreifort		52-64	T3rd	14.0
8-14	Atl.	W	8-1		14	5	Brown	Smoltz		53-64	T3rd	13.0
8-15	Atl.	L	4-5	(11)	12	10	Remlinger	Arnold	Rocker	53-65	4th	14.0
8-16	Fla.	L	5-7		11	8	Nunez	Park		53-66	4th	15.0
8-17	Fla.	L	1-6		7	11	Burnett	Judd	Springer	53-67	4th	16.0
8-18	Fla.	W	7-0		11	7	Dreifort	Meadows		54-67	4th	16.0
8-20	At Phi.	W	8-5	(10)	5	12	Mills	Gomes		55-67	T3rd	15.0
8-21	At Phi.	L	5-6	(11)	12	10	Gomes	Masaoka		55-68	T3rd	16.0
8-22	At Phi.	W	9-7		12	9	Park	Shumaker	Shaw	56-68	3rd	16.0
8-23	At Mil.	W	8-4		8	9	Dreifort	Nomo	Shaw	57-68	3rd	16.0
8-24	At Mil.	W	5-2		11	4	Judd	Karl	Shaw	58-68	3rd	16.0
8-25	At Mil.	L	7-9		9	9	Plunk	Borbon	Wickman	58-69	3rd	17.0
8-27	Chi.	W	9-0		13	7	Valdes	Trachsel		59-69	3rd	16.5
8-28	Chi.	W	4-3		7	8	Park	Lorraine	Shaw	60-69	3rd	16.5
8-29	Chi.	L	0-6		2	9	Farnsworth	Dreifort		60-70	3rd	17.5
8-30	Mil.	W	6-1		8	9	Brown	Pulsipher		61-70	3rd	17.5
8-31	Mil.	W	5-3		12	8	Judd	Peterson	Shaw	62-70	3rd	16.5
9-1	Mil.	L	4-5		7	8	Eldred	Valdes	Wickman	62-71	3rd	16.5
9-3	At Chi.	W	8-6		9	12	Park	Sanders	Shaw	63-71	3rd	15.5
9-4	At Chi.	W	6-0		11	2	Brown	Farnsworth		64-71	3rd	15.5
9-5	At Chi.	W	4-1		6	7	Dreifort	Lieber	Shaw	65-71	3rd	15.5
9-6	At Fla.	L	6-8		10	15	Meadows	Valdes	Alfonseca	65-72	3rd	16.0
9-7	At Fla.	L	1-2		7	6	Sanchez	Herges	Alfonseca	65-73	3rd	17.0
9-8	At Fla.	L	4-5	(13)	13	12	Medina	Masaoka		65-74	3rd	18.0
9-9	N.Y.	L	1-3		2	7	Hershiser	Brown	Benitez	65-75	4th	18.0
9-10	N.Y.	W	3-1		6	6	Dreifort	Leiter	Shaw	66-75	4th	18.0
9-11	N.Y.	L	2-6		7	11	Yoshii	Valdes		66-76	4th	19.0
9-12	N.Y.	L	3-10		14	12	Rogers	Gagne		66-77	4th	20.0
9-13	Mon.	W	12-4		15	10	Park	Smith		67-77	4th	20.0
9-14	Mon.	L	0-3		1	9	Vazquez	Brown		67-78	4th	21.0
9-15	Mon.	L	7-10		14	12	Powell	Arnold	Urbina	67-79	4th	21.0
9-17	At Col.	L	10-18		11	20	Hackman	Checo		67-80	4th	21.0
9-18	At Col.	W	5-4		9	10	Park	Astacio	Shaw	68-80	4th	21.0
9-19	At Col.	W	5-2	(8)	8	7	Brown	Thomson	Borbon	69-80	4th	21.0
9-20	S.F	W	6-5		7	7	Borbon	Embree		70-80	4th	20.0
9-21	S.F	W	9-4		11	6	Williams	Rueter		71-80	4th	20.0
9-22	S.F	L	4-5		6	8	Gardner	Borbon	Nen	71-81	4th	21.0
9-23	S.F	W	5-3		9	5	Park	Hernandez	Shaw	72-81	T3rd	20.5
9-24	S.D.	W	5-1		10	6	Brown	Hitchcock		73-81	3rd	20.5
9-25	S.D.	L	2-3		5	5	Williams	Herges	Hoffman	73-82	T3rd	21.5
9-26	S.D.	W	10-7		13	6	Checo	Miceli		74-82	3rd	21.5
9-28	At S.F	W	6-3		12	5	Park	Nathan		75-82	3rd	22.0
9-29	At S.F	L	1-5		12	7	Hernandez	Brown	Patrick	75-83	3rd	22.0
9-30	At S.F	W	9-4		15	8	Williams	Estes		76-83	3rd	22.0
10-1	At Hou.	W	5-1		9	7	Gagne	Reynolds		77-83	3rd	21.0
10-2	At Hou.	L	0-3		9	6	Lima	Park	Wagner	77-84	3rd	22.0
10-3	At Hou.	L	4-9		7	8	Hampton	Checo		77-85	3rd	23.0

Monthly records: April (13-10), May (13-14), June (8-17), July (11-18), August (17-11), September (14-13), October (1-2).
*Innings, if other than nine. † First game of a doubleheader. ‡ Second game of a doubleheader.

MEMORABLE GAMES

April 5 at Los Angeles

Opening Day featured a marquee matchup between new staff aces Kevin Brown and Randy Johnson. But Raul Mondesi was stole the show, hitting hit two home runs—including a two-out, two-run, 11th-inning blast that capped a dramatic 8-6, comeback victory at Dodger Stadium. Mondesi's three-run homer in the ninth tied the score, sending the game into extra innings.

Arizona	AB	R	H	RBI	Los Angeles	AB	R	H	RBI
S.Finley, cf	6	1	2	0	E.Young, 2b	3	1	1	0
J.Bell, 2b	5	1	2	3	Grudzilnk, ss	2	0	0	0
T.Lee, 1b	6	1	2	0	Masaoka, p	0	0	0	0
M.Williams, 3b	4	0	1	1	Mills, p	0	0	0	0
L.Gonzalez, lf	5	0	1	0	D.Hansen, ph	1	1	1	0
Dellucci, lf	0	0	0	0	Shaw, p	0	0	0	0
Gilkey, rf	5	2	3	2	R.Wilkins, ph	1	0	0	0
D.Powell, rf	0	0	0	0	Sheffield, lf	5	2	1	0
T.Batista, ss	4	0	0	0	Mondesi, rf	5	2	4	6
Stinnett, c	5	1	1	0	D.White, cf	5	1	2	1
Ra.Johnson, p	3	0	0	0	Karros, 1b	4	0	1	1
E.Young, ph	0	0	0	0	Hundley, c	5	0	1	0
Holmes, p	0	0	0	0	Beltre, 3b	5	0	1	0
Swindell, p	0	0	0	0	K.Brown, p	2	0	0	0
Reynoso, p	0	0	0	0	Borbon, p	0	0	0	0
Olson, p	0	0	0	0	Rojas, p	0	0	0	0
A.Fox, ph	1	0	0	0	J.Vizcno, ph-ss	3	1	1	0
Frascatore, p	0	0	0	0					
Totals	**44**	**6**	**12**	**6**	**Totals**	**41**	**8**	**13**	**8**

Arizona....................................0 0 0 1 0 5 0 0 0 0 0—6
Los Angeles..............................1 0 0 1 0 0 0 1 3 0 2—8

E—L.Gonzalez (1). DP—Arizona 2, Los Angeles 1. LOB—Arizona 10, Los Angeles 9. 2B—T.Lee (1), L.Gonzalez (1), Sheffield (1). HR—J.Bell (1), Gilkey 2 (2), Mondesi 2 (2), D.White (1). SB—T.Lee (1), E.Young 2 (2), Karros (1). CS—E.Young (1).

Arizona	IP	H	R	ER	BB	SO
Ra.Johnson	7	5	2	2	6	9
Holmes	0.1	3	1	1	0	1
Swindell (H, 1)	0.1	0	0	0	0	1
Reynoso (H, 1)	0.2	2	2	2	0	0
Olson (BS 1)	0.2	1	1	1	0	2
Frascatore (L, 0-1)	1.2	2	2	2	1	3

Los Angeles	IP	H	R	ER	BB	SO
K.Brown	5.2	10	5	5	2	7
Borbon	0.1	2	1	1	0	0
Rojas	1	0	0	0	0	2
Masaoka	1	0	0	0	2	0
Mills	1	0	0	0	0	1
Shaw (W, 1-0)	2	0	0	0	0	2

HBP—M.Williams by K.Brown, E.Young by Ra.Johnson. U—HP, Froemming. 1B, M.Hirschbeck. 2B, Rapuano. 3B, Wegner. T—3:45. A—53,109.

October 3 at Houston

The Dodgers closed their season with an embarrassing performance, helping the Astros clinch the N.L. Central division title on the final day of the season. Pitcher Robinson Checo, starting for the first time in two months after recovering from a strained right groin, was unable to get out of the first inning in a 9-4 loss. Manager Davey Johnson was criticized for starting the overmatched Checo with the Astros competing for a playoff spot.

Los Angeles	AB	R	H	RBI	Houston	AB	R	H	RBI
E.Young, 2b	4	1	0	0	Biggio, 2b	3	0	1	0
Grudzielnk, ss	5	0	2	1	Javier, rf-lf	4	2	1	1
Mondesi, rf	5	0	2	1	Bagwell, 1b	3	3	1	1
Karros, 1b	4	0	0	0	Everett, cf-rf	4	1	1	0
D.White, cf	3	0	0	0	Caminiti, 3b	2	2	1	2
Beltre, 3b	4	1	1	0	D.Ward, lf	2	0	1	3
Hubbard, lf	3	1	0	0	Mieske, ph	0	0	0	0
LoDuca, c	3	0	0	0	G.Barkr, pr-cf	2	0	1	1
Checo, p	0	0	0	0	Eusebio, c	3	0	0	1
Herges, p	1	0	0	0	Gutierrez, ss	4	0	0	0
Cromer, ph	0	0	0	0	Hampton, p	3	1	1	0
Masaoka, p	0	0	0	0	Spiers, ph	1	0	0	0
Arnold, p	0	0	0	0	J.Cabrera, p	0	0	0	0
Borbon, p	0	0	0	0	Ja.Powell, p	0	0	0	0
J.Vizcaino, ph	1	0	1	0					
Mills, p	0	0	0	0					
M.Maddux, p	0	0	0	0					
D.Hansen, ph	1	1	1	2					
Totals	**34**	**4**	**7**	**4**	**Totals**	**31**	**9**	**8**	**9**

Los Angeles..............................0 0 1 0 0 0 0 0 3 —4
Houston...................................4 0 1 0 1 3 0 0 x —9

E—Arnold (2), D.Ward (2), G.Barker (1). LOB—Los Angeles 8, Houston 9. 2B—D.Hansen (8), Biggio (56), Javier (4), D.Ward (6). HR—Caminiti (13). SB—E.Young (51), D.White (19), Bagwell (30). CS—Biggio (14). S—Biggio.

Los Angeles	IP	H	R	ER	BB	SO
Checo (L, 2-2)	0.1	1	4	4	5	1
Herges	3.2	2	1	1	1	5
Masaoka	0.1	1	1	1	2	1
Arnold	1.1	2	3	2	1	1
Borbon	0.1	1	0	0	0	1
Mills	1	0	0	0	0	2
M.Maddux	1	1	0	0	1	1

Houston	IP	H	R	ER	BB	SO
Hampton (W, 22-4)	7	3	1	1	4	8
J.Cabrera	1	1	0	0	0	2
Ja.Powell	1	3	3	3	1	1

WP—Arnold, M.Maddux, Hampton. U—HP, Gorman. 1B, Cuzzi. 2B, Crawford. 3B, Marquez. T—3:06. A—52,033.

INDIVIDUAL STATISTICS

BATTING

Name	G	TPA	AB	R	H	TB	2B	3B	HR	RBI	Avg.	Obp.	Slg.	SH	SF	HP	BB	IBB	SO	SB	CS	GDP	vs RHP AB	vs RHP Avg.	vs RHP HR	vs RHP RBI	vs LHP AB	vs LHP Avg.	vs LHP HR	vs LHP RBI
Mondesi, Raul	159	680	601	98	152	290	29	5	33	99	.253	.332	.483	0	5	3	71	6	134	36	9	3	462	.247	27	79	139	.273	6	20
Karros, Eric	153	639	578	74	176	318	40	0	34	112	.304	.362	.550	0	6	2	53	0	119	8	5	18	432	.303	23	78	146	.308	11	34
Sheffield, Gary	152	663	549	103	165	287	20	0	34	101	.301	.407	.523	0	9	4	101	4	64	11	5	10	403	.288	26	68	146	.336	8	33
Beltre, Adrian	152	614	538	84	148	230	27	5	15	67	.275	.352	.428	4	5	6	61	12	105	18	7	4	403	.290	14	52	135	.230	1	15
Grudzielanek, Mark	123	534	488	72	159	213	23	5	7	46	.326	.376	.436	2	3	10	31	1	65	6	6	13	344	.299	5	32	144	.389	2	14
White, Devon	134	526	474	60	127	193	20	2	14	68	.268	.337	.407	0	2	11	39	2	88	19	5	10	335	.260	9	46	139	.288	5	22
Young, Eric	119	534	456	73	128	162	24	2	2	41	.281	.371	.355	6	4	5	63	0	26	51	22	12	324	.275	1	30	132	.295	1	11
Hundley, Todd	114	428	376	49	78	164	14	0	24	55	.207	.295	.436	1	3	4	44	3	113	3	0	5	319	.226	24	50	57	.105	0	5
Vizcaino, Jose	94	298	266	27	67	79	9	0	1	29	.252	.304	.297	9	2	1	20	0	23	2	1	9	196	.224	1	20	70	.329	0	9
Hollandsworth, Todd	92	287	261	39	74	117	12	2	9	32	.284	.345	.448	0	1	1	24	1	61	5	2	2	232	.280	7	26	29	.310	2	6
Pena, Angel	43	135	120	14	25	43	6	0	4	21	.208	.276	.358	1	2	0	12	0	24	0	1	6	68	.191	0	6	52	.231	4	15
Counsell, Craig	50	122	108	20	28	34	6	0	0	9	.259	.311	.315	3	2	0	9	0	14	1	0	1	93	.247	0	5	15	.333	0	4
Hansen, Dave	100	136	107	14	27	43	8	1	2	17	.252	.404	.402	0	1	2	26	0	20	0	0	2	92	.250	2	12	15	.267	0	5
Hubbard, Trenidad	82	120	105	23	33	41	5	0	1	13	.314	.387	.390	1	1	0	13	1	24	4	3	2	51	.353	0	7	54	.278	1	6
LoDuca, Paul	36	110	95	11	22	32	1	0	3	11	.232	.312	.337	1	2	2	10	4	9	1	2	3	41	.171	1	5	54	.278	2	6
Brown, Kevin	35	94	78	1	5	5	0	0	0	3	.064	.086	.064	13	1	0	2	0	24	0	0	0	54	.037	0	0	24	.125	0	3
Dreifort, Darren	30	69	62	7	13	20	4	0	1	9	.210	.246	.323	4	0	0	3	0	23	1	0	2	46	.239	1	8	16	.125	0	1
Park, Chan Ho	33	69	59	4	9	11	2	0	0	6	.153	.175	.186	6	2	0	2	0	26	0	0	0	47	.128	0	4	12	.250	0	2
Valdes, Ismael	32	69	58	1	5	5	0	0	0	2	.086	.102	.086	10	0	0	1	0	18	1	0	2	47	.085	0	2	11	.091	0	0
Cromer, Tripp	33	57	52	5	10	16	0	0	2	8	.192	.263	.308	0	0	0	5	0	10	0	0	4	38	.158	1	5	14	.286	1	3
Cora, Alex	11	31	30	2	5	6	1	0	0	3	.167	.194	.200	0	0	1	0	0	4	0	0	1	27	.148	0	3	3	.333	0	0
Perez, Carlos	17	32	27	2	8	13	2	0	1	2	.296	.345	.481	3	0	0	2	0	8	0	0	0	15	.400	0	1	12	.167	1	1
Brumfield, Jacob	18	17	17	4	5	7	0	1	0	1	.294	.294	.412	0	0	0	0	0	5	0	0	0	10	.400	0	1	7	.143	0	0
Arnold, Jamie	36	11	10	1	2	2	0	0	0	1	.200	.200	.200	1	0	0	0	0	3	0	0	0	4	.500	0	1	6	.000	0	0
Gagne, Eric	5	10	10	1	2	2	0	0	0	1	.200	.200	.200	0	0	0	0	0	3	0	0	0	8	.125	0	0	2	.500	0	1
Sanford, Chance	5	8	8	1	2	2	0	0	0	2	.250	.250	.250	0	0	0	0	0	1	0	0	0	8	.250	0	2	0	.000	0	0
Cookson, Brent	3	5	5	0	1	1	0	0	0	0	.200	.200	.200	0	0	0	0	0	1	0	0	0	2	.500	0	0	3	.000	0	0
Williams, Jeff	5	7	5	2	1	1	0	0	0	0	.200	.333	.200	1	0	0	1	0	4	0	0	0	3	.000	0	0	2	.500	0	0
Judd, Mike	7	9	5	0	0	0	0	0	0	0	.000	.167	.000	3	0	0	1	0	1	0	0	0	4	.000	0	0	1	.000	0	0
Wilkins, Rick	3	4	4	0	0	0	0	0	0	0	.000	.000	.000	0	0	0	0	0	2	0	0	0	3	.000	0	0	1	.000	0	0
Masaoka, Onan	54	5	4	0	0	0	0	0	0	0	.000	.000	.000	1	0	0	0	0	2	0	0	0	3	.000	0	0	1	.000	0	0
Checo, Robinson	9	4	3	0	1	1	0	0	0	2	.333	.333	.333	1	0	0	0	0	2	0	0	0	1	.000	0	0	2	.500	0	2
Mills, Alan	68	2	2	0	0	0	0	0	0	0	.000	.000	.000	0	0	0	0	0	1	0	0	0	2	.000	0	0	0	.000	0	0
Borbon, Pedro	70	3	2	0	0	0	0	0	0	0	.000	.000	.000	1	0	0	0	0	1	0	0	0	2	.000	0	0	0	.000	0	0
Mlicki, Dave	2	3	1	0	1	1	0	0	0	0	1.000	1.000	1.000	2	0	0	0	0	0	0	0	0	0	.000	0	0	1	1.000	0	0
Kubenka, Jeff	6	1	1	1	1	1	0	0	0	0	1.000	1.000	1.000	0	0	0	0	0	0	0	0	0	0	.000	0	0	1	1.000	0	0
Castro, Juan	2	1	1	0	0	0	0	0	0	0	.000	.000	.000	0	0	0	0	0	1	0	0	0	1	.000	0	0	0	.000	0	0
Herges, Matt	17	1	1	0	0	0	0	0	0	0	.000	.000	.000	0	0	0	0	0	1	0	0	0	0	.000	0	0	1	.000	0	0
Maddux, Mike	49	0	0	0	0	0	0	0	0	0	.000	.000	.000	0	0	0	0	0	0	0	0	0	0	.000	0	0	0	.000	0	0
Shaw, Jeff	64	0	0	0	0	0	0	0	0	0	.000	.000	.000	0	0	0	0	0	0	0	0	0	0	.000	0	0	0	.000	0	0
Rojas, Mel	5	0	0	0	0	0	0	0	0	0	.000	.000	.000	0	0	0	0	0	0	0	0	0	0	.000	0	0	0	.000	0	0
Osuna, Antonio	5	0	0	0	0	0	0	0	0	0	.000	.000	.000	0	0	0	0	0	0	0	0	0	0	.000	0	0	0	.000	0	0
Bochtler, Doug	12	0	0	0	0	0	0	0	0	0	.000	.000	.000	0	0	0	0	0	0	0	0	0	0	.000	0	0	0	.000	0	0

Players with more than one N.L. team

Name	G	TPA	AB	R	H	TB	2B	3B	HR	RBI	Avg.	Obp.	Slg.	SH	SF	HP	BB	IBB	SO	SB	CS	GDP	vs RHP AB	vs RHP Avg.	vs RHP HR	vs RHP RBI	vs LHP AB	vs LHP Avg.	vs LHP HR	vs LHP RBI
Counsell, Fla.	37	73	66	4	10	11	1	0	0	2	.152	.211	.167	2	0	0	5	0	10	0	0	1	93	.247	0	5	15	.333	0	4
Counsell, Fla.-L.A.	87	195	174	24	38	45	7	0	0	11	.218	.274	.259	5	2	0	14	0	24	1	0	2	150	.213	0	7	24	.250	0	4
Maddux, Mon.	4	0	0	0	0	0	0	0	0	0	.000	.000	.000	0	0	0	0	0	0	0	0	0	0	.000	0	0	0	.000	0	0
Maddux, Mon.-L.A.	53	0	0	0	0	0	0	0	0	0	.000	.000	.000	0	0	0	0	0	0	0	0	0	0	.000	0	0	0	.000	0	0
Rojas, Mon.	3	0	0	0	0	0	0	0	0	0	.000	.000	.000	0	0	0	0	0	0	0	0	0	0	.000	0	0	0	.000	0	0
Rojas, L.A.-Mon.	8	0	0	0	0	0	0	0	0	0	.000	.000	.000	0	0	0	0	0	0	0	0	0	0	.000	0	0	0	.000	0	0

PITCHING

Name	W	L	Pct.	ERA	IP	H	R	ER	HR	SH	SF	HB	BB	IBB	SO	G	GS	CG	ShO	GF	Sv	vs. RH AB	vs. RH Avg.	vs. RH HR	vs. RH RBI	vs. LH AB	vs. LH Avg.	vs. LH HR	vs. LH RBI
Brown, Kevin	18	9	.667	3.00	252.1	210	99	84	19	7	1	7	59	1	221	35	35	5	1	0	0	466	.189	12	40	478	.255	7	51
Valdes, Ismael	9	14	.391	3.98	203.1	213	97	90	32	9	8	6	58	2	143	32	32	2	1	0	0	454	.269	18	51	336	.271	14	39
Park, Chan Ho	13	11	.542	5.23	194.1	208	120	113	31	10	5	14	100	4	174	33	33	0	0	0	0	410	.207	13	50	344	.358	18	58
Dreifort, Darren	13	13	.500	4.79	178.2	177	105	95	20	8	2	7	76	2	140	30	29	1	1	0	0	372	.250	9	42	308	.273	11	48
Perez, Carlos	2	10	.167	7.43	89.2	116	77	74	23	6	3	6	39	1	40	17	16	0	0	0	0	270	.311	15	52	96	.333	8	18
Mills, Alan	3	4	.429	3.73	72.1	70	33	30	10	3	4	4	43	4	49	68	0	0	0	18	0	165	.230	7	29	103	.311	3	12
Arnold, Jamie	2	4	.333	5.48	69.0	81	50	42	6	3	0	6	34	2	26	36	3	0	0	18	1	157	.268	4	29	113	.345	2	21
Shaw, Jeff	2	4	.333	2.78	68.0	64	25	21	6	1	2	1	15	1	43	64	0	0	0	56	34	131	.282	3	16	134	.201	3	12
Masaoka, Onan	2	4	.333	4.32	66.2	55	33	32	8	1	2	2	47	3	61	54	0	0	0	12	1	156	.224	6	22	92	.217	2	11
Maddux, Mike	1	1	.500	3.29	54.2	54	21	20	5	2	2	4	19	2	41	49	0	0	0	19	0	123	.268	4	21	84	.250	1	6
Borbon, Pedro	4	3	.571	4.09	50.2	39	23	23	5	0	3	1	29	1	33	70	0	0	0	11	1	97	.258	3	16	90	.156	2	8
Gagne, Eric	1	1	.500	2.10	30.0	18	8	7	3	1	0	0	15	0	30	5	5	0	0	0	0	52	.154	2	6	51	.196	1	1
Judd, Mike	3	1	.750	5.46	28.0	30	17	17	4	0	0	1	12	0	22	7	4	0	0	0	0	65	.292	3	12	42	.262	1	4
Herges, Matt	0	2	.000	4.07	24.1	24	13	11	5	1	0	1	8	0	18	17	0	0	0	9	0	58	.259	2	5	36	.250	3	6
Williams, Jeff	2	0	1.000	4.08	17.2	12	10	8	2	1	0	0	9	0	7	5	3	0	0	1	0	46	.217	1	7	17	.118	1	2
Checo, Robinson	2	2	.500	10.34	15.2	24	20	18	5	0	0	0	13	1	11	9	2	0	0	1	0	50	.320	3	14	22	.364	2	9
Bochtler, Doug	0	0	.000	5.54	13.0	11	8	8	3	1	1	1	6	1	7	12	0	0	0	4	0	32	.094	2	3	17	.471	1	5
Kubenka, Jeff	0	1	.000	11.74	7.2	13	12	10	1	2	1	0	4	0	2	6	0	0	0	2	0	28	.393	1	7	7	.286	0	2
Mlicki, Dave	0	1	.000	4.91	7.1	10	4	4	1	0	0	0	2	0	1	2	0	0	0	0	0	18	.278	1	2	13	.385	0	1
Rojas, Mel	0	0	.000	12.60	5.0	5	7	7	3	0	0	0	3	1	3	5	0	0	0	2	0	13	.308	2	6	7	.143	1	1
Osuna, Antonio	0	0	.000	7.71	4.2	4	5	4	0	0	0	1	3	0	5	5	0	0	0	1	0	12	.333	0	3	6	.000	0	0

PITCHERS WITH MORE THAN ONE N.L. TEAM

Name	W	L	Pct.	ERA	IP	H	R	ER	HR	SH	SF	HB	BB	IBB	SO	G	GS	CG	ShO	GF	Sv	vs. RH AB	vs. RH Avg.	vs. RH HR	vs. RH RBI	vs. LH AB	vs. LH Avg.	vs. LH HR	vs. LH RBI
Maddux, Mon.	0	0	.000	9.00	5.0	9	5	5	1	0	0	1	3	0	4	4	0	0	0	2	0	123	.268	4	21	84	.250	1	6
Maddux, Mon.-L.A.	1	1	.500	3.77	59.2	63	26	25	6	2	2	5	22	2	45	53	0	0	0	2	0	129	.279	4	22	100	.270	2	9
Rojas, Mon.	0	0	.000	16.88	2.2	5	5	5	0	0	1	2	2	0	1	3	0	0	0	1	0	13	.308	2	6	7	.143	1	1
Rojas, L.A.-Mon.	0	0	.000	14.09	7.2	10	12	12	3	0	1	2	5	1	4	8	0	0	0	1	0	21	.333	2	9	11	.273	1	2

INDIVIDUAL STATISTICS

FIELDING

FIRST BASEMEN

Player	Pct.	G	PO	A	E	TC	DP
Karros, Eric	.991	151	1291	126	13	1430	108
Hansen, Dave	.982	20	52	4	1	57	6
Hollandsworth, Todd	.990	13	91	9	1	101	12
Cromer, Tripp	1.000	1	1	0	0	1	0

SECOND BASEMEN

Player	Pct.	G	PO	A	E	TC	DP
Young, Eric	.984	116	216	321	9	546	62
Counsell, Craig	.993	38	54	85	1	140	13
Vizcaino, Jose	.991	30	36	70	1	107	9
Cromer, Tripp	1.000	9	7	18	0	25	5
Cora, Alex	.857	3	3	9	2	14	2
Sanford, Chance	1.000	2	1	1	0	2	0
Castro, Juan	1.000	1	1	4	0	5	1
Hubbard, Trenidad	-	1	0	0	0	0	0

THIRD BASEMEN

Player	Pct.	G	PO	A	E	TC	DP
Beltre, Adrian	.932	152	121	274	29	424	24
Hansen, Dave	.900	13	5	13	2	20	0
Vizcaino, Jose	1.000	9	2	13	0	15	2
Cromer, Tripp	1.000	2	2	1	0	3	0

SHORTSTOPS

Player	Pct.	G	PO	A	E	TC	DP
Grudzielanek, Mark	.973	119	171	306	13	490	66
Vizcaino, Jose	.966	44	60	109	6	175	20
Cromer, Tripp	1.000	9	10	17	0	27	4
Cora, Alex	1.000	8	10	11	0	21	2
Counsell, Craig	1.000	2	0	1	0	1	0
Castro, Juan	-	1	0	0	0	0	0

OUTFIELDERS

Player	Pct.	G	PO	A	E	TC	DP
Mondesi, Raul	.982	158	315	7	6	328	5
Sheffield, Gary	.972	145	235	7	7	249	1
White, Devon	.986	128	273	3	4	280	1
Hollandsworth, Todd	.984	67	120	2	2	124	0
Hubbard, Trenidad	.980	51	49	1	1	51	0
Brumfield, Jacob	1.000	11	11	0	0	11	0
Cookson, Brent	1.000	3	4	0	0	4	0
Cromer, Tripp	1.000	2	1	0	0	1	0
Hansen, Dave	1.000	2	1	0	0	1	0
Vizcaino, Jose	-	1	0	0	0	0	0

CATCHERS

Player	Pct.	G	PO	A	E	TC	DP	PB
Hundley, Todd	.979	108	681	51	16	748	5	7
Pena, Angel	.989	43	233	26	3	262	5	6
LoDuca, Paul	.990	34	178	21	2	201	3	0
Hubbard, Trenidad	1.000	1	1	0	0	1	0	0
Wilkins, Rick	1.000	1	1	0	0	1	0	0

PITCHERS

Player	Pct.	G	PO	A	E	TC	DP
Borbon, Pedro	1.000	70	2	6	0	8	0
Mills, Alan	.833	68	3	7	2	12	2
Shaw, Jeff	1.000	64	10	4	0	14	1
Masaoka, Onan	.833	54	1	4	1	6	0
Maddux, Mike	.917	49	5	6	1	12	1
Arnold, Jamie	.917	36	4	18	2	24	5
Brown, Kevin	.935	35	41	46	6	93	2
Park, Chan Ho	1.000	33	15	33	0	48	4
Valdes, Ismael	.978	32	12	33	1	46	1
Dreifort, Darren	.936	30	18	26	3	47	2
Perez, Carlos	.905	17	4	15	2	21	0
Herges, Matt	1.000	17	2	2	0	4	0
Bochtler, Doug	1.000	12	1	3	0	4	0
Checo, Robinson	-	9	0	0	0	0	0
Judd, Mike	1.000	7	0	4	0	4	1
Kubenka, Jeff	1.000	6	0	3	0	3	0
Williams, Jeff	1.000	5	1	3	0	4	1
Gagne, Eric	1.000	5	2	0	0	2	0
Osuna, Antonio	1.000	5	0	1	0	1	0
Rojas, Mel	1.000	5	0	1	0	1	0
Mlicki, Dave	1.000	2	1	0	0	1	0

PITCHING AGAINST EACH CLUB

Pitcher	Ari. W-L	Atl. W-L	Chi. W-L	Cin. W-L	Col. W-L	Fla. W-L	Hou. W-L	Mil. W-L	Mon. W-L	N.Y. W-L	Phi. W-L	Pit. W-L	S.D. W-L	S.F. W-L	StL. W-L	A.L. W-L	Total W-L
Arnold, J.	0-0	0-1	1-0	0-0	0-1	0-0	0-0	0-0	1-1	0-0	0-0	0-0	0-0	0-0	0-0	0-0	2-4
Bochtler, D.	0-0	0-0	0-0	0-0	0-0	0-0	0-0	0-0	0-0	0-0	0-0	0-0	0-0	0-0	0-0	0-0	0-0
Borbon, P.	0-0	1-0	0-0	0-0	0-0	0-1	0-0	0-1	0-0	1-0	0-0	1-0	0-0	1-1	0-0	0-0	4-3
Brown, K.	1-0	1-0	1-0	0-1	2-1	1-0	2-0	2-0	0-1	1-1	1-1	1-2	1-1	1-0	0-0	2-0	18-9
Checo, R.	0-0	0-0	0-0	1-0	0-1	0-0	0-0	0-0	0-0	0-0	1-0	0-0	0-0	0-0	0-0	0-0	2-2
Dreifort, D.	1-1	1-2	1-1	0-1	1-1	0-1	0-1	1-0	2-0	2-0	1-1	0-2	0-0	1-1	0-0	1-1	13-13
Gagne, Eric	0-0	0-0	0-0	0-0	0-0	0-0	1-0	0-0	0-1	0-0	0-0	0-0	0-0	0-0	0-0	0-0	1-1
Herges, M.	0-0	0-0	0-0	0-0	0-0	0-0	0-0	0-0	0-0	0-0	0-0	0-1	0-0	0-1	0-0	0-0	0-2
Judd, Mike	0-0	0-1	0-0	0-0	0-0	0-0	0-0	0-0	0-0	0-0	0-0	0-0	0-0	0-0	0-0	0-0	3-1
Kubenka, J.	0-0	0-1	0-0	0-0	0-0	0-0	0-0	0-0	0-0	0-0	0-0	0-0	0-0	0-0	0-0	0-0	0-1
Maddux, M.	1-0	0-0	0-0	0-0	0-1	0-0	0-0	0-0	0-0	0-0	0-0	0-0	0-0	0-0	0-0	0-0	1-1
Masaoka, O.	1-0	0-0	0-0	0-0	0-1	0-0	0-0	0-1	0-0	0-0	0-0	0-1	0-0	0-1	0-0	1-0	2-4
Mills, A.	1-0	0-0	0-0	0-1	0-0	0-0	0-0	0-0	0-0	1-0	0-0	0-0	0-1	0-0	0-0	0-2	3-4
Mlicki, Dav.	0-1	0-0	0-0	0-0	0-0	0-0	0-0	0-0	0-0	0-0	0-0	0-0	0-0	0-1	0-0	0-0	0-2
Osuna, An.	0-0	0-0	0-0	0-0	0-0	0-0	0-0	0-0	0-0	0-0	0-0	0-0	0-0	0-0	0-0	0-0	0-0
Park, Chan Ho	0-1	0-0	2-0	1-0	2-1	0-0	0-1	0-1	1-0	2-0	0-1	1-0	1-1	2-2	0-0	1-0	13-11
Perez, Ca.	0-2	1-1	0-1	0-0	0-1	0-0	1-0	0-1	0-1	1-0	0-1	0-0	0-1	0-1	1-0	0-2	2-10
Rojas, M.	0-0	0-0	0-0	0-0	0-0	0-0	0-0	0-0	0-0	0-0	0-0	0-0	0-0	0-0	0-0	0-0	0-0
Shaw, J.	1-1	0-0	0-0	0-0	0-1	0-0	0-0	0-0	0-0	0-0	0-0	0-0	0-1	0-0	0-0	1-0	1-1
Valdes, I.	1-1	0-0	2-0	1-0	0-1	0-1	0-1	1-1	0-2	0-1	0-1	0-1	1-0	1-1	0-0	2-2	9-14
Williams, J.	0-0	0-0	0-0	0-0	0-0	0-1	0-0	0-0	0-0	0-0	0-0	0-0	0-0	0-1	0-0	0-0	0-2
Totals	6-7	4-5	7-2	3-4	5-8	2-7	3-6	7-2	5-4	4-4	6-3	3-6	3-9	8-5	3-6	8-7	77-85

INTERLEAGUE: Perez 0-1, Valdes 0-1, Dreifort 0-1 vs. Athletics; Valdes 1-0, Shaw 1-0, Dreifort 1-0 vs. Mariners; Brown 1-0, Valdes 0-1, Mills 0-1 vs. Rangers; Brown 1-0, Park 1-0, Masaoka 1-0, Valdes 1-0, Mills 0-1, Perez 0-1 vs. Angels. Total: 8-7.

MISCELLANEOUS

HOME RUNS BY PARK

At Anaheim (6): Karros 2, White 1, Mondesi 1, Hollandsworth 1, Pena 1.
At Arizona (6): Sheffield 3, Karros 2, Grudzielanek 1.
At Atlanta (3): White 1, Mondesi 1, Beltre 1.
At Chicago (NL) (7): Hundley 2, Grudzielanek 2, Sheffield 1, Karros 1, Mondesi 1.
At Cincinnati (5): Sheffield 1, Karros 1, Mondesi 1, Cromer 1, Beltre 1.
At Colorado (11): Karros 3, Sheffield 2, White 1, Hundley 1, Mondesi 1, Perez 1, Beltre 1, Pena 1.
At Florida (3): Mondesi 2, Karros 1.
At Houston (3): White 1, Sheffield 1, Beltre 1.
At Los Angeles (92): Mondesi 18, Karros 17, Sheffield 15, Hundley 10, White 8, Beltre 6, Hollandsworth 5, Grudzielanek 4, Hansen 2, Young 2, Pena 2, Vizcaino 1, Cromer 1, LoDuca 1.
At Milwaukee (4): Mondesi 1, Hubbard 1, LoDuca 1, Beltre 1.
At Montreal (8): Sheffield 3, Hundley 2, Beltre 2, Karros 1.
At New York (NL) (5): Mondesi 2, Sheffield 1, Dreifort 1, LoDuca 1.
At Oakland (2): Karros 2.
At Philadelphia (5): Mondesi 2, Sheffield 1, Hundley 1, Karros 1.
At Pittsburgh (10): Hundley 4, Hollandsworth 2, Sheffield 1, Karros 1, Mondesi 1, Beltre 1.
At San Diego (7): Sheffield 2, Karros 2, White 1, Hundley 1, Mondesi 1.
At San Francisco (10): Sheffield 3, Hundley 3, White 1, Mondesi 1, Hollandsworth 1, Beltre 1.
At St. Louis (0).

LOW-HIT GAMES

No-hitters: None.
One-hitters: None.
Two-hitters: Kevin Brown, September 4 vs. Chicago, W 6-0.

10-STRIKEOUT GAMES

Ismael Valdes 2, Kevin Brown 1, **Total:** 3.

FOUR OR MORE HITS IN ONE GAME

Devon White 2, Raul Mondesi 2, Mark Grudzielanek 2 (including one five-hit game), Jose Vizcaino 1, Eric Karros 1, Adrian Beltre 1, **Total:** 9.

MULTI-HOMER GAMES

Raul Mondesi 5, Gary Sheffield 4, Eric Karros 4, Todd Hundley 2, **Total:** 15.

GRAND SLAMS

6-5: Devon White (off Anaheim's Tim Belcher).
7-19: Todd Hundley (off Pittsburgh's Jose Silva).
8-11: Eric Karros (off Montreal's Anthony Telford).
8-22: Gary Sheffield (off Philadelphia's Steve Montgomery).

PINCH HITTERS

(Minimum 5 at-bats)

Name	AB	Avg.	HR	RBI
Hansen, Dave	48	.271	1	8
Hubbard, Trenidad	27	.222	0	3
Hollandsworth, Todd	23	.304	1	4
Vizcaino, Jose	20	.350	0	7
Cromer, Tripp	13	.231	1	2
Counsell, Craig	10	.400	0	0
Hundley, Todd	9	.222	0	3
White, Devon	8	.250	1	4

DEBUTS

4-5: Onan Masaoka, P.
4-20: Jamie Arnold, P.
8-3: Matt Herges, P.
9-7: Eric Gagne, P.
9-12: Jeff Williams, P.

GAMES BY POSITION

Catcher: Todd Hundley 108, Angel Pena 43, Paul LoDuca 34, Rick Wilkins 1, Trenidad Hubbard 1.
First base: Eric Karros 151, Dave Hansen 20, Todd Hollandsworth 13, Tripp Cromer 1.
Second base: Eric Young 116, Craig Counsell 38, Jose Vizcaino 30, Tripp Cromer 9, Alex Cora 3, Chance Sanford 2, Trenidad Hubbard 1, Juan Castro 1.
Third base: Adrian Beltre 152, Dave Hansen 13, Jose Vizcaino 9, Tripp Cromer 2.
Shortstop: Mark Grudzielanek 119, Jose Vizcaino 44, Tripp Cromer 9, Alex Cora 8, Craig Counsell 2, Juan Castro 1.
Outfield: Raul Mondesi 158, Gary Sheffield 145, Devon White 128, Todd Hollandsworth 67, Trenidad Hubbard 51, Jacob Brumfield 11, Brent Cookson 3, Dave Hansen 2, Tripp Cromer 2, Jose Vizcaino 1.
Designated hitter: Gary Sheffield 3, Dave Hansen 2, Devon White 1.

STREAKS

Wins: 5 (April 25-May 1).
Losses: 6 (June 27-July 3).
Consecutive games with at least one hit: 12, Eric Karros (September 19-October 2).
Wins by pitcher: 4, Chan Ho Park (September 13-28).

ATTENDANCE

Home: 3,064,251.
Road: 2,621,419.
Highest (home): 54,731 (July 4 vs. San Francisco).
Highest (road): 61,389 (September 30 vs. San Francisco).
Lowest (home): 23,616 (September 1 vs. Milwaukee).
Lowest (road): 5,132 (May 3 vs. Montreal).

MILWAUKEE BREWERS

DAY BY DAY

Date	Opp.	Res.	Score	(inn.*)	Hits	Opp. hits	Winning pitcher	Losing pitcher	Save	Record	Pos.	GB
4-5	At StL.	W	10-8		11	11	Weathers	Busby		1-0	1st	+0.5
4-7	At StL.	L	1-4		5	7	Bottenfield	Woodard	Acevedo	1-1	T1st	...
4-8	At StL.	L	4-9		13	8	Mercker	Abbott		1-2	T3rd	1.0
4-9	At Hou.	L	2-3		5	7	Elarton	Wickman	Wagner	1-3	T5th	1.0
4-10	At Hou.	W	8-2		13	7	Pulsipher	Holt	Weathers	2-3	T3rd	1.0
4-11	At Hou.	L	2-5		8	13	Reynolds	Roque	Wagner	2-4	T4th	2.0
4-13	At Mon.	W	8-4		14	12	Woodard	Vazquez		3-4	T4th	1.0
4-14	At Mon.	L	1-15		6	17	Batista	Abbott		3-5	T4th	2.0
4-15	At Mon.	W	9-4		11	12	Karl	Ayala		4-5	4th	1.5
4-16	Chi.	L	4-9		8	13	Heredia	Pulsipher		4-6	6th	2.5
4-17	Chi.	W	5-4		8	9	Myers	Beck		5-6	T3rd	2.5
4-18	Chi.	L	5-6	(10)	11	13	Beck	de los Santos	Serafini	5-7	5th	2.5
4-19	StL.	L	2-6		7	12	Bottenfield	Abbott		5-8	5th	3.5
4-20	StL.	L	3-8		6	12	Mercker	Karl		5-9	6th	4.5
4-21	StL.	W	2-1		5	6	Reyes	Painter	Wickman	6-9	4th	3.5
4-23	At Pit.	W	9-1		13	8	Woodard	Peters		7-9	4th	3.5
4-24	At Pit.	W	5-3		7	6	Reyes	Ritchie	Wickman	8-9	4th	2.5
4-25	At Pit.	W	4-2		10	8	Karl	Benson	Wickman	9-9	3rd	2.5
4-27	L.A.	L	2-3		6	7	Brown	Roque	Shaw	9-10	4th	3.5
4-28	L.A.	L	2-3		11	10	Park	Woodard	Shaw	9-11	4th	3.5
4-29	L.A.	L	4-10		8	13	Valdes	Eldred		9-12	6th	3.5
4-30	Ari.	L	2-3		7	10	Holmes	Myers	Olson	9-13	6th	4.0
5-1	Ari.	L	3-5		8	10	Stottlemyre	Abbott	Olson	9-14	6th	5.0
5-2	Ari.	W	6-5		13	8	Weathers	Olson	Wickman	10-14	5th	5.0
5-3	At Fla.	W	6-4	(13)	12	11	Wickman	Corbin		11-14	5th	4.0
5-4	At Fla.	W	8-1		10	7	Eldred	Sanchez		12-14	5th	4.0
5-5	At Fla.	W	2-0		7	8	Karl	Meadows	Wickman	13-14	5th	4.0
5-7	At S.F	L	3-4		8	7	Brock	Roque	Nen	13-15	5th	5.0
5-8	At S.F	L	4-6		7	13	Rueter	Woodard	Nen	13-16	5th	5.0
5-9	At S.F	W	3-2		7	7	Nomo	Gardner	Wickman	14-16	5th	4.0
5-11	At Cin.	L	1-9		4	12	Avery	Eldred		14-17	6th	5.5
5-12	At Cin.	W	8-7		15	12	Karl	Harnisch	Wickman	15-17	5th	5.5
5-14	Fla.	L	6-14		8	14	Sanchez	Roque	Mantei	15-18	5th	6.5
5-15	Fla.	W	7-2		11	4	Woodard	Meadows		16-18	5th	6.5
5-16	Fla.	L	2-3		14	9	Hernandez	Nomo	Mantei	16-19	6th	6.5
5-17	At N.Y.	W	7-6		13	11	Karl	Jones	Wickman	17-19	6th	6.0
5-18	At N.Y.	W	4-2		8	11	Weathers	Cook	Wickman	18-19	6th	6.0
5-20†	At N.Y.	L	10-11		13	12	Leiter	Abbott	Franco	18-20		
5-20‡	At N.Y.	L	1-10		9	12	Yoshii	Woodard		18-21	7th	7.0
5-21	At Mon.	W	5-3	(11)	9	6	Wickman	Ayala	Weathers	19-21	5th	6.0
5-22	At Mon.	L	4-12		7	14	Vazquez	Karl	Telford	19-22	6th	6.0
5-23	At Mon.	W	13-4		13	7	Weathers	Urbina		20-22	6th	6.0
5-24	Atl.	W	10-7		13	13	Woodard	Glavine		21-22	6th	6.0
5-25	Atl.	L	2-5		8	12	Seanez	Wickman	Rocker	21-23	6th	7.0
5-26	Atl.	L	2-3	(10)	6	11	Seanez	Weathers	Rocker	21-24	6th	8.0
5-27	Atl.	L	7-8		13	11	Millwood	Karl	Seanez	21-25	6th	8.0
5-28	S.D.	L	8-10		11	13	Reyes	Eldred	Hoffman	21-26	6th	8.0
5-29	S.D.	L	3-12		10	15	Clement	Woodard		21-27	6th	8.0
5-30	S.D.	W	10-3		11	10	Abbott	Hitchcock		22-27	6th	7.0
5-31	S.D.	W	8-2		14	5	Nomo	Williams		23-27	6th	6.5
6-1	Hou.	L	0-3	(8)	6	5	Bergman	Karl		23-28	6th	7.5
6-2	Hou.	L	1-9		4	9	Lima	Eldred		23-29	6th	8.5
6-3	Hou.	W	4-1		10	7	Woodard	Reynolds	Wickman	24-29	6th	7.5
6-4	At Col.	L	8-9	(10)	17	17	Veres	Wickman		24-30	6th	8.5
6-5	At Col.	L	11-12		14	13	DeJean	Plunk	Dipoto	24-31	6th	9.5
6-6	At Col.	L	5-10		9	14	Astacio	Karl		24-32	6th	9.5
6-8	At Cle.	W	2-1	(10)	10	13	Roque	Assenmacher	Wickman	25-32	6th	9.0
6-9	At Cle.	L	5-6	(10)	9	9	Jackson	Roque		25-33	6th	10.0
6-10	At Cle.	W	15-9		14	14	Nomo	Colon		26-33	6th	9.5
6-11	Min.	L	7-9		13	16	Wells	Weathers	Trombley	26-34	6th	10.5
6-12	Min.	L	6-8		15	15	Sampson	Eldred	Trombley	26-35	6th	11.5
6-14	Chi.	W	5-1		11	9	Woodard	Farnsworth		27-35	6th	11.5
6-15	Chi.	L	4-7		10	9	Lieber	Abbott	Adams	27-36	6th	11.5
6-16	Chi.	W	11-4		12	6	Nomo	Trachsel		28-36	6th	10.5
6-17	At Cin.	L	0-2		4	8	Harnisch	Karl	Williamson	28-37	6th	10.5
6-18	At Cin.	L	1-7		3	11	Avery	Roque		28-38	6th	11.5
6-19	At Cin.	W	10-1		12	4	Woodard	Villone		29-38	6th	11.5
6-20	At Cin.	W	7-4		10	9	Weathers	Reyes	Wickman	30-38	6th	11.5
6-21	At S.F	W	8-1		11	7	Nomo	Gardner		31-38	6th	10.5
6-22	At S.F	W	5-1		13	8	Karl	Rueter		32-38	6th	9.5
6-23	At S.F	W	9-6		12	13	Woodard	Ortiz	Wickman	33-38	6th	9.5
6-25	Pit.	L	3-5		10	11	Schmidt	Abbott	Christiansen	33-39	6th	9.0
6-26	Pit.	W	7-4		11	10	Nomo	Ritchie	Wickman	34-39	6th	8.0
6-27	Pit.	L	5-6		9	7	Cordova	Karl	Christiansen	34-40	6th	8.0
6-29	At Chi.	W	17-6		21	9	Woodard	Tapani		35-40	6th	8.0
6-30	At Chi.	L	4-5		10	7	Karchner	Weathers	Aguilera	35-41	6th	9.0
7-1	At Chi.	W	19-12		21	11	Myers	Trachsel		36-41	6th	9.0
7-2	At Pit.	W	5-2		11	9	Karl	Cordova	Wickman	37-41	6th	8.0
7-3	At Pit.	W	9-4		11	11	Pulsipher	Benson		38-41	5th	8.0

HIGHLIGHTS

High point: After falling 10 games below .500 on June 18 in Cincinnati, the Brewers won five consecutive road games to ignite a 17-7 run that enabled them to reach the break-even mark on July 18.

Low point: On July 14, the day before the second half of the season was to start, a crane collapsed at the Miller Park construction site, killing three ironworkers and severely damaging the new stadium. After several weeks, officials determined that the opening of the new ballpark—scheduled for 2000—would be set back a full year.

Turning point: With a 47-47 record and hopes of climbing back into the wild-card race, the team went to Florida for a three-game series July 23 and was swept by the lowly Marlins. The pratfall kicked off a stretch in which the Brewers lost 11 of 13 games and waved goodbye to the .500 mark for the rest of the season.

Most valuable player: Despite missing more than a month with a hand fracture, right fielder Jeromy Burnitz led the club in homers (33), RBIs (103), walks (91) and on-base percentage (.402).

Most valuable pitcher: Bob Wickman, who managed a franchise-record 37 saves despite blowing eight chances.

Most improved player: After playing just 84 games as a rookie in 1998, left fielder Geoff Jenkins emerged with a .313 average, 21 homers, 43 doubles and 82 RBIs. He also improved his defense, recording 14 assists.

Most pleasant surprise: Plucked off the scrap heap, righthander Hideo Nomo joined the team May 9 and revived his career. He was 12-8 in 28 starts, with shaky run support costing him a chance for more victories.

Key injuries: Second baseman Fernando Vina injured his right knee in May and was sidelined for most of the season. Righthander Steve Woodard broke his left wrist July 25 and was out for nearly a month. Catcher David Nilsson missed most of the last month with a broken right thumb.

Notable: After 7 1/2 years as manager, Phil Garner was fired August 12 and replaced by Jim Lefebvre. With a 563-617 record, Garner is the winningest and losingest manager in club history. ... GM Sal Bando was reassigned within the organization the day Garner was fired. ... The club was 42-39 on the road but a horrendous 32-48 at home. ... Jeff Cirillo's .326 batting average tied for fifth in the N.L. ... The team turned a triple play against the Cubs in the April 16 home opener. ... The team allowed 177 stolen bases, the most in the major leagues. ... Shortstop Jose Valentin hit two-run homers from both sides of the plate in a 19-12 victory over the Cubs on July 1 at Wrigley Field.

—DREW OLSON

MISCELLANEOUS

RECORDS

1999 regular-season record: 74-87 (5th in N.L. Central); 32-48 at home; 42-39 on road; 18-23 vs. N.L. East; 32-30 vs. N.L. Central; 16-28 vs. N.L. West; 8-6 vs. A.L. Central; 21-27 vs. lefthanded starters; 53-60 vs. righthanded starters; 58-75 on grass; 16-12 on turf; 31-28 in daytime; 43-59 at night; 22-27 in one-run games; 8-9 in extra-inning games; 0-1-2 in double-headers.

Team record past five years: 371-419 (.470).

TEAM LEADERS

Batting average: Jeff Cirillo (.326).
At-bats: Jeff Cirillo (607).
Runs: Jeff Cirillo (98).
Hits: Jeff Cirillo (198).
Total bases: Jeff Cirillo (280).
Doubles: Geoff Jenkins (43).
Triples: Mark Loretta, Jose Valentin (5).
Home runs: Jeromy Burnitz (33).
Runs batted in: Jeromy Burnitz (103).
Stolen bases: Marquis Grissom (24).
Slugging percentage: Jeromy Burnitz (.561).
On-base percentage: Jeromy Burnitz (.402).
Wins: Hideo Nomo (12).
Earned-run average: Steve Woodard (4.52).
Complete games: Steve Woodard (2).
Shutouts: None.
Saves: Bob Wickman (37).
Innings pitched: Scott Karl (197.2).
Strikeouts: Hideo Nomo (161).

Date	Opp.	Res.	Score	(inn.*)	Hits	Opp. hits	Winning pitcher	Losing pitcher	Save	Record	Pos.	GB
7-4	At Pit.	W	4-3		8	6	Weathers	Clontz	Wickman	39-41	4th	7.0
7-5	At Phi.	W	5-0		10	6	Abbott	Ogea	Roque	40-41	T3rd	7.0
7-6	At Phi.	L	0-1		5	4	Person	Nomo	Gomes	40-42	5th	7.0
7-7	At Phi.	L	4-5		8	10	Gomes	Wickman		40-43	5th	7.0
7-9	At Det.	W	4-1		9	6	Woodard	Cruz	Wickman	41-43	T4th	7.5
7-10	At Det.	L	3-9		6	14	Thompson	Abbott		41-44	5th	7.5
7-11	At Det.	W	3-2		6	9	Nomo	Moehler	Wickman	42-44	T4th	7.5
7-16†	K.C.	W	2-0		9	4	Woodard	Appier	Wickman	43-44		
7-16‡	K.C.	L	10-12		13	15	Ray	Pittsley	Service	43-45	6th	8.5
7-17	K.C.	W	11-3		17	7	Nomo	Rosado		44-45	T4th	8.5
7-18	Chi. (AL)	W	5-4		13	9	Plunk	Rizzo		45-45	4th	8.5
7-19	Chi. (AL)	L	8-10	(12)	11	18	Simas	Coppinger	Foulke	45-46	T4th	9.5
7-20	Chi. (AL)	W	5-4		10	9	Plunk	Lowe	Wickman	46-46	3rd	8.5
7-21	Phi.	L	0-7		7	15	Person	Karl	Poole	46-47	3rd	8.5
7-22	Phi.	W	5-0		6	5	Nomo	Wolf		47-47	3rd	7.5
7-23	At Fla.	L	4-5		8	13	Nunez	Wickman		47-48	T3rd	9.0
7-24	At Fla.	L	1-4		6	9	Meadows	Peterson	Alfonseca	47-49	4th	10.0
7-25	At Fla.	L	3-4		8	10	Sanchez	Weathers	Alfonseca	47-50	5th	11.0
7-26	At Atl.	L	1-6		6	8	Maddux	Karl		47-51	5th	12.0
7-27	At Atl.	L	2-10		6	14	Millwood	Nomo		47-52	6th	13.0
7-28	At Atl.	W	10-4		13	9	Pulsipher	Chen		48-52	5th	13.0
7-30	Mon.	W	1-0		7	5	Peterson	Powell	Wickman	49-52	4th	12.5
7-31	Mon.	L	2-4		5	12	Telford	Plunk	Urbina	49-53	5th	13.5
8-1	Mon.	L	4-10		7	13	Smith	Karl		49-54	5th	13.5
8-2	N.Y.	L	2-7		8	12	Reed	Nomo		49-55	5th	14.0
8-3	N.Y.	L	3-10		6	13	Hershiser	Pulsipher		49-56	5th	15.0
8-4	N.Y.	L	5-9		7	17	Rogers	Peterson		49-57	6th	15.0
8-6	Cin.	L	2-9		4	15	Villone	Woodard	Sullivan	49-58	6th	16.0
8-7	Cin.	W	6-4		11	9	Weathers	Graves	Wickman	50-58	5th	16.0
8-8	Cin.	L	2-8		7	11	Harnisch	Nomo	Belinda	50-59	5th	17.0
8-9	Col.	W	7-6		11	9	Wickman	Veres		51-59	5th	16.0
8-10	Col.	W	2-1	(10)	3	6	Coppinger	Veres		52-59	5th	15.0
8-11	Col.	L	5-8		10	14	Jones	Woodard		52-60	5th	15.0
8-13	At Ari.	W	3-1		7	4	Nomo	Benes	Wickman	53-60	5th	14.0
8-14	At Ari.	W	4-2		6	10	Karl	Reynoso	Wickman	54-60	5th	14.0
8-15	At Ari.	L	0-4		7	7	Daal	Pulsipher		54-61	5th	14.0
8-16	At Hou.	L	0-2		2	8	Lima	Peterson	Wagner	54-62	5th	15.0
8-17	At Hou.	L	6-8		11	9	Elarton	Eldred	Wagner	54-63	5th	16.0
8-18	At Hou.	L	4-6		8	9	Williams	Plunk	Wagner	54-64	5th	17.0
8-19	At Hou.	W	6-5		17	10	Coppinger	Powell	Wickman	55-64	5th	16.0
8-20	S.F	L	3-10		9	14	Rueter	Pulsipher		55-65	5th	17.0
8-21	S.F	L	1-5		7	7	Hernandez	Peterson		55-66	5th	18.0
8-22	S.F	L	3-7		12	12	Nathan	Eldred		55-67	5th	18.5
8-23	L.A.	L	4-8		9	8	Dreifort	Nomo	Shaw	55-68	5th	18.5
8-24	L.A.	L	2-5		4	11	Judd	Karl	Shaw	55-69	5th	19.5
8-25	L.A.	W	9-7		9	9	Plunk	Borbon	Wickman	56-69	5th	18.5
8-26	At S.D.	L	3-4		8	8	Ashby	Coppinger	Hoffman	56-70	5th	19.0
8-27	At S.D.	L	7-8		15	9	Whiteside	Wickman		56-71	5th	19.5
8-28	At S.D.	W	6-4		11	9	Nomo	Williams	Wickman	57-71	5th	18.5
8-29	At S.D.	L	4-5	(10)	3	10	Hoffman	Wickman		57-72	5th	19.5
8-30	At L.A.	L	1-6		9	8	Brown	Pulsipher		57-73	5th	19.5
8-31	At L.A.	L	3-5		8	12	Judd	Peterson	Shaw	57-74	5th	20.5
9-1	At L.A.	W	5-4		8	7	Eldred	Valdes	Wickman	58-74	5th	19.5
9-2	StL.	L	3-4		8	9	Painter	Ramirez	Bottalico	58-75	5th	20.0
9-3	StL.	W	5-4	(11)	12	12	Coppinger	Acevedo		59-75	5th	20.0
9-4	StL.	W	4-2		6	3	Pulsipher	Thompson	Wickman	60-75	5th	20.0
9-5	StL.	L	9-13	(10)	12	18	Bottalico	Wickman		60-76	5th	21.0
9-7	Ari.	L	9-11		13	12	Holmes	Dale	Mantei	60-77	5th	22.5
9-8	Ari.	L	1-9		7	14	Daal	Nomo		60-78	5th	23.5
9-9	Ari.	W	9-8		14	11	Karl	Reynoso	Wickman	61-78	5th	23.5
9-10	At Col.	L	3-15		9	14	Bohanon	Pulsipher		61-79	5th	24.5
9-11	At Col.	L	6-7		8	12	Dipoto	Coppinger	Veres	61-80	5th	25.5
9-12	At Col.	W	12-9		16	13	Plunk	Veres	Wickman	62-80	5th	25.5
9-13	At StL.	W	4-3		9	8	Nomo	Thompson	Wickman	63-80	5th	25.5
9-14	At StL.	W	4-1		7	8	Karl	Aybar	Wickman	64-80	5th	25.5
9-15	At StL.	W	10-8	(12)	15	13	Ramirez	Acevedo		65-80	5th	24.5
9-17	At Chi.	L	5-6	(10)	11	7	Aguilera	Peterson		65-81	5th	24.5
9-18	At Chi.	W	7-4	(14)	9	10	Peterson	Guthrie		66-81	5th	23.5
9-19	At Chi.	L	7-8	(10)	10	12	Aguilera	Ramirez		66-82	5th	24.5
9-20	Phi.	W	5-4		8	14	Coppinger	Loewer	Wickman	67-82	5th	23.5
9-21	Phi.	W	8-6		11	9	Pulsipher	Shumaker	Wickman	68-82	5th	23.5
9-22	Phi.	L	3-12		4	16	Telemaco	Peterson		68-83	5th	23.5
9-23	Phi.	W	11-6		12	8	Bere	Grace		69-83	5th	23.0
9-24	Hou.	L	4-9		8	7	Miller	Plunk	Powell	69-84	5th	24.0
9-25	Hou.	W	3-2		9	10	Karl	Reynolds	Wickman	70-84	5th	23.0
9-26	Hou.	W	11-3		16	9	Peterson	Elarton		71-84	5th	22.0
9-29†	Pit.	L	5-7		9	11	Ritchie	Woodard	Williams	71-85		
9-29‡	Pit.	W	5-2		7	7	Bere	Peters	Wickman	72-85	5th	22.0
9-30	Pit.	L	2-3		5	8	Garcia	Nomo	Sauerbeck	72-86	5th	22.5
10-1	Cin.	W	4-3	(10)	10	5	Coppinger	Sullivan		73-86	5th	21.5
10-2	Cin.	W	10-6		14	12	Peterson	Guzman		74-86	T4th	21.5
10-3	Cin.	L	1-7		6	12	Harnisch	Eldred	Villone	74-87	5th	22.5

Monthly records: April (9-13), May (14-14), June (12-14), July (14-12), August (8-21), September (15-12), October (2-1).
*Innings, if other than nine. † First game of a doubleheader. ‡ Second game of a doubleheader.

MEMORABLE GAMES

July 17 at Milwaukee

This one was about symbolism and foreshadowing. In the fourth inning, Brewers rightfielder Jeromy Burnitz was hit in the hand by a Jose Rosado fastball. In the top of the seventh, a power failure caused the lights to go out, forcing a 25-minute delay. Burnitz went to a hospital and was diagnosed with a broken bone in his left hand. He was sidelined more than a month and the club's offense suffered through a dismal stretch without Burnitz.

Kansas City	AB	R	H	RBI	Milwaukee	AB	R	H	RBI
Damon, lf	3	1	2	1	Loretta, 1b	6	3	5	4
Febles, 2b	4	0	0	0	Belliard, 2b	3	1	2	3
C.Beltran, cf	4	1	2	0	Cirillo, 3b	3	0	1	0
Mi.Sweeney, 1b	4	0	0	0	Collier, ph-3b	1	0	0	0
Dye, rf	3	1	1	2	Burnitz, rf	2	0	0	0
Pose, ph-rf	1	0	0	0	Jenkins, lf	2	1	1	0
Randa, 3b	3	0	1	0	Nilsson, c	5	1	2	0
Scarsone, 3b	1	0	0	0	J.Abbott, p	0	0	0	0
Kreuter, c	4	0	0	0	Grissom, cf	3	1	0	1
J.Hansen, ss	4	0	1	0	Ochoa, lf-rf	5	2	2	3
Rosado, p	2	0	0	0	Jos.Valntin, ss	5	2	3	0
Morman, p	0	0	0	0	Nomo, p	2	0	1	0
Je.Giambi, ph	1	0	0	0	Hughes, c	0	0	0	0
Suzuki, p	0	0	0	0					
Whisenant, p	0	0	0	0					
Spehr, ph	1	0	0	0					
Totals	**35**	**3**	**7**	**3**	**Totals**	**37**	**11**	**17**	**11**

Kansas City ....1 0 0 0 0 2 0 0 0 —3
Milwaukee ....0 2 0 3 4 1 1 0 x—11

E—Loretta (9). LOB—Kansas City 6, Milwaukee 13. 2B—Damon (24), Loretta (23), Belliard (13), Jenkins (20). HR—Damon (9), Dye (18), Loretta (4), Belliard (5), Ochoa 2 (5). SB—Damon (16), C.Beltran (14). S—Nomo 2. SF—Grissom.

Kansas City	IP	H	R	ER	BB	SO
Rosado (L, 5-7)	4.2	12	9	9	3	4
Morman	1.1	3	1	1	0	0
Suzuki	1	1	1	1	2	0
Whisenant	1	1	0	0	2	0

Milwaukee	IP	H	R	ER	BB	SO
Nomo (W, 8-2)	7	6	3	3	1	7
J.Abbott	2	1	0	0	0	0

HBP—Burnitz by Rosado. WP—Rosado 2. U—HP, Froemming. 1B, Nelson. 2B, M.Hirschbeck. 3B, Bell. T—3:15. A—29,273.

September 22 at Milwaukee

A three-run double by Jeromy Burnitz and a solid outing by starter Steve Woodard gave the Brewers a 3-1 lead heading into the eighth. But facing a battle-weary Milwaukee bullpen, the Phillies exploded for 11 runs in the inning and cruised to victory. The loss dropped Milwaukee to 15 games below .500.

Philadelphia	AB	R	H	RBI	Milwaukee	AB	R	H	RBI
Glanville, cf	5	1	2	0	Grissom, cf	4	1	2	0
Loewer, p	0	0	0	0	Loretta, 1b	3	1	1	0
Gant, lf	5	2	3	2	Barker, ph-1b	1	0	0	0
Abreu, rf	5	2	2	1	Cirillo, 3b	2	1	0	0
Lieberthal, c	4	2	2	1	Zosky, ph-3b	1	0	0	0
Brogna, 1b	5	2	2	3	Burnitz, rf	3	0	1	3
K.Jordan, 3b	4	1	0	0	L.Mouton, rf	1	0	0	0
M.Anderson, 2b	5	1	3	3	Ochoa, lf	2	0	0	0
S.Montgmry, p	0	0	0	0	Belliard, 2b	4	0	0	0
Magee, cf	0	0	0	0	Collier, ss	4	0	0	0
Relaford, ss	4	0	0	0	Cancel, c	3	0	0	0
Wolf, p	2	0	1	0	C.Greene, c	0	0	0	0
Ducey, ph	1	0	0	0	Woodard, p	3	0	0	0
Telemaco, p	0	0	0	0	Peterson, p	0	0	0	0
A.Arias, ph	1	1	1	2	Weathers, p	0	0	0	0
Doster, 2b	1	0	0	0	Roque, p	0	0	0	0
Totals	**42**	**12**	**16**	**12**	**Totals**	**31**	**3**	**4**	**3**

Philadelphia ....0 0 0 1 0 0 0 (11) 0—12
Milwaukee ....0 0 0 0 0 3 0 0 0 —3

E—Belliard (13), Collier (5). DP—Milwaukee 1. LOB—Philadelphia 7, Milwaukee 4. 2B—Glanville (35), Gant (26), Lieberthal (32), M.Anderson (25), A.Arias (19), Grissom (25), Burnitz (32). SB—Gant (11), Brogna (8). S—Glanville, Relaford.

Philadelphia	IP	H	R	ER	BB	SO
Wolf	6	4	3	3	2	4
Telemaco (W, 4-0)	1	0	0	0	0	2
S.Montgomery	1	0	0	0	0	0
Loewer	1	0	0	0	1	0

Milwaukee	IP	H	R	ER	BB	SO
Woodard	7	8	3	2	0	5
Peterson (BS 1; L 2-7)	0.1	2	4	4	0	0
Weathers	0	5	5	5	0	0
Roque	1.2	1	0	0	0	0

HBP—Lieberthal by Peterson, K.Jordan by Peterson. U—HP, Randazzo.1B, Danley. 2B, Bell. 3B, Montague. T—3:05. A—13,043.

1999 REVIEW

INDIVIDUAL STATISTICS

BATTING

Name	G	TPA	AB	R	H	TB	2B	3B	HR	RBI	Avg.	Obp.	Slg.	SH	SF	HP	BB	IBB	SO	SB	CS	GDP	vs RHP AB	vs RHP Avg.	vs RHP HR	vs RHP RBI	vs LHP AB	vs LHP Avg.	vs LHP HR	vs LHP RBI
Cirillo, Jeff	157	697	607	98	198	280	35	1	15	88	.326	.401	.461	3	7	5	75	4	83	7	4	15	449	.327	6	55	158	.323	9	33
Grissom, Marquis	154	661	603	92	161	250	27	1	20	83	.267	.320	.415	4	5	0	49	4	109	24	6	12	432	.245	16	63	171	.322	4	20
Loretta, Mark	153	664	587	93	170	229	34	5	5	67	.290	.354	.390	9	6	10	52	1	59	4	1	14	427	.286	5	50	160	.300	0	17
Burnitz, Jeromy	130	580	467	87	126	262	33	2	33	103	.270	.402	.561	0	6	16	91	7	124	7	3	11	305	.282	22	62	162	.247	11	41
Belliard, Ron	124	531	457	60	135	196	29	4	8	58	.295	.379	.429	6	4	0	64	0	59	4	5	16	336	.304	4	41	121	.273	4	17
Jenkins, Geoff	135	493	447	70	140	252	43	3	21	82	.313	.371	.564	3	1	7	35	7	87	5	1	10	362	.326	19	67	85	.259	2	15
Nilsson, Dave	115	404	343	56	106	190	19	1	21	62	.309	.400	.554	2	4	2	53	6	64	1	2	7	252	.329	16	47	91	.253	5	15
Ochoa, Alex	119	329	277	47	83	129	16	3	8	40	.300	.404	.466	0	2	5	45	2	43	6	4	4	139	.281	3	15	138	.319	5	25
Berry, Sean	106	281	259	26	59	78	11	1	2	23	.228	.281	.301	0	2	3	17	0	50	0	0	4	179	.251	2	16	80	.175	0	7
Valentin, Jose	89	313	256	45	58	107	9	5	10	38	.227	.347	.418	2	5	2	48	7	52	3	2	3	181	.215	9	27	75	.253	1	11
Banks, Brian	105	249	219	34	53	77	7	1	5	22	.242	.317	.352	3	2	0	25	5	59	6	1	2	165	.248	4	17	54	.222	1	5
Vina, Fernando	37	177	154	17	41	51	7	0	1	16	.266	.339	.331	3	2	4	14	0	6	5	2	1	110	.236	1	10	44	.341	0	6
Becker, Rich	89	174	139	15	35	59	5	2	5	16	.252	.395	.424	2	0	0	33	0	38	5	0	4	128	.266	5	16	11	.091	0	0
Collier, Lou	74	152	135	18	35	50	9	0	2	21	.259	.325	.370	1	2	0	14	0	32	3	2	2	70	.214	1	12	65	.308	1	9
Barker, Kevin	38	127	117	13	33	45	3	0	3	23	.282	.331	.385	0	1	0	9	1	19	1	0	0	100	.310	3	23	17	.118	0	0
Hughes, Bobby	48	106	101	10	26	37	2	0	3	8	.257	.292	.366	0	0	0	5	0	28	0	0	3	52	.288	1	2	49	.224	2	6
Karl, Scott	33	76	60	5	11	19	2	0	2	7	.183	.219	.317	12	1	0	3	0	17	0	0	0	44	.182	2	6	16	.188	0	1
Nomo, Hideo	29	64	56	3	12	16	2	1	0	5	.214	.228	.286	7	0	0	1	0	22	0	0	0	36	.167	0	3	20	.300	0	2
Woodard, Steve	31	69	53	5	7	8	1	0	0	0	.132	.220	.151	10	0	0	6	0	16	0	0	1	36	.167	0	0	17	.059	0	0
Cancel, Robinson	15	48	44	5	8	10	2	0	0	5	.182	.234	.227	1	0	1	2	0	12	0	0	0	31	.194	0	3	13	.154	0	2
Greene, Charlie	32	49	42	4	8	9	1	0	0	1	.190	.271	.214	1	1	0	5	0	11	0	0	0	26	.192	0	1	16	.188	0	0
Eldred, Cal	23	30	24	3	2	3	1	0	0	2	.083	.154	.125	4	0	0	2	0	13	0	0	0	15	.133	0	2	9	.000	0	0
Peterson, Kyle	17	25	22	2	3	3	0	0	0	1	.136	.174	.136	2	0	0	1	0	9	0	0	0	21	.143	0	1	1	.000	0	0
Pulsipher, Bill	19	29	21	1	3	3	0	0	0	0	.143	.143	.143	8	0	0	0	0	14	0	0	1	13	.077	0	0	8	.250	0	0
Abbott, Jim	20	24	21	0	2	2	0	0	0	3	.095	.095	.095	3	0	0	0	0	10	0	0	0	15	.133	0	3	6	.000	0	0
Mouton, Lyle	14	19	17	2	3	7	1	0	1	3	.176	.263	.412	0	0	0	2	0	3	0	0	0	9	.111	0	1	8	.250	1	2
Roque, Rafael	43	20	17	0	1	1	0	0	0	0	.059	.158	.059	1	0	0	2	0	10	0	0	0	10	.100	0	0	7	.000	0	0
Bere, Jason	5	10	8	1	3	3	0	0	0	0	.375	.500	.375	0	0	0	2	0	2	0	0	0	5	.400	0	0	3	.333	0	0
Weathers, Dave	63	8	7	1	1	1	0	0	0	0	.143	.250	.143	0	0	0	1	0	4	0	0	0	4	.250	0	0	3	.000	0	0
Zosky, Eddie	8	8	7	1	1	1	0	0	0	0	.143	.250	.143	0	0	0	1	0	2	0	0	0	5	.200	0	0	2	.000	0	0
Ramirez, Hector	15	3	3	0	0	0	0	0	0	0	.000	.000	.000	0	0	0	0	0	2	0	0	0	2	.000	0	0	1	.000	0	0
Reyes, Al	26	2	2	0	0	0	0	0	0	0	.000	.000	.000	0	0	0	0	0	0	0	0	0	2	.000	0	0	0	.000	0	0
Coppinger, Rocky	29	2	2	0	0	0	0	0	0	0	.000	.000	.000	0	0	0	0	0	2	0	0	0	1	.000	0	0	1	.000	0	0
Estrada, Horacio	4	2	2	0	0	0	0	0	0	0	.000	.000	.000	0	0	0	0	0	0	0	0	0	2	.000	0	0	0	.000	0	0
Harris, Reggie	8	1	1	0	0	0	0	0	0	0	.000	.000	.000	0	0	0	0	0	1	0	0	0	1	.000	0	0	0	.000	0	0
Wickman, Bob	71	1	1	0	0	0	0	0	0	0	.000	.000	.000	0	0	0	0	0	0	0	0	0	1	.000	0	0	0	.000	0	0
Myers, Mike	71	1	1	0	0	0	0	0	0	0	.000	.000	.000	0	0	0	0	0	1	0	0	0	0	.000	0	0	1	.000	0	0
Pittsley, Jim	15	2	1	0	0	0	0	0	0	0	.000	.500	.000	0	0	0	1	0	1	0	0	0	1	.000	0	0	0	.000	0	0
Fox, Chad	6	1	1	0	0	0	0	0	0	0	.000	.000	.000	0	0	0	0	0	0	0	0	0	1	.000	0	0	0	.000	0	0
Falteisek, Steve	11	1	1	1	0	0	0	0	0	0	.000	.000	.000	0	0	0	0	0	1	0	0	0	0	.000	0	0	1	.000	0	0
Plunk, Eric	68	0	0	0	0	0	0	0	0	0	.000	.000	.000	0	0	0	0	0	0	0	0	0	0	.000	0	0	0	.000	0	0
D'Amico, Jeff	1	0	0	0	0	0	0	0	0	0	.000	.000	.000	0	0	0	0	0	0	0	0	0	0	.000	0	0	0	.000	0	0
de los Santos, Valerio	7	0	0	0	0	0	0	0	0	0	.000	.000	.000	0	0	0	0	0	0	0	0	0	0	.000	0	0	0	.000	0	0
Dale, Carl	4	0	0	0	0	0	0	0	0	0	.000	.000	.000	0	0	0	0	0	0	0	0	0	0	.000	0	0	0	.000	0	0

Players with more than one N.L. team

Name	G	TPA	AB	R	H	TB	2B	3B	HR	RBI	Avg.	Obp.	Slg.	SH	SF	HP	BB	IBB	SO	SB	CS	GDP	vs RHP AB	vs RHP Avg.	vs RHP HR	vs RHP RBI	vs LHP AB	vs LHP Avg.	vs LHP HR	vs LHP RBI
Bere, Cin.	12	17	14	2	4	4	0	0	0	1	.286	.333	.286	2	0	1	0	0	7	0	0	0	5	.400	0	0	3	.333	0	0
Bere, Cin.-Mil.	17	27	22	3	7	7	0	0	0	1	.318	.400	.318	2	0	1	2	0	9	0	0	0	14	.286	0	0	8	.375	0	1

PITCHING

Name	W	L	Pct.	ERA	IP	H	R	ER	HR	SH	SF	HB	BB	IBB	SO	G	GS	CG	ShO	GF	Sv	vs. RH AB	vs. RH Avg.	vs. RH HR	vs. RH RBI	vs. LH AB	vs. LH Avg.	vs. LH HR	vs. LH RBI
Karl, Scott	11	11	.500	4.78	197.2	246	121	105	21	12	7	8	69	4	74	33	33	0	0	0	0	659	.317	19	94	130	.285	2	11
Woodard, Steve	11	8	.579	4.52	185.0	219	101	93	23	9	4	6	36	7	119	31	29	2	0	0	0	416	.305	14	53	330	.279	9	39
Nomo, Hideo	12	8	.600	4.54	176.1	173	96	89	27	5	5	3	78	2	161	28	28	0	0	0	0	357	.235	16	49	319	.279	11	40
Weathers, Dave	7	4	.636	4.65	93.0	102	49	48	14	4	4	2	38	3	74	63	0	0	0	14	2	242	.273	7	32	124	.290	7	21
Pulsipher, Bill	5	6	.455	5.98	87.1	100	65	58	19	6	4	2	36	2	42	19	16	0	0	1	0	273	.275	14	40	76	.329	5	15
Roque, Rafael	1	6	.143	5.34	84.1	96	52	50	16	1	3	4	42	1	66	43	9	0	0	7	1	245	.278	14	39	91	.308	2	13
Abbott, Jim	2	8	.200	6.91	82.0	110	71	63	14	2	1	2	42	3	37	20	15	0	0	3	0	257	.323	11	41	90	.300	3	22
Eldred, Cal	2	8	.200	7.79	82.0	101	75	71	19	2	3	1	46	0	60	20	15	0	0	2	0	183	.246	14	35	157	.357	5	31
Peterson, Kyle	4	7	.364	4.56	77.0	87	46	39	3	4	3	4	25	2	34	17	12	0	0	2	0	169	.272	1	22	136	.301	2	16
Plunk, Eric	4	4	.500	5.02	75.1	71	44	42	15	5	2	5	43	5	63	68	0	0	0	13	0	192	.245	11	32	91	.264	4	15
Wickman, Bob	3	8	.273	3.39	74.1	75	31	28	6	3	2	2	38	6	60	71	0	0	0	63	37	159	.314	4	19	127	.197	2	13
Myers, Mike	2	1	.667	5.23	41.1	46	24	24	7	5	0	3	13	1	35	71	0	0	0	14	0	78	.397	5	15	80	.188	2	10
Coppinger, Rocky	5	3	.625	3.68	36.2	35	16	15	5	0	1	0	23	3	39	29	0	0	0	10	0	80	.288	2	16	60	.200	3	5
Reyes, Al	2	0	1.000	4.25	36.0	27	17	17	5	1	1	3	25	1	39	26	0	0	0	6	0	81	.247	3	19	50	.140	2	9
Bere, Jason	2	0	1.000	4.63	23.1	23	15	12	3	1	1	0	10	0	19	5	4	0	0	0	0	46	.304	3	10	44	.205	0	1
Ramirez, Hector	1	2	.333	3.43	21.0	19	8	8	1	0	0	0	11	2	9	15	0	0	0	5	0	42	.238	1	9	35	.257	0	4
Pittsley, Jim	0	1	.000	4.82	18.2	20	12	10	3	0	1	1	10	0	13	15	0	0	0	5	0	45	.244	1	3	28	.321	2	8
Harris, Reggie	0	0	.000	3.00	12.0	8	4	4	1	0	1	2	7	0	11	8	0	0	0	2	0	33	.152	1	5	10	.300	0	1
Falteisek, Steve	0	0	.000	7.50	12.0	18	10	10	3	0	1	0	3	0	5	10	0	0	0	3	0	31	.387	3	9	17	.353	0	2
de los Santos, Valerio	0	1	.000	6.48	8.1	12	6	6	1	0	0	1	7	0	5	7	0	0	0	3	0	28	.357	1	6	7	.286	0	1
Estrada, Horacio	0	0	.000	7.36	7.1	10	6	6	4	0	0	0	4	0	5	4	0	0	0	2	0	27	.296	2	3	5	.400	2	6
Fox, Chad	0	0	.000	10.80	6.2	11	8	8	1	0	0	1	4	0	12	6	0	0	0	2	0	22	.409	1	5	9	.222	0	3
Dale, Carl	0	1	.000	20.25	4.0	8	9	9	2	0	0	1	6	0	4	4	0	0	0	1	0	9	.333	0	2	11	.455	2	4
D'Amico, Jeff	0	0	.000	0.00	1.0	1	0	0	0	0	0	0	0	0	1	1	0	0	0	1	0	2	.000	0	0	2	.500	0	0

PITCHERS WITH MORE THAN ONE N.L. TEAM

Name	W	L	Pct.	ERA	IP	H	R	ER	HR	SH	SF	HB	BB	IBB	SO	G	GS	CG	ShO	GF	Sv	vs. RH AB	vs. RH Avg.	vs. RH HR	vs. RH RBI	vs. LH AB	vs. LH Avg.	vs. LH HR	vs. LH RBI
Bere, Cin.	3	0	1.000	6.85	43.1	56	37	33	6	5	1	2	40	3	28	12	10	0	0	0	0	46	.304	3	10	44	.205	0	1
Bere, Cin.-Mil.	5	0	1.000	6.08	66.2	79	52	45	9	6	2	2	50	3	47	17	14	0	0	2	0	131	.336	8	24	131	.267	1	17

INDIVIDUAL STATISTICS

FIELDING

FIRST BASEMEN

Player	Pct.	G	PO	A	E	TC	DP
Loretta, Mark	.994	66	474	31	3	508	44
Berry, Sean	.989	64	438	27	5	470	50
Banks, Brian	.992	44	221	20	2	243	18
Barker, Kevin	.996	31	254	18	1	273	19

SECOND BASEMEN

Player	Pct.	G	PO	A	E	TC	DP
Belliard, Ron	.978	119	247	330	13	590	75
Vina, Fernando	.995	37	84	104	1	189	31
Loretta, Mark	.956	17	28	37	3	68	8
Collier, Lou	1.000	4	7	0	0	7	0
Zosky, Eddie	1.000	2	1	3	0	4	0

THIRD BASEMEN

Player	Pct.	G	PO	A	E	TC	DP
Cirillo, Jeff	.967	155	124	312	15	451	35
Loretta, Mark	.900	14	11	16	3	30	2
Collier, Lou	.800	7	0	4	1	5	0
Zosky, Eddie	1.000	4	0	1	0	1	0
Belliard, Ron	1.000	1	1	0	0	1	0

SHORTSTOPS

Player	Pct.	G	PO	A	E	TC	DP
Valentin, Jose	.937	85	113	214	22	349	38
Loretta, Mark	.986	74	112	176	4	292	40
Collier, Lou	.948	31	21	52	4	77	7
Belliard, Ron	1.000	1	2	3	0	5	0

OUTFIELDERS

Player	Pct.	G	PO	A	E	TC	DP
Grissom, Marquis	.987	149	374	1	5	380	2
Jenkins, Geoff	.974	128	250	14	7	271	4
Burnitz, Jeromy	.982	127	262	8	5	275	2
Ochoa, Alex	.979	85	133	5	3	141	0
Becker, Rich	.970	50	62	3	2	67	1
Collier, Lou	1.000	10	14	0	0	14	0
Banks, Brian	1.000	5	1	0	0	1	0
Mouton, Lyle	1.000	3	1	0	0	1	0

CATCHERS

Player	Pct.	G	PO	A	E	TC	DP	PB
Nilsson, Dave	.991	101	531	44	5	580	3	2
Hughes, Bobby	.988	44	149	15	2	166	2	5
Banks, Brian	.982	40	148	14	3	165	3	5
Greene, Charlie	.991	31	104	8	1	113	0	1
Cancel, Robinson	.980	15	84	12	2	98	2	0

PITCHERS

Player	Pct.	G	PO	A	E	TC	DP
Wickman, Bob	.840	71	6	15	4	25	2
Myers, Mike	1.000	71	5	7	0	12	0
Plunk, Eric	.857	68	0	6	1	7	0
Weathers, Dave	1.000	63	6	13	0	19	0
Roque, Rafael	.895	43	3	14	2	19	0
Karl, Scott	.931	33	10	44	4	58	4
Woodard, Steve	1.000	31	12	24	0	36	0
Coppinger, Rocky	.667	29	2	0	1	3	0
Nomo, Hideo	1.000	28	11	11	0	22	3
Reyes, Al	1.000	26	1	3	0	4	0
Abbott, Jim	.963	20	3	23	1	27	1
Eldred, Cal	1.000	20	5	3	0	8	0
Pulsipher, Bill	1.000	19	2	19	0	21	1
Peterson, Kyle	.833	17	3	7	2	12	0
Pittsley, Jim	1.000	15	3	3	0	6	0
Ramirez, Hector	1.000	15	2	1	0	3	0
Falteisek, Steve	-	10	0	0	0	0	0
Harris, Reggie	1.000	8	1	0	0	1	1
de los Santos, Valerio	1.000	7	0	2	0	2	0
Fox, Chad	1.000	6	2	0	0	2	0
Bere, Jason	1.000	5	0	1	0	1	0
Estrada, Horacio	1.000	4	0	1	0	1	0
Dale, Carl	-	4	0	0	0	0	0
D'Amico, Jeff	-	1	0	0	0	0	0

PITCHING AGAINST EACH CLUB

Pitcher	Ari. W-L	Atl. W-L	Chi. W-L	Cin. W-L	Col. W-L	Fla. W-L	Hou. W-L	L.A. W-L	Mon. W-L	N.Y. W-L	Phi. W-L	Pit. W-L	S.D. W-L	S.F. W-L	StL. W-L	A.L. W-L	Total W-L
Abbott, J.	0-1	0-0	0-1	0-0	0-0	0-0	0-0	0-0	0-1	0-1	1-0	0-0	1-0	0-0	0-2	0-1	2-8
Bere, J.	0-0	0-0	0-0	0-0	0-0	0-0	0-0	0-0	0-0	0-0	0-0	2-0	0-0	0-0	0-0	0-0	2-0
Coppinger, R.	0-0	0-0	0-0	1-0	1-1	0-0	1-0	0-0	0-0	0-0	0-1	0-0	1-0	0-0	0-1	0-0	5-3
D'Amico, J.	0-0	0-0	0-0	0-0	0-0	0-0	0-0	0-0	0-0	0-0	0-0	0-0	0-0	0-0	0-0	0-1	0-1
Dale, C.	0-1	0-0	0-0	0-0	0-0	0-0	0-0	0-0	0-0	0-0	0-0	0-0	0-0	0-0	0-0	0-0	0-1
delosSantos, V.	0-0	0-0	0-1	0-0	0-0	0-0	0-0	0-0	0-0	0-0	0-0	0-0	0-0	0-0	0-0	0-0	0-1
Eldred, C.	0-0	0-0	0-0	0-2	0-0	1-0	0-2	1-1	0-0	0-0	0-0	0-1	0-1	0-0	0-0	0-1	2-8
Estrada, H.	0-0	0-0	0-0	0-0	0-0	0-0	0-0	0-0	0-0	0-0	0-0	0-0	0-0	0-0	0-0	0-0	0-0
Falteisek, S.	0-0	0-0	0-0	0-0	0-0	0-0	0-0	0-0	0-0	0-0	0-0	0-0	0-0	0-0	0-0	0-0	0-0
Fox, C.	0-0	0-0	0-0	0-0	0-0	0-0	0-0	0-0	0-0	0-0	0-0	0-0	0-0	0-0	0-0	0-0	0-0
Harris, R.	0-0	0-0	0-0	0-0	0-0	0-0	0-0	0-0	0-0	0-0	0-0	0-0	0-0	0-0	0-0	0-0	0-0
Karl, S.	2-0	0-2	0-0	1-1	0-1	1-0	1-1	0-1	1-2	1-0	0-1	2-1	0-0	1-0	1-1	0-0	11-11
Myers, M.	0-1	0-0	2-0	0-0	0-0	0-0	0-0	0-0	0-0	0-0	0-0	0-0	0-0	0-0	0-0	0-0	2-1
Nomo, H.	1-0	0-1	0-0	0-1	0-0	0-1	0-1	0-1	0-0	0-1	1-1	1-1	2-0	1-0	3-0	3-0	12-8
Peterson, K.	0-0	0-0	1-1	1-0	0-0	0-1	1-1	0-1	0-0	0-1	1-1	2-0	0-1	0-0	0-0	0-0	4-7
Pittsley, J.	0-0	0-0	0-0	0-0	0-0	0-0	0-0	0-0	0-0	0-0	0-0	0-0	0-0	0-0	0-0	0-1	0-1
Plunk, E.	0-0	0-0	0-0	0-0	1-0	0-0	0-2	1-0	0-1	0-0	1-0	0-0	0-0	0-0	2-0	0-1	5-4
Pulsipher, B.	0-1	1-0	0-1	0-1	0-0	0-1	0-0	0-0	0-1	0-0	1-0	0-0	0-1	1-0	1-0	0-0	5-6
Ramirez, H.	0-0	0-0	0-0	0-0	0-0	0-0	0-0	0-1	0-0	0-0	0-0	0-0	0-0	1-1	0-0	0-0	1-2
Reyes, A.	0-0	0-0	0-0	0-0	0-0	0-1	0-0	0-0	0-0	0-0	0-0	0-0	0-0	1-0	0-0	0-0	2-0
Roque, R.	1-0	0-1	0-0	2-0	0-0	0-1	0-1	0-1	0-0	0-0	1-0	0-0	0-0	0-0	0-0	1-1	1-6
Weathers, D.	1-0	0-1	0-0	0-0	0-0	0-1	0-0	0-1	1-0	0-0	0-0	0-0	0-0	0-0	1-0	0-1	7-4
Wickman, B.	0-1	0-1	0-0	0-0	1-1	1-1	0-1	0-0	1-0	0-0	0-1	0-0	0-2	0-0	0-0	0-0	3-8
Woodard, S.	0-0	1-0	2-0	1-0	0-1	1-0	0-0	0-1	1-0	0-1	0-0	1-1	0-1	1-1	0-1	2-0	11-8
Totals	4-5	2-5	6-6	6-6	3-6	4-5	5-8	2-7	5-4	2-5	5-4	8-4	3-5	4-5	7-6	8-6	74-87

INTERLEAGUE: Plunk 2-0, Coppinger 0-1 vs. White Sox; Roque 1-1, Nomo 1-0 vs. Indians; Woodard 1-0, Nomo 1-0, Abbott 0-1 vs. Tigers; Woodard 1-0, Nomo 1-0, Pittsley 0-1 vs. Royals; Weathers 0-1, Eldred 0-1 vs. Twins. Total: 8-6.

MISCELLANEOUS

HOME RUNS BY PARK

At Arizona: (0).
At Atlanta (2): Cirillo 1, Jenkins 1.
At Chicago (NL) (14): Grissom 4, Valentin 2, Burnitz 2, Cirillo 2, Nilsson 1, Becker 1, Belliard 1, Barker 1.
At Cincinnati (10): Nilsson 3, Valentin 2, Burnitz 1, Cirillo 1, Banks 1, Belliard 1, Jenkins 1.
At Cleveland (6): Nilsson 2, Jenkins 2, Burnitz 1, Loretta 1.
At Colorado (9): Burnitz 3, Grissom 2, Nilsson 1, Karl 1, Belliard 1, Hughes 1.
At Detroit (3): Burnitz 2, Jenkins 1.
At Florida (6): Nilsson 1, Valentin 1, Vina 1, Burnitz 1, Hughes 1, Jenkins 1.
At Houston (4): Jenkins 2, Burnitz 1, Loretta 1.
At Los Angeles (1): Burnitz 1.
At Milwaukee (77): Burnitz 12, Jenkins 10, Grissom 9, Nilsson 9, Ochoa 8, Cirillo 6, Belliard 5, Becker 4, Banks 4, Valentin 3, Loretta 2, Collier 2, Karl 1, Mouton 1, Barker 1.
At Montreal (5): Burnitz 2, Grissom 1, Nilsson 1, Loretta 1.
At New York (NL) (3): Grissom 1, Cirillo 1, Jenkins 1.
At Philadelphia (3): Nilsson 1, Burnitz 1, Cirillo 1.
At Pittsburgh (8): Cirillo 3, Burnitz 2, Grissom 1, Nilsson 1, Jenkins 1.
At San Diego (2): Grissom 1, Jenkins 1.
At San Francisco (6): Burnitz 3, Grissom 1, Berry 1, Valentin 1.
At St. Louis (6): Berry 1, Nilsson 1, Valentin 1, Burnitz 1, Hughes 1, Barker 1.

LOW-HIT GAMES

No-hitters: None.
One-hitters: None.
Two-hitters: None.

10-STRIKEOUT GAMES

Hideo Nomo 1, Steve Woodard 1, **Total:** 2.

FOUR OR MORE HITS IN ONE GAME

Marquis Grissom 3, Jeff Cirillo 3 (including two five-hit games), Mark Loretta 3 (including one five-hit game), Jeromy Burnitz 2, Dave Nilsson 1, Brian Banks 1, Ron Belliard 1, **Total:** 14.

MULTI-HOMER GAMES

Dave Nilsson 3, Jeromy Burnitz 2, Marquis Grissom 1, Jose Valentin 1, Rich Becker 1, Alex Ochoa 1, Geoff Jenkins 1, **Total:** 10.

GRAND SLAMS

6-27: Jeromy Burnitz (off Pittsburgh's Scott Sauerbeck).
8-25: Jose Valentin (off Los Angeles's Kevin Brown).

PINCH HITTERS

(Minimum 5 at-bats)

Name	AB	Avg.	HR	RBI
Berry, Sean	42	.190	0	3
Becker, Rich	38	.263	1	4
Ochoa, Alex	37	.270	0	5
Banks, Brian	25	.200	0	1
Collier, Lou	24	.250	2	6
Nilsson, Dave	14	.071	0	0
Jenkins, Geoff	12	.250	0	2
Mouton, Lyle	10	.000	0	2
Grissom, Marquis	8	.500	1	4
Hughes, Bobby	7	.286	0	0
Barker, Kevin	7	.143	0	0
Valentin, Jose	6	.500	0	3
Loretta, Mark	6	.000	0	0

DEBUTS

5-4: Horacio Estrada, P.
7-19: Kyle Peterson, P.
8-19: Kevin Barker, 1B.
8-28: Hector Ramirez, P.
9-3: Robinson Cancel, C.
9-7: Carl Dale, P.

GAMES BY POSITION

Catcher: Dave Nilsson 101, Bobby Hughes 44, Brian Banks 40, Charlie Greene 31, Robinson Cancel 15.
First base: Mark Loretta 66, Sean Berry 64, Brian Banks 44, Kevin Barker 31.
Second base: Ron Belliard 119, Fernando Vina 37, Mark Loretta 17, Lou Collier 4, Eddie Zosky 2.
Third base: Jeff Cirillo 155, Mark Loretta 14, Lou Collier 7, Eddie Zosky 4, Ron Belliard 1.
Shortstop: Jose Valentin 85, Mark Loretta 74, Lou Collier 31, Ron Belliard 1.
Outfield: Marquis Grissom 149, Geoff Jenkins 128, Jeromy Burnitz 127, Alex Ochoa 85, Rich Becker 50, Lou Collier 10, Brian Banks 5, Lyle Mouton 3.
Designated hitter: Jeromy Burnitz 3, Rich Becker 2, Dave Nilsson 1, Alex Ochoa 1, Bobby Hughes 1.

STREAKS

Wins: 5 (June 17-23, June 30-July 5).
Losses: 6 (July 31-August 6).
Consecutive games with at least one hit: 13, Jeff Cirillo (April 23-May 7).
Wins by pitcher: 4, Hideo Nomo (June 10-26), Steve Woodard (June 14-29).

ATTENDANCE

Home: 1,701,790.
Road: 2,055,797.
Highest (home): 55,992 (October 3 vs. Cincinnati).
Highest (road): 47,806 (April 5 vs. St. Louis).
Lowest (home): 10,575 (April 19 vs. St. Louis).
Lowest (road): 5,589 (April 13 vs. Montreal).

MONTREAL EXPOS

1999 REVIEW

DAY BY DAY

Date	Opp.	Res.	Score	(inn.*)	Hits	Opp. hits	Winning pitcher	Losing pitcher	Save	Record	Pos.	GB
4-5	At Pit.	W	9-2		17	7	Hermanson	Cordova		1-0	T1st	...
4-6	At Pit.	L	2-8		3	10	Schmidt	Pavano		1-1	T1st	...
4-7	At Pit.	W	4-3		7	11	Urbina	Loiselle		2-1	T1st	...
4-8	N.Y.	W	5-1		10	6	Batista	Hershiser	Urbina	3-1	1st	+1.0
4-9	N.Y.	L	3-10		5	11	Yoshii	Thurman		3-2	T1st	...
4-10	N.Y.	L	3-4	(11)	7	8	Cook	Telford	Franco	3-3	T2nd	1.0
4-11	N.Y.	L	3-6		7	14	Watson	Pavano	Franco	3-4	4th	2.0
4-13	Mil.	L	4-8		12	14	Woodard	Vazquez		3-5	4th	3.0
4-14	Mil.	W	15-1		17	6	Batista	Abbott		4-5	T3rd	3.0
4-15	Mil.	L	4-9		12	11	Karl	Ayala		4-6	4th	3.0
4-16	At N.Y.	W	6-4		7	7	Hermanson	Leiter	Urbina	5-6	4th	2.0
4-17	At N.Y.	L	2-3		7	6	Jones	Pavano	Franco	5-7	4th	3.0
4-18	At N.Y.	W	4-2		11	6	Vazquez	Watson	Urbina	6-7	4th	2.0
4-19	At Col.	L	10-11		20	11	Veres	Urbina		6-8	4th	3.0
4-23	Phi.	L	2-6		6	10	Ogea	Hermanson		6-9	4th	4.0
4-24	Phi.	L	5-6		12	11	Grace	Ayala	Gomes	6-10	4th	4.0
4-25	Phi.	L	6-8		8	10	Byrd	Urbina		6-11	4th	5.0
4-27	S.F	L	2-3	(10)	10	6	Johnstone	Kline	Nen	6-12	4th	5.5
4-28	S.F	L	3-4		9	7	Nathan	Hermanson	Nen	6-13	4th	6.5
4-29	S.F	L	5-6		9	13	Ortiz	Pavano	Nen	6-14	4th	7.5
4-30	StL.	W	3-2		8	6	Urbina	Acevedo		7-14	4th	7.5
5-1	StL.	L	5-16		8	19	Osborne	Thurman	Mohler	7-15	4th	8.5
5-2	StL.	L	7-8	(10)	14	11	Acevedo	Urbina	Radinsky	7-16	4th	9.5
5-3	L.A.	L	0-7		7	13	Park	Hermanson		7-17	4th	10.5
5-4	L.A.	W	2-1		7	4	Pavano	Valdes	Urbina	8-17	4th	9.5
5-5	L.A.	L	2-8		4	13	Arnold	Vazquez		8-18	4th	10.5
5-7	At Hou.	L	2-5		9	8	Lima	Batista		8-19	4th	10.5
5-8	At Hou.	W	6-5		12	9	Hermanson	Reynolds	Urbina	9-19	4th	10.5
5-9	At Hou.	W	4-2		13	9	Pavano	Holt	Urbina	10-19	4th	9.5
5-10	At Ari.	L	6-7		13	11	Olson	Ayala		10-20	4th	9.5
5-11	At Ari.	L	3-4	(10)	9	7	Olson	Mota		10-21	4th	10.5
5-12	At Ari.	L	6-8		10	10	Telemaco	Smart		10-22	4th	10.5
5-14	At Pit.	L	3-5		5	10	Benson	Hermanson	Williams	10-23	4th	10.5
5-15	At Pit.	L	6-17		11	17	Silva	Pavano		10-24	4th	10.5
5-16	At Pit.	L	4-9		10	8	Schourek	Vazquez		10-25	5th	11.5
5-17	Phi.	L	3-4		9	8	Schilling	Thurman		10-26	5th	12.5
5-18	Phi.	W	7-4		9	9	Batista	Bennett	Urbina	11-26	4th	12.5
5-19	Phi.	W	10-9		13	8	Kline	Brantley		12-26	4th	12.5
5-21	Mil.	L	3-5	(11)	6	9	Wickman	Ayala	Weathers	12-27	5th	12.0
5-22	Mil.	W	12-4		14	7	Vazquez	Karl	Telford	13-27	4th	12.0
5-23	Mil.	L	4-13		7	13	Weathers	Urbina		13-28	4th	12.0
5-24	At Phi.	L	4-5		7	7	Perez	Batista	Gomes	13-29	5th	12.0
5-25	At Phi.	W	4-2	(11)	10	6	Urbina	Montgomery		14-29	5th	12.0
5-26	At Phi.	W	5-2		8	6	Pavano	Loewer	Urbina	15-29	4th	12.0
5-28	S.F	W	4-2		9	6	Telford	Ortiz	Urbina	16-29	4th	12.5
5-29	S.F	W	7-4		11	7	Thurman	Estes	Urbina	17-29	4th	11.5
5-30	S.F	W	6-4		12	10	Batista	Brock	Urbina	18-29	4th	10.5
5-31	Ari.	L	5-8	(10)	10	16	Holmes	Kline	Olson	18-30	4th	11.5
6-1	Ari.	W	10-8		12	14	Mota	Frascatore	Urbina	19-30	4th	11.5
6-2	Ari.	L	2-15		5	20	Daal	Vazquez		19-31	4th	11.5
6-4	At Tor.	L	2-6		6	9	Wells	Ayala		19-32	4th	11.5
6-5	At Tor.	W	5-0		6	3	Batista	Hamilton		20-32	4th	11.5
6-6	At Tor.	L	2-9		8	13	Escobar	Hermanson		20-33	4th	12.5
6-7	Bos.	W	8-2		13	6	Pavano	Saberhagen		21-33	4th	12.5
6-8	Bos.	W	5-1		9	4	Smith	Wakefield		22-33	4th	12.5
6-9	Bos.	W	13-1		14	5	Thurman	Martinez		23-33	4th	12.5
6-11	T.B.	W	5-4		9	9	Batista	Witt	Urbina	24-33	4th	11.5
6-12	T.B.	L	3-5		9	14	Callaway	Hermanson	Hernandez	24-34	4th	11.5
6-13	T.B.	W	4-0		8	3	Pavano	Rekar		25-34	4th	10.5
6-14	At StL.	W	7-5		11	9	Telford	Oliver	Urbina	26-34	4th	9.5
6-15	At StL.	L	2-3		5	5	Jimenez	Thurman	Bottalico	26-35	4th	10.5
6-16	At StL.	L	4-5		6	9	Bottenfield	Batista	Bottalico	26-36	4th	11.5
6-18	At Hou.	L	0-5		6	6	Reynolds	Hermanson		26-37	4th	13.0
6-19	At Hou.	L	2-5		8	10	Hampton	Pavano	Wagner	26-38	4th	13.0
6-20	At Hou.	L	3-11		11	9	Holt	Smith		26-39	4th	14.0
6-22	At Atl.	W	2-1		8	9	Thurman	Maddux	Urbina	27-39	4th	13.0
6-23	At Atl.	L	3-7		7	13	Millwood	Batista		27-40	4th	14.0
6-24	At Atl.	L	2-3	(11)	7	13	McGlinchy	Mota		27-41	4th	15.0
6-25	Fla.	W	4-3		12	5	Pavano	Fernandez	Urbina	28-41	4th	14.0
6-26	Fla.	L	3-9		8	12	Dempster	Smith		28-42	4th	15.0
6-27	Fla.	L	3-4		8	6	Springer	Thurman	Mantei	28-43	4th	16.0
6-28	Atl.	L	5-13		11	16	Millwood	Batista		28-44	4th	17.0
6-29	Atl.	W	6-5		10	10	Urbina	Rocker		29-44	4th	16.0
6-30	Atl.	W	7-5		10	8	Kline	McGlinchy	Urbina	30-44	4th	15.0
7-1	Atl.	L	1-4		7	12	Glavine	Smith		30-45	4th	16.0
7-3	At Fla.	L	1-6		7	9	Meadows	Batista		30-46	4th	17.5
7-4	At Fla.	L	1-5		8	8	Hernandez	Powell		30-47	4th	17.5
7-5	At N.Y.	L	1-2		6	9	Wendell	Mota	Benitez	30-48	4th	18.5
7-6	At N.Y.	L	0-10		6	13	Hershiser	Pavano	Isringhausen	30-49	4th	18.5

HIGHLIGHTS

High point: A three-game sweep of the Red Sox June 7-9 at Olympic Stadium. The Expos defeated Bret Saberhagen, Tim Wakefield and former Expos standout Pedro Martinez, prevailing by a cumulative score of 26-4.

Low point: David Cone's perfect game for the Yankees against the Expos on July 18 came on a Sunday afternoon after the club had played in sapping heat in Baltimore the night before. The Expos might have been dragging that day at Yankee Stadium, but comments minimizing Cone's achievement still had to hurt. The oft-heard line: It wasn't much of an accomplishment to shut down lowly Montreal.

Turning point: A draining five-game series against the Rockies in Colorado August 13-15 (including two doubleheaders in three days) was made necessary by the April postponement of two games in the aftermath of the Columbine High School shootings in suburban Denver. The Expos swept the first doubleheader, but lost the last three games and tumbled into last place on August 16.

Most valuable player: Vladimir Guerrero solved many of his early fielding problems and again proved why he's the player the team is building around. Guerrero set eight single-season Expos offensive records, including highs in home runs (42) and RBIs (131). His 31-game hitting streak was the longest in the National League since 1987.

Most valuable pitcher: Ugueth Urbina led the N.L. in saves with 41 despite playing for a team that lost 94 games. In 75.2 innings, he struck out 100 batters and yielded only 59 hits.

Most improved player: Jose Vidro worked on his hitting in winter ball—and it showed. Despite a poor September, he finished with a .304 average and 45 doubles. The second baseman went back to winter ball after the 1999 season to work on his defense.

Most pleasant surprise: Javier Vazquez was struggling again in 1999 when he was sent to the minors in June. Upon his return in July, he was the loser in Cone's perfect game but then pitched complete-game victories in his next two starts. He finished with a 9-8 record.

Key injuries: The loss of shortstop Orlando Cabrera (ankle sprain) for the final two months was a setback. Righthander Carl Pavano (elbow problems) made only one appearance after the All-Star break—and that was in relief.

Notable: Lefthanded reliever Steve Kline led the majors in appearances with 82, and righthander Anthony Telford worked 79 times out of the bullpen. ... Guerrero again was a constant in the lineup (159 games in 1998, 160 in 1999), avoiding injuries despite his aggressive play. ... Rondell White, who split time between left and center field, batted .312 with 22 homers.

—STEPHANIE MYLES

MISCELLANEOUS

RECORDS

1999 regular-season record: 68-94 (4th in N.L. East); 35-46 at home; 33-48 on road; 19-31 vs. N.L. East; 22-28 vs. N.L. Central; 19-25 vs. N.L. West; 8-10 vs. A.L. East; 18-21 vs. lefthanded starters; 50-73 vs. righthanded starters; 23-35 on grass; 45-59 on turf; 14-32 in daytime; 54-62 at night; 16-28 in one-run games; 3-11 in extra-inning games; 1-2-0 in doubleheaders.

Team record past five years: 365-427 (.461, ranks 13th in league in that span).

TEAM LEADERS

Batting average: Vladimir Guerrero (.316).
At-bats: Vladimir Guerrero (610).
Runs: Vladimir Guerrero (102).
Hits: Vladimir Guerrero (193).
Total bases: Vladimir Guerrero (366).
Doubles: Jose Vidro (45).
Triples: Wilton Guerrero, Manny Martinez (7).
Home runs: Vladimir Guerrero (42).
Runs batted in: Vladimir Guerrero (131).
Stolen bases: Manny Martinez (19).
Slugging percentage: Vladimir Guerrero (.600).
On-base percentage: Vladimir Guerrero (.378).
Wins: Dustin Hermanson, Javier Vazquez (9).
Earned-run average: Dustin Hermanson (4.20).
Complete games: Javier Vazquez (3).
Shutouts: Miguel Batista, Carl Pavano, Javier Vazquez (1).
Saves: Ugueth Urbina (41).
Innings pitched: Dustin Hermanson (216.1).
Strikeouts: Dustin Hermanson (145).

Date	Opp.	Res.	Score	(inn.*)	Hits	Opp. hits	Winning pitcher	Losing pitcher	Save	Record	Pos.	GB
7-7	At N.Y.	W	3-1		8	7	Kline	Wendell	Urbina	31-49	4th	18.5
7-8	At N.Y.	W	4-3		6	6	Ayala	Cook	Urbina	32-49	4th	18.5
7-9	Tor.	W	4-3		16	9	Urbina	Lloyd		33-49	4th	17.5
7-10	Tor.	L	6-7		11	9	Quantrill	Telford	Koch	33-50	4th	18.5
7-11	Tor.	L	0-1		2	4	Wells	Pavano		33-51	4th	19.5
7-15	At Bal.	L	2-8		11	9	Ponson	Thurman		33-52	4th	20.5
7-16	At Bal.	L	4-9		9	17	Mussina	Smith		33-53	4th	21.5
7-17	At Bal.	L	1-2		6	4	Erickson	Hermanson		33-54	4th	21.5
7-18	At N.Y. (AL)	L	0-6		0	8	Cone	Vazquez		33-55	4th	21.5
7-19	At N.Y. (AL)	W	6-4		12	10	Kline	Mendoza	Urbina	34-55	4th	20.5
7-20	At N.Y. (AL)	L	4-7		9	9	Clemens	Thurman	Rivera	34-56	4th	20.5
7-21	N.Y.	L	3-7		12	12	Reed	Smith		34-57	5th	20.5
7-22	N.Y.	L	4-7		9	12	Hershiser	Hermanson		34-58	5th	21.5
7-23	Pit.	W	5-1		9	4	Vazquez	Ritchie		35-58	5th	21.0
7-24	Pit.	L	2-7		7	11	Schourek	Powell		35-59	5th	21.0
7-25	Pit.	L	1-6		4	11	Schmidt	Kline		35-60	5th	22.0
7-26	Chi.	W	6-1		9	9	Smith	Lieber		36-60	5th	22.0
7-27	Chi.	L	2-4		10	8	Mulholland	Hermanson	Adams	36-61	4th	23.0
7-28	Chi.	W	8-2		10	3	Vazquez	Tapani		37-61	5th	22.0
7-30	At Mil.	L	0-1		5	7	Peterson	Powell	Wickman	37-62	5th	22.5
7-31	At Mil.	W	4-2		12	5	Telford	Plunk	Urbina	38-62	5th	22.0
8-1	At Mil.	W	10-4		13	7	Smith	Karl		39-62	5th	22.0
8-2	At Chi.	W	5-1		7	6	Hermanson	Tapani	Urbina	40-62	4th	21.5
8-3	At Chi.	W	9-4		13	12	Vazquez	Bowie		41-62	4th	21.5
8-4	At Chi.	L	1-5		5	7	Trachsel	Powell		41-63	4th	22.5
8-5	At Chi.	W	5-2		10	10	Thurman	Lieber	Urbina	42-63	4th	22.0
8-6	S.D.	L	10-12		9	17	Hitchcock	Smith	Hoffman	42-64	4th	23.0
8-7	S.D.	W	3-1		8	4	Hermanson	Williams	Urbina	43-64	4th	22.0
8-8	S.D.	W	4-2		13	7	Kline	Reyes	Urbina	44-64	4th	21.0
8-9	S.D.	W	8-0		11	7	Powell	Clement		45-64	4th	20.5
8-10	L.A.	W	6-4		8	7	Thurman	Valdes	Urbina	46-64	4th	20.5
8-11	L.A.	L	7-9		15	11	Maddux	Ayala	Shaw	46-65	4th	21.5
8-12	L.A.	L	5-10		10	11	Judd	Hermanson		46-66	4th	22.0
8-13†	At Col.	W	14-13	(10)	14	15	Urbina	Dipoto	Telford	47-66		
8-13‡	At Col.	W	8-6		13	11	Vazquez	Bohanon	Urbina	48-66	4th	21.5
8-14	At Col.	L	8-11		11	18	Kile	Powell	Veres	48-67	4th	21.5
8-15†	At Col.	L	2-8		7	9	Thomson	Thurman	Ramirez	48-68		
8-15‡	At Col.	L	4-12		12	14	Astacio	Bennett		48-69	4th	23.0
8-16	At S.F	L	4-7		8	12	Nathan	Armas Jr.	Nen	48-70	5th	24.0
8-17	At S.F	W	2-1	(12)	10	7	Smith	Johnstone	Urbina	49-70	5th	23.0
8-18	At S.F	L	4-5		12	7	Ortiz	Vazquez	Nen	49-71	5th	24.0
8-20	At Cin.	W	5-3		9	8	Batista	Sullivan	Urbina	50-71	4th	23.5
8-21	At Cin.	L	3-9		8	11	Guzman	Thurman		50-72	4th	25.5
8-22	At Cin.	L	3-4	(11)	11	12	Sullivan	Urbina		50-73	T4th	25.5
8-23	StL.	W	11-7		14	11	Telford	Croushore		51-73	4th	25.5
8-24	StL.	W	8-4		12	10	Vazquez	Bottenfield	Urbina	52-73	4th	25.5
8-25	StL.	W	4-1		8	7	Powell	Luebbers	Urbina	53-73	4th	25.5
8-26	Cin.	L	4-10		8	14	Guzman	Thurman	Williamson	53-74	4th	26.0
8-27	Cin.	L	1-4		4	10	Villone	Hermanson	Graves	53-75	4th	27.0
8-28	Cin.	W	8-6		11	9	Kline	Williamson		54-75	4th	27.0
8-29	Cin.	W	8-6		8	10	Mota	Harnisch	Urbina	55-75	4th	27.0
8-30	At Ari.	L	4-5		8	9	Chouinard	Batista	Mantei	55-76	4th	27.0
8-31	At Ari.	W	2-1		6	6	Thurman	Johnson	Urbina	56-76	4th	27.0
9-1	At Ari.	W	8-1		11	7	Hermanson	Daal		57-76	4th	27.0
9-3	Hou.	L	1-8		7	11	Hampton	Smith		57-77	4th	28.0
9-4	Hou.	L	2-5	(10)	8	6	Cabrera	Urbina		57-78	4th	28.0
9-5	Hou.	L	2-6		9	12	Elarton	Telford		57-79	4th	28.0
9-6	Col.	L	3-5		9	10	Astacio	Thurman	Veres	57-80	4th	29.0
9-7	Col.	W	4-1		5	6	Hermanson	Thomson	Urbina	58-80	4th	29.0
9-8	Col.	L	1-5		6	7	Wright	Smith		58-81	4th	30.0
9-9	At S.D.	L	3-10		6	17	Carlyle	Vazquez		58-82	4th	30.5
9-10	At S.D.	L	3-10		8	10	Clement	Powell		58-83	4th	31.5
9-11	At S.D.	W	5-4		7	10	Thurman	Ashby	Urbina	59-83	4th	30.5
9-12	At S.D.	W	8-4		12	12	Hermanson	Hitchcock	Urbina	60-83	4th	29.5
9-13	At L.A.	L	4-12		10	15	Park	Smith		60-84	4th	29.5
9-14	At L.A.	W	3-0		9	1	Vazquez	Brown		61-84	4th	29.5
9-15	At L.A.	W	10-7		12	14	Powell	Arnold	Urbina	62-84	4th	28.5
9-17	At Atl.	L	5-6	(10)	12	5	Remlinger	Kline		62-85	4th	29.5
9-18	At Atl.	W	4-3		8	11	Hermanson	Maddux	Urbina	63-85	4th	28.5
9-19	At Atl.	L	1-5		7	7	Millwood	Lilly		63-86	4th	29.5
9-21†	At Fla.	L	3-5		11	8	Springer	Telford	Alfonseca	63-87		
9-21‡	At Fla.	L	0-4		7	8	Cornelius	Powell		63-88	4th	31.0
9-22	At Fla.	W	5-3		7	7	Batista	Nunez	Urbina	64-88	4th	31.0
9-23	At Fla.	L	1-2		9	4	Burnett	Hermanson	Alfonseca	64-89	4th	32.0
9-24	Atl.	L	3-5	(10)	4	9	Bergman	Mota	Remlinger	64-90	4th	33.0
9-25	Atl.	L	3-5		10	9	Mulholland	Vazquez	Rocker	64-91	4th	34.0
9-26	Atl.	L	0-10		6	13	Smoltz	Powell		64-92	4th	35.0
9-27	Fla.	W	8-4		7	8	Telford	Almonte		65-92	4th	34.5
9-28	Fla.	L	3-5		8	11	Nunez	Hermanson	Alfonseca	65-93	4th	35.5
9-29	Fla.	W	5-3		8	6	Kline	Looper	Urbina	66-93	4th	34.5
10-1	At Phi.	W	7-4		13	11	Vazquez	Grahe	Urbina	67-93	4th	35.0
10-2	At Phi.	W	13-3		14	8	Powell	Byrd	Batista	68-93	4th	34.0
10-3	At Phi.	L	5-6		8	9	Politte	Strickland	Montgomery	68-94	4th	35.0

Monthly records: April (7-14), May (11-16), June (12-14), July (8-18), August (18-14), September (10-17), October (2-1).
*Innings, if other than nine. † First game of a doubleheader. ‡ Second game of a doubleheader.

MEMORABLE GAMES

June 9 at Montreal

It was not a fair fight, it seemed. Former hero Pedro Martinez returned "home" with one loss on the season; Expos starter Mike Thurman had one win. But the Expos got to Pedro for four runs, and broke it open with an eight-run eighth inning to delight one of the largest crowds of the season.

Boston	AB	R	H	RBI	Montreal	AB	R	H	RBI
Offerman, 2b	4	0	2	1	O.Cabrera, ss	4	2	1	0
Frye, 3b	4	0	0	0	Vidro, 2b	4	1	2	1
Garciaparra, ss	3	0	1	0	Mota, p	1	1	1	3
Stanley, 1b	4	0	0	0	Ro.White, cf-lf	5	3	3	1
Buford, lf-cf	3	0	0	0	Merced, lf	3	1	1	0
Varitek, c	4	0	0	0	M.Martinz, cf	2	2	2	2
D.Lewis, cf	3	0	0	0	V.Guerrero, rf	4	0	2	1
Portugal, p	0	0	0	0	Barrett, c	3	1	0	0
Guthrie, p	0	0	0	0	Andrews, 3b	2	1	0	0
Wasdin, p	0	0	0	0	McGuire, 1b	4	1	1	2
T.Nixon, rf	3	0	1	0	Thurman, p	3	0	0	0
P.Martinez, p	2	0	0	0	Mordecai, 2b	0	0	0	1
O'Leary, lf	1	1	1	0					
Totals	31	1	5	1	Totals	36	13	14	13

Boston ....0 0 0   0 0 0   0 1 0 —1
Montreal ....0 0 0   2 0 2   1 8 x—13

DP—Montreal 1. LOB—Boston 5, Montreal 4. 2B—Offerman (21), O.Cabrera (14), Vidro (15), Merced (3), McGuire (5), M.Martinez (9). 3B—Garciaparra (3). HR—M.Martinez (2), Mota (1). SB—Garciaparra (8), V.Guerrero (4). CS—V.Guerrero (2). SF—Mordecai.

Boston	IP	H	R	ER	BB	SO
P.Martinez (L, 11-2)	6	6	4	4	2	10
Portugal	1.1	4	4	4	1	2
Guthrie	0.1	3	4	4	1	0
Wasdin	0.1	1	1	1	0	0

Montreal	IP	H	R	ER	BB	SO
Thurman (W, 2-3)	7.1	5	1	1	2	3
Mota	1.2	0	0	0	0	0

U—HP, Bucknor. 1B—Gorman. 2B—Crawford. 3B—Nauert. T—2:40. A—19,012.

July 18 at New York

Lost amid the commotion of David Cone's perfect game was the performance by Javier Vazquez. It was Vazquez's return to the big leagues after six weeks at Class AAA, and he went seven innings, the last five scoreless. He built on that momentum to record complete-game victories in his next two starts, ending the season as the only Expos starter above .500.

Montreal	AB	R	H	RBI	NY Yankees	AB	R	H	RBI
W.Guerrero, dh	3	0	0	0	Knoblauch, 2b	2	1	1	0
Te.Jones, cf	2	0	0	0	Jeter, ss	4	1	1	2
J.Mouton, cf	1	0	0	0	O'Neill, rf	4	1	1	0
Ro.White, lf	3	0	0	0	B.Williams, cf	4	0	1	1
V.Guerrero, rf	3	0	0	0	T.Martinez, 1b	4	0	1	0
Vidro, 2b	3	0	0	0	C.Davis, dh	3	1	0	0
Fullmer, 1b	3	0	0	0	Ledee, lf	4	1	1	2
Widger, c	3	0	0	0	Brosius, 3b	2	1	0	0
Andrews, 3b	2	0	0	0	Girardi, c	3	0	1	1
McGuire, ph	1	0	0	0					
O.Cabrera, ss	3	0	0	0					
Totals	27	0	0	0	Totals	30	6	8	6

Montreal ....0 0 0   0 0 0   0 0 0 —0
NY Yankees ....0 5 0   0 0 0   0 1 x —6

DP—Montreal 1. LOB—Montreal 0, NY Yankees 4. 2B—O'Neill (20), Girardi (9). HR—Jeter (16), Ledee (3).

Montreal	IP	H	R	ER	BB	SO
Vazquez (L, 2-5)	7	7	6	6	2	3
Ayala	1	1	0	0	0	0

NY Yankees	IP	H	R	ER	BB	SO
Cone (W, 10-4)	9	0	0	0	0	10

HBP—Knoblauch by Vazquez, Brosius by Vazquez. U—HP, Barrett. 1B. McCoy. 2B. Evans. 3B. Meriwether. T—2:16. A—41,930.

BATTING

																							vs RHP				vs LHP			
Name	G	TPA	AB	R	H	TB	2B	3B	HR	RBI	Avg.	Obp.	Slg.	SH	SF	HP	BB	IBB	SO	SB	CS	GDP	AB	Avg.	HR	RBI	AB	Avg.	HR	RBI
Guerrero, Vladimir	160	674	610	102	193	366	37	5	42	131	.316	.378	.600	0	2	7	55	14	62	14	7	18	481	.324	30	104	129	.287	12	27
White, Rondell	138	588	539	83	168	272	26	6	22	64	.312	.359	.505	0	6	11	32	2	85	10	6	17	416	.293	14	42	123	.374	8	22
Vidro, Jose	140	531	494	67	150	235	45	2	12	59	.304	.346	.476	2	2	4	29	2	51	0	4	12	394	.315	11	49	100	.260	1	10
Barrett, Michael	126	469	433	53	127	189	32	3	8	52	.293	.345	.436	0	1	3	32	4	39	0	2	18	317	.303	6	38	116	.267	2	14
Widger, Chris	124	419	383	42	101	169	24	1	14	56	.264	.325	.441	0	1	7	28	0	86	1	4	5	283	.233	9	37	100	.350	5	19
Cabrera, Orlando	104	407	382	48	97	154	23	5	8	39	.254	.293	.403	4	0	3	18	4	38	2	2	9	289	.228	7	31	93	.333	1	8
Fullmer, Brad	100	374	347	38	96	161	34	2	9	47	.277	.321	.464	0	3	2	22	6	35	2	3	14	297	.283	7	34	50	.240	2	13
Martinez, Manny	137	357	331	48	81	113	12	7	2	26	.245	.279	.341	6	3	0	17	0	51	19	6	5	225	.231	2	18	106	.274	0	8
Guerrero, Wilton	132	340	315	42	92	127	15	7	2	31	.292	.324	.403	10	0	2	13	0	38	7	6	4	218	.275	1	20	97	.330	1	11
Andrews, Shane	98	328	281	28	51	92	8	0	11	37	.181	.287	.327	0	4	0	43	2	88	1	0	10	204	.181	8	31	77	.182	3	6
Mordecai, Mike	109	250	226	29	53	82	10	2	5	25	.235	.297	.363	1	2	1	20	0	31	2	5	1	159	.226	3	18	67	.254	2	7
Merced, Orlando	93	221	194	25	52	90	12	1	8	26	.268	.353	.464	0	1	0	26	0	27	2	1	5	184	.266	8	25	10	.300	0	1
McGuire, Ryan	88	171	140	17	31	48	7	2	2	18	.221	.347	.343	3	0	0	27	0	33	1	1	9	122	.213	2	16	18	.278	0	2
Blum, Geoff	45	154	133	21	32	67	7	2	8	18	.241	.327	.504	3	0	0	17	3	25	1	0	3	112	.250	6	16	21	.190	2	2
Mouton, James	95	146	122	18	32	45	5	1	2	13	.262	.364	.369	3	1	2	18	1	31	6	2	2	65	.246	2	6	57	.281	0	7
Seguignol, Fernando	35	119	105	14	27	51	9	0	5	10	.257	.328	.486	0	2	7	5	1	33	0	0	1	83	.265	4	7	22	.227	1	3
Hermanson, Dustin	34	75	64	1	3	3	0	0	0	2	.047	.090	.047	8	0	0	3	0	39	0	0	0	47	.021	0	2	17	.118	0	0
Jones, Terry	17	66	63	4	17	20	1	1	0	3	.270	.303	.317	0	0	0	3	0	14	1	2	0	57	.281	0	2	6	.167	0	1
Coquillette, Trace	17	55	49	2	13	16	3	0	0	4	.265	.333	.327	1	0	1	4	0	7	1	0	3	37	.216	0	1	12	.417	0	3
Bergeron, Peter	16	55	45	12	11	13	2	0	0	1	.244	.370	.289	1	0	0	9	0	5	0	0	0	44	.250	0	1	1	.000	0	0
Vazquez, Javier	26	53	42	4	12	14	2	0	0	5	.286	.333	.333	8	0	0	3	0	8	0	0	1	27	.259	0	3	15	.333	0	2
Thurman, Mike	29	46	40	1	1	1	0	0	0	0	.025	.071	.025	4	0	1	1	0	31	0	0	0	32	.031	0	0	8	.000	0	0
Batista, Miguel	39	41	35	6	7	11	1	0	1	3	.200	.243	.314	4	0	0	2	0	19	0	0	0	30	.167	1	3	5	.400	0	0
Pavano, Carl	19	39	33	1	2	2	0	0	0	2	.061	.088	.061	5	0	0	1	0	14	0	0	0	27	.037	0	2	6	.167	0	0
Powell, Jeremy	17	34	30	2	4	5	1	0	0	0	.133	.212	.167	1	0	0	3	0	8	0	0	0	26	.154	0	0	4	.000	0	0
Cox, Darron	15	27	25	2	6	10	1	0	1	2	.240	.296	.400	0	0	2	0	0	5	0	0	0	14	.214	0	1	11	.273	1	1
Fernandez, Jose	8	25	24	0	5	7	2	0	0	1	.208	.240	.292	0	0	0	1	0	7	0	0	1	23	.217	0	1	1	.000	0	0
Smith, Dan	20	30	24	3	2	2	0	0	0	1	.083	.185	.083	3	0	0	3	0	15	0	0	1	14	.000	0	0	10	.200	0	1
Machado, Robert	17	24	22	3	4	5	1	0	0	0	.182	.250	.227	0	0	0	2	0	6	0	0	0	16	.250	0	0	6	.000	0	0
Lilly, Ted	9	6	5	0	1	1	0	0	0	0	.200	.200	.200	1	0	0	0	0	1	0	0	0	4	.250	0	0	1	.000	0	0
Urbina, Ugueth	71	5	5	0	0	0	0	0	0	0	.000	.000	.000	0	0	0	0	0	2	0	0	0	3	.000	0	0	2	.000	0	0
Johnson, Mike	3	4	4	1	1	1	0	0	0	0	.250	.250	.250	0	0	0	0	0	1	0	0	0	3	.333	0	0	1	.000	0	0
Smart, J.D.	29	3	3	0	0	0	0	0	0	0	.000	.000	.000	0	0	0	0	0	0	0	0	0	2	.000	0	0	1	.000	0	0
Telford, Anthony	79	5	2	0	0	0	0	0	0	1	.000	.333	.000	2	0	0	1	0	1	0	0	0	1	.000	0	1	1	.000	0	0
Bennett, Shayne	5	2	2	0	0	0	0	0	0	0	.000	.000	.000	0	0	0	0	0	1	0	0	0	1	.000	0	0	1	.000	0	0
Stowers, Chris	4	2	2	0	0	0	0	0	0	0	.000	.000	.000	0	0	0	0	0	0	0	0	0	2	.000	0	0	0	.000	0	0
Armas Jr., Tony	1	2	2	0	0	0	0	0	0	0	.000	.000	.000	0	0	0	0	0	1	0	0	0	2	.000	0	0	0	.000	0	0
Mota, Guillermo	51	1	1	1	1	4	0	0	1	3	1.000	1.000	4.000	0	0	0	0	0	0	0	0	0	0	.000	0	0	1	1.000	1	3
Ayala, Bobby	53	1	1	0	0	0	0	0	0	0	.000	.000	.000	0	0	0	0	0	0	0	0	0	1	.000	0	0	0	.000	0	0
Kline, Steve	82	2	1	0	0	0	0	0	0	0	.000	.000	.000	1	0	0	0	0	1	0	0	0	1	.000	0	0	0	.000	0	0
Maddux, Mike	4	0	0	0	0	0	0	0	0	0	.000	.000	.000	0	0	0	0	0	0	0	0	0	0	.000	0	0	0	.000	0	0
Rojas, Mel	3	0	0	0	0	0	0	0	0	0	.000	.000	.000	0	0	0	0	0	0	0	0	0	0	.000	0	0	0	.000	0	0
DeHart, Rick	3	0	0	0	0	0	0	0	0	0	.000	.000	.000	0	0	0	0	0	0	0	0	0	0	.000	0	0	0	.000	0	0
Strickland, Scott	17	0	0	0	0	0	0	0	0	0	.000	.000	.000	0	0	0	0	0	0	0	0	0	0	.000	0	0	0	.000	0	0

Players with more than one N.L. team

																							vs RHP				vs LHP			
Name	G	TPA	AB	R	H	TB	2B	3B	HR	RBI	Avg.	Obp.	Slg.	SH	SF	HP	BB	IBB	SO	SB	CS	GDP	AB	Avg.	HR	RBI	AB	Avg.	HR	RBI
Andrews, Chi.	19	76	67	13	17	36	4	0	5	14	.254	.329	.537	0	1	1	7	1	21	0	1	0	204	.181	8	31	77	.182	3	6
Andrews, Mon.-Chi.	117	404	348	41	68	128	12	0	16	51	.195	.295	.368	0	5	1	50	3	109	1	1	10	257	.183	12	42	91	.231	4	9
Ayala, Chi.	13	0	0	0	0	0	0	0	0	0	.000	.000	.000	0	0	0	0	0	0	0	0	0	1	.000	0	0	0	.000	0	0
Ayala, Mon.-Chi.	66	1	1	0	0	0	0	0	0	0	.000	.000	.000	0	0	0	0	0	0	0	0	0	1	.000	0	0	0	.000	0	0
Maddux, L.A.	49	0	0	0	0	0	0	0	0	0	.000	.000	.000	0	0	0	0	0	0	0	0	0	0	.000	0	0	0	.000	0	0
Maddux, Mon.-L.A.	53	0	0	0	0	0	0	0	0	0	.000	.000	.000	0	0	0	0	0	0	0	0	0	0	.000	0	0	0	.000	0	0
Rojas, L.A.	5	0	0	0	0	0	0	0	0	0	.000	.000	.000	0	0	0	0	0	0	0	0	0	0	.000	0	0	0	.000	0	0
Rojas, L.A.-Mon.	8	0	0	0	0	0	0	0	0	0	.000	.000	.000	0	0	0	0	0	0	0	0	0	0	.000	0	0	0	.000	0	0

PITCHING

																					vs. RH				vs. LH			
Name	W	L	Pct.	ERA	IP	H	R	ER	HR	SH	SF	HB	BB	IBB	SO	G	GS	CG	ShO	GF	Sv	AB	Avg.	HR	RBI	AB	Avg.	HR	RBI
Hermanson, Dustin	9	14	.391	4.20	216.1	225	110	101	20	16	7	7	69	4	145	34	34	0	0	0	0	451	.271	10	55	378	.272	10	45
Vazquez, Javier	9	8	.529	5.00	154.2	154	98	86	20	3	3	4	52	4	113	26	26	3	1	0	0	331	.272	12	43	274	.234	8	40
Thurman, Mike	7	11	.389	4.05	146.2	140	84	66	17	8	3	7	52	4	85	29	27	0	0	1	0	294	.221	11	41	263	.285	6	22
Batista, Miguel	8	7	.533	4.88	134.2	146	88	73	10	8	11	7	58	2	95	39	17	2	1	3	1	283	.230	8	50	239	.339	2	27
Pavano, Carl	6	8	.429	5.63	104.0	117	66	65	8	5	2	4	35	1	70	19	18	1	1	0	0	204	.279	3	29	207	.290	5	24
Powell, Jeremy	4	8	.333	4.73	97.0	113	60	51	14	9	3	8	44	2	44	17	17	0	0	0	0	210	.343	10	38	164	.250	4	14
Telford, Anthony	5	4	.556	3.94	96.0	112	52	42	3	3	5	3	38	3	69	79	0	0	0	21	2	209	.268	2	32	171	.327	1	26
Smith, Dan	4	9	.308	6.02	89.2	104	64	60	12	7	2	4	39	0	72	20	17	0	0	0	0	209	.273	4	32	146	.322	8	26
Urbina, Ugueth	6	6	.500	3.69	75.2	59	35	31	6	1	2	0	36	6	100	71	0	0	0	62	41	163	.215	3	20	121	.198	3	19
Kline, Steve	7	4	.636	3.75	69.2	56	32	29	8	3	1	3	33	6	69	82	0	0	0	18	0	164	.232	7	17	93	.194	1	9
Ayala, Bobby	1	6	.143	3.68	66.0	60	36	27	6	4	3	4	34	1	64	53	0	0	0	17	0	137	.219	4	25	118	.254	2	22
Mota, Guillermo	2	4	.333	2.93	55.1	54	24	18	5	3	3	2	25	3	27	51	0	0	0	18	0	122	.262	2	15	88	.250	3	9
Smart, J.D.	0	1	.000	5.02	52.0	56	30	29	4	2	1	0	17	0	21	29	0	0	0	6	0	115	.261	2	21	88	.295	2	18
Lilly, Ted	0	1	.000	7.61	23.2	30	20	20	7	0	1	3	9	0	28	9	3	0	0	1	0	85	.294	7	19	12	.417	0	4
Strickland, Scott	0	1	.000	4.50	18.0	15	10	9	3	2	0	0	11	0	23	17	0	0	0	5	0	45	.156	0	0	20	.400	3	6
Bennett, Shayne	0	1	.000	14.29	11.1	24	18	18	4	0	1	1	3	0	4	5	1	0	0	1	0	32	.406	3	9	22	.500	1	8
Johnson, Mike	0	0	.000	8.64	8.1	12	8	8	2	0	0	0	7	1	6	3	1	0	0	0	0	23	.261	1	4	14	.429	1	4
Armas Jr., Tony	0	1	.000	1.50	6.0	8	4	1	0	0	1	0	2	1	2	1	1	0	0	0	0	17	.353	0	3	8	.250	0	1
Maddux, Mike	0	0	.000	9.00	5.0	9	5	5	1	0	0	1	3	0	4	4	0	0	0	2	0	6	.500	0	1	16	.375	1	3
Rojas, Mel	0	0	.000	16.88	2.2	5	5	5	0	0	1	2	2	0	1	3	0	0	0	1	0	8	.375	0	3	4	.500	0	1
DeHart, Rick	0	0	.000	21.60	1.2	6	4	4	2	0	0	0	3	1	1	3	0	0	0	0	0	5	.800	1	3	6	.333	1	1

PITCHERS WITH MORE THAN ONE N.L. TEAM

																					vs. RH				vs. LH			
Name	W	L	Pct.	ERA	IP	H	R	ER	HR	SH	SF	HB	BB	IBB	SO	G	GS	CG	ShO	GF	Sv	AB	Avg.	HR	RBI	AB	Avg.	HR	RBI
Ayala, Chi.	0	1	.000	2.81	16.0	11	7	5	4	1	0	2	5	1	15	13	0	0	0	4	0	137	.219	4	25	118	.254	2	22
Ayala, Mon.-Chi.	1	7	.125	3.51	82.0	71	43	32	10	5	3	6	39	2	79	66	0	0	0	3	0	181	.215	7	31	131	.244	3	24
Maddux, L.A.	1	1	.500	3.29	54.2	54	21	20	5	2	2	4	19	2	41	49	0	0	0	19	0	6	.500	0	1	16	.375	1	3
Maddux, Mon.-L.A.	1	1	.500	3.77	59.2	63	26	25	6	2	2	5	22	2	45	53	0	0	0	2	0	129	.279	4	22	100	.270	2	9
Rojas, L.A.	0	0	.000	12.60	5.0	5	7	7	3	0	0	0	3	1	3	5	0	0	0	2	0	8	.375	0	3	4	.500	0	1
Rojas, L.A.-Mon.	0	0	.000	14.09	7.2	10	12	12	3	0	1	2	5	1	4	8	0	0	0	1	0	21	.333	2	9	11	.273	1	2

INDIVIDUAL STATISTICS

FIELDING

FIRST BASEMEN

Player	Pct.	G	PO	A	E	TC	DP
Fullmer, Brad	.991	94	700	41	7	748	48
McGuire, Ryan	.997	58	267	37	1	305	19
Seguignol, Fernando	.989	23	172	11	2	185	20
Andrews, Shane	.985	18	122	7	2	131	12
Vidro, Jose	.970	14	59	5	2	66	7
Merced, Orlando	.917	7	21	1	2	24	2
Mordecai, Mike	1.000	1	2	0	0	2	0

SECOND BASEMEN

Player	Pct.	G	PO	A	E	TC	DP
Vidro, Jose	.982	121	208	291	9	508	61
Guerrero, Wilton	.931	54	65	98	12	175	17
Mordecai, Mike	.962	38	17	33	2	52	11
Coquillette, Trace	1.000	6	10	14	0	24	4
Blum, Geoff	1.000	2	0	2	0	2	0

THIRD BASEMEN

Player	Pct.	G	PO	A	E	TC	DP
Andrews, Shane	.932	82	37	127	12	176	9
Barrett, Michael	.943	66	45	104	9	158	4
Mordecai, Mike	.984	32	15	48	1	64	4
Coquillette, Trace	.944	11	3	14	1	18	1
Fernandez, Jose	.889	6	7	9	2	18	0
Vidro, Jose	1.000	2	1	0	0	1	0

SHORTSTOPS

Player	Pct.	G	PO	A	E	TC	DP
Cabrera, Orlando	.979	102	186	289	10	485	61
Blum, Geoff	.928	42	47	82	10	139	11
Mordecai, Mike	.966	38	38	75	4	117	20
Barrett, Michael	1.000	2	0	1	0	1	0

OUTFIELDERS

Player	Pct.	G	PO	A	E	TC	DP
Guerrero, Vladimir	.948	160	332	15	19	366	3
White, Rondell	.964	135	286	7	11	304	2
Martinez, Manny	.968	126	234	10	8	252	1
Mouton, James	.981	56	50	2	1	53	1
Merced, Orlando	.963	44	74	3	3	80	0
McGuire, Ryan	.960	23	23	1	1	25	0
Guerrero, Wilton	1.000	22	21	0	0	21	0
Jones, Terry	1.000	17	47	2	0	49	0
Bergeron, Peter	.967	13	27	2	1	30	1
Seguignol, Fernando	1.000	8	11	0	0	11	0
Vidro, Jose	1.000	3	2	0	0	2	0
Stowers, Chris	1.000	2	1	0	0	1	0

CATCHERS

Player	Pct.	G	PO	A	E	TC	DP	PB
Widger, Chris	.992	117	662	54	6	722	6	8
Barrett, Michael	.986	59	329	25	5	359	2	7
Machado, Robert	1.000	17	33	3	0	36	0	1
Cox, Darron	.963	14	48	4	2	54	1	0

PITCHERS

Player	Pct.	G	PO	A	E	TC	DP
Kline, Steve	.957	82	5	17	1	23	2
Telford, Anthony	.862	79	10	15	4	29	0
Urbina, Ugueth	1.000	71	5	2	0	7	0
Ayala, Bobby	.810	53	7	10	4	21	1
Mota, Guillermo	1.000	51	4	10	0	14	1
Batista, Miguel	.926	39	5	20	2	27	1
Hermanson, Dustin	1.000	34	20	21	0	41	1
Thurman, Mike	.955	29	9	12	1	22	0
Smart, J.D.	1.000	29	2	8	0	10	0
Vazquez, Javier	1.000	26	9	33	0	42	1
Smith, Dan	.846	20	4	7	2	13	0
Pavano, Carl	1.000	19	10	24	0	34	0
Powell, Jeremy	.957	17	9	13	1	23	0
Strickland, Scott	1.000	17	0	4	0	4	0
Lilly, Ted	1.000	9	0	3	0	3	0
Bennett, Shayne	-	5	0	0	0	0	0
Maddux, Mike	-	4	0	0	0	0	0
Johnson, Mike	1.000	3	1	1	0	2	0
Rojas, Mel	1.000	3	0	1	0	1	0
DeHart, Rick	-	3	0	0	0	0	0
Armas Jr., Tony	1.000	1	1	0	0	1	0

PITCHING AGAINST EACH CLUB

Pitcher	Ari. W-L	Atl. W-L	Chi. W-L	Cin. W-L	Col. W-L	Fla. W-L	Hou. W-L	L.A. W-L	Mil. W-L	N.Y. W-L	Phi. W-L	Pit. W-L	S.D. W-L	S.F. W-L	StL. W-L	A.L. W-L	Total W-L
Armas Jr., T.	0-0	0-0	0-0	0-0	0-0	0-0	0-0	0-0	0-0	0-0	0-0	0-0	0-0	0-1	0-0	0-0	0-1
Ayala, B.	0-1	0-0	0-0	1-0	0-0	0-0	0-0	0-1	0-2	0-1	0-0	0-0	0-0	0-0	0-0	0-1	1-6
Batista, M.	0-1	0-2	0-0	1-0	0-0	1-1	0-1	0-0	1-0	1-1	0-0	0-0	0-0	1-0	0-1	2-0	8-7
Bennett, S.	0-0	0-0	0-0	0-0	0-1	0-0	0-0	0-0	0-0	0-0	0-0	0-0	0-0	0-0	0-0	0-0	0-1
DeHart, R.	0-0	0-0	0-0	0-0	0-0	0-0	0-0	0-0	0-0	0-0	0-0	0-0	0-0	0-0	0-0	0-0	0-0
Hermanson, D.	1-0	1-0	1-1	0-1	1-0	0-2	1-1	0-2	0-0	1-1	1-1	2-0	0-1	0-1	0-0	0-3	9-14
Johnson, M.	0-0	0-0	0-0	0-0	0-0	0-0	0-0	0-0	0-0	0-0	0-0	0-0	0-0	0-0	0-0	0-0	0-0
Kline, S.	0-1	1-1	0-0	1-0	0-0	1-0	0-0	0-0	1-0	0-0	0-1	1-0	0-1	0-0	1-0	1-0	7-4
Lilly, T.	0-0	0-0	0-0	0-0	0-0	0-0	0-0	0-0	0-0	0-0	0-1	0-0	0-0	0-0	0-0	0-0	0-1
Maddux, M.	0-0	0-0	0-0	0-0	0-0	0-0	0-0	0-0	0-0	0-0	0-0	0-0	0-0	0-0	0-0	0-0	0-0
Mota, G.	1-1	0-2	0-0	1-0	0-0	0-0	0-0	0-1	0-0	0-0	0-0	0-0	0-0	0-0	0-0	0-0	2-4
Pavano, C.	0-0	0-0	0-0	0-0	0-0	1-0	1-1	0-0	0-0	0-3	1-0	0-2	0-1	0-1	0-0	2-0	6-8
Powell, J.	0-0	0-0	0-1	1-0	0-0	0-1	0-2	0-0	1-0	1-0	1-1	0-1	0-1	0-0	0-0	0-0	4-8
Rojas, M.	0-0	0-0	0-0	0-0	0-0	0-0	1-0	0-0	0-0	0-0	0-0	0-0	0-0	0-0	0-0	0-0	1-0
Smart, J.D.	0-1	0-0	0-0	0-0	0-0	0-0	0-0	0-0	0-0	0-0	0-0	0-0	0-0	0-0	0-0	0-0	0-1
Smith, D.	0-1	1-0	0-0	0-0	0-1	0-1	0-2	0-1	1-0	0-0	0-1	0-0	1-0	0-0	0-0	1-1	4-9
Strickland, S.	0-0	0-0	0-0	0-0	0-0	0-0	0-0	0-1	1-0	0-1	0-0	0-1	0-0	0-0	0-0	0-0	0-1
Telford, M.	1-0	1-0	1-0	0-0	0-0	0-0	0-0	0-0	0-0	0-0	0-1	0-0	0-0	2-0	0-1	0-1	5-4
Thurman, M.	1-0	1-0	1-0	0-2	0-2	0-0	0-0	0-0	0-0	0-0	0-0	1-0	0-0	0-2	1-0	1-2	7-11
Urbina, U.	0-0	1-0	0-0	0-1	1-1	0-0	0-0	0-1	0-0	1-1	1-0	0-0	0-1	0-0	1-1	1-0	6-6
Vazquez, J.	0-0	0-1	1-0	0-1	1-1	0-0	0-0	1-1	1-0	1-0	1-1	0-0	1-0	1-0	0-1	0-1	9-8
Totals	3-6	4-9	5-2	3-4	3-6	4-8	2-7	4-5	4-5	5-8	6-6	3-6	5-3	4-5	5-4	8-10	68-94

INTERLEAGUE: Thurman 0-1, Smith 0-1, Hermanson 0-1 vs. Orioles; Pavano 1-0, Smith 1-0, Thurman 1-0 vs. Red Sox; Kline 1-0, Vazquez 0-1, Thurman 0-1 vs. Yankees; Batista 1-0, Urbina 1-0, Ayala 0-1, Telford 0-1, Hermanson 0-1 vs. Blue Jays; Batista 1-0, Pavano 1-0, Hermanson 0-1 vs. Devil Rays. Total: 8-10.

MISCELLANEOUS

HOME RUNS BY PARK

At Arizona (6): Blum 2, White 1, Guerrero 1, Guerrero 1, Vidro 1.
At Atlanta (5): Merced 2, Seguignol 1, Barrett 1, Blum 1.
At Baltimore (1): Guerrero 1.
At Chicago (NL) (5): Widger 2, Andrews 1, Guerrero 1, Cabrera 1.
At Cincinnati (3): White 1, Guerrero 1, Barrett 1.
At Colorado (15): White 3, Andrews 3, Guerrero 3, Blum 3, Fullmer 2, Vidro 1.
At Florida (1): Guerrero 1.
At Houston (1): Andrews 1.
At Los Angeles (3): Guerrero 2, Blum 1.
At Milwaukee (1): White 1.
At Montreal (84): Guerrero 23, Widger 11, White 10, Cabrera 6, Andrews 5, Vidro 5, Barrett 5, Mordecai 4, Fullmer 4, Merced 3, Seguignol 3, Mouton 1, Martinez 1, McGuire 1, Cox 1, Mota 1.
At New York (AL) (2): Andrews 1, Fullmer 1.
At New York (NL) (5): White 2, Guerrero 1, Vidro 1, Cabrera 1.
At Philadelphia (13): Guerrero 4, Merced 1, Batista 1, White 1, Mordecai 1, Martinez 1, Guerrero 1, McGuire 1, Vidro 1, Seguignol 1.
At Pittsburgh (6): Guerrero 3, Merced 1, Widger 1, Vidro 1.
At San Diego (4): White 1, Guerrero 1, Fullmer 1, Barrett 1.
At San Francisco (4): White 1, Vidro 1, Fullmer 1, Blum 1.
At St. Louis (2): Mouton 1, Vidro 1.
At Toronto (2): Merced 1, White 1.

LOW-HIT GAMES

No-hitters: None.
One-hitters: Javier Vazquez, September 14 vs. Los Angeles, W 3-0.
Two-hitters: None.

10-STRIKEOUT GAMES

Javier Vazquez 1, **Total:** 1.

FOUR OR MORE HITS IN ONE GAME

Wilton Guerrero 4, Jose Vidro 2, Rondell White 1, Chris Widger 1, Brad Fullmer 1, **Total:** 9.

MULTI-HOMER GAMES

Vladimir Guerrero 3, Orlando Merced 1, Rondell White 1, Shane Andrews 1, Chris Widger 1, Geoff Blum 1, **Total:** 8.

GRAND SLAMS

8-9: Jose Vidro (off San Diego's Carlos Almanzar).
10-2: Wilton Guerrero (off Philadelphia's Paul Byrd).

PINCH HITTERS

(Minimum 5 at-bats)

Name	AB	Avg.	HR	RBI
Guerrero, Wilton	50	.340	0	7
Merced, Orlando	35	.286	2	10
Mouton, James	34	.324	0	6
Vidro, Jose	14	.357	1	5
McGuire, Ryan	13	.154	0	2
Mordecai, Mike	7	.000	0	1
Martinez, Manny	7	.000	0	0
Seguignol, Fernando	6	.333	0	0
Widger, Chris	6	.167	0	0
Fullmer, Brad	6	.000	0	1
Andrews, Shane	5	.400	0	1
Barrett, Michael	5	.000	0	0

DEBUTS

4-6: Darron Cox, C.
4-6: J.D. Smart, P.
5-2: Guillermo Mota, P.
5-14: Ted Lilly, P.
6-8: Dan Smith, P.
7-3: Jose Fernandez, 3B.
7-10: Chris Stowers, PH.
8-9: Geoff Blum, SS.
8-14: Scott Strickland, P.
8-16: Tony Armas Jr., P.
9-7: Trace Coquillette, 3B.
9-7: Peter Bergeron, LF.

GAMES BY POSITION

Catcher: Chris Widger 117, Michael Barrett 59, Robert Machado 17, Darron Cox 14.
First base: Brad Fullmer 94, Ryan McGuire 58, Fernando Seguignol 23, Shane Andrews 18, Jose Vidro 14, Orlando Merced 7, Mike Mordecai 1.
Second base: Jose Vidro 121, Wilton Guerrero 54, Mike Mordecai 38, Trace Coquillette 6, Geoff Blum 2.
Third base: Shane Andrews 82, Michael Barrett 66, Mike Mordecai 32, Trace Coquillette 11, Jose Fernandez 6, Jose Vidro 2.
Shortstop: Orlando Cabrera 102, Geoff Blum 42, Mike Mordecai 38, Michael Barrett 2.
Outfield: Vladimir Guerrero 160, Rondell White 135, Manny Martinez 126, James Mouton 56, Orlando Merced 44, Ryan McGuire 23, Wilton Guerrero 22, Terry Jones 17, Peter Bergeron 13, Fernando Seguignol 8, Jose Vidro 3, Chris Stowers 2.
Designated hitter: Wilton Guerrero 5, Orlando Merced 2, James Mouton 1, Shane Andrews 1.

STREAKS

Wins: 5 (May 23-30).
Losses: 7 (April 19-29, May 10-17).
Consecutive games with at least one hit: 31, Vladimir Guerrero (July 27-August 26).
Wins by pitcher: 4, Dustin Hermanson (September 1-18).

ATTENDANCE

Home: 773,267.
Road: 2,224,414.
Highest (home): 43,918 (April 8 vs. New York).
Highest (road): 55,086 (September 11 vs. San Diego).
Lowest (home): 4,660 (May 18 vs. Philadelphia).
Lowest (road): 8,468 (September 21 vs. Florida).

NEW YORK METS

DAY BY DAY

Date	Opp.	Res.	Score	(inn.*)	Hits	Opp. hits	Winning pitcher	Losing pitcher	Save	Record	Pos.	GB
4-5	At Fla.	L	2-6		9	12	Fernandez	Leiter		0-1	T4th	1.0
4-6	At Fla.	W	12-3		13	8	Reed	Hernandez	Watson	1-1	T1st	...
4-7	At Fla.	W	6-0		13	6	Jones	Sanchez		2-1	T1st	...
4-8	At Mon.	L	1-5		6	10	Batista	Hershiser	Urbina	2-2	T2nd	1.0
4-9	At Mon.	W	10-3		11	5	Yoshii	Thurman		3-2	T1st	...
4-10	At Mon.	W	4-3	(11)	8	7	Cook	Telford	Franco	4-2	1st	+1.0
4-11	At Mon.	W	6-3		14	7	Watson	Pavano	Franco	5-2	1st	+1.0
4-12	Fla.	W	8-1		9	5	Jones	Hernandez		6-2	1st	+1.0
4-14	Fla.	W	4-1		3	5	Hershiser	Sanchez	Franco	7-2	1st	+1.0
4-15	Fla.	L	4-11		9	18	Meadows	Yoshii		7-3	1st	+0.5
4-16	Mon.	L	4-6		7	7	Hermanson	Leiter	Urbina	7-4	2nd	...
4-17	Mon.	W	3-2		6	7	Jones	Pavano	Franco	8-4	1st	+1.0
4-18	Mon.	L	2-4		6	11	Vazquez	Watson	Urbina	8-5	2nd	...
4-20	At Cin.	W	3-2		8	8	Cook	Harnisch	Franco	9-5	1st	+0.5
4-21	At Cin.	L	4-7		3	7	Sullivan	Yoshii	Graves	9-6	2nd	0.5
4-22	At Cin.	W	4-1		7	6	Leiter	Tomko	Franco	10-6	2nd	...
4-23	At Chi.	W	6-5		13	8	Cook	Beck	Franco	11-6	1st	+1.0
4-24	At Chi.	L	0-2		8	5	Mulholland	Watson	Beck	11-7	2nd	...
4-25	At Chi.	L	4-8		11	8	Myers	Hershiser		11-8	2nd	1.0
4-27	S.D.	L	2-6		5	8	Ashby	Yoshii		11-9	3rd	1.5
4-28	S.D.	W	4-3		11	6	Wendell	Hoffman		12-9	2nd	1.5
4-29	S.D.	W	8-5		6	11	Cook	Boehringer	Franco	13-9	2nd	1.5
4-30	S.F.	W	7-2		14	6	Watson	Estes	Wendell	14-9	2nd	1.5
5-1	S.F.	W	9-4		12	7	Hershiser	Brock		15-9	2nd	1.5
5-2	S.F.	W	2-0		5	7	Cook	Johnstone	Franco	16-9	2nd	1.5
5-3	Hou.	W	5-3		9	6	Reed	Holt	Franco	17-9	2nd	1.5
5-4	Hou.	L	1-6		3	13	Hampton	Leiter		17-10	2nd	1.5
5-5	Hou.	L	4-5		11	8	Powell	Benitez	Wagner	17-11	2nd	2.5
5-7	At Ari.	L	7-14		12	15	Stottlemyre	Hershiser		17-12	2nd	2.5
5-8	At Ari.	W	4-2		11	6	Yoshii	Benes	Benitez	18-12	2nd	2.5
5-9	At Ari.	L	6-11		16	13	Daal	Reed		18-13	2nd	2.5
5-10	At Col.	L	3-10		7	12	Astacio	Leiter		18-14	2nd	2.5
5-11	At Col.	L	5-8		11	12	Jones	Jones		18-15	3rd	3.5
5-12	At Col.	W	10-5		15	10	Reed	Thomson		19-15	3rd	2.5
5-14	At Phi.	W	7-3		9	5	Yoshii	Ogea		20-15	2nd	1.5
5-15	At Phi.	W	9-7		12	13	Mahomes	Ryan	Franco	21-15	2nd	0.5
5-16	At Phi.	L	2-5		8	10	Byrd	Hershiser	Brantley	21-16	2nd	1.5
5-17	Mil.	L	6-7		11	13	Karl	Jones	Wickman	21-17	3rd	2.5
5-18	Mil.	L	2-4		11	8	Weathers	Cook	Wickman	21-18	3rd	3.5
5-20†	Mil.	W	11-10		12	13	Leiter	Abbott	Franco	22-18		
5-20‡	Mil.	W	10-1		12	9	Yoshii	Woodard		23-18	2nd	2.5
5-21	Phi.	W	7-5		13	10	Hershiser	Loewer	Franco	24-18	2nd	1.5
5-22	Phi.	L	3-9		7	13	Byrd	Jones		24-19	2nd	2.5
5-23	Phi.	W	5-4		12	9	Beltran	Schilling		25-19	2nd	1.5
5-24	At Pit.	L	4-7		7	8	Silva	Isringhausen	Williams	25-20	2nd	1.5
5-25	At Pit.	W	8-3		11	6	Yoshii	Benson		26-20	2nd	1.5
5-26	At Pit.	W	5-2		10	5	Hershiser	Schourek	Franco	27-20	2nd	1.5
5-28	Ari.	L	1-2		6	6	Daal	Reed	Olson	27-21	2nd	3.0
5-29	Ari.	L	7-8		11	13	Reynoso	Beltran	Kim	27-22	2nd	3.0
5-30	Ari.	L	1-10		6	15	Johnson	Yoshii		27-23	2nd	3.0
5-31	Cin.	L	3-5		6	8	Villone	Leiter	Williamson	27-24	2nd	4.0
6-1	Cin.	L	0-4		7	10	Harnisch	Hershiser		27-25	2nd	5.0
6-2	Cin.	L	7-8		8	11	Williamson	Franco	Sullivan	27-26	3rd	5.0
6-4	At N.Y. (AL)	L	3-4		7	5	Grimsley	Reed	Rivera	27-27	3rd	5.0
6-5	At N.Y. (AL)	L	3-6		9	11	Hernandez	Yoshii	Rivera	27-28	3rd	6.0
6-6	At N.Y. (AL)	W	7-2		8	6	Leiter	Clemens		28-28	3rd	6.0
6-7	Tor.	W	8-2		14	8	Hershiser	Halladay		29-28	3rd	6.0
6-8	Tor.	W	11-3		14	4	Isringhausen	Hentgen		30-28	3rd	6.0
6-9	Tor.	W	4-3	(14)	11	15	Mahomes	Davey		31-28	2nd	6.0
6-11	Bos.	L	2-3	(12)	8	11	Corsi	Franco	Wasdin	31-29	3rd	6.0
6-12	Bos.	W	4-2		8	7	Leiter	Rapp	Franco	32-29	3rd	5.0
6-13	Bos.	W	5-4		11	8	Hershiser	Portugal	Wendell	33-29	2nd	4.0
6-14	At Cin.	L	4-8		5	10	Williamson	McMichael		33-30	T2nd	4.0
6-15	At Cin.	W	11-3		12	9	Reed	Tomko		34-30	2nd	4.0
6-16	At Cin.	W	5-2		10	8	Yoshii	Parris	Franco	35-30	2nd	4.0
6-17	At StL.	W	4-3		10	6	Leiter	Mercker	Cook	36-30	2nd	4.0
6-18	At StL.	W	6-2		14	3	Hershiser	Acevedo	Benitez	37-30	2nd	4.0
6-19	At StL.	L	6-7		9	10	Aybar	Isringhausen	Bottalico	37-31	2nd	4.0
6-20	At StL.	W	9-6		12	10	Reed	Croushore	Franco	38-31	2nd	4.0
6-22	Fla.	W	8-2		14	4	McMichael	Springer	Benitez	39-31	2nd	3.0
6-23	Fla.	W	6-3		8	7	Leiter	Meadows	Franco	40-31	2nd	3.0
6-24	Fla.	W	3-2		8	9	Cook	Hernandez	Franco	41-31	2nd	3.0
6-25	At Atl.	W	10-2		13	8	Reed	Perez		42-31	2nd	2.0
6-26	At Atl.	L	2-7		7	7	Glavine	Dotel		42-32	2nd	3.0
6-27	At Atl.	L	0-1		3	4	Maddux	Yoshii	Rocker	42-33	2nd	4.0
6-28	At Fla.	W	10-4		14	11	Leiter	Meadows		43-33	2nd	4.0
6-29	At Fla.	W	5-1		9	5	Hershiser	Hernandez		44-33	2nd	3.0
6-30	At Fla.	L	3-4	(10)	8	9	Alfonseca	Benitez		44-34	2nd	3.0

HIGHLIGHTS

High point: It was a grand slam that turned into a grand single. Robin Ventura drove a Kevin McGlinchy pitch over the wall in right-center at Shea Stadium to cap a 15th-inning comeback against the Braves in Game 5 of the NLCS. The bases were loaded, but Ventura was credited with only a run-scoring single when Todd Pratt raised him in celebration before he reached second base. The Mets won, 4-3, to force Game 6 in Atlanta.

Low point: Kenny Rogers' high-and-outside fastball to Andruw Jones may have been his last pitch as a Met. It forced home Gerald Williams with the winning run in the 11th inning of Game 6 of the NLCS, sending the Braves to the World Series and the Mets home.

Turning point: Al Leiter's win over the Yankees and Roger Clemens on June 6 at Yankee Stadium. The victory, which ended an eight-game losing streak and came on the heels of the messy firing of three Mets coaches, ignited a 40-15 run that vaulted the club from a 27-28 record to a 67-43 mark, the best in the majors.

Most valuable player: Third baseman Robin Ventura. (Any "most valuable" honor really should go to G.M. Steve Phillips, whose signing of Ventura was a masterstroke in itself and also triggered the move of Edgardo Alfonzo from third to second base, thereby creating one of baseball's best-ever infields.) Ventura won his sixth Gold Glove, batted .301 with 32 homers and 120 RBIs and provided protection for Mike Piazza in the lineup.

Most valuable pitcher: Armando Benitez, who quickly emerged as one of the N.L.'s most overpowering relievers and then replaced John Franco as the closer after an injury sidelined Franco for two months.

Most improved player: Alfonzo. He handled the move to second without a problem, teaming with shortstop Rey Ordonez to form a dazzling double-play combination. Alfonzo also continued to mature as a power hitter, posting career highs with 27 homers and 108 RBIs.

Most pleasant surprise: Roger Cedeno, targeted as a fourth outfielder, made 82 starts in right and appeared in 155 games overall. He batted .313 and blossomed as a basestealer, setting a Mets record with 66 steals.

Key injuries: Franco's absence because of a torn tendon in his finger cost the Mets bullpen depth. And Bonilla, who had only 119 at-bats, was hobbled by a bad knee.

Notable: The Mets set a major league record for fewest errors in a season, 68. ... Ventura became the first player in major league history to hit a grand slam in each game of a doubleheader, connecting against the Brewers on May 20. ... The Mets made the postseason for the first time since 1988.

—RAFAEL HERMOSO

MISCELLANEOUS

RECORDS

1999 regular-season record: 97-66 (2nd in N.L. East); 49-32 at home; 48-34 on road; 27-23 vs. N.L. East; 33-18 vs. N.L. Central; 25-19 vs. N.L. West; 12-6 vs. A.L. East; 22-18 vs. lefthanded starters; 75-48 vs. righthanded starters; 79-56 on grass; 18-10 on turf; 33-23 in daytime; 64-43 at night; 27-19 in one-run games; 6-5 in extra-inning games; 1-0-1 in double-headers.

Team record past five years: 413-380 (.521, ranks 5th in league in that span).

TEAM LEADERS

Batting average: Rickey Henderson (.315).
At-bats: Edgardo Alfonzo (628).
Runs: Edgardo Alfonzo (123).
Hits: Edgardo Alfonzo (191).
Total bases: Edgardo Alfonzo (315).
Doubles: Edgardo Alfonzo (41).
Triples: Roger Cedeno (4).
Home runs: Mike Piazza (40).
Runs batted in: Mike Piazza (124).
Stolen bases: Roger Cedeno (66).
Slugging percentage: Mike Piazza (.575).
On-base percentage: John Olerud (.427).
Wins: Orel Hershiser, Al Leiter (13).
Earned-run average: Al Leiter (4.23).
Complete games: Kenny Rogers (2).
Shutouts: Al Leiter, Rick Reed, Kenny Rogers (1).
Saves: Armando Benitez (22).
Innings pitched: Al Leiter (213.0).
Strikeouts: Al Leiter (162).

Date	Opp.	Res.	Score	(inn.*)	Hits	Opp. hits	Winning pitcher	Losing pitcher	Save	Record	Pos.	GB
7-1	At Fla.	W	12-8		12	13	Dotel	Dempster		45-34	2nd	3.0
7-2	Atl.	L	0-16		3	15	Maddux	Yoshii		45-35	2nd	4.0
7-3	Atl.	L	0-3		3	7	Millwood	Leiter	Rocker	45-36	2nd	5.0
7-4	Atl.	W	7-6		11	8	Cook	Smoltz	Benitez	46-36	2nd	4.0
7-5	Mon.	W	2-1		9	6	Wendell	Mota	Benitez	47-36	2nd	4.0
7-6	Mon.	W	10-0		13	6	Hershiser	Pavano	Isringhausen	48-36	2nd	3.0
7-7	Mon.	L	1-3		7	8	Kline	Wendell	Urbina	48-37	2nd	4.0
7-8	Mon.	L	3-4		6	6	Ayala	Cook	Urbina	48-38	2nd	5.0
7-9	N.Y. (AL)	W	5-2		12	5	Leiter	Clemens	Benitez	49-38	2nd	4.0
7-10	N.Y. (AL)	W	9-8		9	11	Mahomes	Rivera		50-38	2nd	4.0
7-11	N.Y. (AL)	L	3-6		8	13	Irabu	Hershiser	Rivera	50-39	2nd	5.0
7-15	At T.B.	W	8-7	(10)	8	13	Benitez	Charlton		51-39	2nd	5.0
7-16	At T.B.	W	9-7		15	11	Reed	Eiland	Cook	52-39	2nd	5.0
7-17	At T.B.	L	2-3		8	8	Alvarez	Hershiser	Hernandez	52-40	2nd	5.0
7-18	At Bal.	W	8-6		12	12	Yoshii	Guzman	Benitez	53-40	2nd	4.0
7-19	At Bal.	W	4-1		9	4	Dotel	Johnson	Benitez	54-40	2nd	3.0
7-20	At Bal.	L	1-4		6	9	Ponson	Leiter		54-41	2nd	3.0
7-21	At Mon.	W	7-3		12	12	Reed	Smith		55-41	2nd	2.0
7-22	At Mon.	W	7-4		12	9	Hershiser	Hermanson		56-41	2nd	2.0
7-23	Chi.	W	5-4		9	7	Cook	Tapani	Benitez	57-41	2nd	1.5
7-24	Chi.	W	2-1		5	6	Dotel	Trachsel	Benitez	58-41	2nd	0.5
7-25	Chi.	W	5-1		5	8	Leiter	Serafini		59-41	2nd	0.5
7-26	Pit.	W	7-5		9	10	Reed	Cordova	Wendell	60-41	2nd	0.5
7-27	Pit.	L	1-5		6	9	Benson	Hershiser		60-42	2nd	1.5
7-28	Pit.	W	9-2		10	3	Cook	Wilkins		61-42	2nd	0.5
7-30	At Chi.	W	10-9		14	13	Mahomes	Farnsworth	Benitez	62-42	1st	+0.5
7-31	At Chi.	L	10-17		18	14	Serafini	Isringhausen		62-43	2nd	0.5
8-1	At Chi.	W	5-4	(13)	10	10	Mahomes	Sanders		63-43	2nd	0.5
8-2	At Mil.	W	7-2		12	8	Reed	Nomo		64-43	T1st	...
8-3	At Mil.	W	10-3		13	6	Hershiser	Pulsipher		65-43	1st	+1.0
8-4	At Mil.	W	9-5		17	7	Rogers	Peterson		66-43	1st	+2.0
8-6	L.A.	W	2-1		4	5	Dotel	Park	Benitez	67-43	1st	+1.5
8-7	L.A.	L	6-7		11	13	Borbon	Taylor	Shaw	67-44	1st	+0.5
8-8	L.A.	L	3-14		7	14	Dreifort	Reed		67-45	1st	+0.5
8-9	L.A.	L	2-9		6	13	Brown	Hershiser		67-46	2nd	0.5
8-10	S.D.	W	4-3		15	9	Wendell	Ashby	Benitez	68-46	2nd	0.5
8-11	S.D.	W	12-5		14	6	Mahomes	Hitchcock		69-46	2nd	0.5
8-12	S.D.	W	9-3		11	5	Leiter	Williams		70-46	T1st	...
8-13	At S.F	L	2-3		9	5	Ortiz	Yoshii	Nen	70-47	2nd	1.0
8-14	At S.F	W	6-1		16	5	Hershiser	Rueter		71-47	T1st	...
8-15	At S.F	W	12-5		16	12	Rogers	Hernandez		72-47	T1st	...
8-16	At S.D.	W	4-3	(10)	10	2	Cook	Cunnane	Benitez	73-47	T1st	...
8-17	At S.D.	L	2-3		5	5	Williams	Leiter	Hoffman	73-48	T1st	...
8-18	At S.D.	W	9-1		15	6	Yoshii	Spencer		74-48	1st	+1.0
8-21	StL.	W	7-4		9	8	Mahomes	Mercker	Benitez	75-48	1st	...
8-22†	StL.	W	8-7		11	12	Benitez	Bottalico		76-48		
8-22‡	StL.	L	5-7		11	10	Stephenson	Hershiser	Acevedo	76-49	2nd	0.5
8-23	Hou.	W	3-2		8	10	Benitez	Powell		77-49	2nd	0.5
8-24	Hou.	L	1-5	(10)	5	8	Wagner	Cook		77-50	2nd	1.5
8-25	Hou.	W	4-0		12	7	Rogers	Reynolds	Cook	78-50	2nd	1.5
8-27	At Ari.	W	6-3		11	8	Dotel	Daal	Benitez	79-50	2nd	1.5
8-28	At Ari.	L	3-5		6	8	Reynoso	Cook	Mantei	79-51	2nd	2.5
8-29	At Ari.	L	4-8		10	12	Anderson	Leiter	Olson	79-52	2nd	3.5
8-30	At Hou.	W	17-1		21	5	Yoshii	Reynolds		80-52	2nd	2.5
8-31	At Hou.	L	2-6		7	7	Lima	Wendell		80-53	2nd	3.5
9-1	At Hou.	W	9-5		18	7	Dotel	Holt		81-53	2nd	3.5
9-3	Col.	L	2-5	(10)	10	8	Leskanic	Wendell	Veres	81-54	2nd	4.5
9-4	Col.	W	4-2		5	11	Leiter	Bohanon	Benitez	82-54	2nd	3.5
9-5	Col.	W	6-2		9	9	Yoshii	Kile		83-54	2nd	2.5
9-6	S.F	W	3-0		4	4	Rogers	Gardner		84-54	2nd	2.5
9-7	S.F	L	4-7		4	12	Rodriguez	Wendell	Nen	84-55	2nd	3.5
9-8	S.F	W	7-5		10	7	Dotel	Estes	Benitez	85-55	2nd	3.5
9-9	At L.A.	W	3-1		7	2	Hershiser	Brown	Benitez	86-55	2nd	3.0
9-10	At L.A.	L	1-3		6	6	Dreifort	Leiter	Shaw	86-56	2nd	4.0
9-11	At L.A.	W	6-2		11	7	Yoshii	Valdes		87-56	2nd	3.0
9-12	At L.A.	W	10-3		12	14	Rogers	Gagne		88-56	2nd	2.0
9-13	At Col.	W	6-5		9	13	Wendell	Veres	Benitez	89-56	2nd	1.0
9-14	At Col.	L	2-7		7	10	Wright	Dotel		89-57	2nd	2.0
9-15	At Col.	W	10-5		13	11	Wendell	Dipoto	Benitez	90-57	2nd	1.0
9-17	Phi.	L	5-8		9	11	Wolf	Leiter	Brewer	90-58	2nd	2.0
9-18	Phi.	W	11-1		15	5	Yoshii	Grace		91-58	2nd	1.0
9-19	Phi.	W	8-6		9	9	Dotel	Byrd	Benitez	92-58	2nd	1.0
9-21	At Atl.	L	1-2		6	8	Remlinger	Cook	Rocker	92-59	2nd	2.0
9-22	At Atl.	L	2-5		8	6	Glavine	Hershiser	Rocker	92-60	2nd	3.0
9-23	At Atl.	L	3-6		7	13	Maddux	Leiter	Rocker	92-61	2nd	4.0
9-24	At Phi.	L	2-3		9	6	Grahe	Benitez	Aldred	92-62	2nd	5.0
9-25	At Phi.	L	2-4		4	6	Person	Rogers	Gomes	92-63	2nd	6.0
9-26	At Phi.	L	2-3		6	4	Byrd	Reed	Montgomery	92-64	2nd	7.0
9-28	Atl.	L	3-9		9	13	Glavine	Hershiser		92-65	2nd	8.0
9-29	Atl.	W	9-2		13	5	Leiter	Maddux		93-65	2nd	7.0
9-30	Atl.	L	3-4	(11)	6	8	Mulholland	Dotel		93-66	2nd	8.0
10-1	Pit.	W	3-2	(11)	10	7	Mahomes	Sauerbeck		94-66	2nd	8.0
10-2	Pit.	W	7-0		9	3	Reed	Cordova		95-66	2nd	7.0
10-3	Pit.	W	2-1		9	3	Benitez	Hansell		96-66	2nd	7.0
10-4	At Cin.	W	5-0		9	2	Leiter	Parris		97-66	2nd	6.5

Monthly records: April (14-9), May (13-15), June (17-10), July (18-9), August (18-10), September (13-13), October (4-0).
*Innings, if other than nine. † First game of a doubleheader. ‡ Second game of a doubleheader.

MEMORABLE GAMES

August 30 at Houston

Edgardo Alfonzo put together one of the best offensive performances of this decade. The second baseman was 6-for-6 with three homers, a double, six runs and five RBIs. The 17-1 thrashing of Houston also proved the Mets were a legitimate playoff opponent, as they proved to be.

NY Mets	AB	R	H	RBI	Houston	AB	R	H	RBI
Henderson, lf	4	2	2	1	Biggio, 2b	2	0	0	0
Agbayani, lf	2	1	1	0	Gutrrez, ph-ss	2	0	1	0
Alfonzo, 2b	6	6	6	5	Spiers, cf-lf	4	0	0	0
Olerud, 1b	2	2	1	2	Bagwell, 1b	2	0	1	0
Piazza, c	3	2	1	2	R.Thmpsn, ph-cf	2	0	0	0
Tam, p	0	0	0	0	Caminiti, 3b	3	0	0	0
Dunston, ph-cf	2	0	2	3	D.Ward, lf-1b	4	0	1	0
Ventura, 3b	3	1	1	0	Berkman, rf	4	1	1	1
M.Frnco, ph-3b	3	0	0	0	Bako, c	3	0	1	0
D.Hamilton, cf	5	1	4	3	Bogar, ss-2b	3	0	0	0
Taylor, p	0	0	0	0	Reynolds, p	0	0	0	0
Mahomes, ph	1	0	0	0	Ru.Johnsn, ph	1	0	0	0
McElroy, p	0	0	0	0	B.Williams, p	0	0	0	0
R.Cedeno, rf	5	1	1	0	Mieske, ph	1	0	0	0
R.Ordonez, ss	3	0	1	1	Bergman, p	0	0	0	0
L.Lopez, ph-ss	2	0	0	0	Eusebio, ph	1	0	0	0
Yoshii, p	2	0	0	0	Tre.Miller, p	0	0	0	0
Pratt, ph-c	2	1	1	0					
Totals	**45**	**17**	**21**	**17**	**Totals**	**32**	**1**	**5**	**1**

NY Mets.......................................160 212 023—17
Houston.......................................000 000 100 —1

DP—Houston 2. LOB—NY Mets 7, Houston 5. 2B—Alfonzo (37), Olerud (30), D.Ward (3). HR—Alfonzo 3 (23), Piazza (32), D.Hamilton (3), Berkman (4). SB—R.Cedeno (59). S—Yoshii.

NY Mets	IP	H	R	ER	BB	SO
Yoshii (W, 9-8)	6	2	0	0	1	8
Tam	1	1	1	1	0	0
Taylor	1	1	0	0	0	1
McElroy	1	1	0	0	0	1

Houston	IP	H	R	ER	BB	SO
Reynolds (L, 14-11)	3	7	7	7	2	3
B.Williams	2	5	3	3	0	2
Bergman	3	5	4	4	2	0
Tre.Miller	1	4	3	3	1	2

U—HP, Montague. 1B, Winters. 2B, Davidson. 3B, Danley. T—2:51. A—28,032.

October 4 at Cincinnati

The Mets needed 163 games to make the playoffs and Al Leiter made the final one count. He threw a two-hit shutout of the Reds in Cincinnati to give the Mets a 5-0 win and their first playoff appearance since 1988. Leiter salvaged an up-and-down year by finishing 13-12 and the Mets completed their miraculous comeback after losing seven straight games and eight of nine in the final two weeks of the season. They were two games out with three to play before they began their rally.

NY Mets	AB	R	H	RBI	Cincinnati	AB	R	H	RBI
Henderson, lf	5	2	2	1	Reese, 2b	3	0	1	0
Mora, lf	0	0	0	0	Larkin, ss	3	0	0	0
Alfonzo, 2b	4	2	2	3	Casey, 1b	4	0	0	0
Olerud, 1b	5	0	2	0	G.Vaughn, lf	3	0	0	0
Piazza, c	2	0	0	0	D.Young, rf	4	0	0	0
Ventura, 3b	3	0	1	1	Hammnds, cf	3	0	1	0
D.Hamilton, cf	4	0	1	0	Taubensee, c	2	0	0	0
R.Cedeno, rf	4	0	1	0	A.Boone, 3b	3	0	0	0
R.Ordonez, ss	3	1	0	0	Parris, p	0	0	0	0
A.Leiter, p	3	0	0	0	Neagle, p	1	0	0	0
					Stynes, ph	1	0	0	0
					Graves, p	0	0	0	0
					M.Lewis, ph	1	0	0	0
					D.Reyes, p	0	0	0	0
Totals	**33**	**5**	**9**	**5**	**Totals**	**28**	**0**	**2**	**0**

NY Mets.......................................201 011 000— 5
Cincinnati....................................000 000 000— 0

DP—NY Mets 1, Cincinnati 2. LOB—NY Mets 10, Cincinnati 5. 2B—Alfonzo (41), Olerud (39), Reese (37). HR—Henderson (12), Alfonzo (27). S—A.Leiter.

NY Mets	IP	H	R	ER	BB	SO
A.Leiter (W, 13-12)	9	2	0	0	4	7

Cincinnati	IP	H	R	ER	BB	SO
Parris (L, 11-4)	2.2	3	3	3	3	1
Neagle	2.1	2	1	1	3	2
Graves	3	2	1	1	2	2
D.Reyes	1	2	0	0	0	0

U—HP, Froemming. 1B, Davis. 2B, M.Hirschbeck. 3B, Rapuano. T—3:03. A—54,621.

BATTING

Name	G	TPA	AB	R	H	TB	2B	3B	HR	RBI	Avg.	Obp.	Slg.	SH	SF	HP	BB	IBB	SO	SB	CS	GDP	vs RHP AB	vs RHP Avg.	vs RHP HR	vs RHP RBI	vs LHP AB	vs LHP Avg.	vs LHP HR	vs LHP RBI
Alfonzo, Edgardo	158	726	628	123	191	315	41	1	27	108	.304	.385	.502	1	9	3	85	2	85	9	2	14	490	.314	21	88	138	.268	6	20
Ventura, Robin	161	671	588	88	177	311	38	0	32	120	.301	.379	.529	1	5	3	74	10	109	1	1	14	407	.314	23	81	181	.271	9	39
Olerud, John	162	723	581	107	173	269	39	0	19	96	.298	.427	.463	0	6	11	125	5	66	3	0	22	415	.318	17	76	166	.247	2	20
Piazza, Mike	141	593	534	100	162	307	25	0	40	124	.303	.361	.575	0	7	1	51	11	70	2	2	27	403	.305	29	97	131	.298	11	27
Ordonez, Rey	154	588	520	49	134	165	24	2	1	60	.258	.319	.317	11	7	1	49	12	59	8	4	16	390	.267	1	46	130	.231	0	14
Cedeno, Roger	155	525	453	90	142	185	23	4	4	36	.313	.396	.408	7	2	3	60	3	100	66	17	5	386	.334	1	28	67	.194	3	8
Henderson, Rickey	121	526	438	89	138	204	30	0	12	42	.315	.423	.466	1	3	2	82	1	82	37	14	4	333	.306	6	33	105	.343	6	9
McRae, Brian	96	344	298	35	66	104	12	1	8	36	.221	.320	.349	0	2	5	39	1	57	2	6	6	237	.219	8	34	61	.230	0	2
Agbayani, Benny	101	314	276	42	79	145	18	3	14	42	.286	.363	.525	0	3	3	32	4	60	6	4	8	172	.279	9	31	104	.298	5	11
Hamilton, Darryl	55	189	168	19	57	82	8	1	5	21	.339	.410	.488	1	0	1	19	0	18	2	3	2	129	.372	5	18	39	.231	0	3
Pratt, Todd	71	160	140	18	41	54	4	0	3	21	.293	.369	.386	0	2	3	15	0	32	2	0	1	97	.299	1	13	43	.279	2	8
Franco, Matt	122	161	132	18	31	48	5	0	4	21	.235	.366	.364	0	1	0	28	3	21	0	0	9	125	.248	4	21	7	.000	0	0
Bonilla, Bobby	60	141	119	12	19	36	5	0	4	18	.160	.277	.303	0	2	1	19	1	16	0	1	4	88	.170	2	11	31	.129	2	7
Lopez, Luis	68	121	104	11	22	32	4	0	2	13	.212	.308	.308	1	1	3	12	0	33	1	1	1	81	.222	1	9	23	.174	1	4
Dunston, Shawon	42	97	93	12	32	40	6	1	0	16	.344	.354	.430	1	1	2	0	0	16	4	1	4	49	.286	0	10	44	.409	0	6
Allensworth, Jermaine	40	86	73	14	16	27	2	0	3	9	.219	.310	.370	2	1	1	9	0	23	2	1	1	42	.214	1	5	31	.226	2	4
Hershiser, Orel	32	68	62	3	9	10	1	0	0	3	.145	.154	.161	3	2	0	1	0	18	1	0	3	47	.128	0	2	15	.200	0	1
Leiter, Al	32	70	57	1	6	8	2	0	0	5	.105	.136	.140	11	0	0	2	0	29	0	0	0	40	.125	0	5	17	.059	0	0
Yoshii, Masato	31	61	55	1	9	9	0	0	0	2	.164	.164	.164	6	0	0	0	0	16	0	1	3	49	.122	0	2	6	.500	0	0
Kinkade, Mike	28	51	46	3	9	19	2	1	2	6	.196	.275	.413	0	0	2	3	0	9	1	0	1	27	.185	1	2	19	.211	1	4
Reed, Rick	27	54	45	2	11	13	2	0	0	5	.244	.261	.289	8	0	0	1	0	14	0	0	1	36	.250	0	5	9	.222	0	0
Mora, Melvin	66	39	31	6	5	5	0	0	0	1	.161	.278	.161	3	0	1	4	0	7	2	1	0	14	.214	0	0	17	.118	0	1
Rogers, Kenny	12	30	25	2	3	3	0	0	0	1	.120	.185	.120	3	0	0	2	0	10	0	0	0	24	.125	0	1	1	.000	0	0
Dotel, Octavio	19	30	24	2	3	3	0	0	0	1	.125	.276	.125	1	0	1	4	0	17	0	0	0	12	.083	0	1	12	.167	0	0
Mahomes, Pat	41	16	16	2	5	8	3	0	0	3	.313	.313	.500	0	0	0	0	0	6	0	0	0	8	.375	0	2	8	.250	0	1
Jones, Bobby	12	17	16	1	5	8	0	0	1	1	.313	.313	.500	1	0	0	0	0	4	0	0	0	10	.400	1	1	6	.167	0	0
Isringhausen, Jason	13	13	12	2	1	2	1	0	0	1	.083	.083	.167	1	0	0	0	0	4	0	0	0	6	.167	0	1	6	.000	0	0
Watson, Allen	14	10	10	0	3	4	1	0	0	0	.300	.300	.400	0	0	0	0	0	1	0	0	3	6	.333	0	0	4	.250	0	0
Payton, Jay	13	9	8	1	2	3	1	0	0	1	.250	.333	.375	0	0	1	0	0	2	1	2	0	2	.500	0	0	6	.167	0	1
Wendell, Turk	80	7	6	0	0	0	0	0	0	0	.000	.143	.000	0	0	0	1	0	3	0	0	0	5	.000	0	0	1	.000	0	0
Benitez, Armando	77	5	5	0	0	0	0	0	0	1	.000	.000	.000	0	0	0	0	0	2	0	0	0	2	.000	0	1	3	.000	0	0
Toca, Jorge	4	3	3	0	1	1	0	0	0	0	.333	.333	.333	0	0	0	0	0	2	0	0	0	0	.000	0	0	3	.333	0	0
Long, Terrence	3	3	3	0	0	0	0	0	0	0	.000	.000	.000	0	0	0	0	0	2	0	0	1	3	.000	0	0	0	.000	0	0
Manzanillo, Josias	13	1	1	0	1	1	0	0	0	0	1.000	1.000	1.000	0	0	0	0	0	0	0	0	0	1	1.000	0	0	0	.000	0	0
Cook, Dennis	71	1	1	0	0	0	0	0	0	0	.000	.000	.000	0	0	0	0	0	1	0	0	0	1	.000	0	0	0	.000	0	0
Beltran, Rigo	21	1	1	0	0	0	0	0	0	0	.000	.000	.000	0	0	0	0	0	0	0	0	1	0	.000	0	0	1	.000	0	0
Franco, John	46	0	0	0	0	0	0	0	0	0	.000	.000	.000	0	0	0	0	0	0	0	0	0	0	.000	0	0	0	.000	0	0
McElroy, Chuck	15	0	0	0	0	0	0	0	0	0	.000	.000	.000	0	0	0	0	0	0	0	0	0	0	.000	0	0	0	.000	0	0
McMichael, Greg	19	0	0	0	0	0	0	0	0	0	.000	.000	.000	0	0	0	0	0	0	0	0	0	0	.000	0	0	0	.000	0	0
Taylor, Billy	18	0	0	0	0	0	0	0	0	0	.000	.000	.000	0	0	0	0	0	0	0	0	0	0	.000	0	0	0	.000	0	0
Rusch, Glendon	1	0	0	0	0	0	0	0	0	0	.000	.000	.000	0	0	0	0	0	0	0	0	0	0	.000	0	0	0	.000	0	0
Halter, Shane	7	0	0	0	0	0	0	0	0	0	.000	.000	.000	0	0	0	0	0	0	0	0	0	0	.000	0	0	0	.000	0	0
Tam, Jeff	9	0	0	0	0	0	0	0	0	0	.000	.000	.000	0	0	0	0	0	0	0	0	0	0	.000	0	0	0	.000	0	0
Wilson, Vance	1	0	0	0	0	0	0	0	0	0	.000	.000	.000	0	0	0	0	0	0	0	0	0	0	.000	0	0	0	.000	0	0
Murray, Dan	1	0	0	0	0	0	0	0	0	0	.000	.000	.000	0	0	0	0	0	0	0	0	0	0	.000	0	0	0	.000	0	0

Players with more than one N.L. team

Name	G	TPA	AB	R	H	TB	2B	3B	HR	RBI	Avg.	Obp.	Slg.	SH	SF	HP	BB	IBB	SO	SB	CS	GDP	vs RHP AB	vs RHP Avg.	vs RHP HR	vs RHP RBI	vs LHP AB	vs LHP Avg.	vs LHP HR	vs LHP RBI
Beltran, Col.	12	2	2	0	1	1	0	0	0	0	.500	.500	.500	0	0	0	0	0	0	0	0	0	0	.000	0	0	1	.000	0	0
Beltran, N.Y.-Col.	33	3	3	0	1	1	0	0	0	0	.333	.333	.333	0	0	0	0	0	0	0	0	1	1	1.000	0	0	2	.000	0	0
Dunston, StL.	62	158	150	23	46	70	5	2	5	25	.307	.327	.467	2	1	3	2	0	23	6	3	4	49	.286	0	10	44	.409	0	6
Dunston, StL.-N.Y.	104	255	243	35	78	110	11	3	5	41	.321	.337	.453	3	2	5	2	0	39	10	4	8	149	.309	4	27	94	.340	1	14
Hamilton, Col.	91	379	337	63	102	131	11	3	4	24	.303	.374	.389	2	1	1	38	0	21	4	5	7	129	.372	5	18	39	.231	0	3
Hamilton, Col.-N.Y.	146	568	505	82	159	213	19	4	9	45	.315	.386	.422	3	1	2	57	0	39	6	8	9	358	.327	7	36	147	.286	2	9
McElroy, Col.	41	2	1	0	0	0	0	0	0	0	.000	.000	.000	1	0	0	0	0	0	0	0	0	0	.000	0	0	0	.000	0	0
McElroy, Col.-N.Y.	56	2	1	0	0	0	0	0	0	0	.000	.000	.000	1	0	0	0	0	0	0	0	0	1	.000	0	0	0	.000	0	0
McRae, Col.	7	27	23	1	6	11	2	0	1	1	.261	.370	.478	0	0	2	2	0	7	0	0	0	237	.219	8	34	61	.230	0	2
McRae, N.Y.-Col.	103	371	321	36	72	115	14	1	9	37	.224	.323	.358	0	2	7	41	1	64	2	6	6	259	.224	9	35	62	.226	0	2

PITCHING

Name	W	L	Pct.	ERA	IP	H	R	ER	HR	SH	SF	HB	BB	IBB	SO	G	GS	CG	ShO	GF	Sv	vs. RH AB	vs. RH Avg.	vs. RH HR	vs. RH RBI	vs. LH AB	vs. LH Avg.	vs. LH HR	vs. LH RBI
Leiter, Al	13	12	.520	4.23	213.0	209	107	100	19	13	10	9	93	8	162	32	32	1	1	0	0	675	.262	17	83	123	.260	2	17
Hershiser, Orel	13	12	.520	4.58	179.0	175	92	91	14	6	8	11	77	2	89	32	32	0	0	0	0	383	.243	5	37	291	.282	9	39
Yoshii, Masato	12	8	.600	4.40	174.0	168	86	85	25	7	6	6	58	3	105	31	29	1	0	1	0	354	.251	14	49	292	.271	11	31
Reed, Rick	11	5	.688	4.58	149.1	163	77	76	23	6	3	1	47	2	104	26	26	1	1	0	0	330	.270	10	39	250	.296	13	34
Wendell, Turk	5	4	.556	3.05	85.2	80	31	29	9	2	1	2	37	8	77	80	0	0	0	14	3	200	.230	7	23	127	.268	2	11
Dotel, Octavio	8	3	.727	5.38	85.1	69	52	51	12	3	5	6	49	1	85	19	14	0	0	1	0	167	.240	10	31	138	.210	2	15
Benitez, Armando	4	3	.571	1.85	78.0	40	17	16	4	0	0	0	41	4	128	77	0	0	0	42	22	158	.127	2	11	113	.177	2	10
Rogers, Kenny	5	1	.833	4.03	76.0	71	35	34	8	3	1	4	28	1	58	12	12	2	1	0	0	228	.263	4	22	53	.208	4	11
Mahomes, Pat	8	0	1.000	3.68	63.2	44	26	26	7	1	2	2	37	5	51	39	0	0	0	12	0	132	.189	6	14	90	.211	1	13
Cook, Dennis	10	5	.667	3.86	63.0	50	27	27	11	1	2	1	27	1	68	71	0	0	0	12	3	160	.219	11	28	71	.211	0	6
Jones, Bobby	3	3	.500	5.61	59.1	69	37	37	3	3	3	2	11	0	31	12	9	0	0	0	0	143	.273	0	18	91	.330	3	17
Franco, John	0	2	.000	2.88	40.2	40	14	13	1	3	1	2	19	1	41	46	0	0	0	34	19	127	.244	1	12	30	.300	0	3
Watson, Allen	2	2	.500	4.08	39.2	36	18	18	5	3	4	1	22	3	32	14	4	0	0	6	1	109	.257	5	16	34	.235	0	2
Isringhausen, Jason	1	3	.250	6.41	39.1	43	29	28	7	0	1	2	22	2	31	13	5	0	0	2	1	85	.294	3	16	69	.261	4	8
Beltran, Rigo	1	1	.500	3.48	31.0	30	15	12	5	2	0	0	12	2	35	21	0	0	0	10	0	75	.213	4	12	45	.311	1	5
McMichael, Greg	1	1	.500	4.82	18.2	20	10	10	3	1	1	0	8	3	18	19	0	0	0	4	0	44	.273	1	6	30	.267	2	3
Manzanillo, Josias	0	0	.000	5.79	18.2	19	12	12	5	1	1	2	4	1	25	12	0	0	0	1	0	41	.268	3	7	31	.258	2	6
McElroy, Chuck	0	0	.000	3.38	13.1	12	5	5	0	1	1	1	8	1	7	15	0	0	0	7	0	28	.250	0	7	20	.250	0	7
Taylor, Billy	0	1	.000	8.10	13.1	20	12	12	2	1	0	0	9	5	14	18	0	0	0	5	0	46	.261	2	5	12	.667	0	1
Tam, Jeff	0	0	.000	3.18	11.1	6	4	4	3	0	0	0	3	0	8	9	0	0	0	3	0	26	.154	2	2	14	.143	1	1
Murray, Dan	0	0	.000	13.50	2.0	4	3	3	0	0	1	0	2	0	1	1	0	0	0	1	0	5	.400	0	2	4	.500	0	1
Franco, Matt	0	0	.000	13.50	1.1	3	2	2	1	0	0	0	3	0	2	2	0	0	0	2	0	4	.500	1	3	3	.333	0	1
Rusch, Glendon	0	0	.000	0.00	1.0	1	0	0	0	0	0	0	0	0	0	1	0	0	0	1	0	2	.000	0	0	1	1.000	0	0

PITCHERS WITH MORE THAN ONE N.L. TEAM

Name	W	L	Pct.	ERA	IP	H	R	ER	HR	SH	SF	HB	BB	IBB	SO	G	GS	CG	ShO	GF	Sv	vs. RH AB	vs. RH Avg.	vs. RH HR	vs. RH RBI	vs. LH AB	vs. LH Avg.	vs. LH HR	vs. LH RBI
Beltran, Col.	0	0	.000	7.36	11.0	20	9	9	2	1	0	1	7	1	15	12	0	0	0	2	0	75	.213	4	12	45	.311	1	5
Beltran, N.Y.-Col.	1	1	.500	4.50	42.0	50	24	21	7	3	0	1	19	3	50	33	0	0	0	0	0	99	.253	5	18	73	.342	2	10
McElroy, Col.	3	1	.750	6.20	40.2	48	29	28	9	0	2	0	28	3	37	41	0	0	0	12	0	28	.250	0	7	20	.250	0	7
McElroy, Col.-N.Y.	3	1	.750	5.50	54.0	60	34	33	9	1	3	1	36	4	44	56	0	0	0	3	0	131	.298	5	30	79	.266	4	20

INDIVIDUAL STATISTICS

FIELDING

FIRST BASEMEN

Player	Pct.	G	PO	A	E	TC	DP
Olerud, John	.994	160	1344	105	9	1458	127
Franco, Matt	1.000	19	41	5	0	46	8
Bonilla, Bobby	.962	4	23	2	1	26	2
Toca, Jorge	1.000	1	2	0	0	2	0
Ventura, Robin	1.000	1	1	0	0	1	0
Kinkade, Mike	-	1	0	0	0	0	0
Pratt, Todd	-	1	0	0	0	0	0

SECOND BASEMEN

Player	Pct.	G	PO	A	E	TC	DP
Alfonzo, Edgardo	.993	158	298	409	5	712	98
Lopez, Luis	.966	16	8	20	1	29	5
Mora, Melvin	1.000	4	1	1	0	2	1
Cedeno, Roger	-	1	0	0	0	0	0

THIRD BASEMEN

Player	Pct.	G	PO	A	E	TC	DP
Ventura, Robin	.980	160	123	320	9	452	33
Franco, Matt	.950	12	1	18	1	20	1
Lopez, Luis	.857	9	3	3	1	7	1
Mora, Melvin	1.000	3	2	5	0	7	1
Kinkade, Mike	1.000	3	1	1	0	2	0
Dunston, Shawon	1.000	1	1	1	0	2	0

SHORTSTOPS

Player	Pct.	G	PO	A	E	TC	DP
Ordonez, Rey	.994	154	220	416	4	640	91
Lopez, Luis	.971	33	23	45	2	70	8
Mora, Melvin	1.000	1	0	1	0	1	0
Halter, Shane	-	1	0	0	0	0	0

OUTFIELDERS

Player	Pct.	G	PO	A	E	TC	DP
Cedeno, Roger	.989	149	256	9	3	268	2
Henderson, Rickey	.988	116	168	0	2	170	0
McRae, Brian	.994	87	152	1	1	154	0
Agbayani, Benny	.984	80	121	2	2	125	0
Hamilton, Darryl	1.000	52	100	2	0	102	0
Mora, Melvin	1.000	45	18	0	0	18	0
Allensworth, Jermaine	1.000	33	47	1	0	48	1
Dunston, Shawon	.978	27	43	1	1	45	0
Bonilla, Bobby	.974	25	36	2	1	39	0
Franco, Matt	1.000	18	13	0	0	13	0
Kinkade, Mike	1.000	17	14	1	0	15	0
Payton, Jay	1.000	6	3	0	0	3	0
Halter, Shane	-	2	0	0	0	0	0
McElroy, Chuck	1.000	1	1	0	0	1	0
Pratt, Todd	1.000	1	1	0	0	1	0
Reed, Rick	-	1	0	0	0	0	0

CATCHERS

Player	Pct.	G	PO	A	E	TC	DP	PB
Piazza, Mike	.989	137	953	47	11	1011	5	7
Pratt, Todd	.996	52	262	13	1	276	1	3
Kinkade, Mike	1.000	1	3	0	0	3	0	0
Wilson, Vance	-	1	0	0	0	0	0	0

PITCHERS

Player	Pct.	G	PO	A	E	TC	DP
Wendell, Turk	.833	80	4	6	2	12	0
Benitez, Armando	1.000	77	2	6	0	8	0
Cook, Dennis	1.000	71	2	8	0	10	0
Franco, John	1.000	46	4	4	0	8	0
Mahomes, Pat	1.000	39	2	6	0	8	0
Hershiser, Orel	.947	32	19	35	3	57	1
Leiter, Al	.840	32	3	18	4	25	1
Yoshii, Masato	1.000	31	7	10	0	17	1
Reed, Rick	.976	26	11	29	1	41	4
Beltran, Rigo	1.000	21	2	6	0	8	1
Dotel, Octavio	.944	19	8	9	1	18	0
McMichael, Greg	1.000	19	2	1	0	3	0
Taylor, Billy	1.000	18	0	2	0	2	0
McElroy, Chuck	1.000	15	1	0	0	1	0
Watson, Allen	1.000	14	3	2	0	5	0
Isringhausen, Jason	.889	13	3	5	1	9	1
Rogers, Kenny	.958	12	4	19	1	24	2
Jones, Bobby	1.000	12	4	7	0	11	0
Manzanillo, Josias	1.000	12	2	2	0	4	0
Tam, Jeff	1.000	9	3	1	0	4	0
Franco, Matt	-	2	0	0	0	0	0
Murray, Dan	1.000	1	0	1	0	1	0
Rusch, Glendon	-	1	0	0	0	0	0

PITCHING AGAINST EACH CLUB

Pitcher	Ari. W-L	Atl. W-L	Chi. W-L	Cin. W-L	Col. W-L	Fla. W-L	Hou. W-L	L.A. W-L	Mil. W-L	Mon. W-L	Phi. W-L	Pit. W-L	S.D. W-L	S.F. W-L	StL. W-L	A.L. W-L	Total W-L
Beltran, R.	0-1	0-0	0-0	0-0	0-0	0-0	0-0	0-0	0-0	0-0	1-0	0-0	0-0	0-0	0-0	0-0	1-1
Benitez, A.	0-0	0-0	0-0	0-0	0-0	0-1	1-1	0-0	0-0	0-0	0-1	1-0	0-0	0-0	1-0	1-0	4-3
Cook, D.	0-1	1-1	2-0	1-0	0-0	1-0	0-1	0-0	0-1	1-1	0-0	1-0	2-0	1-0	0-0	0-0	10-5
Dotel, O.	1-0	0-2	1-0	0-0	0-1	1-0	1-0	1-0	0-0	0-0	1-0	0-0	0-0	1-0	0-0	1-0	8-3
Franco, J.	0-0	0-0	0-0	0-1	0-0	0-0	0-0	0-0	0-0	0-0	0-0	0-0	0-0	0-0	0-0	0-1	0-2
Franco, M.	0-0	0-0	0-0	0-0	0-0	0-0	0-0	0-0	0-0	0-0	0-0	0-0	0-0	0-0	0-0	0-0	0-0
Hershiser, O.	0-1	0-2	0-1	0-1	0-0	2-0	0-0	1-1	1-0	2-1	1-1	1-1	0-0	2-0	1-1	2-2	13-12
Isringhausen, J.	0-0	0-0	0-1	0-0	0-0	0-0	0-0	0-0	0-0	0-0	0-0	0-1	0-0	0-0	0-1	1-0	1-3
Jones, B.	0-0	0-0	0-0	0-0	0-1	2-0	0-0	0-0	0-1	1-0	0-1	0-0	0-0	0-0	0-0	0-0	3-3
Leiter, Al	0-1	1-2	1-0	2-1	1-1	2-1	0-1	0-1	1-0	0-1	0-1	0-0	1-1	0-0	1-0	3-1	13-12
Mahomes, P.	0-0	0-0	2-0	0-0	0-0	0-0	0-0	0-0	0-0	0-0	1-0	1-0	1-0	0-0	1-0	2-0	8-0
Manzanillo, J.	0-0	0-0	0-0	0-0	0-0	0-0	0-0	0-0	0-0	0-0	0-0	0-0	0-0	0-0	0-0	0-0	0-0
McElroy, C.	0-0	0-0	0-0	0-0	0-0	0-0	0-0	0-0	0-0	0-0	0-0	0-0	0-0	0-0	0-0	0-0	0-0
McMichael, G.	0-0	0-0	0-0	0-1	0-0	1-0	0-0	0-0	0-0	0-0	0-0	0-0	0-0	0-0	0-0	0-0	1-1
Murray, D.	0-0	0-0	0-0	0-0	0-0	0-0	0-0	0-0	0-0	0-0	0-0	0-0	0-0	0-0	0-0	0-0	0-0
Reed, R.	0-2	1-0	0-0	1-0	1-0	1-0	1-0	0-1	1-0	1-0	0-1	2-0	0-0	0-0	1-0	1-1	11-5
Rogers, K.	0-0	0-0	0-0	0-0	0-0	0-0	1-0	1-0	1-0	0-0	0-1	0-0	0-0	2-0	0-0	0-0	5-1
Rusch, G.	0-0	0-0	0-0	0-0	0-0	0-0	0-0	0-0	0-0	0-0	0-0	0-0	0-0	0-0	0-0	0-0	0-0
Tam, J.	0-0	0-0	0-0	0-0	0-0	0-0	0-0	0-0	0-0	0-0	0-0	0-0	0-0	0-0	0-0	0-0	0-0
Taylor, B.	0-0	0-0	0-0	0-0	0-0	0-0	0-0	0-1	0-0	0-0	0-0	0-0	0-0	0-0	0-0	0-0	0-1
Watson, A.	0-0	0-0	0-1	0-0	0-0	0-0	0-0	0-0	0-0	1-1	0-0	0-0	0-0	1-0	0-0	0-0	2-2
Wendell, T.	0-0	0-0	0-0	0-0	2-1	0-0	0-1	0-0	0-0	1-1	0-0	0-0	2-0	0-1	0-0	0-0	5-4
Yoshii, M.	1-1	0-2	0-0	1-1	1-0	0-1	1-0	1-0	1-0	1-0	2-0	1-0	1-1	0-1	0-0	1-1	12-8
Totals	2-7	3-9	6-3	5-5	5-4	10-3	5-4	4-4	5-2	8-5	6-6	7-2	7-2	7-2	5-2	12-6	97-66

INTERLEAGUE: Yoshii 1-0, Dotel 1-0, Leiter 0-1 vs. Orioles; Leiter 1-0, Hershiser 1-0, Franco 0-1 vs. Red Sox; Leiter 2-0, Mahomes 1-0, Reed 0-1, Yoshii 0-1, Hershiser 0-1 vs. Yankees; Hershiser 1-0, Mahomes 1-0, Isringhausen 1-0 vs. Blue Jays; Benitez 1-0, Reed 1-0, Hershiser 0-1 vs. Devil Rays. Total: 12-6.

MISCELLANEOUS

HOME RUNS BY PARK

At Arizona (6): Olerud 1, Piazza 1, Alfonzo 1, Franco 1, Allensworth 1, Kinkade 1.
At Atlanta (4): Piazza 2, Olerud 1, Agbayani 1.
At Baltimore (3): Henderson 1, Ventura 1, Alfonzo 1.
At Chicago (NL) (8): Ventura 3, Henderson 2, Olerud 1, Piazza 1, Alfonzo 1.
At Cincinnati (13): Henderson 3, Bonilla 2, Pratt 2, Alfonzo 2, Olerud 1, Ventura 1, Piazza 1, Franco 1.
At Colorado (6): Agbayani 2, Henderson 1, Lopez 1, Alfonzo 1, Allensworth 1.
At Florida (7): Henderson 2, Ventura 2, Olerud 1, Piazza 1, Alfonzo 1.
At Houston (7): Alfonzo 3, Hamilton 1, Olerud 1, Ventura 1, Piazza 1.
At Los Angeles (3): Piazza 2, Alfonzo 1.
At Milwaukee (7): Ventura 3, Piazza 2, Hamilton 1, Alfonzo 1.
At Montreal (5): Ventura 2, Piazza 2, Alfonzo 1.
At New York (AL) (2): McRae 1, Piazza 1.
At New York (NL) (84): Piazza 18, Ventura 13, Olerud 11, Alfonzo 11, Agbayani 10, McRae 5, Cedeno 4, Hamilton 3, Bonilla 2, Henderson 1, Pratt 1, Jones 1, Lopez 1, Ordonez 1, Allensworth 1, Kinkade 1.
At Philadelphia (7): Ventura 3, Olerud 2, McRae 1, Alfonzo 1.
At Pittsburgh (4): McRae 1, Piazza 1, Franco 1, Agbayani 1.
At San Diego (5): Piazza 2, Henderson 1, Ventura 1, Alfonzo 1.
At San Francisco (5): Piazza 3, Ventura 1, Alfonzo 1.
At St. Louis (4): Piazza 2, Henderson 1, Ventura 1.
At Tampa Bay (1): Franco 1.

LOW-HIT GAMES

No-hitters: None.
One-hitters: None.
Two-hitters: Al Leiter, October 4 vs. Cincinnati, W 5-0.

10-STRIKEOUT GAMES

Kenny Rogers 1, Al Leiter 1, Rick Reed 1, Octavio Dotel 1, **Total:** 4.

FOUR OR MORE HITS IN ONE GAME

Rickey Henderson 3, Mike Piazza 3, Edgardo Alfonzo 3 (including one six-hit game), John Olerud 2, Robin Ventura 2, Rey Ordonez 2, Darryl Hamilton 1, Roger Cedeno 1, Benny Agbayani 1, **Total:** 18.

MULTI-HOMER GAMES

Rickey Henderson 2, Robin Ventura 2, Benny Agbayani 2, John Olerud 1, Edgardo Alfonzo 1, **Total:** 8.

GRAND SLAMS

5-1: Brian McRae (off San Francisco's Jerry Spradlin).
5-20: Robin Ventura (off Milwaukee's Jim Abbott).
5-20: Robin Ventura (off Milwaukee's Horacio Estrada).
8-15: Robin Ventura (off San Francisco's Livan Hernandez).
8-22: John Olerud (off St. Louis's Rich Croushore).
9-5: Darryl Hamilton (off Colorado's Darryl Kile).
9-18: Rey Ordonez (off Philadelphia's Carlton Loewer).
9-29: John Olerud (off Atlanta's Greg Maddux).

PINCH HITTERS

(Minimum 5 at-bats)

Name	AB	Avg.	HR	RBI
Franco, Matt	59	.237	1	11
Lopez, Luis	28	.107	0	0
Bonilla, Bobby	26	.192	0	1
Pratt, Todd	24	.208	0	0
Agbayani, Benny	20	.150	0	0
Cedeno, Roger	18	.222	0	0
Dunston, Shawon	18	.222	0	1
Mora, Melvin	12	.167	0	0
McRae, Brian	11	.182	0	1
Kinkade, Mike	9	.111	0	2
Allensworth, Jermaine	6	.333	1	3
Payton, Jay	5	.400	0	1
Hamilton, Darryl	5	.200	0	1

DEBUTS

4-14: Terrence Long, PH.
4-24: Vance Wilson, C.
5-30: Melvin Mora, SS.
6-26: Octavio Dotel, P.
8-9: Dan Murray, P.
9-12: Jorge Toca, PH.

GAMES BY POSITION

Catcher: Mike Piazza 137, Todd Pratt 52, Vance Wilson 1, Mike Kinkade 1.
First base: John Olerud 160, Matt Franco 19, Bobby Bonilla 4, Robin Ventura 1, Todd Pratt 1, Mike Kinkade 1, Jorge Toca 1.
Second base: Edgardo Alfonzo 158, Luis Lopez 16, Melvin Mora 4, Roger Cedeno 1.
Third base: Robin Ventura 160, Matt Franco 12, Luis Lopez 9, Mike Kinkade 3, Melvin Mora 3, Shawon Dunston 1.
Shortstop: Rey Ordonez 154, Luis Lopez 33, Shane Halter 1, Melvin Mora 1.
Outfield: Roger Cedeno 149, Rickey Henderson 116, Brian McRae 87, Benny Agbayani 80, Darryl Hamilton 52, Melvin Mora 45, Jermaine Allensworth 33, Shawon Dunston 27, Bobby Bonilla 25, Matt Franco 18, Mike Kinkade 17, Jay Payton 6, Shane Halter 2, Rick Reed 1, Chuck McElroy 1, Todd Pratt 1.
Designated hitter: Matt Franco 4, Bobby Bonilla 3, Benny Agbayani 2, Rickey Henderson 1, Mike Piazza 1.

STREAKS

Wins: 6 (April 28-May 3, July 20-26).
Losses: 8 (May 28-June 5).
Consecutive games with at least one hit: 24, Mike Piazza (May 25-June 22).
Wins by pitcher: 5, Al Leiter (June 6-28).

ATTENDANCE

Home: 2,725,908.
Road: 2,600,427.
Highest (home): 53,869 (July 11 vs. New York).
Highest (road): 57,853 (August 14 vs. San Francisco).
Lowest (home): 14,155 (April 15 vs. Florida).
Lowest (road): 8,044 (July 22 vs. Montreal).

DAY BY DAY

Date	Opp.	Res.	Score	(inn.*)	Hits	Opp. hits	Winning pitcher	Losing pitcher	Save	Record	Pos.	GB
4-5	At Atl.	W	7-4		8	8	Schilling	Glavine	Brantley	1-0	T1st	...
4-6	At Atl.	L	3-11		13	17	Maddux	Ogea	Ebert	1-1	T1st	...
4-7	At Atl.	L	0-4		5	7	Smoltz	Loewer		1-2	T4th	1.0
4-8	At Atl.	W	6-3		7	4	Byrd	Millwood	Brantley	2-2	T2nd	1.0
4-9	At Fla.	L	4-7		5	9	Meadows	Spoljaric		2-3	5th	1.0
4-10	At Fla.	W	5-2		8	6	Schilling	Springer	Brantley	3-3	T2nd	1.0
4-11	At Fla.	W	2-1		6	5	Ogea	Fernandez	Brantley	4-3	T2nd	1.0
4-12	Atl.	L	6-8		10	9	Cather	Ryan	Seanez	4-4	3rd	2.0
4-14	Atl.	L	4-10		9	12	Millwood	Byrd		4-5	T3rd	3.0
4-16	Fla.	W	17-3		16	7	Schilling	Springer		5-5	3rd	1.5
4-17	Fla.	W	2-1		7	7	Gomes	Alfonseca		6-5	3rd	1.5
4-18	Fla.	W	7-2		14	8	Loewer	Ojala		7-5	3rd	0.5
4-19	At Ari.	L	2-3		4	8	Daal	Perez	Swindell	7-6	3rd	1.5
4-20	At Ari.	L	1-8		7	10	Johnson	Spoljaric		7-7	3rd	2.0
4-21	At Ari.	L	2-4		7	8	Stottlemyre	Schilling	Olson	7-8	3rd	2.5
4-23	At Mon.	W	6-2		10	6	Ogea	Hermanson		8-8	3rd	2.5
4-24	At Mon.	W	6-5		11	12	Grace	Ayala	Gomes	9-8	3rd	1.5
4-25	At Mon.	W	8-6		10	8	Byrd	Urbina		10-8	3rd	1.5
4-27	Cin.	W	1-0	(10)	7	5	Brantley	White		11-8	2nd	1.0
4-28	Cin.	L	8-12		13	13	Williamson	Brantley		11-9	3rd	2.0
4-29	Cin.	L	3-7		8	13	Bere	Loewer		11-10	3rd	3.0
4-30	L.A.	L	3-4		9	8	Perez	Byrd	Shaw	11-11	3rd	4.0
5-1	L.A.	L	6-12		13	12	Dreifort	Spoljaric		11-12	3rd	5.0
5-2	L.A.	W	12-3		13	8	Schilling	Brown		12-12	3rd	5.0
5-3	S.D.	L	3-9		13	14	Hitchcock	Ogea		12-13	3rd	6.0
5-4	S.D.	W	3-0		4	5	Loewer	Williams		13-13	3rd	5.0
5-5	S.D.	W	11-1		14	3	Byrd	Spencer		14-13	3rd	4.0
5-7	At Col.	W	8-1		14	7	Schilling	Thomson		15-13	3rd	4.0
5-8	At Col.	W	7-2		12	9	Bennett	Bohanon		16-13	3rd	4.0
5-9	At Col.	W	10-8		17	12	Ryan	Veres	Gomes	17-13	3rd	3.0
5-10	At StL.	L	2-5		7	9	Bottenfield	Loewer	Radinsky	17-14	3rd	3.0
5-11	At StL.	W	9-4		13	7	Byrd	Mercker		18-14	2nd	3.0
5-12	At StL.	W	8-4		12	7	Schilling	Oliver		19-14	2nd	2.0
5-14	N.Y.	L	3-7		5	9	Yoshii	Ogea		19-15	3rd	2.0
5-15	N.Y.	L	7-9		13	12	Mahomes	Ryan	Franco	19-16	3rd	2.0
5-16	N.Y.	W	5-2		10	8	Byrd	Hershiser	Brantley	20-16	3rd	2.0
5-17	At Mon.	W	4-3		8	9	Schilling	Thurman		21-16	2nd	2.0
5-18	At Mon.	L	4-7		9	9	Batista	Bennett	Urbina	21-17	2nd	3.0
5-19	At Mon.	L	9-10		8	13	Kline	Brantley		21-18	T2nd	4.0
5-21	At N.Y.	L	5-7		10	13	Hershiser	Loewer	Franco	21-19	3rd	3.5
5-22	At N.Y.	W	9-3		13	7	Byrd	Jones		22-19	3rd	3.5
5-23	At N.Y.	L	4-5		9	12	Beltran	Schilling		22-20	3rd	3.5
5-24	Mon.	W	5-4		7	7	Perez	Batista	Gomes	23-20	3rd	2.5
5-25	Mon.	L	2-4	(11)	6	10	Urbina	Montgomery		23-21	3rd	3.5
5-26	Mon.	L	2-5		6	8	Pavano	Loewer	Urbina	23-22	3rd	4.5
5-28	Col.	L	3-5		12	7	Leskanic	Byrd	Veres	23-23	3rd	6.0
5-29	Col.	W	2-0		4	4	Schilling	Bohanon		24-23	3rd	5.0
5-30	Col.	L	0-1		5	7	Kile	Poole	Veres	24-24	3rd	5.0
5-31	S.F.	W	4-3		9	12	Perez	Johnstone	Gomes	25-24	3rd	5.0
6-1	S.F.	L	5-6	(12)	13	8	Nen	Gomes		25-25	3rd	6.0
6-2	S.F.	W	7-6		11	10	Byrd	Ortiz	Gomes	26-25	2nd	5.0
6-3	S.F.	L	4-7		5	11	Spradlin	Schilling	Nen	26-26	3rd	5.5
6-4	At Bal.	W	9-5		18	9	Ogea	Erickson		27-26	2nd	4.5
6-5	At Bal.	L	6-7	(10)	7	12	Timlin	Montgomery		27-27	2nd	5.5
6-6	At Bal.	W	11-7		19	14	Bennett	Bones		28-27	2nd	5.5
6-7	N.Y. (AL)	W	6-5		9	7	Byrd	Pettitte		29-27	2nd	5.5
6-8	N.Y. (AL)	W	11-5		11	8	Perez	Grimsley		30-27	2nd	5.5
6-9	N.Y. (AL)	L	5-11		9	13	Cone	Ogea		30-28	3rd	6.5
6-11	Tor.	W	8-4		9	9	Wolf	Hamilton		31-28	2nd	5.5
6-12	Tor.	W	7-2		9	6	Byrd	Escobar		32-28	2nd	4.5
6-13	Tor.	L	2-7		4	13	Hentgen	Schilling		32-29	3rd	4.5
6-15	At S.D.	L	1-6		6	11	Clement	Ogea		32-30	3rd	5.0
6-16	At S.D.	W	4-2		9	7	Wolf	Hitchcock	Gomes	33-30	3rd	5.0
6-17	At S.D.	W	7-5		12	12	Byrd	Williams	Gomes	34-30	3rd	5.0
6-18	At L.A.	W	2-1		6	4	Schilling	Valdes	Gomes	35-30	3rd	5.0
6-19	At L.A.	L	1-8		7	13	Dreifort	Person		35-31	3rd	5.0
6-20	At L.A.	L	2-3		5	6	Brown	Ogea	Shaw	35-32	3rd	5.0
6-22	Pit.	W	3-2		7	6	Wolf	Cordova	Gomes	36-32	3rd	5.0
6-23	Pit.	L	6-8		11	12	Benson	Byrd	Williams	36-33	3rd	6.0
6-24	Pit.	W	7-5		10	10	Schilling	Silva	Gomes	37-33	3rd	6.0
6-25	At Chi.	W	3-2		6	3	Ogea	Lieber	Gomes	38-33	3rd	5.0
6-26	At Chi.	W	6-2		11	8	Person	Trachsel		39-33	3rd	5.0
6-27	At Chi.	L	7-13		11	15	Mulholland	Grace		39-34	3rd	6.0
6-28	At Pit.	L	2-3	(10)	6	7	Hansell	Montgomery		39-35	3rd	7.0
6-29	At Pit.	W	7-4		11	7	Schilling	Silva		40-35	3rd	6.0
6-30	At Pit.	L	1-9		9	12	Schmidt	Ogea		40-36	3rd	6.0
7-1	At Pit.	L	7-12		9	14	Ritchie	Person		40-37	3rd	7.0
7-2	Chi.	W	14-1		17	6	Wolf	Mulholland		41-37	3rd	7.0
7-3	Chi.	W	21-8		21	11	Byrd	Farnsworth		42-37	3rd	7.0

HIGHLIGHTS

High point: On August 6, the Phillies climbed a season-best 13 games over .500 with a victory over eventual N.L. West- champion Arizona. At 61-48, the team also was in the thick of the N.L. East race. The rest of the season was a disaster, however, as the Phils won just 16 of their last 53 games.

Low point: When a doubleheader loss to the Rockies triggered a slide of 18 defeats in 19 games. Included in the stretch was a 22-3 loss to the Reds, who went on a nine-homer barrage against Phillies pitching.

Turning point: Third baseman Scott Rolen wrenched his lower back during a hard slide at Milwaukee on July 21. He was on a tear at the time, having had back-to-back two-homer games at Tampa Bay in the previous series. He played only 23 games after the injury before being shut down for the season.

Most valuable player: Right fielder Bobby Abreu, who emerged as a contender for the batting title and wound up hitting .335. He tied for the N.L. lead in triples with 11 and also contributed 118 runs, 109 walks, 35 doubles, 20 home runs and 93 RBIs. Abreu reached base in 52 of his last 54 games.

Most valuable pitcher: Curt Schilling. He started the All-Star Game and seemed to be a lock for his first 20-win season—until biceps tendinitis limited him to a total of three starts after July 23. Schilling finished with a 15-6 record and eight complete games, but his 152 strikeouts were barely half of his total in 1998.

Most improved player: Catcher Mike Lieberthal became the first Phillies player to bat .300 with 30 homers since Mike Schmidt accomplished the feat in 1981. Lieberthal drove in 96 runs and committed just three errors in 143 games, including a 100-game errorless streak.

Most pleasant surprise: All-Star Paul Byrd, who won 15 games and came within one-third of an inning of reaching his spring goal of 200 innings pitched. Byrd allowed 34 home runs and had a league-high 17 hit batsmen, but he tied Schilling for the team victory lead.

Key injuries: Shortstop Desi Relaford, who underwent wrist surgery in late June, played only 65 games. Rolen missed almost one-third of the season, and Schilling had only 24 starts after making 35 in 1997 and 1998. Closer Jeff Brantley recorded just five saves before undergoing season-ending shoulder surgery in late May.

Notable: With 204 hits, center fielder Doug Glanville was the first Phillie to reach 200 since Pete Rose did it in 1979. ... Rico Brogna became the first Philadelphia first baseman to record consecutive 100-RBI seasons (102 in '99, 104 in '98). ... The team established a franchise record with only 100 errors.

—CHRIS EDWARDS

MISCELLANEOUS

RECORDS

1999 regular-season record: 77-85 (3rd in N.L. East); 41-40 at home; 36-45 on road; 28-22 vs. N.L. East; 22-28 vs. N.L. Central; 16-28 vs. N.L. West; 11-7 vs. A.L. East; 19-22 vs. lefthanded starters; 58-63 vs. righthanded starters; 27-35 on grass; 50-50 on turf; 25-25 in daytime; 52-60 at night; 25-19 in one-run games; 4-9 in extra-inning games; 0-1-1 in double-headers.

Team record past five years: 356-436 (.449, ranks 16th in league in that span).

TEAM LEADERS

Batting average: Bobby Abreu (.335).
At-bats: Doug Glanville (628).
Runs: Bobby Abreu (118).
Hits: Doug Glanville (204).
Total bases: Bobby Abreu (300).
Doubles: Doug Glanville (38).
Triples: Bobby Abreu (11).
Home runs: Mike Lieberthal (31).
Runs batted in: Rico Brogna (102).
Stolen bases: Doug Glanville (34).
Slugging percentage: Mike Lieberthal (.551).
On-base percentage: Bobby Abreu (.446).
Wins: Paul Byrd, Curt Schilling (15).
Earned-run average: Curt Schilling (3.54).
Complete games: Curt Schilling (8).
Shutouts: Carlton Loewer, Curt Schilling (1).
Saves: Wayne Gomes (19).
Innings pitched: Paul Byrd (199.2).
Strikeouts: Curt Schilling (152).

Date	Opp.	Res.	Score	(inn.*)	Hits	Opp. hits	Winning pitcher	Losing pitcher	Save	Record	Pos.	GB
7-4	Chi.	W	6-2		12	7	Schilling	Tapani		43-37	3rd	6.0
7-5	Mil.	L	0-5		6	10	Abbott	Ogea	Roque	43-38	3rd	7.0
7-6	Mil.	W	1-0		4	5	Person	Nomo	Gomes	44-38	3rd	6.0
7-7	Mil.	W	5-4		10	8	Gomes	Wickman		45-38	3rd	6.0
7-9	Bal.	W	4-2		5	8	Schilling	Guzman		46-38	3rd	5.5
7-10	Bal.	L	4-8		6	13	Mussina	Byrd		46-39	3rd	6.5
7-11	Bal.	L	2-6		6	12	Erickson	Ogea		46-40	3rd	7.5
7-15	At Bos.	L	4-6		9	12	Rose	Byrd	Wakefield	46-41	3rd	8.5
7-16	At Bos.	W	5-4		10	8	Person	Saberhagen	Gomes	47-41	3rd	8.5
7-17	At Bos.	W	11-3		18	7	Wolf	Portugal		48-41	3rd	7.5
7-18	At T.B.	W	3-2		7	4	Schilling	Lopez		49-41	3rd	6.5
7-19	At T.B.	W	16-3		22	7	Ogea	Rekar		50-41	3rd	5.5
7-20	At T.B.	L	4-5	(13)	10	12	Charlton	Schrenk		50-42	3rd	5.5
7-21	At Mil.	W	7-0		15	7	Person	Karl	Poole	51-42	3rd	4.5
7-22	At Mil.	L	0-5		5	6	Nomo	Wolf		51-43	3rd	5.5
7-23†	Atl.	W	6-5		7	9	Telemaco	Seanez	Gomes	52-43		
7-23‡	Atl.	L	1-3		5	7	Chen	Shumaker	Rocker	52-44	3rd	5.5
7-24	Atl.	W	4-3		11	6	Montgomery	Bowie	Gomes	53-44	3rd	4.5
7-25	Atl.	L	4-5	(10)	8	12	Rocker	Montgomery		53-45	3rd	5.5
7-26	Fla.	W	9-1		15	7	Person	Nunez		54-45	3rd	5.5
7-27	Fla.	L	2-6		7	12	Fernandez	Wolf	Alfonseca	54-46	3rd	6.5
7-28	Fla.	W	9-4		13	8	Schrenk	Dempster		55-46	3rd	5.5
7-29	Fla.	W	12-1		13	6	Ogea	Meadows		56-46	3rd	5.0
7-30	At Atl.	W	9-2		12	5	Byrd	Smoltz		57-46	3rd	4.5
7-31	At Atl.	L	6-8		11	12	Glavine	Person	Rocker	57-47	3rd	5.0
8-1	At Atl.	L	4-12		8	10	Maddux	Wolf		57-48	3rd	6.0
8-3	At Fla.	W	6-5		12	9	Telemaco	Edmondson	Gomes	58-48	3rd	6.0
8-4	At Fla.	W	4-1		9	10	Byrd	Springer	Schrenk	59-48	3rd	6.0
8-5	At Fla.	W	9-3		12	10	Person	Nunez		60-48	3rd	5.5
8-6	Ari.	W	4-2	(11)	8	6	Gomes	Chouinard		61-48	3rd	5.5
8-7	Ari.	L	2-8		7	9	Benes	Schilling		61-49	3rd	5.5
8-8	Ari.	L	4-7		10	13	Reynoso	Ogea	Mantei	61-50	3rd	5.5
8-9	StL.	L	6-12		11	15	Mercker	Schrenk		61-51	3rd	6.0
8-10	StL.	W	7-5		6	10	Poole	Bottalico	Gomes	62-51	3rd	6.0
8-11	StL.	L	1-5		6	9	Stephenson	Wolf	Slocumb	62-52	3rd	7.0
8-13	At Cin.	L	4-5		13	11	Williamson	Schrenk		62-53	3rd	8.0
8-14	At Cin.	L	1-4		4	14	Harnisch	Ogea	Graves	62-54	3rd	8.0
8-15	At Cin.	W	9-3		10	7	Person	Neagle		63-54	3rd	8.0
8-16	At StL.	L	3-4		9	4	Mercker	Wolf	Bottalico	63-55	3rd	9.0
8-17	At StL.	L	5-6		10	10	Acevedo	Gomes		63-56	3rd	9.0
8-18	At StL.	W	6-5		17	8	Aldred	Croushore	Gomes	64-56	3rd	9.0
8-20	L.A.	L	5-8	(10)	12	5	Mills	Gomes		64-57	3rd	9.5
8-21	L.A.	W	6-5	(11)	10	12	Gomes	Masaoka		65-57	3rd	9.5
8-22	L.A.	L	7-9		9	12	Park	Shumaker	Shaw	65-58	3rd	10.5
8-23	S.D.	L	6-7		9	12	Williams	Ogea	Hoffman	65-59	3rd	11.5
8-24	S.D.	W	18-2		22	5	Byrd	Spencer		66-59	3rd	11.5
8-25	S.D.	W	15-1		14	6	Person	Clement		67-59	3rd	11.5
8-28†	At Col.	L	6-11		9	15	Lee	Aldred		67-60		
8-28‡	At Col.	L	0-4		4	11	Bohanon	Grahe		67-61	3rd	13.5
8-29	At Col.	L	5-6		9	14	Kile	Byrd	Veres	67-62	3rd	14.5
8-30	At S.F	L	4-6	(10)	9	9	Rodriguez	Brewer		67-63	3rd	14.5
8-31	At S.F	L	1-8		7	11	Rueter	Wolf		67-64	3rd	15.5
9-1	At S.F	L	3-5	(11)	6	11	Rodriguez	Gomes		67-65	3rd	16.5
9-2	At S.F	L	2-3		7	8	Nathan	Grahe	Nen	67-66	3rd	17.0
9-3	Cin.	W	10-2		12	6	Schilling	Parris		68-66	3rd	17.0
9-4	Cin.	L	3-22		11	19	Harnisch	Byrd	Belinda	68-67	3rd	17.0
9-5	Cin.	L	7-9		7	13	Neagle	Person	Sullivan	68-68	3rd	17.0
9-6	Hou.	L	5-6		12	6	Lima	Wolf	Wagner	68-69	3rd	18.0
9-7	Hou.	L	6-8		10	12	Powell	Gomes	Henry	68-70	3rd	19.0
9-8	Hou.	L	2-10		8	12	Hampton	Schilling		68-71	3rd	20.0
9-9	Hou.	L	1-3		4	9	Reynolds	Montgomery	Wagner	68-72	3rd	20.5
9-10	At Ari.	L	1-3		6	7	Johnson	Person		68-73	3rd	21.5
9-11	At Ari.	L	0-4		6	12	Benes	Wolf		68-74	3rd	21.5
9-12	At Ari.	L	0-5		7	11	Stottlemyre	Grace		68-75	3rd	21.5
9-13	At Hou.	L	2-13		6	10	Hampton	Grahe		68-76	3rd	21.5
9-14	At Hou.	L	2-12		8	16	Reynolds	Byrd		68-77	3rd	22.5
9-15	At Hou.	W	8-6	(10)	14	12	Gomes	Henry	Brewer	69-77	3rd	21.5
9-17	At N.Y.	W	8-5		11	9	Wolf	Leiter	Brewer	70-77	3rd	21.5
9-18	At N.Y.	L	1-11		5	15	Yoshii	Grace		70-78	3rd	21.5
9-19	At N.Y.	L	6-8		9	9	Dotel	Byrd	Benitez	70-79	3rd	22.5
9-20	At Mil.	L	4-5		14	8	Coppinger	Loewer	Wickman	70-80	3rd	23.0
9-21	At Mil.	L	6-8		9	11	Pulsipher	Shumaker	Wickman	70-81	3rd	24.0
9-22	At Mil.	W	12-3		16	4	Telemaco	Peterson		71-81	3rd	24.0
9-23	At Mil.	L	6-11		8	12	Bere	Grace		71-82	3rd	25.0
9-24	N.Y.	W	3-2		6	9	Grahe	Benitez	Aldred	72-82	3rd	25.0
9-25	N.Y.	W	4-2		6	4	Person	Rogers	Gomes	73-82	3rd	25.0
9-26	N.Y.	W	3-2		4	6	Byrd	Reed	Montgomery	74-82	3rd	25.0
9-28	Chi.	L	2-8		9	10	Trachsel	Wolf		74-83	3rd	26.0
9-29	Chi.	W	5-0		12	4	Brewer	Bowie		75-83	3rd	25.0
9-30	Chi.	W	2-1		7	3	Person	McNichol	Montgomery	76-83	3rd	25.0
10-1	Mon.	L	4-7		11	13	Vazquez	Grahe	Urbina	76-84	3rd	26.0
10-2	Mon.	L	3-13		8	14	Powell	Byrd	Batista	76-85	3rd	26.0
10-3	Mon.	W	6-5		9	8	Politte	Strickland	Montgomery	77-85	3rd	26.0

Monthly records: April (11-11), May (14-13), June (15-12), July (17-11), August (10-17), September (9-19), October (1-2).
*Innings, if other than nine. † First game of a doubleheader. ‡ Second game of a doubleheader.

MEMORABLE GAMES

August 6 at Philadelphia

Trailing Randy Johnson and the Diamondbacks, 2-0, after seven innings, the Phillies rallied to send the contest into extra innings on a two-run homer by left fielder Ron Gant. The Phillies captured a 4-2 victory with one out in the 11th inning when reserve shortstop Domingo Cedeno clubbed a two-run homer off reliever Bobby Chouinard. The win moved the team a season-high 13 games over .500 at 61-48.

Arizona	AB	R	H	RBI	Philadelphia	AB	R	H	RBI
Womack, ss-rf	5	0	0	0	Glanville, cf	5	1	1	0
J.Bell, 2b	3	0	2	0	Gant, lf	3	1	1	2
L.Gonzalez, lf	4	0	0	0	K.Jordan, 1b	5	0	1	0
M.Williams, 3b	4	1	1	0	Rolen, 3b	4	0	1	0
Colbrunn, 1b	1	1	1	2	Lieberthal, c	5	0	0	0
T.Lee, 1b	1	0	0	0	Sefcik, rf	4	1	2	0
Gilkey, rf	3	0	0	0	D.Cedeno, ss	4	1	1	2
A.Fox, ss	1	0	0	0	Doster, 2b	4	0	1	0
S.Finley, cf	5	0	1	0	Wolf, p	1	0	0	0
D.Miller, c	5	0	1	0	Aldred, p	0	0	0	0
Ra.Johnson, p	3	0	0	0	A.Arias, ph	1	0	0	0
Durazo, ph	1	0	0	0	Telemaco, p	0	0	0	0
Swindell, p	0	0	0	0	Abreu, ph	1	0	0	0
Chouinard, p	0	0	0	0	Gomes, p	0	0	0	0
Totals	**36**	**2**	**6**	**2**	**Totals**	**37**	**4**	**8**	**4**

Arizona..000 200 000 00— 2
Philadelphia..................................000 000 020 02— 4

E—D.Miller (6). DP—Arizona 1, Philadelphia 2. LOB—Arizona 9, Philadelphia 8. 2B—D.Miller (15), Sefcik (12). HR—Colbrunn (3), Gant (12), D.Cedeno (1). SB—Gant (8), Rolen (11). S—D.Cedeno.

Arizona	IP	H	R	ER	BB	SO
Ra.Johnson	8	5	2	2	3	10
Swindell	1	1	0	0	0	1
Chouinard (L, 4-2)	1.1	2	2	2	1	0

Philadelphia	IP	H	R	ER	BB	SO
Wolf	7.1	5	2	2	5	7
Aldred	0.2	0	0	0	1	1
Telemaco	1	0	0	0	0	2
Gomes (W, 3-1)	2	1	0	0	2	1

HBP—Rolen by Johnson. U—HP, Hernandez. 1B, West. 2B, Vanover. 3B, Bucknor. T—3:08. A—27,742.

September 4 at Philadelphia

The Reds established an N.L. single-game record with nine home runs during a 22-3 drubbing at Veterans Stadium. All-Star Paul Byrd lasted just 3 2/3 innings for the Phillies. Perhaps fittingly, the record-setting homer was an eighth-inning blow by former Phillies second baseman Mark Lewis.

Cincinnati	AB	R	H	RBI	Philadelphia	AB	R	H	RBI
Reese, 2b	4	2	3	3	Glanville, cf	3	1	2	0
Stynes, 2b	2	1	1	0	Prince, c	2	0	0	0
Larkin, ss	2	1	0	0	Ducey, lf	5	0	1	0
Dawkins, ss	2	1	1	0	Abreu, rf	3	1	1	0
Casey, 1b	5	2	2	1	K.Jrdn, 3b-1b	4	0	0	0
Ma.Sweeny, 1b	0	0	0	0	Telemaco, p	0	0	0	0
D.Young, rf	6	3	3	4	Schrenk, p	0	0	0	0
G.Vaughn, lf	3	3	1	3	G.Bennett, ph	1	0	0	0
Robinson, lf	1	0	0	0	Brogna, 1b	3	1	2	2
Taubensee, c	5	3	4	3	Doster, 3b	1	0	0	0
Belinda, p	1	0	0	0	Lieberthal, c	2	0	1	0
A.Boone, 3b	4	1	1	3	Sefcik, cf	2	0	2	0
M.Lewis, 3b	2	1	1	3	Anderson, 2b	4	0	2	0
Hammonds, cf	5	2	1	1	A.Arias, ss	2	0	0	0
Harnisch, p	3	1	0	0	Politte, p	0	0	0	0
B.Johnson, c	2	1	1	1	Ogea, p	1	0	0	0
					Lovullo, 1b	1	0	0	0
					Byrd, p	1	0	0	0
					Brewer, p	0	0	0	0
					D.Cedeno, ss	2	0	0	0
Totals	**47**	**22**	**19**	**22**	**Totals**	**37**	**3**	**11**	**2**

Cincinnati....................................031 191 160—22
Philadelphia..................................200 001 000 —3

E—G.Vaughn (3), K.Jordan 2 (8). LOB—Cincinnati 7, Philadelphia 10. 2B—D.Young 2 (25), Taubensee (17), Lieberthal (27), Mar.Anderson (24). HR—Reese (9), D.Young (9), G.Vaughn (30), Taubensee 2 (16), A.Boone (11), Hammonds (13), M.Lewis (6), B.Johnson (5), Brogna (20). CS—Brogna (5).

Cincinnati	IP	H	R	ER	BB	SO
Harnisch (W, 14-8)	6	8	3	1	2	4
Belinda (S, 2)	3	3	0	0	1	2

Philadelphia	IP	H	R	ER	BB	SO
Byrd (L, 14-8)	3.2	7	5	5	3	3
Brewer	0.1	1	2	2	1	0
Politte	0.1	2	6	6	3	0
Ogea	2.2	4	3	3	1	3
Telemaco	1	5	6	6	0	1
Schrenk	1	0	0	0	0	1

HBP—Dawkins by Telemaco. WP—Harnisch, Politte. U—HP, Emmel. 1B, Rieker. 2B, Davis. 3B, Wegner. T—3:17. A—16,357.

INDIVIDUAL STATISTICS

BATTING

Name	G	TPA	AB	R	H	TB	2B	3B	HR	RBI	Avg.	Obp.	Slg.	SH	SF	HP	BB	IBB	SO	SB	CS	GDP	vs RHP AB	vs RHP Avg.	vs RHP HR	vs RHP RBI	vs LHP AB	vs LHP Avg.	vs LHP HR	vs LHP RBI
Glanville, Doug	150	692	628	101	204	287	38	6	11	73	.325	.376	.457	5	5	6	48	1	82	34	2	9	488	.346	9	62	140	.250	2	11
Brogna, Rico	157	679	619	90	172	281	29	4	24	102	.278	.336	.454	0	4	2	54	7	132	8	5	19	433	.284	15	69	186	.263	9	33
Abreu, Bobby	152	662	546	118	183	300	35	11	20	93	.335	.446	.549	0	4	3	109	8	113	27	9	13	405	.348	20	73	141	.298	0	20
Gant, Ron	138	605	516	107	134	222	27	5	17	77	.260	.364	.430	0	3	1	85	0	112	13	3	6	386	.246	12	55	130	.300	5	22
Lieberthal, Mike	145	574	510	84	153	281	33	1	31	96	.300	.363	.551	1	8	11	44	7	86	0	0	15	388	.276	21	67	122	.377	10	29
Anderson, Marlon	129	484	452	48	114	163	26	4	5	54	.252	.292	.361	4	2	2	24	1	61	13	2	6	388	.245	5	44	64	.297	0	10
Rolen, Scott	112	497	421	74	113	221	28	1	26	77	.268	.368	.525	0	6	3	67	2	114	12	2	8	330	.252	17	55	91	.330	9	22
Arias, Alex	118	390	347	43	105	139	20	1	4	48	.303	.373	.401	1	2	4	36	6	31	2	2	12	252	.321	4	39	95	.253	0	9
Jordan, Kevin	120	380	347	36	99	134	17	3	4	51	.285	.339	.386	0	3	6	24	1	34	0	0	12	224	.277	2	32	123	.301	2	19
Relaford, Desi	65	242	211	31	51	69	11	2	1	26	.242	.322	.327	6	0	6	19	2	34	4	3	5	167	.240	1	19	44	.250	0	7
Sefcik, Kevin	111	242	209	28	58	82	15	3	1	11	.278	.368	.392	3	0	1	29	0	24	9	4	4	118	.229	0	5	91	.341	1	6
Ducey, Rob	104	227	188	29	49	87	10	2	8	33	.261	.383	.463	0	1	0	38	1	57	2	1	1	181	.265	8	31	7	.143	0	2
Doster, David	99	112	97	9	19	30	2	0	3	10	.196	.282	.309	2	1	0	12	1	23	1	0	2	50	.160	1	5	47	.234	2	5
Bennett, Gary	36	94	88	7	24	31	4	0	1	21	.273	.298	.352	0	2	0	4	0	11	0	0	7	66	.273	1	17	22	.273	0	4
Cedeno, Domingo	32	72	66	5	10	17	4	0	1	5	.152	.211	.258	1	0	0	5	0	22	0	1	2	45	.200	1	4	21	.048	0	1
Byrd, Paul	32	71	55	6	7	7	0	0	0	4	.127	.200	.127	11	0	0	5	0	11	0	0	2	38	.132	0	2	17	.118	0	2
Schilling, Curt	24	66	50	5	5	8	1	1	0	3	.100	.211	.160	9	0	0	7	0	28	0	0	0	35	.114	0	3	15	.067	0	0
Ogea, Chad	36	55	44	1	4	4	0	0	0	0	.091	.167	.091	7	0	0	4	0	25	0	0	1	39	.077	0	0	5	.200	0	0
Person, Robert	31	47	41	3	3	3	0	0	0	1	.073	.116	.073	4	0	1	1	0	23	0	0	0	25	.040	0	0	16	.125	0	1
Lovullo, Torey	17	41	38	3	8	14	0	0	2	5	.211	.268	.368	0	0	0	3	0	11	0	0	1	19	.158	1	2	19	.263	1	3
Wolf, Randy	22	39	30	2	7	8	1	0	0	0	.233	.281	.267	7	0	0	2	0	8	0	0	0	19	.211	0	0	11	.273	0	0
Loewer, Carlton	20	25	22	0	5	5	0	0	0	1	.227	.261	.227	2	0	0	1	0	9	0	0	0	16	.250	0	0	6	.167	0	1
Estalella, Bobby	9	22	18	2	3	3	0	0	0	1	.167	.318	.167	0	0	0	4	0	7	0	1	0	15	.133	0	1	3	.333	0	0
Magee, Wendell	12	15	14	4	5	12	1	0	2	5	.357	.400	.857	0	0	0	1	0	4	0	0	1	8	.250	0	1	6	.500	2	4
Grahe, Joe	13	8	7	1	1	1	0	0	0	0	.143	.250	.143	0	0	0	1	0	3	0	0	0	5	.200	0	0	2	.000	0	0
Grace, Mike	27	11	7	1	0	0	0	0	0	0	.000	.125	.000	3	0	0	1	0	4	0	0	0	7	.000	0	0	0	.000	0	0
Prince, Tom	4	7	6	1	1	1	0	0	0	0	.167	.286	.167	0	0	0	1	0	1	0	0	1	3	.333	0	0	3	.000	0	0
Shumaker, Anthony	8	6	5	0	1	1	0	0	0	0	.200	.333	.200	0	0	0	1	0	3	0	0	0	2	.500	0	0	3	.000	0	0
Bennett, Joel	5	6	4	1	0	0	0	0	0	0	.000	.200	.000	1	0	0	1	0	1	0	0	0	3	.000	0	0	1	.000	0	0
Schrenk, Steve	32	4	3	0	0	0	0	0	0	0	.000	.000	.000	1	0	0	0	0	2	0	0	0	2	.000	0	0	1	.000	0	0
Poole, Jim	51	2	2	0	0	0	0	0	0	0	.000	.000	.000	0	0	0	0	0	1	0	0	0	1	.000	0	0	1	.000	0	0
Perez, Yorkis	35	2	2	0	0	0	0	0	0	0	.000	.000	.000	0	0	0	0	0	2	0	0	0	2	.000	0	0	0	.000	0	0
Spoljaric, Paul	5	4	2	0	0	0	0	0	0	0	.000	.000	.000	2	0	0	0	0	0	0	0	0	1	.000	0	0	1	.000	0	0
Montgomery, Steve	53	1	1	1	1	1	0	0	0	0	1.000	1.000	1.000	0	0	0	0	0	0	0	0	0	0	.000	0	0	1	1.000	0	0
Aldred, Scott	29	1	1	0	0	0	0	0	0	0	.000	.000	.000	0	0	0	0	0	1	0	0	0	1	.000	0	0	0	.000	0	0
Gomes, Wayne	73	1	1	0	0	0	0	0	0	0	.000	.000	.000	0	0	0	0	0	1	0	0	0	1	.000	0	0	0	.000	0	0
Brantley, Jeff	10	0	0	0	0	0	0	0	0	0	.000	.000	.000	0	0	0	0	0	0	0	0	0	0	.000	0	0	0	.000	0	0
Ryan, Ken	15	0	0	0	0	0	0	0	0	0	.000	.000	.000	0	0	0	0	0	0	0	0	0	0	.000	0	0	0	.000	0	0
Brewer, Billy	25	0	0	0	0	0	0	0	0	0	.000	.000	.000	0	0	0	0	0	0	0	0	0	0	.000	0	0	0	.000	0	0
Telemaco, Amaury	44	0	0	0	0	0	0	0	0	0	.000	.000	.000	0	0	0	0	0	0	0	0	0	0	.000	0	0	0	.000	0	0
Politte, Cliff	13	0	0	0	0	0	0	0	0	0	.000	.000	.000	0	0	0	0	0	0	0	0	0	0	.000	0	0	0	.000	0	0

Players with more than one N.L. team

Name	G	TPA	AB	R	H	TB	2B	3B	HR	RBI	Avg.	Obp.	Slg.	SH	SF	HP	BB	IBB	SO	SB	CS	GDP	vs RHP AB	vs RHP Avg.	vs RHP HR	vs RHP RBI	vs LHP AB	vs LHP Avg.	vs LHP HR	vs LHP RBI
Telemaco, Ari.	5	0	0	0	0	0	0	0	0	0	.000	.000	.000	0	0	0	0	0	0	0	0	0	0	.000	0	0	0	.000	0	0
Telemaco, Ari.-Phi.	49	0	0	0	0	0	0	0	0	0	.000	.000	.000	0	0	0	0	0	0	0	0	0	0	.000	0	0	0	.000	0	0

PITCHING

Name	W	L	Pct.	ERA	IP	H	R	ER	HR	SH	SF	HB	BB	IBB	SO	G	GS	CG	ShO	GF	Sv	vs. RH AB	vs. RH Avg.	vs. RH HR	vs. RH RBI	vs. LH AB	vs. LH Avg.	vs. LH HR	vs. LH RBI
Byrd, Paul	15	11	.577	4.60	199.2	205	119	102	34	5	6	17	70	2	106	32	32	1	0	0	0	409	.230	17	48	365	.304	17	57
Schilling, Curt	15	6	.714	3.54	180.1	159	74	71	25	11	3	5	44	0	152	24	24	8	1	0	0	338	.225	13	34	334	.249	12	37
Ogea, Chad	6	12	.333	5.63	168.0	192	110	105	36	10	4	4	61	1	77	36	28	0	0	3	0	386	.264	20	49	281	.320	16	54
Person, Robert	10	5	.667	4.27	137.0	130	72	65	23	7	4	2	70	1	127	31	22	0	0	1	0	284	.229	11	30	232	.280	12	40
Wolf, Randy	6	9	.400	5.55	121.2	126	78	75	20	5	1	5	67	0	116	22	21	0	0	0	0	388	.278	16	62	86	.209	4	11
Loewer, Carlton	2	6	.250	5.12	89.2	100	54	51	9	5	6	0	26	0	48	20	13	2	1	2	0	192	.276	5	28	156	.301	4	22
Gomes, Wayne	5	5	.500	4.26	74.0	70	38	35	5	5	3	2	56	2	58	73	0	0	0	58	19	161	.255	5	22	114	.254	0	11
Montgomery, Steve	1	5	.167	3.34	64.2	54	25	24	10	1	0	0	31	3	55	53	0	0	0	21	3	146	.247	6	16	90	.200	4	7
Grace, Mike	1	4	.200	7.69	55.0	80	48	47	5	3	3	6	30	0	28	27	5	0	0	1	0	136	.331	4	31	95	.368	1	16
Schrenk, Steve	1	3	.250	4.29	50.1	41	24	24	6	3	1	7	14	4	36	32	2	0	0	8	1	124	.194	2	11	60	.283	4	11
Telemaco, Amaury	3	0	1.000	5.55	47.0	45	29	29	8	3	1	2	20	3	41	44	0	0	0	7	0	119	.244	6	21	61	.262	2	10
Poole, Jim	1	1	.500	4.33	35.1	48	20	17	3	1	0	3	15	1	22	51	0	0	0	12	1	73	.397	1	14	74	.257	2	13
Grahe, Joe	1	4	.200	3.86	32.2	40	16	14	1	0	3	3	17	0	16	13	5	0	0	4	0	64	.234	0	7	66	.379	1	9
Aldred, Scott	1	1	.500	3.90	32.1	33	15	14	1	1	5	0	15	3	19	29	0	0	0	5	1	76	.224	0	12	43	.372	1	9
Perez, Yorkis	3	1	.750	3.94	32.0	29	15	14	4	2	1	0	15	1	26	35	0	0	0	4	0	71	.239	3	10	48	.250	1	8
Brewer, Billy	1	1	.500	7.01	25.2	30	20	20	4	1	1	0	14	1	28	25	0	0	0	8	2	62	.274	2	11	40	.325	2	10
Shumaker, Anthony	0	3	.000	5.96	22.2	23	17	15	3	2	0	1	14	0	17	8	4	0	0	2	0	68	.265	3	13	20	.250	0	1
Politte, Cliff	1	0	1.000	7.13	17.2	19	14	14	2	1	0	0	15	0	15	13	0	0	0	0	0	43	.279	2	8	26	.269	0	3
Bennett, Joel	2	1	.667	9.00	17.0	26	17	17	10	2	0	0	7	0	13	5	3	0	0	0	0	46	.391	8	14	28	.286	2	3
Ryan, Ken	1	2	.333	6.32	15.2	16	11	11	2	0	0	0	11	2	9	15	0	0	0	5	0	44	.318	2	11	16	.125	0	0
Spoljaric, Paul	0	3	.000	15.09	11.1	23	24	19	1	1	1	1	7	0	10	5	3	0	0	1	0	40	.350	1	12	14	.643	0	7
Brantley, Jeff	1	2	.333	5.19	8.2	5	6	5	0	0	1	0	8	0	11	10	0	0	0	9	5	19	.211	0	3	12	.083	0	2

PITCHERS WITH MORE THAN ONE N.L. TEAM

Name	W	L	Pct.	ERA	IP	H	R	ER	HR	SH	SF	HB	BB	IBB	SO	G	GS	CG	ShO	GF	Sv	vs. RH AB	vs. RH Avg.	vs. RH HR	vs. RH RBI	vs. LH AB	vs. LH Avg.	vs. LH HR	vs. LH RBI
Telemaco, Ari.	1	0	1.000	7.50	6.0	7	5	5	2	1	0	0	6	1	2	5	0	0	0	3	0	119	.244	6	21	61	.262	2	10
Telemaco, Ari.-Phi.	4	0	1.000	5.77	53.0	52	34	34	10	4	1	2	26	4	43	49	0	0	0	1	0	132	.235	7	24	69	.304	3	13

INDIVIDUAL STATISTICS

FIELDING

FIRST BASEMEN

Player	Pct.	G	PO	A	E	TC	DP
Brogna, Rico	.995	157	1240	123	7	1370	119
Jordan, Kevin	1.000	13	55	4	0	59	6
Lovullo, Torey	1.000	6	22	5	0	27	3

SECOND BASEMEN

Player	Pct.	G	PO	A	E	TC	DP
Anderson, Marlon	.979	121	234	284	11	529	59
Doster, David	.993	77	69	72	1	142	21
Jordan, Kevin	.984	33	56	67	2	125	22
Sefcik, Kevin	.977	15	25	17	1	43	4
Lovullo, Torey	1.000	6	14	8	0	22	0
Cedeno, Domingo	1.000	1	1	2	0	3	0
Arias, Alex	-	1	0	0	0	0	0

THIRD BASEMEN

Player	Pct.	G	PO	A	E	TC	DP
Rolen, Scott	.960	112	111	227	14	352	21
Jordan, Kevin	.943	62	40	93	8	141	10
Doster, David	1.000	6	3	7	0	10	1
Arias, Alex	1.000	2	1	1	0	2	0

SHORTSTOPS

Player	Pct.	G	PO	A	E	TC	DP
Arias, Alex	.988	95	119	207	4	330	43
Relaford, Desi	.952	63	97	182	14	293	43
Cedeno, Domingo	.982	19	19	35	1	55	6
Doster, David	1.000	5	6	9	0	15	3

OUTFIELDERS

Player	Pct.	G	PO	A	E	TC	DP
Glanville, Doug	.980	148	385	13	8	406	3
Abreu, Bobby	.989	146	260	8	3	271	0
Gant, Ron	.993	133	260	7	2	269	2
Sefcik, Kevin	.986	64	68	1	1	70	0
Ducey, Rob	1.000	58	89	1	0	90	0
Magee, Wendell	1.000	4	5	0	0	5	0

CATCHERS

Player	Pct.	G	PO	A	E	TC	DP	PB
Lieberthal, Mike	.997	143	881	62	3	946	12	11
Bennett, Gary	.971	32	129	6	4	139	0	2
Estalella, Bobby	.976	7	38	2	1	41	0	1
Prince, Tom	1.000	4	13	1	0	14	0	0
Bennett, Joel	-	0	0	0	0	0	0	0

PITCHERS

Player	Pct.	G	PO	A	E	TC	DP
Gomes, Wayne	1.000	73	4	5	0	9	0
Montgomery, Steve	1.000	53	1	6	0	7	0
Poole, Jim	.800	51	1	3	1	5	0
Telemaco, Amaury	.923	44	5	7	1	13	0
Ogea, Chad	.960	36	8	16	1	25	1
Perez, Yorkis	1.000	35	1	0	0	1	0
Byrd, Paul	.854	32	10	25	6	41	3
Schrenk, Steve	1.000	32	4	7	0	11	1
Person, Robert	.955	31	8	13	1	22	0
Aldred, Scott	1.000	29	2	6	0	8	0
Grace, Mike	1.000	27	5	5	0	10	0
Brewer, Billy	1.000	25	0	1	0	1	0
Schilling, Curt	1.000	24	11	19	0	30	1
Wolf, Randy	.889	22	3	13	2	18	2
Loewer, Carlton	.929	20	3	10	1	14	0
Ryan, Ken	1.000	15	2	2	0	4	0
Grahe, Joe	1.000	13	3	5	0	8	1
Politte, Cliff	1.000	13	1	1	0	2	0
Brantley, Jeff	1.000	10	0	1	0	1	0
Shumaker, Anthony	.833	8	0	5	1	6	0
Bennett, Joel	1.000	5	2	3	0	5	0
Spoljaric, Paul	.667	5	1	1	1	3	0

PITCHING AGAINST EACH CLUB

Pitcher	Ari. W-L	Atl. W-L	Chi. W-L	Cin. W-L	Col. W-L	Fla. W-L	Hou. W-L	L.A. W-L	Mil. W-L	Mon. W-L	N.Y. W-L	Pit. W-L	S.D. W-L	S.F. W-L	StL. W-L	A.L. W-L	Total W-L
Aldred, S.	0-0	0-0	0-0	0-0	0-1	0-0	0-0	0-0	0-0	0-0	0-0	0-0	0-0	0-0	0-0	1-0	1-1
Bennett, J.	0-0	0-0	0-0	0-0	1-0	0-0	0-0	0-0	0-0	0-0	0-0	0-0	0-0	0-0	0-0	1-0	2-1
Brantley, J.	0-0	0-0	0-0	1-1	0-0	0-0	0-0	0-0	0-0	0-0	0-0	0-0	0-0	0-0	0-0	0-0	1-2
Brewer, B.	0-0	0-0	1-0	0-0	0-0	0-0	0-0	0-0	0-0	0-0	0-0	0-0	0-1	0-0	0-0	0-0	1-1
Byrd, P.	0-0	2-1	1-0	0-1	0-2	1-0	0-1	0-1	0-0	1-1	3-1	0-1	3-0	1-0	1-0	2-2	15-11
Gomes, W.	1-0	0-0	0-0	0-0	0-0	0-0	0-0	0-0	1-0	0-0	0-0	0-0	0-0	0-0	0-0	0-0	5-5
Grace, Mi.	0-1	0-0	0-1	0-0	0-0	0-0	0-0	0-1	1-0	0-1	0-0	0-0	0-0	0-0	0-0	0-0	1-4
Grahe, J.	0-0	0-0	0-0	0-0	0-1	0-0	0-1	0-0	0-0	0-1	1-0	0-0	0-0	0-1	0-0	0-0	1-4
Loewer, C.	0-0	0-1	0-1	0-0	0-0	1-0	0-0	0-0	0-1	0-1	0-0	0-1	1-0	0-0	0-1	0-0	2-6
Montgomery, S.	0-0	1-1	0-0	0-0	0-0	0-0	0-0	0-0	0-0	0-0	0-1	0-0	0-1	0-0	0-1	0-1	1-5
Ogea, C.	0-1	0-1	1-0	0-1	0-0	2-0	0-0	0-1	0-1	0-0	1-0	0-3	0-0	0-0	0-0	2-2	6-12
Perez, Y.	0-1	0-0	0-0	0-1	0-0	0-1	0-0	0-0	0-1	0-0	0-1	0-0	1-0	0-0	0-0	1-0	3-5
Person, R.	0-1	2-0	2-1	1-1	0-2	0-1	0-0	0-1	2-0	0-0	1-0	1-0	1-0	0-0	0-1	1-0	10-5
Politte, C.	0-0	0-0	0-0	0-0	0-0	0-0	0-0	0-0	0-0	0-0	0-0	0-0	0-0	0-0	0-0	1-0	1-0
Poole, J.	0-0	0-0	0-0	0-0	0-1	0-0	0-0	0-0	0-0	0-0	0-0	0-0	0-0	0-0	1-0	0-0	1-1
Ryan, K.	0-0	0-1	0-0	0-0	1-0	0-0	0-0	0-0	0-0	0-0	0-0	0-0	0-0	0-0	0-0	0-0	1-2
Schilling, C.	0-2	1-0	1-0	1-0	2-0	2-0	0-1	2-0	0-0	1-0	0-1	0-1	2-0	0-1	1-0	2-1	15-6
Schrenk, S.	0-0	0-0	0-0	0-1	0-0	1-0	0-0	0-0	0-0	0-0	0-0	0-0	0-0	0-1	0-1	0-0	1-3
Shumaker, A.	0-0	0-1	0-0	0-0	0-0	0-0	0-0	0-1	0-0	0-0	0-0	0-0	0-0	0-0	0-0	0-0	0-3
Spoljaric, P.	0-1	0-0	0-0	0-0	0-0	0-0	0-1	0-0	0-0	0-0	0-0	0-0	0-0	0-0	0-0	0-0	0-3
Telemaco, A.	0-0	1-0	0-0	0-0	0-0	1-0	0-0	0-0	1-0	0-0	0-0	0-0	0-0	0-0	0-0	0-0	3-0
Wolf, R.	0-1	0-1	1-1	0-0	0-0	0-0	0-1	0-0	0-0	1-0	1-0	0-1	0-0	0-1	0-2	2-0	7-9
Totals	1-8	5-8	7-2	3-6	4-5	11-2	1-6	3-6	4-5	6-6	6-6	3-4	6-3	2-6	4-5	11-7	77-85

INTERLEAGUE: Ogea 1-1, Bennett 1-0, Schilling 1-0, Montgomery 0-1, Byrd 0-1 vs. Orioles; Person 1-0, Wolf 1-0, Byrd 0-1 vs. Red Sox; Byrd 1-0, Perez 1-0, Ogea 0-1 vs. Yankees; Wolf 1-0, Byrd 1-0, Schilling 0-1 vs. Blue Jays; Schilling 1-0, Ogea 1-0, Schrenk 0-1 vs. Devil Rays. Total: 11-7.

MISCELLANEOUS

HOME RUNS BY PARK

At Arizona (2): Gant 1, Rolen 1.
At Atlanta (7): Rolen 3, Brogna 2, Lieberthal 1, Anderson 1.
At Baltimore (5): Lieberthal 3, Ducey 1, Rolen 1.
At Boston (5): Gant 2, Glanville 1, Rolen 1, Abreu 1.
At Chicago (NL) (5): Lieberthal 2, Gant 1, Brogna 1, Abreu 1.
At Cincinnati (4): Ducey 1, Gant 1, Lieberthal 1, Rolen 1.
At Colorado (14): Lieberthal 3, Ducey 2, Gant 2, Jordan 2, Brogna 1, Glanville 1, Relaford 1, Rolen 1, Abreu 1.
At Florida (7): Brogna 3, Lieberthal 2, Bennett 1, Rolen 1.
At Houston (1): Glanville 1.
At Los Angeles (2): Brogna 1, Lieberthal 1.
At Milwaukee (3): Gant 1, Glanville 1, Magee 1.
At Montreal (7): Lieberthal 2, Abreu 2, Gant 1, Brogna 1, Rolen 1.
At New York (NL) (4): Gant 1, Brogna 1, Lieberthal 1, Abreu 1.
At Philadelphia (77): Brogna 14, Abreu 13, Lieberthal 10, Rolen 9, Gant 6, Glanville 5, Arias 4, Anderson 4, Ducey 3, Lovullo 2, Jordan 2, Doster 2, Cedeno 1, Sefcik 1, Magee 1.
At Pittsburgh (2): Rolen 1, Abreu 1.
At San Diego (4): Gant 1, Lieberthal 1, Glanville 1, Rolen 1.
At San Francisco (2): Ducey 1, Lieberthal 1.
At St. Louis (6): Lieberthal 3, Glanville 1, Doster 1, Rolen 1.
At Tampa Bay (4): Rolen 4.

LOW-HIT GAMES

No-hitters: None.
One-hitters: None.
Two-hitters: None.

10-STRIKEOUT GAMES

Curt Schilling 2, Robert Person 2, Randy Wolf 2, **Total:** 6.

FOUR OR MORE HITS IN ONE GAME

Bobby Abreu 4 (including one five-hit game), Rico Brogna 3, Mike Lieberthal 3, Doug Glanville 3 (including one five-hit game), Rob Ducey 2 (including one five-hit game), Scott Rolen 2, Marlon Anderson 2 (including one five-hit game), Ron Gant 1, Kevin Jordan 1, **Total:** 21.

MULTI-HOMER GAMES

Mike Lieberthal 3, Scott Rolen 3, Ron Gant 1, Rico Brogna 1, Bobby Abreu 1, **Total:** 9.

GRAND SLAMS

4-16: Bobby Abreu (off Florida's Rafael Medina).
5-19: Mike Lieberthal (off Montreal's Dustin Hermanson).
7-3: Scott Rolen (off Chicago's Scott Sanders).

PINCH HITTERS

(Minimum 5 at-bats)

Name	AB	Avg.	HR	RBI
Sefcik, Kevin	45	.311	0	5
Ducey, Rob	43	.186	2	4
Jordan, Kevin	25	.200	0	2
Arias, Alex	22	.545	0	9
Doster, David	17	.235	1	3
Cedeno, Domingo	15	.067	0	1
Magee, Wendell	9	.333	2	5
Bennett, Gary	7	.571	0	0
Anderson, Marlon	5	.000	0	0
Lovullo, Torey	5	.000	0	0

DEBUTS

6-11: Randy Wolf, P.
7-3: Steve Schrenk, P.
7-23: Anthony Shumaker, P.

GAMES BY POSITION

Catcher: Mike Lieberthal 143, Gary Bennett 32, Bobby Estalella 7, Tom Prince 4.
First base: Rico Brogna 157, Kevin Jordan 13, Torey Lovullo 6.
Second base: Marlon Anderson 121, David Doster 77, Kevin Jordan 33, Kevin Sefcik 15, Torey Lovullo 6, Alex Arias 1, Domingo Cedeno 1.
Third base: Scott Rolen 112, Kevin Jordan 62, David Doster 6, Alex Arias 2.
Shortstop: Alex Arias 95, Desi Relaford 63, Domingo Cedeno 19, David Doster 5.
Outfield: Doug Glanville 148, Bobby Abreu 146, Ron Gant 133, Kevin Sefcik 64, Rob Ducey 58, Wendell Magee 4.
Designated hitter: Bobby Abreu 5, Rob Ducey 2, Ron Gant 2.

STREAKS

Wins: 5 (May 4-9).
Losses: 11 (September 4-14).
Consecutive games with at least one hit: 14, Bobby Abreu (August 17-September 1).
Wins by pitcher: 6, Curt Schilling (June 18-July 18).

ATTENDANCE

Home: 1,825,337.
Road: 2,253,879.
Highest (home): 58,086 (July 3 vs. Chicago).
Highest (road): 51,560 (September 19 vs. New York).
Lowest (home): 11,032 (May 3 vs. San Diego).
Lowest (road): 4,660 (May 18 vs. Montreal).

1999 REVIEW

PITTSBURGH PIRATES

1999 REVIEW

DAY BY DAY

Date	Opp.	Res.	Score	(inn.*)	Hits	Opp. hits	Winning pitcher	Losing pitcher	Save	Record	Pos.	GB
4-5	Mon.	L	2-9		7	17	Hermanson	Cordova		0-1	T4th	1.0
4-6	Mon.	W	8-2		10	3	Schmidt	Pavano		1-1	3rd	0.5
4-7	Mon.	L	3-4		11	7	Urbina	Loiselle		1-2	5th	0.5
4-9	Chi.	W	2-1		2	4	Benson	Sanders	Williams	2-2	T1st	...
4-10	Chi.	W	9-3		9	5	Sauerbeck	Woodall		3-2	T1st	...
4-11	Chi.	W	9-6		12	13	Schmidt	Trachsel		4-2	1st	+1.0
4-13	StL.	L	2-4		10	9	Bottenfield	Schourek	Acevedo	4-3	T1st	...
4-14	StL.	L	5-9		14	12	Aybar	Benson		4-4	3rd	1.0
4-16	At Cin.	L	5-6		9	9	Graves	Christiansen		4-5	T3rd	2.0
4-17	At Cin.	W	7-6	(10)	11	9	Christiansen	White		5-5	2nd	2.0
4-18	At Cin.	W	4-2		8	7	Loiselle	Graves	Williams	6-5	2nd	1.0
4-19	At S.D.	W	3-0		6	5	Schourek	Spencer	Christiansen	7-5	2nd	1.0
4-20	At S.D.	W	7-3	(10)	10	8	Williams	Hoffman		8-5	2nd	1.0
4-21	At S.D.	L	0-2		3	8	Ashby	Schmidt	Hoffman	8-6	T2nd	1.0
4-23	Mil.	L	1-9		8	13	Woodard	Peters		8-7	T2nd	2.0
4-24	Mil.	L	3-5		6	7	Reyes	Ritchie	Wickman	8-8	3rd	2.0
4-25	Mil.	L	2-4		8	10	Karl	Benson	Wickman	8-9	4th	3.0
4-27	At Atl.	W	5-3		10	7	Schmidt	Perez	Williams	9-9	3rd	3.0
4-28	At Atl.	L	4-5		8	9	Glavine	Christiansen		9-10	3rd	3.0
4-29	At Atl.	L	1-8		11	10	Maddux	Silva		9-11	T4th	3.0
4-30	Col.	L	2-7		8	8	Astacio	Schourek		9-12	T4th	3.5
5-1	Col.	W	9-3		9	8	Ritchie	Wright		10-12	4th	3.5
5-2	Col.	W	8-5		12	8	Schmidt	Thomson	Williams	11-12	4th	3.5
5-3	S.F.	W	9-8		13	13	Loiselle	Nen		12-12	4th	2.5
5-4	S.F.	L	4-7		10	13	Ortiz	Silva		12-13	4th	3.5
5-5	S.F.	W	4-3	(12)	8	7	Loiselle	Rodriguez		13-13	4th	3.5
5-6	At StL.	W	13-3		15	7	Ritchie	Osborne		14-13	4th	3.0
5-7	At StL.	L	2-4		13	6	Radinsky	Loiselle		14-14	T3rd	4.0
5-8	At StL.	W	7-0		10	4	Benson	Jimenez		15-14	4th	3.0
5-9	At StL.	W	12-9		15	9	Peters	Aybar	Williams	16-14	T2nd	2.0
5-10	At Hou.	L	0-6		5	13	Hampton	Schourek		16-15	3rd	3.0
5-11	At Hou.	L	8-19		14	18	Bergman	Ritchie		16-16	T3rd	4.0
5-12	At Hou.	L	2-6		8	10	Lima	Schmidt		16-17	3rd	5.0
5-14	Mon.	W	5-3		10	5	Benson	Hermanson	Williams	17-17	T2nd	5.0
5-15	Mon.	W	17-6		17	11	Silva	Pavano		18-17	T3rd	5.0
5-16	Mon.	W	9-4		8	10	Schourek	Vazquez		19-17	T2nd	4.0
5-17	At Atl.	L	1-2		5	7	Millwood	Ritchie	Rocker	19-18	4th	4.5
5-18	At Atl.	L	4-12		12	16	Perez	Schmidt		19-19	T4th	5.5
5-19	At Atl.	L	3-7		6	6	Glavine	Cordova		19-20	5th	5.5
5-20	At Fla.	L	3-4	(14)	12	12	Alfonseca	Williams		19-21	5th	6.5
5-21	At Fla.	L	1-8		4	10	Hernandez	Schourek		19-22	6th	6.5
5-22	At Fla.	W	11-4		14	8	Ritchie	Springer		20-22	5th	5.5
5-23	At Fla.	W	6-5		10	11	Wallace	Darensbourg	Williams	21-22	5th	5.5
5-24	N.Y.	W	7-4		8	7	Silva	Isringhausen	Williams	22-22	5th	5.5
5-25	N.Y.	L	3-8		6	11	Yoshii	Benson		22-23	5th	6.5
5-26	N.Y.	L	2-5		5	10	Hershiser	Schourek	Franco	22-24	5th	7.5
5-28	Hou.	W	6-5		9	6	Ritchie	Lima	Williams	23-24	5th	6.0
5-29	Hou.	W	5-1		8	5	Cordova	Reynolds		24-24	5th	5.0
5-30	Hou.	W	7-3		11	4	Benson	Hampton		25-24	4th	4.0
5-31	L.A.	W	5-4		7	9	Wilkins	Arnold	Williams	26-24	4th	3.5
6-1	L.A.	W	4-2		8	7	Schmidt	Valdes	Williams	27-24	4th	3.5
6-2	L.A.	W	8-4		11	8	Ritchie	Dreifort		28-24	4th	3.5
6-4	At Chi. (AL)	W	6-3	(11)	9	10	Wilkins	Simas		29-24	4th	3.0
6-5	At Chi. (AL)	L	5-6		8	15	Parque	Benson	Foulke	29-25	4th	4.0
6-6	At Chi. (AL)	L	3-4		8	8	Sirotka	Silva	Howry	29-26	4th	4.0
6-7	At Det.	L	4-9		8	10	Brunson	Schmidt		29-27	T4th	5.0
6-8	At Det.	L	4-11		7	15	Cruz	Ritchie		29-28	T4th	5.0
6-9	At Det.	W	15-3		17	10	Cordova	Moehler		30-28	4th	5.0
6-11	K.C.	L	3-10		8	9	Rosado	Benson		30-29	4th	6.0
6-12	K.C.	W	9-8		17	13	Christiansen	Whisenant		31-29	4th	6.0
6-13	K.C.	W	8-4		8	9	Schmidt	Whisenant	Williams	32-29	4th	5.5
6-15	At L.A.	W	11-1		14	7	Ritchie	Brown		33-29	4th	5.0
6-16	At L.A.	L	5-6		11	12	Borbon	Clontz	Shaw	33-30	T3rd	5.0
6-17	At L.A.	W	8-3		14	5	Benson	Park		34-30	3rd	4.0
6-18	At S.D.	L	2-4		8	8	Boehringer	Silva	Hoffman	34-31	3rd	5.0
6-19	At S.D.	L	4-5		5	10	Cunnane	Schmidt	Hoffman	34-32	3rd	6.0
6-20	At S.D.	L	3-6		8	12	Clement	Ritchie	Hoffman	34-33	3rd	7.0
6-22	At Phi.	L	2-3		6	7	Wolf	Cordova	Gomes	34-34	T4th	6.5
6-23	At Phi.	W	8-6		12	11	Benson	Byrd	Williams	35-34	3rd	6.5
6-24	At Phi.	L	5-7		10	10	Schilling	Silva	Gomes	35-35	4th	6.5
6-25	At Mil.	W	5-3		11	10	Schmidt	Abbott	Christiansen	36-35	3rd	5.5
6-26	At Mil.	L	4-7		10	11	Nomo	Ritchie	Wickman	36-36	T3rd	5.5
6-27	At Mil.	W	6-5		7	9	Cordova	Karl	Christiansen	37-36	3rd	4.5
6-28	Phi.	W	3-2	(10)	7	6	Hansell	Montgomery		38-36	3rd	4.0
6-29	Phi.	L	4-7		7	11	Schilling	Silva		38-37	3rd	5.0
6-30	Phi.	W	9-1		12	9	Schmidt	Ogea		39-37	3rd	5.0
7-1	Phi.	W	12-7		14	9	Ritchie	Person		40-37	3rd	5.0
7-2	Mil.	L	2-5		9	11	Karl	Cordova	Wickman	40-38	3rd	5.0
7-3	Mil.	L	4-9		11	11	Pulsipher	Benson		40-39	3rd	6.0

HIGHLIGHTS

High point: The Pirates won seven consecutive games from May 28 through June 4, which put them a season-best five games over .500 (29-24) and three games behind N.L. Central-leading Houston. It was the closest they would get to first place in the final four months of the season.

Low point: Beginning July 2, Pittsburgh dropped seven of nine games—and lost catcher Jason Kendall for the season on July 4. Hopes of contending were dashed.

Turning point: Kendall's gruesome ankle dislocation changed the season, robbing the team of a vital component. The Pirates were 38-43 in the 81 games without Kendall, and the catcher's primary replacements (Keith Osik and Joe Oliver) combined for a sub-.200 batting average. Kendall had batted .327 in 1998 and was hitting .332 when he went down.

Most valuable player: Outfielder Brian Giles, who had been obtained from the Indians. He became a force, clubbing 39 home runs, knocking in 115 runs and batting .315. His career highs entering the season were 17 homers and 66 RBIs. Giles also played well in center field after Brant Brown faltered defensively.

Most valuable pitcher: Todd Ritchie, who was signed as a minor league free agent after pitching without distinction in the Twins' bullpen. The righthander won a staff-high 15 games, and his 3.49 ERA was the sixth-best in the N.L.

Most improved player: Left fielder Al Martin rebounded from a career-worst season, thanks to laser eye surgery and a reworked batting stance. Martin batted .277 with 24 homers and 20 stolen bases.

Most pleasant surprise: Ritchie was supposed to work in relief in Class AAA, but injuries helped change all that. After one start at Nashville, he was summoned by Pittsburgh in mid-April. Rule 5 draftee Scott Sauerbeck also deserves mention as a reliever.

Key injuries: Kendall's ankle injury headed the list. Shortstop Pat Meares played in only 21 games because of a hand injury that required surgery. Reliever Rich Loiselle needed elbow surgery and was lost for much of the season. Reliever Jason Christiansen was on the disabled list three times with neck and back problems. Giles missed the final 11 games with a broken finger. And starters Francisco Cordova and Chris Peters had D.L. time.

Notable: The Pirates hit 171 home runs, breaking the team record of 158 set in 1966. ... For the first time in franchise history, four players had at least 20 home runs: Giles (39), Kevin Young (26), Martin (24) and Ed Sprague (22). ... Righthander Kris Benson led N.L. rookie pitchers in ERA (4.07), innings (196⅔) and strikeouts (139).

—JOHN MEHNO

MISCELLANEOUS

RECORDS

1999 regular-season record: 78-83 (3rd in N.L. Central); 45-36 at home; 33-47 on road; 19-22 vs. N.L. East; 30-32 vs. N.L. Central; 22-21 vs. N.L. West; 7-8 vs. A.L. Central; 17-30 vs. lefthanded starters; 61-53 vs. righthanded starters; 24-34 on grass; 54-49 on turf; 25-22 in daytime; 53-61 at night; 20-22 in one-run games; 9-4 in extra-inning games; 0-0-2 in double-headers.

Team record past five years: 357-434 (.451, ranks 14th in league in that span).

TEAM LEADERS

Batting average: Brian S. Giles (.315).
At-bats: Kevin Young (584).
Runs: Brian S. Giles (109).
Hits: Kevin Young (174).
Total bases: Brian S. Giles (320).
Doubles: Kevin Young (41).
Triples: Al Martin (8).
Home runs: Brian S. Giles (39).
Runs batted in: Brian S. Giles (115).
Stolen bases: Jason Kendall, Kevin Young (22).
Slugging percentage: Brian S. Giles (.614).
On-base percentage: Brian S. Giles (.418).
Wins: Todd Ritchie (15).
Earned-run average: Todd Ritchie (3.50).
Complete games: Kris Benson, Francisco Cordova, Todd Ritchie, Jason Schmidt (2).
Shutouts: None.
Saves: Mike Williams (23).
Innings pitched: Jason Schmidt (212.2).
Strikeouts: Jason Schmidt (148).

Date	Opp.	Res.	Score	(inn.*)	Hits	Opp. hits	Winning pitcher	Losing pitcher	Save	Record	Pos.	GB
7-4	Mil.	L	3-4		6	8	Weathers	Clontz	Wickman	40-40	3rd	6.0
7-5	Chi.	L	2-5		11	9	Lieber	Schmidt	Aguilera	40-41	T3rd	7.0
7-6	Chi.	W	6-1		8	9	Ritchie	Trachsel		41-41	3rd	6.0
7-7	Chi.	W	4-1		8	5	Cordova	Mulholland		42-41	3rd	5.0
7-8	Chi.	L	4-9		5	11	Serafini	Benson	Sanders	42-42	3rd	6.0
7-9	At Min.	L	4-5		8	9	Radke	Silva	Trombley	42-43	3rd	7.0
7-10	At Min.	L	4-5		12	10	Guardado	Williams		42-44	3rd	7.0
7-11	At Min.	W	10-2		17	5	Ritchie	Mays		43-44	3rd	7.0
7-15	Cle.	L	0-2		3	7	Colon	Schmidt	Jackson	43-45	T4th	8.0
7-16	Cle.	W	11-3		13	12	Cordova	Burba		44-45	T3rd	8.0
7-17	Cle.	W	13-10		16	16	Benson	Nagy	Williams	45-45	3rd	8.0
7-18	L.A.	W	6-5	(10)	11	14	Sauerbeck	Mills		46-45	3rd	8.0
7-19	L.A.	L	7-12		6	14	Dreifort	Silva		46-46	3rd	9.0
7-20	L.A.	L	4-8		7	13	Brown	Clontz		46-47	4th	9.0
7-21	At Chi.	L	1-2		6	9	Aguilera	Christiansen		46-48	T4th	9.0
7-22	At Chi.	L	3-5		8	10	Mulholland	Benson	Adams	46-49	6th	9.0
7-23	At Mon.	L	1-5		4	9	Vazquez	Ritchie		46-50	6th	10.5
7-24	At Mon.	W	7-2		11	7	Schourek	Powell		47-50	T5th	10.5
7-25	At Mon.	W	6-1		11	4	Schmidt	Kline		48-50	4th	10.5
7-26	At N.Y.	L	5-7		10	9	Reed	Cordova	Wendell	48-51	4th	11.5
7-27	At N.Y.	W	5-1		9	6	Benson	Hershiser		49-51	4th	11.5
7-28	At N.Y.	L	2-9		3	10	Cook	Wilkins		49-52	4th	12.5
7-30	Fla.	L	7-8		11	14	Edmondson	Hansell	Alfonseca	49-53	5th	13.0
7-31	Fla.	W	4-2		5	8	Schmidt	Edmondson	Williams	50-53	4th	13.0
8-1	Fla.	W	2-1		10	5	Cordova	Fernandez		51-53	4th	12.0
8-3	Atl.	W	7-1		7	4	Benson	Millwood		52-53	4th	12.0
8-4	Atl.	W	3-2		5	5	Ritchie	Smoltz	Williams	53-53	4th	11.0
8-5	Atl.	L	3-6		7	9	Remlinger	Hansell	Rocker	53-54	4th	12.0
8-6†	StL.	W	5-1		10	6	Anderson	Jimenez	Silva	54-54		
8-6‡	StL.	L	1-5		3	10	Stephenson	Schmidt	Croushore	54-55	4th	12.0
8-7	StL.	W	3-1		11	7	Cordova	Bottenfield	Williams	55-55	T3rd	12.0
8-8	StL.	W	5-1		8	4	Benson	Oliver		56-55	3rd	12.0
8-9	Cin.	L	2-4		2	7	Neagle	Ritchie	Williamson	56-56	T3rd	12.0
8-10	Cin.	L	1-6		6	13	Guzman	Schourek		56-57	T3rd	12.0
8-11	Cin.	W	5-4		9	9	Williams	Williamson		57-57	T3rd	11.0
8-13	At Hou.	W	6-5	(13)	8	11	Clontz	Miller	Williams	58-57	T3rd	10.0
8-14	At Hou.	L	1-7		6	6	Holt	Benson		58-58	T3rd	11.0
8-15	At Hou.	W	2-0		5	7	Ritchie	Reynolds	Williams	59-58	3rd	10.0
8-16	At Cin.	L	2-9		5	10	Guzman	Schourek		59-59	4th	11.0
8-17	At Cin.	L	4-7	(12)	8	7	Graves	Williams		59-60	4th	12.0
8-18	At Cin.	W	12-6		13	11	Cordova	Tomko		60-60	4th	12.0
8-19	At Cin.	L	0-1		1	7	Harnisch	Benson	Williamson	60-61	4th	12.0
8-20	Ari.	W	5-4		11	5	Ritchie	Stottlemyre	Williams	61-61	4th	12.0
8-21	Ari.	L	2-4		6	9	Johnson	Anderson		61-62	4th	13.0
8-22	Ari.	L	5-7		7	10	Daal	Schmidt	Mantei	61-63	4th	13.5
8-23	Ari.	L	1-2		7	8	Reynoso	Cordova	Mantei	61-64	4th	13.5
8-24	Col.	L	2-3		7	8	Leskanic	Williams	Veres	61-65	4th	14.5
8-25	Col.	W	9-3		14	7	Peters	Kile		62-65	4th	13.5
8-26	Col.	W	8-4		15	8	Anderson	Astacio		63-65	T3rd	13.0
8-27	At S.F	W	4-1		9	6	Schmidt	Nathan	Williams	64-65	3rd	12.5
8-28	At S.F	L	2-6		4	13	Gardner	Cordova		64-66	3rd	12.5
8-29	At S.F	L	3-5		7	7	Estes	Benson	Nen	64-67	3rd	13.5
8-30	At Col.	W	11-8		16	16	Peters	Ramirez	Williams	65-67	3rd	12.5
8-31	At Col.	W	9-8	(10)	14	18	Williams	Lee	Silva	66-67	3rd	12.5
9-1	At Col.	W	9-8		12	12	Sauerbeck	Veres	Clontz	67-67	3rd	11.5
9-3	S.F	L	2-12		7	10	Estes	Cordova		67-68	3rd	12.5
9-4	S.F	L	2-9		5	9	Ortiz	Benson		67-69	3rd	13.5
9-5	S.F	W	8-4		10	8	Peters	Rueter		68-69	3rd	13.5
9-6	S.D.	L	3-4		8	6	Ashby	Ritchie	Hoffman	68-70	3rd	14.5
9-7	S.D.	W	3-1		7	4	Schmidt	Hitchcock	Silva	69-70	3rd	14.5
9-8	S.D.	L	4-7	(10)	10	11	Hoffman	Wilkins		69-71	3rd	15.5
9-10	At StL.	L	5-11		10	13	Bottenfield	Benson		69-72	3rd	17.0
9-11	At StL.	W	8-5		11	10	Peters	Jimenez	Silva	70-72	3rd	17.0
9-13	At Ari.	L	1-5		10	8	Daal	Schmidt	Chouinard	70-73	3rd	18.5
9-14	At Ari.	L	1-2		4	3	Swindell	Wilkins	Mantei	70-74	3rd	19.5
9-15	At Ari.	W	5-1		7	7	Benson	Reynoso		71-74	3rd	18.5
9-17	Cin.	W	3-1		4	7	Ritchie	Villone	Sauerbeck	72-74	3rd	17.5
9-18	Cin.	L	0-3		6	7	Parris	Peters		72-75	3rd	17.5
9-19	Cin.	W	8-5		8	9	Schmidt	Harnisch	Clontz	73-75	3rd	17.5
9-20	Hou.	W	11-5		14	9	Schourek	Reynolds		74-75	3rd	16.5
9-21	Hou.	L	3-6		10	8	Elarton	Benson	Henry	74-76	3rd	17.5
9-22	Hou.	W	3-2		5	6	Ritchie	Lima		75-76	3rd	16.5
9-23	At Chi.	L	5-8		7	13	Bowie	Peters	Aguilera	75-77	3rd	17.0
9-24	At Chi.	L	0-9		5	14	Farnsworth	Schmidt		75-78	3rd	18.0
9-25	At Chi.	L	1-3		3	5	Lieber	Cordova		75-79	3rd	18.0
9-26	At Chi.	W	8-4	(11)	15	8	Sauerbeck	Guthrie		76-79	3rd	17.0
9-29†	At Mil.	W	7-5		11	9	Ritchie	Woodard	Williams	77-79		
9-29‡	At Mil.	L	2-5		7	7	Bere	Peters	Wickman	77-80	3rd	17.0
9-30	At Mil.	W	3-2		8	5	Garcia	Nomo	Sauerbeck	78-80	3rd	16.5
10-1	At N.Y.	L	2-3	(11)	7	10	Mahomes	Sauerbeck		78-81	3rd	16.5
10-2	At N.Y.	L	0-7		3	9	Reed	Cordova		78-82	3rd	17.5
10-3	At N.Y.	L	1-2		3	9	Benitez	Hansell		78-83	3rd	18.5

Monthly records: April (9-12), May (17-12), June (13-13), July (11-16), August (16-14), September (12-13), October (0-3).
*Innings, if other than nine. † First game of a doubleheader. ‡ Second game of a doubleheader.

MEMORABLE GAMES

May 3 at Pittsburgh

Giants closer Robb Nen was in for a save in a comfortable situation, holding an 8-5 lead in the ninth. But Warren Morris led off with a home run. Nen had two outs and a runner on first when Brian Giles hit a game-tying two-run homer. Kevin Young walked, Jason Kendall singled and Brant Brown completed the four-run comeback with an RBI single.

San Fran.	AB	R	H	RBI	Pittsburgh	AB	R	H	RBI
Javier, lf	4	1	1	0	A.Martin, lf	5	2	2	1
R.Martinez, 2b	4	1	1	0	Benjamin, ss	4	1	0	0
Snow, ph-1b	1	0	0	0	Giles, rf	5	2	3	5
Burks, rf	4	2	3	0	K.Young, 1b	4	2	1	1
Embree, p	0	0	0	0	Kendall, c	5	0	5	0
Spradlin, p	0	0	0	0	B.Brown, cf	4	0	1	1
Johnstone, p	0	0	0	0	Sprague, 3b	4	0	0	0
E.Guzman, ph	1	0	0	0	W.Morris, 2b	3	1	1	1
Nen, p	0	0	0	0	Peters, p	2	0	0	0
Kent, 1b-2b	5	2	5	5	M.Wilkins, p	0	0	0	0
Hayes, 3b	5	0	1	1	A.Brown, ph	0	1	0	0
Aurilia, ss	3	2	1	1	Loiselle, p	0	0	0	0
Santangelo, cf	3	0	0	0	T.Ward, ph	1	0	0	0
Servais, c	4	0	1	1					
Nathan, p	3	0	0	0					
Rios, rf	1	0	0	0					
Totals	**38**	**8**	**13**	**8**	**Totals**	**37**	**9**	**13**	**9**

San Francisco ....104 020 010 —8
Pittsburgh ....310 000 104 —9

E—Aurilia (7), Benjamin (1), W.Morris (3). DP—San Francisco 3, Pittsburgh 1. LOB—San Francisco 7, Pittsburgh 7. 2B—Kent (10), Servais (2), Kendall 2 (9). 3B—Kent (1). HR—Kent (4), Aurilia (5), A.Martin (1), Giles 2 (9), K.Young (3), W.Morris (2). SB—A.Martin (2). CS—R.Martinez (2), Burks (2). S—Santangelo.

San Francisco	IP	H	R	ER	BB	SO
Nathan	6	6	4	3	3	4
Embree (H, 2)	0.2	1	1	1	1	0
Spradlin (H, 2)	0.1	0	0	0	0	1
Johnstone (H, 7)	1	1	0	0	0	0
Nen (BS 1; L 0-1)	0.2	5	4	4	1	1

Pittsburgh	IP	H	R	ER	BB	SO
Peters	5	8	7	6	1	3
M.Wilkins	2	2	0	0	0	1
Loiselle (W, 2-1)	2	3	1	1	2	1

U—HP, J.Nelson. 1B, Pulli. 2B, C.Williams. 3B, Bonin. T—2:59. A—11,099.

August 11 at Pittsburgh

Reds reliever Scott Williamson, the 1999 N.L. Rookie of the Year, had a 4-3 lead in the ninth when light-hitting Abraham Nunez worked a leadoff walk. After a bunt, pinch hitter Al Martin walked. Brian Giles doubled to right field to score both and give the Pirates a 5-4 win.

Cincinnati	AB	R	H	RBI	Pittsburgh	AB	R	H	RBI
Cameron, cf	5	1	1	0	A.Brown, rf	3	0	0	0
Tucker, rf	5	1	2	0	Wehner, lf	3	0	0	0
H.Morris, 1b	4	0	1	1	A.Martin, ph	0	1	0	0
G.Vaughn, lf	4	1	2	1	Giles, cf	4	0	1	2
Taubensee, c	4	0	1	0	K.Young, 1b	4	1	1	0
A.Boone, 3b	4	1	1	1	Sprague, 3b	4	1	2	1
Reese, ss	4	0	0	0	W.Morris, 2b	4	0	2	0
Stynes, 2b	2	0	0	0	J.Oliver, c	3	0	1	1
D.Young, ph	1	0	1	1	Benjamin, ss	3	1	1	0
M.Lewis, 2b	0	0	0	0	M.Williams, p	0	0	0	0
Villone, p	3	0	0	0	Schmidt, p	1	0	0	0
Sullivan, p	0	0	0	0	Sveum, ph	1	0	1	0
D.Reyes, p	0	0	0	0	M.Wilkins, p	0	0	0	0
Graves, p	0	0	0	0	A.Nunez, ss	0	1	0	0
Casey, ph	0	0	0	0					
Williamson, p	0	0	0	0					
Totals	**36**	**4**	**9**	**4**	**Totals**	**30**	**5**	**9**	**4**

Cincinnati....................................100 101 001 —4
Pittsburgh ....000 200 102 —5

E—Stynes (5), M.Williams (4), A.Nunez (11). DP—Cincinnati 2, Pittsburgh 1. LOB—Cincinnati 7, Pittsburgh 9. 2B—D.Young (18), Giles (27), K.Young (35), Benjamin (13). 3B—Tucker (4). SB—Stynes (4). S—A.Brown, Wehner, Schmidt.

Cincinnati	IP	H	R	ER	BB	SO
Villone	6	7	3	2	2	2
Sullivan (BS 2)	0.2	0	0	0	0	0
D.Reyes	0	0	0	0	1	0
Graves	1.1	1	0	0	1	1
Williamsn (BS 6; L, 10-5)	0.1	1	2	2	2	0

Pittsburgh	IP	H	R	ER	BB	SO
Schmidt	7	8	3	3	1	4
M.Wilkins	1	0	0	0	0	0
M.Williams (W, 2-2)	1	1	1	0	1	2

WP—Sullivan. Balks—Schmidt. U—HP, Davis. 1B, Layne. 2B, Dreckman. 3B, Rieker. T—3:06. A—23,728.

INDIVIDUAL STATISTICS

BATTING

Name	G	TPA	AB	R	H	TB	2B	3B	HR	RBI	Avg.	Obp.	Slg.	SH	SF	HP	BB	IBB	SO	SB	CS	GDP	vs RHP AB	vs RHP Avg.	vs RHP HR	vs RHP RBI	vs LHP AB	vs LHP Avg.	vs LHP HR	vs LHP RBI
Young, Kevin	156	675	584	103	174	305	41	6	26	106	.298	.387	.522	0	4	12	75	5	124	22	10	13	425	.294	21	81	159	.308	5	25
Martin, Al	143	593	541	97	150	274	36	8	24	63	.277	.337	.506	0	2	1	49	5	119	20	3	8	421	.287	22	54	120	.242	2	9
Giles, Brian S.	141	627	521	109	164	320	33	3	39	115	.315	.418	.614	0	8	3	95	7	80	6	2	14	344	.323	30	87	177	.299	9	28
Morris, Warren	147	581	511	65	147	218	20	3	15	73	.288	.360	.427	4	5	2	59	3	88	3	7	12	401	.274	13	56	110	.336	2	17
Sprague, Ed	137	564	490	71	131	228	27	2	22	81	.267	.352	.465	1	6	17	50	6	93	3	6	12	353	.289	16	58	137	.212	6	23
Benjamin, Mike	110	404	368	42	91	134	26	7	1	37	.247	.288	.364	11	3	2	20	3	90	10	1	3	226	.239	1	21	142	.261	0	16
Brown, Brant	130	371	341	49	79	153	20	3	16	58	.232	.283	.449	0	4	4	22	3	114	3	4	4	294	.235	16	57	47	.213	0	1
Kendall, Jason	78	334	280	61	93	143	20	3	8	41	.332	.428	.511	0	4	12	38	3	32	22	3	8	221	.348	4	32	59	.271	4	9
Nunez, Abraham	90	301	259	25	57	65	8	0	0	17	.220	.299	.251	13	0	1	28	0	54	9	1	2	178	.213	0	13	81	.235	0	4
Brown, Adrian	116	267	226	34	61	82	5	2	4	17	.270	.364	.363	6	1	1	33	2	39	5	3	5	114	.289	2	9	112	.250	2	8
Osik, Keith	66	181	167	12	31	42	3	1	2	13	.186	.239	.251	1	1	1	11	0	30	0	0	8	106	.170	2	7	61	.213	0	6
Oliver, Joe	45	146	134	10	27	38	8	0	1	13	.201	.253	.284	0	2	0	10	0	33	2	0	4	92	.196	0	7	42	.214	1	6
Garcia, Freddy	55	135	130	16	30	53	5	0	6	23	.231	.252	.408	0	1	0	4	0	41	0	0	3	46	.174	1	8	84	.262	5	15
Guillen, Jose	40	132	120	18	32	41	6	0	1	18	.267	.321	.342	1	1	0	10	1	21	1	0	7	84	.226	1	13	36	.361	0	5
Meares, Pat	21	104	91	15	28	32	4	0	0	7	.308	.382	.352	2	0	2	9	0	20	0	0	1	47	.277	0	4	44	.341	0	3
Ward, Turner	49	109	91	2	19	21	2	0	0	8	.209	.311	.231	3	1	1	13	0	9	2	2	2	58	.224	0	2	33	.182	0	6
Sveum, Dale	49	80	71	7	15	31	5	1	3	13	.211	.278	.437	1	1	0	7	1	28	0	0	0	56	.179	1	6	15	.333	2	7
Wehner, John	39	75	65	6	12	17	2	0	1	4	.185	.264	.262	3	0	0	7	0	12	1	0	1	26	.192	0	1	39	.179	1	3
Benson, Kris	31	75	65	7	10	13	3	0	0	7	.154	.191	.200	6	0	0	3	0	24	0	0	1	47	.128	0	2	18	.222	0	5
Hermansen, Chad	19	69	60	5	14	20	3	0	1	1	.233	.324	.333	1	0	1	7	1	19	2	2	0	42	.214	0	0	18	.278	1	1
Schmidt, Jason	33	77	60	2	5	5	0	0	0	1	.083	.154	.083	12	0	0	5	0	33	0	0	0	39	.103	0	1	21	.048	0	0
Ramirez, Aramis	18	64	56	2	10	14	2	1	0	7	.179	.254	.250	1	1	0	6	0	9	0	0	0	46	.174	0	5	10	.200	0	2
Ritchie, Todd	29	62	53	3	8	9	1	0	0	1	.151	.167	.170	8	0	0	1	0	16	0	0	1	38	.132	0	1	15	.200	0	0
Cordova, Francisco	27	56	49	2	8	8	0	0	0	2	.163	.196	.163	5	0	0	2	0	15	0	0	0	31	.161	0	1	18	.167	0	1
Schourek, Pete	30	31	25	1	0	0	0	0	0	1	.000	.107	.000	3	0	0	3	0	13	0	0	1	20	.000	0	1	5	.000	0	0
Peters, Chris	19	25	22	5	6	6	0	0	0	1	.273	.333	.273	1	0	0	2	0	10	1	0	1	15	.200	0	0	7	.429	0	1
Silva, Jose	34	22	20	0	2	2	0	0	0	3	.100	.100	.100	2	0	0	0	0	10	0	0	0	20	.100	0	3	0	.000	0	0
Brown, Emil	6	14	14	0	2	3	1	0	0	0	.143	.143	.214	0	0	0	0	0	3	0	0	0	10	.100	0	0	4	.250	0	0
Tremie, Chris	9	16	14	1	1	1	0	0	0	1	.071	.188	.071	0	0	0	2	0	4	0	0	0	11	.091	0	1	3	.000	0	0
Cruz, Ivan	5	10	10	3	4	7	0	0	1	2	.400	.400	.700	0	0	0	0	0	2	0	0	0	9	.333	1	2	1	1.000	0	0
Laker, Tim	6	9	9	0	3	3	0	0	0	0	.333	.333	.333	0	0	0	0	0	2	0	0	0	5	.200	0	0	4	.500	0	0
Anderson, Jimmy	13	9	9	2	3	4	1	0	0	1	.333	.333	.444	0	0	0	0	0	2	0	0	0	5	.400	0	1	4	.250	0	0
Clontz, Brad	56	3	3	0	0	0	0	0	0	0	.000	.000	.000	0	0	0	0	0	2	0	0	0	3	.000	0	0	0	.000	0	0
Williams, Mike	58	2	2	0	0	0	0	0	0	0	.000	.000	.000	0	0	0	0	0	0	0	0	0	2	.000	0	0	0	.000	0	0
Hansell, Greg	33	2	2	0	0	0	0	0	0	0	.000	.000	.000	0	0	0	0	0	2	0	0	0	2	.000	0	0	0	.000	0	0
Christiansen, Jason	40	1	1	0	0	0	0	0	0	0	.000	.000	.000	0	0	0	0	0	1	0	0	0	1	.000	0	0	0	.000	0	0
Wilkins, Marc	46	1	1	0	0	0	0	0	0	0	.000	.000	.000	0	0	0	0	0	1	0	0	0	0	.000	0	0	1	.000	0	0
Sauerbeck, Scott	65	2	1	0	0	0	0	0	0	0	.000	.000	.000	1	0	0	0	0	1	0	0	0	1	.000	0	0	0	.000	0	0
Haad, Yamid	1	1	1	0	0	0	0	0	0	0	.000	.000	.000	0	0	0	0	0	0	0	0	0	1	.000	0	0	0	.000	0	0
Boyd, Jason	4	1	1	0	0	0	0	0	0	0	.000	.000	.000	0	0	0	0	0	1	0	0	0	1	.000	0	0	0	.000	0	0
Dougherty, Jim	2	1	0	0	0	0	0	0	0	0	.000	1.000	.000	0	0	0	1	0	0	0	0	0	0	.000	0	0	0	.000	0	0
Loiselle, Rich	13	1	0	0	0	0	0	0	0	0	.000	.000	.000	1	0	0	0	0	0	0	0	0	0	.000	0	0	0	.000	0	0
Wallace, Jeff	41	1	0	0	0	0	0	0	0	0	.000	1.000	.000	0	0	0	1	0	0	0	0	0	0	.000	0	0	0	.000	0	0
Phillips, Jason	6	0	0	0	0	0	0	0	0	0	.000	.000	.000	0	0	0	0	0	0	0	0	0	0	.000	0	0	0	.000	0	0
Garcia, Mike	7	0	0	0	0	0	0	0	0	0	.000	.000	.000	0	0	0	0	0	0	0	0	0	0	.000	0	0	0	.000	0	0

PLAYERS WITH MORE THAN ONE N.L. TEAM

Name	G	TPA	AB	R	H	TB	2B	3B	HR	RBI	Avg.	Obp.	Slg.	SH	SF	HP	BB	IBB	SO	SB	CS	GDP	vs RHP AB	vs RHP Avg.	vs RHP HR	vs RHP RBI	vs LHP AB	vs LHP Avg.	vs LHP HR	vs LHP RBI
Garcia, Atl.	2	3	2	1	1	4	0	0	1	1	.500	.667	2.000	0	0	0	1	0	1	0	0	0	46	.174	1	8	84	.262	5	15
Garcia, Pit.-Atl.	57	138	132	17	31	57	5	0	7	24	.235	.261	.432	0	1	0	5	0	42	0	0	3	46	.174	1	8	86	.267	6	16
Ward, Ari.	10	26	23	6	8	15	1	0	2	7	.348	.385	.652	0	1	0	2	0	6	0	0	0	58	.224	0	2	33	.182	0	6
Ward, Pit.-Ari.	59	135	114	8	27	36	3	0	2	15	.237	.326	.316	3	2	1	15	0	15	2	2	2	71	.254	2	6	43	.209	0	9

PITCHING

Name	W	L	Pct.	ERA	IP	H	R	ER	HR	SH	SF	HB	BB	IBB	SO	G	GS	CG	ShO	GF	Sv	vs RH AB	vs RH Avg.	vs RH HR	vs RH RBI	vs LH AB	vs LH Avg.	vs LH HR	vs LH RBI
Schmidt, Jason	13	11	.542	4.19	212.2	219	110	99	24	7	7	3	85	4	148	33	33	2	0	0	0	456	.241	7	37	379	.288	17	58
Benson, Kris	11	14	.440	4.07	196.2	184	105	89	16	6	7	6	83	5	139	31	31	2	0	0	0	399	.226	9	50	339	.277	7	40
Ritchie, Todd	15	9	.625	3.50	172.1	169	79	67	17	3	2	4	54	3	107	28	26	2	0	0	0	377	.244	9	35	275	.280	8	34
Cordova, Francisco	8	10	.444	4.43	160.2	166	83	79	16	7	4	4	59	6	98	27	27	2	0	0	0	323	.266	9	43	285	.281	7	29
Schourek, Pete	4	7	.364	5.34	113.0	128	75	67	20	3	8	5	49	5	94	30	17	0	0	2	0	366	.290	16	53	80	.275	4	15
Silva, Jose	2	8	.200	5.73	97.1	108	70	62	10	3	3	3	39	0	77	34	12	0	0	9	4	224	.317	5	42	161	.230	5	22
Peters, Chris	5	4	.556	6.59	71.0	98	59	52	17	4	4	4	27	0	46	19	11	0	0	2	0	254	.354	15	48	50	.160	2	10
Sauerbeck, Scott	4	1	.800	2.00	67.2	53	19	15	6	4	0	4	38	5	55	65	0	0	0	16	2	151	.252	1	8	90	.167	5	20
Williams, Mike	3	4	.429	5.09	58.1	63	36	33	9	2	1	1	37	7	76	58	0	0	0	50	23	149	.289	6	30	79	.253	3	11
Wilkins, Marc	2	3	.400	4.24	51.0	49	28	24	3	4	2	4	26	1	44	46	0	0	0	14	0	120	.283	2	20	71	.211	1	5
Clontz, Brad	1	3	.250	2.74	49.1	49	21	15	6	2	1	3	24	5	40	56	0	0	0	16	2	147	.197	3	15	46	.435	3	7
Hansell, Greg	1	3	.250	3.89	39.1	42	20	17	5	3	1	3	11	3	34	33	0	0	0	9	0	94	.255	1	15	56	.321	4	14
Wallace, Jeff	1	0	1.000	3.69	39.0	26	17	16	2	4	1	0	38	1	41	41	0	0	0	7	0	87	.161	1	3	46	.261	1	10
Christiansen, Jason	2	3	.400	4.06	37.2	26	17	17	2	2	1	2	22	4	35	39	0	0	0	17	3	88	.193	2	10	44	.205	0	3
Anderson, Jimmy	2	1	.667	3.99	29.1	25	15	13	2	2	1	1	16	2	13	13	4	0	0	2	0	81	.235	1	5	26	.231	1	5
Loiselle, Rich	3	2	.600	5.28	15.1	16	9	9	2	1	0	2	9	2	14	13	0	0	0	6	0	37	.351	2	7	20	.150	0	3
Garcia, Mike	1	0	1.000	1.29	7.0	2	1	1	1	0	0	0	3	0	9	7	0	0	0	2	0	18	.111	1	1	4	.000	0	0
Phillips, Jason	0	0	.000	11.57	7.0	11	9	9	2	2	1	0	6	1	7	6	0	0	0	0	0	22	.364	2	6	6	.500	0	3
Boyd, Jason	0	0	.000	3.38	5.1	5	2	2	0	0	1	1	2	0	4	4	0	0	0	0	0	18	.222	0	2	2	.500	0	1
Dougherty, Jim	0	0	.000	9.00	2.0	3	3	2	0	0	0	0	3	0	1	2	0	0	0	0	0	7	.143	0	0	2	1.000	0	2
Osik, Keith	0	0	.000	36.00	1.0	2	4	4	0	0	0	1	2	0	1	1	0	0	0	1	0	2	.500	0	3	3	.333	0	1

INDIVIDUAL STATISTICS

FIELDING

FIRST BASEMEN
Player	Pct.	G	PO	A	E	TC	DP
Young, Kevin	.985	155	1413	97	23	1533	148
Brown, Brant	1.000	7	37	3	0	40	2
Sveum, Dale	1.000	4	23	2	0	25	5
Cruz, Ivan	1.000	1	13	1	0	14	3
Garcia, Freddy	-	1	0	0	0	0	0

SECOND BASEMEN
Player	Pct.	G	PO	A	E	TC	DP
Morris, Warren	.979	144	263	403	14	680	102
Nunez, Abraham	.985	14	24	42	1	67	13
Benjamin, Mike	1.000	12	21	31	0	52	5
Sveum, Dale	1.000	2	1	2	0	3	1
Wehner, John	1.000	1	4	2	0	6	2

THIRD BASEMEN
Player	Pct.	G	PO	A	E	TC	DP
Sprague, Ed	.920	134	79	254	29	362	22
Ramirez, Aramis	.930	17	11	29	3	43	2
Sveum, Dale	.944	12	2	15	1	18	0
Garcia, Freddy	.938	9	1	14	1	16	1
Benjamin, Mike	1.000	6	1	5	0	6	0
Wehner, John	1.000	2	1	1	0	2	0

SHORTSTOPS
Player	Pct.	G	PO	A	E	TC	DP
Benjamin, Mike	.982	93	140	298	8	446	77
Nunez, Abraham	.953	65	89	172	13	274	37
Meares, Pat	.939	21	26	67	6	99	13
Sveum, Dale	1.000	4	1	5	0	6	1
Wehner, John	1.000	2	0	1	0	1	0

OUTFIELDERS
Player	Pct.	G	PO	A	E	TC	DP
Giles, Brian S.	.990	138	294	8	3	305	2
Martin, Al	.952	133	196	3	10	209	0
Brown, Adrian	.966	96	111	3	4	118	2
Brown, Brant	.981	82	150	4	3	157	0
Guillen, Jose	.952	37	58	1	3	62	1
Ward, Turner	.955	34	41	1	2	44	0
Garcia, Freddy	.977	24	43	0	1	44	0
Hermansen, Chad	1.000	18	29	0	0	29	0
Wehner, John	.958	17	23	0	1	24	0
Brown, Emil	1.000	6	8	0	0	8	0
Sveum, Dale	1.000	1	2	0	0	2	0
Cruz, Ivan	-	1	0	0	0	0	0

CATCHERS
Player	Pct.	G	PO	A	E	TC	DP	PB
Kendall, Jason	.988	75	505	48	7	560	13	6
Osik, Keith	.997	50	289	22	1	312	4	1
Oliver, Joe	.993	44	285	12	2	299	4	1
Tremie, Chris	1.000	8	29	2	0	31	0	1
Laker, Tim	1.000	2	9	0	0	9	0	0

PITCHERS
Player	Pct.	G	PO	A	E	TC	DP
Sauerbeck, Scott	1.000	65	4	8	0	12	1
Williams, Mike	.765	58	4	9	4	17	1
Clontz, Brad	1.000	56	1	7	0	8	0
Wilkins, Marc	1.000	46	2	11	0	13	0
Wallace, Jeff	1.000	41	0	3	0	3	0
Christiansen, Jason	1.000	39	0	7	0	7	1
Silva, Jose	1.000	34	6	16	0	22	2
Schmidt, Jason	.929	33	10	16	2	28	0
Hansell, Greg	1.000	33	1	5	0	6	1
Benson, Kris	.955	31	15	27	2	44	6
Schourek, Pete	.900	30	3	15	2	20	0
Ritchie, Todd	1.000	28	9	25	0	34	0
Cordova, Francisco	.975	27	14	25	1	40	2
Peters, Chris	1.000	19	5	14	0	19	0
Anderson, Jimmy	1.000	13	1	5	0	6	2
Loiselle, Rich	1.000	13	2	3	0	5	1
Garcia, Mike	-	7	0	0	0	0	0
Phillips, Jason	1.000	6	0	2	0	2	0
Boyd, Jason	1.000	4	1	0	0	1	0
Dougherty, Jim	-	2	0	0	0	0	0
Osik, Keith	-	1	0	0	0	0	0
Brown, Adrian	-	0	0	0	0	0	0

PITCHING AGAINST EACH CLUB

Pitcher	Ari. W-L	Atl. W-L	Chi. W-L	Cin. W-L	Col. W-L	Fla. W-L	Hou. W-L	L.A. W-L	Mil. W-L	Mon. W-L	N.Y. W-L	Phi. W-L	S.D. W-L	S.F. W-L	StL. W-L	A.L. W-L	Total W-L
Anderson, J.	0-1	0-0	0-0	0-0	1-0	0-0	0-0	0-0	0-0	0-0	0-0	0-0	0-0	0-0	1-0	0-0	2-1
Benson, K.	1-0	1-0	1-2	0-1	0-0	0-0	1-2	1-0	0-2	1-0	1-1	1-0	0-0	0-2	2-2	1-2	11-14
Boyd, J.	0-0	0-0	0-0	0-0	0-0	0-0	0-0	0-0	0-0	0-0	0-0	0-0	0-0	0-0	0-0	0-0	0-0
Brown, A.	0-0	0-0	0-0	0-0	0-0	0-0	0-0	0-0	0-0	0-0	0-0	0-0	0-0	0-0	0-0	0-0	0-0
Christiansen, J.	0-0	0-1	0-1	1-1	0-0	0-0	0-0	0-0	0-0	0-0	0-0	0-0	0-0	0-0	0-0	1-0	2-3
Clontz, B.	0-0	0-0	0-0	0-0	0-0	0-0	0-0	0-2	0-1	0-0	0-0	0-0	0-0	0-0	0-0	0-0	1-3
Cordova, F.	0-0	0-1	1-1	0-0	0-0	1-0	1-0	0-0	1-1	0-1	0-2	0-1	0-0	0-2	1-0	2-0	8-10
Dougherty, J.	0-0	0-0	0-0	0-0	0-0	0-0	0-0	0-0	0-0	0-0	0-0	0-0	0-0	0-0	0-0	0-0	0-0
Garcia, M.	0-0	0-0	0-0	0-0	0-0	0-0	1-0	0-0	0-0	0-0	0-0	0-0	0-0	0-0	0-0	0-0	1-0
Hansell, G.	0-0	0-1	0-0	0-0	0-0	0-1	0-0	0-0	0-0	0-1	1-0	0-0	0-0	0-0	0-0	0-0	1-3
Loiselle, R.	0-0	0-0	0-0	0-0	0-0	0-0	0-0	0-0	0-1	0-0	0-0	0-0	0-0	2-0	0-1	0-0	2-3
Osik, K.	0-0	0-0	0-0	0-0	0-0	0-0	0-0	0-0	0-0	0-0	0-0	0-0	0-0	0-0	0-0	0-0	0-0
Peters, C.	0-0	0-0	0-1	0-1	2-0	0-0	0-0	0-2	0-0	0-0	0-0	0-0	1-0	2-0	0-0	0-0	5-4
Phillips, J.	0-0	0-0	0-0	0-0	0-0	0-0	0-0	0-0	0-0	0-0	0-0	0-0	0-0	0-0	0-0	0-0	0-0
Ritchie, T.	1-0	1-1	1-0	1-1	1-0	1-0	3-1	2-0	1-2	0-1	0-0	1-0	0-2	0-0	1-0	1-1	15-9
Sauerbeck, S.	0-0	2-0	0-0	0-0	1-0	0-0	0-0	1-0	0-0	0-0	0-1	0-0	0-0	0-0	0-0	0-0	4-1
Schmidt, J.	0-2	1-1	1-2	0-1	1-0	1-0	0-1	0-1	1-0	2-0	1-0	1-2	1-2	0-1	0-0	1-2	13-11
Schourek, P.	0-0	0-0	0-0	0-2	0-1	0-1	1-1	0-0	0-0	2-0	1-0	0-0	0-1	0-1	0-0	0-0	4-7
Silva, J.	0-0	0-1	0-0	0-0	0-0	0-0	0-0	0-1	0-0	0-1	1-0	1-0	0-2	0-1	0-1	0-2	2-8
Wallace, J.	0-0	0-0	0-0	0-0	0-0	0-0	1-0	0-0	0-0	0-0	0-0	0-0	0-0	0-0	0-0	0-0	1-0
Wilkins, M.	0-0	0-0	0-0	0-0	0-0	0-0	0-0	0-0	1-0	0-0	0-0	0-1	0-0	0-0	0-0	1-0	2-3
Williams, M.	0-0	0-0	0-0	0-0	1-1	0-1	0-1	0-0	0-0	0-0	0-0	0-0	0-0	0-0	0-0	0-1	3-4
Totals	2-5	3-6	6-7	6-7	7-2	4-3	7-5	6-3	4-8	6-3	2-7	4-3	3-6	4-5	7-5	7-8	78-83

INTERLEAGUE: Wilkins 1-0, Benson 0-1, Silva 0-1 vs. White Sox; Cordova 1-0, Benson 1-0, Schmidt 0-1 vs. Indians; Cordova 1-0, Schmidt 0-1, Ritchie 0-1 vs. Tigers; Christiansen 1-0, Schmidt 1-0, Benson 0-1 vs. Royals; Ritchie 1-0, Silva 0-1, Williams 0-1 vs. Twins. Total: 7-8.

MISCELLANEOUS

HOME RUNS BY PARK

At Arizona (3): Young 1, Giles 1, Brown 1.
At Atlanta (2): Sprague 1, Giles 1.
At Chicago (AL) (3): Garcia 1, Kendall 1, Morris 1.
At Chicago (NL) (2): Young 1, Hermansen 1.
At Cincinnati (8): Sprague 4, Sveum 2, Martin 1, Giles 1.
At Colorado (9): Giles 3, Martin 2, Brown 2, Young 1, Morris 1.
At Detroit (5): Sprague 2, Giles 1, Brown 1, Guillen 1.
At Florida (1): Giles 1.
At Houston (6): Martin 2, Morris 2, Young 1, Giles 1.
At Los Angeles (7): Brown 3, Sprague 1, Young 1, Martin 1, Kendall 1.
At Milwaukee (8): Young 4, Sprague 1, Martin 1, Brown 1, Morris 1.
At Minnesota (4): Giles 2, Martin 1, Brown 1.
At Montreal (0).
At New York (NL) (6): Martin 2, Brown 2, Wehner 1, Young 1.
At Philadelphia (4): Sprague 1, Giles 1, Brown 1, Morris 1.
At Pittsburgh (91): Giles 24, Young 16, Martin 12, Sprague 10, Morris 9, Garcia 6, Kendall 5, Brown 4, Brown 2, Benjamin 2, Oliver 1, Osik 1, Cruz 1.
At San Diego (3): Sprague 1, Martin 1, Giles 1.
At San Francisco (4): Sveum 1, Martin 1, Giles 1, Brown 1.
At St. Louis (5): Sprague 1, Giles 1, Kendall 1, Osik 1, Brown 1.

LOW-HIT GAMES

No-hitters: None.
One-hitters: None.
Two-hitters: None.

10-STRIKEOUT GAMES

Francisco Cordova 2, Jason Schmidt 1, Todd Ritchie 1, **Total:** 4.

FOUR OR MORE HITS IN ONE GAME

Jason Kendall 2 (including one five-hit game), Al Martin 1, Pat Meares 1 (including one five-hit game), Brian S. Giles 1, Brant Brown 1 (including one five-hit game), Warren Morris 1, **Total:** 7.

MULTI-HOMER GAMES

Brian S. Giles 5, Kevin Young 3, Al Martin 3, Dale Sveum 1, Ed Sprague 1, Brant Brown 1, **Total:** 14.

GRAND SLAMS

4-10: Ed Sprague (off Chicago's Kurt Miller).
5-8: Brian S. Giles (off St. Louis's Jose Jimenez).
8-31: Kevin Young (off Colorado's Dave Veres).

PINCH HITTERS

(Minimum 5 at-bats)
Name	AB	Avg.	HR	RBI
Brown, Brant	35	.114	1	1
Sveum, Dale	28	.321	1	7
Brown, Adrian	24	.250	0	2
Garcia, Freddy	20	.050	0	1
Wehner, John	15	.400	1	2
Osik, Keith	15	.267	0	4
Ward, Turner	15	.067	0	1
Martin, Al	10	.600	0	1
Nunez, Abraham	10	.100	0	0
Benjamin, Mike	7	.429	0	1
Laker, Tim	5	.400	0	0

DEBUTS

4-5: Warren Morris, 2B.
4-5: Jason Phillips, P.
4-5: Scott Sauerbeck, P.
4-9: Kris Benson, P.
7-4: Jimmy Anderson, P.
7-5: Yamid Haad, PH.
9-7: Chad Hermansen, LF.
9-10: Jason Boyd, P.
9-10: Mike Garcia, P.

GAMES BY POSITION

Catcher: Jason Kendall 75, Keith Osik 50, Joe Oliver 44, Chris Tremie 8, Tim Laker 2.
First base: Kevin Young 155, Brant Brown 7, Dale Sveum 4, Freddy Garcia 1, Ivan Cruz 1.
Second base: Warren Morris 144, Abraham Nunez 14, Mike Benjamin 12, Dale Sveum 2, John Wehner 1.
Third base: Ed Sprague 134, Aramis Ramirez 17, Dale Sveum 12, Freddy Garcia 9, Mike Benjamin 6, John Wehner 2.
Shortstop: Mike Benjamin 93, Abraham Nunez 65, Pat Meares 21, Dale Sveum 4, John Wehner 2.
Outfield: Brian S. Giles 138, Al Martin 133, Adrian Brown 96, Brant Brown 82, Jose Guillen 37, Turner Ward 34, Freddy Garcia 24, Chad Hermansen 18, John Wehner 17, Emil Brown 6, Dale Sveum 1, Ivan Cruz 1.
Designated hitter: Brant Brown 6, Brian S. Giles 3, Freddy Garcia 2.

STREAKS

Wins: 7 (May 28-June 4).
Losses: 5 (May 17-21, July 19-23).
Consecutive games with at least one hit: 19, Al Martin (June 23-July 11).
Wins by pitcher: 4, Chris Peters (August 25-September 11).

ATTENDANCE

Home: 1,638,023.
Road: 2,170,274.
Highest (home): 43,519 (July 16 vs. Cleveland).
Highest (road): 60,799 (June 18 vs. San Diego).
Lowest (home): 10,051 (April 6 vs. Montreal).
Lowest (road): 7,510 (July 23 vs. Montreal).

St. Louis Cardinals

1999 REVIEW

Date	Opp.	Res.	Score	(inn.*)	Hits	Opp. hits	Winning pitcher	Losing pitcher	Save	Record	Pos.	GB
4-5	Mil.	L	8-10		11	11	Weathers	Busby		0-1	T4th	1.0
4-7	Mil.	W	4-1		7	5	Bottenfield	Woodard	Acevedo	1-1	T1st	...
4-8	Mil.	W	9-4		8	13	Mercker	Abbott		2-1	T1st	...
4-9	Cin.	L	0-3		6	5	Harnisch	Oliver		2-2	T1st	...
4-10	Cin.	W	4-2		6	7	Acevedo	Williamson		3-2	T1st	...
4-11	Cin.	L	2-4		10	6	Bere	Osborne	Graves	3-3	T2nd	1.0
4-13	At Pit.	W	4-2		9	10	Bottenfield	Schourek	Acevedo	4-3	T1st	...
4-14	At Pit.	W	9-5		12	14	Aybar	Benson		5-3	T1st	...
4-16	At Hou.	W	5-3		9	11	Oliver	Reynolds	Bottalico	6-3	1st	+1.5
4-17	At Hou.	W	8-5		10	11	Jimenez	Holt		7-3	1st	+2.0
4-18	At Hou.	L	4-8		9	16	Powell	Painter		7-4	1st	+1.0
4-19	At Mil.	W	6-2		12	7	Bottenfield	Abbott		8-4	1st	+1.0
4-20	At Mil.	W	8-3		12	6	Mercker	Karl		9-4	1st	+1.0
4-21	At Mil.	L	1-2		6	5	Reyes	Painter	Wickman	9-5	1st	+1.0
4-23	At L.A.	W	12-5		11	11	Jimenez	Park		10-5	1st	+2.0
4-24	At L.A.	L	1-6		6	8	Valdes	Osborne		10-6	1st	+1.0
4-25	At L.A.	W	6-4		9	8	Bottenfield	Dreifort	Acevedo	11-6	1st	+2.0
4-27	Col.	W	7-5		8	10	Oliver	Thomson	Radinsky	12-6	1st	+1.5
4-28	Col.	L	7-9		14	11	Bohanon	Jimenez	Veres	12-7	1st	+1.5
4-29	Col.	L	2-6		8	11	Kile	Mercker		12-8	1st	+0.5
4-30	At Mon.	L	2-3		6	8	Urbina	Acevedo		12-9	2nd	0.5
5-1	At Mon.	W	16-5		19	8	Osborne	Thurman	Mohler	13-9	2nd	0.5
5-2	At Mon.	W	8-7	(10)	11	14	Acevedo	Urbina	Radinsky	14-9	2nd	0.5
5-3	At Atl.	L	2-4		10	8	Remlinger	Jimenez	Rocker	14-10	2nd	0.5
5-4	At Atl.	W	9-1		16	4	Aybar	Maddux		15-10	2nd	0.5
5-5	At Atl.	L	3-12		7	16	Smoltz	Bottenfield		15-11	2nd	1.5
5-6	Pit.	L	3-13		7	15	Ritchie	Osborne		15-12	2nd	2.0
5-7	Pit.	W	4-2		6	13	Radinsky	Loiselle		16-12	2nd	2.0
5-8	Pit.	L	0-7		4	10	Benson	Jimenez		16-13	2nd	2.0
5-9	Pit.	L	9-12		9	15	Peters	Aybar	Williams	16-14	T2nd	2.0
5-10	Phi.	W	5-2		9	7	Bottenfield	Loewer	Radinsky	17-14	2nd	2.0
5-11	Phi.	L	4-9		7	13	Byrd	Mercker		17-15	2nd	3.0
5-12	Phi.	L	4-8		7	12	Schilling	Oliver		17-16	2nd	4.0
5-14	L.A.	L	3-7		8	10	Brown	Jimenez		17-17	T2nd	5.0
5-15	L.A.	W	8-5		12	12	Bottenfield	Park		18-17	T3rd	5.0
5-16	L.A.	W	5-4		8	9	Bottalico	Shaw		19-17	T2nd	4.0
5-18	At S.D.	W	5-2		9	4	Oliver	Clement	Bottalico	20-17	2nd	4.0
5-19	At S.D.	L	6-7		9	8	Boehringer	Bottalico		20-18	3rd	4.0
5-20	At S.D.	W	6-4		9	9	Bottenfield	Hitchcock	Bottalico	21-18	3rd	4.0
5-21	At L.A.	W	10-6		10	7	Acevedo	Valdes	Aybar	22-18	3rd	3.0
5-22	At L.A.	L	7-10		12	14	Dreifort	Sodowsky	Shaw	22-19	3rd	3.0
5-23	At L.A.	W	8-3		14	11	Oliver	Perez		23-19	3rd	3.0
5-25	S.F	L	1-17		5	17	Brock	Jimenez		23-20	T3rd	4.5
5-26	S.F	L	6-7		9	12	Rueter	Bottenfield	Nen	23-21	4th	5.5
5-27	S.F	W	3-2	(12)	6	8	Slocumb	Spradlin		24-21	3rd	4.5
5-28	At Chi.	L	3-6		7	14	Tapani	Painter	Aguilera	24-22	3rd	4.5
5-29	At Chi.	L	3-4		5	9	Heredia	Bottalico		24-23	4th	4.5
5-30	At Chi.	L	4-7		10	12	Lieber	Jimenez		24-24	5th	4.5
5-31	At Fla.	W	5-2		11	10	Bottenfield	Meadows	Bottalico	25-24	5th	4.0
6-1	At Fla.	W	8-4		11	8	Acevedo	Hernandez		26-24	5th	4.0
6-2	At Fla.	L	2-10		8	14	Dempster	Painter		26-25	5th	5.0
6-3	At Fla.	L	2-4		8	5	Looper	Oliver	Mantei	26-26	5th	5.0
6-4	At Det.	L	1-4		4	7	Moehler	Jimenez	Jones	26-27	5th	6.0
6-5	At Det.	W	7-2		15	5	Bottenfield	Blair	Bottalico	27-27	5th	6.0
6-6	At Det.	W	8-4		14	9	Croushore	Nitkowski	Aybar	28-27	5th	5.0
6-7	At K.C.	W	7-5		12	7	Slocumb	Appier	Bottalico	29-27	T4th	5.0
6-8	At K.C.	L	10-11		14	15	Service	Oliver	Montgomery	29-28	T4th	5.0
6-9	At K.C.	L	13-17		18	19	Whisenant	Radinsky		29-29	5th	6.0
6-11	Det.	L	2-8		10	7	Mlicki	Bottenfield		29-30	5th	7.0
6-12	Det.	W	8-7	(14)	17	8	Radinsky	Blair		30-30	5th	7.0
6-13	Det.	L	1-3	(10)	9	11	Jones	Bottalico	Brocail	30-31	5th	7.5
6-14	Mon.	L	5-7		9	11	Telford	Oliver	Urbina	30-32	5th	8.5
6-15	Mon.	W	3-2		5	5	Jimenez	Thurman	Bottalico	31-32	5th	7.5
6-16	Mon.	W	5-4		9	6	Bottenfield	Batista	Bottalico	32-32	5th	6.5
6-17	N.Y.	L	3-4		6	10	Leiter	Mercker	Cook	32-33	5th	6.5
6-18	N.Y.	L	2-6		3	14	Hershiser	Acevedo	Benitez	32-34	5th	7.5
6-19	N.Y.	W	7-6		10	9	Aybar	Isringhausen	Bottalico	33-34	5th	7.5
6-20	N.Y.	L	6-9		10	12	Reed	Croushore	Franco	33-35	5th	8.5
6-21	Hou.	W	5-3		10	5	Bottenfield	Bergman	Bottalico	34-35	5th	7.5
6-22	Hou.	W	4-3	(14)	13	11	Mohler	McCurry		35-35	T4th	6.5
6-23	Hou.	L	4-8		14	12	Reynolds	Acevedo		35-36	5th	7.5
6-24	At Ari.	L	7-8		14	11	Nunez	Bottalico		35-37	5th	7.5
6-25	At Ari.	W	1-0		5	0	Jimenez	Johnson		36-37	5th	6.5
6-26	At Ari.	W	2-1	(10)	5	7	Aybar	Nunez		37-37	T3rd	5.5
6-27	At Ari.	L	2-3	(10)	7	8	Nunez	Bottalico		37-38	5th	6.5
6-29	At Hou.	L	4-5		8	7	Elarton	Aybar	Wagner	37-39	5th	6.5
6-30	At Hou.	L	3-11		8	13	Hampton	Jimenez		37-40	5th	7.5

High point: Mark McGwire had another monster season, finishing only five home runs short of his record total of 70. He hit 50 or more homers for a record fourth consecutive season and reached the 500-mark faster than anyone in history. Also, he won his first RBI crown, driving in 147 runs.

Low point: After being two games over .500 at 62-60 on August 20, the Cardinals lost 26 of their last 39 games.

Turning point: The season went downhill in spring training. Emerging staff ace Matt Morris went down with an elbow injury and had to undergo Tommy John surgery, which cost him the season and dealt the rotation a crippling blow.

Most valuable player: McGwire, although the Cardinals lost 24 of the 56 games in which he homered and, almost unbelievably, were 2-7 in games in which he homered twice. His run-production exploits nonetheless were extraordinary—and his presence spurred the Cardinals to a record attendance of 3.23 million.

Most valuable pitcher: Entering the season with only 18 victories in his major league career, Kent Bottenfield matched that in one season as he developed into the Cardinals' No. 1 pitcher.

Most improved player: Bottenfield. The righthander had been only mediocre in his career as a longtime reliever and spot starter, but he prospered when installed in the rotation and left there. He lost a chance at 20 wins when, because of shoulder fatigue, he was shut down with 10 days left in the season.

Most pleasant surprise: The Cardinals knew third baseman Fernando Tatis was a promising player, but they never envisioned he'd have such a standout season. Tatis hit .298 with 34 homers and 107 RBIs, and he stole 21 bases. He also showed quickness and range at third base.

Key injuries: Morris was joined on the sidelines by Osborne (shoulder surgery after one win), starter Alan Benes (just two innings after shoulder problems), outfielder Eric Davis (shoulder surgery, missed three months), outfielder Darren Bragg (knee surgery, out two months) and reliever Scott Radinsky (elbow surgery, sidelined two months).

Notable: Tatis became the first player in major league history to hit two grand slams in one inning, accomplishing the feat on April 23 in Los Angeles. ... Righthander Jose Jimenez pitched a no-hit game—at Arizona on June 25—in his first full season in the majors. ... Bottenfield was the staff's lone double-figure winner. ... Utilityman Joe McEwing set a club rookie record with a 25-game hitting streak and was a constant spark.

—RICK HUMMEL

MISCELLANEOUS

RECORDS

1999 regular-season record: 75-86 (4th in N.L. Central); 38-42 at home; 37-44 on road; 16-25 vs. N.L. East; 27-34 vs. N.L. Central; 25-19 vs. N.L. West; 7-8 vs. A.L. Central; 17-29 vs. lefthanded starters; 58-57 vs. righthanded starters; 64-70 on grass; 11-16 on turf; 25-28 in daytime; 50-58 at night; 26-27 in one-run games; 9-8 in extra-inning games; 1-0-2 in doubleheaders.

Team record past five years: 381-409 (.482, ranks 10th in league in that span).

TEAM LEADERS

Batting average: Fernando Tatis (.298).
At-bats: Edgar Renteria (585).
Runs: Mark McGwire (118).
Hits: Edgar Renteria (161).
Total bases: Mark McGwire (363).
Doubles: Edgar Renteria (36).
Triples: J.D. Drew (6).
Home runs: Mark McGwire (65).
Runs batted in: Mark McGwire (147).
Stolen bases: Edgar Renteria (37).
Slugging percentage: Mark McGwire (.697).
On-base percentage: Mark McGwire (.424).
Wins: Kent Bottenfield (18).
Earned-run average: Kent Bottenfield (3.97).
Complete games: Jose Jimenez, Darren Oliver (2).
Shutouts: Jose Jimenez (2).
Saves: Ricky Bottalico (20).
Innings pitched: Darren Oliver (196.1).
Strikeouts: Kent Bottenfield (124).

Date	Opp.	Res.	Score	(inn.*)	Hits	Opp. hits	Winning pitcher	Losing pitcher	Save	Record	Pos.	GB
7-1	At Hou.	W	10-4		12	10	Bottenfield	Holt		38-40	5th	7.5
7-2	Ari.	L	5-9		9	15	Anderson	Oliver		38-41	5th	7.5
7-3	Ari.	W	2-1	(10)	5	4	Painter	Kim		39-41	4th	7.5
7-4	Ari.	L	5-17		13	19	Benes	Croushore		39-42	5th	7.5
7-5	Ari.	W	1-0		4	2	Jimenez	Johnson		40-42	5th	7.5
7-6	Cin.	W	6-5		10	9	Bottenfield	Tomko	Bottalico	41-42	4th	6.5
7-7	Cin.	W	2-1		7	9	Croushore	Williamson		42-42	4th	5.5
7-8	Cin.	L	5-8		10	11	Harnisch	Mercker	Graves	42-43	4th	6.5
7-9	At S.F	L	4-5	(11)	11	9	Rodriguez	Aybar		42-44	T4th	7.5
7-10	At S.F	L	2-4		2	7	Ortiz	Jimenez	Johnstone	42-45	4th	7.5
7-11	At S.F	W	5-4		7	8	Bottenfield	Gardner	Bottalico	43-45	T4th	7.5
7-15	Chi. (AL)	W	3-2	(13)	10	8	Croushore	Rizzo		44-45	3rd	7.5
7-16	Chi. (AL)	L	8-9		11	15	Navarro	Acevedo	Howry	44-46	5th	8.5
7-17	Chi. (AL)	W	8-6		9	8	Stephenson	Ward	Bottalico	45-46	T4th	8.5
7-18	Min.	L	2-5		9	7	Hawkins	Oliver		45-47	5th	9.5
7-19	Min.	W	8-4		14	9	Mercker	Lincoln	Bottalico	46-47	T4th	9.5
7-20	Min.	L	2-4		7	7	Radke	Luebbers	Trombley	46-48	5th	9.5
7-21	At Cin.	L	0-1		1	3	Villone	Jimenez	Williamson	46-49	6th	9.5
7-22	At Cin.	W	6-5		5	8	Painter	Graves	Bottalico	47-49	5th	8.5
7-23	At Col.	W	6-4		11	12	Oliver	Ramirez	Slocumb	48-49	T3rd	9.0
7-24	At Col.	W	10-2		15	11	Mercker	Kile		49-49	3rd	9.0
7-25	At Col.	W	6-4		8	9	Luebbers	Astacio	Aybar	50-49	3rd	9.0
7-26	At S.F	L	8-10		11	14	Rodriguez	Slocumb	Nen	50-50	3rd	10.0
7-27	At S.F	L	1-2		4	7	Rueter	Bottenfield	Johnstone	50-51	3rd	11.0
7-28	At S.F	W	6-3		7	7	Oliver	Hernandez	Bottalico	51-51	3rd	11.0
7-30	Col.	L	4-5		7	9	Astacio	Aybar	Veres	51-52	3rd	11.5
7-31	Col.	W	6-5		10	11	Painter	Leskanic	Bottalico	52-52	3rd	11.5
8-1	Col.	L	4-5		10	13	Bohanon	Jimenez	Veres	52-53	3rd	11.5
8-2	S.D.	W	6-5		9	10	Bottenfield	Williams	Croushore	53-53	3rd	11.0
8-3	S.D.	W	6-0		9	4	Oliver	Boehringer		54-53	3rd	11.0
8-4	S.D.	W	7-6		13	6	Slocumb	Wall	Croushore	55-53	3rd	10.0
8-5	S.D.	L	3-10		6	10	Ashby	Luebbers	Hoffman	55-54	3rd	11.0
8-6†	At Pit.	L	1-5		6	10	Anderson	Jimenez	Silva	55-55		
8-6‡	At Pit.	W	5-1		10	3	Stephenson	Schmidt	Croushore	56-55	3rd	11.0
8-7	At Pit.	L	1-3		7	11	Cordova	Bottenfield	Williams	56-56	T3rd	12.0
8-8	At Pit.	L	1-5		4	8	Benson	Oliver		56-57	4th	13.0
8-9	At Phi.	W	12-6		15	11	Mercker	Schrenk		57-57	T3rd	12.0
8-10	At Phi.	L	5-7		10	6	Poole	Bottalico	Gomes	57-58	T3rd	12.0
8-11	At Phi.	W	5-1		9	6	Stephenson	Wolf	Slocumb	58-58	T3rd	11.0
8-13	Chi.	W	7-1		7	8	Bottenfield	Farnsworth		59-58	T3rd	10.0
8-14	Chi.	L	7-9		10	10	Adams	Slocumb		59-59	T3rd	11.0
8-15	Phi.	W	6-5		13	9	Bottalico	Adams		60-59	4th	10.0
8-16	Phi.	W	4-3		4	9	Mercker	Wolf	Bottalico	61-59	3rd	10.0
8-17	Phi.	W	6-5		10	10	Acevedo	Gomes		62-59	3rd	10.0
8-18	Phi.	L	5-6		8	17	Aldred	Croushore	Gomes	62-60	3rd	11.0
8-21	At N.Y.	L	4-7		8	9	Mahomes	Mercker	Benitez	62-61	4th	12.0
8-22†	At N.Y.	L	7-8		12	11	Benitez	Bottalico		62-62		
8-22‡	At N.Y.	W	7-5		10	11	Stephenson	Hershiser	Acevedo	63-62	3rd	12.0
8-23	At Mon.	L	7-11		11	14	Telford	Croushore		63-63	3rd	12.0
8-24	At Mon.	L	4-8		10	12	Vazquez	Bottenfield	Urbina	63-64	3rd	13.0
8-25	At Mon.	L	1-4		7	8	Powell	Luebbers	Urbina	63-65	3rd	13.0
8-27	Atl.	L	1-2		8	8	Springer	Acevedo	Rocker	63-66	4th	13.5
8-28	Atl.	L	0-3	(13)	4	7	Remlinger	Painter	Rocker	63-67	4th	13.5
8-29	Atl.	L	3-4	(12)	8	9	McGlinchy	Acevedo		63-68	4th	14.5
8-30	Fla.	L	2-4		5	13	Nunez	Bottenfield	Alfonseca	63-69	4th	14.5
8-31	Fla.	W	8-1		12	5	Luebbers	Meadows		64-69	4th	14.5
9-1	Fla.	W	9-3		10	9	Stephenson	Dempster		65-69	4th	13.5
9-2	At Mil.	W	4-3		9	8	Painter	Ramirez	Bottalico	66-69	4th	13.0
9-3	At Mil.	L	4-5	(11)	12	12	Coppinger	Acevedo		66-70	4th	14.0
9-4	At Mil.	L	2-4		3	6	Pulsipher	Thompson	Wickman	66-71	4th	15.0
9-5	At Mil.	W	13-9	(10)	18	12	Bottalico	Wickman		67-71	4th	15.0
9-6	At Atl.	L	1-4		3	9	Maddux	Stephenson		67-72	4th	16.0
9-7	At Atl.	L	2-3		6	9	Remlinger	Oliver		67-73	4th	17.0
9-8	At Atl.	L	4-5		9	7	Millwood	Ankiel	Rocker	67-74	4th	18.0
9-10	Pit.	W	11-5		13	10	Bottenfield	Benson		68-74	4th	18.5
9-11	Pit.	L	5-8		10	11	Peters	Jimenez	Silva	68-75	4th	19.5
9-13	Mil.	L	3-4		8	9	Nomo	Thompson	Wickman	68-76	4th	21.0
9-14	Mil.	L	1-4		8	7	Karl	Aybar	Wickman	68-77	4th	22.0
9-15	Mil.	L	8-10	(12)	13	15	Ramirez	Acevedo		68-78	4th	22.0
9-17	Hou.	W	11-8		18	8	Stephenson	Lima	Bottalico	69-78	4th	21.0
9-18	Hou.	W	13-6		13	11	Oliver	Hampton		70-78	4th	20.0
9-19	Hou.	L	3-4		7	10	Holt	Croushore	Wagner	70-79	4th	21.0
9-20	At Chi.	W	7-2		9	8	Thompson	Lieber		71-79	4th	20.0
9-21	At Chi.	W	7-2		8	3	Bottenfield	Lorraine		72-79	4th	20.0
9-22	At Chi.	L	3-5		7	8	Trachsel	Stephenson	Aguilera	72-80	4th	20.0
9-24	At Cin.	L	4-5		7	10	Parris	Croushore	Graves	72-81	4th	21.0
9-25	At Cin.	L	1-6		4	9	Neagle	Jimenez	Graves	72-82	4th	21.0
9-26	At Cin.	L	5-7	(12)	9	10	Williamson	Mohler		72-83	4th	21.0
9-27	At Cin.	L	7-9		8	14	Belinda	Croushore	Reyes	72-84	4th	21.5
9-29†	S.D.	W	4-3		8	5	Oliver	Wall	Painter	73-84		
9-29‡	S.D.	W	6-5	(10)	9	10	Acevedo	Guzman		74-84	4th	20.5
10-1	Chi.	L	2-3		7	7	Lieber	Thompson		74-85	4th	20.5
10-2	Chi.	L	3-6		6	10	Lorraine	Stephenson	Aguilera	74-86	T4th	21.5
10-3	Chi.	W	9-5	(5)	10	6	Luebbers	Trachsel	Ankiel	75-86	4th	21.5

Monthly records: April (12-9), May (13-15), June (12-16), July (15-12), August (12-17), September (10-15), October (1-2).
*Innings, if other than nine. † First game of a doubleheader. ‡ Second game of a doubleheader.

MEMORABLE GAMES

April 23 at Los Angeles

Third baseman Fernando Tatis became the first player in history to hit two grand slams in the same inning with an amazing fourth inning against the Dodgers. The odd part about it was that Tatis hit both off the same pitcher, Dodgers righthander Chan Ho Park, who was left in to absorb the unprecedented beating.

St. Louis	AB	R	H	RBI	Los Angeles	AB	R	H	RBI
Bragg, rf	5	2	3	0	E.Young, 2b	4	1	2	1
Renteria, ss	5	2	1	1	Cromer, rf	1	0	0	0
McGwire, 1b	5	1	1	0	J.Vizcno, ss-2b	3	0	2	0
Aybar, p	0	0	0	0	Sheffield, lf	2	0	0	0
Tatis, 3b	5	2	2	8	Hlndswrth, ph-lf	2	0	0	0
Drew, cf	4	1	2	1	Mondesi, rf	4	0	0	0
Marrero, c-1b	5	1	2	1	Kubenka, p	0	0	0	0
D.Howard, 2b	0	0	0	0	LoDuca, ph	1	0	0	0
Polanco, ph-2b	3	1	0	0	Karros, 1b	3	0	1	0
McEwing, lf	4	1	0	0	D.Hansen, 1b	1	1	1	0
J.Jimenez, p	3	1	0	0	D.White, cf	3	1	2	0
A.Castillo, c	1	0	0	0	Brumfield, cf	1	0	0	0
					Beltre, 3b	4	1	2	1
					Hundley, c	3	0	0	1
					Park, p	1	0	0	0
					C.Perez, p	1	0	0	0
					Grudzinek, ph-s	1	1	1	0
Totals	40	12	11	11	Totals	35	5	11	5

St. Louis ....0 0 (11)   001   000—12
Los Angeles 110   000   210— 5

E—Bragg (1), J.Vizcaino 2 (3), Karros (1). LOB—St. Louis 8, Los Angeles 8. 2B—Bragg (1), Drew (2), D.Hansen (1). HR—Tatis 2 (6), Drew (2), Marrero (1). SB—Marrero (3), McEwing (2). S—J.Jimenez, J.Vizcaino. SF—Sheffield, Hundley.

St. Louis	IP	H	R	ER	BB	SO
J.Jimenez (W, 2-0)	7	9	4	3	1	6
Aybar	2	2	1	1	0	2

Los Angeles	IP	H	R	ER	BB	SO
Park (L, 1-2)	2.2	8	11	6	3	2
C.Perez	4.1	3	1	1	0	4
Kubenka	2	0	0	0	2	1

HBP—Renteria by Park, Grudzielanek by Aybar. U—HP, Bonin. 1B, Nelson. 2B, Pulli. 3B, C.Williams. T—3:05. A—46,687.

June 25 at Phoenix

Rookie Jose Jimenez, who would go on to win just five games, pitched a 1-0, no-hit win against the Diamondbacks' Randy Johnson, whom he shut out again 10 days later. Jimenez later was sent to the minors. Right fielder Eric Davis saved the no-hitter with two diving catches, but re-injured his shoulder and didn't play again the rest of the season.

St. Louis	AB	R	H	RBI	Arizona	AB	R	H	RBI
McEwing, 2b	4	0	1	0	Womack, rf	4	0	0	0
Bragg, cf-lf	2	1	0	0	J.Bell, 2b	3	0	0	0
McGwire, 1b	3	0	0	0	L.Gonzalez, lf	2	0	0	0
E.Davis, rf	4	0	0	0	M.Willms, 3b	3	0	0	0
T.Howard, lf	4	0	1	1	S.Finley, cf	2	0	0	0
Lankford, cf	0	0	0	0	T.Lee, 1b	3	0	0	0
Renteria, ss	3	0	1	0	D.Miller, c	3	0	0	0
A.Castillo, c	3	0	1	0	A.Fox, ss	2	0	0	0
D.Howard, 3b	3	0	1	0	Ra.Johnson, p	2	0	0	0
J.Jimenez, p	3	0	0	0	Dellucci, ph	1	0	0	0
Totals	29	1	5	1	Totals	25	0	0	0

St. Louis 000   000   001 —1
Arizona 000   000   000 —0

DP—St. Louis 2, Arizona 1. LOB—St. Louis 4, Arizona 1. 2B—McEwing (14), Renteria (18), D.Howard (1). S—Bragg.

St. Louis	IP	H	R	ER	BB	SO
J.Jimenez (W, 4-7)	9	0	0	0	2	8

Arizona	IP	H	R	ER	BB	SO
Ra.Johnson (L, 9-4)	9	5	1	1	2	14

HBP—A.Fox by J.Jimenez. U—HP, Froemming. 1B, Nelson. 2B, Wegner. 3B, Bell. T—2:10. A—45,540.

BATTING

Name	G	TPA	AB	R	H	TB	2B	3B	HR	RBI	Avg.	Obp.	Slg.	SH	SF	HP	BB	IBB	SO	SB	CS	GDP	vs RHP AB	Avg.	HR	RBI	vs LHP AB	Avg.	HR	RBI
Renteria, Edgar	154	653	585	92	161	234	36	2	11	63	.275	.334	.400	6	7	2	53	0	82	37	8	16	445	.283	9	47	140	.250	2	16
Tatis, Fernando	149	639	537	104	160	297	31	2	34	107	.298	.404	.553	0	4	16	82	4	128	21	9	11	399	.301	24	78	138	.290	10	29
McGwire, Mark	153	661	521	118	145	363	21	1	65	147	.278	.424	.697	0	5	2	133	21	141	0	0	12	399	.286	49	117	122	.254	16	30
McEwing, Joe	152	575	513	65	141	204	28	4	9	44	.275	.333	.398	9	5	6	41	8	87	7	4	3	359	.267	7	33	154	.292	2	11
Lankford, Ray	122	476	422	77	129	208	32	1	15	63	.306	.380	.493	0	2	3	49	3	110	14	4	6	308	.331	13	47	114	.237	2	16
Drew, J.D.	104	430	368	72	89	156	16	6	13	39	.242	.340	.424	3	3	6	50	0	77	19	3	4	262	.233	8	27	106	.264	5	12
Marrero, Eli	114	343	317	32	61	94	13	1	6	34	.192	.236	.297	4	3	1	18	4	56	11	2	14	243	.189	5	27	74	.203	1	7
Bragg, Darren	93	325	273	38	71	103	12	1	6	26	.260	.369	.377	5	0	3	44	1	67	3	0	5	212	.269	5	22	61	.230	1	4
McGee, Willie	132	290	271	25	68	75	7	0	0	20	.251	.293	.277	0	2	0	17	3	60	7	4	5	169	.308	4	30	86	.174	0	1
Castillo, Alberto	93	290	255	21	67	87	8	0	4	31	.263	.326	.341	5	4	2	24	1	48	0	0	6	139	.237	0	12	81	.346	1	7
Polanco, Placido	88	240	220	24	61	79	9	3	1	19	.277	.321	.359	3	2	0	15	1	24	1	3	7	158	.278	5	21	37	.351	1	7
Howard, Thomas	98	215	195	16	57	85	10	0	6	28	.292	.353	.436	0	1	2	17	0	26	1	1	3	158	.278	5	21	37	.286	1	7
Davis, Eric	58	223	191	27	49	77	9	2	5	30	.257	.359	.403	0	1	1	30	1	49	5	4	1	142	.246	3	22	49	.286	2	8
Paquette, Craig	48	166	157	21	45	81	6	0	10	37	.287	.309	.516	1	2	0	6	0	38	1	0	6	103	.330	7	27	54	.204	3	10
Dunston, Shawon	62	158	150	23	46	70	5	2	5	25	.307	.327	.467	2	1	3	2	0	23	6	3	4	100	.320	4	17	50	.280	1	8
Kennedy, Adam	33	110	102	12	26	41	10	1	1	16	.255	.284	.402	1	2	2	3	0	8	0	1	1	90	.256	1	12	12	.250	0	4
Howard, David	52	92	82	3	17	24	4	0	1	6	.207	.286	.293	1	0	2	7	3	27	0	2	0	51	.196	1	5	31	.226	0	1
Oliver, Darren	35	84	73	7	20	24	4	0	0	6	.274	.303	.329	8	0	0	3	0	23	0	0	1	51	.275	0	5	22	.273	0	1
Bottenfield, Kent	31	70	61	4	9	12	3	0	0	5	.148	.161	.197	8	0	0	1	0	26	0	0	0	47	.170	0	4	14	.071	0	1
Jimenez, Jose	31	55	53	5	5	7	0	1	0	2	.094	.094	.132	2	0	0	0	0	22	0	0	1	31	.129	0	2	22	.045	0	0
Jensen, Marcus	16	42	34	5	8	16	5	0	1	1	.235	.350	.471	2	0	0	6	1	12	0	0	1	27	.222	1	1	7	.286	0	0
Perez, Eduardo	21	39	32	6	11	16	2	0	1	9	.344	.462	.500	0	0	0	7	0	6	0	0	0	16	.313	1	5	16	.375	0	4
Mercker, Kent	26	34	28	5	5	6	1	0	0	2	.179	.233	.214	4	0	0	2	0	10	0	0	0	16	.250	0	1	12	.083	0	1
Stephenson, Garrett	18	30	27	1	2	3	1	0	0	0	.074	.074	.111	3	0	0	0	0	5	0	0	2	16	.125	0	0	11	.000	0	0
Acevedo, Juan	50	22	20	0	1	1	0	0	0	0	.050	.050	.050	2	0	0	0	0	16	0	0	0	18	.000	0	0	2	.500	0	0
Luebbers, Larry	8	18	16	1	2	2	0	0	0	0	.125	.176	.125	1	0	0	1	0	2	0	0	1	13	.154	0	0	3	.000	0	0
Aybar, Manny	67	13	12	0	1	1	0	0	0	1	.083	.083	.083	1	0	0	0	0	7	0	0	0	10	.100	0	1	2	.000	0	0
Osborne, Donovan	6	11	10	1	1	2	1	0	0	0	.100	.100	.200	1	0	0	0	0	2	0	0	0	7	.143	0	0	3	.000	0	0
Ankiel, Rick	9	11	10	0	1	1	0	0	0	0	.100	.100	.100	1	0	0	0	0	3	0	0	0	6	.000	0	0	4	.250	0	0
Ordaz, Luis	10	11	9	3	1	1	0	0	0	2	.111	.200	.111	1	0	0	1	0	2	1	0	0	4	.250	0	2	5	.000	0	0
Thompson, Mark	5	9	8	0	0	0	0	0	0	0	.000	.000	.000	1	0	0	0	0	6	0	0	0	7	.000	0	0	1	.000	0	0
Painter, Lance	56	7	7	0	0	0	0	0	0	0	.000	.000	.000	0	0	0	0	0	5	0	0	1	5	.000	0	0	2	.000	0	0
Croushore, Rich	59	4	3	1	1	1	0	0	0	0	.333	.500	.333	0	0	0	1	0	1	0	0	0	1	.000	0	0	2	.500	0	0
Mohler, Mike	48	3	3	0	0	0	0	0	0	0	.000	.000	.000	0	0	0	0	0	1	0	0	0	2	.000	0	0	1	.000	0	0
Bottalico, Ricky	68	3	3	0	0	0	0	0	0	0	.000	.000	.000	0	0	0	0	0	1	0	0	0	3	.000	0	0	0	.000	0	0
Sodowsky, Clint	3	1	1	0	0	0	0	0	0	0	.000	.000	.000	0	0	0	0	0	1	0	0	0	1	.000	0	0	0	.000	0	0
Heiserman, Rick	3	1	1	0	0	0	0	0	0	0	.000	.000	.000	0	0	0	0	0	0	0	0	0	1	.000	0	0	0	.000	0	0
Radinsky, Scott	43	0	0	0	0	0	0	0	0	0	.000	.000	.000	0	0	0	0	0	0	0	0	0	0	.000	0	0	0	.000	0	0
Slocumb, Heathcliff	40	0	0	0	0	0	0	0	0	0	.000	.000	.000	0	0	0	0	0	0	0	0	0	0	.000	0	0	0	.000	0	0
Benes, Alan	2	0	0	0	0	0	0	0	0	0	.000	.000	.000	0	0	0	0	0	0	0	0	0	0	.000	0	0	0	.000	0	0
Busby, Mike	15	0	0	0	0	0	0	0	0	0	.000	.000	.000	0	0	0	0	0	0	0	0	0	0	.000	0	0	0	.000	0	0
King, Curtis	2	0	0	0	0	0	0	0	0	0	.000	.000	.000	0	0	0	0	0	0	0	0	0	0	.000	0	0	0	.000	0	0

Players with more than one N.L. team

Name	G	TPA	AB	R	H	TB	2B	3B	HR	RBI	Avg.	Obp.	Slg.	SH	SF	HP	BB	IBB	SO	SB	CS	GDP	vs RHP AB	Avg.	HR	RBI	vs LHP AB	Avg.	HR	RBI
Dunston, N.Y.	42	97	93	12	32	40	6	1	0	16	.344	.354	.430	1	1	2	0	0	16	4	1	4	100	.320	4	17	50	.280	1	8
Dunston, StL.-N.Y.	104	255	243	35	78	110	11	3	5	41	.321	.354	.453	3	2	5	2	0	39	10	4	8	149	.309	4	27	94	.340	1	14

PITCHING

Name	W	L	Pct.	ERA	IP	H	R	ER	HR	SH	SF	HB	BB	IBB	SO	G	GS	CG	ShO	GF	Sv	vs. RH AB	Avg.	HR	RBI	vs. LH AB	Avg.	HR	RBI
Oliver, Darren	9	9	.500	4.26	196.1	197	96	93	16	11	4	11	74	4	119	30	30	2	1	0	0	616	.253	14	68	126	.325	2	15
Bottenfield, Kent	18	7	.720	3.97	190.1	197	91	84	21	11	9	5	89	5	124	31	31	0	0	0	0	407	.290	14	51	322	.245	7	34
Jimenez, Jose	5	14	.263	5.85	163.0	173	114	106	16	10	6	11	71	2	113	29	28	2	2	0	0	333	.249	5	35	296	.304	11	57
Mercker, Kent	6	5	.545	5.12	103.2	125	73	59	16	8	3	2	51	3	64	25	18	0	0	2	0	300	.307	14	53	112	.295	2	13
Acevedo, Juan	6	8	.429	5.89	102.1	115	71	67	17	4	6	4	48	3	52	50	12	0	0	21	4	246	.301	11	50	149	.275	6	19
Aybar, Manny	4	5	.444	5.47	97.0	104	67	59	13	4	3	4	36	3	74	65	1	0	0	22	3	242	.252	9	43	141	.305	4	23
Stephenson, Garrett	6	3	.667	4.22	85.1	90	43	40	11	5	5	5	29	1	59	18	12	0	0	1	0	174	.236	5	17	153	.320	6	24
Bottalico, Ricky	3	7	.300	4.91	73.1	83	45	40	8	3	0	3	49	1	66	68	0	0	0	40	20	179	.268	5	28	113	.310	3	18
Croushore, Rich	3	7	.300	4.14	71.2	68	42	33	9	7	1	3	43	4	88	59	0	0	0	12	3	154	.279	7	31	121	.207	2	20
Painter, Lance	4	5	.444	4.83	63.1	63	37	34	6	4	3	2	25	1	56	56	4	0	0	10	1	148	.291	3	23	90	.222	3	11
Slocumb, Heathcliff	3	2	.600	2.36	53.1	49	16	14	3	4	1	1	30	5	48	40	0	0	0	12	2	118	.220	3	17	84	.274	0	5
Mohler, Mike	1	1	.500	4.38	49.1	47	26	24	3	1	1	1	23	2	31	48	0	0	0	16	1	126	.270	3	20	58	.224	0	6
Luebbers, Larry	3	3	.500	5.12	45.2	46	27	26	8	4	0	3	16	0	16	8	8	1	0	0	0	99	.242	4	14	77	.286	4	10
Ankiel, Rick	0	1	.000	3.27	33.0	26	12	12	2	1	0	1	14	0	39	9	5	0	0	1	1	104	.212	2	11	17	.235	0	0
Thompson, Mark	1	3	.250	4.91	29.1	26	12	9	1	3	0	2	17	1	22	5	5	0	0	0	0	65	.292	0	5	43	.163	1	5
Osborne, Donovan	1	1	.250	5.52	29.1	34	18	18	4	3	1	2	10	0	21	6	6	0	0	0	0	105	.305	4	14	9	.222	0	2
Radinsky, Scott	2	1	.667	4.88	27.2	27	16	15	2	2	5	1	18	3	17	43	0	0	0	13	3	56	.268	0	13	44	.273	2	9
Busby, Mike	0	1	.000	7.13	17.2	21	15	14	2	0	0	2	14	0	7	15	0	0	0	3	0	44	.341	0	7	25	.240	2	8
Sodowsky, Clint	0	1	.000	15.63	6.1	15	11	11	1	0	0	0	6	0	2	3	1	0	0	0	0	19	.474	0	8	14	.429	1	4
Heiserman, Rick	0	0	.000	8.31	4.1	8	4	4	2	0	0	0	4	0	4	3	0	0	0	0	0	14	.500	2	5	6	.167	0	0
Benes, Alan	0	0	.000	0.00	2.0	2	0	0	0	0	0	0	2	2	0	0	0	0	0	2	0	5	.400	0	0	2	.000	0	0
King, Curtis	0	0	.000	18.00	1.0	3	2	2	0	0	0	0	1	0	1	2	0	0	0	1	0	3	1.000	0	0	3	.000	0	0

INDIVIDUAL STATISTICS

FIELDING

FIRST BASEMEN

Player	Pct.	G	PO	A	E	TC	DP
McGwire, Mark	.990	151	1180	80	13	1273	119
Marrero, Eli	1.000	20	47	5	0	52	2
Howard, David	1.000	9	33	1	0	34	4
Dunston, Shawon	1.000	8	37	2	0	39	3
Paquette, Craig	1.000	6	19	3	0	22	1
Perez, Eduardo	.952	5	18	2	1	21	2
McGee, Willie	1.000	3	9	0	0	9	0
McEwing, Joe	1.000	2	5	0	0	5	0

SECOND BASEMEN

Player	Pct.	G	PO	A	E	TC	DP
McEwing, Joe	.980	96	202	238	9	449	51
Polanco, Placido	.979	66	116	122	5	243	32
Kennedy, Adam	.971	29	68	64	4	136	14
Howard, David	1.000	9	10	16	0	26	4
Paquette, Craig	.962	7	10	15	1	26	4
Ordaz, Luis	1.000	1	0	1	0	1	0

THIRD BASEMEN

Player	Pct.	G	PO	A	E	TC	DP
Tatis, Fernando	.958	147	101	267	16	384	30
Paquette, Craig	1.000	10	4	24	0	28	0
Polanco, Placido	.889	9	0	8	1	9	0
McEwing, Joe	.875	6	2	5	1	8	2
Dunston, Shawon	.909	5	2	8	1	11	2
Howard, David	1.000	4	3	6	0	9	1
Ordaz, Luis	-	1	0	0	0	0	0

SHORTSTOPS

Player	Pct.	G	PO	A	E	TC	DP
Renteria, Edgar	.959	151	219	393	26	638	88
Howard, David	.966	13	10	18	1	29	2
Polanco, Placido	.931	9	7	20	2	29	5
Ordaz, Luis	.786	8	4	7	3	14	4
Dunston, Shawon	.929	7	1	12	1	14	3
McEwing, Joe	-	1	0	0	0	0	0

OUTFIELDERS

Player	Pct.	G	PO	A	E	TC	DP
Lankford, Ray	.987	106	214	6	3	223	0
Drew, J.D.	.972	98	235	9	7	251	6
McGee, Willie	.972	89	103	2	3	108	1
Bragg, Darren	.982	88	155	7	3	165	1
McEwing, Joe	.991	66	111	3	1	115	1
Davis, Eric	1.000	51	93	4	0	97	0
Howard, Thomas	.987	48	77	0	1	78	0
Paquette, Craig	.955	27	42	0	2	44	0
Dunston, Shawon	1.000	23	38	1	0	39	0
Perez, Eduardo	1.000	6	11	1	0	12	1
Howard, David	1.000	5	3	0	0	3	0

CATCHERS

Player	Pct.	G	PO	A	E	TC	DP	PB
Marrero, Eli	.987	96	490	42	7	539	12	2
Castillo, Alberto	.991	91	514	38	5	557	10	5
Jensen, Marcus	.988	14	71	9	1	81	1	1

PITCHERS

Player	Pct.	G	PO	A	E	TC	DP
Bottalico, Ricky	1.000	68	4	9	0	13	2
Aybar, Manny	1.000	65	5	11	0	16	0
Croushore, Rich	.750	59	2	4	2	8	0
Painter, Lance	.938	56	3	12	1	16	1
Acevedo, Juan	.857	50	5	7	2	14	0
Mohler, Mike	1.000	48	0	4	0	4	0
Radinsky, Scott	.833	43	1	4	1	6	1
Slocumb, Heathcliff	1.000	40	4	7	0	11	0
Bottenfield, Kent	1.000	31	10	30	0	40	3
Oliver, Darren	.952	30	7	33	2	42	1
Jimenez, Jose	.975	29	10	29	1	40	2
Mercker, Kent	.810	25	1	16	4	21	1
Stephenson, Garrett	1.000	18	6	9	0	15	1
Busby, Mike	1.000	15	1	2	0	3	1
Ankiel, Rick	1.000	9	2	0	0	2	0
Luebbers, Larry	1.000	8	4	7	0	11	0
Osborne, Donovan	.889	6	1	7	1	9	0
Thompson, Mark	1.000	5	3	4	0	7	0
Heiserman, Rick	1.000	3	1	0	0	1	1
Sodowsky, Clint	1.000	3	1	0	0	1	0
Benes, Alan	1.000	2	1	0	0	1	0
King, Curtis	-	2	0	0	0	0	0

PITCHING AGAINST EACH CLUB

Pitcher	Ari. W-L	Atl. W-L	Chi. W-L	Cin. W-L	Col. W-L	Fla. W-L	Hou. W-L	L.A. W-L	Mil. W-L	Mon. W-L	N.Y. W-L	Phi. W-L	Pit. W-L	S.D. W-L	S.F. W-L	A.L. W-L	Total W-L
Acevedo, J.	0-0	0-2	0-0	1-0	0-0	1-0	0-1	1-0	0-2	1-1	0-1	0-0	0-0	1-0	0-0	1-1	6-8
Ankiel, R.	0-0	0-1	0-0	0-0	0-0	0-0	0-0	0-0	0-0	0-0	0-0	0-0	0-0	0-0	0-0	0-0	0-1
Aybar, M.	1-0	1-0	0-0	0-0	0-1	0-0	0-1	0-0	0-1	1-0	0-0	1-1	0-0	0-1	0-0	0-0	4-5
Benes, Al.	0-0	0-0	0-0	0-0	0-0	0-0	0-0	0-0	0-0	0-0	0-0	0-0	0-0	0-0	0-0	0-0	0-0
Bottalico, R.	0-2	0-0	1-1	0-0	0-0	0-0	0-0	0-0	0-0	0-0	0-1	0-0	0-1	0-0	0-0	0-1	3-7
Bottenfield, K.	0-0	0-1	2-0	1-0	0-0	1-0	1-0	2-0	2-0	1-1	0-0	1-0	2-1	2-0	1-2	1-1	18-7
Busby, M.	0-0	0-0	0-0	0-0	0-0	0-0	0-1	0-0	0-1	0-0	0-1	0-0	0-1	0-0	0-1	0-0	0-7
Croushore, R.	0-1	0-0	0-0	1-2	0-0	0-0	0-0	0-0	0-0	0-0	0-0	0-0	0-0	0-0	2-0	0-2	3-7
Heiserman, R.	0-0	0-0	0-0	0-0	0-0	0-0	0-0	0-0	0-0	0-0	0-0	0-0	0-0	0-0	0-0	0-0	0-0
Jimenez, J.	2-0	0-1	0-1	0-2	0-2	0-0	1-1	1-1	0-0	1-0	0-0	0-3	0-0	0-0	0-2	0-1	5-14
King, C.	0-0	0-0	0-0	0-0	0-0	0-0	0-0	0-0	0-0	0-0	0-0	0-0	0-0	0-0	0-0	0-0	0-0
Luebbers, L.	0-0	0-0	1-0	0-0	0-0	1-0	0-0	0-0	0-1	0-0	0-0	0-0	0-0	0-1	0-0	0-1	3-3
Mercker, K.	0-0	0-0	0-0	0-1	1-1	0-0	0-0	0-0	2-0	0-0	0-2	2-1	0-0	0-0	0-0	1-0	6-5
Mohler, M.	0-0	0-0	0-0	0-0	0-0	0-0	1-0	0-0	0-0	0-0	0-0	0-0	0-0	0-0	0-0	0-0	1-0
Oliver, D.	0-1	0-1	0-0	0-1	2-0	0-1	0-0	1-0	0-0	0-1	0-0	0-1	3-0	1-0	0-1	2-2	9-9
Osborne, D.	0-0	0-0	0-0	0-0	0-0	0-0	0-0	0-1	0-1	0-0	0-0	0-0	0-0	0-0	0-0	0-0	0-3
Painter, L.	1-0	0-1	1-0	1-0	1-0	0-1	0-1	0-0	0-0	0-0	0-0	0-0	0-1	0-0	0-0	0-0	4-5
Radinsky, S.	0-0	0-0	0-0	0-0	0-0	0-0	0-0	0-0	0-0	0-0	1-0	0-0	0-0	0-0	0-1	1-1	2-1
Slocumb, H.	0-0	0-0	0-0	0-0	0-0	0-0	0-0	0-0	0-0	0-0	0-0	0-0	0-0	1-1	1-0	1-0	3-2
Sodowsky, C.	0-0	0-0	0-0	0-0	0-0	0-0	0-1	0-0	0-0	0-0	0-0	0-0	0-0	0-0	0-0	0-0	0-1
Stephenson, G.	0-0	0-1	0-2	0-0	0-0	0-0	1-0	1-0	0-0	0-0	1-0	1-0	1-0	0-0	0-0	1-0	6-3
Thompson, M.	0-0	0-0	0-0	1-1	0-0	0-0	0-0	0-2	0-0	0-0	0-0	0-0	0-0	0-0	0-0	0-0	1-3
Totals	4-4	1-8	5-7	4-8	5-4	4-3	7-5	6-3	6-7	4-5	2-5	5-4	5-7	7-2	3-6	7-8	75-86

INTERLEAGUE: Croushore 1-0, Stephenson 1-0, Acevedo 0-1 vs. White Sox; Bottenfield 1-1, Croushore 1-0, Radinsky 1-0, Jimenez 0-1, Bottalico 0-1 vs. Tigers; Slocumb 1-0, Radinsky 0-1, Oliver 0-1 vs. Royals; Mercker 1-0, Oliver 0-1, Luebbers 0-1 vs. Twins. Total: 7-8.

MISCELLANEOUS

HOME RUNS BY PARK

At Arizona (1): McGwire 1.
At Atlanta (6): McGwire 1, Lankford 1, Paquette 1, Renteria 1, Tatis 1, Polanco 1.
At Chicago (NL) (11): McGwire 2, Howard 2, Lankford 2, Jensen 1, Renteria 1, Tatis 1, Marrero 1, Drew 1.
At Cincinnati (8): Tatis 4, McGwire 3, Perez 1.
At Colorado (4): McGwire 2, McEwing 1, Drew 1.
At Detroit (1): Davis 1.
At Florida (5): McGwire 2, Renteria 2, Lankford 1.
At Houston (3): McGwire 1, Tatis 1, Drew 1.
At Kansas City (6): McGwire 2, Dunston 1, Renteria 1, Tatis 1, Marrero 1.
At Los Angeles (13): Tatis 5, McGwire 2, Lankford 2, Davis 1, Howard 1, Marrero 1, Drew 1.
At Milwaukee (4): McGwire 2, Tatis 1, Drew 1.
At Montreal (4): Tatis 2, McGwire 1, Castillo 1.
At New York (NL) (5): McGwire 2, Paquette 1, Castillo 1, McEwing 1.
At Philadelphia (4): Lankford 1, Paquette 1, Tatis 1, Drew 1.
At Pittsburgh (5): McGwire 2, Bragg 2, McEwing 1.
At San Diego (4): McGwire 2, Davis 1, McEwing 1.
At San Francisco (6): McGwire 3, Drew 2, Tatis 1.
At St. Louis (104): McGwire 37, Tatis 16, Lankford 8, Paquette 7, Renteria 6, McEwing 5, Drew 5, Dunston 4, Bragg 4, Howard 3, Marrero 3, Davis 2, Castillo 2, Howard 1, Kennedy 1.

LOW-HIT GAMES

No-hitters: Jose Jimenez, June 25 vs. Arizona, W 1-0.
One-hitters: None.
Two-hitters: Jose Jimenez, July 5 vs. Arizona, W 1-0.

10-STRIKEOUT GAMES

Kent Bottenfield 1, Darren Oliver 1, **Total:** 2.

FOUR OR MORE HITS IN ONE GAME

Edgar Renteria 2, Eric Davis 1, Thomas Howard 1, Darren Bragg 1, Fernando Tatis 1, Adam Kennedy 1, **Total:** 7

MULTI-HOMER GAMES

Mark McGwire 9, Fernando Tatis 4, Ray Lankford 3, Darren Bragg 1, Edgar Renteria 1, **Total:** 18.

GRAND SLAMS

4-23: Fernando Tatis (off Los Angeles's Chan Ho Park).
4-23: Fernando Tatis (off Los Angeles's Chan Ho Park).
5-4: Mark McGwire (off Atlanta's Greg Maddux).
5-9: Shawon Dunston (off Pittsburgh's Jose Silva).
8-9: Fernando Tatis (off Philadelphia's Billy Brewer).
9-17: Mark McGwire (off Houston's Jose Lima).

PINCH HITTERS

(Minimum 5 at-bats)

Name	AB	Avg.	HR	RBI
McGee, Willie	50	.160	0	5
Howard, Thomas	47	.255	1	8

Name	AB	Avg.	HR	RBI
Dunston, Shawon	23	.174	0	2
Polanco, Placido	13	.308	0	1
Lankford, Ray	13	.154	0	0
Howard, David	13	.077	1	0
McEwing, Joe	9	.333	0	1
Bragg, Darren	9	.222	1	3
Perez, Eduardo	8	.375	0	1
Marrero, Eli	7	.143	0	1
Drew, J.D.	6	.167	0	2
Davis, Eric	5	.600	0	0
Paquette, Craig	5	.400	0	1
Kennedy, Adam	5	.200	0	0
Renteria, Edgar	5	.000	0	1

DEBUTS

5-23: Rick Heiserman, P.
8-21: Adam Kennedy, 2B.
8-23: Rick Ankiel, P.

GAMES BY POSITION

Catcher: Eli Marrero 96, Alberto Castillo 91, Marcus Jensen 14.

First base: Mark McGwire 151, Eli Marrero 20, David Howard 9, Shawon Dunston 8, Craig Paquette 6, Eduardo Perez 5, Willie McGee 3, Joe McEwing 2.

Second base: Joe McEwing 96, Placido Polanco 66, Adam Kennedy 29, David Howard 9, Craig Paquette 7, Luis Ordaz 1.

Third base: Fernando Tatis 147, Craig Paquette 10, Placido Polanco 9, Joe McEwing 6, Shawon Dunston 5, David Howard 4, Luis Ordaz 1.

Shortstop: Edgar Renteria 151, David Howard 13, Placido Polanco 9, Luis Ordaz 8, Shawon Dunston 7, Joe McEwing 1.

Outfield: Ray Lankford 106, J.D. Drew 98, Willie McGee 89, Darren Bragg 88, Joe McEwing 66, Eric Davis 51, Thomas Howard 48, Craig Paquette 27, Shawon Dunston 23, Eduardo Perez 6, David Howard 5.

Designated hitter: Eric Davis 2, Shawon Dunston 2, Thomas Howard 1, Ray Lankford 1.

STREAKS

Wins: 4 (April 11-17, July 20-25).
Losses: 7 (August 23-30).
Consecutive games with at least one hit: 25, Joe McEwing (June 8-July 4).
Wins by pitcher: 4, Kent Bottenfield (April 7-25).

ATTENDANCE

Home: 3,236,103.
Road: 2,820,339.
Highest (home): 49,085 (October 1 vs. Chicago).
Highest (road): 54,514 (May 23 vs. Los Angeles).
Lowest (home): 27,476 (August 31 vs. Florida).
Lowest (road): 10,575 (April 19 vs. Milwaukee).

SAN DIEGO PADRES

DAY BY DAY

Date	Opp.	Res.	Score	(inn.*)	Hits	Opp. hits	Winning pitcher	Losing pitcher	Save	Record	Pos.	GB
4-4	Col.§	L	2-8		6	18	Kile	Ashby		0-1	5th	1.0
4-6	Col.	W	4-3		9	9	Hitchcock	Astacio	Hoffman	1-1	T3rd	1.0
4-7	Col.	W	2-1		8	8	Rivera	Jones		2-1	3rd	1.0
4-8	At S.F	L	4-12		9	16	Estes	Spencer		2-2	T3rd	2.0
4-9	At S.F	L	3-8		8	11	Brock	Clement		2-3	T3rd	3.0
4-10	At S.F	W	11-1		12	7	Ashby	Gardner		3-3	3rd	2.0
4-11	At S.F	L	6-8		8	11	Johnstone	Rivera	Nen	3-4	3rd	3.0
4-12	At Col.	W	8-5	(11)	13	10	Wall	Veres	Reyes	4-4	3rd	2.5
4-15	At Col.	L	4-6		4	10	Bohanon	Clement	Veres	4-5	3rd	2.5
4-16	L.A.	W	3-0		11	5	Ashby	Brown		5-5	3rd	1.5
4-17	L.A.	L	3-7		9	8	Park	Reyes		5-6	3rd	2.5
4-18	L.A.	W	4-3		8	8	Miceli	Masaoka	Hoffman	6-6	3rd	1.5
4-19	Pit.	L	0-3		5	6	Schourek	Spencer	Christiansen	6-7	4th	2.5
4-20	Pit.	L	3-7	(10)	8	10	Williams	Hoffman		6-8	5th	2.5
4-21	Pit.	W	2-0		8	3	Ashby	Schmidt	Hoffman	7-8	4th	2.5
4-23	Ari.	L	6-10		10	11	Benes	Hitchcock		7-9	5th	3.0
4-24	Ari.	W	7-2		11	7	Williams	Daal		8-9	4th	3.0
4-25	Ari.	L	3-5	(11)	5	12	Swindell	Miceli	Olson	8-10	4th	4.0
4-27	At N.Y.	W	6-2		8	5	Ashby	Yoshii		9-10	4th	4.0
4-28	At N.Y.	L	3-4		6	11	Wendell	Hoffman		9-11	4th	5.0
4-29	At N.Y.	L	5-8		11	6	Cook	Boehringer	Franco	9-12	5th	6.0
4-30	At Chi.	L	5-6		10	9	Mulholland	Spencer	Beck	9-13	5th	6.0
5-1	At Chi.	L	1-2		3	7	Tapani	Clement	Heredia	9-14	5th	6.0
5-2	At Chi.	L	2-3		6	12	Myers	Rivera	Beck	9-15	5th	6.0
5-3	At Phi.	W	9-3		14	13	Hitchcock	Ogea		10-15	5th	5.0
5-4	At Phi.	L	0-3		5	4	Loewer	Williams		10-16	5th	6.0
5-5	At Phi.	L	1-11		3	14	Byrd	Spencer		10-17	5th	6.0
5-7	Atl.	W	4-3		9	4	Boehringer	Rocker	Hoffman	11-17	5th	6.0
5-8	Atl.	L	1-11		8	14	Glavine	Ashby		11-18	5th	7.0
5-9	Atl.	W	5-0		12	5	Hitchcock	Maddux		12-18	5th	6.0
5-10	Fla.	W	7-5		12	8	Miceli	Alfonseca	Hoffman	13-18	5th	6.0
5-11	Fla.	L	4-5		10	15	Dempster	Spencer	Mantei	13-19	5th	6.0
5-12	Fla.	W	8-7		10	15	Wall	Edmondson	Hoffman	14-19	5th	6.0
5-14	At Cin.	W	7-3		8	9	Ashby	Neagle	Hoffman	15-19	5th	5.0
5-15	At Cin.	L	2-6		8	4	Parris	Hitchcock	Williamson	15-20	5th	5.0
5-16	At Cin.	L	0-3		4	6	Tomko	Williams	Williamson	15-21	5th	6.0
5-18	StL.	L	2-5		4	9	Oliver	Clement	Bottalico	15-22	5th	6.5
5-19	StL.	W	7-6		8	9	Boehringer	Bottalico		16-22	4th	5.5
5-20	StL.	L	4-6		9	9	Bottenfield	Hitchcock	Bottalico	16-23	5th	6.0
5-21	Cin.	W	5-4		10	10	Williams	Tomko	Hoffman	17-23	5th	6.0
5-22	Cin.	L	0-3		3	9	Harnisch	Murray		17-24	5th	7.0
5-23	Cin.	L	2-6		2	7	Avery	Clement	Williamson	17-25	5th	7.0
5-24	At Ari.	L	5-6		13	13	Benes	Ashby	Olson	17-26	5th	7.5
5-25	At Ari.	L	0-4		6	6	Johnson	Hitchcock		17-27	5th	8.5
5-26	At Ari.	L	2-3	(11)	8	8	Olson	Miceli		17-28	5th	9.5
5-28	At Mil.	W	10-8		13	11	Reyes	Eldred	Hoffman	18-28	5th	8.5
5-29	At Mil.	W	12-3		15	10	Clement	Woodard		19-28	5th	8.5
5-30	At Mil.	L	3-10		10	11	Abbott	Hitchcock		19-29	5th	9.5
5-31	At Mil.	L	2-8		5	14	Nomo	Williams		19-30	5th	10.5
6-1	At Chi.	W	1-0	(6)	4	3	Ashby	Trachsel		20-30	5th	9.5
6-2	At Chi.	L	8-9		11	14	Sanders	Hoffman		20-31	5th	10.5
6-3	At Chi.	L	2-7		10	7	Tapani	Clement		20-32	5th	11.0
6-4	Sea.	W	3-2		6	7	Wall	Paniagua	Hoffman	21-32	5th	11.0
6-5	Sea.	W	3-2	(10)	7	9	Reyes	Mesa		22-32	5th	10.0
6-6	Sea.	L	1-4		4	7	Garcia	Ashby	Paniagua	22-33	5th	11.0
6-8	Oak.	W	5-3		11	8	Wall	Groom	Hoffman	23-33	3rd	9.5
6-9	Oak.	L	0-3		4	8	Haynes	Clement	Taylor	23-34	5th	10.5
6-10	Oak.	W	2-1		7	4	Hitchcock	Heredia	Hoffman	24-34	5th	10.0
6-11	At Hou.	L	1-2		4	5	Bergman	Williams	Wagner	24-35	5th	11.0
6-12	At Hou.	L	2-3		7	7	Lima	Wall	Wagner	24-36	5th	11.0
6-13	At Hou.	L	3-4		8	9	Reynolds	Murray	Wagner	24-37	5th	11.5
6-15	Phi.	W	6-1		11	6	Clement	Ogea		25-37	5th	12.0
6-16	Phi.	L	2-4		7	9	Wolf	Hitchcock	Gomes	25-38	5th	13.0
6-17	Phi.	L	5-7		12	12	Byrd	Williams	Gomes	25-39	5th	13.5
6-18	Pit.	W	4-2		8	8	Boehringer	Silva	Hoffman	26-39	5th	12.5
6-19	Pit.	W	5-4		10	5	Cunnane	Schmidt	Hoffman	27-39	5th	12.5
6-20	Pit.	W	6-3		12	8	Clement	Ritchie	Hoffman	28-39	5th	11.5
6-22	At L.A.	W	4-1		7	7	Hitchcock	Park	Hoffman	29-39	5th	10.0
6-23	At L.A.	W	6-2		7	5	Williams	Valdes	Hoffman	30-39	5th	9.0
6-24	At L.A.	W	2-1		6	5	Ashby	Dreifort	Miceli	31-39	5th	9.0
6-25	Col.	W	10-1		10	7	Boehringer	Bohanon		32-39	5th	8.0
6-26	Col.	W	13-6		9	10	Clement	Brownson		33-39	5th	7.0
6-27	Col.	W	5-3		8	7	Hitchcock	Kile	Hoffman	34-39	4th	7.0
6-28	Col.	W	8-7		10	14	Williams	Astacio	Hoffman	35-39	3rd	6.5
6-29	L.A.	W	4-3	(12)	13	5	Wall	Maddux		36-39	3rd	5.5
6-30	L.A.	W	11-2		14	8	Boehringer	Brown		37-39	3rd	4.5
7-1	L.A.	W	6-3		10	5	Clement	Dreifort	Hoffman	38-39	3rd	4.5
7-2	At Col.	W	15-3		19	8	Hitchcock	Astacio		39-39	3rd	4.5

Date	Opp.	Res.	Score	(inn.*)	Hits	Opp. hits	Winning pitcher	Losing pitcher	Save	Record	Pos.	GB
7-3†	At Col.	L	10-12		13	17	Ramirez	Williams	Veres	39-40		
7-3‡	At Col.	L	6-8		9	15	Jones	Murray	Veres	39-41	3rd	6.0
7-4	At Col.	W	11-0		17	6	Ashby	Bohanon		40-41	3rd	5.0
7-5	S.F	L	1-4		6	9	Ortiz	Boehringer		40-42	3rd	6.0
7-6	S.F	L	9-10		15	10	Estes	Clement	Johnstone	40-43	3rd	7.0
7-7	S.F	W	5-2		7	10	Hitchcock	Brock	Hoffman	41-43	3rd	6.0
7-9	Tex.	L	2-7		9	8	Sele	Williams		41-44	3rd	7.0
7-10	Tex.	W	5-4		8	9	Wall	Wetteland		42-44	3rd	7.0
7-11	Tex.	W	6-2		11	4	Miceli	Loaiza		43-44	3rd	6.0
7-15	At Sea.	W	3-2		7	8	Cunnane	Mesa	Miceli	44-44	3rd	5.0
7-16	At Sea.	W	2-1		8	9	Hitchcock	Fassero	Hoffman	45-44	3rd	4.0
7-17	At Sea.	L	1-9		5	11	Garcia	Williams		45-45	3rd	5.0
7-18	At Ana.	W	6-3		14	10	Boehringer	Fyhrie	Hoffman	46-45	3rd	4.0
7-19	At Ana.	W	4-1	(10)	8	9	Miceli	Hasegawa	Hoffman	47-45	3rd	3.0
7-20	At Ana.	W	2-1		5	6	Ashby	Petkovsek	Hoffman	48-45	3rd	2.0
7-21	At S.F	L	2-10		7	12	Ortiz	Hitchcock		48-46	3rd	3.0
7-22	At S.F	W	8-7		11	7	Williams	Rueter	Hoffman	49-46	3rd	2.0
7-23	At Hou.	L	4-7		8	7	Hampton	Wall		49-47	3rd	3.5
7-24	At Hou.	L	2-5		8	10	Holt	Clement	Wagner	49-48	3rd	4.0
7-25	At Hou.	L	2-5		8	11	Reynolds	Ashby		49-49	3rd	4.0
7-26	Ari.	L	0-2		6	7	Reynoso	Hitchcock	Mantei	49-50	3rd	5.0
7-27	Ari.	L	3-4		7	10	Olson	Reyes	Mantei	49-51	3rd	6.0
7-28	Ari.	L	4-7		6	10	Daal	Boehringer	Plesac	49-52	3rd	7.0
7-30	Hou.	L	1-5		6	8	Reynolds	Clement		49-53	3rd	8.0
7-31	Hou.	L	5-8		7	10	Henry	Miceli		49-54	3rd	9.0
8-1	Hou.	W	10-3		15	6	Hitchcock	Lima		50-54	3rd	8.0
8-2	At StL.	L	5-6		10	9	Bottenfield	Williams	Croushore	50-55	3rd	9.0
8-3	At StL.	L	0-6		4	9	Oliver	Boehringer		50-56	3rd	9.0
8-4	At StL.	L	6-7		6	13	Slocumb	Wall	Croushore	50-57	3rd	10.0
8-5	At StL.	W	10-3		10	6	Ashby	Luebbers	Hoffman	51-57	3rd	9.5
8-6	At Mon.	W	12-10		17	9	Hitchcock	Smith	Hoffman	52-57	3rd	8.5
8-7	At Mon.	L	1-3		4	8	Hermanson	Williams	Urbina	52-58	3rd	9.5
8-8	At Mon.	L	2-4		7	13	Kline	Reyes	Urbina	52-59	3rd	10.5
8-9	At Mon.	L	0-8		7	11	Powell	Clement		52-60	3rd	11.5
8-10	At N.Y.	L	3-4		9	15	Wendell	Ashby	Benitez	52-61	3rd	12.5
8-11	At N.Y.	L	5-12		6	14	Mahomes	Hitchcock		52-62	3rd	13.5
8-12	At N.Y.	L	3-9		5	11	Leiter	Williams		52-63	T3rd	14.0
8-13	Fla.	L	3-4		10	13	Meadows	Boehringer	Alfonseca	52-64	T3rd	14.0
8-14	Fla.	W	6-4		10	9	Clement	Sanchez	Hoffman	53-64	T3rd	13.0
8-15	Fla.	W	7-6		15	10	Ashby	Springer	Hoffman	54-64	3rd	13.0
8-16	N.Y.	L	3-4	(10)	2	10	Cook	Cunnane	Benitez	54-65	3rd	14.0
8-17	N.Y.	W	3-2		5	5	Williams	Leiter	Hoffman	55-65	3rd	14.0
8-18	N.Y.	L	1-9		6	15	Yoshii	Spencer		55-66	3rd	15.0
8-20	At Atl.	L	3-4	(11)	6	7	Remlinger	Reyes		55-67	T3rd	15.0
8-21	At Atl.	L	2-6		8	10	Maddux	Ashby		55-68	T3rd	16.0
8-22	At Atl.	L	2-3		6	9	Rocker	Miceli		55-69	5th	17.0
8-23	At Phi.	W	7-6		12	9	Williams	Ogea	Hoffman	56-69	4th	17.0
8-24	At Phi.	L	2-18		5	22	Byrd	Spencer		56-70	5th	18.0
8-25	At Phi.	L	1-15		6	14	Person	Clement		56-71	5th	19.0
8-26	Mil.	W	4-3		8	8	Ashby	Coppinger	Hoffman	57-71	4th	19.0
8-27	Mil.	W	8-7		9	15	Whiteside	Wickman		58-71	4th	18.0
8-28	Mil.	L	4-6		9	11	Nomo	Williams	Wickman	58-72	5th	19.0
8-29	Mil.	W	5-4	(10)	10	3	Hoffman	Wickman		59-72	5th	19.0
8-30	Chi.	W	8-4		10	11	Wall	Heredia		60-72	4th	19.0
8-31	Chi.	W	7-3		9	5	Ashby	Bowie		61-72	4th	18.0
9-1	Chi.	L	0-1		4	2	Trachsel	Hitchcock	Adams	61-73	4th	18.0
9-3	At Fla.	W	6-3		9	8	Williams	Burnett	Hoffman	62-73	4th	17.0
9-4	At Fla.	L	4-6		3	6	Fernandez	Carlyle	Alfonseca	62-74	4th	18.0
9-5	At Fla.	W	5-2		9	6	Clement	Nunez	Hoffman	63-74	4th	18.0
9-6	At Pit.	W	4-3		6	8	Ashby	Ritchie	Hoffman	64-74	4th	17.5
9-7	At Pit.	L	1-3		4	7	Schmidt	Hitchcock	Silva	64-75	4th	18.5
9-8	At Pit.	W	7-4	(10)	11	10	Hoffman	Wilkins		65-75	4th	18.5
9-9	Mon.	W	10-3		17	6	Carlyle	Vazquez		66-75	3rd	17.5
9-10	Mon.	W	10-3		10	8	Clement	Powell		67-75	3rd	17.5
9-11	Mon.	L	4-5		10	7	Thurman	Ashby	Urbina	67-76	3rd	18.5
9-12	Mon.	L	4-8		12	12	Hermanson	Hitchcock	Urbina	67-77	3rd	19.5
9-13	Atl.	W	3-0		11	4	Williams	Mulholland	Hoffman	68-77	3rd	19.5
9-14	Atl.	L	4-11		7	14	Millwood	Carlyle		68-78	3rd	20.5
9-15	Atl.	W	4-1		9	4	Clement	Smoltz	Hoffman	69-78	3rd	19.5
9-17	S.F	L	2-4		8	8	Nathan	Ashby	Nen	69-79	3rd	19.5
9-18	S.F	W	11-5		13	8	Hitchcock	Gardner		70-79	3rd	19.5
9-19	S.F	W	6-3		9	9	Williams	Estes	Hoffman	71-79	3rd	19.5
9-20	Cin.	L	1-12		3	15	Neagle	Carlyle		71-80	3rd	19.5
9-21	Cin.	W	6-2		9	7	Clement	Williamson		72-80	3rd	19.5
9-22	Cin.	L	3-4		9	8	Villone	Ashby	Graves	72-81	3rd	20.5
9-24	At L.A.	L	1-5		6	10	Brown	Hitchcock		72-82	4th	21.5
9-25	At L.A.	W	3-2		5	5	Williams	Herges	Hoffman	73-82	T3rd	21.5
9-26	At L.A.	L	7-10		6	13	Checo	Miceli		73-83	4th	22.5
9-29†	At StL.	L	3-4		5	8	Oliver	Wall	Painter	73-84		
9-29‡	At StL.	L	5-6	(10)	10	9	Acevedo	Guzman		73-85	4th	24.0
9-30	At Ari.	L	3-5		6	11	Johnson	Hitchcock	Mantei	73-86	4th	25.0
10-1	At Ari.	W	6-1		12	6	Williams	Stottlemyre		74-86	4th	24.0
10-2	At Ari.	L	5-7		7	7	Kim	Whisenant	Mantei	74-87	4th	25.0
10-3	At Ari.	L	3-10		7	11	Anderson	Murray		74-88	4th	26.0

Monthly records: April (9-13), May (10-17), June (18-9), July (12-15), August (12-18), September (12-14), October (1-2).
*Innings, if other than nine. †First game of a doubleheader. ‡Second game of a doubleheader. §At Monterrey, Mex.

MEMORABLE GAMES

June 28 at San Diego

Damian Jackson stole five bases as the Padres conducted a track meet against the bumbling Colorado Rockies. The club stole nine bases, a franchise record, in the 8-7 win. Jackson's total matched the club record shared by Alan Wiggins (May 17, 1984) and Tony Gwynn (Sept. 20, 1986). The victory was San Diego's 10th in a row en route to 14 consecutive wins.

Colorado	AB	R	H	RBI	San Diego	AB	R	H	RBI
D.Hamilton, cf	5	1	2	0	Q.Veras, 2b	4	1	0	0
N.Perez, ss	5	1	1	1	Owens, cf-lf	5	2	2	0
L.Walker, rf	4	1	2	3	R.Sanders, rf	4	1	1	3
Bichette, lf	5	2	2	2	Vander Wal, lf	2	1	2	2
Castilla, 3b	5	0	2	0	R.Rivera, cf	1	0	0	0
Helton, 1b	5	1	1	0	Joyner, 1b	3	1	1	0
K.Abbott, 2b	4	0	1	0	G.Myers, c	1	0	0	0
Blanco, c	2	0	0	0	B.Davis, c	3	0	2	2
J.Reed, ph-c	1	0	0	0	G.Arias, 3b	4	0	0	0
Astacio, p	2	1	1	0	D.Jackson, ss	3	1	1	0
L.Harris, ph	1	0	1	1	W.Williams, p	2	1	1	0
Dipoto, p	0	0	0	0	Newhan, ph	1	0	0	0
Echevarria, ph	1	0	1	0	Wall, p	0	0	0	0
D.Lee, p	0	0	0	0	Nevin, ph	1	0	0	0
					Cunnane, p	0	0	0	0
					Hoffman, p	0	0	0	0
Totals	**40**	**7**	**14**	**7**	**Totals**	**34**	**8**	**10**	**7**

Colorado ....100 011 103 —7
San Diego ....101 042 00x —8

E—Castilla 2 (14), Blanco (3), Helton (3), Q.Veras (7). DP—Colorado 1. LOB—Colorado 9, San Diego 6. 2B—Castilla (14), B.Davis (1). 3B—D.Hamilton (3). HR—L.Walker (20), Bichette 2 (16), Vander Wal (6). SB—Q.Veras (11), Owens 2 (15), R.Sanders (18), D.Jackson 5 (20). CS—R.Sanders (4). SF—L.Walker, Vander Wal.

Colorado	IP	H	R	ER	BB	SO
Astacio (L, 7-6)	5	8	6	5	1	4
Dipoto	2	2	2	0	0	3
D.Lee	1	0	0	0	1	0

San Diego	IP	H	R	ER	BB	SO
W.Williams (W, 4-5)	6	8	3	2	2	3
Wall	2	3	1	1	0	3
Cunnane	0	2	2	2	0	0
Hoffman (S, 19)	1	1	1	1	0	0

HBP—Q.Veras by Dipoto. WP—Dipoto. U—HP, Bell. 1B, Froemming. 2B, Hu.Wendelstedt. 3B, Nelson. T—3:03. A—41,107.

August 6 at Montreal

Tony Gwynn becomes the 22nd player in history to record 3,000 hits in his career with a first-inning single off of Dan Smith. He was joined in the modest festivities by his proud mother as he calmly waved to the crowd. And in typical Tony Gwyyn fashion, the hit was only the first of four on the night in a San Diego win.

San Diego	AB	R	H	RBI	Montreal	AB	R	H	RBI
Q.Veras, 2b	5	4	3	0	M.Martinz, cf	4	0	0	0
C.Reyes, p	0	0	0	0	Mota, p	0	0	0	0
Hoffman, p	0	0	0	0	Telford, p	0	0	0	0
Gwynn, rf	5	1	4	0	W.Gurrero, ph	1	0	1	2
R.Rivera, pr-cf	0	1	0	0	Barrett, 3b	5	1	1	0
R.Sanders, lf-rf	5	1	2	1	Ro.White, lf	3	0	0	1
Nevin, 3b	5	2	2	4	V.Guerrero, rf	4	2	2	1
Joyner, 1b	4	0	1	0	Widger, c	4	2	2	1
Owens, cf-lf	5	2	2	1	Fullmer, 1b	2	0	0	0
B.Davis, c	5	1	2	1	Ayala, p	0	0	0	0
D.Jackson, ss	4	0	1	1	J.Motn, ph-cf	2	2	2	1
Hitchcock, p	3	0	0	0	O.Cabrera, ss	3	1	1	3
Cunnane, p	0	0	0	0	Mordecai, 2b	3	0	0	0
Vander Wal, ph	1	0	0	0	Merced, ph	1	1	0	0
Miceli, p	0	0	0	0	D.Smith, p	0	0	0	0
Magadan, ph	0	0	0	1	Smart, p	1	0	0	0
Giovanola, 2b	0	0	0	0	Andrews, 1b	3	1	0	0
Totals	**42**	**12**	**17**	**9**	**Totals**	**36**	**10**	**9**	**9**

San Diego ....410 201 022—12
Montreal ....200 100 403—10

E—Q.Veras (11), Nevin (4), Giovanola (2), Ro.White (7), V.Guerrero 2 (15), D.Smith (2), Barrett (10). DP—San Diego 2, Montreal 2. LOB—San Diego 7, Montreal 1. 2B—Q.Veras (19), R.Sanders (15), Nevin (13), B.Davis (10), J.Mouton (4). 3B—Barrett (2), W.Guerrero (5). HR—Nevin (15), V.Guerrero (23), Widger (12), O.Cabrera (7). SB—R.Sanders (27), Owens (27), D.Jackson (25), R.Rivera (10). SF—Magadan, Ro.White.

San Diego	IP	H	R	ER	BB	SO
Hitchcock (W, 11-8)	6	6	6	6	0	5
Cunnane (H, 5)	1	1	1	1	0	1
Miceli (H, 7)	1	0	0	0	0	0
C.Reyes	0.2	1	3	0	1	0
Hoffman (S, 28)	0.1	1	0	0	0	0

Montreal	IP	H	R	ER	BB	SO
D.Smith (L, 3-6)	0.2	5	4	4	1	0
Smart	3.1	6	3	3	1	1
Ayala	3	2	1	0	0	3
Mota	1.2	4	4	4	1	3
Telford	0.1	0	0	0	0	0

WP—Ayala. Balks—Mota. U—HP, Davidson. 1B, Danley. 2B, Montague. 3B, Winters. T—3:18. A—13,540.

BATTING

Name	G	TPA	AB	R	H	TB	2B	3B	HR	RBI	Avg.	Obp.	Slg.	SH	SF	HP	BB	IBB	SO	SB	CS	GDP	vs RHP AB	vs RHP Avg.	vs RHP HR	vs RHP RBI	vs LHP AB	vs LHP Avg.	vs LHP HR	vs LHP RBI
Sanders, Reggie	133	550	478	92	136	252	24	7	26	72	.285	.376	.527	0	1	6	65	1	108	36	13	10	336	.277	18	56	142	.303	8	16
Veras, Quilvio	132	545	475	95	133	180	25	2	6	41	.280	.368	.379	1	2	2	65	0	88	30	17	7	343	.277	4	29	132	.288	2	12
Owens, Eric	149	485	440	55	117	172	22	3	9	61	.266	.327	.391	2	2	3	38	2	50	33	7	12	310	.281	5	40	130	.231	4	21
Gwynn, Tony	111	446	411	59	139	196	27	0	10	62	.338	.381	.477	0	4	2	29	5	14	7	2	15	272	.346	4	36	139	.324	6	26
Rivera, Ruben	147	475	411	65	80	167	16	1	23	48	.195	.295	.406	0	4	5	55	1	143	18	7	9	271	.192	15	30	140	.200	8	18
Jackson, Damian	133	447	388	56	87	138	20	2	9	39	.224	.320	.356	0	3	3	53	3	105	34	10	2	271	.240	7	33	117	.188	2	6
Nevin, Phil	128	441	383	52	103	202	27	0	24	85	.269	.352	.527	1	5	1	51	1	82	1	0	7	246	.268	13	47	137	.270	11	38
Joyner, Wally	110	386	323	34	80	113	14	2	5	43	.248	.363	.350	0	3	2	58	6	54	0	1	8	242	.248	2	27	81	.247	3	16
Davis, Ben	76	293	266	29	65	96	14	1	5	30	.244	.307	.361	0	2	0	25	3	70	2	1	9	199	.246	4	19	67	.239	1	11
Magadan, Dave	116	300	248	20	68	88	12	1	2	30	.274	.377	.355	0	7	0	45	2	36	1	3	10	210	.286	2	27	38	.211	0	3
Vander Wal, John	132	288	246	26	67	103	18	0	6	41	.272	.368	.419	0	3	2	37	1	59	2	1	5	228	.285	6	39	18	.111	0	2
Gomez, Chris	76	265	234	20	59	72	8	1	1	15	.252	.331	.308	2	1	1	27	3	49	1	2	6	166	.235	1	8	68	.294	0	7
Arias, George	55	170	164	20	40	69	8	0	7	20	.244	.271	.421	0	0	0	6	0	54	0	0	6	97	.247	4	13	67	.239	3	7
Leyritz, Jim	50	154	134	17	32	61	5	0	8	21	.239	.331	.455	0	1	4	15	1	37	0	0	4	79	.266	3	10	55	.200	5	11
Myers, Greg	50	141	128	9	37	50	4	0	3	15	.289	.355	.391	0	0	0	13	2	14	0	0	5	110	.300	3	14	18	.222	0	1
Gonzalez, Wiki	30	85	83	7	21	34	2	1	3	12	.253	.271	.410	0	0	1	1	0	8	0	0	5	43	.349	2	8	40	.150	1	4
Baerga, Carlos	33	89	80	6	20	27	1	0	2	5	.250	.318	.338	1	0	2	6	0	14	1	0	2	70	.243	2	4	10	.300	0	1
Williams, Woody	34	80	73	4	13	17	4	0	0	6	.178	.197	.233	4	1	0	2	0	19	0	1	0	57	.193	0	3	16	.125	0	3
Ashby, Andy	31	72	62	3	8	10	2	0	0	2	.129	.169	.161	7	0	0	3	0	25	0	0	1	52	.096	0	1	10	.300	0	1
Hitchcock, Sterling	33	71	61	4	5	5	0	0	0	0	.082	.125	.082	7	0	0	3	0	34	0	0	1	45	.111	0	0	16	.000	0	0
Giovanola, Ed	56	69	58	10	11	13	0	1	0	3	.190	.294	.224	1	1	0	9	0	8	2	0	1	46	.196	0	3	12	.167	0	0
Clement, Matt	31	62	52	7	4	4	0	0	0	1	.077	.143	.077	6	0	0	4	0	28	0	0	1	39	.103	0	1	13	.000	0	0
Darr, Mike	25	53	48	6	13	20	1	0	2	3	.271	.340	.417	0	0	0	5	0	18	2	1	1	43	.279	2	3	5	.200	0	0
Newhan, David	32	44	43	7	6	13	1	0	2	6	.140	.159	.302	0	0	0	1	0	11	2	1	0	37	.135	2	6	6	.167	0	0
Matthews Jr., Gary	23	45	36	4	8	8	0	0	0	7	.222	.378	.222	0	0	0	9	0	9	2	0	1	16	.438	0	5	20	.050	0	2
Boehringer, Brian	33	20	16	0	1	1	0	0	0	0	.063	.167	.063	2	0	0	2	0	9	0	0	1	10	.100	0	0	6	.000	0	0
Murray, Heath	22	15	13	1	2	2	0	0	0	0	.154	.214	.154	1	0	0	1	0	9	0	0	0	11	.182	0	0	2	.000	0	0
Garcia, Carlos	6	12	11	1	2	2	0	0	0	0	.182	.250	.182	0	0	0	1	0	3	0	0	2	2	.500	0	0	9	.111	0	0
Spencer, Stan	9	12	10	0	0	0	0	0	0	0	.000	.091	.000	1	0	1	0	0	3	0	0	0	2	.000	0	0	8	.000	0	0
Carlyle, Buddy	7	11	9	1	2	2	0	0	0	1	.222	.364	.222	0	0	0	2	0	3	0	0	1	5	.000	0	0	4	.500	0	1
Hoffman, Trevor	64	3	3	0	1	2	1	0	0	2	.333	.333	.667	0	0	0	0	0	0	0	0	0	3	.333	0	2	0	.000	0	0
Cunnane, Will	24	3	3	0	0	0	0	0	0	0	.000	.000	.000	0	0	0	0	0	1	0	0	0	2	.000	0	0	1	.000	0	0
Miceli, Dan	66	1	1	0	0	0	0	0	0	0	.000	.000	.000	0	0	0	0	0	1	0	0	0	0	.000	0	0	1	.000	0	0
Reyes, Carlos	65	1	1	0	0	0	0	0	0	0	.000	.000	.000	0	0	0	0	0	1	0	0	0	1	.000	0	0	0	.000	0	0
Wall, Donne	55	1	1	0	0	0	0	0	0	0	.000	.000	.000	0	0	0	0	0	1	0	0	0	0	.000	0	0	1	.000	0	0
Almanzar, Carlos	28	1	1	0	0	0	0	0	0	0	.000	.000	.000	0	0	0	0	0	1	0	0	0	1	.000	0	0	0	.000	0	0
Vosberg, Ed	15	0	0	0	0	0	0	0	0	0	.000	.000	.000	0	0	0	0	0	0	0	0	0	0	.000	0	0	0	.000	0	0
Whiteside, Matt	10	0	0	0	0	0	0	0	0	0	.000	.000	.000	0	0	0	0	0	0	0	0	0	0	.000	0	0	0	.000	0	0
Rivera, Roberto	12	0	0	0	0	0	0	0	0	0	.000	.000	.000	0	0	0	0	0	0	0	0	0	0	.000	0	0	0	.000	0	0
Whisenant, Matt	19	0	0	0	0	0	0	0	0	0	.000	.000	.000	0	0	0	0	0	0	0	0	0	0	.000	0	0	0	.000	0	0
Guzman, Domingo	7	0	0	0	0	0	0	0	0	0	.000	.000	.000	0	0	0	0	0	0	0	0	0	0	.000	0	0	0	.000	0	0

Players with more than one N.L. team

Name	G	TPA	AB	R	H	TB	2B	3B	HR	RBI	Avg.	Obp.	Slg.	SH	SF	HP	BB	IBB	SO	SB	CS	GDP	vs RHP AB	vs RHP Avg.	vs RHP HR	vs RHP RBI	vs LHP AB	vs LHP Avg.	vs LHP HR	vs LHP RBI
Myers, Atl.	34	86	72	10	16	24	2	0	2	9	.222	.337	.333	0	1	0	13	2	16	0	0	1	110	.300	3	14	18	.222	0	1
Myers, S.D.-Atl.	84	227	200	19	53	74	6	0	5	24	.265	.348	.370	0	1	0	26	4	30	0	0	6	171	.269	5	21	29	.241	0	3
Vosberg, Ari.	4	0	0	0	0	0	0	0	0	0	.000	.000	.000	0	0	0	0	0	0	0	0	0	0	.000	0	0	0	.000	0	0
Vosberg, S.D.-Ari.	19	0	0	0	0	0	0	0	0	0	.000	.000	.000	0	0	0	0	0	0	0	0	0	0	.000	0	0	0	.000	0	0

PITCHING

Name	W	L	Pct.	ERA	IP	H	R	ER	HR	SH	SF	HB	BB	IBB	SO	G	GS	CG	ShO	GF	Sv	vs. RH AB	vs. RH Avg.	vs. RH HR	vs. RH RBI	vs. LH AB	vs. LH Avg.	vs. LH HR	vs. LH RBI
Williams, Woody	12	12	.500	4.41	208.1	213	106	102	33	9	9	2	73	5	137	33	33	0	0	0	0	438	.276	23	60	356	.258	10	41
Ashby, Andy	14	10	.583	3.80	206.0	204	95	87	26	10	1	7	54	4	132	31	31	4	3	0	0	434	.240	17	50	356	.281	9	35
Hitchcock, Sterling	12	14	.462	4.11	205.2	202	99	94	29	9	6	5	76	6	194	33	33	1	0	0	0	638	.254	22	72	158	.253	7	18
Clement, Matt	10	12	.455	4.48	180.2	190	106	90	18	7	6	9	86	2	135	31	31	0	0	0	0	375	.235	7	31	320	.319	11	57
Boehringer, Brian	6	5	.545	3.24	94.1	97	38	34	10	6	4	1	35	4	64	33	11	0	0	8	0	215	.298	7	26	148	.223	3	12
Reyes, Carlos	2	4	.333	3.72	77.1	76	38	32	11	5	3	0	24	4	57	65	0	0	0	23	1	171	.228	7	26	128	.289	4	24
Wall, Donne	7	4	.636	3.07	70.1	58	31	24	11	1	1	0	23	3	53	55	0	0	0	12	0	157	.242	8	26	108	.185	3	9
Miceli, Dan	4	5	.444	4.46	68.2	67	39	34	7	4	2	2	36	5	59	66	0	0	0	28	2	159	.264	5	21	93	.269	2	13
Hoffman, Trevor	2	3	.400	2.14	67.1	48	23	16	5	1	3	0	15	2	73	64	0	0	0	54	40	137	.182	4	11	107	.215	1	12
Murray, Heath	0	4	.000	5.76	50.0	60	33	32	7	3	2	1	26	4	25	22	8	0	0	1	0	152	.289	6	24	50	.320	1	7
Spencer, Stan	0	7	.000	9.16	38.1	56	44	39	11	4	0	1	11	1	36	9	8	0	0	1	0	85	.353	5	17	82	.317	6	20
Carlyle, Buddy	1	3	.250	5.97	37.2	36	28	25	7	1	2	2	17	0	29	7	7	0	0	0	0	78	.205	4	14	62	.323	3	13
Almanzar, Carlos	0	0	.000	7.47	37.1	48	32	31	6	2	1	3	15	2	30	28	0	0	0	11	0	91	.275	4	19	61	.377	2	12
Cunnane, Will	2	1	.667	5.23	31.0	34	19	18	8	2	0	0	12	3	22	24	0	0	0	2	0	78	.231	6	14	38	.421	2	6
Whisenant, Matt	0	1	.000	3.68	14.2	10	6	6	0	0	0	0	10	1	10	19	0	0	0	4	0	25	.240	0	6	25	.160	0	2
Whiteside, Matt	1	0	1.000	13.91	11.0	19	17	17	1	1	1	0	5	0	9	10	0	0	0	4	0	32	.375	0	8	16	.438	1	6
Vosberg, Ed	0	0	.000	9.72	8.1	16	11	9	1	2	2	2	3	0	6	15	0	0	0	3	0	18	.444	0	5	20	.400	1	7
Rivera, Roberto	1	2	.333	3.86	7.0	6	4	3	1	1	1	0	3	0	3	12	0	0	0	3	0	7	.571	1	1	18	.111	0	3
Guzman, Domingo	0	1	.000	21.60	5.0	13	12	12	1	2	0	0	3	2	4	7	0	0	0	2	0	14	.500	1	6	14	.429	0	2
Giovanola, Ed	0	0	.000	0.00	1.1	1	0	0	0	0	0	0	2	0	0	1	0	0	0	1	0	5	.200	0	0	0	.000	0	0

PITCHERS WITH MORE THAN ONE N.L. TEAM

Name	W	L	Pct.	ERA	IP	H	R	ER	HR	SH	SF	HB	BB	IBB	SO	G	GS	CG	ShO	GF	Sv	vs. RH AB	vs. RH Avg.	vs. RH HR	vs. RH RBI	vs. LH AB	vs. LH Avg.	vs. LH HR	vs. LH RBI
Vosberg, Ari.	0	1	.000	3.38	2.2	6	1	1	0	0	0	0	0	0	2	4	0	0	0	0	0	18	.444	0	5	20	.400	1	7
Vosberg, S.D.-Ari.	0	1	.000	8.18	11.0	22	12	10	1	2	2	2	3	0	8	19	0	0	0	2	0	25	.400	0	5	26	.462	1	8

INDIVIDUAL STATISTICS

FIELDING

FIRST BASEMEN

Player	Pct.	G	PO	A	E	TC	DP
Joyner, Wally	.995	105	731	66	4	801	83
Magadan, Dave	.985	42	186	15	3	204	19
Vander Wal, John	.994	28	156	8	1	165	14
Leyritz, Jim	.984	19	116	7	2	125	10
Owens, Eric	1.000	12	77	4	0	81	7
Nevin, Phil	.988	11	74	9	1	84	5
Baerga, Carlos	-	2	0	0	0	0	0
Garcia, Carlos	1.000	1	2	0	0	2	0
Newhan, David	-	1	0	0	0	0	0

SECOND BASEMEN

Player	Pct.	G	PO	A	E	TC	DP
Veras, Quilvio	.981	118	271	334	12	617	78
Jackson, Damian	.988	21	37	44	1	82	13
Newhan, David	.970	19	28	36	2	66	10
Giovanola, Ed	.982	19	26	28	1	55	9
Baerga, Carlos	1.000	13	16	20	0	36	7
Owens, Eric	1.000	1	1	0	0	1	0

THIRD BASEMEN

Player	Pct.	G	PO	A	E	TC	DP
Nevin, Phil	.982	67	36	131	3	170	12
Magadan, Dave	.969	52	23	70	3	96	5
Arias, George	.941	50	35	93	8	136	4
Giovanola, Ed	.938	25	4	11	1	16	0
Baerga, Carlos	.882	13	5	10	2	17	2
Garcia, Carlos	.778	4	4	3	2	9	0
Owens, Eric	.714	4	1	4	2	7	0
Leyritz, Jim	-	1	0	0	0	0	0
Newhan, David	-	1	0	0	0	0	0

SHORTSTOPS

Player	Pct.	G	PO	A	E	TC	DP
Jackson, Damian	.940	100	136	258	25	419	57
Gomez, Chris	.961	75	101	195	12	308	48
Giovanola, Ed	1.000	7	6	8	0	14	2

OUTFIELDERS

Player	Pct.	G	PO	A	E	TC	DP
Rivera, Ruben	.976	143	312	8	8	328	2
Sanders, Reggie	.975	129	233	4	6	243	0
Owens, Eric	.990	116	199	4	2	205	1
Gwynn, Tony	.993	104	147	4	1	152	0
Vander Wal, John	1.000	48	71	2	0	73	1
Darr, Mike	1.000	22	28	0	0	28	0
Matthews Jr., Gary	1.000	17	22	0	0	22	0
Nevin, Phil	1.000	13	11	0	0	11	0
Jackson, Damian	1.000	3	1	1	0	2	0

CATCHERS

Player	Pct.	G	PO	A	E	TC	DP	PB
Davis, Ben	.986	74	471	29	7	507	7	4
Myers, Greg	.986	41	199	14	3	216	0	0
Nevin, Phil	.994	31	155	14	1	170	0	4
Leyritz, Jim	.994	24	150	16	1	167	0	6
Gonzalez, Wiki	.992	17	109	15	1	125	2	1

PITCHERS

Player	Pct.	G	PO	A	E	TC	DP
Miceli, Dan	.909	66	4	6	1	11	0
Reyes, Carlos	1.000	65	3	15	0	18	2
Hoffman, Trevor	1.000	64	3	5	0	8	0
Wall, Donne	.909	55	9	11	2	22	1
Hitchcock, Sterling	.969	33	7	24	1	32	0
Williams, Woody	.966	33	11	17	1	29	0
Boehringer, Brian	.944	33	8	9	1	18	0
Ashby, Andy	.961	31	14	35	2	51	4
Clement, Matt	.923	31	12	12	2	26	0
Almanzar, Carlos	.714	28	2	3	2	7	1
Cunnane, Will	1.000	24	1	4	0	5	0
Murray, Heath	1.000	22	0	8	0	8	0
Whisenant, Matt	1.000	19	2	2	0	4	0
Vosberg, Ed	.800	15	1	3	1	5	0
Rivera, Roberto	1.000	12	0	3	0	3	0
Whiteside, Matt	1.000	10	0	3	0	3	0
Spencer, Stan	1.000	9	3	2	0	5	0
Guzman, Domingo	.800	7	1	3	1	5	0
Carlyle, Buddy	1.000	7	0	3	0	3	1
Giovanola, Ed	-	1	0	0	0	0	0

PITCHING AGAINST EACH CLUB

Pitcher	Ari. W-L	Atl. W-L	Chi. W-L	Cin. W-L	Col. W-L	Fla. W-L	Hou. W-L	L.A. W-L	Mil. W-L	Mon. W-L	N.Y. W-L	Phi. W-L	Pit. W-L	S.F. W-L	StL. W-L	A.L. W-L	Total W-L
Almanzar, C.	0-0	0-0	0-0	0-0	0-0	0-0	0-0	0-0	0-0	0-0	0-0	0-0	0-0	0-0	0-0	0-0	0-0
Ashby, A.	0-1	0-2	2-0	1-1	1-1	1-0	0-1	2-0	1-0	0-1	1-1	0-0	2-0	1-1	1-0	1-1	14-10
Boehringer, B.	0-1	1-0	0-0	0-0	0-0	0-1	0-0	1-0	0-0	0-0	0-0	1-0	0-1	0-1	1-1	1-0	6-5
Carlyle, B.	0-0	0-1	0-0	0-0	0-0	0-1	0-0	0-0	0-0	0-0	0-0	0-0	0-0	0-0	0-0	0-0	1-3
Clement, M.	0-0	1-0	0-2	1-1	1-1	2-0	0-2	1-0	1-0	1-1	0-0	1-1	0-0	0-0	0-1	0-1	10-12
Cunnane, W.	0-0	0-0	0-0	0-0	0-0	0-0	0-0	0-0	0-0	0-0	0-0	0-0	0-0	0-0	0-0	1-0	2-1
Giovanola, Ed	0-0	0-0	0-0	0-0	0-0	0-0	0-0	0-0	0-0	0-0	0-0	0-0	0-0	0-0	0-0	0-0	0-0
Guzman, D.	0-0	0-0	0-0	0-0	0-0	0-0	0-0	0-0	0-0	0-0	0-0	0-0	0-0	0-1	0-0	0-0	0-1
Hitchcock, S.	0-4	1-0	0-1	0-1	3-0	0-0	1-0	1-1	0-1	1-1	0-1	1-0	0-1	2-1	0-1	2-0	12-14
Hoffman, T.	0-0	0-1	0-0	0-0	0-0	0-0	1-0	0-0	1-0	0-0	0-0	0-0	0-1	0-0	0-0	0-0	2-3
Miceli, D.	0-2	0-1	0-0	0-0	0-0	0-0	1-0	1-1	0-0	0-0	0-0	0-0	0-0	0-0	2-0	1-0	4-5
Murray, H.	0-1	0-0	0-0	0-0	0-1	0-0	0-1	0-0	0-0	0-0	0-0	0-0	0-0	0-0	0-0	0-0	0-4
Reyes, C.	0-1	0-1	0-1	0-0	0-0	0-0	0-0	0-0	0-1	1-0	0-0	0-0	0-0	0-0	1-0	0-0	2-4
Rivera, R.	0-0	0-0	0-0	0-0	0-1	0-0	0-0	0-0	0-0	0-0	0-0	0-0	0-0	0-0	0-0	0-0	1-2
Spencer, S.	0-0	0-0	0-1	0-0	0-0	0-0	0-1	0-0	0-0	0-0	0-2	0-1	0-0	0-1	0-0	0-1	0-7
Vosberg, Ed	0-0	0-0	0-0	0-0	0-0	0-0	0-0	0-0	0-0	0-0	0-0	0-0	0-0	0-0	0-0	0-0	0-0
Wall, D.	0-0	0-0	1-0	0-0	0-0	1-0	0-0	1-0	0-2	0-0	0-0	1-0	0-0	0-0	0-0	1-0	5-2
Whisenant, M.	0-1	0-0	0-0	0-0	0-0	0-0	0-0	0-0	0-0	0-0	0-0	0-0	0-0	0-0	0-0	0-0	0-1
Whiteside, M.	0-0	0-0	0-0	0-0	0-0	0-0	0-0	0-0	1-0	0-0	0-0	0-0	0-0	0-0	0-0	0-0	1-0
Williams, W.	2-0	1-0	0-0	1-1	1-1	1-0	0-1	0-0	2-0	0-2	0-1	1-1	1-2	0-0	2-0	0-1	12-12
Totals	2-11	4-5	3-6	3-6	9-4	6-3	1-8	9-3	5-3	3-5	2-7	3-6	6-3	5-7	2-7	11-4	74-88

INTERLEAGUE: Wall 1-0, Hitchcock 1-0, Clement 0-1 vs. Athletics; Hitchcock 1-0, Wall 1-0, Cunnane 1-0, Reyes 1-0, Williams 0-1, Ashby 0-1 vs. Mariners; Miceli 1-0, Wall 1-0, Williams 0-1 vs. Rangers; Boehringer 1-0, Miceli 1-0, Ashby 1-0 vs. Angels. Total: 11-4.

MISCELLANEOUS

HOME RUNS BY PARK

At Anaheim (3): Vander Wal 1, Rivera 1, Davis 1.
At Arizona (6): Gwynn 1, Veras 1, Owens 1, Nevin 1, Rivera 1, Newhan 1.
At Atlanta (1): Nevin 1.
At Chicago (NL) (8): Nevin 2, Rivera 2, Arias 2, Vander Wal 1, Owens 1.
At Cincinnati (3): Leyritz 1, Owens 1, Arias 1.
At Colorado (15): Nevin 3, Sanders 2, Rivera 2, Gwynn 1, Joyner 1, Baerga 1, Leyritz 1, Vander Wal 1, Owens 1, Arias 1, Jackson 1.
At Florida (2): Gwynn 1, Davis 1.
At Houston (5): Rivera 2, Myers 1, Sanders 1, Nevin 1.
At Los Angeles (8): Sanders 2, Rivera 2, Gonzalez 2, Joyner 1, Owens 1.
At Milwaukee (8): Sanders 2, Rivera 2, Magadan 1, Leyritz 1, Owens 1, Arias 1.
At Montreal (1): Nevin 1.
At New York (NL) (2): Sanders 1, Owens 1.
At Philadelphia (5): Sanders 2, Nevin 1, Rivera 1, Jackson 1.
At Pittsburgh (3): Gwynn 1, Sanders 1, Veras 1.
At San Diego (69): Nevin 12, Sanders 11, Rivera 10, Jackson 6, Gwynn 5, Leyritz 4, Veras 4, Joyner 2, Myers 2, Vander Wal 2, Owens 2, Arias 2, Magadan 1, Baerga 1, Gomez 1, Davis 1, Darr 1, Newhan 1, Gonzalez 1.
At San Francisco (9): Sanders 2, Davis 2, Joyner 2, Leyritz 1, Vander Wal 1, Nevin 1, Jackson 1.
At Seattle (0).
At St. Louis (5): Sanders 2, Gwynn 1, Nevin 1, Darr 1.

LOW-HIT GAMES

No-hitters: None.
One-hitters: None.
Two-hitters: None.

10-STRIKEOUT GAMES

Woody Williams 1, **Total:** 1.

FOUR OR MORE HITS IN ONE GAME

Tony Gwynn 2, Reggie Sanders 2, Wally Joyner 1, Dave Magadan 1, Chris Gomez 1, Quilvio Veras 1, Ben Davis 1, **Total:** 9.

MULTI-HOMER GAMES

Reggie Sanders 2, Tony Gwynn 1, Phil Nevin 1, Ruben Rivera 1, George Arias 1, **Total:** 6.

GRAND SLAMS

8-4: Tony Gwynn (off St. Louis's Kent Mercker).

PINCH HITTERS

(Minimum 5 at-bats)

Name	AB	Avg.	HR	RBI
Vander Wal, John	52	.231	0	12
Magadan, Dave	32	.219	0	3
Owens, Eric	26	.154	0	3
Nevin, Phil	20	.300	2	8
Veras, Quilvio	13	.000	0	0

Name	AB	Avg.	HR	RBI
Gonzalez, Wiki	12	.333	1	4
Baerga, Carlos	12	.167	1	1
Leyritz, Jim	11	.364	2	3
Rivera, Ruben	9	.111	0	1
Arias, George	8	.375	0	0
Myers, Greg	8	.250	1	2
Joyner, Wally	8	.000	0	1
Jackson, Damian	7	.143	0	0
Giovanola, Ed	6	.167	0	1
Matthews Jr., Gary	6	.000	0	1
Darr, Mike	5	.000	0	0
Newhan, David	5	.000	0	0

DEBUTS

5-23: Mike Darr, PH.
6-4: David Newhan, PR.
6-4: Gary Matthews Jr., RF.
8-14: Wiki Gonzalez, C.
8-29: Buddy Carlyle, P.
9-9: Domingo Guzman, P.

GAMES BY POSITION

Catcher: Ben Davis 74, Greg Myers 41, Phil Nevin 31, Jim Leyritz 24, Wiki Gonzalez 17.
First base: Wally Joyner 105, Dave Magadan 42, John Vander Wal 28, Jim Leyritz 19, Eric Owens 12, Phil Nevin 11, Carlos Baerga 2, Carlos Garcia 1, David Newhan 1.
Second base: Quilvio Veras 118, Damian Jackson 21, Ed Giovanola 19, David Newhan 19, Carlos Baerga 13, Eric Owens 1.
Third base: Phil Nevin 67, Dave Magadan 52, George Arias 50, Ed Giovanola 25, Carlos Baerga 13, Carlos Garcia 4, Eric Owens 4, Jim Leyritz 1, David Newhan 1.
Shortstop: Damian Jackson 100, Chris Gomez 75, Ed Giovanola 7.
Outfield: Ruben Rivera 143, Reggie Sanders 129, Eric Owens 116, Tony Gwynn 104, John Vander Wal 48, Mike Darr 22, Gary Matthews Jr. 17, Phil Nevin 13, Damian Jackson 3.
Designated hitter: Tony Gwynn 2, Wally Joyner 1, Carlos Baerga 1, Reggie Sanders 1, John Vander Wal 1, Phil Nevin 1.

STREAKS

Wins: 14 (June 18-July 2).
Losses: 8 (July 23-31).
Consecutive games with at least one hit: 17, Eric Owens (June 19-July 6).
Wins by pitcher: 5, Sterling Hitchcock (June 22-July 16).

ATTENDANCE

Home: 2,523,538.
Road: 2,408,844.
Highest (home): 61,674 (April 24 vs. Arizona).
Highest (road): 57,430 (April 8 vs. San Francisco).
Lowest (home): 12,713 (May 10 vs. Florida).
Lowest (road): 7,545 (August 9 vs. Montreal).

SAN FRANCISCO GIANTS

DAY BY DAY

Date	Opp.	Res.	Score	(inn.*)	Hits	Opp. hits	Winning pitcher	Losing pitcher	Save	Record	Pos.	GB
4-5	At Cin.	W	11-8		15	12	Embree	Hudek	Nen	1-0	T1st	...
4-6	At Cin.	W	7-6		11	11	Tavarez	Graves	Nen	2-0	T1st	...
4-7	At Cin.	W	8-3		7	6	Ortiz	Avery		3-0	T1st	...
4-8	S.D.	W	12-4		16	9	Estes	Spencer		4-0	1st	+1.0
4-9	S.D.	W	8-3		11	8	Brock	Clement		5-0	1st	+1.0
4-10	S.D.	L	1-11		7	12	Ashby	Gardner		5-1	T1st	...
4-11	S.D.	W	8-6		11	8	Johnstone	Rivera	Nen	6-1	1st	+0.5
4-13	Hou.	L	3-7		6	12	Hampton	Ortiz	Powell	6-2	1st	+1.0
4-14	Hou.	L	3-6		8	14	Lima	Estes	Wagner	6-3	1st	+1.0
4-15	Hou.	W	5-2		9	6	Brock	Bergman	Nen	7-3	1st	+1.0
4-16	At Ari.	L	4-10		8	14	Stottlemyre	Gardner	Anderson	7-4	1st	+1.0
4-17	At Ari.	W	8-5		9	10	Rueter	Benes		8-4	1st	+1.0
4-18	At Ari.	L	3-12		6	11	Reynoso	Ortiz		8-5	1st	+1.0
4-19	Fla.	W	5-4		5	7	Johnstone	Alfonseca	Nen	9-5	1st	+2.0
4-20	Fla.	L	2-7		7	11	Meadows	Brock	Edmondson	9-6	1st	+1.0
4-21	Fla.	W	4-0		5	5	Nathan	Springer		10-6	1st	+1.0
4-22	Col.	L	5-8		9	13	Bohanon	Rueter	Veres	10-7	1st	+0.5
4-23	Col.	W	7-2		10	6	Ortiz	Kile		11-7	1st	+0.5
4-24	Col.	W	8-4		11	4	Estes	Astacio		12-7	1st	+1.5
4-25	Col.	W	7-6	(10)	10	9	Embree	DeJean	Nen	13-7	1st	+1.5
4-27	At Mon.	W	3-2	(10)	6	10	Johnstone	Kline	Nen	14-7	1st	+3.0
4-28	At Mon.	W	4-3		7	9	Nathan	Hermanson	Nen	15-7	1st	+3.0
4-29	At Mon.	W	6-5		13	9	Ortiz	Pavano	Nen	16-7	1st	+3.5
4-30	At N.Y.	L	2-7		6	14	Watson	Estes	Wendell	16-8	1st	+2.5
5-1	At N.Y.	L	4-9		7	12	Hershiser	Brock		16-9	1st	+1.5
5-2	At N.Y.	L	0-2		7	5	Cook	Johnstone	Franco	16-10	1st	+1.5
5-3	At Pit.	L	8-9		13	13	Loiselle	Nen		16-11	1st	+0.5
5-4	At Pit.	W	7-4		13	10	Ortiz	Silva		17-11	1st	+1.5
5-5	At Pit.	L	3-4	(12)	7	8	Loiselle	Rodriguez		17-12	1st	+0.5
5-7	Mil.	W	4-3		7	8	Brock	Roque	Nen	18-12	1st	+1.5
5-8	Mil.	W	6-4		13	7	Rueter	Woodard	Nen	19-12	1st	+1.5
5-9	Mil.	L	2-3		7	7	Nomo	Gardner	Wickman	19-13	1st	+1.5
5-10	Atl.	W	4-1		7	4	Ortiz	Smoltz	Nen	20-13	1st	+1.5
5-11	Atl.	L	8-9	(12)	9	10	Rocker	Rodriguez		20-14	1st	+1.0
5-12	Atl.	W	5-1		12	7	Brock	Millwood		21-14	1st	+1.0
5-14	At Hou.	L	4-7		7	14	Reynolds	Rueter	Wagner	21-15	1st	+0.5
5-15	At Hou.	L	5-10		9	12	Hampton	Gardner		21-16	T1st	...
5-16	At Hou.	W	5-4	(11)	10	9	Nen	Elarton	Nathan	22-16	1st	+1.0
5-17	Ari.	L	1-12		4	13	Frascatore	Estes		22-17	T1st	...
5-18	Ari.	L	3-7		11	11	Reynoso	Brock		22-18	2nd	1.0
5-19	Ari.	W	8-3		9	6	Rueter	Benes		23-18	T1st	...
5-21	Hou.	W	4-3		12	7	Johnstone	Powell	Nen	24-18	1st	+1.5
5-22	Hou.	W	3-1		7	4	Ortiz	Holt	Nen	25-18	1st	+1.5
5-23	Hou.	L	1-4		4	5	Lima	Nathan	Wagner	25-19	1st	+1.5
5-25	At StL.	W	17-1		17	5	Brock	Jimenez		26-19	1st	+1.0
5-26	At StL.	W	7-6		12	9	Rueter	Bottenfield	Nen	27-19	1st	+1.0
5-27	At StL.	L	2-3	(12)	8	6	Slocumb	Spradlin		27-20	1st	+0.5
5-28	At Mon.	L	2-4		6	9	Telford	Ortiz	Urbina	27-21	2nd	0.5
5-29	At Mon.	L	4-7		7	11	Thurman	Estes	Urbina	27-22	2nd	1.5
5-30	At Mon.	L	4-6		10	12	Batista	Brock	Urbina	27-23	2nd	2.5
5-31	At Phi.	L	3-4		12	9	Perez	Johnstone	Gomes	27-24	2nd	3.5
6-1	At Phi.	W	6-5	(12)	8	13	Nen	Gomes		28-24	2nd	2.5
6-2	At Phi.	L	6-7		10	11	Byrd	Ortiz	Gomes	28-25	2nd	3.5
6-3	At Phi.	W	7-4		11	5	Spradlin	Schilling	Nen	29-25	2nd	3.0
6-4	Oak.	W	4-3	(15)	9	9	Spradlin	Taylor		30-25	2nd	3.0
6-5	Oak.	W	8-0		10	8	Rueter	Oquist		31-25	2nd	2.0
6-6	Oak.	L	6-7		12	8	Groom	Johnstone	Taylor	31-26	2nd	3.0
6-7	Ana.	W	5-2		5	7	Ortiz	Finley	Nen	32-26	2nd	2.0
6-8	Ana.	W	6-2		12	5	Estes	Sparks		33-26	2nd	1.0
6-9	Ana.	L	1-2		4	7	Belcher	Brock	Percival	33-27	2nd	2.0
6-11	At Sea.	L	3-7		9	10	Moyer	Gardner	Mesa	33-28	2nd	3.0
6-12	At Sea.	W	15-11		22	15	Rueter	Garcia		34-28	2nd	2.0
6-13	At Sea.	W	8-4		13	7	Tavarez	Paniagua		35-28	2nd	2.0
6-14	At Col.	L	4-5		8	7	Leskanic	Johnstone	Veres	35-29	2nd	3.0
6-15	At Col.	L	6-15		15	16	Bohanon	Brock		35-30	2nd	4.0
6-16	At Col.	W	15-2		19	6	Gardner	Kile		36-30	2nd	4.0
6-17	Chi.	W	3-2		10	4	Nen	Serafini		37-30	2nd	3.5
6-18	Chi.	W	8-5		10	8	Ortiz	Tapani	Nen	38-30	2nd	2.5
6-19	Chi.	W	11-5		9	6	Estes	Farnsworth		39-30	2nd	2.5
6-20	Chi.	W	7-6		9	11	Embree	Aguilera		40-30	2nd	1.5
6-21	Mil.	L	1-8		7	11	Nomo	Gardner		40-31	2nd	1.5
6-22	Mil.	L	6-8		8	13	Karl	Rueter		40-32	2nd	1.5
6-23	Mil.	L	6-9		13	12	Woodard	Ortiz	Wickman	40-33	2nd	1.5
6-25	L.A.	L	2-4		6	9	Brown	Estes	Shaw	40-34	2nd	2.0
6-26	L.A.	L	6-7		11	15	Mills	Nen	Shaw	40-35	2nd	2.0
6-27	L.A.	W	8-7		14	12	Gardner	Park	Nen	41-35	2nd	2.0
6-29	Col.	W	10-1		13	6	Rueter	Jones		42-35	2nd	1.0
6-30	Col.	W	4-1		8	7	Ortiz	Bohanon	Nen	43-35	T1st	...

HIGHLIGHTS

High point: With Russ Ortiz giving up only two hits over 8.2 innings, the Giants beat St. Louis, 4-2, on July 10 and took a 3 1/2-game lead in the N.L. West. It was a sizable accomplishment, considering Barry Bonds' 47-game absence after elbow surgery in April.

Low point: Reality came on September 17, when the Giants won for the 22nd time in 28 games but still trailed Arizona by six games in the division race. The club had gained only 2 1/2 games on the Diamondbacks despite the surge, dashing hopes of overtaking the front-runners.

Turning point: On August 9-11, the Giants ended a 3-9 trip in horrific fashion, blowing four-run leads in three consecutive losses to the lowly Marlins. When the Giants started the trip, they were 1.5 games out of first place; when they ended it, they were 7.5 behind.

Most valuable player: Despite being hobbled by a bad toe, second baseman Jeff Kent finished with a .290 average, 23 homers and 101 RBIs. He had one of his best months in May (.304, four homers, 20 RBIs) even though Bonds wasn't in the lineup to protect him.

Most valuable pitcher: In his first full season in the majors, righthander Ortiz emerged as one of the league's best. Displaying great stuff, he finished 18-9. One negative: He had control problems after the All-Star break, walking 66 batters in 88.1 innings.

Most improved player: First baseman J.T. Snow. Batting only from the left side, the former switch hitter improved his overall average by 26 points, to .274, from the year before. Also, he hit .231 against lefthanders compared to his .164 figure of 1998, and the improvement helped keep him—and his Gold Glove—in the lineup against lefties.

Most pleasant surprise: Rookie righthander Joe Nathan, who shored up the rotation by going 7-4 with a 4.18 ERA.

Key injuries: Just two weeks into the season, left fielder Bonds went down with his elbow injury and didn't return until June 9. The injury bothered him even after he returned. Third baseman Bill Mueller suffered a toe fracture in his first at-bat of the season and was out for six weeks. Rookie outfielder Armando Rios, projected as a key reserve, hurt his shoulder in June and was sidelined nearly 2.5 months. And Chris Brock, an effective fifth starter, suffered a season-ending knee injury in late July.

Notable: The Giants closed out 40 years at Candlestick/3Com Park by drawing 2 million-plus fans for only the third time in franchise history. The final game at Candlestick was a 9-4 loss to the Dodgers on September 30. ... Bonds collected his 2,000th career hit against Atlanta's Tom Glavine on September 11. ... Five Giants hit at least 20 homers—Bonds, Kent, Snow, Rich Aurilia and Ellis Burks. ... Snow won his fifth consecutive Gold Glove.

—HENRY SCHULMAN

MISCELLANEOUS

RECORDS

1999 regular-season record: 86-76 (2nd in N.L. West); 49-32 at home; 37-44 on road; 23-21 vs. N.L. East; 32-21 vs. N.L. Central; 24-26 vs. N.L. West; 7-8 vs. A.L. West; 18-28 vs. lefthanded starters; 68-48 vs. righthanded starters; 71-63 on grass; 15-13 on turf; 40-34 in daytime; 46-42 at night; 27-23 in one-run games; 7-7 in extra-inning games; 1-0-0 in double-headers.

Team record past five years: 400-393 (.504, ranks 8th in league in that span).

TEAM LEADERS

Batting average: Marvin Benard (.290).
At-bats: J.T. Snow (570).
Runs: Marvin Benard (100).
Hits: Marvin Benard (163).
Total bases: Jeff Kent (261).
Doubles: Jeff Kent (40).
Triples: Marvin Benard (5).
Home runs: Barry Bonds (34).
Runs batted in: Jeff Kent (101).
Stolen bases: Marvin Benard (27).
Slugging percentage: Jeff Kent (.511).
On-base percentage: J.T. Snow (.370).
Wins: Russ Ortiz (18).
Earned-run average: Russ Ortiz (3.81).
Complete games: Russ Ortiz (3).
Shutouts: Shawn Estes (1).
Saves: Robb Nen (37).
Innings pitched: Russ Ortiz (207.2).
Strikeouts: Russ Ortiz (164).

Date	Opp.	Res.	Score	(inn.*)	Hits	Opp. hits	Winning pitcher	Losing pitcher	Save	Record	Pos.	GB
7-1	Col.	W	7-1		9	6	Estes	Kile		44-35	1st	+1.0
7-2	At L.A.	W	6-3		8	9	Brock	Perez	Nen	45-35	1st	+1.0
7-3	At L.A.	W	9-1		12	4	Gardner	Park		46-35	1st	+2.0
7-4	At L.A.	L	1-7		5	11	Valdes	Rueter		46-36	1st	+1.0
7-5	At S.D.	W	4-1		9	6	Ortiz	Boehringer		47-36	1st	+2.0
7-6	At S.D.	W	10-9		10	15	Estes	Clement	Johnstone	48-36	1st	+3.0
7-7	At S.D.	L	2-5		10	7	Hitchcock	Brock	Hoffman	48-37	1st	+2.0
7-9	StL.	W	5-4	(11)	9	11	Rodriguez	Aybar		49-37	1st	+2.5
7-10	StL.	W	4-2		7	2	Ortiz	Jimenez	Johnstone	50-37	1st	+3.5
7-11	StL.	L	4-5		8	7	Bottenfield	Gardner	Bottalico	50-38	1st	+2.5
7-15	At Oak.	L	9-11		10	12	Jones	Nen		50-39	1st	+2.5
7-16	At Oak.	L	2-4		5	5	Heredia	Ortiz	Taylor	50-40	1st	+2.5
7-17	At Oak.	W	7-2		10	6	Rueter	Groom		51-40	1st	+2.5
7-18	At Tex.	L	4-5		9	7	Morgan	Gardner	Wetteland	51-41	1st	+2.5
7-19	At Tex.	L	7-14		10	17	Loaiza	Brock		51-42	1st	+2.5
7-20	At Tex.	L	3-6		7	10	Helling	Estes		51-43	1st	+1.5
7-21	S.D.	W	10-2		12	7	Ortiz	Hitchcock		52-43	1st	+1.5
7-22	S.D.	L	7-8		7	11	Williams	Rueter	Hoffman	52-44	1st	+0.5
7-23	Cin.	W	6-5		7	9	Spradlin	Sullivan	Nen	53-44	1st	+0.5
7-24	Cin.	L	6-7		8	6	Williamson	Nen	Graves	53-45	2nd	0.5
7-25	Cin.	L	1-2	(14)	4	5	Belinda	Nen		53-46	2nd	0.5
7-26	StL.	W	10-8		14	11	Rodriguez	Slocumb	Nen	54-46	2nd	0.5
7-27	StL.	W	2-1		7	4	Rueter	Bottenfield	Johnstone	55-46	2nd	0.5
7-28	StL.	L	3-6		7	7	Oliver	Hernandez	Bottalico	55-47	2nd	1.5
7-30	At Cin.	L	4-7		9	10	Neagle	Gardner	Williamson	55-48	2nd	2.5
7-31	At Cin.	W	11-1		15	8	Estes	Villone		56-48	2nd	2.5
8-1	At Cin.	L	1-9		6	12	Tomko	Ortiz		56-49	2nd	2.5
8-2	At Ari.	L	6-16		16	14	Reynoso	Rueter		56-50	2nd	3.5
8-3	At Ari.	W	3-1		6	3	Hernandez	Daal	Nen	57-50	2nd	2.5
8-4	At Ari.	L	4-8		8	10	Anderson	Nathan		57-51	2nd	3.5
8-6	At Atl.	L	3-7		11	10	Maddux	Estes		57-52	2nd	3.5
8-7	At Atl.	L	4-15		11	16	Mulholland	Ortiz		57-53	2nd	4.5
8-8	At Atl.	W	5-2		8	8	Rueter	Millwood	Nen	58-53	2nd	4.5
8-9	At Fla.	L	4-5		12	12	Sanchez	Johnstone		58-54	2nd	5.5
8-10	At Fla.	L	7-8	(12)	13	13	Edmondson	Rodriguez		58-55	2nd	6.5
8-11	At Fla.	L	5-6	(10)	9	12	Sanchez	Nen		58-56	2nd	7.5
8-13	N.Y.	W	3-2		5	9	Ortiz	Yoshii	Nen	59-56	2nd	6.5
8-14	N.Y.	L	1-6		5	16	Hershiser	Rueter		59-57	2nd	6.5
8-15	N.Y.	L	5-12		12	16	Rogers	Hernandez		59-58	2nd	7.5
8-16	Mon.	W	7-4		12	8	Nathan	Armas Jr.	Nen	60-58	2nd	7.5
8-17	Mon.	L	1-2	(12)	7	10	Smith	Johnstone	Urbina	60-59	2nd	8.5
8-18	Mon.	W	5-4		7	12	Ortiz	Vazquez	Nen	61-59	2nd	8.5
8-20	At Mil.	W	10-3		14	9	Rueter	Pulsipher		62-59	2nd	7.5
8-21	At Mil.	W	5-1		7	7	Hernandez	Peterson		63-59	2nd	7.5
8-22	At Mil.	W	7-3		12	12	Nathan	Eldred		64-59	2nd	7.5
8-24	At Chi.	W	12-4		18	9	Estes	Lorraine		65-59	2nd	8.0
8-25†	At Chi.	W	11-5		14	7	Ortiz	Tapani		66-59		
8-25‡	At Chi.	W	6-5		9	10	Rueter	Lieber	Nen	67-59	2nd	7.5
8-26	At Chi.	L	10-11		11	16	Adams	Nen		67-60	2nd	8.5
8-27	Pit.	L	1-4		6	9	Schmidt	Nathan	Williams	67-61	2nd	8.5
8-28	Pit.	W	6-2		13	4	Gardner	Cordova		68-61	2nd	8.5
8-29	Pit.	W	5-3		7	7	Estes	Benson	Nen	69-61	2nd	8.5
8-30	Phi.	W	6-4	(10)	9	9	Rodriguez	Brewer		70-61	2nd	8.5
8-31	Phi.	W	8-1		11	7	Rueter	Wolf		71-61	2nd	7.5
9-1	Phi.	W	5-3	(11)	11	6	Rodriguez	Gomes		72-61	2nd	6.5
9-2	Phi.	W	3-2		8	7	Nathan	Grahe	Nen	73-61	2nd	6.0
9-3	At Pit.	W	12-2		10	7	Estes	Cordova		74-61	2nd	5.0
9-4	At Pit.	W	9-2		9	5	Ortiz	Benson		75-61	2nd	5.0
9-5	At Pit.	L	4-8		8	10	Peters	Rueter		75-62	2nd	6.0
9-6	At N.Y.	L	0-3		4	4	Rogers	Gardner		75-63	2nd	6.5
9-7	At N.Y.	W	7-4		12	4	Rodriguez	Wendell	Nen	76-63	2nd	6.5
9-8	At N.Y.	L	5-7		7	10	Dotel	Estes	Benitez	76-64	2nd	7.5
9-10	Atl.	L	2-4		8	10	Remlinger	Ortiz	Rocker	76-65	2nd	8.0
9-11	Atl.	W	3-2		8	7	Rueter	Glavine	Nen	77-65	2nd	8.0
9-12	Atl.	W	8-4		13	9	Nathan	Maddux		78-65	2nd	8.0
9-14	Fla.	W	3-0		8	4	Estes	Dempster		79-65	2nd	8.5
9-15	Fla.	W	4-3		9	5	Ortiz	Springer	Nen	80-65	2nd	7.5
9-16	Fla.	W	6-5		9	9	Patrick	Nunez	Nen	81-65	2nd	7.0
9-17	At S.D.	W	4-2		8	8	Nathan	Ashby	Nen	82-65	2nd	6.0
9-18	At S.D.	L	5-11		8	13	Hitchcock	Gardner		82-66	2nd	7.0
9-19	At S.D.	L	3-6		9	9	Williams	Estes	Hoffman	82-67	2nd	8.0
9-20	At L.A.	L	5-6		7	7	Borbon	Embree		82-68	2nd	8.0
9-21	At L.A.	L	4-9		6	11	Williams	Rueter		82-69	2nd	9.0
9-22	At L.A.	W	5-4		8	6	Gardner	Borbon	Nen	83-69	2nd	9.0
9-23	At L.A.	L	3-5		5	9	Park	Hernandez	Shaw	83-70	2nd	9.5
9-24	Ari.	L	3-11		5	17	Johnson	Estes		83-71	2nd	10.5
9-25	Ari.	L	3-7		8	14	Olson	Nen		83-72	2nd	11.5
9-26	Ari.	L	1-7		6	14	Daal	Rueter		83-73	2nd	12.5
9-28	L.A.	L	3-6		5	12	Park	Nathan		83-74	2nd	14.0
9-29	L.A.	W	5-1		7	12	Hernandez	Brown	Patrick	84-74	2nd	13.0
9-30	L.A.	L	4-9		8	15	Williams	Estes		84-75	2nd	14.0
10-1	At Col.	W	9-4		11	7	Ortiz	Thomson		85-75	2nd	13.0
10-2	At Col.	W	16-7		18	13	Rueter	Wright		86-75	2nd	13.0
10-3	At Col.	L	8-9		12	11	Veres	Embree		86-76	2nd	14.0

Monthly records: April (16-8), May (11-16), June (16-11), July (13-13), August (15-13), September (13-14), October (2-1).
*Innings, if other than nine. † First game of a doubleheader. ‡ Second game of a doubleheader.

MEMORABLE GAMES

May 25 at St. Louis

Local boy Bill Mueller hit a grand slam for one of his three hits, and Jeff Kent and J.T. Snow also homered as the Giants went into Busch Stadium and pounded the St. Louis Cardinals. Kent and Snow each had three-quarters of the cycle by the fifth inning, both lacking a triple. The only Cardinals run came, appropriately, on a Mark McGwire homer.

San Fran.	AB	R	H	RBI	St. Louis	AB	R	H	RBI
Benard, cf	3	2	0	0	Bragg, cf	4	0	3	0
Mueller, 3b	5	3	2	4	Renteria, ss	3	0	0	0
Snow, 1b	4	2	3	3	McGee, lf	1	0	1	0
Hayes, 1b	2	0	0	0	McGwire, 1b	3	1	1	1
Kent, 2b	4	2	3	3	Marrro, pr-1b	1	0	0	0
W.Dlgdo, 2b-ss	1	1	0	0	Lankford, lf	3	0	0	0
Burks, rf	3	2	1	1	Polanco, 3b	1	0	0	0
Rios, rf	2	0	0	0	Tatis, 3b	2	0	0	0
Javier, lf	5	1	3	2	Dunston, ss	1	0	0	0
Aurilia, ss	4	1	1	0	E.Davis, rf	2	0	0	0
Santngelo, 2b	1	0	0	0	Heiserman, p	1	0	0	0
Servais, c	5	2	3	2	Mohler, p	0	0	0	0
Brock, p	3	1	1	0	Radinsky, p	0	0	0	0
Estes, ph	1	0	0	0	D.Oliver, ph	1	0	0	0
R.Rodrguez, p	0	0	0	0	A.Castillo, c	4	0	0	0
Spradlin, p	0	0	0	0	McEwing, 2b	4	0	0	0
Embree, p	0	0	0	0	J.Jimenez, p	1	0	0	0
					Mercker, p	0	0	0	0
					T.Howard, rf	1	0	0	0
Totals	**43**	**17**	**17**	**15**	**Totals**	**33**	**1**	**5**	**1**

San Francisco ....104 370 200—17
St. Louis ....000 100 000 —1

E—W.Delgado (1), Mercker (2), Renteria (8). DP—St. Louis 1. LOB—San Francisco 8, St. Louis 7. 2B—Snow (10), Kent (12), Javier 2 (8), Servais (5). HR—Mueller (1), Snow (3), Kent (7), Burks (6), McGwire (13). CS—Javier (3). S—Brock.

San Francisco	IP	H	R	ER	BB	SO
Brock (W, 5-3)	6	4	1	1	1	4
R.Rodriguez	1	0	0	0	1	0
Spradlin	1	1	0	0	0	1
Embree	1	0	0	0	0	1

St. Louis	IP	H	R	ER	BB	SO
J.Jimenez (L, 2-5)	3.2	6	7	7	3	1
Mercker	1	4	6	1	1	2
Heiserman	2.1	6	4	4	3	1
Mohler	1	0	0	0	0	1
Radinsky	1	1	0	0	0	0

HBP—Burks by J.Jimenez. WP—Heiserman. PB—A.Castillo. U—HP, Poncino. 1B, Meals. 2B, Rippley. 3B, Darling. T—2:58. A—45,029.

August 11 at Florida

The Giants blew a four-run lead for the third straight game against the Florida Marlins and lost 6-5. The sweep at Miami ended a disastrous 3-9 road trip and left the Giants $7^1/_2$ games out of first place in the N.L. West. The Giants stranded 11 runners on the afternoon, which ended with Mike Lowell's 10th-inning single off Robb Nen.

San Fran.	AB	R	H	RBI	Florida	AB	R	H	RBI
Benard, cf	5	1	1	0	L.Castillo, 2b	5	0	1	0
R.Martinez, 2b	3	1	0	0	Berg, ss	3	0	0	0
Santngelo, 2b	1	0	0	0	Edmndson, p	0	0	0	0
Snow, 1b	4	1	0	0	Kotsay, rf	1	0	0	0
Bonds, lf	3	1	2	1	J.Sanchez, p	0	0	0	0
Hayes, 3b	5	0	1	0	Aven, lf	4	1	1	0
Nen, p	0	0	0	0	Millar, 1b	4	0	0	0
Javier, rf	5	1	1	2	P.Wilson, cf	4	1	1	0
Mayne, c	3	0	1	0	Bautista, rf	3	1	3	1
Aurilia, ss	5	0	2	2	Almanza, p	0	0	0	0
Estes, p	3	0	1	0	Looper, p	0	0	0	0
Spradlin, p	0	0	0	0	Dunwoody, rf	1	0	1	1
Burks, ph	1	0	0	0	Clpnski, 3b-ss	4	2	2	0
Johnstone, p	0	0	0	0	Fabregas, c	4	0	1	0
Embree, p	0	0	0	0	A.Fernndez, p	2	0	0	0
Mueller, 3b	1	0	0	0	Lowll, ph-3b	3	1	2	4
Totals	**39**	**5**	**9**	**5**	**Totals**	**38**	**6**	**12**	**6**

San Francisco...............000 005 000 0 —5
Florida...........................010 003 001 1 —6

E—Aurilia (24), A.Fernandez (1), P.Wilson (6). LOB—San Francisco 11, Florida 11. 3B—P.Wilson (4). HR—Lowell (7). SB—Berg (2), Millar (1), Clapinski (1). CS—Berg (1). S—R.Martinez, Fabregas.

San Francisco	IP	H	R	ER	BB	SO
Estes	6	7	4	4	4	4
Spradlin (H, 8)	1	1	0	0	0	1
Johnstone (H, 25)	0.2	1	0	0	0	0
Embree (H, 13)	0.1	0	0	0	0	0
Nen (BS 7; L 3-6)	1.1	3	2	1	1	0

Florida	IP	H	R	ER	BB	SO
A.Fernandez	6	5	5	4	4	4
Edmondson	1	1	0	0	0	0
Almanza	0.1	1	0	0	1	1
Looper	1	0	0	0	0	0
J.Sanchez (W, 4-4)	1.2	2	0	0	1	1

HBP—Millar by Spradlin. PB—Mayne. Balks— J.Sanchez. U—HP, Meals. 1B, Poncino. 2B, Darling. 3B, Rippley. T—3:27. A—16,709.

1999 REVIEW

BATTING

Name	G	TPA	AB	R	H	TB	2B	3B	HR	RBI	Avg.	Obp.	Slg.	SH	SF	HP	BB	IBB	SO	SB	CS	GDP	vs RHP AB	Avg.	HR	RBI	vs LHP AB	Avg.	HR	RBI
Snow, J.T.	161	668	570	93	156	257	25	2	24	98	.274	.370	.451	1	6	5	86	7	121	0	4	16	401	.292	21	75	169	.231	3	23
Benard, Marvin	149	625	562	100	163	257	36	5	16	64	.290	.359	.457	1	1	6	55	2	97	27	14	5	448	.297	13	53	114	.263	3	11
Aurilia, Rich	152	614	558	68	157	248	23	1	22	80	.281	.336	.444	3	5	5	43	3	71	2	3	16	416	.276	17	58	142	.296	5	22
Kent, Jeff	138	585	511	86	148	261	40	2	23	101	.290	.366	.511	0	8	5	61	3	112	13	6	12	379	.296	16	71	132	.273	7	30
Mueller, Bill	116	492	414	61	120	150	24	0	2	36	.290	.388	.362	8	2	3	65	1	52	4	2	11	301	.306	0	22	113	.248	2	14
Burks, Ellis	120	469	390	73	110	222	19	0	31	96	.282	.394	.569	0	4	6	69	2	86	7	5	11	274	.255	22	66	116	.345	9	30
Bonds, Barry	102	434	355	91	93	219	20	2	34	83	.262	.389	.617	0	3	3	73	9	62	15	2	6	227	.260	22	58	128	.266	12	25
Javier, Stan	112	371	333	49	92	118	15	1	3	30	.276	.335	.354	7	1	1	29	4	55	13	6	4	239	.251	0	19	94	.340	3	11
Mayne, Brent	117	374	322	39	97	135	32	0	2	39	.301	.389	.419	1	3	5	43	5	65	2	2	16	266	.305	2	31	56	.286	0	8
Hayes, Charlie	95	301	264	33	54	83	9	1	6	48	.205	.292	.314	0	3	1	33	0	41	3	1	8	147	.211	2	25	117	.197	4	23
Santangelo, F.P.	113	326	254	49	66	98	17	3	3	26	.260	.406	.386	5	2	11	53	0	54	12	4	1	122	.238	1	14	132	.280	2	12
Servais, Scott	69	217	198	21	54	79	10	0	5	21	.273	.327	.399	3	0	3	13	2	31	0	0	7	109	.248	2	12	89	.303	3	9
Rios, Armando	72	177	150	32	49	79	9	0	7	29	.327	.420	.527	1	1	1	24	1	35	7	4	3	124	.339	5	21	26	.269	2	8
Martinez, Ramon E.	61	165	144	21	38	59	6	0	5	19	.264	.327	.410	6	1	0	14	0	17	1	2	2	90	.267	3	12	54	.259	2	7
Mirabelli, Doug	33	98	87	10	22	31	6	0	1	10	.253	.327	.356	0	1	1	9	1	25	0	0	1	62	.258	0	9	25	.240	1	1
Delgado, Wilson	35	78	71	7	18	22	2	1	0	3	.254	.312	.310	1	0	1	5	0	9	1	0	2	47	.213	0	2	24	.333	0	1
Ortiz, Russ	33	81	71	7	14	19	2	0	1	8	.197	.230	.268	7	0	0	3	0	17	0	0	1	56	.196	0	7	15	.200	1	1
Estes, Shawn	42	75	61	8	10	14	4	0	0	5	.164	.215	.230	10	0	1	3	0	21	0	1	0	47	.170	0	4	14	.143	0	1
Rueter, Kirk	33	70	58	6	9	11	2	0	0	5	.155	.194	.190	8	1	0	3	0	6	0	0	3	37	.216	0	4	21	.048	0	1
Gardner, Mark	29	48	39	2	4	7	0	0	1	3	.103	.167	.179	6	0	0	3	0	15	0	0	3	27	.111	1	2	12	.083	0	1
Brock, Chris	19	42	35	4	7	7	0	0	0	4	.200	.262	.200	4	0	0	3	0	8	0	0	0	25	.200	0	1	10	.200	0	3
Nathan, Joe	19	35	28	1	5	6	1	0	0	1	.179	.233	.214	5	0	0	2	0	6	0	0	0	26	.192	0	1	2	.000	0	0
Murray, Calvin	15	21	19	1	5	7	2	0	0	5	.263	.333	.368	0	0	0	2	0	4	1	0	0	7	.429	0	3	12	.167	0	2
Canizaro, Jay	12	19	18	5	8	13	2	0	1	9	.444	.474	.722	0	0	0	1	0	2	1	0	0	8	.750	1	6	10	.200	0	3
Hernandez, Livan	11	26	18	1	4	4	0	0	0	1	.222	.300	.222	6	0	1	1	0	5	0	0	0	10	.100	0	1	8	.375	0	0
Guzman, Edwards	14	16	15	0	0	0	0	0	0	0	.000	.000	.000	1	0	0	0	0	4	0	0	0	14	.000	0	0	1	.000	0	0
Rodriguez, Felix	47	8	6	3	2	6	1	0	1	3	.333	.429	1.000	1	0	1	0	0	1	0	0	0	3	.333	1	1	3	.333	0	2
Tavarez, Julian	47	5	5	0	1	1	0	0	0	0	.200	.200	.200	0	0	0	0	0	2	0	0	0	4	.250	0	1	0	.000	0	0
del Toro, Miguel	14	5	4	0	0	0	0	0	0	0	.000	.000	.000	1	0	0	0	0	3	0	0	1	3	.000	0	0	1	.000	0	0
Rodriguez, Rich	62	2	1	1	1	1	0	0	0	1	1.000	1.000	1.000	1	0	0	0	0	0	0	0	0	1	1.000	0	1	0	.000	0	0
Spradlin, Jerry	59	1	1	0	0	0	0	0	0	0	.000	.000	.000	0	0	0	0	0	0	0	0	0	1	.000	0	0	0	.000	0	0
Patrick, Bronswell	6	1	1	0	0	0	0	0	0	0	.000	.000	.000	0	0	0	0	0	1	0	0	0	0	.000	0	0	1	.000	0	0
Nen, Robb	72	0	0	0	0	0	0	0	0	0	.000	.000	.000	0	0	0	0	0	0	0	0	0	0	.000	0	0	0	.000	0	0
Embree, Alan	68	0	0	0	0	0	0	0	0	0	.000	.000	.000	0	0	0	0	0	0	0	0	0	0	.000	0	0	0	.000	0	0
Johnstone, John	62	0	0	0	0	0	0	0	0	0	.000	.000	.000	0	0	0	0	0	0	0	0	0	0	.000	0	0	0	.000	0	0

PLAYERS WITH MORE THAN ONE N.L. TEAM

Name	G	TPA	AB	R	H	TB	2B	3B	HR	RBI	Avg.	Obp.	Slg.	SH	SF	HP	BB	IBB	SO	SB	CS	GDP	vs RHP AB	Avg.	HR	RBI	vs LHP AB	Avg.	HR	RBI
Hernandez, Fla.	20	47	45	5	13	21	2	0	2	7	.289	.283	.467	1	1	0	0	0	5	0	0	2	10	.100	0	1	8	.375	0	0
Hernandez, Fla.-S.F.	31	73	63	6	17	25	2	0	2	8	.270	.288	.397	7	1	1	1	0	10	0	0	2	47	.234	1	3	16	.375	1	3
Javier, Hou.	20	75	64	12	21	27	4	1	0	4	.328	.405	.422	1	1	0	9	0	8	3	1	2	239	.251	0	19	94	.340	3	11
Javier, S.F.-Hou.	132	446	397	61	113	145	19	2	3	34	.285	.347	.365	8	2	1	38	4	63	16	7	6	288	.271	0	23	109	.321	3	11

PITCHING

Name	W	L	Pct.	ERA	IP	H	R	ER	HR	SH	SF	HB	BB	IBB	SO	G	GS	CG	ShO	GF	Sv	vs RH AB	Avg.	HR	RBI	vs LH AB	Avg.	HR	RBI
Ortiz, Russ	18	9	.667	3.81	207.2	189	109	88	24	11	6	6	125	5	164	33	33	3	0	0	0	413	.237	14	61	361	.252	10	35
Estes, Shawn	11	11	.500	4.92	203.0	209	121	111	21	14	3	5	112	2	159	32	32	1	1	0	0	658	.267	17	90	122	.270	4	12
Rueter, Kirk	15	10	.600	5.41	184.2	219	118	111	28	6	4	2	55	2	94	33	33	1	0	0	0	589	.312	27	99	148	.236	1	10
Gardner, Mark	5	11	.313	6.47	139.0	142	103	100	27	6	10	8	57	2	86	29	21	1	0	2	0	306	.258	16	63	226	.279	11	31
Brock, Chris	6	8	.429	5.48	106.2	124	69	65	18	5	3	4	41	2	76	19	19	0	0	0	0	203	.261	11	28	213	.318	7	32
Nathan, Joe	7	4	.636	4.18	90.1	84	45	42	17	2	0	1	46	0	54	19	14	0	0	2	1	216	.250	9	23	130	.231	8	19
Nen, Robb	3	8	.273	3.98	72.1	79	36	32	8	5	1	0	27	3	77	72	0	0	0	64	37	157	.210	3	17	130	.354	5	23
Rodriguez, Felix	2	3	.400	3.80	66.1	67	32	28	6	2	3	2	29	2	55	47	0	0	0	26	0	153	.288	5	30	103	.223	1	14
Johnstone, John	4	6	.400	2.60	65.2	48	24	19	8	4	0	1	20	5	56	62	0	0	0	11	3	149	.208	4	12	88	.193	4	8
Hernandez, Livan	3	3	.500	4.38	63.2	66	32	31	6	4	2	0	21	2	47	10	10	0	0	0	0	132	.258	3	18	115	.278	3	9
Embree, Alan	3	2	.600	3.38	58.2	42	22	22	6	3	2	5	26	2	53	68	0	0	0	13	0	120	.200	2	9	90	.200	4	17
Spradlin, Jerry	3	1	.750	4.19	58.0	59	31	27	4	1	0	10	29	6	52	59	0	0	0	14	0	161	.255	3	24	67	.269	1	10
Rodriguez, Rich	3	0	1.000	5.24	56.2	60	33	33	8	5	2	1	28	5	44	62	0	0	0	8	0	123	.276	5	19	96	.271	5	20
Tavarez, Julian	2	0	1.000	5.93	54.2	65	38	36	7	3	2	8	25	3	33	47	0	0	0	12	0	136	.265	4	21	84	.345	3	20
del Toro, Miguel	0	0	.000	4.18	23.2	24	11	11	5	0	0	0	11	0	20	14	0	0	0	2	0	61	.246	3	7	30	.300	2	6
Patrick, Bronswell	1	0	1.000	10.13	5.1	9	7	6	1	0	1	0	3	0	6	6	0	0	0	2	1	19	.421	1	4	5	.200	0	2

PITCHERS WITH MORE THAN ONE N.L. TEAM

Name	W	L	Pct.	ERA	IP	H	R	ER	HR	SH	SF	HB	BB	IBB	SO	G	GS	CG	ShO	GF	Sv	vs RH AB	Avg.	HR	RBI	vs LH AB	Avg.	HR	RBI
Hernandez, Fla.	5	9	.357	4.76	136.0	161	78	72	17	3	4	2	55	3	97	20	20	2	0	0	0	132	.258	3	18	115	.278	3	9
Hernandez, Fla.-S.F.	8	12	.400	4.64	199.2	227	110	103	23	7	6	2	76	5	144	30	30	2	0	6	0	411	.280	11	52	384	.292	12	44

INDIVIDUAL STATISTICS

FIELDING

FIRST BASEMEN

Player	Pct.	G	PO	A	E	TC	DP
Snow, J.T.	.996	160	1221	122	6	1349	123
Hayes, Charlie	1.000	20	103	8	0	111	9
Kent, Jeff	1.000	1	7	2	0	9	2
Servais, Scott	1.000	1	1	0	0	1	0

SECOND BASEMEN

Player	Pct.	G	PO	A	E	TC	DP
Kent, Jeff	.984	133	279	326	10	615	90
Martinez, Ramon E.	.992	27	50	68	1	119	15
Delgado, Wilson	.963	15	17	9	1	27	2
Santangelo, F.P.	1.000	11	13	21	0	34	1
Canizaro, Jay	1.000	4	2	5	0	7	1
Mueller, Bill	1.000	3	2	0	0	2	0

THIRD BASEMEN

Player	Pct.	G	PO	A	E	TC	DP
Mueller, Bill	.958	108	81	195	12	288	17
Hayes, Charlie	.940	55	27	83	7	117	3
Martinez, Ramon E.	1.000	11	5	9	0	14	0
Guzman, Edwards	1.000	5	2	7	0	9	0
Santangelo, F.P.	1.000	3	1	0	0	1	0

SHORTSTOPS

Player	Pct.	G	PO	A	E	TC	DP
Aurilia, Rich	.957	150	218	411	28	657	97
Delgado, Wilson	.932	20	22	33	4	59	10
Martinez, Ramon E.	.878	12	11	25	5	41	4
Santangelo, F.P.	-	1	0	0	0	0	0

OUTFIELDERS

Player	Pct.	G	PO	A	E	TC	DP
Benard, Marvin	.988	142	323	5	4	332	1
Burks, Ellis	.991	107	210	3	2	215	2
Bonds, Barry	.984	96	177	4	3	184	2
Javier, Stan	.976	94	158	4	4	166	3
Santangelo, F.P.	.993	81	130	4	1	135	1
Rios, Armando	.978	53	84	5	2	91	1
Murray, Calvin	1.000	9	6	0	0	6	0
Hayes, Charlie	-	1	0	0	0	0	0

CATCHERS

Player	Pct.	G	PO	A	E	TC	DP	PB
Mayne, Brent	.995	105	597	47	3	647	9	2
Servais, Scott	.992	62	362	23	3	388	5	6
Mirabelli, Doug	1.000	30	156	11	0	167	2	0
Guzman, Edwards	1.000	1	1	0	0	1	0	0

PITCHERS

Player	Pct.	G	PO	A	E	TC	DP
Nen, Robb	.857	72	2	10	2	14	1
Embree, Alan	1.000	68	2	3	0	5	0
Rodriguez, Rich	1.000	62	6	11	0	17	1
Johnstone, John	1.000	62	5	8	0	13	0
Spradlin, Jerry	.750	59	2	4	2	8	1
Rodriguez, Felix	1.000	47	5	11	0	16	1
Tavarez, Julian	.929	47	7	6	1	14	1
Rueter, Kirk	.978	33	15	30	1	46	5
Ortiz, Russ	1.000	33	13	31	0	44	2
Estes, Shawn	.980	32	18	31	1	50	1
Gardner, Mark	1.000	29	7	18	0	25	1
Brock, Chris	.952	19	11	9	1	21	2
Nathan, Joe	1.000	19	3	11	0	14	0
del Toro, Miguel	1.000	14	1	3	0	4	2
Hernandez, Livan	1.000	10	6	13	0	19	1
Patrick, Bronswell	.500	6	0	1	1	2	0

PITCHING AGAINST EACH CLUB

Pitcher	Ari. W-L	Atl. W-L	Chi. W-L	Cin. W-L	Col. W-L	Fla. W-L	Hou. W-L	L.A. W-L	Mil. W-L	Mon. W-L	N.Y. W-L	Phi. W-L	Pit. W-L	S.D. W-L	StL. W-L	A.L. W-L	Total W-L
Brock, C.	0-1	0-0	0-0	0-0	0-0	0-1	1-0	1-0	1-0	0-1	0-1	0-0	0-0	1-1	1-0	0-2	6-8
del Toro, M.	0-0	0-0	0-0	0-0	0-0	0-0	0-0	0-0	0-0	0-0	0-0	0-0	0-0	0-0	0-0	0-0	0-0
Embree, A.	0-0	0-0	1-0	1-0	1-1	0-0	0-0	0-1	0-0	0-0	0-0	0-0	0-0	0-0	0-0	0-0	3-2
Estes, S.	0-2	0-1	2-0	1-0	2-0	1-0	0-1	0-2	0-0	0-1	0-2	0-0	2-0	2-1	0-0	1-1	11-11
Gardner, M.	0-1	0-0	0-0	0-1	1-0	0-0	0-0	3-0	0-2	0-0	0-1	0-0	0-1	0-2	0-2	0-2	5-11
Hernandez, L.	1-0	0-0	0-0	0-0	0-0	0-0	0-1	1-1	1-0	0-0	0-1	0-0	0-0	0-0	0-1	0-0	3-5
Johnstone, J.	0-0	0-0	0-0	0-0	0-0	1-1	0-0	0-0	1-1	0-1	0-1	0-0	1-0	0-0	0-1	0-1	4-6
Nathan, J.	0-1	1-0	0-0	0-0	0-1	0-0	1-0	0-1	1-0	2-0	1-0	0-0	0-0	1-0	0-0	0-0	7-4
Nen, R.	0-1	0-0	1-1	0-2	0-0	0-1	1-0	0-1	0-0	0-0	0-0	0-0	0-1	0-1	0-0	0-1	3-8
Ortiz, R.	0-1	1-2	2-0	1-1	3-0	1-0	1-1	0-0	0-1	2-1	1-0	0-1	0-1	2-0	1-1	1-1	18-9
Patrick, B.	0-0	0-0	0-0	0-0	0-0	0-0	1-0	0-0	0-0	0-0	0-0	0-0	0-0	0-0	0-0	0-0	1-0
Rodriguez, F.	0-0	0-1	0-0	0-0	0-0	0-0	0-0	0-1	0-0	0-0	0-0	1-0	0-0	0-0	0-0	0-0	1-3
Rodriguez, R.	0-0	0-0	0-0	0-0	0-0	0-0	0-0	0-0	0-1	0-0	0-0	2-0	0-0	0-0	0-0	0-0	2-3
Rueter, K.	2-2	2-0	1-0	0-0	2-1	0-0	0-1	0-2	2-1	0-0	0-1	0-0	0-0	0-1	2-0	3-0	15-10
Spradlin, J.	0-0	0-0	0-0	1-0	0-0	0-0	0-0	0-0	0-0	0-0	0-0	0-0	0-0	0-0	0-1	1-0	3-1
Tavarez, Ju.	0-0	0-0	0-0	1-0	0-0	0-0	0-0	0-1	0-0	0-0	0-0	0-0	0-0	0-0	1-0	1-0	2-0
Totals	3-9	5-4	7-1	5-4	9-4	5-4	4-5	5-8	5-4	5-4	2-7	6-2	5-4	7-5	6-3	7-8	86-76

INTERLEAGUE: Rueter 2-0, Spradlin 1-0, Johnstone 0-1, Nen 0-1, Ortiz 0-1 vs. Athletics; Tavarez 1-0, Rueter 1-0, Gardner 0-1 vs. Mariners; Gardner 0-1, Brock 0-1, Estes 0-1 vs. Rangers; Ortiz 1-0, Estes 1-0, Brock 0-1 vs. Angels. Total: 7-8.

MISCELLANEOUS

HOME RUNS BY PARK

At Arizona (10): Aurilia 3, Snow 2, Benard 2, Burks 1, Hayes 1, Servais 1.
At Atlanta (3): Burks 1, Hayes 1, Santangelo 1.
At Chicago (NL) (8): Bonds 3, Snow 2, Hayes 1, Kent 1, Benard 1.
At Cincinnati (11): Bonds 5, Javier 1, Burks 1, Hayes 1, Kent 1, Aurilia 1, Martinez 1.
At Colorado (11): Snow 4, Kent 2, Aurilia 2, Rios 2, Burks 1.
At Florida (3): Burks 2, Snow 1.
At Houston (3): Servais 1, Aurilia 1, Rios 1.
At Los Angeles (9): Bonds 4, Benard 2, Burks 1, Snow 1, Aurilia 1.
At Milwaukee (7): Bonds 3, Burks 2, Kent 1, Martinez 1.
At Montreal (1): Aurilia 1.
At New York (NL) (2): Burks 1, Servais 1.
At Oakland (2): Snow 1, Aurilia 1.
At Philadelphia (4): Burks 1, Mayne 1, Servais 1, Snow 1.
At Pittsburgh (7): Kent 3, Burks 1, Servais 1, Snow 1, Aurilia 1.
At San Diego (8): Burks 2, Kent 2, Bonds 1, Aurilia 1, Benard 1, Canizaro 1.
At San Francisco (87): Bonds 16, Burks 16, Kent 11, Aurilia 9, Benard 9, Snow 7, Rios 4, Martinez 3, Javier 2, Hayes 2, Santangelo 2, Gardner 1, Mayne 1, Rodriguez 1, Mueller 1, Mirabelli 1, Ortiz 1.
At St. Louis (6): Snow 2, Burks 1, Kent 1, Aurilia 1, Mueller 1.
At Texas (3): Bonds 2, Snow 1.

LOW-HIT GAMES

No-hitters: None.
One-hitters: None.
Two-hitters: None.

10-STRIKEOUT GAMES

Russ Ortiz 2, Kirk Rueter 1, **Total:** 3.

FOUR OR MORE HITS IN ONE GAME

Brent Mayne 3, Jeff Kent 3 (including two five-hit games), Marvin Benard 3 (including one five-hit game), Rich Aurilia 2, Stan Javier 1, Barry Bonds 1, Ellis Burks 1, J.T. Snow 1, **Total:** 15.

MULTI-HOMER GAMES

Barry Bonds 7, Ellis Burks 3, Stan Javier 1, Jeff Kent 1, Rich Aurilia 1, Marvin Benard 1, Armando Rios 1, **Total:** 15.

GRAND SLAMS

5-25: Bill Mueller (off St. Louis's Kent Mercker).
6-18: Armando Rios (off Chicago's Doug Creek).
7-21: Ellis Burks (off San Diego's Sterling Hitchcock).
9-3: Jeff Kent (off Pittsburgh's Francisco Cordova).

PINCH HITTERS

(Minimum 5 at-bats)

Name	AB	Avg.	HR	RBI
Javier, Stan	20	.150	0	1
Hayes, Charlie	19	.105	0	4
Mayne, Brent	18	.389	0	4
Rios, Armando	18	.333	2	3
Santangelo, F.P.	18	.167	0	1
Martinez, Ramon E.	15	.133	0	0
Servais, Scott	11	.364	1	3
Benard, Marvin	11	.364	0	2
Burks, Ellis	9	.222	0	3
Canizaro, Jay	8	.500	1	2
Murray, Calvin	7	.143	0	2
Guzman, Edwards	7	.000	0	0
Delgado, Wilson	6	.333	0	0
Mueller, Bill	6	.000	0	0
Mirabelli, Doug	5	.200	0	1
Kent, Jeff	5	.000	0	0

DEBUTS

4-6: Miguel del Toro, P.
4-6: Edwards Guzman, PH.
4-21: Joe Nathan, P.
6-22: Calvin Murray, PH.

GAMES BY POSITION

Catcher: Brent Mayne 105, Scott Servais 62, Doug Mirabelli 30, Edwards Guzman 1.
First base: J.T. Snow 160, Charlie Hayes 20, Scott Servais 1, Jeff Kent 1.
Second base: Jeff Kent 133, Ramon E. Martinez 27, Wilson Delgado 15, F.P. Santangelo 11, Jay Canizaro 4, Bill Mueller 3.
Third base: Bill Mueller 108, Charlie Hayes 55, Ramon E. Martinez 11, Edwards Guzman 5, F.P. Santangelo 3.
Shortstop: Rich Aurilia 150, Wilson Delgado 20, Ramon E. Martinez 12, F.P. Santangelo 1.
Outfield: Marvin Benard 142, Ellis Burks 107, Barry Bonds 96, Stan Javier 94, F.P. Santangelo 81, Armando Rios 53, Calvin Murray 9, Charlie Hayes 1.
Designated hitter: Barry Bonds 4, Ellis Burks 3, Charlie Hayes 2, Stan Javier 1, Ramon E. Martinez 1.

STREAKS

Wins: 8 (August 28-September 4).
Losses: 5 (May 27-31, June 21-26, September 23-28).
Consecutive games with at least one hit: 12, Jeff Kent (August 30-September 11), Marvin Benard (July 31-August 14).
Wins by pitcher: 4, Russ Ortiz (April 23-May 10).

ATTENDANCE

Home: 2,078,095.
Road: 2,430,510.
Highest (home): 61,389 (September 30 vs. Los Angeles).
Highest (road): 58,333 (July 5 vs. San Diego).
Lowest (home): 9,425 (April 13 vs. Houston).
Lowest (road): 4,998 (April 28 vs. Montreal).

TEAM STATISTICS

AMERICAN LEAGUE

BATTING

Team	Avg.	G	PA	AB	R	H	TB	2B	3B	HR	RBI	SH	SF	HP	BB	IBB	SO	SB	CS	GI DP	LOB	SHO	SLG	OBP
Texas	.293	162	6388	5651	945	1653	2705	304	29	230	897	35	62	29	611	41	937	111	54	147	1176	7	.479	.361
Cleveland	.289	162	6553	5634	1009	1629	2629	309	32	209	960	54	67	55	743	41	1099	147	50	136	1234	3	.467	.373
Kansas City	.282	161	6325	5624	856	1584	2435	294	52	151	800	46	56	64	535	25	932	127	39	156	1165	4	.433	.348
New York	.282	162	6416	5568	900	1568	2521	302	36	193	855	22	53	55	718	47	978	104	57	137	1244	6	.453	.366
Toronto	.280	162	6369	5642	883	1580	2581	337	14	212	856	28	45	76	578	29	1077	119	48	129	1177	8	.457	.352
Baltimore	.279	162	6409	5637	851	1572	2522	299	21	203	804	41	55	61	615	34	890	107	46	146	1241	8	.447	.353
Boston	.278	162	6321	5579	836	1551	2497	334	42	176	808	34	56	55	597	27	928	67	39	131	1213	5	.448	.350
Chicago	.277	162	6262	5644	777	1563	2421	298	37	162	742	40	45	34	499	22	810	110	50	138	1157	7	.429	.337
Tampa Bay	.274	162	6272	5586	772	1531	2296	272	29	145	728	30	48	64	544	24	1042	73	49	157	1169	7	.411	.343
Seattle	.269	162	6310	5572	859	1499	2536	263	21	244	825	38	48	42	610	38	1095	130	45	114	1147	9	.455	.343
Minnesota	.264	161	6124	5495	686	1450	2110	285	30	105	643	24	56	49	500	28	978	118	60	151	1118	10	.384	.328
Detroit	.261	161	6095	5481	747	1433	2426	289	34	212	704	35	39	82	458	19	1049	108	70	108	1061	12	.443	.326
Oakland	.259	162	6440	5519	893	1430	2462	287	20	235	845	39	41	71	770	32	1129	70	37	129	1246	4	.446	.355
Anaheim	.256	162	6131	5494	711	1404	2170	248	22	158	673	41	42	43	511	24	1022	71	45	135	1097	11	.395	.322
Totals	.275	1133	88415	78126	11725	21447	34311	4121	419	2635	11140	507	713	780	8289	431	13966	1462	689	1914	16445	101	.439	.347

PITCHING

Team	W	L	Pct.	ERA	G	ShO	Rel.	Sv.	IP	H	TBF	R	ER	HR	SH	SF	HB	BB	IBB	SO	WP	Bk.
Boston	94	68	.580	4.00	162	12	412	50	1436.2	1396	6120	718	638	160	27	43	55	469	25	1131	28	0
New York	98	64	.605	4.13	162	10	359	50	1439.2	1402	6233	731	661	158	42	47	57	581	27	1111	49	4
Oakland	87	75	.537	4.69	162	5	406	48	1435.0	1537	6309	846	750	160	34	39	54	569	45	967	57	8
Baltimore	78	84	.481	4.77	162	11	393	33	1435.0	1468	6259	815	760	198	47	49	49	647	34	982	55	6
Anaheim	70	92	.432	4.79	162	7	400	37	1431.1	1472	6258	826	762	177	36	65	56	624	17	877	65	5
Cleveland	97	65	.599	4.89	162	6	466	46	1450.1	1503	6374	860	788	197	41	39	54	634	55	1120	54	3
Chicago	75	86	.466	4.92	162	3	409	39	1438.1	1608	6452	870	786	210	39	56	61	596	31	968	60	9
Toronto	84	78	.519	4.92	162	9	377	39	1439.0	1582	6368	862	787	191	39	57	53	575	25	1009	55	4
Minnesota	63	97	.394	5.00	161	8	417	34	1423.1	1591	6216	845	791	208	32	48	28	487	22	927	57	6
Tampa Bay	69	93	.426	5.06	162	5	453	45	1433.0	1606	6482	913	805	172	42	53	79	695	25	1055	52	5
Texas	95	67	.586	5.07	162	9	439	47	1436.1	1626	6313	859	809	186	34	52	40	509	23	979	50	2
Detroit	69	92	.429	5.17	161	6	421	33	1421.0	1528	6286	882	817	209	39	60	70	583	26	976	43	4
Seattle	79	83	.488	5.24	162	6	346	40	1433.2	1613	6471	905	834	191	34	54	71	684	39	980	63	3
Kansas City	64	97	.398	5.35	161	3	416	29	1420.2	1607	6387	921	844	202	44	53	68	643	34	831	60	6
Totals	1122	1141	.496	4.86	1133	100	5714	570	20076.2	21539	88528	11853	10832	2619	530	715	795	8296	428	13913	748	65

FIELDING

Team	PCT	G	PO	A	E	TC	DP	TP	PB
Baltimore	.986	162	4305	1781	89	6175	191	0	5
Minnesota	.985	161	4270	1613	92	5975	150	0	12
Cleveland	.983	162	4351	1739	106	6196	154	0	8
Anaheim	.983	162	4294	1723	106	6123	156	0	20
Toronto	.983	162	4317	1664	106	6087	165	0	13
Detroit	.982	161	4263	1623	106	5992	156	0	12
New York	.982	162	4319	1577	111	6007	132	0	18
Seattle	.981	162	4301	1690	113	6104	182	0	8
Texas	.981	162	4309	1730	119	6158	169	1	2
Oakland	.980	162	4315	1700	122	6137	166	0	18
Kansas City	.980	161	4262	1727	125	6114	188	0	10
Boston	.979	162	4310	1548	127	5985	132	0	31
Tampa Bay	.978	162	4299	1776	135	6210	198	0	12
Chicago	.977	162	4315	1563	136	6014	149	0	14
Totals	.981	1133	60230	23454	1593	85277	2288	1	183

PINCH HITTING

Team	BA	AB	R	H	2B	3B	HR	RBI	BB	SO	SLG
Boston	.287	101	12	29	5	0	4	22	15	28	.455
Baltimore	.276	123	15	34	3	1	4	25	13	31	.415
Oakland	.270	115	17	31	8	0	0	22	23	31	.339
Cleveland	.267	86	12	23	7	0	1	14	9	21	.384
Anaheim	.255	98	15	25	6	0	2	11	17	30	.378
Chicago	.250	72	7	18	4	0	0	11	5	11	.306
Minnesota	.250	132	15	33	5	1	2	26	23	29	.348
Texas	.244	45	9	11	2	0	1	6	9	10	.356
Toronto	.238	84	9	20	4	0	4	13	5	23	.429
New York	.234	94	5	22	4	0	1	17	17	30	.309
Detroit	.194	98	9	19	6	1	2	10	2	24	.337
Seattle	.182	99	7	18	3	0	2	12	15	17	.273
Kansas City	.156	96	8	15	2	0	0	10	11	24	.177
Tampa Bay	.145	55	7	8	4	1	0	1	8	15	.255
Totals	.236	1298	147	306	63	4	23	200	172	324	.344

DESIGNATED HITTING

Team	Avg.	AB	R	H	2B	3B	HR	RBI	BB	SO	Slg.
Texas	.323	566	104	183	28	1	43	138	94	79	.604
Seattle	.318	556	99	177	38	1	25	95	104	113	.525
Baltimore	.303	588	93	178	38	1	28	115	66	76	.514
Kansas City	.296	577	94	171	30	1	18	97	68	93	.445
Boston	.281	612	83	172	43	7	21	91	55	138	.477
Chicago	.281	573	80	161	40	1	18	93	77	83	.449
New York	.275	561	87	154	32	1	23	84	99	124	.458
Oakland	.274	562	117	154	30	0	40	125	114	155	.541
Cleveland	.265	566	82	150	31	1	24	114	87	130	.451
Minnesota	.259	572	79	148	35	5	14	82	67	123	.411
Anaheim	.258	590	66	152	29	0	29	106	51	118	.454
Tampa Bay	.257	588	92	151	19	1	39	109	78	166	.491
Detroit	.252	603	79	152	39	4	21	68	50	86	.434
Toronto	.249	610	80	152	27	0	24	81	46	130	.411
Totals	.278	8124	1235	2255	459	24	367	1398	1056	1614	.476

BATTING

Team	Avg.	G	PA	AB	R	H	TB	2B	3B	HR	RBI	SH	SF	HP	BB	IBB	SO	SB	CS	GI DP	LOB	SHO	SLG	OBP
Colorado	.288	162	6368	5717	906	1644	2696	305	39	223	863	54	46	43	508	31	863	70	43	125	1144	3	.472	.348
New York	.279	163	6454	5572	853	1553	2421	297	14	181	814	63	54	48	717	53	994	150	61	149	1267	5	.434	.363
Arizona	.277	162	6415	5658	908	1566	2595	289	46	216	865	61	60	48	588	52	1045	137	39	94	1169	6	.459	.347
Philadelphia	.275	162	6386	5598	841	1539	2412	302	44	161	797	70	41	46	631	37	1081	125	35	127	1221	7	.431	.351
Milwaukee	.273	161	6433	5582	815	1524	2378	299	30	165	777	87	51	55	658	44	1065	81	33	110	1276	6	.426	.353
Cincinnati	.272	163	6377	5649	865	1536	2549	312	37	209	820	70	44	45	569	37	1125	164	54	107	1168	3	.451	.341
San Francisco	.271	162	6448	5563	872	1507	2414	307	18	188	828	87	42	60	696	40	1028	109	56	129	1230	2	.434	.356
Houston	.267	162	6402	5485	823	1463	2306	293	23	168	784	79	58	52	728	57	1138	166	75	127	1252	5	.420	.355
Atlanta	.266	162	6351	5569	840	1481	2427	309	23	197	791	74	47	53	608	62	962	148	66	120	1155	6	.436	.341
Los Angeles	.266	162	6338	5567	793	1480	2340	253	23	187	761	74	51	52	594	34	1030	167	68	109	1173	6	.420	.339
Montreal	.265	162	6149	5559	718	1473	2376	320	47	163	680	71	28	53	438	39	939	70	51	138	1094	8	.427	.323
Florida	.263	162	6216	5578	691	1465	2203	266	44	128	655	44	56	59	479	30	1145	92	46	119	1159	7	.395	.325
St. Louis	.262	161	6353	5570	809	1461	2371	274	27	194	763	75	44	51	613	51	1202	134	48	110	1188	4	.426	.338
Pittsburgh	.259	161	6233	5468	775	1417	2292	282	40	171	735	87	45	60	573	40	1197	112	44	111	1157	7	.419	.334
Chicago	.257	162	6201	5482	747	1411	2303	255	35	189	717	65	44	39	571	38	1170	60	44	120	1130	7	.420	.329
San Diego	.252	162	6136	5394	710	1360	2119	256	22	153	671	36	40	35	631	31	1169	174	67	132	1139	7	.393	.332
Totals	.268	1296	101260	89011	12966	23880	38202	4619	512	2893	12321	1097	751	799	9602	676	17153	1959	830	1927	18922	92	.429	.342

PITCHING

Team	W	L	Pct.	ERA	G	ShO	Rel.	Sv.	IP	H	TBF	R	ER	HR	SH	SF	HB	BB	IBB	SO	WP	Bk.
Atlanta	103	59	.636	3.63	162	9	394	45	1471.0	1398	6218	661	593	142	74	41	26	507	55	1197	34	3
Arizona	100	62	.617	3.77	162	9	382	42	1467.1	1387	6233	676	615	176	46	30	49	543	48	1198	39	10
Houston	97	65	.599	3.83	162	8	339	48	1458.2	1485	6199	675	620	128	60	49	40	478	17	1204	54	0
Cincinnati	96	67	.589	3.98	163	11	381	55	1462.0	1309	6221	711	647	190	71	43	45	636	46	1081	65	3
New York	97	66	.595	4.27	163	7	439	49	1456.2	1372	6232	711	691	167	57	51	52	617	53	1172	38	4
Pittsburgh	78	83	.484	4.33	161	3	425	34	1433.1	1444	6271	782	689	160	59	45	51	633	54	1083	54	10
Los Angeles	77	85	.475	4.45	162	6	399	37	1453.0	1438	6317	787	718	192	56	34	62	594	26	1077	53	9
San Diego	74	88	.457	4.47	162	6	403	43	1420.1	1454	6147	781	705	193	70	44	35	529	48	1078	73	5
Montreal	68	94	.420	4.69	162	4	432	44	1434.1	1505	6321	853	748	152	74	50	60	572	39	1043	46	8
San Francisco	86	76	.531	4.71	162	3	450	42	1456.1	1486	6430	831	762	194	71	39	51	655	41	1076	62	7
St. Louis	75	86	.466	4.74	161	3	454	38	1445.1	1519	6427	838	761	161	85	48	63	667	38	1025	60	9
Florida	64	98	.395	4.90	162	5	453	33	1435.2	1560	6389	852	781	171	69	69	54	655	54	943	46	12
Philadelphia	77	85	.475	4.92	162	6	441	32	1438.1	1494	6348	846	787	212	69	44	58	627	24	1030	67	10
Milwaukee	74	87	.460	5.07	161	5	453	40	1442.2	1618	6477	886	813	213	60	44	51	616	42	987	64	10
Chicago	67	95	.414	5.27	162	6	441	32	1430.2	1619	6359	920	837	221	79	66	27	529	48	980	59	9
Colorado	72	90	.444	6.01	162	2	420	33	1429.0	1700	6574	1028	955	237	74	52	60	737	46	1032	70	3
Totals	1305	1286	.504	4.56	1296	93	6706	647	23134.2	23788	101163	12838	11722	2909	1074	749	784	9595	679	17206	884	112

FIELDING

Team	PCT	G	PO	A	E	TC	DP	TP	PB
New York	.989	163	4370	1607	68	6045	147	0	10
Philadelphia	.983	162	4315	1598	100	6013	144	1	13
Houston	.983	162	4376	1732	106	6214	175	0	9
Arizona	.983	162	4402	1590	104	6096	132	0	17
San Francisco	.983	162	4369	1630	105	6104	155	1	8
Cincinnati	.983	163	4386	1551	105	6042	139	0	11
Atlanta	.982	162	4413	1658	111	6182	127	0	10
Colorado	.981	162	4287	1737	118	6142	189	0	9
Milwaukee	.979	161	4328	1669	127	6124	146	1	13
Florida	.979	162	4307	1687	127	6121	150	0	10
San Diego	.979	162	4261	1633	129	6023	151	0	15
St. Louis	.978	161	4336	1634	132	6102	163	0	8
Los Angeles	.978	162	4359	1725	137	6221	137	0	13
Chicago	.977	162	4292	1597	139	6028	135	0	14
Pittsburgh	.976	161	4300	1746	147	6193	179	0	9
Montreal	.974	162	4303	1618	160	6081	125	0	16
Totals	.980	1296	69404	26412	1915	97731	2394	3	185

PINCH HITTING

Team	BA	AB	R	H	2B	3B	HR	RBI	BB	SO	SLG
Arizona	.319	188	29	60	10	1	5	41	20	47	.463
Colorado	.278	259	36	72	14	0	9	45	24	61	.436
Los Angeles	.271	188	22	51	9	2	4	32	31	42	.404
Cincinnati	.257	214	25	55	11	0	6	37	25	56	.393
Philadelphia	.255	204	31	52	13	2	5	29	29	50	.412
Montreal	.254	205	21	52	8	4	3	34	30	37	.376
Houston	.234	209	22	49	11	1	5	30	27	65	.368
Pittsburgh	.229	210	21	48	7	2	6	25	25	76	.367
Milwaukee	.227	247	22	56	7	1	4	30	31	69	.312
San Francisco	.216	194	21	42	8	0	4	29	28	47	.320
Chicago	.211	270	28	57	8	0	9	28	30	88	.330
Atlanta	.208	226	16	47	8	0	3	30	26	51	.283
St. Louis	.208	231	14	48	9	0	3	26	24	56	.286
Florida	.205	229	21	47	12	0	8	26	23	64	.362
San Diego	.203	251	21	51	8	0	7	41	33	69	.319
New York	.198	257	26	51	15	1	2	24	42	82	.288
Totals	.234	3582	376	838	158	14	82	507	448	960	.355

DESIGNATED HITTING

Team	Avg.	AB	R	H	2B	3B	HR	RBI	BB	SO	Slg.
Houston	.387	31	6	12	4	0	0	8	9	6	.516
Philadelphia	.359	39	10	14	2	0	1	6	4	5	.487
Florida	.325	40	8	13	4	0	0	5	4	4	.425
St. Louis	.320	25	4	8	2	0	0	3	2	6	.400
Atlanta	.289	38	6	11	2	0	1	9	2	6	.421
Cincinnati	.289	38	6	11	1	0	2	8	3	8	.474
Arizona	.263	38	5	10	1	0	2	4	7	8	.447
Pittsburgh	.243	37	4	9	3	0	2	6	3	9	.486
Montreal	.242	33	4	8	1	0	1	4	2	5	.364
Chicago	.227	22	4	5	1	0	1	2	3	7	.409
San Diego	.208	24	1	5	1	0	1	2	4	5	.375
New York	.194	31	7	6	2	0	1	5	8	8	.355
San Francisco	.167	36	4	6	0	0	1	7	5	7	.250
Milwaukee	.148	27	4	4	1	0	1	3	1	11	.296
Los Angeles	.143	21	4	3	0	0	0	0	4	3	.143
Colorado	.143	21	2	3	0	0	1	2	2	4	.286
Totals	.255	501	79	128	25	0	15	74	66	102	.395

TRANSACTIONS

1999 REVIEW

January 4
Twins organization signed 3B Brian Richardson.
Athletics organization signed P Kevin Jarvis.

January 5
Red Sox organization signed P Rheal Cormier, P Kip Gross.
Indians organization signed P Dave Telgheder, P Mike Walker, 3B Jeff Manto, SS Orlando Miller and C Chris Turner.

January 6
Blue Jays organization signed OF Wayne Kirby and OF Jimmy Hurst.
Reds traded OF Pat Watkins to Marlins for P Pedro Minaya.
Dodgers organization signed P Chris Haney, P Pedro Borbon, P Jaime Arnold, 3B Pete Rose Jr., C Tim Laker and C Hector Ortiz.

January 7
Athletics organization signed OF Marc Newfield.
Expos claimed P Roberto Duran on waivers from Tigers.

January 8
Giants claimed P Steve Connelly on waivers from Red Sox.

January 11
Red Sox signed P Pat Rapp.
Indians organization signed P Jim Brower and C Angelo Encarnacion.
Athletics signed P Doug Jones.
Reds signed C Brian Johnson.
Dodgers signed 3B Dave Hansen.
Brewers signed OF Rick Becker.

January 12
Angels signed OF Matt Luke.
Red Sox organization signed OF Pedro Valdes.
Dodgers traded P Darren Hall to White Sox for C Joe Sutton.
Indians organization signed P Jeff Schmidt.
Diamondbacks organization signed P Frank Castillo.
Dodgers signed P Greg Cadaret.
Mets organization signed C-IF-OF Jerry Brooks.
Cardinals signed OF Darren Bragg.

January 13
Expos organization signed C Darron Cox.
Devil Rays organization signed OF Billy Ashley.
Rangers organization signed C John Marzano.

January 14
Reds signed 1B Hal Morris.
Astros traded C Brad Ausmus and P C.J. Nitkowski to Tigers for C Paul Bako, P Dean Crow, P Mark Persails, P Brian Powell and 3B Carlos Villalobos.
Royals signed P Terry Mathews.

January 15
Angels organization signed SS-2B Luis Rivera.
Orioles organization signed P Heathcliff Slocumb.
Dodgers signed P Carlos Perez, 3B Scott Livingstone and P Ricardo Jordan.
Cardinals signed P Mike Mohler.

January 17
Giants signed C Scott Servais.

January 18
Rangers organization signed P Joe Hudson to a minor league contract.
Blue Jays signed 2B Joey Cora and 3B Willie Greene.

January 19
Twins signed P Bob Wells.
Blue Jays signed P Vincente Palacios.
Mets signed P Allen Watson.

January 20
Mariners organization signed P Brien Taylor.
Devil Rays organization signed P Bobby Witt, P Steve Ontiveros, P Marc Valdes, P Steve Cooke and P Norm Charlton.
Twins announced retirement of P Bob Tewksbury.

January 21
Astros organization signed P Brian Williams, P Jeff McCurry, C Randy Knorr, IF-OF Casey Candaele, OF Alex Diaz and OF Ryan Thompson.

January 22
Athletics organization signed 1B Jeff Ball.
Mets organization signed 2B Mariano Duncan.

January 25
Angels organization signed IF Andy Stankiewicz, P Christian Michalak and P Stephen Mintz.
Royals organization signed P Pete Smith, OF Tony Tarasco and IF Steve Scarsone.
Athletics signed OF Tim Raines.
Astros organization signed P Xavier Hernandez.

January 26
Red Sox organization signed 1B-DH Bob Hamelin. White Sox organization signed OF John Cangelosi and OF Darrin Jackson.
Indians organization signed P Dave Stevens and P Scott Klingenbeck.
Royals organization signed P Tim Scott.
Rangers organization signed P Mike Morgan.

January 27
Angels signed P Mike Magnante.
Brewers signed P Jim Abbott.
Cardinals signed 2B Carlos Baerga.

January 28
Tigers claimed P Mike Grzanich on waivers from Astros.
Expos signed OF Orlando Merced.

January 29
Cubs organization signed P Doug Creek.
Orioles announced retirement of P Jimmy Key.

February 1
Twins traded P Chris Cumberland to Red Sox for cash considerations.
Yankees traded 3B Mike Lowell to Marlins for P Ed Yarnall, P Mark Johnson and P Todd Noel.
Padres organization signed OF Chris Jones.

February 2
Red Sox organization signed P Seung Jun Song.
Expos organization signed P Mike Maddux.
Phillies organization signed P Joe Grahe.
Padres traded OF Greg Vaughn and 1B-OF Mark Sweeney to Reds for OF Reggie Sanders, SS Damian Jackson and P Josh Harris.

February 3
Indians signed IF-OF Wil Cordero, IF Bill Selby, P Jamie Brewington and P Paul Wagner.
Devil Rays organization signed C Joe Oliver.
Cubs organization signed OF Tarrik Brock.

February 4
Orioles organization signed P Mike Fetters.
Mets traded IF Ralph Milliard to Reds for P Mark Corey.
Padres organization signed P Carlos Reyes.

February 7
Braves announced retirement of P Dennis Martinez.

February 8
Blue Jays organization signed 1B-DH Cecil Fielder.

February 9
Cubs organization signed C Danny Sheaffer.
Cardinals traded P Sean Lowe to White Sox for P John Ambrose.

February 12
Blue Jays released OF Patrick Lennon.
Expos organization signed P Jose Bautista.
Padres organization signed C Mark Parent.

February 16
Cardinals signed SS Shawon Dunston.
Cardinals organization signed 1B Eduardo Perez.

February 17
Athletics signed 1B John Jaha.
Blue Jays announced retirement of P Dave Stieb.

February 18
Yankees traded P David Wells, P Graeme Lloyd and 2B

Homer Bush to Blue Jays for P Roger Clemens.
Devil Rays organization signed P Ben McDonald.

February 19
Devil Rays organization signed 1B-DH Julio Franco.
Diamondbacks organization signed P Byung-Hyun Kim.

February 20
Indians signed P Orel Hershiser.
Pirates signed SS Pat Meares.

February 24
Royals organization signed OF Curtis Pride.

February 25
Pirates traded 2B Tony Womack to Diamondbacks for OF Paul Weichard and a player to be named; Diamondbacks sent P Jason Boyd to complete deal (August 25).

February 27
Reds organization signed 3B Tim Naehring.

March 3
Dodgers organization signed C Rick Wilkins.

March 4
Royals released OF Curtis Pride.

March 7
Angels announced retirement of INF Craig Shipley.

March 11
Red Sox organization signed P Ramon Martinez.
Reds released P Joey Eischen and SS Pat Listach.
Blue Jays announced retirement of 2B Joey Cora.

March 12
Royals released P Jamie Walker, P Allen McDill, P John Cummings and P Brian Bevil.

March 16
Giants released P Trevor Wilson.

March 17
Red Sox released 1B-DH Bob Hamelin.
Reds released P Todd Williams.
Mets released P Oscar Henriquez.
Cardinals released 2B Carlos Baerga.

March 18
Royals released OF Tony Tarasco.

March 19
Royals sold contract of P Ricky Pickett to Rangers.

March 20
Tigers organization signed 1B-DH Bob Hamelin.
Twins sold contract of OF Melvin Nieves to Daiei of Japanese Pacific League.

March 22
Mets organization signed P Oscar Henriquez. Mets traded OF Jonathan Guzman to Royals for SS Shane Halter.

March 23
Indians traded OF Jim Betzhold to Astros for a player to be named.
Royals released P Pete Smith.
Yankees organization signed P Trevor Wilson.
Reds organization signed 2B Carlos Baerga.

March 24
Tigers claimed IF Jason Maxwell on waivers from Cubs.
Rangers released P Tony Fossas.
Phillies released P Chris Eddy, P Greg Whiteman and C-3B James Fritz.

March 25
Reds traded OF Jon Nunnally to Red Sox for P Pat Flury.
Reds traded C Brook Fordyce to White Sox for P Jake Meyer.
Yankees organization signed P Tony Fossas.
Astros traded C Marc Ronan to Phillies for future considerations.
Mets signed P Orel Hershiser.

March 26
Royals released P Tim Scott and P Dario Veras.
Mariners released IF Randy Jorgensen, P Rafael Batista, P

Albert Derenches, P Jose Gonzalez, P Orin Kawahara, P Dallas Mahan, P Matt Massimi, P Kristofer Totten, OF Anton French, IF David Dallospedale, IF Chris Dean, IF Kip Garcia, IF Domingo Pacheco and IF Felix Rosario.
Dodgers traded C Tim Laker to Pirates for a player to be named.
Mets released P Hideo Nomo.

March 27
Yankees released OF Jerome Walton.
Expos released P Erik Bennett, OF Ed Brady, OF Dax Jones, C Luis Rivera, OF Mo Blakeney, OF Jermaine Swinton, OF Trovin Valdez, P Jason Woodring, P Andrew Frierson and P Raymond Plummer.
Mets released 2B Mariano Duncan.
Pirates released IF Rafael Bournigal.

March 29
Royals released 1B Cary Coffee, P Scott Taylor and P Roland De La Maza.
Mariners released P Bill Swift.
Orioles traded OF Danny Clyburn and a player to be named to Devil Rays for P Jason Johnson; Orioles sent SS Angel Bolivar Volquez to complete deal (April 22).
Cubs claimed OF Curtis Goodwin on waivers from Colorado.
Marlins traded OF Pat Watkins to Rockies for a player to be named; Rockies sent P Kevin Gordon to complete deal (July 16).
Astros released P Xavier Hernandez and OF Dave Clark.
Angels traded C Phil Nevin and P Keith Volkman to Padres for IF Andy Sheets and of Gus Kennedy.
Padres released C Mark Parent and OF Chris Jones.
Angels announced retirement of INF Luis Rivera.
Padres announced retirement of P Mark Langston.

March 30
Angels organization released IF Andy Stankiewicz and P Rich DeLucia.
Red Sox released OF Midre Cummings.
White Sox released OF John Cangelosi.
Indians released P John Burke.
Indians traded 1B Mike Glavine to Braves for future considerations.
Yankees traded P Darren Holmes and cash to Diamondbacks for C Izzy Molina and P Ben Ford.
Athletics claimed P Ron Mahay on waivers from Red Sox.
Athletics traded P Jay Witasick to Royals for a player to be named and cash.
Rangers organization signed IF Rafael Bournigal.
Angels traded 3B-1B Dave Hollins and cash Blue Jays for SS Tomas Perez.
Cardinals traded P John Frascatore to Diamondbacks for P Clint Sodowsky.
Diamondbacks released P Aaron Small.
Cubs released P Marc Pisciotta.

March 31
Royals released P Erik Hanson and P A.J. Sager.
Twins traded P Dan Serafini to Cubs for cash.
Devil Rays released OF Mike Kelly, P Steve Cooke, P Larry Casian, P Mark Hutton, P Steve Ontiveros, P Mark Sievert and OF Billy Ashley.
Blue Jays released 1B-DH Cecil Fielder.
Braves released OF Danny Bautista and 2B Tony Graffanino.
Cubs claimed P Brad Woodall on waivers from Brewers.
Brewers released P William Van Landingham.

April 1
Yankees released P Tony Fossas and P Jim Bruske.
Athletics released P Mark Holzemer.
Blue Jays organization signed P Doug Bochtler.
Marlins traded P Justin Speier to Braves for a player to be named; Braves sent P Matthew Targac to complete deal (June 11).
Cubs organization signed P Hideo Nomo.
Padres released P Mark Langston.

April 2
Angels claimed P Al Levine on waivers from Rangers.
Royals traded 1B-OF Jeff Conine to Orioles for P Chris Fussell.
Orioles released C-1B Chris Hoiles.
Orioles organization signed OF Jose Herrera. Indians released P Ron Villone.
Mariners claimed 1B-OF Ryan Jackson on waivers from Marlins.
Ranngers claimed 3B Tom Evans on waivers from Blue Jays.
Braves organization signed P Marc Pisciotta. Rockies organization signed OF Mike Kelly.

April 3
Indians organization signed P Mark Langston.
Yankees organization signed P Tony Fossas.
Mariners traded P Bobby Ayala to Expos for P Jimmy Turman.

April 5
Indians organization signed P Rich DeLucia.
Reds organization signed P Ron Villone.
Expos released OF Terry Jones.

April 6
Indians organization signed P Chris Haney.
Reds organization signed P A.J. Sager.

April 8
Expos released OF Derrick May.

April 9
Devil Rays organization signed 2B Tony Graffanino.
Devil Rays released SS Dave Silvestri.

April 10
Mariners signed 2B-SS Domingo Cedeno.

April 15
Tigers claimed 3B Rob Sasser on waivers from Rangers.
Blue Jays signed 2B Pat Kelly.

April 16
Braves traded P Mark Wohlers and cash to Reds for P John Hudek.
Marlins claimed P Eric Ludwick on waivers from Blue Jays.
Dodgers traded P Dave Mlicki and P Mel Rojas to Tigers for P Robinson Checo, P Aposto Garcia and P Richard Roberts.

April 20
Reds purchased contract of C Guillermo Garcia from Marlins.

April 22
Twins claimed P Jack Cressend on waivers from Red Sox.
Indians traded P Jerry Spradlin to Giants for OF Dan McKinley and a player to be named; Giants sent P Josh Santos to complete deal (June 27).

April 23
Cubs released P Hideo Nomo.

April 25
Dodgers organization signed P Mike Maddux.

April 27
Rangers traded IF Rafael Bournigal to Mariners for cash.

April 28
Tigers traded OF Brian Hunter to Mariners for two players to be named; Mariners sent P Andrew Vanhekken (June 27) and OF Jerry Amador (August 26) to complete deal.

April 29
Brewers signed P Hideo Nomo.

April 30
Orioles released P Heathcliff Slocumb.

May 3
Expos organization signed P Charles Debuc.

MAY 5
Phillies traded P Paul Spoljaric to Blue Jays for P Robert Person.

May 7
Blue Jays claimed OF Jacob Brumfield on waivers from Dodgers.

May 11
Tigers released P Mel Rojas.

May 12
Blue Jays traded P Luis Arroya to Marlins for a player to be named.

May 14
Mets organization signed P Xavier Hernandez.

May 15
Cardinals organization signed P Heathcliff Slocumb.

May 17
Expos organization signed P Mel Rojas.
Pirates organization signed IF Dale Sveum.

May 19
Blue Jays traded P Doug Bochtler to Dodgers for cash considerations.

May 21
Twins traded P Rick Aguilera and P Scott Downs to Cubs for P Kyle Lohse and P Jason Ryan.

May 23
Brewers claimed P Jim Pittsley on waivers from Royals.
Expos organization released P Jose Bautista.
Royals announced retirement of 1B Jeff King.

May 26
Mariners claimed P Frankie Rodriguez on waivers from Twins.

May 28
Yankees claimed P Greg McCarthy on waivers from Mariners.
Blue Jays claimed 3B Willis Otanez on waivers from Orioles.

June 1
Orioles traded OF Lyle Mouton to Brewers for OF Todd Dunn.

June 3
Orioles claimed C Mike Figga on waivers from Yankees.

June 4
Reds released 2B Carlos Baerga.
Mets organization signed P Jose Bautista.

June 5
Padres organization released P Ed Vosberg. Padres organization signed 2B Carlos Baerga and OF Wayne Kirby.

June 8
Phillies claimed P Amaury Telemaco on waivers from Diamondbacks.

June 10
Expos claimed OF Scott Hunter on waivers from Mets.

June 11
Expos sold P Rick DeHart to the Hiroshima Carp of Japan League.

June 12
Blue Jays traded P Dan Plesac to Diamondbacks for SS Tony Batista and P John Frascatore.

June 14
Phillies claimed P Jason Brester on waivers from Rockies.

June 15
Marlins traded IF Craig Counsell to Dodgers for a player to be named; Dodgers sent P Ryan Moskau to complete deal (July 15).

June 16
Athletics released P Tom Candiotti.

June 18
Indians claimed P Jeff Tam on waivers from Mets.
Indians traded P Tony Dougherty to Pirates for a player to be named.
Indians organization signed P Paul Menhart.
Royals traded IF Jose Cepada to Braves for P Marc Pisciotta.
Mariners traded P Mac Suzuki and a player to be named to Mets for P Allen Watson and cash; Mariners sent P Justin Dunning to complete deal (September 14).

June 19
Mariners traded OF Matt Mieske to Astros for P Kevin Hodges.

June 21
Indians released P Dave Stevens.
Blue Jays released 1B-3B Dave Hollins.

June 22
Royals claimed P Mac Suzuki on waivers from the Mets.

June 23
Red Sox claimed P Travis Baptist on waivers from Twins.

June 27
Mariners released P Brien Taylor.

June 28
Mariners released P Allen Watson.
Diamondbacks traded OF Mike Stoner to Angels for OF Jason Herrick.

June 29
Indians signed P Tom Candiotti.

July 2
Orioles organization signed P Jim Corsi.
Yankees claimed 3B Jeff Manto on waivers from Indians.

July 3

Yankees signed P Allen Watson.
Rockies released C Jeff Reed.

July 6

Devil Rays released P Roger Bailey.
Expos released P Mel Rojas.

July 7

Mariners traded 2B-SS Domingo Cedeno to Phillies for IF Jose Flores.

July 8

Blue Jays traded P Isabel Giron to Padres for SS Juan Melo.

July 9

Marlins traded P Matt Mantei to Diamondbacks for P Vladimir Nunez, P Brad Penny and a player to be named; Diamondbacks sent OF Abraham Nunez to complete deal (December 13).

July 16

Orioles traded P Rocky Coppinger to the Milwaukee Brewers for a player to be named; Brewers sent P Al Reyes to complete deal (July 21).
Royals released P Don Wengert.

July 17

Mariners organization signed C Ryan Christianson.

July 20

Phillies traded P Marty Barnett to Devil Rays for a player to be named; Devil Ray sent P Scott Aldred to complete deal (July 25).
Marlins organization signed P Paul Menhart and 2B Mariano Duncan.

July 21

Devil Rays traded P Julio Santana to Red Sox for a player to be named.

July 22

Mariners traded OF Kerry Robinson to Reds for P Todd Williams.

July 23

Angels released 1B-3B Tim Unroe.
Brewers released P Jim Abbott.
Athletics traded P Kenny Rogers to Mets for OF Terrence Long and P Leo Vasquez.
Pirates traded OF Jose Guillen and P Jeff Sparks to Devil Rays for C Joe Oliver and C Humberto Cota.

July 25

Marlins traded P Livan Hernandez to San Francisco for P Jason Grilli and P Nathan Bump.

July 26

Mariners traded OF Butch Huskey to Boston for P Robert Ramsay.
Braves traded P Doug Dent to San Diego for C Greg Myers.
Rockies traded 3B Tal Light to the Brewers for a player to be named.

July 27

Mets organization signed 3B Scott Livingstone and P Jimmy Myers.

July 28

Red Sox signed C Lenny Webster.
Mariners traded 1B David Segui to Blue Jays for P Tom Davey and P Steve Sinclair.

July 29

White Sox traded P Mario Iglesias to Orioles for IF Esteban Beltre.
Angels traded 2B Randy Velarde and P Omar Olivares to Athletics for P Elvin Nina, OF Jeff DaVanon and OF Nathan Haynes.

July 30

Indians organization signed C Jesse Levis.
Mets organization signed P Vicente Palacios.
Red Sox traded C Mandy Romero to Mets for a player to be named.

July 31

Orioles traded P Juan Guzman and cash to Reds for P B.J. Ryan and P Jacobo Sequea. Tigers traded P Bryce Florie to Red Sox for P Mike Maroth.
Royals traded P Kevin Appier to Athletics for P Blake Stein, P Jeff D'Amico and P Brad Rigby.
Athletics traded P Billy Taylor to Mets for P Jason Isringhausen and P Greg McMichael.

Blue Jays organization signed P John Hudek.
Cubs traded P Terry Mulholland and IF Jose Hernandez to Braves for P Micah Bowie, P Ruben Quevedo and a minor league player to be named; Braves sent P Joey Nation to complete deal (August 24).
Marlins traded P Brandon Villafuerte to Tigers for P Mike Drumright.
Mets traded OF Brian McRae, P Rigo Beltran and OF Thomas Johnson to Rockies for OF Darryl Hamilton and P Chuck McElroy.
Cardinals traded IF Shawon Dunston to Mets for IF Craig Paquette.
Padres traded C-1B Jim Leyritz to Yankees for P Geraldo Padua.

August 4

Reds released P Jason Bere.

August 6

Angels released C Charlie O'Brien.
Blue Jays claimed OF Curtis Goodwin on waivers from Cubs.

August 9

Angels released P Jack McDowell.
Rockies traded OF Brian McRae to Blue Jays for a player to be named; Blue Jays sent P Pat Lynch to complete deal (August 23).

August 11

Mets claimed P Jeff Tam on waivers from Indians.
Pirates released OF Turner Ward.

August 12

Blue Jays announced retirement of OF Curtis Goodwin.

August 13

Indians organization signed 3B Jeff Manto. Royals traded P Jeremy Jackson to the Mets for P Derek Wallace.
Brewers organization signed P Jason Bere.

August 15

Royals released P Matt Whisenant and P Terry Mathews.

August 16

Padres traded 2B Carlos Baerga to Indians for cash.

August 18

Brewers traded OF Rich Becker to Athletics for a player to be named; Athletics sent P Carl Dale to complete deal (August 20).

August 20

Orioles released P Ricky Bones.
Padres signed P Matt Whisenant.

August 24

Cardinals traded P Kent Mercker to Red Sox for P Mike Matthews and C David Benham.

August 26

Indians organization signed P Jim Poole.
Marlins released C Jorge Fabregas.

August 27

Orioles traded DH Harold Baines to Indians for P Juan Aracena and a player to be named; Indians sent P Jimmy Hamilton to complete deal (August 31).
Mariners traded P Jeff Fassero to Rangers for a player to be named; Rangers sent OF Adrian Myers to complete deal (September 22).
Expos released P Bobby Ayala.

August 30

Blue Jays released OF Geronimo Berroa.

August 31

Angels released OF Reggie Williams.
Red Sox traded P Mark Guthrie to Cubs for P Rod Beck and a player to named; Red Sox sent 3B Cole Liniak to complete deal (September 1).
Cubs traded C Tyler Houston to Indians for P Richard Negrette.
Blue Jays signed C Pat Borders.
Rockies traded IF Lenny Harris to Diamondbacks for IF Belvani Martinez.
Braves signed C Jorge Fabregas.
Astros released OF Alex Diaz and P Sean Bergman.
Astros traded P Joe Messman to Giants for OF Stan Javier.

September 5

Braves organization signed P Sean Bergman.
Expos released 3B Shane Andrews.

September 9

Pirates traded IF Freddy Garcia to Braves for P Greg Dukeman.
Cubs signed 3B Shane Andrews.

September 10

Dodgers claimed P Dwayne Jacobs on waivers from White Sox.

September 12

Royals released IF Steve Scarsone.
Phillies released 2B-SS Domingo Cedeno.

September 14

Royals traded P Glendon Rusch to Mets for P Dan Murray.

September 20

Diamondbacks claimed P Jeff Kubenka on waivers from Dodgers.

September 24

Red Sox released P Mark Portugal.
Rockies announced retirement of OF John Cangelosi.

September 29

Twins claimed 1B Mario Valdez on waivers from White Sox.
Phillies released P Matt Beech.

October 1

Athletics announced retirement of C Mike Macfarlane.

October 5

Marlins organization signed IF Chris Clapinski.

October 6

Cubs released OF Lance Johnson.
Reds claimed P Heath Murray on waivers from Padres.
Phillies claimed SS Felix Martinez on waivers from Royals.
Phillies claimed P Carlos Reyes on waivers from Padres.
Padres claimed IF Jed Hanson on waivers from Royals.

October 8

Twins released OF Marty Cordova and IF Brent Gates.
Reds released C Brian Johnson.

October 13

Padres organization signed OF Ethan Faggett, P Brian Doughty, P Len Hart and P Ryan Lynch.
Giants claimed SS Nelson Castro on waivers from Angels.

October 14

Reds claimed 1B Ron Wright on waivers from Pirates.

October 15

Cardinals organization signed P Mike James and OF Steve Bieser.

October 18

Royals claimed P David Lundquist on waivers from White Sox.
Cubs released 3B Gary Gaetti.

October 20

Blue Jays released P John Hudek.

October 22

Dodgers organization signed P Kris Foster.
Phillies claimed P Manny Barrios on waivers from Reds.

October 25

Padres organization signed P Matt Whiteside.

October 26

Indians organization signed P Jamie Brewington, P Cameron Cairncross and P Roy Padilla.

October 28

Rangers released P Eric Gunderson and INF Jon Shave.
Phillies claimed P Hideo Nomo on waivers from Brewers.

October 30

Rockies traded OF Dante Bichette and cash to Reds for OF Jeffrey Hammonds and P Stan Belinda.

November 2

Rangers traded OF Juan Gonzalez, P Danny Patterson and C Gregg Zaun to Tigers for P Justin Thompson, P Francisco Cordero, OF Gabe Kapler, C Bill Haselman, 2B Frank Catalanotto and P Alan Webb.
Marlins organization signed C Chris Tremie and P Jake Benz.

November 3

Reds organization signed INF Mike Bell, INF Chris Sexton and OF Pat Watkins.

November 4

Padres organization signed P Oscar Henriquez, P Luis Andujar, P Eric Moody, P Vicente Palacios, P Anthony Runion, P Derek Root, P Matt Dunbar, OF Ryan Radmanovich and INF Ralph Milliard.

November 7

Indians signed P Danys Baez.

November 8

Blue Jays traded OF Shawn Green and 2B Jorge Nunez to Dodgers for OF Raul Mondesi and P Pedro Borbon.

November 9

Rangers claimed P Brian Sikorski on waivers from Astros.

November 10

Tigers claimed INF Carlos Villalobos on waivers from Astros.
Padres traded P Andy Ashby to Phillies for P Carlton Loewer, P Steve Montgomery and P Adam Eaton.

November 11

Devil Rays announced retirement of 3B Wade Boggs.
Blue Jays traded P Pat Hentgen and P Paul Spoljaric to Cardinals for P Lance Painter, C Alberto Castillo and P Matt DeWitt.
Dodgers organization signed INF Dave Hansen.

November 12

Marlins traded INF Kevin Orie to Dodgers for a minor league player to be named.
Red Sox traded OF Jon Nunnally to Mets for OF Jermaine Allensworth.

November 15

Padres traded P Dan Miceli to Marlins for P Brian Meadows.
Pirates organization signed P Pep Harris and 3B Jarrod Patterson.

November 16

Twins announced retirement of C Terry Steinbach.
Reds organization signed P Larry Luebbers, P Neil Weber, P Tom Fordham, P Bobby Munoz, P Terrell Wade, P Joe Borowski and INF Brooks Kieschnick.
Rockies claimed P Julian Tavarez on waivers from Giants.
Rockies traded P Darryl Kile, RHP Dave Veres and RHP Luther Hackman to Cardinals for RHP Jose Jimenez, RHP Manny Aybar, RHP Rick Croushore and INF Brent Butler.

November 17

Orioles signed P Mike Trombley.
Royals claimed P Jason Rakers on waivers from Indians.
Mariners organization signed OF Rich Butler, C Robert Machada, INF Steven Goodell and INF Robert Gandolfo.
Blue Jays released C Mike Matheny.
Rockies traded P Curtis Leskanic to Brewers for P Mike Myers.
Mets organization signed INF Maurice Bruce.

November 18

Twins claimed P Sean Bergman on waivers from Braves.
Twins claimed P Mike Kusiewicz on waivers from Rockies
Twins claimed 1B Mario Valdez on waivers from Cubs.
Athletics signed P Mike Magnante.
Devil Rays claimed C Mike Figga on waivers from Orioles.
Expos claimed P Brent Billingsley on waivers from Marlins.
Phillies claimed P Mark Brownson on waivers from Rockies.

November 22

Cubs organization signed P Todd Van Poppel, P Daniel Garibay, P Dave Zancanaro, P Mike Heathcott, P Kerry Lacy, C Angelo Encarnacion, C Alan Zinter, INF Chris Peterson, OF Tarrik Brock, OF Raul Gonzalez and OF Chris Hatcher.
Padres organization signed 1B Joe Vitiello, P Jayson Durocher, P Stan Spencer, C George Williams and C John Roskos.

November 23

Indians claimed P Justin Speier on waivers from Braves.
Tigers organization signed P Chad Ogea.
Athletics organization signed P Frank Lankford, P Jon Ratliff, P Jeff Tam, P Will Brunson, P Terry Burrows, P Rich Sauveur, C Chris Norton, OF Greg Martinez and OF David McCarty.
Diamondbacks signed P Russ Springer.

November 24

Tigers claimed P Ramon Tatis on waivers from Devil Rays.
Reds claimed P Eddie Gaillard on waivers from Devil Rays.

November 29

Tigers organization signed P Mike Oquist.
Rockies sold the contract of P Roberto Ramirez to Hanshin Tigers of Japan Central League.

December 1

Yankees released DH Chili Davis.
Brewers organization signed P Rod Bolton, P Ricardo Jordan, 1B Kurt Bierek, SS Norberto Martin, OF Damon Hollins, OF Matt Luke and OF Brad Tyler.
Phillies signed P Mike Jackson.

December 2

White Sox announced retirement of OF Darrin Jackson.
Indians signed P Scott Kamienecki.
Mets signed OF Mike Kelly, INF Orlando Miller, P Brian Shouse and P Jim Baron.

December 3

Indians organization signed P Brian Barber.

December 6

Braves claimed P Rafael Medina on waivers from Marlins.

December 7

Rockies traded P Scott Randall to Twins for OF Chris Latham.
Mariners signed 1B John Olerud.
Brewers organization signed P Michael Busby, P Mike Iglesias, P Greg Mix, P Mike Rossiter, P Travis Smith, P Eric Ludwick, P Greg McCarthy, P David West, P Joe Crawford and C Kade Johnson.
Pirates organization signed OF Adam Hyzdu, INF Jason Wood, P Jose Lopez and OF Daren Hooper.
Pirates released P Michael Chaney, P Mario Cordoba, P Danny Crawford, P Manuel Helena, P Jose Sanchez, C Alvaro Zambrano, 3B Victor Araujo, SS Digno Delarosa, OF Santos Cortez, OF Mo Douglas, OF Juan Hernandez and OF Alvin Hidalgo. Pirates sold contract of P Greg Hansell to Hanshin Tigers of Japanese Central League.

December 8

Orioles released P Doug Linton.
Twins signed P Sean Bergman.
Rockies signed OF Tom Goodwin.
Cardinals signed 1B/OF Larry Sutton.

December 9

Orioles signed DH Harold Baines.
Rockies signed C Brent Mayne.

December 10

Cubs organization signed C Kweon Yoon-min.
Reds released INF Juan Melo.
Mets traded P Chuck McElroy to Orioles for P Jesse Orosco.

December 12

Red Sox traded OF Damon Buford to Cubs for INF Manny Alexander.
Orioles traded INF Jeff Reboulet to Royals for a player to be named.
Rangers organization signed P Koichi Taniguchi.
Dodgers traded P Ismael Valdes and 2B Eric Young to Cubs for P Terry Adams, P Chad Ricketts and a player to be named; Cubs sent P Brian Stephenson to complete deal (December 16).
Rockies organization signed P Butch Henry.
Tigers traded OF Kimera Bartee to Reds for a player to be named or cash.
Reds released C Guillermo Garcia.
Mets signed 3B Todd Zeile.
Giants traded P Chris Brock to Phillies for C Bobby Estalella.

December 13

Giants traded P Jerry Spradlin to Royals for a player to be named.
Marlins traded P Johan Santana to Twins for P Jared Camp and cash.
Yankees traded OF Chad Curtis to Rangers for P Brandon Knight and P Sam Marsonek.
Devil Rays signed OF Greg Vaughn.
Reds organization signed P Elmer Dessens.
Cubs traded P Richard Negrette to Orioles for SS Augie Ojeda.
Rockies traded 3B Vinny Castilla to Devil Rays for P Rolando Arrojo and INF Aaron Ledesma.
Athletics traded P Jimmy Haynes to Brewers. Rockies traded C Henry Blanco and P Jamey Wright to Brewers for 3B Jeff Cirillo, P Scott Karl and cash.
Rockies traded P Justin Miller and cash to Athletics.
Brewers organization signed OF James Mouton.
Expos released INF Jose Fernandez.
Mets organization signed 1B Ryan McGuire, P Johan Lopez and OF Juan Moreno.

December 14

Reds traded 1B Stephen Larkin to Orioles for a player to be named.
Royals signed C Brian Johnson.
Yankees traded P Dan Naulty to Dodgers for 1B Nicholas Leach.
Pirates signed OF-INF Wil Cordero.

December 15

Diamondbacks traded OF Dante Powell to Cardinals for SS Luis Ordaz.
Cubs signed C Joe Girardi.
Marlins traded OF Todd Dunwoody to Royals for INF Sean McNally.
Astros traded OF Carl Everett to Red Sox for SS Adam Everett and P Greg Miller.
Dodgers organization signed P Mike Fetters.

December 16

Indians signed P Chuck Finley.
Tigers organization signed P Allen McDill, P Anthony Chavez, P Edgar Ramos, P Danny Rios, INF Jesus Azuaje, INF Tilson Brito and INF Carlos Mendez.
Rangers organization signed OF David Hulse and C Reed Secrist.
Brewers signed INF Jose Hernandez.
Cardinals signed C Mike Matheny.

December 17

Orioles signed C Greg Myers.
Cubs organization signed P Andy Larkin.
Rockies organization signed C Scott Servais.
Dodgers signed P Orel Hershiser.

December 19

Mariners signed P Kazuhiro Sasaki on a two-year contract.
Devil Rays signed OF Gerald Williams.

December 20

Tigers organization signed P Jim Poole, INF Marty Malloy, INF Kevin Polcovich, P Bart Evans, P Douglas Walls and INF Giomar Guevara.
Twins signed LHP Todd Rizzo.
Mariners signed 2B Mark McLemore and OF Stan Javier.
Rangers organization signed C B.J. Waszgis and INF Edwin Diaz.
Diamondbacks organization signed 1B Alex Cabrera, P David Evans, P Alfredo Garcia, SS Cesar Morillo and 3B Bryant Nelson.
Cubs signed SS Ricky Gutierrez.
Expos signed P Graeme Lloyd.
Cardinals traded P Juan Acevedo and two minor leaguers to be named to Brewers for 2B Fernando Vina.

December 21

Orioles signed P Buddy Groom.
Mariners signed P Arthur Rhodes.
Blue Jays organizations signed P Frank Castillo.
Astros organization signed INF Tripp Cromer.

December 22

Red Sox signed P Jeff Fassero.
Indians organization signed P Kane Davis, C Mandy Romero, C Kevin Lidle, INF Ryan Jones and P Ernie Delgado.
Yankees traded P Hideki Irabu to Expos for P Jake Westbrook and two players to be named.
Cubs traded P Dan Serafini to Padres for OF Brandon Pernell.
Marlins organization signed P Ricardo Bones.
Braves traded 1B Ryan Klesko, 2B Bret Boone and P Jason Shiell to Padres for 2B Quilvio Veras, 1B Wally Joyner and OF Reggie Sanders.

December 23

Red Sox signed P Sang Lee.
Indians organization signed OF Ruben Sierra, INF Bill Selby, P Jim Dedrick, P Jose Pett and P Joey Eischen.
Astros traded P Mike Hampton and OF Derek Bell to Mets for OF Roger Cedeno, P Octavio Dotel and P Kyle Kessel.

December 29

Rangers signed Kenny Rogers.

December 30

Athletics signed Scott Service.

Pirates traded P Brad Clontz to Diamondbacks for a player to be named; Diamondbacks sent P Robert Manzueta to complete deal (December 15).
Pirates traded OF Brant Brown to Marlins for OF Bruce Aven.

ALL-STAR GAME

AT FENWAY PARK, BOSTON, JULY 13, 1999

1999 REVIEW

AMERICAN LEAGUE 4, NATIONAL LEAGUE 1

Why the American League won: Its pitchers, led by starter and MVP Pedro Martinez, held N.L. batters at bay while its own hitters came up with timely hits and its defense turned three double plays and made a couple of sparkling plays. Martinez, Boston's star righthander and the winningest pitcher in the majors (15) in the first half of 1999, set an All-Star Game record by striking out the first four batters he faced. Five of the six outs he recorded were by strikeout.

Why the National League lost: It never could mount a sustained offensive attack. Seven A.L. pitchers scattered seven hits, just two that went for extra bases (both doubles). Sluggers Mark McGwire of the Cardinals and Sammy Sosa of the Cubs combined for four strikeouts in five at-bats. All told, the N.L. left eight runners on base, five of them in scoring position with two out, and struck out 12 times.

TURNING POINTS:

1. After Martinez struck out the side in the top of the first, the A.L. scored two runs against N.L. starter Curt Schilling of Philadelphia in the bottom of the inning. Cleveland's Kenny Lofton led off with an infield single and, two outs later, stole second. Indians teammate Manny Ramirez walked, setting the tables for yet another Cleveland player, Jim Thome, who singled to score Lofton. Baltimore's Cal Ripken then singled home Ramirez.

2. After the N.L. halved the deficit with a run in the third, the A.L. bounced back with two runs in the fourth inning against Cardinals righthander Kent Bottenfield. Thome led off with a walk and Bottenfield then hit Ripken with a pitch. The next batter, Rafael Palmeiro of the Rangers, singled to right to drive home Thome. Bottenfield struck out Texas' Ivan Rodriguez but N.L. third baseman Matt Williams of the Diamondbacks was unable to backhand a grounder by Cleveland's Roberto Alomar, allowing Ripken to score.

3. With runners at second and third with one out in the fifth, the N.L.'s last and best scoring opportunity ends as Baltimore righthander Mike Mussina strikes out Sosa and McGwire in successive at-bats.

WORTH NOTING:

The pregame ceremonies included the appearance of 41 baseball legends walking in from the outfield at Fenway Park, a la the scene from Field of Dreams. Former Red Sox outfielder Ted Williams, 80, shook hands and shared hugs with many past and current players before throwing out the first pitch. ... There were no homers in the game despite the fact the 16 non-pitching starters had hit a combined 363 home runs in the first half of the season. ... The two teams combined to strike out 22 times, an All-Star record. ... Alomar became the fifth player to appear in the All-Star Game with four different teams. He previously represented the Padres, Blue Jays and Orioles, joining Walker Cooper, Rich "Goose" Gossage, George Kell and Lee Smith as four-club All-Stars. ... Martinez became only the third starting pitcher to win an All-Star Game in his home park, joining Johnny Vander Meer of the 1938 Reds (Crosley Field) and Steve Rogers of the 1982 Expos (Olympic Stadium). ... The All-Star win was the A.L.'s third straight, ninth in 12 games and cut the N.L.'s all-time advantage in the midsummer classic to 40-29-1.

WORTH QUOTING:

A.L. shortstop Nomar Garciaparra of Boston, on the delayed start of the game due to the emotion-packed pregame ceremonies: "Nobody wanted to leave. What time was the first pitch? Nobody cared."... A.L. catcher Rodriguez, on the overpowering Martinez: "He's the best in the game. His first two pitches (were so hard), I wasn't able to even see them."... A.L. manager Joe Torre of the Yankees: "When you have a guy like Pedro Martinez out there, it's like hitting in a darkroom."... McGwire, who now is 4-for-20 in All-Star competition with no home runs and eight strikeouts: "I have my two strikeouts every All-Star Game."... Milwaukee outfielder Jeromy Burnitz, on the pregame festivities: "It was a pretty awesome experience. It was something I'll remember a long, long time."

PLAY BY PLAY

FIRST INNING

N.L.—Larkin, Walker and Sosa struck out.

A.L.—Lofton singled to first. Garciaparra flied to Walker. Griffey struck out. With Ramirez batting, Lofton stole second. Ramirez walked. Thome singled to center, scoring Lofton as Ramirez went to second. Ripken singled to right, scoring Ramirez as Thome went to second. Palmeiro grounded to McGwire. A.L. 2, N.L. 0.

SECOND INNING

N.L.—McGwire struck out. M. Williams reached first on an error by R. Alomar. Bagwell struck out as M. Williams was caught stealing, Rodriguez to R. Alomar, to complete a double play.

A.L.—Rodriguez grounded out, Bell to McGwire. R. Alomar and Lofton struck out.

THIRD INNING

N.L.—Cone now pitching. Piazza struck out. Burnitz doubled to right. Bell struck out. Larkin singled to center, scoring Burnitz. Walker grounded out, Cone to Thome. A.L. 2, N.L. 1.

A.L.—Johnson now pitching. Garciaparra popped to Sosa. Griffey grounded to McGwire. Ramirez struck out.

FOURTH INNING

N.L.—Jeter now at short, Surhoff in left field, Lofton in center field and Green in right field. Sosa popped to Thome. McGwire walked. M. Williams struck out. Bagwell singled to right as McGwire went to second. Piazza singled to right as McGwire went to third and Bagwell to second. Burnitz grounded to Thome.

A.L.—Bottenfield now pitching, L. Gonzalez in left field and Burnitz in right field. Thome walked. Ripken was hit by a pitch. Palmeiro singled to right, scoring Thome as Ripken went to third. Rodriguez struck out. Alomar reached first on an error by M. Williams as Ripken scored and Palmeiro went to second. Lofton popped to M. Williams in foul territory. Jeter struck out. A.L. 4, N.L. 1.

FIFTH INNING

N.L.—Mussina now pitching and Fernandez at third. Bell walked. Larkin forced Bell at second, R. Alomar to Jeter. L. Gonzalez doubled to left as Larkin went to third. Sosa and McGwire struck out.

A.L.—Lima now pitching, Jordan in center field, V. Guerrero in right field, Casey at first, Kent at second and Lieberthal catching. Surhoff grounded to Casey. Green singled to second. Thome flied to V. Guerrero. Fernandez grounded out, Kent to Larkin.

SIXTH INNING

N.L.—Rosado now pitching, B. Williams now in center field and Ausmus now catching. M. Williams singled to left. Bagwell struck out. Lieberthal grounded into a double play, Fernandez to R. Alomar to Thome.

A.L.—Millwood now pitching and Sprague at third. Baines, pinch-hitting for Palmeiro, singled to left. Ausmus forced Baines at second, Larkin to Kent. Offerman, pinch-hitting for R. Alomar, grounded out, Millwood to Casey, as Ausmus went to second. B. Williams struck out.

SEVENTH INNING

N.L.—Zimmerman now pitching, Coomer at first, Offerman at second, Vizquel at shortstop and Ordonez in right field. Jordan walked. Jordan caught stealing, Ausmus to Jordan. Kent walked. A. Gonzalez, pinch-hitting for Larkin, popped to Offerman. L. Gonzalez reached first base on a throwing error by Offerman. Guerrero grounded out, Vizquel to Offerman.

A.L.—Ashby now pitching and A. Gonzalez at shortstop. Vizquel grounded to Casey. Hampton now pitching. Surhoff grounded out, Kent to Casey. Ordonez flied to A. Gonzalez.

EIGHTH INNING

N.L.—Hernandez now pitching. Casey grounded out, Vizquel to Coomer. Sprague grounded out, Fernandez to Coomer. Sheffield, pinch-hitting for Bagwell, grounded out, Vizquel to Coomer.

A.L.—Hoffman now pitching and Nilsson catching. Coomer struck out. Wagner now pitching. Fernandez struck out. Jaha, pinch-hitting for Baines, struck out.

NINTH INNING

N.L.—Wetteland now pitching. Nilsson struck out. Jordan singled to right. Kent grounded into a double play, Wetteland to Vizquel to Coomer. Final score: A.L. 4, N.L. 1.

BOX SCORE

National League	AB	R	H	RBI	PO	A
Larkin, ss (Reds)	3	0	1	1	1	1
‡A. Gonzalez, ph-ss (Marlins)	1	0	0	0	1	0
Walker, rf (Rockies)	2	0	0	0	1	0
L. Gonzalez, lf (D'backs)	2	0	1	0	0	0
Sosa, cf (Cubs)	3	0	0	0	1	0
Guerrero, rf (Expos)	1	0	0	0	1	0
McGwire, 1b (Cardinals)	2	0	0	0	3	0
Casey, 1b (Reds)	1	0	0	0	4	0
M. Williams, 3b (D'backs)	3	0	1	0	1	0
Sprague, 3b (Pirates)	1	0	0	0	0	0
Bagwell, dh (Astros)	3	0	1	0	0	0
§Sheffield, ph-dh (Dodgers)	1	0	0	0	0	0
Piazza, c (Mets)	2	0	1	0	6	0
Lieberthal, c (Phillies)	1	0	0	0	1	0
Nilsson, c (Brewers)	1	0	0	0	3	0
Burnitz, lf-rf (Brewers)	2	1	1	0	0	0
Jordan, cf (Braves)	1	0	1	0	0	0
Bell, 2b (Diamondbacks)	1	0	0	0	0	1
Kent, 2b (Giants)	1	0	0	0	1	2
Schilling, p (Phillies)	0	0	0	0	0	0
Johnson, p (D'backs)	0	0	0	0	0	0
Bottenfield, p (Cardinals)	0	0	0	0	0	0
Lima, p (Astros)	0	0	0	0	0	0
Millwood, p (Braves)	0	0	0	0	0	1
Ashby, p (Padres)	0	0	0	0	0	0
Hampton, p (Astros)	0	0	0	0	0	0
Hoffman, p (Padres)	0	0	0	0	0	0
Wagner, p (Astros)	0	0	0	0	0	0
Totals	**32**	**1**	**7**	**1**	**24**	**5**

American League	AB	R	H	RBI	PO	A
Lofton, lf-cf (Indians)	3	1	1	0	0	0
B. Williams, cf (Yankees)	1	0	0	0	0	0
Garciaparra, ss (Red Sox)	2	0	0	0	0	0
Jeter, ss (Yankees)	1	0	0	0	1	0
Vizquel, ss (Indians)	1	0	0	0	1	4
Griffey, cf (Mariners)	2	0	0	0	0	0
Surhoff, lf (Orioles)	2	0	0	0	0	0
Ramirez, rf (Indians)	1	1	0	0	0	0
Green, rf (Blue Jays)	1	0	1	0	0	0
Ordonez, rf (White Sox)	1	0	0	0	0	0
Thome, 1b (Indians)	2	1	1	1	4	0
Coomer, 1b (Twins)	1	0	0	0	4	0
Ripken, 3b (Orioles)	1	1	1	1	0	0
Fernandez, 3b (Blue Jays)	2	0	0	0	0	2
Palmeiro, dh (Rangers)	2	0	1	1	0	0
*Baines, ph-dh (Orioles)	1	0	1	0	0	0
∞Jaha, ph-dh (Athletics)	1	0	0	0	0	0
Rodriguez, c (Rangers)	2	0	0	0	10	1
Ausmus, c (Tigers)	1	0	0	0	2	1
R. Alomar, 2b (Indians)	2	0	0	1	2	2
†Offerman, ph-2b (Red Sox)	1	0	0	0	3	0
Martinez, p (Red Sox)	0	0	0	0	0	0
Cone, p (Yankees)	0	0	0	0	0	1
Mussina, p (Orioles)	0	0	0	0	0	0
Rosado, p (Royals)	0	0	0	0	0	0
Zimmerman, p (Rangers)	0	0	0	0	0	0
Hernandez, p (Devil Rays)	0	0	0	0	0	0
Wetteland, p (Rangers)	0	0	0	0	0	1
Totals	**31**	**4**	**6**	**4**	**27**	**12**

National League	0 0 1	0 0 0	0 0 0—1
American League	2 0 0	2 0 0	0 0 x—4

National League	IP	H	R	ER	BB	SO
Schilling (Phillies)	2.0	3	2	2	1	3
Johnson (Diamondbacks)	1.0	0	0	0	0	1
Bottenfield (Cardinals)	1.0	1	2	2	1	2
Lima (Astros)	1.0	1	0	0	0	0
Millwood (Braves)	1.0	1	0	0	0	1
Ashby (Padres)	0.1	0	0	0	0	0
Hampton (Astros)	0.2	0	0	0	0	0
Hoffman (Padres)	0.1	0	0	0	0	1
Wagner (Astros)	0.2	0	0	0	0	2

American League	IP	H	R	ER	BB	SO
Martinez (Red Sox)	2.0	0	0	0	0	5
Cone (Yankees)	2.0	4	1	1	1	3
Mussina (Orioles)	1.0	1	0	0	1	2
Rosado (Royals)	1.0	1	0	0	0	1
Zimmerman (Rangers)	1.0	0	0	0	2	0
Hernandez (Devil Rays)	1.0	0	0	0	0	0
Wetteland (Rangers)	1.0	1	0	0	0	1

Winning pitcher—Martinez. Losing pitcher—Schilling. Save—Wetteland.

*Singled for Palmeiro in sixth. †Grounded out for Alomar in sixth. ‡Popped out for Larkin in seventh. §Grounded out for Bagwell in eighth. ∞Struck out for Baines in eighth. E—M. Williams, Alomar, Offerman. DP—A.L. 3. LOB—N.L. 8, A.L. 6. 2B—L. Gonzalez, Burnitz. SB—Lofton. CS—M. Williams, Jordan. HBP—By Bottenfield (Ripken). BB—Off Schilling 1 (Ramirez), off Bottenfield 1 (Thome), off Cone 1 (McGwire), off Mussina 1 (Bell), off Zimmerman 2 (Jordan, Kent). SO—By Schilling 3 (Griffey, R. Alomar, Lofton), by Johnson 1 (Ramirez), by Bottenfield 2 (Rodriguez, Jeter), by Millwood 1 (B. Williams), by Hoffman 1 (Coomer), by Wagner 2 (Fernandez, Jaha), by Martinez 5 (Larkin, Walker, Sosa, McGwire, Bagwell), by Cone 3 (Piazza, Bell, M. Williams), by Mussina 2 (Sosa, McGwire), by Rosado 1 (Bagwell), by Wetteland 1 (Nilsson). T—2:53. A—34,187. U—Evans (A.L.), plate; Tata (N.L.), first; Ford (A.L.), second; Hernandez (N.L.), third; Johnson (A.L.), left field; Vanover (N.L.), right field. Official scorers—Bob Elliott, Dave O'Hara and Charlie Scoggins.

Players listed on rosters but not used: N.L.—Byrd (Phillies), Williamson (Reds); A.L.—Nagy (Indians), Percival (Angels).

NEW YORK VS. ARIZONA

The bottom line: Both franchises were fresh on the playoffs scene. The wild-card New York Mets hadn't been to the post-season since 1988, and the Arizona Diamondbacks, with the best one-year turnaround for a team, won the N.L. West in just their second year of existence. The big reason for the Mets' resurgence? All-Star catcher Mike Piazza's bat in the lineup. The big reason for Arizona's turnaround? They had the one pitcher no one in the National League wanted to face: Randy Johnson. But neither player was a factor in the series, as the Mets proved it takes a team effort to win in the postseason. The club shellacked Johnson in Game 1, then relied on standouts such as John Olerud and Edgardo Alfonzo to fill the void with Piazza on the bench because of an injury in Game 3 and the series-clinching Game 4. Not bad for a team that was all but out of the playoffs picture when the final weekend of the season began. Then the Mets won their final three games, forcing a one-game playoff with the Cincinnati Reds. They shut out the Reds, advancing into the postseason.

Why the Mets won: Timely hitting and a different hero each game. In Game 1, Edgardo Alfonzo provided the heroics. In Game 3, it was a combination of Rickey Henderson and John Olerud, and in Game 4 it was backup catcher Todd Pratt. Outside of Kenny Rogers' shaky outing in Game 2, the starting pitchers outperformed an outstanding Diamondbacks rotation. Costly errors by Tony Womack, one each in Games 3 and 4, cost the Diamondbacks a chance to win each game and take the momentum back from the Mets at Shea Stadium. The Diamondbacks had a plethora of veteran players, but at times in this series, they played like a second-year franchise.

TURNING POINTS:

Game 1: Edgardo Alfonzo's ninth-inning grand slam off Arizona reliever Bobby Chouinard broke a 4-4 tie and gave the Mets an 8-4 victory in Phoenix. Surprisingly, seven of the eight runs were charged to Randy Johnson, who led the NL with a 2.48 ERA in the regular season. Johnson allowed singles by Robin Ventura and Rey Ordonez before walking young Melvin Mora, which loaded the bases with one out in the ninth. Chouinard got one out on a sparkling defensive play by Matt Williams on Rickey Henderson's grounder which forced Ventura at the plate, but Alfonzo clocked his second homer of the game just inside the left field foul pole. Mets reliever Turk Wendell followed a hitless eighth inning with a perfect ninth for a save in his first postseason appearance.

Game 2: With the bases loaded in the bottom of the third inning, Steve Finley, a career .091 hitter in Division Series games, singled in two runs off Mets starter Kenny Rogers, giving the Diamondbacks a 3-1 lead. Finley added a two-run double in the fifth inning and a bases-loaded walk in the seventh inning for a five-RBI game. Todd Stottlemyre didn't need any more than the three third-inning runs, pitching 6.2 strong innings in Arizona's 7-1 victory.

Game 3: John Olerud's two-run single in the sixth inning broke open the game, propelling the Mets to a 9-2 victory at Shea Stadium. With the Mets leading 4-2 and one out in the sixth, Arizona manager Buck Showalter played the odds, bringing in lefty reliever Dan Plesac to face the lefthanded-hitting Olerud. Plesac specialized all season in getting out lefthanded hitters—they hit just .186 against him. But Olerud lined a two-run single to right, Roger Cedeno followed with an RBI single, and lefthanded Darryl Hamilton added a two-run single to center. The Mets were without catcher Mike Piazza, who was nursing an injured thumb.

Game 4: Todd Pratt hit a 10th-inning pitch from Matt Mantei that just cleared Finley's glove and the center field wall for a game-winning and series-ending homer. Pratt, replacing Piazza behind the plate, lifted Mantei's fastball to center field where Finley, a two-time Gold Glove winner, nearly made a leaping grab. The 4-3 win kept the Mets from traveling back to Arizona for Game 5. Defense made a difference earlier in the game. Mora, a rookie left fielder, gunned down Jay Bell at the plate in the top of the eighth inning as the Diamondbacks tried to add to a 3-2 lead. Then in the bottom of the frame, Tony Womack missed catching Olerud's fly ball, setting up the game-tying sacrifice fly by Cedeno.

WORTH NOTING:

Mets: John Olerud's Game 1 homer was the first homer by a lefthander off Randy Johnson since September 23, 1997. In fact, the only two lefthanders in the Mets lineup, Olerud and Robin Ventura, went a combined 4-for-8 in Game 1 against Johnson, who allowed just nine hits to lefties during the regular season. ... Rickey Henderson, 40, batted .400 in the Division Series and broke a Division Series record with six stolen bases. ... Kenny Rogers is winless in four career postseason starts. ... John Franco broke a string of 878 career games played with no postseason appearances, a major league record, with his Game 2 appearance. His Game 4 win was his first since September 13, 1997. ... Todd Pratt was 0-for-7 in the series before hitting the series-clinching home run. He was only the fourth player to end a postseason series with a home run, the most recent being Toronto's Joe Carter in the 1993 World Series.

Diamondbacks: The Diamondbacks had won seven of the nine games against the Mets during the regular season. ... Johnson lost a major league record sixth straight postseason decision. ... The Diamondbacks compiled a 32-16 record against lefthanded starters during the regular season. That didn't bode well for Kenny Rogers in Game 2. ... Todd Stottlemyre improved to 2-1 with a 1.69 ERA in three career Division Series starts. ... The Diamondbacks committed three errors and walked eight batters in Game 3. Of those eight walks, three came in the sixth inning, and all three runners scored in the six-run inning. ... Matt Mantei gave up Pratt's homer in his first postseason appearance. ... Arizona hadn't lost consecutive road games since July 18 and 19 at Seattle. ... During the regular season, Womack made only two errors in 258 chances while playing in the outfield. He equalled that total with an error each in Games 3 and 4.

WORTH QUOTING:

Mets: Mike Piazza, who had a hit and two strikeouts in four at-bats against Randy Johnson in Game 1: "Maybe he threw his best pitches to me and made some mistakes to the other guys. In that case, I'll be the whipping boy. It's no problem." ... Rogers on his pitching performance in Game 2: "With the stuff I had, pretty much from the first inning, I knew I'd have to battle." ... Todd Pratt on replacing Mike Piazza in Game 3: "I'm not Mike. I can handle the bat. I can handle myself defensively. But I'm not Mike. We all know that." ... Orel Hershiser, on Rickey Henderson's performance in the Division Series: "I think he's genetically blessed in the same way that Nolan Ryan was genetically blessed." ... Pratt again, on the Division Series win: "It was a team effort, and we really haven't done anything yet." ... John Franco, on winning Game 4: "Growing up as a Mets fan, getting the win in probably the biggest game here in 11 years . . . I am ecstatic right now."

Diamondbacks: Bobby Chouinard, on giving up the game-winning grand slam in Game 1: "I was trying to throw too hard. I threw a 3-1 fastball right down the middle. I fell behind and paid for it." ... Stottlemyre, on how he is pitching with a 70 percent tear of his rotator cuff: "Regardless of what people think, my arm feels good. I consider myself healthy, although medically I have two tears in my shoulder." ... Buck Showalter talking about his team's three-error, eight-walk performance in Game 3: "It certainly wasn't characteristic of the way we've been playing." ... Showalter again, on Tony Womack's second error in as many games, "He's one of the big reasons we're here today. It would be very unfeeling for me or anybody to forget that."

Game 1 at Arizona

NEW YORK 8, ARIZONA 4

HOW THEY SCORED

First Inning

New York—Henderson flied to Finley. Alfonzo homered to left-center. Olerud singled to center. Piazza singled to center, Olerud went to second. Agbayani and Ventura struck out. One run. New York 1, Arizona 0.

Third Inning

New York—Henderson walked. Alfonzo struck out. With Olerud batting, Henderson stole second. Olerud homered to right, scoring Henderson. Piazza flied to Finley. Agbayani struck out. Two runs. New York 3, Arizona 0.

Arizona—Johnson grounded out, Alfonzo to Olerud. Womack tripled to left-center. Bell hit a sacrifice fly to Dunston, scoring Womack. Gonzalez flied to Dunston. One run. New York 3, Arizona 1.

Fourth Inning

New York—Ventura doubled to right. Dunston singled to third as Ventura went to third. Ordonez hit a sacrifice bunt, scoring Ventura as Dunston went to second. Ordonez was out on the play, Johnson to Durazo. Yoshii grounded out, Williams to Durazo. Henderson flied to Womack. One run. New York 4, Arizona 1.

Arizona—Williams grounded out, Ordonez to Olerud. Durazo homered to left-center. Finley flied to Dunston. Frias flied to Agbayani. One run. New York 4, Arizona 2.

Sixth Inning

Arizona—Bell singled to right. Gonzalez homered to right, scoring Bell. Williams struck out. Mora now in center field and Cook pitching. Durazo popped to Cook. Finley walked. Frias struck out. Two runs. New York 4, Arizona 4.

Ninth Inning

New York—Ventura singled to right. Cedeno popped to Johnson. Ordonez singled to left as Ventura went to second. Mora walked. Chouinard now pitching. Henderson forced Ventura at home, Williams to Stinnett, as Ordonez went to third and Mora to second. Alfonzo homered to left, scoring Ordonez, Mora and Henderson. Piazza grounded to Durazo. Four runs. New York 8, Arizona 4.

BOX SCORE

New York	AB	R	H	RBI	PO	A
Henderson, lf	3	2	0	0	1	1
Benitez, p	0	0	0	0	0	0
Alfonzo, 2b	5	2	2	5	2	2
Olerud, 1b	5	1	3	2	5	0
Piazza, c	5	0	1	0	4	0
Agbayani, rf	4	0	0	0	2	0
Wendell, p	0	0	0	0	0	0
Hamilton, cf	0	0	0	0	1	0
Ventura, 3b	4	1	2	0	2	0
Dunston, cf	3	0	1	0	5	0
Cook, p	0	0	0	0	1	0
Cedeno, rf	1	0	0	0	1	0
Ordonez, ss	3	1	1	1	2	2
Yoshii, p	2	0	0	0	0	1
Mora, cf-lf	1	1	0	0	1	0
Totals	36	8	10	8	27	6

Arizona	AB	R	H	RBI	PO	A
Womack, rf	4	1	1	0	3	0
Bell, 2b	3	1	1	1	0	3
Gonzalez, lf	3	1	2	2	0	0
Williams, 3b	4	0	0	0	1	3
Durazo, 1b	4	1	1	1	7	0
Finley, cf	3	0	1	0	3	0
Frias, ss	4	0	0	0	0	0
Stinnett, c	3	0	0	0	12	0
Johnson, p	3	0	1	0	1	2
Chouinard, p	0	0	0	0	0	0
Totals	31	4	7	4	27	8

New York	1 0 2	1 0 0	0 0 4—8
Arizona	0 0 1	1 0 2	0 0 0—4

New York	IP	H	R	ER	BB	SO
Yoshii	5.1	6	4	4	0	3
Cook	1.2	1	0	0	1	1
Wendell (W)	1.0	0	0	0	1	0
Benitez	1.0	0	0	0	0	0
Arizona	**IP**	**H**	**R**	**ER**	**BB**	**SO**
Johnson (L)	8.1	8	7	7	3	11
Chouinard	0.2	2	1	1	0	0

DP—New York 2. LOB—New York 5, Arizona 3. 2B—Ventura, Gonzalez, Johnson. 3B—Womack. HR—Alfonzo 2, Olerud, Durazo, Gonzalez. SH—Ordonez. SF—Bell. SB—Henderson 2. T—2:53. A—49,584. U—Gorman, plate; Bell, first; Hirschbeck, second; DeMuth, third; Marsh, left field; Schrieber, right field.

Game 2 at Arizona

ARIZONA 7, NEW YORK 1

HOW THEY SCORED

Third Inning

New York—Henderson singled to left. Henderson stole second. Alfonzo

flied to Gilkey as Henderson went to third. Olerud grounded out, Womack to Colbrunn, as Henderson scored. Piazza struck out. One run. New York 1, Arizona 0.

Arizona—Stottlemyre grounded out, Rogers to Olerud. Womack struck out. Bell singled to left. Gonzalez hit by a pitch. Williams singled to the mound as Bell went to third and Gonzalez to second. Colbrunn walked, scoring Bell. Finley singled to right and went to second on the throw from the outfield as Gonzalez and Williams scored, and Colbrunn went to third. Gilkey grounded out, Ventura to Olerud. Three runs. Arizona 3, New York 1.

Fifth Inning

Arizona—Bell singled to left. Gonzalez struck out. Mahomes now pitching. Williams singled to center as Bell went to second. Colbrunn struck out. Finley doubled to left-center, scoring Bell and Williams. Gilkey popped to Piazza in foul territory. Two runs. Arizona 5, New York 1.

Seventh Inning

Arizona—Dotel now pitching. Bell flied to Henderson. Gonzalez walked. Williams doubled to left as Gonzalez went to third. Colbrunn hit by a pitch. Finley walked, scoring Gonzalez. Ward pinch-hitting for Gilkey against new pitcher J. Franco, grounded out, Alfonzo to Olerud, as Williams scored, Colbrunn went to third and Finley to second. Stinnett grounded out, Ventura to Olerud. Two runs. Arizona 7, New York 1.

BOX SCORE

New York	AB	R	H	RBI	PO	A
Henderson, lf	3	1	2	0	2	0
Alfonzo, 2b	4	0	0	0	1	2
Olerud, 1b	3	0	0	1	8	1
Piazza, c	4	0	1	0	9	0
Ventura, 3b	2	0	0	0	0	4
Hamilton, cf	2	0	0	0	2	0
Agbayani, ph-rf	1	0	0	0	0	0
Cedeno, rf-cf	3	0	1	0	0	0
Dunston, ph	1	0	0	0	0	0
Ordonez, ss	4	0	1	0	1	2
Rogers, p	2	0	0	0	0	2
Mahomes, p	0	0	0	0	0	0
Bonilla, ph	1	0	0	0	0	0
Dotel, p	0	0	0	0	0	0
J. Franco, p	0	0	0	0	1	0
Pratt, ph	1	0	0	0	0	0
Totals	31	1	5	1	24	11

Arizona	AB	R	H	RBI	PO	A
Womack, ss-rf	5	0	0	0	1	3
Bell, 2b	5	2	2	0	3	4
Gonzalez, lf	1	2	0	0	1	0
Williams, 3b	4	3	3	0	1	3
Colbrunn, 1b	2	0	1	1	12	0
Finley, cf	3	0	2	5	0	0
Gilkey, rf	3	0	0	0	2	0
Ward, ph	1	0	0	1	0	0
Swindell, p	0	0	0	0	0	1
Stinnett, c	4	0	1	0	7	1
Stottlemyre, p	3	0	0	0	0	0
Olson, p	0	0	0	0	0	0
Frias, ss	1	0	0	0	0	1
Totals	32	7	9	7	27	13

New York	0 0 1	0 0 0	0 0 0	—1
Arizona	0 0 3	0 2 0	2 0 x	—7

New York	IP	H	R	ER	BB	SO
Rogers (L)	4.1	5	4	4	2	6
Mahomes	1.2	3	1	1	0	1
Dotel	0.1	1	2	2	2	0
J. Franco	1.2	0	0	0	0	1
Arizona	**IP**	**H**	**R**	**ER**	**BB**	**SO**
Stottlemyre (W)	6.2	4	1	1	5	6
Olson	0.1	0	0	0	0	0
Swindell	2.0	1	0	0	0	1

E—Bell. DP—New York 1, Arizona 1. LOB—New York 8, Arizona 7. 2B—Ordonez, Colbrunn, Finley, Williams. SB—Henderson 3, Ordonez. HBP—By Rogers (Gonzalez), by Dotel (Colbrunn). T—3:13. A—49,328. U—Bell, plate; Hirschbeck, first; DeMuth, second; Marsh, third; Schrieber, left field; Gorman, right field.

Game 3 at New York

NEW YORK 9, ARIZONA 2

HOW THEY SCORED

Second Inning

New York—Agbayani singled to right. Ventura walked. Dunston grounded into a double play, Fox to Bell to Durazo, as Agbayani went to third. Pratt walked. Ordonez singled to right, scoring Agbayani as Pratt went to second. Reed struck out. One run. New York 1, Arizona 0.

Third Inning

New York—Henderson struck out. Alfonzo doubled to left. Olerud singled to left and advanced to second on the throw from the outfield ad Alfonzo scored. Agbayani singled to left as Olerud went to third. Ventura forced Agbayani at second, Durazo to Fox, as Olerud scored and Ventura went to second on a throwing error by Fox. Dunston grounded out, Fox to Durazo. Two runs. New York 3, Arizona 0.

Fifth Inning

Arizona—Stinnett doubled to center. Ward, pinch-hitting for Daal, homered to right, scoring Stinnett. Womack grounded out, Alfonzo to Olerud. Bell flied to Agbayani. Gonzalez grounded out, Alfonzo to Olerud. Two runs. New York 3, Arizona 2.

Sixth Inning

New York—Pratt walked. Ordonez sacrificed Pratt to second, Durazo, unassisted. Bonilla, pinch-hitting for Reed, walked. Henderson singled to right and went to second on Womack's fielding error, as Pratt scored and Bonilla went to third. Alfonzo was walked intentionally. Frias now at shortstop and Plesac pitching. Olerud singled to right, scoring Bonilla and Henderson as Alfonzo went to second. Cedeno singled to left-center, scoring Alfonzo as Olerud went to third. Cedeno stole second. Ventura grounded out, Bell to Durazo. Hamilton singled to center, scoring Olerud and Cedeno. Chouinard now pitching. Pratt grounded out, Chouinard to Durazo. Six runs. New York 9, Arizona 2.

BOX SCORE

Arizona	AB	R	H	RBI	PO	A
Womack, rf	4	0	0	0	0	0
Bell, 2b	4	0	0	0	4	3
Gonzalez, lf	3	0	0	0	1	0
Williams, 3b	4	0	2	0	0	1
Durazo, 1b	3	0	0	0	8	1
Finley, cf	3	0	1	0	3	0
Fox, ss	3	0	0	0	1	2
Plesac, p	0	0	0	0	0	0
Chouinard, p	0	0	0	0	0	0
Swindell, p	0	0	0	0	0	0
Harris, ph	1	0	0	0	0	0
Stinnett, c	3	1	1	0	5	1
Daal, p	1	0	0	0	0	1
Ward, ph	1	1	1	2	0	0
Holmes, p	0	0	0	0	0	0
Frias, ss	1	0	0	0	2	0
Totals	31	2	5	2	24	9

New York	AB	R	H	RBI	PO	A
Henderson, lf	5	1	3	1	1	0
Mora, lf	0	0	0	0	0	0
Alfonzo, 2b	3	2	1	0	1	5
Olerud, 1b	4	2	2	3	10	3
Agbayani, rf	2	1	2	0	1	0
Cedeno, ph-rf	2	1	1	1	2	0
Ventura, 3b	4	0	0	1	1	0
Dunston, cf	2	0	0	0	2	0
Hamilton, ph-cf	3	0	1	2	2	0
Pratt, c	2	1	0	0	3	0
Ordonez, ss	3	0	1	1	2	4
Reed, p	1	0	0	0	2	1
Bonilla, ph	0	1	0	0	0	0
Wendell, p	1	0	0	0	0	0
J. Franco, p	0	0	0	0	0	0
Hershiser, p	0	0	0	0	0	0
Totals	32	9	11	9	27	13

Arizona	0 0 0	0 2 0	0 0 0	—2
New York	0 1 2	0 0 6	0 0 x	—9

Arizona	IP	H	R	ER	BB	SO
Daal (L)	4.0	6	3	3	3	4
Holmes	1.1	1	4	4	3	0
Plesac	0.1	3	2	2	0	0
Chouinard	1.1	1	0	0	0	1
Swindell	1.0	0	0	0	2	0
New York	**IP**	**H**	**R**	**ER**	**BB**	**SO**
Reed (W)	6.0	4	2	2	3	2
Wendell	1.0	0	0	0	1	0
J. Franco	1.0	1	0	0	0	0
Hershiser	1.0	0	0	0	0	1

E—Fox, Daal, Womack. DP—Arizona 1, New York 1. LOB—Arizona 6, New York 9. 2B—Stinnett, Alfonzo. HR—Ward. SH—Reed, Ordonez. SB—Henderson, Cedeno. WP—Reed. T—3:05. A—56,180. U—Rieker, plate; Davis, first; Froemming, second; Meals, third; Winters, left field; Williams, right field.

Game 4 at New York

NEW YORK 4, ARIZONA 3 (10 INNINGS)

HOW THEY SCORED

Fourth Inning

New York—Alfonzo homered to left. Olerud flied to Finley. Agbayani flied to Finley. Ventura doubled to right. Pratt grounded out, Womack to Colbrunn. One run. New York 1, Arizona 0.

Fifth Inning

Arizona—Williams flied to Henderson. Colbrunn homered to left. Finley singled to left-center. Gilkey flied to Henderson. Stinnett struck out. One run. Arizona 1, New York 1.

Sixth Inning

New York—Henderson singled to right. Alfonzo popped to Williams. Olerud singled to left-center as Henderson went to third. Agbayani doubled to right-center, scoring Henderson as Olerud went to third. Ventura grounded out, Anderson to Colbrunn. Pratt grounded out, Williams to Colbrunn. One run. New York 2, Arizona 1.

Eighth Inning

Arizona—Mora now in left field. Gilkey flied to Mora. Stinnett grounded out, Ventura to Olerud. Ward, pinch-hitting for Anderson, walked. Womack singled to second as Ward went to second. Benitez now pitching. Bell doubled to left, scoring Ward and Womack. Gonzalez was walked intentionally. Williams singled to left, but Bell was thrown out at the plate, Mora to Pratt as Gonzalez went to second. Two runs. Arizona 3, New York 2.

New York—Frias now at shortstop, Olson pitching and Womack moves to right field. Alfonzo walked. Swindell now pitching. Olerud reached second on a fielding error by Womack as Alfonzo went to third. Cedeno hit a sacrifice fly to Finley, scoring Alfonzo as Olerud went to third. Ventura was walked intentionally. Harris now at third and Mantei pitching. Pratt reached first on a fielder's choice as Olerud was tagged out by Mantei, unassisted. Ventura went to second on the play. Hamilton walked. Ordonez struck out. One run. Arizona 3, New York 3.

Tenth Inning

New York—Ventura flied to Womack. Pratt homered to center. One run. New York 4, Arizona 3.

BOX SCORE

Arizona	AB	R	H	RBI	PO	A
Womack, ss-rf	5	1	1	0	1	2
Bell, 2b	2	0	1	2	1	1
Gonzalez, lf	3	0	0	0	4	0
Williams, 3b	4	0	1	0	1	2
Mantei, p	0	0	0	0	1	1
Colbrunn, 1b	3	1	1	1	5	0
Finley, cf	4	0	1	0	4	0
Gilkey, rf	3	0	0	0	3	0
Frias, ss	1	0	0	0	2	0
Stinnett, c	4	0	0	0	5	0
Anderson, p	2	0	0	0	1	1
Ward, ph	0	1	0	0	0	0
Olson, p	0	0	0	0	0	0
Swindell, p	0	0	0	0	0	0
Harris, 3b	1	0	0	0	0	0
Totals	32	3	5	3	28	7

New York	AB	R	H	RBI	PO	A
Henderson, lf	4	1	1	0	3	0
Mora, lf	0	0	0	0	1	1
Alfonzo, 2b	4	2	1	1	1	2
Olerud, 1b	4	0	2	0	8	0
Agbayani, rf	3	0	1	1	2	0
Cedeno, rf	1	0	0	1	1	0
Ventura, 3b	4	0	1	0	0	4
Pratt, c	5	1	1	1	8	1
Hamilton, cf	3	0	0	0	4	0
Ordonez, ss	4	0	1	0	2	1
Leiter, p	3	0	0	0	0	1
Benitez, p	0	0	0	0	0	0
M. Franco, ph	0	0	0	0	0	0
Dunston, pr	0	0	0	0	0	0
J. Franco, p	0	0	0	0	0	1
Totals	35	4	8	4	30	11

Arizona	0 0 0	0 1 0	0 2 0	0	—3
New York	0 0 0	1 0 1	0 1 0	1	—4

One out when winning run scored.

Arizona	IP	H	R	ER	BB	SO
Anderson	7.0	7	2	2	0	4
Olson	*0.0	0	1	0	1	0
Swindell	0.1	0	0	0	1	0
Mantei (L)	2.0	1	1	1	3	1
New York	**IP**	**H**	**R**	**ER**	**BB**	**SO**
Leiter	7.2	3	3	3	3	4
Benitez	1.1	2	0	0	1	2
J. Franco (W)	1.0	0	0	0	0	1

*Pitched to one batter in eighth.

E—Womack. DP—New York 1. LOB—Arizona 4, New York 10. 2B—Bell, Ventura, Agbayani. HR—Colbrunn, Alfonzo, Pratt. SH—Mora. SF—Cedeno. CS—Bell. HBP—By Leiter (Bell). T—3:23. A—56,177. U—Davis, plate; Froemming, first; Meals, second; Winters, third; Williams, left field; Rieker, right field.

COMPOSITE

BATTING AVERAGES

New York Mets

Player, position	G	AB	R	H	2B	3B	HR	RBI	Avg.
Olerud, 1b	4	16	3	7	0	0	1	6	.438
Henderson, lf	4	15	5	6	0	0	0	1	.400
Agbayani, rf-ph	4	10	1	3	1	0	0	1	.300
Ordonez, ss	4	14	1	4	1	0	0	2	.286
Cedeno, rf-cf-ph	4	7	1	2	0	0	0	2	.286
Alfonzo, 2b	4	16	6	4	1	0	3	6	.250
Piazza, c	2	9	0	2	0	0	0	0	.222

Player, position	G	AB	R	H	2B	3B	HR	RBI	Avg.
Ventura, 3b	4	14	1	3	2	0	0	1	.214
Dunston, cf-ph-pr	4	6	0	1	0	0	0	0	.167
Hamilton, cf-ph	4	8	0	1	0	0	0	2	.125
Pratt, ph-c	3	8	2	1	0	0	1	1	.125
Bonilla, ph	2	1	1	0	0	0	0	0	.000
Mora, cf-lf	3	1	1	0	0	0	0	0	.000
Benitez, p	2	0	0	0	0	0	0	0	.000
Cook, p	1	0	0	0	0	0	0	0	.000
Dotel, p	1	0	0	0	0	0	0	0	.000
M. Franco, ph	1	0	0	0	0	0	0	0	.000
J. Franco, p	3	0	0	0	0	0	0	0	.000
Hershiser, p	1	0	0	0	0	0	0	0	.000
Mahomes, p	1	0	0	0	0	0	0	0	.000
Reed, p	1	1	0	0	0	0	0	0	.000
Wendell, p	2	1	0	0	0	0	0	0	.000
Rogers, p	1	2	0	0	0	0	0	0	.000
Yoshii, p	1	2	0	0	0	0	0	0	.000
Leiter, p	1	3	0	0	0	0	0	0	.000
Totals	4	134	22	34	5	0	5	22	.254

Arizona Diamondbacks

Player, position	G	AB	R	H	2B	3B	HR	RBI	Avg.
Ward, ph	3	2	2	1	0	0	1	3	.500
Colbrunn, 1b	2	5	1	2	1	0	1	2	.400
Finley, cf	4	13	0	5	1	0	0	5	.385
Williams, 3b	4	16	3	6	1	0	0	0	.375
Johnson, p	1	3	0	1	1	0	0	0	.333
Bell, 2b	4	14	3	4	1	0	0	3	.286
Gonzalez, lf	4	10	3	2	1	0	1	2	.200

Player, position	G	AB	R	H	2B	3B	HR	RBI	Avg.
Stinnett, c	4	14	1	2	1	0	0	0	.143
Durazo, 1b	2	7	1	1	0	0	1	1	.143
Womack, rf-ss	4	18	2	2	0	1	0	0	.111
Chouinard, p	2	0	0	0	0	0	0	0	.000
Holmes, p	1	0	0	0	0	0	0	0	.000
Mantei, p	1	0	0	0	0	0	0	0	.000
Olson, p	2	0	0	0	0	0	0	0	.000
Plesac, p	1	0	0	0	0	0	0	0	.000
Swindell, p	3	0	0	0	0	0	0	0	.000
Daal, p	1	1	0	0	0	0	0	0	.000
Anderson, p	1	2	0	0	0	0	0	0	.000
Harris, ph-3b	2	2	0	0	0	0	0	0	.000
Fox, ss	1	3	0	0	0	0	0	0	.000
Stottlemyre, p	1	3	0	0	0	0	0	0	.000
Gilkey, rf	2	6	0	0	0	0	0	0	.000
Frias, ss	4	7	0	0	0	0	0	0	.000
Totals	4	126	16	26	7	1	4	16	.206

PITCHING AVERAGES

New York Mets

Pitcher	G	IP	H	R	ER	BB	SO	W	L	ERA
J. Franco	3	3.2	1	0	0	0	2	1	0	0.00
Benitez	2	2.1	2	0	0	1	2	0	0	0.00
Wendell	2	2.0	0	0	0	2	0	1	0	0.00
Cook	1	1.2	1	0	0	1	1	0	0	0.00
Hershiser	1	1.0	0	0	0	0	1	0	0	0.00
Reed	1	6.0	4	2	2	3	2	1	0	3.00
Leiter	1	7.2	3	3	3	3	4	0	0	3.52
Mahomes	1	1.2	3	1	1	0	1	0	0	5.40
Yoshii	1	5.1	6	4	4	0	3	0	0	6.75
Rogers	1	4.1	5	4	4	2	6	0	1	8.31
Dotel	1	0.1	1	2	2	2	0	0	0	54.00
Totals	4	36.0	26	16	16	14	22	3	1	4.00

No shutouts or saves.

Arizona Diamondbacks

Pitcher	G	IP	H	R	ER	BB	SO	W	L	ERA
Swindell	3	3.1	1	0	0	3	1	0	0	0.00
Olson	2	0.1	0	1	0	1	0	0	0	0.00
Stottlemyre	1	6.2	4	1	1	5	6	1	0	1.35
Anderson	1	7.0	7	2	2	0	4	0	0	2.57
Chouinard	2	2.0	3	1	1	0	1	0	0	4.50
Mantei	1	2.0	1	1	1	3	1	0	1	4.50
Daal	1	4.0	6	3	3	3	4	0	1	6.75
Johnson	1	8.1	8	7	7	3	11	0	1	7.56
Holmes	1	1.1	1	4	4	3	0	0	0	27.00
Plesac	1	0.1	3	2	2	0	0	0	0	54.00
Totals	4	35.1	34	22	21	21	28	1	3	5.35

No shutouts or saves.

The bottom line: What figured to be an outstanding series between two similar teams turned out to be something very different—a relatively easy 3-1 victory for the Atlanta Braves. For the sixth time, Houston failed to get its first postseason series victory, and Atlanta advanced to its eighth consecutive National League Championship Series. On paper, the Astros' starting rotation looked every bit as strong as the Braves' heralded rotation. The three-man heart of the Astros' rotation—Shane Reynolds, Jose Lima and Mike Hampton—won 59 games during the regular season, only three fewer than Atlanta's four stalwarts, Greg Maddux, Kevin Millwood, Tom Glavine and John Smoltz. But it was Atlanta, as it has all decade, that continually made the big pitches and kept the big hitters off the bases. The Braves also got the necessary timely hitting for a victory. The Braves were relatively subdued after the Division Series victory. They realized that this was just a first step—the Braves had just one championship to show for their decade of dominance. And they wanted that to change.

Why the Braves won: The Braves continually kept the top two Astros hitters off the bases. Craig Biggio and Jeff Bagwell combined for a .299 batting average, 149 extra-base hits and 199 RBIs during the regular season. In this series, the two combined for a .125 average and no RBIs or extra-base hits. Ken Caminiti had the only productive series at the plate for Houston, batting .471 with three home runs and eight RBIs. The Braves got plenty of production from the center of their lineup. Brian Jordan led the way, batting .471 with seven RBIs, and Ryan Klesko had a .333 average. In addition, No. 2 hitter Bret Boone batted .474. National League MVP Chipper Jones hit just .231, but he was pitched around and walked much of the series, setting up RBI opportunities for Jordan and Klesko. The Braves bullpen also was tough in the crunch, allowing just two runs in eight innings in the final two games of the series.

TURNING POINTS:

Game 1: Shane Reynolds struck out Ryan Klesko swinging with the bases loaded and two outs in the fifth inning, killing a Braves rally and keeping the game tied 1-1. Daryle Ward's booming homer to right an inning later gave the Astros a 2-1 lead and sent them toward a 6-1 victory in Atlanta. Reynolds and Maddux locked into a pitching duel, with both pitchers getting out of several jams. The Braves' only serious threat was the fifth inning, tying the game on an RBI single from Gerald

Brian Jordan led the Braves to the 3-1 series victory by batting .471 with three homers and eight RBIs.

Williams with two outs. But Reynolds' lone strikeout of the game kept the Braves from scoring more.

Game 2: After giving up a solo home run to Ken Caminiti in the second inning, Atlanta starter Kevin Millwood dominated the Astros lineup. Millwood didn't allow another runner to reach base until Chipper Jones' error in the seventh, and he faced just two batters over the minimum and pitched a one-hit complete game. It was the first complete game one-hitter in the postseason since Jim Lonborg of the Red Sox pitched a one-hitter against the Cardinals in the 1967 World Series. Brian Jordan continued his strong play in the series with two RBIs in the 5-1 victory.

Game 3: The Astros were one deep fly ball or a seeing-eye single or even a soft grounder from winning Game 3. Braves reliever John Rocker didn't allow it. With the bases loaded and no outs and the game tied 3-3 in the bottom of the tenth, Rocker came in and shut down the Astros. The first batter, Carl Everett, grounded to Klesko who threw to catcher Eddie Perez for the first out. Next, Tony Eusebio grounded a ball up the middle, but Walt Weiss made a diving stab, scrambled to his feet and threw another runner out at home. Then Rocker struck out Ricky Gutierrez, ending the inning and leaving Astros fans in agony. Brian Jordan picked up where he left off in Game 2 by driving in the winning run with a two-run double in the 12th inning, giving the Braves a 5-3 victory. It was Jordan's fifth RBI of the day and seventh in the last two games.

Game 4: The Astros, just as they had in their two previous losses, had a chance to win this game—as late as the bottom of the ninth inning. Down 7-5 in the final frame with a runner on and nobody out, John Rocker struck out National League MVP runner-up Jeff Bagwell and streaky hitter Carl Everett, then he coaxed hot-hitting Ken Caminiti, who had homered earlier, to hit a fly ball to center field for the series-clinching out. Two-run singles by Eddie Perez and Gerald Williams in the sixth inning put the Braves in front 7-0 before Houston rallied.

WORTH NOTING:

Astros: The Astros surpassed their entire run total—five—from their 1997 Division Series loss to the Braves by scoring six runs in Game 1. ... Jose Lima, pitching on three days rest, gave up four runs on nine hits in 6.2 innings of Game 2. This was his first start with three days rest all season. ... The Astros left 12 runners on base in Game 3. ... There was not a sellout in the series at either place. ... The Astros have never hit above .233 in any postseason appearance.

Braves: The Braves had been 12-1, with 10 straight wins in Division Series play going into Game 1. ... In losing Game 1 the Braves had lost four straight home playoff games, only scoring three runs in that span. ... There were 20,024 unsold tickets for Games 1 and 2 at Turner Field. ... Tom Glavine had not lost at the Astrodome since June 25, 1991. True to form, he didn't lose Game 3 either; the Braves won in extra innings. ... Both Game 1 starter Greg Maddux and Game 2 starter Kevin Millwood pitched in Game 3 out of the bullpen. ... Atlanta became the first team to win a Division Series after losing Game 1. (Boston matched the feat two days later with a series win over Cleveland.)

WORTH QUOTING:

Astros: Shane Reynolds on his decision to walk Chipper Jones to load the bases in the fifth: "If there are runners in scoring position, if it's a crucial situation, don't give him anything to hit. If you get behind in the count, take a chance on walking him and getting the next guy." ... Manager Larry Dierker, speaking to whether the Braves had momentum going into Game 3: "I don't know what momentum is. (Twins manager) Tom Kelly said it's your next game's starting pitcher and our next starting pitcher is Mike Hampton. So I feel pretty good about our chances." ... Tony Eusebio, on Walt Weiss's game-saving stab in the bottom of the tenth: "There's no way he should have made that play. He made a heck of a play. When I saw the ball go past the pitcher, I thought it was a hit for sure." ... Jeff Bagwell, on losing the series: "We had a chance, but it wasn't enough. It just goes to show you how big Game 3 is." ... Craig Biggio, also on losing the series: "It's frustrating beyond belief. We really didn't start playing relaxed until it was too late."

Braves: Chipper Jones on the Astros' decision to pitch around him: "It's frustrating. I hope to go up there in situations where

they have to pitch to me. Other teams have been doing this for awhile now and mostly the guys behind me have made them pay." ... Kevin Millwood on Caminiti's home run, the only hit Millwood allowed in Game 2: "That pitch was a mistake. I was trying to go away and threw it right over the middle of the plate. But it was one of the few mistakes I made all day." ... Braves closer John Rocker about his being brought in with the bases loaded and no outs in the bottom of the tenth: "If you can think of a tougher situation than that, let me know." ... John Smoltz on Tony Eusebio's ground ball in the tenth inning: "When he hit it, I got up and started to walk out of the dugout." ... John Smoltz on Ken Caminiti's Division Series performance: "He's just got me baffled when it comes to this time of the year. He almost won the game single-handedly."

Game 1 at Atlanta

HOUSTON 6, ATLANTA 1

HOW THEY SCORED

Second Inning

Houston—Everett singled in front of the plate. Caminiti walked. Ward struck out. Eusebio singled to center, scoring Everett as Caminiti went to third. Gutierrez walked. With Reynolds batting, Caminiti caught stealing home, Perez to C. Jones, as Eusebio went to third and Gutierrez to second on the play. Reynolds grounded out, Hernandez to Klesko. One run. Houston 1, Atlanta 0.

Fifth Inning

Atlanta—Perez grounded out, Caminiti to Bagwell. Hernandez singled to center. Hernandez stole second. Maddux grounded out, Gutierrez to Bagwell. Williams singled to center, scoring Hernandez. Boone singled to short as Williams went to second. C. Jones walked. Klesko struck out. One run. Houston 1, Atlanta 1.

Sixth Inning

Houston—Ward homered to right. Eusebio singled to right. Gutierrez grounded into a double play, Hernandez to Boone to Klesko. Reynolds singled to center. Biggio singled to right and went to second as Reynolds was thrown out at third, Jordan to C. Jones. One run. Houston 2, Atlanta 1.

Ninth Inning

Houston—Mieske pinch-hitting for Henry, walked. Biggio struck out. Javier, pinch-hitting for Spiers, singled to right. Bagwell walked to third. Everett hit a sacrifice fly to A. Jones, scoring Mieske. Caminiti homered to left-center, scoring Javier and Bagwell. Barker grounded out, Remlinger to Klesko. Four runs. Houston 6, Atlanta 1.

BOX SCORE

Houston	AB	R	H	RBI	PO	A
Biggio, 2b	5	0	1	0	4	6
Spiers, rf-lf	4	0	2	0	2	0
Javier, ph-lf	1	1	1	0	0	0
Bagwell, 1b	4	1	1	0	14	1
Everett, cf-rf	3	1	1	1	2	0
Caminiti, 3b	4	1	3	3	0	3
Ward, lf	3	1	1	1	2	0
Barker, cf	1	0	0	0	0	0
Eusebio, c	4	0	2	1	3	0
Gutierrez, ss	2	0	0	0	0	6
Reynolds, p	3	0	1	0	0	0
Miller, p	0	0	0	0	0	0
Henry, p	0	0	0	0	0	0
Mieske, ph	0	1	0	0	0	0
Wagner, p	0	0	0	0	0	0
Totals	34	6	13	6	27	16
Atlanta	AB	R	H	RBI	PO	A
Williams, lf	4	0	2	1	0	0
Boone, 2b	4	0	1	0	2	4
C. Jones, 3b	2	0	0	0	2	0
Klesko, 1b	4	0	0	0	9	0
Jordan, rf	4	0	2	0	2	1
A. Jones, cf	4	0	0	0	4	0
Perez, c	4	0	1	0	7	1
Hernandez, ss	4	1	1	0	1	4
Maddux, p	1	0	0	0	0	1
Lockhart, ph	0	0	0	0	0	0
Battle, ph	1	0	0	0	0	0
Remlinger, p	0	0	0	0	0	2
Totals	32	1	7	1	27	13

```
Houston ...........................  0 1 0  0 0 1  0 0 4—6
Atlanta ...........................  0 0 0  0 1 0  0 0 x—1
```

Houston	IP	H	R	ER	BB	SO
Reynolds (W)	6.0	7	1	1	2	1
Miller	0.1	0	0	0	0	0
Henry	1.2	0	0	0	0	0
Wagner	1.0	0	0	0	0	0
Atlanta	IP	H	R	ER	BB	SO
Maddux (L)	7.0	10	2	2	4	5
Remlinger	2.0	3	4	4	2	2

DP—Houston 1, Atlanta 2. LOB—Houston 9, Atlanta 7. HR—Ward, Caminiti. SH—Barker, Maddux. SF—Everett. SB—Spiers, Hernandez. CS—Caminiti. T—3:03. A—39,119. U—Winters, plate; Williams, first; Rieker, second; Davis, third; Froemming, left field; Meals, right field.

Game 2 at Atlanta

ATLANTA 5, HOUSTON 1

HOW THEY SCORED

First Inning

Atlanta—Williams singled to short. Boone struck out. Williams stole second. C. Jones grounded to Bagwell as Williams went to third. Jordan singled to center, scoring Williams. Klesko flied to Ward. One run. Atlanta 1, Houston 0.

Second Inning

Houston—Everett struck out. Caminiti homered to right. Ward popped to Hernandez. Eusebio grounded out, Hernandez to Klesko. One run. Houston 1, Atlanta 1.

Sixth Inning

Atlanta—Jordan grounded out, Lima to Bagwell. Klesko singled to left-center. A. Jones doubled to left as Klesko went to third. Perez hit a sacrifice fly to Everett, scoring Klesko. Hernandez was walked intentionally. Millwood struck out. One run. Atlanta 2, Houston 1.

Seventh Inning

Atlanta—Williams flied to Everett. Boone doubled to left-center and went to third on Ward's fielding error. C. Jones was walked intentionally. Jordan hit a sacrifice fly to Everett, scoring Boone as C. Jones went to second. Elarton now pitching. Klesko singled to left, scoring C. Jones. Klesko went to second on a wild pitch. Klesko went to third on a wild pitch. A. Jones singled to left, scoring Klesko. Perez grounded out, Gutierrez to Bagwell. Three runs. Atlanta 5, Houston 1.

BOX SCORE

Houston	AB	R	H	RBI	PO	A
Biggio, 2b	4	0	0	0	2	1
Javier, rf	4	0	0	0	1	0
Bagwell, 1b	3	0	0	0	7	1
Everett, cf	3	0	0	0	5	0
Caminiti, 3b	3	1	1	1	0	2
Ward, lf	3	0	0	0	1	0
Eusebio, c	3	0	0	0	5	0
Gutierrez, ss	3	0	0	0	2	4
Lima, p	2	0	0	0	0	1
Elarton, p	0	0	0	0	0	0
Powell, p	0	0	0	0	0	0
Spiers, ph	1	0	0	0	0	0
Totals	29	1	1	1	24	9

Atlanta	AB	R	H	RBI	PO	A
Williams, lf	5	1	1	0	3	0
Boone, 2b	4	1	2	0	2	3
C. Jones, 3b	3	1	1	0	0	1
Jordan, rf	3	0	1	2	2	0
Klesko, 1b	4	2	3	1	8	0
Hunter, 1b	0	0	0	0	1	0
A. Jones, cf	4	0	2	1	0	0
Perez, c	3	0	0	1	8	0
Hernandez, ss	2	0	0	0	2	2
Weiss, ss	1	0	0	0	0	0
Millwood, p	4	0	1	0	1	4
Totals	33	5	11	5	27	11

Houston .... 0 1 0 0 0 0 0 0 0—1
Atlanta .... 1 0 0 0 0 1 3 0 x—5

Houston	IP	H	R	ER	BB	SO
Lima (L)	6.2	9	4	4	2	4
Elarton	0.1	2	1	1	0	0
Powell	1.0	0	0	0	0	1
Atlanta	IP	H	R	ER	BB	SO
Millwood (W)	9.0	1	1	1	0	8

E—Ward, C. Jones. LOB—Houston 1, Atlanta 8. 2B—A. Jones, Boone. HR—Caminiti. SF—Perez, Jordan. SB—Williams. WP—Elarton 2. T—2:13. A—41,913. U—Williams, plate; Rieker, first; Davis, second; Froemming, third; Meals, left field; Winters, right field.

Game 3 at Houston

ATLANTA 5, HOUSTON 3 (12 INNINGS)

HOW THEY SCORED

First Inning

Houston—Biggio singled to left. Bell grounded out, Boone to Hunter, as Biggio went to second. Bagwell hit by a pitch. Caminiti singled to left, scoring Biggio as Bagwell went to second. Mieske flied to A. Jones. Everett walked. Eusebio walked, scoring Bagwell. Gutierrez flied to Jordan. Two runs. Houston 2, Atlanta 0.

Sixth Inning

Atlanta—Glavine grounded out, Hampton to Bagwell. Williams popped to Biggio. Boone singled to left. C. Jones walked. Jordan homered to left-center, scoring Boone and C. Jones. A. Jones struck out. Three runs. Atlanta 3, Houston 2.

Seventh Inning

Houston—Weiss now at shortstop and Mulholland pitching. Gutierrez grounded out, Weiss to Hunter. Johnson, pinch-hitting for Hampton,

Atlanta's John Rocker was sterling in the Division Series, picking up a win and a save in his two outings.

doubled to left. Maddux now pitching. Barker now pinch-running for Johnson. Barker stole third. Biggio walked. Spiers now pinch-hitting for Bell and Remlinger now pitching. Spiers singled to left, scoring Barker as Biggio went to third. Bagwell was walked intentionally. Caminiti struck out. Mieske flied to A. Jones. One run. Atlanta 3, Houston 3.

Twelfth Inning

Atlanta—Powell now pitching. Weiss struck out. Nixon singled to left. Boone singled to right as Nixon went to second. C. Jones grounded out, Caminiti to Bagwell, as Nixon went to third and Boone to second. Jordan doubled to right, scoring Nixon and Boone. A. Jones was walked intentionally. Guillen, pinch-hitting for Rocker, flied to Javier. Two runs. Atlanta 5, Houston 3.

BOX SCORE

Atlanta	AB	R	H	RBI	PO	A
Williams, lf	5	0	2	0	0	0
Nixon, pr-lf	1	1	1	0	0	0
Boone, 2b	6	2	3	0	3	6
C. Jones, 3b	4	1	1	0	1	1
Jordan, rf	5	1	3	5	4	0
A. Jones, cf	5	0	1	0	2	0
Hunter, 1b	3	0	0	0	9	0
Lockhart, ph	1	0	0	0	0	0
Springer, p	0	0	0	0	0	0
Rocker, p	0	0	0	0	0	0
Guillen, ph	1	0	0	0	0	0
Millwood, p	0	0	0	0	0	0
Perez, c	5	0	1	0	14	0
Hernandez, ss	3	0	0	0	2	3
Mulholland, p	0	0	0	0	0	0
Maddux, p	0	0	0	0	0	0
Remlinger, p	0	0	0	0	0	0
Klesko, ph-1b	2	0	0	0	1	1
Glavine, p	2	0	0	0	0	0
Weiss, ph-ss	3	0	0	0	0	3
Totals	46	5	12	5	36	14

Houston	AB	R	H	RBI	PO	A
Biggio, 2b	5	1	1	0	4	1
Bell, rf	3	0	1	0	1	0
Spiers, ph-lf	2	0	1	1	0	0
Henry, p	0	0	0	0	0	0
Bogar, ph	0	0	0	0	0	0
Powell, p	0	0	0	0	0	0
Bagwell, 1b	2	1	0	0	10	1
Caminiti, 3b	6	1	3	1	0	4
Mieske, lf	4	0	0	0	0	0
Cabrera, p	0	0	0	0	0	0
Javier, lf	2	0	1	0	2	0
Houston	AB	R	H	RBI	PO	A
Everett, cf-rf	5	0	1	0	0	0
Eusebio, c	4	0	1	1	16	2
Gutierrez, ss	5	0	0	0	2	6
Hampton, p	2	0	0	0	0	1
Johnson, ph	1	0	1	0	0	0
Barker, pr-cf	2	1	0	0	1	0
Totals	43	3	9	3	36	15

Atlanta ....0 0 0 0 0 3 0 0 0 0 0 2—5
Houston ....2 0 0 0 0 0 1 0 0 0 0 0—3

Atlanta	IP	H	R	ER	BB	SO
Glavine	6.0	5	2	2	3	6
Mulholland	0.1	1	1	1	0	0
Maddux	*0.0	0	0	0	1	0
Remlinger	1.2	1	0	0	1	2
Springer	†1.0	2	0	0	1	1
Rocker (W)	2.0	0	0	0	1	2
Millwood (S)	1.0	0	0	0	0	1

Houston	IP	H	R	ER	BB	SO
Hampton	7.0	6	3	3	1	9
Cabrera	2.0	2	0	0	0	6
Henry	2.0	1	0	0	3	2
Powell (L)	1.0	3	2	2	1	1

*Pitched to one batter in seventh. †Pitched to three batters in 10th. E—Gutierrez, Eusebio. DP—Atlanta 2, Houston 2. LOB—Atlanta 10, Houston 12. 2B—Jordan, Johnson. HR—Jordan. SB—Nixon, Barker. HBP—By Glavine (Bagwell). WP—Hampton. T—4:19. A—48,625. U—Hirschbeck, plate; DeMuth, first; Marsh, second; Schrieber, third; Gorman, left field; Bell, right field.

Game 4 at Houston

ATLANTA 7, HOUSTON 5

HOW THEY SCORED

First Inning

Atlanta—Williams doubled to left. Boone flied to Everett as Williams went to third. C. Jones hit a sacrifice fly to Everett, scoring Williams. Jordan singled to left. Jordan caught stealing, Eusebio to Bogar. One run. Atlanta 1, Houston 0.

Third Inning

Atlanta—Smoltz doubled to right. Williams sacrificed Smoltz to third, Reynolds to Biggio. Boone singled to left, scoring Smoltz. C. Jones popped to Bogar. Boone stole second. Jordan struck out. One run. Atlanta 2, Houston 0.

Dejected Houston pitcher Jose Lima remains in the dugout well after the series-clinching Game 4 loss.

Sixth Inning

Atlanta—Jordan singled to the mound. Klesko singled to right as Jordan went to third. Holt now pitching. A. Jones singled to left and went to second on Spiers' fielding error. Jordan scored on the play and Klesko went to third. Perez singled to center, scoring Klesko and A. Jones. Weiss singled to right as Perez went to second. Elarton now pitching. Smoltz sacrificed Perez to third and Weiss to second, Caminiti to Biggio. Williams singled to center, scoring Perez and Weiss. Boone forced Williams at second, Elarton to Bogar. C. Jones singled to center as Boone went to third. Jordan struck out. Five runs. Atlanta 7, Houston 0.

Seventh Inning

Houston—Eusebio homered to left. Bogar flied to A. Jones. Johnson, pinch-hitting for Elarton, walked. Biggio forced Johnson at second, Weiss to Boone. Javier forced Biggio at second, Weiss to Boone. One run. Atlanta 7, Houston 1.

Eighth Inning

Houston—Bagwell singled to center. Everett hit by a pitch. Caminiti homered to center, scoring Bagwell and Everett. Mulholland now pitching. Spiers flied to A. Jones. Eusebio singled to left-center. Bogar doubled to left, scoring Eusebio. Bell announced as pinch-hitter for Miller. McGlinchy now pitching. Ward, pinch-hitting for Bell, grounded to Hunter as Bogar went to third. Lockhart now at second and Rocker pitching. Biggio struck out. Four runs. Atlanta 7, Houston 5.

BOX SCORE

Atlanta	AB	R	H	RBI	PO	A
Williams, lf	4	1	2	2	1	0
Boone, 2b	5	0	3	1	4	2
Rocker, p	0	0	0	0	0	0
C. Jones, 3b	4	0	1	1	0	2
Jordan, rf	5	1	2	0	4	0
Klesko, 1b	2	1	1	0	4	1
Hunter, 1b	1	0	0	0	1	0
A. Jones, cf	5	1	1	1	6	0
Perez, c	4	1	2	2	6	0
Hernandez, ss	2	0	0	0	1	0
Weiss, ss	2	1	1	0	0	2
Smoltz, p	3	1	2	0	0	1
Mulholland, p	0	0	0	0	0	0
McGlinchy, p	0	0	0	0	0	0
Lockhart, 2b	0	0	0	0	0	0
Totals	37	7	15	7	27	8

Houston	AB	R	H	RBI	PO	A
Biggio, 2b	5	0	0	0	4	2
Javier, rf	4	0	1	0	1	0
Bagwell, 1b	4	1	1	0	5	0
Everett, cf	4	1	0	0	1	0
Caminiti, 3b	4	1	1	3	1	1
Spiers, lf	4	0	0	0	1	0
Eusebio, c	4	2	2	1	10	1
Bogar, ss	4	0	3	1	4	4
Reynolds, p	1	0	0	0	0	1
Holt, p	0	0	0	0	0	0
Elarton, p	0	0	0	0	0	1
Johnson, ph	0	0	0	0	0	0
Miller, p	0	0	0	0	0	0
Bell, ph	0	0	0	0	0	0
Ward, ph	1	0	0	0	0	0
Powell, p	0	0	0	0	0	0
Totals	35	5	8	5	27	10

Atlanta					
Atlanta	1 0 1	0 0 5	0 0 0	—	7
Houston	0 0 0	0 0 0	1 4 0	—	5

Atlanta	IP	H	R	ER	BB	SO
Smoltz (W)	‡7.0	6	4	4	3	3
Mulholland	0.1	2	1	1	0	0
McGlinchy	0.1	0	0	0	0	0
Rocker (S)	1.1	0	0	0	1	3

Houston	IP	H	R	ER	BB	SO
Reynolds (L)	*5.0	9	4	4	1	4
Holt	†0.0	3	3	3	0	0
Elarton	2.0	2	0	0	1	3
Miller	1.0	1	0	0	0	2
Powell	1.0	0	0	0	1	1

*Pitched to two batters in sixth. †Pitched to three batters in sixth. ‡Pitched to three batters in eighth.

E—Hernandez, Spiers. DP—Houston 1. LOB—Atlanta 8, Houston 9. 2B—Williams, Smoltz, Bogar. HR—Eusebio, Caminiti. SH—Williams, Smoltz, Reynolds. SF—C. Jones. SB—Boone, Everett. CS—Jordan. HBP—By Smoltz (Everett). WP—Miller, Rocker. T—3:12. A—48,553. U—DeMuth, plate; Marsh, first; Schrieber, second; Gorman, third; Bell, left field; Hirschbeck, right field.

COMPOSITE

BATTING AVERAGES

Atlanta Braves

Player, position	G	AB	R	H	2B	3B	HR	RBI	Avg.
Nixon, pr-lf	1	1	1	1	0	0	0	0	1.000
Smoltz, p	1	3	1	2	1	0	0	0	.667
Boone, 2b	4	19	3	9	1	0	0	1	.474
Jordan, rf	4	17	2	8	1	0	1	7	.471
Williams, lf	4	18	2	7	1	0	0	3	.389
Klesko, 1b-ph	4	12	3	4	0	0	0	1	.333
Perez, c	4	16	1	4	0	0	0	3	.250
Millwood, p	2	4	0	1	0	0	0	0	.250
C. Jones, 3b	4	13	2	3	0	0	0	1	.231
A. Jones, cf	4	18	1	4	1	0	0	2	.222
Weiss, ss-ph	3	6	1	1	0	0	0	0	.167

Player, position	G	AB	R	H	2B	3B	HR	RBI	Avg.
Hernandez, ss	4	11	1	1	0	0	0	0	.091
McGlinchy, p	1	0	0	0	0	0	0	0	.000
Mulholland, p	2	0	0	0	0	0	0	0	.000
Remlinger, p	2	0	0	0	0	0	0	0	.000
Rocker, p	2	0	0	0	0	0	0	0	.000
Springer, p	1	0	0	0	0	0	0	0	.000
Battle, ph	1	1	0	0	0	0	0	0	.000
Guillen, ph	1	1	0	0	0	0	0	0	.000
Lockhart, ph-2b	3	1	0	0	0	0	0	0	.000
Maddux, p	2	1	0	0	0	0	0	0	.000
Glavine, p	1	2	0	0	0	0	0	0	.000
Hunter, 1b	3	4	0	0	0	0	0	0	.000
Totals	4	148	18	45	5	0	1	18	.304

Houston Astros

Player, position	G	AB	R	H	2B	3B	HR	RBI	Avg.
Johnson, ph	2	1	0	1	0	0	0	0	1.000
Bogar, ph-ss	2	4	0	3	1	0	0	1	.750
Caminiti, 3b	4	17	3	8	0	0	3	8	.471
Bell, rf-ph	2	3	0	1	0	0	0	0	.333
Javier, ph-lf-rf	4	11	1	3	0	0	0	0	.273
Spiers, rf-lf-ph	4	11	0	3	0	0	0	1	.273
Eusebio, c	4	15	2	4	0	0	1	3	.267
Reynolds, p	2	4	0	1	0	0	0	0	.250
Bagwell, 1b	4	13	2	2	0	0	0	1	.154
Ward, lf-ph	3	7	1	1	0	0	1	1	.143
Everett, cf-rf	4	15	2	2	0	0	0	1	.133
Biggio, 2b	4	19	1	2	0	0	0	0	.105
Cabrera, p	1	0	0	0	0	0	0	0	.000
Elarton, p	2	0	0	0	0	0	0	0	.000
Henry, p	2	0	0	0	0	0	0	0	.000
Holt, p	1	0	0	0	0	0	0	0	.000
Miller, p	2	0	0	0	0	0	0	0	.000
Powell, p	3	0	0	0	0	0	0	0	.000
Wagner, p	1	0	0	0	0	0	0	0	.000
Hampton, p	1	2	0	0	0	0	0	0	.000
Lima, p	1	2	0	0	0	0	0	0	.000
Barker, cf-pr	2	3	1	0	0	0	0	0	.000
Mieske, ph-lf	2	4	1	0	0	0	0	0	.000
Gutierrez, ss	3	10	0	0	0	0	0	0	.000
Totals	4	141	15	31	2	0	5	15	.220

PITCHING AVERAGES

Atlanta Braves

Pitcher	G	IP	H	R	ER	BB	SO	W	L	ERA
Rocker	2	3.1	0	0	0	2	5	1	0	0.00
Springer	1	1.0	2	0	0	1	1	0	0	0.00
McGlinchy	1	0.1	0	0	0	0	0	0	0	0.00
Millwood	2	10.0	1	1	1	0	9	1	0	0.90
Maddux	2	7.0	10	2	2	5	5	0	1	2.57
Glavine	1	6.0	5	2	2	3	6	0	0	3.00
Smoltz	1	7.0	6	4	4	3	3	1	0	5.14
Remlinger	2	3.2	4	4	4	3	2	0	0	9.82
Mulholland	2	0.2	3	2	2	0	0	0	0.	27.00
Totals	4	39.0	31	15	15	17	33	3	1	3.46

No shutouts. Saves—Millwood, Rocker.

Houston Astros

Pitcher	G	IP	H	R	ER	BB	SO	W	L.	ERA
Henry	2	3.2	1	0	0	3	2	0	0	0.00
Cabrera	1	2.0	2	0	0	6	6	0	0	0.00
Miller	2	1.1	1	0	0	0	2	0	0	0.00
Wagner	1	1.0	0	0	0	1	1	0	0	0.00
Hampton	1	7.0	6	3	3	1	9	0	0	3.86
Elarton	2	2.1	4	1	1	1	3	0	0	3.86
Reynolds	2	11.0	16	5	5	3	5	1	1	4.09
Lima	1	6.2	9	4	4	2	4	0	1	5.40
Powell	3	3.0	3	2	2	1	3	0	1	6.00
Holt	1	0.0	3	3	3	0	0	0	0	Inf.
Totals	4	38.0	45	18	18	11	35	1	3	4.26

No shutouts or saves.

A.L. DIVISION SERIES

BOSTON VS. CLEVELAND

The bottom line: The Boston Red Sox avenged last year's Division Series loss to the Cleveland Indians with a stunning five-game series victory. Not only did they beat a team that won 97 games in the regular season, they beat them three consecutive times with the series on the brink. After the Indians drubbed the Red Sox 11-1 at Jacobs Field in Game 2 for a 2-0 series lead, Boston's morale and shear firepower appeared diminished as they went home to Fenway Park for Game 3. But the team responded impressively, ending a five-series losing streak and sending the team to the A.L. Championship Series for the first time since 1986.

Why the Red Sox won: In their most critical time of need, ace righthander Pedro Martinez came through, pitching six innings of no-hit relief in the 12-8 series-clinching win. Martinez, baseball's most dominant pitcher during the regular season, had not pitched in the series after he was forced out of Game 1 with a sore back after working four shutout innings. It looked doubtful that he would pitch again in 1999, but he did—masterfully. After Boston forged an 8-8 tie in Game 5, Martinez came in and helped settle down a series that had become a slugfest.

TURNING POINTS:

Game 1: The Red Sox led, 2-0, after four innings when Martinez was forced to leave, and the Indians took advantage of his successors. Righthander Derek Lowe retired Cleveland in order in the fifth and got two outs in the sixth before trouble erupted. Manny Ramirez hit a grounder to third that John Valentin fielded cleanly, but his throw went into the dirt at first, and Ramirez was safe. Cleanup hitter Jim Thome then crushed Lowe's next pitch 434 feet for a home run that tied the game. That was the score when Travis Fryman singled with one out and the bases loaded in the ninth inning, giving Cleveland a 3-2 win.

Game 2: Although Thome's grand slam in the fourth inning made the highlight shows, the biggest hit belonged to 40-year-old DH Harold Baines, a late-season acquisition from Baltimore. After Boston starter Bret Saberhagen, working with a 1-0 lead, walked Fryman leading off the third inning, second baseman Jose Offerman botched a potential double-play grounder by Sandy Alomar, pulling first baseman Mike Stanley off the bag with a poor relay throw. Kenny Lofton walked, and Omar Vizquel drove in two runs with a triple. Roberto Alomar doubled in a run, and Thome walked, setting the stage for Baines' three-run blast that gave the Indians a 6-1 lead. Thome's grand slam was the icing on an 11-1 triumph.

Game 3: With star shortstop Nomar Garciaparra sidelined with a bruised right wrist and the Indians primed for a sweep, the Red Sox kept the series alive with a 9-3 victory. Boston broke open a 3-3 game with six runs in the seventh inning. The big blows were a two-run double by Valentin and a three-run homer by Brian Daubach. Just as Martinez's early exit proved pivotal in Game 1, an early departure by Cleveland righthander Dave Burba—who retired the first nine batters he faced before leaving with numbness in his pitching arm—affected Game 3. Burba's replacement, Jaret Wright, gave up two runs and three hits in the fifth inning, then a solo home run to Valentin in the sixth.

Game 4: A cynic might say there's not much of a turning point after the national anthem in a 23-7 game, but the biggest blow might have been Offerman's two-run homer into the screen above Fenway Park's Green Monster with no outs in the second inning. Offerman's blast increased Boston's lead to 7-2 and chased ineffective Cleveland starter Bartolo Colon, pitching on three days rest for the first time in his career. It was the first of two five-run innings for Boston.

Game 5: With the score tied 8-8 in the seventh, Indians manager Mike Hargrove elected to walk Garciaparra and pitch to Troy O'Leary with one out and one on. The strategy backfired as O'Leary—who in the third inning had clubbed the first postseason grand slam in Red Sox history after an intentional pass to Garciaparra—drove righthander Paul Shuey's first pitch over the right field wall, giving Boston an 11-8 lead. That was more than enough support for Martinez, who held Cleveland hitless the remainder of the game. The Indians gave up leads of 5-2 and 8-7.

WORTH NOTING:

Indians: Cleveland's Game 1 victory snapped a streak of eight consecutive losses in playoff openers. ... Thome ended the series with 16 postseason home runs, third on the all-time list behind Reggie Jackson (18) and Mickey Mantle (18). He passed Babe Ruth (15). ... Thome's two postseason grand slams are the most of any player. ... The Indians and Red Sox combined for 79 runs in the five-game series, three shy of the record for one postseason series, set by the Yankees and Pirates in the 1960 World Series. However, the 1960 Series lasted seven games. ... Nagy had been 3-0 with a 1.23 ERA against the Red Sox in postseason play before getting tagged for eight runs in three innings in Game 5.

Red Sox: Boston became the second team (after the 1995 Mariners) to rebound from a two-games-to-none deficit and win a Division Series. The Red Sox became just the fifth team to come from two down in any best-of-five playoff series. ... Before their Game 3 win, the Red Sox had lost 18 of 19 postseason games, beginning with Bill Buckner's infamous error in Game 6 of the 1986 World Series. ... The 11-1 loss in Game 2 was the most lopsided in Red Sox playoffs history. ... Boston's 23 runs and 24 hits in Game 4 were the most in postseason history for any team. So was the 16-run margin of victory.

WORTH QUOTING:

Indians: Travis Fryman, after Martinez's exit in Game 1: "We got a break with Pedro getting hurt. Any time you face Pedro, he's tough. He's the best pitcher I ever faced. You look up there in the sixth inning and you don't see him out there, it gives you a little pick-me-up." ... Thome, on the same subject: "We were excited. Pedro was pitching a real good game. To get him out of the game like that, it livened us up." ...Thome, on his Game 1 homer off Derek Lowe: "I figured he wasn't going to start me off with a fastball over the plate. So I looked for a changeup and there it was." ... Hargrove, after Game 2: "I don't think there is any danger of being overconfident. We have a tremendous amount of respect for the Red Sox. We know that we still have a fight on our hands. We haven't finished the job by any stretch of the imagination." ... Roberto Alomar, after Game 2: "Teams have been down 2-0 and come back before." ... Burba, after being forced to leave Game 3 with an injury and the Indians thinking sweep: "What frustrated me is that I felt I let my team down. I felt I let the air out of the balloon." ... Sandy Alomar, after the 23-7 loss in Game 4: "It was embarrassing. It was humiliating. But the good part about it is that none of those runs mean anything tomorrow." ... Hargrove, on Martinez's Game 5 performance: "He was outstanding. His velocity wasn't used to what we were seeing, but his off-speed pitches were good. He pitched. He made his pitches when he needed to."

Red Sox: Manager Jimy Williams, on Martinez telling him he felt pain in his back after the fourth inning of Game 1: "He never says anything, so for him to say something, we knew it meant something was wrong." ... Bret Saberhagen, on Harold Baines' big hit in Game 2: "I thought I made a real good pitch on Baines—down and away—and he deposited it in the right-field seats. It's going to be a long flight home." ... Red Sox outfielder Trot Nixon, after Game 5: "There ain't no scale that can measure the heart of this team. Whether we're down two games or three games, there is no quit in this team." ... Saberhagen, after Game 5: "You might say we're celebrating a little too hard. But after a series like this, you have to kick off your shoes a little bit."

Game 1 at Cleveland

CLEVELAND 3, BOSTON 2

HOW THEY SCORED

Second Inning

Boston—Garciaparra homered to center. O'Leary grounded to Thome. Stanley singled to left. Daubach struck out. Lewis lined to R. Alomar. One run. Boston 1, Cleveland 0.

Fourth Inning

Boston—Garciaparra doubled to left. O'Leary struck out. Stanley singled to left and went to second as Garciaparra scored ahead of the throw from the outfield. Daubach struck out. Lewis grounded out, R. Alomar to Thome. One run. Boston 2, Cleveland 0.

Sixth Inning

Cleveland—Vizquel grounded out, Garciaparra to Stanley. R. Alomar grounded out, Lowe to Stanley. Ramirez reached first on a throwing error by Valentin. Thome homered to right-center, scoring Ramirez. Baines grounded out, Offerman to Stanley. Two runs. Boston 2, Cleveland 2.

Ninth Inning

Cleveland—Ramirez hit by a pitch. Cormier now pitching. Thome flied to O'Leary. Cordero, pinch-hitting for Baines, singled to right as Ramirez went to second. Sexson, pinch-hitting for Justice off new Boston pitcher Garces, walked. Fryman singled to left, scoring Ramirez as Cordero went to third and Sexson to second. One run. Cleveland 3, Boston 2.

BOX SCORE

Boston	AB	R	H	RBI	PO	A
Offerman, 2b	2	0	0	0	3	5
Valentin, 3b	4	0	0	0	1	3
Varitek, c	4	0	0	0	7	0
Garciaparra, ss	3	2	2	1	0	1
O'Leary, lf	4	0	0	0	1	0
Stanley, 1b	4	0	3	1	9	1
Daubach, dh	3	0	0	0	0	0
Lewis, cf	3	0	0	0	3	0
Nixon, rf	3	0	0	0	0	0
P. Martinez, p	0	0	0	0	1	0
Lowe, p	0	0	0	0	0	2
Cormier, p	0	0	0	0	0	0
Garces, p	0	0	0	0	0	0
Totals	30	2	5	2	25	12

Cleveland	AB	R	H	RBI	PO	A
Lofton, cf	3	0	0	0	1	0
Vizquel, ss	4	0	0	0	1	2
R. Alomar, 2b	4	0	2	0	3	4
Ramirez, rf	3	2	0	0	0	0
Thome, 1b	4	1	1	2	7	0
Baines, dh	3	0	1	0	0	0
Cordero, ph-dh	1	0	1	0	0	0
Justice, lf	3	0	0	0	3	1
Sexson, ph	0	0	0	0	0	0
Fryman, 3b	4	0	1	1	0	2
S. Alomar, c	3	0	0	0	12	0
Colon, p	0	0	0	0	0	0
Shuey, p	0	0	0	0	0	0
Totals	32	3	6	3	27	9

Boston	0 1 0	1 0 0	0 0 0	—2
Cleveland	0 0 0	0 0 2	0 0 1	—3

One out when winning run scored.

Boston	IP	H	R	ER	BB	SO
P. Martinez	4.0	3	0	0	1	3
Lowe (L)	*4.0	1	3	1	0	4
Cormier	0.1	1	0	0	0	0
Garces	0.0	1	0	0	1	0

Cleveland	IP	H	R	ER	BB	SO
Colon	8.0	5	2	2	3	11
Shuey (W)	1.0	0	0	0	0	1

*Pitched to one batter in ninth.

E—Valentin, R. Alomar. DP—Cleveland 2. LOB—Boston 4, Cleveland 7. 2B—Garciaparra. HR—Garciaparra, Thome. SB—R. Alomar. HBP—By Lowe (Ramirez). T—2:53. A—45,182. U—Roe, plate; Young, first; Hirschbeck, second; Brinkman, third; Reilly, left field; Cousins, right field.

Game 2 at Cleveland

CLEVELAND 11, BOSTON 1

HOW THEY SCORED

Third Inning

Boston— Huskey lined to R. Alomar. Nixon doubled right. Buford struck out. Offerman singled to right, scoring Nixon. Offerman was out trying for second on the play, Ramirez to Thome to Vizquel. One run. Boston 1, Cleveland 0.

Cleveland—Fryman walked. S. Alomar forced Fryman at second, Garciaparra to Offerman. Lofton walked. Vizquel tripled to right, scoring

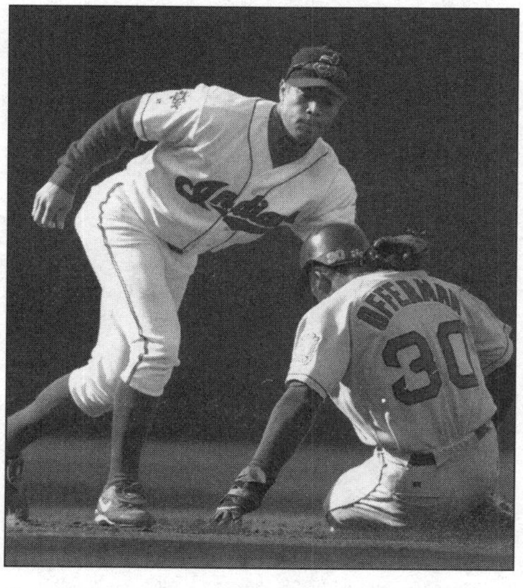

Roberto Alomar tags out Jose Offerman in Game 1. Alomar also recorded a .368 average in the series.

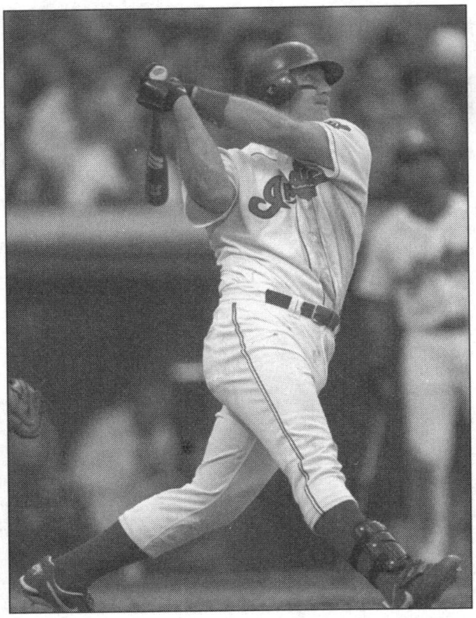

Jim Thome had a huge offensive series—.353 average with four homers and 10 RBIs in 17 at-bats.

S. Alomar and Lofton. R. Alomar doubled to right, scoring Vizquel. Ramirez flied to Buford as R. Alomar went to third. Thome walked. Baines homered to right-center, scoring R. Alomar and Thome. Wasdin now pitching. Justice flied to Nixon. Six runs. Cleveland 6, Boston 1.

Fourth Inning

Cleveland—Fryman walked. S. Alomar struck out. With Lofton batting, Fryman stole second. Lofton walked. Vizquel singled to left as Fryman went to third and Lofton to second. R. Alomar hit a sacrifice fly to O'Leary, scoring Fryman. Ramirez walked. Thome homered to right-center, scoring Lofton, Vizquel and Ramirez. Baines flied to O'Leary. Five runs. Cleveland 11, Boston 1.

BOX SCORE

Boston	AB	R	H	RBI	PO	A
Offerman, 2b	4	0	2	1	2	1
Valentin, 3b	4	0	0	0	1	0
Varitek, c	4	0	0	0	9	0
Garciaparra, ss	3	0	0	0	2	3
Merloni, ss	1	0	0	0	0	0
O'Leary, lf	3	0	1	0	3	0
Stanley, 1b	3	0	2	0	2	1
Huskey, dh	3	0	0	0	0	0
Nixon, rf	2	1	1	0	1	0
Buford, cf	3	0	0	0	3	0
Saberhagen, p	0	0	0	0	0	0
Wasdin, p	0	0	0	0	0	0
Wakefield, p	0	0	0	0	0	0
Gordon, p	0	0	0	0	0	0
Beck, p	0	0	0	0	1	0
Totals	30	1	6	1	24	5
Cleveland	**AB**	**R**	**H**	**RBI**	**PO**	**A**
Lofton, cf	3	2	0	0	4	0
Vizquel, ss	4	2	2	2	1	2
R. Alomar, 2b	4	1	3	2	3	1
Wilson, 2b	0	0	0	0	2	0
Ramirez, rf	4	1	0	0	1	1
Thome, 1b	3	2	1	4	5	4
Sexson, 1b	1	0	0	0	0	0
Baines, dh	4	1	2	3	0	0
Justice, lf	4	0	0	0	3	0
Fryman, 3b	0	1	0	0	0	2
S. Alomar, c	4	1	0	0	5	1
Diaz, c	0	0	0	0	0	0
Nagy, p	0	0	0	0	3	0
Karsay, p	0	0	0	0	0	0
Jackson, p	0	0	0	0	0	0
Totals	31	11	8	11	27	11

Boston	0 0 1	0 0 0	0 0 0	—1
Cleveland	0 0 6	5 0 0	0 0 x	—11

Boston	IP	H	R	ER	BB	SO
Saberhagen (L)	2.2	5	6	6	3	2
Wasdin	1.1	2	5	5	3	1
Wakefield	2.0	1	0	0	2	4
Gordon	1.0	0	0	0	1	2
Beck	1.0	0	0	0	0	1
Cleveland	**IP**	**H**	**R**	**ER**	**BB**	**SO**
Nagy (W)	7.0	5	1	1	0	4
Karsay	1.0	1	0	0	1	1
Jackson	1.0	0	0	0	0	0

DP—Boston 1, Cleveland 1. LOB—Boston 3, Cleveland 7. 2B—R. Alomar 2, Nixon, Stanley. 3B—Vizquel. HR—Baines, Thome. SF—R. Alomar. SB—Fryman. CS—Offerman. HBP—By Gordon (Fryman). PB—Varitek. T—2:47. A—45,184. U—Young, plate; Hirschbeck, first; Brinkman, second; Reilly, third; Cousins, left field; Roe, right field.

Game 3 at Boston

BOSTON 9, CLEVELAND 3

HOW THEY SCORED

Fourth Inning

Cleveland—Ramirez grounded out, Valentin to Stanley. Thome singled to left-center. Baines singled to right-center as Thome went to third. Justice hit a sacrifice fly to Lewis, scoring Thome. Fryman struck out. One run. Cleveland 1, Boston 0.

Fifth Inning

Boston—Wright now pitching. O'Leary grounded out, Wright to Fryman to Thome. Merloni singled to right. Varitek doubled to left as Merloni went to third. Lewis singled to right-center, scoring Merloni as Varitek went to third. Nixon hit a sacrifice fly to Ramirez, scoring Varitek. Offerman grounded to Thome. Two runs. Boston 2, Cleveland 1.

Sixth Inning

Cleveland—R. Alomar doubled to left. Ramirez grounded to Stanley as R. Alomar went to third. Thome walked. Baines forced Thome at second, Stanley to Merloni, and Baines went to second on a throwing error by Merloni as R. Alomar scored. Justice was walked intentionally. Lowe now pitching. Fryman grounded to Valentin. One run. Boston 2, Cleveland 2.

Boston—Valentin homered to center. Daubach, pinch-hitting for Huskey, struck out. Stanley grounded out, Vizquel to Thome. O'Leary flied to Ramirez. One run. Boston 3, Cleveland 2.

Seventh Inning

Cleveland—S. Alomar lined to Stanley. Lofton singled to left. Vizquel grounded out, Lowe to Stanley, as Lofton went to second. With R. Alomar batting, Lofton stole third. R. Alomar walked. Ramirez reached on Valentin's throwing error, scoring Lofton, as R. Alomar went to third. Thome struck out. One run. Boston 3, Cleveland 3.

Boston—Merloni walked. Varitek hit by a pitch. Rincon now pitching. Lewis forced Merloni at third, Fryman to Vizquel, as Varitek went to second. Nixon struck out. Offerman walked. Valentin doubled to left, scoring Varitek and Lewis, as Offerman went to third. Daubach homered to left-center, scoring Offerman and Valentin. DePaula now pitching. Stanley walked. O'Leary singled to left as Stanley went to second. Merloni singled to center and went to second on the throw from the outfield as Stanley scored. O'Leary went to third on Lofton's wild throw on the play. Varitek popped to R. Alomar. Six runs. Boston 9, Cleveland 3.

BOX SCORE

Cleveland	AB	R	H	RBI	PO	A
Lofton, cf	5	1	1	0	4	0
Vizquel, ss	5	0	2	0	1	2
R. Alomar, 2b	4	1	1	0	3	3
Ramirez, rf	5	0	0	0	5	0
Thome, 1b	3	1	1	0	7	0
Baines, dh	4	0	2	1	0	0
Justice, lf	1	0	0	1	1	1
Fryman, 3b	4	0	1	0	0	2
S. Alomar, c	4	0	1	0	3	0
Burba, p	0	0	0	0	0	1
Wright, p	0	0	0	0	0	1
Rincon, p	0	0	0	0	0	0
DePaula, p	0	0	0	0	0	0
Reed, p	0	0	0	0	0	0
Totals	35	3	9	2	24	10
Boston	**AB**	**R**	**H**	**RBI**	**PO**	**A**
Offerman, 2b	3	1	1	0	2	1
Valentin, 3b	5	2	2	3	2	4
Huskey, dh	2	0	1	0	0	0
Daubach, ph-dh	2	1	1	3	0	0
Stanley, 1b	3	1	0	0	9	2
O'Leary, lf	4	0	1	0	1	0
Merloni, ss	3	1	2	1	3	1
Varitek, c	3	2	1	0	8	0
Lewis, cf	4	1	2	1	1	0
Nixon, rf	3	0	0	1	1	0
R. Martinez, p	0	0	0	0	0	1
Lowe, p	0	0	0	0	0	1
Beck, p	0	0	0	0	0	0
Totals	32	9	11	9	27	10

Cleveland	0 0 0	1 0 1	1 0 0	—3
Boston	0 0 0	0 2 1	6 0 x	—9

Cleveland	IP	H	R	ER	BB	SO
Burba	4.0	1	0	0	1	0
Wright (L)	*2.0	4	5	5	1	1
Rincon	0.2	2	2	2	1	1
DePaula	0.1	2	1	1	1	0
Reed	1.0	2	0	0	0	0
Boston	**IP**	**H**	**R**	**ER**	**BB**	**SO**
R. Martinez	5.2	5	2	2	3	6
Lowe (W)	2.1	2	1	0	1	1
Beck	1.0	2	0	0	0	1

*Pitched to two batters in seventh.

E—Lofton, Merloni, Valentin. DP—Cleveland 1, Boston 1. LOB—Cleveland 10, Boston 5. 2B—R. Alomar, Varitek, Valentin, Offerman. HR—Valentin, Daubach. SF—Justice, Nixon. SB—Lofton. HBP—By Wright (Varitek). T—3:08. A—33,539. U—Welke, plate; McKean, first; Shulock, second; Merrill, third; Joyce, left field; Meriwether, right field.

Game 4 at Boston

BOSTON 23, CLEVELAND 7

HOW THEY SCORED

First Inning

Cleveland—Lofton doubled to left. Vizquel sacrificed Lofton to third, Mercker to Stanley. R. Alomar grounded out, Garciaparra to Stanley, as Lofton scored. Ramirez walked. Cordero singled to left as Ramirez went to second. Sexson struck out. One run. Cleveland 1, Boston 0.

Boston—Offerman walked. Valentin homered, scoring Offerman. Daubach struck out. Garciaparra popped to R. Alomar. O'Leary grounded out, Thome to Colon. Two runs. Boston 2, Cleveland 1.

Second Inning

Cleveland—Thome walked. Fryman singled to left as Thome went to second. Thome went to third on a passed ball. S. Alomar hit a sacrifice fly to Lewis, scoring Thome as Fryman went to second. Lofton flied to O'Leary. Vizquel walked. Garces now pitching. R. Alomar grounded out, Stanley to Garces. One run. Boston 2, Cleveland 2.

Boston—Stanley singled to right-center. Varitek singled to right as Stanley went to third. Lewis singled to right, scoring Stanley as Varitek went to second. Nixon doubled to center, scoring Varitek and Lewis. Offerman homered to left, scoring Nixon. Karsay now pitching. Valentin singled to left-center. Daubach struck out. Garciaparra lined to Lofton. O'Leary struck out, but reached first on a wild pitch, as Valentin went to second. Stanley forced O'Leary at second, Vizquel to Thome. Five runs. Boston 7, Cleveland 2.

Third Inning

Boston—Varitek doubled to left. Lewis singled to right as Varitek went to third. Nixon hit a sacrifice fly to Sexson, scoring Varitek. Offerman flied to Ramirez. With Valentin batting, Lewis stole second. Lewis went to third on a wild pitch. Valentin homered to left, scoring Lewis. Daubach popped to Lofton. Three runs. Boston 10, Cleveland 2.

Fourth Inning

Boston—Reed now pitching. Garciaparra hit by a pitch. O'Leary popped to Vizquel. Stanley singled to center as Garciaparra went to second. Varitek hit a ground rule double to right, scoring Garciaparra as Stanley went to third. Lewis struck out. Nixon walked. Offerman singled to right, scoring Stanley as Varitek went to third and Nixon to second. Valentin doubled to left, scoring Varitek, Nixon and Offerman. Daubach grounded out, R. Alomar to Thome. Five runs. Boston 15, Cleveland 2.

Fifth Inning

Cleveland—R. Alomar walked. Wakefield now pitching. R. Alomar went to second on a passed ball. Ramirez walked. With Cordero batting, R. Alomar stole third. Cordero singled to right, scoring R. Alomar as Ramirez went to third. Sexson singled to center, scoring Ramirez as Cordero went to second. Thome walked. Wasdin now pitching. Fryman hit a sacrifice fly to Lewis, scoring Cordero. S. Alomar walked. Cormier now pitching. Lofton walked, scoring Sexson. Vizquel and R. Alomar struck out. Four runs. Boston 15, Cleveland 6.

Boston—Garciaparra singled to left. O'Leary forced Garciaparra at second, Thome to Vizquel. Stanley tripled to right, scoring O'Leary. Varitek homered to right, scoring Stanley. Lewis hit by a pitch. DePaula now pitching. Nixon struck out. Offerman flied to Lofton. Three runs. Boston 18, Cleveland 6.

Seventh Inning

Boston—Wilson now at second, Diaz catching and Assenmacher pitching. O'Leary grounded out, Thome to Assenmacher. Stanley singled to third. Varitek forced Stanley at second, Fryman to Wilson. Lewis singled to left as Varitek went to second. Nixon doubled to left-center, scoring Varitek and Lewis. Offerman singled to center, scoring Nixon. Sadler, pinch-hitting for Valentin, singled to left-center as Offerman went to third. Daubach grounded out, Vizquel to Thome. Three runs. Boston 21, Cleveland 6.

Eighth Inning

Boston—Roberts now in center field and Shuey pitching. Merloni struck out. O'Leary walked. Stanley doubled to left as O'Leary went to third. Hatteberg singled to left-center, scoring O'Leary as Stanley went to third. Lewis reached first on a fielder's choice as Stanley was tagged out, Fryman to Diaz to Fryman to Diaz. Hatteberg went to second on the play. Nixon walked. Offerman walked, scoring Hatteberg. Sadler struck out. Two runs. Boston 23, Cleveland 6.

Ninth Inning

Cleveland—Daubach now at first and Gordon pitching. Ramirez struck out. Cordero homered to left. Sexson grounded out, Merloni to Daubach. Thome popped to Sadler in foul territory. One run. Boston 23, Cleveland 7.

BOX SCORE

Cleveland	AB	R	H	RBI	PO	A
Lofton, cf	3	1	1	1	4	0
Roberts, ph-cf	1	0	0	0	0	0
Vizquel, ss	3	0	0	0	2	2
R. Alomar, 2b	3	1	0	1	2	1
Wilson, 2b	1	0	0	0	1	0
Ramirez, rf	3	1	0	0	1	0
Cordero, dh	4	2	3	2	0	0
Sexson, lf	5	1	1	1	1	0
Thome, 1b	3	1	1	0	2	3
Fryman, 3b	3	0	1	1	0	2
S. Alomar, c	1	0	1	1	6	0
Diaz, ph-c	1	0	0	0	3	1
Colon, p	0	0	0	0	1	0
Karsay, p	0	0	0	0	0	0
Reed, p	0	0	0	0	0	0
DePaula, p	0	0	0	0	0	0
Assenmacher, p	0	0	0	0	1	0
Shuey, p	0	0	0	0	0	0
Totals	31	7	8	7	24	9
Boston	**AB**	**R**	**H**	**RBI**	**PO**	**A**
Offerman, 2b	5	3	3	5	2	1
Valentin, 3b	5	2	4	7	1	2
Sadler, ph-3b	2	0	1	0	1	1
Daubach, dh-1b	6	0	0	0	1	0
Garciaparra, ss	3	1	1	0	1	3
Merloni, ph-ss	2	0	0	0	0	1
O'Leary, lf	5	2	0	0	2	0
Stanley, 1b	6	3	5	1	8	1
Gordon, p	0	0	0	0	0	0
Varitek, c	5	5	4	3	6	0
Hatteberg, c	1	1	1	1	2	0

Boston	AB	R	H	RBI	PO	A
Lewis, cf	5	3	3	1	2	0
Nixon, rf	3	3	2	5	0	0
Mercker, p	0	0	0	0	0	1
Garces, p	0	0	0	0	1	0
Wakefield, p	0	0	0	0	0	0
Wasdin, p	0	0	0	0	0	0
Cormier, p	0	0	0	0	0	0
Totals	48	23	24	23	27	10

Cleveland .... 1 1 0 0 4 0 0 0 1—7
Boston .... 2 5 3 5 3 0 3 2 x—23

Cleveland	IP	H	R	ER	BB	SO
Colon (L)	*1.0	6	7	7	1	1
Karsay	2.0	4	3	3	0	2
Reed	1.1	7	8	8	1	1
DePaula	1.2	0	0	0	0	3
Assenmacher	1.0	5	3	3	0	0
Shuey	1.0	2	2	2	3	2
Boston	**IP**	**H**	**R**	**ER**	**BB**	**SO**
Mercker	1.2	3	2	2	3	1
Garces (W)	†2.1	1	1	1	2	2
Wakefield	‡0.0	2	3	3	2	0
Wasdin	0.1	0	0	0	1	0
Cormier	3.2	1	0	0	1	4
Gordon	1.0	1	1	1	0	1

*Pitched to five batters in second. †Pitched to one batter in fifth. ‡Pitched to four batters in fifth.

DP—Boston 1. LOB—Cleveland 9, Boston 9. 2B—Nixon 2, Varitek 2, Lofton, Valentin, Sadler, Stanley. 3B—Stanley. HR—Valentin 2, Cordero, Offerman, Varitek. SH—Vizquel. SF—S. Alomar, Fryman, Nixon. SB—R. Alomar, Lewis. HBP—By Reed (Garciaparra, Lewis). WP—Karsay 2. PB—Varitek 2. T—3:49. A—33,898. U—McKean, plate; Shulock, first; Merrill, second; Joyce, third; Meriwether, left field; Welke, right field.

Game 5 at Cleveland

BOSTON 12, CLEVELAND 8

HOW THEY SCORED

First Inning

Boston—Offerman grounded out, Vizquel to Thome. Valentin grounded out, Nagy to Thome. Daubach singled to right. Garciaparra homered to center, scoring Daubach. O'Leary struck out. Two runs, Boston 2, Cleveland 0.

Cleveland—Lofton walked. Lofton stole second. Vizquel doubled to left, scoring Lofton. R. Alomar lined to Stanley. Ramirez flied to Nixon. Thome homered to center, scoring Vizquel. Baines grounded to Stanley. Three runs. Cleveland 3, Boston 2.

Second Inning

Cleveland—Cordero singled to left. Fryman homered to left, scoring Cordero. Lowe now pitching. S. Alomar struck out. Lofton popped to Offerman. Vizquel grounded to Stanley. Two runs. Cleveland 5, Boston 2.

Third Inning

Boston—Nixon walked. Offerman singled to center, Nixon went to third. Valentin forced Offerman at second, Fryman to R. Alomar, as Nixon scored. Daubach doubled to left as Valentin went to third. Garciaparra was walked intentionally. O'Leary homered to right-center, scoring Valentin, Daubach and Garciaparra. Stanley grounded out, Fryman to Thome. Varitek flied to Cordero. Five runs. Boston 7, Cleveland 5.

Cleveland—R. Alomar doubled to right-center. Ramirez doubled to right-center, scoring R. Alomar. Thome homered to center, scoring Ramirez. Baines grounded out, Offerman to Stanley. Cordero struck out. Fryman grounded out, Garciaparra to Stanley. Three runs. Cleveland 8, Boston 7.

Fourth Inning

Boston—Lewis doubled to left. DePaula now pitching. Nixon flied to Lofton. Offerman walked. Lewis reached third on a throwing error by S. Alomar. Valentin hit a sacrifice fly to Cordero, scoring Lewis. Daubach flied to Cordero. One run. Boston 8, Cleveland 8.

Seventh Inning

Boston—Shuey now pitching. Valentin singled to short. Daubach grounded out, R. Alomar to Thome, as Valentin went to second. Garciaparra was walked intentionally. O'Leary homered to right, scoring Valentin and Garciaparra. Stanley struck out. Varitek lined to Thome. Three runs. Boston 11, Cleveland 8.

Ninth Inning

Boston—Jackson now pitching. Valentin lined to Roberts. Daubach doubled to left. Sadler now pinch-running for Daubach. Garciaparra doubled to left, scoring Sadler. O'Leary was walked intentionally. Stanley struck out. Varitek forced O'Leary at second, R. Alomar to Vizquel. One run. Boston 12, Cleveland 8.

BOX SCORE

Boston	AB	R	H	RBI	PO	A
Offerman, 2b	4	0	1	0	2	1
Valentin, 3b	4	2	1	2	2	2
Daubach, dh	5	2	3	0	0	0
Sadler, pr-dh	0	1	0	0	0	0
Garciaparra, ss	3	3	2	3	2	4
O'Leary, lf	4	2	2	7	0	0
Stanley, 1b	4	0	0	0	10	1
Varitek, c	5	0	0	0	10	0
Lewis, cf	4	1	1	0	1	0
Nixon, rf	3	1	0	0	1	0
Saberhagen, p	0	0	0	0	0	0
Lowe, p	0	0	0	0	0	0
P. Martinez, p	0	0	0	0	1	0
Totals	36	12	10	12	27	8

Cleveland	AB	R	H	RBI	PO	A
Lofton, cf	2	1	0	0	1	0
Roberts, cf	2	0	0	0	3	0
Vizquel, ss	5	1	1	1	2	1
R. Alomar, 2b	4	1	1	0	2	5
Ramirez, rf	3	1	1	1	1	0
Thome, 1b	4	2	2	4	8	0
Baines, dh	3	0	0	0	0	0
Cordero, lf	4	1	1	0	3	0
Fryman, 3b	4	1	1	2	0	2
S. Alomar, c	2	0	0	0	7	0
Wilson, ph	1	0	0	0	0	0
Nagy, p	0	0	0	0	0	0
DePaula, p	0	0	0	0	0	1
Shuey, p	0	0	0	0	0	0
Jackson, p	0	0	0	0	0	0
Totals	34	8	7	8	27	9

Boston .... 2 0 5 1 0 0 3 0 1—12
Cleveland .... 3 2 3 0 0 0 0 0 0—8

Boston	IP	H	R	ER	BB	SO
Saberhagen	*1.0	4	5	5	1	0
Lowe	2.0	3	3	3	0	2
P. Martinez (W)	6.0	0	0	0	3	8
Cleveland	**IP**	**H**	**R**	**ER**	**BB**	**SO**
Nagy	†3.0	6	8	7	2	2
DePaula	3.0	0	0	0	0	2
Shuey (L)	2.0	2	3	3	1	2
Jackson	1.0	2	1	1	1	1

*Pitched to two batters in second. †Pitched to one batter in fourth.

E—S. Alomar. LOB—Boston 4, Cleveland 3. 2B—Daubach 2, Lewis, Garciaparra, Vizquel, R. Alomar, Ramirez. HR—O'Leary 2, Thome 2, Garciaparra, Fryman. SF—Valentin. SB—Lofton. T—3:12. A—45,114. U—Shulock, plate; Merrill, first; Joyce, second; Meriwether, third; Welke, left field; McKean, right field.

COMPOSITE

BATTING AVERAGES

Boston Red Sox

Player, position	G	AB	R	H	2B	3B	HR	RBI	Avg.
Hatteberg, c	1	1	1	1	0	0	0	1	1.000
Stanley, 1b	5	20	4	10	2	1	0	2	.500
Sadler, ph-3b-pr-dh	2	2	1	1	1	0	0	0	.500
Garciaparra, ss	4	12	6	5	2	0	2	4	.417
Offerman, 2b	5	18	4	7	1	0	1	6	.389
Lewis, cf	4	16	5	6	1	0	0	2	.375
Merloni, ss-ph	3	6	1	2	0	0	0	1	.333
Valentin, 3b	5	22	6	7	2	0	3	12	.318
Daubach, dh-ph-1b	4	16	3	4	2	0	1	3	.250
Varitek, c	5	21	7	5	3	0	1	3	.238
Nixon, rf	5	14	5	3	0	0	0	6	.214
O'Leary, lf	5	20	4	4	0	0	2	7	.200
Huskey, dh	2	5	0	1	0	0	0	0	.200
Lowe, p	3	0	0	0	0	0	0	0	.000
Beck, p	2	0	0	0	0	0	0	0	.000
Cormier, p	2	0	0	0	0	0	0	0	.000
Garces, p	2	0	0	0	0	0	0	0	.000
Gordon, p	2	0	0	0	0	0	0	0	.000
P. Martinez, p	2	0	0	0	0	0	0	0	.000
Saberhagen, p	2	0	0	0	0	0	0	0	.000
Wakefield, p	2	0	0	0	0	0	0	0	.000
Wasdin, p	2	0	0	0	0	0	0	0	.000
R. Martinez, p	1	0	0	0	0	0	0	0	.000
Mercker, p	1	0	0	0	0	0	0	0	.000
Buford, cf	1	3	0	0	0	0	0	0	.000
Totals	5	176	47	56	17	1	10	47	.318

Cleveland Indians

Player, position	G	AB	R	H	2B	3B	HR	RBI	Avg.
Cordero, ph-dh-lf	3	9	3	5	0	0	1	2	.556
R. Alomar, 2b	5	19	4	7	4	0	0	3	.368
Baines, dh	4	14	1	5	0	0	1	4	.357

Bret Saberhagen had few fist-pumps in the series. He allowed 11 earned runs in three-plus innings.

Player, position	G	AB	R	H	2B	3B	HR	RBI	Avg.
Thome, 1b	5	17	7	6	0	0	4	10	.353
Fryman, 3b	5	15	2	4	0	0	1	4	.267
Vizquel, ss	5	21	3	5	1	1	0	3	.238
Sexson, ph-1b-lf	3	6	1	1	0	0	0	1	.167
S. Alomar, c	5	14	1	2	0	0	1	1	.143
Lofton, cf	5	16	5	2	1	0	0	1	.125
Ramirez, rf	5	18	5	1	1	0	0	1	.056
DePaula, p	3	0	0	0	0	0	0	0	.000
Shuey, p	3	0	0	0	0	0	0	0	.000
Colon, p	2	0	0	0	0	0	0	0	.000
Jackson, p	2	0	0	0	0	0	0	0	.000
Karsay, p	2	0	0	0	0	0	0	0	.000
Nagy, p	2	0	0	0	0	0	0	0	.000
Reed, p	2	0	0	0	0	0	0	0	.000
Assenmacher, p	1	0	0	0	0	0	0	0	.000
Burba, p	1	0	0	0	0	0	0	0	.000
Rincon, p	1	0	0	0	0	0	0	0	.000
Wright, p	1	0	0	0	0	0	0	0	.000
Diaz, c-ph	2	1	0	0	0	0	0	0	.000
Wilson, 2b-ph	3	2	0	0	0	0	0	0	.000
Roberts, ph-cf	2	3	0	0	0	0	0	0	.000
Justice, lf	3	8	0	0	0	0	0	1	.000
Totals	5	163	32	38	7	1	7	31	.233

PITCHING AVERAGES

Boston Red Sox

Pitcher	G	IP	H	R	ER	BB	SO	W	L	ERA
P. Martinez	2	10.0	3	0	0	4	11	1	0	0.00
Cormier	2	4.0	2	0	0	1	4	0	0	0.00
Beck	2	2.0	0	0	0	0	0	0	0	0.00
R. Martinez	1	5.2	5	2	2	3	6	0	0	3.18
Garces	2	2.1	2	1	1	3	2	1	0	3.86
Lowe	3	8.1	6	7	4	1	7	1	1	4.32
Gordon	2	2.0	1	1	1	3	0	0	0	4.50
Mercker	1	1.2	3	2	2	3	1	0	0	10.80
Wakefield	2	2.0	3	3	4	4	0	0	0	13.50
Saberhagen	2	3.2	9	11	11	4	0	0	2	27.00
Wasdin	2	1.2	2	5	5	4	1	0	0	27.00
Totals	5	43.1	38	32	29	28	43	3	2	6.02

No shutouts or saves.

Cleveland Indians

Pitcher	G	IP	H	R	ER	BB	SO	W	L	ERA
Burba	1	4.0	1	0	0	1	0	0	0	0.00
DePaula	3	5.0	2	1	1	3	5	0	0	1.80
Jackson	2	2.0	2	1	1	1	1	0	0	4.50
Nagy	2	10.0	11	9	8	2	6	1	0	7.20
Colon	2	9.0	11	9	9	4	12	0	1	9.00
Karsay	2	3.0	5	3	3	1	3	0	0	9.00
Shuey	3	4.0	4	5	5	4	5	1	1	11.25
Wright	1	2.0	4	5	5	1	1	0	1	22.50
Assenmacher	1	1.0	5	3	3	0	0	0	0	27.00
Reed	2	2.1	9	8	8	1	1	0	0	30.86
Rincon	1	0.2	2	3	3	1	1	0	0	40.50
Totals	5	53.0	56	47	46	19	35	2	3	9.63

No shutouts or saves.

A.L. Division Series

NEW YORK VS. TEXAS

The bottom line: Going into the playoffs, baseball experts were saying the '99 version of the New York Yankees wasn't nearly as strong as the miracalous 125-win championship team of 1998. While that may be true, the Yankees appeared every bit as good, if not better, in the 3-0 A.L. Division Series sweep of the Texas Rangers. For the second year in a row, Yankees pitching was far superior to the mighty Rangers offense, holding a team that scored more than 5.8 runs a game during the regular season to just one run in three playoff games. The Yankees sparkled with the bats, the gloves and the arms, certainly turning it up a notch from a so-so final month of the regular season and putting themselves one step closer to their major league record 36th pennant and 25th World Series victory.

Why the Yankees won: Pitching, pitching, pitching. It was Orlando Hernandez's gem in Game 1, Andy Pettitte's in Game 2 and Roger Clemens' in Game 3. The Rangers appeared befuddled—a solo homer by Juan Gonzalez in the fourth inning of Game 2 was the only run the team scored. They couldn't hit the ball solidly, and when they did, Yankee heroes such as Bernie Williams and Derek Jeter found a way to put a glove around it. The Rangers hit .293 with plenty of power in the regular season, but they managed just a .152 average (14-for-92, three extra-base hits) against Yankees hurlers in the three games. This on the heels of a similar performance in the 1998 season—a .141 mark in a 3-0 sweep. The Yankees got clutch performances from their veteran players. Williams had a six-RBI performance in Game 1 and Darryl Strawberry a three-run homer in the first inning of Game 3 that gave Roger Clemens plenty to work with.

TURNING POINTS:

Game 1: Bernie Williams lined Aaron Sele's 3-2 fastball off the base of the centerfield wall, scoring Derek Jeter and Paul O'Neill, in a two-run fifth inning that paced the Yankees to an 8-0 win at Yankee Stadium. Williams not only took over the game offensively, but defensively. In the third inning, he made a sliding grab of Juan Gonzalez's liner in right-center with two runners on, then hauled in Rafael Palmeiro's deep fly one batter later, preserving the Yankees 1-0 lead. Then he got busy at the plate, roping a two-run double over Tom Goodwin's head in the fifth; hammering a three-run homer to right off Rangers rookie reliever Mike Venafro in the sixth, and adding an RBI single off Jeff Fassero in the eighth for a six-RBI night. Yankees Game 1 starter Orlando Hernandez really didn't need that much offense. Hernandez continued the playoffs dominance of Yankees pitchers over the Rangers with an eight-inning, two-hit outing. The Rangers didn't get a runner past first base after Williams' defensive gems in the third inning.

Game 2: When Lee Stevens' double put runners on second and third with nobody out in the fifth inning, the Rangers threatened to blow the game open. Juan Gonzalez had homered an inning earlier and Rick Helling had the Yankees in check for a 1-0 lead. But Yankees hurler Andy Pettitte took care of the situation. After falling behind 3-0, he came back to strike out contact-hitting Mark McLemore, then he coaxed Royce Clayton into a weak groundout to third and struck out Rusty Greer. Killing the rally—which prompted a hard fist-pump from Pettitte as he walked off the mound—appeared to energize the Yankees and their raucous fans. The Rangers did not threaten again, and the Yankees finally got to Helling with three runs in the next four innings for a 3-1 win in Yankee Stadium. Another crucial moment came in the New York seventh inning. With two runners on and one out, rookie outfielder Ricky Ledee lined a ball to right-center. Roberto Kelly, starting in place of speedy centerfielder Tom Goodwin against the lefthanded Pettitte, appeared to give up on the ball early, letting it drop in front of him in the gap for an RBI double. That knocked out Helling and gave the Yankees a one-run lead they did not lose.

Game 3: The Yankees turned to a pair of 37-year-old veterans for heroics in Game 3. Five-time Cy Young Award winner Roger Clemens fired seven shutout innings and Darryl Strawberry clouted a three-run homer in the first inning for a 3-0 game—and series—victory at The Ballpark in Arlington. It was sweet vindication for both players. Clemens had a below-normal 1999 season, posting a career-high 4.60 ERA during the regular season. Against the Rangers he allowed just five runners (three hits, two walks) to reach base. Meanwhile, Strawberry, who hadn't joined the team until September because of a March arrest and suspension, hammered an Esteban Loaiza offering 415 feet over the left-centerfield wall for the decisive total.

WORTH NOTING:

Rangers: Since beating the Yankees in the A.L. Division Series opener in 1996, the Rangers have lost nine straight postseason games, scoring just two runs in their last 60 innings. After leading the A.L. in hitting in 1998 and 1999, the team was a combined .147 (27-for-184) in the two Division Series sweeps, going just 1-for-30 with runners in scoring position. ... Aaron Sele threw Bernie Williams seven straight curveballs before Williams lined a 3-2 fastball to center for the two-run double in the fifth inning of Game 1. Sele hopped off the mound, expecting a strikeout, after Williams took a 1-2 curveball, but the call didn't go the Rangers' way. ... Rangers outfielders had trouble with the Yankee Stadium lighting. Left fielder Rusty Greer lost Ricky Ledee's liner in Game 1, and it went past him for an RBI double. He also lost a high drive by Scott Brosius, also an RBI double, in Game 2. Roberto Kelly claimed he had trouble picking up Ledee's RBI double in Game 2. ... In the days leading up to Game 3, Esteban Loaiza was quoted saying he would use his fastball to beat the Yankees. While that theory worked for him in six of his seven innings of work, it was a fastball that Strawberry hit for the first-inning homer.

Yankees: Don Zimmer sustained cuts to the left jaw and ear when he was hit by Chuck Knoblauch's liner into the Yankees dugout in the fifth inning of Game 1. The 68-year-old Zimmer slumped to the dugout floor and appeared wobbly as he left the dugout, but he returned before the inning concluded. In Game 2, he wore a military helmet with a Yankees logo for a gag. ... Bernie Williams' Game 1 heroics were a redemption of sorts. He was 0-for-11 against Texas in the 1998 A.L. Division Series. ... Orlando Hernandez improved to 3-0 with a 0.41 ERA in postseason play. ... The Yankees' sweep gave them victories in 10 straight postseason games. ... Clemens' Game 3 win was just his second in 10 postseason starts; the other was in 1986 with Boston. He made the start after not pitching for 12 days. ... Paul O'Neill missed the final game of the series with a side injury he suffered late in the regular season. He found out later he had a small displaced rib fracture.

WORTH QUOTING:

Rangers: Manager Johnny Oates, frustrated after the Rangers bats again were quiet in Game 1: "I don't care, Yankee Stadium, Yellowstone Park, it doesn't matter. We can score more runs than this by accident." ... Oates, again, recapping his team's miserable offense in the series: "I've got a few months to analyze what happened in this playoff and see how we can score at will pretty much in the season and then in three games not even smell home plate." ... Mark McLemore, with the same frustration: "This is very hard to take. We came in this year with a better ball club, and the same thing happened." ... Tom Goodwin, about Yankees pitching: "They make other teams look not as good as they really are."

Yankees: Hernandez, after holding the Rangers hitters to just two hits in eight innings in Game 1: "I like to have pressure when I pitch." ... Bernie Williams, after his Game 1 heroics: "I thought I was going to have a terrible night. I was sleepy and dragging, and it was cold. Something happened when they said the lineups. Something inside of me just woke up, said it's time to play." ... Darryl Strawberry, speaking of Williams' Game 1 performance: "Tonight's an example of the type of team we have. You don't look to any one person. Tonight it was Bernie. Next time it could be anyone else." ... Torre, on deciding to start Andy Pettitte over Roger Clemens and David Cone in Game 2: "I've seen Andy do it before. When you need him, he doesn't disappoint. He makes big plays, he makes big pitches."

Game 1 at New York

NEW YORK 8, TEXAS 0

HOW THEY SCORED

Second Inning

New York—Martinez singled to right. Strawberry forced Martinez at second, McLemore to Clayton. Posada flied to Greer. Ledee doubled to left, scoring Strawberry. Brosius grounded out, McLemore to Stevens. One run. New York 1, Texas 0.

Fifth Inning

New York—Brosius grounded out, Zeile to Stevens. Knoblauch grounded out, Clayton to Stevens. Jeter singled to center. O'Neill singled to right as Jeter went to third. Williams doubled to center, scoring Jeter and O'Neill. Martinez was walked intentionally. Williams went to third and Martinez to second on a wild pitch. Strawberry was walked intentionally. Posada flied to Greer. Two runs. New York 3, Texas 0.

Sixth Inning

New York—Ledee walked. Crabtree now pitching. Brosius sacrificed Ledee to second, Stevens to McLemore. Knoblauch struck out. Jeter walked. Venafro now pitching. O'Neill reached first on a fielding error by Zeile as Ledee scored and Jeter went to third. Williams homered to right, scoring Jeter and O'Neill. Martinez popped to Stevens. Four runs. New York 7, Texas 0.

Eighth Inning

New York—Fassero now pitching. Knoblauch singled to left. Jeter walked. O'Neill struck out. Williams singled to left, scoring Knoblauch as Jeter went to second. Martinez flied to Gonzalez as Jeter went to third. Leyritz flied to Goodwin. One run. New York 8, Texas 0.

BOX SCORE

Texas	AB	R	H	RBI	PO	A
McLemore, 2b	3	0	0	0	1	3
Rodriguez, c	4	0	2	0	5	0
Greer, lf	2	0	0	0	3	0
Gonzalez, rf	3	0	0	0	1	0
Palmeiro, dh	3	0	0	0	0	0
Zeile, 3b	3	0	0	0	0	2
Stevens, 1b	3	0	0	0	8	1
Clayton, ss	3	0	0	0	2	3
Goodwin, cf	3	0	0	0	3	0
Sele, p	0	0	0	0	1	0
Crabtree, p	0	0	0	0	0	0
Venafro, p	0	0	0	0	0	0
Patterson, p	0	0	0	0	0	0
Fassero, p	0	0	0	0	0	0
Totals	27	0	2	0	24	9

New York	AB	R	H	RBI	PO	A
Knoblauch, 2b	4	1	2	0	0	2
Jeter, ss	3	2	1	0	2	2
O'Neill, rf	4	2	1	0	3	0
Curtis, lf	0	0	0	0	0	0
Williams, cf	5	1	3	6	7	0
Martinez, 1b	4	0	1	0	7	0
Strawberry, dh	2	1	0	0	0	0
Leyritz, ph-dh	2	0	0	0	0	0
Posada, c	4	0	1	0	5	0
Ledee, lf-rf	3	1	1	1	3	0
Brosius, 3b	3	0	0	0	0	1
Hernandez, p	0	0	0	0	0	1
Nelson, p	0	0	0	0	0	0
Totals	34	8	10	7	27	6

Texas	0 0 0	0 0 0	0 0 0—0
New York	0 1 0	0 2 4	0 1 x—8

Texas	IP	H	R	ER	BB	SO
Sele (L)	*5.0	6	4	3	5	3
Crabtree	0.2	0	1	0	1	1
Venafro	0.1	1	2	0	0	0
Patterson	1.0	1	0	0	0	0
Fassero	1.0	2	1	1	1	1

New York	IP	H	R	ER	BB	SO
Hernandez (W)	8.0	2	0	0	6	4
Nelson	1.0	0	0	0	1	1

*Pitched to one batter in sixth.

E—Zeile. DP—New York 2. LOB—Texas 7, New York 10. 2B—Rodriguez, Ledee, Williams, Posada. HR—Williams. SH—Brosius. SB—Rodriguez. WP—Sele. T—3:37. A—57,099. U—Joyce, plate, Meriwether, first; Welke, second; McKean, third; Shulock, left field; Merrill, right field.

Game 2 at New York

NEW YORK 3, TEXAS 1

HOW THEY SCORED

Fourth Inning

Texas—Rodriguez grounded to Martinez. Gonzalez homered to left. Palmeiro flied to Williams. Zeile grounded out, Jeter to Martinez. One run. Texas 1, New York 0.

Fifth Inning

New York—Martinez singled to right. Davis and Ledee struck out. Brosius doubled to left, scoring Martinez. Girardi popped to Clayton. One run. Texas 1, New York 1.

Seventh Inning

New York—Williams flied to Gonzalez. Martinez walked. Davis singled to right as Martinez went to third. Bellinger now pinch-running for Davis. Crabtree now pitching. Brosius grounded out, Zeile to Stevens. Girardi grounded out, Clayton to Stevens. One run. New York 2, Texas 1.

Eighth Inning

New York—Goodwin now in center field. Knoblauch grounded out, Crabtree to Stevens. Jeter singled to right. Venafro now pitching. O'Neill singled to left as Jeter went to second. Curtis now pinch-running for O'Neill. Williams hit by a pitch. Martinez forced Jeter at home, Stevens to Rodriguez, as Curtis went to third and Williams to second. Leyritz, pinch-hitting for Bellinger, walked, scoring Curtis. Ledee grounded out, Venafro to Stevens. One run. New York 3, Texas 1.

BOX SCORE

Texas	AB	R	H	RBI	PO	A
Clayton, ss	4	0	0	0	1	3
Greer, lf	4	0	0	0	4	0
Rodriguez, c	4	0	1	0	10	0
Gonzalez, rf	4	1	1	1	2	0
Palmeiro, dh	4	0	2	0	0	0
Zeile, 3b	4	0	1	0	1	1
Kelly, cf	3	0	1	0	1	0
Goodwin, cf	1	0	0	0	0	0
Stevens, 1b	3	0	1	0	5	1
McLemore, 2b	3	0	0	0	0	0
Helling, p	0	0	0	0	0	0
Crabtree, p	0	0	0	0	0	1
Venafro, p	0	0	0	0	0	1
Totals	34	1	7	1	24	7

New York	AB	R	H	RBI	PO	A
Knoblauch, 2b	4	0	0	0	1	5
Jeter, ss	4	0	2	0	2	4
O'Neill, rf	4	0	1	0	1	0
Curtis, pr-lf	0	1	0	0	0	0
Williams, cf	3	0	0	0	4	0
Martinez, 1b	3	2	1	0	8	0
Davis, dh	3	0	1	0	0	0
Bellinger, pr-dh	0	0	0	0	0	0
Leyritz, ph-dh	0	0	0	1	0	0
Ledee, lf-rf	4	0	1	1	2	0
Brosius, 3b	3	0	1	1	0	1
Girardi, c	3	0	0	0	9	0
Pettitte, p	0	0	0	0	0	0
Nelson, p	0	0	0	0	0	0
Rivera, p	0	0	0	0	0	0
Totals	31	3	7	3	27	10

Texas .... 0 0 0 1 0 0 0 0 0—1
New York .... 0 0 0 0 1 0 1 1 x—3

Texas	IP	H	R	ER	BB	SO
Helling (L)	6.1	5	2	2	1	8
Crabtree	1.0	1	1	1	0	0
Venafro	0.2	1	0	0	1	0

New York	IP	H	R	ER	BB	SO
Pettitte (W)	7.1	7	1	1	0	5
Nelson	0.2	0	0	0	0	2
Rivera (S)	1.0	0	0	0	0	2

E—Martinez, Knoblauch. DP—New York 2. LOB—Texas 6, New York 7. 2B—Stevens, Jeter, Brosius, Ledee. HR—Gonzalez. HBP—By Venafro (Williams). T—3:32. A—57,485. U—Meriwether, plate; Welke, first; McKean, second; Shulock, third; Merrill, left field; Joyce, right field.

Game 3 at Texas

NEW YORK 3, TEXAS 0

HOW THEY SCORED

First Inning

New York—Knoblauch struck out. Jeter tripled to left. Williams walked. Martinez struck out. Strawberry homered to left-center, scoring Jeter and Williams. Ledee grounded out, McLemore to Stevens. Three runs. New York 3, Texas 0.

BOX SCORE

New York	AB	R	H	RBI	PO	A
Knoblauch, 2b	4	0	0	0	1	4
Jeter, ss	4	1	2	0	1	4
Williams, cf	3	1	1	0	4	0
Martinez, 1b	4	0	0	0	14	0
Strawberry, dh	4	1	2	3	0	0
Ledee, rf	4	0	1	0	1	0
Brosius, 3b	4	0	0	0	2	1
Curtis, lf	3	0	0	0	0	0
Girardi, c	3	0	0	0	3	0
Clemens, p	0	0	0	0	1	3
Nelson, p	0	0	0	0	0	0
Rivera, p	0	0	0	0	0	0
Totals	33	3	6	3	27	13

Texas	AB	R	H	RBI	PO	A
McLemore, 2b	4	0	1	0	1	6
Rodriguez, c	4	0	0	0	6	0
Greer, lf	3	0	1	0	2	0
Gonzalez, rf	4	0	1	0	2	0
Palmeiro, dh	4	0	1	0	0	0
Zeile, 3b	3	0	0	0	0	1
Stevens, 1b	3	0	0	0	12	0
Clayton, ss	3	0	0	0	1	4
Goodwin, cf	3	0	1	0	3	0
Loaiza, p	0	0	0	0	0	0
Zimmerman, p	0	0	0	0	0	0
Wetteland, p	0	0	0	0	0	0
Totals	31	0	5	0	27	11

New York .... 3 0 0 0 0 0 0 0 0—3
Texas .... 0 0 0 0 0 0 0 0 0—0

New York	IP	H	R	ER	BB	SO
Clemens (W)	7.0	3	0	0	2	2
Nelson	*0.0	1	0	0	0	0
Rivera (S)	2.0	1	0	0	0	1

Texas	IP	H	R	ER	BB	SO
Loaiza (L)	7.0	5	3	3	1	4
Zimmerman	1.0	1	0	0	0	1
Wetteland	1.0	0	0	0	0	1

*Pitched to one batter in eighth.

E—Zeile. DP—New York 1, Texas 1. LOB—New York 4, Texas 6. 3B—Jeter. HR—Strawberry. WP—Rivera. T—3:00. A—50,269. U—Hirschbeck, plate; Brinkman, first; Reilly, second; Cousins, third; Roe, left field; Young, right field.

COMPOSITE

BATTING AVERAGES

New York Yankees

Player, position	G	AB	R	H	2B	3B	HR	RBI	Avg.
Jeter, ss	3	11	3	5	1	1	0	0	.455
Williams, cf	3	11	2	4	1	0	1	6	.364
Strawberry, dh	2	6	2	2	0	0	1	3	.333
Davis, dh	1	3	0	1	0	0	0	0	.333
Ledee, lf-rf	3	11	1	3	2	0	0	2	.273
O'Neill, rf	2	8	2	2	0	0	0	0	.250
Posada, c	1	4	0	1	1	0	0	0	.250
Martinez, 1b	3	11	2	2	0	0	0	0	.182
Knoblauch, 2b	3	12	1	2	0	0	0	0	.167
Brosius, 3b	3	10	0	1	1	0	0	1	.100
Nelson, p	3	0	0	0	0	0	0	0	.000
Rivera, p	2	0	0	0	0	0	0	0	.000
Bellinger, pr-dh	1	0	0	0	0	0	0	0	.000
Clemens, p	1	0	0	0	0	0	0	0	.000
Hernandez, p	1	0	0	0	0	0	0	0	.000
Pettitte, p	1	0	0	0	0	0	0	0	.000
Leyritz, ph-dh	2	2	0	0	0	0	0	1	.000
Curtis, lf-pr	3	3	1	0	0	0	0	0	.000
Girardi, c	2	6	0	0	0	0	0	0	.000
Totals	3	98	14	23	6	1	2	13	.235

Texas Rangers

Player, position	G	AB	R	H	2B	3B	HR	RBI	Avg.
Kelly, cf	1	3	0	1	0	0	0	0	.333
Palmeiro, dh	3	11	0	3	0	0	0	0	.273
Rodriguez, c	3	12	0	3	1	0	0	0	.250
Gonzalez, rf	3	11	1	2	0	0	1	1	.182
Goodwin, cf	3	7	0	1	0	0	0	0	.143
Greer, lf	3	9	0	1	0	0	0	0	.111
Stevens, 1b	3	9	0	1	0	0	0	0	.111
McLemore, 2b	3	10	0	1	0	0	0	0	.100
Zeile, 3b	3	10	0	1	0	0	0	0	.100
Crabtree, p	2	0	0	0	0	0	0	0	.000
Venafro, p	2	0	0	0	0	0	0	0	.000
Fassero, p	1	0	0	0	0	0	0	0	.000
Helling, p	1	0	0	0	0	0	0	0	.000
Loaiza, p	1	0	0	0	0	0	0	0	.000
Patterson, p	1	0	0	0	0	0	0	0	.000
Sele, p	1	0	0	0	0	0	0	0	.000
Wetteland, p	1	0	0	0	0	0	0	0	.000
Zimmerman, p	1	0	0	0	0	0	0	0	.000
Clayton, ss	3	10	0	0	0	0	0	0	.000
Totals	3	92	1	14	2	0	1	1	.152

PITCHING AVERAGES

New York Yankees

Pitcher	G	IP	H	R	ER	BB	SO	W	L	ERA
Hernandez	1	8.0	2	0	0	6	4	1	0	0.00
Clemens	1	7.0	3	0	0	2	2	1	0	0.00
Rivera	2	3.0	1	0	0	0	3	0	0	0.00
Nelson	3	1.2	1	0	0	0	3	0	0	0.00
Pettitte	1	7.1	7	1	1	0	5	1	0	1.23
Totals	3	27.0	14	1	1	9	17	3	0	0.33

Shutouts—Hernandez and Nelson (combined); Clemens, Nelson and Rivera (combined). Saves—Rivera 2.

Texas Rangers

Pitcher	G	IP	H	R	ER	BB	SO	W	L	ERA
Patterson	1	1.0	1	0	0	0	0	0	0	0.00
Venafro	2	1.2	2	0	0	1	0	0	0	0.00
Wetteland	1	1.0	0	0	0	0	1	0	0	0.00
Zimmerman	1	1.0	1	0	0	0	1	0	0	0.00
Helling	1	6.1	5	2	2	1	8	0	1	2.84
Loaiza	1	7.0	5	3	3	1	4	0	1	3.86
Sele	1	5.0	6	4	3	5	3	0	1	5.40
Crabtree	2	1.2	2	1	1	1	0	0	0	5.40
Fassero	1	1.0	2	1	1	1	1	0	0	9.00
Totals	3	25.0	23	14	10	10	19	0	3	3.60

No shutouts or saves.

N.L. CHAMPIONSHIP SERIES

ATLANTA VS. NEW YORK

The bottom line: The Braves dominated the Mets in the regular season (winning nine of 12 games) on their way to their eighth straight division title. Atlanta continued that domination by taking the first three games of the NLCS, getting clutch hitting from unexpected sources and great pitching performances from their reliable starters and bullpen. But the wild-card Mets made a series of it, winning the final two games in New York before losing a 10-9, 11-inning Game 6 in Atlanta. This heated rivalry between division foes was entertaining—close games, off-the-field trash talk, unlikely heroes—as Atlanta gained its fifth trip to the World Series in the '90s.

Why the Braves won: No surprise here, but Atlanta won this series with its superior pitching. The Braves continually got outs when they needed to, and the Mets gave up big hits to generally light-hitting players such as Eddie Perez and Keith Lockhart in the series. The Braves won three games by one run, and the fourth by two runs. John Rocker's 6.2 scoreless innings (he appeared in all six games), including two saves, may have been the difference on the mound. Eddie Perez's .500 average with two homers and five RBIs was the difference at the plate. The Mets, who committed a major league low 68 errors during the regular season, didn't help themselves with eight errors in the series. As the season displayed, the Mets had the firepower and talent to hang with the Braves, they just didn't have the big-game experience.

TURNING POINTS:

Game 1: When you're facing Greg Maddux, a four-time Cy Young winner, you must score every chance you have runners in scoring position. And though it was just the third inning, the Mets botched their best opportunity of the night. After Roger Cedeno advanced to third after a double and Gerald Williams' throwing error, the Braves' 1-0 lead appeared in jeopardy. But Rey Ordonez's weak groundout to third and starting pitcher Masato Yoshii's failed suicide squeeze attempt (Cedeno was trapped and tagged out) got the Braves out of the mess. The Mets were able to get only a run off Maddux in his seven innings of work, and weren't able to overcome a 3-1 lead in a 4-2 loss.

Game 2: Though Kenny Rogers already had given up a two-run homer to Brian Jordan and a single to Andruw Jones in the sixth inning, Mets manager Bobby Valentine inexplicably decided to stay with Rogers over reliever Turk Wendell against hot-hitting Eddie Perez. The move backfired as Perez homered into the left field bleachers, giving the Braves a 4-2 lead. Chipper Jones' eighth-inning error opened the door for a Mets rally, but John Rocker struck out both John Olerud and Robin Ventura, preserving the Braves' 4-3 victory.

Game 3: The Mets hadn't committed two errors in the same inning all season until Game 3—and it was the first inning. They paid for it, too. Throwing errors by Al Leiter and Mike Piazza led to an unearned Braves run, the only run Tom Glavine needed. Glavine was brilliant, hitting spot after spot and inducing groundout after groundout in his seven innings of work. The Mets scattered seven hits, but never really got a good scoring chance.

Game 4: After back-to-back homers by Jordan and Ryan Klesko gave the Braves a 2-1 lead in the top of the eighth inning, the Mets' season appeared to be over, especially given the dominant Braves bullpen. But Olerud's single up the middle off the outstretched glove of Atlanta reserve shortstop Ozzie Guillen drove in the tying and game-winning runs in the bottom of the inning and kept the Mets alive in the best-of-7 series. The two-out single followed a well-executed double steal by Cedeno and Melvin Mora.

Game 5: Robin Ventura sent the exhausted Mets fans home happy and the series back to Atlanta with a game-ending grand slam in the 15th inning off Kevin McGlinchy. The grand slam officially was a single, making it a 4-3 Mets victory, because Ventura was not able to complete his trip around the base-paths. He was mobbed after rounding first base by his teammates, who were relieved still to be in the series. Nobody was more relieved than Ventura, who was 1-for-18 in the series to that point. The Mets tied the scored 3-3 earlier in the inning when McGlinchy issue a bases-loaded walk to Todd Pratt.

Game 6: Andruw Jones drew a bases-loaded walk from Kenny Rogers in the 11th inning, giving the Braves a 10-9 victory and a berth in the World Series. What started as a Braves fan's dream and a Mets fan's worst nightmare, ended in the same fashion. But there were plenty of twists and turns along the way. The Braves jumped out to early 5-0 and 7-3 leads, highlighted by two-run singles by Perez and Jose Hernandez. But the Mets came back, eventually tying the game 8-8 and knocking around dependable hurlers Kevin Millwood and John Smoltz in the process. Each team scored a 10th-inning run before the 11th-inning game-winner with one out.

WORTH NOTING:

Braves: The Braves were appearing in their eighth straight National League Championship Series. ... Series MVP Eddie Perez, who hadn't homered all season at Turner Field, had two in three games there. Perez batted .500 in the NLCS after batting .249 during the regular season. ... John Smoltz made his first career postseason relief appearance in Game 2, picking up his first career save. ... John Rocker set a record in every game he appeared. He now has appeared in 12 consecutive NLCS games, six each from the '98 and '99 seasons. ... During the regular season, the Braves were 74-8 when leading after seven innings. They were 3-0 in this series. ... The Braves left 19 runners on base in Game 5, a postseason record. ... Turner Field's Game 6 attendance of 52,335 was the first sellout of the '99 postseason for the Braves and set a Turner Field record. ... Atlanta was 14-for-17 in stolen bases during the series. The 14 stolen bases is an NLCS record. The previous record was 11 by the Cincinnati Reds in 1975.

Mets: Melvin Mora homered for the first time in his major league career in Game 2. ... In six career postseason starts, Kenny Rogers has given up 20 runs in 19 innings. ... Before getting the game-winning hit in the eighth inning of Game 4, Olerud had been hitless in nine at-bats against Rocker. ... The Mets were trying to become the first team ever to come back from a 3-0 deficit in a playoff series. ... The Mets have been involved in two of the longest postseason games in history. They were involved in a 16-inning game in 1986 against the Astros and in Game 5, which lasted 15 innings and took five hours and 46 minutes to complete. ... As a team, the Mets batted .340 in Game 6. In Games 1-5, the Mets batted .188. ... Mike Piazza's home run in Game 6 was his only extra-base hit of the series.

WORTH QUOTING:

Braves: Eddie Perez, on the Braves' winning Game 1: "I think winning the first game is important. I remember the Padres won the first game and went on to win the series. Two years ago the Marlins won the first game and then won the series." ... Manager Bobby Cox, on John Rocker's verbal sparring with Mets fans throughout the series: "He's a great pitcher, a great competitor, but he needs to work on his player-fan relationships." ... Rocker's take on the Mets fans: "A majority of Mets fans aren't human. The bottom line is that 80 percent of Mets fans are Neanderthal." ... Bobby Cox, on John Olerud's two-run single that was the eventual game-winning hit in Game 4: "I don't think any of our shortstops catch that ball. It ends up the same way." ... Cox again, on Kevin McGlinchy's struggle to get batters out in the bottom of the 15th: "McGlinchy is a big leaguer. He should be able to throw strikes and get them out. We thought he would." ... Rocker, on pitching in the high-intensity Game 6: "When I went out for my second inning, I really didn't have much mentally. I was so mentally exhausted from just being in a nail-biting game every single day. It was two weeks of just constant mental anguish and torture. Games hinging on one pitch night after night. Without ever stepping on the field, you walk out there exhausted already."

Mets: Bobby Valentine, on his decision not to pull Kenny Rogers from Game 2: "I should have done it. No doubt about that. I had no reason to keep him in, and it was absolutely the wrong move." ... Valentine, on the Braves pitching staff: "I don't think we have to wait for any historians. The Braves pitchers are as good as there is—in any era, in any decade." ... Al Leiter, on his costly first-inning error in Game 3: "I was thinking I should be throwing to second while I was throwing to first. To think that my bonehead mistake, a poor throw, was the difference between a win and a loss. It was a total brain cramp." ... Robin Ventura, after notified he only was awarded a single, despite hitting the ball over the fence to end Game 5: "As long as I touch first, we won. That's fine with me." ... Valentine, on what he told his players after Game 6, "I told them they played like champions. We don't have a trophy, but they did everything they had to." ... Rogers, about giving up the Game 6 winning run on a bases-loaded walk: "I'm a big boy. I can handle it. God thinks I can handle a lot. He can lay off me now."

Game 1 at Atlanta

ATLANTA 4, NEW YORK 2

HOW THEY SCORED

First Inning

Atlanta—Williams singled to center. Williams stole second. Boone singled to center, scoring Williams. C. Jones walked. Jordan flied to Cedeno. Klesko flied to Cedeno as Boone went to third. A. Jones grounded out, Ventura to Olerud. One run. Atlanta 1, New York 0.

Fourth Inning

New York—Henderson struck out. Alfonzo doubled to left-center. Olerud singled to right as Alfonzo went to third. Piazza grounded out, C. Jones to Klesko, as Alfonzo scored and Olerud went to second. Ventura walked. Hamilton grounded out, Maddux to Klesko. One run. New York 1, Atlanta 1.

Fifth Inning

Atlanta—Weiss doubled to right. Maddux sacrificed Weiss to third, Yoshii to Alfonzo. Williams singled to left and went to second on Henderson's fielding error as Weiss scored. Boone flied to Cedeno. C. Jones was walked intentionally. Mahomes now pitching. Jordan flied to Hamilton. One run. Atlanta 2, New York 1.

Sixth Inning

Atlanta—Klesko reached first on a fielding error by Olerud. A. Jones grounded into a double play, Mahomes to Alfonzo to Ordonez to Olerud. Perez homered to left. Weiss singled to left. Maddux struck out. One run. Atlanta 3, New York 1.

Eighth Inning

Atlanta—Wendell now pitching. A. Jones walked. Perez sacrificed A. Jones to second, Wendell, unassisted. Weiss singled to left, scoring A. Jones. Hunter struck out as Weiss stole second. Williams struck out. One run. Atlanta 4, New York 1.

Ninth Inning

New York—Piazza grounded out, Boone to Hunter. Ventura struck out. Dunston, pinch-hitting for Hamilton, reached first on a fielding error by C. Jones. Pratt now pinch-hitting for Cedeno. Dunston went to second on a wild pitch. Pratt singled to left, scoring Dunston. Ordonez grounded out, C. Jones to Hunter. One run. Atlanta 4, New York 2.

BOX SCORE

New York	AB	R	H	RBI	PO	A
Henderson, lf	4	0	0	0	2	0
Alfonzo, 2b	4	1	2	0	2	1
Olerud, 1b	4	0	1	0	8	0
Piazza, c	4	0	0	1	5	0
Ventura, 3b	3	0	0	0	0	2
Hamilton, cf	3	0	0	0	2	0
Dunston, ph	1	1	0	0	0	0
Cedeno, rf	3	0	2	0	3	0
Pratt, ph	1	0	1	1	0	0
Ordonez, ss	4	0	0	0	1	3
Yoshii, p	2	0	0	0	0	3
Mahomes, p	0	0	0	0	0	1
Cook, p	0	0	0	0	0	0
M. Franco, ph	0	0	0	0	0	0
Mora, ph	0	0	0	0	0	0
Wendell, p	0	0	0	0	1	0
Totals	33	2	6	2	24	10

Atlanta	AB	R	H	RBI	PO	A
Williams, lf	5	1	2	1	2	0
Boone, 2b	4	0	1	1	0	3
C. Jones, 3b	1	0	0	0	1	5
Jordan, rf	3	0	0	0	0	0
Klesko, 1b	3	0	0	0	12	0
Battle, ph-1b	1	0	0	0	0	0
Remlinger, p	0	0	0	0	0	1
Rocker, p	0	0	0	0	0	0
A. Jones, cf	3	1	0	0	2	0
Perez, c	3	1	2	1	5	1
Weiss, ss	4	1	3	1	0	1
Maddux, p	2	0	0	0	1	4
Hunter, 1b	1	0	0	0	4	0
Totals	30	4	8	4	27	15

New York	0 0 0	1 0 0	0 0 1	—2
Atlanta	1 0 0	0 1 1	0 1 x	—4

New York	IP	H	R	ER	BB	SO
Yoshii (L)	4.2	5	2	2	2	1
Mahomes	1.1	2	1	1	0	1
Cook	1.0	0	0	0	2	1
Wendell	1.0	1	1	1	1	2

Atlanta	IP	H	R	ER	BB	SO
Maddux (W)	7.0	5	1	1	1	2
Remlinger	0.2	0	0	0	1	0
Rocker (S)	1.1	1	0	0	0	2

E—Henderson, Olerud, Williams, C. Jones. DP—New York 1. LOB—New York 6, Atlanta 9. 2B—Alfonzo 2, Perez, Cedeno, Weiss. HR—Perez, Maddux, Perez. SB—Williams, C. Jones, Weiss. CS—Cedeno. WP—Rocker. T—3:09. A—44,172. U—Montague, plate; Kellogg, first; Reliford, second; Rapuano, third; Layne, left field; Crawford, right field.

Game 2 at Atlanta

ATLANTA 4, NEW YORK 3

HOW THEY SCORED

Second Inning

New York—Ventura walked. Hamilton singled to center as Ventura went to second. Cedeno singled to center, scoring Ventura as Hamilton went to third. Ordonez lined to Hunter. Rogers sacrificed Cedeno to second, Millwood to Hunter. Henderson grounded out, Boone to Millwood. One run. New York 1, Atlanta 0.

Fifth Inning

New York—Ordonez flied to Jordan. Rogers struck out. Mora homered to left. Alfonzo grounded out, Boone to Hunter. One run. New York 2, Atlanta 0.

Sixth Inning

Atlanta—Boone grounded out, Ordonez to Olerud. C. Jones walked. Jordan homered to right, scoring C. Jones. A. Jones singled to left. Perez homered to left, scoring A. Jones. Wendell now pitching. Hunter flied to Hamilton. Weiss reached first on a fielding error by Alfonzo. Millwood grounded out, Ordonez to Olerud. Four runs. Atlanta 4, New York 2.

Eighth Inning

New York—M. Franco, pinch-hitting for Wendell, lined to Hunter. Mora reached first on a fielding error by C. Jones. Alfonzo doubled to center, scoring Mora. Rocker now pitching. Olerud struck out. Piazza was walked intentionally. Ventura struck out. One run. Atlanta 4, New York 3.

BOX SCORE

New York	AB	R	H	RBI	PO	A
Henderson, lf	2	0	0	0	0	0
Mora, lf	2	2	1	1	1	0
Alfonzo, 2b	4	0	2	1	3	3
Olerud, 1b	4	0	0	0	12	1
Piazza, c	3	0	0	0	4	0
Ventura, 3b	3	1	0	0	1	1
Hamilton, cf	3	0	1	0	2	0
Dunston, ph	1	0	0	0	0	0
Cedeno, rf	4	0	1	1	1	0
Ordonez, ss	3	0	0	0	0	7
Bonilla, ph	1	0	0	0	0	0
Rogers, p	1	0	0	0	0	4
Wendell, p	0	0	0	0	0	0
M. Franco, ph	1	0	0	0	0	0
Benitez, p	0	0	0	0	0	0
Totals	32	3	5	3	24	16
Atlanta	AB	R	H	RBI	PO	A
Williams, lf	4	0	1	0	1	0
Boone, 2b	4	0	1	0	0	2
C. Jones, 3b	2	1	0	0	0	0
Jordan, rf	4	1	1	2	5	0
A. Jones, cf	4	1	3	0	3	0
Perez, c	4	1	2	2	7	0
Hunter, 1b	3	0	0	0	7	1
Weiss, ss	3	0	1	0	2	1
Millwood, p	2	0	0	0	2	2
Rocker, p	0	0	0	0	0	0
Smoltz, p	0	0	0	0	0	0
Totals	30	4	9	4	27	6

New York .... 0 1 0 0 1 0 0 1 0—3
Atlanta .... 0 0 0 0 0 4 0 0 0—4

New York	IP	H	R	ER	BB	SO
Rogers (L)	5.1	9	4	4	3	1
Wendell	1.2	0	0	0	1	1
Benitez	1.0	0	0	0	0	2
Atlanta	IP	H	R	ER	BB	SO
Millwood (W)	7.1	5	3	2	1	4
Rocker	0.2	0	0	0	1	0
Smoltz (S)	1.0	0	0	0	0	1

E—Alfonzo, C. Jones. DP—New York 2. LOB—New York 5, Atlanta 6. 2B—Alfonzo. HR—Mora, Jordan, Perez. SH—Rogers. CS—A. Jones. T—2:42. A—44,624. U—Kellogg, plate; Reliford, first; Rapuano, second; Layne, third; Crawford, left field; Montague, right field.

Game 3 at New York

ATLANTA 1, NEW YORK 0

HOW THEY SCORED

First Inning

Atlanta—Williams walked. Boone reached first on a throwing error by Leiter as Williams went to second. A. Jones popped to Alfonzo. Williams stole third and scored on a throwing error by Piazza as Boone stole second and reached third on the play. Jordan flied into a double play, Mora to Piazza. One run. Atlanta 1, New York 0.

BOX SCORE

Atlanta	AB	R	H	RBI	PO	A
Williams, lf	3	1	0	0	0	0
Boone, 2b	4	0	0	0	3	3
C. Jones, 3b	4	0	1	0	0	0
Jordan, rf	4	0	0	0	4	0
A. Jones, cf	3	0	0	0	3	0
Perez, c	3	0	2	0	9	1
Hunter, 1b	2	0	0	0	6	0
Weiss, ss	2	0	0	0	2	2
Glavine, p	2	0	0	0	0	1
Remlinger, p	0	0	0	0	0	0
Rocker, p	0	0	0	0	0	0
Totals	27	1	3	0	27	7
New York	AB	R	H	RBI	PO	A
Henderson, lf	4	0	1	0	2	2
Olerud, 1b	3	0	1	0	6	0
Alfonzo, 2b	4	0	0	0	5	2
Piazza, c	4	0	2	0	8	0
Agbayani, rf	4	0	0	0	1	0
Ventura, 3b	3	0	0	0	1	1
Pratt, ph	1	0	0	0	0	0
Mora, cf	4	0	2	0	3	1
Ordonez, ss	4	0	1	0	2	4
Leiter, p	2	0	0	0	1	1
Dunston, ph	1	0	0	0	0	0
J. Franco, p	0	0	0	0	0	1
Benitez, p	0	0	0	0	0	0
Totals	34	0	7	0	27	12

Atlanta .... 1 0 0 0 0 0 0 0 0—1
New York .... 0 0 0 0 0 0 0 0 0—0

Atlanta	IP	H	R	ER	BB	SO
Glavine (W)	7.0	7	0	0	1	8
Remlinger	1.0	0	0	0	0	1
Rocker (S)	1.0	0	0	0	0	1
New York	IP	H	R	ER	BB	SO
Leiter (L)	7.0	3	1	0	3	5
J. Franco	0.1	0	0	0	1	0
Benitez	1.2	0	0	0	0	3

E—Weiss, Leiter, Piazza. DP—Atlanta 1, New York 2. LOB—Atlanta 4, New York 8. SH—Glavine. SB—Williams, Boone. CS—Dunston. WP—Leiter. PB—Perez. T—3:04. A—55,911. U—Reliford, plate; Rapuano, first; Layne, second; Crawford, third; Montague, left field; Kellogg, right field.

Game 4 at New York

NEW YORK 3, ATLANTA 2

HOW THEY SCORED

Sixth Inning

New York—Reed popped to Boone. Henderson popped to Klesko. Olerud homered to right. Alfonzo struck out. One run. New York 1, Atlanta 0.

Eighth Inning

Atlanta—Mora now in left field. Jordan homered to left-center. Klesko homered to right. Wendell now pitching. A. Jones flied to Cedeno. Perez grounded out, Ventura to Olerud. Weiss grounded out, Alfonzo to Olerud. Two runs. Atlanta 2, New York 1.

New York—Hunter now at first. Cedeno singled to center. Ordonez popped to Hunter in foul territory. M. Franco now pinch-hitting for Wendell. Remlinger now pitching. Agbayani, pinch-hitting for M. Franco, struck out. Cedeno stole second and Mora walked. Guillen now at shortstop and Rocker pitching. Cedeno stole third and Mora stole second. Olerud singled to center, scoring Cedeno and Mora. Alfonzo struck out. Two runs. New York 3, Atlanta 2.

BOX SCORE

Atlanta	AB	R	H	RBI	PO	A
Williams, lf	4	0	0	0	4	0
Boone, 2b	3	0	1	0	1	1
Lockhart, ph	1	0	0	0	0	0
C. Jones, 3b	3	0	0	0	1	0
Jordan, rf	3	1	1	1	1	0
Klesko, 1b	3	1	1	1	5	1
Hunter, 1b	0	0	0	0	1	0
A. Jones, cf	3	0	0	0	1	0
Perez, c	3	0	0	0	9	0
Weiss, ss	3	0	0	0	0	2
Rocker, p	0	0	0	0	0	0
Smoltz, p	2	0	0	0	0	0
Remlinger, p	0	0	0	0	0	0
Guillen, ss	1	0	0	0	0	0
Totals	29	2	3	2	24	4
New York	AB	R	H	RBI	PO	A
Henderson, lf	3	0	0	0	0	0
Mora, lf	2	1	0	0	0	0
Olerud, 1b	4	1	2	3	10	0
Alfonzo, 2b	4	0	0	0	1	3
Piazza, c	3	0	0	0	7	1
Ventura, 3b	3	0	0	0	1	4
Hamilton, cf	3	0	0	0	1	0
Cedeno, rf	3	1	3	0	6	0
Ordonez, ss	3	0	0	0	1	3
Reed, p	2	0	0	0	0	0
Wendell, p	0	0	0	0	0	0
M. Franco, ph	0	0	0	0	0	0
Agbayani, ph	1	0	0	0	0	0
Benitez, p	0	0	0	0	0	0
Totals	29	3	5	3	27	11

Atlanta's Keith Lockhart (left) is tagged out at the plate by Mike Piazza in the 13th inning of Game 5.

Atlanta .... 0 0 0 0 0 0 0 2 0—2
New York .... 0 0 0 0 0 1 0 2 x—3

Atlanta	IP	H	R	ER	BB	SO
Smoltz	7.1	4	2	2	0	7
Remlinger (L)	0.1	0	1	1	1	1
Rocker	0.1	1	0	0	0	1
New York	IP	H	R	ER	BB	SO
Reed	*7.0	3	2	2	0	5
Wendell (W)	1.0	0	0	0	0	0
Benitez (S)	1.0	0	0	0	0	1

*Pitched to two batters in eighth.

LOB—Atlanta 0, New York 3. HR—Olerud, Jordan, Klesko. SB—Cedeno 2, Mora. CS—Boone. T—2:20. A—55,872. U—Rapuano, plate; Layne, first; Crawford, second; Montague, third; Kellogg, left field; Reliford, right field.

Game 5 at New York

NEW YORK 4, ATLANTA 3 (15 INNINGS)

HOW THEY SCORED

First Inning

New York—Henderson singled to short. Alfonzo lined to A. Jones. Olerud homered to right-center, scoring Henderson. Piazza singled to left. Ventura popped out to C. Jones in foul territory. Two runs. New York 2, Atlanta 0.

Fourth Inning

Atlanta—Boone doubled to left. C. Jones doubled to left, scoring Boone. Jordan singled to left, scoring C. Jones. Klesko walked. Hershiser now pitching. A. Jones and Perez struck out. Weiss grounded out, Olerud to Hershiser. Two runs. Atlanta 2, New York 2.

Fifteenth Inning

Atlanta—Weiss singled to left-center. McGlinchy struck out as Weiss stole second. Williams flied to Agbayani. Lockhart tripled to center, scoring Weiss. C. Jones was walked intentionally. Jordan struck out. One run. Atlanta 3, New York 2.

New York—Dunston singled to center. M. Franco now pinch-hitting for Dotel. Dunston stole second. M. Franco walked. Alfonzo sacrificed Dunston to third and M. Franco to second, McGlinchy to Lockhart. Olerud was walked intentionally. Cedeno now pinch-running for M. Franco. Pratt walked, scoring Dunston. Ventura singled to right-center, scoring Cedeno as Olerud went to third and Pratt to second. Two runs. New York 4, Atlanta 3.

BOX SCORE

Atlanta	AB	R	H	RBI	PO	A
Williams, lf	7	0	1	0	2	0
Boone, 2b	3	1	1	0	0	3
Nixon, pr	0	0	0	0	0	0
Lockhart, 2b	4	0	2	1	1	3
C. Jones, 3b	6	1	3	1	0	2
Jordan, rf	7	0	2	1	4	0
Klesko, 1b	2	0	0	0	8	1
Hunter, ph-1b	3	0	0	0	7	0
A. Jones, cf	5	0	0	0	2	0
Perez, c	4	0	2	0	7	0
Battle, pr	0	0	0	0	0	0
Myers, c	1	0	0	0	7	0
Weiss, ss	6	1	2	0	2	7
Maddux, p	3	0	0	0	1	0
Hernandez, ph	1	0	0	0	0	0
Mulholland, p	0	0	0	0	0	0
Guillen, ph	1	0	0	0	0	0
Remlinger, p	0	0	0	0	0	0
Springer, p	0	0	0	0	0	0

Atlanta	AB	R	H	RBI	PO	A
Fabregas, ph	1	0	0	0	0	0
Rocker, p	0	0	0	0	0	0
McGlinchy, p	1	0	0	0	0	1
Totals	55	3	13	3	43	17

New York	AB	R	H	RBI	PO	A
Henderson, lf	5	1	1	0	2	0
Rogers, p	0	0	0	0	0	0
Bonilla, ph	1	0	0	0	0	0
Dotel, p	0	0	0	0	0	0
M. Franco, ph	0	0	0	0	0	0
Cedeno, pr	0	1	0	0	0	0
Alfonzo, 2b	6	0	1	0	2	5
Olerud, 1b	6	1	2	2	12	1
Piazza, c	6	0	1	0	16	2
Pratt, c	0	0	0	1	4	0
Ventura, 3b	7	0	2	1	0	7
Mora, rf-cf-rf	6	0	1	0	3	1
Hamilton, cf	3	0	2	0	2	0
Agbayani, ph-rf-lf	1	0	0	0	1	0
Ordonez, ss	6	0	0	0	1	2
Yoshii, p	1	0	0	0	0	0
Hershiser, p	1	0	0	0	2	0
Wendell, p	0	0	0	0	0	0
Cook, p	0	0	0	0	0	0
Mahomes, p	1	0	0	0	0	0
J. Franco, p	0	0	0	0	0	0
Benitez, p	0	0	0	0	0	0
Dunston, ph-cf	3	1	1	0	0	0
Totals	53	4	11	4	45	18

Atlanta ....0 0 0 2 0 0 0 0 0 0 0 0 0 0 1—3

New York ....2 0 0 0 0 0 0 0 0 0 0 0 0 0 2—4

One out when winning run scored.

Atlanta	IP	H	R	ER	BB	SO
Maddux	7.0	7	2	2	0	5
Mulholland	2.0	1	0	0	0	2
Remlinger	2.0	1	0	0	0	2
Springer	1.0	0	0	0	1	1
Rocker	1.1	0	0	0	0	2
McGlinchy (L)	1.0	2	2	2	4	1

New York	IP	H	R	ER	BB	SO
Yoshii	*3.0	4	2	2	1	3
Hershiser	3.1	1	0	0	3	5
Wendell	0.1	0	0	0	1	1
Cook	0.0	0	0	0	0	0
Mahomes	1.0	1	0	0	2	1
J. Franco	1.1	1	0	0	0	2
Benitez	1.0	1	0	0	0	1
Rogers	2.0	1	0	0	1	1
Dotel (W)	3.0	4	1	1	2	5

*Pitched to four batters in fourth.

E—Klesko 2, Olerud. DP—Atlanta 2, New York 2. LOB—Atlanta 19, New York 12. 2B—C. Jones 2, Hamilton, Perez, Boone, Williams, Weiss. 3B—Lockhart. HR—Olerud. SH—A. Jones, Alfonzo. SB—Nixon, Battle, Weiss, Agbayani, Dunston. CS—Klesko. HBP—By Hershiser (Boone). T—5:46. A—55,723. U—Layne, plate; Crawford, first; Montague, second; Kellogg, third; Reliford, left field, Rapuano, right field.

Game 6 at Atlanta

ATLANTA 10, NEW YORK 9 (11 INNINGS)

HOW THEY SCORED

First Inning

Atlanta—Williams hit by a pitch. Boone walked. Williams stole third and scored on a throwing error by Piazza as Boone stole second. C. Jones hit by a pitch. Jordan singled to left, scoring Boone as C. Jones went to second. A. Jones reached first on a fielder's choice as C. Jones went to third and Jordan to second. Perez singled to right-center, scoring C. Jones and Jordan as A. Jones went to third. Mahomes now pitching. Hunter hit a sacrifice fly to Hamiltonc scoring A. Jones. Weiss grounded into a double play, Alfonzo to Ordonez to Olerud. Five runs. Atlanta 5, New York 0.

Sixth Inning

New York—Alfonzo doubled to left-center. Olerud singled to center as Alfonzo went to third. Piazza hit a sacrifice fly to Williams, scoring Alfonzo. Ventura doubled to right as Olerud went to third. Hamilton singled to center, scoring Olerud and Ventura. Mulholland now pitching. Agbayani, pinch-hitting for Cedeno, walked. Ordonez lined into a double play, Weiss, unassisted. Three runs. Atlanta 5, New York 3.

Atlanta—Agbayani now in right field. Jordan hit by a pitch. A. Jones singled to the mound as Jordan went to second. Perez sacrificed Jordan to third and A. Jones to second, Olerud to Alfonzo. Hunter was walked intentionally. Weiss forced Jordan at home, Olerud to Piazza, as A. Jones went to third and Hunter to second. Lockhart announced as pinch-hitter for Mulholland. Cook now pitching. Hernandez, pinch-hitting for Lockhart, singled to left, scoring A. Jones and Hunter as Weiss went to second. Williams popped to Ordonez. Two runs. Atlanta 7, New York 3.

Seventh Inning

New York—Smoltz now pitching. M. Franco, pinch-hitting for Cook, doubled to center. Henderson doubled to left, scoring M. Franco. Alfonzo flied to Jordan as Henderson went to third. Olerud singled to right, scoring Henderson. Piazza homered to right-center, scoring Olerud. Remlinger now pitching. Ventura flied to Jordan. Hamilton grounded to Hunter. Four runs. New York 7, Atlanta 7.

Eighth Inning

New York—Agbayani singled to right. Ordonez sacrificed Agbayani to second, Remlinger, unassisted. Mora, pinch-hitting for Hershiser, singled to center, scoring Agbayani. Henderson forced Mora at second, Weiss to Boone. Henderson stole second. Alfonzo walked. Olerud flied to Williams. One run. New York 8, Atlanta 7.

Atlanta—Mora now in right field, J. Franco pitching and Agbayani moved to left. A. Jones grounded out, Ordonez to Olerud. Perez singled to left. Nixon now pinch-running for Perez. Nixon stole second and reached third ona throwing error by Piazza. Hunter singled to center, scoring Nixon. Weiss sacrificed Hunter to second, J. Franco to Alfonzo. Battle, pinch-hitting for Remlinger, struck out. One run. New York 8, Atlanta 8.

Tenth Inning

New York—Agbayani walked. Ordonez popped to Hunter. Agbayani caught stealing second, but was safe and reached on a throwing error by Hunter (assist by Rocker). Mora singled to center as Agbayani went to third. Pratt hit a sacrifice fly to A. Jones, scoring Agbayani as Mora went to second. Mora stole third. Alfonzo struck out. One run. New York 9, Atlanta 8.

Atlanta—A. Jones singled to center. Myers flied to Agbayani. Klesko, pinch-hitting for Hunter, walked. Guillen, pinch-hitting for Weiss, singled to right, scoring A. Jones, but Klesko was thrown out at third, Mora to Ventura. Fabregas, pinch-hitting for Rocker, flied to Agbayani. One run. New York 9, Atlanta 9.

Eleventh Inning

Atlanta—Rogers now pitching. Williams doubled to left. Boone sacrificed Williams to third, Olerud, unassisted. C. Jones and Jordan were walked intentionally. A. Jones walked, scoring Williams. One run. Atlanta 10, New York 9.

BOX SCORE

New York	AB	R	H	RBI	PO	A
Henderson, lf	5	1	2	1	1	0
J. Franco, p	0	0	0	0	0	1
Pratt, c	0	0	0	1	2	0
Alfonzo, 2b	5	1	1	0	2	4
Olerud, 1b	6	2	2	1	11	2
Piazza, c	4	1	1	3	4	0
Benitez, p	0	0	0	0	0	0
Dunston, ph	1	0	0	0	0	0
Rogers, p	0	0	0	0	0	0
Ventura, 3b	6	1	1	0	2	1
Hamilton, cf	5	0	3	2	1	0
Cedeno, rf	2	0	0	0	2	0
Agbayani, ph-rf-lf	1	2	1	0	3	0
Ordonez, ss	4	0	0	0	2	5
Leiter, p	0	0	0	0	0	0
Mahomes, p	1	0	0	0	1	1
Bonilla, ph	1	0	1	0	0	0
Wendell, p	0	0	0	0	0	0
Cook, p	0	0	0	0	0	0
M. Franco, ph	1	1	1	0	0	0
Hershiser, p	0	0	0	0	0	0
Mora, ph-rf	2	0	2	1	0	1
Totals	44	9	15	9	31	15

Atlanta	AB	R	H	RBI	PO	A
Williams, lf	5	2	1	0	3	0
Boone, 2b	4	1	0	0	1	2
C. Jones, 3b	3	1	1	0	1	1
Jordan, rf	4	1	1	1	3	0
A. Jones, cf	5	3	2	1	6	0
Perez, c	3	0	2	2	5	0
Nixon, pr	0	1	0	0	0	0
Myers, c	1	0	0	0	1	0
Hunter, 1b	1	1	1	2	6	1
Klesko, ph-1b	0	0	0	0	2	0
Weiss, ss	3	0	0	0	3	1
Guillen, ph-ss	1	0	1	1	0	0
Millwood, p	2	0	0	0	1	0
Mulholland, p	0	0	0	0	0	0
Lockhart, ph	0	0	0	0	0	0
Hernandez, ph	1	0	1	2	0	0
Smoltz, p	0	0	0	0	0	0
Remlinger, p	0	0	0	0	1	0
Battle, ph	1	0	0	0	0	0
Rocker, p	0	0	0	0	0	1
Fabregas, ph	1	0	0	0	0	0
Springer, p	0	0	0	0	0	0
Totals	35	10	10	9	33	6

New York ....0 0 0 0 0 3 4 1 0 1 0— 9
Atlanta ....5 0 0 0 0 2 0 1 0 1 1—10

One out when winning run scored.

New York	IP	H	R	ER	BB	SO
Leiter	*0.0	2	5	5	1	0
Mahomes	4.0	1	0	0	1	1
Wendell	1.2	1	2	2	1	1
Cook	0.1	1	0	0	0	0
Hershiser	1.0	0	0	0	0	0
J. Franco	1.0	2	1	1	0	1
Benitez	2.0	2	1	1	2	2
Rogers (L)	0.1	1	1	1	3	0

Atlanta	IP	H	R	ER	BB	SO
Millwood	5.1	8	3	3	0	5
Mulholland	0.2	0	0	0	1	0
Smoltz	0.1	4	4	4	0	0
Remlinger	1.2	2	1	1	1	0
Rocker	2.0	1	1	0	1	1
Springer (W)	1.0	0	0	0	0	0

*Pitched to six batters in first.

E—Piazza 2, Hunter. DP—New York 2, Atlanta 1. LOB—New York 8, Atlanta 9. 2B—Alfonzo, Ventura, M. Franco, Henderson, Williams. HR—Piazza. SH—Ordonez, Perez, Weiss, Boone. SF—Piazza, Pratt, Hunter. SB—C. Jones 2, Henderson, Mora, Williams, Boone, Hunter, Nixon. CS—Agbayani. HBP—Leiter 2 (Williams, C. Jones), Wendell (Jordan). T—4:25. A—52,335. U—Crawford, plate; Montague, first; Kellogg, second; Reliford, third; Rapuano, left field; Layne, right field.

COMPOSITE

BATTING AVERAGES

Atlanta Braves

Player, position	G	AB	R	H	2B	3B	HR	RBI	Avg.
Perez, c	6	20	2	10	2	0	2	1	.500
Hernandez, ph	2	2	0	1	0	0	0	0	.500
Lockhart, ph-2b	3	5	0	2	0	1	0	0	.400
Guillen, ss-ph	3	3	0	1	0	0	0	0	.333
Weiss, ss	6	21	2	6	2	0	0	2	.286
C. Jones, 3b	6	19	3	5	2	0	0	9	.263
A. Jones, cf	6	23	5	5	0	0	0	4	.217
Jordan, rf	6	25	3	5	0	0	2	3	.200
Boone, 2b	6	22	2	4	1	0	0	1	.182
Williams, lf	6	28	4	5	2	0	0	2	.179
Klesko, 1b-ph	4	8	1	1	0	0	1	2	.125
Hunter, 1b-ph	6	10	1	1	0	0	0	5	.100
Mulholland, p	2	0	0	0	0	0	0	0	.000
Nixon, pr	2	0	1	0	0	0	0	0	.000
Remlinger, p	5	0	0	0	0	0	0	0	.000
Rocker, p	6	0	0	0	0	0	0	0	.000
Springer, p	2	0	0	0	0	0	0	0	.000
McGlinchy, p	1	1	0	0	0	0	0	0	.000
Battle, ph-1b-pr	3	2	0	0	0	0	0	0	.000
Fabregas, ph	2	2	0	0	0	0	0	0	.000
Glavine, p	1	2	0	0	0	0	0	0	.000
Myers, c	2	2	0	0	0	0	0	1	.000
Smoltz, p	3	2	0	0	0	0	0	0	.000
Millwood, p	2	4	0	0	0	0	0	1	.000
Maddux, p	2	5	0	0	0	0	0	0	.000
Totals	6	206	24	46	9	1	5	31	.223

New York Mets

Player, position	G	AB	R	H	2B	3B	HR	RBI	Avg.
Cedeno, rf-pr	5	12	2	6	1	0	0	0	.500
M. Franco, ph	5	2	1	1	1	0	0	1	.500
Pratt, ph-c	4	2	0	1	0	0	0	1	.500
Mora, ph-lf-cf-rf	6	14	3	6	0	0	1	2	.429
Hamilton, cf	5	17	0	6	1	0	0	0	.353
Bonilla, ph	3	3	0	1	0	0	0	0	.333
Olerud, 1b	6	27	4	8	0	0	2	2	.296
Alfonzo, 2b	6	27	2	6	4	0	0	1	.222
Henderson, lf	6	23	2	4	1	0	0	0	.174
Piazza, c	6	24	1	4	0	0	1	1	.167
Agbayani, rf-ph-lf	4	7	2	1	0	0	0	4	.143
Dunston, ph-cf	5	7	2	1	0	0	0	0	.143
Ventura, 3b	6	25	2	3	1	0	0	2	.120
Ordonez, ss	6	24	0	1	0	0	0	0	.042
Benitez, p	5	0	0	0	0	0	0	0	.000
Cook, p	3	0	0	0	0	0	0	0	.000
Dotel, p	1	0	0	0	0	0	0	0	.000
J. Franco, p	3	0	0	0	0	0	0	0	.000
Wendell, p	5	0	0	0	0	0	0	0	.000
Hershiser, p	2	1	0	0	0	0	0	0	.000
Rogers, p	3	1	0	0	0	0	0	0	.000
Leiter, p	2	2	0	0	0	0	0	0	.000
Mahomes, p	3	2	0	0	0	0	0	0	.000
Reed, p	1	2	0	0	0	0	0	0	.000
Yoshii, p	2	3	0	0	0	0	0	0	.000
Totals	6	225	21	49	9	0	4	14	.218

PITCHING AVERAGES

Atlanta Braves

Pitcher	G	IP	H	R	ER	BB	SO	W	L	ERA
Glavine	1	7.0	7	0	0	1	8	1	0	0.00
Rocker	6	6.2	3	2	0	2	9	0	0	0.00
Mulholland	2	2.2	1	0	0	1	2	0	0	0.00
Springer	2	2.0	0	0	0	1	1	1	0	0.00
Maddux	2	14.0	12	3	3	1	7	1	0	1.93
Remlinger	5	5.2	3	2	2	3	4	0	1	3.18
Millwood	2	12.2	13	6	5	1	9	1	0	3.55
Smoltz	3	8.2	8	6	6	0	8	0	0	6.23
McGlinchy	1	1.0	2	2	2	4	1	0	1	18.00
Totals	6	60.1	49	21	18	14	49	4	2	2.69

Shutout—Glavine, Remlinger and Rocker (combined). Saves—Rocker 2, Smoltz.

New York Mets

Pitcher	G	IP	H	R	ER	BB	SO	W	L	ERA
Hershiser	2	4.1	1	0	0	3	5	0	0	0.00
Cook	3	1.1	1	0	0	2	1	0	0	0.00
Benitez	5	6.2	3	1	1	2	9	0	0	1.35
Mahomes	3	6.1	4	1	1	3	3	0	0	1.42
Reed	1	7.0	3	2	2	0	5	0	0	2.57
Dotel	1	3.0	4	1	1	2	5	1	0	3.00
J. Franco	3	2.2	3	1	1	1	3	0	0	3.38
Yoshii	2	7.2	9	4	4	3	4	0	1	4.70
Wendell	5	5.2	2	3	3	4	5	1	0	4.76
Rogers	3	7.2	11	5	5	7	2	0	2	5.87
Leiter	2	7.0	5	6	5	4	5	0	1	6.43
Totals	6	59.1	46	24	23	31	1	2	4	3.49

No shutouts. Save—Benitez.

The bottom line: Much of the drama for the Yankees-Red Sox championship series was rooted in events that took place long before any of the players were born. The so-called "Curse of the Bambino" claims that the Red Sox were cursed after selling Babe Ruth to the Yankees before the 1920 season. Indeed, Boston has not won a World Series since, and the Yankees now have won 25. That history, coupled with the proximity of the two division foes, has fueled one of the fiercest rivalries in sports. For the first time, the teams met in a postseason series. The Yankees, the A.L. East champs, were seeking a return trip to the World Series, and the scrappy Red Sox, the American League wild-card winners, were going for their first World Series appearance in 13 years. But except for their surreal, 13-1 victory in Game 3 at Fenway Park, it was curses for the Red Sox. Again.

Why the Yankees won: They did little wrong. They had depth at the plate and on the mound, and they were flawless in the field. And, they allowed the Red Sox to sink themselves with mistakes and missed opportunities. Boston stranded 45 runners and made 10 errors in the five games, failures that seemed to happen at the most opportune times for the Yankees. The Yankees, sparked by Bernie Williams' 10th-inning, game-winning home run in Game 1, got strong starting pitching from Orlando Hernandez, David Cone and Andy Pettitte. Shortstop Derek Jeter hit .350 in the series, and the Yankees' short relievers did not allow a run in nine innings.

TURNING POINTS:

Game 1: All-Star center fielder Bernie Williams hit the second pitch from Red Sox reliever Rod Beck for a home run to center field in the bottom of the 10th inning, capping the Yankees' 4-3 comeback win at Yankee Stadium. The Red Sox jumped out to a 2-0 lead in the first and added a run in the second inning, but in both innings they wasted one-out, first-and-second opportunities against Yankees hurler Orlando Hernandez. Hernandez got stronger as the game continued, and the Red Sox had just five hits and no runs the rest of the way. After a two-run home run by Scott Brosius in the second, the Yankees tied it in the seventh when Brosius scored on a single by Derek Jeter, despite a perfect throw from right fielder Trot Nixon that catcher Jason Varitek could not handle.

Game 2: Yankees lefthander Paul O'Neill, who had struggled against lefthanded pitching all season, faced Boston lefty Rheal Cormier in the seventh inning with the score 2-2, and came through with a game-winning single that scored Chuck Knoblauch. New York again used a late-inning rally to snuff the Red Sox at Yankee Stadium, 3-2. Boston starter Ramon Martinez, who missed most of the last two seasons recovering from shoulder surgery, pitched 6.2 innings, but he was outdone by David Cone of the Yankees, who struck out nine in seven innings. The Red Sox led, 2-1, on Nomar Garciaparra's home run, but the Yankees got a run in the seventh on Knoblauch's double before O'Neill's single.

Game 3: John Valentin's first-inning home run after Jose Offerman's leadoff triple set the tone for the Red Sox. With ace Pedro Martinez as their anchor on the mound, the Red Sox breezed to a 13-1 win in the series moved to Fenway Park. Oozing with subplots, it was among the most heavily hyped games in Championship Series history. There was Martinez, a shoo-in for the Cy Young Award, the hero of the Red Sox's series win over the Indians. There was pitcher Roger Clemens, who won three Cy Young Awards in 13 seasons with the Red Sox before he returned to Fenway Park in a crucial playoff game—now as a member of the Yankees. Clemens flopped, though, giving up five runs in two-plus innings, helping the Red Sox on their way to a rout.

Game 4: With the Yankees ahead, 3-2, in the bottom of the eighth, Jose Offerman of the Red Sox was called out on a tag play that umpire Tim Tschida later admitted was the wrong call. It was the second time in the series an umpire admitted a call that went against Boston was incorrect, and the Red Sox did not recover. They allowed six runs in the top of the ninth, losing 9-2. In that inning, Offerman threw away a double-play ball that could have ended the Yankees threat, and the next batter, Ricky Ledee, hit a grand slam that sealed the win.

Game 5: After Derek Jeter put the Yankees ahead, 2-0, with a home run, series MVP Orlando Hernandez again defused some

early Boston rallies. He held the Red Sox to one run over seven innings, and the Yankees closed out the series with a 6-1 victory. The Red Sox had runners on first and third with no outs in the first inning, then had runners on first and second in the second, but Hernandez held them scoreless both times. The Yankees secured the game with two runs in the seventh, getting three hits and some help from three Red Sox errors.

WORTH NOTING:

Yankees: The Yankees were outscored, 11-5, in the first three innings over the five games, but they outscored the Red Sox, 15-5, from the seventh inning on. ... New York turned seven double plays, and Boston turned none. ... Closer Mariano Rivera made three appearances, getting a win and two saves. He threw 74 pitches—only 21 were balls. ... Series MVP Orlando Hernandez's brother, Livan, was the 1997 NLCS MVP for the Marlins. ... The Yankees finished the century with a 1,011-826 advantage against the rival Red Sox. ... Paul O'Neill was a standout in the series despite playing with a broken rib.

Red Sox: Boston's 10 errors—in just five games—were a League Championship Series record. Five of the 23 runs allowed by Red Sox pitchers were unearned. ... After manager Jimy Williams was ejected arguing a call in the ninth inning of Game 4, fans at Fenway Park threw debris onto the field, causing the players to be cleared from the Yankees bullpen. A forfeit was threatened over stadium loudspeakers. ... Babe Ruth's daughter threw out the first pitch for Game 5 at Fenway Park. ... In their Game 3 win, the Red Sox were 7-for-17 (.412) with runners in scoring position. In the other four games, Boston was 6-for 36 (.167). ... The Red Sox had lost 10 straight ALCS games before winning Game 3.

WORTH QUOTING:

Red Sox: Rod Beck, after allowing Bernie Williams' game-winning home run in Game 1: "It was a bad time for a bad pitch." ... Umpire Rick Reed, whose missed call in the top of the 10th inning in Game 1 blunted a Red Sox rally: "As an umpire, it was my job to get it right. I didn't. I feel awful." ... Boston's Game 2 starter Ramon Martinez, after the Yankees' 3-2 win: "This is one of the greatest teams. That is the reason why they are here. I know I am going to have a tough game. I did the best that I could." ... John Valentin, after the Red Sox's Game 3 win: "We had to win today. Going down 3-0 against the New York Yankees would have been almost impossible to come back from. It would have been like going down 2-0 to Cleveland." ... Darren Lewis, after umpire Tim Tschida admittedly made a bad call, ending a Red Sox threat, in the eighth inning of Game 4: "We made some mistakes. But at the same time, they're taking away something we've worked for all year. With calls like this, we feel like we're being cheated."

Yankees: Bernie Williams after his game-winning, 10th-inning home run in Game 1: "If it took a break like that to get us going, it is welcomed." ... Yankee manager Joe Torre after Boston's Pedro Martinez struck out 12 in seven innings in Game 3: "He is an artist out there, except he has a baseball instead of a paint brush." ... Torre, after frustrated fans threw debris on the field at Fenway Park during Game 4: "The sad part about it is you have a ballclub, the Boston Red Sox, who have busted their butts to give this city something to be proud of. I think it's inexcusable." ... MVP Orlando Hernandez, after the series-ending Game 5: "This is a beautiful moment."

Game 1 at New York

NEW YORK 4, BOSTON 3 (10 INNINGS)

HOW THEY SCORED

First Inning

Boston—Offerman singled to center. Valentin reached first on a fielder's choice and went to third on a throwing error by Jeter as Offerman scored. Daubach singled to right, scoring Valentin. Garciaparra flied to Spencer. O'Leary walked. Stanley flied to O'Neill as Daubach went to third. Varitek popped to Knoblauch. Two runs. Boston 2, New York 0.

Second Inning

Boston—Lewis walked. Nixon singled to right-center as Lewis went to third. Valentin singled to short, scoring Lewis as Nixon went to second. Valentin flied to Williams. Daubach popped to Brosius in foul territory. Garciaparra flied to Spencer. One run. Boston 3, New York 0.

New York—Martinez flied to Nixon. Posada grounded out, Garciaparra to Stanley. Spencer singled to left-center. Brosius homered to left, scoring Spencer. Knoblauch flied to O'Leary. Two runs. Boston 3, New York 2.

Seventh Inning

New York—Lowe now pitching. Brosius singled to left. Knoblauch sacrificed Brosius to second, Lowe to Offerman. Jeter singled to right and went to second on the throw to the plate as Brosius scored. O'Neill reached first on a fielding error by Garciaparra. Williams forced O'Neill at second, Garciaparra to Offerman, as Jeter went to third. Williams stole second. Davis struck out. One run. Boston 3, New York 3.

Tenth Inning

New York—Beck now pitching. Williams homered to center. One run. New York 4, Boston 3.

BOX SCORE

Boston	AB	R	H	RBI	PO	A
Offerman, 2b	5	1	3	1	5	2
Valentin, 3b	5	1	1	0	0	2
Daubach, dh	5	0	1	1	0	0
Garciaparra, ss	4	0	0	0	2	3
O'Leary, lf	3	0	0	0	1	0
Stanley, 1b	4	0	1	0	8	0
Varitek, c	4	0	1	0	7	0
Lewis, cf	3	1	0	0	2	0
Nixon, rf	4	0	1	0	2	0
Mercker, p	0	0	0	0	0	2
Garces, p	0	0	0	0	0	1
Lowe, p	0	0	0	0	0	1
Cormier, p	0	0	0	0	0	1
Beck, p	0	0	0	0	0	0
Totals	37	3	8	2	27	12
New York	**AB**	**R**	**H**	**RBI**	**PO**	**A**
Knoblauch, 2b	3	0	1	0	4	1
Jeter, ss	4	0	2	1	4	1
O'Neill, rf	5	0	1	0	4	0
Williams, cf	5	1	2	1	5	0
Davis, dh	4	0	0	0	0	0
T. Martinez, 1b	4	0	0	0	5	1
Posada, c	4	0	0	0	6	1
Spencer, lf	4	1	1	0	3	0
Brosius, 3b	4	2	3	2	1	1
Hernandez, p	0	0	0	0	0	0
Rivera, p	0	0	0	0	0	2
Totals	37	4	10	4	30	7

Boston	2	1	0	0	0	0	0	0	0—3
New York	0	2	0	0	0	0	1	0	1—4

None out when winning run scored.

Boston	IP	H	R	ER	BB	SO
Mercker	4.0	6	2	2	2	2
Garces	2.0	0	0	0	0	1
Lowe	2.2	3	1	1	0	4
Cormier	0.1	0	0	0	0	0
Beck (L)	0.0	1	1	1	0	0
New York	**IP**	**H**	**R**	**ER**	**BB**	**SO**
Hernandez	8.0	7	3	2	2	4
Rivera (W)	2.0	1	0	0	0	2

E—Garciaparra 2, Varitek. DP—New York 2. LOB—Boston 6, New York 9. 2B—Jeter, Valentin. 3B—Brosius. HR—Brosius, Williams. SH—Knoblauch. SB—Williams, Lewis. CS—Lewis. T—3:39. A—57,181. U—McClelland, plate; Morrison, first; Reed, second; Clark, third; Scott, left field; Tschida, right field.

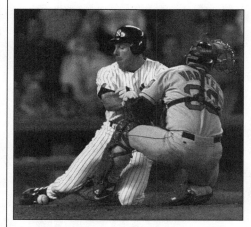

New York's Scott Brosius (left) and Jason Varitek collide at the plate in the seventh inning of Game 1.

Derek Jeter led the Yankees offense by hitting .350 in the series, including a home run and three RBIs.

New York	IP	H	R	ER	BB	SO
Cone (W)	7.0	7	2	2	3	9
Stanton	†0.0	1	0	0	0	0
Nelson	0.1	0	0	0	0	0
Watson	†0.0	0	0	0	1	0
Mendoza	0.2	0	0	0	0	0
Rivera (S)	1.0	2	0	0	0	1

*Pitched to one batter in seventh. †Pitched to one batter in eighth.

LOB—Boston 13, New York 8. 2B—Varitek, Knoblauch, O'Leary. 3B—Varitek. HR—T. Martinez, Garciaparra. SH—Varitek, Brosius. SB—Offerman, Knoblauch. CS—Ledee. HBP—By Nelson (Stanley). PB—Girardi. T—3:46. A—57,180. U—Morrison, plate; Reed, first; Clark, second; Scott, third; Tschida, left field; McClelland, right field.

Game 3 at Boston

BOSTON 13, NEW YORK 1

HOW THEY SCORED

First Inning

Boston—Offerman tripled to right. Valentin homered to left-center, scoring Offerman. Varitek grounded out, Knoblauch to Martinez. Garciaparra reached first on a throwing error by Knoblauch. O'Leary flied to Williams. Stanley walked. Daubach struck out. Two runs. Boston 2, New York 0.

Second Inning

Boston—Lewis grounded out, Jeter to Martinez. Nixon doubled to left. Offerman singled to left as Nixon went to third. Valentin grounded out, Jeter to Martinez, as Nixon scored and Offerman went to second. Varitek walked. Garciaparra doubled to left, scoring Offerman as Varitek went to third. O'Leary struck out. Two runs. Boston 4, New York 0.

Third Inning

Boston—Stanley singled to left. Irabu now pitching. Daubach homered to right, scoring Stanley. Lewis grounded out, Jeter to Martinez. Nixon doubled to right. Offerman grounded out, Martinez to Irabu, as Nixon went to third. Valentin flied to Williams. Two runs. Boston 6, New York 0.

Fifth Inning

Boston—Daubach doubled to right. Lewis doubled to right, scoring Daubach. Nixon and Offerman struck out. Valentin singled to left and went to second as Posada made a fielding error on the throw to the plate as Lewis scored. Varitek struck out swinging. Two runs. Boston 8, New York 0.

Sixth Inning

Boston—Garciaparra singled to right. O'Leary forced Garciaparra at second, Martinez to Jeter. Stanley flied to Ledee. Daubach reached second on a fielding error by Ledee, scoring O'Leary. Lewis popped to Williams. One run. Boston 9, New York 0.

Seventh Inning

Boston—Curtis now in left field and Ledee moves to right. Nixon singled to first. Offerman grounded out, Martinez to Irabu, as Nixon went to second. Valentin singled to left, scoring Nixon. Varitek popped to Jeter. Garciaparra homered to left-center, scoring Valentin. O'Leary doubled to left. Stanley singled to center, scoring O'Leary. Stanton now pitching. Huskey, pinch-hitting for Daubach, grounded out, Stanton to Martinez. Four runs. Boston 13, New York 0.

Eighth Inning

New York—Gordon now pitching. Brosius homered to left-center. Posada flied to Lewis. Sojo, pinch-hitting for Knoblauch, grounded out, Gordon to Stanley. Bellinger, pinch-hitting for Jeter, struck out. One run. Boston 13, New York 1.

BOX SCORE

New York	AB	R	H	RBI	PO	A
Knoblauch, 2b	2	0	0	0	1	2
Sojo, ph-2b	1	0	0	0	1	1
Jeter, ss	3	0	1	0	2	4
Bellinger, ph-ss	1	0	0	0	0	1
O'Neill, rf	3	0	0	0	1	0
Curtis, lf-cf	1	0	0	0	0	0
Williams, cf	3	0	0	0	3	0
Spencer, lf	0	0	0	0	0	0
T. Martinez, 1b	4	0	1	0	7	3
Davis, dh	3	0	0	0	0	0
Ledee, lf-rf	4	0	0	0	1	0
Brosius, 3b	3	1	1	1	1	0
Girardi, c	1	0	0	0	2	0
Posada, c	2	0	0	0	4	0
Clemens, p	0	0	0	0	0	0
Irabu, p	0	0	0	0	0	0
Stanton, p	0	0	0	0	0	1
Watson, p	0	0	0	0	0	0
Totals	31	1	3	1	24	12

Boston	AB	R	H	RBI	PO	A
Offerman, 2b	6	2	3	0	1	1
Valentin, 3b	6	2	3	5	1	1
Varitek, c	4	0	0	0	13	0
Hatteberg, c	0	0	0	0	0	0
Garciaparra, ss	5	1	4	3	1	0
O'Leary, lf	5	2	2	2	2	0
Stanley, 1b	4	1	2	1	5	0
Daubach, dh	4	2	2	2	0	0
Huskey, ph-dh	1	0	0	0	0	0
Lewis, cf-rf	5	1	2	1	3	0
Nixon, rf	4	2	3	0	1	0
Buford, ph-cf	1	0	0	0	0	0
P. Martinez, p	0	0	0	0	0	0
Gordon, p	0	0	0	0	0	1
Rapp, p	0	0	0	0	0	0
Totals	45	13	21	12	27	3

New York .... 000 000 010—1
Boston .... 222 021 40x—13

New York	IP	H	R	ER	BB	SO
Clemens (L)	*2.0	6	5	5	2	2
Irabu	4.2	13	8	7	0	3
Stanton	0.1	0	0	0	0	0
Watson	1.0	2	0	0	0	1

Boston	IP	H	R	ER	BB	SO
P. Martinez (W)	7.0	2	0	0	2	12
Gordon	1.0	1	1	1	0	1
Rapp	1.0	0	0	0	1	0

*Pitched to one batter in third.

E—Knoblauch, Posada, Ledee, Garciaparra. DP—New York 2. LOB—New York 6, Boston 10. 2B—Nixon 2, Garciaparra, Daubach, Lewis, O'Leary. 3B—Offerman. HR—Valentin, Daubach, Garciaparra, Brosius. T—3:14. A—33,190. U—Reed, plate; Clark, first; Scott, second; Tschida, third; McClelland, left field; Morrison, right field.

Game 4 at Boston

NEW YORK 9, BOSTON 2

HOW THEY SCORED

Second Inning

New York—Martinez popped to Garciaparra. Strawberry homered to right. Brosius grounded out, Saberhagen to Stanley. Curtis grounded out, Offerman to Stanley. One run. New York 1, Boston 0.

Boston—Stanley grounded out, Jeter to Martinez. Huskey doubled to left. O'Leary singled to center, scoring Huskey. Varitek grounded into a double play, Knoblauch to Jeter to Martinez. One run. New York 1, Boston 1.

Third Inning

Boston—Lewis grounded out, Knoblauch to Martinez. Buford singled to center. Buford stole second. Offerman singled to center, scoring Buford. Valentin doubled to left, but Offerman was thrown out at the plate, Williams to Jeter to Girardi. Garciaparra walked. Stanley struck out. One run. Boston 2, New York 1.

Fourth Inning

New York—O'Neill struck out. Williams singled to short and went to second on a throwing error by Garciaparra. Martinez doubled to right, scoring Williams. Strawberry was walked intentionally. Brosius struck out. Curtis reached first on a fielding error by Saberhagen in which Stanley received an assist. Martinez scored on the play and Strawberry went to third. Girardi struck out. Two runs. New York 3, Boston 2.

Ninth Inning

New York—Girardi flied to Buford. Knoblauch singled to the mound. Jeter singled to left as Knoblauch went to second. O'Neill reached first on a fielder's choice as Knoblauch scored and Jeter went to second on Offerman's throwing error. Williams singled to right and went to second on Lewis' throwing error as Jeter scored and O'Neill went to third. Martinez was walked intentionally. Beck now pitching. Ledee, pinch-hitting for Bellinger, homered to center, scoring O'Neill, Williams and Martinez. Brosius popped to Offerman. Curtis struck out. Six runs. New York 9, Boston 2.

BOX SCORE

New York	AB	R	H	RBI	PO	A
Knoblauch, 2b	4	1	2	0	3	5
Jeter, ss	5	1	1	0	2	5
O'Neill, rf	5	1	2	0	5	0
Williams, cf	5	2	3	1	0	1
T. Martinez, 1b	4	2	1	1	10	0
Strawberry, dh	2	1	1	1	0	0
Davis, ph	0	0	0	0	0	0
Bellinger, pr-dh	0	0	0	0	0	0
Ledee, ph-dh	1	1	1	4	0	0
Brosius, 3b	5	0	0	0	0	1
Curtis, lf	5	0	0	0	0	0
Girardi, c	4	0	0	0	7	0
Pettitte, p	0	0	0	0	0	0
Rivera, p	0	0	0	0	0	0
Totals	40	9	11	7	27	12

Boston	AB	R	H	RBI	PO	A
Offerman, 2b	4	0	2	1	4	2
Valentin, 3b	4	0	2	0	1	1
Garciaparra, ss	3	0	0	0	2	4
Stanley, 1b	4	0	1	0	9	1
Huskey, dh	3	1	1	0	0	0
Daubach, ph-dh	1	0	0	0	0	0
O'Leary, lf	4	0	2	1	2	0
Varitek, c	4	0	0	0	7	0
Lewis, rf	3	1	2	0	2	0
Buford, cf	3	1	1	0	2	0
Saberhagen, p	0	0	0	0	0	0
Lowe, p	0	0	0	0	0	0
Cormier, p	0	0	0	0	0	0

Game 2 at New York

NEW YORK 3, BOSTON 2

HOW THEY SCORED

Fourth Inning

New York—Williams flied to Nixon. Martinez homered to right. Strawberry and Ledee struck out. One run. New York 1, Boston 0.

Fifth Inning

Boston—Offerman singled to left. Offerman stole second. Valentin struck out. Daubach popped to Jeter. Garciaparra homered to left, scoring Offerman. O'Leary singled to right-center. O'Leary went to second on a passed ball. Stanley struck out. Two runs. Boston 2, New York 1.

Seventh Inning

New York—Ledee walked. Brosius sacrificed Ledee to second, Martinez to Offerman. Girardi popped to Offerman. Knoblauch doubled to left, scoring Ledee. Gordon now pitching. Knoblauch stole third. Jeter walked. Cormier now pitching. O'Neill singled to left-center, scoring Knoblauch as Jeter went to third. Williams walked. Martinez grounded to Stanley. Two runs. New York 3, Boston 2.

BOX SCORE

Boston	AB	R	H	RBI	PO	A
Offerman, 2b	5	1	2	0	4	0
Valentin, 3b	3	0	0	0	1	1
Daubach, dh-1b	5	0	0	0	0	0
Garciaparra, ss	4	1	3	2	0	1
O'Leary, lf	5	0	3	0	1	0
Stanley, 1b	3	0	0	0	5	0
Buford, pr-cf	1	0	0	0	2	0
Varitek, c	3	0	2	0	6	1
Lewis, cf	3	0	0	0	1	0
Hatteberg, ph	0	0	0	0	0	0
Merloni, ph	0	0	0	0	0	0
Sadler, pr-rf	0	0	0	0	0	0
Nixon, rf	3	0	0	0	4	0
Huskey, ph-dh	1	0	0	0	0	0
R. Martinez, p	0	0	0	0	0	2
Gordon, p	0	0	0	0	0	0
Cormier, p	0	0	0	0	0	0
Totals	36	2	10	2	24	5

New York	AB	R	H	RBI	PO	A
Knoblauch, 2b	4	1	1	1	1	1
Jeter, ss	3	0	1	0	2	0
O'Neill, rf	3	0	1	1	5	0
Williams, cf	3	0	1	0	3	0
T. Martinez, 1b	3	1	1	1	3	0
Strawberry, dh	3	0	0	0	0	0
Davis, ph-dh	1	0	0	0	0	0
Ledee, lf	3	1	1	0	2	0
Brosius, 3b	3	0	0	0	0	0
Girardi, c	3	0	2	0	11	1
Cone, p	0	0	0	0	0	0
Stanton, p	0	0	0	0	0	0
Nelson, p	0	0	0	0	0	1
Watson, p	0	0	0	0	0	0
Mendoza, p	0	0	0	0	0	0
Rivera, p	0	0	0	0	0	0
Totals	29	3	7	3	27	3

Boston .... 000 020 000—2
New York .... 000 100 20x—3

Boston	IP	H	R	ER	BB	SO
R. Martinez (L)	6.2	6	3	3	3	5
Gordon	*0.0	0	0	0	1	0
Cormier	1.1	1	0	0	1	1

Boston	AB	R	H	RBI	PO	A
Garces, p	0	0	0	0	0	0
Beck, p	0	0	0	0	0	0
Totals	33	2	10	2	27	10

New York	0 1 0	2 0 0	0 0 6—9		
Boston	0 1 1	0 0 0	0 0 0—2		

New York	IP	H	R	ER	BB	SO
Pettitte (W)	7.1	8	2	2	1	5
Rivera (S)	1.2	2	0	0	0	1

Boston	IP	H	R	ER	BB	SO
Saberhagen (L)	6.0	5	3	1	1	5
Lowe	*1.0	2	0	0	1	0
Cormier	0.1	0	0	0	1	0
Garces	1.0	3	5	4	1	1
Beck	0.2	1	1	1	0	1

*Pitched to two batters in eighth.

E—Garciaparra, Saberhagen, Offerman, Lewis. DP—New York 3. LOB—New York 8, Boston 5. 2B—Huskey, Valentin, T. Martinez, Williams, O'Leary. HR—Strawberry, Ledee. SB—Buford. T—3:39. A—33,586. U—Clark, plate; Scott, first; Tschida, second; McClelland, third; Morrison, left field; Reed, right field.

Game 5 at Boston

NEW YORK 6, BOSTON 1

HOW THEY SCORED

First Inning

New York—Knoblauch singled to right. Jeter homered to center, scoring Knoblauch. O'Neill flied to Lewis. Williams struck out. Davis singled to left. Martinez singled to left as Davis went to second. Posada struck out. Two runs. New York 2, Boston 0.

Seventh Inning

New York—Knoblauch grounded out, Garciaparra to Stanley. Jeter reached second on a fielding error by Stanley in which Garciaparra received an assist. O'Neill singled to right as Jeter went to third. Cormier now pitching. Williams walked. Davis reached first on a fielder's choice in which Offerman made a fielding error as Jeter scored, O'Neill went to third and Williams to second. Bellinger now pinch-running for Davis. Martinez singled to center, scoring O'Neill as Williams went to third and Bellinger to second. Posada and Spencer struck out. Two runs. New York 4, Boston 0.

Eighth Inning

Boston—Sojo now at second. Varitek homered to right. Garciaparra doubled to left. Stanton now pitching. O'Leary walked. Nelson now pitching. Stanley flied to Williams. Watson now pitching. Huskey, pinch-hitting for Daubach, walked. Sadler now pinch-running for Huskey. Mendoza now pitching. Hatteberg, pinch-hitting for Lewis, struck out. Nixon popped to Brosius in foul territory. One run. New York 4, Boston 1.

Ninth Inning

New York—Buford now in center and Gordon pitching. Williams popped to Valentin. Strawberry, pinch-hitting for Bellinger, singled to right. Curtis now pinch-running for Strawberry. Curtis stole second. Martinez struck out. Posada homered to right, scoring Curtis. Spencer struck out. Two runs. New York 6, Boston 1.

BOX SCORE

New York	AB	R	H	RBI	PO	A
Knoblauch, 2b	5	1	2	0	1	1
Sojo, 2b	0	0	0	0	0	0
Jeter, ss	5	2	2	2	0	0
O'Neill, rf	5	1	2	0	4	0
Williams, cf	4	0	0	0	2	0
Davis, dh	3	0	1	1	0	0
Bellinger, pr-dh	0	0	0	0	0	0
Strawberry, ph	1	0	1	0	0	0
Curtis, pr-dh	0	1	0	0	0	0
T. Martinez, 1b	4	0	2	1	4	1
Posada, c	4	1	1	2	10	0
Spencer, lf	5	0	0	0	2	0
Brosius, 3b	3	0	0	0	3	2
Hernandez, p	0	0	0	0	0	0
Stanton, p	0	0	0	0	0	0
Nelson, p	0	0	0	0	0	0
Watson, p	0	0	0	0	0	0
Mendoza, p	0	0	0	0	1	0
Totals	39	6	11	6	27	4

Boston	AB	R	H	RBI	PO	A
Offerman, 2b	4	0	1	0	1	1
Valentin, 3b	5	0	2	0	2	2
Varitek, c	5	1	1	1	11	0
Garciaparra, ss	4	0	1	0	2	5
O'Leary, lf	3	0	0	0	1	0
Stanley, 1b	3	0	0	0	8	1
Daubach, dh	2	0	0	0	0	0
Huskey, ph	0	0	0	0	0	0
Sadler, pr-dh	0	0	0	0	0	0
Lewis, cf	3	0	0	0	1	0
Hatteberg, ph	1	0	0	0	0	0
Buford, cf	0	0	0	0	0	0
Nixon, rf	3	0	0	0	0	0
Mercker, p	0	0	0	0	1	1
Lowe, p	0	0	0	0	0	0
Cormier, p	0	0	0	0	0	0
Gordon, p	0	0	0	0	0	0
Totals	33	1	5	1	27	10

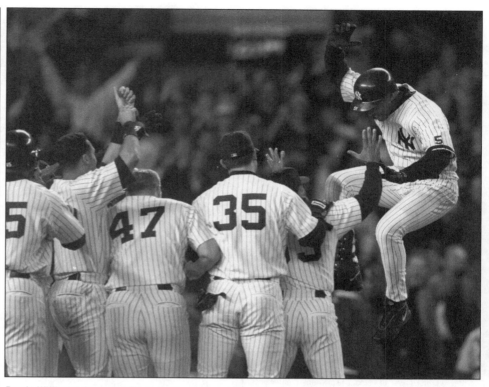

Bernie Williams' dramatic 10th-inning homer to center off Boston's Rod Beck gave the Yankees a 4-3 victory in Game 1 of the A.L. Championship Series. The Yankees won the first two games of the series by a run.

New York	2 0 0	0 0 0	2 0 2—6		
Boston	0 0 0	0 0 0	0 1 0—1		

New York	IP	H	R	ER	BB	SO
Hernandez (W)	*7.0	5	1	1	4	9
Stanton	†0.0	0	0	0	1	0
Nelson	0.1	0	0	0	0	0
Watson	†0.0	0	0	0	1	0
Mendoza (S)	1.2	0	0	0	0	1

Boston	IP	H	R	ER	BB	SO
Mercker (L)	3.2	6	2	2	2	3
Lowe	2.2	1	2	0	1	3
Cormier	1.2	2	0	0	1	3
Gordon	1.0	2	2	2	0	2

*Pitched to two batters in eighth. †Pitched to one batter in eighth.

E—Jeter, Stanley, Offerman. LOB—New York 11, Boston 11. 2B—Garciaparra. HR—Jeter, Varitek, Posada. SB—Curtis, Garciaparra. HBP—By Mercker (T. Martinez). U—Scott, plate; Tschida, first; McClelland, second; Morrison, third; Reed, left field; Clark, right field. T—4:09. A—33,589.

COMPOSITE

BATTING AVERAGES

New York Yankees

Player, position	G	AB	R	H	2B	3B	HR	RBI	Avg.
Jeter, ss	5	20	3	7	1	0	1	3	.350
Knoblauch, 2b	5	18	3	6	1	0	0	1	.333
Strawberry, dh-ph	3	6	1	2	0	0	1	1	.333
O'Neill, rf	5	21	3	6	0	0	0	1	.286
T. Martinez, 1b	5	19	3	5	1	0	1	3	.263
Williams, cf	5	20	3	5	1	0	1	2	.250
Girardi, c	3	8	0	2	0	0	0	0	.250
Ledee, lf-rf-ph-dh	3	8	2	2	0	0	1	4	.250
Brosius, 3b	5	18	3	4	0	1	2	3	.222
Spencer, lf	3	9	1	1	0	0	0	0	.111
Posada, c	3	10	1	1	0	0	1	2	.100
Davis, dh-ph	5	11	0	1	0	0	0	1	.091
Clemens, p	1	0	0	0	0	0	0	0	.000
Cone, p	1	0	0	0	0	0	0	0	.000
Hernandez, p	2	0	0	0	0	0	0	0	.000
Irabu, p	1	0	0	0	0	0	0	0	.000
Mendoza, p	2	0	0	0	0	0	0	0	.000
Nelson, p	2	0	0	0	0	0	0	0	.000
Pettitte, p	1	0	0	0	0	0	0	0	.000
Rivera, p	3	0	0	0	0	0	0	0	.000
Stanton, p	3	0	0	0	0	0	0	0	.000
Watson, p	3	0	0	0	0	0	0	0	.000
Bellinger, ph-ss-dh	3	1	0	0	0	0	0	0	.000
Sojo, ph-2b	2	1	0	0	0	0	0	0	.000
Curtis, lf-cf-pr-dh	3	6	1	0	0	0	0	0	.000
Totals	5	176	23	42	4	1	8	21	.239

Boston Red Sox

Player, position	G	AB	R	H	2B	3B	HR	RBI	Avg.
Offerman, 2b	5	24	4	11	0	1	0	2	.458
Garciaparra, ss	5	20	2	8	2	0	2	5	.400
Buford, pr-cf-ph	4	5	1	2	0	0	0	0	.400
O'Leary, lf	5	20	2	7	3	0	0	1	.350
Valentin, 3b	5	23	3	8	2	0	1	5	.348
Nixon, rf	4	14	2	4	2	0	0	0	.286
Stanley, 1b	5	18	1	4	0	0	0	1	.222
Varitek, c	5	20	1	4	1	1	1	1	.200
Huskey, ph-dh	4	5	1	1	0	0	0	3	.200
Daubach, dh-1b-ph	5	17	2	3	1	0	1	3	.176
Lewis, cf-rf	5	17	2	2	1	0	0	1	.118
Beck, p	2	0	0	0	0	0	0	0	.000
Cormier, p	4	0	0	0	0	0	0	0	.000
Garces, p	2	0	0	0	0	0	0	0	.000
Gordon, p	3	0	0	0	0	0	0	0	.000
Lowe, p	3	0	0	0	0	0	0	0	.000
P. Martinez, p	1	0	0	0	0	0	0	0	.000
R. Martinez, p	1	0	0	0	0	0	0	0	.000
Mercker, p	2	0	0	0	0	0	0	0	.000
Merloni, ph	1	0	0	0	0	0	0	0	.000
Rapp, p	1	0	0	0	0	0	0	0	.000
Saberhagen, p	1	0	0	0	0	0	0	0	.000
Sadler, pr-rf-dh	2	0	0	0	0	0	0	0	.000
Hatteberg, ph-c	3	1	0	0	0	0	0	0	.000
Totals	5	184	21	54	13	2	5	19	.293

PITCHING AVERAGES

New York Yankees

Pitcher	G	IP	H	R	ER	BB	SO	W	L	ERA
Stanton	3	0.1	1	0	0	1	0	0	0	0.00
Nelson	2	0.2	0	0	0	0	0	0	0	0.00
Watson	3	1.0	2	0	0	2	1	0	0	0.00
Mendoza	2	2.1	0	0	0	0	2	0	0	0.00
Rivera	3	4.2	5	0	0	0	3	1	0	0.00
Hernandez	2	15.0	12	4	3	6	13	1	0	1.80
Pettitte	1	7.1	8	2	2	1	5	1	0	2.45
Cone	1	7.0	7	2	2	3	9	1	0	2.57
Irabu	1	4.2	13	8	7	0	3	0	0	13.50
Clemens	1	2.0	6	5	5	2	2	0	1	22.50
Totals	3	45.0	54	21	19	15	38	4	1	3.80

No shutouts. Saves—Rivera 2, Mendoza.

Boston Red Sox

Pitcher	G	IP	H	R	ER	BB	SO	W	L	ERA
Cormier	4	3.2	3	0	0	3	4	0	0	0.00
P. Martinez	1	7.0	2	0	0	2	12	1	0	0.00
Rapp	1	1.0	0	0	0	1	0	0	0	0.00
Lowe	3	6.1	6	3	1	2	7	0	0	1.42
Saberhagen	2	6.0	5	3	1	5	1	0	1	1.50
R. Martinez	1	6.2	6	3	3	3	5	0	1	4.05
Mercker	2	7.2	12	4	4	4	5	0	1	4.70
Garces	2	3.0	3	5	4	1	2	0	1	12.00
Gordon	3	2.0	3	3	3	1	3	0	0	13.50
Beck	2	0.2	2	2	2	0	1	0	1	27.00
Totals	5	44.0	42	23	18	18	44	1	4	3.68

No shutouts or saves.

WORLD SERIES

NEW YORK VS. ATLANTA

Game 1 at Atlanta

NEW YORK 4, ATLANTA 1

Why the Yankees won: Starting pitcher Orlando Hernandez threw seven innings of one-hit ball, showing off a dazzling assortment of pitches and arm angles that kept the Braves off-stride. Hernandez is 5-0 in six career playoff starts.

Why the Braves lost: Their inability to make what should be routine plays, a must in the postseason, proved costly late in the game. Brian Hunter, inserted into the lineup as a defensive replacement at first base for Ryan Klesko, committed two errors in the eighth inning as the Yankees turned a 1-0 deficit into a 4-1 lead.

TURNING POINTS:

Braves starter Greg Maddux had given up only three singles going into the eighth. With the bases loaded and no outs (thanks in part to Hunter's dropping Chuck Knoblauch's bunt) in the eighth, Maddux got ahead of Derek Jeter, 0-2. Jeter singled to left, tying the score, 1-1. After John Rocker relieved, Paul O'Neill singled through a drawn-in infield that would have been playing back had Hunter gotten an out on Knoblauch's bunt.

WORTH NOTING:

Tom Glavine was scheduled to open the series for Atlanta, but he came down with the flu, forcing scheduled Game 2 starter Maddux to step in. ... Hernandez's postseason ERA stands at 1.02 ERA, trailing only Sandy Koufax and teammate Mariano Rivera among players with at least 40 postseason innings. ... Hunter made four errors in 114 regular-season games, but became the first player to commit two in one World Series inning since the Milwaukee Braves' Frank Torre (Joe's brother) did it in 1958 against, yep, the Yankees. ... Though Yankees catcher Jorge Posada was envisioning a 1-0, one-hit loss because of Chipper Jones' home run, Atlanta managed only one other hit, Bret Boone's ninth-inning single. You couldn't even pin the problem on the top, middle or bottom of the order. No one hit, thus no one scored.

WORTH QUOTING:

"You don't want to come in for defense and make errors," Atlanta's Hunter said. "That makes you look stupid." ... Joe Torre, marveling over the two-run, eighth-inning single by O'Neill, a lefthanded hitter who had batted .190 against left-handers in the regular season: "Rocker is tough on righthanders, much less lefthanders." ... Atlanta's Cox, on why he left Maddux in as long as he did: "Maddux was still throwing well. The only ball that was hit well was Jeter's. Even when I took him out, he was still throwing well. He didn't get a whole lot of help, that's for sure. I thought he was as good as he's ever been." ... Torre, on Hernandez: "He continues to make you shake your head. He took control early, as did Maddux." ... Cox, on Glavine's coming down with the flu: "There's absolutely nothing you can do to prevent it except keep Tommy home for a day or two and hope nobody else gets it."

BOX SCORE

New York	AB	R	H	RBI	PO	A
Knoblauch, 2b	4	1	0	0	1	1
Jeter, ss	4	1	2	1	1	1
O'Neill, rf	4	0	1	2	3	0
B. Williams, cf	2	0	0	0	0	0
Martinez, 1b	3	0	0	0	4	1
Posada, c	4	0	0	0	13	1
Ledee, lf	3	0	0	0	0	0
‡Leyritz, ph	0	0	0	1	0	0
Nelson, p	0	0	0	0	0	0
Stanton, p	0	0	0	0	0	0
Rivera, p	0	0	0	0	0	0
Brosius, 3b	4	1	3	0	3	0
O. Hernandez, p	1	0	0	0	2	1
*Strawberry, ph	0	0	0	0	0	0
†Curtis, pr-lf	1	1	0	0	0	0
Totals	30	4	6	4	27	5

Atlanta	AB	R	H	RBI	PO	A
G. Williams, lf	4	0	0	0	3	0
Boone, 2b	4	0	1	0	1	5
C. Jones, 3b	2	1	1	1	0	2
Jordan, rf	4	0	0	0	2	0
Klesko, 1b	3	0	0	0	7	0
Hunter, 1b	0	0	0	0	1	1
nMyers, ph	1	0	0	0	0	0
A. Jones, cf	2	0	0	0	1	0
Perez, c	2	0	0	0	7	1
Weiss, ss	2	0	0	0	3	1
§Guillen, ph	0	0	0	0	0	0
∞J. Hernandez, ph-ss	1	0	0	0	1	0
Maddux, p	2	0	0	0	1	0
Rocker, p	0	0	0	0	0	0
sBattle, ph	0	0	0	0	0	0
uLockhart, ph	1	0	0	0	0	0
Remlinger, p	0	0	0	0	0	1
Totals	28	1	2	1	27	11

New York .... 000 000 040—4
Atlanta .... 000 100 000—1

New York	IP	H	R	ER	BB	SO
O. Hernandez (W)	7.0	1	1	1	2	10
Nelson	0.1	0	0	0	1	1
Stanton	0.1	0	0	0	0	1
Rivera (S)	0.1	1	0	0	1	1

Atlanta	IP	H	R	ER	BB	SO
Maddux (L)	*7.0	5	4	2	3	5
Rocker	1.0	1	0	0	2	3
Remlinger	1.0	0	0	0	1	0

*Pitched to four batters in eighth.

Bases on balls—Off O. Hernandez 2 (A. Jones, C. Jones), off Nelson 1 (Perez), off River 1 (C. Jones), off Maddux 3 (Martinez, B. Williams, Strawberry), off Rocker 2 (B. Williams, Leyritz), off Remlinger 1 (Jeter).

Strikeouts—By O. Hernandez 10 (G. Williams 2, Boone 2, Perez 2, Maddux 2, C. Jones, Weiss), by Nelson 1 (A. Jones), by Stanton 1 (J. Hernandez), by Rivera 1 (Jordan), by Maddux 5 (B. Williams, O'Neill, Jeter, Martinez, Ledee), by Rocker 3 (Martinez, Posada, Brosius).

*Walked for O. Hernandez in eighth. †Ran for Strawberry in eighth. ‡Walked for Ledee in eighth. §Announced for Weiss in eighth. ∞Struck out for Guillen in eighth. ▲Announced for Rocker in eighth. ◆Grounded out for Battle in eighth. ■Fouled out for Hunter in ninth. E—Hunter 2. DP—Atlanta 1. LOB—New York 7, Atlanta 4. HR—C. Jones. SH—O. Hernandez, Knoblauch. SB—Jeter, B. Williams. T—2:57. A—51,342. U—Marsh (N.L.), plate; Roe (A.L.), first; Rippley (N.L.), second; Cousins (A.L.), third; Davis (N.L.), left field; Joyce (A.L.), right field.

PLAY BY PLAY

FIRST INNING

New York—Knoblauch flied to Jordan. Jeter singled to center. O'Neill flied to G. Williams. Jeter stole second. B. Williams struck out.

Atlanta—G. Williams, Boone and C. Jones struck out.

SECOND INNING

New York—Martinez walked. Posada grounded into a double play, Boone to Weiss to Klesko. Ledee flied to G. Williams.

Atlanta—Jordan and Klesko flied to O'Neill. A. Jones walked. Perez struck out.

THIRD INNING

New York—Brosius singled to right. O. Hernandez sacrificed, C. Jones to Boone, as Brosius went to second. Knoblauch flied to A. Jones. Jeter grounded out, Boone to Klesko.

Atlanta—Weiss, Maddux and G. Williams struck out.

FOURTH INNING

New York—O'Neill struck out. B. Williams lined to Klesko. Martinez flied to G. Williams.

Atlanta—Boone struck out. C. Jones homered to right. Jordan flied to O'Neill. Klesko grounded out, O. Hernandez to Martinez. Atl. 1, N.Y. 0

FIFTH INNING

New York—Posada grounded out, Boone to Klesko. Ledee popped to Weiss. Brosius singled to center. O. Hernandez grounded out, Boone to Klesko.

Atlanta—A. Jones lined to Brosius. Perez struck out. Weiss grounded out, Martinez to O. Hernandez.

SIXTH INNING

New York—Knoblauch grounded out, C. Jones to Klesko. Jeter struck out. O'Neill grounded to Maddux.

Atlanta—Maddux struck out. G. Williams grounded to O. Hernandez. Boone grounded out, Jeter to Martinez.

SEVENTH INNING

New York—B. Williams walked and stole second. Martinez struck out, Perez threw to Klesko on the dropped third strike. Posada popped to Weiss. Ledee struck out.

Atlanta—C. Jones walked. Jordan popped to Jeter. Klesko popped to Brosius. C. Jones caught stealing, Posada to Knoblauch.

EIGHTH INNING

New York—Hunter now at first. Brosius singled to left. Strawberry, pinch-hitting for O. Hernandez, walked. Curtis now pinch-running for Strawberry. Knoblauch sacrificed, but was safe at first on an error by Hunter, as Brosius went to third and Curtis to second. Jeter singled to left, scoring Brosius as Curtis went to third and Knoblauch to second. Rocker now pitching. O'Neill singled to right and reached second on a wild throw error by Hunter, as Curtis and Knoblauch scored and Jeter went to third. B. Williams was walked intentionally. Martinez and Posada struck out. Leyritz, pinch-hitting for Ledee, walked, scoring Jeter. Brosius struck out. N.Y. 4, Atl. 1.

Atlanta—Curtis now in left field and Nelson pitching. A. Jones struck out. Perez walked. Guillen was announced as a pinch-hitter for Weiss. Stanton now pitching. J. Hernandez, pinch-hitting for Guillen, struck out. Battle was announced as a pinch-hitter for Rocker. Rivera now pitching. Lockhart, pinch-hitting for Battle, grounded to Martinez.

NINTH INNING

New York—J. Hernandez now at shortstop and Remlinger pitching. Curtis flied to Jordan. Knoblauch grounded out, Boone to Hunter. Jeter walked. Jeter caught stealing, Remlinger to Hunter to J. Hernandez. Final score: N.Y. 4, Atl. 1.

Orlando Hernandez used his unusual windup and delivery to baffle Braves hitters in Game 1. A fourth-inning Chipper Jones homer to right field was the only hit the Yankee hurler allowed in seven innings.

Game 2 at Atlanta

NEW YORK 7, ATLANTA 2

Why the Yankees won: Pitching continued to be the key for New York. David Cone, who had a roller-coaster season, had a roller-coaster game. He didn't give up a hit until the fifth, but allowed a baserunner in every inning until retiring the Braves in order in the sixth. He walked more (five) than he struck out (four), but Greg Myers' fifth-inning single to center was Atlanta's only hit off Cone in his seven innings, and Myers was erased in a double play.

Why the Braves lost: Starting pitcher Kevin Millwood allowed five runs in two-plus innings in his first World Series start, taking the Braves out of the game before they were ever in it. Millwood, who had been scheduled to start Game 3 but was moved up because of the ripple effect of Tom Glavine's flu, allowed eight hits and walked two, and, again, shoddy defense didn't help.

TURNING POINTS:

Up-the-middle run-scoring singles by Tino Martinez and Scott Brosius with two outs in the first inning just eluded shortstop Ozzie Guillen, starting instead of Walt Weiss. The Yankees put together five singles and a walk in the first to build a 3-0 lead. Guillen also missed a soft flare right to him in the third, allowing a run to score on the error.

WORTH NOTING:

In Cone's last two Series starts against the Braves (1999 and 1996), he allowed no runs on five hits. ... Seventeen of the Yankees' 20 hits in the first two games were singles. ... Braves manager Bobby Cox shuffled his lineup (Guillen for Weiss at short and Keith Lockhart for Bret Boone at second) in hopes of injecting some life into the order that got only one run on two hits in Game 1. The result: no runs on two hits . ... Having fallen behind 3-0 after one inning and 5-0 after two, the Braves needed to be patient at the plate, work the count and get baserunners. That's not the strong suit of an Atlanta lineup littered with free swingers. That trait was all the more evident against a veteran pitcher like the Yankees' Cone.

WORTH QUOTING:

"You run into good pitching," Atlanta's Cox said of his team's offensive struggles, "you're not going to score no matter who you run out there." ... "Everyone talks about the Braves' pitchers, and rightly so," New York's Chuck Knoblauch said. "But I think our pitching staff is very comparable, or even, with the Braves." ... "We've had periods of inconsistency with our at-bats before," Braves batting coach Don Baylor said. "But right now is the one that counts the most. You can get by in the season, but right now they're halfway to the World Series title. We've had minimal hits and runs, and that had better change quickly." ... "They've got a lot of veteran hitters who work the count and make you throw the ball over the plate," Atlanta's Millwood said. "I just threw it over the middle, instead of the corners. My job is to go out and give us a chance to win, and I didn't do that." ... "This is the way we score runs, keep pounding away, get a break here or there and make them pay," the Yankees' Paul O'Neill said. "We don't have guys who hit 40 or 50 homers, but we have a team full of guys who scrap and claw and get on base." ... "The pitching pretty much sets the tone for what we do, and David Cone was terrific," New York manager Joe Torre said. ... "I thought I caught a break on that one," Cone said of Brian Jordan's drive caught on the warning track in the first inning. "That's easily a home run on a warmer day."

BOX SCORE

New York	AB	R	H	RBI	PO	A
Knoblauch, 2b	4	1	2	1	3	4
Jeter, ss	5	2	2	0	3	4
O'Neill, rf	4	0	1	1	3	0
B. Williams, cf	4	1	3	0	1	0
Martinez, 1b	5	2	2	2	9	1
Ledee, lf	4	0	2	1	1	0
Brosius, 3b	5	1	2	1	2	2
Girardi, c	4	0	0	0	4	0
Cone, p	4	0	0	0	0	0
Mendoza, p	1	0	0	0	0	1
Nelson, p	0	0	0	0	0	0
Totals	40	7	14	6	27	12

Atlanta	AB	R	H	RBI	PO	A
G. Williams, lf	4	0	0	0	1	0
Guillen, ss	4	0	0	0	4	3
C. Jones, 3b	3	1	1	0	0	2
Jordan, rf	3	0	0	0	0	0
Klesko, 1b	4	0	0	0	8	0
Lockhart, 2b	2	1	0	0	1	2
Myers, c	3	0	2	1	8	0
A. Jones, cf	3	0	0	0	4	0
McGlinchy, p	0	0	0	0	0	0
†Boone, ph	1	0	1	1	0	0
Millwood, p	0	0	0	0	0	0
Mulholland, p	0	0	0	0	1	0
*Fabregas, ph	1	0	0	0	0	0
Springer, p	0	0	0	0	0	1
Nixon, cf	2	0	1	0	0	0
Totals	30	2	5	2	27	8

Atlanta closer John Rocker first verbally battled with the raucous New York Mets fans in the N.L. Championship Series, then crossed the East River to battle the diehard Yankee fans in the World Series.

New York				3 0 2	1 1 0	0 0 0—7	
Atlanta				0 0 0	0 0 0	0 0 2—2	

New York	IP	H	R	ER	BB	SO
Cone (W)	7.0	1	0	0	5	4
Mendoza	1.2	3	2	2	1	0
Nelson	0.1	1	0	0	0	0

Atlanta	IP	H	R	ER	BB	SO
Millwood (L)	*2.0	8	5	4	2	2
Mulholland	3.0	3	2	2	1	3
Springer	2.0	1	0	0	0	1
McGlinchy	2.0	2	0	0	1	2

*Pitched to three batters in third.

Bases on balls—Off Cone 5 (Myers, Mulholland, C. Jones, Jordan, Lockhart), off Mendoza 1 (Lockhart), off Millwood 2 (Ledee, Knoblauch), off Mulholland 1 (B. Williams), off McGlinchy 1 (O'Neill).

Strikeouts—By Cone 4 (Klesko, Fabregas, G. Williams, A. Jones), by Millwood 2 (Girardi, Jeter), by Mulholland 3 (Brosius, Knoblauch, Ledee), by Springer 1 (Ledee), by McGlinchy 2 (Martinez, Brosius).

*Struck out for Mulholland in fifth. †Doubled for McGlinchy in ninth. E—Cone, Guillen. DP—New York 3, Atlanta 1. LOB—New York 11, Atlanta 7. 2B—Jeter, Ledee, Brosius, Boone. SH—Girardi. SB—Knoblauch. T—3:14. A—51,226. U—Roe (A.L.), plate; Rippley (N.L.), first; Cousins (A.L.), second; Davis (N.L.), third; Joyce (A.L.), left field; Marsh (N.L.), right field.

PLAY BY PLAY

FIRST INNING

New York—Knoblauch singled to left-center. Jeter singled to left as Knoblauch went to second. O'Neill singled to center, scoring Knoblauch as Jeter went to second. B. Williams grounded into a double play, Guillen to Klesko, as Jeter went to third. Martinez singled to center, scoring Jeter. Ledee walked. Brosius singled to center, scoring Martinez as Ledee went to second. Girardi struck out. N.Y. 3, Atl. 0.

Atlanta—G. Williams grounded out, Jeter to Martinez. Guillen went to second on a throwing error by Cone. C. Jones grounded out, Knoblauch to Martinez, as Guillen went to third. Jordan flied to Ledee.

SECOND INNING

New York—Cone grounded to Klesko. Knoblauch walked. Jeter struck out as Knoblauch stole second. O'Neill grounded out, C. Jones to Klesko.

Atlanta—Klesko grounded out, Martinez to Cone. Lockhart popped to Brosius. Myers walked. A. Jones popped to Jeter.

THIRD INNING

New York—B. Williams singled to center. Martinez singled to left as B. Williams went to second. Ledee doubled to left-center, scoring B. Williams as Martinez went to third. Mulholland now pitching. Brosius struck out. Girardi grounded out, Guillen to Klesko. Cone reached on an error by Guillen, as Martinez scored and Ledee went to third. Knoblauch struck out. N.Y. 5, Atl. 0.

Atlanta—Mulholland walked. G. Williams flied to O'Neill. Guillen grounded into a double play, Jeter to Martinez.

FOURTH INNING

New York—Jeter doubled to left-center. O'Neill flied to A. Jones as Jeter went to third. B. Williams was walked intentionally. Martinez forced B. Williams at second, Guillen to Lockhart, as Jeter scored. Ledee struck out. N.Y. 6, Atl. 0.

Atlanta—C. Jones walked. Jordan flied to O'Neill. Klesko struck out. Lockhart grounded out, Knoblauch to Martinez.

FIFTH INNING

New York—Brosius doubled to right. Girardi sacrificed Brosius to third, Mulholland made the unassisted putout. Cone popped to Guillen. Knoblauch singled to left, scoring Brosius. Jeter forced Knoblauch at second, Lockhart to Guillen. N.Y. 7, Atl. 0.

Atlanta—Myers singled to center. A. Jones grounded into a double play, Brosius to Knoblauch to Martinez. Fabregas, pinch-hitting for Mulholland, struck out.

SIXTH INNING

New York—Springer now pitching. O'Neill flied to G. Williams. B. Williams singled to right. Martinez forced B. Williams at second, Springer to Guillen. Ledee struck out.

Atlanta—G. Williams struck out. Guillen lined to Knoblauch. C. Jones popped to Brosius.

SEVENTH INNING

New York—Brosius, Girardi and Cone flied to A. Jones.

Atlanta—Jordan walked. Klesko popped to Knoblauch. Lockhart walked. Myers flied to B. Williams as Jordan went to third. A. Jones struck out.

EIGHTH INNING

New York—Nixon now in center field and McGlinchy pitching. Knoblauch popped foul to Klesko. Jeter grounded to Klesko. O'Neill walked. B. Williams singled to center as O'Neill went to second. Martinez struck out.

Atlanta—Mendoza now pitching. Nixon singled to second. G. Williams grounded into a double play, Knoblauch to Jeter to Martinez. Guillen grounded out, Mendoza to Martinez.

NINTH INNING

New York—Ledee singled to right. Brosius struck out. Girardi grounded out, C. Jones to Klesko, as Ledee went to second. Mendoza grounded out, Lockhart to Klesko.

Atlanta—C. Jones singled to center. Jordan grounded out, Brosius to Martinez, as C. Jones went to second. Klesko flied to O'Neill. Lockhart walked. Myers singled to center, scoring C. Jones, as Lockhart went to second. Boone now pinch-hitting for McGlinchy. Nelson now pitching. Boone doubled to left, scoring Lockhart, as Myers went to third. Nixon grounded out, Jeter to Martinez. Final score: N.Y. 7, Atl. 2.

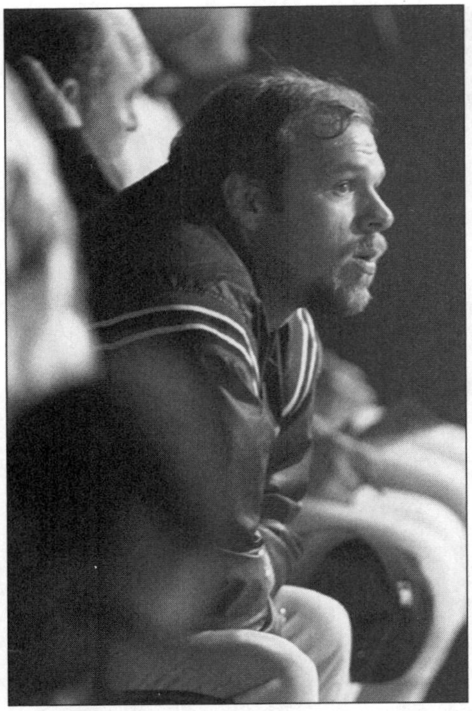

Young Atlanta starter Kevin Millwood lasted just two innings in the Game 2 loss to the Yankees.

Game 3 at New York

NEW YORK 6, ATLANTA 5

Why the Yankees won: Journeyman Chad Curtis etched his name in Yankees and World Series lore with two home runs after hitting five all season. His second was the game-winner, coming in the bottom of the 10th off Braves reliever Mike Remlinger.

Why the Braves lost: Atlanta built a 5-1 lead by the fifth inning, with every batter getting at least one hit in that span, but the Braves lineup went silent from there. Down 0-2 in the Series, Atlanta jumped on New York starter Andy Pettitte and needed to pour it on for a convincing road victory.

TURNING POINTS:

Braves manager Bobby Cox, who was looking for seven strong innings from starter Tom Glavine, got it. But Cox pushed his and Atlanta's luck by letting Glavine, pushed back from a scheduled Game 1 start because of the flu, come out for the eighth inning after the Yankees had cut the lead to two, 5-3. Joe Girardi singled to start the eighth, and Chuck Knoblauch sent a tying two-run homer over the short porch in right, ending Glavine's night.

WORTH NOTING:

The victory was the Yankees' 200th in World Series play; the Cardinals rank second with 96 Series wins. ... If New York relievers Jason Grimsley, Jeff Nelson and winner Mariano Rivera hadn't shut down the Braves' offense, holding Atlanta scoreless after New York starter Andy Pettitte gave up five runs in $3\frac{2}{3}$ innings, then a comeback would have been impossible. ... Although this Yankees team wasn't known for its power, Glavine allowed three home runs in only 76 pitches. Of course, that was a better number than loser Remlinger, who gave up one home run in three pitches. ... The Series victory was the 11th in a row for Yankees manager Joe Torre, breaking the record set by Joe McCarthy of the Yankees.

WORTH QUOTING:

"I'm still amazed, and yet I'm not amazed," New York's Torre said of the come-from-behind victory. "We go out there and play nine innings, and good things happen." ... Said Torre's counterpart, Atlanta's Bobby Cox: "It would've been nice to have won. It would have gotten us going real good. This was a big one to lose." ... "I have a tendency when I get up there in that situation, I try to hit a home run," Curtis said of game-winner in the 10th. "So I went up there and tried to hit it up the middle, and I hit a home run." ... Cox on Curtis, the Yankees' unlikely hero: "Always someone you don't expect. You never know where it's going to come from." ... "It was a changeup," Atlanta's Remlinger said of the 10th-inning pitch Curtis hit. "It looked like it got too much of the plate." ... "I never stepped on the field," Curtis said, recalling not having played in the 1998 World Series victory over the Padres. "I wasn't pouting; we won the World Series. By the same token, I felt like I was more congratulating my teammates than celebrating with them." ... "Every time Joe Torre takes a guy out of the game when we're losing, he tells the new pitcher to hold them here and get a win," the Yankees' Knoblauch said. "That's the way we have to think. It's not cockiness. It's having a great deal of confidence in the guys we have on our team to come back." ... "When we saw Andy struggle a little bit, we knew it was going to be one of those games we were going to need a lot of middle relief," said Yankees reliever Jeff Nelson, who pitched two perfect innings.

BOX SCORE

Atlanta	AB	R	H	RBI	PO	A
G. Williams, lf	5	2	2	0	2	0
Boone, 2b	5	1	4	1	1	2
*Nixon, pr	0	0	0	0	0	0
Lockhart, 2b	0	0	0	0	0	0
C. Jones, 3b	4	0	1	1	1	0
Jordan, rf	3	1	1	1	4	0
A. Jones, cf	5	1	1	0	4	0
J. Hernandez, dh	4	0	1	2	0	0
†Guillen, ph-dh	1	0	0	0	0	0
Perez, c	4	0	1	0	5	0
‡Klesko, ph-1b	1	0	1	0	0	0
Hunter, 1b	4	0	1	0	8	1
§Myers, ph-c	1	0	0	0	0	0
Weiss, ss	4	0	1	0	2	3
Glavine, p	0	0	0	0	0	2
Rocker, p	0	0	0	0	0	0
Remlinger, p	0	0	0	0	0	0
Totals	41	5	14	5	27	8

New York	AB	R	H	RBI	PO	A
Knoblauch, 2b	4	2	2	2	2	2
Jeter, ss	4	0	1	0	2	4
O'Neill, rf	4	0	1	1	2	0
B. Williams, cf	4	0	0	0	1	0
Davis, dh	4	0	0	0	0	0
Martinez, 1b	4	1	1	1	12	0
Brosius, 3b	4	0	0	0	2	2
Curtis, lf	4	2	2	2	4	0
Girardi, c	3	1	2	0	5	2
Pettitte, p	0	0	0	0	0	3
Grimsley, p	0	0	0	0	0	0
Nelson, p	0	0	0	0	0	1
Rivera, p	0	0	0	0	0	0
Totals	35	6	9	6	30	14

Atlanta	1 0 3	1 0 0	0 0 0	0—5
New York	1 0 0	0 1 0	1 2 0	1—6

Atlanta	IP	H	R	ER	BB	SO
Glavine	*7.0	7	5	4	0	3
Rocker	2.0	1	0	0	0	1
Remlinger (L)	0.0	1	1	1	0	0

New York	IP	H	R	ER	BB	SO
Pettitte	3.2	10	5	5	1	1
Grimsley	2.1	2	0	0	2	0
Nelson	2.0	0	0	0	0	2
Rivera (W)	2.0	2	0	0	0	2

*Pitched to two batters in eighth.

Bases on balls—Off Pettitte 1 (Jordan), off Grimsley 2 (Jordan, C. Jones).

Strikeouts—By Glavine 3 (Jeter, Brosius, Davis), by Rocker 1 (Davis), by Pettitte 1 (Perez), by Nelson 2 (J. Hernandez, Hunter), by Rivera 2 (C. Jones, Guillen).

*Ran for Boone in ninth. †Struck out for J. Hernandez in 10th. ‡Singled for Perez in 10th. §Grounded out for Hunter in 10th. E—Jordan. DP—Atlanta 2, New York 1. LOB—Atlanta 9, New York 2. 2B—Boone 3, J. Hernandez, Knoblauch. 3B—G. Williams. HR—Curtis 2, Knoblauch, Martinez. SB—J. Hernandez. WP—Pettitte. T—3:16. A—56,794. U—Rippley (N.L.), plate; Cousins (A.L.), first; Davis (N.L.), second; Joyce (A.L.), third; Marsh (N.L.), left field; Roe (A.L.), right field.

PLAY BY PLAY

FIRST INNING

Atlanta—G. Williams singled to right. Boone doubled to right as G. Williams went to third. C. Jones grounded out, Brosius to Martinez, as G. Williams scored. Jordan walked. A. Jones grounded out, Pettitte to Martinez, as Boone went to third and Jordan to second. J. Hernandez grounded out, Jeter to Martinez. Atl. 1, N.Y. 0.

New York—Knoblauch reached second on an error by Jordan. Jeter flied to Jordan as Knoblauch went to third. O'Neill singled to left, scoring Knoblauch. B. Williams lined to Hunter, who doubled O'Neill off first, unassisted. Atl. 1, N.Y. 1.

SECOND INNING

Atlanta—Perez struck out. Hunter singled to left and went to second on a wild pitch. Weiss grounded out, Knoblauch to Martinez, as Hunter went to third. G. Williams grounded out, Pettitte to Martinez.

New York—Davis grounded out, Weiss to Hunter. Martinez and Brosius flied to A. Jones.

THIRD INNING

Atlanta—Boone doubled to right-center. C. Jones grounded out, Jeter to Martinez, as Boone went to third. Jordan singled to right, scoring Boone. A. Jones singled to left, as Jordan went to second. J. Hernandez doubled to left, scoring Jordan and A. Jones. Perez flied to Curtis. J. Hernandez stole third. Hunter flied to O'Neill. Atl. 4, N.Y. 1.

New York—Curtis flied to G. Williams. Girardi flied to Jordan. Knoblauch doubled to left. Jeter struck out.

FOURTH INNING

Atlanta—Weiss grounded out, Pettitte to Martinez. G. Williams tripled to center. Boone doubled to left, scoring G. Williams. Boone caught stealing third, Girardi to Brosius. C. Jones singled to center. Grimsley now pitching. Jordan walked. A. Jones popped to Knoblauch. Atl. 5, N.Y. 1.

New York—O'Neill grounded to Perez. B. Williams grounded out, Boone to Hunter. Davis flied to Jordan.

FIFTH INNING

Atlanta—J. Hernandez flied to O'Neill. Perez singled to center. Hunter forced Perez at second, Brosius to Knoblauch. Weiss singled to right as Hunter went to second. G. Williams flied to Curtis.

New York—Martinez grounded out, Boone to Hunter. Brosius struck out. Curtis homered to right. Girardi singled to left-center. Knoblauch grounded out, Glavine to Hunter. Atl. 5, N.Y. 2.

SIXTH INNING

Atlanta—Boone flied to B. Williams, C. Jones walked. Jordan grounded into a double play, Jeter to Martinez.

New York—Jeter flied to G. Williams. O'Neill grounded out, Glavine to Hunter. B. Williams flied to Jordan.

SEVENTH INNING

Atlanta—Nelson now pitching. A. Jones popped to Brosius. J. Hernandez struck out. Perez grounded out, Nelson to Martinez.

New York—Davis struck out. Martinez homered to right. Brosius flied to A. Jones. Curtis grounded out, Weiss to Hunter. Atl. 5, N.Y. 3.

EIGHTH INNING

Atlanta—Hunter struck out. Weiss and G. Williams flied to Curtis.

New York—Girardi singled to right. Knoblauch homered to right, scoring Girardi. Rocker now pitching. Jeter singled to center. O'Neill bunted into a double play, Hunter to Weiss to Boone. B. Williams flied to A. Jones. Atl. 5, N.Y. 5.

NINTH INNING

Atlanta—Rivera now pitching. Boone singled to right. Nixon now pinch-running for Boone. Nixon caught stealing second, Girardi to Jeter. C. Jones struck out. Jordan grounded out, Jeter to Martinez.

New York—Lockhart now at second. Davis struck out. Martinez popped foul to C. Jones. Brosius popped to Weiss.

10TH INNING

Atlanta—A. Jones grounded out, Knoblauch to Martinez. Guillen, pinch-hitting for J. Hernandez, struck out. Klesko, pinch-hitting for Perez, singled to right. Myers, pinch-hitting for Hunter, grounded to Martinez.

New York—Klesko now at first, Myers catching and Remlinger pitching. Curtis homered to left. Final score: N.Y. 6, Atl. 5.

Game 4 at New York

NEW YORK 4, ATLANTA 1

Why the Yankees won: Roger Clemens, 37, put to rest any talk of his being a postseason bust (247 lifetime victories, but none in the World Series) by looking like "The Rocket" of his prime. He hit 96 mph on the radar gun and allowed one run on four hits in $7\frac{2}{3}$ innings. In fact, if he hadn't gotten hurt while covering first base on an eighth-inning play, Clemens might have gone the distance.

Why the Braves lost: Defense wins championships, and Atlanta's inability to make plays—routine and otherwise—hurt again. Singles off Walt Weiss' and Ryan Klesko's gloves set up the Yankees' three-run third and proved that when the box scores showed only four errors charged to the Braves in the four-game series, it was deceiving.

TURNING POINTS:

Braves starter John Smoltz intentionally walked Bernie Williams, loading the bases with one out in the third inning. Tino Martinez's sharp grounder to Klesko's right could have become the inning-ending double play the Braves needed, but the ball ricocheted off Klesko's arm, allowing two runs to score. One batter later, Jorge Posada lined a single to right, knocking in the third Yankees run of the inning.

WORTH NOTING:

The Yankees became the first team in 60 years to sweep consecutive World Series. ... Only No. 2 hitter Bret Boone (1-for-3 in Game 4, but .538 for the Series) hit the ball with any regularity for Atlanta. The Braves got 26 hits in four games, and few of those were in key situations. That spelled trouble against a team as effective and opportunistic as the Yankees. ... With a record-tying 12-game World Series winning streak intact, the Yankees' most visible constant was manager Joe Torre, who not only has the perfect personality to buffer his clubhouse from principal owner George Steinbrenner, but he also has outmanaged Bobby Cox twice (1996 and '99) and Bruce Bochy once (1998) in winning three championships in four years. ... New York's Jim Leyritz hit the 18th pinch-hit home run in World Series play, the first since Ed Sprague did it for the Blue Jays in Game 2 of the '92 Series against Atlanta. ... The Braves joined the New York Giants (1910-9) as the only teams to have lost four World Series in a decade. ... New York's Derek Jeter extended his postseason hitting streak to 17 games, tying the Yankees' Hank Bauer for the longest ever; Bauer's streak was in World Series games from 1956-58. Jeter has hit in nine consecutive World Series games.

WORTH QUOTING:

Afterward, New York's Clemens, acquired in February recalled seeing teammates receive their 1998 Series rings in spring training: "I was sitting there watching them receive them. They said, 'We're going to get you one.' " ... "It seemed like a perfect setup," New York's Torre said of Clemens' opportunity to complete the sweep, "I couldn't see it *not* happening, not with the way his career had gone." ... Series MVP Mariano Rivera, who pitched 12⅓ scoreless innings in eight postseason appearances, on the first repeat championship since Toronto in 1992-93: "Everybody talked about last year, but this is unbelievable, back-to-back." ... "I think they think in their minds that they had a tremendous year with all the ballclub went through," the Braves' Cox said of his team. "They're disappointed just like I am." ... "The best team won," said Atlanta's Smoltz, who fell to 12-4 in postseason play. "The Yankees are head and shoulders above most when it comes to this time of the year. We lost to the best team. The Yankees are a model of how to win." ... The Yankees' Jeter on his team's place in history: "I'd have to rank it at the top. Three tiers of playoffs doesn't make it twice as hard or three times as hard, it makes it five times as hard." ... "To win three in four years," Yankees principal owner George Steinbrenner said, "these guys have to be put up there with the old, great Yankees teams."

BOX SCORE

Atlanta	AB	R	H	RBI	PO	A
G. Williams, lf	4	0	1	0	0	0
Boone, 2b	3	0	1	1	2	2
C. Jones, 3b	4	0	0	0	0	1
Jordan, rf	3	0	0	0	2	0
Klesko, 1b	4	0	1	0	6	0
Lockhart, dh	4	0	1	0	0	0
Perez, c	2	0	0	0	11	0
*Myers, ph-c	1	0	0	0	1	0
A. Jones, cf	3	0	0	0	1	0
Weiss, ss	3	1	1	0	0	1
Smoltz, p	0	0	0	0	0	0
Mulholland, p	0	0	0	0	0	0
Springer, p	0	0	0	0	0	0
Totals	31	1	5	1	24	4
New York	**AB**	**R**	**H**	**RBI**	**PO**	**A**
Knoblauch, 2b	4	1	1	0	4	3
Sojo, 2b	0	0	0	0	1	1
Jeter, ss	4	1	1	0	1	6
O'Neill, rf	3	0	0	0	0	0
B. Williams, cf	3	1	0	0	0	0
Martinez, 1b	3	0	1	2	16	0
Strawberry, dh	3	0	1	0	0	0
†Leyritz, ph-dh	1	1	1	1	0	0
Posada, c	4	0	2	1	4	0
Ledee, lf	3	0	0	0	0	0
‡Curtis, ph-lf	1	0	0	0	1	0
Brosius, 3b	3	0	1	0	1	3
Clemens, p	0	0	0	0	0	3
Nelson, p	0	0	0	0	0	0
Rivera, p	0	0	0	0	0	1
Totals	32	4	8	4	27	17

Atlanta	0 0 0	0 0 0	0 1 0—1
New York	0 0 3	0 0 0	0 1 x—4

Atlanta	IP	H	R	ER	BB	SO
Smoltz (L)	7.0	6	3	3	3	11
Mulholland	0.2	2	1	1	0	0
Springer	0.1	0	0	0	0	0
New York	**IP**	**H**	**R**	**ER**	**BB**	**SO**
Clemens (W)	7.2	4	1	1	2	4
Nelson	*0.0	1	0	0	0	0
Rivera (S)	1.1	0	0	0	0	0

*Pitched to one batter in eighth.
Bases on balls—Off Smoltz 3 (O'Neill, Martinez, B. Williams), off Clemens 2 (Jordan, Boone).
Strikeouts—By Smoltz 11 (Knoblauch 2, Posada 2, Strawberry 2, Ledee, Brosius, O'Neill, B. Williams, Martinez), by Clemens 4 (G. Williams, Boone, A. Jones, Jordan).
*Grounded out for Perez in eighth. †Homered for Strawberry in eighth. ‡Fouled out for Ledee in eighth. DP—New York 1. LOB—Atlanta 5, New York 7. 2B—Posada. HR—Leyritz. SB—Jeter 2. T—2:58. A—56,752.
U—Cousins (A.L.), plate; Davis (N.L.), first; Joyce (A.L.), second; Marsh (N.L.), third; Roe (A.L.), left field; Rippley (N.L.), right field.

PLAY BY PLAY

FIRST INNING

Atlanta—G. Williams struck out. Boone and C. Jones grounded out, Jeter to Martinez.

New York—Knoblauch struck out. Jeter grounded to Klesko. O'Neill walked. B. Williams grounded out, Boone to Klesko.

SECOND INNING

Atlanta—Jordan grounded out, Knoblauch to Martinez. Klesko singled to right-center. Lockhart forced Klesko at second, Brosius to Knoblauch. Perez forced Lockhart at second, Jeter to Knoblauch.

New York—Martinez walked. Strawberry singled to left as Martinez went to second. Posada, Ledee and Brosius struck out.

THIRD INNING

Atlanta—A. Jones grounded out, Jeter to Martinez. Weiss grounded to Martinez. G. Williams popped to Knoblauch.

New York's Chuck Knoblauch hit .313 in the series, scoring five runs and driving in three. More importantly for the Yankees, the second baseman didn't commit any errors.

New York—Knoblauch singled to short. Jeter singled to right as Knoblauch went to third. O'Neill struck out as Jeter stole second. B. Williams was walked intentionally. Martinez singled to first, scoring Knoblauch and Jeter, as B. Williams went to third. Strawberry grounded to first. Posada singled to right, scoring B. Williams, as Martinez went to third. Ledee popped to Weiss. N.Y. 3, Atl. 0.

FOURTH INNING

Atlanta—Boone struck out. C. Jones grounded out, Clemens to Martinez. Jordan walked. Klesko grounded to Martinez.

New York—Brosius and Knoblauch flied to Jordan. Jeter grounded out, C. Jones to Klesko.

FIFTH INNING

Atlanta—Lockhart singled to center. Perez grounded into a double play, Brosius to Knoblauch to Martinez. A. Jones struck out.

New York—O'Neill grounded out, Boone to Klesko. B. Williams and Martinez struck out.

SIXTH INNING

Atlanta—Weiss grounded out, Clemens to Martinez. G. Williams grounded out, Jeter to Martinez. Boone walked. C. Jones grounded out, Brosius to Martinez.

New York—Strawberry and Posada struck out. Ledee grounded to Klesko.

SEVENTH INNING

Atlanta—Jordan struck out. Klesko grounded out, Knoblauch to Martinez. Lockhart popped to Brosius.

New York—Brosius singled to right-center. Knoblauch struck out. Jeter forced Brosius at second, Weiss to Boone. Jeter stole second. O'Neill flied to A. Jones.

EIGHTH INNING

Atlanta—Sojo now at second. Myers, pinch-hitting for Perez, grounded out, Clemens to Martinez. A. Jones grounded out, Jeter to Martinez. Weiss singled to first. G. Williams singled to left as Weiss went to second. Nelson now pitching. Boone singled to center, scoring Weiss, as G. Williams went to third. Rivera now pitching. C. Jones grounded out, Sojo to Martinez. N.Y. 3, Atl. 1.

New York—Myers now catching and Mulholland pitching. B. Williams popped to Myers. Leyritz, pinch-hitting for Strawberry, homered to left. Posada doubled to center. Curtis was announced as a pinch-hitter for Ledee. Springer now pitching. Curtis popped foul to Klesko. N.Y. 4, Atl. 1.

NINTH INNING

Atlanta—Curtis now in left field. Jordan grounded out, Rivera to Martinez. Klesko popped to Sojo. Lockhart flied to Curtis. Final score: N.Y. 4, Atl. 1.

COMPOSITE

BATTING AVERAGES

New York Yankees

Player, position	G	AB	R	H	2B	3B	HR	RBI	Avg.
Leyritz, ph-dh	2	1	1	1	0	0	1	2	1.000
Brosius, 3b	4	16	2	6	1	0	0	1	.375
Jeter, ss	4	17	4	6	1	0	0	1	.353
Curtis, pr-lf-ph	3	6	3	2	0	0	2	2	.333
Strawberry, ph-dh	2	3	0	1	0	0	0	0	.333
Knoblauch, 2b	4	16	5	5	1	0	1	3	.313
Girardi, c	2	7	1	2	0	0	0	0	.286
Martinez, 1b	4	15	3	4	0	0	1	5	.267
Posada, c	2	8	0	2	1	0	0	1	.250

Joe Torre and the Yankees battled adversity on and off the field to earn their 25th World Series title.

Player, position	G	AB	R	H	2B	3B	HR	RBI	Avg.
B. Williams, cf	4	13	2	3	0	0	0	0	.231
Ledee, lf	3	10	0	2	1	0	0	1	.200
O'Neill, rf	4	15	0	3	0	0	0	4	.200
Clemens, p	1	0	0	0	0	0	0	0	.000
Grimsley, p	1	0	0	0	0	0	0	0	.000
Nelson, p	4	0	0	0	0	0	0	0	.000
Pettitte, p	1	0	0	0	0	0	0	0	.000
Rivera, p	3	0	0	0	0	0	0	0	.000
Sojo, 2b	1	0	0	0	0	0	0	0	.000
Stanton, p	1	0	0	0	0	0	0	0	.000
O. Hernandez, p	1	1	0	0	0	0	0	0	.000
Mendoza, p	1	1	0	0	0	0	0	0	.000
Davis, dh	1	4	0	0	0	0	0	0	.000
Cone, p	1	4	0	0	0	0	0	0	.000
Totals	4	137	21	37	5	0	5	20	.270

Atlanta Braves

Player, position	G	AB	R	H	2B	3B	HR	RBI	Avg.
Boone, 2b-ph	4	13	1	7	4	0	0	3	.538
Nixon, cf-pr	2	2	0	1	0	0	0	0	.500
Myers, ph-c	4	6	0	2	0	0	0	1	.333
Hunter, 1b	2	4	0	1	0	0	0	0	.250
Weiss, ss	3	9	1	2	0	0	0	0	.222
J. Hernandez, ss-dh	2	5	0	1	1	0	0	2	.200
C. Jones, 3b	4	13	2	3	0	0	1	2	.231
G. Williams, lf	4	17	2	3	0	1	0	0	.176
Klesko, 1b-ph	4	12	0	2	0	0	0	0	.167
Lockhart, ph-2b-dh	4	7	1	1	0	0	0	0	.143
Perez, c	3	8	0	1	0	0	0	0	.125
A. Jones, cf	4	13	1	1	0	0	0	0	.077
Jordan, rf	4	13	1	1	0	0	0	1	.077
Battle, ph	1	0	0	0	0	0	0	0	.000
Glavine, p	1	0	0	0	0	0	0	0	.000
McGlinchy, p	1	0	0	0	0	0	0	0	.000
Millwood, p	1	0	0	0	0	0	0	0	.000
Mulholland, p	2	0	0	0	0	0	0	0	.000
Remlinger, p	2	0	0	0	0	0	0	0	.000
Rocker, p	2	0	0	0	0	0	0	0	.000
Smoltz, p	1	0	0	0	0	0	0	0	.000
Springer, p	2	0	0	0	0	0	0	0	.000
Fabregas, ph	1	1	0	0	0	0	0	0	.000
Maddux, p	1	2	0	0	0	0	0	0	.000
Guillen, ph-ss-dh	3	5	0	0	0	0	0	0	.000
Totals	4	130	9	26	5	1	1	9	.200

PITCHING AVERAGES

New York Yankees

Pitcher	G	IP	H	R	ER	BB	SO	W	L	ERA
Cone	1	7.0	1	0	0	5	4	1	0	0.00
Rivera	3	4.2	3	0	0	1	3	1	0	0.00
Nelson	4	2.2	2	0	0	1	3	0	0	0.00
Grimsley	1	2.1	2	0	0	2	0	0	0	0.00
Stanton	1	0.1	0	0	0	0	1	0	0	0.00
Clemens	1	7.2	4	1	1	2	4	1	0	1.17
O. Hernandez	1	7.0	1	1	1	2	10	1	0	1.29
Mendoza	1	1.2	3	2	2	1	0	0	0	10.80
Pettitte	1	3.2	10	5	5	1	1	0	0	12.27
Totals	4	37.0	26	9	9	15	26	4	0	2.19

Shutouts—None. Saves—Rivera 2.

Atlanta Braves

Pitcher	G	IP	H	R	ER	BB	SO	W	L	ERA
Rocker	2	3.0	2	0	0	2	4	0	0	0.00
Springer	2	2.1	1	0	0	0	1	0	0	0.00
McGlinchy	1	2.0	2	0	0	1	2	0	0	0.00
Maddux	1	7.0	5	4	2	3	5	0	1	2.57
Smoltz	1	7.0	6	3	3	3	11	0	1	3.86
Glavine	1	7.0	7	5	4	0	3	0	0	5.14
Mulholland	2	3.2	5	3	3	1	3	0	0	7.36
Remlinger	2	1.0	1	1	1	1	0	0	1	9.00
Millwood	1	2.0	8	5	4	2	2	0	1	18.00
Totals	4	35.0	37	21	17	13	31	0	4	4.37

No shutouts or saves.

Who's Who

This Hall of Fame gathering at the 1939 Cooperstown induction ceremonies included (front row from left) Eddie Collins, Babe Ruth, Connie Mack, Cy Young and (back row) Honus Wagner, Grover Alexander, Tris Speaker, Nap Lajoie, George Sisler and Walter Johnson.

INTRODUCTION

NO EASY TICKET TO COOPERSTOWN

It's not easy to join this club—just ask Don Sutton.

Winning 300 games as a big-league pitcher is a remarkable feat—worthy, it seems, of a ticket into the Hall of Fame in the first year of eligibility. Occasionally, though, all it means is a rain check. Try again some time in the future.

Sutton, elected in 1998, knows all about that. Winner of 324 games, he didn't gain the necessary votes until his fifth year on the ballot. Phil Niekro and Gaylord Perry are other 1990s inductees who could speak to the issue. Niekro posted 318 victories but he, too, wasn't elected until his fifth year of eligibility, 1997. And Perry, who won 314 games, made the Hall in 1991—his third try.

Winning 500 games is another story, right? Automatic induction, to be sure. Denton True "Cy" Young must have thought so, anyway, as the Hall—destined for Cooperstown, N.Y., but not yet a physical reality—prepared to take in its first class in 1936. Young had finished his career with a record 511 victories and tossed 76 shutouts.

But not even the great Cy Young, who eventually had baseball's preeminent pitching award named in his honor, was a Hall of Fame first-timer. When the balloting for the first Hall enshrinement was announced, those receiving the votes necessary for election—75 percent or more of the ballots cast—were Ty Cobb (the leading vote-getter), Babe Ruth, Honus Wagner, Christy Mathewson and Walter Johnson. Young's pitching brethren Mathewson and Johnson had won 373 and 417 games, respectively.

The skills of The Select Five, as reported at the time by the Spalding Official Base Ball Guide:

"He (Mathewson, who died in 1925) alone, of the five so far chosen, has been called to the great beyond, brought low before his time. ... Who is there who approaches him in daring when, at a critical stage of the game, he never hesitated to put the ball 'across the plate'? Over it would come, but never, if he could help it, at the place where the batter hoped it would.

"Cobb, most elusive of batters as well as most effective, who did not rely on strength alone ... was as clever with the short, powerful hit as with the long and ground-covering one.

"Ruth, possessor of the stout arms, the stout heart, the sharp eye that picked only the best of the pitched balls to hit; Wagner, who has never been equaled as batter and fielder, not even in the five who have been selected as worthy of being put in this Hall of Fame, which is to recognize the greatest of the base ball world since 1900; and Walter Johnson, of fabulous pitching speed, round up the first five chosen."

The Spalding publication also noted that "only the fact there have been so many good second basemen kept the vote divided so that (Nap) Lajoie did not get a higher count," with Rogers Hornsby and Eddie Collins being the spoilers. Tris Speaker and Willie Keeler were "highly placed" in the voting, the guide said, with Grover Cleveland Alexander and Young earning mention along with Mickey Cochrane and Roger Bresnahan.

It was obvious, from the initial balloting in '36, that baseball's Hall of Fame would be a truly selective shrine. Cy Young could have expounded on that.

No, the Hall didn't yet have a gleaming building to house its plaques and myriad treasures. But it did have a lustrous membership of five.

THE ROSTER GROWS

Young and seven other baseball notables were elected to the Hall in the second year of balloting—but baseball's winningest pitcher was named on only 76.1 percent of the ballots. Others in the second class of honorees were Nap Lajoie, Tris Speaker, John McGraw, Connie Mack, George Wright and the first presidents of the National and American leagues,

Detroit's Ty Cobb, the game's premier batsman of the early century, was the leading vote-getter for the first Hall of Fame enshrinement.

Morgan Bulkeley and Ban Johnson. The Hall, whose special-election procedures and waiting-period rules would vary over the years, was already well on its way to including a wide range of baseball personalities in its mix—players, managers, executives, organizers, founders and umpires. Voting for the honorees was being done by the nation's baseball writers and various special committees—much the same as it is today (with the Baseball Writers' Association of America and the Hall's Committee on Veterans currently holding forth). ... Grover Cleveland Alexander, whose career victory total matched Mathewson's, was voted into the Hall in 1938, along with Alexander J. Cartwright, considered by some as the game's real founder and by most as its foremost organizer, and Henry Chadwick, baseball's leading chronicler in its formative years. ... Lou Gehrig was the headliner and sentimental choice in a 10-man addition in 1939, the year the Hall of Fame and Museum became part of the Cooperstown landscape in June dedication ceremonies. Gehrig, forced to retire during the '39 season because of an illness that would take his life within two years, was joined by such luminaries as Willie Keeler, Eddie Collins and George Sisler. ... Rogers Hornsby and the late commissioner Kenesaw Mountain Landis (enshrined shortly after his death in 1944) were the only new inductees from 1940-44. ... Hugh Duffy, who compiled the highest single-season batting average in big-league history (.440, in 1894), was among 10 new members in 1945, and the Tinker-to-Evers-to-Chance double-play unit accounted for three of the 11 enshrinees the next year. ... The Hall classes were downsized in the ensuing six years, with a total of only 13 players winning admission. ... In 1953, Bill Klem gained the distinction of being the first umpire to reach Cooperstown. ... In 1962, Jackie Robinson, the first black player in modern big-league baseball, became the first black to make the Hall. ... Satchel Paige, confined to the Negro leagues, the barnstorming circuit and foreign leagues for most of his career because of the color barrier, was the first player voted to the shrine (1971) by the Special Committee on Negro Leagues, which was formed to honor players whose careers were victimized by racial policies in existence for nearly half of this century. ... Roberto Clemente, killed in an airplane crash on December 31, 1972, and Gehrig are the only players for whom waiting-period guidelines have been waived. Clemente was enshrined in 1973. ... It took until 1979 for Hack Wilson, who holds the big-league record for RBIs in one year and owned the N.L. season homer mark until Mark McGwire broke it in 1998, to achieve Cooperstown induction. ... Defensive skills and leadership qualities seemed to be appreciated more than usual in 1984 when Luis Aparicio, Pee Wee Reese and Rick Ferrell were among those selected. ... Nellie Fox missed election to the Hall by the slimmest margin in history. He was named on 74.7 percent of the ballots in 1985, but 75 percent is required—and, sorry, there's no rounding off. But Fox made it in March 1997, thanks to the veterans committee. ... Voters paid tribute to the age of the relief specialist in 1992, adding Rollie Fingers to the pantheon. Also in '92, Tom Seaver set a record for the highest percentage of votes received, 98.84. ... Nolan Ryan, the majors' runaway leader in career strikeouts (5,714) and no-hitters (seven), threatened Seaver's mark last year, being named on 491 of 497 ballots, or 98.79 percent. Besides electing Ryan, who like Sutton won 324 games, baseball writers also made George Brett (named on 488 ballots) and Robin Yount members of their 1999 Cooperstown class. All three players were ballot first-timers, bringing the total of those reaching the Hall in their initial attempt to 29. ... And, proving that Hall voters attempt to honor anyone truly deserving, regardless of the time frame, the veterans committee chose William Hulbert in 1995—119 years after the Chicago businessman played a pivotal role in the founding of the National League.

—JOE HOPPEL

1936

TY COBB OF
6-1, 175. **B:** L. **T:** R.
Born: Dec. 18, 1886. **Died:** July 17, 1961.
Career: .366 avg., 1st on all-time list; 117 HR; 1,937 RBIs; 4,189 hits; 891 SB.
Teams: Tigers 1905-26; Athletics 1927-28.
How elected: 98.2 percent of vote.

WALTER JOHNSON P
6-1, 200. **B:** R. **T:** R.
Born: Nov. 6, 1887. **Died:** Dec. 10, 1946.
Career: 417-279; 2.16 ERA; 3,509 SO.
Team: Senators 1907-27.
How elected: 83.6 percent of vote.

CHRISTY MATHEWSON P
6-1, 195. **B:** R. **T:** R.
Born: Aug. 12, 1880. **Died:** Oct. 7, 1925.
Career: 373-188; 2.13 ERA; 2,502 SO.
Teams: Giants 1900-16; Reds 1916.
How elected: 90.7 percent of vote.

BABE RUTH OF
6-2, 215. **B:** L. **T:** L.
Born: Feb. 6, 1895. **Died:** Aug. 16, 1948.
Career: .342 avg.; 714 HR; 2,213 RBIs.
Teams: Red Sox 1914-19; Yankees 1920-34; Braves 1935.
How elected: 95.1 percent of vote.

HONUS WAGNER SS
5-11, 200. **B:** R. **T:** R.
Born: Feb. 24, 1874. **Died:** Dec. 6, 1955.
Career: .327 avg.; 101 HR; 1,732 RBIs; 3,415 hits.
Teams: Louisville (Nat.) 1897-99; Pirates 1900-17.
How elected: 95.1 percent of vote.

1937

MORGAN BULKELEY EXECUTIVE
First president of N.L.
Born: Dec. 26, 1837. **Died:** Nov. 6, 1922.
Career: Former Connecticut governor and U.S. senator; helped N.L. organize its first league.
How elected: Centennial Commission.

BAN JOHNSON EXECUTIVE
A.L. founder/president.
Born: Jan. 5, 1864. **Died:** March 28, 1931.
Career: A former sportswriter who revived the old Western League and later renamed it the American League; A.L. president 1901-27.
How elected: Centennial Commission.

NAPOLEON LAJOIE 2B
6-1, 195. **B:** R. **T:** R.
Born: Sept. 5, 1874. **Died:** Feb. 7, 1959.
Career: .338 avg.; 83 HR; 1,599 RBIs; 3,242 hits.
Teams: Phillies 1896-1900; Athletics 1901-02, 1915-16; Indians 1902-14.
How elected: 83.6 percent of vote.

CONNIE MACK C, MAN.
6-1, 150. **B:** R. **T:** R.
Born: Dec. 22, 1862. **Died:** Feb. 8, 1956.
Managing career: 3,731-3,948, 53 years; 3 World Series championships.
Teams: Pirates 1894-96; Athletics 1901-50.
How elected: Centennial Commission.

JOHN MCGRAW IF, MAN.
5-7, 155. **B:** L. **T:** R.
Born: April 7, 1873. **Died:** Feb. 25, 1934.
Playing career: .334 avg.; 13 HR; 462 RBIs.
Managing career: 2,784-1,959, 33 years; 3 World Series championships.
Teams (player): Baltimore (A.A.) 1891; Baltimore (Nat.) 1892-99; St. Louis (Nat.) 1900; Baltimore (Amer.) 1901-02; Giants 1902-06.
Teams (manager): Baltimore (Nat.) 1899; Baltimore (Amer.) 1901-02; Giants 1902-32.
How elected: Centennial Commission.

TRIS SPEAKER OF
5-11, 193. **B:** L. **T:** L.
Born: April 4, 1888. **Died:** Dec. 8, 1958.
Career: .345 avg.; 117 HR; 1,529 RBIs; 3,514 hits.
Teams: Red Sox 1907-15; Indians 1916-26; Senators 1927; Athletics 1928.
How elected: 82.1 percent of vote.

GEORGE WRIGHT SS
5-9, 150. **B:** R. **T:** R.
Born: Jan. 28, 1847. **Died:** Aug. 21, 1937.
Career: .256 avg.; 2 HR; 132 RBIs.
Teams: Boston (Nat.) 1876-78, 1880-81; Providence (Nat.) 1879, 1882.
How elected: Centennial Commission.

CY YOUNG P
6-2, 210. **B:** R. **T:** R.
Born: March 29, 1867. **Died:** Nov. 4, 1955.
Career: 511-316, 1st on all-time win list; 2.63 ERA; 2,800 SO.
Teams: Cleveland (Nat.) 1890-98; St. Louis (Nat.) 1899-1900; Red Sox 1901-08; Indians 1909-11; Braves 1911.
How elected: 76.1 percent of vote.

1938

GROVER CLEVELAND ALEXANDER P
6-1, 185. **B:** R. **T:** R.
Born: Feb. 26, 1887. **Died:** Nov. 4, 1950.
Career: 373-208; 2.56 ERA; 2,198 SO.
Teams: Phillies 1911-17, 1930; Cubs 1918-26; Cardinals 1926-29.
How elected: 80.9 percent of vote.

ALEXANDER CARTWRIGHT ORGANIZER
Organized 1st baseball club in 1845.
Born: April 17, 1820. **Died:** July 12, 1892.
Career: Formed the Knickerbocker Ball Club in 1845 and taught the new game to Americans from coast to coast; served as unofficial ambassador for the game until his death.
How elected: Centennial Commission.

HENRY CHADWICK ORGANIZER
Known as "Father of Baseball."
Born: Oct. 5, 1824. **Died:** April 29, 1908.
Career: A longtime New York baseball writer and contributor to numerous statistical publications dealing with the game; longtime chairman of baseball's committee on rules and author of many significant rules changes during the game's formative years.
How elected: Centennial Commission.

WHO'S WHO

Pirates shortstop Honus Wagner was a member of baseball's first Hall of Fame class.

1939

CAP ANSON   1B
6-1, 227.
B: R. **T:** R.
Born: April 17, 1852.   **Died:** April 14, 1922.
Career: .329 avg.; 97 HR; 1,879 RBIs.
Team: Chicago (Nat.) 1876-97.
How elected: Committee old-time players and writers.

EDDIE COLLINS   2B
5-9, 175.
B: L. **T:** R.
Born: May 2, 1887.   **Died:** March 25, 1951.
Career: .333 avg.; 47 HR; 1,300 RBIs; 3,312 hits.
Teams: Athletics 1906-14; White Sox 1915-26;
Athletics 1927-30.
How elected: 77.7 percent of vote.

CHARLES COMISKEY   1B, MAN., EXEC.
Founder/owner of Chicago White Sox.
6-0, 180.
B: R. **T:** R.
Born: Aug. 15, 1859.   **Died:** Oct. 26, 1931.
Playing career: .264 avg.; 29 HR; revolutionized art of
playing first base by playing off the bag.
Managing career: 839-542, 12 years.
Teams: St. Louis (A.A.) 1882-89, 1891; Chicago (P.L.)
1890; Cincinnati (Nat.) 1892-94.
How elected: Committee old-time players and writers.

CANDY CUMMINGS   P
5-9, 120.
B: R. **T:** R.
Born: Oct. 17, 1948.   **Died:** May 17, 1924.
Career: 21-22; 2.78 ERA; credited with throwing
the first curveball.
Teams: Hartford (Nat.) 1876; Cincinnati (Nat.) 1877.
How elected: Committee old-time players and writers.

BUCK EWING   C, IF, MAN.
5-10, 188.
B: R. **T:** R.
Born: Oct. 27, 1859.   **Died:** Oct. 20, 1906.
Playing career: .303 avg.; 71 HR; 883 RBIs.
Managing career: 489-395, 7 years.
Teams (player): Troy (Nat.) 1880-82; New York (Nat.)
1883-89, 1891-92; New York (P.L.) 1890; Cleveland
(Nat.) 1893-94; Cincinnati (Nat.) 1895-97.
Teams (manager): New York (P.L.) 1890; Cincinnati
(Nat.) 1895-99; New York (Nat.) 1900.
How elected: Committee old-time players and writers.

LOU GEHRIG   1B
6-1, 200.
B: L. **T:** L.
Born: June 19, 1903.   **Died:** June 2, 1941.
Career: .340 avg.; 493 HR; 1,995 RBIs.
Team: Yankees 1923-39.
How elected: Special election Baseball Writers.

WILLIE KEELER   OF
5-4, 140.
B: L. **T:** L.
Born: March 3, 1872.   **Died:** Jan. 1, 1923.
Career: .341 avg.; 33 HR; 810 RBIs; 495 SB.
Teams: New York (Nat.) 1892-93, 1910; Brooklyn (Nat.)
1893, 1899-1902; Baltimore (Nat.) 1894-98;
Yankees 1903-09.
How elected: 75.5 percent of vote.

HOSS RADBOURN   P
5-9, 168.
B: R. **T:** R.
Born: Dec. 9, 1853.   **Died:** Feb. 5, 1897.
Career: 309-195; 2.67 ERA; 1,830 SO.
Teams: Providence (Nat.) 1881-85; Boston (Nat.) 1886-
90; Cincinnati (Nat.) 1891.
How elected: Committee old-time players and writers.

GEORGE SISLER   1B
5-11, 170.
B: L. **T:** L.
Born: March 24, 1893.   **Died:** March 26, 1973.
Career: .340 avg.; 102 HR; 1,175 RBIs.
Teams: Browns 1915-27; Senators 1928; Braves 1928-30.
How elected: 85.8 percent of vote.

AL SPALDING   P, MAN., OWNER
Founder A.G. Spalding & Bros. sporting goods.
6-1, 170.
B: R. **T:** R.
Born: Sept. 2, 1850.   **Died:** Sept. 9, 1915.
Career: 48-12; 1.78 ERA.
Team (player): Chicago (Nat.) 1876-77.
Team (manager): Chicago (Nat.) 1876-78.
Team (owner): Chicago (Nat.) 1882-91.
How elected: Committee old-time players and writers.

1942

ROGERS HORNSBY   2B
5-11, 200.
B: R. **T:** R.
Born: April 27, 1896.   **Died:** Jan. 5, 1963.
Career: .358 avg.; 301 HR; 1,584 RBIs.
Teams: Cardinals 1915-26, 1933; Giants 1927; Braves
1928; Cubs 1929-32; Browns 1933-37.
How elected: 78.1 percent of vote.

1944

KENESAW MOUNTAIN LANDIS   EXEC.
First baseball commissioner.
Born: Nov. 20, 1866.   **Died:** Nov. 25, 1944.
Career: Former U.S. District judge; became baseball's
first commissioner in 1921 and served until his death.
How elected: Committee on Old-Timers.

1945

ROGER BRESNAHAN   C
5-9, 190.
B: R. **T:** R.
Born: June 11, 1879.   **Died:** Dec. 4, 1944.
Career: .279 avg.; 26 HR; 530 RBIs; credited with intro-
ducing shinguards for catchers.
Teams: Washington (Nat.) 1897; Chicago (Nat.) 1900;
Orioles 1901-02; Giants 1902-08; Cardinals 1909-12;
Cubs 1913-15.
How elected: Committee on Old-Timers.

DAN BROUTHERS   1B
6-2, 200.
B: L. **T:** L.
Born: May 8, 1858.   **Died:** Aug. 3, 1932.
Career: .342 avg.; 106 HR; 1,296 RBIs.
Teams: Troy (Nat.) 1879-80; Buffalo (Nat.) 1881-85;
Detroit (Nat.) 1886-88; Boston (Nat.) 1889; Boston (P.L.)
1890; Boston (A.A.) 1891; Brooklyn (Nat.) 1892-93;
Baltimore (Nat.) 1894-95; Louisville (Nat.) 1895;
Philadelphia (Nat.) 1896; Giants 1904.
How elected: Committee on Old-Timers.

FRED CLARKE   OF, MAN.
5-10, 165.
B: L. **T:** R.
Born: Oct. 3, 1872.   **Died:** Aug. 14, 1960.
Playing career: .312 avg.; 67 HR; 1,015 RBIs.
Managing career: 1,602-1,181, 19 years.
Teams (player): Louisville (Nat.) 1894-99;
Pirates 1900-15.
Teams (manager): Louisville (Nat.) 1897-99;
Pirates 1900-15.
How elected: Committee on Old-Timers.

JIMMY COLLINS   3B
5-9, 178.
B: R. **T:** R.
Born: Jan. 16, 1873.   **Died:** March 6, 1943.
Career: .294 avg.; 65 HR; 983 RBIs.
Teams: Boston (Nat.) 1895, 1896-1900; Louisville 1895;
Red Sox 1901-07; Athletics 1907-08.
How elected: Committee on Old-Timers.

ED DELAHANTY   1B, OF
6-1, 170.
B: R. **T:** R.
Born: Oct. 30, 1867.   **Died:** July 2, 1903.
Career: .346 avg.; 101 HR; 1,464 RBIs.
Teams: Philadelphia (Nat.) 1888-89, 1891-1901;
Cleveland (P.L) 1890; Senators 1902-03.
How elected: Committee on Old-Timers.

HUGH DUFFY   OF
5-7, 168.
B: R. **T:** R.
Born: Nov. 26, 1866.   **Died:** Oct. 19, 1954.
Career: .324 avg.; 106 HR; 1,302 RBIs.
Teams: Chicago (Nat.) 1888-89; Chicago (P.L.) 1890;
Boston (A.A.) 1891; Boston (Nat.) 1892-1900;
Milwaukee (Amer.) 1901; Phillies 1904-06.
How elected: Committee on Old-Timers.

HUGH JENNINGS   IF
5-8, 165.
B: R. **T:** R.
Born: April 2, 1869.   **Died:** Feb. 1, 1928.
Career: .311 avg.; 18 HR; 840 RBIs.

Teams: Louisville (A.A.) 1891; Louisville (Nat.) 1892-93;
Baltimore (Nat.) 1893-99; Brooklyn (Nat.) 1899-1900,
1903; Phillies 1901-02; Tigers 1907-1909, 1912, 1918.
How elected: Committee on Old-Timers.

MIKE (KING) KELLY   C, IF
5-10, 180.
B: R. **T:** R.
Born: Dec. 31, 1857.   **Died:** Nov. 8, 1894.
Career: .308 avg.; 69 HR; 950 RBIs.
Teams: Cincinnati (Nat.) 1878-79; Chicago (Nat.) 1880-
86; Boston (Nat.) 1887-90, 1891-92; Cincinnati (A.A.)
1891; New York (Nat.) 1893.
How elected: Committee on Old-Timers.

JIM O'ROURKE   OF, IF
5-8, 185.
B: R. **T:** R.
Born: Aug. 24, 1852.   **Died:** Jan. 8, 1919.
Career: .310 avg.; 50 HR; 1,010 RBIs.
Teams: Boston (Nat.) 1876-78, 1880; Providence (Nat.)
1879; Buffalo (Nat.) 1881-84; New York (Nat.) 1885-89,
1891-92, 1904; New York (P.L.) 1890; Washington
(Nat.) 1893.
How elected: Committee on Old-Timers.

WILBERT ROBINSON   C, MAN.
5-8, 215.
B: R. **T:** R.
Born: June 2, 1864.   **Died:** Aug. 8, 1934.
Playing career: .273 avg.; 18 HR; 622 RBIs.
Managing career: 1,399-1,398, 19 years.
Teams (player): Philadelphia (A.A.) 1886-90; Baltimore
(A.A.) 1890-91; Baltimore (Nat.) 1892-99; St. Louis
(Nat.) 1900; Baltimore (Amer.) 1901-02.
Teams (manager): Baltimore (Amer.) 1902;
Dodgers 1914-31.
How elected: Committee on Old-Timers.

1946

JESSE BURKETT   OF
5-8, 155.
B: L. **T:** L.
Born: Dec. 4, 1868.   **Died:** May 27, 1953.
Career: .338 avg.; 75 HR; 952 RBIs.
Teams: New York (Nat.) 1890; Cleveland (Nat.) 1891-98;
St. Louis (Nat.) 1899-1901; Browns 1902-04;
Red Sox 1905.
How elected: Committee on Old-Timers.

FRANK CHANCE   1B, MAN.
6-0, 190.
B: R. **T:** R.
Born: Sept. 9, 1877.   **Died:** Sept. 15, 1924.
Playing career: .296 avg.; 20 HR; 596 RBIs.
Managing career: 946-648, 11 years.
Teams (player): Cubs 1898-1912; Yankees 1913-14.
Teams (manager): Cubs 1905-12; Yankees 1913-14;
Red Sox 1923.
How elected: Committee on Old-Timers.

JACK CHESBRO   P
5-9, 180.
B: R. **T:** R.
Born: June 5, 1874.   **Died:** Nov. 6, 1931.
Career: 198-132; 2.68 ERA; 1,265 SO.
Teams: Pirates 1899-1902; Yankees 1903-09;
Red Sox 1909.
How elected: Committee on Old-Timers.

JOHNNY EVERS   2B
5-9, 130.
B: R. **T:** R.
Born: July 21, 1881.   **Died:** March 28, 1947.
Career: .270 avg.; 12 HR; 538 RBIs.
Teams: Cubs 1902-13; Braves 1914-17, 1929; Phillies
1917; White Sox 1922.
How elected: Committee on Old-Timers.

CLARK GRIFFITH   P, MAN., EXEC.
5-7, 156.
B: R. **T:** R.
Born: Nov. 20, 1869.   **Died:** Oct. 27, 1955.
Playing career: 237-146; 3.31 ERA; 955 SO.
Managing career: 1,491-1,367, 20 years.
Teams (player): St. Louis (A.A.) 1891; Boston (A.A.)
1891; Chicago (Nat.) 1893-1900; White Sox 1901-02;
Yankees 1903-07; Reds 1909-10; Senators 1912-14.
Teams (manager): White Sox 1901-02; Yankees 1903-
08; Reds 1909-11; Senators 1912-20.
How elected: Committee on Old-Timers.

TOMMY McCARTHY OF, IF
5-7, 170. **B:** R. **T:** R.
Born: July 24, 1864 **Died:** Aug. 5, 1922.
Career: .292 avg.; 44 HR, 666 RBIs.
Teams: Boston (U.A.) 1884; Boston (Nat.) 1885; Philadelphia (Nat.) 1886-87; St. Louis (A.A.) 1888-91; Boston (Nat.) 1892-95; Brooklyn (Nat.) 1896.
How elected: Committee on Old-Timers.

JOE McGINNITY P
5-11, 206. **B:** R. **T:** R.
Born: March 19, 1871. **Died:** Nov. 14, 1929.
Career: 246-142; 2.66 ERA; 1,068 SO.
Teams: Baltimore (Nat.) 1899; Brooklyn (Nat.) 1900; Orioles 1901-02; Giants 1902-08.
How elected: Committee on Old-Timers.

EDDIE PLANK P
5-11, 175. **B:** L. **T:** L.
Born: Aug. 31, 1875. **Died:** Feb. 24, 1926.
Career: 326-194; 2.35 ERA; 2,246 SO.
Teams: Athletics 1901-14; St. Louis (Fed.) 1915; Browns 1916-17.
How elected: Committee on Old-Timers.

JOE TINKER SS
5-9, 175. **B:** R. **T:** R.
Born: July 27, 1880. **Died:** July 27, 1948.
Career: .262 avg.; 31 HR; 782 RBIs.
Teams: Cubs 1902-13, 1916; Chicago (Fed.) 1914-15.
How elected: Committee on Old-Timers.

RUBE WADDELL P
6-1, 196.
Born: Oct. 13, 1876. **Died:** April 1, 1914.
Career: 193-143; 2.16 ERA; 2,316 SO.
Teams: Louisville (Nat.) 1897, 1899; Pirates 1900-01; Cubs 1901; Athletics 1902-07; Browns 1908-10.
How elected: Committee on Old-Timers.

ED WALSH P
6-1, 193. **B:** R. **T:** R.
Born: May 14, 1881. **Died:** May 26, 1959.
Career: 195-126; 1.82 ERA; 1,736 SO.
Teams: White Sox 1904-16; Braves 1917.
How elected: Committee on Old-Timers.

1947

MICKEY COCHRANE C
5-10, 180. **B:** L. **T:** R.
Born: April 6, 1903. **Died:** June 28, 1962.
Career: .320 avg.; 119 HR; 832 RBIs.
Teams: Athletics 1925-33; Tigers 1934-37.
How elected: 79.5 percent of vote.

FRANK FRISCH 2B, MAN.
5-11, 165. **B:** B. **T:** R.
Born: Sept. 9, 1898. **Died:** March 12, 1973.
Playing career: .316 avg.; 105 HR; 1,244 RBIs.
Managing career: 1,138-1,078, 16 years.
Teams (player): Giants 1919-26; Cardinals 1927-37.
Teams (manager): Cardinals 1933-38; Pirates 1940-46; Cubs 1949-51.
How elected: 84.5 percent of vote.

LEFTY GROVE P
6-3, 200. **B:** L. **T:** L.
Born: March 6, 1900. **Died:** May 22, 1975.
Career: 300-141; 3.06 ERA; 2,266 SO.
Teams: Athletics 1925-33; Red Sox 1934-41.
How elected: 76.4 percent of vote.

CARL HUBBELL P
6-0, 170. **B:** R. **T:** L.
Born: June 22, 1903. **Died:** Nov. 21, 1988.
Career: 253-154; 2.98 ERA; 1,677 SO.
Teams: Giants 1928-43.
How elected: 87 percent of vote.

1948

HERB PENNOCK P
6-0, 160. **B:** B. **T:** L.
Born: Feb. 10, 1894. **Died:** Jan. 30, 1948.

Career: 240-162; 3.60 ERA; 1,227 SO.
Teams: Athletics 1912-15; Red Sox 1915-22; Yankees 1923-33; Red Sox 1934.
How elected: 77.7 percent of vote.

PIE TRAYNOR 3B
6-0, 170. **B:** R. **T:** R.
Born: Nov. 11, 1899. **Died:** March 16, 1972.
Career: .320 avg.; 58 HR; 1,273 RBIs.
Team: Pirates 1920-37.
How elected: 76.9 percent of vote.

1949

MORDECAI (THREE FINGER) BROWN P
5-10, 175. **B:** B. **T:** R.
Born: Oct. 19, 1876. **Died:** Feb. 14, 1948.
Career: 239-130; 2.06 ERA; 1,375 SO.
Teams: Cardinals 1903; Cubs 1904-12, 1916; Reds 1913; St. Louis (Fed.) 1914; Brooklyn (Fed.) 1914; Chicago (Fed.) 1915.
How elected: Committee on Old-Timers.

CHARLEY GEHRINGER 2B
5-11, 180. **B:** L. **T:** R.
Born: May 11, 1903. **Died:** Jan. 21, 1993.
Career: .320 avg.; 184 HR; 1,427 RBIs.
Team: Tigers 1924-42.
How elected: 85 percent of vote.

KID NICHOLS P
5-10, 175. **B:** R. **T:** R.
Born: Sept. 14, 1869. **Died:** April 11, 1953.
Career: 361-208; 2.95 ERA; 1,868 SO.
Teams: Boston (Nat.) 1890-1901; Cardinals 1904-05; Phillies 1905-06.
How elected: Committee on Old-Timers.

1951

JIMMIE FOXX C, 3B, 1B
6-0, 195. **B:** R. **T:** R.
Born: Oct. 22, 1907. **Died:** July 21, 1967.
Career: .325 avg.; 534 HR; 1,922 RBIs.
Teams: Athletics 1925-35; Red Sox 1936-42; Cubs 1942, 1944; Phillies 1945.
How elected: 79.2 percent of vote.

MEL OTT OF
5-9, 170. **B:** L. **T:** R.
Born: March 2, 1909. **Died:** Nov. 21, 1958.
Career: .304 avg.; 511 HR; 1,860 RBIs.
Team: Giants 1926-47.
How elected: 87.2 percent of vote.

1952

HARRY HEILMANN OF, 1B
6-1, 195. **B:** R. **T:** R.
Born: Aug. 3, 1894. **Died:** July 9, 1951.
Career: .342 avg.; 183 HR; 1,539 RBIs.
Teams: Tigers 1914-29; Reds 1930-32.
How elected: 86.8 percent of vote.

PAUL WANER OF
5-8, 153. **B:** L. **T:** L.
Born: April 16, 1903. **Died:** Aug. 29, 1965.
Career: .333 avg.; 113 HR; 1,309 RBIs; 3,152 hits.
Teams: Pirates 1926-40; Dodgers 1941, 1943-44; Braves 1941-42; Yankees 1944-45.
How elected: 83.3 percent of vote.

1953

ED BARROW MAN., EXEC.
Born: May 10, 1868. **Died:** Dec. 15, 1953.
Managing career: 310-320, 5 years.
Executive career: Architect of Yankees dynasty that produced 14 A.L. pennants and 10 World Series championships as business manager and president from 1921-45; managed Red Sox to 1918 World Series title and started conversion of Babe Ruth from a pitcher to an outfielder.
How elected: Committee on Veterans.

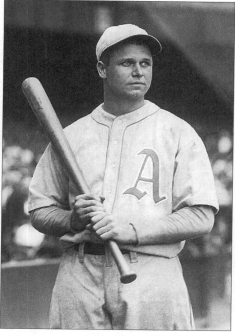

Athletics slugger Jimmie Foxx was the second player to reach the 500-home run plateau.

CHIEF BENDER P
6-2, 185. **B:** R. **T:** R.
Born: May 5, 1884. **Died:** May 22, 1954.
Career: 212-127; 2.46 ERA; 1,711 SO.
Teams: Athletics 1903-14; Baltimore (Fed.) 1915; Phillies 1916-17; White Sox 1925.
How elected: Committee on Veterans.

TOMMY CONNOLLY UMPIRE
Born: Dec. 31, 1870. **Died:** April 28, 1961.
Career: Umpired from 1901, the A.L.'s first season, until 1931; served as A.L. umpires' chief of staff until retirement in 1954; an influential member of baseball's rules committee for many years.
How elected: Committee on Veterans.

DIZZY DEAN P
6-2, 200. **B:** R. **T:** R.
Born: Jan. 16, 1911. **Died:** July 17, 1974.
Career: 150-83; 3.03 ERA; 1,155 SO.
Teams: Cardinals 1930, 1932-37; Cubs 1938-41; Browns 1947.
How elected: 79.2 percent of vote.

BILL KLEM UMPIRE
Born: Feb. 22, 1874. **Died:** Sept. 1, 1951.
Career: Joined N.L. as an umpire in 1905 and served with distinction until 1941; called 18 World Series, more than any other umpire; served as N.L. umpires' chief of staff from 1941 until death; responsible for many umpiring innovations; generally considered the greatest arbiter of all time.
How elected: Committee on Veterans.

AL SIMMONS OF
5-11, 190. **B:** R. **T:** R.
Born: May 22, 1902. **Died:** May 26, 1956.
Career: .334 avg.; 307 HR; 1,827 RBIs.
Teams: Athletics 1924-32, 1940-41, 1944; White Sox 1933-35; Tigers 1936; Senators 1937-38; Braves 1939; Reds 1939; Red Sox 1943.
How elected: 75.4 percent of vote.

BOBBY WALLACE SS
5-8, 170. **B:** R. **T:** R.
Born: Nov. 4, 1874. **Died:** Nov. 3, 1960.
Career: .268 avg.; 34 HR; 1,121 RBIs.
Teams: Cleveland (Nat.) 1894-98; St. Louis (Nat.) 1899-1901, 1917-18; Browns 1902-16;
How elected: Committee on Veterans.

HARRY WRIGHT   MANAGER
Born: Jan. 10, 1835.   Died: Oct. 3, 1895.
Career: 933-660, 18 years.
Teams: Boston (Nat.) 1876-81; Providence (Nat.) 1882-83; Philadelphia (Nat.) 1884-93.
How elected: Committee on Veterans.

1954

BILL DICKEY   C
6-1, 185.   B: L. T: R.
Born: June 6, 1907.   Died: Nov. 12, 1993.
Career: .313 avg.; 202 HR; 1,210 RBIs.
Teams: Yankees 1928-43, 1946.
How elected: 80.2 percent of vote.

RABBIT MARANVILLE   SS
5-5, 155.   B: R. T: R.
Born: Nov. 11, 1891.   Died: Jan. 5, 1954.
Career: .258 avg.; 28 HR; 884 RBIs.
Teams: Braves 1912-20, 1929-35; Pirates 1921-24; Cubs 1925; Dodgers 1926; Cardinals 1927-28.
How elected: 82.9 percent of vote.

BILL TERRY   1B, MAN.
6-1, 200.   B: L. T: L.
Born: Oct. 30, 1898.   Died: Jan. 9, 1989.
Playing career: .341 avg.; 154 HR; 1,078 RBIs.
Managing career: 823-661, 10 years.
Team (player): Giants 1923-36.
Team (manager): Giants 1932-41.
How elected: 77.4 percent of vote.

1955

FRANK (HOME RUN) BAKER   3B
5-11, 173.   B: L. T: R.
Born: March 13, 1886.   Died: June 28, 1963.
Career: .307 avg.; 96 HR; 987 RBIs.
Teams: Athletics 1908-14; Yankees 1916-19, 1921-22.
How elected: Committee on Veterans.

JOE DiMAGGIO   OF
6-2, 193.   B: R. T: R.
Born: Nov. 25, 1914.   Died: March 8, 1999.
Career: .325 avg.; 361 HR; 1,537 RBIs.
Team: Yankees 1936-42, 1946-51.
How elected: 88.8 percent of vote.

GABBY HARTNETT   C
6-1, 200.   B: R. T: R.
Born: Dec. 20, 1900.   Died: Dec. 20, 1972.
Career: .297 avg.; 236 HR; 1,179 RBIs.
Teams: Cubs 1922-40; Giants 1941.
How elected: 77.7 percent of vote.

TED LYONS   P
5-11, 200.   B: B. T: R.
Born: Dec. 28, 1900.   Died: July 25, 1986.
Career: 260-230; 3.67 ERA; 1,073 SO.
Team: White Sox 1923-42, 1946.
How elected: 86.5 percent of vote.

RAY SCHALK   C
5-9, 165.   B: R. T: R.
Born: Aug. 12, 1892.   Died: May 19, 1970.
Career: .253 avg.; 11 HR; 594 RBIs.
Teams: White Sox 1912-28; Giants 1929.
How elected: Committee on Veterans.

DAZZY VANCE   P
6-2, 200.   B: R. T: R.
Born: March 4, 1891.   Died: Feb. 16, 1961.
Career: 197-140; 3.24 ERA; 2,045 SO.
Teams: Pirates 1915; Yankees 1915, 1918; Dodgers 1922-32, 1935; Cardinals 1933, 1934; Reds 1934.
How elected: 81.7 percent of vote.

1956

JOE CRONIN   IF, MAN., EXEC.
6-0, 180.   B: R. T: R.
Born: Oct. 12, 1906.   Died: Sept. 7, 1984.
Playing career: .301 avg.; 170 HR; 1,424 RBIs.

Managing career: 1,236-1,055, 15 years.
Teams (player): Pirates 1926-27; Senators 1928-34; Red Sox 1935-45.
Teams (manager): Senators 1933-34; Red Sox 1935-47.
Executive career: President of A.L. 1959-73.
How elected: 78.8 percent of vote.

HANK GREENBERG   1B, OF
6-3, 210.   B: R. T: R.
Born: Jan. 1, 1911.   Died: Sept. 4, 1986.
Career: .313 avg.; 331 HR; 1,276 RBIs.
Teams: Tigers 1930, 1933-41, 1945-46; Pirates 1947.
How elected: 85.0 percent of vote.

1957

SAM CRAWFORD   OF
6-0, 190.   B: L. T: L.
Born: April 18, 1880.   Died: June 15, 1968.
Career: .309 avg.; 98 HR; 1,525 RBIs.
Teams: Reds 1899-1902; Tigers 1903-17.
How elected: Committee on Veterans.

JOE McCARTHY   MANAGER
Born: April 21, 1887.   Died: Jan. 13, 1978.
Career: 2,125-1,333, 24 years; 7 World Series championships.
Teams: Cubs 1926-30; Yankees 1931-46; Red Sox 1948-50.
How elected: Committee on Veterans.

1959

ZACK WHEAT   OF
5-10, 170.   B: L. T: R.
Born: May 23, 1888.   Died: March 11, 1972.
Career: .317 avg.; 132 HR; 1,248 RBIs.
Teams: Dodgers 1909-26; Athletics 1927.
How elected: Committee on Veterans.

1961

MAX CAREY   OF
5-11, 170.   B: B. T: R.
Born: Jan. 11, 1890.   Died: May 30, 1976.
Career: .285 avg.; 69 HR; 800 RBIs.
Teams: Pirates 1910-26; Dodgers 1926-29.
How elected: Committee on Veterans.

BILLY HAMILTON   OF
5-6, 165.   B: L. T: R.
Born: Feb. 16, 1866.   Died: Dec. 16, 1940.
Career: .344 avg.; 40 HR; 736 RBIs; 912 SB.
Teams: Kansas City (A.A.) 1888-89; Philadelphia (Nat.) 1890-95; Boston (Nat.) 1896-1901.
How elected: Committee on Veterans.

1962

BOB FELLER   P
6-0, 185.   B: R. T: R.
Born: Nov. 3, 1918.
Career: 266-162; 3.25 ERA; 2,581 SO.
Team: Indians 1936-41, 1945-56.
How elected: 93.8 percent of vote.

BILL McKECHNIE   MANAGER
Born: Aug. 7, 1887.   Died: Oct. 29, 1965.
Career: 1,896-1,723, 25 years; 2 World Series championships.
Teams: Newark (Fed.) 1915; Pirates 1922-26; Cardinals 1928-29; Braves 1930-37; Reds 1938-46.
How elected: Committee on Veterans.

JACKIE ROBINSON   IF
5-11, 195.   B: R. T: R.
Born: Jan. 31, 1919.   Died: Oct. 24, 1972.
Career: .311 avg.; 137 HR; 734 RBIs.
Team: Dodgers 1947-56.
How elected: 77.5 percent of vote.

EDD ROUSH   OF
5-11, 170.   B: L. T: L.
Born: May 8, 1893.   Died: March 21, 1988.

Career: .323 avg.; 67 HR; 981 RBIs.
Teams: White Sox 1913; Indianapolis (Fed.) 1914; Newark (Fed.) 1915; Giants 1916, 1927-29; Reds 1916-26, 1931.
How elected: Committee on Veterans.

1963

JOHN CLARKSON   P
5-10, 165.   B: R. T: R.
Born: July 1, 1861.   Died: Feb. 4, 1909.
Career: 328-178; 2.81 ERA; 1,978 SO.
Teams: Worcester (Nat.) 1882; Chicago (Nat.) 1884-87; Boston (Nat.) 1888-92; Cleveland (Nat.) 1892-94.
How elected: Committee on Veterans.

ELMER FLICK   OF
5-9, 168.   B: L. T: R.
Born: Jan. 11, 1876.   Died: Jan. 9, 1971.
Career: .313 avg.; 48 HR; 756 RBIs.
Teams: Philadelphia (Nat.) 1898-1902; Indians 1902-10.
How elected: Committee on Veterans.

SAM RICE   OF
5-9, 150.   B: L. T: L.
Born: Feb. 20, 1890.   Died: Oct. 13, 1974.
Career: .322 avg.; 34 HR; 1,078 RBIs.
Teams: Senators 1915-33; Indians 1934.
How elected: Committee on Veterans.

EPPA RIXEY   P
6-5, 210.   B: R. T: L.
Born: May 3, 1891.   Died: Feb. 28, 1963.
Career: 266-251; 3.15 ERA; 1,350 SO.
Teams: Phillies 1912-1917, 1919-20; Reds 1921-33.
How elected: Committee on Veterans.

1964

LUKE APPLING   SS
5-10, 183.   B: R. T: R.
Born: April 2, 1907.   Died: Jan. 3, 1991.
Career: .310 avg.; 45 HR; 1,116 RBIs.
Team: White Sox 1930-43, 1945-50.
How elected: 84 percent of vote.

RED FABER   P
6-2, 180.   B: B. T: R.
Born: Sept. 6, 1888.   Died: Sept. 25, 1976.
Career: 254-213; 3.15 ERA; 1,471 SO.
Team: White Sox 1914-33.
How elected: Committee on Veterans.

BURLEIGH GRIMES   P
5-10, 175.   B: R. T: R.
Born: Aug. 18, 1893.   Died: Dec. 6, 1985.
Career: 270-212; 3.53 ERA; 1,512 SO.
Teams: Pirates 1916-17, 1928-29, 1934; Dodgers 1918-26; Giants 1927; Braves 1930; Cardinals 1930-31, 1933-34; Cubs 1932-33; Yankees 1934.
How elected: Committee on Veterans.

MILLER HUGGINS   MANAGER
Born: March 27, 1880.   Died: Sept. 25, 1929.
Career: 1,413-1,134, 17 years.
Teams: Cardinals 1913-17; Yankees 1918-29.
How elected: Committee on Veterans.

TIM KEEFE   P
5-10, 185.   B: R. T: R.
Born: Jan. 1, 1857.   Died: April 23, 1933.
Career: 342-225; 2.62 ERA; 2,527 SO.
Teams: Troy (Nat.) 1880-82; Metropolitan (A.A.) 1883-84; New York (Nat.) 1885-91; Philadelphia (Nat.) 1891-93.
How elected: Committee on Veterans.

HEINIE MANUSH   OF
6-1, 200.   B: L. T: L.
Born: July 20, 1901.   Died: May 12, 1971.
Career: .330 avg.; 110 HR; 1,183 RBIs.
Teams: Tigers 1923-27; Browns 1928-30; Senators 1930-35; Red Sox 1936; Dodgers 1937-38; Pirates 1938-39.
How elected: Committee on Veterans.

JOHN MONTGOMERY WARD   IF, P
5-9, 165.   **B:** L. **T:** R.
Born: March 3, 1860.   **Died:** March 4, 1925.
Playing career: .275 avg.; 26 HR; 867 RBIs.
Pitching career: 164-102; 2.10 ERA; 920 SO.
Teams: Providence (Nat.) 1878-82; New York (Nat.) 1883-89, 1893-94; Brooklyn 1890-92.
How elected: Committee on Veterans.

1965

PUD GALVIN   P
5-8, 190.   **B:** R. **T:** R.
Born: Dec. 25, 1856.   **Died:** March 7, 1902.
Career: 360-308; 2.87 ERA; 1,799 SO.
Teams: Buffalo (Nat.) 1879-85; Allegheny (A.A.) 1885-86; Pittsburgh (Nat.) 1887-89, 1891-92; Pittsburgh (P.L.) 1890; St. Louis (Nat.) 1892.
How elected: Committee on Veterans.

1966

CASEY STENGEL   OF, MAN.
5-11, 175.   **B:** L. **T:** L.
Born: July 30, 1890.   **Died:** Sept. 29, 1975.
Playing career: .284 avg.; 60 HR; 535 RBIs.
Managing career: 1,905-1,842, 25 years; 7 World Series championships.
Teams (player): Dodgers 1912-17; Pirates 1918-19; Phillies 1920-21; Giants 1921-23; Braves 1924-25.
Teams (manager): Dodgers 1934-36; Braves 1938-43; Yankees 1949-60; Mets 1962-65.
How elected: Committee on Veterans.

TED WILLIAMS   OF
6-3, 205.   **B:** L. **T:** R.
Born: Aug. 30, 1918.
Career: .344 avg.; 521 HR; 1,839 RBIs.
Team: Red Sox 1939-42, 1946-60.
How elected: 93.4 percent of vote.

1967

BRANCH RICKEY   EXECUTIVE
Born: Dec. 20, 1881.   **Died:** Dec. 9, 1965.
Career: Began baseball association as a minor league catcher in 1903 and played briefly for the Cardinals in three seasons; advanced through the chains of the Browns, Cardinals, Dodgers and Pirates in various front-office positions; introduced concept of a farm system as a member of Cardinals organization; broke baseball's color barrier when he brought Jackie Robinson to the Dodgers in 1947.
How elected: Committee on Veterans.

RED RUFFING   P
6-1, 205.   **B:** R. **T:** R.
Born: May 5, 1905.   **Died:** Feb. 17, 1986.
Career: 273-225; 3.80 ERA; 1,987 SO.
Teams: Red Sox 1924-30; Yankees 1930-42, 1945-46; White Sox 1947.
How elected: 86.9 percent of vote.

LLOYD WANER   OF
5-9, 150.   **B:** L. **T:** R.
Born: March 16, 1906.   **Died:** July 22, 1982.
Career: .316 avg.; 27 HR; 598 RBIs.
Teams: Pirates 1927-41, 1944-45; Braves 1941; Reds 1941; Phillies 1942; Dodgers 1944.
How elected: Committee on Veterans.

1968

KIKI CUYLER   OF
5-10, 180.   **B:** R. **T:** R.
Born: Aug. 30, 1899.   **Died:** Feb. 11, 1950.
Career: .321 avg.; 128 HR; 1,065 RBIs.
Teams: Pirates 1921-27; Cubs 1928-35; Reds 1935-37; Dodgers 1938.
How elected: Committee on Veterans.

GOOSE GOSLIN   OF
5-11, 185.   **B:** L. **T:** R.
Born: Oct. 16, 1900.   **Died:** May 15, 1971.
Career: .316 avg.; 248 HR; 1,609 RBIs.
Teams: Senators 1921-30, 1933, 1938; Browns 1930-32; Tigers 1934-37.
How elected: Committee on Veterans.

JOE MEDWICK   OF
5-10, 187.   **B:** R. **T:** R.
Born: Nov. 24, 1911.   **Died:** March 21, 1975.
Career: .324 avg.; 205 HR; 1,383 RBIs.
Teams: Cardinals 1932-40, 1947-48; Dodgers 1940-43, 1946; Giants 1943-45; Braves 1945.
How elected: 84.8 percent of vote.

1969

ROY CAMPANELLA   C
5-9, 200.   **B:** R. **T:** R.
Born: Nov. 19, 1921.   **Died:** June 26, 1993.
Career: .276 avg.; 242 HR; 856 RBIs.
Team: Dodgers 1948-57.
How elected: 79.4 percent of vote.

STAN COVELESKI   P
5-11, 166.   **B:** R. **T:** R.
Born: July 13, 1890.   **Died:** March 20, 1984.
Career: 215-142; 2.89 ERA; 981 SO.
Teams: Athletics 1912; Indians 1916-24; Senators 1925-27; Yankees 1928.
How elected: Committee on Veterans.

WAITE HOYT   P
6-0, 180.   **B:** R. **T:** R.
Born: Sept. 9, 1899.   **Died:** Aug. 25, 1984.
Career: 237-182; 3.59 ERA; 1,206 SO.
Teams: Giants 1918, 1932; Red Sox 1919-20; Yankees 1921-30; Tigers 1930-31; Athletics 1931; Dodgers 1932, 1937-38; Pirates 1933-37.
How elected: Committee on Veterans.

STAN MUSIAL   OF, 1B
6-0, 175.   **B:** L. **T:** L.
Born: Nov. 21, 1920.
Career: .331 avg.; 475 HR; 1,951 RBIs; 3,630 hits.
Team: Cardinals 1941-44, 1946-63.
How elected: 93.2 percent of vote.

1970

LOU BOUDREAU   SS, MAN.
5-11, 185.   **B:** R. **T:** R.
Born: July 17, 1917.
Playing career: .295 avg.; 68 HR; 789 RBIs.
Managing career: 1,162-1,224, 16 years.
Teams (player): Indians 1938-50; Red Sox 1951-52.
Teams (manager): Indians 1942-50; Red Sox 1952-54; Athletics 1955-57; Cubs 1960.
How elected: 77.3 percent of vote.

EARLE COMBS   OF
6-0, 185.   **B:** L. **T:** R.
Born: May 14, 1899.   **Died:** July 21, 1976.
Career: .325 avg.; 58 HR; 632 RBIs.
Team: Yankees 1924-35.
How elected: Committee on Veterans.

FORD FRICK   EXECUTIVE
Baseball's third commissioner.
Born: Dec. 19, 1894.   **Died:** April 8, 1978.
Career: Newspaper reporter and sportswriter; N.L. president from 1934-51; elected as baseball's third commissioner following resignation of Happy Chandler in 1951; served until retirement Dec. 14, 1965.
How elected: Committee on Veterans.

JESSE HAINES   P
6-0, 190.   **B:** R. **T:** R.
Born: July 22, 1893.   **Died:** Aug. 5, 1978.
Career: 210-158; 3.64 ERA; 981 SO.
Teams: Reds 1918; Cardinals 1920-37.
How elected: Committee on Veterans.

Red Sox left fielder Ted Williams compiled a lofty .344 career batting average.

1971

DAVE BANCROFT   SS
5-9, 160.   **B:** B. **T:** R.
Born: April 20, 1892.   **Died:** Oct. 9, 1972.
Career: .279 avg.; 32 HR; 591 RBIs.
Teams: Phillies 1915-20; Giants 1920-23, 1930; Braves 1924-27; Dodgers 1928-29.
How elected: Committee on Veterans.

JAKE BECKLEY   1B
5-10, 200.   **B:** L. **T:** L.
Born: Aug. 4, 1867.   **Died:** June 25, 1918.
Career: .308 avg.; 86 HR; 1,575 RBIs.
Teams: Pittsburgh (Nat.) 1888-89, 1891-96; Pittsburgh (P.L.) 1890; New York (Nat.) 1896-97; Cincinnati (Nat.) 1897-1903; Cardinals 1904-07.
How elected: Committee on Veterans.

CHICK HAFEY   OF
6-0, 185.   **B:** R. **T:** R.
Born: Feb. 12, 1903.   **Died:** July 2, 1973.
Career: .317 avg.; 164 HR; 833 RBIs.
Teams: Cardinals 1924-31; Reds 1932-35, 1937.
How elected: Committee on Veterans.

HARRY HOOPER   OF
5-10, 168.   **B:** L. **T:** R.
Born: Aug. 24, 1887.   **Died:** Dec. 18, 1974.
Career: .281 avg.; 75 HR; 817 RBIs.
Teams: Red Sox 1909-20; White Sox 1921-25.
How elected: Committee on Veterans.

JOE KELLEY   OF
5-11, 190.   **B:** R. **T:** R.
Born: Dec. 9, 1871.   **Died:** Aug. 14, 1943.
Career: .317 avg.; 65 HR; 1,194 RBIs.
Teams: Boston (Nat.) 1891; Pittsburgh (Nat.) 1891-92; Baltimore (Nat.) 1892-98; Brooklyn (Nat.) 1899-1901; Orioles 1902; Reds 1902-06; Braves 1908.
How elected: Committee on Veterans.

RUBE MARQUARD   P
6-3, 180.   **B:** B. **T:** L.
Born: Oct. 9, 1889.   **Died:** June 1, 1980.
Career: 201-177; 3.08 ERA; 1,593 SO.
Teams: Giants 1908-15; Dodgers 1915-20; Reds 1921; Braves 1922-25.
How elected: Committee on Veterans.

SATCHEL PAIGE   P
6-3, 180.   **B:** R. **T:** R.
Born: July 7, 1906.   **Died:** June 8, 1982.
Career: 28-31; 3.29 ERA; 290 SO.
Teams: Indians 1948-49; Browns 1951-53; Athletics 1965.
How elected: Special Committee on Negro Leagues.

GEORGE WEISS   **EXECUTIVE**
Born: June 23, 1895. **Died:** Aug. 13, 1972.
Career: Joined Yankees as farm director in 1932 after impressive career as minor league executive; built Yankees farm system that stocked pennant-winning machines of the 1930s, '40s and '50s; became general manager in 1948 and led Yankees to 10 pennants and seven World Series championships in 13 seasons; the man who hired Casey Stengel as manager; president of the expansion Mets from 1961-66.
How elected: Committee on Veterans.

1972

YOGI BERRA   **C**
5-8, 194.   **B:** L. **T:** R.
Born: May 12, 1925.
Career: .285 avg.; 358 HR; 1,430 RBIs.
Teams: Yankees 1946-63; Mets 1965.
How elected: 85.6 percent of vote.

JOSH GIBSON   **C**
6-1, 215.   **B:** R. **T:** R.
Born: Dec. 21, 1911. **Died:** Jan. 20, 1947.
Career: Negro League star; statistics not available.
How elected: Special Committee on Negro Leagues.

LEFTY GOMEZ   **P**
6-2, 173.   **B:** L. **T:** L.
Born: Nov. 26, 1910. **Died:** Feb. 17, 1989.
Career: 189-102; 3.34 ERA; 1,468 SO.
Teams: Yankees 1930-42; Senators 1943.
How elected: Committee on Veterans.

WILL HARRIDGE   **EXECUTIVE**
Born: Oct. 16, 1883. **Died:** April 9, 1971.
Career: Private secretary to A.L. President Ban Johnson; A.L. secretary after Johnson's retirement; became A.L. president when Ernest Barnard died suddenly in 1931; served with distinction until retirement in 1958.
How elected: Committee on Veterans.

SANDY KOUFAX   **P**
6-2, 210.   **B:** R. **T:** L.
Born: Dec. 30, 1935.
Career: 165-87; 2.76 ERA; 2,396 SO.
Team: Dodgers 1955-66.
How elected: 86.9 percent of vote.

WALTER (BUCK) LEONARD   **1B**
5-10, 185   **B:** L. **T:** L.
Born: Sept. 8, 1907. **Died:** Nov. 27, 1997.
Career: Negro League star; statistics not available.
How elected: Special Committee on Negro Leagues.

EARLY WYNN   **P**
6-0, 200.   **B:** B. **T:** R.
Born: Jan. 6, 1920. **Died:** April 4, 1999.
Career: 300-244; 3.54 ERA; 2,334 SO.
Teams: Senators 1939, 1941-44, 1946-48; Indians 1949-57, 1963; White Sox 1958-62.
How elected: 76.0 percent of vote.

ROSS YOUNGS   **OF**
5-8, 162.   **B:** B. **T:** R.
Born: April 10, 1897. **Died:** Oct. 22, 1927.
Career: .322 avg.; 42 HR; 592 RBIs.
Team: Giants 1917-26.
How elected: Committee on Veterans.

1973

ROBERTO CLEMENTE   **OF**
5-11, 175.   **B:** R. **T:** R.
Born: Aug. 18, 1934. **Died:** Dec. 31, 1972.
Career: .317 avg.; 240 HR; 1,305 RBIs; 3,000 hits.
Team: Pirates 1955-72.
How elected: 92.7 percent of vote.

BILLY EVANS   **UMPIRE**
Born: Feb. 10, 1884. **Died:** Jan. 23, 1956.
Career: A.L. umpire from 1906-27; considered a master of the rules book and an expert at rules applications on tricky plays; front-office executive for the Indians,

Red Sox and Tigers; president of Southern League from 1942-46.
How elected: Committee on Veterans.

MONTE IRVIN   **OF**
6-1, 195.   **B:** R. **T:** R.
Born: Feb. 25, 1919.
Career: .293 avg.; 99 HR; 443 RBIs; Negro League statistics not available.
Teams: Giants 1949-55; Cubs 1956.
How elected: Special Committee on Negro Leagues.

GEORGE KELLY   **1B**
6-4, 190.   **B:** R. **T:** R.
Born: Sept. 10, 1895. **Died:** Oct. 13, 1984.
Career: .297 avg.; 148 HR; 1,020 RBIs.
Teams: Giants 1915-17, 1919-26; Pirates 1917; Reds 1927-30; Cubs 1930; Dodgers 1932.
How elected: Committee on Veterans.

WARREN SPAHN   **P**
6-0, 175.   **B:** L. **T:** L.
Born: April 23, 1921.
Career: 363-245; 3.09 ERA; 2,583 SO.
Teams: Braves 1942, 1946-64; Mets 1965; Giants 1965.
How elected: 83.2 percent of vote.

MICKEY WELCH   **P**
5-8, 160.   **B:** R. **T:** R.
Born: July 4, 1859. **Died:** July 30, 1941.
Career: 307-210; 2.71 ERA; 1,850 SO.
Teams: Troy (Nat.) 1880-82; New York (Nat.) 1883-92.
How elected: Committee on Veterans.

1974

COOL PAPA BELL   **OF**
6-0, 143.   **B:** B. **T:** L.
Born: May 17, 1903. **Died:** March 7, 1991.
Career: Negro League star; statistics not available.
How elected: Special Committee on Negro Leagues.

JIM BOTTOMLEY   **1B**
6-0, 180.   **B:** L. **T:** L.
Born: April 23, 1900. **Died:** Dec. 11, 1959.
Career: .310 avg.; 219 HR; 1,422 RBIs.
Teams: Cardinals 1922-32; Reds 1933-35; Browns 1936-37.
How elected: Committee on Veterans.

JOCKO CONLAN   **UMPIRE**
Born: Dec. 6, 1899. **Died:** April 1, 1989.
Career: N.L. umpire from 1941-64; worked 5 World Series and 6 All-Star Games; a master of the rules book known for fair and impartial decisions.
How elected: Committee on Veterans.

WHITEY FORD   **P**
5-10, 181.   **B:** L. **T:** L.
Born: Oct. 21, 1928.
Career: 236-106; 2.75 ERA; 1,956 SO.
Team: Yankees 1950, 1953-67.
How elected: 77.8 percent of vote.

MICKEY MANTLE   **OF**
6-0, 198.   **B:** B. **T:** R.
Born: Oct. 20, 1931. **Died:** Aug. 13, 1995.
Career: .298 avg.; 536 HR; 1,509 RBIs.
Team: Yankees 1951-68.
How elected: 88.2 percent of vote.

SAM THOMPSON   **OF**
6-2, 207.   **B:** L. **T:** L.
Born: March 5, 1860. **Died:** Nov. 7, 1922.
Career: .331 avg.; 127 HR; 1,299 RBIs.
Teams: Detroit (Nat.) 1885-88; Philadelphia (Nat.) 1889-98; Tigers 1906.
How elected: Committee on Veterans.

1975

EARL AVERILL   **OF**
5-9, 172.   **B:** L. **T:** R.
Born: May 21, 1902. **Died:** Aug. 16, 1983.
Career: .318 avg.; 238 HR; 1,164 RBIs.

Teams: Indians 1929-39; Tigers 1939-40; Braves 1941.
How elected: Committee on Veterans.

BUCKY HARRIS   **2B, MAN.**
5-9, 156.   **B:** R. **T:** R.
Born: Nov. 8, 1896. **Died:** Nov. 8, 1977.
Playing career: .274 avg.; 9 HR; 506 RBIs.
Managing career: 2,157-2,218, 29 years; 2 World Series championships.
Teams (player): Senators 1919-28; Tigers 1929, 1931.
Teams (manager): Senators 1924-28, 1935-42, 1950-54; Tigers 1929-33, 1955-56; Red Sox 1934; Phillies 1943; Yankees 1947-48.
How elected: Committee on Veterans.

BILLY HERMAN   **2B**
5-11, 180.   **B:** R. **T:** R.
Born: July 7, 1909. **Died:** Sept. 5, 1992.
Career: .304 avg.; 47 HR; 839 RBIs.
Teams: Cubs 1931-41; Dodgers 1941-43, 1946; Braves 1946; Pirates 1947.
How elected: Committee on Veterans.

JUDY JOHNSON   **3B**
5-11, 150.   **B:** R. **T:** R.
Born: Oct. 26, 1899. **Died:** June 14, 1989.
Career: Negro League star; statistics not available.
How elected: Special Committee on Negro Leagues.

RALPH KINER   **OF**
6-2, 195.   **B:** R. **T:** R.
Born: Oct. 27, 1922.
Career: .279 avg.; 369 HR; 1,015 RBIs.
Teams: Pirates 1946-53; Cubs 1953-54; Indians 1955.
How elected: 75.4 percent of vote.

1976

OSCAR CHARLESTON   **OF**
5-11, 190.   **B:** L. **T:** L.
Born: Oct. 14, 1896. **Died:** Oct. 5, 1954.
Career: Negro League star; statistics not available.
How elected: Special Committee on Negro Leagues.

ROGER CONNOR   **1B**
6-3, 220.   **B:** L. **T:** L.
Born: July 1, 1857. **Died:** Jan. 4, 1931.
Career: .317 avg.; 138 HR; 1,322 RBIs.
Teams: Troy (Nat.) 1880-82; New York (Nat.) 1883-89, 1891, 1893-94; New York (P.L.) 1890; Philadelphia (Nat.) 1892; St. Louis (Nat.) 1894-97.
How elected: Committee on Veterans.

CAL HUBBARD   **UMPIRE**
Born: Oct. 31, 1900. **Died:** Oct. 17, 1977.
Career: A.L. umpire from 1936-50; assistant to A.L. supervisor of umpires 1952-53; supervisor of umpires 1954-69; a former pro football player and a member of the National Football League Hall of Fame.
How elected: Committee on Veterans.

BOB LEMON   **P**
6-0, 185.   **B:** L. **T:** R.
Born: Sept. 22, 1920. **Died:** Jan. 11, 2000.
Career: 207-128; 3.23 ERA; 1,277 SO.
Team: Indians 1946-58.
How elected: 78.6 percent of vote.

FRED LINDSTROM   **3B**
5-11, 170.   **B:** R. **T:** R.
Born: Nov. 21, 1905. **Died:** Oct. 4, 1981.
Career: .311 avg.; 103 HR; 779 RBIs.
Teams: Giants 1924-32; Pirates 1933-34; Cubs 1935; Dodgers 1936.
How elected: Committee on Veterans.

ROBIN ROBERTS   **P**
6-0, 190.   **B:** B. **T:** R.
Born: Sept. 30, 1926.
Career: 286-245; 3.41 ERA; 2,357 SO.
Teams: Phillies 1948-61; Orioles 1962-65; Astros 1965-66; Cubs 1966.
How elected: 86.9 percent of vote.

1977

ERNIE BANKS   **SS**
6-1, 180.   **B:** R. **T:** R.
Born: Jan. 31, 1931.
Career: .274 avg.; 512 HR; 1,636 RBIs.
Team: Cubs 1953-71.
How elected: 83.8 percent of vote.

MARTIN DIHIGO   **P, IF, OF**
6-3, 225.   **B:** R. **T:** R.
Born: May 24, 1905.   **Died:** May 20, 1971.
Career: Negro League star; statistics not available.
How elected: Special Committee on Negro Leagues.

JOHN HENRY LLOYD   **SS**
5-11, 180.   **B:** L. **T:** R.
Born: April 25, 1884.   **Died:** March 19, 1965.
Career: Negro League star; statistics not available.
How elected: Special Committee on Negro Leagues.

AL LOPEZ   **C, MAN.**
5-11, 165.   **B:** R. **T:** R.
Born: Aug. 20, 1908.
Playing career: .261 avg.; 51 HR; 652 RBIs.
Managing career: 1,410-1,004, 17 years.
Teams (player): Dodgers 1928, 1930-35; Braves 1936-40; Pirates 1940-46; Indians 1947.
Teams (manager): Indians 1951-56; White Sox 1957-65, 1968-69.
How elected: Committee on Veterans.

AMOS RUSIE   **P**
6-1, 200.   **B:** R. **T:** R.
Born: May 30, 1871.   **Died:** Dec. 6, 1942.
Career: 245-174; 3.07 ERA; 1,934 SO.
Teams: Indianapolis (Nat.) 1889; New York (Nat.) 1890-95, 1897-98; Reds 1901.
How elected: Committee on Veterans.

JOE SEWELL   **SS, 3B**
5-7, 155.   **B:** L. **T:** R.
Born: Oct. 9, 1898.   **Died:** March 6, 1990.
Career: .312 avg.; 49 HR; 1,055 RBIs.
Teams: Indians 1920-30; Yankees 1931-33.
How elected: Committee on Veterans.

1978

ADDIE JOSS   **P**
6-3, 185.   **B:** R. **T:** R.
Born: April 12, 1880.   **Died:** April 14, 1911.
Career: 160-97; 1.89 ERA; 920 SO.
Team: Indians 1902-10.
How elected: Committee on Veterans.

LARRY MACPHAIL   **EXECUTIVE**
Born: Feb. 3, 1890.   **Died:** Oct. 1, 1975.
Career: A franchise builder and innovator; built championship teams for the Reds, Dodgers and Yankees; introduced night baseball in 1935 at Cincinnati; first to use radio broadcasts to increase revenues for his teams.
How elected: Committee on Veterans.

EDDIE MATHEWS   **3B**
6-1, 200.   **B:** L. **T:** R.
Born: Oct. 13, 1931.
Career: .271 avg.; 512 HR; 1,453 RBIs.
Teams: Braves 1952-66; Astros 1967; Tigers 1967-68.
How elected: 79.4 percent of vote.

1979

WARREN GILES   **EXECUTIVE**
Born: May 28, 1896.   **Died:** Feb. 7, 1979.
Career: Reds general manager from 1937-47; Reds president from 1947-52; N.L. president from 1952-69.
How elected: Committee on Veterans.

WILLIE MAYS   **OF**
5-11, 180.   **B:** R. **T:** R.
Born: May 6, 1931.
Career: .302 avg.; 660 HR; 1,903 RBIs; 3,283 hits.

Teams: Giants 1951-52, 1954-72; Mets 1972-73.
How elected: 94.7 percent of vote.

HACK WILSON   **OF**
5-6, 190.   **B:** R. **T:** R.
Born: April 26, 1900.   **Died:** Nov. 23, 1948.
Career: .307 avg.; 244 HR; 1,062 RBIs.
Teams: Giants 1923-25; Cubs 1926-31; Dodgers 1932-34; Phillies 1934.
How elected: Committee on Veterans.

1980

AL KALINE   **OF**
6-2, 180.   **B:** R. **T:** R.
Born: Dec. 19, 1934.
Career: .297 avg.; 399 HR; 1,583 RBIs; 3,007 hits.
Team: Tigers 1953-74.
How elected: 88.3 percent of vote.

CHUCK KLEIN   **OF**
6-0, 185.   **B:** L. **T:** R.
Born: Oct. 7, 1905.   **Died:** March 28, 1958.
Career: .320 avg.; 300 HR; 1,201 RBIs.
Teams: Phillies 1928-33, 1936-39, 1940-44; Cubs 1934-36; Pirates 1939.
How elected: Committee on Veterans.

DUKE SNIDER   **OF**
6-0, 190.   **B:** L. **T:** R.
Born: Sept. 19, 1926.
Career: .295 avg.; 407 HR; 1,333 RBIs.
Teams: Dodgers 1947-62; Mets 1963; Giants 1964.
How elected: 86.5 percent of vote

TOM YAWKEY   **EXECUTIVE**
Born: Feb. 21, 1903.   **Died:** July 9, 1976.
Career: Owner of Red Sox franchise from 1933 until death; longtime champion of the A.L. and one of the most respected figures in the game.
How elected: Committee on Veterans.

1981

RUBE FOSTER   **P, MAN., EXEC.**
6-4, 240.
Born: Sept. 17, 1879.   **Died:** Dec. 9, 1930.
Playing career: Negro League star; statistics not available.
Executive career: Founder of Negro American and Negro National leagues; owner of Chicago-based American Giants, the model from which all other Negro clubs were built.
How elected: Committee on Veterans.

BOB GIBSON   **P**
6-1, 195.   **B:** R. **T:** R.
Born: Nov. 9, 1935.
Career: 251-174; 2.91 ERA; 3,117 SO.
Team: Cardinals 1959-75.
How elected: 84 percent of vote.

JOHNNY MIZE   **1B**
6-2, 215.   **B:** L. **T:** R.
Born: Jan. 7, 1913.   **Died:** June 2, 1993.
Career: .312 avg.; 359 HR; 1,337 RBIs.
Teams: Cardinals 1936-41; Giants 1942, 1946-49; Yankees 1949-53.
How elected: Committee on Veterans.

1982

HANK AARON   **OF**
6-0, 180.   **B:** R. **T:** R.
Born: Feb. 5, 1934.
Career: .305 avg.; 755 HR, 1st on all-time list; 2,297 RBIs, 1st on all-time list; 3,771 hits.
Teams: Braves 1954-74; Brewers 1975-76.
How elected: 97.8 percent of vote.

HAPPY CHANDLER   **EXECUTIVE**
Second commissioner of baseball.
Born: July 14, 1898.   **Died:** June 15, 1991.

Hank Aaron's Hall of Fame credentials include record totals of 755 home runs and 2,297 RBIs.

Career: Former U.S. senator from Kentucky; was elected commissioner in 1945 after the death of Kenesaw Mountain Landis; served until his forced retirement in 1950; returned to Kentucky and won two terms as the state's governor.
How elected: Committee on Veterans.

TRAVIS JACKSON   **SS**
5-11, 160.   **B:** R. **T:** R.
Born: Nov. 2, 1903.   **Died:** July 17, 1987.
Career: .291 avg.; 135 HR; 929 RBIs.
Team: Giants 1922-36.
How elected: Committee on Veterans.

FRANK ROBINSON   **OF**
6-1, 195.   **B:** R. **T:** R.
Born: Aug. 31, 1935.
Career: .294 avg.; 586 HR; 1,812 RBIs.
Teams: Reds 1956-65; Orioles 1966-71; Dodgers 1972; Angels 1973-74; Indians 1974-76.
How elected: 89.2 percent of vote.

1983

WALTER ALSTON   **MANAGER**
Born: Dec. 1, 1911.   **Died:** Oct. 1, 1984.
Career: 2,040-1,613, 23 years; 4 World Series championships.
Team: Dodgers 1954-76.
How elected: Committee on Veterans.

GEORGE KELL   **3B**
5-9, 175.   **B:** R. **T:** R.
Born: Aug. 23, 1922.
Career: .306 avg.; 78 HR; 870 RBIs.
Teams: Athletics 1943-46; Tigers 1946-52; Red Sox 1952-54; White Sox 1954-56; Orioles 1956-57.
How elected: Committee on Veterans.

JUAN MARICHAL   **P**
6-0, 185.   **B:** R. **T:** R.
Born: Oct. 20, 1938.
Career: 243-142; 2.89 ERA; 2,303 SO.
Teams: Giants 1960-73; Red Sox 1974; Dodgers 1975.
How elected: 83.7 percent of vote.

BROOKS ROBINSON   **3B**
6-1, 190.   **B:** R. **T:** R.
Born: May 18, 1937.
Career: .267 avg.; 268 HR; 1,357 RBIs.
Team: Orioles 1955-77.
How elected: 92 percent of vote

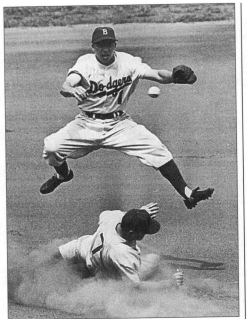

Shortstop Pee Wee Reese anchored the Dodgers infield through two glorious decades.

1984

LUIS APARICIO SS
5-9, 160. **B:** R. **T:** R.
Born: April 29, 1934.
Career: .262 avg.; 83 HR; 791 RBIs.
Teams: White Sox 1956-62, 1968-70; Orioles 1963-67; Red Sox 1971-73.
How elected: 84.6 percent of vote.

DON DRYSDALE P
6-6, 216. **B:** R. **T:** R.
Born: July 23, 1936. **Died:** July 3, 1993.
Career: 209-166; 2.95 ERA; 2,486 SO.
Team: Dodgers 1956-69.
How elected: 78.4 percent of vote.

RICK FERRELL C
5-10, 160. **B:** R. **T:** R.
Born: Oct. 12, 1906. **Died:** July 27, 1995.
Career: .281 avg.; 28 HR; 734 RBIs.
Teams: Browns 1929-33, 1941-43; Red Sox 1933-37; Senators 1937-41, 1944-45, 1947.
How elected: Committee on Veterans.

HARMON KILLEBREW 3B, 1B
5-11, 213. **B:** R. **T:** R.
Born: June 29, 1936.
Career: .256 avg.; 573 HR; 1,584 RBIs.
Teams: Senators 1954-60; Twins 1961-74; Royals 1975.
How elected: 83.1 percent of vote.

PEE WEE REESE SS
5-10, 175. **B:** R. **T:** R.
Born: July 23, 1918. **Died:** August 14, 1999.
Career: .269 avg.; 126 HR; 885 RBIs.
Teams: Dodgers 1940-42, 1946-58.
How elected: Committee on Veterans.

1985

LOU BROCK OF
5-11, 170. **B:** L. **T:** L.
Born: June 18, 1939.
Career: .293 avg.; 149 HR; 900 RBIs; 3,023 hits; 938 SB.
Teams: Cubs 1961-64; Cardinals 1964-79.
How elected: 79.7 percent of vote.

ENOS SLAUGHTER OF
5-9, 192. **B:** L. **T:** R.
Born: April 27, 1916.
Career: .300 avg.; 169 HR; 1,304 RBIs.

Teams: Cardinals 1938-42, 1946-53; Yankees 1954-55, 1956-59; Athletics 1955-56; Braves 1959.
How elected: Committee on Veterans.

ARKY VAUGHAN IF
5-11, 175. **B:** L. **T:** R.
Born: March 9, 1912. **Died:** Aug. 30, 1952.
Career: .318 avg.; 96 HR; 926 RBIs.
Teams: Pirates 1932-41; Dodgers 1942-43, 1947-48.
How elected: Committee on Veterans.

HOYT WILHELM P
6-0, 195. **B:** R. **T:** R.
Born: July 26, 1923.
Career: 143-122; 2.52 ERA; 1,610 SO; 1,070 games, 1st on all-time list; 227 saves.
Teams: Giants 1952-56; Cardinals 1957; Indians 1957-58; Orioles 1958-62; White Sox 1963-68; Angels 1969; Braves 1969-70, 1971; Cubs 1970; Dodgers 1971-72.
How elected: 83.8 percent of vote.

1986

BOBBY DOERR 2B
5-11, 175. **B:** R. **T:** R.
Born: April 7, 1918.
Career: .288 avg.; 223 HR; 1,247 RBIs.
Team: Red Sox 1937-44, 1946-51.
How elected: Committee on Veterans.

ERNIE LOMBARDI C
6-3, 230. **B:** R. **T:** R.
Born: April 6, 1908. **Died:** Sept. 26, 1977.
Career: .306 avg.; 190 HR; 990 RBIs.
Teams: Dodgers 1931; Reds 1932-41; Braves 1942; Giants 1943-47.
How elected: Committee on Veterans.

WILLIE McCOVEY 1B
6-4, 210. **B:** L. **T:** L.
Born: Jan. 10, 1938.
Career: .270 avg.; 521 HR; 1,555 RBIs.
Teams: Giants 1959-73, 1977-80; Padres 1974-76; Athletics 1976.
How elected: 81.4 percent of vote.

1987

RAY DANDRIDGE 3B
5-7, 175. **B:** R. **T:** R.
Born: Aug. 31, 1913. **Died:** Feb. 12, 1994.
Career: Negro League star; statistics not available.
How elected: Committee on Veterans.

JIM (CATFISH) HUNTER P
6-0, 195. **B:** R. **T:** R.
Born: April 8, 1946. **Died:** September 9, 1999.
Career: 224-166; 3.26 ERA; 2,012 SO.
Teams: Athletics 1965-74; Yankees 1975-79.
How elected: 76.3 percent of vote.

BILLY WILLIAMS OF
6-1, 175. **B:** L. **T:** R.
Born: June 15, 1938.
Career: .290 avg.; 426 HR; 1,475 RBIs.
Teams: Cubs 1959-74; Athletics 1975-76.
How elected: 85.7 percent of vote.

1988

WILLIE STARGELL OF, 1B
6-2, 225. **B:** L. **T:** L.
Born: March 6, 1940.
Career: .282 avg.; 475 HR; 1,540 RBIs.
Team: Pirates 1962-82.
How elected: 82.4 percent of vote.

1989

AL BARLICK UMPIRE
Born: April 2, 1915. **Died:** December 27, 1995.
Career: N.L. umpire from 1940-1971; worked as N.L. umpire supervisor after retirement.
How elected: Committee on Veterans.

JOHNNY BENCH C
6-1, 208. **B:** R. **T:** R.
Born: Dec. 7, 1947.
Career: .267 avg.; 389 HR; 1,376 RBIs.
Team: Reds 1967-83.
How elected: 96.4 percent of vote.

RED SCHOENDIENST 2B
6-0, 170. **B:** B. **T:** R.
Born: Feb. 2, 1923.
Career: .289 avg.; 84 HR; 773 RBIs.
Teams: Cardinals 1945-56, 1961-63; Giants 1956-57; Braves 1957-60.
How elected: Committee on Veterans.

CARL YASTRZEMSKI OF
5-11, 182. **B:** L. **T:** R.
Born: Aug. 22, 1939.
Career: .285 avg.; 452 HR; 1,844 RBIs; 3,419 hits.
Team: Red Sox 1961-83.
How elected: 94.6 percent of vote.

1990

JOE MORGAN 2B
5-7, 160. **B:** L. **T:** R.
Born: Sept. 19, 1943.
Career: .271 avg.; 268 HR; 1,133 RBIs.
Teams: Astros 1963-71, 1980; Reds 1972-79; Giants 1981-82; Phillies 1983; Athletics 1984.
How elected: 81.8 percent of vote.

JIM PALMER P
6-3, 196. **B:** R. **T:** R.
Born: Oct. 15, 1945.
Career: 268-152; 2.86 ERA; 2,212 SO.
Team: Orioles 1965-67; 1969-84.
How elected: 92.6 percent of vote.

1991

ROD CAREW 2B, 1B
6-0, 182. **B:** L. **T:** R.
Born: Oct. 1, 1945.
Career: .328 avg.; 92 HR; 1,015 RBIs; 3,053 hits.
Teams: Twins 1967-78; Angels 1979-85.
How elected: 89.7 percent of vote.

FERGUSON JENKINS P
6-5, 210. **B:** R. **T:** R.
Born: Dec. 13, 1943.
Career: 284-226; 3.34 ERA; 3,192 SO.
Teams: Phillies 1965-66; Cubs 1966-73, 1982-83; Rangers 1974-75, 1978-81; Red Sox 1976-77.
How elected: 74.7 percent of vote.

TONY LAZZERI 2B
6-0, 170. **B:** R. **T:** R.
Born: Dec. 6, 1903. **Died:** Aug. 6, 1946.
Career: .292 avg.; 178 HR; 1,191 RBIs.
Teams: Yankees 1926-37; Cubs 1938; Dodgers 1939; Giants 1939.
How elected: Committee on Veterans.

GAYLORD PERRY P
6-4, 215. **B:** R. **T:** R.
Born: Sept. 15, 1938.
Career: 314-265; 3.11 ERA; 3,534 SO.
Teams: Giants 1962-71; Indians 1972-75; Rangers 1975-77, 1980; Padres 1978-79; Yankees 1980; Braves 1981; Mariners 1982-83; Royals 1983.
How elected: 76.5 percent of vote.

BILL VEECK EXECUTIVE
Born: Feb. 9, 1914. **Died:** Jan. 2, 1986.
Career: A three-time major league owner best known for his showmanship and promotional stunts; owned Indians, Browns and White Sox franchises; broke A.L. color barrier in 1947 by signing Larry Doby to an Indians contract; remembered as the man who sent a midget to the plate for the Browns in a 1951 promotional stunt.
How elected: Committee on Veterans.

1992

ROLLIE FINGERS   P
6-4, 195.   **B:** R. **T:** R.
Born: Aug. 25, 1946.
Career: 114-118; 2.90 ERA; 1,299 SO; 341 saves.
Teams: Athletics 1968-76; Padres 1977-80; Brewers
1981-82, 1984-85.
How elected: 81.2 percent of vote.

BILL MCGOWAN   UMPIRE
Born: Jan. 18, 1896.   **Died:** Dec. 9, 1954.
Career: Served as an A.L. umpire from 1925-53;
worked 8 World Series and 4 All-Star Games; worked
2,541 consecutive games over a 16½-year period.
How elected: Committee on Veterans.

HAL NEWHOUSER   P
6-2, 192.   **B:** L. **T:** L.
Born: May 20, 1921.   **Died:** November 10, 1998.
Career: 207-150; 3.06 ERA; 1,796 SO.
Teams: Tigers 1939-53; Indians 1954-55.
How elected: Committee on Veterans.

TOM SEAVER   P
6-1, 206.   **B:** R. **T:** R.
Born: Nov. 17, 1944.
Career: 311-205; 2.86 ERA; 3,640 SO.
Teams: Mets 1967-77, 1983; Reds 1977-82; White Sox
1984-86; Red Sox 1986.
How elected: 98.8 percent of vote.

1993

REGGIE JACKSON   OF
6-0, 200.   **B:** L. **T:** L.
Born: May 18, 1946.
Career: .262 avg.; 563 HR; 1,702 RBIs.
Teams: Athletics 1967-75, 1987; Orioles 1976; Yankees
1977-81; Angels 1982-86.
How elected: 93.6 percent of vote.

1994

STEVE CARLTON   P
6-4, 210.   **B:** L. **T:** L.
Born: Dec. 22, 1944.
Career: 329-244; 3.22 ERA; 4,136 SO.
Teams: Cardinals 1965-71; Phillies 1972-86; Giants
1986; White Sox 1986; Indians 1987; Twins 1987-88.
How elected: 95.8 percent of vote.

LEO DUROCHER   SS, MAN.
5-10, 160.   **B:** R. **T:** R.
Born: July 27, 1905.   **Died:** Oct. 7, 1991.
Playing career: .247 avg.; 24 HR; 567 RBIs.
Managing career: 2,008-1,709, 24 years; 1 World Series
championship.
Teams (player): Yankees 1925, 1928-29; Reds 1930-33;
Cardinals 1933-37; Dodgers 1938-41, 1943, 1945.
Teams (manager): Dodgers 1939-46, 1948; Giants
1948-55; Cubs 1966-72; Astros 1972-73.
How elected: Committee on Veterans.

PHIL RIZZUTO   SS
5-6, 160.   **B:** R. **T:** R.
Born: Sept. 25, 1917.
Career: .273 avg.; 38 HR; 563 RBIs.
Team: Yankees 1941-42, 1946-56.
How elected: Committee on Veterans.

1995

RICHIE ASHBURN   OF
5-10, 170   **B:** L. **T:** R.
Born: March 19, 1927.   **Died:** September 9, 1997.
Career: .308 avg.; 29 HR; 586 RBIs.
Teams: Phillies 1948-59; Cubs 1960-61; Mets 1962.
How elected: Committee on Veterans.

More than a decade of Tom Seaver's outstanding career was spent in New York.

LEON DAY   P
5-10, 180.   **B:** R. **T:** R.
Born: Oct. 30, 1916.   **Died:** March 13, 1995.
Career: Negro League star; statistics not available.
How elected: Committee on Veterans.

WILLIAM HULBERT   EXECUTIVE
Born: Oct. 23, 1832.   **Died:** April 10, 1882.
Career: A former National Association executive and
founder of the National League in 1876; served as
second president of the new circuit when Morgan
Bulkeley left the job after 10 months; he also is credited
with hiring baseball's first umpiring staff.
How elected: Committee on Veterans.

MIKE SCHMIDT   3B
6-2, 203.   **B:** R. **T:** R.
Born: Sept. 27, 1949.
Career: .267 avg.; 548 HR; 1,595 RBIs.
Team: Phillies 1972-89.
How elected: 96.5 percent of vote.

VIC WILLIS   P
6-2, 185.   **B:** R. **T:** R.
Born: April 12, 1876.   **Died:** Aug. 3, 1947.
Career: 249-205; 2.63 ERA; 1,651 SO.
Teams: Braves 1898-1905; Pirates 1906-09;
Cardinals 1910.
How elected: Committee on Veterans.

1996

JIM BUNNING   P
6-3, 195.   **B:** R. **T:** R.
Born: Oct. 23, 1931.
Career: 224-184; 3.27 ERA; 2,855 SO.
Teams: Tigers 1955-63; Phillies 1964-67, 1970-71;
Pirates 1968-69; Dodgers 1969.
How elected: Committee on Veterans.

BILL FOSTER   P
6-1, 196.   **B:** B. **T:** L.
Born: June 12, 1904.   **Died:** Sept. 16, 1978.
Career: Negro League star; statistics not available.
How elected: Committee on Veterans.

NED HANLON   OF, MAN.
5-10, 170.   **B:** L. **T:** R.
Born: Aug. 22, 1857.   **Died:** April 14, 1937.
Playing career: .260 avg.; 30 HR; 517 RBIs.
Managing career: 1,313-1,164, 19 years; 5
championships.
Teams (player): Cleveland 1880; Detroit 1881-88;
Pittsburgh (N.L.) 1889, 1891; Pittsburgh (P.L.) 1890;
Baltimore (N.L.) 1892.
Teams (manager): Pittsburgh (N.L.) 1889, 1891;
Pittsburgh (P.L.) 1890; Baltimore (N.L.) 1892-98;
Dodgers 1899-1905; Reds 1906-07.
How elected: Committee on Veterans.

EARL WEAVER   MANAGER
Born: Aug. 14, 1930.
Career: 1,480-1,060, 17 years; 1 World Series
championship.
Team: Orioles 1968-82, 1985-86.
How elected: Committee on Veterans.

1997

NELLIE FOX   2B
5-9,150.   **B:** L. **T:** R
Born: Dec. 25, 1927.   **Died:** Dec. 1, 1975.
Career: .288 avg.; 35 HR; 790 RBIs.
Teams: Athletics 1947-49; White Sox 1950-63; Astros
1964-65.
How elected: Committee on Veterans.

Larry Doby, baseball's second black player, began his career in 1947 under Hall of Fame Cleveland player-manager Lou Boudreau (left).

TOM LASORDA   MANAGER
Born: Sept. 22, 1927.
Career: 1,599-1,439, 21 years; 2 World Series championships.
Team: Dodgers, 1976-96.
How elected: Committee on Veterans.

PHIL NIEKRO   P
6-1,180.   **B:** R. **T:** R
Born: April 1, 1939.
Career: 318-274; 3.35 ERA; 3,342 strikeouts.
Teams: Braves 1964-83, 1987; Yankees 1984-85; Indians 1986, 1987; Blue Jays 1987.
How elected: 80.3 percent of vote.

WILLIE WELLS   SS, 3B, 2B, P
5-8, 160.   **B:** R. **T:** R.
Born: Aug. 10, 1905.   **Died:** Jan. 22, 1989.
Career: Negro League star; statistics not available.
How elected: Committee on Veterans.

1998

GEORGE DAVIS   3B, OF, SS
5-9, 180.   **B:** B. **T:** R.
Born: Aug. 23, 1870.   **Died:** Oct. 17, 1940.
Career: .295 avg.; 73 HR; 1,437 RBIs.
Teams: Cleveland N.L. 1890-92; Giants 1893-1901, 1903; White Sox 1902, 1904-09.
How elected: Committee on Veterans.

LARRY DOBY   OF
6-1, 182.   **B:** L. **T:** R.
Born: Dec. 13, 1924.
Career: .283 avg.; 253 HR; 970 RBIs.
Teams: Indians 1947-55, 1958; White Sox 1956-57, 1959; Tigers 1959.
How elected: Committee on Veterans.

LEE MACPHAIL   EXECUTIVE
Born: Oct. 25, 1917.
Career: A former minor league executive, major league executive and president of the American League (1974-83); as director of player personnel for the New York Yankees, he helped build the farm system that fueled seven World Series titles in 10 years; as general manager of the Baltimore Orioles, he helped build another championship organization; the son of Larry MacPhail, a Hall of Fame executive and innovator who paved the way for his son's career.
How elected: Committee on Veterans.

JOE ROGAN   P, OF, IF
5-7, 180.   **B:** R. **T:** R.
Born: July 28, 1889.   **Died:** March 4, 1967.
Career: Negro League star; statistics not available.
How elected: Committee on Veterans.

DON SUTTON   P
6-1, 185   **B:** R. **T:** R.
Born: April 2, 1945.
Career: 324-256; 3.26 ERA; 3,574 strikeouts.
Teams: Dodgers 1966-80, 1988; Astros 1981-82; Brewers 1982-84; Athletics 1985; Angels 1985-87.
How elected: 81.6 percent of vote.

1999

GEORGE BRETT   3B
6-0, 200.   **B:** L. **T:** R.
Born: May 15, 1953.
Career: .305 avg.; 317 HR; 1,595 RBIs.
Teams: Royals 1973-93.
How elected: 98.2 percent of vote.

ORLANDO CEPEDA   1B, OF
6-2, 210.   **B:** R. **T:** R.
Born: September 17, 1937.
Career: .297 avg.; 379 HR; 1,365 RBIs.
Teams: Giants 1958-66, Cardinals 1966-68, Braves 1969-72, Athletics 1972, Red Sox 1973, Royals 1974.
How elected: Committee on Veterans.

NESTOR CHYLAK   UMPIRE
Born: May 11, 1922.   **Died:** February 17, 1982.
Career: Served as an A.L. umpire from 1954-78; worked 5 World Series and 6 All-Star Games; known as an excellent teacher of umpires.
How elected: Committee on Veterans.

NOLAN RYAN   P
6-2, 195   **B:** R. **T:** R.
Born: January 31, 1947.
Career: 324-292; 3.19 ERA; 5,714 strikeouts.
Teams: Mets 1966-71, Angels 1972-79, Astros 1980-88; Rangers 1989-93.
How elected: 98.8 percent of vote.

FRANK SELEE   MANAGER
Born: Oct. 26, 1859.   **Died:** July 5, 1909.
Career: 1,284-862, 16 years.
Teams: Braves 1890-1901, Cubs 1902-1905.
How elected: Committee on Veterans.

SMOKEY JOE WILLIAMS   P, OF, 1B, MAN.
6-4, 200.   **B:** R. **T:** R.
Born: April 6, 1885.   **Died:** March 12, 1946.
Career: Negro League star; statistics not available.
How elected: Committee on Veterans.

ROBIN YOUNT   SS, OF
6-0, 170.   **B:** R. **T:** R.
Born: September 16, 1955.
Career: .285 avg.; 251 HR; 1,406 RBIs.
Teams: Brewers 1974-93.
How elected: 77.5 percent of vote.

2000

CARLTON FISK   C
6-2, 220.   **B:** R. **T:** R.
Born: December 26, 1947.
Career: .269 avg.; 376 HR; 1,330 RBIs.
Teams: Red Sox 1969-80; White Sox 1982-93.
How elected: 79.6 percent of vote.

TONY PEREZ   1B
6-2, 190   **B:** R. **T:** R.
Born: May 14, 1942.
Career: .279 avg.; 379 HR; 1,652 RBIs.
Teams: Reds 1964-76, 1984-86; Expos 1977-79; Red Sox 1980-82; Phillies 1983.
How elected: 77.15 percent of vote.

Award Winners

1931

LEFTY GROVE A.L. MVP
Team: Athletics. **Position:** Pitcher.
Season: 31-4; 2.06 ERA; 175 SO.
(See Hall of Fame section, 1947.)

FRANK FRISCH N.L. MVP
Team: Cardinals. **Position:** Second base.
Season: .311 avg.; 4 HR; 82 RBIs; 28 SB.
(See Hall of Fame section, 1947.)

1932

JIMMIE FOXX A.L. MVP
Team: Athletics. **Position:** First base.
Season: .364 avg.; 58 HR; 169 RBIs.
(See Hall of Fame section, 1951.)

CHUCK KLEIN N.L. MVP
Team: Phillies. **Position:** Outfield.
Season: .348 avg.; 38 HR; 137 RBIs.
(See Hall of Fame section, 1980.)

1933

JIMMIE FOXX A.L. MVP
Team: Athletics. **Position:** First base.
Season: .356 avg.; 48 HR; 163 RBIs.
(See Hall of Fame section, 1951.)

CARL HUBBELL N.L. MVP
Team: Giants. **Position:** Pitcher.
Season: 23-12; 1.66 ERA; 156 SO.
(See Hall of Fame section, 1947.)

1934

MICKEY COCHRANE A.L. MVP
Team: Tigers. **Position:** Catcher.
Season: .320 avg.; 2 HR; 76 RBIs.
(See Hall of Fame section, 1947.)

DIZZY DEAN N.L. MVP
Team: Cardinals. **Position:** Pitcher.
Season: 30-7; 2.66 ERA; 195 SO.
(See Hall of Fame section, 1953.)

1935

HANK GREENBERG A.L. MVP
Team: Tigers. **Position:** First base.
Season: .328 avg.; 36 HR; 170 RBIs.
(See Hall of Fame section, 1956.)

GABBY HARTNETT N.L. MVP
Team: Cubs. **Position:** Catcher.
Season: .344 avg.; 13 HR; 91 RBIs.
(See Hall of Fame section, 1955.)

1936

LOU GEHRIG A.L. MVP
Team: Yankees. **Position:** First base.
Season: .354 avg.; 49 HR; 152 RBIs.
(See Hall of Fame section, 1939.)

CARL HUBBELL N.L. MVP
Team: Giants. **Position:** Pitcher.
Season: 26-6; 2.31 ERA; 123 SO.
(See Hall of Fame section, 1947.)

Hank Greenberg (left) and Charley Gehringer were Tigers teammates for 10 seasons.

1937

CHARLEY GEHRINGER A.L. MVP
Team: Tigers. **Position:** Second base.
Season: .371 avg.; 14 HR; 96 RBIs.
(See Hall of Fame section, 1949.)

JOE MEDWICK N.L. MVP
Team: Cardinals. **Position:** Outfield.
Season: .374 avg.; 31 HR; 154 RBIs; Triple Crown
winner.
(See Hall of Fame section, 1968.)

1938

JIMMIE FOXX A.L. MVP
Team: Red Sox. **Position:** First base.
Season: .349 avg.; 50 HR; 175 RBIs.
(See Hall of Fame section, 1951.)

ERNIE LOMBARDI N.L. MVP
Team: Reds. **Position:** Catcher.
Season: .342 avg.; 19 HR; 95 RBIs.
(See Hall of Fame section, 1986.)

1939

JOE DiMAGGIO A.L. MVP
Team: Yankees. **Position:** Outfield.
Season: .381 avg.; 30 HR; 126 RBIs.
(See Hall of Fame section, 1955.)

BUCKY WALTERS N.L. MVP
Team: Reds. **Position:** Pitcher.
6-1, 180. **B:** R. **T:** R.
Born: April 19, 1909.

Season: 27-11; 2.29 ERA; 137 SO.
Career: 198-160; 3.30 ERA; 1,107 SO.
Teams: Phillies 1934-38; Reds 1938-48; Braves 1950.

1940

HANK GREENBERG A.L. MVP
Team: Tigers. **Position:** Outfield.
Season: .340 avg.; 41 HR; 150 RBIs.
(See Hall of Fame section, 1956.)

FRANK McCORMICK N.L. MVP
Team: Reds. **Position:** First base.
6-4, 205. **B:** R. **T.** R.
Born: June 9, 1911. **Died:** Nov. 21, 1982.
Season: .309 avg.; 19 HR; 127 RBIs.
Career: .299 avg.; 128 HR; 951 RBIs.
Teams: Reds 1934, 1937-45; Phillies 1946-47;
Braves 1947-48.

1941

JOE DiMAGGIO A.L. MVP
Team: Yankees. **Position:** Outfield.
Season: .357 avg.; 30 HR; 125 RBIs.
(See Hall of Fame section, 1955.)

DOLPH CAMILLI N.L. MVP
Team: Dodgers. **Position:** First base.
5-10, 185. **B:** L. **T:** L.
Born: April 23, 1907.
Season: .285 avg.; 34 HR; 120 RBIs.
Career: .277 avg.; 239 HR; 950 RBIs.
Teams: Cubs 1933-34; Phillies 1934-37; Dodgers 1938-43; Red Sox 1945.

WHO'S WHO

Jackie Robinson was the first Rookie of the Year after his barrier-breaking 1947 season.

1942

JOE GORDON   A.L. MVP
Team: Yankees.   **Position:** Second base.
5-10, 180.   **B:** R. **T:** R.
Born: Feb. 18, 1915.   **Died:** April 14, 1978.
Season: .322 avg.; 18 HR; 103 RBIs.
Career: .268 avg.; 253 HR; 975 RBIs.
Teams: Yankees 1938-43, 1946; Indians 1947-50.

MORT COOPER   N.L. MVP
Team: Cardinals.   **Position:** Pitcher.
6-2, 210.   **B:** R. **T:** R.
Born: March 2, 1913.   **Died:** Nov. 17, 1958.
Season: 22-7; 1.78 ERA; 152 SO.
Career: 128-75; 2.97 ERA; 913 SO.
Teams: Cardinals 1938-45; Braves 1945-47; Giants 1947; Cubs 1949.

1943

SPUD CHANDLER   A.L. MVP
Team: Yankees.   **Position:** Pitcher.
6-0, 181.   **B:** R. **T:** R.
Born: Sept. 12, 1907.   **Died:** Jan. 9, 1990.
Season: 20-4; 1.64 ERA; 134 SO.
Career: 109-43; 2.84 ERA; 614 SO.
Team: Yankees 1937-47.

STAN MUSIAL   N.L. MVP
Team: Cardinals.   **Position:** Outfield.
Season: .357 avg.; 13 HR; 81 RBIs.
(See Hall of Fame section, 1969.)

1944

HAL NEWHOUSER   A.L. MVP
Team: Tigers.   **Position:** Pitcher.
Season: 29-9; 2.22 ERA; 187 SO.
(See Hall of Fame section, 1992.)

MARTY MARION   N.L. MVP
Team: Cardinals.   **Position:** Shortstop.
6-2, 170.   **B:** R. **T:** R.
Born: Dec. 1, 1917.
Season: .267 avg.; 6 HR; 63 RBIs.
Career: .263 avg.; 36 HR; 624 RBIs.
Team: Cardinals 1940-50, 1952-53.

1945

HAL NEWHOUSER   A.L. MVP
Team: Tigers.   **Position:** Pitcher.
Season: 25-9; 1.81 ERA; 212 SO.
(See Hall of Fame section, 1992.)

PHIL CAVARRETTA   N.L. MVP
Team: Cubs.   **Position:** First base.
5-11, 175.   **B:** L. **T:** L.
Born: July 19, 1916.
Season: .355 avg.; 6 HR; 97 RBIs.
Career: .293 avg.; 95 HR; 920 RBIs.
Team: Cubs 1934-55.

1946

TED WILLIAMS   A.L. MVP
Team: Red Sox.   **Position:** Outfield.
Season: .342 avg.; 38 HR; 123 RBIs.
(See Hall of Fame section, 1966.)

STAN MUSIAL   N.L. MVP
Team: Cardinals.   **Position:** First base.
Season: .365 avg.; 16 HR; 103 RBIs.
(See Hall of Fame section, 1969.)

1947

JOE DiMAGGIO   A.L. MVP
Team: Yankees.   **Position:** Outfield.
Season: .315 avg.; 20 HR; 97 RBIs.
(See Hall of Fame section, 1955.)

BOB ELLIOTT   N.L. MVP
Team: Braves.   **Position:** Third base.
6-0, 185.   **B:** R. **T:** R.
Born: Nov. 26, 1916.   **Died:** May 4, 1966.
Season: .317 avg.; 22 HR; 113 RBIs.
Career: .289 avg.; 170 HR; 1,195 RBIs.
Teams: Pirates 1939-46; Braves 1947-51; Giants 1952; Browns 1953; White Sox 1953.

JACKIE ROBINSON   ROOKIE
Team: Dodgers.   **Position:** First base.
Season: .297 avg.; 12 HR; 48 RBIs; 29 SB.
(See Hall of Fame section, 1962.)

1948

LOU BOUDREAU   A.L. MVP
Team: Indians.   **Position:** Shortstop.
Season: .355 avg.; 18 HR; 106 RBIs.
(See Hall of Fame section, 1970.)

STAN MUSIAL   N.L. MVP
Team: Cardinals.   **Position:** Outfield.
Season: .376 avg.; 39 HR; 131 RBIs.
(See Hall of Fame section, 1969.)

ALVIN DARK   ROOKIE
Team: Braves.   **Position:** Shortstop.
5-11, 185.   **B:** R. **T:** R.
Born: Jan. 7, 1922.
Season: .322 avg.; 3 HR; 48 RBIs.
Career: .289 avg.; 126 HR; 757 RBIs.
Teams: Braves 1946, 1948-49, 1960; Giants 1950-56; Cardinals 1956-58; Cubs 1958-59; Phillies 1960.

1949

TED WILLIAMS   A.L. MVP
Team: Red Sox.   **Position:** Outfield.
Season: .343 avg.; 43 HR; 159 RBIs.
(See Hall of Fame section, 1966.)

JACKIE ROBINSON   N.L. MVP
Team: Dodgers.   **Position:** Second base.
Season: .342 avg.; 16 HR; 124 RBIs; 37 SB.
(See Hall of Fame section, 1962.)

ROY SIEVERS   A.L. ROOKIE
Team: Browns.   **Position:** Outfield.
6-1, 195.   **B:** R. **T:** R.
Born: Nov. 18, 1926.
Season: .306 avg.; 16 HR; 91 RBIs.
Career: .267 avg.; 318 HR; 1,147 RBIs.
Teams: Browns 1949-53; Senators 1954-59, 1964-65; White Sox 1960-61; Phillies 1962-64.

DON NEWCOMBE   N.L. ROOKIE
Team: Dodgers.   **Position:** Pitcher.
6-4, 225.   **B:** L. **T:** R.
Born: June 14, 1926.
Season: 17-8; 3.17 ERA; 149 SO.
Career: 149-90; 3.56 ERA; 1,129 SO.
Teams: Dodgers 1949-51, 1954-58; Reds 1958-60; Indians 1960.

1950

PHIL RIZZUTO   A.L. MVP
Team: Yankees.   **Position:** Shortstop.
Season: .324 avg.; 7 HR; 66 RBIs.
(See Hall of Fame section, 1994.)

JIM KONSTANTY   N.L. MVP
Team: Phillies.   **Position:** Pitcher.
6-2, 202.   **B:** R. **T:** R.
Born: March 2, 1917.   **Died:** June 11, 1976.
Season: 16-7; 2.66 ERA; 56 SO.
Career: 66-48; 3.46 ERA; 268 SO.
Teams: Reds 1944; Braves 1946; Phillies 1948-54; Yankees 1954-56; Cardinals 1956.

WALT DROPO   A.L. ROOKIE
Team: Red Sox.   **Position:** First base.
6-5, 220.   **B:** R. **T:** R.
Born: Jan. 30, 1923.
Season: .322 avg.; 34 HR; 144 RBIs.
Career: .270 avg.; 152 HR; 704 RBIs.
Teams: Red Sox 1949-52; Tigers 1952-54; White Sox 1955-58; Reds 1958-59; Orioles 1959-61.

SAM JETHROE   N.L. ROOKIE
Team: Braves.   **Position:** Outfield.
6-1, 178.   **B:** B. **T:** R.
Born: Jan. 20, 1922.
Season: .273 avg.; 18 HR; 58 RBIs.
Career: .261 avg.; 49 HR; 181 RBIs.
Teams: Braves 1950-52; Pirates 1954.

1951

YOGI BERRA   A.L. MVP
Team: Yankees.   **Position:** Catcher.
Season: .294 avg.; 27 HR; 88 RBIs.
(See Hall of Fame section, 1972.)

ROY CAMPANELLA   N.L. MVP
Team: Dodgers.   **Position:** Catcher.
Season: .325 avg.; 33 HR; 108 RBIs.
(See Hall of Fame section, 1969.)

GIL McDOUGALD   A.L. ROOKIE
Team: Yankees.   **Position:** Third base.
6-1, 180.   **B:** R. **T:** R.
Born: May 19, 1928.
Season: .306 avg.; 14 HR; 63 RBIs.
Career: .276 avg.; 112 HR; 576 RBIs.
Team: Yankees 1951-60.

WILLIE MAYS   N.L. ROOKIE
Team: Giants.   **Position:** Outfield.
Season: .274 avg.; 20 HR; 68 RBIs.
(See Hall of Fame section, 1979.)

1952

BOBBY SHANTZ   A.L. MVP
Team: Athletics.   **Position:** Pitcher.
5-6, 142.   **B:** R. **T:** L.
Born: Sept. 26, 1925.
Season: 24-7; 2.48 ERA; 152 SO.
Career: 119-99; 3.38 ERA; 1,072 SO.
Teams: Athletics 1949-56; Yankees 1957-60; Pirates 1961; Colt .45s 1962; Cardinals 1962-64; Cubs 1964; Phillies 1964.

HANK SAUER   **N.L. MVP**
Team: Cubs.   **Position:** Outfield.
6-4, 199.   **B:** R. **T:** R.
Born: March 17, 1919.
Season: .270 avg.; 37 HR; 121 RBIs.
Career: .266 avg.; 288 HR; 876 RBIs.
Teams: Reds 1941-42, 1945, 1948-49; Cubs 1949-55; Cardinals 1956; Giants 1957-59.

HARRY BYRD   **A.L. ROOKIE**
Team: Athletics.   **Position:** Pitcher.
6-1, 188.   **B:** R. **T:** R.   **Died:** May 14, 1985.
Born: Feb. 3, 1925.
Season: 15-15; 3.31 ERA; 116 SO.
Career: 46-54; 4.35 ERA; 381 SO.
Teams: Athletics 1950, 1952-53; Yankees 1954; Orioles 1955; White Sox 1955-56; Tigers 1957.

JOE BLACK   **N.L. ROOKIE**
Team: Dodgers.   **Position:** Pitcher.
6-2, 220.   **B:** R. **T:** R.
Born: Feb. 8, 1924.
Season: 15-4; 2.15 ERA; 85 SO.
Career: 30-12; 3.91 ERA; 222 SO.
Teams: Dodgers 1952-55; Reds 1955-56; Senators 1957.

1953

AL ROSEN   **A.L. MVP**
Team: Indians.   **Position:** Third base.
5-11, 180.   **B:** R. **T:** R.
Born: Feb. 29, 1924.
Season: .336 avg.; 43 HR; 145 RBIs.
Career: .285 avg.; 192 HR; 717 RBIs.
Team: Indians 1947-56.

ROY CAMPANELLA   **N.L. MVP**
Team: Dodgers.   **Position:** Catcher.
Season: .312 avg.; 41 HR; 142 RBIs.
(See Hall of Fame section, 1969.)

HARVEY KUENN   **A.L. ROOKIE**
Team: Tigers.   **Position:** Shortstop.
6-2, 190.   **B:** R. **T:** R.
Born: Dec. 4, 1930.   **Died:** Feb. 28, 1988.
Season: .308 avg.; 2 HR; 48 RBIs.
Career: .303 avg.; 87 HR; 671 RBIs.
Teams: Tigers 1952-59; Indians 1960; Giants 1961-65; Cubs 1965-66; Phillies 1966.

JIM GILLIAM   **N.L. ROOKIE**
Team: Dodgers.   **Position:** Second base.
5-11, 175.   **B:** B. **T:** R.
Born: Oct. 17, 1928.   **Died:** Oct. 8, 1978.
Season: .278 avg.; 6 HR; 63 RBIs; 21 SB.
Career: .265 avg.; 65 HR; 558 RBIs; 203 SB.
Team: Dodgers 1953-66.

1954

YOGI BERRA   **A.L. MVP**
Team: Yankees.   **Position:** Catcher.
Season: .307 avg.; 22 HR; 125 RBIs.
(See Hall of Fame section, 1972.)

WILLIE MAYS   **N.L. MVP**
Team: Giants.   **Position:** Outfield.
Season: .345 avg.; 41 HR; 110 RBIs.
(See Hall of Fame section, 1979.)

BOB GRIM   **A.L. ROOKIE**
Team: Yankees.   **Position:** Pitcher.
6-1, 185.   **B:** R. **T:** R.
Born: March 8, 1930.
Season: 20-6; 3.26 ERA; 108 SO.
Career: 61-41; 3.61 ERA; 443 SO.
Teams: Yankees 1954-58; Athletics 1958-59, 1962; Indians 1960; Reds 1960; Cardinals 1960.

WALLY MOON   **N.L. ROOKIE**
Team: Cardinals.   **Position:** Outfield.
6-0, 175.   **B:** L. **T:** R.
Born: April 3, 1930.
Season: .304 avg.; 12 HR; 76 RBIs.
Career: .289 avg.; 142 HR; 661 RBIs.
Teams: Cardinals 1954-58; Dodgers 1959-65.

1955

YOGI BERRA   **A.L. MVP**
Team: Yankees.   **Position:** Catcher.
Season: .272 avg.; 27 HR; 108 RBIs.
(See Hall of Fame section, 1972.)

ROY CAMPANELLA   **N.L. MVP**
Team: Dodgers.   **Position:** Catcher.
Season: .318 avg.; 32 HR; 107 RBIs.
(See Hall of Fame section, 1969.)

HERB SCORE   **A.L. ROOKIE**
Team: Indians.   **Position:** Pitcher.
6-2, 185.   **B:** L. **T:** L.
Born: June 7, 1933.
Season: 16-10; 2.85 ERA; 245 SO.
Career: 55-46; 3.36 ERA; 837 SO.
Teams: Indians 1955-59; White Sox 1960-62.

BILL VIRDON   **N.L. ROOKIE**
Team: Cardinals.   **Position:** Outfield.
6-0, 175.   **B:** L. **T:** R.
Born: June 9, 1931.
Season: .281 avg.; 17 HR; 68 RBIs.
Career: .267 avg.; 91 HR; 502 RBIs.
Teams: Cardinals 1955-56; Pirates 1956-65, 1968.

1956

MICKEY MANTLE   **A.L. MVP**
Team: Yankees.   **Position:** Outfield.
Season: .353 avg.; 52 HR; 130 RBIs; Triple Crown winner.
(See Hall of Fame section, 1974.)

DON NEWCOMBE   **N.L. MVP, CY YOUNG**
Team: Dodgers.   **Position:** Pitcher.
Season: 27-7; 3.06 ERA; 139 SO.
(See 1949 N.L. Rookie of Year.)

LUIS APARICIO   **A.L. ROOKIE**
Team: White Sox.   **Position:** Shortstop.
Season: .266 avg.; 3 HR; 56 RBIs; 21 SB.
(See Hall of Fame section, 1984.)

FRANK ROBINSON   **N.L. ROOKIE**
Team: Reds.   **Position:** Outfield.
Season: .290 avg.; 38 HR; 83 RBIs.
(See Hall of Fame section, 1982.)

1957

MICKEY MANTLE   **A.L. MVP**
Team: Yankees.   **Position:** Outfield.
Season: .365 avg.; 34 HR; 94 RBIs.
(See Hall of Fame section, 1974.)

HANK AARON   **N.L. MVP**
Team: Braves.   **Position:** Outfield.
Season: .322 avg.; 44 HR; 132 RBIs.
(See Hall of Fame section, 1982.)

WARREN SPAHN   **CY YOUNG**
Team: Braves.
Season: 21-11; 2.69 ERA; 111 SO.
(See Hall of Fame section, 1973.)

TONY KUBEK   **A.L. ROOKIE**
Team: Yankees.   **Position:** Infield, outfield.
6-3, 190.   **B:** L. **T:** R.
Born: Oct. 12, 1936.

Giants star Willie Mays was named N.L. MVP after his second full Major League season.

Season: .297 avg.; 3 HR; 39 RBIs.
Career: .266 avg.; 57 HR; 373 RBIs.
Team: Yankees 1957-65.

JACK SANFORD   **N.L. ROOKIE**
Team: Phillies.   **Position:** Pitcher.
6-0, 190.   **B:** R. **T:** R.
Born: May 18, 1929.
Season: 19-8; 3.08 ERA; 188 SO.
Career: 137-101; 3.69 ERA; 1,182 SO.
Teams: Phillies 1956-58; Giants 1959-65; Angels 1965-67; Athletics 1967.

1958

JACKIE JENSEN   **A.L. MVP**
Team: Red Sox.   **Position:** Outfield.
5-11, 190.   **B:** R. **T:** R.
Born: March 9, 1927.   **Died:** July 14, 1982.
Season: .286 avg.; 35 HR; 122 RBIs.
Career: .279 avg.; 199 HR; 929 RBIs.
Teams: Yankees 1950-52; Senators 1952-53; Red Sox 1954-59, 1961.

ERNIE BANKS   **N.L. MVP**
Team: Cubs.   **Position:** Shortstop.
Season: .313 avg.; 47 HR; 129 RBIs.
(See Hall of Fame section, 1977.)

BOB TURLEY   **CY YOUNG**
Team: Yankees.
6-2, 215.   **B:** R. **T:** R.
Born: Sept. 19, 1930.
Season: 21-7; 2.97 ERA; 168 SO.
Career: 101-85; 3.64 ERA; 1,265 SO.
Teams: Browns 1951, 1953; Orioles 1954; Yankees 1955-62; Angels 1963; Red Sox 1963.

ALBIE PEARSON   **A.L. ROOKIE**
Team: Senators.   **Position:** Outfield.
5-5, 140.   **B:** L. **T:** L.
Born: Sept. 12, 1934.
Season: .275 avg.; 3 HR; 33 RBIs.
Career: .270 avg.; 28 HR; 214 RBIs.
Teams: Senators 1958-59; Orioles 1959-60; Angels 1961-66.

ORLANDO CEPEDA   **N.L. ROOKIE**
Team: Giants.   **Position:** First base.
Season: .312 avg.; 25 HR; 96 RBIs.
(See Hall of Fame section, 1999.)

Dodgers ace Sandy Koufax swept N.L. Cy Young and MVP honors in 1963.

1959

NELLIE FOX   **A.L. MVP**
Team: White Sox.   **Position:** Second base.
Season: .306 avg.; 2 HR; 70 RBIs.
(See Hall of Fame section, 1999.)

ERNIE BANKS   **N.L. MVP**
Team: Cubs.   **Position:** Shortstop.
Season: .304 avg.; 45 HR; 143 RBIs.
(See Hall of Fame section, 1977.)

EARLY WYNN   **CY YOUNG**
Team: White Sox.
Season: 22-10; 3.17 ERA; 179 SO.
(See Hall of Fame section, 1972.)

BOB ALLISON   **A.L. ROOKIE**
Team: Senators.   **Position:** Outfield.
6-4, 215.   **B:** R. **T:** R.
Born: July 11, 1934.
Season: .261 avg.; 30 HR; 85 RBIs.
Career: .255 avg.; 256 HR; 796 RBIs.
Teams: Senators 1958-60; Twins 1961-70.

WILLIE MCCOVEY   **N.L. ROOKIE**
Team: Giants.   **Position:** First base.
Season: .354 avg.; 13 HR; 38 RBIs.
(See Hall of Fame section, 1986.)

1960

ROGER MARIS   **A.L. MVP**
Team: Yankees.   **Position:** Outfield.
6-0, 203.   **B:** L. **T:** R.
Born: Sept. 10, 1934.   **Died:** Dec. 14, 1985.
Season: .283 avg.; 39 HR; 112 RBIs.
Career: .260 avg.; 275 HR; 851 RBIs.
Teams: Indians 1957-58; Athletics 1958-59; Yankees 1960-66; Cardinals 1967-68.

DICK GROAT   **N.L. MVP**
Team: Pirates.   **Position:** Shortstop.
6-0, 180.   **B:** R. **T:** R.
Born: Nov. 4, 1930.
Season: .325 avg.; 2 HR; 50 RBIs.
Career: .286 avg.; 39 HR; 707 RBIs.
Teams: Pirates 1952, 1955-62; Cardinals 1963-65; Phillies 1966-67; Giants 1967.

VERNON LAW   **CY YOUNG**
Team: Pirates.
6-2, 195.   **B:** R. **T:** R.

Born: March 12, 1930.
Season: 20-9; 3.08 ERA; 120 SO.
Career: 162-147; 3.77 ERA; 1,092 SO.
Team: Pirates 1950-51, 1954-67.

RON HANSEN   **A.L. ROOKIE**
Team: Orioles.   **Position:** Shortstop.
6-3, 200.   **B:** R. **T:** R.
Born: April 5, 1938.
Season: .255 avg.; 22 HR; 86 RBIs.
Career: .234 avg.; 106 HR; 501 RBIs.
Teams: Orioles 1958-62; White Sox 1963-67, 1968-69; Senators 1968; Yankees 1970-71; Royals 1972.

FRANK HOWARD   **N.L. ROOKIE**
Team: Dodgers.   **Position:** Outfield.
6-7, 255.   **B:** R. **T:** R.
Born: Aug. 8, 1936.
Season: .268 avg.; 23 HR; 77 RBIs.
Career: .273 avg.; 382 HR; 1,119 RBIs.
Teams: Dodgers 1958-64; Senators 1965-71; Rangers 1972; Tigers 1972-73.

1961

ROGER MARIS   **A.L. MVP**
Team: Yankees.   **Position:** Outfield.
Season: .269 avg.; 61 HR; 142 RBIs.
(See 1960 A.L. MVP.)

FRANK ROBINSON   **N.L. MVP**
Team: Reds.   **Position:** Outfield.
Season: .323 avg.; 37 HR; 124 RBIs.
(See Hall of Fame section, 1982.)

WHITEY FORD   **CY YOUNG**
Team: Yankees.
Season: 25-4; 3.21 ERA; 209 SO.
(See Hall of Fame section, 1974.)

DON SCHWALL   **A.L. ROOKIE**
Team: Red Sox.   **Position:** Pitcher.
6-6, 200.   **B:** R. **T:** R.
Born: March 2, 1936.
Season: 15-7; 3.22 ERA; 91 SO.
Career: 49-48; 3.72 ERA; 408 SO.
Teams: Red Sox 1961-62; Pirates 1963-66; Braves 1966-67.

BILLY WILLIAMS   **N.L. ROOKIE**
Team: Cubs.   **Position:** Outfield.
Season: .278 avg.; 25 HR; 86 RBIs.
(See Hall of Fame section, 1987.)

1962

MICKEY MANTLE   **A.L. MVP**
Team: Yankees.   **Position:** Outfield.
Season: .321 avg.; 30 HR; 89 RBIs.
(See Hall of Fame section, 1974.)

MAURY WILLS   **N.L. MVP**
Team: Dodgers.   **Position:** Shortstop.
5-11, 170.   **B:** B. **T:** R.
Born: Oct. 2, 1932.
Season: .299 avg.; 6 HR; 48 RBIs; 104 SB.
Career: .281 avg.; 20 HR; 458 RBIs; 586 SB.
Teams: Dodgers 1959-66, 1969-72; Pirates 1967-68; Expos 1969.

DON DRYSDALE   **CY YOUNG**
Team: Dodgers.
Season: 25-9; 2.83 ERA; 232 SO.
(See Hall of Fame section, 1984.)

TOM TRESH   **A.L. ROOKIE**
Team: Yankees.   **Position:** Shortstop, Outfield.
6-1, 190.   **B:** B. **T:** R.
Born: Sept. 20, 1937.
Season: .286 avg.; 20 HR; 93 RBIs.
Career: .245 avg.; 153 HR; 530 RBIs.
Teams: Yankees 1961-69; Tigers 1969.

KEN HUBBS   **N.L. ROOKIE**
Team: Cubs.   **Position:** Second base.
6-2, 175.   **B:** R. **T:** R.
Born: Dec. 23, 1941.   **Died:** Feb. 13, 1964.
Season: .260 avg.; 5 HR; 49 RBIs.
Career: .247 avg.; 14 HR; 98 RBIs.
Team: Cubs 1961-63.

1963

ELSTON HOWARD   **A.L. MVP**
Team: Yankees.   **Position:** Catcher.
6-2, 200.   **B:** R. **T:** R.
Born: Feb. 23, 1929.   **Died:** Dec. 14, 1980.
Season: .287 avg.; 28 HR; 85 RBIs.
Career: .274 avg.; 167 HR; 762 RBIs.
Teams: Yankees 1955-67; Red Sox 1967-68.

SANDY KOUFAX   **N.L. MVP, CY YOUNG**
Team: Dodgers.   **Position:** Pitcher.
Season: 25-5; 1.88 ERA; 306 SO.
(See Hall of Fame section, 1972.)

GARY PETERS   **A.L. ROOKIE**
Team: White Sox.   **Position:** Pitcher.
6-2, 200.   **B:** L. **T:** L.
Born: April 21, 1937.
Season: 19-8; 2.33 ERA; 189 SO.
Career: 124-103; 3.25 ERA; 1,420 SO.
Teams: White Sox 1959-69; Red Sox 1970-72.

PETE ROSE   **N.L. ROOKIE**
Team: Reds.   **Position:** Second base.
5-11, 200.   **B:** B. **T:** R.
Born: April 14, 1941.
Season: .273 avg.; 6 HR; 41 RBIs.
Career: .303 avg.; 160 HR; 1,314 RBIs; 4,256 hits, 1st on all-time list.
Teams: Reds 1963-78, 1984-86; Phillies 1979-83; Expos 1984.

1964

BROOKS ROBINSON   **A.L. MVP**
Team: Orioles.   **Position:** Third base.
Season: .317 avg.; 28 HR; 118 RBIs.
(See Hall of Fame section, 1983.)

KEN BOYER   **N.L. MVP**
Team: Cardinals.   **Position:** Third base.
6-2, 200.   **B:** R. **T:** R.
Born: May 20, 1931.   **Died:** Sept. 7, 1982.
Season: .295 avg.; 24 HR; 119 RBIs.
Career: .287 avg.; 282 HR; 1,141 RBIs.
Teams: Cardinals 1955-65; Mets 1966-67; Cubs 1967-68; Dodgers 1968-69.

DEAN CHANCE   **CY YOUNG**
Team: Angels.
6-3, 200.   **B:** R. **T:** R.
Born: June 1, 1941.
Season: 20-9; 1.65 ERA; 207 SO.
Career: 128-115; 2.92 ERA; 1,534 SO.
Teams: Angels 1961-66; Twins 1967-69; Indians 1970; Mets 1970; Tigers 1971.

TONY OLIVA   **A.L. ROOKIE**
Team: Twins.   **Position:** Outfield.
6-2, 190.   **B:** L. **T:** R.
Born: July 20, 1940.
Season: .323 avg.; 32 HR; 94 RBIs; 217 hits.
Career: .304 avg.; 220 HR; 947 RBIs.
Team: Twins 1962-76.

DICK ALLEN   **N.L. ROOKIE**
Team: Phillies.   **Position:** Third base.
5-11, 190.   **B:** R. **T:** R.
Born: March 8, 1942.
Season: .318 avg.; 29 HR; 91 RBIs.

Career: .292 avg.; 351 HR; 1,119 RBIs.
Teams: Phillies 1963-69, 1975-76; Cardinals 1970; Dodgers 1971; White Sox 1972-74; Athletics 1977.

1965

ZOILO VERSALLES — A.L. MVP
Team: Twins. **Position:** Shortstop.
5-10, 150. **B:** R. **T:** R.
Born: Dec. 18, 1939.
Season: .273 avg.; 19 HR; 77 RBIs; 27 SB.
Career: .242 avg.; 95 HR; 471 RBIs.
Teams: Senators 1959-60, 1969; Twins 1961-67; Dodgers 1968; Indians 1969; Braves 1971.

WILLIE MAYS — N.L. MVP
Team: Giants. **Position:** Outfield.
Season: .317 avg.; 52 HR; 112 RBIs.
(See Hall of Fame section, 1979.)

SANDY KOUFAX — CY YOUNG
Team: Dodgers.
Season: 26-8; 2.04 ERA; 382 SO.
(See Hall of Fame section, 1972.)

CURT BLEFARY — A.L. ROOKIE
Team: Orioles. **Position:** Outfield.
6-2, 195. **B:** L. **T:** R.
Born: July 5, 1943.
Season: .260 avg.; 22 HR; 70 RBIs.
Career: .237 avg.; 112 HR; 382 RBIs.
Teams: Orioles 1965-68; Astros 1969; Yankees 1970-71; Athletics 1971-72; Padres 1972.

JIM LEFEBVRE — N.L. ROOKIE
Team: Dodgers. **Position:** Second base.
6-0, 185. **B:** B. **T:** R.
Born: Jan. 7, 1942.
Season: .250 avg.; 12 HR; 69 RBIs.
Career: .251 avg.; 74 HR; 404 RBIs.
Team: Dodgers 1965-72.

1966

FRANK ROBINSON — A.L. MVP
Team: Orioles. **Position:** Outfield.
Season: .316 avg.; 49 HR; 122 RBIs.
(See Hall of Fame section, 1982.)

ROBERTO CLEMENTE — N.L. MVP
Team: Pirates. **Position:** Outfield.
Season: .317 avg.; 29 HR; 119 RBIs.
(See Hall of Fame section, 1973.)

SANDY KOUFAX — CY YOUNG
Team: Dodgers.
Season: 27-9; 1.73 ERA; 317 SO.
(See Hall of Fame section, 1972.)

TOMMIE AGEE — A.L. ROOKIE
Team: White Sox. **Position:** Outfield.
5-11, 195. **B:** R. **T:** R.
Born: Aug. 9, 1942.
Season: .273 avg.; 22 HR; 86 RBIs.
Career: .255 avg.; 130 HR; 433 RBIs.
Teams: Indians 1962-64; White Sox 1965-67; Mets 1968-72; Astros 1973; Cardinals 1973.

TOMMY HELMS — N.L. ROOKIE
Team: Reds. **Position:** Third base.
5-10, 175. **B:** R. **T:** R.
Born: May 5, 1941.
Season: .284 avg.; 9 HR; 49 RBIs.
Career: .269 avg.; 34 HR; 477 RBIs.
Teams: Reds 1964-71; Astros 1972-75; Pirates 1976-77; Red Sox 1977.

1967

CARL YASTRZEMSKI — A.L. MVP
Team: Red Sox. **Position:** Outfield.
Season: .326 avg.; 44 HR; 121 RBIs; Triple Crown winner.
(See Hall of Fame section, 1989.)

ORLANDO CEPEDA — N.L. MVP
Team: Cardinals. **Position:** First base.
Season: .325 avg.; 25 HR; 111 RBIs.
(See Hall of Fame section, 1999.)

JIM LONBORG — A.L. CY YOUNG
Team: Red Sox.
6-5, 210. **B:** R. **T:** R.
Born: April 16, 1942.
Season: 22-9; 3.16 ERA; 246 SO.
Career: 157-137; 3.86 ERA; 1,475 SO.
Teams: Red Sox 1965-71; Brewers 1972; Phillies 1973-79.

MIKE McCORMICK — N.L. CY YOUNG
Team: Giants.
6-2, 195. **B:** L. **T:** L.
Born: Sept. 29, 1938.
Season: 22-10; 2.85 ERA; 150 SO.
Career: 134-128; 3.73 ERA; 1.321 SO.
Teams: Giants 1956-62, 1967-70; Orioles 1963-64; Senators 1965-66; Yankees 1970; Royals 1971.

ROD CAREW — A.L. ROOKIE
Team: Twins. **Position:** Second base.
Season: .292 avg.; 8 HR; 51 RBIs.
(See Hall of Fame section, 1991.)

TOM SEAVER — N.L. ROOKIE
Team: Mets. **Position:** Pitcher.
Season: 16-13; 2.76 ERA; 170 SO.
(See Hall of Fame section, 1992.)

1968

DENNY McLAIN — A.L. MVP, CY YOUNG
Team: Tigers. **Position:** Pitcher.
6-1, 185. **B:** R. **T:** R.
Born: March 29, 1944.
Season: 31-6; 1.96 ERA; 280 SO.
Career: 131-91; 3.39 ERA; 1,282 SO.
Teams: Tigers 1963-70; Senators 1971; Athletics 1972; Braves 1972.

BOB GIBSON — N.L. MVP, CY YOUNG
Team: Cardinals. **Position:** Pitcher.
Season: 22-9; 1.12 ERA; 268 SO.
(See Hall of Fame section, 1981.)

STAN BAHNSEN — A.L. ROOKIE
Team: Yankees. **Position:** Pitcher.
6-2, 203. **B:** R. **T:** R.
Born: Dec. 15, 1944.
Season: 17-12; 2.05 ERA; 162 SO.
Career: 146-149; 3.60 ERA; 1,359 SO.
Teams: Yankees 1966, 1968-71; White Sox 1972-75; Athletics 1975-77; Expos 1977-81; Angels 1982; Phillies 1982.

JOHNNY BENCH — N.L. ROOKIE
Team: Reds. **Position:** Catcher.
Season: .275 avg.; 15 HR; 82 RBIs.
(See Hall of Fame section, 1989.)

1969

HARMON KILLEBREW — A.L. MVP
Team: Twins. **Position:** First base, third base.
Season: .276 avg.; 49 HR; 140 RBIs.
(See Hall of Fame section, 1984.)

WILLIE McCOVEY — N.L. MVP
Team: Giants. **Position:** First base.
Season: .320 avg.; 45 HR; 126 RBIs.
(See Hall of Fame section, 1986.)

DENNY McLAIN — A.L. CO-CY YOUNG
Team: Tigers.
Season: 24-9; 2.80 ERA; 181 SO.
(See 1968 A.L. MVP.)

MIKE CUELLAR — A.L. CO-CY YOUNG
Team: Orioles.
5-11, 175. **B:** L. **T:** L.
Born: May 8, 1937.
Season: 23-11; 2.38 ERA; 182 SO.
Career: 185-130; 3.14 ERA; 1,632 SO.
Teams: Reds 1959; Cardinals 1964; Astros 1965-68; Orioles 1969-76; Angels 1977.

TOM SEAVER — N.L. CY YOUNG
Team: Mets.
Season: 25-7; 2.21 ERA; 208 SO.
(See Hall of Fame section, 1992.)

LOU PINIELLA — A.L. ROOKIE
Team: Royals. **Position:** Outfield.
6-2, 198. **B:** R. **T:** R.
Born: Aug. 28, 1943.
Season: .282 avg.; 11 HR; 68 RBIs.
Career: .291 avg.; 102 HR; 766 RBIs.
Teams: Orioles 1964; Indians 1968; Royals 1969-73; Yankees 1974-84.

TED SIZEMORE — N.L. ROOKIE
Team: Dodgers. **Position:** Second base.
5-10, 165. **B:** R. **T:** R.
Born: April 15, 1945.
Season: .271 avg.; 4 HR; 46 RBIs.
Career: .262 avg.; 23 HR; 430 RBIs.
Teams: Dodgers 1969-70, 1976; Cardinals 1971-75; Phillies 1977-78; Cubs 1979; Red Sox 1979-80.

1970

BOOG POWELL — A.L. MVP
Team: Orioles. **Position:** First base.
6-4, 240. **B:** L. **T:** R.
Born: Aug. 17, 1941.
Season: .297 avg.; 35 HR; 114 RBIs.
Career: .266 avg.; 339 HR; 1,187 RBIs.
Teams: Orioles 1961-74; Indians 1975-76; Dodgers 1977.

JOHNNY BENCH — N.L. MVP
Team: Reds. **Position:** Catcher.
Season: .293 avg.; 45 HR; 148 RBIs.
(See Hall of Fame section, 1989.)

JIM PERRY — A.L. CY YOUNG
Team: Twins.
6-4, 200. **B:** B. **T:** R.
Born: Oct. 30, 1936.
Season: 24-12; 3.04 ERA; 168 SO.
Career: 215-174; 3.45 ERA; 1,576.
Teams: Indians 1959-63, 1974-75; Twins 1963-72; Tigers 1973; Athletics 1975.

BOB GIBSON — N.L. CY YOUNG
Team: Cardinals.
Season: 23-7; 3.12 ERA; 274 SO.
(See Hall of Fame section, 1981.)

THURMAN MUNSON — A.L. ROOKIE
Team: Yankees. **Position:** Catcher.
5-11, 190. **B:** R. **T:** R.
Born: June 7, 1947. **Died:** Aug. 2, 1979.
Season: .302 avg.; 6 HR; 53 RBIs.
Career: .292 avg.; 113 HR; 701 RBIs.
Team: Yankees 1969-79.

CARL MORTON — N.L. ROOKIE
Team: Expos. **Position:** Pitcher.
6-0, 200. **B:** R. **T:** R.
Born: Jan. 18, 1944. **Died:** April 12, 1983.
Season: 18-11; 3.60 ERA; 154 SO.
Career: 87-92; 3.73 ERA; 650 SO.
Teams: Expos 1969-72; Braves 1973-76.

Cincinnati catcher Johnny Bench won the first of two N.L. MVP awards in 1970.

1971

VIDA BLUE A.L. MVP, CY YOUNG
Team: Athletics. **Position:** Pitcher.
6-0, 189. **B:** B. **T:** L.
Born: July 28, 1949.
Season: 24-8; 1.82 ERA; 301 SO.
Career: 209-161; 3.27 ERA; 2,175 SO.
Teams: Athletics 1969-77; Giants 1978-81, 1985-86; Royals 1982-83.

JOE TORRE N.L. MVP
Team: Cardinals. **Position:** Third base.
6-2, 212. **B:** R. **T:** R.
Born: July 18, 1940.
Season: .363 avg.; 24 HR; 137 RBIs.
Career: .297 avg.; 252 HR; 1,185 RBIs.
Teams: Braves 1960-68; Cardinals 1969-74; Mets 1975-77.

FERGUSON JENKINS N.L. CY YOUNG
Team: Cubs.
Season: 24-13; 2.77 ERA; 263 SO.
(See Hall of Fame section, 1991.)

CHRIS CHAMBLISS A.L. ROOKIE
Team: Indians. **Position:** First base.
6-1, 215. **B:** L. **T:** R.
Born: Dec. 26, 1948.
Season: .275 avg.; 9 HR; 48 RBIs.
Career: .279 avg.; 185 HR; 972 RBIs.
Teams: Indians 1971-74; Yankees 1974-79, 1988; Braves 1980-86.

EARL WILLIAMS N.L. ROOKIE
Team: Braves. **Position:** Catcher.
6-3, 220. **B:** R. **T:** R.
Born: July 14, 1948.
Season: .260 avg.; 33 HR; 87 RBIs.
Career: .247 avg.; 138 HR; 457 RBIs.
Teams: Braves 1970-72, 1975-76; Orioles 1973-74; Expos 1976; Athletics 1977.

1972

DICK ALLEN A.L. MVP
Team: White Sox. **Position:** First base.
Season: .308 avg.; 37 HR; 113 RBIs.
(See 1964 N.L. Rookie of Year.)

JOHNNY BENCH N.L. MVP
Team: Reds. **Position:** Catcher.
Season: .270 avg.; 40 HR; 125 RBIs.
(See Hall of Fame section, 1989.)

GAYLORD PERRY A.L. CY YOUNG
Team: Indians.
Season: 24-16; 1.92 ERA; 234 SO.
(See Hall of Fame section, 1991.)

STEVE CARLTON N.L. CY YOUNG
Team: Phillies.
Season: 27-10; 1.97 ERA; 310 SO.
(See Hall of Fame section, 1994.)

CARLTON FISK A.L. ROOKIE
Team: Red Sox. **Position:** Catcher.
6-2, 220. **B:** R. **T:** R.
Born: Dec. 26, 1947.
Season: .293 avg.; 22 HR; 61 RBIs.
Career: .269 avg.; 376 HR; 1,330 RBIs.
Teams: Red Sox 1969, 1971-80; White Sox 1981-93.

JON MATLACK N.L. ROOKIE
Team: Mets. **Position:** Pitcher.
6-3, 205. **B:** L. **T:** L.
Born: Jan. 19, 1950.
Season: 15-10; 2.32 ERA; 169 SO.
Career: 125-126; 3.18 ERA; 1,516 SO.
Teams: Mets 1971-77; Rangers 1978-83.

1973

REGGIE JACKSON A.L. MVP
Team: Athletics. **Position:** Outfield.
Season: .293 avg.; 32 HR; 117 RBIs.
(See Hall of Fame section, 1993.)

PETE ROSE N.L. MVP
Team: Reds. **Position:** Outfield.
Season: .338 avg.; 5 HR; 64 RBIs; 230 hits.
(See 1963 N.L. Rookie of Year.)

JIM PALMER A.L. CY YOUNG
Team: Orioles.
Season: 22-9; 2.40 ERA; 158 SO.
(See Hall of Fame section, 1990.)

TOM SEAVER N.L. CY YOUNG
Team: Mets.
Season: 19-10; 2.08 ERA; 251 SO.
(See Hall of Fame section, 1992.)

AL BUMBRY A.L. ROOKIE
Team: Orioles. **Position:** Outfield.
5-8, 175. **B:** L. **T:** R.
Born: April 21, 1947.
Season: .337 avg.; 7 HR; 34 RBIs; 23 SB.
Career: .281 avg.; 54 HR; 402 RBIs; 254 SB.
Teams: Orioles 1972-84; Padres 1985.

GARY MATTHEWS N.L. ROOKIE
Team: Giants. **Position:** Outfield.
6-3, 190. **B:** R. **T:** R.
Born: July 5, 1950.
Season: .300 avg.; 12 HR; 58 RBIs.
Career: .281 avg.; 234 HR; 978 RBIs.
Teams: Giants 1972-76; Braves 1977-80; Phillies 1981-83; Cubs 1984-87; Mariners 1987.

1974

JEFF BURROUGHS A.L. MVP
Team: Rangers. **Position:** Outfield.
6-1, 200. **B:** R. **T:** R.
Born: March 7, 1951.
Season: .301 avg.; 25 HR; 118 RBIs.
Career: .261 avg.; 240 HR; 882 RBIs.
Teams: Senators 1970-71; Rangers 1972-76; Braves 1977-80; Mariners 1981; Athletics 1982-84; Blue Jays 1985.

STEVE GARVEY N.L. MVP
Team: Dodgers. **Position:** First base.
5-10, 192. **B:** R. **T:** R.
Born: Dec. 22, 1948.

Season: .312 avg.; 21 HR; 111 RBIs.
Career: .294 avg.; 272 HR; 1,308 RBIs.
Teams: Dodgers 1969-82; Padres 1983-87.

JIM (CATFISH) HUNTER A.L. CY YOUNG
Team: Athletics.
Season: 25-12; 2.49 ERA; 143 SO.
(See Hall of Fame section, 1987.)

MIKE MARSHALL N.L. CY YOUNG
Team: Dodgers.
5-10, 180. **B:** R. **T:** R.
Born: Jan. 15, 1943.
Season: 15-12; 2.42 ERA; 143 SO; 21 saves; 106 games.
Career: 97-112; 3.14 ERA; 880 SO; 188 saves.
Teams: Tigers 1967; Mariners 1969; Astros 1970; Expos 1970-73; Dodgers 1974-76; Braves 1976-77; Rangers 1977; Twins 1978-80; Mets 1981.

MIKE HARGROVE A.L. ROOKIE
Team: Rangers. **Position:** First base.
6-0, 195. **B:** L. **T:** L.
Born: Oct. 26, 1949.
Season: .323 avg.; 4 HR; 66 RBIs.
Career: .290 avg.; 80 HR; 686 RBIs.
Teams: Rangers 1974-78; Padres 1979; Indians 1979-85.

BAKE McBRIDE N.L. ROOKIE
Team: Cardinals. **Position:** Outfield.
6-2, 190. **B:** L. **T:** R.
Born: Feb. 3, 1949.
Season: .309 avg.; 6 HR; 56 RBIs.
Career: .299 avg.; 63 HR; 430 RBIs.
Teams: Cardinals 1973-77; Phillies 1977-81; Indians 1982-83.

1975

FRED LYNN A.L. MVP, ROOKIE
Team: Red Sox. **Position:** Outfield.
6-1, 190. **B:** L. **T:** L.
Born: Feb. 3, 1952.
Season: .331 avg.; 21 HR; 105 RBIs.
Career: .283 avg.; 306 HR; 1,111 RBIs.
Teams: Red Sox 1974-80; Angels 1981-84; Orioles 1985-88; Tigers 1988-89; Padres 1990.

JOE MORGAN N.L. MVP
Team: Reds. **Position:** Second base.
Season: .327 avg.; 17 HR; 94 RBIs; 67 SB.
(See Hall of Fame section, 1990.)

JIM PALMER A.L. CY YOUNG
Team: Orioles.
Season: 23-11; 2.09 ERA; 193 SO.
(See Hall of Fame section, 1990.)

TOM SEAVER N.L. CY YOUNG
Team: Mets.
Season: 22-9; 2.38 ERA; 243 SO.
(See Hall of Fame section, 1992.)

JOHN MONTEFUSCO N.L. ROOKIE
Team: Giants. **Position:** Pitcher.
6-1, 180. **B:** R. **T:** R.
Born: May 25, 1950.
Season: 15-9; 2.88 ERA; 215 SO.
Career: 90-83; 3.54 ERA; 1,081 SO.
Teams: Giants 1974-80; Braves 1981; Padres 1982-83; Yankees 1983-86.

1976

THURMAN MUNSON A.L. MVP
Team: Yankees. **Position:** Catcher.
Season: .302 avg.; 17 HR; 105 RBIs.
(See 1970 A.L. Rookie of Year.)

JOE MORGAN N.L. MVP
Team: Reds. **Position:** Second base.
Season: .320 avg.; 27 HR; 111 RBIs; 60 SB.
(See Hall of Fame section, 1990.)

WHO'S WHO

JIM PALMER   **A.L. CY YOUNG**
Team: Orioles.
Season: 22-13; 2.51 ERA; 159 SO.
(See Hall of Fame section, 1990.)

RANDY JONES   **N.L. CY YOUNG**
Team: Padres.
6-0, 178.   B: R. T: L.
Born: Jan. 12, 1950.
Season: 22-14; 2.74 ERA; 93 SO.
Career: 100-123; 3.42 ERA; 735 SO.
Teams: Padres 1973-80; Mets 1981-82.

MARK FIDRYCH   **A.L. ROOKIE**
Team: Tigers.   Position: Pitcher.
6-3, 175.   B: R. T: R.
Born: Aug. 14, 1954.
Season: 19-9; 2.34 ERA; 97 SO.
Career: 29-19; 3.10 ERA; 170 SO.
Team: Tigers 1976-80.

BUTCH METZGER   **N.L. CO-ROOKIE**
Team: Padres.   Position: Pitcher.
6-1, 185.   B: R. T: R.
Born: May 23, 1952.
Season: 11-4; 2.92 ERA; 89 SO.
Career: 18-9; 3.74 ERA; 175 SO.
Teams: Giants 1974; Padres 1975-77; Cardinals 1977; Mets 1978.

PAT ZACHRY   **N.L. CO-ROOKIE**
Team: Reds.   Position: Pitcher.
6-5, 180.   B: R. T: R.
Born: April 24, 1952.
Season: 14-7; 2.74 ERA; 143 SO.
Career: 69-67; 3.52 ERA; 669 SO.
Teams: Reds 1976-77; Mets 1977-82; Dodgers 1983-84; Phillies 1985.

1977

ROD CAREW   **A.L. MVP**
Team: Twins.   Position: First base.
Season: .388 avg.; 14 HR; 100 RBIs; 239 hits.
(See Hall of Fame section, 1991.)

GEORGE FOSTER   **N.L. MVP**
Team: Reds.   Position: Outfield.
6-1, 185.   B: R. T: R.
Born: Dec. 1, 1948.
Season: .320 avg.; 52 HR; 149 RBIs.
Career: .274 avg.; 348 HR; 1,239 RBIs.
Teams: Giants 1969-71; Reds 1971-81; Mets 1982-86; White Sox 1986.

SPARKY LYLE   **A.L. CY YOUNG**
Team: Yankees.
6-1, 192.   B: L. T: L.
Born: July 22, 1944.
Season: 13-5; 2.17 ERA; 68 SO; 26 saves.
Career: 99-76; 2.88 ERA; 873 SO; 238 saves.
Teams: Red Sox 1967-71; Yankees 1972-78; Rangers 1979-80; Phillies 1980-82; White Sox 1982.

STEVE CARLTON   **N.L. CY YOUNG**
Team: Phillies.
Season: 23-10; 2.64 ERA; 198 SO.
(See Hall of Fame section, 1994.)

EDDIE MURRAY   **A.L. ROOKIE**
Team: Orioles.   Position: First base.
6-2, 200.   B: B. T: R.
Born: Feb. 24, 1956.
Season: .283 avg.; 27 HR; 88 RBIs.
Career: .287 avg.; 504 HR; 1,917 RBIs.
Teams: Orioles 1977-88, 1996; Dodgers 1989-91, 1997; Mets 1992-93; Indians 1994-96; Angels 1997.

ANDRE DAWSON   **N.L. ROOKIE**
Team: Expos.   Position: Outfield.
6-3, 195.   B: R. T: R.

Born: July 10, 1954.
Season: .282 avg.; 19 HR; 65 RBIs.
Career: .279 avg.; 438 HR; 1,591 RBIs; still active.
Teams: Expos 1976-86; Cubs 1987-92; Red Sox 1993-94; Marlins 1995-96.

1978

JIM RICE   **A.L. MVP**
Team: Red Sox.   Position: Outfield.
6-2, 205.   B: R. T: R.
Born: March 8, 1953.
Season: .315 avg.; 46 HR; 139 RBIs.
Career: .298 avg.; 382 HR; 1,451 RBIs.
Team: Red Sox 1974-89.

DAVE PARKER   **N.L. MVP**
Team: Pirates.   Position: Outfield.
6-5, 230.   B: L. T: R.
Born: June 9, 1951.
Season: .334 avg.; 30 HR; 117 RBIs.
Career: .290 avg.; 339 HR; 1,493 RBIs.
Teams: Pirates 1973-83; Reds 1984-87; Athletics 1988-89; Brewers 1990; Angels 1991; Blue Jays 1991.

RON GUIDRY   **A.L. CY YOUNG**
Team: Yankees.
5-11, 161.   B: L. T: L.
Born: Aug. 28, 1950.
Season: 25-3; 1.74 ERA; 248 SO.
Career: 170-91; 3.29 ERA; 1,778 SO.
Team: Yankees 1975-88.

GAYLORD PERRY   **N.L. CY YOUNG**
Team: Padres.
Season: 21-6; 2.73 ERA; 154 SO.
(See Hall of Fame section, 1991.)

LOU WHITAKER   **A.L. ROOKIE**
Team: Tigers.   Position: Second base.
5-11, 160.   B: L. T: R.
Born: May 12, 1957.
Season: .285 avg.; 3 HR; 58 RBIs.
Career: .276 avg.; 244 HR; 1,084 RBIs.
Team: Tigers 1977-95.

BOB HORNER   **N.L. ROOKIE**
Team: Braves.   Position: Third base.
6-1, 210.   B: R. T: R.
Born: Aug. 6, 1957.
Season: .266 avg.; 23 HR; 63 RBIs.
Career: .277 avg.; 218 HR; 685 RBIs.
Teams: Braves 1978-86; Cardinals 1988.

1979

DON BAYLOR   **A.L. MVP**
Team: Angels.   Position: Outfield.
6-1, 200.   B: R. T: R.
Born: June 28, 1949.
Season: .296 avg.; 36 HR; 139 RBIs.
Career: .260 avg.; 338 HR; 1,276 RBIs.
Teams: Orioles 1970-75; Athletics 1976, 1988; Angels 1977-82; Yankees 1983-85; Red Sox 1986-87; Twins 1987.

WILLIE STARGELL   **N.L. CO-MVP**
Team: Pirates.   Position: First base.
Season: .281 avg.; 32 HR; 82 RBIs.
(See Hall of Fame section, 1988.)

KEITH HERNANDEZ   **N.L. CO-MVP**
Team: Cardinals.   Position: First base.
6-0, 195.   B: L. T: L.
Born: Oct. 20, 1953.
Season: .344 avg.; 11 HR; 105 RBIs.
Career: .296 avg.; 162 HR; 1,071 RBIs.
Teams: Cardinals 1974-83; Mets 1983-89; Indians 1990.

MIKE FLANAGAN   **A.L. CY YOUNG**
Team: Orioles.
6-0, 195.   B: L. T: L.

Pittsburgh first baseman Willie Stargell had to share N.L. MVP honors in 1979.

Born: Dec. 16, 1951.
Season: 23-9; 3.08 ERA; 190 SO.
Career: 167-143; 3.90 ERA; 1,491 SO.
Teams: Orioles 1975-87, 1991-92; Blue Jays 1987-90.

BRUCE SUTTER   **N.L. CY YOUNG**
Team: Cubs.
6-2, 190.   B: R. T: R.
Born: Jan. 8, 1953.
Season: 6-6; 2.22 ERA; 110 SO; 37 saves.
Career: 68-71; 2.83 ERA; 861 SO; 300 saves.
Teams: Cubs 1976-80; Cardinals 1981-84; Braves 1985-88.

JOHN CASTINO   **A.L. CO-ROOKIE**
Team: Twins.   Position: Third base.
5-11, 175.   B: R. T: R.
Born: Oct. 23, 1954.
Season: .285 avg.; 5 HR; 52 RBIs.
Career: .278 avg.; 41 HR; 249 RBIs.
Team: Twins 1979-84.

ALFREDO GRIFFIN   **A.L. CO-ROOKIE**
Team: Blue Jays.   Position: Shortstop.
5-11, 165.   B: B. T: R.
Born: Oct. 6, 1957.
Season: .287 avg.; 2 HR; 31 RBIs; 21 SB.
Career: .249 avg.; 24 HR; 527 RBIs.
Teams: Indians 1976-78; Blue Jays 1979-84, 1992-93; Athletics 1985-87; Dodgers 1988-91.

RICK SUTCLIFFE   **N.L. ROOKIE**
Team: Dodgers.   Position: Pitcher.
6-7, 220.   B: L. T: R.
Born: June 21, 1956.
Season: 17-10; 3.46 ERA; 117 SO.
Career: 171-139; 4.08 ERA; 1,679 SO.
Teams: Dodgers 1976, 1978-81; Indians 1982-84; Cubs 1984-91; Orioles 1992-93; Cardinals 1994.

1980

GEORGE BRETT   **A.L. MVP**
Team: Royals.   Position: Third base.
Season: .390 avg.; 24 HR; 118 RBIs.
(See Hall of Fame section, 1999.)

MIKE SCHMIDT   **N.L. MVP**
Team: Phillies.   Position: Third base.
Season: .286 avg.; 48 HR; 121 RBIs.
(See Hall of Fame section, 1995.)

STEVE STONE   **A.L. CY YOUNG**
Team: Orioles.

Atlanta outfielder Dale Murphy won consecutive MVP awards in 1982 and '83.

5-10, 175.   **B:** R. **T:** R.
Born: July 14, 1947.
Season: 25-7; 3.23 ERA; 149 SO.
Career: 107-93; 3.97 ERA; 1,065 SO.
Teams: Giants 1971-72; White Sox 1973, 1977-78; Cubs 1974-76; Orioles 1979-81.

STEVE CARLTON   **N.L. CY YOUNG**
Team: Phillies.
Season: 24-9; 2.34 ERA; 286 SO.
(See Hall of Fame section, 1994.)

JOE CHARBONEAU   **A.L. ROOKIE**
Team: Indians.   **Position:** Outfield.
6-2, 205.   **B:** R. **T:** R.
Born: June 17, 1955.
Season: .289 avg.; 23 HR; 87 RBIs.
Career: .266 avg.; 29 HR; 114 RBIs.
Team: Indians 1980-82.

STEVE HOWE   **N.L. ROOKIE**
Team: Dodgers.   **Position:** Pitcher.
6-1, 180.   **B:** L. **T:** L.
Born: March 10, 1958.
Season: 7-9; 2.66 ERA; 39 SO; 17 saves.
Career: 47-41; 3.03 ERA; 328 SO; 91 saves.
Teams: Dodgers 1980-83, 1985; Twins 1985; Rangers 1987; Yankees 1991-95.

1981

ROLLIE FINGERS   **A.L. MVP, CY YOUNG**
Team: Brewers.   **Position:** Pitcher.
Season: 6-3; 1.04 ERA; 61 SO; 28 saves.
(See Hall of Fame section, 1992.)

MIKE SCHMIDT   **N.L. MVP**
Team: Phillies.   **Position:** Third base.
Season: .316 avg.; 31 HR; 91 RBIs.
(See Hall of Fame section, 1995.)

FERNANDO VALENZUELA   **N.L. ROOKIE, CY YOUNG**
Team: Dodgers.
5-11, 195.   **B:** L. **T:** L.
Born: Nov. 1, 1960.
Season: 13-7; 2.48 ERA; 180 SO.

Career: 173-153; 3.54 ERA; 2,074 SO.
Teams: Dodgers 1980-90; Angels 1991; Orioles 1993; Phillies 1994; Padres 1995-97; Cardinals 1997.

DAVE RIGHETTI   **A.L. ROOKIE**
Team: Yankees.   **Position:** Pitcher.
6-3, 205.   **B:** L. **T:** L.
Born: Nov. 28, 1958.
Season: 8-4; 2.05 ERA; 89 SO.
Career: 82-79; 3.46 ERA; 1,112 SO.
Teams: Yankees 1979, 1981-90; Giants 1991-93; Athletics 1994; White Sox 1995.

1982

ROBIN YOUNT   **A.L. MVP**
Team: Brewers.   **Position:** Shortstop.
Season: .331 avg.; 29 HR; 114 RBIs.
(See Hall of Fame section, 1999.)

DALE MURPHY   **N.L. MVP**
Team: Braves.   **Position:** Outfield.
6-4, 215.   **B:** R. **T:** R.
Born: March 12, 1956.
Season: .281 avg; 36 HR; 109 RBIs.
Career: .265 avg.; 398 HR; 1,266 RBIs.
Teams: Braves 1976-90; Phillies 1990-92; Rockies 1993.

PETE VUCKOVICH   **A.L. CY YOUNG**
Team: Brewers.
6-4, 220.   **B:** R. **T:** R.
Born: Oct. 27, 1952.
Season: 18-6; 3.34 ERA; 105 SO.
Career: 93-69; 3.66 ERA; 882 SO.
Teams: White Sox 1975-76; Blue Jays 1977; Cardinals 1978-80; Brewers 1981-83, 1985-86.

STEVE CARLTON   **N.L. CY YOUNG**
Team: Phillies.
Season: 23-11; 3.10 ERA; 286 SO.
(See Hall of Fame section, 1994.)

CAL RIPKEN   **A.L. ROOKIE**
Team: Orioles.   **Position:** Shortstop, third base.
6-4, 210.   **B:** R. **T:** R.
Born: Aug. 24, 1960.

Season: .264 avg.; 28 HR; 93 RBIs.
Career: .278 avg.; 402 HR; 1,571 RBIs; still active.
Team: Orioles 1981-99.

STEVE SAX   **N.L. ROOKIE**
Team: Dodgers.   **Position:** Second base.
5-11, 185.   **B:** R. **T:** R.
Born: Jan. 29, 1960.
Season: .282 avg.; 4 HR; 47 RBIs; 49 SB.
Career: .281 avg.; 54 HR; 550 RBIs; 444 SB.
Teams: Dodgers 1981-88; Yankees 1989-91; White Sox 1992-93; Athletics 1994.

1983

CAL RIPKEN   **A.L. MVP**
Team: Orioles.   **Position:** Shortstop.
Season: .318 avg.; 27 HR; 102 RBIs.
(See 1982 A.L. Rookie.)

DALE MURPHY   **N.L. MVP**
Team: Braves.   **Position:** Outfield.
Season: .302 avg.; 36 HR; 121 RBIs.
(See 1982 N.L. MVP.)

LAMARR HOYT   **A.L. CY YOUNG**
Team: White Sox.
6-1, 222.   **B:** R. **T:** R.
Born: Jan. 1, 1955.
Season: 24-10; 3.66 ERA; 148 SO.
Career: 98-68; 3.99 ERA; 681 SO.
Teams: White Sox 1979-84; Padres 1985-86.

JOHN DENNY   **N.L. CY YOUNG**
Team: Phillies.
6-3, 190.   **B:** R. **T:** R.
Born: Nov. 8, 1952.
Season: 19-6; 2.37 ERA; 139 SO.
Career: 123-108; 3.59 ERA; 1,146 SO.
Teams: Cardinals 1974-79; Indians 1980-82; Phillies 1982-85; Reds 1986.

RON KITTLE   **A.L. ROOKIE**
Team: White Sox.   **Position:** Outfield.
6-4, 220.   **B:** R. **T:** R.
Born: Jan. 5, 1958.
Season: .254 avg.; 35 HR; 100 RBIs.
Career: .239 avg.; 176 HR; 460 RBIs.
Teams: White Sox 1982-86, 1989-91; Yankees 1986-87; Indians 1988; Orioles 1990.

DARRYL STRAWBERRY   **N.L. ROOKIE**
Team: Mets.   **Position:** Outfield.
6-6, 200.   **B:** L. **T:** L.
Born: March 12, 1962.
Season: .257 avg.; 26 HR; 74 RBIs.
Career: .259 avg.; 335 HR; 1,000 RBIs; still active.
Teams: Mets 1983-90; Dodgers 1991-93; Giants 1994; Yankees 1995-99.

1984

WILLIE HERNANDEZ   **A.L. MVP, CY YOUNG**
Team: Tigers.   **Position:** Pitcher.
6-3, 180.   **B:** L. **T:** L.
Born: Nov. 14, 1954.
Season: 9-3; 1.92 ERA; 112 SO; 32 saves.
Career: 70-63; 3.38 ERA; 788 SO; 147 saves.
Teams: Cubs 1977-83; Phillies 1983; Tigers 1984-89.

RYNE SANDBERG   **N.L. MVP**
Team: Cubs.   **Position:** Second base.
6-2, 180.   **B:** R. **T:** R.
Born: Sept. 18, 1959.
Season: .314 avg.; 19 HR; 84 RBIs.
Career: .285 avg.; 282 HR; 1,061 RBIs.
Teams: Phillies 1981; Cubs 1982-94, 1996-97.

RICK SUTCLIFFE N.L. CY YOUNG
Team: Cubs.
Season: 16-1; 2.69 ERA; 155 SO.
(See 1979 N.L. Rookie of Year.)

ALVIN DAVIS A.L. ROOKIE
Team: Mariners. **Position:** First base.
6-1, 195. **B:** L. **T:** R.
Born: Sept. 9, 1960.
Season: .284 avg.; 27 HR; 116 RBIs.
Career: .280 avg.; 160 HR; 683 RBIs.
Team: Mariners 1984-91; Angels 1992.

DWIGHT GOODEN N.L. ROOKIE
Team: Mets. **Position:** Pitcher.
6-3, 200. **B:** R. **T:** R.
Born: Nov. 16, 1964.
Season: 17-9; 2.60 ERA; 276 SO.
Career: 188-107; 3.46 ERA; 2,238 SO; still active.
Team: Mets 1984-94; Yankees 1996-97; Indians 1998-99.

1985

DON MATTINGLY A.L. MVP
Team: Yankees. **Position:** First base.
6-0, 185. **B:** L. **T:** L.
Born: April 20, 1961.
Season: .324 avg.; 35 HR; 145 RBIs.
Career: .307 avg.; 222 HR; 1,099 RBIs.
Team: Yankees 1982-95.

WILLIE MCGEE N.L. MVP
Team: Cardinals. **Position:** Outfield.
6-1, 185. **B:** B. **T:** R.
Born: Nov. 2, 1958.
Season: .353 avg.; 10 HR; 82 RBIs; 216 hits; 56 SB.
Career: .295 avg.; 79 HR; 856 RBIs; 352 SB.
Teams: Cardinals 1982-90, 1996-99; Athletics 1990; Giants 1991-94; Red Sox 1995.

BRET SABERHAGEN A.L. CY YOUNG
Team: Royals.
6-1, 195. **B:** R. **T:** R.
Born: April 11, 1964.
Season: 20-6; 2.87 ERA; 158 SO.
Career: 166-115; 3.33 ERA; 1,705 SO; still active.
Teams: Royals 1984-91; Mets 1992-95; Rockies 1995-96; Red Sox 1997-99.

DWIGHT GOODEN N.L. CY YOUNG
Team: Mets.
Season: 24-4; 1.53 ERA; 268 SO.
(See 1984 N.L. Rookie of Year.)

OZZIE GUILLEN A.L. ROOKIE
Team: White Sox. **Position:** Shortstop.
5-11, 160. **B:** L. **T:** R.
Born: Jan. 20, 1964.
Season: .273 avg.; 1 HR; 33 RBIs.
Career: .264 avg.; 26 HR; 607 RBIs; still active.
Team: White Sox 1985-97; Orioles 1998; Braves 1998-99.

VINCE COLEMAN N.L. ROOKIE
Team: Cardinals. **Position:** Outfield
6-0, 170. **B:** B. **T:** R.
Born: Sept. 22, 1961.
Season: .267 avg.; 1 HR; 40 RBIs; 110 SB.
Career: .264 avg.; 28 HR; 346 RBIs; 752 SB.
Teams: Cardinals 1985-90; Mets 1991-93; Royals 1994-95; Mariners 1995; Reds 1996; Tigers 1997.

1986

ROGER CLEMENS A.L. MVP, CY YOUNG
Team: Red Sox. **Position:** Pitcher.
6-4, 215. **B:** R. **T:** R.
Born: Aug. 4, 1962.
Season: 24-4; 2.48 ERA; 238 SO.

Willie McGee's .353 average, 56 stolen bases and outstanding defense in center field for the '85 pennant-winning Cardinals won him the N.L. MVP award.

Career: 247-134; 3.04 ERA; 3,316 SO; still active.
Team: Red Sox 1984-96; Blue Jays 1997-98; Yankees 1999.

MIKE SCHMIDT N.L. MVP
Team: Phillies. **Position:** Third base.
Season: .290 avg.; 37 HR; 119 RBIs.
(See Hall of Fame section, 1995.)

MIKE SCOTT N.L. CY YOUNG
Team: Astros.
6-3, 215. **B:** R. **T:** R.
Born: April 26, 1955.
Season: 18-10; 2.22 ERA; 306 SO.
Career: 124-108; 3.54 ERA; 1,469 SO.
Teams: Mets 1979-82; Astros 1983-91.

JOSE CANSECO A.L. ROOKIE
Team: Athletics. **Position:** Outfield.
6-4, 240. **B:** R. **T:** R.
Born: July 2, 1964.
Season: .240 avg.; 33 HR; 117 RBIs.
Career: .267 avg.; 431 HR; 1,309 RBIs; still active.
Teams: Athletics 1985-92, 1997; Rangers 1992-94; Red Sox 1995-96; Blue Jays 1998; Devil Rays 1999.

TODD WORRELL N.L. ROOKIE
Team: Cardinals. **Position:** Pitcher.
6-5, 215. **B:** R. **T:** R.
Born: Sept. 28, 1959.
Season: 9-10; 2.08 ERA; 73 SO; 36 saves.
Career: 50-52; 3.09 ERA; 628 SO; 256 saves.
Teams: Cardinals 1985-89, 1992; Dodgers 1993-97.

1987

GEORGE BELL A.L. MVP
Team: Blue Jays. **Position:** Outfield.
6-1, 200. **B:** R. **T:** R.
Born: Oct. 21, 1959.
Season: .308 avg.; 47 HR; 134 RBIs.

Career: .278 avg.; 265 HR; 1,002 RBIs.
Teams: Blue Jays 1981, 1983-90; Cubs 1991; White Sox 1992-93.

ANDRE DAWSON N.L. MVP
Team: Cubs. **Position:** Outfield.
Season: .287 avg.; 49 HR; 137 RBIs.
(See 1977 N.L. Rookie of Year.)

ROGER CLEMENS A.L. CY YOUNG
Team: Red Sox.
Season: 20-9; 2.97 ERA; 256 SO.
(See 1986 A.L. MVP.)

STEVE BEDROSIAN N.L. CY YOUNG
Team: Phillies.
6-3, 200. **B:** R. **T:** R.
Born: Dec. 6, 1957.
Season: 5-3; 2.83 ERA; 74 SO; 40 saves.
Career: 76-79; 3.38 ERA; 921 SO; 184 saves.
Teams: Braves 1981-85, 1993-95; Phillies 1986-89; Giants 1989-90; Twins 1991.

MARK MCGWIRE A.L. ROOKIE
Team: Athletics. **Position:** First base.
6-5, 225. **B:** R. **T:** R.
Born: Oct. 1, 1963.
Season: .289 avg.; 49 HR; 118 RBIs.
Career: .265 avg.; 522 HR; 1,277 RBIs; still active.
Team: Athletics 1986-97; Cardinals 1997-99.

BENITO SANTIAGO N.L. ROOKIE
Team: Padres. **Position:** Catcher.
6-1, 185. **B:** R. **T:** R.
Born: March 9, 1965.
Season: .300 avg.; 18 HR; 79 RBIs.
Career: .260 avg.; 170 HR; 677 RBIs; still active.
Teams: Padres 1986-92; Marlins 1993-94; Reds 1995; Phillies 1996; Blue Jays 1997-98; Cubs 1999.

Red Sox ace Roger Clemens won the first of five Cy Youngs in 1986.

1988

JOSE CANSECO   **A.L. MVP**
Team: Athletics.   **Position:** Outfield.
Season: .307 avg.; 42 HR; 124 RBIs; 40 SB.
(See 1986 A.L. Rookie of Year.)

KIRK GIBSON   **N.L. MVP**
Team: Dodgers.   **Position:** Outfield.
6-3, 215.   **B:** L. **T:** L.
Born: May 28, 1957.
Season: .290 avg.; 25 HR; 76 RBIs; 31 SB.
Career: .268 avg.; 255 HR; 870 RBIs.
Teams: Tigers 1979-87, 1993-95; Dodgers 1988-90; Royals 1991; Pirates 1992.

FRANK VIOLA   **A.L. CY YOUNG**
Team: Twins.
6-4, 210.   **B:** L. **T:** L.
Born: April 19, 1960.
Season: 24-7; 2.64 ERA; 193 SO.
Career: 176-150; 3.73 ERA; 1,844 SO.
Teams: Twins 1982-89; Mets 1989-91; Red Sox 1992-94; Reds 1995; Blue Jays 1996.

OREL HERSHISER   **N.L. CY YOUNG**
Team: Dodgers.
6-3, 190.   **B:** R. **T:** R.
Born: Sept. 16, 1958.
Season: 23-8; 2.26 ERA; 178 SO.
Career: 203-145; 3.41 ERA; 2,001 SO; still active.
Team: Dodgers 1983-94; Indians 1995-97; Giants 1998; Mets 1999.

WALT WEISS   **A.L. ROOKIE**
Team: Athletics.   **Position:** Shortstop.
6-0, 175.   **B:** B. **T:** R.
Born: Nov. 28, 1963.
Season: .250 avg.; 3 HR; 39 RBIs.
Career: .257 avg.; 25 HR; 368 RBIs; still active.
Teams: Athletics 1987-92; Marlins 1993; Rockies 1994-97.

CHRIS SABO   **N.L. ROOKIE**
Team: Reds.   **Position:** Third base.
5-11, 185.   **B:** R. **T:** R.
Born: Jan. 19, 1962.
Season: .271 avg.; 11 HR; 44 RBIs; 46 SB.
Career: .268 avg.; 116 HR; 426 RBIs; 120 SB.
Teams: Reds 1988-93, 1996; Orioles 1994; White Sox 1995; Cardinals 1995.

1989

ROBIN YOUNT   **A.L. MVP**
Team: Brewers.   **Position:** Outfield.
Season: .318 avg.; 21 HR; 103 RBIs.
(See Hall of Fame section, 1999.)

KEVIN MITCHELL   **N.L. MVP**
Team: Giants.   **Position:** Outfield.
5-11, 220.   **B:** R. **T:** R.
Born: Jan. 13, 1962.
Season: .291 avg.; 47 HR; 125 RBIs.
Career: .284 avg.; 234 HR; 760 RBIs.
Teams: Mets 1984, 1986; Padres 1987; Giants 1987-91; Mariners 1992; Reds 1993-94, 1996; Red Sox 1996; Indians 1997; Athletics 1998.

BRET SABERHAGEN   **A.L. CY YOUNG**
Team: Royals.
Season: 23-6, 2.16 ERA; 193 SO.
(See 1985 A.L. Cy Young.)

MARK DAVIS   **N.L. CY YOUNG**
Team: Padres.
6-4, 205.   **B:** L. **T:** L.
Born: Oct. 19, 1960.
Season: 4-3; 1.85 ERA; 92 SO; 44 saves.
Career: 51-84; 4.15 ERA; 993 SO; 96 saves.
Teams: Phillies 1980-81; Giants 1983-87; Padres 1987-89, 1993-94; Royals 1990-92; Braves 1992; Phillies 1993.

GREGG OLSON   **A.L. ROOKIE**
Team: Orioles.   **Position:** Pitcher.
6-4, 210.   **B:** R. **T:** R.
Born: Oct. 11, 1966.
Season: 5-2; 1.69 ERA; 90 SO; 27 saves.
Career: 40-37; 3.23 ERA; 549 SO; 217 saves; still active.
Teams: Orioles 1988-93; Braves 1994; Indians 1995; Royals 1995, 1997; Tigers 1996; Astros 1996; Twins 1997; Diamondbacks 1998-99.

JEROME WALTON   **N.L. ROOKIE**
Team: Cubs.   **Position:** Outfield.
6-1, 175.   **B:** R. **T:** R.
Born: July 8, 1965.
Season: .293 avg.; 5 HR; 46 RBIs; 24 SB.
Career: .268 avg.; 25 HR; 129 RBIs; still active.
Teams: Cubs 1989-92; Angels 1993; Reds 1994-95; Braves 1996; Orioles 1997.

1990

RICKEY HENDERSON   **A.L. MVP**
Team: Athletics.   **Position:** Outfield.
5-10, 195.   **B:** R. **T:** L.
Born: Dec. 25, 1958.
Season: .325 avg.; 28 HR; 61 RBIs; 65 SB.
Career: .284 avg.; 278 HR; 1,020 RBIs; 1,334 SB; still active.
Teams: Athletics 1979-84, 1989-93, 1994-95, 1998; Yankees 1985-89; Blue Jays 1993; Padres 1996-97; Angels 1997; Mets 1999.

BARRY BONDS   **N.L. MVP**
Team: Pirates.   **Position:** Outfield.
6-1, 185.   **B:** L. **T:** L.
Born: July 24, 1964.
Season: .301 avg.; 33 HR; 114 RBIs; 52 SB.
Career: .288 avg.; 445 HR; 1,299 RBIs; 460 SB; still active.
Teams: Pirates 1986-92; Giants 1993-99.

BOB WELCH   **A.L. CY YOUNG**
Team: Athletics.
6-3, 190.   **B:** R. **T:** R.
Born: Nov. 3, 1956.
Season: 27-6; 2.95 ERA; 127 SO.
Career: 211-146; 3.47 ERA; 1,969 SO.
Teams: Dodgers 1978-87; Athletics 1988-94.

DOUG DRABEK   **N.L. CY YOUNG**
Team: Pirates.
6-1, 185.   **B:** R. **T:** R.
Born: July 25, 1962.
Season: 22-6; 2.76 ERA; 131 SO.
Career: 155-134; 3.73 ERA; 1,594 SO.
Teams: Yankees 1986; Pirates 1987-92; Astros 1993-96; White Sox 1997; Orioles 1998.

SANDY ALOMAR JR.   **A.L. ROOKIE**
Team: Indians.   **Position:** Catcher.
6-5, 200.   **B:** R. **T:** R.
Born: June 18, 1966.
Season: .290 avg.; 9 HR; 66 RBIs.
Career: .275 avg.; 86 HR; 417 RBIs; still active.
Teams: Padres 1988-89; Indians 1990-99.

DAVID JUSTICE   **N.L. ROOKIE**
Team: Braves.   **Position:** Outfield.
6-3, 195.   **B:** L. **T:** L.
Born: April 14, 1966.
Season: .282 avg.; 28 HR; 78 RBIs.
Career: .283 avg.; 235 HR; 799 RBIs; still active.
Team: Braves 1989-96; Indians 1997-99.

1991

CAL RIPKEN   **A.L. MVP**
Team: Orioles.   **Position:** Shortstop.
Season: .323 avg.; 34 HR; 114 RBIs.
(See 1982 A.L. Rookie of Year.)

TERRY PENDLETON   **N.L. MVP**
Team: Braves.   **Position:** Third base.
5-9, 190.   **B:** B. **T:** R.
Born: July 16, 1960.
Season: .319 avg.; 22 HR; 86 RBIs.
Career: .270 avg.; 140 HR; 946 RBIs.
Teams: Cardinals 1984-90; Braves 1991-94, 1996; Marlins 1995-96; Reds 1997; Royals 1998.

ROGER CLEMENS   **A.L. CY YOUNG**
Team: Red Sox.
Season: 18-10; 2.62 ERA; 241 SO.
(See 1986 A.L. MVP.)

TOM GLAVINE   **N.L. CY YOUNG**
Team: Braves.
6-1, 190.   **B:** L. **T:** L.
Born: March 25, 1966.
Season: 20-11; 2.55 ERA; 192 SO.
Career: 187-116; 3.38 ERA; 1,659 SO; still active.
Team: Braves 1987-99.

CHUCK KNOBLAUCH   **A.L. ROOKIE**
Team: Twins.   **Position:** Second base.
5-9, 175.   **B:** R. **T:** R.
Born: July 7, 1968.
Season: .281 avg.; 1 HR; 50 RBIs; 25 SB.
Career: .298 avg.; 78 HR; 523 RBIs; 335 SB; still active.
Team: Twins 1991-97; Yankees 1998-99.

JEFF BAGWELL   **N.L. ROOKIE**
Team: Astros.   **Position:** First base.
6-0, 195.   **B:** R. **T:** R.
Born: May 27, 1968.
Season: .294 avg.; 15 HR; 82 RBIs.
Career: .304 avg.; 263 HR; 961 RBIs; still active.
Team: Astros 1991-99.

1992

DENNIS ECKERSLEY   **A.L. MVP,**
                                     CY YOUNG
Team: Athletics.   **Position:** Pitcher.
6-2, 190.   **B:** R. **T:** R.
Born: Oct. 3, 1954.

–254–

Season: 7-1; 1.91 ERA; 93 SO; 51 saves.
Career: 197-171; 3.50 ERA; 2,401 SO; 390 saves; still active.
Teams: Indians 1975-77; Red Sox 1978-84, 1998; Cubs 1984-86; Athletics 1987-95; Cardinals 1996-97.

BARRY BONDS — N.L. MVP
Team: Pirates.   **Position:** Outfield.
Season: .311 avg.; 34 HR; 103 RBIs; 39 SB.
(See 1990 N.L. MVP.)

GREG MADDUX — N.L. CY YOUNG
Team: Cubs.
6-0, 175.   **B:** R. **T:** R.
Born: April 14, 1966.
Season: 20-11; 2.18 ERA; 199 SO.
Career: 221-126; 2.81 ERA; 2,160 SO.
Teams: Cubs 1986-92; Braves 1993-99.

PAT LISTACH — A.L. ROOKIE
Team: Brewers.   **Position:** Shortstop.
5-9, 170.   **B:** B. **T:** R.
Born: Sept. 12, 1967.
Season: .290 avg.; 1 HR; 47 RBIs; 54 SB.
Career: .251 avg.; 5 HR; 143 RBIs; 116 SB; still active.
Team: Brewers 1992-96; Astros 1997.

ERIC KARROS — N.L. ROOKIE
Team: Dodgers.   **Position:** First base.
6-4, 216.   **B:** R. **T:** R.
Born: Nov. 4, 1967.
Season: .257 avg.; 20 HR; 88 RBIs.
Career: .273 avg.; 211 HR; 734 RBIs; still active.
Team: Dodgers 1991-99.

1993

FRANK THOMAS — A.L. MVP
Team: White Sox.   **Position:** First base.
6-5, 240.   **B:** R. **T:** R.
Born: May 27, 1968.
Season: .317 avg.; 41 HR; 128 RBIs.
Career: .320 avg.; 301 HR; 1,040 RBIs; still active.
Team: White Sox 1990-99.

BARRY BONDS — N.L. MVP
Team: Giants.   **Position:** Outfield.
Season: .336 avg.; 46 HR; 123 RBIs; 29 SB.
(See 1990 N.L. MVP.)

JACK MCDOWELL — A.L. CY YOUNG
Team: White Sox.
6-5, 188.   **B:** R. **T:** R.
Born: Jan. 16, 1966.
Season: 22-10; 3.37 ERA; 158 SO.
Career: 127-87; 3.85 ERA; 1,311 SO; still active.
Teams: White Sox 1987-88, 1990-94; Yankees 1995; Indians 1996-97; Angels 1998-99.

GREG MADDUX — N.L. CY YOUNG
Team: Braves.
Season: 20-10; 2.36 ERA; 197 SO.
(See 1992 N.L. Cy Young.)

TIM SALMON — A.L. ROOKIE
Team: Angels.   **Position:** Outfield.
6-3, 220.   **B:** R. **T:** R.
Born: Aug. 24, 1968.
Season: .283 avg.; 31 HR; 95 RBIs.
Career: .291 avg.; 196 HR; 660 RBIs; still active.
Team: Angels 1992-99.

MIKE PIAZZA — N.L. ROOKIE
Team: Dodgers.   **Position:** Catcher.
6-3, 197.   **B:** R. **T:** R.
Born: Sept. 4, 1968.
Season: .318 avg.; 35 HR; 112 RBIs.
Career: .328 avg.; 240 HR; 768 RBIs; still active.
Team: Dodgers 1992-98; Marlins 1998; Mets 1998-99.

1994

FRANK THOMAS — A.L. MVP
Team: White Sox.   **Position:** First base.
Season: .353 avg.; 38 HR; 101 RBIs.
(See 1993 A.L. MVP.)

JEFF BAGWELL — N.L. MVP
Team: Astros.   **Position:** First base.
Season: .368 avg.; 39 HR; 116 RBIs.
(See 1991 N.L. Rookie of Year.)

DAVID CONE — A.L. CY YOUNG
Team: Royals.
6-1, 190.   **B:** L. **T:** R.
Born: Jan. 2, 1963.
Season: 16-5; 2.94 ERA; 132 SO.
Career: 180-102; 3.19 ERA; 2,420 SO; still active.
Teams: Royals 1986, 1993-94; Mets 1987-92; Blue Jays 1992, 1995; Yankees 1995-99.

GREG MADDUX — N.L. CY YOUNG
Team: Braves.
Season: 16-6; 1.56 ERA; 156 SO.
(See 1992 N.L. Cy Young.)

BOB HAMELIN — A.L. ROOKIE
Team: Royals.   **Position:** Designated hitter.
6-0, 235.   **B:** L. **T:** L.
Born: Nov. 29, 1967.
Season: .282 avg.; 24 HR; 65 RBIs.
Career: .246 avg.; 67 HR; 209 RBIs; still active.
Team: Royals 1993-96; Tigers 1997; Brewers 1998.

RAUL MONDESI — N.L. ROOKIE
Team: Dodgers.   **Position:** Outfield.
5-11, 202.   **B:** R. **T:** R.
Born: March 12, 1971.
Season: .306 avg.; 16 HR; 56 RBIs.
Career: .288 avg.; 163 HR; 518 RBIs; still active.
Team: Dodgers 1993-99.

1995

MO VAUGHN — A.L. MVP
Team: Red Sox.   **Position:** First base.
6-1, 230.   **B:** L. **T:** R.
Born: Dec. 15, 1967.
Season: .300 avg.; 39 HR; 126 RBIs.
Career: .301 avg.; 263 HR; 860 RBIs; still active.
Team: Red Sox 1991-98; Angels 1999.

BARRY LARKIN — N.L. MVP
Team: Reds.   **Position:** Shortstop.
6-0, 196.   **B:** R. **T:** R.
Born: April 28, 1964.
Season: .319 avg.; 15 HR; 66 RBIs; 51 SBs.
Career: .299 avg.; 168 HR; 793 RBIs; 345 SBs; still active.
Team: Reds 1986-99.

RANDY JOHNSON — A.L. CY YOUNG
Team: Mariners.
6-10, 225.   **B:** R. **T:** L.
Born: Sept. 10, 1963.
Season: 18-2; 2.48 ERA; 294 SO.
Career: 160-88; 3.26 ERA; 2,693 SO; still active.
Teams: Expos 1988-89; Mariners 1989-98; Astros 1998; Diamondbacks 1999.

GREG MADDUX — N.L. CY YOUNG
Team: Braves.
Season: 19-2; 1.63 ERA; 181 SO.
(See 1992 N.L. Cy Young.)

MARTY CORDOVA — A.L. ROOKIE
Team: Twins.   **Position:** Outfield.
6-0, 200.   **B:** R. **T:** R.

Oakland's Dennis Eckersley spelled relief with a 1992 MVP-Cy Young sweep.

Born: July 10, 1969.
Season: .277 avg.; 24 HR; 84 RBIs.
Career: .277 avg.; 79 HR; 385 RBIs; still active.
Team: Twins 1995-99.

HIDEO NOMO — N.L. ROOKIE
Team: Dodgers.   **Position:** Pitcher.
6-2, 210.   **B:** R. **T:** R.
Born: Aug. 31, 1968.
Season: 13-6; 2.54 ERA; 236 SO.
Career: 61-49; 3.82 ERA; 1,031 SO; still active.
Team: Dodgers 1995-98; Mets 1998; Brewers 1999.

1996

JUAN GONZALEZ — A.L. MVP
Team: Rangers.   **Position:** Outfield.
6-3, 215.   **B:** R. **T:** R.
Born: Oct. 16, 1969.
1996 season: .314 avg.; 47 HR; 144 RBIs.
Career: .294 avg.; 340 HR; 1,075 RBIs.
Teams: Rangers 1989-99.

KEN CAMINITI — N.L. MVP
Team: Padres.   **Position:** Third base.
6-0, 200.   **B:** B. **T:** R.
Born: April 21, 1963.
Season: .326 avg.; 40 HR; 130 RBIs.
Career: .274 avg.; 209 HR; 897 RBIs; still active.
Teams: Astros 1987-94, 1999; Padres 1995-98.

PAT HENTGEN — A.L. CY YOUNG
Team: Blue Jays.
6-2, 200.   **B:** R. **T:** R.
Born: Nov. 13, 1968
Season: 20-10; 3.22 ERA; 177 SO.
Career: 105-76; 4.14 ERA; 995 SO; still active.
Teams: Blue Jays 1991-99.

JOHN SMOLTZ — N.L. CY YOUNG
Team: Braves.
6-3, 185.   **B:** R. **T:** R.
Born: May 15, 1967.
Season: 24-8; 2.94 ERA; 276 SO.
Career: 157-113; 3.35 ERA; 2,098 SO; still active.
Teams: Braves 1988-99.

DEREK JETER — A.L. ROOKIE
Team: Yankees.   **Position:** Shortstop.
6-3, 185.   **B:** R. **T:** R.
Born: June 26, 1974.
Season: .314 avg.; 10 HR; 78 RBIs.
Career: .318 avg.; 63 HR; 341 RBIs; still active.
Team: Yankees 1995-99.

Arizona's Randy Johnson overpowered hitters in his first full season in the National League. He struck out 364 hitters, recorded a 2.48 ERA and brought home his second Cy Young Award.

TODD HOLLANDSWORTH   N.L. ROOKIE
Team: Dodgers.   **Position:** Outfield.
6-2, 193.   **B:** L. **T:** L.
Born: April 20, 1973.
Season: .291 avg.; 12 HR; 59 RBIs.
Career: .272 avg.; 33 HR; 155 RBIs; still active.
Team: Dodgers 1995-99.

1997

KEN GRIFFEY JR.   A.L. MVP
Team: Mariners.   **Position:** Outfield.
6-3, 205.   **B:** L. **T:** L.
Born: November 21, 1969.
Season: .304 avg.; 56 HR; 147 RBIs.
Career: .299 avg.; 398 HR; 1,152 RBIs; still active.
Team: Mariners 1989-99.

LARRY WALKER   N.L. MVP
Team: Rockies.   **Position:** Outfield.
6-3, 225.   **B:** L. **T:** R.
Born: December 1, 1966.
Season: .366 avg.; 49 HR; 130 RBIs; 33 SBs.
Career: .312 avg.; 262 HR; 855 RBIs; still active.
Team: Expos 1989-94; Rockies 1995-99.

ROGER CLEMENS   A.L. CY YOUNG
Team: Blue Jays.
Season: 21-7; 2.05 ERA; 292 SO.
(See 1986 A.L. MVP.)

PEDRO MARTINEZ   N.L. CY YOUNG
Team: Expos.
5-11, 175.   **B:** R. **T:** R.
Born: October 25, 1971.
Season: 17-8; 1.90 ERA; 305 SO.
Career: 107-50; 2.83 ERA; 1,534 SO; still active.
Team: Dodgers 1992-93; Expos 1994-97; Red Sox 1998-99.

NOMAR GARCIAPARRA   A.L. ROOKIE
Team: Red Sox.   **Position:** Shortstop.
6-0, 167.   **B:** R. **T:** R.
Born: July 23, 1973.
Season: .306 avg.; 30 HR; 98 RBIs; 22 SB.
Career: .322 avg.; 96 HR; 340 RBIs; 53 SB; still active.
Team: Red Sox 1996-99.

SCOTT ROLEN   N.L. ROOKIE
Team: Phillies.   **Position:** Third base.
6-4, 195.   **B:** R. **T:** R.
Born: April 4, 1975.
Season: .283 avg.; 21 HR; 92 RBIs.
Career: .280 avg.; 82 HR; 297 RBIs; still active.
Team: Phillies 1996-99.

1998

JUAN GONZALEZ   A.L. MVP
Team: Rangers.   **Position:** Outfield.
Season: .318 avg.; 45 HR; 157 RBIs.
(See 1997 A.L. MVP.)

SAMMY SOSA   N.L. MVP
Team: Cubs.   **Position:** Outfield.
6-0, 200.   **B:** R. **T:** R.
Born: November 12, 1968.
Season: .307 avg.; 66 HR; 158 RBIs.
Career: .267 avg.; 336 HR; 941 RBIs; still active.
Team: Rangers 1989; White Sox 1989-91; Cubs 1992-99.

ROGER CLEMENS   A.L. CY YOUNG
Team: Blue Jays.
Season: 20-6; 2.65 ERA; 271 SO.
(See 1986 A.L. MVP.)

TOM GLAVINE   N.L. CY YOUNG
Team: Braves.
Season: 20-6; 2.47 ERA; 157 SO.
(See 1991 N.L. Cy Young.)

BEN GRIEVE   A.L. ROOKIE
Team: Athletics.   **Position:** Outfield.
6-4, 200.   **B:** L. **T:** R.
Born: May 4, 1976.
Season: .288 avg.; 18 HR; 89 RBIs.
Career: .281 avg.; 49 HR; 199 RBIs; still active.
Team: Athletics 1997-99.

KERRY WOOD   N.L. ROOKIE
Team: Cubs.   **Position:** Pitcher.
6-5, 195.   **B:** R. **T:** R.
Born: June 16, 1977.
Season: 13-6; 3.40 ERA; 233 SO.
Career: 13-6; 3.40 ERA; 233 SO; still active.
Team: Cubs 1998.

1999

IVAN RODRIGUEZ   A.L. MVP
Team: Rangers.   **Position:** Catcher.
5-9, 205.   **B:** R. **T:** R.
Born: November 30, 1971.
Season: .332 avg.; 35 HR; 113 RBIs; 25 SBs.
Career: .300 avg.; 144 HR; 621 RBIs; 60 SBs; still active.
Team: Rangers 1991-99.

CHIPPER JONES   N.L. MVP
Team: Braves.   **Position:** Third base.
6-4, 210.   **B:** B. **T:** R.
Born: April 24, 1972.
Season: .319 avg.; 45 HR; 110 RBIs; 25 SBs.
Career: .301 avg.; 153 HR; 524 RBIs; 83 SBs; still active.
Team: Braves 1993-99.

PEDRO MARTINEZ   A.L. CY YOUNG
Team: Red Sox.
Season: 23-4; 2.07 ERA; 313 SO.
(See 1997 N.L. Cy Young.)

RANDY JOHNSON   N.L. CY YOUNG
Team: Diamondbacks.
Season: 17-9; 2.48 ERA; 364 SO.
(See 1995 A.L. Cy Young.)

CARLOS BELTRAN   A.L. ROOKIE
Team: Royals.   **Position:** Outfield.
6-0, 175.   **B:** B. **T:** R.
Born: April 24, 1977.
Season: .293 avg.; 22 HR; 108 RBIs; 27 SBs.
Career: .291 avg.; 22 HR; 115 RBIs; 27 SBs; still active.
Team: Royals 1998-99.

SCOTT WILLIAMSON   N.L. ROOKIE
Team: Reds.   **Position:** Pitcher.
6-2, 210.   **B:** R. **T:** R.
Born: February 17, 1976.
Season: .12-7; 2.41 ERA; 107 SO; 19 saves.
Career: .12-7; 2.41 ERA; 107 SO; 19 saves.
Team: Reds 1999.

2000 PROMINENT FACES

PLAYERS

BATTERS

BOBBY ABREU   **PHILLIES**
6-0, 186   **B:** L. **T:** R.
Position: Outfield.
Born: March 11, 1974.
1999 season: .335 avg.; 20 HR; 93 RBIs; 27 SB.
Career: .311 avg; 40 HR; 194 RBIs; 53 SB.
Teams: Astros 1996-97; Phillies 1998-99.

BENNY AGBAYANI   **METS**
5-11, 225   **B:** R. **T:** R.
Position: Outfield.
Born: December 28, 1971.
1999 season: .286 avg.; 14 HR; 42 RBIs.
Career: .278 avg.; 14 HR; 42 RBIs.
Team: Mets 1998-99.

EDGARDO ALFONZO   **METS**
5-11, 187   **B:** R. **T:** R.
Position: Second base.
Born: November 8, 1973.
1999 season: .304 avg.; 27 HR; 108 RBIs.
Career: .290 avg.; 62 HR; 339 RBIs.
Team: Mets 1995-99.

ROBERTO ALOMAR   **INDIANS**
6-0, 185   **B:** B. **T:** R.
Position: Second base.
Born: February 5, 1968.
1999 season: .323 avg.; 24 HR; 120 RBIs; 37 SB.
Career: .304 avg.; 151 HR; 829 RBIs; 377 SB.
Teams: Padres 1988-90; Blue Jays 1991-95; Orioles 1996-98; Indians 1999.

SANDY ALOMAR JR.   **INDIANS**
6-5, 220   **B:** R. **T:** R.
Position: Catcher.
1999 season: .307 avg.; 6 HR; 25 RBIs.
Awards: See A.L. Rookie of the Year 1990.

MOISES ALOU   **ASTROS**
6-3, 195   **B:** R. **T:** R.
Position: Outfield.
Born: July 3, 1966.
1999 season: Did not play due to injury.
Career: .295 avg.; 145 HR; 612 RBIs.
Teams: Pirates 1990; Expos 1990, 1992-96; Marlins 1997; Astros 1998.

BRADY ANDERSON   **ORIOLES**
6-1, 190   **B:** L. **T:** L.
Position: Outfield.
Born: January 18, 1964.
1999 season: .282 avg.; 24 HR; 81 RBIs; 36 SB.
Career: .261 avg.; 182 HR; 661 RBIs; 283 SB.
Teams: Red Sox, 1988; Orioles 1988-99.

GARRET ANDERSON   **ANGELS**
6-3, 190   **B:** L. **T:** L.
Position: Outfield.
Born: June 30, 1972.
1999 season: .303 avg.; 21 HR; 80 RBIs.
Career: .300 avg.; 72 HR; 393 RBIs.
Team: Angels 1994-99.

RICH AURILIA   **GIANTS**
6-1, 185   **B:** R. **T:** R.
Position: Shortstop.
Born: September 2, 1971.
1999 season: .281 avg.; 22 HR; 80 RBIs.
Career: .270 avg.; 41 HR; 178 RBIs.
Team: Giants 1995-99.

BRAD AUSMUS   **TIGERS**
5-11, 195   **B:** R. **T:** R.
Position: Catcher.
Born: April 14, 1969.
1999 season: .275 avg.; 9 HR; 54 RBIs.
Career: .262 avg.; 41 HR; 248 RBIs.
Teams: Padres 1993-96; Tigers 1996, 1999; Astros 1997-98.

JEFF BAGWELL   **ASTROS**
Position: First base.
1999 season: .304 avg.; 42 HR; 126 RBIs; 30 SB.
Awards: See N.L. Rookie of the Year 1991; N.L. MVP 1994.

HAROLD BAINES   **ORIOLES**
6-2, 200   **B:** L. **T:** L.
Position: Designated hitter.
Born: March 15, 1959.
1999 season: .312 avg.; 25 HR; 103 RBIs.
Career: .292 avg.; 373 HR; 1583 RBIs.
Teams: White Sox 1980-89, 1996-97; Rangers 1989-90; Athletics 1990-92; Orioles 1993-95, 1997-99; Indians 1999.

MICHAEL BARRETT   **EXPOS**
6-0, 195   **B:** R. **T:** R.
Position: Third base, catcher.
Born: October 22, 1976.
1999 season: .293 avg.; 8 HR; 52 RBIs.
Career: .294 avg.; 9 HR; 54 RBIs.
Team: Expos 1998-99.

TONY BATISTA   **BLUE JAYS**
6-0, 195   **B:** R. **T:** R.
Position: Shortstop.
Born: December 9, 1973.
1999 season: .285 avg.; 26 HR; 79 RBIs.
Career: .269 avg.; 59 HR; 184 RBIs.
Teams: Athletics 1996-97; Diamondbacks 1998-99; Blue Jays 1999.

JAY BELL   **DIAMONDBACKS**
6-0, 184   **B:** R. **T:** R.
Position: Second base.
Born: December 11, 1965.
1999 season: .289 avg.; 38 HR; 112 RBIs.
Career: .269 avg.; 162 HR; 732 RBIs.
Teams: Indians 1986-88; Pirates 1989-96; Royals 1997; Diamondbacks 1998-99.

ALBERT BELLE   **ORIOLES**
6-2, 225   **B:** R. **T:** R.
Position: Outfield.
Born: August 25, 1966.
1999 season: .297 avg.; 37 HR; 117 RBIs.
Career: .296 avg.; 358 HR; 1136 RBIs.
Teams: Indians 1989-96; White Sox 1997-98; Orioles 1999.

CARLOS BELTRAN   **ROYALS**
Position: Outfield.
1999 season: .293 avg.; 22 HR; 108 RBIs; 27 SB.
Awards .See A.L. Rookie of the Year 1999.

ADRIAN BELTRE   **DODGERS**
5-11, 170   **B:** R. **T:** R.
Position: Third base.
Born: April 7, 1978.
1999 season: .275 avg.; 15 HR; 67 RBIs.
Career: .259 avg.; 22 HR; 89 RBIs.
Team: Dodgers 1998-99.

DANTE BICHETTE   **REDS**
6-3, 238   **B:** R. **T:** R.
Position: Outfield.

Craig Biggio (left) and Jeff Bagwell have anchored the right side of Houston's infield since 1991.

Born: November 18, 1963.
1999 season: .298 avg.; 34 HR; 133 RBIs.
Career: .300 avg.; 239 HR; 1002 RBIs.
Teams: Angels 1988-90; Brewers 1991-92; Rockies 1993-99.

CRAIG BIGGIO   **ASTROS**
5-11, 180   **B:** R. **T:** R.
Position: Second base.
Born: December 14, 1965.
1999 season: .294 avg.; 16 HR; 73 RBIs; 28 SB.
Career: .292 avg.; 152 HR; 706 RBIs; 346 SB.
Team: Astros 1988-99.

BARRY BONDS   **GIANTS**
Position: Outfield.
1999 season: .262 avg.; 34 HR; 83 RBIs.
Awards: See N.L. MVP 1990, 1992, 1993.

BRET BOONE   **PADRES**
5-10, 180   **B:** R. **T:** R.
Position: Second base.
Born: April 6, 1969.
1999 season: .252 avg.; 20 HR; 63 RBIs.
Career: .255 avg.; 106 HR; 462 RBIs.
Teams: Mariners 1992-93; Reds 1994-98; Braves 1999.

RICO BROGNA   **PHILLIES**
6-2, 205   **B:** L. **T:** L.
Position: First base.
Born: April 18, 1970.
1999 season: .278 avg.; 24 HR; 102 RBIs.
Career: .273 avg; 101 HR; 416 RBIs.
Teams: Tigers 1992; Mets 1994-96; Phillies 1997-99.

JAY BUHNER   **MARINERS**
6-3, 215   **B:** R **T:** R.
Position: Outfield.
Born: August 13, 1964.
1999 season: .222 avg.; 14 HR; 38 RBIs.
Career; .254 avg.; 282 HR; 878 RBIs.
Teams: Yankees 1987-88; Mariners 1988-99.

Carlos Delgado has quietly hit 82 homers and driven in 249 runs the last two seasons for the Jays.

ELLIS BURKS   **GIANTS**
6-2, 205   **B:** R. **T:** R.
Position: Outfield.
Born: September 11, 1964.
1999 season: .282 avg.; 31 HR; 96 RBIs.
Career: .289 avg.; 261 HR; 916 RBIs.
Teams: Red Sox 1987-92; White Sox 1993; Rockies 1994-98; Giants 1998-99.

JEROMY BURNITZ   **BREWERS**
6-0, 205   **B:** L. **T:** R.
Position: Outfield.
Born: April 15, 1969.
1999 season: .270 avg.; 33 HR; 103 RBIs.
Career: .266 avg.; 123 HR; 406 RBIs.
Teams: Mets 1993-94; Indians 1995-96; Brewers 1996-99.

HOMER BUSH   **BLUE JAYS**
5-10, 180   **B:** R. **T:** R.
Position: Second base.
Born: November 12, 1972.
1999 season: .320 avg.; 5 HR; 55 RBIs; 32 SB.
Career: .328 avg.; 6 HR; 63 RBIs; 38 SB.
Teams: Yankees 1997-98; Blue Jays 1999.

MIKE CAMERON   **REDS**
6-2, 190   **B:** R. **T:** R.
Position: Outfield.
Born: January 8, 1973.
1999 season: .256 avg.; 21 HR; 66 RBIs.
Career: .240 avg.; 44 HR; 166 RBIs.
Teams: White Sox 1995-98; Reds 1999.

KEN CAMINITI   **ASTROS**
Position: Third Base.
1999 season: .286 avg.; 13 HR; 56 RBIs.
Awards: See N.L. MVP 1996.

JOSE CANSECO   **DEVIL RAYS**
Position: Designated hitter.
1999 season: .279 avg.; 34 HR; 95 RBIs.
Awards: See A.L. Rookie of the Year 1986; A.L. MVP 1988.

SEAN CASEY   **REDS**
6-4, 225   **B:** L. **T:** R.
Position: First base.
Born: July 2, 1974.
1999 season: .332 avg.; 25 HR; 99 RBIs.
Career: .310 avg.; 32 HR; 152 RBIs.
Teams: Indians 1997; Reds 1998-99.

VINNY CASTILLA   **DEVIL RAYS**
6-1, 200   **B:** R. **T:** R.
Position: Third base.
Born: July 4, 1967.
1999 season: .275 avg; 33 HR; 102 RBIs.
Career: .298 avg.; 203 HR; 611 RBIs.
Teams: Braves 1991-92; Rockies 1993-99.

LUIS CASTILLO   **MARLINS**
5-11, 175   **B:** B. **T:** R.
Position: Second base.
Born: September 12, 1975.
1999 season: .302 avg.; 0 HR; 28 RBIs; 50 SB.
Career: .266 avg.; 2 HR; 54 RBIs; 86 SB.
Team: Marlins 1996-99.

ROGER CEDENO   **ASTROS**
6-1, 205   **B:** B. **T:** R.
Position: Outfield.
Born: August 16, 1974.
1999 season: .313 avg.; 4 HR; 36 RBIs; 66 SB.
Career: .276 avg.; 11 HR; 91 RBIs; 89 SB.
Teams: Dodgers 1995-98; Mets 1999.

JEFF CIRILLO   **ROCKIES**
6-2, 195   **B:** R. **T:** R.
Position: Third base.
Born: September 23, 1969.
1999 season: .326 avg.; 15 HR; 88 RBIs.
Career: .307 avg.; 66 HR; 372 RBIs.
Team: Brewers 1994-99.

TONY CLARK   **TIGERS**
6-8, 250   **B:** B. **T:** R.
Position: First base.
Born: June 15, 1972.
1999 season: .280 avg.; 31 HR; 99 RBIs.
Career: .275 avg.; 127 HR; 402 RBIs.
Team: Tigers 1995-99.

RON COOMER   **TWINS**
5-11, 206   **B:** R. **T:** R.
Position: Third base.
Born: November 18, 1966.
1999 season: .265 avg.; 16 HR; 65 RBIs.
Career: .281 avg.; 61 HR; 282 RBIs.
Team: Twins 1995-99.

MARTY CORDOVA   **TWINS**
6-0, 206   **B:** R. **T:** R.
Position: Outfield.
Born: July 10, 1969.
1999 season: .285 avg.; 14 HR; 70 RBIs.
Career: .277 avg.; 79 HR; 385 RBIs.
Team: Twins 1995-99.

JOHNNY DAMON   **ROYALS**
6-2, 190   **B:** L. **T:** L.
Position: Outfield.
Born: November 5, 1973.
1999 season: .307 avg.; 14 HR; 77 RBIs; 36 SB.
Career: .283 avg.; 49 HR; 264 RBIs; 110 SB.
Team: Royals 1995-99.

ERIC DAVIS   **CARDINALS**
6-3, 185   **B:** R. **T:** R.
Position: Outfield.
Born: May 29, 1962.
1999 season: .257 avg.; 5 HR; 30 RBIs.
Career: .269 avg.; 272 HR; 872 RBIs.
Teams: Reds 1984-91, 1996; Dodgers 1992-93; Tigers 1993-94; Orioles 1997-98; Cardinals 1999.

CARLOS DELGADO   **BLUE JAYS**
6-3, 225   **B:** L. **T:** R.
Position: First base.
Born: June 25, 1972.
1999 season: .272 avg.; 44 HR; 134 RBIs.
Career: .267 avg.; 149 HR; 467 RBIs.
Team: Blue Jays 1993-99.

J.D. DREW   **CARDINALS**
6-1, 195   **B:** L. **T:** R.
Position: Outfield.
Born: November 20, 1975.
1999 season: .242 avg.; 13 HR. 39 RBIs; 19 SB.
Career: .257 avg.; 18 HR; 52 RBIs; 19 SB.
Team: Cardinals 1998-99.

RAY DURHAM   **WHITE SOX**
5-8, 170   **B:** B. **T:** R.
Position: Second base.
Born: November 30, 1971.
1999 season: .296 avg.; 13 HR; 60 RBIs; 34 SB.
Career: .278 avg.; 60 HR; 296 RBIs; 151 SB.
Team: White Sox 1995-99.

JERMAINE DYE   **ROYALS**
6-4, 210   **B:** R. **T:** R.
Position: Outfield.
Born: January 28, 1974.
1999 season: .294 avg.; 27 HR; 119 RBIs.
Career: .271 avg.; 51 HR; 201 RBIs.
Teams: Braves 1996; Royals 1997-99.

DAMION EASLEY   **TIGERS**
5-11, 185   **B:** R. **T:** R.
Position: Second base.
Born: November 11, 1969.
1999 season: .266 avg.; 20 HR; 65 RBIs.
Career: .258 avg.; 86 HR; 353 RBIs.
Teams: Angels 1992-96; Tigers 1996-99.

JIM EDMONDS   **ANGELS**
6-1, 190   **B:** L. **T:** L.
Position: Outfield.
Born: June 27, 1970.
1999 season: .250 avg.; 5 HR; 23 RBIs.
Career: .290 avg.; 121 HR; 408 RBIs.
Team: Angels 1993-99.

JUAN ENCARNACION   **TIGERS**
6-3, 187   **B:** R. **T:** R.
Position: Outfield.
Born: March 8, 1976.
1999 season: .255 avg.; 19 HR; 74 RBIs; 33 SB.
Career: .271 avg.; 27 HR; 100 RBIs; 43 SB.
Team: Tigers 1997-99.

CARL EVERETT   **RED SOX**
6-0, 190   **B:** B. **T:** R.
Position: Outfield.
Born: June 3, 1971.
1999 season: .325 avg.; 25 HR; 108 RBIs; 27 SB.
Career: .277 avg; 69 HR; 317 RBIs; 71 SB.
Teams: Marlins 1993-94; Mets 1995-97; Astros 1998-99.

TONY FERNANDEZ   **FREE AGENT**
6-2, 175   **B:** B. **T:** R.
Position: Third base.
Born: June 30, 1962.
1999 season: .328 avg.; 6HR; 75 RBIs.
Career: .288 avg.; 92 HR; 829 RBIs.
Teams: Blue Jays 1983-90, 1993, 1998-99; Padres 1991-92; Mets 1993; Reds 1994; Yankees 1995; Indians 1997.

STEVE FINLEY   **DIAMONDBACKS**
6-2, 180   **B:** L. **T:** L.
Position: Outfield.
Born: March 12, 1965.
1999 season: .264 avg.; 34 HR; 103 RBIs.
Career: .274 avg.; 153 HR; 649 RBIs.
Teams: Orioles 1989-90; Astros 1991-94; Padres 1995-98; Diamondbacks 1999.

JOHN FLAHERTY   **DEVIL RAYS**
6-1, 200   **B:** R. **T:** R.
Position: Catcher.
Born: October 21, 1967.
1999 season: .278 avg.; 14 HR; 71 RBIs.
Career: .255 avg.; 50 HR; 253 RBIs.
Teams: Red Sox 1992-93; Tigers 1994-96; Padres 1996-97; Devil Rays 1998-99.

CLIFF FLOYD   **MARLINS**
6-4, 235   **B:** L. **T:** R.
Position: Outfield.
Born: December 5, 1972.
1999 season: .303 avg.; 11 HR; 49 RBIs.
Career: .268 avg.; 51 HR; 235 RBIs.
Teams: Expos 1993-96; Marlins 1997-99.

TRAVIS FRYMAN   **INDIANS**
6-1, 195   **B:** R. **T:** R.
Position: Third base.
Born: March 25, 1969.
1999 season: .255 avg.; 10 HR; 48 RBIs.
Career: .274 avg.; 187 HR; 823 RBIs.
Teams: Tigers 1990-97; Indians 1998-99.

ANDRES GALARRAGA   **BRAVES**
6-3, 235   **B:** R. **T:** R.
Position: First base.
Born: June 18, 1961.
1999 season: Did not play due to injury.
Career: .290 avg.; 332 HR; 1,172 RBIs.
Teams: Expos 1985-91; Cardinals 1992; Rockies 1993-97; Braves 1998-99.

NOMAR GARCIAPARRA   **RED SOX**
Position: Shortstop.
1999 season: .357 avg.; 27 HR; 104 RBIs.
Awards: See A.L. Rookie of the Year 1997.

JASON GIAMBI   **ATHLETICS**
6-2, 218   **B:** L. **T:** R.
Position: First base.
Born: January 8, 1971.
1999 season: .315 avg.; 33 HR; 123 RBIs.
Career: .296 avg.; 106 HR; 418 RBIs.
Team: Athletics 1995-99.

BRIAN GILES   **PIRATES**
5-11, 200   **B:** L. **T:** L.
Position: Outfield.
Born: January 20, 1971.
1999 season: .315 avg.; 39 HR; 115 RBIs.
Career: .295 avg.; 78 HR; 272 RBIs.
Teams: Indians 1995-98; Pirates 1999.

DOUG GLANVILLE   **PHILLIES**
6-2, 180   **B:** R. **T:** R.
Position: Outfield.
Born: August 25, 1970.
1999 season: .325 avg.; 11 HR; 73 RBIs; 34 SB.
Career: .298 avg.; 24 HR; 167 RBIs; 78 SB.
Teams: Cubs 1996-97; Phillies 1998-99.

TROY GLAUS   **ANGELS**
6-5, 229   **B:** R. **T:** R.
Position: Third base.
Born: August 3, 1976.
1999 season: .240 avg.; 29 HR; 79 RBIs.
Career: .235 avg.; 30 HR; 102 RBIs.
Team: Angels 1998-99.

ALEX GONZALEZ   **MARLINS**
6-0, 170   **B:** R. **T:** R.
Position: Shortstop.
Born: February 15, 1977.
1999 season: .277 avg.; 14 HR; 59 RBIs.
Career: .260 avg.; 17 HR; 66 RBIs.
Team: Marlins 1998-99.

JUAN GONZALEZ   **TIGERS**
Position: Outfield, designated hitter.
1999 season: .326 avg.; 39 HR; 128 RBIs.
Awards: See A.L. MVP 1996, 1998.

LUIS GONZALEZ   **DIAMONDBACKS**
6-2, 190   **B:** L. **T:** R.
Position: Outfield.
Born: September 3, 1967.
1999 season: .336 avg.; 26 HR; 111 RBIs.
Career: .277 avg.; 133 HR; 661 RBIs.
Teams: Astros 1990-95, 1997; Cubs 1995-96; Tigers 1998; Diamondbacks 1999.

MARK GRACE   **CUBS**
6-2, 200   **B:** L. **T:** L.
Position: First base.
Born: June 28, 1964.
1999 season: .309 avg.;16 HR; 91 RBIs.
Career: .310 avg.; 137 HR; 922 RBIs.
Team: Cubs 1988-99.

SHAWN GREEN   **DODGERS**
6-4, 195   **B:** L. **T:** L.
Position: Outfield.
Born: November 10, 1972.
1999 season: .309 avg.; 42 HR; 123 RBIs; 20 SB.
Career: .286 avg.; 119 HR; 376 RBIs; 76 SB.
Team: Blue Jays 1993-99.

RUSTY GREER   **RANGERS**
6-0, 190   **B:** L. **T:** L.
Position: Outfield.
Born: January 21, 1969.
1999 season: .300 avg.; 20 HR; 101 RBIs.
Career: .309 avg.; 103 HR; 503 RBIs.
Team: Rangers 1994-99.

BEN GRIEVE   **ATHLETICS**
6-4, 200   **B:** L. **T:** R.
Position: Outfield.
Born: May 4, 1976.
1999 season: .265 avg.; 28 HR; 86 RBIs.
Career: .281 avg.; 49 HR; 199 RBIs.
Team: Athletics 1997-99.

KEN GRIFFEY JR.   **MARINERS**
Position: Outfield.
1999 season: .285 avg.; 48 HR; 134 RBIs; 24 SB.
Awards: See A.L. MVP 1997.

MARQUIS GRISSOM   **BREWERS**
5-11, 188   **B:** R. **T:** R.
Position: Outfield.
Born: April 17, 1967.
1999 season: .267 avg.; 20 HR; 83 RBIs; 24 SB.
Career: .277 avg.; 131 HR; 601 RBIs; 382 SB.
Teams: Expos 1989-94; Braves 1995-96; Indians 1997; Brewers 1998-99.

MARK GRUDZIELANEK   **DODGERS**
6-1, 185   **B:** R. **T:** R.
Position: Shortstop.
Born: June 30, 1970.
1999 season: .326 avg.; 7 HR; 46 RBIs.
Career: .288 avg.; 28 HR; 228 RBIs.
Teams: Expos 1995-98; Dodgers 1998-99.

VLADIMIR GUERRERO   **EXPOS**
6-2, 195   **B:** R. **T:** R.
Position: Outfield.
Born: February 9, 1976.
1999 season: .316 avg.; 42 HR; 131 RBIs.
Career: .314 avg.; 92 HR; 281 RBIs.
Team: Expos 1996-99.

TONY GWYNN   **PADRES**
5-11, 225   **B:** L. **T:** L.
Position: Outfield.
Born: May 9, 1960.
1999 season: .338 avg.; 10 HR; 62 RBIs.
Career: .339 avg.; 133 HR; 1104 RBIs.
Team: Padres 1982-99.

TODD HELTON   **ROCKIES**
6-2, 190   **B:** L. **T:** L.
Position: First base.
Born: August 20, 1973.
1999 season: .320 avg.; 35 HR; 113 RBIs.

Nomar Garciaparra's slick fielding and dependable bat paced the Red Sox to ALCS play in 1999.

Career: .315 avg.; 65 HR; 221 RBIs.
Team: Rockies 1997-99.

RICKEY HENDERSON   **METS**
Position: Outfield.
1999 season: .315 avg.; 12 HR; 42 RBIs; 37 SB.
Awards: See A.L. MVP 1990.

GLENALLEN HILL   **CUBS**
6-3, 230   **B:** R. **T:** R.
Position: Outfield.
Born: March 22, 1965.
1999 season: .300 avg.; 20 HR; 55 RBIs.
Career: .271 avg.; 158 HR; 526 RBIs.
Teams: Blue Jays 1989-91; Indians 1991-93; Cubs 1993-94, 1998-99; Giants 1995-97; Mariners 1998.

BRIAN L. HUNTER   **MARINERS**
6-4, 180   **B:** R. **T:** R.
Position: Outfield.
Born: March 5, 1971.
1999 season: .232 avg.; 4 HR; 34 RBIs; 44 SB.
Career: .263 avg.; 19 HR; 178 RBIs.; 221 SB.
Teams: Astros 1994-96; Tigers 1997-99; Mariners 1999.

JOHN JAHA   **ATHLETICS**
6-1, 224   **B:** R. **T:** R.
Position: Designated hitter.
Born: May 27, 1966.
1999 season: .276 avg.; 35 HR; 111 RBIs.
Career: .269 avg.; 140 HR; 477 RBIs.
Teams: Brewers 1992-98; Athletics 1999.

GEOFF JENKINS   **BREWERS**
6-1, 204   **B:** L. **T:** R.
Position: Outfield.
Born: July 21, 1974.
1999 season: .313 avg.; 21 HR; 82 RBIs.
Career: .282 avg.; 30 HR; 110 RBIs.
Team: Brewers 1998-99.

DEREK JETER   **YANKEES**
Position: Shortstop.
1999 season: .349 avg.; 24 HR; 102 RBIs; 19 SB.
Awards: See A.L. Rookie of the Year 1996.

CHARLES JOHNSON   **ORIOLES**
6-2, 220   **B:** R. **T:** R.
Position: Catcher.
Born: July 20, 1971.
1999 season: .251 avg.; 16 HR; 54 RBIs.
Career: .238 avg.; 79 HR; 255 RBIs.
Teams: Marlins 1994-98; Dodgers 1998; Orioles 1999.

Third baseman Chipper Jones parlayed his dependable defense and devastating bat into an MVP performance in 1999.

ANDRUW JONES   BRAVES
6-1, 185   **B:** R. **T:** R.
Position: Outfield.
Born: April 23, 1977.
1999 season: .275 avg.; 26 HR; 84 RBIs; 24 SB.
Career: .260 avg.; 80 HR; 257 RBIs.; 74 SB.
Team: Braves 1996-99.

CHIPPER JONES   BRAVES
Position: Third base.
1999 season: .319 avg.; 45 HR; 110 RBIs; 25 SB.
Awards: See N.L. MVP 1999.

BRIAN JORDAN   BRAVES
6-1, 205   **B:** R. **T:** R.
Position: Outfield.
Born: March 29, 1967.
1999 season: .283 avg.; 23 HR; 115 RBIs.
Career: .289 avg; 107 HR; 482 RBIs.
Teams: Cardinals 1992-98; Braves 1999.

WALLY JOYNER   BRAVES
6-2, 200   **B:** L. **T:** L.
Position: First base.
Born: June 16, 1962.
1999 season: .248 avg.; 5 HR; 43 RBIs.
Career: .290 avg.; 196 HR; 1060 RBIs.
Teams: Angels 1986-91; Royals 1992-95; Padres 1996-99.

DAVID JUSTICE   INDIANS
Position: Outfield, designated hitter.
1999 season: .287 avg.; 21 HR; 88 RBIs.
Awards: See N.L. Rookie of the Year 1990.

GABE KAPLER   RANGERS
6-2, 208   **B:** R. **T:** R.
Position: Outfield.
Born: August 31, 1975.
1999 Season: .245 avg.; 18 HR; 49 RBIs.
Career: .243 avg.; 18 HR; 49 RBIs.
Team: Tigers 1998-99.

ERIC KARROS   DODGERS
Position: First base.
1999 season: .304 avg.; 34 HR; 112 RBIs.
Awards: See N.L. Rookie of the Year 1992.

JASON KENDALL   PIRATES
6-0, 190   **B:** R. **T:** R.
Position: Catcher.
Born: June 26, 1974.
1999 season: .332 avg.; 8 HR; 41 RBIs; 22 SB.

Career: .312 avg.; 31 HR; 207 RBIs; 71 SB.
Team: Pirates 1996-99.

JEFF KENT   GIANTS
6-1, 205   **B:** R. **T:** R.
Position: Second base.
Born: March 7, 1968.
1999 season: .290 avg.; 23 HR; 101 RBIs.
Career: .276 avg.; 161 HR; 668 RBIs.
Teams: Blue Jays 1992; Mets 1992-96; Indians 1996; Giants 1997-99.

RYAN KLESKO   PADRES
6-3, 220   **B:** L. **T:** L.
Position: First base, outfield.
Born: June 12, 1971.
1999 season: .297 avg.; 21 HR; 80 RBIs.
Career: .281 avg.; 139 HR; 450 RBIs.
Team: Braves 1992-99.

CHUCK KNOBLAUCH   YANKEES
Position: Second base.
1999 season: .292 avg.; 18 HR; 68 RBIs; 28 SB.
Awards: See A.L. Rookie of the Year 1991.

PAUL KONERKO   WHITE SOX
6-3, 211   **B:** R. **T:** R.
Position: Third base.
Born: March 5, 1976.
1999 season: .294 avg.; 24 HR; 81 RBIs.
Career: .270 avg.; 31 HR; 110 RBIs.
Teams: Dodgers 1997-98; Reds 1998; White Sox 1999.

RAY LANKFORD   CARDINALS
5-11, 198   **B:** L. **T:** L.
Position: Outfield.
Born: June 5, 1967.
1999 season: .306 avg.; 15 HR; 63 RBIs.
Career: .278 avg.; 181 HR; 703 RBIs.
Team: Cardinals 1990-99.

BARRY LARKIN   REDS
Position: Shortstop.
1999 season: .293 avg.; 12 HR; 75 RBIs; 30 SB.
Awards: See N.L. MVP 1995.

RICKY LEDEE   YANKEES
6-1, 160   **B:** L. **T:** L.
Position: Outfield.
Born: November 22, 1973.
1999 season: .276 avg.; 9 HR; 40 RBIs.
Career: .267 avg.; 10 HR; 52 RBIs.
Team: Yankees 1998-99.

CARLOS LEE   WHITE SOX
6-2, 202   **B:** R. **T:** R.
Position:
Born: June 20, 1976.
1999 season: .293 avg.; 16 HR; 84 RBIs.
Career: .293 avg.; 16 HR; 84 RBIs.
Team: White Sox 1999.

TRAVIS LEE   DIAMONDBACKS
6-3, 210   **B:** L. **T:** L.
Position: First base.
Born: May 26, 1975.
1999 season: .237 avg.; 9 HR; 50 RBIs.
Career: .256 avg.; 31 HR; 122 RBIs.
Team: Diamonbacks 1998-99.

MIKE LIEBERTHAL   PHILLIES
6-0. 186   **B:** R. **T:** R.
Position: Catcher.
Born: January 18, 1972.
1999 season: .300 avg.; 31 HR; 96 RBIs.
Career: .268 avg.; 67 HR; 250 RBIs.
Team: Phillies 1994-99.

KENNY LOFTON   INDIANS
6-0, 180   **B:** L. **T:** L
Position: Outfield.
Born: May 31, 1967.
1999 season: .301 avg.; 7 HR; 39 RBIs; 25 SB.

Career: .310 avg.; 63 HR; 412 RBIs; 433 SB.
Teams: Astros 1991; Indians 1992-96, 1998-99; Braves 1997.

JAVY LOPEZ   BRAVES
6-3, 200   **B:** R. **T:** R.
Position: Catcher.
Born: November 5, 1970.
1999 season: .317 avg.; 11 HR; 45 RBIs.
Career: .290 avg.; 119 HR; 378 RBIs.
Team: Braves 1992-99.

AL MARTIN   PIRATES
6-2, 210   **B:** L. **T:** L.
Position: Outfield.
Born: November 24, 1967.
1999 season: .277 avg.; 24 HR; 63 RBIs; 20 SB.
Career: .280 avg.; 107 HR; 381 RBIs; 152 SB.
Team: Pirates 1992-99.

EDGAR MARTINEZ   MARINERS
5-11, 190   **B:** R. **T:** R.
Position: Designated hitter.
Born: January 2, 1963.
1999 season: .337 avg.; 24 HR; 86 RBIs.
Career: .320 avg.; 198 HR; 780 RBIs.
Team: Mariners 1987-99.

TINO MARTINEZ   YANKEES
6-2, 210   **B:** L. **T:** R.
Position: First base.
Born: December 7, 1967.
1999 season: .263 avg.; 28 HR; 105 RBIs.
Career: .275 avg.; 213 HR; 798 RBIs.
Teams: Mariners 1990-95; Yankees 1996-99.

FRED MCGRIFF   DEVIL RAYS
6-3, 215   **B:** L. **T:** L.
Position: First base, designated hitter.
Born: October 31, 1963.
1999 season: .310 avg.; 32 HR; 104 RBIs.
Career: .287 avg.; 390 HR; 1192 RBIs.
Teams: Blue Jays1986-90; Padres 1991-93; Braves 1993-97; Devil Rays 1998-99.

MARK MCGWIRE   CARDINALS
Position: First base.
1999 season: .278 avg.; 65 HR; 147 RBIs.
Awards: See A.L. Rookie of the Year 1987.

RAUL MONDESI   BLUE JAYS
Position: Outfield.
1999 season: .253 avg.; 33 HR; 99 RBIs; 36 SB.
Awards: See N.L. Rookie of the Year 1994.

WARREN MORRIS   PIRATES
5-10, 175   **B:** L. **T:** R.
Position: Second base.
Born: January 11, 1974.
1999 season: .288 avg.; 15 HR; 73 RBIs.
Career: .288 avg.; 15 HR; 73 RBIs.
Team: Pirates 1999.

PHIL NEVIN   PADRES
6-2, 231   **B:** R. **T:** R.
Position: Third base, catcher.
Born: January 19, 1971.
1999 season: .269 avg.; 24 HR; 85 RBIs.
Career: .243 avg.; 51 HR; 179 RBIs.
Teams: Astros 1995; Tigers 1995-97; Angels 1998; Padres 1999.

DAVID NILSSON   FREE AGENT
6-3, 240   **B:** L. **T:** R.
Position: Catcher.
Born: December 14, 1969.
1999 season: .309 avg.; 21 HR; 62 RBIs.
Career: .284 avg.; 105 HR; 470 RBIs.
Team: Brewers 1992-99.

JOSE OFFERMAN   RED SOX
6-0, 190   **B:** B. **T:** R.
Position: Second base.

Born: November 8, 1968.
1999 season: .294 avg.; 8 HR; 69 RBIs; 18 SB.
Career: .280 avg.; 30 HR; 381 RBIs; 157 SB.
Teams: Dodgers 1990-95; Royals 1996-98; Red Sox 1999.

TROY O'LEARY · RED SOX
6-0, 198 **B:** L. **T:** L.
Position: Outfield.
Born: August 4, 1969.
1999 season: .280 avg.; 28 HR; 103 RBIs.
Career: .283 avg.; 93 HR; 406 RBIs.
Teams: Brewers 1993-94; Red Sox 1995-99.

JOHN OLERUD · MARINERS
6-5, 220 **B:** L. **T:** L.
Position: First base.
Born: August 5, 1968.
1999 season: .298 avg.; 19 HR; 96 RBIs.
Career: .301 avg.; 172 HR; 762 RBIs.
Teams: Blue Jays 1989-96; Mets 1997-99.

PAUL O'NEILL · YANKEES
6-4, 215 **B:** L. **T:** L.
Position: Outfield.
Born: February 25, 1963.
1999 season: .285 avg.; 19 HR; 110 RBIs.
Career: .290 avg.; 242 HR; 1099 RBIs.
Teams: Reds 1985-92; Yankees 1993-99.

MAGGLIO ORDONEZ · WHITE SOX
5-11, 170 **B:** R. **T:** R.
Position: Outfield.
Born: January 24, 1974.
1999 season: .301 avg.; 30 HR; 117 RBIs.
Career: .294 avg.; 48 HR; 193 RBIs.
Team: White Sox 1997-99.

REY ORDONEZ · METS
5-9, 159 **B:** R. **T:** R.
Position: Shortstop.
Born: November 11, 1972.
1999 season: .258 avg.; 1 HR; 60 RBIs.
Career: .246 avg.; 4 HR; 165 RBIs.
Team: Mets 1996-99.

RAFAEL PALMEIRO · RANGERS
6-0. 225 **B:** L. **T:** L.
Position: Designated hitter, first base.
Born: September 24, 1964.
1999 season: .324 avg.; 47 HR; 148 RBIs.
Career: .296 avg.; 361 HR; 1227 RBIs.
Teams: Cubs 1986-88; Rangers 1989-93, 1999; Orioles 1994-98.

DEAN PALMER · TIGERS
6-1, 210 **B:** R. **T:** R.
Position: Third base.
Born: December 27, 1968.
1999 season: .263 avg.; 38 HR; 100 RBIs.
Career: .255 avg.; 235 HR; 701 RBIs.
Teams: Rangers 1989-97; Royals 1997-98; Tigers 1999.

MIKE PIAZZA · METS
Position: Catcher.
1999 season: .303 avg.; 40 HR; 124 RBIs.
Awards: See N.L. Rookie of the Year 1993.

JORGE POSADA · YANKEES
6-2, 205 **B:** B. **T:** R.
Position: Catcher.
Born: August 17, 1971.
1999 season: .245 avg.; 12 HR; 57 RBIs.
Career: .252 avg.; 35 HR; 145 RBIs.
Team: Yankees 1995-99.

MANNY RAMIREZ · INDIANS
6-0, 215 **B:** R. **T:** R.
Position: Outfield.
Born: May 30, 1972.
1999 season: .333 avg.; 44 HR; 165 RBIs.
Career: .307 avg. 198 HR; 682 RBIs.
Team: Indians 1993-99.

JOE RANDA · ROYALS
5-11, 190 **B:** R. **T:** R.
Position: Third base.
Born: December 18, 1969.
1999 season: .314 avg.; 16 HR; 84 RBIs.
Career: .290 avg.; 39 HR; 246 RBIs.
Teams: Royals 1995-96, 1999; Pirates 1997; Tigers 1998.

POKEY REESE · REDS
5-11, 180 **B:** R. **T:** R.
Position: Second base.
Born: June 10, 1973.
1999 season: .285 avg.; 10 HR; 52 RBIs.
Career: .258 avg.; 15 HR; 94 RBIs.
Team: Reds 1997-99.

EDGAR RENTERIA · CARDINALS
6-1, 180 **B:** R. **T:** R.
Position: Shortstop.
Born: August 7, 1975.
1999 season: .275 avg.; 11 HR; 63 RBIs; 37 SB.
Career: .284 avg.; 23 HR; 177 RBis; 126 SB.
Teams: Marlins 1996-98; Cardinals 1999.

CAL RIPKEN · ORIOLES
Position: Third base.
1999 season: .340 avg.; 18 HR; 57 RBIs.
Awards: See A.L. Rookie of the Year 1982; A.L. MVP 1983, 1991.

RUBEN RIVERA · PADRES
6-3, 200 **B:** R. **T:** R.
Position: Outfield.
Born: November 14, 1973.
1999 season: .195 avg.; 23 HR; 48 RBIs.
Career: .211 avg.; 31 HR; 94 RBIs.
Teams: Yankees 1995-96; Padres 1997-99.

ALEX RODRIGUEZ · MARINERS
6-3, 190 **B:** R. **T:** R.
Position: Shortstop.
Born: July 27, 1975.
1999 season: .285 avg.; 42 HR; 111 RBIs; 21 SB.
Career: .308 avg.; 148 HR; 463 RBIs; 118 SB.
Team: Mariners 1994-99.

HENRY RODRIGUEZ · CUBS
6-2, 225 **B:** L. **T:** L.
Position: Outfield.
Born: November 8, 1967.
1999 season: .304 avg.; 26 HR; 87 RBIs.
Career: .261 avg.; 140 HR; 459 RBIs.
Team: Dodgers 1992-95; Expos 1995-97; Cubs 1998-99.

IVAN RODRIGUEZ · RANGERS
Position: Catcher.
1999 season: .332 avg.; 35 HR; 113 RBIs; 25 SB.
Awards: See A.L. MVP 1999.

SCOTT ROLEN · PHILLIES
Position: Third base.
1999 season: .268 avg.; 26 HR; 77 RBIs.
Awards: See N.L. Rookie of the Year 1997.

TIM SALMON · ANGELS
Position: Outfield.
1999 season: .266 avg.; 17 HR; 69 RBIs.
Awards: See A.L. Rookie of the Year 1993.

REGGIE SANDERS · BRAVES
6-1, 185 **B:** R. **T:** R.
Position: Outfield.
Born: December 1, 1967.
1999 season: .285 avg.; 26 HR; 72 RBIs; 36 SB.
Career: .273 avg.; 151 HR; 503 RBIs; 194 SB.
Teams: Reds 1991-98; Padres 1999.

DAVID SEGUI · BLUE JAYS
6-1, 202 **B:** B. **T:** L.
Position: First base.
Born: July 19, 1966.

Rafael Palmeiro put up MVP-like numbers last season—.324 average, 47 homers and 148 RBIs.

1999 season: .298 avg.; 14 HR; 52 RBIs.
Career: .285 avg.; 102 HR; 487 RBIs.
Teams: Orioles 1990-93; Mets 1994-95; Expos 1995-97; Mariners 1998-99; Blue Jays 1999.

RICHIE SEXSON · INDIANS
6-7, 225 **B:** R. **T:** R.
Position: First base, outfield, designated hitter.
Born: December 29, 1974.
1999 season: .255 avg.; 31 HR; 116 RBIs.
Career: .270 avg.; 42 HR; 151 RBIs.
Team: Indians 1997-99.

GARY SHEFFIELD · DODGERS
5-11, 205 **B:** R. **T:** R.
Position: Outfield.
Born: November 18, 1968.
1999 season: .301 avg.; 34 HR; 101 RBIs.
Career: .290 avg; 236 HR; 807 RBIs.
Teams: Brewers 1988-91; Padres 1992-93; Marlins 1993-98; Dodgers 1998-99.

CHRIS SINGLETON · WHITE SOX
6-2, 195 **B:** L. **T:** L.
Position: Outfield.
Born: August 15, 1972.
1999 season: .300 avg.; 17 HR; 72 RBIs; 20 SB.
Career: .300 avg; 17 HR; 72 RBIs; 20 SB.
Team: White Sox 1999.

J.T. SNOW · GIANTS
6-2, 205 **B:** L. **T:** L.
Position: First base.
Born: February 26, 1968.
1999 season: .274 avg. 24 HR; 98 RBIs.
Career: .263 avg.; 132 HR; 539 RBIs.
Teams: Yankees 1992; Angels 1993-96; Giants 1997-99.

SAMMY SOSA · CUBS
Position: Outfield.
1999 season: .288 avg.; 63 HR; 141 RBIs.
Award: See N.L. MVP 1998.

SHANE SPENCER · YANKEES
5-11, 210 **B:** R. **T:** R.
Position: Outfield.
Born: February 20, 1972.
1999 season: .234 avg.; 8 HR; 20 RBIs.
Career: .268 avg.; 18 HR; 47 RBIs.
Team: Yankees 1998-99.

Coors Field or not, Larry Walker has put up impressive offensive numbers in his five seasons for the Rockies.

ED SPRAGUE   **FREE AGENT**
6-2, 205   **B:** R. **T:** R.
Position: Third base.
Born: July 25, 1967.
1999 season: .267 avg.; 22 HR; 81 RBIs.
Career: .246 avg; 138 HR; 506 RBIs.
Teams: Blue Jays 1991-98; Athletics 1998; Pirates 1999.

MATT STAIRS   **ATHLETICS**
5-9, 212   **B:** L. **T:** R.
Position: Outfield.
Born: February 27, 1968.
1999 season: .258 avg; 38 HR; 102 RBIs.
Career: .279 avg; 102 HR; 328 RBIs.
Teams: Expos 1992-93; Red Sox 1995; Athletics 1996-99.

MIKE STANLEY   **RED SOX**
6-0, 190   **B:** R. **T:** R.
Position: First base.
Born: June 25, 1963.
1999 season: .281 avg; 19 HR; 72 RBIs.
Career: .272 avg.; 173 HR; 656 RBIs.
Teams: Rangers 1986-91; Yankees 1992-95, 1997; Red Sox 1996-99; Blue Jays 1998.

SHANNON STEWART   **BLUE JAYS**
6-1, 194   **B:** R. **T:** R.
Position: Outfield.
Born: February 25, 1974.
1999 season: .304 avg.; 11 HR; 67 RBIs; 37 SB.
Career: .288 avg.; 23 HR; 147 RBIs; 101 SB.
Team: Blue Jays 1995-99.

DARRYL STRAWBERRY   **YANKEES**
6-6, 215   **B:** L. **T:** L.
Position: Designated hitter.
Born: March 12, 1962.
1999 season: .327 avg.; 3 HR; 6 RBIs.
Career: .259 avg.; 335 HR; 1000 RBIs.
Teams: Mets 1983-90; Dodgers 1991-93; Giants 1994; Yankees 1995-99.

B.J. SURHOFF   **ORIOLES**
6-1, 200   **B:** L. **T:** R.
Position: Outfield.
Born: August 4, 1964.
1999 season: .308 avg.; 28 HR; 107 RBIs.
Career: .281 avg; 146 HR; 893 RBIs.
Teams: Brewers 1987-95; Orioles 1996-99.

MIKE SWEENEY   **ROYALS**
6-2, 215   **B:** R. **T:** R.
Position: First base, designated hitter.
Born: July 22, 1973.
1999 season: .322 avg.; 22 HR; 102 RBIs.
Career: .287 avg.; 41 HR; 192 RBIs.
Team: Royals 1995-99.

FERNANDO TATIS   **CARDINALS**
6-1, 175   **B:** R. **T:** R.
Position: Third base.
Born: January 1, 1975.
1999 season: .298 avg.; 34 HR; 107 RBIs; 21 SB.
Career: .282 avg.; 53 HR; 194 RBIs; 37 SB.
Teams: Rangers 1997-98; Cardinals 1998-99.

EDDIE TAUBENSEE   **REDS**
6-3, 200   **B:** L. **T:** R.
Position: Catcher.
Born: October 31, 1968.
1999 season: .311 avg.; 21 HR; 87 RBIs.
Career: .274 avg.; 85 HR; 384 RBIs.
Teams: Indians 1991; Astros 1992-94; Reds 1994-99.

MIGUEL TEJADA   **ATHLETICS**
5-9, 192   **B:** R. **T:** R.
Position: Shortstop.
Born: May 25, 1976.
1999 season: .251 avg.; 21 HR; 84 RBIs.
Career: .240 avg.; 34 HR; 139 RBIs.
Team: Athletics 1997-99.

FRANK THOMAS   **WHITE SOX**
Position: Designated hitter, first base.
1999 season: .305 avg.; 15 HR; 77 RBIs.
Awards: See A.L. MVP 1993, 1994.

JIM THOME   **INDIANS**
6-4, 225   **B:** L. **T:** R.
Position: First base.
Born: August 27, 1970.
1999 season: .277 avg.; 33 HR; 108 RBIs.
Career: .287 avg.; 196 HR; 646 RBIs.
Team: Indians 1991-99.

JOHN VALENTIN   **RED SOX**
6-0, 185   **B:** R. **T:** R.
Position: Third base.
Born: February 18, 1967.
1999 season: .253 avg.; 12 HR; 70 RBIs.
Career: .283 avg.; 118 HR; 521 RBIs.
Team: Red Sox 1992-99.

JASON VARITEK   **RED SOX**
6-2, 220   **B:** R. **T:** R.
Position: Catcher.
Born: April 11, 1972.
1999 season: .269 avg.; 20 HR; 76 RBIs.
Career: .265 avg.; 27 HR; 109 RBIs.
Team: Red Sox 1997-99.

GREG VAUGHN   **DEVIL RAYS**
6-0, 202   **B:** R. **T:** R.
Position: Outfield.
Born: July 3, 1965.
1999 season: .245 avg.; 45 HR; 118 RBIs.
Career: .246 avg.; 292 HR; 882 RBIs.
Teams: Brewers 1989-96; Padres 1996-98; Reds 1999.

MO VAUGHN   **ANGELS**
Position: First base, designated hitter.
1999 season: .281 avg.; 33 HR; 108 RBIs.
Awards: See A.L. MVP 1995.

RANDY VELARDE   **ATHLETICS**
6-0, 200   **B:** R. **T:** R.
Position: Second base.
Born: November 24, 1962.
1999 season: .317 avg.; 16 HR; 76 RBIs; 24 SB.
Career: .277 avg.; 77 HR; 364 RBIs; 60 SB.
Teams: Yankees 1987-95; Angels 1996-99; Athletics 1999.

ROBIN VENTURA   **METS**
6-1, 198   **B:** L. **T:** R.
Position: Third base.
Born: July 14, 1967.
1999 season: .301 avg.; 32 HR; 120 RBIs.
Career: .277 avg. 203 HR; 861 RBIs.
Teams: White Sox 1989-98; Mets 1999.

QUILVIO VERAS   **BRAVES**
5-9, 166   **B:** B. **T:** R.
Position: Second base.
Born: April 3, 1971.
1999 season: .280 avg.; 6 HR; 41 RBIs; 30 SB.
Career: .267 avg.; 24 HR; 177 RBIs; 151 SB.
Teams: Marlins 1995-96; Padres 1997-99.

JOSE VIDRO   **EXPOS**
5-11, 190   **B:** B. **T:** R.
Position: Second base.
Born: August 27, 1974.
1999 season: .304 avg.;12 HR; 59 RBIs.
Career: .273 avg.; 14 HR; 94 RBIs.
Team: Expos 1997-99.

FERNANDO VINA   **CARDINALS**
5-9, 170   **B:** L. **T:** R.
Position: Second base.
Born: April 16, 1969.
1999 season: .266 avg.; 1 HR; 16 RBIs.
Career: .282 avg.; 22 HR; 172 RBIs.
Teams: Mariners 1993; Mets 1994; Brewers 1995-99.

OMAR VIZQUEL   **INDIANS**
5-9, 170   **B:** B. **T:** R.
Position: Shortstop.
Born: April 24, 1967.
1999 season: .333 avg.; 5 HR; 66 RBIs; 42 SB.
Career: .275 avg.; 34 HR; 449 RBIs; 238 SB.
Teams: Mariners 1989-93; Indians 1994-99.

LARRY WALKER   **ROCKIES**
Position: Outfield.
1999 season: .379 avg.; 37 HR; 115 RBis.
Awards: See N.L. MVP 1997.

DEVON WHITE   **DODGERS**
6-2, 190   **B:** B. **T:** R.
Position: Outfield.
Born: December 29, 1962.
1999 season: .268 avg.; 14 HR; 68 RBIs; 19 SB.
Career: .263 avg.; 190 HR; 786 RBIs; 325 SB.
Teams: Angels 1985-90; Blue Jays 1991-95; Marlins 1996-97; Diamondbacks 1998; Dodgers 1999.

RONDELL WHITE   **EXPOS**
6-0, 210   **B:** R. **T:** R.
Position: Outfield.
Born: February 23, 1972.
1999 season: .312 avg.; 22 HR; 64 RBIs.
Career: .292 avg.; 90 HR; 330 RBIs.
Team: Expos 1993-99.

BERNIE WILLIAMS   **YANKEES**
6-2, 205   **B:** B. **T:** R.
Position: Outfield.
Born: September 13, 1968.
1999 season: .342 avg.; 25 HR; 115 RBIs.
Career: .304 avg.; 151 HR; 681 RBIs.
Team: Yankees 1991-99.

GERALD WILLIAMS   **DEVIL RAYS**
6-2, 187   **B:** R. **T:** R.
Position: Outfield.
Born: August 10, 1966.
1999 season: .275 avg.; 17 HR; 68 RBIs.
Career: .263 avg.; 55 HR; 240 RBIs.
Teams: Yankees 1992-96; Brewers 1996-97; Braves 1998-99.

MATT WILLIAMS   **DIAMONDBACKS**
6-2, 214   **B:** R. **T:** R.
Position: Third base.

Born: November 28, 1965.
1999 season: .303 avg.; 35 HR; 142 RBIs.
Career: .268 avg.; 334 HR; 1050 RBIs.
Teams: Giants 1987-96; Indians 1997; Diamondbacks 1998-99.

PRESTON WILSON   MARLINS
6-2, 193   **B:** R. **T:** R.
Position: Outfield.
Born: July 19, 1974.
1999 season: .280 avg.; 26 HR; 71 RBIs.
Career: .268 avg.; 27 HR; 74 RBIs.
Teams: Mets 1998; Marlins 1998-99.

TONY WOMACK   DIAMONDBACKS
5-9, 155   **B:** L. **T:** R.
Position: Outfield, shortstop, second base.
Born: September 25, 1969.
1999 season: .277 avg; 4 HR; 41 RBIs; 72 SB.
Career: .278 avg.; 13 HR; 144 RBIs; 194 SB.
Teams: Pirates 1993-98; Diamondbacks 1999.

DMITRI YOUNG   REDS
6-2, 210   **B:** B. **T:** R.
Position: Outfield.
Born: October 11, 1973.
1999 season: .300 avg.; 14 HR; 56 RBIs.
Career: .292 avg.; 33 HR; 175 RBIs.
Teams: Cardinals 1996-97; Reds 1998-99.

ERIC YOUNG   CUBS
5-9, 170   **B:** R. **T:** R.
Position: Second base.
Born: May 18, 1967.
1999 season: .281 avg.; 2 HR; 41 RBIs; 51 SB.
Career: .289 avg.; 43 HR; 338 RBIs; 292 SB.
Teams: Dodgers 1991, 1997-99; Rockies 1993-97.

KEVIN YOUNG   PIRATES
6-3, 221   **B:** R. **T:** R.
Position: First base.
Born: June 16, 1969.
1999 season: .298 avg.; 26 HR; 106 RBIs; 22 SB.
Career: .268 avg.; 92 HR; 395 RBIs; 55 SB.
Teams: Pirates 1992-95, 1997-99; Royals 1996.

TODD ZEILE   METS
6-1, 205   **B:** R. **T:** R.
Position: Third base.
Born: September 9, 1965.
1999 season: .293 avg.; 24 HR; 98 RBIs.
Career: .268 avg.; 183 HR; 805 RBIs.
Teams: Cardinals 1989-95; Cubs 1995; Phillies 1996; Orioles 1996; Dodgers 1997-98; Marlins 1998; Rangers 1998-99.

PITCHERS

WILSON ALVAREZ   DEVIL RAYS
6-1, 235   **Throws:** Left.
Status: Starter.
Born: March 24, 1970.
1999 season: 9-9; 4.22 ERA; 128 SO.
Career: 86-77; 3.96 ERA; 1074 SO.
Teams: Rangers 1989; White Sox 1991-97; Giants 1997; Devil Rays 1998-99.

RICK ANKIEL   CARDINALS
6-1, 210   **Throws:** Left.
Status: Starter.
Born: July 19, 1979.
1999 season: 0-1; 3.27 ERA; 39 SO.
Career: 0-1; 3.27 ERA; 39 SO.
Team: Cardinals 1999.

KEVIN APPIER   ATHLETICS
6-2, 200   **Throws:** Right.
Status: Starter.
Born: December 6, 1967.
1999 season: 16-14; 5.17 ERA; 131 SO.
Career: 121-94; 3.54 ERA; 1504 SO.
Teams: Royals 1989-99; Athletics 1999.

Kevin Brown signed a contract with the Dodgers worth over $100 million before the 1999 season. Thus far, he has been worth every penny. He tallied an 18-9 record in 1999 with a 3.00 ERA and 221 strikeouts.

ROLANDO ARROJO   ROCKIES
6-4, 220   **Throws:** Right.
Status: Starter.
Born: July 18, 1968.
1999 season: 7-12; 5.18 ERA; 107 SO.
Career: 21-24; 4.23 ERA; 259 SO.
Team: Devil Rays 1998-99.

ANDY ASHBY   PHILLIES
6-5, 190   **Throws:** Right.
Status: Starter.
Born: July 11, 1967.
1999 season: 14-10; 3.80 ERA; 132 SO.
Career: 72-74; 3.98 ERA; 910 SO.
Teams: Phillies 1991-92; Rockies 1993; Padres 1993-99.

PEDRO ASTACIO   ROCKIES
6-2, 208   **Throws:** Right.
Status: Starter.
Born: November 28, 1969.
1999 season: 17-11; 5.04 ERA; 210 SO.
Career: 83-73; 4.32 ERA; 1029 SO.
Teams: Dodgers 1992-96; Rockies 1997-99.

ROD BECK   RED SOX
6-1, 235   **Throws:** Right.
Status: Reliever.
Born: August 3, 1968.
1999 season: 2-5; 5.93 ERA; 22 saves.
Career: 26-37; 3.20 ERA; 260 saves.
Team: Giants 1991-97; Cubs 1998-99; Red Sox 1999.

ANDY BENES   CARDINALS
6-6, 245   **Throws:** Right.
Status: Starter.
Born: August 20, 1967.
1999 season: 13-12; 4.81 ERA; 141 SO.
Career: 131-119; 4.13 ERA; 1719 SO.
Teams: Padres 1989-95; Mariners 1995; Cardinals 1996-97; Diamondbacks 1998-99.

ARMANDO BENITEZ   METS
6-4, 229   **Throws:** Right.
Status: Reliever.
Born: November 3, 1972.
1999 season: 4-3; 1.85 ERA; 22 saves.

Career: 15-19; 3.15 ERA; 59 saves.
Teams: Orioles 1994-98; Mets 1999.

KENT BOTTENFIELD   CARDINALS
6-3, 240   **Throws:** Right.
Status: Starter.
Born: November 14, 1968.
1999 season: 18-7; 3.97 ERA; 124 SO.
Career: 36-34; 4.19 ERA; 421 SO.
Teams: Expos 1992-93; Rockies 1993-94; Giants 1994; Cubs 1996-97; Cardinals 1998-99.

KEVIN BROWN   DODGERS
6-4, 200   **Throws:** Right.
Status: Starter.
Born: March 14, 1965.
1999 season: 18-9; 3.00 ERA; 221 SO.
Career: 157-108; 3.27 ERA; 1701 SO.
Teams: Rangers 1986-94; Orioles 1995; Marlins 1996-97; Padres 1998; Dodgers 1999.

DAVE BURBA   INDIANS
6-4, 240   **Throws:** Right.
Status: Starter.
Born: July 7, 1966.
1999 season: 15-9; 4.25 ERA; 174 SO.
Career: 79-64; 4.23 ERA; 920 SO.
Teams: Mariners 1990-91; Giants 1992-95; Reds 1995-97; Indians 1998-99.

PAUL BYRD   PHILLIES
6-1, 185   **Throws:** Right.
Status: Starter.
Born: December 3, 1970.
1999 season: 15-11; 4.60 ERA; 106 SO.
Career: 27-19; 4.21 ERA; 239 SO.
Teams: Mets 1995-96; Braves 1997-98; Phillies 1998-99.

CHRIS CARPENTER   BLUE JAYS
6-6, 215   **Throws:** Right.
Status: Starter.
Born: April 27, 1975.
1999 season: 9-8; 4.38 ERA; 106 SO.
Career: 24-22; 4.52 ERA; 297 SO.
Team: Blue Jays 1997-99.

After winning just 11 games in his first four major league seasons, Texas' Rick Helling has won 33 games the last two years.

BRUCE CHEN   **BRAVES**
6-1, 180   **Throws:** Left.
Status: Starter.
Born: June 6, 1977.
1999 season: 2-2; 5.47 ERA; 45 SO.
Career: 4-2; 5.05 ERA; 62 SO.
Team: Braves 1998-99.

ROGER CLEMENS   **YANKEES**
Status: Starter.
1999 season: 14-10; 4.60 ERA; 163 SO.
Awards: See A.L. Cy Young 1986, 1987, 1991, 1997, 1998; A.L. MVP 1986.

BARTOLO COLON   **INDIANS**
6-0, 230   **Throws:** Right.
Status: Starter.
Born: May 24, 1975.
1999 season: 18-5; 3.95 ERA; 161 SO.
Career: 36-21; 4.17 ERA; 385 SO.
Team: Indians 1997-99.

DAVID CONE   **YANKEES**
Status: Starter.
1999 season: 12-9; 3.44 ERA; 177 SO.
Awards: See A.L. Cy Young 1994.

FRANCISCO CORDOVA   **PIRATES**
6-1, 197   **Throws:** Right.
Status: Starter.
Born: April 26, 1972.
1999 season: 8-10; 4.43 ERA; 98 SO.
Career: 36-39; 3.78 ERA; 471 SO.
Team: Pirates 1996-99.

OMAR DAAL   **DIAMONDBACKS**
6-3, 195   **Throws:** Left.
Status: Starter.
Born: February 23, 1972.
1999 season: 16-9; 3.65 ERA; 148 SO.
Career: 36-32; 4.02 ERA; 445 SO.
Teams: Dodgers 1993-95; Expos 1996-97; Blue Jays 1997; Diamondbacks 1998-99.

OCTAVIO DOTEL   **ASTROS**
6-0, 175   **Throws:** Right.
Status: Starter.
Born: November 25, 1975.
1999 season: 8-3; 5.38 ERA; 85 SO.
Career: 8-3; 5.38 ERA; 85 SO.
Team: Mets 1999.

SCOTT ERICKSON   **ORIOLES**
6-4, 230   **Throws:** Right.
Status: Starter.
Born: February 2, 1968.
1999 season: 15-12; 4.81 ERA; 106 SO.
Career: 130-108; 4.27 ERA; 1111 SO.
Teams: Twins 1990-95; Orioles 1996-99.

KELVIM ESCOBAR   **BLUE JAYS**
6-1, 195   **Throws:** Right.
Status: Starter.
Born: April 11, 1976.
1999 season: 14-11; 5.69 ERA; 129 SO.
Career: 24-16; 4.84 ERA; 237 SO.
Team: Blue Jays 1997-99.

SHAWN ESTES   **GIANTS**
6-2, 192   **Throws:** Left.
Status: Starter.
Born: February 18, 1973.
1999 season: 11-11; 4.92 ERA; 159 SO.
Career: 40-36; 4.31 ERA; 550 SO.
Team: Giants 1995-99.

ALEX FERNANDEZ   **MARLINS**
6-1, 225   **Throws:** Right.
Status: Starter.
Born: August 13, 1969.
1999 season: 7-8; 3.38 ERA; 91 SO.
Career: 103-83; 3.73 ERA; 1225 SO.
Teams: White Sox 1990-96; Marlins 1997, 1999.

CHUCK FINLEY   **INDIANS**
6-6, 226   **Throws:** Left.
Status: Starter.
Born: November 26, 1962.
1999 season: 12-11; 4.43 ERA; 200 SO.
Career: 165-140; 3.72 ERA; 2151 SO.
Team: Angels 1986-99.

JOHN FRANCO   **METS**
5-10. 185   **Throws:** Left.
Status: Reliever.
Born: September 17, 1960.
1999 season: 0-2; 2.88 ERA; 19 saves.
Career: 77-70; 2.64 ERA; 416 saves.
Teams: Reds 1984-89; Mets 1990-99.

FREDDY GARCIA   **MARINERS**
6-4, 235   **Throws:** Right.
Status: Starter.
Born: October 6, 1976.
1999 season: 17-8; 4.07 ERA; 170 SO.
Career: 17-8; 4.07 ERA; 170 SO.
Team: Mariners 1999.

TOM GLAVINE   **BRAVES**
Status: Starter.
1999 season: 14-11; 4.12 ERA; 138 SO.
Awards: See N.L. Cy Young 1991, 1998.

TOM GORDON   **RED SOX**
5-9, 180   **Throws:** Right.
Status: Reliever.
Born: November 18, 1967.
1999 season: 0-2; 5.60 ERA; 11 saves.
Career: 104-96; 4.15 ERA; 71 saves.
Teams: Royals 1988-95; Red Sox 1996-99.

DANNY GRAVES   **REDS**
5-11, 185   **Throws:** Right.
Status: Reliever.
Born: August 7, 1973.
1999 season: 8-7; 3.08 ERA; 27 saves.
Career: 12-8; 3.59 ERA; 35 saves.
Teams: Indians 1996-97; Reds 1997-99.

JOHN HALAMA   **MARINERS**
6-5, 220   **Throws:** Left.
Status: Starter.
Born: February 22, 1972.
1999 season: 11-10; 4.22 ERA; 105 SO.
Career: 12-11; 4.47 ERA; 126 SO.
Teams: Astros 1998; Mariners 1999.

ROY HALLADAY   **BLUE JAYS**
6-6, 205   **Throws:** Right.
Status: Starter, Reliever.
Born: May 14, 1977.
1999 season: 8-7; 3.92 ERA; 82 SO.
Career: 9-7; 3.75 ERA; 95 SO.
Team: Blue Jays 1998-99.

JOEY HAMILTON   **BLUE JAYS**
6-4, 230   **Throws:** Right.
Status: Starter.
Born: September 9, 1970.
1999 season: 7-8; 6.52 ERA; 56 SO.
Career: 62-52; 4.09 ERA; 695 SO.
Teams: Padres 1994-98; Blue Jays 1999.

MIKE HAMPTON   **METS**
5-10, 180   **Throws:** Left.
Status: Starter.
Born: September 9, 1972.
1999 season: 22-4; 2.90 ERA; 177 SO.
Career: 70-43; 3.50 ERA; 701 SO.
Teams: Mariners 1993; Astros 1994-99.

PETE HARNISCH   **REDS**
6-0, 228   **Throws:** Right.
Status: Starter.
Born: September 23, 1966.
1999 season: 16-10; 3.68 ERA; 120 SO.
Career: 102-94; 3.78 ERA; 1280 SO.
Teams: Orioles 1988-90; Astros 1991-94; Mets 1995-97; Brewers 1997; Reds 1998-99.

RICK HELLING   **RANGERS**
6-3, 220   **Throws:** Right.
Status: Starter.
Born: December 15, 1970.
1999 season: 13-11; 4.84 ERA; 131 SO.
Career: 44-34; 4.71 ERA; 466 SO.
Teams: Rangers 1994-99; Marlins 1996-97.

PAT HENTGEN   **CARDINALS**
6-2, 195   **Throws:** Right.
Status: Starter.
Born: November 13, 1968.
1999 season: 11-12; 4.79 ERA; 118 SO.
Career: 105-76; 4.14 ERA; 995 SO.
Team: Blue Jays 1991-99.

DUSTIN HERMANSON   **EXPOS**
6-0, 205   **Throws:** Right.
Status: Starter.
Born: December 21, 1972.
1999 season: 9-14; 4.20 ERA; 145 SO.
Career: 35-34; 3.97 ERA; 465 SO.
Teams: Padres 1995-96; Expos 1997-99.

LIVAN HERNANDEZ   **GIANTS**
6-2, 222   **Throws:** Right.
Status: Starter.
Born: February 20, 1975.
1999 season: 8-12; 4.64 ERA; 144 SO.
Career: 27-27; 4.39 ERA; 380 SO.
Teams: Marlins 1996-99; Giants 1999.

ORLANDO HERNANDEZ   **YANKEES**
6-2, 210   **Throws:** Right.
Status: Starter.
Born: October 11, 1965.
1999 season: 17-9; 4.12 ERA; 157 SO.
Career: 29-13; 3.72 ERA; 288 SO.
Team: Yankees 1998-99.

ROBERTO HERNANDEZ   **DEVIL RAYS**
6-4, 235   **Throws:** Right.
Status: Reliever.
Born: November 11, 1964.
1999 season: 2-3; 3.07 ERA; 43 saves.
Career: 38-35; 3.02 ERA; 234 saves.
Teams: White Sox 1991-97; Giants 1997; Devil Rays 1998-99.

OREL HERSHISER   **DODGERS**
Status: Starter.
1999 season: 13-12; 4.58 ERA; 89 SO.
Awards: See N.L. Cy Young 1988.

STERLING HITCHCOCK   **PADRES**
6-1, 192   **Throws:** Left.
Status: Starter.
Born: April 29, 1971.
1999 season: 12-14; 4.11 ERA; 194 SO.
Career: 60-56; 4.67 ERA; 780 SO.
Teams: Yankees 1992-95; Mariners 1996; Padres 1997-99.

TREVOR HOFFMAN   **PADRES**
6-0, 205   **Throws:** Right.
Status: Reliever.
Born: October 13, 1967.
1999 season: 2-3; 2.14 ERA; 40 saves.
Career: 36-28; 2.69 ERA; 228 saves.
Teams: Marlins 1993; Padres 1993-99.

TIM HUDSON   **ATHLETICS**
6-0, 160   **Throws:** Right.
Status: Starter.
Born: July 14, 1975.
1999 season: 11-2; 3.23 ERA; 132 SO.
Career: 11-2; 3.23 ERA; 132 SO.
Team: Athletics 1999.

HIDEKI IRABU   **EXPOS**
6-4, 240   **Throws:** Right.
Status: Starter.
Born: May 5, 1969.
1999 season: 11-7; 4.84 ERA; 133 SO.
Career: 29-20; 4.80 ERA; 315 SO.
Team: Yankees 1997-99.

MIKE JACKSON   **PHILLIES**
6-2, 225   **Throws:** Right.
Status: Reliever.
Born: December 22, 1964.
1999 season: 3-4; 4.06 ERA; 39 saves.
Career: 53-61; 3.26 ERA; 138 saves.
Teams: Phillies 1986-87; Mariners 1988-91; Giants 1992-94; Reds 1995; Indians 1997-99.

RANDY JOHNSON   **DIAMONDBACKS**
Status: Starter.
1999 season: 17-9; 2.48 ERA; 364 SO.
Awards: See A.L. Cy Young 1995; N.L. Cy Young 1999.

DARRYL KILE   **CARDINALS**
6-5, 212   **Throws:** Right.
Status: Starter.
Born: December 2, 1968.
1999 season: 8-13; 6.61 ERA; 116 SO.
Career: 92-95; 4.32 ERA; 1247 SO.
Teams: Astros 1991-97; Rockies 1998-99.

BILLY KOCH   **BLUE JAYS**
6-3, 218   **Throws:** Right.
Status: Reliever.
Born: December 14, 1974.
1999 season: 0-5; 3.39 ERA; 31 saves.
Career: 0-5; 3.39 ERA; 31 saves.
Team: Blue Jays 1999.

AL LEITER   **METS**
6-3, 220   **Throws:** Left.
Status: Starter.
Born: October 23, 1965.
1999 season: 13-12; 4.23 ERA; 162 SO.
Career: 90-71; 4.07 ERA; 1107 SO.
Teams: Yankees 1987-89; Blue Jays 1989-95; Marlins 1996-97; Mets 1998-99.

JON LIEBER   **CUBS**
6-3, 225   **Throws:** Right.
Status: Starter.
Born: April 2, 1970.
1999 season: 10-11; 4.07 ERA; 186 SO.
Career: 48-58; 4.30 ERA; 694 SO.
Teams: Pirates 1994-98; Cubs 1999.

KERRY LIGTENBERG   **BRAVES**
6-2, 205   **Throws:** Right.
Status: Reliever.
Born: May 11, 1971.
1999 season: Did not play due to injury.
Career: 4-2; 2.76 ERA; 31 saves.
Team: Braves 1997-98.

JOSE LIMA   **ASTROS**
6-2, 205   **Throws:** Right.
Status: Starter.
Born: September 30, 1972.
1999 season: 21-10; 3.58 ERA; 187 SO.
Career: 46-40; 4.37 ERA; 522 SO.
Teams: Tigers 1994-96; Astros 1997-99.

GRAEME LLOYD   **EXPOS**
6-7, 234   **Throws:** Left.
Status: Reliever.
Born: April 9, 1967.
1999 season: 5-3; 3.63 ERA; 47 SO.
Career: 16-22; 3.62 ERA; 198 SO.
Teams: Brewers 1993-96; Yankees 1996-98; Blue Jays 1999.

ESTEBAN LOAIZA   **RANGERS**
6-3, 210   **Throws:** Right.
Status: Starter.
Born: December 31, 1971.
1999 season: 9-5; 4.56 ERA; 77 SO.
Career: 39-39; 4.76 ERA; 424 SO.
Teams: Pirates 1995-98; Rangers 1998-99.

DEREK LOWE   **RED SOX**
6-6, 170   **Throws:** Right.
Status: Reliever.
Born: June 1, 1973.
1999 season: 6-3; 2.63 ERA; 15 saves.
Career: 11-18; 4.00 ERA; 19 saves.
Teams: Mariners 1997; Red Sox 1997-99.

GREG MADDUX   **BRAVES**
Status: Starter.
1999 season: 19-9; 3.57 ERA; 136 SO.
Awards: See N.L. Cy Young 1992, 1993, 1994, 1995.

MATT MANTEI   **DIAMONDBACKS**
6-1, 190   **Throws:** Right.
Status: Reliever.
Born: July 7, 1973.
1999 season: 1-3; 2.76 ERA; 32 saves.
Career: 5-8; 3.44 ERA; 41 saves.
Teams: Marlins 1995-99; Diamondbacks 1999.

PEDRO MARTINEZ   **RED SOX**
Status: Starter.
1999 season: 23-4; 2.07 ERA; 313 SO.
Awards: See N.L. Cy Young 1997; A.L. Cy Young 1999.

RAMON MARTINEZ   **RED SOX**
6-4, 184.   **Throws:** Right.
Status: Starter.
Born: March 22, 1968.
1999 season: 2-1; 3.05 ERA; 15 SO.
Career: 125-78; 3.44 ERA; 1329 SO.
Teams: Dodgers 1988-98; Red Sox 1999.

BRIAN MEADOWS   **MARLINS**
6-4, 210   **Throws:** Right.
Status: Starter.
Born: November 21, 1975.

Roberto Hernandez has recorded 69 saves in his two seasons for the expansion Devil Rays.

1999 season: 11-15; 5.60 ERA; 72 SO.
Career: 22-28; 5.41 ERA; 160 SO.
Team: Marlins 1998-99.

RAMIRO MENDOZA   **YANKEES**
6-2, 155   **Throws:** Right.
Status: Starter, reliever.
Born: June 15, 1972.
1999 season: 9-9; 4.29 ERA; 80 SO.
Career: 31-22; 4.27 ERA; 252 SO.
Team: Yankees 1996-99.

KEVIN MILLWOOD   **BRAVES**
6-4, 220   **Throws:** Right.
Status: Starter.
Born: December 24, 1974.
1999 season: 18-7; 2.68 ERA; 205 SO.
Career: 40-18; 3.37 ERA; 410 SO.
Team: Braves 1997-99.

ERIC MILTON   **TWINS**
6-3, 220   **Throws:** Left.
Status: Starter.
Born: August 4, 1975.
1999 season: 7-11; 4.49 ERA; 163 SO.
Career: 15-25; 5.02 ERA; 270 SO.
Team: Twins 1998-99.

JEFF MONTGOMERY   **ROYALS**
5-11, 175   **Throws:** Right.
Status: Reliever.
Born: January 7, 1962.
1999 season: 1-4; 6.84 ERA; 12 saves.
Career: 46-52; 3.27 ERA; 304 saves.
Teams: Reds 1987; Royals 1988-99.

MATT MORRIS   **CARDINALS**
6-5, 210   **Throws:** Right.
Status: Starter.
Born: August 9, 1974.
1999 season: Did not play due to injury.
Career: 19-14; 2.97 ERA; 228 SO.
Team: Cardinals 1997-98.

JAMIE MOYER   **MARINERS**
6-0, 170   **Throws:** Left.
Status: Starter.
Born: November 18, 1962.
1999 season: 14-8; 3.87 ERA; 137 SO.
Career: 118-101; 4.21 ERA; 1164 SO.
Teams: Cubs 1986-88; Rangers 1989-90; Cardinals 1991; Orioles 1993-95; Red Sox 1996; Mariners 1996-99.

Mike Mussina's .673 career winning percentage ranks him second among active pitchers.

MIKE MUSSINA   ORIOLES
6-2, 185   **Throws:** Right.
Status: Starter.
Born: December 8, 1968.
1999 season: 18-7; 3.50 ERA; 172 SO.
Career: 136-66; 3.50 ERA; 1325 SO.
Team: Orioles 1991-99.

CHARLES NAGY   INDIANS
6-3, 220   **Throws:** Right.
Status: Starter.
Born: May 5, 1967.
1999 season: 17-11; 4.95 ERA; 126 SO.
Career: 121-86; 4.20 ERA; 1143 SO.
Team: Indians 1990-99.

JOE NATHAN   GIANTS
6-4, 195   **Throws:** Right.
Status: Starter.
Born: November 22, 1974.
1999 season: 7-4; 4.18 ERA; 54 SO.
Career: 7-4; 4.18 ERA; 54 SO.
Team: Giants 1999.

DENNY NEAGLE   REDS
6-2, 225   **Throws:** Left.
Status: Starter.
Born: September 13, 1968.
1999 season: 9-5; 4.27 ERA; 76 SO.
Career: 90-60; 3.82 ERA; 998 SO.
Teams: Twins 1991; Pirates 1992-96; Braves 1996-98; Reds 1999.

ROBB NEN   GIANTS
6-5, 215   **Throws:** Right.
Status: Reliever.
Born: November 28, 1969.
1999 season: 3-8; 3.98 ERA; 37 saves.
Career: 31-32; 2.74 ERA; 185 saves.
Teams: Rangers 1993; Marlins 1993-97; Giants 1998-99.

HIDEO NOMO   PHILLIES
Status: Starter.
1999 season: 12-8; 4.54 ERA; 161 SO.
Awards: See N.L. Rookie of the Year 1995.

OMAR OLIVARES   ATHLETICS
6-0, 205   **Throws:** Right.
Status: Starter.
Born: July 6, 1967.
1999 season: 15-11; 4.16 ERA; 85 SO.
Career: 67-69; 4.36 ERA; 727 SO.

Teams: Cardinals 1990-94; Rockies 1995; Phillies 1995; Tigers 1996-97; Mariners 1997; Angels 1998-99; Athletics 1999.

DARREN OLIVER   FREE AGENT
6-2, 210   **Throws:** Left.
Status: Starter.
Born: October 6, 1970.
1999 season: 9-9; 4.26 ERA; 119 SO.
Career: 54-40; 4.55 ERA; 515 SO.
Teams: Rangers 1993-98; Cardinals 1998-99.

RUSS ORTIZ   GIANTS
6-1, 210   **Throws:** Right.
Status: Starter.
Born: June 5, 1974.
1999 season: 18-9; 3.81 ERA; 164 SO.
Career: 22-13; 4.17 ERA; 239 SO.
Team: Giants 1998-99.

CHAN HO PARK   DODGERS
6-2, 204   **Throws:** Right.
Status: Starter.
Born: June 30, 1973.
1999 season: 13-11; 5.23 ERA; 174 SO.
Career: 47-33; 4.07 ERA; 663 SO.
Team: Dodgers 1994-99.

TROY PERCIVAL   ANGELS
6-3, 230   **Throws:** Right.
Status: Reliever.
Born: August 9, 1969.
1999 season: 4-6; 3.79 ERA; 31 saves.
Career: 14-22; 2.95 ERA; 139 saves.
Team: Angels 1995-99.

ANDY PETTITTE   YANKEES
6-5, 235   **Throws:** Left.
Status: Starter.
Born: June 15, 1972.
1999 season: 14-11; 4.70 ERA; 121 SO.
Career: 81-46; 3.92 ERA; 709 SO.
Team: Yankees 1995-99.

SIDNEY PONSON   ORIOLES
6-1, 220   **Throws:** Right.
Status: Starter.
Born: November 2, 1976.
1999 season: 12-12; 4.71 ERA; 112 SO.
Career: 20-21; 4.93 ERA; 197 SO.
Team: Orioles 1998-99.

BRAD RADKE   TWINS
6-2, 184   **Throws:** Right.
Status: Starter.
Born: October 27, 1972.
1999 season: 12-14; 3.75 ERA; 121 SO.
Career: 66-68; 4.30 ERA; 664 SO.
Team: Twins 1995-99.

RICK REED   METS
6-1, 195   **Throws:** Right.
Status: Starter.
Born: August 16, 1965.
1999 season: 11-5; 4.58 ERA; 104 SO.
Career: 49-40; 3.90 ERA; 515 SO.
Teams: Pirates 1988-91; Royals 1992-93; Rangers 1993-94; Reds 1995; Mets 1997-99.

SHANE REYNOLDS   ASTROS
6-3, 210   **Throws:** Right.
Status: Starter.
Born: March 26, 1968.
1999 season: 16-14; 3.85 ERA; 197 SO.
Career: 79-61; 3.70 ERA; 1067 SO.
Team: Astros 1992-99.

ARMANDO REYNOSO   DIAMONDBACKS
6-0, 204   **Throws:** Right.
Status: Starter.
Born: May 1, 1966.

1999 season: 10-6; 4.37 ERA; 79 SO.
Career: 56-44; 4.56 ERA; 448 SO.
Teams: Braves 1991-92; Rockies 1993-96; Mets 1997-98; Diamondbacks 1999.

TODD RITCHIE   PIRATES
6-3, 219   **Throws:** Right.
Status: Starter.
Born: November 7, 1971.
1999 season: 15-9; 3.49 ERA; 107 SO.
Career: 17-12; 3.98 ERA; 172 SO.
Teams: Twins 1997-98; Pirates 1999.

MARIANO RIVERA   YANKEES
6-2, 170   **Throws:** Right.
Status: Reliever.
Born: November 29, 1969.
1999 season: 4-3; 1.83 ERA; 45 saves.
Career: 26-13; 2.58 ERA; 129 saves.
Team: Yankees 1995-99.

JOHN ROCKER   BRAVES
6-4, 210   **Throws:** Left.
Status: Reliever.
Born: October 17, 1974.
1999 season: 4-5; 2.49 ERA; 38 saves.
Career: 5-8; 2.37 ERA; 40 saves.
Team: Braves 1998-99.

KENNY ROGERS   RANGERS
6-1, 217   **Throws:** Left.
Status: Starter.
Born: November 10, 1964.
1999 season: 10-4; 4.20 ERA; 126 SO.
Career: 114-78; 4.05 ERA; 1056 SO.
Team: Rangers 1989-95; Yankees 1996-97; Athletics 1998-99; Mets 1999.

JOSE ROSADO   ROYALS
6-0, 185   **Throws:** Left.
Status: Starter.
Born: November 9, 1974.
1999 season: 10-14; 3.85 ERA; 141 SO.
Career: 35-43; 4.21 ERA; 469 SO.
Team: Royals 1996-99.

BRIAN ROSE   RED SOX
6-3, 212   **Throws:** Right.
Status: Starter.
Born: February 13, 1976.
1999 season: 7-6; 4.87 ERA; 51 SO.
Career: 8-10; 5.58 ERA; 72 SO.
Team: Red Sox 1997-99.

KIRK RUETER   GIANTS
6-2, 205   **Throws:** Left.
Status: Starter.
Born: December 1, 1970.
1999 season: 15-10; 5.41 ERA; 94 SO.
Career: 70-39; 4.21 ERA; 466 SO.
Team: Expos 1993-96; Giants 1996-99.

BRET SABERHAGEN   RED SOX
Status: Starter.
1999 season: 10-6; 2.95 ERA; 81 SO.
Awards: See A.L. Cy Young 1985, 1989.

CURT SCHILLING   PHILLIES
6-4, 228   **Throws:** Right.
Status: Starter.
Born: November 14, 1966.
1999 season: 15-6; 3.54 ERA; 152 SO.
Career: 99-83; 3.38 ERA; 1571 SO.
Teams: Orioles 1988-90; Astros 1991; Phillies 1992-99.

JASON SCHMIDT   PIRATES
6-5, 211   **Throws:** Right.
Status: Starter.
Born: January 29, 1973.
1999 season: 13-11; 4.19 ERA; 148 SO.
Career: 41-42; 4.51 ERA; 535 SO.
Teams: Braves 1995-96; Pirates 1996-99.

AARON SELE   **MARINERS**
6-5, 215   **Throws:** Right.
Status: Starter.
Born: June 25, 1970.
1999 season: 18-9; 4.79 ERA; 186 SO.
Career: 75-53; 4.45 ERA; 831 SO.
Teams: Red Sox 1993-97; Rangers 1998-99.

JEFF SHAW   **DODGERS**
6-2, 200   **Throws:** Right.
Status: Reliever.
Born: July 7, 1966.
1999 season: 2-4; 2.78 ERA; 34 saves.
Career: 28-45; 3.48 ERA; 133 saves.
Teams: Indians 1990-92; Expos 1993-95; White Sox 1995; Reds 1996-98; Dodgers 1998-99.

JOHN SMOLTZ   **BRAVES**
Status: Starter.
1999 season: 11-8; 3.19 ERA; 156 SO.
Awards: See N.L. Cy Young 1996.

TODD STOTTLEMYRE   **DIAMONDBACKS**
6-3, 200   **Throws:** Right.
Status: Starter.
Born: May 20, 1965.
1999 season: 6-3; 4.09 ERA; 74 SO.
Career: 129-113; 4.22 ERA; 1499 SO.
Teams: Blue Jays 1988-94; Athletics 1995; Cardinals 1996-98; Rangers 1998; Diamondbacks 1999.

JUSTIN THOMPSON   **RANGERS**
6-4, 215   **Throws:** Left.
Status: Starter.
Born: March 8, 1973.
1999 season: 9-11; 5.11 ERA; 83 SO.
Career: 36-43; 3.98 ERA; 427 SO.
Team: Tigers 1996-99.

MIKE TIMLIN   **ORIOLES**
6-4, 210   **Throws:** Right.
Status: Reliever.
Born: March 10, 1966.
1999 season: 3-9; 3.57 ERA; 27 saves.
Career: 32-36; 3.53 ERA; 99 saves.
Teams: Blue Jays 1991-97; Mariners 1997-98; Orioles 1999.

BRETT TOMKO   **REDS**
6-4, 215   **Throws:** Right.
Status: Starter.
Born: April 7, 1973.
1999 season: 5-7; 4.92 ERA; 132 SO.
Career: 29-26; 4.35 ERA; 389 SO.
Team: Reds 1997-99.

MIKE TROMBLEY   **ORIOLES**
6-2, 210   **Throws:** Right.
Status: Reliever.
Born: April 14, 1967.
1999 season: 2-8; 4.33 ERA; 24 saves.
Career: 30-33; 4.46 ERA; 34 saves.
Team: Twins 1992-99.

UGUETH URBINA   **EXPOS**
6-2, 205   **Throws:** Right.
Status: Reliever.
Born: February 15, 1974.
1999 season: 6-6; 3.69 ERA; 41 saves.
Career: 29-24; 3.40 ERA; 102 saves.
Team: Expos 1995-99.

ISMAEL VALDES   **CUBS**
6-3, 215   **Throws:** Right.
Status: Starter.
Born: August 21, 1973.
1999 season: 9-14; 3.98 ERA; 143 SO.
Career: 61-54; 3.38 ERA; 756 SO.
Team: Dodgers 1994-99.

DAVE VERES   **CARDINALS**
6-2, 220   **Throws:** Right.
Status: Reliever.
Born: October 19, 1966.
1999 season: 4-8; 5.14 ERA; 31 saves.
Career: 23-19; 3.40 ERA; 46 saves.
Teams: Astros 1994-95; Expos 1996-97; Rockies 1998-99.

RON VILLONE   **REDS**
6-3, 237   **Throws:** Left.
Status: Starter.
Born: January 16, 1970.
1999 season: 9-7; 4.23 ERA; 97 SO.
Career: 13-11; 4.32 ERA; 253 SO.
Teams: Mariners 1995; Padres 1995-96; Brewers 1996-97; Indians 1998; Reds 1999.

BILLY WAGNER   **ASTROS**
5-11, 180   **Throws:** Left.
Status: Reliever.
Born: July 25, 1971.
1999 season: 4-1; 1.57 ERA; 39 saves.
Career: 17-14; 2.35 ERA; 101 saves.
Team: Astros 1995-99.

TIM WAKEFIELD   **RED SOX**
6-2, 206   **Throws:** Right.
Status: Starter, Reliever.
Born: August 2, 1966.
1999 season: 6-11; 5.08 ERA; 15 saves; 104 SO.
Career: 79-67; 4.34 ERA; 15 saves; 770 SO.
Teams: Pirates 1992-93; Red Sox 1995-99.

JEFF WEAVER   **TIGERS**
6-5, 200   **Throws:** Right.
Status: Starter.
Born: August 22, 1976.
1999 season: 9-12; 5.55 ERA; 114 SO.
Career: 9-12; 5.55 ERA; 114 SO.
Team: Tigers 1999.

DAVID WELLS   **BLUE JAYS**
6-4, 225   **Throws:** Left.
Status: Starter.
Born: May 20, 1963.
1999 season: 17-10; 4.82 ERA; 169 SO.
Career: 141-99; 4.05 ERA; 1410 SO.
Teams: Blue Jays 1987-92, 1999; Tigers 1993-95; Reds 1995; Orioles 1996; Yankees 1997-98.

JOHN WETTELAND   **RANGERS**
6-2, 215   **Throws:** Reliever.
Status: Reliever.

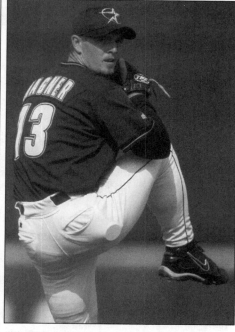

Billy Wagner's 100-mph fastball is the primary reason he averaged 1.7 strikeouts per inning in '99.

Born: August 21, 1966.
1999 season: 4-4; 3.68 ERA; 43 saves.
Career: 42-40; 2.82 ERA; 296 saves.
Teams: Dodgers 1989-91; Expos 1992-94; Yankees 1995-96; Rangers 1997-99.

SCOTT WILLIAMSON   **REDS**
Status: Reliever.
1999 season: 12-7; 2.41 ERA; 40 saves.
Awards: See N.L. Rookie of the Year 1999.

JARET WRIGHT   **INDIANS**
6-2, 230   **Throws:** Right.
Status: Starter.
Born: December 29, 1975.
1999 season: 8-10; 6.06 ERA; 91 SO.
Career: 28-23; 5.08 ERA; 294 SO.
Team: Indians 1997-99.

MASATO YOSHII   **METS**
6-2, 210   **Throws:** Right.
Status: Starter.
Born: April 20, 1965.
1999 season: 12-8; 4.40 ERA; 105 SO.
Career: 18-16; 4.17 ERA; 222 SO.
Team: Mets 1998-99.

JEFF ZIMMERMAN   **RANGERS**
6-1, 200   **Throws:** Right.
Status: Reliever.
Born: August 9, 1972.
1999 season: 9-3; 2.36 ERA; 3 saves.
Career: 9-3; 2.36 ERA; 3 saves.
Team: Rangers 1999.

AMERICAN LEAGUE

JIM FREGOSI　　　　**BLUE JAYS**
6-2, 197　　　　　**Born:** April 4, 1942.
1999 record: 84-78, 3rd place A.L. East.
Career: 237-248 Angels 1978-81; 193-226 White Sox 1986-88; 364-368 Phillies 1991-95; 84-78 Blue Jays, 1999.
Position as player: Infielder.

PHIL GARNER　　　　**TIGERS**
5-10, 177　　　　　**Born:** April 30, 1949.
1999 record: 52-60, April 5-August 11, 1999 with Brewers.
Career: 563-617 Brewers 1992-99.
Position as player: Second base, third base.

MIKE HARGROVE　　　　**ORIOLES**
6-0, 195　　　　　**Born:** October 26, 1949.
1999 record: 97-65, 1st place A.L. Central with Indians.
Career: 721-591 Indians 1991-99.
Position as player: First base, DH.

ART HOWE　　　　**ATHLETICS**
6-1, 185　　　　　**Born:** December 15, 1946.
1999 record: 87-75, 2nd place A.L. West.
Career: 391-418 Astros 1989-93; 304-344 Athletics 1996-99.
Position as player: Third base, first base.

TOM KELLY　　　　**TWINS**
5-11, 185　　　　　**Born:** August 15, 1950.
1999 record: 63-97, 5th place A.L. Central.
Career: 986-1,074 Twins 1986-99.
Position as player: First base, outfield.

CHARLIE MANUEL　　　　**INDIANS**
6-3, 200　　　　　**Born:** January 4, 1944.
1999 record: Did not manage.
Career: Beginning first year as manager.
Position as player: Outfield.

JERRY MANUEL　　　　**WHITE SOX**
5-11, 180　　　　　**Born:** December 23, 1953.
1999 record: 75-86, 2nd place A.L. Central.
Career: 155-168 White Sox 1998-99.
Position as player: Second base, shortstop.

Jack McKeon's 96-win season with the upstart Reds earned him his first Manager of the Year Award.

TONY MUSER　　　　**ROYALS**
6-2, 190　　　　　**Born:** August 1, 1947.
1999 record: 64-97, 4th place A.L. Central.
Career: 167-234 Royals 1997-99.
Position as player: First base, outfield.

JOHNNY OATES　　　　**RANGERS**
5-11, 185　　　　　**Born:** January 21, 1946.
1999 record: 95-67, 1st place A.L. West.
Career: 291-270 Orioles 1991-94; 424-368 Rangers 1995-99.
Position as player: Catcher.

LOU PINEILLA　　　　**MARINERS**
6-2, 199　　　　　**Born:** August 28, 1943.
1999 record: 79-83, 3rd place A.L. West.
Career: 224-193 Yankees 1986-88; 255-231 Reds 1990-92; 540-525 Mariners 1993-99.
Position as player: Oufield, DH.

LARRY ROTHSCHILD　　　　**DEVIL RAYS**
6-2, 185　　　　　**Born:** March 12, 1954.
1999 record: 69-93, 5th place A.L. East.
Career: 132-192 Devil Rays 1998-99.
Position as player: Pitcher.

MIKE SCIOSCIA　　　　**ANGELS**
6-2, 220　　　　　**Born:** November 27, 1958.
1999 record: Did not manage.
Career: Beginning first year as manager.
Position as player: Catcher.

JOE TORRE　　　　**YANKEES**
6-1, 210　　　　　**Born:** July 18, 1940.
1999 record: 98-64, 1st place A.L. East.
Career: 286-420 Mets 1977-81; 257-229 Braves 1982-84; 351-354 Cardinals 1990-95; 400-248 Yankees 1996-99.
Position as player: Catcher, first base, third base.

JIMY WILLIAMS　　　　**RED SOX**
5-11, 170　　　　　**Born:** October 4, 1943.
1999 record: 94-68, 2nd place A.L. East.
Career: 281-241 Blue Jays; 264-222 Red Sox 1997-99.
Position as player: Shortstop.

NATIONAL LEAGUE

FELIPE ALOU　　　　**EXPOS**
6-1, 195　　　　　**Born:** May 12, 1935.
1999 record: 68-94, 4th place N.L. East.
Career: 603-590 Expos 1992-99.
Position as player: Outfield.

DUSTY BAKER　　　　**GIANTS**
6-2, 200　　　　　**Born:** June 15, 1949.
1999 record: 86-76, 2nd place N.L. West.
Career: 558-512 Giants 1993-99.
Position as player: Outfield.

DON BAYLOR　　　　**CUBS**
6-1, 220　　　　　**Born:** June 28, 1949.
1999 record: Did not manage.
Career: 440-469 Rockies 1993-98.
Position as player: Outfield, DH.

BUDDY BELL　　　　**ROCKIES**
6-3, 200　　　　　**Born:** August 27, 1951.
1999 record: Did not manage.
Career: 184-277 Tigers 1996-98.
Position as player: Third base, first base.

BRUCE BOCHY　　　　**PADRES**
6-4, 225　　　　　**Born:** April 16, 1955.
1999 record: 74-88, 4th place N.L. West.
Career: 409-383 Padres 1995-99
Position as player: Catcher.

JOHN BOLES　　　　**MARLINS**
5-10, 165　　　　　**Born:** August 19, 1948.
1999 record: 64-98, 5th place N.L. East.
Career: 40-35 Marlins 1996, 64-98 1999.
Position as player: No Major League Experience.

BOBBY COX　　　　**BRAVES**
6-0, 185　　　　　**Born:** May 21, 1941.
1999 record: 103-59, 1st place N.L. East.
Career: 266-323 Braves 1978-81, 900-589 1990-99; 355-292 Blue Jays 1982-85.
Position as player: Third base, second base.

LARRY DIERKER　　　　**ASTROS**
6-4, 215　　　　　**Born:** Sept. 22, 1946.
1999 record: 97-65, 1st place N.L. Central.
Career: 283-203 Astros 1997-99.
Position as player: Pitcher.

TERRY FRANCONA　　　　**PHILLIES**
6-1, 175　　　　　**Born:** April 22, 1959.
1999 record: 77-85, 3rd place N.L. East.
Career: 220-266 Phillies 1997-99.
Position as player: First base, outfield.

DAVEY JOHNSON　　　　**DODGERS**
6-1, 182　　　　　**Born:** January 30, 1943.
1999 record: 77-85, 3rd place N.L. West.
Career: 595-417 Mets 1984-90; 204-172 Reds 1993-95; 186-138 Orioles 1996-97; 77-85 Dodgers 1999.
Position as player: Second base.

GENE LAMONT　　　　**PIRATES**
6-1, 190　　　　　**Born:** December 25, 1946.
1999 record: 78-83, 3rd place N.L. Central.
Career: 258-210 White Sox 1992-95; 226-259 Pirates 1997-99.
Position as player: Catcher.

TONY LA RUSSA　　　　**CARDINALS**
6-0, 185　　　　　**Born:** October 4, 1944.
1999 record: 75-86, 4th place N.L. Central.
Career: 522-510 White Sox 1979-86; 798-673 Athletics 1986-95; 319-328 Cardinals 1996-99.
Position as player: Infield.

DAVEY LOPES　　　　**BREWERS**
5-9, 170　　　　　**Born:** May 3, 1945.
1999 record: Did not manage.
Career: Beginning first year as manager.
Position as player: Second base.

JACK McKEON　　　　**REDS**
5-8, 205　　　　　**Born:** November 23, 1930.
1999 record: 96-67, 2nd place in N.L. Central.
Career: 215-205 Royals 1973-75; 71-105 Athletics 1977-78; 231-208 Padres 1988-90; 206-182 Reds 1997-99.
Position as player: No Major League experience.

BUCK SHOWALTER　　　　**DIAMONDBACKS**
5-10, 185　　　　　**Born:** May 23, 1956.
1999 record: 100-62, 1st place N.L. West.
Career: 313-268 Yankees 1992-95; 165-159 Diamondbacks 1998-99.
Position as player: No Major League experience.

BOBBY VALENTINE　　　　**METS**
5-10, 189　　　　　**Born:** May 13, 1950.
1999 record: 97-66, 2nd place N.L. East.
Career: 581-605 Rangers 1985-92; 285-233 Mets 1996-99.
Position as player: Infield.

GENERAL MANAGERS

AMERICAN LEAGUE

GORD ASH — BLUE JAYS
Born: December 20, 1951.
Blue Jays general manager: 1994-2000.
Career path: Joined the Blue Jays organization in 1978; Blue Jays assistant director, operations 1980-84; Blue Jays administrator, player personnel 1984-89; Blue Jays assistant G.M. 1989-94; Blue Jays V.P. baseball and G.M. 1994-2000.

BILLY BEANE — ATHLETICS
Born: March 29, 1962.
Athletics general manager: 1996-2000.
Career path: Major League player with Mets, Twins, Tigers and Athletics 1984-89; joined Athletics as advance scout in 1990; Athletics assistant general manager 1993-96; Athletics general manager 1996-2000.

BRIAN CASHMAN — YANKEES
Born: July 3, 1967.
Yankees general manager: 1998-2000.
Career path: Joined Yankees as a college intern in 1986; became a full-time assistant in baseball operations department in 1989; served as assistant G.M. 1992-98; Yankees G.M. 1998-2000.

DAN DUQUETTE — RED SOX
Born: May 26, 1958.
Red Sox general manager: 1994-2000.
Career path: Joined Brewers front office in 1980 as assistant in scouting and player development; Brewers scouting director 1986-87; joined Expos organization in 1987 as director of player development; named Expos assistant G.M. 1990; Expos vice-president and general manager 1991-94; Red Sox G.M. 1994-2000.

PAT GILLICK — MARINERS
Born: August 22, 1937.
Mariners general manager: 2000.
Career path: Joined Astros organization as assistant farm director in 1964; advanced to director of scouting in 10 years with Houston; joined the Yankees as coordinator of player development and scouting in 1974; joined Blue Jays front office in the expansion season of 1976 as vice-president of player personnel; Blue Jays vice-president of baseball operations 1977-84; Blue Jays executive vice-president/baseball 1984-94; Orioles G.M. 1995-98; Mariners executive vice president and general manager of baseball operations 1999-2000.

JOHN HART — INDIANS
Born: July 21, 1948.
Indians general manager: 1991-2000.
Career path: Minor league manager in Orioles organization 1982-87; Orioles third base coach 1988; joined Indians front office in 1989 and served as director of baseball operations 1990-91; Indians executive V.P. and G.M. 1991-2000.

CHUCK LaMAR — DEVIL RAYS
Born: July 22, 1956.
Devil Rays general manager: 1995-2000.
Career path: Scouting supervisor for Reds 1985-89; director of minor league operations for Pirates 1989-90; director of scouting and player development for Braves 1990-93; assistant G.M. for player personnel for Braves 1993-95; Devil Rays senior V.P. for Baseball Operations and G.M. 1995-2000.

DOUG MELVIN — RANGERS
Born: August 8, 1952.
Rangers general manager: 1994-2000.
Career path: Coordinator of advance scouting reports for Yankees 1979-85; Yankees scouting director 1985; Orioles special assistant to club owner 1986-87; Orioles director of player personnel 1987-88; Orioles assistant G.M. 1988-94; Rangers V.P. and G.M. 1994-2000.

HERK ROBINSON — ROYALS
Born: June 25, 1940.
Royals general manager: 1990-2000.
Career path: Began career in Reds organization 1962-67; Orioles organization 1968; Royals assistant scouting director 1969-73; Royals director of stadium operations 1973-75; Royals vice-president 1975-81; Royals executive V.P. for administration 1981-90; Royals executive V.P. and G.M. 1990-2000.

TERRY RYAN — TWINS
Born: October 26, 1953.
Twins general manager: 1994-2000.
Career path: Mets Midwest scouting supervisor 1980-86; Twins scouting director 1986-91; Twins V.P. of player personnel 1991-94; Twins V.P. and G.M. 1994-2000.

RON SCHUELER — WHITE SOX
Born: April 18, 1948.
White Sox general manager: 1990-2000.
Career path: Major League pitcher with Braves, Phillies, Twins and White Sox 1972-79; White Sox pitching coach 1979-81; A's pitching coach 1982-84; Pirates pitching coach 1986; A's special assistant to G.M. 1986-89; White Sox V.P., Major League operations 1990-2000.

RANDY SMITH — TIGERS
Born: June 15, 1953.
Tigers general manager: 1995-2000.
Career path: Administrative assistant in Padres minor league system 1984; Padres assistant director of scouting 1985-88; Rockies assistant G.M. 1991-93; Padres V.P. baseball operations and G.M. 1993-95; Tigers V.P. baseball operations and G.M. 1995-2000.

BILL STONEMAN — ANGELS
Born: April 7, 1944.
Angels general manager: 2000.
Career path: Major League pitcher with Cubs, Expos and Angels 1967-74; Expos assistant to the President 1983; Expos vice president, baseball administration 1984-99; Angels vice president and general manager 1999-2000.

SYD THRIFT — ORIOLES
Born: February 25, 1929.
Orioles general manager: 2000.
Career path: Pitcher/first baseman in Yankees farm system 1949-50; part-time scout with Pirates and Yankees 1953-56; Pirates scouting supervisor and spring training instructor 1957-67; Royals scouting director and founding director of Royals Baseball Academy 1967-75; worked with Athletics scouting department 1975-76; Pirates general manager 1985-88; Yankees senior vice president, baseball operations 1989; consultant to the Dodgers, Mets and Giants organizations 1991; Cubs assistant general manager 1991-94; Orioles director of player development 1995-98; Orioles director of player personnel 1999-2000.

NATIONAL LEAGUE

JIM BEATTIE — EXPOS
Born: July 4, 1954.
Expos general manager: 1995-2000.
Career path: Major League pitcher with Yankees and Mariners 1978-86; Mariners director of player development 1989-95; Expos V.P and G.M. 1995-2000.

CAM BONIFAY — PIRATES
Born: February 12, 1952.
Pirates general manager: 1993-2000.
Career path: Served as a scout in Reds organization 1976-77; Cardinals scout 1978-80; Reds scouting supervisor 1982-87; Pirates scout 1988-90; Pirates assistant G.M. 1990-93; Pirates senior V.P. and G.M. 1993-2000.

Manager Bobby Cox (right) and general manager John Schuerholz call the shots for the Braves.

JIM BOWDEN   REDS
Born: May 18, 1961.
Reds general manager: 1992-2000.
Career path: Joined Pirates organization in 1984; Pirates assistant director of player development 1985-88; Yankees assistant to the senior V.P. 1989; Reds administrative assistant for scouting 1990; Reds director of player development 1991-92; Reds G.M. 1992-2000.

DAVE DOMBROWSKI   MARLINS
Born: July 27, 1956.
Marlins general manager: 1991-2000.
Career path: Joined White Sox organization in 1978 as a minor league administrative assistant; White Sox assistant director of player development 1979-81; White Sox assistant G.M. 1981-85; White Sox V.P., baseball operations 1985-86; joined Expos front office 1986; Expos assistant to the G.M. 1987-88; Expos V.P./player personnel 1988-90; Expos G.M. 1990-91; Marlins executive V.P. and G.M. 1991-2000.

JOE GARAGIOLA JR.   DIAMONDBACKS
Born: August 6, 1950.
Diamondbacks general manager: 1995-2000.
Career path: Began baseball association in 1970s as general counsel and assistant to the president for the Yankees; practiced law with a Phoenix firm from 1982-95; chairman of Phoenix Metropolitan Sports Foundation 1985-87; vice chairman of Governor's Cactus League Task Force 1988-90; as member of Mayor's Professional Baseball Committee, he helped get an expansion team for Phoenix; Diamondbacks vice president and G.M. 1995-2000.

GERRY HUNSICKER   ASTROS
Born: June 10, 1950.
Astros general manager: 1995-2000.
Career path: Held a variety of jobs in Astros organization 1978-81, including assistant to the G.M.; Mets director of minor league operations 1988-90; Mets director of baseball operations 1990-91; Mets assistant to the executive V.P. 1991-95; Astros G.M. 1995-2000.

WALT JOCKETTY   CARDINALS
Born: February 19, 1951.
Cardinals general manager: 1994-2000.
Career path: A's director of minor league operations and scouting 1980-83; A's director of baseball administration 1983-93; Rockies assistant G.M./player personnel 1993-94; Cardinals V.P./G.M. 1994-2000.

ED LYNCH   CUBS
Born: February 25, 1956.
Cubs general manager: 1994-2000.
Career path: Major League pitcher with Mets and Cubs 1980-87; Padres director of minor leagues 1990-93; Mets special assistant to executive V.P. of baseball operations 1993-94; Cubs G.M. 1994-2000.

KEVIN MALONE   DODGERS
Born: Aug. 6, 1957.
Dodgers general manager: 1999-2000.
Career path: Served as the Angels' Southern California scout from 1985-87; worked as Expos' Southern California scout and a minor league instructor in 1988; worked as Twins' East Coast scouting supervisor from 1989-91; Expos' director of scouting from 1991-94; Expos' G.M. from 1994-95; Orioles' assistant G.M. from 1995-98; Dodgers' executive V.P and G.M. September 1998-2000.

DAN O'DOWD   ROCKIES
Born: 1959.
Rockies general manager: 2000.
Career path: Worked in Orioles broadcasting and marketing departments 1983-85; Orioles assistant director of player development and scouting 1985-87; Indians director of player development 1988-92; Indians director of baseball operations and assistant general manager 1993-98.; Rockies executive vice president-general manager, 1999-2000.

STEVE PHILLIPS   METS
Born: May 18, 1963, 1949.
Mets general manager: 1998-2000.
Career path: Mets administrative assistant to the minor leagues and scouting 1990-91; Mets director of minor leagues 1991-97; Mets senior vice president and general manager 1998-2000.

BRIAN SABEAN   GIANTS
Born: July 1, 1956.
Giants general manager: 1996-2000.
Career path: Former college baseball coach at St. Leo College and University of Tampa; head coach at Tampa 1983-84; joined Yankees organization and served as director of scouting 1986-90; Yankees vice president player development/scouting 1990-92; joined Giants and served as assistant general manager and vice president of scouting/player personnel 1993-95; served as senior vice president, player personnel 1995-96; Giants senior V.P. and G.M. 1996-2000.

JOHN SCHUERHOLZ   BRAVES
Born: October 1, 1940.
Braves general manager: 1990-2000.
Career path: Worked in Orioles organization 1966-68; Royals administrative assistant 1968-70; Royals assistant farm director 1970-75; Royals farm director 1975-76; Royals director of player procurement 1976-79; Royals V.P./player personnel 1979-81; Royals executive V.P and G.M. 1981-90; Braves executive V.P. and G.M. 1990-2000.

DEAN TAYLOR   BREWERS
Born: April 19, 1951.
Brewers general manager: 2000.
Career path: Minor league general manager 1976-80; Royals administrative assistant for minor league operations and assistant director of scouting and player development 1980-85; Royals assistant to the general manager 1985-90; Braves assistant general manager 1990-99; Brewers senior vice president/baseball operations and General Manager 1999-2000.

KEVIN TOWERS   PADRES
Born: November 11, 1961.
Padres general manager: 1995-2000.
Career path: Padres scout 1989-91; Padres scouting director 1993-95; Padres senior V.P. and G.M. 1995-2000.

ED WADE   PHILLIES
Born: January 31, 1956.
Phillies general manager: 1997-2000.
Career path: Began baseball career as public relations assistant 1977-79; Astros public relations director 1979-81; joined Pirates as public relations director 1981-85; became an associate for Tal Smith Enterprises 1985-89; Phillies assistant general manager 1989-97; Phillies G.M. 1997-2000.

History

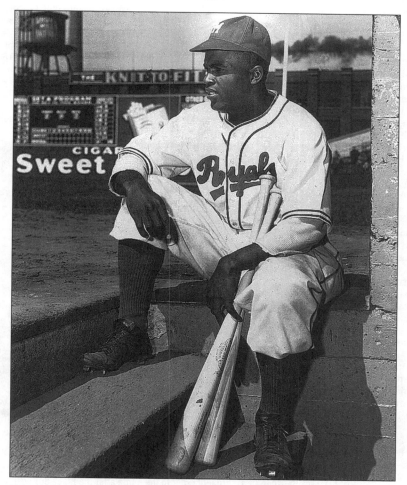

The year before Jackie Robinson became the first black player in modern baseball history, he performed his magic for the Montreal Royals, Brooklyn's Class AAA farm team.

INTRODUCTION

IN THE BEGINNING

When Chicago businessman William Ambrose Hulbert set out to cure the ills that had afflicted his favorite sport in its formative years, he called a meeting in New York.

And what a meeting it turned out to be. When all was said and done, Major League Baseball—in the form of the National League—had become a part of the American sports landscape.

It all happened at the Grand Central Hotel on February 2, 1876. Hulbert, a baseball fan of the first rank, was determined to end the rowdyism, alcohol abuse and gambling that had troubled baseball. What he ended up with was the founding of the National League of Professional Baseball Clubs, with franchises awarded to Chicago, Cincinnati, St. Louis, Louisville, New York, Hartford, Boston and Philadelphia.

Hulbert, who had headed the Chicago club in baseball's first professional league, the wild and woolly National Association (1871-75), wanted the new league to exhibit a higher caliber of play and, just as important, be beyond reproach in terms of integrity and orderliness. To help achieve his goals, Hulbert named prominent businessman Morgan Bulkeley—the son of the founder of the Aetna Insurance Co.—as the National League's first president.

Bulkeley indicated his reign would be brief, and it was. His one year on the job was long enough, though, to get the National League off on a firm footing. And this new league, with strong leadership and outstanding talent, won billing as baseball's first major league.

Franchises came and went in the National League's first 24 years, but the alignment in place for 1900—Brooklyn, Boston, New York, Philadelphia, Pittsburgh, Chicago, Cincinnati and St. Louis—remained intact through the 1952 season.

Rivals to the N.L. came and went, too, with only the American League surviving. The A.L., with Ban Johnson as its first president, was founded in 1901. And, from 1903 through 1953, the American League was another model of stability, with its membership (New York, Boston, Washington, Cleveland, Detroit, Chicago, Philadelphia and St. Louis) holding firm.

Spurred by franchise shifts and expansion, the major league landscape has changed dramatically since '52. The leagues have grown from two entities of eight teams each to two of 16 and 14 clubs, and the majors have moved into Milwaukee, Baltimore, Kansas City, Los Angeles, San Francisco, Minneapolis-St. Paul, Houston, Anaheim, Atlanta, Oakland, Seattle, Montreal, San Diego, Arlington, Toronto, Miami, Denver, Tampa-St. Petersburg and Phoenix. The latter two areas were new to the big-league map in 1998.

Major League Baseball's growth since that 1876 meeting in New York has mirrored that of the nation. It has been an exhilarating and frenetic 124 years in America's ballparks—and as season No. 125 unfolds in 2000, fans are expecting more of the same.

THE WAY IT WAS ... AND IS

When the first pitch in major league history was thrown on April 22, 1876 (in a game matching the Boston and Philadelphia teams in the fledgling National League), Ulysses S. Grant was serving as the 18th president of the United States, the Union consisted of 37 states, George Armstrong Custer and his troops had yet to meet their fate at the Battle of the Little Bighorn, the Statue of Liberty was eight years away from completion in France and aviation's Wright brothers were 9 and 4 years old. In that first game, another Wright—Harry, known as the "father of professional baseball" because he organized the first pro team, the 1869 Cincinnati Red Stockings—managed Boston to a 6-5 victory. ... The Boston franchise, later to be known as the Braves, lives on today in Atlanta and is one of only two big-league clubs to have been in continuous operation since the start of major league ball. Of course, the franchise has bounced from Beantown to Milwaukee to Atlanta, leaving Chicago's N.L. team as the only franchise to be operated continuously in one city from Day One of the majors' inception. ... Other "big leagues" sprung up in 1882 (the American Association, which lasted through 1891), 1884 (the Union Association), 1890 (the Players League, like the UA, a one-season operation), 1901 (the American League) and 1914 (the Federal League, which lasted two years). ... Although the Cubs and Red Sox will be among teams hoping to end long World Series droughts in 2000, those clubs were among the scourges of baseball in the early part of the 20th century. The Cubs, who haven't even played in a Series since 1945 and last won one in 1908, took two consecutive Series crowns while making four fall classic appearances in five years (1906-1910). The Red Sox, who haven't claimed a Series title since 1918, won the first-ever fall classic in 1903 and were champions in their first five Series ('03, 1912, 1915, 1916, 1918). Boston has lost in its last four Series. The Red Sox qualified for the playoffs for the second consecutive year in 1999 (the first time they had made back-to-back postseason appearances since '15-'16), but New England fans were disappointed once more when the Sox were eliminated in the League Championship Series by the Yankees. ... The Yankees, who won their 36th A.L. pennant in 1999, won their first flag in the club's pre-Bronx Bombers days. Yes, the Yanks had Babe Ruth and other robust hitters when they copped their first pennant in 1921, but the club was still playing at the Polo Grounds—in the borough of Manhattan—in those days. The move to the Bronx and

Commissioner Kenesaw Mountain Landis, pictured with American League president Will Harridge (left), brought order to the game after the Black Sox scandal.

Yankee Stadium came in 1923, the year the Yankees won their first of 25 World Series championships. ... The Athletics and Giants also fielded powerhouse teams in the century's first three decades. Connie Mack's A's were World Series champions three times in a four-year span (1910-13) and ruled again in 1929 and 1930. John McGraw's Giants won it all in 1905, 1921 and 1922 and appeared in six other Series. ... Commissioner Kenesaw Mountain Landis' unyielding stewardship, Ruth's slugging (and accompanying gate appeal) and the presence of great Yankees teams helped baseball overcome the Black Sox mess of 1919. Starting in '23, the Yanks won eight Series titles in 17 years. ... In the 18 seasons from 1947 through 1964, the Yankees rolled to 15 pennants in a run that included a record-setting five consecutive Series championships (1949-53). ... Since '64, the Oakland A's (three straight Series crowns in the early 1970s) and Cincinnati's Big Red Machine (1975 and 1976 Series championships and strong clubs before and after) have been in the spotlight, joined in recent years by the Series-winning Toronto Blue Jays of 1992 and 1993 and the Yankees, whose '99 Series title was their third in four years. Also rating mention are the Atlanta Braves, who have won divisional crowns in the last eight non-strike seasons; the Florida Marlins, who won the World Series in only the fifth season in franchise history, 1997, before being dismantled in a payroll-reduction move; and the Arizona Diamondbacks, who won a division title last season in only their second year of existence.

—JOE HOPPEL

HISTORY

1876

FINAL STANDINGS

National League

Team	W	L	Pct.	GB
Chicago	52	14	.788	...
St. Louis	45	19	.703	6
Hartford	47	21	.691	6
Boston	39	31	.557	15
Louisville	30	36	.455	22
New York	21	35	.375	26
Philadelphia	14	45	.237	34.5
Cincinnati	9	56	.138	42.5

SIGNIFICANT EVENTS

■ William Hulbert, president of the National Association's Chicago franchise, presided over a February meeting that signaled the official beginning of a new National League. Morgan Bulkeley was selected as the new circuit's first president.

■ The New York Mutuals, following the lead of the Philadelphia Athletics, announced they would not make their season-ending Western trip, forcing cancellation of a major chunk of the N.L.'s September schedule.

■ During a December meeting in Cleveland, the Athletics and Mutuals were expelled from the N.L. lineup and William Hulbert was elected president.

MEMORABLE MOMENTS

■ Boston 6, Philadelphia 5 in the first N.L. game. Jim O'Rourke entered the record books as the first player to get a hit in the April 22 battle at Athletic Park.

■ Chicago's Ross Barnes became the first N.L. player to hit a home run—an inside-the-park drive in a game at Cincinnati.

■ St. Louis' George Bradley pitched the first no-hitter in N.L. history, defeating Hartford, 2-0.

■ Hartford 14-8, Cincinnati 4-1 in baseball's first doubleheader.

■ Chicago clinched the N.L.'s first pennant with a victory over Hartford.

LEADERS

BA: Ross Barnes, Chi., .429.
Runs: Ross Barnes, Chi., 126.
Hits: Ross Barnes, Chi., 138.
TB: Ross Barnes, Chi., 190.
HR: George Hall, Phil., 5.
RBI: Deacon White, Chi., 60.
Wins: Al Spalding, Chi., 47.
ERA: George Bradley, St.L., 1.23.
CG: Jim Devlin, Lou., 66.
IP: Jim Devlin, Lou., 622.
SO: Jim Devlin, Lou., 122.

20-game winners

Al Spalding, Chi., 47-12
George Bradley, St.L., 45-19
Tommy Bond, Hart., 31-13
Jim Devlin, Lou., 30-35
Bobby Mathews, N.Y., 21-34

THE RULES

■ The new National League adopted a detailed rule book that included these interesting variations to the rules we use today:

■ The Strike Zone: The batter, upon stepping into position, had to call for a high or low pitch and the umpire notified the pitcher to deliver the ball as requested, making his calls accordingly.

■ The Strikeout: When a batter with two strikes failed to swing at the next good pitch, the umpire warned him by calling "good ball." If the batter swung and missed or failed to swing at the next "good ball," the umpire called "three strikes" and the batter was expected to run to first as if he had hit a fair ball.

■ Substitutions: No player could be replaced after the fourth inning, except those giving way temporarily for a pinch runner.

■ Batter/Position: When batters stepped outside the box while striking at the ball, the umpire would call "foul balk and out," allowing all runners to return to their bases.

■ Pitchers threw underhanded from a box with a front line that was 45 feet from the center of home base.

1877

FINAL STANDINGS

National League

Team	W	L	Pct.	GB
Boston	42	18	.700	...
Louisville	35	25	.583	7
Hartford	31	27	.534	10
St. Louis	28	32	.467	14
Chicago	26	33	.441	15.5
Cincinnati	15	42	.263	25.5

SIGNIFICANT EVENTS

■ The Hartford club announced in March that it would play its 1877 "home games" in Brooklyn while retaining its "home base" of Hartford.

■ Without enough money to finance a mid-season trip, the Cincinnati club disbanded. It was reorganized three days later under new ownership.

■ The Louisville team expelled players George Hall, Jim Devlin, Al Nichols and Bill Craver for fixing games, a move that later would be supported by league officials.

■ At its December meeting, the N.L. dropped franchises in Hartford and St. Louis and admitted teams in Indianapolis and Milwaukee.

MEMORABLE MOMENTS

■ Boston and Hartford opened the N.L.'s second season with an 11-inning 1-1 tie at Brooklyn.

■ Boston clinched the N.L. pennant with a victory over Hartford.

LEADERS

BA: Deacon White, Bos., .387.
Runs: Jim O'Rourke, Bos., 68.
Hits: Deacon White, Bos., 103.
TB: Deacon White, Bos., 145.
HR: Lip Pike, Cin., 4.
RBI: Deacon White, Bos., 49.
Wins: Tommy Bond, Bos., 40.
ERA: Tommy Bond, Bos., 2.11.
CG: Jim Devlin, Lou., 61.
IP: Jim Devlin, Lou., 559.
SO: Tommy Bond, Bos., 170.

20-game winners

Tommy Bond, Bos., 40-17
Jim Devlin, Lou., 35-25
Terry Larkin, Hart., 29-25

MAJOR RULES CHANGES

■ Any batted ball that bounced into foul territory before passing first or third base became a "foul" ball instead of a "fair" ball.

■ Home base was repositioned entirely in fair territory, two sides laying flush with the foul lines. The 17-inch move forward forced a corresponding move back of the pitcher's box.

■ The batter's box was changed to 6 feet in length—3 feet in front and 3 feet in back of the home-base line.

■ The size of bases was enlarged to 15 square inches, with their sides positioned parallel to the base lines.

■ An at-bat was not charged when a batter drew a base on balls.

1878

FINAL STANDINGS

National League

Team	W	L	Pct.	GB
Boston	41	19	.683	...
Cincinnati	37	23	.617	4
Providence	33	27	.550	8
Chicago	30	30	.500	11
Indianapolis	24	36	.400	17
Milwaukee	15	45	.250	26

SIGNIFICANT EVENTS

■ The N.L. increased its membership to seven with the addition of the Grays, a new franchise in Providence, R.I., but the field was reduced back to six when Louisville, unable to put together a competitive roster, resigned from the league.

■ At its winter meetings, the N.L. admitted new members Syracuse, Buffalo and Cleveland while dropping Indianapolis and Milwaukee.

MEMORABLE MOMENTS

■ Defending-champion Boston spoiled the Major League debut of the Grays, 1-0, in an opening day game at Providence's new Messer Street Park.

■ Tommy Bond defeated Providence for his 40th victory and brought Boston within range of its second consecutive pennant.

LEADERS

BA: Abner Dalrymple, Mil., .354.
Runs: Dick Higham, Pro., 60.
Hits: Joe Start, Chi., 100.
TB: Paul Hines, Pro.; Joe Start, Chi.; Tom York, Pro., 125.
HR: Paul Hines, Pro., 4.
RBI: Paul Hines, Pro., 50.
Wins: Tommy Bond, Bos., 40.
ERA: Monte Ward, Pro., 1.51.
CG: Tommy Bond, Bos., 57.
IP: Tommy Bond, Bos., 532.2.
SO: Tommy Bond, Bos., 182.

20-game winners

Tommy Bond, Bos., 40-19
Will White, Cin., 30-21
Terry Larkin, Chi. 29-26
Monte Ward, Pro., 22-13

MAJOR RULES CHANGES

■ Captains were required to position their players and after one at-bat, the batting order could no longer be changed.

■ Pinch runners were not allowed except in cases of illness or injury. The emergency substitute could enter the game only after the original player had reached base.

1879

FINAL STANDINGS

National League

Team	W	L	Pct.	GB
Providence	59	25	.702	...
Boston	54	30	.643	5
Buffalo	46	32	.590	10
Chicago	46	33	.582	10.5
Cincinnati	43	37	.538	14
Cleveland	27	55	.329	31
Syracuse	22	48	.314	30
Troy	19	56	.253	35.5

SIGNIFICANT EVENTS

■ The N.L. beefed up its preseason roster by admitting a new Troy franchise.

■ The Syracuse Stars, facing bankruptcy in mid-September, resigned from the N.L., leaving the league with an incomplete schedule.

■ The financially strapped Cincinnati club ended the season and folded operation, refusing to pay its players their final month's salary.

■ A new Cincinnati club gained quick N.L. acceptance during the annual winter meetings.

MEMORABLE MOMENTS

■ John Montgomery Ward's streak of having pitched every inning of 73 consecutive Providence games ended in mid-July when he was relieved in the fourth inning of a 9-0 loss to Cincinnati.

■ The Providence Grays scored a ninth-inning run and claimed a pennant-clinching victory over Boston.

■ Cincinnati pitcher Will White completed the season with 75 complete games and 680 innings—still-standing Major League records.

LEADERS

BA: Cap Anson, Chi., .317.
Runs: Charley Jones, Bos., 85.
Hits: Paul Hines, Pro., 146.
TB: Paul Hines, Pro., 197.
HR: Charley Jones, Bos., 9.
RBI: Charley Jones, Bos.; Jim O'Rourke, Bos., 62.
Wins: Monte Ward, Pro., 47.
ERA: Tommy Bond, Bos., 1.96.
CG: Will White, Cin., 75.
IP: Will White, Cin., 680.
SO: Monte Ward, Pro., 239.

20-game winners

Monte Ward, Pro., 47-19
Tommy Bond, Bos., 43-19
Will White, Cin., 43-31
Pud Galvin, Buf., 37-27
Terry Larkin, Chi., 31-23
Jim McCormick, Cle., 20-40

MAJOR RULES CHANGES

■ The size of the pitcher's box was enlarged to 4-by-6 feet.

■ A batter was declared out after three strikes if the pitch was caught before touching the ground.

■ Any pitcher who, in the opinion of the umpire, intentionally hit a batter with a pitch was fined from $10 to $50.

■ The "Spalding League Ball" was adopted as the official ball.

FINAL STANDINGS

National League

Team	W	L	Pct.	GB
Chicago	67	17	.798	...
Providence	52	32	.619	15
Cleveland	47	37	.560	20
Troy	41	42	.494	25.5
Worcester	40	43	.482	26.5
Boston	40	44	.476	27
Buffalo	24	58	.293	42
Cincinnati	21	59	.263	44

SIGNIFICANT EVENTS

■ The preseason addition of a team in Worcester brought the N.L. field back to eight.

■ After kicking Cincinnati out of the league for rules violations, the N.L. admitted a new franchise from Detroit.

MEMORABLE MOMENTS

■ A Major League first—Worcester's Lee Richmond was perfect in a 1-0 victory over Cleveland.

■ Providence ace John Montgomery Ward matched the perfect-game feat of Lee Richmond five days earlier, retiring all 27 Buffalo batters he faced in a 5-0 victory.

■ Fred Dunlap's ninth-inning home run broke a scoreless tie and gave Cleveland a victory over Chicago, snapping the White Stockings' record 21-game inning streak.

■ Chicago completed its season with a 67-17 record and a 15-game bulge over second-place Providence.

LEADERS

BA: George Gore, Chi., .360.
Runs: Abner Dalrymple, Chi., 91.
Hits: Abner Dalrymple, Chi., 126.
TB: Abner Dalrymple, Chi., 175.
HR: Jim O'Rourke, Bos.; Harry Stovey, Wor., 6.
RBI: Cap Anson, Chi., 74.
Wins: Jim McCormick, Cle., 45.
ERA: Tim Keefe, Troy, 0.86.
CG: Jim McCormick, Cle., 72.
IP: Jim McCormick, Cle., 657.2.
SO: Larry Corcoran, Chi., 268.

20-game winners

Jim McCormick, Cle., 45-28
Larry Corcoran, Chi., 43-14
Monte Ward, Pro., 39-24
Mickey Welch, Troy, 34-30
Lee Richmond, Wor., 32-32
Tommy Bond, Bos., 26-29
Fred Goldsmith, Chi., 21-3
Pud Galvin, Buf., 20-35

MAJOR RULES CHANGES

■ A walk was awarded after eight balls instead of nine.

■ A runner was declared out if hit by a batted ball, and no run was allowed to score on the play.

■ The batter was required to run for first base immediately after "strike three" was called by the umpire.

FINAL STANDINGS

National League

Team	W	L	Pct.	GB
Chicago	56	28	.667	...
Providence	47	37	.560	9
Buffalo	45	38	.542	10.5
Detroit	41	43	.488	15
Troy	39	45	.464	17
Boston	38	45	.458	17.5
Cleveland	36	48	.429	20
Worcester	32	50	.390	23

SIGNIFICANT EVENTS

■ One month after the 1881 season had ended, officials announced the formation of the American Association, a rival Major League with franchises in St. Louis, Cincinnati, Louisville, Philadelphia, Pittsburgh and Brooklyn.

■ American Association officials voted to ignore N.L. rules against Sunday games, liquor sales and 25-cent ticket prices. They also announced their decision not to abide by the N.L.'s restrictive reserve clause in player contracts.

MEMORABLE MOMENTS

■ Troy's Roger Connor hit the first grand slam in N.L. history—a bottom-of-the-ninth blow that handed Worcester an 8-7 defeat.

■ Chicago clinched its second straight pennant with a victory over Boston and White Stockings star Cap Anson put the finishing touches on his league-leading .399 average.

LEADERS

BA: Cap Anson, Chi., .399.
Runs: George Gore, Chi., 86.
Hits: Cap Anson, Chi., 137.
TB: Cap Anson, Chi., 175.
HR: Dan Brouthers, Buf., 8.
RBI: Cap Anson, Chi., 82.
Wins: Larry Corcoran, Chi.;
  Jim Whitney, Bos., 31.
ERA: Stump Weidman, Det., 1.80.
CG: Jim McCormick, Cle.;
  Jim Whitney, Bos., 57.
IP: Jim Whitney, Bos., 552.1.
SO: George Derby, Det., 212.

20-game winners

Larry Corcoran, Chi., 31-14
Jim Whitney, Bos., 31-33
George Derby, Det., 29-26
Pud Galvin, Buf., 28-24
Jim McCormick, Cle., 26-30
Hoss Radbourn, Pro., 25-11
Lee Richmond, Wor., 25-26
Fred Goldsmith, Chi., 24-13
Mickey Welch, Troy, 21-18

MAJOR RULES CHANGES

■ The front line of the pitcher's box was moved from 45 to 50 feet from the center of home base.

■ A batter was awarded first base after seven balls.

■ No substitutes were permitted except in the cases of illness or injury.

■ Umpires no longer gave players the "good ball" warning on called third strikes.

FINAL STANDINGS

American Association

Team	W	L	Pct.	GB
Cincinnati	55	25	.688	...
Philadelphia	41	34	.547	11.5
Louisville	42	38	.525	13
Pittsburgh	39	39	.500	15
St. Louis	37	43	.463	18
Baltimore	19	54	.260	32.5

SIGNIFICANT EVENTS

■ After completing its first season as a six-team circuit, the American Association added franchises in Columbus and New York.

■ A baseball first: The Association formed the first permanent staff of umpires.

MEMORABLE MOMENTS

■ Opening day for the new American Association: St. Louis 9, Louisville 7; Philadelphia 10, Baltimore 7; Allegheny 10, Cincinnati 9.

■ Louisville ace Tony Mullane recorded the league's first no-hitter, beating the Red Stockings 2-0 at Cincinnati.

■ Cincinnati clinched the first A.A. pennant with a 6-1 mid-September victory over Louisville as the second-place Athletics dropped a game at Pittsburgh.

■ In the first post-season matchup of Major League champions, the Red Stockings split a two-game series with N.L. pennant winner Chicago.

LEADERS

BA: Pete Browning, Lou., .378.
Runs: Ed Swartwood, Pit., 86.
Hits: Hick Carpenter, Cin., 120.
TB: Ed Swartwood, Pit., 159.
HR: Oscar Walker, St.L., 7.
Wins: Will White, Cin., 40.
ERA: Denny Driscoll, Pit., 1.21.
CG: Will White, Cin., 52.
IP: Will White, Cin., 480.
SO: Tony Mullane, Lou., 170.

20-game winners

Will White, Cin., 40-12
Tony Mullane, Lou., 30-24
Sam Weaver, Phil., 26-15
George McGinnis, St.L., 25-18
Harry Salisbury, Pit., 20-18

THE RULES

■ The new American Association began its first season with several modifications to the existing rules book. Among the variations:

■ Sunday games were allowed.

■ Teams could charge 25 cents for admission rather than the N.L. price of 50 cents.

■ Liquor could be sold at the ballparks.

■ Pitchers judged to be intentionally throwing at batters were not subject to immediate fines.

FINAL STANDINGS

National League

Team	W	L	Pct.	GB
Chicago	55	29	.655	...
Providence	52	32	.619	3
Boston	45	39	.536	10
Buffalo	45	39	.536	10
Cleveland	42	40	.512	12
Detroit	42	41	.506	12.5
Troy	35	48	.422	19.5
Worcester	18	66	.214	37

SIGNIFICANT EVENTS

■ When N.L. President William Hulbert died of a heart attack in April, Boston team president A.H. Soden was named as his replacement.

■ At the winter meetings, N.L. officials replaced the Troy and Worcester franchises with teams from New York and Philadelphia, keeping the league roster at eight.

MEMORABLE MOMENTS

■ Chicago 35, Cleveland 4: a record rout in which seven White Stockings got four or more hits.

■ Chicago ace Larry Corcoran pitched his second career no-hitter, beating Worcester, 5-0.

■ Chicago finished with a 55-29 record and claimed its third straight N.L. pennant by three games over Providence.

LEADERS

BA: Dan Brouthers, Buf., .368.
Runs: George Gore, Chi., 99.
Hits: Dan Brouthers, Buf., 129.
TB: Dan Brouthers, Buf., 192.
HR: George Wood, Det., 7.
RBI: Cap Anson, Chi., 83.
Wins: Jim McCormick, Cle., 36.
ERA: Larry Corcoran, Chi., 1.95.
CG: Jim McCormick, Cle., 65.
IP: Jim McCormick, Cle., 595.2.
SO: Hoss Radbourn, Pro., 201.

20-game winners

Jim McCormick, Cle., 36-30
Hoss Radbourn, Pro., 33-20
Fred Goldsmith, Chi., 28-17
Pud Galvin, Buf., 28-23
Larry Corcoran, Chi., 27-12
George Weidman, Det., 25-20
Jim Whitney, Bos., 24-21

MAJOR RULES CHANGES

■ Umpires could call for a new ball at the end of even innings, provided the old ball was unfit for fair use.

■ The home team was required to provide a players' bench, 12 feet in length and fastened to the ground. Racks that held at least 20 bats became mandatory.

■ A baserunner obstructing a player attempting to field a batted ball was called out for interference.

■ Spectators caught hissing or hooting at the umpire were ejected from the park.

FINAL STANDINGS

American Association

Team	W	L	Pct.	GB
Philadelphia	66	32	.673	...
St. Louis	65	33	.663	1
Cincinnati	61	37	.622	5
New York	54	42	.563	11
Louisville	52	45	.536	13.5
Columbus	32	65	.330	33.5
Pittsburgh	31	67	.316	35
Baltimore	28	68	.292	37

SIGNIFICANT EVENTS

■ In a significant February meeting, baseball officials drafted the first National Agreement, ensuring peaceful co-existence and respect for player contracts between the N.L. and American Association. Both leagues embraced the controversial reserve clause.

■ The Association announced post-season plans to expand to 12 teams with new franchises in Brooklyn, Washington, Indianapolis and Toledo.

MEMORABLE MOMENTS

■ New York's Tim Keefe celebrated Independence Day by winning both ends of a doubleheader against Columbus. Keefe allowed only three total hits.

■ The Athletics posted a late-September victory over Louisville and claimed the American Association's second pennant.

LEADERS

BA: Ed Swartwood, Pit., .357.
Runs: Harry Stovey, Phil., 110.
Hits: Ed Swartwood, Pit., 147.
TB: Harry Stovey, Phil., 213.
HR: Harry Stovey, Phil., 14.
Wins: Will White, Cin., 43.
ERA: Will White, Cin., 2.09.
CG: Tim Keefe, N.Y., 68.
IP: Tim Keefe, N.Y., 619.
SO: Tim Keefe, N.Y., 359.

20-game winners

Will White, Cin., 43-22
Tim Keefe, N.Y., 41-27
Tony Mullane, St.L., 35-15
Bobby Mathews, Phil., 30-13
George McGinnis, St.L., 28-16
Sam Weaver, Lou., 26-22
Guy Hecker, Lou., 26-23
Frank Mountain, Col., 26-33

MAJOR RULES CHANGES

■ Pitchers were allowed to deliver the ball from a shoulder-length position instead of the former below-the-waist position.

■ A runner touching and overrunning first base put himself at risk of being tagged out if he turned to his left while returning to the bag.

■ Pinch runners were allowed in cases of illness and injury.

FINAL STANDINGS

National League

Team	W	L	Pct.	GB
Boston	63	35	.643	...
Chicago	59	39	.602	4
Providence	58	40	.592	5
Cleveland	55	42	.567	7.5
Buffalo	52	45	.536	10.5
New York	46	50	.479	16
Detroit	40	58	.408	23
Philadelphia	17	81	.173	46

SIGNIFICANT EVENTS

■ Peace prevails: The N.L. and American Association signed a new National Agreement, ensuring respect for player contracts under the controversial reserve system.

MEMORABLE MOMENTS

■ Philadelphia 28, Providence 0—the most lopsided shutout in Major League history.

■ The White Stockings exploded for a record 18 runs in the seventh inning of a victory over Detroit.

■ Boston broke Chicago's three-year stranglehold on the N.L. pennant with a clinching victory over Cleveland.

LEADERS

BA: Dan Brouthers, Buf., .374.
Runs: Joe Hornung, Bos., 107.
Hits: Dan Brouthers, Buf., 159.
TB: Dan Brouthers, Buf., 243.
HR: Buck Ewing, N.Y., 10.
RBI: Dan Brouthers, Buf., 97.
Wins: Hoss Radbourn, Pro., 48.
ERA: Jim McCormick, Cle., 1.84.
CG: Pud Galvin, Buf., 72.
IP: Pud Galvin, Buf., 656.1.
SO: Jim Whitney, Bos., 345.

20-game winners

Hoss Radbourn, Pro., 48-25
Pud Galvin, Buf., 46-29
Jim Whitney, Bos., 37-21
Larry Corcoran, Chi., 34-20
Jim McCormick, Cle., 28-12
Charlie Buffinton, Bos., 25-14
Fred Goldsmith, Chi., 25-19
Mickey Welch, N.Y., 25-23
Hugh Daily, Cle., 23-19

MAJOR RULES CHANGES

■ Pitchers working within the confines of the box and facing the batter could deliver the ball with more forceful motion. The ball, on delivery, had to pass below the line of the pitcher's shoulder instead of below his waist.

■ A batted ball caught in foul territory was declared an out. Previously, balls caught on one bounce in foul territory were outs.

■ A player batting out of order was declared out.

■ Umpires became salaried employees.

FINAL STANDINGS

Union Association

Team	W	L	Pct.	GB
St. Louis	94	19	.832	...
Milwaukee	8	4	.667	35.5
Cincinnati	69	36	.657	21
Baltimore	58	47	.552	32
Boston	58	51	.532	34
Chicago-Pitt.	41	50	.451	42
Washington	47	65	.420	46.5
Philadelphia	21	46	.313	50
St. Paul	2	6	.250	39.5
Altoona	6	19	.240	44
Kansas City	16	63	.203	61
Wilmington	2	16	.111	44.5

SIGNIFICANT EVENTS

■ The new Union Association, organized the previous September as a third Major League, added a Boston team to its roster while preparing for its first season.

■ U.A. casualties: Altoona (6-19) ceased operations in May, Philadelphia (21-46) disbanded in August and Chicago transferred operations in late August to Pittsburgh. Wilmington and Pittsburgh later were replaced by Milwaukee and Omaha—a franchise that lasted eight days and was replaced by St. Paul.

■ Only five teams attended the U.A.'s winter meetings, setting the stage for the league to disband in January.

MEMORABLE MOMENTS

■ Boston defeated St. Louis and ended the Maroons' 20-game winning streak

■ Boston's Fred Shaw held St. Louis to one hit and struck out 18, but he still lost a 1-0 decision to the pennant-bound Maroons.

LEADERS

BA: Fred Dunlap, St.L., .412.
Runs: Fred Dunlap, St.L., 160.
Hits: Fred Dunlap, St.L., 185.
TB: Fred Dunlap, St.L., 279.
HR: Fred Dunlap, St.L., 13.
Wins: Bill Sweeney, Bal., 40.
ERA: Jim McCormick, Cin., 1.54.
CG: Bill Sweeney, Bal., 58.
IP: Bill Sweeney, Bal., 538.
SO: Hugh Daily, CP-Wash., 483.

20-game winners

Bill Sweeney, Bal., 40-21
Hugh Daily, C-W-P, 28-28
Billy Taylor, St.L., 25-4
George Bradley, Cin., 25-15
Charlie Sweeney, St.L., 24-7
Dick Burns, Cin., 23-15
Bill Wise, Wash., 23-18
Jim McCormick, Cin., 21-3
Fred Shaw, Bos., 21-15

THE RULES

■ The Union Association, in its only Major League season, adopted the American Association rules book, which still included the shoulder-length restriction on pitching deliveries and seven-ball walks. The U.A., however, did adopt the N.L. rule on foul flies. The A.A.'s new hit-by-pitch rule was not adopted by the U.A.

FINAL STANDINGS

American Association

Team	W	L	Pct.	GB
New York	75	32	.701	...
Columbus	69	39	.639	6.5
Louisville	68	40	.630	7.5
St. Louis	67	40	.626	8
Cincinnati	68	41	.624	8
Baltimore	63	43	.594	11.5
Philadelphia	61	46	.570	14
Toledo	46	58	.442	27.5
Brooklyn	40	64	.385	33.5
Richmond	12	30	.286	30.5
Pittsburgh	30	78	.278	45.5
Indianapolis	29	78	.271	46
Washington	12	51	.190	41

SIGNIFICANT EVENTS

■ Toledo's Fleetwood Walker became the Major League's first black player when he went 0-for-3 in an opening day loss to Louisville.

■ Columbus, a second-place finisher in its only season, sold its players and dropped out of the league.

MEMORABLE MOMENTS

■ Louisville ace Guy Hecker, en route to Association season-high totals of 52 wins and 72 complete games, pitched both ends of a Fourth of July doubleheader sweep of Brooklyn.

■ The Metropolitans captured their first A.A. pennant with a 4-1 victory over Columbus.

■ The N.L.'s Providence Grays posted a 6-0 victory over New York in a post-season matchup of pennant winners. The Grays would go on to win three straight games and an unofficial world championship.

LEADERS

BA: Dude Esterbrook, N.Y., .314.
Runs: Harry Stovey, Phil., 124.
Hits: Dave Orr, N.Y., 162.
TB: Dave Orr, N.Y.; John Reilly, Cin., 247.
HR: John Reilly, Cin., 11.
Wins: Guy Hecker, Lou., 52.
ERA: Guy Hecker, Lou., 1.80.
CG: Guy Hecker, Lou., 72.
IP: Guy Hecker, Lou., 670.2.
SO: Guy Hecker, Lou., 385.

20-game winners

Guy Hecker, Lou., 52-20
Jack Lynch, N.Y., 37-15
Tim Keefe, N.Y., 37-17
Tony Mullane, Tol., 36-26
Ed Morris, Col., 34-13
Will White, Cin., 34-18
Bob Emslie, Bal., 32-17
Bobby Mathews, Phil., 30-18
Hardie Henderson, Bal., 27-23
George McGinnis, St.L., 24-16
Frank Mountain, Col., 23-17

MAJOR RULES CHANGES

■ Any batter hit by a pitch after trying to avoid the ball was awarded first base.

■ Each team was allowed an extra person on the field to take charge of bats—the equivalent of a modern-day bat boy.

1884

FINAL STANDINGS

National League

Team	W	L	Pct.	GB
Providence	84	28	.750	...
Boston	73	38	.658	10.5
Buffalo	64	47	.577	19.5
Chicago	62	50	.554	22
New York	62	50	.554	22
Philadelphia	39	73	.348	45
Cleveland	35	77	.313	49
Detroit	28	84	.250	56

SIGNIFICANT EVENTS

■ N.L. officials legalized overhand pitching, stipulating that pitchers must keep both feet on the ground through their delivery.

MEMORABLE MOMENTS

■ Providence pitcher Charlie Sweeney struck out a record 19 Boston batters in a 2-1 victory over the Red Stockings.

■ Chicago ace Larry Corcoran pitched his record third career no-hitter, ending a 10-game Providence winning streak with a 6-0 victory.

■ New York's Mickey Welch opened a game against Philadelphia with a record nine consecutive strikeouts.

■ September 11: Hoss Radbourn, who would finish the season with a record 59 wins, pitched pennant-bound Providence to a victory over Cleveland—the Grays' 20th consecutive triumph.

■ Providence completed a three-game sweep of the American Association's New York Metropolitans with an 12-2 victory, punctuating baseball's second post-season matchup between pennant winners.

LEADERS

BA: Jim O'Rourke, Buf., .347.
Runs: King Kelly, Chi., 120.
Hits: Jim O'Rourke, Buf.; Ezra Sutton, Bos., 162.
TB: Abner Dalrymple, Chi., 263.
HR: Ned Williamson, Chi., 27.
RBI: Cap Anson, Chi., 102.
Wins: Hoss Radbourn, Pro., 59.
ERA: Hoss Radbourn, Pro., 1.38.
CG: Hoss Radbourn, Pro., 73.
IP: Hoss Radbourn, Pro., 678.2.
SO: Hoss Radbourn, Pro., 441.

20-game winners

Hoss Radbourn, Pro., 59-12
Charlie Buffinton, Bos., 48-16
Pud Galvin, Buf., 46-22
Mickey Welch, N.Y., 39-21
Larry Corcoran, Chi., 35-23
Jim Whitney, Bos., 23-14
Charlie Ferguson, Phil., 21-25

POST-SEASON PLAYOFF

(Providence N.L. 3, New York A.A. 0)

Game 1—Providence 6, New York 0

Game 2—Providence 3, New York 1

Game 3—Providence 12, New York 2 (6 innings, darkness)

MAJOR RULES CHANGES

■ All restrictions against pitching deliveries were lifted, meaning pitchers could throw overhand for the first time.

■ Batters were awarded first base after six balls.

■ Any ball leaving the park was declared either fair or foul, depending on its position within the foul lines.

1885

FINAL STANDINGS

American Association

Team	W	L	Pct.	GB
St. Louis	79	33	.705	...
Cincinnati	63	49	.563	16
Pittsburgh	56	55	.505	22.5
Philadelphia	55	57	.491	24
Louisville	53	59	.473	26
Brooklyn	53	59	.473	26
New York	44	64	.407	33
Baltimore	41	68	.376	36.5

SIGNIFICANT EVENTS

■ The reorganized American Association began play with teams located in St. Louis, Philadelphia, Cincinnati, Pittsburgh, Brooklyn, Louisville, New York and Baltimore.

MEMORABLE MOMENTS

■ St. Louis jumped into first place with an early May victory over Philadelphia—a position the Browns would hold the remainder of the season.

■ Baltimore snapped St. Louis' A.A.-record 17-game winning streak with a 7-1 victory.

■ The Browns, refusing to acknowledge a controversial Game 2 forfeit loss to N.L.-champion Chicago, "claimed" status as baseball world champions after beating the White Stockings and knotting the post-season series at three games apiece.

LEADERS

BA: Pete Browning, Lou., .362.
Runs: Harry Stovey, Phil., 130.
Hits: Pete Browning, Lou., 174.
TB: Pete Browning, Lou., 255.
HR: Harry Stovey, Phil., 13.
Wins: Bob Caruthers, St.L., 40.
ERA: Bob Caruthers, St.L., 2.07.
CG: Ed Morris, Pit., 63.
IP: Ed Morris, Pit., 581.
SO: Ed Morris, Pit., 298.

20-game winners

Bob Caruthers, St.L., 40-13
Ed Morris, Pit., 39-24
Dave Foutz, St.L., 33-14
Henry Porter, Brk., 33-21
Bobby Mathews, Phil., 30-17
Guy Hecker, Lou., 30-23
Hardie Henderson, Bal., 25-35
Jack Lynch, N.Y., 23-21
Larry McKeon, Cin., 20-13

MAJOR RULES CHANGES

■ The one-bounce rule was dropped and fielders were required to catch foul balls on the fly to record an out.

■ Home-team captains were given the option of batting first or second.

■ The overhand delivery was permitted, bringing league pitchers in line with their N.L. counterparts.

■ Every team was required to wear a neat and attractive uniform.

1885

FINAL STANDINGS

National League

Team	W	L	Pct.	GB
Chicago	87	25	.777	...
New York	85	27	.759	2
Philadelphia	56	54	.509	30
Providence	53	57	.482	33
Boston	46	66	.411	41
Detroit	41	67	.380	44
Buffalo	38	74	.339	49
St. Louis	36	72	.333	49

SIGNIFICANT EVENTS

■ Providence ace Hoss Radbourn, the N.L.'s highest paid player, was suspended for poor pitching after a lopsided loss to New York.

■ The Washington Nationals were accepted into the league, replacing Providence.

MEMORABLE MOMENTS

■ Philadelphia snapped Chicago's 18-game winning streak—the White Stockings' first loss at new West Side Park.

■ John Clarkson, en route to a Major League-high 53 wins, held Providence hitless in an 4-0 victory.

■ Game 2 of a post-season "World's Series" between Chicago and American Association-champion St. Louis ended in controversy when the Browns refused to continue the game in the sixth inning because of umpiring decisions. The White Stockings were declared forfeit winners.

■ The Browns defeated the White Stockings 13-4 in the championship finale, tying the series at 3-3. The Browns claimed victory, refusing to accept the forfeit decision.

LEADERS

BA: Roger Connor, N.Y., .371.
Runs: King Kelly, Chi., 124.
Hits: Roger Connor, N.Y., 169.
TB: Roger Connor, N.Y., 225.
HR: Abner Dalrymple, Chi., 11.
RBI: Cap Anson, Chi., 108.
Wins: John Clarkson, Chi., 53.
ERA: Tim Keefe, N.Y., 1.58.
CG: John Clarkson, Chi., 68.
IP: John Clarkson, Chi., 623.
SO: John Clarkson, Chi., 308.

20-game winners

John Clarkson, Chi., 53-16
Mickey Welch, N.Y., 44-11
Tim Keefe, N.Y., 32-13
Hoss Radbourn, Pro., 28-21
Charlie Ferguson, Phil., 26-20
Ed Daily, Phil., 26-23
Fred Shaw, Pro., 23-26
Charlie Buffinton, Bos., 22-27
Jim McCormick, Pro.-Chi., 21-7

POST-SEASON PLAYOFF

(Chicago N.L. 3, St. Louis A.A. 3; 1 tie)

Game 1—Chicago 5, St. Louis 5 (8 innings, darkness)

Game 2—Chicago awarded 5-4 forfeit victory

Game 3—St. Louis 7, Chicago 4

Game 4—St. Louis 3, Chicago 2

Game 5—Chicago 9, St. Louis 2 (7 innings, darkness)

Game 6—Chicago 9, St. Louis 2

Game 7—St. Louis 13, Chicago 4 (8 innings, darkness)

MAJOR RULES CHANGES

■ The batter's box was resized to 4 feet wide by 6 feet long and moved a foot closer to home base.

■ Pitchers were required to keep both feet in contact with the ground during delivery. Batters were awarded first base after two "foul balks," a rule that was eliminated at midseason.

■ Players were permitted to use bats with one flat side.

■ Any ball leaving the park at a distance of less than 210 feet was declared an automatic double.

1886

FINAL STANDINGS

American Association

Team	W	L	Pct.	GB
St. Louis	93	46	.669	...
Pittsburgh	80	57	.584	12
Brooklyn	76	61	.555	16
Louisville	66	70	.485	25.5
Cincinnati	65	73	.471	27.5
Philadelphia	63	72	.467	28
New York	53	82	.393	38
Baltimore	48	83	.366	41

SIGNIFICANT EVENTS

■ When Pittsburgh defected to the rival N.L. in November, the American Association filled the void with a new Cleveland franchise.

MEMORABLE MOMENTS

■ Louisville pitcher Guy Hecker belted a record-tying three home runs and scored a Major League-record seven times in a victory over Brooklyn.

■ The St. Louis Browns posted a 4-3 victory over the N.L.'s Chicago White Stockings in Game 6 of the "World's Series," staking their undisputed claim as king of baseball.

LEADERS

BA: Dave Orr, N.Y., .338.
Runs: Arlie Latham, St.L., 152.
Hits: Dave Orr, N.Y., 193.
TB: Dave Orr, N.Y., 301.
HR: Bid McPhee, Cin., 8.
SB: Harry Stovey, Phil., 68.
Wins: Dave Foutz, St.L.; Ed Morris, Pit., 41.
ERA: Dave Foutz, St.L., 2.11.
CG: Matt Kilroy, Bal.; Toad Ramsey, Lou., 66.
IP: Toad Ramsey, Lou., 588.2.
SO: Matt Kilroy, Bal., 513.

20-game winners

Dave Foutz, St.L., 41-16
Ed Morris, Pit., 41-20
Tom Ramsey, Lou., 38-27
Tony Mullane, Cin., 33-27
Bob Caruthers, St.L., 30-14
Pud Galvin, Pit., 29-21
Matt Kilroy, Bal., 29-34
Henry Porter, Brk., 27-19
Guy Hecker, Lou., 26-23
Al Atkinson, Phil., 25-17
Jack Lynch, N.Y., 20-30

MAJOR RULES CHANGES

■ A 4-by-1 foot smooth stone slab was placed at the front end of the pitcher's box, helping umpires determine if the pitcher had stepped beyond the front line.

■ The number of balls required for a walk was decreased from seven to six.

■ The A.A. adopted the reshaped 6-by-3 foot batter's box and 4-by-7 foot pitcher's box.

■ Stolen bases were credited for any base a runner was able to gain on his own volition, such as a first-to-third dash on a single.

1886

FINAL STANDINGS

National League

Team	W	L	Pct.	GB
Chicago	90	34	.726	...
Detroit	87	36	.707	2.5
New York	75	44	.630	12.5
Philadelphia	71	43	.623	14
Boston	56	61	.479	30.5
St. Louis	43	79	.352	46
Kansas City	30	91	.248	58.5
Washington	28	92	.233	60

SIGNIFICANT EVENTS

■ The N.L. increased its preseason roster to eight with the addition of a Kansas City team on a one-year trial basis.

■ The N.L. adopted the stolen base as an official statistic and reshaped the pitcher's box to 4-by-7 feet.

■ New rules: 4 strikes for an out; 5 balls for a walk; a standardized strike zone from the knees to the shoulders, and a 55½-foot pitching distance.

■ Pittsburgh made a November jump from the American Association to the N.L., replacing Kansas City.

MEMORABLE MOMENTS

■ The White Stockings clinched another N.L. pennant with a final-day victory over Boston. The final lead was 2½ games over Detroit.

■ Chicago dropped a 4-3 decision to the American Association-champion Browns and lost the best-of-seven "World's Series" in six games.

LEADERS

BA: King Kelly, Chi., .388.
Runs: King Kelly, Chi., 155.
Hits: Hardy Richardson, Det., 189.
TB: Dan Brouthers, Det., 284.
HR: Dan Brouthers, Det.;
  Hardy Richardson, Det., 11.
RBI: Cap Anson, Chi., 147.
SB: Ed Andrews, Phil., 56.
Wins: Lady Baldwin, Det.; Tim Keefe, N.Y., 42.
ERA: Henry Boyle, St.L., 1.76.
CG: Tim Keefe, N.Y., 62.
IP: Tim Keefe, N.Y., 535.
SO: Lady Baldwin, Det., 323.

20-game winners

Lady Baldwin, Det., 42-13
Tim Keefe, N.Y., 42-20
John Clarkson, Chi., 36-17]
Mickey Welch, N.Y., 33-22
Charlie Ferguson, Phil., 30-9
Charlie Getzien, Det., 30-11
Jim McCormick, Chi., 31-11
Hoss Radbourn, Bos., 27-31
Dan Casey, Phil., 24-18
Jocko Flynn, Chi., 23-6
Bill Stemmeyer, Bos., 22-18

POST-SEASON PLAYOFF

(St. Louis A.A. 4, Chicago N.L. 2)

Game 1—Chicago 6, St. Louis 0

Game 2—St. Louis 12, Chicago 0 (8 innings, darkness)

Game 3—Chicago 11, St. Louis 4 (8 innings, darkness)

Game 4—St. Louis 8, Chicago 5 (7 innings, darkness)

Game 5—St. Louis 10, Chicago 3 (8 innings, darkness)

Game 6—St. Louis 4, Chicago 3 (10 innings)

MAJOR RULES CHANGES

■ The number of balls required for a walk was increased from six to seven.

■ The shape of the pitcher's box was changed from 6-by-6 to 4-by-7 feet.

■ Pitchers no longer were required to keep both feet on the ground during delivery. "Foul balks" were eliminated.

■ The batter's box was reshaped to its 6-by-3 shape, 12 inches from home base.

■ Stolen bases were credited for any base a runner was able to gain on his own volition, such as a first-to-third dash on a single.

1887

FINAL STANDINGS

American Association

Team	W	L	Pct.	GB
St. Louis	95	40	.704	...
Cincinnati	81	54	.600	14
Baltimore	77	58	.570	18
Louisville	76	60	.559	19.5
Philadelphia	64	69	.481	30
Brooklyn	60	74	.448	34.5
New York	44	89	.331	50
Cleveland	39	92	.298	54

SIGNIFICANT EVENTS

■ The 4-strike rule was eliminated in a November meeting and officials reversed their preseason decision to count walks as "hits."

MEMORABLE MOMENTS

■ St. Louis, en route to 95 victories and its third straight A.A. pennant, defeated the Athletics for its 15th consecutive victory.

■ The 52-game hitting streak of Athletics star Denny Lyons came to an end in late August. Lyons' streak included two games in which he managed only walks, which were counted as hits in the 1887 season.

■ The Browns defeated New York for their 12th straight victory and increased their lead over second-place Cincinnati to a whopping 19½ games.

■ The Browns closed their best-of-15 "World's Series" battle against Detroit with a 9-2 victory, but they still lost the war, 10 games to 5.

LEADERS

BA: Tip O'Neill, St.L., .435.
Runs: Tip O'Neill, St.L., 167.
Hits: Tip O'Neill, St.L., 225.
TB: Tip O'Neill, St.L., 357.
HR: Tip O'Neill, St.L., 14.
SB: Hugh Nicol, Cin., 138.
Wins: Matt Kilroy, Bal., 46.
ERA: Elmer Smith, Cin., 2.94.
CG: Matt Kilroy, Bal., 66.
IP: Matt Kilroy, Bal., 589.1.
SO: Toad Ramsey, Lou., 355.

20-game winners

Matt Kilroy, Bal., 46-19
Toad Ramsey, Lou., 37-27
Silver King, St.L., 32-12
Elmer Smith, Cin., 34-17
Tony Mullane, Cin., 31-17
Bob Caruthers, St.L., 29-9
John Smith, Bal., 25-30
Gus Weyhing, Phil., 26-28
Ed Seward, Phil., 25-25
Dave Foutz, St.L., 25-12

MAJOR RULES CHANGES

■ The National League and American Association agreed to abide by a uniform rules book and several rules were rewritten. Here are some of the more significant changes:

■ Batters no longer were allowed to call for high or low pitches and the strike zone was defined as the area in which he could hit the ball.

■ The pitcher's box was reshaped to 4-by-5½ feet.

■ Batters hit by a pitch were awarded first base and not charged with an at-bat.

■ The number of balls required for a walk was dropped to five.

■ The batter was declared out after four strikes.

■ Batters drawing a base on balls were credited with a hit and charged with a time at-bat.

1887

FINAL STANDINGS

National League

Team	W	L	Pct.	GB
Detroit	79	45	.637	...
Philadelphia	75	48	.610	3.5
Chicago	71	50	.587	6.5
New York	68	55	.553	10.5
Boston	61	60	.504	16.5
Pittsburgh	55	69	.444	24
Washington	46	76	.377	32
Indianapolis	37	89	.294	43

SIGNIFICANT EVENTS

■ The N.L.'s St. Louis franchise was sold to Indianapolis interests.

■ The Phillies christened their new ballpark, which would remain in use as the "Baker Bowl" until 1938.

■ N.L. officials held a November meeting with the Brotherhood of Professional Base Ball Players, an organization set up to protect players' contract interests.

MEMORABLE MOMENTS

■ Detroit posted a doubleheader sweep of Chicago, increasing its N.L. lead to seven games and putting the city on the verge of its first pennant.

■ The best-of-15 "World's Series" opened with the Browns posting a 6-1 victory over Detroit.

■ The post-season title series ended with Detroit holding a commanding 10 games to 5 advantage.

LEADERS

BA: Sam Thompson, Det., .372.
Runs: Dan Brouthers, Det., 153.
Hits: Sam Thompson, Det., 203.
TB: Sam Thompson, Det., 311.
HR: Billy O'Brien, Wash., 19.
RBI: Sam Thompson, Det., 166.
SB: Monte Ward, N.Y., 111.
Wins: John Clarkson, Chi., 38.
ERA: Dan Casey, Phil., 2.86.
CG: John Clarkson, Chi., 56.
IP: John Clarkson, Chi., 523.
SO: John Clarkson, Chi., 237.

20-game winners

John Clarkson, Chi., 38-21
Tim Keefe, N.Y., 35-19
Charlie Getzien, Det., 29-13
Dan Casey, Phil., 28-13
Pud Galvin, Pit., 28-21
Jim Whitney, Wash., 24-21
Hoss Radbourn, Bos., 24-23
Charlie Ferguson, Phil., 22-10
Mickey Welch, N.Y., 22-15
Kid Madden, Bos., 21-14
Charlie Buffinton, Phil., 21-17

POST-SEASON PLAYOFF

(Detroit N.L. 10, St. Louis A.A. 5)

Game 1—St. Louis 6, Detroit 1
Game 2—Detroit 5, St. Louis 3
Game 3—Detroit 2, St. Louis 1(13 innings)
Game 4—Detroit 8, St. Louis 0
Game 5—St. Louis 5, Detroit 2
Game 6—Detroit 9, St. Louis 0
Game 7—Detroit 3, St. Louis 1
Game 8—Detroit 9, St. Louis 2
Game 9—Detroit 4, St. Louis 2
Game 10—St. Louis 11, Detroit 4
Game 11—Detroit 13, St. Louis 3
Game 12—St. Louis 5, Detroit 1 (7 innings, darkness)
Game 13—Detroit 6, St. Louis 3
Game 14—Detroit 4, St. Louis 3
Game 15—St. Louis 9, Detroit 2 (6 innings, cold)

MAJOR RULES CHANGES

■ The National League and American Association agreed to abide by a uniform rules book and several rules were rewritten. Here are some of the more significant changes:

■ Batters no longer were allowed to call for high or low pitches and the strike zone was defined as the area between the top of the shoulder and the bottom of the knees.

■ The pitcher's box was reshaped to 4-by-5½ feet.

■ Batters hit by a pitch were awarded first base and not charged with an at-bat.

■ The number of balls required for a walk was dropped to five.

■ The batter was declared out after four strikes.

■ Batters drawing a base on balls were credited with a hit and charged with a time at-bat.

1888

FINAL STANDINGS

American Association

Team	W	L	Pct.	GB
St. Louis	92	43	.681	...
Brooklyn	88	52	.629	6.5
Philadelphia	81	52	.609	10
Cincinnati	80	54	.597	11.5
Baltimore	57	80	.416	36
Cleveland	50	82	.379	40.5
Louisville	48	87	.356	44
Kansas City	43	89	.326	47.5

SIGNIFICANT EVENTS

■ Columbus became a member of the American Association roster in December, replacing Cleveland.

MEMORABLE MOMENTS

■ The St. Louis Browns, seeking their fourth straight A.A. pennant, moved into first place with a mid-July victory over Kansas City—a position they would not relinquish the rest of the season.

■ St. Louis ace Silver King posted his 45th victory and raised his league-leading totals in games (66), innings (585⅔), complete games (64) and ERA (1.64).

■ The Browns fell to N.L.-champion New York in a best-of-10 "World's Series," despite winning the finale, 18-7.

LEADERS

BA: Tip O'Neill, St.L., .335.
Runs: George Pinkney, Brk., 134.
Hits: Tip O'Neill, St.L., 177.
TB: John Reilly, Cin., 264.
HR: John Reilly, Cin., 13.
RBI: John Reilly, Cin., 103.
SB: Arlie Latham, St.L., 109.
Wins: Silver King, St.L., 45.
ERA: Silver King, St.L., 1.64.
CG: Silver King, St.L., 64.
IP: Silver King, St.L., 585.2.
SO: Ed Seward, Phil., 272.

20-game winners

Silver King, St.L., 45-21
Ed Seward, Phil., 35-19
Bob Caruthers, Brk., 29-15
Gus Weyhing, Phil., 28-18
Lee Viau, Cin., 27-14
Tony Mullane, Cin., 26-16
Nat Hudson, St.L., 25-10
Elton Chamberlain, Lou.-St.L., 25-11
Mickey Hughes, Brk., 25-13
Ed Bakely, Cle., 25-33
Elmer Smith, Cin., 22-17
Bert Cunningham, Bal., 22-29

MAJOR RULES CHANGES

■ The rule awarding the batter a hit on a base on balls was reversed.

■ The batter was credited with a "hit" on any batted ball that struck a baserunner, even though the runner was declared out.

■ The number of strikes required for a strikeout was reduced to three.

■ Pitchers were charged with an error for walks, wild pitches, hit batters and balks.

1888

FINAL STANDINGS

National League

Team	W	L	Pct.	GB
New York	84	47	.641	...
Chicago	77	58	.570	9
Philadelphia	69	61	.531	14.5
Boston	70	64	.522	15.5
Detroit	68	63	.519	16
Pittsburgh	66	68	.493	19.5
Indianapolis	50	85	.370	36
Washington	48	86	.358	37.5

SIGNIFICANT EVENTS

■ Rules changes: 4 balls for a walk and 3 strikes for a strikeout—standards that would hold up for more than a century.
■ Cleveland, a former American Association franchise, was admitted to the N.L., replacing Detroit.

MEMORABLE MOMENTS

■ With more than 10,000 fans watching at New York's Polo Grounds, Giants pitcher Tim Keefe dropped a 4-2 decision to Pittsburgh, snapping his record 19-game winning streak.
■ Pittsburgh ace Ed Morris pitched his record fourth consecutive shutout—a 1-0 victory over New York.
■ The Giants clinched the first of many N.L. pennants.
■ The Giants clinched their best-of-10 "World's Series" against St. Louis in Game 8 with an 11-3 victory.

LEADERS

BA: Cap Anson, Chi., .344.
Runs: Dan Brouthers, Det., 118.
Hits: Jimmy Ryan, Chi., 182.
TB: Jimmy Ryan, Chi., 283.
HR: Jimmy Ryan, Chi., 16.
RBI: Cap Anson, Chi., 84.
SB: Dummy Hoy, Wash., 82.
Wins: Tim Keefe, N.Y., 35.
ERA: Tim Keefe, N.Y., 1.74.
CG: Ed Morris, Pit., 54.
IP: John Clarkson, Bos., 483.1.
SO: Tim Keefe, N.Y., 333.

20-game winners

Tim Keefe, N.Y., 35-12
John Clarkson, Bos., 33-20
Pete Conway, Det., 30-14
Ed Morris, Pit., 29-25
Charlie Buffinton, Phil., 28-17
Mickey Welch, N.Y., 26-19
Gus Krock, Chi., 25-14
Pud Galvin, Pit., 23-25

POST-SEASON PLAYOFF

(New York N.L. 6, St. Louis A.A. 4)
Game 1—New York 2, St. Louis 1
Game 2—St. Louis 3, New York 0
Game 3—New York 4, St. Louis 2
Game 4—New York 6, St. Louis 3
Game 5—St. Louis 6, New York 4 (8 innings, darkness)
Game 6—New York 12, St. Louis 5 (8 innings, darkness)
Game 7—St. Louis 7, New York 5 (8 innings, darkness)
Game 8—New York 11, St. Louis 3
Game 9—St. Louis 14, New York 11 (10 innings)
Game 10—St. Louis 18, New York 7

MAJOR RULES CHANGES

■ The rule awarding the batter a hit on a base on balls was reversed.
■ The batter was credited with a "hit" on any batted ball that struck a baserunner, even though the runner was declared out.
■ Pitchers were charged with an error for walks, wild pitches, hit batters and balks.

1889

FINAL STANDINGS

American Association

Team	W	L	Pct.	GB
Brooklyn	93	44	.679	...
St. Louis	90	45	.667	2
Philadelphia	75	58	.564	16
Cincinnati	76	63	.547	18
Baltimore	70	65	.519	22
Columbus	60	78	.435	33.5
Kansas City	55	82	.401	38
Louisville	27	111	.196	66.5

SIGNIFICANT EVENTS

■ A record Association crowd of 22,122 showed up for a May 30 game in Brooklyn to watch the Bridegrooms play the Browns.
■ Baltimore, following the lead of Brooklyn, Cincinnati and Kansas City, dropped out of the American Association.

MEMORABLE MOMENTS

■ Toad Ramsey pitched Louisville to a victory over St. Louis, snapping the Colonels' Major League-record losing streak at 26 games.
■ The Browns, leading 4-2 in the ninth inning of a September 7 game, walked off the field in Brooklyn, claiming it was too dark to continue. The Bridegrooms were declared forfeit winners, a ruling that later would be reversed.
■ The Browns, claiming they feared for the personal safety amid unruly Brooklyn fans, forfeited their September 8 game to the Bridegrooms—a defeat that would help Brooklyn claim the A.A. pennant.
■ The Bridegrooms dropped a 3-2 decision to the N.L.-champion Giants in the decisive Game 9 of the "World's Series."

LEADERS

BA: Tommy Tucker, Bal., .372.
Runs: Mike Griffin, Bal.; Harry Stovey, Phil., 152.
Hits: Tommy Tucker, Bal., 196.
TB: Harry Stovey, Phil., 292.
HR: Bug Holliday, Cin.; Harry Stovey, Phil., 19.
RBI: Harry Stovey, Phil., 119.
SB: Billy Hamilton, K.C., 111.
Wins: Bob Caruthers, Brk., 40.
ERA: Jack Stivetts, St.L., 2.25.
CG: Matt Kilroy, Bal., 55.
IP: Mark Baldwin, Col., 513.2.
SO: Mark Baldwin, Col., 368.

20-game winners

Bob Caruthers, Brk., 40-11
Silver King, St.L., 35-16
Elton Chamberlain, St.L., 32-15
Jesse Duryea, Cin., 32-19
Gus Weyhing, Phil., 30-21
Matt Kilroy, Bal., 29-25
Mark Baldwin, Col., 27-34
Frank Foreman, Bal., 23-21
Adonis Terry, Brk., 22-15
Lee Viau, Cin., 22-20
Ed Seward, Phil., 21-15

MAJOR RULES CHANGES

■ The number of balls required for a walk was reduced to four.
■ A foul tip was defined as a foul hit that did not rise above the batter's head and was caught within 10 feet of home base. Batters could not be declared out on a caught foul tip and runners were permitted to return safely to their bases.
■ Pitchers were required to get into pitching position by placing one foot on the back line of the pitching box and only one step was allowed during delivery.
■ One "extra player" could be substituted at the end of any complete inning, but the player leaving the game could not return. Substitutions could be made at any time for a disabled player.
■ Pitchers no longer were charged with errors for walks, wild pitches, hit batsmen and balks.
■ The sacrifice bunt was recognized for the first time, although the hitter still was charged with an at-bat.

FINAL STANDINGS

National League

Team	W	L	Pct.	GB
New York	83	43	.659	...
Boston	83	45	.648	1
Chicago	67	65	.508	19
Philadelphia	63	64	.496	20.5
Pittsburgh	61	71	.462	25
Cleveland	61	72	.459	25.5
Indianapolis	59	75	.440	28
Washington	41	83	.331	41

SIGNIFICANT EVENTS

■ Brooklyn and Cincinnati made a November jump from the American Association to the N.L., creating a 10-team circuit.
■ A threat becomes official: The Brotherhood of Professional Base Ball Players formally organized the Players League, a third major circuit partially operated by the players themselves.

MEMORABLE MOMENTS

■ The Giants christened their new Polo Grounds with a victory over Pittsburgh.
■ The New York Giants captured their second straight pennant on the final day of the season, beating Cleveland while Boston was losing to Pittsburgh.
■ The Giants reigned as world champions again, thanks to a 6 games to 3 post-season victory over the American Association's Brooklyn Bridegrooms. New York won Game 9, 3-2.

LEADERS

BA: Dan Brouthers, Bos., .373.
Runs: Mike Tiernan, N.Y., 147.
Hits: Jack Glasscock, N.Y., 205.
TB: Jimmy Ryan, Chi., 287.
HR: Sam Thompson, Phil., 20.
RBI: Roger Connor, N.Y., 130.
SB: Jim Fogarty, Phil., 99.
Wins: John Clarkson, Bos., 49.
ERA: John Clarkson, Bos., 2.73.
CG: John Clarkson, Bos., 68.
IP: John Clarkson, Bos., 620.
SO: John Clarkson, Bos., 284.

20-game winners

John Clarkson, Bos., 49-19
Tim Keefe, N.Y., 28-13
Charlie Buffinton, Phil., 28-16
Mickey Welch, N.Y., 27-12
Pud Galvin, Pit., 23-16
Darby O'Brien, Cle., 22-17
Henry Boyle, Ind., 21-23
Harry Staley, Pit., 21-26
Hoss Radbourn, Bos., 20-11
Ed Beatin, Cle., 20-15

POST-SEASON PLAYOFF

(New York N.L. 6, Brooklyn A.A. 3)
Game 1—Brooklyn 12, New York 10 (8 innings, darkness)
Game 2—New York 6, Brooklyn 2
Game 3—Brooklyn 8, New York 7 (8 innings, darkness)
Game 4—Brooklyn 10, New York 7 (6 innings, darkness)
Game 5—New York 11, Brooklyn 3
Game 6—New York 2, Brooklyn 1 (11 innings)
Game 7—New York 11, Brooklyn 7
Game 8—New York 16, Brooklyn 7
Game 9—New York 3, Brooklyn 2

MAJOR RULES CHANGES

■ The number of balls required for a walk was reduced to four.
■ A foul tip was defined as a foul hit that did not rise above the batter's head and was caught within 10 feet of home base. Batters could not be declared out on a caught foul tip and runners were permitted to return safely to their bases.
■ Pitchers were required to get into pitching position by placing one foot on the back line of the pitching box and only one step was allowed during delivery.
■ One "extra player" could be substituted at the end of any complete inning, but the player leaving the game could not return. Substitutions could be made at any time for a disabled player.
■ Pitchers no longer were charged with errors for walks, wild pitches, hit batsmen and balks.
■ The sacrifice bunt was recognized for the first time, although the hitter still was charged with an at-bat.

1890

FINAL STANDINGS

Players League

Team	W	L	Pct.	GB
Boston	81	48	.628	...
Brooklyn	76	56	.576	6.5
New York	74	57	.565	8
Chicago	75	62	.547	10
Philadelphia	68	63	.519	14
Pittsburgh	60	68	.469	20.5
Cleveland	55	75	.423	26.5
Buffalo	36	96	.273	46.5

SIGNIFICANT EVENTS

■ The new Players League won the first of many lawsuits it would have to endure when a judge refused to grant a January injunction against Brotherhood president John Montgomery Ward.
■ The Players League began its inaugural season in a war-like atmosphere, thanks to the league-jumping antics of many big-name stars from the National League and American Association.
■ The New York and Pittsburgh teams combined with the same-city franchises from the N.L., pronouncing last rites for the one-year circuit. The December defections would prompt Players League backers to seek their own deals in a scramble to remain solvent.

MEMORABLE MOMENTS

■ Willie McGill, a 16-year-old Cleveland hurler, became the youngest Major League pitcher to throw a complete game when he defeated Buffalo.
■ Boston closed out the first and last Players League season with an 81-48 record, capturing the pennant by 6½ games over Brooklyn.

LEADERS

BA: Pete Browning, Cle., .373.
Runs: Hugh Duffy, Chi., 161.
Hits: Hugh Duffy, Chi., 191.
TB: Billy Shindle, Phil., 281.
HR: Roger Connor, N.Y., 14.
RBI: Hardy Richardson, Bos., 146.
SB: Harry Stovey, Bos., 97.
Wins: Mark Baldwin, Chi., 34.
ERA: Silver King, Chi., 2.69.
CG: Mark Baldwin, Chi., 54.
IP: Mark Baldwin, Chi., 501.
SO: Mark Baldwin, Chi., 211.

20-game winners

Mark Baldwin, Chi., 34-24
Gus Weyhing, Brk., 30-16
Silver King, Chi., 30-22
Hoss Radbourn, Bos., 27-12
Addison Gumbert, Bos., 23-12
Phil Knell, Phil., 22-11
Hank O'Day, N.Y., 22-13
Henry Gruber, Cle., 22-23
Harry Staley, Pit., 21-25

THE RULES

■ The one-season Players League adopted its own rules book with only slight variations to the ones used by the American Association and National League. The most significant was a resized pitcher's box that reverted to the 6-by-4 foot rectangle last used in 1885 with a front line 51 feet from the center of home base. Other key variations:
■ If a team failed to begin play within one minute after the umpire called "play" at the start of a game, a forfeit was declared.
■ Each corner of the reshaped pitcher's box was marked by a wooden peg, a variation from the flat rubber plates used by the other leagues.
■ Two umpires were required for each championship game, one behind the plate and the other standing in the field.

FINAL STANDINGS

American Association

Team	W	L	Pct.	GB
Louisville	88	44	.667	...
Columbus	79	55	.590	10
St. Louis	78	58	.574	12
Toledo	68	64	.515	20
Rochester	63	63	.500	22
Baltimore	15	19	.441	24
Syracuse	55	72	.433	30.5
Philadelphia	54	78	.409	34
Brooklyn	26	73	.263	45.5

SIGNIFICANT EVENTS

■ Brooklyn joined Syracuse, Rochester and Toledo as new American Association cities.

■ The bankrupt Athletics disbanded, releasing and selling their players. A patchwork Philadelphia club would close the season with 22 consecutive losses.

■ The Athletics were expelled, a new Philadelphia franchise was admitted and new teams from Boston, Washington and Chicago replaced Syracuse, Rochester and Toledo in action at the winter meetings.

MEMORABLE MOMENT

■ Louisville defeated N.L.-champion Brooklyn 6-2 to salvage a "World's Series" split. Each team won three games and one ended in a tie.

LEADERS

BA: Jimmy Wolf, Lou., .363.
Runs: Jim McTamany, Col., 140.
Hits: Jimmy Wolf, Lou., 197.
TB: Jimmy Wolf, Lou., 260.
HR: Count Campau, St.L., 9.
SB: Tommy McCarthy, St.L., 83.
Wins: Sadie McMahon, Phil.-Bal., 36.
ERA: Scott Stratton, Lou., 2.36.
CG: Sadie McMahon, Phil.-Bal., 55.
IP: Sadie McMahon, Phil.-Bal., 509.
SO: Sadie McMahon, Phil.-Bal., 291.

20-game winners

Sadie McMahon, Phil.-Bal., 36-21
Scott Stratton, Lou., 34-14
Hank Gastright, Col., 30-14
Bob Barr, Rch., 28-24
Jack Stivetts, St.L., 27-21
Red Ehret, Lou., 25-14
Toad Ramsey, St.L., 24-17
John Healy, Tol., 22-21

MAJOR RULES CHANGES

■ Pitchers and other players were no longer allowed to discolor the ball by rubbing it with soil or other foreign substances.

■ Each team was allowed a second "extra player" and substitutions could be made at any time with retiring players unable to return.

FINAL STANDINGS

National League

Team	W	L	Pct.	GB
Brooklyn	86	43	.667	...
Chicago	84	53	.613	6
Philadelphia	78	54	.591	9.5
Cincinnati	77	55	.583	10.5
Boston	76	57	.571	12
New York	63	68	.481	24
Cleveland	44	88	.333	43.5
Pittsburgh	23	113	.169	66.5

SIGNIFICANT EVENTS

■ Committees from the three rival Major Leagues began October peace negotiations that eventually would signal the end of the Players League.

MEMORABLE MOMENTS

■ N.L. newcomer Brooklyn moved into first place with a victory over Cincinnati. The Bridegrooms would win the pennant with a six-game edge over Chicago.

■ Brooklyn swept a tripleheader from hapless Pittsburgh and stretched its losing streak to 22 games. Pittsburgh would finish the season with a record 113 losses.

■ Brooklyn (N.L.) and Louisville (A.A.) began play in a "World's Series" that did not include Players League champion Boston. The Bridegrooms won the opener, 9-0, but the series would end in a 3-3 deadlock with one tie.

LEADERS

BA: Jack Glasscock, N.Y., .336.
Runs: Hub Collins, Brk., 148.
Hits: Jack Glasscock, N.Y.;
    Sam Thompson, Phil., 172.
TB: Mike Tiernan, N.Y., 274.
HR: Oyster Burns, Brk.; Mike Tiernan, N.Y.;
    Walt Wilmot, Chi., 13.
RBI: Oyster Burns, Brk., 128.
SB: Billy Hamilton, Phil., 102.
Wins: Bill Hutchinson, Chi., 42.
ERA: Billy Rhines, Cin., 1.95.
CG: Bill Hutchinson, Chi., 65.
IP: Bill Hutchinson, Chi., 603.
SO: Amos Rusie, N.Y., 341.

20-game winners

Bill Hutchinson, Chi., 42-25
Kid Gleason, Phil., 38-17
Tom Lovett, Brk., 30-11
Amos Rusie, N.Y., 29-34
Billy Rhines, Cin., 28-17
Kid Nichols, Bos., 27-19
Adonis Terry, Brk., 26-16
John Clarkson, Bos., 26-18
Tom Vickery, Phil., 24-22
Bob Caruthers, Brk., 23-11
Charlie Getzien, Bos., 23-17
Ed Beatin, Cle., 22-30
Pat Luby, Chi., 20-9

POST-SEASON PLAYOFF

(Brooklyn N.L. 3, Louisville A.A. 3; 1 tie)

Game 1—Brooklyn 9, Louisville 0 (8 innings, darkness)

Game 2—Brooklyn 5, Louisville 3

Game 3—Brooklyn 7, Louisville 7 (8 innings, darkness)

Game 4—Louisville 5, Brooklyn 4

Game 5—Brooklyn 7, Louisville 2

Game 6—Louisville 9, Brooklyn 8

Game 7—Louisville 6, Brooklyn 2

MAJOR RULES CHANGES

■ Pitchers and other players were no longer allowed to discolor the ball by rubbing it with soil or other foreign substances.

■ Each team was allowed a second "extra player" and substitutions could be made at any time with retiring players unable to return.

FINAL STANDINGS

American Association

Team	W	L	Pct.	GB
Boston	93	42	.689	...
St. Louis	86	52	.623	8.5
Milwaukee	21	15	.583	22.5
Baltimore	71	64	.526	22
Philadelphia	73	66	.525	22
Columbus	61	76	.445	33
Cincinnati	43	57	.430	32.5
Louisville	55	84	.396	40
Washington	44	91	.326	49

SIGNIFICANT EVENTS

■ In a February declaration of war, the American Association withdrew from the National Agreement and moved its Chicago franchise to Cincinnati to compete with the N.L.'s Reds.

■ The Association's Cincinnati franchise folded in mid-August and was replaced by the Western Association's Milwaukee Brewers.

■ The Boston Reds, en route to the A.A. pennant, were shocked by the August defection of star King Kelly to their Boston N.L. rival.

■ A "World's Series" challenge by Reds owners was turned down by the the N.L.-champion Boston team. N.L. officials cited the A.A.'s withdrawal from the National Agreement.

■ After 10 Major League seasons, the Association died when four of its eight teams joined the N.L. and the other four accepted buyouts.

MEMORABLE MOMENTS

■ The Boston Reds defeated Baltimore and clinched the final A.A. pennant.

■ Browns rookie Ted Breitenstein, making his first Major League start on the final day of the season, pitched an 8-0 no-hitter against Louisville.

LEADERS

BA: Dan Brouthers, Bos., .350.
Runs: Tom Brown, Bos., 177.
Hits: Tom Brown, Bos., 189.
TB: Tom Brown, Bos., 276.
HR: Duke Farrell, Bos., 12.
RBI: Hugh Duffy, Bos.; Duke Farrell, Bos., 110.
SB: Tom Brown, Bos., 106.
Wins: Sadie McMahon, Bal., 35.
ERA: Ed Crane, Cin., 2.45.
CG: Sadie McMahon, Bal., 53.
IP: Sadie McMahon, Bal., 503.
SO: Jack Stivetts, St.L., 259.

20-game winners

Sadie McMahon, Bal., 35-24
George Haddock, Bos., 34-11
Jack Stivetts, St.L., 33-22
Gus Weyhing, Phil., 31-20
Charlie Buffinton, Bos., 29-9
Phil Knell, Col., 28-27
Elton Chamberlain, Phil., 22-23
Willie McGill, Cin.-St.L., 21-15

MAJOR RULES CHANGE

■ All teams were required to have one or more substitutes available for each game.

FINAL STANDINGS

National League

Team	W	L	Pct.	GB
Boston	87	51	.630	...
Chicago	82	53	.607	3.5
New York	71	61	.538	13
Philadelphia	68	69	.496	18.5
Cleveland	65	74	.468	22.5
Brooklyn	61	76	.445	25.5
Cincinnati	56	81	.409	30.5
Pittsburgh	55	80	.407	30.5

SIGNIFICANT EVENTS

■ The American Association withdrew from the National Agreement in February and declared war, moving its Chicago franchise to Cincinnati to compete with the N.L.'s Reds.

■ Pittsburgh secured its nickname as "Pirates" when it lured stars Pete Browning and Scott Stratton away from the A.A.'s Louisville team.

■ With August peace talks between the National League and American Association in progress, the N.L. Boston team shattered the calm by pirating King Kelly away from its A.A. Boston rival.

■ The American Association ceased operations in December when four A.A. clubs (St. Louis, Louisville, Washington and Baltimore) joined the N.L., creating "The National League and American Association of Professional Base Ball Clubs."

MEMORABLE MOMENTS

■ Cy Young christened Cleveland's new League Park, pitching the Spiders to an easy victory over the Reds.

■ Chicago's Wild Bill Hutchison defeated Boston for his 40th victory en route to a Major League-high 44.

■ Boston clinched the N.L. pennant with a victory over Philadelphia—its 17th in a row.

LEADERS

BA: Billy Hamilton, Phil., .340.
Runs: Billy Hamilton, Phil., 141.
Hits: Billy Hamilton, Phil., 179.
TB: Harry Stovey, Bos., 271.
HR: Harry Stovey, Bos.; Mike Tiernan, N.Y., 16.
RBI: Cap Anson, Chi., 120.
SB: Billy Hamilton, Phil., 111.
Wins: Bill Hutchinson, Chi., 44.
ERA: John Ewing, N.Y., 2.27.
CG: Bill Hutchinson, Chi., 56.
IP: Bill Hutchinson, Chi., 561.
SO: Amos Rusie, N.Y., 337.

20-game winners

Bill Hutchison, Chi., 44-19
John Clarkson, Bos., 33-19
Amos Rusie, N.Y., 33-20
Kid Nichols, Bos., 30-17
Cy Young, Cle., 27-22
Harry Staley, Pit.-Bos., 24-13
Kid Gleason, Phil., 24-22
Tom Lovett, Brk., 23-19
Tony Mullane, Cin., 23-26
Mark Baldwin, Pit., 22-28
John Ewing, N.Y., 21-8
Duke Esper, Phil., 20-15

MAJOR RULES CHANGE

■ All teams were required to have one or more substitutes available for each game.

HISTORY

1892

FINAL STANDINGS

National League

Team	W	L	Pct.	GB
Boston	102	48	.680	...
Cleveland	93	56	.624	8.5
Brooklyn	95	59	.617	9
Philadelphia	87	66	.569	16.5
Cincinnati	82	68	.547	20
Pittsburgh	80	73	.523	23.5
Chicago	70	76	.479	30
New York	71	80	.470	31.5
Louisville	63	89	.414	40
Washington	58	93	.384	44.5
St. Louis	56	94	.373	46
Baltimore	46	101	.313	54.5

SIGNIFICANT EVENTS

■ The new 12-team N.L. adopted a 154-game split schedule featuring first-half and second-half champions.

■ Cincinnati, playing host to the first Sunday game in N.L. history, defeated the Browns, 5-1.

■ N.L. owners, holding a mid-November meeting in Chicago, shortened the 1893 schedule to 132 games and dropped the split-season format.

MEMORABLE MOMENTS

■ Baltimore catcher Wilbert Robinson collected a record seven hits during a 25-7 victory over the Browns.

■ Cincinnati's Bumpus Jones made his Major League debut a spectacular one, holding Pittsburgh hitless in a 7-1 victory.

■ First-half champion Boston swept aside second-half champion Cleveland in a post-season playoff. The Beaneaters won five of the six games and the other ended in a tie.

LEADERS

BA: Dan Brouthers, Brk., .335.
Runs: Cupid Childs, Cle., 136.
Hits: Dan Brouthers, Brk., 197.
TB: Dan Brouthers, Brk., 282.
HR: Bug Holliday, Cin., 13.
RBI: Dan Brouthers, Brk., 124.
SB: Monte Ward, Brk., 88.
Wins: Bill Hutchinson, Chi.; Cy Young, Cle., 36.
ERA: Cy Young, Cle., 1.93.
CG: Bill Hutchinson, Chi., 67.
IP: Bill Hutchinson, Chi., 627.
SO: Bill Hutchinson, Chi., 316.

20-game winners

Bill Hutchinson, Chi., 36-36
Cy Young, Cle., 36-12
Kid Nichols, Bos., 35-16
Jack Stivetts, Bos., 35-16
Gus Weyhing, Phil., 32-21
Amos Rusie, N.Y., 31-31
George Haddock, Brk., 29-13
Frank Killen, Wash., 29-26
George Cuppy, Cle., 28-13
Ed Stein, Brk., 27-16
Mark Baldwin, Pit., 26-27
John Clarkson, Bos.-Cle., 25-16
Silver King, N.Y., 23-24
Harry Staley, Bos., 22-10
Ad Gumbert, Chi., 22-19
Tony Mullane, Cin., 21-13
Frank Dwyer, St.L.-Cin., 21-18
Scott Stratton, Lou., 21-19
Kid Gleason, St.L., 20-24

POST-SEASON PLAYOFF

(Boston 5, Cleveland 0; 1 tie)
Game 1—Boston 0, Cleveland 0 (11 innings, darkness)
Game 2—Boston 4, Cleveland 3
Game 3—Boston 3, Cleveland 2
Game 4—Boston 4, Cleveland 0
Game 5—Boston 12, Cleveland 7
Game 6—Boston 8, Cleveland 3

MAJOR RULES CHANGES

■ Games were declared "official" after five full innings or 4½ if the home team was leading.

■ An umpire was given authority to declare a forfeit when he believed players were using delay tactics to gain suspension of a game.

■ Any ball hit over an outfield fence was declared a home run, except in cases where the distance was less than 235 feet from home base. Such drives were called ground-rule doubles.

■ Any batter obstructing or interfering with a catcher's throw was declared out.

1893

FINAL STANDINGS

National League

Team	W	L	Pct.	GB
Boston	86	43	.667	...
Pittsburgh	81	48	.628	5
Cleveland	73	55	.570	12.5
Philadelphia	72	57	.558	14
New York	68	64	.515	19.5
Brooklyn	65	63	.508	20.5
Cincinnati	65	63	.508	20.5
Baltimore	60	70	.462	26.5
Chicago	56	71	.441	29
St. Louis	57	75	.432	30.5
Louisville	50	75	.400	34
Washington	40	89	.310	46

SIGNIFICANT EVENT

■ A revolutionary rules change: The pitching box was eliminated and a pitcher's rubber was placed 5 feet behind the back line of the box—60 feet, 6 inches from home plate.

MEMORABLE MOMENTS

■ Boston defeated Baltimore 6-2 in a late July game and took over permanent posession of first place en route to its third consecutive pennant.

■ Cleveland ended the 33-game hitting streak of George Davis during an 8-6 victory over the Giants.

LEADERS

BA: Hugh Duffy, Bos., .363.
Runs: Herman Long, Bos., 149.
Hits: Sam Thompson, Phil., 222.
TB: Ed Delahanty, Phil., 347.
HR: Ed Delahanty, Phil., 19.
RBI: Ed Delahanty, Phil., 146.
SB: Tom Brown, Lou., 66.
Wins: Frank Killen, Pit., 36.
ERA: Ted Breitenstein, St.L., 3.18.
CG: Amos Rusie, N.Y., 50.
IP: Amos Rusie, N.Y., 482.
SO: Amos Rusie, N.Y., 208.

20-game winners

Frank Killen, Pit., 36-14
Kid Nichols, Bos., 34-14
Cy Young, Cle., 34-16
Amos Rusie, N.Y., 33-21
Brickyard Kennedy, Brk., 25-20
Gus Weyhing, Phil., 23-16
Sadie McMahon, Bal., 23-18
Kid Gleason, St.L., 21-22
Jack Stivetts, Bos., 20-12

MAJOR RULES CHANGES

■ The pitcher's box was eliminated and the pitching distance was lengthened to 60 feet, 6 inches from the outer corner of home base. The distance was marked by a rubber slab (a pitching rubber) 12 inches long and 4 inches wide.

■ Pitchers were required to deliver the ball with one foot remaining in contact with the rubber.

■ Bats with a flat surface were outlawed. Bats were required to be completely round.

■ Lineups were submitted before each game and the batting order was followed throughout the contest. Each new inning started with the batter whose name followed the man who had made the final out of the previous inning.

1894

FINAL STANDINGS

National League

Team	W	L	Pct.	GB
Baltimore	89	39	.695	...
New York	88	44	.667	3
Boston	83	49	.629	8
Philadelphia	71	57	.555	18
Brooklyn	70	61	.534	20.5
Cleveland	68	61	.527	21.5
Pittsburgh	65	65	.500	25
Chicago	57	75	.432	34
St. Louis	56	76	.424	35
Cincinnati	55	75	.423	35
Washington	45	87	.341	46
Louisville	36	94	.277	54

SIGNIFICANT EVENT

■ Rules changes: Foul bunts became strikes and the infield fly rule was entered into the books.

MEMORABLE MOMENTS

■ Boston second baseman Bobby Lowe became baseball's first four-homer man when he connected in consecutive at-bats during a rout of Cincinnati.

■ Chicago shortstop Bill Dahlen failed to get a hit in six at-bats against Cincinnati, ending his 42-game hitting streak.

■ Philadelphia star Billy Hamilton tied a Major League record with seven stolen bases in a victory over Washington.

■ The Orioles clinched the first of three consecutive pennants with a victory over Cleveland.

■ Second-place New York defeated regular-season champion Baltimore 16-3 and concluded its sweep of the best-of-seven Temple Cup series—a new post-season playoff.

LEADERS

BA: Hugh Duffy, Bos., .440.
Runs: Billy Hamilton, Phil., 192.
Hits: Hugh Duffy, Bos., 237.
TB: Hugh Duffy, Bos., 374.
HR: Hugh Duffy, Bos., 18.
RBI: Hugh Duffy, Bos., 145.
SB: Billy Hamilton, Phil., 98.
Wins: Amos Rusie, N.Y., 36.
ERA: Amos Rusie, N.Y., 2.78.
CG: Ted Breitenstein, St.L., 46.
IP: Ted Breitenstein, St.L., 447.1.
SO: Amos Rusie, N.Y., 195.

20-game winners

Amos Rusie, N.Y., 36-13
Jouett Meekin, N.Y., 33-9
Kid Nichols, Bos., 32-13
Ted Breitenstein, St.L., 27-23
Ed Stein, Brk., 26-14
Jack Stivetts, Bos., 26-14
Cy Young, Cle., 26-21
Sadie McMahon, Bal., 25-8
George Cuppy, Cle., 24-15
Brickyard Kennedy, Brk., 24-20
Jack Taylor, Phil., 23-13
Clark Griffith, Chi., 21-14

TEMPLE CUP

(New York 4, Baltimore 0)
Game 1—New York 4, Baltimore 1
Game 2—New York 9, Baltimore 6
Game 3—New York 4, Baltimore 1
Game 4—New York 16, Baltimore 3

MAJOR RULES CHANGES

■ Batters were charged with a strike when bunting the ball into foul territory.

■ Batters who advanced a runner with a bunt while being put out were credited with a sacrifice and not charged with an at-bat.

1895

FINAL STANDINGS

National League

Team	W	L	Pct.	GB
Baltimore	87	43	.669	...
Cleveland	84	46	.646	3
Philadelphia	78	53	.595	9.5
Chicago	72	58	.554	15
Boston	71	60	.542	16.5
Brooklyn	71	60	.542	16.5
Pittsburgh	71	61	.538	17
Cincinnati	66	64	.508	21
New York	66	65	.504	21.5
Washington	43	85	.336	43
St. Louis	39	92	.298	48.5
Louisville	35	96	.267	52.5

SIGNIFICANT EVENT

■ N.L. officials, reacting to player complaints, restricted the size of gloves for everybody but first basemen and catchers to 10 ounces and 14 inches in circumference around the palm.

MEMORABLE MOMENTS

■ Louisville defeated Washington, but Colonels star Fred Clarke saw his 35-game hitting streak come to an end.

■ Baltimore clinched its second straight pennant with a victory over New York—two days before the regular season ended.

■ Cleveland captured the Temple Cup with a fifth-game, 5-2 victory over Baltimore.

LEADERS

BA: Jesse Burkett, Cle., .409.
Runs: Billy Hamilton, Phil., 166.
Hits: Jesse Burkett, Cle., 225.
TB: Sam Thompson, Phil., 352.
HR: Sam Thompson, Phil., 18.
RBI: Sam Thompson, Phil., 165.
SB: Billy Hamilton, Phil., 97.
Wins: Cy Young, Cle., 35.
ERA: Al Maul, Wash., 2.45.
CG: Ted Breitenstein, St.L., 46.
IP: Pink Hawley, Pit., 444.1.
SO: Amos Rusie, N.Y., 201.

20-game winners

Cy Young, Cle., 35-10
Bill Hoffer, Bal., 31-6
Pink Hawley, Pit., 31-22
George Cuppy, Cle., 26-14
Clark Griffith, Chi., 26-14
Jack Taylor, Phil., 26-14
Kid Nichols, Bos., 26-16
Kid Carsey, Phil., 24-16
Amos Rusie, N.Y., 23-23
Adonis Terry, Chi., 21-14
George Hemming, Bal., 20-13

TEMPLE CUP

(Cleveland 4, Baltimore 1)
Game 1—Cleveland 5, Baltimore 4
Game 2—Cleveland 7, Baltimore 2
Game 3—Cleveland 7, Baltimore 1
Game 4—Baltimore 5, Cleveland 0
Game 5—Cleveland 5, Baltimore 2

MAJOR RULES CHANGES

■ The pitching rubber was enlarged to 24-by-6 inches, its current size.

■ A foul tip caught by the catcher became a strike.

■ The infield fly rule became official.

■ Bats were limited to 2¾ inches in diameter.

■ Catchers and first basemen were given permission to use oversized gloves. Other fielders still were restricted to gloves weighing 10 ounces with a hand size not more than 14 inches.

1896

FINAL STANDINGS

National League

Team	W	L	Pct.	GB
Baltimore	90	39	.698	...
Cleveland	80	48	.625	9.5
Cincinnati	77	50	.606	12
Boston	74	57	.565	17
Chicago	71	57	.555	18.5
Pittsburgh	66	63	.512	24
New York	64	67	.489	27
Philadelphia	62	68	.477	28.5
Brooklyn	58	73	.443	33
Washington	58	73	.443	33
St. Louis	40	90	.308	50.5
Louisville	38	93	.290	53

SIGNIFICANT EVENT

■ Cleveland's Jesse Burkett collected three final-day hits and finished with a league-leading .410 average—his record second consecutive .400 season.

MEMORABLE MOMENTS

■ Philadelphia star Ed Delahanty matched Bobby Lowe's 1894 record of four home runs in a game—all inside-the-park shots in a loss to Chicago.

■ Baltimore clinched its third straight pennant with a victory over Brooklyn.

■ Regular-season champion Baltimore defeated Cleveland 5-0 and capped its four-game sweep of the Temple Cup series.

LEADERS

BA: Jesse Burkett, Cle., .410.
Runs: Jesse Burkett, Cle., 160.
Hits: Jesse Burkett, Cle., 240.
TB: Jesse Burkett, Cle., 317.
HR: Ed Delahanty, Phil.;
  Bill Joyce, Wash.-N.Y., 13.
RBI: Ed Delahanty, Phil., 126.
SB: Joe Kelley, Bal., 87.
Wins: Frank Killen, Pit.; Kid Nichols, Bos., 30.
ERA: Billy Rhines, Cin., 2.45.
CG: Frank Killen, Pit., 44.
IP: Frank Killen, Pit., 432.1.
SO: Cy Young, Cle., 140.

20-game winners
Kid Nichols, Bos., 30-14
Frank Killen, Pit., 30-18
Cy Young, Cle., 28-15
Jouett Meekin, N.Y., 26-14
Bill Hoffer, Bal., 25-7
George Cuppy, Cle., 25-14
George Mercer, Wash., 25-18
Frank Dwyer, Cin., 24-11
Clark Griffith, Chi., 23-11
Jack Stivetts, Bos., 22-14
Pink Hawley, Pit., 22-21
Jack Taylor, Phil., 20-21

TEMPLE CUP

(Baltimore 4, Cleveland 0)
Game 1—Baltimore 7, Cleveland 1
Game 2—Baltimore 7, Cleveland 2 (8 innings, darkness)
Game 3—Baltimore 6, Cleveland 2
Game 4—Baltimore 5, Cleveland 0

MAJOR RULES CHANGES

■ Pitchers were no longer required to hold the ball in full sight of the umpire up to delivery.

■ Umpires were given authority to eject players using vulgar language and fine them $25. Umpires also were allowed to fine players $5 to $10 for specified misconduct.

■ Home teams were required to have at least 12 regulation balls available for each game.

1897

FINAL STANDINGS

National League

Team	W	L	Pct.	GB
Boston	93	39	.705	...
Baltimore	90	40	.692	2
New York	83	48	.634	9.5
Cincinnati	76	56	.576	17
Cleveland	69	62	.527	23.5
Brooklyn	61	71	.462	32
Washington	61	71	.462	32
Pittsburgh	60	71	.458	32.5
Chicago	59	73	.447	34
Philadelphia	55	77	.417	38
Louisville	52	78	.400	40
St. Louis	29	102	.221	63.5

SIGNIFICANT EVENT

■ The 4-year-old Temple Cup series, which failed to attract fan interest, died a quiet death after regular-season champion Boston lost a five-game series to second-place Baltimore.

MEMORABLE MOMENTS

■ Pittsburgh pitcher Frank Killen defeated Baltimore and ended Willie Keeler's 44-game hitting streak.

■ Chicago set an N.L. single-game scoring record during a 36-7 demolition of Louisville.

■ Boston's victory over Brooklyn, coupled with Baltimore's same-day loss to Washington, gave the Beaneaters the N.L. pennant.

LEADERS

BA: Willie Keeler, Bal., .424.
Runs: Billy Hamilton, Bos., 152.
Hits: Willie Keeler, Bal., 239.
TB: Nap Lajoie, Phil., 310.
HR: Hugh Duffy, Bos., 11.
RBI: George Davis, N.Y., 136.
SB: Bill Lange, Chi., 73.
Wins: Kid Nichols, Bos., 31.
ERA: Amos Rusie, N.Y., 2.54.
CG: Red Donahue, St.L.; Clark Griffith, Chi.;
  Frank Killen, Pit., 38.
IP: Kid Nichols, Bos., 368.
SO: Doc McJames, Wash., 156.

20-game winners
Kid Nichols, Bos., 31-11
Amos Rusie, N.Y., 28-10
Fred Klobedanz, Bos., 26-7
Joe Corbett, Bal., 24-8
Ted Breitenstein, Cin., 23-12
Bill Hoffer, Bal., 22-11
Ted Lewis, Bos., 21-12
Bill Rhines, Cin., 21-15
Clark Griffith, Chi., 21-18
Cy Young, Cle., 21-19
Jerry Nops, Bal., 20-6
Jouett Meekin, N.Y., 20-11
George Mercer, Wash., 20-20

TEMPLE CUP

(Baltimore 4, Boston 1)
Game 1—Boston 13, Baltimore 12
Game 2—Baltimore 13, Boston 11
Game 3—Baltimore 8, Boston 3 (7 innings, rain)
Game 4—Baltimore 12, Boston 11
Game 5—Baltimore 9, Boston 3

MAJOR RULES CHANGES

■ Runners who were held or obstructed by fielders without the ball were given the base they were trying to reach. Any fielder stopping a ball in any way other than with his hands was guilty of obstruction and runners were allowed to advance.

■ Runners returning to their original base after a caught fly ball were required to retouch all bases they had passed in reverse order.

■ Any judgement call by the umpire was final and could not be reversed.

■ Earned runs were defined as runs scored without the aid of errors.

1898

FINAL STANDINGS

National League

Team	W	L	Pct.	GB
Boston	102	47	.685	...
Baltimore	96	53	.644	6
Cincinnati	92	60	.605	11.5
Chicago	85	65	.567	17.5
Cleveland	81	68	.544	21
Philadelphia	78	71	.523	24
New York	77	73	.513	25.5
Pittsburgh	72	76	.486	29.5
Louisville	70	81	.464	33
Brooklyn	54	91	.372	46
Washington	51	101	.336	52.5
St. Louis	39	111	.260	63.5

SIGNIFICANT EVENT

■ Cap Anson, who compiled a 1,293-932 record over 19 seasons as a Chicago manager, was fired.

MEMORABLE MOMENTS

■ A Major League first: Baltimore's Jim Hughes and Cincinnati's Ted Breitenstein pitched nine-inning no-hitters on the same day.

■ Philadelphia pitcher Bill Duggleby hit a grand slam in his first Major League at-bat—a feat never since duplicated.

■ Boston, en route to a record-tying 102 wins, clinched its second straight pennant with a victory over Washington.

LEADERS

BA: Willie Keeler, Bal., .385.
Runs: John McGraw, Bal., 143.
Hits: Willie Keeler, Bal., 216.
TB: Jimmy Collins, Bos., 286.
HR: Jimmy Collins, Bos., 15.
RBI: Nap Lajoie, Phil., 127.
SB: Ed Delahanty, Phil., 58.
Wins: Kid Nichols, Bos., 31.
ERA: Clark Griffith, Chi., 1.88.
CG: Jack Taylor, St.L., 42.
IP: Jack Taylor, St.L., 397.1.
SO: Cy Seymour, N.Y., 239.

20-game winners
Kid Nichols, Bos., 31-12
Bert Cunningham, Lou., 28-15
Pink Hawley, Cin., 27-11
Doc McJames, Bal., 27-15
Ted Lewis, Bos., 26-8
Jesse Tannehill, Pit., 25-13
Vic Willis, Bos., 25-13
Cy Young, Cle., 25-13
Cy Seymour, N.Y., 25-19
Clark Griffith, Chi., 24-10
Wiley Piatt, Phil., 24-14
Jim Hughes, Bal., 23-12
Jack Powell, Cle., 23-15
Al Maul, Bal., 20-7
Jim Callahan, Chi., 20-10
Amos Rusie, N.Y., 20-11
Ted Breitenstein, Cin., 20-14

MAJOR RULES CHANGES

■ Penalties were specified for teams batting out of order.

■ Detailed definitions were provided for pitchers committing balks, including illegal motions to home base and to the bases.

■ Stolen bases were awarded for bases attained without the aid of batted balls or errors.

1899

FINAL STANDINGS

National League

Team	W	L	Pct.	GB
Brooklyn	101	47	.682	...
Boston	95	57	.625	8
Philadelphia	94	58	.618	9
Baltimore	86	62	.581	15
St. Louis	84	67	.556	18.5
Cincinnati	83	67	.553	19
Pittsburgh	76	73	.510	25.5
Chicago	75	73	.507	26
Louisville	75	77	.493	28
New York	60	90	.400	42
Washington	54	98	.355	49
Cleveland	20	134	.130	84

SIGNIFICANT EVENTS

■ John McGraw made his managerial debut a successful one, leading Baltimore to a victory over New York.

■ The Western League changed its name to the American Baseball League, setting the stage for Ban Johnson's circuit to gain "Major League" credibility.

MEMORABLE MOMENTS

■ Cleveland defeated Washington and snapped its 24-game losing streak.

■ The Brooklyn Superbas, en route to 101 victories, clinched the pennant with a win over New York.

■ Cincinnati posted a season-closing sweep of Cleveland, handing the Spiders their 133rd and 134th losses.

LEADERS

BA: Ed Delahanty, Phil., .410.
Runs: Willie Keeler, Brk.;
  John McGraw, Bal., 140.
Hits: Ed Delahanty, Phil., 238.
TB: Ed Delahanty, Phil., 338.
HR: Buck Freeman, Wash., 25.
RBI: Ed Delahanty, Phil., 137.
SB: Jimmy Sheckard, Bal., 77.
Wins: Jim Hughes, Brk.; Joe McGinnity, Bal., 28.
ERA: Vic Willis, Bos., 2.50.
CG: Bill Carrick, N.Y.; Jack Powell, St.L.;
  Cy Young, St.L., 40.
IP: Sam Leever, Pit., 379.
SO: Noodles Hahn, Cin., 145.

20-game winners
Jim Hughes, Brk., 28-6
Joe McGinnity, Bal., 28-16
Vic Willis, Bos., 27-8
Cy Young, St.L., 26-16
Jesse Tannehill, Pit., 24-14
Noodles Hahn, Cin., 23-8
Jack Dunn, Brk., 23-13
Wiley Piatt, Phil., 23-15
Jack Powell, St.L., 23-19
Brickyard Kennedy, Brk., 22-9
Clark Griffith, Chi., 22-14
Frank Kitson, Bal., 22-16
Red Donahue, Phil., 21-8
Jim Callahan, Chi., 21-12
Chick Fraser, Phil., 21-12
Deacon Phillippe, Lou., 21-17
Kid Nichols, Bos., 21-19
Sam Leever, Pit., 21-23

MAJOR RULES CHANGES

■ The score of any game suspended or called before the full nine innings had been played reverted back to the last full inning completed.

■ Batters were awarded first base for catcher's interference.

■ The 1898 balk rules were further defined.

■ Each team was required to wear uniforms that conformed in color and style.

HISTORY

1900

FINAL STANDINGS

National League

Team	W	L	Pct.	GB
Brooklyn	82	54	.603	...
Pittsburgh	79	60	.568	4.5
Philadelphia	75	63	.543	8
Boston	66	72	.478	17
Chicago	65	75	.464	19
St. Louis	65	75	.464	19
Cincinnati	62	77	.446	21.5
New York	60	78	.435	23

SIGNIFICANT EVENTS

■ **March 8:** The National League streamlined its product, reducing from 12 to eight teams.

■ **March 9:** N.L. officials expanded the strike zone by reshaping home plate from a 12-inch square to a 17-inch-wide, five-sided figure.

■ **March 16:** Ban Johnson announced formation of a franchise in Chicago, giving his young American League teams in eight cities. The others were Kansas City, Minneapolis, Milwaukee, Indianapolis, Detroit, Cleveland and Buffalo.

■ **October 11:** Ban Johnson's new American League, claiming status as an equal to the National League, announced plans to locate franchises in Baltimore and Washington.

■ **November 14:** The N.L. declared war when it rejected the A.L. as an equal and pronounced it an "outlaw league" outside the National Agreement.

■ **December 15:** The Giants traded aging Amos Rusie to the Reds for a young pitcher named Christy Mathewson.

MEMORABLE MOMENTS

■ **April 19:** Ban Johnson's new American League opened with a bang when Buffalo's Doc Amole pitched an 8-0 no-hitter against the Tigers.

■ **July 7:** Boston's Kid Nichols defeated the Cubs 11-4 for his 300th career victory.

■ **October 3:** Brooklyn clinched the N.L. pennant with a 6-4, 5-4 sweep at Boston, giving manager Ned Hanlon his fifth championship in seven years.

LEADERS

BA: Honus Wagner, Pit., .381.
Runs: Roy Thomas, Phil., 132.
Hits: Willie Keeler, Brk., 204.
TB: Honus Wagner, Pit., 302.
HR: Herman Long, Bos., 12.
RBI: Elmer Flick, Phil., 110.

SB: Patsy Donovan, St.L.; George Van Haltren, N.Y., 45.
Wins: Joe McGinnity, Brk., 28.
ERA: Rube Waddell, Pit., 2.37.
CG: Pink Hawley, N.Y., 34.
IP: Joe McGinnity, Brk., 343.
SO: Noodles Hahn, Cin., 132.

20-game winners
Joe McGinnity, Brk., 28-8
Jesse Tannehill, Pit., 20-6
Brickyard Kennedy, Brk., 20-13
Deacon Phillippe, Pit., 20-13
Bill Dinneen, Bos., 20-14

100 RBIs
Elmer Flick, Phil., 110
Ed Delahanty, Phil., 109
Honus Wagner, Pit., 100

CHRONICLE-TELEGRAPH CUP

(Brooklyn 3, Pittsburgh 1)
Game 1—Brooklyn 5, Pittsburgh 2
Game 2—Brooklyn 4, Pittsburgh 2
Game 3—Pittsburgh 10, Brooklyn 0
Game 4—Brooklyn 6, Pittsburgh 1

MAJOR RULES CHANGES

■ Home "base" became home "plate" when its shape was changed from a 12-inch square to a five-sided flat surface 17 inches wide.

■ A batter was not awarded first base on a pitcher's balk.

1901

FINAL STANDINGS

American League

Team	W	L	Pct.	GB
Chicago	83	53	.610	...
Boston	79	57	.581	4
Detroit	74	61	.548	8.5
Philadelphia	74	62	.544	9
Baltimore	68	65	.511	13.5
Washington	61	72	.459	20.5
Cleveland	54	82	.397	29
Milwaukee	48	89	.350	35.5

National League

Team	W	L	Pct.	GB
Pittsburgh	90	49	.647	...
Philadelphia	83	57	.593	7.5
Brooklyn	79	57	.581	9.5
St. Louis	76	64	.543	14.5
Boston	69	69	.500	20.5
Chicago	53	86	.381	37
New York	52	85	.380	37
Cincinnati	52	87	.374	38

SIGNIFICANT EVENTS

■ **January 28:** When the A.L. formally organized as an eight-team "Major League," it placed franchises in Chicago, Philadelphia and Boston—N.L. strongholds.

■ **February 27:** Among a series of N.L. rules changes was the declaration that all foul balls will count as strikes, except when the batter already has two.

■ **March 28:** In a move to keep Napoleon Lajoie from jumping to the A.L.'s Athletics, the Phillies filed for an injunction to keep him from playing for any other team.

■ **September 19:** The baseball schedule was canceled because of the funeral of President William McKinley, who was killed by an assassin's bullet.

■ **October 20:** Seven Cardinals, including top hitters Jesse Burkett and Bobby Wallace, jumped to the American League's new St. Louis franchise.

■ **November 20:** A.L. President Ban Johnson shifted his Milwaukee franchise to St. Louis for a head-to-head battle with the N.L.'s Cardinals.

MEMORABLE MOMENTS

■ **April 24:** Chicago played host to the A.L.'s first Major League game, defeating Cleveland, 8-2.

■ **April 25:** Detroit celebrated its A.L. debut by scoring 10 ninth-inning runs and beating Milwaukee, 14-13.

■ **July 15:** Christy Mathewson, the Giants' 21-year-old rookie righthander, held the Cardinals hitless in a 5-0 New York victory at St. Louis.

■ **September 29:** The White Stockings captured the first A.L. pennant, but Philadelphia's Napoleon Lajoie compiled Triple Crown totals of .426, 14 homers and 125 RBI.

LEADERS

American League
BA: Nap Lajoie, Phil., .426.
Runs: Nap Lajoie, Phil., 145.
Hits: Lajoie, Phil., 232.
TB: Nap Lajoie, Phil., 350.
HR: Nap Lajoie, Phil., 14.
RBI: Nap Lajoie, Phil., 125.
SB: Frank Isbell, Chi., 52.
Wins: Cy Young, Bos., 33
ERA: Cy Young, Bos., 1.62
CG: Joe McGinnity, Balt., 39.
IP: Joe McGinnity, Balt., 382.
SO: Cy Young, Bos., 158.

National League
BA: Jesse Burkett, St.L., .376.
Runs: Jesse Burkett, St.L., 142.
Hits: Jesse Burkett, St.L., 226.
TB: Jesse Burkett, St.L., 306.
HR: Sam Crawford, Cin., 16.
RBI: Honus Wagner, Pit., 126.
SB: Honus Wagner, Pit., 49.
Wins: Bill Donovan, Brk., 25.
ERA: Jesse Tannehill, Pit., 2.18.
CG: Noodles Hahn, Cin., 41.
IP: Noodles Hahn, Cin., 375.1.
SO: Noodles Hahn, Cin., 239.

A.L. 20-game winners
Cy Young, Bos., 33-10
Joe McGinnity, Bal., 26-20
Clark Griffith, Chi., 24-7
Roscoe Miller, Det., 23-13
Chick Fraser, Phil., 22-16
Roy Patterson, Chi., 20-15

N.L. 20-game winners
Bill Donovan, Brk., 25-15
Jack Harper, St.L., 23-13
Deacon Phillippe, Pit., 22-12
Noodles Hahn, Cin., 22-19
Jack Chesbro, Pit., 21-10

Red Donahue, Phil., 21-13
Al Orth, Phil., 20-12
Christy Mathewson, N.Y., 20-17
Vic Willis, Bos., 20-17

A.L. 100 RBIs
Nap Lajoie, Phil., 125
Buck Freeman, Bos., 114

N.L. 100 RBIs
Honus Wagner, Pit., 126
Ed Delahanty, Phil., 108
Jimmy Sheckard, Brk., 104
Sam Crawford, Cin., 104

1902

FINAL STANDINGS

American League

Team	W	L	Pct.	GB
Philadelphia	83	53	.610	...
St. Louis	78	58	.574	5
Boston	77	60	.562	6.5
Chicago	74	60	.552	8
Cleveland	69	67	.507	14
Washington	61	75	.449	22
Detroit	52	83	.385	30.5
Baltimore	50	88	.362	34

National League

Team	W	L	Pct.	GB
Pittsburgh	103	36	.741	...
Brooklyn	75	63	.543	27.5
Boston	73	64	.533	29
Cincinnati	70	70	.500	33.5
Chicago	68	69	.496	34
St. Louis	56	78	.418	44.5
Philadelphia	56	81	.409	46
New York	48	88	.353	53.5

SIGNIFICANT EVENTS

■ **April 21:** The Pennsylvania Supreme Court granted an injunction barring league-jumper Napoleon Lajoie from playing for any team but the Phillies.

■ **May 27:** To keep Lajoie from returning to the N.L., A.L. president Ban Johnson shifted his contract from the Athletics to the Indians, getting him out of Pennsylvania.

■ **July 8:** The A.L. lost Baltimore manager John McGraw, who jumped to the N.L. as manager of the Giants and took five players with him.

■ **September 28:** Philadelphia Athletics star Socks Seybold completed the American League season with a Major League single-season record 16 home runs.

■ **December 9:** The A.L. announced plans to locate a franchise in New York for the 1903 season.

■ **December 12:** Owners elected Harry Pulliam as N.L. president.

MEMORABLE MOMENTS

■ **April 26:** In a stirring Major League debut, Cleveland's Addie Joss fired a one-hitter and beat the Browns, 3-0.

■ **July 19:** The New York Giants, en route to a last-place finish in the N.L., dropped a 5-3 decision to Philadelphia in the managerial debut of John McGraw.

■ **October 4:** The Pirates completed their 103-36 season with a 27½-game lead over second-place Brooklyn in the N.L.

LEADERS

American League
BA: Nap Lajoie, Phil-Cle., .378.
Runs: Dave Fultz, Phil.; Topsy Hartsel, Phil., 109.
Hits: Charlie Hickman, Bos.-Cle., 193.
TB: Charlie Hickman, Bos.-Cle., 288.
HR: Socks Seybold, Phil., 16.
RBI: Buck Freeman, Bos., 121.
SB: Topsy Hartsel, Phil., 47.
Wins: Cy Young, Bos., 32.
ERA: Ed Siever, Det., 1.91.
CG: Cy Young, Bos., 41.
IP: Cy Young, Bos., 384.2.
SO: Rube Waddell, Phil., 210.

National League
BA: Ginger Beaumont, Pit., .357.
Runs: Honus Wagner, Pit., 105.
Hits: Ginger Beaumont, Pit., 193.
TB: Sam Crawford, Cin., 256.
HR: Tommy Leach, Pit., 6.
RBI: Honus Wagner, Pit., 91.
SB: Honus Wagner, Pit., 42.
Wins: Jack Chesbro, Pit., 28.
ERA: Jack Taylor, Chi., 1.33.
CG: Vic Willis, Bos., 45.
IP: Vic Willis, Bos., 410.
SO: Vic Willis, Bos., 225.

A.L. 20-game winners
Cy Young, Bos., 32-11
Rube Waddell, Phil., 24-7
Red Donahue, St.L., 22-11
Jack Powell, St.L., 22-17
Bill Dinneen, Bos., 21-21
Eddie Plank, Phil., 20-15

N.L. 20-game winners
Jack Chesbro, Pit., 28-6
Togie Pittinger, Bos., 27-16

Vic Willis, Bos., 27-20
Jack Taylor, Chi., 23-11
Noodles Hahn, Cin., 23-12
Jesse Tannehill, Pit., 20-6
Deacon Phillippe, Pit., 20-9

A.L. 100 RBIs
Buck Freeman, Bos., 121
Charlie Hickman, Bos.-Cle., 110
Lave Cross, Phil., 108

FINAL STANDINGS

American League

Team	W	L	Pct.	GB
Boston	91	47	.659	...
Philadelphia	75	60	.556	14.5
Cleveland	77	63	.550	15
New York	72	62	.537	17
Detroit	65	71	.478	25
St. Louis	65	74	.468	26.5
Chicago	60	77	.438	30.5
Washington	43	94	.314	47.5

National League

Team	W	L	Pct.	GB
Pittsburgh	91	49	.650	...
New York	84	55	.604	6.5
Chicago	82	56	.594	8
Cincinnati	74	65	.532	16.5
Brooklyn	70	66	.515	19
Boston	58	80	.420	32
Philadelphia	49	86	.363	39.5
St. Louis	43	94	.314	46.5

SIGNIFICANT EVENTS

■ **January 9:** A peace treaty was signed with the N.L. agreeing to recognize the A.L. as a Major League and both parties agreeing to honor the reserve clause in player contracts.
■ **July 2:** Washington star Ed Delahanty died when he fell off a railroad bridge spanning the Niagara River at Fort Erie, Ontario.
■ **August 8:** A bleacher overhang at Philadelphia's N.L. park collapsed, killing 12 and injuring 282.
■ **September 16:** The presidents of the A.L. Boston and N.L. Pittsburgh teams agreed to a best-of-nine championship playoff—baseball's first World Series.

MEMORABLE MOMENTS

■ **April 22:** The A.L.'s new New York team officially opened play, but the Highlanders dropped a 3-1 decision at Washington.
■ **April 30:** The A.L.'s New York team opened new Hilltop Park with a 6-2 victory over Washington.
■ **September 17:** Boston clinched the A.L. pennant with a victory over Cleveland and set up a championship showdown with N.L.-winner Pittsburgh.

LEADERS

American League
BA: Nap Lajoie, Cle., .344.
Runs: Patsy Dougherty, Bos., 107.
Hits: Patsy Dougherty, Bos., 195.
TB: Buck Freeman, Bos., 281.
HR: Buck Freeman, Bos., 13.
RBI: Buck Freeman, Bos., 104.
SB: Harry Bay, Cle., 45.
Wins: Cy Young, Bos., 28.
ERA: Earl Moore, Cle., 1.74.
CG: Bill Donovan, Det.; Rube Waddell, Phil.; Cy Young, Bos., 34.
IP: Cy Young, Bos., 341.2.
SO: Rube Waddell, Phil., 302.

National League
BA: Honus Wagner, Pit., .355.
Runs: Ginger Beaumont, Pit., 137.
Hits: Ginger Beaumont, Pit., 209.
TB: Ginger Beaumont, Pit., 272.
HR: Jimmy Sheckard, Brk., 9.
RBI: Sam Mertes, N.Y., 104.
SB: Frank Chance, Chi.; Jimmy Sheckard, Brk., 67.
Wins: Joe McGinnity, N.Y., 31.
ERA: Sam Leever, Pit., 2.06.
CG: Joe McGinnity, N.Y., 44.
IP: Joe McGinnity, N.Y., 434.
SO: Christy Mathewson, N.Y., 267.

A.L. 20-game winners
Cy Young, Bos., 28-9
Eddie Plank, Phil., 23-16
Bill Dinneen, Bos., 21-13
Jack Chesbro, N.Y., 21-15
Willie Sudhoff, St.L., 21-15
Rube Waddell, Phil., 21-16
Tom Hughes, Bos., 20-7
Earl Moore, Cle., 20-8

N.L. 20-game winners
Joe McGinnity, N.Y., 31-20
Christy Mathewson, N.Y., 30-13
Sam Leever, Pit., 25-7
Deacon Phillippe, Pit., 25-9
Noodles Hahn, Cin., 22-12
Henry Schmidt, Brk., 22-13
Jack Taylor, Chi., 21-14
Jake Weimer, Chi., 20-8

Bob Wicker, St.L.-Chi., 20-9

A.L. 100 RBIs
Buck Freeman, Bos., 104

N.L. 100 RBIs
Sam Mertes, N.Y., 104
Honus Wagner, Pit., 101

WORLD SERIES

■ **Winner:** The Red Sox captured the first modern World Series with a five-games-to-three victory over the N.L.-champion Pirates.
■ **Turning point:** A 7-3 Game 7 victory in which the Red Sox claimed a 4-3 Series lead and finally showed they could beat Pirates starter Deacon Phillippe.
■ **Memorable moments:** Pirates right fielder Jimmy Sebring's Game 1 home run—the first in World Series history.
■ **Top guns:** Bill Dinneen (35 IP, 3-1, 2.06 ERA), Cy Young (34 IP, 2-1, 1.59), Red Sox; Phillippe (44 IP, 3-2), Pirates.

Linescores

Game 1—October 1, at Boston
Pittsburgh ...... 4 0 1 1 0 0 1 0 0 — 7 12 2
Boston .... 0 0 0 0 0 0 2 0 1 — 3 6 4
Phillippe; Young. W—Phillippe. L—Young. HR—Sebring (Pit.).

Game 2—October 2, at Boston
Pittsburgh ...... 0 0 0 0 0 0 0 0 0 — 0 3 2
Boston .... 2 0 0 1 0 0 0 0 x — 3 9 0
Leever, Veil (2); Dinneen. W—Dinneen. L—Leever. HR—Dougherty 2 (Bos.).

Game 3—October 3, at Boston
Pittsburgh ...... 0 1 2 0 0 0 0 1 0 — 4 7 0
Boston .... 0 0 0 1 0 0 0 1 0 — 2 4 2
Phillippe; Hughes, Young (3). W—Phillippe. L—Hughes.

Game 4—October 6, at Pittsburgh
Boston .... 0 0 0 0 1 0 0 0 3 — 4 9 1
Pittsburgh ...... 1 0 0 0 1 0 3 0 x — 5 12 1
Dinneen; Phillippe. W—Phillippe. L—Dinneen.

Game 5—October 7, at Pittsburgh
Boston .... 0 0 0 0 0 6 4 1 0 — 11 14 2
Pittsburgh ...... 0 0 0 0 0 0 0 2 0 — 2 6 4
Young; Kennedy, Thompson (8). W—Young. L—Kennedy.

Game 6—October 8, at Pittsburgh
Boston .... 0 0 3 0 2 0 1 0 0 — 6 10 1
Pittsburgh ...... 0 0 0 0 0 0 3 0 0 — 3 10 3
Dinneen; Leever. W—Dinneen. L—Leever.

Game 7—October 10, at Pittsburgh
Boston .... 2 0 0 2 0 2 0 1 0 — 7 11 4
Pittsburgh ...... 0 0 0 1 0 1 0 0 1 — 3 10 3
Young; Phillippe. W—Young. L—Phillippe.

Game 8—October 13, at Boston
Pittsburgh ...... 0 0 0 0 0 0 0 0 0 — 0 4 3
Boston .... 0 0 0 2 0 1 0 0 x — 3 8 0
Phillippe; Dinneen. W—Dinneen. L—Phillippe.

FINAL STANDINGS

American League

Team	W	L	Pct.	GB
Boston	95	59	.617	...
New York	92	59	.609	1.5
Chicago	89	65	.578	6
Cleveland	86	65	.570	7.5
Philadelphia	81	70	.536	12.5
St. Louis	65	87	.428	29
Detroit	62	90	.408	32
Washington	38	113	.252	55.5

National League

Team	W	L	Pct.	GB
New York	106	47	.693	...
Chicago	93	60	.608	13
Cincinnati	88	65	.575	18
Pittsburgh	87	66	.569	19
St. Louis	75	79	.487	31.5
Brooklyn	56	97	.366	50
Boston	55	98	.359	51
Philadelphia	52	100	.342	53.5

SIGNIFICANT EVENT

■ **October 10:** Chastising the A.L. as a "minor circuit," Giants owner John T. Brush and manager John McGraw refused to meet the A.L.-champion Red Sox in a second "World Series."

MEMORABLE MOMENTS

■ **May 5:** Boston great Cy Young pitched the century's first perfect game, retiring all 27 Athletics he faced in a 3-0 victory.
■ **July 5:** The Phillies defeated the Giants 6-5 in 10 innings, ending New York's winning streak at 18 games.
■ **October 6:** Cardinals pitcher Jack Taylor pitched his Major League-record 39th consecutive complete game, but dropped a 6-3 decision to Pittsburgh.
■ **October 10:** The Red Sox captured their second straight A.L. pennant when New York's Jack Chesbro uncorked a final-day wild pitch that allowed the winning run to score in a 3-2 victory.

LEADERS

American League
BA: Nap Lajoie, Cle., .376.
Runs: Patsy Dougherty, Bos.-N.Y., 113.
Hits: Nap Lajoie, Cle., 208.
TB: Nap Lajoie, Cle., 305.
HR: Harry Davis, Phil., 10.
RBI: Nap Lajoie, Cle., 102.
SB: Harry Bay, Cle.; Elmer Flick, Cle., 38.
Wins: Jack Chesbro, N.Y., 41.
ERA: Addie Joss, Cle., 1.59.
CG: Jack Chesbro, N.Y., 48.
IP: Jack Chesbro, N.Y., 454.2.
SO: Rube Waddell, Phil., 349.

National League
BA: Honus Wagner, Pit., .349.
Runs: George Browne, N.Y., 99.
Hits: Ginger Beaumont, Pit., 185.
TB: Honus Wagner, Pit., 255.
HR: Harry Lumley, Brk., 9.
RBI: Bill Dahlen, N.Y., 80.
SB: Honus Wagner, Pit., 53.
Wins: Joe McGinnity, N.Y., 35.
ERA: Joe McGinnity, N.Y., 1.61.
CG: Jack Taylor, St.L.; Vic Willis, Bos., 39.
IP: Joe McGinnity, N.Y., 408.
SO: Christy Mathewson, N.Y., 212.

A.L. 20-game winners
Jack Chesbro, N.Y., 41-12
Cy Young, Bos., 26-16
Eddie Plank, Phil., 26-17
Rube Waddell, Phil., 25-19
Bill Bernhard, Cle., 23-13
Bill Dinneen, Bos., 23-14

Jack Powell, N.Y., 23-19
Jesse Tannehill, Bos., 21-11
Frank Owen, Chi., 21-15

N.L. 20-game winners
Joe McGinnity, N.Y., 35-8
Christy Mathewson, N.Y., 33-12
Jack Harper, Cin., 23-9

Kid Nichols, St.L., 21-13
Dummy Taylor, N.Y., 21-15
Jake Weimer, Chi., 20-14
Jack Taylor, St.L., 20-19

A.L. 100 RBIs
Nap Lajoie, Cle., 102

No World Series in 1904.

Cleveland's Nap Lajoie won his fourth consecutive A.L. batting championship in 1904.

FINAL STANDINGS

American League

Team	W	L	Pct.	GB
Philadelphia	92	56	.622	...
Chicago	92	60	.605	2
Detroit	79	74	.516	15.5
Boston	78	74	.513	16
Cleveland	76	78	.494	19
New York	71	78	.477	21.5
Washington	64	87	.424	29.5
St. Louis	54	99	.353	40.5

National League

Team	W	L	Pct.	GB
New York	105	48	.686	...
Pittsburgh	96	57	.627	9
Chicago	92	61	.601	13
Philadelphia	83	69	.546	21.5
Cincinnati	79	74	.516	26
St. Louis	58	96	.377	47.5
Boston	51	103	.331	54.5
Brooklyn	48	104	.316	56.5

SIGNIFICANT EVENTS

■ **October 3:** The National Commission adopted the John T. Brush rules for World Series play: a seven-game format, four umpires, two from each league, to work the Series and a revenue-sharing formula for the teams involved.

MEMORABLE MOMENTS

■ **June 13:** New York's Christy Mathewson pitched his second career no-hitter, but the Giants needed a ninth-inning run off Chicago's Mordecai Brown to post a 1-0 victory.
■ **August 30:** Detroit's Ty Cobb made his Major League debut, doubling off New York's Jack Chesbro in a 5-3 Tigers victory.
■ **September 27:** Boston's Bill Dinneen pitched the fourth no-hitter of the season, beating Chicago 2-0 in the first game of a doubleheader.
■ **October 6:** Despite losing to Washington 10-4, the Athletics clinched the A.L. pennant when the Browns defeated the White Sox 6-2 on the next-to-last day of the season.

LEADERS

American League

BA: Elmer Flick, Cle., .308
Runs: Harry Davis, Phil., 93.
Hits: George Stone, St.L., 187.
TB: George Stone, St.L., 259.
HR: Harry Davis, Phil., 8.
RBI: Harry Davis, Phil., 83.
SB: Danny Hoffman, Phil., 46.
Wins: Rube Waddell, Phil., 27.
ERA: Rube Waddell, Phil., 1.48.
CG: Harry Howell, St.L.; George Mullin, Det.; Eddie Plank, Phil., 35.
IP: George Mullin, Det., 347.2.
SO: Rube Waddell, Phil., 287.

National League

BA: Cy Seymour, Cin., .377.
Runs: Mike Donlin, N.Y., 124.
Hits: Cy Seymour, Cin., 219.
TB: Cy Seymour, Cin., 325.
HR: Fred Odwell, Cin., 9.
RBI: Cy Seymour, Cin., 121.
SB: Art Devlin, N.Y.; Billy Maloney, Chi., 59.
Wins: Christy Mathewson, N.Y., 31.
ERA: Christy Mathewson, N.Y., 1.28.
CG: Irv Young, Bos., 41.
IP: Irv Young, Bos., 378.
SO: Christy Mathewson, N.Y., 206.

A.L. 20-game winners

Rube Waddell, Phil., 27-10
Eddie Plank, Phil., 24-12
Nick Altrock, Chi., 23-12
Ed Killian, Det., 23-14
Jesse Tannehill, Bos., 22-9
Frank Owen, Chi., 21-13
George Mullin, Det., 21-21
Addie Joss, Cle., 20-12
Frank Smith, Chi., 20-14

N.L. 20-game winners

Christy Mathewson, N.Y., 31-9
Togie Pittinger, Phil., 23-14
Red Ames, N.Y., 22-8
Joe McGinnity, N.Y., 21-15
Sam Leever, Pit., 20-5
Bob Ewing, Cin., 20-11
Deacon Phillippe, Pit., 20-13
Irv Young, Bos., 20-21

N.L. 100 RBIs

Cy Seymour, Cin., 121
Sam Mertes, N.Y., 108
Honus Wagner, Pit., 101

WORLD SERIES

■ **Winner:** The Giants prevailed over the Athletics in an all-shutout fall classic.
■ **Turning point:** Joe McGinnity's five-hit, 1-0 victory over Athletics lefthander Eddie Plank in Game 4. Plank allowed only four hits.
■ **Memorable moment:** New York's John McGraw and Philadelphia's Connie Mack exchanging lineups before Game 1. The two managers would dominate baseball for more than three decades.
■ **Top guns:** Christy Mathewson (3 shutouts, 0.00 ERA), Joe McGinnity, (17 IP, 0.00), Giants; Chief Bender (17 IP, 1.06), Athletics.

Linescores

Game 1—October 9, at Philadelphia
New York....... 0 0 0 0 2 0 0 0 1 — 3 10 1
Philadelphia.... 0 0 0 0 0 0 0 0 0 — 0 4 0
Mathewson; Plank. W—Mathewson. L—Plank.

Game 2—October 10, at New York
Philadelphia.... 0 0 1 0 0 0 0 2 0 — 3 6 2
New York....... 0 0 0 0 0 0 0 0 0 — 0 4 2
Bender; McGinnity, Ames (9). W—Bender. L—McGinnity.

Game 3—October 12, at Philadelphia
New York........ 2 0 0 0 5 0 0 0 2 — 9 9 1
Philadelphia.... 0 0 0 0 0 0 0 0 0 — 0 4 5
Mathewson; Coakley. W—Mathewson. L—Coakley.

Game 4—October 13, at New York
Philadelphia.... 0 0 0 0 0 0 0 0 0 — 0 5 2
New York........ 0 0 0 1 0 0 0 0 x — 1 4 1
Plank; McGinnity. W—McGinnity. L—Plank.

Game 5—October 14, at New York
Philadelphia.... 0 0 0 0 0 0 0 0 0 — 0 6 0
New York........ 0 0 0 0 1 0 0 1 x — 2 5 1
Bender; Mathewson. W—Mathewson. L—Bender.

FINAL STANDINGS

American League

Team	W	L	Pct.	GB
Chicago	93	58	.616	...
New York	90	61	.596	3
Cleveland	89	64	.582	5
Philadelphia	78	67	.538	12
St. Louis	76	73	.510	16
Detroit	71	78	.477	21
Washington	55	95	.367	37.5
Boston	49	105	.318	45.5

National League

Team	W	L	Pct.	GB
Chicago	116	36	.763	...
New York	96	56	.632	20
Pittsburgh	93	60	.608	23.5
Philadelphia	71	82	.464	45.5
Brooklyn	66	86	.434	50
Cincinnati	64	87	.424	51.5
St. Louis	52	98	.347	63
Boston	49	102	.325	66.5

SIGNIFICANT EVENTS

■ **August 13:** When Chicago's Jack Taylor failed to last through the third inning of a game against Brooklyn, it ended his record complete-game streak at 187.
■ **October 7:** The Cubs ended an amazing regular season with a Major League-record 116 victories and a team ERA of 1.76.

MEMORABLE MOMENTS

■ **May 25:** Jesse Tannehill snapped Boston's A.L.-record 20-game losing streak with a 3-0 victory over the White Sox.
■ **June 9:** The Boston Beaneaters ended their 19-game losing streak with a 6-3 victory over the Cardinals.
■ **August 23:** Washington ended the Chicago White Stockings' A.L.-record winning streak at 19 games.
■ **September 1:** The Athletics scored three times in the top of the 24th inning and claimed a 4-1 victory over Boston in the longest game in Major League history.
■ **October 3:** Chicago's "Hitless Wonders" clinched the A.L. pennant when the Athletics posted a 3-0 victory over New York in the second game of a doubleheader.

LEADERS

American League

BA: George Stone, St.L.,.358.
Runs: Elmer Flick, Cle., 98.
Hits: Nap Lajoie, Cle., 214.
TB: George Stone, St.L., 291.
HR: Harry Davis, Phil., 12.
RBI: Harry Davis, Phil., 96.
SB: John Anderson, Wash.; Elmer Flick, Cle., 39.
Wins: Al Orth, N.Y., 27.
ERA: Doc White, Chi., 1.52.
CG: Al Orth, N.Y., 36.
IP: Al Orth, N.Y., 338.2.
SO: Rube Waddell, Phil., 196.

National League

BA: Honus Wagner, Pit., .339.
Runs: Frank Chance, Chi.; Honus Wagner, Pit., 103.
Hits: Harry Steinfeldt, Chi., 176.
TB: Honus Wagner, Pit., 237.
HR: Tim Jordan, Brk., 12.
RBI: Jim Nealon, Pit.; Harry Steinfeldt, Chi., 83.
SB: Frank Chance, Chi., 57.
Wins: Joe McGinnity, N.Y., 27.
ERA: Mordecai Brown, Chi., 1.04.
CG: Irv Young, Bos., 37.
IP: Irv Young, Bos., 358.1.
SO: Fred Beebe, Chi.-St.L., 171.

A.L. 20-game winners

Al Orth, N.Y., 27-17
Jack Chesbro, N.Y., 23-17
Bob Rhoades, Cle., 22-10
Frank Owen, Chi., 22-13
Addie Joss, Cle., 21-9
George Mullin, Det., 21-18
Nick Altrock, Chi., 20-13
Otto Hess, Cle., 20-17

N.L. 20-game winners

Joe McGinnity, N.Y., 27-12
Mordecai Brown, Chi., 26-6
Vic Willis, Pit., 23-13
Sam Leever, Pit., 22-7
Christy Mathewson, N.Y., 22-12
Jack Pfiester, Chi., 20-8
Jack Taylor, St.L.-Chi., 20-12
Jake Weimer, Cin., 20-14

WORLD SERIES

■ **Winner:** Chicago's "Hitless Wonders" pulled an intra-city shocker with a six-game victory over the powerful Cubs.
■ **Turning point:** An eight-run Game 5 explosion by the light-hitting White Sox, which was spiced by Frank Isbell's four doubles and two RBIs.
■ **Memorable moment:** Big Ed Walsh's two-hit Game 3 shutout. The Cubs were held hitless after getting a first-inning single and double.
■ **Top guns:** Walsh (2-0, 1.80 ERA), George Rohe (.333, 4 RBIs), White Sox; Ed Reulbach (Game 2 1-hitter), Cubs.

Linescores

Game 1—October 9, at Chicago Cubs
White Sox....... 0 0 0 0 1 1 0 0 0 — 2 4 1
Cubs.............. 0 0 0 0 0 1 0 0 0 — 1 4 2
Altrock; Brown. W—Altrock. L—Brown.

Game 2—October 10, at Chicago White Sox
Cubs.............. 0 3 1 0 0 1 0 2 0 — 7 10 2
White Sox....... 0 0 0 0 1 0 0 0 0 — 1 1 2
Reulbach; White, Owen (4). W—Reulbach. L—White.

Game 3—October 11, at Chicago Cubs
White Sox....... 0 0 0 0 0 3 0 0 0 — 3 4 1
Cubs.............. 0 0 0 0 0 0 0 0 0 — 0 2 2
Walsh; Pfiester. W—Walsh. L—Pfiester.

Game 4—October 12, at Chicago White Sox
Cubs.............. 0 0 0 0 0 0 1 0 0 — 1 7 1
White Sox....... 0 0 0 0 0 0 0 0 0 — 0 2 1
Brown; Altrock. W—Brown. L—Altrock.

Game 5—October 13, at Chicago Cubs
White Sox....... 1 0 2 4 0 1 0 0 0 — 8 12 6
Cubs.............. 3 0 0 1 0 2 0 0 0 — 6 6 0
Walsh, White (7); Reulbach, Pfiester (3), Overall (4). W—Walsh. L—Pfiester.

Game 6—October 14, at Chicago White Sox
Cubs.............. 1 0 0 0 1 0 0 0 0 — 3 7 0
White Sox....... 3 4 0 0 0 0 0 1 x — 8 14 3
Brown, Overall (2); White. W—White. L—Brown.

FINAL STANDINGS

American League

Team	W	L	Pct.	GB
Detroit	92	58	.613	...
Philadelphia	88	57	.607	1.5
Chicago	87	64	.576	5.5
Cleveland	85	67	.559	8
New York	70	78	.473	21
St. Louis	69	83	.454	24
Boston	59	90	.396	32.5
Washington	49	102	.325	43.5

National League

Team	W	L	Pct.	GB
Chicago	107	45	.704	...
Pittsburgh	91	63	.591	17
Philadelphia	83	64	.565	21.5
New York	82	71	.536	25.5
Brooklyn	65	83	.439	40
Cincinnati	66	87	.431	41.5
Boston	58	90	.392	47
St. Louis	52	101	.340	55.5

SIGNIFICANT EVENTS

■ **April 11:** Giants catcher Roger Bresnahan introduced his newest innovation in a game against the Phillies: wooden shinguards to protect his legs and knees.
■ **August 2:** Washington fireballer Walter Johnson dropped a 3-2 decision to Detroit in his Major League debut.

MEMORABLE MOMENTS

■ **May 20:** The Cardinals ended New York's 17-game winning streak with a 6-4 victory at the Polo Grounds.
■ **October 3:** The seventh-place Boston Red Sox edged sixth-place St. Louis 1-0 and ended their 16-game losing streak.
■ **October 5:** The Tigers, locked in a tight A.L. pennant race with Philadelphia, clinched the title with a 10-2 victory over St. Louis.

LEADERS

American League

BA: Ty Cobb, Det., .350.
Runs: Sam Crawford, Det., 102.
Hits: Ty Cobb, Det., 212.
TB: Ty Cobb, Det., 283.
HR: Harry Davis, Phil., 8.
RBI: Ty Cobb, Det., 119.
SB: Ty Cobb, Det., 49.
Wins: Addie Joss, Cle.; Doc White, Chi., 27.
ERA: Ed Walsh, Chi., 1.60.
CG: Ed Walsh, Chi., 37.
IP: Ed Walsh, Chi., 422.1.
SO: Rube Waddell, Phil., 232.

National League

BA: Honus Wagner, Pit., .350.
Runs: Spike Shannon, N.Y., 104.
Hits: Ginger Beaumont, Bos., 187.
TB: Honus Wagner, Pit., 264.
HR: Dave Brain, Bos., 10.
RBI: Sherry Magee, Phil., 85.
SB: Honus Wagner, Pit., 61.
Wins: Christy Mathewson, N.Y., 24.
ERA: Jack Pfiester, Chi., 1.15.
CG: Stoney McGlynn, St.L., 33.
IP: Stoney McGlynn, St.L., 352.1.
SO: Christy Mathewson, N.Y., 178.

A.L. 20-game winners
Addie Joss, Cle., 27-11
Doc White, Chi., 27-13
Bill Donovan, Det., 25-4
Ed Killian, Det., 25-13
Eddie Plank, Phil., 24-16
Ed Walsh, Chi., 24-18
Frank Smith, Chi., 23-10
Jimmy Dygert, Phil., 21-8
Cy Young, Bos., 21-15
George Mullin, Det., 20-20

N.L. 20-game winners
Christy Mathewson, N.Y., 24-12
Orval Overall, Chi., 23-7
Tully Sparks, Phil., 22-8
Vic Willis, Pit., 21-11
Mordecai Brown, Chi., 20-6
Lefty Leifield, Pit., 20-16

A.L. 100 RBIs
Ty Cobb, Det., 119

WORLD SERIES

■ **Winner:** The powerful Cubs, atoning for their shocking loss to the White Sox in 1906, made short work of the A.L.-champion Tigers.

■ **Turning point:** A ninth-inning passed ball by Tigers catcher Charlie Schmidt that allowed the Cubs to score the tying run in a Game 1 battle that would end in a 3-3 deadlock.

■ **Memorable moment:** Schmidt's passed ball, which awoke the Cubs and set the stage for their sweeping finish.

■ **Top guns:** Harry Steinfeldt (.471), Johnny Evers (.350), Cubs; Claude Rossman (.400), Tigers.

Linescores

Game 1—October 8, at Chicago
Detroit ...0 0 0 0 0 0 0 3 0 0 0 0 — 3 9 3
Chicago .0 0 0 1 0 0 0 2 0 0 0 0 — 3 10 5
Donovan; Overall, Reulbach (10). Game called after 12 innings because of darkness.

Game 2—October 9, at Chicago
Detroit .... 0 1 0 0 0 0 0 0 0 — 1 9 1
Chicago .... 0 1 0 2 0 0 0 0 x — 3 9 1
Mullin; Pfiester. W—Pfiester. L—Mullin.

Game 3—October 10, at Chicago
Detroit .... 0 0 0 0 0 1 0 0 0 — 1 6 1
Chicago .... 0 1 0 3 1 0 0 0 x — 5 10 1
Siever, Killian (5); Reulbach. W—Reulbach. L—Siever.

Game 4—October 11, at Detroit
Chicago .... 0 0 0 0 2 0 3 0 1 — 6 7 2
Detroit .... 0 0 0 1 0 0 0 0 0 — 1 5 2
Overall; Donovan. W—Overall. L—Donovan.

Game 5—October 12, at Detroit
Chicago .... 1 1 0 0 0 0 0 0 0 — 2 7 1
Detroit .... 0 0 0 0 0 0 0 0 0 — 0 7 2
Brown; Mullin. W—Brown. L—Mullin.

FINAL STANDINGS

American League

Team	W	L	Pct.	GB
Detroit	90	63	.588	...
Cleveland	90	64	.584	.5
Chicago	88	64	.579	1.5
St. Louis	83	69	.546	6.5
Boston	75	79	.487	15.5
Philadelphia	68	85	.444	22
Washington	67	85	.441	22.5
New York	51	103	.331	39.5

National League

Team	W	L	Pct.	GB
Chicago	99	55	.643	...
New York	98	56	.636	1
Pittsburgh	98	56	.636	1
Philadelphia	83	71	.539	16
Cincinnati	73	81	.474	26
Boston	63	91	.409	36
Brooklyn	53	101	.344	46
St. Louis	49	105	.318	50

SIGNIFICANT EVENTS

■ **February 27:** Baseball adopted the sacrifice fly rule, stating that a batter will not be charged with an at-bat if a runner tags up and scores after the catch of his fly ball.

MEMORABLE MOMENTS

■ **June 30:** Boston's 41-year-old Cy Young became the first pitcher to notch three career no-hitters when he defeated New York, 8-0.
■ **September 23:** The outcome of an important Giants-Cubs game was thrown into confusion when New York baserunner Fred Merkle failed to touch second base on an apparent game-ending hit, prompting the Cubs' claims of a game-prolonging forceout.
■ **September 24:** N.L. President Harry Pulliam declared the September 23 Cubs-Giants game a tie.
■ **September 26:** Chicago's Ed Reulbach made baseball history when he shut out Brooklyn twice—5-0 and 3-0—on the same day.
■ **October 2:** Cleveland's Addie Joss became the second modern-era pitcher to throw a perfect game, retiring all 27 Chicago batters he faced in a 1-0 victory.
■ **October 6:** The Tigers defeated the White Sox, 7-0, and claimed the A.L. pennant on the season's final day.
■ **October 8:** In an N.L. pennant-deciding matchup dictated by the controversial September 23 tie game, Chicago defeated the Giants, 4-2.

LEADERS

American League

BA: Ty Cobb, Det., .324.
Runs: Matty McIntyre, Det., 105.
Hits: Ty Cobb, Det., 188.
TB: Ty Cobb, Det., 276.
HR: Sam Crawford, Det., 7.
RBI: Ty Cobb, Det., 108.
SB: Patsy Dougherty, Chi., 47.
Wins: Ed Walsh, Chi., 40.
ERA: Addie Joss, Cle., 1.16.
CG: Ed Walsh, Chi., 42.
IP: Ed Walsh, Chi., 464.
SO: Ed Walsh, Chi., 269.

National League

BA: Honus Wagner, Pit., .354.
Runs: Fred Tenney, N.Y., 101.
Hits: Honus Wagner, Pit., 201.
TB: Honus Wagner, Pit., 308.
HR: Tim Jordan, Brk., 12.
RBI: Honus Wagner, Pit., 109.
SB: Honus Wagner, Pit., 53.
Wins: Christy Mathewson, N.Y., 37.
ERA: Christy Mathewson, N.Y., 1.43.
CG: Christy Mathewson, N.Y., 34.
IP: Christy Mathewson, N.Y., 390.2.
SO: Christy Mathewson, N.Y., 259.

A.L. 20-game winners
Ed Walsh, Chi., 40-15
Addie Joss, Cle., 24-11
Ed Summers, Det., 24-12
Cy Young, Bos., 21-11

N.L. 20-game winners
Christy Mathewson, N.Y., 37-11
Mordecai Brown, Chi., 29-9
Ed Reulbach, Chi., 24-7
Nick Maddox, Pit., 23-8
Vic Willis, Pit. 23-11
Hooks Wiltse, N.Y., 23-14

George McQuillan, Phil., 23-17

A.L. 100 RBIs
Ty Cobb, Det., 108

N.L. 100 RBIs
Honus Wagner, Pit., 109
Mike Donlin, N.Y., 106

WORLD SERIES

■ **Winner:** The Cubs became the first two-time Series champs by defeating Detroit for the second consecutive year.

■ **Turning point:** A five-run ninth-inning rally that turned a 6-5 Game 1 deficit into a 10-6 Cubs victory.

■ **Memorable moment:** A two-run eighth-inning home run by Chicago's Joe Tinker that broke up a scoreless Game 2 pitching duel and gave Orval Overall a 6-1 victory over Bill Donovan.

■ **Top guns:** Overall (2-0, 0.98 ERA), Frank Chance (.421), Cubs; Ty Cobb (.368), Tigers.

Linescores

Game 1—October 10, at Detroit
Chicago .... 0 0 4 0 0 0 1 0 5 — 10 14 2
Detroit .... 1 0 0 0 0 0 3 2 0 — 6 10 4
Reulbach, Overall (7), Brown (8); Killian, Summers (3). W—Brown. L—Summers.

Game 2—October 11, at Chicago
Detroit .... 0 0 0 0 0 0 0 0 1 — 1 4 1
Chicago .... 0 0 0 0 0 0 0 6 x — 6 7 1
Donovan; Overall. W—Overall. L—Donovan. HR—Tinker (Chi.).

Game 3—October 12, at Chicago
Detroit .... 1 0 0 0 0 5 0 2 0 — 8 11 4
Chicago .... 0 0 0 3 0 0 0 0 0 — 3 7 2
Mullin; Pfiester, Reulbach (9). W—Mullin. L—Pfiester.

Game 4—October 13, at Detroit
Chicago .... 0 0 2 0 0 0 0 0 1 — 3 10 0
Detroit .... 0 0 0 0 0 0 0 0 0 — 0 4 1
Brown; Summers, Winter (9). W—Brown. L—Summers.

Game 5—October 14, at Detroit
Chicago .... 1 0 0 0 1 0 0 0 0 — 2 10 0
Detroit .... 0 0 0 0 0 0 0 0 0 — 0 3 0
Overall; Donovan. W—Overall. L—Donovan.

FINAL STANDINGS

American League

Team	W	L	Pct.	GB
Detroit	98	54	.645	...
Philadelphia	95	58	.621	3.5
Boston	88	63	.583	9.5
Chicago	78	74	.513	20
New York	74	77	.490	23.5
Cleveland	71	82	.464	27.5
St. Louis	61	89	.407	36
Washington	42	110	.276	56

National League

Team	W	L	Pct.	GB
Pittsburgh	110	42	.724	...
Chicago	104	49	.680	6.5
New York	92	61	.601	18.5
Cincinnati	77	76	.503	33.5
Philadelphia	74	79	.484	36.5
Brooklyn	55	98	.359	55.5
St. Louis	54	98	.355	56
Boston	45	108	.294	65.5

SIGNIFICANT EVENTS

■ **April 12:** The Athletics and pitcher Eddie Plank christened Philadelphia's new Shibe Park with an 8-1 victory over Boston.
■ **June 30:** The Cubs spoiled Pittsburgh's opening of new Forbes Field, posting a 3-2 victory over the Pirates.
■ **July 29:** N.L. President Harry Pulliam shocked the baseball world when he shot himself to death.
■ **October 5:** Detroit's Ty Cobb finished his Triple Crown season with a .377 average, 9 home runs and 107 RBIs.

MEMORABLE MOMENTS

■ **April 15:** New York's Red Ames lost his Opening Day no-hit bid in the 10th inning and the game in the 13th when Brooklyn scored a 3-0 victory.
■ **July 16:** A Detroit-Washington game ended 0-0 after 18 innings—the longest scoreless tie in A.L. history.
■ **July 19:** Cleveland shortstop Neal Ball pulled off the first unassisted triple play of the century in a game against the Red Sox.

LEADERS

American League
BA: Ty Cobb, Det., .377.
Runs: Ty Cobb, Det., 116.
Hits: Ty Cobb, Det., 216.
TB: Ty Cobb, Det., 296.
HR: Ty Cobb, Det., 9.
RBI: Ty Cobb, Det., 107.
SB: Ty Cobb, Det., 76.
Wins: George Mullin, Det., 29.
ERA: Harry Krause, Phil., 1.39.
CG: Frank Smith, Chi., 37.
IP: Frank Smith, Chi., 365.
SO: Frank Smith, Chi., 177.

National League
BA: Honus Wagner, Pit., .339.
Runs: Tommy Leach, Pit., 126.
Hits: Larry Doyle, N.Y., 172.
TB: Honus Wagner, Pit., 242.
HR: Red Murray, N.Y., 7.
RBI: Honus Wagner, Pit., 100.
SB: Bob Bescher, Cin., 54.
Wins: Mordecai Brown, Chi., 27.
ERA: Christy Mathewson, N.Y., 1.14.
CG: Mordecai Brown, Chi., 32.
IP: Mordecai Brown, Chi., 342.2.
SO: Orval Overall, Chi., 205.

A.L. 20-game winners
George Mullin, Det., 29-8
Frank Smith, Chi., 25-17
Ed Willett, Det., 21-10

N.L. 20-game winners
Mordecai Brown, Chi., 27-9
Howie Camnitz, Pit., 25-6
Christy Mathewson, N.Y., 25-6
Vic Willis, Pit., 22-11
Orval Overall, Chi., 20-11

Hooks Wiltse, N.Y., 20-11

A.L. 100 RBIs
Ty Cobb, Det., 107

N.L. 100 RBIs
Honus Wagner, Pit., 100

WORLD SERIES

■ **Winner:** The Pirates, losers in baseball's first World Series, bounced back to hand the Tigers their third straight post-season loss.
■ **Turning point:** A tie-breaking three-run homer by Pirates player/manager Fred Clarke that keyed an 8-4 victory in the pivotal fifth game.
■ **Memorable moment:** When Pirates pitcher Babe Adams retired the final Tiger in Game 7 and ended the first Series to go the distance.
■ **Top guns:** Adams (3-0, 1.33 ERA), Honus Wagner (.333, 7 RBIs, 6 SB), Pirates; Jim Delahanty (.346), Tigers.

Linescores
Game 1—October 8, at Pittsburgh
Detroit........... 1 0 0 0 0 0 0 0 0 — 1 6 4
Pittsburgh..... 0 0 0 1 2 1 0 0 x — 4 5 0
Mullin; Adams. W—Adams. L—Mullin. HR—Clarke (Pit.).

Game 2—October 9, at Pittsburgh
Detroit........... 0 2 3 0 2 0 0 0 0 — 7 9 3
Pittsburgh..... 2 0 0 0 0 0 0 0 0 — 2 5 1
Donovan; Camnitz, Willis (3). W—Donovan. L—Camnitz.

Game 3—October 11, at Detroit
Pittsburgh..... 5 1 0 0 0 0 0 0 2 — 8 10 3
Detroit........... 0 0 0 0 0 0 4 0 2 — 6 10 5
Maddox; Summers, Willett (1), Works (8). W—Maddox. L—Summers.

Game 4—October 12, at Detroit
Pittsburgh..... 0 0 0 0 0 0 0 0 0 — 0 5 6
Detroit........... 0 2 0 3 0 0 0 0 x — 5 8 0
Leifield, Phillippe (5); Mullin. W—Mullin. L—Leifield.

Game 5—October 13, at Pittsburgh
Detroit........... 1 0 0 0 0 2 0 1 0 — 4 6 1
Pittsburgh..... 1 1 1 0 0 0 4 1 x — 8 10 1
Summers, Willett (8); Adams. W—Adams. L—Summers. HR—D. Jones, Crawford (Det.); Clarke (Pit.).

Game 6—October 14, at Detroit
Pittsburgh..... 3 0 0 0 0 0 0 0 1 — 4 7 3
Detroit........... 1 0 0 2 1 1 0 0 x — 5 10 3
Willis, Camnitz (6); Phillippe (7); Mullin. W—Mullin. L—Willis.

Game 7—October 16, at Detroit
Pittsburgh..... 0 2 0 2 0 3 0 1 0 — 8 7 0
Detroit........... 0 0 0 0 0 0 0 0 0 — 0 6 3
Adams; Donovan, Mullin (4). W—Adams. L—Donovan.

FINAL STANDINGS

American League

Team	W	L	Pct.	GB
Philadelphia	102	48	.680	...
New York	88	63	.583	14.5
Detroit	86	68	.558	18
Boston	81	72	.529	22.5
Cleveland	71	81	.467	32
Chicago	68	85	.444	35.5
Washington	66	85	.437	36.5
St. Louis	47	107	.305	57

National League

Team	W	L	Pct.	GB
Chicago	104	50	.675	...
New York	91	63	.591	13
Pittsburgh	86	67	.562	17.5
Philadelphia	78	75	.510	25.5
Cincinnati	75	79	.487	29
Brooklyn	64	90	.416	40
St. Louis	63	90	.412	40.5
Boston	53	100	.346	50.5

SIGNIFICANT EVENTS

■ **February 18:** The N.L. approved a 154-game schedule, a plan already adopted by the A.L.
■ **April 14:** William Howard Taft became the first U.S. President to throw out the first ball at a season opener in Washington.
■ **April 21:** Detroit spoiled the opening of Cleveland's League Park with a 5-0 victory over the Indians.
■ **July 1:** Chicago unveiled White Sox Park (Comiskey Park), but the Browns spoiled the occasion with a 2-0 victory.

MEMORABLE MOMENTS

■ **July 19:** The incredible Cy Young earned his 500th career victory when he pitched Cleveland to an 11-inning, 5-2 win over Washington.
■ **August 30:** The Highlanders' Tom Hughes lost his no-hit bid against Cleveland with one out in the 10th and lost the game, 5-0, in the 11th.
■ **September 25:** The scoreless streak of Philadelphia's Jack Coombs ended at 53 innings in a darkness-shortened 5-2 loss to Chicago in the second game of a doubleheader.
■ **October 9:** Cleveland's Napoleon Lajoie collected eight final-day hits, seven of them bunt singles, in a doubleheader against the Browns and lifted his final average to .384—one point ahead of Detroit's Ty Cobb.
■ **October 15:** A.L. President Ban Johnson adjusted Cobb's final average to .385 and declared him winner of the A.L. batting title.

LEADERS

American League
BA: Ty Cobb, Det., .383.
Runs: Ty Cobb, Det., 106.
Hits: Nap Lajoie, Cle., 227.
TB: Nap Lajoie, Cle., 304.
HR: Jake Stahl, Bos., 10.
RBI: Sam Crawford, Det., 120.
SB: Eddie Collins, Phil., 81.
ERA: Ed Walsh, Chi., 1.27.
CG: Walter Johnson, Wash., 38.
IP: Walter Johnson, Wash., 370.
SO: Walter Johnson, Wash., 313.

National League
BA: Sherry Magee, Phil., .331.
Runs: Sherry Magee, Phil., 110.
Hits: Bobby Byrne, Pit.; Honus Wagner, Pit., 178.
TB: Sherry Magee, Phil., 263.
HR: Fred Beck, Bos.; Frank Schulte, Chi., 10.
RBI: Sherry Magee, Phil., 123.
SB: Bob Bescher, Cin., 70.
Wins: Christy Mathewson, N.Y., 27.
ERA: King Cole, Chi., 1.80.
CG: Mordecai Brown, Chi.; Christy Mathewson, N.Y.; Nap Rucker, Brk., 27.
IP: Nap Rucker, Brk., 320.1.
SO: Earl Moore, Phil., 185.

A.L. 20-game winners
Jack Coombs, Phil., 31-9
Russ Ford, N.Y., 26-6
Walter Johnson, Wash., 25-17
Chief Bender, Phil., 23-5
George Mullin, Det., 21-12

N.L. 20-game winners
Christy Mathewson, N.Y., 27-9
Mordecai Brown, Chi., 25-14
Earl Moore, Phil., 22-15
King Cole, Chi., 20-4
George Suggs, Cin., 20-12

A.L. 100 RBIs
Sam Crawford, Det., 120

N.L. 100 RBIs
Sherry Magee, Phil., 123

WORLD SERIES

■ **Winner:** Philadelphia won their first Series championship and thwarted the Cubs' bid to become a three-time winner.
■ **Turning point:** The Cubs' failure to take advantage of the less-than-artistic Jack Coombs in Game 2. Coombs allowed eight hits and nine walks but still won, 9-3.
■ **Memorable moment:** A three-run homer by Danny Murphy that broke up a tight Game 3 and helped Philadelphia to a 12-5 victory.
■ **Top guns:** Eddie Collins (.429), Murphy (.350, 8 RBIs), Frank Baker (.409), Athletics; Frank Chance (.353), Frank Schulte (.353), Cubs.

Linescores
Game 1—October 17, at Philadelphia
Chicago.......... 0 0 0 0 0 0 0 0 1 — 1 3 1
Philadelphia.... 0 2 1 0 0 0 1 x — 4 7 2
Overall, McIntire (4); Bender. W—Bender. L—Overall.

Game 2—October 18, at Philadelphia
Chicago.......... 0 1 0 0 0 0 1 0 1 — 3 8 3
Philadelphia.... 0 0 2 0 1 0 6 0 x — 9 14 4
Brown, Richie (8); Coombs. W—Coombs. L—Brown.

Game 3—October 20, at Chicago
Philadelphia.... 1 2 5 0 0 0 4 0 0 — 12 15 1
Chicago.......... 1 2 0 0 0 0 2 0 — 5 6 5
Coombs; Reulbach, McIntre (3), Pfiester (3). W—Coombs. L—McIntire. HR—Murphy (Phil.).

Game 4—October 22, at Chicago
Philadelphia.... 0 0 1 2 0 0 0 0 0 — 3 11 3
Chicago.......... 1 0 0 1 0 0 0 0 1 — 4 9 1
Bender; Cole, Brown (9). W—Brown. L—Bender.

Game 5—October 23, at Chicago
Philadelphia.... 1 0 0 0 1 0 0 5 0 — 7 9 1
Chicago.......... 0 1 0 0 0 0 1 0 — 2 9 2
Coombs; Brown. W—Coombs. L—Brown.

HISTORY

FINAL STANDINGS

American League

Team	W	L	Pct.	GB
Philadelphia	101	50	.669	...
Detroit	89	65	.578	13.5
Cleveland	80	73	.523	22
Chicago	77	74	.510	24
Boston	78	75	.510	24
New York	76	76	.500	25.5
Washington	64	90	.416	38.5
St. Louis	45	107	.296	56.5

National League

Team	W	L	Pct.	GB
New York	99	54	.647	...
Chicago	92	62	.597	7.5
Pittsburgh	85	69	.552	14.5
Philadelphia	79	73	.520	19.5
St. Louis	75	74	.503	22
Cincinnati	70	83	.458	29
Brooklyn	64	86	.427	33.5
Boston	44	107	.291	54

SIGNIFICANT EVENTS

■ **April 14:** New York's Polo Grounds burned down, forcing the Giants to play a big stretch of their schedule at the Highlanders' Hilltop Park.
■ **June 28:** The Giants defeated the Braves, 3-0, in the first game at the new Polo Grounds.
■ **October 11:** Chalmers automobile recipients as baseball's first MVPs: Detroit's Ty Cobb in the A.L. and Chicago's Frank Schulte in the N.L.

MEMORABLE MOMENTS

■ **May 13:** The Giants exploded for a record 13 first-inning runs, 10 before the first out was recorded, in a 19-5 victory over St. Louis.
■ **July 4:** Chicago ace Ed Walsh stopped Detroit, 7-3, and ended Ty Cobb's hitting streak at 40 games.
■ **September 29:** Phillies righthander Grover Cleveland Alexander defeated Pittsburgh 7-4 and claimed his rookie-record 28th victory.
■ **September 22:** Cy Young, ending his career with the Braves, won his 511th and final game, beating Pittsburgh 1-0.

LEADERS

American League

BA: Ty Cobb, Det., .420.
Runs: Ty Cobb, Det., 147.
Hits: Ty Cobb, Det., 248.
TB: Ty Cobb, Det., 367.
HR: Frank Baker, Phil., 11.
RBI: Ty Cobb, Det., 127.
SB: Ty Cobb, Det., 83.
Wins: Jack Coombs, Phil., 28.
ERA: Vean Gregg, Cle., 1.80.
CG: Walter Johnson, Wash., 36.
IP: Ed Walsh, Chi., 368.2.
SO: Ed Walsh, Chi., 255.

National League

BA: Honus Wagner, Pit., .334.
Runs: Jimmy Sheckard, Chi., 121.
Hits: Doc Miller, Bos., 192.
TB: Frank Schulte, Chi., 308.
HR: Frank Schulte, Chi., 21.
RBI: Frank Schulte, Chi.; Chief Wilson, Pit., 107.
SB: Bob Bescher, Cin., 80.
Wins: Grover Alexander, Phil., 28.
ERA: Christy Mathewson, N.Y., 1.99.
CG: Grover Alexander, Phil., 31.
IP: Grover Alexander, Phil., 367.
SO: Rube Marquard, N.Y., 237.

A.L. 20-game winners

Jack Coombs, Phil., 28-12
Ed Walsh, Chi., 27-18
Walter Johnson, Wash., 25-13
Vean Gregg, Cle., 23-7
Eddie Plank, Phil., 23-8
Joe Wood, Bos., 23-17
Russ Ford, N.Y., 22-11

N.L. 20-game winners

Grover Alexander, Phil., 28-13
Christy Mathewson, N.Y., 26-13
Rube Marquard, N.Y., 24-7
Bob Harmon, St.L., 23-16
Babe Adams, Pit., 22-12
Nap Rucker, Brk., 22-18
Mordecai Brown, Chi., 21-11
Howie Camnitz, Pit., 20-15

A.L. 100 RBIs

Ty Cobb, Det., 127
Frank Baker, Phil., 115
Sam Crawford, Det., 115

N.L. 100 RBIs

Frank Schulte, Chi., 107
Chief Wilson, Pit., 107

Chalmers MVP

A.L.: Ty Cobb, OF, Det.
N.L.: Frank Schulte, OF, Chi.

WORLD SERIES

■ **Winner:** The Athletics became baseball's second back-to-back winners and gained revenge for their 1905 loss to the Giants.

■ **Turning point:** A ninth-inning Game 3 homer by Frank Baker off Christy Mathewson. The solo shot tied the game at 1-1 and the A's won in 11 innings, 3-2.

■ **Memorable moment:** Baker's homer off Mathewson.

■ **Top guns:** Chief Bender (2-1, 1.04 ERA), Baker (.375, 2 HR), Jack Barry (.368), Athletics; Mathewson (27 IP, 2.00), Giants.

Linescores

Game 1—October 14, at New York
Philadelphia.... 0 1 0 0 0 0 0 0 0 — 1 6 2
New York........ 0 0 0 1 0 0 1 0 x — 2 5 0
Bender; Mathewson. W—Mathewson. L—Bender.

Game 2—October 16, at Philadelphia
New York........ 0 1 0 0 0 0 0 0 0 — 1 5 3
Philadelphia.... 1 0 0 0 0 2 0 0 x — 3 4 0
Marquard, Crandall (8); Plank. W—Plank.
L—Marquard. HR—Baker (Phil.).

Game 3—October 17, at New York
Philadelphia ....0 0 0 0 0 0 0 0 1 0 2—3 9 2
New York ....0 0 1 0 0 0 0 0 0 0 1—2 3 5
Coombs; Mathewson. W—Coombs.
L—Mathewson. HR—Baker (Phil.).

Game 4—October 24, at Philadelphia
New York....... 2 0 0 0 0 0 0 0 0 — 2 7 3
Philadelphia... 0 0 0 3 1 0 0 0 x — 4 1 1
Mathewson, Wiltse (8); Bender. W—Bender.
L—Mathewson.

Game 5—October 25, at New York
Philadelphia ... 0 0 3 0 0 0 0 0 0 — 3 7 1
New York....... 0 0 0 0 0 1 0 2 1 — 4 9 2
Coombs, Plank (10); Marquard, Ames (4), Crandall (9). W—Crandall. L—Plank. HR—Oldring (Phil.).

Game 6—October 26, at Philadelphia
New York....... 1 0 0 0 0 0 0 0 1 — 2 4 3
Philadelphia... 0 0 1 4 0 1 7 0 x — 13 3 5
Ames, Wiltse (5), Marquard (7); Bender. W—Bender. L—Ames.

FINAL STANDINGS

American League

Team	W	L	Pct.	GB
Boston	105	47	.691	...
Washington	91	61	.599	14
Philadelphia	90	62	.592	15
Chicago	78	76	.506	28
Cleveland	75	78	.490	30.5
Detroit	69	84	.451	36.5
St. Louis	53	101	.344	53
New York	50	102	.329	55

National League

Team	W	L	Pct.	GB
New York	103	48	.682	...
Pittsburgh	93	58	.616	10
Chicago	91	59	.607	11.5
Cincinnati	75	78	.490	29
Philadelphia	73	79	.480	30.5
St. Louis	63	90	.412	41
Brooklyn	58	95	.379	46
Boston	52	101	.340	52

SIGNIFICANT EVENTS

■ **April 11:** Cincinnati celebrated the opening of new Redland Field with a 10-6 victory over the Cubs.
■ **April 20:** The Red Sox christened Fenway Park with an 11-inning 7-6 victory over New York and the Tigers opened Navin Field with an 11-inning 6-5 victory over Cleveland.
■ **May 16:** A.L. President Ban Johnson handed Detroit's Ty Cobb an indefinite suspension after Cobb entered the stands at New York's Hilltop Park to fight a heckler.
■ **May 18:** A team of amateur Tigers dropped a 24-2 decision to the Athletics when the regular Tigers went on strike to protest Cobb's suspension.
■ **May 20:** The Tigers, facing the threat of lifetime suspensions from Johnson, returned to uniform.

MEMORABLE MOMENTS

■ **June 13:** New York's Christy Mathewson earned his 300th career victory and 20th win of the season when he defeated the Cubs, 3-2.
■ **July 3:** Giants lefty Rube Marquard earned his record 19th consecutive victory of the season and 21st straight over two years, stopping Brooklyn, 2-1.
■ **August 26:** The Browns handed Washington's Walter Johnson a 3-2 loss and ended his A.L.-record winning streak at 16 games.
■ **September 20:** Joe Wood's record-tying 16-game winning streak ended when Detroit handed Boston a 6-4 loss.
■ **September 22:** For the second time in 11 days, Athletics star Eddie Collins stole a modern-record six bases in a game—an 8-2 victory over the Browns.

LEADERS

American League

BA: Ty Cobb, Det., .409.
Runs: Eddie Collins, Phil., 137.
Hits: Ty Cobb, Det.; Joe Jackson, Cle., 226.
TB: Joe Jackson, Cle., 331.
HR: Frank Baker, Phil.; Tris Speaker, Bos., 10.
RBI: Frank Baker, Phil., 130.
SB: Clyde Milan, Wash., 88.
Wins: Joe Wood, Bos., 34.
ERA: Walter Johnson, Wash., 1.39.
CG: Joe Wood, Bos., 35.
IP: Ed Walsh, Chi., 393.
SO: Walter Johnson, Wash., 303.

National League

BA: Heinie Zimmerman, Chi., .372.
Runs: Bob Bescher, Cin., 120.
Hits: Heinie Zimmerman, Chi., 207.
TB: Heinie Zimmerman, Chi., 318.
HR: Heinie Zimmerman, Chi., 14.
RBI: Honus Wagner, Pit., 102.
SB: Bob Bescher, Cin., 67.
Wins: Larry Cheney, Chi.; Rube Marquard, N.Y., 26.
ERA: Jeff Tesreau, N.Y., 1.96.
CG: Larry Cheney, Chi., 28.
IP: Grover Alexander, Phil., 310.1.
SO: Grover Alexander, Phil., 195.

A.L. 20-game winners

Joe Wood, Bos., 34-5
Walter Johnson, Wash., 33-12
Ed Walsh, Chi., 27-17
Eddie Plank, Phil., 26-6
Bob Groom, Wash., 24-13
Jack Coombs, Phil., 21-10
Hugh Bedient, Bos., 20-9
Vean Gregg, Cle., 20-13
Buck O'Brien, Bos., 20-13

N.L. 20-game winners

Larry Cheney, Chi., 26-10
Rube Marquard, N.Y., 26-11
Claude Hendrix, Pit., 24-9
Christy Mathewson, N.Y., 23-12
Howie Camnitz, Pit., 22-12

A.L. 100 RBIs

Frank Baker, Phil., 130
Sam Crawford, Det., 109

N.L. 100 RBIs

Duffy Lewis, Bos., 109
Stuffy McInnis, Phil., 101

N.L. 100 RBIs

Honus Wagner, Pit., 102
Bill Sweeney, Bos., 100

Chalmers MVP

A.L.: Tris Speaker, OF, Bos.
N.L.: Larry Doyle, 2B, N.Y.

WORLD SERIES

■ **Winners:** The Red Sox, who had not made a Series appearance since beating Pittsburgh in the 1903 inaugural, made it two for two with a victory over the Giants.

■ **Turning point:** A dropped fly ball by Giants center fielder Fred Snodgrass in the Series-deciding eighth game. The Red Sox wiped out a 2-1 deficit against Christy Mathewson and claimed a 3-2 victory.

■ **Memorable moment:** Snodgrass' muff and the failure of catcher Chief Meyers and first baseman Fred Merkle to catch a foul pop in the same inning.

■ **Top guns:** Joe Wood (3-1), Red Sox; Buck Herzog (.400), Meyers (.357), Giants.

Linescores

Game 1—October 8, at New York
Boston ....0 0 0 0 0 1 3 0 0 — 4 6 1
New York ....0 0 2 0 0 0 0 0 1 — 3 8 1
Wood; Tesreau, Crandall (8). W—Wood.
L—Tesreau.

Game 2—October 9, at Boston
New York......0 1 0 1 0 0 0 3 0 1 0 — 6 11 5
Boston........3 0 0 1 0 0 0 1 0 — 6 10 1
Mathewson; Collins, Hall (8), Bedient (11). Game called after 11 innings because of darkness.

Game 3—October 10, at Boston
New York ....0 1 0 0 1 0 0 0 0 — 2 7 1
Boston ....0 0 0 0 0 0 0 0 1 — 1 7 0
Marquard; O'Brien, Bedient (9). W—Marquard.
L—O'Brien.

Game 4—October 11, at New York
Boston ....0 1 0 1 0 0 0 0 1 — 3 8 1
New York ....0 0 0 0 0 0 1 0 0 — 1 9 1
Wood; Tesreau, Ames (8). W—Wood. L—Tesreau.

Game 5—October 12, at Boston
New York ....0 0 0 0 0 0 1 0 0 — 1 3 11
Boston ....0 0 2 0 0 0 0 0 x — 2 5 1
Mathewson; Bedient. W—Bedient.
L—Mathewson.

Game 6—October 14, at New York
Boston ....0 2 0 0 0 0 0 0 0 — 2 7 2
New York ....5 0 0 0 0 0 0 0 x — 5 11 2
O'Brien, Collins (2); Marquard. W—Marquard.
L—O'Brien.

Game 7—October 15, at Boston
New York ....6 1 0 0 0 2 1 0 1 — 11 16 4
Boston ....0 1 0 0 0 0 2 1 0 — 4 9 3
Tesreau; Wood, Hall (2). W—Tesreau. L—Wood.
HR—Doyle (N.Y.); Gardner (Bos.).

Game 8—October 16, at Boston
New York ....0 0 1 0 0 0 0 0 0 1 — 2 9 2
Boston ....0 0 1 0 0 0 1 0 0 2 — 3 8 5
Mathewson; Bedient, Wood (8). W—Wood.
L—Mathewson.

HISTORY

FINAL STANDINGS

American League

Team	W	L	Pct.	GB
Philadelphia	96	57	.627	...
Washington	90	64	.584	6.5
Cleveland	86	66	.566	9.5
Boston	79	71	.527	15.5
Chicago	78	74	.513	17.5
Detroit	66	87	.431	30
New York	57	94	.377	38
St. Louis	57	96	.373	39

National League

Team	W	L	Pct.	GB
New York	101	51	.664	...
Philadelphia	88	63	.583	12.5
Chicago	88	65	.575	13.5
Pittsburgh	78	71	.523	21.5
Boston	69	82	.457	31.5
Brooklyn	65	84	.436	34.5
Cincinnati	64	89	.418	37.5
St. Louis	51	99	.340	49

SIGNIFICANT EVENTS

■ **January 22:** The Yankees, no longer tenants of Hilltop Park, received permission from the New York Giants to use the Polo Grounds as co-tenants.

■ **April 9:** The Dodgers lost their Ebbets Field debut to the Phillies, 1-0.

■ **April 10:** The A.L.'s New York team began life anew as the "Yankees," losing to Washington, 2-1, in the season opener.

■ **November 2:** The outlaw Federal League began its challenge as a third Major League when its Kansas City entry enticed Browns manager George Stovall to jump.

■ **December 9:** N.L. owners elected Pennsylvania Governor John K. Tener as their new president.

MEMORABLE MOMENTS

■ **May 14:** Walter Johnson's Major League-record 56-inning scoreless streak ended when the Washington righthander yielded a fourth-inning run to the Browns.

■ **August 28:** Johnson's 14-game winning streak came to an end when the Senators fell to Boston, 1-0, in 11 innings.

■ **September 29:** Johnson defeated the Athletics, 1-0, and closed his incredible season with a 36-7 record, 11 shutouts and a 1.14 ERA.

LEADERS

American League

BA: Ty Cobb, Det., .390.
Runs: Eddie Collins, Phil., 125.
Hits: Joe Jackson, Cle., 197.
TB: Sam Crawford, Det., 298.
HR: Frank Baker, Phil., 12.
RBI: Frank Baker, Phil., 117.
SB: Clyde Milan, Wash., 75.
Wins: Walter Johnson, Wash., 36.
ERA: Walter Johnson, Wash., 1.14.
CG: Walter Johnson, Wash., 29.
IP: Walter Johnson, Wash., 346.
SO: Walter Johnson, Wash., 243.

National League

BA: Jake Daubert, Brk., .350.
Runs: Max Carey, Pit.; Tommy Leach, Chi., 99.
Hits: Gavvy Cravath, Phil., 179.
TB: Gavvy Cravath, Phil., 298.
HR: Gavvy Cravath, Phil., 19.
RBI: Gavvy Cravath, Phil., 128.
SB: Max Carey, Pit., 61.
Wins: Tom Seaton, Phil., 27.
ERA: Christy Mathewson, N.Y., 2.06.
CG: Lefty Tyler, Bos., 28.
IP: Tom Seaton, Phil., 322.1.
SO: Tom Seaton, Phil., 168.

A.L. 20-game winners
Walter Johnson, Wash., 36-7
Cy Falkenberg, Cle., 23-10
Reb Russell, Chi., 22-16
Chief Bender, Phil., 21-10
Vean Gregg, Cle., 20-13
Jim Scott, Chi., 20-21

N.L. 20-game winners
Tom Seaton, Phil., 27-12
Christy Mathewson, N.Y., 25-11
Rube Marquard, N.Y., 23-10
Grover Alexander, Phil., 22-8
Jeff Tesreau, N.Y., 22-13
Babe Adams, Pit., 21-10
Larry Cheney, Chi., 21-14

A.L. 100 RBIs
Frank Baker, Phil., 117

N.L. 100 RBIs
Gavvy Cravath, Phil., 128

Chalmers MVP
A.L.: Walter Johnson, P, Wash.
N.L.: Jake Daubert, 1B, Brk.

WORLD SERIES

■ **Winner:** The Athletics needed only five games to win their third Series in four years and hand the Giants their third straight loss.

■ **Turning point:** Complete-game victories by A's pitchers Joe Bush and Chief Bender in Games 3 and 4, setting up Eddie Plank for the kill.

■ **Memorable moment:** A Game 2 pitching duel between Plank and Christy Mathewson. The Giants scored three runs in the 10th for a 3-0 win.

■ **Top guns:** Frank Baker (.450, 7 RBIs), Eddie Collins (.421), Athletics; Mathewson (19 IP, 0.95 ERA), Giants.

Linescores

Game 1—October 7, at New York
Philadelphia.... 0 0 0 3 2 0 0 1 0 — 6 11 1
New York........ 0 0 1 0 3 0 0 0 0 — 4 11 0
Bender; Marquard, Crandall (6), Tesreau (8).
W—Bender. L—Marquard. HR—Baker (Phil.).

Game 2—October 8, at Philadelphia
New York......... 0 0 0 0 0 0 0 0 0 3 — 3 7 2
Philadelphia..... 0 0 0 0 0 0 0 0 0 0 — 0 8 2
Mathewson; Plank. W—Mathewson. L—Plank.

Game 3—October 9, at New York
Philadelphia........ 3 2 0 0 0 0 2 1 0 — 8 12 1
New York............ 0 0 0 0 1 0 1 0 0 — 2 5 1
Bush; Tesreau, Crandall (7). W—Bush.
L—Tesreau. HR—Schang (Phil.).

Game 4—October 10, at Philadelphia
New York........... 0 0 0 0 0 0 3 2 0 — 5 8 2
Philadelphia....... 0 1 0 3 2 0 0 0 x — 6 9 0
Demaree, Marquard (5); Bender. W—Bender.
L—Demaree. HR—Merkle (N.Y.).

Game 5—October 11, at New York
Philadelphia........ 1 0 2 0 0 0 0 0 0 — 3 6 1
New York........... 0 0 0 0 1 0 0 0 0 — 1 2 2
Plank; Mathewson. W—Plank. L—Mathewson.

FINAL STANDINGS

American League

Team	W	L	Pct.	GB
Philadelphia	99	53	.651	...
Boston	91	62	.595	8.5
Washington	81	73	.526	19
Detroit	80	73	.523	19.5
St. Louis	71	82	.464	28.5
Chicago	70	84	.455	30
New York	70	84	.455	30
Cleveland	51	102	.333	48.5

National League

Team	W	L	Pct.	GB
Boston	94	59	.614	...
New York	84	70	.545	10.5
St. Louis	81	72	.529	13
Chicago	78	76	.506	16.5
Brooklyn	75	79	.487	19.5
Philadelphia	74	80	.481	20.5
Pittsburgh	69	85	.448	25.5
Cincinnati	60	94	.390	34.5

SIGNIFICANT EVENTS

■ **April 13:** The outlaw Federal League, claiming to be a Major League equal, opened play with Baltimore defeating Buffalo, 3-2.

■ **November 1:** Philadelphia's Connie Mack began dismantling his powerful Athletics team by asking waivers on Jack Coombs, Eddie Plank and Chief Bender.

■ **December 8:** Connie Mack continued his housecleaning by selling star second baseman Eddie Collins to the White Sox for $50,000.

MEMORABLE MOMENTS

■ **May 14:** Chicago's Jim Scott lost his no-hit bid and the game when the Senators scored on two 10th-inning hits for a 1-0 victory.

■ **July 11:** Young Babe Ruth pitched the Red Sox to a 4-3 victory over Cleveland in his Major League debut.

■ **July 17:** Giants 3, Pirates 1 as Rube Marquard outpitched Babe Adams in a 21-inning marathon.

■ **September 23:** The Reds snapped their team-record 19-game losing streak with a 3-0 victory over the Braves.

■ **September 27:** Cleveland's Napoleon Lajoie collected career hit No. 3,000, a double, and the Indians defeated the Yankees.

■ **September 29:** The Miracle Braves, who would finish with an incredible 68-19 rush, clinched their first N.L. pennant with a 3-2 victory over the Cubs.

■ **October 7:** The Indianapolis Hoosiers defeated St. Louis, 4-0, and claimed the Federal League pennant.

LEADERS

American League

BA: Ty Cobb, Det., .368.
Runs: Eddie Collins, Phil., 122.
Hits: Tris Speaker, Bos., 193.
TB: Tris Speaker, Bos., 287.
HR: Frank Baker, Phil., 9.
RBI: Sam Crawford, Det., 104.
SB: Fritz Maisel, N.Y., 74.
Wins: Walter Johnson, Wash., 28.
ERA: Dutch Leonard, Bos., 0.96.
CG: Walter Johnson, Wash., 33.
IP: Walter Johnson, Wash., 371.2.
SO: Walter Johnson, Wash., 225.

National League

BA: Jake Daubert, Brk., .329.
Runs: George Burns, N.Y., 100.
Hits: Sherry Magee, Phil., 171.
TB: Sherry Magee, Phil., 277.
HR: Gavvy Cravath, Phil., 19.
RBI: Sherry Magee, Phil., 103.
SB: George Burns, N.Y., 62.
Wins: Grover Alexander, Phil., 27.
ERA: Bill Doak, St.L., 1.72.
CG: Grover Alexander, Phil., 32.
IP: Grover Alexander, Phil., 355.
SO: Grover Alexander, Phil., 214.

A.L. 20-game winners
Walter Johnson, Wash., 28-18
Harry Coveleski, Det., 22-12
Ray Collins, Bos., 20-13

N.L. 20-game winners
Grover Alexander, Phil., 27-15
Bill James, Bos., 26-7
Dick Rudolph, Bos., 26-10

Jeff Tesreau, N.Y., 26-10
Christy Mathewson, N.Y., 24-13
Jeff Pfeffer, Brk., 23-12
Hippo Vaughn, Chi., 21-13
Erskine Mayer, Phil., 21-19
Larry Cheney, Chi., 20-18

A.L. 100 RBIs
Sam Crawford, Det., 104

N.L. 100 RBIs
Sherry Magee, Phil., 103
Gavvy Cravath, Phil., 100

Chalmers MVP
A.L.: Eddie Collins, 2B, Phil.
N.L.: Johnny Evers, 2B, Bos.

WORLD SERIES

■ **Winner:** The Braves punctuated their miracle pennant run with a shocking four-game sweep of the powerful Athletics.

■ **Turning point:** Boston's come-from-behind effort in Game 3 that produced a 5-4 victory in 12 innings. The Braves stayed alive by scoring two 10th-inning runs after falling behind in the top of the inning.

■ **Memorable moment:** A dramatic Game 2 pitching duel between Boston's Bill James and Eddie Plank. James won 1-0 on Les Mann's ninth-inning single.

■ **Top guns:** James (2-0, 0.00 ERA), Dick Rudolph (2-0, 0-50), Hank Gowdy (.545), Johnny Evers (.438), Braves.

Linescores

Game 1—October 9, at Philadelphia
Boston........... 0 2 0 0 1 3 0 1 0 — 7 11 2
Phil............. 0 1 0 0 0 0 0 0 1 — 1 5 0
Rudolph; Bender, Wyckoff (6). W—Rudolph.
L—Bender.

Game 2—October 10, at Philadelphia
Boston........... 0 0 0 0 0 0 0 0 1 — 1 7 1
Phil............. 0 0 0 0 0 0 0 2 1 — 0 2 1
James; Plank. W—James. L—Plank.

Game 3—October 12, at Boston
Phil........ 1 0 0 1 0 0 2 0 0 — 4 8 2
Boston...... 0 1 0 1 0 0 2 0 1 — 5 9 1
Bush; Tyler, James (11). W—James. L—Bush.
HR—Gowdy (Bos.).

Game 4—October 13, at Boston
Phil. .....0 0 0 0 1 0 0 0 0 — 1 7 0
Boston ....0 0 0 1 2 0 0 0 x — 3 6 0
Shawkey, Pennock (6); Rudolph. W—Rudolph.
L—Shawkey.

1914—Federal League

FINAL STANDINGS

Team	W	L	Pct.	GB
Indianapolis	88	65	.575	...
Chicago	87	67	.565	1.5
Baltimore	84	70	.545	4.5
Buffalo	80	71	.530	7
Brooklyn	77	77	.500	11.5
Kansas City	67	84	.444	20
Pittsburgh	64	86	.427	22.5
St. Louis	62	89	.411	25

SIGNIFICANT EVENT

■ **November 1:** After being released by A's boss Connie Mack, pitchers Eddie Plank (St. Louis) and Chief Bender (Baltimore) signed contracts to play in the second-year Federal League.

MEMORABLE MOMENTS

■ **April 13:** Baltimore pitcher Jack Quinn, working before an estimated crowd of 28,000 at new Terrapin Park, posted a 3-2 victory over Buffalo in the Federal League inaugural.

■ **April 23:** The Chicago Whales christened new Weeghman Park—the future Wrigley Field—with a 9-1 victory over the Kansas City Packers.

■ **September 19:** Brooklyn's Ed Lafitte pitched the Federal League's first no-hitter, beating the Packers 6-2.

■ **October 6:** An Indianapolis victory over St. Louis combined with a Chicago loss to Kansas City clinched the first Federal League pennant for the Hoosiers, who finished with an 88-65 record.

LEADERS

BA: Benny Kauff, Ind., .370
Runs: Benny Kauff, Ind., 120
Hits: Benny Kauff, Ind., 211
TB: Benny Kauff, Ind., 305
HR: Dutch Zwilling, Chi., 16
RBI: Frank LaPorte, Ind., 107
SB: Benny Kauff, Ind., 75
Wins: Claude Hendrix, Chi., 29
ERA: Claude Hendrix, Chi., 1.69
CG: Claude Hendrix, Chi., 34
IP: Cy Falkenberg, Ind., 377.1
SO: Cy Falkenberg, Ind., 236

20-game winners
Claude Hendrix, Chi., 29-10
Jack Quinn, Bal., 26-14
Tom Seaton, Brk., 25-14
Cy Falkenberg, Ind., 25-16
George Suggs, Bal., 24-14
Russ Ford, Buf., 21-6
Elmer Knetzer, Pit., 20-12
Gene Packard, K.C., 20-14

100 RBIs
Frank LaPorte, Ind., 107

1915—Federal League

FINAL STANDINGS

Team	W	L	Pct.	GB
Chicago	86	66	.566	...
St. Louis	87	67	.565	...
Pittsburgh	86	67	.562	0.5
Kansas City	81	72	.529	5.5
Newark	80	72	.526	6
Buffalo	74	78	.487	12
Brooklyn	70	82	.461	16
Baltimore	47	107	.305	40

SIGNIFICANT EVENTS

■ **January 5:** The Federal League filed a lawsuit challenging Organized Baseball as an illegal trust that should be dissolved.
■ **December 22:** Organized Baseball's costly two-year battle against the Federal League ended when a peace treaty was arranged and the outlaw circuit was disbanded.

MEMORABLE MOMENTS

■ **April 24:** Pittsburgh's Frank Allen held St. Louis hitless in the Rebels' 2-0 victory.
■ **May 15:** Chicago's Claude Hendrix pitched a Whale of a game—a 10-0 no-hitter against Pittsburgh.
■ **July 31:** St. Louis' Dave Davenport pitched a pair of 1-0 games on the same day against Buffalo, winning the opener and dropping the nightcap.
■ **August 16, September 7:** Kansas City's Miles Main and St. Louis' Dave Davenport joined the no-hit fraternity. Main stopped Buffalo 5-0 and Davenport beat Chicago 3-0.
■ **October 3:** Chicago's season-ending victory over Pittsburgh clinched the second Federal League pennant—by an incredible .001 over St. Louis and a half game over the Rebels.

LEADERS

BA: Benny Kauff, Brk., .342
Runs: Babe Borton, St.L., 97
Hits: Jack Tobin, St.L., 184
TB: Ed Konetchy, Pit., 278
HR: Hal Chase, Buf., 17
RBI: Dutch Zwilling, Chi., 94
SB: Benny Kauff, Brk., 55
Wins: George McConnell, Chi., 25
ERA: Earl Moseley, New., 1.91
CG: Dave Davenport, St.L., 30
IP: Dave Davenport, St.L., 392.2
SO: Dave Davenport, St.L., 229

20-game winners
George McConnell, Chi., 25-10
Frank Allen, Pit., 23-13
Nick Cullop, K.C., 22-11
Dave Davenport, St.L., 22-18
Ed Reulbach, New., 21-10
Eddie Plank, St.L., 21-11
Al Schulz, Buf., 21-14
Doc Crandall, St.L., 21-15
Gene Packard, K.C., 20-12

1915

FINAL STANDINGS

American League

Team	W	L	Pct.	GB
Boston	101	50	.669	...
Detroit	100	54	.649	2.5
Chicago	93	61	.604	9.5
Washington	85	68	.556	17
New York	69	83	.454	32.5
St. Louis	63	91	.409	39.5
Cleveland	57	95	.375	44.5
Philadelphia	43	109	.283	58.5

National League

Team	W	L	Pct.	GB
Philadelphia	90	62	.592	...
Boston	83	69	.546	7
Brooklyn	80	72	.526	10
Chicago	73	80	.477	17.5
Pittsburgh	73	81	.474	18
St. Louis	72	81	.471	18.5
Cincinnati	71	83	.461	20
New York	69	83	.454	21

SIGNIFICANT EVENTS

■ **August 18:** Boston defeated St. Louis, 3-1, in the first game at new Braves Field.
■ **December 22:** Organized Baseball's costly two-year battle against the Federal League ended when a peace treaty was arranged and the outlaw circuit was disbanded.

MEMORABLE MOMENTS

■ **September 29:** Grover Cleveland Alexander pitched a one-hitter and his 12th shutout of the season as the Phillies clinched their first N.L. pennant with a 5-0 victory over the Braves.
■ **September 30:** The Red Sox clinched the A.L. pennant when the St. Louis Browns handed the Tigers an 8-2 loss in a game at Detroit.
■ **October 3:** Detroit's Ty Cobb, on his way to a record ninth consecutive A.L. batting title, stole his record 96th base in a 6-5 victory over Cleveland.

LEADERS

American League
BA: Ty Cobb, Det., .369.
Runs: Ty Cobb, Det., 144.
Hits: Ty Cobb, Det., 208.
TB: Ty Cobb, Det., 274.
HR: Braggo Roth, Chi.-Cle., 7.
RBI: Sam Crawford, Det.; Bobby Veach, Det., 112.
SB: Ty Cobb, Det., 96.
Wins: Walter Johnson, Wash., 27.
ERA: Joe Wood, Bos., 1.49.
CG: Walter Johnson, Wash., 35.
IP: Walter Johnson, Wash., 336.2.
SO: Walter Johnson, Wash., 203.

National League
BA: Larry Doyle, N.Y., .320.
Runs: Gavvy Cravath, Phil., 89.
Hits: Larry Doyle, N.Y., 189.
TB: Gavvy Cravath, Phil., 266.
HR: Gavvy Cravath, Phil., 24.
RBI: Gavvy Cravath, Phil., 115.
SB: Max Carey, Pit., 36.
Wins: Grover Alexander, Phil., 31.
ERA: Grover Alexander, Phil., 1.22.
CG: Grover Alexander, Phil., 36.
IP: Grover Alexander, Phil, 376.1
SO: Grover Alexander, Phil., 241.

A.L. 20-game winners
Walter Johnson, Wash., 27-13
Jim Scott, Chi., 24-11
Hooks Dauss, Det., 24-13
Red Faber, Chi., 24-14
Harry Coveleski, Det., 22-13

N.L. 20-game winners
Grover Alexander, Phil., 31-10
Dick Rudolph, Bos., 22-19
Al Mamaux, Pit., 21-8
Erskine Mayer, Phil., 21-15
Hippo Vaughn, Chi., 20-12

A.L. 100 RBIs
Sam Crawford, Det., 112
Bobby Veach, Det., 112

N.L. 100 RBIs
Gavvy Cravath, Phil., 115

WORLD SERIES

■ **Winner:** The Red Sox matched the Athletics as three-time Series winners with a five-game romp past another Philadelphia team — the Phillies.

■ **Turning point:** Dutch Leonard's 2-1 Game 3 victory over Phillies ace Grover Cleveland Alexander. The game was decided in the ninth inning on Duffy Lewis' RBI single.

■ **Memorable moment:** Harry Hooper's Series-deciding ninth-inning home run in Game 5 off Philadelphia reliever Eppa Rixey.

■ **Top guns:** Rube Foster (2-0, 2.00 ERA), Lewis (.444), Red Sox; Fred Luderus (.438), Phillies.

Linescores

Game 1—October 8, at Philadelphia
Boston........... 0 0 0 0 0 0 0 1 0 — 1 8 1
Philadelphia... 0 0 0 1 0 0 0 2 x — 3 5 1
Shore; Alexander. W—Alexander. L—Shore.

Game 2—October 9, at Philadelphia
Boston........... 1 0 0 0 0 0 0 0 1 — 2 10 0
Philadelphia... 0 0 0 0 1 0 0 0 0 — 1 3 1
Foster; Mayer. W—Foster. L—Mayer.

Game 3—October 11, at Boston
Philadelphia... 0 0 1 0 0 0 0 0 0 — 1 3 0
Boston........... 0 0 0 1 0 0 0 0 1 — 2 6 1
Alexander; Leonard. W—Leonard. L—Alexander.

Game 4—October 12, at Boston
Philadelphia... 0 0 0 0 0 0 0 1 0 — 1 7 0
Boston........... 0 0 1 0 0 1 0 0 x — 2 8 1
Chalmers; Shore. W—Shore. L—Chalmers.

Game 5—October 13, at Philadelphia
Boston........... 0 1 1 0 0 0 0 2 1 — 5 10 1
Philadelphia... 2 0 0 2 0 0 0 0 0 — 4 9 1
Foster; Mayer, Rixey (3). W—Foster. L—Rixey. HR—Hooper 2, Lewis (Bos.); Luderus (Phil.).

1916

FINAL STANDINGS

American League

Team	W	L	Pct.	GB
Boston	91	63	.591	...
Chicago	89	65	.578	2
Detroit	87	67	.565	4
New York	80	74	.519	11
St. Louis	79	75	.513	12
Cleveland	77	77	.500	14
Washington	76	77	.497	14.5
Philadelphia	36	117	.235	54.5

National League

Team	W	L	Pct.	GB
Brooklyn	94	60	.610	...
Philadelphia	91	62	.595	2.5
Boston	89	63	.586	4
New York	86	66	.566	7
Chicago	67	86	.438	26.5
Pittsburgh	65	89	.422	29
Cincinnati	60	93	.392	33.5
St. Louis	60	93	.392	33.5

SIGNIFICANT EVENTS

■ **July 20:** Giants great Christy Mathewson was traded to Cincinnati in a career-prolonging deal that allowed him to become manager of the Reds.
■ **November 1:** Harry Frazee, a New York theater owner and producer, bought the Red Sox for $675,000.

MEMORABLE MOMENTS

■ **August 9:** The Athletics' 20-game losing streak came to a merciful end when they defeated the Tigers, 7-1.
■ **September 30:** The Braves ended New York's winning streak at a Major League-record 26 games with an 8-3 victory in the second game of a doubleheader.
■ **October 2:** Grover Cleveland Alexander pitched the Phillies to a 2-0 victory over the Braves—his modern record 16th shutout of the season.

LEADERS

American League
BA: Tris Speaker, Cle., .386.
Runs: Ty Cobb, Det., 113.
Hits: Tris Speaker, Cle., 211.
TB: Joe Jackson, Chi., 293.
HR: Wally Pipp, N.Y., 12.
RBI: Del Pratt, St.L., 103.
SB: Ty Cobb, Det., 68.
Wins: Walter Johnson, Wash., 25.
ERA: Babe Ruth, Bos., 1.75.
CG: Walter Johnson, Wash., 36.
IP: Walter Johnson, Wash., 369.2.
SO: Walter Johnson, Wash., 228.

National League
BA: Hal Chase, Cin., .339.
Runs: George Burns, N.Y., 105.
Hits: Hal Chase, Cin., 184.
TB: Zack Wheat, Brk., 262.
HR: Dave Robertson, N.Y.; Cy Williams, Chi., 12.
RBI: Heinie Zimmerman, Chi.-N.Y., 83.
SB: Max Carey, Pit., 63.
Wins: Grover Alexander, Phil., 33.
ERA: Grover Alexander, Phil., 1.55.
CG: Grover Alexander, Phil., 38.
IP: Grover Alexander, Phil., 389.
SO: Grover Alexander, Phil., 167.

A.L. 20-game winners
Walter Johnson, Wash., 25-20
Bob Shawkey, N.Y., 24-14
Babe Ruth, Bos., 23-12
Harry Coveleski, Det., 21-11

N.L. 20-game winners
Grover Alexander, Phil., 33-12
Jeff Pfeffer, Brk., 25-11
Eppa Rixey, Phil., 22-10
Al Mamaux, Pit., 21-15

A.L. 100 RBIs
Del Pratt, St.L., 103

WORLD SERIES

■ **Winner:** Stingy Boston pitchers allowed only eight earned runs and the Red Sox closed down the Dodgers to become the first four-time Series winners.

■ **Turning point:** Larry Gardner's three-run Game 4 homer propelled Dutch Leonard to a 6-2 victory and the Red Sox to a 3-1 Series advantage.

■ **Memorable moment:** A 14-inning Game 2 pitching duel between Boston's Babe Ruth and Brooklyn's Sherry Smith. Ruth won 2-1 on Del Gainor's pinch-hit single.

■ **Top guns:** Eddie Shore (2-0, 1.53 ERA), Duffy Lewis (.353), Red Sox; Casey Stengel (.364), Dodgers.

Linescores

Game 1—October 7, at Boston
Brooklyn ....0 0 0 1 0 0 0 0 4 — 5 10 4
Boston ....0 0 1 0 1 0 3 1 x — 6 8 1
Marquard, Pfeffer (8); Shore, Mays (9). W—Shore. L—Marquard.

Game 2—October 9, at Boston
Brooklyn........1 0 0 0 0 0 0 0 0 0 0 0 0 0 — 1 6 2
Boston...........0 0 1 0 0 0 0 0 0 0 0 0 0 1 — 2 7 1
Smith; Ruth. W—Ruth. L—Smith. HR—Myers (Brk.).

Game 3—October 10, at Brooklyn
Boston ....0 0 0 0 0 2 1 0 0 — 3 7 1
Brooklyn..........................0 0 1 1 2 0 0 0 x — 4 10 0
Mays, Foster (6); Coombs, Pfeffer (7). W—Coombs. L—Mays. HR—Gardner (Bos.).

Game 4—October 11, at Brooklyn
Boston ....0 3 0 1 1 0 1 0 0 — 6 10 1
Brooklyn ....2 0 0 0 0 0 0 0 0 — 2 5 4
Leonard; Marquard, Cheney (5), Rucker (8). W—Leonard. L—Marquard. HR—Gardner (Bos.).

Game 5—October 12, at Boston
Brooklyn ....0 1 0 0 0 0 0 0 0 — 1 3 3
Boston ....0 1 2 0 1 0 0 0 x — 4 7 2
Pfeffer, Dell (8); Shore. W—Shore. L—Pfeffer.

FINAL STANDINGS

American League

Team	W	L	Pct.	GB
Chicago	100	54	.649	...
Boston	90	62	.592	9
Cleveland	88	66	.571	12
Detroit	78	75	.510	21.5
Washington	74	79	.484	25.5
New York	71	82	.464	28.5
St. Louis	57	97	.370	43
Philadelphia	55	98	.359	44.5

National League

Team	W	L	Pct.	GB
New York	98	56	.636	...
Philadelphia	87	65	.572	10
St. Louis	82	70	.539	15
Cincinnati	78	76	.506	20
Chicago	74	80	.481	24
Boston	72	81	.471	25.5
Brooklyn	70	81	.464	26.5
Pittsburgh	51	103	.331	47

SIGNIFICANT EVENTS

■ **October 26:** New York owner Jacob Ruppert took a dynastic step when he signed former Cardinals manager Miller Huggins to manage the Yankees.

MEMORABLE MOMENTS

■ **April 14:** Chicago ace Eddie Cicotte kicked off the season's no-hitter parade with an 11-0 victory over St. Louis. Cicotte's no-hitter was the first of five in the American League.

■ **May 2:** Cincinnati's Fred Toney and Chicago's Hippo Vaughn matched no-hitters for an unprecedented nine innings before Vaughn wilted in the 10th and the Reds scored a 1-0 victory.

■ **May 6:** Browns pitcher Bob Groom pitched a 3-0 no-hitter against the White Sox, matching the previous-day feat of teammate Ernie Koob in a 1-0 victory over Chicago.

■ **June 23:** Boston's Ernie Shore retired 27 consecutive Senators after replacing starter Babe Ruth, who was ejected after walking the first batter of the game. The runner was thrown out trying to steal and Shore went on to claim a 4-0 victory.

■ **September 3:** Grover Alexander, en route to a Major League-leading 30 victories, pitched both ends of the Phillies' 6-0 and 9-3 doubleheader sweep of Brooklyn.

LEADERS

American League

BA: Ty Cobb, Det., .383.
Runs: Donie Bush, Det., 112.
Hits: Ty Cobb, Det., 225.
TB: Ty Cobb, Det., 335.
HR: Wally Pipp, N.Y., 9.
RBI: Bobby Veach, Det., 103.
SB: Ty Cobb, Det., 55.
Wins: Eddie Cicotte, Chi., 28.
ERA: Eddie Cicotte, Chi., 1.53.
CG: Babe Ruth, Bos., 35.
IP: Eddie Cicotte, Chi., 346.2.
SO: Walter Johnson, Wash., 188.

National League

BA: Edd Roush, Cin., .341.
Runs: George Burns, N.Y., 103.
Hits: Heinie Groh, Cin., 182.
TB: Rogers Hornsby, St.L., 253.
HR: Gavvy Cravath, Phil.; Dave Robertson, N.Y., 12.
RBI: Heinie Zimmerman, N.Y., 102.
SB: Max Carey, Pit., 46.
Wins: Grover Alexander, Phil., 30.
ERA: Fred Anderson, N.Y., 1.44.
CG: Grover Alexander, Phil., 34.
IP: Grover Alexander, Phil., 388.
SO: Grover Alexander, Phil., 200.

A.L. 20-game winners

Ed Cicotte, Chi., 28-12
Babe Ruth, Bos., 24-13
Jim Bagby, Cle., 23-13
Walter Johnson, Wash., 23-16
Carl Mays, Bos., 22-9

N.L. 20-game winners

Grover Alexander, Phil., 30-13
Fred Toney, Cin., 24-16
Hippo Vaughn, Chi., 23-13
Ferdie Schupp, N.Y., 21-7
Pete Schneider, Cin., 20-19

A.L. 100 RBIs

Bobby Veach, Det., 103
Ty Cobb, Det., 102
Happy Felsch, Chi., 102

N.L. 100 RBIs

Heinie Zimmerman, N.Y., 102

WORLD SERIES

■ **Winner:** The White Sox, making their first Series appearance since 1906, took advantage of the Giants' sloppy play for a six-game victory.

■ **Turning point:** The White Sox rallied for six seventh and eighth-inning runs to claim an 8-5 victory in the pivotal fifth game.

■ **Memorable moment:** Third baseman Heinie Zimmerman giving futile chase to Chicago's Eddie Collins as he bolted toward the uncovered plate on one of several Game 6 fielding gaffes by the Giants. The White Sox closed out the Series with a 4-2 victory.

■ **Top guns:** Red Faber (3-1), Collins (.409), White Sox; Dave Robertson (.500), Giants.

Linescores

Game 1—October 6, at Chicago
New York........ 0 0 0 0 1 0 0 0 0 — 1 7 1
Chicago .... 0 0 1 1 0 0 0 0 x — 2 7 1
Sallee; Cicotte. W—Cicotte. L—Sallee. HR—Felsch (Chi.).

Game 2—October 7, at Chicago
New York........ 0 2 0 0 0 0 0 0 0 — 2 8 1
Chicago .... 0 2 0 5 0 0 0 0 x — 7 14 1
Schupp, Anderson (2), Perritt (4), Tesreau (8); Faber. W—Faber. L—Anderson.

Game 3—October 10, at New York
Chicago.......... 0 0 0 0 0 0 0 0 0 — 0 5 3
New York........ 0 0 0 2 0 0 0 0 x — 2 8 2
Cicotte; Benton. W—Benton. L—Cicotte.

Game 4—October 11, at New York
Chicago.......... 0 0 0 0 0 0 0 0 0 — 0 7 0
New York........ 0 0 0 1 1 0 1 2 x — 5 10 1
Faber, Danforth (8); Schupp. W—Schupp. L—Faber. HR—Kauff 2 (N.Y.).

Game 5—October 13, at Chicago
New York........ 2 0 0 2 0 0 1 0 0 — 5 12 3
Chicago .... 0 0 1 0 0 1 3 3 x — 8 14 6
Sallee, Perritt (8); Russell, Cicotte (1), Williams (7), Faber (8). W—Faber. L—Sallee.

Game 6—October 15, at New York
Chicago.......... 0 0 0 3 0 0 0 0 1 — 4 7 1
New York........ 0 0 0 0 0 0 2 0 0 — 2 6 3
Faber; Benton, Perritt (6). W—Faber. L—Benton.

FINAL STANDINGS

American League

Team	W	L	Pct.	GB
Boston	75	51	.595	...
Cleveland	73	54	.575	2.5
Washington	72	56	.563	4
New York	60	63	.488	13.5
St. Louis	58	64	.475	15
Chicago	57	67	.460	17
Detroit	55	71	.437	20
Philadelphia	52	76	.406	24

National League

Team	W	L	Pct.	GB
Chicago	84	45	.651	...
New York	71	53	.573	10.5
Cincinnati	68	60	.531	15.5
Pittsburgh	65	60	.520	17
Brooklyn	57	69	.452	25.5
Philadelphia	55	68	.447	26
Boston	53	71	.427	28.5
St. Louis	51	78	.395	33

SIGNIFICANT EVENTS

■ **April 30:** Cubs great Grover Cleveland Alexander answered the draft call and reported for World War I duty with the Army.

■ **May 14:** Washington D.C. officials repealed the ban against night baseball in the nation's capital, citing the need for more wartime recreational outlets.

■ **July 19:** U.S. Secretary of War Newton Baker issued a "Work or Fight" order forcing all able-bodied Americans into jobs considered essential to the war.

■ **August 2:** A.L. and N.L. officials voted to close down the regular season by September 2 (Labor Day) with the World Series to follow immediately.

■ **October 5:** Infielder Eddie Grant became baseball's first war casualty when he was killed during action in France.

■ **December 10:** N.L. secretary John Heydler was selected to replace John K. Tener as the league's new president.

MEMORABLE MOMENTS

■ **April 15:** Babe Ruth got the Red Sox's season off to a rousing start with an opening day 7-1 victory over the A's.

■ **June 3:** Boston's Dutch Leonard pitched the season's only no-hitter, beating the Tigers 5-0 with the aide of a Babe Ruth home run.

■ **August 31:** Babe Ruth pitched the Red Sox to an A.L. pennant-clinching 6-1 victory over the Athletics.

LEADERS

American League

BA: Ty Cobb, Det., .382.
Runs: Ray Chapman, Cle., 84.
Hits: George Burns, Phil., 178.
TB: George Burns, Phil., 236.
HR: Babe Ruth, Bos.; Tilly Walker, Phil., 11.
RBI: Bobby Veach, Det., 78.
SB: George Sisler, St.L., 45.
Wins: Walter Johnson, Wash., 23.
ERA: Walter Johnson, Wash., 1.27.
CG: Carl Mays, Bos.; Scott Perry, Phil., 30.
IP: Scott Perry, Phil., 332.1.
SO: Walter Johnson, Wash., 162.

National League

BA: Zack Wheat, Brk., .335.
Runs: Heinie Groh, Cin., 86.
Hits: Charlie Hollocher, Chi., 161.
TB: Charlie Hollocher, Chi., 202.
HR: Gavvy Cravath, Phil., 8.
RBI: Sherry Magee, Cin., 76.
SB: Max Carey, Pit., 58.
Wins: Hippo Vaughn, Chi., 22.
ERA: Hippo Vaughn, Chi., 1.74.
CG: Art Nehf, Bos., 28.
IP: Hippo Vaughn, Chi., 290.1.
SO: Hippo Vaughn, Chi., 148.

A.L. 20-game winners

Walter Johnson, Wash., 23-13
Stan Coveleski, Cle., 22-13
Carl Mays, Bos., 21-13
Scott Perry, Phil., 20-19

N.L. 20-game winners

Hippo Vaughn, Chi., 22-10
Claude Hendrix, Chi., 20-7

WORLD SERIES

■ **Winner:** The Red Sox ended baseball's war-depleted season by defeating the Cubs and winning their fifth Series in as many tries.

■ **Turning point:** Babe Ruth's second victory, a 3-2 Game 4 decision that gave the Red Sox a three games to one advantage.

■ **Memorable moment:** A Game 6 delay while players haggled with the owners over gate receipts. The Red Sox closed out the Cubs with a 2-1 victory.

■ **Top guns:** Carl Mays (2-0, 1.00 ERA), Ruth (2-0, 1.06), Red Sox; Charlie Pick (.389), Cubs.

Linescores

Game 1—September 5, at Chicago
Boston ....0 0 0 1 0 0 0 0 0 — 1 5 0
Chicago ....0 0 0 0 0 0 0 0 0 — 0 6 0
Ruth; Vaughn. W—Ruth. L—Vaughn.

Game 2—September 6, at Chicago
Boston ....0 0 0 0 0 0 0 0 1 — 1 6 1
Chicago ....0 3 0 0 0 0 0 0 x — 3 7 1
Bush; Tyler. W—Tyler. L—Bush.

Game 3—September 7, at Chicago
Boston ....0 0 0 2 0 0 0 0 0 — 2 7 0
Chicago ....0 0 0 0 1 0 0 0 0 — 1 7 1
Mays; Vaughn. W—Mays. L—Vaughn.

Game 4—September 9, at Boston
Chicago.........0 0 0 0 0 0 0 2 0 — 2 7 1
Boston...........0 0 0 2 0 0 1 0 x — 3 4 0
Tyler, Douglas (8); Ruth, Bush (9). W—Ruth. L—Douglas.

Game 5—September 10, at Boston
Chicago.........0 0 1 0 0 0 0 2 0 — 3 7 0
Boston ....0 0 0 0 0 0 0 0 0 — 0 5 0
Vaughn; Jones. W—Vaughn. L—Jones.

Game 6—September 11, at Boston
Chicago.........0 0 0 1 0 0 0 0 0 — 1 3 2
Boston...........0 0 2 0 0 0 0 0 x — 2 5 0
Tyler, Hendrix (8); Mays. W—Mays. L—Tyler.

1919

FINAL STANDINGS

American League

Team	W	L	Pct.	GB
Chicago	88	52	.629	...
Cleveland	84	55	.604	3.5
New York	80	59	.576	7.5
Detroit	80	60	.571	8
St. Louis	67	72	.482	20.5
Boston	66	71	.482	20.5
Washington	56	84	.400	32
Philadelphia	36	104	.257	52

National League

Team	W	L	Pct.	GB
Cincinnati	96	44	.686	...
New York	87	53	.621	9
Chicago	75	65	.536	21
Pittsburgh	71	68	.511	24.5
Brooklyn	69	71	.493	27
Boston	57	82	.410	38.5
St. Louis	54	83	.394	40.5
Philadelphia	47	90	.343	47.5

SIGNIFICANT EVENTS

■ **April 19:** New York Governor Al Smith signed a bill permitting Sunday baseball throughout the state.
■ **April 23:** The slimmed-down 140-game Major League schedule opened in Washington, where Walter Johnson shut out the A's, 1-0.
■ **September 2:** Major League officials approved a best-of-nine World Series format, replacing the long-running seven-game format.

MEMORABLE MOMENTS

■ **September 16:** The Reds defeated the Giants, 4-3, and clinched their first N.L. pennant of the century.
■ **September 24:** The White Sox captured their second A.L. pennant in three years when they defeated St. Louis, 6-5.
■ **September 27:** Boston's Babe Ruth stretched his one-season home run record to 29 in a game at Washington.

LEADERS

American League
BA: Ty Cobb, Det., .384.
Runs: Babe Ruth, Bos., 103.
Hits: Ty Cobb, Det.; Bobby Veach, Det., 191.
TB: Babe Ruth, Bos., 284.
HR: Babe Ruth, Bos., 29.
RBI: Babe Ruth, Bos., 114.
SB: Eddie Collins, Chi., 33.
Wins: Eddie Cicotte, Chi., 29.
ERA: Walter Johnson, Wash., 1.49.
CG: Eddie Cicotte, Chi., 30.
IP: Eddie Cicotte, Chi.; Jim Shaw, Wash., 306.2.
SO: Walter Johnson, Wash., 147.

National League
BA: Gavvy Cravath, Phil., .341.
Runs: George Burns, N.Y., 86.
Hits: Ivy Olson, Brk., 164.
TB: Hy Myers, Brk., 223.
HR: Gavvy Cravath, Phil., 12.
RBI: Hy Myers, Brk., 73.
SB: George Burns, N.Y., 40.
Wins: Jesse Barnes, N.Y., 25.
ERA: Grover Alexander, Chi., 1.72.
CG: Wilbur Cooper, Pit., 27.
IP: Hippo Vaughn, Chi., 306.2.
SO: Hippo Vaughn, Chi., 141.

A.L. 20-game winners
Ed Cicotte, Chi., 29-7
Stan Coveleski, Cle., 24-12
Lefty Williams, Chi., 23-11
Hooks Dauss, Det., 21-9
Allen Sothoron, St.L., 20-12
Bob Shawkey, N.Y., 20-11
Walter Johnson, Wash., 20-14

N.L. 20-game winners
Jess Barnes, N.Y., 25-9
Slim Sallee, Cin., 21-7
Hippo Vaughn, Chi., 21-14

A.L. 100 RBIs
Babe Ruth, Bos., 114
Bobby Veach, Det., 101

WORLD SERIES

■ **Winner:** The Reds earned their first Series victory amid suspicions the White Sox were consorting with gamblers in a fall classic fix.

■ **Turning point:** The Series' first pitch, when Chicago starter Eddie Cicotte hit Cincinnati leadoff man Morrie Rath, reportedly signaling to bettors the fix was on.

■ **Memorable moment:** White Sox lefthander Dickey Kerr, suspecting something was brewing among his teammates, fired a heroic three-hit shutout in Game 3.

■ **Top guns:** Hod Eller (2-0, 2.00 ERA), Greasy Neale (.357), Reds; Kerr (2-0, 1.42), White Sox.

Linescores
Game 1—October 1, at Cincinnati
Chicago .... 0 1 0 0 0 0 0 0 0 — 1 6 1
Cincinnati .... 1 0 0 5 0 0 2 1 x — 9 14 1
Cicotte, Wilkinson (4), Lowdermilk (8); Ruether.
W—Ruether. L—Cicotte.

Game 2—October 2, at Cincinnati
Chicago .... 0 0 0 0 0 0 2 0 0 — 2 10 1
Cincinnati .... 0 0 0 3 0 1 0 0 x — 4 4 2
Williams; Sallee. W—Sallee. L—Williams.

Game 3—October 3, at Chicago
Cincinnati .... 0 0 0 0 0 0 0 0 0 — 0 3 1
Chicago .... 0 2 0 1 0 0 0 0 x — 3 7 0
Fisher, Luque (8); Kerr. W—Kerr. L—Fisher.

Game 4—October 4, at Chicago
Cincinnati .... 0 0 0 0 2 0 0 0 0 — 2 5 2
Chicago .... 0 0 0 0 0 0 0 0 0 — 0 3 2
Ring; Cicotte. W—Ring. L—Cicotte.

Game 5—October 6, at Chicago
Cincinnati .... 0 0 0 0 0 4 0 0 1 — 5 4 0
Chicago .... 0 0 0 0 0 0 0 0 0 — 0 3 3
Eller; Williams, Mayer (9). W—Eller. L—Williams.

Game 6—October 7, at Cincinnati
Chicago .... 0 0 0 0 1 3 0 0 0 1—5 10 3
Cincinnati .... 0 0 2 2 0 0 0 0 0—4 11 0
Kerr; Ruether, Ring (6). W—Kerr. L—Ring.

Game 7—October 8, at Cincinnati
Chicago .... 1 0 1 0 2 0 0 0 0 — 4 10 1
Cincinnati .... 0 0 0 0 0 1 0 0 0 — 1 7 4
Cicotte; Sallee, Fisher (5), Luque (6). W—Cicotte.
L—Sallee.

Game 8—October 9, at Chicago
Cincinnati .... 4 1 0 0 1 3 0 1 0 — 10 16 2
Chicago .... 0 0 1 0 0 0 0 4 0 — 5 10 1
Eller; Williams, James (1), Wilkinson (6).
W—Eller. L—Williams. HR—Jackson (Chi.).

1920

FINAL STANDINGS

American League

Team	W	L	Pct.	GB
Cleveland	98	56	.636	...
Chicago	96	58	.623	2
New York	95	59	.617	3
St. Louis	76	77	.497	21.5
Boston	72	81	.471	25.5
Washington	68	84	.447	29
Detroit	61	93	.396	37
Philadelphia	48	106	.312	50

National League

Team	W	L	Pct.	GB
Brooklyn	93	61	.604	...
New York	86	68	.558	7
Cincinnati	82	71	.536	10.5
Pittsburgh	79	75	.513	14
Chicago	75	79	.487	18
St. Louis	75	79	.487	18
Boston	62	90	.408	30
Philadelphia	62	91	.405	30.5

SIGNIFICANT EVENTS

■ **January 5:** The New York Yankees acquired pitcher-outfielder Babe Ruth from Boston Red Sox owner Harry Frazee for the incredible price of $125,000.
■ **February 9:** Baseball's joint rules committee banned the use of all foreign substances and ball-doctoring methods used by pitchers.
■ **September 28:** A Chicago grand jury indicted eight White Sox players, including star center fielder Joe Jackson, for conspiring to fix the 1919 World Series. All eight were immediately suspended by Chicago owner Charles Comiskey.

MEMORABLE MOMENTS

■ **May 1:** Boston's Joe Oeschger and Brooklyn's Leon Cadore traded pitches for a Major League-record 26 innings in a game that ended in a 1-1 tie at Braves Field.
■ **May 14:** Washington great Walter Johnson defeated Detroit for his 300th career victory.
■ **August 17:** Cleveland shortstop Ray Chapman died a day after he was hit on the head by a pitch from Yankee righthander Carl Mays.
■ **October 2:** Pittsburgh and Cincinnati played the century's only tripleheader.
■ **October 3:** Browns first baseman George Sisler collected his record-setting 257th hit of the season.

LEADERS

American League
BA: George Sisler, St.L., .407.
Runs: Babe Ruth, N.Y., 158.
Hits: George Sisler, St.L., 257.
TB: George Sisler, St.L., 399.
HR: Babe Ruth, N.Y., 54.
RBI: Babe Ruth, N.Y., 137.
SB: Sam Rice, Wash., 63.
Wins: Jim Bagby, Cle., 31.
ERA: Bob Shawkey, N.Y., 2.45.
CG: Jim Bagby, Cle., 30.
IP: Jim Bagby, Cle., 339.2.
SO: Stan Coveleski, Cle., 133.

National League
BA: Rogers Hornsby, St.L., .370.
Runs: George Burns, N.Y., 115.
Hits: Rogers Hornsby, St.L., 218.
TB: Rogers Hornsby, St.L., 329.
HR: Cy Williams, Phil., 15.
RBI: Rogers Hornsby, St.L.; George Kelly, N.Y., 94.
SB: Max Carey, Pit., 52.
Wins: Grover Alexander, Chi., 27.
ERA: Grover Alexander, Chi., 1.91.
CG: Grover Alexander, Chi., 33.
IP: Grover Alexander, Chi., 363.1.
SO: Grover Alexander, Chi., 173.

A.L. 20-game winners
Jim Bagby, Cle., 31-12
Carl Mays, N.Y., 26-11
Stan Coveleski, Cle., 24-14
Red Faber, Chi., 23-13
Lefty Williams, Chi., 22-14
Dickie Kerr, Chi., 21-9
Ed Cicotte, Chi., 21-10
Ray Caldwell, Cle., 20-10
Urban Shocker, St.L., 20-10
Bob Shawkey, N.Y., 20-13

N.L. 20-game winners
Grover Alexander, Chi., 27-14
Wilbur Cooper, Pit., 24-15
Burleigh Grimes, Brk., 23-11
Fred Toney, N.Y., 21-11
Art Nehf, N.Y., 21-12
Bill Doak, St.L., 20-12
Jess Barnes, N.Y., 20-15

A.L. 100 RBIs
Babe Ruth, N.Y., 137
Bill Jacobson, St.L., 122
George Sisler, St.L., 122
Joe Jackson, Chi., 121
Larry Gardner, Cle., 118
Happy Felsch, Chi., 115
Bobby Veach, Det., 113
Tris Speaker, Cle., 107
Elmer Smith, Cle., 103

A.L. 40 homers
Babe Ruth, N.Y., 54

WORLD SERIES

■ **Winner:** The Indians, Series newcomers, held off the Dodgers in a seven-game fall classic filled with memorable firsts.

■ **Turning point:** Stan Coveleski's second win, a 5-1 Game 4 decision, that knotted the Series at two and set up a dramatic Game 5.

■ **Memorable moments:** There were several for the Indians in Game 5. Elmer Smith hit the first grand slam in Series history, Jim Bagby became the first pitcher to hit a Series homer and second baseman Bill Wambsganss pulled off the first Series triple play — unassisted.

■ **Top guns:** Coveleski (3-0, 0.67 ERA), Smith (.308, 5 RBIs), Indians; Zack Wheat (.333), Dodgers.

Linescores
Game 1—October 5, at Brooklyn
Cleveland .... 0 2 0 1 0 0 0 0 0 — 3 5 0
Brooklyn .... 0 0 0 0 0 0 1 0 0 — 1 5 1
Coveleski; Marquard, Mamaux (7), Cadore (9).
W—Coveleski. L—Marquard.

Game 2—October 6, at Brooklyn
Cleveland .... 0 0 0 0 0 0 0 0 0 — 0 7 1
Brooklyn .... 1 0 1 0 1 0 0 0 x — 3 7 0
Bagby, Uhle (7); Grimes. W—Grimes. L—Bagby.

Game 3—October 7, at Brooklyn
Cleveland .... 0 0 0 1 0 0 0 0 0 — 1 3 1
Brooklyn .... 2 0 0 0 0 0 0 0 x — 2 6 1
Caldwell, Mails (1), Uhle (8); S. Smith.
W—S. Smith. L—Caldwell.

Game 4—October 9, at Cleveland
Brooklyn .... 0 0 0 1 0 0 0 0 0 — 1 5 1
Cleveland .... 2 0 2 0 0 1 0 0 x — 5 12 2
Cadore, Mamaux (2), Marquard (3), Pfeffer (6);
Coveleski. W—Coveleski. L—Cadore.

Game 5—October 10, at Cleveland
Brooklyn .... 0 0 0 0 0 0 0 0 1 — 1 13 1
Cleveland .... 4 0 0 3 1 0 0 0 x — 8 12 2
Grimes, Mitchell (4); Bagby. W—Bagby.
L—Grimes. HR—E. Smith, Bagby (Cle.).

Game 6—October 11, at Cleveland
Brooklyn .... 0 0 0 0 0 0 0 0 0 — 0 3 0
Cleveland .... 0 0 0 0 0 1 0 0 x — 1 7 3
S. Smith; Mails. W—Mails. L—S. Smith.

Game 7—October 12, at Cleveland
Brooklyn .... 0 0 0 0 0 0 0 0 0 — 0 5 2
Cleveland .... 0 0 0 1 1 0 1 0 x — 3 7 3
Grimes, Mamaux (8); Coveleski. W—Coveleski.
L—Grimes.

HISTORY

FINAL STANDINGS

American League

Team	W	L	Pct.	GB
New York	98	55	.641	...
Cleveland	94	60	.610	4.5
St. Louis	81	73	.526	17.5
Washington	80	73	.523	18
Boston	75	79	.487	23.5
Detroit	71	82	.464	27
Chicago	62	92	.403	36.5
Philadelphia	53	100	.346	45

National League

Team	W	L	Pct.	GB
New York	94	59	.614	...
Pittsburgh	90	63	.588	4
St. Louis	87	66	.569	7
Boston	79	74	.516	15
Brooklyn	77	75	.507	16.5
Cincinnati	70	83	.458	24
Chicago	64	89	.418	30
Philadelphia	51	103	.331	43.5

SIGNIFICANT EVENTS

■ **January 21:** Federal Judge Kenesaw Mountain Landis began his seven-year contract as baseball's first commissioner.
■ **August 3:** Commissioner Landis banned eight Chicago White Sox players from baseball for life, even though a Chicago jury had cleared them of charges that they conspired to fix the 1919 World Series.
■ **August 5:** Pittsburgh radio station KDKA did the first Major League baseball broadcast—a Pirates-Phillies game at Forbes Field.
■ **October 5:** Pittsburgh radio station KDKA broadcast the opening game of the Yankees-Giants World Series.
■ **October 21:** Commissioner Landis suspended Babe Ruth and Yankee teammates Bob Meusel and Bill Piercy for their illegal barnstorming tour after the 1921 World Series.

MEMORABLE MOMENTS

■ **August 19:** Detroit's Ty Cobb collected career hit No. 3,000 off Boston pitcher Elmer Myers.
■ **October 2:** Babe Ruth connected for record home run No. 59 off Boston's Curt Fullerton.

LEADERS

American League

BA: Harry Heilmann, Det., .394.
Runs: Babe Ruth, N.Y., 177.
Hits: Harry Heilmann, Det., 237.
TB: Babe Ruth, N.Y., 457.
HR: Babe Ruth, N.Y., 59.
RBI: Babe Ruth, N.Y., 171.
SB: George Sisler, St.L., 35.
Wins: Carl Mays, N.Y.; Urban Shocker, St.L., 27.
ERA: Red Faber, Chi., 2.48.
CG: Red Faber, Chi., 32.
IP: Carl Mays, N.Y., 336.2.
SO: Walter Johnson, Wash., 143.

National League

BA: Rogers Hornsby, St.L., .397.
Runs: Rogers Hornsby, St.L., 131.
Hits: Rogers Hornsby, St.L., 235.
TB: Rogers Hornsby, St.L., 378.
HR: George Kelly, N.Y., 23.
RBI: Rogers Hornsby, St.L., 126.
SB: Frank Frisch, N.Y., 49.
Wins: Wilbur Cooper, Pit.; Burleigh Grimes, Brk., 22.
ERA: Bill Doak, St.L., 2.59.
CG: Burleigh Grimes, Brk., 30.
IP: Wilbur Cooper, Pit., 327.
SO: Burleigh Grimes, Brk., 136.

A.L. 20-game winners
Carl Mays, N.Y., 27-9
Urban Shocker, St.L., 27-12
Red Faber, Chi., 25-15
Stan Coveleski, Cle., 23-13
Sam Jones, Bos., 23-16

N.L. 20-game winners
Burleigh Grimes, Brk., 22-13
Wilbur Cooper, Pit., 22-14
Art Nehf, N.Y., 20-10
Joe Oeschger, Bos., 20-14

A.L. 100 RBIs
Babe Ruth, N.Y., 170
Harry Heilmann, Det., 139
Bob Meusel, N.Y., 135
Bobby Veach, Det., 128
Ken Williams, St.L., 117
Larry Gardner, Cle., 115
George Sisler, St.L., 104
Ty Cobb, Det., 101
Tilly Walker, Phil., 101
Del Pratt, Bos., 100

N.L. 100 RBIs
Rogers Hornsby, St.L., 126
George Kelly, N.Y., 122
Austin McHenry, St.L., 102
Ross Youngs, N.Y., 102
Frank Frisch, N.Y., 100

A.L. 40 homers
Babe Ruth, N.Y., 59

WORLD SERIES

■ **Winner:** The Giants shook the ghosts of Series past and rallied for an eight-game victory in the battle of New York.

■ **Turning point:** Down two games to none and trailing 4-0 in the third inning of Game 3, the Giants rallied for a 13-5 victory.

■ **Memorable moment:** An unusual 4-3-5 double play that finished off Art Nehf's 1-0 Game 8 victory over Yankee Waite Hoyt and provided a dramatic conclusion to the Series.

■ **Top guns:** Jesse Barnes (2-0, 1.65 ERA), Frank Snyder (.364), Irish Meusel (.345, 7 RBIs), Giants; Hoyt (2-1, 0.00), Yankees.

Linescores

Game 1—October 5, at Polo Grounds
Yankees.......... 1 0 0 0 1 1 0 0 0 — 3 7 0
Giants............ 0 0 0 0 0 0 0 0 0 — 0 5 0
Mays; Douglas, Barnes (9). W—Mays. L—Douglas.

Game 2—October 6, at Polo Grounds
Giants............ 0 0 0 0 0 0 0 0 0 — 0 2 3
Yankees.......... 0 0 0 1 0 0 0 2 x — 3 3 0
Nehf; Hoyt. W—Hoyt. L—Nehf.

Game 3—October 7, at Polo Grounds
Yankees.......... 0 0 4 0 0 0 0 1 0 — 5 8 0
Giants............ 0 0 4 0 0 0 8 1 x — 13 20 0
Shawkey, Quinn (3), Collins (7), Rogers (7); Toney, Barnes (3). W—Barnes. L—Quinn.

Game 4—October 9, at Polo Grounds
Giants............ 0 0 0 0 0 0 0 3 1 — 4 9 1
Yankees.......... 0 0 0 0 1 0 0 0 1 — 2 7 1
Douglas; Mays. W—Douglas. L—Mays. HR—Ruth (NYY).

Game 5—October 10, at Polo Grounds
Yankees.......... 0 0 1 2 0 0 0 0 0 — 3 6 1
Giants............ 1 0 0 0 0 0 0 0 0 — 1 10 1
Hoyt; Nehf. W—Hoyt. L—Nehf.

Game 6—October 11, at Polo Grounds
Giants............ 0 3 0 4 0 1 0 0 0 — 8 13 0
Yankees.......... 3 2 0 0 0 0 0 0 0 — 5 7 2
Toney, Barnes (1); Harper, Shawkey (2), Piercy (9). W—Barnes. L—Shawkey. HR—E. Meusel, Snyder (NYG); Fewster (NYY).

Game 7—October 12, at Polo Grounds
Yankees.......... 0 1 0 0 0 0 0 0 0 — 1 8 1
Giants............ 0 0 0 1 0 0 1 0 x — 2 6 0
Mays; Douglas. W—Douglas. L—Mays.

Game 8—October 13, at Polo Grounds
Giants............ 1 0 0 0 0 0 0 0 0 — 1 6 0
Yankees.......... 0 0 0 0 0 0 0 0 0 — 0 4 1
Nehf; Hoyt. W—Nehf. L—Hoyt.

FINAL STANDINGS

American League

Team	W	L	Pct.	GB
New York	94	60	.610	...
St. Louis	93	61	.604	1
Detroit	79	75	.513	15
Cleveland	78	76	.506	16
Chicago	77	77	.500	17
Washington	69	85	.448	25
Philadelphia	65	89	.422	29
Boston	61	93	.396	33

National League

Team	W	L	Pct.	GB
New York	93	61	.604	...
Cincinnati	86	68	.558	7
Pittsburgh	85	69	.552	8
St. Louis	85	69	.552	8
Chicago	80	74	.519	13
Brooklyn	76	78	.494	17
Philadelphia	57	96	.373	35.5
Boston	53	100	.346	39.5

SIGNIFICANT EVENTS

■ **March 5:** Babe Ruth signed a three-year Yankee contract for a record $52,000 per season.
■ **September 21:** Browns first baseman George Sisler, a .420 hitter, was the choice of A.L. baseball writers for the first MVP award presented since 1914.
■ **October:** The World Series returned to a best-of-seven format and the entire Series was broadcast over the radio.

MEMORABLE MOMENTS

■ **April 30:** Chicago rookie Charlie Robertson became the third modern-era pitcher to throw a perfect game, retiring all 27 Tigers he faced in a 2-0 victory at Detroit.
■ **May 7:** Giants righthander Jesse Barnes pitched a 6-0 no-hitter against Philadelphia, an effort blemished only by a fifth-inning walk.
■ **June 28:** Washington fireballer Walter Johnson outdueled New York ace Waite Hoyt and recorded his 95th career shutout with a 1-0 victory at Griffith Stadium.
■ **August 25:** Chicago and Philadelphia combined for a record 49 runs and 51 hits in the Cubs' 26-23 victory at Wrigley Field.
■ **September 18:** The New York Yankees ended George Sisler's modern-era record hitting streak at 41 games during a 3-2 victory over the Browns.
■ **October 1:** Cardinals second baseman Rogers Hornsby became baseball's third Triple Crown winner when he finished the season at .401 with 42 homers and 152 RBI.

LEADERS

American League

BA: George Sisler, St.L., .420.
Runs: George Sisler, St.L., 134.
Hits: George Sisler, St.L., 246.
TB: Ken Williams, St.L., 367.
HR: Ken Williams, St.L., 39.
RBI: Ken Williams, St.L., 155.
SB: George Sisler, St.L., 51.
Wins: Eddie Rommel, Phil., 27.
ERA: Red Faber, Chi., 2.81.
CG: Red Faber, Chi., 31.
IP: Red Faber, Chi., 352.
SO: Urban Shocker, St.L., 149.

National League

BA: Rogers Hornsby, St.L., .401.
Runs: Rogers Hornsby, St.L., 141.
Hits: Rogers Hornsby, St.L., 250.
TB: Rogers Hornsby, St.L., 450.
HR: Rogers Hornsby, St.L., 42.
RBI: Rogers Hornsby, St.L., 152.
SB: Max Carey, Pit., 51.
Wins: Eppa Rixey, Cin., 25.
ERA: Phil Douglas, N.Y., 2.63.
CG: Wilbur Cooper, Pit., 27.
IP: Eppa Rixey, Cin., 313.1.
SO: Dazzy Vance, Brk., 134.

A.L. 20-game winners
Eddie Rommel, Phil., 27-13
Joe Bush, N.Y., 26-7
Urban Shocker, St.L., 24-17
George Uhle, Cle., 22-16
Red Faber, Chi., 21-17
Bob Shawkey, N.Y., 20-12

N.L. 20-game winners
Eppa Rixey, Cin., 25-13

Wilbur Cooper, Pit., 23-14
Dutch Ruether, Brk., 21-12

A.L. 100 RBIs
Ken Williams, St.L., 155
Bobby Veach, Det., 126
Marty McManus, St.L., 109
George Sisler, St.L., 105
Bill Jacobson, St.L., 102

N.L. 100 RBIs
Rogers Hornsby, St.L., 152
Irish Meusel, N.Y., 132
Zack Wheat, Brk., 112
George Kelly, N.Y., 107

N.L 40 homers
Rogers Hornsby, St.L., 42

League MVP
A.L.: George Sisler, 1B, St.L.
N.L.: No selection.

WORLD SERIES

■ **Winner:** The all-New York rematch had the same result, the Giants winning this time in five games.

■ **Turning point:** A 3-3 Game 2 tie that took away the Yankees' best hope for a victory.

■ **Memorable moment:** Giants lefthander Art Nehf closing out the Yankees in the Series finale for the second straight year.

■ **Top guns:** Heinie Groh (.474), Frankie Frisch (.471), Irish Meusel (7 RBIs), Giants.

Linescores

Game 1—October 4, at Polo Grounds
Yankees.......... 0 0 0 0 0 1 1 0 0 — 2 7 0
Giants............ 0 0 0 0 0 0 0 3 x — 3 11 3
Bush, Hoyt (8); Nehf, Ryan (8). W—Ryan. L—Bush.

Game 2—October 5, at Polo Grounds
Giants............ 3 0 0 0 0 0 0 0 0 — 3 8 1
Yankees.......... 1 0 0 1 0 0 1 0 0 — 3 8 0
J. Barnes; Shawkey. HR—E. Meusel (NYG); Ward (NYY). Game called after 10 innings because of darkness.

Game 3—October 6, at Polo Grounds
Yankees.......... 0 0 0 0 0 0 0 0 0 — 0 4 1
Giants............ 0 0 2 0 0 0 1 0 x — 3 12 1
Hoyt, Jones (8); J. Scott. W—J. Scott. L—Hoyt.

Game 4—October 7, at Polo Grounds
Giants............ 0 0 0 0 4 0 0 0 0 — 4 9 1
Yankees.......... 2 0 0 0 0 0 1 0 0 — 3 8 0
McQuillan; Mays, Jones (9). W—McQuillan. L—Mays. HR—Ward (NYY).

Game 5—October 8, at Polo Grounds
Yankees.......... 1 0 0 0 1 0 1 0 0 — 3 5 0
Giants............ 0 2 0 0 0 0 0 3 x — 5 10 0
Bush; Nehf. W—Nehf. L—Bush.

FINAL STANDINGS

American League

Team	W	L	Pct.	GB
New York	98	54	.645	...
Detroit	83	71	.539	16
Cleveland	82	71	.536	16.5
Washington	75	78	.490	23.5
St. Louis	74	78	.487	24
Philadelphia	69	83	.454	29
Chicago	69	85	.448	30
Boston	61	91	.401	37

National League

Team	W	L	Pct.	GB
New York	95	58	.621	...
Cincinnati	91	63	.591	4.5
Pittsburgh	87	67	.565	8.5
Chicago	83	71	.539	12.5
St. Louis	79	74	.516	16
Brooklyn	76	78	.494	19.5
Boston	54	100	.351	41.5
Philadelphia	50	104	.325	45.5

SIGNIFICANT EVENTS

■ **April 18:** A Major League-record 74,217 fans watched Babe Ruth christen new Yankee Stadium with a three-run homer that sparked a 4-1 victory over Boston.

MEMORABLE MOMENTS

■ **May 2:** New York Yankee shortstop Everett Scott was honored when his ironman streak reached 1,000 games.

■ **May 11:** The Phillies defeated the Cardinals 20-14 in a game that featured 10 homers—three by Philadelphia's Cy Williams.

■ **July 7:** Cleveland, scoring in each of its eight at-bats, set an A.L. record for runs in a 27-3 victory over Boston.

■ **July 22:** Washington's Walter Johnson fanned five Indians and became the first pitcher to record 3,000 career strikeouts.

■ **September 7:** Boston's Howard Ehmke, duplicating the no-hit feat of New York Yankee Sam Jones three days earlier in the same stadium, stopped the Athletics 4-0 at Philadelphia.

■ **October 7:** St. Louis ended the regular season with a doubleheader split against the Cubs and Cardinals star Rogers Hornsby captured his fourth straight batting title with a .384 average.

LEADERS

American League

BA: Harry Heilmann, Det., .403.
Runs: Babe Ruth, N.Y., 151.
Hits: Charlie Jamieson, Cle., 222.
TB: Babe Ruth, N.Y., 399.
HR: Babe Ruth, N.Y., 41.
RBI: Babe Ruth, N.Y., 131.
SB: Eddie Collins, Chi., 49.
Wins: George Uhle, Cle., 26.
ERA: Stan Coveleski, Cle., 2.76.
CG: George Uhle, Cle., 29.
IP: George Uhle, Cle., 357.2.
SO: Walter Johnson, Wash., 130.

National League

BA: Rogers Hornsby, St.L., .384.
Runs: Ross Youngs, N.Y., 121.
Hits: Frank Frisch, N.Y., 223.
TB: Frank Frisch, N.Y., 311.
HR: Cy Williams, Phil., 41.
RBI: Irish Meusel, N.Y., 125.
SB: Max Carey, Pit., 51.
Wins: Dolf Luque, Cin., 27.
ERA: Dolf Luque, Cin., 1.93.
CG: Burleigh Grimes, Brk., 33.
IP: Burleigh Grimes, Brk., 327.
SO: Dazzy Vance, Brk., 197.

A.L. 20-game winners
George Uhle, Cle., 26-16
Sam Jones, N.Y., 21-8
Hooks Dauss, Det., 21-13
Urban Shocker, St.L., 20-12
Howard Ehmke, Bos., 20-17

N.L. 20-game winners
Dolf Luque, Cin., 27-8
Johnny Morrison, Pit., 25-13
Grover Alexander, Chi., 22-12
Pete Donohue, Cin., 21-15
Burleigh Grimes, Brk., 21-18

Jesse Haines, St.L., 20-13
Eppa Rixey, Cin., 20-15

A.L. 100 RBIs
Babe Ruth, N.Y., 130
Tris Speaker, Cle., 130
Harry Heilmann, Det., 115
Joe Sewell, Cle., 109
Wally Pipp, N.Y., 108

N.L. 100 RBIs
Irish Meusel, N.Y., 125
Cy Williams, Phil., 114

Frank Frisch, N.Y., 111
George Kelly, N.Y., 103
Jack Fournier, Brk., 102
Pie Traynor, Pit., 101

A.L. 40 homers
Babe Ruth, N.Y., 41

N.L. 40 homers
Cy Williams, Phil., 41

League MVP
A.L.: Babe Ruth, OF, N.Y.
N.L.: No selection.

WORLD SERIES

■ **Winner:** The third Series was a charm for the Yankees, who ascended to baseball's throne with a six-game victory over the Giants.

■ **Turning point:** A three-hit Game 5 performance by Joe Bush that helped the Yankees claim an 8-1 victory and a 3-2 Series lead.

■ **Memorable moment:** Veteran Casey Stengel chugging around the bases on a ninth-inning inside-the-park home run that gave the Giants a 5-4 Game 1 victory in the first Series contest at new Yankee Stadium.

■ **Top guns:** Aaron Ward (.417), Babe Ruth (.368, 3 HR), Yankees; Stengel (.417, 2 HR), Giants.

Linescores

Game 1—October 10, at Yankee Stadium
Giants............ 0 0 4 0 0 0 0 0 1 — 5 8 0
Yankees......... 1 2 0 0 0 0 1 0 0 — 4 12 1
Watson, Ryan (3); Bush (3). W—Ryan.
L—Bush. HR—Stengel (NYG).

Game 2—October 11, at Polo Grounds
Yankees........ 0 1 0 2 1 0 0 0 0 — 4 10 0
Giants........... 0 1 0 1 0 0 0 0 0 — 2 9 2
Pennock; McQuillan, Bentley (4). W—Pennock.
L—McQuillan. HR—Ward, Ruth 2 (NYY); E. Meusel (NYG).

Game 3—October 12, at Yankee Stadium
Giants............ 0 0 0 0 0 0 1 0 0 — 1 4 0
Yankees........ 0 0 0 0 0 0 0 0 0 — 0 6 1
Nehf; Jones, Bush (9). W—Nehf. L—Jones.
HR—Stengel (NYG).

Game 4—October 13, at Polo Grounds
Yankees............ 0 6 1 1 0 0 0 0 0 — 8 13 1
Giants............ 0 0 0 0 0 0 3 1 — 4 13 1
Shawkey, Pennock (8); J. Scott, Ryan (2), McQuillan (2), Jonnard (8), Barnes (8).
W—Shawkey. L—J. Scott. HR—Youngs (NYG).

Game 5—October 14, at Yankee Stadium
Giants............ 0 1 0 0 0 0 0 — 1 3 2
Yankees......... 3 4 0 1 0 0 0 x — 8 14 0
Bentley, J. Scott (2), Barnes (4), Jonnard (8).
Bush. W—Bush. L—Bentley. HR—Dugan (NYY).

Game 6—October 15, at Polo Grounds
Yankees......... 1 0 0 0 0 0 5 0 — 6 5 0
Giants............ 1 0 0 1 1 1 0 0 0 — 4 10 1
Pennock, Jones (8); Nehf, Ryan (8). W—Pennock.
L—Nehf. HR—Ruth (NYY); Snyder (NYG).

FINAL STANDINGS

American League

Team	W	L	Pct.	GB
Washington	92	62	.597	...
New York	89	63	.586	2
Detroit	86	68	.558	6
St. Louis	74	78	.487	17
Philadelphia	71	81	.467	20
Cleveland	67	86	.438	24.5
Boston	67	87	.435	25
Chicago	66	87	.431	25.5

National League

Team	W	L	Pct.	GB
New York	93	60	.608	...
Brooklyn	92	62	.597	1.5
Pittsburgh	90	63	.588	3
Cincinnati	83	70	.542	10
Chicago	81	72	.529	12
St. Louis	65	89	.422	28.5
Philadelphia	55	96	.364	37
Boston	53	100	.346	40

SIGNIFICANT EVENTS

■ **March 7:** Reds manager Pat Moran died of Bright's disease at a hospital in Orlando, Fla., the team's spring training home.

■ **December 10:** National League owners accepted a proposal to go to a 2-3-2 World Series format.

MEMORABLE MOMENTS

■ **June 13:** The Yankees were awarded a 9-0 forfeit victory over the Tigers when a ninth-inning players' fight escalated into a full-scale fan riot at Detroit's Navin Field, creating a life-threatening situation for players, umpires and police.

■ **July 16:** Giants first baseman George Kelly set a Major League record when he homered in his sixth consecutive game—an 8-7 victory over the Pirates.

■ **September 16:** Jim Bottomley collected six hits, belted two homers and drove in a single-game record 12 runs in St. Louis' 17-3 victory over Brooklyn.

■ **September 28:** Cardinals second baseman Rogers Hornsby finished the season with the highest average in baseball history—.424.

LEADERS

American League

BA: Babe Ruth, N.Y., .378.
Runs: Babe Ruth, N.Y., 143.
Hits: Sam Rice, Wash., 216.
TB: Babe Ruth, N.Y., 391.
HR: Babe Ruth, N.Y., 46.
RBI: Goose Goslin, Wash., 129.
SB: Eddie Collins, Chi., 42.
Wins: Walter Johnson, Wash., 23.
ERA: Walter Johnson, Wash., 2.72.
CG: Sloppy Thurston, Chi., 28.
IP: Howard Ehmke, Bos., 315.
SO: Walter Johnson, Wash., 158.

National League

BA: Rogers Hornsby, St.L., .424.
Runs: Frank Frisch, N.Y.;
Rogers Hornsby, St.L., 121.
Hits: Rogers Hornsby, St.L., 227.
TB: Rogers Hornsby, St.L., 373.
HR: Jack Fournier, Brk., 27.
RBI: George Kelly, N.Y., 136.
SB: Max Carey, Pit., 49.
Wins: Dazzy Vance, Brk., 28.
ERA: Dazzy Vance, Brk., 2.16.
CG: Burleigh Grimes, Brk.; Dazzy Vance, Brk., 30.
IP: Burleigh Grimes, Brk., 310.2.
SO: Dazzy Vance, Brk., 262.

A.L. 20-game winners
Walter Johnson, Wash., 23-7
Herb Pennock, N.Y., 21-9
Sloppy Thurston, Chi., 20-14
Joe Shaute, Cle., 20-17

N.L. 20-game winners
Dazzy Vance, Brk., 28-6
Burleigh Grimes, Brk., 22-13
Carl Mays, Cin., 20-9
Wilbur Cooper, Pit., 20-14

A.L. 100 RBIs
Goose Goslin, Wash., 129
Babe Ruth, N.Y., 121
Bob Meusel, N.Y., 120
Joe Hauser, Phil., 115
Harry Heilmann, Det., 113
Wally Pipp, N.Y., 113
Joe Sewell, Cle., 104
Earl Sheely, Chi., 103
Al Simmons, Phil., 102

N.L. 100 RBIs
George Kelly, N.Y., 136
Jack Fournier, Brk., 116
Jim Bottomley, St.L., 111
Glenn Wright, Pit., 111
Irish Meusel, N.Y., 102

A.L. 40 homers
Babe Ruth, N.Y., 46

League MVP
A.L.: Walter Johnson, P, Wash.
N.L.: Dazzy Vance, P, Brk.

WORLD SERIES

■ **Winner:** The Senators made their first appearance in baseball's fall classic a successful one.

■ **Turning point:** A dramatic 2-1 Game 6 victory that kept Washington's hopes alive. Tom Zachary allowed seven hits and player/manager Bucky Harris drove in both runs with a fifth-inning single.

■ **Memorable moment:** Earl McNeely's 12th-inning Game 7 ground ball that took an inexplicable bad hop over third baseman Fred Lindstrom's head and gave the Senators a Series-ending 4-3 victory.

■ **Top guns:** Zachary (2-0, 2.04 ERA), Goose Goslin (.344, 3 HR, 7 RBIs), Harris (.333, 7 RBIs), Senators; Bill Terry (.429), Giants.

Linescores

Game 1—October 4, at Washington
N.Y.,........0 1 0 1 0 0 0 0 2 — 4 14 1
Wash....0 0 0 0 0 1 0 0 1 0 0 1 — 3 10 1
Nehf; Johnson. W—Nehf. L—Johnson.
HR—Kelly, Terry (N.Y.).

Game 2—October 5, at Washington
N.Y. .... 0 0 0 0 0 0 1 0 2 — 3 6 0
Wash........... 2 0 0 1 0 0 0 0 1 — 4 6 1
Bentley; Zachary, Marberry (9). W—Zachary.
L—Bentley. HR—Goslin, Harris (Wash.).

Game 3—October 6, at New York
Wash............. 0 0 0 2 0 0 0 1 1 — 4 9 2
N.Y. .... 0 2 1 1 0 1 0 1 x — 6 12 0
Marberry, Russell (4), Martina (7), Speece (8);
McQuillan, Ryan (4), Jonnard (9), Watson (9).
W—McQuillan. L—Marberry. HR—Ryan (N.Y.).

Game 4—October 7, at New York
Wash............. 0 0 3 0 2 0 0 2 0 — 7 13 3
N.Y. .... 1 0 0 0 0 1 1 — 4 6 1
Mogridge, Marberry (8); Barnes, Baldwin (6),
Dean (8). W—Mogridge. L—Barnes. HR—Goslin
(Wash.).

Game 5—October 8, at New York
Wash............. 0 0 0 0 1 0 0 1 0 — 2 9 1
N.Y. .... 0 0 1 0 2 0 0 3 x — 6 13 0
Johnson; Bentley, McQuillan (8). W—Bentley.
L—Johnson. HR—Bentley (N.Y.); Goslin (Wash.).

Game 6—October 9, at Washington
N.Y. .... 1 0 0 0 0 0 0 0 0 — 1 7 1
Wash............. 0 0 0 2 0 0 0 0 x — 2 4 0
Nehf, Ryan (8); Zachary. W—Zachary. L—Nehf.

Game 7—October 10, at Washington
N.Y.,........0 0 0 0 0 3 0 0 0 0 0 1 — 3 8 3
Wash....0 0 0 1 0 0 0 2 0 0 0 1 — 4 10 4
Barnes, Nehf (8), McQuillan (9), Bentley (11);
Ogden, Mogridge (1), Marberry (6), Johnson (9).
W—Johnson. L—Bentley. HR—Harris (Wash.).

HISTORY

FINAL STANDINGS

American League

Team	W	L	Pct.	GB
Washington	96	55	.636	...
Philadelphia	88	64	.579	8.5
St. Louis	82	71	.536	15
Detroit	81	73	.526	16.5
Chicago	79	75	.513	18.5
Cleveland	70	84	.455	27.5
New York	69	85	.448	28.5
Boston	47	105	.309	49.5

National League

Team	W	L	Pct.	GB
Pittsburgh	95	58	.621	...
New York	86	66	.566	8.5
Cincinnati	80	73	.523	15
St. Louis	77	76	.503	18
Boston	70	83	.458	25
Brooklyn	68	85	.444	27
Philadelphia	68	85	.444	27
Chicago	68	86	.442	27.5

SIGNIFICANT EVENTS

■ **April 17:** Yankee slugger Babe Ruth underwent surgery for an intestinal abscess, an injury that would sideline him until June 1.

■ **April 18:** Brooklyn owner Charles Ebbets died on the morning of his Dodgers' home opener against the Giants at Ebbets Field.

■ **October 7:** Christy Mathewson, considered by many the greatest pitcher in history, died after a five-year bout with tuberculosis at age 45.

MEMORABLE MOMENTS

■ **May 5:** Detroit's Ty Cobb enjoyed a six-hit, three-homer game against the Browns, setting a modern Major League record with 16 total bases.

■ **May 6:** Yankee manager Miller Huggins benched shortstop Everett Scott, ending his record consecutive-games streak at 1,307.

■ **May 17:** Cleveland's Tris Speaker collected career hit No. 3,000 off Washington lefthander Tom Zachary.

■ **June 3:** White Sox manager Eddie Collins joined baseball's select 3,000-hit circle in a game against Detroit.

■ **June 15:** The Philadelphia Athletics, trailing 15-4 in the eighth inning, exploded for 13 runs and a 17-15 victory over the Indians.

■ **October 4:** St. Louis manager Rogers Hornsby matched his 1922 Triple Crown feat when he finished with a .403 average, 39 home runs and 143 RBIs.

LEADERS

American League

BA: Harry Heilmann, Det., .393.
Runs: Johnny Mostil, Chi., 135.
Hits: Al Simmons, Phil., 253.
TB: Al Simmons, Phil., 392.
HR: Bob Meusel, N.Y., 33.
RBI: Bob Meusel, N.Y., 138.
SB: Johnny Mostil, Chi., 43.
Wins: Ted Lyons, Chi.; Eddie Rommel, Phil., 21.
ERA: Stan Coveleski, Wash., 2.84.
CG: Howard Ehmke, Bos.; Sherry Smith, Cle., 22.
IP: Herb Pennock, N.Y., 277.
SO: Lefty Grove, Phil., 116.

National League

BA: Rogers Hornsby, St.L., .403.
Runs: Kiki Cuyler, Pit., 144.
Hits: Jim Bottomley, St.L., 227.
TB: Rogers Hornsby, St.L., 381.
HR: Rogers Hornsby, St.L., 39.
RBI: Rogers Hornsby, St.L., 143.
SB: Max Carey, Pit., 46.
Wins: Dazzy Vance, Brk., 22.
ERA: Dolf Luque, Cin., 2.63.
CG: Pete Donohue, Cin., 27.
IP: Pete Donohue, Cin., 301.
SO: Dazzy Vance, Brk., 221.

A.L. 20-game winners
Eddie Rommel, Phil., 21-10
Ted Lyons, Chi., 21-11
Stan Coveleski, Wash., 20-5
Walter Johnson, Wash., 20-7

N.L. 20-game winners
Dazzy Vance, Brk., 22-9
Eppa Rixey, Cin., 21-11
Pete Donohue, Cin., 21-14

A.L. 100 RBIs
Bob Meusel, N.Y., 138
Harry Heilmann, Det., 133
Al Simmons, Phil., 129
Goose Goslin, Wash., 113
Earl Sheely, Phil., 111
George Sisler, St.L., 105
Ken Williams, St.L., 105
Ty Cobb, Det., 102

N.L. 100 RBIs
Rogers Hornsby, St.L., 143

Jack Fournier, Brk., 130
Jim Bottomley, St.L., 128
Glenn Wright, Pit., 121
Clyde Barnhart, Pit., 114
Irish Meusel, N.Y., 111
Pie Traynor, Pit., 106
Zack Wheat, Brk., 103
Kiki Cuyler, Pit., 102

League MVP
A.L.: Roger Peckinpaugh, SS, Wash.
N.L.: Rogers Hornsby, 2B, St.L.

WORLD SERIES

■ **Winner:** The Pirates became the first team to rally from a three-games-to-one Series deficit and ruined Washington's hopes for a repeat victory.

■ **Turning point:** A Game 6 home run by Eddie Moore that gave Pittsburgh a 3-2 victory and knotted the Series at three games apiece.

■ **Memorable moment:** Washington's 37-year-old Walter Johnson battling valiantly but coming up short in Pittsburgh's 9-7 Game 7 victory.

■ **Top guns:** Max Carey (.458), Pirates; Joe Harris (.440, 3 HR, 6 RBIs), Goose Goslin (3 HR, 6 RBIs), Senators.

Linescores

Game 1—October 7, at Pittsburgh
Washington.... 0 1 0 0 2 0 0 0 1 — 4 8 1
Pittsburgh ..... 0 0 0 0 1 0 0 0 0 — 1 5 0
Johnson; Meadows, Morrison (9). W—Johnson. L—Meadows. HR—J. Harris (Wash.); Traynor (Pit.).

Game 2—October 8, at Pittsburgh
Washington ... 0 1 0 0 0 0 0 0 1 — 2 8 2
Pittsburgh ..... 0 0 0 1 0 0 0 2 x — 3 7 0
Coveleski; Aldridge. W—Aldridge. L—Coveleski. HR—Judge (Wash.); Wright (Pit.).

Game 3—October 10, at Washington
Pittsburgh ..... 0 1 0 1 0 1 0 0 0 — 3 8 3
Washington ... 0 0 1 0 0 1 2 0 x — 4 10 1
Kremer; Ferguson, Marberry (8). W—Ferguson. L—Kremer. HR—Goslin (Wash.).

Game 4—October 11, at Washington
Pittsburgh ..... 0 0 0 0 0 0 0 0 0 — 0 6 1
Washington ... 0 0 4 0 0 0 0 0 x — 4 12 0
Yde, Morrison (3), C. Adams (8); Johnson. W—Johnson. L—Yde. HR—Goslin, J. Harris (Wash.).

Game 5—October 12, at Washington
Pittsburgh ..... 0 0 2 0 0 0 2 1 1 — 6 13 0
Washington ... 1 0 0 1 0 0 1 0 0 — 3 8 1
Aldridge; Coveleski, Ballou (7), Zachary (8), Marberry (9). W—Aldridge. L—Coveleski. HR—J. Harris (Wash.).

Game 6——October 13, at Pittsburgh
Washington ... 1 1 0 0 0 0 0 0 0 — 2 6 2
Pittsburgh ..... 0 0 2 0 1 0 0 0 x — 3 7 1
Ferguson, Ballou (8); Kremer. W—Kremer. L—Ferguson. HR—Goslin (Wash.); Moore (Pit.).

Game 7——October 15, at Pittsburgh
Washington ... 4 0 0 2 0 0 0 1 0 — 7 7 2
Pittsburgh ..... 0 0 3 0 1 0 2 3 x — 9 15 2
Johnson; Aldridge, Morrison (1), Kremer (5), Oldham (8). W—Kremer. L—Johnson. HR—Peckinpaugh (Wash.).

FINAL STANDINGS

American League

Team	W	L	Pct.	GB
New York	91	63	.591	...
Cleveland	88	66	.571	3
Philadelphia	83	67	.553	6
Washington	81	69	.540	8
Chicago	81	72	.529	9.5
Detroit	79	75	.513	12
St. Louis	62	92	.403	29
Boston	46	107	.301	44.5

National League

Team	W	L	Pct.	GB
St. Louis	89	65	.578	...
Cincinnati	87	67	.565	2
Pittsburgh	84	69	.549	4.5
Chicago	82	72	.532	7
New York	74	77	.490	13.5
Brooklyn	71	82	.464	17.5
Boston	66	86	.434	22
Philadelphia	58	93	.384	29.5

SIGNIFICANT EVENTS

■ **January 30:** The Major League rules committee granted pitchers permission to use a resin bag during the course of games.

■ **October 13:** Cleveland first baseman George Burns, who batted .358 with a record 64 doubles, captured A.L. MVP honors, even though the Yankees' Babe Ruth batted .372 with 47 homers and 146 RBIs.

■ **December 16:** Commissioner Kenesaw Mountain Landis was elected to a second seven-year term.

■ **December 20:** In a trade billed as the biggest in baseball history, Cardinals manager Rogers Hornsby was dealt to the Giants for second baseman Frank Frisch and pitcher Jimmy Ring.

■ **December 22:** Baseball greats Ty Cobb and Tris Speaker denied accusations by former Detroit pitcher Dutch Leonard that they had conspired to throw 1919 Tigers-Indians games and had bet on their outcome. The charges would be investigated by Commissioner Kenesaw Mountain Landis and later dismissed for lack of evidence.

MEMORABLE MOMENTS

■ **May 12:** Washington fireballer Walter Johnson defeated St. Louis, 7-4, and became baseball's second 400-game winner.

■ **May 21:** Chicago's Earl Sheely belted a home run and three doubles in a game against Boston, giving him a record seven consecutive extra-base hits.

LEADERS

American League

BA: Heinie Manush, Det., .378.
Runs: Babe Ruth, N.Y., 139.
Hits: George Burns, Cle.; Sam Rice, Wash., 216.
TB: Babe Ruth, N.Y., 365.
HR: Babe Ruth, N.Y., 47.
RBI: Babe Ruth, N.Y., 146.
SB: Johnny Mostil, Chi., 35.
Wins: George Uhle, Cle., 27.
ERA: Lefty Grove, Phil., 2.51.
CG: George Uhle, Cle., 32.
IP: George Uhle, Cle., 318.1.
SO: Lefty Grove, Phil., 194.

National League

BA: Paul Waner, Pit., .336.
Runs: Kiki Cuyler, Pit., 113.
Hits: Eddie Brown, Bos., 201.
TB: Jim Bottomley, St.L., 305.
HR: Hack Wilson, Chi., 21.
RBI: Jim Bottomley, St.L., 120.
SB: Kiki Cuyler, Pit., 35.
Wins: Pete Donohue, Cin.; Ray Kremer, Pit.; Lee Meadows, Pit.; Flint Rhem, St.L., 20.
ERA: Ray Kremer, Pit., 2.61.
CG: Carl Mays, Cin., 24.
IP: Pete Donohue, Cin., 285.2.
SO: Dazzy Vance, Brk., 140.

A.L. 20-game winners
George Uhle, Cle., 27-11
Herb Pennock, N.Y., 23-11

N.L. 20-game winners
Remy Kremer, Pit., 20-6
Flint Rhem, St.L., 20-7
Lee Meadows, Pit., 20-9
Pete Donohue, Cin., 20-14

A.L. 100 RBIs
Babe Ruth, N.Y., 146
George Burns, Cle., 114
Tony Lazzeri, N.Y., 114
Al Simmons, Phil., 109
Goose Goslin, Wash., 108
Lou Gehrig, N.Y., 107
Harry Heilmann, Det., 103

N.L. 100 RBIs
Jim Bottomley, St.L., 120
Hack Wilson, Chi., 109
Les Bell, St.L., 100

A.L. 40 homers
Babe Ruth, N.Y., 47

League MVP
A.L.: George Burns, 1B, Cle.
N.L.: Bob O'Farrell, C, St.L.

WORLD SERIES

■ **Winner:** The Cardinals, making their first Series appearance, outlasted the Yankees in a seven-game classic.

■ **Turning point:** A Series-squaring 10-2 Cardinals victory in Game 6. Lester Bell homered and drove in four runs.

■ **Memorable moment:** The aging Grover Cleveland Alexander striking out Yankee slugger Tony Lazzeri with the bases loaded in the seventh inning of Game 7, saving the Cardinals.

■ **Top guns:** Jesse Haines (2-0, 1.08 ERA), Alexander (2-0, 1.33), Tommy Thevenow (.417), Cardinals; Babe Ruth (4 HR), Yankees.

Linescores

Game 1—October 2, at New York
St. Louis........ 1 0 0 0 0 0 0 0 0 — 1 3 1
New York........ 1 0 0 1 0 0 0 0 x — 2 6 0
Sherdel, Haines (8); Pennock. W—Pennock. L—Sherdel.

Game 2—October 3, at New York
St. Louis........ 0 0 2 0 0 0 3 0 1 — 6 12 1
New York........ 2 0 0 0 0 0 0 2 0 — 4 10 4
Alexander; Shocker, Shawkey (8), Jones (9). W—Alexander. L—Shawkey. HR—Southworth, Thevenow (St.L.).

Game 3—October 5, at St. Louis
New York........ 0 0 0 0 0 0 0 0 0 — 0 5 1
St. Louis........ 0 0 0 3 1 0 0 0 x — 4 8 0
Ruether, Shawkey (5), Thomas (8); Haines. W—Haines. L—Ruether. HR—Haines (St.L.).

Game 4—October 6, at St. Louis
New York........ 1 0 1 1 4 2 1 0 0 — 10 14 1
St. Louis........ 1 0 0 3 0 0 0 0 1 — 5 14 0
Hoyt; Rhem, Reinhart (5), H. Bell (5), Hallahan (7), Keen (9). W—Hoyt. L—Reinhart. HR—Ruth 3 (N.Y.).

Game 5—October 7, at St. Louis
New York........ 0 0 0 0 0 1 0 0 1 1—3 9 1
St. Louis........ 0 0 0 1 0 0 1 0 0 0—2 7 1
Pennock; Sherdel. W—Pennock. L—Sherdel.

Game 6—October 9, at New York
St. Louis........ 3 0 0 0 1 0 5 0 1 — 10 13 2
New York........ 0 0 0 1 0 0 1 0 0 — 2 8 1
Alexander; Shawkey, Shocker (7), Thomas (8). W—Alexander. L—Shawkey. HR—L. Bell (St.L.).

Game 7—October 10, at New York
St. Louis........ 0 0 0 3 0 0 0 0 0 — 3 8 0
New York........ 0 0 1 0 0 1 0 0 0 — 2 8 3
Haines, Alexander (7); Hoyt, Pennock (7). W—Haines. L—Hoyt. HR—Ruth (N.Y.).

FINAL STANDINGS

American League					National League				
Team	W	L	Pct.	GB	Team	W	L	Pct.	GB
New York	110	44	.714	...	Pittsburgh	94	60	.610	...
Philadelphia	91	63	.591	19	St. Louis	92	61	.601	1.5
Washington	85	69	.552	25	New York	92	62	.597	2
Detroit	82	71	.536	27.5	Chicago	85	68	.556	8.5
Chicago	70	83	.458	39.5	Cincinnati	75	78	.490	18.5
Cleveland	66	87	.431	43.5	Brooklyn	65	88	.425	28.5
St. Louis	59	94	.386	50.5	Boston	60	94	.390	34
Boston	51	103	.331	59	Philadelphia	51	103	.331	43

SIGNIFICANT EVENTS

■ **March 3:** The Yankees made slugger Babe Ruth the highest paid player in baseball history, signing him for three years at a reported $70,000 per season.
■ **October 17:** A.L. founder and 28-year president Ban Johnson retired, three days after 416-game winner Walter Johnson called it quits after 21 seasons with Washington.
■ **October 22:** Ross Youngs, a .322 hitter over 10 seasons with the Giants, died of Bright's disease at age 30.
■ **November 2:** E.S. Barnard was named new A.L. president, replacing Ban Johnson.

MEMORABLE MOMENTS

■ **May 30-31:** Cubs shortstop Jimmy Cooney and Detroit first baseman Johnny Neun pulled off rare unassisted triple plays on consecutive days.
■ **July 18:** Philadelphia's Ty Cobb opened a new club when he doubled against his former Detroit team-mates for hit No. 4,000.
■ **July 19:** The Cubs spoiled John McGraw Day at the Polo Grounds by beating the Giants. But fans enjoyed festivities honoring McGraw for his 25 years as New York manager.
■ **September 30:** Yankee slugger Babe Ruth broke his own one-season record when he blasted home run No. 60 off Washington lefty Tom Zachary.

LEADERS

American League
BA: Harry Heilmann, Det., .398.
Runs: Babe Ruth, N.Y., 158.
Hits: Earle Combs, N.Y., 231.
TB: Lou Gehrig, N.Y., 447.
HR: Babe Ruth, N.Y., 60.
RBI: Lou Gehrig, N.Y., 175.
SB: George Sisler, St.L., 27.
Wins: Waite Hoyt, N.Y.; Ted Lyons, Chi., 22.
ERA: Wilcy Moore, N.Y., 2.28.
CG: Ted Lyons, Chi., 30.
IP: Ted Lyons, Chi.; Tommy Thomas, Chi., 307.2
SO: Lefty Grove, Phil., 174.

National League
BA: Paul Waner, Pit., .380.
Runs: Rogers Hornsby, N.Y.; Lloyd Waner, Pit., 133.
Hits: Paul Waner, Pit., 237.
TB: Paul Waner, Pit., 342.
HR: Cy Williams, Phil.; Hack Wilson, Chi., 30.
RBI: Paul Waner, Pit., 131.
SB: Frank Frisch, St.L., 48.
Wins: Charlie Root, Chi., 26.
ERA: Ray Kremer, Pit., 2.47.
CG: Jesse Haines, St.L.; Lee Meadows, Pit.; Dazzy Vance, Brk., 25.
IP: Charlie Root, Chi., 309.
SO: Dazzy Vance, Brk., 184.

A.L. 20-game winners
Waite Hoyt, N.Y., 22-7
Ted Lyons, Chi., 22-14
Lefty Grove, Phil., 20-13
N.L. 20-game winners
Charlie Root, Chi., 26-15
Jesse Haines, St.L., 24-10
Carmen Hill, Pit., 22-11
Grover Alexander, St.L., 21-10

A.L. 100 RBIs
Lou Gehrig, N.Y., 175
Babe Ruth, N.Y., 164
Goose Goslin, Wash., 120
Harry Heilmann, Det., 120
Bob Fothergill, Det., 114
Al Simmons, Phil., 108
Bob Meusel, N.Y., 103
Tony Lazzeri, N.Y., 102
N.L. 100 RBIs
Paul Waner, Pit., 131
Hack Wilson, Chi., 129

Rogers Hornsby, N.Y., 125
Jim Bottomley, St.L., 124
Bill Terry, N.Y., 121
Pie Traynor, Pit., 106
Glenn Wright, Pit., 105

A.L. 40 homers
Babe Ruth, N.Y., 60
Lou Gehrig, N.Y., 47

League MVP
A.L.: Lou Gehrig, 1B, N.Y.
N.L.: Paul Waner, OF, Pit.

WORLD SERIES

■ **Winner:** The powerful Yankees made short work of the overmatched Pirates.
■ **Turning point:** When the Pirates watched the Yankees take batting practice before Game 1.
■ **Memorable moment:** Yankee Earle Combs dancing across the plate with the Series-ending run after a John Miljus wild pitch.
■ **Top guns:** Wilcy Moore (1-0, 0.84 ERA), Herb Pennock (1-0, 1.00), Mark Koenig (.500), Babe Ruth (.400, 2 HR, 7 RBIs), Yankees; Lloyd Waner (.400), Pirates.

Linescores
Game 1—October 5, at Pittsburgh
New York....... 1 0 3 0 1 0 0 0 0 — 5 6 1
Pittsburgh ...... 1 0 1 0 1 0 0 1 0 — 4 9 2
Hoyt, Moore (8); Kremer, Miljus (6). W—Hoyt. L—Kremer.

Game 2—October 6, at Pittsburgh
New York ...... 0 0 3 0 0 0 0 3 0 — 6 11 0
Pittsburgh ...... 1 0 0 0 0 0 0 1 0 — 2 7 2
Pipgras; Aldridge, Cvengros (8), Dawson (9). W—Pipgras. L—Aldridge.

Game 3—October 7, at New York
Pittsburgh ...... 0 0 0 0 0 0 0 1 0 — 1 3 1
New York ...... 2 0 0 0 0 0 6 0 x — 8 9 0
Meadows, Cvengros (7); Pennock. W—Pennock. L—Meadows. HR—Ruth (N.Y.).

Game 4—October 8, at New York
Pittsburgh ...... 1 0 0 0 0 0 2 0 0 — 3 10 1
New York....... 1 0 0 0 2 0 0 0 1 — 4 12 2
Hill, Miljus (7); Moore. W—Moore. L—Miljus. HR—Ruth (N.Y.).

FINAL STANDINGS

American League					National League				
Team	W	L	Pct.	GB	Team	W	L	Pct.	GB
New York	101	53	.656	...	St. Louis	95	59	.617	...
Philadelphia	98	55	.641	2.5	New York	93	61	.604	2
St. Louis	82	72	.532	19	Chicago	91	63	.591	4
Washington	75	79	.487	26	Pittsburgh	85	67	.559	9
Chicago	72	82	.468	29	Cincinnati	78	74	.513	16
Detroit	68	86	.442	33	Brooklyn	77	76	.503	17.5
Cleveland	62	92	.403	39	Boston	50	103	.327	44.5
Boston	57	96	.373	43.5	Philadelphia	43	109	.283	51

SIGNIFICANT EVENTS

■ **May 14:** Giants manager John McGraw was hit by a car while crossing a street outside Chicago's Wrigley Field, an injury that would sideline him for six weeks.
■ **September 9:** Urban Shocker, a 187-game winner for the Yankees and Browns, died of pneumonia at age 38.
■ **November 7:** Massachusetts voters cleared the way for Sunday baseball in Boston, leaving Pennsylvania as the only state still enforcing the blue law.
■ **December 13:** National League President John Heydler, contending fans were tired of watching weak-hitting pitchers try to bat, proposed a designated hitter rule that was voted down at the annual winter meetings.

MEMORABLE MOMENTS

■ **July 21:** Philadelphia's Jimmie Foxx became the first player to hit a ball over the double-decked left-field stands of Shibe Park during a game against St. Louis.
■ **September 3:** Athletics pinch-hitter Ty Cobb stroked his 724th career double and final career hit—No. 4,191—in a game against Washington.
■ **September 28-29:** The New York Yankees clinched the A.L. pennant with a victory over the Tigers and the Cardinals closed out a tight N.L. race with a next-day win over the Braves.

LEADERS

American League
BA: Goose Goslin, Wash., .379.
Runs: Babe Ruth, N.Y., 163.
Hits: Heinie Manush, St.L., 241.
TB: Babe Ruth, N.Y., 380.
HR: Babe Ruth, N.Y., 54.
RBI: Lou Gehrig, N.Y.; Babe Ruth, N.Y., 142.
SB: Buddy Myer, Bos., 30.
Wins: Lefty Grove, Phil.; George Pipgras, N.Y., 24.
ERA: Garland Braxton, Wash., 2.51.
CG: Red Ruffing, Bos., 25.
IP: George Pipgras, N.Y., 300.2.
SO: Lefty Grove, Phil., 183.

National League
BA: Rogers Hornsby, Bos., .387.
Runs: Paul Waner, Pit., 142.
Hits: Fred Lindstrom, N.Y., 231.
TB: Jim Bottomley, St.L., 362.
HR: Jim Bottomley, St.L.; Hack Wilson, Chi., 31.
RBI: Jim Bottomley, St.L., 136.
SB: Kiki Cuyler, Chi., 37.
Wins: Larry Benton, N.Y.; Burleigh Grimes, Pit., 25.
ERA: Dazzy Vance, Brk., 2.09.
CG: Larry Benton, N.Y.; Burleigh Grimes, Pit., 28.
IP: Burleigh Grimes, Pit., 330.2.
SO: Dazzy Vance, Brk., 200.

A.L. 20-game winners
Lefty Grove, Phil., 24-8
George Pipgras, N.Y., 24-13
Waite Hoyt, N.Y., 23-7
General Crowder, St.L., 21-5
Sam Gray, St.L., 20-12
N.L. 20-game winners
Larry Benton, N.Y., 25-9
Burleigh Grimes, Pit., 25-14
Dazzy Vance, Brk., 22-10
Bill Sherdel, St.L., 21-10
Jesse Haines, St.L., 20-8
Fred Fitzsimmons, N.Y., 20-9

A.L. 100 RBIs
Lou Gehrig, N.Y., 142
Babe Ruth, N.Y., 142
Bob Meusel, N.Y., 113
Heinie Manush, St.L., 108
Harry Heilmann, Det., 107
Al Simmons, Phil., 107
Goose Goslin, Wash., 102
N.L. 100 RBIs
Jim Bottomley, St.L., 136
Pie Traynor, Pit., 124
Hack Wilson, Chi., 120

Chick Hafey, St.L., 111
Fred Lindstrom, N.Y., 107
Del Bissonette, Brk., 106
Pinky Whitney, Phil., 103
Bill Terry, N.Y., 101

A.L. 40 homers
Babe Ruth, N.Y., 54

League MVP
A.L.: Mickey Cochrane, C, Phil.
N.L.: Jim Bottomley, 1B, St.L.

WORLD SERIES

■ **Winner:** The muscular Yankees swept aside St. Louis for their third Series victory of the decade.
■ **Turning point:** A 9-3 second-game romp that made it clear the Cardinals were overmatched.
■ **Memorable moment:** Babe Ruth's show-stealing three-home run performance in Game 4 at St. Louis' Sportsman's Park.
■ **Top guns:** Waite Hoyt (2-0, 1.50 ERA), Ruth (.625, 3 HR), Lou Gehrig, (.545, 4 HR, 9 RBIs).

Linescores
Game 1—October 4, at New York
St. Louis......... 0 0 0 0 0 0 1 0 0 — 1 3 1
New York....... 1 0 0 2 0 0 0 1 x — 4 7 0
Sherdel, Johnson (8); Hoyt. W—Hoyt. L—Sherdel. HR—Meusel (N.Y.); Bottomley (St.L.).

Game 2—October 5, at New York
St. Louis......... 0 3 0 0 0 0 0 0 0 — 3 4 1
New York....... 3 1 4 0 0 0 1 0 x — 9 8 2
Alexander, Mitchell (3); Pipgras. W—Pipgras. L—Alexander. HR—Gehrig (N.Y.).

Game 3—October 7, at St. Louis
New York....... 0 1 0 2 0 3 1 0 0 — 7 7 2
St. Louis......... 2 0 0 0 1 0 0 0 0 — 3 9 3
Zachary; Haines, Johnson (7), Rhem (8). W—Zachary. L—Haines. HR—Gehrig 2 (N.Y.).

Game 4—October 9, at St. Louis
New York....... 0 0 0 1 0 0 4 2 0 — 7 15 2
St. Louis......... 0 0 1 1 0 0 0 0 1 — 3 11 0
Hoyt; Sherdel, Alexander (7). W—Hoyt. L—Sherdel. HR—Ruth 3, Durst, Gehrig (N.Y.).

HISTORY

FINAL STANDINGS

American League

Team	W	L	Pct.	GB
Philadelphia	104	46	.693	...
New York	88	66	.571	18
Cleveland	81	71	.533	24
St. Louis	79	73	.520	26
Washington	71	81	.467	34
Detroit	70	84	.455	36
Chicago	59	93	.388	46
Boston	58	96	.377	48

National League

Team	W	L	Pct.	GB
Chicago	98	54	.645	...
Pittsburgh	88	65	.575	10.5
New York	84	67	.556	13.5
St. Louis	78	74	.513	20
Philadelphia	71	82	.464	27.5
Brooklyn	70	83	.458	28.5
Cincinnati	66	88	.429	33
Boston	56	98	.364	43

SIGNIFICANT EVENTS

■ **January 22:** The Yankees announced an innovation: permanent numbers on the backs of uniforms corresponding to players' positions in the batting order.

■ **September 25:** New York manager Miller Huggins, who led the Yankees to six pennants and three World Series championships in 12 seasons, died suddenly of blood poisoning at age 49.

MEMORABLE MOMENTS

■ **July 6:** The Cardinals set a modern Major League record for runs and an N.L. record for hits (28) when they pounded the Phillies, 28-6.

■ **August 10:** Cardinals great Grover Cleveland Alexander shut out Philadelphia in four innings of relief and was credited with an 11-9 victory—the 373rd and last of his career.

■ **August 11:** Yankee Babe Ruth drove a Willis Hudlin pitch out of Cleveland's League Park for career homer No. 500.

■ **October 5:** Philadelphia slugger Chuck Klein hit home run No. 43 in a final-day doubleheader against New York, setting a one-season N.L. record and edging Giants outfielder Mel Ott by one.

■ **October 6:** Cleveland third baseman Joe Sewell finished the season with an amazing four strikeouts in 578 official at-bats.

LEADERS

American League
BA: Lew Fonseca, Cle., .369.
Runs: Charley Gehringer, Det., 131.
Hits: Dale Alexander, Det.; Charley Gehringer, Det., 215.
TB: Al Simmons, Phil., 373.
HR: Babe Ruth, N.Y., 46.
RBI: Al Simmons, Phil., 157.
SB: Charley Gehringer, Det., 27.
Wins: George Earnshaw, Phil., 24.
ERA: Lefty Grove, Phil., 2.81.
CG: Tommy Thomas, Chi., 24.
IP: Sam Gray, St.L., 305.
SO: Lefty Grove, Phil., 170.

National League
BA: Lefty O'Doul, Phil., .398.
Runs: Rogers Hornsby, Chi., 156.
Hits: Lefty O'Doul, Phil., 254.
TB: Rogers Hornsby, Chi., 409.
HR: Chuck Klein, Phil., 43.
RBI: Hack Wilson, Chi., 159.
SB: Kiki Cuyler, Chi., 43.
Wins: Pat Malone, Chi., 22.
ERA: Bill Walker, N.Y., 3.09.
CG: Red Lucas, Cin., 28.
IP: Watty Clark, Brk., 279.
SO: Pat Malone, Chi., 166.

A.L. 20-game winners
George Earnshaw, Phil., 24-8
Wes Ferrell, Cle., 21-10
Lefty Grove, Phil., 20-6

N.L. 20-game winners
Pat Malone, Chi., 22-10

A.L. 100 RBIs
Al Simmons, Phil., 157
Babe Ruth, N.Y., 154
Dale Alexander, Det., 137
Lou Gehrig, N.Y., 126
Harry Heilmann, Det., 120
Jimmie Foxx, Phil., 117
Red Kress, St.L., 107

Charlie Gehringer, Det., 106
Tony Lazzeri, N.Y., 106
Lew Fonseca, Cle., 103

N.L. 100 RBIs
Hack Wilson, Chi., 159
Mel Ott, N.Y., 151
Rogers Hornsby, Chi., 149
Chuck Klein, Phil., 145
Jim Bottomley, St.L., 137
Chick Hafey, St.L., 125
Don Hurst, Phil., 125
Lefty O'Doul, Phil., 122
Bill Terry, N.Y., 117
Pinky Whitney, Phil., 115
Babe Herman, Brk., 113

Riggs Stephenson, Chi., 110
Pie Traynor, Pit., 108
George Kelly, Cin., 103
Kiki Cuyler, Chi., 102
Paul Waner, Pit., 100

A.L. 40 homers
Babe Ruth, N.Y., 46

N.L. 40 homers
Chuck Klein, Phil., 43
Mel Ott, N.Y., 42

League MVP
A.L.: No selection.
N.L.: Rogers Hornsby, 2B, Chi.

WORLD SERIES

■ **Winner:** The Athletics, an A.L. doormat since their last Series appearance in 1914, re-emerged as baseball's dominant team.

■ **Turning point:** The seventh inning of Game 4. Leading the Series two games to one but trailing the Cubs 8-0, the A's exploded for an incredible 10 runs.

■ **Memorable moments:** Mule Haas' three-run inside-the-park home run in the 10-run seventh inning and his ninth-inning game-tying homer in the Series-ending fifth game; surprise starter Howard Ehmke's record 13 strikeouts in Game 1.

■ **Top guns:** Jimmie Dykes (.421), Jimmie Foxx (.350, 2 HR, 5 RBIs), Haas (2 HR, 6 RBIs), Athletics; Hack Wilson (.471), Cubs.

Linescores

Game 1—October 8, at Chicago
Philadelphia.... 0 0 0   0 0 0   1 0 2 — 3 6 1
Chicago.......... 0 0 0   0 0 0   0 0 1 — 1 8 2
Ehmke; Root, Bush (8). W—Ehmke. L—Root. HR—Foxx (Phil.).

Game 2—October 9, at Chicago
Philadelphia... 0 0 3   3 0 0   1 2 0 — 9 12 0
Chicago.......... 0 0 0   0 3 0   0 0 0 — 3 11 1
Earnshaw, Grove (5); Malone, Blake (4), Carlson (6), Nehf (9). W—Earnshaw. L—Malone. HR—Simmons, Foxx (Phil.).

Game 3—October 11, at Philadelphia
Chicago .... 0 0 0   0 0 3   0 0 0 — 3 6 1
Philadelphia.... 0 0 0   0 1 0   0 0 0 — 1 9 1
Bush; Earnshaw. W—Bush. L—Earnshaw.

Game 4—October 12, at Philadelphia
Chicago.......... 0 0 0   2 0 5   1 0 0 — 8 10 2
Philadelphia.... 0 0 0   0 0 0   10 0 x — 10 15 2
Root, Nehf (7), Blake (7), Malone (7), Carlson (8); Quinn, Walberg (6), Rommel (7), Grove (8). W—Rommel. L—Blake. HR—Grimm (Chi.); Haas, Simmons (Phil.).

Game 5—October 14, at Philadelphia
Chicago .... 0 0 0   2 0 0   0 0 0 — 2 8 1
Philadelphia.... 0 0 0   0 0 0   0 0 3 — 3 6 0
Malone; Ehmke, Walberg (4). W—Walberg. L—Malone. HR—Haas (Phil.).

FINAL STANDINGS

American League

Team	W	L	Pct.	GB
Philadelphia	102	52	.662	...
Washington	94	60	.610	8
New York	86	68	.558	16
Cleveland	81	73	.526	21
Detroit	75	79	.487	27
St. Louis	64	90	.416	38
Chicago	62	92	.403	40
Boston	52	102	.338	50

National League

Team	W	L	Pct.	GB
St. Louis	92	62	.597	...
Chicago	90	64	.584	2
New York	87	67	.565	5
Brooklyn	86	68	.558	6
Pittsburgh	80	74	.519	12
Boston	70	84	.455	22
Cincinnati	59	95	.383	33
Philadelphia	52	102	.338	40

SIGNIFICANT EVENTS

■ **March 8:** Yankee slugger Babe Ruth signed a record two-year contract at $80,000 per season.

■ **December 11:** Major League officials granted the Baseball Writers Association of America permission to conduct future MVP balloting—a practice that would continue without interruption.

■ **December 12:** Rules changes: The sacrifice fly was eliminated and balls bouncing into the stands were classified as ground-rule doubles instead of home runs.

MEMORABLE MOMENTS

■ **May 2:** Commissioner Kenesaw Mountain Landis attended Organized Baseball's first game under permanently installed lights at Des Moines (Iowa) of the Western League.

■ **September 27:** Chicago's Hack Wilson hit home runs 55 and 56—an N.L. record—in a game against the Reds.

■ **September 28:** Wilson drove in his Major League-record 189th and 190th runs in Chicago's season-finale victory over the Reds.

■ **September 28:** New York's Bill Terry finished with a .401 average and N.L. hitters closed with a composite .303 mark.

LEADERS

American League
BA: Al Simmons, Phil., .381.
Runs: Al Simmons, Phil., 152.
Hits: Johnny Hodapp, Cle., 225.
TB: Lou Gehrig, N.Y., 419.
HR: Babe Ruth, N.Y., 49.
RBI: Lou Gehrig, N.Y., 174.
SB: Marty McManus, Det., 23.
Wins: Lefty Grove, Phil., 28.
ERA: Lefty Grove, Phil., 2.54.
CG: Ted Lyons, Chi., 29.
IP: Lyons, Chi., 297.2.
SO: Lefty Grove, Phil., 209.

National League
BA: Bill Terry, N.Y., .401.
Runs: Chuck Klein, Phil., 158.
Hits: Bill Terry, N.Y., 254.
TB: Chuck Klein, Phil., 445.
HR: Hack Wilson, Chi., 56.
RBI: Hack Wilson, Chi., 190.
SB: Kiki Cuyler, Chi., 37.
Wins: Ray Kremer, Pit.; Pat Malone, Chi., 20.
ERA: Dazzy Vance, Brk., 2.61.
CG: Erv Brame, Pit.; Pat Malone, Chi., 22.
IP: Ray Kremer, Pit., 276.
SO: Bill Hallahan, St.L., 177.

A.L. 20-game winners
Lefty Grove, Phil., 28-5
Wes Ferrell, Cle., 25-13
George Earnshaw, Phil., 22-13
Ted Lyons, Chi., 22-15
Lefty Stewart, St.L., 20-12

N.L. 20-game winners
Pat Malone, Chi., 20-9
Remy Kremer, Pit., 20-12

A.L. 100 RBIs
Lou Gehrig, N.Y., 174
Al Simmons, Phil., 165
Jimmie Foxx, Phil., 156
Babe Ruth, N.Y., 153
Goose Goslin, Wash.-St.L., 138
Ed Morgan, Cle., 136

Dale Alexander, Det., 135
Joe Cronin, Wash., 126
Johnny Hodapp, Cle., 121
Tony Lazzeri, N.Y., 121
Earl Averill, Cle., 119
Smead Jolley, Chi., 114
Red Kress, St.L., 112
Carl Reynolds, Chi., 104
Bing Miller, Phil., 100

N.L. 100 RBIs
Hack Wilson, Chi., 190
Chuck Klein, Phil., 170
Kiki Cuyler, Chi., 134
Babe Herman, Brk., 130
Bill Terry, N.Y., 129
Glenn Wright, Brk., 126
Gabby Hartnett, Chi., 122

Wally Berger, Bos., 119
Adam Comorosky, Pit., 119
Mel Ott, N.Y., 119
Pie Traynor, Pit., 119
Pinky Whitney, Pit., 117
Frank Frisch, St.L., 114
Del Bissonette, Brk., 113
Chick Hafey, St.L., 107
Gus Suhr, Pit., 107
Fred Lindstrom, N.Y., 106

A.L. 40 homers
Babe Ruth, N.Y., 49
Lou Gehrig, N.Y., 41

N.L. 40 homers
Hack Wilson, Chi., 56
Chuck Klein, Phil., 40

WORLD SERIES

■ **Winner:** The Athletics became the first team to win back-to-back Series twice.

■ **Turning point:** Jimmie Foxx's two-run ninth-inning home run off Burleigh Grimes, which broke open a scoreless Game 5 and put Philadelphia in the driver's seat.

■ **Memorable moment:** Foxx's Game 5-winning home run.

■ **Top guns:** George Earnshaw (2-0, 0.72 ERA), Al Simmons (.364, 2 HR, 4 RBIs), Athletics; Jesse Haines (1-0, 1.00), Cardinals.

Linescores

Game 1—October 1, at Philadelphia
St. Louis ....0 0 2   0 0 0   0 0 0—2 9 0
Philadelphia........0 1 0   1 0 1   1 1 x—5 5 0
Grimes; Grove. W—Grove. L—Grimes. HR—Cochrane, Simmons (Phil.).

Game 2—October 2, at Philadelphia
St. Louis ....0 1 0   0 0 0   0 0 0—1 6 2
Philadelphia........2 0 2   2 0 0   0 0 x—6 7 2
Rhem, Lindsey (4), Johnson (7); Earnshaw. W—Earnshaw. L—Rhem. HR—Cochrane (Phil.); Watkins (St.L.).

Game 3—October 4, at St. Louis
Philadelphia......0 0 0   0 0 0   0 0 0—0 7 0
St. Louis ....0 0 0   1 1 0   2 1 x—5 10 0
Walberg, Shores (5), Quinn (7); Hallahan. W—Hallahan. L—Walberg. HR—Douthit (St.L.).

Game 4—October 5, at St. Louis
Philadelphia........1 0 0   0 0 0   0 0 0—1 4 1
St. Louis ....0 0 1   2 0 0   0 x—3 5 1
Grove; Haines. W—Haines. L—Grove.

Game 5—October 6, at St. Louis
Philadelphia........0 0 0   0 0 0   0 0 2—2 5 0
St. Louis ....0 0 0   0 0 0   0 0 0—0 3 1
Earnshaw, Grove (8); Grimes. W—Grove. L—Grimes. HR—Foxx (Phil.).

Game 6—October 8, at Philadelphia
St. Louis ....0 0 0   0 0 0   0 0 1—1 5 1
Philadelphia........2 0 1   2 1 1   0 0 x—7 7 0
Hallahan, Johnson (3), Lindsey (6), Bell (8); Earnshaw. W—Earnshaw. L—Hallahan. HR—Dykes, Simmons (Phil.).

FINAL STANDINGS

American League

Team	W	L	Pct.	GB
Philadelphia	107	45	.704	...
New York	94	59	.614	13.5
Washington	92	62	.597	16
Cleveland	78	76	.506	30
St. Louis	63	91	.409	45
Boston	62	90	.408	45
Detroit	61	93	.396	47
Chicago	56	97	.366	51.5

National League

Team	W	L	Pct.	GB
St. Louis	101	53	.656	...
New York	87	65	.572	13
Chicago	84	70	.545	17
Brooklyn	79	73	.520	21
Pittsburgh	75	79	.487	26
Philadelphia	66	88	.429	35
Boston	64	90	.416	37
Cincinnati	58	96	.377	43

SIGNIFICANT EVENTS

■ **March 27-28:** Former A.L. president and founder Ban Johnson died at age 67, 16 hours after E.S. Barnard, the man who succeeded him, died of a heart attack at age 56.
■ **October 20, 28:** The Baseball Writers Association of America named its first MVPs: Cardinals infielder Frank Frisch and Athletics 31-game winner Lefty Grove.
■ **October 26:** Charles Comiskey, one of the A.L.'s founding fathers and longtime owner of the White Sox, died at age 72.

MEMORABLE MOMENTS

■ **May 26:** The Yankees ended Philadelphia's winning streak at 17 games with a 6-2 victory.
■ **August 21:** Yankee Babe Ruth belted his historic 600th career home run off Browns righthander George Blaeholder.
■ **August 23:** Philadelphia's Lefty Grove, bidding to break the A.L. record of 16 straight victories, dropped a 1-0 decision to the Browns.
■ **September 1:** Yankee Lou Gehrig, en route to an A.L.-record 184 RBIs, became the third player to hit home runs in six straight games — a streak that included three grand slams in five days.

LEADERS

American League

BA: Al Simmons, Phil., .390.
Runs: Lou Gehrig, N.Y., 163.
Hits: Lou Gehrig, N.Y., 211.
TB: Lou Gehrig, N.Y., 410.
HR: Lou Gehrig, N.Y.; Babe Ruth, N.Y., 46.
RBI: Lou Gehrig, N.Y., 184.
SB: Ben Chapman, N.Y., 61.
Wins: Lefty Grove, Phil., 31.
ERA: Lefty Grove, Phil., 2.06.
CG: Wes Ferrell, Cle.; Lefty Grove, Phil., 27.
IP: Rube Walberg, Phil., 291.
SO: Lefty Grove, Phil., 175.

National League

BA: Chick Hafey, St.L., .349.
Runs: Chuck Klein, Phil.; Bill Terry, N.Y., 121.
Hits: Lloyd Waner, Pit., 214.
TB: Chuck Klein, Phil., 347.
HR: Chuck Klein, Phil., 31.
RBI: Chuck Klein, Phil., 121.
SB: Frank Frisch, St.L., 28.
Wins: Jumbo Elliott, Phil.; Bill Hallahan, St.L.; Heinie Meine, Pit., 19.
ERA: Bill Walker, N.Y., 2.26.
CG: Red Lucas, Cin., 24.
IP: Heinie Meine, Pit., 284.
SO: Bill Hallahan, St.L., 159.

A.L. 20-game winners

Lefty Grove, Phil., 31-4
Wes Ferrell, Cle., 22-12
George Earnshaw, Phil., 21-7
Lefty Gomez, N.Y., 21-9
Rube Walberg, Phil., 20-12

A.L. 100 RBIs

Lou Gehrig, N.Y., 184
Babe Ruth, N.Y., 163
Earl Averill, Cle., 143

Al Simmons, Phil., 128
Joe Cronin, Wash., 126
Ben Chapman, N.Y., 122
Jimmie Foxx, Phil., 120
Joe Vosmik, Cle., 117
Red Kress, St.L., 114
Lyn Lary, N.Y., 107
Goose Goslin, St.L., 105
Earl Webb, Bos., 103

N.L. 100 RBIs

Chuck Klein, Phil., 121

Mel Ott, N.Y., 115
Bill Terry, N.Y., 112
Pie Traynor, Pit., 103

A.L. 40 homers

Lou Gehrig, N.Y., 46
Babe Ruth, N.Y., 46

Most Valuable Player

A.L.: Lefty Grove, P, Phil.
N.L.: Frank Frisch, 2B, St.L.

WORLD SERIES

■ **Winner:** The Cardinals spoiled Philadelphia's bid to win a record third consecutive Series.
■ **Turning point:** A pair of two-run innings that staked Cardinals spitballer Burleigh Grimes to a 4-0 lead in Game 7.
■ **Memorable moment:** The Series-long do-everything performance of exciting Cardinals center fielder Pepper Martin.
■ **Top guns:** Grimes (2-0, 2.04 ERA), Bill Hallahan (2-0, 0.49), Martin (.500, 12 hits, 5 RBIs, 5 SB), Cardinals; Al Simmons (.333, 2 HR, 8 RBIs), Athletics.

Linescores

Game 1—October 1, at St. Louis
Philadelphia......0 0 4 0 0 0 2 0 0—6 11 0
St. Louis ....2 0 0 0 0 0 0 0 0—2 12 0
Grove; Derringer, Johnson (8). W—Grove. L—Derringer. HR—Simmons (Phil.).

Game 2—October 2, at St. Louis
Philadelphia.......0 0 0 0 0 0 0 0 0—0 3 0
St. Louis ....0 1 0 0 0 0 1 0 x—2 6 1
Earnshaw; Hallahan. W—Hallahan. L—Earnshaw.

Game 3—October 5, at Philadelphia
St. Louis ....0 2 0 2 0 0 0 0 1—5 12 0
Philadelphia.....0 0 0 0 0 0 0 0 2—2 2 0
Grimes; Grove, Mahaffey (9). W—Grimes.
L—Grove. HR—Simmons (Phil.).

Game 4—October 6, at Philadelphia
St. Louis ....0 0 0 0 0 0 0 0 0—0 2 1
Philadelphia.....1 0 0 0 0 2 0 0 x—3 10 0
Johnson, Lindsey (6); Derringer (8); Earnshaw.
W—Earnshaw. L—Johnson. HR—Foxx (Phil.).

Game 5—October 7, at Philadelphia
St. Louis ....1 0 0 0 0 2 0 1 1—5 12 0
Philadelphia.....0 0 0 0 0 1 0 0—1 9 0
Hallahan; Hoyt, Walberg (7), Rommel (9).
W—Hallahan. L—Hoyt. HR—Martin (St.L.).

Game 6—October 9, at St. Louis
Philadelphia.......0 0 0 0 4 0 4 0 0—8 8 1
St. Louis ....0 0 0 0 0 1 0 0—1 5 2
Grove; Derringer, Johnson (5), Lindsey (7), Rhem (9). W—Grove. L—Derringer.

Game 7—October 10, at St. Louis
Philadelphia.......0 0 0 0 0 0 0 2—2 7 1
St. Louis ....2 0 2 0 0 0 0 x—4 5 0
Earnshaw, Walberg (8); Grimes, Hallahan (9).
W—Grimes. L—Earnshaw. HR—Watkins (St.L.).

FINAL STANDINGS

American League

Team	W	L	Pct.	GB
New York	107	47	.695	...
Philadelphia	94	60	.610	13
Washington	93	61	.604	14
Cleveland	87	65	.572	19
Detroit	76	75	.503	29.5
St. Louis	63	91	.409	44
Chicago	49	102	.325	56.5
Boston	43	111	.279	64

National League

Team	W	L	Pct.	GB
Chicago	90	64	.584	...
Pittsburgh	86	68	.558	4
Brooklyn	81	73	.526	9
Philadelphia	78	76	.506	12
Boston	77	77	.500	13
New York	72	82	.468	18
St. Louis	72	82	.468	18
Cincinnati	60	94	.390	30

SIGNIFICANT EVENTS

■ **June 22:** N.L. officials, after a long holdout, approved the use of numbers to identify their players.
■ **July 31:** The 76,979 fans who turned out for Cleveland's unveiling of Municipal Stadium watched the Indians lose a 1-0 decision to the Athletics and Lefty Grove.
■ **September 28:** Connie Mack began dismantling his powerful Athletics with the sale of Al Simmons, Jimmie Dykes and Mule Haas to the White Sox for $150,000.
■ **October 19:** A Philadelphia double: Athletics slugger Jimmie Foxx earned A.L. MVP honors and Phillies slugger Chuck Klein captured the N.L. award.

MEMORABLE MOMENTS

■ **June 3:** An historic day: Yankee Lou Gehrig belted four home runs in a game at Philadelphia and John McGraw retired after 31 seasons as manager of the Giants.
■ **July 4:** In a Fourth of July battle between the Yankees and Senators, New York catcher Bill Dickey punched Washington outfielder Carl Reynolds and broke his jaw, a tantrum that would cost him a 30-day suspension and $1,000.
■ **September 25:** Athletics slugger Jimmie Foxx hit home run No. 58 in the season finale against Washington, falling two short of Babe Ruth's single-season record.

LEADERS

American League

BA: Dale Alexander, Det.-Bos., .367.
Runs: Jimmie Foxx, Phil., 151.
Hits: Al Simmons, Phil., 216.
TB: Jimmie Foxx, Phil., 438.
HR: Jimmie Foxx, Phil., 58.
RBI: Jimmie Foxx, Phil., 169.
SB: Ben Chapman, N.Y., 38.
Wins: General Crowder, Wash., 26.
ERA: Lefty Grove, Phil., 2.84.
CG: Lefty Grove, Phil., 27.
IP: General Crowder, Wash., 327.
SO: Red Ruffing, N.Y., 190.

National League

BA: Lefty O'Doul, Brk., .368.
Runs: Chuck Klein, Phil., 152.
Hits: Chuck Klein, Phil., 226.
TB: Chuck Klein, Phil., 420.
HR: Chuck Klein, Phil.; Mel Ott, N.Y., 38.
RBI: Don Hurst, Phil., 143.
SB: Chuck Klein, Phil., 20.
Wins: Lon Warneke, Chi., 22.
ERA: Lon Warneke, Chi., 2.37.
CG: Red Lucas, Cin., 28.
IP: Dizzy Dean, St.L., 286.
SO: Dizzy Dean, St.L., 191.

A.L. 20-game winners

General Crowder, Wash., 26-13
Lefty Grove, Phil., 25-10
Lefty Gomez, N.Y., 24-7
Wes Ferrell, Cle., 23-13
Monte Weaver, Wash., 22-10

N.L. 20-game winners

Lon Warneke, Chi., 22-6
Watty Clark, Brk., 20-12

A.L. 100 RBIs

Jimmie Foxx, Phil., 169
Lou Gehrig, N.Y., 151

Al Simmons, Phil., 151
Babe Ruth, N.Y., 137
Earl Averill, Cle., 124
Joe Cronin, Wash., 116
Heinie Manush, Wash., 116
Tony Lazzeri, N.Y., 113
Mickey Cochrane, Phil., 112
John Stone, Det., 108
Ben Chapman, N.Y., 107
Charlie Gehringer, Det., 107
Smead Jolley, Chi.-St.L., 106
Goose Goslin, St.L., 104

N.L. 100 RBIs

Don Hurst, Phil., 143
Chuck Klein, Phil., 137
Pinky Whitney, Phil., 124
Mel Ott, N.Y., 123
Hack Wilson, Brk., 123
Bill Terry, N.Y., 117

A.L. 40 homers

Jimmie Foxx, Phil., 58
Babe Ruth, N.Y., 41

Most Valuable Player

A.L.: Jimmie Foxx, 1B, Phil.
N.L.: Chuck Klein, OF, Phil.

WORLD SERIES

■ **Winner:** The Yankees played long ball in their sweep of the Cubs.
■ **Turning point:** A fourth-inning Game 1 homer by Lou Gehrig that gave the Yankees a 3-2 lead and propelled them to their sweep.
■ **Memorable moment:** Babe Ruth's second homer in Game 3 off Cubs righthander Charlie Root — whether it was a "called shot" or not.
■ **Top guns:** Gehrig (.529, 3 HR, 8 RBIs), Ruth (.333, 2 HR, 6 RBIs), Yankees; Riggs Stephenson (.444), Cubs.

Linescores

Game 1—September 28, at New York
Chicago..........2 0 0 0 0 2 2 0—6 10 1
New York........0 0 0 3 0 5 3 1 x—12 8 2
Bush, Grimes (6), Smith (8); Ruffing. W—Ruffing.
L—Bush. HR—Gehrig (N.Y.).

Game 2—September 29, at New York
Chicago..........1 0 1 0 0 0 0 0—2 9 0
New York.........2 0 2 0 1 0 0 x—5 10 1
Warneke; Gomez. W—Gomez. L—Warneke.

Game 3—October 1, at Chicago
New York ....3 0 1 0 2 0 0 0 1—7 8 1
Chicago.............1 0 2 1 0 0 0 0 1—5 9 4
Pipgras, Pennock (9); Root, Malone (5), May (8), Tinning (9). W—Pipgras. L—Root. HR—Ruth 2, Gehrig 2 (N.Y.); Cuyler, Hartnett (Chi.).

Game 4—October 2, at Chicago
New York ......1 0 2 0 0 2 4 0 4—13 19 4
Chicago..........4 0 0 0 0 1 0 0 1—6 9 1
Allen, W. Moore (1), Pennock (7); Bush, Warneke (1), May (4), Tinning (7), Grimes (9). W—W. Moore. L—May. HR—Demaree (Chi.); Lazzeri 2, Combs (N.Y.).

1933

FINAL STANDINGS

American League

Team	W	L	Pct.	GB
Washington	99	53	.651	...
New York	91	59	.607	7
Philadelphia	79	72	.523	19.5
Cleveland	75	76	.497	23.5
Detroit	75	79	.487	25
Chicago	67	83	.447	31
Boston	63	86	.423	34.5
St. Louis	55	96	.364	43.5

National League

Team	W	L	Pct.	GB
New York	91	61	.599	...
Pittsburgh	87	67	.565	5
Chicago	86	68	.558	6
Boston	83	71	.539	9
St. Louis	82	71	.536	9.5
Brooklyn	65	88	.425	26.5
Philadelphia	60	92	.395	31
Cincinnati	58	94	.382	33

SIGNIFICANT EVENTS

■ **January 7:** Commissioner Kenesaw Mountain Landis, sending a Depression-era message to owners and players, took a voluntary $25,000 cut in salary.
■ **November 7:** A referendum was passed by Pennsylvania voters legalizing Sunday baseball for Pittsburgh and Philadelphia — the only Major League cities still observing the blue law.

MEMORABLE MOMENTS

■ **July 30:** Cardinals ace Dizzy Dean set a modern record with 17 strikeouts in an 8-2 victory over Chicago.
■ **July 2:** Giants pitchers Carl Hubbell (18) and Roy Parmelee (9) combined for 27 scoreless innings in a doubleheader shutout of the St. Louis Cardinals. Both games ended 1-0.
■ **August 1:** Giants lefty Carl Hubbell extended his N.L.-record scoreless-innings streak to 45 in a game eventually won by Boston, 3-1.
■ **August 17:** Yankee Lou Gehrig broke Everett Scott's Major League record when he played in his 1,308th consecutive game — a 7-6 loss at St. Louis.
■ **October 1:** Philadelphia stars Jimmie Foxx (.356, 48 homers, 163 RBIs) and Chuck Klein (.368, 28, 120) completed an unprecedented one-season double, becoming the fifth and sixth Triple Crown winners of the century.

LEADERS

American League
BA: Jimmie Foxx, Phil., .356.
Runs: Lou Gehrig, N.Y., 138.
Hits: Heinie Manush, Wash., 221.
TB: Jimmie Foxx, Phil., 403.
HR: Jimmie Foxx, Phil., 48.
RBI: Jimmie Foxx, Phil., 163.
SB: Ben Chapman, N.Y., 27.
Wins: General Crowder, Wash.; Lefty Grove, Phil., 24.
ERA: Mel Harder, Cle., 2.95.
CG: Lefty Grove, Phil., 21.
IP: Bump Hadley, St.L., 316.2.
SO: Lefty Gomez, N.Y., 163.

National League
BA: Chuck Klein, Phil., .368.
Runs: Pepper Martin, St.L., 122.
Hits: Chuck Klein, Phil., 223.
TB: Chuck Klein, Phil., 365.
HR: Chuck Klein, Phil., 28.
RBI: Chuck Klein, Phil., 120.
SB: Pepper Martin, St.L., 26.
Wins: Carl Hubbell, N.Y., 23.
ERA: Carl Hubbell, N.Y., 1.66.
CG: Dizzy Dean, St.L.; Lon Warneke, Chi., 26.
IP: Carl Hubbell, N.Y., 308.2.
SO: Dizzy Dean, St.L., 199.

A.L. 20-game winners
Lefty Grove, Phil., 24-8
General Crowder, Wash., 24-15
Earl Whitehill, Wash., 22-8

N.L. 20-game winners
Carl Hubbell, N.Y., 23-12
Ben Cantwell, Bos., 20-10
Guy Bush, Chi., 20-12
Dizzy Dean, St.L., 20-18

A.L. 100 RBIs
Jimmie Foxx, Phil., 163
Lou Gehrig, N.Y., 139
Al Simmons, Chi., 119
Joe Cronin, Wash., 118
Joe Kuhel, Wash., 107
Bruce Campbell, St.L., 106
Charlie Gehringer, Det., 105
Tony Lazzeri, N.Y., 104
Babe Ruth, N.Y., 103

N.L. 100 RBIs
Chuck Klein, Phil., 120
Wally Berger, Bos., 106
Mel Ott, N.Y., 103

A.L. 40 homers
Jimmie Foxx, Phil., 48

Most Valuable Player
A.L.: Jimmie Foxx, 1B, Phil.
N.L.: Carl Hubbell, P, N.Y.

ALL-STAR GAME

■ **Winner:** The American League prevailed 4-2 in baseball's "Game of the Century," which gathered the biggest stars from both leagues for an unprecedented meeting at Chicago's Comiskey Park.
■ **Key inning:** The third, when Yankee slugger Babe Ruth pounded a two-run homer and gave the A.L. a 3-0 lead.
■ **Memorable moment:** The star-studded pregame introductions for baseball's first All-Star classic.
■ **Top guns:** Lefty Gomez (Yankees), Ruth (Yankees), Jimmie Dykes (White Sox), A.L.; Frank Frisch (Cardinals), Bill Terry (Giants), N.L.
■ **MVP:** Ruth.

Linescore

July 6, at Chicago's Comiskey Park
N.L. ....0 0 0 0 0 2 0 0 0—2 8 0
A.L. ....0 1 2 0 0 1 0 0 x—4 9 1
Hallahan (Cardinals), Warneke (Cubs) 3, Hubbell (Giants) 7; Gomez (Yankees), Crowder (Senators) 4, Grove (Athletics) 7. W—Gomez. L—Hallahan. HR—Ruth, A.L.; Frisch (N.L.).

WORLD SERIES

■ **Winner:** The pitching-rich Giants, now under the direction of player/manager Bill Terry, captured their first Series without John McGraw at the helm.
■ **Turning point:** Carl Hubbell's 2-1, 11-inning victory that gave the Giants a three-games-to-one edge.
■ **Memorable moment:** A 10th-inning home run by Mel Ott that gave the Giants a Series-ending 4-3 victory.
■ **Top guns:** Hubbell (2-0, 0.00 ERA), Ott (.389, 2 HR, 4 RBIs), Giants; Fred Schulte (.333), Senators.

Linescores

Game 1—October 3, at New York
Washington.............0 0 0 1 0 0 0 0 1—2 5 3
New York..................2 0 2 0 0 0 0 0 x—4 10 2
Stewart, Russell (3), Thomas (8); Hubbell. W—Hubbell. L—Stewart. HR—Ott (N.Y.).

Game 2—October 4, at New York
Washington.............0 0 1 0 0 0 0 0 0—1 5 0
New York..................0 0 0 0 0 6 0 0 x—6 10 0
Crowder, Thomas (6), McColl (7); Schumacher. W—Schumacher. L—Crowder. HR—Goslin (Wash.).

Game 3—October 5, at Washington
New York...................0 0 0 0 0 0 0 0 0—0 5 0
Washington...............2 1 0 0 0 0 1 0 x—4 9 1
Fitzsimmons, Bell (8); Whitehill. W—Whitehill. L—Fitzsimmons.

Game 4—October 6, at Washington
New York........0 0 0 1 0 0 0 0 0 0 1—2 11 1
Washington....0 0 0 0 0 0 1 0 0 0 0—1 8 0
Hubbell; Weaver, Russell (11). W—Hubbell. L—Weaver. HR—Terry (N.Y.).

Game 5—October 7, at Washington
New York...........0 2 0 0 0 1 0 0 0 1—4 11 1
Washington........0 0 0 0 0 3 0 0 0 0—3 10 0
Schumacher, Luque (6); Crowder, Russell (6). W—Luque. L—Russell. HR—Schulte (Wash.); Ott (N.Y.).

1934

FINAL STANDINGS

American League

Team	W	L	Pct.	GB
Detroit	101	53	.656	...
New York	94	60	.610	7
Cleveland	85	69	.552	16
Boston	76	76	.500	24
Philadelphia	68	82	.453	31
St. Louis	67	85	.441	33
Washington	66	86	.434	34
Chicago	53	99	.349	47

National League

Team	W	L	Pct.	GB
St. Louis	95	58	.621	...
New York	93	60	.608	2
Chicago	86	65	.570	8
Boston	78	73	.517	16
Pittsburgh	74	76	.493	19.5
Brooklyn	71	81	.467	23.5
Philadelphia	56	93	.376	37
Cincinnati	52	99	.344	42

SIGNIFICANT EVENTS

■ **February 25:** John McGraw, considered by many the greatest manager of all time, died of cancer at age 60.
■ **November 9:** N.L. officials selected Ford Frick as league president, six days after John Heydler resigned for health reasons.
■ **December 12:** The N.L., acting independently of the A.L., voted to allow night baseball on a limited basis.

MEMORABLE MOMENTS

■ **July 13:** Yankee outfielder Babe Ruth opened the 700-homer club when he connected off righthander Tommy Bridges in a game at Detroit.
■ **August 25:** Detroit rookie Schoolboy Rowe defeated Washington 4-2 for his A.L. record-tying 16th consecutive victory.
■ **September 21:** Cardinals ace Dizzy Dean shut out Brooklyn on three hits in the first game of a doubleheader and brother Paul pitched a no-hitter against the Dodgers in the nightcap.

LEADERS

American League
BA: Lou Gehrig, N.Y., .363.
Runs: Charley Gehringer, Det., 134.
Hits: Charley Gehringer, Det., 214.
TB: Lou Gehrig, N.Y., 409.
HR: Lou Gehrig, N.Y., 49.
RBI: Lou Gehrig, N.Y., 165.
SB: Billy Werber, Bos., 40.
Wins: Lefty Gomez, N.Y., 26.
ERA: Lefty Gomez, N.Y., 2.33.
CG: Lefty Gomez, N.Y., 25.
IP: Lefty Gomez, N.Y., 281.2.
SO: Lefty Gomez, N.Y., 158.

National League
BA: Paul Waner, Pit., .362.
Runs: Paul Waner, Pit., 122.
Hits: Paul Waner, Pit., 217.
TB: Ripper Collins, St.L., 369.
HR: Ripper Collins, St.L.; Mel Ott, N.Y., 35.
RBI: Mel Ott, N.Y., 135.
SB: Pepper Martin, St.L., 23.
Wins: Dizzy Dean, St.L., 30.
ERA: Carl Hubbell, N.Y., 2.30.
CG: Carl Hubbell, N.Y., 25.
IP: Van Lingle Mungo, Brk., 315.1.
SO: Dizzy Dean, St.L., 195.

A.L. 20-game winners
Lefty Gomez, N.Y., 26-5
Schoolboy Rowe, Det., 24-8
Tommy Bridges, Det., 22-11
Mel Harder, Cle., 20-12

N.L. 20-game winners
Dizzy Dean, St.L., 30-7
Hal Schumacher, N.Y., 23-10
Lon Warneke, Chi., 22-10
Carl Hubbell, N.Y., 21-12

A.L. 100 RBIs
Lou Gehrig, N.Y., 165
Hal Trosky, Cle., 142
Hank Greenberg, Det., 139
Jimmie Foxx, Phil., 130
Charlie Gehringer, Det., 127
Roy Johnson, Bos., 119
Earl Averill, Cle., 113
Zeke Bonura, Chi., 110
Al Simmons, Chi., 104
Joe Cronin, Wash., 101
Odell Hale, Cle., 101
Roy Pepper, St.L., 101
Goose Goslin, Det., 100
Billy Rogell, Det., 100

N.L. 100 RBIs
Mel Ott, N.Y., 135
Ripper Collins, St.L., 128
Wally Berger, Bos., 121
Joe Medwick, St.L., 106
Gus Suhr, Pit., 103
Sam Leslie, Brk., 102
Travis Jackson, N.Y., 101

A.L. 40 homers
Lou Gehrig, N.Y., 49
Jimmie Foxx, Phil., 44

Most Valuable Player
A.L.: Mickey Cochrane, C, Det.
N.L.: Dizzy Dean, P, St.L.

ALL-STAR GAME

■ **Winner:** The A.L. made it two in a row by roaring back from a 4-0 deficit for a 9-7 victory.
■ **Key inning:** The fifth, when the A.L. scored six times to take command. Cleveland's Earl Averill doubled home two runs and Yankee pitcher Red Ruffing singled in two more.
■ **Memorable moment:** The first- and second-inning performance of Giants lefthander Carl Hubbell, who struck out A.L. bashers Babe Ruth (Yankees), Lou Gehrig (Yankees), Jimmie Foxx (Athletics), Al Simmons (White Sox) and Joe Cronin (Senators) consecutively.
■ **Top guns:** Mel Harder (Indians), Averill (Indians), Cronin (Senators), Simmons (White Sox), A.L.; Hubbell (Giants), Joe Medwick (Cardinals), Frank Frisch (Cardinals), N.L.
■ **MVP:** Averill.

Linescore

July 10, at New York's Polo Grounds
A.L. ....0 0 0 2 6 1 0 0 0—9 14 1
N.L. ....1 0 3 0 3 0 0 0 0—7 8 1
Gomez (Yankees), Ruffing (Yankees) 4, Harder (Indians) 5, A.L.; Hubbell (Giants), Warneke (Cubs) 4, Mungo (Dodgers) 5, Dean (Cardinals) 6, Frankhouse (Braves) 9. W—Harder. L—Mungo. HR—Frisch, Medwick, N.L.

WORLD SERIES

■ **Winner:** St. Louis' Gas House Gang defeated the Tigers in the infamous "Garbage" World Series.
■ **Turning point:** Paul Dean's pitching and hitting gave the Cardinals a 4-3 Game 6 victory that set up a winner-take-all seventh game.
■ **Memorable moment:** A seventh-game outburst by frustrated Tigers fans who pelted Cardinals left fielder Joe Medwick with garbage and other debris, forcing a long delay. The Cardinals were leading 9-0 en route to an 11-0 victory.
■ **Top guns:** Paul Dean (2-0, 1.00 ERA), Dizzy Dean (2-1, 1.73), Medwick (.379, 5 RBIs), Cardinals; Charley Gehringer (.379), Tigers.

Linescores

Game 1—October 3, at Detroit
St. Louis ....0 2 1 0 1 4 0 0 0—8 13 2
Detroit.....................0 0 1 0 0 1 0 1 0—3 8 5
D. Dean; Crowder, Marberry (6), Hogsett (6). W—D. Dean. L—Crowder. HR—Medwick (St.L.); Greenberg (Det.).

Game 2—October 4, at Detroit
St. Louis ......0 1 1 0 0 0 0 0 0 0 0 0—2 7 3
Detroit.........0 0 0 1 0 0 0 0 1 0 0 1—3 7 0
Hallahan, W. Walker (9); Rowe. W—Rowe. L—W. Walker.

Game 3—October 5, at St. Louis
Detroit........................0 0 0 0 0 0 0 0 1—1 8 2
St. Louis ....1 1 0 0 2 0 0 0 x—4 9 1
Bridges, Hogsett (5); P. Dean. W—P. Dean. L—Bridges.

Game 4—October 6, at St. Louis
Detroit.....................0 0 3 1 0 0 1 5 0—10 13 1
St. Louis ....0 1 1 2 0 0 0 0 0— 4 10 5
Auker; Carleton, Vance (3), W. Walker (5), Haines (8), Mooney (9). W—Auker. L—W. Walker.

Game 5—October 7, at St. Louis
Detroit........................0 1 0 0 0 2 0 0 0—3 7 0
St. Louis ....0 0 0 0 0 0 1 0 0—1 7 1
Bridges; D. Dean, Carleton (9). W—Bridges. L—D. Dean. HR—Gehringer (Det.); DeLancey (St.L.).

Game 6—October 8, at Detroit
St. Louis ....1 0 0 0 2 0 1 0 0—4 10 2
Detroit......................0 0 1 0 0 2 0 0 0—3 7 1
P. Dean; Rowe. W—P. Dean. L—Rowe.

Game 7—October 9, at Detroit
St. Louis ....0 0 7 0 0 2 2 0 0—11 17 1
Detroit....................0 0 0 0 0 0 0 0 0— 0 6 3
D. Dean; Auker, Rowe (3), Hogsett (3), Bridges (3), Marberry (8), Crowder (9). W—D. Dean. L—Auker.

1935

FINAL STANDINGS

American League

Team	W	L	Pct.	GB
Detroit	93	58	.616	...
New York	89	60	.597	3
Cleveland	82	71	.536	12
Boston	78	75	.510	16
Chicago	74	78	.487	19.5
Washington	67	86	.438	27
St. Louis	65	87	.428	28.5
Philadelphia	58	91	.389	34

National League

Team	W	L	Pct.	GB
Chicago	100	54	.649	...
St. Louis	96	58	.623	4
New York	91	62	.595	8.5
Pittsburgh	86	67	.562	13.5
Brooklyn	70	83	.458	29.5
Cincinnati	68	85	.444	31.5
Philadelphia	64	89	.418	35.5
Boston	38	115	.248	61.5

SIGNIFICANT EVENTS

■ **February 26:** Babe Ruth ended his long love affair with New York fans when the Yankees granted him a release to sign with the Braves.

■ **December 10:** A.L. owners attending the winter meetings voted not to sanction night baseball.

MEMORABLE MOMENTS

■ **May 24:** Larry MacPhail's Reds staged the first night game in Major League history and defeated the Phillies, 2-1, at Crosley Field.

■ **June 2:** Braves slugger Babe Ruth retired, eight days after a three-homer game at Pittsburgh had raised his career total to 714.

■ **August 31:** Chicago pitcher Vern Kennedy pitched the first no-hitter in Comiskey Park history and punctuated his 5-0 victory over Cleveland with a bases-loaded triple.

■ **September 22:** The lowly Braves lost their Major League-record 110th game en route to 115 losses.

■ **September 27:** The Cubs clinched the N.L. pennant with a 6-2 victory over St. Louis — their 20th straight win in a streak that would end at 21.

LEADERS

American League

BA: Buddy Myer, Wash., .349.
Runs: Lou Gehrig, N.Y., 125.
Hits: Joe Vosmik, Cle., 216.
TB: Hank Greenberg, Det., 389.
HR: Jimmie Foxx, Phil.; Hank Greenberg, Det., 36.
RBI: Hank Greenberg, Det., 170.
SB: Billy Werber, Bos., 29.
Wins: Wes Ferrell, Bos., 25.
ERA: Lefty Grove, Bos., 2.70.
CG: Wes Ferrell, Bos., 31.
IP: Wes Ferrell, Bos., 322.1.
SO: Tommy Bridges, Det., 163.

National League

BA: Arky Vaughan, Pit., .385.
Runs: Augie Galan, Chi., 133.
Hits: Billy Herman, Chi., 227.
TB: Joe Medwick, St.L., 365.
HR: Wally Berger, Bos., 34.
RBI: Wally Berger, Bos., 130.
SB: Augie Galan, Chi., 22.
Wins: Dizzy Dean, St.L., 28.
ERA: Cy Blanton, Pit., 2.58.
CG: Dizzy Dean, St.L., 29.
IP: Dizzy Dean, St.L., 325.1
SO: Dizzy Dean, St.L., 190.

A.L. 20-game winners

Wes Ferrell, Bos., 25-14
Mel Harder, Cle., 22-11
Tommy Bridges, Det., 21-10
Lefty Grove, Bos., 20-12

N.L. 20-game winners

Dizzy Dean, St.L., 28-12
Carl Hubbell, N.Y., 23-12
Paul Derringer, Cin., 22-13
Bill Lee, Chi., 20-6
Lon Warneke, Chi., 20-13

A.L. 100 RBIs

Hank Greenberg, Det., 170
Lou Gehrig, N.Y., 119
Jimmie Foxx, Phil., 115
Hal Trosky, Cle., 113
Moose Solters, Bos.-St.L., 112
Joe Vosmik, Cle., 110
Goose Goslin, Det., 109
Bob Johnson, Phil., 109
Charlie Gehringer, Det., 108
Odell Hale, Cle., 101
Buddy Myer, Wash., 100

N.L. 100 RBIs

Wally Berger, Bos., 130
Joe Medwick, St.L., 126
Ripper Collins, St.L., 122
Mel Ott, N.Y., 114
Hank Leiber, N.Y., 107

Most Valuable Player

A.L.: Hank Greenberg, 1B, Det.
N.L.: Gabby Hartnett, C, Chi.

ALL-STAR GAME

■ **Winner:** New York's Lefty Gomez and Cleveland's Mel Harder combined on a four-hitter and the A.L. recorded its third straight All-Star victory, 4-1.

■ **Key inning:** The first, when Athletics slugger Jimmie Foxx belted a two-run homer off Bill Walker, giving Gomez and Harder all the runs they would need.

■ **Memorable moment:** The ovation for hometown favorite Harder after his three-inning, one-hit pitching to close out the N.L.

■ **Top guns:** Gomez (Yankees), Harder (Indians), Foxx (Athletics), Charley Gehringer (Tigers), A.L.; Bill Terry (Giants), N.L.

■ **MVP:** Foxx.

Linescore

July 8, at Cleveland Stadium
N.L. ....0 0 0 1 0 0 0 0 0—1 4 1
A.L. ....2 1 0 0 1 0 0 0 x—4 8 0
Walker (Cardinals), Schumacher (Giants) 3, Derringer (Reds) 7, Dean (Cardinals) 8; Gomez (Yankees), Harder (Indians) 7. W—Gomez. L—Walker. HR—Foxx, A.L.

WORLD SERIES

■ **Winner:** The Tigers, four-time Series losers, won their first in a six-game battle with the Cubs.

■ **Turning point:** Detroit's 6-5 Game 3 victory. Jo Jo White drove in the game-winner with an 11th-inning single, giving the Tigers a two-games-to-one edge.

■ **Memorable moment:** Detroit pitcher Tommy Bridges' dramatic ninth-inning escape in Game 7 after giving up a leadoff triple to Stan Hack with the game tied, 3-3. The Tigers ended the Series in the bottom of the inning.

■ **Top guns:** Bridges (2-0, 2.50 ERA), Pete Fox (.385), Tigers; Lon Warneke (2-0, 0.54), Billy Herman (.333, 6 RBIs), Cubs.

Linescores

Game 1—October 2, at Detroit
Chicago......................2 0 0 0 0 0 0 0 1—3 7 0
Detroit.......................0 0 0 0 0 0 0 0 0—0 4 3
Warneke; Rowe. W—Warneke. L—Rowe. HR—Demaree (Chi.).

Game 2—October 3, at Detroit
Chicago......................0 0 0 0 1 0 2 0 0—3 6 1
Detroit.......................4 0 0 3 0 0 1 0 x—8 9 2
Root, Henshaw (1), Kowalik (4); Bridges. W—Bridges. L—Root. HR—Greenberg (Det.).

Game 3—October 4, at Chicago
Detroit............0 0 0 0 0 1 0 4 0 0 1—6 12 2
Chicago..........0 2 0 0 1 0 0 0 2 0 0—5 10 3
Auker, Hogsett (7), Rowe (8); Lee, Warneke (8), French (10). W—Rowe. L—French. HR—Demaree (Chi.).

Game 4—October 5, at Chicago
Detroit.......................0 0 1 0 0 1 0 0 0—2 7 0
Chicago......................0 1 0 0 0 0 0 0 0—1 5 2
Crowder; Carleton, Root (8). W—Crowder. L—Carleton. HR—Hartnett (Chi.).

Game 5—October 6, at Chicago
Detroit.......................0 0 0 0 0 0 0 0 1—1 7 1
Chicago......................0 0 2 0 0 0 1 0 x—3 8 0
Rowe; Warneke, Lee (7). W—Warneke. L—Rowe. HR—Klein (Chi.).

Game 6—October 7, at Detroit
Chicago....................0 0 1 0 2 0 0 0 0—3 12 0
Detroit.....................1 0 0 1 0 1 0 0 1—4 12 1
French; Bridges. W—Bridges. L—French. HR—Herman (Chi.).

1936

FINAL STANDINGS

American League

Team	W	L	Pct.	GB
New York	102	51	.667	...
Detroit	83	71	.539	19.5
Chicago	81	70	.536	20
Washington	82	71	.536	20
Cleveland	80	74	.519	22.5
Boston	74	80	.481	28.5
St. Louis	57	95	.375	44.5
Philadelphia	53	100	.346	49

National League

Team	W	L	Pct.	GB
New York	92	62	.597	...
Chicago	87	67	.565	5
St. Louis	87	67	.565	5
Pittsburgh	84	70	.545	8
Cincinnati	74	80	.481	18
Boston	71	83	.461	21
Brooklyn	67	87	.435	25
Philadelphia	54	100	.351	38

SIGNIFICANT EVENTS

■ **February 2:** Ty Cobb, Babe Ruth, Honus Wagner, Walter Johnson and Christy Mathewson were named charter members of baseball's new Hall of Fame.

■ **June 4:** Detroit player/manager Mickey Cochrane collapsed in a Shibe Park dugout and was hospitalized on the threshhold of a career-threatening nervous breakdown.

■ **December 9:** A.L. owners granted the Browns permission to play night baseball in St. Louis and ruled that players must have at least 400 at-bats to qualify for a batting championship.

MEMORABLE MOMENTS

■ **May 24:** Tony Lazzeri drilled three home runs, including a single-game record two grand slams, and drove in an A.L.-record 11 runs in the Yankees' 25-2 pounding of the Athletics.

■ **July 10:** Philadelphia's Chuck Klein became the fourth Major Leaguer to hit four homers in one game, completing his big day with a solo blast leading off the 10th inning of a 9-6 victory over Pittsburgh.

■ **September 13:** Cleveland 17-year-old Bob Feller tied a Major League record when he struck out 17 Athletics in a 5-2 victory.

LEADERS

American League

BA: Luke Appling, Chi., .388.
Runs: Lou Gehrig, N.Y., 167.
Hits: Earl Averill, Cle., 232.
TB: Hal Trosky, Cle., 405.
HR: Lou Gehrig, N.Y., 49.
RBI: Hal Trosky, Cle., 162.
SB: Lyn Lary, St.L., 37.
Wins: Tommy Bridges, Det., 23.
ERA: Lefty Grove, Bos., 2.81.
CG: Wes Ferrell, Bos., 28.
IP: Wes Ferrell, Bos., 301.
SO: Tommy Bridges, Det., 175.

National League

BA: Paul Waner, Pit., .373.
Runs: Arky Vaughan, Pit., 122.
Hits: Joe Medwick, St.L., 223.
TB: Joe Medwick, St.L., 367.
HR: Mel Ott, N.Y., 33.
RBI: Joe Medwick, St.L., 138.
SB: Pepper Martin, St.L., 23.
Wins: Carl Hubbell, N.Y., 26.
ERA: Carl Hubbell, N.Y., 2.31.
CG: Dizzy Dean, St.L., 28.
IP: Dizzy Dean, St.L., 315.
SO: Van Lingle Mungo, Brk., 238.

A.L. 20-game winners

Tommy Bridges, Det., 23-11
Vern Kennedy, Chi., 21-9
Johnny Allen, Cle., 20-10
Red Ruffing, N.Y., 20-12
Wes Ferrell, Bos., 20-15

N.L. 20-game winners

Carl Hubbell, N.Y., 26-6
Dizzy Dean, St.L., 24-13

A.L. 100 RBIs

Hal Trosky, Cle., 162
Lou Gehrig, N.Y., 152
Jimmie Foxx, Bos., 143
Zeke Bonura, Chi., 138
Moose Solters, St.L., 134
Luke Appling, Chi., 128
Earl Averill, Cle., 126
Joe DiMaggio, N.Y., 125
Goose Goslin, Det., 125
Beau Bell, St.L., 123
Bob Johnson, Phil., 121
Joe Kuhel, Wash., 118
Charlie Gehringer, Det., 116
Al Simmons, Det., 112
Tony Lazzeri, N.Y., 109
Bill Dickey, N.Y., 107
George Selkirk, N.Y., 107
Marv Owen, Det., 105

N.L. 100 RBIs

Joe Medwick, St.L., 138
Mel Ott, N.Y., 135
Gus Suhr, Pit., 118
Chuck Klein, Chi.-Phil.,, 104
Bill Brubaker, Pit., 102
Dolph Camilli, Phil., 102

A.L. 40 homers

Lou Gehrig, N.Y., 49
Hal Trosky, Cle., 42
Jimmie Foxx, Bos., 41

Most Valuable Player

A.L.: Lou Gehrig, 1B, N.Y.
N.L.: Carl Hubbell, P, N.Y.

Hall of Fame additions

Charter Class

Ty Cobb, OF, 1905-28
Walter Johnson, P, 1907-27
Christy Mathewson, P, 1900-16
Babe Ruth, P/OF, 1914-35
Honus Wagner, SS, 1897-1917

ALL-STAR GAME

■ **Winner:** The N.L. recorded its first All-Star victory, thanks to the work of three Cubs — Gabby Hartnett (a run-scoring triple), Augie Galan (a solo home run) and pitcher Lon Warneke.

■ **Key inning:** After the A.L. had cut its deficit to 4-3 in the seventh, Warneke retired Yankee slugger Joe DiMaggio on a line drive with the bases loaded.

■ **Memorable moment:** Galan's fifth-inning blast into the right-field bleachers. It drew a vehement protest from A.L. manager Joe McCarthy, who thought it was foul.

■ **Top guns:** Dizzy Dean (Cardinals), Warneke (Cubs), Galan (Cubs), Hartnett (Cubs), N.L.; Lou Gehrig (Yankees), Luke Appling (White Sox), A.L.

■ **MVP:** Warneke.

Linescore

July 7, at Boston's Braves Field
A.L. ....0 0 0 0 0 0 3 0 0—3 7 1
N.L. ....0 2 0 0 2 0 0 0 x—4 9 0
Grove (Red Sox), Rowe (Tigers) 4, Harder (Indians) 7; D. Dean (Cardinals), Hubbell (Giants) 4, Davis (Cubs) 7, Warneke (Cubs) 7. W—D. Dean. L—Grove. HR—Galan, N.L.; Gehrig, A.L.

WORLD SERIES

■ **Winner:** Renewing an old New York rivalry, the Yankees prevailed in their first Series without Babe Ruth.

■ **Turning point:** Lou Gehrig's two-run Game 4 homer off Giants ace Carl Hubbell propelled the Yankees to a 5-2 victory and a three-games-to-one Series lead.

■ **Memorable moment:** Yankee slugger Tony Lazzeri's Game 2 grand slam, only the second in Series history.

■ **Top guns:** Jake Powell (.455), Gehrig (2 HR, 7 RBIs), Red Rolfe (.400), Yankees; Dick Bartell (.381), Giants.

Linescores

Game 1—September 30, at Polo Grounds
Yankees......................0 0 1 0 0 0 0 0 0—1 7 2
Giants ....0 0 0 0 1 1 0 4 x—6 9 1
Ruffing; Hubbell. W—Hubbell. L—Ruffing. HR—Bartell (NYG); Selkirk (NYY).

Game 2—October 2, at Polo Grounds
Yankees..................2 0 7 0 0 1 2 0 6—18 17 0
Giants ....0 1 0 3 0 0 0 0 0— 4 6 1
Gomez; Schumacher, Smith (3), Coffman (3), Gabler (5), Gumbert (9). W—Gomez. L—Schumacher. HR—Dickey, Lazzeri (NYY).

Game 3—October 3, at Yankee Stadium
Giants ....0 0 0 0 1 0 0 0 0—1 11 0
Yankees....................0 1 0 0 0 0 0 1 x—2 4 0
Fitzsimmons; Hadley, Malone (9). W—Hadley. L—Fitzsimmons. HR—Gehrig (NYY); Ripple (NYG).

Game 4—October 4, at Yankee Stadium
Giants ....0 0 0 1 0 0 0 1 0—2 7 1
Yankees....................0 1 3 0 0 0 0 1 x—5 10 1
Hubbell, Gabler (8); Pearson. W—Pearson. L—Hubbell. HR—Gehrig (NYY).

Game 5—October 5, at Yankee Stadium
Giants ....3 0 0 0 0 1 0 0 0 1—5 8 3
Yankees................0 1 1 0 0 2 0 0 0 0—4 10 1
Schumacher; Ruffing, Malone (7). W—Schumacher. L—Malone. HR—Selkirk (NYY).

Game 6—October 6, at Polo Grounds
Yankees..................0 2 1 2 0 0 0 1 7—13 17 2
Giants ....2 0 0 0 1 0 1 1 0— 5 9 1
Gomez, Murphy (7); Fitzsimmons, Castleman (4), Coffman (9), Gumbert (9). W—Gomez. L—Fitzsimmons. HR—Moore, Ott (NYG); Powell (NYY).

1937

FINAL STANDINGS

American League

Team	W	L	Pct.	GB
New York	102	52	.662	...
Detroit	89	65	.578	13
Chicago	86	68	.558	16
Cleveland	83	71	.539	19
Boston	80	72	.526	21
Washington	73	80	.477	28.5
Philadelphia	54	97	.358	46.5
St. Louis	46	108	.299	56

National League

Team	W	L	Pct.	GB
New York	95	57	.625	...
Chicago	93	61	.604	3
Pittsburgh	86	68	.558	10
St. Louis	81	73	.526	15
Boston	79	73	.520	16
Brooklyn	62	91	.405	33.5
Philadelphia	61	92	.399	34.5
Cincinnati	56	98	.364	40

SIGNIFICANT EVENTS

- **May 25:** Detroit player/manager Mickey Cochrane suffered a career-ending skull fracture when he was struck by a pitch from Yankee Bump Hadley.
- **May 26:** Commissioner Kenesaw Mountain Landis took the All-Star vote away from the fans and decreed that the two managers would select future teams.

MEMORABLE MOMENTS

- **April 20:** Detroit outfielder Gee Walker carved out his own piece of the Major League record book when he hit a single, double, triple and home run in a season-opening victory over Cleveland—the first player to hit for the cycle on Opening Day.
- **May 27:** Giants lefty Carl Hubbell, asked to make a rare relief appearance, pitched two scoreless innings and earned a 3-2 victory over the Reds, his record 24th straight over two seasons.
- **August 31:** Detroit rookie Rudy York hit two home runs against Washington, capping the biggest home run-hitting month in baseball history with 18.
- **October 3:** Cleveland's Johnny Allen, 15-0 and one win from tying the A.L. record for consecutive victories, dropped a 1-0 final-day decision to Detroit.
- **October 3:** St. Louis' Joe Medwick captured an N.L. Triple Crown, batting .374, driving in 154 runs and tying New York's Mel Ott with 31 homers.

LEADERS

American League

BA: Charley Gehringer, Det., .371.
Runs: Joe DiMaggio, N.Y., 151.
Hits: Beau Bell, St.L., 218.
TB: Joe DiMaggio, N.Y., 418.
HR: Joe DiMaggio, N.Y., 46.
RBI: Hank Greenberg, Det., 183.
SB: Ben Chapman, Wash.-Bos.; Billy Werber, Phil., 35.
Wins: Lefty Gomez, N.Y., 21.
ERA: Lefty Gomez, N.Y., 2.33.
CG: Wes Ferrell, Wash.-Bos., 26.
IP: Wes Ferrell, Wash.-Bos., 281.
SO: Lefty Gomez, N.Y., 194.

National League

BA: Joe Medwick, St.L., .374.
Runs: Joe Medwick, St.L., 111.
Hits: Joe Medwick, St.L., 237.
TB: Joe Medwick, St.L., 406.
HR: Joe Medwick, St.L.; Mel Ott, N.Y., 31.
RBI: Joe Medwick, St.L., 154.
SB: Augie Galan, Chi., 23.
Wins: Carl Hubbell, N.Y., 22.
ERA: Jim Turner, Bos., 2.38.
CG: Jim Turner, Bos., 24.
IP: Claude Passeau, Phil., 292.1.
SO: Carl Hubbell, N.Y., 159.

A.L. 20-game winners
Lefty Gomez, N.Y., 21-11
Red Ruffing, N.Y., 20-7

N.L. 20-game winners
Carl Hubbell, N.Y., 22-8
Cliff Melton, N.Y., 20-9
Lou Fette, Bos., 20-10
Jim Turner, Bos., 20-11

A.L. 100 RBIs
Hank Greenberg, Det., 183
Joe DiMaggio, N.Y., 167
Lou Gehrig, N.Y., 159
Bill Dickey, N.Y., 133
Hal Trosky, Cle., 128
Jimmie Foxx, Bos., 127
Harlond Clift, St.L., 118
Beau Bell, St.L., 117
Gee Walker, Det., 113
Joe Cronin, Bos., 110
Moose Solters, Cle., 109
Bob Johnson, Phil., 108
Pinky Higgins, Bos., 106
Rudy York, Det., 103
Zeke Bonura, Chi., 100

N.L. 100 RBIs
Joe Medwick, St.L., 154
Frank Demaree, Chi., 115
Johnny Mize, St.L., 113

A.L. 40 homers
Joe DiMaggio, N.Y., 46
Hank Greenberg, Det., 40

Most Valuable Player
A.L.: Charley Gehringer, 2B, Det.
N.L.: Joe Medwick, OF, St.L.

Hall of Fame additions
Morgan Bulkeley, executive
Ban Johnson, executive
Napoleon Lajoie, 2B, 1896-1916
Connie Mack, manager/owner
John McGraw, manager
Tris Speaker, OF, 1907-28
George Wright, player/manager
Cy Young, P, 1890-1911

ALL-STAR GAME

- **Winner:** Yankees Lou Gehrig, Red Rolfe and Bill Dickey combined for seven RBIs and teammate Lefty Gomez claimed his third All-Star victory as the A.L. won for the fourth time in five years.
- **Key inning:** The third, when Gehrig blasted a Dizzy Dean pitch for a two-run homer. The Yankee first baseman later added a two-run double.
- **Memorable moment:** A third-inning Earl Averill line drive that deflected off the foot of Dean. The Cardinals' righthander suffered a broken toe that would begin to unravel his outstanding career.
- **Top guns:** Gomez (Yankees), Gehrig (Yankees), Rolfe (Yankees), Dickey (Yankees), Charley Gehringer (Tigers), A.L.; Joe Medwick (Cardinals), Billy Herman (Cubs), N.L.
- **MVP:** Gehrig.

Linescore

July 7, at Washington's Griffith Stadium
N.L. ....0 0 0 1 1 1 0 0 0—3 13 0
A.L. ....0 0 2 3 1 2 0 0 x—8 13 2
D. Dean (Cardinals), Hubbell (Giants) 4, Blanton (Pirates) 4, Grissom (Reds) 5, Mungo (Dodgers) 6, Walters (Phillies) 8; Gomez (Yankees), Bridges (Tigers) 4, Harder (Indians) 7. W—Gomez. L—D. Dean. HR—Gehrig, A.L.

WORLD SERIES

- **Winner:** Two in a row. The first of several big Yankee World Series runs began to take shape.
- **Turning point:** The Yankees' 8-1 pounding of Giants ace Carl Hubbell in Game 1.
- **Memorable moment:** Yankee pitcher Lefty Gomez, a notoriously poor hitter, driving in the Game 5 winner with a fifth-inning single.
- **Top guns:** Gomez (2-0, 1.50 ERA), Tony Lazzeri (.400), Yankees; Joe Moore (.391), Giants.

Linescores

Game 1—October 6, at Yankee Stadium
Giants ....0 0 0 0 1 0 0 0 0—1 6 2
Yankees ....0 0 0 0 0 7 0 1 x—8 7 0
Hubbell, Gumbert (6), Coffman (6), Smith (8); Gomez. W—Gomez. L—Hubbell. HR—Lazzeri (NYY).

Game 2—October 7, at Yankee Stadium
Giants ....1 0 0 0 0 0 0 0 0—1 7 0
Yankees ....0 0 0 0 2 4 2 0 x—8 12 0
Melton, Gumbert (5), Coffman (6); Ruffing. W—Ruffing. L—Melton.

Game 3—October 8, at Polo Grounds
Yankees ....0 1 2 1 1 0 0 0 0—5 9 0
Giants ....0 0 0 0 0 0 1 0 0—1 5 4
Pearson, Murphy (9); Schumacher, Melton (7), Brennan (9). W—Pearson. L—Schumacher.

Game 4—October 9, at Polo Grounds
Yankees ....1 0 1 0 0 0 0 0 1—3 6 0
Giants ....0 6 0 0 0 0 1 0 x—7 12 3
Hadley, Andrews (2), Wicker (8); Hubbell. W—Hubbell. L—Hadley. HR—Gehrig (NYY).

Game 5—October 10, at Polo Grounds
Yankees ....0 1 1 0 2 0 0 0 0—4 8 0
Giants ....0 0 2 0 0 0 0 0 0—2 10 0
Gomez; Melton, Smith (6), Brennan (8). W—Gomez. L—Melton. HR—DiMaggio, Hoag (NYY); Ott (NYG).

1938

FINAL STANDINGS

American League

Team	W	L	Pct.	GB
New York	99	53	.651	...
Boston	88	61	.591	9.5
Cleveland	86	66	.566	13
Detroit	84	70	.545	16
Washington	75	76	.497	23.5
Chicago	65	83	.439	32
St. Louis	55	97	.362	44
Philadelphia	53	99	.349	46

National League

Team	W	L	Pct.	GB
Chicago	89	63	.586	...
Pittsburgh	86	64	.573	2
New York	83	67	.553	5
Cincinnati	82	68	.547	6
Boston	77	75	.507	12
St. Louis	71	80	.470	17.5
Brooklyn	69	80	.463	18.5
Philadelphia	45	105	.300	43

SIGNIFICANT EVENTS

- **April 16:** The Cardinals sent shockwaves through baseball when they traded ace Dizzy Dean to the Cubs for two pitchers and an outfielder.
- **May 31:** Yankee Lou Gehrig stretched his ironman streak to an incredible 2,000 games during a victory over Boston.
- **December 14:** The N.L. granted Cincinnati, baseball's first professional team, permission to play its traditional season opener.

MEMORABLE MOMENTS

- **June 15:** Cincinnati's Johnny Vander Meer pitched his record second consecutive no-hitter, a 6-0 victory that stole the spotlight from the Dodgers in the first night game at Brooklyn's Ebbets Field.
- **June 21:** Boston third baseman Pinky Higgins etched his name in the record books when he collected 12 consecutive hits over a two-day, four-game stretch against Chicago and Detroit.
- **September 28:** Moments away from a suspended game, Chicago catcher Gabby Hartnett stroked a ninth-inning homer into the thickening darkness of Wrigley Field, giving the Cubs a crucial 6-5 victory over Pittsburgh and half-game lead in the tense N.L. pennant race.
- **October 2:** Cleveland's Bob Feller struck out a Major League-record 18 batters while losing a 4-1 decision to the Tigers.

LEADERS

American League

BA: Jimmie Foxx, Bos., .349.
Runs: Hank Greenberg, Det., 144.
Hits: Joe Vosmik, Bos., 201.
TB: Jimmie Foxx, Bos., 398.
HR: Hank Greenberg, Det., 58.
RBI: Jimmie Foxx, Bos., 175.
SB: Frank Crosetti, N.Y., 27.
Wins: Red Ruffing, N.Y., 21.
ERA: Lefty Grove, Bos., 3.08.
CG: Bobo Newsom, St.L., 31.
IP: Bobo Newsom, St.L., 329.2.
SO: Bob Feller, Cle., 240.

National League

BA: Ernie Lombardi, Cin., .342.
Runs: Mel Ott, N.Y., 116.
Hits: Frank McCormick, Cin., 209.
TB: Johnny Mize, St.L., 326.
HR: Mel Ott, N.Y., 36.
RBI: Joe Medwick, St.L., 122.
SB: Stan Hack, Chi., 16.
Wins: Bill Lee, Chi., 22.
ERA: Bill Lee, Chi., 2.66.
CG: Paul Derringer, Cin., 26.
IP: Paul Derringer, Cin., 307.
SO: Clay Bryant, Chi., 135.

A.L. 20-game winners
Red Ruffing, N.Y., 21-7
Bobo Newsom, St.L., 20-16

N.L. 20-game winners
Bill Lee, Chi., 22-9
Paul Derringer, Cin., 21-14

A.L. 100 RBIs
Jimmie Foxx, Bos., 175
Hank Greenberg, Det., 146
Joe DiMaggio, N.Y., 140
Rudy York, Det., 127
Harlond Clift, St.L., 118
Bill Dickey, N.Y., 115
Zeke Bonura, Wash., 114
Lou Gehrig, N.Y., 114
Bob Johnson, Phil., 113
Ken Keltner, Cle., 113
Jeff Heath, Cle., 112
Hal Trosky, Cle., 110
Charlie Gehringer, Det., 107
Pinky Higgins, Bos., 106

N.L. 100 RBIs
Joe Medwick, St.L., 122
Mel Ott, N.Y., 116
Johnny Rizzo, Pit., 111
Frank McCormick, Cin., 106
Johnny Mize, St.L., 102
Dolph Camilli, Brk., 100

A.L. 40 homers
Hank Greenberg, Det., 58
Jimmie Foxx, Bos., 50

Most Valuable Player
A.L.: Jimmie Foxx, 1B, Bos.
N.L.: Ernie Lombardi, C, Cin.

Hall of Fame additions
Grover Alexander, P, 1911-30
Alexander Cartwright, executive
Henry Chadwick, historian, executive

ALL-STAR GAME

- **Winner:** Cincinnati's Johnny Vander Meer, Chicago's Bill Lee and Pittsburgh's Mace Brown held the A.L. to seven hits as the N.L. claimed its second All-Star victory.
- **Key inning:** The first, when the N.L. took a lead it never surrendered on Red Sox shortstop Joe Cronin's error.
- **Memorable moment:** A seventh-inning sacrifice bunt by Brooklyn's Leo Durocher that resulted in two N.L. runs. Durocher circled the bases when third baseman Jimmie Foxx and right fielder Joe DiMaggio made wild throws on the play.
- **Top guns:** Vander Meer (Reds), Lee (Cubs), Ernie Lombardi (Reds), N.L.; Cronin (Red Sox), A.L.
- **MVP:** Vander Meer.

Linescore

July 6, at Cincinnati's Crosley Field
A.L. ....0 0 0 0 0 0 0 0 1—1 7 4
N.L. ....1 0 0 1 0 0 2 0 x—4 8 0
Gomez (Yankees), Allen (Indians) 4, Grove (Red Sox) 7; Vander Meer (Reds), Lee (Cubs) 4, Brown (Pirates) 7. W—Vander Meer. L—Gomez.

WORLD SERIES

- **Winner:** Three in a row. Another Series first for the vaunted Yankee machine of Joe McCarthy.
- **Turning point:** Light-hitting Frankie Crosetti hit an eighth-inning Game 2 homer, helping the Yankees rally to a 6-3 victory over Chicago veteran Dizzy Dean.
- **Memorable moment:** Lou Gehrig's fourth-game single — his last hit in World Series competition.
- **Top guns:** Red Ruffing (2-0, 1.50 ERA), Bill Dickey (.400), Joe Gordon (.400, 6 RBIs), Crosetti (6 RBIs), Yankees; Stan Hack (.471), Cubs.

Linescores

Game 1—October 5, at Chicago
New York ....0 2 0 0 0 0 1 0 0—3 12 1
Chicago ....0 0 1 0 0 0 0 0 0—1 9 1
Ruffing; Lee, Russell (9). W—Ruffing. L—Lee.

Game 2—October 6, at Chicago
New York ....0 2 0 0 0 0 0 2 2—6 7 2
Chicago ....1 0 2 0 0 0 0 0 0—3 11 0
Gomez, Murphy (8); Dean, French (9). W—Gomez. L—Dean. HR—Crosetti, DiMaggio (N.Y.).

Game 3—October 8, at New York
Chicago ....0 0 0 0 1 0 0 1 0—2 5 1
New York ....0 0 0 0 2 2 0 1 x—5 7 2
Bryant, Russell (6), French (7); Pearson. W—Pearson. L—Bryant. HR—Dickey, Gordon (N.Y.); Marty (Chi.).

Game 4—October 9, at New York
Chicago ....0 0 0 1 0 0 0 2 0—3 8 1
New York ....0 3 0 0 0 1 0 4 x—8 11 1
Lee, Root (4), Page (7), French (8), Carleton (8), Dean (8); Ruffing. W—Ruffing. L—Lee. HR—Henrich (N.Y.); O'Dea (Chi.).

1939

FINAL STANDINGS

American League

Team	W	L	Pct.	GB
New York	106	45	.702	...
Boston	89	62	.589	17
Cleveland	87	67	.565	20.5
Chicago	85	69	.552	22.5
Detroit	81	73	.526	26.5
Washington	65	87	.428	41.5
Philadelphia	55	97	.362	51.5
St. Louis	43	111	.279	64.5

National League

Team	W	L	Pct.	GB
Cincinnati	97	57	.630	...
St. Louis	92	61	.601	4.5
Brooklyn	84	69	.549	12.5
Chicago	84	70	.545	13
New York	77	74	.510	18.5
Pittsburgh	68	85	.444	28.5
Boston	63	88	.417	32.5
Philadelphia	45	106	.298	50.5

SIGNIFICANT EVENTS

■ **June 12:** Baseball dignitaries, gathering in Cooperstown, N.Y., for a centennial celebration, dedicated the sport's new Hall of Fame museum and inducted its first four classes of Hall of Famers.

■ **August 26:** Red Barber handled the play-by-play as experimental station W2XBS presented Major League baseball's first telecast, a game between the Dodgers and Reds at Ebbets Field.

MEMORABLE MOMENTS

■ **May 16:** The visiting Indians recorded a 10-inning 8-3 victory in the A.L.'s first night game at Philadelphia's Shibe Park.

■ **June 27:** Brooklyn and Boston battled for 23 innings and more than five hours before settling for a 2-2 tie in a marathon game at Braves Field.

■ **June 28:** The New York Yankees rocketed a doubleheader-record 13 home runs out of Shibe Park in a 23-2 and 10-0 sweep of the Athletics.

■ **July 4:** Lou Gehrig, forced to end his incredible ironman streak at 2,130 games and retire because of a life-threatening disease, was honored in an emotional farewell at Yankee Stadium.

■ **July 4:** Boston's Jim Tabor tied a Major League record with two grand slams during an 18-12 victory over the Athletics.

LEADERS

American League

BA: Joe DiMaggio, N.Y., .381.
Runs: Red Rolfe, N.Y., 139.
Hits: Red Rolfe, N.Y., 213.
TB: Ted Williams, Bos., 344.
HR: Jimmie Foxx, Bos., 35.
RBI: Ted Williams, Bos., 145.
SB: George Case, Wash., 51.
Wins: Bob Feller, Cle., 24.
ERA: Lefty Grove, Bos., 2.54.
CG: Bob Feller, Cle.; Bobo Newsom, St.L.-Det., 24.
IP: Bob Feller, Cle., 296.2.
SO: Bob Feller, Cle., 246.

National League

BA: Johnny Mize, St.L., .349.
Runs: Billy Werber, Cin., 115.
Hits: Frank McCormick, Cin., 209.
TB: Johnny Mize, St.L., 353.
HR: Johnny Mize, St.L., 28.
RBI: Frank McCormick, Cin., 128.
SB: Stan Hack, Chi.; Lee Handley, Pit., 17.
Wins: Bucky Walters, Cin., 27.
ERA: Bucky Walters, Cin., 2.29.
CG: Bucky Walters, Cin., 31.
IP: Bucky Walters, Cin., 319.
SO: Claude Passeau, Phil.-Chi.; Bucky Walters, Cin., 137.

A.L. 20-game winners
Bob Feller, Cle., 24-9
Red Ruffing, N.Y., 21-7
Dutch Leonard, Wash., 20-8
Bobo Newsom, St.L.-Det., 20-11

N.L. 20-game winners
Bucky Walters, Cin., 27-11
Paul Derringer, Cin., 25-7
Curt Davis, St.L., 22-16
Luke Hamlin, Brk., 20-13

A.L. 100 RBIs
Ted Williams, Bos., 145
Joe DiMaggio, N.Y., 126
Bob Johnson, Phil., 114
Hank Greenberg, Det., 112
Joe Gordon, N.Y., 111
Gee Walker, Chi., 111
Joe Cronin, Bos., 107
Bill Dickey, N.Y., 105
Jimmie Foxx, Bos., 105
Hal Trosky, Cle., 104
George Selkirk, N.Y., 101

N.L. 100 RBIs
Frank McCormick, Cin., 128
Joe Medwick, St.L., 117
Johnny Mize, St.L., 108
Dolph Camilli, Brk., 104

Most Valuable Player
A.L.: Joe DiMaggio, OF, N.Y.
N.L.: Bucky Walters, P, Cin.

Hall of Fame additions
Cap Anson, 1B, 1876-97
Eddie Collins, 2B, 1906-30
Charles Comiskey, manager/exec.
Candy Cummings, P, 1872-77
Buck Ewing, C, 1880-97
Lou Gehrig, 1B, 1923-39
Willie Keeler, OF, 1892-1910
Hoss Radbourn, P, 1880-91
George Sisler, 1B, 1915-30
Al Spalding, pitcher/executive

ALL-STAR GAME

■ **Winner:** The A.L.'s Yankee-studded lineup posted a ho-hum 3-1 victory before 62,892 fans at Yankee Stadium.

■ **Key inning:** The sixth, when the N.L. loaded the bases with one out. Indians fireballer Bob Feller was summoned and got Pittsburgh's Arky Vaughan to hit into a first-pitch double play. Feller allowed one hit the rest of the way.

■ **Memorable moment:** Joe DiMaggio's fifth-inning home run, which touched off a celebration among ecstatic Yankee fans.

■ **Top guns:** Tommy Bridges (Tigers), Feller (Indians), George Selkirk (Yankees), DiMaggio (Yankees), A.L.; Paul Derringer (Reds), Lonny Frey (Reds), N.L.

■ **MVP:** Feller.

Linescore

July 11, at New York's Yankee Stadium
N.L. ....0 0 1 0 0 0 0 0 0 — 1 7 1
A.L. ....0 0 0 2 1 0 0 0 x — 3 6 1
Derringer (Reds), Lee (Cubs) 4, Fette (Braves) 7; Ruffing (Yankees), Bridges (Tigers) 4, Feller (Indians) 6. W—Bridges. L—Lee. HR—DiMaggio, A.L.

WORLD SERIES

■ **Winner:** Four in a row. The Yankees recorded their second straight sweep and 13th victory in 14 Series games.

■ **Turning point:** Bill Dickey's ninth-inning single gave New York a 2-1 victory in Game 1 and momentum the Reds could not stop.

■ **Memorable moment:** A strange Game 4 play that helped produce three 10th-inning Yankee runs. Joe DiMaggio singled to right with two runners aboard and circled the bases when Reds catcher Ernie Lombardi lay dazed after a home-plate collision with Yankee runner Charlie Keller. "Lombardi's Snooze."

■ **Top guns:** Keller (.438, 3 HR, 6 RBIs), Dickey (2 HR, 5 RBIs), Yankees; Frank McCormick (.400), Reds.

Linescores

Game 1—October 4, at New York
Cincinnati 0 0 0 1 0 0 0 0 0 — 1 4 0
New York 0 0 0 0 1 0 0 0 1 — 2 6 0
Derringer; Ruffing. W—Ruffing. L—Derringer.

Game 2—October 5, at New York
Cincinnati 0 0 0 0 0 0 0 0 0 — 0 2 0
New York 0 0 3 1 0 0 0 0 x — 4 9 0
Walters; Pearson. W—Pearson. L—Walters. HR—Dahlgren (N.Y.).

Game 3—October 7, at Cincinnati
New York 2 0 2 0 3 0 0 0 0 — 7 5 1
Cincinnati 1 2 0 0 0 0 0 0 0 — 3 10 0
Gomez, Hadley (2); Thompson, Grissom (5), Moore (7). W—Hadley. L—Thompson. HR—Keller 2, DiMaggio, Dickey (N.Y.).

Game 4—October 8, at Cincinnati
New York 0 0 0 0 0 0 2 0 2 3—7 7 1
Cincinnati 0 0 0 0 0 0 3 1 0 0—4 11 4
Hildebrand, Sundra (5), Murphy (7); Derringer, Walters (8). W—Murphy. L—Walters. HR—Keller, Dickey (N.Y.).

1940

FINAL STANDINGS

American League

Team	W	L	Pct.	GB
Detroit	90	64	.584	...
Cleveland	89	65	.578	1
New York	88	66	.571	2
Boston	82	72	.532	8
Chicago	82	72	.532	8
St. Louis	67	87	.435	23
Washington	64	90	.416	26
Philadelphia	54	100	.351	36

National League

Team	W	L	Pct.	GB
Cincinnati	100	53	.654	...
Brooklyn	88	65	.575	12
St. Louis	84	69	.549	16
Pittsburgh	78	76	.506	22.5
Chicago	75	79	.487	25.5
New York	72	80	.474	27.5
Boston	65	87	.428	34.5
Philadelphia	50	103	.327	50

SIGNIFICANT EVENTS

■ **January 14:** In the biggest free-agency ruling ever handed down, Commissioner Kenesaw Mountain Landis freed 91 members of the Tigers organization, citing player-movement coverup.

■ **May 7:** The Dodgers became the first N.L. team to travel by air, flying in two planes from St. Louis to Chicago.

■ **May 24, June 4:** The first night games were played at New York's Polo Grounds, St. Louis' Sportsman's Park and Pittsburgh's Forbes Field.

■ **August 3:** Reds catcher Willard Hershberger, despondent over what he considered inadequate play, committed suicide in his Boston hotel room.

MEMORABLE MOMENTS

■ **April 16:** Cleveland's Bob Feller fired the first Opening Day no-hitter in baseball history, beating the White Sox, 1-0, at Chicago's Comiskey Park.

■ **September 24:** Jimmie Foxx became baseball's second 500-homer man when he hit one of Boston's four sixth-inning blasts in a 16-8 victory over the Athletics.

■ **September 27:** Detroit rookie Floyd Giebell ignored near-riotous Cleveland fans and outpitched Bob Feller in an A.L. pennant-clinching 2-0 Tigers victory.

LEADERS

American League

BA: Joe DiMaggio, N.Y., .352.
Runs: Ted Williams, Bos., 134.
Hits: Doc Cramer, Bos.; Barney McCosky, Det.; Rip Radcliff, St.L., 200.
TB: Hank Greenberg, Det., 384.
HR: Hank Greenberg, Det., 41.
RBI: Hank Greenberg, Det., 150.
SB: George Case, Wash., 35.
Wins: Bob Feller, Cle., 27.
ERA: Bob Feller, Cle., 2.61.
CG: Bob Feller, Cle., 31.
IP: Bob Feller, Cle., 320.1.
SO: Bob Feller, Cle., 261.

National League

BA: Stan Hack, Chi., .317.
Runs: Arky Vaughan, Pit., 113.
Hits: Stan Hack, Chi.; Frank McCormick, Cin., 191.
TB: Johnny Mize, St.L., 368.
HR: Johnny Mize, St.L., 43.
RBI: Johnny Mize, St.L., 137.
SB: Lonny Frey, Cin., 22.
Wins: Bucky Walters, Cin., 22.
ERA: Bucky Walters, Cin., 2.48.
CG: Bucky Walters, Cin., 29.
IP: Bucky Walters, Cin., 305.
SO: Kirby Higbe, Phil., 137.

A.L. 20-game winners
Bob Feller, Cle., 27-11
Bobo Newsom, Det., 21-5

N.L. 20-game winners
Bucky Walters, Cin., 22-10
Paul Derringer, Cin., 20-12
Claude Passeau, Chi., 20-13

A.L. 100 RBIs
Hank Greenberg, Det., 150
Rudy York, Det., 134
Joe DiMaggio, N.Y., 133
Jimmie Foxx, Bos., 119
Ted Williams, Bos., 113
Joe Cronin, Bos, 111
Bobby Doerr, Bos., 105
Joe Gordon, N.Y., 103
Bob Johnson, Phil., 103
Lou Boudreau, Cle., 101

N.L. 100 RBIs
Johnny Mize, St.L., 137
Frank McCormick, Cin., 127
Maurice Van Robays, Pit., 116
Elbie Fletcher, Pit., 104
Babe Young, N.Y., 101

A.L. 40 homers
Hank Greenberg, Det., 41

N.L. 40 homers
Johnny Mize, St.L., 43

Most Valuable Player
A.L.: Hank Greenberg, OF, Det.
N.L.: Frank McCormick, 1B, Cin.

ALL-STAR GAME

■ **Winner:** Five N.L. pitchers shut down the A.L. on three hits and recorded the first shutout in All-Star Game history.

■ **Key inning:** The first, when Boston's Max West connected with a Red Ruffing delivery for a three-run homer.

■ **Memorable moment:** An inning after his home run, West crashed into the outfield wall while chasing a fly ball and had to be helped off the field.

■ **Top guns:** Paul Derringer (Reds), Bucky Walters (Reds), Whitlow Wyatt (Dodgers), Larry French (Cubs), Carl Hubbell (Giants), West (Braves), Billy Herman (Cubs), N.L.; Luke Appling (White Sox), A.L.

■ **MVP:** West.

Linescore

July 9, at St. Louis' Sportsman's Park
A.L. ....0 0 0 0 0 0 0 0 0—0 3 1
N.L. ....3 0 0 0 0 0 0 1 x—4 7 0
Ruffing (Yankees), Newsom (Tigers) 4, Feller (Indians) 7; Derringer (Reds), Walters (Reds) 3, Wyatt (Dodgers) 5, French (Cubs) 7, Hubbell (Giants) 9. W—Derringer. L—Ruffing. HR—West, N.L.

WORLD SERIES

■ **Winner:** The Reds needed seven games to dispatch the Tigers and capture their first non-tainted World Series.

■ **Turning point:** The Reds' Game 6 victory in which Bucky Walters pitched a 4-0 shutout and also hit a home run.

■ **Memorable moment:** Reds pitcher Paul Derringer retiring Detroit in order in a tense ninth inning of Game 7.

■ **Top guns:** Walters (2-0, 1.50 ERA), Jimmy Ripple (.333, 6 RBIs), Reds; Hank Greenberg (.357, 6 RBIs), Pinky Higgins (.333, 6 RBIs), Tigers.

Linescores

Game 1—October 2, at Cincinnati
Detroit ....0 5 0 0 2 0 0 0 0—7 10 1
Cincinnati...............0 0 0 1 0 0 0 1 0—2 8 3
Newsom; Derringer, Moore (2), Riddle (9). W—Newsom. L—Derringer. HR—Campbell (Det.).

Game 2—October 3, at Cincinnati
Detroit ....2 0 0 0 0 1 0 0 0—3 3 1
Cincinnati.................0 2 2 1 0 0 0 0 x—5 9 0
Rowe, Gorsica (4); Walters. W—Walters. L—Rowe. HR—Ripple (Cin.).

Game 3—October 4, at Detroit
Cincinnati...............1 0 0 0 0 0 0 1 2—4 10 1
Detroit ....0 0 0 1 0 0 4 2 x—7 13 1
Turner, Moore (7), Beggs (8); Bridges. W—Bridges. L—Turner. HR—York, Higgins (Det.).

Game 4—October 5, at Detroit
Cincinnati...............2 0 1 1 0 0 0 1 0—5 11 1
Detroit ....0 0 1 0 0 1 0 0 0—2 5 1
Derringer; Trout, Smith (3), McKain (7). W—Derringer. L—Trout.

Game 5—October 6, at Detroit
Cincinnati...............0 0 0 0 0 0 0 0 0—0 3 0
Detroit ....0 0 3 4 0 0 0 1 x—8 13 0
Thompson, Moore (4), Vander Meer (5), Hutchings (8); Newsom. W—Newsom. L—Thompson. HR—Greenberg (Det.).

Game 6—October 7, at Cincinnati
Detroit ....0 0 0 0 0 0 0 0 0—0 5 0
Cincinnati...............2 0 0 0 0 1 0 1 x—4 10 2
Rowe, Gorsica (1), Hutchinson (8); Walters. W—Walters. L—Rowe. HR—Walters (Cin.).

Game 7—October 8, at Cincinnati
Detroit ....0 0 1 0 0 0 0 0 0—1 7 0
Cincinnati.................0 0 0 0 0 0 2 0 x—2 7 1
Newsom; Derringer. W—Derringer. L—Newsom.

HISTORY

1941

FINAL STANDINGS

American League

Team	W	L	Pct.	GB
New York	101	53	.656	...
Boston	84	70	.545	17
Chicago	77	77	.500	24
Cleveland	75	79	.487	26
Detroit	75	79	.487	26
St. Louis	70	84	.455	31
Washington	70	84	.455	31
Philadelphia	64	90	.416	37

National League

Team	W	L	Pct.	GB
Brooklyn	100	54	.649	...
St. Louis	97	56	.634	2.5
Cincinnati	88	66	.571	12
Pittsburgh	81	73	.526	19
New York	74	79	.484	25.5
Chicago	70	84	.455	30
Boston	62	92	.403	38
Philadelphia	43	111	.279	57

SIGNIFICANT EVENTS

■ **May 1:** Dodgers President Larry MacPhail submitted a patent application on the "Brooklyn Safety Cap," a hat lined with plastic to protect players from bean balls.

■ **May 7:** Detroit slugger Hank Greenberg reported for duty in the U.S. Army—one of many Major Leaguers who would leave baseball to fight in World War II.

■ **June 2:** Former Yankee great Lou Gehrig died at age 37 from the incurable disease that had forced his retirement two years earlier.

■ **May 28:** The Senators dropped a 6-5 decision to the Yankees in the first night game at Washington's Griffith Stadium.

MEMORABLE MOMENTS

■ **July 17:** Yankee center fielder Joe DiMaggio's record 56-game hitting streak was stopped by pitchers Al Smith and Jim Bagby Jr. at Cleveland Stadium.

■ **July 25:** Boston's Lefty Grove joined the 300-victory club when he staggered to a 10-6 victory over Cleveland at Fenway Park.

■ **September 4:** The Yankees recorded the earliest pennant-clinching date in history when they defeated Boston, 6-3.

■ **November 27:** Yankee Joe DiMaggio won the A.L. MVP by a slim 37-point margin over Boston's Ted Williams, baseball's first .400 hitter (.406) since 1930.

LEADERS

American League

BA: Ted Williams, Bos., .406.
Runs: Ted Williams, Bos., 135.
Hits: Cecil Travis, Wash., 218.
TB: Joe DiMaggio, N.Y., 348.
HR: Ted Williams, Bos., 37.
RBI: Joe DiMaggio, N.Y., 125.
SB: George Case, Wash., 33.
Wins: Bob Feller, Cle., 25.
ERA: Thornton Lee, Chi., 2.37.
CG: Thornton Lee, Chi., 30.
IP: Bob Feller, Cle., 343.
SO: Bob Feller, Cle., 260.

National League

BA: Pete Reiser, Brk., .343.
Runs: Pete Reiser, Brk., 117.
Hits: Stan Hack, Chi., 186.
TB: Pete Reiser, Brk., 299.
HR: Dolph Camilli, Brk., 34.
RBI: Dolph Camilli, Brk., 120.
SB: Danny Murtaugh, Phil., 18.
Wins: Kirby Higbe, Brk.; Whitlow Wyatt, Brk., 22.
ERA: Elmer Riddle, Cin., 2.24.
CG: Bucky Walters, Cin., 27.
IP: Bucky Walters, Cin., 302.
SO: Johnny Vander Meer, Cin., 202.

A.L. 20-game winners
Bob Feller, Cle., 25-13
Thornton Lee, Chi., 22-11

N.L. 20-game winners
Kirby Higbe, Brk., 22-9
Whitlow Wyatt, Brk., 22-10

A.L. 100 RBIs
Joe DiMaggio, N.Y., 125
Jeff Heath, Cle., 123
Charlie Keller, N.Y., 122
Ted Williams, Bos., 120
Rudy York, Det., 111
Bob Johnson, Phil., 107
Sam Chapman, Phil., 106
Jimmie Foxx, Bos., 105
Jim Tabor, Bos., 101
Cecil Travis, Wash., 101

N.L. 100 RBIs
Dolph Camilli, Brk., 120
Babe Young, N.Y., 104
Vince DiMaggio, Pit., 100
Johnny Mize, St.L., 100

Most Valuable Player
A.L.: Joe DiMaggio, OF, N.Y.
N.L.: Dolf Camilli, 1B, Brk.

ALL-STAR GAME

■ **Winner:** The A.L. scored four ninth-inning runs and overcame a pair of home runs by Pittsburgh's Arky Vaughan for a 7-5 victory in the most exciting All-Star Game in the classic's nine-year history.

■ **Key inning:** The ninth, when the A.L. overcame a 5-3 deficit to claim its sixth victory in nine All-Star Games.

■ **Memorable moment:** A dramatic game-ending, three-run homer by Boston slugger Ted Williams with two out in the ninth. Williams connected off Chicago's Claude Passeau after the N.L. had botched what could have been a game-ending double play.

■ **Top guns:** Bob Feller (Indians), Williams (Red Sox), Lou Boudreau (Indians), A.L.; Vaughan (Pirates), N.L.

■ **MVP:** Williams.

Linescore

July 8, at Detroit's Briggs Stadium
N.L. ....0 0 0 0 0 1 2 2 0—5 10 2
A.L. ....0 0 0 1 0 1 0 1 4—7 11 3
Wyatt (Dodgers), Derringer (Reds) 3, Walters (Reds) 5, Passeau (Cubs) 7; Feller (Indians), Lee (White Sox) 4, Hudson (Senators) 7, Smith (White Sox) 8. W—Smith. L—Passeau. HR—Vaughan 2, N.L.; Williams, A.L.

WORLD SERIES

■ **Winner:** The Yankees returned to the top and won the first of many memorable meetings with the Dodgers.

■ **Turning point:** A two-out, ninth-inning passed ball by Dodgers catcher Mickey Owen that could have finished off a 4-3 Brooklyn victory in Game 4. Given new life, the Yanks scored four times and took a three-games-to-one Series lead.

■ **Memorable moment:** Owen's passed ball.

■ **Top guns:** Joe Gordon (.500, 5 RBIs), Charlie Keller (.389, 5 RBIs), Yankees.

Linescores

Game 1—October 1, at New York
Brooklyn ....0 0 0 0 1 0 1 0 0—2 6 0
New York....................0 1 0 1 0 1 0 0 x—3 6 1
Davis, Casey (6), Allen (7); Ruffing. W—Ruffing. L—Davis. HR—Gordon (N.Y.).

Game 2—October 2, at New York
Brooklyn ....0 0 0 0 2 1 0 0 0—3 6 2
New York....................0 1 1 0 0 0 0 0 0—2 9 1
Wyatt; Chandler, Murphy (6). W—Wyatt. L—Chandler.

Game 3—October 4, at Brooklyn
New York....................0 0 0 0 0 0 0 2 0—2 8 0
Brooklyn ....0 0 0 0 0 0 0 1 0—1 4 0
Russo; Fitzsimmons, Casey (8), French (8), Allen (9). W—Russo. L—Casey.

Game 4—October 5, at Brooklyn
New York..................1 0 0 2 0 0 0 0 4—7 12 0
Brooklyn ....0 0 0 2 2 0 0 0 0—4 9 1
Donald, Breuer (5), Murphy (8); Higbe, French (4), Allen (5), Casey (5). W—Murphy. L—Casey. HR—Reiser (Brk.).

Game 5—October 6, at Brooklyn
New York....................0 2 0 0 1 0 0 0 0—3 6 0
Brooklyn ....0 0 1 0 0 0 0 0 0—1 4 1
Bonham; Wyatt. W—Bonham. L—Wyatt. HR—Henrich (N.Y.).

1942

FINAL STANDINGS

American League

Team	W	L	Pct.	GB
New York	103	51	.669	...
Boston	93	59	.612	9
St. Louis	82	69	.543	19.5
Cleveland	75	79	.487	28
Detroit	73	81	.474	30
Chicago	66	82	.446	34
Washington	62	89	.411	39.5
Philadelphia	55	99	.357	48

National League

Team	W	L	Pct.	GB
St. Louis	106	48	.688	...
Brooklyn	104	50	.675	2
New York	85	67	.559	20
Cincinnati	76	76	.500	29
Pittsburgh	66	81	.449	36.5
Chicago	68	86	.442	38
Boston	59	89	.399	44
Philadelphia	42	109	.278	62.5

SIGNIFICANT EVENTS

■ **January 6:** Cleveland ace Bob Feller became the second high-profile star to leave baseball for the armed services when he enlisted in the Navy and reported for duty.

■ **January 16:** U.S. President Franklin D. Roosevelt gave baseball the "green light" to continue wartime play as a needed diversion for hard-working Americans.

■ **February 3:** In response to President Roosevelt's request for more night games, baseball owners softened restrictions and more than doubled the nocturnal schedule.

■ **October 29:** Cardinals Vice-President Branch Rickey resigned to become president of the Dodgers.

■ **November 4:** Yankee second baseman Joe Gordon edged out Boston Triple Crown winner Ted Williams by 21 votes for A.L. MVP.

MEMORABLE MOMENTS

■ **June 19:** Boston's Paul Waner became baseball's seventh 3,000-hit man when he singled off Pittsburgh's Rip Sewell.

■ **July 7:** One day after defeating the N.L. in the annual All-Star Game, the A.L. beat Mickey Cochrane's Armed Service All-Stars, 5-0, in a game to raise money for the war effort.

■ **September 27:** The Cardinals recorded a final-day sweep of the Cubs and finished with 106 victories, two more than the Dodgers in an amazing N.L. pennant battle.

LEADERS

American League

BA: Ted Williams, Bos., .356.
Runs: Ted Williams, Bos., 141.
Hits: Johnny Pesky, Bos., 205.
TB: Ted Williams, Bos., 338.
HR: Ted Williams, Bos., 36.
RBI: Ted Williams, Bos., 137.
SB: George Case, Wash., 44.
Wins: Tex Hughson, Bos., 22.
ERA: Ted Lyons, Chi., 2.10.
CG: Tiny Bonham, N.Y.; Tex Hughson, Bos., 22.
IP: Tex Hughson, Bos., 281.
SO: Tex Hughson, Bos.;
Bobo Newsom, Wash., 113.

National League

BA: Enos Slaughter, St.L., .318.
Runs: Mel Ott, N.Y., 118.
Hits: Enos Slaughter, St.L., 188.
TB: Enos Slaughter, St.L., 292.
HR: Mel Ott, N.Y., 30.
RBI: Johnny Mize, N.Y., 110.
SB: Pete Reiser, Brk., 20.
Wins: Mort Cooper, St.L., 22.
ERA: Mort Cooper, St.L., 1.78.
CG: Jim Tobin, Bos., 28.
IP: Jim Tobin, Bos., 287.2.
SO: Johnny Vander Meer, Cin., 186.

A.L. 20-game winners
Tex Hughson, Bos., 22-6
Tiny Bonham, N.Y., 21-5

N.L. 20-game winners
Mort Cooper, St.L., 22-7
Johnny Beazley, St.L., 21-6

A.L. 100 RBIs
Ted Williams, Bos., 137
Joe DiMaggio, N.Y., 114
Charlie Keller, N.Y., 108
Joe Gordon, N.Y., 103
Bobby Doerr, Bos., 102

N.L. 100 RBIs
Johnny Mize, N.Y., 110
Dolph Camilli, Brk., 109

Most Valuable Player
A.L.: Joe Gordon, 2B, N.Y.
N.L.: Mort Cooper, P, St.L.

Hall of Fame addition
Rogers Hornsby, 2B, 1915-37

ALL-STAR GAME

■ **Winner:** Spud Chandler and Al Benton combined on a six-hitter and the A.L. made it 7 for 10 with a rainy-day victory in an All-Star Game played with war-depleted rosters.

■ **Key inning:** The first, when the A.L. scored all of its runs, one coming on a leadoff home run by Cleveland's Lou Boudreau.

■ **Memorable moment:** After New York's Tommy Henrich had followed Boudreau's home run with a double, Detroit slugger Rudy York lined an opposite-field shot that settled into the right-field bleachers for a two-run homer.

■ **Top guns:** Chandler (Yankees), Benton (Tigers), Boudreau (Indians), York (Tigers), A.L.; Johnny Vander Meer (Reds), Mickey Owen (Dodgers), N.L.

■ **MVP:** York.

Linescore

July 7, at New York's Polo Grounds
A.L. ....3 0 0 0 0 0 0 0 0—3 7 0
N.L. ....0 0 0 0 0 0 0 1 0—1 6 1
Chandler (Yankees), Benton (Tigers) 5; M. Cooper (Cardinals), Vander Meer (Reds) 4, Passeau (Cubs) 7, Walters (Reds) 9. W—Chandler. L—M. Cooper. HR—Boudreau, York, A.L.; Owen, N.L.

WORLD SERIES

■ **Winner:** After losing the opener, the Cardinals tamed the powerful Yankees with four consecutive victories.

■ **Turning point:** The ninth inning of Game 1. Although the Cardinals' four-run rally fell short in a 7-4 Yankee victory, they delivered a message that would become more clear as the Series progressed.

■ **Memorable moment:** A two-run, ninth-inning home run by Whitey Kurowski that gave St. Louis a Series-ending 4-2 victory.

■ **Top guns:** Johnny Beazley (2-0, 2.50 ERA), Kurowski (5 RBIs), Cardinals; Phil Rizzuto (.381), Yankees.

Linescores

Game 1—September 30, at St. Louis
New York..................0 0 0 1 1 0 0 3 2—7 11 0
St. Louis ....0 0 0 0 0 0 0 0 4—4 7 4
Ruffing, Chandler (9); M. Cooper, Gumbert (8), Lanier (9). W—Ruffing. L—M. Cooper.

Game 2—October 1, at St. Louis
New York..................0 0 0 0 0 0 0 3 0—3 10 2
St. Louis ....2 0 0 0 0 0 1 1 x—4 6 0
Bonham; Beazley. W—Beazley. L—Bonham. HR—Keller (N.Y.).

Game 3—October 3, at New York
St. Louis ....0 0 1 0 0 0 0 0 1—2 5 1
New York....................0 0 0 0 0 0 0 0 0—0 6 1
White; Chandler, Breuer (9), Turner (9). W—White. L—Chandler.

Game 4—October 4, at New York
St. Louis ....0 0 0 6 0 0 2 0 1—9 12 1
New York..................1 0 0 0 0 5 0 0 0—6 10 1
M. Cooper, Gumbert (6), Pollet (6), Lanier (7); Borowy, Donald (4), Bonham (7). W—Lanier. L—Donald. HR—Keller (N.Y.).

Game 5—October 5, at New York
St. Louis ....0 0 0 1 0 1 0 0 2—4 9 4
New York....................1 0 0 1 0 0 0 0 0—2 7 1
Beazley; Ruffing. W—Beazley. L—Ruffing. HR—Rizzuto (N.Y.); Slaughter, Kurowski (St.L.).

1943

FINAL STANDINGS

American League

Team	W	L	Pct.	GB
New York	98	56	.636	...
Washington	84	69	.549	13.5
Cleveland	82	71	.536	15.5
Chicago	82	72	.532	16
Detroit	78	76	.506	20
St. Louis	72	80	.474	25
Boston	68	84	.447	29
Philadelphia	49	105	.318	49

National League

Team	W	L	Pct.	GB
St. Louis	105	49	.682	...
Cincinnati	87	67	.565	18
Brooklyn	81	72	.529	23.5
Pittsburgh	80	74	.519	25
Chicago	74	79	.484	30.5
Boston	68	85	.444	36.5
Philadelphia	64	90	.416	41
New York	55	98	.359	49.5

SIGNIFICANT EVENTS

■ **January 5:** In concessions to the war and travel restrictions, Major League owners agreed to open the season a week late and to conduct spring training in northern cities.
■ **February 28:** The Texas League suspended operations, cutting the minor league ranks to nine circuits—down from the 41 that operated in 1941.
■ **April 20:** Boston Braves manager Casey Stengel suffered a broken leg when he was hit by a Boston taxicab—an injury that would sideline him for much of the season.
■ **May 8:** Baseball's two-week "dead ball" era came to an end when A.G. Spalding's "war ball" was replaced with a more lively ball.

MEMORABLE MOMENTS

■ **June 4:** Cardinals ace Mort Cooper stopped Philadelphia 5-0 at Sportsman's Park—his second consecutive one-hit shutout.
■ **June 17:** Boston player-manager Joe Cronin made history when he blasted three-run pinch-hit homers in both ends of a doubleheader against Philadelphia at Fenway Park.
■ **August 24:** The Athletics ended their A.L. record-tying losing streak at 20 with an 8-1 victory in the second game of a doubleheader at Chicago.

LEADERS

American League
BA: Luke Appling, Chi., .328.
Runs: George Case, Wash., 102.
Hits: Dick Wakefield, Det., 200.
TB: Rudy York, Det., 301.
HR: Rudy York, Det., 34.
RBI: Rudy York, Det., 118.
SB: George Case, Wash., 61.
Wins: Spud Chandler, N.Y.; Dizzy Trout, Det., 20.
ERA: Spud Chandler, N.Y., 1.64.
CG: Spud Chandler, N.Y.; Tex Hughson, Bos., 20.
IP: Jim Bagby, Cle., 273.
SO: Allie Reynolds, Cle., 151.

National League
BA: Stan Musial, St.L., .357.
Runs: Arky Vaughan, Brk., 112.
Hits: Stan Musial, St.L., 220.
TB: Stan Musial, St.L., 347.
HR: Bill Nicholson, Chi., 29.
RBI: Bill Nicholson, Chi., 128.
SB: Arky Vaughan, Brk., 20.
Wins: Mort Cooper, St.L.; Elmer Riddle, Cin.; Rip Sewell, Pit., 21.
ERA: Max Lanier, St.L., 1.90.
CG: Rip Sewell, Pit., 25.
IP: Al Javery, Bos., 303.
SO: Johnny Vander Meer, Cin., 174.

A.L. 20-game winners
Spud Chandler, N.Y., 20-4
Dizzy Trout, Det., 20-12

N.L. 20-game winners
Mort Cooper, St.L., 21-8
Rip Sewell, Pit., 21-9
Elmer Riddle, Cin., 21-11

A.L. 100 RBIs
Rudy York, Det., 118
Nick Etten, N.Y., 107

N.L. 100 RBIs
Bill Nicholson, Chi., 128
Bob Elliott, Pit., 101
Billy Herman, Brk., 100

Most Valuable Player
A.L.: Spud Chandler, P, N.Y.
N.L.: Stan Musial, OF, St.L.

ALL-STAR GAME

■ **Winner:** A.L. manager Joe McCarthy, tired of complaints that he favored his own Yankee players in All-Star competition, guided his team to a Yankeeless victory.
■ **Key inning:** The second, when Boston's Bobby Doerr belted a three-run homer that gave the A.L. a lead it never relinquished.
■ **Memorable moments:** A seventh-inning run-scoring triple and a ninth-inning home run by Pittsburgh's Vince DiMaggio, brother of Yankee great Joe DiMaggio.
■ **Top guns:** Hal Newhouser (Tigers), Doerr (Red Sox), Dick Wakefield (Tigers), A.L.; V. DiMaggio (Pirates), Stan Hack (Cubs), N.L.
■ **MVP:** Doerr.

Linescore

July 13, at Philadelphia's Shibe Park
N.L. ....1 0 0 000 1 0 1—3 10 3
A.L. ....0 3 1 010 0 0 x—5 8 1
M. Cooper (Cardinals), Vander Meer (Reds) 3, Sewell (Pirates) 6, Javery (Braves) 7; Leonard (Senators), Newhouser (Tigers) 4, Hughson (Red Sox) 7. W—Leonard. L—M. Cooper. HR—Doerr, A.L.; DiMaggio, N.L.

WORLD SERIES

■ **Winner:** Joe McCarthy managed his seventh and final Series champion as the Yankees avenged their 1942 loss to the Cardinals.
■ **Turning point:** Billy Johnson's bases-loaded triple that keyed a five-run eighth inning and helped the Yankees to a 6-2 victory in Game 3.
■ **Memorable moment:** Bill Dickey's two-run, sixth-inning home run in New York's 2-0 Series-ending victory.
■ **Top guns:** Spud Chandler (2-0, 0.50 ERA), Dickey (4 RBIs), Yankees; Marty Marion (.357), Cardinals.

Linescores

Game 1—October 5, at New York
St. Louis....................0 1 0 0 1 0 0 0 0—2 7 2
New York ....0 0 0 2 0 2 0 0 x—4 8 2
Lanier, Brecheen (8); Chandler. W—Chandler. L—Lanier. HR—Gordon (N.Y.).

Game 2—October 6, at New York
St. Louis....................0 0 1 3 0 0 0 0 0—4 7 2
New York ....0 0 0 1 0 0 0 0 2—3 6 0
M. Cooper; Bonham, Murphy (9). W—M. Cooper. L—Bonham. HR—Marion, Sanders (St.L.).

Game 3—October 7, at New York
St. Louis....................0 0 0 2 0 0 0 0 0—2 6 4
New York ....0 0 0 0 0 1 0 5 x—6 8 0
Brazle, Krist (8), Brecheen (8); Borowy, Murphy (9). W—Borowy. L—Brazle.

Game 4—October 10, at St. Louis
New York ....0 0 0 1 0 0 0 1 0—2 6 2
St. Louis....................0 0 0 0 0 0 1 0 0—1 7 1
Russo; Lanier, Brecheen (8). W—Russo. L—Brecheen.

Game 5—October 11, at St. Louis
New York ....0 0 0 0 0 2 0 0 0—2 7 1
St. Louis..................0 0 0 0 0 0 0 0 0—0 10 1
Chandler; M. Cooper, Lanier (8), Dickson (9). W—Chandler. L—M. Cooper. HR—Dickey (N.Y.).

1944

FINAL STANDINGS

American League

Team	W	L	Pct.	GB
St. Louis	89	65	.578	...
Detroit	88	66	.571	1
New York	83	71	.539	6
Boston	77	77	.500	12
Cleveland	72	82	.468	17
Philadelphia	72	82	.468	17
Chicago	71	83	.461	18
Washington	64	90	.416	25

National League

Team	W	L	Pct.	GB
St. Louis	105	49	.682	...
Pittsburgh	90	63	.588	14.5
Cincinnati	89	65	.578	16
Chicago	75	79	.487	30
New York	67	87	.435	38
Boston	65	89	.422	40
Brooklyn	63	91	.409	42
Philadelphia	61	92	.399	43.5

SIGNIFICANT EVENTS

■ **June 6:** Baseball canceled its schedule as Americans braced for D-day—the invasion of Europe on the beaches of Normandy, France.
■ **October:** Major League baseball raised $329,555 for the National War Fund Inc. and the American Red Cross through its 16 war relief games.
■ **November 25:** Kenesaw Mountain Landis, baseball's first commissioner, died of a heart attack at age 78.

MEMORABLE MOMENTS

■ **April 30:** Giants first baseman Phil Weintraub drove in 11 runs, one short of the Major League record, in a 26-8 victory over the Dodgers.
■ **June 10:** Reds pitcher Joe Nuxhall, at 15 years and 10 months, became the youngest player to compete in a Major League game when he worked 2/3 of an inning against the Cardinals.
■ **August 10:** Braves righthander Red Barrett threw a record-low 58 pitches in a 2-0 victory over the Reds.
■ **October 1:** The Browns recorded a final-day 5-2 victory over the Yankees and clinched the first pennant of their frustrating 44-year history.

LEADERS

American League
BA: Lou Boudreau, Cle., .327.
Runs: Snuffy Stirnweiss, N.Y., 125.
Hits: Snuffy Stirnweiss, N.Y., 205.
TB: Johnny Lindell, N.Y., 297.
HR: Nick Etten, N.Y., 22.
RBI: Vern Stephens, St.L., 109.
SB: Snuffy Stirnweiss, N.Y., 55.
Wins: Hal Newhouser, Det., 29.
ERA: Dizzy Trout, Det., 2.12.
CG: Dizzy Trout, Det., 33.
IP: Dizzy Trout, Det., 352.1.
SO: Hal Newhouser, Det., 187.

National League
BA: Dixie Walker, Brk., .357.
Runs: Bill Nicholson, Chi., 116.
Hits: Phil Cavarretta, Chi.; Stan Musial, St.L., 197.
TB: Bill Nicholson, Chi., 317.
HR: Bill Nicholson, Chi., 33.
RBI: Bill Nicholson, Chi., 122.
SB: Johnny Barrett, Pit., 28.
Wins: Bucky Walters, Cin., 23.
ERA: Ed Heusser, Cin., 2.38.
CG: Jim Tobin, Bos., 28.
IP: Bill Voiselle, N.Y., 312.2.
SO: Bill Voiselle, N.Y., 161.

A.L. 20-game winners
Hal Newhouser, Det., 29-9
Dizzy Trout, Det., 27-14

N.L. 20-game winners
Bucky Walters, Cin., 23-8
Mort Cooper, St.L., 22-7
Rip Sewell, Pit., 21-12
Bill Voiselle, N.Y., 21-16

A.L. 100 RBIs
Vern Stephens, St.L., 109
Bob Johnson, Bos., 106
Johnny Lindell, N.Y., 103
Stan Spence, Wash., 100

N.L. 100 RBIs
Bill Nicholson, Chi., 122
Bob Elliott, Pit., 108
Ron Northey, Phil., 104
Frank McCormick, Cin., 102
Ray Sanders, St.L., 102
Babe Dahlgren, Pit., 101

Most Valuable Player
A.L.: Hal Newhouser, P, Det.
N.L.: Marty Marion, SS, St.L.

Hall of Fame addition
Kenesaw M. Landis, commissioner

ALL-STAR GAME

■ **Winner:** With many of baseball's stars serving their country in World War II, four pitchers held the A.L. to six hits and the N.L. claimed a 7-1 victory.
■ **Key inning:** The fifth, when the N.L. scored four times on RBI hits by Chicago's Bill Nicholson, St. Louis' Walker Cooper and Dodgers' Augie Galan and Dixie Walker.
■ **Memorable moment:** Pittsburgh's Rip Sewell threw two "ephus pitches" to Browns first baseman George McQuinn, who took one for a called strike and bunted the other for an out.
■ **Top guns:** Sewell (Pirates), Phil Cavarretta (Cubs), Cooper (Cardinals), Walker (Dodgers), Whitey Kurowski (Cardinals), Nicholson (Cubs), N.L.; Hank Borowy (Yankees), A.L.
■ **MVP:** Sewell.

Linescore

July 11, at Pittsburgh's Forbes Field
A.L. ....0 1 0 000 000—1 6 3
N.L. ....0 0 0 040 2 1 x—7 12 1
Borowy (Yankees), Hughson (Red Sox) 4, Muncrief (Browns) 5, Newhouser (Tigers) 7, Newsom (Athletics) 8; Walters (Reds), Raffensberger (Phillies) 4, Sewell (Pirates) 6, Tobin (Braves) 9. W—Raffensberger. L—Hughson.

WORLD SERIES

■ **Winner:** Playing with a war-depleted roster, the Cardinals won the all-Sportsman's Park Series and the Battle of St. Louis.
■ **Turning point:** Game 5 homers by Ray Sanders and Danny Litwhiler that gave the Cardinals a 2-0 victory and a three-games-to-two edge.
■ **Memorable moment:** A two-run George McQuinn homer that gave the long-suffering Browns a 2-1 victory in their first-ever Series game.
■ **Top guns:** Emil Verban (.412), Walker Cooper (.318), Cardinals; McQuinn (.438, 5 RBIs), Browns.

Linescores

Game 1—October 4, at St. Louis
Browns ....0 0 0 2 0 0 0 0 0—2 2 0
Cardinals....................0 0 0 0 0 0 0 0 1—1 7 0
Galehouse; M. Cooper, Donnelly (8). W—Galehouse. L—M. Cooper. HR—McQuinn (Browns).

Game 2—October 5, at St. Louis
Browns ....0 0 0 0 0 0 2 0 0 0 0—2 7 4
Cardinals..........0 0 1 1 0 0 0 0 0 0 1—3 7 0
Potter, Muncrief (7); Lanier, Donnelly (8). W—Donnelly. L—Muncrief.

Game 3—October 6, at St. Louis
Cardinals....................1 0 0 0 0 0 1 0 0—2 7 0
Browns ....0 0 4 0 0 0 2 0 x—6 8 2
Wilks, Schmidt (3), Jurisich (7), Byerly (7); Kramer. W—Kramer. L—Wilks.

Game 4—October 7, at St. Louis
Cardinals..................2 0 2 0 0 1 0 0 0—5 12 0
Browns ....0 0 0 0 0 0 0 1 0—1 9 1
Brecheen; Jakucki, Hollingsworth (4), Shirley (8). W—Brecheen. L—Jakucki. HR—Musial (Cardinals).

Game 5—October 8, at St. Louis
Cardinals....................0 0 0 0 0 1 0 1 0—2 6 1
Browns ....0 0 0 0 0 0 0 0 0—0 7 1
M. Cooper; Galehouse. W—M. Cooper. L—Galehouse. HR—Sanders, Litwhiler (Cardinals).

Game 6—October 9, at St. Louis
Browns ....0 1 0 0 0 0 0 0 0—1 3 2
Cardinals..................0 0 0 3 0 0 0 0 0—3 10 0
Potter, Muncrief (4), Kramer (7); Lanier, Wilks (6). W—Lanier. L—Potter.

1945

FINAL STANDINGS

American League

Team	W	L	Pct.	GB
Detroit	88	65	.575	...
Washington	87	67	.565	1.5
St. Louis	81	70	.536	6
New York	81	71	.533	6.5
Cleveland	73	72	.503	11
Chicago	71	78	.477	15
Boston	71	83	.461	17.5
Philadelphia	52	98	.347	34.5

National League

Team	W	L	Pct.	GB
Chicago	98	56	.636	...
St. Louis	95	59	.617	3
Brooklyn	87	67	.565	11
Pittsburgh	82	72	.532	16
New York	78	74	.513	19
Boston	67	85	.441	30
Cincinnati	61	93	.396	37
Philadelphia	46	108	.299	52

SIGNIFICANT EVENTS

■ **January 26:** The Yankees were sold to the triumvirate of Larry MacPhail, Dan Topping and Del Webb for $2.8 million.

■ **April 24:** Kentucky Senator Albert B. (Happy) Chandler was the unanimous selection as baseball's second commissioner.

■ **July 10:** The All-Star Game, a baseball fixture since 1933, was not played because of wartime travel restrictions.

■ **October 23:** Brooklyn President Branch Rickey signed Jackie Robinson to a minor league contract, giving Organized Baseball its first black player since the turn of the century.

MEMORABLE MOMENTS

■ **April 18:** One-armed St. Louis outfielder Pete Gray collected one hit in his Major League debut—a 7-1 Browns victory over Detroit.

■ **July 12:** Boston's Tommy Holmes failed to get a hit during a 6-1 loss to the Cubs, ending his modern-era N.L.-record 37-game hitting streak.

■ **August 1:** Giants slugger Mel Ott became baseball's third 500-homer man when he connected off Boston's Johnny Hutchings.

■ **September 9:** Philadelphia's Dick Fowler, released from military duty nine days earlier, pitched a 1-0 no-hitter against the Browns in his first post-war appearance.

LEADERS

American League

BA: Snuffy Stirnweiss, N.Y., .309.
Runs: Snuffy Stirnweiss, N.Y., 107.
Hits: Snuffy Stirnweiss, N.Y., 195.
TB: Snuffy Stirnweiss, N.Y., 301.
HR: Vern Stephens, St.L., 24.
RBI: Nick Etten, N.Y., 111.
SB: Snuffy Stirnweiss, N.Y., 33.
Wins: Hal Newhouser, Det., 25.
ERA: Hal Newhouser, Det., 1.81.
CG: Hal Newhouser, Det., 29.
IP: Hal Newhouser, Det., 313.1.
SO: Hal Newhouser, Det., 212.

National League

BA: Phil Cavarretta, Chi., .355.
Runs: Eddie Stanky, Brk., 128.
Hits: Tommy Holmes, Bos., 224.
TB: Tommy Holmes, Bos., 367.
HR: Tommy Holmes, Bos., 28.
RBI: Dixie Walker, Brk., 124.
SB: Red Schoendienst, St.L., 26.
Wins: Red Barrett, Bos.-St.L., 23.
ERA: Ray Prim, Chi., 2.40.
CG: Red Barrett, Bos.-St.L., 24.
IP: Red Barrett, Bos.-St.L., 284.2.
SO: Preacher Roe, Pit., 148.

A.L. 20-game winners
Hal Newhouser, Det., 25-9
Boo Ferriss, Bos., 21-10
Roger Wolff, Wash., 20-10

N.L. 20-game winners
Red Barrett, Bos.-St.L., 23-12
Hank Wyse, Chi., 22-10

A.L. 100 RBIs
Nick Etten, N.Y., 111

N.L. 100 RBIs
Dixie Walker, Brk., 124
Tommy Holmes, Bos., 117
Luis Olmo, Brk., 110
Andy Pafko, Chi., 110
Buster Adams, Phil.-St.L., 109
Bob Elliott, Pit., 108
Whitey Kurowski, St.L., 102

Most Valuable Player
A.L.: Hal Newhouser, P, Det.
N.L.: Phil Cavarretta, 1B, Chi.

Hall of Fame additions
Roger Bresnahan, C, 1897-1915
Dan Brouthers, 1B, 1879-1904
Fred Clarke, OF, 1894-1915
Jimmy Collins, 3B, 1895-1908
Ed Delahanty, OF, 1888-1903
Hugh Duffy, OF, 1888-1906
Hugh Jennings, SS, 1891-1918
Mike (King) Kelly, C, 1878-93
Jim O'Rourke, OF, 1876-1904
Wilbert Robinson, manager

ALL-STAR GAME

The scheduled 13th All-Star Game was called off because of wartime travel restrictions.

WORLD SERIES

■ **Winner:** The Tigers won only their second Series and the Cubs lost their seventh straight in the last of the wartime fall classics.

■ **Turning point:** A four-run, sixth-inning explosion that broke a 1-1 tie and helped the Tigers to an 8-4 victory in the pivotal fifth game.

■ **Memorable moment:** Stan Hack's 12th-inning bad-hop double that gave the Cubs an 8-7 victory in a must-win sixth game.

■ **Top guns:** Roger Cramer (.379), Hank Greenberg (.304, 2 HR, 7 RBIs), Tigers; Phil Cavarretta (.423, 5 RBIs), Cubs.

Linescores

Game 1—October 3, at Detroit
Chicago....................4 0 3 0 0 0 2 0 0—9 13 0
Detroit......................0 0 0 0 0 0 0 0 0—0 6 0
Borowy; Newhouser, Benton (3), Tobin (5), Mueller (8). W—Borowy. L—Newhouser. HR—Cavarretta (Chi.).

Game 2—October 4, at Detroit
Chicago......................0 0 0 1 0 0 0 0 0—1 7 0
Detroit.......................0 0 0 0 4 0 0 0 x—4 7 0
Wyse, Erickson (7); Trucks. W—Trucks. L—Wyse. HR—Greenberg (Det.).

Game 3—October 5, at Detroit
Chicago.....................0 0 0 2 0 0 1 0 0—3 8 0
Detroit.......................0 0 0 0 0 0 0 0 0—0 1 2
Passeau; Overmire, Benton (7). W—Passeau. L—Overmire.

Game 4—October 6, at Chicago
Detroit........................0 0 0 4 0 0 0 0 0—4 7 1
Chicago......................0 0 0 0 0 1 0 0 0—1 5 1
Trout; Prim, Derringer (4), Vandenberg (6), Erickson (8). W—Trout. L—Prim.

Game 5—October 7, at Chicago
Detroit......................0 0 1 0 0 4 1 0 2—8 11 0
Chicago...................0 0 1 0 0 0 2 0 1—4 7 2
Newhouser; Borowy, Vandenberg (6), Chipman (6), Derringer (7), Erickson (9). W—Newhouser. L—Borowy.

Game 6—October 8, at Chicago
Detroit........0 1 0 0 0 0 2 4 0 0 0 0—7 13 1
Chicago......0 0 0 0 4 1 2 0 0 0 0 1—8 15 3
Trucks, Caster (5), Bridges (6), Benton (7), Trout (8); Passeau, Wyse (7), Prim (8), Borowy (9). W—Borowy. L—Trout. HR—Greenberg (Det.).

Game 7—October 10, at Chicago
Detroit.......................5 1 0 0 0 0 1 2 0—9 9 1
Chicago.....................1 0 0 1 0 0 0 1 0—3 10 0
Newhouser; Borowy, Derringer (1), Vandenberg (2), Erickson (6), Passeau (8), Wyse (9). W—Newhouser. L—Borowy.

1946

FINAL STANDINGS

American League

Team	W	L	Pct.	GB
Boston	104	50	.675	...
Detroit	92	62	.597	12
New York	87	67	.565	17
Washington	76	78	.494	28
Chicago	74	80	.481	30
Cleveland	68	86	.442	36
St. Louis	66	88	.429	38
Philadelphia	49	105	.318	55

National League

Team	W	L	Pct.	GB
*St. Louis	98	58	.628	...
Brooklyn	96	60	.615	2
Chicago	82	71	.536	14.5
Boston	81	72	.529	15.5
Philadelphia	69	85	.448	28
Cincinnati	67	87	.435	30
Pittsburgh	63	91	.409	34
New York	61	93	.396	36

*Defeated Brooklyn 2-0 in pennant playoff.

SIGNIFICANT EVENTS

■ **February 19:** Giants outfielder Danny Gardella jumped to the outlaw Mexican League, the first in a group of Major Leaguers who would fall victim to big-money inducements.

■ **April 18:** Jackie Robinson broke Organized Baseball's color barrier with a four-hit debut for the International League's Montreal Royals.

■ **September 16:** Among the benefits awarded players in a history-making New York meeting were a $5,000 minimum salary, upgraded hospital and medical expenses and salary-cut guarantees.

■ **December 6:** Baseball owners decided to return the All-Star vote to the fans.

MEMORABLE MOMENTS

■ **July 27:** Boston's Rudy York belted a record-tying two grand slams and drove in 10 runs in a 13-6 victory over the Browns.

■ **October 3:** The Cardinals capped their two-game sweep of the Dodgers with an 8-4 victory in baseball's first pennant playoff.

LEADERS

American League

BA: Mickey Vernon, Wash., .353.
Runs: Ted Williams, Bos., 142.
Hits: Johnny Pesky, Bos., 208.
TB: Ted Williams, Bos., 343.
HR: Hank Greenberg, Det., 44.
RBI: Hank Greenberg, Det., 127.
SB: George Case, Cle., 28.
Wins: Bob Feller, Cle.; Hal Newhouser, Det., 26.
ERA: Hal Newhouser, Det., 1.94.
CG: Bob Feller, Cle., 36.
IP: Bob Feller, Cle., 371.1.
SO: Bob Feller, Cle., 348.

National League

BA: Stan Musial, St.L., .365.
Runs: Stan Musial, St.L., 124.
Hits: Stan Musial, St.L., 228.
TB: Stan Musial, St.L., 366.
HR: Ralph Kiner, Pit., 23.
RBI: Enos Slaughter, St.L., 130.
SB: Pete Reiser, Brk., 34.
Wins: Howie Pollet, St.L., 21.
ERA: Howie Pollet, St.L., 2.10.
CG: Johnny Sain, Bos., 24.
IP: Howie Pollet, St.L., 266.
SO: Johnny Schmitz, Chi., 135.

A.L. 20-game winners
Hal Newhouser, Det., 26-9
Bob Feller, Cle., 26-15
Boo Ferriss, Bos., 25-6
Spud Chandler, N.Y., 20-8
Tex Hughson, Bos., 20-11

N.L. 20-game winners
Howie Pollet, St.L., 21-10
Johnny Sain, Bos., 20-14

A.L. 100 RBIs
Hank Greenberg, Det., 127
Ted Williams, Bos., 123
Rudy York, Bos., 119
Bobby Doerr, Bos., 116
Charlie Keller, N.Y., 101

N.L. 100 RBIs
Enos Slaughter, St.L., 130
Dixie Walker, Brk., 116
Stan Musial, St.L., 103

A.L. 40 homers
Hank Greenberg, Det., 44

Most Valuable Player
A.L.: Ted Williams, OF, Bos.
N.L.: Stan Musial, 1B, St.L.

Hall of Fame additions
Jesse Burkett, OF, 1890-1905
Frank Chance, 1B, 1898-1914
Jack Chesbro, P, 1899-1909
Johnny Evers, 2B, 1902-29
Clark Griffith, P/Man./Exec.
Tommy McCarthy, OF, 1884-96
Joe McGinnity, P, 1899-1908
Eddie Plank, P, 1901-17
Joe Tinker, SS, 1902-16
Rube Waddell, P, 1897-1910
Ed Walsh, P, 1904-17

ALL-STAR GAME

■ **Winner:** War hero Ted Williams rewarded his home fans with a four-hit, two-homer, five-RBI performance and three pitchers — Cleveland's Bob Feller, Detroit's Hal Newhouser and St. Louis' Jack Kramer — combined on a three-hitter that produced a 12-0 victory.

■ **Key inning:** The first, when Yankee Charlie Keller hit a two-run homer that ignited the A.L. charge.

■ **Memorable moment:** Williams' three-run, eighth-inning homer off Rip Sewell's famed "ephus pitch"—one of the All-Star Game's classic moments.

■ **Top guns:** Feller (Indians), Newhouser (Tigers), Kramer (Browns), Williams (Red Sox), Keller (Yankees), Vern Stephens (Browns), A.L.

■ **MVP:** Williams.

Linescore

July 9, at Boston's Fenway Park
N.L. ....0 0 0 0 0 0 0 0 0— 0 3 0
A.L. ....2 0 0 1 3 0 2 4 x—12 14 1
Passeau (Cubs), Higbe (Dodgers) 4, Blackwell (Reds) 5, Sewell (Pirates) 8; Feller (Indians), Newhouser (Tigers) 4, Kramer (Browns) 7. W—Feller. L—Passeau. HR—Keller, Williams 2, A.L.

WORLD SERIES

■ **Winner:** The Cardinals celebrated the end of wartime baseball with seven-game victory over the Red Sox.

■ **Turning point:** Harry Brecheen's seven-hit pitching gave the Cardinals a 4-1 victory in a must-win sixth game.

■ **Memorable moments:** The eighth inning of Game 7, when Enos Slaughter made his game-winning "Mad Dash" around the bases on Harry Walker's double. The ninth inning of Game 7, when Brecheen pitched out of a two-on, nobody out jam to secure the victory.

■ **Top guns:** Brecheen (3-0, 0.45 ERA), Slaughter (.320), Walker (.412, 6 RBIs), Cardinals; Bobby Doerr (.409), Rudy York (2 HR, 5 RBIs), Red Sox.

Linescores

Game 1—October 6, at St. Louis
Boston ....0 1 0 0 0 0 0 0 1 1—3 9 2
St. Louis ....0 0 0 0 0 1 0 1 0 0—2 7 0
Hughson, Johnson (9); Pollet. W—Johnson. L—Pollet. HR—York (Bos.).

Game 2—October 7, at St. Louis
Boston ....0 0 0 0 0 0 0 0 0—0 4 1
St. Louis ....0 0 1 0 2 0 0 0 x—3 6 0
Harris, Dobson (8); Brecheen. W—Brecheen. L—Harris.

Game 3—October 9, at Boston
St. Louis ....0 0 0 0 0 0 0 0 0—0 6 1
Boston........................3 0 0 0 0 0 0 1 x—4 8 0
Dickson, Wilks (8); Ferriss. W—Ferriss. L—Dickson. HR—York (Bos.).

Game 4—Ocotber 10, at Boston
St. Louis ....0 3 3 0 1 0 1 0 4—12 20 1
Boston ....0 0 0 1 0 0 0 2 0— 3 9 4
Munger; Hughson, Bagby (3), Zuber (6), Brown (8), Ryba (9), Driesewerd (9). W—Munger. L—Hughson. HR—Slaughter (St.L.); Doerr (Bos.).

Game 5—October 11, at Boston
St. Louis ....0 1 0 0 0 0 0 0 2—3 4 1
Boston.....................1 1 0 0 0 1 3 0 x—6 11 3
Pollet, Brazle (1), Beazley (8); Dobson. W—Dobson. L—Brazle. HR—Culberson (Bos.).

Game 6—October 13, at St. Louis
Boston ....0 0 0 0 0 0 1 0 0—1 7 0
St. Louis ....0 0 3 0 0 0 0 1 x—4 8 0
Harris, Hughson (3), Johnson (8); Brecheen. W—Brecheen. L—Harris.

Game 7—October 15, at St. Louis
Boston ....1 0 0 0 0 0 0 2 0—3 8 0
St. Louis ....0 1 0 0 2 0 0 1 x—4 9 1
Ferriss, Dobson (5), Klinger (8), Johnson (8); Dickson, Brecheen (8). W—Brecheen. L—Klinger.

1947

FINAL STANDINGS

American League

Team	W	L	Pct.	GB
New York	97	57	.630	...
Detroit	85	69	.552	12
Boston	83	71	.539	14
Cleveland	80	74	.519	17
Philadelphia	78	76	.506	19
Chicago	70	84	.455	27
Washington	64	90	.416	33
St. Louis	59	95	.383	38

National League

Team	W	L	Pct.	GB
Brooklyn	94	60	.610	...
St. Louis	89	65	.578	5
Boston	86	68	.558	8
New York	81	73	.526	13
Cincinnati	73	81	.474	21
Chicago	69	85	.448	25
Philadelphia	62	92	.403	32
Pittsburgh	62	92	.403	32

SIGNIFICANT EVENTS

■ **April 9:** Brooklyn manager Leo Durocher was suspended by Commissioner Happy Chandler for the entire 1947 season for "conduct detrimental to baseball."

■ **April 15:** The Major League color barrier came tumbling down when Jackie Robinson went hitless in the Dodgers' 5-3 Opening Day victory over the Braves at Ebbets Field.

■ **April 27:** Cancer-stricken Babe Ruth was honored throughout baseball on "Babe Ruth Day" and in special ceremonies at Yankee Stadium.

■ **July 5:** Cleveland's Larry Doby became the A.L.'s first black player when he struck out as a pinch-hitter in a 6-5 loss at Chicago.

■ **November 12:** Dodgers first baseman Jackie Robinson capped his historic season by capturing the first Rookie of the Year award.

MEMORABLE MOMENTS

■ **June 22:** Cincinnati's Ewell Blackwell fell two outs short of matching Johnny Vander Meer's back-to-back no-hitter feat when Brooklyn's Eddie Stanky stroked a ninth-inning single.

■ **September 28:** The greatest home run battle in history ended with neither Pittsburgh's Ralph Kiner nor New York's Johnny Mize adding to their 51-homer totals.

LEADERS

American League

BA: Ted Williams, Bos., .343.
Runs: Ted Williams, Bos., 125.
Hits: Johnny Pesky, Bos., 207.
TB: Ted Williams, Bos., 335.
HR: Ted Williams, Bos., 32.
RBI: Ted Williams, Bos., 114.
SB: Bob Dillinger, St.L., 34.
Wins: Bob Feller, Cle., 20.
ERA: Joe Haynes, Chi., 2.42.
CG: Hal Newhouser, Det., 24.
IP: Bob Feller, Cle., 299.
SO: Bob Feller, Cle., 196.

National League

BA: Harry Walker, St.L.-Phil., .363.
Runs: Johnny Mize, N.Y., 137.
Hits: Tommy Holmes, Bos., 191.
TB: Ralph Kiner, Pit., 361.
HR: Ralph Kiner, Pit.; Johnny Mize, N.Y., 51.
RBI: Johnny Mize, N.Y., 138.
SB: Jackie Robinson, Brk., 29.
Wins: Ewell Blackwell, Cin., 22.
ERA: Warren Spahn, Bos., 2.33.
CG: Ewell Blackwell, Cin., 23.
IP: Warren Spahn, Bos., 289.2.
SO: Ewell Blackwell, Cin., 193.

A.L. 20-game winners
Bob Feller, Cle., 20-11

N.L. 20-game winners
Ewell Blackwell, Cin., 22-8
Larry Jansen, N.Y., 21-5
Warren Spahn, Bos., 21-10
Ralph Branca, Brk., 21-12
Johnny Sain, Bos., 21-12

A.L. 100 RBIs
Ted Williams, Bos., 114

N.L. 100 RBIs
Johnny Mize, N.Y., 138
Ralph Kiner, Pit., 127
Walker Cooper, N.Y., 122
Bob Elliott, Bos., 113
Willard Marshall, N.Y., 107
Whitey Kurowski, St.L., 104

N.L. 40 homers
Ralph Kiner, Pit., 51
Johnny Mize, N.Y., 51

Most Valuable Player
A.L.: Joe DiMaggio, OF, N.Y.
N.L.: Bob Elliott, 3B, Bos.

Rookie of the Year
A.L.-N.L.: Jackie Robinson, 1B, Brk.

Hall of Fame additions
Mickey Cochrane, C, 1925-37
Frank Frisch, 2B, 1919-37
Lefty Grove, P, 1925-41
Carl Hubbell, P, 1928-43

ALL-STAR GAME

■ **Winner:** The A.L. won its 10th All-Star Game in 14 tries with a 2-1 decision at windswept Wrigley Field.

■ **Key inning:** The seventh, when Washington pinch-hitter Stan Spence singled home Boston's Bobby Doerr with the eventual winning run.

■ **Memorable moment:** A game-saving defensive play by Cleveland shortstop Lou Boudreau in the eighth inning on a ball hit by St. Louis' Enos Slaughter with two men on base.

■ **Top guns:** Hal Newhouser (Tigers), Spec Shea (Yankees), Ted Williams (Red Sox), Spence (Senators), A.L.; Ewell Blackwell (Reds), Johnny Mize (Giants), N.L.

■ **MVP:** Spence.

Linescore

July 8, at Chicago's Wrigley Field
A.L. ....0 0 0 0 0 1 1 0 0—2 8 0
N.L. ....0 0 0 1 0 0 0 0 0—1 5 1
Newhouser (Tigers), Shea (Yankees) 4, Masterson (Senators) 7, Page (Yankees) 8; Blackwell (Reds), Brecheen (Cardinals) 4, Sain (Braves) 7, Spahn (Braves) 8. W—Shea. L—Sain. HR—Mize, N.L.

WORLD SERIES

■ **Winner:** After a three-year drought, the Yankees returned to the top in a memorable seven-game battle against the Dodgers.

■ **Turning point:** Spec Shea's 2-1 Game 5 victory — the day after teammate Bill Bevens, one out away from victory and the first no-hitter in Series history, had surrendered a game-deciding two-run double to Dodgers pinch-hitter Cookie Lavagetto.

■ **Memorable moments:** Lavagetto's Game 4 hit and a spectacular Game 6 catch by Dodgers left fielder Al Gionfriddo that robbed Joe DiMaggio of a home run and helped secure an 8-6 must victory for Brooklyn.

■ **Top guns:** Shea (2-0, 2.35 ERA), Johnny Lindell (.500, 7 RBIs), Yankees; Hugh Casey (2-0, 0.87), Carl Furillo (.353), Dodgers.

Linescores

Game 1—September 30, at New York
Brooklyn ....1 0 0 0 0 1 1 0 0—3 6 0
New York....................0 0 0 0 5 0 0 0 x—5 4 0
Branca, Behrman (5), Casey (7); Shea, Page (6). W—Shea. L—Branca.

Game 2—October 1, at New York
Brooklyn ....0 0 1 1 0 0 0 0 1— 3 9 2
New York................1 0 1 1 2 1 4 0 x—10 15 1
Lombardi, Gregg (5), Behrman (7), Barney (7); Reynolds. W—Reynolds. L—Lombardi. HR—Walker (Brk.); Henrich (N.Y.).

Game 3—October 2, at Brooklyn
New York..................0 0 2 2 2 1 1 0 0—8 13 0
Brooklyn ....0 6 1 2 0 0 0 0 x—9 13 1
Newsom, Raschi (2), Drews (3), Chandler (4), Page (6); Hatten, Branca (5), Casey (7). W—Casey. L—Newsom. HR—DiMaggio, Berra (N.Y.).

Game 4—October 3, at Brooklyn
New York....................1 0 0 1 0 0 0 0 0—2 8 1
Brooklyn ....0 0 0 0 1 0 0 0 2—3 1 3
Bevens; Taylor, Gregg (1), Behrman (8), Casey (9). W—Casey. L—Bevens.

Game 5—October 4, at Brooklyn
New York....................0 0 0 1 1 0 0 0 0—2 5 0
Brooklyn ....0 0 0 0 0 1 0 0 0—1 4 1
Shea; Barney, Hatten (5), Behrman (7), Casey (8). W—Shea. L—Barney. HR—DiMaggio (N.Y.).

Game 6—October 5, at New York
Brooklyn ....2 0 2 0 0 4 0 0 0—8 12 1
New York..................0 0 4 1 0 0 0 0 1—6 15 2
Lombardi, Branca (3), Hatten (6), Casey (9); Reynolds, Drews (3), Page (5), Newsom (6), Raschi (7), Wensloff (8). W—Branca. L—Page.

Game 7—October 6, at New York
Brooklyn ....0 2 0 0 0 0 0 0 0—2 7 0
New York....................0 1 0 2 0 1 1 0 x—5 7 0
Gregg, Behrman (4), Hatten (6), Barney (6), Casey (7); Shea, Bevens (2), Page (5). W—Page. L—Gregg.

1948

FINAL STANDINGS

American League

Team	W	L	Pct.	GB
*Cleveland	97	58	.626	...
Boston	96	59	.619	1
New York	94	60	.610	2.5
Philadelphia	84	70	.545	12.5
Detroit	78	76	.506	18.5
St. Louis	59	94	.386	37
Washington	56	97	.366	40
Chicago	51	101	.336	44.5

*Defeated Boston in one-game pennant playoff.

National League

Team	W	L	Pct.	GB
Boston	91	62	.595	...
St. Louis	85	69	.552	6.5
Brooklyn	84	70	.545	7.5
Pittsburgh	83	71	.539	8.5
New York	78	76	.506	13.5
Philadelphia	66	88	.429	25.5
Cincinnati	64	89	.418	27
Chicago	64	90	.416	27.5

SIGNIFICANT EVENTS

■ **June 15:** The Tigers became the final A.L. team to host a night game when they posted a 4-1 victory over the Athletics at Briggs Stadium.

■ **August 16:** Babe Ruth, whose uniform No. 3 had been retired by the Yankees two months earlier, died of throat cancer at age 53.

■ **October 3:** The Indians finished the season with a record attendance of 2,620,627.

■ **October 12:** Casey Stengel brought his colorful antics to New York when he signed a two-year contract to manage the Yankees.

MEMORABLE MOMENTS

■ **July 18:** Chicago's Pat Seerey joined a select club when he pounded an 11th-inning home run, his fourth of the game, to give the White Sox a 12-11 victory over the Athletics.

■ **October 4:** Player-manager Lou Boudreau belted two home runs and the Indians posted an 8-3 victory over Boston in a one-game playoff to decide the A.L. pennant.

LEADERS

American League

BA: Ted Williams, Bos., .369.
Runs: Tommy Henrich, N.Y., 138.
Hits: Bob Dillinger, St.L., 207.
TB: Joe DiMaggio, N.Y., 355.
HR: Joe DiMaggio, N.Y., 39.
RBI: Joe DiMaggio, N.Y., 155.
SB: Bob Dillinger, St.L., 28.
Wins: Hal Newhouser, Det., 21.
ERA: Gene Bearden, Cle., 2.43.
CG: Bob Lemon, Cle., 20.
IP: Bob Lemon, Cle., 293.2.
SO: Bob Feller, Cle., 164.

National League

BA: Stan Musial, St.L., .376.
Runs: Stan Musial, St.L., 135.
Hits: Stan Musial, St.L., 230.
TB: Stan Musial, St.L., 429.
HR: Ralph Kiner, Pit.; Johnny Mize, N.Y., 40.
RBI: Stan Musial, St.L., 131.
SB: Richie Ashburn, Phil., 32.
Wins: Johnny Sain, Bos., 24.
ERA: Harry Brecheen, St.L., 2.24.
CG: Johnny Sain, Bos., 28.
IP: Johnny Sain, Bos., 314.2.
SO: Harry Brecheen, St.L., 149.

A.L. 20-game winners
Hal Newhouser, Det., 21-12
Gene Bearden, Cle., 20-7
Bob Lemon, Cle., 20-14

N.L. 20-game winners
Johnny Sain, Bos., 24-15
Harry Brecheen, St.L., 20-7

A.L. 100 RBIs
Joe DiMaggio, N.Y., 155
Vern Stephens, Bos., 137
Ted Williams, Bos., 127
Joe Gordon, Cle., 124
Hank Majeski, Phil., 120
Ken Keltner, Cle., 119
Bobby Doerr, Bos., 111
Lou Boudreau, Cle., 106
Hoot Evers, Det., 103
Tommy Henrich, N.Y., 100

N.L. 100 RBIs
Stan Musial, St.L., 131
Johnny Mize, N.Y., 125
Ralph Kiner, Pit., 123
Sid Gordon, N.Y., 107
Andy Pafko, Chi., 101
Bob Elliott, Bos., 100

N.L. 40 homers
Ralph Kiner, Pit., 40
Johnny Mize, N.Y., 40

Most Valuable Player
A.L.: Lou Boudreau, SS, Cle.
N.L.: Stan Musial, OF, St.L.

Rookie of the Year
A.L.-N.L.: Alvin Dark, SS, Bos. (N.L.).

Hall of Fame additions
Herb Pennock, P, 1912-34
Pie Traynor, 3B, 1920-37

ALL-STAR GAME

■ **Winner:** Yankee Vic Raschi and Philadelphia's Joe Coleman pitched six innings of shutout relief and the A.L. won for the 11th time in 15 All-Star classics.

■ **Key inning:** The fourth, when the A.L. broke a 2-2 tie with three runs. Two scored on a bases-loaded single by pitcher Raschi.

■ **Memorable moment:** A first-inning home run by hometown favorite Stan Musial — the first of a record six All-Star homers he would hit.

■ **Top guns:** Raschi (Yankees), Coleman (Athletics), Hoot Evers (Tigers), A.L.; Musial (Cardinals), Richie Ashburn (Phillies).

■ **MVP:** Raschi.

Linescore

July 13, at St. Louis' Sportsman's Park
N.L. ....2 0 0 0 0 0 0 0 0—2 8 0
A.L. ....0 1 1 3 0 0 0 0 x—5 6 0
Branca (Dodgers), Schmitz (Cubs) 4, Sain (Braves) 4, Blackwell (Reds) 6; Masterson (Senators), Raschi (Yankees) 4, Coleman (Athletics) 7. W—Raschi. L—Schmitz. HR—Musial, N.L.; Evers, A.L.

WORLD SERIES

■ **Winner:** The Indians, survivors of a pennant playoff against the Red Sox, needed six games to dispatch Boston's other team in the Series.

■ **Turning point:** Gene Bearden's 2-0 Game 3 shutout, which put the Indians in the driver's seat.

■ **Memorable moment:** The Game 5 appearance of Indians pitcher Satchel Paige, the 42-year-old former Negro Leagues legend. Paige became the first black pitcher in Series history.

■ **Top guns:** Bob Lemon (2-0, 1.65 ERA), Larry Doby (.318), Indians; Bob Elliott (.333, 2 HR, 5 RBIs), Braves.

Linescores

Game 1—October 6, at Boston
Cleveland ....0 0 0 0 0 0 0 0 0—0 4 0
Boston........................0 0 0 0 0 0 0 1 x—1 2 2
Feller; Sain. W—Sain. L—Feller.

Game 2—October 7, at Boston
Cleveland ....0 0 0 2 1 0 0 0 1—4 8 1
Boston ....1 0 0 0 0 0 0 0 0—1 8 3
Lemon; Spahn, Barrett (5), Potter (8). W—Lemon. L—Spahn.

Game 3—October 8, at Cleveland
Boston ....0 0 0 0 0 0 0 0 0—0 5 1
Cleveland...................0 0 1 1 0 0 0 0 x—2 5 0
Bickford, Voiselle (4), Barrett (8); Bearden. W—Bearden. L—Bickford.

Game 4—October 9, at Cleveland
Boston ....0 0 0 0 0 0 1 0 0—1 7 0
Cleveland...................1 0 1 0 0 0 0 0 x—2 5 0
Sain; Gromek. W—Gromek. L—Sain. HR—Doby (Cle.); Rickert (Bos.).

Game 5—October 10, at Cleveland
Boston ....3 0 1 0 0 1 6 0 0—11 12 0
Cleveland ....1 0 0 4 0 0 0 0 0— 5 6 2
Potter, Spahn (4); Feller, Klieman (7), Christopher (7), Paige (7), Muncrief (8). W—Spahn. L—Feller. HR—Elliott 2, Salkeld (Bos.); Mitchell, Hegan (Cle.).

Game 6—October 11, at Boston
Cleveland ....0 0 1 0 0 2 0 1 0—4 10 0
Boston ....0 0 0 1 0 0 0 2 0—3 9 0
Lemon, Bearden (8); Voiselle, Spahn (8). W—Lemon. L—Voiselle. HR—Gordon (Cle.).

1949

FINAL STANDINGS

American League

Team	W	L	Pct.	GB
New York	97	57	.630	...
Boston	96	58	.623	1
Cleveland	89	65	.578	8
Detroit	87	67	.565	10
Philadelphia	81	73	.526	16
Chicago	63	91	.409	34
St. Louis	53	101	.344	44
Washington	50	104	.325	47

National League

Team	W	L	Pct.	GB
Brooklyn	97	57	.630	...
St. Louis	96	58	.623	1
Philadelphia	81	73	.526	16
Boston	75	79	.487	22
New York	73	81	.474	24
Pittsburgh	71	83	.461	26
Cincinnati	62	92	.403	35
Chicago	61	93	.396	36

SIGNIFICANT EVENTS

■ **February 7:** Yankee star Joe DiMaggio signed baseball's first $100,000 contract.

■ **April 19:** In ceremonies at Yankee Stadium, the Yankees unveiled center-field granite monuments honoring Babe Ruth, Lou Gehrig and Miller Huggins.

■ **June 5:** Commissioner Happy Chandler lifted the five-year suspensions of the 18 players who jumped to the outlaw Mexican League in 1946.

■ **June 15:** Phillies star Eddie Waitkus was shot and seriously wounded in a Chicago hotel room by a 19-year-old woman who professed to having a secret crush on him.

■ **December 12:** Baseball's Rules Committee redefined the strike zone as the area over home plate between the batter's armpits and the top of his knees.

MEMORABLE MOMENTS

■ **September 30:** Pittsburgh's Ralph Kiner, the first N.L. player to top the 50-homer plateau twice, blasted No. 54 in a 3-2 victory over the Reds.

■ **October 2:** The Yankees posted a 5-3 final-day victory over Boston in a pennant-deciding battle at Yankee Stadium.

■ **October 2:** The Dodgers held off the Cardinals and claimed the N.L. pennant with a 10-inning, 9-7 final-day victory over Philadelphia.

LEADERS

American League

BA: George Kell, Det., .343.
Runs: Ted Williams, Bos., 150.
Hits: Dale Mitchell, Cle., 203.
TB: Ted Williams, Bos., 368.
HR: Ted Williams, Bos., 43.
RBI: Vern Stephens, Bos,; Ted Williams, Bos., 159.
SB: Bob Dillinger, St.L., 20.
Wins: Mel Parnell, Bos., 25.
ERA: Mike Garcia, Cle., 2.36.
CG: Mel Parnell, Bos., 27.
IP: Mel Parnell, Bos., 295.1.
SO: Virgil Trucks, Det., 153.

National League

BA: Jackie Robinson, Brk., .342.
Runs: Pee Wee Reese, Brk., 132.
Hits: Stan Musial, St.L., 207.
TB: Stan Musial, St.L., 382.
HR: Ralph Kiner, Pit., 54.
RBI: Ralph Kiner, Pit., 127.
SB: Jackie Robinson, Brk., 37.
Wins: Warren Spahn, Bos., 21.
ERA: Dave Koslo, N.Y., 2.50.
CG: Warren Spahn, Bos., 25.
IP: Warren Spahn, Bos., 302.1.
SO: Warren Spahn, Bos., 151.

A.L. 20-game winners
Mel Parnell, Bos., 25-7
Ellis Kinder, Bos., 23-6
Bob Lemon, Cle., 22-10
Vic Raschi, N.Y., 21-10
Alex Kellner, Phil., 20-12

N.L. 20-game winners
Warren Spahn, Bos., 21-14
Howie Pollet, St.L., 20-9

A.L. 100 RBIs
Vern Stephens, Bos., 159
Ted Williams, Bos., 159
Vic Wertz, Det., 133
Bobby Doerr, Bos., 109
Sam Chapman, Phil., 108

N.L. 100 RBIs
Ralph Kiner, Pit., 127
Jackie Robinson, Brk., 124
Stan Musial, St.L., 123
Gil Hodges, Brk., 115
Del Ennis, Phil., 110
Bobby Thomson, N.Y., 109
Carl Furillo, Brk., 106
Wally Westlake, Pit., 104

A.L. 40 homers
Ted Williams, Bos., 43

N.L. 40 homers
Ralph Kiner, Pit., 54

Most Valuable Player
A.L.: Ted Williams, OF, Bos.
N.L.: Jackie Robinson, 2B, Brk.

Rookie of the Year
A.L.: Roy Sievers, OF, St.L.
N.L.: Don Newcombe, P, Brk.

Hall of Fame additions
Three Finger Brown, P, 1903-16
Charley Gehringer, 2B, 1924-42
Kid Nichols, P, 1890-1906

ALL-STAR GAME

■ **Winner:** The DiMaggios, Boston's Dom and New York's Joe, combined for four RBIs and Yankee pitcher Vic Raschi shut down the N.L. over the last three innings as the A.L. prevailed in a sloppy game at Brooklyn.

■ **Key inning:** The seventh, when the A.L. broke open a close game with a three-run rally.

■ **Memorable moment:** Jackie Robinson's first-inning double — the first hit by a black player in the first integrated All-Star Game.

■ **Top guns:** Raschi (Yankees), D. DiMaggio (Red Sox), J. DiMaggio (Yankees), George Kell (Tigers), A.L.; Stan Musial (Cardinals), Ralph Kiner (Pirates), N.L.

■ **MVP:** Joe DiMaggio.

Linescore

July 12, at Brooklyn's Ebbets Field
A.L. ....4 0 0 2 0 2 3 0 0—1 13 1
N.L. ....2 1 2 0 0 2 0 0 0—7 12 5
Parnell (Red Sox), Trucks (Tigers) 2, Brissie (Athletics) 4, Raschi (Yankees) 7; Spahn (Braves), Newcombe (Dodgers) 2, Munger (Cardinals) 5, Bickford (Braves) 6, Pollet (Cardinals) 7, Blackwell (Reds) 8, Roe (Dodgers) 9. W—Trucks. L—Newcombe. HR—Musial, Kiner, N.L.

WORLD SERIES

■ **Winner:** The Yankee machine was back, this time with a new driver. Casey Stengel made his Series managerial debut a successful one.

■ **Turning point:** A three-run ninth inning that produced a 4-3 Yankee victory in Game 3.

■ **Memorable moment:** Tommy Henrich's leadoff ninth-inning home run that decided a 1-0 pitching duel between Dodgers ace Don Newcombe and Yankee righthander Allie Reynolds in Game 1.

■ **Top guns:** Reynolds (12⅓ IP, 0.00 ERA), Bobby Brown (.500, 5 RBIs), Yankees; Pee Wee Reese (.316), Dodgers.

Linescores

Game 1—Oct. 5, at New York
Brooklyn ....0 0 0 0 0 0 0 0 0—0 2 0
New York...................0 0 0 0 0 0 0 0 1—1 5 1
Newcombe; Reynolds. W—Reynolds. L—Newcombe. HR—Henrich (N.Y.).

Game 2—October 6, at New York
Brooklyn ....0 1 0 0 0 0 0 0 0—1 7 2
New York...................0 0 0 0 0 0 0 0 0—0 6 1
Roe; Raschi, Page (9). W—Roe. L—Raschi.

Game 3—October 7, at Brooklyn
New York...................0 0 1 0 0 0 0 0 3—4 5 0
Brooklyn ....0 0 0 1 0 0 0 0 2—3 5 0
Byrne, Page (4); Branca, Banta (9). W—Page. L—Branca. HR—Reese, Olmo, Campanella (Brk.).

Game 4—October 8, at Brooklyn
New York...................0 0 0 3 3 0 0 0 0—6 10 0
Brooklyn ....0 0 0 0 0 4 0 0 0—4 9 1
Lopat, Reynolds (6); Newcombe, Hatten (4), Erskine (6), Banta (7). W—Lopat. L—Newcombe.

Game 5—October 9, at Brooklyn
New York................2 0 3 1 1 3 0 0 0—10 11 1
Brooklyn ....0 0 1 0 0 1 4 0 0— 6 11 2
Raschi, Page (7); Barney, Banta (3), Erskine (6), Hatten (6), Palica (7), Minner (9). W—Raschi. L—Barney. HR—DiMaggio (N.Y.); Hodges (Brk.).

1950

FINAL STANDINGS

American League

Team	W	L	Pct.	GB
New York	98	56	.636	...
Detroit	95	59	.617	3
Boston	94	60	.610	4
Cleveland	92	62	.597	6
Washington	67	87	.435	31
Chicago	60	94	.390	38
St. Louis	58	96	.377	40
Philadelphia	52	102	.338	46

National League

Team	W	L	Pct.	GB
Philadelphia	91	63	.591	...
Brooklyn	89	65	.578	2
New York	86	68	.558	5
Boston	83	71	.539	8
St. Louis	78	75	.510	12.5
Cincinnati	66	87	.431	24.5
Chicago	64	89	.418	26.5
Pittsburgh	57	96	.373	33.5

SIGNIFICANT EVENTS

■ **January 31:** Pittsburgh made 18-year-old pitcher Paul Pettit baseball's first $100,000 bonus baby.

■ **October 18:** Connie Mack retired after 50 years as manager and owner of the Athletics, the team he built in 1901 when the American League was organized.

■ **December 11:** Major League owners pulled a shocker when they voted not to renew the contract of Commissioner Happy Chandler.

■ **December 26:** Chandler announced that the Gillette Safety Razor Company had agreed to pay a six-year fee of $6 million for rights to the World Series and All-Star Game.

MEMORABLE MOMENTS

■ **June 8:** The Red Sox, in the biggest single-game explosion in history, defeated the Browns 29-4 at Boston's Fenway Park.

■ **August 31:** Brooklyn's Gil Hodges became the sixth player to hit four home runs in a game during a 19-3 rout of the Braves at Ebbets Field. Hodges also singled and tied the single-game record of 17 total bases.

■ **October 1:** Dick Sisler crashed a three-run 10th-inning home run to give the Phillies a 4-1 victory over the Dodgers and their first N.L. pennant in 35 years.

LEADERS

American League

BA: Billy Goodman, Bos., .354.
Runs: Dom DiMaggio, Bos., 131.
Hits: George Kell, Det., 218.
TB: Walt Dropo, Bos., 326.
HR: Al Rosen, Cle., 37.
RBI: Walt Dropo, Bos.; Vern Stephens, Bos., 144.
SB: Dom DiMaggio, Bos., 15.
Wins: Bob Lemon, Cle., 23.
ERA: Early Wynn, Cle., 3.20.
CG: Ned Garver, St.L.; Bob Lemon, Cle., 22.
IP: Bob Lemon, Cle., 288.
SO: Bob Lemon, Cle., 170.

National League

BA: Stan Musial, St.L., .346.
Runs: Earl Torgeson, Bos., 120.
Hits: Duke Snider, Brk., 199.
TB: Duke Snider, Brk., 343.
HR: Ralph Kiner, Pit., 47.
RBI: Del Ennis, Phil., 126.
SB: Sam Jethroe, Bos., 35.
Wins: Warren Spahn, Bos., 21.
ERA: Sal Maglie, N.Y., 2.71.
CG: Vern Bickford, Bos., 27.
IP: Vern Bickford, Bos., 311.2.
SO: Warren Spahn, Bos., 191.

A.L. 20-game winners
Bob Lemon, Cle., 23-11
Vic Raschi, N.Y., 21-8

N.L. 20-game winners
Warren Spahn, Bos., 21-17
Robin Roberts, Phil., 20-11
Johnny Sain, Bos., 20-13

A.L. 100 RBIs
Walt Dropo, Bos., 144
Vern Stephens, Bos., 144
Yogi Berra, N.Y., 124
Vic Wertz, Det., 123
Joe DiMaggio, N.Y., 122
Bobby Doerr, Bos., 120
Al Rosen, Cle., 116
Luke Easter, Cle., 107
Hoot Evers, Det., 103
Larry Doby, Cle., 102
George Kell, Det., 101

N.L. 100 RBIs
Del Ennis, Phil., 126
Ralph Kiner, Pit., 118
Gil Hodges, Brk., 113
Ted Kluszewski, Cin., 111
Stan Musial, St.L., 109
Bob Elliott, Bos., 107
Duke Snider, Brk., 107
Carl Furillo, Brk., 106
Sid Gordon, Bos., 103
Hank Sauer, Chi., 103
Enos Slaughter, St.L., 101

N.L. 40 homers
Ralph Kiner, Pit., 47

Most Valuable Player
A.L.: Phil Rizzuto, SS, N.Y.
N.L.: Jim Konstanty, P, Phil.

Rookie of the Year
A.L.: Walt Dropo, 1B, Bos.
N.L.: Sam Jethroe, OF, Bos.

ALL-STAR GAME

■ **Winner:** The N.L. broke a four-game losing streak with a 4-3 victory in the first extra-inning All-Star Game.

■ **Key inning:** The ninth, when Tigers pitcher Art Houtteman, trying to close out a 3-2 A.L. victory, surrendered a game-tying home run to Pirates slugger Ralph Kiner.

■ **Memorable moment:** A dramatic 14th-inning home run by Cardinals second baseman Red Schoendienst that gave the N.L. its first win since 1944. Schoendienst was an 11th-inning defensive replacement.

■ **Top guns:** Larry Jansen (Giants), Ewell Blackwell (Reds), Kiner (Pirates), Schoendienst (Cardinals), N.L.; Bob Lemon (Indians), Larry Doby (Indians), A.L.

■ **MVP:** Schoendienst.

Linescore

July 11, at Chicago's Comiskey Park
N.L.......0 2 0 0 0 0 0 0 1 0 0 0 0 1—4 10 0
A.L.......0 0 1 0 2 0 0 0 0 0 0 0 0 0—3 8 1
Roberts (Phillies), Newcombe (Dodgers) 4, Konstanty (Phillies) 6, Jansen (Giants) 7, Blackwell (Reds) 12; Raschi (Yankees), Lemon (Indians) 4, Houtteman (Tigers) 7, Reynolds (Yankees) 10, Gray (Tigers) 13, Feller (Indians) 14. W—Blackwell. L—Gray. HR—Kiner, Schoendienst, N.L.

WORLD SERIES

■ **Winner:** Rekindling memories of New York's 1936-39 machine, the Bronx Bombers captured their second straight Series with a sweep of the Phillies.

■ **Turning point:** Joe DiMaggio's 10th-inning homer that gave the Yankees and Allie Reynolds a 2-1 victory in Game 2.

■ **Memorable moment:** Rookie Whitey Ford's first Series victory — a 5-2 Game 4 decision.

■ **Top guns:** Gene Woodling (.429), Bobby Brown (.333), Yankees; Granny Hamner (.429), Phillies.

Linescores

Game 1—October 4, at Philadelphia
New York ....0 0 0 1 0 0 0 0 0—1 5 0
Philadelphia ....0 0 0 0 0 0 0 0 0—0 2 1
Raschi; Konstanty, Meyer (9). W—Raschi. L—Konstanty.

Game 2—October 5, at Philadelphia
New York ....0 1 0 0 0 0 0 0 0 1—2 10 0
Philadelphia ....0 0 0 0 1 0 0 0 0 0—1 7 0
Reynolds; Roberts. W—Reynolds. L—Roberts. HR—DiMaggio (N.Y.).

Game 3—October 6, at New York
Philadelphia ....0 0 0 0 0 1 1 0 0—2 10 2
New York ....0 0 1 0 0 0 0 1 1—3 7 0
Heintzelman, Konstanty (8), Meyer (9); Lopat, Ferrick (9). W—Ferrick. L—Meyer.

Game 4—October 7, at New York
Philadelphia ....0 0 0 0 0 0 0 0 2—2 7 1
New York ....2 0 0 0 0 3 0 0 x—5 8 2
Miller, Konstanty (1), Roberts (8); Ford, Reynolds (9). W—Ford. L—Miller. HR—Berra (N.Y.).

1951

FINAL STANDINGS

American League

Team	W	L	Pct.	GB
New York	98	56	.636	...
Cleveland	93	61	.604	5
Boston	87	67	.565	11
Chicago	81	73	.526	17
Detroit	73	81	.474	25
Philadelphia	70	84	.455	28
Washington	62	92	.403	36
St. Louis	52	102	.338	46

National League

Team	W	L	Pct.	GB
*New York	98	59	.624	...
Brooklyn	97	60	.618	1
St. Louis	81	73	.526	15.5
Boston	76	78	.494	20.5
Philadelphia	73	81	.474	23.5
Cincinnati	68	86	.442	28.5
Pittsburgh	64	90	.416	32.5
Chicago	62	92	.403	34.5

*Defeated Brooklyn 2-1 in pennant playoff.

SIGNIFICANT EVENTS

■ **August 19:** Browns owner Bill Veeck pulled off a wild promotional stunt when he sent midget Eddie Gaedel to the plate as a surprise pinch-hitter in a Sportsman's Park game against the Tigers.

■ **September 20:** N.L. President Ford Frick was selected as baseball's third commissioner during a marathon meeting in Chicago.

■ **December 11:** Yankee center fielder Joe DiMaggio, a three-time A.L. MVP, announced his retirement.

MEMORABLE MOMENTS

■ **September 14:** Browns outfielder Bob Nieman became the first player to hit home runs in his first two big-league at-bats. Both came off Mickey McDermott in a game at Boston.

■ **September 28:** New York's Allie Reynolds fired his record-tying second no-hitter of the season in the opener of a doubleheader against Boston, earning an 8-0 decision and clinching at least a tie for the A.L. pennant. The Yankees clinched their third straight flag with an 11-3 win in the nightcap.

■ **October 3:** Bobby Thomson smashed a three-run, ninth-inning homer—giving the Giants a dramatic 5-4 victory over the Dodgers in the decisive third game of an N.L. pennant playoff.

LEADERS

American League

BA: Ferris Fain, Phil., .344.
Runs: Dom DiMaggio, Bos., 113.
Hits: George Kell, Det., 191.
TB: Ted Williams, Bos., 295.
HR: Gus Zernial, Chi.-Phil., 33.
RBI: Gus Zernial, Chi.-Phil., 129.
SB: Minnie Minoso, Cle.-Chi., 31.
Wins: Bob Feller, Cle., 22.
ERA: Saul Rogovin, Det.-Chi., 2.78.
CG: Ned Garver, St.L., 24.
IP: Early Wynn, Cle., 274.1.
SO: Vic Raschi, N.Y., 164.

National League

BA: Stan Musial, St.L., .355.
Runs: Ralph Kiner, Pit.; Stan Musial, St.L., 124.
Hits: Richie Ashburn, Phil., 221.
TB: Stan Musial, St.L., 355.
HR: Ralph Kiner, Pit., 42.
RBI: Monte Irvin, N.Y., 121.
SB: Sam Jethroe, Bos., 35.
Wins: Larry Jansen, N.Y.; Sal Maglie, N.Y., 23.
ERA: Chet Nichols, Bos., 2.88.
CG: Warren Spahn, Bos., 26.
IP: Robin Roberts, Phil., 315.
SO: Don Newcombe, Brk.; Warren Spahn, Bos., 164.

A.L. 20-game winners

Bob Feller, Cle., 22-8
Eddie Lopat, N.Y., 21-9
Vic Raschi, N.Y., 21-10
Ned Garver, St.L., 20-12
Mike Garcia, Cle., 20-13
Early Wynn, Cle., 20-13

N.L. 20-game winners

Sal Maglie, N.Y., 23-6
Larry Jansen, N.Y., 23-11
Preacher Roe, Brk., 22-3
Warren Spahn, Bos., 22-14
Robin Roberts, Phil., 21-15
Don Newcombe, Brk., 20-9
Murry Dickson, Pit., 20-16

A.L. 100 RBIs

Gus Zernial, Chi.-Phil., 129
Ted Williams, Bos., 126
Eddie Robinson, Chi., 117
Luke Easter, Cle., 103
Al Rosen, Cle., 102

N.L. 100 RBIs

Monte Irvin, N.Y., 121
Sid Gordon, Bos., 109
Ralph Kiner, Pit., 109
Roy Campanella, Brk., 108
Stan Musial, St.L., 108
Gil Hodges, Brk., 103
Duke Snider, Brk., 101
Bobby Thomson, N.Y., 101

N.L. 40 homers

Ralph Kiner, Pit., 42
Gil Hodges, Brk., 40

Most Valuable Player

A.L.: Yogi Berra, C, N.Y.
N.L.: Roy Campanella, C, Brk.

Rookie of the Year

A.L.: Gil McDougald, 3B, N.Y.
N.L.: Willie Mays, OF, N.Y.

Hall of Fame additions

Jimmie Foxx, 1B, 1925-45
Mel Ott, OF, 1926-47

ALL-STAR GAME

■ **Winner:** The N.L. hit an All-Star Game-record four home runs in an 8-3 victory. It marked the first time the senior circuit had recorded back-to-back wins.

■ **Key inning:** A three-run fourth, when St. Louis' Stan Musial and Boston's Bob Elliott connected off Yankee lefty Eddie Lopat.

■ **Memorable moments:** A.L. home runs by Vic Wertz and George Kell before their home fans at Detroit's Briggs Stadium.

■ **Top guns:** Don Newcombe (Dodgers), Musial (Cardinals), Elliott (Braves), Jackie Robinson (Dodgers), Ralph Kiner (Pirates), Gil Hodges (Dodgers), N.L.; Wertz (Tigers), Kell (Tigers), A.L.

■ **MVP:** Elliott.

Linescore

July 10, at Detroit's Briggs Stadium
N.L. ....1 0 0 3 0 2 1 1 0—8 12 1
A.L. ....0 1 0 1 1 0 0 0 0—3 10 2
Roberts (Phillies), Maglie (Giant) 3, Newcombe (Dodgers) 6, Blackwell (Reds) 9; Garver (Browns), Lopat (Yankees) 4, Hutchinson (Tigers) 5, Parnell (Red Sox) 8, Lemon (Indians) 9. W—Maglie. L—Lopat. HR—Musial, Elliott, Hodges, Kiner, N.L.; Wertz, Kell, A.L.

WORLD SERIES

■ **Winner:** The Yankees' third straight Series victory came at the expense of the torrid Giants, who had beaten Brooklyn in a memorable pennant playoff series.

■ **Turning point:** Infielder Gil McDougald's Game 5 grand slam, which sparked a momentum-turning 13-1 Yankee victory.

■ **Memorable moment:** Yankee right fielder Hank Bauer's Game 6 heroics: a bases-loaded triple and a spectacular Series-ending catch in a 4-3 victory.

■ **Top guns:** Eddie Lopat (2-0, 0.50 ERA), Bobby Brown (.357), McDougald (7 RBIs), Yankees; Monte Irvin (.458), Alvin Dark (.417), Giants.

Linescores

Game 1—October 4, at Yankee Stadium
Giants ....2 0 0 0 0 3 0 0 0—5 10 1
Yankees ....0 1 0 0 0 0 0 0 0—1 7 1
Koslo; Reynolds, Hogue (7), Morgan (8). W—Koslo. L—Reynolds. HR—Dark (Giants).

Game 2—October 5, at Yankee Stadium
Giants ....0 0 0 0 0 0 1 0 0—1 5 1
Yankees ....1 1 0 0 0 0 0 1 x—3 6 0
Jansen, Spencer (7); Lopat. W—Lopat. L—Jansen. HR—Collins (Yankees).

Game 3—October 6, at Polo Grounds
Yankees ....0 0 0 0 0 0 0 1 1—2 5 2
Giants ....0 1 0 0 5 0 0 0 x—6 7 2
Raschi, Hogue (5), Ostrowski (8); Hearn, Jones (8). W—Hearn. L—Raschi. HR—Lockman (Giants); Woodling (Yankees).

Game 4—October 8, at Polo Grounds
Yankees ....0 1 0 1 2 0 2 0 0—6 12 0
Giants ....1 0 0 0 0 0 0 0 1—2 8 2
Reynolds; Maglie, Jones (6), Kennedy (9). W—Reynolds. L—Maglie. HR—DiMaggio (Yankees).

Game 5—October 9, at Polo Grounds
Yankees ....0 0 5 2 0 2 4 0 0—13 12 1
Giants ....1 0 0 0 0 0 0 0 0— 1 5 3
Lopat; Jansen, Kennedy (4), Spencer (6), Corwin (7), Konikowski (9). W—Lopat. L—Jansen. HR—McDougald, Rizzuto (Yankees).

Game 6—October 10, at Yankee Stadium
Giants ....0 0 0 0 1 0 0 0 2—3 11 1
Yankees ....1 0 0 0 0 3 0 0 x—4 7 0
Koslo, Hearn (7), Jansen (8); Raschi, Sain (7), Kuzava (9). W—Raschi. L—Koslo.

1952

FINAL STANDINGS

American League

Team	W	L	Pct.	GB
New York	95	59	.617	...
Cleveland	93	61	.604	2
Chicago	81	73	.526	14
Philadelphia	79	75	.513	16
Washington	78	76	.506	17
Boston	76	78	.494	19
St. Louis	64	90	.416	31
Detroit	50	104	.325	45

National League

Team	W	L	Pct.	GB
Brooklyn	96	57	.627	...
New York	92	62	.597	4.5
St. Louis	88	66	.571	8.5
Philadelphia	87	67	.565	9.5
Chicago	77	77	.500	19.5
Cincinnati	69	85	.448	27.5
Boston	64	89	.418	32
Pittsburgh	42	112	.273	54.5

SIGNIFICANT EVENTS

■ **May 2:** Boston's Ted Williams, who lost three years to military service in World War II, returned to a 17-month tour of duty with the U.S. Marines as a fighter pilot in Korea.

■ **May-June-July:** Joining Williams on the Korean front were such name players as Don Newcombe, Willie Mays, Jerry Coleman, Bob Kennedy, Bobby Brown and Tom Morgan.

MEMORABLE MOMENTS

■ **April 23:** Browns lefty Bob Cain outdueled Cleveland ace Bob Feller, 1-0, in a record-tying battle of one-hitters at St. Louis' Sportsman's Park.

■ **May 21:** The Dodgers exploded for a Major League-record 15 first-inning runs and coasted to a 19-1 victory over the Reds at Ebbets Field.

■ **July 15:** Detroit first baseman Walt Dropo doubled in the second game of a doubleheader against Washington for his 12th consecutive hit, tying the 1938 record set by Boston's Pinky Higgins.

■ **August 25:** Detroit's Virgil Trucks became the third pitcher to throw two no-hitters in one season when he stopped New York, 1-0, at Yankee Stadium.

LEADERS

American League

BA: Ferris Fain, Phil., .327.
Runs: Larry Doby, Cle., 104.
Hits: Nellie Fox, Chi., 192.
TB: Al Rosen, Cle., 297.
HR: Larry Doby, Cle., 32.
RBI: Al Rosen, Cle., 105.
SB: Minnie Minoso, Chi., 22.
Wins: Bobby Shantz, Phil., 24.
ERA: Allie Reynolds, N.Y., 2.06.
CG: Bob Lemon, Cle., 28.
IP: Bob Lemon, Cle., 309.2.
SO: Allie Reynolds, N.Y., 160.

National League

BA: Stan Musial, St.L., .336.
Runs: Solly Hemus, St.L.; Stan Musial, St.L., 105.
Hits: Stan Musial, St.L., 194.
TB: Stan Musial, St.L., 311.
HR: Ralph Kiner, Pit.; Hank Sauer, Chi., 37.
RBI: Hank Sauer, Chi., 121.
SB: Pee Wee Reese, Brk., 30.
Wins: Robin Roberts, Phil., 28.
ERA: Hoyt Wilhelm, N.Y., 2.43.
CG: Robin Roberts, Phil., 30.
IP: Robin Roberts, Phil., 330.
SO: Warren Spahn, Bos., 183.

A.L. 20-game winners

Bobby Shantz, Phil., 24-7
Early Wynn, Cle., 23-12
Mike Garcia, Cle., 22-11
Bob Lemon, Cle., 22-11
Allie Reynolds, N.Y., 20-8

N.L. 20-Game Winner

Robin Roberts, Phil., 28-7

A.L. 100 RBIs

Al Rosen, Cle., 105
Larry Doby, Cle., 104
Eddie Robinson, Chi., 104
Gus Zernial, Phil., 100

N.L. 100 RBIs

Hank Sauer, Chi., 121
Bobby Thomson, N.Y., 108
Del Ennis, Phil., 107
Gil Hodges, Brk., 102
Enos Slaughter, St.L., 101

Most Valuable Player

A.L.: Bobby Shantz, P, Phil.
N.L.: Hank Sauer, OF, Chi.

Rookie of the Year

A.L.: Harry Byrd, P, Phil.
N.L.: Joe Black, P, Brk.

Hall of Fame additions

Harry Heilmann, OF/1B, 1914-32
Paul Waner, OF, 1926-45

ALL-STAR GAME

■ **Winner:** The N.L. recorded a rain-shortened 3-2 victory and closed its All-Star deficit to 12-7.

■ **Key inning:** The fourth, when the A.L. scored twice for a 2-1 lead and the N.L. answered with a two-run homer by the Cubs' Hank Sauer.

■ **Memorable moments:** The pitching of Philadelphia stars Curt Simmons (Phillies) and Bobby Shantz (Athletics) before their home fans. Simmons pitched three scoreless innings for the N.L. and Shantz struck out all three batters he faced in a scoreless fifth.

■ **Top guns:** Simmons (Phillies), Jackie Robinson (Dodgers), Sauer (Cubs), N.L.; Shantz (Athletics), Bobby Avila (Indians), A.L.

■ **MVP:** Sauer.

Linescore

July 8, at Philadelphia's Shibe Park
A.L. ....0 0 0 2 0—2 5 0
N.L. ....1 0 0 2 0—3 3 0
Raschi (Yankees), Lemon (Indians) 3, Shantz (Athletics) 5; Simmons (Phillies), Rush (Cubs) 4. W—Rush. L—Lemon. HR—J. Robinson, Sauer, N.L.

WORLD SERIES

■ **Winner:** The Yankees tied their own previous best run of four consecutive Series championships with a seven-game thriller against the Dodgers.

■ **Turning point:** Game 6 home runs by Yogi Berra and Mickey Mantle that keyed a 3-2 victory and tied the Series at three games apiece.

■ **Memorable moment:** Yankee second baseman Billy Martin's Series-saving shoetop catch of Jackie Robinson's bases-loaded infield popup, which appeared destined to fall untouched. Martin's mad-dash catch saved a 4-2 victory.

■ **Top guns:** Vic Raschi (2-0, 1.59 ERA), Johnny Mize (.400, 3 HR, 6 RBIs), Mantle (.345, 2 HR), Yankees; Duke Snider (.345, 4 HR, 8 RBIs), Pee Wee Reese (.345), Dodgers.

Linescores

Game 1—October 1, at Brooklyn
New York ....0 0 1 0 0 0 0 1 0—2 6 2
Brooklyn ....0 1 0 0 0 2 0 1 x—4 6 0
Reynolds, Scarborough (8); Black. W—Black. L—Reynolds. HR—Robinson, Snider, Reese (Brk.); McDougald (N.Y.).

Game 2—October 2, at Brooklyn
New York ....0 0 0 1 1 5 0 0 0—7 10 0
Brooklyn ....0 0 1 0 0 0 0 0 0—1 3 1
Raschi; Erskine, Loes (6), Lehman (8). W—Raschi. L—Erskine. HR—Martin (N.Y.).

Game 3—October 3, at New York
Brooklyn ....0 0 1 0 1 0 0 1 2—5 11 0
New York ....0 1 0 0 0 0 0 1 1—3 6 2
Roe; Lopat, Gorman (9). W—Roe. L—Lopat. HR—Berra, Mize (N.Y.).

Game 4—October 4, at New York
Brooklyn ....0 0 0 0 0 0 0 0 0—0 4 1
New York ....0 0 0 1 0 0 0 1 x—2 4 1
Black, Rutherford (8); Reynolds. W—Reynolds. L—Black. HR—Mize (N.Y.).

Game 5—October 5, at New York
Brooklyn ....0 1 0 0 3 0 1 0 0 0 1—6 10 0
New York ....0 0 0 0 5 0 0 0 0 0 0—5 5 1
Erskine; Blackwell, Sain (6). W—Erskine. L—Sain. HR—Snider (Brk.); Mize (N.Y.).

Game 6—October 6, at Brooklyn
New York ....0 0 0 0 0 0 2 1 0—3 9 0
Brooklyn ....0 0 0 0 0 1 0 1 0—2 8 1
Raschi, Reynolds (8); Loes, Roe (9). W—Raschi. L—Loes. HR—Mantle, Berra (N.Y.); Snider 2 (Brk.).

Game 7—October 7, at Brooklyn
New York ....0 0 0 1 1 1 1 0 0—4 10 4
Brooklyn ....0 0 0 1 1 0 0 0 0—2 8 1
Lopat, Reynolds (4), Raschi (7), Kuzava (7); Black, Roe (6), Erskine (8). W—Reynolds. L—Black. HR—Woodling, Mantle (N.Y.).

1953

FINAL STANDINGS

American League

Team	W	L	Pct.	GB
New York	99	52	.656	...
Cleveland	92	62	.597	8.5
Chicago	89	65	.578	11.5
Boston	84	69	.549	16
Washington	76	76	.500	23.5
Detroit	60	94	.390	40.5
Philadelphia	59	95	.383	41.5
St. Louis	54	100	.351	46.5

National League

Team	W	L	Pct.	GB
Brooklyn	105	49	.682	...
Milwaukee	92	62	.597	13
Philadelphia	83	71	.539	22
St. Louis	83	71	.539	22
New York	70	84	.455	35
Cincinnati	68	86	.442	37
Chicago	65	89	.422	40
Pittsburgh	50	104	.325	55

SIGNIFICANT EVENTS

■ **March 18:** The Braves, a fixture in Boston for 77 years, received unanimous approval for a move to Milwaukee—baseball's first franchise shift since 1903.

■ **September 29:** Bill Veeck sold his St. Louis Browns to a syndicate that received quick approval to move the franchise to Baltimore.

■ **November 9:** Baseball won a major victory when the U.S. Supreme Court ruled that it is a sport, not an interstate business, and therefore not subject to federal antitrust laws.

MEMORABLE MOMENTS

■ **May 6:** Browns rookie Bobo Holloman made baseball history when he pitched a 6-0 no-hitter against Philadelphia in his first Major League start.

■ **May 25:** Milwaukee's Max Surkont struck out a modern-record eight consecutive Reds en route to a 10-3 victory.

■ **June 18:** The Red Sox scored a record 17 runs in the seventh inning of a 23-3 victory over the Tigers.

LEADERS

American League

BA: Mickey Vernon, Wash., .337.
Runs: Al Rosen, Cle., 115.
Hits: Harvey Kuenn, Det., 209.
TB: Al Rosen, Cle., 367.
HR: Al Rosen, Cle., 43.
RBI: Al Rosen, Cle., 145.
SB: Minnie Minoso, Chi., 25.
Wins: Bob Porterfield, Wash., 22.
ERA: Eddie Lopat, N.Y., 2.42.
CG: Bob Porterfield, Wash., 24.
IP: Bob Lemon, Cle., 286.2.
SO: Billy Pierce, Chi., 186.

National League

BA: Carl Furillo, Brk., .344.
Runs: Duke Snider, Brk., 132.
Hits: Richie Ashburn, Phil., 205.
TB: Duke Snider, Brk., 370.
HR: Eddie Mathews, Mil., 47.
RBI: Roy Campanella, Brk., 142.
SB: Bill Bruton, Mil., 26.
Wins: Robin Roberts, Phil.; Warren Spahn, Mil., 23.
ERA: Warren Spahn, Mil., 2.10.
CG: Robin Roberts, Phil., 33.
IP: Robin Roberts, Phil., 346.2.
SO: Robin Roberts, Phil., 198.

A.L. 20-game winners

Bob Porterfield, Wash., 22-10
Mel Parnell, Bos., 21-8
Bob Lemon, Cle., 21-15
Virgil Trucks, St.L.-Chi., 20-10

N.L. 20-game winners

Warren Spahn, Mil., 23-7
Robin Roberts, Phil., 23-16
Carl Erskine, Brk., 20-6
Harvey Haddix, St.L., 20-9

A.L. 100 RBIs

Al Rosen, Cle., 145
Mickey Vernon, Wash., 115
Ray Boone, Cle.-Det., 114
Yogi Berra, N.Y., 108
Gus Zernial, Phil., 108
Minnie Minoso, Chi., 104
Larry Doby, Cle., 102
Eddie Robinson, Phil., 102

N.L. 100 RBIs

Roy Campanella, Brk., 142
Eddie Mathews, Mil., 135
Duke Snider, Brk., 126
Del Ennis, Phil., 125
Gil Hodges, Brk., 122
Ralph Kiner, Pit.-Chi., 116
Stan Musial, St.L., 113
Ray Jablonski, St.L., 112
Ted Kluszewski, Cin., 108
Bobby Thomson, N.Y., 106
Gus Bell, Cin., 105
Frank Thomas, Pit., 102
Jim Greengrass, Cin., 100

A.L. 40 homers

Al Rosen, Cle., 43
Gus Zernial, Phil., 42

N.L. 40 homers

Eddie Mathews, Mil., 47
Duke Snider, Brk., 42
Roy Campanella, Brk., 41
Ted Kluszewski, Cin., 40

Most Valuable Player

A.L.: Al Rosen, 3B, Cle.
N.L.: Roy Campanella, C, Brk.

Rookie of the Year

A.L.: Harvey Kuenn, SS, Det.
N.L.: Jim Gilliam, 2B, Brk.

Hall of Fame additions

Ed Barrow, manager/executive
Chief Bender, P, 1903-25
Tommy Connolly, umpire
Dizzy Dean, P, 1930-47
Bill Klem, umpire
Al Simmons, OF, 1924-44
Bobby Wallace, SS, 1894-1918
Harry Wright, manager

ALL-STAR GAME

■ **Winner:** Robin Roberts (Phillies), Warren Spahn (Braves), Curt Simmons (Phillies) and Murry Dickson (Pirates) combined on a six-hitter and the N.L. rolled to its fourth consecutive victory.

■ **Key inning:** The N.L.'s two-run fifth, when Philadelphia's Richie Ashburn and Brooklyn's Pee Wee Reese singled home runs.

■ **Memorable moment:** The eighth-inning appearance of Browns righthander Satchel Paige, a former Negro League legend and the oldest man (47) ever to play in an All-Star Game.

■ **Top guns:** Roberts (Phillies), Spahn (Braves), Simmons (Phillies), Reese (Dodgers), N.L.; Billy Pierce (White Sox), Minnie Minoso (White Sox), A.L.

■ **MVP:** Reese.

Linescore

July 14, at Cincinnati's Crosley Field

A.L. ....0 0 0 0 0 0 0 0 1—1 5 0
N.L. ....0 0 0 0 2 0 1 2 x—5 10 0

Pierce (White Sox), Reynolds (Yankees) 4, Garcia (Indians) 6, Paige (Browns) 8; Roberts (Phillies), Spahn (Braves) 4, Simmons (Phillies) 6, Dickson (Pirates) 8. W—Spahn. L—Reynolds.

WORLD SERIES

■ **Winner:** The Yankees earned their record fifth consecutive Series victory and remained perfect in post-season play under manager Casey Stengel.

■ **Turning point:** Billy Martin's two-run homer and Mickey Mantle's grand slam in the Yankees' 11-7 fifth-game Series-turning triumph.

■ **Memorable moment:** Martin's ninth-inning Series-ending single in Game 6 — his record-tying 12th hit of the fall classic.

■ **Top guns:** Martin (.500, 12 hits, 2 HR, 8 RBIs), Mantle (2 HR, 7 RBIs), Yankees; Gil Hodges (.364), Carl Furillo (.333), Dodgers.

Linescores

Game 1—September 30, at New York

Brooklyn ....0 0 0 0 1 3 1 0 0—5 12 2
New York..................4 0 0 0 1 0 1 3 x—9 12 0

Erskine, Hughes (2), Labine (6), Wade (7); Reynolds, Sain (6). W—Sain. L—Labine. HR—Berra, Collins (N.Y.); Gilliam, Hodges, Shuba (Brk.).

Game 2—October 1, at New York

Brooklyn ....0 0 0 2 0 0 0 0 0—2 9 1
New York....................1 0 0 0 0 0 1 2 x—4 5 0

Roe; Lopat. W—Lopat. L—Roe. HR—Martin, Mantle (N.Y.).

Game 3—October 2, at Brooklyn

New York....................0 0 0 0 1 0 0 1 0—2 6 0
Brooklyn ....0 0 0 0 1 1 0 1 x—3 9 0

Raschi; Erskine. W—Erskine. L—Raschi. HR—Campanella (Brk.).

Game 4—October 3, at Brooklyn

New York..................0 0 0 0 2 0 0 0 1—3 9 0
Brooklyn ....3 0 0 1 0 2 1 0 x—7 12 0

Ford, Gorman (2), Sain (5), Schallock (7); Loes, Labine (9). W—Loes. L—Ford. HR—McDougald (N.Y.); Snider (Brk.).

Game 5—October 4, at Brooklyn

New York................1 0 5 0 0 0 3 1 1—11 11 1
Brooklyn ....0 1 0 0 1 0 0 4 1— 7 14 1

McDonald, Kuzava (8), Reynolds (9); Podres, Meyer (3), Wade (8), Black (9). W—McDonald. L—Podres. HR—Woodling, Mantle, Martin, McDougald (N.Y.); Cox, Gilliam (Brk.).

Game 6—October 5, at New York

Brooklyn ....0 0 0 0 0 1 0 0 2—3 8 3
New York..................2 1 0 0 0 0 0 0 1—4 13 0

Erskine, Milliken (5), Labine (7); Ford, Reynolds (8). W—Reynolds. L—Labine. HR—Furillo (Brk.).

1954

FINAL STANDINGS

American League

Team	W	L	Pct.	GB
Cleveland	111	43	.721	...
New York	103	51	.669	8
Chicago	94	60	.610	17
Boston	69	85	.448	42
Detroit	68	86	.442	43
Washington	66	88	.429	45
Baltimore	54	100	.351	57
Philadelphia	51	103	.331	60

National League

Team	W	L	Pct.	GB
New York	97	57	.630	...
Brooklyn	92	62	.597	5
Milwaukee	89	65	.578	8
Philadelphia	75	79	.487	22
Cincinnati	74	80	.481	23
St. Louis	72	82	.468	25
Chicago	64	90	.416	33
Pittsburgh	53	101	.344	44

SIGNIFICANT EVENTS

■ **July 12:** Big league players organized into a group called the Major League Baseball Players Association and hired J. Norman Lewis to represent it in negotiations with owners.

■ **November 8:** A.L. owners approved the sale of the Athletics to Chicago industrialist Arnold Johnson and transfer of the team to Kansas City.

■ **December 1:** The finishing touches were put on a record 17-player trade between the Orioles and Yankees.

MEMORABLE MOMENTS

■ **April 15:** Baltimore welcomed its new Orioles with a huge celebration and the team responded with a 3-1 victory over Chicago at Memorial Stadium.

■ **May 2:** Cardinals slugger Stan Musial hit a doubleheader-record five home runs in a split with the Giants at Busch Stadium.

■ **July 31:** Milwaukee's Joe Adcock joined the exclusive four-homer club in a 15-7 victory over Brooklyn and set a record for total bases (18) when he added a double to his offensive explosion.

■ **September 25:** Early Wynn fired a two-hitter and the Indians defeated Detroit, 11-1, for their A.L.-record 111th victory of the season.

LEADERS

American League

BA: Bobby Avila, Cle., .341.
Runs: Mickey Mantle, N.Y., 129.
Hits: Nellie Fox, Chi.; Harvey Kuenn, Det., 201.
TB: Minnie Minoso, Chi., 304.
HR: Larry Doby, Cle., 32.
RBI: Larry Doby, Cle., 126.
SB: Jackie Jensen, Bos., 22.
Wins: Bob Lemon, Cle.; Early Wynn, Cle., 23.
ERA: Mike Garcia, Cle., 2.64.
CG: Bob Lemon, Cle.; Bob Porterfield, Wash., 21.
IP: Early Wynn, Cle., 270.2.
SO: Bob Turley, Bal., 185.

National League

BA: Willie Mays, N.Y., .345.
Runs: Stan Musial, St.L.; Duke Snider, Brk., 120.
Hits: Don Mueller, N.Y., 212.
TB: Duke Snider, Brk., 378.
HR: Ted Kluszewski, Cin., 49.
RBI: Ted Kluszewski, Cin., 141.
SB: Bill Bruton, Mil., 34.
Wins: Robin Roberts, Phil., 23.
ERA: Johnny Antonelli, N.Y., 2.30.
CG: Robin Roberts, Phil., 29.
IP: Robin Roberts, Phil., 336.2.
SO: Robin Roberts, Phil., 185.

A.L. 20-game winners

Bob Lemon, Cle., 23-7
Early Wynn, Cle., 23-11
Bob Grim, N.Y., 20-6

N.L. 20-game winners

Robin Roberts, Phil., 23-15
Johnny Antonelli, N.Y., 21-7
Warren Spahn, Mil., 21-12

A.L. 100 RBIs

Larry Doby, Cle., 126
Yogi Berra, N.Y., 125
Jackie Jensen, Bos., 117
Minnie Minoso, Chi., 116
Mickey Mantle, N.Y., 102
Al Rosen, Cle., 102
Roy Sievers, Wash., 102

N.L. 100 RBIs

Ted Kluszewski, Cin., 141
Gil Hodges, Brk., 130
Duke Snider, Brk., 130
Stan Musial, St.L., 126
Del Ennis, Phil., 119
Willie Mays, N.Y., 110
Ray Jablonski, St.L., 104
Eddie Mathews, Mil., 103
Hank Sauer, Chi., 103
Gus Bell, Cin., 101

N.L. 40 homers

Ted Kluszewski, Cin., 49
Gil Hodges, Brk., 42
Willie Mays, N.Y., 41
Hank Sauer, Chi., 41
Eddie Mathews, Mil., 40
Duke Snider, Brk., 40

Most Valuable Player

A.L.: Yogi Berra, C, N.Y.
N.L.: Willie Mays, OF, N.Y.

Rookie of the Year

A.L.: Bob Grim, P, N.Y.
N.L.: Wally Moon, OF, St.L.

Hall of Fame additions

Bill Dickey, C, 1928-46
Rabbit Maranville, SS, 1912-35
Bill Terry, 1B, 1923-36

ALL-STAR GAME

■ **Winner:** Chicago's Nellie Fox looped a two-run eighth-inning single to spark the A.L. in a game that featured two home runs and five RBIs by Cleveland fan favorite Al Rosen.

■ **Key inning:** The eighth. Before Fox's game-winning single, Cleveland's Larry Doby excited the home fans with a game-tying home run.

■ **Memorable moment:** Senators lefthander Dean Stone's no-pitch victory. Stone entered the game with two out in the eighth and retired St. Louis' Red Schoendienst trying to steal home.

■ **Top guns:** Rosen (Indians), Bobby Avila (Indians), Doby (Indians), Ray Boone (Tigers), Fox (White Sox), Yogi Berra (Yankees), A.L.; Duke Snider (Dodgers), Ted Kluszewski (Reds), Gus Bell (Reds), N.L.

■ **MVP:** Rosen.

Linescore

July 13, at Cleveland Stadium

N.L. ....0 0 0 5 2 0 0 2 0— 9 14 0
A.L. ....0 0 4 1 2 1 0 3 x—11 17 1

Roberts (Phillies), Antonelli (Giants) 4, Spahn (Braves) 6, Grissom (Giants) 6, Conley (Braves) 8, Erskine (Dodgers) 8; Ford (Yankees), Consuegra (White Sox) 4, Lemon (Indians) 4, Porterfield (Senators) 5, Keegan (White Sox) 8, Stone (Senators) 8, Trucks (White Sox) 9. W—Stone. L—Conley. HR—Rosen 2, Boone, Doby, A.L.; Kluszewski, Bell, N.L.

WORLD SERIES

■ **Winner:** The Giants pulled off a surprising sweep of the Indians, who had won an A.L.-record 111 games.

■ **Turning point:** A three-run 10th-inning home run by pinch-hitter Dusty Rhodes that decided Game 1. Rhodes' pop-fly homer traveled 260 feet.

■ **Memorable moment:** Center fielder Willie Mays' over-the-shoulder catch of a Game 1 blast by Cleveland's Vic Wertz — perhaps the greatest defensive play in Series history.

■ **Top guns:** Rhodes (.667, 2 HR, 7 RBIs), Alvin Dark (.412), Don Mueller (.389), Giants; Wertz (.500), Indians.

Linescores

Game 1—September 29, at New York

Cleveland ....2 0 0 0 0 0 0 0 0 0—2 8 0
New York.............0 0 2 0 0 0 0 0 0 3—5 9 3

Lemon; Maglie, Liddle (8), Grissom (8). W—Grissom. L—Lemon. HR—Rhodes (N.Y.).

Game 2—September 30, at New York

Cleveland ....1 0 0 0 0 0 0 0 0—1 8 0
New York...................0 0 0 0 2 0 1 0 x—3 4 0

Wynn, Mossi (8); Antonelli. W—Antonelli. L—Wynn. HR—Smith (Cle.); Rhodes (N.Y.).

Game 3—October 1, at Cleveland

New York..................1 0 3 0 1 1 0 0 0—6 10 1
Cleveland ....0 0 0 0 0 0 1 1 0—2 4 2

Gomez, Wilhelm (8); Garcia, Houtteman (4), Narleski (6), Mossi (9). W—Gomez. L—Garcia. HR—Wertz (Cle.).

Game 4—October 2, at Cleveland

New York..................0 2 1 0 4 0 0 0 0—7 10 3
Cleveland ....0 0 0 0 3 0 1 0 0—4 6 2

Liddle, Wilhelm (7), Antonelli (8); Lemon, Newhouser (5), Narleski (5), Mossi (6), Garcia (8). W—Liddle. L—Lemon. HR—Majeski (Cle.).

1955

FINAL STANDINGS

American League

Team	W	L	Pct.	GB
New York	96	58	.623	...
Cleveland	93	61	.604	3
Chicago	91	63	.591	5
Boston	84	70	.545	12
Detroit	79	75	.513	17
Kansas City	63	91	.409	33
Baltimore	57	97	.370	39
Washington	53	101	.344	43

National League

Team	W	L	Pct.	GB
Brooklyn	98	55	.641	...
Milwaukee	85	69	.552	13.5
New York	80	74	.519	18.5
Philadelphia	77	77	.500	21.5
Cincinnati	75	79	.487	23.5
Chicago	72	81	.471	26
St. Louis	68	86	.442	30.5
Pittsburgh	60	94	.390	38.5

SIGNIFICANT EVENT

- **April 14:** The New York Yankees, one of four non-integrated teams, broke the color barrier when Elston Howard singled in his first big-league at-bat in a game at Boston.

MEMORABLE MOMENTS

- **April 12:** The Athletics made their Kansas City debut with a 6-2 victory over the Tigers.
- **April 23:** The White Sox hit seven home runs and tied a modern run-scoring record with a 29-6 victory at Kansas City.
- **September 25:** Giants slugger Willie Mays, baseball's seventh 50-homer man, belted No. 51 in a 5-2 victory over the Phillies.
- **September 25:** 20-year-old Tigers outfielder Al Kaline became baseball's youngest batting champ when he finished with an A.L.-best .340 average.

LEADERS

American League

BA: Al Kaline, Det., .340.
Runs: Al Smith, Cle., 123.
Hits: Al Kaline, Det., 200.
TB: Al Kaline, Det., 321.
HR: Mickey Mantle, N.Y., 37.
RBI: Ray Boone, Det.; Jackie Jensen, Bos., 116.
SB: Jim Rivera, Chi., 25.
Wins: Whitey Ford, N.Y.; Bob Lemon, Cle.; Frank Sullivan, Bos., 18.
ERA: Billy Pierce, Chi., 1.97.
CG: Whitey Ford, N.Y., 18.
IP: Frank Sullivan, Bos., 260.
SO: Herb Score, Cle., 245.

National League

BA: Richie Ashburn, Phil., .338.
Runs: Duke Snider, Brk., 126.
Hits: Ted Kluszewski, Cin., 192.
TB: Willie Mays, N.Y., 382.
HR: Willie Mays, N.Y., 51.
RBI: Duke Snider, Brk., 136.
SB: Bill Bruton, Mil., 25.
Wins: Robin Roberts, Phil., 23.
ERA: Bob Friend, Pit., 2.83.
CG: Robin Roberts, Phil., 26.
IP: Robin Roberts, Phil., 305.
SO: Sam Jones, Chi., 198.

N.L. 20-game winners
Robin Roberts, Phil., 23-14
Don Newcombe, Brk., 20-5

A.L. 100 RBIs
Ray Boone, Det., 116
Jackie Jensen, Bos., 116
Yogi Berra, N.Y., 108
Roy Sievers, Wash., 106
Al Kaline, Det., 102

N.L. 100 RBIs
Duke Snider, Brk., 136
Willie Mays, N.Y., 127
Del Ennis, Phil., 120
Ernie Banks, Chi., 117
Ted Kluszewski, Cin., 113
Wally Post, Cin., 109
Stan Musial, St.L., 108
Roy Campanella, Brk., 107
Hank Aaron, Mil., 106
Gus Bell, Cin., 104
Gil Hodges, Brk., 102
Eddie Mathews, Mil., 101

N.L. 40 homers
Willie Mays, N.Y., 51
Ted Kluszewski, Cin., 47
Ernie Banks, Chi., 44
Duke Snider, Brk., 42
Eddie Mathews, Mil., 41
Wally Post, Cin., 40

Most Valuable Player
A.L.: Yogi Berra, C, N.Y.
N.L.: Roy Campanella, C, Brk.

Rookie of the Year
A.L.: Herb Score, P, Cle.
N.L.: Bill Virdon, OF, St.L.

Hall of Fame additions
Home Run Baker, 3B, 1908-22
Joe DiMaggio, OF, 1936-51
Gabby Hartnett, C, 1922-41
Ted Lyons, P, 1923-46
Ray Schalk, C, 1912-29
Dazzy Vance, P, 1915-35

ALL-STAR GAME

- **Winner:** The N.L., down 5-0 entering the seventh inning, rallied for a 6-5 victory in 12 innings — the second longest All-Star Game.
- **Key inning:** The N.L.'s three-run eighth, which tied the score and forced extra innings. The tying run scored on right fielder Al Kaline's wild throw.
- **Memorable moment:** Stan Musial's first-pitch home run in the 12th off Boston's Frank Sullivan. It was Musial's record fourth All-Star homer.
- **Top guns:** Joe Nuxhall (Reds), Gene Conley (Braves), Willie Mays (Giants), Hank Aaron (Braves), Musial (Cardinals), N.L.; Billy Pierce (White Sox), Chico Carrasquel (White Sox), Mickey Mantle (Yankees), A.L.
- **MVP:** Musial.

Linescore

July 12, at Milwaukee's County Stadium
A.L. ....4 0 0 0 0 1 0 0 0 0 0 0—5 10 2
N.L. ....0 0 0 0 0 0 2 3 0 0 0 1—6 13 1
Pierce (White Sox), Wynn (Indians) 4, Ford (Yankees) 7, Sullivan (Red Sox) 8; Roberts (Phillies), Haddix (Cardinals) 4, Newcombe (Dodgers) 7, Jones (Cubs) 8, Nuxhall (Reds) 8, Conley (Braves) 12. W—Conley. L—Sullivan. HR—Mantle, A.L.; Musial, N.L.

WORLD SERIES

- **Winner:** Brooklyn's long wait finally ended as the Dodgers won a Series on their eighth try — beating the hated Yankees in the process.

Turning point: Hot-hitting Duke Snider's two home runs powered the Dodgers to within a game of their first championship in a 5-3 Game 5 victory.
- **Memorable moment:** A spectacular Series-saving catch by Dodgers outfielder Sandy Amoros in the sixth inning of Game 7. The two-on, nobody-out catch of Yogi Berra's line drive resulted in a double play and preserved Johnny Podres' 2-0 shutout.
- **Top guns:** Podres (2-0, 1.00 ERA), Snider (.320, 4 HR, 7 RBIs), Dodgers; Whitey Ford (2-0, 2.12), Hank Bauer (.429), Berra (.417), Yankees.
- **MVP:** Podres.

Linescores

Game 1—September 28, at New York
Brooklyn ....0 2 1 0 0 0 0 2 0—5 10 0
New York..................0 2 1 1 0 2 0 0 x—6 9 1
Newcombe, Bessent (6), Labine (8); Ford, Grim (9). W—Ford. L—Newcombe. HR—Collins 2, Howard (N.Y.); Furillo, Snider (Brk.).

Game 2—September 29, at New York
Brooklyn ....0 0 0 1 1 0 0 0 0—2 5 2
New York....................0 0 0 4 0 0 0 0 x—4 8 0
Loes, Bessent (4), Spooner (5), Labine (8); Byrne. W—Byrne. L—Loes.

Game 3—September 30, at Brooklyn
New York..................0 2 0 0 0 0 1 0 0—3 7 0
Brooklyn ....2 2 0 2 0 0 2 0 x—8 11 1
Turley, Morgan (2), Kucks (5), Sturdivant (7); Podres. W—Podres. L—Turley. HR—Campanella (Brk.); Mantle (N.Y.).

Game 4—October 1, at Brooklyn
New York..................1 1 0 1 0 2 0 0 0—5 9 0
Brooklyn ....0 0 1 3 3 0 1 0 x—8 14 0
Larsen, Kucks (5), R. Coleman (6), Morgan (7), Sturdivant (8); Erskine, Bessent (4), Labine (5). W—Labine. L—Larsen. HR—McDougald (N.Y.); Campanella, Hodges, Snider (Brk).

Game 5—October 2, at Brooklyn
New York....................0 0 0 1 0 0 1 1 0—3 6 0
Brooklyn ....0 2 1 0 1 0 0 1 x—5 9 2
Grim, Turley (7); Craig, Labine (7). W—Craig. L—Grim. HR—Snider 2, Amoros (Brk.); Cerv, Berra (N.Y.).

Game 6—October 3, at New York
Brooklyn ....0 0 0 1 0 0 0 0 0—1 4 1
New York....................5 0 0 0 0 0 0 0 x—5 8 0
Spooner, Meyer (1), Roebuck (7); Ford. W—Ford. L—Spooner. HR—Skowron (N.Y.).

Game 7—October 4, at New York
Brooklyn ....0 0 0 1 0 1 0 0 0—2 5 0
New York....................0 0 0 0 0 0 0 0 0—0 8 1
Podres; Byrne, Grim (6), Turley (8). W—Podres. L—Byrne.

1956

FINAL STANDINGS

American League

Team	W	L	Pct.	GB
New York	97	57	.630	...
Cleveland	88	66	.571	9
Chicago	85	69	.552	12
Boston	84	70	.545	13
Detroit	82	72	.532	15
Baltimore	69	85	.448	28
Washington	59	95	.383	38
Kansas City	52	102	.338	45

National League

Team	W	L	Pct.	GB
Brooklyn	93	61	.604	...
Milwaukee	92	62	.597	1
Cincinnati	91	63	.591	2
St. Louis	76	78	.494	17
Philadelphia	71	83	.461	22
New York	67	87	.435	26
Pittsburgh	66	88	.429	27
Chicago	60	94	.390	33

SIGNIFICANT EVENTS

- **April 19:** The Dodgers played the first of seven "home-away-from-home" games at Jersey City's Roosevelt Stadium and posted a 10-inning, 5-4 victory over the Phillies.
- **September 30:** Yankee slugger Mickey Mantle finished his Triple Crown journey with a .353 average, 52 home runs and 130 RBIs.
- **November 21:** N.L. MVP Don Newcombe, who finished 27-7 for the Dodgers, captured the inaugural Cy Young Award as baseball's top pitcher.

MEMORABLE MOMENTS

- **May 28:** Pittsburgh first baseman Dale Long hit a home run in his record eighth consecutive game as the Pirates defeated Brooklyn, 3-2.
- **September 11:** Cincinnati's Frank Robinson tied the rookie home run record when he hit No. 38 in an 11-5 victory over the Giants.
- **September 30:** The Dodgers posted a final-day 8-6 victory over Pittsburgh and captured their second straight N.L. pennant by one game over Milwaukee.

LEADERS

American League

BA: Mickey Mantle, N.Y., .353.
Runs: Mickey Mantle, N.Y., 132.
Hits: Harvey Kuenn, Det., 196.
TB: Mickey Mantle, N.Y., 376.
HR: Mickey Mantle, N.Y., 52.
RBI: Mickey Mantle, N.Y., 130.
SB: Luis Aparicio, Chi., 21.
Wins: Frank Lary, Det., 21.
ERA: Whitey Ford, N.Y., 2.47.
CG: Bob Lemon, Cle.; Billy Pierce, Chi., 21.
IP: Frank Lary, Det., 294.
SO: Herb Score, Cle., 263.

National League

BA: Hank Aaron, Mil., .328.
Runs: Frank Robinson, Cin., 122.
Hits: Hank Aaron, Mil., 200.
TB: Hank Aaron, Mil., 340.
HR: Duke Snider, Brk., 43.
RBI: Stan Musial, St.L., 109.
SB: Willie Mays, N.Y., 40.
Wins: Don Newcombe, Brk., 27.
ERA: Lew Burdette, Mil., 2.70.
CG: Robin Roberts, Phil., 22.
IP: Bob Friend, Pit., 314.1
SO: Sam Jones, Chi., 176.

A.L. 20-game winners
Frank Lary, Det., 21-13
Herb Score, Cle., 20-9
Early Wynn, Cle., 20-9
Billy Pierce, Chi., 20-9
Bob Lemon, Cle., 20-14
Billy Hoeft, Det., 20-14

N.L. 20-game winners
Don Newcombe, Brk., 27-7
Warren Spahn, Mil., 20-11
Johnny Antonelli, N.Y., 20-13

A.L. 100 RBIs
Mickey Mantle, N.Y., 130
Al Kaline, Det., 128
Vic Wertz, Cle., 106
Yogi Berra, N.Y., 105
Harry Simpson, K.C., 105
Larry Doby, Chi., 102

N.L. 100 RBIs
Stan Musial, St.L., 109
Joe Adcock, Mil., 103
Ted Kluszewski, Cin., 102
Duke Snider, Brk., 101

A.L. 40 homers
Mickey Mantle, N.Y., 52

N.L. 40 homers
Duke Snider, Brk., 43

Most Valuable Player
A.L.: Mickey Mantle, OF, N.Y.
N.L.: Don Newcombe, P, Brk.

Cy Young Award
A.L.-N.L.: Don Newcombe, Brk.

Rookie of the Year
A.L.: Luis Aparicio, SS, Chi.
N.L.: Frank Robinson, OF, Cin.

Hall of Fame additions
Joe Cronin, SS/Man./Exec.
Hank Greenberg, 1B, 1930-47

ALL-STAR GAME

- **Winner:** Third baseman Ken Boyer singled three times and made three outstanding defensive plays to lead the N.L. to victory — its sixth in seven years.
- **Key inning:** The fourth, when the N.L. stretched its 1-0 lead on a two-run pinch-hit homer by Willie Mays.
- **Memorable moment:** Stan Musial's fifth All-Star home run, a seventh-inning shot that offset sixth-inning blasts by A.L. stars Ted Williams and Mickey Mantle.
- **Top guns:** Bob Friend (Pirates), Boyer (Cardinals), Mays (Giants), Ted Kluszewski (Reds), Musial (Cardinals), N.L.; Williams (Red Sox), Mantle (Yankees), Yogi Berra (Yankees), A.L.
- **MVP:** Boyer.

Linescore

July 10, at Washington's Griffith Stadium
N.L. ....0 0 1 2 1 1 2 0 0—7 11 0
A.L. ....0 0 0 0 0 3 0 0 0—3 11 0
Friend (Pirates), Spahn (Braves) 4, Antonelli (Giants) 6; Pierce (White Sox), Ford (Yankees) 4, Wilson (White Sox) 5, Brewer (Red Sox) 6, Score (Indians) 8, Wynn (Indians) 9. W—Friend. L—Pierce. HR—Mays, Musial, N.L.; Williams, Mantle, A.L.

WORLD SERIES

- **Winner:** The Yankees turned the tables on the Dodgers in a Series featuring one of baseball's most incredible pitching performances.
- **Turning point:** 5-3 and 6-2 Yankee victories in Games 3 and 4 after the Dodgers had won the first two games.
- **Memorable moment:** The final pitch of Yankee righthander Don Larsen's Game 5 perfect game — the first no-hitter in Series history. Larsen struck out pinch-hitter Dale Mitchell to complete his 2-0 shutout.
- **Top guns:** Larsen (1-0, 0.00 ERA), Yogi Berra (.360, 3 HR, 10 RBIs), Enos Slaughter (.350), Yankees; Gil Hodges (.304, 8 RBIs), Dodgers.
- **MVP:** Larsen.

Linescores

Game 1—October 3, at Brooklyn
New York....................2 0 0 1 0 0 0 0 0—3 9 1
Brooklyn ....0 2 3 1 0 0 0 0 x—6 9 0
Ford, Kucks (4), Morgan (6), Turley (8); Maglie. W—Maglie. L—Ford. HR—Mantle, Martin (N.Y.); Robinson, Hodges (Brk.).

Game 2—October 5, at Brooklyn
New York................1 5 0 1 0 0 0 0 1— 8 12 2
Brooklyn ....0 6 1 2 2 0 0 2 x—13 12 0
Larsen, Kucks (2), Byrne (2), Sturdivant (3), Morgan (3), Turley (5), McDermott (6); Newcombe, Roebuck (2), Bessent (3). W—Bessent. L—Morgan. HR—Berra (N.Y.); Snider (Brk.).

Game 3—October 6, at New York
Brooklyn ....0 1 0 0 0 1 1 0 0—3 8 1
New York....................0 1 0 0 0 3 0 1 x—5 8 1
Craig, Labine (7); Ford. W—Ford. L—Craig. HR—Martin, Slaughter (N.Y.).

Game 4—October 7, at New York
Brooklyn ....0 0 0 1 0 0 0 0 1—2 6 0
New York....................1 0 0 2 0 1 2 0 x—6 7 2
Erskine, Roebuck (5), Drysdale (7); Sturdivant. W—Sturdivant. L—Erskine. HR—Mantle, Bauer (N.Y.).

Game 5—October 8, at New York
Brooklyn ....0 0 0 0 0 0 0 0 0—0 0 0
New York....................0 0 0 1 0 1 0 0 x—2 5 0
Maglie; Larsen. W—Larsen. L—Maglie. HR—Mantle (N.Y.).

Game 6—October 9, at Brooklyn
New York.............0 0 0 0 0 0 0 0 0 0—0 7 0
Brooklyn ....0 0 0 0 0 0 0 0 0 1—1 4 0
Turley; Labine. W—Labine. L—Turley.

Game 7—October 10, at Brooklyn
New York.................2 0 2 1 0 0 4 0 0—9 10 0
Brooklyn ....0 0 0 0 0 0 0 0 0—0 3 1
Kucks; Newcombe, Bessent (4), Craig (7), Roebuck (7), Erskine (9). W—Kucks. L—Newcombe. HR—Berra 2, Howard, Skowron (N.Y.).

1957

FINAL STANDINGS

American League

Team	W	L	Pct.	GB
New York	98	56	.636	...
Chicago	90	64	.584	8
Boston	82	72	.532	16
Detroit	78	76	.506	20
Baltimore	76	76	.500	21
Cleveland	76	77	.497	21.5
Kansas City	59	94	.386	38.5
Washington	55	99	.357	43

National League

Team	W	L	Pct.	GB
Milwaukee	95	59	.617	...
St. Louis	87	67	.565	8
Brooklyn	84	70	.545	11
Cincinnati	80	74	.519	15
Philadelphia	77	77	.500	18
New York	69	85	.448	26
Chicago	62	92	.403	33
Pittsburgh	62	92	.403	33

SIGNIFICANT EVENTS

■ **February 2:** Baseball owners approved a five-year pension plan offering more liberal benefits to players, coaches and trainers.
■ **April 22:** The Phillies became the final N.L. team to break the color barrier when John Kennedy was inserted as a pinch-runner in a 5-1 loss to Brooklyn.
■ **May 28:** N.L. owners approved the proposed moves of the Dodgers and Giants to the West Coast, opening the door for relocations that would become official in the fall.
■ **June 28:** Commissioner Ford Frick infuriated ballot-stuffing Cincinnati fans when he replaced three members of an all-Reds starting lineup for the All-Star Game.

MEMORABLE MOMENTS

■ **May 7:** Young Cleveland ace Herb Score suffered a career-threatening injury when he was hit in the eye by Yankee Gil McDougald's line drive.
■ **September 23:** Hank Aaron belted a two-run, 11th-inning homer to give the Braves a 4-2 victory over St. Louis and their first pennant since moving to Milwaukee.

LEADERS

American League

BA: Ted Williams, Bos., .388.
Runs: Mickey Mantle, N.Y., 121.
Hits: Nellie Fox, Chi., 196.
TB: Roy Sievers, Wash., 331.
HR: Roy Sievers, Wash., 42.
RBI: Roy Sievers, Wash., 114.
SB: Luis Aparicio, Chi., 28.
Wins: Jim Bunning, Det.; Billy Pierce, Chi., 20.
ERA: Bobby Shantz, N.Y., 2.45.
CG: Dick Donovan, Chi.; Billy Pierce, Chi., 16.
IP: Jim Bunning, Det., 267.1.
SO: Early Wynn, Cle., 184.

National League

BA: Stan Musial, St.L., .351.
Runs: Hank Aaron, Mil., 118.
Hits: Red Schoendienst, N.Y.-Mil., 200.
TB: Hank Aaron, Mil., 369.
HR: Hank Aaron, Mil., 44.
RBI: Hank Aaron, Mil., 132.
SB: Willie Mays, N.Y., 38.
Wins: Warren Spahn, Mil., 21.
ERA: Johnny Podres, Brk., 2.66.
CG: Warren Spahn, Mil., 18.
IP: Bob Friend, Pit., 277.
SO: Jack Sanford, Phil., 188.

A.L. 20-game winners
Jim Bunning, Det., 20-8
Billy Pierce, Chi., 20-12

N.L. 20-game winners
Warren Spahn, Mil., 21-11

A.L. 100 RBIs
Roy Sievers, Wash., 114
Vic Wertz, Cle., 105
Jackie Jensen, Bos., 103
Frank Malzone, Bos., 103
Minnie Minoso, Chi., 103

N.L. 100 RBIs
Hank Aaron, Mil., 132
Del Ennis, St.L., 105
Ernie Banks, Chi., 102
Stan Musial, St.L., 102

A.L. 40 homers
Roy Sievers, Wash., 42

N.L. 40 homers
Hank Aaron, Mil., 44
Ernie Banks, Chi., 43
Duke Snider, Brk., 40

Most Valuable Player
A.L.: Mickey Mantle, OF, N.Y.
N.L.: Hank Aaron, OF, Mil.

Cy Young Award
A.L.-N.L.: Warren Spahn, Mil.

Rookie of the Year
A.L.: Tony Kubek, IF/OF, N.Y.
N.L.: Jack Sanford, P, Phil.

Hall of Fame additions
Sam Crawford, OF, 1899-1917
Joe McCarthy, manager

ALL-STAR GAME

■ **Winner:** Minnie Minoso, who had doubled home a run in the top of the ninth, made two outstanding defensive plays in the bottom of the inning to preserve the A.L.'s victory.

■ **Key inning:** The ninth. After the A.L. had scored three times in the top of the frame for a 6-2 lead, the N.L. answered with three runs and had the tying run on second when the game ended.

■ **Memorable moment:** Left fielder Minoso, who had just thrown out a runner trying to advance to third, made an outstanding game-ending catch of a Gil Hodges drive into left-center field.

■ **Top guns:** Jim Bunning (Tigers), Al Kaline (Tigers), Bill Skowron (Yankees), Minoso (White Sox), A.L.; Lew Burdette (Braves), Willie Mays (Giants), Gus Bell (Reds), N.L.

■ **MVP:** Minoso.

Linescore

July 9, at St. Louis' Busch Stadium
A.L. ....0 2 0 0 0 1 0 0 3—6 10 0
N.L. ....0 0 0 0 0 0 2 0 3—5 9 1
Bunning (Tigers), Loes (Orioles) 4, Wynn (Indians) 7, Pierce (White Sox) 7, Mossi (Indians) 9, Grim (Yankees) 9; Simmons (Phillies), Burdette (Braves) 2, Sanford (Phillies) 6, Jackson (Cardinals) 7, Labine (Dodgers) 9. W—Bunning. L—Simmons.

WORLD SERIES

■ **Winner:** The Braves' fifth Milwaukee season produced the franchise's first Series winner since the miracle of 1914.

■ **Turning point:** A two-run 10th-inning home run by Eddie Mathews that gave Milwaukee a 7-5 victory in Game 4 and evened the Series at two games apiece.

■ **Memorable moment:** The final pitch of Milwaukee righthander Lew Burdette's 5-0 seventh-game shutout, giving Milwaukee its first Series championship.

■ **Top guns:** Burdette (3-0, 0-67 ERA), Hank Aaron (.393, 3 HR, 7 RBIs), Frank Torre (.300, 2 HR), Braves; Jerry Coleman (.364), Yankees.

■ **MVP:** Burdette.

Linescores

Game 1—October 2, at New York
Milwaukee..................0 0 0 0 0 0 1 0 0—1 5 0
New York....................0 0 0 0 1 2 0 0 x—3 9 1
Spahn, Johnson (6), McMahon (7); Ford. W—Ford. L—Spahn.

Game 2—October 3, at New York
Milwaukee..................0 1 1 2 0 0 0 0 0—4 8 0
New York....................0 1 1 0 0 0 0 0 0—2 7 2
Burdette; Shantz, Ditmar (4), Grim (8). W—Burdette. L—Shantz. HR—Logan (Mil.); Bauer (N.Y.).

Game 3—October 5, at Milwaukee
New York.................3 0 2 2 0 0 5 0 0—12 9 0
Milwaukee................0 1 0 0 2 0 0 0 0— 3 8 1
Turley, Larsen (2); Buhl, Pizarro (1), Conley (3), Johnson (5), Trowbridge (7), McMahon (8). W—Larsen. L—Buhl. HR—Kubek 2, Mantle (N.Y.); Aaron (Mil.).

Game 4—October 6, at Milwaukee
New York...........1 0 0 0 0 0 0 0 3 1—5 11 0
Milwaukee..........0 0 0 4 0 0 0 0 0 3—7 7 0
Sturdivant, Shantz (5), Kucks (8), Byrne (8), Grim (10); Spahn. W—Spahn. L—Grim. HR—Aaron, Torre, Mathews (Mil.); Howard (N.Y.).

Game 5—October 7, at Milwaukee
New York...................0 0 0 0 0 0 0 0 0—0 7 0
Milwaukee..................0 0 0 0 0 1 0 0 x—1 6 1
Ford, Turley (8); Burdette. W—Burdette. L—Ford.

Game 6—October 9, at New York
Milwaukee..................0 0 0 0 1 0 1 0 0—2 4 0
New York....................0 0 2 0 0 0 1 0 x—3 7 0
Buhl, Johnson (3), McMahon (8); Turley. W—Turley. L—Johnson. HR—Berra, Bauer (N.Y.); Torre, Aaron (Mil.).

Game 7—October 10, at New York
Milwaukee..................0 0 4 0 0 0 0 1 0—5 9 1
New York....................0 0 0 0 0 0 0 0 0—0 7 3
Burdette; Larsen, Shantz (3), Ditmar (4), Sturdivant (6), Byrne (8). W—Burdette. L—Larsen. HR—Crandall (Mil.).

1958

FINAL STANDINGS

American League

Team	W	L	Pct.	GB
New York	92	62	.597	...
Chicago	82	72	.532	10
Boston	79	75	.513	13
Cleveland	77	76	.503	14.5
Detroit	77	77	.500	15
Baltimore	74	79	.484	17.5
Kansas City	73	81	.474	19
Washington	61	93	.396	31

National League

Team	W	L	Pct.	GB
Milwaukee	92	62	.597	...
Pittsburgh	84	70	.545	8
San Francisco	80	74	.519	12
Cincinnati	76	78	.494	16
Chicago	72	82	.468	20
St. Louis	72	82	.468	20
Los Angeles	71	83	.461	21
Philadelphia	69	85	.448	23

SIGNIFICANT EVENTS

■ **January 28:** Dodgers catcher Roy Campanella suffered a broken neck and paralysis from his shoulders down when the car he was driving overturned on a slippery road in Glen Cove, N.Y.
■ **January 29:** Stan Musial became the N.L.'s first six-figure star when he signed with the Cardinals for $100,000.
■ **January 30:** Commissioner Ford Frick took the All-Star vote away from the fans, handing it back to the players, coaches and managers.
■ **September 28:** Boston's 40-year-old Ted Williams used a 7-for-11 closing surge to win his sixth A.L. batting title with a .328 average.
■ **December 3:** Will Harridge, who served as A.L. president for more than 27 years, retired at age 72.

MEMORABLE MOMENTS

■ **April 15:** The Giants rolled to an 8-0 victory over the Dodgers in the first West Coast game at San Francisco's Seals Stadium.
■ **April 18:** The Dodgers rewarded a record Los Angeles Coliseum crowd of 78,672 with a 6-5 victory over the Giants in their West Coast home debut.
■ **May 13:** Stan Musial became the eighth member of baseball's 3,000-hit club when he stroked a pinch-hit double off Moe Drabowsky in a 5-3 Cardinals' victory at Chicago.

LEADERS

American League

BA: Ted Williams, Bos., .328.
Runs: Mickey Mantle, N.Y., 127.
Hits: Nellie Fox, Chi., 187.
TB: Mickey Mantle, N.Y., 307.
HR: Mickey Mantle, N.Y., 42.
RBI: Jackie Jensen, Bos., 122.
SB: Luis Aparicio, Chi., 29.
Wins: Bob Turley, N.Y., 21.
ERA: Whitey Ford, N.Y., 2.01.
CG: Frank Lary, Det.; Billy Pierce, Chi.; Bob Turley, N.Y., 19.
IP: Frank Lary, Det., 260.1.
SO: Early Wynn, Chi., 179.

National League

BA: Richie Ashburn, Phil., .350.
Runs: Willie Mays, S.F., 121.
Hits: Richie Ashburn, Phil., 215.
TB: Ernie Banks, Chi., 379.
HR: Ernie Banks, Chi., 47.
RBI: Ernie Banks, Chi., 129.
SB: Willie Mays, S.F., 31.
Wins: Bob Friend, Pit.; Warren Spahn, Mil., 22.
ERA: Stu Miller, S.F., 2.47.
CG: Warren Spahn, Mil., 23.
IP: Warren Spahn, Mil., 290.
SO: Sam Jones, St.L., 225.

A.L. 20-game winners
Bob Turley, N.Y., 21-7

N.L. 20-game winners
Warren Spahn, Mil., 22-11
Bob Friend, Pit., 22-14
Lew Burdette, Mil., 20-10

A.L. 100 RBIs
Jackie Jensen, Bos., 122
Rocky Colavito, Cle., 113
Roy Sievers, Wash., 108
Bob Cerv, K.C., 104

N.L. 100 RBIs
Ernie Banks, Chi., 129
Frank Thomas, Pit., 109

A.L. 40 homers
Mickey Mantle, N.Y., 42
Rocky Colavito, Cle., 41

N.L. 40 homers
Ernie Banks, Chi., 47

Most Valuable Player
A.L.: Jackie Jensen, OF, Bos.
N.L.: Ernie Banks, SS, Chi.

Cy Young Award
A.L.-N.L.: Bob Turley, N.Y. (AL).

Rookie of the Year
A.L.: Albie Pearson, OF, Wash.
N.L.: Orlando Cepeda, 1B, S.F.

ALL-STAR GAME

■ **Winner:** After spotting the N.L. a 3-1 lead, the A.L. rallied for a 4-3 victory in the first All-Star Game without an extra-base hit. Ray Narleski, Early Wynn and Billy O'Dell allowed one hit over the final 7 1/3 innings.

■ **Key inning:** The sixth, when the A.L. scored the go-ahead run on a single by Gil McDougald.

■ **Memorable moment:** The last out of the game — the ninth consecutive batter retired by hometown favorite O'Dell.

■ **Top guns:** Narleski (Indians), Wynn (White Sox), O'Dell (Orioles), Nellie Fox (White Sox), McDougald (Yankees), A.L.; Willie Mays (Giants), N.L.

■ **MVP:** O'Dell.

Linescore

July 8, at Baltimore's Memorial Stadium
N.L. ....2 1 0 0 0 0 0 0 0—3 4 2
A.L. ....1 1 0 0 1 1 0 0 x—4 9 2
Spahn (Braves), Friend (Pirates) 4, Jackson (Cardinals) 6, Farrell (Phillies) 7; Turley (Yankees), Narleski (Indians) 2, Wynn (White Sox) 6, O'Dell (Orioles) 7. W—Wynn. L—Friend.

WORLD SERIES

■ **Winner:** The Yankees became only the second team to recover from a three-games-to-one deficit en route to their seventh Series victory in 10 years under manager Casey Stengel.

■ **Turning point:** Bob Turley's five-hit 7-0 victory in Game 5 with his Yankees on the brink of elimination.

■ **Memorable moment:** A 10th-inning Game 6 home run by Gil McDougald that lifted the Yankees to a 4-3 victory and forced a seventh game.

■ **Top guns:** Turley (2-1, 2.76 ERA), Hank Bauer (.323, 4 HR, 8 RBIs), McDougald (.321, 2 HR, 4 RBIs), Yankees; Bill Bruton (.412), Braves.

■ **MVP:** Turley.

Linescores

Game 1—October 1, at Milwaukee
New York...........0 0 0 1 2 0 0 0 0 0—3 8 1
Milwaukee..........0 0 0 2 0 0 0 1 0 1—4 10 0
Ford, Duren (8); Spahn. W—Spahn. L—Duren. HR—Skowron, Bauer (N.Y.).

Game 2—October 2, at Milwaukee
New York................1 0 0 1 0 0 0 0 3— 5 7 0
Milwaukee..............7 1 0 0 0 0 2 3 x—13 15 1
Turley, Maas (1), Kucks (1), Dickson (5), Monroe (8); Burdette. W—Burdette. L—Turley. HR—Bruton, Burdette (Mil.); Mantle 2, Bauer (N.Y.).

Game 3—October 4, at New York
Milwaukee..................0 0 0 0 0 0 0 0 0—0 6 0
New York....................0 0 0 0 2 0 2 0 x—4 4 0
Rush, McMahon (7); Larsen, Duren (8). W—Larsen. L—Rush. HR—Bauer (N.Y.).

Game 4—October 5, at New York
Milwaukee..................0 0 0 0 0 1 1 1 0—3 9 0
New York....................0 0 0 0 0 0 0 0 0—0 2 1
Spahn; Ford, Kucks (8), Dickson (9). W—Spahn. L—Ford.

Game 5—October 6, at New York
Milwaukee................0 0 0 0 0 0 0 0 0—0 5 0
New York..................0 0 1 0 0 6 0 0 x—7 10 0
Burdette, Pizarro (6), Willey (8); Turley. W—Turley. L—Burdette. HR—McDougald (N.Y.).

Game 6—October 8, at Milwaukee
New York...........1 0 0 0 0 1 0 0 0 2—4 10 1
Milwaukee..........1 1 0 0 0 0 0 0 0 1—3 10 4
Ford, Ditmar (2), Duren (6), Turley (10); Spahn, McMahon (10). W—Duren. L—Spahn. HR—Bauer, McDougald (N.Y.).

Game 7—October 9, at Milwaukee
New York...................0 2 0 0 0 0 0 4 0—6 8 0
Milwaukee.................1 0 0 0 0 1 0 0 0—2 5 2
Larsen, Turley (3); Burdette, McMahon (9). W—Turley. L—Burdette. HR—Crandall (Mil.); Skowron (N.Y.).

1959

FINAL STANDINGS

American League

Team	W	L	Pct.	GB
Chicago	94	60	.610	...
Cleveland	89	65	.578	5
New York	79	75	.513	15
Detroit	76	78	.494	18
Boston	75	79	.487	19
Baltimore	74	80	.481	20
Kansas City	66	88	.429	28
Washington	63	91	.409	31

National League

Team	W	L	Pct.	GB
*Los Angeles	88	68	.564	...
Milwaukee	86	70	.551	2
San Francisco	83	71	.539	4
Pittsburgh	78	76	.506	9
Chicago	74	80	.481	13
Cincinnati	74	80	.481	13
St. Louis	71	83	.461	16
Philadelphia	64	90	.416	23

*Defeated Milwaukee 2-0 in pennant playoff.

SIGNIFICANT EVENT

■ **July 21:** The Red Sox became the last Major League team to break the color barrier when infielder Pumpsie Green played briefly in a game at Chicago.

MEMORABLE MOMENTS

■ **May 26:** In an amazing pitching exhibition, Pittsburgh's Harvey Haddix worked 12 perfect innings before losing to the Braves, 1-0, in the 13th.
■ **June 10:** Cleveland's Rocky Colavito became the eighth member of an exclusive club when he belted four home runs during the Indians' 11-8 victory over Baltimore.
■ **September 11:** The Dodgers ended the two-year, 22-game winning streak of Pittsburgh reliever Elroy Face when they scored two ninth-inning runs for a 5-4 victory.
■ **September 29:** The Dodgers completed their two-game sweep of a pennant-playoff series against Milwaukee with a 12-inning, 6-5 victory at Los Angeles.

LEADERS

American League
BA: Harvey Kuenn, Det., .353.
Runs: Eddie Yost, Det., 115.
Hits: Harvey Kuenn, Det., 198.
TB: Rocky Colavito, Cle., 301.
HR: Rocky Colavito, Cle.; Harmon Killebrew, Wash., 42.
RBI: Jackie Jensen, Bos., 112.
SB: Luis Aparicio, Chi., 56.
Wins: Early Wynn, Chi., 22.
ERA: Hoyt Wilhelm, Bal., 2.19.
CG: Camilo Pascual, Wash., 17.
IP: Early Wynn, Chi., 255.2.
SO: Jim Bunning, Det., 201.

National League
BA: Hank Aaron, Mil., .355.
Runs: Vada Pinson, Cin., 131.
Hits: Hank Aaron, Mil., 223.
TB: Hank Aaron, Mil., 400.
HR: Eddie Mathews, Mil., 46.
RBI: Ernie Banks, Chi., 143.
SB: Willie Mays, S.F., 27.
Wins: Lew Burdette, Mil.; Sam Jones, S.F.; Warren Spahn, Mil., 21.
ERA: Sam Jones, S.F., 2.83.
CG: Warren Spahn, Mil., 21.
IP: Warren Spahn, Mil., 292.
SO: Don Drysdale, L.A., 242.

A.L. 20-game winners
Early Wynn, Chi., 22-10

N.L. 20-game winners
Lew Burdette, Mil., 21-15
Warren Spahn, Mil., 21-15
Sam Jones, S.F., 21-15

A.L. 100 RBIs
Jackie Jensen, Bos., 112
Rocky Colavito, Cle., 111
Harmon Killebrew, Wash., 105
Jim Lemon, Wash., 100

N.L. 100 RBIs
Ernie Banks, Chi., 143
Frank Robinson, Cin., 125
Hank Aaron, Mil., 123
Gus Bell, Cin., 115
Eddie Mathews, Mil., 114
Orlando Cepeda, S.F., 105
Willie Mays, S.F., 104

A.L. 40 homers
Rocky Colavito, Cle., 42
Harmon Killebrew, Wash., 42

N.L. 40 homers
Eddie Mathews, Mil., 46
Ernie Banks, Chi., 45

Most Valuable Player
A.L.: Nellie Fox, 2B, Chi.
N.L.: Ernie Banks, SS, Chi.

Cy Young Award
A.L.-N.L.: Early Wynn, Chi. (AL)

Rookie of the Year
A.L.: Bob Allison, OF, Wash.
N.L.: Willie McCovey, 1B, S.F.

Hall of Fame addition
Zack Wheat, OF, 1909-27

ALL-STAR GAMES

■ **Winner:** Home runs by Frank Malzone, Yogi Berra and Rocky Colavito helped the A.L. to a 5-3 victory and a split of the first All-Star doubleheader. The N.L. had won the first game four weeks earlier, 5-4.

■ **Key Innings:** The eighth in Game 1, when San Francisco's Willie Mays tripled home the winning run. The third in Game 2, when Berra pounded a two-run homer to give the A.L. a lead it never relinquished.

■ **Memorable moment:** The final out of Game 2. With hometown favorite Jim Gilliam at bat and the potential tying runs on second and third, Los Angeles fans roared. But Gilliam grounded out.

■ **Top guns:** Game 1: Don Drysdale (Dodgers), Eddie Mathews (Braves), Hank Aaron (Braves), N.L.; Al Kaline (Tigers), Gus Triandos (Orioles), A.L.; Game 2: Berra (Yankees), Malzone (Red Sox), Colavito (Indians), A.L.; Frank Robinson (Reds), Gilliam (Dodgers), N.L.

■ **MVPs:** Game 1: Drysdale. Game 2: Berra.

Linescores

Game 1, July 7, at Pittsburgh's Forbes Field
A.L. ....0 0 0 1 0 0 0 3 0—4 8 0
N.L. ....1 0 0 0 0 0 2 2 x—5 9 1
Wynn (White Sox), Duren (Yankees) 4, Bunning (Tigers) 7, Ford (Yankees) 8, Daley (Athletics) 8; Drysdale (Dodgers), Burdette (Braves) 4, Face (Pirates) 7, Antonelli (Giants) 8, Elston (Cubs) 9. W—Antonelli. L—Ford. HR—Mathews, N.L.; Kaline, A.L.

Game 2, August 3, at Los Angeles Coliseum
A.L. ....0 1 2 0 0 0 1 1 0—5 6 0
N.L. ....1 0 0 0 1 0 1 0 0—3 6 3
Walker (Orioles), Wynn (White Sox) 4, Wilhelm (Orioles) 6, O'Dell (Orioles) 7, McLish (Indians) 8; Drysdale (Dodgers), Conley (Phillies) 4, Jones (Giants) 6, Face (Pirates) 8. W—Walker. L—Drysdale. HR—Malzone, Berra, Colavito, A.L.; Robinson, Gilliam, N.L.

WORLD SERIES

■ **Winner:** The Dodgers, winners of a pennant playoff against Milwaukee, defeated the "Go-Go" White Sox for their first Series victory in Los Angeles.

■ **Turning point:** The Dodgers' 5-4 fourth-game victory, which was decided by Gil Hodges' home run.

■ **Memorable moment:** The first West Coast World Series contest — a 3-1 Dodger victory in Game 3.

■ **Top guns:** Larry Sherry (2-0, 0.71 ERA), Charlie Neal (.370, 2 HR, 6 RBIs), Chuck Essegian (2 PH HR), Dodgers; Ted Kluszewski (.391, 3 HR, 10 RBIs), Nellie Fox (.375), White Sox.

■ **MVP:** Sherry.

Linescores

Game 1—October 1, at Chicago
Los Angeles ....0 0 0 0 0 0 0 0 0— 0 8 3
Chicago.................2 0 7 2 0 0 0 0 x—11 11 0
Craig, Churn (3), Labine (4), Koufax (5), Klippstein (7); Wynn, Staley (8). W—Wynn. L—Craig. HR—Kluszewski 2 (Chi.).

Game 2—October 2, at Chicago
Los Angeles ....0 0 0 0 1 0 3 0 0—4 9 1
Chicago.....................2 0 0 0 0 0 0 1 0—3 8 0
Podres, Sherry (7); Shaw, Lown (7). W—Podres. L—Shaw. HR—Neal 2, Essegian (L.A.).

Game 3—October 4, at Los Angeles.
Chicago...................0 0 0 0 0 0 0 1 0—1 12 0
Los Angeles ....0 0 0 0 0 0 2 1 x—3 5 0
Donovan, Staley (7); Drysdale, Sherry (8). W—Drysdale. L—Donovan.

Game 4—October 5, at Los Angeles
Chicago...................0 0 0 0 0 0 4 0 0—4 10 3
Los Angeles ....0 0 4 0 0 0 0 1 x—5 9 0
Wynn, Lown (3), Pierce (4), Staley (7); Craig, Sherry (8). W—Sherry. L—Staley. HR—Lollar (Chi.); Hodges (L.A.).

Game 5—October 6, at Los Angels
Chicago.....................0 0 0 1 0 0 0 0 0—1 5 0
Los Angeles ....0 0 0 0 0 0 0 0 0—0 9 0
Shaw, Pierce (8), Donovan (8); Koufax, Williams (8). W—Shaw. L—Koufax.

Game 6—October 8, at Chicago
Los Angeles ....0 0 2 6 0 0 0 0 1—9 13 0
Chicago...................0 0 0 3 0 0 0 0 0—3 6 1
Podres, Sherry (4); Wynn, Donovan (4), Lown (4), Staley (5), Pierce (8), Moore (9). W—Sherry. L—Wynn. HR—Snider, Moon, Essegian (L.A.); Kluszewski (Chi.).

1960

FINAL STANDINGS

American League

Team	W	L	Pct.	GB
New York	97	57	.630	...
Baltimore	89	65	.578	8
Chicago	87	67	.565	10
Cleveland	76	78	.494	21
Washington	73	81	.474	24
Detroit	71	83	.461	26
Boston	65	89	.422	32
Kansas City	58	96	.377	39

National League

Team	W	L	Pct.	GB
Pittsburgh	95	59	.617	...
Milwaukee	88	66	.571	7
St. Louis	86	68	.558	9
Los Angeles	82	72	.532	13
San Francisco	79	75	.513	16
Cincinnati	67	87	.435	28
Chicago	60	94	.390	35
Philadelphia	59	95	.383	36

SIGNIFICANT EVENTS

■ **August 3:** In baseball's most bizarre trade, the Indians swapped manager Joe Gordon to Detroit for manager Jimmie Dykes.
■ **October 18:** Casey Stengel, who managed the Yankees to 10 pennants and seven World Series titles in 12 years, was fired.
■ **October 26:** The A.L. announced relocation of the Senators to Minneapolis-St. Paul and 1961 expansion to Los Angeles and Washington.

MEMORABLE MOMENTS

■ **June 17:** Ted Williams became the fourth member of the 500-homer fraternity when he connected off Cleveland's Wynn Hawkins in a 3-1 Boston victory.
■ **September 28:** Williams belted career homer No. 521 in Boston's 5-4 victory over Baltimore and promptly retired.

LEADERS

American League
BA: Pete Runnels, Bos., .320.
Runs: Mickey Mantle, N.Y., 119.
Hits: Minnie Minoso, Chi., 184.
TB: Mickey Mantle, N.Y., 294.
HR: Mickey Mantle, N.Y., 40.
RBI: Roger Maris, N.Y., 112.
SB: Luis Aparicio, Chi., 51.
Wins: Chuck Estrada, Bal.; Jim Perry, Cle., 18.
ERA: Frank Baumann, Chi., 2.67.
CG: Frank Lary, Det., 15.
IP: Frank Lary, Det., 274.1.
SO: Jim Bunning, Det., 201.

National League
BA: Dick Groat, Pit., .325.
Runs: Bill Bruton, Mil., 112.
Hits: Willie Mays, S.F., 190.
TB: Hank Aaron, Mil., 334.
HR: Ernie Banks, Chi., 41.
RBI: Hank Aaron, Mil., 126.
SB: Maury Wills, L.A., 50.
Wins: Ernie Broglio, St.L.; Warren Spahn, Mil., 21.
ERA: Mike McCormick, S.F., 2.70.
CG: Lew Burdette, Mil.; Vernon Law, Pit.; Warren Spahn, Mil., 18.
IP: Larry Jackson, St.L., 282.
SO: Don Drysdale, L.A., 246.

N.L. 20-game winners
Ernie Broglio, St.L., 21-9
Warren Spahn, Mil., 21-10
Vernon Law, Pit., 20-9

A.L. 100 RBIs
Roger Maris, N.Y., 112
Minnie Minoso, Chi., 105
Vic Wertz, Bos., 103
Jim Lemon, Wash., 100

N.L. 100 RBIs
Hank Aaron, Mil., 126
Eddie Mathews, Mil., 124
Ernie Banks, Chi., 117
Willie Mays, S.F., 103

A.L. 40 homers
Mickey Mantle, N.Y., 40

N.L. 40 homers
Ernie Banks, Chi., 41
Hank Aaron, Mil., 40

Most Valuable Player
A.L.: Roger Maris, OF, N.Y.
N.L.: Dick Groat, SS, Pit.

Cy Young Award
A.L.-N.L.: Vernon Law, Pit.

Rookie of the Year
A.L.: Ron Hansen, SS, Bal.
N.L.: Frank Howard, OF, L.A.

ALL-STAR GAMES

■ **Winner:** In a three-day All-Star doubleheader, the N.L. pulled off a 5-3 and 6-0 sweep and narrowed its once-embarrassing overall deficit to 16-13.

■ **Key Innings:** The first in Game 1, when a Willie Mays triple and an Ernie Banks homer sparked the N.L. to a 3-0 lead; the second in Game 2, when Eddie Mathews opened the N.L. scoring with a two-run homer.

■ **Memorable moment:** A third-inning Game 2 home run by Mays, who was 6 for 8 in the two games. The homer gave Mays a perfect 6-for-6 All-Star ledger against Yankee great Ford.

■ **Top guns:** Game 1: Bob Friend (Pirates), Mays (Giants), Banks (Cubs), N.L.; Al Kaline (Tigers), A.L.; Game 2: Vernon Law (Pirates), Mays (Giants), Mathews (Braves), Ken Boyer (Cardinals), N.L.

■ **MVPs:** Games 1 and 2 : Mays.

Linescores

Game 1, July 11, at Kansas City's Municipal Stadium
N.L. ....3 1 1 0 0 0 0 0 0—5 12 4
A.L. ....0 0 0 0 0 1 0 2 0—3 6 1
Friend (Pirates), McCormick (Giants) 4, Face (Pirates) 6, Buhl (Braves) 8, Law (Pirates) 9; Monbouquette (Red Sox), Estrada (Orioles) 3, Coates (Yankees) 4, Bell (Indians) 6, Lary (Tigers) 8, Daley (Athletics) 9. W—Friend. L—Monbouquette. HR—Banks, Crandall, N.L.; Kaline, A.L.

Game 2, July 13, at New York's Yankee Stadium
N.L. ....0 2 1 0 0 0 1 0 2—6 10 0
A.L. ....0 0 0 0 0 0 0 0 0—0 8 0
Law (Pirates), Podres (Dodgers) 3, S. Williams (Dodgers) 5, Jackson (Cardinals) 7, Henry (Reds) 8, McDaniel (Cardinals) 9; Ford (Yankees), Wynn (White Sox) 4, Staley (White Sox) 6, Lary (Tigers) 8, Bell (Indians) 9. W—Law. L—Ford. HR—Mathews, Mays, Musial, Boyer, N.L.

WORLD SERIES

■ **Winner:** Despite being outscored 55-27, the Pirates edged the Yankees in a seven-game Series that will be long remembered for its classic ending.

■ **Turning point:** The Pirates' 3-2 fourth-game victory after suffering successive 16-3 and 10-0 losses to the hard-hitting Yankees.

■ **Memorable moment:** Bill Mazeroski's Series-ending ninth-inning home run that broke a 9-9 tie after the Yankees had rallied for two runs in the top of the frame. One of the classic moments in Series history.

■ **Top guns:** Vernon Law (2-0), Mazeroski (.320, 2 HR, 5 RBIs), Pirates; Whitey Ford (2-0, 0.00 ERA), Mickey Mantle (.400, 3 HR, 11 RBIs), Bobby Richardson (.367, 12 RBIs), Yankees.

■ **MVP:** Richardson.

Linescores

Game 1—October 5, at Pittsburgh
New York.................1 0 0 1 0 0 0 0 2—4 13 2
Pittsburgh ....3 0 0 2 0 1 0 0 x—6 8 0
Ditmar, Coates (1), Maas (5), Duren (7); Law, Face (8). W—Law. L—Ditmar. HR—Maris, Howard (N.Y.); Mazeroski (Pit.).

Game 2—October 6, at Pittsburgh
New York...............0 0 2 1 2 7 3 0 1—16 19 1
Pittsburgh ....0 0 0 1 0 0 0 0 2— 3 13 1
Turley, Shantz (9); Friend, Green (5), Labine (6), Witt (6), Gibbon (7), Cheney (9). W—Turley. L—Friend. HR—Mantle 2 (N.Y.).

Game 3—October 8, at New York
Pittsburgh ....0 0 0 0 0 0 0 0 0— 0 4 0
New York...............6 0 0 4 0 0 0 0 x—10 16 1
Mizell, Labine (1), Green (1), Witt (4), Cheney (6), Gibbon (8); Ford. W—Ford. L—Mizell. HR—Richardson, Mantle (N.Y.).

Game 4—October 9, at New York
Pittsburgh ....0 0 0 0 3 0 0 0 0—3 7 0
New York...................0 0 0 1 0 0 1 0 0—2 8 0
Law, Face (7); Terry, Shantz (7), Coates (8). W—Law. L—Terry. HR—Skowron (N.Y.).

Game 5—October 10, at New York
Pittsburgh ....0 3 1 0 0 0 0 0 1—5 10 2
New York.................0 1 1 0 0 0 0 0 0—2 5 2
Haddix, Face (7); Ditmar, Arroyo (2), Stafford (3), Duren (8). W—Haddix. L—Ditmar. HR—Maris (N.Y.).

Game 6—October 12, at Pittsburgh
New York...............0 1 5 0 0 2 2 2 0—12 17 1
Pittsburgh ....0 0 0 0 0 0 0 0 0— 0 7 1
Ford; Friend, Cheney (3), Mizell (4), Green (6), Labine (6), Witt (9). W—Ford. L—Friend.

Game 7—October 13, at Pittsburgh
New York...............0 0 0 0 1 4 0 2 2— 9 13 1
Pittsburgh ....2 2 0 0 0 0 0 5 1—10 11 0
Turley, Stafford (2), Shantz (3), Coates (8), Terry (8); Law, Face (6), Friend (9), Haddix (9). W—Haddix. L—Terry. HR—Skowron, Berra (N.Y.); Nelson, Smith, Mazeroski (Pit.).

HISTORY

1961

FINAL STANDINGS

American League

Team	W	L	Pct.	GB
New York	109	53	.673	...
Detroit	101	61	.623	8
Baltimore	95	67	.586	14
Chicago	86	76	.531	23
Cleveland	78	83	.484	30.5
Boston	76	86	.469	33
Minnesota	70	90	.438	38
Los Angeles	70	91	.435	38.5
Kansas City	61	100	.379	47.5
Washington	61	100	.379	47.5

National League

Team	W	L	Pct.	GB
Cincinnati	93	61	.604	...
Los Angeles	89	65	.578	4
San Francisco	85	69	.552	8
Milwaukee	83	71	.539	10
St. Louis	80	74	.519	13
Pittsburgh	75	79	.487	18
Chicago	64	90	.416	29
Philadelphia	47	107	.305	46

SIGNIFICANT EVENTS

■ **April 6:** The Cubs designated Vedie Himsl as the first of nine coaches who would rotate as the team's manager during the season.
■ **July 17:** Commissioner Ford Frick ruled that nobody could be credited with breaking Babe Ruth's 60-homer record unless he did it in the first 154 games of a season.
■ **October 10:** The Mets and Colt .45s combined to pick 45 players in the N.L.'s first expansion draft.

MEMORABLE MOMENTS

■ **April 30:** Willie Mays became the ninth player to hit four homers in a game during the Giants' 14-4 victory at Milwaukee.
■ **August 11:** Warren Spahn pitched Milwaukee to a 2-1 victory over Chicago and claimed his 300th career victory.
■ **August 20:** The Phillies defeated Milwaukee, 7-4, and ended their modern-era record losing streak at 23.
■ **October 1:** Roger Maris drove a pitch from Boston's Tracy Stallard for his record-setting 61st home run, giving New York a 1-0 victory at Yankee Stadium.

LEADERS

American League
BA: Norm Cash, Det., .361.
Runs: Mickey Mantle, N.Y.; Roger Maris, N.Y., 132.
Hits: Norm Cash, Det., 193.
TB: Roger Maris, N.Y., 366.
HR: Roger Maris, N.Y., 61.
RBI: Roger Maris, N.Y., 142.
SB: Luis Aparicio, Chi., 53.
Wins: Whitey Ford, N.Y., 25.
ERA: Dick Donovan, Wash., 2.40.
CG: Frank Lary, Det., 22.
IP: Whitey Ford, N.Y., 283.
SO: Camilo Pascual, Min., 221.

National League
BA: Roberto Clemente, Pit., .351.
Runs: Willie Mays, S.F., 129.
Hits: Vada Pinson, Cin., 208.
TB: Hank Aaron, Mil., 358.
HR: Orlando Cepeda, S.F., 46.
RBI: Orlando Cepeda, S.F., 142.
SB: Maury Wills, L.A., 35.
Wins: Joey Jay, Cin.; Warren Spahn, Mil., 21.
ERA: Warren Spahn, Mil., 3.02.
CG: Warren Spahn, Mil., 21.
IP: Lew Burdette, Mil., 272.1.
SO: Sandy Koufax, L.A., 269.

A.L. 20-game winners
Whitey Ford, N.Y., 25-4
Frank Lary, Det., 23-9

N.L. 20-game winners
Joey Jay, Cin., 21-10
Warren Spahn, Mil., 21-13

A.L. 100 RBIs
Roger Maris, N.Y., 142
Jim Gentile, Bal., 141
Rocky Colavito, Det., 140
Norm Cash, Det., 132
Mickey Mantle, N.Y., 128
Harmon Killebrew, Min., 122
Bob Allison, Min., 105

N.L. 100 RBIs
Orlando Cepeda, S.F., 142
Frank Robinson, Cin., 124
Willie Mays, S.F., 123
Hank Aaron, Mil., 120
Dick Stuart, Pit., 117
Joe Adcock, Mil., 108

A.L. 40 homers
Roger Maris, N.Y., 61
Mickey Mantle, N.Y., 54
Jim Gentile, Bal., 46
Harmon Killebrew, Min., 46
Rocky Colavito, Det., 45
Norm Cash, Det., 41

N.L. 40 homers
Orlando Cepeda, S.F., 46
Willie Mays, S.F., 40

Most Valuable Player
A.L.: Roger Maris, OF, N.Y.
N.L.: Frank Robinson, OF, Cin.

Cy Young Award
A.L.-N.L.: Whitey Ford, N.Y. (AL)

Rookie of the Year
A.L.: Don Schwall, P, Bos.
N.L.: Billy Williams, OF, Chi.

Hall of Fame additions
Max Carey, OF, 1910-29
Billy Hamilton, OF, 1888-1901

ALL-STAR GAMES

■ **Winner:** The N.L. captured a wind-blown 5-4 victory in the All-Star opener at Candlestick Park and played to a 1-1 tie in a second game that was halted by a Boston rainstorm after nine innings.

■ **Key inning:** The 10th in Game 1, when the A.L. took a 4-3 lead and the N.L. answered with two runs. The winner was driven home by a Roberto Clemente single.

■ **Memorable moment:** The ninth inning of Game 1 when the A.L's two-run, game-tying rally received a big assist from a gust of wind that blew Giants reliever Stu Miller off the mound in mid delivery for a balk.

■ **Top guns:** Game 1: Warren Spahn (Braves), Willie Mays (Giants), Clemente (Pirates), N.L.; Harmon Killebrew (Twins), A.L.; Game 2: Jim Bunning (Tigers), Camilo Pascual (Twins), Rocky Colavito (Tigers), A.L.; Miller (Giants), Bill White (Cardinals), N.L.

■ **MVPs:** Game 1: Clemente; Game 2: Bunning.

Linescores

Game 1, July 11, at San Francisco's Candlestick Park
A.L. ....0 0 0 0 0 1 0 0 2 1—4 4 2
N.L. ....0 1 0 1 0 0 0 1 0 2—5 11 5
Ford (Yankees), Lary (Tigers) 4, Donovan (Senators) 4, Bunning (Tigers) 6, Fornieles (Red Sox) 8, Wilhelm (Orioles) 8; Spahn (Braves), Purkey (Reds) 4, McCormick (Giants) 6, Face (Pirates) 9, Koufax (Dodgers) 9, Miller (Giants) 9. W—Miller. L—Wilhelm. HR—Killebrew, A.L.; Altman, N.L.

Game 2, July 31, at Boston's Fenway Park
N.L. ....0 0 0 0 0 1 0 0 0—1 5 1
A.L. ....1 0 0 0 0 0 0 0 0—1 4 0
Purkey (Reds), Mahaffey (Phillies) 3, Koufax (Dodgers) 5, Miller (Giants) 7; Bunning (Tigers), Schwall (Red Sox) 4, Pascual (Twins) 7. HR—Colavito, A.L.

WORLD SERIES

■ **Winner:** The Yankee machine, powered by 61-homer man Roger Maris, earned its first Series championship since 1947 without Casey Stengel at the helm.

■ **Turning point:** A ninth-inning Maris home run that lifted the Yankees to a 3-2 victory in Game 3.

■ **Memorable moment:** Yankee lefthander Whitey Ford's five shutout innings in Game 4, which lifted his consecutive-inning scoreless streak to a Series-record 32.

■ **Top guns:** Ford (2-0, 0.00 ERA), John Blanchard (.400, 2 HR), Bill Skowron (.353, 5 RBIs), Hector Lopez (.333, 7 RBIs), Yankees; Wally Post (.333), Reds.

■ **MVP:** Ford.

Linescores

Game 1—October 4, at New York
Cincinnati ....0 0 0 0 0 0 0 0 0—0 2 0
New York....................0 0 0 1 0 1 0 0 x—2 6 0
O'Toole, Brosnan (8); Ford. W—Ford. L—O'Toole. HR—Howard, Skowron (N.Y.).

Game 2—October 5, at New York
Cincinnati ....0 0 0 2 1 1 0 2 0—6 9 0
New York....................0 0 0 2 0 0 0 0 0—2 4 3
Jay; Terry, Arroyo (8). W—Jay. L—Terry. HR—Coleman (Cin.); Berra (N.Y.).

Game 3—October 7, at Cincinnati
New York....................0 0 0 0 0 0 1 1 1—3 6 1
Cincinnati ....0 0 1 0 0 0 1 0 0—2 8 0
Stafford, Daley (7), Arroyo (8); Purkey. W—Arroyo. L—Purkey. HR—Blanchard, Maris (N.Y.).

Game 4—October 8, at Cincinnati
New York..................0 0 0 1 1 2 3 0 0—7 11 0
Cincinnati ....0 0 0 0 0 0 0 0 0—0 5 1
Ford, Coates (6); O'Toole, Brosnan (6), Henry (9). W—Ford. L—O'Toole.

Game 5—October 9, at Cincinnati
New York...............5 1 0 5 0 2 0 0 0—13 15 1
Cincinnati ....0 0 3 0 2 0 0 0 0— 5 11 3
Terry, Daley (3); Jay, Maloney (1), K. Johnson (2), Henry (3), Jones (4), Purkey (5), Brosnan (7), Hunt (9). W—Daley. L—Jay. HR—Blanchard, Lopez (N.Y.); Robinson, Post (Cin.).

1962

FINAL STANDINGS

American League

Team	W	L	Pct.	GB
New York	96	66	.593	...
Minnesota	91	71	.562	5
Los Angeles	86	76	.531	10
Detroit	85	76	.528	10.5
Chicago	85	77	.525	11
Cleveland	80	82	.494	16
Baltimore	77	85	.475	19
Boston	76	84	.475	19
Kansas City	72	90	.444	24
Washington	60	101	.373	35.5

National League

Team	W	L	Pct.	GB
*San Francisco	103	62	.624	...
Los Angeles	102	63	.618	1
Cincinnati	98	64	.605	3.5
Pittsburgh	93	68	.578	8
Milwaukee	86	76	.531	15.5
St. Louis	84	78	.519	17.5
Philadelphia	81	80	.503	20
Houston	64	96	.400	36.5
Chicago	59	103	.364	42.5
New York	40	120	.250	60.5

*Defeated Los Angeles 2-1 in pennant playoff.

SIGNIFICANT EVENTS

■ **April 9-10:** The Senators christened their $20-million D.C. Stadium with a 4-1 victory over Detroit, but Cincinnati beat Los Angeles 6-3 in the first game at Dodger Stadium.
■ **November 23:** Dodgers shortstop Maury Wills, who ran his way to a record 104 stolen bases, walked away with the N.L. MVP.

MEMORABLE MOMENTS

■ **September 12:** Washington's Tom Cheney set a single-game record when he struck out 21 batters in a 16-inning 2-1 victory over the Orioles.
■ **October 3:** The Giants captured the N.L. pennant with a 6-4 victory over the Dodgers in the third game of a three-game playoff.

LEADERS

American League
BA: Pete Runnels, Bos., .326.
Runs: Albie Pearson, L.A., 115.
Hits: Bobby Richardson, N.Y., 209.
TB: Rocky Colavito, Det., 309.
HR: Harmon Killebrew, Min., 48.
RBI: Harmon Killebrew, Min., 126.
SB: Luis Aparicio, Chi., 31.
Wins: Ralph Terry, N.Y., 23.
ERA: Hank Aguirre, Det., 2.21.
CG: Camilo Pascual, Min., 18.
IP: Ralph Terry, N.Y., 298.2.
SO: Camilo Pascual, Min., 206.

National League
BA: Tommy Davis, L.A., .346.
Runs: Frank Robinson, Cin., 134.
Hits: Tommy Davis, L.A., 230.
TB: Willie Mays, S.F., 382.
HR: Willie Mays, S.F., 49.
RBI: Tommy Davis, L.A., 153.
SB: Maury Wills, L.A., 104.
Wins: Don Drysdale, L.A., 25.
ERA: Sandy Koufax, L.A., 2.54.
CG: Warren Spahn, Mil., 22.
IP: Don Drysdale, L.A., 314.1.
SO: Don Drysdale, L.A., 232.

A.L. 20-game winners
Ralph Terry, N.Y., 23-12
Ray Herbert, Chi., 20-9
Dick Donovan, Cle., 20-10
Camilo Pascual, Min., 20-11

N.L. 20-game winners
Don Drysdale, L.A., 25-9
Jack Sanford, S.F., 24-7
Bob Purkey, Cin., 23-5
Joey Jay, Cin., 21-14

A.L. 100 RBIs
Harmon Killebrew, Min., 126
Norm Siebern, K.C., 117
Rocky Colavito, Det., 112
Floyd Robinson, Chi., 109
Leon Wagner, L.A., 107
Lee Thomas, L.A., 104
Bob Allison, Min., 102
Roger Maris, N.Y., 100

N.L. 100 RBIs
Tommy Davis, L.A., 153
Willie Mays, S.F., 141
Frank Robinson, Cin., 136
Hank Aaron, Mil., 128
Frank Howard, L.A., 119
Orlando Cepeda, S.F., 114
Don Demeter, Phil., 107
Ernie Banks, Chi., 104
Bill White, St.L., 102
Vada Pinson, Cin., 100

N.L. 40 homers
Willie Mays, S.F., 49
Hank Aaron, Mil., 45

A.L. 40 homers
Harmon Killebrew, Min., 48

Most Valuable Player
A.L.: Mickey Mantle, OF, N.Y.
N.L.: Maury Wills, SS, L.A.

Cy Young Award
A.L.-N.L.: Don Drysdale, L.A. (NL)

Rookie of the Year
A.L.: Tom Tresh, SS, N.Y.
N.L.: Ken Hubbs, 2B, Chi.

Hall of Fame additions
Bob Feller, P, 1936-56
Bill McKechnie, manager
Jackie Robinson, 2B, 1947-56
Edd Roush, OF, 1913-31

ALL-STAR GAMES

■ **Winner:** The N.L. narrowed its series deficit to 16-15 with a 3-1 victory in the All-Star opener, but the A.L. pulled out its heavy artillery in a 9-4 second-game rout.

■ **Key Innings:** The sixth in Game 1, when pinch-runner Maury Wills sparked a two-run rally with a stolen base; the seventh in Game 2, when Rocky Colavito belted a three-run homer.

■ **Memorable moment:** The final out of the second game. The A.L. would not win again in the 1960s.

■ **Top guns:** Game 1: Don Drysdale (Dodgers), Juan Marichal (Giants), Roberto Clemente (Pirates), Wills (Dodgers), N.L.; Game 2: Leon Wagner (Angels), Pete Runnels (Red Sox), Colavito (Tigers), A.L.

■ **MVPs:** Game 1: Wills; Game 2: Wagner.

Linescores

Game 1, July 10, at Washington's D.C. Stadium
N.L. ....0 0 0 0 0 2 0 1 0—3 8 0
A.L. ....0 0 0 0 0 1 0 0 0—1 4 0
Drysdale (Dodgers), Marichal (Giants) 4, Purkey (Reds) 6, Shaw (Braves) 8; Bunning (Tigers), Pascual (Twins) 4, Donovan (Indians) 7, Pappas (Orioles) 9. W—Marichal. L—Pascual.

Game 2, July 30, at Chicago's Wrigley Field
A.L. ....0 0 1 2 0 1 3 0 2—9 10 0
N.L. ....0 1 0 0 0 0 1 1 1—4 10 4
Stenhouse (Senators), Herbert (White Sox) 3, Aguirre (Tigers) 6, Pappas (Orioles) 9; Podres (Dodgers), Mahaffey (Phillies) 3, Gibson (Cardinals) 5, Farrell (Colts) 7, Marichal (Giants) 8. W—Herbert. L—Mahaffey. HR—Runnels, Wagner, Colavito, A.L.; Roseboro, N.L.

WORLD SERIES

■ **Winner:** The Yankees prevailed over the Giants, who were making their first Series appearance since moving from New York to San Francisco.

■ **Turning point:** A three-run eighth-inning homer by rookie Tom Tresh that lifted Ralph Terry and the Yankees to a 5-3 Game 5 victory.

■ **Memorable moment:** Yankee second baseman Bobby Richardson snagging Willie McCovey's vicious seventh-game line drive with runners on second and third base, preserving Terry's 1-0 shutout and ending the Series. A slight variation in the path of McCovey's shot would have given the Giants a championship.

■ **Top guns:** Terry (2-1, 1.80 ERA), Tresh (.321, 4 RBIs), Yankees; Jose Pagan (.368), Giants.

■ **MVP:** Terry.

Linescores

Game 1—October 4, at San Francisco
New York..................2 0 0 0 0 0 1 2 1—6 11 0
San Francisco ....0 1 1 0 0 0 0 0 0—2 10 0
Ford; O'Dell, Larsen (8), Miller (9). W—Ford. L—O'Dell. HR—Boyer (N.Y.).

Game 2—October 5, at San Francisco
New York....................0 0 0 0 0 0 0 0 0—0 3 1
San Francisco ....1 0 0 0 0 0 1 0 x—2 6 0
Terry, Daley (8); Sanford. W—Sanford. L—Terry. HR—McCovey (S.F.).

Game 3—October 7, at New York
San Francisco ....0 0 0 0 0 0 0 0 2—2 4 3
New York....................0 0 0 0 0 0 3 0 x—3 5 1
Pierce, Larsen (7), Bolin (8); Stafford. W—Stafford. L—Pierce. HR—Bailey (S.F.).

Game 4—October 8, at New York
San Francisco ....0 2 0 0 0 0 4 0 1—7 9 1
New York....................0 0 0 0 0 2 0 0 1—3 9 1
Marichal, Bolin (5), Larsen (6), O'Dell (7); Ford, Coates (7), Bridges (7). W—Larsen. L—Coates. HR—Haller, Hiller (S.F.).

Game 5—October 10, at New York
San Francisco ....0 0 1 0 1 0 0 0 1—3 8 2
New York....................0 0 0 1 0 1 0 3 x—5 6 0
Sanford, Miller (8); Terry. W—Terry. L—Sanford. HR—Pagan (S.F.); Tresh (N.Y.).

Game 6—October 15, at San Francisco
New York...................0 0 0 0 1 0 0 1 0—2 3 2
San Francisco ....0 0 0 3 2 0 0 0 x—5 10 1
Ford, Coates (5), Bridges (8); Pierce. W—Pierce. L—Ford. HR—Maris (N.Y.).

Game 7—October 16, at San Francisco
New York....................0 0 0 0 1 0 0 0 0—1 7 0
San Francisco ....0 0 0 0 0 0 0 0 0—0 4 1
Terry; Sanford, O'Dell (8). W—Terry. L—Sanford.

1963

FINAL STANDINGS

American League

Team	W	L	Pct.	GB
New York	104	57	.646	...
Chicago	94	68	.580	10.5
Minnesota	91	70	.565	13
Baltimore	86	76	.531	18.5
Cleveland	79	83	.488	25.5
Detroit	79	83	.488	25.5
Boston	76	85	.472	28
Kansas City	73	89	.451	31.5
Los Angeles	70	91	.435	34
Washington	56	106	.346	48.5

National League

Team	W	L	Pct.	GB
Los Angeles	99	63	.611	...
St. Louis	93	69	.574	6
San Francisco	88	74	.543	11
Philadelphia	87	75	.537	12
Cincinnati	86	76	.531	13
Milwaukee	84	78	.519	15
Chicago	82	80	.506	17
Pittsburgh	74	88	.457	25
Houston	66	96	.407	33
New York	51	111	.315	48

SIGNIFICANT EVENTS

- **January 26:** Baseball's Rules Committee expanded the strike zone—from the top of the shoulders to the bottom of the knees.
- **September 29:** Cardinals great Stan Musial retired with N.L. records for hits (3,630) and RBIs (1,951).
- **November 7:** Yankee catcher Elston Howard became the first black MVP in A.L. history.

MEMORABLE MOMENTS

- **July 13:** Cleveland's Early Wynn struggled through five rocky innings but still won his 300th career game, a 7-4 victory over Kansas City.
- **August 21:** Pittsburgh's Jerry Lynch hit his record-setting 15th career pinch-hit homer in a 7-6 victory at Chicago.
- **September 8:** 42-year-old Braves lefty Warren Spahn tied the N.L. record when he stopped Philadelphia 3-2, becoming a 20-game winner for the 13th time.

LEADERS

American League

BA: Carl Yastrzemski, Bos., .321.
Runs: Bob Allison, Min., 99.
Hits: Carl Yastrzemski, Bos., 183.
TB: Dick Stuart, Bos., 319.
HR: Harmon Killebrew, Min., 45.
RBI: Dick Stuart, Bos., 118.
SB: Luis Aparicio, Bal., 40.
Wins: Whitey Ford, N.Y., 24.
ERA: Gary Peters, Chi., 2.33.
CG: Camilo Pascual, Min.; Ralph Terry, N.Y., 18.
IP: Whitey Ford, N.Y., 269.1.
SO: Camilo Pascual, Min., 202.

National League

BA: Tommy Davis, L.A., .326.
Runs: Hank Aaron, Mil., 121.
Hits: Vada Pinson, Cin., 204.
TB: Hank Aaron, Mil., 370.
HR: Hank Aaron, Mil.; Willie McCovey, S.F., 44.
RBI: Hank Aaron, Mil., 130.
SB: Maury Wills, L.A., 40.
Wins: Sandy Koufax, L.A.; Juan Marichal, S.F., 25.
ERA: Sandy Koufax, L.A., 1.88.
CG: Warren Spahn, Mil., 22.
IP: Juan Marichal, S.F., 321.1.
SO: Sandy Koufax, L.A., 306.

A.L. 20-game winners
Whitey Ford, N.Y., 24-7
Jim Bouton, N.Y., 21-7
Camilo Pascual, Min., 21-9
Bill Monbouquette, Bos., 20-10
Steve Barber, Bal., 20-13

N.L. 20-game winners
Sandy Koufax, L.A., 25-5
Juan Marichal, S.F., 25-8
Jim Maloney, Cin., 23-7
Warren Spahn, Mil., 23-7
Dick Ellsworth, Chi., 22-10

A.L. 100 RBIs
Dick Stuart, Bos., 118
Al Kaline, Det., 101

N.L. 100 RBIs
Hank Aaron, Mil., 130
Ken Boyer, St.L., 111
Bill White, St.L., 109
Vada Pinson, Cin., 106
Willie Mays, S.F., 103
Willie McCovey, S.F., 102

A.L. 40 homers
Harmon Killebrew, Min., 45
Dick Stuart, Bos., 42

N.L. 40 homers
Hank Aaron, Mil., 44
Willie McCovey, S.F., 44

Most Valuable Player
A.L.: Elston Howard, C, N.Y.
N.L.: Sandy Koufax, P, L.A.

Cy Young Award
A.L.-N.L.: Sandy Koufax, L.A. (NL)

Rookie of the Year
A.L.: Gary Peters, P, Chi.
N.L.: Pete Rose, 2B, Cin.

Hall of Fame additions
John Clarkson, P, 1882-94
Elmer Flick, OF, 1898-1910
Sam Rice, OF, 1915-35
Eppa Rixey, P, 1912-33

ALL-STAR GAME

- **Winner:** The N.L. unleashed secret weapon Willie Mays on the A.L. again and claimed a 5-3 victory in a return to the single All-Star Game format.
- **Key inning:** The third, when Mays singled home a run, stole his second base and scored on a single by Dick Groat. Mays scored two runs, drove in two and made an outstanding catch.
- **Memorable moment:** Pinch-hitter Stan Musial lining out to right field in his 24th, and last, All-Star appearance. Musial batted .317 and hit a record six home runs.
- **Top guns:** Mays (Giants), Ron Santo (Cubs), N.L.; Albie Pearson (Angels), Leon Wagner (Angels), A.L.
- **MVP:** Mays.

Linescore

July 9, at Cleveland Stadium
N.L. ....0 1 2 0 1 0 0 1 0—5 6 0
A.L. ....0 1 2 0 0 0 0 0 0—3 11 1
O'Toole (Reds), Jackson (Cubs) 3, Culp (Phillies) 5, Woodeshick (Colts) 6, Drysdale (Dodgers) 8; McBride (Angels), Bunning (Tigers) 4, Bouton (Yankees) 6, Pizarro (White Sox) 7, Radatz (Red Sox) 8. W—Jackson. L—Bunning.

WORLD SERIES

- **Winner:** The Dodgers cut down their old nemesis in an impressive pitching-dominated sweep.
- **Turning point:** The first two innings of Game 1. Dodgers lefthander Sandy Koufax set the tone for the Series when he struck out the first five Yankees he faced en route to a record-setting 15-strikeout performance.
- **Memorable moment:** The first World Series game at new Dodger Stadium — a three-hit 1-0 victory for Los Angeles righthander Don Drysdale in Game 3.
- **Top guns:** Koufax (2-0, 1.50 ERA), Tommy Davis (.400), Bill Skowron (.385), Dodgers; Elston Howard (.333), Yankees.
- **MVP:** Koufax.

Linescores

Game 1—October 2, at New York
Los Angeles ....0 4 1 0 0 0 0 0 0—5 9 0
New York...................0 0 0 0 0 0 0 2 0—2 6 0
Koufax; Ford, Williams (6), Hamilton (9). W—Koufax. L—Ford. HR—Roseboro (L.A.); Tresh (N.Y.).

Game 2—October 3, at New York
Los Angeles ....2 0 0 1 0 0 0 1 0—4 10 1
New York...................0 0 0 0 0 0 0 0 1—1 7 0
Podres, Perranoski (9); Downing, Terry (6), Reniff (9). W—Podres. L—Downing. HR—Skowron (L.A.).

Game 3—October 5, at Los Angeles
New York...................0 0 0 0 0 0 0 0 0—0 3 0
Los Angeles ....1 0 0 0 0 0 0 0 x—1 4 1
Bouton, Reniff (8); Drysdale. W—Drysdale. L—Bouton.

Game 4—October 6, at Los Angeles
New York...................0 0 0 0 0 0 1 0 0—1 6 1
Los Angeles.................0 0 0 0 1 0 1 0 x—2 2 1
Ford, Reniff (8); Koufax. W—Koufax. L—Ford. HR—F. Howard (L.A.); Mantle (N.Y.).

1964

FINAL STANDINGS

American League

Team	W	L	Pct.	GB
New York	99	63	.611	...
Chicago	98	64	.605	1
Baltimore	97	65	.599	2
Detroit	85	77	.525	14
Los Angeles	82	80	.506	17
Cleveland	79	83	.488	20
Minnesota	79	83	.488	20
Boston	72	90	.444	27
Washington	62	100	.383	37
Kansas City	57	105	.352	42

National League

Team	W	L	Pct.	GB
St. Louis	93	69	.574	...
Cincinnati	92	70	.568	1
Philadelphia	92	70	.568	1
San Francisco	90	72	.556	3
Milwaukee	88	74	.543	5
Los Angeles	80	82	.494	13
Pittsburgh	80	82	.494	13
Chicago	76	86	.469	17
Houston	66	96	.407	27
New York	53	109	.327	40

SIGNIFICANT EVENTS

- **February 13:** Ken Hubbs, the Cubs' 22-year-old second baseman, died when the single-engine plane he was flying crashed near Provo, Utah.
- **April 17:** The Mets opened $25-million Shea Stadium with a 4-3 loss to the Pirates.
- **November 7:** The Braves received N.L. permission to move their sagging franchise from Milwaukee to Atlanta after the 1965 season.

MEMORABLE MOMENTS

- **April 23:** Houston's Ken Johnson became the first pitcher to lose a game in which he had thrown a complete-game no-hitter. Johnson dropped a 1-0 decision to the Reds.
- **June 4:** Dodgers lefty Sandy Koufax joined Bob Feller as the only three-time no-hit pitchers of the 20th Century when he stopped the Phillies, 3-0.
- **June 21:** Philadelphia's Jim Bunning fired baseball's first regular-season perfect game in 42 years, beating the Mets, 6-0.

LEADERS

American League

BA: Tony Oliva, Min., .323.
Runs: Tony Oliva, Min., 109.
Hits: Tony Oliva, Min., 217.
TB: Tony Oliva, Min., 374.
HR: Harmon Killebrew, Min., 49.
RBI: Brooks Robinson, Bal., 118.
SB: Luis Aparicio, Bal., 57.
Wins: Dean Chance, L.A.; Gary Peters, Chi., 20.
ERA: Dean Chance, L.A., 1.65.
CG: Dean Chance, L.A., 15.
IP: Dean Chance, L.A., 278.1.
SO: Al Downing, N.Y., 217.

National League

BA: Roberto Clemente, Pit., .339.
Runs: Dick Allen, Phil., 125.
Hits: Roberto Clemente, Pit.; Curt Flood, St.L., 211.
TB: Dick Allen, Phil., 352.
HR: Willie Mays, S.F., 47.
RBI: Ken Boyer, St.L., 119.
SB: Maury Wills, L.A., 53.
Wins: Larry Jackson, Chi., 24.
ERA: Sandy Koufax, L.A., 1.74.
CG: Juan Marichal, S.F., 22.
IP: Don Drysdale, L.A., 321.1.
SO: Bob Veale, Pit., 250.

A.L. 20-game winners
Dean Chance, L.A., 20-9
Gary Peters, Chi., 20-8

N.L. 20-game winners
Larry Jackson, Chi., 24-11
Juan Marichal, S.F., 21-8
Ray Sadecki, St.L., 20-11

A.L. 100 RBIs
Brooks Robinson, Bal., 118
Dick Stuart, Bos., 114
Harmon Killebrew, Min., 111
Mickey Mantle, N.Y., 111
Rocky Colavito, K.C., 102
Joe Pepitone, N.Y., 100
Leon Wagner, Cle., 100

N.L. 100 RBIs
Ken Boyer, St.L., 119
Ron Santo, Chi., 114
Willie Mays, S.F., 111
Joe Torre, Mil., 109
Johnny Callison, Phil., 104
Bill White, St.L., 102

A.L. 40 homers
Harmon Killebrew, Min., 49

N.L. 40 homers
Willie Mays, S.F., 47

Most Valuable Player
A.L.: Brooks Robinson, 3B, Bal.
N.L.: Ken Boyer, 3B, St.L.

Cy Young Award
A.L.-N.L.: Dean Chance, L.A. (AL)

Rookie of the Year
A.L.: Tony Oliva, OF, Min.
N.L.: Dick Allen, 3B, Phil.

Hall of Fame additions
Luke Appling, SS, 1930-50
Red Faber, P, 1914-33
Burleigh Grimes, P, 1916-34
Miller Huggins, manager
Tim Keefe, P, 1880-93
Heinie Manush, OF, 1923-39
Monte Ward, IF/P, 1878-94

ALL-STAR GAME

- **Winner:** In a game that rekindled memories of 1941, the N.L. struck for four ninth-inning runs and escaped with a stunning 7-4 victory.
- **Key inning:** The ninth, when Willie Mays walked, stole second moved to third on Orlando Cepeda's bloop single and scored the tying run on a wild throw. But the N.L. was far from finished.
- **Memorable moment:** Johnny Callison's stunning three-run homer that finished off the A.L. in the ninth. The blast was hit off Boston relief ace Dick Radatz.
- **Top guns:** Billy Williams (Cubs), Ken Boyer (Cardinals), Callison (Phillies), N.L.; Dean Chance (Angels), Harmon Killebrew (Twins), A.L.
- **MVP:** Callison.

Linescore

July 7, at New York's Shea Stadium
A.L. ....1 0 0 0 0 2 1 0 0—4 9 1
N.L. ....0 0 0 2 1 0 0 0 4—7 8 0
Chance (Angels), Wyatt (Athletics) 4, Pascual (Twins) 5, Radatz (Red Sox) 7; Drysdale (Dodgers), Bunning (Phillies) 4, Short (Phillies) 6, Farrell (Colts) 7, Marichal (Giants) 9. W—Marichal. L—Radatz. HR—Williams, Boyer, Callison, N.L.

WORLD SERIES

- **Winner:** The Cardinals brought down the curtain on the Yankee dynasty with a seven-game triumph.
- **Turning point:** Trailing two games to one and 3-0 in the sixth inning of Game 4, the Cardinals rallied to a 4-3 victory when Ken Boyer connected for a grand slam.
- **Memorable moment:** A dramatic Game 3-ending homer by Mickey Mantle on the first ninth-inning pitch by St. Louis reliever Barney Schultz.
- **Top guns:** Bob Gibson (2-1, 3.00 ERA), Tim McCarver (.478, 5 RBIs), Boyer (2 HR, 6 RBIs), Lou Brock (.300, 5 RBIs), Cardinals; Bobby Richardson (13 hits, .406), Mantle (.333, 3 HR, 8 RBIs), Yankees.
- **MVP:** Gibson.

Linescores

Game 1—October 7, at St. Louis
New York..................0 3 0 0 1 0 0 1 0—5 12 2
St. Louis ....1 1 0 0 0 4 0 3 x—9 12 0
Ford, Downing (6), Sheldon (8), Mikkelsen (8); Sadecki, Schultz (7). W—Sadecki. L—Ford. HR—Tresh (N.Y.); Shannon (St.L.).

Game 2—October 8, at St. Louis
New York..................0 0 0 1 0 1 2 0 4—8 12 0
St. Louis ....0 0 1 0 0 0 0 1 1—3 7 0
Stottlemyre; Gibson, Schultz (9); G. Richardson (9); Craig (9). W—Stottlemyre. L—Gibson. HR—Linz (N.Y.).

Game 3—October 10, at New York
St. Louis ....0 0 0 0 1 0 0 0 0—1 6 0
New York....................0 1 0 0 0 0 0 0 1—2 5 2
Simmons, Schultz (9); Bouton. W—Bouton. L—Schultz. HR—Mantle (N.Y.).

Game 4—October 11, at New York
St. Louis ....0 0 0 0 0 4 0 0 0—4 6 1
New York....................3 0 0 0 0 0 0 0 0—3 6 1
Sadecki, Craig (1), Taylor (6); Downing, Mikkelsen (7), Terry (8). W—Craig. L—Downing. HR—K. Boyer (St.L.).

Game 5—October 12, at New York
St. Louis ....0 0 0 0 2 0 0 0 0 3—5 10 1
New York............0 0 0 0 0 0 0 0 2 0—2 6 2
Gibson; Stottlemyre, Reniff (8), Mikkelsen (8). W—Gibson. L—Mikkelsen. HR—Tresh (N.Y.); McCarver (St.L.).

Game 6—October 14, at St. Louis
New York..................0 0 0 0 1 2 0 5 0—8 10 0
St. Louis ....1 0 0 0 0 0 0 1 1—3 10 1
Bouton, Hamilton (9); Simmons, Taylor (7), Schultz (8), G. Richardson (8), Humphreys (9). W—Bouton. L—Simmons. HR—Maris, Mantle, Pepitone (N.Y.).

Game 7—October 15, at St. Louis
New York..................0 0 0 0 0 3 0 0 2—5 9 2
St. Louis ....0 0 0 3 3 0 1 0 x—7 10 1
Stottlemyre, Downing (5), Sheldon (5), Hamilton (7), Mikkelsen (8); Gibson. W—Gibson. L—Stottlemyre. HR—Brock, K. Boyer (St.L.); Mantle, C. Boyer, Linz (N.Y.).

1965

FINAL STANDINGS

American League

Team	W	L	Pct.	GB
Minnesota	102	60	.630	...
Chicago	95	67	.586	7
Baltimore	94	68	.580	8
Detroit	89	73	.549	13
Cleveland	87	75	.537	15
New York	77	85	.475	25
California	75	87	.463	27
Washington	70	92	.432	32
Boston	62	100	.383	40
Kansas City	59	103	.364	43

National League

Team	W	L	Pct.	GB
Los Angeles	97	65	.599	...
San Francisco	95	67	.586	2
Pittsburgh	90	72	.556	7
Cincinnati	89	73	.549	8
Milwaukee	86	76	.531	11
Philadelphia	85	76	.528	11.5
St. Louis	80	81	.497	16.5
Chicago	72	90	.444	25
Houston	65	97	.401	32
New York	50	112	.309	47

SIGNIFICANT EVENTS

■ **April 9:** The Houston Astrodome, baseball's first domed stadium, was unveiled for an exhibition game between the Astros and Yankees.

■ **August 22:** Giants pitcher Juan Marichal touched off a wild 14-minute brawl when he attacked Dodgers catcher John Roseboro with a bat.

■ **August 29:** Citing poor health, Casey Stengel stepped down as Mets manager and ended his 56-year baseball career.

■ **September 2:** The Los Angeles Angels, preparing to move to Anaheim, changed their name to the California Angels.

MEMORABLE MOMENTS

■ **August 19:** Cincinnati's Jim Maloney, who had no-hit the Mets two months earlier only to lose in the 11th, fired another 10-inning no-hitter and beat the Cubs, 1-0.

■ **September 13:** San Francisco's Willie Mays, en route to his second 50-homer season, became the fifth member of the 500 club when he connected off Houston's Don Nottebart in a game at the Astrodome.

■ **September 29:** Dodgers ace Sandy Koufax reached perfection when he retired all 27 Cubs he faced in a 1-0 victory—his record fourth career no-hitter.

LEADERS

American League

BA: Tony Oliva, Min., .321.
Runs: Zoilo Versalles, Min., 126.
Hits: Tony Oliva, Min., 185.
TB: Zoilo Versalles, Min., 308.
HR: Tony Conigliaro, Bos., 32.
RBI: Rocky Colavito, Cle., 108.
SB: Campy Campaneris, K.C., 51.
Wins: Jim (Mudcat) Grant, Min., 21.
ERA: Sam McDowell, Cle., 2.18.
CG: Mel Stottlemyre, N.Y., 18.
IP: Mel Stottlemyre, N.Y., 291.
SO: Sam McDowell, Cle., 325.

National League

BA: Roberto Clemente, Pit., .329.
Runs: Tommy Harper, Cin., 126.
Hits: Pete Rose, Cin., 209.
TB: Willie Mays, S.F., 360.
HR: Willie Mays, S.F., 52.
RBI: Deron Johnson, Cin., 130.
SB: Maury Wills, L.A., 94.
Wins: Sandy Koufax, L.A., 26.
ERA: Sandy Koufax, L.A., 2.04.
CG: Sandy Koufax, L.A., 27.
IP: Sandy Koufax, L.A., 335.2.
SO: Sandy Koufax, L.A., 382.

A.L. 20-game winners

Jim (Mudcat) Grant, Min., 21-7
Mel Stottlemyre, N.Y., 20-9

N.L. 20-game winners

Sandy Koufax, L.A., 26-8
Tony Cloninger, Mil., 24-11
Don Drysdale, L.A., 23-12
Sammy Ellis, Cin., 22-10
Juan Marichal, S.F., 22-13
Jim Maloney, Cin., 20-9
Bob Gibson, St.L., 20-12

A.L. 100 RBIs

Rocky Colavito, Cle., 108
Willie Horton, Det., 104

N.L. 100 RBIs

Deron Johnson, Cin., 130
Frank Robinson, Cin., 113
Willie Mays, S.F., 112
Billy Williams, Chi., 108
Willie Stargell, Pit., 107
Ernie Banks, Chi., 106
Johnny Callison, Phil., 101
Ron Santo, Chi., 101

N.L. 40 homers

Willie Mays, S.F., 52

Most Valuable Player

A.L: Zoilo Versalles, SS, Min.
N.L.: Willie Mays, OF, S.F.

Cy Young Award

A.L.-N.L.: Sandy Koufax, L.A. (NL)

Rookie of the Year

A.L.: Curt Blefary, OF, Bal.
N.L.: Jim Lefebvre, 2B, L.A.

Hall of Fame addition

Pud Galvin, P, 1879-92

ALL-STAR GAME

■ **Winner:** The N.L. took its first All-Star lead when Ron Santo drove home Willie Mays with a seventh-inning infield single that produced the winning run.

■ **Key Innings:** An N.L. first that featured home runs by Mays and Joe Torre and an A.L. fifth that featured Dick McAuliffe and Harmon Killebrew homers.

■ **Memorable moment:** Bob Gibson striking out Killebrew and New York's Joe Pepitone in the ninth inning with the tying run on second base.

■ **Top guns:** Juan Marichal (Giants), Mays (Giants), Willie Stargell (Pirates), Joe Torre (Braves), N.L.; McAuliffe (Tigers), Killebrew (Twins), A.L.

■ **MVP:** Marichal.

Linescore

July 13, at Minnesota's Metropolitan Stadium
N.L. ....3 2 0 0 0 0 1 0 0—6 11 0
A.L. ....0 0 0 1 4 0 0 0 0—5 8 0
Marichal (Giants), Maloney (Reds) 4, Drysdale (Dodgers) 5, Koufax (Dodgers) 6, Farrell (Astros) 7, Gibson (Cardinals) 8; Pappas (Orioles), Grant (Twins) 2, Richert (Senators) 4, McDowell (Indians) 6, Fisher (White Sox) 8. W—Koufax. L—McDowell. HR—Mays, Torre, Stargell, N.L.; McAuliffe, Killebrew, A.L.

WORLD SERIES

■ **Winner:** The pitching-rich Dodgers prevailed after dropping the first two games to the Twins — Minnesota's first World Series representative.

■ **Turning point:** A 4-0 shutout by Dodgers lefthander Claude Osteen in Game 3, after the Twins had beaten Don Drysdale and Sandy Koufax in Games 1 and 2.

■ **Memorable moment:** A three-hit seventh-game shutout by Koufax, who struck out 10 in his 2-0 victory.

■ **Top guns:** Koufax (2-1, 0.38 ERA), Ron Fairly (2 HR, 6 RBIs), Dodgers; Jim Grant (2-1, 2.74), Twins.

■ **MVP:** Koufax.

Linescores

Game 1—October 6, at Minnesota
Los Angeles ....0 1 0 0 0 0 0 0 1—2 10 1
Minnesota ....0 1 6 0 0 1 0 0 x—8 10 0
Drysdale, Reed (3), Brewer (5), Perranoski (7); Grant. W—Grant. L—Drysdale. HR—Fairly (L.A.); Mincher, Versalles (Min.).

Game 2—October 7, at Minnesota
Los Angeles ....0 0 0 0 0 0 1 0 0—1 7 3
Minnesota ....0 0 0 0 0 2 1 2 x—5 9 0
Koufax, Perranoski (7), Miller (8); Kaat. W—Kaat. L—Koufax.

Game 3—October 9, at Los Angeles
Minnesota ....0 0 0 0 0 0 0 0 0—0 5 0
Los Angeles.............0 0 0 2 1 1 0 0 x—4 10 1
Pascual, Merritt (6), Klippstein (8); Osteen. W—Osteen. L—Pascual.

Game 4—October 10, at Los Angeles
Minnesota ....0 0 0 1 0 1 0 0 0—2 5 2
Los Angeles.............1 1 0 1 0 3 0 1 x—7 10 0
Grant, Worthington (6), Pleis (8); Drysdale. W—Drysdale. L—Grant. HR—Killebrew, Oliva (Min.); Parker, Johnson (L.A.).

Game 5—October 11, at Los Angeles
Minnesota ....0 0 0 0 0 0 0 0 0—0 4 1
Los Angeles.............2 0 2 1 0 0 2 0 x—7 14 0
Kaat, Boswell (3), Perry (6); Koufax. W—Koufax. L—Kaat.

Game 6—October 13, at Minnesota
Los Angeles ....0 0 0 0 0 0 1 0 0—1 6 1
Minnesota ....0 0 0 2 0 3 0 0 x—5 6 1
Osteen, Reed (6), Miller (8); Grant. W—Grant. L—Osteen. HR—Fairly (L.A.); Allison, Grant (Min.).

Game 7—October 14, at Minnesota
Los Angeles ....0 0 0 2 0 0 0 0 0—2 7 0
Minnesota ....0 0 0 0 0 0 0 0 0—0 3 1
Koufax; Kaat, Worthington (4), Klippstein (6), Merritt (7), Perry (9). W—Koufax. L—Kaat. HR—Johnson (L.A.).

1966

FINAL STANDINGS

American League

Team	W	L	Pct.	GB
Baltimore	97	63	.606	...
Minnesota	89	73	.549	9
Detroit	88	74	.543	10
Chicago	83	79	.512	15
Cleveland	81	81	.500	17
California	80	82	.494	18
Kansas City	74	86	.463	23
Washington	71	88	.447	25.5
Boston	72	90	.444	26
New York	70	89	.440	26.5

National League

Team	W	L	Pct.	GB
Los Angeles	95	67	.586	...
San Francisco	93	68	.578	1.5
Pittsburgh	92	70	.568	3
Philadelphia	87	75	.537	8
Atlanta	85	77	.525	10
St. Louis	83	79	.512	12
Cincinnati	76	84	.475	18
Houston	72	90	.444	23
New York	66	95	.410	28.5
Chicago	59	103	.364	36

SIGNIFICANT EVENTS

■ **March 30:** The joint 32-day holdout of Dodger pitchers Sandy Koufax and Don Drysdale ended when they agreed to a combined package worth more than $210,000.

■ **April 11:** Another barrier fell when Emmett Ashford, baseball's first black umpire, worked the season opener at Washington.

■ **April 12:** The Braves dropped a 3-2 verdict to the Pirates in their debut at the new $18-million Atlanta Stadium.

■ **November 18:** Sandy Koufax, baseball's only three-time Cy Young Award winner, stunned the Dodgers when he announced his retirement at age 30 because of an arthritic elbow.

MEMORABLE MOMENTS

■ **June 9:** Rich Rollins, Zoilo Versalles, Tony Oliva, Don Mincher and Harmon Killebrew hit home runs in a seventh-inning explosion against Kansas City, matching a Major League record.

■ **August 17:** San Francisco's Willie Mays belted career homer No. 535 off St. Louis' Ray Washburn and moved into second place on the all-time list.

■ **September 22:** The Orioles clinched their first A.L. pennant with a 6-1 victory over Kansas City.

■ **October 2:** Sandy Koufax, working on two days rest, beat Philadelphia 6-3 for his 27th victory and clinched the Dodgers' third pennant in four years.

■ **November 8:** Baltimore's Frank Robinson, baseball's 13th Triple Crown winner, became the first player to win MVP honors in both leagues.

LEADERS

American League

BA: Frank Robinson, Bal., .316.
Runs: Frank Robinson, Bal., 122.
Hits: Tony Oliva, Min., 191.
TB: Frank Robinson, Bal., 367.
HR: Frank Robinson, Bal., 49.
RBI: Frank Robinson, Bal., 122.
SB: Campy Campaneris, K.C., 52.
Wins: Jim Kaat, Min., 25.
ERA: Gary Peters, Chi., 1.98.
CG: Jim Kaat, Min., 19.
IP: Jim Kaat, Min., 304.2.
SO: Sam McDowell, Cle., 225.

National League

BA: Matty Alou, Pit., .342.
Runs: Felipe Alou, Atl., 122.
Hits: Felipe Alou, Atl., 218.
TB: Felipe Alou, Atl., 355.
HR: Hank Aaron, Atl., 44.
RBI: Hank Aaron, Atl., 127.
SB: Lou Brock, St.L., 74.
Wins: Sandy Koufax, L.A., 27.
ERA: Sandy Koufax, L.A., 1.73.
CG: Sandy Koufax, L.A., 27.
IP: Sandy Koufax, L.A., 323.
SO: Sandy Koufax, L.A., 317.

A.L. 20-game winners

Jim Kaat, Min., 25-13
Denny McLain, Det., 20-14

N.L. 20-game winners

Sandy Koufax, L.A., 27-9
Juan Marichal, S.F., 25-6
Gaylord Perry, S.F., 21-8
Bob Gibson, St.L., 21-12
Chris Short, Phil., 20-10

A.L. 100 RBIs

Frank Robinson, Bal., 122
Harmon Killebrew, Min., 110
Boog Powell, Bal., 109
Willie Horton, Det., 100
Brooks Robinson, Bal., 100

N.L. 100 RBIs

Hank Aaron, Atl., 127
Roberto Clemente, Pit., 119
Dick Allen, Phil., 110
Willie Mays, S.F., 103
Bill White, Phil., 103
Willie Stargell, Pit., 102
Joe Torre, Atl., 101

A.L. 40 homers

Frank Robinson, Bal., 49

N.L. 40 homers

Hank Aaron, Atl., 44
Dick Allen, Phil., 40

Most Valuable Player

A.L.: Frank Robinson, OF, Bal.
N.L.: Roberto Clemente, OF, Pit.

Cy Young Award

A.L.-N.L.: Sandy Koufax, L.A. (NL)

Rookie of the Year

A.L.: Tommie Agee, OF, Chi.
N.L.: Tommy Helms, 3B, Cin.

Hall of Fame additions

Casey Stengel, manager
Ted Williams, OF, 1939-60

ALL-STAR GAME

■ **Winner:** The N.L. needed 10 innings to win its fourth consecutive All-Star Game in the blistering 105-degree heat of St. Louis.

■ **Key inning:** The 10th, when Maury Wills singled home Tim McCarver with the game-ending run.

■ **Memorable moment:** The almost-constant sight of fans being helped in the stands after passing out because of the heat.

■ **Top guns:** Gaylord Perry (Giants), Roberto Clemente (Pirates), Wills (Dodgers), N.L.; Denny McLain (Tigers), Brooks Robinson (Orioles), A.L.

■ **MVP:** Robinson.

Linescore

July 12, at St. Louis' Busch Stadium
A.L. ....0 1 0 0 0 0 0 0 0 0—1 6 0
N.L. ....0 0 0 1 0 0 0 0 0 1—2 6 0
McLain (Tigers), Kaat (Twins) 4, Stottlemyre (Yankees) 6, Siebert (Indians) 8, Richert (Senators) 10; Koufax (Dodgers), Bunning (Phillies) 4, Marichal (Giants) 6, Perry (Giants) 9. W—Perry. L—Richert.

WORLD SERIES

■ **Winner:** The Orioles, making only the second Series appearance in franchise history and first since moving from St. Louis to Baltimore, allowed only two Dodger runs — none after the third inning of Game 1.

■ **Turning point:** Game 1, when Moe Drabowsky relieved Baltimore lefty Dave McNally with the bases loaded in the third inning. Drabowsky worked 6⅔ innings of shutout relief and struck out 11 Dodgers in a 5-2 victory.

■ **Memorable moments:** Series-ending 1-0 victories by Wally Bunker (six-hitter) and McNally (four-hitter).

■ **Top guns:** Boog Powell (.357), Frank Robinson (2 HR, 3 RBIs), Orioles.

■ **MVP:** Frank Robinson.

Linescores

Game 1—October 5, at Los Angeles
Baltimore ....3 1 0 1 0 0 0 0 0—5 9 0
Los Angeles ....0 1 1 0 0 0 0 0 0—2 3 0
McNally, Drabowsky (3); Drysdale, Moeller (3), R. Miller (5), Perranoski (8). W—Drabowsky. L—Drysdale. HR—F. Robinson, B. Robinson (Bal.); Lefebvre (L.A.).

Game 2—October 6, at Los Angeles
Baltimore ....0 0 0 0 3 1 0 2 0—6 8 0
Los Angeles ....0 0 0 0 0 0 0 0 0—0 4 6
Palmer; Koufax, Perranoski (7), Regan (8), Brewer (9). W—Palmer. L—Koufax.

Game 3—October 8, at Baltimore
Los Angeles ....0 0 0 0 0 0 0 0 0—0 6 0
Baltimore....................0 0 0 0 1 0 0 0 x—1 3 0
Osteen, Regan (8); Bunker. W—Bunker. L—Osteen. HR—Blair (Bal.).

Game 4—October 9, at Baltimore
Los Angeles ....0 0 0 0 0 0 0 0 0—0 4 0
Baltimore....................0 0 0 1 0 0 0 0 x—1 4 0
Drysdale; McNally. W—McNally. L—Drysdale. HR—F. Robinson.

1967

FINAL STANDINGS

American League

Team	W	L	Pct.	GB
Boston	92	70	.568	...
Detroit	91	71	.562	1
Minnesota	91	71	.562	1
Chicago	89	73	.549	3
California	84	77	.522	7.5
Baltimore	76	85	.472	15.5
Washington	76	85	.472	15.5
Cleveland	75	87	.463	17
New York	72	90	.444	20
Kansas City	62	99	.385	29.5

National League

Team	W	L	Pct.	GB
St. Louis	101	60	.627	...
San Francisco	91	71	.562	10.5
Chicago	87	74	.540	14
Cincinnati	87	75	.537	14.5
Philadelphia	82	80	.506	19.5
Pittsburgh	81	81	.500	20.5
Atlanta	77	85	.475	24.5
Los Angeles	73	89	.451	28.5
Houston	69	93	.426	32.5
New York	61	101	.377	40.5

SIGNIFICANT EVENT

■ **October 18:** The A.L. approved the Athletics' move to Oakland and 1969 expansion to Kansas City and Seattle.

MEMORABLE MOMENTS

■ **April 14:** Boston lefthander Bill Rohr, making his Major League debut, lost a no-hit bid when Yankee Elston Howard singled with two out in the ninth inning of a 3-0 Red Sox victory.
■ **April 30:** Baltimore's Steve Barber and Stu Miller combined to pitch a no-hitter, but the Orioles lost, 2-1, when Detroit scored two ninth-inning runs.
■ **May 14, July 14:** New York's Mickey Mantle and Houston's Eddie Mathews became the sixth and seventh members of the 500-homer club exactly two months apart.

LEADERS

American League
BA: Carl Yastrzemski, Bos., .326.
Runs: Carl Yastrzemski, Bos., 112.
Hits: Carl Yastrzemski, Bos., 189.
TB: Carl Yastrzemski, Bos., 360.
HR: Harmon Killebrew, Min.; Carl Yastrzemski, Bos., 44.
RBI: Carl Yastrzemski, Bos., 121.
SB: Campy Campaneris, K.C., 55.
Wins: Jim Lonborg, Bos.; Earl Wilson, Det., 22.
ERA: Joel Horlen, Chi., 2.06.
CG: Dean Chance, Min., 18.
IP: Dean Chance, Min., 283.2.
SO: Jim Lonborg, Bos., 246.

National League
BA: Roberto Clemente, Pit., .357.
Runs: Hank Aaron, Atl.; Lou Brock, St.L., 113.
Hits: Roberto Clemente, Pit., 209.
TB: Hank Aaron, Atl., 344.
HR: Hank Aaron, Atl., 39.
RBI: Orlando Cepeda, St.L., 111.
SB: Lou Brock, St.L., 52.
Wins: Mike McCormick, S.F., 22.
ERA: Phil Niekro, Atl., 1.87.
CG: Ferguson Jenkins, Chi., 20.
IP: Jim Bunning, Phil., 302.1.
SO: Jim Bunning, Phil., 253.

A.L. 20-game winners
Jim Lonborg, Bos., 22-9
Earl Wilson, Det., 22-11
Dean Chance, Min., 20-14

N.L. 20-game winners
Mike McCormick, S.F., 22-10
Ferguson Jenkins, Chi., 20-13

A.L. 100 RBIs
Carl Yastrzemski, Bos., 121
Harmon Killebrew, Min., 113

N.L. 100 RBIs
Orlando Cepeda, St.L., 111
Roberto Clemente, Pit., 110
Hank Aaron, Atl., 109
Jim Wynn, Hou., 107
Tony Perez, Cin., 102

A.L. 40 homers
Harmon Killebrew, Min., 44
Carl Yastrzemski, Bos., 44

Most Valuable Player
A.L.: Carl Yastrzemski, OF, Bos.
N.L.: Orlando Cepeda, 1B, St.L.

Cy Young Award
A.L.: Jim Lonborg, Bos.
N.L.: Mike McCormick, S.F.

Rookie of the Year
A.L.: Rod Carew, 2B, Min.
N.L.: Tom Seaver, P, N.Y.

Hall of Fame additions
Branch Rickey, executive
Red Ruffing, P, 1924-47
Lloyd Waner, OF, 1927-45

ALL-STAR GAME

■ **Winner:** The N.L. continued its All-Star hex with a pulsating 15-inning 2-1 victory — the longest game in the classic's 35-year history.
■ **Key inning:** The 15th, when Cincinnati's Tony Perez deposited a Catfish Hunter pitch over the left-field fence, ending the N.L.'s 12-inning scoreless run.
■ **Memorable moment:** The overall performance of 12 pitchers, who gave up only 17 hits and two bases on balls while recording 30 strikeouts.
■ **Top guns:** Juan Marichal (Giants), Don Drysdale (Dodgers), Richie Allen (Phillies), Perez (Reds), N.L.; Gary Peters (White Sox), Hunter (Athletics), Carl Yastrzemski (Red Sox), Brooks Robinson (Orioles), A.L.
■ **MVP:** Perez.

Linescore

July 11, at California's Anaheim Stadium
N.L. ..0 1 0 0 0 0 0 0 0 0 0 0 0 0 1—2 9 0
A.L. ..0 0 0 0 0 1 0 0 0 0 0 0 0 0 0—1 8 0
Marichal (Giants), Jenkins (Cubs) 4, Gibson (Cardinals) 7, Short (Phillies) 9, Cuellar (Astros) 11, Drysdale (Dodgers) 13, Seaver (Mets) 15; Chance (Twins), McGlothlin (Angels) 4, Peters (White Sox) 6, Downing (Yankees) 9, Hunter (Athletics) 11. W—Drysdale. L—Hunter. HR—Allen, Perez, N.L.; Robinson, A.L.

WORLD SERIES

■ **Winner:** It took seven games for the Cardinals to ruin Boston's "impossible dream" of winning its first Series championship since 1918.
■ **Turning point:** The seventh-game heroics of Bob Gibson, who belted a home run and pitched the Cardinals to a 7-2 victory.
■ **Memorable moment:** A two-out eighth-inning double by St. Louis' Julian Javier in Game 2, ending Boston righthander Jim Lonborg's no-hit bid. Lonborg finished with a one-hit 5-0 victory.
■ **Top guns:** Gibson (3-0, 1.00 ERA), Lou Brock (.414), Roger Maris (.385, 7 RBIs), Cardinals; Lonborg (2-1), Carl Yastrzemski (.400, 3 HR, 5 RBIs), Red Sox.
■ **MVP:** Gibson.

Linescores

Game 1—October 4, at Boston
St. Louis ....0 0 1 0 0 0 1 0 0—2 10 0
Boston ....0 0 1 0 0 0 0 0 0—1 6 0
Gibson; Santiago, Wyatt (8). W—Gibson. L—Santiago. HR—Santiago (Bos.).

Game 2—October 5, at Boston
St. Louis ....0 0 0 0 0 0 0 0 0—0 1 1
Boston.......................0 0 0 1 0 1 3 0 x—5 9 0
Hughes, Willis (6), Hoerner (7), Lamabe (7); Lonborg. W—Lonborg. L—Hughes. HR—Yastrzemski 2 (Bos.).

Game 3—Ocotber 7, at St. Louis
Boston ....0 0 0 0 0 1 1 0 0—2 7 1
St. Louis ....1 2 0 0 0 1 0 1 x—5 10 0
Bell, Waslewski (3), Stange (6), Osinski (8); Briles. W—Briles. L—Bell. HR—Shannon (St.L.); Smith (Bos.).

Game 4—October 8, at St. Louis
Boston ....0 0 0 0 0 0 0 0 0—0 5 0
St. Louis ....4 0 2 0 0 0 0 0 x—6 9 0
Santiago, Bell (1), Stephenson (3), Morehead (5), Brett (8); Gibson. W—Gibson. L—Santiago.

Game 5—October 9, at St. Louis
Boston ....0 0 1 0 0 0 0 0 2—3 6 1
St. Louis ....0 0 0 0 0 0 0 0 1—1 3 2
Lonborg; Carlton, Washburn (7), Willis (9), Lamabe (9). W—Lonborg. L—Carlton. HR—Maris.

Game 6—October 11, at Boston
St. Louis ....0 0 2 0 0 0 2 0 0— 4 8 0
Boston.......................0 1 0 3 0 0 4 0 x—8 12 1
Hughes, Willis (4), Briles (5), Lamabe (7), Hoerner (7), Jaster (7), Washburn (7), Woodeshick (8); Waslewski, Wyatt (6), Bell (8). W—Wyatt. L—Lamabe. HR—Petrocelli 2, Yastrzemski, Smith (Bos.); Brock (St.L.).

Game 7—October 12, at Boston
St. Louis ....0 0 2 0 2 3 0 0 0—7 10 1
Boston ....0 0 0 0 1 0 0 1 0—2 3 1
Gibson; Lonborg, Santiago (7), Morehead (9), Osinski (9), Brett (9). W—Gibson. L—Lonborg. HR—Gibson, Javier (St.L.).

1968

FINAL STANDINGS

American League

Team	W	L	Pct.	GB
Detroit	103	59	.636	...
Baltimore	91	71	.562	12
Cleveland	86	75	.534	16.5
Boston	86	76	.531	17
New York	83	79	.512	20
Oakland	82	80	.506	21
Minnesota	79	83	.488	24
California	67	95	.414	36
Chicago	67	95	.414	36
Washington	65	96	.404	37.5

National League

Team	W	L	Pct.	GB
St. Louis	97	65	.599	...
San Francisco	88	74	.543	9
Chicago	84	78	.519	13
Cincinnati	83	79	.512	14
Atlanta	81	81	.500	16
Pittsburgh	80	82	.494	17
Los Angeles	76	86	.469	21
Philadelphia	76	86	.469	21
New York	73	89	.451	24
Houston	72	90	.444	25

SIGNIFICANT EVENTS

■ **May 27:** The N.L. crossed the Canadian border when it awarded 1969 expansion franchises to Montreal and San Diego.
■ **July 10:** A.L. and N.L. officials agreed to uniformity in their 1969 expansions: two-division formats, 162-game schedules and best-of-five League Championship Series.
■ **December 3:** The Rules Committee lowered the mound, shrunk the strike zone and cracked down on illegal pitches in an effort to increase offense.
■ **December 6:** Baseball owners forced William Eckert to resign as commissioner.

MEMORABLE MOMENTS

■ **May 8:** A's righthander Catfish Hunter fired baseball's ninth perfect game, retiring all 27 Twins he faced in a 4-0 victory at Oakland.
■ **July 30:** Washington shortstop Ron Hansen pulled off baseball's eighth unassisted triple play in the first inning of a 10-1 loss at Cleveland.
■ **September 14:** The Tigers rallied for two ninth-inning runs and defeated Oakland 5-4, allowing Denny McLain to become baseball's first 30-game winner since 1934.

LEADERS

American League
BA: Carl Yastrzemski, Bos., .301.
Runs: Dick McAuliffe, Det., 95.
Hits: Campy Campaneris, Oak., 177.
TB: Frank Howard, Wash., 330.
HR: Frank Howard, Wash., 44.
RBI: Ken Harrelson, Bos., 109.
SB: Campy Campaneris, Oak., 62.
Wins: Denny McLain, Det., 31.
ERA: Luis Tiant, Cle., 1.60.
CG: Denny McLain, Det., 28.
IP: Denny McLain, Det., 336.
SO: Sam McDowell, Cle., 283.

National League
BA: Pete Rose, Cin., .335.
Runs: Glenn Beckert, Chi., 98.
Hits: Felipe Alou, Atl.; Pete Rose, Cin., 210.
TB: Billy Williams, Chi., 321.
HR: Willie McCovey, S.F., 36.
RBI: Willie McCovey, S.F., 105.
SB: Lou Brock, St.L., 62.
Wins: Juan Marichal, S.F., 26.
ERA: Bob Gibson, St.L., 1.12.
CG: Juan Marichal, S.F., 30.
IP: Juan Marichal, S.F., 326.
SO: Bob Gibson, St.L., 268.

A.L. 20-game winners
Denny McLain, Det., 31-6
Dave McNally, Bal., 22-10
Luis Tiant, Cle., 21-9
Mel Stottlemyre, N.Y., 21-12

N.L. 20-game winners
Juan Marichal, S.F., 26-9
Bob Gibson, St.L., 22-9
Ferguson Jenkins, Chi., 20-15

A.L. 100 RBIs
Ken Harrelson, Bos., 109
Frank Howard, Wash., 106

N.L. 100 RBIs
Willie McCovey, S.F., 105

A.L. 40 homers
Frank Howard, Wash., 44

Most Valuable Player
A.L.: Denny McLain, P, Det.
N.L.: Bob Gibson, P, St.L.

Cy Young Award
A.L.: Denny McLain, Det.
N.L.: Bob Gibson, St.L.

Rookie of the Year
A.L.: Stan Bahnsen, P, N.Y.
N.L.: Johnny Bench, C, Cin.

Hall of Fame additions
Kiki Cuyler, OF, 1921-38
Goose Goslin, OF, 1921-38
Joe Medwick, OF, 1932-48

ALL-STAR GAME

■ **Winner:** The N.L. stretched its winning streak to six with the first 1-0 game in All-Star history. It also was the first played indoors and on an artificial surface.
■ **Key inning:** The first, when the N.L. scored the game's only run on a double-play grounder.
■ **Memorable moment:** The performance of a six-man N.L. staff that held the A.L. to three hits.
■ **Top guns:** Don Drysdale (Dodgers), Juan Marichal (Giants), Steve Carlton (Cardinals), Tom Seaver (Mets), Willie Mays (Giants), N.L.; Blue Moon Odom (Athletics), Denny McLain (Tigers), A.L.
■ **MVP:** Mays.

Linescore

July 9, at Houston's Astrodome
A.L. ....0 0 0 0 0 0 0 0 0—0 3 1
N.L. ....1 0 0 0 0 0 0 0 x—1 5 0
Tiant (Indians), Odom (Athletics) 3, McLain (Tigers) 5, McDowell (Indians) 7, Stottlemyre (Yankees) 8, John (White Sox) 8; Drysdale (Dodgers), Marichal (Giants) 4, Carlton (Cardinals) 6, Seaver (Mets) 7, Reed (Braves) 9, Koosman (Mets) 9. W—Drysdale. L—Tiant.

WORLD SERIES

■ **Winner:** The Tigers, down three games to one, rallied to win their first World Series since 1945.
■ **Turning point:** With the Tigers on the brink of elimination entering Game 5, lefthander Mickey Lolich pitched them to a 5-3 victory.
■ **Memorable moments:** Bob Gibson striking out 17 Tigers in Game 1. Cardinals center fielder Curt Flood misjudging Jim Northrup's seventh-game fly ball, which became a Series-deciding two-run triple.
■ **Top guns:** Lolich (3-0, 1.67 ERA), Norm Cash (.385, 5 RBIs); Al Kaline (.379, 2 HR, 8 RBIs), Tigers; Gibson (2-1, 1.67), Lou Brock (.464, 2 HR, 5 RBIs), Cardinals.
■ **MVP:** Lolich.

Linescores

Game 1—October 2, at St. Louis
Detroit.......................0 0 0 0 0 0 0 0 0—0 5 3
St. Louis ....0 0 0 3 0 0 1 0 x—4 6 0
McLain, Dobson (6), McMahon (8); Gibson. W—Gibson. L—McLain. HR—Brock (St.L.).

Game 2—October 3, at St. Louis
Detroit.......................0 1 1 0 0 3 1 0 2—8 13 1
St. Louis ....0 0 0 0 0 1 0 0 0—1 6 1
Lolich; Briles, Carlton (6), Willis (7), Hoerner (9). W—Lolich. L—Briles. HR—Horton, Lolich, Cash (Det.).

Game 3—October 5, at Detroit
St. Louis ....0 0 0 0 4 0 3 0 0—7 13 0
Detroit.......................0 0 2 0 1 0 0 0 0—3 4 0
Washburn, Hoerner (6); Wilson, Dobson (5), McMahon (6), Patterson (7), Hiller (8). W—Washburn. L—Wilson. HR—Kaline, McAuliffe (Det.); McCarver, Cepeda (St.L.).

Game 4—October 6, at Detroit
St. Louis ....2 0 2 2 0 0 0 4 0—10 13 0
Detroit....................0 0 0 1 0 0 0 0 0— 1 5 4
Gibson; McLain, Sparma (3), Patterson (4), Lasher (6), Hiller (8), Dobson (8). W—Gibson. L—McLain. HR—Brock, Gibson (St.L.); Northrup (Det.).

Game 5—October 7, at Detroit
St. Louis ....3 0 0 0 0 0 0 0 0—3 9 0
Detroit.........................0 0 0 2 0 0 3 0 x—5 9 1
Briles, Hoerner (7), Willis (7); Lolich. W—Lolich. L—Hoerner. HR—Cepeda (St.L.).

Game 6—October 9, at St. Louis
Detroit..................0 2 10 0 1 0 0 0 0—13 12 1
St. Louis ....0 0 0 0 0 0 0 0 1— 1 9 1
McLain; Washburn, Jaster (3), Willis (3), Hughes (3), Carlton (4), Granger (7), Nelson (9). W—McLain. L—Washburn. HR—Northrup, Kaline (Det.).

Game 7—October 10, at St. Louis
Detroit.......................0 0 0 0 0 0 3 0 1—4 8 1
St. Louis ....0 0 0 0 0 0 0 0 1—1 5 0
Lolich; Gibson. W—Lolich. L—Gibson. HR—Shannon (St.L.).

1969

FINAL STANDINGS

American League

East Division

Team	Bal.	Det.	Bos.	Wash.	N.Y.	Cle.	Min.	Oak.	Cal.	K.C.	Chi.	Sea.	W	L	Pct.	GB
Baltimore	...	11	10	13	11	13	8	8	6	11	9	9	109	53	.673	...
Detroit	7	...	8	7	10	11	6	7	7	8	9	10	90	72	.556	19
Boston	8	10	...	6	11	12	7	4	8	10	5	6	87	75	.537	22
Washington	5	11	12	...	8	15	6	4	7	5	8	5	86	76	.531	23
New York	7	8	7	10	...	8	2	6	9	7	9	7	80	81	.497	28.5
Cleveland	5	7	6	3	9	...	5	5	4	7	4	7	62	99	.385	46.5

West Division

Team	Min.	Oak.	Cal.	K.C.	Chi.	Sea.	Bal.	Det.	Bos.	Wash.	N.Y.	Cle.	W	L	Pct.	GB
Minnesota	...	13	11	10	13	12	4	6	5	6	10	7	97	65	.599	...
Oakland	5	...	12	10	10	13	4	5	8	8	6	7	88	74	.543	9
California	7	6	...	9	9	9	6	5	4	5	3	8	71	91	.438	26
Kansas City	8	8	9	...	10	10	1	4	2	7	5	5	69	93	.426	28
Chicago	5	8	9	8	...	10	3	3	7	4	3	8	68	94	.420	29
Seattle	6	5	9	8	8	...	3	2	6	7	5	5	64	98	.395	33

National League

East Division

Team	N.Y.	Chi.	Pit.	St.L.	Phi.	Mon.	Atl.	S.F.	Cin.	L.A.	Hou.	S.D.	W	L	Pct.	GB
New York	...	10	10	12	12	13	8	8	6	8	2	11	100	62	.617	...
Chicago	8	...	7	9	12	10	9	6	6	6	8	11	92	70	.568	8
Pittsburgh	8	11	...	9	8	13	4	5	7	4	9	10	88	74	.543	12
St. Louis	6	9	9	...	11	11	6	9	4	9	5	8	87	75	.537	13
Philadelphia	6	6	10	7	...	7	6	3	2	4	4	8	63	99	.389	37
Montreal	5	8	5	7	11	...	4	1	4	2	1	4	52	110	.321	48

West Division

Team	Atl.	S.F.	Cin.	L.A.	Hou.	S.D.	N.Y.	Chi.	Pit.	St.L	Phi.	Mon.	W	L	Pct.	GB
Atlanta	...	9	12	9	15	13	4	3	8	6	6	8	93	69	.574	...
San Fran.	9	...	8	13	8	12	4	6	7	3	9	11	90	72	.556	3
Cincinnati	6	10	...	10	9	11	6	6	5	8	10	8	89	73	.549	4
Los Angeles	9	5	8	...	12	12	4	6	8	3	8	10	85	77	.525	8
Houston	3	10	9	6	...	10	10	4	3	7	8	11	81	81	.500	12
San Diego	5	6	7	6	8	...	1	1	2	4	4	8	52	110	.321	41

SIGNIFICANT EVENTS

■ **February 4:** Bowie Kuhn, a little-known attorney, was handed a one-year term as a compromise choice to succeed William Eckert as commissioner.

■ **February 25:** Baseball owners avoided a strike by increasing player pension plan contributions and granting improvements in other important benefits.

■ **April 8:** The four expansion teams—Kansas City, Seattle, Montreal and San Diego—recorded Opening Day victories.

■ **April 14:** The first Major League game on foreign soil: Montreal defeated the Cardinals, 8-7, at Jarry Park.

■ **December 4:** Chub Feeney was named to succeed Warren Giles as N.L. president.

MEMORABLE MOMENTS

■ **April 30-May 1:** Cincinnati's Jim Maloney and Houston's Don Wilson fired back-to-back no-hitters at Crosley Field, matching the Gaylord Perry-Ray Washburn feat of 1968.

■ **September 15:** Cardinals lefty Steve Carlton struck out a record 19 batters, but the Mets won the game 4-3 on a pair of two-run homers by Ron Swoboda.

■ **September 22:** San Francisco's Willie Mays became the second batter to hit 600 home runs when he connected off Mike Corkins in a 4-2 victory over San Diego.

LEADERS

American League
BA: Rod Carew, Min., .332.
Runs: Reggie Jackson, Oak., 123.
Hits: Tony Oliva, Min., 197.
TB: Frank Howard, Wash., 340.
HR: Harmon Killebrew, Min., 49.
RBI: Harmon Killebrew, Min., 140.
SB: Tommy Harper, Sea., 73.
Wins: Denny McLain, Det., 24.
ERA: Dick Bosman, Wash., 2.19.
CG: Mel Stottlemyre, N.Y., 24.
IP: Denny McLain, Det., 325.
SO: Sam McDowell, Cle., 279.
SV: Ron Perranoski, Min., 31.

National League
BA: Pete Rose, Cin., .348.
Runs: Bobby Bonds, S.F.; Pete Rose, Cin., 120.
Hits: Matty Alou, Pit., 231.
TB: Hank Aaron, Atl., 332.
HR: Willie McCovey, S.F., 45.
RBI: Willie McCovey, S.F., 126.
SB: Lou Brock, St.L., 53.
Wins: Tom Seaver, N.Y., 25.
ERA: Juan Marichal, S.F., 2.10.
CG: Bob Gibson, St.L., 28.
IP: Gaylord Perry, S.F., 325.1.
SO: Ferguson Jenkins, Chi., 273.
SV: Fred Gladding, Hou., 29.

A.L. 20-game winners
Denny McLain, Det., 24-9
Mike Cuellar, Bal., 23-11
Jim Perry, Min., 20-6
Dave McNally, Bal., 20-7
Dave Boswell, Min., 20-12
Mel Stottlemyre, N.Y., 20-14

N.L. 20-game winners
Tom Seaver, N.Y., 25-7
Phil Niekro, Atl., 23-13
Juan Marichal, S.F., 21-11
Ferguson Jenkins, Chi., 21-15
Bill Singer, L.A., 20-12
Larry Dierker, Hou., 20-13
Bob Gibson, St.L., 20-13
Bill Hands, Chi., 20-14
Claude Osteen, L.A., 20-15

A.L. 100 RBIs
Harmon Killebrew, Min., 140
Boog Powell, Bal., 121
Reggie Jackson, Oak., 118
Sal Bando, Oak., 113
Frank Howard, Wash., 111
Carl Yastrzemski, Bos., 111
Tony Oliva, Min., 101
Frank Robinson, Bal., 100

N.L. 100 RBIs
Willie McCovey, S.F., 126
Ron Santo, Chi., 123
Tony Perez, Cin., 122
Lee May, Cin., 110
Ernie Banks, Chi., 106
Joe Torre, St.L., 101

A.L. 40 homers
Harmon Killebrew, Min., 49
Frank Howard, Wash., 48
Reggie Jackson, Oak., 47
Rico Petrocelli, Bos., 40
Carl Yastrzemski, Bos., 40

N.L. 40 homers
Willie McCovey, S.F., 45
Hank Aaron, Atl., 44

Most Valuable Player
A.L.: Harmon Killebrew, 3B, Min.
N.L.: Willie McCovey, 1B, S.F.

Cy Young Award
A.L.: Denny McLain, Det.
Mike Cuellar, Bal.
N.L.: Tom Seaver, N.Y.

Rookie of the Year
A.L.: Lou Piniella, OF, K.C.
N.L.: Ted Sizemore, 2B, L.A.

Hall of Fame additions
Roy Campanella, C, 1948-57
Stan Coveleski, P, 1912-28
Waite Hoyt, P, 1918-38
Stan Musial, OF/1B, 1941-63

ALL-STAR GAME

■ **Winner:** Willie McCovey belted a pair of home runs and Johnny Bench hit another as the N.L. stretched its winning streak to seven.

■ **Key inning:** A five-run N.L. third, fueled by the first of McCovey's two blasts. The explosion broke open a 3-1 contest.

■ **Memorable moment:** A sensational leaping catch by A.L. left fielder Carl Yastrzemski in the sixth inning, robbing Bench of another home run.

■ **Top guns:** McCovey (Giants), Bench (Reds), Cleon Jones (Mets), Felix Millan (Braves), N.L.; Frank Howard (Senators), Bill Freehan (Tigers), A.L.

■ **MVP:** McCovey.

Linescore
July 22, at Washington's RFK Stadium
N.L............1 2 5 1 0 0 0 0 0—9 11 0
A.L............0 1 1 1 0 0 0 0 0—3 6 2
Carlton (Cardinals), Gibson (Cardinals) 4, Singer (Dodgers) 5, Koosman (Mets) 7, Dierker (Astros) 8, Niekro (Braves) 9; Stottlemyre (Yankees), Odom (Athletics) 3, Knowles (Senators) 3, McLain (Tigers) 4, McNally (Orioles) 5, McDowell (Indians) 7, Culp (Red Sox) 9. W—Carlton. L—Stottlemyre. HR—McCovey 2, Bench, N.L.; Howard, Freehan, A.L.

ALCS

■ **Winner:** The Baltimore Orioles, hailed by many as the best A.L. team since the Yankee pennant-winning machines of yesteryear, swept past Minnesota in baseball's first season of League Championship Series play.

■ **Turning point:** Paul Blair's 12th-inning squeeze bunt gave the Orioles a 4-3 Game 1 victory after Boog Powell had tied the contest with a ninth-inning home run.

■ **Memorable moment:** An 11th-inning Curt Motton pinch-hit single that put the capper on a second-game, three-hit, 1-0 shutout by Orioles lefthander Dave McNally.

■ **Top guns:** McNally (1-0, 0.00 ERA), Brooks Robinson (.500), Blair (.400, 6 RBIs), Orioles; Tony Oliva (.385), Twins.

■ **MVP:** McNally.

Linescores

Game 1—October 4, at Baltimore
Minn.0 0 0 0 1 0 2 0 0 0 0 0—3 4 2
Balt. ..0 0 0 1 1 0 0 0 1 0 0 1—4 10 1
Perry, Perranoski (9); Cuellar, Richert (9), Watt (10), Lopez (12), Hall (12). W—Hall. L—Perranoski. HR—F. Robinson, Belanger, Powell (Bal.); Oliva (Min.).

Game 2—October 5, at Baltimore
Minn. ....0 0 0 0 0 0 0 0 0 0 0—0 3 1
Balt. ......0 0 0 0 0 0 0 0 0 0 1—1 8 0
Boswell, Perranoski (11); McNally. W—McNally. L—Boswell.

Game 3—October 6, at Minnesota
Balt. ....0 3 0 2 0 1 0 2 3—11 18 0
Minn. ......1 0 0 0 1 0 0 0 0— 2 10 2
Palmer; Miller, Woodson (2), Hall (4), Worthington (5), Grzenda (6), Chance (7), Perranoski (9). W—Palmer. L—Miller. HR—Blair (Bal.).

NLCS

■ **Winner:** The Mets completed their stunning pennant run by sweeping the Braves in the N.L.'s first League Championship Series.

■ **Turning point:** A five-run eighth-inning rally that produced a 9-5 Mets victory in Game 1 and set the tone for the rest of the series.

■ **Memorable moment:** Young Nolan Ryan's Game 3 heroics. Ryan took over for starter Gary Gentry in the third inning with runners on second and third, none out and the Braves leading 2-0. He pitched out of the jam and recorded the series-ending victory with seven innings of three-hit pitching.

■ **Top guns:** Art Shamsky (.538), Cleon Jones (.429), Ken Boswell (.333, 2 HR, 5 RBIs), Mets; Orlando Cepeda (.455), Hank Aaron (.357, 3 HR, 7 RBIs), Braves.

■ **MVP:** Boswell.

Linescores

Game 1—October 4, at Atlanta
New York ..0 2 0 2 0 0 0 5 0—9 10 1
Atlanta ......0 1 2 0 1 0 1 0 0—5 10 2
Seaver, Taylor (8); Niekro, Upshaw (9). W—Seaver. L—Niekro. S—Taylor. HR—Gonzalez, H. Aaron (Atl.).

Game 2—October 5, at Atlanta
New York 1 3 2 2 1 0 2 0 0—11 13 1
Atlanta ....0 0 0 1 5 0 0 0 0— 6 9 3
Koosman, Taylor (5), McGraw (7); Reed, Doyle (2), Pappas (3), Britton (6), Upshaw (6), Neibauer (9). W—Taylor. L—Reed. S—McGraw. HR—Agee, Boswell, Jones (N.Y.); H. Aaron (Atl.).

Game 3—October 6, at New York
Atlanta ......2 0 0 0 2 0 0 0 0—4 8 1
New York ..0 0 1 2 3 1 0 0 x—7 14 0
Jarvis, Stone (5), Upshaw (6); Gentry, Ryan (3). W—Ryan. L—Jarvis. HR—H. Aaron, Cepeda (Atl.); Agee, Boswell, Garrett (N.Y.).

WORLD SERIES

■ **Winner:** The Amazing Mets completed their Cinderella season with a shocking five-game victory over the powerful Orioles.

■ **Turning point:** A ninth-inning RBI single by light-hitting Al Weis that gave the Mets and Jerry Koosman a Series-evening 2-1 victory in Game 2.

■ **Memorable moments:** Tommie Agee's Game 3 performance. Center fielder Agee hit a first-inning home run and made two spectacular catches that saved five runs and preserved a 5-0 victory.

■ **Top guns:** Koosman (2-0, 2.04 ERA), Weis (.455), Donn Clendenon (.357, 3 HR, 4 RBIs), Mets.

■ **MVP:** Clendenon.

Linescores

Game 1—October 11, at Baltimore
NY...............0 0 0 0 0 0 1 0 0—1 6 1
Balt. ....1 0 0 3 0 0 0 0 x—4 6 0
Seaver, Cardwell (6), Taylor (7); Cuellar. W—Cuellar. L—Seaver. HR—Buford (Bal.).

Game 2—October 12, at Baltimore
NY...............0 0 0 1 0 0 0 0 1—2 6 0
Balt. ....0 0 0 0 0 0 1 0 0—1 2 0
Koosman, Taylor (9); McNally. W—Koosman. L—McNally. HR—Clendenon (N.Y.).

Game 3—October 14, at New York
Balt. ....0 0 0 0 0 0 0 0 0—0 4 1
NY...............1 2 0 0 0 1 0 1 x—5 6 0
Palmer, Leonhard (7); Gentry, Ryan (7). W—Gentry. L—Palmer. S—Ryan. HR—Agee, Kranepool (N.Y.).

Game 4—Ocotber 15, at New York
Balt. ....0 0 0 0 0 0 0 0 1 0—1 6 1
NY ....0 1 0 0 0 0 0 0 0 1—2 10 1
Cuellar, Watt (8), Hall (10), Richert (10); Seaver. W—Seaver. L—Hall. HR—Clendenon (N.Y.).

Game 5—October 16, at New York
Balt. ....0 0 3 0 0 0 0 0 0—3 5 2
NY...............0 0 0 0 0 2 1 2 x—5 7 0
McNally, Watt (8); Koosman. W—Koosman. L—Watt. HR—McNally, F. Robinson (Bal.); Clendenon, Weis (N.Y.).

FINAL STANDINGS

American League

East Division

Team	Bal.	N.Y.	Bos.	Det.	Cle.	Wsh.	Min.	Oak.	Cal.	K.C.	Mil.	Chi.	W	L	Pct.	GB
Baltimore	...	11	13	11	14	12	5	7	7	12	7	9	108	54	.667	...
New York	7	...	8	11	10	10	7	6	7	11	9	7	93	69	.574	15
Boston	5	10	...	9	12	12	7	7	5	7	5	8	87	75	.537	21
Detroit	7	7	9	...	11	9	4	6	6	6	8	6	79	83	.488	29
Cleveland	4	8	6	7	...	11	6	7	6	8	7	6	76	86	.469	32
Washington	6	8	6	9	7	...	6	2	5	6	7	8	70	92	.432	38

West Division

Team	Min.	Oak.	Cal.	K.C.	Mil.	Chi.	Bal.	N.Y.	Bos.	Det.	Cle.	Wsh.	W	L	Pct.	GB
Minnesota	...	13	10	13	13	12	7	5	5	8	6	6	98	64	.605	...
Oakland	5	...	10	11	10	16	5	6	5	6	5	10	89	73	.549	9
California	8	8	...	10	12	12	5	5	7	6	6	7	86	76	.531	12
Kansas City	5	7	8	...	12	11	0	1	5	6	4	6	65	97	.401	33
Milwaukee	5	8	6	6	...	11	5	3	7	4	5	5	65	97	.401	33
Chicago	6	2	6	7	7	...	3	5	4	6	6	4	56	106	.346	42

National League

East Division

Team	Pit.	Chi.	N.Y.	St.L.	Phi.	Mon.	Cin.	L.A.	S.F.	Hou.	Atl.	S.D.	W	L	Pct.	GB
Pittsburgh	...	10	12	12	14	9	4	6	4	6	6	6	89	73	.549	...
Chicago	8	...	7	7	9	13	7	6	7	7	4	9	84	78	.519	5
New York	6	11	...	12	13	8	4	5	6	6	6	6	83	79	.512	6
St. Louis	6	11	6	...	10	11	3	5	5	6	5	8	76	86	.469	13
Philadelphia	4	9	5	8	...	7	5	5	8	8	5	9	73	88	.453	15.5
Montreal	9	5	10	7	11	...	5	4	6	4	6	6	73	89	.451	16

West Division

Team	Cin.	L.A.	S.F.	Hou.	Atl.	S.D.	Pit.	Chi.	N.Y.	St.L.	Phi.	Mon.	W	L	Pct.	GB
Cincinnati	...	13	9	15	13	8	8	5	8	9	7	7	102	60	.630	...
Los Angeles	5	...	9	10	12	11	6	6	7	7	6	8	87	74	.540	14.5
San Fran.	9	9	...	8	11	13	8	5	6	7	4	6	86	76	.531	16
Houston	3	8	10	...	9	14	6	5	6	6	4	8	79	83	.488	23
Atlanta	5	6	7	9	...	9	6	8	6	7	7	6	76	86	.469	26
San Diego	10	7	5	4	9	...	6	3	6	4	3	6	63	99	.389	39

LEADERS

American League

BA: Alex Johnson, Cal., .329.
Runs: Carl Yastrzemski, Bos., 125.
Hits: Tony Oliva, Min., 204.
TB: Carl Yastrzemski, Bos., 335.
HR: Frank Howard, Wash., 44.
RBI: Frank Howard, Wash., 126.
SB: Campy Campaneris, Oak., 42.
Wins: Mike Cuellar, Bal.; Dave McNally, Bal.; Jim Perry, Min., 24.
ERA: Diego Segui, Oak., 2.56.
CG: Mike Cuellar, Bal., 21.
IP: Sam McDowell, Cle.; Jim Palmer, Bal., 305.
SO: Sam McDowell, Cle., 304.
SV: Ron Perranoski, Min., 34.

National League

BA: Rico Carty, Atl., .366.
Runs: Billy Williams, Chi., 137.
Hits: Pete Rose, Cin.; Billy Williams, Chi., 205.
TB: Billy Williams, Chi., 373.
HR: Johnny Bench, Cin., 45.
RBI: Johnny Bench, Cin., 148.
SB: Bobby Tolan, Cin., 57.
Wins: Bob Gibson, St.L.; Gaylord Perry, S.F., 23.
ERA: Tom Seaver, N.Y., 2.82.
CG: Ferguson Jenkins, Chi., 24.
IP: Gaylord Perry, S.F., 328.2.
SO: Tom Seaver, N.Y., 283.
SV: Wayne Granger, Cin., 35.

A.L. 20-game winners
Mike Cuellar, Bal., 24-8
Dave McNally, Bal., 24-9
Jim Perry, Min., 24-12
Clyde Wright, Cal., 22-12
Jim Palmer, Bal., 20-10
Fred Peterson, N.Y., 20-11
Sam McDowell, Cle., 20-12

N.L. 20-game winners
Bob Gibson, St.L., 23-7
Gaylord Perry, S.F., 23-13
Ferguson Jenkins, Chi., 22-16
Jim Merritt, Cin., 20-12

A.L. 100 RBIs
Frank Howard, Wash., 126
Tony Conigliaro, Bos., 116
Boog Powell, Bal., 114
Harmon Killebrew, Min., 113
Tony Oliva, Min., 107
Rico Petrocelli, Bos., 103
Carl Yastrzemski, Bos., 102

N.L. 100 RBIs
Johnny Bench, Cin., 148
Tony Perez, Cin., 129
Billy Williams, Chi., 129
Willie McCovey, S.F., 126
Hank Aaron, Atl., 118
Jim Hickman, Chi., 115
Ron Santo, Chi., 114
Orlando Cepeda, Atl., 111
Wes Parker, L.A., 111
Dick Dietz, S.F., 107
Dick Allen, St.L., 101
Rico Carty, Atl., 101
Joe Torre, St.L., 100

A.L. 40 homers
Frank Howard, Wash., 44
Harmon Killebrew, Min., 41
Carl Yastrzemski, Bos., 40

N.L. 40 homers
Johnny Bench, Cin., 45
Billy Williams, Chi., 42
Tony Perez, Cin., 40

Most Valuable Player
A.L.: Boog Powell, 1B, Bal.
N.L.: Johnny Bench, C, Cin.

Cy Young Award
A.L.: Jim Perry, Min.
N.L.: Bob Gibson, St.L.

Rookie of the Year
A.L.: Thurman Munson, C, N.Y.
N.L.: Carl Morton, P, Mon.

Hall of Fame additions
Lou Boudreau, SS, 1938-52
Earle Combs, OF, 1924-35
Ford Frick, exec./commissioner
Jesse Haines, P, 1918-37

SIGNIFICANT EVENTS

■ **January 16:** Outfielder Curt Flood, who refused to report to Philadelphia after being traded by the Cardinals, filed a federal lawsuit challenging baseball's reserve clause.

■ **March 28:** Commissioner Bowie Kuhn returned the All-Star selection to the fans, with voting to be done on punch cards and processed by computer.

■ **March 31:** The financially strapped Pilots ended their one-year Seattle existence when the team was sold and moved to Milwaukee.

■ **June 30, July 16:** The Reds lost in their Riverfront Stadium debut to Atlanta, 8-2, but spoiled the Pirates' Three Rivers Stadium inaugural, 3-2.

■ **September 3:** Exhausted Cubs star Billy Williams ended his N.L.-record ironman streak at 1,117 games.

■ **October 4:** Umpires ended their unprecedented one-day strike when they accepted a four-year contract and returned to work for the second games of the League Championship Series.

MEMORABLE MOMENTS

■ **April 22:** Mets righthander Tom Seaver tied the Major League record when he struck out 19 Padres, including a record 10 in succession, during a 2-1 victory at Shea Stadium.

■ **May 10:** Atlanta knuckleballer Hoyt Wilhelm became the first pitcher to appear in 1,000 Major League games.

■ **May 12:** Cubs shortstop Ernie Banks hit his 500th career home run off Atlanta's Pat Jarvis in a 4-3 victory at Wrigley Field.

■ **May 17, July 18:** Two new members of baseball's 3,000-hit club: Atlanta's Hank Aaron and San Francisco's Willie Mays.

■ **June 21:** Detroit's Cesar Gutierrez performed a 20th Century first when he collected seven hits (six singles and a double) in a 12-inning 9-8 victory over Cleveland.

■ **June 26:** Baltimore's Frank Robinson belted a record-tying two grand slams in the Orioles' 12-2 victory over the Senators.

■ **October 1:** California's Alex Johnson collected two final-day hits and edged Boston's Carl Yastrzemski, .3289 to .3286, in the tightest A.L. batting race since 1946.

ALL-STAR GAME

■ **Winner:** Chicago's Jim Hickman singled home Pete Rose in the 12th inning, giving the N.L. a come-from-behind victory that pushed its All-Star winning streak to eight games.
■ **Key inning:** The bottom of the ninth, when a Dick Dietz home run, an RBI single by Willie McCovey and Roberto Clemente's sacrifice fly brought the N.L. back from a 4-1 deficit and forced extra innings.
■ **Memorable moment:** A game-ending collision between Rose and A.L. catcher Ray Fosse. Rose, playing before his home fans, jarred the ball free and sent Fosse sprawling with a nasty body block.
■ **Top guns:** Tom Seaver (Mets), Bud Harrelson (Mets), Dietz (Giants), McCovey (Giants), Rose (Reds), Hickman (Cubs), N.L.; Jim Palmer (Orioles), Sam McDowell (Indians), Carl Yastrzemski (Red Sox), Brooks Robinson (Orioles), A.L.
■ **MVP:** Yastrzemski

Linescore
July 14, at Cincinnati's Riverfront Stadium
A.L...0 0 0 0 0 1 1 2 0 0 0 0—4 12 0
N.L. 0 0 0 0 0 0 1 0 3 0 0 1—5 10 0
Palmer (Orioles), McDowell (Indians) 4, J. Perry (Twins) 7, Hunter (Athletics) 9, Peterson (Yankees) 9, Stottlemyre (Yankees) 9, Wright (Angels) 11; Seaver (Mets), Merritt (Reds) 4, G. Perry (Giants) 6, Gibson (Cardinals) 8, Osteen (Dodgers) 10. W—Osteen. L—Wright. HR—Dietz, N.L.

ALCS

■ **Winner:** Powerful Baltimore made it two straight over the Twins, who were outscored by an average of almost six runs per game.
■ **Turning point:** The fourth inning of Game 1. The Orioles scored seven times and broke the only tie the Twins could manage in the entire series.
■ **Memorable moment:** A fourth-inning Game 1 grand slam homer by light-hitting pitcher Mike Cuellar. He pulled the pitch down the right-field line, clearly foul, but a gusty wind brought the ball back inside the foul pole.
■ **Top guns:** Jim Palmer (1-0, 1.00 ERA), Brooks Robinson (.583), Boog Powell (.429, 6 RBIs), Don Buford (.429), Orioles; Tony Oliva (.500), Twins.
■ **MVP:** Powell.

Linescores
Game 1—October 3, at Minnesota
Balt. ....0 2 0 7 0 1 0 0 0—10 13 0
Minn. ......1 1 0 1 3 0 0 0 0— 6 11 2
Cuellar, Hall (5); Perry, Zepp (4), Woodson (5), Williams (6), Perranoski (9). W—Hall. L—Perry. HR—Cuellar, Buford, Powell (Bal.); Killebrew (Min.).

Game 2—October 4, at Minnesota
Balt. ....1 0 2 1 0 0 0 0 7—11 13 0
Minn. ......0 0 0 3 0 0 0 0 0— 3 6 2
McNally; Hall, Zepp (4), Williams (5), Perranoski (8), Tiant (9). W—McNally. L—Hall. HR—F. Robinson, Johnson (Bal.); Killebrew, Oliva (Min.).

Game 3—October 5, at Baltimore
Minn. ....0 0 0 0 1 0 0 0 0—1 7 2
Balt. ....1 1 3 0 0 0 1 0 x—6 10 0
Kaat, Blyleven (3), Hall (5), Perry (7); Palmer. W—Palmer. L—Kaat. HR—Johnson (Bal.).

NLCS

■ **Winner:** Power-packed Cincinnati's sweep of Pittsburgh was orchestrated by an oft-maligned pitching staff that recorded a 0.96 series ERA.
■ **Turning point:** Don Gullett's 3⅓ innings of hitless relief in Game 2. He secured a 3-1 Cincinnati victory and struck out the side in an impressive seventh inning.
■ **Memorable moment:** Back-to-back Game 3 homers by Tony Perez and Johnny Bench — the Reds' only power display of the series.
■ **Top guns:** Gary Nolan (1-0, 0-00 ERA), Bobby Tolan (.417), Reds; Richie Hebner (.667), Willie Stargell (.500), Pirates.
■ **MVP:** Reds' pitching staff (0.96 ERA).

Linescores
Game 1—October 3, at Pittsburgh
Cin. ....0 0 0 0 0 0 0 0 0 3—3 9 0
Pitt. ....0 0 0 0 0 0 0 0 0 0—0 8 0
Nolan, Carroll (10); Ellis, Gibbon (10). W—Nolan. L—Ellis S—Carroll.

Game 2—October 4, at Pittsburgh
Cincinnati ....0 0 1 0 1 0 0 1 0—3 8 1
Pittsburgh....0 0 0 0 0 1 0 0 0—1 5 2
Merritt, Carroll (6), Gullett (6); Walker, Giusti (8). W—Merritt. L—Walker. HR—Tolan (Cin.).

Game 3—October 5, at Cincinnati
Pittsburgh..1 0 0 0 1 0 0 0 0—2 10 0
Cincinnati ..2 0 0 0 0 0 0 1 x—3 5 0
Moose, Gibbon (8), Giusti (8); Cloninger, Wilcox (6), Granger (9), Gullett (9). W—Wilcox. L—Moose. S—Gullett. HR—Perez, Bench (Cin.).

WORLD SERIES

■ **Winner:** The Orioles, still reeling from their five-game 1969 loss to the Mets, turned the tables on the young Reds.
■ **Turning point:** Game 1. The Orioles, down 3-0 in the first Series game at new Riverfront Stadium, rallied on home runs by Boog Powell, Brooks Robinson and Elrod Hendricks for a 4-3 victory.
■ **Memorable moments:** The incredible fielding artistry of Orioles third baseman Brooks Robinson, who constantly foiled the Reds with big plays, and Baltimore pitcher Dave McNally's third-game grand slam.
■ **Top guns:** Brooks Robinson (.429, 6 RBIs), Paul Blair (.474), Orioles; Hal McRae (.455), Lee May (.389, 2 HR, 8 RBIs), Reds.
■ **MVP:** Brooks Robinson.

Linescores
Game 1—October 10, at Cincinnati
Balt. ....0 0 0 2 1 0 1 0 0—4 7 2
Cin. ....1 0 2 0 0 0 0 0 0—3 5 0
Palmer, Richert (9); Nolan, Carroll (7). W—Palmer. L—Nolan. S—Richert. HR—May (Cin.); Powell, Hendricks, B. Robinson (Bal.).

Game 2—October 11, at Cincinnati
Balt. ....0 0 0 1 5 0 0 0 0—6 10 2
Cin. ....3 0 1 0 0 1 0 0 0—5 7 0
Cuellar, Phoebus (3), Drabowsky (5), Lopez (7), Hall (7); McGlothlin, Wilcox (5), Carroll (5), Gullett (8). W—Phoebus. L—Wilcox. S—Hall. HR—Tolan, Bench (Cin.); Powell (Bal.).

Game 3—October 13, at Baltimore
Cin. ....0 1 0 0 0 0 2 0 0—3 9 0
Balt. ....2 0 1 0 1 4 1 0 x—9 10 1
Cloninger, Granger (6), Gullett (7); McNally. W—McNally. L—Cloninger. HR—F. Robinson, Buford, McNally (Bal.).

Game 4—October 14, at Baltimore
Cin. ....0 1 1 0 1 0 0 3 0—6 8 3
Balt. ....0 1 3 0 0 1 0 0 0—5 8 0
Nolan, Gullett (3), Carroll (6); Palmer, Watt (8), Drabowsky (9). W—Carroll. L—Watt. HR—B. Robinson (Bal.); Rose, May (Cin.).

Game 5—October 15, at Baltimore
Cin. ....3 0 0 0 0 0 0 0 0—3 6 0
Balt. ....2 2 2 0 1 0 0 2 x—9 15 0
Merritt, Granger (2), Wilcox (3), Cloninger (5), Washburn (7), Carroll (8); Cuellar. W—Cuellar. L—Merritt. HR—F. Robinson, Rettenmund (Bal.).

FINAL STANDINGS

American League

East Division

Team	Bal.	Det.	Bos.	N.Y.	Wash.	Cle.	Oak.	K.C.	Chi.	Cal.	Min.	Mil.	W	L	Pct.	GB
Baltimore	...	8	9	11	13	13	7	6	8	7	10	9	101	57	.639	—
Detroit	10	...	6	10	14	12	4	8	5	6	6	10	91	71	.562	12
Boston	9	12	...	7	12	11	3	1	10	6	8	6	85	77	.525	18
New York	7	8	11	...	7	10	5	7	7	6	4	10	82	80	.506	21
Washington	3	4	6	11	...	11	3	3	2	8	6	6	63	96	.396	38.5
Cleveland	5	6	7	8	7	...	4	2	9	4	4	4	60	102	.370	43

West Division

Team	Oak.	K.C.	Chi.	Cal.	Min.	Mil.	Bal.	Det.	Bos.	N.Y.	Wash.	Cle.	W	L	Pct.	GB
Oakland	...	13	7	11	10	15	4	8	9	7	9	8	101	60	.627	—
Kansas City	5	...	9	10	9	8	5	4	11	5	9	10	85	76	.528	16
Chicago	11	9	...	10	7	11	4	7	2	5	10	3	79	83	.488	22.5
California	7	8	8	...	12	6	5	6	6	6	4	7	76	86	.469	25.5
Minnesota	8	9	11	6	...	7	2	6	4	8	5	8	74	86	.463	26.5
Milwaukee	3	10	7	12	10	...	3	2	6	2	6	8	69	92	.429	32

National League

East Division

Team	Pit.	St.L.	Chi.	N.Y.	Mon.	Phi.	S.F.	L.A.	Atl.	Cin.	Hou.	S.D.	W	L	Pct.	GB
Pittsburgh	...	11	12	8	11	12	3	6	8	7	8	9	97	65	.599	—
St. Louis	7	...	9	8	14	11	7	6	4	10	8	9	90	72	.556	7
Chicago	6	9	...	11	8	13	4	5	8	7	5	7	83	79	.512	14
New York	10	10	7	...	9	13	4	7	5	4	7	7	83	79	.512	14
Montreal	7	4	10	9	...	7	4	3	5	6	7	9	71	90	.441	25.5
Philadelphia	6	7	7	5	12	...	6	5	4	7	4	6	67	95	.414	30

West Division

Team	S.F.	L.A.	Atl.	Cin.	Hou.	S.D.	Pit.	St.L.	Chi.	N.Y.	Mon.	Phi.	W	L	Pct.	GB
San Fran.	...	6	11	9	13	9	3	5	8	8	5	6	90	72	.556	—
L.A.	12	...	9	11	10	13	4	6	4	5	8	7	89	73	.549	1
Atlanta	7	9	...	9	9	11	4	6	5	7	7	8	82	80	.506	8
Cincinnati	9	7	9	...	5	10	5	8	6	8	7	5	79	83	.488	11
Houston	9	8	9	13	...	10	4	2	7	5	4	9	79	83	.488	11
San Diego	5	5	7	8	8	...	4	3	5	5	8	7	61	100	.379	28.5

SIGNIFICANT EVENTS

■ **April 10:** The Phillies made their Veterans Stadium debut a successful one, defeating Montreal, 4-1.

■ **May 6:** Commissioner Bowie Kuhn closed a deal with NBC-TV that would net the 24 teams $72 million over four years.

■ **September 21:** Baseball ended its 71-year association with the nation's capital when owners approved the Senators' transfer to the Dallas-Fort Worth area.

MEMORABLE MOMENTS

■ **April 27:** The 600-homer club welcomed its third member when Atlanta's Hank Aaron connected off Gaylord Perry in a 10-inning 6-5 loss to the Giants.

■ **June 23:** Philadelphia's Rick Wise pitched a no-hitter and spiced his 4-0 victory over Cincinnati with two home runs.

■ **August 10, September 13:** Minnesota's Harmon Killebrew and Baltimore's Frank Robinson became the 10th and 11th players to hit 500 career home runs.

■ **September 26:** When Jim Palmer blanked Cleveland 5-0 for his 20th victory, the Orioles joined the 1920 White Sox as the only teams to boast four 20-game winners in one season. Palmer joined Dave McNally, Mike Cuellar and Pat Dobson in the select circle.

■ **September 30:** The Senators had to forfeit their final game in Washington to the Yankees when fans swarmed out of the stands in the ninth inning and began tearing up RFK Stadium.

LEADERS

American League
BA: Tony Oliva, Min., .337.
Runs: Don Buford, Bal., 99.
Hits: Cesar Tovar, Min., 204.
TB: Reggie Smith, Bos., 302.
HR: Bill Melton, Chi., 33.
RBI: Harmon Killebrew, Min., 119.
SB: Amos Otis, K.C., 52.
Wins: Mickey Lolich, Det., 25.
ERA: Vida Blue, Oak., 1.82.
CG: Mickey Lolich, Det., 29.
IP: Mickey Lolich, Det., 376.
SO: Mickey Lolich, Det., 308.
SV: Ken Sanders, Mil., 31.

National League
BA: Joe Torre, St.L., .363.
Runs: Lou Brock, St.L., 126.
Hits: Joe Torre, St.L., 230.
TB: Joe Torre, St.L., 352.
HR: Willie Stargell, Pit., 48.
RBI: Joe Torre, St.L., 137.
SB: Lou Brock, St.L., 64.
Wins: Ferguson Jenkins, Chi., 24.
ERA: Tom Seaver, N.Y., 1.76.
CG: Ferguson Jenkins, Chi., 30.
IP: Ferguson Jenkins, Chi., 325.
SO: Tom Seaver, N.Y., 289.
SV: Dave Giusti, Pit., 30.

A.L. 20-game winners
Mickey Lolich, Det., 25-14
Vida Blue, Oak., 24-8
Wilbur Wood, Chi., 22-13
Dave McNally, Bal., 21-5
Catfish Hunter, Oak., 21-11
Pat Dobson, Bal., 20-8
Jim Palmer, Bal., 20-9
Mike Cuellar, Bal., 20-9
Joe Coleman, Det., 20-9
Andy Messersmith, Cal., 20-13

N.L. 20-game winners
Ferguson Jenkins, Chi., 24-13
Al Downing, L.A., 20-9
Steve Carlton, St.L., 20-9
Tom Seaver, N.Y., 20-10

A.L. 100 RBIs
Harmon Killebrew, Min., 119

N.L. 100 RBIs
Joe Torre, St.L., 137
Willie Stargell, Pit., 125
Hank Aaron, Mil., 118
Bobby Bonds, S.F., 102

N.L. 40 homers
Willie Stargell, Pit., 48
Hank Aaron, Atl., 47

Most Valuable Player
A.L.: Vida Blue, P, Oak.
N.L.: Joe Torre, 3B, St.L.

Cy Young Award
A.L.: Vida Blue, Oak.
N.L.: Ferguson Jenkins, Chi.

Rookie of the Year
A.L.: Chris Chambliss, 1B, Cle.
N.L.: Earl Williams, C, Atl.

Hall of Fame additions
Dave Bancroft, SS, 1915-30
Jake Beckley, 1B, 1888-1907
Chick Hafey, OF, 1924-37
Harry Hooper, OF, 1909-25
Joe Kelley, OF, 1891-1908
Rube Marquard, P, 1908-25
Satchel Paige, P, 1948-65
George Weiss, executive

ALL-STAR GAME

■ **Winner:** The A.L. ended its eight-year All-Star drought with a three-homer barrage that produced a 6-4 victory.

■ **Key inning:** After falling behind 3-0 on Johnny Bench and Hank Aaron home runs, the A.L. struck for four third-inning runs on two-run homers by Reggie Jackson and Frank Robinson.

■ **Memorable moment:** The titanic third-inning blast by Jackson, which struck a light tower on the roof of Tiger Stadium, 520 feet from home plate in right-center field.

■ **Top guns:** Jackson (Athletics), F. Robinson (Orioles), Harmon Killebrew (Twins), A.L.; Bench (Reds), Aaron (Braves), Roberto Clemente (Pirates), N.L.

■ **MVP:** F. Robinson.

Linescore
July 13, at Detroit's Tiger Stadium
N.L. ....0 2 1 0 0 0 0 1 0—4 5 0
A.L. ....0 0 4 0 0 2 0 0 x—6 7 0
Ellis (Pirates), Marichal (Giants) 4, Jenkins (Cubs) 4, Wilson (Astros) 7; Blue (Athletics), Palmer (Orioles) 4, Cuellar (Orioles) 6, Lolich (Tigers) 8. W—Blue. L—Ellis. HR—Bench, Aaron, Clemente, N.L.; Jackson, F. Robinson, Killebrew, A.L.

ALCS

■ **Winner:** The Orioles recorded their third consecutive Championship Series sweep, turning aside the up-and-coming Oakland Athletics.

■ **Turning point:** A four-run seventh-inning Game 1 rally that wiped out a 3-1 deficit and marked the last time Baltimore trailed in the series.

■ **Memorable moments:** A four-homer Game 2 salvo and Mike Cuellar's six-hit pitching added up to a 5-1 Orioles' victory.

■ **Top guns:** Cuellar (1-0, 1.00 ERA), Brooks Robinson (.364, 3 RBIs), Boog Powell (2 HR, 3 RBIs), Orioles; Sal Bando (.364), Reggie Jackson (.333, 2 HR), Athletics.

■ **MVP:** Cuellar.

Linescores
Game 1—October 3, at Baltimore
Oakland........0 2 0 1 0 0 0 0 0—3 9 0
Baltimore ....0 0 0 1 0 0 4 0 x—5 7 1
Blue, Fingers (8); McNally, Watt (8).
W—McNally. L—Blue. S—Watt.

Game 2—October 4, at Baltimore
Oakland........0 0 0 1 0 0 0 0 0—1 6 0
Baltimore ....0 1 1 0 0 0 1 2 x—5 7 0
Hunter; Cuellar. W—Cuellar. L—Hunter.
HR—B. Robinson, Powell 2, Hendricks (Bal.).

Game 3—October 5, at Oakland
Baltimore ..1 0 0 0 2 0 2 0 0—5 12 0
Oakland........0 0 1 0 0 1 0 1 0—3 7 0
Palmer; Segui, Fingers (5), Knowles (7), Locker (7), Grant (8). W—Palmer. L—Segui. HR—Jackson 2, Bando (Oak.).

NLCS

■ **Winner:** Pittsburgh defeated San Francisco to claim its first pennant since 1960. The Pirates needed four games to win the first LCS not decided by a sweep.

■ **Turning point:** Richie Hebner's eighth-inning Game 3 home run, which gave substitute starter Bob Johnson a 2-1 victory and the Pirates a 2-1 series edge.

■ **Memorable moment:** Pittsburgh first baseman Bob Robertson's ninth-inning Game 2 home run — his record-setting third of the game — capping a 9-4 Pirates victory.

■ **Top guns:** Robertson (.438, 4 HR, 6 RBIs), Dave Cash (.421), Hebner (2 HR, 4 RBIs), Pirates; Willie McCovey (.429, 2 HR, 6 RBIs), Chris Speier (.357), Giants.

■ **MVP:** Robertson.

Linescores
Game 1—October 2, at San Francisco
Pitt. ....0 0 2 0 0 0 2 0 0—4 9 0
San Fran.......0 0 1 0 4 0 0 0 x—5 7 2
Blass, Moose (6), Giusti (8); Perry. W—Perry. L—Blass. HR—Fuentes, McCovey (S.F.).

WORLD SERIES

■ **Winner:** The Pirates, absent from Series competition for a decade, rebounded after losing the first two games.

■ **Turning point:** After Pittsburgh starter Luke Walker surrendered three first-inning runs in Game 4, Bruce Kison and Dave Giusti pitched 8½ scoreless innings and the Pirates rallied for a 4-3 victory.

■ **Memorable moments:** The Game 7 performances of Roberto Clemente, who homered, and Steve Blass, who shut down the Orioles 2-1 on a gritty four-hitter.

■ **Top guns:** Blass (2-0, 1.00 ERA), Clemente (.414, 12 hits, 2 HR, 4 RBIs), Manny Sanguillen (.379), Pirates; Dave McNally (2-1, 1.98), Orioles.

■ **MVP:** Clemente.

Linescores
Game 1—October 9, at Baltimore
Pitt. ....0 3 0 0 0 0 0 0 0—3 3 0
Balt. ....0 1 3 0 1 0 0 x—5 10 3
Ellis, Moose (3), Miller (7); McNally.
W—McNally. L—Ellis. HR—F. Robinson, Rettenmund, Buford (Bal.).

Game 2—October 11, at Baltimore
Pitt. ....0 0 0 0 0 0 0 3 0—3 8 1
Balt. ....0 1 0 3 6 1 0 0 x—11 14 1
R. Johnson, Moose (4), Miller (6), Giusti (8); Palmer, Hall (9).
W—Palmer. L—R. Johnson. S—Hall.
HR—Hebner (Pit.).

Game 3—October 12, at Pittsburgh
Balt. ....0 0 0 0 0 0 1 0 0—1 3 3
Pitt. ....1 0 0 0 0 1 3 0 x—5 7 0
Cuellar, Dukes (7), Watt (8); Blass. W—Blass. L—Cuellar. HR—F. Robinson (Bal.); Robertson (Pit.).

Game 4—October 13, at Pittsburgh
Balt. ....3 0 0 0 0 0 0 0 0—3 4 1
Pitt. ....2 0 1 0 0 0 1 0 x—4 14 0
Dobson, Jackson (6), Watt (7), Richert (8); Walker, Kison (1), Giusti (8). W—Kison.
L—Watt. S—Giusti.

Game 5—October 14, at Pittsburgh
Balt. ....0 0 0 0 0 0 0 0 0—0 2 1
Pitt. ....0 2 1 0 1 0 0 0 x—4 9 0
McNally, Leonhard (5), Dukes (6); Briles.
W—Briles. L—McNally. HR—Robertson (Pit.).

Game 6—October 16, at Baltimore
Pitt. ....0 1 1 0 0 0 0 0 0—2 9 1
Balt. ....0 0 0 0 0 1 1 0 0 1—3 8 0
Moose, R. Johnson (6), Giusti (10), Miller (10); Palmer, Dobson (10), McNally (10).
W—McNally. L—Miller. HR—Clemente (Pit.); Buford (Bal.).

Game 7—October 17, at Baltimore
Pitt. ....0 0 0 1 0 0 0 1 0—2 6 1
Balt. ....0 0 0 0 0 0 1 0 0—1 4 0
Blass; Cuellar, Dobson (9), McNally (9).
W—Blass. L—Cuellar. HR—Clemente (Pit.).

FINAL STANDINGS

American League

East Division

Team	Det.	Bos.	Bal.	N.Y.	Cle.	Mil.	Oak.	Chi.	Min.	K.C.	Cal.	Tex.	W	L	Pct.	GB
Detroit	...	9	8	7	8	10	4	7	9	7	7	10	86	70	.551	...
Boston	5	...	11	9	8	11	9	6	4	6	8	8	85	70	.548	.5
Baltimore	10	7	...	7	8	10	6	8	6	6	6	6	80	74	.519	5
New York	9	9	6	...	11	9	3	5	6	5	8	8	79	76	.510	6.5
Cleveland	10	7	10	7	...	5	2	4	8	6	4	9	72	84	.462	14
Milwaukee	8	7	5	9	10	...	4	3	4	5	5	5	65	91	.417	21

West Division

Team	Oak.	Chi.	Min.	K.C.	Cal.	Tex.	Det.	Bos.	Bal.	N.Y.	Cle.	Mil	W	L	Pct.	GB
Oakland	...	8	9	11	10	11	8	3	6	9	10	8	93	62	.600	...
Chicago	7	...	8	8	11	14	5	6	4	7	8	9	87	67	.565	5.5
Minnesota	8	6	...	9	8	11	3	8	6	6	4	8	77	77	.500	15.5
Kansas City	7	9	9	...	6	8	5	6	6	7	6	7	76	78	.494	16.5
California	8	7	7	9	...	10	5	4	6	4	8	7	75	80	.484	18
Texas	4	4	7	6	7	...	2	4	6	4	3	7	54	100	.351	38.5

National League

East Division

Team	Pit.	Chi.	N.Y.	St.L.	Mon.	Phi.	Cin.	Hou.	L.A.	Atl.	S.F.	S.D.	W	L	Pct.	GB
Pittsburgh	...	12	6	10	12	13	4	9	5	6	9	10	96	59	.619	...
Chicago	3	...	10	10	10	10	8	3	8	7	7	9	85	70	.548	11
New York	8	8	...	7	12	13	4	6	5	5	8	7	83	73	.532	13.5
St. Louis	8	8	9	...	8	7	2	8	4	6	7	8	75	81	.481	21.5
Montreal	6	5	6	9	...	10	4	4	6	8	6	6	70	86	.449	26.5
Philadelphia	5	7	5	8	6	...	2	3	5	6	6	6	59	97	.378	37.5

West Division

Team	Cin.	Hou.	L.A.	Atl.	S.F.	S.D.	Pit.	Chi.	N.Y.	St.L.	Mon.	Phi.	W	L	Pct.	GB
Cincinnati	...	11	9	9	10	8	8	4	8	10	8	10	95	59	.617	...
Houston	6	...	7	7	13	12	3	9	6	4	8	9	84	69	.549	10.5
Los Angeles	5	11	...	8	9	13	7	4	7	8	6	7	85	70	.548	10.5
Atlanta	9	7	7	...	7	6	6	5	7	6	4	6	70	84	.455	25
San Fran.	5	5	9	11	...	10	3	5	4	5	6	6	69	86	.445	26.5
San Diego	10	2	5	11	4	...	2	3	5	4	6	6	58	95	.379	36.5

SIGNIFICANT EVENTS

■ **April 2:** Gil Hodges, completing spring training preparations for his fifth season as Mets manager, died from a heart attack at West Palm Beach, Fla., at age 47.

■ **April 13:** The first players' strike in baseball history was settled after 13 days and 86 cancelled games.

■ **April 21:** The Rangers celebrated their Texas debut with a 7-6 victory over California at Arlington Stadium.

■ **June 19:** The U.S. Supreme Court upheld baseball's antitrust exemption and ended Curt Flood's long, frustrating challenge to the sport's reserve clause.

■ **November 2:** Steve Carlton, who posted 27 of the last-place Phillies' 59 victories, captured the N.L. Cy Young Award.

■ **December 31:** Pirates outfielder Roberto Clemente, the newest member of baseball's 3,000-hit club, died when a cargo plane carrying supplies to Nicaraguan earthquake victims crashed near San Juan, Puerto Rico.

MEMORABLE MOMENTS

■ **May 14:** Willie Mays, returning to New York after more than 14 seasons in San Francisco, belted a game-winning solo home run against the Giants in his first game with the Mets.

■ **June 10:** Atlanta's Hank Aaron hit his N.L. record-tying 14th grand slam in a 15-3 victory over the Phillies and moved into second place on the all-time home run list.

■ **August 1:** San Diego's Nate Colbert belted a record-tying five homers and drove in a doubleheader-record 13 runs in a 9-0 and 11-7 sweep of the Braves.

LEADERS

American League
BA: Rod Carew, Min., .318.
Runs: Bobby Murcer, N.Y., 102.
Hits: Joe Rudi, Oak., 181.
TB: Bobby Murcer, N.Y., 314.
HR: Dick Allen, Chi., 37.
RBI: Dick Allen, Chi., 113.
SB: Campy Campaneris, Oak., 52.
Wins: Gaylord Perry, Cle.; Wilbur Wood, Chi., 24.
ERA: Luis Tiant, Bos., 1.91.
CG: Gaylord Perry, Cle., 29.
IP: Wilbur Wood, Chi., 376.2.
SO: Nolan Ryan, Cal., 329.
SV: Sparky Lyle, N.Y., 35.

National League
BA: Billy Williams, Chi., .333.
Runs: Joe Morgan, Cin., 122.
Hits: Pete Rose, Cin., 198.
TB: Billy Williams, Chi., 348.
HR: Johnny Bench, Cin., 40.
RBI: Johnny Bench, Cin., 125.
SB: Lou Brock, St.L., 63.
Wins: Steve Carlton, Phil., 27.
ERA: Steve Carlton, Phil., 1.97.
CG: Steve Carlton, Phil., 30.
IP: Steve Carlton, Phil., 346.1.
SO: Steve Carlton, Phil., 310.
SV: Clay Carroll, Cin., 37.

A.L. 20-game winners
Gaylord Perry, Cle., 24-16
Wilbur Wood, Chi., 24-17
Mickey Lolich, Det., 22-14
Catfish Hunter, Oak., 21-7
Jim Palmer, Bal., 21-10
Stan Bahnsen, Chi., 21-16

N.L. 20-game winners
Steve Carlton, Phil., 27-10
Tom Seaver, N.Y., 21-12
Claude Osteen, L.A., 20-11
Ferguson Jenkins, Chi., 20-12

A.L. 100 RBIs
Dick Allen, Chi., 113
John Mayberry, K.C., 100

N.L. 100 RBIs
Johnny Bench, Cin., 125
Billy Williams, Chi., 122
Willie Stargell, Pit., 112
Nate Colbert, S.D., 111

N.L. 40 homers
Johnny Bench, Cin., 40

Most Valuable Player
A.L.: Dick Allen, 1B, Chi.
N.L.: Johnny Bench, C, Cin.

Cy Young Award
A.L.: Gaylord Perry, Cle.
N.L.: Steve Carlton, Phil.

Rookie of the Year
A.L.: Carlton Fisk, C, Bos.
N.L.: Jon Matlack, P, N.Y.

Hall of Fame additions
Yogi Berra, C, 1946-65
Josh Gibson, C, Negro Leagues
Lefty Gomez, P, 1930-43
Will Harridge, executive
Sandy Koufax, P, 1955-66
Buck Leonard, 1B, Negro Leagues
Early Wynn, P, 1939-63
Ross Youngs, OF, 1917-26

ALL-STAR GAME

■ **Winner:** Joe Morgan's 10th-inning single capped another N.L. comeback that produced a 4-3 victory — the senior circuit's seventh consecutive extra-inning All-Star decision.
■ **Key inning:** The ninth, when the N.L. tied the game 3-3 on a pair of singles and Lee May's ground-ball out.
■ **Memorable moment:** Hank Aaron, who entered the game with 659 career home runs, sent the Atlanta crowd into a frenzy when he hit a two-run shot in the sixth inning.
■ **Top guns:** Tug McGraw (Mets), Aaron (Braves), Morgan (Reds), N.L.; Jim Palmer (Orioles), Cookie Rojas (Royals), Rod Carew (Twins), A.L.
■ **MVP:** Morgan.

Linescore
July 25, at Atlanta Stadium
A.L. ....0 0 1 0 0 0 0 2 0 0—3 6 0
N.L. ....0 0 0 0 0 2 0 0 1 1—4 8 0
Palmer (Orioles), Lolich (Tigers) 4, Perry (Indians) 6, Wood (White Sox) 8, McNally (Orioles) 10; Gibson (Cardinals), Blass (Pirates) 3, Sutton (Dodgers) 4, Carlton (Phillies) 6, Stoneman (Expos) 7, McGraw (Mets) 9. W—McGraw. L—McNally. HR—Aaron, N.L.; Rojas, A.L.

ALCS

■ **Winner:** The Athletics claimed their first pennant in 41 years and first since moving to Oakland. The A's victory over Detroit marked the first ALCS to go beyond three games.
■ **Turning point:** The Game 5 pitching of left-hander Vida Blue, who worked four scoreless innings in relief of Blue Moon Odom to secure the A's series-ending 2-1 victory.
■ **Memorable moment:** A seventh-inning melee triggered by A's shortstop Bert Campaneris in Game 2. When Campaneris was hit by a Lerrin LaGrow pitch, he threw his bat at the pitcher and both benches emptied. Campaneris was suspended for the remainder of the series.
■ **Top guns:** Odom (2-0, 0.00 ERA), Blue (0.00), Matty Alou (.381), Athletics; Joe Coleman (1-0, 0-00 ERA), Jim Northrup (.357), Tigers.
■ **MVP:** Odom.

Linescores

Game 1—October 7, at Oakland
Det...0 1 0 0 0 0 0 0 0 0 1—2 6 2
Oak. 0 0 1 0 0 0 0 0 0 0 2—3 10 1
Lolich, Seelbach (11); Hunter, Blue (9), Fingers (9). W—Fingers. L—Lolich. HR—Cash, Kaline (Det.).

Game 2—October 8, at Oakland
Det. ....0 0 0 0 0 0 0 0 0—0 3 1
Oak. ....1 0 0 4 0 0 0 0 x—5 8 0
Fryman, Zachary (5), Scherman (5), LaGrow (6), Hiller (7); Odom. W—Odom. L—Fryman.

Game 3—October 10, at Detroit
Oak. ....0 0 0 0 0 0 0 0 0—0 7 0
Det. ....0 0 0 2 0 0 0 1 x—3 8 1
Holtzman, Fingers (5), Blue (6), Locker (7); Coleman. W—Coleman. L—Holtzman. HR—Freehan (Det.).

Game 4—October 11, at Detroit
Oak. ......0 0 0 0 0 0 1 0 0 2—3 9 2
Det.........0 0 1 0 0 0 0 0 0 3—4 10 1
Hunter, Fingers (8), Blue (9), Locker (10), Horlen (10), Hamilton (10); Lolich, Seelbach (10), Hiller (10). W—Hiller. L—Horlen. HR—McAuliffe (Det.); Epstein (Oak.).

Game 5—October 12, at Detroit
Oak. ....0 1 0 1 0 0 0 0 0—2 4 0
Det...............1 0 0 0 0 0 0 0 0—1 5 2
Odom, Blue (6); Fryman, Hiller (9). W—Odom. L—Fryman. S—Blue.

NLCS

■ **Winner:** Cincinnati needed an N.L.-record five games to get past Pittsburgh and claim its second pennant in three years.
■ **Turning point:** Down two games to one and facing elimination, the Reds got two-hit pitching from Ross Grimsley and forged a 7-1 victory that forced a decisive fifth game.
■ **Memorable moment:** Cincinnati's George Foster racing across the plate with the series-ending run on a Bob Moose wild pitch with two out in the ninth inning of Game 5. The Reds had tied the game moments earlier on a Johnny Bench home run.
■ **Top guns:** Pete Rose (.450), Bench (.333), Reds; Manny Sanguillen (.313), Pirates.
■ **MVP:** Rose.

Linescores

Game 1—October 7, at Pittsburgh
Cin. ....1 0 0 0 0 0 0 0 0—1 8 0
Pitt. ....3 0 0 0 2 0 0 0 x—5 6 0
Gullett, Borbon (7); Blass, R. Hernandez (9). W—Blass. L—Gullett. S—R. Hernandez. HR—Morgan (Cin.); Oliver (Pit.).

Game 2—October 8, at Pittsburgh
Cin. ....4 0 0 0 0 0 0 1 0—5 8 1
Pitt...............0 0 0 1 1 1 0 0 0—3 7 1
Billingham, Hall (5); Moose, Johnson (1), Kison (6), R. Hernandez (7), Giusti (9). W—Hall. L—Moose. HR—Morgan (Cin.).

Game 3—October 9, at Cincinnati
Pitt...............0 0 0 0 1 0 1 1 0—3 7 0
Cin. ....0 0 2 0 0 0 0 0 0—2 8 1
Briles, Kison (7), Giusti (8); Nolan, Borbon (7), Carroll (7), McGlothlin (9). W—Kison. L—Carroll. S—Giusti. HR—Sanguillen (Pit.).

Game 4—October 10, at Cincinnati
Pitt.............0 0 0 0 0 0 1 0 0—1 2 3
Cin. ....1 0 0 2 0 2 2 0 x—7 11 1
Ellis, Johnson (6), Walker (7), Miller (8); Grimsley. W—Grimsley. L—Ellis. HR—Clemente (Pit.).

Game 5—October 11, at Cincinnati
Pitt...............0 2 0 1 0 0 0 0 0—3 8 0
Cin. ....0 0 1 0 1 0 0 0 2—4 7 1
Blass, R. Hernandez (8), Giusti (9), Moose (9); Gullett, Borbon (4), Hall (6), Carroll (9). W—Carroll. L—Giusti. HR—Geronimo, Bench (Cin.).

WORLD SERIES

■ **Winner:** The Athletics, who had not played in a World Series since 1931 when the franchise was located in Philadelphia, began a run that would put them in select company.
■ **Turning point:** A Game 4 ninth-inning rally that gave Oakland a three games to one lead. Down 2-1 with one out, the A's scored two runs on four consecutive singles.
■ **Memorable moment:** A's catcher Gene Tenace blasting home runs in his first two Series at-bats — and a record-tying four overall.
■ **Top guns:** Catfish Hunter (2-0, 2.81 ERA), Tenace (.348, 4 HR, 9 RBIs), Athletics; Tony Perez (.435), Bobby Tolan (6 RBIs), Reds.
■ **MVP:** Tenace.

Linescores

Game 1—October 14, at Cincinnati
Oakland........0 2 0 0 1 0 0 0 0—3 4 0
Cincinnati ....0 1 0 1 0 0 0 0 0—2 7 0
Holtzman, Fingers (6), Blue (7); Nolan, Borbon (7), Carroll (8). W—Holtzman. L—Nolan. S—Blue. HR—Tenace 2 (Oak.).

Game 2—October 15, at Cincinnati
Oakland........0 1 1 0 0 0 0 0 0—2 9 2
Cincinnati ....0 0 0 0 0 0 0 0 1—1 6 0
Hunter, Fingers (9); Grimsley, Borbon (6), Hall (8). W—Hunter. L—Grimsley. S—Fingers. HR—Rudi (Oak.).

Game 3—October 18, at Oakland
Cincinnati ....0 0 0 0 0 0 1 0 0—1 4 2
Oakland........0 0 0 0 0 0 0 0 0—0 3 2
Billingham, Carroll (9); Odom, Blue (8), Fingers (8). W—Billingham. L—Odom. S—Carroll.

Game 4—October 19, at Oakland
Cincinnati ..0 0 0 0 0 0 0 2 0—2 7 1
Oakland......0 0 0 0 1 0 0 0 2—3 10 1
Gullett, Borbon (8), Carroll (9); Holtzman, Blue (8), Fingers (9). W—Fingers. L—Carroll. HR—Tenace (Oak.).

Game 5—October 20, at Oakland
Cincinnati ....1 0 0 1 1 0 0 1 1—5 8 0
Oakland........0 3 0 1 0 0 0 0 0—4 7 2
McGlothlin, Borbon (4), Hall (5), Carroll (7), Grimsley (8), Billingham (9); Hunter, Fingers (5), Hamilton (9). W—Grimsley. L—Fingers. S—Billingham. HR—Rose, Menke (Cin.); Tenace (Oak.).

Game 6—October 21, at Cincinnati
Oakland......0 0 0 0 1 0 0 0 0—1 7 1
Cincinnati ..0 0 0 1 1 1 5 0 x—8 10 0
Blue, Locker (6), Hamilton (7), Horlen (7); Nolan, Grimsley (5), Borbon (6), Hall (7). W—Grimsley. L—Blue. S—Hall. HR—Bench (Cin.).

Game 7—October 22, at Cincinnati
Oakland........1 0 0 0 0 2 0 0 0—3 6 1
Cincinnati ....0 0 0 0 1 0 0 1 0—2 4 2
Odom, Hunter (5), Holtzman (8), Fingers (8); Billingham, Borbon (6), Carroll (6), Grimsley (7), Hall (8). W—Hunter. L—Borbon. S—Fingers.

HISTORY

FINAL STANDINGS

American League

East Division

Team	Bal.	Bos.	Det.	N.Y.	Mil.	Cle.	Cal.	Chi.	K.C.	Min.	Oak.	Tex.	W	L	Pct.	GB
Baltimore	...	7	9	9	15	12	6	8	8	8	5	10	97	65	.599	...
Boston	11	...	3	14	12	9	7	6	8	6	4	9	89	73	.549	8
Detroit	9	15	...	7	12	9	5	7	4	5	7	5	85	77	.525	12
New York	9	4	11	...	8	11	6	4	6	9	4	8	80	82	.494	17
Milwaukee	3	6	6	10	...	9	7	9	4	8	4	8	74	88	.457	23
Cleveland	6	9	9	7	9	...	7	5	2	7	3	7	71	91	.438	26

West Division

Team	Oak.	K.C.	Min.	Cal.	Chi.	Tex.	Bal.	Bos.	Cle.	Det.	Mil.	N.Y.	W	L	Pct.	GB
Oakland	...	10	4	12	12	11	7	8	9	5	8	8	94	68	.580	...
Kansas City	8	...	9	8	12	11	4	4	10	8	8	6	88	74	.543	6
Minnesota	14	9	...	8	9	12	4	6	5	7	4	3	81	81	.500	13
California	6	10	10	...	8	11	6	5	5	7	5	6	79	83	.488	15
Chicago	6	6	9	10	...	13	4	6	7	5	3	8	77	85	.475	17
Texas	7	7	6	7	5	...	2	3	5	7	4	4	57	105	.352	37

National League

East Division

Team	N.Y.	St.L.	Pit.	Mon.	Chi.	Phi.	Atl.	Cin.	Hou.	L.A.	S.D.	S.F.	W	L	Pct.	GB
New York	...	10	13	9	7	9	6	4	6	5	8	5	82	79	.509	...
St. Louis	8	...	8	10	9	9	6	6	7	4	8	6	81	81	.500	1.5
Pittsburgh	5	10	...	12	12	10	5	5	6	2	8	5	80	82	.494	2.5
Montreal	9	8	6	...	9	13	6	4	6	5	7	6	79	83	.488	3.5
Chicago	10	9	6	9	...	10	5	8	6	5	7	2	77	84	.478	5
Philadelphia	9	9	8	5	8	...	6	4	5	3	9	5	71	91	.438	11.5

West Division

Team	Cin.	L.A.	S.F.	Hou.	Atl.	S.D.	Chi.	Mon.	N.Y.	Phi.	Pit.	St.L.	W	L	Pct.	GB
Cincinnati	...	11	10	11	13	13	4	8	8	8	7	6	99	63	.611	...
Los Angeles	7	...	9	7	15	9	7	7	7	9	10	8	95	66	.590	3.5
San Fran.	8	9	...	7	10	11	10	6	7	7	7	6	88	74	.543	11
Houston	7	11	11	...	7	10	6	6	6	7	6	5	82	80	.506	17
Atlanta	5	2	8	11	...	12	7	6	6	6	7	6	76	85	.472	22.5
San Diego	5	9	7	8	6	...	5	5	4	3	4	4	60	102	.370	39

SIGNIFICANT EVENTS

- **January 3:** An investment group headed by shipbuilder George Steinbrenner purchased the Yankees from CBS for $10 million.
- **February 25:** Owners and players approved a three-year Basic Agreement that included binding arbitration and modifications of the controversial reserve clause.
- **April 6:** The A.L. began its designated hitter experiment when Yankee Ron Blomberg drew a first-inning walk in a game at Boston's Fenway Park.
- **April 10:** New Royals Stadium received a rousing welcome when Kansas City pounded Texas, 12-1.

MEMORABLE MOMENTS

- **July 15:** Angels ace Nolan Ryan held Detroit hitless in a 6-0 victory, becoming the fourth pitcher to throw two no-hitters in one season.
- **July 21:** Atlanta's Hank Aaron inched closer to Babe Ruth's all-time record when he belted homer No. 700 off Philadelphia's Ken Brett in an 8-4 loss.
- **September 28:** Ryan struck out 16 Twins in his final start, raising his record season strikeout total to 383.
- **October 1:** The Mets posted a final-day 6-4 victory over Chicago and clinched the N.L. East championship with an 82-79 record.

LEADERS

American League
BA: Rod Carew, Min., .350.
Runs: Reggie Jackson, Oak., 99.
Hits: Rod Carew, Min., 203.
TB: Sal Bando, Oak.; Dave May, Mil.; George Scott, Mil., 295.
HR: Reggie Jackson, Oak., 32.
RBI: Reggie Jackson, Oak., 117.
SB: Tommy Harper, Bos., 54.
Wins: Wilbur Wood, Chi., 24.
ERA: Jim Palmer, Bal., 2.40.
CG: Gaylord Perry, Cle., 29.
IP: Wilbur Wood, Chi., 359.1.
SO: Nolan Ryan, Cal., 383.
SV: John Hiller, Det., 38.

National League
BA: Pete Rose, Cin., .338.
Runs: Bobby Bonds, S.F., 131.
Hits: Pete Rose, Cin., 230.
TB: Bobby Bonds, S.F., 341.
HR: Willie Stargell, Pit., 44.
RBI: Willie Stargell, Pit., 119.
SB: Lou Brock, St.L., 70.
Wins: Ron Bryant, S.F., 24.
ERA: Tom Seaver, N.Y., 2.08.
CG: Steve Carlton, Phil.; Tom Seaver, N.Y., 18.
IP: Jack Billingham, Cin.; Steve Carlton, Phil., 293.1.
SO: Tom Seaver, N.Y., 251.
SV: Mike Marshall, Mon., 31.

A.L. 20-game winners
Wilbur Wood, Chi., 24-20
Joe Coleman, Det., 23-15
Jim Palmer, Bal., 22-9
Catfish Hunter, Oak., 21-5
Ken Holtzman, Oak., 21-13
Nolan Ryan, Cal., 21-16
Vida Blue, Oak., 20-9
Paul Splittorff, K.C., 20-11
Jim Colborn, Mil., 20-12
Luis Tiant, Bos., 20-13
Bill Singer, Cal., 20-14
Bert Blyleven, Min., 20-17

N.L. 20-game winners
Ron Bryant, S.F., 24-12

A.L. 100 RBIs
Reggie Jackson, Oak., 117
George Scott, Mil., 107
John Mayberry, K.C., 100

N.L. 100 RBIs
Willie Stargell, Pit., 119
Lee May, Hou., 105
Johnny Bench, Cin., 104
Darrell Evans, Atl., 104
Ken Singleton, Mon., 103
Tony Perez, Cin., 101

N.L. 40 homers
Willie Stargell, Pit., 44
Dave Johnson, Atl., 43
Darrell Evans, Atl., 41
Hank Aaron, Atl., 40

Most Valuable Player
A.L.: Reggie Jackson, OF, Oak.
N.L.: Pete Rose, OF, Cin.

Cy Young Award
A.L.: Jim Palmer, Bal.
N.L.: Tom Seaver, N.Y.

Rookie of the Year
A.L.: Al Bumbry, OF, Bal.
N.L.: Gary Matthews, OF, S.F.

Hall of Fame additions
Roberto Clemente, OF, 1955-72
Billy Evans, umpire
Monte Irvin, OF, 1949-56
George Kelly, 1B, 1915-32
Warren Spahn, P, 1942-65
Mickey Welch, P, 1880-92

ALL-STAR GAME

- **Winners:** Johnny Bench, Bobby Bonds and Willie Davis powered the N.L. to its 10th All-Star victory in 11 years in the 40th anniversary of the midsummer classic.
- **Key innings:** The fourth, fifth and sixth, when the N.L.'s Big Three hit home runs that accounted for five runs.
- **Memorable moment:** An eighth-inning strikeout by pinch-hitter Willie Mays, who was making his 24th and final appearance in the baseball classic he had dominated like no other player.
- **Top guns:** Bonds (Giants), Bench (Reds), Davis (Dodgers), N.L.; Amos Otis (Royals), A.L.
- **MVP:** Bonds.

Linescore
July 24, at Kansas City's Royals Stadium
N.L. ....0 0 2 1 2 2 0 0 0—7 10 0
A.L. ....0 1 0 0 0 0 0 0 1—1 5 0
Wise (Cardinals), Osteen (Dodgers) 3, Sutton (Dodgers) 5, Twitchell (Phillies) 6, Giusti (Pirates) 7, Seaver (Mets) 8, Brewer (Dodgers) 9; Hunter (Athletics), Holtzman (Athletics) 2, Blyleven (Twins) 3, Singer (Angels) 4, Ryan (Angels) 6, Lyle (Yankees) 8, Fingers (Athletics) 9. W—Wise. L—Blyleven. HR—Bench, Bonds, Davis, N.L.

ALCS

- **Winner:** The Athletics earned their second consecutive pennant and the Orioles lost their first ALCS after three previous sweeps.
- **Turning point:** An 11th-inning Game 3 home run by Bert Campaneris that broke up a pitching duel between Oakland's Ken Holtzman and Baltimore's Mike Cuellar. The 2-1 victory gave the A's a 2-1 series advantage.
- **Memorable moment:** A game-tying three-run seventh-inning home run by catcher Andy Etchebarren that kept Baltimore's hopes alive in Game 4. The Orioles won, 5-4, and forced a fifth game.
- **Top guns:** Catfish Hunter (2-0, 1.65 ERA), Vic Davalillo (.625), Campaneris (.333, 2 HR), Athletics; Etchebarren (.357, 4 RBIs), Orioles.
- **MVP:** Hunter.

Linescores

Game 1—October 6, at Baltimore
Oak. ....0 0 0 0 0 0 0 0 0—0 5 1
Balt. ....4 0 0 0 0 0 1 1 x—6 12 0
Blue, Pina (1), Odom (3), Fingers (8); Palmer. W—Palmer. L—Blue.

Game 2—October 7, at Baltimore
Oak. ....1 0 0 0 0 2 0 2 1—6 9 0
Balt. ....1 0 0 0 0 1 0 1 0—3 8 0
Hunter, Fingers (8); McNally, Reynolds (8), G. Jackson (9). W—Hunter. L—McNally. S—Fingers. HR—Campaneris, Rudi, Bando 2 (Oak.).

Game 3—October 9, at Oakland
Balt. ....0 1 0 0 0 0 0 0 0 0 0—1 3 0
Oak. ....0 0 0 0 0 0 0 1 0 0 1—2 4 3
Cuellar; Holtzman. W—Holtzman. L—Cuellar. HR—Williams (Bal.); Campaneris (Oak.).

Game 4—October 10, at Oakland
Balt. ....0 0 0 0 0 0 4 1 0—5 8 0
Oak. ....0 3 0 0 0 1 0 0 0—4 7 0
Palmer, Reynolds (2), Watt (7), G. Jackson (7); Blue, Fingers (7). W—G. Jackson. L—Fingers. HR—Etchebarren, Grich (Bal.).

Game 5—October 11, at Oakland
Balt. ....0 0 0 0 0 0 0 0 0—0 5 2
Oak. ....0 0 1 2 0 0 0 0 x—3 7 0
Alexander, Palmer (4); Hunter. W—Hunter. L—Alexander.

NLCS

- **Winner:** The New York Mets captured their second pennant in five years and kept Cincinnati from repeating as N.L. champion.
- **Turning point:** New York's 9-2 Game 3 victory that was spiced by a fifth-inning fight between Mets shortstop Bud Harrelson and Cincinnati leftfielder Pete Rose. Reds manager Sparky Anderson had to temporarily pull his team from the field in the next half inning when fans began pelting Rose with garbage and other debris.
- **Memorable moment:** Rose's 12th-inning Game 4 home run that kept the Reds alive and forced a fifth game.
- **Top guns:** Jon Matlack (1-0, 0.00 ERA), Felix Millan (.316), Rusty Staub (3 HR, 5 RBIs), Mets; Rose (.381, 2 HR), Reds.
- **MVP:** Staub.

Linescores

Game 1—October 6, at Cincinnati
N.Y. ....0 1 0 0 0 0 0 0 0—1 3 0
Cin. ....0 0 0 0 0 0 0 1 1—2 6 0
Seaver; Billingham, Hall (9), Borbon (9). W—Borbon. L—Seaver. HR—Rose, Bench (Cin.).

Game 2—October 7, at Cincinnati
N.Y. ....0 0 0 1 0 0 0 0 4—5 7 0
Cin. ....0 0 0 0 0 0 0 0 0—0 2 0
Matlack; Gullett, Carroll (6), Hall (9), Borbon (9). W—Matlack. L—Gullett. HR—Staub (N.Y.).

Game 3—October 8, at New York
Cin. ....0 0 2 0 0 0 0 0 0—2 8 1
N.Y. ....1 5 1 2 0 0 0 0 x—9 11 1
Grimsley, Hall (2), Tomlin (3), Nelson (4), Borbon (7); Koosman. W—Koosman. L—Grimsley. HR—Staub 2 (N.Y.); Menke (Cin.).

Game 4—October 9, at New York
Cin.......0 0 0 0 0 0 1 0 0 0 0 1—2 8 0
N.Y.......0 0 1 0 0 0 0 0 0 0 0 0—1 3 2
Norman, Gullett (6), Carroll (10), Borbon (12); Stone, McGraw (7), Parker (12). W—Carroll. L—Parker. S—Borbon. HR—Perez, Rose (Cin.).

Game 5—October 10, at New York
Cin. ....0 0 1 0 1 0 0 0 0—2 7 1
N.Y. ....2 0 0 0 4 1 0 0 x—7 13 1
Billingham, Gullett (5), Carroll (5), Grimsley (7); Seaver, McGraw (9). W—Seaver. L—Billingham. S—McGraw.

WORLD SERIES

- **Winner:** The Athletics made it two in a row with a seven-game scramble against the resilient Mets.
- **Turning point:** In a valiant Game 6 performance that staved off elimination, the A's prevailed 3-1 behind Catfish Hunter's pitching and the two-RBI hitting of Reggie Jackson.
- **Memorable moment:** The "firing" of A's second baseman Mike Andrews by owner Charles O. Finley. Andrews' two 12th-inning errors in Game 2 enabled the Mets to post a 10-7 victory.
- **Top guns:** Joe Rudi (.333), Jackson (.310, 6 RBIs), Athletics; Rusty Staub (.423, 6 RBIs), Mets.
- **MVP:** Jackson.

Linescores

Game 1—October 13, at Oakland
N.Y. ....0 0 0 1 0 0 0 0 0—1 7 2
Oak. ....0 0 2 0 0 0 0 0 x—2 4 0
Matlack, McGraw (7); Holtzman, Fingers (6), Knowles (9). W—Holtzman. L—Matlack. S—Knowles.

Game 2—October 14, at Oakland
N.Y. ....0 1 1 0 0 4 0 0 0 0 0 4—10 15 1
Oak. ....2 1 0 0 0 0 1 0 2 0 0 1— 7 13 5
Koosman, Sadecki (3), Parker (5), McGraw (6), Stone (12); Blue, Pina (6), Knowles (6), Odom (8), Fingers (10), Lindblad (12). W—McGraw. L—Fingers. S—Stone. HR—Jones, Garrett (N.Y.).

Game 3—October 16, at New York
Oak. ....0 0 0 0 0 1 0 1 0 0 1—3 10 1
N.Y. ....2 0 0 0 0 0 0 0 0 0 0—2 10 2
Hunter, Knowles (7), Lindblad (9), Fingers (11); Seaver, Sadecki (9), McGraw (9), Parker (11). W—Lindblad. L—Parker. S—Fingers. HR—Garrett (N.Y.).

Game 4—October 17, at New York
Oak. ....0 0 0 1 0 0 0 0 0—1 5 1
N.Y. ....3 0 0 3 0 0 0 0 x—6 13 1
Holtzman, Odom (1), Knowles (4), Pina (5), Lindblad (8); Matlack, Sadecki (9). W—Matlack. L—Holtzman. S—Sadecki. HR—Staub (N.Y.).

Game 5—October 18, at New York
Oak. ....0 0 0 0 0 0 0 0 0—0 3 1
N.Y. ....0 1 0 0 0 1 0 0 x—2 7 1
Blue, Knowles (6), Fingers (7); Koosman, McGraw (7). W—Koosman. L—Blue. S—McGraw.

Game 6—October 20, at Oakland
N.Y. ....0 0 0 0 0 0 0 1 0—1 6 2
Oak. ....1 0 1 0 0 0 0 1 x—3 7 0
Seaver, McGraw (8); Hunter, Knowles (8), Fingers (8). W—Hunter. L—Seaver. S—Fingers.

Game 7—October 21, at Oakland
N.Y. ....0 0 0 0 0 1 0 0 1—2 8 1
Oak. ....0 0 4 0 1 0 0 0 x—5 9 1
Matlack, Parker (3), Sadecki (5), Stone (7); Holtzman, Fingers (6), Knowles (9). W—Holtzman. L—Matlack. S—Knowles. HR—Campaneris, Jackson (Oak.).

FINAL STANDINGS

American League

East Division

Team	Bal.	N.Y.	Bos.	Cle.	Mil.	Det.	Cal.	Chi.	K.C.	Min.	Oak.	Tex.	W	L	Pct.	GB
Baltimore	...	11	10	12	8	14	7	5	8	6	6	4	91	71	.562	...
New York	7	...	7	11	9	7	9	8	8	8	7	8	89	73	.549	2
Boston	8	11	...	9	10	11	4	8	4	6	8	5	84	78	.519	7
Cleveland	6	7	9	...	10	9	9	4	8	6	5	4	77	85	.475	14
Milwaukee	10	9	8	8	..	9	9	4	1	6	5	7	76	86	.469	15
Detroit	4	11	7	9	9	...	7	5	7	3	5	5	72	90	.444	19

West Division

Team	Oak.	Tex.	Min.	Chi.	K.C.	Cal.	Bal.	Bos.	Cle.	Det.	Mil.	N.Y.	W	L	Pct.	GB
Oakland	...	8	13	11	10	12	6	4	7	7	7	5	90	72	.556	...
Texas	10	...	9	7	10	9	8	7	8	7	5	4	84	76	.525	5
Minnesota	5	9	...	11	10	10	6	6	6	9	6	4	82	80	.506	8
Chicago	7	9	7	...	11	8	7	4	8	7	8	4	80	80	.500	9
Kansas City	8	8	8	7	...	10	4	8	4	5	11	4	77	85	.475	13
California	6	9	8	10	8	...	5	8	3	5	3	3	68	94	.420	22

National League

East Division

Team	Pit.	St.L.	Phi.	Mon.	N.Y.	Chi.	Atl.	Cin.	Hou.	L.A.	S.D.	S.F.	W	L	Pct.	GB
Pittsburgh	...	7	8	9	11	9	8	4	7	8	9	8	88	74	.543	...
St. Louis	11	...	9	9	12	13	3	6	4	6	7	6	86	75	.534	1.5
Philadelphia	10	9	...	7	11	10	4	4	6	6	5	8	80	82	.494	8
Montreal	9	8	11	...	9	13	3	6	6	4	6	4	79	82	.491	8.5
New York	7	6	7	9	...	10	4	3	6	7	6	6	71	91	.438	17
Chicago	9	5	8	5	8	...	8	5	4	2	6	6	66	96	.407	22

West Division

Team	L.A.	Cin.	Atl.	Hou.	S.F.	S.D.	Chi.	Mon.	N.Y.	Phi.	Pit.	St.L.	W	L	Pct.	GB
Los Angeles	...	12	10	13	12	16	10	8	5	6	4	6	102	60	.630	...
Cincinnati	6	...	11	14	11	12	7	6	9	8	8	6	98	64	.605	4
Atlanta	8	7	...	6	8	17	4	9	8	8	4	9	88	74	.543	14
Houston	5	4	12	...	10	11	8	6	6	6	5	8	81	81	.500	21
San Fran.	6	7	10	8	...	7	6	8	6	4	4	6	72	90	.444	30
San Diego	2	6	1	7	11	...	6	6	6	7	3	5	60	102	.370	42

SIGNIFICANT EVENTS

- **January 1:** Lee MacPhail took the reins as A.L. president, succeeding retiring Joe Cronin.
- **February 11:** Baseball's first arbitration hearing was decided in favor of Twins pitcher Dick Woodson.
- **October 3:** The Indians crossed another color barrier when they named Frank Robinson as baseball's first black manager and the game's first player-manager since 1959.
- **November 2:** The Braves honored the request of home run king Hank Aaron when they traded him to Milwaukee, the city where he started his career in 1954.
- **November 6:** Mike Marshall, who appeared in a record 106 games for the Dodgers, became the first relief pitcher to earn a Cy Young Award.
- **December 31:** The Yankees won the most celebrated free-agent chase in history when they signed former Oakland ace Catfish Hunter to a five-year, $3.75-million contract.

MEMORABLE MOMENTS

- **April 8:** Atlanta's Hank Aaron overtook Babe Ruth as baseball's all-time greatest slugger when he connected off Al Downing for record home run No. 715 in a 7-4 victory over the Dodgers.
- **July 17:** Bob Gibson became the second pitcher to reach 3,000 strikeouts when he fanned Cincinnati's Cesar Geronimo in a game at St. Louis.
- **August 12:** California's Nolan Ryan tied the single-game record when he struck out 19 Red Sox in a 4-2 victory.
- **September 24:** Al Kaline doubled off Baltimore's Dave McNally for hit No. 3,000 in Detroit's 5-4 loss.
- **September 29:** St. Louis speedster Lou Brock swiped his record 118th base in a 7-3 victory over the Cubs.
- **October 1:** The Orioles, who finished the season on a 28-6 run, clinched the A.L. East with a 7-6 victory over the Tigers.

LEADERS

American League
BA: Rod Carew, Min., .364.
Runs: Carl Yastrzemski, Bos., 93.
Hits: Rod Carew, Min., 218.
TB: Joe Rudi, Oak., 287.
HR: Dick Allen, Chi., 32.
RBI: Jeff Burroughs, Tex., 118.
SB: Bill North, Oak., 54.
Wins: Catfish Hunter, Oak.; Ferguson Jenkins, Tex., 25.
ERA: Catfish Hunter, Oak., 2.49.
CG: Ferguson Jenkins, Tex., 29.
IP: Nolan Ryan, Cal., 332.2.
SO: Nolan Ryan, Cal., 367.
SV: Terry Forster, Chi., 24.

National League
BA: Ralph Garr, Atl., .353.
Runs: Pete Rose, Cin., 110.
Hits: Ralph Garr, Atl., 214.
TB: Johnny Bench, Cin., 315.
HR: Mike Schmidt, Phil., 36.
RBI: Johnny Bench, Cin., 129.
SB: Lou Brock, St.L., 118.
Wins: Andy Messersmith, L.A.; Phil Niekro, Atl., 20.
ERA: Buzz Capra, Atl., 2.28.
CG: Phil Niekro, Atl., 18.
IP: Phil Niekro, Atl., 302.1.
SO: Steve Carlton, Phil., 240.
SV: Mike Marshall, L.A., 21.

A.L. 20-game winners
Catfish Hunter, Oak., 25-12
Ferguson Jenkins, Tex., 25-12
Mike Cuellar, Bal., 22-10
Luis Tiant, Bos., 22-13
Steve Busby, K.C., 22-14
Nolan Ryan, Cal., 22-16
Jim Kaat, Chi., 21-13
Gaylord Perry, Cle., 21-13
Wilbur Wood, Chi., 20-19

N.L. 20-game winners
Andy Messersmith, L.A., 20-6
Phil Niekro, Atl., 20-13

A.L. 100 RBIs
Jeff Burroughs, Tex., 118
Sal Bando, Oak., 103

N.L. 100 RBIs
Johnny Bench, Cin., 129
Mike Schmidt, Phil., 116
Steve Garvey, L.A., 111
Jim Wynn, L.A., 108
Ted Simmons, St.L., 103
Cesar Cedeno, Hou., 102
Tony Perez, Cin., 101
Reggie Smith, St.L., 100
Richie Zisk, Pit., 100

Most Valuable Player
A.L.: Jeff Burroughs, OF, Tex.
N.L.: Steve Garvey, 1B, L.A.

Cy Young Award
A.L.: Catfish Hunter, Oak.
N.L.: Mike Marshall, L.A.

Rookie of the Year
A.L.: Mike Hargrove, 1B, Tex.
N.L.: Bake McBride, OF, St.L.

Hall of Fame additions
Cool Papa Bell, OF, Negro Leagues
Jim Bottomley, 1B, 1922-37
Jocko Conlan, umpire
Whitey Ford, P, 1950-67
Mickey Mantle, OF, 1951-68
Sam Thompson, OF, 1885-1906

ALL-STAR GAME

- **Winner:** The N.L. continued its amazing All-Star run with a 7-2 victory fashioned by five pitchers who had never worked in a mid-summer classic.
- **Key inning:** A two-run N.L. fourth, when Steve Garvey doubled home the tying run and the lead run scored on Ron Cey's groundout.
- **Memorable moment:** A third-inning diving stop by N.L. first baseman Garvey on a smash by Bobby Murcer. The play saved at least two A.L. runs and possibly the game.
- **Top guns:** Mike Marshall (Dodgers), Reggie Smith (Cardinals), Garvey (Dodgers), Cey (Dodgers), N.L.; Dick Allen (White Sox), A.L.
- **MVP:** Garvey.

Linescore
July 23, at Pittsburgh's Three Rivers Stadium
A.L. ....0 0 2 0 0 0 0 0 0—2 4 1
N.L. ....0 1 0 2 1 0 1 2 x—7 10 1
Perry (Indians), Tiant (Red Sox) 4, Hunter (Athletics) 6, Fingers (Athletics) 8; Messersmith (Dodgers), Brett (Pirates) 4, Matlack (Mets) 6, McGlothen (Cardinals) 7, Marshall (Dodgers) 8. W—Brett. L—Tiant. HR—Smith, N.L.

ALCS

- **Winner:** The Athletics needed only four games to earn their third consecutive A.L. pennant and second straight ALCS victory over Baltimore.
- **Turning point:** Oakland's 1-0 Game 3 victory, which was decided by a fourth-inning Sal Bando home run. A's lefty Vida Blue allowed only two hits and gave his team a 2-1 series advantage.
- **Memorable moment:** Reggie Jackson's seventh-inning double in Game 4. The A's only hit in a 2-1 series-ending victory drove in the winning run.
- **Top guns:** Blue (1-0, 0-00 ERA), Ken Holtzman (1-0, 0.00), Bando (2 HR), Athletics; Andy Etchebarren (.333), Orioles.
- **MVP:** Blue.

Linescores

Game 1—October 5, at Oakland
Baltimore ..1 0 0 1 4 0 0 0 0—6 10 0
Oakland......0 0 1 0 1 0 0 0 1—3 9 0
Cuellar, Grimsley (9); Hunter, Odom (5), Fingers (9). W—Cuellar. L—Hunter. HR—Blair, Robinson, Grich (Bal.).

Game 2—October 6, at Oakland
Baltimore ....0 0 0 0 0 0 0 0 0—0 5 2
Oakland........0 0 0 1 0 1 0 3 x—5 8 0
McNally, Garland (6), Reynolds (7), G. Jackson (8); Holtzman. W—Holtzman. L—McNally. HR—Bando, Fosse (Oak.).

Game 3—October 8, at Baltimore
Oakland........0 0 0 1 0 0 0 0 0—1 4 2
Baltimore ....0 0 0 0 0 0 0 0 0—0 2 1
Blue; Palmer. W—Blue. L—Palmer. HR—Bando (Oak.).

Game 4—October 9, at Baltimore
Oakland........0 0 0 0 1 0 1 0 0—2 1 0
Baltimore ....0 0 0 0 0 0 0 0 1—1 5 1
Hunter, Fingers (8); Cuellar, Grimsley (5). W—Hunter. L—Cuellar. S—Fingers.

NLCS

- **Winner:** Los Angeles, making its first Championship Series appearance, overpowered Pittsburgh and claimed its first pennant since 1966.
- **Turning point:** Pitchers Don Sutton, Andy Messersmith and Mike Marshall held the Pirates scoreless in 17 of the first 18 innings as the Dodgers forged a 2-0 series advantage.
- **Memorable moment:** The Game 4 performance of Los Angeles first baseman Steve Garvey, who collected four hits, belted two home runs and drove in four runs in a 12-1 series-ending victory.
- **Top guns:** Sutton (2-0, 0.53 ERA), Garvey (.389, 2 HR, 5 RBIs), Bill Russell (.389), Dodgers; Bruce Kison (1-0, 0.00), Willie Stargell (.400, 2 HR, 4 RBIs), Pirates.
- **MVP:** Sutton.

Linescores

Game 1—October 5, at Pittsburgh
L.A. ....0 1 0 0 0 0 0 0 2—3 9 2
Pitt...............0 0 0 0 0 0 0 0 0—0 4 0
Sutton; Reuss, Giusti (8). W—Sutton. L—Reuss.

Game 2—October 6, at Pittsburgh
L.A. ....1 0 0 1 0 0 0 3 0—5 12 0
Pitt.............0 0 0 0 0 0 2 0 0—2 8 3
Messersmith, Marshall (8); Rooker, Giusti (8), Demery (8), Hernandez (8). W—Messersmith. L—Giusti. HR—Cey (L.A.).

Game 3—October 8, at Los Angeles
Pitt.............5 0 2 0 0 0 0 0 0—7 10 0
L.A. ....0 0 0 0 0 0 0 0 0—0 4 5
Kison, Hernandez (7); Rau, Hough (1), Downing (4), Solomon (8). W—Kison. L—Rau. HR—Stargell, Hebner (Pit.).

Game 4—October 9, at Los Angeles
Pitt...........0 0 0 0 0 0 1 0 0— 1 3 1
L.A. ....1 0 2 0 2 2 2 3 x—12 12 0
Reuss, Brett (3), Demery (6), Giusti (7), Pizarro (8); Sutton, Marshall (9). W—Sutton. L—Reuss. HR—Garvey 2 (L.A.); Stargell (Pit.).

WORLD SERIES

- **Winner:** Manager Alvin Dark's Athletics, who had won the previous two years under Dick Williams, became only the second team to win three consecutive World Series.
- **Turning point:** The A's 5-2 Game 4 victory, which featured a home run by pitcher Ken Holtzman, who had not batted all season because of the A.L.'s designated hitter rule.
- **Memorable moment:** Joe Rudi's tie-breaking solo home run off Dodger ironman reliever Mike Marshall in the seventh inning of Game 5.
- **Top guns:** Rollie Fingers (1-0, 2 saves, 1.93 ERA), Holtzman (1-0, 1.50, 1 HR), Rudi (.333, 4 RBIs), A's; Steve Garvey (.381), Dodgers.
- **MVP:** Fingers.

Linescores

Game 1—October 12, at Los Angeles
Oakland......0 1 0 0 1 0 0 1 0—3 6 2
L.A. ....0 0 0 0 1 0 0 0 1—2 11 1
Holtzman, Fingers (5), Hunter (9); Messersmith, Marshall (9). W—Fingers. L—Messersmith. S—Hunter. HR—Jackson (Oak.); Wynn (L.A.).

Game 2—October 13, at Los Angeles
Oakland........0 0 0 0 0 0 0 0 2—2 6 0
L.A. ....0 1 0 0 0 2 0 0 x—3 6 1
Blue, Odom (8); Sutton, Marshall (9). W—Sutton. L—Blue. S—Marshall. HR—Ferguson (L.A.).

Game 3—October 15, at Oakland
L.A. ....0 0 0 0 0 0 0 1 1—2 7 2
Oakland........0 0 2 1 0 0 0 0 x—3 5 2
Downing, Brewer (4), Hough (5), Marshall (7); Hunter, Fingers (8). W—Hunter. L—Downing. S—Fingers. HR—Buckner, Crawford (L.A.).

Game 4—October 16, at Oakland
L.A. ....0 0 0 2 0 0 0 0 0—2 7 1
Oakland........0 0 1 0 0 4 0 0 x—5 7 0
Messersmith, Marshall (7); Holtzman, Fingers (8). W—Holtzman. L—Messersmith. S—Fingers. HR—Holtzman.

Game 5—October 17, at Oakland
L.A. ....0 0 0 0 0 2 0 0 0—2 5 1
Oakland........1 1 0 0 0 0 1 0 x—3 6 1
Sutton, Marshall (6); Blue, Odom (7), Fingers (8). W—Odom. L—Marshall. S—Fingers. HR—Fosse, Rudi (Oak.).

FINAL STANDINGS

American League

East Division

Team	Bos.	Bal.	N.Y.	Cle.	Mil.	Det.	Cal.	Chi.	K.C.	Min.	Oak.	Tex.	W	L	Pct.	GB
Boston	...	9	11	7	10	13	6	8	7	10	6	8	95	65	.594	...
Baltimore	9	...	8	10	14	12	6	7	7	6	4	7	90	69	.566	4.5
New York	5	10	...	9	9	12	5	6	5	8	6	8	83	77	.519	12
Cleveland	11	8	9	...	9	12	9	5	6	3	2	5	79	80	.497	15.5
Milwaukee	8	4	9	9	...	11	5	4	5	2	5	6	68	94	.420	28
Detroit	5	4	6	6	7	...	5	7	6	4	6	1	57	102	.358	37.5

West Division

Team	Oak.	K.C.	Tex.	Min.	Chi.	Cal.	Bal.	Bos.	Cle.	Det.	Mil.	N.Y.	W	L	Pct.	GB
Oakland	...	11	12	12	9	11	8	6	10	6	7	6	98	64	.605	...
Kansas City	7	...	14	11	9	14	5	5	6	6	7	7	91	71	.562	7
Texas	6	4	...	10	13	9	5	4	7	11	6	4	79	83	.488	19
Minnesota	6	7	8	...	9	10	6	2	6	8	10	4	76	83	.478	20.5
Chicago	9	9	5	9	...	9	4	4	7	5	8	6	75	86	.466	22.5
California	7	4	9	8	9	...	6	6	3	6	7	7	72	89	.447	25.5

National League

East Division

Team	Pit.	Phi.	N.Y.	St.L.	Chi.	Mon.	Atl.	Cin.	Hou.	L.A.	S.D.	S.F.	W	L	Pct.	GB
Pittsburgh	...	7	13	10	12	11	8	6	5	7	8	5	92	69	.571	...
Philadelphia	11	...	11	10	6	11	7	5	6	5	7	7	86	76	.531	6.5
New York	5	7	...	9	11	8	8	4	8	6	8	8	82	80	.506	10.5
St. Louis	8	8	9	...	7	7	9	4	8	7	8	7	82	80	.506	10.5
Chicago	6	12	7	11	...	9	7	1	7	5	5	5	75	87	.463	17.5
Montreal	7	7	10	11	9	...	4	4	4	7	7	5	75	87	.463	17.5

West Division

Team	Cin.	L.A.	S.F.	S.D.	Atl.	Hou.	Chi.	Mon.	N.Y.	Phi.	Pit.	St.L.	W	L	Pct.	GB
Cincinnati	...	8	13	11	15	13	11	8	8	7	6	8	108	54	.667	...
L.A.	10	...	10	11	10	12	7	5	6	7	5	5	88	74	.543	20
San Fran.	5	8	...	10	9	13	7	7	4	5	7	5	80	81	.497	27.5
San Diego	7	7	8	...	11	9	7	5	4	5	4	4	71	91	.438	37
Atlanta	3	8	8	7	...	12	5	8	4	5	4	3	67	94	.416	40.5
Houston	5	6	5	9	6	...	5	8	4	6	6	4	64	97	.398	43.5

SIGNIFICANT EVENTS

■ **January 5:** Houston righthander Don Wilson died of carbon monoxide poisoning in the garage of his Houston home, an apparent suicide victim at age 29.

■ **November 26:** Boston's Fred Lynn became the first rookie MVP winner in baseball history.

■ **December 23:** Baseball's reserve system was shattered when labor arbitrator Peter Seitz handed pitchers Andy Messersmith and Dave McNally their unqualified free agency.

MEMORABLE MOMENTS

■ **April 8:** Frank Robinson belted a dramatic home run and led the Indians to a 5-3 Opening Day victory over the Yankees in his historic debut as baseball's first black manager.

■ **May 1:** Milwaukee's Hank Aaron drove in two runs in a 17-3 victory over Detroit and became baseball's all-time RBI leader with 2,211.

■ **June 1:** California's Nolan Ryan tied Sandy Koufax's record when he pitched his fourth career no-hitter, a 1-0 victory over the Orioles.

■ **June 18:** Boston rookie Fred Lynn drove in 10 runs with three home runs, a triple and a single in a 15-1 victory over the Tigers.

■ **September 16:** Pirates second baseman Rennie Stennett became the first modern-era player to collect seven hits in a nine-inning game—a 22-0 victory over the Cubs.

■ **September 28:** Oakland's Vida Blue, Glenn Abbott, Paul Lindblad and Rollie Fingers combined for the first multi-pitcher no-hitter in baseball history—a final-day 5-0 victory over the Angels.

LEADERS

American League
BA: Rod Carew, Min., .359.
Runs: Fred Lynn, Bos., 103.
Hits: George Brett, K.C., 195.
TB: George Scott, Mil., 318.
HR: Reggie Jackson, Oak.; George Scott, Mil., 36.
RBI: George Scott, Mil., 109.
SB: Mickey Rivers, Cal., 70.
Wins: Catfish Hunter, N.Y.; Jim Palmer, Bal., 23.
ERA: Jim Palmer, Bal., 2.09.
CG: Catfish Hunter, N.Y., 30.
IP: Catfish Hunter, N.Y., 328.
SO: Frank Tanana, Cal., 269.
SV: Goose Gossage, Chi., 26.

National League
BA: Bill Madlock, Chi., .354.
Runs: Pete Rose, Cin., 112.
Hits: Dave Cash, Phil., 213.
TB: Greg Luzinski, Phil., 322.
HR: Mike Schmidt, Phil., 38.
RBI: Greg Luzinski, Phil., 120.
SB: Dave Lopes, L.A., 77.
Wins: Tom Seaver, N.Y., 22.
ERA: Randy Jones, S.D., 2.24.
CG: Andy Messersmith, L.A., 19.
IP: Andy Messersmith, L.A., 321.2.
SO: Tom Seaver, N.Y., 243.
SV: Rawly Eastwick, Cin.; Al Hrabosky, St.L., 22.

A.L. 20-game winners
Jim Palmer, Bal., 23-11
Catfish Hunter, N.Y., 23-14
Vida Blue, Oak., 22-11
Mike Torrez, Bal., 20-9
Jim Kaat, Chi., 20-14

N.L. 20-game winners
Tom Seaver, N.Y., 22-9
Randy Jones, S.D., 20-12

A.L. 100 RBIs
George Scott, Mil., 109
John Mayberry, K.C., 106
Fred Lynn, Bos., 105
Reggie Jackson, Oak., 104
Thurman Munson, N.Y., 102
Jim Rice, Bos., 102

N.L. 100 RBIs
Greg Luzinski, Phil., 120
Johnny Bench, Cin., 110
Tony Perez, Cin., 109
Rusty Staub, N.Y., 105
Ron Cey, L.A., 101
Willie Montanez, Phil.-S.F., 101
Dave Parker, Pit., 101
Ted Simmons, St.L., 100

Most Valuable Player
A.L.: Fred Lynn, OF, Bos.
N.L.: Joe Morgan, 2B, Cin.

Cy Young Award
A.L.: Jim Palmer, Bal.
N.L.: Tom Seaver, N.Y.

Rookie of the Year
A.L.: Fred Lynn, OF, Bos.
N.L.: John Montefusco, P, S.F.

Hall of Fame additions
Earl Averill, OF, 1929-41
Bucky Harris, manager
Billy Herman, 2B, 1931-47
Judy Johnson, 3B, Negro Leagues
Ralph Kiner, OF, 1946-55

ALL-STAR GAME

■ **Winner:** The N.L., having uncharacteristically squandered a 3-0 lead, scored three ninth-inning runs and escaped with a 6-3 victory, its 12th in 13 years.

■ **Key inning:** The ninth, when Bill Madlock delivered the big blow with a two-run single and Pete Rose added an insurance run with a sacrifice fly.

■ **Memorable moment:** A long sixth-inning three-run homer by Carl Yastrzemski that wiped away the 3-0 deficit and gave the A.L. brief hope for a victory.

■ **Top guns:** Steve Garvey (Dodgers), Jim Wynn (Dodgers), Rose (Reds), Madlock (Cubs), N.L.; Yastrzemski (Red Sox), Bert Campaneris (Athletics), A.L.

■ **MVP:** Madlock.

Linescore
July 15, at Milwaukee's County Stadium
N.L............0 2 1 0 0 0 0 0 3—6 13 1
A.L............0 0 0 0 0 3 0 0 0—3 10 1
Reuss (Pirates), Sutton (Dodgers) 4, Seaver (Mets) 6, Matlack (Mets) 7, Jones (Padres) 9; Blue (Athletics), Busby (Royals) 3, Kaat (White Sox) 5, Hunter (Yankees) 7, Gossage (White Sox) 9. W—Matlack. L—Hunter. HR—Garvey, Wynn, N.L.; Yastrzemski, A.L.

ALCS

■ **Winner:** The Boston Red Sox brought a surprising end to Oakland's three-year championship reign and made it look as easy as 1-2-3.

■ **Turning point:** Oakland's four-error first-game performance that helped Boston to a 7-1 victory and set the tone for the series.

■ **Memorable moment:** Reggie Jackson's first-inning Game 2 home run, which gave Oakland its only lead of the series.

■ **Top guns:** Luis Tiant (1-0, 0.00 ERA), Carl Yastrzemski (.455), Rick Burleson (.444), Carlton Fisk (.417), Red Sox; Sal Bando (.500), Jackson (.417), Athletics.

■ **MVP:** Yastrzemski.

Linescores

Game 1—October 4, at Boston
Oakland........0 0 0 0 0 0 0 1 0—1 3 4
Boston ....2 0 0 0 0 0 5 0 x—7 8 3
Holtzman, Todd (7), Lindblad (7), Bosman (7), Abbott (8); Tiant. W—Tiant. L—Holtzman.

Game 2—October 5, at Boston
Oakland......2 0 0 1 0 0 0 0 0—3 10 0
Boston ......0 0 0 3 0 1 1 1 x—6 12 0
Blue, Todd (4), Fingers (5); Cleveland, Moret (6), Drago (7). W—Moret. L—Fingers. S—Drago. HR—Jackson (Oak.); Yastrzemski, Petrocelli (Bos.)

Game 3—October 7, at Oakland
Boston ......0 0 0 1 3 0 0 1 0—5 11 1
Oakland......0 0 0 0 0 1 0 2 0—3 6 2
Wise, Drago (8); Holtzman, Todd (5), Lindblad (5). W—Wise. L—Holtzman. S—Drago.

NLCS

■ **Winner:** Cincinnati's Big Red Machine rolled over Pittsburgh in a quick and easy Championship Series.

■ **Turning point:** Reds pitcher Don Gullett hit a homer, drove in three runs and pitched an eight-hit, first-game victory.

■ **Memorable moment:** A two-run eighth-inning home run by Cincinnati's Pete Rose erased a 2-1, Game 3 deficit in a contest eventually won by the Reds in 10 innings, 5-3.

■ **Top guns:** Gullett (1-0, 1 HR, 3 RBIs), Dave Concepcion (.455), Tony Perez (.417, 4 RBIs), Reds; Richie Zisk (.500), Pirates.

■ **MVP:** Gullett.

Linescores

Game 1—October 4, at Cincinnati
Pitt.............0 2 0 0 0 0 0 0 1—3 8 0
Cin. ....0 1 3 0 4 0 0 0 x—8 11 0
Reuss, Brett (3), Demery (5), Ellis (7); Gullett. W—Gullett. L—Reuss. HR—Gullett (Cin.).

Game 2—October 5, at Cincinnati
Pitt.............0 0 0 1 0 0 0 0 0—1 5 0
Cin. ....2 0 0 2 0 1 1 0 x—6 12 1
Rooker, Tekulve (5), Brett (6), Kison (7); Norman, Eastwick (7). W—Norman. L—Rooker. S—Eastwick. HR—Perez (Cin.).

Game 3—October 7, at Pittsburgh
Cin. ....0 1 0 0 0 0 0 2 0 2—5 6 0
Pitt............0 0 0 0 0 2 0 0 1 0—3 7 2
Nolan, Carroll (7), McEnaney (8), Eastwick (9), Borbon (10); Candelaria, Giusti (8), Hernandez (10), Tekulve (10). W—Eastwick. L—Hernandez. S—Borbon. HR—Concepcion, Rose (Cin.); Oliver (Pit.).

WORLD SERIES

■ **Winner:** Cincinnati's Big Red Machine held off the gritty Red Sox in one of the most exciting Series in baseball history.

■ **Turning point:** Reds second baseman Joe Morgan's Series-deciding single in the ninth inning of Game 7. The Series was that close.

■ **Memorable moments:** In the Red Sox's 7-6 Game 6 victory: Boston pinch-hitter Bernie Carbo's game-tying, three-run homer in the eighth inning; Boston right fielder Dwight Evans' spectacular, leaping, 11th-inning catch that he turned into a rally-killing double play; Boston catcher Carlton Fisk's dramatic, game-ending, "fair-or-foul" home run in the 12th inning.

■ **Top guns:** Pete Rose (.370), Tony Perez (3 HR, 7 RBIs), Reds; Carbo (2 PH HR), Carl Yastrzemski (.310, 4 RBIs), Rico Petrocelli (.308, 4 RBIs), Red Sox.

■ **MVP:** Rose.

Linescores

Game 1—October 11, at Boston
Cin. ....0 0 0 0 0 0 0 0 0—0 5 0
Bos. ....0 0 0 0 0 0 6 0 x—6 12 0
Gullett, Carroll (7), McEnaney (7); Tiant. W—Tiant. L—Gullett.

Game 2—October 12, at Boston
Cin. ....0 0 0 1 0 0 0 0 2—3 7 1
Bos. ....1 0 0 0 0 1 0 0 0—2 7 0
Billingham, Borbon (6), McEnaney (7), Eastwick (8); Lee, Drago (9). W—Eastwick. L—Drago.

Game 3—October 14, at Cincinnati
Bos. ......0 1 0 0 0 1 1 0 2 0—5 10 2
Cin. ....0 0 0 2 3 0 0 0 0 1—6 7 0
Wise, Burton (5), Cleveland (5), Willoughby (7), Moret (10); Nolan, Darcy (5), Carroll (7), McEnaney (7), Eastwick (9). W—Eastwick. L—Willoughby. HR—Fisk, Carbo, Evans (Bos.); Bench, Concepcion, Geronimo (Cin.).

Game 4—October 15, at Cincinnati
Bos. ....0 0 0 5 0 0 0 0 0—5 11 1
Cin. ....2 0 0 2 0 0 0 0 0—4 9 1
Tiant; Norman, Borbon (4), Carroll (5), Eastwick (7). W—Tiant. L—Norman.

Game 5—October 16, at Cincinnati
Bos. ....1 0 0 0 0 0 0 0 1—2 5 0
Cin. ....0 0 0 1 1 3 0 1 x—6 8 0
Cleveland, Willoughby (6), Pole (8), Segui (8); Gullett, Eastwick (9). W—Gullett. L—Cleveland. S—Eastwick. HR—Perez 2 (Cin.).

Game 6—October 21, at Boston
Cin.....0 0 0 0 3 0 2 1 0 0 0 0—6 14 0
Bos. ..3 0 0 0 0 0 0 3 0 0 0 1—7 10 1
Nolan, Norman (3), Billingham (3), Carroll (5), Borbon (6), Eastwick (8), McEnaney (9), Darcy (10); Tiant, Moret (8), Drago (9), Wise (12). W—Wise. L—Darcy. HR—Lynn, Carbo, Fisk (Bos.); Geronimo (Cin.).

Game 7—October 22, at Boston
Cin. ....0 0 0 0 0 2 1 0 1—4 9 0
Bos. ....0 0 3 0 0 0 0 0 0—3 5 2
Gullett, Billingham (5), Carroll (7), McEnaney (9); Lee, Moret (7), Willoughby (7), Burton (9), Cleveland (9). W—Carroll. L—Burton. S—McEnaney. HR—Perez (Cin.).

FINAL STANDINGS

American League

East Division

Team	N.Y.	Bal.	Bos.	Cle.	Det.	Mil.	Cal.	Chi.	K.C.	Min.	Oak.	Tex.	W	L	Pct.	GB
New York	...	5	11	12	8	13	7	11	5	10	6	9	97	62	.610	...
Baltimore	13	...	7	7	12	11	8	8	6	4	4	8	88	74	.543	10.5
Boston	7	11	...	9	14	12	7	6	3	7	4	3	83	79	.512	15.5
Cleveland	4	11	9	...	6	11	5	9	6	9	4	7	81	78	.509	16
Detroit	9	6	4	12	...	12	6	6	4	4	6	5	74	87	.460	24
Milwaukee	5	7	6	6	6	...	8	5	4	5	5	10	66	95	.410	32

West Division

Team	K.C.	Oak.	Min.	Cal.	Tex.	Chi.	Bal.	Bos.	Cle.	Det.	Mil.	N.Y.	W	L	Pct.	GB
Kansas City	...	9	10	10	7	10	6	9	6	8	8	7	90	72	.556	...
Oakland	9	...	7	12	7	9	8	8	8	6	7	8	87	74	.540	2.5
Minnesota	8	11	...	10	11	11	8	5	3	8	8	2	85	77	.525	5
California	8	6	8	...	12	11	4	5	7	6	4	5	76	86	.469	14
Texas	11	11	7	6	...	11	4	9	5	7	2	3	76	86	.469	14
Chicago	8	8	7	7	7	...	4	6	3	6	7	1	64	97	.398	25.5

National League

East Division

Team	Phi.	Pit.	N.Y.	Chi.	St.L.	Mon.	Atl.	Cin.	Hou.	L.A.	S.D.	S.F.	W	L	Pct.	GB
Philadelphia	...	8	13	10	12	15	7	7	8	7	8	6	101	61	.623	...
Pittsburgh	10	...	8	10	12	10	9	4	10	3	7	9	92	70	.568	9
New York	5	10	...	13	9	10	8	6	6	5	7	7	86	76	.531	15
Chicago	8	8	5	...	12	11	6	3	5	3	6	8	75	87	.463	26
St. Louis	6	6	9	6	...	11	8	6	3	2	8	7	72	90	.444	29
Montreal	3	8	8	7	7	...	4	3	2	2	4	7	55	107	.340	46

West Division

Team	Cin.	L.A.	Hou.	S.F.	S.D.	Atl.	Chi.	Mon.	N.Y.	Phi.	Pit.	St.L.	W	L	Pct.	GB
Cincinnati	...	13	12	9	13	12	9	9	6	5	8	6	102	60	.630	...
L.A.	5	...	13	8	6	10	9	10	7	5	9	10	92	70	.568	10
Houston	6	5	...	10	10	11	7	10	6	4	2	9	80	82	.494	22
San Fran.	9	10	8	...	10	9	4	5	5	6	3	5	74	88	.457	28
San Diego	5	12	8	8	...	8	6	8	5	4	5	4	73	89	.451	29
Atlanta	6	8	7	9	10	...	6	8	4	5	3	4	70	92	.432	32

SIGNIFICANT EVENTS

■ **January 14:** N.L. owners approved the sale of the Braves to Ted Turner, head of Turner Communications, for $12 million.

■ **April 10:** Free-agent pitcher Andy Messersmith signed a "lifetime contract" to pitch for new Braves owner Turner.

■ **April 25:** Cubs center fielder Rick Monday dashed into left field at Dodger Stadium and snatched an American flag away from two protestors who were trying to set it on fire.

■ **June 18:** Commissioner Bowie Kuhn voided Oakland owner Charles O. Finley's sale of Vida Blue to the Yankees and Joe Rudi and Rollie Fingers to the Red Sox.

■ **September 29:** Walter Alston, who compiled 2,040 victories over 23 seasons as manager of the Dodgers, retired at age 64.

■ **November 5:** The A.L. conducted its third expansion draft to fill rosters of new teams in Seattle and Toronto.

■ **November 6:** Reliever Bill Campbell, one of the plums of baseball's first free-agent reentry draft, signed a four-year, $1 million contract with the Red Sox.

MEMORABLE MOMENTS

■ **April 17:** Mike Schmidt's two-run, 10th-inning home run, his record-tying fourth of the game, gave the Phillies an 18-16 victory over the Cubs at Wrigley Field.

■ **October 3:** George Brett collected three final-day hits and edged Kansas City teammate Hal McRae, .3333 to .3326, for the A.L. batting title.

LEADERS

American League
BA: George Brett, K.C., .333.
Runs: Roy White, N.Y., 104.
Hits: George Brett, K.C., 215.
TB: George Brett, K.C., 298.
HR: Graig Nettles, N.Y., 32.
RBI: Lee May, Bal., 109.
SB: Bill North, Oak., 75.
Wins: Jim Palmer, Bal., 22.
ERA: Mark Fidrych, Det., 2.34.
CG: Mark Fidrych, Det., 24.
IP: Jim Palmer, Bal., 315.
SO: Nolan Ryan, Cal., 327.
SV: Sparky Lyle, N.Y., 23.

National League
BA: Bill Madlock, Chi., .339.
Runs: Pete Rose, Cin., 130.
Hits: Pete Rose, Cin., 215.
TB: Mike Schmidt, Phil., 306.
HR: Mike Schmidt, Phil., 38.
RBI: George Foster, Cin., 121.
SB: Dave Lopes, L.A., 63.
Wins: Randy Jones, S.D., 22.
ERA: John Denny, St.L., 2.52.
CG: Randy Jones, S.D., 25.
IP: Randy Jones, S.D., 315.1.
SO: Tom Seaver, N.Y., 235.
SV: Rawly Eastwick, Cin., 26.

A.L. 20-game winners
Jim Palmer, Bal., 22-13
Luis Tiant, Bos., 21-12
Wayne Garland, Bal., 20-7

N.L. 20-game winners
Randy Jones, S.D., 22-14
Jerry Koosman, N.Y., 21-10
Don Sutton, L.A., 21-10
Steve Carlton, Phil., 20-7
J.R. Richard, Hou., 20-15

A.L. 100 RBIs
Lee May, Bal., 109
Thurman Munson, N.Y., 105
Carl Yastrzemski, Bos., 102

N.L. 100 RBIs
George Foster, Cin., 121
Joe Morgan, Cin., 111
Mike Schmidt, Phil., 107
Bob Watson, Hou., 102

Most Valuable Player
A.L.: Thurman Munson, C, N.Y.
N.L.: Joe Morgan, 2B, Cin.

Cy Young Award
A.L.: Jim Palmer, Bal.
N.L.: Randy Jones, S.D.

Rookie of the Year
A.L.: Mark Fidrych, P, Det.
N.L.: Butch Metzger, P, S.D.
Pat Zachry, P, Cin.

Hall of Fame additions
Oscar Charleston, OF, Negro Leagues
Roger Connor, 1B, 1880-97
Cal Hubbard, umpire
Bob Lemon, P, 1946-58
Fred Lindstrom, 3B, 1924-36
Robin Roberts, P, 1948-66

ALL-STAR GAME

■ **Winner:** Baseball celebrated the nation's Bicentennial with another N.L. All-Star victory — a 7-1 rout sparked by George Foster and Cesar Cedeno.

■ **Key innings:** The third, when Foster blasted a two-run homer, and the eighth, when Cedeno secured the outcome with another two-run shot.

■ **Memorable moment:** The five-hit pitching of an N.L. staff that surrendered the A.L.'s lone run on a homer by Fred Lynn.

■ **Top guns:** Randy Jones (Padres), Foster (Reds), Cedeno (Astros), Pete Rose (Reds), N.L.; Lynn (Red Sox), Rusty Staub (Tigers), A.L.

■ **MVP:** Foster.

Linescore
July 13, at Philadelphia's Veterans Stadium
A.L............0 0 0 1 0 0 0 0 0—1 5 0
N.L............2 0 2 0 0 0 0 3 x—7 10 0
Fidrych (Tigers), Hunter (Yankees) 3, Tiant (Red Sox) 5, Tanana (Angels) 7, Jones (Padres), Seaver (Mets) 4, Montefusco (Giants) 6, Rhoden (Dodgers) 8, Forsch (Astros) 9. W—Jones. L—Fidrych. HR—Foster, Cedeno, N.L.; Lynn, A.L.

ALCS

■ **Winner:** The New York Yankees, absent from post-season play since 1964, qualified for their 30th World Series with a riveting five-game victory over postseason newcomer Kansas City.

■ **Turning point:** The Yankees' 5-3 Game 3 victory, which was fueled by a homer and three RBIs by first baseman Chris Chambliss.

■ **Memorable moment:** Chambliss' dramatic series-ending home run leading off the ninth inning of Game 5. The blast off Royals reliever Mark Littell gave the Yankees a 7-6 victory and touched off a wild mob scene at Yankee Stadium.

■ **Top guns:** Chambliss (.524, 2 HR, 8 RBIs), Thurman Munson (.435), Mickey Rivers (.348), Yankees; Paul Splittorff (1-0, 1.93 ERA), George Brett (.444, 5 RBIs), Royals.

■ **MVP:** Chambliss.

Linescores
Game 1—October 9, at Kansas City
N.Y.............2 0 0 0 0 0 0 0 2—4 12 0
K.C.............0 0 0 0 0 0 0 1 0—1 5 2
Hunter; Gura, Littell (9). W—Hunter. L—Gura.

Game 2—October 10, at Kansas City
N.Y.............0 1 2 0 0 0 0 0 0—3 12 5
K.C.............2 0 0 0 0 2 0 3 x—7 9 0
Figueroa, Tidrow (6); Leonard, Splittorff (3), Mingori (6). W—Splittorff. L—Figueroa.

Game 3—October 12, at New York
K.C.............3 0 0 0 0 0 0 0 0—3 6 0
N.Y.............0 0 0 2 0 3 0 0 x—5 9 0
Hassler, Pattin (6), Hall (6), Mingori (6), Littell (6); Ellis, Lyle (9). W—Ellis. L—Hassler. S—Lyle. HR—Chambliss (N.Y.).

Game 4—October 13, at New York
K.C.............0 3 0 2 0 1 0 1 0—7 9 1
N.Y.............0 2 0 0 0 1 0 1—4 11 0
Gura, Bird (3), Mingori (7); Hunter, Tidrow (4), Jackson (7). W—Bird. L—Hunter. S—Mingori. HR—Nettles 2 (N.Y.).

Game 5—October 14, at New York
K.C.............2 1 0 0 0 0 0 3 0—6 11 1
N.Y.............2 0 2 0 0 2 0 0 1—7 11 1
Leonard, Splittorff (1), Pattin (4), Hassler (5), Littell (7); Figueroa, Jackson (8), Tidrow (9). W—Tidrow. L—Littell. HR—Mayberry, Brett (K.C.); Chambliss (N.Y.).

NLCS

■ **Winner:** Philadelphia was no match for the powerful Reds, who were being hailed as one of the great teams in baseball history.

■ **Turning point:** The Reds took quick control with a 6-3 first-game victory over the Phillies and ace lefthander Steve Carlton.

■ **Memorable moment:** The ninth inning of Game 3. After tying the game with consecutive home runs by George Foster and Johnny Bench, the Reds claimed a 7-6 victory when Ken Griffey singled with the bases loaded off reliever Tom Underwood.

■ **Top guns:** Don Gullett (1-0, 1.13 ERA), Pete Rose (.429), Griffey (.385), Foster (2 HR, 4 RBIs), Reds; Jay Johnstone (.778), Phillies.

■ **MVP:** Griffey.

Linescores
Game 1—October 9, at Philadelphia
Cin. ....0 0 1 0 0 2 0 3 0—6 10 0
Phil. ....1 0 0 0 0 0 0 0 2—3 6 1
Gullett, Eastwick (9); Carlton, McGraw (8). W—Gullett. L—Carlton. HR—Foster (Cin.).

Game 2—October 10, at Philadelphia
Cin. ....0 0 0 0 0 4 2 0 0—6 6 0
Phil. ....0 1 0 0 1 0 0 0 0—2 10 1
Zachry, Borbon (6); Lonborg, Garber (6), McGraw (7), Reed (7). W—Zachry. L—Lonborg. S—Borbon. HR—Luzinski (Phil.).

Game 3—October 12, at Cincinnati
Phil. ....0 0 0 1 0 0 2 2 1—6 11 0
Cin. ....0 0 0 0 0 0 4 0 3—7 9 2
Kaat, Reed (7), Garber (9), Lonborg (8); Nolan, Sarmiento (6), Borbon (7), Eastwick (8). W—Eastwick. L—Garber. HR—Foster, Bench (Cin.).

WORLD SERIES

■ **Winner:** Cincinnati's Big Red Machine was in full gear as it rolled over the Yankees, who were making their first Series appearance since 1964.

■ **Turning point:** Joe Morgan's first-inning home run in Game 1. The Reds never looked back.

■ **Memorable moment:** Game 3 at refurbished Yankee Stadium. Despite a 6-2 New York loss, the atmosphere was electric and baseball's most revered ballpark was the stately host for its 28th World Series.

■ **Top guns:** Johnny Bench (.533, 2 HR, 6 RBIs), George Foster (.429), Dave Concepcion (.357), Dan Driessen (.357), Reds; Thurman Munson (.529), Yankees.

■ **MVP:** Bench.

Linescores
Game 1—October 16, at Cincinnati
N.Y.............0 1 0 0 0 0 0 0 0—1 5 1
Cin. ....1 0 1 0 0 1 2 0 x—5 10 1
Alexander, Lyle (7); Gullett, Borbon (8). W—Gullett. L—Alexander. HR—Morgan (Cin.).

Game 2—October 17, at Cincinnati
N.Y.............0 0 0 1 0 0 2 0 0—3 9 1
Cin. ....0 3 0 0 0 0 0 1—4 10 0
Hunter; Norman, Billingham (7). W—Billingham. L—Hunter.

Game 3—October 19, at New York
Cin. ....0 3 0 1 0 0 2 0—6 13 2
N.Y.............0 0 0 1 0 0 1 0 0—2 8 0
Zachry, McEnaney (7); Ellis, Jackson (4), Tidrow (8). W—Zachry. L—Ellis. S—McEnaney. HR—Driessen (Cin.); Mason (N.Y.).

Game 4—October 21, at New York
Cin. ....0 0 0 3 0 0 0 0 4—7 9 2
N.Y.............1 0 0 0 1 0 0 0 0—2 8 0
Nolan, McEnaney (7); Figueroa, Tidrow (9), Lyle (9). W—Nolan. L—Figueroa. S—McEnaney. HR—Bench 2 (Cin.).

HISTORY

1977

FINAL STANDINGS

American League

East Division

Team	N.Y.	Bos.	Bal.	Det.	Cle.	Mil.	Tor.	Cal.	Chi.	K.C.	Min.	Oak.	Sea.	Tex.	W	L	Pct.	GB
New York	...	7	7	9	12	7	9	7	7	5	8	9	6	7	100	62	.617	...
Boston	8	...	8	9	8	9	12	7	3	5	4	8	10	6	97	64	.602	2.5
Baltimore	8	6	...	12	11	11	10	5	5	4	6	8	7	4	97	64	.602	2.5
Detroit	6	6	3	...	7	10	10	6	6	3	5	5	5	2	74	88	.457	26
Cleveland	3	7	4	8	...	11	9	4	4	3	2	7	7	2	71	90	.441	28.5
Milwaukee	8	6	4	5	4	...	8	5	5	2	3	5	7	5	67	95	.414	33
Toronto	6	3	5	5	5	7	...	4	3	2	1	3	6	4	54	107	.335	45.5

West Division

Team	K.C.	Tex.	Chi.	Min.	Cal.	Sea.	Oak.	Bal.	Bos.	Cle.	Det.	Mil.	N.Y.	Tor.	W	L	Pct.	GB
Kansas City	...	8	7	10	9	11	9	7	5	7	8	8	5	8	102	60	.630	...
Texas	7	...	9	7	10	6	13	6	4	9	8	5	3	7	94	68	.580	8
Chicago	8	6	...	10	7	10	10	5	7	6	4	6	3	8	90	72	.556	12
Minnesota	5	8	5	...	8	7	8	4	6	9	5	8	2	9	84	77	.522	17.5
California	6	5	8	7	...	9	5	6	3	6	4	5	4	6	74	88	.457	28
Seattle	4	9	5	8	6	...	8	3	1	3	6	3	4	4	64	98	.395	38
Oakland	6	2	5	6	10	7	...	2	3	3	5	5	2	7	63	98	.391	38.5

National League

East Division

Team	Phi.	Pit.	St.L.	Chi.	Mon.	N.Y.	Atl.	Cin.	Hou.	L.A.	S.D.	S.F.	W	L	Pct.	GB
Philadelphia	...	8	11	12	11	13	10	4	8	6	9	9	101	61	.623	...
Pittsburgh	10	...	9	11	11	14	9	9	8	3	10	2	96	66	.593	5
St.Louis	7	9	...	11	6	10	11	7	7	6	4	5	83	79	.512	18
Chicago	6	7	7	...	10	9	7	7	6	6	7	9	81	81	.500	20
Montreal	7	7	12	8	...	10	6	5	4	5	5	6	75	87	.463	26
New York	5	4	8	9	8	...	5	2	6	4	6	7	64	98	.395	37

West Division

Team	L.A.	Cin.	Hou.	S.F.	S.D.	Atl.	Chi.	Mon.	N.Y.	Phi.	Pit.	St.L.	W	L	Pct.	GB
Los Angeles	...	8	9	14	12	13	6	7	8	6	9	6	98	64	.605	...
Cincinnati	10	...	5	10	11	14	5	7	10	8	3	5	88	74	.543	10
Houston	9	13	...	9	8	9	6	8	6	4	4	5	81	81	.500	17
San Fran.	4	8	9	..	10	10	3	6	5	3	10	7	75	87	.463	23
San Diego	6	7	10	8	...	7	5	7	6	3	2	8	69	93	.426	29
Atlanta	5	4	9	8	11	...	5	6	7	2	3	1	61	101	.377	37

SIGNIFICANT EVENTS

■ **January 2:** Commissioner Bowie Kuhn suspended Braves owner Ted Turner for a year and fined him $10,000 for "tampering" with free-agent outfielder Gary Matthews.

■ **April 6-7:** The expansion Mariners lost their debut, 7-0, to the Angels, but the Blue Jays won their Toronto inaugural, 9-5, over the White Sox.

■ **April 15:** The Expos opened new Olympic Stadium, but the Phillies spoiled the occasion with a 7-2 victory.

■ **March 28:** Texas second baseman Lenny Randle, frustrated over losing his starting job, sent 50-year-old manager Frank Lucchesi to the hospital with a vicious beating before a spring training game.

■ **October 25:** Yankees lefty Sparky Lyle became the first A.L. reliever to win a Cy Young Award.

■ **November 8:** Cincinnati's George Foster, the first player to top the 50-homer barrier since 1965, earned N.L. MVP honors.

MEMORABLE MOMENTS

■ **June 8:** California's Nolan Ryan struck out 19 Blue Jays in a 10-inning performance, reaching that single-game plateau for the fourth time.

■ **August 29:** St. Louis' Lou Brock swiped two bases in a game against San Diego, lifting his career total to 893 and passing Ty Cobb as baseball's greatest modern-era basestealer.

LEADERS

American League
BA: Rod Carew, Min., .388.
Runs: Rod Carew, Min., 128.
Hits: Rod Carew, Min., 239.
TB: Jim Rice, Bos., 382.
HR: Jim Rice, Bos., 39.
RBI: Larry Hisle, Min., 119.
SB: Fred Patek, K.C., 53.
Wins: Dave Goltz, Min.; Dennis Leonard, K.C.; Jim Palmer, Bal., 20.
ERA: Frank Tanana, Cal., 2.54.
CG: Jim Palmer, Bal.; Nolan Ryan, Cal., 22.
IP: Jim Palmer, Bal., 319.
SO: Nolan Ryan, Cal., 341.
SV: Bill Campbell, Bos., 31.

National League
BA: Dave Parker, Pit., .338.
Runs: George Foster, Cin., 124.
Hits: Dave Parker, Pit., 215.
TB: George Foster, Cin., 388.
HR: George Foster, Cin., 52.
RBI: George Foster, Cin., 149.
SB: Frank Taveras, Pit., 70.
Wins: Steve Carlton, Phil., 23.
ERA: John Candelaria, Pit., 2.34.
CG: Phil Niekro, Atl., 20.
IP: Phil Niekro, Atl., 330.1.
SO: Phil Niekro, Atl., 262.
SV: Rollie Fingers, S.D., 35.

A.L. 20-game winners
Jim Palmer, Bal., 20-11
Dave Goltz, Min., 20-11
Dennis Leonard, K.C., 20-12

N.L. 20-game winners
Steve Carlton, Phil., 23-10
Tom Seaver, N.Y.-Cin., 21-6
John Candelaria, Pit., 20-5
Bob Forsch, St.L., 20-7
Tommy John, L.A., 20-7
Rick Reuschel, Chi., 20-10

A.L. 100 RBIs
Larry Hisle, Min., 119
Bobby Bonds, Cal., 115
Jim Rice, Bos., 114
Al Cowens, K.C., 112
Butch Hobson, Bos., 112
Reggie Jackson, N.Y., 110
Graig Nettles, N.Y., 107
Jason Thompson, Det., 105
Carlton Fisk, Bos., 102
Carl Yastrzemski, Bos., 102
Rusty Staub, Det., 101
Richie Zisk, Chi., 101
Rod Carew, Min., 100
Thurman Munson, N.Y., 100

N.L. 100 RBIs
George Foster, Cin., 149
Greg Luzinski, Phil., 130
Steve Garvey, L.A., 115
Jeff Burroughs, Atl., 114
Ron Cey, L.A., 110
Bob Watson, Hou., 110
Johnny Bench, Cin., 109
Bill Robinson, Pit., 104
Mike Schmidt, Phil., 101

N.L. 40 homers
George Foster, Cin., 52
Jeff Burroughs, Atl., 41

Most Valuable Player
A.L.: Rod Carew, 1B, Min.
N.L.: George Foster, OF, Cin.

Cy Young Award
A.L.: Sparky Lyle, N.Y.
N.L.: Steve Carlton, Phil.

Rookie of the Year
A.L.: Eddie Murray, 1B, Bal.
N.L.: Andre Dawson, OF, Mon.

Hall of Fame additions
Ernie Banks, SS, 1953-71
Martin Dihigo, P/IF, Negro Leagues
John Henry Lloyd, SS, Negro Leagues
Al Lopez, manager
Amos Rusie, P, 1889-1901
Joe Sewell, SS, 1920-33

ALL-STAR GAME

■ **Winner:** The N.L. continued its All-Star mastery with a 7-5 victory — its sixth in a row and 14th in 15 contests.

■ **Key inning:** The first, when the N.L. struck for four quick runs. A leadoff homer by Joe Morgan and a two-run shot by Greg Luzinski were the big blows.

■ **Memorable moment:** Watching the N.L. close out another All-Star victory at venerable Yankee Stadium, where so much A.L. glory had been achieved.

■ **Top guns:** Don Sutton (Dodgers), Morgan (Reds), Luzinski (Phillies), Dave Winfield (Padres), Steve Garvey (Dodgers), N.L.; Dennis Eckersley (Indians), Richie Zisk (White Sox), George Scott (Red Sox), A.L.

■ **MVP:** Sutton.

Linescore

July 19, at New York's Yankee Stadium
N.L. ....4 0 1 0 0 0 0 2 0—7 9 1
A.L. ....0 0 0 0 0 2 1 0 2—5 8 0
Sutton (Dodgers), Lavelle (Giants) 4, Seaver (Reds) 6, R. Reuschel (Cubs) 8, Gossage (Pirates) 9; Palmer (Orioles), Kern (Indians) 3, Eckersley (Indians) 4, LaRoche (Angels) 6, Campbell (Red Sox) 7, Lyle (Yankees) 8. W—Sutton. L—Palmer. HR—Morgan, Luzinski, Garvey, N.L.; Scott, A.L.

ALCS

■ **Winner:** The Yankees, bidding to return to the World Series for a second consecutive season, needed a three-run ninth-inning rally to defeat Kansas City in the decisive fifth game.

■ **Turning point:** Sparky Lyle's 5⅓ innings of scoreless Game 4 relief after the Royals, bidding to close out the series, had cut a 4-0 Yankee lead to 5-4. The Yanks evened the series with a 6-4 win.

■ **Memorable moment:** A bloop single by light-hitting Yankee Paul Blair leading off the ninth inning of Game 5. Blair's hit off Royals ace Dennis Leonard set up the Yankees' series-winning rally.

■ **Top guns:** Lyle (2-0, 0.96 ERA), Cliff Johnson (.400), Mickey Rivers (.391), Yankees; Hal McRae (.444), Fred Patek (.389), Royals.

■ **MVP:** Lyle.

Linescores

Game 1—October 5, at New York
K.C. ....2 2 2 0 0 0 0 1 0—7 9 0
N.Y. ....0 0 2 0 0 0 0 0 0—2 9 0
Splittorff, Bird (9); Gullett, Tidrow (3), Lyle (9). W—Splittorff. L—Gullett. HR—McRae, Mayberry, Cowens (K.C.); Munson (N.Y.).

Game 2—October 6, at New York
K.C. ....0 0 1 0 0 1 0 0 0—2 3 1
N.Y. ....0 0 0 0 2 3 0 1 x—6 10 1
Hassler, Littell (6), Mingori (8); Guidry. W—Guidry. L—Hassler. HR—Johnson (N.Y.).

Game 3—October 7, at Kansas City
N.Y. ....0 0 0 0 1 0 0 0 1—2 4 1
K.C. ....0 1 1 0 1 2 1 0 x—6 12 1
Torrez, Lyle (6); Leonard. W—Leonard. L—Torrez.

Game 4—October 8, at Kansas City
N.Y. ....1 2 1 1 0 0 0 0 1—6 13 0
K.C. ....0 0 2 2 0 0 0 0 0—4 8 2
Figueroa, Tidrow (4), Lyle (4); Gura, Pattin (3), Mingori (9), Bird (9). W—Lyle. L—Gura.

Game 5—October 9, at Kansas City
N.Y. ....0 0 1 0 0 0 0 1 3—5 10 0
K.C. ....2 0 1 0 0 0 0 0 0—3 10 1
Guidry, Torrez (3), Lyle (8); Splittorff, Bird (8), Mingori (8), Leonard (9), Gura (9), Littell (9). W—Lyle. L—Leonard.

NLCS

■ **Winner:** The Dodgers returned to the World Series for the second time in four years and denied Philadelphia its first pennant since 1950.

■ **Turning point:** The ninth inning of Game 3. With the series tied at a game apiece and the Phillies holding a 5-3 lead with two out and nobody on base in the final inning, the Dodgers collected four straight hits, scored three runs and escaped with a 6-5 victory.

■ **Memorable moment:** Dusty Baker's two-run fourth-game homer that helped Dodgers lefty Tommy John record a 4-1 series-ending victory in a steady rain.

■ **Top guns:** John (1-0, 0.66 ERA), Baker (.357, 2 HR, 8 RBIs), Ron Cey (.308, 4 RBIs), Dodgers; Bob Boone (.400), Richie Hebner (.357), Phillies.

■ **MVP:** Baker.

Linescores

Game 1—October 4, at Los Angeles
Phil. ....2 0 0 0 2 1 0 0 2—7 9 0
L.A. ....0 0 0 0 1 0 4 0 0—5 9 2
Carlton, Garber (7), McGraw (9); John, Garman (5), Hough (6), Sosa (8). W—Garber. L—Sosa. S—McGraw. HR—Luzinski (Phil.); Cey (L.A.).

Game 2—October 5, at Los Angeles
Phil. ....0 0 1 0 0 0 0 0 0—1 9 1
L.A. ....0 0 1 4 0 1 1 0 x—7 9 1
Lonborg, Reed (5), Brusstar (7); Sutton. W—Sutton. L—Lonborg. HR—McBride (Phil.); Baker (L.A.).

Game 3—October 7, at Philadelphia
L.A. ....0 2 0 1 0 0 0 0 3—6 12 2
Phil. ....0 3 0 0 0 0 0 2 0—5 6 2
Hooton, Rhoden (2), Rau (7), Sosa (8), Rautzhan (8), Garman (9); Christenson, Brusstar (4), Reed (5), Garber (7). W—Rautzhan. L—Garber. S—Garman.

Game 4—October 8, at Philadelphia
L.A. ....0 2 0 0 2 0 0 0 0—4 5 0
Phil. ....0 0 0 1 0 0 0 0 0—1 7 0
John; Carlton, Reed (6), McGraw (7), Garber (9). W—John. L—Carlton. HR—Baker (L.A.).

WORLD SERIES

■ **Winner:** The Yankees won their record 21st World Series — but first since 1962.

■ **Turning point:** Ron Guidry's four-hit pitching in Game 4 — a 4-2 victory that gave the Yankees a three-games-to-one edge.

■ **Memorable moment:** Reggie Jackson's eighth-inning Game 6 blast into the center field bleachers — his record-tying third home run of the contest. The Yankees ended the classic with an 8-4 victory and Jackson finished with a Series-record five homers.

■ **Top guns:** Mike Torrez (2-0, 2.50 ERA), Jackson (.450, 5 HR, 8 RBIs), Yankees; Steve Garvey (.375), Steve Yeager (.316, 2 HR, 5 RBIs), Dodgers.

■ **MVP:** Jackson.

Linescores

Game 1—October 11, at New York
L.A.....2 0 0 0 0 0 0 0 1 0 0 0—3 6 0
N.Y.....1 0 0 0 0 1 0 1 0 0 0 1—4 11 0
Sutton, Rautzhan (8), Sosa (8), Garman (9), Rhoden (12); Gullett, Lyle (9). W—Lyle. L—Rhoden. HR—Randolph (N.Y.).

Game 2—October 12, at New York
L.A. ....2 1 2 0 0 0 0 0 1—6 9 0
N.Y. ....0 0 0 1 0 0 0 0 0—1 5 0
Hooton; Hunter, Tidrow (3), Clay (6), Lyle (9). W—Hooton. L—Hunter. HR—Cey, Yeager, Smith, Garvey (L.A.).

Game 3——October 14, at Los Angeles
N.Y. ....3 0 0 1 1 0 0 0 0—5 10 0
L.A. ....0 0 3 0 0 0 0 0 0—3 7 1
Torrez; John, Hough (7). W—Torrez. L—John. HR—Baker (L.A.).

Game 4—October 15, at Los Angeles
N.Y. ....0 3 0 0 0 1 0 0 0—4 7 0
L.A. ....0 0 2 0 0 0 0 0 0—2 4 0
Guidry; Rau, Rhoden (2), Garman (9). W—Guidry. L—Rau. HR—Lopes (L.A.); Jackson (N.Y.).

Game 5—October 16, at Los Angeles
N.Y. ....0 0 0 0 0 0 2 2 0— 4 9 2
L.A. ....1 0 0 4 3 2 0 0 x—10 13 0
Gullett, Clay (5), Tidrow (6), Hunter (7); Sutton. W—Sutton. L—Gullett. HR—Yeager, Smith (L.A.); Munson, Jackson (N.Y.).

Game 6—October 18, at New York
L.A. ....2 0 1 0 0 0 0 0 1—4 9 0
N.Y. ....0 2 0 3 2 0 0 1 x—8 8 1
Hooton, Sosa (4), Rau (5), Hough (7); Torrez. W—Torrez. L—Hooton. HR—Chambliss, Jackson 3 (N.Y.); Smith (L.A.).

HISTORY

FINAL STANDINGS

American League

East Division

Team	N.Y.	Bos.	Mil.	Bal.	Det.	Cle.	Tor.	Cal.	Chi.	K.C.	Min.	Oak.	Sea.	Tex.	W	L	Pct.	GB
New York	...	9	5	9	11	9	11	5	9	5	7	8	6	6	100	63	.613	...
Boston	7	...	10	8	12	7	11	9	7	4	9	5	7	3	99	64	.607	1
Milwaukee	10	5	...	8	8	10	12	5	7	4	4	9	5	6	93	69	.574	6.5
Baltimore	6	7	7	...	7	9	8	4	8	2	5	11	9	7	90	71	.559	9
Detroit	4	3	7	8	...	10	9	7	9	4	4	6	8	7	86	76	.531	13.5
Cleveland	6	8	5	6	5	...	10	4	2	5	5	4	8	1	69	90	.434	29
Toronto	4	4	3	7	6	4	...	3	6	5	4	4	2	7	59	102	.366	40

West Division

Team	K.C.	Cal.	Tex.	Min.	Chi.	Oak.	Sea.	Bal.	Bos.	Cle.	Det.	Mil.	N.Y.	Tor.	W	L	Pct.	GB
Kansas City	...	6	7	7	7	10	12	8	6	6	6	6	6	5	92	70	.568	...
California	9	...	5	12	8	9	9	6	2	6	4	5	5	7	87	75	.537	5
Texas	8	10	...	9	4	9	12	4	7	9	3	4	4	4	87	75	.537	5
Minnesota	8	3	6	...	7	9	6	5	2	5	6	7	3	6	73	89	.451	19
Chicago	8	7	11	8	...	7	7	1	3	8	2	4	1	4	71	90	.441	20.5
Oakland	5	6	6	6	8	...	13	0	5	6	4	1	2	7	69	93	.426	23
Seattle	3	6	3	9	8	2	...	1	3	1	2	5	5	8	56	104	.350	35

National League

East Division

Team	Phi.	Pit.	Chi.	Mon.	St.L.	N.Y.	Atl.	Cin.	Hou.	L.A.	S.D.	S.F.	W	L	Pct.	GB
Philadelphia	...	11	14	9	10	12	4	5	6	5	8	6	90	72	.556	...
Pittsburgh	7	...	11	11	9	11	10	7	8	5	5	4	88	73	.547	1.5
Chicago	4	7	...	7	15	11	7	7	6	4	7	4	79	83	.488	11
Montreal	9	7	11	...	9	8	7	4	6	4	6	5	76	86	.469	14
St. Louis	8	9	3	9	...	11	7	4	5	7	3	3	69	93	.426	21
New York	6	7	7	10	7	...	6	5	5	5	5	3	66	96	.407	24

West Division

Team	L.A.	Cin.	S.F.	S.D.	Hou.	Atl.	Chi.	Mon.	N.Y.	Phi.	Pit.	St.L.	W	L	Pct.	GB
Los Angeles	...	9	11	9	11	13	8	8	7	7	7	5	95	67	.586	...
Cincinnati	9	...	12	9	11	12	5	8	7	7	4	8	92	69	.571	2.5
San Fran.	7	6	...	10	12	7	8	7	9	6	8	9	89	73	.549	6
San Diego	9	9	8	...	10	10	5	6	7	4	7	9	84	78	.519	11
Houston	7	7	6	8	...	10	6	6	7	6	4	7	74	88	.457	21
Atlanta	5	6	11	8	8	...	5	5	6	8	2	5	69	93	.426	26

SIGNIFICANT EVENTS

■ **June 31:** Larry Doby, baseball's second black player in 1947, became the game's second black manager when he took the White Sox reins from Bob Lemon.

■ **August 26:** Major League umpires were forced back to work by a restraining order after a one-day strike.

■ **September 23:** Angels outfielder Lyman Bostock, a .311 career hitter, was killed by an errant shotgun blast while riding in a car in Gary, Ind.

■ **October 24:** Padres ace Gaylord Perry became the first pitcher to win a Cy Young Award in both leagues.

■ **December 5:** Pete Rose completed his high-profile free-agency showcase by signing with the Phillies for $3.2 million over four years.

MEMORABLE MOMENTS

■ **May 5:** Cincinnati's Pete Rose collected career hit No. 3,000 in a 4-3 loss to the Expos.

■ **June 30:** Giants first baseman Willie McCovey crashed his 500th career home run off Jamie Easterly in a 10-9 loss to the Braves.

■ **August 1:** Atlanta pitchers Larry McWilliams and Gene Garber stopped Rose's N.L. record-tying hitting streak at 44 games in a 16-4 victory over the Reds.

■ **October 2:** The Yankees capped their incredible comeback from a 14-game A.L. East Division deficit with a 5-4 victory over Boston in a one-game playoff to decide the A.L. East Division title.

LEADERS

American League
BA: Rod Carew, Min., .333.
Runs: Ron LeFlore, Det., 126.
Hits: Jim Rice, Bos., 213.
TB: Jim Rice, Bos., 406.
HR: Jim Rice, Bos., 46.
RBI: Jim Rice, Bos., 139.
SB: Ron LeFlore, Det., 68.
Wins: Ron Guidry, N.Y., 25.
ERA: Ron Guidry, N.Y., 1.74.
CG: Mike Caldwell, Mil., 23.
IP: Jim Palmer, Bal., 296.
SO: Nolan Ryan, Cal., 260.
SV: Goose Gossage, N.Y., 27.

National League
BA: Dave Parker, Pit., .334.
Runs: Ivan DeJesus, Chi., 104.
Hits: Steve Garvey, L.A., 202.
TB: Dave Parker, Pit., 340.
HR: George Foster, Cin., 40.
RBI: George Foster, Cin., 120.
SB: Omar Moreno, Pit., 71.
Wins: Gaylord Perry, S.D., 21.
ERA: Craig Swan, N.Y., 2.43.
CG: Phil Niekro, Atl., 22.
IP: Phil Niekro, Atl., 334.1.
SO: J.R. Richard, Hou., 303.
SV: Rollie Fingers, S.D., 37.

A.L. 20-game winners
Ron Guidry, N.Y., 25-3
Mike Caldwell, Mil., 22-9
Jim Palmer, Bal., 21-12
Dennis Leonard, K.C., 21-17
Dennis Eckersley, Bos., 20-8
Ed Figueroa, N.Y., 20-9

N.L. 20-game winners
Gaylord Perry, S.D., 21-6
Ross Grimsley, Mon., 20-11

A.L. 100 RBIs
Jim Rice, Bos., 139
Rusty Staub, Det., 121
Larry Hisle, Mil., 115
Andre Thornton, Cle., 105

N.L. 100 RBIs
George Foster, Cin., 120
Dave Parker, Pit., 117
Steve Garvey, L.A., 113
Greg Luzinski, Phil., 101

A.L. 40 homers
Jim Rice, Bos., 46

N.L. 40 homers
George Foster, Cin., 40

Most Valuable Player
A.L.: Jim Rice, OF, Bos.
N.L.: Dave Parker, OF, Pit.

Cy Young Award
A.L.: Ron Guidry, N.Y.
N.L.: Gaylord Perry, S.D.

Rookie of the Year
A.L.: Lou Whitaker, 2B, Det.
N.L.: Bob Horner, 3B, Atl.

Hall of Fame additions
Addie Joss, P, 1902-10
Larry MacPhail, executive
Eddie Mathews, 3B, 1952-68

ALL-STAR GAME

■ **Winner:** The N.L. varied its approach, spotting the A.L. a 3-0 lead before roaring to its seventh straight All-Star victory.

■ **Key inning:** The eighth, when the N.L. broke a 3-3 deadlock with four runs. The tie-breaker scored on a Goose Gossage wild pitch and two more came home on Bob Boone's single.

■ **Memorable moment:** A stunning third-inning collapse by A.L. starting pitcher Jim Palmer, who issued consecutive two-out walks to Joe Morgan, George Foster and Greg Luzinski to force in a run and then gave up a game-tying, two-run single to Steve Garvey.

■ **Top guns:** Bruce Sutter (Cubs), Garvey (Dodgers), Boone (Phillies), N.L.; Lary Sorensen (Brewers), George Brett (Royals), Rod Carew (Twins), A.L.

■ **MVP:** Garvey.

Linescore
July 11, at San Diego Stadium
A.L. ....2 0 1 0 0 0 0 0 0—3 8 1
N.L. ....0 0 3 0 0 0 0 4 x—7 10 0
Palmer (Orioles), Keough (Athletics) 3, Sorensen (Brewers) 4, Kern (Indians) 7, Guidry (Yankees) 7, Gossage (Yankees) 8; Blue (Giants), Rogers (Expos) 4, Fingers (Padres) 6, Sutter (Cubs) 8, Niekro (Braves) 9. W—Sutter. L—Gossage.

ALCS

■ **Winner:** The Yankees, extended to the limit by the Royals in 1976 and '77, needed only four games to claim their third consecutive A.L. pennant.

■ **Turning point:** Yankee catcher Thurman Munson's two-run, eighth-inning home run off Royals reliever Doug Bird in Game 3. The shot turned a 5-4 New York deficit into a 6-5 victory.

■ **Memorable moment:** The three-home run performance of Kansas City's George Brett in the pivotal third game. Brett's three solo shots off Yankee ace Catfish Hunter were wasted.

■ **Top guns:** Reggie Jackson (.462, 2 HR, 6 RBIs), Mickey Rivers (.455), Chris Chambliss (.400), Yankees; Amos Otis (.429), Brett (.389, 3 HR), Royals.

■ **MVP:** Munson.

Linescores

Game 1—October 3, at Kansas City
N.Y. ....0 1 1 0 2 0 0 3 0—7 16 0
K.C. ....0 0 0 0 0 1 0 0 0—1 2 2
Beattie, Clay (6); Leonard, Mingori (5), Hrabosky (8), Bird (9). W—Beattie. L—Leonard. S—Clay. HR—Jackson (N.Y.).

Game 2—October 4, at Kansas City
N.Y. ....0 0 0 0 0 0 2 2 0— 4 12 1
K.C. ....1 4 0 0 0 0 3 2 0—10 16 1
Figueroa, Tidrow (2), Lyle (7); Gura, Pattin (7), Hrabosky (8). W—Gura. L—Figueroa. HR—Patek (K.C.).

Game 3—October 6, at New York
K.C. ....1 0 1 0 1 0 0 2 0—5 10 1
N.Y. ....0 1 0 2 0 1 0 2 x—6 10 0
Splittorff, Bird (8), Hrabosky (8); Hunter, Gossage (7). W—Gossage. L—Bird. \HR—Brett 3 (K.C.); Jackson, Munson (N.Y.).

Game 4—October 7, at New York
K.C. ....1 0 0 0 0 0 0 0 0—1 7 0
N.Y. ....0 1 0 0 0 1 0 0 x—2 4 0
Leonard; Guidry, Gossage (9). W—Guidry. L—Leonard. S—Gossage. HR—Nettles, R. White (N.Y.).

NLCS

■ **Winner:** Los Angeles earned its second consecutive pennant and handed Philadelphia its third straight NLCS defeat.

■ **Turning point:** The first inning of Game 4, when the Phillies loaded the bases against Dodgers starter Doug Rau with nobody out — and failed to score.

■ **Memorable moment:** The two-out, 10th-inning line drive that sure-handed Phillies center fielder Garry Maddox dropped. Dodger shortstop Bill Russell followed with a game- and series-winning single.

■ **Top guns:** Tommy John (1-0, 0.00 ERA), Dusty Baker (.467), Russell (.412), Steve Garvey (.389, 4 HR, 7 RBIs), Dodgers; Ted Sizemore (.385), Greg Luzinski (.375, 2 HR), Phillies.

■ **MVP:** Garvey.

Linescores

Game 1—October 4, at Philadelphia
L.A. ....0 0 4 2 1 1 0 0 1—9 13 1
Phil. ....0 1 0 0 3 0 0 0 1—5 12 1
Hooton, Welch (5); Christenson, Brusstar (5), Eastwick (6), McGraw (7). W—Welch. L—Christenson. HR—Garvey 2, Lopes, Yeager (L.A.); Martin (Phil.).

Game 2—October 5, at Philadelphia
L.A. ....0 0 0 1 2 0 1 0 0—4 8 0
Phil. ....0 0 0 0 0 0 0 0 0—0 4 0
John; Ruthven, Brusstar (5), Reed (7), McGraw (9). W—John. L—Ruthven. HR—Lopes (L.A.).

Game 3—October 6, at Los Angeles
Phil. ....0 4 0 0 0 3 1 0 1—9 11 1
L.A. ....0 1 2 0 0 0 0 1 0—4 8 2
Carlton; Sutton, Rautzhan (6), Hough (8). W—Carlton. L—Sutton. HR—Carlton, Luzinski (Phil.); Garvey (L.A.).

Game 4—October 7, at Los Angeles
Phil. ......0 0 2 0 0 0 1 0 0 0—3 8 2
L.A. ....0 1 0 1 0 1 0 0 0 1—4 13 0
Lerch, Brusstar (6), Reed (7), McGraw (9); Rau, Rhoden (6), Forster (10). W—Forster. L—McGraw. HR—Luzinski, McBride (Phil.); Cey, Garvey (L.A.).

WORLD SERIES

■ **Winner:** The Yankees became the first team to win a six-game Series after losing the first two games. The Dodgers became their Series victim for the eighth time.

■ **Turning point:** A 10th-inning RBI single by Lou Piniella that gave the Yankees a 4-3 Game 4 victory and tied the Series at two games.

■ **Memorable moment:** A Bob Welch-Reggie Jackson battle in Game 2. With the Dodgers leading 4-3 and two out in the ninth, Dodger rookie Welch needed nine pitches to strike out Yankee slugger Jackson in a classic duel with two men on base.

■ **Top guns:** Denny Doyle (.438), Bucky Dent (.417, 7 RBIs), Jackson (.391, 2 HR, 8 RBIs), Yankees; Bill Russell (.423), Dave Lopes (3 HR, 7 RBIs), Dodgers.

■ **MVP:** Dent.

Linescores

Game 1—October 10, at Los Angeles
N.Y. ....0 0 0 0 0 0 3 2 0— 5 9 1
L.A. ....0 3 0 3 1 0 3 1 x—11 15 2
Figueroa, Clay (2), Lindblad (5), Tidrow (7); John, Forster (8). W—John. L—Figueroa. HR—Jackson (N.Y.); Baker, Lopes 2 (L.A.).

Game 2—October 11, at Los Angeles
N.Y. ....0 0 2 0 0 0 1 0 0—3 11 0
L.A. ....0 0 0 1 0 3 0 0 x—4 7 0
Hunter, Gossage (7); Hooton, Forster (7), Welch (9). W—Hooton. L—Hunter. S—Welch. HR—Cey (L.A.).

Game 3—October 13, at New York
L.A. ....0 0 1 0 0 0 0 0 0—1 8 0
N.Y. ....1 1 0 0 0 0 3 0 x—5 10 1
Sutton, Rautzhan (7), Hough (8); Guidry. W—Guidry. L—Sutton. HR—White (N.Y.).

Game 4—October 14, at New York
L.A. ....0 0 0 0 3 0 0 0 0 0—3 6 1
N.Y. ....0 0 0 0 0 2 0 1 0 1—4 9 0
John, Forster (8), Welch (8); Figueroa, Tidrow (6), Gossage (9). W—Gossage. L—Welch. HR—Smith (L.A.).

Game 5—October 15, at New York
L.A. ....1 0 1 0 0 0 0 0 0— 2 9 3
N.Y. ....0 0 4 3 0 0 4 1 x—12 18 0
Hooton, Rautzhan (3), Hough (4); Beattie. W—Beattie. L—Hooton.

Game 6—October 17, at Los Angeles
N.Y. ....0 3 0 0 0 2 2 0 0—7 11 0
L.A. ....1 0 1 0 0 0 0 0 0—2 7 1
Hunter, Gossage (8); Sutton, Welch (6), Rau (8). W—Hunter. L—Sutton. HR—Lopes (L.A.); Jackson (N.Y.).

HISTORY

1979

FINAL STANDINGS

American League

East Division

Team	Bal.	Mil.	Bos.	N.Y.	Det.	Cle.	Tor.	Cal.	Chi.	K.C.	Min.	Oak.	Sea.	Tex.	W	L	Pct.	GB
Baltimore	...	8	8	5	7	8	11	9	8	6	8	8	10	6	102	57	.642	...
Milwaukee	5	...	4	9	7	9	10	5	7	7	8	6	9	9	95	66	.590	8
Boston	5	8	...	5	8	6	9	5	5	8	9	9	8	6	91	69	.569	11.5
New York	6	4	8	...	6	8	9	5	8	7	5	9	6	8	89	71	.556	13.5
Detroit	6	6	5	7	...	6	9	8	9	5	4	7	7	6	85	76	.528	18
Cleveland	5	4	7	5	6	...	8	6	6	6	8	8	7	5	81	80	.503	22
Toronto	2	3	4	4	4	5	...	5	5	3	1	8	4	5	53	109	.327	50.5

West Division

Team	Cal.	K.C.	Tex.	Min.	Chi.	Sea.	Oak.	Bal.	Bos.	Cle.	Det.	Mil.	N.Y.	Tor.	W	L	Pct.	GB
California	...	7	5	9	9	7	10	3	7	6	4	7	7	7	88	74	.543	...
Kansas City	6	...	6	7	8	7	9	6	4	6	7	5	5	9	85	77	.525	3
Texas	8	7	...	9	2	7	11	6	6	7	6	3	4	7	83	79	.512	5
Minnesota	4	6	4	...	8	10	9	4	3	4	8	4	7	11	82	80	.506	6
Chicago	4	5	11	5	...	5	9	3	6	6	3	5	4	7	73	87	.456	14
Seattle	6	6	6	3	8	...	5	2	4	5	5	3	6	8	67	95	.414	21
Oakland	3	4	2	4	4	8	...	4	3	4	5	6	3	4	54	108	.333	34

National League

East Division

Team	Pit.	Mon.	St.L.	Phi.	Chi.	N.Y.	Atl.	Cin.	Hou.	L.A.	S.D.	S.F.	W	L	Pct.	GB
Pittsburgh	...	11	11	10	12	10	8	4	8	8	7	9	98	64	.605	...
Montreal	7	...	10	11	12	15	9	6	5	6	7	7	95	65	.594	2
St. Louis	7	8	...	11	10	11	8	4	6	6	8	7	86	76	.531	12
Philadelphia	8	7	7	...	9	13	5	4	7	9	9	6	84	78	.519	14
Chicago	6	6	8	9	...	8	8	7	6	5	9	8	80	82	.494	18
New York	8	3	7	5	10	...	8	4	3	3	4	8	63	99	.389	35

West Division

Team	Cin.	Hou.	L.A.	S.F.	S.D.	Atl.	Chi.	Mon.	N.Y.	Phi.	Pit.	St.L.	W	L	Pct.	GB
Cincinnati	...	8	11	6	10	12	5	6	8	8	8	8	90	71	.559	...
Houston	10	...	10	7	14	11	6	7	9	5	4	6	89	73	.549	1.5
Los Angeles	7	8	...	14	9	6	7	6	9	3	4	6	79	83	.488	11.5
San Fran.	12	11	4	...	10	7	4	5	4	6	3	5	71	91	.438	19.5
San Diego	7	4	9	8	...	12	3	5	8	3	5	4	68	93	.422	22
Atlanta	6	7	12	11	6	...	4	1	4	7	4	4	66	94	.413	23.5

SIGNIFICANT EVENTS

■ **May 19:** Major League umpires returned to work after a six-week strike that forced baseball to play its games with amateur and minor league arbiters.

■ **July 12:** Bill Veeck's "Disco Demolition Night" promotion turned into Comiskey Park bedlam when fans refused to leave the field, and the White Sox were forced to forfeit the second game of a doubleheader to Detroit.

■ **August 2:** Yankee catcher Thurman Munson, the 1976 A.L. MVP, died at age 32 when the plane he was flying crashed short of the runway at the Akron-Canton Airport in Ohio.

■ **October 29:** Willie Mays was banned from baseball after accepting a job with a corporation that operates gambling casinos.

■ **November 13:** The N.L. crowned baseball's first co-MVPs—Pittsburgh's Willie Stargell and St. Louis' Keith Hernandez.

MEMORABLE MOMENTS

■ **May 17:** The Phillies beat the Cubs, 23-22, in an 11-homer, 50-hit slugfest at wind-swept Wrigley Field.

■ **August 13, September 12:** St. Louis' Lou Brock and Boston's Carl Yastrzemski became baseball's 14th and 15th 3,000-hit men in games against the Cubs and Yankees.

■ **September 23:** Brock stole his 938th and final base in a 7-4 victory over the Mets, moving past Billy Hamilton into first place on the all-time list.

LEADERS

American League
BA: Fred Lynn, Bos., .333.
Runs: Don Baylor, Cal., 120.
Hits: George Brett, K.C., 212.
TB: Jim Rice, Bos., 369.
HR: Gorman Thomas, Mil., 45.
RBI: Don Baylor, Cal., 139.
SB: Willie Wilson, K.C., 83.
Wins: Mike Flanagan, Bal., 23.
ERA: Ron Guidry, N.Y., 2.78.
CG: Dennis Martinez, Bal., 18.
IP: Dennis Martinez, Bal., 292.1.
SO: Nolan Ryan, Cal., 223.
SV: Mike Marshall, Min., 32.

National League
BA: Keith Hernandez, St.L., .344.
Runs: Keith Hernandez, St.L., 116.
Hits: Garry Templeton, St.L., 211.
TB: Dave Winfield, S.D., 333.
HR: Dave Kingman, Chi., 48.
RBI: Dave Winfield, S.D., 118.
SB: Omar Moreno, Pit., 77.
Wins: Joe Niekro, Hou.; Phil Niekro, Atl., 21.
ERA: J.R. Richard, Hou., 2.71.
CG: Phil Niekro, Atl., 23.
IP: Phil Niekro, Atl., 342.
SO: J.R. Richard, Hou., 313.
SV: Bruce Sutter, Chi., 37.

A.L. 20-game winners
Mike Flanagan, Bal., 23-9
Tommy John, N.Y., 21-9
Jerry Koosman, Min., 20-13

N.L. 20-game winners
Joe Niekro, Hou., 21-11
Phil Niekro, Atl., 21-20

A.L. 100 RBIs
Don Baylor, Cal., 139
Jim Rice, Bos., 130
Gorman Thomas, Mil., 123
Fred Lynn, Bos., 122
Darrell Porter, K.C., 112
Ken Singleton, Bal., 111
George Brett, K.C., 107
Cecil Cooper, Mil., 106
Willie Horton, Sea., 106
Steve Kemp, Det., 105
Buddy Bell, Tex., 101
Dan Ford, Cal., 101
Bobby Grich, Cal., 101
Sixto Lezcano, Mil., 101
Bruce Bochte, Sea., 100

N.L. 100 RBIs
Dave Winfield, S.D., 118
Dave Kingman, Chi., 115
Mike Schmidt, Phil., 114
Steve Garvey, L.A., 110
Keith Hernandez, St.L., 105

A.L. 40 homers
Gorman Thomas, Mil., 45

N.L. 40 homers
Dave Kingman, Chi., 48
Mike Schmidt, Phil., 45

Most Valuable Player
A.L.: Don Baylor, OF, Cal.
N.L.: Willie Stargell, 1B, Pit.
Keith Hernandez, 1B, St.L.

Cy Young Award
A.L.: Mike Flanagan, Bal.
N.L.: Bruce Sutter, Chi.

Rookie of the Year
A.L.: John Castino, 3B, Min.
Alfredo Griffin, SS, Tor.
N.L.: Rick Sutcliffe, P, L.A.

Hall of Fame additions
Warren Giles, executive
Willie Mays, OF, 1951-73
Hack Wilson, OF, 1923-34

ALL-STAR GAME

■ **Winner:** Lee Mazzilli tied the game with an eighth-inning homer and drove in the winner in the ninth with a bases-loaded walk as the N.L. recorded a 7-6 victory in the 50th All-Star Game.

■ **Key innings:** The eighth, when Mazzilli erased a 6-5 deficit with an opposite-field blast, and the ninth, when he drew a base on balls off Ron Guidry after Jim Kern had walked the bases loaded.

■ **Memorable moments:** Game-saving seventh- and eighth-inning throws by right fielder Dave Parker that cut down A.L. runners at third base and home plate.

■ **Top guns:** Steve Rogers (Expos), Mazzilli (Mets), Mike Schmidt (Phillies), Parker (Pirates), N.L.; Fred Lynn (Red Sox), Don Baylor (Angels), Carl Yastrzemski (Red Sox), A.L.

■ **MVP:** Parker.

Linescore
July 17, at Seattle's Kingdome
N.L. ....2 1 1 0 0 1 0 1 1—7 10 1
A.L. ....3 0 2 0 0 1 0 0 0—6 10 0
Carlton (Phillies), Andujar (Astros) 2, Rogers (Expos) 4, Perry (Padres) 6, Sambito (Astros) 6, LaCoss (Reds) 6, Sutter (Cubs) 8; Ryan (Angels), Stanley (Red Sox) 3, Clear (Angels) 5, Kern (Rangers) 7, Guidry (Yankees) 9. W—Sutter. L—Kern. HR—Lynn, A.L.; Mazzilli, N.L.

ALCS

■ **Winner:** Baltimore, winner of the first three A.L. Championship Series, ruined California's first experience in the post-season spotlight.

■ **Turning point:** A dramatic three-run homer by Baltimore pinch-hitter John Lowenstein in the 10th inning of Game 1. Lowenstein's opposite-field shot broke a 3-3 deadlock and propelled the Orioles to their first pennant since 1971.

■ **Memorable moment:** A dramatic defensive play by Orioles third baseman Doug DeCinces. With one out and the bases loaded in the fifth inning of Game 4, DeCinces made a diving stop of Jim Anderson's shot down the third-base line, stepped on third and fired to first for a rally-killing double play that preserved a 3-0 lead.

■ **Top guns:** Scott McGregor (1-0, 0.00 ERA), Eddie Murray (.417, 5 RBIs), Rick Dempsey (.400), Orioles; Rod Carew (.412), Dan Ford (2 HR, 4 RBIs), Angels.

■ **MVP:** Murray.

Linescores

Game 1—October 3, at Baltimore
Cal. ....1 0 1 0 0 1 0 0 0 0—3 7 1
Balt. ....0 0 2 1 0 0 0 0 0 3—6 6 0
Ryan, Montague (8); Palmer, Stanhouse (10). W—Stanhouse. L—Montague. HR—Ford (Cal.); Lowenstein (Bal.).

Game 2—October 4, at Baltimore
Cal. ....1 0 0 0 0 1 1 3 2—8 10 1
Balt. ....4 4 1 0 0 0 0 0 x—9 11 1
Frost, Clear (2), Aase (8); Flanagan, Stanhouse (8). W—Flanagan. L—Frost. HR—Ford (Cal.); Murray (Bal.).

Game 3—October 5, at California
Balt. ....0 0 0 1 0 1 1 0 0—3 8 3
Cal. ....1 0 0 1 0 0 0 0 2—4 9 0
D. Martinez, Stanhouse (9); Tanana, Aase (6). W—Aase. L—Stanhouse. HR—Baylor (Cal.).

Game 4—October 6, at California
Balt. ....0 0 2 1 0 0 5 0 0—8 12 1
Cal. ....0 0 0 0 0 0 0 0 0—0 6 0
McGregor; Knapp, LaRoche (3), Frost (4), Montague (7), Barlow (9). W—McGregor. L—Knapp. HR—Kelly (Bal.).

NLCS

■ **Winner:** Pittsburgh, which had been swept by Cincinnati in the 1970 and '75 NLCS, turned the tables on the Reds and earned its first World Series berth since 1971.

■ **Turning point:** A 10th-inning single by Dave Parker that gave the Pirates a 3-2 victory in Game 2.

■ **Memorable moment:** Willie Stargell's three-run, 11th-inning home run, which gave the Pirates a 5-2 Game 1 victory and all the momentum they needed.

■ **Top guns:** Stargell (.455, 2 HR, 6 RBIs), Phil Garner (.417), Pirates; Dave Concepcion (.429), Reds.

■ **MVP:** Stargell.

Linescores

Game 1—October 2, at Cincinnati
Pitt. ....0 0 2 0 0 0 0 0 0 0 3—5 10 0
Cin. ....0 0 0 2 0 0 0 0 0 0 0—2 7 0
Candelaria, Romo (8), Tekulve (8), Jackson (10), D. Robinson (11); Seaver, Hume (9), Tomlin (11). W—Jackson. L—Hume. S—D. Robinson. HR—Garner, Stargell (Pit); Foster (Cin.).

Game 2—October 3, at Cincinnati
Pitt. ....0 0 0 1 1 0 0 0 0 1—3 11 0
Cin. ....0 1 0 0 0 0 0 0 1 0—2 8 0
Bibby, Jackson (8), Romo (8), Tekulve (8), Roberts (9), D. Robinson (9); Pastore, Tomlin (8), Hume (8), Bair (10). W—D. Robinson. L—Bair.

Game 3—October 5, at Pittsburgh
Cin. ....0 0 0 0 0 1 0 0 0—1 8 1
Pitt. ....1 1 2 2 0 0 0 1 x—7 7 0
LaCoss, Norman (2), Leibrandt (4), Soto (5), Tomlin (7), Hume (8); Blyleven. W—Blyleven. L—LaCoss. HR—Stargell, Madlock (Pit.); Bench (Cin.).

WORLD SERIES

■ **Winner:** Pittsburgh's "Family" beat the Orioles and became the fourth team to recover from a three-games-to-one deficit.

■ **Turning point:** After blowing a 6-3, eighth-inning lead in Game 4 to fall within a game of elimination, the Pirates regrouped to win Game 5, 7-1, behind the six-hit pitching of Jim Rooker and Bert Blyleven.

■ **Memorable moment:** Willie Stargell's two-run, sixth-inning homer that put the Pirates ahead to stay in a 4-1 Series-ending victory.

■ **Top guns:** Phil Garner (.500, 12 hits), Stargell (.400, 12 hits, 3 HR, 7 RBIs), Bill Madlock (.375), Pirates; Kiko Garcia (.400, 6 RBIs), Orioles.

■ **MVP:** Stargell.

Linescores

Game 1—October 10, at Baltimore
Pitt. ....0 0 0 1 0 2 0 1 0—4 11 3
Balt. ....5 0 0 0 0 0 0 0 x—5 6 3
Kison, Rooker (1), Romo (5), D. Robinson (6), Jackson (8); Flanagan. W—Flanagan. L—Kison. HR—DeCinces (Bal.); Stargell (Pit.).

Game 2—October 11, at Baltimore
Pitt. ....0 2 0 0 0 0 0 0 1—3 11 2
Balt. ....0 1 0 0 0 1 0 0 0—2 6 1
Blyleven, D. Robinson (7), Tekulve (9); Palmer, T. Martinez (8), Stanhouse (9). W—D. Robinson. L—Stanhouse. S—Tekulve. HR—Murray (Bal.).

Game 3—October 12, at Pittsburgh
Balt. ....0 0 2 5 0 0 1 0 0—8 13 0
Pitt. ....1 2 0 0 0 1 0 0 0—4 9 2
McGregor; Candelaria, Romo (4), Jackson (7), Tekulve (8). W—McGregor. L—Candelaria. HR—Ayala (Bal.).

Game 4—October 13, at Pittsburgh
Balt. ....0 0 3 0 0 0 0 6 0—9 12 0
Pitt. ....0 4 0 0 1 1 0 0 0—6 17 1
D. Martinez, Stewart (2), Stone (5), Stoddard (7); Bibby, Jackson (7), D. Robinson (8), Tekulve (8). W—Stoddard. L—Tekulve. HR—Stargell (Pit.).

Game 5—October 14, at Pittsburgh
Balt. ....0 0 0 0 1 0 0 0 0—1 6 2
Pitt. ....0 0 0 0 0 2 2 3 x—7 13 1
Flanagan, Stoddard (7), T. Martinez (7), Stanhouse (8); Rooker, Blyleven (6). W—Blyleven. L—Flanagan.

Game 6—October 16, at Baltimore
Pitt. ....0 0 0 0 0 0 2 2 0—4 10 0
Balt. ....0 0 0 0 0 0 0 0 0—0 7 1
Candelaria, Tekulve (7); Palmer, Stoddard (9). W—Candelaria. L—Palmer. S—Tekulve.

Game 7—October 17, at Baltimore
Pitt. ....0 0 0 0 0 2 0 0 2—4 10 0
Balt. ....0 0 1 0 0 0 0 0 0—1 4 2
Bibby, D. Robinson (5), Jackson (5), Tekulve (8); McGregor, Stoddard (9), Flanagan (9), Stanhouse (9), T. Martinez (9), D. Martinez (9). W—Jackson. L—McGregor. S—Tekulve. HR—Dauer (Bal.); Stargell (Pit.).

FINAL STANDINGS

American League

East Division

Team	N.Y.	Bal.	Mil.	Bos.	Det.	Cle.	Tor.	Cal.	Chi.	K.C.	Min.	Oak.	Sea.	Tex.	W	L	Pct.	GB
New York	...	6	8	10	8	8	10	10	7	4	8	8	9	7	103	59	.636	...
Baltimore	7	...	7	8	10	6	11	10	6	6	10	7	6	6	100	62	.617	3
Milwaukee	5	6	...	7	6	10	5	6	7	6	7	7	9	5	86	76	.531	17
Boston	3	5	6	...	8	7	7	9	6	5	6	9	7	5	83	77	.519	19
Detroit	5	3	7	5	...	10	9	7	10	2	6	6	10	4	84	78	.519	19
Cleveland	5	7	3	6	3	...	8	6	7	5	9	6	8	6	79	81	.494	23
Toronto	3	2	8	6	4	5	...	9	7	3	5	4	6	5	67	95	.414	36

West Division

Team	K.C.	Oak.	Min.	Tex.	Chi.	Cal.	Sea.	Bal.	Bos.	Cle.	Det.	Mil.	N.Y.	Tor.	W	L	Pct.	GB
Kansas City	...	6	5	10	8	8	7	6	7	7	10	6	8	9	97	65	.599	...
Oakland	7	...	7	7	7	10	8	5	3	6	6	5	4	8	83	79	.512	14
Minnesota	8	6	...	9	8	6	7	2	6	3	6	5	4	7	77	84	.478	19.5
Texas	3	6	3	...	7	2	9	6	7	6	8	7	5	7	76	85	.472	20.5
Chicago	5	6	5	6	...	10	6	6	4	5	2	5	5	5	70	90	.438	26
California	5	3	7	11	3	...	11	2	3	4	5	6	2	3	65	95	.406	31
Seattle	6	5	6	4	7	2	...	6	5	4	2	3	3	6	59	103	.364	38

National League

East Division

Team	Phi.	Mon.	Pit.	St.L.	N.Y.	Chi.	Atl.	Cin.	Hou.	L.A.	S.D.	S.F.	W	L	Pct.	GB
Philadelphia	...	9	7	9	12	13	7	5	9	6	8	6	91	71	.562	...
Montreal	9	...	6	12	10	12	7	9	7	1	10	7	90	72	.556	1
Pittsburgh	11	12	...	10	8	10	1	6	5	6	6	8	83	79	.512	8
St. Louis	9	6	8	...	9	9	6	7	5	5	5	5	74	88	.457	17
New York	6	8	10	9	...	8	9	4	4	5	1	3	67	95	.414	24
Chicago	5	6	8	9	10	...	4	7	1	5	4	5	64	98	.395	27

West Division

Team	Hou.	L.A.	Cin.	Atl.	S.F.	S.D.	Chi.	Mon.	N.Y.	Phi.	Pit.	St.L.	W	L	Pct.	GB
Houston	...	9	10	11	11	11	11	5	8	3	7	7	93	70	.571	...
Los Angeles	10	...	9	7	13	9	7	11	7	6	6	7	92	71	.564	1
Cincinnati	8	9	...	16	7	15	5	3	8	7	6	5	89	73	.549	3.5
Atlanta	7	11	2	...	11	12	8	5	3	5	11	6	81	80	.503	11
San Fran.	7	5	11	6	...	8	7	5	9	6	4	7	75	86	.466	17
San Diego	7	9	3	6	10	...	8	2	11	4	6	7	73	89	.451	19.5

SIGNIFICANT EVENTS

■ **January 24:** Nelson Doubleday and Fred Wilpon headed a group that bought the New York Mets for a reported $21.1 million.

■ **May 23:** The owners and players agreed to defer settlement of the free-agent compensation issue, thus avoiding the first player in-season walkout in baseball history.

■ **July 30:** Houston ace J.R. Richard was rushed to the hospital after suffering a career-ending stroke during a light workout at the Astrodome.

■ **November 18:** Kansas City's George Brett, who finished the season with the highest average (.390) since 1941, captured A.L. MVP honors.

MEMORABLE MOMENTS

■ **September 30:** Oakland's Rickey Henderson, en route to the A.L.'s first 100-steal season, passed Ty Cobb's A.L. record of 96 in a 5-1 victory over Chicago.

■ **October 6:** The Astros, who allowed the Dodgers to force a division playoff with a three-game season-closing sweep, rebounded to win their first N.L. West title with a 7-1 victory.

LEADERS

American League
BA: George Brett, K.C., .390.
Runs: Willie Wilson, K.C., 133.
Hits: Willie Wilson, K.C., 230.
TB: Cecil Cooper, Mil., 335.
HR: Reggie Jackson, N.Y.; Ben Oglivie, Mil., 41.
RBI: Cecil Cooper, Mil., 122.
SB: Rickey Henderson, Oak., 100.
Wins: Steve Stone, Bal., 25.
ERA: Rudy May, N.Y., 2.46.
CG: Rick Langford, Oak., 28.
IP: Rick Langford, Oak., 290.
SO: Len Barker, Cle., 187.
SV: Goose Gossage, N.Y.; Dan Quisenberry, K.C., 33.

National League
BA: Bill Buckner, Chi., .324.
Runs: Keith Hernandez, St.L., 111.
Hits: Steve Garvey, L.A., 200.
TB: Mike Schmidt, Phil., 342.
HR: Mike Schmidt, Phil., 48.
RBI: Mike Schmidt, Phil., 121.
SB: Ron LeFlore, Mon., 97.
Wins: Steve Carlton, Phil., 24.
ERA: Don Sutton, L.A., 2.20.
CG: Steve Rogers, Mon., 14.
IP: Steve Carlton, Phil., 304.
SO: Steve Carlton, Phil., 286.
SV: Bruce Sutter, Chi., 28.

A.L. 20-game winners
Steve Stone, Bal., 25-7
Tommy John, N.Y., 22-9
Mike Norris, Oak., 22-9
Scott McGregor, Bal., 20-8
Dennis Leonard, K.C., 20-11

N.L. 20-game winners
Steve Carlton, Phil., 24-9
Joe Niekro, Hou., 20-12

A.L. 100 RBIs
Cecil Cooper, Mil., 122
George Brett, K.C., 118
Ben Oglivie, Mil., 118
Al Oliver, Tex., 117
Eddie Murray, Bal., 116
Reggie Jackson, N.Y., 111
Tony Armas, Oak., 109
Tony Perez, Bos., 105
Gorman Thomas, Mil., 105
Ken Singleton, Bal., 104
Steve Kemp, Det., 101

N.L. 100 RBIs
Mike Schmidt, Phil., 121
George Hendrick, St.L., 109
Steve Garvey, L.A., 106
Gary Carter, Mon., 101

A.L. 40 homers
Reggie Jackson, N.Y., 41
Ben Oglivie, Mil., 41

N.L. 40 homers
Mike Schmidt, Phil., 48

Most Valuable Player
A.L.: George Brett, 3B, K.C.
N.L.: Mike Schmidt, 3B, Phil.

Cy Young Award
A.L.: Steve Stone, Bal.
N.L.: Steve Carlton, Phil.

Rookie of the Year
A.L.: Joe Charboneau, OF, Cle.
N.L.: Steve Howe, P, L.A.

Hall of Fame additions
Al Kaline, OF, 1953-74
Chuck Klein, OF, 1928-44
Duke Snider, OF, 1947-64
Tom Yawkey, executive/owner

ALL-STAR GAME

■ **Winner:** The N.L., held hitless for 4⅔ innings, scored the go-ahead run on a sixth-inning error and started the new decade with a 4-2 victory, its ninth straight in All-Star competition.

■ **Key inning:** The sixth, when the N.L. took a 3-2 lead on George Hendrick's single and second baseman Willie Randolph's error on a smash hit by Dave Winfield.

■ **Memorable moment:** Ken Griffey's two-out homer in the fifth. Before the solo blast, the N.L. had not even managed a baserunner against A.L. hurlers Steve Stone and Tommy John.

■ **Top guns:** J.R. Richard (Astros), Griffey (Reds), Hendrick (Cardinals), N.L.; Stone (Orioles), Rod Carew (Angels), Fred Lynn (Red Sox), A.L.

■ **MVP:** Griffey.

Linescore
July 8, at Los Angeles' Dodger Stadium
A.L. ....0 0 0 0 2 0 0 0 0—2 7 2
N.L. ....0 0 0 0 1 2 1 0 x—4 7 0
Stone (Orioles), John (Yankees) 4, Farmer (White Sox) 6, Stieb (Blue Jays) 7, Gossage (Yankees) 8; Richard (Astros), Welch (Dodgers) 3, Reuss (Dodgers) 6, Bibby (Pirates) 7, Sutter (Cubs) 8. W—Reuss. L—John. S—Sutter. HR—Lynn, A.L.; Griffey, N.L.

ALCS

■ **Winner:** Kansas City, a Championship Series loser to the Yankees in 1976, '77 and '78, qualified for its first World Series with an impressive sweep.

■ **Turning point:** The eighth inning of Game 2, when the Royals threw out Yankee Willie Randolph at the plate, preserving a 3-2 victory. Randolph was trying to score on a two-out double by Bob Watson.

■ **Memorable moment:** A titanic three-run homer by George Brett that produced a 4-2 series-ending victory. Brett's seventh-inning blast off relief ace Goose Gossage landed in the third deck at Yankee Stadium.

■ **Top guns:** Dan Quisenberry (1-0, 1 save, 0.00 ERA), Frank White (.545), Brett (2 HR, 4 RBIs), Royals; Watson (.500), Randolph (.385), Yankees.

■ **MVP:** White.

Linescores

Game 1—October 8, at Kansas City
N.Y. ....0 2 0 0 0 0 0 0 0—2 10 1
K.C. ....0 2 2 0 0 0 1 2 x—7 10 0
Guidry, Davis (4), Underwood (8); Gura. W—Gura. L—Guidry. HR—Cerone, Piniella (N.Y.); Brett (K.C.).

Game 2—October 9, at Kansas City
N.Y. ....0 0 0 0 2 0 0 0 0—2 8 0
K.C. ....0 0 3 0 0 0 0 0 x—3 6 0
May; Leonard, Quisenberry (9). W—Leonard. L—May. S—Quisenberry. HR—Nettles (N.Y.).

Game 3—October 10, at New York
K.C. ....0 0 0 0 1 0 3 0 0—4 12 1
N.Y. ....0 0 0 0 0 2 0 0 0—2 8 0
Splittorff, Quisenberry (6); John, Gossage (7), Underwood (8). W—Quisenberry. L—Gossage. HR—White, Brett (K.C.).

NLCS

■ **Winner:** Philadelphia scored in the 10th inning of Game 5 to dispatch Houston, 8-7, and qualify for its first World Series since 1950.

■ **Turning point:** A Game 4 collision in which Pete Rose bowled over Houston catcher Bruce Bochy. Rose scored the winning run on the 10th-inning play, giving the Phillies a series-tying victory.

■ **Memorable moment:** A fourth-game controversy that wiped out Houston claims of a triple play and sparked protests by both teams. The fourth-inning confusion revolved around the "catch" or "trap" of a line drive by Astros pitcher Vern Ruhle and stopped play for 20 minutes.

■ **Top guns:** Rose (.400), Manny Trillo (.381), Phillies; Joe Niekro (10 IP, 0.00 ERA), Terry Puhl (.526), Jose Cruz (.400), Astros.

■ **MVP:** Trillo.

Linescores

Game 1—October 7, at Philadelphia
Hou. ....0 0 1 0 0 0 0 0 0—1 7 0
Phil. ....0 0 0 0 0 2 1 0 x—3 8 1
Forsch; Carlton, McGraw (8). W—Carlton. L—Forsch. S—McGraw. HR—Luzinski (Phil.).

Game 2—October 8, at Philadelphia
Hou. ......0 0 1 0 0 0 1 1 0 4—7 8 1
Phil. ......0 0 0 2 0 0 0 1 0 1—4 14 2
Ryan, Sambito (7), D. Smith (7), LaCorte (9), Andujar (10); Ruthven, McGraw (8), Reed (9), Saucier (10). W—LaCorte. L—Reed. S—Andujar.

Game 3—October 10, at Houston
Phil. ..0 0 0 0 0 0 0 0 0 0 0—0 7 1
Hou. ..0 0 0 0 0 0 0 0 0 0 1—1 6 1
Christenson, Noles (7), McGraw (8); Niekro, D. Smith (11). W—D. Smith. L—McGraw.

Game 4—October 11, at Houston
Phil. ......0 0 0 0 0 0 0 3 0 2—5 13 0
Hou. ......0 0 0 1 1 0 0 0 1 0—3 5 1
Carlton, Noles (6), Saucier (7), Reed (7), Brusstar (8), McGraw (10); Ruhle, D. Smith (8), Sambito (8). W—Brusstar. L—Sambito. S—McGraw.

Game 5—October 12, at Houston
Phil. ......0 2 0 0 0 0 0 5 0 1—8 13 2
Hou. ......1 0 0 0 0 1 3 2 0 0—7 14 0
Bystrom, Brusstar (6), Christenson (7), Reed (7), McGraw (8), Ruthven (9); Ryan, Sambito (8), Forsch (8), LaCorte (9). W—Ruthven. L—LaCorte.

WORLD SERIES

■ **Winner:** The Phillies, two-time Series qualifiers in their 97-year history, won their first fall classic with a six-game victory over the Royals — first-time Series participants.

■ **Turning point:** A two-run, ninth-inning rally that gave the Phillies a 4-3 victory in Game 5 and a three-games-to-two Series lead.

■ **Memorable moments:** The clutch pitching of Phillies reliever Tug McGraw, who recorded bases-loaded, game-ending strikeouts in Games 5 and 6.

■ **Top guns:** Steve Carlton (2-0, 2.40 ERA), McGraw (2 saves, 1.17), Mike Schmidt (.381, 2 HR, 7 RBIs), Phillies; Amos Otis (.478, 3 HR, 7 RBIs), Willie Aikens (.400, 4 HR, 8 RBIs), Royals.

■ **MVP:** Schmidt.

Linescores

Game 1—October 14, at Philadelphia
K.C. ....0 2 2 0 0 0 0 2 0—6 9 1
Phil. ....0 0 5 1 1 0 0 0 x—7 11 0
Leonard, Martin (4), Quisenberry (8); Walk, McGraw (8). W—Walk. L—Leonard. S—McGraw. HR—Otis, Aikens 2 (K.C.); McBride (Phil.).

Game 2—October 15, at Philadelphia
K.C. ....0 0 0 0 0 1 3 0 0—4 11 0
Phil. ....0 0 0 0 2 0 0 4 x—6 8 1
Gura, Quisenberry (7); Carlton, Reed (9). W—Carlton. L—Quisenberry. S—Reed.

Game 3—October 17, at Kansas City
Phil. ......0 1 0 0 1 0 0 1 0 0—3 14 0
K.C. ....1 0 0 1 0 0 1 0 0 1—4 11 0
Ruthven, McGraw (10); Gale, Martin (5), Quisenberry (8). W—Quisenberry. L—McGraw. HR—Brett, Otis (K.C.); Schmidt (Phil.).

Game 4—October 18, at Kansas City
Phil. ....0 1 0 0 0 0 1 1 0—3 10 1
K.C. ....4 1 0 0 0 0 0 0 x—5 10 2
Christenson, Noles (1), Saucier (6), Brusstar (6); Leonard, Quisenberry (8). W—Leonard. L—Christenson. S—Quisenberry. HR—Aikens 2 (K.C.).

Game 5—October 19, at Kansas City
Phil. ....0 0 0 2 0 0 0 0 2—4 7 0
K.C. ....0 0 0 0 1 2 0 0 0—3 12 2
Bystrom, Reed (6), McGraw (7); Gura, Quisenberry (7). W—McGraw. L—Quisenberry. HR—Schmidt (Phil.); Otis (K.C.).

Game 6—October 21, at Philadelphia
K.C. ....0 0 0 0 0 0 0 1 0—1 7 2
Phil. ....0 0 2 0 1 1 0 0 x—4 9 0
Gale, Martin (3), Splittorff (5), Pattin (7), Quisenberry (8); Carlton, McGraw (8). W—Carlton. L—Gale. S—McGraw.

FINAL STANDINGS

American League

East Division

Team	Mil.	Bal.	N.Y.	Det.	Bos.	Cle.	Tor.	Oak.	Tex.	Chi.	K.C.	Cal.	Sea.	Min.	W	L	Pct.	GB
Milwaukee†	...	4	3	8	7	6	6	4	4	1	5	3	2	9	62	47	.569	...
Baltimore	2	...	7	6	2	4	5	7	2	3	5	6	4	6	59	46	.562	1
New York*	3	6	...	7	3	5	2	4	5	7	10	2	2	3	59	48	.551	2
Detroit	5	7	3	...	1	5	6	1	9	3	3	3	5	9	60	49	.550	2
Boston	6	2	3	6	...	7	4	7	3	5	3	2	9	2	59	49	.546	2.5
Cleveland	3	2	7	1	6	...	4	3	2	5	4	5	8	2	52	51	.505	7
Toronto	4	2	3	4	0	2	...	2	2	5	3	6	3	1	37	69	.349	23.5

West Division

Team	Oak.	Tex.	Chi.	K.C.	Cal.	Sea.	Min.	Mil.	Bal.	N.Y.	Det.	Bos.	Cle.	Tor.	W	L	Pct.	GB
Oakland*	...	4	6	3	8	6	8	2	5	3	2	5	2	10	64	45	.587	...
Texas	2	...	4	4	4	8	8	5	1	4	3	6	2	6	57	48	.543	5
Chicago	7	2	...	2	7	3	2	4	6	5	3	4	2	7	54	52	.509	8.5
Kansas City†	3	3	0	...	6	6	9	4	3	2	2	3	4	5	50	53	.485	11
California	2	2	6	0	...	6	3	4	6	2	3	4	7	6	51	59	.464	13.5
Seattle	1	5	3	7	4	...	6	2	2	3	1	3	4	3	44	65	.404	20
Minnesota	2	5	4	4	3	3	...	3	0	3	3	5	1	5	41	68	.376	23

National League

East Division

Team	St.L.	Mon.	Phi.	Pit.	N.Y.	Chi.	Cin.	L.A.	Hou.	S.F.	Atl.	S.D.	W	L	Pct.	GB
St.Louis	...	9	6	8	5	4	5	5	4	3	3	7	59	43	.578	...
Montreal†	6	...	7	10	9	7	4	2	2	2	7	4	60	48	.556	2
Philadelphia*	7	4	...	7	7	10	2	3	6	4	5	4	59	48	.551	2.5
Pittsburgh	3	3	5	...	6	10	2	1	4	3	3	6	46	56	.451	13
New York	6	3	7	3	...	8	3	1	3	2	3	2	41	62	.398	18.5
Chicago	5	4	2	4	5	...	1	6	1	5	2	3	38	65	.369	21.5

West Division

Team	Cin.	L.A.	Hou.	S.F.	Atl.	S.D.	St.L.	Mon.	Phi.	Pit.	N.Y.	Chi.	W	L	Pct.	GB
Cincinnati	...	8	8	9	5	10	0	5	5	4	7	5	66	42	.611	...
Los Angeles*	8	...	8	7	7	6	5	5	3	5	5	4	63	47	.573	4
Houston†	4	4	...	9	8	11	2	5	4	2	6	6	61	49	.555	6
San Fran.	5	5	6	...	7	7	2	5	3	7	4	5	56	55	.505	11.5
Atlanta	6	7	4	5	...	9	4	3	4	2	3	3	50	56	.472	15
San Diego	2	5	3	6	6	...	3	2	2	4	5	3	41	69	.373	26

* Won first-half division title † Won second-half division title

SIGNIFICANT EVENTS

■ **February 12:** Boston catcher Carlton Fisk was declared a free agent because the Red Sox violated the Basic Agreement by mailing his contract two days beyond the deadline.

■ **July 31:** Baseball's 50-day strike, the longest in American sports history, ended when owners and players reached agreement on the free-agent compensation issue.

■ **November 11:** Dodgers lefty Fernando Valenzuela became the first rookie to win a Cy Young when he outpointed the Reds' Tom Seaver for N.L. honors.

■ **November 25:** Milwaukee's Rollie Fingers, who earlier was named A.L. Cy Young winner, became the first relief pitcher to win an A.L. MVP.

MEMORABLE MOMENTS

■ **May 15:** Cleveland's Len Barker retired 27 consecutive Blue Jays in a 3-0 victory and pitched the first Major League perfect game in 13 years.

■ **August 10:** Philadelphia's Pete Rose collected career hit No. 3,631 in a 6-2 loss to St. Louis and moved into third place on the all-time list.

■ **September 26:** Houston's Nolan Ryan stepped into uncharted territory when he fired his record-setting fifth no-hitter, beating the Dodgers, 5-0.

■ **October 11:** The Dodgers, Expos and Yankees won decisive fifth games of special post-season series set up to determine division champions because of the 50-day baseball strike.

LEADERS

American League
BA: Carney Lansford, Bos., .336.
Runs: Rickey Henderson, Oak., 89.
Hits: Rickey Henderson, Oak., 135.
TB: Dwight Evans, Bos., 215.
HR: Tony Armas, Oak.; Dwight Evans, Bos.; Bobby Grich, Cal.; Eddie Murray, Bal., 22.
RBI: Eddie Murray, Bal., 78.
SB: Rickey Henderson, Oak., 56.
Wins: Dennis Martinez, Bal.; Steve McCatty, Oak.; Jack Morris, Det.; Pete Vuckovich, Mil., 14.
ERA: Dave Righetti, N.Y., 2.05
CG: Rick Langford, Oak., 18.
IP: Dennis Leonard, K.C., 201.2.
SO: Len Barker, Cle., 127.
SV: Rollie Fingers, Mil., 28.

National League
BA: Bill Madlock, Pit., .341.
Runs: Mike Schmidt, Phil., 78.
Hits: Pete Rose, Phil., 140.
TB: Mike Schmidt, Phil., 228.
HR: Mike Schmidt, Phil., 31.
RBI: Mike Schmidt, Phil., 91.
SB: Tim Raines, Mon., 71.
Wins: Tom Seaver, Cin., 14.
ERA: Nolan Ryan, Hou., 1.69.
CG: Fernando Valenzuela, L.A., 11.
IP: Fernando Valenzuela, L.A., 192.1.
SO: Fernando Valenzuela, L.A., 180.
SV: Bruce Sutter, St.L., 25.

Most Valuable Player
A.L.: Rollie Fingers, P, Mil.
N.L.: Mike Schmidt, 3B, Phil.

Cy Young Award
A.L.: Rollie Fingers, Mil.
N.L.: Fernando Valenzuela, L.A.

Rookie of the Year
A.L.: Dave Righetti, P, N.Y.
N.L.: Fernando Valenzuela, P, L.A.

Hall of Fame additions
Rube Foster, manager/executive, Negro Leagues
Bob Gibson, P, 1959-75
Johnny Mize, 1B, 1936-53

ALL-STAR GAME

■ **Winner:** With the All-Star Game serving as the official resumption of the season after a 50-day players' strike, the N.L. continued its winning ways by belting four home runs and stretching its winning streak to 10.

■ **Key inning:** The eighth, when Mike Schmidt drilled a two-run homer off Rollie Fingers, giving the N.L. its tying and winning runs.

■ **Memorable moment:** Gary Carter's solo blast in the seventh inning, his second home run of the game. Carter became the fifth All-Star performer to homer twice.

■ **Top guns:** Schmidt (Phillies), Carter (Expos), Dave Parker (Pirates), N.L.; Len Barker (Indians), Fred Lynn (Angels), Ken Singleton (Orioles), A.L.

■ **MVP:** Carter.

Linescore
August 9, at Cleveland Stadium
N.L. ....0 0 0 0 1 1 1 2 0—5 9 1
A.L. ....0 1 0 0 0 3 0 0 0—4 11 1
Valenzuela (Dodgers), Seaver (Reds) 2, Knepper (Astros) 3, Hooton (Dodgers) 5, Ruthven (Phillies) 6, Blue (Giants) 7, Ryan (Astros) 8, Sutter (Cardinals) 9; Morris (Tigers), Barker (Indians) 3, Forsch (Angels) 5, Norris (Athletics) 6, Davis (Yankees) 7, Fingers (Brewers) 8, Stieb (Blue Jays) 8. W—Blue. L—Fingers. S—Sutter. HR—Singleton, A.L.; Carter 2, Parker, Schmidt, N.L.

DIVISIONAL PLAYOFFS

Los Angeles defeated Houston, 3 games to 2
Montreal defeated Philadelphia, 3 games to 2
NY Yankees defeated Milwaukee, 3 games to 2
Oakland defeated Kansas City, 3 games to 0

ALCS

■ **Winner:** The New York Yankees captured their 33rd pennant with a 1-2-3 Championship Series victory over Oakland.

■ **Turning point:** The first inning of Game 1, when Yankee third baseman Graig Nettles drilled a three-run double, giving lefty Tommy John and two relievers all the runs they needed for a 3-1 victory.

■ **Memorable moment:** The ninth inning of Game 3, when Nettles drilled another three-run double, putting the wraps on a 4-0 series-ending victory.

■ **Top guns:** Nettles (.500, 1 HR, 9 RBIs), Jerry Mumphrey (.500), Larry Milbourne (.462), Yankees; Rickey Henderson (.364), Athletics.

■ **MVP:** Nettles.

Linescores

Game 1—October 13 at New York
Oakland........0 0 0 0 1 0 0 0 0—1 6 1
N.Y. ....3 0 0 0 0 0 0 0 x—3 7 1
Norris, Underwood (8); John, Davis (7), Gossage (8). W—John. L—Norris. S—Gossage.

Game 2—October 14, at New York
Oakland....0 0 1 2 0 0 0 0 0— 3 11 1
N.Y. ....1 0 0 7 0 1 4 0 x—13 19 0
McCatty, Beard (4), Jones (5), Kingman (7), Owchinko (7); May, Frazier (4). W—Frazier. L—McCatty. HR—Piniella, Nettles (N.Y.).

Game 3—October 15, at Oakland
N.Y. ....0 0 0 0 0 1 0 0 3—4 10 0
Oakland......0 0 0 0 0 0 0 0 0—0 5 2
Righetti, Davis (7), Gossage (9); Keough, Underwood (9). W—Righetti. L—Keough. HR—Randolph (N.Y.).

NLCS

■ **Winner:** The Los Angeles Dodgers ruined Montreal's bid to become the first Canadian qualifier for a World Series with a dramatic ninth-inning home run in the fifth game.

■ **Turning point:** An eighth-inning Game 4 home run by Steve Garvey that broke a 1-1 tie and propelled the Dodgers to an elimination-saving 7-1 victory.

■ **Memorable moment:** A ninth-inning series-winning home run by Dodgers outfielder Rick Monday off Expos ace Steve Rogers in Game 5 at frigid Montreal.

■ **Top guns:** Burt Hooton (2-0, 0.00 ERA), Monday (.333), Dusty Baker (.316), Dodgers; Ray Burris (1-0, 0.53 ERA), Gary Carter (.438), Expos.

■ **MVP:** Hooton.

Linescores

Game 1—October 13, at Los Angeles
Montreal ......0 0 0 0 0 0 0 0 1—1 9 0
L.A. ....0 2 0 0 0 0 0 3 x—5 8 0
Gullickson, Reardon (8); Hooton, Welch (8), Howe (9). W—Hooton. L—Gullickson. HR—Guerrero, Scioscia (L.A.).

Game 2—October 14, at Los Angeles
Montreal ....0 2 0 0 0 1 0 0 0—3 10 1
L.A. ....0 0 0 0 0 0 0 0 0—0 5 1
Burris; Valenzuela, Niedenfuer (7), Forster (7), Pena (7), Castillo (9). W—Burris. L—Valenzuela.

Game 3—October 16, at Montreal
L.A. ....0 0 0 1 0 0 0 0 0—1 7 0
Montreal ......0 0 0 0 0 4 0 0 x—4 7 1
Reuss, Pena (8); Rogers. W—Rogers. L—Reuss. HR—White (Mon.).

Game 4—October 17, at Montreal
L.A. ....0 0 1 0 0 0 0 2 4—7 12 1
Montreal ....0 0 0 1 0 0 0 0 0—1 5 1
Hooton, Welch (8), Howe (9); Gullickson, Fryman (8), Sosa (9), Lee (9). W—Hooton. L—Gullickson. HR—Garvey (L.A.).

Game 5—October 19, at Montreal
L.A. ....0 0 0 0 1 0 0 0 1—2 6 0
Montreal ......1 0 0 0 0 0 0 0 0—1 3 1
Valenzuela, Welch (9); Burris, Rogers (9). W—Valenzuela. L—Rogers. S—Welch. HR—Monday (L.A.).

WORLD SERIES

■ **Winner:** The Dodgers brought the strike-shortened season to an end by duplicating the Yankees' 1978 feat against them—four straight victories after two opening losses.

■ **Turning point:** After falling behind 4-0 and 6-3 in Game 4, the Dodgers rallied for an 8-7 victory that squared the Series at two games.

■ **Memorable moment:** Back-to-back, seventh-inning home runs by Pedro Guerrero and Steve Yeager that gave Jerry Reuss a 2-1 victory over Ron Guidry and the Yankees in the pivotal fifth game.

■ **Top guns:** Steve Garvey (.417), Ron Cey (.350, 6 RBIs), Guerrero (.333, 2 HR, 7 RBIs), Dodgers; Bob Watson (.318, 2 HR, 7 RBIs), Yankees.

■ **Co-MVPs:** Guerrero, Yeager, Cey.

Linescores

Game 1—October 20, at New York
L.A. ....0 0 0 0 1 0 0 2 0—3 5 0
N.Y. ....3 0 1 1 0 0 0 0 x—5 6 0
Reuss, Castillo (3), Goltz (4), Niedenfuer (5), Stewart (8); Guidry, Davis (8), Gossage (8). W—Guidry. L—Reuss. S—Gossage. HR—Yeager (L.A.); Watson (N.Y.).

Game 2—October 21, at New York
L.A. ....0 0 0 0 0 0 0 0 0—0 4 2
N.Y. ....0 0 0 0 1 0 0 2 x—3 6 1
Hooton, Forster (7), Howe (8), Stewart (8); John, Gossage (8). W—John. L—Hooton. S—Gossage.

Game 3—October 23, at Los Angeles
N.Y. ....0 2 2 0 0 0 0 0 0—4 9 0
L.A. ....3 0 0 0 2 0 0 0 x—5 11 1
Righetti, Frazier (3), May (5), Davis (8); Valenzuela. W—Valenzuela. L—Frazier. HR—Cey (L.A.); Watson, Cerone (N.Y.).

Game 4—October 24, at Los Angeles
N.Y. ....2 1 1 0 0 2 0 1 0—7 13 1
L.A. ....0 0 2 0 1 3 2 0 x—8 14 2
Reuschel, May (4), Davis (5), Frazier (6), John (7); Welch, Goltz (1), Forster (4), Niedenfuer (5), Howe (7). W—Howe. L—Frazier. HR—Randolph, Jackson (N.Y.); Johnstone (L.A.).

Game 5—October 25, at Los Angeles
N.Y. ....0 1 0 0 0 0 0 0 0—1 5 0
L.A. ....0 0 0 0 0 0 2 0 x—2 4 3
Guidry, Gossage (8); Reuss. W—Reuss. L—Guidry. HR—Guerrero, Yeager (L.A.).

Game 6—October 28, at New York
L.A. ....0 0 0 1 3 4 0 1 0—9 13 1
N.Y. ....0 0 1 0 0 1 0 0 0—2 7 2
Hooton, Howe (6); John, Frazier (5), Davis (6), Reuschel (6), May (7), LaRoche (9). W—Hooton. L—Frazier. S—Howe. HR—Randolph (N.Y.); Guerrero (L.A.).

1982

FINAL STANDINGS

American League

East Division

Team	Mil.	Bal.	Bos.	Det.	N.Y.	Tor.	Cle.	Cal.	Chi.	K.C.	Min.	Oak.	Sea.	Tex.	W	L	Pct.	GB
Milwaukee	...	4	9	10	8	9	6	6	9	5	7	7	8	7	95	67	.586	...
Baltimore	9	...	4	7	11	10	6	7	5	4	8	7	7	9	94	68	.580	1
Boston	4	9	...	8	7	7	6	7	4	6	6	8	7	10	89	73	.549	6
Detroit	3	6	5	...	8	6	7	7	3	6	9	9	6	8	83	79	.512	12
New York	5	2	6	5	...	6	9	5	4	7	10	7	6	7	79	83	.488	16
Toronto	4	3	6	7	7	...	6	4	4	8	7	9	5	8	78	84	.481	17
Cleveland	7	7	7	6	4	7	...	4	6	2	8	4	9	7	78	84	.481	17

West Division

Team	Cal.	K.C.	Chi.	Sea.	Oak.	Tex.	Min.	Bal.	Bos.	Cle.	Det.	Mil.	N.Y.	Tor.	W	L	Pct.	GB
California	...	7	8	10	9	8	7	5	5	8	5	6	7	8	93	69	.574	...
Kansas City	6	...	10	7	7	7	7	8	6	10	6	7	5	4	90	72	.556	3
Chicago	5	3	...	6	9	8	7	7	8	6	9	3	8	8	87	75	.537	6
Seattle	3	6	7	...	7	9	8	5	5	3	6	4	6	7	76	86	.469	17
Oakland	4	6	4	6	...	5	10	5	4	8	3	5	5	3	68	94	.420	25
Texas	5	6	5	4	8	...	8	3	2	5	4	5	5	4	64	98	.395	29
Minnesota	6	6	6	5	3	5	...	4	6	4	3	5	2	5	60	102	.370	33

National League

East Division

Team	St.L.	Phi.	Mon.	Pit.	Chi.	N.Y.	Atl.	Cin.	Hou.	L.A.	S.D.	S.F.	W	L	Pct	.GB
St. Louis	...	11	8	11	12	12	5	7	6	5	8	7	92	70	.568	...
Philadelphia	7	...	10	9	9	11	6	7	5	8	7	10	89	73	.549	3
Montreal	10	8	...	7	12	11	7	8	8	4	7	4	86	76	.531	6
Pittsburgh	7	9	11	...	9	10	8	8	3	7	6	6	84	78	.519	8
Chicago	6	9	6	9	...	9	4	6	9	5	4	6	73	89	.451	19
New York	6	7	7	8	9	...	3	5	4	6	6	4	65	97	.401	27

West Division

Team	Atl.	L.A.	S.F.	S.D.	Hou.	Cin.	Chi.	Mon.	N.Y.	Phi.	Pit.	St.L.	W	L	Pct.	GB
Atlanta	...	7	8	11	10	14	8	5	9	6	4	7	89	73	.549	...
Los Angeles	11	..	9	9	11	11	7	8	6	4	5	7	88	74	.543	1
San Fran.	10	9	...	8	13	12	6	8	8	2	6	5	87	75	.537	2
San Diego	7	9	10	...	9	12	8	5	6	5	6	4	81	81	.500	8
Houston	8	7	5	9	...	11	3	4	8	7	9	6	77	85	.475	12
Cincinnati	4	7	6	6	7	...	6	4	7	5	4	5	61	101	.377	28

SIGNIFICANT EVENTS

■ **April 6:** Seattle spoiled the Metrodome inaugural for Minnesota fans with an 11-7 Opening Day victory over the Twins.

■ **April 22:** The Reds defeated Atlanta, 2-1, handing the Braves their first loss after a season-opening record 13 consecutive victories.

■ **October 3:** The Brewers captured their first A.L. East title when they defeated Baltimore, 10-2, in a winner-take-all final-day battle.

■ **October 3:** The Braves, final-day losers to San Diego, clinched their first division title since 1969 when San Francisco defeated the Dodgers, 5-3, on Joe Morgan's three-run homer.

■ **October 26:** Phillies ace Steve Carlton captured his record fourth N.L. Cy Young Award.

■ **November 1:** Owners ended the 14-year reign of commissioner Bowie Kuhn when they voted not to renew his contract at a meeting in Chicago.

MEMORABLE MOMENTS

■ **May 6:** Gaylord Perry pitched the Mariners to a 7-3 victory over the Yankees and became the 15th member of baseball's 300-win club.

■ **June 22:** Philadelphia's Pete Rose doubled off the Cardinals' John Stuper and moved into second place on the all-time hit list with 3,772.

■ **August 27:** Oakland's Rickey Henderson claimed the one-season basestealing record when he swiped four in a game at Milwaukee, giving him 122 en route to a final total of 130.

LEADERS

American League
BA: Willie Wilson, K.C., .332.
Runs: Paul Molitor, Mil., 136.
Hits: Robin Yount, Mil., 210.
TB: Robin Yount, Mil., 367.
HR: Reggie Jackson, Cal.; Gorman Thomas, Mil., 39.
RBI: Hal McRae, K.C., 133.
SB: Rickey Henderson, Oak., 130.
Wins: LaMarr Hoyt, Chi., 19.
ERA: Rick Sutcliffe, Cle., 2.96.
CG: Dave Stieb, Tor., 19.
IP: Dave Stieb, Tor., 288.1.
SO: Floyd Bannister, Sea., 209.
SV: Dan Quisenberry, K.C., 35.

National League
BA: Al Oliver, Mon., .331.
Runs: Lonnie Smith, St.L., 120.
Hits: Al Oliver, Mon., 204.
TB: Al Oliver, Mon., 317.
HR: Dave Kingman, N.Y., 37.
RBI: Dale Murphy, Atl.; Al Oliver, Mon., 109.
SB: Tim Raines, Mon., 78.
Wins: Steve Carlton, Phil., 23.
ERA: Steve Rogers, Mon., 2.40.
CG: Steve Carlton, Phil., 19.
IP: Steve Carlton, Phil., 295.2.
SO: Steve Carlton, Phil., 286.
SV: Bruce Sutter, St.L., 36.

N.L. 20-game winner
Steve Carlton, Phil., 23-11

A.L. 100 RBIs
Hal McRae, K.C., 133
Cecil Cooper, Mil., 121
Andre Thornton, Cle., 116
Robin Yount, Mil., 114
Gorman Thomas, Mil., 112
Eddie Murray, Bal., 110
Dave Winfield, N.Y., 106
Harold Baines, Chi., 105
Greg Luzinski, Chi., 102
Ben Oglivie, Mil., 102
Reggie Jackson, Cal., 101

N.L. 100 RBIs
Dale Murphy, Atl., 109
Al Oliver, Mon., 109
Bill Buckner, Chi., 105
George Hendrick, St.L., 104
Jack Clark, S.F., 103
Jason Thompson, Pit., 101
Pedro Guerrero, L.A., 100

Most Valuable Player
A.L.: Robin Yount, SS, Mil.
N.L.: Dale Murphy, OF, Atl.

Cy Young Award
A.L.: Pete Vuckovich, Mil.
N.L.: Steve Carlton, Phil.

Rookie of the Year
A.L.: Cal Ripken, SS, Bal.
N.L.: Steve Sax, 2B, L.A.

Hall of Fame additions
Hank Aaron, OF, 1954-76
Happy Chandler, commissioner
Travis Jackson, SS, 1922-36
Frank Robinson, OF, 1956-76

ALL-STAR GAME

■ **Winner:** The N.L. made it 11 in a row and 19 of 20 with a 4-1 victory at Montreal — the first midsummer classic played on foreign soil.

■ **Key inning:** The second, when Dave Concepcion pounded a two-run homer, giving N.L. pitchers all the runs they would need.

■ **Memorable moment:** A sixth-inning run manufactured by a pair of Expos. Al Oliver thrilled the home fans with a double and Gary Carter singled him home.

■ **Top guns:** Steve Carlton (Phillies), Oliver (Expos), Concepcion (Reds), N.L.; Rickey Henderson (Athletics), George Brett (Royals), A.L.

■ **MVP:** Concepcion.

Linescore
July 13, at Montreal's Olympic Stadium
A.L. ....1 0 0 0 0 0 0 0 0—1 8 2
N.L. ....0 2 1 0 0 1 0 0 x—4 8 1
Eckersley (Red Sox), Clancy (Blue Jays) 4, Bannister (Mariners) 5, Quisenberry (Royals) 6, Fingers (Brewers) 8; Rogers (Expos), Carlton (Phillies) 4, Soto (Reds) 6, Valenzuela (Dodgers) 8, Minton (Giants) 8, Howe (Dodgers) 9, Hume (Reds) 9. W—Rogers. L—Eckersley. S—Hume. HR—Concepcion, N.L.

ALCS

■ **Winner:** In a battle of first-time pennant hopefuls, the Milwaukee Brewers defeated California and became the first team to recover from a two-games-to-one deficit in a League Championship Series.

■ **Turning point:** The unexpected Game 4 boost the Brewers received from substitute left fielder Mark Brouhard, who collected three hits, belted a home run and drove in three runs in Milwaukee's elimination-saving 9-5 victory.

■ **Memorable moment:** Cecil Cooper's two-run, seventh-inning single that wiped out a 3-2 Angels lead and gave the Brewers a 4-3 Game 5 victory and the franchise's first World Series berth.

■ **Top guns:** Charlie Moore (.462), Paul Molitor (.316, 2 HR, 5 RBIs), Brouhard (.750), Brewers; Bruce Kison (1-0, 1.93 ERA), Fred Lynn (.611, 5 RBIs), Don Baylor (10 RBIs), Angels.

■ **MVP:** Lynn.

Linescores

Game 1—October 5, at California
Mil. ....0 2 1 0 0 0 0 0 0—3 7 2
Cal. ....1 0 4 2 1 0 0 0 x—8 10 0
Caldwell, Slaton (4), Ladd (7), Bernard (8); John. W—John. L—Caldwell. HR—Thomas (Mil.); Lynn (Cal.).

Game 2—October 6, at California
Mil. ....0 0 0 0 2 0 0 0 0—2 5 0
Cal. ....0 2 1 1 0 0 0 0 x—4 6 0
Vuckovich; Kison. W—Kison. L—Vuckovich. HR—Re. Jackson (Cal.); Molitor (Mil.).

Game 3—October 8, at Milwaukee
Cal. ....0 0 0 0 0 0 0 3 0—3 8 0
Mil. ....0 0 0 3 0 0 2 0 x—5 6 0
Zahn, Witt (4), Hassler (7); Sutton, Ladd (8). W—Sutton. L—Zahn. S—Ladd. HR—Molitor (Mil.); Boone (Cal).

Game 4—October 9, at Milwaukee
Cal. ....0 0 0 0 0 1 0 4 0—5 5 3
Mil. ....0 3 0 3 0 1 0 2 x—9 9 2
John, Goltz (4), Sanchez (8); Haas, Slaton (8). W—Haas. L—John. S—Slaton. HR—Baylor (Cal.); Brouhard (Mil.).

Game 5—October 10, at Milwaukee
Cal. ....1 0 1 1 0 0 0 0 0—3 11 1
Mil. ....1 0 0 1 0 0 2 0 x—4 6 4
Kison, Sanchez (6), Hassler (7); Vuckovich, McClure (7), Ladd (9). W—McClure. L—Sanchez. S—Ladd. HR—Oglivie (Mil.).

NLCS

■ **Winner:** The Atlanta Braves, who were swept by the New York Mets in the first NLCS in 1969, suffered the same fate against St. Louis in the franchise's second post-season appearance.

■ **Turning point:** A Game 1 rainstorm that wiped out a 1-0 Braves lead after 4½ innings and forced Atlanta to bypass ace Phil Niekro in the rescheduled opener.

■ **Memorable moment:** Ken Oberkfell's ninth-inning line drive that eluded Braves center fielder Brett Butler and drove home David Green, giving the Cardinals a 4-3 Game 2 victory.

■ **Top guns:** Bob Forsch (1-0, 0.00 ERA), Darrell Porter (.556), Ozzie Smith (.556), Cardinals; Claudell Washington (.333), Braves.

■ **MVP:** Porter.

Linescores

Game 1—October 7, at St. Louis
Atlanta ....0 0 0 0 0 0 0 0 0—0 3 0
St. Louis ....0 0 1 0 0 5 0 1 x—7 13 1
Perez, Bedrosian (6), Moore (6), Walk (8); Forsch. W—Forsch. L—Perez.

Game 2—October 9, at St. Louis
Atlanta ....0 0 2 0 1 0 0 0 0—3 6 0
St. Louis ......1 0 0 0 0 1 0 1 1—4 9 1
Niekro, Garber (7); Stuper, Bair (7), Sutter (8). W—Sutter. L—Garber.

Game 3—October 10, at Atlanta
St. Louis ....0 4 0 0 1 0 0 0 1—6 12 0
Atlanta ......0 0 0 0 0 0 2 0 0—2 6 1
Andujar, Sutter (7); Camp, Perez (2), Moore (5), Mahler (7), Bedrosian (8), Garber (9). W—Andujar. L—Camp. S—Sutter. HR—McGee (St.L.).

WORLD SERIES

■ **Winner:** The resilient Cardinals tamed "Harvey's Wallbangers" and spoiled the Brewers' first World Series.

■ **Turning point:** A special Game 3 performance by center fielder Willie McGee, who stepped out of character to hit two home runs and added two spectacular catches in a 6-2 victory that gave the Cardinals their first Series lead.

■ **Memorable moment:** A two-run single by Keith Hernandez and a run-scoring single by George Hendrick in a three-run sixth inning that rallied the Cardinals to a seventh-game 6-3 victory.

■ **Top guns:** Joaquin Andujar (2-0, 1.35 ERA), Dane Iorg (.529), Darrell Porter (5 RBIs), Hernandez (8 RBIs), Cardinals; Mike Caldwell (2-0, 2.04), Robin Yount (.414, 12 hits, 6 RBIs), Paul Molitor (.355), Brewers.

■ **MVP:** Porter.

Linescores

Game 1—October 12, at St. Louis
Mil. ....2 0 0 1 1 2 0 0 4—10 17 0
St. Louis ..0 0 0 0 0 0 0 0 0— 0 3 1
Caldwell; Forsch, Kaat (6), LaPoint (8), Lahti (9). W—Caldwell. L—Forsch. HR—Simmons (Mil.).

Game 2—October 13, at St. Louis
Mil. ....0 1 2 0 1 0 0 0 0—4 10 1
St. Louis ....0 0 2 0 0 2 0 1 x—5 8 0
Sutton, McClure (7), Ladd (8); Stuper, Kaat (5), Bair (5), Sutter (7). W—Sutter. L—McClure. HR—Simmons (Mil.).

Game 3—October 15, at Milwaukee
St. Louis ......0 0 0 0 3 0 2 0 1—6 6 1
Mil. ....0 0 0 0 0 0 0 2 0—2 5 3
Andujar, Kaat (7), Bair (7), Sutter (7); Vuckovich, McClure (9). W—Andujar. L—Vuckovich. S—Sutter. HR—McGee 2 (St.L.); Cooper (Mil.).

Game 4—October 16, at Milwaukee
St. Louis ....1 3 0 0 0 1 0 0 0—5 8 1
Mil. ....0 0 0 0 1 0 6 0 x—7 10 2
LaPoint, Bair (7), Kaat (7), Lahti (7); Haas, Slaton (6), McClure (8). W—Slaton. L—Bair. S—McClure.

Game 5—October 17, at Milwaukee
St. Louis ....0 0 1 0 0 0 1 0 2—4 15 2
Mil. ....1 0 1 0 1 0 1 2 x—6 11 1
Forsch, Sutter (8); Caldwell, McClure (9). W—Caldwell. L—Forsch. S—McClure. HR—Yount (Mil.).

Game 6—October 19, at St. Louis
Mil. ....0 0 0 0 0 0 0 0 1— 1 4 4
St. Louis ..0 2 0 3 2 6 0 0 x—13 12 1
Sutton, Slaton (5), Medich (6), Bernard (8); Stuper. W—Stuper. L—Sutton. HR—Porter, Hernandez (St.L.).

Game 7—October 20, at St. Louis
Mil. ....0 0 0 0 1 2 0 0 0—3 7 0
St. Louis ....0 0 0 1 0 3 0 2 x—6 15 1
Vuckovich, McClure (6), Haas (6), Caldwell (8); Andujar, Sutter (8). W—Andujar. L—McClure. S—Sutter. HR—Oglivie (Mil.).

HISTORY

FINAL STANDINGS

American League

East Division

Team	Bal.	Det.	N.Y.	Tor.	Mil.	Bos.	Cle.	Cal.	Chi.	K.C.	Min.	Oak.	Sea.	Tex.	W	L	Pct.	GB
Baltimore	...	5	6	7	11	8	6	7	7	8	8	8	8	9	98	64	.605	...
Detroit	8	...	5	6	6	9	8	8	4	7	9	6	8	8	92	70	.568	6
New York	7	8	...	7	9	6	7	7	4	6	8	8	7	7	91	71	.562	7
Toronto	6	7	6	...	5	6	9	8	7	6	7	6	8	8	89	73	.549	9
Milwaukee	2	7	4	8	...	9	10	6	8	6	8	6	5	8	87	75	.537	11
Boston	5	4	7	7	4	...	7	6	6	5	5	8	7	7	78	84	.481	20
Cleveland	7	5	6	4	3	6	...	4	4	7	6	7	8	3	70	92	.432	28

West Division

Team	Chi.	K.C.	Tex.	Oak.	Cal.	Min.	Sea.	Bal.	Bos.	Cle.	Det.	Mil.	N.Y.	Tor.	W	L	Pct.	GB
Chicago	...	9	8	8	10	8	12	5	6	8	8	4	8	5	99	63	.611	...
Kansas City	4	...	8	7	7	6	8	4	7	5	5	6	6	6	79	83	.488	20
Texas	5	5	...	11	7	8	7	3	5	9	4	4	5	4	77	85	.475	22
Oakland	5	6	2	...	8	9	9	4	4	5	6	6	4	6	74	88	.457	25
California	3	6	6	5	...	6	6	5	6	8	4	6	5	4	70	92	.432	29
Minnesota	5	7	5	4	7	...	9	4	7	6	3	4	4	5	70	92	.432	29
Seattle	1	5	6	4	7	4	...	4	5	4	4	7	5	4	60	102	.370	39

National League

East Division

Team	Phi.	Pit.	Mon.	St.L.	Chi.	N.Y.	Atl.	Cin.	Hou.	L.A.	S.D.	S.F.	W	L	Pct.	GB
Philadelphia	...	11	10	14	13	12	5	6	8	1	5	5	90	72	.556	...
Pittsburgh	7	...	10	10	9	9	6	6	6	6	9	6	84	78	.519	6
Montreal	8	8	...	9	11	8	5	8	4	5	8	8	82	80	.506	8
St. Louis	4	8	9	...	8	12	5	6	10	3	6	8	79	83	.488	11
Chicago	5	9	7	10	...	9	7	4	5	6	5	4	71	91	.438	19
New York	6	9	10	6	9	...	4	5	3	5	6	5	68	94	.420	22

West Division

Team	L.A.	Atl.	Hou.	S.D.	S.F.	Cin.	Chi.	Mon.	N.Y.	Phi.	Pit.	St.L.	W	L	Pct.	GB
Los Angeles	...	11	12	6	5	11	6	7	7	11	6	9	91	71	.562	...
Atlanta	7	...	11	9	9	12	5	7	8	7	6	7	88	74	.543	3
Houston	6	7	...	11	12	13	7	8	9	4	6	2	85	77	.525	6
San Diego	12	9	7	...	11	9	7	4	6	7	3	6	81	81	.500	10
San Fran.	13	9	6	7	...	8	8	4	7	7	6	4	79	83	.488	12
Cincinnati	7	6	5	9	10	...	8	4	7	6	6	6	74	88	.457	17

SIGNIFICANT EVENTS

■ **April 7:** ABC and NBC agreed to share a lucrative six-year television contract that would pay baseball $1.2 billion.

■ **February 8:** Former Yankee great Mickey Mantle was ordered to sever ties with baseball after taking a job with an Atlantic City hotel and casino.

■ **July 29:** The N.L.-record ironman streak of San Diego's Steve Garvey ended at 1,207 games when he dislocated his thumb in a home-plate collision against the Braves.

■ **November 17:** A U.S. magistrate handed three members of the 1983 Royals, Willie Wilson, Willie Aikens and Jerry Martin, three-month prison sentences for attempting to purchase cocaine.

■ **December 8:** Dr. Bobby Brown was elected as the successor to retiring A.L. president Lee MacPhail.

■ **December 19:** Former Cy Young winner Vida Blue became the fourth Kansas City player to receive a three-month prison sentence for attempting to purchase cocaine.

MEMORABLE MOMENTS

■ **July 24:** A two-out, game-winning home run by Kansas City's George Brett off Yankee reliever Goose Gossage was nullified by umpires who said Brett's bat was illegally covered by pine tar—a controversial ruling that later would be overturned.

■ **June 26:** Mets veteran Rusty Staub collected his record-tying eighth consecutive pinch hit in an 8-4 loss to the Phillies.

■ **September 23:** Philadelphia lefty Steve Carlton became baseball's 16th 300-game winner when he defeated St. Louis, 6-2.

LEADERS

American League
BA: Wade Boggs, Bos., .361.
Runs: Cal Ripken, Bal., 121.
Hits: Cal Ripken, Bal., 211.
TB: Jim Rice, Bos., 344.
HR: Jim Rice, Bos., 39.
RBI: Cecil Cooper, Mil.; Jim Rice, Bos., 126.
SB: Rickey Henderson, Oak., 108.
Wins: LaMarr Hoyt, Chi., 24.
ERA: Rick Honeycutt, Tex., 2.42.
CG: Ron Guidry, N.Y., 21.
IP: Jack Morris, Det., 293.2.
SO: Jack Morris, Det., 232.
SV: Dan Quisenberry, K.C., 45.

National League
BA: Bill Madlock, Pit., .323.
Runs: Tim Raines, Mon., 133.
Hits: Jose Cruz, Hou.; Andre Dawson, Mon., 189.
TB: Andre Dawson, Mon., 341.
HR: Mike Schmidt, Phil., 40.
RBI: Dale Murphy, Atl., 121.
SB: Tim Raines, Mon., 90.
Wins: John Denny, Phil., 19.
ERA: Atlee Hammaker, S.F., 2.25.
CG: Mario Soto, Cin., 18.
IP: Steve Carlton, Phil., 283.2.
SO: Steve Carlton, Phil., 275.
SV: Lee Smith, Chi., 29.

A.L. 20-game winners
LaMarr Hoyt, Chi., 24-10
Rich Dotson, Chi., 22-7
Ron Guidry, N.Y., 21-9
Jack Morris, Det., 20-13

A.L. 100 RBIs
Cecil Cooper, Mil., 126
Jim Rice, Bos., 126
Dave Winfield, N.Y., 116
Lance Parrish, Det., 114
Eddie Murray, Bal., 111
Ted Simmons, Mil., 108
Tony Armas, Bos., 107
Willie Upshaw, Tor., 104
Cal Ripken, Bal., 102
Ron Kittle, Chi., 100

N.L. 100 RBIs
Dale Murphy, Atl., 121
Andre Dawson, Mon., 113
Mike Schmidt, Phil., 109
Pedro Guerrero, L.A., 103

N.L. 40 homers
Mike Schmidt, Phil., 40

Most Valuable Player
A.L.: Cal Ripken, SS, Bal.
N.L.: Dale Murphy, OF, Atl.

Cy Young Award
A.L.: LaMarr Hoyt, Chi.
N.L.: John Denny, Phil.

Rookie of the Year
A.L.: Ron Kittle, OF, Chi.
N.L.: Darryl Strawberry, OF, N.Y.

Manager of the Year
A.L.: Tony La Russa, Chi.
N.L.: Tommy Lasorda, L.A.

Hall of Fame additions
Walter Alston, manager
George Kell, 3B, 1943-57
Juan Marichal, P, 1960-75
Brooks Robinson, 3B, 1955-77

ALL-STAR GAME

■ **Winner:** The A.L. snapped its frustrating 11-game All-Star losing streak with a 13-3 rout in a special 50th-anniversary celebration of the midsummer classic at Chicago's Comiskey Park.

■ **Key inning:** A record seven-run third that gave the A.L. a 9-1 lead and set the course for its first victory since 1971.

■ **Memorable moment:** Fred Lynn's third-inning bases-loaded homer off Atlee Hammaker — the first grand slam in 54 All-Star Games.

■ **Top guns:** Dave Stieb (Blue Jays), Lynn (Angels), Jim Rice (Red Sox), George Brett (Royals), Dave Winfield (Yankees), A.L.; Steve Sax (Dodgers), N.L.

■ **MVP:** Lynn.

Linescore
July 6, Chicago's Comiskey Park
N.L. ....1 0 0 1 1 0 0 0 0— 3 8 3
A.L. ....1 1 7 0 0 0 2 2 x—13 15 2
Soto (Reds), Hammaker (Giants) 3, Dawley (Astros) 3, Dravecky (Padres) 5, Perez (Braves) 7, Orosco (Mets) 7, L. Smith (Cubs) 8; Stieb (Blue Jays), Honeycutt (Rangers) 4, Stanley (Red Sox) 6, Young (Mariners) 8, Quisenberry (Royals) 9. W—Stieb. L—Soto. HR—Rice, Lynn, A.L.

ALCS

■ **Winner:** Baltimore, a 2-1 loser to the Chicago White Sox in the opener, roared to three consecutive victories and claimed its fifth pennant since LCS play began in 1969.

■ **Turning point:** Mike Boddicker's five-hit, 4-0 shutout in Game 2. Orioles pitchers would finish the series with a 0.49 ERA.

■ **Memorable moment:** A 10th-inning home run by unlikely Baltimore hero Tito Landrum off Chicago lefty Britt Burns in Game 4. The blast broke up a scoreless battle and propelled the Orioles to a series-ending 3-0 victory.

■ **Top guns:** Boddicker (1-0, 0.00 ERA), Tippy Martinez (1-0, 0.00), Cal Ripken (.400), Orioles; LaMarr Hoyt (1-0, 1.00), Rudy Law (.389), White Sox.

■ **MVP:** Boddicker.

Linescores

Game 1—October 5, at Baltimore
Chi. ....0 0 1 0 0 1 0 0 0—2 7 0
Balt. ....0 0 0 0 0 0 0 0 1—1 5 1
Hoyt; McGregor, Stewart (7), T. Martinez (8). W—Hoyt. L—McGregor.

Game 2—October 6, at Baltimore
Chi. ....0 0 0 0 0 0 0 0 0—0 5 2
Balt. ....0 1 0 1 0 2 0 0 x—4 6 0
Bannister, Barojas (7), Lamp (8); Boddicker. W—Boddicker. L—Bannister. HR—Roenicke (Bal.).

Game 3—October 7, at Chicago
Balt. ....3 1 0 0 2 0 0 1 4—11 8 1
Chi. ....0 1 0 0 0 0 0 0 0— 1 6 1
Flanagan, Stewart (6); Dotson, Tidrow (6), Koosman (9), Lamp (9). W—Flanagan. L—Dotson. S—Stewart. HR—Murray (Bal.).

Game 4—October 8, at Chicago
Balt. ....0 0 0 0 0 0 0 0 0 3—3 9 0
Chi. ......0 0 0 0 0 0 0 0 0 0—0 10 0
Davis, T. Martinez (7); Burns, Barojas (10), Agosto (10), Lamp (10). W—T. Martinez. L—Burns. HR—Landrum (Bal.).

NLCS

■ **Winner:** The Philadelphia Phillies advanced to their second World Series in four years and settled an old NLCS score with the Dodgers, who had defeated them in 1977 and '78.

■ **Turning point:** The Game 3 performance of veteran outfielder Gary Matthews: three hits, a home run and four RBIs in a 7-2 Phillies victory.

■ **Memorable moment:** A three-run, first-inning home run by Matthews in Game 4. Matthews' third homer in as many games propelled the Phillies to a series-ending 7-2 victory.

■ **Top guns:** Steve Carlton (2-0, 0.66 ERA), Mike Schmidt (.467), Matthews (.429, 3 HR, 8 RBIs), Phillies; Fernando Valenzuela (1-0, 1.13), Dusty Baker (.357), Dodgers.

■ **MVP:** Matthews.

Linescores

Game 1—October 4, at Los Angeles
Phil. ....1 0 0 0 0 0 0 0 0—1 5 1
L.A. ....0 0 0 0 0 0 0 0 0—0 7 0
Carlton, Holland (8); Reuss, Niedenfuer (9). W—Carlton. L—Reuss. S—Holland. HR—Schmidt (Phil.).

Game 2—October 5, at Los Angeles
Phil. ....0 1 0 0 0 0 0 0 0—1 7 2
L.A. ....1 0 0 0 2 0 0 1 x—4 6 1
Denny, Reed (7); Valenzuela, Niedenfuer (9). W—Valenzuela. L—Denny. S—Niedenfuer. HR—Matthews (Phil.).

Game 3—October 7, at Philadelphia
L.A. ....0 0 0 2 0 0 0 0 0—2 4 0
Phil. ....0 2 1 1 2 0 1 0 x—7 9 1
Welch, Pena (2), Honeycutt (5), Beckwith (5), Zachry (7); Hudson. W—Hudson. L—Welch. HR—Marshall (L.A.); Matthews (Phil.).

Game 4—October 8, at Philadelphia
L.A. ....0 0 0 1 0 0 0 1 0—2 10 0
Phil. ....3 0 0 0 2 2 0 0 x—7 13 1
Reuss, Beckwith (5), Honeycutt (5), Zachry (7); Carlton, Reed (7), Holland (8). W—Carlton. L—Reuss. HR—Matthews, Lezcano (Phil.); Baker (L.A.).

WORLD SERIES

■ **Winner:** The Orioles lost the opener and then sprinted past the Phillies for their first championship since 1970.

■ **Turning point:** When Phillies manager Paul Owens let starting pitcher Steve Carlton bat with two runners on base in the sixth inning of Game 3. Carlton struck out and then yielded two seventh-inning runs that vaulted the Orioles to a 3-2 victory.

■ **Memorable moment:** Garry Maddox's game-deciding eighth-inning homer in Game 1. Maddox connected on the first pitch from Scott McGregor, who stood on the mound for about five minutes while President Ronald Reagan was being interviewed for television.

■ **Top guns:** Rick Dempsey (.385), John Lowenstein (.385), Orioles; Bo Diaz (.333), Phillies.

■ **MVP:** Dempsey.

Linescores

Game 1—October 11, at Baltimore
Phil. ....0 0 0 0 0 1 0 1 0—2 5 0
Baltimore ....1 0 0 0 0 0 0 0 0—1 5 1
Denny, Holland (8); McGregor, Stewart (9), T. Martinez (9). W—Denny. L—McGregor. S—Holland. HR—Dwyer (Bal.); Morgan, Maddox (Phil.).

Game 2—October 12, at Baltimore
Phil. ....0 0 0 1 0 0 0 0 0—1 3 0
Baltimore ....0 0 0 0 3 0 1 0 x—4 9 1
Hudson, Hernandez (5), Andersen (6), Reed (8); Boddicker. W—Boddicker. L—Hudson. HR—Lowenstein (Bal.).

Game 3—October 14, at Philadelphia
Baltimore ....0 0 0 0 0 1 2 0 0—3 6 1
Phil. ....0 1 1 0 0 0 0 0 0—2 8 2
Flanagan, Palmer (5), Stewart (7), T. Martinez (9); Carlton, Holland (7). W—Palmer. L—Carlton. S—T. Martinez. HR—Matthews, Morgan (Phil.); Ford (Bal.).

Game 4—October 15, at Philadelphia
Baltimore ..0 0 0 2 0 2 1 0 0—5 10 1
Phil. ....0 0 0 1 2 0 0 0 1—4 10 0
Davis, Stewart (6), T. Martinez (8); Denny, Hernandez (6), Reed (6), Andersen (8). W—Davis. L—Denny. S—T. Martinez.

Game 5—October 16, at Philadelphia
Baltimore ....0 1 1 2 1 0 0 0 0—5 5 0
Phil. ....0 0 0 0 0 0 0 0 0—0 5 1
McGregor; Hudson, Bystrom (5), Hernandez (6), Reed (9). W—McGregor. L—Hudson. HR—Murray 2, Dempsey (Bal.).

1984

FINAL STANDINGS

American League

East Division

Team	Det.	Tor.	N.Y.	Bos.	Bal.	Cle.	Mil.	Cal.	Chi.	K.C.	Min.	Oak.	Sea.	Tex.	W	L	Pct.	GB
Detroit	...	8	7	6	6	9	11	8	8	7	9	9	6	10	104	58	.642	...
Toronto	5	...	5	8	9	7	3	5	8	7	11	8	7	6	89	73	.549	15
New York	6	8	...	6	8	11	7	4	5	7	4	8	7	6	87	75	.537	17
Boston	7	5	7	...	7	10	9	9	7	3	6	7	4	5	86	76	.531	18
Baltimore	7	4	5	6	...	7	7	8	7	5	5	6	9	9	85	77	.525	19
Cleveland	4	6	2	3	6	...	9	4	4	6	7	7	8	9	75	87	.463	29
Milwaukee	2	10	6	4	6	4	...	4	5	6	5	4	6	5	67	94	.416	36.5

West Division

Team	K.C.	Cal.	Min.	Oak.	Chi.	Sea.	Tex.	Bal.	Bos.	Cle.	Det.	Mil.	N.Y.	Tor.	W	L	Pct.	GB
Kansas City	...	7	6	5	8	9	6	7	9	6	5	6	5	5	84	78	.519	...
California	6	...	4	7	8	9	5	4	3	8	4	8	8	7	81	81	.500	3
Minnesota	7	9	...	8	5	7	8	7	6	5	3	7	8	1	81	81	.500	3
Oakland	8	6	5	...	7	8	8	6	5	5	3	8	4	4	77	85	.475	7
Chicago	5	5	8	6	...	5	5	5	5	8	4	7	7	4	74	88	.457	10
Seattle	4	4	6	5	8	...	10	3	8	4	6	6	5	5	74	88	.457	10
Texas	7	8	5	5	8	3	...	3	7	3	2	6	6	6	69	92	.429	14.5

National League

East Division

Team	Chi.	N.Y.	St.L.	Phi.	Mon.	Pit.	Atl.	Cin.	Hou.	L.A.	S.D.	S.F.	W	L	Pct.	GB
Chicago	...	12	13	9	10	8	9	7	6	7	6	9	96	65	.596	...
New York	6	...	7	10	11	12	8	9	8	9	6	4	90	72	.556	6.5
St. Louis	5	11	...	10	9	14	7	8	4	6	5	5	84	78	.519	12.5
Philadelphia	9	8	8	...	7	7	5	7	6	9	7	8	81	81	.500	15.5
Montreal	7	7	9	11	...	7	7	5	5	6	7	7	78	83	.484	18
Pittsburgh	10	6	4	11	11	...	4	5	6	8	4	6	75	87	.463	21.5

West Division

Team	S.D.	Atl.	Hou.	L.A.	Cin.	S.F.	Chi.	Mon.	N.Y.	Phi.	Pit.	St.L.	W	L	Pct.	GB
San Diego	...	11	12	8	11	13	6	5	6	5	8	7	92	70	.568	...
Atlanta	7	...	12	6	13	10	3	5	4	7	8	5	80	82	.494	12
Houston	6	6	...	9	10	12	6	7	4	6	6	8	80	82	.494	12
L.A.	10	12	9	...	11	10	5	6	3	3	4	6	79	83	.488	13
Cincinnati	7	5	8	7	...	12	5	7	3	5	7	4	70	92	.432	22
San Fran.	5	8	6	8	6	...	3	5	8	4	6	7	66	96	.407	26

SIGNIFICANT EVENTS

■ **March 3:** Baseball's owners selected businessman Peter V. Ueberroth as the sixth commissioner, succeeding Bowie Kuhn.

■ **August 16:** Pete Rose, who joined the select 4,000-hit circle early in the season as a member of the Expos, returned to his hometown Cincinnati as the Reds' player-manager.

■ **September 20, 24:** The Padres clinched their first-ever division title and the Cubs clinched their first post-season appearance since 1945.

■ **October 7:** Major League umpires, agreeing to let Commissioner Ueberroth arbitrate their dispute over post-season pay, ended a one-week strike and returned for the final game of the NLCS.

■ **November 6:** Detroit reliever Willie Hernandez capped his big season with an A.L. Cy Young-MVP sweep.

MEMORABLE MOMENTS

■ **September 17:** Kansas City posted a 10-1 victory, but the night belonged to Angels slugger Reggie Jackson, who belted his 500th homer off lefty Bud Black.

■ **September 28:** Cardinals reliever Bruce Sutter notched his 45th save in a 4-1 victory over the Cubs, matching the 1-year-old record of Kansas City's Dan Quisenberry.

■ **September 30:** California's Mike Witt brought a dramatic end to the regular season when he fired baseball's 11th perfect game, beating Texas, 1-0.

LEADERS

American League
BA: Don Mattingly, N.Y., .343.
Runs: Dwight Evans, Bos., 121.
Hits: Don Mattingly, N.Y., 207.
TB: Tony Armas, Bos., 339.
HR: Tony Armas, Bos., 43.
RBI: Tony Armas, Bos., 123.
SB: Rickey Henderson, Oak., 66.
Wins: Mike Boddicker, Bal., 20.
ERA: Mike Boddicker, Bal., 2.79.
CG: Charlie Hough, Tex., 17.
IP: Dave Stieb, Tor., 267.
SO: Mark Langston, Sea., 204.
SV: Dan Quisenberry, K.C., 44.

National League
BA: Tony Gwynn, S.D., .351.
Runs: Ryne Sandberg, Chi., 114.
Hits: Tony Gwynn, S.D., 213.
TB: Dale Murphy, Atl., 332.
HR: Dale Murphy, Atl.; Mike Schmidt, Phil., 36.
RBI: Gary Carter, Mon.; Mike Schmidt, Phil., 106.
SB: Tim Raines, Mon., 75.
Wins: Joaquin Andujar, St.L., 20.
ERA: Alejandro Pena, L.A., 2.48.
CG: Mario Soto, Cin., 13.
IP: Joaquin Andujar, St.L., 261.1.
SO: Dwight Gooden, N.Y., 276.
SV: Bruce Sutter, St.L., 45.

A.L. 20-game winner
Mike Boddicker, Bal., 20-11

N.L. 20-game winner
Joaquin Andujar, St.L., 20-14

A.L. 100 RBIs
Tony Armas, Bos., 123
Jim Rice, Bos., 122
Dave Kingman, Oak., 118
Alvin Davis, Sea., 116
Don Mattingly, N.Y., 110
Eddie Murray, Bal., 110
Kent Hrbek, Min., 107
Dwight Evans, Bos., 104
Larry Parrish, Tex., 101
Dave Winfield, N.Y., 100

N.L. 100 RBIs
Gary Carter, Mon., 106
Mike Schmidt, Phil., 106
Dale Murphy, Atl., 100

A.L. 40 homers
Tony Armas, Bos., 43

Most Valuable Player
A.L.: Willie Hernandez, P, Det.
N.L.: Ryne Sandberg, 2B, Chi.

Cy Young Award
A.L.: Willie Hernandez, Det.
N.L.: Rick Sutcliffe, Chi.

Rookie of the Year
A.L.: Alvin Davis, 1B, Sea.
N.L.: Dwight Gooden, P, N.Y.

Manager of the Year
A.L.: Sparky Anderson, Det.
N.L.: Jim Frey, Chi.

Hall of Fame additions
Luis Aparicio, SS, 1956-73
Don Drysdale, P, 1956-69
Rick Ferrell, C, 1929-47
Harmon Killebrew, 1B/3B, 1954-75
Pee Wee Reese, SS, 1940-58

ALL-STAR GAME

■ **Winner:** After a one-year lull, it was business as usual for the N.L., which used home runs by Gary Carter and Dale Murphy to post a 3-1 All-Star victory.

■ **Key inning:** The second, when Carter belted a solo shot to give the N.L. a 2-1 lead after the A.L. had tied in the top of the inning on George Brett's home run.

■ **Memorable moment:** A fourth and fifth-inning strikeout flurry by the N.L.'s Fernando Valenzuela and Dwight Gooden. Consecutive victims Dave Winfield, Reggie Jackson, Brett, Lance Parrish, Chet Lemon and Alvin Davis broke the 50-year-old record of five straight.

■ **Top guns:** Valenzuela (Dodgers), Gooden (Mets), Carter (Expos), Murphy (Braves), N.L.; Brett (Royals), Lou Whitaker (Tigers), A.L.

■ **MVP:** Carter.

Linescore

July 10, at San Francisco's Candlestick Park

A.L. ....0 1 0 0 0 0 0 0 0—1 7 2
N.L. ....1 1 0 0 0 0 0 1 x—3 8 0

Stieb (Blue Jays), Morris (Tigers) 3, Dotson (White Sox) 5, Caudill (Athletics) 7, W. Hernandez (Tigers) 8; Lea (Expos), Valenzuela (Dodgers) 3, Gooden (Mets) 5, Soto (Reds) 7, Gossage (Padres) 9. W—Lea. L—Steib. S—Gossage. HR—Brett, A.L.; Carter, Murphy, N.L.

ALCS

■ **Winner:** The Detroit Tigers capped their 104-victory regular season with a sweep of Kansas City and claimed their first pennant since 1968.

■ **Turning point:** The 11th inning of Game 2, when Johnny Grubb's one-out double off Royals relief ace Dan Quisenberry drove in two runs and gave the Tigers a 5-3 victory and a two-games-to-none series edge.

■ **Memorable moment:** The Game 3 pitching performance of Tigers veteran Milt Wilcox, who allowed only two hits in eight innings of a series-clinching 1-0 victory.

■ **Top guns:** Wilcox (1-0, 0.00 ERA), Jack Morris (1-0, 1.29), Kirk Gibson (.417), Alan Trammell (.364), Tigers; Don Slaught (.364), Royals.

■ **MVP:** Gibson.

Linescores

Game 1—October 2, at Kansas City

Det. ....2 0 0 1 1 0 1 2 1—8 14 0
K.C. ....0 0 0 0 0 0 1 0 0—1 5 1

Morris, Hernandez (8); Black, Huismann (6), M. Jones (8). W—Morris. L—Black. HR—Herndon, Trammell, Parrish (Det.).

Game 2—October 3, at Kansas City

Det...2 0 1 0 0 0 0 0 0 0 2—5 8 1
K.C...0 0 0 1 0 0 1 1 0 0 0—3 10 3

Petry, Hernandez (8), Lopez (9); Saberhagen, Quisenberry (9). W—Lopez. L—Quisenberry. HR—Gibson (Det.).

Game 3—October 5, at Detroit

K.C. ....0 0 0 0 0 0 0 0 0—0 3 3
Det. ....0 1 0 0 0 0 0 0 x—1 3 0

Leibrandt; Wilcox, Hernandez (9). W—Wilcox. L—Leibrandt. S—Hernandez.

NLCS

■ **Winner:** The San Diego Padres became the first N.L. team to recover from a two-game deficit and captured their first-ever pennant, denying the Cubs their first World Series appearance since 1945.

■ **Turning point:** The seventh inning of Game 5. The key blows in San Diego's four-run series-deciding rally were an error by Cubs first baseman Leon Durham and a bad-hop double by Tony Gwynn that drove in two runs and broke a 3-3 tie.

■ **Memorable moment:** Steve Garvey's two-run ninth-inning home run that gave the Padres an elimination-saving 7-5 victory in Game 4.

■ **Top guns:** Craig Lefferts (2-0, 0.00 ERA), Garvey (.400, 7 RBIs), Gwynn (.368), Padres; Jody Davis (.389, 2 HR, 6 RBIs), Gary Matthews (2 HR, 5 RBIs), Cubs.

■ **MVP:** Garvey.

Linescores

Game 1—October 2, at Chicago

S.D...........0 0 0 0 0 0 0 0 0— 0 6 1
Chicago....2 0 3 0 6 2 0 0 x—13 16 0

Show, Harris (5), Booker (7); Sutcliffe, Brusstar (8). W—Sutcliffe. L—Show. HR—Dernier, Matthews 2, Sutcliffe, Cey (Chi.).

Game 2—October 3, at Chicago

S.D..............0 0 0 1 0 1 0 0 0—2 5 0
Chicago........1 0 2 1 0 0 0 0 x—4 8 1

Thurmond, Hawkins (4), Dravecky (6), Lefferts (8); Trout, Smith (9). W—Trout. L—Thurmond. S—Smith.

Game 3—October 4, at San Diego

Chicago......0 1 0 0 0 0 0 0 0—1 5 0
S.D............0 0 0 0 3 4 0 0 x—7 11 0

Eckersley, Frazier (6), Stoddard (8); Whitson, Gossage (9). W—Whitson. L—Eckersley. HR—McReynolds (S.D.).

Game 4—October 6, at San Diego

Chicago......0 0 0 3 0 0 0 2 0—5 8 1
S.D............0 0 2 0 1 0 2 0 2—7 11 0

Sanderson, Brusstar (5), Stoddard (7), Smith (8); Lollar, Hawkins (5), Dravecky (6), Gossage (8), Lefferts (9). W—Lefferts. L—Smith. HR—Davis, Durham (Chi.); Garvey (S.D.).

Game 5—October 7, at San Diego

Chicago ....2 1 0 0 0 0 0 0 0—3 5 1
S.D..............0 0 0 0 0 2 4 0 x—6 8 0

Sutcliffe, Trout (7), Brusstar (8); Show, Hawkins (2), Dravecky (4), Lefferts (6), Gossage (8). W—Lefferts. L—Sutcliffe. S—Gossage. HR—Durham, Davis (Chi.).

WORLD SERIES

■ **Winner:** The Tigers made short work of first-time Series qualifier San Diego and Sparky Anderson became the first man to manage champions in both leagues.

■ **Turning point:** Jack Morris pitched a five-hitter and Alan Trammell drove in all of Detroit's runs with two homers in a 4-2 Game 4 victory.

■ **Memorable moment:** The ever-intense Kirk Gibson stomping on home plate after an eighth-inning upper-deck home run in the Series finale — his second of the game. Gibson also drove in five runs and scored three times in the Tigers' 8-4 victory.

■ **Top guns:** Morris (2-0, 2.00 ERA), Trammell (.450, 2 HR, 6 RBIs), Gibson (.333, 2 HR, 7 RBIs), Tigers; Kurt Bevacqua (.412), Alan Wiggins (.364), Padres.

■ **MVP:** Trammell.

Linescores

Game 1—October 9, at San Diego

Detroit..........1 0 0 0 2 0 0 0 0—3 8 0
San Diego ....2 0 0 0 0 0 0 0 0—2 8 1

Morris; Thurmond, Hawkins (6), Dravecky (8). W—Morris. L—Thurmond. HR—Herndon (Det.).

Game 2—October 10, at San Diego

Detroit........3 0 0 0 0 0 0 0 0—3 7 3
San Diego ..1 0 0 1 3 0 0 0 x—5 11 0

Petry, Lopez (5), Scherrer (6), Bair (7), Hernandez (8); Whitson, Hawkins (1), Lefferts (7). W—Hawkins. L—Petry. S—Lefferts. HR—Bevacqua (S.D.).

Game 3—October 12, at Detroit

San Diego ..0 0 1 0 0 0 1 0 0—2 10 0
Detroit........0 4 1 0 0 0 0 0 x—5 7 0

Lollar, Booker (2), Harris (3); Wilcox, Scherrer (7), Hernandez (7). W—Wilcox. L—Lollar. S—Hernandez. HR—Castillo (Det.).

Game 4—October 13, at Detroit

San Diego ....0 1 0 0 0 0 0 0 1—2 5 2
Detroit..........2 0 2 0 0 0 0 0 x—4 7 0

Show, Dravecky (3), Lefferts (7), Gossage (8); Morris. W—Morris. L—Show. HR—Trammell 2 (Det.); Kennedy (S.D.).

Game 5—October 14, at Detroit

San Diego ..0 0 1 2 0 0 0 1 0—4 10 1
Detroit........3 0 0 0 1 0 1 3 x—8 11 1

Thurmond, Hawkins (1), Lefferts (5), Gossage (7); Petry, Scherrer (4), Lopez (5), Hernandez (8). W—Lopez. L—Hawkins. S—Hernandez. HR—Gibson 2, Parrish (Det.); Bevacqua (S.D.).

HISTORY

FINAL STANDINGS

American League

East Division

Team	Tor.	N.Y.	Det.	Bal.	Bos.	Mil.	Cle.	K.C.	Cal.	Chi.	Min.	Oak.	Sea.	Tex.	W	L	Pct.	GB
Toronto	...	7	7	8	4	9	9	5	7	9	8	7	10	9	99	62	.615	...
New York	6	...	3	12	8	6	7	7	9	6	9	7	9	8	97	64	.602	2
Detroit	6	9	...	7	7	9	8	5	4	6	3	8	5	7	84	77	.522	15
Baltimore	4	1	6	...	5	9	8	6	7	8	6	7	6	10	83	78	.516	16
Boston	9	5	6	8	...	5	8	5	5	4	7	8	6	5	81	81	.500	18.5
Milwaukee	4	7	4	4	8	...	6	4	3	7	9	3	4	8	71	90	.441	28
Cleveland	4	6	5	5	5	7	...	2	4	2	4	3	6	7	60	102	.370	39.5

West Division

Team	K.C.	Cal.	Chi.	Min.	Oak.	Sea.	Tex.	Tor.	N.Y.	Det.	Bal.	Bos.	Mil.	Cle.	W	L	Pct.	GB
Kansas City	...	9	8	7	8	3	6	7	5	7	6	7	8	10	91	71	.562	...
California	4	...	8	9	6	9	9	5	3	8	5	7	9	8	90	72	.556	1
Chicago	5	5	...	6	8	9	10	3	6	6	4	8	5	10	85	77	.525	6
Minnesota	6	4	7	...	8	6	8	4	3	9	6	5	3	8	77	85	.475	14
Oakland	5	7	5	5	...	8	6	5	5	4	5	4	9	9	77	85	.475	14
Seattle	10	4	4	7	5	...	6	2	3	7	6	6	8	6	74	88	.457	17
Texas	7	4	3	5	7	7	...	3	4	5	2	7	3	5	62	99	.385	28.5

National League

East Division

Team	St.L.	N.Y.	Mon.	Chi.	Phi.	Pit.	L.A.	Cin.	Hou.	S.D.	Atl.	S.F.	W	L	Pct.	GB
St. Louis	...	10	7	14	10	15	5	7	6	8	9	10	101	61	.623	...
New York	8	...	9	14	11	10	5	8	8	7	10	8	98	64	.605	3
Montreal	11	9	...	11	8	9	5	4	6	5	9	7	84	77	.522	16.5
Chicago	4	4	7	...	13	13	5	5	5	8	7	6	77	84	.478	23.5
Philadelphia	8	7	10	5	...	11	8	5	8	5	2	6	75	87	.463	26
Pittsburgh	3	8	8	5	7	...	4	3	6	4	6	3	57	104	.354	43.5

West Division

Team	L.A.	Cin.	Hou.	S.D.	Atl.	S.F.	St.L.	N.Y.	Mon.	Chi.	Phi.	Pit.	W	L	Pct.	GB
Los Angeles	...	11	12	8	13	11	7	7	7	7	4	8	95	67	.586	...
Cincinnati	7	...	11	9	11	12	5	4	8	6	7	9	89	72	.553	5.5
Houston	6	7	...	12	10	15	6	4	6	7	4	6	83	79	.512	12
San Diego	10	9	6	...	11	12	4	5	7	4	7	8	83	79	.512	12
Atlanta	5	7	8	7	...	10	3	2	3	5	10	6	66	96	.407	29
San Fran.	7	6	3	6	8	...	2	4	5	6	6	9	62	100	.383	33

LEADERS

American League
BA: Wade Boggs, Bos., .368.
Runs: Rickey Henderson, N.Y., 146.
Hits: Wade Boggs, Bos., 240.
TB: Don Mattingly, N.Y., 370.
HR: Darrell Evans, Det., 40.
RBI: Don Mattingly, N.Y., 145.
SB: Rickey Henderson, N.Y., 80.
Wins: Ron Guidry, N.Y., 22.
ERA: Dave Stieb, Tor., 2.48.
CG: Bert Blyleven, Cle.-Min., 24.
IP: Bert Blyleven, Cle.-Min., 293.2.
SO: Bert Blyleven, Cle.-Min., 206.
SV: Dan Quisenberry, K.C., 37.

National League
BA: Willie McGee, St.L., .353.
Runs: Dale Murphy, Atl., 118.
Hits: Willie McGee, St.L., 216.
TB: Dave Parker, Cin., 350.
HR: Dale Murphy, Atl., 37.
RBI: Dave Parker, Cin., 125.
SB: Vince Coleman, St.L., 110.
Wins: Dwight Gooden, N.Y., 24.
ERA: Dwight Gooden, N.Y., 1.53.
CG: Dwight Gooden, N.Y., 16.
IP: Dwight Gooden, N.Y., 276.2.
SO: Dwight Gooden, N.Y., 268.
SV: Jeff Reardon, Mon., 41.

A.L. 20-game winners
Ron Guidry, N.Y., 22-6
Bret Saberhagen, K.C., 20-6

N.L. 20-game winners
Dwight Gooden, N.Y., 24-4
John Tudor, St.L., 21-8
Joaquin Andujar, St.L., 21-12
Tom Browning, Cin., 20-9

A.L. 100 RBIs
Don Mattingly, N.Y., 145
Eddie Murray, Bal., 124
Dave Winfield, N.Y., 114
Harold Baines, Chi., 113
George Brett, K.C., 112
Bill Buckner, Bos., 110
Cal Ripken, Bal., 110
Carlton Fisk, Chi., 107
Jim Rice, Bos., 103

N.L. 100 RBIs
Dave Parker, Cin., 125
Dale Murphy, Atl., 111
Tommy Herr, St.L., 110
Keith Moreland, Chi., 106
Glenn Wilson, Phil., 102
Hubie Brooks, Mon., 100
Gary Carter, N.Y., 100

A.L. 40 homers
Darrell Evans, Det., 40

Most Valuable Player
A.L.: Don Mattingly, 1B, N.Y.
N.L.: Willie McGee, OF, St.L.

Cy Young Award
A.L.: Bret Saberhagen, K.C.
N.L.: Dwight Gooden, N.Y.

Rookie of the Year
A.L.: Ozzie Guillen, SS, Chi.
N.L.: Vince Coleman, OF, St.L.

Manager of the Year
A.L.: Bobby Cox, Tor.
N.L.: Whitey Herzog, St.L.

Hall of Fame additions
Lou Brock, OF, 1961-79
Enos Slaughter, OF, 1938-59
Arky Vaughan, IF, 1932-48
Hoyt Wilhelm, P, 1952-72

SIGNIFICANT EVENTS

■ **April 25:** Denny McLain, a 31-game winner in 1968, was sentenced to 23 years in prison after his conviction on racketeering, extortion and cocaine-possession charges in Tampa, Fla.
■ **March 18:** The baseball bans against former greats Mickey Mantle and Willie Mays were lifted by Commissioner Peter V. Ueberroth.
■ **April 3:** The owners and players agreed to expand the League Championship Series from a best-of-five to best-of-seven format.
■ **August 7:** Major League players ended their two-day, 25-game strike when owners dropped their demand for an arbitration salary cap.

MEMORABLE MOMENTS

■ **July 11:** Houston's Nolan Ryan became the first pitcher to record 4,000 career strikeouts when he fanned Danny Heep in a 4-3 victory over the Mets.
■ **August 4:** Chicago's Tom Seaver earned career win No. 300 against the Yankees and California's Rod Carew got hit No. 3,000 against the Twins in games played a continent apart on the same day.
■ **September 11:** Reds player-manager Pete Rose overtook all-time hit leader Ty Cobb when he singled off San Diego's Eric Show for career hit No. 4,192.
■ **October 6:** Yankee knuckleballer Phil Niekro fired a final-day 8-0 shutout at the Blue Jays and joined baseball's 300-win club.

ALL-STAR GAME

■ **Winner:** The N.L. made it 21 of 23 and two in a row as five pitchers shut down the A.L. on five hits.
■ **Key inning:** The third, when the N.L. took the lead on a double by Tommy Herr and Steve Garvey's single.
■ **Memorable moment:** The performance of the N.L. pitchers, who did not even allow an extra-base hit.
■ **Top guns:** LaMarr Hoyt (Padres), Nolan Ryan (Astros), Garvey (Dodgers), Willie McGee (Cardinals), Ozzie Virgil (Phillies), N.L.; Rickey Henderson (Yankees), A.L.
■ **MVP:** Hoyt.

Linescore
July 16, at Minnesota's Metrodome
N.L. ....0 1 1 0 2 0 0 0 2—6 9 1
A.L. ....1 0 0 0 0 0 0 0 0—1 5 0
Hoyt (Padres), Ryan (Astros) 4, Valenzuela (Dodgers) 7, Reardon (Expos) 8, Gossage (Padres) 9; Morris (Tigers), Key (Blue Jays) 3, Blyleven (Indians) 4, Stieb (Blue Jays) 6, Moore (Angels) 7, Petry (Tigers) 9, Hernandez (Tigers) 9. W—Hoyt. L—Morris.

ALCS

■ **Winner:** The Kansas City Royals, taking advantage of baseball's expanded seven-game playoff format, rallied from a three-games-to-one deficit to deny Toronto's bid for a first Canadian pennant.
■ **Turning point:** One day after the Blue Jays had rallied for three ninth-inning runs and a 3-1 series edge, Danny Jackson steadied the Royals with an eight-hit, 2-0 shutout at Royals Stadium.
■ **Memorable moment:** A bases-loaded, opposite-field Jim Sundberg blast that bounded high off the wall and resulted in a three-run, sixth-inning triple — the big blow in Kansas City's seventh-game 6-2 victory.
■ **Top guns:** Jackson (1-0, 0.00 ERA), George Brett (.348, 3 HR, 5 RBIs), Willie Wilson (.310), Royals; Al Oliver (.375), Cliff Johnson (.368), Blue Jays.
■ **MVP:** Brett.

Linescores

Game 1—October 8, at Toronto
K.C. ....0 0 0 0 0 0 0 0 1—1 5 1
Tor. ....0 2 3 1 0 0 0 0 x—6 11 0
Leibrandt, Farr (3), Gubicza (5), Jackson (8); Stieb, Henke (9). W—Stieb. L—Leibrandt.

Game 2—October 9, at Toronto
K.C. ....0 0 2 1 0 0 0 0 1 1—5 10 3
Tor. ....0 0 0 1 0 2 0 1 0 2—6 10 0
Black, Quisenberry (8); Key, Lamp (4), Lavelle (8), Henke (8). W—Henke. L—Quisenberry. HR—Wilson, Sheridan (K.C.).

Game 3—October 11, at Kansas City
Tor. ....0 0 0 0 5 0 0 0 0—5 13 1
K.C. ....1 0 0 1 1 2 0 1 x—6 10 1
Alexander, Lamp (6), Clancy (8); Saberhagen, Black (5), Farr (5). W—Farr. L—Clancy. HR—Brett 2, Sundberg (K.C.); Barfield, Mulliniks (Tor.)

Game 4—October 12, at Kansas City
Tor. ....0 0 0 0 0 0 0 0 3—3 7 0
K.C. ....0 0 0 0 0 1 0 0 0—1 2 0
Stieb, Henke (7); Leibrandt, Quisenberry (9). W—Henke. L—Leibrandt.

Game 5—October 13, at Kansas City
Tor. ....0 0 0 0 0 0 0 0 0—0 8 0
K.C. ....1 1 0 0 0 0 0 0 x—2 8 0
Key, Acker (6); Jackson. W—Jackson. L—Key.

Game 6—October 15, at Toronto
K.C. ....1 0 1 0 1 2 0 0 0—5 8 1
Tor. ....1 0 1 0 0 1 0 0 0—3 8 2
Gubicza, Black (6), Quisenberry (9); Alexander, Lamp (6). W—Gubicza. L—Alexander. S—Quisenberry. HR—Brett (K.C.).

Game 7—October 16, at Toronto
K.C. ....0 1 0 1 0 4 0 0 0—6 8 0
Tor. ....0 0 0 0 1 0 0 0 1—2 8 1
Saberhagen, Leibrandt (4), Quisenberry (9); Stieb, Acker (6). W—Leibrandt. L—Stieb. HR—Sheridan (K.C.).

NLCS

■ **Winner:** The speed-and-pitching oriented St. Louis Cardinals used a new weapon — the dramatic home run — to post a six-game NLCS victory over Los Angeles.
■ **Turning point:** The ninth inning of Game 5 when light-hitting Ozzie Smith, who had hit only 14 career home runs, stunned the Dodgers with a shot down the right-field line against Tom Niedenfuer that produced a 3-2 Cardinals victory and a 3-2 series edge.
■ **Memorable moment:** A three-run, series-clinching home run by Cardinals first baseman Jack Clark in the ninth inning of Game 6. The shot off Niedenfuer gave St. Louis a 7-5 victory — its fourth straight after the Dodgers had won Games 1 and 2.
■ **Top guns:** Ken Dayley (6 IP, 2 saves, 0.00 ERA), Smith (.435), Clark (.381), Cardinals; Fernando Valenzuela (1-0, 1.88), Bill Madlock (.333, 3 HR, 7 RBIs), Dodgers.
■ **MVP:** Smith.

Linescores

Game 1—October 9, at Los Angeles
St. Louis ......0 0 0 0 0 0 1 0 0—1 8 1
L.A. ....0 0 0 1 0 3 0 0 x—4 8 0
Tudor, Dayley (6), Campbell (7), Worrell (8); Valenzuela, Niedenfuer (7). W—Valenzuela. L—Tudor. S—Niedenfuer.

Game 2—October 10, at Los Angeles
St. Louis ....0 0 1 0 0 0 0 0 1—2 8 1
L.A. ....0 0 3 2 1 2 0 0 x—8 13 1
Andujar, Horton (5), Campbell (6), Dayley (7), Lahti (8); Hershiser. W—Hershiser. L—Andujar. HR—Brock (L.A.).

Game 3—October 12, at St. Louis
L.A. ....0 0 0 1 0 0 1 0 0—2 7 2
St. Louis ......2 2 0 0 0 0 0 0 x—4 8 0
Welch, Honeycutt (3), Diaz (5), Howell (7); Cox, Horton (7), Worrell (7), Dayley (9). W—Cox. L—Welch. S—Dayley. HR—Herr (St.L.).

Game 4—October 13, at St. Louis
L.A. ....0 0 0 0 0 0 1 1 0— 2 5 2
St. Louis ..0 9 0 1 1 0 0 1 x—12 15 0
Reuss, Honeycutt (2), Castillo (2), Diaz (8); Tudor, Horton (8), Campbell (9). W—Tudor. L—Reuss. HR—Madlock (L.A.).

Game 5—October 14, at St. Louis
L.A. ....0 0 0 2 0 0 0 0 0—2 5 1
St. Louis ......2 0 0 0 0 0 0 0 1—3 5 1
Valenzuela, Niedenfuer (9); Forsch, Dayley (4), Worrell (7), Lahti (9). W—Lahti. L—Niedenfuer. HR—Madlock (L.A.); Smith (St.L.).

Game 6—October 16, at Los Angeles
St. Louis ....0 0 1 0 0 0 3 0 3—7 12 1
L.A. ....1 1 0 0 2 0 0 1 0—5 8 0
Andujar, Worrell (7), Dayley (9); Hershiser, Niedenfuer (7). W—Worrell. L—Niedenfuer. S—Dayley. HR—Madlock, Marshall (L.A.); Clark (St.L.).

WORLD SERIES

■ **Winner:** The Royals needed three consecutive victories and a controversial sixth-game decision to claim their first Series triumph in an all-Missouri fall classic.
■ **Turning point:** A blown call at first base by umpire Don Denkinger in the Royals' ninth inning of Game 6. After arguing vehemently, the Cardinals unraveled and the Royals scored twice, claiming a 2-1 victory and forcing a seventh game.
■ **Memorable moment:** Royals catcher Jim Sundberg sliding around the tag of Cardinals catcher Darrell Porter with the winning run in Game 6. Sundberg and Onix Concepcion scored on Dane Iorg's one-out single.
■ **Top guns:** Bret Saberhagen (2-0, 0.50 ERA), George Brett (.370), Willie Wilson (.367), Royals; Tito Landrum (.360), Cardinals.
■ **MVP:** Saberhagen.

Linescores

Game 1—October 19, at Kansas City
St. Louis ......0 0 1 1 0 0 0 0 1—3 7 1
K.C. ....0 1 0 0 0 0 0 0 0—1 8 0
Tudor, Worrell (7); Jackson, Quisenberry (8), Black (9). W—Tudor. L—Jackson. S—Worrell.

Game 2—October 20, at Kansas City
St. Louis ......0 0 0 0 0 0 0 0 4—4 6 0
K.C. ....0 0 0 2 0 0 0 0 0—2 9 0
Cox, Dayley (8), Lahti (9); Leibrandt, Quisenberry (9). W—Dayley. L—Leibrandt. S—Lahti.

Game 3—October 22, at St. Louis
K.C. ....0 0 0 2 2 0 2 0 0—6 11 0
St. Louis ....0 0 0 0 0 1 0 0 0—1 6 0
Saberhagen; Andujar, Campbell (5), Horton (6), Dayley (8). W—Saberhagen. L—Andujar. HR—White (K.C.).

Game 4—October 23, at St. Louis
K.C. ....0 0 0 0 0 0 0 0 0—0 5 1
St. Louis ......0 1 1 0 1 0 0 0 x—3 6 0
Black, Beckwith (6), Quisenberry (8); Tudor. W—Tudor. L—Black. HR—Landrum, McGee (St.L.).

Game 5—October 24, at St. Louis
K.C. ....1 3 0 0 0 0 0 1 1—6 11 2
St. Louis ......1 0 0 0 0 0 0 0 0—1 5 1
Jackson; Forsch, Horton (2), Campbell (4), Worrell (6), Lahti (8). W—Jackson. L—Forsch.

Game 6—October 26, at Kansas City
St. Louis ....0 0 0 0 0 0 0 1 0—1 5 0
K.C. ....0 0 0 0 0 0 0 0 2—2 10 0
Cox, Dayley (8), Worrell (9); Leibrandt, Quisenberry (8). W—Quisenberry. L—Worrell.

Game 7—October 27, at Kansas City
St. Louis ..0 0 0 0 0 0 0 0 0— 0 5 0
K.C. ....0 2 3 0 6 0 0 0 x—11 14 0
Tudor, Campbell (3), Lahti (5), Horton (5), Andujar (5), Forsch (5), Dayley (7); Saberhagen. W—Saberhagen. L—Tudor. HR—Motley (K.C.).

FINAL STANDINGS

American League

East Division

Team	Bos.	N.Y.	Det.	Tor.	Cle.	Mil.	Bal.	Cal.	Tex.	K.C.	Oak.	Chi.	Min.	Sea.	W	L	Pct.	GB
Boston	...	5	7	7	10	6	9	5	8	6	7	7	10	8	95	66	.590	...
New York	8	...	7	7	8	5	8	5	7	8	5	6	8	8	90	72	.556	5.5
Detroit	6	6	...	4	9	8	12	5	7	5	6	6	7	6	87	75	.537	8.5
Toronto	6	6	9	...	10	6	5	6	7	7	4	6	8	6	86	76	.531	9.5
Cleveland	3	5	4	3	...	8	9	6	6	8	10	7	6	9	84	78	.519	11.5
Milwaukee	6	8	5	7	5	...	7	7	4	6	5	7	4	6	77	84	.478	18
Baltimore	4	5	1	8	4	6	...	6	5	6	5	9	8	6	73	89	.451	22.5

West Division

Team	Cal.	Tex.	K.C.	Oak.	Chi.	Min.	Sea.	Bos.	N.Y.	Det.	Tor.	Cle.	Mil.	Bal.	W	L	Pct.	GB
California	...	8	8	10	7	7	8	7	7	7	6	6	5	6	92	70	.568	...
Texas	5	...	5	10	11	7	9	4	5	5	5	6	8	7	87	75	.537	5
Kansas City	5	8	...	8	6	6	5	6	4	7	5	4	6	6	76	86	.469	16
Oakland	3	3	5	...	6	7	10	5	7	6	8	2	7	7	76	86	.469	16
Chicago	6	2	7	7	...	6	8	5	6	6	6	5	5	3	72	90	.444	20
Minnesota	6	6	7	6	7	...	6	2	4	5	4	6	8	4	71	91	.438	21
Seattle	5	4	8	3	5	7	...	4	4	6	6	3	6	6	67	95	.414	25

National League

East Division

Team	N.Y.	Phi.	St.L.	Mon.	Chi.	Pit.	Hou.	Cin.	S.F.	S.D.	L.A.	Atl.	W	L	Pct.	GB
New York	...	8	12	10	12	17	7	8	7	10	9	8	108	54	.667	...
Phil.	10	...	6	10	8	11	6	5	9	6	7	8	86	75	.534	21.5
St. Louis	6	12	...	9	7	11	5	5	7	7	4	6	79	82	.491	28.5
Montreal	8	8	9	...	10	11	4	5	5	4	7	7	78	83	.484	29.5
Chicago	6	9	10	8	...	7	4	5	6	6	6	3	70	90	.438	37
Pittsburgh	1	7	7	7	11	...	6	2	4	8	4	7	64	98	.395	44

West Division

Team	Hou.	Cin.	S.F.	S.D.	L.A.	Atl.	N.Y.	Phi.	St.L.	Mon.	Chi.	Pit.	W	L	Pct.	GB
Houston	...	14	9	10	10	13	5	6	7	8	8	6	96	66	.593	...
Cincinnati	4	...	9	9	10	12	4	7	7	7	7	10	86	76	.531	10
San Fran.	9	9	...	10	10	11	5	3	5	7	6	8	83	79	.512	13
San Diego	8	9	8	...	12	6	2	6	5	8	6	4	74	88	.457	22
Los Angeles	8	8	8	6	...	8	3	5	8	5	6	8	73	89	.451	23
Atlanta	5	6	7	12	10	...	4	4	6	4	9	5	72	89	.447	23.5

LEADERS

American League
BA: Wade Boggs, Bos., .357.
Runs: Rickey Henderson, N.Y., 130.
Hits: Don Mattingly, N.Y., 238.
TB: Don Mattingly, N.Y., 388.
HR: Jesse Barfield, Tor., 40.
RBI: Joe Carter, Cle., 121.
SB: Rickey Henderson, N.Y., 87.
Wins: Roger Clemens, Bos., 24.
ERA: Roger Clemens, Bos., 2.48.
CG: Tom Candiotti, Cle., 17.
IP: Bert Blyleven, Min., 271.2.
SO: Mark Langston, Sea., 245.
SV: Dave Righetti, N.Y., 46.

National League
BA: Tim Raines, Mon., .334.
Runs: Tony Gwynn, S.D.; Von Hayes, Phil., 107.
Hits: Tony Gwynn, S.D., 211.
TB: Dave Parker, Cin., 304.
HR: Mike Schmidt, Phil., 37.
RBI: Mike Schmidt, Phil., 119.
SB: Vince Coleman, St.L., 107.
Wins: Fernando Valenzuela, L.A., 21.
ERA: Mike Scott, Hou., 2.22.
CG: Fernando Valenzuela, L.A., 20.
IP: Mike Scott, Hou., 275.1.
SO: Mike Scott, Hou., 306.
SV: Todd Worrell, St.L., 36.

A.L. 20-game winners
Roger Clemens, Bos., 24-4
Jack Morris, Det., 21-8
Ted Higuera, Mil., 20-11

N.L. 20-game winners
Fernando Valenzuela, L.A., 21-11
Mike Krukow, S.F., 20-9

A.L. 100 RBIs
Joe Carter, Cle., 121
Jose Canseco, Oak., 117
Don Mattingly, N.Y., 113
Jim Rice, Bos., 110
Jesse Barfield, Tor., 108
George Bell, Tor., 108
Gary Gaetti, Min., 108
Jim Presley, Sea., 107
Dave Winfield, N.Y., 104
Bill Buckner, Bos., 102
Wally Joyner, Cal., 100

N.L. 100 RBIs
Mike Schmidt, Phil., 119
Dave Parker, Cin., 116
Gary Carter, N.Y., 105
Glenn Davis, Hou., 101

A.L. 40 homers
Jesse Barfield, Tor., 40

Most Valuable Player
A.L.: Roger Clemens, P, Bos.
N.L.: Mike Schmidt, 3B, Phil.

Cy Young Award
A.L.: Roger Clemens, Bos.
N.L.: Mike Scott, Hou.

Rookie of the Year
A.L.: Jose Canseco, OF, Oak.
N.L.: Todd Worrell, P, St.L.

Manager of the Year
A.L.: John McNamara, Bos.
N.L.: Hal Lanier, Hou.

Hall of Fame additions
Bobby Doerr, 2B, 1937-51
Ernie Lombardi, C, 1931-47
Willie McCovey, 1B, 1959-80

SIGNIFICANT EVENTS

■ **February 28:** Commissioner Peter V. Ueberroth handed one-year suspensions to players Dave Parker, Keith Hernandez, Lonnie Smith, Dale Berra, Jeffrey Leonard, Enos Cabell and Joaquin Andujar for drug-related activities.
■ **June 20:** Bo Jackson, the 1985 Heisman Trophy winner from Auburn, stunningly signed with the Royals instead of the NFL's Tampa Bay Buccaneers.

MEMORABLE MOMENTS

■ **April 29:** Boston's Roger Clemens broke a long-standing Major League record when he struck out 20 Mariners in a 3-1 victory at Fenway Park.
■ **June 18:** California's Don Sutton became a 300-game winner when he defeated the Rangers, 5-1.
■ **July 6:** Bob Horner became the 11th Major Leaguer to hit four homers in a game, but his Braves still dropped an 11-8 decision to the Expos.
■ **August 5:** Giants lefty Steve Carlton joined Nolan Ryan in the exclusive 4,000-strikeout club, but dropped an 11-6 decision to the Reds.
■ **September 25:** Houston righthander Mike Scott pitched the first pennant-clinching no-hitter in baseball history, beating the Giants, 2-0.
■ **October 4:** Yankee closer Dave Righetti set a one-season record when he recorded his 45th and 46th saves in a doubleheader sweep of the Red Sox.

ALL-STAR GAME

■ **Winner:** The A.L., looking to break its one-win-per-decade streak, got home runs from second basemen Lou Whitaker and Frank White and scored a 3-2 victory — its second of the 1980s.
■ **Key inning:** The second, when Whitaker followed a Dave Winfield double with a two-run shot off Dwight Gooden.
■ **Memorable moment:** Fernando Valenzuela tied Carl Hubbell's 1934 All-Star record when he struck out, consecutively, Don Mattingly, Cal Ripken, Jesse Barfield, Whitaker and Ted Higuera.
■ **Top guns:** Roger Clemens (Red Sox), Higuera (Brewers), Whitaker (Tigers), White (Royals), A.L.; Valenzuela (Dodgers), Steve Sax (Dodgers), N.L.
■ **MVP:** Clemens.

Linescore
July 15, at Houston's Astrodome
A.L. ....0 2 0 0 0 0 1 0 0—3 5 0
N.L. ....0 0 0 0 0 0 0 2 0—2 5 1
Clemens (Red Sox), Higuera (Brewers) 4, Hough (Rangers) 7, Righetti (Yankees) 8, Aase (Orioles) 9; Gooden (Mets), Valenzuela (Dodgers) 4, Scott (Astros) 7, Fernandez (Mets) 8, Krukow (Giants) 9. W—Clemens. L—Gooden. HR—Whitaker, White, A.L.

ALCS

■ **Winner:** Boston, on the verge of elimination in the ninth inning of Game 5, roared back to post a seven-game triumph over the stunned California Angels.
■ **Turning point:** Dave Henderson, one strike away from becoming the final out in the Angels' pennant-clinching victory, stroked a Donnie Moore pitch into the left-field bleachers for a two-run homer. The blast gave the Red Sox a 6-5 lead and they went on to post a series-turning 7-6 victory in 11 innings.
■ **Memorable moment:** Henderson dancing triumphantly around the bases as a crowd of 64,223 watched in stunned silence at Anaheim Stadium.
■ **Top guns:** Spike Owen (.429), Marty Barrett (.367, 5 RBIs), Rich Gedman (.357, 6 RBIs), Jim Rice (2 HR, 6 RBIs), Red Sox; Bob Boone (.455), Wally Joyner (.455), Angels.
■ **MVP:** Barrett.

Linescores
Game 1—October 7, at Boston
Cal. ....0 4 1 0 0 0 0 3 0—8 11 0
Boston ......0 0 0 0 0 1 0 0 0—1 5 1
Witt; Clemens, Sambito (8), Stanley (8). W—Witt. L—Clemens.
Game 2—October 8, at Boston
Cal. ....0 0 0 1 1 0 0 0 0—2 11 3
Boston ......1 1 0 0 1 0 3 3 x—9 13 2
McCaskill, Lucas (8), Corbett (8); Hurst. W—Hurst. L—McCaskill. HR—Joyner (Cal.); Rice (Bos.).
Game 3—October 10, at California
Boston ....0 1 0 0 0 0 0 2 0—3 9 1
Cal. ....0 0 0 0 0 1 3 1 x—5 8 0
Boyd, Sambito (7), Schiraldi (8); Candelaria, Moore (8). W—Candelaria. L—Boyd. S—Moore. HR—Schofield, Pettis (Cal.).
Game 4—October 11, at California
Boston....0 0 0 0 0 1 0 2 0 0 0—3 6 1
Cal. ....0 0 0 0 0 0 0 0 3 0 1—4 11 2
Clemens, Schiraldi (9); Sutton, Lucas (7), Ruhle (7), Finley (8), Corbett (8). W—Corbett. L—Schiraldi. HR—DeCinces (Cal.).
Game 5—October 12, at California
Boston....0 2 0 0 0 0 0 0 4 0 1—7 12 0
Cal. ....0 0 1 0 0 2 2 0 1 0 0—6 13 0
Hurst, Stanley (7), Sambito (9), Crawford (9), Schiraldi (11); Witt, Lucas (9), Moore (9), Finley (11). W—Crawford. L—Moore. S—Schiraldi. HR—Gedman, Baylor, Henderson (Bos.); Boone, Grich (Cal.).
Game 6—October 14, at Boston
Cal. ....2 0 0 0 0 0 1 1 0— 4 11 1
Boston ....2 0 5 0 1 0 2 0 x—10 16 1
McCaskill, Lucas (3), Corbett (4), Finley (7); Boyd, Stanley (8). W—Boyd. L—McCaskill. HR—Downing (Cal.).
Game 7—October 15, at Boston
Cal. ....0 0 0 0 0 0 0 1 0—1 6 2
Boston ....0 3 0 4 0 0 1 0 x—8 8 1
Candelaria, Sutton (4), Moore (8); Clemens, Schiraldi (8). W—Clemens. L—Candelaria. HR—Rice, Evans (Bos.).

NLCS

■ **Winner:** The New York Mets overcame the outstanding pitching of Houston's Mike Scott and denied the Astros their first-ever pennant.
■ **Turning point:** The Mets claimed a 6-5 Game 3 victory when Lenny Dykstra stroked a two-run homer in the bottom of the ninth inning.
■ **Memorable moment:** Mets relief ace Jesse Orosco fired a pennant-winning third strike past Houston's Kevin Bass with two runners on base in the bottom of the 16th inning, preserving New York's 7-6 victory in the longest Championship Series game ever played.
■ **Top guns:** Orosco (3-0), Dykstra (.304), Darryl Strawberry (2 HR, 5 RBIs), Mets; Scott (2-0, 0.50 ERA), Craig Reynolds (.333), Astros.
■ **MVP:** Scott.

Linescores
Game 1—October 8, at Houston
N.Y. ....0 0 0 0 0 0 0 0 0—0 5 0
Hou. ....0 1 0 0 0 0 0 0 x—1 7 1
Gooden, Orosco (8); Scott. W—Scott. L—Gooden. HR—Davis (Hou.).
Game 2—October 9, at Houston
N.Y. ....0 0 0 2 3 0 0 0 0—5 10 0
Hou. ....0 0 0 0 0 0 1 0 0—1 10 2
Ojeda; Ryan, Andersen (6), Lopez (8), Kerfeld (9). W—Ojeda. L—Ryan.
Game 3—October 11, at New York
Hou. ....2 2 0 0 0 0 1 0 0—5 8 1
N.Y. ....0 0 0 0 0 4 0 0 2—6 10 1
Knepper, Kerfeld (8), Smith (9); Darling, Aguilera (6), Orosco (8). W—Orosco. L—Smith. HR—Doran (Hou.); Strawberry, Dykstra (N.Y.).
Game 4—October 12, at New York
Hou. ....0 2 0 0 1 0 0 0 0—3 4 1
N.Y. ....0 0 0 0 0 0 0 1 0—1 3 0
Scott; Fernandez, McDowell (7), Sisk (9). W—Scott. L—Fernandez. HR—Ashby, Thon (Hou.).
Game 5—October 14, at New York
Hou. ......0 0 0 0 1 0 0 0 0 0 0 0—1 9 1
N.Y. ....0 0 0 0 1 0 0 0 0 0 0 1—2 4 0
Ryan, Kerfeld (10); Gooden, Orosco (11). W—Orosco. L—Kerfeld. HR—Strawberry (N.Y.).
Game 6—October 15, at Houston
N.Y. ....0 0 0 0 0 0 0 0 3 0 0 0 0 1 0 3—7 11 0
Hou.....3 0 0 0 0 0 0 0 0 0 0 0 0 1 0 2—6 11 1
Ojeda, Aguilera (6), McDowell (9), Orosco (14); Knepper, Smith (9), Andersen (11), Lopez (14), Calhoun (16). W—Orosco. L—Lopez. HR—Hatcher (Hou.).

WORLD SERIES

■ **Winner:** The Mets, on the brink of elimination, made a wild Game 6 recovery and kept the Red Sox without a Series victory since 1918.
■ **Turning point:** The bottom of the 10th inning of Game 6. One out away from elimination and trailing 5-3 with nobody on base, the Mets amazingly rallied for three runs and a 6-5, Game 7-forcing victory.
■ **Memorable moments:** A tense, 10-pitch battle between Mets batter Mookie Wilson and Boston pitcher Bob Stanley in the fateful 10th inning of Game 6. One Stanley pitch was wild, allowing the tying run to score, and Wilson slapped the final one to first baseman Bill Buckner, who let the ball dribble between his legs for a game-deciding error.
■ **Top guns:** Ray Knight (.391), Gary Carter (2 HR, 9 RBIs), Mets; Bruce Hurst (2-0, 1.96 ERA), Dwight Evans (2 HR, 9 RBIs), Red Sox.
■ **MVP:** Knight.

Linescores
Game 1—October 18, at New York
Boston ....0 0 0 0 0 0 1 0 0—1 5 0
N.Y. ....0 0 0 0 0 0 0 0 0—0 4 1
Hurst, Schiraldi (9); Darling, McDowell (8). W—Hurst. L—Darling. S—Schiraldi.
Game 2—October 19, at New York
Boston ......0 0 3 1 2 0 2 0 1—9 18 0
N.Y. ....0 0 2 0 1 0 0 0 0—3 8 1
Clemens, Crawford (5), Stanley (7); Gooden, Aguilera (6), Orosco (7), Fernandez (9), Sisk (9). W—Crawford. L—Gooden. S—Stanley. HR—Henderson, Evans (Bos.).
Game 3—October 21, at Boston
N.Y. ....4 0 0 0 0 0 2 1 0—7 13 0
Boston ......0 0 1 0 0 0 0 0 0—1 5 0
Ojeda, McDowell (8); Boyd, Sambito (8), Stanley (8). W—Ojeda. L—Boyd. HR—Dykstra (N.Y.).
Game 4—October 22, at Boston
N.Y. ....0 0 0 3 0 0 2 1 0—6 12 0
Boston ......0 0 0 0 0 0 0 2 0—2 7 1
Darling, McDowell (8), Orosco (8); Nipper, Crawford (7), Stanley (9). W—Darling. L—Nipper. S—Orosco. HR—Carter 2, Dykstra (N.Y.).
Game 5—October 23, at Boston
N.Y. ....0 0 0 0 0 0 0 1 1—2 10 1
Boston ......0 1 1 0 2 0 0 0 x—4 12 0
Gooden, Fernandez (5); Hurst. W—Hurst. L—Gooden. HR—Teufel (N.Y.).
Game 6—October 25, at New York
Boston ..1 1 0 0 0 0 1 0 0 2—5 13 3
N.Y. ....0 0 0 0 2 0 0 1 0 3—6 8 2
Clemens, Schiraldi (8), Stanley (10); Ojeda, McDowell (7), Orosco (8), Aguilera (9). W—Aguilera. L—Schiraldi. HR—Henderson (Bos.).
Game 7—October 27, at New York
Boston ......0 3 0 0 0 0 0 2 0—5 9 0
N.Y. ....0 0 0 0 0 3 3 2 x—8 10 0
Hurst, Schiraldi (7), Sambito (7), Stanley (7), Nipper (8), Crawford (8); Darling, Fernandez (4), McDowell (7), Orosco (8). W—McDowell. L—Schiraldi. S—Orosco. HR—Evans, Gedman (Bos.); Knight, Strawberry (N.Y.).

FINAL STANDINGS

American League

East Division

Team	Det.	Tor.	Mil.	N.Y.	Bos.	Bal.	Cle.	Min.	K.C.	Oak.	Sea.	Chi.	Tex.	Cal.	W	L	Pct.	GB
Detroit	...	7	6	5	11	9	9	8	5	5	7	9	8	9	98	64	.605	...
Toronto	6	...	4	7	7	12	8	9	4	5	10	8	9	7	96	66	.593	2
Milwaukee	7	9	...	7	7	11	9	3	8	6	4	6	9	5	91	71	.562	7
New York	8	6	6	...	6	10	7	6	7	5	7	7	5	9	89	73	.549	9
Boston	2	6	6	7	...	12	7	7	6	4	7	3	7	4	78	84	.481	20
Baltimore	4	1	2	3	1	...	7	5	9	7	4	8	7	9	67	95	.414	31
Cleveland	4	5	4	6	6	6	...	3	6	4	5	5	2	5	61	101	.377	37

West Division

Team	Min.	K.C.	Oak.	Sea.	Chi.	Tex.	Cal.	Det.	Tor.	Mil.	N.Y.	Bos.	Bal.	Cle.	W	L	Pct.	GB
Minnesota	...	5	10	9	7	6	5	4	3	9	6	5	7	9	85	77	.525	...
Kansas City	8	...	5	9	7	7	8	7	8	4	5	6	3	6	83	79	.512	2
Oakland	3	8	...	5	4	6	7	7	7	6	7	8	5	8	81	81	.500	4
Seattle	4	4	8	...	7	9	6	5	2	8	5	5	8	7	78	84	.481	7
Chicago	6	6	9	6	...	7	5	3	4	6	5	9	4	7	77	85	.475	8
Texas	7	6	7	4	6	...	8	4	3	3	7	5	5	10	75	87	.463	10
California	8	5	6	7	8	5	...	3	5	7	3	8	3	7	75	87	.463	10

National League

East Division

Team	St.L.	N.Y.	Mon.	Phi.	Pit.	Chi.	S.F.	Cin.	Hou.	L.A.	Atl.	S.D.	W	L	Pct.	GB
St. Louis	...	9	7	10	11	12	5	8	7	9	9	8	95	67	.586	...
New York	9	...	10	13	12	9	9	5	6	6	5	8	92	70	.568	3
Montreal	11	8	...	10	11	8	5	6	5	9	9	9	91	71	.562	4
Philadelphia	8	5	8	...	11	10	2	7	6	10	5	8	80	82	.494	15
Pittsburgh	7	6	7	7	...	14	6	8	6	6	5	8	80	82	.494	15
Chicago	6	9	10	8	4	...	5	6	8	6	5	9	76	85	.472	18.5

West Division

Team	S.F.	Cin.	Hou.	L.A.	Atl.	S.D.	St.L.	N.Y.	Mon.	Phi.	Pit.	Chi.	W	L	Pct.	GB
San Fran.	...	11	8	8	10	13	7	3	7	10	6	7	90	72	.556	...
Cincinnati	7	...	13	10	10	12	4	7	6	5	4	6	84	78	.519	6
Houston	10	5	...	12	10	5	5	6	7	6	6	4	76	86	.469	14
Los Angeles	10	8	6	...	12	11	3	6	3	2	6	6	73	89	.451	17
Atlanta	8	8	8	6	...	6	3	7	3	7	7	6	69	92	.429	20.5
San Diego	5	6	13	7	12	...	4	4	3	4	4	3	65	97	.401	25

SIGNIFICANT EVENTS

■ **April 8:** Dodgers vice president Al Campanis, reeling from criticism he had generated two days earlier with his nationally televised comments about the role of blacks in sports, resigned.

■ **July 14:** Kansas City's Bo Jackson became a two-sport star when he signed a five-year contract to play football for the Los Angeles Raiders.

MEMORABLE MOMENTS

■ **April 18:** Mike Schmidt joined the 500-homer club with a dramatic three-run ninth-inning shot that gave the Phillies an 8-6 victory over the Pirates.

■ **July 18:** Yankee Don Mattingly tied a 31-year-old Major League record when he hit a home run in his eighth consecutive game—a 7-2 loss to the Rangers.

■ **August 26:** Cleveland pitcher John Farrell stopped Paul Molitor's 39-game hitting streak, but Milwaukee won in 10 innings, 1-0.

■ **September 14:** Catcher Ernie Whitt belted three home runs to lead a Toronto assault that produced a record 10 homers and an 18-3 rout of the Orioles.

■ **September 29:** Oakland's Mark McGwire pounded his 49th home run in a 5-4 victory over Cleveland, giving him 11 more than the previous rookie record.

■ **October 3:** Dodgers ace Orel Hershiser ended Padres catcher Benito Santiago's rookie-record 34-game hitting streak.

■ **October 4:** The Tigers defeated Toronto, 1-0, and completed a season-ending, A.L. East-deciding sweep of the Blue Jays.

LEADERS

American League
BA: Wade Boggs, Bos., .363.
Runs: Paul Molitor, Mil., 114.
Hits: Kirby Puckett, Min.; Kevin Seitzer, K.C., 207.
TB: George Bell, Tor., 369.
HR: Mark McGwire, Oak., 49.
RBI: George Bell, Tor., 134.
SB: Harold Reynolds, Sea., 60.
Wins: Roger Clemens, Bos.; Dave Stewart, Oak., 20.
ERA: Jimmy Key, Tor., 2.76.
CG: Roger Clemens, Bos., 18.
IP: Charlie Hough, Tex., 285.1.
SO: Mark Langston, Sea., 262.
SV: Tom Henke, Tor., 34.

National League
BA: Tony Gwynn, S.D., .370.
Runs: Tim Raines, Mon., 123.
Hits: Tony Gwynn, S.D., 218.
TB: Andre Dawson, Chi., 353.
HR: Andre Dawson, Chi., 49.
RBI: Andre Dawson, Chi., 137.
SB: Vince Coleman, St.L., 109.
Wins: Rick Sutcliffe, Chi., 18.
ERA: Nolan Ryan, Hou., 2.76.
CG: Rick Reuschel, Pit.-S.F.; Fernando Valenzuela, L.A., 12.
IP: Orel Hershiser, L.A., 264.2.
SO: Nolan Ryan, Hou., 270.
SV: Steve Bedrosian, Phil., 40.

A.L. 20-game winners
Roger Clemens, Bos., 20-9
Dave Stewart, Oak., 20-13

A.L. 100 RBIs
George Bell, Tor., 134
Dwight Evans, Bos., 123
Mark McGwire, Oak., 118
Wally Joyner, Cal., 117
Don Mattingly, N.Y., 115
Jose Canseco, Oak., 113
Gary Gaetti, Min., 109
Ruben Sierra, Tex., 109
Joe Carter, Cle., 106
Alan Trammell, Det., 105
Robin Yount, Mil., 103
Danny Tartabull, K.C., 101
Alvin Davis, Sea., 100
Larry Parrish, Tex., 100

N.L. 100 RBIs
Andre Dawson, Chi., 137
Tim Wallach, Mon., 123
Mike Schmidt, Phil., 113
Jack Clark, St.L., 106
Willie McGee, St.L., 105
Dale Murphy, Atl., 105
Darryl Strawberry, N.Y., 104
Eric Davis, Cin., 100
Juan Samuel, Phil., 100

A.L. 40 homers
Mark McGwire, Oak., 49
George Bell, Tor., 47

N.L. 40 homers
Andre Dawson, Chi., 49
Dale Murphy, Atl., 44

Most Valuable Player
A.L.: George Bell, OF, Tor.
N.L.: Andre Dawson, OF, Chi.

Cy Young Award
A.L.: Roger Clemens, Bos.
N.L.: Steve Bedrosian, Phil.

Rookie of the Year
A.L.: Mark McGwire, 1B, Oak.
N.L.: Benito Santiago, C, S.D.

Manager of the Year
A.L.: Sparky Anderson, Det.
N.L.: Buck Rodgers, Mon.

Hall of Fame additions
Ray Dandridge, 3B, Negro Leagues
Catfish Hunter, P, 1965-79
Billy Williams, OF, 1959-76

ALL-STAR GAME

■ **Winner:** The N.L. broke a scoreless deadlock in the 13th inning to claim a 2-0 victory.

■ **Key inning:** The 13th, when Tim Raines drilled a two-out Jay Howell pitch for a two-run triple, scoring Ozzie Virgil and Hubie Brooks.

■ **Memorable moment:** A violent collision between Dave Winfield and N.L. catcher Virgil in the ninth. Winfield, trying to score from second on a failed double-play attempt, was called out when Virgil held onto the ball.

■ **Top guns:** Mike Scott (Astros), Rick Sutcliffe (Cubs), Orel Hershiser (Dodgers), Raines (Expos), N.L.; Bret Saberhagen (Royals), Mark Langston (Mariners), A.L.

■ **MVP:** Raines.

Linescore

July 14, at the Oakland Coliseum
N.L. ....000 000 000 0002—2 8 2
A.L. ....000 000 000 0000—0 6 1
Scott (Astros), Sutcliffe (Cubs) 3, Hershiser (Dodgers) 5, Reuschel (Pirates) 7, Franco (Reds) 8, Bedrosian (Phillies) 9, L. Smith (Cubs) 10, S. Fernandez (Mets) 13; Saberhagen (Royals), Morris (Tigers) 4, Langston (Mariners) 6, Plesac (Brewers) 8, Righetti (Yankees) 9, Henke (Blue Jays) 9, Howell (Athletics) 12. W—L. Smith. L—Howell. S—S. Fernandez.

ALCS

■ **Winner:** Minnesota, a loser in the A.L.'s first two LCS in 1969 and '70, surprised the favored Detroit Tigers in a five-game romp.

■ **Turning point:** The sixth inning of Game 4. With the Twins leading the series 2-1 and the game 4-3, Detroit's Darrell Evans let Minnesota catcher Tim Laudner pick him off third base — a mistake that doomed the Tigers' pennant hopes.

■ **Memorable moment:** The Game 5 hitting of Twins right fielder Tom Brunansky, who collected a single, double, homer and three RBIs in Minnesota's series-closing 9-5 victory.

■ **Top guns:** Brunansky (.412, 2 HR, 9 RBIs), Dan Gladden (.350), Gary Gaetti (.300, 2 HR, 5 RBIs), Twins; Johnny Grubb (.571), Chet Lemon (2 HR, 4 RBIs), Tigers.

■ **MVP:** Gaetti.

Linescores

Game 1—October 7, at Minnesota
Detroit........0 0 1 0 0 1 1 2 0—5 10 0
Minnesota..0 1 0 0 3 0 0 4 x—8 10 0
Alexander, Henneman (8), Hernandez (8), King (8); Viola, Reardon (8). W—Reardon. L—Alexander. HR—Gaetti 2 (Min.); Heath, Gibson (Det.).

Game 2—October 8, at Minnesota
Detroit..........0 2 0 0 0 0 0 1 0—3 7 1
Minnesota....0 3 0 2 1 0 0 0 x—6 6 0
Morris; Blyleven, Berenguer (8). W—Blyleven. L—Morris. S—Berenguer. HR—Lemon, Whitaker (Det.); Hrbek (Min.).

Game 3—October 10, at Detroit
Minnesota....0 0 0 2 0 2 2 0 0—6 8 1
Detroit..........0 0 5 0 0 0 0 2 x—7 7 0
Straker, Schatzeder (3), Berenguer (7), Reardon (8); Terrell, Henneman (7). W—Henneman. L—Reardon. HR—Gagne, Brunansky (Min.); Sheridan (Det.).

Game 4—October 11, at Detroit
Minnesota....0 0 1 1 1 1 0 1 0—5 7 1
Detroit..........1 0 0 0 1 1 0 0 0—3 7 3
Viola, Atherton (6), Berenguer (6), Reardon (9); Tanana, Petry (6), Thurmond (9). W—Viola. L—Tanana. S—Reardon. HR—Puckett, Gagne (Min.).

Game 5—October 12, at Detroit
Minnesota..0 4 0 0 0 0 1 1 3—9 15 1
Detroit........0 0 0 3 0 0 0 1 1—5 9 1
Blyleven, Schatzeder (7), Berenguer (8), Reardon (8); Alexander, King (2), Henneman (7), Robinson (9). W—Blyleven. L—Alexander. S—Reardon. HR—Nokes, Lemon (Det.); Brunansky (Min.).

NLCS

■ **Winner:** The Cardinals had to overcome the lusty hitting of San Francisco's Jeffrey Leonard to claim their third pennant of the decade.

■ **Turning point:** The combined six-hit pitching of Cardinals John Tudor, Todd Worrell and Ken Dayley in a 1-0 Game 6 victory.

■ **Memorable moment:** Leonard's two-run homer in the fifth inning of Game 4—his record-tying fourth in the series.

■ **Top guns:** Tony Pena (.381), Willie McGee (.308), Cardinals; Dave Dravecky (1-1, 0.60 ERA), Leonard (.417, 4 HR, 5 RBIs), Giants.

■ **MVP:** Leonard.

Linescores

Game 1—October 6, at St. Louis
San Fran. ....1 0 0 1 0 0 0 1 0—3 7 1
St. Louis ......0 0 1 1 0 3 0 0 x—5 10 1
Reuschel, Lefferts (7), Garrelts (8); Mathews, Worrell (8), Dayley (8). W—Mathews. L—Reuschel. S—Dayley. HR—Leonard (S.F.).

Game 2—October 7, at St. Louis
San Fran. ....0 2 0 1 0 0 0 2 0—5 10 0
St. Louis ......0 0 0 0 0 0 0 0 0—0 2 1
Dravecky; Tudor, Forsch (9). W—Dravecky. L—Tudor. HR—W. Clark, Leonard (S.F.).

Game 3—October 9, at San Francisco
St. Louis ......0 0 0 0 0 2 4 0 0—6 11 1
San Fran. ....0 3 1 0 0 0 0 0 1—5 7 1
Magrane, Forsch (5), Worrell (7); Hammaker, D. Robinson (7), Lefferts (7), LaCoss (8). W—Forsch. L—D. Robinson. S—Worrell. HR—Leonard, Spilman (S.F.); Lindeman (St.L.).

Game 4—October 10, at San Francisco
St. Louis ....0 2 0 0 0 0 0 0 0—2 9 0
San Fran.........0 0 0 1 2 0 0 1 x—4 9 2
Cox; Krukow. W—Krukow. L—Cox. HR—Thompson, Leonard, Brenly (S.F.).

Game 5—October 11, at San Francisco
St. Louis ....1 0 1 1 0 0 0 0 0—3 7 0
San Fran. ......1 0 1 4 0 0 0 0 x—6 7 1
Mathews, Forsch (4), Horton (4), Dayley (7); Reuschel, Price (5). W—Price. L—Forsch. HR—Mitchell (S.F.).

Game 6—October 13, at St. Louis
San Fran. ......0 0 0 0 0 0 0 0 0—0 6 0
St. Louis ....0 1 0 0 0 0 0 0 x—1 5 0
Dravecky, D. Robinson (7); Tudor, Worrell (8), Dayley (9). W—Tudor. L—Dravecky. S—Dayley.

Game 7—October 14, at St. Louis
San Fran. ....0 0 0 0 0 0 0 0 0—0 8 1
St. Louis ......0 4 0 0 0 2 0 0 x—6 12 0
Hammaker, Price (3), Downs (3), Garrelts (5), Lefferts (6), LaCoss (6), D. Robinson (8); Cox. W—Cox. L—Hammaker. HR—Oquendo (St.L.).

WORLD SERIES

■ **Winner:** The Twins held off the Cardinals and captured a Series in which the home team won every game.

■ **Turning point:** Don Baylor's two-run fifth-inning homer and Kent Hrbek's grand slam, blows that turned a 5-2 deficit into an 11-5 sixth-game victory for the Twins.

■ **Memorable moment:** Hrbek's arm-pumping jaunt around the bases after his Game 6 slam.

■ **Top guns:** Frank Viola (2-1), Steve Lombardozzi (.412), Twins; Tony Pena (.409), Willie McGee (.370), Cardinals.

■ **MVP:** Viola.

Linescores

Game 1—October 17, at Minnesota
St. Louis ..0 1 0 0 0 0 0 0 0— 1 5 1
Minn. ......0 0 0 7 2 0 1 0 x—10 11 0
Magrane, Forsch (4), Horton (7); Viola, Atherton (9). W—Viola. L—Magrane. HR—Gladden, Lombardozzi (Min.).

Game 2—October 18, at Minnesota
St. Louis ....0 0 0 0 1 0 1 2 0—4 9 0
Minn. ....0 1 0 6 0 1 0 0 x—8 10 0
Cox, Tunnell (4), Dayley (7), Worrell (8); Blyleven, Berenguer (8), Reardon (9). W—Blyleven. L—Cox. HR—Gaetti, Laudner (Min.).

Game 3—October 20, at St. Louis
Minn. ....0 0 0 0 0 1 0 0 0—1 5 1
St. Louis ......0 0 0 0 0 0 3 0 x—3 9 1
Straker, Berenguer (7), Schatzeder (7); Tudor, Worrell (8). W—Tudor. L—Berenguer. S—Worrell.

Game 4—October 21, at St. Louis
Minn. ....0 0 1 0 1 0 0 0 0—2 7 1
St. Louis ....0 0 1 6 0 0 0 0 x—7 10 1
Viola, Schatzeder (4), Niekro (5), Frazier (7); Mathews, Forsch (4), Dayley (7). W—Forsch. L—Viola. S—Dayley. HR—Gagne (Min.); Lawless (St.L.).

Game 5—October 22, at St. Louis
Minn. ....0 0 0 0 0 0 0 2 0—2 6 1
St. Louis ....0 0 0 0 0 3 1 0 x—4 10 0
Blyleven, Atherton (7), Reardon (7); Cox, Dayley (8), Worrell (8). W—Cox. L—Blyleven. S—Worrell.

Game 6—October 24, at Minnesota
St. Louis ..1 1 0 2 1 0 0 0 0— 5 11 2
Minn. ......2 0 0 0 4 4 0 1 x—11 15 0
Tudor, Horton (5), Forsch (6), Dayley (6), Tunnell (7); Straker, Schatzeder (4), Berenguer (6), Reardon (9). W—Schatzeder. L—Tudor. HR—Herr (St.L.); Baylor, Hrbek (Min.).

Game 7—October 25, at Minnesota
St. Louis ....0 2 0 0 0 0 0 0 0—2 6 1
Minn. ....0 1 0 0 1 1 0 1 x—4 10 0
Magrane, Cox (5), Worrell (6); Viola, Reardon (9). W—Viola. L—Cox. S—Reardon.

FINAL STANDINGS

American League

East Division

Team	Bos.	Det.	Mil.	Tor.	N.Y.	Cle.	Bal.	Oak.	Min.	K.C.	Cal.	Chi.	Tex.	Sea.	W	L	Pct.	GB
Boston	...	6	10	2	9	8	9	3	7	6	8	7	8	6	89	73	.549	...
Detroit	7	...	5	5	8	9	8	4	1	8	7	9	8	9	88	74	.543	1
Milwaukee	3	8	...	7	6	4	9	3	7	9	9	6	8	8	87	75	.537	2
Toronto	11	8	6	...	7	7	8	3	5	8	6	5	6	7	87	75	.537	2
New York	4	5	7	6	...	7	10	6	9	6	6	9	5	5	85	76	.528	3.5
Cleveland	5	4	9	6	6	...	9	4	5	6	4	9	6	5	78	84	.481	11
Baltimore	4	5	4	5	3	4	...	4	3	0	5	4	6	7	54	107	.335	34.5

West Division

Team	Oak.	Min.	K.C.	Cal.	Chi.	Tex.	Sea.	Bos.	Det.	Mil.	Tor.	N.Y.	Cle.	Bal.	W	L	Pct.	GB
Oakland	...	8	5	9	8	8	9	9	8	9	9	6	8	8	104	58	.642	...
Minnesota	5	...	6	9	9	7	8	5	11	5	7	3	7	9	91	71	.562	13
Kansas City	8	7	...	8	6	7	7	6	4	3	4	6	6	12	84	77	.522	19.5
California	4	4	5	...	9	8	6	4	5	3	6	6	8	7	75	87	.463	29
Chicago	5	4	7	4	...	8	9	5	3	6	7	3	3	7	71	90	.441	32.5
Texas	5	6	6	5	5	...	7	4	4	4	6	6	6	6	70	91	.435	33.5
Seattle	4	5	5	7	4	6	...	6	3	4	5	7	7	5	68	93	.422	35.5

National League

East Division

Team	N.Y.	Pit.	Mon.	Chi.	St.L.	Phi.	L.A.	Cin.	S.D.	S.F.	Hou.	Atl.	W	L	Pct.	GB
New York	...	12	12	9	14	10	10	7	7	4	7	8	100	60	.625	...
Pittsburgh	6	...	10	11	11	11	6	5	8	8	4	5	85	75	.531	15
Montreal	6	8	...	9	13	9	4	7	4	7	6	8	81	81	.500	20
Chicago	9	7	9	...	7	8	4	6	8	5	7	7	77	85	.475	24
St. Louis	4	7	5	11	...	12	5	6	6	5	6	9	76	86	.469	25
Philadelphia	8	7	9	10	6	...	1	3	4	7	4	6	65	96	.404	35.5

West Division

Team	L.A.	Cin.	S.D.	S.F.	Hou.	Atl.	N.Y.	Pit.	Mon.	Chi.	St.L.	Phi.	W	L	Pct.	GB
Los Angeles	...	11	7	12	9	14	1	6	8	8	7	11	94	67	.584	...
Cincinnati	7	...	10	11	9	13	4	7	5	6	6	9	87	74	.540	7
San Diego	11	8	...	8	12	10	5	4	8	4	6	7	83	78	.516	11
San Fran.	6	7	10	...	11	13	8	4	5	7	7	5	83	79	.512	11.5
Houston	9	9	6	7	...	13	5	8	6	5	6	8	82	80	.506	12.5
Atlanta	4	5	8	5	5	...	4	5	4	5	3	6	54	106	.338	39.5

SIGNIFICANT EVENTS

■ **January 22:** Kirk Gibson and Carlton Fisk were among seven players declared free agents by an arbitrator who ruled that owners had acted in collusion against free agents after the 1985 season.
■ **June 23:** Yankee owner George Steinbrenner fired manager Billy Martin for a fifth time and replaced him with the man he had replaced—Lou Piniella.
■ **August 9:** The Cubs defeated the Mets, 6-4, in the first official night game at Chicago's 74-year-old Wrigley Field.
■ **August 31:** Major League owners were stunned when a labor arbitrator found them guilty of collusion for a second time—this time against the 1986 class of free agents.
■ **September 8:** N.L. President A. Bartlett Giamatti was elected to succeed Peter V. Ueberroth as baseball's seventh commissioner.

MEMORABLE MOMENTS

■ **April 29:** The Orioles defeated Chicago, 9-0, and ended their record season-opening losing streak at 21 games.
■ **June 25:** Orioles shortstop Cal Ripken stretched his ironman streak to 1,000 games in a 10-3 loss to Boston.
■ **September 16:** Cincinnati's Tom Browning retired 27 consecutive Dodgers in a 1-0 victory—baseball's 12th perfect game.
■ **September 23:** Oakland's Jose Canseco swiped two bases in a victory over Milwaukee and became the first player to hit 40 homers and record 40 steals in the same season.
■ **September 28:** Dodgers righthander Orel Hershiser worked 10 shutout innings against the Padres in his final regular-season start and stretched his scoreless-innings streak to a record 59.

ALL-STAR GAME

■ **Winner:** A.L. pitchers held the N.L. to five hits and catcher Terry Steinbach supplied all the offense they needed for a 2-1 All-Star Game victory.
■ **Key inning:** The third, when Steinbach drove a Dwight Gooden pitch over the right-field wall, giving the A.L. a lead it never relinquished.
■ **Memorable moment:** Steinbach, maligned by the media as an unworthy starter because of his .217 season average, drove in the winning run with a fourth-inning sacrifice fly and walked away with MVP honors.
■ **Top guns:** Frank Viola (Twins), Dennis Eckersley (Athletics), Steinbach (Athletics), A.L.; Vince Coleman (Cardinals), N.L.
■ **MVP:** Steinbach.

Linescore

July 12, at Cincinnati's Riverfront Stadium
A.L. ....0 0 1 1 0 0 0 0 0—2 6 2
N.L. ....0 0 0 1 0 0 0 0 0—1 5 0
Viola (Twins), Clemens (Red Sox) 3, Gubicza (Royals) 4, Stieb (Blue Jays) 6, Russell (Rangers) 7, Jones (Indians) 8, Plesac (Brewers) 8, Eckersley (Athletics) 9; Gooden (Mets), Knepper (Astros) 4, Cone (Mets) 5, Gross (Dodgers) 6, Davis (Padres) 7, Walk (Phillies) 7, Hershiser (Dodgers) 8, Worrell (Cardinals) 9. W—Viola. L—Gooden. S—Eckersley. HR—Steinbach, A.L.

ALCS

■ **Winner:** The Oakland Athletics, making their first Championship Series appearance since 1975, recorded the first sweep in the best-of-seven format and claimed their first pennant since 1974.
■ **Turning point:** Amid a flurry of Oakland home runs, the Athletics actually took control on a ninth-inning Walt Weiss single that produced a 4-3 Game 2 victory over the Red Sox at Fenway Park.
■ **Memorable moment:** Jose Canseco's first-inning home run in the fourth game, his third of the series and Oakland's seventh. The A's went on to close out the Red Sox with a 4-1 victory.
■ **Top guns:** Dennis Eckersley (4 games, 4 saves, 0.00 ERA), Gene Nelson (2-0, 0.00), Rickey Henderson (.375), Canseco (.313, 3 HR, 4 RBIs), Athletics; Wade Boggs (.385), Rich Gedman (.357), Red Sox.
■ **MVP:** Eckersley.

Linescores

Game 1—October 5, at Boston
Oakland........0 0 0 1 0 0 0 1 0—2 6 0
Boston ....0 0 0 0 0 0 1 0 0—1 6 0
Stewart, Honeycutt (7), Eckersley (8); Hurst. W—Honeycutt. L—Hurst. S—Eckersley. HR—Canseco (Oak.).

Game 2—October 6, at Boston
Oakland......0 0 0 0 0 0 3 0 1—4 10 1
Boston ......0 0 0 0 0 2 1 0 0—3 4 1
Davis, Cadaret (7), Nelson (7), Eckersley (9); Clemens, Stanley (8), Smith (8). W—Nelson. L—Smith. S—Eckersley. HR—Canseco (Oak.); Gedman (Bos.).

Game 3—October 8, at Oakland
Boston ....3 2 0 0 0 0 1 0 0— 6 12 0
Oakland....0 4 2 0 1 0 1 2 x—10 15 1
Boddicker, Gardner (3), Stanley (8); Welch, Nelson (2), Young (6), Plunk (7), Honeycutt (7), Eckersley (8). W—Nelson. L—Boddicker. S—Eckersley. HR—Greenwell (Bos.); McGwire, Lansford, Hassey, Henderson (Oak.).

Game 4—October 9, at Oakland
Boston ......0 0 0 0 0 1 0 0 0—1 4 0
Oakland......1 0 1 0 0 0 0 2 x—4 10 1
Hurst, Smithson (5), Smith (7); Stewart, Honeycutt (8), Eckersley (9). W—Stewart. L—Hurst. S—Eckersley. HR—Canseco (Oak.).

LEADERS

American League
BA: Wade Boggs, Bos., .366.
Runs: Wade Boggs, Bos., 128.
Hits: Kirby Puckett, Min., 234.
TB: Kirby Puckett, Min., 358.
HR: Jose Canseco, Oak., 42.
RBI: Jose Canseco, Oak., 124.
SB: Rickey Henderson, N.Y., 93.
Wins: Frank Viola, Min., 24.
ERA: Allan Anderson, Min., 2.45.
CG: Roger Clemens, Bos.; Dave Stewart, Oak., 14.
IP: Dave Stewart, Oak., 275.2.
SO: Roger Clemens, Bos., 291.
SV: Dennis Eckersley, Oak., 45.

National League
BA: Tony Gwynn, S.D., .313.
Runs: Brett Butler, S.F., 109.
Hits: Andres Galarraga, Mon., 184.
TB: Andres Galarraga, Mon., 329.
HR: Darryl Strawberry, N.Y., 39.
RBI: Will Clark, S.F., 109.
SB: Vince Coleman, St.L., 81.
Wins: Orel Hershiser, L.A.; Danny Jackson, Cin., 23.
ERA: Joe Magrane, St.L., 2.18.
CG: Orel Hershiser, L.A.; Danny Jackson, Cin., 15.
IP: Orel Hershiser, L.A., 267.
SO: Nolan Ryan, Hou., 228.
SV: John Franco, Cin., 39.

A.L. 20-game winners
Frank Viola, Min., 24-7
Dave Stewart, Oak., 21-12
Mark Gubicza, K.C., 20-8

N.L. 20-game winners
Orel Hershiser, L.A., 23-8
Danny Jackson, Cin., 23-8
David Cone, N.Y., 20-3

A.L. 100 RBIs
Jose Canseco, Oak., 124
Kirby Puckett, Min., 121
Mike Greenwell, Bos., 119
Dwight Evans, Bos., 111
Dave Winfield, N.Y, 107
George Brett, K.C., 103
Danny Tartabull, K.C., 102

N.L. 100 RBIs
Will Clark, S.F., 109
Darryl Strawberry, N.Y., 101
Bobby Bonilla, Pit., 100
Andy Van Slyke, Pit., 100

A.L. 40 homers
Jose Canseco, Oak., 42

Most Valuable Player
A.L.: Jose Canseco, OF, Oak.
N.L.: Kirk Gibson, OF, L.A.

Cy Young Award
A.L.: Frank Viola, Min.
N.L.: Orel Hershiser, L.A.

Rookie of the Year
A.L.: Walt Weiss, SS, Oak.
N.L.: Chris Sabo, 3B, Cin.

Manager of the Year
A.L.: Tony La Russa, Oak.
N.L.: Tommy Lasorda, L.A.

Hall of Fame addition
Willie Stargell, OF/1B, 1962-82

NLCS

■ **Winner:** Los Angeles ace Orel Hershiser denied New York's bid for its second pennant in three years with a 6-0 shutout in Game 7.
■ **Turning point:** Game 4, when Dodgers catcher Mike Scioscia hit a game-tying two-run homer in the ninth inning and Kirk Gibson settled matters with a solo shot in the 12th, knotting the series at two games apiece.
■ **Memorable moment:** The eighth inning of Game 3, when Dodgers relief ace Jay Howell was thrown out of the game because a foreign substance was found in his glove. The Mets scored five runs in the inning and claimed an 8-4 victory.
■ **Top guns:** Hershiser (1-0, 1.09 ERA), Scioscia (.364), Gibson (2 HR, 6 RBIs), Dodgers; Randy Myers (2-0, 0.00), Lenny Dykstra (.429), Darryl Strawberry (.300, 6 RBIs), Mets.
■ **MVP:** Hershiser.

Linescores

Game 1—October 4, at Los Angeles
N.Y. ....0 0 0 0 0 0 0 0 3—3 8 1
L.A. ....1 0 0 0 0 0 1 0 0—2 4 0
Gooden, Myers (8); Hershiser, J. Howell (9). W—Myers. L—J. Howell.

Game 2—October 5, at Los Angeles
N.Y. ....0 0 0 2 0 0 0 0 1—3 6 0
L.A. ....1 4 0 0 1 0 0 0 x—6 7 0
Cone, Aguilera (3), Leach (6), McDowell (8); Belcher, Orosco (9), Pena (9). W—Belcher. L—Cone. S—Pena. HR—Hernandez (N.Y.).

Game 3—October 8, at New York
L.A. ....0 2 1 0 0 0 0 1 0—4 7 2
N.Y. ....0 0 1 0 0 2 0 5 x—8 9 2
Hershiser, J. Howell (8), Pena (8), Orosco (8), Horton (8); Darling, McDowell (7), Myers (8), Cone (9). W—Myers. L—Pena.

Game 4—October 9, at New York
L.A. ......2 0 0 0 0 0 0 0 2 0 0 1—5 7 1
N.Y. ......0 0 0 3 0 1 0 0 0 0 0 0—4 10 2
Tudor, Holton (6), Horton (7), Pena (9), Leary (12), Orosco (12), Hershiser (12); Gooden, Myers (9), McDowell (11). W—Pena. L—McDowell. S—Hershiser. HR—Strawberry, McReynolds (N.Y.); Scioscia, Gibson (L.A.).

Game 5—October 10, at New York
L.A. ....0 0 0 3 3 0 0 0 1—7 12 0
N.Y. ....0 0 0 0 3 0 0 1 0—4 9 1
Belcher, Horton (8), Holton (8); Fernandez, Leach (5), Aguilera (6), McDowell (8). W—Belcher. L—Fernandez. S—Holton. HR—Gibson (L.A.); Dykstra (N.Y.).

Game 6—October 11, at Los Angeles
N.Y. ....1 0 1 0 2 1 0 0 0—5 11 0
L.A. ....0 0 0 0 1 0 0 0 0—1 5 2
Cone; Leary, Holton (5), Horton (6), Orosco (8). W—Cone. L—Leary. HR—McReynolds (N.Y.).

Game 7—October 12, at Los Angeles
N.Y. ....0 0 0 0 0 0 0 0 0—0 5 2
L.A. ....1 5 0 0 0 0 0 0 x—6 10 0
Darling, Gooden (2), Leach (5), Aguilera (7); Hershiser. W—Hershiser. L—Darling.

WORLD SERIES

■ **Winner:** The Cinderella Dodgers pulled off a five-game surprise against the powerful Athletics.
■ **Turning point:** A two-out, ninth-inning, two-run homer by Kirk Gibson that gave the Dodgers a shocking 5-4 victory in Game 1.
■ **Memorable moment:** The gimpy Gibson, wincing in pain with every swing, connecting with a Dennis Eckersley pitch and then limping triumphantly around the bases with the winning run in the Series opener.
■ **Top guns:** Orel Hershiser (2-0, 1.00 ERA), Gibson (1 AB, 1 hit, 1 HR, 2 RBIs), Mickey Hatcher (.368, 5 RBIs), Dodgers; Terry Steinbach (.364), Athletics.
■ **MVP:** Hershiser.

Linescores

Game 1—October 15, at Los Angeles
Oakland........0 4 0 0 0 0 0 0 0—4 7 0
L.A. ....2 0 0 0 0 1 0 0 2—5 7 0
Stewart, Eckersley (9); Belcher, Leary (3), Holton (6), Pena (8). W—Pena. L—Eckersley. HR—Hatcher, Gibson (L.A.); Canseco (Oak.).

Game 2—October 16, at Los Angeles
Oakland......0 0 0 0 0 0 0 0 0—0 3 0
L.A. ....0 0 5 1 0 0 0 0 x—6 10 1
S. Davis, Nelson (4), Young (6), Plunk (7), Honeycutt (8); Hershiser. W—Hershiser. L—S. Davis. HR—Marshall (L.A.).

Game 3—October 18, at Oakland
L.A. ....0 0 0 0 1 0 0 0 0—1 8 1
Oakland........0 0 1 0 0 0 0 0 1—2 5 0
Tudor, Leary (2), Pena (6), J. Howell (9); Welch, Cadaret (6), Nelson (6), Honeycutt (8). W—Honeycutt. L—J. Howell. HR—McGwire (Oak.).

Game 4—October 19, at Oakland
L.A. ....2 0 1 0 0 0 1 0 0—4 8 1
Oakland........1 0 0 0 0 1 1 0 0—3 9 2
Belcher, J. Howell (7); Stewart, Cadaret (7), Eckersley (9). W—Belcher. L—Stewart. S—J. Howell.

Game 5—October 20, at Oakland
L.A. ....2 0 0 2 0 1 0 0 0—5 8 0
Oakland........0 0 1 0 0 0 0 1 0—2 4 0
Hershiser; S. Davis, Cadaret (5), Nelson (5), Honeycutt (8), Plunk (9), Burns (9). W—Hershiser. L—S. Davis. HR—Hatcher, M. Davis (L.A.).

FINAL STANDINGS

American League

East Division

Team	Tor.	Bal.	Bos.	Mil.	N.Y.	Cle.	Det.	Oak.	K.C.	Cal.	Tex.	Min.	Sea.	Chi.	W	L	Pct.	GB
Toronto	...	6	8	7	6	8	11	5	5	5	7	3	7	11	89	73	.549	...
Baltimore	7	...	6	7	8	7	10	5	6	6	9	4	6	6	87	75	.537	2
Boston	5	7	...	6	7	8	11	7	4	4	6	6	5	7	83	79	.512	6
Milwaukee	6	6	7	...	8	10	7	5	4	5	5	9	7	2	81	81	.500	8
New York	7	5	6	5	...	4	7	3	6	6	5	6	8	6	74	87	.460	14.5
Cleveland	5	6	5	3	9	...	5	2	8	7	7	5	6	5	73	89	.451	16
Detroit	2	3	2	6	6	8	...	4	6	1	4	5	4	8	59	103	.364	30

West Division

Team	Oak.	K.C.	Cal.	Tex.	Min.	Sea.	Chi.	Tor.	Bal.	Bos.	Mil.	N.Y.	Cle.	Det.	W	L	Pct.	GB
Oakland	...	6	8	8	7	9	8	7	7	5	7	9	10	8	99	63	.611	...
Kansas City	7	...	9	8	7	9	7	7	6	8	8	6	4	6	92	70	.568	7
California	5	4	...	6	11	7	8	7	6	8	7	6	5	11	91	71	.562	8
Texas	5	5	7	...	8	7	10	5	3	6	7	7	5	8	83	79	.512	16
Minnesota	6	6	2	5	...	7	8	9	8	6	3	6	7	7	80	82	.494	19
Seattle	4	4	6	6	6	...	6	5	6	7	5	4	6	8	73	89	.451	26
Chicago	5	6	5	3	5	7	...	1	6	5	10	5	7	4	69	92	.429	29.5

National League

East Division

Team	Chi.	N.Y.	St.L.	Mon.	Pit.	Phi.	S.F.	S.D.	Hou.	L.A.	Cin.	Atl.	W	L	Pct.	GB
Chicago	...	10	11	10	12	10	6	8	5	7	7	7	93	69	.574	...
New York	8	...	10	9	9	12	3	5	6	7	8	10	87	75	.537	6
St. Louis	7	8	...	13	5	11	5	10	5	9	4	9	86	76	.531	7
Montreal	8	9	5	...	11	9	7	5	8	5	8	6	81	81	.500	12
Pittsburgh	6	9	13	7	...	8	5	3	5	5	5	8	74	88	.457	19
Philadelphia	8	6	7	9	10	...	4	2	3	6	8	4	67	95	.414	26

West Division

Team	S.F.	S.D.	Hou.	L.A.	Cin.	Atl.	Chi.	N.Y.	St.L.	Mon.	Pit.	Phi.	W	L	Pct.	GB
San Fran.	...	10	10	8	10	12	6	9	7	5	7	8	92	70	.568	...
San Diego	8	...	10	12	9	11	4	7	2	7	9	10	89	73	.549	3
Houston	8	8	...	10	10	10	7	6	7	4	7	9	86	76	.531	6
Los Angeles	10	6	8	...	10	10	5	5	3	7	7	6	77	83	.481	14
Cincinnati	8	9	8	8	...	10	5	4	8	4	7	4	75	87	.463	17
Atlanta	6	7	8	6	8	...	5	2	3	6	4	8	63	97	.394	28

SIGNIFICANT EVENTS

■ **January 5:** Commissioner Peter Ueberroth signed a $400-million cable television package with ESPN, a month after signing a four-year, $1.06-billion contract with CBS-TV.

■ **February 3:** Bill White became the highest ranking black executive in professional sports when he was tabbed to succeed A. Bartlett Giamatti as N.L. president.

■ **June 5:** The Blue Jays opened SkyDome with a 5-3 loss to the Brewers.

■ **August 24:** Commissioner A. Bartlett Giamatti handed all-time hits leader Pete Rose, who had been implicated in a gambling scandal, a lifetime ban from baseball.

■ **September 1:** Giamatti, 51, died of a heart attack at his Massachusetts summer cottage, eight days after handing Rose his lifetime ban.

■ **September 13:** Giamatti assistant Fay Vincent was elected as baseball's eighth commissioner.

■ **December 25:** Former player and manager Billy Martin died when a pickup truck in which he was riding crashed near his home in Binghamton, N.Y.

MEMORABLE MOMENTS

■ **August 15:** Giants lefty Dave Dravecky, on the comeback trail from cancer surgery, broke his arm while throwing a pitch in a game at Montreal.

■ **August 22:** Nolan Ryan fired a fastball past Oakland's Rickey Henderson and became the first Major Leaguer to record 5,000 career strikeouts.

LEADERS

American League
BA: Kirby Puckett, Min., .339.
Runs: Wade Boggs, Bos.; Rickey Henderson, N.Y.-Oak., 113.
Hits: Kirby Puckett, Min., 215.
TB: Ruben Sierra, Tex., 344.
HR: Fred McGriff, Tor., 36.
RBI: Ruben Sierra, Tex., 119.
SB: Rickey Henderson, N.Y.-Oak., 77.
Wins: Bret Saberhagen, K.C., 23.
ERA: Bret Saberhagen, K.C., 2.16.
CG: Bret Saberhagen, K.C., 12.
IP: Bret Saberhagen, K.C., 262.1.
SO: Nolan Ryan, Tex., 301.
SV: Jeff Russell, Tex., 38.

National League
BA: Tony Gwynn, S.D., .336.
Runs: Will Clark, S.F.; Howard Johnson, N.Y.; Ryne Sandberg, Chi., 104.
Hits: Tony Gwynn, S.D., 203.
TB: Kevin Mitchell, S.F., 345.
HR: Kevin Mitchell, S.F., 47.
RBI: Kevin Mitchell, S.F., 125.
SB: Vince Coleman, St.L., 65.
Wins: Mike Scott, Hou., 20.
ERA: Scott Garrelts, S.F., 2.28.
CG: Tim Belcher, L.A.; Bruce Hurst, S.D., 10.
IP: Orel Hershiser, L.A., 256.2.
SO: Jose DeLeon, St.L., 201.
SV: Mark Davis, S.D., 44.

A.L. 20-game winners
Bret Saberhagen, K.C., 23-6
Dave Stewart, Oak., 21-9

N.L. 20-game winner
Mike Scott, Hou., 20-10

A.L. 100 RBIs
Ruben Sierra, Tex., 119
Don Mattingly, N.Y., 113
Nick Esasky, Bos., 108
Joe Carter, Cle., 105
Bo Jackson, K.C., 105
George Bell, Tor., 104
Robin Yount, Mil., 103
Dwight Evans, Bos., 100

N.L. 100 RBIs
Kevin Mitchell, S.F., 125
Pedro Guerrero, St.L., 117
Will Clark, S.F., 111
Eric Davis, Cin., 101
Howard Johnson, N.Y., 101

N.L. 40 homers
Kevin Mitchell, S.F., 47

Most Valuable Player
A.L.: Robin Yount, OF, Mil.
N.L.: Kevin Mitchell, OF, S.F.

Cy Young Award
A.L.: Bret Saberhagen, K.C.
N.L.: Mark Davis, S.D.

Rookie of the Year
A.L.: Gregg Olson, P, Bal.
N.L.: Jerome Walton, OF, Chi.

Manager of the Year
A.L.: Frank Robinson, Bal.
N.L.: Don Zimmer, Chi.

Hall of Fame additions
Al Barlick, umpire
Johnny Bench, C, 1967-83
Red Schoendienst, 2B, 1945-63
Carl Yastrzemski, OF, 1961-83

ALL-STAR GAME

■ **Winner:** The A.L.'s 5-3 victory marked its first back-to-back All-Star wins since 1957-58.
■ **Key inning:** The third, when the A.L. added to its 3-2 advantage with run-scoring singles by Harold Baines and Ruben Sierra.
■ **Memorable moment:** Consecutive home runs by Bo Jackson and Wade Boggs to lead off the A.L. first inning. That was an All-Star first.
■ **Top guns:** Nolan Ryan (Rangers), Jackson (Royals), Boggs (Red Sox), Sierra (Rangers), A.L.; Kevin Mitchell (Giants), Bobby Bonilla (Pirates), N.L.
■ **MVP:** Jackson.

Linescore
July 11, at California's Anaheim Stadium
N.L.............2 0 0 0 0 0 0 1 0—3 9 1
A.L. ....2 1 2 0 0 0 0 0 x—5 12 0
Reuschel (Giants), Smoltz (Braves) 2, Sutcliffe (Cubs) 3, Burke (Expos) 4, M. Davis (Padres) 6, Howell (Dodgers) 7, Williams (Cubs) 8; Stewart (Athletics), Ryan (Rangers) 2, Gubicza (Royals) 4, Moore (Athletics) 5, Swindell (Indians) 6, Russell (Rangers) 7, Plesac (Brewers) 8, Jones (Indians) 8. W—Ryan. L—Smoltz. S—Jones. HR—Jackson, Boggs, A.L.

ALCS

■ **Winner:** The Oakland Athletics ran and muscled their way past Toronto in a series dominated by leadoff hitter Rickey Henderson.
■ **Turning point:** After killing the Blue Jays in Games 1 and 2 with his speed, Henderson muscled up for two home runs in a 6-5 Game 4 victory that gave Oakland a 3-1 series edge.
■ **Memorable moment:** A mammoth Game 4 home run by Oakland slugger Jose Canseco that landed in the fifth tier of the left-field bleachers at SkyDome. The ball officially was measured at 490 feet, but most observers claimed it traveled well beyond 500.
■ **Top guns:** Dennis Eckersley (4 games, 3 saves, 1.59 ERA), Carney Lansford (.455), Henderson (.400, 8 SB, 8 runs, 2 HR, 5 RBIs), Mark McGwire (.389), Athletics; Tony Fernandez (.350), Blue Jays.
■ **MVP:** Henderson.

Linescores

Game 1—October 3, at Oakland
Toronto......0 2 0 1 0 0 0 0 0—3 5 1
Oakland......0 1 0 0 1 3 0 2 x—7 11 0
Stieb, Acker (6), Ward (8); Stewart, Eckersley (9). W—Stewart. L—Stieb. HR—D. Henderson, McGwire (Oak.); Whitt (Tor.).

Game 2—October 4, at Oakland
Toronto ....0 0 1 0 0 0 0 2 0—3 5 1
Oakland........0 0 0 2 0 3 1 0 x—6 9 1
Stottlemyre, Acker (6), Wells (6), Henke (7), Cerutti (8); Moore, Honeycutt (8), Eckersley (8). W—Moore. L—Stottlemyre. S—Eckersley. HR—Parker (Oak.).

Game 3—October 6, at Toronto
Oakland........1 0 1 1 0 0 0 0 0—3 8 1
Toronto ....0 0 0 4 0 0 3 0 x—7 8 0
Davis, Honeycutt (7), Nelson (7), M. Young (8); Key, Acker (7), Henke (9). W—Key. L—Davis. HR—Parker (Oak.).

Game 4—October 7, at Toronto
Oakland......0 0 3 0 2 0 1 0 0—6 11 1
Toronto ......0 0 0 1 0 1 1 2 0—5 13 0
Welch, Honeycutt (6), Eckersley (8); Flanagan, Ward (5), Cerutti (8), Acker (9). W—Welch. L—Flanagan. S—Eckersley. HR—R. Henderson 2, Canseco (Oak.).

Game 5—October 8, at Toronto
Oakland........1 0 1 0 0 0 2 0 0—4 4 0
Toronto ....0 0 0 0 0 0 0 1 2—3 9 0
Stewart, Eckersley (9); Stieb, Acker (7), Henke (9). W—Stewart. L—Stieb. S—Eckersley. HR—Moseby, Bell (Tor.).

NLCS

■ **Winner:** First basemen Will Clark and Mark Grace took center stage as San Francisco won its first pennant since 1962 and stretched Chicago's pennant drought to 44 years.
■ **Turning point:** The seventh inning of Game 3 when Giants second baseman Robby Thompson belted a two-run homer off reliever Les Lancaster, giving San Francisco a 5-4 victory and a 2-1 series edge.
■ **Memorable moment:** Game 1 at Chicago — the first post-season game played under the lights of Wrigley Field. San Francisco's Clark stole the show with four hits, a grand slam and six RBIs in the Giants' 11-3 victory.
■ **Top guns:** Steve Bedrosian (3 saves), Clark (.650, 13 hits, 2 HR, 8 RBIs), Kevin Mitchell (.353, 2 HR, 7 RBIs), Matt Williams (2 HR, 9 RBIs), Giants; Grace (.647, 8 RBIs), Ryne Sandberg (.400), Cubs.
■ **MVP:** Clark.

Linescores

Game 1—October 4, at Chicago
S.F. ....3 0 1 4 0 0 0 3 0—11 13 0
Chicago....2 0 1 0 0 0 0 0 0— 3 10 1
Garrelts, Brantley (8), Hammaker (9); Maddux, Kilgus (5), Wilson (8). W—Garrelts. L—Maddux. HR—Grace, Sandberg (Chi.); Clark 2, Mitchell (S.F.).

Game 2—October 5, at Chicago
S.F. ....0 0 0 2 0 0 0 2 1—5 10 0
Chicago......6 0 0 0 0 3 0 0 x—9 11 0
Reuschel, Downs (1), Lefferts (6), Brantley (7), Bedrosian (8); Bielecki, Assenmacher (5), Lancaster (6). W—Lancaster. L—Reuschel. HR—Mitchell, Ma. Williams, Thompson (S.F.).

Game 3—October 7, at San Francisco
Chicago......2 0 0 1 0 0 1 0 0—4 10 0
S.F. ....3 0 0 0 0 0 2 0 x—5 8 3
Sutcliffe, Assenmacher (7), Lancaster (7); LaCoss, Brantley (4), Robinson (7), Lefferts (8), Bedrosian (9). W—Robinson. L—Lancaster. S—Bedrosian. HR—Thompson (S.F.).

Game 4—October 8, at San Francisco
Chicago......1 1 0 0 2 0 0 0 0—4 12 1
S.F. ....1 0 2 1 2 0 0 0 x—6 9 1
Maddux, Wilson (4), Sanderson (6), Mi. Williams (8); Garrelts, Downs (5), Bedrosian (9). W—Downs. L—Wilson. S—Bedrosian. HR—Salazar (Chi.); Ma. Williams (S.F.).

Game 5—October 9, at San Francisco
Chicago......0 0 1 0 0 0 0 0 1—2 10 1
S.F. ....0 0 0 0 0 0 1 2 x—3 4 1
Bielecki, Mi. Williams (8), Lancaster (8); Reuschel, Bedrosian (9). W—Reuschel. L—Bielecki. S—Bedrosian.

WORLD SERIES

■ **Winner:** Oakland's four-game sweep of San Francisco in the first Bay Area Series was overshadowed by a massive earthquake that rocked parts of California, causing death and destruction and forcing postponement of the fall classic's final two games for 10 days.
■ **Turning point:** The second inning of Game 1, when Oakland jumped on the Giants for three runs en route to a 5-0 victory. That outburst set the pattern for the rest of the Series.
■ **Memorable moment:** The moments leading up to Game 3, when an earthquake measuring 7.1 on the Richter scale shook San Francisco and Candlestick Park. With the power out and incoming reports of mass destruction, Commissioner Fay Vincent ordered postponement of the game and told officials to clear the park.
■ **Top guns:** Dave Stewart (2-0, 1.69 ERA), Mike Moore (2-0, 2.08), Rickey Henderson (.474), Carney Lansford (.438), Athletics; Kevin Mitchell (.294), Giants.
■ **MVP:** Stewart.

Linescores

Game 1—October 14, at Oakland
S.F. ....0 0 0 0 0 0 0 0 0—0 5 1
Oakland......0 3 1 1 0 0 0 0 x—5 11 1
Garrelts, Hammaker (5), Brantley (6), LaCoss (8); Stewart. W—Stewart. L—Garrelts. HR—Parker, Weiss (Oak.).

Game 2—October 15, at Oakland
S.F. ....0 0 1 0 0 0 0 0 0—1 4 0
Oakland........1 0 0 4 0 0 0 0 x—5 7 0
Reuschel, Downs (5), Lefferts (7), Bedrosian (8); Moore, Honeycutt (8), Eckersley (9). W—Moore. L—Reuschel. HR—Steinbach (Oak.).

Game 3—October 27, at San Francisco
Oakland....2 0 0 2 4 1 0 4 0—13 14 0
S.F. ....0 1 0 2 0 0 0 0 4— 7 10 3
Stewart, Honeycutt (8), Nelson (9), Burns (9); Garrelts, Downs (4), Brantley (5), Hammaker (8), Lefferts (8). W—Stewart. L—Garrelts. HR—Williams, Bathe (S.F.); D. Henderson 2, Phillips, Canseco, Lansford (Oak.).

Game 4—October 28, at San Francisco
Oakland......1 3 0 0 3 1 0 1 0—9 12 0
S.F. ....0 0 0 0 0 2 4 0 0—6 9 0
Moore, Nelson (7), Honeycutt (7), Burns (7), Eckersley (9); Robinson, LaCoss (2), Brantley (6), Downs (4), Lefferts (8), Bedrosian (8). W—Moore. L—Robinson. S—Eckersley. HR—R. Henderson (Oak.); Mitchell, Litton (S.F.).

FINAL STANDINGS

American League

East Division

Team	Bos.	Tor.	Det.	Cle.	Bal.	Mil.	N.Y.	Oak.	Chi.	Tex.	Cal.	Sea.	K.C.	Min.	W	L	Pct.	GB
Boston	...	10	8	9	9	5	9	4	6	5	7	8	4	4	88	74	.543	...
Toronto	3	...	8	9	8	6	8	5	7	5	5	6	7	9	86	76	.531	2
Detroit	5	5	...	8	7	3	7	6	7	6	7	7	5	6	79	83	.488	9
Cleveland	4	4	5	...	7	9	5	4	7	7	5	7	6	7	77	85	.475	11
Baltimore	4	5	6	6	...	7	6	4	6	8	7	3	8	6	76	85	.472	11.5
Milwaukee	8	7	10	4	6	...	6	5	2	5	5	4	8	4	74	88	.457	14
New York	4	5	6	8	7	7	...	0	2	3	6	9	4	6	67	95	.414	21

West Division

Team	Oak.	Chi.	Tex.	Cal.	Sea.	K.C.	Min.	Bos.	Tor.	Det.	Cle.	Bal.	Mil.	N.Y.	W	L	Pct.	GB
Oakland	...	5	8	9	9	9	7	8	7	6	8	8	7	12	103	59	.636	...
Chicago	8	...	7	8	8	9	7	6	5	5	5	6	10	10	94	68	.580	9
Texas	5	6	...	5	6	8	8	7	7	6	5	4	7	9	83	79	.512	20
California	4	5	8	...	5	7	9	5	7	5	7	5	7	6	80	82	.494	23
Seattle	4	5	7	8	...	6	7	4	6	5	5	9	8	3	77	85	.475	26
Kansas City	4	4	5	6	7	...	8	8	5	7	6	3	4	8	75	86	.466	27.5
Minnesota	6	6	5	4	6	5	...	8	3	6	5	6	8	6	74	88	.457	29

National League

East Division

Team	Pit.	N.Y.	Mon.	Chi.	Phi.	St.L.	Cin.	L.A.	S.F.	Hou.	S.D.	Atl.	W	L	Pct.	GB
Pittsburgh	...	8	5	14	12	10	6	8	8	7	10	7	95	67	.586	...
New York	10	...	10	9	10	12	6	7	7	7	5	8	91	71	.562	4
Montreal	13	8	...	7	10	11	3	6	7	7	7	6	85	77	.525	10
Chicago	4	9	11	...	11	8	4	3	7	6	8	6	77	85	.475	18
Philadelphia	6	8	8	7	...	10	5	4	8	7	7	7	77	85	.475	18
St. Louis	8	6	7	10	8	...	3	5	3	6	9	5	70	92	.432	25

West Division

Team	Cin.	L.A.	S.F.	Hou.	S.D.	Atl.	Pit.	N.Y.	Mon.	Chi.	Phi.	St.L.	W	L	Pct.	GB
Cincinnati	...	9	7	11	9	10	6	6	9	8	7	9	91	71	.562	...
Los Angeles	9	...	8	9	9	12	4	5	6	9	8	7	86	76	.531	5
San Fran.	11	10	...	8	11	13	4	5	5	5	4	9	85	77	.525	6
Houston	7	9	10	...	4	13	5	5	5	6	5	6	75	87	.463	16
San Diego	9	9	7	14	...	10	2	7	5	4	5	3	75	87	.463	16
Atlanta	8	6	5	5	8	...	5	4	6	6	5	7	65	97	.401	26

SIGNIFICANT EVENTS

■ **March 18:** Players and owners reached agreement on a four-year contract that ended a 32-day lockout and cleared the way for spring training camps to open.
■ **June 14:** The N.L. announced plans to expand from 12 to 14 teams for the 1993 season.
■ **July 30:** Commissioner Fay Vincent banned George Steinbrenner from involvement with the Yankees for actions "not in the best interests of baseball."
■ **August 8:** Former baseball great Pete Rose reported to a federal work camp at Marion, Ill., to begin serving his five-month sentence for income tax evasion.

MEMORABLE MOMENTS

■ **June 11:** Rangers ace Nolan Ryan fired his record sixth no-hitter, defeating Oakland 5-0.
■ **June 12:** Baltimore's Cal Ripken Jr. moved into second place on the all-time ironman list when he pushed his consecutive-games streak to 1,308 in a 4-3 victory over Milwaukee.
■ **June 29:** A baseball first: Oakland's Dave Stewart and Dodgers lefthander Fernando Valenzuela threw no-hitters on the same day.
■ **July 1:** Yankees righthander Andy Hawkins became the second Major League pitcher to throw a complete-game no-hitter and lose when the White Sox stumbled to a 4-0 victory.
■ **July 31:** Ryan became baseball's 20th 300-game winner when the Rangers pounded the Brewers, 11-3.
■ **August 31:** The Griffeys, 20-year-old Ken Jr. and 40-year-old Ken Sr., became baseball's first father-son combination when both played for Seattle in a game against Kansas City.
■ **September 2:** Dave Stieb held Cleveland without a hit in a 3-0 victory—the first no-hitter in Blue Jays history and the record ninth of the season in the Major Leagues.
■ **October 3:** Detroit's Cecil Fielder became the first player in 13 years to break the 50-homer barrier when he crashed Nos. 50 and 51 in a final-day 10-3 victory over the Yankees.

LEADERS

American League
BA: George Brett, K.C., .329.
Runs: Rickey Henderson, Oak., 119.
Hits: Rafael Palmeiro, Tex., 191.
TB: Cecil Fielder, Det., 339.
HR: Cecil Fielder, Det., 51.
RBI: Cecil Fielder, Det., 132.
SB: Rickey Henderson, Oak., 65.
Wins: Bob Welch, Oak., 27.
ERA: Roger Clemens, Bos., 1.93.
CG: Jack Morris, Det.; Dave Stewart, Oak., 11.
IP: Dave Stewart, Oak., 267.
SO: Nolan Ryan, Tex., 232.
SV: Bobby Thigpen, Chi., 57.

National League
BA: Willie McGee, St.L., .335.
Runs: Ryne Sandberg, Chi., 116.
Hits: Brett Butler, S.F.; Lenny Dykstra, Phil., 192.
TB: Ryne Sandberg, Chi., 344.
HR: Ryne Sandberg, Chi., 40.
RBI: Matt Williams, S.F., 122.
SB: Vince Coleman, St.L., 77.
Wins: Doug Drabek, Pit., 22.
ERA: Danny Darwin, Hou., 2.21.
CG: Ramon Martinez, L.A., 12.
IP: Frank Viola, N.Y., 249.2.
SO: David Cone, N.Y., 233.
SV: John Franco, N.Y., 33.

A.L. 20-game winners
Bob Welch, Oak., 27-6
Dave Stewart, Oak., 22-11
Roger Clemens, Bos., 21-6

N.L. 20-game winners
Doug Drabek, Pit., 22-6
Ramon Martinez, L.A., 20-6
Frank Viola, N.Y., 20-12

A.L. 100 RBIs
Cecil Fielder, Det., 132
Kelly Gruber, Tor., 118
Mark McGwire, Oak., 108
Jose Canseco, Oak., 101

N.L. 100 RBIs
Matt Williams, S.F., 122
Bobby Bonilla, Pit., 120
Joe Carter, S.D., 115
Barry Bonds, Pit., 114
Darryl Strawberry, N.Y., 108
Andre Dawson, Chi., 100
Ryne Sandberg, Chi., 100

A.L. 40 homers
Cecil Fielder, Det., 51

N.L. 40 homers
Ryne Sandberg, Chi., 40

Most Valuable Player
A.L.: Rickey Henderson, OF, Oak.
N.L.: Barry Bonds, OF, Pit.

Cy Young Award
A.L.: Bob Welch, Oak.
N.L.: Doug Drabek, Pit.

Rookie of the Year
A.L.: Sandy Alomar Jr., C, Cle.
N.L.: Dave Justice, OF, Atl.

Manager of the Year
A.L.: Jeff Torborg, Chi.
N.L.: Jim Leyland, Pit.

Hall of Fame additions
Joe Morgan, 2B, 1963-84
Jim Palmer, P, 1965-84

ALL-STAR GAME

■ **Winner:** Six pitchers held the N.L. to an All-Star record-low two hits and the A.L. won for the third straight year, 2-0.

■ **Key inning:** The seventh, when the A.L. broke a scoreless deadlock on a two-run double by Julio Franco off fireballer Rob Dibble. Franco was the first batter after a 68-minute rain delay.

■ **Memorable moment:** The performance of an A.L. staff that allowed only a first-inning single by Will Clark and a ninth-inning single by Lenny Dykstra and retired 16 consecutive batters at one point.

■ **Top guns:** Bob Welch (Athletics), Dave Stieb (Blue Jays), Bret Saberhagen (Royals), Franco (Rangers), Wade Boggs (Red Sox), A.L.

■ **MVP:** Franco.

Linescore
July 10, at Chicago's Wrigley Field
A.L..............0 0 0 0 0 0 2 0 0—2 7 0
N.L..............0 0 0 0 0 0 0 0 0—0 2 1
Welch (Athletics), Stieb (Blue Jays) 3, Saberhagen (Royals) 5, Thigpen (White Sox) 7, Finley (Angels) 8, Eckersley (Athletics) 9; Armstrong (Reds), R. Martinez (Dodgers) 3, D. Martinez (Expos) 4, Viola (Mets) 5, D. Smith (Astros) 6, Brantley (Giants) 6, Dibble (Reds) 7, Myers (Reds) 8, Jo. Franco (Mets) 9. W—Saberhagen. L—Brantley. S—Eckersley.

ALCS

■ **Winner:** The powerful Athletics swept to their third consecutive pennant without benefit of a home run — their trademark offensive weapon.

■ **Turning point:** The final three innings of Game 1. Trailing 1-0 when Boston starter Roger Clemens left the game, the A's pounded five Red Sox relievers for nine runs and set the pattern for the series.

■ **Memorable moment:** The second inning of Game 4 when Clemens, frustrated by his team's 3-0 series deficit and the calls of umpire Terry Cooney, was ejected during an angry exchange, killing any hopes for a Boston comeback.

■ **Top guns:** Dave Stewart (2-0, 1.13 ERA), Terry Steinbach (.455), Carney Lansford (.438), Athletics; Wade Boggs (.438), Red Sox.

■ **MVP:** Stewart.

Linescores

Game 1—October 6, at Boston
Oakland......0 0 0 0 0 0 1 1 7—9 13 0
Boston ......0 0 0 1 0 0 0 0 0—1 5 1
Stewart, Eckersley (9); Clemens, Andersen (7), Bolton (8), Gray (8), Lamp (9), Murphy (9). W—Stewart. L—Andersen. HR—Boggs (Bos.).

Game 2—October 7, at Boston
Oakland......0 0 0 1 0 0 1 0 2—4 13 1
Boston ......0 0 1 0 0 0 0 0 0—1 6 0
Welch, Honeycutt (8), Eckersley (8); Kiecker, Harris (6), Andersen (7), Reardon (8). W—Welch. L—Harris. S—Eckersley.

Game 3—October 9, at Oakland
Boston ....0 1 0 0 0 0 0 0 0—1 8 3
Oakland........0 0 0 2 0 2 0 0 x—4 6 0
Boddicker; Moore, Nelson (7), Honeycutt (8), Eckersley (9). W—Moore. L—Boddicker. S—Eckersley.

Game 4—October 10, at Oakland
Boston ....0 0 0 0 0 0 0 0 1—1 4 1
Oakland........0 3 0 0 0 0 0 0 x—3 6 0
Clemens, Bolton (2), Gray (5), Andersen (8); Stewart, Honeycutt (9). W—Stewart. L—Clemens. S—Honeycutt.

NLCS

■ **Winner:** Cincinnati prevailed over Pittsburgh in a matchup of teams that dominated in the 1970s and failed to qualify for post-season play in the 1980s.
■ **Turning point:** The pivotal third game when the Reds got unlikely home runs from Billy Hatcher and Mariano Duncan and recorded a 6-3 victory.
■ **Memorable moment:** Glenn Braggs, a defensive replacement in right field, made a sensational over-the-wall catch in the ninth inning of Game 6, robbing Pittsburgh's Carmelo Martinez of a two-run homer and preserving the Reds' series-ending 2-1 victory.
■ **Top guns:** Randy Myers (3 saves, 7 SO, 0.00 ERA), Rob Dibble (1 save, 10 SO, 0.00), Paul O'Neill (.471), Hal Morris (.417), Reds; Doug Drabek (1-1, 1.65), Pirates.
■ **MVPs:** Dibble and Myers.

Linescores

Game 1—October 4, at Cincinnati
Pitt..............0 0 1 2 0 0 1 0 0—4 7 1
Cin. ....3 0 0 0 0 0 0 0 0—3 5 0
Walk, Belinda (7), Patterson (9), Power (9); Rijo, Charlton (6), Dibble (9). W—Walk. L—Charlton. S—Power. HR—Bream (Pit.).

Game 2—October 5, at Cincinnati
Pitt..............0 0 0 0 1 0 0 0 0—1 6 0
Cin. ....1 0 0 0 1 0 0 0 x—2 5 0
Drabek; Browning, Dibble (7), Myers (8). W—Browning. L—Drabek. S—Myers. HR—Lind (Pit.).

Game 3—October 8, at Pittsburgh
Cin. ....0 2 0 0 3 0 0 0 1—6 13 1
Pitt.............0 0 0 2 0 0 0 1 0—3 8 0
Jackson, Dibble (6), Charlton (8), Myers (9); Smith, Landrum (6), Smiley (7), Belinda (9). W—Jackson. L—Smith. S—Myers. HR—Hatcher, Duncan (Cin.).

Game 4—October 9, at Pittsburgh
Cin. ....0 0 0 2 0 0 2 0 1—5 10 1
Pitt.............1 0 0 1 0 0 0 1 0—3 8 0
Rijo, Myers (8), Dibble (9); Walk, Power (8). W—Rijo. L—Walk. S—Dibble. HR—O'Neill, Sabo (Cin.); Bell (Pit.).

Game 5—October 10, at Pittsburgh
Cin. ....1 0 0 0 0 0 0 1 0—2 7 0
Pitt. ....2 0 0 1 0 0 0 0 x—3 6 1
Browning, Mahler (6), Charlton (7), Scudder (8); Drabek, Patterson (9). W—Drabek. L—Browning. S—Patterson.

Game 6—October 12, at Cincinnati
Pitt..............0 0 0 0 1 0 0 0 0—1 1 3
Cin. ....1 0 0 0 0 0 1 0 x—2 9 0
Power, Smith (3), Belinda (7), Landrum (8); Jackson, Charlton (7), Myers (8). W—Charlton. L—Smith. S—Myers.

WORLD SERIES

■ **Winner:** The Oakland Athletics' aura of invincibility was shattered by the Cincinnati Reds in a startling sweep. The A's, who were looking for a second straight championship, entered the Series with a 10-game post-season winning streak.
■ **Turning point:** Game 1. Eric Davis' first-inning home run and the combined nine-hit pitching of Jose Rijo, Rob Dibble and Randy Myers in a 7-0 victory served notice that the A's had their hands full.
■ **Memorable moment:** Relief ace Myers retiring Jose Canseco and Carney Lansford in the ninth inning of Game 4 to preserve a 2-1 victory for Rijo and complete the sweep.
■ **Top guns:** Rijo (2-0, 0.59 ERA), Myers (3 games, 0.00), Dibble (1-0, 0.00), Billy Hatcher (.750), Chris Sabo (.563, 2 HR, 5 RBIs), Reds; Rickey Henderson (.333), Athletics.
■ **MVP:** Rijo.

Linescores

Game 1—October 16, at Cincinnati
Oak. ....0 0 0 0 0 0 0 0 0—0 9 1
Cin. ....2 0 2 0 3 0 0 0 x—7 10 0
Stewart, Burns (5), Nelson (5), Sanderson (7), Eckersley (8); Rijo, Dibble (8), Myers (9). W—Rijo. L—Stewart. HR—Davis (Cin.).

Game 2—October 17, at Cincinnati
Oak. ......1 0 3 0 0 0 0 0 0 0—4 10 2
Cin. ....2 0 0 1 0 0 0 1 0 1—5 14 2
Welch, Honeycutt (8), Eckersley (10); Jackson, Scudder (3), Armstrong (5), Charlton (8), Dibble (9). W—Dibble. L—Eckersley. HR—Canseco (Oak.).

Game 3—October 19, at Oakland
Cin. ....0 1 7 0 0 0 0 0 0—8 14 1
Oak. ....0 2 1 0 0 0 0 0 0—3 7 1
Browning, Dibble (7), Myers (8); Moore, Sanderson (3), Klink (4), Nelson (4), Burns (8), Young (9). W—Browning. L—Moore. HR—Sabo 2 (Cin.); Baines, R. Henderson (Oak.).

Game 4—October 20, at Oakland
Cin. ....0 0 0 0 0 0 0 2 0—2 7 1
Oak. ....1 0 0 0 0 0 0 0 0—1 2 1
Rijo, Myers (9); Stewart. W—Rijo. L—Stewart. S—Myers.

FINAL STANDINGS

American League

East Division

Team	Tor.	Det.	Bos.	Mil.	N.Y.	Bal.	Cle.	Min.	Chi.	Tex.	Oak.	Sea.	K.C.	Cal.	W	L	Pct.	GB
Toronto	...	8	4	7	7	8	12	8	5	6	6	7	7	6	91	71	.562	...
Detroit	5	...	8	4	8	8	6	4	8	6	4	8	8	7	84	78	.519	7
Boston	9	5	...	7	6	5	9	3	7	5	8	9	7	4	84	78	.519	7
Milwaukee	6	9	6	...	6	10	8	6	5	7	8	3	3	6	83	79	.512	8
New York	6	5	7	7	...	8	7	2	4	5	6	3	5	6	71	91	.438	20
Baltimore	5	5	8	3	5	...	7	4	4	9	3	4	4	6	67	95	.414	24
Cleveland	1	7	4	5	6	6	...	2	6	4	5	2	4	5	57	105	.352	34

West Division

Team	Min.	Chi.	Tex.	Oak.	Sea.	K.C.	Cal.	Tor.	Det.	Bos.	Mil.	N.Y.	Bal.	Cle.	W	L	Pct.	GB
Minnesota	...	5	6	8	9	7	5	4	8	9	6	10	8	10	95	67	.586	...
Chicago	8	...	8	7	7	7	5	7	4	5	7	8	8	6	87	75	.537	8
Texas	7	5	...	9	8	6	8	6	6	7	5	7	3	8	85	77	.525	10
Oakland	5	6	4	...	6	7	12	6	8	4	4	6	9	7	84	78	.519	11
Seattle	4	6	5	7	...	6	7	5	4	3	9	9	8	10	83	79	.512	12
Kansas City	6	6	7	6	7	...	4	5	4	5	9	7	8	8	82	80	.506	13
California	8	8	5	1	6	9	...	6	5	8	6	6	6	7	81	81	.500	14

National League

East Division

Team	Pit.	St.L.	Phi.	Chi.	N.Y.	Mon.	Atl.	L.A.	S.D.	S.F.	Cin.	Hou.	W	L	Pct.	GB
Pittsburgh	...	11	12	11	12	12	3	5	7	7	10	8	98	64	.605	...
St. Louis	7	...	12	8	11	11	3	6	3	8	8	7	84	78	.519	14
Philadelphia	6	6	...	10	7	14	7	5	9	6	3	5	78	84	.481	20
Chicago	7	10	8	...	11	10	6	2	4	6	4	9	77	83	.481	20
New York	6	7	11	6	...	14	3	5	7	6	7	5	77	84	.478	20.5
Montreal	6	7	4	7	4	...	7	7	6	7	6	10	71	90	.441	26.5

West Division

Team	Atl.	L.A.	S.D.	S.F.	Cin.	Hou.	Pit.	St.L.	Phi.	Chi.	N.Y.	Mon.	W	L	Pct.	GB
Atlanta	...	7	11	9	11	13	9	9	5	6	9	5	94	68	.580	...
Los Angeles	11	...	10	8	12	10	7	6	7	10	7	5	93	69	.574	1
San Diego	7	8	...	11	10	12	5	9	3	8	5	6	84	78	.519	10
San Fran.	9	10	7	...	8	9	5	4	6	6	6	5	75	87	.463	19
Cincinnati	7	6	8	10	...	9	2	4	9	8	5	6	74	88	.457	20
Houston	5	8	6	9	9	...	4	5	7	3	7	2	65	97	.401	29

LEADERS

American League
BA: Julio Franco, Tex., .341.
Runs: Paul Molitor, Mil., 133.
Hits: Paul Molitor, Mil., 216.
TB: Cal Ripken, Bal., 368.
HR: Jose Canseco, Oak.; Cecil Fielder, Det., 44.
RBI: Cecil Fielder, Det., 133.
SB: Rickey Henderson, Oak., 58.
Wins: Scott Erickson, Min.; Bill Gullickson, Det., 20.
ERA: Roger Clemens, Bos., 2.62.
CG: Jack McDowell, Chi., 15.
IP: Roger Clemens, Bos., 271.1.
SO: Roger Clemens, Bos., 241.
SV: Bryan Harvey, Cal., 46.

National League
BA: Terry Pendleton, Atl., .319.
Runs: Brett Butler, L.A., 112.
Hits: Terry Pendleton, Atl., 187.
TB: Will Clark, S.F.; Terry Pendleton, Atl., 303.
HR: Howard Johnson, N.Y., 38.
RBI: Howard Johnson, N.Y., 117.
SB: Marquis Grissom, Mon., 76.
Wins: Tom Glavine, Atl.; John Smiley, Pit., 20.
ERA: Dennis Martinez, Mon., 2.39.
CG: Tom Glavine, Atl.; Dennis Martinez, Mon., 9.
IP: Greg Maddux, Chi., 263.
SO: David Cone, N.Y., 241.
SV: Lee Smith, St.L., 47.

A.L. 20-game winners
Scott Erickson, Min., 20-8
Bill Gullickson, Det., 20-9

N.L. 20-game winners
John Smiley, Pit., 20-8
Tom Glavine, Atl., 20-11

A.L. 100 RBIs
Cecil Fielder, Det., 133
Jose Canseco, Oak., 122
Ruben Sierra, Tex., 116
Cal Ripken, Bal., 114
Frank Thomas, Chi., 109
Joe Carter, Tor., 108
Juan Gonzalez, Tex., 102
Ken Griffey Jr., Sea., 100
Danny Tartabull, K.C., 100
Robin Ventura, Chi., 100

N.L. 100 RBIs
Howard Johnson, N.Y., 117
Barry Bonds, Pit., 116
Will Clark, S.F., 116
Fred McGriff, S.D., 106
Ron Gant, Atl., 105
Andre Dawson, Chi., 104
Ryne Sandberg, Chi., 100
Bobby Bonilla, Pit., 100

A.L. 40 homers
Jose Canseco, Oak., 44
Cecil Fielder, Det., 44

Most Valuable Player
A.L.: Cal Ripken, SS, Bal.
N.L.: Terry Pendleton, 3B, Atl.

Cy Young Award
A.L.: Roger Clemens, Bos.
N.L.: Tom Glavine, Atl.

Rookie of the Year
A.L.: Chuck Knoblauch, 2B, Min.
N.L.: Jeff Bagwell, 1B, Hou.

Manager of the Year
A.L.: Tom Kelly, Min.
N.L.: Bobby Cox, Atl.

Hall of Fame additions
Rod Carew, 2B/1B, 1967-85
Ferguson Jenkins, P, 1965-83
Tony Lazzeri, 2B, 1926-39
Gaylord Perry, P, 1962-83
Bill Veeck, executive/owner

SIGNIFICANT EVENTS

■ **April 18:** The Tigers spoiled the dedication of Chicago's new Comiskey Park when they routed the White Sox, 16-0.
■ **June 10:** Miami and Denver were declared winners by a four-man N.L. expansion committee.

MEMORABLE MOMENTS

■ **May 1:** Oakland's Rickey Henderson swiped his 939th base in a game against the Yankees, passing Lou Brock as baseball's all-time greatest base stealer.
■ **May 1:** Nolan Ryan, stealing the day's headlines from Henderson, fired his seventh career no-hitter, striking out 16 Blue Jays in a 3-0 victory.
■ **July 28:** Montreal's Dennis Martinez became the 14th pitcher to throw a perfect game when he retired all 27 Dodgers he faced in a 2-0 victory.
■ **October 2:** Cardinals closer Lee Smith, who had notched his 300th career save earlier in the year, recorded his single-season N.L-record 47th in a 6-4 victory over Montreal.
■ **October 6:** Mets righthander David Cone tied the N.L. single-game record when he struck out 19 Phillies in a 7-0 victory.

ALL-STAR GAME

■ **Winner:** The A.L. ran its winning streak to four with a 4-2 victory and the N.L. ran its four-year run total to a paltry six.
■ **Key inning:** The third, when Cal Ripken followed singles by Rickey Henderson and Wade Boggs with a home run.
■ **Memorable moment:** A first-inning line drive by Bobby Bonilla that struck A.L. starter Jack Morris on the ankle, reviving All-Star memories of the 1937 Earl Averill shot that broke Dizzy Dean's toe.
■ **Top guns:** Ripken (Orioles), Ken Griffey Jr. (Mariners), Henderson (Athletics), Boggs (Red Sox), A.L.; Tom Glavine (Braves), Bonilla (Pirates), Andre Dawson (Cubs), N.L.
■ **MVP:** Ripken.

Linescore
July 9, at Toronto's SkyDome
N.L. ....1 0 0 1 0 0 0 0 0—2 10 1
A.L. ....0 0 3 0 0 0 1 0 x—4 8 0
Glavine (Braves), De. Martinez (Expos) 3, Viola (Mets) 5, Harnisch (Astros) 6, Smiley (Pirates) 7, Dibble (Reds) 7, Morgan (Dodgers) 8; Morris (Twins), Key (Blue Jays) 3, Clemens (Red Sox) 4, McDowell (White Sox) 5, Reardon (Red Sox) 7, Aguilera (Twins) 7, Eckersley (Athletics) 9. W—Key. L—De. Martinez. S—Eckersley. HR—Ripken, A.L.; Dawson, N.L.

ALCS

■ **Winner:** Minnesota won an LCS-record three road games and its second pennant in five years while handing Toronto its third Championship Series defeat.
■ **Turning point:** The 10th inning of Game 3 when Minnesota's Mike Pagliarulo homered off Toronto reliever Mike Timlin, giving the Twins a 3-2 victory and a 2-1 series advantage.
■ **Memorable moment:** Minnesota first baseman Kent Hrbek delivered a two-run single off David Wells in the eighth inning of Game 5 to cap a series-ending 8-5 victory.
■ **Top guns:** Rick Aguilera (3 saves, 0.00 ERA), Kirby Puckett (.429, 2 HR, 6 RBIs), Twins; Roberto Alomar (.474), Blue Jays.
■ **MVP:** Puckett.

Linescores
Game 1—October 8, at Minnesota
Toronto ......0 0 0 1 0 3 0 0 0—4 9 3
Minn. ....2 2 1 0 0 0 0 0 x—5 11 0
Candiotti, Wells (3), Timlin (6); Morris, Willis (6), Aguilera (8). W—Morris. L—Candiotti. S—Aguilera.
Game 2—October 9, at Minnesota
Toronto ....1 0 2 0 0 0 2 0 0—5 9 0
Minn. ....0 0 1 0 0 1 0 0 0—2 5 1
Guzman, Henke (6), Ward (8); Tapani, Bedrosian (7), Guthrie (7). W—Guzman. L—Tapani. S—Ward.
Game 3—October 11, at Toronto
Minn. ......0 0 0 0 1 1 0 0 0 1—3 7 0
Tor. ....2 0 0 0 0 0 0 0 0 0—2 5 1
Erickson, West (5), Willis (7), Guthrie (9), Aguilera (10); Key, Wells (7), Henke (8), Timlin (10). W—Guthrie. L—Timlin. S—Aguilera. HR—Carter (Tor.); Pagliarulo (Min.).
Game 4—October 12, at Toronto
Minn. ....0 0 0 4 0 2 1 1 1—9 13 1
Toronto ......0 1 0 0 0 1 0 0 1—3 11 2
Morris, Bedrosian (9); Stottlemyre, Wells (4), Acker (6), Timlin (7), MacDonald (9). W—Morris. L—Stottlemyre. HR—Puckett (Min.).
Game 5—October 13, at Toronto
Minn. ....1 1 0 0 0 3 0 3 0—8 14 2
Toronto ......0 0 3 2 0 0 0 0 0—5 9 1
Tapani, West (5), Willis (8), Aguilera (9); Candiotti, Timlin (6), Ward (6), Wells (8). W—West. L—Ward. S—Aguilera. HR—Puckett (Min.).

NLCS

■ **Winner:** The young Braves, last-place N.L. West finishers in 1990, defeated the Pirates and won their first Atlanta pennant.
■ **Turning point:** Greg Olson's run-scoring double in the ninth inning of Game 6, which gave Braves lefthander Steve Avery his second 1-0 victory.
■ **Memorable moment:** The final pitch of John Smoltz's 4-0 Game 7 victory. The shutout, the Braves' third, gave Atlanta fans their first World Series qualifier.
■ **Top guns:** Avery (2-0, 0.00 ERA), Smoltz (2-0, 1.76), Olson (.333), Brian Hunter (.333), Braves; Doug Drabek (1-1, 0.60), Zane Smith (1-1, 0.61), Jay Bell (.414), Pirates.
■ **MVP:** Avery.

Linescores
Game 1—October 9, at Pittsburgh
Atlanta ....0 0 0 0 0 0 0 0 1—1 5 1
Pit. ....1 0 2 0 0 1 0 1 x—5 8 1
Glavine, Wohlers (7), Stanton (8); Drabek, Walk (7). W—Drabek. L—Glavine. S—Walk. HR—Van Slyke (Pit.); Justice (Atl.).
Game 2—October 10, at Pittsburgh
Atlanta ....0 0 0 0 0 1 0 0 0—1 8 0
Pit. ....0 0 0 0 0 0 0 0 0—0 6 0
Avery, Pena (9); Z. Smith, Mason (8), Belinda (9). W—Avery. L—Z. Smith. S—Pena.
Game 3—October 12, at Atlanta
Pit. ....1 0 0 1 0 0 1 0 0— 3 10 2
Atlanta......4 1 1 0 0 0 1 3 x—10 11 0
Smiley, Landrum (3), Patterson (4), Kipper (6), Rodriguez (8); Smoltz, Stanton (7), Wohlers (8), Pena (8). W—Smoltz. L—Smiley. S—Pena. HR—Gant, Olson, Bream (Atl.); Merced, Bell (Pit.).
Game 4—October 13, at Atlanta
Pit. ......0 1 0 0 1 0 0 0 0 1—3 11 1
Atlanta 2 0 0 0 0 0 0 0 0 0—2 7 1
Tomlin, Walk (7), Belinda (9); Leibrandt, Clancy (7), Stanton (8), Mercker (10), Wohlers (10). W—Belinda. L—Mercker.
Game 5—October 14, at Atlanta
Pit. ....0 0 0 0 1 0 0 0 0—1 6 2
Atlanta ....0 0 0 0 0 0 0 0 0—0 9 1
Z. Smith, Mason (8); Glavine, Pena (9). W—Z. Smith. L—Glavine. S—Mason.
Game 6—October 16, at Pittsburgh
Atlanta ....0 0 0 0 0 0 0 0 1—1 7 0
Pit. ....0 0 0 0 0 0 0 0 0—0 4 0
Avery, Pena (9); Drabek. W—Avery. L—Drabek. S—Pena.
Game 7—October 17, at Pittsburgh
Atlanta ....3 0 0 0 1 0 0 0 0—4 6 1
Pit. ....0 0 0 0 0 0 0 0 0—0 6 0
Smoltz; Smiley, Walk (1), Mason (6), Belinda (8). W—Smoltz. L—Smiley. HR—Hunter (Atl.).

WORLD SERIES

■ **Winner:** Minnesota defeated Atlanta in the "worst-to-first" World Series, which featured teams that had risen from last-place 1990 finishes to win pennants.
■ **Turning point:** The 11th-inning of Game 6, when Kirby Puckett greeted Braves reliever Charlie Leibrandt with a game-ending home run, squaring the Series. Puckett had made an outstanding leaping catch earlier in the 4-3 victory.
■ **Memorable moment:** A seventh-game baserunning blunder by Atlanta's Lonnie Smith, who failed to score on Terry Pendleton's eighth-inning double. The Twins and Jack Morris went on to post a 1-0 Series-ending victory on Gene Larkin's 12th-inning single.
■ **Top guns:** Morris (2-0, 1.17 ERA), Brian Harper (.381), Puckett (2 HR, 4 RBIs), Twins; David Justice (2 HR, 6 RBIs), Braves.
■ **MVP:** Morris.

Linescores
Game 1—October 19, at Minnesota
Atlanta ....0 0 0 0 0 1 0 1 0—2 6 1
Minn. ....0 0 1 0 3 1 0 0 x—5 9 1
Leibrandt, Clancy (5), Wohlers (7), Stanton (8); Morris, Guthrie (8), Aguilera (8). W—Morris. L—Leibrandt. S—Aguilera. HR—Gagne, Hrbek (Min.).
Game 2—October 20, at Minnesota
Atlanta ....0 1 0 0 1 0 0 0 0—2 8 1
Minn. ....2 0 0 0 0 0 0 1 x—3 4 1
Glavine; Tapani, Aguilera (9). W—Tapani. L—Glavine. S—Aguilera. HR—Davis, Leius (Min.).
Game 3—October 22, at Atlanta
Minn. ....1 0 0 0 0 0 1 2 0 0 0 0—4 10 1
Atl. ....0 1 0 1 2 0 0 0 0 0 0 1—5 8 2
Erickson, West (5), Leach (5), Bedrosian (6), Willis (8), Guthrie (10), Aguilera (12); Avery, Pena (8), Stanton (10), Wohlers (12), Mercker (12), Clancy (12). W—Clancy. L—Aguilera. HR—Justice, Smith (Atl.); Puckett, Davis (Min.).
Game 4—October 23, at Atlanta
Minn. ....0 1 0 0 0 0 1 0 0—2 7 0
Atlanta ....0 0 1 0 0 0 1 0 1—3 8 0
Morris, Willis (7), Guthrie (8), Bedrosian (9); Smoltz, Wohlers (8), Stanton (8). W—Stanton. L—Guthrie. HR—Pendleton, Smith (Atl.); Pagliarulo (Min.).
Game 5—October 24, at Atlanta
Minn. ......0 0 0 0 0 3 0 1 1— 5 7 1
Atlanta......0 0 0 4 1 0 6 3 x—14 17 1
Tapani, Leach (5), West (7), Bedrosian (7), Willis (8); Glavine, Mercker (6), Clancy (7), St. Claire (9). W—Glavine. L—Tapani. HR—Justice, Smith, Hunter (Atl.).
Game 6—October 26, at Minnesota
Atl. ....0 0 0 0 2 0 1 0 0 0 0—3 9 0
Minn. 2 0 0 0 1 0 0 0 0 0 1—4 9 1
Avery, Stanton (7), Pena (9), Leibrandt (11); Erickson, Guthrie (7), Willis (7), Aguilera (10). W—Aguilera. L—Leibrandt. HR—Pendleton (Atl.); Puckett (Min.).
Game 7—October 27, at Minnesota
Atl. ....0 0 0 0 0 0 0 0 0 0—0 7 0
Minn. ....0 0 0 0 0 0 0 0 0 1—1 10 0
Smoltz, Stanton (8), Pena (9); Morris. W—Morris. L—Pena.

FINAL STANDINGS

American League

East Division

Team	Tor.	Mil.	Bal.	Cle.	N.Y.	Det.	Bos.	Oak.	Min.	Chi.	Tex.	Cal.	K.C.	Sea.	W	L	Pct.	GB
Toronto	...	5	8	7	11	8	6	6	7	7	9	7	7	8	96	66	.593	...
Milwaukee	8	...	7	8	6	8	8	7	6	7	7	7	5	8	92	70	.568	4
Baltimore	5	6	...	7	5	10	8	6	6	6	7	8	8	7	89	73	.549	7
Cleveland	6	5	6	...	7	5	7	6	6	5	5	6	5	7	76	86	.469	20
New York	2	7	8	6	...	8	6	6	5	4	6	5	7	6	76	86	.469	20
Detroit	5	5	3	8	5	...	9	6	3	2	8	5	7	9	75	87	.463	21
Boston	7	5	5	6	7	4	...	5	3	6	4	8	7	6	73	89	.451	23

West Division

Team	Oak.	Min.	Chi.	Tex.	Cal.	K.C.	Sea.	Tor.	Mil.	Bal.	Cle.	N.Y.	Det.	Bos.	W	L	Pct.	GB
Oakland	...	8	8	9	8	9	12	6	5	6	6	6	6	7	96	66	.593	...
Minnesota	5	...	5	6	11	7	8	5	6	6	6	7	9	9	90	72	.556	6
Chicago	5	8	...	5	10	7	4	5	5	6	7	8	10	6	86	76	.531	10
Texas	4	7	8	...	4	7	9	3	5	5	7	6	4	8	77	85	.475	19
California	5	2	3	9	...	8	7	5	5	4	6	7	7	4	72	90	.444	24
Kansas City	4	6	6	6	5	...	7	5	7	4	7	5	5	5	72	90	.444	24
Seattle	1	5	9	4	6	6	...	4	4	5	5	6	3	6	64	98	.395	32

National League

East Division

Team	Pit.	Mon.	St.L.	Chi.	N.Y.	Phi.	Atl.	Cin.	S.D.	Hou.	S.F.	L.A.	W	L	Pct.	GB
Pittsburgh	...	9	15	10	14	13	5	6	5	6	6	7	96	66	.593	...
Montreal	9	...	6	11	12	9	8	7	8	4	5	8	87	75	.537	9
St. Louis	3	12	...	7	9	11	6	5	8	7	7	8	83	79	.512	13
Chicago	8	7	11	...	9	9	2	5	5	8	8	6	78	84	.481	18
New York	4	6	9	9	...	6	5	5	4	7	10	7	72	90	.444	24
Philadelphia	5	9	7	9	12	...	6	5	3	4	3	7	70	92	.432	26

West Division

Team	Atl.	Cin.	S.D.	Hou.	S.F.	L.A.	Pit.	Mon.	St.L.	Chi.	N.Y.	Phi.	W	L	Pct.	GB
Atlanta	...	9	13	13	11	12	7	4	6	10	7	6	98	64	.605	...
CIncinnati	9	...	11	10	10	11	6	5	7	7	7	7	90	72	.556	8
San Diego	5	7	...	11	11	9	7	4	4	7	8	9	82	80	.506	16
Houston	5	8	7	...	12	13	6	8	5	4	5	8	81	81	.500	17
San Fran.	7	8	7	6	...	11	6	7	5	4	2	9	72	90	.444	26
Los Angeles	6	7	9	5	7	...	5	4	4	6	5	5	63	99	.389	35

LEADERS

American League
BA: Edgar Martinez, Sea., .343.
Runs: Tony Phillips, Det., 114.
Hits: Kirby Puckett, Min., 210.
TB: Kirby Puckett, Min., 313.
HR: Juan Gonzalez, Tex., 43.
RBI: Cecil Fielder, Det., 124.
SB: Kenny Lofton, Cle., 66.
Wins: Kevin Brown, Tex.; Jack Morris, Tor., 21.
ERA: Roger Clemens, Bos., 2.41.
CG: Jack McDowell, Chi., 13.
IP: Kevin Brown, Tex., 265.2.
SO: Randy Johnson, Sea., 241.
SV: Dennis Eckersley, Oak., 51.

National League
BA: Gary Sheffield, S.D., .330.
Runs: Barry Bonds, Pit., 109.
Hits: Terry Pendleton, Atl.; Andy Van Slyke, Pit., 199.
TB: Gary Sheffield, S.D., 323.
HR: Fred McGriff, S.D., 35.
RBI: Darren Daulton, Phil., 109.
SB: Marquis Grissom, Mon., 78.
Wins: Tom Glavine, Atl.; Greg Maddux, Chi., 20.
ERA: Bill Swift, S.F., 2.08.
CG: Terry Mulholland, Phil., 12.
IP: Greg Maddux, Chi., 268.
SO: John Smoltz, Atl., 215.
SV: Lee Smith, St.L., 43.

A.L. 20-game winners
Jack Morris, Tor., 21-6
Kevin Brown, Tex., 21-11
Jack McDowell, Chi., 20-10

N.L. 20-game winners
Tom Glavine, Atl., 20-8
Greg Maddux, Chi., 20-11

A.L. 100 RBIs
Cecil Fielder, Det., 124
Joe Carter, Tor., 119
Frank Thomas, Chi., 115
George Bell, Chi., 112
Albert Belle, Cle., 112
Kirby Puckett, Min., 110
Juan Gonzalez, Tex., 109
Dave Winfield, Tor., 108
Mike Devereaux, Bal., 107
Carlos Baerga, Cle., 105
Mark McGwire, Oak., 104
Ken Griffey Jr., Sea., 103

N.L. 100 RBIs
Darren Daulton, Phil., 109
Terry Pendleton, Atl., 105
Fred McGriff, S.D., 104
Barry Bonds, Pit., 103
Gary Sheffield, S.D., 100

A.L. 40 homers
Juan Gonzalez, Tex., 43
Mark McGwire, Oak., 42

Most Valuable Player
A.L.: Dennis Eckersley, P, Oak.
N.L.: Barry Bonds, OF, Pit.

Cy Young Award
A.L.: Dennis Eckersley, Oak.
N.L.: Greg Maddux, Chi.

Rookie of the Year
A.L.: Pat Listach, SS, Mil.
N.L.: Eric Karros, 1B, L.A.

Manager of the Year
A.L.: Tony La Russa, Oak.
N.L.: Jim Leyland, Pit.

Hall of Fame additions
Rollie Fingers, P, 1968-85
Bill McGowan, umpire
Hal Newhouser, P, 1939-55
Tom Seaver, P, 1967-86

SIGNIFICANT EVENTS

■ **April 6:** The Orioles opened their new Camden Yards home with a 2-0 victory over Cleveland.
■ **September 7:** Fay Vincent, reacting to an 18-9 no-confidence vote by the owners, resigned his post as baseball's eighth commissioner.
■ **November 17:** The Florida Marlins and Colorado Rockies selected 36 players apiece in baseball's first expansion draft since 1976.

MEMORABLE MOMENTS

■ **April 12:** Boston's Matt Young became the third pitcher in history to lose a complete-game no-hitter when he dropped a 2-1 decision to Cleveland.
■ **September 9, 30:** Milwaukee's Robin Yount and Kansas City's George Brett became the 17th and 18th members of baseball's 3,000-hit club.
■ **September 20:** Philadelphia second baseman Mickey Morandini pulled off baseball's ninth unassisted triple play and the N.L.'s first since 1927 in the sixth inning of a game against Pittsburgh.

ALL-STAR GAME

■ **Winner:** Ken Griffey Jr. went 3 for 3 as the suddenly dominant A.L. pounded out 19 hits and romped to an easy 13-6 victory.
■ **Key inning:** The A.L. first, when N.L. starter Tom Glavine was touched for four runs on seven consecutive singles.
■ **Memorable moment:** Ruben Sierra's two-run sixth-inning homer, which lifted the A.L.'s lead to 10-0.
■ **Top guns:** Griffey Jr. (Mariners), Sierra (Rangers), Robin Ventura (White Sox), Joe Carter (Blue Jays), Will Clark (Giants), Fred McGriff (Padres), N.L.
■ **MVP:** Griffey Jr.

Linescore
July 14, at San Diego's Jack Murphy Stadium
A.L. ....4 1 1 0 0 4 0 3 0—13 19 1
N.L. ....0 0 0 0 0 1 0 3 2— 6 12 1
Brown (Rangers), McDowell (White Sox) 2, Guzman (Blue Jays) 3, Clemens (Red Sox) 4, Mussina (Orioles) 5, Langston (Angels) 6, Nagy (Indians) 7, Montgomery (Royals) 8, Aguilera (Twins) 8, Eckersley (Athletics) 9; Glavine (Braves), Maddux (Braves) 2, Cone (Mets) 4, Tewksbury (Cardinals) 5, Smoltz (Braves) 6, D. Martinez (Expos) 7, Jones (Astros) 8, Charlton (Reds) 9. W—Brown. L—Glavine. HR—Griffey, Sierra, A.L.; Clark, N.L.

ALCS

■ **Winner:** The Toronto Blue Jays, three-time Championship Series losers, brought Canada its first pennant with a rousing six-game victory over Oakland.
■ **Turning point:** Down 6-1 entering the eighth inning of Game 4, the Blue Jays rallied to tie against A's relief ace Dennis Eckersley and won in the 11th on Pat Borders' sacrifice fly. Instead of a 2-2 series tie, Toronto was up 3-1.
■ **Memorable moment:** Roberto Alomar's stunning game-tying homer off Eckersley in the ninth inning of Game 4. The two-run shot forced extra innings.
■ **Top guns:** Juan Guzman (2-0, 2.08 ERA), Alomar (.423, 2 HR), Candy Maldonado (2 HR, 6 RBIs), Blue Jays; Harold Baines (.440), Ruben Sierra (.333, 7 RBIs), Athletics.
■ **MVP:** Alomar.

Linescores
Game 1—October 7, at Toronto
Oak. ....0 3 0 0 0 0 0 0 1—4 6 1
Tor. ....0 0 0 0 1 1 0 1 0—3 9 0
Stewart, Russell (8), Eckersley (9); Morris. W—Russell. L—Morris. S—Eckersley. HR—McGwire, Steinbach, Baines (Oak.); Borders, Winfield (Tor.).
Game 2—October 8, at Toronto
Oak. ....0 0 0 0 0 0 0 0 1—1 6 0
Tor. ....0 0 0 0 2 0 1 0 x—3 4 0
Moore, Corsi (8), Parrett (8); Cone, Henke (9). W—Cone. L—Moore. S—Henke. HR—Gruber (Tor.).
Game 3—October 10, at Oakland
Tor. ....0 1 0 1 1 0 2 1 1—7 9 1
Oak. ....0 0 0 2 0 0 2 1 0—5 13 3
Guzman, Ward (7), Timlin (8), Henke (8); Darling, Downs (7), Corsi (8), Russell (8), Honeycutt (9), Eckersley (9). W—Guzman. L—Darling. S—Henke. HR—Alomar, Maldonado (Tor.).
Game 4—October 11, at Oakland
Tor. ....0 1 0 0 0 0 0 3 2 0 1—7 17 4
Oak. ....0 0 5 0 0 1 0 0 0 0 0—6 12 2
Morris, Stottlemyre (4), Timlin (8), Ward (9), Henke (11); Welch, Parrett (8), Eckersley (8), Corsi (9), Downs (10). W—Ward. L—Downs. S—Henke. HR—Olerud, Alomar (Tor.).
Game 5—October 12, at Oakland
Tor. ....0 0 0 1 0 0 1 0 0—2 7 3
Oak. ....2 0 1 0 3 0 0 0 x—6 8 0
Cone, Key (5), Eichhorn (8); Stewart. W—Stewart. L—Cone. HR—Sierra (Oak.); Winfield (Tor.).
Game 6—October 14, at Toronto
Oak. ....0 0 0 0 0 1 0 1 0—2 7 1
Tor. ....2 0 4 0 1 0 0 2 x—9 13 0
Moore, Parrett (3), Honeycutt (5), Russell (7), Witt (8); Guzman, Ward (8), Henke (9). W—Guzman. L—Moore. HR—Carter, Maldonado (Tor.).

NLCS

■ **Winner:** Atlanta won its rematch with Pittsburgh and captured its second straight pennant in a stirring Championship Series that was decided on the final pitch.
■ **Turning point:** The incredible ninth inning of Game 7. Down 2-0 to Pirates ace Doug Drabek after eight innings and on the brink of blowing what had once been a three-games- to-one advantage, the Braves rallied for three runs.
■ **Memorable moment:** With two out and the bases loaded in the bottom of the ninth inning of Game 7, pinch-hitter Francisco Cabrera delivered a two-run, pennant-deciding single to left field off Stan Belinda.
■ **Top guns:** John Smoltz (2-0, 2.66 ERA), Mark Lemke (.333), David Justice (2 HR, 6 RBIs), Ron Gant (2 HR, 6 RBIs), Braves; Tim Wakefield (2-0, 3.00), Lloyd McClendon (.727), Gary Redus (.438), Pirates.
■ **MVP:** Smoltz.

Linescores
Game 1—October 6, at Atlanta
Pitt. ....0 0 0 0 0 0 0 1 0—1 5 1
Atlanta..........0 1 0 2 1 0 1 0 x—5 8 0
Drabek, Patterson (5), Neagle (7), Cox (8); Smoltz, Stanton (9). W—Smoltz. L—Drabek. HR—Blauser (Atl.); Lind (Pit.).
Game 2—October 7, at Atlanta
Pitt. ....0 0 0 0 0 0 4 1 0— 5 7 0
Atlanta......0 4 0 0 4 0 5 0 x—13 14 0
Jackson, Mason (2), Walk (3), Tomlin (5), Neagle (7), Patterson (7), Belinda (8); Avery, Freeman (7), Stanton (7), Wohlers (8), Reardon (9). W—Avery. L—Jackson. HR—Gant (Atl.).
Game 3—October 9, at Pittsburgh
Atlanta ....0 0 0 1 0 0 1 0 0—2 5 0
Pitt. ....0 0 0 0 1 1 1 0 x—3 8 1
Glavine, Stanton (7), Wohlers (8); Wakefield. W—Wakefield. L—Glavine. HR—Slaught (Pit.); Bream, Gant (Atl.).
Game 4—October 10, at Pittsburgh
Atlanta ......0 2 0 0 2 2 0 0 0—6 11 1
Pitt. ....0 2 1 0 0 0 1 0 0—4 6 1
Smoltz, Stanton (7), Reardon (9); Drabek, Tomlin (5), Cox (6), Mason (7). W—Smoltz. L—Drabek. S—Reardon.
Game 5—October 11, at Pittsburgh
Atlanta ......0 0 0 0 0 0 0 1 0—1 3 0
Pitt. ....4 0 1 0 0 1 1 0 x—7 13 0
Avery, P. Smith (1), Leibrandt (5), Freeman (6), Mercker (8); Walk. W—Walk. L—Avery.
Game 6—October 13, at Atlanta
Pitt. ....0 8 0 0 4 1 0 0 0—13 13 1
Atlanta ....0 0 0 1 0 0 1 0 2— 4 9 1
Wakefield; Glavine, Leibrandt (2), Freeman (5), Mercker (7), Wohlers (9). W—Wakefield. L—Glavine. HR—Bonds, Bell, McClendon (Pit.); Justice 2 (Atl.).
Game 7—October 14, at Atlanta
Pitt. ....1 0 0 0 0 1 0 0 0—2 7 1
Atlanta ....0 0 0 0 0 0 0 0 3—3 7 0
Drabek, Belinda (9); Smoltz, Stanton (7), P. Smith (7), Avery (7), Reardon (9). W—Reardon. L—Drabek.

WORLD SERIES

■ **Winner:** Toronto brought a baseball championship to Canada and the Braves failed to give Atlanta its long-awaited title for the second year in a row.
■ **Turning point:** The Blue Jays took a three-games-to-one advantage with a 2-1 victory in Game 4, thanks to the combined five-hit pitching of Jimmy Key, Duane Ward and Tom Henke and a home run by Pat Borders.
■ **Memorable moment:** Dave Winfield's two-run double in the 11th inning of Game 6 , which gave Toronto a 4-3 Series-clinching win.
■ **Top guns:** Key (2-0, 1.00 ERA), Borders (.450), Joe Carter (2 HR), Blue Jays; Deion Sanders (.533), Braves.
■ **MVP:** Borders.

Linescores
Game 1—October 17, at Atlanta
Tor. ....0 0 0 1 0 0 0 0 0—1 4 0
Atl. ....0 0 0 0 0 3 0 0 x—3 4 0
Morris, Stottlemyre (7), Wells (8); Glavine. W—Glavine. L—Morris. HR—Carter (Tor.); Berryhill (Atl.).
Game 2—October 18, at Atlanta
Tor. ....0 0 0 0 2 0 0 1 2—5 9 2
Atl. ....0 1 0 1 2 0 0 0 0—4 5 1
Cone, Wells (5), Stottlemyre (7), Ward (8), Henke (9); Smoltz, Stanton (8), Reardon (8). W—Ward. L—Reardon. S—Henke. HR—Sprague (Tor.).
Game 3—October 20, at Toronto
Atl. ....0 0 0 0 0 1 0 1 0—2 9 0
Tor. ....0 0 0 1 0 0 0 1 1—3 6 1
Avery, Wohlers (9), Stanton (9), Reardon (9); Guzman, Ward (9). W—Ward. L—Avery. HR—Carter, Gruber (Tor.).
Game 4—October 21, at Toronto
Atl. ....0 0 0 0 0 0 0 1 0—1 5 0
Tor. ....0 0 1 0 0 0 1 0 x—2 6 0
Glavine; Key, Ward (8), Henke (9). W—Key. L—Glavine. S—Henke. HR—Borders (Tor.).
Game 5—October 22, at Toronto
Atl. ....1 0 0 1 5 0 0 0 0—7 13 0
Tor. ....0 1 0 1 0 0 0 0 0—2 6 0
Smoltz, Stanton (7); Morris, Wells (5), Timlin (7), Eichhorn (8), Stottlemyre (9). W—Smoltz. L—Morris. S—Stanton. HR—Justice, L. Smith (Atl.).
Game 6—October 24, at Atlanta
Tor. ..1 0 0 1 0 0 0 0 0 0 2—4 14 1
Atl. ..0 0 1 0 0 0 0 0 1 0 1—3 8 1
Cone, Stottlemyre (7), Wells (7), Ward (8), Henke (9), Key (10), Timlin (11); Avery, P. Smith (5), Stanton (8), Wohlers (9), Leibrandt (10). W—Key. L—Leibrandt. S—Timlin. HR—Maldonado (Tor.).

FINAL STANDINGS

American League

East Division

Team	Tor.	N.Y.	Det.	Bal.	Bos.	Cle.	Mil.	Chi.	Tex.	K.C.	Sea.	Min.	Cal.	Oak.	W	L	Pct.	GB
Toronto	...	8	7	8	10	9	8	6	5	4	5	10	8	7	95	67	.586	...
New York	5	...	9	7	7	7	9	8	3	6	7	8	6	6	88	74	.543	7
Detroit	6	4	...	8	7	7	8	5	6	5	7	6	8	8	85	77	.525	10
Baltimore	5	6	5	...	6	8	8	4	4	7	7	8	7	10	85	77	.525	10
Boston	3	6	6	7	...	5	5	7	6	5	7	7	7	9	80	82	.494	15
Cleveland	4	6	6	5	8	...	8	3	7	7	3	4	7	8	76	86	.469	19
Milwaukee	5	4	5	5	8	5	...	3	4	7	4	7	5	7	69	93	.426	26

West Division

Team	Chi.	Tex.	K.C.	Sea.	Min.	Cal.	Oak.	Tor.	N.Y.	Det.	Bal.	Bos.	Cle.	Mil.	W	L	Pct.	GB
Chicago	...	8	6	9	10	6	7	6	4	7	8	5	9	9	94	68	.580	...
Texas	5	...	6	5	6	7	8	7	9	6	8	6	5	8	86	76	.531	8
Kansas City	7	7	...	7	7	7	6	8	6	7	5	7	5	5	84	78	.519	10
Seattle	4	8	6	...	9	7	4	7	5	5	5	5	9	8	82	80	.506	12
Minnesota	3	7	6	4	...	9	8	2	4	6	4	5	8	5	71	91	.438	23
California	7	6	6	6	4	...	6	4	6	4	5	5	5	7	71	91	.438	23
Oakland	6	5	7	9	5	7	...	5	6	4	2	3	4	5	68	94	.420	26

National League

East Division

Team	Phi.	Mon.	St.L.	Chi.	Pit.	Fla.	N.Y.	Atl.	S.F.	Hou.	L.A.	Cin.	Col.	S.D.	W	L	Pct.	GB
Philadelphia	...	7	8	6	7	9	10	6	4	7	10	8	9	6	97	65	.599	...
Montreal	6	...	7	8	8	8	9	5	3	7	6	8	9	10	94	68	.580	3
St. Louis	5	6	...	5	9	9	8	6	8	6	6	7	7	5	87	75	.537	10
Chicago	7	5	8	...	5	6	8	5	6	4	7	7	8	8	84	78	.519	13
Pittsburgh	6	5	4	8	...	7	9	5	5	5	4	4	4	9	75	87	.463	22
Florida	4	5	4	7	6	...	4	5	4	3	5	5	5	7	64	98	.395	33
New York	3	4	5	5	4	9	...	3	4	1	4	6	6	5	59	103	.364	38

West Division

Team	Atl.	S.F.	Hou.	L.A.	Cin.	Col.	S.D.	Phi.	Mon.	St.L.	Chi.	Pit.	Fla.	N.Y.	W	L	Pct.	GB
Atlanta	...	7	8	8	10	13	9	6	7	6	7	7	7	9	104	58	.642	...
San Fran.	6	...	10	6	11	10	10	8	9	4	6	7	8	8	103	59	.636	1
Houston	5	3	...	9	7	2	8	5	5	6	8	7	9	11	85	77	.525	19
Los Angeles	5	7	4	...	8	6	9	2	6	6	5	8	7	8	81	81	.500	23
Cincinnati	3	2	6	5	...	9	9	4	4	5	5	8	7	6	73	89	.451	31
Colorado	0	3	11	7	4	...	6	3	3	5	4	8	7	6	67	95	.414	37
San Diego	4	3	5	4	4	7	...	6	2	7	4	3	5	7	61	101	.377	43

LEADERS

American League
BA: John Olerud, Tor., .363.
Runs: Rafael Palmeiro, Tex., 124.
Hits: Paul Molitor, Tor., 211.
TB: Ken Griffey, Jr., Sea., 359.
HR: Juan Gonzalez, Tex., 46.
RBI: Albert Belle, Cle., 129.
SB: Kenny Lofton, Cle., 70.
Wins: Jack McDowell, Chi., 22.
ERA: Kevin Appier, K.C., 2.56.
CG: Chuck Finley, Cal., 13.
IP: Cal Eldred, Mil., 258.
SO: Randy Johnson, Sea., 308.
SV: Jeff Montgomery, K.C.;
Duane Ward, Tor., 45.

National League
BA: Andres Galarraga, Col., .370.
Runs: Lenny Dykstra, Phil., 143.
Hits: Lenny Dykstra, Phil., 194.
HR: Barry Bonds, S.F., 46.
RBI: Barry Bonds, S.F., 123.
SB: Chuck Carr, Fla., 58.
Wins: John Burkett, S.F.;
Tom Glavine, Atl., 22.
ERA: Greg Maddux, Atl., 2.36.
CG: Greg Maddux, Atl., 8.
IP: Greg Maddux, Atl., 267.
SO: Jose Rijo, Cin., 227.
SV: Randy Myers, Chi., 53.

A.L. 20-game winner
Jack McDowell, Chi., 22-10

N.L. 20-game winners
Tom Glavine, Atl., 22-6
John Burkett, S.F., 22-7
Bill Swift, S.F., 21-8
Greg Maddux, Atl., 20-10

A.L. 100 RBIs
Albert Belle, Cle., 129
Frank Thomas, Chi., 128
Joe Carter, Tor., 121
Juan Gonzalez, Tex., 118
Cecil Fielder, Det., 117
Carlos Baerga, Cle., 114
Chili Davis, Cal., 112
Paul Molitor, Tor., 111
Mickey Tettleton, Det., 110
Ken Griffey Jr., Sea., 109
John Olerud, Tor., 107
Rafael Palmeiro, Tex., 105
Danny Tartabull, N.Y., 102
Mo Vaughn, Bos., 101
Ruben Sierra, Oak., 101

N.L. 100 RBIs
Barry Bonds, S.F., 123
David Justice, Atl., 120
Ron Gant, Atl., 117
Mike Piazza, L.A., 112
Matt Williams, S.F., 110
Darren Daulton, Phil., 105
Todd Zeile, St.L., 103
Fred McGriff, S.D.-Atl., 101
Eddie Murray, N.Y., 100
Phil Plantier, S.D., 100

A.L. 40 homers
Juan Gonzalez, Tex., 46
Ken Griffey Jr., Sea., 45
Frank Thomas, Chi., 41

N.L. 40 homers
Barry Bonds, S.F., 46
David Justice, Atl., 40

Most Valuable Player
A.L.: Frank Thomas, 1B, Chi.
N.L.: Barry Bonds, OF, S.F.

Cy Young Award
A.L.: Jack McDowell, Chi.
N.L.: Greg Maddux, Atl.

Rookie of the Year
A.L.: Tim Salmon, OF, Cal.
N.L.: Mike Piazza, C, L.A.

Manager of the Year
A.L.: Gene Lamont, Chi.
N.L.: Dusty Baker, S.F.

Hall of Fame addition
Reggie Jackson, OF, 1967-87

SIGNIFICANT EVENTS

■ **March 22:** Cleveland players Steve Olin and Tim Crews were killed and pitcher Bob Ojeda was seriously injured in a spring training boating accident near Orlando, Fla.
■ **September 9:** Owners and players agreed to split the A.L. and N.L. into three divisions and expand the number of playoff qualifiers from four to eight teams.
■ **October 3:** The Braves clinched the N.L. West Division title with a final-day 5-3 victory over Colorado while the Giants were losing to the Dodgers, 12-1.

MEMORABLE MOMENTS

■ **July 28:** Seattle's Ken Griffey Jr. tied a long-standing record when he homered in his eighth consecutive game—a 5-1 loss to Minnesota.
■ **July 28:** The Mets scored two ninth-inning runs against Florida, handing Anthony Young a 5-4 victory and ending his record 27-game losing streak.
■ **September 7:** St. Louis' Mark Whiten tied a pair of records when he hit four homers and drove in 12 runs in a 15-2 victory over Cincinnati.
■ **September 16:** Minnesota's Dave Winfield joined baseball's exclusive 3,000-hit club in a game against Oakland.

ALL-STAR GAME

■ **Winner:** Kirby Puckett fueled the high-powered A.L. offense to a 9-3 victory — its sixth straight.
■ **Key inning:** The fifth. After hitting a solo home run in the second, Puckett contributed a run-scoring double in a three-run fifth that broke a 2-2 tie.
■ **Memorable moment:** Hard-throwing A.L. lefty Randy Johnson striking out John Kruk, who bailed out on three straight pitches, swinging feebly at the third.
■ **Top guns:** Johnson (Mariners), Puckett (Twins), Roberto Alomar (Blue Jays), Albert Belle (Indians), A.L.; Gary Sheffield (Marlins), Barry Bonds (Giants), N.L.
■ **MVP:** Puckett.

Linescore
July 13, at Baltimore's Camden Yards
N.L. ....2 0 0 0 0 1 0 0 0—3 7 2
A.L. ....0 1 1 0 3 3 1 0 x—9 11 0
Mulholland (Phillies), Benes (Padres) 3, Burkett (Giants) 5, Avery (Braves) 5, Smoltz (Braves) 6, Beck (Giants) 7, Harvey (Marlins) 8; Langston (Angels), Johnson (Mariners) 3, McDowell (White Sox) 5, Key (Yankees) 6, Montgomery (Royals) 7, Aguilera (Twins) 8, Ward (Blue Jays) 9. W—McDowell. L—Burkett. HR—Sheffield, N.L.; Puckett, Alomar, A.L.

ALCS

■ **Winner:** Toronto kept the A.L. pennant on Canadian soil and denied Chicago's bid for its first World Series appearance since 1959.
■ **Turning point:** The Blue Jays defeated the White Sox, 5-3, in the pivotal fifth game, which wasn't decided until reliever Duane Ward struck out Bo Jackson with a man on base in the ninth inning.
■ **Memorable moment:** A 6-3 finale in which Toronto's Dave Stewart lifted his LCS record to 8-0 and pitched his fourth pennant-clinching victory in six seasons.
■ **Top guns:** Stewart (2-0, 2.03 ERA), Juan Guzman (2-0, 2.08), Devon White (.444), Blue Jays; Tim Raines (.444), White Sox.
■ **MVP:** Stewart.

Linescores
Game 1—October 5, at Chicago
Toronto......0 0 0 2 3 0 2 0 0—7 17 1
Chicago......0 0 0 3 0 0 0 0 0—3 6 1
Guzman, Cox (7), Ward (9); McDowell, DeLeon (7), Radinsky (8), McCaskill (9). W—Guzman. L—McDowell. HR—Molitor (Tor.).

Game 2—October 6, at Chicago
Toronto........1 0 0 2 0 0 0 0 0—3 8 0
Chicago........1 0 0 0 0 0 0 0 0—1 7 2
Stewart, Leiter (7), Ward (9); A. Fernandez, Hernandez (9). W—Stewart. L—A. Fernandez. S—Ward.

Game 3—October 8, at Toronto
Chicago......0 0 5 1 0 0 0 0 0—6 12 0
Toronto......0 0 1 0 0 0 0 0 0—1 7 1
Alvarez; Hentgen, Cox (4), Eichhorn (7), Castillo (9). W—Alvarez. L—Hentgen.

Game 4—October 9, at Toronto
Chicago......0 2 0 0 0 3 1 0 1—7 11 0
Toronto......0 0 3 0 0 1 0 0 0—4 9 0
Bere, Belcher (3), McCaskill (7), Radinsky (8), Hernandez (9); Stottlemyre, Leiter (7), Timlin (7). W—Belcher. L—Stottlemyre. S—Hernandez. HR—Thomas, Johnson (Chi.).

Game 5—October 10, at Toronto
Chicago......0 0 0 0 1 0 0 0 2—3 5 1
Toronto ......1 1 1 1 0 0 1 0 x—5 14 0
McDowell, DeLeon (3), Radinsky (7), Hernandez (7); Guzman, Castillo (8), Ward (9). W—Guzman. L—McDowell. HR—Burks, Ventura (Chi.).

Game 6—October 12, at Chicago
Toronto......0 2 0 1 0 0 0 0 3—6 10 0
Chicago......0 0 2 0 0 0 0 0 1—3 5 3
Stewart, Ward (8); A. Fernandez, McCaskill (8), Radinsky (9), Hernandez (9). W—Stewart. L—A. Fernandez. S—Ward. HR—White (Tor.); Newson (Chi.).

NLCS

■ **Winner:** Philadelphia needed six games to ruin Atlanta's bid for a third consecutive pennant.
■ **Turning point:** The pivotal fifth game, when Curt Schilling pitched eight innings of four-hit ball and Lenny Dykstra hit a game-winning 10th-inning home run.
■ **Memorable moment:** The ninth inning of Game 6. Phillies lefthander Mitch Williams, also known as "Wild Thing," pulled a shocker when he retired the Braves 1-2-3 for his second series save and a 6-3 pennant-clinching victory.
■ **Top guns:** Schilling (1.69 ERA), Williams (2-0, 2 saves, 1.69), Dykstra (2 HR), Phillies; Fred McGriff (.435), Otis Nixon (.348), Terry Pendleton (.346), Braves.
■ **MVP:** Schilling.

Linescores
Game 1—October 6, at Philadelphia
Atlanta ....0 0 1 1 0 0 0 0 1 0—3 9 0
Phil. ....1 0 0 1 0 1 0 0 0 1—4 9 1
Avery, Mercker (7), McMichael (9); Schilling, Williams (9). W—Williams. L—McMichael. HR—Incaviglia (Phil.).
Game 2—October 7, at Philadelphia
Atlanta ....2 0 6 0 1 0 0 4 1—14 16 0
Phil. ....0 0 0 2 0 0 0 0 1— 3 7 2
Maddux, Stanton (8), Wohlers (9); Greene, Thigpen (3), Rivera (4), Mason (6), West (8), Andersen (9). W—Maddux. L—Greene. HR—McGriff, Blauser, Berryhill, Pendleton (Atl.); Hollins, Dykstra (Phil.).
Game 3—October 9, at Atlanta
Phil. ....0 0 0 1 0 1 0 1 1—4 10 1
Atlanta........0 0 0 0 0 5 4 0 x—9 12 0
Mulholland, Mason (6), Andersen (7), West (7), Thigpen (8); Glavine, Mercker (8), McMichael (9). W—Glavine. L—Mulholland. HR—Kruk (Phil.)
Game 4—October 10, at Atlanta
Phil. ....0 0 0 2 0 0 0 0 0—2 8 1
Atlanta ......0 1 0 0 0 0 0 0 0—1 10 1
Jackson, Williams (8); Smoltz, Mercker (7), Wohlers (8). W—Jackson. L—Smoltz. S—Williams.
Game 5—October 11, at Atlanta
Phil. ....1 0 0 1 0 0 0 0 1 1—4 6 1
Atlanta ....0 0 0 0 0 0 0 0 3 0—3 7 1
Schilling, Williams (9), Andersen (10); Avery, Mercker (8), McMichael (9), Wohlers (10). W—Williams. L—Wohlers. S—Andersen. HR—Daulton, Dykstra (Phil.).
Game 6—October 13, at Philadelphia
Atlanta ....0 0 0 0 1 0 2 0 0—3 5 3
Phil. ....0 0 2 0 2 2 0 0 x—6 7 1
Maddux, Mercker (6), McMichael (7), Wohlers (7); Greene, West (8), Williams (9). W—Greene. L—Maddux. S—Williams. HR—Hollins (Phil.); Blauser (Atl.).

WORLD SERIES

■ **Winner:** Toronto defeated Philadelphia to become the first back-to-back Series winner since the Yankees of 1977-78.
■ **Turning point:** The Blue Jays' six-run, eighth-inning rally that turned a 14-9 Game 4 deficit into a 15-14 victory and a 3-1 Series lead.
■ **Memorable moment:** Joe Carter's three-run, ninth-inning home run that turned a 6-5 Game 6 deficit into one of the most dramatic victories in World Series history.
■ **Top guns:** Paul Molitor (.500, 2 HR, 8 RBIs), Roberto Alomar (.480), Tony Fernandez (.333, 9 RBIs), Carter (2 HR, 8 RBIs), Blue Jays; Lenny Dykstra (.348, 4 HR, 8 RBIs), John Kruk (.348), Phillies.
■ **MVP:** Molitor.

Linescores
Game 1—October 16, at Toronto
Phil. ....2 0 1 0 1 0 0 0 1—5 11 1
Toronto ......0 2 1 0 1 1 3 0 x—8 10 3
Schilling, West (7), Andersen (7), Mason (8); Guzman, Leiter (6), Ward (8). W—Leiter. L—Schilling. S—Ward. HR—White, Olerud (Tor.).
Game 2—October 17, at Toronto
Phil. ....0 0 5 0 0 0 1 0 0—6 12 0
Toronto ......0 0 0 2 0 1 0 1 0—4 8 0
Mulholland, Mason (6), Williams (7); Stewart, Castillo (7), Eichhorn (8), Timlin (8). W—Mulholland. L—Stewart. S—Williams. HR—Carter (Tor.); Dykstra, Eisenreich (Phil.).
Game 3—October 19, at Philadelphia
Toronto ....3 0 1 0 0 1 3 0 2—10 13 1
Phil. ....0 0 0 0 1 0 1 0 1— 3 9 0
Hentgen, Cox (7), Ward (9); Jackson, Rivera (6), Thigpen (7), Andersen (9). W—Hentgen. L—Jackson. HR—Thompson (Phil.); Molitor (Tor.).
Game 4—October 20, at Philadelphia
Toronto ....3 0 4 0 0 2 0 6 0—15 18 0
Phil. ....4 2 0 1 5 1 1 0 0—14 14 0
Stottlemyre, Leiter (3), Castillo (5), Timlin (8), Ward (8); Greene, Mason (3), West (6), Andersen (7), Williams (8), Thigpen (9). W—Castillo. L—Williams. S—Ward. HR—Dykstra 2, Daulton (Phil.).
Game 5—October 21, at Philadelphia
Toronto ....0 0 0 0 0 0 0 0 0—0 5 1
Phil. ....1 1 0 0 0 0 0 0 x—2 5 1
Guzman, Cox (8); Schilling. W—Schilling. L—Guzman.
Game 6—October 23, at Toronto
Phil. ....0 0 0 1 0 0 5 0 0—6 7 0
Toronto ......3 0 0 1 1 0 0 0 3—8 10 2
Mulholland, Mason (6), West (8), Andersen (8), Williams (9); Stewart, Cox (7), Leiter (7), Ward (9). W—Ward. L—Williams. HR—Molitor, Carter (Tor.); Dykstra (Phil.).

FINAL STANDINGS

American League

East Division

Team	N.Y.	Bal.	Tor.	Bos.	Det.	Chi.	Cle.	K.C.	Min.	Mil.	Tex.	Oak.	Sea.	Cal.	W	L	Pct.	GB
New York	...	6	3	7	3	2	9	2	5	7	3	7	8	8	70	43	.619	...
Baltimore	4	...	7	4	3	2	4	4	4	7	3	7	6	8	63	49	.563	6.5
Toronto	4	2	...	3	4	3	4	6	8	3	8	1	5	4	55	60	.478	16
Boston	3	2	7	...	4	2	3	4	1	5	1	9	6	7	54	61	.470	17
Detroit	3	4	5	2	...	4	2	4	3	6	5	5	6	4	53	62	.461	18

Central Division

Team	Chi.	Cle.	K.C.	Min.	Mil.	N.Y.	Bal.	Tor.	Bos.	Det.	Tex.	Oak.	Sea.	Cal.	W	L	Pct.	GB
Chicago	...	7	3	9	4	4	2	4	8	4	6	9	5		67	46	.593	...
Cleveland	5	...	1	9	5	0	6	6	7	8	5	6	3	5	66	47	.584	1
Kansas City	7	4	...	6	5	4	1	6	2	8	4	7	6	4	64	51	.557	4
Minnesota	4	3	4	...	6	4	5	4	8	3	4	2	3	3	53	60	.469	14
Milwaukee	3	2	7	6	...	2	3	7	5	4	3	4	4	3	53	62	.461	15

West Division

Team	Tex.	Oak.	Sea.	Cal.	N.Y.	Bal.	Tor.	Bos.	Det.	Chi.	Cle.	K.C.	Min.	Mil.	W	L	Pct.	GB
Texas	...	3	1	4	2	3	4	5	7	5	7	3	5	3	52	62	.456	...
Oakland	7	...	4	6	5	5	5	3	4	3	0	3	5	1	51	63	.447	1
Seattle	9	3	...	7	4	4	1	6	3	1	2	4	3	2	49	63	.438	2
California	6	3	2	...	4	4	3	5	3	5	0	6	3	3	47	68	.409	5.5

National League

East Division

Team	Mon.	Atl.	N.Y.	Phi.	Fla.	Cin.	Hou.	Pit.	St.L.	Chi.	L.A.	S.F.	Col.	S.D.	W	L	Pct.	GB
Montreal	...	5	4	5	7	2	4	8	7	4	9	5	2	12	74	40	.649	...
Atlanta	4	...	5	6	8	5	3	3	5	4	6	5	8	6	68	46	.596	6
New York	3	4	...	4	4	4	3	4	6	4	6	6	1	6	55	58	.487	18.5
Philadelphia	4	3	6	...	6	2	1	5	4	6	5	4	1	6	54	61	.470	20.5
Florida	2	4	6	4	...	5	2	1	3	5	3	2	9	5	51	64	.443	23.5

Central Division

Team	Cin.	Hou.	Pit.	St.L.	Chi.	Mon.	Atl.	N.Y.	Phi.	Fla.	L.A.	S.F.	Col.	S.D.	W	L	Pct.	GB
Cincinnati	...	4	9	2	7	4	5	4	7	3	7	4	8		66	48	.579	...
Houston	6	...	8	8	3	2	3	3	5	4	1	8	5	5	66	49	.574	.5
Pittsburgh	3	4	...	5	5	2	9	5	4	6	3	1	3	3	53	61	.465	13
St. Louis	2	4	5	...	5	3	7	3	3	7	4	4	4	2	53	61	.465	13
Chicago	5	4	5	5	...	2	2	1	1	4	3	5	6	6	49	64	.434	16.5

West Division

Team	L.A.	S.F.	Col.	S.D.	Mon.	Atl.	N.Y.	Phi.	Fla.	Cin.	Hou.	Pit.	St.L.	Chi.	W	L	Pct.	GB
Los Angeles	...	5	6	6	3	0	6	7	3	6	8	3	2	3	58	56	.509	...
San Fran.	5	...	7	2	7	1	6	8	4	2	2	5	2	4	55	60	.478	3.5
Colorado	4	3	...	5	4	2	5	2	3	4	5	2	8	6	53	64	.453	6.5
San Diego	4	5	5	...	0	1	6	8	1	2	5	3	4	3	47	70	.402	12.5

SIGNIFICANT EVENTS

■ **March 1, June 7:** The N.L. elected Leonard Coleman as its new president and the A.L. opted for Gene Budig.

■ **April 4, 11:** Two parks were dedicated: The Indians needed 11 innings to beat Seattle, 4-3, in their Jacobs Field opener and the Rangers lost their debut at The Ballpark in Arlington to Milwaukee, 4-3.

■ **August 12:** Major League players brought the season to a skidding halt when they called a general strike—baseball's eighth work stoppage since 1972.

■ **September 14:** Baseball owners announced cancellation of the regular season and Post Season, rubber-stamping the first uncompleted season in the game's long history.

■ **December 28:** The Astros and Padres completed a 12-player trade, baseball's largest since 1957.

Despite the short season and a late injury, hot-hitting Houston first baseman Jeff Bagwell drove in a Major League-leading 116 runs.

Atlanta righthander Greg Maddux claimed the third of his four consecutive Cy Young Awards during the strike-shortened season.

MEMORABLE MOMENTS

■ **April 4:** Tuffy Rhodes became the first player to homer in his first three Opening Day at-bats, but the Cubs still dropped a 12-8 decision to the Mets.

■ **July 8:** Boston shortstop John Valentin pulled off baseball's 10th unassisted triple play and the Red Sox beat Seattle, 4-3.

■ **July 28:** When Kenny Rogers retired all 27 Minnesota hitters in a 4-0 victory, he became the first A.L. lefthander to throw a perfect game.

■ **August 1:** Cal Ripken stretched his ironman streak to 2,000 games and the Orioles celebrated with a 1-0 victory over Minnesota.

■ **August 6:** The Mariners routed Kansas City, 11-2, and ended the Royals' winning streak at 14 games.

LEADERS

American League
BA: Paul O'Neill, N.Y., .359.
Runs: Frank Thomas, Chi., 106.
Hits: Kenny Lofton, Cle., 160.
TB: Albert Belle, Cle., 294.
HR: Ken Griffey, Jr., Sea., 40.
RBI: Kirby Puckett, Min., 112.
SB: Lofton, Cle., 60.
Wins: Jimmy Key, N.Y., 17.
ERA: Steve Ontiveros, Oak., 2.65.
CG: Randy Johnson, Sea., 9.
IP: Chuck Finley, Cal., 183.1.
SO: Randy Johnson, Sea., 204.
SV: Lee Smith, Bal., 33.

National League
BA: Tony Gwynn, S.D., .394.
Runs: Jeff Bagwell, Hou., 104.
Hits: Gwynn, S.D., 165.
TB: Bagwell, Hou., 300.
HR: Matt Williams, S.F., 43.
RBI: Bagwell, Hou., 116.
SB: Craig Biggio, Hou., 39.
Wins: Ken Hill, Mon.; Greg Maddux, Atl., 16.
ERA: Greg Maddux, Atl., 1.56.
CG: Maddux, Atl., 10.
IP: Maddux, Atl., 202.
SO: Andy Benes, S.D., 189.
SV: John Franco, N.Y., 30.

A.L. 100 RBIs
Kirby Puckett, Min., 112
Joe Carter, Tor., 103
Albert Belle, Cle., 101
Frank Thomas, Chi., 101

N.L. 100 RBIs
Jeff Bagwell, Hou., 116

A.L. 40 homers
Ken Griffey Jr., Sea., 40

N.L. 40 homers
Matt Williams, S.F., 43

Most Valuable Player
A.L.: Frank Thomas, 1B, Chi.
N.L.: Jeff Bagwell, 1B, Hou.

Cy Young Award
A.L.: David Cone, K.C.
N.L.: Greg Maddux, Atl.

Rookie of the Year
A.L.: Bob Hamelin, DH, K.C.
N.L.: Raul Mondesi, OF, L.A.

Manager of the Year
A.L.: Buck Showalter, N.Y.
N.L.: Felipe Alou, Mon.

Hall of Fame additions
Steve Carlton, P, 1965-88
Leo Durocher, manager
Phil Rizzuto, SS, 1941-56

ALL-STAR GAME

■ **Winner:** The N.L. scored two runs in the ninth and one in the 10th to snap the A.L.'s six-game All-Star winning streak with an 8-7 victory.

■ **Key inning:** The 10th, when the N.L. scored its winning run on a single by Tony Gwynn and a game-ending double by Moises Alou.

■ **Memorable moment:** Fred McGriff's two-run, game-tying homer in the ninth off relief ace Lee Smith.

■ **Top guns:** Ken Hill (Expos), Gwynn (Padres), Alou (Expos), Marquis Grissom (Expos), McGriff (Braves), Gregg Jefferies (Cardinals), N.L.; Ken Griffey Jr. (Mariners), Kenny Lofton (Indians), Frank Thomas (White Sox), A.L.

■ **MVP:** McGriff.

Linescore
July 12, at Pittsburgh's Three Rivers Stadium
A.L........1 0 0 0 0 3 3 0 0—7 15 0
N.L........1 0 3 0 0 1 0 0 2 1—8 12 1
Key (Yankees), Cone (Royals) 3, Mussina (Orioles) 5, Johnson (Mariners) 6, Hentgen (Blue Jays) 7, Alvarez (White Sox) 8, L. Smith (Orioles) 9, Bere (White Sox) 10; Maddux (Braves), Hill (Expos) 4, Drabek (Astros) 6, Hudek (Astros) 7, Jackson (Phillies) 7, Beck (Giants) 7, Myers (Cubs) 9, Jones (Phillies) 10. W—Jones. L—Bere. HR—Grissom, McGriff, N.L.

FINAL STANDINGS

American League

East Division

Team	Bos.	N.Y.	Bal.	Det.	Tor.	Cle.	K.C.	Chi.	Mil.	Min.	Sea.	Cal.	Tex.	Oak.	W	L	Pct.	GB
Boston	...	5	9	8	8	6	3	5	8	5	7	11	3	8	86	58	.597	...
New York	8	...	7	8	12	6	7	2	6	4	4	5	6	4	79	65	.549	7
Baltimore	4	6	...	8	7	2	4	6	7	3	6	9	4	5	71	73	.493	15
Detroit	5	5	5	...	7	3	3	4	8	7	5	2	4	2	60	84	.417	26
Toronto	5	1	6	6	...	3	5	5	5	4	4	2	3	7	56	88	.389	30

Central Division

Team	Cle.	K.C.	Chi.	Mil.	Min.	Bos.	N.Y.	Bal.	Det.	Tor.	Sea.	Cal.	Tex.	Oak.	W	L	Pct.	GB
Cleveland	...	11	8	9	9	7	6	10	10	10	5	2	6	7	100	44	.694	...
Kansas City	1	...	5	10	6	2	3	5	4	7	7	7	8	5	70	74	.486	30
Chicago	5	8	...	6	10	3	3	1	8	6	4	2	5	7	68	76	.472	32
Milwaukee	4	2	7	...	9	4	5	5	5	7	3	2	5	7	65	79	.451	35
Minnesota	4	7	3	4	...	4	3	6	5	1	4	5	5	5	56	88	.389	44

West Division

Team	Sea.	Cal.	Tex.	Oak.	Bos.	N.Y.	Bal.	Det.	Tor.	Cle.	K.C.	Chi.	Mil.	Min.	W	L	Pct.	GB
Seattle	...	6	10	6	5	9	7	5	3	4	5	9	2	8	79	66	.545	...
California	7	...	6	6	3	7	4	6	8	3	5	10	5	8	78	67	.538	1
Texas	3	7	...	8	4	3	1	8	9	3	6	7	7	8	74	70	.514	4.5
Oakland	7	7	5	...	4	9	7	3	3	0	8	5	2	7	67	77	.465	11.5

National League

East Division

Team	Atl.	Phi.	N.Y.	Fla.	Mon.	Cin.	Hou.	Chi.	St.L.	Pit.	L.A.	Col.	S.D.	S.F.	W	L	Pct.	GB
Atlanta	...	7	5	10	9	8	6	8	7	4	5	9	5	7	90	54	.625	...
Philadelphia	6	...	6	7	5	3	7	1	5	6	9	2	6	6	69	75	.479	21
New York	8	7	...	6	6	5	6	3	3	4	6	4	6	5	69	75	.479	21
Florida	3	6	7	...	6	6	8	4	4	5	3	7	3	5	67	76	.469	22.5
Montreal	4	8	7	7	...	4	3	5	4	4	5	1	7	7	66	78	.458	24

Central Division

Team	Cin.	Hou.	Chi.	St.L.	Pit.	Atl.	Phi.	N.Y.	Fla.	Mon.	L.A.	Col.	S.D.	S.F.	W	L	Pct.	GB
Cincinnati	...	12	7	8	8	5	9	7	6	8	4	5	3	3	85	59	.590	...
Houston	1	...	8	9	9	6	5	6	4	9	3	4	7	5	76	68	.528	9
Chicago	3	5	...	9	8	4	6	4	8	3	7	6	5	5	73	71	.507	12
St. Louis	5	4	4	...	7	5	4	4	3	3	5	7	5	6	62	81	.434	22.5
Pittsburgh	5	4	5	6	...	2	3	3	8	4	4	4	4	6	58	86	.403	27

West Division

Team	L.A.	Col.	S.D.	S.F.	Atl.	Phi.	N.Y.	Fla.	Mon.	Cin.	Hou.	Chi.	St.L.	Pit.	W	L	Pct.	GB
Los Angeles	...	9	7	8	4	4	6	7	7	3	2	5	7	9	78	66	.542	...
Colorado	4	...	9	8	4	4	5	5	7	7	4	7	5	8	77	67	.535	1
San Diego	6	4	...	6	2	6	7	2	5	6	4	7	7	8	70	74	.486	8
San Fran.	5	5	7	...	1	6	8	3	6	3	3	7	7	6	67	77	.465	11

LEADERS

American League
BA: Edgar Martinez, Sea., .356.
Runs: Albert Belle, Cle.; Edgar Martinez, Sea., 121.
Hits: Lance Johnson, Chi., 186.
TB: Albert Belle, Cle., 377.
HR: Albert Belle, Cle., 50.
RBI: Albert Belle, Cle.; Mo Vaughn, Bos., 126.
SB: Kenny Lofton, Cle., 54.
Wins: Mike Mussina, Bal., 19.
ERA: Randy Johnson, Sea., 2.48.
CG: Jack McDowell, N.Y., 8.
IP: David Cone, Tor.-N.Y., 229.1.
SO: Randy Johnson, Sea., 294.
SV: Jose Mesa, Cle., 46.

National League
BA: Tony Gwynn, S.D., .368.
Runs: Craig Biggio, Hou., 123.
Hits: Dante Bichette, Col.; Tony Gwynn, S.D., 197.
TB: Dante Bichette, Col., 359.
HR: Dante Bichette, Col., 40.
RBI: Dante Bichette, Col., 128.
SB: Quilvio Veras, Fla., 56.
Wins: Greg Maddux, Atl., 19.
ERA: Greg Maddux, Atl., 1.63.
CG: Greg Maddux, Atl., 10.
IP: Greg Maddux, Atl.; Denny Neagle, Pit., 209.2.
SO: Hideo Nomo, L.A., 236.
SV: Randy Myers, Chi., 38.

A.L. 100 RBIs
Albert Belle, Cle., 126
Mo Vaughn, Bos., 126
Jay Buhner, Sea., 121
Edgar Martinez, Sea., 113
Tino Martinez, Sea., 111
Frank Thomas, Chi., 111
Jim Edmonds, Cal., 107
Manny Ramirez, Cle., 107
Tim Salmon, Cal., 105
Rafael Palmeiro, Bal., 104
J.T. Snow, Cal., 102
John Valentin, Bos., 102

N.L. 100 RBIs
Dante Bichette, Col., 128
Sammy Sosa, Chi., 119
Andres Galarraga, Col., 106
Jeff Conine, Fla., 105
Eric Karros, L.A., 105
Barry Bonds, S.F., 104
Larry Walker, Col., 101

A.L. 40 homers
Albert Belle, Cle., 50
Jay Buhner, Sea., 40
Frank Thomas, Chi., 40

N.L. 40 homers
Dante Bichette, Col., 40

Most Valuable Player
A.L.: Mo Vaughn, 1B, Bos.
N.L.: Barry Larkin, SS, Cin.

Cy Young Award
A.L.: Randy Johnson, Sea.
N.L.: Greg Maddux, Atl.

Rookie of the Year
A.L.: Marty Cordova, OF, Min.
N.L.: Hideo Nomo, P, L.A.

Manager of the Year
A.L.: Lou Piniella, Sea.
N.L.: Don Baylor, Col.

Hall of Fame additions
Richie Ashburn, OF, 1948-62
Leon Day, P, Negro Leagues
William Hulbert, Executive
Mike Schmidt, 3B, 1972-89
Vic Willis, P, 1898-1910

SIGNIFICANT EVENTS

■ **April 2:** Baseball owners, blocked by an injunction preventing them from imposing new work rules and using replacement players in the 1995 season, invited striking players to return to work, ending the 234-day work stoppage. Opening Day was pushed back to April 25 and the schedule was reduced to 144 games.

■ **April 30:** Major League Baseball agreed to a new contract with its umpires, ending a lockout that had extended a week into the regular season and forced use of replacement arbiters.

■ **March 9:** Major League owners approved expansion franchises for Tampa Bay (Devil Rays) and Phoenix (Arizona Diamondbacks), with play to begin in 1998.

■ **August 13:** Baseball was stung by the loss of former Yankee great Mickey Mantle, who died at age 63 of lung cancer.

■ **October 2:** Sparky Anderson, whose 2,194 managerial victories ranked third all-time to Connie Mack and John McGraw, retired after nine seasons with the Reds and 17 with the Tigers.

■ **November 13:** Atlanta righthander Greg Maddux won his record-setting fourth consecutive N.L. Cy Young after a 19-2, 1.63-ERA season. Maddux joined Steve Carlton as the only four-time Cy Young winners.

MEMORABLE MOMENTS

■ **June 3:** Montreal's Pedro Martinez pitched nine perfect innings before giving up a 10th-inning double to San Diego's Bip Roberts after the Expos had scored in the top of the inning. Martinez did not finish his 1-0 victory.

■ **June 30:** Cleveland's Eddie Murray joined baseball's 3,000-hit club when he singled off Minnesota righthander Mike Trombley.

■ **September 6:** Baltimore shortstop Cal Ripken passed Lou Gehrig's ironman streak when he played in his 2,131st consecutive game — a 4-2 victory over California at Camden Yards.

■ **September 8:** Cleveland defeated Baltimore 3-2 and clinched the team's first title of any kind in 41 years. The Indians' final 30-game A.L. Central Division margin over Kansas City was the largest in modern baseball history.

■ **October 2:** The Mariners defeated California 9-1 in a one-game playoff, giving Seattle its first division title in the franchise's 19-year history.

ALL-STAR GAME

■ **Winner:** The N.L. managed only three hits off seven A.L. pitchers, but all were solo home runs and produced an unlikely 3-2 victory.

■ **Key inning:** The seventh, when Los Angeles catcher Mike Piazza collected the N.L.'s second hit, a game-tying homer off Texas' Kenny Rogers, and Phillies reliever Heathcliff Slocumb pitched the N.L. out of a two-on, one-out jam.

■ **Memorable moment:** Pinch-hitter Jeff Conine's eighth-inning blast off Oakland's Steve Ontiveros, which broke the 2-2 tie and gave the N.L. its first lead. Conine became the 10th player to hit a homer in his first All-Star at-bat.

■ **Top guns:** Randy Johnson (Mariners), Kevin Appier (Royals), Frank Thomas (White Sox), Carlos Baerga (Indians), A.L.; Hideo Nomo (Dodgers), Slocumb (Phillies), Craig Biggio (Astros), Piazza (Dodgers), Conine (Marlins), N.L.

■ **MVP:** Conine.

Linescore

July 11, at Texas' The Ballpark in Arlington
N.L.................0 0 0 0 0 1 1 1 0—3 3 0
A.L.................0 0 0 2 0 0 0 0 0—2 8 0
Nomo (Dodgers), Smiley (Reds) 3, Green (Phillies) 5, Neagle (Pirates) 6, C. Perez (Expos) 7, Slocumb (Phillies) 7, Henke (Cardinals) 8, Myers (Cubs) 9; Johnson (Mariners), Appier (Royals) 3, Martinez (Indians) 5, Rogers (Rangers) 7, Ontiveros (A's) 8, Wells (Tigers) 8, Mesa (Indians) 9. W—Slocumb. L—Ontiveros. S—Myers. HR—Thomas, A.L.; Biggio, Piazza, Conine, N.L.

A.L. DIVISION SERIES

■ **Winners:** Cleveland swept past Boston, but Seattle needed five games and extra innings to defeat New York in baseball's inaugural Division Series. The Mariners could not secure victory until the 11th inning of Game 5.

■ **Turning points:** For Cleveland, catcher Tony Pena's Game 1-ending home run in the bottom of the 13th inning. For Seattle, Edgar Martinez's two-homer, seven-RBI Game 4 effort that kept the Mariners' title hopes alive.

■ **Memorable moments:** Martinez's tie-breaking eighth-inning grand slam in Game 4 and his Series-ending two-run double in the 11th inning of Game 5.

■ **Memorable performances:** The playoff-record five-home run effort of Seattle outfielder Ken Griffey and Martinez's 10-RBI effort.

Linescores

Cleveland vs. Boston

Game 1—October 3, at Cleveland
Bos. ....0 0 2 0 0 0 0 1 0 0 1 0 0—4 11 2
Cle.............0 0 0 0 0 3 0 0 0 0 1 0 1—5 10 2
Clemens, Cormier (8), Belinda (8), Stanton (8), Aguilera (11), Maddux (11), Smith (13); Martinez, Tavarez (7), Assenmacher (8), Plunk (8), Mesa (10), Poole (11), Hill (12). W—Hill. L—Smith. HR—Valentin, Alicea, Naehring (Bos.); Belle, Pena (Cle.).

Game 2—October 4, at Cleveland
Bos. ....0 0 0 0 0 0 0 0 0—0 3 1
Cle. ....0 0 0 0 2 0 0 2 x—4 4 2
Hanson; Hershiser, Tavarez (8), Assenmacher (8), Mesa (9). W—Hershiser. L—Hanson. HR—Murray (Cle.).

Game 3—October 6, at Boston
Cle. ....0 2 1 0 0 5 0 0 0—8 11 2
Bos. ....0 0 0 1 0 0 0 1 0—2 7 1
Nagy, Tavarez (8), Assenmacher (9); Wakefield, Cormier (6), Maddux (6), Hudson (9). W—Nagy. L—Wakefield. HR—Thome (Cle.).

Seattle vs. New York

Game 1—October 3, at New York
Seattle........0 0 0 1 0 1 2 0 2—6 9 0
N.Y. ....0 0 2 0 0 2 4 1 x—9 13 0
Bosio, Nelson (6), Ayala (7), Risley (7), Wells (8); Cone, Wetteland (9). W—Cone. L—Nelson. HR—Griffey 2 (Sea.); Boggs, Sierra (N.Y.).

Game 2—October 4, at New York
Seattle......0 0 1 0 0 1 2 0 0 0 0 1 0 0 0—5 16 2
N.Y...........0 0 0 0 1 2 1 0 0 0 0 1 0 0 2—7 11 0
Benes, Risley (6), Charlton (7), Nelson (11), Belcher (12); Pettitte, Wickman (8), Wetteland (9), Rivera (12). W—Rivera. L—Belcher. HR—Coleman, Griffey (Sea.); Sierra, Mattingly, O'Neill, Leyritz (N.Y.).

Game 3—October 6, at Seattle
N.Y. ....0 0 0 1 0 0 1 2 0—4 6 2
Seattle..........0 0 0 0 2 4 1 0 x—7 7 0
McDowell, Howe (6), Wickman (6), Hitchcock (7), Rivera (7); Johnson, Risley (8), Charlton (8). W—Johnson. L—McDowell. S—Charlton. HR—B. Williams 2, Stanley (N.Y.); T. Martinez (Sea.).

Game 4—October 7, at Seattle
N.Y...........3 0 2 0 0 0 0 1 2— 8 14 1
Seattle......0 0 4 0 1 1 0 5 x—11 16 0
Kamieniecki, Hitchcock (6), Wickman (7), Wetteland (8), Howe (8); Bosio, Nelson (3), Belcher (7), Charlton (8), Ayala (9), Risley (9). W—Charlton. L—Wetteland. S—Risley. HR—O'Neill (N.Y.); E. Martinez 2, Griffey, Buhner (Sea.).

Game 5—October 8, at Seattle
N.Y.......0 0 0 2 0 2 0 0 0 0 1—5 6 0
Seattle 0 0 1 1 0 0 0 2 0 0 2—6 15 0
Cone, Rivera (8), McDowell (9); Benes, Charlton (7), Johnson (9). W—Johnson. L—McDowell. HR—O'Neill (N.Y.); Cora, Griffey (Sea.).

N.L. DIVISION SERIES

■ **Winners:** Atlanta and Cincinnati powered past West Division opponents in the N.L.'s first Division Series.

■ **Turning points:** For the Braves, a four-run ninth-inning Game 2 rally that produced a 7-4 victory and a two-games-to-none edge over the Rockies. For the Reds, a 5-4 Game 2 victory, despite being outhit by the Dodgers, 14-6.

■ **Memorable moment:** Colorado pitcher Lance Painter striking out with the bases loaded in the ninth inning of a 5-4 Game 1 loss to the Braves. Painter was pinch-hitting because Colorado manager Don Baylor had no more position players on his bench.

■ **Top performances:** Atlanta third baseman Chipper Jones belted two Game 1 homers, including the game-winner in the top of the ninth inning; Braves first baseman Fred McGriff broke out of a slump with a two-homer, five-RBI Game 5 effort; Reds infielder Mark Lewis broke open Game 3 against the Dodgers with the first pinch-hit grand slam in playoff history.

Linescores

Atlanta vs. Colorado

Game 1—October 3, at Colorado
Atlanta ......0 0 1 0 0 2 0 1 1—5 12 1
Colorado....0 0 0 3 0 0 0 1 0—4 13 4
Maddux, McMichael (8), Pena (8), Wohlers (9); Ritz, Reed (6), Ruffin (7), Munoz (8), Holmes (8), Leskanic (9). W—Pena. L—Leskanic. S—Wohlers. HR—Jones 2, Grissom (Atl.); Castilla (Col.).

Game 2—October 4, at Colorado
Atlanta ......1 0 1 1 0 0 0 0 4—7 13 1
Colorado ....0 0 0 0 0 3 0 1 0—4 8 2
Glavine, Avery (8), Pena (8), Wohlers (9); Painter, Reed (6), Ruffin (7), Leskanic (8), Munoz (9), Holmes (9). W—Munoz. S—Wohlers. HR—Grissom 2 (Atl.); Walker (Col.).

Game 3—October 6, at Atlanta
Colorado......1 0 2 0 0 2 0 0 0 2—7 9 0
Atlanta ....0 0 0 3 0 0 1 0 1 0—5 11 0
Swift, Reed (7), Munoz (7), Leskanic (7), Ruffin (8), Holmes (9), Thompson (10); Smoltz, Clontz (6), Borbon (8), McMichael (9), Wohlers (10), Mercker (10). W—Holmes. L—Wohlers. S—Thompson. HR—Young, Castilla (Col.).

Game 4— October 7, at Atlanta
Colorado......0 0 3 0 0 1 0 0 0— 4 11 1
Atlanta ....0 0 4 2 1 3 0 0 x—10 15 0
Saberhagen, Ritz (5), Munoz (6), Reynoso (7), Ruffin (8), Maddux, Pena (8). W—Maddux. L—Saberhagen. HR—Bichette, Castilla (Col.); McGriff 2 (Atl.).

Cincinnati vs. Los Angeles

Game 1—October 3, at Los Angeles
Cincinnati ....4 0 0 0 3 0 0 0 0—7 12 0
Los Angeles ......0 0 0 0 1 1 0 0 0—2 8 0
Schourek, Jackson (8), Brantley (9); Martinez, Cummings (6), Astacio (6), Guthrie (8), Osuna (9). W—Schourek. L—Martinez. HR—Santiago (Cin.); Piazza (L.A.).

Game 2—October 4, at Los Angeles
Cincinnati ....0 0 0 2 0 0 0 1 2—5 6 0
Los Angeles ......1 0 0 1 0 0 0 0 2—4 14 2
Smiley, Burba (7), Jackson (8), Brantley (9); Valdes, Osuna (8), Tapani (9), Guthrie (9), Astacio (9). W—Burba. L—Osuna. S—Brantley. HR—Sanders (Cin.); Karros 2 (L.A.).

Game 3—October 6, at Cincinnati
Los Angeles ...0 0 0 1 0 0 0 0 0— 1 9 1
Cincinnati ....0 0 2 1 0 4 3 0 x—10 11 2
Nomo, Tapani (6), Guthrie (6), Astacio (6), Cummings (7), Osuna (7); Wells, Jackson (7), Brantley (9). W—Wells. L—Nomo. HR—Gant, Boone, M. Lewis (Cin.).

ALCS

■ **Winner:** The Cleveland Indians needed six games and a hard-fought victory over Seattle ace lefthander Randy Johnson to secure their first World Series berth in 41 years.

■ **Turning point:** With the intimidating Johnson scheduled to pitch Game 6 in Seattle, the Indians won the pivotal fifth game, 3-2, on Jim Thome's two-run sixth-inning homer. The victory gave them a three-games-to-two advantage.

■ **Memorable moment:** A two-run passed ball in the eighth inning of Cleveland's 4-0 pennant-clinching victory. Ruben Amaro scored from third base and speedy Kenny Lofton surprised the Mariners with a mad dash from second, extending the Indians' lead to 3-0.

■ **Top guns:** Orel Hershiser (2-0, 1.29 ERA), Lofton (.458, 5 SB), Carlos Baerga (.400), Thome (2 HR, 5 RBI), Indians; Ken Griffey (.333), Jay Buhner (3 HR, 5 RBI), Norm Charlton (1-0, 0.00, 1 sv), Mariners.

■ **MVP:** Hershiser.

Linescores
Game 1—October 10, at Seattle
Cleveland ....0 0 1 0 0 0 1 0 0—2 10 1
Seattle ....0 2 0 0 0 0 1 0 x—3 7 0
D. Martinez, Tavarez (7), Assenmacher (8), Plunk (8); Wolcott, Nelson (8), Charlton (8). W—Wolcott. L—D. Martinez. S—Charlton. HR—Belle (Cle.); Blowers (Sea.).

Game 2—October 11, at Seattle
Cleveland ....0 0 0 0 2 2 0 1 0—5 12 0
Seattle ....0 0 0 0 0 0 1 0 1—2 6 1
Hershiser, Mesa (9); Belcher, Ayala (6), Risley (9). W—Hershiser. L—Belcher. HR—Ramirez 2 (Cle.); Griffey, Buhner (Sea.).

Game 3—October 13, at Cleveland
Seattle ......0 1 1 0 0 0 0 0 0 0 3—5 9 1
Cleveland ..0 0 0 1 0 0 0 1 0 0 0—2 4 2
Johnson, Charlton (9); Nagy, Mesa, Tavarez

(10), Assenmacher (11), Plunk (11). W—Charlton. L—Tavarez. HR—Buhner 2 (Sea.).

Game 4—October 14, at Cleveland
Seattle ....0 0 0 0 0 0 0 0 0—0 6 1
Cleveland ....3 1 2 0 0 1 0 0 x—7 9 0
Benes, Wells (3), Ayala (6), Nelson (7), Risley (8); Hill, Poole (8), Ogea (9), Embree (9). W—Hill. L—Benes. HR—Murray, Thome (Cle.).

Game 5—October 15, at Cleveland
Seattle ....0 0 1 0 1 0 0 0 0—2 5 2
Cleveland ....1 0 0 0 0 2 0 0 x—3 10 4
Bosio, Nelson (6), Risley (7); Hershiser, Tavarez (7), Assenmacher (7), Plunk (8), Mesa (9). W—Hershiser. L—Bosio. S—Mesa. HR—Thome (Cle.).

Game 6—October 17, at Seattle
Cleveland ....0 0 0 0 1 0 0 3 0—4 8 0
Seattle ....0 0 0 0 0 0 0 0 0—0 4 1
D. Martinez, Tavarez (8), Mesa (9); Johnson, Charlton (8). W—D. Martinez. L—Johnson. HR—Baerga (Cle.).

NLCS

■ **Winner:** Atlanta pitchers limited Cincinnati to five total runs and the Braves swept past the Reds and claimed their third World Series berth of the decade.

■ **Turning point:** It came early, in the 11th inning of Game 1. Mike Devereaux singled home the winner in a 2-1 victory and the Braves cruised the rest of the way.

■ **Memorable moment:** A three-run, 10th-inning blast off the left-field foul pole by Atlanta catcher Javier Lopez that secured Atlanta's 6-2 victory in Game 2.

■ **Top guns:** Greg Maddux (1-0, 1.13 ERA), Steve Avery (1-0, 0.00), Fred McGriff (.438), Chipper Jones (.438), Lopez (.357), Devereaux (5 RBI), Braves; Barry Larkin (.389), Reds.

■ **MVP:** Devereaux.

Linescores
Game 1—October 10, at Cincinnati
Atlanta ......0 0 0 0 0 0 0 0 1 0 1—2 7 0
Cincinnati ..0 0 0 1 0 0 0 0 0 0 0—1 8 0
Glavine, Pena (8), Wohlers (9), Clontz (11), Avery (11), McMichael (11); Schourek, Brantley (9), Jackson (11). W—Wohlers. L—Jackson. S—McMichael.

Game 2—October 11, at Cincinnati
Atlanta ....1 0 0 1 0 0 0 0 0 4—6 11 1
Cincinnati ...0 0 0 0 2 0 0 0 0 0—2 9 1
Smoltz, Pena (8), McMichael (9), Wohlers (10); Smiley, Burba (6), Jackson (8), Brantley (9), Portugal (10). W—McMichael. L—Portugal. HR—Lopez (Atl.).

Game 3—October 13, at Atlanta
Cincinnati ....0 0 0 0 0 0 0 1 1—2 8 0
Atlanta ....0 0 0 0 0 3 2 0 x—5 12 1
Wells, Hernandez (7), Carrasco (7); Maddux, Wohlers (9). W—Maddux. L—Wells. HR: O'Brien, Jones (Atl.).

Game 4—October 14, at Atlanta
Cincinnati ....0 0 0 0 0 0 0 0 0—0 3 1
Atlanta ....0 0 1 0 0 0 0 5 x—6 12 1
Schourek, Jackson (7), Burba (7); Avery, McMichael (7), Pena (8), Wohlers (9). W—Avery. L—Schourek. HR—Devereaux (Atl.).

WORLD SERIES

■ **Winner:** The Braves needed six games to give Atlanta its first championship in any major sport and the franchise its first World Series title since 1957. The loss extended Cleveland's championship drought to 47 years.

■ **Turning point:** A two-run, sixth-inning homer by Javier Lopez in Game 2. It gave the Braves a 4-3 victory and put the Indians in a two-games-to-none hole.

■ **Memorable moment:** A Series-opening two-hitter by Braves ace Greg Maddux and a Series-closing combined one-hitter by Tom Glavine and Mark Wohlers. The 1-0 finale was decided by a Dave Justice home run.

■ **Top guns:** Glavine (2-0, 1.29 ERA), Wohlers (1.80, 2 sv), Marquis Grissom (.360), Ryan Klesko (.313, 3 HR), Braves; Albert Belle (2 HR), Indians.

■ **MVP:** Glavine.

Linescores
Game 1—October 21, at Atlanta
Cleveland ....1 0 0 0 0 0 0 0 1—2 2 0
Atlanta ....0 1 0 0 0 0 2 0 x—3 3 2
Hershiser, Assenmacher (7), Tavarez, Embree (8); Maddux. W—Maddux. L—Hershiser. HR—McGriff (Atl.).

Game 2—October 22, at Atlanta
Cleveland ....0 0 0 0 0 0 1 0 0—3 6 2
Atlanta ....0 0 2 0 0 2 0 0 x—4 8 2
Martinez, Embree (6), Poole (7), Tavarez (8); Glavine, McMichael (7), Pena (7), Wohlers (8). W—Glavine. L—Martinez. S—Wohlers. HR—Murray (Cle.), Lopez (Atl.).

Game 3—October 24, at Cleveland
Atlanta ....1 0 0 0 0 1 1 3 0 0 0—6 12 1
Cleveland ....2 0 2 0 0 0 1 1 0 0 1—7 12 2
Smoltz, Clontz (3), Mercker (5), McMichael (7), Wohlers (8), Pena (11); Nagy, Assenmacher (8), Tavarez (8), Mesa (9). W—Mesa. L—Pena. HR—McGriff, Klesko (Atl.).

Game 4—October 25, at Cleveland
Atlanta ....0 0 0 0 0 1 3 0 1—5 11 1
Cleveland ....0 0 0 0 0 1 0 0 1—2 6 0
Avery, McMichael (7), Wohlers (9), Borbon (9); Hill, Assenmacher (7), Tavarez (8), Embree (8). W—Avery. L—Hill. S—Borbon. HR—Klesko (Atl.); Belle, Ramirez (Cle.).

Game 5—October 26, at Cleveland
Atlanta ....0 0 0 1 1 0 0 0 2—4 7 0
Cleveland ....2 0 0 0 0 2 0 1 x—5 8 1
Maddux, Clontz (8); Hershiser, Mesa (8). W—Hershiser. L—Maddux. S—Mesa. HR—Polonia, Klesko (Atl.); Belle, Thome (Cle.).

Game 6—October 28, at Atlanta
Cleveland..........0 0 0 0 0 0 0 0 0—0 1 1
Atlanta ....0 0 0 0 0 1 0 0 x—1 6 0
Martinez, Poole (5), Hill (7), Embree (7), Tavarez (8), Assenmacher (8); Glavine, Wohlers (9). W—Glavine. L—Poole. S—Wohlers. HR—Justice (Atl.).

Despite the strike-shortened schedule, Cleveland outfielder Albert Belle became the 12th 50-homer man in Major League history.

FINAL STANDINGS

American League

East Division

Team	N.Y.	Bal.	Bos.	Tor.	Det.	Cle.	Chi.	Mil.	Min.	K.C.	Tex.	Sea.	Oak.	Cal.	W	L	Pct.	GB
New York	—	10	6	8	8	9	7	6	7	8	5	3	9	6	92	70	.568	—
Baltimore	3	—	7	8	11	5	4	9	7	9	3	7	9	6	88	74	.543	4.0
Boston	7	6	—	8	12	1	6	7	6	3	6	7	8	8	85	77	.525	7.0
Toronto	5	5	5	—	7	5	5	7	5	8	2	7	8	5	74	88	.457	18.0
Detroit	5	2	1	6	—	3	4	6	6	0	4	6	4	6	53	109	.327	39.0

Central Division

Team	Cle.	Chi.	Mil.	Min.	K.C.	N.Y.	Bal.	Bos.	Tor.	Det.	Tex.	Sea.	Oak.	Cal.	W	L	Pct.	GB
Cleveland	—	8	7	10	7	3	7	11	7	12	4	8	6	9	99	62	.615	—
Chicago	5	—	6	6	7	6	8	6	7	10	8	5	5	6	85	77	.525	14.5
Milwaukee	6	7	—	9	9	6	3	5	5	8	6	4	7	5	80	82	.494	19.5
Minnesota	3	7	4	—	7	5	5	6	8	6	7	6	6	8	78	84	.481	21.5
Kansas City	6	6	4	6	—	4	3	9	5	6	6	7	5	8	75	86	.466	24

West Division

Team	Tex.	Sea.	Oak.	Cal.	N.Y.	Bal.	Bos.	Tor.	Det.	Cle.	Chi.	Mil.	Min.	K.C.	W	L	Pct.	GB
Texas	—	3	6	9	7	10	6	10	9	8	4	7	5	6	90	72	.556	—
Seattle	10	—	5	8	9	5	6	5	6	4	7	9	6	5	85	76	.528	4.5
Oakland	7	8	—	7	3	4	5	4	8	6	7	5	7	7	78	84	.481	12
California	4	5	6	—	7	6	4	7	6	4	6	7	4	4	70	91	.435	19.5

National League

East Division

Team	Atl.	Mon.	Fla.	N.Y.	Phil.	St.L.	Hou.	Cin.	Chi.	Pit.	S.D.	L.A.	Col.	S.F.	W	L	Pct.	GB
Atlanta	—	10	6	7	9	9	6	7	7	9	9	5	5	7	96	66	.593	—
Montreal	3	—	8	7	6	8	9	9	6	7	4	3	9	9	88	74	.543	8
Florida	7	5	—	7	6	6	7	9	6	5	3	6	8	5	80	82	.494	16
New York	6	6	6	—	7	5	4	6	5	8	3	4	5	6	71	91	.438	25
Philadelphia	4	7	7	6	—	4	2	2	6	7	4	6	6	6	67	95	.414	29

Central Division

Team	St.L.	Hou.	Cin.	Chi.	Pit.	Atl.	Mon.	Fla.	N.Y.	Phil.	S.D.	L.A.	Col.	S.F.	W	L	Pct.	GB
St. Louis	—	11	8	8	10	4	4	6	7	8	8	4	4	6	88	74	.543	—
Houston	2	—	6	8	8	6	4	5	8	10	6	6	5	8	82	80	.506	6
Cincinnati	5	7	—	8	5	5	3	3	6	10	9	4	7	9	81	81	.500	7
Chicago	5	5	5	—	4	5	6	6	7	7	6	8	5	7	76	86	.469	12
Pittsburgh	3	5	8	9	—	3	5	7	5	5	4	6	5	8	73	89	.451	15

West Division

Team	S.D.	L.A.	Col.	S.F.	Atl.	Mon.	Fla.	N.Y.	Phil.	St.L.	Hou.	Cin.	Chi.	Pit.	W	L	Pct.	GB
San Diego	—	8	5	11	4	8	9	10	8	4	6	3	6	9	91	71	.562	—
Los Angeles	5	—	7	7	7	9	7	8	7	8	6	8	5	6	90	72	.556	1
Colorado	8	6	—	5	7	3	5	7	6	8	8	6	7	7	83	79	.512	8
San Fran.	2	6	8	—	5	4	7	6	6	7	4	4	5	4	68	94	.420	23

LEADERS

American League
BA: Alex Rodriguez, Sea., .358.
Runs: Alex Rodriguez, Sea., .358.
Hits: Paul Molitor, Min., 225.
TB: Alex Rodriguez, Sea., 379.
HR: Mark McGwire, Oak., 52.
RBI: Albert Belle, Cle., 148.
SB: Kenny Lofton, Cle., 75.
Wins: Andy Pettitte, N.Y., 21.
ERA: Juan Guzman, Tor., 2.93.
CG: Pat Hentgen, Tor., 10.
IP: Pat Hentgen, Tor., 265.2.
SO: Roger Clemens, Bos., 257.
SV: John Wetteland, N.Y., 43.

National League
BA: Tony Gwynn, S.D., .353.
Runs: Ellis Burks, Col., 142.
Hits: Lance Johnson, N.Y., 227.
TB: Ellis Burks, Col., 392
HR: Andres Galarraga, Col., 47.
RBI: Andres Galarraga, Col., 150
SB: Eric Young, Col., 53.
Wins: John Smoltz, Atl., 24.
ERA: Kevin Brown, Fla., 1.89.
CG: Curt Schilling, Phi., 8.
IP: John Smoltz, Atl., 253.2
SO: John Smoltz, Atl., 276.
SV: Jeff Brantley, Cin.;
Todd Worrell, L.A., 44.

A.L. 100 RBIs
Albert Belle, Cle., 148
Juan Gonzalez, Tex., 144
Mo Vaughn, Bos., 143
Rafael Palmeiro, Bal., 142
Ken Griffey Jr., Sea., 140
Jay Buhner, Sea., 138
Frank Thomas, Chi., 134
Alex Rodriguez, Sea., 123
John Jaha, Mil., 118
Cecil Fielder, Det.-N.Y., 117
Tino Martinez, N.Y., 117
Bobby Bonilla, Bal., 116
Jim Thome, Cle., 116
Mark McGwire, Oak., 113
Paul Molitor, Min., 113
Manny Ramirez, Cle., 112
Marty Cordova, Min., 111
Brady Anderson, Bal., 110
Joe Carter, Tor., 107
Dean Palmer, Tex., 107
Geronimo Berroa, Oak., 106
Robin Ventura, Chi., 105
Edgar Martinez, Sea., 103
Cal Ripken, Bal., 102
Bernie Williams, N.Y., 102
Ed Sprague, Tor., 101
Danny Tartabull, Chi., 101
Travis Fryman, Det., 100
Rusty Greer, Tex., 100
Terry Steinbach, Oak., 100

N.L. 100 RBIs
Andres Galarraga, Col., 150
Dante Bichette, Col., 141
Ken Caminiti, S.D., 130
Barry Bonds, S.F., 129
Ellis Burks, Col., 128
Jeff Bagwell, Hou., 120
Gary Sheffield, Fla., 120
Bernard Gilkey, N.Y., 117
Derek Bell, Hou., 113
Vinny Castilla, Col., 113
Todd Hundley, N.Y., 112
Eric Karros, L.A., 111
Jeff King, Pit., 111
Chipper Jones, Atl., 110
Fred McGriff, Atl., 107
Mike Piazza, L.A., 105
Brian Jordan, St.L., 104
Henry Rodriguez, Mon., 103
Sammy Sosa, Chi., 100

A.L./N.L. 100 RBIs
Greg Vaughn, Mil.-S.D., 117

A.L. 40 homers
Mark McGwire, Oak., 52
Brady Anderson, Bal., 50
Ken Griffey Jr., Sea., 49
Albert Belle, Cle., 48
Juan Gonzalez, Tex., 47
Jay Buhner, Sea., 44
Mo Vaughn, Bos., 44
Frank Thomas, Chi., 40

N.L. 40 homers
Andres Galarraga, Col., 47
Barry Bonds, S.F., 42
Gary Sheffield, Fla., 42
Todd Hundley, N.Y., 41
Ellis Burks, Col., 40
Ken Caminiti, S.D., 40
Vinny Castilla, Col., 40
Sammy Sosa, Chi., 40

A.L./N.L. 40 homers
Greg Vaughn, Mil.-S.D., 41

Most Valuable Player
A.L.: Juan Gonzalez, OF, Tex.
N.L.: Ken Caminiti, 3B, Hou.

Cy Young Award
A.L.: Pat Hentgen, Tor.
N.L.: John Smoltz, Atl.

Rookie of the Year
A.L.: Derek Jeter, SS, N.Y.
N.L.: Todd Hollandsworth, OF, L.A.

Manager of the Year
A.L.: Johnny Oates, Tex.; Joe Torre, N.Y.
N.L.: Bruce Bochy, S.D.

Hall of Fame additions
Jim Bunning, P, 1955-71
Bill Foster, P, Negro Leagues
Ned Hanlon, manager
Earl Weaver, manager

SIGNIFICANT EVENTS

■ **January:** The Official Playing Rules Committee lowered the strike zone from "a line at the top of the knees" to "a line at the hollow beneath the kneecap."
■ **April 1:** Umpire John McSherry collapsed seven pitches into the opening day game between the Expos and Reds at Cincinnati and died about an hour later from a heart problem. The game was postponed.
■ **June 12:** Reds owner Marge Schott agreed to surrender day-to-day control of the team through the 1998 season as discipline for actions and statements detrimental to baseball.
■ **September 27:** In what would develop into one of the most controversial player-umpire disputes in baseball history, Baltimore second baseman Roberto Alomar spat in the face of umpire John Hirshbeck during a called-strike argument.
■ **November 19:** White Sox owner Jerry Reinsdorf signed Cleveland slugger Albert Belle to the richest contract in baseball history—$50 million over five years.
■ **November 26:** After completing the first full-schedule season since 1993, Major League Baseball and the players' association agreed on a contract that would run through October 31, 2000.

MEMORABLE MOMENTS

■ **September 6:** Baltimore's Eddie Murray connected for his 500th career home run against Detroit and joined 14 other players in that exclusive circle.
■ **September 16:** Minnesota's Paul Molitor became the 21st player to record 3,000 career hits when he tripled in the fifth inning of a game at Kansas City.
■ **September 18:** Boston ace Roger Clemens matched his own major league record when he struck out 20 Tigers in a nine-inning game.
■ **September 29:** Giants slugger Barry Bonds completed the season with 42 homers and 40 stolen bases, joining Jose Canseco as the only members of the 40-40 club.
■ **September 29:** The Orioles, led by Brady Anderson's 50 home runs, finished the season with a one-season record 257.
■ **September 29:** San Diego's Tony Gwynn finished the season with a .353 average and won his seventh N.L. batting title.

ALL-STAR GAME

■ **Winner:** Nine N.L. pitchers combined on a seven hitter as the A.L. lost its third consecutive midsummer classic and saw the N.L.'s All-Star domination grow to 40-26-1.
■ **Key inning:** The second, when the A.L. failed to score after putting its leadoff man on second base and the N.L. stretched its lead to 2-0 on Dodgers catcher Mike Piazza's solo home run.
■ **Memorable moment:** Piazza, who drove in two runs with his homer and a double, holding up the MVP trophy for a large hometown contingent at Philadelphia. Piazza was born in nearby Norristown, Pa., and once served as a bat boy at Veterans Stadium.
■ **Top guns:** Piazza (Dodgers), Lance Johnson (Mets), John Smoltz (Braves), Steve Trachsel (Cubs), N.L.; Kenny Lofton (Indians), A.L.
■ **MVP:** Piazza.

Linescore
July 9, at Philadelphia's Veterans Stadium
A.L. ....0 0 0 0 0 0 0 0 0—0 7 0
N.L. ....1 2 1 0 0 2 0 0 x—6 12 1
Smoltz (Braves), Brown (Marlins) 3, Glavine (Braves) 4, Bottalico (Phillies) 5, P. Martinez (Expos) 6, Trachsel (Cubs) 7, Worrell (Dodgers) 8, Wohlers (Braves) 9, Leiter (Marlins) 9; Nagy (Indians), Finley (Angels) 3, Pavlik (Rangers) 5, Percival (Angels) 7, Hernandez (White Sox) 8. W—Smoltz. L—Nagy. HR—Piazza, Caminiti, N.L.

A.L. DIVISION SERIES

■ **Winners:** The Yankees, bidding for their 34th World Series appearance, ruined the Rangers' Post Season debut with a four-game victory; the wild-card Orioles pulled off a surprising four-game upset of the Indians.
■ **Turning points:** Throwing errors turned the tide for both the Yankees and Orioles. New York took control in the 10th inning of Game 2 when the Rangers failed to score after loading the bases in the top of the inning and the Yankees won in the bottom of the frame on third baseman Dean Palmer's wild throw. The Orioles took control when Cleveland catcher Sandy Alomar fired wildly on an eighth-inning home-to-first double-play attempt in Game 2, allowing the winning run to score in an eventual 7-4 victory. The Indians argued that batter B.J. Surhoff ran out of the baseline, causing Alomar's miscue.
■ **Memorable moments:** The final out of Texas' 6-2 Game 1 victory over the Yankees—the first postseason win in Rangers history. The Game 4 heroics of Baltimore second baseman Roberto Alomar, who tied the game with a ninth-inning single and clinched the series victory with a 12th-inning home run. It was sweet vindication for Alomar, who had been the center of controversy since a late-season spitting incident involving umpire John Hirschbeck.
■ **Memorable performances:** Bernie Williams batted .467, hit three home runs, including two in the decisive fourth game, and drove in five runs for the Yankees; Yankee relievers Mariano Rivera, David Weathers, Jeff Nelson and John Wetteland combined for 17⅓ scoreless innings, allowing only five hits; Juan Gonzalez set a record pace for the Rangers, hitting .438 with five home runs and nine RBIs; B.J. Surhoff hit three home runs and Bobby Bonilla hit two, including a grand slam, for the Orioles; Albert Belle hit a Game 3 grand slam for the Indians.

Linescores
Baltimore vs. Cleveland

Game 1—October 1, at Baltimore
Cleveland ..0 1 0 2 0 0 1 0 0— 4 10 0
Baltimore....1 1 2 0 0 5 1 0 x—10 12 1
Nagy, Embree (6), Shuey (6), Tavarez (8); Wells, Orosco (7), Mathews (7), Rhodes (8), Myers (9). W—Wells. L—Nagy. HR—Ramirez (Cle.); Anderson, Bonilla, Surhoff 2 (Bal.).

Game 2—October 2, at Baltimore
Cleveland ......0 0 0 0 0 3 0 1 0—4 8 2
Baltimore........1 0 0 0 3 0 0 3 x—7 9 0
Hershiser, Plunk (6), Assenmacher (8), Tavaraz (8); Erickson, Orosco (7), Benitez (8), Myers (9). W—Benitez. L—Plunk. S—Myers. HR—Belle (Cle.); Anderson (Bal.).

Game 3—October 4, at Cleveland
Baltimore ....0 1 0 3 0 0 0 0 0—4 8 2
Cleveland......1 2 0 1 0 0 4 1 x—9 10 0
Mussina, Orosco (7), Benitez (7), Rhodes (8), Mathews (8); McDowell, Embree (6), Shuey (7), Assenmacher (7), Plunk (8), Mesa (9). W—Assenmacher. L—Orosco. HR—Surhoff (Bal.); Belle, Ramirez (Cle.).

Game 4—October 5, at Cleveland
Bal. 0 2 0 0 0 0 0 0 1 0 0 1—4 14 1
Cle. ..0 0 0 2 1 0 0 0 0 0 0 0—3 7 1
Wells, Mathews (8), Orosco (9), Benitez (10), Myers (12); Nagy, Embree (7), Shuey (7), Assenmacher (7), Plunk (8), Mesa (9), Ogea (12). W—Benitez. L—Mesa. S—Myers. HR—R. Alomar, Palmeiro, Bonilla (Bal.).

New York vs. Texas

Game 1—October 1, at New York
Texas ....0 0 0 5 0 1 0 0 0—6 8 0
New York......1 0 0 1 0 0 0 0 0—2 10 0
Burkett; Cone, Lloyd (7), Weathers (8). W—Burkett. L—Cone. HR—Gonzalez, Palmer (Tex.).

Game 2—October 2, at New York
Texas 0 1 3 0 0 0 0 0 0 0 0 0—4 8 1
N.Y. ..0 1 0 1 0 0 1 1 0 0 0 1—5 8 0
Hill, Cook (7), Russell (8), Stanton (10), Henneman (12); Pettitte, M. Rivera (7), Wetteland (10), Lloyd (12), Nelson (12), Rogers (12), Boehringer (12). W—Boehringer. L—Stanton. HR—Gonzalez 2 (Tex.); Fielder (N.Y.).

Game 3—October 4, at Texas
New York........1 0 0 0 0 0 0 0 2—3 7 1
Texas ....0 0 0 1 1 0 0 0 0—2 6 1
Key, Nelson (6), Wetteland (9); Oliver, Henneman (9), Stanton (9). W—Nelson. L—Oliver. S–Wetteland. HR—Williams (N.Y.); Gonzalez (Tex.).

Game 4—October 5, at Texas
New York......0 0 0 3 1 0 1 0 1—6 12 1
Texas ....0 2 2 0 0 0 0 0 0—4 9 0
Rogers, Boehringer (3), Weathers (4), M. Rivera (7), Wetteland (9); Witt, Patterson (4), Cook (4), Pavlik (5), Vosberg (7), Russell (7), Stanton (8), Henneman (9). W—Weathers. L—Pavlik. S—Wetteland. HR—Williams 2 (N.Y.); Gonzalez (Tex.).

N.L. DIVISION SERIES

■ **Winners:** The Braves continued their quest for back-to-back World Series titles with a sweep of the Dodgers; St. Louis matched that 1-2-3 effort against San Diego.
■ **Turning points:** For the Braves, catcher Javy Lopez's Game 1-winning 10th-inning home run

in a 2-1 victory. The Cardinals took control of their series in the opening inning of Game 1 when Gary Gaetti hit a three-run homer, giving pitcher Todd Stottlemyre all the runs he would need for a 3-1 victory.

■ **Memorable moments:** The Braves put the Dodgers away in the seventh inning of Game 2 when Fred McGriff and Jermaine Dye hit solo home runs, wiping out a 2-1 deficit and setting up Greg Maddux for a 3-2 victory. Cardinals right fielder Brian Jordan finished off the Padres in Game 3 with a great run-saving catch in the eighth inning and a game-winning two-run homer in the ninth.

■ **Top performances:** The Braves' pitching staff, with starters John Smoltz, Maddux and Tom Glavine working 22⅔ innings, posted a sparkling 0.96 ERA against the Dodgers.
St. Louis' Ron Gant batted .400, hit a home run and drove in four runs against the Padres and closer Dennis Eckersley saved all three victories.

Linescores
St. Louis vs. San Diego

Game 1—October 1, at St. Louis
San Diego ......0 0 0 0 0 1 0 0 0—1 8 1
St. Louis ....3 0 0 0 0 0 0 0 x—3 6 0
Hamilton, Blair (7); Stottlemyre, Honeycutt (7), Eckersley (8). W—Stottlemyre. L—Hamilton. S—Eckersley. HR—Henderson (S.D.); Gaetti (St.L.).

Game 2—October 3, at St. Louis
San Diego ....0 0 0 0 1 2 0 1 0—4
St. Louis ....0 0 1 0 3 0 0 1 x—5
Sanders, Veras (5), Worrell (6), Bochtler (8), Hoffman (9); An. Benes, Honeycutt (8), Eckersley (9). W—Honeycutt. L—Bochtler. S—Eckersley. HR—Caminiti (S.D.).

Game 3—October 5, at San Diego
St. Louis ....1 0 0 0 0 3 1 0 2—7
San Diego ....0 0 0 1 0 0 1 0 0—5
Osborne, Petkovsek (5), Honeycutt (7), Mathews (8), Eckersley (9); Ashby, Worrell (6), Valenzuela (8), Veras (8), Hoffman (9). W—Mathews. L—Hoffman. S—Eckersley. HR—Gant, Jordan (St.L.); Caminiti 2 (S.D.).

Atlanta vs. Los Angeles

Game 1—October 2, at Los Angeles
Atlanta ....0 0 0 1 0 0 0 0 0 1—2 4 1
Los Angeles ....0 0 0 0 1 0 0 0 0 0—1 5 0
Smoltz, Wohlers (10); Martinez, Radinsky (9), Osuna (9). W—Smoltz. L—Osuna. S—Wohlers. HR—Lopez (Atl.).

Game 2—October 3, at Los Angeles
Atlanta ....0 1 0 0 0 0 2 0 0—3 5 2
Los Angeles ....0 1 0 0 1 0 0 0 0 0—2 3 0
Maddux, McMichael (8), Wohlers (9); Valdes, Astacio (7), Worrell (8). W—Maddux. L—Valdes. S—Wohlers. HR—McGriff, Klesko, Dye (Atl.).

Game 3—October 5, at Atlanta
Los Angeles....0 0 0 0 0 0 1 1 0—2 6 1
Atlanta ....1 0 0 4 0 0 0 0 x—5 7 0
Nomo, Guthrie (4), Candiotti (5), Radinsky (7), Osuna (8), Dreifort (8); Glavine, McMichael (7), Bielecki (8), Wohlers (9). W—Glavine. L—Nomo. S—Wohlers. HR—C. Jones (Atl.).

ALCS

■ **Winner:** The Yankees overpowered Baltimore, the most prolific home run team in baseball history, and earned the franchise's 34th pennant. The five-game victory set up the Yankees' first World Series appearance since 1981.

■ **Turning point:** The eighth inning of Game 3, when the Yankees, trailing 2-1, struck for four two-out runs against Orioles ace Mike Mussina. The key plays were Bernie Williams' game-tying single, third baseman Todd Zeile's error and Cecil Fielder's two-run homer.

■ **Memorable moment:** The eighth inning of Game 1, when 12-year-old fan Jeff Maier reached over Yankee Stadium's right field wall and unwittingly set the course for the series. The Orioles held a 4-3 advantage when shortstop Derek Jeter hit a fly ball to deep right that backed Baltimore outfielder Tony Tarasco to the wall. As Tarasco reached up in an attempt to make the catch, Maier stuck his glove over the wall and pulled the ball into the stands. The Orioles argued vehemently for fan interference, but umpire Richie Garcia ruled it a game-tying home run and the Yankees won in the 11th on a Williams home run. Maier became an instant national celebrity.

■ **Top guns:** Williams (.474, 2 HR, 6 RBI), Jeter (.417), Darryl Strawberry (.417, 3 HR), Cecil Fielder (8 RBI), Mariano Rivera (0.00 ERA), Yankees; Zeile (3 HR, 5 RBI), Rafael Palmeiro (2 HR), Orioles. MVP: Williams.

Linescores

Game 1—October 9, at New York
Bal. ....0 1 1 1 0 1 0 0 0 0 0—4 11 1
N.Y. ....1 1 0 0 0 0 1 1 0 0 1—5 11 0
Erickson, Orosco (7), Benitez (7), Rhodes (8), Mathews (9), Myers (9); Pettitte, Nelson (8), Wetteland (9), M. Rivera (10). W—M. Rivera. L—Myers. HR—Anderson, Palmeiro (Bal.); Jeter, Williams (N.Y.).

Game 2—October 10, at New York
Baltimore......0 0 2 0 0 0 2 1 0—5 10 0
New York......2 0 0 0 0 0 1 0 0—3 11 1
Cone, Nelson (7), Lloyd (8), Weathers (9). W—Wells. L—Nelson. S—Benitez. HR—Zeile, Palmeiro (Bal.).

Game 3—October 11, at Baltimore
New York......0 0 0 1 0 0 0 4 0—5 8 0
Baltimore.......2 0 0 0 0 0 0 0 0—2 3 2
Key, Wetteland (9); Mussina, Orosco (8), Mathews (9). W—Key. L—Mussina. S—Wetteland. HR—Fielder (N.Y.); Zeile (Bal.).

Game 4—October 12, at Baltimore
New York......2 1 0 2 0 0 0 3 0—8 9 0
Baltimore......1 0 1 2 0 0 0 0 0—4 11 0
Rogers, Weathers (4), Lloyd (6), M. Rivera (7), Wetteland (9); Coppinger, Rhodes (6), Mills (7), Orosco (8), Benitez (8), Mathews (9). W—Weathers. L—Coppinger. HR—Williams, Strawberry 2, O'Neill (N.Y.); Hoiles (Bal.).

Game 5—October 13, at Baltimore
New York......0 0 6 0 0 0 0 0 0—6 11 0
Baltimore......0 0 0 0 0 1 0 1 2—4 4 1
Pettitte, Wetteland (9); Erickson, Rhodes (6), Mills (7), Myers (8). W—Pettitte. L—Erickson. HR—Fielder, Strawberry, Leyritz (N.Y.); Zeile, Bonilla, Murray (Bal.).

NLCS

■ **Winner:** The Braves, hoping to become the N.L.'s first repeat World Series champion in 20 years, recovered from a three-games-to-one deficit in a tense seven-game victory over the Cardinals. The Braves, on the brink of elimination, outscored St. Louis 32-1 over the final three games to earn their eighth fall classic appearance and fourth of the decade.

■ **Turning point:** The first inning of Game 5, when the Braves scored five runs off Cardinals starter Todd Stottlemyre. That 14-0 victory served notice that rumors of the Braves' demise were premature.

■ **Memorable moment:** An eighth-inning Game 4 home run by St. Louis' Brian Jordan, the blow that gave ecstatic home fans a 4-3 victory and put the Cardinals on the brink of a 16th World Series appearance.

■ **Top guns:** Javier Lopez (.542, 6 RBI), Mark Lemke (.444), Fred McGriff (2 HR, 7 RBI), John Smoltz (2-0, 1.20 ERA), Braves; Royce Clayton (.350), Ron Gant (2 HR, 4 RBI), Cardinals.

■ **MVP:** Lopez.

Linescores

Game 1—October 9, at Atlanta
St. Louis ....0 1 0 0 0 0 1 0 0—2 5 1
Atlanta ....0 0 0 2 0 0 2 0 x—4 9 0
An. Benes, Petkovsek (7), Fossas (8), Mathews (8); Smoltz, Wohlers (9). W—Smoltz. L—Petkovsek. S—Wohlers.

Game 2—October 10, at Atlanta
St. Louis ......1 0 2 0 0 0 5 0 0—8 11 0
Atlanta..........0 0 2 0 0 1 0 0 0—3 5 2
Stottlemyre, Petkovsek (7), Honeycutt (8), Eckersley (8); Maddux, McMichael (7), Neagle (8), Avery (9). W—Stottlemyre. L—Maddux. HR—Gaetti (St.L.); Grissom (Atl.).

Game 3—October 12, at St. Louis
Atlanta............1 0 0 0 0 0 0 1 0—2 8 1
St. Louis ....2 0 0 0 0 1 0 0 x—3 7 0
Glavine, Bielecki (7), McMichael (8); Osborne, Petkovsek (8), Honeycutt (9), Eckersley (9). W—Osborne. L—Glavine. S—Eckersley. HR—Gant 2 (St.L.).

Game 4—October 13, at St. Louis
Atlanta............0 1 0 0 0 2 0 1 0—3 9 1
St. Louis ....0 0 0 0 0 0 3 1 x—4 5 0
Neagle, McMichael (7), Wohlers (8); An. Benes, Fossas (6), Mathews (6), Al. Benes, Honeycutt (8), Eckersley (8). W—Eckersley. L—McMichael. HR—Lemke, Klesko (Atl.); Jordan (St.L.).

Game 5—October 14, at St. Louis
Atlanta........5 2 0 3 1 0 0 1 2—14 22 0
St. Louis ......0 0 0 0 0 0 0 0 0—0 7 0
Smoltz, Bielecki (8), Wade (9), Clontz (9); Stottlemyre, Jackson (2), Fossas (5), Petkovsek (7), Honeycutt (9). W—Smoltz. L—Stottlemyre. HR—McGriff, Lopez (Atl.).

Game 6—October16, at Atlanta
St. Louis ....0 0 0 0 0 0 0 1 0—1 6 1
Atlanta ....0 1 0 0 1 0 0 1 x—3 7 0
Al. Benes, Fossas (6), Petkovsek (6), Stottlemyre (8); Maddux, Wohlers (8). W—Maddux. L—Al. Benes. S—Wohlers.

Game 7—October 17, at Atlanta
St. Louis ....0 0 0 0 0 0 0 0 0—0 4 2
Atlanta........6 0 0 4 0 3 2 0 x—15 17 0
Osborne, An. Benes (1), Petkovsek (6), Honeycutt (6), Fossas (8); Glavine, Bielecki (8), Avery (9). W—Glavine. L—Osborne. HR—McGriff, Lopez, A. Jones (Atl.).

WORLD SERIES

■ **Winner:** The Yankees, missing from the World Series scene since 1981, collected their franchise-record 23rd championship when they spotted Atlanta two wins and stormed back to post an impressive six-game victory. The New York triumph dashed the Braves' hope of becoming the N.L.'s first back-to-back fall classic winner in 20 years.

■ **Turning point:** The eighth inning of Game 4, when catcher Jim Leyritz rocked Braves closer Mark Wohlers for a three-run, game-tying homer that set up an eventual 8-6 Yankees victory. The Braves had led the game 6-0 and appeared on the verge of taking a three games-to-one series lead.

■ **Memorable moment:** Right fielder Paul O'Neill's over-the-shoulder Game 5-ending catch that saved a 1-0 victory for the Yankees and Andy Pettitte. The catch denied pinch-hitter Luis Polonia extra bases with runners on first and third.

■ **Top guns:** Cecil Fielder (.391), Jeff Nelson (3 games, 0.00 ERA), Mariano Rivera, 4 games, 1.59 ERA), John Wetteland (4 saves, 2.08 ERA), Yankees; Grissom (.444), A. Jones (.400, 2 HR, 6 RBI), Fred McGriff (2 HR, 6 RBI), John Smoltz (1-1, 0.64 ERA), Braves.

■ **MVP:** Wetteland.

Talented Yankees lefthander Andy Pettitte won an American League-high 21 games in 1996 and earned a World Series ring to boot.

Linescores

Game 1—October 20, at New York
Atlanta........0 2 6 0 1 3 0 0 0—12 13 0
New York....0 0 0 0 1 0 0 0 0—1 4 1
Smoltz, McMichael (7), Neagle (8), Wade (9), Clontz (9); Pettitte, Boehringer (3), Weathers (6), Nelson (8), Wetteland (9). W—Smoltz. L—Pettitte. HR—McGriff, A. Jones 2 (Atl.).

Game 2—October 21, at New York
Atlanta ....1 0 1 0 1 1 0 0 0—4 10 0
New York......0 0 0 0 0 0 0 0 0—0 7 1
Maddux, Wohlers (9); Key, Lloyd (7), Nelson (7), M. Rivera (9). W—Maddux. L—Key.

Game 3—October 22, at Atlanta
New York........1 0 0 1 0 0 0 3 0—5 8 1
Atlanta ....0 0 0 0 0 1 0 1 0—2 6 1
Cone, M. Rivera (7), Lloyd (8), Wetteland (9); Glavine, McMichael (8), Clontz (8), Bielecki (9). W—Cone. L—Glavine. S—Wetteland. HR—Williams (N.Y.).

Game 4—October 23, at Atlanta
N.Y. ....0 0 0 0 0 3 0 3 0 2—8 12 0
Atlanta ....0 4 1 0 1 0 0 0 0 0—6 9 2
Rogers, Boehringer (3), Weathers (5), Nelson (6), M. Rivera (8), Lloyd (9), Wetteland (10); Neagle, Wade (6), Bielecki (6), Wohlers (8), Avery (10), Clontz (10). W—Lloyd. L—Avery. S—Wetteland. HR—Leyritz (N.Y.); McGriff (Atl.).

Game 5—October 24, at Atlanta
New York.........0 0 0 1 0 0 0 0 0—1 4 1
Atlanta ....0 0 0 0 0 0 0 0 0—0 5 1
Pettitte, Wetteland (9); Smoltz, Wohlers (9). W—Pettitte. L—Smoltz. S—Wetteland.

Game 6—October 26, at New York
Atlanta.............0 0 0 1 0 0 0 0 1—2 8 0
New York.........0 0 3 0 0 0 0 0 x—3 8 1
Maddux, Wohlers (8); Key, Weathers (6), Lloyd (6), M. Rivera (7), Wetteland (9). W—Key. L—Maddux. S—Wetteland.

FINAL STANDINGS

American League

East Division

Team	Bal.	NYY	Det.	Bos.	Tor.	Cle.	ChW	Mil.	Min.	K.C.	Sea.	Ana.	Tex.	Oak.	Atl.	Fla.	NYM	Mtl.	Phi.	W	L	Pct.	GB
Baltimore	—	8	6	5	6	6	5	5	10	7	7	7	10	8	3	0	1	1	3	98	64	.605	—
New York	4	—	10	8	7	6	9	7	8	8	4	7	7	6	1	1	2	1	0	96	66	.593	2
Detroit	6	2	—	7	6	5	7	4	4	6	4	6	7	7	2	1	3	0	2	79	83	.488	19
Boston	7	4	5	—	6	6	3	8	8	3	7	5	3	7	0	1	2	0	3	78	84	.481	20
Toronto	6	5	6	6	—	5	6	4	8	6	3	5	7	5	1	0	0	1	2	76	86	.469	22

Central Division

Team	Bal.	NYY	Det.	Bos.	Tor.	Cle.	ChW	Mil.	Min.	K.C.	Sea.	Ana.	Tex.	Oak.	Hou.	Pit.	Cin.	St.L.	ChC	W	L	Pct.	GB
Cleveland	5	5	6	5	6	—	7	8	8	8	3	4	5	7	2	2	1	2	2	86	75	.534	—
Chicago	6	2	4	8	5	5	—	4	6	11	5	5	3	8	3	0	2	1	2	80	81	.497	6
Milwaukee	6	4	7	3	7	4	7	—	5	6	5	4	7	5	2	2	0	3	1	78	83	.484	8
Minnesota	1	3	7	3	3	4	6	7	—	5	5	7	3	7	2	2	2	0	1	68	94	.420	18½
Kansas City	4	3	5	8	5	3	1	6	7	—	5	5	6	3	2	2	1	1	0	67	94	.416	19

West Division

Team	Bal.	NYY	Det.	Bos.	Tor.	Cle.	ChW	Mil.	Min.	K.C.	Sea.	Ana.	Tex.	Oak.	S.F.	L.A.	Col.	S.D.	W	L	Pct.	GB
Seattle	4	7	7	4	8	8	6	6	6	6	—	6	8	7	1	3	2	1	90	72	.556	—
Anaheim	4	4	5	6	6	7	6	7	4	6	6	—	8	11	1	0	1	2	84	78	.519	6
Texas	1	4	4	8	4	6	8	4	8	5	4	4	—	7	2	3	3	2	77	85	.475	13
Oakland	3	5	4	4	6	4	3	6	4	8	5	1	5	—	2	1	1	3	65	97	.401	25

National League

East Division

Team	Atl.	Fla.	NYM	Mtl.	Phi.	Hou.	Pit.	Cin.	St.L.	ChC	S.F.	L.A.	Col.	S.D.	Bal.	NYY	Det.	Bos.	Tor.	W	L	Pct.	GB
Atlanta	—	4	5	10	10	7	5	9	8	9	7	6	5	8	0	2	1	3	2	101	61	.623	—
Florida	8	—	4	7	6	7	7	6	5	9	5	7	4	5	3	2	2	2	3	92	70	.568	9
New York	7	8	—	7	7	4	7	9	9	5	3	5	5	5	2	1	0	1	3	88	74	.543	13
Montreal	2	5	5	—	6	3	5	5	6	7	6	4	4	8	2	2	3	3	2	78	84	.481	23
Philadelphia	2	6	5	6	—	7	5	3	6	5	3	1	7	7	0	3	1	0	1	68	94	.420	33

Central Division

Team	Atl.	Fla.	NYM	Mtl.	Phi.	Hou.	Pit.	Cin.	St.L.	ChC	S.F.	L.A.	Col.	S.D.	Cle.	ChW	Mil.	Min.	K.C.	W	L	Pct.	GB
Houston	4	4	7	8	4	—	6	7	9	9	3	7	6	6	1	0	1	1	1	84	78	.519	—
Pittsburgh	6	4	4	6	6	6	—	4	9	5	8	2	7	5	1	3	1	1	1	79	83	.488	5
Cincinnati	2	5	2	6	8	5	8	—	6	5	4	6	5	5	2	1	3	1	2	76	86	.469	8
St. Louis	3	6	2	5	5	3	3	6	—	8	8	6	4	6	1	2	0	3	2	73	89	.451	11
Chicago	2	2	6	4	6	3	7	7	4	—	5	5	2	6	1	1	2	2	3	68	94	.420	16

West Division

Team	Atl.	Fla.	NYM	Mtl.	Phi.	Hou.	Pit.	Cin.	St.L.	ChC	S.F.	L.A.	Col.	S.D.	Sea.	Ana.	Tex.	Oak.	W	L	Pct.	GB
San Fran.	4	6	8	5	8	8	3	7	3	6	—	6	8	8	3	3	2	2	90	72	.556	—
Los Angeles	5	4	6	7	10	4	9	5	5	6	6	—	7	5	1	4	1	3	88	74	.543	2
Colorado	6	7	6	7	4	5	4	6	7	9	4	5	—	4	2	3	1	3	83	79	.512	7
San Diego	3	6	6	3	4	5	6	6	5	5	4	7	8	—	3	2	2	1	76	86	.469	14

LEADERS

American League
BA: Frank Thomas, Chi., .347.
Runs: Ken Griffey Jr., Sea., 125.
Hits: Nomar Garciaparra, Bos., 209.
TB: Ken Griffey Jr., Sea., 393.
HR: Ken Griffey Jr., Sea., 56.
RBI: Ken Griffey Jr., Sea., 147.
SB: Brian Hunter, Det., 74.
Wins: Roger Clemens, Tor., 21.
ERA: Roger Clemens, Tor., 2.05.
CG: Roger Clemens, Tor.; Pat Hentgen, Tor., 9.
IP: Roger Clemens, Tor.; Pat Hentgen, Tor., 264.0.
SO: Roger Clemens, Tor., 292.
SV: Randy Myers, Bal., 45.

National League
BA: Tony Gwynn, S.D., .372.
Runs: Craig Biggio, Hou., 146.
Hits: Tony Gwynn, S.D., 220.
TB: Larry Walker, Col., 409.
HR: Larry Walker, Col., 49.
RBI: Larry Walker, Col., 140.
SB: Tony Womack, Pit., 60.
Wins: Denny Neagle, Atl., 20.
ERA: Pedro J. Martinez, Mon., 1.90.
CG: Pedro J. Martinez, Mon., 13.
IP: John Smoltz, Atl., 256.0.
SO: Curt Schilling, Phi., 319.
SV: Jeff Shaw, Cin., 42.

A.L. 100 RBIs
Ken Griffey Jr., Sea., 147
Tino Martinez, N.Y., 141
Juan Gonzalez, Tex., 131
Tim Salmon, Ana., 129
Frank Thomas, Chi., 125
Tony Clark, Det., 117
Paul O'Neill, N.Y., 117
Albert Belle, Chi., 116
Jeff King, K.C., 112
Rafael Palmeiro, Bal., 110
Jay Buhner, Sea., 109
Edgar Martinez, Sea., 108
Matt Williams, Cle., 105
Joe Carter, Tor., 102
Travis Fryman, Det., 102
Jim Thome, Cle., 102
Bobby Higginson, Det., 101
David Justice, Cle., 101
Bernie Williams, N.Y., 100

N.L. 100 RBIs
Andres Galarraga, Col., 140
Jeff Bagwell, Hou., 135
Larry Walker, Col., 130
Mike Piazza, L.A., 124
Jeff Kent, S.F., 121
Tony Gwynn, S.D., 119
Sammy Sosa, Chi., 119
Dante Bichette, Col., 118
Moises Alou, Fla., 115
Vinny Castilla, Col., 113
Chipper Jones, Atl., 111
Eric Karros, L.A., 104
J.T. Snow, S.F., 104
John Olerud, N.Y., 102
Barry Bonds, S.F., 101

A.L./N.L. 100 RBIs
Mark McGwire, Oak.-St.L., 123

A.L. 40 homers
Ken Griffey Jr., Sea., 56
Tino Martinez, N.Y., 44
Juan Gonzalez, Tex., 42
Jay Buhner, Sea., 40
Jim Thome, Cle., 40

N.L. 40 homers
Larry Walker, Col., 49
Jeff Bagwell, Hou., 43
Andres Galarraga, Col., 41
Barry Bonds, S.F., 40
Vinny Castilla, Col., 40
Mike Piazza, L.A., 40

A.L./N.L. 40 homers
Mark McGwire, Oak.-St.L., 58

Most Valuable Player
A.L.: Ken Griffey Jr., OF, Sea.
N.L.: Larry Walker, OF, Col.

Cy Young Award
A.L.: Roger Clemens, Tor.
N.L.: Pedro Martinez, Mon.

Rookie of the Year
A.L.: Nomar Garciaparra, SS, Bos.
N.L.: Scott Rolen, 3B, Phi.

Manager of the Year
A.L.: Davey Johnson, Bal.
N.L.: Dusty Baker, S.F.

Hall of Fame additions
George Davis, SS, 1890-1909
Larry Doby, OF, 1947-59.
Lee MacPhail, Executive
Joe Rogan, P, Negro Leagues
Don Sutton, P, 1966-88

SIGNIFICANT EVENTS

■ **April 4:** The Atlanta Braves christened new Turner Field with a 5-4 come-from-behind victory over Chicago.
■ **April 15:** Celebrating the 50th anniversary of Jackie Robinson's debut as the first black Major League player of the century, baseball announced every team would retire Robinson's uniform No. 42.
■ **April 19:** St. Louis recorded a 1-0 victory over San Diego in the opener of the three-game Paradise Series—the first Major League regular-season game ever played in Hawaii.
■ **April 20:** The Chicago Cubs defeated the New York Mets in the second game of a doubleheader, ending their season-opening losing streak at 14 games.
■ **June 12:** The San Francisco Giants posted a 4-3 victory at Texas in the first interleague game in baseball history.
■ **November 5:** The Milwaukee Brewers agreed to move from the American League to the National League Central Division, completing a re-alignment that placed Tampa Bay in the A.L. East, moved Detroit to the A.L. Central and positioned Arizona in the N.L. West.
■ **November 18:** Tampa Bay opened the expansion draft by selecting pitcher Tony Saunders off the Florida roster and Arizona followed by grabbing Cleveland pitcher Brian Anderson.

MEMORABLE MOMENTS

■ **June 30:** Texas' Bobby Witt became the first American League pitcher to hit a home run since October 1972 when he connected off Los Angeles' Ismael Valdes in an interleague contest.
■ **August 8:** For the second time in six weeks, Seattle lefthander Randy Johnson struck out 19 batters in a game—the first time a pitcher had reached that plateau twice in a season. Johnson shut out Chicago, 5-0.
■ **September 20:** Colorado's Larry Walker doubled during a victory over Los Angeles, becoming the first National League player to reach 400 total bases in a season since Hank Aaron in 1959.
■ **September 26:** Philadelphia's Curt Schilling struck out six Marlins in a 5-3 victory over Florida, setting a National League record for most strikeouts by a righthander with 319.
■ **September 27:** San Francisco clinched the N.L. West title with a 6-1 victory over San Diego, becoming the fourth last-to-first team of the century.
■ **September 28:** St. Louis' Mark McGwire, the second player in history to record back-to-back 50-homer seasons, connected for No. 58 in a final-day victory over Chicago—matching Jimmie Foxx and Hank Greenberg for the single-season record by a righthanded hitter. The total topped Seattle's Ken Griffey Jr. by two and was the highest in one season since Roger Maris hit his record 61 in 1961.
■ **September 28:** San Diego's Tony Gwynn completed a .372 season and captured his N.L.-record tying eighth batting championship.

ALL-STAR GAME

■ **Winner:** The A.L. snapped a three-year losing streak with a 3-1 victory behind the late-inning heroics of hometown Cleveland catcher Sandy Alomar and the three-hit work of an eight-man pitching parade.
■ **Key inning:** The fourth, when the N.L. ran itself out of a potential big inning that opened with walks to San Francisco's Barry Bonds and Los Angeles' Mike Piazza. After Bonds had advanced to third on a fly ball by Houston's Jeff Bagwell, Piazza was caught trying to advance to second on a ball that momentarily eluded Rangers catcher Ivan Rodriguez. Larry Walker grounded out to end the N.L.'s only serious threat of the game.
■ **Memorable moment:** Alomar, who entered the mid-summer classic with a 30-game hitting streak, broke a 1-1 tie with a seventh-inning two-run homer—in his only at-bat. The blow wiped out a game-tying solo homer in the top of the inning by Atlanta catcher Javy Lopez and earned Alomar home-field MVP honors.
■ **Top guns:** S. Alomar (Indians), Edgar Martinez (Mariners), Brady Anderson (Orioles), Randy Johnson (Mariners), A.L.; Lopez (Braves), Curt Schilling (Phillies), N.L.
■ **MVP:** S. Alomar.

Linescore
July 8 at Cleveland's Jacobs Field
N.L. ....0 0 0 0 0 0 1 0 0—1 3 0
A.L. ....0 1 0 0 0 0 2 0 x—3 7 0
Maddux (Braves), Schilling (Phillies) 3, Brown (Marlins) 5, P. Martinez (Expos) 6, Estes (Giants) 7, B. Jones (Mets) 8; R. Johnson (Mariners), Clemens (Blue Jays) 3, Cone (Yankees) 4, Thompson (Tigers) 5, Hentgen (Blue Jays) 6, Rosado (Royals) 7, Myers (Orioles) 8, Rivera (Yankees) 9. W—Rosado. L—Estes. HR—E. Martinez, S. Alomar, A.L.; Lopez, N.L.

A.L. DIVISION SERIES

■ **Winners:** Baltimore claimed a surprisingly easy four-game victory over Seattle and Cleveland survived a comeback-filled five-game battle against the wild-card New York Yankees. The Indians' victory set up a grudge match with the Orioles, who had eliminated them in a 1996 Division Series.
■ **Turning points:** The Orioles claimed their second straight A.L. Championship Series berth because of their ability to beat Mariners ace Randy Johnson. Baltimore scored five earned runs in Johnson's five Game 1 innings en route to a 9-3 victory and then handed the big left-hander a 3-1 defeat in the Game 4 clincher. The Indians advanced because they finally were able to break the stranglehold of a powerful New York bullpen that had worked 11 2/3 scoreless innings entering Game 4. Cleveland scored single runs in the eighth and ninth innings off Mariano Rivera and Ramiro Mendoza to claim a 3-2 Game 4 win and prevailed in a 4-3 clincher behind the pitching of rookie Jaret Wright.
■ **Memorable moments:** The Game 4 home run of light-hitting Baltimore second baseman Jeff Reboulet, who also hit two regular-season homers off the intimidating Johnson. The consecutive Game 1 home runs by Yankees Tim Raines, Derek Jeter and Paul O'Neill, a post-season record that helped the New Yorkers rally for an 8-6 victory. Omar Vizquel's ninth-inning single that completed the Indians' rally for a series-tying Game 4 victory.
■ **Memorable performances:** Geronimo Berroa hit a pair of home runs, including one in the decisive 3-1 series-clinching victory, and batted .385 for the Orioles; Baltimore right-hander Mike Mussina recorded two wins and a 1.93 ERA while outdueling Mariners ace Johnson; Yankees right fielder O'Neill batted .421 with two homers, including a Game 3 grand slam, and seven RBIs against the Indians; catcher Sandy Alomar hit a pair of home runs and the 21-year-old Wright won twice for Cleveland.

Linescores
Baltimore vs. Seattle

Game 1—October 1, at Seattle
Baltimore......0 0 1 0 4 4 0 0 0—9 13 0
Seattle ....0 0 0 1 0 0 1 0 1—3 7 1
Mussina, Orosco (8), Benitez (9); Johnson, Timlin (6), Spoljaric (6), Wells (7), Charlton (8). W—Mussina. L—Johnson. HR—Berroa, Hoiles (Bal.); Martinez, Buhner, Rodriguez (Sea.).

Game 2—October 2, at Seattle
Baltimore......0 1 0 0 2 0 2 4 0—9 14 0
Seattle ....2 0 0 0 0 0 1 0 0—3 9 0
Erickson, Benitez (7), Orosco (8), Myers (9); Moyer, Spoljaric (5), Ayala (7), Charlton (8), Slocumb (9). W—Erickson. L—Moyer. HR—Baines, Anderson (Bal.).

Game 3—October 4, at Baltimore
Seattle ....0 0 1 0 1 0 0 0 2—4 11 0
Baltimore......0 0 0 0 0 0 0 0 2—2 5 0
Fassero, Slocumb (9); Key, Mills (5), Rhodes (6), Mathews (9). W—Fassero. L—Key. HR—Buhner, Sorrento (Sea.).

Game 4—October 5, at Baltimore
Seattle ....0 1 0 0 0 0 0 0 0—1 2 0
Baltimore........2 0 0 0 1 0 0 0 x—3 7 0
Johnson; Mussina, Benitez (8), Myers (9). W—Mussina. L—Johnson. S—Myers. HR—Reboulet, Berroa (Bal.); Martinez (Sea.).

Cleveland vs. New York

Game 1—September 30, at New York
Cleveland.......5 0 0 1 0 0 0 0 0—6 11 0
New York......0 1 0 1 1 5 0 0 0—8 11 0
Hershiser, Morman (5), Plunk (5), Assenmacher (6), Jackson (7); Cone, Mendoza (4), Stanton (7), Nelson (7), Rivera (8). W—Mendoza. L—Plunk. S—Rivera. HR—Alomar (Cle.); Martinez, Raines, Jeter, O'Neill (N.Y.).

Game 2—October 2, at New York
Cleveland......0 0 0 5 2 0 0 0 0—7 11 1
New York......3 0 0 0 0 0 0 1 1—5 7 2
Wright, Jackson (7), Assenmacher (7), Mesa (8); Pettitte, Boehringer (6), Lloyd (7), Nelson (9). W—Wright. L—Pettitte. HR—M. Williams (Cle.); Jeter (N.Y.).

Game 3—October 4, at Cleveland
New York.......1 0 1 4 0 0 0 0 0—6 4 1
Cleveland........0 1 0 0 0 0 0 0 0—1 5 1
Wells; Nagy, Ogea (4). W—Wells. L—Nagy. HR—O'Neill (N.Y.).

Game 4—October 5, at Cleveland
New York........2 0 0 0 0 0 0 0 0—2 9 1
Cleveland........0 1 0 0 0 0 0 1 1—3 9 0

1997

Gooden, Lloyd (6), Nelson (6), Stanton (7), Rivera (8), Mendoza (8); Hershiser, Assenmacher (8), Jackson (8). W—Jackson. L—Mendoza. HR—Justice, Alomar (Cle.).

Game 5—October 6, at Cleveland
New York......0 0 0 0 2 1 0 0 0—3 12 0
Cleveland......0 0 3 1 0 0 0 0 x—4 7 2
Pettitte, Nelson (7), Stanton (8); Wright, Jackson (6), Assenmacher (7), Mesa (8). W—Wright. L—Pettitte. S—Mesa.

N.L. DIVISION SERIES

■ **Winners:** The Atlanta Braves and the wild-card Florida Marlins set up an NLCS showdown of East Division teams with convincing sweeps of the Houston Astros and San Francisco Giants. The Braves earned a record sixth straight LCS appearance behind the outstanding pitching of Greg Maddux, John Smoltz and Tom Glavine. The 5-year-old Marlins became the youngest expansion team to win a playoff series behind the near-perfect combination of clutch hitting and pitching.
■ **Turning points:** Maddux set the tone for Atlanta's victory by throwing a Game 1 seven-hitter and outdueling Houston ace Darryl Kile for a 2-1 victory. Edgar Renteria gave the Marlins a 2-1 Game 1 victory with a bases-loaded, ninth-inning single and Moises Alou singled home the winning run in the ninth inning of a 7-6 Game 2 win—a two-games-to-none hole from which the Giants could not recover.
■ **Memorable moments:** Smoltz took Atlanta honors with an 11-strikeout three-hitter in a 4-1 Game 3 victory that completed the Braves' sweep of Houston. Florida's 6-2 third-game victory over the Giants was keyed by Devon White's sixth-inning grand slam, which erased a 1-0 deficit.
■ **Memorable performances:** Third baseman Chipper Jones batted .500 with a home run and Jeff Blauser had a home run and four RBIs for the Braves, who also got a victory from each of their Big Three—Maddux, Glavine and Smoltz. The Marlins rode the clutch hitting of Renteria, Alou and White and the outstanding pitching of Kevin Brown and Alex Fernandez. The Giants got two home runs from second baseman Jeff Kent and a nice pitching effort from Kirk Rueter, who failed to get a decision.

Linescores

Atlanta vs. Houston

Game 1—September 30, at Atlanta
Houston.................0 0 0 0 1 0 0 0 0—1 7 1
Atlanta..................1 1 0 0 0 0 0 0 x—2 2 0
Kile, Springer (8), Martin (8); Maddux. W—Maddux. L—Kile. HR—Klesko (Atl.).

Game 2—October 1, at Atlanta
Houston............0 0 0 3 0 0 0 0 0— 3 6 2
Atlanta..............0 0 3 0 3 5 0 2 x—13 10 1
Hampton, Magnante (5), Garcia (6), Lima (7), Wagner (8); Glavine, Cather (7), Wohlers (9). W—Glavine. L—Hampton. HR—Blauser (Atl.).

Game 3—October 3, at Houston
Atlanta..................1 1 0 0 0 0 1 1 0—4 8 2
Houston................0 0 0 0 0 0 1 0 0—1 3 1
Smoltz; Reynolds, Springer (7), Martin (8), Garcia (8), Magnante (9). W—Smoltz. L—Reynolds. HR—C. Jones (Atl.), Carr (Hou.).

Florida vs. San Francisco

Game 1—September 30, at Florida
San Francisco ......0 0 0 0 0 0 1 0 0—1 4 0
Florida..................0 0 0 0 0 0 1 0 1—2 7 0
Rueter, Tavarez (8), R. Hernandez (9); Brown, Cook (8). W—Cook. L—Tavarez. HR—Mueller (S.F.), C. Johnson (Fla.).

Game 2—October 1, at Florida
San Francisco ....1 1 1 1 0 0 1 0 1—6 11 0
Florida................2 0 1 2 0 1 0 0 1—7 10 2
Estes, Henry (3), Tavarez (6), Rodriguez (8), R. Hernandez (9); Leiter, L. Hernandez (5), Nen (9). W—Nen. L—R. Hernandez. HR—Bonilla, Sheffield (Fla.), B. Johnson (S.F.).

Game 3—October 3, at San Francisco
Florida................0 0 0 0 0 4 0 2 0—6 10 2
San Francisco ....0 0 0 1 0 1 0 0 0—2 7 0
Fernandez, Cook (8), Nen (9); Alvarez, Tavarez (7), R. Hernandez (8), Rodriguez (8), Beck (8). W—Fernandez. L—Alvarez. HR—Kent 2 (S.F.), White (Fla.).

ALCS

■ **Winner:** The Indians, looking for their first championship since 1948, earned their second World Series appearance in three years with a six-game victory over the Orioles. The Indians overcame a .193 team average to claim the franchise's fifth pennant behind clutch pitching and timely hitting that produced four one-run wins over the A.L.'s winningest regular-season team.
■ **Turning point:** The fifth inning of Game 4, when Indians catcher Sandy Alomar took center stage with a baserunning gamble. The bases were loaded and the score was tied when Alomar, stationed at second, alertly raced home after an Arthur Rhodes wild pitch led to a home-plate collision between lead runner Dave Justice and catcher Lenny Webster. The Orioles fought back for a 7-7 tie, but Alomar decided the game with a ninth-inning single off Baltimore closer Armando Benitez to give the Indians a three-games-to-one series advantage.
■ **Memorable moment:** The 11th inning of Game 6 when shortstop Tony Fernandez drove a Benitez pitch into the right field seats at Camden Yards and gave the Indians a 1-0 series-clinching win. The Indians had managed only one hit through eight innings off Orioles starter Mike Mussina while Baltimore stranded 14 baserunners and was 0-for-12 with men in scoring position against Cleveland starter Charles Nagy and four relievers.
■ **Top guns:** Manny Ramirez (2 HR, 3 RBI), Fernandez (.357, 1 HR, 2 RBI), Marquis Grissom (1 HR, 4 RBI), S. Alomar (1 HR, 4 RBI), Mike Jackson (5 games, 0.00 ERA), Indians; Brady Anderson (.360, 2 HR, 3 RBI), Cal Ripken (.348, 1 HR, 3 RBI), Harold Baines (.353, 1 HR), Mussina (15 IP, 0.60 ERA), Orioles.
■ **MVP:** Marquis Grissom.

Linescores

Game 1—October 8, at Baltimore
Cleveland........0 0 0 0 0 0 0 0 0—0 4 1
Baltimore........1 0 2 0 0 0 0 0 x—3 6 1
Ogea, Bri. Anderson (7); Erickson, Myers (9). W—Erickson. L—Ogea. S—Myers. HR—Bra. Anderson, R. Alomar (Bal.).

Game 2—October 9, at Baltimore
Cleveland........2 0 0 0 0 0 0 3 0—5 6 3
Baltimore........0 2 0 0 0 2 0 0 0—4 8 1
Nagy, Morman (6), Juden (7), Assenmacher (7), Jackson (8), Mesa (9); Key, Kamieniecki (5), Benitez (8), Mills (9). W—Assenmacher. L—Benitez. S—Mesa. HR—Ramirez, Grissom (Cle.); Ripken (Bal.).

Game 3—October 11, at Cleveland
Bal. ....0 0 0 0 0 0 0 0 1 0 0 0—1 8 1
Cle. ....0 0 0 0 0 0 1 0 0 0 0 1—2 6 0
Mussina, Benitez (8), Orosco (9), Mills (9), Rhodes (10), Myers (11); Hershiser, Assenmacher (8), Jackson (8), Mesa (9), Juden (11), Morman (11), Plunk (12). W—Plunk. L—Myers.

Game 4—October 12, at Cleveland
Baltimore ....0 1 4 0 0 0 1 0 1—7 12 2
Cleveland......0 2 0 1 4 0 0 0 1—8 13 0
Erickson, Rhodes (5), Mills (7), Orosco (9), Benitez (9); Wright, Bri. Anderson (4), Juden (7), Assenmacher (7), Jackson (7), Mesa (8). W—Mesa. L—Mills. HR—S. Alomar, Ramirez (Cle.); Bra. Anderson, Baines, Palmeiro (Bal.).

Game 5—October 13, at Cleveland
Baltimore......0 0 2 0 0 0 0 0 2—4 10 0
Cleveland......0 0 0 0 0 0 0 0 2—2 8 1
Kamieniecki, Key (6), Myers (9); Ogea, Assenmacher (9), Jackson (9). W—Kamieniecki. L—Ogea. HR—Davis (Bal.).

Game 6—October 15, at Baltimore
Cle. ....0 0 0 0 0 0 0 0 0 0 1—1 3 0
Bal. ....0 0 0 0 0 0 0 0 0 0 0—0 10 0
Nagy, Assenmacher (8), Jackson (8), Bri. Anderson (10), Mesa (11); Mussina, Myers (9), Benitez (11). W—Bri. Anderson. L—Benitez. S—Mesa. HR—Fernandez (Cle.).

NLCS

■ **Winner:** The Marlins became the first wild-card team to reach the World Series when they upended the defending-N.L. champion Braves in a six-game NLCS. The 5-year-old Marlins also became the youngest expansion team to reach the fall classic while giving the spring training haven of South Florida its first World Series. The Marlins, who finished nine games behind Atlanta in the N.L. East, didn't even exist in 1991 when the Braves began their long playoff run.
■ **Turning point:** After righthander Livan Hernandez surrendered a Game 5-opening triple to Kenny Lofton and a walk to Keith Lockhart, he came back to strike out Chipper Jones, Fred McGriff and Ryan Klesko in a scoreless first inning. Bolstered by that great escape, Hernandez surrendered only two more hits and tied the LCS record with 15 strikeouts while outdueling Greg Maddux in a 2-1 victory at Pro Player Stadium.
■ **Memorable moment:** Kevin Brown's final pitch of Game 6, which extended the Marlins' Cinderella run and gave manager Jim Leyland his first World Series appearance in a career that spanned 33 years. Brown, the Game 1 winner, struggled through an 11-hit, complete-game 7-4 victory while fighting a stomach flu.
■ **Top guns:** Craig Counsell (.429), Bobby Bonilla (4 RBI), Charles Johnson (5 RBI), Jeff Conine (5 RBI), Hernandez (2-0, 0.84 ERA), Brown (2-0), Marlins; Lockhart (.500), Andruw Jones (.444), McGriff (.333, 4 RBI), Chipper Jones (2 HR, 4 RBI), Ryan Klesko (2 HR, 4 RBI), Denny Neagle (12 IP, 1-0, 0.00 ERA), Maddux (13 IP, 0-2, 1.38 ERA), Braves.
■ **MVP:** Hernandez.

Linescores

Game 1—October 7, at Atlanta
Florida............3 0 2 0 0 0 0 0 0—5 6 0
Atlanta............1 0 1 0 0 1 0 0 0—3 5 2
Brown, Cook (7), Powell (8), Nen (9); Maddux, Neagle (7). W—Brown. L—Maddux. S—Nen. HR—C. Jones, Klesko (Atl.).

Game 2—October 8, at Atlanta
Florida..........0 0 0 0 0 0 0 1 0—1 3 1
Atlanta..........3 0 2 0 0 0 2 0 x—7 13 0
Fernandez, Leiter (3), Heredia (6), Vosberg (7); Glavine, Cather (8), Wohlers (9). W—Glavine. L—Fernandez. HR—Klesko, C. Jones (Atl.).

Game 3—October 10, at Florida
Atlanta............0 0 0 1 0 1 0 0 0—2 6 1
Florida............0 0 0 1 0 4 0 0 x—5 8 1
Smoltz, Cather (7), Ligtenberg (8); Saunders, Hernandez (6), Cook (8), Nen (9). W—Hernandez. L—Smoltz. S—Nen. HR—Sheffield (Fla.).

Game 4—October 11, at Florida
Atlanta..........1 0 1 0 2 0 0 0 0—4 11 0
Florida..........0 0 0 0 0 0 0 0 0—0 4 0
Neagle; Leiter, Heredia (7), Vosberg (9). W—Neagle. L—Leiter. HR—Blauser (Atl.).

Game 5—October 12, at Florida
Atlanta............0 1 0 0 0 0 0 0 0—1 3 0
Florida............1 0 0 0 0 0 1 0 x—2 5 0
Maddux, Cather (8); Hernandez. W—Hernandez. L—Maddux. HR—Tucker (Atl.).

Game 6—October 14, at Atlanta
Florida..........4 0 0 0 0 3 0 0 0—7 10 1
Atlanta..........1 2 0 0 0 0 0 0 1—4 11 1
Brown; Glavine, Cather (6), Ligtenberg (7), Embree (9). W—Brown. L—Glavine.

WORLD SERIES

■ **Winner:** The expansion Marlins, who had undergone an $89 million offseason facelift, made the investment pay off when they outlasted the Indians in an exciting World Series that was decided in the 11th inning of Game 7 at Pro Player Stadium. The victory gave the 5-year-old Marlins distinction as the youngest team ever to win a fall classic and the only wild-card team to earn a championship. The Indians failed to win their first World Series since 1948 for the second time in three years.
■ **Turning point:** It didn't arrive until the ninth inning of Game 7, when the Indians were leading 2-1 and two outs away from an elusive championship. That's when the Marlins scored the tying run on Craig Counsell's sacrifice fly, setting the stage for a dramatic finish to a closely contested series in which the teams alternated victories.
■ **Memorable moment:** The bases-loaded, 11th-inning single by shortstop Edgar Renteria that gave the Marlins their unlikely victory and sent 67,204 fans at Pro Player Stadium into a frenzy. The two-out hit completed a gutsy comeback after the Marlins had been limited to two hits over eight innings by starter Jaret Wright and three Cleveland relievers. It also made a winner out of Jay Powell, who completed the six-pitcher six-hitter with a scoreless top of the 11th.
■ **Top guns:** Darren Daulton (.389), Charles Johnson (.357), Moises Alou (.321, 3 HR, 9 RBI), Livan Hernandez (2-0), Marlins; Matt Williams (.385), Sandy Alomar (.367, 2 HR, 10 RBI), Manny Ramirez (2 HR, 6 RBI); Chad Ogea (2-0, 1.54 ERA), Wright (1-0, 2.92), Indians.
■ **MVP:** Hernandez.

Linescores

Game 1—October 18, at Florida
Cleveland......1 0 0 0 1 1 0 1 0—4 11 0
Florida..........0 0 1 4 2 0 0 0 x—7 7 1
Hershiser, Juden (5), Plunk (6), Assenmacher (8); Hernandez, Cook (6), Powell (8), Nen (9). W—Hernandez. L—Hershiser. S—Nen. HR—Alou, Johnson (Fla.), Ramirez, Thome (Cle.).

Game 2—October 19, at Florida
Cleveland......1 0 0 0 3 2 0 0 0—6 14 0
Florida..........1 0 0 0 0 0 0 0 0—1 8 0
Ogea, Jackson (7), Mesa (9); Brown, Heredia (7), Alfonseca (8). W—Ogea. L—Brown. HR—Alomar (Cle.).

Game 3—October 21, at Cleveland
Florida........1 0 1 1 0 2 2 0 7—14 16 3
Cleveland....2 0 0 3 2 0 0 0 4—11 10 3
Leiter, Heredia (5), Cook (8), Nen (9); Nagy, Anderson (7), Jackson (7), Assenmacher (8), Plunk (8), Morman (9), Mesa (9). W—Cook. L—Plunk. HR—Sheffield, Daulton, Eisenreich (Fla.), Thome (Cle.).

Game 4—October 22, at Cleveland
Florida........0 0 0 1 0 2 0 0 0— 3 6 2
Cleveland....3 0 3 0 0 1 1 2 x—10 15 0
Saunders, Alfonseca (3), Vosberg (6), Powell (8); Wright, Anderson (7). W—Wright. L—Saunders. S—Anderson. HR—Ramirez, Williams (Cle.), Alou (Fla.).

Game 5—October 23, at Cleveland
Florida..........0 2 0 0 0 4 0 1 1—8 15 2
Cleveland......0 1 3 0 0 0 0 0 3—7 9 0
Hernandez, Nen (9); Hershiser, Morman (6), Plunk (6), Juden (7), Assenmacher (8), Mesa (9). W—Hernandez. L—Hershiser. S—Nen. HR—Alomar (Cle.), Alou (Fla.).

Game 6—October 25, at Florida
Cleveland........0 2 1 0 1 0 0 0 0—4 8 0
Florida............0 0 0 0 1 0 0 0 0—1 8 0
Ogea, Jackson (6), Assenmacher (8), Mesa (9); Brown, Heredia (6), Powell (8), Vosberg (9). W—Ogea. L—Brown. S—Mesa.

Game 7—October 26, at Florida
Cle. ......0 0 2 0 0 0 0 0 0 0 0—2 6 2
Fla. ......0 0 0 0 0 0 1 0 1 0 1—3 8 0
Wright, Assenmacher (7), Jackson (8), Anderson (8), Mesa (9), Nagy (10); Leiter, Cook (7), Alfonseca (8), Heredia (9), Nen (9), Powell (11). W—Powell. L—Nagy. HR—Bonilla (Fla.).

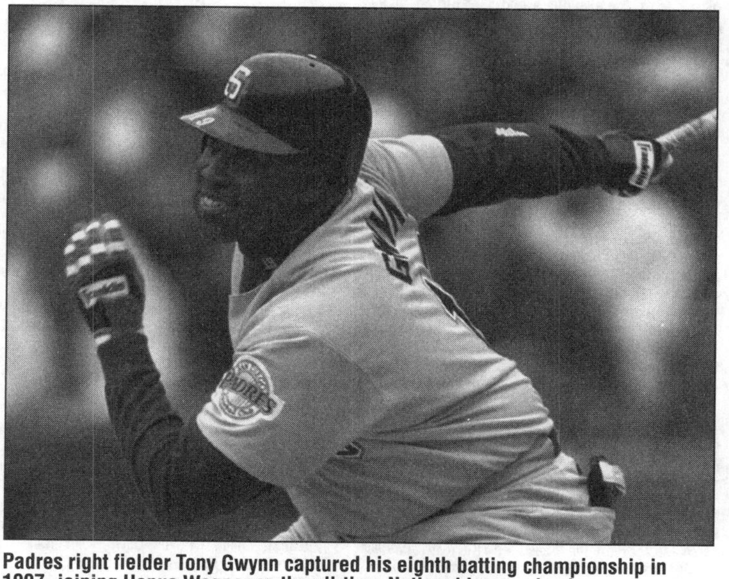

Padres right fielder Tony Gwynn captured his eighth batting championship in 1997, joining Honus Wagner as the all-time National League leader.

HISTORY

FINAL STANDINGS

American League

EAST DIVISION

Team	N.Y.	Bos.	Tor.	Bal.	T.B.	Cle.	Chi.	K.C.	Min.	Det.	Tex.	Ana.	Sea.	Oak.	Atl.	NYM	Phi.	Mtl.	Fla.	W	L	Pct.	GB
New York	—	7	6	9	11	7	7	10	7	8	8	5	8	8	3	2	3	2	3	114	48	.704	—
Boston	5	—	5	6	9	8	5	8	5	5	6	5	7	9	2	1	1	3	2	92	70	.568	22
Toronto	6	7	—	7	7	4	6	5	7	6	4	7	7	6	1	2	1	4	1	88	74	.543	26
Baltimore	3	6	5	—	5	5	2	5	7	10	6	6	6	8	1	1	2	0	1	79	83	.488	35
Tampa Bay	1	3	5	7	—	3	6	3	4	6	4	5	5	6	0	1	2	1	1	63	99	.389	51

CENTRAL DIVISION

Team	N.Y.	Bos.	Tor.	Bal.	T.B.	Cle.	Chi.	K.C.	Min.	Det.	Tex.	Ana.	Sea.	Oak.	Hou.	ChC	Stl.	Cin.	Mil.	Pit.	W	L	Pct.	GB
Cleveland	4	3	7	6	7	—	6	8	6	9	4	7	9	3	1	2	2	2	2	1	89	73	.549	—
Chicago	4	6	4	9	5	6	—	8	6	6	5	6	4	4	1	0	2	1	1	2	80	82	.494	9
Kansas City	0	3	6	6	8	4	4	—	7	6	3	5	4	7	1	2	2	2	1	1	72	89	.447	16.5
Minnesota	4	6	4	3	7	6	6	5	—	4	7	5	2	4	1	2	2	1	0	1	70	92	.432	19
Detroit	3	5	5	1	5	3	6	6	8	—	3	3	3	7	0	2	1	0	2	2	65	97	.401	24

WEST DIVISION

Team	N.Y.	Bos.	Tor.	Bal.	T.B.	Cle.	Chi.	K.C.	Min.	Det.	Tex.	Ana.	Sea.	Oak.	S.D.	S.F.	L.A.	Col.	Ari.	W	L	Pct.	GB
Texas	3	5	7	5	7	7	6	8	4	8	—	7	7	6	2	1	0	2	3	88	74	.543	—
Anaheim	6	6	4	5	6	4	5	6	6	8	5	—	9	5	1	1	3	3	2	85	77	.525	3
Seattle	3	4	4	5	6	2	7	6	9	8	5	3	—	7	2	1	1	2	1	76	85	.472	11.5
Oakland	3	2	5	3	5	8	7	4	7	4	6	7	5	—	2	2	1	1	2	74	88	.457	14

National League

EAST DIVISION

Team	Atl.	N.Y.	Phi.	Mtl.	Fla.	Hou.	Chi.	Stl.	Cin.	Mil.	Pit.	S.D.	S.F.	L.A.	Col.	Ari.	NYY	Bos.	Tor.	Bal.	T.B.	W	L	Pct.	GB
Atlanta	—	9	8	6	7	4	3	6	7	7	7	5	7	8	5	8	1	1	2	2	3	106	56	.654	—
New York	3	—	8	4	7	4	5	6	6	8	4	4	4	5	6	5	1	2	1	3	2	88	74	.543	18
Philadelphia	4	4	—	7	6	2	6	3	5	5	8	1	2	4	4	7	0	3	2	1	1	75	87	.463	31
Montreal	6	8	5	—	7	2	2	3	1	3	2	4	3	4	2	7	1	0	0	3	2	65	97	.401	41
Florida	5	5	6	5	—	3	2	4	0	0	3	4	0	4	3	2	0	1	2	2	3	54	108	.333	52

CENTRAL DIVISION

Team	Atl.	N.Y.	Phi.	Mtl.	Fla.	Hou.	Chi.	Stl.	Cin.	Mil.	Pit.	S.D.	S.F.	L.A.	Col.	Ari.	Cle.	ChW	K.C.	Min.	Det.	W	L	Pct.	GB
Houston	5	5	7	7	6	—	7	5	8	9	9	5	6	3	5	5	2	2	2	1	3	102	60	.630	—
Chicago	6	4	3	7	7	4	—	4	6	6	8	5	7	4	7	7	0	3	1	1	0	90	73	.552	12.5
St. Louis	3	3	6	6	5	7	7	—	3	8	5	3	5	5	6	7	0	1	1	1	1	83	79	.512	19
Cincinnati	2	3	4	8	9	3	5	8	—	6	5	1	2	5	4	5	1	1	0	2	3	77	85	.475	25
Milwaukee	2	1	4	6	9	2	6	3	5	—	6	3	5	4	7	3	1	2	2	2	1	74	88	.457	28
Pittsburgh	2	5	1	7	6	2	3	6	7	5	—	5	2	5	4	3	2	0	1	2	1	69	93	.426	33

WEST DIVISION

Team	Atl.	N.Y.	Phi.	Mtl.	Fla.	Hou.	Chi.	Stl.	Cin.	Mil.	Pit.	S.D.	S.F.	L.A.	Col.	Ari.	Tex.	Ana.	Sea.	Oak.	W	L	Pct.	GB
San Diego	4	5	8	4	5	4	4	6	11	6	4	—	8	7	7	9	1	2	2	1	98	64	.605	—
San Fran.	2	5	6	6	9	3	3	7	7	4	7	4	—	6	5	7	2	2	2	2	89	74	.546	9.5
Los Angeles	1	3	5	5	5	6	5	4	4	5	7	5	6	—	6	8	3	1	2	2	83	79	.512	15
Colorado	3	3	5	7	6	6	2	3	5	4	5	5	7	6	—	6	1	0	1	2	77	85	.475	21
Arizona	1	4	2	2	6	4	5	2	4	6	6	3	5	4	6	—	1	1	2	1	65	97	.401	33

SIGNIFICANT EVENTS

■ **March 31:** Two expansion teams made their major league debut, Arizona losing 9-2 to the Colorado Rockies at new Bank One Ballpark in Phoenix and Tampa Bay dropping an 11-6 decision to Detroit at new Tropicana Field.

■ **March 31:** The Milwaukee Brewers, transplanted to the National League because of expansion, lost their first N.L. game, 2-1, at Atlanta. The Brewers became the first modern-era team in baseball history to switch leagues.

■ **April 15:** The New York Yankees, forced to temporarily abandon Yankee Stadium when a steel beam fell from beneath the upper deck to the empty seats below, posted a 6-3 win over the Angels at Shea Stadium, home of the Mets. The Mets came back that night to beat the Cubs 2-1—the first time this century that two regular-season games involving four teams were played in the same stadium on the same day.

■ **July 9:** After serving as chairman of the Executive Committee and interim commissioner for almost six years, Allan (Bud) Selig, the Milwaukee Brewers' president and chief executive officer, accepted a five-year term as baseball's ninth commissioner.

■ **August 9:** Atlanta veteran Dennis Martinez posted his 244th career victory in a relief role against San Francisco, making him the winningest Latin pitcher in major league history.

■ **September 28:** Gary Gaetti's two-run homer lifted Chicago to a 5-3 win over San Francisco in the first-ever playoff to decide a league's wild-card representative.

■ **December 12:** The Los Angeles Dodgers broke new ground when they signed pitcher Kevin Brown to a seven-year contract worth $105 million—the first $100 million deal in baseball history.

MEMORABLE MOMENTS

■ **May 6:** Chicago Cubs rookie Kerry Wood tied Roger Clemens' single-game strikeout record when he fanned 20 Houston batters in a one-hit, 2-0 shutout at Wrigley Field.

■ **May 17:** Lefthander David Wells fired the first regular-season perfect game in New York Yankees history and the 13th perfecto of the modern era when he retired all 27 Minnesota Twins he faced in a 4-0 win before 49,820 fans at Yankee Stadium.

■ **September 8:** St. Louis first baseman Mark McGwire broke Roger Maris' 37-year-old single-season home run record when he drove a pitch from Chicago righthander Steve Trachsel over the left field fence at Busch Stadium for homer No. 62.

■ **September 13:** Chicago right fielder Sammy Sosa, following McGwire's home run lead, hit Nos. 61 and 62 during a Sunday night victory over Milwaukee at Wrigley Field.

■ **September 20:** Baltimore third baseman Cal Ripken ended his record ironman streak at 2,632 consecutive games when he sat out against the New York Yankees in the Orioles' final home contest of the season.

■ **September 25:** The Yankees posted a 6-1 victory over Tampa Bay at Yankee Stadium for their 112th win, topping the American League record of 111 set by the 1954 Cleveland Indians. The Yanks would go on to win 114 times.

■ **September 27:** McGwire, who trailed Sosa briefly on the final Friday of the great 1998 home run race, capped a five-homer final weekend with two final-day shots against Montreal, bringing his record season total to 70.

ALL-STAR GAME

■ **Winner:** The A.L. obliterated the N.L. with a 19-hit, five-stolen base barrage that resulted in a 13-8 victory. The A.L.'s second straight win featured home runs by Alex Rodriguez and Roberto Alomar and a surprising running attack.

■ **Key inning:** The sixth, when the A.L. broke out its ugly game and scored three times for an 8-6 lead. The rally off Montreal righthander Ugueth Urbina featured four stolen bases and runners crossing the plate on a wild pitch and a passed ball. The uprising wiped out a three-run fifth-inning homer by San Francisco's Barry Bonds.

■ **Memorable moment:** A towering two-run double to right by third baseman Cal Ripken in the fourth. The double was Ripken's 11th hit in his 16th All-Star Game.

■ **Top guns:** Rafael Palmeiro (Orioles), Alex Rodriguez (Mariners), Ken Griffey Jr. (Mariners), Roberto Alomar (Indians), Ripken (Orioles), David Wells (Yankees), A.L.; Bonds (Giants), Tony Gwynn (Padres), N.L.

■ **MVP** Roberto Alomar.

LEADERS

American League
BA: Bernie Williams, N.Y., .339.
Runs: Derek Jeter, N.Y., 127.
Hits: Alex Rodriguez, Sea., 213.
TB: Albert Belle, Chi., 399.
HR: Ken Griffey Jr., Sea., 56.
RBI: Juan Gonzalez, Tex., 157.
SB: Rickey Henderson, Oak., 66.
Wins: Roger Clemens, Tor., David Cone, N.Y., Rick Helling, Tex., 20.
ERA: Roger Clemens, Tor., 2.65.
CG: Scott Erickson, Bal., 11.
IP: Scott Erickson, Bal., 251.1.
SO: Roger Clemens, Tor., 271.
Sv.: Tom Gordon, Bos., 46.

National League
BA: Larry Walker, Col., .363.
Runs: Sammy Sosa, Chi., 134.
Hits: Dante Bichette, Col., 219.
TB: Sammy Sosa, Chi., 416.
HR: Mark McGwire, St.L., 70.
RBI: Sammy Sosa, Chi., 158.
SB: Tony Womack, Pit., 58.
Wins: Tom Glavine, Atl., 20.
ERA: Greg Maddux, Atl., 2.22.
CG: Curt Schilling, Phi., 15.
IP: Curt Schilling, Phi., 268.2.
SO: Curt Schilling, Phi., 300.
Sv.: Trevor Hoffman, S.D., 53.

A.L. 100 RBIs
Juan Gonzalez, Tex., 157
Albert Belle, Chi., 152
Ken Griffey Jr., Sea., 146
Manny Ramirez, Cle., 145
Alex Rodriguez, Sea., 124
Tino Martinez, N.Y., 123
Nomar Garciaparra, Bos., 122
Rafael Palmeiro, Bal., 121
Dean Palmer, K.C., 119
Paul O'Neill, N.Y., 116
Carlos Delgado, Tor., 115
Mo Vaughn, Bos., 115
Jason Giambi, Oak., 110
Frank Thomas, Chi., 109
Rusty Greer, Tex., 108
Jose Canseco, Tor., 107
Matt Stairs, Oak., 106
Tony Clark, Det., 103
Will Clark, Tex., 102
Edgar Martinez, Sea., 102
Damion Easley, Det., 100
Shawn Green, Tor., 100

N.L. 100 RBIs
Sammy Sosa, Chi., 158
Mark McGwire, St.L., 147
Vinny Castilla, Col., 144
Jeff Kent, S.F., 128
Jeromy Burnitz, Mil., 125
Moises Alou, Hou., 124
Dante Bichette, Col., 122
Barry Bonds, S.F., 122
Andres Galarraga, Atl., 121
Greg Vaughn, S.D., 119
Jeff Bagwell, Hou., 111
Mike Piazza, L.A., Fla., N.Y., 111
Scott Rolen, Phi., 110
Vladimir Guerrero, Mon., 109
Derek Bell, Hou., 108
Kevin Young, Pit., 108
Chipper Jones, Atl., 107
Javy Lopez, Atl., 106
Ray Lankford, St.L., 105
Rico Brogna, Phi., 104

A.L. 40 homers
Ken Griffey Jr., Sea., 56
Albert Belle, Chi., 49
Jose Canseco, Tor., 46
Juan Gonzalez, Tex., 45
Manny Ramirez, Cle., 45
Rafael Palmeiro, Bal., 43
Alex Rodriguez, Sea., 42
Mo Vaughn, Bos., 40

N.L. 40 homers
Mark McGwire, St.L., 70
Sammy Sosa, Chi., 66
Greg Vaughn, S.D., 50
Vinny Castilla, Col., 46
Andres Galarraga, Atl., 44

Most Valuable Player
A.L.: Juan Gonzalez, OF, Tex.
N.L.: Sammy Sosa, OF, Chi.

Cy Young Award
A.L.: Roger Clemens, Tor.
N.L.: Tom Glavine, Atl.

Rookie of the Year
A.L.: Ben Grieve, OF, Oak.
N.L.: Kerry Wood, P, Chi.

Manager of the Year
A.L.: Joe Torre, N.Y.
N.L.: Larry Dierker, Hou.

Hall of Fame additions
George Brett, 3B, 1973-93
Orlando Cepeda, OF-1B, 1958-74
Nestor Chylak, umpire
Nolan Ryan, P, 1966-93
Frank Selee, M, 1890-1905
Smokey Joe Williams, P, Negro Leagues
Robin Yount, SS-OF, 1974-93

Linescore

July 7 at Colorado's Coors Field

A.L. ....0 0 0 4 1 3 1 1 3—13 19 2
N.L. ....0 0 2 1 3 0 0 2 0— 8 12 1

Wells (Yankees), Clemens (Blue Jays) 3, Radke (Twins) 4, Colon (Indians) 5, Arrojo (Devil Rays) 6, Wetteland (Rangers) 7, Gordon (Red Sox) 8, Percival (Angels) 9 and I. Rodriguez (Rangers), S. Alomar (Indians); Maddux (Braves), Glavine (Braves) 3, Brown (Padres) 4, Ashby (Padres) 5, Urbina (Expos) 6, Hoffman (Padres) 7, Shaw (Dodgers) 8, Nen (Giants) 9 and Piazza (Mets), Lopez (Braves). W—Colon. L—Urbina. HR—A. Rodriguez, R. Alomar, A.L.; Bonds, N.L.

A.L. DIVISION SERIES

■ **Winners:** The New York Yankees, who won an A.L.-record 114 regular-season games, carried that dominance into the postseason with a three-game Division Series sweep of the Texas Rangers, and the Cleveland Indians earned their third ALCS berth in four years with an exciting four-game victory over the wild-card Boston Red Sox. Yankee pitchers shut down the A.L.'s top-hitting team (a .141 average) en route to their second ALCS opportunity in three years and the Indians overcame an 11-3 series-opening loss while extending Boston's 80-year World Series championship drought.

■ **Turning points:** What little offense the Yankees needed in 2-0, 3-1 and 4-0 victories was provided by unlikely sources: Third baseman Scott Brosius singled in the go-ahead run in Game 1 and hit a lead-extending two-run homer in Game 2; backup outfielder Shane Spencer homered in Game 2 and hit a key three-run shot in Game 3. A Game 2 first-inning ejection of Cleveland manager Mike Hargrove and starting pitcher Dwight Gooden seemed to energize the lethargic Indians, who erupted for six runs in the first two innings and went on to a 9-5 series-squaring win.

■ **Memorable moments:** A Game 3 Texas-type downpour that forced a 3-hour, 16-minute rain delay in Game 3, but merely delayed the inevitable for the Rangers. The delay knocked Yankee starter David Cone out of the game, but three relievers came on to complete his shutout and Spencer delivered the big blow. Left fielder David Justice provided the big plays in Game 4 for the Indians, a sixth-inning throw that cut down Boston runner John Valentin at the plate and a two-run, eighth-inning double that secured a 2-1 victory.

■ **Memorable performances:** Brosius and Spencer combined for seven of the Yankees' eight RBIs in the series, but the real heroes were pitchers David Wells, Andy Pettitte, Cone, Mariano Rivera, Jeff Nelson and Graeme Lloyd, who combined for a 0.33 ERA—allowing only one run in three games. Texas starters—Todd Stottlemyre, Rick Helling, Aaron Sele—all pitched well, but got little run support. Kenny Lofton, Manny Ramirez, Jim Thome and Justice provided the bulk of Cleveland's offense and the Indians got good pitching from starters Charles Nagy and Bartolo Colon and three saves from Mike Jackson. First baseman Mo Vaughn (2 homers, 7 RBIs) and shortstop Nomar Garciaparra (3, 11) were prolific offensively for the losing Red Sox.

Linescores

New York vs. Texas

Game 1—September 29, at New York

Texas..............0 0 0 0 0 0 0 0 0—0 5 0
New York........0 2 0 0 0 0 0 0 x—2 6 0

Stottlemyre and Rodriguez; Wells, Rivera (9) and Posada. W—Wells. L—Stottlemyre. S—Rivera.

Game 2—September 30, at New York

Texas..............0 0 0 0 1 0 0 0 0—1 5 0
New York........0 1 0 2 0 0 0 0 x—3 8 0

Helling, Crabtree (7) and Rodriguez; Pettitte, Nelson (8), Rivera (8) and Girardi. W—Pettitte. L—Helling. S—Rivera. HR—Spencer, Brosius (N.Y.).

Game 3—October 2, at Texas

New York........0 0 0 0 0 4 0 0 0—4 9 1
Texas..............0 0 0 0 0 0 0 0 0—0 3 1

Cone, Lloyd (6), Nelson (7), Rivera (9) and Girardi; Sele, Crabtree (7), Wetteland (9) and Rodriguez. W—Cone. L—Sele. HR—O'Neill, Spencer (N.Y.).

Boston vs. Cleveland

Game 1—September 29, at Cleveland
Boston........3 0 0 0 3 2 0 3 0—11 12 0
Cleveland....0 0 0 0 0 2 1 0 0— 3 7 0
Martinez, Corsi (8) and Hatteberg; Wright, Jones (5), Reed (8), Poole (8), Shuey (8), Assenmacher (9) and Alomar. W—Martinez. L—Wright. HR—Vaughn 2, Garciaparra (Bos.); Lofton, Thome (Cle.).

Game 2—September 30, at Cleveland
Boston..........2 0 1 0 0 2 0 0 0—5 10 0
Cleveland......1 5 1 0 0 1 0 1 x—9 9 1
Wakefield, Wasdin (2), Lowe (4), Swindell (6), Gordon (8) and Varitek; Gooden, Burba (1), Shuey (6), Assenmacher (8), Jackson (8) and Alomar. W—Burba. L—Wakefield. S—Jackson. HR—Justice (Cle.).

Game 3—October 2, at Boston
Cleveland........0 0 0 0 1 1 1 0 1—4 5 0
Boston............0 0 0 1 0 0 0 0 2—3 6 0
Nagy, Jackson (9) and Alomar; Saberhagen, Corsi (8), Eckersley (9) and Hatteberg. W—Nagy. L—Saberhagen. S—Jackson. HR—Thome, Lofton, M. Ramirez 2 (Cle.); Garciaparra (Bos.).

Game 4—October 3, at Boston
Cleveland........0 0 0 0 0 0 0 2 0—2 5 0
Boston............0 0 0 1 0 0 0 0 0—1 6 0
Colon, Poole (6), Reed (7), Assenmacher (8), Shuey (8), Jackson (9) and Alomar; Schourek, Lowe (6), Gordon (8) and Hatteberg. W—Reed. L—Gordon. S—Jackson. HR—Garciaparra (Bos.).

N.L. DIVISION SERIES

■ **Winners:** The Atlanta Braves earned their seventh straight N.L. Championship Series berth by sweeping past the wild-card Chicago Cubs, and the San Diego Padres reached the NLCS for the first time since 1984 by throttling the Houston Astros and their N.L.-leading offense. Braves pitchers simply were too much for the overmatched Cubs, who scored only four runs in the three games, and the Padres followed that lead by holding the high-powered Astros to a .182 average in a surprising four-game victory.

■ **Turning points:** The Braves took control of the series in Game 2 when they tied the game at 1-1 in the bottom of the ninth and then won in the 10th on a Chipper Jones single down the left field line. The Padres served notice to the Astros in Game 1 when starter Kevin Brown struck out 16 batters and allowed two hits over eight innings while outdueling Houston ace Randy Johnson, 2-1.

■ **Memorable moments:** The ninth inning of Game 2, when Atlanta catcher Javy Lopez connected off Chicago pitcher Kevin Tapani for a one-out home run that tied the game 1-1. The Padres got a dramatic Game 2-tying home run from Jim Leyritz off Houston closer Billy Wagner in the ninth inning, but the Astros rebounded in the bottom of the ninth to post a 5-4 victory—their only win of the series.

■ **Memorable performances:** Atlanta catchers Lopez and Eddie Perez combined for eight RBIs and Braves pitchers, led by starters John Smoltz, Tom Glavine and Greg Maddux, posted a 1.29 ERA. Tapani and rookie Kerry Wood had outstanding starting efforts for the Cubs, but there was too little offensive support. San Diego's biggest offensive gun was Leyritz, who came off the bench to hit three home runs, while pitchers Brown and Sterling Hitchcock led a staff that compiled a 1.78 ERA. Johnson allowed only three earned runs in two starts covering 14 innings for the Astros, but all he had to show for his efforts were two losses.

Linescores

Chicago vs. Atlanta

Game 1—September 30, at Atlanta
Chicago..........0 0 0 0 0 0 0 1 0—1 5 1
Atlanta ....0 2 0 0 0 1 4 0 x—7 8 0
Clark, Heredia (7), Karchner (7), Morgan (8) and Houston; Smoltz, Rocker (8), Ligtenberg (9) and Lopez. W—Smoltz. L—Clark. HR—Houston (Chi.); Tucker, Klesko (Atl.).

Game 2—October 1, at Atlanta
Chicago....0 0 0 0 0 1 0 0 0 0—1 4 1
Atlanta ....0 0 0 0 0 0 0 0 1 1—2 6 0
Tapani, Mulholland (10) and Servais, Houston; Glavine, Rocker (8), Seanez (9), O. Perez (10) and Lopez. W—O. Perez. L—Mulholland. HR—Lopez (Atl.).

Game 3—October 3, at Chicago
Atlanta............0 0 1 0 0 0 0 5 0—6 9 0
Chicago..........0 0 0 0 0 0 0 2 0—2 8 2
Maddux, Ligtenberg (8) and E. Perez; Wood, Mulholland (6), Beck (8), Morgan (9) and Houston, Martinez. W—Maddux. L—Wood. HR—E. Perez (Atl.).

Houston vs. San Diego

Game 1—September 29, at Houston
San Diego ......0 0 0 0 0 1 0 1 0—2 9 1
Houston ....0 0 0 0 0 0 0 0 1—1 4 0
Brown, Hoffman (9) and Hernandez; Johnson, Powell (9), Henry (9) and Ausmus. W—Brown. L—Johnson. S—Hoffman. HR—Vaughn (S.D.).

Game 2—October 1, at Houston
San Diego ....0 0 0 0 0 2 0 0 2—4 8 1
Houston ......1 0 2 0 0 0 0 1 1—5 11 1
Ashby, Hamilton (5), Wall (8), Miceli (9), Hoffman (9) and Hernandez, Myers; Reynolds, Powell (8), Wagner (9) and Eusebio, Ausmus. W—Wagner. L—Miceli. HR—Leyritz (S.D.); Bell (Hou.).

Game 3—October 3, at San Diego
Houston ....0 0 0 0 0 0 1 0 0—1 4 0
San Diego ......0 0 0 0 0 1 1 0 x—2 3 0
Hampton, Elarton (7) and Ausmus; Brown, Miceli (7), Hoffman (9) and Hernandez. W—Miceli. L—Elarton. S—Hoffman. HR—Leyritz (S.D.).

Game 4—October 4, at San Diego
Houston ....0 0 0 1 0 0 0 0 0—1 3 1
San Diego ......0 1 0 0 0 1 0 4 x—6 7 1
Johnson, Miller (7), Henry (7), Powell (8) and Ausmus; Hitchcock, Hamilton (7), Miceli (7), Hoffman (9) and Leyritz, Hernandez. W—Hitchcock. L—Johnson. HR—Leyritz, Joyner (S.D.).

ALCS

■ **Winner:** The New York Yankees raised their incredible 1998 season record to 121-50 with a surprisingly difficult six-game victory over Cleveland. After watching the Indians jump to a two-games-to-one advantage, the Yankees won three straight times and advanced to the franchise's record 35th World Series.

■ **Turning point:** Down two-games-to-one and in danger of watching an incredible season unravel, the Yankees tied the series at Cleveland's Jacobs Field behind the four-hit pitching of Orlando Hernandez, Mike Stanton and Mariano Rivera, who combined for a 4-0 shutout of the powerful Indians. Paul O'Neill provided all the offense the trio would need with a solo home run in the first inning.

■ **Memorable moment:** The 12th inning of Game 2 at New York, when a sacrifice bunt by Cleveland's Travis Fryman transformed a 1-1 tie into a 4-1 Indians victory. Yankees first baseman Tino Martinez fielded the bunt and fired to second baseman Chuck Knoblauch covering first. But the ball hit Fryman, who appeared to be running illegally inside the line, and caromed about 20 feet away. Instead of chasing the ball, Knoblauch argued the noncall of umpire Ted Hendry as pinch runner Enrique Wilson circled the bases to score the go-ahead run. Kenny Lofton's two-run single finished the Yankees in an ugly and controversial end to what had been a well-played game.

■ **Top guns:** Bernie Williams (.381, 5 RBIs), Scott Brosius (.300, 6 RBIs), Hernandez (1-0, 0.00 ERA), David Wells (2-0, 2.87), Rivera (4 games, 0.00), Yankees; Omar Vizquel (.440), Jim Thome (.304, 4 HRs, 8 RBIs), Manny Ramirez (.333, 2 HRs, 4 RBIs), Bartolo Colon (1-0, 1.00 ERA), Paul Shuey (5 games, 0.00), Indians.

■ **MVP:** Wells.

Linescores

Game 1—October 6, a New York
Cleveland......0 0 0 0 0 0 0 0 2—2 5 0
New York......5 0 0 0 0 1 1 0 x—7 11 0
Wright, Ogea (1), Poole (7), Reed (7), Shuey (8) and Alomar, Diaz; Wells, Nelson (9) and Posada. W—Wells. L—Wright. HR—Ramirez (Cle.); Posada (N.Y.).

Game 2—October 7, at New York
Cleveland0 0 0 1 0 0 0 0 0 0 0 3—4 7 1
New York0 0 0 0 0 0 1 0 0 0 0 0—1 7 1
Nagy, Reed (7), Poole (8), Shuey (8), Assenmacher (10), Burba (11), Jackson (12) and Alomar; Cone, Rivera (9), Stanton (11), Nelson (11), Lloyd (12) and Girardi. W—Burba. L—Nelson. S—Jackson. HR—Justice (Cle.).

Game 3—October 9, at Cleveland
New York......1 0 0 0 0 0 0 0 0—1 4 0
Cleveland......0 2 0 0 4 0 0 0 x—6 12 0
Pettitte, Mendoza (5), Stanton (7) and Girardi, Posada; Colon and Alomar. W—Colon. L—Pettitte. HR—Thome 2, Ramirez, Whiten (Cle.).

Game 4—October 10, at Cleveland
New York........1 0 0 2 0 0 0 0 1—4 4 0
Cleveland........0 0 0 0 0 0 0 0 0—0 4 3
Hernandez, Stanton (8), Rivera (9) and Posada; Gooden, Poole (5), Burba (6), Shuey (9) and Alomar, Diaz. W—Hernandez. L—Gooden. HR—O'Neill (N.Y.).

Game 5—October 11, at Cleveland
New York........3 1 0 1 0 0 0 0 0—5 6 0
Cleveland........2 0 0 0 0 1 0 0 0—3 8 0
Wells, Nelson (8), Rivera (8) and Posada; Ogea, Wright (2), Reed (8), Assenmacher (8), Shuey (9) and Diaz. W—Wells. L—Ogea. S—Rivera. HR—Lofton, Thome (Cle.); Davis (N.Y.).

Game 6—October 13, at New York
Cleveland......0 0 0 0 5 0 0 0 0—5 8 3
New York......2 1 3 0 0 3 0 0 x—9 11 1
Nagy, Burba (4), Poole (6), Shuey (6), Assenmacher (8) and Alomar, Diaz; Cone, Mendoza (6), Rivera (9) and Girardi. W—Cone. L—Nagy. HR—Brosius (N.Y.); Thome (Cle.).

NLCS

■ **Winner:** The San Diego Padres, the dark horse in National League playoffs that featured high-powered teams from Houston and Atlanta, claimed the second pennant of their 30-year existence with a six-game victory over the N.L. East Division-champion Braves, who had won a club-record 106 games during the regular season. The Padres, 98-game winners, beat the Braves at their own game—pitching and defense—and gave them the distinction of becoming the winningest team not to reach the World Series.

■ **Turning point:** Game 3, when the Braves loaded the bases three times—twice with less than two out—and failed to score. Starting pitcher Sterling Hitchcock worked out of the first jam, Dan Miceli came out of the bullpen in the sixth to strike out consecutive pinch hitters and Trevor Hoffman came on in the eighth to strike out catcher Javy Lopez, who represented the potential winning run. The Padres' 4-1 win over Greg Maddux gave them a shocking three-games-to-none advantage over an experienced Braves team appearing in its seventh straight NLCS.

■ **Memorable moment:** Michael Tucker's three-run, eighth-inning homer off Padres ace Kevin Brown in Game 5, a blow that temporarily rescued the Braves from elimination and gave them hope of becoming the first baseball team to come back and win a post-season series after losing the first three games. Brown, who was making a surprise relief appearance after throwing a three-hit shutout in Game 2, escaped a seventh-inning jam but coughed up a 4-2 San Diego lead in the eighth when he walked Ryan Klesko, gave up an infield single to Lopez and then surrendered the game-turning homer to Tucker.

■ **Top guns:** Ozzie Guillen (.417), Tucker (.385, 1 HR, 5 RBIs), John Rocker (6 games, 1-0, 0.00 ERA), Braves; John Vander Wal (.429), Steve Finley (.333), Ken Caminiti (2 HRs, 4 RBIs), Brown (1-1, 2.61 ERA), Hitchcock (2-0, 0-90), Padres.

■ **MVP:** Hitchcock.

Game 1—October 7, at Atlanta
San Diego....0 0 0 0 1 0 0 1 0 1—3 7 0
Atlanta ....0 0 1 0 0 0 0 0 1 0—2 8 3
Ashby, R. Myers (8), Miceli (8), Hoffman (8), Wall (10) and Hernandez; Smoltz, Rocker (8), Martinez (8), Ligtenberg (9) and Lopez, E. Perez. W—Hoffman. L—Ligtenberg. S—Wall. HR—A. Jones (Atl.); Caminiti (S.D.).

Game 2—October 8, at Atlanta
San Diego ....0 0 0 0 0 1 0 0 2—3 11 0
Atlanta..........0 0 0 0 0 0 0 0—0 3 1
Brown and Hernandez; Glavine, Rocker (7), Seanez (8), O. Perez (9), Ligtenberg (9) and Lopez. W—Brown. L—Glavine.

Game 3—October 10, at San Diego
Atlanta ....0 0 1 0 0 0 0 0 0—1 8 2
San Diego ......0 0 0 0 2 0 0 2 x—4 7 0
Maddux, Martinez (6), Rocker (7), Seanez (8) and E. Perez, Lopez; Hitchcock, Wall (6), Miceli (8) R. Myers (8), Hoffman (8) and Leyritz, Hernandez. W—Hitchcock. L—Maddux. S—Hoffman.

Game 4—October 11, at San Diego
Atlanta..........0 0 0 1 0 1 6 0 0—8 12 0
San Diego ....0 0 2 0 0 1 0 0 0—3 8 0
Neagle, Martinez (6), Rocker (7), O. Perez (8), Seanez (8), Ligtenberg (9) and Lopez; Hamilton, R. Myers (7), Miceli (7), Boehringer (8), Langston (9) and Hernandez. W—Martinez. L—Hamilton. HR—Leyritz (S.D.); Lopez, Galarraga (Atl.).

Game 5—October 12, at San Diego
Atlanta..........0 0 0 1 0 1 0 5 0—7 14 1
San Diego ....2 0 0 0 0 2 0 0 2—6 10 1
Smoltz, Rocker (7), Seanez (8), Ligtengerg (9), Maddux (9) and Lopez, E. Perez; Ashby, Langston (7), Brown (7), Wall (8), Boehringer (9), R. Myers (9) and Hernandez. W—Rocker. L—Brown. S—Maddux. HR—Caminiti, Vander Wal (S.D.); Tucker (Atl.).

Game 6—October 14, at Atlanta
San Diego ....0 0 0 0 0 5 0 0 0—5 10 0
Atlanta..........0 0 0 0 0 0 0 0 0—2 2 1
Hitchcock, Boehringer (6), Langston (7), Hamilton (7), Hoffman (9) and Leyritz, Hernandez; Glavine, Rocker (6), Martinez (6), Neagle (8) and Lopez. W—Hitchcock. L—Glavine.

WORLD SERIES

■ **Winner:** New York closed out its remarkable season with a four-game sweep of San Diego, giving the Yankees a shockingly efficient 125-50 final 1998 record, including regular season and playoffs. The World Series championship was New York's record 24th overall and second in three years. The sweep was the first in Series play since 1990.

■ **Turning point:** A second-inning Chili Davis smash in Game 1 that struck the left shin of Padres righthander Kevin Brown. San Diego's ace went on to pitch 61/3 innings before leaving with a sore leg and the Yankees exploded for seven runs in the seventh inning, turning a 5-2 deficit into a 9-5 advantage. New York's 9-6 win deflated the overmatched Padres.

■ **Memorable moment:** When Scott Brosius, the World Series MVP, hit a three-run, eighth-inning Game 3 home run off San Diego closer Trevor Hoffman, wiping away a 3-2 New York deficit and giving the Yankees a lead they never relinquished. It was Brosius' second homer of the game and he finished the 5-4 victory with four RBIs.

■ **Top guns:** Tony Gwynn (.500, 3 RBIs), Greg Vaughn (2 HR, 4 RBIs), Sterling Hitchcock (1.50 ERA), Padres; Ricky Ledee (.600, 4 RBIs), Brosius (.471, 2 HR, 6 RBIs), Tino Martinez (.385, 1 HR, 4 RBIs), Andy Pettitte (1-0, 0.00 ERA), Orlando Hernandez (1-0, 1.29 ERA), Mariano Rivera (3 games, 0.00 ERA, 3 saves), Yankees.

■ **MVP:** Brosius.

Game 1—October 17, at New York
San Diego ......0 0 2 0 3 0 0 1 0—6 8 1
New York........0 2 0 0 0 0 7 0 x—9 9 1
Brown, Wall (7), Langston (7), Boehringer (8), R. Myers (8) and C. Hernandez; Wells, Nelson (8), Rivera (8) and Posada. W—Wells. L—Wall. S—Rivera. HR—Vaughn 2, Gwynn (S.D.); Knoblauch, Martinez (N.Y.).

Game 2—October 18, at New York
San Diego ....0 0 0 0 1 0 0 2 0—3 10 1
New York........3 3 1 0 2 0 0 0 x—9 16 0
Ashby, Boehringer (3), Wall (5), Miceli (8) and G. Myers; O. Hernandez, Stanton (8), Nelson (8) and Posada. W—O. Hernandez. L—Ashby. HR—Williams, Posada (N.Y.).

Game 3—October 20, at San Diego
New York........0 0 0 0 0 0 2 3 0—5 9 1
San Diego ......0 0 0 0 0 3 0 1 0—4 7 1
Cone, Lloyd (7), Mendoza (7), Rivera (8) and Girardi; Hitchcock, Hamilton (7), R. Myers (8), Hoffman (8) and Leyritz, C. Hernandez. W—Mendoza. L—Hoffman. S—Rivera. HR—Brosius 2 (N.Y.).

Game 4—October 21, at San Diego
New York........0 0 0 0 0 1 0 2 0—3 9 0
San Diego ......0 0 0 0 0 0 0 0 0—0 7 0
Pettitte, Nelson (8), Rivera (8) and Girardi; Brown, Miceli (9), R. Myers (9) and C. Hernandez. W—Pettitte. L—Brown. S—Rivera.

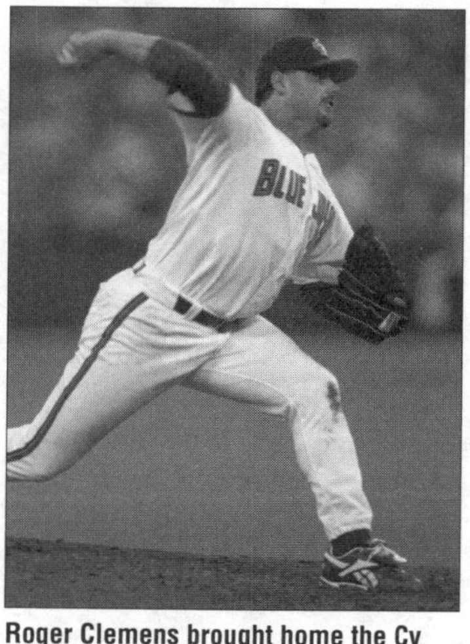

Roger Clemens brought home the Cy Young Award for a record fifth time.

Franchise Histories

The 1930 Athletics, the consecutive World Series champions managed by the incomparable Connie Mack (center, in suit), rank among the great teams in baseball history.

Franchise chronology

Results vs. opponents by decade

Managers and records

World Series champions

Pennant and division winners

Attendance highs, award winners and retired uniforms

Ballpark chronology and firsts

25- and 30-homer men

100-RBI men and 20-game winners

Home run, RBI, batting, ERA and strikeout champions

No-hit pitchers, longest hitting streaks, individual season and single-game records

Career leaders in 21 batting and pitching categories

Team season and single-game records

Team charts showing year-by-year records

Managers and various statistical leaders

Expansion information and draft picks

ANAHEIM ANGELS

FRANCHISE CHRONOLOGY

First season: 1961, as the Los Angeles Angels, with home games played at Los Angeles' Wrigley Field. The Angels, who shared distinction with the second-edition Washington Senators as baseball's first expansion teams, recorded a 7-2 victory at Baltimore in their Major League debut. They went on to post a 70-91 first-season record, good for eighth place in the 10-team A.L.

1962-present: The second-year Angels moved out of tiny Wrigley Field and up in the standings. Sharing new Dodger Stadium with the N.L. Dodgers, they posted a surprising 86-76 record, good for third place behind New York and Minnesota. That success was an illusion. The Angels, who swapped the "Los Angeles" part of their name for "California" in 1965 and moved into new Anaheim Stadium a year later, didn't win their first West Division title until 1979 and failed in their three journeys into the A.L. Championship Series. They were within one pitch of reaching the World Series in the 1986 ALCS when Boston's Dave Henderson hit a dramatic two-run, Game 5 homer that tied the game and propelled the Red Sox to eventual victory. The Angels, under the new ownership flag of Walt Disney Company, changed their name to "Anaheim Angels" after the 1996 season.

First baseman Rod Carew.

ANGELS VS. OPPONENTS BY DECADE

	A's	Indians	Orioles	Red Sox	Tigers	Twins	White Sox	Yankees	Rangers	Brewers	Royals	Blue Jays	Mariners	Devil Rays	Interleague	Decade Record
1961-69	88-74	82-74	72-83	79-76	60-96	79-82	70-92	61-95	76-80	9-9	9-9					685-770
1970-79	72-97	58-58	52-65	53-64	53-63	89-77	90-79	52-65	77-79	61-67	79-87	20-12	25-18			781-831
1980-89	57-70	69-49	49-71	55-59	55-59	66-57	68-62	49-63	68-55	61-54	50-73	57-63	79-48			783-783
1990-99	55-68	44-59	46-73	47-71	54-53	54-61	60-58	59-58	63-61	47-37	64-56	53-58	59-64	13-10	20-30	738-817
Totals	272-309	253-240	219-292	234-270	222-271	288-277	288-291	221-281	284-275	178-167	202-225	130-133	163-130	13-10	20-30	2987-3201

Interleague results: 5-9 vs. Dodgers; 3-7 vs. Padres; 3-7 vs. Giants; 6-4 vs. Rockies; 3-3 vs. Diamondbacks.

MANAGERS

(Los Angeles Angels, 1961-65; California Angels, 1965-96)

Name	Years	Record
Bill Rigney	1961-69	625-707
Lefty Phillips	1969-71	222-225
Del Rice	1972	75-80
Bobby Winkles	1973-74	109-127
Whitey Herzog	1974	2-2
Dick Williams	1974-76	147-194
Norm Sherry	1976-77	76-71
Dave Garcia	1977-78	60-66
Jim Fregosi	1978-81	237-249
Gene Mauch	1981-82, 1985-87	379-332
John McNamara	1983-84, 1996	161-191
Cookie Rojas	1988	75-79
Moose Stubing	1988	0-8
Doug Rader	1989-91	232-216
Buck Rodgers	1991-94	140-172
John Wathan	1992	39-50
Marcel Lachemann	1994-96	161-170
Joe Maddon	1996	8-14
Terry Collins	1997-99	220-237
Joe Maddon	1999	19-10

WEST DIVISION CHAMPIONS

Year	Record	Manager	ALCS Result
1979	88-74	Fregosi	Lost to Orioles
1982	93-69	Mauch	Lost to Brewers
1986	92-70	Mauch	Lost to Red Sox

ALL-TIME RECORD OF EXPANSION TEAMS

Team	W	L	Pct.	DT	P	WS
Arizona	165	159	.509	1	0	0
Kansas City	2,471	2,412	.506	6	2	1
Toronto	1,784	1,818	.495	5	2	2
Houston	2,980	3,048	.494	6	0	0
Montreal	2,387	2,501	.488	2	0	0
Anaheim	2,987	3,201	.483	3	0	0
Milwaukee	2,348	2,542	.480	2	1	0
Colorado	512	559	.478	0	0	0
New York	2,840	3,178	.472	4	3	2
Texas	2,881	3,290	.467	4	0	0
San Diego	2,239	2,656	.457	3	2	0
Seattle	1,624	1,977	.451	2	0	0
Florida	472	596	.442	0	1	1
Tampa Bay	132	192	.407	0	0	0

DT—Division Titles. P—Pennants won. WS—World Series won.

ATTENDANCE HIGHS

Total	Season	Park
2,807,360	1982	Anaheim Stadium
2,696,299	1987	Anaheim Stadium
2,655,892	1986	Anaheim Stadium
2,647,291	1989	Anaheim Stadium
2,567,427	1985	Anaheim Stadium

BALLPARK CHRONOLOGY

Edison International Field of Anaheim, formerly Anaheim Stadium (1966-present)
Capacity: 45,050.
First game: Chicago 3, Angels 1 (April 19, 1966).
First batter: Tommie Agee, White Sox.
First hit: Jim Fregosi, Angels (double).
First run: Rick Reichardt, Angels (2nd inning).
First home run: Rick Reichardt, Angels.
First winning pitcher: Tommy John, White Sox.
First-season attendance: 1,400,321.

Wrigley Field, Los Angeles (1961)
Capacity: 20,457.
First game: Minnesota 4, Angels 2 (April 27, 1961).
First-season attendance: 603,510.

Dodger Stadium (1962-65)
Capacity: 56,000.
First game: Kansas City 5, Angels 3 (April 17, 1962).
First-season attendance: 1,144,063.

A.L. MVP
Don Baylor, OF, 1979

CY YOUNG WINNER
Dean Chance, RH, 1964

ROOKIE OF THE YEAR
Tim Salmon, OF, 1993

RETIRED UNIFORMS

No.	Name	Pos.
11	Jim Fregosi	SS, Manager
26	Gene Autry	Owner
29	Rod Carew	2B-1B
30	Nolan Ryan	P
50	Jimmie Reese	Coach

HISTORY

Righthander Nolan Ryan spent eight record-breaking seasons mowing down hitters for the Angels.

25-plus home runs
39— Reggie Jackson 1982
37— Bobby Bonds 1977
      Leon Wagner 1962
36— Don Baylor 1979
34— Wally Joyner 1987
      Don Baylor 1978
      Tim Salmon 1995
33— Jim Edmonds 1995
      Tim Salmon 1997
      Mo Vaughn 1999
31— Tim Salmon 1993
30— Doug DeCinces 1982
      Bobby Grich 1979
      Frank Robinson 1973
      Tim Salmon 1996
29— Brian Downing 1987
      Troy Glaus 1999
28— Leon Wagner 1961
      Brian Downing 1982
      Dave Winfield 1991
      Chili Davis 1996
27— Reggie Jackson 1985
      Chili Davis 1993
      Tony Phillips................................1995
      Jim Edmonds 1996
26— Lee Thomas 1962
      Leon Wagner 1963
      Doug DeCinces 1986
      Chili Davis 1994
      Jim Edmonds 1997
      Tim Salmon 1998
25— Ken Hunt 1961
      Dan Mincher 1967
      Don Baylor 1977
      Reggie Jackson 1985
      Brian Downing 1988
      Jim Edmonds 1998

100-plus RBIs
139— Don Baylor 1979
129— Tim Salmon 1997
117— Wally Joyner 1987
115— Bobby Bonds 1977
112— Chili Davis 1993
108— Mo Vaughn 1999
107— Leon Wagner 1962
      Jim Edmonds 1995
105— Tim Salmon 1995
104— Lee Thomas 1962
102— J.T. Snow 1995
101— Reggie Jackson 1982
      Dan Ford 1979
      Bobby Grich 1979
100— Wally Joyner 1986

20-plus victories
1964— Dean Chance.............................20-9
1970— Clyde Wright 22-12
1971— Andy Messersmith 20-13
1973— Nolan Ryan 21-16
      Bill Singer 20-14
1974— Nolan Ryan 22-16

A.L. home run champions
1981— Bobby Grich *22
1982— Reggie Jackson *39
* Tied for league lead

A.L. RBI champions
1979— Don Baylor 139

A.L. batting champions
1970— Alex Johnson................................329

A.L. ERA champions
1964— Dean Chance 1.65
1977— Frank Tanana 2.54

A.L. strikeout champions
1972— Nolan Ryan 329
1973— Nolan Ryan 383
1974— Nolan Ryan 367
1975— Frank Tanana 269
1976— Nolan Ryan 327
1977— Nolan Ryan 341
1978— Nolan Ryan 260
1979— Nolan Ryan 223

No-hit pitchers
(9 innings or more)
1962— Bo Belinsky ....2-0 vs. Baltimore
1970— Clyde Wright ....4-0 vs. Oakland
1973— Nolan Ryan ....3-0 vs. Kansas City
1973— Nolan Ryan ....6-0 vs. Detroit
1974— Nolan Ryan ....4-0 vs. Minnesota
1975— Nolan Ryan ....1-0 vs. Baltimore
1984— Mike Witt ....1-0 vs. Texas (Perfect)
1990— Mark Langston-Mike Witt ....1-0 vs. Seattle

Longest hitting streaks
28— Garret Anderson...............................1998
25— Rod Carew 1984
23— Jim Edmonds 1995
22— Sandy Alomar 1970
21— Bobby Grich 1981
      Randy Velarde 1996
20— Bobby Grich 1979
19— Rod Carew 1982
18— Chad Curtis 1993
      Fred Lynn 1982
      Rod Carew 1980
      Sandy Alomar 1971
      Bob Rodgers 1964
17— Ken McMullen 1972
      Brian Downing 1987
      Garret Anderson...........................1997
      Garret Anderson...........................1999
16— Lee Thomas 1961
      Aurelio Rodriguez..........................1968
      Dan Ford 1980
      Johnny Ray 1988
      Wally Joyner 1991
      Garret Anderson...........................1999
15— Felix Torres 1962
      Bobby Knoop 1967
      John Stephenson 1971
      Leo Cardenas 1972
      Dave Collins 1975
      Rick Burleson 1981
      Brian Downing 1985
      Johnny Ray 1989
      Dave Gallagher 1991
      Chad Curtis 1993
      Tim Salmon 1995
      Darin Erstad 1998

Outfielders Leon Wagner (left) and Lee Thomas enjoyed good homer and run-production seasons in the 1960s.

Dean Chance, the A.L.'s 1964 ERA champion, holds the team single-season record for shutouts with 11.

SEASON

Batting
At-bats	689	Sandy Alomar	1971
Runs	120	Don Baylor	1979
		Jim Edmonds	1995
		Alex Johnson	1970
Hits	202	Alex Johnson	1970
Singles	156	Alex Johnson	1970
Doubles	42	3 times	1982
		Last by Jim Edmonds	1998
Triples	13	3 times	
		Last by Devon White	1989
Home runs	39	Reggie Jackson	1982
Home runs, rookie	31	Tim Salmon	1993
Grand slams	3	Joe Rudi	1978, 1979
Total bases	333	Don Baylor	1979
RBIs	139	Don Baylor	1979
Walks	113	Tony Phillips	1995
Most strikeouts	156	Reggie Jackson	1982
Fewest strikeouts	29	Gary DiSarcina	1997
Batting average	.339	Rod Carew	1983
Slugging pct.	.594	Tim Salmon	1995
Stolen bases	70	Mickey Rivers	1975

Pitching
Games	72	Minnie Rojas	1967
Complete games	26	Nolan Ryan	1973, 1974
Innings	332.2	Nolan Ryan	1974
Wins	22	Clyde Wright	1970
		Nolan Ryan	1974
Losses	19	4 times	
		Last by Kirk McCaskill	1991
Winning pct.	.773 (17-5)	Bert Blyleven	1989
Walks	204	Nolan Ryan	1977
Strikeouts	383	Nolan Ryan	1973
Shutouts	11	Dean Chance	1964
Home runs allowed	40	Shawn Boskie	1996
Lowest ERA	1.65	Dean Chance	1964
Saves	46	Bryan Harvey	1991

GAME

Batting
Runs	5	Last by Tim Salmon	10-2-99
Hits	6	Garret Anderson	9-27-96
Doubles	3	Last by Troy Glaus	4-12-99
Triples	2	Last by Reggie Williams	6-30-99
Home runs	3	Last by Dave Winfield	4-13-91
RBIs	8	Last by Don Baylor	8-25-79
Total bases	15	Dave Winfield	4-13-91
Stolen bases	4	Last by Chad Curtis	4-17-93

BATTING

Games

Brian Downing	1,661
Jim Fregosi	1,429
Bobby Grich	1,222
Dick Schofield	1,086
Gary DiSarcina	1,074
Bob Boone	968
Tim Salmon	955
Chili Davis	950
Bob Rodgers	932
Wally Joyner	846

At-bats

Brian Downing	5,854
Jim Fregosi	5,244
Bobby Grich	4,100
Gary DiSarcina	3,706
Chili Davis	3,491
Tim Salmon	3,483
Dick Schofield	3,434
Wally Joyner	3,208
Don Baylor	3,105
Rod Carew	3,080

Runs

Brian Downing	889
Jim Fregosi	691
Tim Salmon	608
Bobby Grich	601
Chili Davis	520
Don Baylor	481
Rod Carew	474
Jim Edmonds	464
Wally Joyner	455
Gary DiSarcina	438

Hits

Brian Downing	1,588
Jim Fregosi	1,408
Bobby Grich	1,103
Tim Salmon	1,015
Chili Davis	973
Rod Carew	968
Gary DiSarcina	951
Wally Joyner	925
Garret Anderson	858
Don Baylor	813

Doubles

Brian Downing	282
Jim Fregosi	219
Tim Salmon	195
Gary DiSarcina	184
Bobby Grich	183
Wally Joyner	170
Chili Davis	167
Garret Anderson	165
Jim Edmonds	161
Doug DeCinces	149

Triples

Jim Fregosi	70
Mickey Rivers	32
Luis Polonia	27
Dick Schofield	27
Bobby Knoop	25
Devon White	24
Gary Pettis	23
Rod Carew	22
Brian Downing	22
Gary DiSarcina	20
Bobby Grich	20

Home runs

Brian Downing	222
Tim Salmon	196
Chili Davis	156
Bobby Grich	154
Don Baylor	141
Doug DeCinces	130
Reggie Jackson	123
Jim Edmonds	121
Jim Fregosi	115
Wally Joyner	114

Total bases

Brian Downing	2,580
Jim Fregosi	2,112
Tim Salmon	1,826
Bobby Grich	1,788
Chili Davis	1,620
Wally Joyner	1,459
Don Baylor	1,390
Doug DeCinces	1,334
Jim Edmonds	1,316
Garret Anderson	1,269

Runs batted in

Brian Downing	846
Tim Salmon	660

SEASON

Batting

Most at-bats	5,686	1996
Most runs	866	1979
Fewest runs	454	1972
Most hits	1,571	1996
Most singles	1,114	1979
Most doubles	314	1998
Most triples	54	1966
Most home runs	192	1996
Fewest home runs	55	1975
Most grand slams	8	1979, 1983
Most pinch-hit home runs	9	1987
Most total bases	2,451	1996
Most stolen bases	220	1975
Highest batting average	.282	1979
Lowest batting average	.227	1968
Highest slugging pct	.448	1995

Pitching

Lowest ERA	2.91	1964
Highest ERA	5.30	1996
Most complete games	72	1973
Most shutouts	28	1964
Most saves	52	1998
Most walks	713	1961
Most strikeouts	1,091	1998

Fielding

Most errors	192	1961
Fewest errors	96	1989
Most double plays	202	1985
Highest fielding average	.985	1989

General

Most games won	93	1982
Most games lost	95	1968, 1980
Highest win pct	.574	1982
Lowest win pct	.406	1980

GAME, INNING

Batting

Most runs, game	24	8-25-79
Most runs, inning	13	9-14-78
		5-12-97
Most hits, game	26	8-25-79, 6-20-80
Most home runs, game	6	Last 7-14-90
Most total bases, game	52	6-20-80

Lefthander Frank Tanana recorded 102 victories in his eight successful seasons with the Angels.

Chili Davis	618
Bobby Grich	557
Jim Fregosi	546
Don Baylor	523
Wally Joyner	518
Doug DeCinces	481
Jim Edmonds	408
Garret Anderson	393

Extra-base hits

Brian Downing	526
Tim Salmon	405
Jim Fregosi	404
Bobby Grich	357
Chili Davis	329
Wally Joyner	295
Doug DeCinces	294
Jim Edmonds	294
Don Baylor	288
Garret Anderson	252

Batting average
(Minimum 500 games)

Rod Carew	.314
Garret Anderson	.300
Luis Polonia	.294
Juan Beniquez	.293
Tim Salmon	.291
Jim Edmonds	.290
Wally Joyner	.288
Chili Davis	.279
Albie Pearson	.275
Brian Downing	.271

Stolen bases

Gary Pettis	186
Luis Polonia	174
Sandy Alomar Sr.	139
Mickey Rivers	126
Devon White	123
Chad Curtis	116
Jerry Remy	110
Dick Schofield	99
Don Baylor	89
Rod Carew	82

PITCHING

Earned-run average
(Minimum 500 innings)

Andy Messersmith	2.78
Dean Chance	2.83
Nolan Ryan	3.07
Frank Tanana	3.08
George Brunet	3.13
Paul Hartzell	3.27
Clyde Wright	3.28
Jim McGlothlin	3.37
Fred Newman	3.41
Geoff Zahn	3.64

Wins

Chuck Finley	165
Nolan Ryan	138
Mike Witt	109
Frank Tanana	102
Mark Langston	88
Clyde Wright	87
Kirk McCaskill	78
Dean Chance	74
Andy Messersmith	59
Jim Abbott	54
George Brunet	54

Losses

Chuck Finley	140
Nolan Ryan	121
Mike Witt	107
Clyde Wright	85
Frank Tanana	78
Rudy May	76
Jim Abbott	74
Mark Langston	74
Kirk McCaskill	74
George Brunet	69

Innings pitched

Chuck Finley	2,675.0
Nolan Ryan	2,181.1
Mike Witt	1,965.1
Frank Tanana	1,615.1
Mark Langston	1,445.1
Clyde Wright	1,403.1
Dean Chance	1,236.2
Kirk McCaskill	1,221.0
Rudy May	1,138.2
Jim Abbott	1,073.2

Strikeouts

Nolan Ryan	2,416
Chuck Finley	2,151
Mike Witt	1,283
Frank Tanana	1,233
Mark Langston	1,112
Dean Chance	857
Rudy May	844

Andy Messersmith	768
Kirk McCaskill	714
George Brunet	678

Bases on balls

Nolan Ryan	1,302
Chuck Finley	1,118
Mike Witt	656
Mark Langston	551
Rudy May	484
Dean Chance	462
Clyde Wright	449
Kirk McCaskill	448
Frank Tanana	422
Andy Messersmith	402

Games

Chuck Finley	436
Mike Witt	314
Troy Percival	306
Dave LaRoche	304
Nolan Ryan	291
Clyde Wright	266
Andy Hassler	259
Bryan Harvey	250
Rudy May	230
Frank Tanana	225

Shutouts

Nolan Ryan	40
Frank Tanana	24
Dean Chance	21
George Brunet	14
Chuck Finley	14
Geoff Zahn	13
Rudy May	12
Kirk McCaskill	11
Andy Messersmith	11
Mike Witt	10

Saves

Troy Percival	139
Bryan Harvey	126
Dave LaRoche	65
Donnie Moore	61
Bob Lee	58
Joe Grahe	45
Minnie Rojas	43
Ken Tatum	39
Lee Smith	37
Don Aase	27
Art Fowler	27
Luis Sanchez	27

Year	W	L	Place	Games Back	Manager	Batting avg.	Hits	Home runs	RBIs	Wins	ERA
										Leaders	
1961	70	91	8th	38½	Rigney	Pearson, .288	L. Thomas, 129	Wagner, 28	Hunt, 84	McBride, 12	Morgan, 2.36
1962	86	76	3rd	10	Rigney	L. Thomas, .290	Moran, 186	Wagner, 37	Wagner, 107	Chance, 14	Chance, 2.96
1963	70	91	9th	34	Rigney	Pearson, .304	Pearson, 176	Wagner, 26	Wagner, 90	Chance, McBride, 13	Navarro, 2.89
1964	82	80	5th	17	Rigney	W. Smith, .301	Fregosi, 140	Adcock, 21	Fregosi, 72	Chance, 20	Lee, 1.51
1965	75	87	7th	27	Rigney	Pearson, .278	Fregosi, 167	Fregosi, 15	Fregosi, 64	Chance, 15	Lee, 1.92
1966	80	82	6th	18	Rigney	Cardenal, .276	Cardenal, 155	Adcock, 18	Knoop, 72	Brunet, Sanford 13	Lee, 2.74
1967	84	77	5th	7½	Rigney	Fregosi, .290	Fregosi, 171	Mincher, 25	Mincher, 76	R. Clark, McGlothlin, Rojas, 12	Rojas, 2.52
1968	67	95	8th	36	Rigney	Reichardt, .255	Fregosi, 150	Reichardt, 21	Reichardt, 73	Brunet, 13	Murphy, 2.17

—WEST DIVISION—

Year	W	L	Place	Games Back	Manager	Batting avg.	Hits	Home runs	RBIs	Wins	ERA
1969	71	91	3rd	26	Rigney, Phillips	Johnstone, .270	Alomar, 153	Reichardt, 13	Reichardt, 68	Messersmith, 16	Messersmith, 2.52
1970	86	76	3rd	12	Phillips	A. Johnson, .329	A. Johnson, 202	Fregosi, 22	A. Johnson, 86	Wright, 22	Wright, 2.83
1971	76	86	4th	25½	Phillips	Alomar, .260	Alomar, 179	McMullen, 21	McMullen, 68	Messersmith, 20	Allen, 2.49
1972	75	80	5th	18	Rice	Berry, .289	Oliver, 154	Oliver, 20	Oliver, 76	Ryan, 19	Ryan, 2.28
1973	79	83	4th	15	Winkles	Berry, .284	Oliver, 144	Robinson, 30	Robinson, 97	Ryan, 21	Ryan, 2.87
1974	68	94	6th	22	Winkles, D. Williams, Herzog	Rivers, .285	Doyle, Rivers, 133	Robinson, 20	Robinson, 63	Ryan, 22	Hassler, 2.61
1975	72	89	6th	25½	D. Williams	Bochte, .285	Rivers, 175	Stanton, 14	Stanton, 82	Figueroa, Tanana, 16	Tanana, 2.62
1976	76	86	*4th	14	D. Williams, Sherry	Bonds, .265	Remy, 132	Bonds, 10	Bonds, 54	Tanana, 19	Tanana, 2.43
1977	74	88	5th	28	Sherry, Garcia	Chalk, .277	Bonds, 156	Bonds, 37	Bonds, 115	Ryan, 19	Tanana, 2.54
1978	87	75	*2nd	5	Garcia, Fregosi	Ro. Jackson, .297	Bostock, 168	Baylor, 34	Baylor, 99	Tanana, 18	LaRoche, 2.82
1979	88	74	†1st	+3	Fregosi	Downing, .326	Lansford, 188	Baylor, 36	Baylor, 139	Frost, Ryan, 16	Frost, 3.57
1980	65	95	6th	31	Fregosi	Carew, .331	Carew, 179	Thompson, 17	Lansford, 80	Clear, Ryan, 11	Clear, 3.30
1981	51	59	‡4th/7th	—	Fregosi, Mauch	Carew, .305	Burleson, 126	Grich, 22	Baylor, 66	Forsch, 11	Forsch, 2.88
1982	93	69	†1st	+3	Mauch	Carew, .319	Downing, 175	Jackson, 39	Jackson, 101	Zahn, 18	Kison, 3.17
1983	70	92	*5th	29	McNamara	Carew, .339	Carew, 160	Lynn, 22	Lynn, 74	Forsch, John, Kison, 11	Zahn, 3.33
1984	81	81	*2nd	3	McNamara	Beniquez, .336	Downing, 148	Jackson, 25	Downing, 91	Witt, 15	Zahn, 3.12
1985	90	72	2nd	1	Mauch	Beniquez, .304	Downing, 137	Jackson, 27	Downing, Jackson, 85	Witt, 15	Moore, 1.92
1986	92	70	†1st	+5	Mauch	Joyner, .290	Joyner, 172	DeCinces, 26	Joyner, 100	Witt, 18	Candelaria, 2.55
1987	75	87	*6th	10	Mauch	Joyner, .285	White, 168	Joyner, 34	Joyner, 117	Witt, 16	Buice, 3.39
1988	75	87	4th	29	Rojas, Stubing	Ray, .306	Ray, 184	Downing, 25	C. Davis, 93	Witt, 13	Witt, 4.15
1989	91	71	3rd	8	Rader	Ray, .289	Joyner, 167	C. Davis, 22	C. Davis, 90	Blyleven, 17	Minton, 2.20
1990	80	82	4th	23	Rader	Polonia, .336	Polonia, 135	Parrish, 24	Winfield, 78	Finley, 18	Finley, 2.40
1991	81	81	7th	14	Rader, Rodgers	Joyner, .301	Polonia, 179	Winfield, 28	Joyner, 96	Langston, 19	J. Abbott, 2.89
1992	72	90	*5th	24	Rodgers, Wathan	Polonia, .286	Polonia, 165	Gaetti, 12	Felix, 72	Langston, 13	J. Abbott, 2.77
1993	71	91	*5th	23	Rodgers	Curtis, .285	Curtis, 166	Salmon, 31	C. Davis, 112	Finley, Langston, 16	Finley, 3.15
1994	47	68	4th	5½	M. Lachemann	C. Davis, .311	C. Davis, 122	C. Davis, 26	C. Davis, 84	Finley, 10	Finley, 4.32
1995	78	66	§2nd	1	M. Lachemann	Salmon, .330	Salmon, 177	Salmon, 34	Edmonds, 107	Finley, Langston, 15	Finley, 4.21
1996	70	91	4th	18½	M. Lachemann, McNamara	Edmonds, .304	Anderson, 173	Salmon, 30	Salmon, 98	Finley, 15	Finley, 4.16
1997	84	78	2nd	6	Collins	Anderson, .303	Anderson, 189	Salmon, 33	Salmon, 129	Finley, Dickson, 13	Hasegawa, 3.93
1998	85	77	2nd	3	Collins	Edmonds, .307	Edmonds, 184	Salmon, 26	Edmonds, 91	Finley, 11	Hasegawa, 3.14
1999	70	92	4th	25	Collins, Maddon	Velarde, .306	Anderson, 188	Vaughn, 33	Vaughn, 108	Finley, 12	Olivares, 4.05

* Tied for position. † Lost Championship Series. ‡ First half 31-29; second half 20-30. § Lost division playoff.

Note: Batting average minimum 350 at-bats; ERA minimum 90 innings pitched.

Eli Grba

THE ANGELS joined an exclusive fraternity in 1960 when actor/singer Gene Autry and partner Bob Reynolds were awarded the Los Angeles franchise in baseball's first expansion. The Angels, based in Los Angeles, joined the new-edition Washington Senators in an American League lineup that increased from eight to 10 teams. The former Washington Senators, owned by Calvin Griffith, were granted permission to transfer operations to Minneapolis-St. Paul.

The Los Angeles Angels participated in baseball's first expansion draft on December 14, 1960, and grabbed righthanded pitcher Eli Grba with their first pick. They went on to select 30 players and opened play on April 11, 1961, with a 7-2 victory over Baltimore.

Expansion draft (December 14, 1960)

Players

Ken Aspromonte ....Cleveland ....second base
Earl Averill......................Chicago ....catcher
Julio Becquer ....Minnesota ....infield
Steve Bilko ....Detroit ....first base
Bob Cerv ....New York ....outfield
Jim Fregosi ....Boston ....shortstop
Ken Hamlin ....Kansas City ....first base
Ken Hunt ....New York ....outfield
Ted Kluszewski ....Chicago ....first base
Gene Leek ....Cleveland ....infield
Jim McAnany ....Chicago ....outfield
Albie Pearson ....Baltimore ....outfield
Bob Rodgers ....Detroit ....catcher
Don Ross ....Baltimore ....infield
Ed Sadowski ....Boston ....catcher
Faye Throneberry ....Minnesota ....outfield
Red Wison ....Cleveland ....catcher
Eddie Yost ....Detroit ....third base

Pitchers

Jerry Casale ....Boston ....righthander
Dean Chance ....Baltimore ....righthander
Tex Clevenger ....Minnesota ....righthander
Bob Davis ....Kansas City ....righthander
Ned Garver ....Kansas City ....righthander
Aubrey Gatewood ....Detroit ....righthander
*Eli Grba ....New York ....righthander
Duke Maas ....New York ....righthander
Ken McBride ....Chicago ....righthander
Ron Moeller ....Baltimore ....lefthander
Fred Newman ....Boston ....righthander
Bob Sprout ....Detroit ....lefthander

*First pick

Opening day lineup

Albie Pearson

April 11, 1961
Eddie Yost, third base
Ken Aspromonte, second base
Albie Pearson, rightfield
Ted Kluszewski, first base
Bob Cerv, left field
Ken Hunt, center field
Fritzie Brickell, shortstop
Del Rice, catcher
Eli Grba, pitcher

Angels firsts
First hit: Ted Kluszewski, April 11, 1961, at Baltimore (home run)
First home run: Ted Kluszewski, April 11, 1961, at Baltimore
First RBI: Ted Kluszewski, April 11, 1961, at Baltimore
First win: Eli Grba, April 11, 1961, at Baltimore
First shutout: Ken McBride, May 23, 1961, 9-0 vs. Cleveland

HISTORY

BALTIMORE ORIOLES

FRANCHISE CHRONOLOGY

First season: 1901, in Milwaukee, as a member of the new American League. The team lost its Major League debut when Detroit rallied for 10 ninth-inning runs and a 14-13 victory and finished its first season in last place with a 48-89 record.

1902-1953: The franchise played its second season in St. Louis and remained there for more than half a century. The Browns moved up to second place in the 1902 standings (78-58), but such success would be elusive. The Browns won their only A.L. pennant in 1944 and lost their only World Series to the cross-town Cardinals. When owner Bill Veeck sold out to Baltimore interests in 1953, the team was relocated and renamed the Orioles.

1954-present: The Orioles posted a 3-1 victory over Chicago at Memorial Stadium in their Baltimore debut but went on to finish seventh in the A.L. standings at 54-100. Over the next four-plus decades, they would become an A.L. power, winning six pennants, three World Series, eight East Division titles and one wild-card playoff berth (1996).

Manager Earl Weaver.

ORIOLES VS. OPPONENTS BY DECADE

	A's	Indians	Red Sox	Tigers	Twins	White Sox	Yankees	Angels	Rangers	Brewers	Royals	Blue Jays	Mariners	Devil Rays	Interleague	Decade Record
1901-09	79-105	82-109	76-114	90-101	108-81	74-112	90-99									599-721
1910-19	93-120	81-130	71-142	90-126	96-119	74-132	92-123									597-892
1920-29	105-114	106-112	137-82	111-109	111-108	114-104	78-140									762-769
1930-39	88-127	64-155	103-117	85-135	84-135	90-127	64-155									578-951
1940-49	115-105	95-124	98-120	90-129	110-110	113-102	77-143									698-833
1950-59	110-109	67-151	77-143	106-114	117-103	86-134	69-151									632-905
1960-69	107-69	99-85	105-79	90-94	91-87	95-83	111-73	83-72	110-52	9-3	11-1					911-698
1970-79	66-50	104-65	83-85	102-65	64-52	74-39	89-73	65-52	77-50	100-54	65-51	29-14	26-6			944-656
1980-89	63-57	59-64	48-73	61-69	63-51	63-53	56-74	71-49	72-39	64-59	55-61	62-61	63-51			800-761
1990-99	65-54	51-67	57-63	69-49	63-45	46-59	50-75	73-46	60-46	52-45	62-43	54-69	58-57	10-14	24-25	794-757
Totals	891-910	808-1062	855-1018	894-991	907-891	829-945	776-1106	292-219	319-187	225-161	193-156	145-144	147-114	10-14	24-25	7315-7943

Interleague results: 7-2 vs. Braves; 4-5 vs. Expos; 3-7 vs. Mets; 8-4 vs. Phillies; 2-7 vs. Marlins.

MANAGERS

(Milwaukee Brewers, 1901)
(St. Louis Browns, 1902-53)

Name	Years	Record
Hugh Duffy	1901	48-89
Jimmy McAleer	1902-09	551-632
Jack O'Connor	1910	47-107
Bobby Wallace	1911-12	57-134
George Stovall	1912-13	91-158
Branch Rickey	1913-15	139-179
Fielder Jones	1916-18	158-196
Jimmy Austin	1913, 1918, 1923	31-44
Jimmy Burke	1918-20	172-180
Lee Fohl	1921-23	226-183
George Sisler	1924-26	218-241
Dan Howley	1927-29	220-239
Bill Killefer	1930-33	224-329
Al Sothoron	1933	2-6
Rogers Hornsby	1933-37, 1952	255-381
Jim Bottomley	1937	21-56
Gabby Street	1938	55-97
Fred Haney	1939-41	125-227
Luke Sewell	1941-46	432-410
Zack Taylor	1946, 1948-51	235-410
Marty Marion	1952-53	96-161
Jimmie Dykes	1954	54-100
Paul Richards	1955-61	517-539
Lum Harris	1961	17-10
Billy Hitchcock	1962-63	163-161
Hank Bauer	1964-68	407-318
Earl Weaver	1968-82, 1985-86	1480-1060
Joe Altobelli	1983-85	212-167
Cal Ripken Sr.	1987-88	68-101
Frank Robinson	1988-91	230-285
Johnny Oates	1991-94	362-343
Phil Regan	1995	71-73
Davey Johnson	1996-97	186-138
Ray Miller	1998-99	157-167

WORLD SERIES CHAMPIONS

Year	Loser	Length	MVP
1966	Los Angeles	4 games	F. Robinson
1970	Cincinnati	5 games	B. Robinson
1983	Philadelphia	5 games	Dempsey

A.L. PENNANT WINNERS

Year	Record	Manager	Series Result
1944	89-65	Sewell	Lost to Cardinals
1966	97-63	Bauer	Defeated Dodgers
1969	109-53	Weaver	Lost to N.Y. Mets
1970	108-54	Weaver	Defeated Reds
1971	101-57	Weaver	Lost to Pirates
1979	102-57	Weaver	Lost to Pirates
1983	98-64	Altobelli	Defeated Phillies

EAST DIVISION CHAMPIONS

Year	Record	Manager	ALCS Result
1969	109-53	Weaver	Defeated Twins
1970	108-54	Weaver	Defeated Twins
1971	101-57	Weaver	Defeated A's
1973	97-65	Weaver	Lost to A's
1974	91-71	Weaver	Lost to A's
1979	102-57	Weaver	Defeated Angels
1983	98-64	Altobelli	Defeated White Sox
1997	98-64	Johnson	Lost to Indians

WILD-CARD QUALIFIERS

Year	Record	Manager	Div. Series Result
1996	88-74	Johnson	Defeated Indians

ALCS Result
Lost to Yankees

ATTENDANCE HIGHS

Total	Season	Park
3,711,132	1997	Camden Yards
3,685,194	1998	Camden Yards
3,646,950	1996	Camden Yards
3,644,965	1993	Camden Yards
3,567,819	1992	Camden Yards

BALLPARK CHRONOLOGY

Oriole Park at Camden Yards (1992-present)
Capacity: 48,876.
First game: Orioles 2, Cleveland 0 (April 6, 1992).
First batter: Kenny Lofton, Indians.
First hit: Paul Sorrento, Indians (single).
First run: Sam Horn, Orioles (5th inning).
First home run: Paul Sorrento, Indians (April 8).
First winning pitcher: Rick Sutcliffe, Orioles.
First-season attendance: 3,567,819.

Lloyd Street Park, Milwaukee (1901)
Capacity: 10,000.
First game: Chicago 11, Brewers 3 (May 4, 1901).
First-season attendance: 139,034.

Sportsman's Park, St. Louis (1902-53)
Capacity: 30,500.
First game: Browns 5, Cleveland 2 (April 23, 1902).
First-season attendance: 272,283.

Memorial Stadium, Baltimore (1954-91)
Capacity: 53,371.
First game: Orioles 3, Chicago 1 (April 15, 1954).
First-season attendance: 1,060,910.

A.L. MVPs

Brooks Robinson, 3B, 1964
Frank Robinson, OF, 1966
Boog Powell, 1B, 1970
Cal Ripken, SS, 1983
Cal Ripken, SS, 1991

CY YOUNG WINNERS

*Mike Cuellar, LH, 1969
Jim Palmer, RH, 1973
Jim Palmer, RH, 1975
Jim Palmer, RH, 1976
Mike Flanagan, LH, 1979
Steve Stone, RH, 1980
* Co-winner.

ROOKIES OF THE YEAR

Roy Sievers, OF, 1949
Ron Hansen, SS, 1960
Curt Blefary, OF, 1965
Al Bumbry, OF, 1973
Eddie Murray, 1B, 1977
Cal Ripken, SS, 1982
Gregg Olson, P, 1989

MANAGER OF THE YEAR

Frank Robinson, 1989
Davey Johnson, 1997

RETIRED UNIFORMS

No.	Name	Position
4	Earl Weaver	Man.
5	Brooks Robinson	3B
20	Frank Robinson	OF
22	Jim Palmer	P
33	Eddie Murray	1B

Third baseman Brooks Robinson excited Orioles fans with his Hall of Fame bat and glove.

MILESTONE PERFORMANCES

30-plus home runs

50— Brady Anderson 1996
49— Frank Robinson 1966
46— Jim Gentile 1961
43— Rafael Palmeiro 1998
39— Ken Williams 1922
    Boog Powell 1964
    Rafael Palmeiro 1995
    Rafael Palmeiro 1996
38— Rafael Palmeiro 1997
37— Boog Powell 1969
    Albert Belle 1999
35— Boog Powell 1970
    Ken Singleton 1979
34— Harlond Clift 1938
    Boog Powell 1966
    Cal Ripken 1991
33— Jim Gentile 1962
    Eddie Murray 1983
32— Frank Robinson 1969
    Eddie Murray 1980, 1982
31— Eddie Murray 1985
    Larry Sheets 1987
30— Goose Goslin 1930
    Gus Triandos 1958
    Frank Robinson 1967
    Eddie Murray 1987

100-plus RBIs

155— Ken Williams 1922
142— Rafael Palmeiro 1996
141— Jim Gentile 1961
134— Moose Solters 1936
124— Eddie Murray 1985
123— Beau Bell.......................................1936
122— George Sisler 1920
    Baby Doll Jacobson 1920
    Frank Robinson 1966
121— Boog Powell 1969
    Rafael Palmeiro 1998
118— Harlond Clift 1937, 1938
    Brooks Robinson 1964
117— Ken Williams 1921
    Beau Bell 1937
    Albert Belle 1999
116— Eddie Murray 1980
    Bobby Bonilla 1996
114— Red Kress 1931
    Boog Powell 1970
    Cal Ripken 1991

112—Red Kress (and following)

112— Red Kress 1930
111— Ken Singleton 1979
    Eddie Murray 1983
110— Eddie Murray 1982, 1984
    Cal Ripken 1985
    Brady Anderson 1996
    Rafael Palmeiro 1997
109— Marty McManus 1922
    Vern Stephens 1944
    Boog Powell 1966
    Lee May 1976
108— Heinie Manush 1928
107— Red Kress 1929
    Mike Devereaux 1992
    B.J. Surhoff 1999
106— Bruce Campbell 1933
105— George Sisler 1922, 1925
    Ken Williams 1925
    Goose Goslin 1931
104— George Sisler 1921
    Goose Goslin 1932
    Moose Solters 1935
    Ken Singleton 1980
    Rafael Palmeiro 1995
103— George Sisler 1916
102— Baby Doll Jacobson 1922
    Cal Ripken 1983
    Cal Ripken 1996
101— Ray Pepper 1934
100— Goose Goslin 1930
    Brooks Robinson 1966
    Frank Robinson 1969

20-plus victories

1902— Red Donahue..............................22-11
    Jack Powell..................................22-17
1903— Willie Sudhoff 21-15
1919— Allen Sothoron 20-12
1920— Urban Shocker 20-10
1921— Urban Shocker 27-12
1922— Urban Shocker 24-17
1923— Urban Shocker 20-12
1928— General Crowder 21-5
    Sam Gray 20-12
1930— Lefty Stewart 20-12
1938— Bobo Newsom 20-16
1951— Ned Garver 20-12
1963— Steve Barber 20-13
1968— Dave McNally 22-10

When slugging outfielder Frank Robinson arrived on the Baltimore scene in 1966, the Orioles took on a championship aura.

INDIVIDUAL SEASON, GAME RECORDS

SEASON

Batting

At-bats	673	B.J. Surhoff	1999
Runs	145	Harlond Clift	1936
Hits	257	George Sisler	1920
Singles	179	Jack Tobin	1921
Doubles	51	Beau Bell	1937
Triples	20	Heinie Manush	1928
Home runs	50	Brady Anderson	1996
Home runs, rookie	28	Cal Ripken	1982
Grand slams	5	Jim Gentile	1961
Total bases	399	George Sisler	1920
RBIs	155	Ken Williams	1922
Walks	126	Lu Blue	1929
Most strikeouts	160	Mickey Tettleton	1990
Fewest strikeouts	13	Jack Tobin	1923
Batting average	.420	George Sisler	1922
Slugging pct.	.646	Jim Gentile	1961
Stolen bases	57	Luis Aparicio	1964

Pitching

Games	76	Tippy Martinez	1982
Complete games	36	Jack Powell	1902
Innings	348	Urban Shocker	1922
Wins	27	Urban Shocker	1922
Losses	25	Fred Glade	1905
Winning pct.	.808	General Crowder	1928
		Dave McNally	1971
Walks	192	Bobo Newsom	1938
Strikeouts	232	Rube Waddell	1908
Shutouts	10	Jim Palmer	1975
Home runs allowed	35	3 times	
		Last by Sidney Ponson	1999
Lowest ERA	1.95	Dave McNally	1968
Saves	45	Randy Myers	1997

GAME

Batting

Runs	5	Last by Cal Ripken	6-13-99
Hits	6	Last by Cal Ripken	6-13-99
Doubles	4	Last by Albert Belle	9-23-99
Triples	3	Last by Al Bumbry	9-22-73
Home runs	3	Last by Albert Belle	7-25-99
RBIs	9	Last by Eddie Murray	8-26-85
Total bases	13	Last by Cal Ripken	6-13-99
Stolen bases	4	Last by Brady Anderson	7-5-98

1969— Mike Cuellar 23-11
    Dave McNally 20-7
1970— Mike Cuellar 24-8
    Dave McNally 24-9
    Jim Palmer 20-10
1971— Dave McNally 21-5
    Pat Dobson 20-8
    Jim Palmer 20-9
    Mike Cuellar 20-9
1972— Jim Palmer 21-10
1973— Jim Palmer 22-9
1974— Mike Cuellar 22-10
1975— Jim Palmer 23-11
    Mike Torrez 20-9
1976— Jim Palmer 22-13
    Wayne Garland 20-7
1977— Jim Palmer 20-11
1978— Jim Palmer 21-12
1979— Mike Flanagan 23-9
1980— Steve Stone 25-7
    Scott McGregor 20-8
1984— Mike Boddicker 20-11

A.L. home run champions

1922— Ken Williams 39
1945— Vern Stephens 24
1966— Frank Robinson 49
1981— Eddie Murray *22

    * Tied for league lead

A.L. RBI champions

1916— Del Pratt 103
1922— Ken Williams 155
1944— Vern Stephens 109
1964— Brooks Robinson 118
1966— Frank Robinson 122
1976— Lee May 109
1981— Eddie Murray 78

A.L. batting champions

1906— George Stone .... .358
1920— George Sisler .... .407
1922— George Sisler .... .420
1966— Frank Robinson .... .316

A.L. ERA champions

1959— Hoyt Wilhelm 2.19
1973— Jim Palmer 2.40
1975— Jim Palmer 2.09
1984— Mike Boddicker 2.79

A.L. strikeout champions

1922— Urban Shocker 149
1954— Bob Turley 185

No-hit pitchers

1912— Earl Hamilton ....5-1 vs. Detroit
1917— Ernie Koob ....1-0 vs. Chicago
1917— Bob Groom ....3-0 vs. Chicago
1953— Bobo Holloman ....6-0 vs. Philadelphia
1958— Hoyt Wilhelm ....1-0 vs. New York
1967— Steve Barber-Stu Miller ....1-2 vs. Detroit
1968— Tom Phoebus ....6-0 vs. Boston
1969— Jim Palmer ....8-0 vs. Oakland
1991— Bob Milacki-Mike Flanagan-Mark
    Williamson-Gregg Olson ....2-0 vs. Oakland

Longest hitting streaks

41— George Sisler 1922
34— George Sisler 1925
    George McQuinn...............................1938
30— Eric Davis 1998
29— Mel Almada 1938
28— Ken Williams 1922
27— Bob Dillinger 1948
26— Hobe Ferris 1908
25— George Sisler 1920
24— Rafael Palmeiro 1994
22— Red Kress 1930
    Eddie Murray 1984
    Roberto Alomar 1996
    Bobby Bonilla *1995-96
21— Jack Tobin 1922
    Beau Bell 1936
    Joe Vosmik....................................1937
    Johnny Berardino 1946
    Doug DeCinces 1978
    Joe Orsulak 1991
    B.J. Surhoff 1999
20— Jack Burns 1932
    Harlond Clift 1937
    Bob Nieman 1956
    Lee Lacy 1985
    Bobby Bonilla 1995

*20 games in 1995; 2 in 1996

BATTING

Games

Brooks Robinson	2,896
Cal Ripken	2,790
Mark Belanger	1,962
Eddie Murray	1,884
Boog Powell	1,763
Paul Blair	1,700
George Sisler	1,647
Bobby Wallace	1,569
Brady Anderson	1,487
Ken Singleton	1,446

At-bats

Cal Ripken	10,765
Brooks Robinson	10,654
Eddie Murray	7,075
George Sisler	6,667
Boog Powell	5,912
Mark Belanger	5,734
Paul Blair	5,606
Bobby Wallace	5,529
Brady Anderson	5,335
Harlond Clift	5,281

Runs

Cal Ripken	1,561
Brooks Robinson	1,232
George Sisler	1,091
Eddie Murray	1,084
Harlond Clift	1,013
Brady Anderson	905
Boog Powell	796
Al Bumbry	772
Ken Williams	757
Paul Blair	737

Hits

Cal Ripken	2,991
Brooks Robinson	2,848
George Sisler	2,295
Eddie Murray	2,080
Boog Powell	1,574
Baby Doll Jacobson	1,508
Harlond Clift	1,463
Ken Singleton	1,455
Paul Blair	1,426
Bobby Wallace	1,424

Doubles

Cal Ripken	571
Brooks Robinson	482
Eddie Murray	363
George Sisler	343
Harlond Clift	294
Brady Anderson	291
Paul Blair	269
Baby Doll Jacobson	269
George McQuinn	254
Boog Powell	243

Triples

George Sisler	145
Baby Doll Jacobson	88
Del Pratt	72
Jack Tobin	72
Ken Williams	70
Brooks Robinson	68
George Stone	68
Jimmy Austin	67
Bobby Wallace	65
Harlond Clift	62

Home runs

Cal Ripken	402
Eddie Murray	343
Boog Powell	303
Brooks Robinson	268
Ken Williams	185
Brady Anderson	182
Rafael Palmeiro	182
Ken Singleton	182
Frank Robinson	179
Harlond Clift	170

Total bases

Cal Ripken	4,856
Brooks Robinson	4,270
Eddie Murray	3,522
George Sisler	3,207
Boog Powell	2,748
Harlond Clift	2,391
Brady Anderson	2,356
Ken Singleton	2,274
Ken Williams	2,239
Baby Doll Jacobson	2,181

Runs batted in

Cal Ripken	1,571
Brooks Robinson	1,357
Eddie Murray	1,224
Boog Powell	1,063

SEASON

Batting

Most at-bats	5,689	1996
Most runs	949	1996
Fewest runs	441	1909
Most hits	1,693	1922
Most singles	1,239	1920
Most doubles	327	1937
Most triples	106	1921
Most home runs	257	1996
Fewest home runs	9	1906
Most grand slams	11	1996
Most pinch-hit home runs	11	1982
Most total bases	2,685	1996
Most stolen bases	234	1916
Highest batting average	.313	1922
Lowest batting average	.216	1910
Highest slugging pct	.472	1996

Pitching

Lowest ERA	2.15	1908
Highest ERA	6.24	1936
Most complete games	135	1904
Most shutouts	21	1909, 1961
Most saves	59	1997
Most walks	801	1951
Most strikeouts	1,139	1997

Fielding

Most errors	378	1910
Fewest errors	81	1998
Most double plays	190	1948
Highest fielding average	.987	1998

General

Most games won	109	1969
Most games lost	111	1939
Highest win pct	.673	1969
Lowest win pct	.279	1939

GAME, INNING

Batting

Most runs, game	22	6-13-99
Most runs, inning	11	Last 7-21-49
Most hits, game	26	8-28-80
Most home runs, game	7	Last 8-26-85
Most total bases, game	44	6-13-99

George Sisler (right) was an early franchise star and a contemporary of Babe Ruth.

George Sisler	959
Ken Williams	808
Harlond Clift	769
Ken Singleton	766
Baby Doll Jacobson	704
Brady Anderson	649

Extra-base hits

Cal Ripken	1,017
Brooks Robinson	818
Eddie Murray	731
George Sisler	581
Boog Powell	557
Brady Anderson	534
Harlond Clift	526
Ken Williams	491
Paul Blair	446
Ken Singleton	436

Batting average

(Minimum 500 games)

George Sisler	.344
Ken Williams	.326
Jack Tobin	.318
Baby Doll Jacobson	.317
Bob Dillinger	.309
Beau Bell	.309
Sam West	.305
Harold Baines	.305
George Stone	.301
Bob Boyd	.301

Stolen bases

George Sisler	351
Brady Anderson	279
Al Bumbry	252
Burt Shotton	247
Jimmy Austin	192
Del Pratt	174
Paul Blair	167
Luis Aparicio	166
Mark Belanger	166
Ken Williams	144

PITCHING

Earned-run average

(Minimum 1,000 innings)

Harry Howell	2.06
Fred Glade	2.52
Barney Pelty	2.62
Jack Powell	2.63
Carl Weilman	2.67

Jim Palmer	2.86
Allen Sothoron	2.98
Earl Hamilton	3.00
Steve Barber	3.12
Mike Cuellar	3.18

Wins

Jim Palmer	268
Dave McNally	181
Mike Cuellar	143
Mike Flanagan	141
Scott McGregor	138
Mike Mussina	136
Urban Shocker	126
Jack Powell	117
Milt Pappas	110
Dennis Martinez	108

Losses

Jim Palmer	152
Jack Powell	143
Mike Flanagan	116
Dave McNally	113
Barney Pelty	113
George Blaeholder	111
Scott McGregor	108
Dennis Martinez	93
Carl Weilman	93
Harry Howell	91
Elam Vangilder	91

Innings pitched

Jim Palmer	3,948.0
Dave McNally	2,652.2
Mike Flanagan	2,317.2
Jack Powell	2,229.2
Scott McGregor	2,140.2
Mike Cuellar	2,028.1
Barney Pelty	1,864.1
Dennis Martinez	1,775.0
Mike Mussina	1,772.0
Urban Shocker	1,749.2

Strikeouts

Jim Palmer	2,212
Dave McNally	1,476
Mike Mussina	1,325
Mike Flanagan	1,297
Mike Cuellar	1,011
Milt Pappas	944
Steve Barber	918
Scott McGregor	904

Jack Powell	884
Dennis Martinez	858

Bases on balls

Jim Palmer	1,311
Dave McNally	790
Mike Flanagan	740
Steve Barber	668
Dixie Davis	640
Elam Vangilder	625
Mike Cuellar	601
Dennis Martinez	583
Milt Pappas	531
Barney Pelty	522

Games

Jim Palmer	558
Tippy Martinez	499
Mike Flanagan	450
Dave McNally	412
Mark Williamson	365
Eddie Watt	363
Scott McGregor	356
Dick Hall	342
Jesse Orosco	336
Elam Vangilder	323

Shutouts

Jim Palmer	53
Dave McNally	33
Mike Cuellar	30
Jack Powell	27
Milt Pappas	26
Scott McGregor	23
Urban Shocker	23
Barney Pelty	22
Steve Barber	19
Mike Flanagan	17

Saves

Gregg Olson	160
Tippy Martinez	105
Stu Miller	100
Randy Myers	76
Eddie Watt	74
Dick Hall	58
Tim Stoddard	57
Don Aase	50
Don Stanhouse	45
Sammy Stewart	42

ORIOLES YEAR-BY-YEAR

Year	W	L	Place	Games Back	Manager	Leaders: Batting avg.	Hits	Home runs	RBIs	Wins	ERA
								MILWAUKEE BREWERS			
1901	48	89	8th	35½	Duffy	Anderson, .330	Anderson, 190	Anderson, 8	Anderson, 99	Reidy, 16	Garvin, 3.46
								ST. LOUIS BROWNS			
1902	78	58	2nd	5	McAleer	Hemphill, .317	Burkett, 169	Hemphill, 6	Anderson, 85	Donahue, Powell, 22	Donahue, 2.76
1903	65	74	6th	26½	McAleer	Burkett, .293	Anderson, 156	Burkett, Hemphill, 3	Anderson, 78	Sudhoff, 21	Sudhoff, 2.27
1904	65	87	6th	29	McAleer	Wallace, .275	T. Jones, 152	4 Tied, 2	Wallace, 69	Glade, 18	Howell, 2.19
1905	54	99	8th	40½	McAleer	Stone, .296	Stone, 187	Stone, 7	Wallace, 59	Howell, 15	Howell, 1.98
1906	76	73	5th	16	McAleer	Stone, .358	Stone, 208	Stone, 6	Stone, 71	Pelty, 16	Pelty, 1.59
1907	69	83	6th	24	McAleer	Stone, .320	Stone, 191	Stone, 4	Wallace, 70	Howell, 16	Howell, 1.93
1908	83	69	4th	6½	McAleer	Stone, .281	Stone, 165	Stone, 5	Ferris, 74	Waddell, 19	Howell, Waddell, 1.89
1909	61	89	7th	36	McAleer	Griggs, .280	Hartzell, 161	Ferris, 3	Ferris, 58	Powell, 12	Powell, 2.11
1910	47	107	8th	57	O'Connor	Wallace, .258	Stone, 144	4 Tied, 2	Stone, 40	Lake, 11	Lake, 2.20
1911	45	107	8th	56½	Wallace	LaPorte, .314	LaPorte, 159	Kutina, Meloan, Murray, 3	LaPorte, 82	Lake, 10	Pelty, 2.97
1912	53	101	7th	53	Wallace, Stovall	Pratt, .302	Pratt, 172	Pratt, 5	Pratt, 69	Baumgardner, Hamilton, 11	E. Brown, 2.99
1913	57	96	8th	39	Stovall, Rickey	Shotton, .297	Pratt, 175	Williams, 5	Pratt, 87	Hamilton, Mitchell, 13	Hamilton, 2.57
1914	71	82	5th	28½	Rickey	T. Walker, .298	Pratt, 165	T. Walker, 6	T. Walker, 78	Weilman, 18	Weilman, 2.08
1915	63	91	6th	39½	Rickey	Pratt, .291	Pratt, 175	T. Walker, 5	Pratt, 78	Weilman, 18	Weilman, 2.34
1916	79	75	5th	12	Jones	Sisler, .305	Sisler, 177	Pratt, 5	Pratt, 103	Weilman, 17	Weilman, 2.15
1917	57	97	7th	43	Jones	Sisler, .353	Sisler, 190	Jacobson, 4	Severeid, 57	Davenport, 17	Plank, 1.79
1918	58	64	5th	15	Jones, Austin, Burke	Sisler, .341	Sisler, 154	Sisler, 2	Demmitt, 61	Sothoron, 12	Shocker, 1.81
1919	67	72	5th	20½	Burke	Sisler, .352	Sisler, 180	Sisler, 10	Sisler, 83	Sothoron, 20	Weilman, 2.07
1920	76	77	4th	21½	Burke	Sisler, .407	Sisler, 257	Sisler, 19	Jacobson, Sisler, 122	Shocker, 20	Shocker, 2.71
1921	81	73	3rd	17½	Fohl	Sisler, .371	Tobin, 236	Williams, 24	Williams, 117	Shocker, 27	Shocker, 3.55
1922	93	61	2nd	1	Fohl	Sisler, .420	Sisler, 246	Williams, 39	Williams, 155	Shocker, 24	Pruett, 2.33
1923	74	78	5th	24	Fohl, Austin	Williams, .357	Tobin, 202	Williams, 29	McManus, 94	Shocker, 20	Vangilder, 3.06
1924	74	78	4th	17	Sisler	McManus, .333	Sisler, 194	Jacobson, 19	Jacobson, 97	Shocker, 16	Wingard, 3.51
1925	82	71	3rd	15	Sisler	Rice, .359	Sisler, 224	Williams, 25	Sisler, Williams, 105	Gaston, 15	Danforth, 4.36
1926	62	92	7th	29	Sisler	B. Miller, .331	Rice, 181	Williams, 17	Williams, 74	Zachary, 14	Wingard, 3.57
1927	59	94	7th	50½	Howley	Sisler, .327	Sisler, 201	Williams, 17	Sisler, 97	Gaston, 13	Stewart, 4.28
1928	82	72	3rd	19	Howley	Manush, .378	Manush, 241	Blue, 14	Manush, 108	Crowder, 21	Gray, 3.19
1929	79	73	4th	26	Howley	Manush, .355	Manush, 204	Kress, 9	Kress, 107	Gray, 18	Stewart, 3.25
1930	64	90	6th	38	Killefer	Goslin, .326	Kress, 192	Goslin, 30	Kress, 112	Stewart, 20	Stewart, 3.45
1931	63	91	5th	45	Killefer	Goslin, .328	Goslin, 194	Goslin, 24	Kress, 114	Stewart, 14	Collins, 3.79
1932	63	91	6th	44	Killefer	Ferrell, .315	Burns, 188	Goslin, 17	Goslin, 104	Stewart, 15	Gray, 4.53
1933	55	96	8th	43½	Killefer, Sothoron, Hornsby	West, .300	Burns, 160	Campbell, 16	Campbell, 106	Blaeholder, Hadley, 15	Hadley, 3.92
1934	67	85	6th	33	Hornsby	West, .326	Pepper, 168	Clift, 14	Pepper, 101	Newsom, 16	Newsom, 4.01
1935	65	87	7th	28½	Hornsby	Solters, .330	Solters, 182	Solters, 18	Solters, 104	Andrews, 13	Andrews, 3.54
1936	57	95	7th	44½	Hornsby	Bell, .344	Bell, 212	Clift, 20	Solters, 134	Hogsett, 13	Andrews, 4.84
1937	46	108	8th	56	Hornsby, Bottomley	Bell, .340	Bell, 218	Clift, 29	Clift, 118	Walkup, 9	Knott, 4.89
1938	55	97	7th	44	Street	Almada, .342	McQuinn, 195	Clift, 34	Clift, 118	Newsom, 20	Newsom, 5.08
1939	43	111	8th	64½	Haney	McQuinn, .316	McQuinn, 195	McQuinn, 20	McQuinn, 94	Kennedy, Kramer, 9	Lawson, 5.32
1940	67	87	6th	23	Haney	Radcliff, .342	Radcliff, 200	Judnich, 24	Judnich, 89	Auker, 16	Trotter, 3.77
1941	70	84	*6th	31	Haney, Sewell	Cullenbine, .317	Cullenbine, 159	McQuinn, 18	Berardino, 89	Auker, 14	Galehouse, 3.64
1942	82	69	3rd	19½	Sewell	Judnich, .313	Stephens, 169	Laabs, 27	Laabs, 99	Niggeling, 15	Niggeling, 2.66
1943	72	80	6th	25	Sewell	Stephens, .289	Stephens, 148	Stephens, 22	Stephens, 91	Sundra, 15	Galehouse, 2.77
1944	89	65	1st	+1	Sewell	Kreevich, .301	Stephens, 164	Stephens, 20	Stephens, 109	Potter, 19	Kramer, 2.49
1945	81	70	3rd	6	Sewell	Stephens, .289	Stephens, 165	Stephens, 24	Stephens, 89	Potter, 15	Potter, 2.47
1946	66	88	7th	38	Sewell, Taylor	Stephens, .307	Berardino, 154	Laabs, 16	Judnich, 72	Kramer, 13	Kramer, 3.19
1947	59	95	8th	38	Ruel	Dillinger, .294	Dillinger, 168	Heath, 27	Heath, 85	Kramer, 11	Zoldak, 3.47
1948	59	94	6th	37	Taylor	Zarilla, .329	Dillinger, 207	Moss, 14	Platt, 82	Sanford, 12	Garver, 3.41
1949	53	101	7th	44	Taylor	Dillinger, .324	Dillinger, 176	Graham, 24	Sievers, 91	Garver, 12	Ferrick, 3.88
1950	58	96	7th	40	Taylor	Lollar, .280	Lenhardt, 131	Lenhardt, 22	Lenhardt, 81	Garver, 13	Garver, 3.39
1951	52	102	8th	46	Taylor	Young, .260	Young, 159	Wood, 15	Coleman, 55	Garver, 20	Garver, 3.73
1952	64	90	7th	31	Hornsby, Marion	Nieman, .289	Young, 142	Nieman, 18	Nieman, 74	Cain, Paige, 12	Paige, 3.07
1953	54	100	8th	46½	Marion	Wertz, .268	Groth, 141	Wertz, 19	Wertz, 70	Stuart, 8	Brecheen, 3.07
								BALTIMORE ORIOLES			
1954	54	100	7th	57	Dykes	Abrams, .293	Abrams, 124	Stephens, 8	Stephens, 46	Turley, 14	Pillette, 3.12
1955	57	97	7th	39	Richards	Triandos, .277	Triandos, 133	Triandos, 12	Triandos, 65	Wilson, 12	Wight, 2.45
1956	69	85	6th	28	Richards	Nieman, .322	Triandos, 126	Triandos, 21	Triandos, 88	Moore, 12	C. Johnson, 3.43
1957	76	76	5th	21	Richards	Boyd, .318	Gardner, 169	Triandos, 19	Triandos, 72	C. Johnson, 14	Zuverink, 2.48
1958	74	79	6th	17½	Richards	Boyd, .309	Gardner, 126	Triandos, 30	Triandos, 79	Portocarrero, 15	Harshman, 2.89
1959	74	80	6th	20	Richards	Woodling, .300	Woodling, 132	Triandos, 25	Woodling, 77	Pappas, Wilhelm, 15	Wilhelm, 2.19
1960	89	65	2nd	8	Richards	B. Robinson, .294	B. Robinson, 175	Hansen, 22	Gentile, 98	Estrada, 18	Brown, 3.06
1961	95	67	3rd	14	Richards, Harris	Gentile, .302	B. Robinson, 192	Gentile, 46	Gentile, 141	Barber, 18	Hoeft, 2.02
1962	77	85	7th	19	Hitchcock	Snyder, .305	B. Robinson, 192	Gentile, 33	Gentile, 87	Pappas, 12	Wilhelm, 1.94
1963	86	76	4th	18½	Hitchcock	Orsino, A. Smith, .272	Aparicio, 150	Powell, 25	Powell, 82	Barber, 20	Miller, 2.24
1964	97	65	3rd	2	Bauer	B. Robinson, .317	B. Robinson, 194	Powell, 39	B. Robinson, 118	Bunker, 19	Haddix, 2.31
1965	94	68	3rd	8	Bauer	B. Robinson, .297	B. Robinson, 166	Blefary, 22	B. Robinson, 80	Barber, 15	Miller, 1.89
1966	97	63	1st	+9	Bauer	F. Robinson, .316	Aparicio, F. Robinson, 182	F. Robinson, 49	F. Robinson, 122	Palmer, 15	Miller, 2.25
1967	76	85	*6th	15½	Bauer	F. Robinson, .311	B. Robinson, 164	F. Robinson, 30	F. Robinson, 94	Phoebus, 14	Drabowsky, 1.60
1968	91	71	2nd	12	Bauer, Weaver	Buford, .282	B. Robinson, 154	B. Robinson, 17	Powell, 85	McNally, 22	McNally, 1.95
								EAST DIVISION			
1969	109	53	†1st	+19	Weaver	F. Robinson, .308	Blair, 178	Powell, 37	Powell, 121	Cuellar, 23	Palmer, 2.34
1970	108	54	†1st	+15	Weaver	F. Robinson, .306	B. Robinson, 168	Powell, 35	Powell, 114	Cuellar, McNally, 24	Palmer, 2.71
1971	101	57	†1st	+12	Weaver	Rettenmund, .318	B. Robinson, 160	F. Robinson, 28	F. Robinson, 99	McNally, 21	Palmer, 2.68
1972	80	74	3rd	5	Weaver	Grich, .278	B. Robinson, 139	Powell, 21	Powell, 81	Palmer, 21	Palmer, 2.07
1973	97	65	‡1st	+8	Weaver	Coggins, .319	T. Davis, 169	Williams, 22	T. Davis, 89	Palmer, 22	Reynolds, 1.95
1974	91	71	‡1st	+2	Weaver	T. Davis, .289	T. Davis, 181	Grich, 19	T. Davis, 84	Cuellar, 22	Garland, 2.97
1975	90	69	2nd	4½	Weaver	Singleton, .300	Singleton, 176	Baylor, 25	L. May, 99	Palmer, 23	Palmer, 2.09
1976	88	74	2nd	10½	Weaver	Singleton, .278	Singleton, 151	R. Jackson, 27	L. May, 109	Palmer, 22	Palmer, 2.51
1977	97	64	*2nd	2½	Weaver	Singleton, .328	Singleton, 176	L. May, Murray, 27	L. May, Singleton, 99	Palmer, 20	Palmer, 2.91
1978	90	71	4th	9	Weaver	Singleton, .293	Murray, 174	DeCinces, 28	Murray, 95	Palmer, 21	Palmer, 2.46
1979	102	57	†1st	+8	Weaver	Murray, Singleton, .295	Murray, 179	Singleton, 35	Singleton, 111	Flanagan, 23	Flanagan, 3.08
1980	100	62	2nd	3	Weaver	Bumbry, .318	Bumbry, 205	Murray, 32	Murray, 116	Stone, 25	Stone, 3.23
1981	59	46	§2nd/4th	—	Weaver	Murray, .294	Murray, 111	Murray, 22	Murray, 78	D. Martinez, 14	Stewart, 2.32
1982	94	68	2nd	1	Weaver	Murray, .316	Murray, 174	Murray, 32	Murray, 110	D. Martinez, 16	Palmer, 3.13
1983	98	64	†1st	+6	Altobelli	C. Ripken, .318	C. Ripken, 211	Murray, 33	Murray, 111	McGregor, 18	T. Martinez, 2.35
1984	85	77	5th	19	Altobelli	Murray, .306	C. Ripken, 195	Murray, 29	Murray, 110	Boddicker, 20	Boddicker, 2.79
1985	83	78	4th	16	Altobelli, Weaver	Rayford, .306	C. Ripken, 181	Murray, 31	Murray, 124	McGregor, 14	Snell, 2.69
1986	73	89	7th	22½	Weaver	Murray, .305	C. Ripken, 177	C. Ripken, 25	Murray, 84	Boddicker, 14	S. Davis, 3.62
1987	67	95	6th	31	C. Ripken, Sr.	Sheets, .316	Murray, 171	Sheets, 31	C. Ripken, 98	Bell, Boddicker, Schmidt, 10	Schmidt, 3.77
1988	54	107	7th	34½	C. Ripken, Sr., F. Robinson	Orsulak, .288	Murray, 171	Murray, 28	Murray, 84	Ballard, Schmidt, 8	Schmidt, 3.40
1989	87	75	2nd	2	F. Robinson	Orsulak, .285	C. Ripken, 166	Tettleton, 26	C. Ripken, 93	Ballard, 18	Williamson, 2.93
1990	76	85	5th	11½	F. Robinson	B. Ripken, .291	C. Ripken, 150	C. Ripken, 21	C. Ripken, 84	D. Johnson, 13	McDonald, 2.43
1991	67	95	6th	24	F. Robinson, Oates	C. Ripken, .323	C. Ripken, 210	C. Ripken, 34	C. Ripken, 114	Milacki, 10	Frohwirth, 1.87
1992	89	73	3rd	7	Oates	Orsulak, .289	Devereaux, 180	Devereaux, 24	Devereaux, 107	Mussina, 18	Frohwirth, 2.46
1993	85	77	*3rd	10	Oates	Baines, .313	McLemore, 165	Hoiles, 29	C. Ripken, 90	Mussina, 14	Mills, 3.23
1994	63	49	2nd	6½	Oates	Palmeiro, .319	C. Ripken, 140	Palmeiro, 23	Palmeiro, 76	Mussina, 16	Mussina, 3.06
1995	71	73	3rd	15	Regan	Palmeiro, .310	Palmeiro, 172	Palmeiro, 39	Palmeiro, 104	Mussina, 19	Mussina, 3.29
1996	88	74	∞‡2nd	4	Johnson	Alomar, .328	Alomar, 193	Anderson, 50	Palmeiro, 142	Mussina, 19	Mussina, 4.81
1997	98	64	∞1st	+2	Johnson	Alomar, .333	Anderson, 170	Palmeiro, 38	Palmeiro, 110	Key, Erickson, 16	Rhodes, 3.02
1998	79	83	4th	35	Miller	E. Davis, .327	Palmeiro, 183	Palmeiro, 43	Palmeiro, 121	Erickson, 16	Mussina, 3.49
1999	78	84	4th	20	Miller	Surhoff, .308	Surhoff, 207	Belle, 37	Belle, 117	Mussina, 18	Mussina, 3.50

* Tied for position. † Won Championship Series. ‡ Lost Championship Series. § First half 31-23; second half 28-23. ∞ Won Division Series.

Note: Batting average minimum 350 at-bats; ERA minimum 90 innings pitched.

HISTORY

BOSTON RED SOX

FRANCHISE CHRONOLOGY

First season: 1901, as a member of the new American League. The Red Sox, who also were known in the early years as the Pilgrims, Puritans and Somersets, dropped a 10-6 decision to Baltimore in their Major League debut and went on to finish 79-57, four games behind pennant-winner Chicago.

1902-present: The Red Sox captured their first pennant in 1903 and defeated the National League's Pirates in the first modern World Series. Boston went on to enjoy distinction as baseball's most successful franchise over its first two decades, winning six A.L. pennants and all five World Series appearances. But the Red Sox's 1918 championship marked the beginning of a dry spell that would last the remainder of the century. They failed to win another pennant until 1946 and have lost their four World Series appearances since World War II, all in dramatic seventh games.

Outfielder Ted Williams.

RED SOX VS. OPPONENTS BY DECADE

	A's	Indians	Orioles	Tigers	Twins	White Sox	Yankees	Angels	Rangers	Brewers	Royals	Blue Jays	Mariners	Devil Rays	Interleague	Decade Record
1901-09	88-102	93-96	114-76	92-97	113-76	90-101	101-86									691-634
1910-19	129-84	115-97	142-71	124-88	115-93	117-97	115-94									857-624
1920-29	86-131	90-130	82-137	81-139	82-135	103-117	71-149									595-938
1930-39	116-99	89-131	117-103	99-121	90-128	114-97	80-136									705-815
1940-49	137-83	105-116	120-98	127-93	133-86	134-85	98-122									854-683
1950-59	141-79	98-122	143-77	121-99	120-100	98-122	93-126									814-725
1960-69	96-82	90-94	79-105	88-95	74-104	76-102	83-101	76-79	86-75	6-6	10-2					764-845
1970-79	63-54	86-80	85-83	96-69	70-47	67-48	89-79	64-53	72-56	93-63	53-63	32-11	25-8			895-714
1980-89	68-52	78-52	73-48	65-59	62-53	56-59	60-63	59-55	64-53	62-67	49-65	59-62	66-54			821-742
1990-99	71-46	61-60	63-57	64-54	48-62	54-54	60-64	71-47	43-61	50-47	52-51	72-52	71-46	13-12	21-28	814-741
Totals	995-812	905-978	1018-855	957-914	907-884	909-882	850-1020	270-234	265-245	211-183	164-181	163-125	162-108	13-12	21-28	7810-7461

Interleague results: 4-8 vs. Braves; 3-6 vs. Expos; 4-5 vs. Mets; 5-5 vs. Phillies; 5-4 vs. Marlins.

MANAGERS

Name	Years	Record
Jimmy Collins	1901-06	455-376
Chick Stahl	1906	14-26
George Huff	1907	2-6
Bob Unglaub	1907	9-20
Cy Young	1907	3-3
Deacon McGuire	1907-08	98-123
Fred Lake	1908-09	110-80
Patsy Donovan	1910-11	159-147
Jake Stahl	1912-13	144-88
Bill Carrigan	1913-16, 1927-29	489-500
Jack Barry	1917	90-62
Ed Barrow	1918-20	213-203
Hugh Duffy	1921-22	136-172
Frank Chance	1923	61-91
Lee Fohl	1924-26	160-299
Heinie Wagner	1930	52-102
Shano Collins	1931-32	73-134
Marty McManus	1932-33	95-153
Bucky Harris	1934	76-76
Joe Cronin	1935-47	1071-916
Joe McCarthy	1948-50	223-145
Steve O'Neill	1950-51	150-99
Lou Boudreau	1952-54	229-232
Pinky Higgins	1955-59, 1960-62	560-556
Rudy York	1959	0-1
Billy Jurges	1959-60	59-63
Del Baker	1960	2-5
Johnny Pesky	1963-64, 1980	147-179
Billy Herman	1964-66	128-182
Pete Runnels	1966	8-8
Dick Williams	1967-69	260-217
Eddie Popowski	1969, 1973	6-4
Eddie Kasko	1970-73	345-295
Darrell Johnson	1974-76	220-188
Don Zimmer	1976-80	411-304
Ralph Houk	1981-84	312-282
John McNamara	1985-88	297-273
Joe Morgan	1988-91	301-252
Butch Hobson	1992-94	207-232
Kevin Kennedy	1995-96	171-135
Jimy Williams	1997-99	264-222

WORLD SERIES CHAMPIONS

Year	Loser	Length	MVP
1903	Pittsburgh	8 games	None
1912	N.Y. Giants	7 games	None
1915	Philadelphia	5 games	None
1916	Brooklyn	5 games	None
1918	Chicago	6 games	None

A.L. PENNANT WINNERS

Year	Record	Manager	Series Result
1903	91-47	J. Collins	Defeated Pirates
1904	95-59	J. Collins	No Series
1912	105-47	J. Stahl	Defeated N.Y. Giants
1915	101-50	Carrigan	Defeated Phillies
1916	91-63	Carrigan	Defeated Dodgers
1918	75-51	Barrow	Defeated Cubs
1946	104-50	Cronin	Lost to Cardinals
1967	92-70	Williams	Lost to Cardinals
1975	95-65	Johnson	Lost to Reds
1986	95-66	McNamara	Lost to N.Y. Mets

EAST DIVISION CHAMPIONS

Year	Record	Manager	ALCS Result
1975	95-65	Johnson	Defeated A's
1986	95-66	McNamara	Defeated Angels
1988	89-73	McNamara, Morgan	Lost to A's
1990	88-74	Morgan	Lost to A's
1995	86-58	Kennedy	Lost in Div. Series

WILD-CARD QUALIFIERS

Year	Record	Manager	ALCS Result
1998	92-70	Williams	Lost in Div. Series
1999	94-68	Williams	Lost to Yankees

ATTENDANCE HIGHS

Total	Season	Park
2,562,435	1991	Fenway Park
2,528,986	1990	Fenway Park
2,510,012	1989	Fenway Park
2,468,574	1992	Fenway Park
2,464,851	1988	Fenway Park

BALLPARK CHRONOLOGY

Fenway Park—(1912-present)

Capacity: 33,455.
First game: Red Sox 7, New York 6, 11 innings (April 20, 1912).
First batter: Guy Zinn, Yankees.
First hit: Harry Wolter, Yankees.
First run: Guy Zinn, Yankees (1st inning).
First home run: Hugh Bradley, Red Sox (April 26).
First winning pitcher: Charley Hall, Red Sox.
First-season attendance: 597,096.

Huntington Avenue Grounds (1901-11)

Capacity: 9,000.
First game: Red Sox 12, Philadelphia 4 (May 8, 1901).
First-season attendance: 289,448.

A.L. MVPs

Jimmie Foxx, 1B, 1938
Ted Williams, OF, 1946
Ted Williams, OF, 1949
Jackie Jensen, OF, 1958
Carl Yastrzemski, OF, 1967
Fred Lynn, OF, 1975
Jim Rice, OF, 1978
Roger Clemens, P, 1986
Mo Vaughn, 1B, 1995

CY YOUNG WINNERS

Jim Lonborg, RH, 1967
Roger Clemens, RH, 1986
Roger Clemens, RH, 1987
Roger Clemens, RH, 1991
Pedro Martinez, RH, 1999

ROOKIES OF THE YEAR

Walt Dropo, 1B, 1950
Don Schwall, P, 1961
Carlton Fisk, C, 1972
Fred Lynn, OF, 1975
Nomar Garciaparra, SS, 1997

MANAGERS OF THE YEAR

John McNamara, 1986
Jimy Williams, 1999

RETIRED UNIFORMS

No.	Name	Pos.
1	Bobby Doerr	2B
4	Joe Cronin	SS
8	Carl Yastrzemski	OF
9	Ted Williams	OF

30-plus home runs
50— Jimmie Foxx 1938
46— Jim Rice 1978
44— Carl Yastrzemski 1967
Mo Vaughn 1996
43— Tony Armas 1984
Ted Williams 1949
42— Dick Stuart 1963
41— Jimmie Foxx 1936
40— Carl Yastrzemski 1969, 1970
Rico Petrocelli 1969
Mo Vaughn 1998
39— Vern Stephens 1949
Jim Rice 1977, 1979, 1983
Fred Lynn 1979
Mo Vaughn 1995
38— Ted Williams 1946, 1957
37— Ted Williams 1941
36— Jimmie Foxx 1937, 1940
Ted Williams 1942
Tony Conigliaro 1970
Tony Armas 1983
35— Jimmie Foxx 1939
Jackie Jensen 1958
Ken Harrelson 1968
Mo Vaughn 1997
Nomar Garciaparra 1998
34— Walt Dropo 1950
Dwight Evans 1987
33— Dick Stuart 1964
George Scott 1977
32— Ted Williams 1947
Tony Conigliaro 1965
Dwight Evans 1982, 1984
31— Ted Williams 1939
Don Baylor 1986
30— Vern Stephens 1950
Ted Williams 1951
Felix Mantilla 1964
Reggie Smith 1971
Butch Hobson 1977
Nick Esasky 1989
Nomar Garciaparra 1997

100-plus RBIs
175— Jimmie Foxx 1938
159— Vern Stephens 1949
Ted Williams 1949
145— Ted Williams 1939
144— Walt Dropo 1950
Vern Stephens 1950
143— Jimmie Foxx 1936
Mo Vaughn 1996
139— Jim Rice 1978
137— Ted Williams 1942
Vern Stephens 1948
130— Jim Rice 1979
127— Jimmie Foxx 1937
Ted Williams 1948
126— Ted Williams 1951
Jim Rice 1983
Mo Vaughn 1995
123— Ted Williams 1946
Tony Armas 1984
Dwight Evans 1987
122— Jackie Jensen 1958
Fred Lynn 1979
Jim Rice 1984
Nomar Garciaparra 1998
121— Buck Freeman 1902
Carl Yastrzemski 1967
120— Ted Williams 1941
Bobby Doerr 1950
119— Roy Johnson 1934
Jimmie Foxx 1940
Rudy York 1946
Mike Greenwell 1988
118— Dick Stuart 1963
117— Jackie Jensen 1954
116— Bobby Doerr 1946
Jackie Jensen 1955
Tony Conigliaro 1970
115— Mo Vaughn 1998
114— Buck Freeman 1901
Babe Ruth 1919
Ted Williams 1947
Dick Stuart 1964
Jim Rice 1977
113— Ted Williams 1940
112— Jackie Jensen 1959
Butch Hobson 1977
111— Joe Cronin 1940
Bobby Doerr 1948
Carl Yastrzemski 1969
Dwight Evans 1988
110— Joe Cronin 1937
Bill Buckner 1985
Jim Rice 1986
109— Duffy Lewis 1912
Bobby Doerr 1949
Ken Harrelson 1968
108— Nick Esasky 1989
107— Joe Cronin 1939
Tony Armas 1983
106— Mike Higgins 1937, 1938
Bob Johnson 1944
105— Jimmie Foxx 1939, 1941
Bobby Doerr 1940
Fred Lynn 1975
Tony Perez 1980
104— Buck Freeman 1903
Dwight Evans 1984
Nomar Garciaparra 1999
103— Earl Webb 1931
Frank Malzone 1957
Jackie Jensen 1957
Vic Wertz 1960
Rico Petrocelli 1970
Jim Rice 1985
Troy O'Leary 1999
102— Bobby Doerr 1942
Carl Yastrzemski 1970, 1976, 1977
Jim Rice 1975
Carlton Fisk 1977
Bill Buckner 1986
John Valentin 1995
101— Jim Tabor 1941
Mo Vaughn 1993
100— Del Pratt 1921
Dwight Evans 1989

20-plus victories
1901— Cy Young 33-10
1902— Cy Young 32-11
Bill Dinneen 21-21
1903— Cy Young 28-9
Bill Dinneen 21-13
Tom Hughes 20-7
1904— Cy Young 26-16
Bill Dinneen 23-14
Jesse Tannehill 21-11
1905— Jesse Tannehill 22-9
1907— Cy Young 21-15
1908— Cy Young 21-11
1911— Joe Wood 23-17
1912— Joe Wood 34-5
Hugh Bedient 20-9
Buck O'Brien 20-13
1914— Ray Collins 20-13
1916— Babe Ruth 23-12
1917— Babe Ruth 24-13
Carl Mays 22-9
1918— Carl Mays 21-13
1921— Sam Jones 23-16
1923— Howard Ehmke 20-17
1935— Wes Ferrell 25-14
Lefty Grove 20-12
1936— Wes Ferrell 20-15
1942— Tex Hughson 22-6
1945— Dave Ferriss 21-10
1946— Dave Ferriss 25-6
Tex Hughson 20-11
1949— Mel Parnell 25-7
Ellis Kinder 23-6
1953— Mel Parnell 21-8
1963— Bill Monbouquette 20-10
1967— Jim Lonborg 22-9
1973— Luis Tiant 20-13
1974— Luis Tiant 22-13
1976— Luis Tiant 21-12
1978— Dennis Eckersley 20-8
1986— Roger Clemens 24-4
1987— Roger Clemens 20-9
1990— Roger Clemens 21-6
1999— Pedro Martinez 23-4

A.L. home run champions
1903— Buck Freeman 13
1910— Jake Stahl 10
1912— Tris Speaker *10
1918— Babe Ruth *11
1919— Babe Ruth 29
1939— Jimmie Foxx 35
1941— Ted Williams 37
1942— Ted Williams 36
1947— Ted Williams 32
1949— Ted Williams 43
1965— Tony Conigliaro 32
1967— Carl Yastrzemski *44
1977— Jim Rice 39
1978— Jim Rice 46
1981— Dwight Evans *22
1983— Jim Rice 39
1984— Tony Armas 43

* Tied for league lead

A.L. RBI champions
1902— Buck Freeman 121
1903— Buck Freeman 104
1919— Babe Ruth 114
1938— Jimmie Foxx 175
1939— Ted Williams 145
1942— Ted Williams 137
1947— Ted Williams 114
1949— Ted Williams *159
Vern Stephens *159
1950— Walt Dropo *144
Vern Stephens *144
1955— Jackie Jensen *116
1958— Jackie Jensen 122
1959— Jackie Jensen 112
1963— Dick Stuart 118
1967— Carl Yastrzemski 121
1968— Ken Harrelson 109
1978— Jim Rice 139
1983— Jim Rice *126
1984— Tony Armas 123
1995— Mo Vaughn *126

* Tied for league lead

A.L. batting champions
1932— Dale Alexander .367
1938— Jimmie Foxx .349
1941— Ted Williams .406
1942— Ted Williams .356
1947— Ted Williams .343
1948— Ted Williams .369
1950— Billy Goodman .354
1957— Ted Williams .388
1958— Ted Williams .328
1960— Pete Runnels .320
1962— Pete Runnels .326
1963— Carl Yastrzemski .321
1967— Carl Yastrzemski .326
1968— Carl Yastrzemski .301
1979— Fred Lynn .333
1981— Carney Lansford .336
1983— Wade Boggs .361
1985— Wade Boggs .368
1986— Wade Boggs .357
1987— Wade Boggs .363
1988— Wade Boggs .366
1999— Nomar Garciaparra .357

A.L. ERA champions
1901— Cy Young 1.62
1914— Dutch Leonard 0.96
1915— Joe Wood 1.49
1916— Babe Ruth 1.75
1935— Lefty Grove 2.70
1936— Lefty Grove 2.81
1938— Lefty Grove 3.08
1939— Lefty Grove 2.54
1949— Mel Parnell 2.78
1972— Luis Tiant 1.91
1986— Roger Clemens 2.48
1990— Roger Clemens 1.93
1991— Roger Clemens 2.62
1992— Roger Clemens 2.41
1999— Pedro Martinez 2.07

A.L. strikeout champions
1901— Cy Young 158
1942— Tex Hughson 113
1967— Jim Lonborg 246
1988— Roger Clemens 291
1991— Roger Clemens 241
1996— Roger Clemens 257
1999— Pedro Martinez 313

No-hit pitchers
(9 innings or more)
1904— Cy Young 3-0 vs. Philadelphia (Perfect)
Jesse Tannehill 6-0 vs. Chicago
1905— Bill Dinneen 2-0 vs. Chicago
1908— Cy Young 8-0 vs. New York
1911— Joe Wood 5-0 vs. St. Louis
1916— George Foster 2-0 vs. New York
Dutch Leonard 4-0 vs. St. Louis
1917— Ernie Shore 4-0 vs. Washington (Perfect)
1918— Dutch Leonard 5-0 vs. Detroit
1923— Howard Ehmke 4-0 vs. Philadelphia
1956— Mel Parnell 4-0 vs. Chicago
1962— Earl Wilson 2-0 vs. Los Angeles
Bill Monbouquette 1-0 vs. Chicago
1965— Dave Morehead 2-0 vs. Cleveland
1992— †Matt Young 1-2 vs. Cleveland

† Pitched 8 innings

Longest hitting streaks
34— Dom DiMaggio 1949
30— Tris Speaker 1912
Nomar Garciaparra 1997
28— Wade Boggs 1985
27— Dom DiMaggio 1951
26— Buck Freeman 1902
Johnny Pesky 1947
25— George Metkovich 1944
Wade Boggs 1987
24— Nomar Garciaparra 1998
23— Gorge Burns 1922
Del Pratt 1922
Buddy Myer 1928
Ted Williams 1941
22— Tris Speaker 1913
Dom DiMaggio 1942
Denny Doyle 1975
Reggie Jefferson 1997
21— Bobby Doerr 1943
Jim Rice 1980
Mike Greenwell 1989
20— Tris Speaker 1912
Tris Speaker 1912
Babe Ruth 1919
Ike Boone 1925
Smead Jolley 1932
Ed Bressoud 1964
Fred Lynn 1975
Fred Lynn 1979
Mike Easler 1984
Wade Boggs 1986

INDIVIDUAL SEASON, GAME RECORDS

SEASON

Batting			
At-bats	684	Nomar Garciaparra	1997
Runs	150	Ted Williams	1949
Hits	240	Wade Boggs	1985
Singles	187	Wade Boggs	1985
Doubles	67	Earl Webb	1931
Triples	22	Tris Speaker	1913
Home runs	50	Jimmie Foxx	1938
Home runs, rookie	34	Walt Dropo	1950
Grand slams	4	Babe Ruth	1919
Total bases	406	Jim Rice	1978
RBIs	175	Jimmie Foxx	1938
Walks	162	Ted Williams	1947, 1949
Most strikeouts	162	Butch Hobson	1977
Fewest strikeouts	9	Stuffy McInnis	1921
Batting average	.406	Ted Williams	1941
Slugging pct.	.735	Ted Williams	1941
Stolen bases	54	Tommy Harper	1973

Pitching			
Games	80	Greg Harris	1993
Complete games	41	Cy Young	1902
Innings	384.2	Cy Young	1902
Wins	34	Joe Wood	1912
Losses	25	Charley Ruffing	1928
Winning pct.	.882 (15-2)	Bob Stanley	1978
Walks	134	Mel Parnell	1949
Strikeouts	313	Pedro Martinez	1999
Shutouts	10	Cy Young	1904
		Joe Wood	1912
Home runs allowed	38	Tim Wakefield	1996
Lowest ERA	0.96	Dutch Leonard	1914
Saves	46	Tom Gordon	1998

GAME

Batting			
Runs	6	Last by Spike Owen	8-21-86
Hits	6	Last by Jerry Remy	9-3-81 (20 innings)
Doubles	4	Last by Rick Miller	5-11-81
Triples	3	Patsy Dougherty	9-5-03
Home runs	3	Last by Mo Vaughn	5-30-97
RBIs	10	Last by Nomar Garciaparra	5-10-99
Total bases	16	Fred Lynn	6-18-75
Stolen bases	4	Jerry Remy	6-14-80

HISTORY

BATTING

Games
Carl Yastrzemski	3,308
Dwight Evans	2,505
Ted Williams	2,292
Jim Rice	2,089
Bobby Doerr	1,865
Harry Hooper	1,647
Wade Boggs	1,625
Rico Petrocelli	1,553
Dom DiMaggio	1,399
Frank Malzone	1,359

At-bats
Carl Yastrzemski	11,988
Dwight Evans	8,726
Jim Rice	8,225
Ted Williams	7,706
Bobby Doerr	7,093
Harry Hooper	6,270
Wade Boggs	6,213
Dom DiMaggio	5,640
Rico Petrocelli	5,390
Frank Malzone	5,273

Runs
Carl Yastrzemski	1,816
Ted Williams	1,798
Dwight Evans	1,435
Jim Rice	1,249
Bobby Doerr	1,094
Wade Boggs	1,067
Dom DiMaggio	1,046
Harry Hooper	988
Johnny Pesky	776
Jimmie Foxx	721

Hits
Carl Yastrzemski	3,419
Ted Williams	2,654
Jim Rice	2,452
Dwight Evans	2,373
Wade Boggs	2,098
Bobby Doerr	2,042
Harry Hooper	1,707
Dom DiMaggio	1,680
Frank Malzone	1,454
Mike Greenwell	1,400

Doubles
Carl Yastrzemski	646
Ted Williams	525
Dwight Evans	474
Wade Boggs	422
Bobby Doerr	381
Jim Rice	373
Dom DiMaggio	308
Mike Greenwell	275
Joe Cronin	270
John Valentin	263

Triples
Harry Hooper	130
Tris Speaker	106
Buck Freeman	90
Bobby Doerr	89
Larry Gardner	87
Jim Rice	79
Hobe Ferris	77
Dwight Evans	72
Ted Williams	71
Jimmy Collins	65

Home runs
Ted Williams	521
Carl Yastrzemski	452
Jim Rice	382
Dwight Evans	379
Mo Vaughn	230
Bobby Doerr	223
Jimmie Foxx	222
Rico Petrocelli	210
Jackie Jensen	170
Tony Conigliaro	162
Carlton Fisk	162

Total bases
Carl Yastrzemski	5,539
Ted Williams	4,884
Jim Rice	4,129
Dwight Evans	4,128
Bobby Doerr	3,270
Wade Boggs	2,869
Dom DiMaggio	2,363
Harry Hooper	2,303
Rico Petrocelli	2,263
Mike Greenwell	2,141

Runs batted in
Carl Yastrzemski	1,844
Ted Williams	1,839
Jim Rice	1,451
Dwight Evans	1,346

SEASON

Batting
Most at-bats	5,781	1997
Most runs	1,027	1950
Fewest runs	463	1906
Most hits	1,684	1997
Most singles	1,156	1905
Most doubles	373	1997
Most triples	112	1903
Most home runs	213	1977
Fewest home runs	12	1906
Most grand slams	9	1941, 1950, 1987
Most pinch-hit home runs	6	1953
Most total bases	2,676	1997
Most stolen bases	215	1909
Highest batting average	.302	1950
Lowest batting average	.234	1905, 1907
Highest slugging pct	.465	1977

Pitching
Lowest ERA	2.12	1904
Highest ERA	5.02	1932
Most complete games	148	1904
Most shutouts	26	1918
Most saves	53	1998
Most walks	748	1950
Most strikeouts	1,165	1996

Fielding
Most errors	373	1901
Fewest errors	93	1988
Most double plays	207	1949
Highest fielding averag	.984	1988

General
Most games won	105	1912
Most games lost	111	1932
Highest win pct	.691	1912
Lowest win pct	.279	1932

GAME, INNING

Batting
Most runs, game	29	6-8-50
Most runs, inning	17	6-18-53
Most hits, game	28	6-8-50
Most home runs, game	8	7-4-77
Most total bases, game	60	6-8-50

Jackie Jensen (left) and Ted Williams formed two-thirds of a prolific outfield for six seasons.

Bobby Doerr	1,247
Jimmie Foxx	788
Rico Petrocelli	773
Mo Vaughn	752
Joe Cronin	737
Jackie Jensen	733

Extra base hits
Carl Yastrzemski	1,157
Ted Williams	1,117
Dwight Evans	925
Jim Rice	834
Bobby Doerr	693
Wade Boggs	554
Rico Petrocelli	469
Dom DiMaggio	452
Jimmie Foxx	448
Mike Greenwell	443

Batting average
(Minimum 500 games)
Ted Williams	.344
Wade Boggs	.338
Tris Speaker	.337
Pete Runnels	.320
Jimmie Foxx	.320
Roy Johnson	.313
Johnny Pesky	.313
Fred Lynn	.308
Billy Goodman	.306
Mo Vaughn	.304

Stolen bases
Harry Hooper	300
Tris Speaker	267
Carl Yastrzemski	168
Heinie Wagner	141
Larry Gardner	134
Freddy Parent	129
Tommy Harper	107
Billy Werber	107
Chick Stahl	105
Jimmy Collins	102
Duffy Lewis	102

PITCHING

Earned-run average
(Minimum 1,000 innings)
Joe Wood	1.99
Cy Young	2.00
Dutch Leonard	2.13
Babe Ruth	2.19

Carl Mays	2.21
Ray Collins	2.51
Bill Dinneen	2.81
George Winter	2.91
Tex Hughson	2.94
Roger Clemens	3.06

Wins
Roger Clemens	192
Cy Young	192
Mel Parnell	123
Luis Tiant	122
Joe Wood	117
Bob Stanley	115
Joe Dobson	106
Lefty Grove	105
Tex Hughson	96
Bill Monbouquette	96

Losses
Cy Young	112
Roger Clemens	111
Bob Stanley	97
George Winter	97
Red Ruffing	96
Jack Russell	94
Bill Monbouquette	91
Bill Dinneen	85
Tom Brewer	82
Luis Tiant	81

Innings pitched
Roger Clemens	2,776.0
Cy Young	2,728.1
Luis Tiant	1,774.2
Mel Parnell	1,752.2
Bob Stanley	1,707.0
Bill Monbouquette	1,622.0
George Winter	1,599.2
Joe Dobson	1,544.0
Lefty Grove	1,539.2
Tom Brewer	1,509.1

Strikeouts
Roger Clemens	2,590
Cy Young	1,341
Luis Tiant	1,075
Bruce Hurst	1,043
Joe Wood	986
Bill Monbouquette	969
Frank Sullivan	821
Ray Culp	794

Jim Lonborg	784
Dennis Eckersley	771
Dutch Leonard	771

Bases on balls
Roger Clemens	856
Mel Parnell	758
Tom Brewer	669
Joe Dobson	604
Jack Wilson	564
Willard Nixon	530
Ike Delock	514
Mickey McDermott	504
Luis Tiant	501
Fritz Ostermueller	491

Games
Bob Stanley	637
Roger Clemens	383
Ellis Kinder	365
Cy Young	327
Ike Delock	322
Bill Lee	321
Mel Parnell	289
Greg Harris	287
Mike Fornieles	286
Dick Radatz	286

Shutouts
Roger Clemens	38
Cy Young	38
Joe Wood	28
Luis Tiant	26
Dutch Leonard	25
Mel Parnell	20
Ray Collins	19
Tex Hughson	19
Sam Jones	18
Joe Dobson	17
Babe Ruth	17

Saves
Bob Stanley	132
Dick Radatz	104
Ellis Kinder	91
Jeff Reardon	88
Sparky Lyle	69
Tom Gordon	68
Lee Smith	58
Bill Campbell	51
Mike Fornieles	48
Heathcliff Slocumb	48

HISTORY

RED SOX YEAR-BY-YEAR

Year	W	L	Place	Games Back	Manager	Leaders: Batting avg.	Hits	Home runs	RBIs	Wins	ERA
1901	79	57	2nd	4	J. Collins	Freeman, .339	J. Collins, 187	Freeman, 12	Freeman, 114	Young, 33	Young, 1.62
1902	77	60	3rd	6½	J. Collins	Dougherty, .342	Freeman, 174	Freeman, 11	Freeman, 121	Young, 32	Young, 2.15
1903	91	47	1st	+14½	J. Collins	Dougherty, .331	Dougherty, 195	Freeman, 13	Freeman, 104	Young, 28	Young, 2.08
1904	95	59	1st	+1½	J. Collins	Parent, .291	Parent, 172	Freeman, 7	Freeman, 84	Young, 26	Young, 1.97
1905	78	74	4th	16	J. Collins	J. Collins, .276	Burkett, 147	Ferris, 6	J. Collins, 65	Tannehill, 22	Young, 1.82
1906	49	105	8th	45½	J. Collins, Stahl	Grimshaw, .290	Stahl, 170	Stahl, 4	Stahl, 51	Tannehill, Young, 13	Dinneen, 2.92
1907	59	90	7th	32½	Huff, Unglaub, McGuire	Congalton, .286	Congalton, 142	Ferris, 4	Unglaub, 62	Young, 21	Morgan, 1.97
1908	75	79	5th	15½	McGuire, Lake	Gessler, .308	Lord, 145	Gessler, 3	Gessler, 63	Young, 21	Young, 1.26
1909	88	63	3rd	9½	Lake	Lord, .311	Speaker, 168	Speaker, 7	Speaker, 77	Arellanes, 16	Cicotte, 1.97
1910	81	72	4th	22½	Donovan	Speaker, .340	Speaker, 183	Stahl, 10	Stahl, 77	Cicotte, 15	R. Collins, 1.62
1911	78	75	5th	24	Donovan	Speaker, .334	Speaker, 167	Speaker, 8	Lewis, 86	Wood, 23	Wood, 2.02
1912	105	47	1st	+14	Stahl	Speaker, .383	Speaker, 222	Speaker, 10	Lewis, 109	Wood, 34	Wood, 1.91
1913	79	71	4th	15½	Stahl, Carrigan	Speaker, .363	Speaker, 189	Hooper, 4	Lewis, 90	R. Collins, 19	Wood, 2.29
1914	91	62	2nd	8½	Carrigan	Speaker, .338	Speaker, 193	Speaker, 4	Speaker, 90	R. Collins, 20	Leonard, 0.96
1915	101	50	1st	+2½	Carrigan	Speaker, .322	Speaker, 176	Ruth, 4	Lewis, 76	Foster, Shore, 19	Wood, 1.49
1916	91	63	1st	+2	Carrigan	Gardner, .308	Hooper, 156	Walker, Ruth, Gainor, 3	Gardner, 62	Ruth, 23	Ruth, 1.75
1917	90	62	2nd	9	Barry	Lewis, .302	Lewis, 167	Hooper, 3	Lewis, 65	Ruth, 24	Mays, 1.74
1918	75	51	1st	+1½	Barrow	Hooper, .289	Hooper, 137	Ruth, 11	Ruth, 66	Mays, 21	Bush, 2.11
1919	66	71	6th	20½	Barrow	Ruth, .322	Scott, 141	Ruth, 29	Ruth, 114	Pennock, 16	Mays, 2.47
1920	72	81	5th	25½	Barrow	Hendryx, .328	Hooper, 167	Hooper, 7	Hendryx, 73	Pennock, 16	Myers, 2.13
1921	75	79	5th	23½	Duffy	Pratt, .324	McInnis, 179	Pratt, 5	Pratt, 100	S. Jones, 23	S. Jones, 3.22
1922	61	93	8th	33	Duffy	J. Harris, .316	Pratt, 183	Burns, 12	Pratt, 86	R. Collins, 14	Quinn, 3.48
1923	61	91	8th	37	Chance	J. Harris, .335	Burns, 181	J. Harris, 13	Burns, 82	Ehmke, 20	Piercy, 3.41
1924	67	87	7th	25	Fohl	Boone, .333	Wambsganss, 174	Boone, 13	Veach, 99	Ehmke, 19	Quinn, 3.27
1925	47	105	8th	49½	Fohl	Boone, .330	Flagstead, 160	Todt, 11	Todt, 75	Wingfield, 12	Ehmke, 3.73
1926	46	107	8th	44½	Fohl	Jacobson, .305	Todt, 153	Todt, 7	Jacobson, Todt, 69	Wingfield, 11	Russell, 3.58
1927	51	103	8th	59	Carrigan	Tobin, .310	Myer, 135	Todt, 6	Flagstead, 69	Harriss, 14	Russell, 4.10
1928	57	96	8th	43½	Carrigan	Myer, .313	Myer, 168	Todt, 12	Regan, 75	Morris, 19	Morris, 3.53
1929	58	96	8th	48	Carrigan	Rothrock, .300	Scarritt, 159	Rothrock, 6	Scarritt, 71	Morris, 14	MacFayden, 3.62
1930	52	102	8th	50	Wagner	Webb, .323	Oliver, 189	Webb, 16	Webb, 66	Gaston, 13	Gaston, 3.92
1931	62	90	6th	45	S. Collins	Webb, .333	Webb, 196	Webb, 14	Webb, 103	MacFayden, 16	Moore, 3.88
1932	43	111	8th	64	S. Collins, McManus	Alexander, .372	Jolley, 164	Jolley, 18	Jolley, 99	Kline, 11	Durham, 3.80
1933	63	86	7th	34½	McManus	R. Johnson, .313	R. Johnson, 151	R. Johnson, 10	R. Johnson, 95	Rhodes, 12	Weiland, 3.87
1934	76	76	4th	24	B. Harris	Werber, .321	Werber, 200	Werber, 11	R. Johnson, 119	Ferrell, 14	Ostermueller, 3.49
1935	78	75	4th	16	Cronin	R. Johnson, .315	Almada, 176	Werber, 14	Cronin, 95	Ferrell, 25	Grove, 2.70
1936	74	80	6th	28½	Cronin	Foxx, .338	Foxx, 198	Foxx, 41	Foxx, 143	Ferrell, 20	Grove, 2.81
1937	80	72	5th	21	Cronin	Chapman,.Cronin, .307	Cronin, 175	Foxx, 36	Foxx, 127	Grove, 17	Grove, 3.02
1938	88	61	2nd	9½	Cronin	Foxx, .349	Vosmik, 201	Foxx, 50	Foxx, 175	Bagby, J. Wilson, 15	Grove, 3.08
1939	89	62	2nd	17	Cronin	Foxx, .360	T. Williams, 185	Foxx, 35	T. Williams, 145	Grove, 15	Grove, 2.54
1940	82	72	4th	8	Cronin	T. Williams, .344	Cramer, 200	Foxx, 36	Foxx, 119	Heving, J. Wilson, 12	Grove, 3.99
1941	84	70	2nd	17	Cronin	T. Williams, .406	T. Williams, 185	T. Williams, 37	T. Williams, 120	D. Newsome, 19	Wagner, 3.07
1942	93	59	2nd	9	Cronin	T. Williams, .356	Pesky, 205	T. Williams, 36	T. Williams, 137	Hughson, 22	Butland, 2.51
1943	68	84	7th	29	Cronin	Fox, .288	Doerr, 163	Doerr, 16	Tabor, 85	Hughson, 12	Brown, 2.12
1944	77	77	4th	12	Cronin	Doerr, .325	B. Johnson, 170	B. Johnson, 17	B. Johnson, 106	Hughson, 18	Hughson, 2.26
1945	71	83	7th	17½	Cronin	S. Newsome, .290	B. Johnson, 148	B. Johnson, 12	B. Johnson, 74	Ferriss, 21	Ryba, 2.49
1946	104	50	1st	+12	Cronin	T. Williams, .342	Pesky, 208	T. Williams, 38	T. Williams, 123	Ferriss, 25	Hughson, 2.75
1947	83	71	3rd	14	Cronin	T. Williams, .343	Pesky, 207	T. Williams, 32	T. Williams, 114	Dobson, 18	Dobson, 2.95
1948	96	59	*2nd	1	McCarthy	T. Williams, .369	T. Williams, 188	Stephens, 29	Stephens, 137	Kramer, 18	Parnell, 3.14
1949	96	58	2nd	1	McCarthy	T. Williams, .343	T. Williams, 194	T. Williams, 43	Stephens, Williams, 159	Parnell, 25	Parnell, 2.77
1950	94	60	3rd	4	McCarthy, O'Neill	Goodman, .354	D. DiMaggio, 193	Dropo, 34	Dropo, Stephens, 144	Parnell, 18	Parnell, 3.61
1951	87	67	3rd	11	O'Neill	T. Williams, .318	D. DiMaggio, 189	T. Williams, 30	T. Williams, 126	Parnell, 18	Kinder, 2.55
1952	76	78	6th	19	Boudreau	Goodman, .306	Goodman, 157	Gernert, 19	Gernert, 67	Parnell, 12	Kinder, 2.58
1953	84	69	4th	16	Boudreau	Goodman, .313	Goodman, 161	Gernert, 21	Kell, 73	Parnell, 21	Kinder, 1.85
1954	69	85	4th	42	Boudreau	T. Williams, .345	Jensen, 160	T. Williams, 29	Jensen, 117	Sullivan, 15	Sullivan, 3.14
1955	84	70	4th	12	Higgins	Goodman, .294	Goodman, 176	T. Williams, 28	Jensen, 116	Sullivan, 18	Kiely, 2.80
1956	84	70	4th	13	Higgins	T. Williams, .345	Jensen, 182	T. Williams, 24	Jensen, 97	Brewer, 19	Sullivan, 3.42
1957	82	72	3rd	16	Higgins	T. Williams, .388	Malzone, 185	T. Williams, 38	Jensen, Malzone, 103	Brewer, 16	Sullivan, 2.73
1958	79	75	3rd	13	Higgins	T. Williams, .328	Malzone, 185	Jensen, 35	Jensen, 122	Delock, 14	Delock, 3.37
1959	75	79	5th	19	Higgins, York, Jurges	Runnels, .314	Runnels, 176	Jensen, 28	Jensen, 112	Casale, 13	DeLock, 2.95
1960	65	89	7th	32	Jurges, Baker, Higgins	Runnels, .320	Runnels, 169	T. Williams, 29	Wertz, 103	Monbouquette, 14	Fornieles, 2.64
1961	76	86	6th	33	Higgins	Runnels, .317	Schilling, 167	Geiger, 18	Malzone, 87	Schwall, 15	Schwall, 3.22
1962	76	84	8th	19	Higgins	Runnels, .326	Yastrzemski, 191	Malzone, 21	Malzone, 95	Conley, Monbouquette, 15	Radatz, 2.24
1963	76	85	7th	28	Pesky	Yastrzemski, .321	Yastrzemski, 183	Stuart, 42	Stuart, 118	Monbouquette, 20	Radatz, 1.97
1964	72	90	8th	27	Pesky, Herman	Bressoud, .293	Stuart, 168	Stuart, 33	Stuart, 114	Radatz, 16	Radatz, 2.29
1965	62	100	9th	40	Herman	Yastrzemski, .312	Yastrzemski, 154	Conigliaro, 32	Mantilla, 92	Wilson, 13	Monbouquette, 3.70
1966	72	90	9th	26	Herman, Runnels	Yastrzemski, .278	Yastrzemski, 165	Conigliaro, 28	Conigliaro, 93	Santiago, 12	Brandon, 3.31
1967	92	70	1st	+1	D. Williams	Yastrzemski, .326	Yastrzemski, 189	Yastrzemski, 44	Yastrzemski, 121	Lonborg, 22	Wyatt, 2.60
1968	86	76	4th	17	D. Williams	Yastrzemski, .301	Yastrzemski, 162	Harrelson, 35	Harrelson, 109	Culp, Ellsworth, 16	Santiago, 2.25
							EAST DIVISION				
1969	87	75	3rd	22	D. Williams, Popowski	R. Smith, .309	R. Smith, 168	Petrocelli, Yastrzemski, 40	Yastrzemski, 111	Culp, 17	Lyle, 2.54
1970	87	75	3rd	21	Kasko	Yastrzemski, .329	Yastrzemski, 186	Yastrzemski, 40	Conigliaro, 116	Culp, 17	Culp, 3.04
1971	85	77	3rd	18	Kasko	R. Smith, .283	R. Smith, 175	R. Smith, 30	R. Smith, 96	Siebert, 16	Lee, 2.74
1972	85	70	2nd	½	Kasko	Fisk, .293	Harper, 141	Fisk, 22	Petrocelli, 75	Pattin, 17	Tiant, 1.91
1973	89	73	2nd	8	Kasko, Popowski	R. Smith, .303	Yastrzemski, 160	Fisk, 26	Yastrzemski, 95	Tiant, 20	Lee, 2.75
1974	84	78	3rd	7	D. Johnson	Yastrzemski, .301	Yastrzemski, 155	Petrocelli, Yastrzemski, 15	Yastrzemski, 79	Tiant, 22	Tiant, 2.92
1975	95	65	†1st	+4½	D. Johnson	Lynn, .331	Lynn, 175	Rice, 22	Lynn, 105	Wise, 19	Moret, 3.60
1976	83	79	3rd	15½	D. Johnson, Zimmer	Lynn, .314	Rice, 164	Rice, 25	Yastrzemski, 102	Tiant, 21	Willoughby, 2.82
1977	97	64	‡2nd	2½	Zimmer	Rice, .320	Rice, 206	Rice, 39	Rice, 114	Campbell, 13	Campbell, 2.96
1978	99	64	§2nd	1	Zimmer	Rice, .315	Rice, 213	Rice, 46	Rice, 139	Eckersley, 20	Stanley, 2.60
1979	91	69	3rd	11½	Zimmer	Lynn, .333	Rice, 201	Lynn, Rice, 39	Rice, 130	Eckersley, 17	Eckersley, 2.99
1980	83	77	4th	19	Zimmer, Pesky	Stapleton, .321	Burleson, 179	Perez, 25	Perez, 105	Eckersley, 12	Burgmeier, 2.00
1981	59	49	∞5th/2nd	—	Houk	Lansford, .336	Lansford, 134	Evans, 22	Evans, 71	Stanley, Torrez, 10	Torrez, 3.68
1982	89	73	3rd	6	Houk	Rice, .309	Evans, Remy, 178	Evans, 32	Evans, 98	Clear, 14	Burgmeier, 2.29
1983	78	84	6th	20	Houk	Boggs, .361	Boggs, 210	Rice, 39	Rice, 126	Tudor, 13	Stanley, 2.85
1984	86	76	4th	18	Houk	Boggs, .325	Boggs, 203	Armas, 43	Armas, 123	Boyd, Hurst, Ojeda, 12	Stanley, 3.54
1985	81	81	5th	18½	McNamara	Boggs, .368	Boggs, 240	Evans, 29	Buckner, 110	Boyd, 15	Clemens, 3.29
1986	95	66	†1st	+5½	McNamara	Boggs, .357	Boggs, 207	Baylor, 31	Rice, 110	Clemens, 24	Clemens, 2.48
1987	78	84	5th	20	McNamara	Boggs, .363	Boggs, 200	Evans, 34	Evans, 123	Clemens, 20	Clemens, 2.97
1988	89	73	▲1st	+1	McNamara, Morgan	Boggs, .366	Boggs, 214	Greenwell, 22	Greenwell, 119	Clemens, Hurst, 18	Clemens, 2.93
1989	83	79	3rd	6	Morgan	Boggs, .330	Boggs, 205	Esasky, 30	Esasky, 108	Clemens, 17	Lamp, 2.32
1990	88	74	▲1st	+2	Morgan	Boggs, .302	Boggs, 187	Burks, 21	Burks, 89	Clemens, 21	Clemens, 1.93
1991	84	78	‡2nd	7	Morgan	Boggs, .332	Boggs, 181	Clark, 28	Clark, 87	Clemens, 18	Clemens, 2.62
1992	73	89	7th	23	Hobson	Zupcic, .276	Reed, 136	Brunansky, 15	Brunansky, 74	Clemens, 18	Clemens, 2.41
1993	80	82	5th	15	Hobson	Greenwell, .315	Greenwell, 170	Vaughn, 29	Vaughn, 101	Darwin, 15	Sele, 2.74
1994	54	61	4th	17	Hobson	Vaughn, .310	Vaughn, 122	Vaughn, 26	Vaughn, 82	Clemens, 9	Clemens, 2.85
1995	86	58	◆1st	+7	Kennedy	O'Leary, .308	Vaughn, 165	Vaughn, 39	Vaughn, 126	Wakefield, 16	Wakefield, 2.95
1996	85	77	3rd	7	Kennedy	Jefferson, .347	Vaughn, 207	Vaughn, 44	Vaughn, 143	Wakefield, 14	Clemens, 3.63
1997	78	84	4th	20	J. Williams	Jefferson, .319	Garciaparra, 209	Vaughn, 35	Garciaparra, 98	Sele, 13	Gordon, 3.74
1998	92	70	◆2nd	22	J. Williams	Vaughn, .337	Vaughn, 205	Vaughn, 40	Garciaparra, 122	P.Martinez, 19	P.Martinez, 2.89
1999	94	68	▲2nd	4	J. Williams	Garciaparra, .357	Garciaparra, 190	O'Leary, 28	Garciaparra, 104	P.Martinez, 23	P.Martinez, 2.07

* Lost pennant playoff. † Won Championship Series. ‡ Tied for position. § Lost division playoff. ∞ First half 30-26, second half 29-23. ▲ Lost Championship Series. ◆ Lost Division Series.
Note: Batting average minimum 350 at-bats; ERA minimum 90 innings pitched.

HISTORY

CHICAGO WHITE SOX

FRANCHISE CHRONOLOGY

First season: 1901, as a member of the new American League. Charles Comiskey's White Sox defeated Cleveland, 8-2, in their Major League debut and proceeded to win the circuit's first pennant. Chicago's 83-53 record was four games better than second-place Boston.

1902-present: The Hitless Wonder White Sox of 1906 won another A.L. pennant and stunned the powerful Cubs in a six-game World Series, and Chicago repeated as Series champion in 1917 with a six-game triumph over the New York Giants. But the franchise would never taste such success again. The team's image was tarnished two years later when the White Sox won another pennant and conspired with gamblers to lose the World Series. In the wake of the infamous "Black Sox" scandal, it would take four decades for the White Sox to win another pennant and another 24 years to qualify again for postseason play. The "Go Go Sox" of 1959 lost to Los Angeles in the World Series and the 1983 and '93 Sox won West Division titles, only to lose in the A.L. Championship Series. Chicago was one of five teams placed in the Central Division when the A.L. adopted a three-division format in 1994.

Shortstop Luis Aparicio.

WHITE SOX VS. OPPONENTS BY DECADE

	A's	Indians	Orioles	Red Sox	Tigers	Twins	Yankees	Angels	Rangers	Brewers	Royals	Blue Jays	Mariners	Devil Rays	Interleague	Decade Record
1901-09	92-98	100-89	112-74	101-90	96-93	130-57	113-74									744-575
1910-19	125-90	114-102	132-74	97-117	103-109	109-106	118-94									798-692
1920-29	100-119	105-114	104-114	117-103	124-95	95-125	86-134									731-804
1930-39	102-118	94-125	127-90	97-114	89-129	101-117	68-148									678-841
1940-49	112-108	103-114	102-113	85-134	95-125	124-93	86-133									707-820
1950-59	124-96	116-104	134-86	122-98	122-98	141-79	88-132									847-693
1960-69	118-66	104-74	83-95	102-76	81-97	83-101	76-102	92-70	95-61	10-8	8-10					852-760
1970-79	76-89	62-54	39-74	48-67	50-67	76-89	44-72	79-90	90-65	68-62	79-89	19-14	22-21			752-853
1980-89	70-60	61-54	53-63	59-56	48-66	57-66	58-61	62-68	59-64	55-58	55-64	50-70	71-52			758-802
1990-99	60-57	58-64	59-46	54-54	69-51	71-48	54-52	58-60	58-59	56-41	72-52	53-54	59-62	11-10	24-25	816-735
Totals	979-901	917-894	945-829	882-909	877-930	987-881	791-1002	291-288	302-249	189-169	214-215	122-138	152-135	11-10	24-25	7683-7575

Interleague results: 6-6 vs. Cubs; 3-2 vs. Reds; 5-4 vs. Astros; 4-4 vs. Pirates; 4-5 vs. Cardinals; 2-4 vs. Brewers.

MANAGERS

Name	Years	Record
Clark Griffith	1901-02	157-113
Nixey Callahan	1903-04, 1912-14	309-329
Fielder Jones	1904-08	426-293
Billy Sullivan	1909	78-74
Hugh Duffy	1910-11	145-159
Pants Rowland	1915-18	339-247
Kid Gleason	1919-23	392-364
Johnny Evers	1924	66-87
Eddie Collins	1925-26	160-147
Ray Schalk	1927-28	102-125
Lena Blackburne	1928-29	99-133
Donie Bush	1930-31	118-189
Lew Fonseca	1932-34	120-196
Jimmie Dykes	1934-46	899-940
Ted Lyons	1946-48	185-245
Jack Onslow	1949-50	71-113
Red Corriden	1950	52-72
Paul Richards	1951-54, 1976	406-362
Marty Marion	1954-56	179-138
Al Lopez	1957-65, 1968-69	840-650
Eddie Stanky	1966-68	206-197
Don Gutteridge	1969-70	109-172
Chuck Tanner	1970-75	401-414
Bob Lemon	1977-78	124-112
Larry Doby	1978	37-50
Don Kessinger	1979	46-60
Tony La Russa	1979-86	522-510

MANAGERS—cont'd.

Name	Years	Record
Jim Fregosi	1986-88	193-226
Jeff Torborg	1989-91	250-235
Gene Lamont	1992-95	258-210
Terry Bevington	1995-97	222-214
Jerry Manuel	1998-99	155-168

WORLD SERIES CHAMPIONS

Year	Loser	Length	MVP
1906	Chicago Cubs	6 games	None
1917	N.Y. Giants	6 games	None

A.L. PENNANT WINNERS

Year	Record	Manager	Series Result
1901	83-53	Griffith	None
1906	93-58	Jones	Defeated Cubs
1917	100-54	Rowland	Defeated Giants
1919	88-52	Gleason	Lost to Reds
1959	94-60	Lopez	Lost to Dodgers

WEST DIVISION CHAMPIONS

Year	Record	Manager	ALCS Result
1983	99-63	La Russa	Lost to Orioles
1993	94-68	Lamont	Lost to Blue Jays
1994	67-46	Lamont	None

BALLPARK CHRONOLOGY

New Comiskey Park (1991-present)

Capacity: 44,321.
First game: Detroit 16, White Sox 0 (April 18, 1991).
First batter: Tony Phillips, Tigers.
First hit: Alan Trammell, Tigers (single).
First run: Travis Fryman, Tigers (3rd inning).
First home run: Cecil Fielder, Tigers.
First winning pitcher: Frank Tanana, Tigers.
First-season attendance: 2,934,154.

Southside Park (1901-10)

Capacity: 15,000.
First game: White Sox 8, Cleveland 2 (April 24, 1901).
First-season attendance: 354,350.

Comiskey Park (1910-90)

Capacity: 43,931.
First game: St. Louis 2, White Sox 0 (July 1, 1910).
First-season attendance (1911): 583,208.

ATTENDANCE HIGHS

Total	Season	Park
2,934,154	1991	New Comiskey Park
2,681,156	1992	New Comiskey Park
2,581,091	1993	New Comiskey Park
2,136,988	1984	Comiskey Park
2,132,821	1983	Comiskey Park

A.L. MVPs

Nellie Fox, 2B, 1959
Dick Allen, 1B, 1972
Frank Thomas, 1B, 1993
Frank Thomas, 1B, 1994

CY YOUNG WINNERS

Early Wynn, RH, 1959
LaMarr Hoyt, RH, 1983
Jack McDowell, RH, 1993

ROOKIES OF THE YEAR

Luis Aparicio, SS, 1956
Gary Peters, P, 1963
Tommie Agee, OF, 1966
Ron Kittle, OF, 1983
Ozzie Guillen, SS, 1985

MANAGERS OF THE YEAR

Tony La Russa, 1983
Jeff Torborg, 1990
Gene Lamont, 1993

RETIRED UNIFORMS

No.	Name	Pos.
2	Nellie Fox	2B
3	Harold Baines	OF
4	Luke Appling	SS
9	Minnie Minoso	OF
11	Luis Aparicio	SS
16	Ted Lyons	P
19	Billy Pierce	P
72	Carlton Fisk	C

Nellie Fox was a second-base fixture for more than a decade in Chicago.

30-plus home runs

49—	Albert Belle	1998
41—	Frank Thomas	1993
40—	Frank Thomas	1995
	Frank Thomas	1996
38—	Frank Thomas	1994
37—	Carlton Fisk	1985
	Dick Allen	1972
35—	Ron Kittle	1983
	Frank Thomas	1997
34—	Robin Ventura	1996
33—	Bill Melton	1971
	Bill Melton	1970
32—	Frank Thomas	1991
	Ron Kittle	1984
	Greg Luzinski	1983
	Dick Allen	1974
31—	Oscar Gamble	1977
30—	Albert Belle	1997
	Magglio Ordonez	1999

100-plus RBIs

152—	Albert Belle	1998
138—	Zeke Bonura	1936
134—	Frank Thomas	1996
128—	Frank Thomas	1993
	Luke Appling	1936
125—	Frank Thomas	1997
121—	Joe Jackson	1920
119—	Al Simmons	1933
117—	Eddie Robinson	1951
	Magglio Ordonez	1999
116—	Minnie Minoso	1954
	Albert Belle	1997
115—	Frank Thomas	1992
	Happy Felsch	1920
114—	Smead Jolley	1930
113—	Harold Baines	1985
	Dick Allen	1972
112—	George Bell	1992
111—	Gee Walker	1939
	Earl Sheely	1925
	Frank Thomas	1995
110—	Zeke Bonura	1934
109—	Frank Thomas	1991, 1998
	Floyd Robinson	1962
108—	Bib Falk	1926
107—	Carlton Fisk	1985
105—	Harold Baines	1982
	Minnie Minoso	1960
	Robin Ventura	1996
104—	Minnie Minoso	1953
	Eddie Robinson	1952
	Al Simmons	1934
	Carl Reynolds	1930
103—	Minnie Minoso	1957
	Earl Sheely	1924
102—	Greg Luzinski	1982
	Larry Doby	1956
	Happy Felsch	1917
101—	Frank Thomas	1994
	Richie Zisk	1977
	Danny Tartabull	1996
100—	Robin Ventura	1991
	Ron Kittle	1983
	Zeke Bonura	1937

20-plus victories

1901—	Clark Griffith	24-7
	Roy Patterson	20-15
1904—	Frank Owen	21-15
1905—	Nick Altrock	23-12
	Frank Owen	21-13
1906—	Frank Owen	22-13
	Nick Altrock	20-13
1907—	Guy White	27-13
	Ed Walsh	24-18
	Frank Smith	23-10
1908—	Ed Walsh	40-15
1909—	Frank Smith	25-17
1911—	Ed Walsh	27-18
1912—	Ed Walsh	27-17
1913—	Reb Russell	22-16
	Jim Scott	20-21
1915—	Jim Scott	24-11
	Urban Faber	24-14
1917—	Ed Cicotte	28-12
1919—	Ed Cicotte	29-7
	Lefty Williams	23-11

Shortstop Luke Appling, who spent 20 seasons with the White Sox, batted a hefty .388 in 1936, still a team record.

SEASON

Batting

At-bats	649	Nellie Fox	1956
Runs	135	John Mostil	1925
Hits	222	Eddie Collins	1920
Singles	169	Eddie Collins	1920
Doubles	48	Albert Belle	1998
Triples	21	Joe Jackson	1916
Home runs	49	Albert Belle	1998
Home runs, rookie	35	Ron Kittle	1983
Grand slams	4	Albert Belle	1997
Total bases	399	Albert Belle	1998
RBIs	152	Albert Belle	1998
Walks	138	Frank Thomas	1991
Most strikeouts	175	Dave Nicholson	1963
Fewest strikeouts	11	Nellie Fox	1958
Batting average	.388	Luke Appling	1936
Slugging pct.	.729	Frank Thomas	1994
Stolen bases	77	Rudy Law	1983

Pitching

Games	88	Wilbur Wood	1968
Complete games	42	Ed Walsh	1908
Innings	464.0	Ed Walsh	1908
Wins	40	Ed Walsh	1908
Losses	25	Patrick Flaherty	1903
Winning pct.	.857 (12-2)	Jason Bere	1994
Walks	147	Vern Kennedy	1936
Strikeouts	269	Ed Walsh	1908
Shutouts	11	Ed Walsh	1908
Home runs allowed	34	3 times	
		Last by James Baldwin	1999
Lowest ERA	1.52	Doc White	1906
Saves	57	Bobby Thigpen	1990

GAME

Batting

Runs	5	Last by Walt Williams	5-31-70
Hits	6	Last by Lance Johnson	9-23-95
Doubles	4	Last by Marv Owen	4-23-39
Triples	3	Lance Johnson	9-23-95
Home runs	4	Pat Seerey	7-18-48
RBIs	8	Last by Robin Ventura	9-4-95
Total bases	16	Pat Seerey	7-18-48
Stolen bases	4	Last by Lou Frazier	4-19-98

1920—	Red Faber	23-13
	Lefty Williams	22-14
	Dickie Kerr	21-9
	Ed Cicotte	21-10
1921—	Red Faber	25-15
1922—	Red Faber	21-17
1924—	Sloppy Thurston	20-14
1925—	Ted Lyons	21-11
1927—	Ted Lyons	22-14
1930—	Ted Lyons	22-15
1936—	Vern Kennedy	21-9
1941—	Thornton Lee	22-11
1953—	Virgil Trucks	*20-10
1956—	Billy Pierce	20-9
1957—	Billy Pierce	20-12
1959—	Early Wynn	22-10
1962—	Ray Herbert	20-9
1964—	Gary Peters	20-8
1971—	Wilbur Wood	22-13
1972—	Wilbur Wood	24-17
	Stan Bahnsen	21-16
1973—	Wilbur Wood	24-20
1974—	Jim Kaat	21-13
	Wilbur Wood	20-19
1975—	Jim Kaat	20-14
1983—	LaMarr Hoyt	24-10
	Rich Dotson	22-7
1992—	Jack McDowell	20-10
1993—	Jack McDowell	22-10

* 15-6 with White Sox; 5-4 with Browns.

A.L. home run champions

1971—	Bill Melton	33
1972—	Dick Allen	37
1974—	Dick Allen	32

A.L. RBI champions

1972—	Dick Allen	113

A.L. batting champions

1936—	Luke Appling	.388
1943—	Luke Appling	.328
1997—	Frank Thomas	.347

A.L. ERA champions

1906—	Doc White	1.52
1907—	Ed Walsh	1.60
1910—	Ed Walsh	1.27
1917—	Ed Cicotte	1.53
1921—	Red Faber	2.48
1922—	Red Faber	2.80
1941—	Thornton Lee	2.37
1942—	Ted Lyons	2.10
1947—	Joe Haynes	2.42
1951—	Saul Rogovin	*2.48
1955—	Billy Pierce	1.97
1960—	Frank Baumann	2.67
1963—	Gary Peters	2.33
1966—	Gary Peters	1.98
1967—	Joel Horlen	2.06

*ERA compiled with two teams.

A.L. strikeout champions

1908—	Ed Walsh	269
1909—	Frank Smith	177
1911—	Ed Walsh	255
1953—	Billy Pierce	186
1958—	Early Wynn	179

No-hit pitchers
(9 innings or more)

1902—	Nixey Callahan	3-0 vs. Detroit
1905—	Frank Smith	15-0 vs. Detroit
1908—	Frank Smith	1-0 vs. Philadelphia
1911—	Ed Walsh	5-0 vs. Boston
1914—	Joe Benz	6-1 vs. Cleveland
1917—	Ed Cicotte	11-0 vs. St. Louis
1922—	Charlie Robertson	2-0 vs. Detroit (Perfect)
1926—	Ted Lyons	6-0 vs. Boston
1935—	Vern Kennedy	5-0 vs. Cleveland
1937—	Bill Dietrich	8-0 vs. St. Louis
1957—	Bob Keegan	6-0 vs. Washington
1967—	Joel Horlen	6-0 vs. Detroit
1976—	Blue Moon Odom-Francisco Barrios	2-1 vs. Oakland
1986—	Joe Cowley	7-1 vs. California
1991—	Wilson Alvarez	7-0 vs. Baltimore

Longest hitting streaks

27—	Luke Appling	1936
	Albert Belle	1997
26—	Guy Cutright	1943
25—	Lance Johnson	1992
24—	Chico Carrasquel	1950
23—	Minnie Minoso	1955
22—	Sam Mele	1953
	Eddie Collins	1920
21—	Roy Sievers	1960
	Frank Thomas	1999
20—	Ken Berry	1967
	Rip Radcliff	1937
	Eddie Collins	1916

BATTING

Games
Luke Appling	2,422
Nellie Fox	2,115
Ray Schalk	1,757
Ozzie Guillen	1,743
Eddie Collins	1,670
Harold Baines	1,614
Luis Aparicio	1,511
Carlton Fisk	1,421
Minnie Minoso	1,373
Frank Thomas	1,371

At-bats
Luke Appling	8,856
Nellie Fox	8,486
Ozzie Guillen	6,067
Eddie Collins	6,065
Harold Baines	6,004
Luis Aparicio	5,856
Ray Schalk	5,304
Minnie Minoso	5,011
Carlton Fisk	4,896
Frank Thomas	4,892

Runs
Luke Appling	1,319
Nellie Fox	1,187
Eddie Collins	1,065
Frank Thomas	968
Minnie Minoso	893
Luis Aparicio	791
Harold Baines	781
Ozzie Guillen	693
Fielder Jones	693
Robin Ventura	658

Hits
Luke Appling	2,749
Nellie Fox	2,470
Eddie Collins	2,007
Harold Baines	1,749
Ozzie Guillen	1,608
Luis Aparicio	1,576
Frank Thomas	1,564
Minnie Minoso	1,523
Ray Schalk	1,345
Buck Weaver	1,308

Doubles
Luke Appling	440
Nellie Fox	335
Frank Thomas	317
Harold Baines	314
Eddie Collins	266
Minnie Minoso	260
Bibb Falk	245
Willie Kamm	243
Ozzie Guillen	240
Shano Collins	230

Triples
Shano Collins	104
Nellie Fox	104
Luke Appling	102
Eddie Collins	102
Johnny Mostil	82
Joe Jackson	79
Minnie Minoso	79
Lance Johnson	77
Buck Weaver	69
Ozzie Guillen	68

Home runs
Frank Thomas	301
Harold Baines	220
Carlton Fisk	214
Robin Ventura	171
Bill Melton	154
Ron Kittle	140
Minnie Minoso	135
Sherm Lollar	124
Greg Walker	113
Pete Ward	97

Total bases
Luke Appling	3,528
Nellie Fox	3,118
Harold Baines	2,811
Frank Thomas	2,804
Eddie Collins	2,570
Minnie Minoso	2,346
Carlton Fisk	2,143
Ozzie Guillen	2,056
Luis Aparicio	2,036
Robin Ventura	2,000

Runs batted in
Luke Appling	1,116
Frank Thomas	1,040
Harold Baines	966
Minnie Minoso	808
Eddie Collins	804
Carlton Fisk	762
Robin Ventura	741
Nellie Fox	740
Sherm Lollar	631
Bibb Falk	627

Extra-base hits
Frank Thomas	628
Luke Appling	587
Harold Baines	578
Nellie Fox	474
Minnie Minoso	474
Carlton Fisk	442
Robin Ventura	402
Eddie Collins	399
Shano Collins	351
Bibb Falk	345

Batting average
(Minimum 500 games)
Joe Jackson	.340
Eddie Collins	.331
Frank Thomas	.320
Zeke Bonura	.317
Bibb Falk	.315
Taffy Wright	.312
Luke Appling	.310
Rip Radcliff	.310
Earl Sheely	.305
Minnie Minoso	.304

Stolen bases
Eddie Collins	368
Luis Aparicio	318
Frank Isbell	250
Lance Johnson	226
Fielder Jones	206
Shano Collins	192
Luke Appling	179
Ray Schalk	177
Johnny Mostil	176
Buck Weaver	172

PITCHING

Earned-run average
(Minimum 1,000 innings)
Ed Walsh	1.81
Frank Smith	2.18
Eddie Cicotte	2.25
Jim Scott	2.30
Doc White	2.30
Reb Russell	2.33
Nick Altrock	2.40
Joe Benz	2.43
Frank Owen	2.48
Roy Patterson	2.75

Wins
Ted Lyons	260
Red Faber	254
Ed Walsh	195
Billy Pierce	186
Wilbur Wood	163
Doc White	159
Eddie Cicotte	156
Joe Horlen	113
Frank Smith	108
Jim Scott	107

Losses
Ted Lyons	230
Red Faber	213
Billy Pierce	152
Wilbur Wood	148
Ed Walsh	125
Doc White	123
Jim Scott	114
Joe Horlen	113
Thornton Lee	104
Eddie Cicotte	101

Innings pitched
Ted Lyons	4,161.0
Red Faber	4,086.2
Ed Walsh	2,946.1
Billy Pierce	2,931.0
Wilbur Wood	2,524.1
Doc White	2,498.1
Eddie Cicotte	2,322.2
Joe Horlen	1,918.0
Jim Scott	1,892.0
Thornton Lee	1,888.0

Strikeouts
Billy Pierce	1,796
Ed Walsh	1,732
Red Faber	1,471
Wilbur Wood	1,332
Gary Peters	1,098
Ted Lyons	1,073
Doc White	1,067
Joe Horlen	1,007
Eddie Cicotte	961
Alex Fernandez	951

Bases on balls
Red Faber	1,213
Ted Lyons	1,121
Billy Pierce	1,052
Wilbur Wood	671
Richard Dotson	637
Thornton Lee	633
Jim Scott	609
Ed Walsh	608
Bill Dietrich	561
Eddie Smith	545

Games
Red Faber	669
Ted Lyons	594
Wilbur Wood	578
Billy Pierce	456
Ed Walsh	426
Bobby Thigpen	424
Hoyt Wilhelm	361
Doc White	360
Eddie Cicotte	353
Roberto Hernandez	345

Shutouts
Ed Walsh	57
Doc White	42
Billy Pierce	35
Red Faber	29
Eddie Cicotte	28
Ted Lyons	27
Jim Scott	26
Frank Smith	25
Reb Russell	24
Wilbur Wood	24

Saves
Bobby Thigpen	201
Roberto Hernandez	161
Hoyt Wilhelm	98
Terry Forster	75
Wilbur Wood	57
Bob James	56
Ed Farmer	54
Clint Brown	53
Bob Locker	48
Turk Lown	45

SEASON

Batting
Most at-bats	5,644	1996, 1999
Most runs	920	1936
Fewest runs	447	1910
Most hits	1,597	1936
Most singles	1,199	1936
Most doubles	314	1926
Most triples	102	1915
Most home runs	198	1998
Fewest home runs	3	1908
Most grand slams	8	1996
Most pinch-hit home runs	9	1984
Most total bases	2,521	1996
Most stolen bases	280	1901
Highest batting average	.295	1920
Lowest batting average	.211	1910
Highest slugging pct	.447	1996

Pitching
Lowest ERA	1.99	1905
Highest ERA	5.41	1934
Most complete games	134	1904
Most shutouts	32	1906
Most saves	68	1990
Most walks	734	1950
Most strikeouts	1,039	1996

Fielding
Most errors	345	1901
Fewest errors	107	1957
Most double plays	187	1970, 1974
Highest fielding average	.982	5 times

General
Most games won	100	1917
Most games lost	106	1970
Highest win pct	.649	1917
Lowest win pct	.325	1932

GAME, INNING

Batting
Most runs, game	29	4-23-55
Most runs, inning	13	9-26-43
Most hits, game	29	4-23-55
Most home runs, game	7	4-23-55
Most total bases, game	55	4-23-55

Durable righthander Ed Walsh recorded a sparkling 1.81 earned-run average over 13 Chicago seasons.

HISTORY

WHITE SOX YEAR-BY-YEAR

Year	W	L	Place	Games Back	Manager	Leaders: Batting avg.	Hits	Home runs	RBIs	Wins	ERA
1901	83	53	1st	+4	Griffith	Jones, .311	Jones, 162	Mertes, 5	Mertes, 98	Griffith, 24	Callahan, 2.42
1902	74	60	4th	8	Griffith	Jones, .321	Jones, 171	Isbell, 4	Davis, 93	Patterson, 19	Garvin, 2.21
1903	60	77	7th	30½	Callahan	Green, .309	Green, 154	Green, 6	Green, 62	White, 17	White, 2.13
1904	89	65	3rd	6	Callahan, Jones	Green, .265	Davis, 143	Jones, 3	Davis, 69	Owen, 21	White, 1.78
1905	92	60	2nd	2	Jones	Donahue, .287	Davis, Donahue, 153	Isbell, Jones, Sullivan, 2	Donahue, 76	Altrock, 23	White, 1.76
1906	93	58	1st	+3	Jones	Isbell, .279	Isbell, 153	Jones, Sullivan, 2	Davis, 80	Altrock, 20	White, 1.52
1907	87	64	3rd	5½	Jones	Dougherty, .270	Donahue, 158	Rohe, 2	Donahue, 68	White, 27	Walsh, 1.60
1908	88	64	3rd	1½	Jones	Dougherty, .278	Dougherty, Jones, 134	Isbell, Jones, Walsh, 1	Jones, 50	Walsh, 40	Walsh, 1.42
1909	78	74	4th	20	Sullivan	Dougherty, .285	Dougherty, 140	4 Tied, 1	Dougherty, 55	Smith, 25	Walsh, 1.41
1910	68	85	6th	35½	Duffy	Dougherty, .248	Dougherty, 110	Gandil, 2	Dougherty, 43	Walsh, 18	Walsh, 1.27
1911	77	74	4th	24	Duffy	McIntyre, .323	McIntyre, 184	Bodie, S. Collins, 4	Bodie, 97	Walsh, 27	Walsh, 2.22
1912	78	76	4th	28	Callahan	Bodie, .294	S. Collins, 168	Bodie, Lord, 5	Collins, 81	Walsh, 27	Walsh, 2.15
1913	78	74	5th	17½	Callahan	Chase, .286	Weaver, 145	Bodie, 8	Weaver, 52	Russell, 22	Cicotte, 1.58
1914	70	84	*6th	30	Callahan	Fournier, .311	S. Collins, 164	Fournier, 6	S. Collins, 65	Benz, Scott, 14	Wolfgang, 1.89
1915	93	61	3rd	9½	Rowland	E. Collins, .332	E. Collins, 173	Fournier, 5	S. Collins, 85	Faber, Scott, 24	Scott, 2.03
1916	89	65	2nd	2	Rowland	Jackson, .341	Jackson, 202	Felsch, 7	Jackson, 78	Russell, 18	Cicotte, 1.78
1917	100	54	1st	+9	Rowland	Felsch, .308	Felsch, 177	Felsch, 6	Felsch, 102	Cicotte, 28	Cicotte, 1.53
1918	57	67	6th	17	Rowland	Weaver, .300	Weaver, 126	E. Collins, 2	S. Collins, 56	Cicotte, 12	Russell, 2.60
1919	88	52	1st	+3½	Gleason	Jackson, .351	Jackson, 181	Felsch, Jackson, 7	Jackson, 96	Cicotte, 29	Cicotte, 1.82
1920	96	58	2nd	2	Gleason	Jackson, .382	E. Collins, 224	Felsch, 14	Jackson, 121	Faber, 23	Faber, 2.99
1921	62	92	7th	36½	Gleason	E. Collins, .337	Johnson, 181	Sheely, 11	Sheely, 95	Faber, 25	Faber, 2.48
1922	77	77	5th	17	Gleason	E. Collins, .324	E. Collins, 194	Falk, 12	Hooper, Sheely, 80	Faber, 21	Faber, 2.81
1923	69	85	7th	30	Gleason	E. Collins, .360	E. Collins, 182	Hooper, 10	Sheely, 88	Faber, 14	Thurston, 3.05
1924	66	87	8th	25½	Evers	Falk, .352	E. Collins, 194	Hooper, 10	Sheely, 103	Thurston, 20	Thurston, 3.80
1925	79	75	5th	18½	E. Collins	E. Collins, .346	Sheely, 189	Sheely, 9	Sheely, 111	Lyons, 21	Blankenship, 3.03
1926	81	72	5th	9½	E. Collins	Falk, .345	Mostil, 197	Falk, 8	Falk, 108	Lyons, 18	Lyons, 3.01
1927	70	83	5th	29½	Schalk	Falk, .327	Falk, 175	Falk, 9	Barrett, Falk, 83	Lyons, 22	Lyons, 2.84
1928	72	82	5th	29	Schalk, Blackburne	Kamm, .308	Kamm, 170	Barrett, Metzler, 3	Kamm, 84	Thomas, 17	Thomas, 3.08
1929	59	93	7th	46	Blackburne	Reynolds, .317	Cissell, 173	Reynolds, 11	Reynolds, 67	Lyons, Thomas, 14	Thomas, 3.19
1930	62	92	7th	40	Bush	Reynolds, .359	Reynolds, 202	Reynolds, 22	Jolley, 114	Lyons, 22	Lyons, 3.78
1931	56	97	8th	51	Bush	Blue, .304	Blue, 179	Reynolds, 6	Reynolds, 77	Frazier, 13	Faber, 3.82
1932	49	102	7th	56½	Fonseca	Seeds, .290	Kress, 147	Kress, 9	Appling, 63	Jones, Lyons, 10	Lyons, 3.28
1933	67	83	6th	31	Fonseca	Simmons, .331	Simmons, 200	Simmons, 14	Simmons, 119	Durham, Jones, Lyons, 10	Heving, 2.67
1934	53	99	8th	47	Fonseca, Dykes	Simmons, .344	Simmons, 192	Bonura, 27	Bonura, 110	Earnshaw, 14	Earnshaw, 4.52
1935	74	78	5th	19½	Dykes	Appling, .307	Radcliff, 178	Bonura, 21	Bonura, 92	Lyons, 15	Lyons, 3.02
1936	81	70	3rd	20	Dykes	Appling, .388	Radcliff, 207	Bonura, 12	Bonura, 138	Kennedy, 21	Kennedy, 4.63
1937	86	68	3rd	16	Dykes	Bonura, .345	Radcliff, 190	Bonura, 19	Bonura, 100	Stratton, 15	Stratton, 2.40
1938	65	83	6th	32	Dykes	Steinbacher, .331	Radcliff, 166	G. Walker, 16	G. Walker, 87	Stratton, 15	Lee, 3.49
1939	85	69	4th	22½	Dykes	McNair, .324	Kreevich, 175	Kuhel, 15	G. Walker, 111	Lee, Rigney, 15	Lyons, 2.76
1940	82	72	*4th	8	Dykes	Appling, .348	Appling, 197	Kuhel, 27	Kuhel, 94	Rigney, Smith, 14	Rigney, 3.11
1941	77	77	3rd	24	Dykes	Wright, .322	Appling, 186	Kuhel, 12	Wright, 97	Lee, 22	Lee, 2.37
1942	66	82	6th	34	Dykes	Kolloway, .273	Kolloway, 164	Moses, 7	Kolloway, 60	Lyons, 14	Lyons, 2.10
1943	82	72	4th	16	Dykes	Appling, .328	Appling, 192	Kuhel, 5	Appling, 80	Grove, 15	Maltzberger, 2.46
1944	71	83	7th	18	Dykes	Hodgin, .295	Moses, 150	Trosky, 10	Trosky, 70	Dietrich, 16	Haynes, 2.57
1945	71	78	6th	15	Dykes	Cuccinello, .308	Moses, 168	Curtright, Dickshot, 4	Schalk, 65	Lee, 15	Lee, 2.44
1946	74	80	5th	30	Dykes	Appling, .309	Appling, 180	Wright, 7	Appling, 55	Caldwell, Lopat, 13	Caldwell, 2.08
1947	70	84	6th	27	Lyons	Wright, .324	Appling, 154	York, 15	York, 64	Lopat, 16	Haynes, 2.42
1948	51	101	8th	44½	Lyons	Appling, .314	Appling, 156	Seerey, 18	Seerey, 64	Haynes, Wight, 9	Gumpert, 3.79
1949	63	91	6th	34	Onslow	Michaels, .308	Michaels, 173	Souchock, 7	Michaels, 83	Wight, 15	Wight, 3.31
1950	60	94	6th	38	Onslow, Corriden	E. Robinson, .314	E. Robinson, 163	Zernial, 29	Zernial, 93	Pierce, 12	Wight, 3.58
1951	81	73	4th	17	Richards	Minoso, .324	Fox, 189	E. Robinson, 29	E. Robinson, 117	Pierce, 15	Rogovin, 2.48
1952	81	73	3rd	14	Richards	Fox, E. Robinson, .296	Fox, 192	E. Robinson, 22	E. Robinson, 104	Pierce, 15	Dorish, 2.47
1953	89	65	3rd	11½	Richards	Minoso, .313	Fox, 178	Minoso, 15	Minoso, 104	Pierce, 18	Consuegra, 2.54
1954	94	60	3rd	17	Richards, Marion	Minoso, .320	Fox, 201	Minoso, 19	Minoso, 116	Trucks, 19	Consuegra, 2.69
1955	91	63	3rd	5	Marion	Kell, .312	Fox, 198	Dropo, 19	Kell, 81	Donovan, Pierce, 15	Pierce, 1.97
1956	85	69	3rd	12	Marion	Minoso, .316	Fox, 192	Doby, 24	Doby, 102	Pierce, 20	Staley, 2.92
1957	90	64	2nd	8	Lopez	Fox, .317	Fox, 196	Doby, Rivera, 14	Minoso, 103	Pierce, 20	Staley, 2.06
1958	82	72	2nd	10	Lopez	Fox, .300	Fox, 187	Lollar, 20	Lollar, 84	Pierce, 17	Pierce, 2.68
1959	94	60	1st	+5	Lopez	Fox, .306	Fox, 191	Lollar, 22	Lollar, 84	Wynn, 22	Staley, 2.24
1960	87	67	3rd	10	Lopez	A. Smith, .315	Minoso, 184	Sievers, 28	Minoso, 105	Pierce, 14	Staley, 2.42
1961	86	76	4th	23	Lopez	F. Robinson, .310	Aparicio, 170	A. Smith, 28	A. Smith, 93	Pizarro, 14	Lown, 2.76
1962	85	77	5th	11	Lopez	F. Robinson, .312	F. Robinson, 187	A. Smith, 16	F. Robinson, 109	Herbert, 20	Fisher, 3.10
1963	94	68	2nd	10½	Lopez	Ward, .295	Ward, 177	Nicholson, Ward, 22	Ward, 84	Peters, 19	Peters, 2.33
1964	98	64	2nd	1	Lopez	F. Robinson, .301	F. Robinson, 158	Ward, 23	Ward, 94	Peters, 20	Horlen, 1.88
1965	95	67	2nd	7	Lopez	Buford, .283	Buford, 166	Romano, Skowron, 18	Skowron, 78	Fisher, 15	Wilhelm, 1.87
1966	83	79	4th	15	Stanky	Agee, .273	Agee, 172	Agee, 22	Agee, 86	John, 14	Peters, 1.98
1967	89	73	4th	3	Stanky	Berry, Buford, .241	Buford, 129	Ward, 18	Ward, 62	Horlen, 19	McMahon, 1.67
1968	67	95	*8th	36	Stanky, Lopez	T. Davis, .268	Aparicio, 164	Ward, 15	T. Davis, Ward, 50	Wood, 13	Wilhelm, 1.73
								WEST DIVISION			
1969	68	94	5th	29	Lopez, Gutteridge	Williams, .304	Aparicio, 168	Melton, 23	Melton, 87	Horlen, 13	Wood, 3.01
1970	56	106	6th	42	Gutteridge, Tanner	Aparicio, .313	Aparicio, 173	Melton, 33	Melton, 96	John, 12	Wood, 2.81
1971	79	83	3rd	22½	Tanner	May, Williams, .294	May, 147	Melton, 33	Melton, 86	Wood, 22	Wood, 1.91
1972	87	67	2nd	5½	Tanner	Allen, May, .308	May, 161	Allen, 37	Allen, 113	Wood, 24	Forster, 2.25
1973	77	85	5th	17	Tanner	Kelly, .280	Melton, 155	May, Melton, 20	May, 96	Wood, 24	Acosta, 2.23
1974	80	80	4th	9	Tanner	Orta, .316	Henderson, 176	Allen, 32	Henderson, 95	Kaat, 21	B. Johnson, 2.74
1975	75	86	5th	22½	Tanner	Orta, .304	Orta, 165	D. Johnson, 18	Orta, 83	Kaat, 20	Gossage, 1.84
1976	64	97	6th	25½	Richards	Garr, .300	Orta, 174	Orta, Spencer, 14	Orta, 72	Brett, 10	Brett, 3.32
1977	90	72	3rd	12	Lemon	L. Johnson, .302	Garr, 163	Gamble, 31	Zisk, 101	Stone, 15	LaGrow, 2.46
1978	71	90	5th	20½	Lemon, Doby	Lemon, .300	Lam. Johnson, 136	Soderholm, 20	Lam. Johnson, 72	Stone, 12	Willoughby, 3.86
1979	73	87	5th	14	Kessinger, La Russa	Lemon, .318	Lemon, 177	Lemon, 17	Lemon, 86	Kravec, 15	Baumgarten, 3.54
1980	70	90	5th	26	La Russa	Lemon, .292	Morrison, 171	Morrison, Nordhagen, 15	Lam. Johnson, 81	Burns, 15	Burns, 2.84
1981	54	52	†3rd/6th	—	La Russa	Bernazard, .276	Bernazard, 106	Luzinski, 21	Luzinski, 62	Burns, 10	Lamp, 2.41
1982	87	75	3rd	6	La Russa	Paciorek, .312	Luzinski, 170	Baines, 25	Baines, 105	Hoyt, 19	Hoyt, 3.53
1983	99	63	‡1st	+20	La Russa	Paciorek, .307	Baines, 167	Kittle, 35	Kittle, 100	Hoyt, 24	Dotson, 3.23
1984	74	88	*5th	10	La Russa	Baines, .304	Baines, 173	Kittle, 32	Baines, 94	Seaver, 15	Dotson, 3.59
1985	85	77	3rd	6	La Russa	Baines, .309	Baines, 196	Fisk, 37	Baines, 113	Burns, 18	James, 2.13
1986	72	90	5th	20	La Russa, Fregosi	Baines, .296	Baines, 169	Baines, 21	Baines, 88	Cowley, 11	Schmidt, 3.31
1987	77	85	5th	8	Fregosi	Baines, Calderon, .293	Calderon, 159	Calderon, 28	Walker, 94	Bannister, 16	Bannister, 3.58
1988	71	90	5th	32½	Fregosi	Baines, .277	Baines, 166	Pasqua, 20	Baines, 81	Reuss, 13	Thigpen, 3.30
1989	69	92	7th	29½	Torborg	Martinez, .300	Calderon, 178	Calderon, 14	Calderon, 87	Perez, 11	Hibbard, 3.21
1990	94	68	2nd	9	Torborg	Fisk, Lan. Johnson, .285	Calderon, 166	Fisk, 18	Calderon, 74	Hibbard, McDowell, 14	Hibbard, 3.16
1991	87	75	2nd	8	Torborg	F. Thomas, .318	F. Thomas, 178	F. Thomas, 32	F. Thomas, 109	McDowell, 17	Perez, 3.12
1992	86	76	3rd	10	Lamont	F. Thomas, .323	F. Thomas, 185	Bell, 25	F. Thomas, 115	McDowell, 20	McDowell, 3.18
1993	94	68	‡1st	+8	Lamont	F. Thomas, .317	F. Thomas, 174	F. Thomas, 41	F. Thomas, 128	McDowell, 22	Alvarez, 2.95
								CENTRAL DIVISION			
1994	67	46	1st	+1	Lamont	F. Thomas, .353	F. Thomas, 141	F. Thomas, 38	F. Thomas, 101	Bere, Alvarez, 12	Alvarez, 3.45
1995	68	76	3rd	32	Lamont, Bevington	F. Thomas, .308	Lan. Johnson, 186	F. Thomas, 40	F. Thomas, 111	Fernandez, 12	Fernandez, 3.80
1996	85	77	∞2nd	14½	Bevington	F. Thomas, .349	F. Thomas, 184	F. Thomas, 40	F. Thomas, 134	Fernandez, 16	Fernandez, 3.45
1997	80	81	2nd	6	Bevington	F. Thomas, .347	F. Thomas, 184	F. Thomas, 35	F. Thomas, 125	Baldwin, Drabek, 12	Alvarez, 3.03
1998	80	82	2nd	9	Manuel	Belle, .328	Belle, 200	Belle, 49	Belle, 152	Sirotka, 14	Sirotka, 5.06
1999	75	86	2nd	21½	Manuel	F. Thomas, .305	Ordonez, 188	Ordonez, 30	Ordonez, 117	Baldwin, 12	Foulke, 2.22

* Tied for position. † First half 31-22, second half 23-30. ‡ Lost Championship Series. ∞ Lost division playoff.

Note: Batting average minimum 350 at-bats, ERA minimum 90 innings pitched.

HISTORY

CLEVELAND INDIANS

FRANCHISE CHRONOLOGY

First season: 1901, as a member of the new American League. Cleveland lost its Major League debut at Chicago, 8-2, and struggled through a difficult first season. The Indians won only 54 games and finished seventh in the eight-team A.L. field.

1902-present: The early decade Indians (also known as the Naps after star second baseman Napoleon Lajoie) were annual contenders, but it took almost two decades before they had anything to show for their efforts. And after the 1920 Indians captured the team's first pennant and defeated Brooklyn in an historic World Series, Cleveland fans had to wait 28 years for another. The 1948 championship was followed by an amazing 1954 season in which the Indians won an A.L.-record 111 games—and then fell to the Giants in a shocking four-game Series sweep. That would be it for more than four decades as the Indians languished in the lower reaches of the A.L. standings, posting only 11 winning records. They finally resurfaced in the strike-shortened 1995 season to claim their first of five consecutive Central Division titles with a league-leading 100 victories. But their fourth pennant in 1995 resulted in a six-game World Series loss to Atlanta and a Cinderella World Series run in 1997 came up short in the seventh game against the Florida Marlins.

Righthander Bob Feller.

INDIANS VS. OPPONENTS BY DECADE

	A's	Orioles	Red Sox	Tigers	Twins	White Sox	Yankees	Angels	Rangers	Brewers	Royals	Blue Jays	Mariners	Devil Rays	Interleague	Decade Record
1901-09	86-105	109-82	96-93	95-95	118-72	89-100	104-85									697-632
1910-19	110-105	130-81	97-115	94-114	92-123	102-114	117-95									742-747
1920-29	113-106	112-106	130-90	109-111	113-106	114-105	95-125									786-749
1930-39	114-106	155-64	131-89	101-118	114-104	125-94	84-133									824-708
1940-49	136-80	124-95	116-105	105-115	115-104	114-103	90-129									800-731
1950-59	153-67	151-67	122-98	136-84	141-79	104-116	97-123									904-634
1960-69	92-85	85-99	94-90	83-101	96-82	74-104	83-100	74-82	88-73	7-5	7-5					783-826
1970-79	46-70	65-104	80-86	78-90	58-56	54-62	64-103	58-58	58-71	75-78	52-65	27-14	22-9			737-866
1980-89	50-63	64-59	52-78	41-82	55-56	54-61	56-73	49-69	55-57	56-62	54-62	52-71	72-48			710-849
1990-99	62-45	67-51	60-61	76-47	70-52	64-58	45-72	59-44	50-63	56-41	64-49	56-65	54-52	12-7	28-21	823-728
Totals	962-832	1062-808	978-905	918-957	972-834	894-917	835-1038	240-253	251-264	194-194	177-181	135-150	148-109	12-7	28-21	7806-7470

Interleague results: 6-2 vs. Cubs; 7-5 vs. Reds; 4-5 vs. Astros; 4-5 vs. Pirates; 4-1 vs. Cardinals; 3-3 vs. Brewers.

MANAGERS

Name	Years	Record
Jimmy McAleer	1901	55-82
Bill Armour	1902-04	232-195
Nap Lajoie	1905-09	377-309
Deacon McGuire	1909-11	91-117
George Stovall	1911	74-62
Harry Davis	1912	54-71
Joe Birmingham	1912-15	170-191
Lee Fohl	1915-19	327-310
Tris Speaker	1919-26	617-520
Jack McCallister	1927	66-87
Roger Peckinpaugh	1928-33, 1941	490-481
Walter Johnson	1933-35	179-168
Steve O'Neill	1935-37	199-168
Oscar Vitt	1938-40	262-198
Lou Boudreau	1942-50	728-649

MANAGERS—cont'd.

Name	Years	Record
Al Lopez	1951-56	570-354
Kerby Farrell	1957	76-77
Bobby Bragan	1958	31-36
Joe Gordon	1958-60	184-151
Jimmie Dykes	1960-61	103-115
Mel McGaha	1962	78-82
Birdie Tebbetts	1963-66	278-259
George Strickland	1964, 1966	48-63
Joe Adcock	1967	75-87
Alvin Dark	1968-71	266-321
Johnny Lipon	1971	18-41
Ken Aspromonte	1972-74	220-260
Frank Robinson	1975-77	186-189
Jeff Torborg	1977-79	157-201
Dave Garcia	1979-82	247-244
Mike Ferraro	1983	40-60
Pat Corrales	1983-87	280-355
Doc Edwards	1987-89	173-207
John Hart	1989	8-11
John McNamara	1990-91	102-137
Mike Hargrove	1991-99	721-591

WORLD SERIES CHAMPIONS

Year	Loser	Length	MVP
1920	Brooklyn	7 games	None
1948	Boston	6 games	None

A.L. PENNANT WINNERS

Year	Record	Manager	Series Result
1920	98-56	Speaker	Defeated Dodgers
1948	97-58	Boudreau	Defeated Braves
1954	111-43	Lopez	Lost to Giants
1995	100-44	Hargrove	Lost to Braves
1997	86-75	Hargrove	Lost to Marlins

CENTRAL DIVISION CHAMPIONS

Year	Record	Manager	ALCS Result
1995	100-44	Hargrove	Defeated Mariners
1996	99-62	Hargrove	Lost in Division Series
1997	86-75	Hargrove	Defeated Orioles
1998	89-73	Hargrove	Lost to Yankees
1999	97-65	Hargrove	Lost in Division Series

ATTENDANCE HIGHS

Total	Season	Park
3,467,299	1998	Jacobs Field
3,404,750	1997	Jacobs Field
3,384,788	1999	Jacobs Field
3,318,174	1996	Jacobs Field
2,842,745	1995	Jacobs Field

BALLPARK CHRONOLOGY

Jacobs Field (1994-present)

Capacity: 43,863.
First game: Indians 4, Seattle 3 (April 4, 1994).
First batter: Rich Amaral, Mariners.
First hit: Eric Anthony, Mariners (home run).
First run: Edgar Martinez, Mariners (1st inning).
First home run: Eric Anthony, Mariners.
First winning pitcher: Eric Plunk, Indians.
First-season attendance: 1,995,174.

League Park I (1901-09)

Capacity: 9,000.
First game: Indians 4, Milwaukee 3 (April 29, 1901).
First-season attendance: 131,380.

League Park II (1910-46)

Capacity: 21,414.
First game: Detroit 5, Indians 0 (April 21, 1910).
First-season attendance: 293,456.

Cleveland (Municipal) Stadium (1932-93)

Capacity: 74,483.
First game: Philadelphia 1, Indians 0 (July 31, 1932).
First-season attendance (1947): 1,521,978.

Note: League Park II was known as Dunn Field from 1920-27; Cleveland Stadium was originally called Municipal Stadium and games were played there on a part-time basis from 1932-46.

A.L. MVPs

Lou Boudreau, SS, 1948
Al Rosen, 3B, 1953

CY YOUNG WINNER

Gaylord Perry, RH, 1972

ROOKIES OF THE YEAR

Herb Score, P, 1955
Chris Chambliss, 1B, 1971
Joe Charboneau, OF, 1980
Sandy Alomar Jr., C, 1990

RETIRED UNIFORMS

No.	Name	Pos.
3	Earl Averill	OF
5	Lou Boudreau	SS
14	Larry Doby	OF
18	Mel Harder	P
19	Bob Feller	P
21	Bob Lemon	P

Third baseman Al Rosen topped the 100-RBI barrier five times in the 1950s.

30-plus home runs
50— Albert Belle ...1995
48— Albert Belle ...1996
45— Manny Ramirez ...1998
44— Manny Ramirez ...1999
43— Al Rosen ...1953
42— Hal Trosky ...1936
    Rocky Colavito ...1959
41— Rocky Colavito ...1958
40— Jim Thome ...1997
38— Albert Belle ...1993
    Jim Thome ...1996
37— Al Rosen ...1950
36— Albert Belle ...1994
    Joe Carter ...1989
35— Hal Trosky ...1934
34— Albert Belle ...1992
33— Andre Thornton ...1978, 1984
    Manny Ramirez ...1996
    David Justice ...1997
    Jim Thome ...1999
32— Earl Averill ...1931, 1932
    Hal Trosky ...1937
    Joe Gordon ...1948
    Larry Doby ...1952, 1954
    Vic Wertz ...1956
    Andre Thornton ...1982
    Joe Carter ...1987
    Brook Jacoby ...1987
    Cory Snyder ...1987
    Matt Williams ...1997
31— Earl Averill ...1934
    Ken Keltner ...1948
    Luke Easter ...1952
    Leon Wagner ...1964
    Manny Ramirez ...1995
    Richie Sexson ...1999
30— Rocky Colavito ...1966
    Jim Thome ...1998

100-plus RBIs
165— Manny Ramirez ...1999
162— Hal Trosky ...1936
148— Albert Belle ...1996
145— Al Rosen ...1953
    Manny Ramirez ...1998
143— Earl Averill ...1931
142— Hal Trosky ...1934
136— Eddie Morgan ...1930
130— Tris Speaker ...1923
129— Albert Belle ...1993
128— Hal Trosky ...1937
126— Earl Averill ...1936
    Larry Doby ...1954
    Albert Belle ...1995
124— Earl Averill ...1932
    Joe Gordon ...1948
123— Jeff Heath ...1941
121— Johnny Hodapp ...1930
    Joe Carter ...1986
120— Roberto Alomar ...1999
119— Earl Averill ...1930
    Ken Keltner ...1948
118— Larry Gardner ...1920
117— Joe Vosmik ...1931
116— Al Rosen ...1950
    Andre Thornton ...1982
    Jim Thome ...1996
    Richie Sexson ...1999
115— Larry Gardner ...1921
114— George Burns ...1926
    Carlos Baerga ...1993
113— Earl Averill ...1934
    Hal Trosky ...1935
    Ken Keltner ...1938
    Rocky Colavito ...1938
112— Jeff Heath ...1938
    Albert Belle ...1992
    Manny Ramirez ...1996
111— Rocky Colavito ...1959
110— Joe Vosmik ...1935
    Hal Trosky ...1938
109— Joe Sewell ...1923
    Julius Solters ...1937
108— Rocky Colavito ...1965
    Jim Thome ...1999
107— Tris Speaker ...1920
    Luke Easter ...1950
    Manny Ramirez ...1995
106— Lou Boudreau ...1948
    Vic Wertz ...1956
    Joe Carter ...1987
105— Al Rosen ...1952
    Vic Wertz ...1957
    Andre Thornton ...1978
    Joe Carter ...1989
    Carlos Baerga ...1992
    Matt Williams ...1997

(continued)
104— Joe Sewell ...1924
    Hal Trosky ...1939
    Larry Doby ...1952
103— Elmer Smith ...1920
    Lew Fonseca ...1929
    Luke Easter ...1951
    Harold Baines ...*1999
102— Nap Lajoie ...1904
    Al Rosen ...1951, 1954
    Larry Doby ...1950, 1953
    Jim Thome ...1997
101— Odell Hale ...1934, 1935
    Lou Boudreau ...1940
    Albert Belle ...1994
    David Justice ...1997
100— Leon Wagner ...1964

*81 with Orioles; 22 with Indians.

20-plus victories
1903— Earl Moore ...20-8
1904— William Bernhard ...23-13
1905— Addie Joss ...20-11
1906— Robert Rhodes ...22-10
    Addie Joss ...21-9
    Otto Hess ...20-17
1907— Addie Joss ...27-10
1908— Addie Joss ...24-11
1911— Vean Gregg ...23-7
1912— Vean Gregg ...20-13
1913— Fred Falkenberg ...23-10
    Vean Gregg ...20-13
1917— Jim Bagby ...23-13
1918— Stan Coveleski ...22-13
1919— Stan Coveleski ...23-17
1920— Jim Bagby ...31-12
    Stanley Coveleski ...24-14
    Ray Caldwell ...20-10
1921— Stan Coveleski ...23-13
1922— George Uhle ...22-16
1923— George Uhle ...26-16
1924— Joe Shaute ...20-17
1926— George Uhle ...27-11
1929— Wesley Ferrell ...21-10
1930— Wesley Ferrell ...25-13
1931— Wesley Ferrell ...22-12
1932— Wesley Ferrell ...23-13
1934— Mel Harder ...20-12
1935— Mel Harder ...22-11
1936— Johnny Allen ...20-10
1939— Bob Feller ...24-9
1940— Bob Feller ...27-11
1941— Bob Feller ...25-12
1946— Bob Feller ...26-15
1947— Bob Feller ...20-11
1948— Gene Bearden ...20-7
    Bob Lemon ...20-14
1949— Bob Lemon ...22-10
1950— Bob Lemon ...23-11
1951— Bob Feller ...22-8
    Mike Garcia ...20-13
    Early Wynn ...20-13
1952— Early Wynn ...23-12
    Mike Garcia ...22-11
    Bob Lemon ...22-11
1953— Bob Lemon ...21-15
1954— Bob Lemon ...23-7
    Early Wynn ...23-11
1956— Herb Score ...20-9
    Early Wynn ...20-9
    Bob Lemon ...20-14
1962— Dick Donovan ...20-10
1968— Luis Tiant ...21-9
1970— Sam McDowell ...20-12
1972— Gaylord Perry ...24-16
1974— Gaylord Perry ...21-13

A.L. home run champions
1915— Bobby Roth ...7
1950— Al Rosen ...37
1952— Larry Doby ...32
1953— Al Rosen ...43
1954— Larry Doby ...32
1959— Rocky Colavito ...*42
1995— Albert Belle ...50
* Tied for league lead

A.L. RBI champions
1904— Nap Lajoie ...102
1936— Hal Trosky ...162
1952— Al Rosen ...105
1953— Al Rosen ...145
1954— Larry Doby ...126
1965— Rocky Colavito ...108
1986— Joe Carter ...121
1993— Albert Belle ...129
1995— Albert Belle ...*126
1996— Albert Belle ...148
1999— Manny Ramirez ...165
* Tied for league lead

SEASON

Batting
Stat	Value	Player	Year
At-bats	663	Joe Carter	1986
Runs	140	Earl Averill	1931
Hits	233	Joe Jackson	1911
Singles	172	Charley Jamieson	1923
Doubles	64	George Burns	1926
Triples	26	Joe Jackson	1912
Home runs	50	Albert Belle	1995
Home runs, rookie	37	Al Rosen	1950
Grand slams	4	Al Rosen	1951
Total bases	405	Hal Trosky	1936
RBIs	165	Manny Ramirez	1999
Walks	127	Jim Thome	1999
Most strikeouts	171	Jim Thome	1999
Fewest strikeouts	4	Joe Sewell	1925, 1929
Batting average	.408	Joe Jackson	1911
Slugging pct.	.714	Albert Belle	1994
Stolen bases	75	Kenny Lofton	1996

Pitching
Stat	Value	Player	Year
Games	76	Sid Monge	1979
Complete games	36	Bob Feller	1946
Innings	371	Bob Feller	1946
Wins	31	Jim Bagby Sr.	1920
Losses	22	Pete Dowling	1901
Winning pct.	.938 (15-1)	Johnny Allen	1937
Walks	208	Bob Feller	1936
Strikeouts	348	Bob Feller	1946
Shutouts	10	Bob Feller	1946
		Bob Lemon	1948
Home runs allowed	37	Luis Tiant	1969
Lowest ERA	1.16	Addie Joss	1908
Saves	46	Jose Mesa	1995

GAME

Batting
Stat	Value	Player	Date
Runs	5	Last by Joe Carter	9-6-86
Hits	6	Last by Jorge Orta	6-15-80
Doubles	4	Last by Sandy Alomar Jr.	6-6-97
Triples	3	Last by Ben Chapman	7-3-39
Home runs	4	Rocky Colavito	6-10-59
RBIs	9	Chris James	5-4-91
Total bases	16	Rocky Colavito	6-10-59
Stolen bases	5	Alex Cole	8-1-90, 5-3-92

A.L. batting champions
1903— Nap Lajoie ...344
1904— Nap Lajoie ...376
1905— Elmer Flick ...306
1914— Tris Speaker ...386
1929— Lew Fonseca ...369
1944— Lou Boudreau ...327
1954— Bobby Avila ...341

A.L. ERA champions
1903— Earl Moore ...1.74
1904— Addie Joss ...1.59
1908— Addie Joss ...1.16
1911— Vean Gregg ...1.80
1923— Stan Coveleski ...2.76
1933— Monte Pearson ...2.33
1940— Bob Feller ...2.61
1948— Gene Bearden ...2.43
1950— Early Wynn ...3.20
1954— Mike Garcia ...2.64
1965— Sam McDowell ...2.18
1968— Luis Tiant ...1.60
1982— Rick Sutcliffe ...2.96

A.L. strikeout champions
1920— Stan Coveleski ...133
1938— Bob Feller ...240
1939— Bob Feller ...246
1940— Bob Feller ...261
1941— Bob Feller ...260
1943— Allie Reynolds ...151
1946— Bob Feller ...348
1947— Bob Feller ...196
1948— Bob Feller ...164
1950— Bob Lemon ...170
1955— Herb Score ...245
1956— Herb Score ...263
1957— Early Wynn ...184
1965— Sam McDowell ...325
1966— Sam McDowell ...225
1968— Sam McDowell ...283
1969— Sam McDowell ...279
1970— Sam McDowell ...304
1980— Len Barker ...187
1981— Len Barker ...127

No-hit pitchers
(9 innings or more)
1908— Robert Rhoads ...2-1 vs. Boston
1908— Addie Joss ...1-0 vs. Chicago (Perfect)
1910— Addie Joss ...1-0 vs. Chicago
1919— Ray Caldwell ...3-0 vs. New York
1931— Wesley Ferrell ...9-0 vs. St. Louis
1940— Bob Feller ...1-0 vs. Chicago
1946— Bob Feller ...1-0 vs. New York
1947— Don Black ...3-0 vs. Philadelphia
1948— Bob Lemon ...2-0 vs. Detroit
1951— Bob Feller ...2-1 vs. Detroit
1966— Sonny Siebert ...2-0 vs. Washington
1974— Dick Bosman ...4-0 vs. Oakland
1977— Dennis Eckersley ...1-0 vs. California
1981— Len Barker ...3-0 vs. Toronto (Perfect)

Longest hitting streaks
31— Nap Lajoie ...1906
30— Sandy Alomar Jr. ...1997
29— Bill Bradley ...1902
28— Joe Jackson ...1911
    Hal Trosky ...1936
27— Dale Mitchell ...1953
26— Harry Bay ...1902
24— Matt Williams ...1997
23— Charlie Jamieson ...1923
    Tris Speaker ...1923
    Dale Mitchell ...1951
    Ray Fosse ...1970
    Mike Hargrove ...1980
22— John Hodapp ...1929
    Dale Mitchell ...1947
    Al Smith ...1956
    John Romano ...1961
    Julio Franco ...1988
21— Nap Lajoie ...1904
    Odell Hale ...1936
    Dale Mitchell ...1948, 1953
    Larry Doby ...1951
    Joe Carter ...1986
    Julio Franco ...1988
    Albert Belle ...1996
20— Earl Averill ...1936
    Roy Weatherly ...1936
    Joe Vosmik ...1936
    Al Rosen ...1953
    Vic Power ...1960

Note: Joey Cora hit in 20 straight games for Seattle (16) and Cleveland (4) in 1998.

HISTORY

BATTING

Games

Terry Turner	1,619
Napoleon Lajoie	1,614
Lou Boudreau	1,560
Jim Hegan	1,526
Tris Speaker	1,519
Ken Keltner	1,513
Joe Sewell	1,513
Earl Averill	1,509
Charlie Jamieson	1,483
Jack Graney	1,402

At-bats

Napoleon Lajoie	6,034
Earl Averill	5,909
Terry Turner	5,787
Lou Boudreau	5,754
Ken Keltner	5,655
Joe Sewell	5,621
Charlie Jamieson	5,551
Tris Speaker	5,546
Jack Graney	4,705
Bill Bradley	4,648

Runs

Earl Averill	1,154
Tris Speaker	1,079
Charlie Jamieson	942
Napoleon Lajoie	865
Joe Sewell	857
Lou Boudreau	823
Larry Doby	808
Hal Trosky	758
Kenny Lofton	753
Ken Keltner	735

Hits

Napoleon Lajoie	2,046
Tris Speaker	1,965
Earl Averill	1,903
Joe Sewell	1,800
Charlie Jamieson	1,753
Lou Boudreau	1,706
Ken Keltner	1,561
Terry Turner	1,472
Hal Trosky	1,365
Julio Franco	1,272

Doubles

Tris Speaker	486
Napoleon Lajoie	424
Earl Averill	377
Joe Sewell	375
Lou Boudreau	367
Ken Keltner	306
Charlie Jamieson	296
Hal Trosky	287
Bill Bradley	238
Odell Hale	235

Triples

Earl Averill	121
Tris Speaker	108
Elmer Flick	106
Joe Jackson	89
Jeff Heath	83
Ray Chapman	81
Jack Graney	79
Napoleon Lajoie	78
Terry Turner	77
Bill Bradley	74
Charlie Jamieson	74

Home runs

Albert Belle	242
Earl Averill	226
Hal Trosky	216
Larry Doby	215
Andre Thornton	214
Manny Ramirez	198
Jim Thome	196
Al Rosen	192
Rocky Colavito	190
Ken Keltner	163

Total bases

Earl Averill	3,200
Tris Speaker	2,886
Napoleon Lajoie	2,725
Ken Keltner	2,494
Hal Trosky	2,406
Lou Boudreau	2,392
Joe Sewell	2,391
Charlie Jamieson	2,251
Larry Doby	2,159
Albert Belle	1,995

Runs batted in

Earl Averill	1,084
Napoleon Lajoie	919
Hal Trosky	911
Tris Speaker	884

Joe Sewell	869
Ken Keltner	850
Larry Doby	776
Albert Belle	751
Andre Thornton	749
Lou Boudeau	740

Extra-base hits

Earl Averill	724
Tris Speaker	667
Hal Trosky	556
Ken Keltner	538
Napoleon Lajoie	535
Lou Boudreau	495
Albert Belle	481
Joe Sewell	468
Larry Doby	450
Andre Thornton	419

Batting average
(Minimum 500 games)

Joe Jackson	.375
Tris Speaker	.354
Napoleon Lajoie	.339
George Burns	.327
Ed Morgan	.323
Earl Averill	.322
Joe Sewell	.320
Johnny Hodapp	.318
Charlie Jamieson	.316
Joe Vosmik	.313

Stolen bases

Kenny Lofton	404
Terry Turner	254
Napoleon Lajoie	240
Ray Chapman	233
Elmer Flick	207
Omar Vizquel	199
Harry Bay	165
Brett Butler	164
Bill Bradley	157
Tris Speaker	151

PITCHING

Earned-run average
(Minimum 1,000 innings)

Addie Joss	1.89
Bob Rhoads	2.39
Bill Bernhard	2.45
Earl Moore	2.58
Gaylord Perry	2.71
Stan Coveleski	2.80

Luis Tiant	2.84
Willie Mitchell	2.89
Sam McDowell	2.99
Jim Bagby	3.02

Wins

Bob Feller	266
Mel Harder	223
Bob Lemon	207
Stan Coveleski	172
Early Wynn	164
Addie Joss	160
Willis Hudlin	157
George Uhle	147
Mike Garcia	142
Jim Bagby	122
Sam McDowell	122

Losses

Mel Harder	186
Bob Feller	162
Willis Hudlin	151
Bob Lemon	128
Stan Coveleski	123
George Uhle	119
Sam McDowell	109
Early Wynn	102
Addie Joss	97
Mike Garcia	96

Innings pitched

Bob Feller	3,827.0
Mel Harder	3,426.1
Bob Lemon	2,850.0
Willis Hudlin	2,557.2
Stan Coveleski	2,502.1
Addie Joss	2,327.0
Early Wynn	2,286.2
George Uhle	2,200.1
Mike Garcia	2,138.0
Sam McDowell	2,109.2

Strikeouts

Bob Feller	2,581
Sam McDowell	2,159
Bob Lemon	1,277
Early Wynn	1,277
Mel Harder	1,161
Charles Nagy	1,143
Gary Bell	1,104
Mike Garcia	1,095
Luis Tiant	1,041
Addie Joss	920

Bases on balls

Bob Feller	1,764
Bob Lemon	1,251
Mel Harder	1,118
Sam McDowell	1,072
Early Wynn	877
Willis Hudlin	832
George Uhle	709
Mike Garcia	696
Gary Bell	670
Stan Coveleski	616

Games

Mel Harder	582
Bob Feller	570
Willis Hudlin	475
Bob Lemon	460
Gary Bell	419
Mike Garcia	397
Eric Plunk	373
Stan Coveleski	360
George Uhle	357
Early Wynn	343

Shutouts

Addie Joss	45
Bob Feller	44
Stan Coveleski	31
Bob Lemon	31
Mike Garcia	27
Mel Harder	25
Early Wynn	24
Sam McDowell	22
Luis Tiant	21
Guy Morton	19
Bob Rhoads	19

Saves

Doug Jones	129
Jose Mesa	104
Mike Jackson	94
Ray Narleski	53
Steve Olin	48
Jim Kern	46
Sid Monge	46
Gary Bell	45
Ernie Camacho	44
Dave LaRoche	42

SEASON

Batting

Most at-bats	5,702	1986
Most runs	1,009	1999
Fewest runs	472	1972
Most hits	1,715	1936
Most singles	1,218	1925
Most doubles	358	1930
Most triples	95	1920
Most home runs	220	1997
Fewest home runs	8	1910
Most grand slams	12	1999
Most pinch-hit home runs	9	1965, 1970
Most total bases	2,700	1996
Most stolen bases	210	1917
Highest batting average	.308	1921
Lowest batting average	.234	1968, 1972
Highest slugging pct	.484	1994

Pitching

Lowest ERA	2.02	1908
Highest ERA	5.28	1987
Most complete games	141	1904
Most shutouts	27	1906
Most saves	50	1995
Most walks	770	1971
Most strikeouts	1,189	1967

Fielding

Most errors	329	1901
Fewest errors	101	1995
Most double plays	197	1953
Highest fielding average	.983	5 times Last in 1999

General

Most games won	111	1954
Most games lost	105	1991
Highest win pct	.721	1954
Lowest win pct	.333	1914

GAME, INNING

Batting

Most runs, game	27	7-7-23
Most runs, inning	14	6-18-50
Most hits, game	33	7-10-32
Most home runs, game	7	7-17-66
Most total bases, game	45	7-10-32

Outfielder Rocky Colavito led the A.L. with 42 home runs in 1959.

HISTORY

INDIANS YEAR-BY-YEAR

Year	W	L	Place	Games Back	Manager	Batting avg.	Hits	Home runs	RBIs	Wins	ERA
						Leaders					
1901	54	82	7th	29	McAleer	Pickering, .309	Pickering, 169	Beck, 6	Beck, 79	Moore, 16	Moore, 2.90
1902	69	67	5th	14	Armour	Hickman, .379	Bradley, 187	Bradley, 11	Hickman, 94	Bernhard, Joss, Moore, 17	Bernhard, 2.20
1903	77	63	3rd	15	Armour	Lajoie, .344	Bradley, Hickman, 171	Hickman, 12	Hickman, 97	Moore, 19	Moore, 1.74
1904	86	65	4th	7½	Armour	Lajoie, .376	Lajoie, 211	Flick, Lajoie, 6	Lajoie, 102	Bernhard, 23	Joss, 1.59
1905	76	78	5th	19	Lajoie	Flick, .306	Bay, 164	Flick, 4	Flick, 64	Joss, 20	Joss, 2.01
1906	89	64	3rd	5	Lajoie	Lajoie, .355	Lajoie, 214	4 Tied, 2	Lajoie, 91	Rhoads, 22	Joss, 1.72
1907	85	67	4th	8	Lajoie	Flick, .302	Flick, 166	Flick, 3	Lajoie, 63	Joss, 27	Joss, 1.83
1908	90	64	2nd	½	Lajoie	Stovall, .292	Lajoie, 168	Hinchman, 6	Lajoie, 74	Joss, 24	Joss, 1.16
1909	71	82	6th	27½	Lajoie, McGuire	Lajoie, .324	Lajoie, 152	Hinchman, Stovall, 6	Hinchman, 53	Young, 19	Joss, 1.71
1910	71	81	5th	32	McGuire	Lajoie, .384	Lajoie, 227	Lajoie, 4	Lajoie, 76	Falkenberg, 14	Kahler, 1.60
1911	80	73	3rd	22	McGuire, Stovall	Jackson, .408	Jackson, 233	Jackson, 7	Jackson, 83	Gregg, 23	Gregg, 1.80
1912	75	78	5th	30½	Davis, Birmingham	Jackson, .395	Jackson, 226	Jackson, 3	Jackson, Lajoie, 90	Gregg, 20	Gregg, 2.59
1913	86	66	3rd	9½	Birmingham	Jackson, .373	Jackson, 197	Jackson, 7	Jackson, 71	Falkenberg, 23	W. Mitchell, 1.91
1914	51	102	8th	48½	Birmingham	Jackson, .338	Jackson, 153	Jackson, 3	Jackson, 53	W. Mitchell, 12	Steen, 2.60
1915	57	95	7th	44½	Birmingham, Fohl	Chapman, .270	Chapman, 154	Roth, 7	Chapman, E. Smith, 67	Morton, 16	Morton, 2.14
1916	77	77	6th	14	Fohl	Speaker, .386	Speaker, 211	Graney, 5	Speaker, 79	Bagby, 16	Coumbe, 2.02
1917	88	66	3rd	12	Fohl	Speaker, .352	Speaker, 184	Graney, E. Smith, 3	Roth, 72	Bagby, 23	Coveleski, 1.81
1918	73	54	2nd	2½	Fohl	Speaker, .318	Speaker, 150	Wood, 5	Wood, 66	Coveleski, 22	Coveleski, 1.82
1919	84	55	2nd	3½	Fohl, Speaker	Chapman, Gardner, .300	Gardner, 157	E. Smith, 9	Gardner, 79	Coveleski, 24	Coveleski, 2.61
1920	98	56	1st	+2	Speaker	Speaker, .388	Speaker, 214	E. Smith, 12	Gardner, 118	Bagby, 31	Coveleski, 2.49
1921	94	60	2nd	4½	Speaker	Speaker, .362	Gardner, 187	E. Smith, 16	Gardner, 115	Coveleski, 23	Morton, 2.76
1922	78	76	4th	16	Speaker	Speaker, .378	Jamieson, 183	Speaker, 11	Wood, 92	Uhle, 22	Coveleski, 3.32
1923	82	71	3rd	16½	Speaker	Speaker, .380	Jamieson, 222	Speaker, 17	Speaker, 130	Uhle, 26	Coveleski, 2.76
1924	67	86	6th	24½	Speaker	Jamieson, .359	Jamieson, 213	Myatt, Speaker, 8	Sewell, 104	Shaute, 20	S. Smith, 3.01
1925	70	84	6th	27½	Speaker	Speaker, .389	Sewell, 204	Speaker, 12	Sewell, 98	Buckeye, Uhle, 13	Miller, 3.31
1926	88	66	2nd	3	Speaker	Burns, .358	Burns, 216	Speaker, 7	Burns, 114	Uhle, 27	Uhle, 2.83
1927	66	87	6th	43½	McAllister	Burns, .319	Sewell, 180	Hodapp, 5	Sewell, 92	Hudlin, 18	Miller, 3.21
1928	62	92	7th	39	Peckinpaugh	Sewell, Hodapp, .323	Lind, 191	Burns, 5	Hodapp, 73	Hudlin, 14	Hudlin, Shaute, 4.04
1929	81	71	3rd	24	Peckinpaugh	Fonseca, .369	Fonseca, 209	Averill, 18	Fonseca, 103	Ferrell, 21	Holloway, 3.03
1930	81	73	4th	21	Peckinpaugh	Hodapp, .354	Hodapp, 225	Morgan, 26	Morgan, 136	Ferrell, 25	Ferrell, 3.31
1931	78	76	4th	30	Peckinpaugh	Morgan, .351	Averill, 209	Averill, 32	Averill, 143	Ferrell, 22	Ferrell, 3.75
1932	87	65	4th	19	Peckinpaugh	Cissell, .320	Averill, 198	Averill, 32	Averill, 124	Ferrell, 23	Ferrell, 3.66
1933	75	76	4th	23½	Peckinpaugh, Johnson	Averill, .301	Averill, 180	Averill, 11	Averill, 92	Hildebrand, 16	Pearson, 2.33
1934	85	69	3rd	16	Johnson	Vosmik, .341	Trosky, 206	Trosky, 35	Trosky, 142	Harder, 20	Harder, 2.61
1935	82	71	3rd	12	Johnson, O'Neill	Vosmik, .348	Vosmik, 216	Trosky, 26	Trosky, 113	Harder, 22	Harder, 3.29
1936	80	74	5th	22½	O'Neill	Averill, .378	Averill, 232	Trosky, 42	Trosky, 162	Allen, 20	Allen, 3.44
1937	83	71	4th	19	O'Neill	Solters, .323	Solters, 190	Trosky, 32	Trosky, 128	Allen, Harder, 15	Allen, 2.55
1938	86	66	3rd	13	Vitt	Heath, .343	Trosky, 185	Keltner, 26	Keltner, 113	Feller, Harder, 17	Harder, 3.83
1939	87	67	3rd	20½	Vitt	Trosky, .335	Keltner, 191	Trosky, 25	Trosky, 104	Feller, 24	Feller, 2.85
1940	89	65	2nd	1	Vitt	Weatherly, .303	Boudreau, 185	Trosky, 25	Boudreau, 101	Feller, 27	Feller, 2.61
1941	75	79	*4th	26	Peckinpaugh	Heath, .340	Heath, 199	Heath, 24	Heath, 123	Feller, 25	Feller, 3.15
1942	75	79	4th	28	Boudreau	Fleming, .292	Keltner, 179	Fleming, 14	Fleming, 82	Bagby, 17	Bagby, 2.96
1943	82	71	3rd	15½	Boudreau	Cullenbine, .289	Hockett, 166	Heath, 18	Heath, 79	Bagby, A. Smith, 17	Kennedy, 2.45
1944	72	82	*5th	17	Boudreau	Boudreau, .327	Boudreau, 191	Cullenbine, 16	Keltner, 91	Harder, 12	Heving, 1.96
1945	73	72	5th	11	Boudreau	Heath, .305	Meyer, 153	Heath, 15	Heath, 61	Gromek, 19	Gromek, 2.55
1946	68	86	6th	36	Boudreau	Edwards, .301	Boudreau, 151	Seerey, 26	Boudreau, Seerey, 62	Feller, 26	Feller, 2.18
1947	80	74	4th	17	Boudreau	D. Mitchell, .316	Boudreau, 165	Gordon, 29	Gordon, 93	Feller, 20	Feller, 2.68
1948	97	58	†1st	+1	Boudreau	Boudreau, .355	D. Mitchell, 204	Gordon, 32	Gordon, 124	Bearden, Lemon, 20	Bearden, 2.43
1949	89	65	3rd	8	Boudreau	D. Mitchell, .317	D. Mitchell, 203	Doby, 24	Doby, 85	Lemon, 22	Benton, 2.12
1950	92	62	4th	6	Boudreau	Doby, .326	Doby, 164	Rosen, 37	Rosen, 116	Lemon, 23	Wynn, 3.20
1951	93	61	2nd	5	Lopez	Avila, .304	Avila, 165	Easter, 27	Easter, 103	Feller, 22	Gromek, 2.77
1952	93	61	2nd	2	Lopez	D. Mitchell, .323	Avila, 179	Doby, 32	Rosen, 105	Wynn, 23	Garcia, 2.37
1953	92	62	2nd	8½	Lopez	Rosen, .336	Rosen, 201	Rosen, 43	Rosen, 145	Lemon, 21	Garcia, 3.25
1954	111	43	1st	+8	Lopez	Avila, .341	Avila, 189	Doby, 32	Doby, 126	Lemon, Wynn, 23	Mossi, 1.94
1955	93	61	2nd	3	Lopez	A. Smith, .306	A. Smith, 186	Doby, 26	Rosen, 81	Lemon, 18	Wynn, 2.82
1956	88	66	2nd	9	Lopez	A. Smith, .274	A. Smith, 144	Wertz, 32	Wertz, 106	Lemon, Score, Wynn 20	Score, 2.53
1957	76	77	6th	21½	Farrell	Woodling, .321	Wertz, 145	Wertz, 28	Wertz, 105	Wynn, 14	McLish, 2.74
1958	77	76	4th	14½	Bragan, Gordon	Power, .317	Minoso, 168	Colavito, 41	Colavito, 113	McLish, 16	Wilhelm, 2.49
1959	89	65	2nd	5	Gordon	Francona, .363	Minoso, Power, 172	Colavito, 42	Colavito, 111	McLish, 19	J. Perry, 2.65
1960	76	78	4th	21	Gordon, Dykes	Kuenn, .308	Power, 167	Held, 21	Power, 84	J. Perry, 18	Locke, 3.37
1961	78	83	5th	30½	Dykes	Piersall, .322	Francona, 178	Kirkland, 27	Kirkland, 95	Grant, 15	Funk, 3.31
1962	80	82	6th	16	McGaha	Francona, .272	Francona, 169	Romano, 25	Romano, 81	Donovan, 20	Donovan, 3.59
1963	79	83	*5th	25½	Tebbetts	Davalillo, .292	Alvis, 165	Alvis, 22	Alvis, 67	Grant, Kralick 13	Kralick, 2.92
1964	79	83	*6th	20	Tebbetts	B. Chance, .279	Howser, 163	Wagner, 31	Wagner, 100	Kralick, 12	McMahon, 2.41
1965	87	75	5th	15	Tebbetts	Davalillo, .301	Colavito, 170	Wagner, 28	Colavito, 108	McDowell, 17	McDowell, 2.18
1966	81	81	5th	17	Tebbetts, Strickland	Wagner, .279	Wagner, 153	Colavito, 30	Whitfield, 78	Siebert, 16	Hargan, 2.48
1967	75	87	8th	17	Adcock	Davalillo, .287	Alvis, 163	Alvis, 21	Alvis, 70	Hargan, 14	Siebert, 2.38
1968	86	75	3rd	16½	Dark	Azcue, .280	Cardenal, 150	Horton, 14	Horton, 59	Tiant, 21	Tiant, 1.60
								EAST DIVISION			
1969	62	99	6th	46½	Dark	Horton, .278	Horton, 174	Harrelson, Horton 27	Horton, 93	McDowell, 18	McDowell, 2.94
1970	76	86	5th	32	Dark	Fosse, .307	Pinson, 164	Nettles, 26	Pinson, 82	McDowell, 20	Hargan, 2.90
1971	60	102	6th	43	Dark, Lipon	Uhlaender, .288	Nettles, 156	Nettles, 28	Nettles, 86	McDowell, 13	Lamb, 3.35
1972	72	84	5th	14	Aspromonte	Chambliss, .292	Nettles, 141	Nettles, 17	Nettles, 70	G. Perry, 24	G. Perry, 1.92
1973	71	91	6th	26	Aspromonte	Williams, .289	B. Bell, 169	Spikes, 23	Spikes, 73	G. Perry, 19	Hilgendorf, 3.14
1974	77	85	4th	14	Aspromonte	Gamble, .291	Spikes, 154	Spikes, 22	Spikes, 80	G. Perry, 21	G. Perry, 2.51
1975	79	80	4th	15½	Robinson	Carty, .308	B. Bell, 150	Powell, 27	Hendrick, Powell ,86	Peterson, 14	Eckersley, 2.60
1976	81	78	4th	16	Robinson	Carty, .310	Carty, 171	Hendrick, 25	Carty, 83	Dobson, 16	LaRoche, 2.24
1977	71	90	5th	28½	Robinson, Torborg	Bochte, .304	Kuiper, 169	Thornton, 28	Carty, 80	Eckersley, 14	Hood, 3.00
1978	69	90	6th	29	Torborg	Kuiper, Norris .283	B. Bell, 157	Thornton, 33	Thornton, 105	Waits, 13	Kern, 3.08
1979	81	80	6th	22	Torborg, Garcia	Harrah, .279	Bonds, 148	Thornton, 26	Thornton, 93	Waits, 16	Monge, 2.40
1980	79	81	6th	23	Garcia	Dilone, .341	Dilone, 180	Charboneau, 23	Charboneau, 87	Barker, 19	Monge, 3.53
1981	52	51	‡6th/5th	—	Garcia	Hargrove, .317	Harrah, 105	Diaz, 7	Hargrove, 49	Blyleven, 11	Blyleven, 2.88
1982	78	84	*6th	17	Garcia	Harrah, .304	Harrah, 183	Thornton, 32	Thornton, 116	Barker, 15	Sutcliffe, 2.96
1983	70	92	7th	28	Ferraro, Corrales	Tabler, .291	Franco, 153	Thomas, 17	Franco, 80	Sutcliffe, 17	Blyleven, 3.91
1984	75	87	6th	29	Corrales	Vukovich, .304	Franco, 188	Thornton, 33	Thornton, 99	Blyleven, 19	Camacho, 2.43
1985	60	102	7th	39½	Corrales	Butler, .311	Butler, 184	Thornton, 22	Franco, 90	Heaton, 9	Blyleven, 3.26
1986	84	78	5th	11½	Corrales	Tabler, .326	Carter, 200	Carter, 29	Carter, 121	Candiotti, 16	Candiotti, 3.57
1987	61	101	7th	37	Corrales, Edwards	Franco, .319	Tabler, 170	Snyder, 33	Carter, 106	Bailes, Candiotti, Niekro, 7	Jones, 3.15
1988	78	84	6th	11	Edwards	Franco, .303	Franco, 186	Carter, 27	Carter, 98	Swindell, 18	Swindell, 3.20
1989	73	89	6th	16	Edwards, Hart	Browne, .299	Browne, 179	Carter, 35	Carter, 95	Candiotti, Swindell 13	Candiotti, 3.10
1990	77	85	4th	11	McNamara	C. James, .299	Jacoby, 162	Maldonado, 22	Maldonado, 95	Candiotti, 15	Olin, 3.41
1991	57	105	7th	34	McNamara, Hargrove	Cole, .295	Baerga, 171	Belle, 28	Belle, 95	Nagy, 10	Candiotti, 2.24
1992	76	86	*4th	20	Hargrove	Baerga, .312	Baerga, 205	Belle, 34	Belle, 112	Nagy, 17	Power, 2.54
1993	76	86	6th	19	Hargrove	Lofton, .325	Baerga, 200	Belle, 38	Belle, 129	Mesa, 10	Kramer, 4.02
								CENTRAL DIVISION			
1994	66	47	2nd	1	Hargrove	Belle, .357	Lofton, 160	Belle, 36	Belle, 101	M. Clark, Martinez, 11	Nagy, 3.45
1995	100	44	§∞1st	+30	Hargrove	Murray, .323	Baerga, 175	Belle, 50	Belle, 126	Hershiser, Nagy 16	Ogea, 3.05
1996	99	62	▲1st	+14½	Hargrove	Franco, .322	Lofton, 210	Belle, 48	Belle, 148	Nagy, 17	Nagy, 3.41
1997	86	75	§∞1st	+6	Hargrove	Justice, .329	Ramirez, 184	Thome, 40	Williams, 105	Nagy, 15	Nagy, 4.28
1998	89	73	§◆1st	+9	Hargrove	Ramirez, .294	Lofton,169	Ramirez, 45	Ramirez, 145	Burba, Nagy, 15	Colon, 3.71
1999	97	65	▲1st	+21½	Hargrove	Ramirez, .333	R.Alomar,138	Ramirez, 44	Ramirez, 165	Colon, 18	Colon, 3.95

* Tied for position. † Won pennant playoff. ‡ First half 26-24; second half 26-27. § Won Division Series. ∞ Won Championship Series. ▲ Lost Division Series. ◆ Lost Championship Series.
Note: Batting average minimum 350 at-bats; ERA minimum 90 innings pitched.

HISTORY

DETROIT TIGERS

FRANCHISE CHRONOLOGY

First season: 1901, as a member of the new American League. The Tigers made a spectacular Major League debut by rallying for 10 ninth-inning runs in a 14-13 victory over Milwaukee and rode that success to a third-place finish (74-61) behind league-champion Chicago and Boston.

1902-present: The Tigers, who have captured nine A.L. pennants and four World Series, have never experienced more than five straight losing seasons and rank behind only the Yankees in sustained A.L. success. After losing three straight fall classics from 1907-09, the Tigers went a quarter of a century before qualifying again. But after a 1934 loss to the Cardinals, they rebounded to defeat the Cubs in 1935 and matched that with another victory over the Cubs in 1945. Their other two championship seasons were 1968 and 1984, an amazing campaign in which they capped their wire-to-wire pennant run with a six-game Series victory over the Padres. After division play began in 1969, the Tigers won three A.L. East titles before moving to the A.L. Central Division in a realignment that sent Milwaukee to the National League.

Right fielder Al Kaline.

TIGERS VS. OPPONENTS BY DECADE

	A's	Indians	Orioles	Red Sox	Twins	White Sox	Yankees	Angels	Rangers	Brewers	Royals	Blue Jays	Mariners	Devil Rays	Interleague	Decade Record
																683-632
1901-09	80-102	95-95	101-90	97-92	114-72	93-96	103-85									790-704
1910-19	116-99	114-94	126-90	88-124	116-100	109-103	121-94									760-778
1920-29	105-114	111-109	109-111	139-81	107-113	95-124	94-126									818-716
1930-39	111-106	118-101	135-85	121-99	118-102	129-89	86-134									834-705
1940-49	130-90	115-105	129-90	93-127	130-90	125-95	112-108									738-802
1950-59	122-98	84-136	114-106	99-121	121-99	98-122	100-120									882-729
1960-69	109-69	101-83	94-90	95-88	88-90	97-81	90-94	96-60	94-68	10-2	8-4					789-820
1970-79	56-60	90-78	65-102	69-96	48-68	67-50	74-92	63-53	64-64	91-66	54-63	28-15	20-13			839-727
1980-89	58-53	82-41	69-61	59-65	66-54	66-48	62-64	59-55	73-47	66-64	54-59	59-68	66-48			702-852
1990-99	53-53	47-76	49-69	54-64	53-60	51-69	47-72	53-54	54-63	42-56	57-56	52-70	58-53	9-11	23-26	702-852
Totals	940-844	957-918	991-894	914-957	961-848	930-877	889-989	271-222	285-242	209-188	173-182	139-153	144-114	9-11	23-26	7835-7465

Interleague results: 2-1 vs. Braves; 0-3 vs. Expos; 3-0 vs. Mets; 2-1 vs. Phillies; 1-2 vs. Marlins; 2-0 vs. Cubs; 2-4 vs. Reds; 0-6 vs. Astros; 4-2 vs. Pirates; 4-4 vs. Cardinals; 3-3 vs. Brewers.

MANAGERS

Name	Years	Record
George Stallings	1901	74-61
Frank Dwyer	1902	52-83
Ed Barrow	1903-04	97-117
Bobby Lowe	1904	30-44
Bill Armour	1905-06	150-152
Hugh Jennings	1907-20	1131-972
Ty Cobb	1921-26	479-444
George Moriarty	1927-28	150-157
Bucky Harris	1929-33, 1955-56	516-557
Del Baker	1933, 1937-42	399-339
Mickey Cochrane	1934-38	366-266
Ralph Perkins	1937	6-9
Steve O'Neill	1943-48	509-414
Red Rolfe	1949-52	278-256
Fred Hutchinson	1952-54	155-235
Jack Tighe	1957-58	99-104
Bill Norman	1958-59	58-64
Jimmie Dykes	1959-60	118-115
Joe Gordon	1960	26-31
Bob Scheffing	1961-63	210-173
Chuck Dressen	1963-65, 1966	221-189
Bob Swift	1965, 1966	56-43
Frank Skaff	1966	40-39
Mayo Smith	1967-70	363-285
Billy Martin	1971-73	248-204
Joe Schultz	1973	14-14
Ralph Houk	1974-78	363-443
Les Moss	1979	27-26

MANAGERS—cont'd.

Name	Years	Record
Sparky Anderson	1979-95	1331-1248
Buddy Bell	1996-98	184-277
Larry Parrish	1998-99	82-104

WORLD SERIES CHAMPIONS

Year	Loser	Length	MVP
1935	Chicago	6 games	None
1945	Chicago	7 games	None
1968	St. Louis	7 games	Lolich
1984	San Diego	5 games	Trammell

A.L. PENNANT WINNERS

Year	Record	Manager	Series Result
1907	92-58	Jennings	Lost to Cubs
1908	90-63	Jennings	Lost to Cubs
1909	98-54	Jennings	Lost to Pirates
1934	101-53	Cochrane	Lost to Cardinals
1935	93-58	Cochrane	Defeated Cubs
1940	90-64	Baker	Lost to Reds
1945	88-65	O'Neill	Defeated Cubs
1968	103-59	Smith	Defeated Cardinals
1984	104-58	Anderson	Defeated Padres

EAST DIVISION CHAMPIONS

Year	Record	Manager	ALCS Result
1972	86-70	Martin	Lost to A's
1984	104-58	Anderson	Defeated Royals
1987	98-64	Anderson	Lost to Twins

ATTENDANCE HIGHS

Total	Season	Park
2,704,794	1984	Tiger Stadium
2,286,609	1985	Tiger Stadium
2,081,162	1988	Tiger Stadium
2,061,830	1987	Tiger Stadium
2,031,847	1968	Tiger Stadium

BALLPARK CHRONOLOGY

Tiger Stadium (1912-present)
Capacity: 46,945.
First game: Tigers 6, Cleveland 5, 11 innings (April 20, 1912).
First batter: Jack Graney, Indians.
First hit: Nap Lajoie, Indians.
First run: Joe Jackson, Indians (1st inning).
First home run: Del Pratt, Browns (May 5).
First winning pitcher: George Mullin, Tigers.
First-season attendance: 402,870.

Bennett Park (1901-11)
Capacity: 8,500.
First game: Tigers 14, Milwaukee 13 (April 25, 1901).
First-season attendance: 259,430.

Note: Tiger Stadium was known as Navin Field from 1912-37 and Briggs Stadium from 1938-60.

A.L. MVPs

Mickey Cochrane, C, 1934
Hank Greenberg, 1B, 1935
Charley Gehringer, 2B, 1937
Hank Greenberg, OF, 1940
Hal Newhouser, P, 1944
Hal Newhouser, P, 1945
Denny McLain, P, 1968
Willie Hernandez, P, 1984

CY YOUNG WINNERS

Denny McLain, RH, 1968
*Denny McLain, RH, 1969
Willie Hernandez, LH, 1984
    * Co-winner.

ROOKIES OF THE YEAR

Harvey Kuenn, SS, 1953
Mark Fidrych, P, 1976
Lou Whitaker, 2B, 1978

MANAGERS OF THE YEAR

Sparky Anderson, 1984
Sparky Anderson, 1987

RETIRED UNIFORMS

No.	Name	Pos.
2	Charley Gehringer	2B
5	Hank Greenberg	1B
6	Al Kaline	OF
16	Hal Newhouser	P

Outfielder Ty Cobb (sliding) played the game with reckless abandon and a devilish commitment.

MILESTONE PERFORMANCES

30-plus home runs

58—	Hank Greenberg	1938
51—	Cecil Fielder	1990
45—	Rocky Colavito	1961
44—	Hank Greenberg	1946
	Cecil Fielder	1991
41—	Hank Greenberg	1940
	Norm Cash	1961
40—	Hank Greenberg	1937
	Darrell Evans	1985
39—	Norm Cash	1962
38—	Dean Palmer	1999
37—	Rocky Colavito	1962
36—	Hank Greenberg	1935
	Willie Horton	1968
35—	Rudy York	1937
	Rocky Colavito	1960
	Cecil Fielder	1992
34—	Rudy York	1943
	Darrell Evans	1987
	Tony Clark	1998
33—	Rudy York	1938, 1940
	Hank Greenberg	1939
	Lance Parrish	1984
32—	Norm Cash	1966, 1971
	Lance Parrish	1982
	Matt Nokes	1987
	Mickey Tettleton	1992, 1993
	Rob Deer	1992
	Tony Clark	1997
31—	Charlie Maxwell	1959
	Jason Thompson	1977
	Mickey Tettleton	1991
	Cecil Fielder	1995
	Tony Clark	1999
30—	Norm Cash	1965
	Cecil Fielder	1993

100-plus RBIs

183—	Hank Greenberg	1937
170—	Hank Greenberg	1935
150—	Hank Greenberg	1940
146—	Hank Greenberg	1938
140—	Rocky Colavito	1961
139—	Harry Heilmann	1921
	Hank Greenberg	1934
137—	Dale Alexander	1929
135—	Dale Alexander	1930
134—	Rudy York	1940
133—	Harry Heilmann	1925
	Vic Wertz	1949
	Cecil Fielder	1991
132—	Norm Cash	1961
	Cecil Fielder	1990
128—	Bobby Veach	1921
	Al Kaline	1956
127—	Ty Cobb	1911
	Charley Gehringer	1934
	Rudy York	1938
	Hank Greenberg	1946
126—	Bobby Veach	1922
125—	Goose Goslin	1936
124—	Cecil Fielder	1992
123—	Vic Wertz	1950
121—	Rusty Staub	1978
120—	Sam Crawford	1910
	Harry Heilmann	1927, 1929
119—	Ty Cobb	1907
118—	Rudy York	1943
117—	Cecil Fielder	1993
	Tony Clark	1997
116—	Charley Gehringer	1936
	Ray Boone	1955
115—	Sam Crawford	1911
	Harry Heilmann	1923
114—	Bob Fothergill	1927
	Lance Parrish	1983
113—	Bobby Veach	1920
	Harry Heilmann	1924
	Gee Walker	1937
112—	Sam Crawford	1915
	Bobby Veach	1915
	Al Simmons	1936
	Hank Greenberg	1939
	Rocky Colavito	1962
111—	Rudy York	1941
110—	Mickey Tettleton	1993
109—	Sam Crawford	1912
	Goose Goslin	1935
108—	Ty Cobb	1908
	John Stone	1932
	Charley Gehringer	1935
107—	Ty Cobb	1909
	Harry Heilmann	1928
	Charley Gehringer	1932, 1938
106—	Charley Gehringer	1929
105—	Charley Gehringer	1933
	Marv Owen	1936
	Jason Thompson	1977
	Steve Kemp	1979
	Alan Trammell	1987
104—	Sam Crawford	1914
	Willie Horton	1965
103—	Bobby Veach	1917
	Harry Heilmann	1926
	Rudy York	1937
	Hoot Evers	1948, 1950
	Tony Clark	1998
102—	Ty Cobb	1917, 1925
	Al Kaline	1955
	Travis Fryman	1997
101—	Ty Cobb	1921
	Bobby Veach	1919
	George Kell	1950
	Al Kaline	1963
	Rusty Staub	1977
	Steve Kemp	1980
	Bobby Higginson	1997
100—	Goose Goslin	1934
	Billy Rogell	1934
	Willie Horton	1966
	Travis Fryman	1996
	Damion Easley	1998
	Dean Palmer	1999

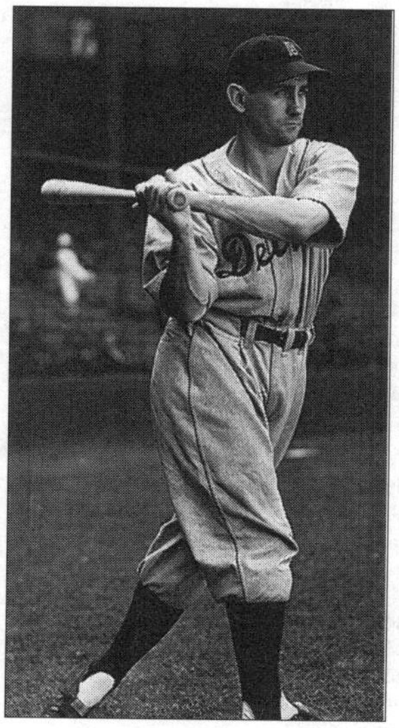

Second baseman Charley Gehringer.

20-plus victories

1901—	Roscoe Miller	23-13
1905—	Ed Killian	23-14
	George Mullin	21-21
1906—	George Mullin	21-18
1907—	Bill Donovan	25-4
	Ed Killian	25-13
	George Mullin	20-20
1908—	Ed Summers	24-12
1909—	George Mullin	29-9
	Edgar Willett	21-10
1910—	George Mullin	21-12
1914—	Harry Coveleski	22-12
1915—	George Dauss	24-13
	Harry Coveleski	22-13
1916—	Harry Coveleski	21-11
1919—	George Dauss	21-9
1923—	George Dauss	21-13
1934—	Schoolboy Rowe	24-8
	Tommy Bridges	22-11
1935—	Tommy Bridges	21-10
1936—	Tommy Bridges	23-11
1939—	Bobo Newsom	*20-11
1940—	Bobo Newsom	21-5
1943—	Dizzy Trout	20-12
1944—	Hal Newhouser	29-9
	Dizzy Trout	27-14
1945—	Hal Newhouser	25-9
1946—	Hal Newhouser	26-9
1948—	Hal Newhouser	21-12
1956—	Frank Lary	21-13
	Billy Hoeft	20-14
1957—	Jim Bunning	20-8
1961—	Frank Lary	23-9
1966—	Denny McLain	20-14
1967—	Earl Wilson	22-11
1968—	Denny McLain	31-6
1969—	Denny McLain	24-9
1971—	Mickey Lolich	25-14
	Joe Coleman	20-9
1972—	Mickey Lolich	22-14
1973—	Joe Coleman	23-15
1983—	Jack Morris	20-13
1986—	Jack Morris	21-8
1991—	Bill Gullickson	20-9

*3-1 with St. Louis; 17-10 with Detroit.

A.L. home run champions

1908—	Sam Crawford	7
1909—	Ty Cobb	9
1935—	Hank Greenberg	*36
1938—	Hank Greenberg	58
1940—	Hank Greenberg	41
1943—	Rudy York	34
1946—	Hank Greenberg	44
1985—	Darrell Evans	40
1990—	Cecil Fielder	51
1991—	Cecil Fielder	*44

* Tied for league lead

A.L. RBI champions

1907—	Ty Cobb	119
1908—	Ty Cobb	108
1909—	Ty Cobb	107
1910—	Sam Crawford	120
1911—	Ty Cobb	127
1914—	Sam Crawford	104
1915—	Sam Crawford	*112
	Bobby Veach	*112
1917—	Bobby Veach	103
1918—	Bobby Veach	78
1935—	Hank Greenberg	170
1937—	Hank Greenberg	183
1940—	Hank Greenberg	150
1943—	Rudy York	118
1946—	Hank Greenberg	127
1955—	Ray Boone	*116
1990—	Cecil Fielder	132
1991—	Cecil Fielder	133
1992—	Cecil Fielder	124

* Tied for league lead

A.L. batting champions

1907—	Ty Cobb	.350
1908—	Ty Cobb	.324
1909—	Ty Cobb	.377
1910—	Ty Cobb	.385
1911—	Ty Cobb	.420
1912—	Ty Cobb	.410
1913—	Ty Cobb	.390
1914—	Ty Cobb	.368
1915—	Ty Cobb	.369
1917—	Ty Cobb	.383
1918—	Ty Cobb	.382
1919—	Ty Cobb	.384
1921—	Harry Heilmann	.394
1923—	Harry Heilmann	.403
1925—	Harry Heilmann	.393
1926—	Heinie Manush	.378
1927—	Harry Heilmann	.398
1937—	Charley Gehringer	.371
1949—	George Kell	.343
1955—	Al Kaline	.340
1959—	Harvey Kuenn	.353
1961—	Norm Cash	.361

INDIVIDUAL SEASON, GAME RECORDS

SEASON

Batting

At-bats	679	Harvey Kuenn	1953
Runs	147	Ty Cobb	1911
Hits	248	Ty Cobb	1911
Singles	169	Ty Cobb	1911
Doubles	63	Hank Greenberg	1934
Triples	26	Sam Crawford	1926
Home runs	58	Hank Greenberg	1938
Home runs, rookie	35	Rudy York	1937
Grand slams	4	3 times	
		Last by Jim Northrup	1968
Total bases	397	Hank Greenberg	1937
RBIs	183	Hank Greenberg	1937
Walks	137	Roy Cullenbine	1947
Most strikeouts	182	Cecil Fielder	1990
Fewest strikeouts	13	Charley Gehringer	1936
		Harvey Kuenn	1954
Batting average	.420	Ty Cobb	1911
Slugging pct.	.683	Hank Greenberg	1938
Stolen bases	96	Ty Cobb	1915

Pitching

Games	88	Mike Myers	1997
		Sean Runyan	1998
Complete games	42	George Mullin	1904
Innings	382.1	George Mullin	1904
Wins	31	Denny McLain	1968
Losses	23	George Mullin	1904
Winning pct.	.862 (25-4)	Bill Donovan	1907
Walks	158	Joe Coleman	1974
Strikeouts	308	Mickey Lolich	1971
Shutouts	9	Denny McLain	1969
Home runs allowed	42	Denny McLain	1966
Lowest ERA	1.64	Ed Summers	1908
Saves	38	John Hiller	1973

GAME

Batting

Runs	5	Last by Travis Fryman	4-17-93
Hits	7	Rocky Colavito	6-24-62
		Cesar Gutierrez	6-21-70
Doubles	4	Frank Dillon	4-25-01
		Bill Bruton	5-19-63
Triples	3	Charley Gehringer	8-5-29
Home runs	3	Last by Bobby Higginson	6-30-97
RBIs	8	Jim Northrup	6-24-68
		Jim Northrup	7-11-73
Total bases	16	Ty Cobb	5-5-25
Stolen bases	5	Johnny Neun	7-9-27

A.L. ERA champions

1902—	Ed Siever	1.91
1944—	Dizzy Trout	2.12
1945—	Hal Newhouser	1.81
1946—	Hal Newhouser	1.94
1962—	Hank Aguirre	2.21
1976—	Mark Fidrych	2.34

A.L. strikeout champions

1935—	Tommy Bridges	163
1936—	Tommy Bridges	175
1944—	Hal Newhouser	187
1945—	Hal Newhouser	212
1949—	Virgil Trucks	153
1959—	Jim Bunning	201
1960—	Jim Bunning	201
1971—	Mickey Lolich	308
1983—	Jack Morris	232

No-hit pitchers

(9 innings or more)

1912—	George Mullin	7-0 vs. St. Louis
1952—	Virgil Trucks	1-0 vs. Washington
	Virgil Trucks	1-0 vs. New York
1958—	Jim Bunning	3-0 vs. Boston
1984—	Jack Morris	4-0 vs. Chicago

Longest hitting streaks

40—	Ty Cobb	1911
35—	Ty Cobb	1917
34—	John Stone	1930
30—	Goose Goslin	1934
	Ron LeFlore	1976
29—	Dale Alexander	1930
	Pete Fox	1935
27—	Gee Walker	1937
	Ron LeFlore	1978
25—	Kid Gleason	1901
	Ty Cobb	1906
23—	Sam Crawford	1909
	Harry Heilmann	1921
	John Stone	1931
22—	Harvey Kuenn	1959
	Al Kaline	1961
21—	Harry Heilmann	1923
	Ty Cobb	1926
	Charley Gehringer	1927
	Dick Wakefield	1943
20—	Kid Gleason	1901
	Sam Crawford	1903
	Charley Gehringer	1937
	Alan Trammell	1984

HISTORY

BATTING

Games
Al Kaline	2,834
Ty Cobb	2,806
Lou Whitaker	2,390
Charley Gehringer	2,323
Alan Trammell	2,293
Sam Crawford	2,114
Norm Cash	2,018
Harry Heilmann	1,991
Donie Bush	1,872
Bill Freehan	1,774

At-bats
Ty Cobb	10,591
Al Kaline	10,116
Charley Gehringer	8,860
Lou Whitaker	8,570
Alan Trammell	8,288
Sam Crawford	7,984
Harry Heilmann	7,297
Donie Bush	6,970
Norm Cash	6,593
Bill Freehan	6,073

Runs
Ty Cobb	2,088
Charley Gehringer	1,774
Al Kaline	1,622
Lou Whitaker	1,386
Donie Bush	1,242
Alan Trammell	1,231
Harry Heilmann	1,209
Sam Crawford	1,115
Norm Cash	1,028
Hank Greenberg	980

Hits
Ty Cobb	3,900
Al Kaline	3,007
Charley Gehringer	2,839
Harry Heilmann	2,499
Sam Crawford	2,466
Lou Whitaker	2,369
Alan Trammell	2,365
Bobby Veach	1,859
Norm Cash	1,793
Donie Bush	1,745

Doubles
Ty Cobb	665
Charley Gehringer	574
Al Kaline	498
Harry Heilmann	497
Lou Whitaker	420
Alan Trammell	412
Sam Crawford	402
Hank Greenberg	366
Bobby Veach	345
Harvey Kuenn	244

Triples
Ty Cobb	284
Sam Crawford	249
Charley Gehringer	146
Harry Heilmann	145
Bobby Veach	136
Al Kaline	75
Donie Bush	73
Dick McAuliffe	70
Hank Greenberg	69
Lu Blue	66

Home runs
Al Kaline	399
Norm Cash	373
Hank Greenberg	306
Willie Horton	262
Cecil Fielder	245
Lou Whitaker	244
Rudy York	239
Lance Parrish	212
Bill Freehan	200
Kirk Gibson	195

Total Bases
Ty Cobb	5,466
Al Kaline	4,852
Charley Gehringer	4,257
Harry Heilmann	3,778
Lou Whitaker	3,651
Sam Crawford	3,576
Alan Trammell	3,442
Norm Cash	3,233
Hank Greenberg	2,950
Bobby Veach	2,653

Runs batted in
Ty Cobb	1,805
Al Kaline	1,583
Harry Heilmann	1,442
Charley Gehringer	1,427
Sam Crawford	1,264
Hank Greenberg	1,202
Norm Cash	1,087
Lou Whitaker	1,084
Bobby Veach	1,042
Alan Trammell	1,003

Extra-base hits
Ty Cobb	1,060
Al Kaline	972
Charley Gehringer	904
Harry Heilmann	806
Hank Greenberg	741
Lou Whitaker	729
Sam Crawford	721
Norm Cash	654
Alan Trammell	652
Bobby Veach	540

Batting average
(Minimum 500 games)
Ty Cobb	.368
Harry Heilmann	.342
Bob Fothergill	.337
George Kell	.325
Heinie Manush	.321
Charley Gehringer	.320
Hank Greenberg	.319
Gee Walker	.317
Harvey Kuenn	.314
Barney McCosky	.312

Stolen bases
Ty Cobb	865
Donie Bush	400
Sam Crawford	317
Ron Leflore	294
Alan Trammell	236
Kirk Gibson	194
George Moriarty	190
Bobby Veach	189
Charley Gehringer	181
Lou Whitaker	143

PITCHING

Earned-run average
(Minimum 1,000 innings)
Harry Coveleski	2.34
Ed Killian	2.38
Bill Donovan	2.49
Ed Siever	2.61
George Mullin	2.76
John Hiller	2.83
Ed Willett	2.89
Jean Dubuc	3.06
Hal Newhouser	3.07
Bernie Boland	3.09

Wins
Hooks Dauss	223
George Mullin	209
Mickey Lolich	207
Hal Newhouser	200
Jack Morris	198
Tommy Bridges	194
Dizzy Trout	161
Bill Donovan	140
Earl Whitehill	133
Frank Lary	123

Losses
Hooks Dauss	182
George Mullin	179
Mickey Lolich	175
Dizzy Trout	153
Jack Morris	150
Hal Newhouser	148
Tommy Bridges	138
Earl Whitehill	119
Frank Lary	110
Vic Sorrell	101

Innings piitched
George Mullin	3,394.0
Hooks Dauss	3,390.2
Mickey Lolich	3,361.2
Jack Morris	3,042.2
Hal Newhouser	2,944.0
Tommy Bridges	2,826.1
Dizzy Trout	2,591.2
Earl Whitehill	2,171.1
Bill Donovan	2,137.1
Frank Lary	2,008.2

Strikeouts
Mickey Lolich	2,679
Jack Morris	1,980
Hal Newhouser	1,770
Tommy Bridges	1,674
Jim Bunning	1,406
George Mullin	1,380
Hooks Dauss	1,201
Dizzy Trout	1,199
Denny McLain	1,150
Bill Donovan	1,079

Bases on balls
Hal Newhouser	1,227
Tommy Bridges	1,192
George Mullin	1,106
Jack Morris	1,086
Hooks Dauss	1,067
Mickey Lolich	1,014
Dizzy Trout	978
Earl Whitehill	831
Dan Petry	744
Virgil Trucks	732

Games
John Hiller	545
Hooks Dauss	538
Mickey Lolich	508
Dizzy Trout	493
Mike Henneman	491
Hal Newhouser	460
George Mullin	435
Jack Morris	430
Tommy Bridges	424
Willie Hernandez	358

Shutouts
Mickey Lolich	39
George Mullin	34
Tommy Bridges	33
Hal Newhouser	33
Bill Donovan	29
Dizzy Trout	28
Denny McLain	26
Jack Morris	24
Hooks Dauss	22
Frank Lary	20
Virgil Trucks	20

Saves
Mike Henneman	154
John Hiller	125
Willie Hernandez	120
Todd Jones	89
Aurelio Lopez	85
Terry Fox	55
Al Benton	45
Hooks Dauss	39
Larry Sherry	37
Fred Scherman	34
Dizzy Trout	34

Batting
Most at-bats	5,664	1998
Most runs	958	1934
Fewest runs	499	1904
Most hits	1,724	1921
Most singles	1,298	1921
Most doubles	349	1934
Most triples	102	1913
Most home runs	225	1987
Fewest home runs	9	1906
Most grand slams	10	1938
Most pinch-hit home runs	8	1971
Most total bases	2,548	1987
Most stolen bases	280	1909
Highest batting average	.316	1921
Lowest batting average	.230	1904
Highest slugging pct.	.453	1929

Pitching
Lowest ERA	2.26	1909
Highest ERA	6.38	1996
Most complete games	143	1904
Most shutouts	22	1917, 1944, 1969
Most saves	51	1984
Most walks	784	1996
Most strikeouts	1,115	1968

Fielding
Most errors	410	1901
Fewest errors	92	1997
Most double plays	194	1950
Highest fielding average	.985	1997

General
Most games won	104	1984
Most games lost	109	1996
Highest win pct.	.656	1934
Lowest win pct.	.325	1952

Batting
Most runs, game	21	Last 7-1-36
Most runs, inning	13	6-17-25
Most hits, game	28	9-29-28
Most home runs, game	7	Last 5-28-95
Most total bases, game	45	8-14-37

Hal Newhouser claimed A.L. MVP citations during the war seasons of 1944 and '45.

HISTORY

TIGERS YEAR-BY-YEAR

Year	W	L	Place	Games Back	Manager	Leaders: Batting avg.	Hits	Home runs	RBIs	Wins	ERA
1901	74	61	3rd	8½	Stallings	Elberfeld, .310	Barrett, 159	Barrett, Holmes, 4	Elberfeld, 76	Miller, 23	Yeager, 2.61
1902	52	83	7th	30½	Dwyer	Barrett, .303	Barrett, 154	Casey, 3	Elberfeld, 64	Mercer, 15	Siever, 1.91
1903	65	71	5th	25	Barrow	Crawford, .335	Crawford, 184	Crawford, 4	Crawford, 89	Mullin, 19	Mullin, 2.25
1904	62	90	7th	32	Barrow, Lowe	Barrett, .268	Barrett, 167	3 Tied, 2	Crawford, 73	Donovan, Mullin, 17	Mullin, 2.40
1905	79	74	3rd	15½	Armour	Crawford, .297	Crawford, 171	Crawford, 6	Crawford, 75	Killian, 23	Killian, 2.27
1906	71	78	6th	21	Armour	Cobb, .316	Crawford, 166	4 Tied, 2	Crawford, 72	Mullin, 21	Siever, 2.71
1907	92	58	1st	+1½	Jennings	Cobb, .350	Cobb, 212	Cobb, 5	Cobb, 119	Donovan, Killian, 25	Killian, 1.78
1908	90	63	1st	+½	Jennings	Cobb, .324	Cobb, 188	Crawford, 7	Cobb, 108	Summers, 24	Summers, 1.64
1909	98	54	1st	+3½	Jennings	Cobb, .377	Cobb, 216	Cobb, 9	Cobb, 107	Mullin, 29	Killian, 1.71
1910	86	68	3rd	18	Jennings	Cobb, .383	Cobb, 196	Cobb, 8	Crawford, 120	Mullin, 21	Willett, 2.37
1911	89	65	2nd	13½	Jennings	Cobb, .420	Cobb, 248	Cobb, 8	Cobb, 144	Mullin, 18	Mullin, 3.07
1912	69	84	6th	36½	Jennings	Cobb, .410	Cobb, 227	Cobb, 7	Crawford, 109	Dubuc, Willett, 17	Dubuc, 2.77
1913	66	87	6th	30	Jennings	Cobb, .390	Crawford, 193	Crawford, 9	Crawford, 83	Dubuc, 15	Dauss, 2.68
1914	80	73	4th	19½	Jennings	Crawford, .314	Crawford, 183	Crawford, 8	Crawford, 104	Coveleski, 21	Cavet, 2.44
1915	100	54	2nd	2½	Jennings	Cobb, .369	Cobb, 208	Burns, 5	Crawford, Veach, 112	Dauss, 24	Coveleski, 2.45
1916	87	67	3rd	4	Jennings	Cobb, .371	Cobb, 201	Cobb, 5	Veach, 91	Coveleski, 21	Coveleski, 1.97
1917	78	75	4th	21½	Jennings	Cobb, .383	Cobb, 225	Veach, 8	Veach, 103	Dauss, 17	James, 2.09
1918	55	71	7th	20	Jennings	Cobb, .382	Cobb, 161	Heilmann, 5	Veach, 78	Boland, 14	Erickson, 2.48
1919	80	60	4th	8	Jennings	Cobb, .384	Cobb, Veach, 191	Heilmann, 8	Veach, 101	Dauss, 21	Ayers, 2.69
1920	61	93	7th	37	Jennings	Cobb, .334	Veach, 188	Veach, 11	Veach, 113	Ehmke, 15	Ehmke, 3.25
1921	71	82	6th	27	Cobb	Heilmann, .394	Heilmann, 237	Heilmann, 19	Heilmann, 139	Ehmke, 13	Leonard, 3.75
1922	79	75	3rd	15	Cobb	Cobb, .401	Cobb, 211	Heilmann, 21	Veach, 126	Pillette, 19	Pillette, 2.85
1923	83	71	2nd	16	Cobb	Heilmann, .403	Heilmann, 211	Heilmann, 18	Heilmann, 115	Dauss, 21	Dauss, 3.62
1924	86	68	3rd	6	Cobb	Bassler, Heilmann, .346	Cobb, 211	Heilmann, 10	Heilmann, 113	Whitehill, 17	Collins, 3.21
1925	81	73	4th	16½	Cobb	Heilmann, .393	Heilmann, 225	Heilmann, 13	Heilmann, 133	Dauss, 16	Dauss, 3.16
1926	79	75	6th	12	Cobb	Manush, .378	Manush, 188	Manush, 14	Heilmann, 103	Whitehill, 16	Collins, 2.73
1927	82	71	4th	27½	Moriarty	Heilmann, .398	Heilmann, 201	Heilmann, 14	Heilmann, 120	Whitehill, 16	Whitehill, 3.36
1928	68	86	6th	33	Moriarty	Heilmann, .328	Gehringer, 193	Heilmann, 14	Heilmann, 107	Carroll, 16	Carroll, 3.27
1929	70	84	6th	36	Harris	Heilmann, .344	Alexander, Gehringer, 215	Alexander, 25	Alexander, 137	Uhle, 15	Uhle, 4.08
1930	75	79	5th	27	Harris	Gehringer, .330	Gehringer, 201	Alexander, 20	Alexander, 135	Whitehill, 17	Uhle, 3.65
1931	61	93	7th	47	Harris	Stone, .327	Stone, 191	Stone, 10	Alexander, 87	Sorrell, Whitehill, 13	Uhle, 3.50
1932	76	75	5th	29½	Harris	Walker, .323	Gehringer, 184	Gehringer, 19	Stone, 108	Whitehill, 16	Bridges, 3.36
1933	75	79	5th	25	Harris, Baker	Gehringer, .325	Gehringer, 204	Gehringer, Greenberg, 12	Gehringer, 105	Marberry, 16	Bridges, 3.09
1934	101	53	1st	+7	Cochrane	Gehringer, .356	Gehringer, 214	Greenberg, 26	Greenberg, 139	Rowe, 24	Auker, 3.42
1935	93	58	1st	+3	Cochrane	Gehringer, .330	Greenberg, 203	Greenberg, 36	Greenberg, 170	Bridges, 21	Bridges, Sullivan, 3.51
1936	83	71	2nd	19½	Cochrane	Gehringer, .354	Gehringer, 227	Goslin, 24	Goslin, 125	Bridges, 23	Bridges, 3.60
1937	89	65	2nd	13	Cochrane, Perkins	Gehringer, .371	Walker, 213	Greenberg, 40	Greenberg, 183	Lawson, 18	Auker, 3.88
1938	84	70	4th	16	Cochrane, Baker	Greenberg, .315	Fox, 186	Greenberg, 58	Greenberg, 146	Bridges, 13	Benton, 3.30
1939	81	73	5th	26½	Baker	Gehringer, .325	McCosky, 190	Greenberg, 33	Greenberg, 112	Bridges, Newsom, 17	Newsom, 3.37
1940	90	64	1st	+1	Baker	Greenberg, McCosky, .340	McCosky, 200	Greenberg, 41	Greenberg, 150	Newsom, 21	Newsom, 2.83
1941	75	79	*4th	26	Baker	McCosky, .324	Higgins, 161	York, 27	York, 111	Benton, 15	Benton, 2.97
1942	73	81	5th	30	Baker	McCosky, .293	McCosky, 176	York, 21	York, 90	Trucks, 14	Newhouser, 2.45
1943	78	76	5th	20	O'Neill	Wakefield, .316	Wakefield, 200	York, 34	York, 118	Trout, 20	Bridges, 2.39
1944	88	66	2nd	1	O'Neill	Higgins, .297	Cramer, 169	York, 18	York, 98	Newhouser, 29	Trout, 2.12
1945	88	65	1st	+1½	O'Neill	Mayo, .285	York, 157	Cullenbine, York, 18	Cullenbine, 93	Newhouser, 25	Newhouser, 1.81
1946	92	62	2nd	12	O'Neill	Kell, .327	Lake, 149	Greenberg, 44	Greenberg, 127	Newhouser, 26	Newhouser, 1.94
1947	85	69	2nd	12	O'Neill	Kell, .320	Kell, 188	Cullenbine, 24	Kell, 93	Hutchinson, 18	Newhouser, 2.87
1948	78	76	5th	18½	O'Neill	Evers, .314	Evers, 169	Mullin, 23	Evers, 103	Newhouser, 21	Newhouser, 3.01
1949	87	67	4th	10	Rolfe	Kell, .343	Wertz, 185	Wertz, 20	Wertz, 133	Trucks, 19	Trucks, 2.81
1950	95	59	2nd	3	Rolfe	Kell, .340	Kell, 218	Wertz, 27	Wertz, 123	Houtteman, 19	Houtteman, 3.54
1951	73	81	5th	25	Rolfe	Kell, .319	Kell, 191	Wertz, 27	Wertz, 94	Trucks, 13	Hutchinson, 3.68
1952	50	104	8th	45	Rolfe, Hutchinson	Groth, .284	Groth, 149	Dropo, 23	Dropo, 70	Gray, 12	Newhouser, 3.74
1953	60	94	6th	40½	Hutchinson	Boone, .312	Kuenn, 209	Boone, 22	Dropo, 96	Garver, 11	Branca, 4.15
1954	68	86	5th	43	Hutchinson	Kuenn, .306	Kuenn, 201	Boone, 20	Boone, 85	Gromek, 18	Gromek, 2.74
1955	79	75	5th	17	Harris	Kaline, .340	Kaline, 200	Kaline, 27	Boone, 116	Hoeft, 16	Hoeft, 2.99
1956	82	72	5th	15	Harris	Kuenn, .332	Kuenn, 196	Maxwell, 28	Kaline, 128	Lary, 21	Lary, 3.15
1957	78	76	4th	20	Tighe	Kaline, .295	Kuenn, 173	Maxwell, 24	Kaline, 90	Bunning, 20	Bunning, 2.69
1958	77	77	5th	15	Tighe, Norman	Kuenn, .319	Kuenn, 179	Harris, 20	Kaline, 85	Lary, 16	Lary, 2.90
1959	76	78	4th	18	Norman, Dykes	Kuenn, .353	Kuenn, 198	Maxwell, 31	Maxwell, 95	Bunning, Lary, Mossi, 17	Mossi, 3.36
1960	71	83	6th	26	Dykes, Gordon	Kaline, .278	Kaline, 153	Colavito, 35	Colavito, 87	Lary, 15	Bunning, 2.79
1961	101	61	2nd	8	Scheffing	Cash, .361	Cash, 193	Colavito, 45	Colavito, 140	Lary, 23	Mossi, 2.96
1962	85	76	4th	10½	Scheffing	Kaline, .304	Colavito, 164	Cash, 39	Colavito, 112	Bunning, 19	Aguirre, 2.21
1963	79	83	*5th	25½	Scheffing, Dressen	Kaline, .312	Kaline, 172	Kaline, 27	Kaline, 101	Regan, 15	Lary, 3.27
1964	85	77	4th	14	Dressen	Freehan, .300	Lumpe, 160	McAuliffe, 24	Cash, 83	Wickersham, 19	Lolich, 3.26
1965	89	73	4th	13	Dressen, Swift	Kaline, .281	Wert, 159	Cash, 30	Horton, 104	McLain, 16	McLain, 2.61
1966	88	74	3rd	10	Dressen, Swift, Skaff	Kaline, .288	Cash, 168	Cash, 32	Horton, 100	McLain, 20	Wilson, 2.59
1967	91	71	*2nd	1	Smith	Kaline, .308	Freehan, 146	Kaline, 25	Kaline, 78	Wilson, 22	Lolich, 3.04
1968	103	59	1st	+12	Smith	Horton, .285	Northrup, 153	Horton, 36	Northrup, 90	McLain, 31	McLain, 1.96
							—EAST DIVISION—				
1969	90	72	2nd	19	Smith	Northrup, .295	Northrup, 160	Horton, 28	Horton, 91	McLain, 24	McLain, 2.80
1970	79	83	4th	29	Smith	Horton, .305	Stanley, 143	Northrup, 24	Northrup, 80	Lolich, 14	Hiller, 3.03
1971	91	71	2nd	12	Martin	Kaline, .294	Rodriguez, 153	Cash, 32	Cash, 91	Lolich, 25	Scherman, 2.71
1972	86	70	†1st	+½	Martin	Freehan, .262	Rodriguez, 142	Cash, 22	Cash, 61	Lolich, 22	Fryman, 2.06
1973	85	77	3rd	12	Martin, Schultz	Horton, .316	Stanley, 147	Cash, 19	Rodriguez, 58	Coleman, 23	Hiller, 1.44
1974	72	90	6th	19	Houk	Freehan, .297	Sutherland, 157	Freehan, 18	Kaline, 64	Hiller, 17	Hiller, 2.64
1975	57	102	6th	37½	Houk	Horton, .275	Horton, 169	Horton, 25	Horton, 92	Lolich, 12	Lolich, 3.78
1976	74	87	5th	24	Houk	LeFlore, .316	Staub, 176	Thompson, 17	Staub, 96	Fidrych, 19	Fidrych, 2.34
1977	74	88	4th	26	Houk	LeFlore, .325	LeFlore, 212	Thompson, 31	Thompson, 105	Rozema, 15	Rozema, 3.09
1978	86	76	5th	13½	Houk	LeFlore, .297	LeFlore, 198	Thompson, 26	Staub, 121	Slaton, 17	Hiller, 2.34
1979	85	76	5th	18	Moss, Anderson	Kemp, .318	LeFlore, 180	Kemp, 26	Kemp, 105	Morris, 17	Lopez, 2.41
1980	84	78	5th	19	Anderson	Trammell, .300	Trammell, 168	Parrish, 24	Kemp, 101	Morris, 16	P. Underwood, 3.59
1981	60	49	‡4th/2nd	—	Anderson	Gibson, .328	Kemp, 103	Parrish, 10	Kemp, 49	Morris, 14	Petry, 3.00
1982	83	79	4th	12	Anderson	Herndon, .292	Herndon, 179	Parrish, 32	Herndon, 88	Morris, 17	Petry, 3.22
1983	92	70	2nd	6	Anderson	Whitaker, .320	Whitaker, 206	Parrish, 27	Parrish, 114	Morris, 20	Lopez, 2.81
1984	104	58	§1st	+15	Anderson	Trammell, .314	Trammell, 174	Parrish, 33	Parrish, 98	Morris, 19	Hernandez, 1.92
1985	84	77	3rd	15	Anderson	K. Gibson, .287	Whitaker, 170	Evans, 40	Parrish, 98	Morris, 16	Hernandez, 2.70
1986	87	75	3rd	8½	Anderson	Trammell, .277	Trammell, 159	Evans, 29	Coles, Gibson, 86	Morris, 21	Morris, 3.27
1987	98	64	†1st	+2	Anderson	Trammell, .343	Trammell, 205	Evans, 34	Trammell, 105	Morris, 18	Henneman, 2.98
1988	88	74	2nd	1	Anderson	Trammell, .311	Trammell, 145	Evans, 22	Trammell, 69	Morris, 15	Henneman, 1.87
1989	59	103	7th	30	Anderson	Bergman, .268	Whitaker, 128	Whitaker, 28	Whitaker, 85	Henneman, 11	Tanana, 3.58
1990	79	83	3rd	9	Anderson	Trammell, .304	Trammell, 170	Fielder, 51	Fielder, 132	Morris, 15	P. Gibson, Henneman, 3.05
1991	84	78	2nd	7	Anderson	Phillips, .284	Fielder, 163	Fielder, 44	Fielder, 133	Gullickson, 20	Tanana, 3.77
1992	75	87	6th	21	Anderson	Livingstone, .282	Fryman, 175	Fielder, 35	Fielder, 124	Gullickson, 14	Doherty, 3.88
1993	85	77	*3rd	10	Anderson	Trammell, .329	Fryman, 182	Tettleton, 32	Tettleton, 117	Doherty, 14	Wells, 4.19
1994	53	62	5th	18	Anderson	Whitaker, .301	Phillips, 123	Fielder, 28	Fielder, 90	Moore, 11	Wells, 3.96
1995	60	84	4th	26	Anderson	Fryman, .275	Curtis, 157	Fielder, 31	Fielder, 82	Wells, 10	Wells, 3.04
1996	53	109	5th	39	Bell	Higginson, .320	Fryman, 165	Clark, 27	Fryman, 100	Olivares, 7	Olivares, 4.89
1997	79	83	3rd	19	Bell	Higginson, .299	Hunter, 177	Clark, 32	Clark, 117	Blair, 16	Thompson, 3.02
1998	65	97	5th	24	Bell, Parrish	Clark, .291	Clark, 175	Clark, 34	Clark, 103	Moehler, 14	Moehler, 3.90
1999	69	92	3rd	27½	Parrish	D.Cruz, .284	Clark, 150	Palmer, 38	Palmer, 100	Mlicki, 14	Mlicki, 4.60

* Tied for position. † Lost Championship Series. ‡ First half 31-26; second half 29-23. § Won Championship Series.

Note: Batting average minimum 350 at-bats; ERA minimum 90 innings pitched.

HISTORY

KANSAS CITY ROYALS

FRANCHISE CHRONOLOGY

First season: 1969, as one of two expansion teams in the American League. The young Royals excited their home fans with a 12-inning, 4-3 victory over the Minnesota Twins in their Major League debut and went on to carve out a respectable 69-93 first-season record, good for a fourth-place finish in the six-team A.L. West Division.

1970-present: It didn't take long for the Royals to become the model for future expansion franchises as they built an A.L. power through minor league player development and an astute series of trades. In 1976, their eighth major league season, the Royals joined the baseball elite by winning the first of three consecutive West Division championships, all of which were followed by heartbreaking losses to the New York Yankees in the A.L. Championship Series. The Royals turned the tables on the Yankees in 1980 for their first pennant, losing to Philadelphia in the World Series. But they captured their first Series championship in 1985 with a seven-game victory over the cross-state Cardinals. The Royals were one of five teams placed in the Central Division when baseball adopted a three-division format in 1994.

Third baseman George Brett.

ROYALS VS. OPPONENTS BY DECADE

	A's	Indians	Orioles	Red Sox	Tigers	Twins	White Sox	Yankees	Angels	Rangers	Brewers	Blue Jays	Mariners	Devil Rays	Interleague	Decade Record
1969	8-10	5-7	1-11	2-10	4-8	8-10	10-8	5-7	9-9	7-5	10-8					69-93
1970-79	79-90	65-52	51-65	63-53	63-54	85-84	89-79	53-64	87-79	84-69	80-48	22-10	30-13			851-760
1980-89	64-59	62-54	61-55	65-49	59-54	68-62	64-55	52-68	73-50	70-54	58-59	60-56	70-59			826-734
1990-99	53-68	49-64	43-62	51-52	56-57	64-61	52-72	45-61	56-64	56-61	50-47	55-62	64-55	10-11	21-28	725-825
Totals	204-227	181-177	156-193	181-164	182-173	225-217	215-214	155-200	225-202	217-189	198-162	137-128	164-127	10-11	21-28	2471-2412

Interleague results: 4-5 vs. Cubs; 3-5 vs. Reds; 3-6 vs. Astros;4-4 vs. Pirates; 5-4 vs. Cardinals; 2-4 vs. Brewers.

MANAGERS

Name	Years	Record
Joe Gordon	1969	69-93
Charlie Metro	1970	19-33
Bob Lemon	1970-72	207-218
Jack McKeon	1973-75	215-205
Whitey Herzog	1974-79	410-304
Jim Frey	1980-81	127-105
Dick Howser	1981-86	404-365
Mike Ferraro	1986	36-38
Billy Gardner	1987	62-64
John Wathan	1987-91	287-270
Bob Schaefer	1991	1-0
Hal McRae	1991-94	286-277
Bob Boone	1995-97	181-206
Tony Muser	1997-99	167-234

WORLD SERIES CHAMPIONS

Year	Loser	Length	MVP
1985	St. Louis	7 games	Saberhagen

A.L. PENNANT WINNERS

Year	Record	Manager	Series Result
1980	97-65	Frey	Lost to Phillies
1985	91-71	Howser	Defeated Cardinals

WEST DIVISION CHAMPIONS

Year	Record	Manager	ALCS Result
1976	90-72	Herzog	Lost to Yankees
1977	102-60	Herzog	Lost to Yankees
1978	92-70	Herzog	Lost to Yankees
1980	97-65	Frey	Defeated Yankees
*1981	50-53	Frey, Howser	None
1984	84-78	Howser	Lost to Tigers
1985	91-71	Howser	Defeated Blue Jays

* Second-half champion; lost division playoff to A's.

ALL-TIME RECORD OF EXPANSION TEAMS

Team	W	L	Pct.	DT	P	WS
Arizona	165	159	.509	1	0	0
Kansas City	2,471	2,412	.506	6	2	1
Toronto	1,784	1,818	.495	5	2	2
Houston	2,980	3,048	.494	6	0	0
Montreal	2,387	2,501	.488	2	0	0
Anaheim	2,987	3,201	.483	3	0	0
Milwaukee	2,348	2,542	.480	2	1	0
Colorado	512	559	.478	0	0	0
New York	2,840	3,178	.472	4	3	2
Texas	2,881	3,290	.467	4	0	0
San Diego	2,239	2,656	.457	3	2	0
Seattle	1,624	1,977	.451	2	0	0
Florida	472	596	.442	0	1	1
Tampa Bay	132	192	.407	0	0	0

DT—Division Titles. P—Pennants won. WS—World Series won.

ATTENDANCE HIGHS

Total	Season	Park
2,477,700	1989	Royals Stadium
2,392,471	1987	Royals Stadium
2,350,181	1988	Royals Stadium
2,320,764	1986	Royals Stadium
2,288,714	1980	Royals Stadium

BALLPARK CHRONOLOGY

Kauffman Stadium (1973-present)
Capacity: 40,529.
First game: Royals 12, Texas 1 (April 10, 1973).
First batter: Dave Nelson, Rangers.
First hit: Amos Oits, Royals (single).
First run: Fred Patek, Royals (1st inning).
First home run: John Mayberry, Royals.
First winning pitcher: Paul Splittorff, Royals.
First-season attendance: 1,345,341.

Municipal Stadium (1969-72)
Capacity: 35,020.
First game: Royals 4, Minnesota 3, 12 innings (April 8, 1969).
First-season attendance: 902,414.

Note: Kauffman Stadium was known as Royals Stadium from 1973-93.

A.L. MVP
George Brett, 3B, 1980

CY YOUNG WINNERS
Bret Saberhagen, RH, 1985
Bret Saberhagen, RH, 1989
David Cone, RH, 1994

ROOKIES OF THE YEAR
Lou Piniella, OF, 1969
Bob Hamelin, DH, 1994
Carlos Beltran, OF, 1999

RETIRED UNIFORMS

No.	Name	Pos.
5	George Brett	3B
10	Dick Howser	Man.
20	Frank White	2B

Hal McRae was a key contributor to the Royals' 1970s success.

MILESTONE PERFORMANCES

25-plus home runs
36— Steve Balboni 1985
35— Gary Gaetti 1995
34— John Mayberry 1975
    Danny Tartabull........................1987
    Dean Palmer 1998
32— Bo Jackson 1989
31— Danny Tartabull......................1991
30— George Brett 1985
    Chili Davis................................1997
29— Steve Balboni 1986
28— Steve Balboni 1984
    Bo Jackson 1990
    Jeff King 1997
27— Hal McRae 1982
    Bob Oliver 1970
    Jermaine Dye 1999
26— John Mayberry 1973
    Amos Otis 1973
    Danny Tartabull........................1988
25— John Mayberry 1972
    George Brett 1983
    Bo Jackson 1988

100-plus RBIs
133— Hal McRae 1982
119— Dean Palmer 1998
     Jermaine Dye 1999
118— George Brett 1980
112— Al Cowens.............................1977
     Darrell Porter 1979
     George Brett 1985
     Jeff King 1997
108— Carlos Beltran 1999
107— George Brett 1979
106— John Mayberry 1975
105— Bo Jackson 1989
103— George Brett 1988
102— Danny Tartabull......................1988
     Mike Sweeney...........................1999
101— Danny Tartabull......................1987
100— John Mayberry 1972, 1973
     Danny Tartabull........................1991

20-plus victories
1973— Paul Splittorff 20-11
1974— Steve Busby 22-14
1977— Dennis Leonard 20-12
1978— Dennis Leonard 21-17
1980— Dennis Leonard 20-11
1985— Bret Saberhagen 20-6
1988— Mark Gubicza 20-8
1989— Bret Saberhagen 23-6

A.L. home run champions
None

A.L. RBI champions
1982— Hal McRae 133

A.L. batting champions
1976— George Brett 333
1980— George Brett 390
1982— Willie Wilson 332
1990— George Brett 329

A.L. ERA champions
1989— Bret Saberhagen 2.16
1993— Kevin Appier 2.56

A.L. strikeout champions
None

No-hit pitchers
(9 innings or more)
1973— Steve Busby ....3-0 vs. Detroit
1974— Steve Busby ....2-0 vs. Milwaukee
1977— Jim Colborn ....6-0 vs. Texas
1991— Bret Saberhagen ....7-0 vs. Chicago

Longest hitting streaks
30— George Brett 1980
27— Jose Offerman 1998
25— George Brett 1983
    Mike Sweeney...........................1999
22— Brian McRae 1991
19— Amos Otis 1974
18— Lou Piniella 1970
    Ed Kirkpatrick 1973
    Willie Wilson.............................1984
    Gregg Jefferies 1992
    Joe Randa 1999
17— Hal McRae 1974
    Willie Wilson.............................1982
    Kevin Seitzer 1990
    Kevin McReynolds 1992
    Vince Coleman 1995
16— John Mayberry 1975
    Al Cowens...............................1977
    George Brett 1987
    George Brett 1990
    Gregg Jefferies 1992
    Jose Lind 1994
    Johnny Damon 1999
    Mike Sweeney...........................1999
15— Willie Wilson............................1981
    George Brett 1985
    Kevin Seitzer 1989

INDIVIDUAL SEASON, GAME RECORDS

Lefthander Paul Splittorff, who spent 15 popular years in Kansas City, holds several career team records.

SEASON

Batting
At-bats	705	Willie Wilson	1980
Runs	133	Willie Wilson	1980
Hits	230	Willie Wilson	1980
Singles	184	Willie Wilson	1980
Doubles	54	Hal McRae	1977
Triples	21	Willie Wilson	1985
Home runs	36	Steve Balboni	1985
Home runs, rookie	24	Bob Hamelin	1994
Grand slams	3	Danny Tartabull	1988
Total bases	363	George Brett	1979
RBIs	133	Hal McRae	1982
Walks	122	John Mayberry	1973
Most strikeouts	172	Bo Jackson	1989
Fewest strikeouts	22	George Brett	1980
Batting average	.390	George Brett	1980
Slugging pct.	.664	George Brett	1980
Stolen bases	83	Willie Wilson	1979

Pitching
Games	84	Dan Quisenberry	1985
Complete games	21	Dennis Leonard	1977
Innings	294.2	Dennis Leonard	1978
Wins	23	Bret Saberhagen	1989
Losses	19	Paul Splittorff	1974
Winning pct.	.793 (23-6)	Bret Saberhagen	1989
Walks	120	Mark Gubicza	1987
Strikeouts	244	Dennis Leonard	1977
Shutouts	6	Roger Nelson	1972
Home runs allowed	37	Tim Belcher	1998
Lowest ERA	2.08	Roger Nelson	1972
Saves	45	Dan Quisenberry	1983
		Jeff Montgomery	1993

GAME

Batting
Runs	5	Tony Solaita	6-18-75
		Tom Poquette	6-15-76
Hits	6	Bob Oliver	5-4-69
		Kevin Seitzer	8-2-87
Doubles	3	Last by Carlos Beltran	5-14-99
Triples	2	Last by Carlos Beltran	9-21-98
Home runs	3	Last by Danny Tartabull	7-6-91
RBIs	7	Last by Johnny Damon	8-10-96
Total bases	13	George Brett	4-20-83
		Kevin Seitzer	8-2-87
Stolen bases	5	Amos Otis	9-7-71

Frank White, an eight-time Gold Glove-winning second baseman, spent his entire 17-year career with the Royals.

CAREER LEADERS

BATTING

Games

George Brett	2,707
Frank White	2,324
Amos Otis	1,891
Hal McRae	1,837
Willie Wilson	1,787
Fred Patek	1,245
John Mayberry	897
Mike Macfarlane	887
Cookie Rojas	880
John Wathan	860

At-bats

George Brett	10,349
Frank White	7,859
Amos Otis	7,050
Willie Wilson	6,799
Hal McRae	6,568
Fred Patek	4,305
John Mayberry	3,131
Cookie Rojas	3,072
Mike Macfarlane	2,794
Al Cowens	2,785

Runs

George Brett	1,583
Amos Otis	1,074
Willie Wilson	1,060
Frank White	912
Hal McRae	873
Fred Patek	571
John Mayberry	459
Kevin Seitzer	408
Al Cowens	373
Johnny Damon	368

Hits

George Brett	3,154
Frank White	2,006
Amos Otis	1,977
Willie Wilson	1,968
Hal McRae	1,924
Fred Patek	1,036
Cookie Rojas	824
John Mayberry	816
Kevin Seitzer	809
Al Cowens	784

Doubles

George Brett	665
Hal McRae	449
Frank White	407
Amos Otis	365
Willie Wilson	241
Fred Patek	182
Mike Macfarlane	174
Danny Tartabull	141
John Mayberry	139
Cookie Rojas	139

Triples

George Brett	137
Willie Wilson	133
Amos Otis	65
Hal McRae	63
Frank White	58
Al Cowens	44
Fred Patek	41
Johnny Damon	37
Brian McRae	32
U.L. Washington	28

Home runs

George Brett	317
Amos Otis	193
Hal McRae	169
Frank White	160
John Mayberry	143
Danny Tartabull	124
Steve Balboni	119
Bo Jackson	109
Mike Macfarlane	103
Willie Aikens	77

Total bases

George Brett	5,044
Amos Otis	3,051
Frank White	3,009
Hal McRae	3,006
Willie Wilson	2,595
John Mayberry	1,404
Fred Patek	1,384
Mike Macfarlane	1,231
Danny Tartabull	1,205
Al Cowens	1,124

Runs batted in

George Brett	1,595
Hal McRae	1,012

TEAM SEASON, GAME RECORDS

SEASON

Batting

Most at-bats	5,714	1980
Most runs	856	1999
Fewest runs	586	1969
Most hits	1,633	1980
Most singles	1,193	1980
Most doubles	316	1990
Most triples	79	1979
Most home runs	168	1987
Fewest home runs	65	1976
Most grand slams	7	1991
Most pinch-hit home runs	6	1995
Most total bases	2,440	1977
Most stolen bases	218	1976
Highest batting average	.286	1980
Lowest batting average	.240	1969
Highest slugging pct	.436	1977

Pitching

Lowest ERA	3.21	1976
Highest ERA	5.35	1999
Most complete games	54	1974
Most shutouts	16	1972
Most saves	50	1984
Most walks	643	1999
Most strikeouts	1,006	1990

Fielding

Most errors	167	1973
Fewest errors	91	1997
Most double plays	192	1973
Highest fielding average	.985	1997

General

Most games won	102	1977
Most games lost	97	1970, 1999
Highest win pct	.630	1977
Lowest win pct	.398	1999

GAME, INNING

Batting

Most runs, game	23	4-6-74
Most runs, inning	11	8-6-79, 8-2-86
Most hits, game	24	6-15-76
Most home runs, game	6	7-14-91
Most total bases, game	37	9-12-82

Center fielder Amos Otis posted career numbers second only to George Brett among Royals players.

Amos Otis	992
Frank White	886
John Mayberry	552
Willie Wilson	509
Danny Tartabull	425
Mike Macfarlane	398
Fred Patek	382
Al Cowens	374

Extra-base hits

George Brett	1,119
Hal McRae	681
Frank White	625
Amos Otis	623
Willie Wilson	414
Mike Macfarlane	293
John Mayberry	292
Danny Tartabull	274
Fred Patek	251
Steve Balboni	214

Batting average
(Minimum 500 games)

George Brett	.305
Kevin Seitzer	.294
Wally Joyner	.293
Hal McRae	.293
Danny Tartabull	.290
Willie Wilson	.289
Lou Piniella	.286
Johnny Damon	.283
Willie Aikens	.282
Al Cowens	.282

Stolen bases

Willie Wilson	612
Amos Otis	340
Fred Patek	336
George Brett	201
Frank White	178
Tom Goodwin	150
U.L. Washington	120
Johnny Damon	110
Hal McRae	105
John Wathan	105

PITCHING

Earned-run average
(Minimum 500 innings)

Dan Quisenberry	2.55
Steve Farr	3.05
Jeff Montgomery	3.20
Bret Saberhagen	3.21

Kevin Appier	3.46
Al Fitzmorris	3.46
Marty Pattin	3.48
Dick Drago	3.52
Doug Bird	3.56
Charlie Leibrandt	3.60

Wins

Paul Splittorff	166
Dennis Leonard	144
Mark Gubicza	132
Kevin Appier	114
Larry Gura	111
Bret Saberhagen	110
Tom Gordon	79
Charlie Leibrandt	76
Steve Busby	70
Al Fitzmorris	70

Losses

Paul Splittorff	143
Mark Gubicza	135
Dennis Leonard	106
Kevin Appier	89
Larry Gura	78
Bret Saberhagen	78
Tom Gordon	71
Dick Drago	70
Charlie Leibrandt	61
Bud Black	57

Innings pitched

Paul Splittorff	2,554.2
Mark Gubicza	2,218.2
Dennis Leonard	2,187.0
Kevin Appier	1,820.2
Larry Gura	1,701.1
Bret Saberhagen	1,660.1
Charlie Leibrandt	1,257.0
Tom Gordon	1,149.2
Dick Drago	1,134.0
Al Fitzmorris	1,098.0

Strikeouts

Kevin Appier	1,451
Mark Gubicza	1,366
Dennis Leonard	1,323
Bret Saberhagen	1,093
Paul Splittorff	1,057
Tom Gordon	999
Jeff Montgomery	720
Steve Busby	659
Larry Gura	633
Charlie Leibrandt	618

Bases on balls

Mark Gubicza	783
Paul Splittorff	780
Kevin Appier	624
Dennis Leonard	622
Tom Gordon	587
Larry Gura	503
Steve Busby	433
Al Fitzmorris	359
Charlie Leibrandt	359
Bret Saberhagen	331

Games

Jeff Montgomery	686
Dan Quisenberry	573
Paul Splittorff	429
Mark Gubicza	382
Dennis Leonard	312
Larry Gura	310
Doug Bird	292
Steve Farr	289
Kevin Appier	281
Hipolito Pichardo	281

Shutouts

Dennis Leonard	23
Paul Splittorff	17
Mark Gubicza	16
Larry Gura	14
Bret Saberhagen	14
Al Fitzmorris	11
Kevin Appier	10
Dick Drago	10
Charlie Leibrandt	10
Steve Busby	7
Roger Nelson	7
Jim Rooker	7

Saves

Jeff Montgomery	304
Dan Quisenberry	238
Doug Bird	58
Steve Farr	49
Ted Abernathy	40
Al Hrabosky	31
Tom Burgmeier	28
Mark Littell	28
Steve Mingori	27
Gene Garber	26

Year	W	L	Place	Games Back	Manager	Batting avg.	Hits	Home runs	RBIs	Wins	ERA
								—WEST DIVISION—			
1969	69	93	4th	28	Gordon	Piniella, .282	Foy, 139	Kirkpatrick, 14	Piniella, 68	Bunker, 12	Drabowsky, 2.94
1970	65	97	*4th	33	Metro, Lemon	Piniella, .301	Otis, 176	Oliver, 27	Oliver, 99	Rooker, 10	Johnson, 3.07
1971	85	76	2nd	16	Lemon	Otis, .301	Otis, 167	Otis, 15	Otis, 79	Drago, 17	Splittorff, 2.68
1972	76	78	4th	16½	Lemon	Piniella, .312	Piniella, 179	Mayberry, 25	Mayberry, 100	Drago, Splittorff, 12	Nelson, 2.08
1973	88	74	2nd	6	McKeon	Otis, .300	Otis, 175	Mayberry, Otis, 26	Mayberry, 100	Splittorff, 20	Bird, 2.99
1974	77	85	5th	13	McKeon	H. McRae, .310	H. McRae, 167	Mayberry, 22	H. McRae, 88	Busby, 22	Bird, 2.73
1975	91	71	2nd	7	McKeon, Herzog	Brett, .308	Brett, 195	Mayberry, 34	Mayberry, 106	Busby, 18	Busby, 3.08
1976	90	72	†1st	+2½	Herzog	Brett, .333	Brett, 215	Otis, 18	Mayberry, 95	Leonard, 17	Littell, 2.08
1977	102	60	†1st	+8	Herzog	Brett, .312	H. McRae, 191	Cowens, Mayberry, 23	Cowens, 112	Leonard, 20	Leonard, 3.04
1978	92	70	†1st	+5	Herzog	Otis, .298	H. McRae, 170	Otis, 22	Otis, 96	Leonard, 21	Gura, 2.72
1979	85	77	2nd	3	Herzog	Brett, .329	Brett, 212	Brett, 23	Porter, 112	Splittorff, 15	Busby, 3.63
1980	97	65	‡1st	+14	Frey	Brett, .390	Wilson, 230	Brett, 24	Brett, 118	Leonard, 20	Gura, 2.95
1981	50	53	§5th/1st	—	Frey, Howser	Brett, .314	Wilson, 133	Aikens, 17	Otis, 57	Leonard, 13	Gura, 2.72
1982	90	72	2nd	3	Howser	Wilson, .332	Wilson, 194	H. McRae, 27	H. McRae, 133	Gura, 18	Quisenberry, 2.57
1983	79	83	2nd	20	Howser	H. McRae, .311	H. McRae, 183	Brett, 25	Brett, 93	Splittorff, 13	Quisenberry, 1.94
1984	84	78	†1st	+3	Howser	Wilson, .301	Wilson, 163	Balboni, 28	Balboni, 77	Black, 17	Quisenberry, 2.64
1985	91	71	‡1st	+1	Howser	Brett, .335	Brett, 184	Balboni, 36	Brett, 112	Saberhagen, 20	Quisenberry, 2.37
1986	76	86	*3rd	16	Howser, Ferraro	Brett, .290	Wilson, 170	Balboni, 29	Balboni, 88	Leibrandt, 14	Farr, 3.13
1987	83	79	2nd	2	Gardner, Wathan	Seitzer, .323	Seitzer, 207	Tartabull, 34	Tartabull, 101	Saberhagen, 18	Saberhagen, 3.36
1988	84	77	3rd	19½	Wathan	Brett, .306	Brett, 180	Tartabull, 26	Brett, 103	Gubicza, 20	Gubicza, 2.70
1989	92	70	2nd	7	Wathan	Eisenreich, .293	Seitzer, 168	Jackson, 32	Jackson 105	Saberhagen, 23	Saberhagen, 2.16
1990	75	86	6th	27½	Wathan	Brett, .329	Brett, 179	Jackson, 28	Brett, 87	Farr, 13	Farr, 1.98
1991	82	80	6th	13	Wathan, Schaefer, H. McRae	Tartabull, .316	B. McRae, 164	Tartabull, 31	Tartabull, 100	Appier, Saberhagen, 13	Montgomery, 2.90
1992	72	90	*5th	24	H. McRae	Brett, Jefferies, .285	Jefferies, 172	Macfarlane, 17	Jefferies, 75	Appier, 15	Appier, 2.46
1993	84	78	3rd	10	H. McRae	Joyner, .292	B. McRae, 177	Macfarlane, 20	Brett, 75	Appier, 18	Appier, 2.56
								—CENTRAL DIVISION—			
1994	64	51	3rd	4	H. McRae	Joyner, .311	B. McRae, 119	Hamelin, 24	Hamelin, 65	Cone, 16	Cone, 2.94
1995	70	74	2nd	30	Boone	Joyner, .310	Joyner, 144	Gaetti, 35	Gaetti, 96	Appier, 15	Gubicza, 3.75
1996	75	86	5th	24	Boone	Offerman, .303	Offerman, 170	Paquette, 22	Paquette, 67	Belcher, 15	Rosado, 3.21
1997	67	94	5th	19	Boone, Muser	Offerman, .297	Bell, 167	Davis, 30	King, 112	Belcher, 13	Appier, 3.40
1998	72	89	3rd	16½	Muser	Offerman, .315	Offerman, 191	Palmer, 34	Palmer, 119	Belcher, 14	Belcher, 4.27
1999	64	97	4th	32½	Muser	Sweeney, .322	Randa, 197	Dye, 27	Dye, 119	Rosado, Suppan, 10	Rosado, 3.85

* Tied for position. † Lost Championship Series. ‡ Won Championship Series. § First half 20-30; second half 30-23.

Note: Batting average minimum 350 at-bats; ERA minimum 90 innings pitched.

Roger Nelson

THE ROYALS were born as part of a four-team 1969 expansion that included the Seattle Pilots in the American League and the San Diego Padres and Montreal Expos in the National League. The franchise came to life on January 11, 1968, when Kansas City businessman Ewing Kauffman was awarded a team that would compete in the A.L.'s newly-created Western Division.

The Royals grabbed righthanded pitcher Roger Nelson with their first pick of the expansion draft and went on to select 30 players, concentrating heavily on youth. The team won its Major League debut on April 8, 1969, when Joe Keough's 12th-inning sacrifice fly produced a 4-3 victory over Minnesota at Kansas City's Municipal Stadium.

Expansion draft (October 15, 1968)

Players
Jerry Adair	Boston	second base
Mike Fiore	Baltimore	first base
Joe Foy	Boston	third base
Bill Harris	Cleveland	second base
Dan Haynes	Chicago	first base
Fran Healy	Cleveland	catcher
Jackie Hernandez	Minnesota	shortstop
Pat Kelly	Minnesota	outfield
Joe Keough	Oakland	outfield
Scott Northey	Chicago	outfield
Bob Oliver	Minnesota	first base
Ellie Rodriguez	New York	catcher
Paul Schaal	California	third base
Steve Whitaker	New York	outfield

Pitchers
Ike Brookens	Washington	righthander
Wally Bunker	Baltimore	righthander
Tom Burgmeier	California	lefthander
Bill Butler	Detroit	lefthander
Jerry Cram	Minnesota	righthander
Moe Drabowsky	Baltimore	righthander
Dick Drago	Detroit	righthander
Al Fitzmorris	Chicago	righthander
Mike Hedlund	Cleveland	righthander
Steve Jones	Washington	lefthander
Dave Morehead	Boston	righthander
*Roger Nelson	Baltimore	righthander
Don O'Riley	Oakland	righthander
Jim Rooker	New York	lefthander
Jon Warden	Detroit	lefthander
Hoyt Wilhelm	Chicago	righthander

*First pick

Opening day lineup
April 8, 1969

Lou Piniella, center field
Jerry Adair, second base
Ed Kirkpatrick, left field
Joe Foy, third base
Chuck Harrison, first base
Bob Oliver, right field
Ellie Rodriguez, catcher
Jackie Hernandez, shortstop
Wally Bunker, pitcher

Lou Piniella

Royals firsts

First hit: Lou Piniella, April 8, 1969, vs. Minnesota (double)
First home run: Mike Fiore, April 13, 1969, vs. Oakland
First RBI: Jerry Adair, April 8, 1969, vs. Minnesota
First win: Moe Drabowsky, April 8, 1969, vs. Minnesota
First shutout: Roger Nelson, May 21, 1969, 4-0 at Cleveland

HISTORY

MINNESOTA TWINS

FRANCHISE CHRONOLOGY

First season: 1901, in Washington, as a member of the new American League. The Senators recorded a 5-1 victory over Philadelphia in their major league debut and went on to post a 61-72 record, good for sixth place in the eight-team A.L. field.

1902-1960: To say the Senators struggled through their 60-year existence is an understatement. Through the 1911 season, the Senators never finished higher than sixth place and they failed to win their first pennant until 1924. In their six Washington decades, they qualified for the World Series three times, winning once—a 1924 victory over the Giants.

1961-present: The Senators were shifted to Minnesota after the 1960 season as part of a complicated A.L. expansion that brought the Angels and another Washington Senators team into existence. The Twins shut out the Yankees, 6-0, in their first game and went on to record a 70-90 record. The change of scenery proved agreeable. By 1965, the Twins were consistent contenders who would win three pennants, two World Series and four West Division titles over the next three decades. The Twins were assigned to the Central Division when baseball adopted its three-division format in 1994.

Third baseman Harmon Killebrew.

TWINS VS. OPPONENTS BY DECADE

	A's	Indians	Orioles	Red Sox	Tigers	White Sox	Yankees	Angels	Rangers	Brewers	Royals	Blue Jays	Mariners	Devil Rays	Interleague	Decade Record
1901-09	56-128	72-118	81-108	76-113	72-114	57-130	66-122									480-833
1910-19	101-108	123-92	119-96	93-115	100-116	106-109	113-101									755-737
1920-29	108-105	106-113	108-111	135-82	113-107	125-95	97-122									792-735
1930-39	124-91	104-114	135-84	128-90	102-118	117-101	96-124									806-722
1940-49	125-95	104-115	110-110	86-133	90-130	93-124	69-151									677-858
1950-59	107-113	79-141	103-117	100-120	99-121	79-141	73-145									640-898
1960-69	105-79	82-96	87-91	104-74	90-88	101-83	90-87	82-79	99-56	12-6	10-8					862-747
1970-79	91-76	56-58	52-64	47-70	68-48	89-76	44-72	77-89	80-76	75-54	84-85	26-6	23-20			812-794
1980-89	58-69	56-55	51-63	53-62	54-66	66-57	43-71	57-66	64-65	52-68	62-68	50-64	67-59			733-833
1990-99	58-60	52-70	45-63	62-48	60-53	48-71	50-58	61-54	50-70	46-52	61-64	38-72	51-65	12-9	24-24	718-833
Totals	933-924	834-972	891-907	884-907	842-955	887-993	741-1053	277-288	293-267	185-180	217-225	114-142	141-144	12-9	24-24	7275-7990

Interleague results: 4-5 vs. Cubs; 5-4 vs. Reds; 4-4 vs. Astros; 5-4 vs. Pirates; 4-5 vs. Cardinals; 2-2 vs. Brewers.

MANAGERS

(Washington Senators, 1901-1960)

Name	Years	Record
Jimmy Manning	1901	61-72
Tom Loftus	1902-03	104-169
Patsy Donovan	1904	38-113
Jake Stahl	1905-06	119-182
Joe Cantillon	1907-09	158-297
Jimmy McAleer	1910-11	130-175
Clark Griffith	1912-20	693-646
George McBride	1921	80-73
Clyde Milan	1922	69-85
Donie Bush	1923	75-78
Bucky Harris	1924-28, 1935-42, 1950-54	1336-1416
Walter Johnson	1929-32	350-264
Joe Cronin	1933-34	165-139
Ossie Bluege	1943-47	375-394
Joe Kuhel	1948-49	106-201
Chuck Dressen	1955-57	116-212
Cookie Lavagetto	1957-61	271-384
Sam Mele	1961-67	524-436
Cal Ermer	1967-68	145-129
Billy Martin	1969	97-65
Bill Rigney	1970-72	208-184
Frank Quilici	1972-75	280-287
Gene Mauch	1976-80	378-394
Johnny Goryl	1980-81	34-38
Billy Gardner	1981-85	268-353
Ray Miller	1985-86	109-130
Tom Kelly	1986-99	986-1074

WORLD SERIES CHAMPIONS

Year	Loser	Length	MVP
1924	N.Y. Giants	7 games	None
1987	St. Louis	7 games	Viola
1991	Atlanta	7 games	Morris

A.L. PENNANT WINNERS

Year	Record	Manager	Series Result
1924	92-62	Harris	Defeated Giants
1925	96-55	Harris	Lost to Pirates
1933	99-53	Cronin	Lost to Giants
1965	102-60	Mele	Lost to Dodgers
1987	85-77	Kelly	Defeated Cardinals
1991	95-67	Kelly	Defeated Braves

WEST DIVISION CHAMPIONS

Year	Record	Manager	ALCS Result
1969	97-65	Martin	Lost to Orioles
1970	98-64	Rigney	Lost to Orioles
1987	85-77	Kelly	Defeated Tigers
1991	95-67	Kelly	Defeated Blue Jays

ATTENDANCE HIGHS

Total	Season	Park
3,030,672	1988	Metrodome
2,482,428	1992	Metrodome
2,293,842	1991	Metrodome
2,277,438	1989	Metrodome
2,081,976	1987	Metrodome

BALLPARK CHRONOLOGY

Hubert H. Humphrey Metrodome (1982-present)
Capacity: 48,678.
First game: Seattle 11, Twins 7 (April 6, 1982).
First batter: Julio Cruz, Mariners.
First hit: Dave Engle, Twins (home run).
First run: Dave Engle, Twins (1st inning).
First home run: Dave Engle, Twins.
First winning pitcher: Floyd Bannister, Mariners.
First-season attendance: 921,186.

American League Park, Washington, D.C. (1901-02)
Capacity: 10,000.
First game: Senators 5, Baltimore 2 (April 29, 1901).
First-season attendance: 161,661.

Griffith Stadium, Washington, D.C. (1903-60)
Capacity: 27,410.
First game: Senators 3, New York 1 (April 22, 1903).
First-season attendance: 128,878.

Metropolitan Stadium, Minnesota (1961-81)
Capacity: 45,919.
First game: Washington 5, Twins 3 (April 21, 1961).
First-season attendance: 1,256,723.

Note: Griffith Stadium was known as National Park from 1901-20.

A.L. MVPs

Zoilo Versalles, SS, 1965
Harmon Killebrew, 1B-3B, 1969
Rod Carew, 1B, 1977

CY YOUNG WINNERS

Jim Perry, RH, 1970
Frank Viola, LH, 1988

ROOKIES OF THE YEAR

Albie Pearson, OF, 1958
Bob Allison, OF, 1959
Tony Oliva, OF, 1964
Rod Carew, 2B, 1967
*John Castino, 3B, 1979
Chuck Knoblauch, 2B, 1991
Marty Cordova, OF, 1995
    * Co-winner

MANAGER OF THE YEAR

Tom Kelly, 1991

RETIRED UNIFORMS

No.	Name	Pos.
3	Harmon Killebrew	3B-1B
6	Tony Oliva	OF
14	Kent Hrbek	1B
29	Rod Carew	2B-1B
34	Kirby Puckett	OF

The Twins' 1970 staff featured (left to right) Dave Boswell, Jim Perry, Jim Kaat and Luis Tiant.

30-plus home runs
49—	Harmon Killebrew	1964, 1969
48—	Harmon Killebrew	1962
46—	Harmon Killebrew	1961
45—	Harmon Killebrew	1963
44—	Harmon Killebrew	1967
42—	Roy Sievers	1957
	Harmon Killebrew	1959
41—	Harmon Killebrew	1970
39—	Roy Sievers	1958
	Harmon Killebrew	1966
38—	Jim Lemon	1960
35—	Bob Allison	1963
34—	Gary Gaetti	1986
	Kent Hrbek	1987
33—	Jim Lemon	1959
	Jimmie Hall	1963
32—	Bob Allison	1964
	Tony Oliva	1964
	Tom Brunansky	1984, 1987
31—	Harmon Killebrew	1960
	Kirby Puckett	1986
	Gary Gaetti	1987
30—	Bob Allison	1959

100-plus RBIs
140—	Harmon Killebrew	1969
129—	Goose Goslin	1924
126—	Joe Cronin	1930, 1931
	Harmon Killebrew	1962
122—	Harmon Killebrew	1961
121—	Kirby Puckett	1988
120—	Goose Goslin	1927
119—	Harmon Killebrew	1971
	Larry Hisle	1977
118—	Joe Cronin	1933
	Joe Kuhel	1936
116—	Joe Cronin	1932
	Heinie Manush	1932
115—	Mickey Vernon	1953
114—	Zeke Bonura	1938
	Roy Sievers	1957
113—	Goose Goslin	1925
	Harmon Killebrew	1967, 1970
	Paul Molitor	1996
112—	Kirby Puckett	1994
111—	Harmon Killebrew	1964
	Marty Cordova	1996
110—	Harmon Killebrew	1966
	Kirby Puckett	1992
109—	Gary Gaetti	1987
108—	Goose Goslin	1926
	Roy Sievers	1958
	Gary Gaetti	1986
107—	Joe Kuhel	1933
	Tony Oliva	1970
	Kent Hrbek	1984
106—	Roy Sievers	1955
105—	Harmon Killebrew	1959
	Bob Allison	1961
102—	Goose Goslin	1928
	Roy Sievers	1954
	Bob Allison	1962
101—	Joe Cronin	1934
	Cecil Travis	1941
	Tony Oliva	1969
100—	Buddy Myer	1935
	Stan Spence	1944
	Jim Lemon	1959, 1960
	Rod Carew	1977

20-plus victories
1910—	Walter Johnson	25-17
1911—	Walter Johnson	25-13
1912—	Walter Johnson	33-12
	Bob Groom	24-13
1913—	Walter Johnson	36-7
1914—	Walter Johnson	28-18
1915—	Walter Johnson	27-13
1916—	Walter Johnson	25-20
1917—	Walter Johnson	23-16
1918—	Walter Johnson	23-13
1919—	Walter Johnson	20-14
1924—	Walter Johnson	23-7
1925—	Stan Coveleski	20-5
	Walter Johnson	20-7
1932—	General Crowder	26-13
	Monte Weaver	22-10
1933—	General Crowder	24-15
	Earl Whitehill	22-8
1939—	Dutch Leonard	20-8
1945—	Roger Wolff	20-10
1953—	Bob Porterfield	22-10
1962—	Camilo Pascual	20-11
1963—	Camilo Pascual	21-9
1965—	Mudcat Grant	21-7
1966—	Jim Kaat	25-13
1967—	Dean Chance	20-14
1969—	Jim Perry	20-6
	Dave Boswell	20-12
1970—	Jim Perry	24-12
1973—	Bert Blyleven	20-17
1977—	Dave Goltz	20-11
1979—	Jerry Koosman	20-13
1988—	Frank Viola	24-7
1991—	Scott Erickson	20-8
1997—	Brad Radke	20-10

A.L. home run champions
1957—	Roy Sievers	42
1959—	Harmon Killebrew	*42
1962—	Harmon Killebrew	48
1963—	Harmon Killebrew	45
1964—	Harmon Killebrew	49
1967—	Harmon Killebrew	*44
1969—	Harmon Killebrew	49

* Tied for league lead

A.L. RBI champions
1924—	Goose Goslin	129
1957—	Roy Sievers	114
1962—	Harmon Killebrew	126
1969—	Harmon Killebrew	140
1971—	Harmon Killebrew	119
1977—	Larry Hisle	119
1994—	Kirby Puckett	112

A.L. batting champions
1902—	Ed Delahanty	.376
1928—	Goose Goslin	.379
1935—	Buddy Myer	.349
1946—	Mickey Vernon	.353
1953—	Mickey Vernon	.337
1964—	Tony Oliva	.323
1965—	Tony Oliva	.321
1969—	Rod Carew	.332
1971—	Tony Oliva	.337
1972—	Rod Carew	.318
1973—	Rod Carew	.350
1974—	Rod Carew	.364
1975—	Rod Carew	.359
1977—	Rod Carew	.388
1978—	Rod Carew	.333
1989—	Kirby Puckett	.339

A.L. ERA champions
1912—	Walter Johnson	1.39
1913—	Walter Johnson	1.09
1918—	Walter Johnson	1.27
1919—	Walter Johnson	1.49
1924—	Walter Johnson	2.72
1925—	Stan Coveleski	2.84
1928—	Garland Braxton	2.51
1988—	Allan Anderson	2.45

A.L. strikeout champions
1910—	Walter Johnson	313
1912—	Walter Johnson	303
1913—	Walter Johnson	243
1914—	Walter Johnson	225
1915—	Walter Johnson	203
1916—	Walter Johnson	228
1917—	Walter Johnson	188
1918—	Walter Johnson	162
1919—	Walter Johnson	147
1921—	Walter Johnson	143
1923—	Walter Johnson	130
1924—	Walter Johnson	158
1942—	Bobo Newsom	*113
1961—	Camilo Pascual	221
1962—	Camilo Pascual	206
1963—	Camilo Pascual	202
1985—	Bert Blyleven	*206

* Tied for league lead

No-hit pitchers
(9 innings or more)
1920—	Walter Johnson	1-0 vs. Boston
1931—	Bobby Burke	5-0 vs. Boston
1962—	Jack Kralick	1-0 vs. Kansas City
1967—	Dean Chance	2-1 vs. Cleveland
1994—	Scott Erickson	6-0 vs. Milwaukee
1999—	Eric Milton	7-0 vs. Anaheim

Longest hitting streaks
33—	Heinie Manush	1933
31—	Sam Rice	1924
	Ken Landreaux	1980
29—	Sam Rice	1920
28—	Sam Rice	1930
26—	Heinie Manush	1933
25—	Goose Goslin	1928
	Brian Harper	1990
24—	Cecil Travis	1941
	Lenny Green	1961
23—	Kent Hrbek	1982
	Marty Cordova	1996
22—	Joe Cronin	1932
	Heinie Manush	1932
	Mickey Vernon	1946
	Shane Mack	1992
21—	Eddie Foster	1918
	Buddy Myer	1935
	Taffy Wright	1938
20—	Joe Cronin	1930
	George Case	1939
	Jackie Jensen	1952
	Mickey Vernon	1953
	Ted Uhlaender	1969
	Chuck Knoblauch	1991

Longtime ace Walter Johnson (left) delivered his powerful fastball to catcher Gabby Steet from 1908-11.

SEASON

Batting
At-bats	691	Kirby Puckett	1985
Runs	140	Chuck Knoblauch	1996
Hits	239	Rod Carew	1977
Singles	182	Sam Rice	1925
Doubles	51	Mickey Vernon	1946
Triples	20	Goose Goslin	1925
Home runs	49	Harmon Killebrew	1964, 1969
Home runs, rookie	33	Jimmie Hall	1963
Grand slams	3	4 times	
		Last by Kirby Puckett	1992
Total bases	374	Tony Oliva	1964
RBIs	140	Harmon Killebrew	1969
Walks	151	Eddie Yost	1956
Most strikeouts	145	Bob Darwin	1972
Fewest strikeouts	9	Sam Rice	1929
Batting average	.388	Rod Carew	1977
Slugging pct.	.614	Goose Goslin	1928
Stolen bases	88	Clyde Milan	1912

Pitching
Games	90	Mike Marshall	1979
Complete games	38	Walter Johnson	1910
Innings	374	Walter Johnson	1910
Wins	36	Walter Johnson	1913
Losses	26	Jack Townsend	1904
		Bob Groom	1909
Winning pct.	.837	Walter Johnson	1913
Walks	146	Bobo Newsom	1936
Strikeouts	313	Walter Johnson	1910
Shutouts	11	Walter Johnson	1913
Home runs allowed	50	Bert Blyleven	1986
Lowest ERA	1.14	Walter Johnson	1913
Saves	42	Jeff Reardon	1988
		Rick Aguilera	1991

GAME

Batting
Runs	5	Last by Tim Teufel	9-16-83
Hits	6	Last by Kirby Puckett	5-23-91
Doubles	4	Kirby Puckett	5-13-89
Triples	3	Last by Ken Landreaux	7-3-80
Home runs	3	Last by Tony Oliva	7-3-73
RBIs	8	Last by Randy Bush	5-20-89
Total bases	14	Kirby Puckett	8-30-87
Stolen bases	5	Clyde Milan	6-14-12

BATTING

Games
Harmon Killebrew	2,329
Sam Rice	2,307
Joe Judge	2,084
Clyde Milan	1,982
Ossie Bluege	1,867
Mickey Vernon	1,805
Kirby Puckett	1,783
Kent Hrbek	1,747
Eddie Yost	1,690
Tony Oliva	1,676

At-bats
Sam Rice	8,934
Harmon Killebrew	7,835
Joe Judge	7,663
Clyde Milan	7,359
Kirby Puckett	7,244
Mickey Vernon	6,930
Ossie Bluege	6,440
Tony Oliva	6,301
Rod Carew	6,235
Kent Hrbek	6,192

Runs
Sam Rice	1,466
Harmon Killebrew	1,258
Joe Judge	1,154
Kirby Puckett	1,071
Buddy Myer	1,037
Clyde Milan	1,004
Eddie Yost	971
Mickey Vernon	956
Rod Carew	950
Kent Hrbek	903

Hits
Sam Rice	2,889
Kirby Puckett	2,304
Joe Judge	2,291
Clyde Milan	2,100
Rod Carew	2,085
Harmon Killebrew	2,024
Mickey Vernon	1,993
Tony Oliva	1,917
Buddy Myer	1,828
Ossie Bluege	1,751

Doubles
Sam Rice	479
Joe Judge	421
Kirby Puckett	414
Mickey Vernon	391
Tony Oliva	329
Kent Hrbek	312
Rod Carew	305
Buddy Myer	305
Goose Goslin	289
Eddie Yost	282

Triples
Sam Rice	183
Joe Judge	157
Goose Goslin	125
Buddy Myer	113
Mickey Vernon	108
Clyde Milan	105
Buddy Lewis	93
Rod Carew	90
Howie Shanks	87
Cecil Travis	78

Home runs
Harmon Killebrew	559
Kent Hrbek	293
Bob Allison	256
Tony Oliva	220
Kirby Puckett	207
Gary Gaetti	201
Roy Sievers	180
Tom Brunansky	163
Jim Lemon	159
Goose Goslin	127

Total bases
Harmon Killebrew	4,026
Sam Rice	3,833
Kirby Puckett	3,453
Joe Judge	3,239
Tony Oliva	3,002
Kent Hrbek	2,976
Mickey Vernon	2,963
Rod Carew	2,792
Clyde Milan	2,601
Goose Goslin	2,579

Runs batted in
Harmon Killebrew	1,540
Kent Hrbek	1,086

SEASON

Batting
Most at-bats	5,677	1969
Most runs	892	1930
Fewest runs	380	1909
Most hits	1,633	1996
Most singles	1,209	1935
Most doubles	332	1996
Most triples	100	1932
Most home runs	225	1963
Fewest home runs	4	1917
Most grand slams	8	1938, 1961
Most pinch-hit home runs	7	1964, 1967
Most total bases	2,413	1996
Most stolen bases	287	1913
Highest batting average	.303	1925
Lowest batting average	.223	1909
Highest slugging pct	.430	1963, 1987

Pitching
Lowest ERA	2.14	1918
Highest ERA	5.76	1995
Most complete games	137	1904
Most shutouts	25	1914
Most saves	58	1970
Most walks	779	1949
Most strikeouts	1,099	1964

Fielding
Most errors	323	1901
Fewest errors	84	1988
Most double plays	203	1979
Highest fielding average	.986	1988

General
Most games won	102	1965
Most games lost	113	1904
Highest win pct	.651	1933
Lowest win pct	.252	1904

GAME, INNING

Batting
Most runs, game	24	4-24-96
Most runs, inning	12	7-10-26
Most hits, game	24	Last 6-4-94
Most home runs, game	8	8-29-63
Most total bases, game	47	8-29-63

Hard-hitting outfielder Tony Oliva was part of the Twins' offensive wrecking crew in the 1960s.

Kirby Puckett	1,085
Sam Rice	1,045
Mickey Vernon	1,026
Joe Judge	1,001
Tony Oliva	947
Goose Goslin	931
Ossie Bluege	848
Bob Allison	796

Extra base hits
Harmon Killebrew	860
Sam Rice	695
Kirby Puckett	678
Joe Judge	649
Kent Hrbek	623
Mickey Vernon	620
Tony Oliva	597
Goose Goslin	541
Bob Allison	525
Gary Gaetti	478

Batting average
(Minimum 500 games)
Rod Carew	.334
Heinie Manush	.328
Sam Rice	.323
Goose Goslin	.323
Kirby Puckett	.318
John Stone	.317
Cecil Travis	.314
Shane Mack	.309
Brian Harper	.306
Joe Cronin	.304

Stolen bases
Clyde Milan	495
Sam Rice	346
George Case	321
Chuck Knoblauch	276
Rod Carew	271
Joe Judge	210
Cesar Tovar	186
Howie Shanks	177
Eddie Foster	166
Bucky Harris	166

PITCHING

Earned-run average
(Minimum 1,000 innings)
Walter Johnson	2.17
Doc Ayers	2.64
Harry Harper	2.75
Tom Hughes	3.02
Bob Groom	3.04
Jim Shaw	3.07
Jim Perry	3.15
Dutch Leonard	3.27
Bert Blyleven	3.28
Mickey Haefner	3.29

Wins
Walter Johnson	417
Jim Kaat	190
Bert Blyleven	149
Camilo Pascual	145
Jim Perry	128
Dutch Leonard	118
Firpo Marberry	117
Frank Viola	112
Case Patten	105
Alvin Crowder	98

Losses
Walter Johnson	279
Jim Kaat	159
Camilo Pascual	141
Bert Blyleven	138
Sid Hudson	130
Case Patten	127
Tom Hughes	125
Pedro Ramos	112
Tom Zachary	103
Dutch Leonard	101

Innings pitched
Walter Johnson	5,914.2
Jim Kaat	3,014.1
Bert Blyleven	2,566.2
Camilo Pascual	2,465.0
Case Patten	2,059.1
Dutch Leonard	1,899.1
Jim Perry	1,883.1
Sid Hudson	1,819.1
Tom Hughes	1,776.0
Frank Viola	1,772.2

Strikeouts
Walter Johnson	3,509
Bert Blyleven	2,035
Camilo Pascual	1,885
Jim Kaat	1,851
Frank Viola	1,214
Jim Perry	1,025

Dave Goltz	887
Tom Hughes	884
Dave Boswell	865
Jim Shaw	767

Bases on balls
Walter Johnson	1,363
Camilo Pascual	909
Jim Kaat	729
Sid Hudson	720
Walt Masterson	694
Jim Shaw	688
Bert Blyleven	674
Bump Hadley	572
Firpo Marberry	568
Tom Hughes	567

Games
Walter Johnson	802
Rick Aguilera	490
Jim Kaat	484
Firpo Marberry	470
Camilo Pascual	432
Jim Perry	376
Eddie Guardado	368
Mike Trombley	360
Bert Blyleven	348
Al Worthington	327

Shutouts
Walter Johnson	110
Camilo Pascual	31
Bert Blyleven	29
Jim Kaat	23
Dutch Leonard	23
Bob Porterfield	19
Tom Hughes	17
Case Patten	17
Jim Perry	17
Jim Shaw	17

Saves
Rick Aguilera	254
Ron Davis	108
Jeff Reardon	104
Firpo Marberry	96
Al Worthington	88
Ron Perranoski	76
Mike Marshall	54
Bill Campbell	51
Doug Corbett	43
Ray Moore	38

TWINS YEAR-BY-YEAR

Year	W	L	Place	Games Back	Manager	Leaders: Batting avg.	Hits	Home runs	RBIs	Wins	ERA
							WASHINGTON SENATORS				
1901	61	72	6th	20½	Manning	Waldron, .322	Dungan, 179	Grady, 9	Dungan, 73	Patten, 18	Carrick, 3.75
1902	61	75	6th	22	Loftus	E. Delahanty, .376	E. Delahanty, 178	E. Delahanty, 10	E. Delahanty, 93	Orth, 19	Orth, 3.97
1903	43	94	8th	47½	Loftus	Selbach, .251	Selbach, 134	Ryan, 7	Selbach, 49	Orth, Patten, 10	Lee, 3.08
1904	38	113	8th	55½	Donovan	Stahl, .262	Cassidy, 140	Stahl, 3	Stahl, 50	Patten, 14	Patten, 3.07
1905	64	87	7th	29½	Stahl	Hickman, .311	Cassidy, 124	Stahl, 5	Stahl, 66	Hughes, 17	Hughes, 2.35
1906	55	95	7th	37½	Stahl	Hickman, .284	Anderson, 158	Hickman, 9	Anderson, 70	Patten, 19	Patten, 2.17
1907	49	102	8th	43½	Cantillon	J. Delahanty, .292	Ganley, 167	Altizer, J. Delahanty, 2	J. Delahanty, 54	Patten, 12	Johnson, 1.88
1908	67	85	7th	22½	Cantillon	Clymer, .253	Freeman, 134	Pickering, 2	Freeman, 45	Hughes, 18	Johnson, 1.64
1909	42	110	8th	56	Cantillon	Lelivelt, .292	Unglaub, 127	Unglaub, 3	Unglaub, 41	Johnson, 13	Johnson, 2.21
1910	66	85	7th	36½	McAleer	Milan, .279	Milan, 148	Elberfeld, Gessler, 2	McBride, 55	Johnson, 25	Johnson, 1.35
1911	64	90	7th	38½	McAleer	Schaefer, .334	Milan, 194	Gessler, 4	Gessler, 78	Johnson, 25	Johnson, 1.89
1912	91	61	2nd	14	Griffith	Milan, .306	Milan, 184	Moeller, 6	Gandil, 81	Johnson, 33	Johnson, 1.39
1913	90	64	2nd	6½	Griffith	Gandil, .318	Gandil, 175	Moeller, 5	Gandil, 72	Johnson, 36	Johnson, 1.14
1914	81	73	3rd	19	Griffith	Milan, .295	Foster, 174	Shanks, 4	Gandil, 75	Johnson, 28	Johnson, 1.72
1915	85	68	4th	17	Griffith	Gandil, .291	Foster, 170	Gandil, Milan, Moeller, 2	Milan, 66	Johnson, 27	Johnson, 1.55
1916	76	77	7th	14½	Griffith	Milan, .273	Milan, 154	E. Smith, 2	Shanks, 48	Johnson, 25	Johnson, 1.89
1917	74	79	5th	25½	Griffith	Rice, .302	Rice, 177	Judge, 2	Rice, 69	Johnson, 23	Ayers, 2.17
1918	72	56	3rd	4	Griffith	Milan, .290	Foster, 147	4 Tied, 1	Milan, Shanks, 56	Johnson, 23	Johnson, 1.27
1919	56	84	7th	32	Griffith	Rice, .321	Rice, 179	Menosky, 6	Rice, 71	Johnson, 20	Johnson, 1.49
1920	68	84	6th	29	Griffith	Rice, .338	Rice, 211	Roth, 9	Roth, 92	Zachary, 15	Johnson, 3.13
1921	80	73	4th	18	McBride	Rice, .330	Judge, 187	B. Miller, 9	Rice, 79	Mogridge, Zachary, 18	Mogridge, 3.00
1922	69	85	6th	25	Milan	Goslin, .324	Rice, 187	Judge, 10	Judge, 81	Mogridge, 18	Johnson, 2.99
1923	75	78	4th	23½	Bush	Rice, .316	Rice, 188	Goslin, 9	Goslin, 99	Johnson, 17	A. Russell, 3.03
1924	92	62	1st	+2	Harris	Goslin, .344	Rice, 216	Goslin, 12	Goslin, 129	Johnson, 23	Ogden, 2.58
1925	96	55	1st	+8½	Harris	Rice, .350	Rice, 227	Goslin, 18	Goslin, 113	Coveleski, Johnson, 20	Coveleski, 2.84
1926	81	69	4th	8	Harris	Goslin, .354	Rice, 216	Goslin, 17	Goslin, 108	Johnson, 15	Marberry, 3.00
1927	85	69	3rd	25	Harris	Goslin, .334	Goslin, 194	Goslin, 13	Goslin, 120	Lisenbee, 18	Hadley, 2.85
1928	75	79	4th	26	Harris	Goslin, .379	Rice, 202	Goslin, 17	Goslin, 102	S. Jones, 17	Braxton, 2.51
1929	71	81	5th	34	Johnson	Rice, .323	Rice, 199	Goslin, 18	Goslin, 91	Marberry, 19	Marberry, 3.06
1930	94	60	2nd	8	Johnson	Manush, .362	Rice, 207	Cronin, 13	Cronin, 126	Brown, 16	Liska, 3.29
1931	92	62	3rd	16	Johnson	West, .333	Manush, 189	Cronin, 12	Cronin, 126	Crowder, 18	Hadley, 3.06
1932	93	61	3rd	14	Johnson	Manush, .342	Manush, 214	Manush, 14	Cronin, Manush, 116	Crowder, 26	Crowder, 3.33
1933	99	53	1st	+7	Cronin	Manush, .336	Manush, 221	Kuhel, 11	Cronin, 118	Crowder, 24	J. Russell, 2.69
1934	66	86	7th	34	Cronin	Manush, .349	Manush, 194	Manush, 11	Cronin, 101	Whitehill, 14	Burke, 3.21
1935	67	86	6th	27	Harris	Myer, .349	Myer, 215	Powell, 6	Myer, 100	Whitehill, 14	Whitehill, 4.29
1936	82	71	4th	20	Harris	Stone, .341	Kuhel, 189	Kuhel, 16	Kuhel, 118	DeShong, 18	Appleton, 3.53
1937	73	80	6th	28½	Harris	Travis, .344	Lewis, 210	Lewis, 10	Stone, 88	DeShong, 14	Ferrell, 3.94
1938	75	76	5th	23½	Harris	Myer, .336	Lewis, 194	Bonura, 22	Bonura, 114	Ferrell, 13	Krakauskas, 3.12
1939	65	87	6th	41½	Harris	Lewis, .319	Lewis, 171	Lewis, 10	Wright, 93	Leonard, 20	Leonard, 3.54
1940	64	90	7th	26	Harris	Travis, .322	Case, 192	Walker, 13	Walker, 96	Hudson, 17	Chase, 3.23
1941	70	84	*6th	31	Harris	Travis, .359	Travis, 218	Early, 10	Travis, 101	Leonard, 18	Carrasquel, 3.44
1942	62	89	7th	39½	Harris	Spence, .323	Spence, 203	Vernon, 9	Vernon, 86	Newsom, 11	Masterson, 3.34
1943	84	69	2nd	13½	Bluege	Case, .294	Case, 180	Spence, 12	Spence, 88	Wynn, 18	Haefner, 2.29
1944	64	90	8th	25	Bluege	Spence, .316	Spence, 187	Spence, 18	Spence, 100	Leonard, 14	Niggeling, 2.32
1945	87	67	2nd	1½	Bluege	Myatt, .296	Binks, 153	Clift, 8	Binks, 81	Wolff, 20	Wolff, 2.12
1946	76	78	4th	28	Bluege	Vernon, .353	Vernon, 207	Spence, 16	Spence, 87	Haefner, 14	Wolff, 2.58
1947	64	90	7th	33	Bluege	Spence, .279	Vernon, 159	Spence, 16	Vernon, 85	Wynn, 17	Masterson, 3.13
1948	56	97	7th	40	Kuhel	Stewart, .279	Kozar, 144	Coan, Stewart, 7	Stewart, 69	Scarborough, 15	Scarborough, 2.82
1949	50	104	8th	47	Kuhel	Robinson, .294	Dente, 161	Robinson, 18	Robinson, 78	Scarborough, 13	Hittle, 4.21
1950	67	87	5th	31	Harris	Vernon, .306	Yost, 169	Noren, 14	Noren, 98	Hudson, 14	Kuzava, 3.95
1951	62	92	7th	36	Harris	Coan, .303	Coan, 163	Yost, 12	Mele, 94	Marrero, 11	Porterfield, 3.24
1952	78	76	5th	17	Harris	Jensen, .286	Jensen, 163	Yost, 12	Jensen, Vernon, 80	Porterfield, 13	Porterfield, 2.72
1953	76	76	5th	23½	Harris	Vernon, .337	Vernon, 205	Vernon, 15	Vernon, 115	Porterfield, 22	Marrero, 3.03
1954	66	88	6th	45	Harris	Busby, .298	Busby, 187	Sievers, 24	Sievers, 102	Porterfield, 13	Schmitz, 2.91
1955	53	101	8th	43	Dressen	Vernon, .301	Vernon, 162	Sievers, 25	Sievers, 106	McDermott, Porterfield, 10	Schmitz, 3.71
1956	59	95	7th	38	Dressen	Runnels, .310	Runnels, 179	Sievers, 29	Lemon, 96	Stobbs, 15	Stobbs, 3.60
1957	55	99	8th	43	Dressen, Lavagetto	Sievers, .301	Sievers, 172	Sievers, 42	Sievers, 114	Ramos, 12	Byerly, 3.13
1958	61	93	8th	31	Lavagetto	Sievers, .295	Sievers, 162	Sievers, 39	Sievers, 108	Ramos, 14	Hyde, 1.75
1959	63	91	8th	31	Lavagetto	Lemon, .279	Allison, 149	Killebrew, 42	Killebrew, 105	Pascual, 17	Pascual, 2.64
1960	73	81	5th	24	Lavagetto	Green, .294	Gardner, 152	Lemon, 38	Lemon, 100	Pascual, Stobbs, 12	Pascual, 3.03
							MINNESOTA TWINS				
1961	70	90	7th	38	Lavagetto, Mele	Battey, .302	Green, 171	Killebrew, 46	Killebrew, 122	Pascual, 15	Pascual, 3.46
1962	91	71	2nd	5	Mele	Rollins, .298	Rollins, 186	Killebrew, 48	Killebrew, 126	Pascual, 20	Kaat, 3.14
1963	91	70	3rd	13	Mele	Rollins, .307	Rollins, 163	Killebrew, 45	Killebrew, 96	Pascual, 21	Dailey, 1.98
1964	79	83	*6th	20	Mele	Oliva, .323	Oliva, 217	Killebrew, 49	Killebrew, 111	Kaat, 17	Grant, 2.82
1965	102	60	1st	+7	Mele	Oliva, .321	Oliva, 185	Killebrew, 25	Oliva, 98	Grant, 21	J. Perry, 2.63
1966	89	73	2nd	9	Mele	Oliva, .307	Oliva, 191	Killebrew, 39	Killebrew, 110	Kaat, 25	Worthington, 2.46
1967	91	71	*2nd	1	Mele, Ermer	Carew, .292	Oliva, 161	Killebrew, 44	Killebrew, 113	Chance, 20	Merritt, 2.53
1968	79	83	7th	24	Ermer	Oliva, .289	Tovar, 167	Allison, 22	Oliva, 68	Chance, 16	J. Perry, 2.27
							WEST DIVISION				
1969	97	65	†1st	+9	Martin	Carew, .332	Oliva, 197	Killebrew, 49	Killebrew, 140	Boswell, J. Perry, 20	Perranoski, 2.11
1970	98	64	†1st	+9	Rigney	Oliva, .325	Oliva, 204	Killebrew, 41	Killebrew, 113	J. Perry, 24	Williams, 1.99
1971	74	86	5th	26½	Rigney	Oliva, .337	Tovar, 204	Killebrew, 28	Killebrew, 119	Perry, 17	Blyleven, 2.81
1972	77	77	3rd	15½	Rigney, Quilici	Carew, .318	Carew, 170	Killebrew, 26	Darwin, 80	Blyleven, 17	Kaat, 2.06
1973	81	81	3rd	13	Quilici	Carew, .350	Carew, 203	Darwin, 18	Oliva, 92	Blyleven, 20	Blyleven, 2.52
1974	82	80	3rd	8	Quilici	Carew, .364	Carew, 218	Darwin, 25	Darwin, 94	Blyleven, 17	Campbell, 2.62
1975	76	83	4th	20½	Quilici	Carew, .359	Carew, 192	Ford, 15	Carew, 80	Hughes, 16	Blyleven, 3.00
1976	85	77	3rd	5	Mauch	Carew, .331	Carew, 200	Ford, 20	Hisle, 96	Campbell, 17	Burgmeier, 2.50
1977	84	77	4th	17½	Mauch	Carew, .388	Carew, 239	Hisle, 28	Hisle, 119	Goltz, 20	Johnson, 3.13
1978	73	89	4th	19	Mauch	Carew, .333	Carew, 188	Smalley, 19	Ford, 82	Goltz, 15	Marshall, 2.45
1979	82	80	4th	6	Mauch	Wilfong, .313	Landreaux, 172	Smalley, 24	Smalley, 95	Koosman, 20	Marshall, 2.65
1980	77	84	3rd	19½	Mauch, Goryl	Castino, .302	Castino, 165	Castino, 13	Castino, 64	Koosman, 16	Corbett, 1.98
1981	41	68	‡7th/4th	–	Goryl, Gardner	Castino, .268	Castino, 102	Smalley, 7	Hatcher, 37	Redfern, 9	Erickson, 3.84
1982	60	102	7th	33	Gardner	Hrbek, .301	Ward, 165	Ward, 28	Hrbek, 92	Castillo, 13	Castillo, 3.66
1983	70	92	*5th	29	Gardner	Hatcher, .317	Ward, 173	Brunansky, 28	Ward, 88	Schrom, 15	Lysander, 3.38
1984	81	81	*2nd	3	Gardner	Hrbek, .311	Hatcher, 174	Brunansky, 32	Hrbek, 107	Viola, 18	Viola, 3.21
1985	77	85	*4th	14	Gardner, Miller	Salas, .300	Puckett, 199	Brunansky, 27	Hrbek, 93	Viola, 18	Blyleven, 3.00
1986	71	91	6th	21	Miller, Kelly	Puckett, .328	Puckett, 223	Gaetti, 34	Gaetti, 108	Blyleven, 17	Heaton, 3.98
1987	85	77	§1st	+2	Kelly	Puckett, .332	Puckett, 207	Hrbek, 34	Gaetti, 109	Viola, 17	Viola, 2.90
1988	91	71	2nd	13	Kelly	Puckett, .356	Puckett, 234	Gaetti, 28	Puckett, 121	Viola, 24	Anderson, 2.45
1989	80	82	5th	19	Kelly	Puckett, .339	Puckett, 215	Hrbek, 25	Puckett, 85	Anderson, 17	Berenguer, 3.48
1990	74	88	7th	29	Kelly	Puckett, .298	Puckett, 164	Hrbek, 22	Gaetti, 85	Tapani, 12	Erickson, 2.87
1991	95	67	§1st	+8	Kelly	Puckett, .319	Puckett, 195	Davis, 29	Davis, 93	Erickson, 20	Tapani, 2.99
1992	90	72	2nd	6	Kelly	Puckett, .329	Puckett, 210	Puckett, 19	Puckett, 110	Smiley, Tapani, 16	Smiley, 3.21
1993	71	91	*5th	23	Kelly	Harper, .304	Puckett, 184	Hrbek, 25	Puckett, 89	Tapani, 12	Banks, 4.04
							CENTRAL DIVISION				
1994	53	60	4th	14	Kelly	Puckett, .317	Knoblauch, Puckett, 139	Puckett, 20	Puckett, 112	Tapani, 11	Tapani, 4.62
1995	56	88	5th	44	Kelly	Knoblauch, .333	Knoblauch, 179	Cordova, 24	Puckett, 99	Radke, 11	Tapani, 4.92
1996	78	84	4th	21½	Kelly	Molitor, .3409	Molitor, 225	Cordova, 16	Molitor, 113	Rodriguez, 13	Radke, 4.46
1997	68	94	4th	18½	Kelly	Molitor, .305	Knoblauch, 178	Cordova, 15	Molitor, 89	Radke, 20	Swindell, 3.58
1998	70	92	4th	19	Kelly	Walker, .316	Walker, 167	Lawton, 21	Lawton, 77	Radke, 12	Trombley, 3.63
1999	63	97	5th	33	Kelly	Cordova, .285	Walker, 148	Coomer, 16	Cordova, 70	Radke, 12	Radke, 3.75

* Tied for position. † Lost Championship Series. ‡ First half 17-39; second half 24-29. § Won Championship Series.

Note: Batting average minimum 350 at-bats; ERA minimum 90 innings pitched.

HISTORY

NEW YORK YANKEES

Outfielder Babe Ruth.

FRANCHISE CHRONOLOGY

First season: 1901, in Baltimore, as a member of the new American League. The Orioles made their Major League debut with a 10-6 victory over Boston en route to a 68-65 record, but dropped to the bottom of the A.L. in their second and final Baltimore season.
1903-present: The Highlanders/Yankees dropped a 3-1 decision to Washington in their New York debut and spent the next 18 seasons languishing among the A.L. also-rans. That would change. With the arrival of Babe Ruth in 1920, the Yankees rose into prominence as baseball's most dominant franchise and began the most glorious success run in sports history. In a 44-year stretch (1921-64), the Bronx Bombers won 29 pennants and 20 World Series. They won four straight fall classics (1936-39) under Joe McCarthy and five in a row (1949-53) under Casey Stengel. After playing in their first Series in 1921, the Yankees never went three years without playing in another through 1964. Though success has been more elusive since that 1964 loss to the Cardinals, the Yankees seem to have found the winning touch once again. The Yanks have taken the championship three of the last four years, including World Series sweeps in 1998 and 1999, for a record 25 World Series titles.

YANKEES VS. OPPONENTS BY DECADE

	A's	Indians	Orioles	Red Sox	Tigers	Twins	White Sox	Angels	Rangers	Brewers	Royals	Blue Jays	Mariners	Devil Rays	Interleague	Decade Record
1901-09	87-94	85-104	99-90	86-101	85-103	122-66	74-113									638-671
1910-19	100-104	95-117	123-92	94-115	94-121	101-113	94-118									701-780
1920-29	137-81	125-95	140-78	149-71	126-94	122-97	134-86									933-602
1930-39	140-76	133-84	155-64	136-80	134-86	124-96	134-86									970-554
1940-49	143-77	129-90	143-77	122-98	108-112	151-69	133-86									929-609
1950-59	158-62	123-97	151-69	126-93	120-100	145-73	132-88									955-582
1960-69	117-61	100-83	73-111	101-83	94-90	87-90	102-76	95-61	104-55	7-5	7-5					887-720
1970-79	63-54	103-64	73-89	79-89	92-74	72-44	72-44	65-52	79-49	83-74	64-53	29-14	18-15			892-715
1980-89	61-54	73-56	74-56	63-60	64-62	71-43	61-58	63-49	62-54	61-62	68-52	65-57	68-45			854-708
1990-99	58-59	72-45	75-50	64-60	72-47	58-50	52-54	58-59	54-54	56-39	61-45	64-57	61-56	19-5	27-22	851-702
Totals	1064-722	1038-835	1106-776	1020-850	989-889	1053-741	1002-791	281-221	299-212	207-180	200-155	158-128	147-116	19-5	27-22	8610-6643

Interleague results: 5-5 vs. Braves; 5-4 vs. Expos; 7-5 vs. Mets; 4-5 vs. Phillies; 6-3 vs. Marlins.

MANAGERS

(Baltimore Orioles, 1901-02)

Name	Years	Record
John McGraw	1901-02	94-96
Wilbert Robinson	1902	24-57
Clark Griffith	1903-08	419-370
Kid Elberfeld	1908	27-71
George Stallings	1909-10	152-136
Hal Chase	1910-11	86-80
Harry Wolverton	1912	50-102
Frank Chance	1913-14	117-168
Roger Peckinpaugh	1914	10-10
Bill Donovan	1915-17	220-239
Miller Huggins	1918-29	1067-719
Art Fletcher	1929	6-5
Bob Shawkey	1930	86-68
Joe McCarthy	1931-46	1460-867
Bill Dickey	1946	57-48
Johnny Neun	1946	8-6
Bucky Harris	1947-48	191-117
Casey Stengel	1949-60	1149-696
Ralph Houk	1961-63, 1966-73	944-806
Yogi Berra	1964, 1984-85	192-148
Johnny Keane	1965-66	81-101
Bill Virdon	1974-75	142-124
Billy Martin	1975-78, 1979, 1983, 1985, 1988	556-385
Bob Lemon	1978-79, 1981-82	99-73
Dick Howser	1978, 1980	103-60
Gene Michael	1981, 1982	92-76
Clyde King	1982	29-33
Lou Piniella	1986-87, 1988	224-193
Dallas Green	1989	56-65
Bucky Dent	1989-90	36-53
Stump Merrill	1990-91	120-155
Buck Showalter	1992-95	313-268
Joe Torre	1996-99	400-248

WORLD SERIES CHAMPIONS

Year	Loser	Length	MVP
1923	N.Y. Giants	6 games	None
1927	Pittsburgh	4 games	None
1928	St. Louis	4 games	None
1932	Chicago	4 games	None
1936	N.Y. Giants	6 games	None
1937	N.Y. Giants	5 games	None
1938	Chicago	4 games	None
1939	Cincinnati	4 games	None
1941	Brooklyn	5 games	None
1943	St. Louis	5 games	None
1947	Brooklyn	7 games	None
1949	Brooklyn	5 games	None
1950	Philadelphia	4 games	None
1951	N.Y. Giants	6 games	None
1952	Brooklyn	7 games	None
1953	Brooklyn	6 games	None
1956	Brooklyn	7 games	Larsen
1958	Milwaukee	7 games	Turley
1961	Cincinnati	5 games	Ford
1962	San Francisco	7 games	Terry
1977	Los Angeles	6 games	Jackson
1978	Los Angeles	6 games	Dent
1996	Atlanta	6 games	Wetteland
1998	San Diego	4 games	Brosius
1999	Atlanta	4 games	Rivera

A.L. PENNANT WINNERS

Year	Record	Manager	Series Result
1921	98-55	Huggins	Lost to Giants
1922	94-60	Huggins	Lost to Giants
1923	98-54	Huggins	Defeated Giants
1926	91-63	Huggins	Lost to Cardinals
1927	110-44	Huggins	Defeated Pirates

A.L. PENNANT WINNERS—cont'd.

Year	Record	Manager	Series Result
1928	101-53	Huggins	Defeated Cardinals
1932	107-47	McCarthy	Defeated Cubs
1936	102-51	McCarthy	Defeated Giants
1937	102-52	McCarthy	Defeated Giants
1938	99-53	McCarthy	Defeated Cubs
1939	106-45	McCarthy	Defeated Reds
1941	101-53	McCarthy	Defeated Dodgers
1942	103-51	McCarthy	Lost to Cardinals
1943	98-56	McCarthy	Defeated Cardinals
1947	97-57	Harris	Defeated Dodgers
1949	97-57	Stengel	Defeated Dodgers
1950	98-56	Stengel	Defeated Phillies
1951	98-56	Stengel	Defeated Giants
1952	95-59	Stengel	Defeated Dodgers
1953	99-52	Stengel	Defeated Dodgers
1955	96-58	Stengel	Lost to Dodgers
1956	97-57	Stengel	Defeated Dodgers
1957	98-56	Stengel	Lost to Braves
1958	92-62	Stengel	Defeated Braves
1960	97-57	Stengel	Lost to Pirates
1961	109-53	Houk	Defeated Reds
1962	96-66	Houk	Defeated Giants
1963	104-57	Houk	Lost to Dodgers
1964	99-63	Berra	Lost to Cardinals
1976	97-62	Martin	Lost to Reds
1977	100-62	Martin	Defeated Dodgers
1978	100-63	Martin, Lemon	Defeated Dodgers
*1981	59-48	Michael, Lemon	Lost to Dodgers
1996	92-70	Torre	Defeated Braves
1998	114-48	Torre	Defeated Padres
1999	98-64	Torre	Defeated Braves

EAST DIVISION CHAMPIONS

Year	Record	Manager	ALCS Result
1976	97-62	Martin	Defeated Royals
1977	100-62	Martin	Defeated Royals
1978	100-63	Martin, Lemon	Defeated Royals
1980	103-59	Howser	Lost to Royals
*1981	59-48	Michael, Lemon	Defeated A's
1994	70-43	Showalter	None
1996	92-70	Torre	Defeated Orioles
1998	114-48	Torre	Defeated Indians
1999	98-64	Torre	Defeated Red Sox

* First-half champion; won division playoff from Brewers.

WILD-CARD QUALIFIERS

Year	Record	Manager	Div. Series Result
1995	79-65	Showalter	Lost to Mariners
1997	96-66	Torre	Lost to Indians

ATTENDANCE HIGHS

Total	Season	Park
3,292,629	1999	Yankee Stadium
2,949,734	1998	Yankee Stadium
2,633,701	1988	Yankee Stadium
2,627,417	1980	Yankee Stadium
2,580,445	1997	Yankee Stadium
2,537,765	1979	Yankee Stadium

BALLPARK CHRONOLOGY

Yankee Stadium (1923-present)

Capacity: 57,546.
First game: Yankees 4, Boston 1 (April 18, 1923).
First batter: Chick Fewster, Red Sox.
First hit: George Burns, Red Sox (single).

First run: Bob Shawkey, Yankees (3rd inning).
First home run: Babe Ruth, Yankees.
First winning pitcher: Bob Shawkey, Yankees.
First-season attendance: 1,007,066.

Oriole Park, Baltimore (1901-02)

First game: Orioles 10, Boston 6 (April 26, 1901).
First-season attendance: 141,952.

Hilltop Park, New York (1903-12)

Capacity: 15,000.
First game: Yankees 6, Washington 2 (May 1, 1903).
First-season attendance: 211,808.

Polo Grounds (1913-22)

Capacity: 38,000.
First game: Washington 9, Yankees 3 (April 17, 1913).
First-season attendance: 357,551.

Shea Stadium (1974-75)

Capacity: 55,101.
First game: Yankees 6, Cleveland 1 (April 6, 1974).
First-season attendance: 1,273,075.

Note: The Yankees played two seasons at Shea Stadium while Yankee Stadium was being refurbished. Before its facelift, Yankee Stadium capacity was 67,224.

A.L. MVPs

Lou Gehrig, 1B, 1936	Mickey Mantle, OF, 1956
Joe DiMaggio, OF, 1939	Mickey Mantle, OF, 1957
Joe DiMaggio, OF, 1941	Roger Maris, OF, 1960
Joe Gordon, 2B, 1942	Roger Maris, OF, 1961
Spud Chandler, P, 1943	Mickey Mantle, OF, 1962
Joe DiMaggio, OF, 1947	Elston Howard, C, 1963
Phil Rizzuto, SS, 1950	Thurman Munson, C, 1976
Yogi Berra, C, 1951	Don Mattingly, 1B, 1985
Yogi Berra, C, 1954	
Yogi Berra, C, 1955	

CY YOUNG WINNERS

Bob Turley, RH, 1958	Sparky Lyle, LH, 1977
Whitey Ford, LH, 1961	Ron Guidry, LH, 1978

ROOKIES OF THE YEAR

Gil McDougald, 3B, 1951	Stan Bahnsen, P, 1968
Bob Grim, P, 1954	Thurman Munson, C, 1970
Tony Kubek, SS/OF, 1957	Dave Righetti, P, 1981
Tom Tresh, SS/OF, 1962	Derek Jeter, SS, 1996

MANAGER OF THE YEAR

Buck Showalter, 1994	Joe Torre, 1998
*Joe Torre, 1996	*Co-winner

RETIRED UNIFORMS

No.	Name	Pos.
1	Billy Martin	2B-Man.
3	Babe Ruth	OF
4	Lou Gehrig	1B
5	Joe DiMaggio	OF
7	Mickey Mantle	OF
8	Bill Dickey	C
	Yogi Berra	C
9	Roger Maris	OF
10	Phil Rizzuto	SS
15	Thurman Munson	C
16	Whitey Ford	P
23	Don Mattingly	1B
32	Elston Howard	C
37	Casey Stengel	Man.
44	Reggie Jackson	OF

HISTORY

MILESTONE PERFORMANCES

30-plus home runs

61— Roger Maris 1961
60— Babe Ruth 1927
59— Babe Ruth 1921
54— Babe Ruth 1920, 1928
Mickey Mantle 1961
52— Mickey Mantle 1956
49— Babe Ruth 1930
Lou Gehrig 1934, 1936
47— Babe Ruth 1926
Lou Gehrig 1927
46— Babe Ruth 1924, 1929, 1931
Lou Gehrig 1931
Joe DiMaggio 1937
44— Tino Martinez 1997
42— Mickey Mantle 1958
41— Babe Ruth 1923, 1932
Lou Gehrig 1930
Reggie Jackson 1980
40— Mickey Mantle 1960
39— Joe DiMaggio 1948
Roger Maris 1960
37— Lou Gehrig 1937
Mickey Mantle 1955
Graig Nettles 1977
Dave Winfield 1982
35— Babe Ruth 1922
Mickey Mantle 1964
Don Mattingly 1985
34— Babe Ruth 1933
Mickey Mantle 1957
33— Bob Meusel 1925
Charlie Keller 1941
Roger Maris 1962
Bobby Murcer 1972
32— Lou Gehrig 1933
Joe DiMaggio 1938, 1950
Bobby Bonds 1975
Graig Nettles 1976
Dave Winfield 1983
Mike Pagliarulo 1987
31— Joe DiMaggio 1940
Tommy Henrich 1941
Charlie Keller 1943
Mickey Mantle 1959
Joe Pepitone 1966
Don Mattingly 1986
Danny Tartabull 1993
30— Lou Gehrig 1935
Joe DiMaggio 1939, 1941
Joe Gordon 1940
Charlie Keller 1946
Yogi Berra 1952
Mickey Mantle 1962
Don Mattingly 1987

100-plus RBIs

184— Lou Gehrig 1931
175— Lou Gehrig 1927
174— Lou Gehrig 1930
171— Babe Ruth 1921
167— Joe DiMaggio 1937
165— Lou Gehrig 1934
164— Babe Ruth 1927
163— Babe Ruth 1931
159— Lou Gehrig 1937
155— Joe DiMaggio 1948
154— Babe Ruth 1929
153— Babe Ruth 1930
152— Lou Gehrig 1936
151— Lou Gehrig 1932
146— Babe Ruth 1926
145— Don Mattingly 1985
142— Lou Gehrig 1928
Babe Ruth 1928
Roger Maris 1961
141— Tino Martinez 1997
140— Joe DiMaggio 1938
139— Lou Gehrig 1933
138— Bob Meusel 1925
137— Babe Ruth 1920, 1932
135— Bob Meusel 1921
133— Bill Dickey 1937
Joe DiMaggio 1940
131— Babe Ruth 1923
130— Mickey Mantle 1956
128— Mickey Mantle 1961
126— Lou Gehrig 1929
Joe DiMaggio 1939
125— Joe DiMaggio 1936, 1941
Yogi Berra 1954
124— Yogi Berra 1950
123— Tino Martinez 1998
122— Ben Chapman 1931
Charlie Keller 1941
Joe DiMaggio 1950
121— Babe Ruth 1924
Tony Lazzeri 1930
120— Bob Meusel 1924
119— Lou Gehrig 1935
117— Tino Martinez 1996
Paul O'Neill 1997
116— Dave Winfield 1983
Paul O'Neill 1998
115— Bill Dickey 1938
Don Mattingly 1987
Bernie Williams 1999
114— Tony Lazzeri 1926
Lou Gehrig 1938
Joe DiMaggio 1942
Dave Winfield 1985
113— Wally Pipp 1924
Bob Meusel 1928
Tony Lazzeri 1932
Don Mattingly 1986, 1989
112— Lou Gehrig 1926
Roger Maris 1960
111— Joe Gordon 1939
Nick Etten 1945
Mickey Mantle 1964
Reggie Jackson 1980
110— Reggie Jackson 1977
Don Mattingly 1984
Paul O'Neill 1999
109— Tony Lazzeri 1936
108— Wally Pipp 1923
Charlie Keller 1942
Yogi Berra 1953, 1955
107— Lyn Lary 1931
Ben Chapman 1932
Bill Dickey 1936
George Selkirk 1936
Nick Etten 1943
Graig Nettles 1977
Dave Winfield 1988
106— Tony Lazzeri 1929
Dave Winfield 1982
105— Bill Dickey 1939
Yogi Berra 1956
Thurman Munson 1976
Tino Martinez 1999
104— Tony Lazzeri 1933
Dave Winfield 1986
103— Bob Meusel 1927
Babe Ruth 1933
Joe Gordon 1940, 1942
Johnny Lindell 1944
102— Tony Lazzeri 1927
Mickey Mantle 1954
Thurman Munson 1975
Danny Tartabull 1993
Bernie Williams 1996
Derek Jeter 1999
101— George Selkirk 1939
Charlie Keller 1946
100— Tommy Henrich 1948
Roger Maris 1962
Joe Pepitone 1964
Thurman Munson 1977
Dave Winfield 1984
Bernie Williams 1997

20-plus victories

1901— Joe McGinnity 26-20
1903— Jack Chesbro 21-15
1904— Jack Chesbro 41-12
Jack Powell 23-19
1906— Albert Orth 27-17
Jack Chesbro 23-17
1910— Russell Ford 26-6
1911— Russell Ford 22-11
1916— Bob Shawkey 24-14
1919— Bob Shawkey 20-11
1920— Carl Mays 26-11
Bob Shawkey 20-13
1921— Carl Mays 27-9
1922— Joe Bush 26-7
Bob Shawkey 20-12
1923— Sad Sam Jones 21-8
1924— Herb Pennock 21-9
1926— Herb Pennock 23-11
1927— Waite Hoyt 22-7
1928— George Pipgras 24-13
Waite Hoyt 23-7
1931— Lefty Gomez 21-9
1932— Lefty Gomez 24-7
1934— Lefty Gomez 26-5
1936— Red Ruffing 20-12
1937— Lefty Gomez 21-11
Red Ruffing 20-7
1938— Red Ruffing 21-7
1939— Red Ruffing 21-7
1942— Ernie Bonham 21-5
1943— Spud Chandler 20-4
1946— Spud Chandler 20-8
1949— Vic Raschi 21-10
1950— Vic Raschi 21-8
1951— Eddie Lopat 21-9
Vic Raschi 21-10
1952— Allie Reynolds 20-8
1954— Bob Grim 20-6
1958— Bob Turley 21-7
1961— Whitey Ford 25-4
1962— Ralph Terry 23-12
1963— Whitey Ford 24-7
Jim Bouton 21-7
1965— Mel Stottlemyre 20-9
1968— Mel Stottlemyre 21-12
1969— Mel Stottlemyre 20-14
1970— Fritz Peterson 20-11
1975— Catfish Hunter 23-14
1978— Ron Guidry 25-3
Ed Figueroa 20-9
1979— Tommy John 21-9
1980— Tommy John 22-9
1983— Ron Guidry 21-9
1985— Ron Guidry 22-6
1996— Andy Pettitte 21-8
1998— David Cone 20-7

INDIVIDUAL SEASON, GAME RECORDS

SEASON

Batting			
At-bats	692	Bobby Richardson	1962
Runs	177	Babe Ruth	1921
Hits	238	Don Mattingly	1986
Singles	171	Steve Sax	1989
Doubles	53	Don Mattingly	1986
Triples	23	Earle Combs	1927
Home runs	61	Roger Maris	1961
Home runs, rookie	29	Joe DiMaggio	1936
Grand slams	6	Don Mattingly	1987
Total bases	457	Babe Ruth	1921
RBIs	184	Lou Gehrig	1931
Walks	170	Babe Ruth	1923
Most strikeouts	156	Danny Tartabull	1993
Fewest strikeouts	3	Joe Sewell	1932
Batting average	.393	Babe Ruth	1923
Slugging pct.	.847	Babe Ruth	1920
Stolen bases	93	Rickey Henderson	1988
Pitching			
Games	77	Jeff Nelson	1997
Complete games	48	Jack Chesbro	1904
Innings	454.2	Jack Chesbro	1904
Wins	41	Jack Chesbro	1904
Losses	22	Joe Lake	1908
Winning pct.	.893 (25-3)	Ron Guidry	1978
Walks	179	Tommy Byrne	1949
Strikeouts	248	Ron Guidry	1978
Shutouts	9	Ron Guidry	1978
Home runs allowed	40	Ralph Terry	1962
Lowest ERA	1.64	Spud Chandler	1943
Saves	46	Dave Righetti	1986

GAME

Batting			
Runs	5	Last by Tino Martinez	4-2-97
Hits	6	Myril Hoag	6-6-34
		Gerald Williams	5-1-96
Doubles	4	Last by Jim Mason	7-8-74
Triples	3	Last by Joe DiMaggio	8-28-38
Home runs	4	Lou Gehrig	6-3-32
RBIs	11	Tony Lazzeri	5-24-36
Total bases	16	Lou Gehrig	6-3-32
Stolen bases	4	Last by Gerald Williams	6-2-96

A.L. home run champions

1916— Wally Pipp 12
1917— Wally Pipp 9
1920— Babe Ruth 54
1921— Babe Ruth 59
1923— Babe Ruth 41
1924— Babe Ruth 46
1925— Bob Meusel 33
1926— Babe Ruth 47
1927— Babe Ruth 60
1928— Babe Ruth 54
1929— Babe Ruth 46
1930— Babe Ruth 49
1931— Lou Gehrig 46
Babe Ruth 46
1934— Lou Gehrig 49
1936— Lou Gehrig 49
1937— Joe DiMaggio 46
1944— Nick Etten 22
1948— Joe DiMaggio 39
1955— Mickey Mantle 37
1956— Mickey Mantle 52
1958— Mickey Mantle 42
1960— Mickey Mantle 40
1961— Roger Maris 61
1976— Graig Nettles 32
1980— Reggie Jackson *41

* Tied for league lead

A.L. RBI champions

1920— Babe Ruth 137
1921— Babe Ruth 171
1923— Babe Ruth 131
1925— Bob Meusel 138
1926— Babe Ruth 146
1927— Lou Gehrig 175
1928— Lou Gehrig *142
Babe Ruth *142
1930— Lou Gehrig 174
1931— Lou Gehrig 184
1934— Lou Gehrig 165
1941— Joe DiMaggio 125
1945— Nick Etten 111
1948— Joe DiMaggio 155
1956— Mickey Mantle 130
1960— Roger Maris 112
1961— Roger Maris 142
1985— Don Mattingly 145

* Tied for league lead

A.L. batting champions

1924— Babe Ruth .378
1934— Lou Gehrig .363
1939— Joe DiMaggio .381
1940— Joe DiMaggio .352
1945— Snuffy Stirnweiss .309
1956— Mickey Mantle .353
1984— Don Mattingly .343
1994— Paul O'Neill .359
1998— Bernie Williams .339

A.L. ERA champions

1920— Bob Shawkey 2.45
1927— Wilcy Moore 2.28
1934— Lefty Gomez 2.33
1937— Lefty Gomez 2.33
1943— Spud Chandler 1.64
1947— Spud Chandler 2.46
1952— Allie Reynolds 2.06
1953— Eddie Lopat 2.42
1956— Whitey Ford 2.47
1957— Bobby Shantz 2.45
1958— Whitey Ford 2.01
1978— Ron Guidry 1.74
1979— Ron Guidry 2.78
1980— Rudy May 2.46

A.L. strikeout champions

1932— Red Ruffing 190
1933— Lefty Gomez 163
1934— Lefty Gomez 158
1937— Lefty Gomez 194
1951— Vic Raschi 164
1952— Allie Reynolds 160
1964— Al Downing 217

No-hit pitchers

(9 innings or more)
1917— George Mogridge 2-1 vs. Boston
1923— Sad Sam Jones 2-0 vs. Philadelphia
1938— Monte Pearson 13-0 vs. Cleveland
1951— Allie Reynolds 1-0 vs. Cleveland
Allie Reynolds 8-0 vs. Boston
1956— *Don Larsen 2-0 vs. Brooklyn (Perfect)
1983— Dave Righetti 4-0 vs. Boston
1990— Andy Hawkins 0-4 vs. Chicago
1993— Jim Abbott 4-0 vs. Cleveland
1996— Dwight Gooden 2-0 vs. Seattle
1998— David Wells 4-0 vs. Minnesota (Perfect)
1999— David Cone 6-0 vs. Montreal (Perfect)

* World Series game

Longest hitting streaks

56— Joe DiMaggio 1941
33— Hal Chase 1907
29— Roger Peckinpaugh 1919
Earle Combs 1931
Joe Gordon 1942
27— Hal Chase 1907
26— Babe Ruth 1921
23— Joe DiMaggio 1940
22— Joe DiMaggio 1937
21— Wally Pipp 1923
Joe DiMaggio 1937
Bernie Williams 1993
20— Buddy Hassett 1942
Mickey Rivers 1976
Dave Winfield 1984
Don Mattingly 1985

HISTORY

BATTING

Games
Mickey Mantle	2,401
Lou Gehrig	2,164
Yogi Berra	2,116
Babe Ruth	2,084
Roy White	1,881
Bill Dickey	1,789
Don Mattingly	1,785
Joe DiMaggio	1,736
Willie Randolph	1,694
Frankie Crosetti	1,683

At-bats
Mickey Mantle	8,102
Lou Gehrig	8,001
Yogi Berra	7,546
Babe Ruth	7,217
Don Mattingly	7,003
Joe DiMaggio	6,821
Roy White	6,650
Willie Randolph	6,303
Bill Dickey	6,300
Frankie Crosetti	6,277

Runs
Babe Ruth	1,959
Lou Gehrig	1,888
Mickey Mantle	1,677
Joe DiMaggio	1,390
Earle Combs	1,186
Yogi Berra	1,174
Willie Randolph	1,027
Don Mattingly	1,007
Frankie Crosetti	1,006
Roy White	964

Hits
Lou Gehrig	2,721
Babe Ruth	2,518
Mickey Mantle	2,415
Joe DiMaggio	2,214
Don Mattingly	2,153
Yogi Berra	2,148
Bill Dickey	1,969
Earle Combs	1,866
Roy White	1,803
Tony Lazzeri	1,784

Doubles
Lou Gehrig	534
Don Mattingly	442
Babe Ruth	424
Joe DiMaggio	389
Mickey Mantle	344
Bill Dickey	343
Bob Meusel	338
Tony Lazzeri	327
Yogi Berra	321
Earle Combs	309

Triples
Lou Gehrig	163
Earle Combs	154
Joe DiMaggio	131
Wally Pipp	121
Tony Lazzeri	115
Babe Ruth	106
Bob Meusel	87
Tommy Henrich	73
Bill Dickey	72
Mickey Mantle	72

Home runs
Babe Ruth	659
Mickey Mantle	536
Lou Gehrig	493
Joe DiMaggio	361
Yogi Berra	358
Graig Nettles	250
Don Mattingly	222
Dave Winfield	205
Roger Maris	203
Bill Dickey	202

Total bases
Babe Ruth	5,131
Lou Gehrig	5,060
Mickey Mantle	4,511
Joe DiMaggio	3,948
Yogi Berra	3,641
Don Mattingly	3,301
Bill Dickey	3,062
Tony Lazzeri	2,848
Roy White	2,685
Earle Combs	2,657

Runs batted in
Lou Gehrig	1,995
Babe Ruth	1,971
Joe DiMaggio	1,537
Mickey Mantle	1,509

TEAM SEASON, GAME RECORDS

SEASON

Batting
Most at-bats	5,710	1997
Most runs	1,067	1931
Fewest runs	459	1908
Most hits	1,683	1930
Most singles	1,237	1988
Most doubles	325	1997
Most triples	111	1901
Most home runs	240	1961
Fewest home runs	8	1913
Most grand slams	10	1987
Most pinch-hit home runs	10	1961
Most total bases	2,703	1936
Most stolen bases	288	1910
Highest batting average	.309	1930
Lowest batting average	.214	1968
Highest slugging pct	.489	1927

Pitching
Lowest ERA	2.57	1904
Highest ERA	4.88	1930
Most complete games	123	1904
Most shutouts	24	1951
Most saves	58	1986
Most walks	812	1949
Most strikeouts	1,165	1997

Fielding
Most errors	401	1901
Fewest errors	91	1996
Most double plays	214	1956
Highest fielding average	.986	1995

General
Most games won	114	1998
Most games lost	103	1908
Highest win pct	.714	1927
Lowest win pct	.329	1912

GAME, INNING

Batting
Most runs, game	25	5-24-36
Most runs, inning	14	7-6-20
Most hits, game	30	9-28-23
Most home runs, game	8	6-28-39
Most total bases, game	53	6-28-39

Mickey Mantle's 536 career home runs rank only second on the Yankees' career list—thanks to Babe Ruth.

Yogi Berra	1,430
Bill Dickey	1,209
Tony Lazzeri	1,154
Don Mattingly	1,099
Bob Meusel	1,005
Graig Nettles	834

Extra-base hits
Lou Gehrig	1,190
Babe Ruth	1,189
Mickey Mantle	952
Joe DiMaggio	881
Yogi Berra	728
Don Mattingly	684
Bill Dickey	617
Tony Lazzeri	611
Bob Meusel	571
Tommy Henrich	525

Batting average
(Minimum 500 games)
Babe Ruth	.349
Lou Gehrig	.340
Earle Combs	.325
Joe DiMaggio	.325
Derek Jeter	.318
Wade Boggs	.313
Bill Dickey	.313
Paul O'Neill	.312
Bob Meusel	.311
Don Mattingly	.307

Stolen bases
Rickey Henderson	326
Willie Randolph	251
Hal Chase	248
Roy White	233
Ben Chapman	184
Wid Conroy	184
Fritz Maisel	183
Mickey Mantle	153
Horace Clarke	151
Roberto Kelly	151

PITCHING

Earned-run average
(Minimum 1,000 innings)
Russ Ford	2.54
Jack Chesbro	2.58
Al Orth	2.72
Tiny Bonham	2.73

Whitey Ford	2.75
Spud Chandler	2.84
Ray Fisher	2.91
Mel Stottlemyre	2.97
Ray Caldwell	3.00
Fritz Peterson	3.10

Wins
Whitey Ford	236
Red Ruffing	231
Lefty Gomez	189
Ron Guidry	170
Bob Shawkey	168
Mel Stottlemyre	164
Herb Pennock	162
Waite Hoyt	157
Allie Reynolds	131
Jack Chesbro	128

Losses
Mel Stottlemyre	139
Bob Shawkey	131
Red Ruffing	124
Whitey Ford	106
Fritz Peterson	106
Lefty Gomez	101
Ray Caldwell	99
Waite Hoyt	98
Jack Chesbro	93
Jack Warhop	92

Innings pitched
Whitey Ford	3,170.1
Red Ruffing	3,168.2
Mel Stottlemyre	2,661.1
Lefty Gomez	2,498.1
Bob Shawkey	2,488.2
Ron Guidry	2,392.0
Waite Hoyt	2,272.1
Herb Pennock	2,203.1
Jack Chesbro	1,952.0
Fritz Peterson	1,857.1

Strikeouts
Whitey Ford	1,956
Ron Guidry	1,778
Red Ruffing	1,526
Lefty Gomez	1,468
Mel Stottlemyre	1,257
Bob Shawkey	1,163
Al Downing	1,028
Allie Reynolds	967

Dave Righetti	940
Jack Chesbro	913

Bases on balls
Lefty Gomez	1,090
Whitey Ford	1,086
Red Ruffing	1,066
Bob Shawkey	855
Allie Reynolds	819
Mel Stottlemyre	809
Tommy Byrne	763
Bob Turley	761
Ron Guidry	633
Waite Hoyt	631

Games
Dave Righetti	522
Whitey Ford	498
Red Ruffing	426
Sparky Lyle	420
Bob Shawkey	415
Johnny Murphy	383
Ron Guidry	368
Lefty Gomez	367
Waite Hoyt	365
Mel Stottlemyre	360

Shutouts
Whitey Ford	45
Red Ruffing	40
Mel Stottlemyre	40
Lefty Gomez	28
Allie Reynolds	27
Spud Chandler	26
Ron Guidry	26
Bob Shawkey	26
Vic Raschi	24
Bob Turley	21

Saves
Dave Righetti	224
Rich Gossage	151
Sparky Lyle	141
Mariano Rivera	129
Johnny Murphy	104
Steve Farr	78
Joe Page	76
John Wetteland	74
Lindy McDaniel	58
Luis Arroyo	43
Ryne Duren	43

HISTORY

YANKEES YEAR-BY-YEAR

Year	W	L	Place	Games Back	Manager	Leaders: Batting avg.	Hits	Home runs	RBIs	Wins	ERA
								BALTIMORE ORIOLES			
1901	68	65	5th	13½	McGraw	Donlin, .341	Seymour, 167	Williams, 7	Williams, 96	McGinnity, 26	McGinnity, 3.56
1902	50	88	8th	34	McGraw, Robinson	Selbach, .320	Selbach, 161	Williams, 8	Williams, 83	McGinnity, 13	McGinnity, 3.44
								HIGHLANDERS/YANKEES			
1903	72	62	4th	17	Griffith	Keeler, .318	Keeler, 164	McFarland, 5	Williams, 82	Chesbro, 21	Griffith, 2.70
1904	92	59	2nd	1½	Griffith	Keeler, .343	Keeler, 185	Ganzel, 6	Anderson, 82	Chesbro, 41	Chesbro, 1.82
1905	71	78	6th	21½	Griffith	Keeler, .302	Keeler, 169	Williams, 6	Williams, 60	Chesbro, 20	Griffity, 1.68
1906	90	61	2nd	3	Griffith	Chase, .323	Chase, 193	Conroy, 4	Williams, 77	Orth, 27	Clarkson, 2.32
1907	70	78	5th	21	Griffith	Chase, .287	Chase, 143	Hoffman, 5	Chase, 68	Orth, 14	Chesbro, 2.53
1908	51	103	8th	39½	Griffith, Elberfeld	Hemphill, .297	Hemphill, 150	Niles, 4	Hemphill, 44	Chesbro, 14	Chesbro, 2.93
1909	74	77	5th	23½	Stallings	Chase, .283	Engle, 137	Chase, Demmitt, 4	Engle, 71	Lake, 14	Lake, 1.88
1910	88	63	2nd	14½	Stallings, Chase	Knight, .312	Chase, 152	Cree, Wolter, 4	Chase, 73	Ford, 26	Ford, 1.65
1911	76	76	6th	25½	Chase	Cree, .348	Cree, 181	Cree, Wolter, 4	Hartzell, 91	Ford, 22	Ford, 2.28
1912	50	102	8th	55	Wolverton	Chase, Daniels, .274	Chase, 143	Zinn, 6	Chase, 58	Ford, 13	McConnell, 2.75
1913	57	94	7th	38	Chance	Cree, .272	Cree, 145	Sweeney, Wolter, 2	Cree, 63	Fisher, Ford, 11	Caldwell, 2.41
1914	70	84	*6th	30	Chance, Peckinpaugh	Cook, .283	Cook, 133	Peckinpaugh, 3	Peckinpaugh, 51	Caldwell, 17	Caldwell, 1.94
1915	69	83	5th	32½	Donovan	Maisel, .281	Maisel, 149	Peckinpaugh, 5	Pipp, 58	Caldwell, 19	Fisher, 2.11
1916	80	74	4th	11	Donovan	Baker, .269	Pipp, 143	Pipp, 12	Pipp, 99	Shawkey, 23	Cullop, 2.05
1917	71	82	6th	28½	Huggins	Baker, .306	Baker, 154	Baker, 6	Baker, 68	Mogridge, 16	Mogridge, 2.18
1918	60	63	4th	13½	Huggins	Baker, .306	Baker, 154	Baker, 6	Baker, 68	Mogridge, 16	Mogridge, 2.18
1919	80	59	3rd	7½	Huggins	Peckinpaugh, .305	Baker, 166	Baker, 10	Baker, 78	Shawkey, 20	Mays, 1.65
1920	95	59	3rd	3	Huggins	Ruth, .376	Pratt, 180	Ruth, 54	Ruth, 137	Mays, 26	Shawkey, 2.45
1921	98	55	1st	+4½	Huggins	Ruth, .378	Ruth, 204	Ruth, 59	Ruth, 171	Mays, 27	Mays, 3.05
1922	94	60	1st	+1	Huggins	Pipp, .329	Pipp, 190	Ruth, 35	Ruth, 96	Bush, 26	Shawkey, 2.91
1923	98	54	1st	+16	Huggins	Ruth, .393	Ruth, 205	Ruth, 41	Ruth, 131	Jones, 21	Hoyt, 3.02
1924	89	63	2nd	2	Huggins	Ruth, .378	Ruth, 200	Ruth, 46	Ruth, 121	Pennock, 21	Pennock, 2.83
1925	69	85	7th	30	Huggins	Combs, .342	Combs, 203	Meusel, 33	Meusel, 138	Pennock, 16	Pennock, 2.96
1926	91	63	1st	+3	Huggins	Ruth, .372	Ruth, 184	Ruth, 47	Ruth, 146	Pennock, 23	Shocker, 3.38
1927	110	44	1st	+19	Huggins	Gehrig, .373	Combs, 231	Ruth, 60	Gehrig, 175	Hoyt, 22	W. Moore, 2.28
1928	101	53	1st	+2½	Huggins	Gehrig, .374	Gehrig, 210	Ruth, 54	Gehrig, Ruth, 142	Pipgras, 24	Pennock, 2.56
1929	88	66	2nd	18	Huggins, Fletcher	Lazzeri, .354	Combs, 202	Ruth, 46	Ruth, 154	Pipgras, 18	Zachary, 2.48
1930	86	68	3rd	16	Shawkey	Gehrig, .379	Gehrig, 220	Ruth, 49	Gehrig, 174	Pipgras, Ruffing, 15	Pipgras, 4.11
1931	94	59	2nd	13½	McCarthy	Ruth, .373	Gehrig, 211	Gehrig, Ruth, 46	Gehrig, 184	Gomez, 21	Gomez, 2.67
1932	107	47	1st	+13	McCarthy	Gehrig, .349	Gehrig, 208	Ruth, 41	Gehrig, 151	Gomez, 24	Ruffing, 3.09
1933	91	59	2nd	7	McCarthy	Gehrig, .334	Gehrig, 198	Ruth, 34	Gehrig, 139	Gomez, 16	Gomez, 3.18
1934	94	60	2nd	7	McCarthy	Gehrig, .363	Gehrig, 210	Gehrig, 49	Gehrig, 165	Gomez, 26	Gomez, 2.33
1935	89	60	2nd	3	McCarthy	Gehrig, .329	Rolfe, 192	Gehrig, 30	Gehrig, 119	Ruffing, 16	Ruffing, 3.12
1936	102	51	1st	+19½	McCarthy	Dickey, .362	DiMaggio, 206	Gehrig, 49	Gehrig, 152	Ruffing, 20	Pearson, 3.71
1937	102	52	1st	+13	McCarthy	Gehrig, .351	DiMaggio, 215	DiMaggio, 46	DiMaggio, 167	Gomez, 21	Gomez, 2.33
1938	99	53	1st	+9½	McCarthy	DiMaggio, .324	Rolfe, 196	DiMaggio, 32	DiMaggio, 140	Ruffing, 21	Ruffing, 3.31
1939	106	45	1st	+17	McCarthy	DiMaggio, .381	Rolfe, 213	DiMaggio, 30	DiMaggio, 126	Ruffing, 21	Russo, 2.41
1940	88	66	3rd	2	McCarthy	DiMaggio, .352	DiMaggio, 179	DiMaggio, 31	DiMaggio, 133	Ruffing, 15	Bonham, 1.90
1941	101	53	1st	+17	McCarthy	DiMaggio, .357	DiMaggio, 193	Keller, 33	DiMaggio, 125	Gomez, Ruffing, 15	Bonham, 2.98
1942	103	51	1st	+9	McCarthy	Gordon, .322	DiMaggio, 186	Keller, 26	DiMaggio, 114	Bonham, 21	Bonham, 2.27
1943	98	56	1st	+13½	McCarthy	B. Johnson, .280	B. Johnson, 166	Keller, 31	Etten, 107	Chandler, 20	Chandler, 1.64
1944	83	71	3rd	6	McCarthy	Stirnweiss, .319	Stirnweiss, 205	Etten, 22	Lindell, 103	Borowy, 17	Borowy, 2.64
1945	81	71	4th	6½	McCarthy	Stirnweiss, .309	Stirnweiss, 195	Etten, 18	Etten, 111	Bevens, 13	Page, 2.82
1946	87	67	3rd	17	McCarthy, Dickey, Neun	DiMaggio, .290	Keller, 148	Keller, 30	Keller, 101	Chandler, 20	Chandler, 2.10
1947	97	57	1st	+12	Harris	DiMaggio, .315	DiMaggio, 168	DiMaggio, 20	Henrich, 98	Reynolds, 19	Chandler, 2.46
1948	94	60	3rd	2½	Harris	DiMaggio, .320	DiMaggio, 190	DiMaggio, 39	DiMaggio, 155	Raschi, 19	Byrne, 3.30
1949	97	57	1st	+1	Stengel	Henrich, .287	Rizzuto, 169	Henrich, 24	Berra, 91	Raschi, 21	Page, 2.59
1950	98	56	1st	+3	Stengel	Rizzuto, .324	Rizzuto, 200	DiMaggio, 32	Berra, 124	Raschi, 21	Ford, 2.81
1951	98	56	1st	+5	Stengel	McDougald, .306	Berra, 161	Berra, 27	Berra, 88	Lopat, Raschi, 21	Lopat, 2.91
1952	95	59	1st	+2	Stengel	Mantle, .311	Mantle, 171	Berra, 30	Berra, 98	Reynolds, 20	Reynolds, 2.06
1953	99	52	1st	+8½	Stengel	Woodling, .306	McDougald, 154	Berra, 27	Berra, 108	Ford, 18	Lopat, 2.42
1954	103	51	2nd	8	Stengel	Noren, .319	Berra, 179	Mantle, 27	Berra, 125	Grim, 20	Ford, 2.82
1955	96	58	1st	+3	Stengel	Mantle, .306	Mantle, 158	Mantle, 37	Berra, 108	Ford, 18	Ford, 2.63
1956	97	57	1st	+9	Stengel	Mantle, .353	Mantle, 188	Mantle, 52	Mantle, 130	Ford, 19	Ford, 2.47
1957	98	56	1st	+8	Stengel	Mantle, .365	Mantle, 173	Mantle, 34	Mantle, 94	Sturdivant, 16	Shantz, 2.45
1958	92	62	1st	+10	Stengel	Howard, .314	Mantle, 158	Mantle, 42	Mantle, 97	Turley, 21	Ford, 2.01
1959	79	75	3rd	15	Stengel	Richardson, .301	Mantle, 154	Mantle, 31	Lopez, 93	Ford, 16	Shantz, 2.38
1960	97	57	1st	+8	Stengel	Skowron, .309	Skowron, 166	Mantle, 40	Maris, 112	Ditmar, 15	Ditmar, 3.06
1961	109	53	1st	+8	Houk	Howard, .348	Richardson, 173	Maris, 61	Maris, 142	Ford, 25	Arroyo, 2.19
1962	96	66	1st	+5	Houk	Mantle, .321	Richardson, 209	Maris, 33	Maris, 100	Terry, 23	Ford, 2.90
1963	104	57	1st	+10½	Houk	Howard, .287	Richardson, 167	Howard, 28	Pepitone, 89	Ford, 24	Bouton, 2.53
1964	99	63	1st	+1	Berra	Howard, .313	Richardson, 181	Mantle, 35	Mantle, 111	Bouton, 18	Stottlemyre, 2.06
1965	77	85	6th	25	Keane	Tresh, .279	Tresh, 168	Tresh, 26	Tresh, 74	Stottlemyre, 20	Stottlemyre, 2.63
1966	70	89	10th	26½	Keane, Houk	Howard, .256	Richardson, 153	Pepitone, 31	Pepitone, 83	Peterson, Stottlemyre, 12	Bouton, 2.69
1967	72	90	9th	20	Houk	Clarke, .272	Clarke, 160	Mantle, 22	Pepitone, 64	Stottlemyre, 15	Monbouquette, 2.36
1968	83	79	5th	20	Houk	White, .267	White, 154	Mantle, 18	White, 62	Stottlemyre, 21	Bahnsen, 2.05
								EAST DIVISION			
1969	80	81	5th	28½	Houk	White, .290	Clarke, 183	Pepitone, 27	Murcer, 62	Stottlemyre, 20	Peterson, 2.55
1970	93	69	2nd	15	Houk	Munson, .302	White, 180	Murcer, 23	White, 94	Peterson, 20	McDaniel, 2.01
1971	82	80	4th	21	Houk	Murcer, .331	Murcer, 175	Murcer, 25	Murcer, 94	Stottlemyre, 16	Stottlemyre, 2.87
1972	79	76	4th	6½	Houk	Murcer, .292	Murcer, 171	Murcer, 33	Murcer, 96	Peterson, 17	Lyle, 1.92
1973	80	82	4th	17	Houk	Murcer, .304	Murcer, 187	Murcer, Nettles, 22	Murcer, 95	Stottlemyre, 16	Beene, 1.68
1974	89	73	2nd	2	Virdon	Piniella, .305	Murcer, 166	Nettles, 22	Murcer, 88	Dobson, Medich, 19	Lyle, 1.66
1975	83	77	3rd	12	Virdon, Martin	Munson, .318	Munson, 190	Bonds, 32	Munson, 102	Hunter, 23	Hunter, 2.58
1976	97	62	†1st	+10½	Martin	Rivers, .312	Chambliss, 188	Nettles, 32	Munson, 105	Figueroa, 19	Lyle, 2.26
1977	100	62	†1st	+2½	Martin	Rivers, .326	Rivers, 184	Nettles, 37	Jackson, 110	Figueroa, Guidry, 16	Lyle, 2.17
1978	100	63	‡†1st	+1	Martin, Lemon	Piniella, .314	Munson, 183	Jackson, Nettles, 27	Jackson, 97	Guidry, 25	Guidry, 1.74
1979	89	71	4th	13½	Lemon, Martin	Jackson, Piniella, .297	Chambliss, Randolph, 155	Jackson, 29	Jackson, 89	John, 21	Guidry, 2.78
1980	103	59	§1st	+3	Howser	Watson, .307	Jackson, 154	Jackson, 41	Jackson, 111	John, 22	May, 2.46
1981	59	48∞	†1st/6th	—	Michael, Lemon	Winfield, .294	Winfield, 114	Jackson, Nettles, 15	Winfield, 68	Guidry, 11	Righetti, 2.05
1982	79	83	5th	16	Lemon, Michael, King	Mumphrey, .300	Randolph, 155	Winfield, 37	Winfield, 106	Guidry, 14	Gossage, 2.23
1983	91	71	3rd	7	Martin	Griffey, .306	Winfield, 169	Winfield, 32	Winfield, 116	Guidry, 21	Fontenot, 3.33
1984	87	75	3rd	17	Berra	Mattingly, .343	Mattingly, 207	Baylor, 27	Mattingly, 110	Niekro, 16	Righetti, 2.34
1985	97	64	2nd	2	Berra, Martin	Mattingly, .324	Mattingly, 211	Mattingly, 35	Mattingly, 145	Guidry, 22	Fisher, 2.38
1986	90	72	2nd	5½	Piniella	Mattingly, .352	Mattingly, 238	Mattingly, 31	Mattingly, 113	Rasmussen, 18	Righetti, 2.45
1987	89	73	4th	9	Piniella	Mattingly, .327	Mattingly, 186	Pagliarulo, 32	Mattingly, 115	Rhoden, 16	Stoddard, 3.50
1988	85	76	5th	3½	Martin, Piniella	Winfield, .322	Mattingly, 186	Clark, 27	Winfield, 107	Candelaria, 13	Candelaria, 3.38
1989	74	87	5th	14½	Green, Dent	Sax, .315	Sax, 205	Mattingly, 23	Mattingly, 113	Hawkins, 15	Guetterman, 2.45
1990	67	95	7th	21	Dent, Merrill	Kelly, .285	Kelly, 183	Barfield, 25	Barfield, 78	Guetterman, 11	Guetterman, 3.39
1991	71	91	5th	20	Merrill	Sax, .304	Sax, 198	Nokes, 24	Hall, 80	Sanderson, 16	Habyan, 2.30
1992	76	86	*4th	20	Showalter	Mattingly, .288	Mattingly, 184	Tartabull, 25	Mattingly, 86	Perez, 13	Perez, 2.87
1993	88	74	2nd	7	Showalter	O'Neill, .311	Boggs, 169	Tartabull, 31	Tartabull, 102	Key, 18	Key, 3.00
1994	70	43	1st	+6½	Showalter	O'Neill, .359	O'Neill, 132	O'Neill, 21	O'Neill, 83	Key, 17	Key, 3.27
1995	79	65	▲2nd	7	Showalter	Boggs, .324	B. Williams, 173	O'Neill, 22	O'Neill, 96	Cone, 18	Cone, 3.57
1996	92	70	◆†1st	+4	Torre	Duncan, .340	Jeter, 183	B. Williams, 29	Martinez, 117	Pettitte, 21	M. Rivera, 2.09
1997	96	66	▲2nd	2	Torre	B. Williams, .328	Jeter, 190	Martinez, 44	Martinez, 141	Pettitte, 18	Cone, 2.82
1998	114	48	◆†1st	+22	Torre	B. Williams, .339	Jeter, 203	Martinez, 28	Martinez, 123	Cone, 20	O. Hernandez, 3.13
1999	98	64	◆†1st	+4	Torre	Jeter, .349	Jeter, 219	Martinez, 28	B. Williams, 115	O. Hernandez, 17	Cone, 3.44

* Tied for position. † Won Championship Series. ‡ Won division playoff. § Lost Championship Series. ∞ First half 34-22; second half 25-26. ▲ Lost Division Series. ◆ Won Division Series.

Note: Batting average minimum 350 at-bats; ERA minimum 90 innings pitched.

HISTORY

OAKLAND ATHLETICS

FRANCHISE CHRONOLOGY

First season: 1901, in Philadelphia, as a member of the new American League. The Athletics lost their big-league debut to Washington, 5-1, and went on to a 74-62 record and fourth-place finish.

1902-54: A team of extremes, Connie Mack's Athletics won nine pennants and five World Series—and finished eighth 18 times. Those first and last-place finishes accounted for 27 of the team's 54 seasons in Philadelphia. The powerful A's won three World Series from 1910 through 1913 and consecutive championships in 1929 and '30. But from 1934 through 1954, the A's never got their heads above fourth place and finished either seventh or eighth 14 times.

1955-1967: The A's defeated Detroit, 6-2, in their Kansas City debut and completed their first season in sixth place with a 63-91 record. That was as good as it got. The A's never finished above seventh place in the remainder of their Kansas City existence and never came closer than 19 games to the A.L. champion.

1968-present: The A's lost their Oakland debut to Baltimore, 3-1, but went on to record their first above-.500 record (82-80) since 1952. Young and talented, they would return to prominence and claim 10 West Division titles, six pennants and four World Series championships, including three straight fall classic titles from 1972 through 1974.

A'S VS. OPPONENTS BY DECADE

	Indians	Orioles	Red Sox	Tigers	Twins	White Sox	Yankees	Angels	Rangers	Brewers	Royals	Blue Jays	Mariners	Devil Rays	Interleague	Decade Record
1901-09	105-86	105-79	102-88	102-80	128-56	98-92	94-87									734-568
1910-19	105-110	120-93	84-129	99-116	108-101	90-125	104-100									710-774
1920-29	106-113	114-105	131-86	114-105	105-108	119-100	81-137									770-754
1930-39	106-114	127-88	99-116	106-111	91-124	118-102	76-140									723-795
1940-49	80-136	105-115	83-137	90-130	95-125	108-112	77-143									638-898
1950-59	67-153	109-110	79-141	98-122	113-107	96-124	62-158									624-915
1960-69	85-92	69-107	82-96	69-109	79-105	66-118	61-117	74-88	78-77	13-5	10-8					686-922
1970-79	70-46	50-66	54-63	60-56	76-91	89-76	54-63	97-72	78-76	74-54	90-79	18-15	28-15			838-772
1980-89	63-50	57-63	52-68	53-58	69-58	60-70	54-61	70-57	57-66	64-50	59-64	67-53	78-46			803-764
1990-99	45-62	54-65	46-71	53-53	60-58	57-60	59-58	68-55	61-63	35-50	68-53	55-53	71-50	14-7	27-23	773-781
Totals	832-962	910-891	812-995	844-940	924-933	901-979	722-1064	309-272	274-282	186-159	227-204	140-121	177-111	14-7	27-23	7299-7943

Interleague results: 5-5 vs. Dodgers; 6-4 vs. Padres; 7-7 vs. Giants; 5-5 vs. Rockies; 4-2 vs. Diamondbacks.

MANAGERS

(Philadelphia Athletics, 1901-54)
(Kansas City Athletics, 1955-67)

Name	Years	Record
Connie Mack	1901-50	3582-3814
Jimmie Dykes	1951-53	208-254
Eddie Joost	1954	51-103
Lou Boudreau	1955-57	151-260
Harry Craft	1957-59	162-196
Bob Elliott	1960	58-96
Joe Gordon	1961	26-33
Hank Bauer	1961-62, 1969	187-226
Eddie Lopat	1963-64	90-124
Mel McGaha	1964-65	45-91
Haywood Sullivan	1965	54-82
Alvin Dark	1966-67, 1974-75	314-291
Luke Appling	1967	10-30
Bob Kennedy	1968	82-80
John McNamara	1969-70	97-78
Dick Williams	1971-73	288-190
Chuck Tanner	1976	87-74
Jack McKeon	1977, 1978	71-105
Bobby Winkles	1977-78	61-86
Jim Marshall	1979	54-108
Billy Martin	1980-82	215-218
Steve Boros	1983-84	94-112
Jackie Moore	1984-86	163-190
Tony La Russa	1986-95	798-673
Art Howe	1996-99	304-344

Outfielder Reggie Jackson found early success with the Athletics in the late '60s.

WORLD SERIES CHAMPIONS

Year	Loser	Length	MVP
1910	Chicago	5 games	None
1911	N.Y. Giants	6 games	None
1913	N.Y. Giants	5 games	None
1929	Chicago	5 games	None
1930	St. Louis	6 games	None
1972	Cincinnati	7 games	Tenace
1973	N.Y. Mets	7 games	Jackson
1974	Los Angeles	5 games	Fingers
1989	San Francisco	4 games	Stewart

A.L. PENNANT WINNERS

Year	Record	Manager	Series Result
1902	83-53	Mack	None
1905	92-56	Mack	Lost to Giants
1910	102-48	Mack	Defeated Cubs
1911	101-50	Mack	Defeated Giants
1913	96-57	Mack	Defeated Giants
1914	99-53	Mack	Lost to Braves
1929	104-46	Mack	Defeated Cubs
1930	102-52	Mack	Defeated Cardinals
1931	107-45	Mack	Lost to Cardinals
1972	93-62	Williams	Defeated Reds
1973	94-68	Williams	Defeated Mets
1974	90-72	Dark	Defeated Dodgers
1988	104-58	La Russa	Lost to Dodgers
1989	99-63	La Russa	Defeated Giants
1990	103-59	La Russa	Lost to Reds

WEST DIVISION CHAMPIONS

Year	Record	Manager	ALCS Result
1971	101-60	Williams	Lost to Orioles
1972	93-62	Williams	Defeated Tigers
1973	94-68	Williams	Defeated Orioles
1974	90-72	Dark	Defeated Orioles
1975	98-64	Dark	Lost to Red Sox
1981*	64-45	Martin	Lost to Yankees
1988	104-58	La Russa	Defeated Red Sox
1989	99-63	La Russa	Defeated Blue Jays
1990	103-59	La Russa	Defeated Red Sox
1992	96-66	La Russa	Lost to Blue Jays

* First-half champion; won division playoff from Royals.

ATTENDANCE HIGHS

Total	Season	Park
2,900,217	1990	Oakland Coliseum
2,713,493	1991	Oakland Coliseum
2,667,255	1989	Oakland Coliseum
2,494,160	1992	Oakland Coliseum
2,287,335	1988	Oakland Coliseum

BALLPARK CHRONOLOGY

Network Associates Coliseum, formerly Oakland Alameda County Coliseum (1968-present)
Capacity: 43,662.
First game: Baltimore 4, A's 1 (April 17, 1968).

First batter: Curt Blefary, Orioles.
First hit: Boog Powell, Orioles (home run).
First run: Boog Powell, Orioles (2nd inning).
First home run: Boog Powell, Orioles.
First winning pitcher: Dave McNally, Orioles.
First-season attendance: 837,466.

Columbia Park, Philadelphia (1901-08)
Capacity: 9,500.
First game: Washington 5, Athletics 1 (April 26, 1901).
First-season attendance: 206,329.

Shibe Park, Philadelphia (1909-54)
Capacity: 33,608.
First game: Athletics 8, Boston 1 (April 12, 1909).
First-season attendance: 517,653.

Municipal Stadium, Kansas City (1955-67)
Capacity: 35,020.
First game: Athletics 6, Detroit 2 (April 12, 1955).
First-season attendance: 1,393,054.

Note: Shibe Park was changed to Connie Mack Stadium in 1953.

A.L. MVPs

Lefty Grove, P, 1931
Jimmie Foxx, 1B, 1932
Jimmie Foxx, 1B, 1933
Bobby Shantz, P, 1952
Vida Blue, P, 1971
Reggie Jackson, OF, 1973
Jose Canseco, OF, 1988
Rickey Henderson, OF, 1990
Dennis Eckersley, P, 1992

CY YOUNG WINNERS

Vida Blue, LH, 1971
Catfish Hunter, RH, 1974
Bob Welch, RH, 1990
Dennis Eckersley, P, 1992

ROOKIES OF THE YEAR

Harry Byrd, P, 1952
Jose Canseco, OF, 1986
Mark McGwire, 1B, 1987
Walt Weiss, SS, 1988
Ben Grieve, OF, 1998

MANAGERS OF THE YEAR

Tony La Russa, 1988
Tony La Russa, 1992

RETIRED UNIFORMS

No.	Name	Pos.
27	Catfish Hunter	P
34	Rollie Fingers	P

HISTORY

30-plus home runs

58—	Jimmie Foxx	1932
52—	Mark McGwire	1996
49—	Mark McGwire	1987
48—	Jimmie Foxx	1933
47—	Reggie Jackson	1969
44—	Jimmie Foxx	1934
	Jose Canseco	1991
42—	Gus Zernial	1953
	Jose Canseco	1988
	Mark McGwire	1992
39—	Mark McGwire	1990
	Mark McGwire	1995
38—	Bob Cerv	1958
	Matt Stairs	1999
37—	Tilly Walker	1922
	Jimmie Foxx	1930
	Jose Canseco	1990
36—	Al Simmons	1930
	Jimmie Foxx	1935
	Reggie Jackson	1975
	Geronimo Berroa	1996
35—	Al Simmons	1932
	Tony Armas	1980
	Dave Kingman	1984, 1986
	Terry Steinbach	1996
	John Jaha	1999
34—	Al Simmons	1929
	Bob Johnson	1934
	Rocky Colavito	1964
	Mark McGwire	1997
33—	Jimmie Foxx	1929
	Gus Zernial	1951
	Dwayne Murphy	1984
	Jose Canseco	1986
	Mark McGwire	1989
	Jason Giambi	1999
32—	Reggie Jackson	1971, 1973
	Mark McGwire	1988
31—	Bob Johnson	1940
	Sal Bando	1969
	Jose Canseco	1987
30—	Jimmie Foxx	1931
	Bob Johnson	1938
	Gus Zernial	1955
	Dave Kingman	1985

100-plus RBIs

169—	Jimmie Foxx	1932
165—	Al Simmons	1930
163—	Jimmie Foxx	1933
157—	Al Simmons	1929
156—	Jimmie Foxx	1930
151—	Al Simmons	1932
130—	Frank Baker	1912
	Jimmie Foxx	1934
129—	Al Simmons	1925
	Gus Zernial	*1951
128—	Al Simmons	1931
125—	Nap Lajoie	1901
124—	Jose Canseco	1988
123—	Jason Giambi	1999
122—	Jose Canseco	1991
121—	Bob Johnson	1936
120—	Jimmie Foxx	1931
	Hank Majeski	1948
118—	Reggie Jackson	1969
	Dave Kingman	1984
	Mark McGwire	1987
117—	Frank Baker	1913
	Jimmie Foxx	1929
	Norm Siebern	1962
	Reggie Jackson	1973
	Jose Canseco	1986
115—	Frank Baker	1911
	Joe Hauser	1924
	Jimmie Foxx	1935
114—	Bob Johnson	1939
113—	Bob Johnson	1938
	Sal Bando	1969
	Jose Canseco	1987
	Mark McGwire	1996
112—	Mickey Cochrane	1932

111—	John Jaha	1999
110—	Jason Giambi	1998
109—	Al Simmons	1926
	Bob Johnson	1935
	Tony Armas	1980
108—	Lave Cross	1902
	Al Simmons	1927
	Bob Johnson	1937
	Sam Chapman	1949
	Gus Zernial	1953
	Mark McGwire	1990
107—	Al Simmons	1928
	Bob Johnson	1941
106—	Sam Chapman	1941
	Geronimo Berroa	1996
	Matt Stairs	1998
105—	Harry Simpson	1956
104—	Bob Cerv	1958
	Reggie Jackson	1975
	Mark McGwire	1992
103—	Bob Johnson	1940
	Sal Bando	1974
102—	Al Simmons	1924
	Eddie Robinson	1953
	Rocky Colavito	1964
	Matt Stairs	1999
101—	Stuffy McInnis	1912
	Tilly Walker	1921
	Jose Canseco	1990
	Ruben Sierra	1993
100—	Bing Miller	1930
	Gus Zernial	1952
	Terry Steinbach	1996

*125 with Athletics; 4 with White Sox.

20-plus victories

1901—	Chick Fraser	22-16
1902—	Rube Waddell	24-7
	Eddie Plank	20-15
1903—	Eddie Plank	23-16
	Rube Waddell	21-16
1904—	Eddie Plank	26-17
	Rube Waddell	25-19
1905—	Rube Waddell	27-10
	Eddie Plank	24-12
1907—	Eddie Plank	24-16
	Jimmy Dygert	21-8
1910—	Jack Coombs	31-9
	Chief Bender	23-5
1911—	Jack Coombs	28-12
	Eddie Plank	23-8
1912—	Eddie Plank	26-6
	Jack Coombs	21-10
1913—	Chief Bender	21-10
1918—	Scott Perry	20-19
1922—	Eddie Rommel	27-13
1925—	Eddie Rommel	21-10
1927—	Lefty Grove	20-13
1928—	Lefty Grove	24-8
1929—	George Earnshaw	24-8
	Lefty Grove	20-6
1930—	Lefty Grove	28-5
	George Earnshaw	22-13
1931—	Lefty Grove	31-4
	George Earnshaw	21-7
	Rube Walberg	20-12
1932—	Lefty Grove	25-10
1933—	Lefty Grove	24-8
1949—	Alex Kellner	20-12
1952—	Bobby Shantz	24-7
1971—	Vida Blue	24-8
	Catfish Hunter	21-11
1972—	Catfish Hunter	21-7
1973—	Catfish Hunter	21-5
	Ken Holtzman	21-13
	Vida Blue	20-9
1974—	Catfish Hunter	25-12
1975—	Vida Blue	22-11
1980—	Mike Norris	22-9
1987—	Dave Stewart	20-13
1988—	Dave Stewart	21-12
1989—	Dave Stewart	21-9
1990—	Bob Welch	27-6
	Dave Stewart	22-11

INDIVIDUAL SEASON, GAME RECORDS

SEASON

Batting

At-bats	670		Al Simmons	1932
Runs	152		Al Simmons	1930
Hits	253		Al Simmons	1925
Singles	174		Al Simmons	1925
Doubles	53		Al Simmons	1926
Triples	21		Frank Baker	1912
Home runs	58		Jimmie Foxx	1932
Home runs, rookie	49		Mark McGwire	1987
Grand slams	3		6 times	
			Last by Dave Kingman	1984
Total bases	438		Jimmie Foxx	1932
RBIs	169		Jimmie Foxx	1932
Walks	149		Ed Joost	1949
Most strikeouts	175		Jose Canseco	1986
Fewest strikeouts	17		Dick Siebert	1942
Batting average	.426		Nap Lajoie	1901
Slugging pct.	.749		Jimmie Foxx	1932
Stolen bases	130		Rickey Henderson	1982

Pitching

Games	81		John Wyatt	1964
Complete games	39		Rube Waddell	1904
Innings	383		Rube Waddell	1904
Wins	31		Jack Coombs	1910
			Lefty Grove	1931
Losses	25		Scott Perry	1920
Winning pct.	.886 (31-4)		Lefty Grove	1931
Walks	168		Elmer Myers	1916
Strikeouts	349		Rube Waddell	1904
Shutouts	13		Jack Coombs	1910
Home runs allowed	40		Orlando Pena	1964
Lowest ERA	1.30		Jack Coombs	1910
Saves	51		Dennis Eckersley	1992

GAME

Batting

Runs	5	Last by Luis Polonia	9-9-88
Hits	6	Last by Joe DeMaestri	7-8-55
Doubles	4	Frankie Hayes	7-25-36
Triples	3	Bert Campaneris	8-29-67
Home runs	3	Last by Miguel Tejada	6-11-99
RBIs	10	Reggie Jackson	6-14-69
Total bases	16	Jimmie Foxx	7-10-32
Stolen bases	6	Eddie Collins	9-11-12, 9-22-12

A.L. home run champions

1901—	Nap Lajoie	14
1902—	Socks Seybold	16
1904—	Harry Davis	10
1905—	Harry Davis	8
1906—	Harry Davis	12
1907—	Harry Davis	8
1911—	Frank Baker	11
1912—	Frank Baker	*10
1913—	Frank Baker	12
1914—	Frank Baker	9
1918—	Tilly Walker	*11
1932—	Jimmie Foxx	58
1933—	Jimmie Foxx	48
1935—	Jimmie Foxx	*36
1951—	Gus Zernial	33
1973—	Reggie Jackson	32
1975—	Reggie Jackson	*36
1981—	Tony Armas	*22
1987—	Mark McGwire	49
1988—	Jose Canseco	42
1991—	Jose Canseco	*44
1996—	Mark McGwire	52

* Tied for league lead

A.L. RBI champions

1901—	Nap Lajoie	125
1905—	Harry Davis	83
1906—	Harry Davis	96
1912—	Frank Baker	130
1913—	Frank Baker	117
1929—	Al Simmons	157
1932—	Jimmie Foxx	169
1933—	Jimmie Foxx	163
1951—	Gus Zernial	*129
1973—	Reggie Jackson	117
1988—	Jose Canseco	124

*125 with Athletics; 4 with White Sox.

A.L. batting champions

1901—	Nap Lajoie	.426
1930—	Al Simmons	.381
1931—	Al Simmons	.390
1933—	Jimmie Foxx	.356
1951—	Ferris Fain	.344
1952—	Ferris Fain	.327

A.L. ERA champions

1905—	Rube Waddell	1.48
1909—	Harry Krause	1.39
1926—	Lefty Grove	2.51
1929—	Lefty Grove	2.81
1930—	Lefty Grove	2.54
1931—	Lefty Grove	2.06
1932—	Lefty Grove	2.84
1970—	Diego Segui	2.56
1971—	Vida Blue	1.82
1974—	Catfish Hunter	2.49
1981—	Steve McCatty	2.32
1994—	Steve Ontiveros	2.65

A.L. strikeout champions

1902—	Rube Waddell	210
1903—	Rube Waddell	302
1904—	Rube Waddell	349
1905—	Rube Waddell	287
1906—	Rube Waddell	196
1907—	Rube Waddell	232
1925—	Lefty Grove	116
1926—	Lefty Grove	194
1927—	Lefty Grove	174
1928—	Lefty Grove	183
1929—	Lefty Grove	170
1930—	Lefty Grove	209
1931—	Lefty Grove	175

No-hit pitchers
(9 innings or more)

1905—	Weldon Henley	6-0 vs. St. Louis
1910—	Chief Bender	4-0 vs. Cleveland
1916—	Joe Bush	5-0 vs. Cleveland
1945—	Dick Fowler	1-0 vs. St. Louis
1947—	Bill McCahan	3-0 vs. Washington
1968—	Catfish Hunter	4-0 vs. Minnesota (Perfect)
1970—	Vida Blue	6-0 vs. Minnesota
1975—	Vida Blue-Glenn Abbott-Paul Lindblad-Rollie Fingers	5-0 vs. California
1983—	Mike Warren	3-0 vs. Chicago
1990—	Dave Stewart	5-0 vs. Toronto

Longest hitting streaks

29—	Bill Lamar	1925
28—	Bing Miller	1929
27—	Socks Seybold	1901
	Al Simmons	1931
26—	Bob Johnson	1938
25—	Jason Giambi	1997
24—	Jimmie Foxx	1929
	Ferris Fain	1952
	Carney Lansford	1984
23—	Al Simmons	1925
22—	Al Simmons	1925
	Doc Cramer	1932
	Hector Lopez	1957
	Vic Power	1958
21—	Ty Cobb	1927
20—	Wally Schang	1916
	Wally Moses	1938
	Dave Philley	1953
	Hal Smith	1958
	Vic Power	*1958
	Jerry Lumpe	1962

*Two teams

Hard-hitting Al Simmons was a key figure on Connie Mack's 1929 and '30 World Series-championship teams.

HISTORY

BATTING

Games
Bert Campaneris	1,795
Rickey Henderson	1,704
Jimmy Dykes	1,702
Sal Bando	1,468
Bob Johnson	1,459
Pete Suder	1,421
Harry Davis	1,413
Danny Murphy	1,412
Bing Miller	1,361
Elmer Valo	1,361

At-bats
Bert Campaneris	7,180
Rickey Henderson	6,140
Jimmy Dykes	6,023
Bob Johnson	5,428
Harry Davis	5,367
Sal Bando	5,145
Danny Murphy	5,138
Al Simmons	5,130
Pete Suder	5,085
Bing Miller	4,762

Runs
Rickey Henderson	1,270
Bob Johnson	997
Bert Campaneris	983
Jimmie Foxx	975
Al Simmons	969
Max Bishop	882
Jimmy Dykes	881
Mickey Cochrane	823
Harry Davis	811
Mark McGwire	773

Hits
Bert Campaneris	1,882
Al Simmons	1,827
Rickey Henderson	1,768
Jimmy Dykes	1,705
Bob Johnson	1,617
Harry Davis	1,500
Jimmie Foxx	1,492
Danny Murphy	1,489
Bing Miller	1,482
Mickey Cochrane	1,317
Carney Lansford	1,317

Doubles
Jimmy Dykes	365
Al Simmons	348
Harry Davis	319
Bob Johnson	307
Bing Miller	292
Rickey Henderson	289
Danny Murphy	279
Wally Moses	274
Bert Campaneris	270
Jimmie Foxx	257

Triples
Danny Murphy	102
Al Simmons	98
Frank Baker	88
Eddie Collins	85
Harry Davis	82
Jimmie Foxx	79
Rube Oldring	75
Topsy Hartsel	74
Bing Miller	74
Jimmy Dykes	73

Home runs
Mark McGwire	363
Jimmie Foxx	302
Reggie Jackson	269
Jose Canseco	254
Bob Johnson	252
Al Simmons	209
Sal Bando	192
Gus Zernial	191
Sam Chapman	174
Rickey Henderson	167

Total bases
Al Simmons	2,998
Bob Johnson	2,824
Jimmie Foxx	2,813
Rickey Henderson	2,640
Bert Campaneris	2,502
Jimmy Dykes	2,474
Mark McGwire	2,451
Reggie Jackson	2,323
Bing Miller	2,202
Harry Davis	2,190

Runs batted in
Al Simmons	1,178
Jimmie Foxx	1,075
Bob Johnson	1,040

SEASON

Batting
Most at-bats	5,630	1996
Most runs	981	1932
Fewest runs	447	1916
Most hits	1,659	1925
Most singles	1,206	1925
Most doubles	323	1928
Most triples	108	1912
Most home runs	243	1996
Fewest home runs	16	1915, 1917
Most grand slams	8	1932, 1999
Most pinch-hit home runs	8	1970
Most total bases	2,546	1996
Most stolen bases	341	1976
Highest batting average	.307	1925
Lowest batting average	.223	1908
Highest slugging pct.	.457	1932

Pitching
Lowest ERA	1.79	1910
Highest ERA	6.08	1936
Most complete games	136	1904
Most shutouts	27	1907, 1909
Most saves	64	1988, 1990
Most walks	827	1915
Most strikeouts	1,042	1987

Fielding
Most errors	337	1901
Fewest errors	87	1990
Most double plays	217	1949
Highest fielding average	.986	1990

General
Most games won	107	1931
Most games lost	117	1916
Highest win pct.	.704	1931
Lowest win pct.	.235	1916

GAME, INNING

Batting
Most runs, game	24	Last 5-1-29
Most runs, inning	13	Last 7-5-96
Most hits, game	29	5-1-29
Most home runs, game	8	6-27-96
Most total bases, game	44	5-1-29, 6-27-96

300-game winner Lefty Grove won 195 times as a member of the Athletics.

Mark McGwire	941
Sal Bando	796
Jose Canseco	793
Reggie Jackson	776
Jimmy Dykes	764
Bing Miller	762
Harry Davis	761

Extra-base hits
Al Simmons	655
Jimmie Foxx	638
Bob Johnson	631
Mark McGwire	563
Reggie Jackson	530
Jimmy Dykes	524
Rickey Henderson	497
Harry Davis	470
Bing Miller	460
Jose Canseco	448

Batting average
(Minimum 500 games)
Al Simmons	.356
Jimmie Foxx	.339
Eddie Collins	.337
Mickey Cochrane	.321
Frank Baker	.321
Stuffy McInnis	.313
Bing Miller	.311
Doc Cramer	.308
Pinky Higgins	.307
Wally Moses	.307

Stolen bases
Rickey Henderson	867
Bert Campaneris	566
Eddie Collins	376
Bill North	232
Harry Davis	223
Topsy Hartsel	196
Rube Oldring	187
Danny Murphy	185
Frank Baker	172
Carney Lansford	146

PITCHING

Earned-run average
(Minimum 1,000 innings)
Rube Waddell	1.97
Chief Bender	2.32
Eddie Plank	2.39
Jack Coombs	2.60
Lefty Grove	2.88

Rollie Fingers	2.91
Ken Holtzman	2.92
Vida Blue	2.95
Catfish Hunter	3.13
Joe Bush	3.19

Wins
Eddie Plank	284
Lefty Grove	195
Chief Bender	193
Eddie Rommel	171
Catfish Hunter	161
Rube Walberg	134
Rube Waddell	131
Vida Blue	124
Dave Stewart	119
Jack Coombs	115

Losses
Eddie Plank	162
Eddie Rommel	119
Rube Walberg	114
Catfish Hunter	113
Alex Kellner	108
Rick Langford	105
Chief Bender	102
Slim Harriss	93
Vida Blue	86
Rollie Naylor	83

Innings pitched
Eddie Plank	3,860.2
Chief Bender	2,602.0
Eddie Rommel	2,556.1
Catfish Hunter	2,456.1
Lefty Grove	2,401.0
Rube Walberg	2,186.2
Vida Blue	1,945.2
Rube Waddell	1,869.1
Alex Kellner	1,730.1
Dave Stewart	1,717.1

Strikeouts
Eddie Plank	1,985
Rube Waddell	1,576
Chief Bender	1,536
Lefty Grove	1,523
Catfish Hunter	1,520
Vida Blue	1,315
Dave Stewart	1,152
Rube Walberg	907
Jack Coombs	870
Blue Moon Odom	799

Bases on balls
Eddie Plank	913
Rube Walberg	853
Lefty Grove	740
Blue Moon Odom	732
Eddie Rommel	724
Alex Kellner	717
Catfish Hunter	687
Phil Marchildon	682
Dave Stewart	655
Vida Blue	617

Games
Dennis Eckersley	525
Eddie Plank	524
Rollie Fingers	502
Eddie Rommel	500
Paul Lindblad	479
Rube Walberg	412
Lefty Grove	402
Rick Honeycutt	387
Chief Bender	385
Catfish Hunter	363

Shutouts
Eddie Plank	59
Rube Waddell	37
Chief Bender	36
Catfish Hunter	31
Vida Blue	28
Jack Coombs	28
Lefty Grove	20
Eddie Rommel	18
Jimmy Dygert	16
Joe Bush	15
Rube Walberg	15

Saves
Dennis Eckersley	320
Rollie Fingers	136
Billy Taylor	100
John Wyatt	73
Jay Howell	61
Jack Aker	58
Lefty Grove	51
Paul Lindblad	41
Bill Caudill	37
Tom Gorman	33

ATHLETICS YEAR-BY-YEAR

Year	W	L	Place	Games Back	Manager	Leaders: Batting avg.	Hits	Home runs	RBIs	Wins	ERA
1901	74	62	4th	9	Mack	Lajoie, .422	Lajoie, 229	Lajoie, 14	Lajoie, 125	Fraser, 22	Plank, 3.31
1902	83	53	1st	+5	Mack	L. Cross, .342	L. Cross, 191	Seybold, 16	L. Cross, 108	Waddell, 24	Waddell, 2.05
1903	75	60	2nd	14½	Mack	Hartsel, .311	L. Cross, 163	Seybold, 8	L. Cross, 90	Plank, 23	Plank, 2.38
1904	81	70	5th	12½	Mack	Davis, .309	L. Cross, 176	Davis, 10	D. Murphy, 77	Plank, 26	Waddell, 1.62
1905	92	56	1st	+2	Mack	Davis, .285	Davis, 173	Davis, 8	Davis, 83	Waddell, 27	Waddell, 1.48
1906	78	67	4th	12	Mack	Seybold, .316	Davis, 161	Davis, 12	Davis, 96	Plank, 19	Waddell, 2.21
1907	88	57	2nd	1½	Mack	Nicholls, .302	Davis, 155	Davis, 8	Davis, 87	Plank, 24	Bender, 2.05
1908	68	85	6th	22	Mack	D. Murphy, .265	D. Murphy, 139	Davis, 5	D. Murphy, 66	Vickers, 18	Bender, 1.75
1909	95	58	2nd	3½	Mack	E. Collins, .346	E. Collins, 198	D. Murphy, 5	Baker, 85	Plank, 19	Krause, 1.39
1910	102	48	1st	+14½	Mack	E. Collins, .322	E. Collins, 188	D. Murphy, Oldring, 4	E. Collins, 81	Coombs, 31	Coombs, 1.30
1911	101	50	1st	+13½	Mack	E. Collins, .365	Baker, 198	Baker, 11	Baker, 115	Coombs, 28	Plank 2.10
1912	90	62	3rd	15	Mack	E. Collins, .348	Baker, 200	Baker, 10	Baker, 130	Plank, 26	Plank 2.22
1913	96	57	1st	+6½	Mack	E. Collins, .345	Baker, 190	Baker, 12	Baker, 117	Bender, 21	Bender, 2.21
1914	99	53	1st	+8½	Mack	E. Collins, .344	Baker, 182	Baker, 9	McInnis, 95	Bender, Bush, 17	Bressler, 1.77
1915	43	109	8th	58½	Mack	McInnis, .314	Strunk, 144	Oldring, 6	Lajoie, 61	Wyckoff, 10	Knowlson, 3.49
1916	36	117	8th	54½	Mack	Strunk, .316	Strunk, 172	Schang, 7	McInnis, 60	Bush, 15	Bush, 2.57
1917	55	98	8th	44½	Mack	McInnis, .303	McInnis, 172	Bodie, 7	Bodie, 74	Bush, 11	Bush, 2.47
1918	52	76	8th	24	Mack	Burns, .352	Burns, 178	T. Walker, 11	Burns, 70	Perry, 21	Perry, 1.98
1919	36	104	8th	52	Mack	Burns, .296	Burns, 139	T. Walker, 10	T. Walker, 64	J. Johnson, Kinney, 9	Naylor, 3.34
1920	48	106	8th	50	Mack	Dugan, .322	Dugan, 158	T. Walker, 17	T. Walker, 82	Perry, 11	Rommel, 2.85
1921	53	100	8th	45	Mack	Witt, .315	Witt, 198	T. Walker, 23	T. Walker, 101	Rommel, 16	Rommel, 3.94
1922	65	89	7th	29	Mack	B. Miller, .335	Galloway, 185	T. Walker, 37	T. Walker, 99	Rommel, 27	Rommel, 3.28
1923	69	83	6th	29	Mack	Hauser, .307	Hauser, 165	Hauser, 17	Hauser, 94	Rommel, 18	Rommel, 3.27
1924	71	81	5th	20	Mack	B. Miller, .342	Simmons, 183	Hauser, 27	Hauser, 115	Rommel, 18	Rommel, 3.95
1925	88	64	2nd	8½	Mack	Simmons, .387	Simmons, 253	Simmons, 24	Simmons, 129	Rommel, 21	Gray, 3.27
1926	83	67	3rd	6	Mack	Simmons, .341	Simmons, 199	Simmons, 19	Simmons, 109	Grove, 13	Grove, 2.51
1927	91	63	2nd	19	Mack	Simmons, .392	Cobb, 175	Simmons, 15	Simmons, 108	Grove, 20	Grove, 3.19
1928	98	55	2nd	2½	Mack	Simmons, .351	B. Miller, 168	Hauser, 16	Simmons, 107	Grove, 24	Grove, 2.58
1929	104	46	1st	+18	Mack	Simmons, .365	Simmons, 212	Simmons, 34	Simmons, 157	Earnshaw, 24	Grove, 2.81
1930	102	52	1st	+8	Mack	Simmons, .381	Simmons, 211	Foxx, 37	Simmons, 165	Grove, 28	Grove, 2.54
1931	107	45	1st	+13½	Mack	Simmons, .390	Simmons, 200	Foxx, 30	Simmons, 128	Grove, 31	Grove, 2.06
1932	94	60	2nd	13	Mack	Foxx, .364	Simmons, 216	Foxx, 58	Foxx, 169	Grove, 25	Grove, 2.84
1933	79	72	3rd	19½	Mack	Foxx, .356	Foxx, 204	Foxx, 48	Foxx, 163	Grove, 24	Grove, 3.20
1934	68	82	5th	31	Mack	Foxx, .334	Cramer, 202	Foxx, 44	Foxx, 130	Marcum, 14	Cain, 4.41
1935	58	91	8th	34	Mack	Foxx, .346	Cramer, 214	Foxx, 36	Foxx, 115	Marcum, 17	Mahaffey, 3.90
1936	53	100	8th	49	Mack	Moses, .345	Moses, 202	B. Johnson, 25	B. Johnson, 121	Kelley, 15	Kelley, 3.86
1937	54	97	7th	46½	Mack	Moses, .320	Moses, 208	B. Johnson, Moses, 25	B. Johnson, 108	Kelley, 13	E. Smith, 3.94
1938	53	99	8th	46	Mack	B. Johnson, .313	Moses, 181	B. Johnson, 30	B. Johnson, 113	Caster, 16	Caster, 4.35
1939	55	97	7th	51½	Mack	B. Johnson, .338	B. Johnson, 184	B. Johnson, 23	B. Johnson, 114	Nelson, 10	Nelson, 4.78
1940	54	100	8th	36	Mack	Moses, .309	Siebert, 170	B. Johnson, 31	B. Johnson, 103	Babich, 14	Babich, 3.73
1941	64	90	8th	37	Mack	Siebert, .334	Chapman, 178	Chapman, 25	B. Johnson, 107	Knott, 13	Marchildon, 3.57
1942	55	99	8th	48	Mack	B. Johnson, .291	B. Johnson, 160	B. Johnson, 13	B. Johnson, 80	Marchildon, 17	Wolff, 3.32
1943	49	105	8th	49	Mack	Hall, .256	Siebert, 140	Estalella, 11	Siebert, 72	Flores, 12	Flores, 3.11
1944	72	82	*5th	17	Mack	Siebert, .306	Estalella, 151	Hayes, 13	Hayes, 78	Christopher, 14	Berry, 1.94
1945	52	98	8th	34½	Mack	Estalella, .299	Hall, 161	Estalella, 8	Kell, 56	Christopher, 13	Berry, 2.35
1946	49	105	8th	55	Mack	McCosky, .354	Chapman, 142	Chapman, 20	Chapman, 67	Marchildon, 13	Flores, 2.32
1947	78	76	5th	19	Mack	McCosky, .328	McCosky, 179	Chapman, 14	Chapman, 83	Marchildon, 19	Fowler, 2.81
1948	84	70	4th	12½	Mack	McCosky, .326	Majeski, 183	Joost, 16	Majeski, 120	Fowler, 15	Fowler, 3.78
1949	81	73	5th	16	Mack	Valo, .283	Chapman, 164	Chapman, 24	Chapman, 108	Kellner, 20	Shantz, 3.40
1950	52	102	8th	46	Mack	Dillinger, Lehner, .309	Fain, 147	Chapman, 23	Chapman, 95	Hooper, 15	Brissie, 4.02
1951	70	84	6th	28	Dykes	Fain, .344	Joost, 160	Zernial, 33	Zernial, 125	Shantz, 18	Zoldak, 3.16
1952	79	75	4th	16	Dykes	Fain, .327	Fain, 176	Zernial, 29	Zernial, 100	Shantz, 24	Shantz, 2.48
1953	59	95	7th	41½	Dykes	Philley, .303	Philley, 188	Zernial, 42	Zernial, 108	Byrd, Kellner, 11	Fricano, 3.88
1954	51	103	8th	60	Joost	Finigan, .302	Finigan, 147	Wilson, 15	Zernial, 62	Portocarrero, 9	Burtschy, 3.80
							—KANSAS CITY ATHLETICS—				
1955	63	91	6th	33	Boudreau	Power, .319	Power, 190	Zernial, 30	Zernial, 84	Ditmar, 12	Gorman, 3.55
1956	52	102	8th	45	Boudreau	Power, .309	Power, 164	Simpson, 21	Simpson, 105	Ditmar, 12	Burnette, 2.89
1957	59	94	7th	38½	Boudreau, Craft	H. Smith, .303	Power, 121	Zernial, 27	Zernial, 69	Morgan, Trucks, 9	Trucks, 3.03
1958	73	81	7th	19	Craft	Cerv, .305	Cerv, 157	Cerv, 38	Cerv, 104	Garver, 12	Dickson, 3.27
1959	66	88	7th	28	Craft	Tuttle, .300	Tuttle, 139	Cerv, 20	Cerv, 87	B. Daley, 16	B. Daley, 3.16
1960	58	96	8th	39	Elliot	Williams, .288	Lumpe, 156	Siebern, 19	Siebern, 69	B. Daley, 16	Herbert, 3.28
1961	61	100	*9th	47½	Gordon, Bauer	Siebern, .296	Howser, 171	Siebern 18	Siebern, 98	Bass, 11	Archer, 3.20
1962	72	90	9th	24	Bauer	Siebern, .308	Lumpe, 193	Siebern, 25	Siebern, 117	Rakow, 14	Pena, 3.01
1963	73	89	8th	31½	Lopat	Causey, .280	Charles, 161	Siebern, Lumpe, 16	Siebern, 83	Pena, Wickersham, 12	Drabowsky, 3.05
1964	57	105	10th	42	Lopat, McGaha	Causey, .281	Causey, 170	Colavito, 34	Colavito, 102	Pena, 12	Stock, 1.94
1965	59	103	10th	43	McGaha, Sullivan	Campaneris, .270	Campaneris, 156	Harrelson, 23	Harrelson, 66	Sheldon, Talbot, 10	O'Donoghue, Sheldon, 3.95
1966	74	86	7th	23	Dark	Cater, .292	Campaneris, 153	Repoz, 11	Green, 62	Krausse, 14	Aker, 1.99
1967	62	99	10th	29½	Dark, Appling	Donaldson, .276	Campaneris, 149	Monday, 14	Monday, 58	Hunter, 13	Hunter, 2.81
							—OAKLAND ATHLETICS—				
1968	82	80	6th	21	Kennedy	Cater, .290	Campaneris, 177	Jackson, 29	Jackson, 74	Odom, 16	Nash, 2.28
							—WEST DIVISION—				
1969	88	74	2nd	9	Bauer, McNamara	Bando, .281	Bando, 171	Jackson, 47	Jackson, 118	Dobson, Odom, 15	Odom, 2.92
1970	89	73	2nd	9	McNamara	Rudi, .309	Campaneris, 168	Mincher, 27	Bando, 75	Hunter, 18	Segui, 2.56
1971	101	60	†1st	+16	Williams	Jackson, .277	Jackson, 157	Jackson, 32	Bando, 94	Blue, 24	Blue, 1.82
1972	93	62	‡1st	+5½	Williams	Rudi, .305	Rudi, 181	Epstein, 26	Bando, 77	Hunter, 21	Hunter, 2.04
1973	94	68	‡1st	+6	Williams	Jackson, .293	Bando, 170	Jackson, 32	Jackson, 117	Holtzman, Hunter, 21	Fingers, 1.92
1974	90	72	‡1st	+5	Dark	Rudi, .293	Rudi, 174	Jackson, 29	Bando, 103	Hunter, 25	Lindblad, 2.06
1975	98	64	†1st	+7	Dark	Washington, .308	Washington, 182	Jackson, 36	Jackson, 104	Blue, 22	Todd, 2.29
1976	87	74	2nd	2½	Tanner	North, .276	North, 163	Bando, 27	Rudi, 94	Blue, 18	Blue, 2.35
1977	63	98	7th	38½	McKeon, Winkles	Page, .307	Sanguillen, 157	Gross, 22	Page, 75	Blue, 14	Torrealba, 2.62
1978	69	93	6th	23	Winkles, McKeon	Page, .285	Page, 147	Page, 17	Page, 70	Johnson, 11	Sosa, 2.64
1979	54	108	7th	34	Marshall	Revering, .288	Revering, 136	Newman, 22	Revering, 77	Langford, 12	McCatty, 4.22
1980	83	79	2nd	14	Martin	R. Henderson, .303	R. Henderson, 179	Armas, 35	Armas, 109	Norris, 22	Norris, 2.53
1981	64	45	∞†1st/2nd	—	Martin	R. Henderson, .319	R. Henderson, 135	Armas, 22	Armas, 76	McCatty, 14	McCatty, 2.32
1982	68	94	5th	25	Martin	Burroughs, .277	R. Henderson, 143	Armas, 28	Murphy, 94	Keough, Langford, 11	Underwood, 3.29
1983	74	88	4th	25	Boros	Lansford, .308	R. Henderson, 150	Lopes, Murphy, 17	Murphy, 75	Codiroli, 12	Burgmeier, 2.81
1984	77	85	4th	7	Boros, Moore	Lansford, .300	Lansford, 179	Kingman, 35	Kingman, 118	Burris, 13	Caudill, 2.71
1985	77	85	*4th	14	Moore	Bochte, .295	Griffin, 166	Kingman, 30	Kingman, 91	Codiroli, 14	Howell, 2.85
1986	76	86	*3rd	16	Moore, La Russa	Griffin, .285	Griffin, 169	Kingman, 35	Canseco, 117	Young, 13	Haas, 2.74
1987	81	81	3rd	4	La Russa	Lansford, McGwire, .289	Canseco, 162	McGwire, 49	McGwire, 118	Stewart, 20	Eckersley, 3.03
1988	104	58	‡1st	+13	La Russa	Canseco, .307	Canseco, 187	Canseco, 42	Canseco, 124	Stewart, 21	Nelson, 3.06
1989	99	63	‡1st	+7	La Russa	Lansford, .336	Lansford, 185	McGwire, 33	Parker, 97	Stewart, 21	Burns, 2.24
1990	103	59	‡1st	+9	La Russa	R. Henderson, .325	R. Henderson, 159	McGwire, 39	McGwire, 108	Welch, 27	Stewart, 2.56
1991	84	78	4th	11	La Russa	Baines, .295	D. Henderson, 158	Canseco, 44	Canseco, 122	Moore, 17	Moore, 2.96
1992	96	66	†1st	+6	La Russa	Bordick, .300	Bordick, 151	McGwire, 42	McGwire, 104	Moore, 17	Parrett, 3.02
1993	68	94	7th	26	La Russa	R. Henderson, .327	Gates, 155	Sierra, 22	Sierra, 101	Witt, 14	Witt, 4.21
1994	51	63	2nd	1	La Russa	Berroa, .306	Javier, 114	Sierra, 23	Sierra, 92	Darling, 10	Ontiveros, 2.65
1995	67	77	4th	11	La Russa	R. Henderson, .300	Berroa, 152	McGwire, 39	McGwire, 90	Stottlemyre, 14	Ontiveros, 4.3
1996	78	84	3rd	12	Howe	McGwire, .312	Berroa, 170	McGwire, 52	McGwire, 113	Wasdin, 8	Prieto, 4.157
1997	65	97	4th	25	Howe	Stairs, .298	Giambi, 152	McGwire, 34	Giambi, McGwire, 81	Small, 9	Small, 4.28
1998	74	88	4th	14	Howe	Giambi, .295	Grieve, 168	Giambi, 27	Giambi, 110	Rogers, 16	Rogers, 3.17
1999	87	75	2nd	8	Howe	Giambi, .315	Giambi, 181	Stairs, 38	Giambi, 123	Heredia, 13	Hudson, 3.23

* Tied for position. † Lost Championship Series. ‡ Won Championship Series. ∞ First half 37-23; second half 27-22.

Note: Batting average minimum 350 at-bats; ERA minimum 90 innings pitched.

HISTORY

SEATTLE MARINERS

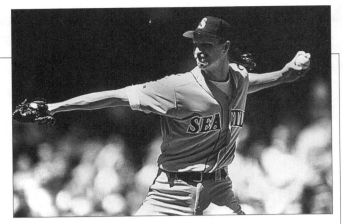

Lefthander Randy Johnson.

FRANCHISE CHRONOLOGY

First season: 1977, as a result of the two-team expansion that increased the American League to 14 teams. The Mariners were shut out by California, 7-0, in their A.L. debut and went on to lose 98 games. They finished their first season in sixth place, 38 games behind A.L. West Division-champion Kansas City.

1978-present: The Mariners have not had much to brag about in their short existence. Before 1995, they had never finished above fourth place and had two winning seasons to show for 18 years. Over that same span, their expansion mate, Toronto, had won five division titles, two pennants and a pair of World Series. But the Mariners' fortunes changed in 1995. They caught California with a late run, earned their first West Division championship in a one-game playoff and captured the A.L.'s first division playoff series in five games over the New York Yankees before losing in the Championship Series. They followed that success with a second division title in 1997 but came up short in the Division Series against Baltimore.

MARINERS VS. OPPONENTS BY DECADE

	A's	Indians	Orioles	Red Sox	Tigers	Twins	White Sox	Yankees	Angels	Rangers	Brewers	Royals	Blue Jays	Devil Rays	Interleague	Decade Record
1977-79	15-28	9-22	6-26	8-25	13-20	20-23	21-22	15-18	18-25	18-25	11-21	13-30	20-12			187-297
1980-89	46-78	48-72	51-63	54-66	48-66	59-67	52-71	45-68	48-79	65-65	53-59	59-70	45-69			673-893
1990-99	50-71	52-54	57-58	46-71	53-58	65-51	62-59	56-61	64-59	71-54	48-35	55-64	50-54	14-9	21-29	764-787
Totals	111-177	109-148	114-147	108-162	114-144	144-141	135-152	116-147	130-163	154-144	112-115	127-164	115-135	14-9	21-29	1624-1977

Interleague results: 4-6 vs. Dodgers; 5-9 vs. Padres; 3-7 vs. Giants; 6-4 vs. Rockies; 3-3 vs. Diamondbacks.

ALL-TIME RECORD OF EXPANSION TEAMS

Team	W	L	Pct.	DT	P	WS
Arizona	165	159	.509	1	0	0
Kansas City	2,471	2,412	.506	6	2	1
Toronto	1,784	1,818	.495	5	2	2
Houston	2,980	3,048	.494	6	0	0
Montreal	2,387	2,501	.488	2	0	0
Anaheim	2,987	3,201	.483	3	0	0
Milwaukee	2,348	2,542	.480	2	1	0
Colorado	512	559	.478	0	0	0
New York	2,840	3,178	.472	4	3	2
Texas	2,881	3,290	.467	4	0	0
San Diego	2,239	2,656	.457	3	2	0
Seattle	1,624	1,977	.451	2	0	0
Florida	472	596	.442	0	1	1
Tampa Bay	132	192	.407	0	0	0

DT—Division Titles. P—Pennants won. WS—World Series won.

MANAGERS

Name	Years	Record
Darrell Johnson	1977-80	226-362
Maury Wills	1980-81	26-56
Rene Lachemann	1981-83	140-180
Del Crandall	1983-84	93-141
Chuck Cottier	1984-86	98-119
Marty Martinez	1986	0-1
Dick Williams	1986-88	159-192
Jimmy Snyder	1988	45-60
Jim Lefebvre	1989-91	233-253
Bill Plummer	1992	64-98
Lou Piniella	1993-99	540-525

WEST DIVISION CHAMPIONS

Year	Record	Manager	ALCS Result
1995	79-66	Piniella	Lost to Indians
1997	90-72	Piniella	Lost Div. Series

BALLPARK CHRONOLOGY

Safeco Field (1999-present)
Capacity: 47,000.
First game: Padres 3, Mariners 2 (July 15, 1999).
First batter: Quilvio Veras, Padres.
First hit: Eric Owens, Padres (single).
First run: Quilvio Veras, Padres (3rd inning).
First home run: Russ Davis, Mariners (July 17).
First winning pitcher: Will Cunnane, Padres.
First-season attendance: 2,915,908 (includes Kingdome attendance prior to July 15).

The Kingdome (1977-99)
Capacity: 59,856.
First game: California 7, Mariners 0 (April 6, 1977).
First batter: Jerry Remy, Angels.
First hit: Don Baylor, Angels (single).
First run: Jerry Remy, Angels (1st inning).
First home run: Joe Rudi, Angels.
First winning pitcher: Frank Tanana, Angels.
First-season attendance: 1,338,511.

ATTENDANCE HIGHS

Total	Season	Park
3,198,995	1997	Kingdome
2,915,908	1999	Kingdome/Safeco Field
2,722,392	1996	Kingdome
2,644,166	1998	Kingdome
2,147,905	1991	Kingdome

A.L. MVP
Ken Griffey Jr. ,OF, 1997

CY YOUNG WINNER
Randy Johnson, LH, 1995

ROOKIE OF THE YEAR
Alvin Davis, 1B, 1984

MANAGER OF THE YEAR
Lou Piniella, 1995

The powerful bat of center fielder Ken Griffey Jr. has helped the Mariners rise out of the American League West cellar.

MILESTONE PERFORMANCES

25-plus home runs
56— Ken Griffey Jr...........................1997, 1998
49— Ken Griffey Jr...............................1996
48— Ken Griffey Jr...............................1999
45— Ken Griffey Jr...............................1993
44— Jay Buhner 1996
42— Alex Rodriguez 1998
      Alex Rodriguez 1999
40— Ken Griffey Jr...............................1994
      Jay Buhner 1995, 1997
36— Alex Rodriguez 1996
32— Gorman Thomas 1985
31— Tino Martinez 1995
      Paul Sorrento 1997
29— Willie Horton 1979
      Alvin Davis 1987
      Edgar Martinez 1995, 1998
28— Jim Presley 1985
      Edgar Martinez 1997
27— Lee Stanton 1977
      Alvin Davis 1984
      Jim Presley 1986
      Ken Phelps 1987
      Jay Buhner 1991, 1993
      Ken Griffey Jr................................1992
26— Phil Bradley 1985
25— Danny Tartabull............................1986
      Jay Buhner 1992

100-plus RBIs
147— Ken Griffey Jr..............................1997
146— Ken Griffey Jr..............................1998
140— Ken Griffey Jr..............................1996
138— Jay Buhner 1996
134— Ken Griffey Jr..............................1999
124— Alex Rodriguez 1998
123— Alex Rodriguez 1996
121— Jay Buhner 1995
116— Alvin Davis 1984
113— Edgar Martinez 1995
111— Tino Martinez 1995
      Alex Rodriguez 1999
109— Ken Griffey Jr..............................1993
      Jay Buhner 1997
108— Edgar Martinez 1997
107— Jim Presley 1986
106— Willie Horton 1979
103— Ken Griffey Jr..............................1992
      Edgar Martinez 1996
102— Edgar Martinez 1998
100— Bruce Bochte 1979
      Alvin Davis 1987
      Ken Griffey Jr................................1991

20-plus victories
1997— Randy Johnson 20-4

A.L. home run champions
1994— Ken Griffey Jr.............................40
1997— Ken Griffey Jr.............................56
1998— Ken Griffey Jr.............................56
1999— Ken Griffey Jr.............................48

A.L. RBI champions
1997— Ken Griffey Jr...........................147

A.L. batting champions
1992— Edgar Martinez 343
1995— Edgar Martinez 356
1996— Alex Rodriguez 358

A.L. ERA champions
1995— Randy Johnson 2.48

A.L. strikeout champions
1982— Floyd Bannister 209
1984— Mark Langston 204
1986— Mark Langston 245
1987— Mark Langston 262
1992— Randy Johnson 241
1993— Randy Johnson 308
1994— Randy Johnson 204
1995— Randy Johnson 294

No-hit pitchers
(9 innings or more)
1990— Randy Johnson ....2-0 vs. Detroit
1993— Chris Bosio ....7-0 vs. Boston

Longest hitting streaks
24— Joey Cora 1997
21— Dan Meyer 1979
      Richie Zisk 1982
20— Alex Rodriguez 1996
19— Phil Bradley 1986
18— Joey Cora 1996
17— Edgar Martinez 1992, 1997
16— Harold Reynolds 1989
      Craig Reynolds 1978
      Alex Rodriguez 1997
      Joey Cora, 2 1998
      Ken Griffey Jr................................1999
15— Willie Horton 1979
      Richie Zisk 1981
      Jack Perconte 1985
      Edgar Martinez 1991
      David Segui 1999

Second baseman Harold Reynolds was an offensive and defensive rock while the Mariners struggled through the 1980s.

INDIVIDUAL SEASON, GAME RECORDS

Speedy Julio Cruz, a second baseman during the team's formative years, holds the club record with 290 career stolen bases.

SEASON

Batting

At-bats	686	Alex Rodriguez	1998
Runs	141	Alex Rodriguez	1996
Hits	215	Alex Rodriguez	1996
Singles	152	Jack Perconte	1984
Doubles	54	Alex Rodriguez	1996
Triples	11	Harold Reynolds	1988
Home runs	56	Ken Griffey Jr.	1997, 1998
Home runs, rookie	27	Alvin Davis	1984
Grand slams	3	6 times	
		Last by Alex Rodriguez	1999
Total bases	393	Ken Griffey Jr..	1997
RBIs	147	Ken Griffey Jr.	1997
Walks	123	Edgar Martinez	1996
Most strikeouts	175	Jay Buhner	1997
Fewest strikeouts	34	Harold Reynolds	1987
Batting average	.358	Alex Rodriguez	1996
Slugging pct.	.674	Ken Griffey Jr.	1994
Stolen bases	60	Harold Reynolds	1987

Pitching

Games	78	Ed Vande Berg	1982
Complete games	14	Mike Moore	1985
		Mark Langston	1987
Innings	272	Mark Langston	1987
Wins	20	Randy Johnson	1997
Losses	19	Matt Young	1985
		Mike Moore	1987
Winning pct.	.900 (18-2)	Randy Johnson	1995
Walks	152	Randy Johnson	1991
Strikeouts	308	Randy Johnson	1993
Shutouts	4	Dave Fleming	1992
		Randy Johnson	1994
Home runs allowed	35	Scott Bankhead	1987
Lowest ERA	2.28	Randy Johnson	1997
Saves	33	Mike Schooler	1989
		Jose Mesa	1999

GAME

Batting

Runs	5	Ken Griffey Jr.	5-24-96
		Edgar Martinez	5-17-99
Hits	5	Last by John Mabry	5-8-99
Doubles	3	Last by David Bell	7-15-99
Triples	2	Last by Joey Cora	6-28-96
Home runs	3	Last by Edgar Martinez	5-18-99
RBIs	8	Alvin Davis	5-9-86
		Mike Blowers	5-24-95
Total bases	14	Mickey Brantley	9-14-87
Stolen bases	4	Last by Henry Cotto	6-23-90

BATTING

Games
Ken Griffey Jr.	1,535
Edgar Martinez	1,387
Jay Buhner	1,309
Alvin Davis	1,166
Harold Reynolds	1,155
Dave Valle	846
Jim Presley	799
Julio Cruz	742
Dan Wilson	713
Bruce Bochte	681

At-bats
Ken Griffey Jr.	5,832
Edgar Martinez	4,876
Jay Buhner	4,513
Alvin Davis	4,136
Harold Reynolds	4,090
Jim Presley	2,946
Julio Cruz	2,667
Alex Rodriguez	2,572
Dave Valle	2,502
Dan Wilson	2,419

Runs
Ken Griffey Jr.	1,063
Edgar Martinez	880
Jay Buhner	736
Alvin Davis	563
Harold Reynolds	543
Alex Rodriguez	493
Julio Cruz	402
Joey Cora	354
Jim Presley	351
Phil Bradley	346

Hits
Ken Griffey Jr.	1,742
Edgar Martinez	1,558
Alvin Davis	1,163
Jay Buhner	1,153
Harold Reynolds	1,063
Alex Rodriguez	791
Jim Presley	736
Bruce Bochte	697
Phil Bradley	649
Julio Cruz	649

Doubles
Edgar Martinez	372
Ken Griffey Jr.	320
Alvin Davis	212
Jay Buhner	209
Harold Reynolds	200
Alex Rodriguez	160
Jim Presley	147
Bruce Bochte	134
Dan Wilson	131
Al Cowens	128

Triples
Harold Reynolds	48
Ken Griffey Jr.	30
Phil Bradley	26
Spike Owen	23
Ruppert Jones	20
Jay Buhner	19
Dan Meyer	19
Joey Cora	18
Al Cowens	17
Julio Cruz	16
Leon Roberts	16

Home runs
Ken Griffey Jr.	398
Jay Buhner	279
Edgar Martinez	198
Alvin Davis	160
Alex Rodriguez	148
Jim Presley	115
Ken Phelps	105
Tino Martinez	88
Dave Henderson	79
Dave Valle	72

Total bases
Ken Griffey Jr.	3,316
Edgar Martinez	2,552
Jay Buhner	2,237
Alvin Davis	1,875
Alex Rodriguez	1,417
Harold Reynolds	1,410
Jim Presley	1,254
Bruce Bochte	1,031
Dan Wilson	973
Phil Bradley	969

Runs batted in
Ken Griffey Jr.	1,152
Jay Buhner	864
Edgar Martinez	780
Alvin Davis	667

SEASON

Batting
Most at-bats	5,668	1996
Most runs	993	1996
Fewest runs	558	1983
Most hits	1,625	1996
Most singles	1,056	1979
Most doubles	343	1996
Most triples	52	1979
Most home runs	264	1997
Fewest home runs	97	1978
Most grand slams	11	1996
Most pinch-hit home runs	5	1994, 1996
Most total bases	2,741	1996
Most stolen bases	174	1987
Highest batting average	.287	1996
Lowest batting average	.240	1983
Highest slugging pct	.485	1997

Pitching
Lowest ERA	3.69	1990
Highest ERA	5.24	1999
Most complete games	39	1987
Most shutouts	13	1991
Most saves	48	1991
Most walks	684	1999
Most strikeouts	1,156	1998

Fielding
Most errors	156	1986
Fewest errors	90	1993
Most double plays	191	1986
Highest fielding average	.985	1993

General
Most games won	90	1997
Most games lost	104	1978
Highest win pct	.556	1997
Lowest win pct	.350	1978

GAME, INNING

Batting
Most runs, game	22	4-29-99
Most runs, inning	11	4-29-99
Most hits, game	24	6-11-96
Most home runs, game	7	4-11-85, 7-31-96, 7-5-99
Most total bases, game	42	5-20-94

Outfielder Jay Buhner ranks second on the Mariners' career home run chart.

Alex Rodriguez	463
Jim Presley	418
Bruce Bochte	329
Dave Valle	318
Dan Wilson	317
Dan Meyer	313

Extra-base hits
Ken Griffey Jr.	748
Edgar Martinez	584
Jay Buhner	507
Alvin Davis	382
Alex Rodriguez	319
Jim Presley	275
Harold Reynolds	265
Bruce Bochte	205
Dave Henderson	205
Al Cowens	201
Dan Wilson	201

Batting average
(Minimum 500 games)
Edgar Martinez	.320
Alex Rodriguez	.308
Phil Bradley	.301
Ken Griffey Jr.	.299
Joey Cora	.293
Bruce Bochte	.290
Alvin Davis	.281
Rich Amaral	.278
Dan Wilson	.265
Dan Meyer	.265
Tino Martinez	.265

Stolen bases
Julio Cruz	290
Harold Reynolds	228
Ken Griffey Jr.	167
Alex Rodriguez	118
Phil Bradley	107
Henry Cotto	102
Rich Amaral	97
John Moses	70
Ruppert Jones	68
Jack Perconte	60

PITCHING

Earned-run average
(Minimum 500 innings)
Randy Johnson	3.42
Erik Hanson	3.69
Jamie Moyer	3.70
Brian Holman	3.73

Floyd Bannister	3.75
Mark Langston	4.01
Matt Young	4.13
Jim Beattie	4.14
Scott Bankhead	4.16
Rick Honeycutt	4.22

Wins
Randy Johnson	130
Mark Langston	74
Mike Moore	66
Erik Hanson	56
Jamie Moyer	52
Matt Young	45
Glenn Abbott	44
Jim Beattie	43
Bill Swift	41
Floyd Bannister	40

Losses
Mike Moore	96
Randy Johnson	74
Jim Beattie	72
Mark Langston	67
Matt Young	66
Glenn Abbott	62
Erik Hanson	54
Floyd Bannister	50
Bill Swift	49
Rick Honeycutt	41

Innings pitched
Randy Johnson	1,838.1
Mike Moore	1,457.0
Mark Langston	1,197.2
Erik Hanson	967.1
Jim Beattie	944.2
Glenn Abbott	904.0
Bill Swift	903.2
Matt Young	864.1
Floyd Bannister	768.1
Jamie Moyer	721.2

Strikeouts
Randy Johnson	2,162
Mark Langston	1,078
Mike Moore	937
Erik Hanson	740
Matt Young	597
Floyd Bannister	564
Jim Beattie	563
Jeff Fassero	466
Jamie Moyer	437
Mike Jackson	383

Bases on balls
Randy Johnson	884
Mark Langston	575
Mike Moore	535
Jim Beattie	369
Matt Young	365
Bill Swift	304
Erik Hanson	285
Floyd Bannister	250
Glenn Abbott	230
Dave Fleming	229

Games
Mike Jackson	335
Bobby Ayala	292
Bill Swift	282
Randy Johnson	274
Ed Vande Berg	272
Mike Schooler	243
Mike Moore	227
Jeff Nelson	227
Norm Charlton	205
Edwin Nunez	205
Shane Rawley	205

Shutouts
Randy Johnson	19
Mark Langston	9
Mike Moore	9
Floyd Bannister	7
Jim Beattie	6
Dave Fleming	5
Brian Holman	5
Matt Young	5
Glenn Abbott	3
Scott Bankhead	3
Erik Hanson	3
Rick Honeycutt	3
Mike Morgan	3
Jamie Moyer	3

Saves
Mike Schooler	98
Norm Charlton	66
Bobby Ayala	56
Bill Caudill	52
Shane Rawley	36
Edwin Nunez	35
Mike Jackson	34
Jose Mesa	33
Enrique Romo	26
Bill Swift	24
Mike Stanton	23

Year	W	L	Place	Games Back	Manager	Batting avg.	Hits	Home runs	RBIs	Wins	ERA
								Leaders			
							—WEST DIVISION—				
1977	64	98	6th	38	Johnson	Stanton, .275	Meyer, 159	Stanton, 27	Meyer, Stanton, 90	Abbott, 12	Romo, 2.83
1978	56	104	7th	35	Johnson	Roberts, .301	Reynolds, 160	Roberts, 22	Roberts, 92	Romo, 11	Romo, 3.69
1979	67	95	6th	21	Johnson	Bochte, .316	Horton, 180	Horton, 29	Horton, 106	Parrott, 14	Parrott, 3.77
1980	59	103	7th	38	Johnson, Wills	Bochte, .300	Bochte, 156	Paciorek, 15	Bochte, 78	Abbott, 12	Rawley, 3.33
1981	44	65	*6th/5th	—	Wills, Lachemann	Paciorek, .326	Paciorek, 132	Zisk, 16	Paciorek, 66	Bannister, 9	Abbott, 3.95
1982	76	86	4th	17	Lachemann	Bochte, .297	Bochte, Cowens, 151	Zisk, 21	Cowens, 78	Bannister, Caudill, 12	Caudill, 2.35
1983	60	102	7th	39	Lachemann, Crandall	S. Henderson, .294	D. Henderson, 136	Putnam, 19	Putnam, 67	Young, 11	Young, 3.27
1984	74	88	†5th	10	Crandall, Cottier	Perconte, .294	Perconte, 180	Davis, 27	Davis, 116	Langston, 17	Langston, 3.40
1985	74	88	6th	17	Cottier	P. Bradley, .300	P. Bradley, 192	G. Thomas, 32	P. Bradley, 88	Moore, 17	Nunez, 3.09
1986	67	95	7th	25	Cottier, Martinez, Williams	P. Bradley, .310	P. Bradley, Presley, 163	Presley, 27	Presley, 107	Langston, 12	Young, 3.82
1987	78	84	4th	7	Williams	Brantley, .302	P. Bradley, 179	Davis, 29	Davis, 100	Langston, 19	Guetterman, 3.81
1988	68	93	7th	35½	Williams, Snyder	Davis, .295	Reynolds, 169	Balboni, 21	Davis, 69	Langston, 15	Jackson, 2.63
1989	73	89	6th	26	Lefebvre	Davis, .305	Reynolds, 184	Leonard, 24	Davis, 95	Bankhead, 14	Jackson, 3.17
1990	77	85	5th	26	Lefebvre	E. Martinez, .302	Griffey Jr., 179	Griffey Jr., 22	Griffey Jr., 80	Hanson, 18	Swift, 2.39
1991	83	79	5th	12	Lefebvre	Griffey Jr., .327	Griffey Jr., 179	Buhner, 27	Griffey Jr., 100	Holman, R. Johnson, 13	Swift, 1.99
1992	64	98	7th	32	Plummer	E. Martinez, .343	E. Martinez, 181	Griffey Jr., 27	Griffey Jr., 103	Fleming, 17	Fleming, 3.39
1993	82	80	4th	12	Piniella	Griffey Jr., .309	Griffey Jr., 180	Griffey Jr., 45	Griffey Jr., 109	R. Johnson, 19	R. Johnson, 3.24
1994	49	63	3rd	2	Piniella	Griffey Jr., .323	Griffey Jr., 140	Griffey Jr., 40	Griffey Jr., 90	R. Johnson, 13	R. Johnson, 3.19
1995	78	66	‡§∞1st	+1	Piniella	E. Martinez, .356	E. Martinez, 182	Buhner, 40	Buhner, 121	Johnson, 18	Johnson, 2.48
1996	85	75	2nd	4½	Piniella	Rodriguez, .358	Rodriguez, 215	Griffey Jr., 49	Griffey Jr., 140	Hitchcock, Moyer, 13	Moyer, 3.98
1997	90	72	▲1st	+6	Piniella	E. Martinez, .330	Griffey Jr., 185	Griffey Jr., 56	Griffey Jr., 147	Johnson, 20	Johnson, 2.28
1998	76	85	3rd	11½	Piniella	E. Martinez, .322	Rodriguez, 213	Griffey Jr., 56	Griffey Jr., 146	Moyer, 15	Moyer, 3.53
1999	79	83	3rd	16	Piniella	E. Martinez, .337	Griffey Jr., 173	Griffey Jr., 48	Griffey Jr., 134	F. Garcia, 17	Moyer, 3.87

* First half 21-36; second half 23-29. † Tied for position. ‡ Won division playoff. § Won Division Series. ∞ Lost Championship Series. ▲ Lost Division Series.   Note: Batting average minimum 350 at-bats; ERA minimum 90 innings pitched.

Ruppert Jones

A PARTNERSHIP that included actor Danny Kaye was granted the American League's 13th franchise on February 6, 1976, as part of a two-team expansion that would increase the A.L. roster to 14. The Mariners represented baseball's second attempt to establish a team in Seattle. The Pilots played the 1969 season there before transferring operations to Milwaukee.

The Mariners stocked their roster with 30 players from the November 5, 1976, expansion draft, including first pick Ruppert Jones, an outfielder from the Kansas City organization. The team made its Major League debut on April 6, 1977, losing, 7-0, to the California Angels at Seattle's Kingdome.

Expansion draft (November 5, 1976)

Players

Juan Bernhardt	New York	infield
Steve Braun	Minnesota	outfield
Dave Collins	California	outfield
Julio Cruz	California	second base
Luis Delgado	Boston	outfield
*Ruppert Jones	Kansas City	outfield
Joe Lis	Cleveland	first base
Carlos Lopez	California	outfield
Tom McMillan	Cleveland	shortstop
Dan Meyer	Detroit	first base
Tommie Smith	Cleveland	outfield
Leroy Stanton	California	outfield
Bill Stein	Chicago	third base
Bob Stinson	Kansas City	catcher

Pitchers

Glenn Abbott	Oakland	righthanded
Steve Barr	Texas	righthanded
Pete Broberg	Milwaukee	righthanded
Steve Burke	Boston	righthanded
Joe Erardi	Milwaukee	righthanded
Bob Galasso	Baltimore	righthanded
Alan Griffin	Oakland	righthanded
Grant Jackson	New York	lefthanded
Rick Jones	Boston	lefthanded
Bill Laxton	Detroit	lefthanded
Frank MacCormack	Detroit	righthanded
Dave Pagan	Baltimore	righthanded
Dick Pole	Boston	righthanded
Roy Thomas	Chicago	righthanded
Stan Thomas	Cleveland	righthanded
Gary Wheelock	California	righthanded

*First pick

Opening day lineup

April 6, 1977

Dave Collins, designated hitter
Jose Baez, second base
Steve Braun, left field
Lee Stanton, right field
Bill Stein, third base
Dan Meyer, first base
Ruppert Jones, center field
Bob Stinson, catcher
Craig Reynolds, shortstop
Diego Segui, pitcher

Craig Reynolds

Mariners firsts

First hit: Jose Baez, April 6, 1977, vs. California
First home run: Juan Bernhardt, April 10, 1977, vs. California
First RBI: Dan Meyer, April 8, 1977 vs. California
First win: Bill Laxton, April 8, 1977, vs. California
First shutout: Dave Pagan, May 19, 1977, 3-0 at Oakland

HISTORY

TAMPA BAY DEVIL RAYS

FRANCHISE CHRONOLOGY

The beginnings: Tampa Bay, a longtime home to minor league baseball, the Gulf Coast Rookie League and spring training, pursued a Major League team for about 19 years before the dream was realized. At a March 9, 1995, owner's meeting, the vote was 28-0 to admit two new franchises, a Phoenix-based team that would be known as the Diamondbacks and a Tampa club, awarded to a local group headed by Tampa businessman Vincent J. Naimoli, that would become the Devil Rays. The franchise became the state's second, only two years after the Florida Marlins had begun play as an expansion team in Miami. Both teams were stocked in a November 1997 expansion draft and began play in the 1998 season—Arizona as a member of the N.L. West Division and the Devil Rays in the rugged A.L. East. The Diamondbacks and Devil Rays were the 13th and 14th expansion teams in baseball's long history.

First season: The March 31, 1998, debut on Florida's west coast was long on pageantry and short on success. The Devil Rays fell behind 11-0 and dropped an 11-6 decision to Detroit at Tropicana Field. Tampa Bay went on to record a 66-99 first-season finish, 51 games behind the record-setting New York Yankees.

1999: Clearly improvement was the goal for the Devil Rays' second season. And it was achieved—a 69-93 record in arguably baseball's best division. For the second year in a row, the A.L. East sported two playoff and three above-.500 teams, leaving the Devil Rays little shot at a division title.

Third baseman Bobby Smith.

DEVIL RAYS VS. OPPONENTS BY DECADE

	A's	Indians	Orioles	Red Sox	Tigers	Twins	White Sox	Yankees	Angels	Rangers	Royals	BlueJays	Mariners	Interleague	Decade Record
1998-99	7-14	7-12	14-10	12-13	11-9	9-12	10-11	5-19	10-13	8-15	11-10	10-15	9-14	9-25	132-192
Totals	7-14	7-12	14-10	12-13	11-9	9-12	10-11	5-19	10-13	8-15	11-10	10-15	9-14	9-25	132-192

Interleague results: 0-6 vs. Braves; 2-4 vs. Expos; 2-4 vs. Mets; 3-3 vs. Phillies; 2-8 vs. Marlins.

ALL-TIME RECORD OF EXPANSION TEAMS

Team	W	L	Pct.	DT	P	WS
Arizona	165	159	.509	1	0	0
Kansas City	2,471	2,412	.506	6	2	1
Toronto	1,784	1,818	.495	5	2	2
Houston	2,980	3,048	.494	6	0	0
Montreal	2,387	2,501	.488	2	0	0
Anaheim	2,987	3,201	.483	3	0	0
Milwaukee	2,348	2,542	.480	2	1	0
Colorado	512	559	.478	0	0	0
New York	2,840	3,178	.472	4	3	2
Texas	2,881	3,290	.467	4	0	0
San Diego	2,239	2,656	.457	3	2	0
Seattle	1,624	1,977	.451	2	0	0
Florida	472	596	.442	0	1	1
Tampa Bay	132	192	.407	0	0	0

DT—Division Titles. P—Pennants won. WS—World Series won.

BALLPARK CHRONOLOGY

Tropicana Field (1998-present)

Capacity: 43,819.
First game: Tigers 11, Devil Rays 6 (March 31, 1998).
First batter: Brian Hunter, Tigers.
First hit: Tony Clark, Tigers (single).
First run: Tony Clark, Tigers (2nd inning).
First home run: Luis Gonzalez, Tigers.
First winning pitcher: Justin Thompson, Tigers..
First-season attendance: 2,506,023.

MANAGERS

Name	Years	Record
Larry Rothschild	1998-99	132-192

ATTENDANCE HIGHS

Total	Season	Park
2,506,023	1998	Tropicana Field
1,749,567	1999	Tropicana Field

LONGEST HITTING STREAKS

18—Quinton McCracken	1998
13—Wade Boggs	1998
Dave Martinez	1999

Expansion draft (November 18, 1998)

Players
Bobby Abreu	Houston	outfield
Rich Butler	Toronto	outfield
Miguel Cairo	Cubs	second base
Steve Cox	Oakland	first base
Mike Difelice	St. Louis	catcher
Brooks Kieschnick	Cubs	first base
Aaron Ledesma	Baltimore	shortstop
Quinton McCracken	Colorado	outfield
Carlos Mendoza	N.Y. Mets	outfield
Herbert Perry	Cleveland	first base
Kerry Robinson	St. Louis	outfield
Andy Sheets	Seattle	shortstop
Bobby Smith	Atlanta	third base
Bubba Trammell	Detroit	outfield
Chris Wilcox	N.Y. Yankees	outfield
Randy Winn	Florida	outfield
Dmitri Young	Cincinnati	outfield/1B

Pitchers
Brian Boehringer	N.Y. Yankees	righthanded
Dan Carlson	San Francisco	righthanded
Mike Duvall	Florida	lefthanded
Vaughn Eshelman	Oakland	lefthanded
Rick Gorecki	Los Angeles	righthanded
Santos Hernandez	San Francisco	righthanded
Jason Johnson	Pittsburgh	righthanded
Ryan Karp	Philadelphia	lefthanded
John LeRoy	Atlanta	righthanded
Albie Lopez	Cleveland	righthanded
Jim Mecir	Boston	righthanded
Jose Paniagua	Montreal	righthanded
Bryan Rekar	Colorado	righthanded
*Tony Saunders	Florida	lefthanded
Dennis Springer	Anaheim	righthanded
Ramon Tatis	Cubs	lefthanded
Terrell Wade	Atlanta	lefthanded
Esteban Yan	Baltimore	righthanded

*First pick

Opening day lineup

March 31, 1998
Quinton McCracken, center field
Miguel Cairo, second base
Wade Boggs, third base
Fred McGriff, first base
Mike Kelly, left field
Paul Sorrento, designated hitter
John Flaherty, catcher
Dave Martinez, right field
Kevin Stocker, shortstop
Wilson Alvarez, pitcher

Tony Saunders

Devil Rays firsts
First hit: Dave Martinez, March 31, 1998, vs. Detroit (single)
First home run: Wade Boggs, March 31, 1998, vs. Detroit
First RBI: Wade Boggs, March 31, 1998, vs. Detroit
First win: Rolando Arrojo, April 1, 1998, vs. Detroit
First shutout: Rolando Arrojo, April 30, 1998, at Minnesota

HISTORY

BATTING

Games
Fred McGriff	295
Miguel Cairo	270
Paul Sorrento	236
Dave Martinez	233
Wade Boggs	213
John Flaherty	208
Quinton McCracken	195
Kevin Stocker	191
Aaron Ledesma	188
Randy Winn	188

At-bats
Fred McGriff	1,093
Miguel Cairo	980
Dave Martinez`	823
Quinton McCracken	762
John Flaherty	750
Paul Sorrento	729
Wade Boggs	727
Randy Winn	641
Aaron Ledesma	593
Kevin Stocker	590

Runs
Fred McGriff	148
Miguel Cairo	110
Dave Martinez	110
Quinton McCracken	97
Randy Winn	95
Wade Boggs	91
Paul Sorrento	80
Bubba Trammell	77
Kevin Stocker	76
Jose Canseco	75

Hits
Fred McGriff	324
Miguel Cairo	275
Dave Martinez	225
Quinton McCracken	216
Wade Boggs	210
John Flaherty	187
Aaron Ledesma	175
Randy Winn	175
Paul Sorrento	167
Kevin Stocker	146

Doubles
Fred McGriff	63
Quinton McCracken	44
Miguel Cairo	41
Paul Sorrento	41
Wade Boggs	37
Bubba Trammell	37
Dave Martinez	36
Aaron Ledesma	31
John Flaherty	30
Randy Winn	25

Triples
Randy Winn	13
Miguel Cairo	10
Quinton McCracken	8
Wade Boggs	5
Dave Martinez	5
Kevin Stocker	5
Tony Graffanino	4
Bobby Smith	4
Rich Butler	3
Mike Difelice	3
Aaron Ledesma	3

Home runs
Fred McGriff	51
Jose Canseco	34
Paul Sorrento	28
Bubba Trammell	26
John Flaherty	17
Bobby Smith	14
Mike Kelly	10
Wade Boggs	9
Mike Difelice	9
Dave Martinez	9

Total bases
Fred McGriff	542
Miguel Cairo	360
Quinton McCracken	300
Dave Martinez	298
Paul Sorrento	294
Wade Boggs	284
John Flaherty	268
Bubba Trammell	256
Jose Canseco	242
Randy Winn	235

Runs batted in
Fred McGriff	185
Paul Sorrento	99
Jose Canseco	95
John Flaherty	95
Dave Martinez	86

Miguel Cairo	82
Wade Boggs	81
Quinton McCracken	77
Bobby Smith	74
Bubba Trammell	74

Extra-base hits
Fred McGriff	115
Paul Sorrento	70
Bubba Trammell	64
Quinton McCracken	60
Miguel Cairo	59
Jose Canseco	53
Wade Boggs	51
Dave Martinez	50
John Flaherty	47
Randy Winn	41

Batting average
(Minimum 125 games)
Fred McGriff	.296
Aaron Ledesma	.295
Wade Boggs	.289
Bubba Trammell	.288
Quinton McCracken	.283
Miguel Cairo	.281
Dave Martinez	.273
Randy Winn	.273
Mike Difelice	.262
John Flaherty	.249

Stolen bases
Miguel Cairo	41
Randy Winn	35
Quinton McCracken	25
Dave Martinez	21
Kevin Stocker	14
Mike Kelly	13
Aaron Ledesma	10
Bobby Smith	9
Fred McGriff	8
Wade Boggs	4
Rich Butler	4

PITCHING

Earned-run average
(Minimum 125 innings)
Albie Lopez	3.51
Roberto Hernandez	3.55
Rick White	3.97
Rolando Arrojo	4.23
Wilson Alvarez	4.46
Tony Saunders	4.53
Ryan Rupe	4.55
Esteban Yan	4.69
Julio Santana	5.11
Bryan Rekar	5.41

Wins
Rolando Arrojo	21
Wilson Alvarez	15
Albie Lopez	10
Tony Saunders	9
Bryan Rekar	8
Ryan Rupe	8
Esteban Yan	8
Jim Mecir	7
Rick White	7
Bobby Witt	7

Losses
Rolando Arrojo	24
Wilson Alvarez	23
Tony Saunders	18
Bobby Witt	15
Bryan Rekar	14
Dennis Springer	11
Julio Santana	10
Dave Eiland	9
Roberto Hernandez	9
Ryan Rupe	9
Rick White	9

Innings pitched
Rolando Arrojo	342.2
Wilson Alvarez	302.2
Tony Saunders	234.1
Julio Santana	195.2
Bryan Rekar	181.1
Bobby Witt	180.1
Rick White	176.2
Esteban Yan	149.2
Roberto Hernandez	144.2
Albie Lopez	143.2

Strikeouts
Rolando Arrojo	259
Wilson Alvarez	235
Tony Saunders	202
Roberto Hernandez	124
Bobby Witt	123
Esteban Yan	123
Rick White	120
Bryan Rekar	110

Fred McGriff has added 51 home runs and 185 RBIs to his career totals as the first baseman for the Devil Rays.

SEASON

Batting
Most at-bats	5,586	1999
Most runs	772	1999
Fewest runs	620	1998
Most hits	1,531	1999
Most singles	1,085	1999
Most doubles	272	1999
Most triples	43	1998
Most home runs	145	1999
Fewest home runs	111	1998
Most grand slams	3	1998
Most pinch-hit home runs	3	1998
Most total bases	2,296	1999
Most stolen bases	120	1998
Highest batting average	.274	1999
Lowest batting average	.261	1998
Highest slugging pct.	.411	1999

Pitching
Lowest ERA	4.35	1998
Highest ERA	5.06	1999
Most complete games	7	1998
Most shutouts	8	1998
Most saves	45	1999
Most walks	695	1999
Most strikeouts	1,055	1999

Fielding
Most errors	135	1999
Fewest errors	94	1998
Most double plays	198	1999
Highest fielding average	.985	1998

General
Most games won	69	1999
Most games lost	99	1998
Highest win pct.	.426	1999
Lowest win pct.	.389	1998

GAME, INNING

Batting
Most runs, game	15	5-30-99, 9-19-99
Most runs, inning	8	5-30-99
Most hits, game	18	4-1-98, 9-4-99
Most home runs, game	4	5-30-99
Most total bases, game	36	5-30-99

Albie Lopez	99
Ryan Rupe	97

Bases on balls
Wilson Alvarez	147
Tony Saunders	140
Rolando Arrojo	125
Bobby Witt	96
Julio Santana	90
Roberto Hernandez	74
Esteban Yan	73
Bryan Rekar	62
Rick White	61
Dennis Springer	60

Games
Roberto Hernandez	139
Esteban Yan	114
Albie Lopez	105

Rick White	101
Scott Aldred	85
Jim Mecir	85
Rolando Arrojo	56
Julio Santana	54
Wilson Alvarez	53
Mike Duvall	43
Bryan Rekar	43

Shutouts
Rolando Arrojo	2
Bobby Witt	2

Saves
Roberto Hernandez	69
Albie Lopez	2
Jeff Sparks	1
Esteban Yan	1

HISTORY

TEXAS RANGERS

FRANCHISE CHRONOLOGY

First season: 1961, in Washington, as part of baseball's first expansion. The Senators, who were replacing a Washington Senators franchise that was relocating to Minnesota, dropped a 4-3 decision to Chicago in their Major League debut en route to a 61-100 first-season record.

1962-1971: The Senators, upholding the long tradition of their Washington predecessors, lost 100 or more games in each of their first four seasons and never finished above fourth place in their 11-year existence. The highlight of their Washington stay was an 86-76 mark in 1969, the first season of divisional play. That Senators team still finished 23 games behind East Division winner Baltimore.

1972-present: The Senators, relocated to Arlington, Texas, as the Texas Rangers, dropped a 1-0 debut to California and struggled to consecutive 100-loss seasons. The Rangers have fared better than their Washington ancestor, but they still are looking for their first pennant and World Series appearance. Their first West Division title was accompanied by an asterisk—the Rangers finished first in the strike-halted 1994 season with a 52-62 record. Their second, third and fourth titles, in 1996, '98 and '99, were all followed by losses to the New York Yankees in the Division Series.

First baseman Frank Howard.

RANGERS VS. OPPONENTS BY DECADE

	A's	Indians	Orioles	Red Sox	Tigers	Twins	White Sox	Yankees	Angels	Brewers	Royals	Blue Jays	Mariners	Devil Rays	Interleague	Decade Record
1961-69	77-78	73-88	52-110	75-86	68-94	56-99	61-95	55-104	80-76	5-7	5-7					607-844
1970-79	76-78	71-58	50-77	56-72	64-64	76-80	65-90	49-79	79-77	49-67	69-84	18-16	25-18			747-860
1980-89	66-57	57-55	39-72	53-64	47-73	65-64	64-59	54-62	55-68	52-63	54-70	49-67	65-65			720-839
1990-99	63-61	63-50	46-60	61-43	63-54	70-50	59-58	54-54	61-63	46-44	61-56	63-53	54-71	15-8	28-22	807-747
Totals	282-274	264-251	187-319	245-265	242-285	267-293	249-302	212-299	275-284	152-181	189-217	130-136	144-154	15-8	28-22	2881-3290

Interleague results: 5-5 vs. Dodgers; 5-5 vs. Padres; 6-4 vs. Giants; 6-4 vs. Rockies; 6-4 vs. Diamondbacks.

MANAGERS

(Washington Senators, 1961-71)

Name	Years	Record
Mickey Vernon	1961-63	135-227
Gil Hodges	1963-67	321-444
Jim Lemon	1968	65-96
Ted Williams	1969-72	273-364
Whitey Herzog	1973	47-91
Del Wilber	1973	1-0
Billy Martin	1973-75	137-141
Frank Lucchesi	1975-77	142-149
Eddie Stanky	1977	1-0
Connie Ryan	1977	2-4
Billy Hunter	1977-78	146-108
Pat Corrales	1978-80	160-164
Don Zimmer	1981-82	95-106
Darrell Johnson	1982	26-40
Doug Rader	1983-85	155-200
Bobby Valentine	1985-92	581-605
Toby Harrah	1992	32-44
Kevin Kennedy	1993-94	138-138
Johnny Oates	1995-99	424-368

WEST DIVISION CHAMPIONS

Year	Record	Manager	Div. Series Result
1994	52-62	Kennedy	None
1996	90-72	Oates	Lost to Yankees
1998	88-74	Oates	Lost to Yankees
1999	95-67	Oates	Lost to Yankees

ALL-TIME RECORD OF EXPANSION TEAMS

Team	W	L	Pct.	DT	P	WS
Arizona	165	159	.509	1	0	0
Kansas City	2,471	2,412	.506	6	2	1
Toronto	1,784	1,818	.495	5	2	2
Houston	2,980	3,048	.494	6	0	0
Montreal	2,387	2,501	.488	2	0	0
Anaheim	2,987	3,201	.483	3	0	0
Milwaukee	2,348	2,542	.480	2	1	0
Colorado	512	559	.478	0	0	0
New York	2,840	3,178	.472	4	3	2
Texas	2,881	3,290	.467	4	0	0
San Diego	2,239	2,656	.457	3	2	0
Seattle	1,624	1,977	.451	2	0	0
Florida	472	596	.442	0	1	1
Tampa Bay	132	192	.407	0	0	0

DT—Division Titles. P—Pennants won. WS—World Series won.

ATTENDANCE HIGHS

Total	Season	Park
2,945,228	1997	The Ballpark in Arlington
2,927,409	1998	The Ballpark in Arlington
2,888,920	1996	The Ballpark in Arlington
2,774,514	1999	The Ballpark in Arlington
2,503,198	1994	The Ballpark in Arlington

BALLPARK CHRONOLOGY

The Ballpark in Arlington (1994-present)
Capacity: 49,166.
First game: Milwaukee 4, Rangers 3 (April 11, 1994).
First batter: Pat Listach, Brewers.
First hit: David Hulse, Rangers (single).
First run: Dave Nilsson, Brewers (5th inning).
First home run: Dave Nilsson, Brewers.
First winning pitcher: Jaime Navarro, Brewers.
First-season attendance: 2,503,198.

Griffith Stadium, Washington, D.C. (1961)
Capacity: 27,410.
First game: Chicago 4, Senators 3 (April 10, 1961).
First-season attendance: 597,287.

RFK Stadium, Washington, D.C. (1962-71)
Capacity: 45,016.
First game: Senators 4, Detroit 1 (April 9, 1962).
First-season attendance: 729,775.

Arlington Stadium, Texas (1972-93)
Capacity: 43,521.
First game: Rangers 7, California 6 (April 21, 1972).
First-season attendance: 662,974.

Note: RFK Stadium was originally called D.C. Stadium.

A.L. MVPs

Jeff Burroughs, OF, 1974
Juan Gonzalez, OF, 1996
Juan Gonzalez, OF, 1998
Ivan Rodriguez, C, 1999

ROOKIE OF THE YEAR

Mike Hargrove, 1B, 1974

MANAGER OF THE YEAR

*Johnny Oates, 1996
*Co-winner

RETIRED UNIFORM

No.	Name	Pos.
34	Nolan Ryan	P

First baseman Pete O'Brien was Mr. Reliable during seven seasons with the Rangers.

25-plus home runs
48— Frank Howard 1969
47— Juan Gonzalez 1996
       Rafael Palmeiro 1999
46— Juan Gonzalez 1993
45— Juan Gonzalez 1998
44— Frank Howard 1968, 1970
43— Juan Gonzalez 1992
42— Juan Gonzalez 1997
39— Juan Gonzalez 1999
38— Dean Palmer 1996
37— Rafael Palmeiro 1993
36— Frank Howard 1967
35— Ivan Rodriguez 1999
33— Dean Palmer 1993
32— Larry Parrish 1987
       Mickey Tettleton 1995
31— Jose Canseco 1994
30— Mike Epstein 1969
       Jeff Burroughs 1973
       Pete Incaviglia 1986
       Ruben Sierra 1987
29— Jeff Burroughs 1975
       Bobby Bonds 1978
       Ruben Sierra 1989
28— Don Lock 1964
       Larry Parrish 1986
27— Don Lock 1963
       Toby Harrah 1977
       Pete Incaviglia 1987
       Juan Gonzalez 1991, 1995
26— Frank Howard 1971
       Larry Parrish 1983
       Rafael Palmeiro 1991
       Dean Palmer 1992
       Rusty Greer 1997
25— Jeff Burroughs 1974
       Ruben Sierra 1991

100-plus RBIs
157— Juan Gonzalez.....................................1998
148— Rafael Palmeiro 1999
144— Juan Gonzalez.....................................1996
131— Juan Gonzalez.....................................1997
128— Juan Gonzalez.....................................1999
126— Frank Howard 1970
119— Ruben Sierra 1989
118— Jeff Burroughs 1974
       Juan Gonzalez.....................................1993
117— Al Oliver 1980
116— Ruben Sierra 1991
113— Ivan Rodriguez 1999
111— Frank Howard 1969
109— Ruben Sierra 1987
       Juan Gonzalez.....................................1992
108— Rusty Greer 1998
107— Dean Palmer 1996
106— Frank Howard 1968
105— Rafael Palmeiro 1993
102— Juan Gonzalez.....................................1991
       Will Clark 1998
101— Buddy Bell 1979
       Larry Parrish 1984
       Rusty Greer 1999

100— Larry Parrish 1987
       Rusty Greer 1996

20-plus victories
1974— Fergie Jenkins 25-12
1992— Kevin Brown 21-11
1998— Rick Helling......................................20-7

A.L. home run champions
1968— Frank Howard 44
1970— Frank Howard 44
1992— Juan Gonzalez....................................43
1993— Juan Gonzalez....................................46

A.L. RBI champions
1970— Frank Howard 126
1974— Jeff Burroughs 118
1989— Ruben Sierra 119
1998— Juan Gonzalez 157

A.L. batting champions
1991— Julio Franco 341

A.L. ERA champions
1961— Dick Donovan 2.40
1969— Dick Bosman 2.19
1983— Rick Honeycutt 2.42

A.L. strikeout champions
1989— Nolan Ryan 301
1990— Nolan Ryan 232

No-hit pitchers
(9 innings or more)
1973— Jim Bibby.......................6-0 vs. Oakland
1977— Bert Blyleven ....6-0 vs. California
1990— Nolan Ryan ....5-0 vs. Oakland
1991— Nolan Ryan ....3-0 vs. Toronto
1994— Kenny Rogers ....4-0 vs. California (Perfect)

Longest hitting streaks
24— Mickey Rivers 1980
22— Jim Sundberg 1978
21— Johnny Grubb 1979
       Buddy Bell 1980
       Al Oliver 1980
       Juan Gonzalez ....1996 (2 times)
20— Mickey Rivers 1980
       Juan Gonzalez 1998
       Ivan Rodriguez 1999
19— Ken McMullen 1967
       Billy Sample 1981
       Scott Fletcher 1986
       Ivan Rodriguez 1996
18— Bill Stein 1981
       Billy Sample 1982
       Ruben Sierra 1991
17— Gene Woodling 1961
       Chuck Hinton 1962
       Ken Hamlin 1965
       Cesar Tovar 1974
       Toby Harrah 1976
       Al Oliver 1980
       Jim Sundberg 1981
       Buddy Bell 1983
       Todd Zeile 1999
16— Juan Beniquez 1977
       Willie Montanez 1979
       Rafael Palmeiro 1993

Venerable righthander Charlie Hough knuckleballed his way to 139 victories with the Rangers, a club career record.

Catcher Jim Sundberg (left) and designated hitter Richie Zisk were teammates on the 1978, '79 and '80 Texas teams.

SEASON

Batting
At-bats	670	Buddy Bell	1979
Runs	124	Rafael Palmeiro	1993
Hits	210	Mickey Rivers	1980
Singles	165	Mickey Rivers	1980
Doubles	50	Juan Gonzalez	1998
Triples	14	Ruben Sierra	1989
Home runs	48	Frank Howard	1969
Home runs, rookie	30	Pete Incaviglia	1986
Grand slams	3	3 times	
		Last by Rafael Palmeiro	1999
Total bases	382	Juan Gonzalez	1998
RBIs	157	Juan Gonzalez	1998
Walks	132	Frank Howard	1970
Most strikeouts	185	Pete Incaviglia	1986
Batting average	.341	Julio Franco	1991
Slugging pct.	.643	Juan Gonzalez	1996
Stolen bases	52	Bump Wills	1978

Pitching
Games	85	Mitch Williams	1987
Complete games	29	Fergie Jenkins	1974
Innings	328.1	Fergie Jenkins	1974
Wins	25	Fergie Jenkins	1974
Losses	22	Denny McLain	1971
Winning pct.	.741 (20-7)	Rick Helling	1998
Walks	143	Bobby Witt	1986
Strikeouts	301	Nolan Ryan	1989
Shutouts	6	Fergie Jenkins	1974
		Bert Blyleven	1976
Home runs allowed	41	Rick Helling	1999
Lowest ERA	2.17	Mike Paul	1972
Saves	43	John Wetteland	1999

GAME

Batting
Runs	5	Pete O'Brien	5-29-87
Hits	5	Last by Ivan Rodriguez	8-1-99
Doubles	3	Last by Rusty Greer	6-15-96
Triples	2	Last by Lee Stevens	7-20-96
Home runs	3	Last by Juan Gonzalez	9-24-99
RBIs	9	Ivan Rodriguez	4-13-99
Total bases	14	Jose Canseco	6-13-94
Stolen bases	4	Dave Hulse	5-1-93

BATTING

Games

Jim Sundberg	1,512
Toby Harrah	1,355
Juan Gonzalez	1,248
Frank Howard	1,172
Ivan Rodriguez	1,169
Ed Brinkman	1,143
Ruben Sierra	1,033
Buddy Bell	958
Pete O'Brien	946
Rafael Palmeiro	946

At-bats

Juan Gonzalez	4,831
Jim Sundberg	4,684
Toby Harrah	4,572
Ivan Rodriguez	4,443
Frank Howard	4,120
Ruben Sierra	4,043
Ed Brinkman	3,847
Buddy Bell	3,623
Rafael Palmeiro	3,558
Pete O'Brien	3,351

Runs

Juan Gonzalez	791
Ivan Rodriguez	649
Toby Harrah	631
Ruben Sierra	571
Rafael Palmeiro	567
Frank Howard	544
Rusty Greer	516
Jim Sundberg	482
Buddy Bell	471
Dean Palmer	425

Hits

Juan Gonzalez	1,421
Ivan Rodriguez	1,333
Jim Sundberg	1,180
Toby Harrah	1,174
Frank Howard	1,141
Ruben Sierra	1,132
Rafael Palmeiro	1,070
Buddy Bell	1,060
Rusty Greer	923
Pete O'Brien	914

Doubles

Juan Gonzalez	282
Ivan Rodriguez	261
Ruben Sierra	226
Rafael Palmeiro	204
Jim Sundberg	200
Buddy Bell	197
Rusty Greer	192
Toby Harrah	187
Pete O'Brien	161
Frank Howard	155

Triples

Ruben Sierra	43
Chuck Hinton	30
Ed Brinkman	27
Jim Sundberg	27
Ed Stroud	24
Toby Harrah	22
Oddibe McDowell	22
Del Unser	22
Buddy Bell	21
Rusty Greer	20
Frank Howard	20
Rafael Palmeiro	20
Ivan Rodriguez	20
Bump Wills	20

Home runs

Juan Gonzalez	340
Frank Howard	246
Rafael Palmeiro	154
Dean Palmer	154
Ruben Sierra	153
Larry Parrish	149
Ivan Rodriguez	144
Toby Harrah	124
Pete Incaviglia	124
Pete O'Brien	114

Total bases

Juan Gonzalez	2,761
Frank Howard	2,074
Ivan Rodriguez	2,066
Ruben Sierra	1,903
Toby Harrah	1,777
Rafael Palmeiro	1,776
Jim Sundberg	1,614
Buddy Bell	1,560
Rusty Greer	1,464
Larry Parrish	1,464

Runs batted in

Juan Gonzalez	1,075

SEASON

Batting

Most at-bats	5,703	1991
Most runs	945	1999
Fewest runs	461	1972
Most hits	1,653	1999
Most singles	1,202	1980
Most doubles	323	1996
Most triples	46	1989
Most home runs	230	1999
Fewest home runs	56	1972
Most grand slams	8	1999
Most pinch-hit home runs	8	1965, 1966
Most total bases	2,705	1999
Most stolen bases	196	1978
Highest batting average	.293	1980, 1996, 1999
Lowest batting average	.217	1972
Highest slugging pct	.479	1999

Pitching

Lowest ERA	3.31	1983
Highest ERA	5.07	1999
Most complete games	63	1976
Most shutouts	17	1977
Most saves	47	1999
Most walks	760	1987
Most strikeouts	1,112	1989

Fielding

Most errors	191	1975
Fewest errors	87	1996
Most double plays	173	1970, 1975
Highest fielding average	.986	1996

General

Most games won	95	1999
Most games lost	106	1963
Highest win pct	.586	1999
Lowest win pct	.346	1963

GAME, INNING

Batting

Most runs, game	26	4-19-96
Most runs, inning	16	4-19-96
Most hits, game	23	4-2-98
Most home runs, game	7	9-13-86
Most total bases, game	43	9-13-86

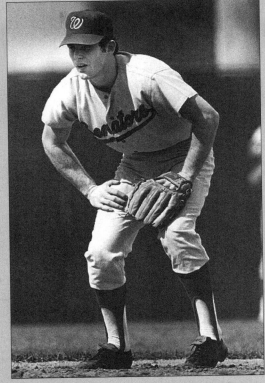

Third baseman Toby Harrah ranks high on most Rangers offensive charts.

Frank Howard	701
Ruben Sierra	656
Ivan Rodriguez	621
Rafael Palmeiro	579
Toby Harrah	568
Larry Parrish	522
Rusty Greer	503
Buddy Bell	499
Pete O'Brien	487

Extra-base hits

Juan Gonzalez	641
Ivan Rodriguez	425
Ruben Sierra	422
Frank Howard	421
Rafael Palmeiro	378
Toby Harrah	333
Rusty Greer	315
Buddy Bell	305
Larry Parrish	305
Dean Palmer	296

Batting average
(Minimum 500 games)

Al Oliver	.319
Rusty Greer	.309
Will Clark	.308
Julio Franco	.307
Mickey Rivers	.303
Rafael Palmeiro	.301
Ivan Rodriguez	.300
Juan Gonzalez	.294
Mike Hargrove	.293
Buddy Bell	.293

Stolen bases

Bump Wills	161
Toby Harrah	153
Dave Nelson	144
Oddibe McDowell	129
Julio Franco	98
Tom Goodwin	93
Chuck Hinton	92
Bill Sample	92
Cecil Espy	91
Ruben Sierra	86

PITCHING

Earned-run average
(Minimum 500 innings)

Gaylord Perry	3.26
Dick Bosman	3.35

Jon Matlack	3.41
Nolan Ryan	3.43
Claude Osteen	3.46
Joe Coleman	3.51
Fergie Jenkins	3.56
Casey Cox	3.67
Charlie Hough	3.68
Danny Darwin	3.72

Wins

Charlie Hough	139
Bobby Witt	104
Fergie Jenkins	93
Kevin Brown	78
Kenny Rogers	70
Jose Guzman	66
Dick Bosman	59
Danny Darwin	55
Nolan Ryan	51
Doc Medich	50

Losses

Charlie Hough	123
Bobby Witt	104
Fergie Jenkins	72
Dick Bosman	64
Kevin Brown	64
Jose Guzman	62
Bennie Daniels	60
Danny Darwin	52
Kenny Rogers	51
Joe Coleman	50

Innings pitched

Charlie Hough	2,308.0
Bobby Witt	1,680.2
Fergie Jenkins	1,410.1
Kevin Brown	1,278.2
Dick Bosman	1,103.1
Jose Guzman	1,013.2
Kenny Rogers	943.1
Jon Matlack	915.0
Danny Darwin	872.0
Joe Coleman	850.1

Strikeouts

Charlie Hough	1,452
Bobby Witt	1,405
Nolan Ryan	939
Fergie Jenkins	895
Kevin Brown	742
Jose Guzman	715
Kenny Rogers	680
Gaylord Perry	575

Dick Bosman	573
Danny Darwin	566

Bases on balls

Bobby Witt	1,001
Charlie Hough	965
Kevin Brown	428
Jose Guzman	395
Jim Hannan	378
Kenny Rogers	370
Nolan Ryan	353
Roger Pavlik	346
Fergie Jenkins	315
Bennie Daniels	309

Games

Jeff Russell	445
Kenny Rogers	376
Charlie Hough	344
Casey Cox	302
Bobby Witt	276
Darold Knowles	271
Ron Kline	260
Jim Hannan	248
Mitch Williams	232
Danny Darwin	224

Shutouts

Fergie Jenkins	17
Gaylord Perry	12
Bert Blyleven	11
Charlie Hough	11
Dick Bosman	9
Jim Bibby	8
Tom Cheney	7
Joe Coleman	7
Doc Medich	7
Kevin Brown	6
Phil Ortega	6
Nolan Ryan	6

Saves

Jeff Russell	134
John Wetteland	116
Ron Kline	83
Darold Knowles	64
Tom Henke	58
Jim Kern	37
Steve Foucault	35
Mitch Williams	32
Greg Harris	31
Mike Henneman	31

HISTORY

Year	W	L	Place	Games Back	Manager	Batting avg.	Hits	Home runs	RBIs	Wins	ERA
								Leaders			
						WASHINGTON SENATORS					
1961	61	100	*9th	47½	Vernon	Green, .280	O'Connell, 128	G. Green, 18	Tasby, 63	Daniels, 12	Donovan, 2.40
1962	60	101	10th	35½	Vernon	Hinton, .310	Hinton, 168	Bright, Hinton, 17	Hinton, 75	Stenhouse, 11	Cheney, 3.17
1963	56	106	10th	48½	Vernon, Hodges	Hinton, .269	Hinton, 152	Lock, 27	Lock, 82	Osteen, 9	Cheney, 2.71
1964	62	100	9th	37	Hodges	Hinton, .274	Hinton, 141	Lock, 28	Lock, 80	Osteen, 15	Ridzik, 2.89
1965	70	92	8th	32	Hodges	Howard, .289	Howard, 149	Howard, 21	Howard, 84	Richert, 15	Richert, 2.60
1966	71	88	8th	25½	Hodges	Howard, .278	Valentine, 140	Howard, 18	Howard, 71	Richert, 14	Kline, 2.39
1967	76	85	*6th	15½	Hodges	Howard, .256	McMullen, 138	Howard, 36	Howard, 89	Pascual, 12	Knowles, 2.70
1968	65	96	10th	37½	Lemon	Howard, .274	Howard, 164	Howard, 44	Howard, 106	Pascual, 13	Pascual, 2.69
						EAST DIVISION					
1969	86	76	4th	23	Williams	Howard, .296	Howard, 175	Howard, 48	Howard, 111	Bosman, 14	Bosman, 2.19
1970	70	92	6th	38	Williams	Howard, .283	Brinkman, 164	Howard, 44	Howard, 126	Bosman, 16	Knowles, 2.04
1971	63	96	5th	38½	Williams	Howard, .279	Howard, 153	Howard, 26	Howard, 83	Bosman, 12	Gogolewski, 2.75
						TEXAS RANGERS					
						WEST DIVISION					
1972	54	100	6th	38½	Williams	Biittner, Harrah, .259	Billings, 119	Ford, 14	Billings, 58	Hand, 10	Paul, 2.17
1973	57	105	6th	37	Herzog, Wilber, Martin	A. Johnson, .287	A. Johnson, 179	Burroughs, 30	Burroughs, 85	Bibby, 9	Bibby, 3.24
1974	84	76	2nd	5	Martin	Hargrove, .323	Burroughs, 167	Burroughs, 25	Burroughs, 118	Jenkins, 25	Foucault, 2.24
1975	79	83	3rd	19	Martin, Lucchesi	Hargrove, .303	Randle, 166	Burroughs, 29	Burroughs, 94	Jenkins, 17	G. Perry, 3.03
1976	76	86	*4th	14	Lucchesi	Hargrove, .287	Hargrove, 155	Grieve, 20	Burroughs, 86	G. Perry, 15	Blyleven, 2.76
1977	94	68	2nd	8	Lucchesi, Stanky, Ryan, Hunter	Hargrove, .305	Hargrove, 160	Harrah, 27	Harrah, 87	Alexander, 17	Blyleven, 2.72
1978	87	75	*2nd	5	Hunter, Corrales	Oliver, .324	Oliver, 170	Bonds, 29	Oliver, 89	Jenkins, 18	Matlack, 2.27
1979	83	79	3rd	5	Corrales	Oliver, .323	Bell, 200	Bell, Putnam, Zisk, 18	Bell, 101	Comer, 17	Kern, 1.57
1980	76	85	4th	20½	Corrales	Rivers, .333	Rivers, 210	Oliver, Zisk, 19	Oliver, 117	Medich, 14	Darwin, 2.63
1981	57	48	†2nd/3rd	—	Zimmer	Oliver, .309	Oliver, 130	Bell, 10	Bell, 64	Honeycutt, 11	Medich, 3.08
1982	64	98	6th	29	Zimmer, Johnson	Bell, .296	Bell, 159	Hostetler, 22	Bell, Hostetler, 67	Hough, 16	Schmidt, 3.20
1983	77	85	3rd	22	Rader	Bell, .277	Wright, 175	Parrish, 26	Parrish, 88	Hough, 15	Honeycutt, 2.42
1984	69	92	7th	14½	Rader	Bell, .315	Parrish, 175	Parrish, 22	Parrish, 101	Hough, 16	Tanana, 3.25
1985	62	99	7th	28½	Rader, Valentine	Ward, .287	Ward, 170	O'Brien, 22	O'Brien, 92	Hough, 14	Harris, 2.47
1986	87	75	2nd	5	Valentine	Ward, .316	O'Brien, 160	Incaviglia, 30	Parrish, 94	Hough, 17	Harris, 2.83
1987	75	87	*6th	10	Valentine	Fletcher, .287	Fletcher, Sierra, 169	Parrish, 32	Sierra, 109	Hough, 18	Mohorcic, 2.99
1988	70	91	6th	33½	Valentine	Petralli, .282	Sierra, 156	Sierra, 23	Sierra, 91	Hough, 15	Hough, 3.32
1989	83	79	4th	16	Valentine	Franco, .316	Sierra, 194	Sierra, 29	Sierra, 119	Ryan, 16	Ryan, 3.20
1990	83	79	3rd	20	Valentine	Palmeiro, .319	Palmeiro, 191	Incaviglia, 24	Sierra, 96	Witt, 17	Rogers, 3.13
1991	85	77	3rd	10	Valentine	Franco, .341	Palmeiro, Sierra, 203	Gonzalez, 27	Sierra, 116	Guzman, 13	Ryan, 2.91
1992	77	85	4th	19	Valentine, Harrah	Sierra, .278	Palmeiro, 163	Gonzalez, 43	Gonzalez, 109	Brown, 21	Brown, 3.32
1993	86	76	2nd	8	Kennedy	Gonzalez, .310	Palmeiro, 176	Gonzalez, 46	Gonzalez, 118	Rogers, 16	Pavlik, 3.41
1994	52	62	1st	+1	Kennedy	Clark, .329	Clark, 128	Canseco, 31	Canseco, 90	Rogers, 11	Rogers, 4.46
1995	74	70	3rd	4	Oates	Rodriguez, .303	Nixon, 174	Tettleton, 32	Clark, 92	Rogers, 17	Rogers, 3.38
1996	90	72	‡1st	+4½	Oates	Greer, .332	Rodriguez, 192	Gonzalez, 47	Gonzalez, 144	Hill, Witt, 16	Hill, 3.63
1997	77	85	3rd	13	Oates	Clark, .326	Greer, 193	Gonzalez, 42	Gonzalez, 131	Oliver, 13	Oliver, 4.20
1998	88	74	‡1st	+3	Oates	Rodriguez, .321	Gonzalez, 193	Gonzalez, 45	Gonzalez, 157	Helling, 20	Sele, 4.23
1999	95	67	‡1st	+8	Oates	Rodriguez, .332	Rodriguez, 199	Palmeiro, 47	Palmeiro, 148	Sele, 18	Loaiza, 4.56

* Tied for position. †First half 33-22; second half 24-26. ‡ Lost Division Series.

Note: Batting average minimum 350 at-bats; ERA minimum 90 innings pitched.

Bobby Shantz

WASHINGTON lost one team and gained another in the two-team 1961 American League expansion that marked the first addition of baseball franchises in more than six decades. The original Senators were granted permission to move to Minneapolis/St. Paul for the 1961 season and the new Senators, under the ownership of Elwood R. Quesada, were admitted to the fold on October 26, 1960, along with the Los Angeles Angels.

The new Senators, who would become the Texas Rangers after 11 Washington seasons, grabbed lefthander Bobby Shantz with their first pick in the December 14, 1960, A.L. expansion draft and 31 players overall. They made their Major League debut on April 10, 1961, dropping a 4-3 decision to the Chicago White Sox.

Expansion draft (December 14, 1960)

Players

Chester Boak	Kansas City	second base
Leo Burke	Baltimore	infield
Pete Daley	Kansas City	catcher
Dutch Dotterer	Kansas City	catcher
Gene Green	Baltimore	catcher
Joe Hicks	Chicago	outfield
Chuck Hinton	Baltimore	outfield
Bob Johnson	Kansas City	infield
Marty Keough	Cleveland	outfield
Jim King	Cleveland	outfield
Billy Klaus	Baltimore	infield
Dale Long	New York	first base
Jim Mahoney	Boston	shortstop
John Schaive	Minnesota	second base
Haywood Sullivan	Boston	catcher
Willie Tasby	Boston	outfield
Coot Veal	Detroit	shortstop
Gene Woodling	Baltimore	outfield
Bud Zipfel	New York	first base

Pitchers

Pete Burnside	Detroit	lefthanded
Dick Donovan	Chicago	righthanded
Rudy Hernandez	Minnesota	righthanded
Ed Hobaugh	Chicago	righthanded
John Klippstein	Cleveland	righthanded
Hector Maestri	Minnesota	righthanded
Carl Mathias	Cleveland	lefthanded
Joe McClain	Minnesota	righthanded
*Bobby Shantz	New York	lefthanded
Dave Sisler	Detroit	righthanded
Tom Sturdivant	Boston	righthanded
Hal Woodeshick	Minnesota	lefthanded

*First pick

Opening day lineup

April 10, 1961

Coot Veal, shortstop
Billy Klaus, third base
Marty Keough, right field
Dale Long, first base
Gene Woodling, left field
Willie Tasby, center field
Danny O'Connell, second base
Pete Daley, catcher
Dick Donovan, pitcher

Senators firsts

First hit: Coot Veal, April 10, 1961, vs. Chicago (single)
First home run: Billy Klaus, April 15, 1961, vs. Cleveland
First RBI: Gene Woodling, April 10, 1961, vs. Chicago
First win: Joe McClain, April 14, 1961, vs. Cleveland
First shutout: Tom Sturdivant, May 13, 1969, 4-0 vs. Boston

Billy Klaus

TORONTO BLUE JAYS

FRANCHISE CHRONOLOGY

First season: 1977, as part of a two-team expansion that increased the American League field to 14 teams. The Blue Jays celebrated the debut of A.L. baseball in Canada with a 9-5 victory over Chicago, but they would go on to lose 107 times and finish last in the A.L. East, 45½ games behind the New York Yankees.

1978-present: The Blue Jays struggled for six seasons as they built the foundation for a franchise that would rise to prominence. Building patiently from within, the Jays topped 100 losses in each of their first three seasons and occupied the basement of the A.L. East Division five consecutive years. But the patience was rewarded in 1985 when the young and talented Blue Jays, playing in their ninth season, captured their first East Division title and began a run that would produce consecutive World Series championships in 1992 and '93. The Blue Jays lost three Championship Series before securing 1992 postseason victories over Oakland and Atlanta—and the first World Series triumph for a Canadian-based team.

Outfielder George Bell.

BLUE JAYS VS. OPPONENTS BY DECADE

	A's	Indians	Orioles	Red Sox	Tigers	Twins	White Sox	Yankees	Angels	Rangers	Brewers	Royals	Mariners	Devil Rays	Interleague	Decade Record
1977-79	15-18	14-27	14-29	11-32	15-28	6-26	14-19	14-29	12-20	16-18	13-30	10-22	12-20			166-318
1980-89	53-67	71-52	61-62	62-59	68-59	64-50	70-50	57-65	63-57	67-49	56-71	56-60	69-45			817-746
1990-99	53-55	65-56	69-54	52-72	70-52	72-38	54-53	57-64	58-53	53-63	45-52	62-55	54-50	15-10	22-27	801-754
Totals	121-140	150-135	144-145	125-163	153-139	142-114	138-122	128-158	133-130	136-130	114-153	128-137	135-115	15-10	22-27	1784-1818

Interleague results: 5-4 vs. Braves; 9-4 vs. Expos; 2-7 vs. Mets; 4-5 vs. Phillies; 2-7 vs. Marlins.

MANAGERS

Name	Years	Record
Roy Hartsfield	1977-79	166-318
Bobby Mattick	1980-81	104-164
Bobby Cox	1982-85	355-292
Jimy Williams	1986-89	281-241
Cito Gaston	1989-97	702-650
Mel Queen	1997	4-1
Tim Johnson	1998	88-74
Jim Fregosi	1999	84-78

WORLD SERIES CHAMPIONS

Year	Loser	Length	MVP
1992	Atlanta	6 games	Borders
1993	Philadelphia	6 games	Molitor

A.L. PENNANT WINNERS

Year	Record	Manager	Series Result
1992	96-66	Gaston	Defeated Braves
1993	95-67	Gaston	Defeated Phillies

EAST DIVISION CHAMPIONS

Year	Record	Manager	ALCS Result
1985	99-62	Cox	Lost to Royals
1989	89-73	Williams, Gaston	Lost to A's
1991	91-71	Gaston	Lost to Twins
1992	96-66	Gaston	Defeated A's
1993	95-67	Gaston	Defeated White Sox

ALL-TIME RECORD OF EXPANSION TEAMS

Team	W	L	Pct.	DT	P	WS
Arizona	165	159	.509	1	0	0
Kansas City	2,471	2,412	.506	6	2	1
Toronto	1,784	1,818	.495	5	2	2
Houston	2,980	3,048	.494	6	0	0
Montreal	2,387	2,501	.488	2	0	0
Anaheim	2,987	3,201	.483	3	0	0
Milwaukee	2,348	2,542	.480	2	1	0
Colorado	512	559	.478	0	0	0
New York	2,840	3,178	.472	4	3	2
Texas	2,881	3,290	.467	4	0	0
San Diego	2,239	2,656	.457	3	2	0
Seattle	1,624	1,977	.451	2	0	0
Florida	472	596	.442	0	1	1
Tampa Bay	132	192	.407	0	0	0

DT—Division Titles. P—Pennants won. WS—World Series won.

ATTENDANCE HIGHS

Total	Season	Park
4,057,098	1993	SkyDome
4,028,318	1992	SkyDome
4,001,526	1991	SkyDome
3,885,284	1990	SkyDome
3,375,883	1989	SkyDome

BALLPARK CHRONOLOGY

SkyDome (1989-present)
Capacity: 50,516.
First game: Milwaukee 5, Blue Jays 3 (June 5, 1989).
First batter: Paul Molitor, Brewers.
First hit: Paul Molitor, Brewers (double).
First run: Paul Molitor, Brewers (1st inning).
First home run: Fred McGriff, Blue Jays.
First winning pitcher: Don August, Brewers.
First-season attendance: 3,375,883 (SkyDome and Exhibition Stadium).

Exhibition Stadium (1977-89)
Capacity: 43,737.
First game: Blue Jays 9, Chicago 5 (April 7, 1977).
First-season attendance: 1,701,052.

A.L. MVP

George Bell, OF, 1987

CY YOUNG WINNER

Pat Hentgen, RH, 1996
Roger Clemens, RH, 1997
Roger Clemens, RH, 1998

ROOKIE OF THE YEAR

Alfredo Griffin, SS, 1979

MANAGER OF THE YEAR

Bobby Cox, 1985

Second baseman Roberto Alomar was a key figure for the 1992 and '93 championship teams.

25-plus home runs

47	George Bell	1987
46	Jose Canseco	1998
44	Carlos Delgado	1999
42	Shawn Green	1999
40	Jesse Barfield	1986
38	Carlos Delgado	1998
36	Fred McGriff	1989
	Ed Sprague	1996
35	Fred McGriff	1990
	Shawn Green	1998
34	Fred McGriff	1988
	Joe Carter	1992
33	Joe Carter	1991, 1993
31	George Bell	1986
	Kelly Gruber	1990
	Tony Batista	*1999
30	John Mayberry	1980
	Joe Carter	1996
	Carlos Delgado	1997
28	George Bell	1985
	Jesse Barfield	1987
27	Willie Upshaw	1983
	Jesse Barfield	1983, 1985
	Joe Carter	1994
26	George Bell	1984
	Lloyd Moseby	1987
	Dave Winfield	1992
25	Joe Carter	1995
	Carlos Delgado	1996

^26 with Blue Jays, 5 with Diamondbacks.

100-plus RBIs

134	George Bell	1987
	Carlos Delgado	1999
123	Shawn Green	1999
121	Joe Carter	1993
119	Joe Carter	1992
118	Kelly Gruber	1990
115	Carlos Delgado	1998
111	Paul Molitor	1993
108	Jesse Barfield	1986
	George Bell	1986
	Joe Carter	1991
	Dave Winfield	1992
107	John Olerud	1993
	Joe Carter	1996
	Jose Canseco	1998
104	Willie Upshaw	1983
	George Bell	1989
103	Joe Carter	1994
102	Joe Carter	1997
101	Ed Sprague	1996
100	Shawn Green	1999
	Tony Batista	*1999

*79 with Blue Jays, 21 with Diamondbacks.

20-plus victories

1992	Jack Morris	21-6
1996	Pat Hentgen	20-10
1997	Roger Clemens	21-7
1998	Roger Clemens	20-6

A.L. home run champions

1986	Jesse Barfield	40
1989	Fred McGriff	36

A.L. RBI champions

1987	George Bell	134

A.L. batting champions

1993	John Olerud	.363

A.L. ERA champions

1985	Dave Stieb	2.48
1987	Jimmy Key	2.76
1996	Juan Guzman	2.93
1997	Roger Clemens	2.05
1998	Roger Clemens	2.65

A.L. strikeout champions

1997	Roger Clemens	292
1998	Roger Clemens	271

No-hit pitchers

(9 innings or more)

1990	Dave Stieb	3-0 vs. Cleveland

Longest hitting streaks

28	Shawn Green	1999
26	John Olerud	1993
	Shannon Stewart	1999
22	George Bell	1989
21	Damaso Garcia	1983
	Lloyd Moseby	1983
20	Damaso Garcia	1982
19	Alfredo Griffin	1980
	Roberto Alomar	1995
	Carlos Delgado	1998
18	Damaso Garcia	1986
	Tony Fernandez	1987
17	John Mayberry	1980
	Damaso Garcia	1982
	George Bell	1987
	Dave Winfield	1992
	Tony Batista	1999
16	Dave McKay	1978
	Jesse Barfield	1985
	Damaso Garcia	1985
	Tony Fernandez	1989
	Roberto Alomar	1992
	Joe Carter	1992
	Ed Sprague	1995
	Shannon Stewart	1999
15	Roy Howell	1977
	George Bell	1986
	Kelly Gruber	1989
	Tony Fernandez	1990
	Kelly Gruber	1990
	Roberto Alomar	1991
	Carlos Delgado	1997

Slick-fielding shortstop Tony Fernandez holds single-season Blue Jays records for at-bats, hits, singles and triples.

SEASON

Batting

At-bats	687	Tony Fernandez	1986
Runs	134	Shawn Green	1999
Hits	213	Tony Fernandez	1986
Singles	161	Tony Fernandez	1986
Doubles	54	John Olerud	1993
Triples	17	Tony Fernandez	1990
Home runs	47	George Bell	1987
Home runs, rookie	20	Fred McGriff	1987
Grand slams	3	Carlos Delgado	1997
Total bases	369	George Bell	1987
RBIs	134	George Bell	1987
		Carlos Delgado	1999
Walks	119	Fred McGriff	1989
Most strikeouts	159	Jose Canseco	1998
Fewest strikeouts	21	Bob Bailor	1978
Batting average	.363	John Olerud	1993
Slugging pct.	.605	George Bell	1987
Stolen bases	60	Dave Collins	1984

Pitching

Games	89	Mark Eichorn	1987
Complete games	19	Dave Stieb	1982
Innings	288.1	Dave Stieb	1982
Wins	21	Jack Morris	1992
		Roger Clemens	1997
Losses	18	Jerry Garvin	1977
		Phil Huffman	1979
Winning pct.	.824	Juan Guzman	1993
Walks	128	Jim Clancy	1980
Strikeouts	292	Roger Clemens	1997
Shutouts	5	Dave Stieb	1982
Home runs allowed	36	Woody Williams	1998
Lowest ERA	2.05	Roger Clemens	1997
Saves	45	Duane Ward	1993

GAME

Batting

Runs	5	Carlos Delgado	5-3-99
Hits	5	Last by Tony Fernandez	5-7-99
Doubles	4	Damaso Garcia	6-27-86
Triples	2	Last by Shannon Stewart	9-20-97
Home runs	3	Last by Carlos Delgado	8-6-99
RBIs	9	Roy Howell	9-10-77
Total bases	13	Roy Howell	9-10-77
Stolen bases	4	Last by Otis Nixon	8-14-96

Workhorse righthander Dave Stieb, a 175-game winner, holds virtually every key Toronto career pitching record.

HISTORY

BATTING

FRANCHISE RECORDS

Games
Tony Fernandez	1,402
Lloyd Moseby	1,392
Ernie Whitt	1,218
George Bell	1,181
Rance Mulliniks	1,115
Willie Upshaw	1,115
Joe Carter	1,039
Jesse Barfield	1,032
Alfredo Griffin	982
Garth Iorg	931

At-bats
Tony Fernandez	5,276
Lloyd Moseby	5,124
George Bell	4,528
Joe Carter	4,093
Willie Upshaw	3,710
Damaso Garcia	3,572
Ernie Whitt	3,514
Jesse Barfield	3,463
Alfredo Griffin	3,396
Ed Sprague	3,156

Runs
Lloyd Moseby	768
Tony Fernandez	699
George Bell	641
Joe Carter	578
Willie Upshaw	538
Jesse Barfield	530
John Olerud	464
Damaso Garcia	453
Devon White	452
Roberto Alomar	451

Hits
Tony Fernandez	1,565
Lloyd Moseby	1,319
George Bell	1,294
Joe Carter	1,051
Damaso Garcia	1,028
Willie Upshaw	982
Jesse Barfield	919
John Olerud	910
Ernie Whitt	888
Alfredo Griffin	844

Doubles
Tony Fernandez	287
Lloyd Moseby	242
George Bell	237
Joe Carter	218
John Olerud	213
Rance Mulliniks	204
Willie Upshaw	177
Damaso Garcia	172
Ed Sprague	170
Shawn Green	164
Ernie Whitt	164

Triples
Tony Fernandez	72
Lloyd Moseby	60
Alfredo Griffin	50
Willie Upshaw	42
Roberto Alomar	36
Devon White	34
George Bell	32
Joe Carter	28
Jesse Barfield	27
Damaso Garcia	26

Home runs
Joe Carter	203
George Bell	202
Jesse Barfield	179
Carlos Delgado	149
Lloyd Moseby	149
Ernie Whitt	131
Fred McGriff	125
Shawn Green	119
Kelly Gruber	114
Ed Sprague	113

Total bases
George Bell	2,201
Tony Fernandez	2,173
Lloyd Moseby	2,128
Joe Carter	1,934
Jesse Barfield	1,672
Willie Upshaw	1,579
Ernie Whitt	1,475
John Olerud	1,462
Damaso Garcia	1,348
Kelly Gruber	1,335

TEAM SEASON, GAME RECORDS

SEASON

Batting
Most at-bats	5,716	1986
Most runs	883	1999
Fewest runs	590	1978
Most hits	1,580	1999
Most singles	1,069	1984
Most doubles	337	1999
Most triples	68	1984
Most home runs	221	1998
Fewest home runs	95	1979
Most grand slams	8	1989
Most pinch-hit home runs	6	1984
Most total bases	2,581	1999
Most stolen bases	193	1984
Highest batting average	.280	1999
Lowest batting average	.244	1997
Highest slugging pct	.457	1999

Pitching
Lowest ERA	3.29	1985
Highest ERA	4.92	1999
Most complete games	44	1979
Most shutouts	17	1988
Most saves	60	1991
Most walks	635	1980
Most strikeouts	1,154	1998

Fielding
Most errors	164	1977
Fewest errors	86	1990
Most double plays	206	1980
Highest fielding average	.986	1990

General
Most games won	99	1985
Most games lost	109	1979
Highest win pct	.615	1985
Lowest win pct	.327	1979

GAME, INNING

Batting
Most runs, game	24	6-26-78
Most runs, inning	11	7-20-84
Most hits, game	25	8-9-99
Most home runs, game	10	9-14-87
Most total bases, game	53	9-14-87

Righthander Jim Clancy ranks second on Toronto's all-time victory chart with 128.

Runs batted in
George Bell	740
Joe Carter	736
Lloyd Moseby	651
Tony Fernandez	601
Jesse Barfield	527
Ernie Whitt	518
Willie Upshaw	478
John Olerud	471
Carlos Delgado	467
Kelly Gruber	434

Extra-base hits
George Bell	471
Lloyd Moseby	451
Joe Carter	449
Tony Fernandez	418
Jesse Barfield	368
Willie Upshaw	331
John Olerud	328
Carlos Delgado	312
Ernie Whitt	310
Shawn Green	298

Batting average
(Minimum 500 games)
Roberto Alomar	.307
Tony Fernandez	.297
John Olerud	.293
Damaso Garcia	.288
George Bell	.286
Shawn Green	.286
Rance Mulliniks	.280
Fred McGriff	.278
Roy Howell	.272
Devon White	.270

Stolen bases
Lloyd Moseby	255
Roberto Alomar	206
Damaso Garcia	194
Tony Fernandez	172
Devon White	126
Otis Nixon	101
Shannon Stewart	101
Dave Collins	91
Kelly Gruber	80
Alfredo Griffin	79

PITCHING

Earned-run average
(Minimum 500 innings)
Tom Henke	2.48

Duane Ward	3.18
Dave Stieb	3.42
Jimmy Key	3.42
Doyle Alexander	3.56
John Cerutti	3.87
Dave Wells	4.04
Jim Acker	4.07
Juan Guzman	4.07
Jim Clancy	4.10

Wins
Dave Stieb	175
Jim Clancy	128
Jimmy Key	116
Pat Hentgen	105
Juan Guzman	76
Todd Stottlemyre	69
David Wells	64
Luis Leal	51
Doyle Alexander	46
John Cerutti	46

Losses
Jim Clancy	140
Dave Stieb	134
Jimmy Key	81
Pat Hentgen	76
Todd Stottlemyre	70
Juan Guzman	62
Luis Leal	58
Jesse Jefferson	56
David Wells	47
Dave Lemanczyk	45

Innings pitched
Dave Stieb	2,873.0
Jim Clancy	2,204.2
Jimmy Key	1,695.2
Pat Hentgen	1,555.2
Juan Guzman	1,215.2
Todd Stottlemyre	1,139.0
Luis Leal	946.0
David Wells	919.0
John Cerutti	772.1
Doyle Alexander	750.0

Strikeouts
Dave Stieb	1,658
Jim Clancy	1,237
Juan Guzman	1,030
Pat Hentgen	995
Jimmy Key	944

Duane Ward	671
Todd Stottlemyre	662
Tom Henke	644
David Wells	618
Roger Clemens	563

Bases on balls
Dave Stieb	1,020
Jim Clancy	814
Pat Hentgen	557
Juan Guzman	546
Todd Stottlemyre	414
Jimmy Key	404
Luis Leal	320
Duane Ward	278
Jesse Jefferson	266
David Wells	263

Games
Duane Ward	452
Tom Henke	446
Dave Stieb	439
Jim Clancy	352
Jimmy Key	317
Mike Timlin	305
Jim Acker	281
Mark Eichhorn	279
David Wells	271
Pat Hentgen	252

Shutouts
Dave Stieb	30
Jim Clancy	11
Jimmy Key	10
Pat Hentgen	9
Roger Clemens	6
Jesse Jefferson	4
Todd Stottlemyre	4
Doyle Alexander	3
Chris Carpenter	3
Jim Gott	3
Luis Leal	3
Dave Lemanczyk	3

Saves
Tom Henke	217
Duane Ward	121
Mike Timlin	52
Billy Koch	31
Joey McLaughlin	31
Roy Lee Jackson	30
Randy Myers	28

BLUE JAYS YEAR-BY-YEAR

Year	W	L	Place	Games Back	Manager	Batting avg.	Hits	Home runs	RBIs	Wins	ERA
								Leaders			
						EAST DIVISION					
1977	54	107	7th	45½	Hartsfield	Howell, .316	Bailor, 154	Fairly, 19	Ault, Fairly, 64	Lemanczyk, 13	Vuckovich, 3.47
1978	59	102	7th	40	Hartsfield	Carty, .284	Bailor, 164	Mayberry, 22	Mayberry, 70	Clancy, 10	Murphy, 3.93
1979	53	109	7th	50½	Hartsfield	Griffin, .287	Griffin, 179	Mayberry, 21	Mayberry, 74	T. Underwood, 9	T. Underwood, 3.69
1980	67	95	7th	36	Mattick	Woods, .300	Griffin, 166	Mayberry, 30	Mayberry, 82	Clancy, 13	Clancy, 3.30
1981	37	69	*7th/7th	—	Mattick	Garcia, .252	Moseby, 88	Mayberry, 17	Mayberry, Moseby, 43	Stieb, 11	Stieb, 3.19
1982	78	84	†6th	17	Cox	Garcia, .310	Garcia, 185	Upshaw, 21	Upshaw, 75	Stieb, 17	Jackson, 3.06
1983	89	73	4th	9	Cox	Bonnell, .318	Upshaw, 177	Barfield, Upshaw, 27	Upshaw, 104	Stieb, 17	Stieb, 3.04
1984	89	73	2nd	15	Cox	Collins, .308	Garcia, 180	Bell, 26	Moseby, 92	Alexander, 17	Stieb, 2.83
1985	99	62	‡1st	+2	Cox	Mulliniks, .295	Bell, 167	Bell, 28	Bell, 95	Alexander, 17	Stieb, 2.48
1986	86	76	4th	9½	J. Williams	Fernandez, .310	Fernandez, 213	Barfield, 40	Barfield, Bell, 108	Clancy, Key, Eichhorn, 14	Eichhorn, 1.72
1987	96	66	2nd	2	J. Williams	Fernandez, .322	Bell, 188	Bell, 47	Bell, 134	Key, 17	Key, 2.76
1988	87	75	†3rd	2	J. Williams	Lee, .291	Fernandez, 186	McGriff, 34	Bell, 97	Stieb, 16	Stieb, 3.04
1989	89	73	‡1st	+2	J. Williams, Gaston	Bell, .297	Bell, 182	McGriff, 36	Bell, 104	Stieb, 17	Cerutti, 3.07
1990	86	76	2nd	2	Gaston	McGriff, .300	Fernandez, 175	McGriff, 35	Gruber, 118	Stieb, 18	Stieb, 2.93
1991	91	71	‡1st	+7	Gaston	Alomar, .295	Alomar, 188	Carter, 33	Carter, 108	Key, 17	Ward, 2.77
1992	96	66	§1st	+4	Gaston	Alomar, .310	Alomar, 177	Carter, 34	Carter, 119	Morris, 21	Ward, 1.95
1993	95	67	§1st	+7	Gaston	Olerud, .363	Molitor, 211	Carter, 33	Carter, 121	Hentgen, 19	Hentgen, 3.87
1994	55	60	3rd	16	Gaston	Molitor, .341	Molitor, 155	Carter, 27	Carter, 103	Hentgen, 13	Hentgen, 3.40
1995	56	88	5th	30	Gaston	Alomar, .300	Alomar, 155	Carter, 25	Carter, 76	Leiter, 11	Leiter, 3.64
1996	74	88	4th	18	Gaston	Nixon, .286	Carter, 158	Sprague, 36	Carter, 107	Hentgen, 20	Guzman, 2.93
1997	76	86	5th	22	Gaston, Queen	Green, .287	Carter, 143	Delgado, 30	Carter, 102	Clemens, 21	Clemens, 2.05
1998	88	74	3rd	26	T. Johnson	Fernandez, .321	Green, 175	Canseco, 46	Delgado, 115	Clemens, 20	Clemens, 2.65
1999	84	78	3rd	14	Fregosi	Fernandez, .328	Green, 190	Delgado, 44	Delgado, 134	Wells, 17	Halladay, 3.92

* First half 16-42; second half 21-27. † Tied for position. ‡ Lost Championship Series. § Won Championship Series.

Note: Batting average minimum 350 at-bats; ERA minimum 90 innings pitched.

Bob Bailor

TORONTO was welcomed into the American League fold on March 26, 1976, when owners granted ownership approval to Labatt Breweries and Imperial Trust, giving the Blue Jays distinction as the first A.L. team outside the continental United States. The Blue Jays, the A.L.'s 14th franchise, joined the league with the Seattle Mariners.

Infielder Bob Bailor gained distinction as the first of 30 Toronto selections in the November 5, 1976, A.L. expansion draft. American League baseball made a successful Canadian debut on April 7, 1977, when the Blue Jays defeated the Chicago White Sox, 9-5, at Exhibition Stadium.

Expansion draft (November 5, 1976)

Players
Doug Ault .... Texas .... first base
*Bob Bailor .... Baltimore .... infield
Steve Bowling .... Milwaukee .... outfield
Rico Carty .... Cleveland .... outfield
Sam Ewing .... Chicago .... first base
Garth Iorg .... New York .... infield
Jim Mason .... New York .... shortstop
Dave McKay .... Minnesota .... third base
Steve Staggs .... Kansas City .... second base
Otto Velez .... New York .... outfield
Ernie Whitt .... Boston .... catcher
Mike Weathers .... Oakland .... infield
Al Woods .... Minnesota .... outfield
Gary Woods .... Oakland .... outfield

Pitchers
Larry Anderson .... Milwaukee .... righthanded
Tom Bruno .... Kansas City .... righthanded
Jeff Byrd .... Texas .... righthanded
Jim Clancy .... Texas .... righthanded
Mike Darr .... Baltimore .... righthanded
Dennis DeBarr .... Detroit .... lefthanded
Butch Edge .... Milwaukee .... righthanded
Al Fitzmorris .... Kansas City .... righthanded
Jerry Garvin .... Minnesota .... lefthanded
Steve Hargan .... Texas .... righthanded
Leon Hooten .... Oakland .... righthanded
Jesse Jefferson .... Chicago .... righthanded
Dave Lemanczyk .... Detroit .... righthanded
Bill Singer .... Minnesota .... righthanded
Pete Vuckovich .... Chicago .... righthanded
Mike Willis .... Baltimore .... lefthanded

*First pick

Opening day lineup

Doug Ault

April 7, 1977
John Scott, left field
Hector Torres, shortstop
Doug Ault, first base
Otto Velez, designated hitter
Gary Woods, center field
Steve Bowling, right field
Pedro Garcia, second base
Dave McKay, third base
Rick Cerone, catcher
Bill Singer, pitcher

Blue Jays firsts
First hit: Doug Ault, April 7, 1977, vs. Chicago
First home run: Doug Ault, April 7, 1977, vs. Chicago
First RBI: Doug Ault, April 7, 1977, vs. Chicago
First win: Jerry Johnson, April 7, 1977, vs. Chicago
First shutout: Pete Vuckovich, June 26, 1977, 2-0 at Baltimore

HISTORY

ARIZONA DIAMONDBACKS

First baseman Travis Lee.

FRANCHISE CHRONOLOGY

The beginnings: Arizona, a longtime bastion of minor league baseball and spring training, joined the Major League ranks on March 9, 1995, when owners unanimously approved expansion to Phoenix and Tampa. The 13th and 14th expansion cubs in Major League history were also the earliest-formed expansion teams, gaining approval more than three years before they would throw their first pitch against big-league competition. The Diamondbacks were awarded to a group headed by Jerry Colangelo, the man who had built the Phoenix Suns into one of the most admired franchises in the NBA. Both teams were stocked in a November 1997 expansion draft and began play in the 1998 season, Arizona as part of the National League West division.

First season: Major League baseball made its Arizona debut on March 31, 1998, at Bank One Ballpark in Phoenix when the Diamondbacks dropped a 9-2 decision to the Rockies. Arizona went on to compile a 65-97 first-year record, two games better than Tampa Bay in its A.L. debut season. The Diamondbacks finished in the N.L. West basement, 33 games behind San Diego.

1999: In only its second year of existence, the Diamondbacks captured its first N.L. West title. Colangelo had a busy offseason, re-stocking the team with high-priced veteran signings. And they didn't let him down, to the tune of a 100-62 mark. However, the wild-card Mets would defeat the Diamondbacks in Division Series play, stopping the team's bid for its first pennant.

DIAMONDBACKS VS. OPPONENTS BY DECADE

	Braves	Cardinals	Cubs	Dodgers	Giants	Phillies	Pirates	Reds	Astros	Mets	Expos	Padres	Marlins	Rockies	Brewers	Interleague	Decade Record
1998-99	5-13	6-11	12-9	11-14	14-10	10-8	11-5	5-13	9-9	11-7	8-10	14-11	14-3	12-13	11-7	12-16	165-159
Totals	5-13	6-11	12-9	11-14	14-10	10-8	11-5	5-13	9-9	11-7	8-10	14-11	14-3	12-13	11-7	12-16	165-159

Interleague results: 3-3 vs. Angels; 2-4 vs. Athletics; 3-3 vs. Mariners; 4-6 vs. Rangers.

ALL-TIME RECORD OF EXPANSION TEAMS

Team	W	L	Pct.	DT	P	WS
Arizona	165	159	.509	1	0	0
Kansas City	2,471	2,412	.506	6	2	1
Toronto	1,784	1,818	.495	5	2	2
Houston	2,980	3,048	.494	6	0	0
Montreal	2,387	2,501	.488	2	0	0
Anaheim	2,987	3,201	.483	3	0	0
Milwaukee	2,348	2,542	.480	2	1	0
Colorado	512	559	.478	0	0	0
New York	2,840	3,178	.472	4	3	2
Texas	2,881	3,290	.467	4	0	0
San Diego	2,239	2,656	.457	3	2	0
Seattle	1,624	1,977	.451	2	0	0
Florida	472	596	.442	0	1	1
Tampa Bay	132	192	.407	0	0	0

DT—Division Titles. P—Pennants won. WS—World Series won.

BALLPARK CHRONOLOGY

Bank One Ballpark (1998-present)
Capacity: 49,075.
First game: Rockies 9, Diamondbacks 2 (March 31, 1998).
First batter: Mike Lansing, Rockies.
First hit: Mike Lansing, Rockies (single).
First run: Vinny Castilla, Rockies (2nd inning).
First home run: Vinny Castilla, Rockies.
First winning pitcher: Darryl Kile, Rockies.
First-season attendance: 3,602,856.

MANAGERS

Name	Years	Record
Buck Showalter	1998-99	165-159

ATTENDANCE HIGHS

Total	Season	Park
3,602,856	1998	Bank One Ballpark
3,017,489	1999	Bank One Ballpark

CY YOUNG WINNER

Randy Johnson, LH, 1999

N.L. ERA champions
1999—Randy Johnson 2.48

N.L. strikeout champions
1999—Randy Johnson 364

LONGEST HITTING STREAKS

30—Luis Gonzalez	....	1999
19—Matt Williams	....	1999
16—Luis Gonzalez	....	1999
14—Tony Womack	....	1999
13—Kelly Stinnett	....	1998
Luis Gonzalez	....	1999
12—Luis Gonzalez	....	1999
11—Travis Lee	....	1998
Jay Bell	....	1999
11—Luis Gonzalez	....	1999

Expansion draft (November 18, 1998)

Players

Gabe Alvarez	San Diego	third base
Tony Batista	Oakland	shortstop
Mike Bell	Anaheim	third base
Yamil Benetez	Kansas City	outfield
Brent Brede	Minnesota	outfield
David Dellucci	Baltimore	outfield
Edwin Diaz	Texas	second base
Jorge Fabregas	White Sox	catcher
Hanley Frias	Texas	shortstop
Karim Garcia	Los Angeles	outfield
Dan Klassen	Milwaukee	shortstop
Damian Miller	Minnesota	catcher
Joe Randa	Pittsburgh	third base
Kelly Stinnett	Milwaukee	catcher

Pitchers

Joel Adamson	Milwaukee	lefthanded
*Brian Anderson	Cleveland	lefthanded
Jason Boyd	Philadelphia	righthanded
Hector Carrasco	Kansas City	righthanded
Chris Clemons	White Sox	righthanded
Bryan Corey	Detroit	righthanded
Omar Daal	Toronto	lefthanded
Matt Drews	Detroit	righthanded
Todd Erdos	San Diego	righthanded
Ben Ford	N.Y. Yankees	righthanded
Marty Janzen	Toronto	righthanded
Cory Lidle	N.Y. Mets	righthanded
Thomas Martin	Houston	lefthanded
Jesus Martinez	Los Angeles	lefthanded
Chuck McElroy	White Sox	lefthanded
Clint Sodowsky	Pittsburgh	righthanded
Russ Springer	Houston	righthanded
Jeff Suppan	Boston	righthanded
Neil Weber	Montreal	lefthanded
Scott Winchester	Cincinnati	righthanded
Bob Wolcott	Seattle	righthanded

*First pick

Opening day lineup

March 31, 1998
Devon White, center field
Jay Bell, shortstop
Travis Lee, first base
Matt Williams, third base
Brent Brede, left field
Karim Garcia, right field
Jorge Fabregas, catcher
Edwin Diaz, second base
Andy Benes, pitcher

Brian Anderson

Diamondbacks firsts
First hit: Travis Lee, March 31, 1998, vs. Colorado (single)
First home run: Travis Lee, March 31, 1998, vs. Colorado
First RBI: Travis Lee, March 31, 1998, vs. Colorado
First win: Andy Benes, April 5, 1998, vs. San Francisco
First shutout: Omar Daal, July 20, 1998, 4-0 vs. Cubs.

HISTORY

BATTING

Games

Jay Bell	306
Matt Williams	289
Travis Lee	266
Andy Fox	238
Dave Dellucci	187
Kelly Stinnett	180
Steve Finley	156
Luis Gonzalez	153
Tony Batista	150
Devon White	146

At-bats

Jay Bell	1,138
Matt Williams	1,137
Travis Lee	937
Andy Fox	776
Luis Gonzalez	614
Tony Womack	614
Steve Finley	590
Devon White	563
Kelly Stinnett	558
Dave Dellucci	525

Runs

Jay Bell	211
Matt Williams	170
Travis Lee	128
Luis Gonzalez	112
Tony Womack	111
Andy Fox	101
Steve Finley	100
Devon White	84
Kelly Stinnett	71
Dave Dellucci	70

Hits

Matt Williams	326
Jay Bell	308
Travis Lee	240
Andy Fox	209
Luis Gonzalez	206
Tony Womack	170
Devon White	157
Steve Finley	156
Dave Dellucci	151
Kelly Stinnett	137

Doubles

Matt Williams	63
Jay Bell	61
Luis Gonzalez	45
Travis Lee	36
Andy Fox	33
Damian Miller	33
Steve Finley	32
Devon White	32
Kelly Stinnett	27
Dave Dellucci	26

Triples

Dave Dellucci	13
Jay Bell	11
Steve Finley	10
Tony Womack	10
Andy Fox	8
Karim Garcia	8
Luis Gonzalez	4
Travis Lee	4
Brent Brede	3
Greg Colbrunn	3
Hanley Frias	3
Matt Williams	3

Home runs

Jay Bell	58
Matt Williams	55
Steve Finley	34
Travis Lee	31
Luis Gonzalez	26
Kelly Stinnett	25
Tony Batista	23
Devon White	22
Andy Fox	15
Damian Miller	14

Total bases

Jay Bell	565
Matt Williams	560
Travis Lee	377
Luis Gonzalez	337
Steve Finley	310
Andy Fox	303
Devon White	257
Kelly Stinnett	241
Tony Womack	227
Dave Dellucci	221

Runs batted in

Matt Williams	213
Jay Bell	179
Travis Lee	122

Luis Gonzalez	111
Steve Finley	103
Devon White	85
Andy Fox	77
Kelly Stinnett	72
Dave Dellucci	66
Tony Batista	62

Extra-base hits

Jay Bell	130
Matt Williams	121
Steve Finley	76
Luis Gonzalez	75
Travis Lee	71
Andy Fox	56
Devon White	55
Kelly Stinnett	53
Damian Miller	49
Tony Batista	45
Dave Dellucci	45

Batting average
(Minimum 125 games)

Luis Gonzalez	.336
Dave Dellucci	.288
Matt Williams	.287
Devon White	.279
Tony Womack	.277
Damian Miller	.276
Jay Bell	.271
Andy Fox	.269
Tony Batista	.268
Steve Finley	.264

Stolen bases

Tony Womack	72
Travis Lee	25
Devon White	22
Andy Fox	18
Jay Bell	10
Luis Gonzalez	9
Steve Finley	8
Matt Williams	7
Bernard Gilkey	6
Dave Dellucci	5
Karim Garcia	5

PITCHING

Earned-run average
(Minimum 125 innings)

Randy Johnson	2.48
Omar Daal	3.32
Gregg Olson	3.34
Amaury Telemaco	4.11
Andy Benes	4.36
Armando Reynoso	4.37
Brian Anderson	4.42
Willie Blair	5.34

Wins

Andy Benes	27
Omar Daal	24
Brian Anderson	20
Randy Johnson	17
Gregg Olson	12
Armando Reynoso	10
Amaury Telemaco	7
Todd Stottlemyre	6
Bobby Chouinard	5
Willie Blair	4
Darren Holmes	4
Russ Springer	4
Greg Swindell	4

Losses

Andy Benes	25
Omar Daal	21
Brian Anderson	15
Willie Blair	15
Randy Johnson	9
Amaury Telemaco	9
Gregg Olson	8
Jeff Suppan	7
Armando Reynoso	6
Clint Sodowsky	6

Innings pitched

Andy Benes	429.2
Omar Daal	377.1
Brian Anderson	338.0
Randy Johnson	271.2
Armando Reynoso	167.0
Willie Blair	146.2
Gregg Olson	129.1
Amaury Telemaco	127.0
Todd Stottlemyre	101.1
Bobby Chouinard	78.2

Strikeouts

Randy Johnson	364
Andy Benes	305
Omar Daal	280
Brian Anderson	170
Gregg Olson	100
Armando Reynoso	79

Jay Bell has provided a veteran presence at shortstop during the Diamondbacks' first two seasons.

SEASON

Batting

Most at-bats	5,658	1999
Most runs	908	1999
Fewest runs	665	1998
Most hits	1,566	1999
Most singles	1,015	1999
Most doubles	289	1999
Most triples	46	1998, 1999
Most home runs	216	1999
Fewest home runs	159	1998
Most grand slams	8	1999
Most pinch-hit home runs	5	1999
Most total bases	2,595	1999
Most stolen bases	137	1999
Highest batting average	.277	1999
Lowest batting average	.246	1998
Highest slugging pct.	.459	1999

Pitching

Lowest ERA	3.77	1999
Highest ERA	4.64	1998
Most complete games	16	1999
Most shutouts	9	1999
Most saves	42	1999
Most walks	543	1999
Most strikeouts	1,198	1999

Fielding

Most errors	104	1999
Fewest errors	100	1998
Most double plays	132	1999
Highest fielding average	.984	1998

General

Most games won	100	1999
Most games lost	97	1998
Highest win pct.	.617	1999
Lowest win pct.	.401	1998

GAME, INNING

Batting

Most runs, game	17	7-4-99
Most runs, inning	8	8-26-99
Most hits, game	20	6-2-99
Most home runs, game	5	Last on 8-4-99
Most total bases, game	37	6-2-99

Todd Stottlemyre	74
Willie Blair	71
Amaury Telemaco	62
Greg Swindell	51

Bases on balls

Andy Benes	156
Omar Daal	130
Randy Johnson	70
Armando Reynoso	67
Brian Anderson	52
Willie Blair	51
Gregg Olson	50
Todd Stottlemyre	40
Clint Sodowsky	39
Amaury Telemaco	39

Games

Gregg Olson	125
Andy Benes	67
Omar Daal	65
Brian Anderson	63
Greg Swindell	63
Bobby Chouinard	58

Clint Sodowsky	45
Darren Holmes	44
Felix Rodriguez	43
Alan Embree	35
Randy Johnson	35

Shutouts

Brian Anderson	2
Omar Daal	2
Randy Johnson	2

Saves

Gregg Olson	44
Matt Mantei	22
Felix Rodriguez	5
Brian Anderson	1
Willie Banks	1
Bobby Chouinard	1
Alan Embree	1
Byung-Hyun Kim	1
Vladimir Nunez	1
Dan Plesac	1
Greg Swindell	1

ATLANTA BRAVES

FRANCHISE CHRONOLOGY

First season: 1876, in Boston, as a member of the new National League. The "Red Stockings" defeated Philadelphia, 6-5, in their franchise debut and went on to finish fourth with a 39-31 first-year record.

1877-1900: Boston's "Beaneaters" were dominant in the pre-1900 era. They won consecutive pennants in 1877 and '78, returned to the top in 1883 and powered their way to five more flags in the 1890s.

1901-1952: Such success did not carry over to the modern era. Over the next 52 seasons, the Braves would win only two more pennants—while finishing sixth, seventh or eighth 33 times. One of the pennants was secured by the Miracle Braves of 1914, who recovered from a 15-game deficit to overtake the Giants with a 68-19 stretch run and then swept past powerful Philadelphia in the World Series. When the financially strapped Braves transferred to Milwaukee after the 1952 season, they broke up a baseball alignment that had existed since 1903.

1953-1965: The Braves were embraced by Milwaukee fans and rewarded them with a 1957 World Series victory and a 1958 pennant. But when the team fell into the second division in the early 1960s, enthusiasm waned and management began another search for greener pastures. After the 1965 season, the Braves made their second franchise shift in 14 years—this time to Atlanta.

1966-present: It has taken another quarter century for the Braves to regain status as an N.L. power. They won West Division titles in 1969 and 1982, but lost N.L. Championship Series both years. Since 1991, the rebuilt Braves have won a record eight straight division titles, five pennants and one World Series—a six-game triumph over Cleveland in 1995.

Outfielder Hank Aaron.

BRAVES VS. OPPONENTS BY DECADE

	Cardinals	Cubs	Dodgers	Giants	Phillies	Pirates	Reds	Astros	Mets	Expos	Padres	Marlins	Rockies	Brewers	D'backs	Interleague	Decade Record
1900-09	98-111	76-135	95-114	83-125	87-119	58-153	90-120										587-877
1910-19	110-100	87-127	105-103	73-137	90-123	104-109	97-116										666-815
1920-29	85-135	80-139	90-128	82-137	100-118	77-141	89-130										603-928
1930-39	98-121	74-146	117-103	89-127	122-97	92-125	108-110										700-829
1940-49	76-144	111-108	90-129	100-116	132-87	105-112	105-112										719-808
1950-59	119-101	126-94	92-129	126-94	118-102	139-81	134-86										854-687
1960-69	88-94	92-90	89-99	97-91	107-75	88-94	85-103	95-49	89-49	8-4	13-5						851-753
1970-79	51-69	54-66	70-106	84-95	62-58	43-77	60-120	85-91	59-61	60-58	97-82						725-883
1980-89	47-68	57-55	69-105	79-94	64-53	58-53	81-92	78-96	46-68	45-72	88-89						712-845
1990-99	71-43	62-43	68-55	69-53	70-50	62-45	82-49	71-53	69-50	70-50	79-44	51-36	50-26	12-4	13-5	26-23	925-629
Totals	843-986	819-1003	885-1071	882-1069	952-882	826-990	931-1038	329-289	263-228	183-184	277-220	51-36	50-26	12-4	13-5	26-23	7342-8054

Interleague results: 2-7 vs. Orioles; 8-4 vs. Red Sox; 1-2 vs. Tigers; 5-5 vs. Yankees; 4-5 vs. Blue Jays; 6-0 vs. Devil Rays.

MANAGERS

(Boston Braves, 1876-1952)
(Milwaukee Braves, 1953-65)

Name	Years	Record
Harry Wright	1876-81	254-187
John Morrill	1882, 1883-86, 1887-88	335-296
Jack Burdock	1883	30-24
King Kelly	1887	49-43
Jim Hart	1889	83-45
Frank Selee	1890-1901	1004-649
Al Buckenberger	1902-04	186-242
Fred Tenney	1905-07, 1911	202-402
Joe Kelley	1908	63-91
Frank Bowerman	1909	22-54
Harry Smith	1909	23-54
Fred Lake	1910	53-100
Johnny Kling	1912	52-101
George Stallings	1913-20	579-597
Fred Mitchell	1921-23	186-274
Dave Bancroft	1924-27	249-363
Jack Slattery	1928	11-20
Rogers Hornsby	1928	39-83
Emil Fuchs	1929	56-98
Bill McKechnie	1930-37	560-666
Casey Stengel	1938-43	373-491
Bob Coleman	1943, 1944-45	128-165
Del Bissonette	1945	25-34
Billy Southworth	1946-51	424-358
Tommy Holmes	1951-52	61-69
Charlie Grimm	1952-56	341-285
Fred Haney	1956-59	341-231
Chuck Dressen	1960-61	159-124
Birdie Tebbetts	1961-62	98-89
Bobby Bragan	1963-66	310-287
Billy Hitchcock	1966-67	110-100
Ken Silvestri	1967	0-3
Lum Harris	1968-72	379-373
Eddie Mathews	1972-74	149-161
Clyde King	1974-75	96-101
Connie Ryan	1975	9-18
Dave Bristol	1976-77	131-192
Ted Turner	1977	0-1
Bobby Cox	1978-81, 1990-99	1,166-912
Joe Torre	1982-84	257-229
Eddie Haas	1985	50-71
Bobby Wine	1985	16-25
Chuck Tanner	1986-88	153-208
Russ Nixon	1988-90	130-216

WORLD SERIES CHAMPIONS

Year	Loser	Length	MVP
1914	Philadelphia	4 games	None
1957	N.Y. Yankees	7 games	Burdette
1995	Cleveland	6 games	Glavine

N.L. PENNANT WINNERS

Year	Record	Manager	Series Result
1877	42-18	Wright	None
1878	41-19	Wright	None
1883	63-35	Burdock, Morrill	None
1891	87-51	Selee	None
1892	102-48	Selee	None
1893	86-43	Selee	None
1897	93-39	Selee	None
1898	102-47	Selee	None
1914	94-59	Stallings	Defeated A's
1948	91-62	Southworth	Lost to Indians
1957	95-59	Haney	Defeated Yankees
1958	92-62	Haney	Lost to Yankees
1991	94-68	Cox	Lost to Twins
1992	98-64	Cox	Lost to Blue Jays
1995	90-54	Cox	Defeated Indians
1996	96-66	Cox	Lost to Yankees
1999	103-59	Cox	Lost to Yankees

WEST DIVISION CHAMPIONS

Year	Record	Manager	NLCS Result
1969	93-69	Harris	Lost to Mets
1982	89-73	Torre	Lost to Cardinals
1991	94-68	Cox	Defeated Pirates
1992	98-64	Cox	Defeated Pirates
1993	104-58	Cox	Lost to Phillies

EAST DIVISION CHAMPIONS

Year	Record	Manager	NLCS Result
1995	90-54	Cox	Defeated Reds
1996	96-66	Cox	Defeated Cardinals
1997	101-61	Cox	Lost to Marlins
1998	106-56	Cox	Lost to Padres
1999	103-59	Cox	Defeated Mets

ATTENDANCE HIGHS

Total	Season	Park
3,884,720	1993	Fulton County Stadium
3,463,988	1997	Turner Field
3,361,350	1998	Turner Field
3,284,901	1999	Turner Field
3,077,400	1992	Fulton County Stadium

RETIRED UNIFORMS

No.	Name	Pos.
3	Dale Murphy	OF
21	Warren Spahn	P
35	Phil Niekro	P
41	Ed Mathews	3B
44	Hank Aaron	OF

BALLPARK CHRONOLOGY

Turner Field (1997-present)
Capacity: 50,062.

First game: Braves 5, Cubs 4 (April 4, 1997).
First batter: Brian McRae, Cubs.
First hit: Chipper Jones, Braves (single).
First run: Michael Tucker, Braves (3rd inning).
First home run: Michael Tucker, Braves.
First winning pitcher: Brad Clontz, Braves.
First-season attendance: 3,463,988.

South End Grounds I and II, Boston (1876-1914)
First game: Boston 6, Philadelphia 5 (April 22, 1876).

Braves Field, Boston (1915-52)
Capacity: 40,000.
First game: Braves 3, St. Louis 1 (August 18, 1915).
First-season attendance (1916): 313,495.

County Stadium, Milwaukee (1953-65)
Capacity: 43,394.
First game: Braves 3, St. Louis 2, 10 innings (April 14, 1953).
First-season attendance: 1,826,397.

Atlanta-Fulton County Stadium (1966-96)
Capacity: 52,710.
First game: Pittsburgh 3, Braves 2, 13 innings (April 12, 1966).
First-season attendance: 1,539,801.

N.L. MVPs

Bob Elliott, 3B, 1947
Hank Aaron, OF, 1957
Dale Murphy, OF, 1982
Dale Murphy, OF, 1983
Terry Pendleton, 3B, 1991
Chipper Jones, 3B, 1999

CY YOUNG WINNERS

Warren Spahn, LH, 1957
Tom Glavine, LH, 1991
Greg Maddux, RH, 1993
Greg Maddux, RH, 1994
Greg Maddux, RH, 1995
John Smoltz, RH, 1996
Tom Glavine, LH, 1998

ROOKIES OF THE YEAR

Alvin Dark, SS, 1948
Sam Jethroe, OF, 1950
Earl Williams, C, 1971
Bob Horner, 3B, 1978
Dave Justice, OF, 1990

MANAGER OF THE YEAR

Bobby Cox, 1991

30-plus home runs

47—	Eddie Mathews	1953
	Hank Aaron	1971
46—	Eddie Mathews	1959
45—	Hank Aaron	1962
	Chipper Jones	1999
44—	Hank Aaron	1957, 1963, 1966, 1969
	Dale Murphy	1987
	Andres Galarraga	1998
43—	Dave Johnson	1973
41—	Eddie Mathews	1955
	Darrell Evans	1973
	Jeff Burroughs	1977
40—	Eddie Mathews	1954
	Hank Aaron	1960, 1973
	Dave Justice	1993
39—	Wally Berger	1930
	Hank Aaron	1959, 1967
	Eddie Mathews	1960
38—	Joe Adcock	1956
	Hank Aaron	1970
37—	Eddie Mathews	1956
	Dale Murphy	1985
	Fred McGriff	*1993
36—	Joe Torre	1966
	Dale Murphy	1982, 1983, 1984
	Ron Gant	1993
35—	Joe Adcock	1961
	Bob Horner	1980
34—	Wally Berger	1934, 1935
	Hank Aaron	1961, 1972
	Orlando Cepeda	1970
	Fred McGriff	1994
	Ryan Klesko	1996
	Chipper Jones	1998
	Javier Lopez	1998
33—	Earl Williams	1971
	Bob Horner	1979
	Dale Murphy	1980
32—	Eddie Mathews	1957, 1961, 1965
	Hank Aaron	1965
	Bob Horner	1982
	Ron Gant	1990, 1991
31—	Eddie Mathews	1958
	Mack Jones	1965
	Felipe Alou	1966
	Andruw Jones	1998
30—	Hank Aaron	1958
	Chipper Jones	1996

*18 with Padres; 19 with Braves.

100-plus RBIs

145—	Hugh Duffy	1894
135—	Eddie Mathews	1953
132—	Hank Aaron	1957
130—	Wally Berger	1935
	Hank Aaron	1963
128—	Hank Aaron	1962
127—	Hank Aaron	1966
126—	Hank Aaron	1960
124—	Eddie Mathews	1960
123—	Hank Aaron	1959
121—	Wally Berger	1934
	Dale Murphy	1983
	Andres Galarraga	1998
120—	Hank Aaron	1961
	Dave Justice	1993
119—	Wally Berger	1930
118—	Hank Aaron	1970, 1971
117—	Tommy Holmes	1945
	Ron Gant	1993
115—	Brian Jordan	1999
114—	Eddie Mathews	1959
	Jeff Burroughs	1977
113—	Bob Elliott	1947
111—	Orlando Cepeda	1970
	Dale Murphy	1985
	Chipper Jones	1997
110—	Chipper Jones	1996
	Chipper Jones	1999
109—	Sid Gordon	1951
	Joe Torre	1964
	Hank Aaron	1967
	Dale Murphy	1982
108—	Joe Adcock	1961
107—	Bob Elliott	1950
	Fred McGriff	1996
	Chipper Jones	1998
106—	Wally Berger	1933
	Hank Aaron	1955
105—	Dale Murphy	1987
	Ron Gant	1991
	Terry Pendleton	1992
104—	Darrell Evans	1973
	Javier Lopez	1998
103—	Sid Gordon	1950
	Eddie Mathews	1954
	Joe Adcock	1956
101—	Eddie Mathews	1955
	Joe Torre	1966
	Rico Carty	1970
100—	Bill Sweeney	1912
	Bob Elliott	1948
	Dale Murphy	1984

20-plus victories

1877—	Tommy Bond	40-17
1878—	Tommy Bond	40-19
1879—	Tommy Bond	43-19
1880—	Tommy Bond	26-29
1881—	Jim Whitney	31-33
1882—	Jim Whitney	24-21
1883—	Jim Whitney	37-21
	Charlie Buffinton	25-14
1884—	Charlie Buffinton	48-16
	Jim Whitney	23-14
1885—	Charlie Buffinton	22-27
1886—	Hoss Radbourn	27-31
	Bill Stemmeyer	22-18
1887—	Hoss Radbourn	24-23
	Michael Madden	21-14
1888—	John Clarkson	33-20
1889—	John Clarkson	49-19
	Hoss Radbourn	20-11
1890—	Kid Nichols	27-19
	John Clarkson	26-18
	Charlie Getzien	23-17
1891—	John Clarkson	33-19
	Kid Nichols	30-17
	Harry Staley	*24-13
1892—	Kid Nichols	35-16
	Jack Stivetts	35-16
	Harry Staley	22-10
1893—	Kid Nichols	34-14
	Jack Stivetts	20-12
1894—	Kid Nichols	32-13
	Jack Stivetts	26-14
1895—	Kid Nichols	26-16
1896—	Kid Nichols	30-14
	Jack Stivetts	22-14
1897—	Kid Nichols	31-11
	Fred Klobedanz	26-7
	Ted Lewis	21-12
1898—	Kid Nichols	31-12
	Ted Lewis	26-8
	Vic Willis	25-13
1899—	Vic Willis	27-8
	Kid Nichols	21-19
1900—	Bill Dinneen	20-14
1901—	Vic Willis	20-17
1902—	Togie Pittinger	27-16
	Vic Willis	27-20
1905—	Irv Young	20-21
1914—	Bill James	26-7
	Dick Rudolph	26-10
1915—	Dick Rudolph	22-19
1921—	Joe Oeschger	20-14
1933—	Ben Cantwell	20-10
1937—	Lou Fette	20-10
	Jim Turner	20-11
1946—	Johnny Sain	20-14
1947—	Warren Spahn	21-10
	Johnny Sain	21-12
1948—	Johnny Sain	24-15
1949—	Warren Spahn	21-14
1950—	Warren Spahn	21-17
	Johnny Sain	20-13
1951—	Warren Spahn	22-14
1953—	Warren Spahn	23-7
1954—	Warren Spahn	21-12
1956—	Warren Spahn	20-11
1957—	Warren Spahn	21-11
1958—	Warren Spahn	22-11
	Lew Burdette	20-10
1959—	Lew Burdette	21-15
	Warren Spahn	21-15
1960—	Warren Spahn	21-10
1961—	Warren Spahn	21-13
1963—	Warren Spahn	23-7
1965—	Tony Cloninger	24-11
1969—	Phil Niekro	23-13
1974—	Phil Niekro	20-13
1979—	Phil Niekro	21-20
1991—	Tom Glavine	20-11
1992—	Tom Glavine	20-8
1993—	Tom Glavine	22-6
	Greg Maddux	20-10
1997—	Denny Neagle	20-5
1998—	Tom Glavine	20-6

* 4-5 with Pittsburgh; 20-8 with Boston.

N.L. home run champions

1879—	Charley Jones	9
1880—	John O'Rourke	*6
1891—	Harry Stovey	*16
1894—	Hugh Duffy	18
1897—	Hugh Duffy	11
1898—	Jimmy Collins	15
1900—	Herman Long	12
1907—	Dave Brain	10
1910—	Fred Beck	*10
1935—	Wally Berger	34
1945—	Tommy Holmes	28
1953—	Eddie Mathews	47
1957—	Hank Aaron	44
1959—	Eddie Mathews	46
1963—	Hank Aaron	*44
1966—	Hank Aaron	44
1967—	Hank Aaron	39
1984—	Dale Murphy	*36
1985—	Dale Murphy	37

* Tied for league lead

N.L. RBI champions

1935—	Wally Berger	130
1957—	Hank Aaron	132
1960—	Hank Aaron	126
1963—	Hank Aaron	130
1966—	Hank Aaron	127
1982—	Dale Murphy	*109
1983—	Dale Murphy	121

* Tied for league lead

N.L. batting champions

1877—	Deacon White	.387
1889—	Dan Brouthers	.373
1893—	Hugh Duffy	.363
1894—	Hugh Duffy	.440
1928—	Rogers Hornsby	.387
1942—	Ernie Lombardi	.330
1956—	Hank Aaron	.328
1959—	Hank Aaron	.355
1970—	Rico Carty	.366
1974—	Ralph Garr	.353
1991—	Terry Pendleton	.319

N.L. ERA champions

1937—	Jim Turner	2.38
1947—	Warren Spahn	2.33
1951—	Chet Nichols	2.88
1953—	Warren Spahn	2.10
1956—	Lew Burdette	2.70
1961—	Warren Spahn	3.02
1967—	Phil Niekro	1.87
1974—	Buzz Capra	2.28
1993—	Greg Maddux	2.36
1994—	Greg Maddux	1.56
1995—	Greg Maddux	1.63
1997—	Greg Maddux	2.22

N.L. strikeout champions

1877—	Tommy Bond	170
1878—	Tommy Bond	182
1883—	Jim Whitney	345
1889—	John Clarkson	284
1902—	Vic Willis	225
1949—	Warren Spahn	151
1950—	Warren Spahn	191
1951—	Warren Spahn	*164
1952—	Warren Spahn	183
1977—	Phil Niekro	262
1992—	John Smoltz	215
1996—	John Smoltz	276

* Tied for league lead

SEASON

Batting

At-bats	671	Marquis Grissom	1996
Runs	160	Hugh Duffy	1894
Hits	236	Hugh Duffy	1894
Singles	180	Ralph Garr	1971
Doubles	50	Hugh Duffy	1894
Triples	20	Dick Johnston	1887
Home runs	47	Eddie Mathews	1953
		Hank Aaron	1971
Home runs, rookie	38	Wally Berger	1930
Grand slams	4	Sid Gordon	1950
Total bases	400	Hank Aaron	1959
RBIs	145	Hugh Duffy	1894
Walks	131	Bob Elliott	1948
Most strikeouts	146	Andres Galarraga	1998
Fewest strikeouts	9	Tommy Holmes	1945
Batting average	.438	Hugh Duffy	1894
Slugging pct.	.679	Hugh Duffy	1894
Stolen bases	93	Billy Hamilton	1896

Pitching

Games	81	Brad Clontz	1996
Complete games	68	John Clarkson	1889
Innings	620	John Clarkson	1889
Wins	49	John Clarkson	1889
Losses	29	Vic Willis	1905
		Tommy Bond	1880
Winning pct.	.905 (19-2)	Greg Maddux	1995
Walks	164	Phil Niekro	1977
Strikeouts	417	Charlie Buffinton	1884
Shutouts	12	Tommy Bond	1879
Home runs allowed	41	Phil Niekro	1979
Lowest ERA	1.56	Greg Maddux	1994
Saves	39	Mark Wohlers	1996

GAME

Batting

Runs	6	Frank Torre	9-2-57
Hits	6	Felix Millan	7-6-70
Doubles	4	Last by Rafael Ramirez	5-21-86
Triples	3	Last by Danny O'Connell	6-13-56
Home runs	4	Last by Bob Horner	7-6-86
RBIs	9	Tony Cloninger	7-3-66
Total bases	18	Joe Adcock	7-31-54
Stolen bases	6	Otis Nixon	6-16-91

No-hit pitchers
(9 innings or more)

1892—	Jack Stivetts	11-0 vs. Brooklyn
1907—	Frank Pfeffer	6-0 vs. Cincinnati
1914—	George Davis	7-0 vs. Philadelphia
1916—	Tom Hughes	2-0 vs. Pittsburgh
1944—	Jim Tobin	2-0 vs. Brooklyn
1950—	Vern Bickford	7-0 vs. Brooklyn
1954—	Jim Wilson	2-0 vs. Philadelphia
1960—	Lew Burdette	1-0 vs. Philadelphia
1960—	Warren Spahn	4-0 vs. Philadelphia
1961—	Warren Spahn	1-0 vs. San Francisco
1973—	Phil Niekro	9-0 vs. San Diego
1991—	Kent Mercker–Mark Wohlers–Alejandro Pena	1-0 vs. San Diego
1994—	Kent Mercker	6-0 vs. Los Angeles

Longest hitting streaks

37—	Tommy Holmes	1945
31—	Rico Carty	1970
29—	Rowland Office	1976
28—	Marquis Grissom	1996
27—	Hugh Duffy	1893
26—	Hugh Duffy	1894, 1895
	Germany Long	1897
	Bill Sweeney	1911
25—	Jimmy Bannon	1894
	Hank Aaron	1956, 1962
23—	Jimmy Collins	1897
	Germany Long	1895
	Gene DeMontreville	1901
	Alvin Dark	1948
	Red Schoendienst	1957
22—	Hugh Duffy	1894
	Earl Torgeson	1950
	Hank Aaron	1959
	Felipe Alou	1968
	Hank Aaron	1971
	Ralph Garr	1971
21—	Jimmy Bannon	1895
	Chick Stahl	1897
	Billy Hamilton	1898
20—	Tommy Holmes	1946, 1949
	Andy Pafko	1953
	Joe Adcock	1959
	Bob Horner	1979
	Otis Nixon	1991

HISTORY

BATTING

Games
Hank Aaron	3,076
Eddie Mathews	2,223
Dale Murphy	1,926
Rabbit Maranville	1,795
Fred Tenney	1,737
Herman Long	1,646
Bobby Lowe	1,410
Del Crandall	1,394
Johnny Logan	1,351
Tommy Holmes	1,289

At-bats
Hank Aaron	11,628
Eddie Mathews	8,049
Dale Murphy	7,098
Herman Long	6,777
Rabbit Maranville	6,724
Fred Tenney	6,637
Bobby Lowe	5,617
Tommy Holmes	4,956
Johnny Logan	4,931
John Morrill	4,759

Runs
Hank Aaron	2,107
Eddie Mathews	1,452
Herman Long	1,291
Fred Tenney	1,134
Dale Murphy	1,103
Hugh Duffy	1,036
Bobby Lowe	999
Billy Nash	855
Rabbit Maranville	801
John Morrill	800

Hits
Hank Aaron	3,600
Eddie Mathews	2,201
Fred Tenney	1,994
Dale Murphy	1,901
Herman Long	1,900
Rabbit Maranville	1,696
Hugh Duffy	1,630
Bobby Lowe	1,606
Tommy Holmes	1,503
Johnny Logan	1,329

Doubles
Hank Aaron	600
Eddie Mathews	338
Dale Murphy	306
Herman Long	295
Tommy Holmes	291
Wally Berger	248
Rabbit Maranville	244
Fred Tenney	242
John Morrill	234
Hugh Duffy	220

Triples
Rabbit Maranville	103
Hank Aaron	96
Herman Long	91
John Morrill	80
Bill Bruton	79
Fred Tenney	74
Hugh Duffy	73
Bobby Lowe	71
Sam Wise	71
Eddie Mathews	70

Home runs
Hank Aaron	733
Eddie Mathews	493
Dale Murphy	371
Joe Adcock	239
Bob Horner	215
Wally Berger	199
Del Crandall	170
David Justice	160
Chipper Jones	153
Ron Gant	147

Total bases
Hank Aaron	6,591
Eddie Mathews	4,158
Dale Murphy	3,394
Herman Long	2,641
Fred Tenney	2,435
Rabbit Maranville	2,215
Wally Berger	2,212
Joe Adcock	2,164
Tommy Holmes	2,152
Bobby Lowe	2,144

Runs batted in
Hank Aaron	2,202
Eddie Mathews	1,388
Dale Murphy	1,143

SEASON

Batting
Most at-bats	5,631	1973
Most runs	1,220	1894
Fewest runs	408	1906
Most hits	1,567	1925
Most singles	1,196	1925
Most doubles	309	1999
Most triples	100	1921
Most home runs	215	1998
Fewest home runs	15	1909
Most grand slams	12	1997
Most pinch-hit home runs	9	1992
Most total bases	2,483	1998
Most stolen bases	189	1902
Highest batting average	.292	1925
Lowest batting average	.223	1909
Highest slugging pct.	.453	1998

Pitching
Lowest ERA	2.19	1916
Highest ERA	5.12	1929
Most complete games	139	1905
Most shutouts	24	1992
Most saves	51	1982
Most walks	701	1977
Most strikeouts	1,245	1996

Fielding
Most errors	361	1903
Fewest errors	91	1998
Most double plays	197	1985
Highest fielding average	.985	1998

General
Most games won	106	1998
Most games lost	115	1935
Highest win pct.	.705	1897
Lowest win pct.	.248	1935

GAME, INNING

Batting
Most runs, game	30	6-9-1883
Most runs, inning	16	6-18-1894
Most hits, game	32	9-3-1896
Most home runs, game	8	8-30-53
Most total bases, game	47	8-30-53

Third baseman Eddie Mathews hit a team-record 47 home runs in 1953.

Herman Long	964
Hugh Duffy	927
Bobby Lowe	872
Billy Nash	809
Joe Adcock	760
Wally Berger	746
Bob Horner	652

Extra-base hits
Hank Aaron	1,429
Eddie Mathews	901
Dale Murphy	714
Wally Berger	499
Herman Long	474
Joe Adcock	458
Tommy Holmes	426
Bob Horner	382
Rabbit Maranville	370
Hugh Duffy	362

Batting average
(Minimum 500 games)
Billy Hamilton	.339
Hugh Duffy	.332
Chick Stahl	.327
Rico Carty	.317
Ralph Garr	.317
Lance Richbourg	.311
Hank Aaron	.310
Jimmy Collins	.309
Wally Berger	.304
Tommy Holmes	.303

Stolen bases
Herman Long	433
Hugh Duffy	331
Billy Hamilton	274
Bobby Lowe	260
Fred Tenney	260
Hank Aaron	240
King Kelly	238
Billy Nash	232
Rabbit Maranville	194
Otis Nixon	186

PITCHING

Earned-run average
(Minimum 1,000 innings)
Tommy Bond	2.21
Greg Maddux	2.34
Jim Whitney	2.49

Dick Rudolph	2.62
John Clarkson	2.82
Vic Willis	2.82
Charlie Buffinton	2.83
Kid Nichols	3.00
Warren Spahn	3.05
Lefty Tyler	3.06

Wins
Warren Spahn	356
Kid Nichols	329
Phil Niekro	268
Tom Glavine	187
Lew Burdette	179
John Smoltz	157
Vic Willis	151
Tommy Bond	149
John Clarkson	149
Jim Whitney	133

Losses
Phil Niekro	230
Warren Spahn	229
Kid Nichols	183
Vic Willis	147
Jim Whitney	121
Lew Burdette	120
Bob Smith	120
Ed Brandt	119
Tom Glavine	116
John Smoltz	113

Innings pitched
Warren Spahn	5,046.0
Phil Niekro	4,622.2
Kid Nichols	4,538.0
Tom Glavine	2,659.2
Lew Burdette	2,638.0
Vic Willis	2,575.0
John Smoltz	2,414.1
Jim Whitney	2,263.2
Tommy Bond	2,127.1
John Clarkson	2,092.2

Strikeouts
Phil Niekro	2,912
Warren Spahn	2,493
John Smoltz	2,098
Kid Nichols	1,672
Tom Glavine	1,659
Greg Maddux	1,223
Vic Willis	1,161

Jim Whitney	1,157
Lew Burdette	923
Charlie Buffinton	911

Bases on balls
Phil Niekro	1,458
Warren Spahn	1,378
Kid Nichols	1,159
Tom Glavine	900
Vic Willis	854
Bob Buhl	782
John Smoltz	774
Lefty Tyler	678
John Clarkson	676
Jack Stivetts	651

Games
Phil Niekro	740
Warren Spahn	714
Gene Garber	557
Kid Nichols	556
Lew Burdette	468
Rick Camp	414
Tom Glavine	399
Mark Wohlers	388
John Smoltz	356
Steve Bedrosian	350

Shutouts
Warren Spahn	63
Kid Nichols	44
Phil Niekro	43
Lew Burdette	30
Tommy Bond	29
Dick Rudolph	27
Vic Willis	26
Lefty Tyler	22
John Clarkson	20
Charlie Buffinton	19

Saves
Gene Garber	141
Mark Wohlers	112
Cecil Upshaw	78
Rick Camp	57
Mike Stanton	55
Don McMahon	50
Greg McMichael	44
Steve Bedrosian	41
John Rocker	40
Bruce Sutter	40

HISTORY

BRAVES YEAR-BY-YEAR

				Games		Leaders					
Year	W	L	Place	Back	Manager	Batting avg.	Hits	Home runs	RBIs	Wins	ERA
BOSTON BRAVES											
1901	69	69	5th	20½	Selee	DeMontreville, .300	DeMontreville, 173	DeMontreville, 5	DeMontreville, 72	Willis, 20	Willis, 2.36
1902	73	64	3rd	29	Buckenberger	Tenney, .315	Cooley, 162	5 Tied, 2	Carney, Gremminger, 65	Pittinger, Willis, 27	Willis, 2.20
1903	58	80	6th	32	Buckenberger	Tenney, .313	Cooley, 160	Moran, 7	Cooley, 70	Pittinger, 18	Willis, 2.98
1904	55	98	7th	51	Buckenberger	J. Delahanty, .285	Abbaticchio, 148	Cooley, 5	Cooley, 70	Willis, 18	Pittinger, 2.66
1905	51	103	7th	54½	Tenney	Tenney, .288	Abbaticchio, 170	J. Delahanty, 5	J. Delahanty, Wolverton, 55	Young, 20	Young, 2.90
1906	49	102	8th	66½	Tenney	Tenney, .283	Tenney, 154	Bates, 6	Bates, Howard, 54	Young, 16	Lindaman, 2.43
1907	58	90	7th	47	Tenney	Beaumont, .322	Beaumont, 187	Brain, 10	Beaumont, 62	Dorner, Flaherty, 12	Flaherty, 2.70
1908	63	91	6th	36	Kelley	Ritchey, 2.73	Beaumont, 127	Dahlen, 3	McGann, 55	Flaherty, Lindaman, Ferguson 12	McCarthy, 1.63
1909	45	108	8th	65½	Bowerman, H. Smith	Beaumont, .263	Becker, 138	Becker, 6	Beaumont, 60	Mattern, 15	Richie, 2.32
1910	53	100	8th	50½	Lake	Miller, .286	Beck, 157	Beck, 10	Beck, 64	Mattern, 16	Brown, 2.67
1911	44	107	8th	54	Tenney	Miller, .333	Miller, 192	Miller, 7	Miller, 91	Brown, 8	Brown, 4.29
1912	52	101	8th	52	Kling	Sweeney, .344	Sweeney, 204	Houser, 8	Sweeney, 100	Perdue, 13	Hess, 3.76
1913	69	82	5th	31½	Stallings	Connolly, .281	Myers, 143	Lord, 6	Connolly, 57	Perdue, Tyler, 16	James, Tyler, 2.79
1914	94	59	1st	+10½	Stallings	Connolly, .306	Schmidt, 153	Connolly, 9	Maranville, 78	Rudolph, James, 26	James, 1.90
1915	83	69	2nd	7	Stallings	Magee, .280	Magee, 160	6 Tied, 2	Magee, 87	Rudolph, 22	Hughes, 2.12
1916	89	63	3rd	4	Stallings	Konetchy, .260	Konetchy, 147	Maranville, 4	Konetchy, 70	Rudolph, 19	Nehf, 2.01
1917	72	81	6th	25½	Stallings	R. Smith, .295	R. Smith, 149	Powell, 4	R. Smith, 62	Nehf, 17	Nehf, 2.16
1918	53	71	7th	28½	Stallings	R. Smith, .298	R. Smith, 128	Wickland, 4	R. Smith, 65	Nehf, 15	Fillingim, 2.23
1919	57	82	6th	38½	Stallings	Holke, .292	Holke, 151	Maranville, 5	Holke, 48	Rudolph, 13	Rudolph, 2.17
1920	62	90	7th	30	Stallings	Holke, .294	Holke, 162	Powell, 6	Holke, 64	Oeschger, 15	Fillingim, 3.11
1921	79	74	4th	15	Mitchell	Boeckel, .313	Powell, 191	Powell, 12	Boeckel, 84	Oeschger, 20	Fillingim, 3.45
1922	53	100	8th	39½	Mitchell	Powell, .296	Powell, 163	Boeckel, Powell, 6	Ford, 60	F. Miller, Marquard, 11	F. Miller, 3.51
1923	54	100	7th	41½	Mitchell	Southworth, .319	Southworth, 195	Boeckel, 7	McInnis, 95	Genewich, 13	Barnes, 2.76
1924	53	100	8th	40	Bancroft	McInnis, .291	McInnis, 169	Tierney, 6	McInnis, 59	Barnes, 15	Cooney, 3.18
1925	70	83	5th	25	Bancroft	Burrus, .340	Burrus, 200	Welsh, 7	Burrus, 87	Benton, Cooney, 14	Benton, 3.09
1926	66	86	7th	22	Bancroft	E. Brown, .328	E. Brown, 201	Burrus, Welsh, 3	E. Brown, 84	Benton, 14	Werts, 3.28
1927	60	94	7th	34	Bancroft, Hornsby	Richbourg, .309	E. Brown, 171	Fournier, 10	E. Brown, 75	Genewich, Greenfield, 11	B. Smith, 3.76
1928	50	103	7th	44½	Slattery	Hornsby, .387	Richbourg, 206	Hornsby, 21	Hornsby, 94	B. Smith, 13	Delaney, 3.79
1929	56	98	8th	43	Fuchs	Sisler, .326	Sisler, 205	Harper, 10	Sisler, 79	Seibold, 12	Cunningham, 4.52
1930	70	84	6th	22	McKechnie	Spohrer, .317	Berger, 172	Berger, 38	Berger, 119	Seibold, 15	Seibold, 4.12
1931	64	90	7th	37	McKechnie	Berger, .323	Berger, 199	Berger, 19	Berger, 84	Brandt, 18	Brandt, 2.92
1932	77	77	5th	13	McKechnie	Berger, .307	Berger, 185	Berger, 17	Berger, 73	Brandt, 16	Betts, 2.80
1933	83	71	4th	9	McKechnie	Berger, .313	Jordan, 168	Berger, 27	Berger, 106	Cantwell, 20	Brandt, 2.60
1934	78	73	4th	16	McKechnie	Jordan, .311	Berger, 183	Berger, 34	Berger, 121	Betts, Frankhouse, 17	Frankhouse, 3.20
1935	38	115	8th	61½	McKechnie	Lee, .303	Berger, 174	Berger, 34	Berger, 130	Frankhouse, 11	B. Smith, 3.94
1936	71	83	6th	21	McKechnie	Jordan, .323	Moore, 185	Berger, 25	Berger, 91	MacFayden, 17	MacFayden, 2.87
1937	79	73	5th	16	McKechnie	Moore, .283	Moore, 159	Moore, 16	Cuccinello, 80	Fette, Turner, 20	Turner, 2.38
1938	77	75	5th	12	Stengel	Garms, .315	Cuccinello, 147	V. DiMaggio, 14	Cuccinello, 76	MacFayden, Turner, 14	Hutchinson, 2.74
1939	63	88	7th	32½	Stengel	Hassett, .308	Hassett, 182	West, 19	West, 82	Posedel, 15	Fette, 2.96
1940	65	87	7th	34½	Stengel	Cooney, .318	E. Miller, 157	Ross, 17	Ross, 89	Errickson, Posedel, 12	Salvo, 3.08
1941	62	92	7th	38	Stengel	Cooney, .319	Cooney, 141	West, 12	E. Miller, West, 68	Tobin, 12	Earley, 2.53
1942	59	89	7th	44	Stengel	Holmes, .278	Holmes, 155	West, 16	West, 56	Javery, Tobin, 12	Javery, Salvo, 3.03
1943	68	85	6th	36½	Stengel	Holmes, .270	Holmes, 170	Workman, 10	Workman, 67	Javery, 17	Andrews, 2.57
1944	65	89	6th	40	Coleman	Holmes, .309	Holmes, 195	Nieman, 16	Holmes, 73	Tobin, 18	Tobin, 3.01
1945	67	85	6th	30	Coleman, Bissonette	Holmes, .352	Holmes, 224	Holmes, 28	Holmes, 117	Tobin, 9	Wright, 2.51
1946	81	72	4th	15½	Southworth	Hopp, .333	Holmes, 176	Litwhiler, 8	Holmes, 79	Sain, 20	Sain, 2.21
1947	86	68	3rd	8	Southworth	Elliott, .317	Holmes, 191	Elliott, 22	Elliott, 113	Sain, Spahn, 21	Spahn, 2.33
1948	91	62	1st	+6½	Southworth	Holmes, .325	Holmes, 190	Elliott, 23	Elliott, 100	Sain, 24	Sain, 2.60
1949	75	79	4th	22	Southworth	Stanky, .285	Dark, 146	Elliott, 17	Elliott, 76	Spahn, 21	Spahn, 3.07
1950	83	71	4th	8	Southworth	Elliott, .305	Torgeson, 167	Gordon, 27	Elliott, 107	Spahn, 21	Spahn, 3.16
1951	76	78	4th	20½	Southworth, Holmes	Gordon, .287	Jethroe, 160	Gordon, 29	Gordon, 109	Spahn, 22	Nichols, 2.88
1952	64	89	7th	32	Holmes, Grimm	Gordon, .289	Gordon, 151	Gordon, Mathews, 25	Gordon, 75	Spahn, 14	Spahn, 2.98
MILWAUKEE BRAVES											
1953	92	62	2nd	13	Grimm	Mathews, .302	Mathews, 175	Mathews, 47	Mathews, 135	Spahn, 23	Spahn, 2.10
1954	89	65	3rd	8	Grimm	Adcock, .308	Bruton, 161	Mathews, 40	Mathews, 103	Spahn, 21	Jolly, 2.43
1955	85	69	2nd	13½	Grimm	Aaron, .314	Aaron, 189	Mathews, 41	Aaron, 106	Spahn, 17	Buhl, 3.21
1956	92	62	2nd	1	Grimm, Haney	Aaron, .328	Aaron, 200	Adcock, 38	Adcock, 103	Spahn, 20	Burdette, 2.70
1957	95	59	1st	+8	Haney	Aaron, .322	Aaron, 198	Aaron, 44	Aaron, 132	Spahn, 21	Spahn, 2.69
1958	92	62	1st	+8	Haney	Aaron, .326	Aaron, 196	Mathews, 31	Aaron, 95	Spahn, 22	Jay, 2.14
1959	86	70	*2nd	2	Haney	Aaron, .355	Aaron 223	Mathews, 46	Aaron, 123	Burdette, Spahn, 21	Rush, 2.40
1960	88	66	2nd	7	Dressen	Adcock, .298	Bruton, 180	Aaron, 40	Aaron, 126	Spahn, 21	Buhl, 3.09
1961	83	71	4th	10	Dressen, Tebbetts	Aaron, .327	Aaron, 197	Adcock, 35	Aaron, 120	Spahn, 21	McMahon, 2.84
1962	86	76	5th	15½	Tebbetts	Aaron, .323	Aaron, 191	Aaron, 45	Aaron, 128	Spahn, 18	Shaw, 2.80
1963	84	78	6th	15	Bragan	Aaron, .319	Aaron, 201	Aaron, 44	Aaron, 130	Spahn, 23	Spahn, 2.60
1964	88	74	5th	5	Bragan	Carty, .330	Torre, 193	Aaron, 24	Torre, 109	Cloninger, 19	Cloninger, 3.56
1965	86	76	5th	11	Bragan	Aaron, .318	Aaron, 181	Aaron, Mathews, 32	Mathews, 95	Cloninger, 24	O'Dell, 2.18
ATLANTA BRAVES											
1966	85	77	5th	10	Bragan, Hitchcock	F. Alou, .327	F. Alou, 218	Aaron, 44	Aaron, 127	Cloninger, Johnson, 14	Carroll, 2.37
1967	77	85	7th	24½	Hitchcock, Silvestri	Aaron, .307	Aaron, 184	Aaron, 39	Aaron, 109	Jarvis, 15	Niekro, 1.87
1968	81	81	5th	16	Harris	F. Alou, .317	F. Alou, 210	Aaron, 29	Aaron, 86	Jarvis, 16	Pappas, 2.37
WEST DIVISION											
1969	93	69	†1st	+3	Harris	Aaron, .300	Millan, 174	Aaron, 44	Aaron, 97	Niekro, 23	Niekro, 2.56
1970	76	86	5th	26	Harris	Carty, .366	Millan, 183	Aaron, 38	Aaron, 118	Jarvis, 16	Jarvis, 3.61
1971	82	80	3rd	8	Harris	Garr, .343	Garr, 219	Aaron, 47	Aaron, 118	Niekro, 15	T. Kelley, 2.96
1972	70	84	4th	25	Harris, Mathews	Garr, .325	Garr, 180	Aaron, 34	Williams, 87	Niekro, 16	Niekro, 3.06
1973	76	85	5th	22½	Mathews	Aaron, .301	Garr, 200	D. Johnson, 43	Evans, 104	Morton, 15	Niekro, 3.31
1974	88	74	3rd	14	Mathews, King	Garr, .353	Garr, 214	Evans, 25	Evans, 79	Niekro, 20	House, 1.93
1975	67	94	5th	40½	King, Ryan	Office, .290	Garr, 174	Evans, 22	Evans, 73	Morton, 17	Niekro, 3.20
1976	70	92	6th	32	Bristol	Montanez, .321	Montanez, 135	Wynn, 17	Wynn, 66	Niekro, 17	Messersmith, 3.04
1977	61	101	6th	37	Bristol , Turner	Bonnell, .300	Burroughs, Matthews, 157	Burroughs, 41	Burroughs, 114	Niekro, 16	Niekro, 4.03
1978	69	93	6th	26	Cox	Burroughs, .301	Burroughs, 147	Burroughs, Horner, 23	Murphy, 79	Niekro, 19	McWilliams, 2.81
1979	66	94	6th	23½	Cox	Horner, .314	Matthews, 192	Horner, 33	Horner, 98	Niekro, 21	Niekro, 3.39
1980	81	80	4th	11	Cox	Chambliss, .282	Chambliss, 170	Horner, 35	Horner, Murphy, 89	Niekro, 15	Camp, 1.91
1981	50	56	‡4th/5th	—	Cox	Washington, .291	Chambliss, 110	Horner, 15	Chambliss, 51	Camp, 9	R. Mahler, 2.80
1982	89	73	†1st	+1	Torre	Murphy, .281	Ramirez, 169	Murphy, 36	Murphy, 109	Niekro, 17	Garber, 2.34
1983	88	74	2nd	3	Torre	Horner, .303	Ramirez, 185	Murphy, 36	Murphy, 121	McMurtry, Perez, 15	McMurtry, 3.08
1984	80	82	§2nd	12	Torre	Murphy, .290	Murphy, 176	Murphy, 36	Murphy, 100	Perez, 14	Garber, 3.06
1985	66	96	5th	29	Haas, Wine	Murphy, .300	Murphy, 185	Murphy, 37	Murphy, 111	R. Mahler, 17	R. Mahler, 3.48
1986	72	89	6th	23½	Tanner	Horner, .273	Murphy, 163	Murphy, 29	Horner, 87	Mahler, 14	Dedmon, 2.98
1987	69	92	5th	20½	Tanner	James, .312	Murphy, 167	Murphy, 44	Murphy, 105	Z. Smith, 15	Dedmon, 3.91
1988	54	106	6th	39½	Tanner, Nixon	Perry, .300	Perry, 164	Murphy, 24	Murphy, 77	Mahler, 9	Alvarez, 2.99
1989	63	97	6th	28	Nixon	L. Smith, .315	L. Smith, 152	L. Smith, 21	Murphy, 84	Glavine, 14	Acker, 2.67
1990	65	97	6th	26	Nixon, Cox	L. Smith, .305	Gant, 174	Gant, 32	Gant, 84	Smoltz, 14	Leibrandt, 3.16
1991	94	68	∞1st	+1	Cox	Pendleton, .319	Pendleton, 187	Gant, 32	Gant, 105	Glavine, 20	Glavine, 2.55
1992	98	64	∞1st	+8	Cox	Pendleton, .311	Pendleton, 199	Justice, Pendleton, 21	Pendleton, 105	Glavine, 20	Glavine, 2.76
1993	104	58	†1st	+1	Cox	Blauser, .305	Blauser, 182	Justice, 40	Justice, 120	Glavine, 22	McMichael, 2.06
EAST DIVISION											
1994	68	46	2nd	6	Cox	McGriff, .318	McGriff, 135	McGriff, 34	McGriff, 94	Maddux, 16	Maddux, 1.56
1995	90	54	▲∞1st	+21	Cox	McGriff, .280	McGriff, 148	McGriff, 27	McGriff, 93	Maddux, 19	Maddux, 1.63
1996	96	66	▲∞1st	+8	Cox	C. Jones, .309	Grissom, 207	Klesko, 34	C. Jones, 110	Smoltz, 24	Maddux, 2.72
1997	101	61	▲†1st	+9	Cox	Lofton, .333	C. Jones, 176	Klesko, 24	C. Jones, 111	Neagle, 20	Maddux, 2.20
1998	106	56	▲†1st	+18	Cox	C. Jones, .313	C. Jones, 188	Galarraga, 44	Galarraga, 121	Glavine, 20	Maddux, 2.22
1999	103	59	▲∞1st	+6½	Cox	C. Jones, .319	C. Jones, 181	C. Jones, 45	B. Jordan, 115	Maddux, 19	Millwood, 2.68

* Lost pennant playoff. † Lost Championship Series. ‡ First half 25-29; second half 25-27. § Tied for position. ∞ Won Championship Series. ▲ Won Division Series.

Note: Batting average minimum 350 at-bats; ERA minimum 90 innings pitched.

HISTORY

CHICAGO CUBS

Shortstop Ernie Banks.

FRANCHISE CHRONOLOGY

First season: 1876, as a member of the new National League. The "White Stockings" defeated Louisville, 4-0, in their first N.L. game and went on to win the league's first pennant with a 52-14 record.

1877-1900: Chicago, under the inspired leadership of player/manager Cap Anson, won five pennants as the premier franchise of the 1880s. But after a second-place finish in 1891, the team sank to seventh place and never mounted another pre-1900 challenge.

1901-present: The 1906 Cubs set a modern Major League record with 116 victories before being upset by the White Sox in the World Series. But that disappointment was followed by consecutive Series victories over Detroit—a success the franchise never would be able to duplicate. Over the next nine decades, the Cubs failed to bring another Series banner to Chicago. Pennants in 1910, 1918, 1929, 1932, 1935, 1938 and 1945 were followed by fall classic defeats, and East Division titles in 1984 and 1989 were followed by Championship Series losses. The Cubs qualified for the playoffs as the N.L. wild-card after the 1998 campaign, but a Division Series loss to Atlanta continued their record streak of consecutive seasons without winning a World Series. Chicago was one of five teams placed in the Central Division when the N.L. adopted its three-division format in 1994.

CUBS VS. OPPONENTS BY DECADE

	Braves	Cardinals	Dodgers	Giants	Phillies	Pirates	Reds	Astros	Mets	Expos	Padres	Marlins	Rockies	Brewers	D'backs	Interleague	Decade Record
1900-09	135-76	144-64	135-74	115-97	119-90	99-112	132-79										879-592
1910-19	127-87	136-78	117-98	99-116	110-101	118-95	119-93										826-668
1920-29	139-80	112-105	115-104	99-121	132-88	95-125	115-105										807-728
1930-39	146-74	111-109	127-89	117-102	147-73	120-100	121-99										889-646
1940-49	108-111	82-138	101-119	110-109	121-99	104-116	110-110										736-802
1950-59	94-126	107-113	85-134	90-130	92-128	114-106	90-129										672-866
1960-69	90-92	73-114	80-102	76-106	93-95	78-110	79-103	66-72	79-65	10-8	11-1						735-868
1970-79	66-54	93-87	52-68	59-61	87-92	66-111	59-61	55-65	86-93	88-89	74-46						785-827
1980-89	55-57	81-89	57-61	57-61	78-95	81-95	54-59	51-64	83-92	77-95	61-53						735-821
1990-99	43-62	71-67	57-61	57-53	60-63	63-76	51-68	51-70	62-57	57-62	59-51	39-36	38-40	12-12	9-12	20-23	739-813
Totals	1003-819	1010-964	916-910	879-956	1039-924	938-1046	930-906	223-271	310-307	232-254	205-151	39-36	38-40	12-12	9-12	20-23	7803-7631

Interleague results: 6-6 vs. White Sox; 2-6 vs. Indians; 5-4 vs. Royals; 2-1 vs. Brewers; 5-4 vs. Twins; 0-2 vs. Tigers.

MANAGERS

Name	Years	Record
Al Spalding	1876-77	78-47
Bob Ferguson	1878	30-30
Silver Flint	1879	5-12
Cap Anson	1879-97	1283-932
Tom Burns	1898-99	160-138
Tom Loftus	1900-01	118-161
Frank Selee	1902-05	280-213
Frank Chance	1905-12	768-389
Johnny Evers	1913, 1921	129-120
Hank O'Day	1914	78-76
Roger Bresnahan	1915	73-80
Joe Tinker	1916	67-86
Fred Mitchell	1917-20	308-269
Bill Killefer	1921-25	300-293
Rabbit Maranville	1925	23-30
George Gibson	1925	12-14
Joe McCarthy	1926-30	442-321
Rogers Hornsby	1930-32	141-116
Charlie Grimm	1932-38, 1944-49, 1960	946-782
Gabby Hartnett	1938-40	203-176
Jimmie Wilson	1941-44	213-258
Roy Johnson	1944	0-1
Frank Frisch	1949-51	141-196
Phil Cavarretta	1951-53	169-213
Stan Hack	1954-56	196-265
Bob Scheffing	1957-59	208-254
Lou Boudreau	1960	54-83
*Vedie Himsl	1961	10-21
*Harry Craft	1961	7-9
*Elvin Tappe	1961-62	46-70
*Lou Klein	1961-62, 1965	65-82
*Charlie Metro	1962	43-69
Bob Kennedy	1963-65	182-198
Leo Durocher	1966-72	535-526
Whitey Lockman	1972-74	157-162
Jim Marshall	1974-76	175-218
Herman Franks	1977-79	238-241
Joe Amalfitano	1979, 1980-81	66-116
Preston Gomez	1980	38-52
Lee Elia	1982-83	127-158
Charlie Fox	1983	17-22
Jim Frey	1984-86	196-182
John Vukovich	1986	1-1
Gene Michael	1986-87	114-124
Frank Lucchesi	1987	8-17
Don Zimmer	1988-91	265-258
Joe Altobelli	1991	0-1
Jim Essian	1991	59-63
Jim Lefebvre	1992-93	162-162
Tom Trebelhorn	1994	49-64
Jim Riggleman	1995-99	374-419

* Members of College of Coaches.

WORLD SERIES CHAMPIONS

Year	Loser	Length	MVP
1907	Detroit	5 games	None
1908	Detroit	5 games	None

N.L. PENNANT WINNERS

Year	Record	Manager	Series Result
1876	52-14	Spalding	None
1880	67-17	Anson	None
1881	56-28	Anson	None
1882	55-29	Anson	None
1885	87-25	Anson	None
1886	90-34	Anson	None
1906	116-36	Chance	Lost to White Sox
1907	107-45	Chance	Defeated Tigers
1908	99-55	Chance	Defeated Tigers
1910	104-50	Chance	Lost to A's
1918	84-45	Mitchell	Lost to Red Sox
1929	98-54	McCarthy	Lost to A's
1932	90-64	Hornsby, Grimm	Lost to Yankees
1935	100-54	Grimm	Lost to Tigers
1938	89-63	Grimm, Hartnett	Lost to Yankees
1945	98-56	Grimm	Lost to Tigers

EAST DIVISION CHAMPIONS

Year	Record	Manager	NLCS Result
1984	96-65	Frey	Lost to Padres
1989	93-69	Zimmer	Lost to Giants

WILD-CARD QUALIFIERS

Year	Record	Manager	Div. Series Result
1998	90-73	Riggleman	Lost to Braves

ATTENDANCE HIGHS

Total	Season	Park
2,813,800	1999	Wrigley Field
2,653,763	1993	Wrigley Field
2,583,444	1998	Wrigley Field
2,491,942	1989	Wrigley Field
2,314,250	1991	Wrigley Field

BALLPARK CHRONOLOGY

Wrigley Field (1916-present)

Capacity: 38,902.
First game: Cubs 7, Cincinnati 6, 11 innings (April 20, 1916).
First batter: Red Killefer, Reds.
First hit: Red Killefer (single).
First run: Red Killefer (5th inning).
First home run: Johnny Beall, Reds.
First winning pitcher: Gene Packard, Cubs.
First-season attendance: 453,685.

State Street Grounds (1876-77)
First game: Chicago 6, Cincinnati 0 (May 10, 1876).

Lakefront Park (1878-84)
First game: Indianapolis 5, Chicago 3 (May 14, 1878).

West Side Park (1885-92)
First game: Chicago 9, St. Louis 2 (June 6, 1885).

South Side Park (1891-94)
First game: Chicago 1, Pittsburgh 0 (May 5, 1891).

West Side Grounds (1893-1915)
First game: Cincinnati 13, Chicago 12 (May 14, 1893).

Note: South Side Park shared home games with West Side Park in 1891 and '92 and West Side Grounds in 1893 and '94.

N.L. MVPs
Gabby Hartnett, C, 1935
Phil Cavarretta, 1B, 1945
Hank Sauer, OF, 1952
Ernie Banks, SS, 1958
Ernie Banks, SS, 1959
Ryne Sandberg, 2B, 1984
Andre Dawson, OF, 1987
Sammy Sosa, OF, 1998

CY YOUNG WINNERS
Ferguson Jenkins, RH, 1971
Bruce Sutter, RH, 1979
Rick Sutcliffe, RH, 1984
Greg Maddux, RH, 1992

ROOKIES OF THE YEAR
Billy Williams, OF, 1961
Ken Hubbs, 2B, 1962
Jerome Walton, OF, 1989
Kerry Wood, P, 1998

MANAGERS OF THE YEAR
Jim Frey, 1984
Don Zimmer, 1989

RETIRED UNIFORMS

No.	Name	Pos.
14	Ernie Banks	SS
23	Ryan Sandberg	2B
26	Billy Williams	OF

MILESTONE PERFORMANCES

30-plus home runs
66— Sammy Sosa 1998
63— Sammy Sosa 1999
56— Hack Wilson 1930
49— Andre Dawson 1987
48— Dave Kingman 1979
47— Ernie Banks 1958
45— Ernie Banks 1959
44— Ernie Banks 1955
43— Ernie Banks 1957
42— Billy Williams 1970
41— Hank Sauer 1954
      Ernie Banks 1960
40— Ryne Sandberg 1990
      Sammy Sosa 1996
39— Rogers Hornsby 1929
      Hack Wilson 1929
37— Gabby Hartnett 1930
      Hank Sauer 1952
      Ernie Banks 1962
      Billy Williams 1972
36— Andy Pafko 1950
      Sammy Sosa 1995, 1997
34— Billy Williams 1965
33— Bill Nicholson 1944
      Billy Williams 1964
      Ron Santo 1965
      Sammy Sosa 1993
32— Hank Sauer 1950
      Ernie Banks 1968
      Jim Hickman 1970
      Rick Monday 1976
31— Hack Wilson 1928
      Ron Santo 1967
      Andre Dawson 1991
      Henry Rodriguez 1998
30— Hack Wilson 1927
      Hank Sauer 1951
      Ron Santo.................................1964, 1966
      Billy Williams 1968
      Ryne Sandberg 1989
      Rick Wilkins 1993

100-plus RBIs
191— Hack Wilson 1930
159— Hack Wilson 1929
158— Sammy Sosa 1998
149— Rogers Hornsby 1929
143— Ernie Banks 1959
141— Sammy Sosa 1999
137— Andre Dawson 1987
134— Kiki Cuyler 1930
129— Hack Wilson 1927
      Ernie Banks 1958
      Billy Williams 1970
128— Bill Nicholson 1943
123— Ron Santo 1969
122— Gabby Hartnett 1930
      Bill Nicholson 1944
      Billy Williams 1972
121— Hank Sauer 1952
120— Hack Wilson 1928
119— Sammy Sosa 1995, 1997
117— Ernie Banks 1955, 1960
115— Frank Demaree 1937
      Jim Hickman 1970
      Dave Kingman 1979
114— Ron Santo.................................1964, 1970
110— Riggs Stephenson 1929
      Andy Pafko 1945
109— Hack Wilson 1926
108— Billy Williams 1965
107— Frank Schulte 1911
106— Ernie Banks 1965, 1969
      Keith Moreland 1985
105— Bill Buckner 1982
104— Ernie Banks 1962
      Andre Dawson 1991
103— Hank Sauer 1950, 1954
102— Ernie Banks 1957
101— Andy Pafko 1948
      Ron Santo 1965

100 home runs
100— Andre Dawson 1990
      Ryne Sandberg 1990, 1991
      Sammy Sosa 1996

20-plus victories
1876— Al Spalding 47-13
1878— Terry Larkin 29-26
1879— Terry Larkin 30-23
1880— Larry Corcoran 43-14
          Fred Goldsmith 22-3
1881— Larry Corcoran 31-14
          Fred Goldsmith 25-13
1882— Fred Goldsmith 28-16
          Larry Corcoran 27-13
1883— Larry Corcoran 31-21
          Fred Goldsmith 28-18
1884— Larry Corcoran 35-23
1885— John Clarkson 53-16
          Jim McCormick *21-7
1886— John Clarkson 36-17
          Jim McCormick 31-11
          John Flynn 23-6
1887— John Clarkson 38-21
1888— Gus Krock 25-14
1890— Bill Hutchinson 42-25
          Pat Luby 20-9
1891— Bill Hutchinson 44-19
1892— Bill Hutchinson 36-36
          Ad Gumbert 22-19
1894— Clark Griffith 21-14
1895— Clark Griffith 26-14
          William Terry 21-14
1896— Clark Griffith 23-11
1897— Clark Griffith 21-18
1898— Clark Griffith 24-10
          Jim Callahan 20-10
1899— Clark Griffith 22-14
          Jim Callahan 21-12
1902— Jack Taylor 23-11
1903— Jack Taylor 21-14
          Jake Weimer 21-9
1904— Jake Weimer 20-14
1906— Mordecai Brown 26-6
          Jack Pfiester 20-8
          Jack Taylor ....† 20-12
1907— Orval Overall 23-7
          Mordecai Brown 20-6
1908— Mordecai Brown 29-9
          Ed Reulbach 24-7
1909— Mordecai Brown 27-9
          Orval Overall 20-11
1910— Mordecai Brown 25-13
          Leonard Cole 20-4
1911— Mordecai Brown 21-11
1912— Larry Cheney 26-10
1913— Larry Cheney 21-14
1914— Hippo Vaughn 21-13
          Larry Cheney 20-18
1915— Hippo Vaughn 20-12
1917— Hippo Vaughn 23-13
1918— Hippo Vaughn 22-10
1919— Hippo Vaughn 21-14
1920— Grover Alexander 27-14
1923— Grover Alexander 22-12
1927— Charlie Root 26-15
1929— Pat Malone 22-10
1930— Pat Malone 20-9
1932— Lon Warneke 22-6
1933— Guy Bush 20-12
1934— Lon Warneke 22-10
1935— Bill Lee 20-6
          Lon Warneke 20-13
1938— Bill Lee 22-9
1940— Claude Passeau 20-13
1945— Hank Wyse 22-10
          Hank Borowy ....‡ 21-7
1963— Dick Ellsworth 22-10
1964— Larry Jackson 24-11
1967— Fergie Jenkins 20-13
1968— Fergie Jenkins 20-15
1969— Fergie Jenkins 21-15
          Bill Hands 20-14
1970— Fergie Jenkins 22-16
1971— Fergie Jenkins 24-13
1972— Fergie Jenkins 20-12
1977— Rick Reuschel 20-10
1984— Rick Sutcliffe ....∞ 20-6
1992— Greg Maddux...............................20-11

*1-3 with Providence; 20-4 with Chicago. †8-9
with Cardinals; 12-3 with Cubs. ‡10-5 with Yankees;
11-2 with Cubs. ∞ 4-5 with Indians; 16-1 with Cubs.

N.L. home run champions
1884— Ned Williamson 27
1885— Abner Dalrymple 11
1888— Jimmy Ryan 16
1890— Walt Wilmot *13
1910— Frank Schulte *10
1911— Frank Schulte 21
1912— Heinie Zimmerman 14
1916— Cy Williams *12
1926— Hack Wilson 21
1927— Hack Wilson *30
1928— Hack Wilson *31
1930— Hack Wilson 56
1943— Bill Nicholson 29
1944— Bill Nicholson 33

1952— Hank Sauer *37
1958— Ernie Banks 47
1960— Ernie Banks 41
1979— Dave Kingman 48
1987— Andre Dawson 49
1990— Ryne Sandberg 40

* Tied for league lead

N.L. RBI champions
1906— Harry Steinfeldt *83
1911— Frank Schulte 121
1929— Hack Wilson 159
1930— Hack Wilson 191
1943— Bill Nicholson 128
1944— Bill Nicholson 122
1952— Hank Sauer 121
1958— Ernie Banks 129
1959— Ernie Banks 143
1987— Andre Dawson 137
1998— Sammy Sosa 158

* Tied for league lead

N.L. batting champions
1876— Ross Barnes .... .429
1880— George Gore .... .360
1881— Cap Anson .... .399
1884— King Kelly .... .354
1886— King Kelly .... .388
1888— Cap Anson .... .344
1912— Heinie Zimmerman .... .372
1945— Phil Cavarretta .... .355
1972— Billy Williams .... .333
1975— Bill Madlock .... .354
1976— Bill Madlock .... .339
1980— Bill Buckner .... .324

N.L. ERA champions
1902— Jack Taylor 1.33
1906— Mordecai Brown 1.04
1907— Jack Pfiester 1.15
1918— Jim Vaughn 1.74
1919— Grover Alexander 1.72
1920— Grover Alexander 1.91
1932— Lon Warneke 2.37
1938— Bill Lee 2.66
1945— Hank Borowy 2.13

N.L. strikeout champions
1880— Larry Corcoran 268
1885— John Clarkson 308
1887— John Clarkson 237

INDIVIDUAL SEASON, GAME RECORDS

SEASON

Batting
At-bats	666		Billy Herman	1935
Runs	156		Rogers Hornsby	1929
Hits	229		Rogers Hornsby	1929
Singles	165		Earl Adams	1927
Doubles	57		Billy Herman	1935, 1936
Triples	21		Frank Schulte	1911
			Vic Saier	1913
Home runs	66		Sammy Sosa	1998
Home runs, rookie	25		Billy Williams	1961
Grand slams	5		Ernie Banks	1955
Total bases	423		Hack Wilson	1930
RBIs	191		Hack Wilson	1930
Walks	147		Jimmy Sheckard	1911
Most strikeouts	174		Sammy Sosa	1997
Fewest strikeouts	5		Charlie Hollocher	1922
Batting average	.388		King Kelly	1886
			Bill Lange	1895
Slugging pct.	.723		Hack Wilson	1930
Stolen bases	67		Frank Chance	1903

Pitching
Games	84		Ted Abernathy	1965
			Dick Tidrow	1980
Complete games	33		Jack Taylor	1902, 1903
			Grover Alexander	1920
Innings	363.1		Grover Alexander	1920
Wins	29		Mordecai Brown	1908
Losses	23		Tom Hughes	1901
Winning pct.	.941 (16-1)		Rick Sutcliffe	1984
Walks	185		Sam Jones	1955
Strikeouts	274		Fergie Jenkins	1970
Shutouts	9		6 times	
			Last by Bill Lee	1938
Home runs allowed	38		Warren Hacker	1955
Lowest ERA	1.04		Mordecai Brown	1906
Saves	53		Randy Myers	1993

GAME

Batting
Runs	6		Cap Anson	8-24-1886
			Jimmy Ryan	7-25-1894
			Last by Sammy Sosa	7-2-93
Hits	6		Last by Billy Williams	4-9-69
Doubles	4		Last by Shawon Dunston	7-28-90
Triples	3		Last by Brant Brown	6-18-98
Home runs	3		Heinie Zimmerman	6-11-11
RBIs	9		Last by George Mitterwald	4-17-74
Total bases	14		George Gore	6-25-1881
Stolen bases	7			

1892— Bill Hutchinson 316
1909— Orval Overall 205
1918— Jim Vaughn 148
1919— Jim Vaughn 141
1920— Grover Alexander 173
1929— Pat Malone 166
1938— Clay Bryant 135
1946— Johnny Schmitz 135
1955— Sam Jones 198
1956— Sam Jones 176
1969— Fergie Jenkins 273

No-hit pitchers
(9 innings or more)
1880— Larry Corcoran ....6-0 vs. Boston
1882— Larry Corcoran ....5-0 vs. Worcester
1884— Larry Corcoran ....6-0 vs. Providence
1885— John Clarkson ....4-0 vs. Providence
1898— Walter Thornton ....2-0 vs. Brooklyn
1915— Jim Lavender ....2-0 vs. New York
1955— Sam Jones ....4-0 vs. Pittsburgh
1960— Don Cardwell ....4-0 vs. St. Louis
1969— Ken Holtzman ....3-0 vs. Atlanta
1971— Ken Holtzman ....1-0 vs. Cincinnati
1972— Burt Hooton ....4-0 vs. Philadelphia
          Milt Pappas ....8-0 vs. San Diego

Longest hitting streaks
42— Bill Dahlen 1894
30— Jerome Walton 1989
      Cal McVey 1876
28— Bill Dahlen 1894
      Ron Santo 1966
27— Hack Wilson 1929
      Glenn Beckert 1968
26— George Decker 1896
      Hack Wilson 1927
      Gabby Hartnett 1937
      Glenn Beckert 1973
25— Hack Wilson 1926
24— Gabby Hartnett 1937
      Stan Hack 1945
23— Heinie Zimmerman 1912
22— Hack Wilson 1930
21— Glenn Beckert 1966
      Lenny Randle 1980
20— Billy Herman 1934
      Rafael Palmeiro 1988

Second baseman Ryne Sandberg.

BATTING

Games

Ernie Banks	2,528
Cap Anson	2,276
Billy Williams	2,213
Ryne Sandberg	2,151
Ron Santo	2,126
Phil Cavarretta	1,953
Stan Hack	1,938
Gabby Hartnett	1,926
Mark Grace	1.767
Jimmy Ryan	1,660

At-bats

Ernie Banks	9,421
Cap Anson	9,101
Billy Williams	8,479
Ryne Sandberg	8,379
Ron Santo	7,768
Stan Hack	7,278
Jimmy Ryan	6,757
Mark Grace	6.646
Phil Cavarretta	6,592
Don Kessinger	6,355

Runs

Cap Anson	1,719
Jimmy Ryan	1,409
Ryne Sandberg	1,316
Billy Williams	1,306
Ernie Banks	1,305
Stan Hack	1,239
Ron Santo	1,109
Mark Grace	982
Phil Cavarretta	968
Bill Dahlen	896

Hits

Cap Anson	2,995
Ernie Banks	2,583
Billy Williams	2,510
Ryne Sandberg	2,385
Stan Hack	2,193
Ron Santo	2,171
Jimmy Ryan	2,073
Mark Grace	2,058
Phil Cavarretta	1,927
Gabby Hartnett	1,867

Doubles

Cap Anson	528
Mark Grace	415
Ernie Banks	407
Ryne Sandberg	403
Billy Williams	402
Gabby Hartnett	391
Stan Hack	363
Jimmy Ryan	362
Ron Santo	353
Billy Herman	346

Triples

Jimmy Ryan	142
Cap Anson	124
Frank Schulte	117
Bill Dahlen	106
Phil Cavarretta	99
Joe Tinker	93
Ernie Banks	90
Billy Williams	87
Stan Hack	81
Bill Lange	80
Ned Williamson	80
Heinie Zimmerman	80

Home runs

Ernie Banks	512
Billy Williams	392
Ron Santo	337
Sammy Sosa	307
Ryne Sandberg	282
Gabby Hartnett	231
Bill Nicholson	205
Hank Sauer	198
Hack Wilson	190
Andre Dawson	174

Total bases

Ernie Banks	4,706
Billy Williams	4,262
Cap Anson	4,062
Ryne Sandberg	3,786
Ron Santo	3,667
Gabby Hartnett	3,079
Jimmy Ryan	3,016
Mark Grace	2,968
Stan Hack	2,889
Phil Cavarretta	2,742

Runs batted in

Cap Anson	1,879
Ernie Banks	1,636
Billy Williams	1,353
Ron Santo	1,290
Gabby Hartnett	1,153

SEASON

Batting

Most at-bats	5,675	1988
Most runs	998	1930
Fewest runs	454	1919
Most hits	1,722	1930
Most singles	1,226	1921
Most doubles	340	1931
Most triples	101	1911
Most home runs	212	1998
Fewest home runs	6	1902
Most grand slams	9	1929
Most pinch-hit home runs	10	1998
Most total bases	2,684	1930
Most stolen bases	283	1906
Highest batting average	.309	1930
Lowest batting average	.238	1963, 1965
Highest slugging pct	.481	1930

Pitching

Lowest ERA	1.73	1907
Highest ERA	5.27	1999
Most complete games	139	1904
Most shutouts	32	1907, 1909
Most saves	56	1993, 1998
Most walks	628	1987
Most strikeouts	1,207	1998

Fielding

Most errors	418	1900
Fewest errors	101	1998
Most double plays	176	1928
Highest fielding average	.984	1998

General

Most games won	116	1906
Most games lost	103	1962, 1966
Highest win pct	.798	1880
Lowest win pct	.364	1962, 1966

GAME, INNING

Batting

Most runs, game	36	6-29-1897
Most runs, inning	18	9-6-1883
Most hits, game	32	7-3-1883, 6-29-1897
Most home runs, game	7	Last 5-17-77
Most total bases, game	54	8-25-1891

Dependable third baseman Ron Santo hit 337 home runs while wearing a Cubs uniform.

Ryne Sandberg	1,061
Mark Grace	922
Jimmy Ryan	914
Phil Cavarretta	896
Bill Nicholson	833

Extra-base hits

Ernie Banks	1,009
Billy Williams	881
Ron Santo	756
Ryne Sandberg	761
Cap Anson	749
Gabby Hartnett	686
Jimmy Ryan	603
Mark Grace	594
Phil Cavarretta	532
Bill Nicholson	503

Batting average
(Minimum 500 games)

Riggs Stephenson	.336
Bill Lange	.330
Cap Anson	.329
Kiki Cuyler	.325
Bill Everitt	.323
Hack Wilson	.322
King Kelly	.316
George Gore	.315
Mark Grace	.310
Frank Demaree	.309

Stolen bases

Frank Chance	400
Bill Lange	399
Jimmy Ryan	369
Ryne Sandberg	344
Joe Tinker	304
Johnny Evers	291
Walt Wilmot	290
Bill Dahlen	285
Fred Pfeffer	263
Cap Anson	247

PITCHING

Earned-run average
(Minimum 1,000 innings)

Mordecai Brown	1.80
Jack Pfiester	1.85
Orval Overall	1.91
Ed Reulbach	2.24
Larry Corcoran	2.26
Hippo Vaughn	2.34
Terry Larkin	2.34

John Clarkson	2.39
Carl Lundgren	2.42
Jack Taylor	2.66

Wins

Charlie Root	201
Mordecai Brown	188
Bill Hutchison	181
Larry Corcoran	175
Fergie Jenkins	167
Guy Bush	152
Clark Griffith	152
Hippo Vaughn	151
Bill Lee	139
John Clarkson	137

Losses

Bill Hutchison	158
Charlie Root	156
Bob Rush	140
Fergie Jenkins	132
Rick Reuschel	127
Bill Lee	123
Dick Ellsworth	110
Hippo Vaughn	105
Guy Bush	101
Clark Griffith	96

Innings pitched

Charles Root	3,137.1
Bill Hutchison	3,021.0
Fergie Jenkins	2,673.2
Larry Corcoran	2,338.1
Mordecai Brown	2,329.0
Rick Reuschel	2,290.0
Bill Lee	2,271.1
Hippo Vaughn	2,216.1
Guy Bush	2,201.2
Clark Griffith	2,188.2

Strikeouts

Fergie Jenkins	2,038
Charles Root	1,432
Rick Reuschel	1,367
Bill Hutchison	1,222
Hippo Vaughn	1,138
Larry Corcoran	1,086
Bob Rush	1,076
Mordecai Brown	1,043
Ken Holtzman	988
John Clarkson	960

Bases on balls

Bill Hutchison	1,109
Charlie Root	871
Guy Bush	734
Bob Rush	725
Bill Lee	704
Sheriff Blake	661
Ed Reulbach	650
Rick Reuschel	640
Hippo Vaughn	621
Fergie Jenkins	600

Games

Charlie Root	605
Lee Smith	458
Don Elston	449
Guy Bush	428
Fergie Jenkins	401
Bill Hutchison	367
Bill Lee	364
Rick Reuschel	358
Mordecai Brown	346
Bob Rush	339

Shutouts

Mordecai Brown	48
Hippo Vaughn	35
Ed Reulbach	31
Fergie Jenkins	29
Orval Overall	28
Bill Lee	25
Grover Alexander	24
Larry Corcoran	22
Claude Passeau	22
Larry French	21
Bill Hutchison	21
Charlie Root	21

Saves

Lee Smith	180
Bruce Sutter	133
Randy Myers	112
Don Elston	63
Phil Regan	60
Rod Beck	58
Mitch Williams	52
Charlie Root	40
Ted Abernathy	39
Mordecai Brown	39
Lindy McDaniel	39

CUBS YEAR-BY-YEAR

Year	W	L	Place	Games Back	Manager	Leaders: Batting avg.	Hits	Home runs	RBIs	Wins	ERA
1901	53	86	6th	37	Loftus	Hartsel, .335	Hartsel, 187	Hartsel, 7	Dexter, 66	Waddell, 14	Waddell, 2.81
1902	68	69	5th	34	Selee	Slagle, .315	Slagle, 143	Dexter, Tinker, 2	Kling, 57	Taylor, 23	Taylor, 1.33
1903	82	56	3rd	8	Selee	Chance, .327	Slagle, 162	Kling, 3	Chance, 81	Taylor, 21	Weimer, 2.30
1904	93	60	2nd	13	Selee	Chance, .310	Casey, 147	Chance, 6	McCarthy, 51	Weimer, 20	M. Brown, 1.86
1905	92	61	3rd	13	Selee, Chance	Chance, .316	Slagle, 153	Chance, Maloney, Tinker, 2	Chance, 70	M. Brown, Reulbach, Weimer, 18	Reulbach, 1.42
1906	116	36	1st	+20	Chance	Steinfeldt, .327	Steinfeldt, 176	Schulte, 7	Steinfeldt, 83	M. Brown, 26	M. Brown, 1.04
1907	107	45	1st	+17	Chance	Chance, .293	Steinfeldt, 144	Evers, Schulte, 2	Steinfeldt, 70	Overall, 23	Pfiester, 1.15
1908	99	55	1st	+1	Chance	Evers, .300	Tinker, 146	Tinker, 6	Tinker, 68	M. Brown, 29	M. Brown, 1.47
1909	104	49	2nd	6½	Chance	Hofman, .285	Hofman, 150	Schulte, Tinker, 4	Schulte, 60	M. Brown, 27	M. Brown, 1.31
1910	104	50	1st	+13	Chance	Hofman, .325	Schulte, 168	Schulte, 10	Hofman, 86	M. Brown, 25	Pfiester, 1.79
1911	92	62	2nd	7½	Chance	Zimmerman, .307	Schulte, 173	Schulte, 21	Schulte, 107	M. Brown, 21	Richie, 2.31
1912	91	59	3rd	11½	Chance	Zimmerman, .372	Zimmerman, 207	Zimmerman, 14	Zimmerman, 99	Cheney, 26	Cheyney, 2.85
1913	88	65	3rd	13½	Evers	Zimmerman, .313	Saier, 149	Saier, 14	Zimmerman, 95	Cheyney, 21	Pearce, 2.31
1914	78	76	4th	16½	O'Day	Zimmerman, .296	Zimmerman, 167	Saier, 18	Zimmerman, 87	Vaughn, 21	Vaughn, 2.05
1915	73	80	4th	17½	Bresnahan	Fisher, .287	Fisher, 163	Williams, 13	Saier, Williams, 64	Vaughn, 20	Humphries, 2.31
1916	67	86	5th	26½	Tinker	Zimmerman, .291	Saier, 126	Williams, 12	Williams, 66	Vaughn, 17	Vaughn, 2.20
1917	74	80	5th	24	Mitchell	Mann, .273	Merkle, 146	Doyle, 6	Doyle, 61	Vaughn, 23	Vaughn, 2.01
1918	84	45	1st	+10½	Mitchell	Hollocher, .316	Hollocher, 161	Flack, 4	Merkle, 65	Vaughn, 22	Vaughn, 1.74
1919	75	65	3rd	21	Mitchell	Flack, .294	Flack, 138	Flack, 6	Merkle, 62	Vaughn, 21	Alexander, 1.72
1920	75	79	*5th	18	Mitchell	Flack, .302	Flack, 157	Robertson, 10	Robertson, 75	Alexander, 27	Alexander, 1.91
1921	64	89	7th	30	Evers, Killefer	Grimes, .321	Flack, 172	Flack, Grimes, 6	Grimes, 79	Alexander, 15	Alexander, 3.39
1922	80	74	5th	13	Killefer	Grimes, .354	Hollocher, 201	Grimes, 14	Grimes, 99	Aldridge, Alexander, 16	Aldridge, 3.52
1923	83	71	4th	12½	Killefer	Statz, O'Farrell, .319	Statz, 209	Miller, 20	Friberg, Miller, 88	Alexander, 22	Keen, 3.00
1924	81	72	5th	12	Killefer	Grantham, .316	Statz, 152	Hartnett, 16	Friberg, 82	Kaufmann, 16	Alexander, 3.03
1925	68	86	8th	27½	Killefer, Maranville, Gibson	Freigau, .307	Adams, 180	Hartnett, 24	Grimm, 76	Alexander, 15	Alexander, 3.39
1926	82	72	4th	7	McCarthy	Wilson, .321	Adams, 193	Wilson, 21	Wilson, 109	Root, 18	Root, 2.82
1927	85	68	4th	8½	McCarthy	Stephenson, .344	Stephenson, 199	Wilson, 30	Wilson, 129	Root, 26	Bush, 3.03
1928	91	63	3rd	4	McCarthy	Stephenson, .324	Stephenson, 166	Wilson, 31	Wilson, 120	Malone, 18	Blake, 2.47
1929	98	54	1st	+10½	McCarthy	Hornsby, .380	Hornsby, 229	Hornsby, Wilson, 39	Wilson, 159	Malone, 22	Root, 3.47
1930	90	64	2nd	2	McCarthy, Hornsby	Wilson, .356	Cuyler, 228	Wilson, 56	Wilson, 190	Malone, 20	Malone, 3.94
1931	84	70	3rd	17	Hornsby	Grimm, Hornsby, .331	Cuyler, English, 202	Hornsby, 16	Hornsby, 90	Root, 17	B. Smith, 3.22
1932	90	64	1st	+4	Hornsby, Grimm	Stephenson, .324	B. Herman, 206	Moore, 13	Stephenson, 85	Warneke, 22	Warneke, 2.37
1933	86	68	3rd	6	Grimm	Herman, .289	B. Herman, 173	Hartnett, B. Herman, 16	B. Herman, 93	Bush, 20	Warneke, 2.00
1934	86	65	3rd	8	Grimm	Cuyler, .338	Cuyler, 189	Hartnett, 22	Hartnett, 90	Warneke, 22	Warneke, 3.21
1935	100	54	1st	+4	Grimm	Hartnett, .344	B. Herman, 227	Klein, 21	Hartnett, 91	Lee, Warneke, 20	French, Lee, 2.96
1936	87	67	*2nd	5	Grimm	Demaree, .350	Demaree, 212	Demaree, 16	Demaree, 96	French, Lee, 18	C. Davis, 3.00
1937	93	61	2nd	3	Grimm	Hartnett, .354	Demaree, 199	Galan, 18	Demaree, 115	Carleton, French, 16	Carleton, 3.15
1938	89	63	1st	+2	Grimm, Hartnett	Hack, .320	Hack, 195	Collins, 13	Galan, 69	Lee, 22	Lee, 2.66
1939	84	70	4th	13	Hartnett	Leiber, .310	Hack, B. Herman, 191	Leiber, 24	Leiber, 88	Lee, 19	Passeau, 3.05
1940	75	79	5th	25½	Hartnett	Hack, .317	Hack, 191	Nicholson, 25	Nicholson, 98	Passeau, 20	Passeau, 2.50
1941	70	84	6th	30	Wilson	Hack, .317	Hack, 186	Nicholson, 26	Nicholson, 98	Passeau, 14	Olsen, 3.15
1942	68	86	6th	38	Wilson	Hack, .Novikoff, .300	Nicholson, 173	Nicholson, 21	Nicholson, 78	Passeau, 19	Warneke, 2.27
1943	74	79	5th	30½	Wilson	Nicholson, .309	Nicholson, 188	Nicholson, 29	Nicholson, 128	Bithorn, 18	Hanyzewski, 2.56
1944	75	79	4th	30	Wilson, Grimm	Cavarretta, .321	Cavarretta, 197	Nicholson, 33	Nicholson, 122	Wyse, 16	Passeau, 2.89
1945	98	56	1st	+3	Grimm	Cavarretta, .355	Hack, 193	Nicholson, 13	Pafko, 110	Wyse, 22	Borowy, 2.13
1946	82	71	3rd	14½	Grimm	Waitkus, .304	Cavarretta, 150	Cavarretta, Nicholson, 8	Cavarretta, 78	Wyse, 14	Erickson, 2.43
1947	69	85	6th	25	Grimm	Cavarretta, .314	Pafko, 155	Nicholson, 26	Nicholson, 75	Schmitz, 13	Schmitz, 3.22
1948	64	90	8th	27½	Grimm	Pafko, .312	Pafko, 171	Pafko, 26	Pafko, 101	Schmitz, 18	Schmitz, 2.64
1949	61	93	8th	36	Grimm, Frisch	Cavarretta, .294	Pafko, 146	Sauer, 27	Sauer, 83	Schmitz, 11	Chapman, 3.98
1950	64	89	7th	26½	Frisch	Pafko, .304	Pafko, 156	Pafko, 36	Sauer, 103	Rush, 13	Hiller, 3.53
1951	62	92	8th	34½	Frisch, Cavarretta	Baumholtz, .284	Baumholtz, 159	Sauer, 30	Sauer, 89	Rush, 11	Leonard, 2.64
1952	77	77	5th	19½	Cavarretta	Baumholtz, .325	Fondy, 166	Sauer, 37	Sauer, 121	Rush, 17	Hacker, 2.58
1953	65	89	7th	40	Cavarretta	Fondy, .309	Fondy, 184	Kiner, 28	Kiner, 87	Hacker, Minner, 12	Pollet, 4.12
1954	64	90	7th	33	Hack	Sauer, .288	Banks, 163	Sauer, 41	Sauer, 103	Rush, 13	Davis, 3.52
1955	72	81	6th	26	Hack	Banks, .295	Banks, 176	Banks, 44	Banks, 117	Jones, 14	Jeffcoat, 2.95
1956	60	94	8th	33	Hack	Banks, .297	Banks, 160	Banks, 28	Banks, 85	Rush, 13	Rush, 3.19
1957	62	92	*7th	33	Scheffing	Long, .305	Banks, 169	Banks, 43	Banks, 102	Drott, 15	Brosnan, 3.38
1958	72	82	*5th	20	Scheffing	Banks, .313	Banks, 193	Banks, 47	Banks, 129	Hobbie, 10	Elston, 2.88
1959	74	80	*5th	13	Scheffing	Banks, .304	Banks, 179	Banks, 45	Banks, 143	Hobbie, 16	Henry, 2.68
1960	60	94	7th	35	Grimm, Boudreau	Ashburn, .291	Banks, 162	Banks, 41	Banks, 117	Hobbie, 16	Elston, 3.40
1961	64	90	7th	29	Himsl, Craft, Tappe, Klein	Altman, .303	Santo, 164	Banks, 29	Altman, 96	Cardwell, 15	Cardwell, 3.82
1962	59	103	9th	42½	Metro, Tappe,Klein	Altman, .318	Williams, 184	Banks, 37	Banks, 104	Buhl, 12	Buhl, 3.69
1963	82	80	7th	17	Kennedy	Santo, .297	Santo, 187	Santo, Williams, 25	Santo, 99	Ellsworth, 22	Ellsworth, 2.11
1964	76	86	8th	17	Kennedy	Santo, .313	Williams, 201	Williams, 33	Santo, 114	Jackson, 24	Jackson, 3.14
1965	72	90	8th	25	Kennedy, Klein	Williams, .315	Williams, 203	Williams, 34	Williams, 108	Ellsworth, Jackson, 14	Abernathy, 2.57
1966	59	103	10th	36	Durocher	Santo, .312	Beckert, 188	Santo, 30	Santo, 94	Holtzman, 11	Jenkins, 3.31
1967	87	74	3rd	14	Durocher	Santo, .300	Santo, Williams, 176	Santo, 31	Santo, 98	Jenkins, 20	Hands, 2.46
1968	84	78	3rd	13	Durocher	Beckert, .294	Beckert, 189	Banks, 32	Santo, Williams, 98	Jenkins, 20	Regan, 2.20
								EAST DIVISION			
1969	92	70	2nd	8	Durocher	Williams, .293	Williams, 188	Santo, 29	Santo, 123	Jenkins, 21	Hands, 2.49
1970	84	78	2nd	5	Durocher	Williams, .322	Williams, 205	Williams, 42	Williams, 129	Jenkins, 22	Pappas, 2.68
1971	83	79	*3rd	14	Durocher	Beckert, .342	Beckert, 181	Williams, 28	Williams, 93	Jenkins, 24	Jenkins, 2.77
1972	85	70	2nd	11	Durocher, Lockman	Williams, .333	Williams, 191	Williams, 37	Williams, 122	Jenkins, 20	Pappas, 2.77
1973	77	84	5th	5	Lockman	Cardenal, .303	Williams, 166	Monday, 26	Williams, 86	Hooton, Jenkins, R. Reuschel, 14	Locker, 2.54
1974	66	96	6th	22	Lockman, Marshall	Madlock, .313	Cardenal, 159	Monday, 20	Morales, 82	R. Reuschel, 13	Bonham, 3.86
1975	75	87	*5th	17½	Marshall	Madlock, .354	Cardenal, Madlock, 182	Thornton, 18	Morales, 91	Burris, 15	R. Reuschel, 3.73
1976	75	87	4th	26	Marshall	Madlock, .339	Madlock, 174	Monday, 32	Madlock, 84	Burris, 15	Burris, 3.11
1977	81	81	4th	20	Franks	Ontiveros, .299	DeJesus, 166	Murcer, 27	Murcer, 89	R. Reuschel, 20	Sutter, 1.34
1978	79	83	3rd	11	Franks	Buckner, .323	DeJesus, 172	Kingman, 28	Kingman, 79	Reuschel, 14	Sutter, 3.18
1979	80	82	5th	18	Franks, Amalfitano	Kingman, .288	DeJesus, 180	Kingman, 48	Kingman, 115	Reuschel, 18	Sutter, 2.22
1980	64	98	6th	27	Gomez, Amalfitano	Buckner, .324	Buckner, 187	Martin, 23	Martin, 73	McGlothen, 12	Caudill, 2.19
1981	38	65	†6th/5th	—	Amalfitano	Buckner, .311	Buckner, 131	Buckner, Durham, 10	Buckner, 75	Krukow, 9	R. Reuschel, 3.47
1982	73	89	5th	19	Elia	Durham, .312	Buckner, 201	Durham, 22	Buckner, 105	Jenkins, 14	L. Smith, 2.69
1983	71	91	5th	19	Elia, Fox	Moreland, .302	Buckner, 175	Cey, J. Davis, 24	Cey, 90	Rainey, 14	L. Smith, 1.65
1984	96	65	‡1st	+6½	Frey	Sandberg, .314	Sandberg, 200	Cey, 25	Cey, 97	Sutcliffe, 16	Sutcliffe, 2.69
1985	77	84	4th	23½	Frey	Moreland, .307	Sandberg, 186	Sandberg, 26	Moreland, 106	Eckersley, 11	L. Smith, 3.04
1986	70	90	5th	37	Frey, Vukovich, Michael	Sandberg, .284	Sandberg, 178	J. Davis, Matthews, 21	Moreland, 79	Sanderson, L. Smith, 9	L. Smith, 3.09
1987	76	85	6th	18½	Michael, Lucchesi	Sandberg, .294	Dawson, 178	Dawson, 49	Dawson, 137	Sutcliffe, 18	Sutcliffe, 3.68
1988	77	85	4th	24	Zimmer	Palmeiro, .307	Dawson, 179	Dawson, 24	Dawson, 79	Maddux, 18	Maddux, 3.18
1989	93	69	‡1st	+6	Zimmer	Grace, .314	Sandberg, 176	Sandberg, 30	Grace, 79	Maddux, 19	Maddux, 2.95
1990	77	85	*4th	18	Zimmer	Dawson, .310	Sandberg, 188	Sandberg, 40	Dawson, Sandberg, 100	Maddux, 15	Assenmacher, 2.80
1991	77	83	4th	20	Zimmer, Altobelli, Essian	Sandberg, .291	Sandberg, 170	Dawson, 31	Dawson, 104	Maddux, 15	McElroy, 1.95
1992	78	84	4th	18	Lefebvre	Grace, .307	Sandberg, 186	Sandberg, 26	Dawson, 90	Maddux, 20	Maddux, 2.18
1993	84	78	4th	13	Lefebvre	Grace, .325	Grace, 193	Sosa, 33	Grace, 98	Hibbard, 15	Bautista, 2.82
								CENTRAL DIVISION			
1994	49	64	5th	16½	Trebelhorn	Sosa, .300	Sosa, 128	Sosa, 25	Sosa, 70	Trachsel, 9	Trachsel, 3.21
1995	73	71	3rd	12	Riggleman	Grace, .326	Grace, 180	Sosa, 36	Sosa, 119	Foster, 12	Castillo, 3.21
1996	76	86	4th	12	Riggleman	Grace, .331	Grace, 181	Sosa, 40	Sosa, 100	Navarro, 15	Adams, 2.94
1997	68	94	5th	16	Riggleman	Grace, .319	Grace, 177	Sosa, 36	Sosa, 119	Gonzalez, 11,	Mulholland, 4.07
1998	90	73	§∞2nd	12½	Riggleman	Grace, Sosa, .307	Sosa, 196	Sosa, 66	Sosa, 158	Tapani, 19	Mulholland, 2.82
1999	67	95	6th	30	Riggleman	Grace, .309	Grace, 183	Sosa, 63	Sosa, 141	Lieber, 10	Lieber, 4.07

* Tied for position. † First half 15-37; second half 23-28. ‡ Lost Championship Series. § Won wild-card playoff. ∞ Lost Division Series.

Note: Batting average minimum 350 at-bats; ERA minimum 90 innings pitched.

CINCINNATI REDS

FRANCHISE CHRONOLOGY

First season: 1876, as a member of the new National League. The Red Stockings won their first N.L. game, beating St. Louis, 2-1. That would be one of the few highlights in a 9-56 debut.

1877-1900: The Reds played five seasons in the N.L., sat out a year and returned as a member of the new American Association in 1882. After eight seasons in the A.A., they transferred back to the N.L., where they remain today. The Reds' only pre-1900 pennant came in 1882, the American Association's inaugural season.

1901-present: Through the first 39 years of the century, the Reds' only success was a tainted one: a victory over Chicago in the infamous "Black Sox" World Series of 1919. But four decades of futility ended in 1940 when the Reds punctuated their second straight pennant with a seven-game World Series victory over Detroit. Although usually competitive, Cincinnati's first sustained success did not occur until the 1970s, when the Big Red Machine of Sparky Anderson won six West Division titles, four pennants and two World Series. The Reds won their fifth fall classic in 1990. Cincinnati was one of five teams placed in the Central Division when the N.L. adopted its three-division format in 1994.

Infielder/outfielder Pete Rose.

REDS VS. OPPONENTS BY DECADE

	Braves	Cardinals	Cubs	Dodgers	Giants	Phillies	Pirates	Astros	Mets	Expos	Padres	Marlins	Rockies	Brewers	D'backs	Interleague	Decade Record
1900-09	120-90	119-91	79-132	114-97	87-123	105-105	81-131										705-769
1910-19	116-97	109-108	93-119	121-93	85-129	91-124	102-109										717-779
1920-29	130-89	105-115	105-115	122-96	86-134	149-68	101-118										798-735
1930-39	110-108	73-147	99-121	108-112	79-139	116-99	79-140										664-866
1940-49	112-105	87-133	110-110	87-133	120-100	136-84	115-104										767-769
1950-59	86-134	96-124	129-90	91-129	92-128	113-107	134-86										741-798
1960-69	103-85	92-90	103-79	94-94	84-103	107-75	90-92	85-59	83-54	8-4	11-7						860-742
1970-79	120-60	74-46	61-59	97-79	99-78	73-47	65-54	105-74	80-40	74-46	105-74						953-657
1980-89	92-81	50-63	59-54	80-98	91-85	60-55	64-50	81-93	55-62	53-64	96-78						781-783
1990-99	49-82	62-51	68-51	57-65	58-66	68-39	64-59	76-63	49-59	57-48	69-61	43-32	41-34	12-11	13-5	23-20	809-746
Totals	1038-931	867-968	906-930	971-996	881-1085	1018-803	895-943	347-289	267-215	192-162	281-220	43-32	41-34	12-11	13-5	23-20	7795-7644

Interleague results: 2-3 vs. White Sox; 5-7 vs. Indians; 5-3 vs. Royals; 3-0 vs. Brewers; 4-5 vs. Twins; 4-2 vs. Tigers..

MANAGERS

Name	Years	Record
Charlie Gould	1876	9-56
Lip Pike	1877	3-11
Bob Addy	1877	5-19
Jack Manning	1877	7-12
Cal McVey	1878, 1879	71-51
Deacon White	1879	9-9
John Clapp	1880	21-59
Pop Snyder	1882-83, 1884	140-76
Will White	1884	44-27
Oliver Caylor	1885-86	128-122
Gus Schmelz	1887-89	237-171
Tom Loftus	1890-91	133-136
Charles Comiskey	1892-94	202-206
Buck Ewing	1895-99	394-297
Bob Allen	1900	62-77
Biddy McPhee	1901-02	79-124
Frank Bancroft	1902	9-7
Joe Kelley	1902-05	275-230
Ned Hanlon	1906-07	130-174
John Ganzel	1908	73-81
Clark Griffith	1909-11	222-238
Hank O'Day	1912	75-78
Joe Tinker	1913	64-89
Buck Herzog	1914-16	165-226
Christy Mathewson	1916-18	164-176
Heinie Groh	1918	7-3
Pat Moran	1919-23	425-329
Jack Hendricks	1924-29	469-450
Dan Howley	1930-32	177-285
Donie Bush	1933	58-94
Bob O'Farrell	1934	30-60
Chuck Dressen	1934-37	214-282
Bobby Wallace	1937	5-20
Bill McKechnie	1938-46	744-631
Hank Gowdy	1946	3-1
Johnny Neun	1947-48	117-137
Bucky Walters	1948-49	81-123
Luke Sewell	1950-52	174-234
Earle Brucker	1952	3-2
Rogers Hornsby	1952-53	91-106
Buster Mills	1953	4-4
Birdie Tebbetts	1954-58	372-357
Jimmie Dykes	1958	24-17
Mayo Smith	1959	35-45
Fred Hutchinson	1959-64	443-372
Dick Sisler	1964-65	121-94
Don Heffner	1966	37-46
Dave Bristol	1966-69	298-265
Sparky Anderson	1970-78	863-586
John McNamara	1979-82	279-244
Russ Nixon	1982-83	101-131
Vern Rapp	1984	51-70
Pete Rose	1984-89	412-373
Tommy Helms	1988, 1989	28-36
Lou Piniella	1990-92	255-231
Tony Perez	1993	20-24
Dave Johnson	1993-95	204-172
Ray Knight	1996-97	124-137
Jack McKeon	1997-99	206-182

WORLD SERIES CHAMPIONS

Year	Loser	Length	MVP
1919	Chicago	8 games	None
1940	Detroit	7 games	None
1975	Boston	7 games	Rose
1976	N.Y. Yankees	4 games	Bench
1990	Oakland	4 games	Rijo

A.A. PENNANT WINNERS

Year	Record	Manager	Series Result
1882	55-25	Snyder	None

N.L. PENNANT WINNERS

Year	Record	Manager	Series Result
1919	96-44	Moran	Defeated White Sox
1939	97-57	McKechnie	Lost to Yankees
1940	100-53	McKechnie	Defeated Tigers
1961	93-61	Hutchinson	Lost to Yankees
1970	102-60	Anderson	Lost to Orioles
1972	95-59	Anderson	Lost to A's
1975	108-54	Anderson	Defeated Red Sox
1976	102-60	Anderson	Defeated Yankees
1990	91-71	Piniella	Defeated A's

WEST DIVISION CHAMPIONS

Year	Record	Manager	NLCS Result
1970	102-60	Anderson	Defeated Pirates
1972	95-59	Anderson	Defeated Pirates
1973	99-63	Anderson	Lost to Mets
1975	108-54	Anderson	Defeated Pirates
1976	102-60	Anderson	Defeated Phillies
1979	90-71	McNamara	Lost to Pirates
1990	91-71	Piniella	Defeated Pirates

CENTRAL DIVISION CHAMPIONS

Year	Record	Manager	NLCS Result
1994	66-48	Johnson	None
1995	85-59	Johnson	Lost to Braves

ATTENDANCE HIGHS

Total	Season	Park
2,629,708	1976	Riverfront Stadium
2,532,497	1978	Riverfront Stadium
2,519,670	1977	Riverfront Stadium
2,453,232	1993	Riverfront Stadium
2,400,892	1990	Riverfront Stadium

BALLPARK CHRONOLOGY

Cinergy Field, formerly Riverfront Stadium (1970-present)
Capacity: 52,953.
First game: Atlanta 8, Reds 2 (June 30, 1970).
First batter: Sonny Jackson, Braves.
First hit: Felix Millan, Braves (single).

First run: Felix Millan, Braves (1st inning).
First home run: Hank Aaron, Braves.
First winning pitcher: Pat Jarvis, Braves.
First-season attendance (1971): 1,501,122.

Avenue Grounds (1876-79)
First game: Cincinnati 2, St. Louis 1 (April 25, 1876).

Bank Street Grounds (1880)
First game: Chicago 4, Cincinnati 3 (May 1, 1880).

Redland Field I (1882-1901)

Palace of the Fans (1902-11)
First game: Chicago 6, Reds 1 (April 17, 1902).
First-season attendance: 217,300.

Crosley Field (1912-70)
Capacity: 29,603.
First game: Reds 10, Chicago 6 (April 11, 1912).
First-season attendance: 344,000.

N.L. MVPs

Ernie Lombardi, C, 1938
Bucky Walters, P, 1939
Frank McCormick, 1B, 1940
Frank Robinson, OF, 1961
Johnny Bench, C, 1970
Johnny Bench, C, 1972
Pete Rose, OF, 1973
Joe Morgan, 2B, 1975
Joe Morgan, 2B, 1976
George Foster, OF, 1977
Barry Larkin, SS, 1995

ROOKIES OF THE YEAR

Frank Robinson, OF, 1956
Pete Rose, 2B, 1963
Tommy Helms, 3B, 1966
Johnny Bench, C, 1968
*Pat Zachry, P, 1976
Chris Sabo, 3B, 1988
Scott Williamson, P, 1999
  * Co-winner.

MANAGER OF THE YEAR

Jack McKeon, 1999

RETIRED UNIFORMS

No.	Name	Pos.
1	Fred Hutchinson	Man.
5	Johnny Bench	C
8	Joe Morgan	2B
18	Ted Kluszewski	OF
20	Frank Robinson	OF

HISTORY

MILESTONE PERFORMANCES

30-plus home runs

52— George Foster 1977
49— Ted Kluszewski 1954
47— Ted Kluszewski 1955
45— Johnny Bench 1970
Greg Vaughn 1999
40— Ted Kluszewski 1953
Wally Post 1955
Tony Perez 1970
Johnny Bench 1972
George Foster 1978
39— Frank Robinson 1956
Lee May 1971
38— Frank Robinson 1956
Lee May 1969
37— Frank Robinson 1961
Tony Perez 1969
Eric Davis 1987
36— Wally Post 1956
Frank Robinson 1959
35— Hank Sauer 1948
Ted Kluszewski 1956
34— Lee May 1970
Dave Parker 1985
Eric Davis 1989
33— Frank Robinson 1965
Johnny Bench 1974
Barry Larkin 1996
32— Deron Johnson 1965
31— George Crowe 1957
Frank Robinson 1958, 1960
Johnny Bench 1977
Dave Parker 1986
30— Ival Goodman 1938
Gus Bell 1953
George Foster 1979
Kevin Mitchell 1994

100-plus RBIs

149— George Foster 1977
148— Johnny Bench 1970
141— Ted Kluszewski 1954
136— Frank Robinson 1962
130— Deron Johnson 1965
129— Tony Perez 1970
Johnny Bench 1974
128— Frank McCormick 1939
127— Frank McCormick 1940
125— Frank Robinson 1959
Johnny Bench 1972
Dave Parker 1985
124— Frank Robinson 1961
122— Tony Perez 1969
121— Cy Seymour 1905
George Foster 1976
120— George Foster 1978
118— Greg Vaughn 1999
116— Dave Parker 1986
115— Gus Bell 1959
113— Ted Kluszewski 1955
Frank Robinson 1965
111— Ted Kluszewski 1950
Joe Morgan 1976
110— Lee May 1969
Johnny Bench 1975
109— Wally Post 1955
Tony Perez 1975
Johnny Bench 1977
108— Ted Kluszewski 1953
106— Frank McCormick 1938
Vada Pinson 1963
105— Gus Bell 1953
104— Sam Crawford 1901
Gus Bell 1955
Johnny Bench 1973
103— George Kelly 1929
102— Frank McCormick 1944
Ted Kluszewski 1956
Tony Perez 1967
101— Gus Bell 1954
Tony Perez 1973, 1974
Eric Davis 1989
100— Jim Greengrass 1953
Vada Pinson 1962
Eric Davis 1987

20-plus victories

1878— Will White 30-21
1879— Will White 43-31
1890— Billy Rhines 28-17
1891— Tony Mullane 23-26
1892— Tony Mullane 21-13
Frank Dwyer *21-18
1896— Frank Dwyer 24-11
1897— Ted Breitenstein 23-12
Billy Rhines 21-15
1898— Pink Hawley 27-11
Ted Breitenstein 20-14
1899— Noodles Hahn 23-8
1901— Noodles Hahn 22-19
1902— Noodles Hahn 23-12
1903— Noodles Hahn 22-12
1904— Charles Harper 23-9
1905— Bob Ewing 20-11
1906— Jake Weimer 20-14
1910— George Suggs 20-12
1917— Fred Toney 24-16
Pete Schneider 20-19
1919— Slim Sallee 21-7
1922— Eppa Rixey 25-13
1923— Dolf Luque 27-8
Pete Donohue 21-15
Eppa Rixey 20-15
1924— Carl Mays 20-9
1925— Eppa Rixey 21-11
Pete Donohue 21-14
1926— Pete Donohue 20-14
1935— Paul Derringer 22-13
1938— Paul Derringer 21-14
1939— Bucky Walters 27-11
Paul Derringer 25-7
1940— Bucky Walters 22-10
Paul Derringer 20-12
1943— Elmer Riddle 21-11
1944— Bucky Walters 23-8
1947— Ewell Blackwell 22-8
1961— Joey Jay 21-10
1962— Bob Purkey 23-5
Joey Jay 21-14
1963— Jim Maloney 23-7
1965— Sammy Ellis 22-10
Jim Maloney 20-9
1970— Jim Merritt 20-12
1977— Tom Seaver ....†21-6
1985— Tom Browning 20-9
1988— Danny Jackson 23-8

*2-8 with St. Louis; 19-10 with Cincinnati; †7-3 with Mets; 14-3 with Reds.

N.L. home run champions

1877— Lip Pike 4
1892— Bug Holliday 13
1901— Sam Crawford 16
1905— Fred Odwell 9
1954— Ted Kluszewski 49
1970— Johnny Bench 45
1972— Johnny Bench 40
1977— George Foster 52
1978— George Foster 40

N.L. RBI champions

1905— Cy Seymour 121
1918— Sherry Magee 76
1939— Frank McCormick 128
1954— Ted Kluszewski 141
1965— Deron Johnson 130
1970— Johnny Bench 148
1972— Johnny Bench 125
1974— Johnny Bench 129
1976— George Foster 121
1977— George Foster 149
1978— George Foster 120
1985— Dave Parker 125

N.L. batting champions

1905— Cy Seymour 377
1916— Hal Chase 339
1917— Edd Roush 341
1919— Edd Roush 321
1926— Bubbles Hargrave 353
1938— Ernie Lombardi 342
1968— Pete Rose 335
1969— Pete Rose 348
1973— Pete Rose 338

N.L. ERA champions

1923— Dolf Luque 1.93
1925— Dolf Luque 2.63
1939— Bucky Walters 2.29
1940— Bucky Walters 2.48
1941— Elmer Riddle 2.24
1944— Ed Heusser 2.38

N.L. strikeout champions

1899— Noodles Hahn 145
1900— Noodles Hahn 132
1901— Noodles Hahn 239
1939— Bucky Walters *137
1941— Johnny Vander Meer 202
1942— Johnny Vander Meer 186
1943— Johnny Vander Meer 174
1947— Ewell Blackwell 193
1993— Jose Rijo 227

* Tied for league lead

No-hit pitchers

1892— Bumpus Jones ....7-1 vs. Pittsburgh
1898— Ted Breitenstein ....11-0 vs. Pittsburgh
1900— Noodles Hahn ....4-0 vs. Philadelphia
1917— Fred Toney ......1-0 vs. Chicago (10 innings)
1919— Hod Eller ....6-0 vs. St. Louis
1938— Johnny Vander Meer ....3-0 vs. Boston
Johnny Vander Meer ....6-0 vs. Brooklyn
1944— Clyde Shoun ....1-0 vs. Boston
1947— Ewell Blackwell ....6-0 vs. Boston
1965— Jim Maloney ..1-0 vs. Chicago (10 innings)
1968— George Culver ....6-1 vs. Philadelphia
1969— Jim Maloney ....10-0 vs. Houston
1978— Tom Seaver ....4-0 vs. St. Louis
1988— Tom Browning1-0 vs. Los Angeles (Perfect)

Longest hitting streaks

44— Pete Rose 1978
30— Elmer Smith 1898
29— Hal Morris 1996
27— Edd Roush 1920, 1924
Vada Pinson 1965
25— Rube Bressler 1927
Pete Rose 1967
24— Cy Seymour 1903
Hughie Critz 1928
Tommy Harper 1966
23— Heinie Groh 1917
Vada Pinson 1965
22— Jake Daubert 1922
Pete Rose 1968
21— Cy Seymour 1905
Ron Oester 1984
Barry Larkin 1988
20— Al Libke 1945
Tony Perez 1968
Pete Rose ....1977 (twice)

Lefthander Johnny Vander Meer was untouchable for two games in 1938, when he fired back-to-back no-hitters at the Braves and Dodgers.

INDIVIDUAL SEASON, GAME RECORDS

SEASON

Batting			
At-bats	680	Pete Rose	1973
Runs	134	Frank Robinson	1962
Hits	230	Pete Rose	1973
Singles	181	Pete Rose	1973
Doubles	51	Frank Robinson	1962
		Pete Rose	1978
Triples	25	Bid McPhee	1890
Home runs	52	George Foster	1977
Home runs, rookie	38	Frank Robinson	1956
Grand slams	3	5 times	
		Last by Chris Sabo	1993
Total bases	388	George Foster	1977
RBIs	149	George Foster	1977
Walks	132	Joe Morgan	1975
Most strikeouts	145	Mike Cameron	1999
Fewest strikeouts	13	Frank McCormick	1941
Batting average	.383	Bug Holliday	1894
Slugging pct.	.681	Kevin Mitchell	1994
Stolen bases	93	Arlie Latham	1891
Pitching (since 1900)			
Games	90	Wayne Granger	1969
Complete games	41	Noodles Hahn	1901
Innings	375.1	Noodles Hahn	1901
Wins	27	Dolf Luque	1923
		Bucky Walters	1939
Losses	25	Paul Derringer	1933
Winning pct.	.875 (14-2)	Tom Seaver	1981
Walks	162	Johnny Vander Meer	1943
Strikeouts	274	Mario Soto	1982
Shutouts	7	4 times	
		Last by Jack Billingham	1973
Home runs allowed	36	Tom Browning	1988
Lowest ERA	1.57	Fred Toney	1915
Saves	44	Jeff Brantley	1996

GAME

Batting			
Runs	5	Last by Jeffrey Hammonds and Sean Casey	5-19-99
Hits	6	Last by Walker Cooper	7-6-49
Doubles	4	Last by Billy Hatcher	8-21-90
Triples	3	Last by Herm Winningham	8-15-90
Home runs	3	Last by Greg Vaughn	9-7-99
RBIs	10	Walker Cooper	7-6-49
Total bases	15	Walker Cooper	7-6-49
Stolen bases	4	Last by Deion Sanders	4-14-97

BATTING

Games
Pete Rose	2,722
Dave Concepcion	2,488
Johnny Bench	2,158
Tony Perez	1,948
Barry Larkin	1,707
Vada Pinson	1,565
Frank Robinson	1,502
Dan Driessen	1,480
Edd Roush	1,399
Roy McMillan	1,348

At-bats
Pete Rose	10,934
Dave Concepcion	8,723
Johnny Bench	7,658
Tony Perez	6,846
Vada Pinson	6,335
Barry Larkin	6,291
Frank Robinson	5,527
Edd Roush	5,384
Ted Kluszewski	4,961
Tommy Corcoran	4,849

Runs
Pete Rose	1,741
Johnny Bench	1,091
Barry Larkin	1,063
Frank Robinson	1,043
Dave Concepcion	993
Vada Pinson	978
Tony Perez	936
Bid McPhee	916
Joe Morgan	816
Edd Roush	815

Hits
Pete Rose	3,358
Dave Concepcion	2,326
Johnny Bench	2,048
Tony Perez	1,934
Barry Larkin	1,884
Vada Pinson	1,881
Edd Roush	1,784
Frank Robinson	1,673
Ted Kluszewski	1,499
Frank McCormick	1,439

Doubles
Pete Rose	601
Dave Concepcion	389
Johnny Bench	381
Vada Pinson	342
Tony Perez	339
Barry Larkin	335
Frank Robinson	318
Frank McCormick	285
Edd Roush	260
Ted Kluszewski	244

Triples
Edd Roush	152
Pete Rose	115
Bid McPhee	112
Vada Pinson	96
Curt Walker	94
Mike Mitchell	88
Ival Goodman	79
Jake Daubert	78
Jake Beckley	77
Heinie Groh	75

Home runs
Johnny Bench	389
Frank Robinson	324
Tony Perez	287
Ted Kluszewski	251
George Foster	244
Eric Davis	203
Vada Pinson	186
Wally Post	172
Barry Larkin	168
Gus Bell	160

Total bases
Pete Rose	4,645
Johnny Bench	3,644
Tony Perez	3,246
Dave Concepcion	3,114
Frank Robinson	3,063
Vada Pinson	2,973
Barry Larkin	2,853
Ted Kluszewski	2,542
Edd Roush	2,489
George Foster	2,289

Runs batted in
Johnny Bench	1,376
Tony Perez	1,192
Pete Rose	1,036
Frank Robinson	1,009

SEASON

Batting
Most at-bats	5,767	1968
Most runs	865	1999
Fewest runs	488	1908
Most hits	1,599	1976
Most singles	1,191	1922
Most doubles	312	1999
Most triples	120	1926
Most home runs	221	1956
Fewest home runs	14	1908, 1916
Most grand slams	7	1974, 1980, 1987
Most pinch-hit home runs	12	1957
Most total bases	2,549	1999
Most stolen bases	310	1910
Highest batting average	.296	1922
Lowest batting average	.227	1908
Highest slugging pct	.451	1999

Pitching
Lowest ERA	2.23	1919
Highest ERA	5.08	1930
Most complete games	142	1904
Most shutouts	23	1919
Most saves	60	1970, 1972
Most walks	640	1949
Most strikeouts	1,159	1997

Fielding
Most errors	355	1901
Fewest errors	95	1977
Most double plays	194	1928, 1931, 1954
Highest fielding average	.986	1995

General
Most games won	108	1975
Most games lost	101	1982
Highest win pct	.686	1919
Lowest win pct	.138	1876

GAME, INNING

Batting
Most runs, game	30	6-18-1893
Most runs, inning	14	6-18-1893, 8-3-89
Most hits, game	32	6-18-1893
Most home runs, game	9	9-4-99
Most total bases, game	55	6-18-1893, 5-19-99

George Foster joined an exclusive club in 1977 when he blasted a team-record 52 home runs.

Dave Concepcion	950
Ted Kluszewski	886
George Foster	861
Vada Pinson	814
Frank McCormick	803
Barry Larkin	793

Extra-base hits
Pete Rose	868
Johnny Bench	794
Frank Robinson	692
Tony Perez	682
Vada Pinson	624
Barry Larkin	568
Dave Concepcion	538
Ted Kluszewski	518
George Foster	488
Edd Roush	459

Batting average
(Minimum 500 games)
Cy Seymour	.332
Edd Roush	.331
Jake Beckley	.325
Bubbles Hargrave	.314
Rube Bressler	.311
Ernie Lombardi	.311
Bug Holliday	.309
Dusty Miller	.308
Pete Rose	.307
Pat Duncan	.307

Stolen bases
Joe Morgan	406
Barry Larkin	345
Arlie Latham	337
Dave Concepcion	321
Bob Bescher	320
Bid McPhee	316
Eric Davis	270
Vada Pinson	221
Bug Holliday	202
Edd Roush	199

PITCHING

Earned-run average
(Minimum 1,000 innings)
Bob Ewing	2.37
Noodles Hahn	2.52
Pete Schneider	2.65
Jose Rijo	2.71

Bucky Walters	2.93
Tony Mullane	2.99
Gary Nolan	3.02
George Suggs	3.03
Don Gullett	3.03
Dolf Luque	3.09

Wins
Eppa Rixey	179
Paul Derringer	161
Bucky Walters	160
Dolf Luque	154
Jim Maloney	134
Frank Dwyer	133
Joe Nuxhall	130
Pete Donohue	127
Noodles Hahn	127
Tom Browning	123

Losses
Dolf Luque	152
Paul Derringer	150
Eppa Rixey	148
Johnny Vander Meer	116
Pete Donohue	110
Joe Nuxhall	109
Bucky Walters	107
Bob Ewing	103
Frank Dwyer	100
Red Lucas	99
Ken Raffensberger	99

Innings pitched
Eppa Rixey	2,890.2
Dolf Luque	2,668.2
Paul Derringer	2,615.1
Bucky Walters	2,355.2
Joe Nuxhall	2,169.1
Johnny Vander Meer	2,028.0
Bob Ewing	2,020.1
Pete Donohue	1,996.1
Frank Dwyer	1,992.2
Noodles Hahn	1,987.1

Strikeouts
Jim Maloney	1,592
Mario Soto	1,449
Joe Nuxhall	1,289
Johnny Vander Meer	1,251
Jose Rijo	1,201
Paul Derringer	1,062
Gary Nolan	1,035
Jim O'Toole	1,002

Tom Browning	997
Dolf Luque	970

Bases on balls
Johnny Vander Meer	1,072
Bucky Walters	806
Jim Maloney	786
Dolf Luque	756
Joe Nuxhall	706
Mario Soto	657
Eppa Rixey	603
Herm Wehmeier	591
Ewell Blackwell	532
Fred Norman	531

Games
Pedro Borbon	531
Clay Carroll	486
Joe Nuxhall	484
Tom Hume	457
Eppa Rixey	440
Dolf Luque	395
Paul Derringer	393
John Franco	393
Rob Dibble	354
Ted Power	349

Shutouts
Bucky Walters	32
Jim Maloney	30
Johnny Vander Meer	29
Ken Raffensberger	25
Paul Derringer	24
Noodles Hahn	24
Dolf Luque	24
Eppa Rixey	23
Joe Nuxhall	20
Jack Billingham	18
Red Lucas	18

Saves
John Franco	148
Clay Carroll	119
Jeff Brantley	88
Rob Dibble	88
Tom Hume	88
Pedro Borbon	76
Wayne Granger	73
Jeff Shaw	69
Bill Henry	64
Rawly Eastwick	57

HISTORY

REDS YEAR-BY-YEAR

Year	W	L	Place	Games Back	Manager	Leaders: Batting avg.	Hits	Home runs	RBIs	Wins	ERA
1901	52	87	8th	38	McPhee	Crawford, .330	Beckley, 178	Crawford, 16	Crawford, 104	Hahn, 22	Hahn, 2.71
1902	70	70	4th	33½	McPhee, Bancroft, Kelley	Crawford, .333	Crawford, 185	Beckley, 5	Crawford, 78	Hahn, 23	Hahn, 1.77
1903	74	65	4th	16½	Kelley	Donlin, .351	Seymour, 191	Donlin, Seymour, 7	Steinfeldt, 83	Hahn, 22	Hahn, 2.52
1904	88	65	3rd	18	Kelley	Seymour, .313	Seymour, 166	Dolan, 6	Corcoran, 74	Harper, 23	Hahn, 2.06
1905	79	74	5th	26	Kelley	Seymour, .377	Seymour, 219	Odwell, 9	Seymour, 121	Ewing, 20	Ewing, 2.51
1906	64	87	6th	51½	Hanlon	Huggins, .292	Huggins, 159	Schlei, Seymour, 4	Schlei, 54	Weimer, 20	Weimer, 2.22
1907	66	87	6th	41½	Hanlon	Mitchell, .292	Mitchell, 163	Kane, Mitchell, 3	Ganzel, 64	Coakley, Ewing, 17	Ewing, 1.73
1908	73	81	5th	26	Ganzel	Lobert, .293	Lobert, 167	Lobert, 4	Lobert, 63	Ewing, Spade, 17	Coakley, 1.86
1909	77	76	4th	33½	Griffith	Mitchell, .310	Mitchell, 162	3 Tied, 4	Mitchell, 86	Fromme, 19	Fromme, 1.90
1910	75	79	5th	29	Griffith	Paskert, .300	Hoblitzell, 170	Mitchell, 5,	Mitchell, 88	Suggs, 20	Suggs, 2.40
1911	70	83	6th	29	Griffith	Bates, .292	Hoblitzell, 180	Hoblitzell, 11	Hoblitzell, 91	Suggs, 15	Keefe, 2.69
1912	75	78	4th	29	O'Day	Marsans, .317	Hoblitzell, 164	Bescher, 4, Mitchell, 4	Hoblitzell, 85	Suggs, 19	Fromme, 2.74
1913	64	89	7th	37½	Tinker	Tinker, .317	Hoblitzell, 143	Bates, 6	Hoblitzell, 62	Johnson, 14	Ames, 2.88
1914	60	94	8th	34½	Herzog	Groh, .288	Herzog, 140	Niehoff, 4	Niehoff, 49	Benton, 16	Douglas, 2.56
1915	71	83	7th	20	Herzog	T. Griffith, .307	T. Griffith, 179	T. Griffith, 4	T. Griffith, 85	Dale, 18	Toney, 1.58
1916	60	93	*7th	33½	Herzog, Mathewson	Chase, .339	Chase, 184	Chase, 4	Chase, 82	Toney, 14	Toney, 2.28
1917	78	76	4th	20	Mathewson	Roush, .341	Groh, 182	Chase, Roush, Thorpe, 4	Chase, 86	Toney, 24	Schneider, 2.10
1918	68	60	3rd	15½	Mathewson, Groh	Roush, .333	Groh, 158	Roush, 5	S. Magee, 76	Eller, 16	Eller, 2.36
1919	96	44	1st	+9	Moran	Roush, .321	Roush, 162	Groh, 5	Roush, 71	Sallee, 21	Ruether, 1.82
1920	82	71	3rd	10½	Moran	Roush, .339	Roush, 196	Daubert, Roush, 4	Roush, 90	Ring, 17	Ruether, 2.47
1921	70	83	6th	24	Moran	Roush, .352	Bohne, 175	Roush, 4	Roush, 71	Rixey, 19	Rixey, 2.78
1922	86	68	2nd	7	Moran	Harper, .340	Daubert, 205	Daubert, 12	Duncan, 94	Rixey, 25	Donohue, 3.12
1923	91	63	2nd	4½	Moran	Roush, .351	Duncan, Roush, 185	Hargrave, 10	Roush, 88	Luque, 27	Luque, 1.93
1924	83	70	4th	10	Hendricks	Roush, .348	Roush, 168	4 Tied, 4	Roush, 72	Mays, 20	Rixey, 2.76
1925	80	73	3rd	15	Hendricks	Roush, .339	Roush, 183	Roush, E. Smith, 8	Roush, 83	Donohue, Rixey, 21	Luque, 2.63
1926	87	67	2nd	2	Hendricks	Roush, .323	Roush, 182	Roush, 7	Pipp, 99	Donohue, 20	Mays, 3.14
1927	75	78	5th	18½	Hendricks	Allen, .295	Dressen, 160	Walker, 6	Walker, 80	Lucas, 18	Luque, 3.20
1928	78	74	5th	16	Hendricks	Allen, .305	Critz, 190	Picinich, 7	Walker, 73	Rixey, 19	Kolp, 3.19
1929	66	88	7th	33	Hendricks	Walker, .313	Swanson, 172	Walker, 7	Kelly, 103	Lucas, 19	Lucas, 3.60
1930	59	95	7th	33	Howley	Heilmann, .333	Heilmann, 153	Heilmann, 19	Heilmann, 91	Lucas, 14	Kolp, 4.22
1931	58	96	8th	43	Howley	Stripp, .324	Cuccinello, 181	Cullop, 8	Cuccinello, 93	Lucas, 14	Benton, 3.35
1932	60	94	8th	30	Howley	Herman, .326	Herman, 188	Herman, 16	Herman, 87	Johnson, Lucas, 13	Rixey, 2.66
1933	58	94	8th	33	Bush	Hafey, .303	Hafey, 172	Bottomley, 13	Bottomley, 83	Benton, Lucas, 10	Rixey, 3.15
1934	52	99	8th	42	O'Farrell, Dressen	Pool, .327	Koenig, 172	Hafey, 18	Bottomley, 78	Derringer, 15	Frey, 3.52
1935	68	85	6th	31½	Dressen	Riggs, .278	Goodman, 159	Goodman, Lombardi, 12	Goodman, 72	Derringer, 22	Brennan, 3.15
1936	74	80	5th	18	Dressen	Lombardi, .333	Cuyler, 185	Goodman, 17	Cuyler, 74	Derringer, 19	Davis, 3.58
1937	56	98	8th	40	Dressen, Wallace	Lombardi, .334	Goodman, 150	Kampouris, 17	Kampouris, 71	Grissom, 12	Schott, 2.97
1938	82	68	4th	6	McKechnie	Lombardi, .342	F. McCormick, 209	Goodman, 30	F. McCormick, 106	Derringer, 21	Derringer, 2.93
1939	97	57	1st	+4½	McKechnie	F. McCormick, .332	F. McCormick, 209	Lombardi, 20	F. McCormick, 128	Walters, 27	Walters, 2.29
1940	100	53	1st	+12	McKechnie	Lombardi, .319	F. McCormick, 191	F. McCormick, 19	F. McCormick, 127	Walters, 22	Walters, 2.48
1941	88	66	3rd	12	McKechnie	M. McCormick, .287	F. McCormick, 162	F. McCormick, 17	F. McCormick, 97	Riddle, Walters, 19	Riddle, 2.24
1942	76	76	4th	29	McKechnie	F. McCormick, .277	F. McCormick, 156	F. McCormick, 13	F. McCormick, 89	Vander Meer, 18	Vander Meer, 2.43
1943	87	67	2nd	18	McKechnie	F. McCormick, .303	Frey, 154	Tipton, 9	Miller, 71	Riddle, 21	Beggs, 2.34
1944	89	65	3rd	16	McKechnie	F. McCormick, .305	F. McCormick, 177	F. McCormick, 20	F. McCormick, 102	Walters, 23	Heusser, 2.38
1945	61	93	7th	37	McKechnie	Libke, .283	Clay, 184	Miller, 13	F. McCormick, 81	Bowman, Heusser, 11	Walters, 2.68
1946	67	87	6th	30	McKechnie	Hatton, .271	Haas, 141	Hatton, 14	Hatton, 69	Beggs, 12	Beggs, 2.32
1947	73	81	5th	21	Neun	Galan, .314	Baumholtz, 182	Miller, 19	Miller, 87	Blackwell, 22	Blackwell, 2.47
1948	64	89	7th	27	Neun, Walters	Adams, .298	Wyrostek, 140	Sauer, 35	Sauer, 97	Vander Meer, 17	Vander Meer, 3.41
1949	62	92	7th	35	Walters	Kluszewski, .309	Kluszewski, 164	Cooper, 16	Hatton, 69	Raffensberger, 18	Erautt, 3.36
1950	66	87	6th	24½	Sewell	Kluszewski, .307	Kluszewski, 165	Kluszewski, 25	Kluszewski, 111	Blackwell, 17	Blackwell, 2.97
1951	68	86	6th	28½	Sewell	Wyrostek, .311	Wyrostek, 167	Ryan, 16	Kluszewski, 77	Blackwell, Raffensberger, 16	Perkowski, 2.82
1952	69	85	6th	27½	Sewell, Hornsby	Kluszewski, .320	Adams, 180	Kluszewski, 16	Kluszewski, 86	Raffensberger, 17	Raffensberger, 2.81
1953	68	86	6th	37	Hornsby, Mills	Kluszewski, .316	G. Bell, 183	Kluszewski, 40	Kluszewski, 108	Perkowski, 12	Baczewski, 3.45
1954	74	80	5th	23	Tebbetts	Kluszewski, .326	Kluszewski, 187	Kluszewski, 49	Kluszewski, 141	Fowler, Nuxhall, Valentine, 12	Fowler, 3.83
1955	75	79	5th	23½	Tebbetts	Kluszewski, .314	Kluszewski, 192	Kluszewski, 47	Kluszewski, 113	Nuxhall, 17	Freeman, 2.16
1956	91	63	3rd	2	Tebbetts	Kluszewski, .302	Temple, 180	Robinson, 38	Kluszewski, 102	Lawrence, 19	Freeman, 3.40
1957	80	74	4th	15	Tebbetts	Robinson, .322	Robinson, 197	Crowe, 31	Crowe, 92	Lawrence, 16	Lawrence, 3.52
1958	76	78	4th	16	Tebbetts, Dykes	Lynch, .312	Temple, 166	Robinson, 31	Robinson, 83	Purkey, 17	Haddix, 3.52
1959	74	80	*5th	13	Smith, Hutchinson	Pinson, .316	Pinson, 205	Robinson, 36	Robinson, 125	Newcombe, Purkey, 13	Newcombe, 3.16
1960	67	87	6th	28	Hutchinson	Robinson, .297	Pinson, 187	Robinson, 31	Robinson, 83	Purkey, 17	Brosnan, 2.36
1961	93	61	1st	+4	Hutchinson	Pinson, .343	Pinson, 208	Robinson, 37	Robinson, 124	Jay, 21	O'Toole, 3.10
1962	98	64	3rd	3½	Hutchinson	Robinson, .342	Robinson, 208	Robinson, 39	Robinson, 136	Purkey, 23	Purkey, 2.81
1963	86	76	5th	13	Hutchinson	Pinson, .313	Pinson, 204	Pinson, 22	Pinson, 106	Maloney, 23	Nuxhall, 2.61
1964	92	70	*2nd	1	Hutchinson, Sisler	Robinson, .306	Robinson, 174	Robinson, 29	Robinson, 96	O'Toole, 17	Ellis, 2.57
1965	89	73	4th	8	Sisler	Rose, .312	Rose, 209	Robinson, 33	De. Johnson, 130	Ellis, 22	Maloney, 2.54
1966	76	84	7th	18	Heffner	Rose, .313	Rose, 205	De. Johnson, 24	Cardenas, De. Johnson, 81	Maloney, 16	McCool, 2.48
1967	87	75	4th	14½	Bristol	Rose, .301	Pinson, 187	Perez, 26	Perez, 102	Pappas, 16	Abernathy, 1.27
1968	83	79	4th	14	Bristol	Rose, .335	Rose, 210	May, 22	Perez, 92	Maloney, 16	Carroll, 2.29
								WEST DIVISION			
1969	89	73	3rd	4	Bristol	Rose, .348	Rose, 218	May, 38	Perez, 122	Merritt, 17	Maloney, 2.77
1970	102	60	†1st	+14½	Anderson	Perez, .317	Rose, 205	Bench, 45	Bench, 148	Merritt, 20	Carroll, 2.59
1971	79	83	*4th	11	Anderson	Rose, .304	Rose, 192	May, 39	May, 98	Gullett, 16	Carroll, 2.50
1972	95	59	†1st	+10½	Anderson	Rose, .307	Rose, 198	Bench, 40	Bench, 125	Nolan, 15	Nolan, 1.99
1973	99	63	‡1st	+3½	Anderson	Rose, .338	Rose, 230	Perez, 27	Bench, 104	Billingham, 19	Borbon, 2.16
1974	98	64	2nd	4	Anderson	Morgan, .293	Rose, 185	Bench, 33	Bench, 129	Billingham, 19	Carroll, 2.15
1975	108	54	†1st	+20	Anderson	Morgan, .327	Rose, 210	Bench, 28	Bench, 110	Billingham, Gullett, Nolan, 15	Gullett, 2.42
1976	102	60	†1st	+10	Anderson	Griffey, .336	Rose, 215	Foster, 29	Foster, 121	Nolan, 15	Eastwick, 2.09
1977	88	74	2nd	10	Anderson	Foster, .320	Rose, 204	Foster, 52	Foster, 149	Norman, Seaver, 14	Seaver, 2.34
1978	92	69	2nd	2½	Anderson	Rose, .302	Rose, 198	Foster, 40	Foster, 120	Seaver, 16	Bair, 1.97
1979	90	71	‡1st	+1½	McNamara	Knight, Collins, .318	Knight, 175	Foster, 30	Foster, 98	Seaver, 16	Hume, 2.76
1980	89	73	3rd	3½	McNamara	Collins, .303	Collins, 167	Foster, 25	Foster, 93	Pastore, 13	Hume, 2.56
1981	66	42	§2nd/2nd	–	McNamara	Griffey, .311	Concepcion, 129	Foster, 22	Foster, 90	Seaver, 14	Seaver, 2.54
1982	61	101	6th	28	McNamara, Nixon	Cedeno, .289	Concepcion, 164	Driessen, 17	Cedeno, Driessen, 57	Soto, 14	Soto, 2.79
1983	74	88	6th	17	Nixon	Driessen, .277	Oester, 145	Redus, 17	Oester, 58	Soto, 17	Soto, 2.70
1984	70	92	5th	22	Rapp, Rose	Parker, .285	Parker, 173	Parker, 16	Parker, 94	Soto, 18	Power, 2.82
1985	89	72	2nd	5½	Rose	Parker, .312	Parker, 198	Parker, 34	Parker, 125	Browning, 20	Franco, 2.18
1986	86	76	2nd	10	Rose	B. Bell, .278	Parker, 174	Parker, 31	Parker, 116	Gullickson, 15	Franco, 2.94
1987	84	78	2nd	6	Rose	Daniels, .334	Davis, 139	Davis, 37	Davis, 100	Browning, Gullickson, Power, 10	Williams, 2.30
1988	87	74	2nd	7	Rose	Larkin, .296	Larkin, 174	Davis, 26	Davis, 93	Jackson, 23	Rijo, 2.39
1989	75	87	5th	17	Rose, Helms	Davis, .281	Benzinger, 154	Davis, 34	Davis, 101	Browning, 15	Dibble, 2.09
1990	91	71	†1st	+5	Piniella	Duncan, .306	Larkin, 185	Sabo, 25	Davis, 86	Browning, 15	Dibble, 1.74
1991	74	88	5th	20	Piniella	Morris, .318	Sabo, 175	O'Neill, 28	O'Neill, 91	Rijo, 15	Rijo, 2.51
1992	90	72	2nd	8	Piniella	Roberts, .323	Roberts, 172	O'Neill, 14	Larkin, 78	Belcher, Rijo, 15	Rijo, 2.56
1993	73	89	5th	31	Perez, Johnson	Morris, .317	Sabo, 143	Sabo, 21	Sanders, 83	Rijo, 14	Rijo, 2.48
								CENTRAL DIVISION			
1994	66	48	1st	+½	Johnson	Morris, .335	Morris, 146	Mitchell, 30	Morris, 78	Smiley, 11	Rijo, 3.08
1995	85	59	∞‡1st	+9	Johnson	Larkin, .319	Larkin, 158	Gant, 29	R. Sanders, 99	Schourek, 18	Schourek, 3.22
1996	81	81	3rd	7	Knight	Morris, .313	Morris, 165	Larkin, 33	Larkin, 89	Smiley, 13	Shaw, 2.49
1997	76	86	3rd	8	Knight, McKeon	D. Sanders, .273	D. Sanders, 127	Greene, 26	Greene, 91	Burba, Tomko, 11	Shaw, 2.38
1998	77	85	4th	25	McKeon	Young, .310	Young, Larkin, 166	B. Boone, 24	B. Boone, 95	Harnisch, 14	Harnisch, 3.14
1999	96	67	◆2nd	1½	McKeon	Casey, .332	Casey, 197	Vaughn, 45	Vaughn, 118	Harnisch, 16	Williamson, 2.41

* Tied for position. † Won Championship Series. ‡ Lost Championship Series. § First half 35-21; second half 31-21. ∞ Won Division Series; ◆ Lost wild-card playoff. Note: Batting average minimum 350 at-bats; ERA minimum 90 innings pitched.

COLORADO ROCKIES

FRANCHISE CHRONOLOGY

First season: 1993, as part of a two-team expansion that increased the National League to 14 teams and the Major Leagues to 28. The Rockies lost their first game at New York, 3-0, and went on to finish sixth in the seven-team N.L. West Division with a 67-95 record, 37 games behind the first-place Braves.

1994-present: The Rockies improved to a 53-64 second-season record and 77-67 in 1995, when they finished one game behind Los Angeles in the realigned West Division. Their second-place record was good enough to earn the N.L.'s first wild-card berth under an expanded playoff format and gave Colorado the distinction of reaching postseason play faster than any previous expansion team. The Rockies' first playoff visit ended with a four-game Division Series loss to the Braves. Colorado made history in its debut season with a Major League-record attendance of 4,483,350 and drew well over 3 million fans in each of the next two strike-shortened campaigns.

Outfielder Dante Bichette.

ROCKIES VS. OPPONENTS BY DECADE

	Braves	Cardinals	Cubs	Dodgers	Giants	Phillies	Pirates	Reds	Astros	Mets	Expos	Padres	Marlins	Brewers	D'backs	Interleague	Decade Record
1993-9	26-50	40-37	40-38	40-46	34-52	29-36	36-34	34-41	41-33	36-32	37-30	41-45	38-40	10-10	13-12	17-23	512-559
Totals	26-50	40-37	40-38	40-46	34-52	29-36	36-34	34-41	41-33	36-32	37-30	41-45	38-40	10-10	13-12	17-23	512-559

Interleague results: 4-6 vs. Angels; 5-5 vs. Athletics; 4-6 vs. Mariners; 4-6 vs. Rangers.

ALL-TIME RECORD OF EXPANSION TEAMS

Team	W	L	Pct.	DT	P	WS
Arizona	165	159	.509	1	0	0
Kansas City	2,471	2,412	.506	6	2	1
Toronto	1,784	1,818	.495	5	2	2
Houston	2,980	3,048	.494	6	0	0
Montreal	2,387	2,501	.488	2	0	0
Anaheim	2,987	3,201	.483	3	0	0
Milwaukee	2,348	2,542	.480	2	1	0
Colorado	512	559	.478	0	0	0
New York	2,840	3,178	.472	4	3	2
Texas	2,881	3,290	.467	4	0	0
San Diego	2,239	2,656	.457	3	2	0
Seattle	1,624	1,977	.451	2	0	0
Florida	472	596	.442	0	1	1
Tampa Bay	132	192	.407	0	0	0

DT—Division Titles. P—Pennants won. WS—World Series won.

BALLPARK CHRONOLOGY

Coors Field (1995-present)
Capacity: 50,381.
First game: Rockies 11, New York 9 (April 26, 1995).
First batter: Brett Butler, Mets.
First hit: Brett Butler, Mets (single).
First run: Walt Weiss, Rockies (1st inning).
First home run: Rico Brogna, Mets.
First winning pitcher: Mark Thompson, Rockies.
First-season attendance: 3,390,037.

Mile High Stadium (1993-94)
Capacity: 76,100.
First game: Rockies 11, Expos 4 (April 9, 1993).
First-season attendance: 4,483,350.

MANAGERS

Name	Years	Record
Don Baylor	1993-98	440-469
Jim Leyland	1999	72-90

WILD-CARD QUALIFIERS

Year	Record	Manager	Div. Series Result
1995	77-67	Baylor	Lost to Braves

ATTENDANCE HIGHS

Total	Season	Park
4,483,350	1993	Mile High Stadium
3,891,014	1996	Coors Field
3,888,453	1997	Coors Field
3,789,347	1998	Coors Field
3,390,037	1995	Coors Field

N.L. MVP
Larry Walker, OF, 1997

MANAGER OF THE YEAR
Don Baylor, 1995

INDIVIDUAL SEASON, GAME RECORDS

SEASON

Batting
At-bats	690	Neifi Perez	1999
Runs	143	Larry Walker	1997
Hits	219	Dante Bichette	1998
Singles	149	Eric Young	1996
Doubles	48	Dante Bichette	1998
Triples	12	Neifi Perez	1999
Home runs	49	Larry Walker	1997
Home runs, rookie	25	Todd Helton	1998
Grand slams	2	5 times	
		Last by Larry Walker	1998
Total bases	409	Larry Walker	1997
RBIs	150	Andres Galarraga	1996
Walks	98	Walt Weiss	1995
Most strikeouts	157	Andres Galarraga	1996
Fewest strikeouts	31	Eric Young	1996
Batting average	.379	Larry Walker	1999
Slugging pct.	.720	Larry Walker	1997
Stolen bases	53	Eric Young	1996

Pitching
Games	78	Chuck McElroy	1998
Complete games	7	Pedro Astacio	1999
Innings	232.0	Pedro Astacio	1999
Wins	17	Kevin Ritz	1996
		Pedro Astacio	1999
Losses	17	Darryl Kile	1998
Winning pct.	.833	Marvin Freeman	1994
Walks	105	Kevin Ritz	1996
Strikeouts	210	Pedro Astacio	1999
Shutouts	2	Roger Bailey	1997
Home runs allowed	39	Pedro Astacio	1998
Lowest ERA	3.83	Dave Veres	1998
Saves	31	Dave Veres	1999

GAME

Batting
Runs	5	Walt Weiss	9-20-95
Hits	6	Andres Galarraga	7-3-95
Doubles	3	Last by Terry Schumpert	9-29-99
Triples	2	Last by Neifi Perez	9-14-99
Home runs	3	Last by Vinny Castilla	6-5-99
RBIs	8	Andres Galarraga	6-27-96
		Larry Walker	4-28-99
Total bases	13	Last by Vinny Castilla	6-5-99
Stolen bases	6	Eric Young	6-30-96

Second baseman Eric Young, an original Rockie, enjoyed a breakthrough 1996 season.

MILESTONE PERFORMANCES

30-plus home runs
49— Larry Walker	1997
46— Vinny Castilla	1998
47— Andres Galarraga	1996
41— Andres Galarraga	1997
40— Dante Bichette	1995
Ellis Burks	1996
Vinny Castilla	1996, 1997
37— Larry Walker	1999
36— Larry Walker	1995
35— Todd Helton	1999
34— Dante Bichette	1999
33— Vinny Castilla	1999
32— Vinny Castilla	1995
Ellis Burks	1997
31— Andres Galarraga	1994
Andres Galarraga	1995
Dante Bichette	1996

100-plus RBIs
150— Andres Galarraga	1996
144— Vinny Castilla	1998
141— Dante Bichette	1996
140— Andres Galarraga	1997
133— Dante Bichette	1999
130— Larry Walker	1997
128— Dante Bichette	1995
Ellis Burks	1996
122— Dante Bichette	1998
118— Dante Bichette	1997
115— Larry Walker	1999
113— Vinny Castilla	1996, 1997
Todd Helton	1999
106— Andres Galarraga	1995
102— Vinny Castilla	1999
101— Larry Walker	1995

20-plus victories
None

N.L. home run champions
1995— Dante Bichette	40
1996— Andres Galarraga	47
1997— Larry Walker	49

N.L. RBI champions
1995— Dante Bichette	128
1996— Andres Galarraga	150
1997— Andres Galarraga	140

N.L. batting champions
1993— Andres Galarraga	.370
1998— Larry Walker	.363
1999— Larry Walker	.379

BATTING

Games
Dante Bichette	1,018
Vinny Castilla	935
Andres Galarraga	679
Larry Walker	624
Eric Young	613
Walt Weiss	523
Ellis Burks	520
John Vander Wal	465
Neifi Perez	419
Jeff Reed	365

At-bats
Dante Bichette	4,050
Vinny Castilla	3,495
Andres Galarraga	2,667
Larry Walker	2,226
Eric Young	2,120
Ellis Burks	1,821
Walt Weiss	1,760
Neifi Perez	1,695
Todd Helton	1,201
Joe Girardi	1,102

Runs
Dante Bichette	665
Larry Walker	518
Vinny Castilla	516
Andres Galarraga	476
Eric Young	378
Ellis Burks	361
Walt Weiss	264
Neifi Perez	238
Todd Helton	205
Joe Girardi	145

Hits
Dante Bichette	1,278
Vinny Castilla	1,044
Andres Galarraga	843
Larry Walker	765
Eric Young	626
Ellis Burks	558
Walt Weiss	469
Neifi Perez	468
Todd Helton	378
Joe Girardi	302

Doubles
Dante Bichette	270
Larry Walker	167
Vinny Castilla	165
Andres Galarraga	155
Ellis Burks	104
Eric Young	102
Todd Helton	78
Walt Weiss	71
Charlie Hayes	68
Neifi Perez	67

Triples
Neifi Perez	30
Eric Young	28
Ellis Burks	24
Larry Walker	20
Dante Bichette	18
Vinny Castilla	17
Walt Weiss	14
Andres Galarraga	13
Mike Kingery	12
Joe Girardi	11

Home runs
Vinny Castilla	203
Dante Bichette	201
Andres Galarraga	172
Larry Walker	163
Ellis Burks	115
Todd Helton	65
Jeff Reed	36
Charlie Hayes	35
Eric Young	30
Neifi Perez	26

Total bases
Dante Bichette	2,187
Vinny Castilla	1,852
Andres Galarraga	1,540
Larry Walker	1,461
Ellis Burks	1,055
Eric Young	874
Neifi Perez	673
Todd Helton	665
Walt Weiss	610
Charlie Hayes	482

Runs batted in
Dante Bichette	826
Vinny Castilla	610
Andres Galarraga	579
Larry Walker	471
Ellis Burks	337
Eric Young	227
Todd Helton	221
Neifi Perez	163
Charlie Hayes	148
Walt Weiss	143

Extra-base hits
Dante Bichette	489
Vinny Castilla	385
Larry Walker	350
Andres Galarraga	340
Ellis Burks	243
Eric Young	160
Todd Helton	150
Neifi Perez	123
Charlie Hayes	109
Walt Weiss	99

Batting average
(Minimum 300 games)
Larry Walker	.344
Andres Galarraga	.316
Dante Bichette	.316
Todd Helton	.315
Ellis Burks	.306
Vinny Castilla	.299
Eric Young	.295
Jeff Reed	.286
Neifi Perez	.276
Joe Girardi	.274

Stolen bases
Eric Young	180
Dante Bichette	105
Larry Walker	92
Andres Galarraga	55
Ellis Burks	52
Quinton McCracken	45
Walt Weiss	42
Alex Cole	30
Neifi Perez	24
Vinny Castilla	22

Longest hitting streaks
23—Dante Bichette		1995
22—Vinny Castilla		1997
21—Larry Walker		1999
20—Larry Walker		1998
19—Eric Young		1995
	Dante Bichette	1995
18—Larry Walker		1999
17—Eric Young		1996
16—Dante Bichette		1994
	Larry Walker	1997
15—Andres Galarraga		1993
	Neifi Perez	1998

PITCHING

Earned-run average
(Minimum 300 innings)
Steve Reed	3.68
Bruce Ruffin	3.84
Darren Holmes	4.42
Armando Reynoso	4.65
Roger Bailey	4.90
Marvin Freeman	4.91
Curtis Leskanic	4.92
Kevin Ritz	5.20
John Thomson	5.28
Pedro Astacio	5.47

Wins
Kevin Ritz	39
Pedro Astacio	35
Curtis Leskanic	31
Armando Reynoso	30
Steve Reed	25
Jamey Wright	25
Darren Holmes	23
Darryl Kile	21
Marvin Freeman	20
Roger Bailey	18

Losses
Kevin Ritz	38
Jamey Wright	33
Armando Reynoso	31
Darryl Kile	30
John Thomson	30
Pedro Astacio	26
Greg Harris	20
Curtis Leskanic	20
Mark Thompson	20
Roger Bailey	19
Bobby Jones	19

Innings pitched
Kevin Ritz	576.1
Jamey Wright	541.2
Armando Reynoso	503.0
Pedro Astacio	490.0
Curt Leskanic	470.0
Darryl Kile	421.0
John Thomson	390.0
Steve Reed	369.2
Roger Bailey	356.0
Marvin Freeman	337.0

Strikeouts
Pedro Astacio	431
Curt Leskanic	415
Kevin Ritz	337
Bruce Ruffin	319
Darren Holmes	297
Steve Reed	275
Darryl Kile	274
Armando Reynoso	270
John Thomson	246
Jamey Wright	239

Bases on balls
Jamey Wright	261
Kevin Ritz	253
Curtis Leskanic	221
Darryl Kile	205
Armando Reynoso	170
Bruce Ruffin	165
Pedro Astacio	163
Roger Bailey	161
Bobby Jones	155
Darren Holmes	136
John Thomson	136

Games
Curtis Leskanic	356
Steve Reed	329
Mike Munoz	300
Darren Holmes	263
Bruce Ruffin	246
Jerry Dipoto	205
Mike DeJean	170
Dave Veres	136
Chuck McElroy	119
Kevin Ritz	101

Shutouts
Roger Bailey	2
Brian Bohanon	1
Mark Brownson	1
Darryl Kile	1
David Nied	1
Mark Thompson	1
John Thomson	1

Saves
Bruce Ruffin	60
Darren Holmes	46
Dave Veres	39
Jerry DiPoto	36
Curtis Leskanic	20
Steve Reed	15
Mike Munoz	8
Mike DeJean	4
Willie Blair	3
Chuck McElroy	2
Kevin Ritz	2
Bill Swift	2

SEASON

Batting
Most at-bats	5,717	1999
Most runs	961	1996
Fewest runs	758	1993
Most hits	1,644	1999
Most singles	1,088	1998
Most doubles	333	1998
Most triples	59	1993
Most home runs	239	1997
Fewest home runs	142	1993
Most grand slams	5	1994, 1998
Most pinch-hit home runs	11	1995
Most total bases	2,677	1997, 1999
Most stolen bases	201	1996
Highest batting average	.291	1998
Lowest batting average	.273	1993
Highest slugging pct	.478	1997

Pitching
Lowest ERA	4.97	1995
Highest ERA	6.01	1999
Most complete games	12	1999
Most shutouts	5	1994, 1997, 1998
Most saves	43	1995
Most walks	737	1999
Most strikeouts	1,032	1999

Fielding
Most errors	167	1993
Fewest errors	84	1994
Most double plays	202	1997
Highest fielding average	.984	1998

General
Most games won	83	1996, 1997
Most games lost	95	1993
Highest win pct.	.535	1995
Lowest win pct.	.414	1993

GAME, INNING

Batting
Most runs, game	19	6-7-96
Most runs, inning	11	7-12-96
Most hits, game	21	Last 5-14-98
Most home runs, game	7	Last 4-5-97
Most total bases, game	41	5-4-96

Year	W	L	Place	Games Back	Manager	Batting avg.	Hits	Home runs	RBIs	Wins	ERA
									Leaders		
								WEST DIVISION			
1993	67	95	6th	37	Baylor	Galarraga, .370	Hayes, 175	Hayes, 25	Galarraga, Hayes, 98	Reynoso, 12	Ruffin, 3.87
1994	53	64	3rd	6½	Baylor	Galarraga, .319	Bichette, 147	Galarraga, 31	Bichette, 95	Freeman, 10	Freeman, 2.80
1995	77	67	*2nd	1	Baylor	Bichette, .340	Bichette, 197	Bichette, 40	Bichette, 128	Ritz, 11	Leskanic, 3.40
1996	83	79	3rd	8	Baylor	Burks, .344	Burks, 211	Galarraga, 47	Galarraga, 150	Ritz, 17	Reynoso, 4.96
1997	83	79	3rd	7	Baylor	Walker, .366	Walker, 208	Walker, 49	Galarraga, 140	Bailey, Holmes, 9	Bailey, 4.29
1998	77	85	4th	21	Baylor	Walker, .363	Bichette, 219	Castilla, 46	Castilla, 144	Kile, Astacio, 13	Thomson, 4.81
1999	72	90	5th	28	Leyland	Walker, .379	Perez, 193	Walker, 37	Bichette, 133	Astacio, 17	Wright, 4.87

* Lost Division Series.

Note: Batting average minimum 350 at-bats; ERA minimum 90 innings pitched.

David Nied

MAJOR LEAGUE Baseball became a Mile High reality on July 5, 1991, when owners tabbed Denver and South Florida for the 13th and 14th franchises in the National League fraternity. With the Colorado Baseball Partnership in place and the proposal for a new stadium approved, the Rockies began preparation for a 1993 season inaugural.

The Rockies selected pitcher David Nied as the first of 36 picks in the November 17, 1992, expansion draft. The team dropped a 3-0 decision in its April 5, 1993, Major League debut at New York, but rebounded for an 11-4 victory over Montreal in its April 9 Mile High Stadium opener.

Expansion draft (November 17, 1992)

Players
Brad Ausmus....................N.Y. Yankees...............catcher
Freddie Benavides ....Cincinnati ....infield
Pedro Castellano ....Chicago Cubs ....infield
Vinny Castilla ....Atlanta ....infield
Braulio Castillo ....Philadelphia................outfield
Jerald Clark.......................San Diego ....outfield
Alex Cole...........................Pittsburgh ....outfield
Joe Girardi........................Chicago Cubs ....catcher
Charlie Hayes ..................N.Y. Yankees..............third base
Roberto Mejia....................Los Angeles...............infield
J. Owens............................Minnesota...................catcher
Jody Reed.........................Boston.........................infield
Kevin Reimer ....Texas...........................outfield
Jim Tatum.........................Milwaukee...................infield
Eric Wedge........................Boston.........................catcher
Eric Young.........................Los Angeles...............infield

Pitchers
Scott Aldred........................Detroit ....lefthanded
Andy Ashby........................Philadelphia ....righthanded
Willie Blair ....Houston ....righthanded
Doug Bochtler ....Montreal ....righthanded
Denis Boucher ....Cleveland ....lefthanded
Scott Fredrickson ....San Diego ....righthanded
Ryan Hawblitzel ....Chicago Cubs ....righthanded
Butch Henry ....Houston ....righthanded
Darren Holmes ....Milwaukee ....righthanded
Calvin Jones ....Seattle ....righthanded
Curt Leskanic ....Minnesota ....righthanded
Brett Merriman ....California ....righthanded
Marcus Moore ....Toronto ....righthanded
*David Nied ....Atlanta ....righthanded
Lance Painter ....San Diego ....lefthanded
Steve Reed ....San Francisco ....righthanded
Armando Reynoso ....Atlanta ....righthanded
Kevin Ritz ....Detroit ....righthanded
Mo Sanford ....Cincinnati ....righthanded
Keith Shepherd ....Philadelphia..................righthanded
  *First pick

Opening day lineup
April 5, 1993
Eric Young, second base
Alex Cole, center field
Dante Bichette, right field
Andres Galarraga, first base
Jerald Clark, left field
Charlie Hayes, third base
Joe Girardi, catcher
Freddie Benavides, shortstop
David Nied, pitcher

Rockies firsts
Charlie Hayes

First hit: Andres Galarraga, April 5, 1993,
   at New York (single)
First home run: Dante Bichette, April 7, 1993, at New York
First RBI: Dante Bichette, April 7, 1993, at New York
First win: Bryn Smith, April 9, 1993, vs. Montreal
First shutout: David Nied (7 inn.), Bruce Ruffin (1),
   Darren Holmes (1), April 14, 1994, 5-0 at Philadelphia
First CG shutout: David Nied, June 21, 1994, 8-0 vs. Houston

HISTORY

FLORIDA MARLINS

FRANCHISE CHRONOLOGY

First season: 1993, as part of a two-team expansion that increased the National League to 14 teams and the Major Leagues to 28. The Marlins collected 14 hits and defeated Los Angeles, 6-3, in their major league debut and went on to post a 64-98 first-year record. That was good for sixth place in the seven-team N.L. East Division, 33 games behind first-place Philadelphia.

1994-present: The Marlins improved to 51-64 in the strike-interrupted 1994 season and climbed to within nine games of .500 in the strike-shortened 1995 campaign. But the real breakthrough came in 1997 when the 5-year-old Marlins, buoyed by an offseason spending spree that beefed up their roster, won 92 games, earned a wild-card berth and made a Cinderella run through the playoffs, beating Atlanta in the NLCS to claim the pennant and defeating Cleveland in a seven-game World Series. In the process, they became the youngest championship team in baseball history.

Outfielder Gary Sheffield.

MARLINS VS. OPPONENTS BY DECADE

	Braves	Cardinals	Cubs	Dodgers	Giants	Phillies	Pirates	Reds	Astros	Mets	Expos	Padres	Rockies	Brewers	D'backs	Interleague	Decade Record
1993-99	36-51	29-40	36-39	35-35	25-42	34-52	30-42	32-43	32-39	36-50	38-46	30-34	40-38	5-13	3-14	31-18	472-498
Totals	36-51	29-40	36-39	35-35	25-42	34-52	30-42	32-43	32-39	36-50	38-46	30-34	40-38	5-13	3-14	31-18	472-596

Interleague results: 7-2 vs. Orioles; 4-5 vs. Red Sox; 2-1 vs. Tigers; 3-6 vs. Yankees; 7-2 vs. Blue Jays; 8-2 vs. Devil Rays.

ALL-TIME RECORD OF EXPANSION TEAMS

Team	W	L	Pct.	DT	P	WS
Arizona	165	159	.509	1	0	0
Kansas City	2,471	2,412	.506	6	2	1
Toronto	1,784	1,818	.495	5	2	2
Houston	2,980	3,048	.494	6	0	0
Montreal	2,387	2,501	.488	2	0	0
Anaheim	2,987	3,201	.483	3	0	0
Milwaukee	2,348	2,542	.480	2	1	0
Colorado	512	559	.478	0	0	0
New York	2,840	3,178	.472	4	3	2
Texas	2,881	3,290	.467	4	0	0
San Diego	2,239	2,656	.457	3	2	0
Seattle	1,624	1,977	.451	2	0	0
Florida	*472*	*596*	*.442*	*0*	*1*	*1*
Tampa Bay	132	192	.407	0	0	0

DT—Division Titles. P—Pennants won. WS—World Series won.

WORLD SERIES CHAMPION

Year	Loser	Length	MVP
1997	Cleveland	7 games	L. Hernandez

N.L. PENNANT WINNER

Year	Record	Manager	Series Result
1997	92-70	Leyland	Defeated Indians

WILD-CARD QUALIFIER

Year	Record	Manager	Div. Series Result
1997	90-72	Leyland	Defeated Giants

NLCS Result
Defeated Braves

MANAGERS

Name	Years	Record
Rene Lachemann	1993-96	221-285
Cookie Rojas	1996	1-0
John Boles	1996, 1999	104-133
Jim Leyland	1997-98	146-178

BALLPARK CHRONOLOGY

Pro Player Stadium, formerly Joe Robbie Stadium (1993-present)
Capacity: 42,530.
First game: Marlins 6, Los Angeles 3 (April 5, 1993).
First batter: Jose Offerman, Dodgers.
First hit: Bret Barberie, Marlins (single).
First run: Benito Santiago, Marlins (2nd inning).
First home run: Tim Wallach, Dodgers.
First winning pitcher: Charlie Hough, Marlins.
First-season attendance: 3,064,847.

ATTENDANCE HIGHS

Total	Season	Park
3,064,847	1993	Joe Robbie Stadium
2,364,387	1997	Joe Robbie Stadium
1,937,467	1994	Joe Robbie Stadium
1,750,395	1998	Joe Robbie Stadium
1,746,767	1996	Joe Robbie Stadium

INDIVIDUAL SEASON, GAME RECORDS

SEASON

Batting

At-bats	617	Edgar Renteria	1997
Runs	118	Gary Sheffield	1996
Hits	175	Jeff Conine	1996
Singles	143	Edgar Renteria	1997
Doubles	45	Cliff Floyd	1998
Triples	9	Mark Kotsay	1999
Home runs	42	Gary Sheffield	1996
Home runs, rookie	26	Preston Wilson	1999
Grand slams	3	Bobby Bonilla	1997
Total bases	324	Gary Sheffield	1996
RBIs	120	Gary Sheffield	1996
Walks	142	Gary Sheffield	1996
Most strikeouts	156	Preston Wilson	1999
Fewest strikeouts	50	Mark Kotsay	1999
Batting average	.319	Jeff Conine	1994
Slugging pct.	.624	Gary Sheffield	1996
Stolen bases	58	Chuck Carr	1993

Pitching

Games	75	Robb Nen	1996
Complete games	9	Livan Hernandez	1998
Innings	237.1	Kevin Brown	1997
Wins	17	Kevin Brown	1996
		Alex Fernandez	1997
Losses	17	Jack Armstrong	1993
Winning pct.	.667	Pat Rapp	1995
		Kevin Brown	1997
Walks	119	Al Leiter	1996
Strikeouts	205	Kevin Brown	1997
Shutouts	3	Kevin Brown	1996
Home runs allowed	37	Livan Hernandez	1998
Lowest ERA	1.89	Kevin Brown	1996
Saves	45	Bryan Harvey	1993

GAME

Batting

Runs	4	Last by Edgar Renteria	8-13-98
Hits	5	Last by Mark Kotsay	6-22-98
Doubles	3	Last by Mark Kotsay	4-22-98
Triples	2	Jesus Tavarez	8-28-95
Home runs	2	Last by Mike Lowell	9-18-99
RBIs	7	Last by Gary Sheffield	9-18-95
Stolen bases	3	Last by Luis Castillo	8-27-99

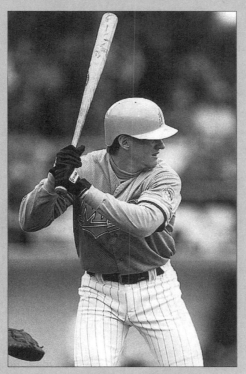

Outfielder Jeff Conine's steady bat helped the Marlins navigate the rough expansion waters.

MILESTONE PERFORMANCES

25-plus home runs
42—	Gary Sheffield	1996
27—	Gary Sheffield	1994
26—	Jeff Conine	1996
	Preston Wilson	1999
25—	Jeff Conine	1995

100-plus RBIs
120—	Gary Sheffield	1996
115—	Moises Alou	1997
105—	Jeff Conine	1995

20-plus victories
None

N.L. home run champions
None

N.L. RBI champions
None

N.L. batting champions
None

N.L. ERA champions
1996— Kevin Brown 1.89

N.L. strikeout champions
None

No-hit pitchers
(9 innings or more)
1996— Al Leiter ....11-0 vs. Colorado
1997— Kevin Brown............................9-0 vs. San Francisco

Longest hitting streaks
22—	Edgar Renteria	1996
	Luis Castillo	1999
21—	Greg Colbrunn	1996
17—	Greg Colbrunn	1995
15—	Bret Barberie	1993
	Chuck Carr	1993

CAREER LEADERS

BATTING

Games
Jeff Conine	718
Gary Sheffield	558
Kurt Abbott	424
Alex Arias	423
Edgar Renteria	393
Charles Johnson	376
Chuck Carr	353
Greg Colbrunn	326
Mark Kotsay	316
Luis Castillo	288

At-bats
Jeff Conine	2,531
Gary Sheffield	1,870
Edgar Renteria	1,565
Kurt Abbott	1,337
Chuck Carr	1,292
Charles Johnson	1,241
Greg Colbrunn	1,194
Mark Kotsay	1,125
Luis Castillo	1,067
Cliff Floyd	976

Runs
Gary Sheffield	365
Jeff Conine	337
Edgar Renteria	237
Chuck Carr	190
Kurt Abbott	173
Luis Castillo	150
Greg Colbrunn	147
Cliff Floyd	145
Charles Johnson	135
Mark Kotsay	134

Hits
Jeff Conine	737
Gary Sheffield	538
Edgar Renteria	450
Kurt Abbott	343
Greg Colbrunn	339
Chuck Carr	331
Mark Kotsay	305
Charles Johnson	297
Luis Castillo	284
Cliff Floyd	274

Doubles
Jeff Conine	122
Gary Sheffield	98
Cliff Floyd	73
Kurt Abbott	71
Charles Johnson	60
Chuck Carr	58
Greg Colbrunn	58
Edgar Renteria	57
Terry Pendleton	52
Devon White	50

Triples
Kurt Abbott	19
Mark Kotsay	17
Jeff Conine	14
Todd Dunwoody	12
Alex Gonzalez	8
Edgar Renteria	8
Benito Santiago	8
Quilvio Veras	8
Luis Castillo	7
Craig Counsell	7
Gary Sheffield	7
Devon White	7

Home runs
Gary Sheffield	122
Jeff Conine	98
Charles Johnson	51
Greg Colbrunn	45
Kurt Abbott	40
Cliff Floyd	39
Preston Wilson	27
Orestes Destrade	25
Benito Santiago	24
Moises Alou	23
Devon White	23

Total bases
Jeff Conine	1,181
Gary Sheffield	1,016
Kurt Abbott	572
Edgar Renteria	559
Greg Colbrunn	538
Charles Johnson	516
Cliff Floyd	474
Mark Kotsay	445
Chuck Carr	421
Terry Pendleton	370

Runs batted in
Jeff Conine	422
Gary Sheffield	380
Greg Colbrunn	189
Charles Johnson	166
Cliff Floyd	158
Kurt Abbott	156
Terry Pendleton	136
Mark Kotsay	122
Devon White	118
Moises Alou	115

Extra-base hits
Jeff Conine	234
Gary Sheffield	227
Kurt Abbott	130
Cliff Floyd	117
Charles Johnson	114
Greg Colbrunn	106
Mark Kotsay	85
Devon White	80
Edgar Renteria	77
Terry Pendleton	75

Batting average
(Minimum 300 games)
Jeff Conine	.291
Gary Sheffield	.288
Edgar Renteria	.288
Greg Colbrunn	.284
Mark Kotsay	.271
Alex Arias	.265
Kurt Abbott	.257
Chuck Carr	.256
Charles Johnson	.239

Stolen bases
Chuck Carr	115
Edgar Renteria	89
Luis Castillo	86
Gary Sheffield	74
Quilvio Veras	64
Cliff Floyd	38
Devon White	35
Mark Kotsay	20
Greg Colbrunn	16
Kurt Abbott	13
Jesus Tavarez	13

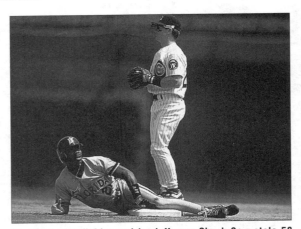

Speedy center fielder and leadoff man **Chuck Carr** stole 58 bases in the Marlins' 1993 expansion debut season.

TEAM SEASON, GAME RECORDS

SEASON

Batting
Most at-bats	5,578	1999
Most runs	740	1997
Fewest runs	581	1993
Most hits	1,465	1999
Most singles	1,034	1993
Most doubles	272	1998
Most triples	44	1999
Most home runs	150	1996
Fewest home runs	94	1993, 1994
Most grand slams	9	1997
Most pinch-hit home runs	8	1999
Most total bases	2,203	1999
Most stolen bases	131	1995
Highest batting average	.266	1994
Lowest batting average	.248	1993
Highest slugging pct.	.406	1995

Pitching
Lowest ERA	3.83	1997
Highest ERA	5.18	1998
Most complete games	12	1995, 1997
Most shutouts	13	1996
Most saves	48	1993
Most walks	715	1998
Most strikeouts	1,188	1997

Fielding
Most errors	129	1998
Fewest errors	111	1996
Most double plays	187	1996
Highest fielding average	.982	1996

General
Most games won	92	1997
Most games lost	108	1998
Highest win pct	.568	1997
Lowest win pct	.333	1998

GAME, INNING

Batting
Most runs, game	17	9-17-95
Most runs, inning	8	Last 6-5-99
Most hits, game	24	7-15-96
Most home runs, game	4	Last 5-24-99
Most total bases, game	39	9-17-95

PITCHING

Earned-run average
(Minimum 300 innings)
Kevin Brown	2.30
Robb Nen	3.41
Alex Fernandez	3.51
Al Leiter	3.51
Pat Rapp	4.18
John Burkett	4.31
Livan Hernandez	4.39
Chris Hammond	4.52
Charlie Hough	4.58
Dave Weathers	5.28

Wins
Pat Rapp	37
Kevin Brown	33
Chris Hammond	29
Al Leiter	27
Alex Fernandez	24
Livan Hernandez	24
Brian Meadows	22
John Burkett	20
Robb Nen	20
Dave Weathers	16

Losses
Pat Rapp	43
Chris Hammond	32
Brian Meadows	28
Charlie Hough	25
John Burkett	24
Livan Hernandez	24
Dave Weathers	22
Al Leiter	21
Alex Fernandez	20
Kevin Brown	19

Innings pitched
Pat Rapp	665.2
Chris Hammond	520.0
Kevin Brown	470.1
Livan Hernandez	469.2
Al Leiter	366.2
Alex Fernandez	361.2
Brian Meadows	352.2
John Burkett	342.1
Dave Weathers	342.1
Charlie Hough	318.0

Strikeouts
Pat Rapp	384
Kevin Brown	364
Livan Hernandez	333
Chris Hammond	332
Al Leiter	332
Robb Nen	328
Alex Fernandez	274
John Burkett	234
Dave Weathers	206
Jesus Sanchez	199

Bases on balls
Pat Rapp	326
Al Leiter	210
Livan Hernandez	199
Chris Hammond	171
Dave Weathers	152
Jesus Sanchez	151
Ryan Dempster	131
Charlie Hough	123
Robb Nen	121
Ryan Bowen	118

Games
Robb Nen	269
Jay Powell	183
Yorkis Perez	177
Antonio Alfonseca	148
Terry Mathews	138
Richie Lewis	123
Felix Heredia	118
Pat Rapp	117
Vic Darensbourg	115
Brian Edmondson	111
Chris Hammond	111

Shutouts
Kevin Brown	5
Pat Rapp	4
Chris Hammond	3
Dennis Springer	2
Ryan Bowen	1
Alex Fernandez	1
Mark Gardner	1
Charlie Hough	1
Al Leiter	1

Saves
Robb Nen	108
Bryan Harvey	51
Antonio Alfonseca	29
Matt Mantei	19
Jeremy Hernandez	9
Matt Mantei	9
Antonio Alfonseca	8
Terry Mathews	7
Jay Powell	7
Felix Heredia	2
Trevor Hoffman	2
Rob Stanifer	2

MARLINS YEAR-BY-YEAR

Year	W	L	Place	Games Back	Manager	Leaders Batting avg.	Hits	Home runs	RBIs	Wins	ERA
						EAST DIVISION					
1993	64	98	6th	33	Lachemann	Conine, .292	Conine, 174	Destrade, 20	Destrade, 87	Hammond, 11	Aquino, 3.42
1994	51	64	5th	23½	Lachemann	Conine, .319	Conine, 144	Sheffield, 27	Conine, 82	Weathers, 8	Rapp, 3.85
1995	67	76	4th	22½	Lachemann	Conine, .302	Pendleton, 149	Conine, 25	Conine, 105	Burkett, Rapp, 14	Rapp, 3.44
1996	80	82	3rd	16	R. Lachemann, Boles	Sheffield, .314	Conine, 175	Sheffield, 42	Sheffield, 120	Brown, 17	Brown, 1.89
1997	92	70	*†2nd	9	Leyland	Bonilla, .297	Renteria, 171	Alou, 23	Alou, 115	Fernandez, 17	Brown, 2.69
1998	54	108	5th	52	Leyland	Renteria, .282	Floyd, 166	Floyd, 22	Floyd, 90	Meadows, 11	Ojala, 4.25
1999	64	98	5th	39	Boles	Castillo, .302	Gonzalez, 155	Wilson, 26	Wilson, 71	Meadows, 11	Fernandez, 3.38

* Won Division Series. † Won Championship Series.

Note: Batting average minimum 350 at-bats; ERA minimum 90 innings pitched.

Nigel Wilson

FLORIDA, long associated with spring training baseball, received its own Major League franchise when National League owners unanimously approved expansion to Denver and Miami. The Marlins, owned by H. Wayne Huizenga, joined the Colorado Rockies as the 13th and 14th N.L. franchises.

The Marlins stocked their roster with 36 selections in the November 17, 1992, expansion draft, grabbing outfielder Nigel Wilson with their first pick. Florida made its April 5, 1993, Major League debut a successful one, beating the Los Angeles Dodgers, 6-3, at Joe Robbie Stadium.

Expansion draft (November 17, 1992)

Players

Bret Barberie	Montreal	infield
Chuck Carr	St. Louis	outfield
Jeff Conine	Kansas City	outfield
Steve Decker	San Francisco	catcher
Chris Donnels	N.Y. Mets	infield
Carl Everett	N.Y. Yankees	outfield
Monty Fariss	Texas	outfield
Junior Felix	California	outfield
Eric Helfand	Oakland	catcher
Ramon Martinez	Pittsburgh	infield
Kerwin Moore	Kansas City	outfield
Bob Natal	Montreal	catcher
Jesus Tavarez	Seattle	outfield
*Nigel Wilson	Toronto	outfield
Darrell Whitmore	Cleveland	outfield

Pitchers

Jack Armstrong	Cleveland	righthanded
Scott Baker	St. Louis	lefthanded
Andres Berumen	Kansas City	righthanded
Ryan Bowen	Houston	righthanded
Cris Carpenter	St. Louis	righthanded
Scott Chiamparino	Texas	righthanded
Jim Corsi	Oakland	righthanded
Tom Edens	Minnesota	righthanded
Brian Harvey	California	righthanded
Greg Hibbard	Chicago White Sox	lefthanded
Trevor Hoffman	Cincinnati	righthanded
Danny Jackson	Pittsburgh	lefthanded
John Johnstone	N.Y. Mets	righthanded
Richie Lewis	Baltimore	righthanded
Jose Martinez	N.Y. Mets	righthanded
Jamie McAndrew	Los Angeles	righthanded
Robert Person	Chicago White Sox	righthanded
Pat Rapp	San Francisco	righthanded
Jeff Tabaka	Milwaukee	lefthanded
Dave Weathers	Toronto	righthanded
Kip Yaughn	Baltimore	righthanded

* First pick

Opening day lineup

April 5, 1993

Chuck Carr, center field
Jerry Browne, third base
Gary Sheffield, right field
Orestes Destrade, first base
Jeff Conine, left field
Bret Barberie, second base
Benito Santiago, catcher
Kurt Abbott, shortstop
Charlie Hough, pitcher

Jeff Conine

Marlins firsts

First hit: Bret Barberie, April 5, 1993, vs. Los Angeles (single)
First home run: Benito Santiago, April 12, 1993, at San Francisco
First RBI: Walt Weiss, April 5, 1993, vs. Los Angeles
First win: Charlie Hough, April 5, 1993, vs. Los Angeles
First shutout: Ryan Bowen, May 15, 1993, 8-0 at St. Louis

HISTORY

HOUSTON ASTROS

FRANCHISE CHRONOLOGY

First season: 1962, as one of two entries in the National League's first modern-era expansion. The Colt .45s, as they were known for three seasons, pounded the Chicago Cubs, 11-2, in their big-league debut and went on to finish with a 64-96 first-year record, good for eighth place in the 10-team N.L. field.

1963-present: The Astros still are looking for their first pennant, an honor the New York Mets, their expansion mate, has claimed three times. They came excruciatingly close in two N.L. Championship Series: 1980, when they dropped a 10-inning Game 5 thriller to Philadelphia; and 1986, when they lost a 16-inning Game 6 decision in an expansion showdown with the Mets. Those two West Division titles and consecutive Central titles that were followed by Division Series losses in 1997, '98 and '99 are all the Astros have to show for more than three decades of Major League Baseball, although they have finished second or third 13 times since division play began in 1969. In a historical sense, Houston will be long remembered as the franchise that brought indoor baseball and AstroTurf to the major leagues.

Righthander Mike Scott.

ASTROS VS. OPPONENTS BY DECADE

	Braves	Cardinals	Cubs	Dodgers	Giants	Phillies	Pirates	Reds	Mets	Expos	Padres	Marlins	Rockies	Brewers	D'backs	Interleague	Decade Record
1962-69	49-95	59-79	72-66	57-87	55-89	51-87	45-93	59-85	87-49	11-1	10-8						555-739
1970-79	91-85	56-64	65-55	76-104	90-90	59-61	44-75	74-105	61-59	71-49	106-70						793-817
1980-89	96-78	56-58	64-51	82-93	98-79	57-61	63-51	93-81	61-56	60-55	89-87						819-750
1990-99	53-71	60-62	70-51	65-57	69-57	62-43	67-54	63-76	61-46	57-51	62-67	39-32	33-41	17-7	9-9	26-18	813-742
Totals	289-329	231-263	271-223	280-341	312-315	229-252	219-273	289-347	270-210	199-156	267-232	39-32	33-41	17-7	9-9	26-18	2980-3048

Interleague results: 4-5 vs. White Sox; 5-4 vs. Indians; 6-3 vs. Royals; 1-2 vs. Brewers; 4-4 vs. Twins; 6-0 vs. Tigers.

MANAGERS

(Houston Colt .45s, 1962-64)

Name	Years	Record
Harry Craft	1962-64	191-280
Lum Harris	1964-65	70-105
Grady Hatton	1966-68	164-221
Harry Walker	1968-72	355-353
Leo Durocher	1972-73	98-95
Salty Parker	1972	1-0
Preston Gomez	1973-75	128-161
Bill Virdon	1975-82	544-522
Bob Lillis	1982-85	276-261
Hal Lanier	1986-88	254-232
Art Howe	1989-93	392-418
Terry Collins	1994-96	224-197
Larry Dierker	1997-99	283-203

WEST DIVISION CHAMPIONS

Year	Record	Manager	NLCS Result
1980	93-70	Virdon	Lost to Phillies
1981*	61-49	Virdon	None
1986	96-66	Lanier	Lost to Mets

* Second-half champion; lost division playoff to Dodgers.

CENTRAL DIVISION CHAMPIONS

Year	Record	Manager	Div. Series Result
1997	84-78	Dierker	Lost to Braves
1998	102-60	Dierker	Lost to Padres
1999	97-65	Dierker	Lost to Braves

ALL-TIME RECORD OF EXPANSION TEAMS

Team	W	L	Pct.	DT	P	WS
Arizona	165	159	.509	1	0	0
Kansas City	2,471	2,412	.506	6	2	1
Toronto	1,784	1,818	.495	5	2	2
Houston	2,980	3,048	.494	6	0	0
Montreal	2,387	2,501	.488	2	0	0
Anaheim	2,987	3,201	.483	3	0	0
Milwaukee	2,348	2,542	.480	2	1	0
Colorado	512	559	.478	0	0	0
New York	2,840	3,178	.472	4	3	2
Texas	2,881	3,290	.467	4	0	0
San Diego	2,239	2,656	.457	3	2	0
Seattle	1,624	1,977	.451	2	0	0
Florida	472	596	.442	0	1	1
Tampa Bay	132	192	.407	0	0	0

DT—Division Titles. P—Pennants won. WS—World Series won.

ATTENDANCE HIGHS

Total	Season	Park
2,706,020	1999	Astrodome
2,450,451	1998	Astrodome
2,278,217	1980	Astrodome
2,151,470	1965	Astrodome
2,084,546	1993	Astrodome

BALLPARK CHRONOLOGY

The Astrodome (1965-present)

Capacity: 54,313.
First game: Philadelphia 2, Astros 0 (April 12, 1965).
First batter: Tony Taylor, Phillies.
First hit: Bob Aspromonte, Astros (double).
First run: Ruben Amaro, Phillies (3rd inning).
First home run: Dick Allen, Phillies.
First winning pitcher: Chris Short, Phillies.
First-season attendance: 2,151,470.

Colt Stadium (1962-64)

Capacity: 32,601.
First game: Astros 11, Chicago 2 (April 10, 1962).
First-season attendance: 924,456.

N.L. MVP

Jeff Bagwell, 1B, 1994

CY YOUNG WINNER

Mike Scott, RH, 1986

ROOKIE OF THE YEAR

Jeff Bagwell, 1B, 1991

MANAGERS OF THE YEAR

Hal Lanier, 1986
Larry Dierker, 1998

RETIRED UNIFORMS

No.	Name	Pos.
25	Jose Cruz	OF
32	Jim Umbricht	P
33	Mike Scott	P
34	Nolan Ryan	P
40	Don Wilson	P

Hard-hitting Jimmy Wynn was Houston's major power source in the late 1960s.

25-plus home runs
43— Jeff Bagwell 1997
42— Jeff Bagwell 1999
39— Jeff Bagwell 1994
38— Moises Alou 1998
37— Jimmy Wynn 1967
34— Glenn Davis 1989
    Jeff Bagwell 1998
33— Jimmy Wynn 1969
31— Glenn Davis 1986
    Jeff Bagwell 1996
30— Glenn Davis 1988
29— Lee May 1972
28— Lee May 1973
27— Jimmy Wynn 1970
    Glenn Davis 1987
26— Jimmy Wynn 1968
    Cesar Cedeno 1974
25— Doug Rader 1970
    Cesar Cedeno 1973
    Carl Everett 1999

100-plus RBIs
135— Jeff Bagwell 1997
126— Jeff Bagwell 1999
124— Moises Alou 1998
120— Jeff Bagwell 1996
116— Jeff Bagwell 1994
113— Derek Bell 1996
111— Jeff Bagwell 1998
110— Bob Watson 1977
108— Derek Bell 1998
     Carl Everett 1999
107— Jimmy Wynn 1967
105— Lee May 1973
102— Cesar Cedeno 1974
     Bob Watson 1976
101— Glenn Davis 1986

20-plus victories
1969—Larry Dierker 20-13
1976—J.R. Richard 20-15
1979—Joe Niekro 21-11
1980—Joe Niekro 20-12
1989—Mike Scott 20-10
1999—Mike Hampton 22-4
     Jose Lima 21-10

N.L. home run champions
None

N.L. RBI champions
1994— Jeff Bagwell 116

N.L. batting champions
None

N.L. ERA champions
1979—J.R. Richard 2.71
1981—Nolan Ryan 1.69
1986—Mike Scott 2.22
1987—Nolan Ryan 2.76
1990—Danny Darwin 2.21

N.L. strikeout champions
1978—J.R. Richard 303
1979—J.R. Richard 313
1986—Mike Scott 306
1987—Nolan Ryan 270
1988—Nolan Ryan 228

No-hit pitchers
(9 innings or more)
1963—Don Nottebart ....4-1 vs. Philadelphia
1964—Ken Johnson ....0-1 vs. Cincinnati
1967—Don Wilson ....2-0 vs. Atlanta
1969—Don Wilson ....4-0 at Cincinnati
1976—Larry Dierker ....6-0 vs. Montreal
1979—Ken Forsch ....6-0 vs. Atlanta
1981—Nolan Ryan ....5-0 vs. Los Angeles
1986—Mike Scott ....2-0 vs. San Francisco
1993—Darryl Kile ....7-1 vs. New York

Longest hitting streaks
23— Art Howe.......................................1981
    Luis Gonzalez 1997
22— Cesar Cedeno 1977
21— Lee May 1973
    Dickie Thon 1982
20— Rusty Staub 1967
    Kevin Bass 1986
19— Bob Watson 1973
    Cesar Cedeno 1976
    Jose Cruz 1983
18— Terry Puhl 1978
    Jeff Bagwell 1994
17— Rusty Staub 1966
    Doug Rader 1970
    Terry Puhl 1977
    Bob Watson 1978
16— Roman Mejias 1962
    Jim Wynn 1968
    Joe Morgan 1971
    Ray Knight 1982
    Billy Hatcher 1987
15— Sonny Jackson 1966
    Enos Cabell 1979
    Jose Cruz 1979
    Craig Reynolds 1979
    Bill Doran 1984

Righthanded knuckleballer Joe Niekro reached the 20-victory plateau for the Astros in the 1979 and '80 seasons.

SEASON

Batting
At-bats	660	Enos Cabell	1978
Runs	146	Craig Biggio	1997
Hits	210	Craig Biggiol	1998
Singles	160	Sonny Jackson	1966
Doubles	56	Craig Biggio	1999
Triples	14	Roger Metzger	1973
Home runs	43	Jeff Bagwell	1997
Home runs, rookie	20	Glenn Davis	1985
Grand slams	2	Last by Sean Berry	1996
Total bases	340	Moises Alou	1998
RBIs	135	Jeff Bagwell	1997
Walks	149	Jeff Bagwell	1999
Most strikeouts	145	Lee May	1972
Fewest strikeouts	39	Greg Gross	1974
Batting average	.368	Jeff Bagwell	1994
Slugging pct.	.750	Jeff Bagwell	1994
Stolen bases	65	Gerald Young	1988

Pitching
Games	82	Juan Agosto	1990
Complete games	20	Larry Dierker	1969
Innings	305.1	Larry Dierker	1969
Wins	22	Mike Hampton	1999
Losses	20	Dick Farrell	1962
Winning pct.	.909 (10-1)	Randy Johnson	1998
Walks	151	J.R. Richard	1976
Strikeouts	313	J.R. Richard	1979
Shutouts	6	Dave A. Roberts	1973
Home runs allowed	34	Jose Lima	1998
Lowest ERA	1.69	Nolan Ryan	1981
Saves	39	Billy Wagner	1999

GAME

Batting
Runs	5	Last by Craig Biggio	6-4-96
Hits	6	Joe Morgan	7-8-65
Doubles	4	Jeff Bagwell	6-14-96
Triples	3	Craig Reynolds	5-16-81
Home runs	3	Last by Jeff Bagwell	7-9-99
RBIs	7	Rafael Ramirez	8-29-89
		Pete Incaviglia	6-14-92
Total bases	13	Lee May	6-21-73
		Jeff Bagwell	6-24-94
Stolen bases	4	Last by Craig Biggio	9-16-95

Center fielder Cesar Cedeno brought a nice blend of power and speed to the Astros' lineup for more than a decade.

HISTORY

BATTING

Games
Jose Cruz	1,870
Craig Biggio	1,699
Terry Puhl	1,516
Cesar Cedeno	1,512
Jimmy Wynn	1,426
Bob Watson	1,381
Jeff Bagwell	1,317
Doug Rader	1,178
Craig Reynolds	1,170
Bill Doran	1,165

At-bats
Jose Cruz	6,629
Craig Biggio	6,389
Cesar Cedeno	5,732
Jimmy Wynn	5,063
Bob Watson	4,883
Terry Puhl	4,837
Jeff Bagwell	4,759
Bill Doran	4,264
Doug Rader	4,232
Enos Cabell	4,005

Runs
Craig Biggio	1,120
Jeff Bagwell	921
Cesar Cedeno	890
Jose Cruz	871
Jimmy Wynn	829
Terry Puhl	676
Bob Watson	640
Bill Doran	611
Joe Morgan	597
Enos Cabell	522

Hits
Jose Cruz	1,937
Craig Biggio	1,868
Cesar Cedeno	1,659
Bob Watson	1,448
Jeff Bagwell	1,447
Terry Puhl	1,357
Jimmy Wynn	1,291
Bill Doran	1,139
Enos Cabell	1,124
Doug Rader	1,060

Doubles
Craig Biggio	389
Cesar Cedeno	343
Jose Cruz	335
Jeff Bagwell	314
Bob Watson	241
Jimmy Wynn	228
Terry Puhl	226
Doug Rader	197
Kevin Bass	194
Ken Caminiti	191

Triples
Jose Cruz	80
Joe Morgan	63
Roger Metzger	62
Terry Puhl	56
Cesar Cedeno	55
Craig Reynolds	55
Enos Cabell	45
Steve Finley	41
Craig Biggio	38
Bill Doran	35

Home runs
Jeff Bagwell	263
Jimmy Wynn	223
Glenn Davis	166
Cesar Cedeno	163
Craig Biggio	152
Bob Watson	139
Jose Cruz	138
Doug Rader	128
Ken Caminiti	88
Kevin Bass	87

Total bases
Jose Cruz	2,846
Craig Biggio	2,789
Cesar Cedeno	2,601
Jeff Bagwell	2,592
Jimmy Wynn	2,252
Bob Watson	2,166
Terry Puhl	1,881
Doug Rader	1,701
Bill Doran	1,596
Enos Cabell	1,524

Runs batted in
Jeff Bagwell	961
Jose Cruz	942
Bob Watson	782

SEASON

Batting
Most at-bats	5,641	1998
Most runs	874	1998
Fewest runs	464	1963
Most hits	1,578	1998
Most singles	1,097	1984
Most doubles	326	1998
Most triples	67	1980, 1984
Most home runs	168	1999
Fewest home runs	49	1979
Most grand slams	6	1989
Most pinch-hit home runs	9	1995
Most total bases	2,458	1998
Most stolen bases	198	1988
Highest batting average	.280	1998
Lowest batting average	.220	1963
Highest slugging pct	.445	1994

Pitching
Lowest ERA	2.66	1981
Highest ERA	4.37	1996
Most complete games	55	1979
Most shutouts	19	1979, 1981, 1986
Most saves	51	1986
Most walks	679	1975
Most strikeouts	1,221	1969

Fielding
Most errors	174	1966
Fewest errors	76	1994
Most double plays	175	1999
Highest fielding average	.983	1971, 1994, 1998, 1999

General
Most games won	102	1998
Most games lost	97	1965, 1975, 1991
Highest win pct	.630	1998
Lowest win pct	.398	1975

GAME, INNING

Batting
Most runs, game	19	6-25-95, 5-11-99
Most runs, inning	12	5-31-75
Most hits, game	25	5-30-76
Most home runs, game	5	Last 6-9-99
Most total bases, game	36	8-17-72, 7-28-99

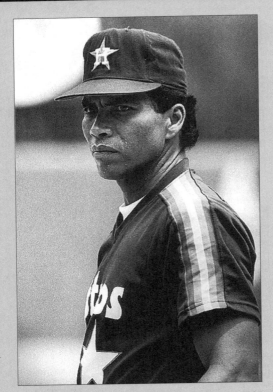

When outfielder Jose Cruz left Houston after the 1987 season, he held many career records.

Cesar Cedeno	778
Jimmy Wynn	719
Craig Biggio	706
Doug Rader	600
Glenn Davis	518
Ken Caminiti	501
Kevin Bass	468

Extra-base hits
Jeff Bagwell	598
Craig Biggio	579
Cesar Cedeno	561
Jose Cruz	553
Jimmy Wynn	483
Bob Watson	410
Doug Rader	355
Terry Puhl	344
Glenn Davis	326
Kevin Bass	311

Batting average
(Minimum 500 games)
Jeff Bagwell	.304
Bob Watson	.297
Craig Biggio	.292
Jose Cruz	.292
Cesar Cedeno	.289
Bill Spiers	.285
Derek Bell	.284
Jesus Alou	.282
Enos Cabell	.281
Terry Puhl	.281
Steve Finley	.281

Stolen bases
Cesar Cedeno	487
Craig Biggio	346
Jose Cruz	288
Joe Morgan	219
Terry Puhl	217
Enos Cabell	191
Bill Doran	191
Jimmy Wynn	180
Jeff Bagwell	158
Gerald Young	153

PITCHING

Earned-run average
(Minimum 500 innings)
Joe Sambito	2.42
Dave Smith	2.53

Mike Cuellar	2.74
Nolan Ryan	3.13
Don Wilson	3.15
J.R. Richard	3.15
Ken Forsch	3.18
Danny Darwin	3.21
Joe Niekro	3.22
Larry Dierker	3.28

Wins
Joe Niekro	144
Larry Dierker	137
Mike Scott	110
J.R. Richard	107
Nolan Ryan	106
Don Wilson	104
Bob Knepper	93
Shane Reynolds	79
Ken Forsch	78
Darryl Kile	71

Losses
Larry Dierker	117
Joe Niekro	116
Bob Knepper	100
Nolan Ryan	94
Don Wilson	92
Ken Forsch	81
Mike Scott	81
J.R. Richard	71
Darryl Kile	65
Dick Farrell	64

Innings pitched
Larry Dierker	2,294.1
Joe Niekro	2,270.0
Nolan Ryan	1,854.2
Don Wilson	1,748.1
Bob Knepper	1,738.0
Mike Scott	1,704.0
J.R. Richard	1,606.0
Ken Forsch	1,493.2
Shane Reynolds	1,234.2
Darryl Kile	1,200.0

Strikeouts
Nolan Ryan	1,866
J.R. Richard	1,493
Larry Dierker	1,487
Mike Scott	1,318
Don Wilson	1,283
Joe Niekro	1,178
Shane Reynolds	1,067

Darryl Kile	973
Bob Knepper	946
Ken Forsch	815

Bases on balls
Joe Niekro	818
Nolan Ryan	796
J.R. Richard	770
Larry Dierker	695
Don Wilson	640
Darryl Kile	562
Bob Knepper	521
Mike Scott	505
Tom Griffin	441
Ken Forsch	428

Games
Dave Smith	563
Ken Forsch	421
Joe Niekro	397
Joe Sambito	353
Larry Dierker	345
Bob Knepper	284
Nolan Ryan	282
Jim Ray	280
Xavier Hernandez	273
Larry Andersen	268

Shutouts
Larry Dierker	25
Joe Niekro	21
Mike Scott	21
Don Wilson	20
J.R. Richard	19
Bob Knepper	18
Nolan Ryan	13
Dave A. Roberts	11
Ken Forsch	9
Tom Griffin	9

Saves
Dave Smith	199
Billy Wagner	101
Fred Gladding	76
Joe Sambito	72
Doug Jones	62
Ken Forsch	50
Frank DiPino	43
Todd Jones	39
Hal Woodeshick	36
John Hudek	29

HISTORY

ASTROS YEAR-BY-YEAR

Year	W	L	Place	Games Back	Manager	Batting avg.	Hits	Home runs	RBIs	Wins	ERA
COLT .45s											
1962	64	96	8th	36½	Craft	Mejias, .286	Mejias, 162	Mejias, 24	Mejias, 76	Bruce, Farrell 10	Farrell, 3.01
1963	66	96	9th	33	Craft	Spangler, .281	Warwick, 134	Bateman, 10	Bateman, 59	Farrell, 14	Woodeshick, 1.97
1964	66	96	9th	27	Craft, Harris	Aspromonte, .280	Aspromonte, 155	Bond, 20	Bond, 85	Bruce, 15	Larsen, 2.26
1965	65	97	9th	32	Harris	Wynn, .275	Morgan, 163	Wynn, 22	Wynn, 73	Farrell, 11	Raymond, 2.90
1966	72	90	8th	23	Hatton	Jackson, .292	Jackson, 174	Wynn, 18	Bateman 70	Giusti, 15	Cuellar, 2.22
1967	69	93	9th	32½	Hatton	Staub, .333	Staub, 182	Wynn, 37	Wynn, 107	Cuellar, 16	Cuellar, 2.79
1968	72	90	10th	25	Hatton, Walker	Staub, .291	Staub, 172	Wynn, 26	Staub, 72	Wilson, 13	Cuellar, 2.74
WEST DIVISION											
1969	81	81	5th	12	Walker	Menke, Wynn, .269	Menke, 149	Wynn, 33	Menke, 90	Dierker, 20	Dierker, 2.33
1970	79	83	4th	23	Walker	Cedeno, .310	Menke, 171	Wynn, 27	Menke, 92	Dierker, 16	Ray, 3.26
1971	79	83	*4th	11	Walker	Watson, .288	Cedeno, 161	Morgan, 13	Cedeno, 81	Wilson, 16	Ray, 2.12
1972	84	69	2nd	10½	Walker, Durocher, Parker	Cedeno, .320	Cedeno, 179	May, 29	May, 98	Dierker, Wilson 15	Wilson, 2.68
1973	82	80	4th	17	Durocher, Gomez	Cedeno, .320	Watson, 179	May, 28	May, 105	Roberts, 17	Roberts, 2.86
1974	81	81	4th	21	Gomez	Gross, .314	Gross, 185	Cedeno, 26	Cedeno, 102	Griffin, 14	Forsch, 2.79
1975	64	97	6th	43½	Gomez, Virdon	Watson, .324	Watson, 157	C. Johnson, 20	Watson, 85	Dierker, 14	Forsch, 3.22
1976	80	82	3rd	22	Virdon	Watson, .313	Watson, 183	Cedeno, 18	Watson, 102	Richard, 20	Forsch, 2.15
1977	81	81	3rd	17	Virdon	Cruz, .299	Cabell, 176	Watson, 22	Watson, 110	Richard, 18	Richard, 2.97
1978	74	88	5th	21	Virdon	Cruz, .315	Cabell, 195	Watson, 14	Cruz, 83	Richard, 18	Forsch, 2.70
1979	89	73	2nd	1½	Virdon	Leonard, .290	Puhl, 172	Cruz, 9	Cruz, 72	Niekro, 21	Sambito, 1.77
1980	93	70	†‡1st	+1	Virdon	Cedeno, .309	Cruz, 185	Puhl, 13	Cruz, 91	Niekro, 20	Richard, 1.89
1981	61	49	§3rd/1st	—	Virdon	Howe, .296	Cruz, 109	Cruz, 13	Cruz, 55	Ryan, Sutton 11	Ryan, 1.69
1982	77	85	5th	12	Virdon, Lillis	Knight, .294	Knight, 179	Garner, 13	Garner, 83	Niekro, 17	Niekro, 2.47
1983	85	77	3rd	6	Lillis	Cruz, .318	Cruz, 189	Thon, 20	Cruz, 92	Niekro, 15	Ryan, 2.98
1984	80	82	*2nd	12	Lillis	Cruz, .312	Cruz, 187	Cruz, 12	Cruz, 95	Niekro, 16	Dawley, 1.93
1985	83	79	*3rd	12	Lillis	Cruz, .300	Doran, 166	Davis, 20	Cruz, 79	Scott, 18	Scott, 3.29
1986	96	66	‡1st	+10	Lanier	Walling, .312	Bass, 184	Davis, 31	Davis, 101	Scott, 18	Scott, 2.22
1987	76	86	3rd	14	Lanier	Hatcher, .296	Doran, 177	Davis, 27	Davis, 93	Scott, 16	Ryan, 2.76
1988	82	80	5th	12½	Lanier	Ramirez, .276	Ramirez, 156	Davis, 30	Davis, 99	Knepper, Scott 14	Agosto, 2.26
1989	86	76	3rd	6	Howe	Davis, .269	Davis, 156	Davis, 34	Davis, 89	Scott, 20	Darwin, 2.36
1990	75	87	*4th	16	Howe	Biggio, .276	Biggio, 153	Stubbs, 23	Stubbs, 71	Darwin, Portugal 11	Darwin, 2.21
1991	65	97	6th	29	Howe	Biggio, .295	Finley, 170	Bagwell, 15	Bagwell, 82	Harnisch, 12	Harnisch, 2.70
1992	81	81	4th	17	Howe	Caminiti, .294	Finley, 177	Anthony, 19	Bagwell, 96	D. Jones, 11	D. Jones, 1.85
1993	85	77	3rd	19	Howe	Bagwell, .320	Biggio, 175	Biggio, 21	Bagwell, 88	Portugal, 18	Hernandez, 2.61
CENTRAL DIVISION											
1994	66	49	2nd	½	Collins	Bagwell, .368	Bagwell, 147	Bagwell, 39	Bagwell, 116	Drabek, 12	Drabek, 2.84
1995	76	68	2nd	9	Collins	Bell, .334	Biggio, 167	Biggio, 22	Bagwell, 87	Reynolds, 10	Veres, 2.26
1996	82	80	2nd	6	Collins	Bagwell, .315	Biggio, 179	Bagwell, 31	Bagwell, 120	Reynolds, 16	Hampton, 3.59
1997	84	78	∞1st	+5	Dierker	Biggio, .309	Biggio, 191	Bagwell, 43	Bagwell, 135	Kile, 19	Kile, 2.57
1998	102	60	∞1st	+12½	Dierker	Biggio, .325	Biggio, 210	Alou, 38	Alou, 124	Reynolds, 19	Hampton, 3.36
1999	97	65	∞1st	+1½	Dierker	Everett, .325	Biggio, 188	Bagwell, 42	Bagwell, 126	Hampton, 22	Hampton, 2.90

* Tied for position. † Won division playoff. ‡ Lost Championship Series. § First half 28-29; second half 33-20. ∞ Lost Division Series.

Note: Batting average minimum 350 at-bats; ERA minimum 90 innings pitched.

Eddie Bressoud

HOUSTON became part of the National League family in a two-team 1962 expansion that marked the first league structural change since 1900. Houston and New York were granted franchise approval on October 16, 1960, bringing the N.L. membership roster to 10.

The Colt .45s stocked their first roster with 23 selections in the October 10, 1961, expansion draft, leading off with infielder Eddie Bressoud. Houston made its Major League debut a successful one, defeating the Chicago Cubs, 11-2, at Colt Stadium en route to a 64-96 first-year record.

Expansion draft (October 10, 1961)

Players

Joe Amalfitano	San Francisco	infield
Bob Aspromonte	Los Angeles	infield
*Eddie Bressoud	San Francisco	infield
Dick Gernert	Cincinnati	infield
Al Heist	Chicago	outfield
Bob Lillis	St. Louis	infield
Norm Larker	Los Angeles	infield
Roman Mejias	Pittsburgh	outfield
Ed Olivares	St. Louis	infield
Merritt Ranew	Milwaukee	catcher
Hal Smith	Pittsburgh	catcher
Al Spangler	Milwaukee	outfield
Don Taussig	St. Louis	outfield
George Williams	Philadelphia	infield

Pitchers

Dick Drott	Chicago	righthanded
Dick Farrell	Los Angeles	righthanded
Jim Golden	Los Angeles	righthanded
Jesse Hickman	Philadelphia	righthanded
Ken Johnson	Cincinnati	righthanded
Sam Jones	San Francisco	righthanded
Paul Roof	Milwaukee	righthanded
Bobby Shantz	Pittsburgh	lefthanded
Jim Umbricht	Pittsburgh	righthanded

*First pick

Opening day lineup

April 10, 1962
Bob Aspromonte, third base
Al Spangler, center field
Roman Mejias, right field
Norm Larker, first base
Jim Pendleton, left field
Hal Smith, catcher
Joe Amalfitano, second base
Don Buddin, shortstop
Bobby Shantz, pitcher

Colt .45s firsts
First hit: Bob Aspromonte, April 10, 1962, vs. Chicago
First home run: Roman Mejias, April 10, 1962, vs. Chicago
First RBI: Al Spangler, April 10, 1962, vs. Chicago
First win: Bobby Shantz, April 10, 1962, vs. Chicago
First shutout: Hal Woodeshick (8 inn.), Dick Farrell (1) April 11, 1962, 2-0 vs. Chicago
First CG shutout: Dean Stone, April 12, 1962, 2-0 vs. Chicago

Bob Aspromonte

LOS ANGELES DODGERS

Manager Walter Alston.

FRANCHISE CHRONOLOGY

First season: 1884, in Brooklyn, as a member of the American Association. The first-year "Bridegrooms" won only 40 games and finished ninth in the league's 13-team field.

1885-1900: Brooklyn celebrated its first A.A. pennant in 1889 by transferring to the more prestigious National League. The Bridegrooms lost their N.L. opener to Boston, 15-9, but went on to claim another pennant with an 86-43 record. Renamed "Superbas," they would close out the century with consecutive pennants under manager Ned Hanlon.

1901-57: The modern-era "Dodgers" might have more aptly been named "Bridesmaids." From 1916 to 1954, they finished second seven times and won seven N.L. pennants, losing every World Series appearance. "Wait til next year" became the rallying cry of frustrated Brooklyn fans, who nevertheless supported their beloved "Bums" with a fervor unmatched in major league baseball. Walter Alston's Dodgers finally broke through with a victory in the 1955 World Series against the hated Yankees, but two years later owner Peter O'Malley moved his franchise to the greener pastures of the West Coast.

1958-present: The Dodgers became less lovable but more efficient in Los Angeles. In 40 seasons, they have claimed nine N.L. pennants, five World Series championships and nine West Division titles while finishing second 13 times. Incredibly, that success has been choreographed by four full-time managers: Alston (1958-76), Tom Lasorda (1976-96), Bill Russell, who replaced the ailing Lasorda midway through the 1996 season, and Davey Johnson last season.

DODGERS VS. OPPONENTS BY DECADE

	Braves	Cardinals	Cubs	Giants	Phillies	Pirates	Reds	Astros	Mets	Expos	Padres	Marlins	Rockies	Brewers	D'backs	Interleague	Decade Record
																	649-809
1900-09	114-95	115-93	74-135	80-128	93-112	76-132	97-114										696-787
1910-19	103-105	105-104	98-117	88-125	99-110	110-105	93-121										765-768
1920-29	128-90	101-119	104-115	106-113	133-87	97-122	96-122										734-793
1930-39	103-117	91-127	89-127	98-120	128-89	113-105	112-108										894-646
1940-49	129-90	90-132	119-101	137-82	162-58	124-96	133-87										913-630
1950-59	129-92	135-85	134-85	117-106	128-92	141-79	129-91										878-729
1960-69	99-89	91-91	102-80	83-108	106-76	100-82	94-94	87-57	94-44	10-2	12-6						910-701
1970-79	106-70	67-53	68-52	108-72	63-56	65-55	79-97	104-76	68-52	73-47	109-71						825-741
1980-89	105-69	62-56	61-57	95-79	55-59	61-53	98-80	93-82	50-63	67-48	78-95						797-757
1990-99	55-68	52-55	61-47	70-70	61-54	61-50	65-57	57-65	58-53	57-56	68-71	35-35	46-40	12-6	14-11	25-19	
Totals	1071-885	909-915	910-916	982-1003	1028-793	948-879	996-971	341-280	270-212	207-153	267-243	35-35	46-40	12-6	14-11	25-19	8061-7361

Interleague results: 9-5 vs. Angels; 5-5 vs. Athletics; 6-4 vs. Mariners; 5-5 vs. Rangers.

MANAGERS

(Brooklyn Dodgers, 1884-1957)

Name	Years	Record
George Taylor	1884	40-64
Charlie Hackett	1885	15-22
Charlie Byrne	1885-87	174-172
Bill McGunnigle	1888-90	268-138
Monte Ward	1891-92	156-135
Dave Foutz	1893-96	264-257
Billy Barnie	1897-98	76-91
Ned Hanlon	1899-1905	511-488
Patsy Donovan	1906-08	184-270
Harry Lumley	1909	55-98
Bill Dahlen	1910-13	251-355
Wilbert Robinson	1914-31	1375-1341
Max Carey	1932-33	146-161
Casey Stengel	1934-36	208-251
Burleigh Grimes	1937-38	131-171
Leo Durocher	1939-46, 1948	738-565
Clyde Sukeforth	1947	2-0
Burt Shotton	1947, 1948-50	326-215
Chuck Dressen	1951-53	298-166
Walter Alston	1954-76	2040-1613
Tom Lasorda	1976-96	1599-1439
Bill Russell	1996-98	173-149
Glenn Hoffman	1998	47-41
Davey Johnson	1999	77-85

WORLD SERIES CHAMPIONS

Year	Loser	Length	MVP
1955	N.Y. Yankees	7 games	Podres
1959	Chicago	6 games	Sherry
1963	N.Y. Yankees	4 games	Koufax
1965	Minnesota	7 games	Koufax
1981	N.Y. Yankees	6 games	Cey, Guerrero, Yeager
1988	Oakland	5 games	Hershiser

A.A. PENNANT WINNERS

Year	Record	Manager	Series Result
1889	93-44	McGunnigle	None

N.L. PENNANT WINNERS

Year	Record	Manager	Series Result
1890	86-43	McGunnigle	None
1899	101-47	Hanlon	None
1900	82-54	Hanlon	None
1916	94-60	Robinson	Lost to Red Sox
1920	93-61	Robinson	Lost to Indians
1941	100-54	Durocher	Lost to Yankees
1947	94-60	Sukeforth, Shotton	Lost to Yankees
1949	97-57	Shotton	Lost to Yankees
1952	96-57	Dressen	Lost to Yankees
1953	105-49	Dressen	Lost to Yankees
1955	98-55	Alston	Defeated Yankees
1956	93-61	Alston	Lost to Yankees
1959	88-68	Alston	Defeated White Sox
1963	99-63	Alston	Defeated Yankees
1965	97-65	Alston	Defeated Twins
1966	95-67	Alston	Lost to Orioles
1974	102-60	Alston	Lost to A's
1977	98-64	Lasorda	Lost to Yankees

N.L. PENNANT WINNERS—cont'd.

Year	Record	Manager	Series Result
1978	95-67	Lasorda	Lost to Yankees
1981	63-47	Lasorda	Defeated Yankees
1988	94-67	Lasorda	Defeated A's

WEST DIVISION CHAMPIONS

Year	Record	Manager	NLCS Result
1974	102-60	Alston	Defeated Pirates
1977	98-64	Lasorda	Defeated Phillies
1978	95-67	Lasorda	Defeated Phillies
*1981	63-47	Lasorda	Defeated Expos
1983	91-71	Lasorda	Lost to Phillies
1985	95-67	Lasorda	Lost to Cardinals
1988	94-67	Lasorda	Defeated Mets
1994	58-56	Lasorda	None
1995	78-66	Lasorda	Lost in Division Series

* First-half champion; won division playoff from Astros.

WILD-CARD QUALIFIERS

Year	Record	Manager	Div. Series Result
1996	90-72	Lasorda, Russell	Lost to Braves

ATTENDANCE HIGHS

Total	Season	Park
3,608,881	1982	Dodger Stadium
3,510,313	1983	Dodger Stadium
3,348,170	1991	Dodger Stadium
3,347,845	1978	Dodger Stadium
3,318,886	1997	Dodger Stadium

BALLPARK CHRONOLOGY

Dodger Stadium (1962-present)
Capacity: 56,000.
First game: Cincinnati 6, Dodgers 3 (April 10, 1962).
First batter: Eddie Kasko, Reds.
First hit: Eddie Kasko, Reds (double).
First run: Eddie Kasko, Reds (1st inning).
First home run: Wally Post, Reds.
First winning pitcher: Bob Purkey, Reds.
First-season attendance: 2,755,184.

Washington Park, Brooklyn (1884-90)
First game: Brooklyn (A.A.) 11, Washington 3 (May 5, 1884).

Eastern Park, Brooklyn (1891-97)
First game: New York 6, Brooklyn 5 (April 27, 1891).

Washington Park II, Brooklyn (1898-1912)
First game: Philadelphia 6, Brooklyn 4 (April 30, 1898).

Ebbets Field, Brooklyn (1913-57)
Capacity: 31,497.
First game: Philadelphia 1, Dodgers 0 (April 9, 1913).
First-season attendance: 347,000.

Roosevelt Stadium, Jersey City (1956-57)
(Site of 15 games over two seasons)
Capacity: 24,167.

First game: Dodgers 5, Philadelphia 4, 10 innings (April 19, 1956).

Los Angeles Memorial Coliseum (1958-61)
Capacity: 93,600.
First game: Dodgers 6, San Francisco 5 (April 18, 1958).
First-season attendance: 1,845,556.

N.L. MVPs

Dolph Camilli, 1B, 1941
Jackie Robinson, 2B, 1949
Roy Campanella, C, 1951
Roy Campanella, C, 1953
Roy Campanella, C, 1955
Don Newcombe, P, 1956
Maury Wills, SS, 1962
Sandy Koufax, P, 1963
Steve Garvey, 1B, 1974
Kirk Gibson, OF, 1988

CY YOUNG WINNERS

Don Newcombe, RH, 1956
Don Drysdale, RH, 1962
Sandy Koufax, LH, 1963
Sandy Koufax, LH, 1965
Sandy Koufax, LH, 1966
Mike Marshall, RH, 1974
Fernando Valenzuela, LH, 1981
Orel Hershiser, RH, 1988

ROOKIES OF THE YEAR

Jackie Robinson, 1B, 1947
Don Newcombe, P, 1949
Joe Black, P, 1952
Jim Gilliam, 2B, 1953
Frank Howard, OF, 1960
Jim Lefebvre, 2B, 1965
Ted Sizemore, 2B, 1969
Rick Sutcliffe, P, 1979
Steve Howe, P, 1980
Fernando Valenzuela, P, 1981
Steve Sax, 2B, 1982
Eric Karros, 1B, 1992
Mike Piazza, C, 1993
Raul Mondesi, OF, 1994
Hideo Nomo, P, 1995
Todd Hollandsworth, OF, 1996

MANAGERS OF THE YEAR

Tom Lasorda, 1983
Tom Lasorda, 1988

RETIRED UNIFORMS

No.	Name	Pos.
1	Pee Wee Reese	SS
2	Tommy Lasorda	Man.
4	Duke Snider	OF
19	Jim Gilliam	IF
20	Don Sutton	P
24	Walter Alston	Man.
32	Sandy Koufax	P
39	Roy Campanella	C
42	Jackie Robinson	2B
53	Don Drysdale	P

MILESTONE PERFORMANCES

30-plus home runs

43— Duke Snider 1956
42— Duke Snider 1953, 1955
Gil Hodges 1954
41— Roy Campanella 1953
40— Gil Hodges 1951
Duke Snider 1954, 1957
Mike Piazza 1997
36— Mike Piazza 1996
35— Babe Herman 1930
Mike Piazza 1993
34— Dolph Camilli 1941
Eric Karros 1996
Eric Karros 1999
Gary Sheffield 1999
33— Roy Campanella 1951
Steve Garvey....................................1977
Pedro Guerrero 1985
Raul Mondesi 1999
32— Gil Hodges 1950, 1952, 1956
Roy Campanella 1955
Jimmy Wynn 1974
Reggie Smith 1977
Pedro Guerrero 1982, 1983
Eric Karros 1995
Mike Piazza 1995
31— Roy Campanella 1950
Duke Snider 1950
Gil Hodges 1953
Frank Howard 1962
Eric Karros 1997
Todd Zeile 1997
30— Dusty Baker 1977
Ron Cey 1977
Raul Mondesi 1997, 1998

100-plus RBIs

153— Tommy Davis 1962
142— Roy Campanella 1953
136— Duke Snider 1955
130— Jack Fournier 1925
Babe Herman 1930
Gil Hodges 1954
Duke Snider 1954
126— Glenn Wright 1930
Duke Snider 1953
124— Dixie Walker 1945
Jackie Robinson 1949
Mike Piazza 1997
123— Hack Wilson 1932
122— Gil Hodges 1953
120— Dolph Camilli 1941
119— Frank Howard 1962
116— Jack Fournier 1924
Dixie Walker 1946
115— Gil Hodges 1949
Steve Garvey....................................1977
113— Babe Herman 1929
Del Bissonette 1930
Gil Hodges 1950
Steve Garvey....................................1978
112— Zack Wheat 1922
Mike Piazza 1993
Eric Karros 1999
111— Wes Parker 1970
Steve Garvey....................................1974
Eric Karros 1996
110— Luis Olmo 1945
Ron Cey 1977
Steve Garvey....................................1979
109— Dolph Camilli 1942
108— Roy Campanella 1951
Jimmy Wynn 1974
107— Duke Snider 1954
Roy Campanella 1955
106— Del Bissonette 1928
Carl Furillo 1949, 1950

(right column, continued)

Steve Garvey....................................1980
105— Eric Karros 1995
Mike Piazza 1996
104— Dolph Camilli 1939
Eric Karros 1997
103— Zack Wheat 1925
Gil Hodges 1951
Pedro Guerrero 1983
102— Jack Fournier 1923
Sam Leslie 1934
Gil Hodges 1952, 1955
101— Duke Snider 1951, 1956
Ron Cey 1975
Gary Sheffield 1999
100— Dolph Camilli 1938
Billy Herman 1943
Pedro Guerrero 1982

20-plus victories

1890— Tom Lovett 30-11
Adonis Terry 26-16
Bob Caruthers 23-11
1891— Tom Lovett 23-19
1892— George Haddock 29-13
Ed Stein 27-16
1893— Brickyard Kennedy 25-20
1894— Ed Stein 26-14
Brickyard Kennedy 24-20
1899— Jim Hughes 28-6
Jack Dunn 23-13
Brickyard Kennedy 22-9
1900— Joseph McGinnity 28-8
Brickyard Kennedy 20-13
1901— William Donovan 25-15
1903— Henry Schmidt 21-13
1911— Nap Rucker 22-18
1914— Jeff Pfeffer 23-12
1916— Jeff Pfeffer 25-11
1920— Burleigh Grimes 23-11
1921— Burleigh Grimes 22-13
1922— Walter Reuther 21-12
1923— Burleigh Grimes 21-18
1924— Dazzy Vance 28-6
Burleigh Grimes 22-13
1925— Dazzy Vance 22-9
1928— Dazzy Vance 22-10
1932— William Clark 20-12
1939— Luke Hamlin 20-13
1941— Kirby Higbe 22-9
Whit Wyatt 22-10
1947— Ralph Branca 21-12
1951— Preacher Roe 22-3
Don Newcombe 20-9
1953— Carl Erskine 20-6
1955— Don Newcombe 20-5
1956— Don Newcombe 27-7
1962— Don Drysdale 25-9
1963— Sandy Koufax 25-5
1965— Sandy Koufax 26-8
Don Drysdale 23-12
1966— Sandy Koufax 27-9
1969— Claude Osteen 20-15
Bill Singer 20-12
1971— Al Downing 20-9
1972— Claude Osteen 20-11
1974— Andy Messersmith 20-6
1976— Don Sutton 21-10
1977— Tommy John 20-7
1986— Fernando Valenzuela 21-11
1988— Orel Hershiser 23-8
1990— Ramon Martinez 20-6

N.L. home run champions

1890— Oyster Burns *13
1903— Jimmy Sheckard............................9
1904— Harry Lumley 9
1906— Tim Jordan 12

Hall of Fame center fielder Duke Snider reached the 40-home run barrier five consecutive years in the 1950s.

INDIVIDUAL SEASON, GAME RECORDS

SEASON

Batting

At-bats	695	Maury Wills		1962
Runs	148	Hub Collins		1890
Hits	241	Babe Herman		1930
Singles	187	Willie Keeler		1899
Doubles	52	John Frederick		1929
Triples	26	George Treadway		1894
Home runs	43	Duke Snider		1956
Home runs, rookie	35	Mike Piazza		1993
		Last by Mike Piazza		1998
Grand slams	3	Babe Herman		1930
Total bases	416	Tommy Davis		1962
RBIs	153	Eddie Stanky		1945
Walks	148	Bill Grabarkewitz		1970
Most strikeouts	149	Jim Johnston		1923
Fewest strikeouts	15	Babe Herman		1930
Batting average	.393	Babe Herman		1930
Slugging pct.	.678	Maury Wills		1962
Stolen bases	104			

Pitching

Games	106	Mike Marshall		1974
Complete games	40	Brickyard Kennedy		1893
Innings	382.2	Brickyard Kennedy		1893
Wins	30	Tom Lovett		1890
Losses	27	George Bell		1910
Winning pct.	.933 (14-1)	Phil Regan		1966
Walks	152	Bill Donovan		1901
Strikeouts	382	Sandy Koufax		1965
Shutouts	11	Sandy Koufax		1963
Home runs allowed	38	Don Sutton		1970
Lowest ERA	1.58	Rube Marquard		1916
Saves	44	Todd Worrell		1996

GAME

Batting

Runs	5	Last by Steve Garvey		8-28-77
Hits	6	Last by Willie Davis		5-24-73
Doubles	3	Last by Eric Karros		4-9-99
Triples	3	Jimmy Sheckard		4-18-01
Home runs	4	Gil Hodges		8-31-50
RBIs	9	Gil Hodges		8-31-50
		Ron Cey		7-31-74
Total bases	17	Gil Hodges		8-31-50
		Davey Lopes		8-20-74
Stolen bases	5	Davey Lopes		8-24-74

1908— Tim Jordan 12
1924— Jack Fournier 27
1941— Dolph Camilli 34
1956— Duke Snider 43

* Tied for league lead

N.L. RBI champions

1919— Hy Myers 73
1941— Dolph Camilli 120
1945— Dixie Walker 124
1953— Roy Campanella 142
1955— Duke Snider 136
1962— Tommy Davis 153

N.L. batting champions

1892— Dan Brouthers 335
1913— Jake Daubert 350
1914— Jake Daubert 329
1918— Zack Wheat 335
1932— Lefty O'Doul 368
1941— Pete Reiser 343
1944— Dixie Walker 357
1949— Jackie Robinson 342
1953— Carl Furillo 344
1962— Tommy Davis 346
1963— Tommy Davis 326

N.L. ERA champions

1924— Dazzy Vance 2.16
1928— Dazzy Vance 2.09
1930— Dazzy Vance 2.61
1957— Johnny Podres 2.66
1962— Sandy Koufax 2.54
1963— Sandy Koufax 1.88
1964— Sandy Koufax 1.74
1965— Sandy Koufax 2.04
1966— Sandy Koufax 1.73
1980— Don Sutton 2.20
1984— Alejandro Pena 2.48

N.L. strikeout champions

1921— Burleigh Grimes 136
1922— Dazzy Vance 134
1923— Dazzy Vance 197
1924— Dazzy Vance 262
1925— Dazzy Vance 221
1926— Dazzy Vance 140
1927— Dazzy Vance 184
1928— Dazzy Vance 200
1936— Van Lingle Mungo 238
1951— Don Newcombe 164
1959— Don Drysdale 242
1960— Don Drysdale 246
1961— Sandy Koufax 269
1962— Don Drysdale 232
1963— Sandy Koufax 306

1965— Sandy Koufax 382
1966— Sandy Koufax 317
1981— Fernando Valenzuela 180
1995— Hideo Nomo 236

No-hit pitchers

(9 innings or more)
1891— Thomas Lovett................4-0 vs. New York
1906— Malcolm Eason ....2-0 vs. St. Louis
1908— Nap Rucker...................6-0 vs. Boston
1925— Dazzy Vance ....10-1 vs. Philadelphia
1940— Tex Carleton ....3-0 vs. Cincinnati
1946— Edward Head ....5-0 vs. Boston
1948— Rex Barney ....2-0 vs. New York
1952— Carl Erskine ....5-0 vs. Chicago
1956— Carl Erskine ....3-0 vs. New York
Sal Maglie ....5-0 vs. Philadelphia
1962— Sandy Koufax ....5-0 vs. New York
1963— Sandy Koufax ....8-0 vs. San Francisco
1964— Sandy Koufax ....3-0 vs. Philadelphia
1965— Sandy Koufax ......1-0 vs. Chicago (Perfect)
1970— Bill Singer ....5-0 vs. Philadelphia
1980— Jerry Reuss ....8-0 vs. San Francisco
1990— Fernando Valenzuela ....6-0 vs. St. Louis
1992— Kevin Gross ....2-0 vs. San Francisco
1995— Ramon Martinez..............7-0 vs. Florida
1996— Hideo Nomo ....9-0 vs. Colorado

Longest hitting streaks

31— Willie Davis 1969
29— Zack Wheat 1916
27— Joe Medwick 1942
Duke Snider 1953
26— Willie Keeler 1902
Zack Wheat 1918
25— Gink Hendrick 1929
Buzz Boyle 1934
Willie Davis 1971
Steve Sax 1986
24— Willie Keeler 1899
Zack Wheat 1924
John Shelby 1988
23— Hy Myers 1915
Brett Butler 1991
22— Duke Snider 1950
Pee Wee Reese 1951
21— Jackie Robinson 1947
Steve Garvey....................................1978
20— Jimmy Johnston 1921
Zack Wheat 1923
Johnny Frederick 1933
Tommy Davis 1960, 1964
Maury Wills 1965
Steve Garvey....................................1978

HISTORY

CAREER LEADERS

BATTING

Games

Zack Wheat	2,322
Bill Russell	2,181
Pee Wee Reese	2,166
Gil Hodges	2,006
Jim Gilliam	1,956
Willie Davis	1,952
Duke Snider	1,923
Carl Furillo	1,806
Steve Garvey	1,727
Maury Wills	1,593

At-bats

Zack Wheat	8,859
Pee Wee Reese	8,058
Willie Davis	7,495
Bill Russell	7,318
Jim Gilliam	7,119
Gil Hodges	6,881
Duke Snider	6,640
Steve Garvey	6,543
Carl Furillo	6,378
Maury Wills	6,156

Runs

Pee Wee Reese	1,338
Zack Wheat	1,255
Duke Snider	1,199
Jim Gilliam	1,163
Gil Hodges	1,088
Willie Davis	1,004
Jackie Robinson	947
Carl Furillo	895
Mike Griffin	881
Maury Wills	876

Hits

Zack Wheat	2,804
Pee Wee Reese	2,170
Willie Davis	2,091
Duke Snider	1,995
Steve Garvey	1,968
Bill Russell	1,926
Carl Furillo	1,910
Jim Gilliam	1,889
Gil Hodges	1,884
Maury Wills	1,732

Doubles

Zack Wheat	464
Duke Snider	343
Steve Garvey	333
Pee Wee Reese	330
Carl Furillo	324
Willie Davis	321
Jim Gilliam	304
Gil Hodges	294
Bill Russell	293
Dixie Walker	274

Triples

Zack Wheat	171
Willie Davis	110
Hy Myers	97
Jake Daubert	87
John Hummel	82
Duke Snider	82
Pee Wee Reese	80
Tom Daly	76
Jimmy Sheckard	76
Jimmy Johnston	73

Home runs

Duke Snider	389
Gil Hodges	361
Roy Campanella	242
Ron Cey	228
Steve Garvey	211
Eric Karros	211
Carl Furillo	192
Mike Piazza	177
Pedro Guerrero	171
Raul Mondesi	163

Total bases

Zack Wheat	4,003
Duke Snider	3,669
Gil Hodges	3,357
Willie Davis	3,094
Pee Wee Reese	3,038
Steve Garvey	3,004
Carl Furillo	2,922
Jim Gilliam	2,530
Bill Russell	2,471
Ron Cey	2,321

Runs batted in

Duke Snider	1,271
Gil Hodges	1,254
Zack Wheat	1,210
Carl Furillo	1,058

SEASON

Batting

Most at-bats	5,642	1982
Most runs	1,021	1894
Fewest runs	375	1908
Most hits	1,654	1930
Most singles	1,223	1925
Most doubles	303	1930
Most triples	130	1894
Most home runs	208	1953
Fewest home runs	14	1915
Most grand slams	8	1952
Most pinch-hit home runs	8	1983, 1992
Most total bases	2,545	1953
Most stolen bases	409	1892
Highest batting average	.313	1894
Lowest batting average	.213	1908
Highest slugging pct.	.474	1953

Pitching

Lowest ERA	2.12	1916
Highest ERA	4.92	1929
Most complete games	135	1904
Most shutouts	24	1963, 1988
Most saves	50	1996
Most walks	671	1946
Most strikeouts	1,212	1996

Fielding

Most errors	432	1891
Fewest errors	106	1952
Most double plays	198	1958
Highest fielding average	.982	1952

General

Most games won	105	1953
Most games lost	104	1905
Highest win pct.	.682	1953
Lowest win pct.	.316	1905

GAME, INNING

Batting

Most runs, game	25	5-20-1896, 9-23-01
Most runs, inning	15	5-21-52
Most hits, game	28	6-23-30, 8-22-17
Most home runs, game	7	5-5-76, 5-25-79
Most total bases, game	48	8-20-74

Smooth-fielding first baseman Steve Garvey was a five-time member of the Dodgers' 100-RBI fraternity.

Steve Garvey	992
Pee Wee Reese	885
Roy Campanella	856
Willie Davis	849
Ron Cey	842
Eric Karros	734
Jackie Robinson	734

Extra-base hits

Duke Snider	814
Zack Wheat	766
Gil Hodges	703
Willie Davis	585
Steve Garvey	579
Carl Furillo	572
Pee Wee Reese	536
Ron Cey	469
Jackie Robinson	464
Eric Karros	445

Batting average
(Minimum 500 games)

Willie Keeler	.352
Babe Herman	.339
Jack Fournier	.337
Mike Piazza	.331
Zack Wheat	.317
Babe Phelps	.315
Manny Mota	.315
Fielder Jones	.313
Jackie Robinson	.311
Dixie Walker	.311

Stolen bases

Maury Wills	490
Davey Lopes	418
Willie Davis	335
Tom Daly	298
Steve Sax	290
Mike Griffin	264
Pee Wee Reese	232
Jimmy Sheckard	212
Jim Gilliam	203
Zack Wheat	203

PITCHING

Earned-run average
(Minimum 1,000 innings)

Jeff Pfeffer	2.31
Nap Rucker	2.42
Sandy Koufax	2.76
George Bell	2.85

Whit Wyatt	2.86
Sherry Smith	2.91
Don Drysdale	2.95
Doc Scanlan	2.96
Tommy John	2.97
Orel Hershiser	3.00

Wins

Don Sutton	233
Don Drysdale	209
Dazzy Vance	190
Brickyard Kennedy	177
Sandy Koufax	165
Burleigh Grimes	158
Claude Osteen	147
Fernando Valenzuela	141
Johnny Podres	136
Orel Hershiser	134
Nap Rucker	134

Losses

Don Sutton	181
Don Drysdale	166
Brickyard Kennedy	149
Nap Rucker	134
Dazzy Vance	131
Claude Osteen	126
Burleigh Grimes	121
Fernando Valenzuela	116
Johnny Podres	104
Orel Hershiser	102

Innings pitched

Don Sutton	3,816.1
Don Drysdale	3,432.0
Brickyard Kennedy	2,857.0
Dazzy Vance	2,757.2
Burleigh Grimes	2,425.2
Claude Osteen	2,396.2
Nap Rucker	2,375.1
Fernando Valenzuela	2,348.2
Sandy Koufax	2,324.1
Orel Hershiser	2,156.0

Strikeouts

Don Sutton	2,696
Don Drysdale	2,486
Sandy Koufax	2,396
Dazzy Vance	1,918
Fernando Valenzuela	1,759
Orel Hershiser	1,443
Johnny Podres	1,331
Ramon Martinez	1,314

Bob Welch	1,292
Nap Rucker	1,217

Bases on balls

Brickyard Kennedy	1,128
Don Sutton	996
Fernando Valenzuela	915
Don Drysdale	855
Sandy Koufax	817
Dazzy Vance	764
Burleigh Grimes	744
Ramon Martinez	704
Nap Rucker	701
Van Lingle Mungo	697

Games

Don Sutton	550
Don Drysdale	518
Jim Brewer	474
Ron Perranoski	457
Clem Labine	425
Charlie Hough	401
Sandy Koufax	397
Brickyard Kennedy	381
Dazzy Vance	378
Johnny Podres	366

Shutouts

Don Sutton	52
Don Drysdale	49
Sandy Koufax	40
Nap Rucker	38
Claude Osteen	34
Fernando Valenzuela	29
Dazzy Vance	29
Jeff Pfeffer	25
Orel Hershiser	24
Johnny Podres	23
Bob Welch	23

Saves

Todd Worrell	127
Jim Brewer	125
Ron Perranoski	101
Jay Howell	85
Clem Labine	83
Tom Niedenfuer	64
Charlie Hough	60
Steve Howe	59
Jeff Shaw	59
Hugh Casey	50
Ed Roebuck	43

DODGERS YEAR-BY-YEAR

Year	W	L	Place	Games Back	Manager	Leaders: Batting avg.	Hits	Home runs	RBIs	Wins	ERA
						BROOKLYN DODGERS					
1901	79	57	3rd	9½	Hanlon	Sheckard, .354	Keeler, 202	Sheckard, 11	Sheckard, 104	Donovan, 25	Donovan, 2.77
1902	75	63	2nd	27½	Hanlon	Keeler, .333	Keeler, 186	McCreery, Sheckard, 4	Dahlen, 74	Kitson, 19	Newton, 2.42
1903	70	66	5th	19	Hanlon	Sheckard, .332	Sheckard, 171	Sheckard, 9	Doyle, 91	Schmidt, 22	O. Jones, 2.94
1904	56	97	6th	50	Hanlon	Lumley, .279	Lumley, 161	Lumley, 9	Lumley, 78	O. Jones, 17	Garvin, 1.68
1905	48	104	8th	56½	Hanlon	Lumley, .293	Lumley, 148	Lumley, 7	Batch, 49	Scanlan, 14	Scanlan, 2.92
1906	66	86	5th	50	Donovan	Lumley, .324	Lumley, 157	Jordan, 12	Jordan, 78	Scanlan, 18	Stricklett, 2.72
1907	65	83	5th	40	Donovan	Jordan, .274	Jordan, 133	Lumley, 9	Lumley, 66	Pastorius, 16	Rucker, 2.06
1908	53	101	7th	46	Donovan	Jordan, .247	Hummel, 143	Jordan, 12	Jordan, 60	Rucker, 17	Wilhelm, 1.87
1909	55	98	6th	55½	Lumley	Hummel, .280	Burch, 163	Hummel, 4	Hummel, 52	Bell, 16	Rucker, 2.24
1910	64	90	6th	40	Dahlen	Wheat, .284	Wheat, 172	Daubert, 8	Hummel, 74	Rucker, 17	Rucker, 2.58
1911	64	86	7th	33½	Dahlen	Daubert, .307	Daubert, 176	Erwin, 7	Wheat, 76	Rucker, 22	Ragan, 2.11
1912	58	95	7th	46	Dahlen	Daubert, .308	Daubert, 172	Wheat, 8	Daubert, 66	Rucker, 18	Rucker, 2.21
1913	65	84	6th	34½	Dahlen	Daubert, .350	Daubert, 178	Cutshaw, Stengel, Wheat, 7	Cutshaw, 80	Ragan, 15	Reulbach, 2.05
1914	75	79	5th	19½	Robinson	Daubert, .329	Wheat, 170	Wheat, 9	Wheat, 89	Pfeffer, 23	Pfeffer, 1.97
1915	80	72	3rd	10	Robinson	Daubert, .301	Daubert, 164	Wheat, 5	Wheat, 66	Pfeffer, 19	Pfeffer, 2.10
1916	94	60	1st	+2½	Robinson	Daubert, .316	Wheat, 177	Wheat, 9	Wheat, 73	Pfeffer, 25	Marquard, 1.58
1917	70	81	7th	26½	Robinson	Wheat, .312	Olson, 156	Hickman, Stengel, 6	Stengel, 73	Marquard, 19	Pfeffer, 2.23
1918	57	69	5th	25½	Robinson	Wheat, .335	Wheat, 137	Myers, 4	Wheat, 51	Grimes, 19	Grimes, 2.14
1919	69	71	5th	27	Robinson	Myers, .307	Olson, 164	Griffith, 6	Myers, 73	Pfeffer, 17	S. Smith, 2.24
1920	93	61	1st	+7	Robinson	Wheat, .328	Wheat, 191	Wheat, 9	Myers, 80	Grimes, 23	S. Smith, 1.85
1921	77	75	5th	16½	Robinson	Kilduff, .388	J. Johnston, 203	Wheat, 14	Wheat, 85	Grimes, 22	Grimes, 2.83
1922	76	78	6th	17	Robinson	Wheat, .335	Wheat, 201	Wheat, 16	Wheat, 112	Ruether, 21	Shriver, 2.99
1923	76	78	6th	19½	Robinson	Fournier, .351	J. Johnston, 203	Fournier, 22	Fournier, 102	Grimes, 21	Decatur, 2.58
1924	92	62	2nd	1½	Robinson	Wheat, .375	Wheat, 212	Fournier, 27	Fournier, 116	Vance, 28	Vance, 2.16
1925	68	85	*6th	27	Robinson	Wheat, .359	Wheat, 221	Fournier, 22	Fournier, 130	Vance, 22	Vance, 3.53
1926	71	82	6th	17½	Robinson	Herman, .319	Herman, 158	Fournier, Herman, 11	Herman, 81	Petty, 17	Petty, 2.84
1927	65	88	6th	28½	Robinson	Hendrick, .310	Partridge, 149	Herman, 14	Herman, 73	Vance, 16	Vance, 2.70
1928	77	76	6th	17½	Robinson	Herman, .340	Bissonette, 188	Bissonette, 25	Bissonette, 106	Vance, 22	Vance, 2.09
1929	70	83	6th	28½	Robinson	Herman, .381	Herman, 217	Frederick, 24	Herman, 113	Clark, 16	Clark, 3.74
1930	86	68	4th	6	Robinson	Herman, .393	Herman, 241	Herman, 35	Herman, 130	Vance, 17	Vance, 2.61
1931	79	73	4th	21	Robinson	O'Doul, .336	Herman, 191	Herman, 18	Herman, 97	Clark, 14	Clark, 3.20
1932	81	73	3rd	9	Carey	O'Doul, .368	O'Doul, 219	H. Wilson, 23	H. Wilson, 123	Clark, 20	Clark, 3.49
1933	65	88	6th	26½	Carey	Frederick, .308	Frederick, 171	Cuccinello, D. Taylor, H. Wilson, 9	Cuccinello, 65	Mungo, 16	Mungo, 2.72
1934	71	81	6th	23½	Stengel	Leslie, .332	Leslie, 181	Cuccinello, Koenecke, 14	Leslie, 102	Mungo, 18	Leonard, 3.28
1935	70	83	5th	29½	Stengel	Leslie, .308	Leslie, 160	Frey, 11	Leslie, 93	Mungo, 16	Clark, 3.30
1936	67	87	7th	25	Stengel	Stripp, .317	Hassett, 197	Phelps, 5	Hassett, 82	Mungo, 18	Mungo, 3.35
1937	62	91	6th	33½	Grimes	Manush, .333	Hassett, 169	Lavagetto, 8	Manush, 73	Butcher, Hamlin, 11	Mungo, 2.91
1938	69	80	7th	18½	Grimes	Koy, .299	Koy, 156	Camilli, 24	Camilli, 100	Hamlin, Tamulis, 12	Fitzsimmons, 3.02
1939	84	69	3rd	12½	Durocher	Lavagetto, .300	Lavagetto, 176	Camilli, 26	Camilli, 104	Hamlin, 20	Wyatt, 2.31
1940	88	65	2nd	12	Durocher	Walker, .308	Walker, 171	Camilli, 23	Camilli, 96	Fitzsimmons, 16	Fitzsimmons, 2.81
1941	100	54	1st	+2½	Durocher	Reiser, .343	Reiser, 184	Camilli, 34	Camilli, 120	Higbe, Wyatt, 22	Wyatt, 2.34
1942	104	50	2nd	2	Durocher	Reiser, .310	Medwick, 166	Camilli, 26	Camilli, 109	Wyatt, 19	French, 1.83
1943	81	72	3rd	23½	Durocher	Herman, .330	Herman, 193	Galan, 9	Herman, 100	Wyatt, 14	Wyatt, 2.49
1944	63	91	7th	42	Durocher	Walker, .357	Walker, 191	Walker, 13	Galan, 93	C. Davis, 10	C. Davis, 3.34
1945	87	67	3rd	11	Durocher	Rosen, .325	Rosen, 197	Rosen, 12	Walker, 124	Gregg, 18	Branca, 3.03
1946	96	60	†2nd	2	Durocher	Walker, .319	Walker, 184	Reiser, 11	Walker, 116	Higbe, 17	Casey, Melton, 1.99
1947	94	60	1st	+5	Sukeforth, Shotton	Reiser, .309	Robinson, 175	Reese, Robinson, 12	Walker, 94	Branca, 21	Branca, 2.67
1948	84	70	3rd	7½	Durocher, Shotton	Furillo, .297	Robinson, 170	Hermanski, 15	Robinson, 85	Barney, 15	Roe, 2.63
1949	97	57	1st	+1	Shotton	Robinson, .342	Robinson, 203	Hodges, Snider, 23	Robinson, 124	Newcombe, 17	Roe, 2.79
1950	89	65	2nd	2	Shotton	Robinson, .328	Snider, 199	Hodges, 32	Hodges, 113	Newcombe, Roe, 19	Roe, 3.30
1951	97	60	†2nd	1	Dressen	Robinson, .338	Furillo, 197	Hodges, 40	Campanella, 108	Roe, 22	Roe, 3.04
1952	96	57	1st	+4½	Dressen	Robinson, .308	Snider, 162	Hodges, 32	Hodges, 102	Black, 15	Black, 2.15
1953	105	49	1st	+13	Dressen	Furillo, .344	Snider, 198	Snider, 42	Campanella, 142	Erskine, 20	Labine, 2.77
1954	92	62	2nd	5	Alston	Snider, .341	Snider, 199	Hodges, 42	Hodges, Snider, 130	Erskine, 18	Meyer, 3.99
1955	98	55	1st	+13½	Alston	Campanella, .318	Snider, 166	Snider, 42	Snider, 136	Newcombe, 20	Craig, 2.78
1956	93	61	1st	+1	Alston	Gilliam, .300	Gilliam, 178	Snider, 43	Snider, 101	Newcombe, 27	Drysdale, 2.64
1957	84	70	3rd	11	Alston	Furillo, .306	Hodges, 173	Snider, 40	Hodges, 98	Drysdale, 17	Podres, 2.66
						LOS ANGELES DODGERS					
1958	71	83	7th	21	Alston	Furillo, .290	Gilliam, 145	Hodges, Neal, 22	Furillo, 83	Podres, 13	Podres, 3.73
1959	88	68	‡1st	+2	Alston	Snider, .308	Neal, 177	Hodges, 25	Snider, 88	Drysdale, 17	Drysdale, 3.45
1960	82	72	4th	13	Alston	Larker, .323	Wills, 152	Howard, 23	Larker, 78	Drysdale, 15	Drysdale, 2.84
1961	89	65	2nd	4	Alston	Moon, .328	Wills, 173	Roseboro, 18	Moon, 88	Koufax, Podres, 18	Perranoski, 2.65
1962	102	63	†2nd	1	Alston	T. Davis, .346	T. Davis, 230	Howard, 31	T. Davis, 153	Drysdale, 25	Koufax, 2.54
1963	99	63	1st	+6	Alston	T. Davis, .326	T. Davis, 181	Howard, 28	T. Davis, 88	Koufax, 25	Koufax, 1.88
1964	80	82	*6th	13	Alston	W. Davis, .294	W. Davis, 180	Howard, 24	T. Davis, 86	Koufax, 19	Koufax, 1.74
1965	97	65	1st	+2	Alston	Wills, .286	Wills, 186	Johnson, Lefebvre, 12	Fairly, 70	Koufax, 26	Koufax, 2.04
1966	95	67	1st	+1½	Alston	Fairly, .288	W. Davis, 177	Lefebvre, 24	Lefebvre, 74	Koufax, 27	Koufax, 1.73
1967	73	89	8th	28½	Alston	Hunt, .263	W. Davis, 146	Ferrara, 16	Fairly, 55	Osteen, 17	Perranoski, 2.45
1968	76	86	7th	21	Alston	Haller, .285	W. Davis, 161	Gabrielson, 10	Haller, 53	Drysdale, 14	Drysdale, 2.15
						WEST DIVISION					
1969	85	77	4th	8	Alston	W. Davis, .311	Sizemore, 160	Kosco, 19	Kosco, 74	Osteen, Singer, 20	Singer, 2.34
1970	87	74	2nd	14½	Alston	Parker, .319	Parker, 196	Grabarkewitz, 17	Parker, 111	Osteen, 16	Singer, Vance, 3.13
1971	89	73	2nd	1	Alston	W. Davis, .309	W. Davis, 198	Allen, 23	Allen, 90	Downing, 20	Brewer, 1.89
1972	85	70	3rd	10½	Alston	Mota, .323	W. Davis, 178	W. Davis, Robinson, 19	W. Davis, 79	Osteen, 20	Sutton, 2.08
1973	95	66	2nd	3½	Alston	Crawford, .295	W. Davis, 171	Ferguson, 25	Ferguson, 88	Sutton, 18	Sutton, 2.42
1974	102	60	§1st	+4	Alston	Buckner, .314	Garvey, 200	Wynn, 32	Garvey, 111	Messersmith, 20	Marshall, 2.42
1975	88	74	2nd	20	Alston	Garvey, .319	Garvey, 210	Cey, 25	Cey, 101	Messersmith, 19	Messersmith, 2.29
1976	92	70	2nd	10	Alston, Lasorda	Garvey, .317	Garvey, 200	Cey, 23	Cey, Garvey, 80	Sutton, 21	Hough, 2.20
1977	98	64	§1st	+10	Lasorda	R. Smith, .307	Garvey, 192	Garvey, 33	Garvey, 115	John, 20	Hooton, 2.62
1978	95	67	§1st	+2½	Lasorda	Garvey, .316	Garvey, 202	R. Smith, 29	Garvey, 113	Hooton, 19	Welch, 2.03
1979	79	83	3rd	11½	Lasorda	Garvey, .315	Garvey, 204	Cey, Garvey, Lopes, 28	Garvey, 110	Sutcliffe, 17	Hooton, 2.97
1980	92	71	∞2nd	1	Lasorda	Garvey, .304	Garvey, 200	Baker, 29	Garvey, 106	Reuss, 18	Sutton, 2.20
1981	63	47	▲§1st/4th	—	Lasorda	Baker, .320	Baker, 128	Cey, 13	Garvey, 64	Valenzuela, 13	Hooton, 2.28
1982	88	74	2nd	1	Lasorda	Guerrero, .304	Sax, 180	Guerrero, 32	Guerrero, 100	Valenzuela, 19	Howe, 2.08
1983	91	71	◆1st	+3	Lasorda	Guerrero, .298	Sax, 175	Guerrero, 32	Guerrero, 103	Valenzuela, Welch, 15	Niedenfuer, 1.90
1984	79	83	4th	13	Lasorda	Guerrero, .303	Guerrero, 162	Marshall, 21	Guerrero, 72	Welch, 13	Pena, 2.48
1985	95	67	◆1st	+5½	Lasorda	Guerrero, .320	Guerrero, 156	Guerrero, 33	Marshall, 95	Hershiser, 19	Hershiser, 2.03
1986	73	89	5th	23	Lasorda	Sax, .332	Sax, 210	Stubbs, 23	Madlock, 60	Valenzuela, 21	Valenzuela, 3.14
1987	73	89	4th	17	Lasorda	Guerrero, .338	Guerrero, 184	Guerrero, 27	Guerrero, 89	Hershiser, 16	Hershiser, 3.06
1988	94	67	§1st	+7	Lasorda	Gibson, .290	Sax, 175	Gibson, 25	Marshall, 82	Hershiser, 23	Pena, 1.91
1989	77	83	4th	14	Lasorda	Randolph, .282	Randolph, 155	Murray, 20	Murray, 88	Belcher, Hershiser, 15	Hershiser, 2.31
1990	86	76	2nd	5	Lasorda	Murray, .330	Murray, 184	Daniels, 27	Murray, 95	R. Martinez, 20	Crews, 2.77
1991	93	69	2nd	1	Lasorda	Butler, .296	Butler, 182	Strawberry, 28	Strawberry, 99	R. Martinez, 17	Belcher, 2.62
1992	63	99	6th	35	Lasorda	Butler, .309	Butler, 171	Karros, 20	Karros, 88	Candiotti, 11	Astacio, 1.98
1993	81	81	4th	23	Lasorda	Piazza, .318	Butler, 181	Piazza, 35	Piazza, 112	Astacio, 14	P. Martinez, 2.61
1994	58	56	1st	+3½	Lasorda	Piazza, .319	Mondesi, 133	Piazza, 24	Piazza, 92	R. Martinez, 12	Gross, 3.60
1995	78	66	■1st	+1	Lasorda	Piazza, .346	Karros, 164	Karros, Piazza, 32	Karros, 105	Martinez, 17	Nomo, 2.54
1996	90	72	■2nd	1	Lasorda, Russell	Piazza, .336	Mondesi, 188	Karros, 36	Karros, 111	Nomo, 16	Nomo, 3.19
1997	88	74	2nd	2	Russell	Piazza, .362	Piazza, 201	Piazza, 40	Piazza, 124	Nomo, Park, 14	Valdes, 2.65
1998	83	79	3rd	15	Russell, Hoffman	Sheffield, .302	Mondesi, 162	Mondesi, 30	Mondesi, 90	Perez, Valdes, 11	Bohanon, 2.67
1999	77	85	3rd	23	Johnson	Grudzielanek, .326	Karros, 176	Karros, Sheffield, 34	Karros, 112	Brown, 18	Brown, 3.00

* Tied for position. † Lost pennant playoff. ‡ Won pennant playoff. § Won Championship Series. ∞ Lost division playoff. ▲ First half 36-21; second half 27-26. ◆ Lost Championship Series. ■ Lost Division Series.

Note: Batting average minimum 350 at-bats; ERA minimum 90 innings pitched.

MILWAUKEE BREWERS

FRANCHISE CHRONOLOGY

First season: 1969, in Seattle, as part of a two-team American League expansion. The Pilots defeated California, 4-3, in their Major League debut, but that's about the only thing that went right. By season's end, the Pilots were resting in the cellar of the A.L. West Division with 98 losses and battling serious financial problems. Before the 1970 campaign could get under way, Seattle already held distinction as a here-today-gone-tomorrow Major League city.

1970-present: Baseball, American League-style, returned to Milwaukee after a four-year absence when the Pilots were shifted from Seattle and renamed the Brewers. Milwaukee, former home of the National League Braves, lost its A.L. debut, 12-0, to the Angels and posted only one more victory in its first season than the Pilots had in Seattle. It would take eight years for the Brewers to enjoy a winning season and 11 before they would qualify for postseason play—a one-time division playoff set up because of the 1981 players' strike. Milwaukee's banner season came a year later when the Brewers won their only A.L. pennant and dropped a seven-game World Series heartbreaker to St. Louis. The team made history after the 1997 season when it switched from the American League to the National League—the first ever to make such a crossover.

Shortstop/outfielder Robin Yount.

BREWERS VS. A.L. OPPONENTS BY DECADE

	A's	Indians	Orioles	Red Sox	Tigers	Twins	White Sox	Yankees	Angels	Rangers	Royals	Blue Jays	Mariners	Interleague	Decade Record
1969	5-13	5-7	3-9	6-6	2-10	6-12	8-10	5-7	9-9	7-5	8-10				64-98
1970-79	54-74	78-75	54-100	63-93	66-91	54-75	62-68	74-83	67-61	67-49	48-80	30-13	21-11		738-873
1980-89	50-64	70-56	59-64	67-62	64-66	68-52	58-55	62-61	54-61	63-52	59-58	71-56	59-53		804-760
1990-97	50-35	41-56	45-52	47-50	56-42	52-46	41-56	39-56	37-47	44-46	47-50	52-45	35-48	8-7	594-636
Totals	159-186	194-194	161-225	183-211	188-209	180-185	169-189	180-207	167-178	181-152	162-198	153-114	115-112	8-7	2200-2367

Interleague results: 1-2 vs. Cubs; 0-3 vs. Reds; 2-1 vs. Astros; 2-1 vs. Pirates; 3-0 vs. Cardinals.

BREWERS VS. N.L. OPPONENTS BY DECADE

	Braves	Cardinals	Cubs	Dodgers	Giants	Phillies	Pirates	Reds	Astros	Mets	Expos	Padres	Marlins	Rockies	D'backs	Interleague	Decade Record
1998-99	4-12	10-14	12-12	6-12	9-9	9-9	14-9	11-12	7-17	3-13	11-7	6-11	13-5	10-10	7-11	16-12	148-175
Totals	4-12	10-14	12-12	6-12	9-9	9-9	14-9	11-12	7-17	3-13	11-7	6-11	13-5	10-10	7-11	16-12	148-175

Interleague results: 4-2 vs. White Sox; 3-3 vs. Indians; 3-3 vs. Tigers; 4-2 vs. Royals; 2-2 vs. Twins.

MANAGERS

(Seattle Pilots, 1969)

Name	Years	Record
Joe Schultz	1969	64-98
Dave Bristol	1970-72	144-209
Del Crandall	1972-75	271-338
Alex Grammas	1976-77	133-190
George Bamberger	1978-80, 1985-86	377-351
Buck Rodgers	1980-82	124-102
Harvey Kuenn	1982-83	160-118
Rene Lachemann	1984	67-94
Tom Trebelhorn	1986-91	422-397
Phil Garner	1992-99	563-617
Jim Lefebvre	1999	22-27

A.L. PENNANT WINNERS

Year	Record	Manager	Series Result
1982	95-67	Rodgers, Kuenn	Lost to Cardinals

EAST DIVISION CHAMPIONS

Year	Record	Manager	ALCS Result
*1981	62-47	Rodgers	None
1982	95-67	Rodgers, Kuenn	Defeated Angels

* Second-half champion; lost division playoff to Yankees.

ALL-TIME RECORD OF EXPANSION TEAMS

Team	W	L	Pct.	DT	P	WS
Arizona	165	159	.509	1	0	0
Kansas City	2,471	2,412	.506	6	2	1
Toronto	1,784	1,818	.495	5	2	2
Houston	2,980	3,048	.494	6	0	0
Montreal	2,387	2,501	.488	2	0	0
Anaheim	2,987	3,201	.483	3	0	0
Milwaukee	2,348	2,542	.480	2	1	0
Colorado	512	559	.478	0	0	0
New York	2,840	3,178	.472	4	3	2
Texas	2,881	3,290	.467	4	0	0
San Diego	2,239	2,656	.457	3	2	0
Seattle	1,624	1,977	.451	2	0	0
Florida	472	596	.442	0	1	1
Tampa Bay	132	192	.407	0	0	0

DT—Division Titles. P—Pennants won. WS—World Series won.

ATTENDANCE HIGHS

Total	Season	Park
2,397,131	1983	County Stadium
1,978,896	1982	County Stadium
1,970,735	1989	County Stadium
1,923,238	1988	County Stadium
1,918,343	1979	County Stadium

BALLPARK CHRONOLOGY

County Stadium (1970-present)

Capacity: 53,192.
First game: California 12, Brewers 0 (April 7, 1970).
First batter: Sandy Alomar, Angels.
First hit: Alex Johnson, Angels (triple).
First run: Alex Johnson, Angels (2nd inning).
First home run: Bobby Knoop, Angels (April 10).
First winning pitcher: Andy Messersmith, Angels.
First-season attendance: 933,690.

Sick's Stadium, Seattle (1969)

Capacity: 25,420.
First game: Pilots 7, Chicago 0 (April 11, 1969).
First-season attendance: 677,944.

A.L. MVPs

Rollie Fingers, P, 1981
Robin Yount, SS, 1982
Robin Yount, OF, 1989

CY YOUNG WINNERS

Rollie Fingers, RH, 1981
Pete Vuckovich, RH, 1982

ROOKIE OF THE YEAR

Pat Listach, SS, 1992

RETIRED UNIFORMS

No.	Name	Pos.
4	Paul Molitor	3B-DH
19	Robin Yount	SS-OF
34	Rollie Fingers	P
44	Hank Aaron	OF

HISTORY

Paul Molitor's journey to 3,000 career hits started in Milwaukee.

MILESTONE PERFORMANCES

25-plus home runs
45—Gorman Thomas 1979
41—Ben Oglivie 1980
39—Gorman Thomas 1982
38—Gorman Thomas 1980
        Jeromy Burnitz 1998
36—George Scott 1975
34—Larry Hisle 1978
        Ben Oglivie 1982
        John Jaha 1996
33—Rob Deer 1986
        Jeromy Burnitz 1999
32—Gorman Thomas 1978
        Cecil Cooper 1982
31—Tommy Harper 1970
        Greg Vaughn 1996
30—Cecil Cooper 1983
        Greg Vaughn 1993
29—Ben Oglivie 1979
        Robin Yount 1982
        Rob Deer 1987
28—Sixto Lezcano 1979
27—Rob Deer 1990
        Greg Vaughn 1991
        Jeromy Burnitz 1997
26—Rob Deer 1989
25—Don Mincher 1969
        Dave May 1973
        Don Money 1977
        Cecil Cooper 1980
        Dale Sveum 1987

100-plus RBIs
126—Cecil Cooper 1983
125—Jeromy Burnitz 1998
123—Gorman Thomas 1979
122—Cecil Cooper 1980
121—Cecil Cooper 1982
118—Ben Oglivie 1980
        John Jaha 1996
115—Larry Hisle 1978
114—Robin Yount 1982
112—Gorman Thomas 1982
109—George Scott 1975
108—Ted Simmons 1983
107—George Scott 1973
106—Cecil Cooper 1979
105—Gorman Thomas 1980
103—Robin Yount 1987, 1989
        Jeromy Burnitz 1999
102—Ben Oglivie 1982
101—Sixto Lezcano 1979

20-plus victories
1973—Jim Colborn 20-12
1978—Mike Caldwell 22-9
1986—Teddy Higuera 20-11

A.L. home run champions
1975—George Scott *36
1979—Gorman Thomas 45
1980—Ben Oglivie *41
1982—Gorman Thomas *39
* Tied for league lead

A.L. RBI champions
1975—George Scott 109
1980—Cecil Cooper 122
1983—Cecil Cooper *126
* Tied for league lead

A.L. batting champions
None

A.L. ERA champions
None

A.L. strikeout champions
None

No-hit pitchers
(9 innings or more)
1987—Juan Nieves ....7-0 vs. Baltimore

Longest hitting streaks
39—Paul Molitor 1987
24—Dave May 1973
22—Cecil Cooper 1980
19—Robin Yount 1989
        Paul Molitor 1989, 1990
        Darryl Hamilton 1991
18—Robin Yount 1980
17—Cecil Cooper 1982
        Paul Molitor 1982
        Pat Listach 1992
16—John Briggs 1974
        Robin Yount 1976
        Cecil Cooper 1979
        Paul Molitor 1979, 1985
        Ben Oglivie 1979, 1983
        Ted Simmons 1983
        Gary Sheffield 1990
        Greg Vaughn 1991
15—Billy Conigliaro 1972
        Don Money 1973
        Paul Molitor 1978
        Darryl Hamilton 1991, 1992
        B.J. Surhoff 1993
        Kevin Seitzer 1994
        Greg Vaughn 1996

Dependable second baseman Jim Gantner played 1,801 games in a Brewers uniform, third on the team's all-time list.

INDIVIDUAL SEASON, GAME RECORDS

Slugging outfielder Gorman Thomas topped the 30-home run plateau four times in the 1970s and '80s.

SEASON

Batting

At-bats	666	Paul Molitor	1982
Runs	136	Paul Molitor	1982
Hits	219	Cecil Cooper	1980
Singles	157	Cecil Cooper	1980
Doubles	49	Robin Yount	1980
Triples	16	Paul Molitor	1979
Home runs	45	Gorman Thomas	1979
Home runs, rookie	17	Danny Walton	1970
		Greg Vaughn	1990
Grand slams	3	John Jaha	1995
Total bases	367	Robin Yount	1982
RBIs	126	Cecil Cooper	1983
Walks	98	Gorman Thomas	1979
Most strikeouts	186	Rob Deer	1987
Fewest strikeouts	35	Fernando Vina	1996
Batting average	.353	Paul Molitor	1987
Slugging pct.	.578	Robin Yount	1982
Stolen bases	73	Tommy Harper	1969

Pitching

Games	83	Ken Sanders	1971
Complete games	23	Mike Caldwell	1978
Innings	314.1	Jim Colborn	1973
Wins	22	Mike Caldwell	1978
Losses	20	Clyde Wright	1974
Winning pct.	.846 (11-2)	Cal Eldred	1992
Walks	106	Pete Broberg	1975
Strikeouts	240	Teddy Higuera	1987
Shutouts	6	Mike Caldwell	1978
Home runs allowed	35	Mike Caldwell	1983
Lowest ERA	2.36	Mike Caldwell	1978
Saves	37	Bob Wickman	1999

GAME

Batting

Runs	4	Last by Jeromy Burnitz	9-23-99
Hits	6	John Briggs	8-4-73
		Kevin Reimer	8-24-93
Doubles	3	Last by Ron Belliard	7-1-99
Triples	2	Last by Jose Valentin	9-29-99
Home runs	3	Last by Jose Valentin	4-3-98
RBIs	7	Ted Kubiak	7-18-70
Total bases	13	Paul Molitor	5-12-82
		Fernando Vina	9-12-96
Stolen bases	4	Tommy Harper	6-18-69
		John Jaha	9-11-92

HISTORY

-435-

BATTING

Games

Robin Yount	2,856
Paul Molitor	1,856
Jim Gantner	1,801
Cecil Cooper	1,490
Charlie Moore	1,283
Don Money	1,196
Ben Oglivie	1,149
B.J. Surhoff	1,102
Gorman Thomas	1,102
Greg Vaughn	903

At-bats

Robin Yount	11,008
Paul Molitor	7,520
Jim Gantner	6,189
Cecil Cooper	6,019
Don Money	4,330
Ben Oglivie	4,136
Charlie Moore	3,926
B.J. Surhoff	3,884
Gorman Thomas	3,544
Greg Vaughn	3,244

Runs

Robin Yount	1,632
Paul Molitor	1,275
Cecil Cooper	821
Jim Gantner	726
Don Money	596
Ben Oglivie	567
Greg Vaughn	528
Gorman Thomas	524
B.J. Surhoff	472
Jeff Cirillo	444

Hits

Robin Yount	3,142
Paul Molitor	2,281
Cecil Cooper	1,815
Jim Gantner	1,696
Don Money	1,168
Ben Oglivie	1,144
B.J. Surhoff	1,064
Charlie Moore	1,029
Jeff Cirillo	864
George Scott	851

Doubles

Robin Yount	583
Paul Molitor	405
Cecil Cooper	345
Jim Gantner	262
Don Money	215
Ben Oglivie	194
B.J. Surhoff	194
Jeff Cirillo	186
Charlie Moore	177
Gorman Thomas	172

Triples

Robin Yount	126
Paul Molitor	86
Charlie Moore	42
Jim Gantner	38
Cecil Cooper	33
Fernando Vina	26
B.J. Surhoff	24
Sixto Lezcano	22
Darryl Hamilton	21
Ben Oglivie	21

Home runs

Robin Yount	251
Gorman Thomas	208
Cecil Cooper	201
Ben Oglivie	176
Greg Vaughn	169
Paul Molitor	160
Rob Deer	137
Don Money	134
George Scott	115
John Jaha	105
Dave Nilsson	105

Total bases

Robin Yount	4,730
Paul Molitor	3,338
Cecil Cooper	2,829
Jim Gantner	2,175
Ben Oglivie	1,908
Don Money	1,825
Gorman Thomas	1,635
Greg Vaughn	1,490
B.J. Surhoff	1,477
Charlie Moore	1,395

Runs batted in

Robin Yount	1,406
Cecil Cooper	944
Paul Molitor	790
Ben Oglivie	685

SEASON

Batting

Most at-bats	5,733	1982
Most runs	894	1996
Fewest runs	494	1972
Most hits	1,599	1982
Most singles	1,107	1991
Most doubles	304	1996
Most triples	57	1983
Most home runs	216	1982
Fewest home runs	82	1992
Most grand slams	10	1995
Most pinch-hit home runs	7	1998
Most total bases	2,605	1982
Most stolen bases	256	1992
Highest batting average	.280	1979
Lowest batting average	.229	1971
Highest slugging pct	.455	1982

Pitching

Lowest ERA	3.38	1971
Highest ERA	5.14	1996
Most complete games	62	1978
Most shutouts	23	1971
Most saves	51	1988
Most walks	653	1969
Most strikeouts	1,063	1998

Fielding

Most errors	180	1975
Fewest errors	89	1992
Most double plays	189	1980
Highest fielding average	.986	1992

General

Most games won	95	1979, 1982
Most games lost	98	1969
Highest win pct	.590	1979
Lowest win pct	.395	1969

GAME, INNING

Batting

Most runs, game	22	8-28-92
Most runs, inning	13	7-8-90
Most hits, game	31	8-28-92
Most home runs, game	7	4-29-80
Most total bases, game	38	8-28-92

The sweet swing of first baseman Cecil Cooper produced 1,815 hits, 201 home runs and 944 RBIs for the Brewers.

Gorman Thomas	605
Jim Gantner	568
Greg Vaughn	566
Don Money	529
B.J. Surhoff	524
Dave Nilsson	470

Extra-base hits

Robin Yount	960
Paul Molitor	651
Cecil Cooper	579
Gorman Thomas	392
Ben Oglivie	391
Don Money	369
Jim Gantner	347
Greg Vaughn	340
B.J. Surhoff	275
Dave Nilsson	272

Batting average
(Minimum 500 games)

Jeff Cirillo	.307
Paul Molitor	.303
Cecil Cooper	.302
Kevin Seitzer	.300
Mark Loretta	.294
Darryl Hamilton	.290
Fernando Vina	.286
Robin Yount	.285
Dave Nilsson	.284
George Scott	.283

Stolen bases

Paul Molitor	412
Robin Yount	271
Jim Gantner	137
Tommy Harper	136
Pat Listach	112
Darryl Hamilton	109
Mike Felder	108
B.J. Surhoff	102
Jose Valentin	78
Cecil Cooper	77

PITCHING

Earned-run average
(Minimum 500 innings)

Dan Plesac	3.21
Chuck Crim	3.47
Teddy Higuera	3.61
Jim Colborn	3.65
Lary Sorensen	3.72
Mike Caldwell	3.74
Skip Lockwood	3.75
Chris Bosio	3.76
Ed Rodriguez	3.78
Marty Pattin	3.82

Wins

Jim Slaton	117
Mike Caldwell	102
Teddy Higuera	94
Moose Haas	91
Bill Wegman	81
Chris Bosio	67
Bill Travers	65
Cal Eldred	64
Jamie Navarro	62
Jim Colborn	57

Losses

Jim Slaton	121
Bill Wegman	90
Mike Caldwell	80
Moose Haas	79
Bill Travers	67
Cal Eldred	65
Teddy Higuera	64
Chris Bosio	62
Jim Colborn	60
Jerry Augustine	59
Jamie Navarro	59

Innings pitched

Jim Slaton	2,025.1
Mike Caldwell	1,604.1
Moose Haas	1,542.0
Bill Wegman	1,482.2
Teddy Higuera	1,380.0
Chris Bosio	1,190.0
Jim Colborn	1,118.0
Cal Eldred	1,078.2
Bill Travers	1,068.1
Jamie Navarro	1,043.0

Strikeouts

Teddy Higuera	1,081
Jim Slaton	929
Moose Haas	800
Chris Bosio	749
Bill Wegman	696
Cal Eldred	686
Mike Caldwell	540
Jamie Navarro	524
Bob McClure	497
Jim Colborn	495

Bases on balls

Jim Slaton	760
Cal Eldred	448
Teddy Higuera	443
Moose Haas	408
Bill Travers	392
Bob McClure	363
Mike Caldwell	353
Bill Wegman	352
Jerry Augustine	340
Scott Karl	324

Games

Dan Plesac	365
Jim Slaton	364
Bob McClure	352
Chuck Crim	332
Mike Fetters	289
Jerry Augustine	279
Bill Wegman	262
Bill Castro	253
Moose Haas	245
Mike Caldwell	239

Shutouts

Jim Slaton	19
Mike Caldwell	18
Teddy Higuera	12
Bill Travers	10
Chris Bosio	8
Moose Haas	8
Jim Colborn	7
Lary Sorensen	7
Jerry Augustine	6
Jamie Navarro	6
Bill Parsons	6
Marty Pattin	6

Saves

Dan Plesac	133
Rollie Fingers	97
Mike Fetters	79
Bob Wickman	63
Doug Henry	61
Ken Sanders	61
Doug Jones	49
Bill Castro	44
Chuck Crim	42
Tom Murphy	41

Year	W	L	Place	Games Back	Manager	Batting avg.	Hits	Home runs	RBIs	Wins	ERA
									Leaders		
						SEATTLE PILOTS					
						WEST DIVISION					
1969	64	98	6th	33	Schultz	T. Davis, .271	Harper, 126	Mincher, 25	T. Davis, 80	Brabender, 13	Gelnar, 3.31
						MILWAUKEE BREWERS					
1970	65	97	4th	33	Bristol	Harper, .296	Harper, 179	Harper, 31	Harper, 82	Pattin, 14	Sanders, 1.75
1971	69	92	6th	32	Bristol	May, .277	Harper, 151	Briggs, 21	May, 65	Pattin, 14	Sanders, 1.91
						EAST DIVISION					
1972	65	91	6th	21	Bristol, Crandall	Rodriguez, .285	Scott, 154	Briggs, 21	Scott, 88	Lonborg, 14	Lonborg, 2.83
1973	74	88	5th	23	Crandall	Scott, .306	May, 189	May, 25	Scott, 107	Colborn, 20	Colborn, 3.18
1974	76	86	5th	15	Crandall	Money, .283	Scott, 170	Briggs, Scott, 17	Scott, 82	Slaton, 13	Murphy, 1.90
1975	68	94	5th	28	Crandall	Scott, .285	Scott, 176	Scott, 36	Scott, 109	Broberg, 14	Hausman, 4.10
1976	66	95	6th	32	Grammas	Lezcano, .285	Scott, 166	Scott, 18	Scott, 77	Travers, 15	Travers, 2.81
1977	67	95	6th	33	Grammas	Cooper, .300	Cooper, 193	Money, 25	Money, 83	Augustine, 12	Slaton, 3.58
1978	93	69	3rd	6½	Bamberger	Cooper, .312	Bando, 154	Hisle, 34	Hisle, 115	Caldwell, 22	Caldwell, 2.37
1979	95	66	2nd	8	Bamberger	Molitor, .322	Molitor, 188	G. Thomas, 45	G. Thomas, 123	Caldwell, 16	Caldwell, 3.29
1980	86	76	3rd	17	Bamberger, Rodgers	Cooper, .352	Cooper, 219	Oglivie, 41	Cooper, 122	Haas, 16	McClure, 3.07
1981	62	47	*3rd/1st	—	Rodgers	Cooper, .320	Cooper, 133	G. Thomas, 21	Oglivie, 72	Vuckovich, 14	Vuckovich, 3.55
1982	95	67	†1st	+1	Rodgers, Kuenn	Yount, .331	Yount, 210	G. Thomas, 39	Cooper, 121	Vuckovich, 18	Slaton, 3.29
1983	87	75	5th	11	Kuenn	Simmons, Yount, .308	Cooper, 203	Cooper, 30	Cooper, 126	Slaton, 14	Tellmann, 2.80
1984	67	94	7th	36½	Lachemann	Yount, .298	Yount, 186	Yount, 16	Yount, 80	Sutton, 14	Sutton, 3.77
1985	71	90	6th	28	Bamberger	Molitor, .297	Cooper, 185	Cooper, 16	Cooper, 99	Higuera, 15	Darwin, 3.80
1986	77	84	6th	18	Bamberger, Trebelhorn	Yount, .312	Yount, 163	Deer, 33	Deer, 86	Higuera, 20	Higuera, 2.79
1987	91	71	3rd	7	Trebelhorn	Molitor, .353	Yount, 198	Deer, 28	Yount, 103	Higuera, 18	Crim, 3.67
1988	87	75	‡3rd	2	Trebelhorn	Molitor, .312	Molitor, Yount, 190	Deer, 23	Yount, 91	Higuera, 16	Higuera, 2.45
1989	81	81	4th	8	Trebelhorn	Yount, .318	Yount, 195	Deer, 26	Yount, 103	Bosio, 15	Crim, 2.83
1990	74	88	6th	14	Trebelhorn	Sheffield, .294	Parker, 176	Deer, 27	Parker, 92	Robinson, 12	Robinson, 2.91
1991	83	79	4th	8	Trebelhorn	Randolph, .327	Molitor, 216	Vaughn, 27	Vaughn, 98	Navarro, Wegman, 15	Wegman, 2.84
1992	92	70	2nd	4	Garner	Molitor, .320	Molitor, 195	Vaughn, 23	Molitor, 89	Navarro, 17	Eldred, 1.79
1993	69	93	7th	26	Garner	Hamilton, .310	Hamilton, 161	Vaughn, 30	Vaughn, 97	Eldred, 16	Miranda, 3.30
						CENTRAL DIVISION					
1994	53	62	5th	15	Garner	Seitzer, .314	Nilsson, 109	Vaughn, 19	Nilsson, 69	Eldred, 11	Bones, 3.43
1995	65	79	4th	35	Garner	Surhoff, .320	Seitzer, 153	Jaha, 20	Surhoff, 73	Bones, 10	Karl, 4.14
1996	80	82	3rd	19½	Garner	Nilsson, .331	Cirillo, 184	Jaha, 34	Jaha, 118	Karl, 13	McDonald, 3.90
1997	78	83	3rd	8	Garner	Cirillo, .288	Cirillo, 167	Burnitz, 27	Burnitz, 85	Eldred, 13	Wickman, 2.73
						NATIONAL LEAGUE					
						CENTRAL DIVISION					
1998	74	88	5th	28	Garner	Cirillo, .321	Vina, 198	Burnitz, 38	Burnitz, 125	Woodard, Karl, 10	Woodard, 4.18
1999	74	87	5th	22½	Garner, Lefebvre	Cirillo, .326	Cirillo, 198	Burnitz, 33	Burnitz, 103	Nomo, 12	Woodard, 4.52

* First half 31-25; second half 31-22. † Won Championship Series. ‡ Tied for position.

Note: Batting average minimum 350 at-bats; ERA minimum 90 innings pitched.

Don Mincher

SEATTLE joined Kansas City, San Diego and Montreal in the four-team 1969 expansion that brought baseball's membership roster to a modern-record 24 teams. The franchise, which would last only one season in Seattle before moving to Milwaukee as the Brewers, came to life December 1, 1967, when the bid by Pacific Northwest Sports, Inc., was officially approved and the name "Pilots" was adopted three months later.

The Pilots selected 30 players in the October 15, 1968, expansion draft, leading off with veteran first baseman Don Mincher. The Pilots defeated the California Angels, 4-3, in their April 8, 1969, debut at Anaheim Stadium—one of 64 victories the team would post in its brief history. One year later on April 7, the Brewers lost their American League debut, 12-0, to the same Angels.

Expansion draft (October 15, 1968)

Players

Wayne Comer	Detroit	outfield
Tommy Davis	Chicago	outfield
Mike Ferraro	New York	infield
Jim Gosger	Oakland	outfield
Larry Haney	Baltimore	catcher
Tommy Harper	Cleveland	outfield
Steve Hovley	California	outfield
Gerry McNertney	Chicago	catcher
*Don Mincher	California	first base
Ray Oyler	Detroit	shortstop
Lou Piniella	Cleveland	outfield
Rich Rollins	Minnesota	third base
Chico Salmon	Cleveland	second base

Pitchers

Jack Aker	Oakland	righthanded
Dick Baney	Boston	righthanded
Steve Barber	New York	lefthanded
Dick Bates	Washington	righthanded
Gary Bell	Boston	righthanded
Darrell Brandon	Boston	righthanded
Paul Click	California	righthanded
Skip Lockwood	Oakland	righthanded
Mike Marshall	Detroit	righthanded
John Miklos	Washington	lefthanded
John Morris	Baltimore	lefthanded
Marty Pattin	California	righthanded
Bob Richmond	Washington	righthanded
Gerry Schoen	Washington	righthanded
Diego Segui	Oakland	righthanded
Lou Stephen	Minnesota	righthanded
Gary Timberlake	New York	lefthanded

*First pick

Opening day lineups

April 8, 1969 (Seattle Pilots)

Tommy Harper, second base
Steve Whitaker, right field
Tommy Davis, left field
Don Mincher, first base
Rich Rollins, third base
Jim Gosger, center field
Jerry McNertney, catcher
Ray Oyler, shortstop
Marty Pattin, pitcher

April 7, 1970 (Milwaukee Brewers)

Tommy Harper, second base
Russ Snyder, center field
Mike Hegan, first base
Danny Walton, left field
Jerry McNertney, catcher
Steve Hovley, right field
Max Alvis, third base
Ted Kubiak, shortstop
Lew Krausse, pitcher

Tommy Harper

Pilots firsts

First hit: Tommy Harper, April 8, 1969, at California (double)
First home run: Mike Hegan, April 8, 1969, at California
First RBI: Mike Hegan, April 8, 1969, at California
First win: Marty Pattin, April 8, 1968, at California
First shutout: Gary Bell, April 11, 1969, 7-0 vs. Chicago

HISTORY

MONTREAL EXPOS

FRANCHISE CHRONOLOGY

First season: 1969, as one of two National League expansion teams and baseball's first Canadian franchise. The Expos rallied for an 11-10 opening day victory over New York and posted an 8-7 victory over St. Louis six days later in the first Major League game on foreign soil, but they stumbled to a 52-110 first-season record and finished 48 games behind the Mets in the new N.L. East Division.

1970-present: The Expos, one of baseball's so-called small-market franchises, still are looking for their first N.L. pennant and World Series appearance. They came close in 1981, when they survived a strike-forced divisional playoff before suffering a heartbreaking N.L. Championship Series loss to the Los Angeles Dodgers. And they were sailing along with baseball's best record in 1994 when another players' strike brought a sudden halt to the season—and realistic hopes for a championship. When the strike finally ended in 1995, the Expos began auctioning off high-priced players and entered the new season with a talented, but inexperienced, team. While the Expos continue to grope for success, their Canadian cousins, the Toronto Blue Jays, have won two World Series since entering the American League in 1977.

Center fielder Andre Dawson.

EXPOS VS. OPPONENTS BY DECADE

	Braves	Cardinals	Cubs	Dodgers	Giants	Phillies	Pirates	Reds	Astros	Mets	Padres	Marlins	Rockies	Brewers	D'backs	Interleague	Decade Record
1969	4-8	7-11	8-10	2-10	1-11	11-7	5-13	4-8	1-11	5-13	4-8						52-110
1970-79	58-60	85-93	89-88	47-73	59-61	88-90	73-107	46-74	49-71	94-86	60-59						748-862
1980-89	72-45	95-82	95-77	48-67	59-56	87-86	88-86	64-53	55-60	85-89	63-51						811-752
1990-99	50-70	64-61	62-57	56-57	56-59	65-73	65-61	48-57	51-57	69-68	71-40	46-38	30-37	7-11	10-8	26-23	776-777
Totals	184-183	251-247	254-232	153-207	175-187	251-256	231-267	162-192	156-199	253-256	198-158	46-38	30-37	7-11	10-8	26-23	2387-2501

Interleague results: 5-4 vs. Orioles; 6-3 vs. Red Sox; 3-0 vs.Tigers; 4-5 vs. Yankees; 4-9 vs. Blue Jays; 4-2 vs. Devil Rays.

MANAGERS

Name	Years	Record
Gene Mauch	1969-75	499-627
Karl Kuehl	1976	43-85
Charlie Fox	1976	12-22
Dick Williams	1977-81	380-347
Jim Fanning	1981-82, 1984	116-103
Bill Virdon	1983-84	146-147
Buck Rodgers	1985-91	520-499
Tom Runnells	1991-92	68-81
Felipe Alou	1992-99	603-590

EAST DIVISION CHAMPIONS

Year	Record	Manager	NLCS Result
*1981	60-48	Williams, Fanning	Lost to Dodgers
1994	74-40	Alou	None

* Second-half champion; won division playoff over Phillies.

ALL-TIME RECORD OF EXPANSION TEAMS

Team	W	L	Pct.	DT	P	WS
Arizona	165	159	.509	1	0	0
Kansas City	2,471	2,412	.506	6	2	1
Toronto	1,784	1,818	.495	5	2	2
Houston	2,980	3,048	.494	6	0	0
Montreal	2,387	2,501	.488	2	0	0
Anaheim	2,987	3,201	.483	3	0	0
Milwaukee	2,348	2,542	.480	2	1	0
Colorado	512	559	.478	0	0	0
New York	2,840	3,178	.472	4	3	2
Texas	2,881	3,290	.467	4	0	0
San Diego	2,239	2,656	.457	3	2	0
Seattle	1,624	1,977	.451	2	0	0
Florida	472	596	.442	0	1	1
Tampa Bay	132	192	.407	0	0	0

DT—Division Titles. P—Pennants won. WS—World Series won.

BALLPARK CHRONOLOGY

Olympic Stadium (1977-present)
Capacity: 46,500.
First game: Philadelphia 7, Expos 2 (April 15, 1977).
First batter: Jay Johnstone, Phillies.
First hit: Dave Cash, Expos (single).
First run: Greg Luzinski, Phillies (2nd inning).
First home run: Ellis Valentine, Expos.
First winning pitcher: Steve Carlton, Phillies.
First-season attendance: 1,433,757.

Jarry Park (1969-76)
Capacity: 28,000.
First game: Expos 8, St. Louis 7 (April 14, 1969).
First-season attendance: 1,212,608.

ATTENDANCE HIGHS

Total	Season	Park
2,320,651	1983	Olympic Stadium
2,318,292	1982	Olympic Stadium
2,208,175	1980	Olympic Stadium
2,102,173	1979	Olympic Stadium
1,850,324	1987	Olympic Stadium

CY YOUNG WINNER

Pedro Martinez, RH, 1997

ROOKIES OF THE YEAR

Carl Morton, P, 1970
Andre Dawson, OF, 1977

MANAGERS OF THE YEAR

Buck Rodgers, 1987
Felipe Alou, 1994

RETIRED UNIFORMS

No.	Name	Pos.
8	Gary Carter	C
10	Rusty Staub	1B-OF
	Andre Dawson	OF

Outfielder/first baseman Rusty Staub was one of the most popular players in Expos history.

25-plus home runs

42	Vladimir Guerrero	1999
38	Vladimir Guerrero	1998
36	Henry Rodriguez	1996
32	Andre Dawson	1983
31	Gary Carter	1977
30	Rusty Staub	1970
	Larry Parrish	1979
29	Rusty Staub	1969
	Gary Carter	1980, 1982
	Andres Galarraga	1988
28	Bob Bailey	1970
	Tim Wallach	1982
	Rondell White	1997
27	Gary Carter	1984
26	Bob Bailey	1973
	Tim Wallach	1987
	Henry Rodriguez	1997
25	Ellis Valentine	1977, 1978
	Andre Dawson	1978, 1979
	Shane Andrews	1998

100-plus RBIs

131	Vladimir Guerrero	1999
123	Tim Wallach	1987
113	Andre Dawson	1983
109	Al Oliver	1982
	Vladimir Guerrero	1998
106	Gary Carter	1984
103	Ken Singleton	1973
	Henry Rodriguez	1996
101	Gary Carter	1981
100	Hubie Brooks	1985

20-plus victories

1978	Ross Grimsley	20-11

N.L. home run champions
None

N.L. RBI champions

1982	Al Oliver	*109
1984	Gary Carter	*106

* Tied for league lead

N.L. batting champions

1982	Al Oliver	.331
1986	Tim Raines	.334

N.L. ERA champions

1982	Steve Rogers	2.40
1991	Dennis Martinez	2.39
1997	Pedro Martinez	1.90

N.L. strikeout champions
None

No-hit pitchers
(9 innings or more)

1969	Bill Stoneman	7-0 vs. Philadelphia
1972	Bill Stoneman	7-0 vs. New York
1981	Charlie Lea	4-0 vs. San Francisco
1991	Dennis Martinez	2-0 vs. Los Angeles

Longest hitting streaks

31	Vladimir Guerrero	1999
21	Delino DeShields	1993
19	Warren Cromartie	1979
	Andre Dawson	1980
18	Pepe Mangual	1975
	Warren Cromartie	1980
	David Segui	1980
	F.P. Santangelo	1997
17	Bob Bailey	1973
	Tim Raines	1986
	Mark Grudzielanek	1996, 1997
16	Rusty Staub	1971
	Tony Perez	1977
	Ellis Valentine	1978
	Andre Dawson	1981
	Henry Rodriguez	1997
	Brad Fullmer	1999
15	Ken Singleton	1973
	Boots Day	1971
	Warren Cromartie	1978
	Larry Parrish	1978
	Al Oliver	1982
	Delino DeShields	1990
	Mike Lansing	1997

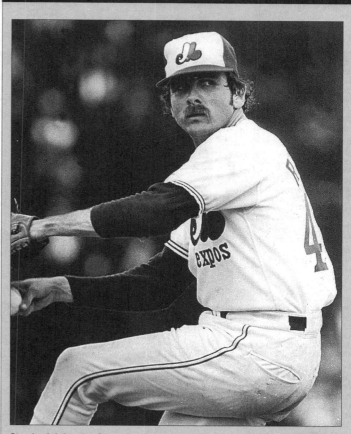

Steady righthander Steve Rogers set a club record when he pitched more than 300 innings in a workhorse 1977 season.

SEASON

Batting

At-bats	659	Warren Cromartie	1979
Runs	133	Tim Raines	1983
Hits	204	Al Oliver	1982
Singles	157	Mark Grudzielanek	1996
Doubles	54	Mark Grudzielanek	1997
Triples	13	3 times	
		Last by Mitch Webster	1986
Home runs	42	Vladimir Guerrero	1999
Home runs, rookie	19	Andre Dawson	1977
		Larry Walker	1990
Grand slams	2	14 times	
		Last by Henry Rodriguez	1997
Total bases	367	Vladimir Guerrero	1998
RBIs	131	Vladimir Guerrero	1999
Walks	123	Ken Singleton	1973
Most strikeouts	169	Andres Galarraga	1990
Fewest strikeouts	29	Dave Cash	1978
Batting average	.339	Moises Alou	1994
Slugging pct.	.600	Vladimir Guerrero	1999
Stolen bases	97	Ron LeFlore	1980

Pitching

Games	92	Mike Marshall	1973
Complete games	20	Bill Stoneman	1971
Innings	301.2	Steve Rogers	1977
Wins	20	Ross Grimsley	1978
Losses	22	Steve Rogers	1974
Winning pct.	.783 (18-5)	Bryn Smith	1985
Walks	146	Bill Stoneman	1971
Strikeouts	305	Pedro Martinez	1997
Shutouts	5	5 times	
		Last by Carlos Perez	1997
Home runs allowed	31	Javier Vazquez	1998
Lowest ERA	1.90	Pedro Martinez	1997
Saves	43	John Wetteland	1993

GAME

Batting

Runs	5	Last by Rondell White	6-11-95
Hits	6	Rondell White	6-11-95
Doubles	3	Last by Wilton Guerrero	6-14-99
Triples	2	Last by Orlando Cabrera	7-30-98
Home runs	3	Last by Tim Wallach	5-4-87
RBIs	8	Last by Tim Wallach	5-13-90
Total bases	14	Larry Parrish	5-29-77, 7-30-78
Stolen bases	4	Last by Marquis Grissom	7-21-92

During Gary Carter's successful 11-year Montreal stay, he ranked as one of the best hitting catchers in the game.

BATTING

Games
Tim Wallach	1,767
Gary Carter	1,503
Andre Dawson	1,443
Tim Raines	1,405
Warren Cromartie	1,038
Larry Parrish	967
Bob Bailey	951
Chris Speier	895
Andres Galarraga	847
Ron Fairly	718

At-bats
Tim Wallach	6,529
Andre Dawson	5,628
Tim Raines	5,305
Gary Carter	5,303
Warren Cromartie	3,796
Larry Parrish	3,411
Andres Galarraga	3,082
Bob Bailey	2,991
Chris Speier	2,902
Marquis Grissom	2,678

Runs
Tim Raines	934
Andre Dawson	828
Tim Wallach	737
Gary Carter	707
Warren Cromartie	446
Marquis Grissom	430
Larry Parrish	421
Bob Bailey	412
Andres Galarraga	394
Larry Walker	368
Rondell White	368

Hits
Tim Wallach	1,694
Tim Raines	1,598
Andre Dawson	1,575
Gary Carter	1,427
Warren Cromartie	1,063
Larry Parrish	896
Andres Galarraga	830
Bob Bailey	791
Marquis Grissom	747
Rondell White	719

Doubles
Tim Wallach	360
Andre Dawson	295
Gary Carter	274
Tim Raines	273
Warren Cromartie	222
Larry Parrish	208
Andres Galarraga	168
Mike Lansing	165
Larry Walker	147
Rondell White	141

Triples
Tim Raines	81
Andre Dawson	67
Tim Wallach	31
Warren Cromartie	30
Delino DeShields	25
Mitch Webster	25
Gary Carter	24
Larry Parrish	24
Bob Bailey	23
Marquis Grissom	23
Rondell White	23

Home Runs
Andre Dawson	225
Gary Carter	220
Tim Wallach	204
Bob Bailey	118
Andres Galarraga	106
Larry Parrish	100
Larry Walker	99
Tim Raines	96
Ellis Valentine	95
Vladimir Guerrero	92

Total bases
Tim Wallach	2,728
Andre Dawson	2,679
Gary Carter	2,409
Tim Raines	2,321
Warren Cromartie	1,525
Larry Parrish	1,452
Andres Galarraga	1,344
Bob Bailey	1,307
Rondell White	1,176
Larry Walker	1,142

SEASON

Batting
Most at-bats	5,675	1977
Most runs	741	1987, 1996
Fewest runs	513	1972
Most hits	1,482	1983
Most singles	1,042	1983
Most doubles	339	1997
Most triples	61	1980
Most home runs	172	1997
Fewest home runs	86	1974
Most grand slams	9	1996
Most pinch-hit home runs	9	1973
Most total bases	2,376	1999
Most stolen bases	237	1980
Highest batting average	.265	1987, 1999
Lowest batting average	.234	1972
Highest slugging pct	.427	1999

Pitching
Lowest ERA	3.08	1988
Highest ERA	4.69	1999
Most complete games	49	1971
Most shutouts	18	1979
Most saves	61	1993
Most walks	716	1970
Most strikeouts	1,206	1996

Fielding
Most errors	184	1969
Fewest errors	110	1990
Most double plays	193	1970
Highest fielding average	.982	1990

General
Most games won	95	1979
Most games lost	110	1969
Highest win pct	.649	1994
Lowest win pct	.321	1969

GAME, INNING

Batting
Most runs, game	21	Last 4-28-96
Most runs, inning	13	5-7-97
Most hits, game	28	7-30-78
Most home runs, game	8	7-30-78
Most total bases, game	58	7-30-78

Third baseman Tim Wallach holds numerous team records, including hits (1,694) and RBIs (905).

Runs batted in
Tim Wallach	905
Andre Dawson	838
Gary Carter	823
Tim Raines	552
Bob Bailey	466
Larry Parrish	444
Andres Galarraga	433
Hubie Brooks	390
Larry Walker	384
Moises Alou	373

Extra-base hits
Tim Wallach	595
Andre Dawson	587
Gary Carter	518
Tim Raines	450
Larry Parrish	332
Warren Cromartie	312
Andres Galarraga	288
Larry Walker	262
Bob Bailey	257
Rondell White	254

Batting average
(Minimum 500 games)
Tim Raines	.301
Rusty Staub	.294
Moises Alou	.292
Rondell White	.292
Ellis Valentine	.288
Larry Walker	.282
Warren Cromartie	.280
Andre Dawson	.280
Marquis Grissom	.279
Hubie Brooks	.279

Stolen bases
Tim Raines	634
Marquis Grissom	266
Andre Dawson	253
Delino DeShields	187
Rodney Scott	139
Otis Nixon	133
Larry Walker	98
Ron LeFlore	97
Mike Lansing	96
Mitch Webster	96

PITCHING

Earned-run average
(Minimum 500 innings)
Tim Burke	2.61
Jeff Reardon	2.84
Ken Hill	3.04
Pedro Martinez	3.06
Dennis Martinez	3.06
Dan Schatzeder	3.09
Mel Rojas	3.11
Steve Rogers	3.17
Jeff Fassero	3.20
Woodie Fryman	3.24

Wins
Steve Rogers	158
Dennis Martinez	100
Bryn Smith	81
Bill Gullickson	72
Steve Renko	68
Jeff Fassero	58
Scott Sanderson	56
Charlie Lea	55
Pedro Martinez	55
Woodie Fryman	51
Bill Stoneman	51

Losses
Steve Rogers	152
Steve Renko	82
Dennis Martinez	72
Bill Stoneman	72
Bryn Smith	71
Bill Gullickson	61
Woodie Fryman	52
Ernie McAnally	49
Jeff Fassero	48
Scott Sanderson	47

Innings pitched
Steve Rogers	2,837.2
Dennis Martinez	1,609.0
Bryn Smith	1,400.1
Steve Renko	1,359.1
Bill Gullickson	1,186.1
Bill Stoneman	1,085.1
Scott Sanderson	883.0
Jeff Fassero	850.0
Pedro Martinez	797.1
Charlie Lea	793.1

Strikeouts
Steve Rogers	1,621
Dennis Martinez	973
Pedro Martinez	843
Bryn Smith	838
Bill Stoneman	831
Steve Renko	810
Jeff Fassero	750
Bill Gullickson	678
Scott Sanderson	603
Woodie Fryman	469

Bases on balls
Steve Rogers	876
Steve Renko	624
Bill Stoneman	535
Dennis Martinez	407
Bryn Smith	341
Mike Torrez	303
Charlie Lea	291
Bill Gullickson	288
Carl Morton	279
Jeff Fassero	274
Woodie Fryman	274

Games
Tim Burke	425
Steve Rogers	399
Mel Rojas	388
Jeff Reardon	359
Woodie Fryman	297
Bryn Smith	284
Jeff Fassero	262
Andy McGaffigan	258
Mike Marshall	247
Dan Schatzeder	241

Shutouts
Steve Rogers	37
Bill Stoneman	15
Dennis Martinez	13
Woodie Fryman	8
Charlie Lea	8
Pedro Martinez	8
Scott Sanderson	8
Bryn Smith	8
5 tied with 6	

Saves
Jeff Reardon	152
Mel Rojas	109
John Wetteland	105
Ugueth Urbina	102
Tim Burke	101
Mike Marshall	75
Woodie Fryman	52
Dale Murray	33
Elias Sosa	30
Claude Raymond	24

EXPOS YEAR-BY-YEAR

Year	W	L	Place	Games Back	Manager	Leaders					
						Batting avg.	Hits	Home runs	RBIs	Wins	ERA
						EAST DIVISION					
1969	52	110	6th	48	Mauch	Staub, .302	Staub, 166	Staub, 29	Laboy, 83	Stoneman, 11	Waslewski, 3.29
1970	73	89	6th	16	Mauch	Fairly, .288	Staub, 156	Staub, 30	Staub, 94	Morton, 18	Morton, 3.60
1971	71	90	5th	25½	Mauch	Staub, .311	Staub, 186	Staub, 19	Staub, 97	Stoneman, 17	Stoneman, 3.15
1972	70	86	5th	26½	Mauch	Fairly, .278	Singleton, 139	Fairly, 17	Fairly, 68	Torrez, 16	Marshall, 1.78
1973	79	83	4th	3½	Mauch	Hunt, .309	Singleton, 169	Bailey, 26	Singleton, 103	Renko, 15	Rogers, 1.54
1974	79	82	4th	8½	Mauch	W. Davis, .295	W. Davis, 180	Bailey, 20	W. Davis, 89	Rogers, Torrez, 15	Taylor, 2.17
1975	75	87	*5th	17½	Mauch	Parrish, .274	Parrish, 146	Jorgensen, 18	Carter, 68	Murray, 15	Warthen, 3.11
1976	55	107	6th	46	Kuehl, Fox	Foli, .264	Foli, 144	Parrish, 11	Parrish, 61	Fryman, 13	Rogers, 3.21
1977	75	87	5th	26	Williams	Valentine, .293	Cash, 188	Carter, 31	Perez, 91	Rogers, 17	Rogers, 3.10
1978	76	86	4th	14	Williams	Cromartie, .297	Cromartie, 180	Dawson, Valentine, 25	Perez, 78	Grimsley, 20	Dues, 2.36
1979	95	65	2nd	2	Williams	Parrish, .307	Cromartie, 181	Parrish, 30	Dawson, 92	Lee, 16	Sosa, 1.96
1980	90	72	2nd	1	Williams	Dawson, .308	Dawson, 178	Carter, 29	Carter, 101	Rogers, Sanderson, 16	Palmer, Rogers, 2.98
1981	60	48	†‡3rd/1st	—	Williams, Fanning	Cromartie, Raines, .304	Dawson, 119	Dawson, 24	Carter, 68	Rogers, 12	Gullickson, 2.80
1982	86	76	3rd	6	Fanning	Oliver, .331	Oliver, 204	Carter, 29	Oliver, 109	Rogers, 19	Reardon, 2.06
1983	82	80	3rd	8	Virdon	Oliver, .300	Dawson, 189	Dawson, 32	Dawson, 113	Gullickson, Rogers, 17	B. Smith, 2.49
1984	78	83	5th	18	Virdon, Fanning	Raines, .309	Raines, 192	Carter, 27	Carter, 106	Lea, 15	Schatzeder, 2.71
1985	84	77	3rd	16½	Rodgers	Raines, .320	Raines, 184	Dawson, 23	Brooks, 100	B. Smith, 18	Burke, 2.39
1986	78	83	4th	29½	Rodgers	Raines, .334	Raines, 194	Dawson, 20	Dawson, 78	Youmans, 13	McGaffigan, 2.65
1987	91	71	3rd	4	Rodgers	Raines, .330	Wallach, 177	Wallach, 26	Wallach, 123	Heaton, 13	Burke, 1.19
1988	81	81	3rd	20	Rodgers	Galarraga, .302	Galarraga, 184	Galarraga, 29	Galarraga, 92	Martinez, 15	P. Perez, 2.44
1989	81	81	4th	12	Rodgers	Raines, .286	Wallach, 159	Galarraga, 23	Galarraga, 85	Martinez, 16	Langston, 2.39
1990	85	77	3rd	10	Rodgers	Wallach, .296	Wallach, 185	Wallach, 21	Wallach, 98	Sampen, 12	Boyd, 2.93
1991	71	90	6th	26½	Rodgers, Runnells	Calderon, .300	Grissom, 149	Calderon, 19	Calderon, 75	Martinez, 14	Martinez, 2.39
1992	87	75	2nd	9	Runnells, F. Alou	Walker, .301	Grissom, 180	Walker, 23	Walker, 93	Hill, Martinez, 16	Rojas, 1.43
1993	94	68	2nd	3	F. Alou	Grissom, .298	Grissom, 188	Walker, 22	Grissom, 95	Martinez, 15	Fassero, 2.29
1994	74	40	1st	+6	F. Alou	M. Alou, .339	M. Alou, 143	M. Alou, 22	Walker, 86	Hill, 16	Henry, 2.43
1995	66	78	5th	24	Alou	Segui, .309	Cordero, 147	Alou, Berry, Tarasco, 14	Segui, 68	Martinez, 14	Henry, 2.84
1996	88	74	2nd	8	Alou	Grudzielanek, .306	Grudzielanek, 201	Rodriguez, 36	Rodriguez, 103	Fassero, 15	Fassero, 3.30
1997	78	84	4th	23	Alou	Segui, .307	Grudzielanek, 177	White, 28	Rodriguez, 83	Martinez, 17	Martinez, 1.90
1998	65	97	4th	41	Alou	V.Guerrero, .324	V.Guerrero, 202	V.Guerrero, 38	V.Guerrero, 109	Hermanson, 14	Hermanson, 3.13
1999	68	94	4th	35	Alou	V.Guerrero, .316	V.Guerrero, 193	V.Guerrero, 42	V.Guerrero, 131	Hermanson, Vazquez, 9	Telford, 3.94

* Tied for position. † First half 30-25; second half 30-23. ‡ Lost Championship Series.

Note: Batting average minimum 350 at-bats; ERA minimum 90 innings pitched.

Manny Mota

MONTREAL made history May 27, 1968, when it was awarded an expansion franchise—the first outside the continental United States. Montreal joined San Diego in the National League and Kansas City and Seattle in the American League as part of a four-team expansion that brought baseball's membership roster to 24 teams.

The infant Expos took their first step when they made versatile Manny Mota their first pick of the October 14, 1968, expansion draft—one of 30 overall selections. Montreal made its Major League debut on April 8, 1969, with an 11-10 victory over the Mets at New York's Shea Stadium. The long-awaited home inaugural at Jarry Park took place on April 14, and the Expos celebrated with an 8-7 victory over St. Louis in the first Major League regular-season game on foreign soil.

Expansion draft (October 14, 1968)

Players
Jesus Alou .... San Francisco .... outfield
John Bateman .... Houston .... catcher
John Boccabella .... Chicago .... catcher
Ron Brand .... Houston .... catcher
Donn Clendenon .... Pittsburgh .... first base
Ty Cline .... San Francisco .... outfield
Jim Fairey .... Los Angeles .... outfield
Angel Hermoso .... Atlanta .... infield
Jose Herrera .... Houston .... infield
Garry Jestadt .... Chicago .... infield
Mack Jones .... Cincinnati .... outfield
Coco Laboy .... St. Louis .... infield
*Manny Mota .... Pittsburgh .... infield/outfield
Gary Sutherland .... Philadelphia .... infield/outfield
Jim Williams .... Cincinnati .... shortstop
Maury Wills .... Pittsburgh .... shortstop

Pitchers
Jack Billingham .... Los Angeles .... righthanded
John Glass .... New York .... righthanded
Jim (Mudcat) Grant .... Los Angeles .... righthanded
Skip Guinn .... Atlanta .... lefthanded
Larry Jackson .... Philadelphia .... righthanded
Larry Jaster .... St. Louis .... lefthanded
Ernie McAnally .... New York .... righthanded
Dan McGinn .... Cincinnati .... lefthanded
Carl Morton .... Atlanta .... righthanded
Bob Reynolds .... San Francisco .... righthanded
Jerry Robertson .... St. Louis .... righthanded
Don Shaw .... New York .... lefthanded
Bill Stoneman .... Chicago .... righthanded
Mike Wegener .... Philadelphia .... righthanded

*First pick

Opening day lineup
April 8, 1969
Maury Wills, shortstop
Gary Sutherland, second base
Rusty Staub, right field
Mack Jones, left field
Bob Bailey, first base
John Batemen, catcher
Coco Laboy, third base
Don Hahn, center field
Mudcat Grant, pitcher

Rusty Staub

Expos firsts
First hit: Maury Wills, April 8, 1969, at New York (single)
First home run: Dan McGinn, April 8, 1969, at New York
First RBI: Bob Bailey, April 8, 1969, at New York
First win: Don Shaw, April 8, 1969, at New York
First shutout: Bill Stoneman (no-hitter), April 17, 1969, 7-0 at Philadelphia

HISTORY

NEW YORK METS

Manager Gil Hodges (14).

FRANCHISE CHRONOLOGY

First season: 1962, as one of two new teams in the National League's first modern-era expansion. The Mets dropped an 11-4 opener to St. Louis and stumbled to 120 first-year losses, a 20th-century record.
1963-present: The early year Mets were bumbling and inept—and lovable. New York, devoid of an N.L. franchise since losing the Dodgers and Giants in 1957, fervently embraced the mistake-prone Mets as they struggled to 452 losses in their first four seasons (an average of 113) under irascible manager Casey Stengel. But that feeling changed in 1969, when the upstart New Yorkers, coming off a ninth-place finish, won 100 games and finished first in the newly created East Division. They punctuated their surprising success with a three-game sweep of Atlanta in the first N.L. Championship Series and a shocking five-game victory over powerful Baltimore in the World Series. The Miracle Mets had risen from ineptitude to the top of the baseball world. No longer lovable losers, the Mets remained consistent contenders, winning another pennant in 1973, another Series championship in 1986 and their fourth division title in 1988.

METS VS. OPPONENTS BY DECADE

	Braves	Cardinals	Cubs	Dodgers	Giants	Phillies	Pirates	Reds	Astros	Expos	Padres	Marlins	Rockies	Brewers	D'backs	Interleague	Decade Record
1962-69	49-89	54-90	65-79	44-94	51-87	53-91	51-93	54-83	49-87	13-5	11-1						494-799
1970-79	61-59	85-93	93-86	52-68	62-58	83-97	78-98	40-80	59-61	86-94	64-56						763-850
1980-89	68-46	87-86	92-83	63-50	49-65	90-86	102-69	62-55	56-61	89-85	58-57						816-743
1990-99	50-69	67-55	57-62	53-58	58-56	69-70	59-49	46-61	68-69	52-63	50-36	32-36	13-3	7-11	28-21		767-786
Totals	228-263	293-324	307-310	212-270	220-266	295-344	289-327	215-267	210-270	256-253	185-177	50-36	32-36	13-3	7-11	28-21	2840-3178

Interleague results: 7-3 vs. Orioles; 5-4 vs. Red Sox; 0-3 vs. Tigers; 5-7 vs. Yankees; 7-2 vs. Blue Jays; 4-2 vs. Devil Rays.

MANAGERS

Name	Years	Record
Casey Stengel	1962-65	175-404
Wes Westrum	1965-67	142-237
Salty Parker	1967	4-7
Gil Hodges	1968-71	339-309
Yogi Berra	1972-75	292-296
Roy McMillan	1975	26-27
Joe Frazier	1976-77	101-106
Joe Torre	1977-81	286-420
George Bamberger	1982-83	81-127
Frank Howard	1983	52-64
Dave Johnson	1984-90	595-417
Bud Harrelson	1990-91	145-129
Mike Cubbage	1991	3-4
Jeff Torborg	1992-93	85-115
Dallas Green	1993-96	229-283
Bobby Valentine	1996-99	285-233

WORLD SERIES CHAMPIONS

Year	Loser	Length	MVP
1969	Baltimore	5 games	Clendenon
1986	Boston	7 games	Knight

N.L. PENNANT WINNERS

Year	Record	Manager	Series Result
1969	100-62	Hodges	Defeated Orioles
1973	82-79	Berra	Lost to A's
1986	108-54	Johnson	Defeated Red Sox

EAST DIVISION CHAMPIONS

Year	Record	Manager	NLCS Result
1969	100-62	Hodges	Defeated Braves
1973	82-79	Berra	Defeated Reds
1986	108-54	Johnson	Defeated Astros
1988	100-60	Johnson	Lost to Dodgers

WILD-CARD QUALIFIERS

Year	Record	Manager	Div. Series Result
1999	97-66	Valentine	Defeated D'backs

			NLCS Result
			Lost to Braves

ALL-TIME RECORD OF EXPANSION TEAMS

Team	W	L	Pct.	DT	P	WS
Arizona	165	159	.509	1	0	0
Kansas City	2,471	2,412	.506	6	2	1
Toronto	1,784	1,818	.495	5	2	2
Houston	2,980	3,048	.494	6	0	0
Montreal	2,387	2,501	.488	2	0	0
Anaheim	2,987	3,201	.483	3	0	0
Milwaukee	2,348	2,542	.480	2	1	0
Colorado	512	559	.478	0	0	0
New York	2,840	3,178	.472	4	3	2
Texas	2,881	3,290	.467	4	0	0
San Diego	2,239	2,656	.457	3	2	0
Seattle	1,624	1,977	.451	2	0	0
Florida	472	596	.442	0	1	1
Tampa Bay	132	192	.407	0	0	0

DT—Division Titles. P—Pennants won. WS—World Series won.

ATTENDANCE HIGHS

Total	Season	Park
3,047,724	1988	Shea Stadium
3,027,121	1987	Shea Stadium
2,918,710	1989	Shea Stadium
2,762,417	1986	Shea Stadium
2,751,437	1985	Shea Stadium

BALLPARK CHRONOLOGY

Shea Stadium (1964-present)

Capacity: 55,601.
First game: Pittsburgh 4, Mets 3 (April 17, 1964).
First batter: Dick Schofield, Pirates.
First hit: Willie Stargell, Pirates (home run).
First run: Willie Stargell, Pirates (2nd inning).
First home run: Willie Stargell, Pirates.
First winning pitcher: Bob Friend, Pirates.
First-season attendance: 1,732,597.

Polo Grounds (1962-63)

First game: Pittsburgh 4, Mets 3 (April 13, 1962).
First-season attendance: 922,530.

CY YOUNG WINNERS

Tom Seaver, RH, 1969
Tom Seaver, RH, 1973
Tom Seaver, RH, 1975
Dwight Gooden, RH, 1985

ROOKIES OF THE YEAR

Tom Seaver, P, 1967
Jon Matlack, P, 1972
Darryl Strawberry, OF, 1983
Dwight Gooden, P, 1984

RETIRED UNIFORMS

No.	Name	Pos.
14	Gil Hodges	Man.
37	Casey Stengel	Man.
41	Tom Seaver	P

Manager Casey Stengel and outfielder Ed Kranepool were New York Mets originals.

MILESTONE PERFORMANCES

25-plus home runs
41— Todd Hundley 1996
40— Mike Piazza..1999
39— Darryl Strawberry 1987, 1988
38— Howard Johnson 1991
37— Dave Kingman 1976, 1982
     Darryl Strawberry 1990
36— Dave Kingman 1975
     Howard Johnson 1987, 1989
34— Frank Thomas 1962
     Bobby Bonilla......................................1993
32— Gary Carter 1985
     Mike Piazza *1998
     Robin Ventura.....................................1999
30— Bernard Gilkey 1996
     Todd Hundley 1997
29— Darryl Strawberry 1985, 1989
     Kevin McReynolds 1987
28— George Foster 1983
27— Darryl Strawberry 1986
     Kevin McReynolds 1987
     Eddie Murray 1993
     Edgardo Alfonzo 1999
26— Tommie Agee 1969
     Darryl Strawberry 1983, 1984
25— Bobby Murcer 1971
*9 with Los Angeles; 23 with Mets.

100-plus RBIs
124— Mike Piazza 1999
120— Robin Ventura......................................1999
117— Howard Johnson 1991
      Bernard Gilkey 1996
112— Todd Hundley 1996
111— Mike Piazza *1998
108— Darryl Strawberry 1990
      Edgardo Alfonzo 1999
105— Rusty Staub 1975
      Gary Carter 1986
104— Darryl Strawberry 1987
102— John Olerud 1997
101— Darryl Strawberry 1988
      Howard Johnson 1989
100— Gary Carter 1985
      Eddie Murray 1993
*30 with Los Angeles; 5 with Florida; 76 with Mets.

20-plus victories
1969— Tom Seaver 25-7
1971— Tom Seaver 20-10
1972— Tom Seaver 21-12
1975— Tom Seaver 22-9
1976— Jerry Koosman 21-10
1985— Dwight Gooden 24-4
1988— David Cone 20-3
1990— Frank Viola 20-12

N.L. home run champions
1982— Dave Kingman 37
1988— Darryl Strawberry 39
1991— Howard Johnson 38

N.L. RBI champion
1991— Howard Johnson 117

N.L. batting champions
None

N.L. ERA champions
1970— Tom Seaver 2.81
1971— Tom Seaver 1.76
1973— Tom Seaver 2.08
1978— Craig Swan 2.43
1985— Dwight Gooden 1.53

N.L. strikeout champions
1970— Tom Seaver 283
1971— Tom Seaver 289
1973— Tom Seaver 251
1975— Tom Seaver 243
1976— Tom Seaver 235
1984— Dwight Gooden 276
1985— Dwight Gooden 268
1990— David Cone 233
1991— David Cone 241

No-hit pitchers
(9 innings or more)
None

Longest hitting streaks
24— Hubie Brooks 1984
     Mike Piazza 1999
23— Cleon Jones 1970
     Mike Vail 1975
     John Olerud 1998
20— Tommie Agee 1970
     Butch Huskey 1997
     Edgardo Alfonzo 1997
19— Tommie Agee 1970
     Lee Mazzilli 1979
     Felix Millan 1975
18— Ed Kranepool 1975
     Lee Mazzilli 1980
     Felix Millan 1973
     Darryl Strawberry 1990
     Frank Thomas.....................................1962
17— Lance Johnson 1996
16— Joe Torre 1975
     John Milner 1976
     Jose Vizcaino 1994
15— Rusty Staub 1973
     John Stearns 1977
     John Stearns 1982
     Mookie Wilson 1984
     Rico Brogna 1994

First baseman Keith Hernandez (right) brought his golden glove and steady bat to New York midway through the 1983 season.

INDIVIDUAL SEASON, GAME RECORDS

Outfielder Darryl Strawberry hit 252 home runs for the Mets before taking his bat to the Los Angeles Dodgers in 1991.

SEASON

Batting
At-bats	682	Lance Johnson	1996
Runs	123	Edgardo Alfonzo	1999
Hits	227	Lance Johnson	1996
Singles	166	Lance Johnson	1996
Doubles	44	Bernard Gilkey	1996
Triples	21	Lance Johnson	1996
Home runs	41	Todd Hundley	1996
Home runs, rookie	26	Darryl Strawberry	1983
Grand slams	3	John Milner	1976
		Robin Ventura	1999
Total bases	327	Lance Johnson	1996
RBIs	124	Mike Piazza	1999
Walks	125	John Olerud	1999
Most strikeouts	156	Tommie Agee	1970
		Dave Kingman	1982
Fewest strikeouts	14	Felix Millan	1974
Batting average	.353	John Olerud	1998
Slugging pct.	.583	Darryl Strawberry	1987
Stolen bases	66	Roger Cedeno	1999

Pitching
Games	80	Turk Wendell	1999
Complete games	21	Tom Seaver	1971
Innings	290.2	Tom Seaver	1970
Wins	25	Tom Seaver	1969
Losses	24	Roger Craig	1962
		Jack Fisher	1965
Winning pct.	.870 (20-3)	David Cone	1988
Walks	116	Nolan Ryan	1971
Strikeouts	289	Tom Seaver	1971
Shutouts	8	Dwight Gooden	1985
Home runs allowed	35	Roger Craig	1962
Lowest ERA	1.53	Dwight Gooden	1985
Saves	38	John Franco	1998

GAME

Batting
Runs	6	Edgardo Alfonzo	8-30-99
Hits	6	Edgardo Alfonzo	8-30-99
Doubles	3	Last by John Olerud	4-11-99
Triples	3	Doug Flynn	8-5-80
Home runs	3	Last by Edgardo Alfonzo	8-30-99
RBIs	8	Dave Kingman	6-4-76
Total bases	16	Edgardo Alfonzo	8-30-99
Stolen bases	4	Last by Roger Cedeno	5-14-99

HISTORY

–443–

BATTING

Games
Ed Kranepool	1,853
Bud Harrelson	1,322
Jerry Grote	1,235
Cleon Jones	1,201
Howard Johnson	1,154
Mookie Wilson	1,116
Darryl Strawberry	1,109
Lee Mazzilli	979
Rusty Staub	942
Wayne Garrett	883

At-bats
Ed Kranepool	5,436
Bud Harrelson	4,390
Cleon Jones	4,223
Mookie Wilson	4,027
Howard Johnson	3,968
Darryl Strawberry	3,903
Jerry Grote	3,881
Keith Hernandez	3,164
Lee Mazzilli	3,013
Kevin McReynolds	2,910

Runs
Darryl Strawberry	662
Howard Johnson	627
Mookie Wilson	592
Cleon Jones	563
Ed Kranepool	536
Bud Harrelson	490
Keith Hernandez	455
Kevin McReynolds	405
Lee Mazzilli	404
Wayne Garrett	389

Hits
Ed Kranepool	1,418
Cleon Jones	1,188
Mookie Wilson	1,112
Bud Harrelson	1,029
Darryl Strawberry	1,025
Howard Johnson	997
Jerry Grote	994
Keith Hernandez	939
Lee Mazzilli	796
Kevin McReynolds	791

Doubles
Ed Kranepool	225
Howard Johnson	214
Darryl Strawberry	187
Cleon Jones	182
Mookie Wilson	170
Keith Hernandez	159
Kevin McReynolds	153
John Stearns	152
Lee Mazzilli	148
Jerry Grote	143

Triples
Mookie Wilson	62
Bud Harrelson	45
Cleon Jones	33
Steve Henderson	31
Darryl Strawberry	30
Lance Johnson	27
Doug Flynn	26
Ed Kranepool	25
Lee Mazzilli	22
Wayne Garrett	20
Ron Swoboda	20

Home runs
Darryl Strawberry	252
Howard Johnson	192
Dave Kingman	154
Todd Hundley	124
Kevin McReynolds	122
Ed Kranepool	118
George Foster	99
Bobby Bonilla	95
John Milner	94
Cleon Jones	93

Total bases
Ed Kranepool	2,047
Darryl Strawberry	2,028
Howard Johnson	1,823
Cleon Jones	1,715
Mookie Wilson	1,586
Keith Hernandez	1,358
Kevin McReynolds	1,338
Jerry Grote	1,278
Bud Harrelson	1,260
Lee Mazzilli	1,192

Runs batted in
Darryl Strawberry	733
Howard Johnson	629
Ed Kranepool	614

SEASON

Batting
Most at-bats	5,618	1996
Most runs	853	1999
Fewest runs	473	1968
Most hits	1,553	1999
Most singles	1,087	1980
Most doubles	297	1999
Most triples	47	1978, 1996
Most home runs	192	1987
Fewest home runs	61	1980
Most grand slams	8	1999
Most pinch-hit home runs	12	1983
Most total bases	2,430	1987
Most stolen bases	159	1987
Highest batting average	.279	1999
Lowest batting average	.219	1963
Highest slugging pct	.434	1987, 1999

Pitching
Lowest ERA	2.72	1968
Highest ERA	5.04	1962
Most complete games	53	1976
Most shutouts	28	1969
Most saves	51	1987
Most walks	617	1999
Most strikeouts	1,217	1990

Fielding
Most errors	210	1962, 1963
Fewest errors	68	1999
Most double plays	171	1966, 1983
Highest fielding average	.989	1999

General
Most games won	108	1986
Most games lost	120	1962
Highest win pct	.667	1986
Lowest win pct	.250	1962

GAME, INNING

Batting
Most runs, game	23	8-16-87
Most runs, inning	10	6-12-79
Most hits, game	28	7-4-85
Most home runs, game	6	4-4-88, 6-15-99
Most total bases, game	38	7-4-85, 8-30-99
Most stolen bases, game	6	Last 4-10-91

Lefthanded starter Jerry Koosman was a key figure in the Mets' 1969 World Series miracle.

Cleon Jones	521
Keith Hernandez	468
Kevin McReynolds	456
Rusty Staub	399
Todd Hundley	397
Dave Kingman	389
George Foster	361

Extra-base hits
Darryl Strawberry	469
Howard Johnson	424
Ed Kranepool	368
Cleon Jones	308
Mookie Wilson	292
Kevin McReynolds	289
Keith Hernandez	249
Todd Hundley	249
Lee Mazzilli	238
Dave Kingman	230

Batting average
(Minimum 500 games)
Keith Hernandez	.297
Dave Magadan	.292
Edgardo Alfonzo	.290
Wally Backman	.283
Cleon Jones	.281
Lenny Dykstra	.278
Felix Millan	.278
Mookie Wilson	.276
Rusty Staub	.276
Joel Youngblood	.274

Stolen bases
Mookie Wilson	281
Howard Johnson	202
Darryl Strawberry	191
Lee Mazzilli	152
Lenny Dykstra	116
Bud Harrelson	115
Wally Backman	106
Vince Coleman	99
Tommie Agee	92
Cleon Jones	91
John Stearns	91

PITCHING

Earned-run average
(Minimum 500 innings)
Tom Seaver	2.57
Jesse Orosco	2.73
John Franco	2.81

Jon Matlack	3.03
David Cone	3.08
Jerry Koosman	3.09
Dwight Gooden	3.10
Bob Ojeda	3.12
Sid Fernandez	3.14
Bret Saberhagen	3.16

Wins
Tom Seaver	198
Dwight Gooden	157
Jerry Koosman	140
Ron Darling	99
Sid Fernandez	98
Jon Matlack	82
David Cone	80
Bobby Jones	63
Craig Swan	59
Bob Ojeda	51

Losses
Jerry Koosman	137
Tom Seaver	124
Dwight Gooden	85
Jon Matlack	81
Al Jackson	80
Sid Fernandez	78
Jack Fisher	73
Craig Swan	71
Ron Darling	70
Tug McGraw	55

Innings pitched
Tom Seaver	3,045.1
Jerry Koosman	2,544.2
Dwight Gooden	2,169.2
Ron Darling	1,620.0
Sid Fernandez	1,584.2
Jon Matlack	1,448.0
Craig Swan	1,230.2
David Cone	1,191.1
Bobby Jones	1,061.0
Al Jackson	980.2

Strikeouts
Tom Seaver	2,541
Dwight Gooden	1,875
Jerry Koosman	1,799
Sid Fernandez	1,449
David Cone	1,159
Ron Darling	1,148
Jon Matlack	1,023

Craig Swan	671
Bobby Jones	629
Tug McGraw	618

Bases on balls
Tom Seaver	847
Jerry Koosman	820
Dwight Gooden	651
Ron Darling	614
Sid Fernandez	596
Jon Matlack	419
David Cone	418
Craig Swan	368
Tug McGraw	350
Nolan Ryan	344

Games
John Franco	485
Tom Seaver	401
Jerry Koosman	376
Jesse Orosco	372
Tug McGraw	361
Dwight Gooden	305
Jeff Innis	288
Roger McDowell	280
Ron Taylor	269
Doug Sisk	263

Shutouts
Tom Seaver	44
Jerry Koosman	26
Jon Matlack	26
Dwight Gooden	23
David Cone	15
Ron Darling	10
Al Jackson	10
Sid Fernandez	9
Bob Ojeda	9
Gary Gentry	8

Saves
John Franco	268
Jesse Orosco	107
Tug McGraw	86
Roger McDowell	84
Neil Allen	69
Skip Lockwood	65
Randy Myers	56
Ron Taylor	49
Doug Sisk	33
Bob Apodaca	26

HISTORY

Year	W	L	Place	Games Back	Manager	Batting avg.	Hits	Home runs	RBIs	Wins	ERA
1962	40	120	10th	60½	Stengel	Ashburn, .306	Thomas, 152	Thomas, 34	Thomas, 94	Craig, 10	Jackson, 4.40
1963	51	111	10th	48	Stengel	Hunt, .272	Hunt, 145	Hickman, 17	Thomas, 60	Jackson, 13	Willey, 3.10
1964	53	109	10th	40	Stengel	Hunt, .303	Christopher, 163	C. Smith, 20	Christopher, 76	Jackson, 11	Wakefield, 3.61
1965	50	112	10th	47	Stengel, Westrum	Kranepool, .253	Kranepool, 133	Swoboda, 19	C. Smith, 62	Fisher, Jackson, 8	McGraw, 3.32
1966	66	95	9th	28½	Westrum	Hunt, .288	Hunt, 138	Kranepool, 16	Boyer, 61	Fisher, Ribant, B. Shaw, 11	Ribant, 3.20
1967	61	101	10th	40½	Westrum, Parker	T. Davis, .302	T. Davis, 174	T. Davis, 16	T. Davis, 73	Seaver, 16	Seaver, 2.76
1968	73	89	9th	24	Hodges	Jones, .297	Jones, 151	Charles, 15	Swoboda, 59	Koosman, 19	Koosman, 2.08
EAST DIVISION											
1969	100	62	*1st	+8	Hodges	Jones, .340	Jones, 164	Agee, 26	Agee, 76	Seaver, 25	Seaver, 2.21
1970	83	79	3rd	6	Hodges	Shamsky, .293	Agee, 182	Agee, 24	Clendenon, 97	Seaver, 18	Seaver, 2.82
1971	83	79	3rd	14	Hodges	Jones, .319	Jones, 161	Agee, Jones, Kranepool, 14	Jones, 69	Seaver, 20	McGraw, 1.70
1972	83	73	3rd	13½	Berra	Jones, .245	Agee, 96	Milner, 17	Jones, 52	Seaver, 21	McGraw, 1.70
1973	82	79	*1st	+1½	Berra	Millan, .290	Millan, 185	Milner, 23	Staub, 76	Seaver, 19	Seaver, 2.08
1974	71	91	5th	17	Berra	Jones, .282	Staub, 145	Milner, 20	Staub, 78	Koosman, 15	Matlack, 2.41
1975	82	80	†3rd	10½	Berra, McMillan	Grote, .295	Millan, 191	Kingman, 36	Staub, 105	Seaver, 22	Seaver, 2.38
1976	86	76	3rd	15	Frazier	Kranepool, .292	Millan, 150	Kingman, 37	Kingman, 86	Koosman, 21	Seaver, 2.59
1977	64	98	6th	37	Frazier, Torre	Randle, .304	Randle, 156	Henderson, Milner, Stearns, 12	Henderson, 65	Espinosa, 10	Seaver, 3.00
1978	66	96	6th	24	Torre	Mazzilli, .273	Henderson, Montanez, 156	Montanez, 17	Montanez, 96	Espinosa, 11	Swan, 2.43
1979	63	99	6th	35	Torre	Henderson, .306	Mazzilli, 181	Youngblood, 16	Hebner, Mazzilli, 79	Swan, 14	Swan, 3.29
1980	67	95	5th	24	Torre	Henderson, .290	Mazzilli, 162	Mazzilli, 16	Mazzilli, 76	Bomback, 10	Reardon, 2.61
1981	41	62	‡5th/4th	—	Torre	Brooks, .307	Brooks, 110	Kingman, 22	Kingman, 59	Allen, Zachry, 7	Falcone, 2.55
1982	65	97	6th	27	Bamberger	Stearns, .293	Wilson, 178	Kingman, 37	Kingman, 99	Swan, 11	Orosco, 2.72
1983	68	94	6th	22	Bamberger, Howard	Wilson, .276	Wilson, 176	Foster, 28	Foster, 90	Orosco, 13	Orosco, 1.47
1984	90	72	2nd	6½	D. Johnson	Hernandez, .311	Hernandez, 171	Strawberry, 26	Strawberry, 97	Gooden, 17	Orosco, 2.59
1985	98	64	2nd	3	D. Johnson	Hernandez, .309	Hernandez, 183	Carter, 32	Carter, 100	Gooden, 24	Gooden, 1.53
1986	108	54	*1st	+21½	D. Johnson	Backman, .320	Hernandez, 171	Strawberry, 27	Carter, 105	Ojeda, 18	Ojeda, 2.57
1987	92	70	2nd	3	D. Johnson	Wilson, .299	Hernandez, 170	Strawberry, 39	Strawberry, 104	Gooden, 15	Gooden, 3.21
1988	100	60	§1st	+15	D. Johnson	Wilson, .296	McReynolds, 159	Strawberry, 39	Strawberry, 101	Cone, 20	Cone, 2.22
1989	87	75	2nd	6	D. Johnson	H. Johnson, .287	H. Johnson, 164	H. Johnson, 36	H. Johnson, 101	Cone, Darling, Fernandez, 14	Fernandez, 2.83
1990	91	71	2nd	4	Johnson, Harrelson	Magadan, .328	Jefferies, 171	Strawberry, 37	Strawberry, 108	Viola, 20	Viola, 2.67
1991	77	84	5th	20½	Harrelson, Cubbage	Jefferies, .272	H. Johnson, 146	H. Johnson, 38	H. Johnson, 117	Cone, 14	Cone, 3.29
1992	72	90	5th	24	Torborg	Murray, .261	Murray, 144	Bonilla, 19	Murray, 93	Fernandez, 14	Fernandez, 2.73
1993	59	103	7th	38	Torborg, Green	Murray, .285	Murray, 174	Bonilla, 34	Murray, 100	Gooden, 12	Fernandez, 2.93
1994	55	58	3rd	18½	Green	Kent, .292	Kent, 121	Bonilla, 20	Kent, 68	Saberhagen, 14	Saberhagen, 2.74
1995	69	75	†2nd	21	Green	Brogna, .289	Vizcaino, 146	Brogna, 22	Brogna, 76	B. Jones, 10	Isringhausen, 2.81
1996	71	91	4th	25	Green, Valentine	Johnson, .333	Johnson, 227	Hundley, 41	Gilkey, 117	Clark, 14	Clark, 3.43
1997	88	74	3rd	13	Valentine	Alfonzo, .315	Alfonzo, 163	Hundley, 30	Olerud, 102	B. Jones, 15	Reed, 2.89
1998	88	74	2nd	18	Valentine	Olerud, .353	Olerud, 197	Piazza, 32	Piazza, 111	Leiter, 17	Leiter, 2.47
1999	97	66	2nd	6½	Valentine	Henderson, .315	Alfonzo, 191	Piazza, 40	Piazza, 124	Leiter, Hershiser, 13	Leiter, 4.23

* Won Championship Series. † Tied for position. ‡ First half 17-34; second half 24-28. § Lost Championship Series. ∞ Won wild-card playoff.　　　　Note: Batting average minimum 350 at-bats; ERA minimum 90 innings pitched.

Hobie Landrith

NATIONAL LEAGUE baseball returned to the nation's largest metropolitan area on October 16, 1960, when owners approved 1962 expansion to New York and Houston. The arrival of the "Mets" filled the void created by the 1958 departures of the Dodgers and Giants to the West Coast, and it set the stage for the triumphant New York return of former Yankees manager Casey Stengel as the lovable boss of New York's expansion bumblers.

The Mets stocked their roster with 22 players from the October 10, 1961, expansion draft, grabbing catcher Hobie Landrith with their first pick. The franchise debut took place on April 11, 1962, when the Mets dropped an 11-4 decision at St. Louis—the first of 120 losses they would suffer in their inaugural season.

Expansion draft (October 10, 1961)

Players

Gus Bell	Cincinnati	outfield
Ed Bouchee	Chicago	first base
Chris Cannizzaro	St. Louis	catcher
Elio Chacon	Cincinnati	second base
Joe Christopher	Pittsburgh	outfield
Clarence Coleman	Philadelphia	catcher
John DeMerit	Milwaukee	outfield
Sammy Drake	Chicago	infield
Jim Hickman	St. Louis	outfield
Gil Hodges	Los Angeles	first base
*Hobie Landrith	San Francisco	catcher
Felix Mantilla	Milwaukee	shortstop
Bobby Gene Smith	Philadelphia	outfield
Lee Walls	Philadelphia	outfield
Don Zimmer	Chicago	second base

Pitchers

Craig Anderson	St. Louis	righthanded
Roger Craig	Los Angeles	righthanded
Ray Daviault	San Francisco	righthanded
Jay Hook	Cincinnati	righthanded
Al Jackson	Pittsburgh	lefthanded
Sherman Jones	Cincinnati	righthanded
Bob Miller	St. Louis	righthanded

*First pick

Opening day lineup

April 11, 1962

Richie Ashburn, center field
Felix Mantilla, shortstop
Charlie Neal, second base
Frank Thomas, left field
Gus Bell, right field
Gil Hodges, first base
Don Zimmer, third base
Hobie Landrith, catcher
Roger Craig, pitcher

Roger Craig

Mets firsts

First hit: Gus Bell, April 11, 1962, at St. Louis (single)
First home run: Gil Hodges, April 11, 1962, at St. Louis
First RBI: Charlie Neal, April 11, 1962, at St. Louis
First win: Jay Hook, April 23, 1962, at Pittsburgh
First shutout: Al Jackson, April 29, 1962, 8-0 vs. Philadelphia

HISTORY

PHILADELPHIA PHILLIES

FRANCHISE CHRONOLOGY

First season: 1883, as a member of the National League. The Phillies dropped an opening 4-3 decision to Providence and went on to lose 81 of 98 games. They finished in last place, 46 games behind first-place Boston and 23 games behind seventh-place Detroit.

1884-1900: The Phillies improved from that first-season disaster, but never enough to claim a pennant. They finished second once and third six times before entering the new century.

1901-present: The modern-era Phillies were not much different from their predecessors. They did not claim their first N.L. pennant until 1915, 32 years after their birth, and failed to win a World Series championship until 1980, at the not-so-tender age of 97. Over their 115-year history, the Phillies have finished last in their league or division 31 times, more than once every four years. They went 34 years between their first and second pennants and 30 more between their second and third. Their most successful run came from 1976 to 1983, when they won five East Division titles, two pennants and their only World Series—a six-game 1980 triumph over Kansas City. Philadelphia fans were treated to their fifth pennant in 1993, but they watched their Phillies lose a six-game World Series to Toronto.

Third baseman Mike Schmidt.

PHILLIES VS. OPPONENTS BY DECADE

	Braves	Cardinals	Cubs	Dodgers	Giants	Pirates	Reds	Astros	Mets	Expos	Padres	Marlins	Rockies	Brewers	D'backs	Interleague	Decade Record
1900-09	119-87	121-90	90-119	112-93	87-121	75-137	105-105										709-752
1910-19	123-90	112-98	101-110	110-99	85-124	107-105	124-91										762-717
1920-29	118-100	69-151	88-132	87-133	65-149	71-148	68-149										566-962
1930-39	97-122	61-159	73-147	89-128	72-145	90-126	99-116										581-943
1940-49	87-132	70-150	99-121	58-162	91-129	95-121	84-136										584-951
1950-59	102-118	107-113	128-92	92-128	99-121	132-88	107-113										767-773
1960-69	75-107	79-108	95-93	76-106	77-105	89-98	75-107	87-51	91-53	7-11	8-4						759-843
1970-79	58-62	91-86	92-87	56-63	67-53	79-101	47-73	61-59	97-83	90-88	74-46						812-801
1980-89	53-64	80-95	95-78	59-55	61-54	91-83	55-60	61-57	86-90	86-87	56-57						783-780
1990-99	50-70	57-67	63-60	54-61	44-67	58-66	39-68	43-62	70-69	73-65	53-60	52-34	36-29	9-9	8-10	23-26	732-823
Totals	882-952	847-1117	924-1039	793-1028	748-1068	887-1073	803-1018	252-229	344-295	256-251	191-167	52-34	36-29	9-9	8-10	23-26	7055-8345

Interleague results: 4-8 vs. Orioles; 5-5 vs. Red Sox; 1-2 vs. Tigers; 5-4 vs. Yankees; 5-4 vs. Blue Jays; 3-3 vs. Devil Rays.

MANAGERS

Name	Years	Record
Bob Ferguson	1883	4-13
Blondie Purcell	1883	13-68
Harry Wright	1884-93	636-566
Jack Clements	1890	13-6
Al Reach	1890	4-7
Bob Allen	1890	25-10
Albert Irwin	1894-95	149-110
Billy Nash	1896	62-68
George Stallings	1897-98	74-104
Bill Shettsline	1898-1902	367-303
Chief Zimmer	1903	49-86
Hugh Duffy	1904-06	206-251
Bill Murray	1907-09	240-214
Red Dooin	1910-14	392-370
Pat Moran	1915-18	323-257
Jack Coombs	1919	18-44
Gavvy Cravath	1919-20	91-137
Bill Donovan	1921	25-62
Kaiser Wilhelm	1921-22	83-137
Art Fletcher	1923-26	231-378
Stuffy McInnis	1927	51-103
Burt Shotton	1928-33	370-549

MANAGERS—cont'd.

Name	Years	Record
Jimmy Wilson	1934-38	280-477
Hans Lobert	1938, 1942	42-111
Doc Prothro	1939-41	138-320
Bucky Harris	1943	38-52
Fred Fitzsimmons	1943-45	105-181
Ben Chapman	1945-48	196-276
Dusty Cooke	1948	6-6
Eddie Sawyer	1948-52, 1958-60	390-423
Steve O'Neill	1952-54	182-140
Terry Moore	1954	35-42
Mayo Smith	1955-58	264-282
Andy Cohen	1960	1-0
Gene Mauch	1960-68	646-684
George Myatt	1968, 1969	20-35
Bob Skinner	1968-69	92-123
Frank Lucchesi	1970-72	166-233
Paul Owens	1972, 1983-84	161-158
Danny Ozark	1973-79	594-510
Dallas Green	1979-81	169-130
Pat Corrales	1982-83	132-115
John Felske	1985-87	190-194
Lee Elia	1987-88	111-142
John Vukovich	1988	5-4
Nick Leyva	1989-91	148-189
Jim Fregosi	1991-96	431-463
Terry Francona	1997-99	220-266

WORLD SERIES CHAMPIONS

Year	Loser	Length	MVP
1980	Kansas City	6 games	Schmidt

N.L. PENNANT WINNERS

Year	Record	Manager	Series Result
1915	90-62	Moran	Lost to Red Sox
1950	91-63	Sawyer	Lost to Yankees
1980	91-71	Green	Defeated Royals
1983	90-72	Corrales, Owens	Lost to Orioles
1993	97-65	Fregosi	Lost to Blue Jays

EAST DIVISION CHAMPIONS

Year	Record	Manager	NLCS Result
1976	101-61	Ozark	Lost to Reds
1977	101-61	Ozark	Lost to Dodgers
1978	90-72	Ozark	Lost to Dodgers
1980	91-71	Green	Defeated Astros
*1981	59-48	Green	None
1983	90-72	Corrales, Owens	Defeated Dodgers
1993	97-65	Fregosi	Defeated Braves

* First-half champion; lost division series to Expos.

ATTENDANCE HIGHS

Total	Season	Park
3,137,674	1993	Veterans Stadium
2,775,011	1979	Veterans Stadium
2,700,007	1977	Veterans Stadium
2,651,650	1980	Veterans Stadium
2,583,389	1978	Veterans Stadium

BALLPARK CHRONOLOGY

Veterans Stadium (1971-present)
Capacity: 62,409.
First game: Phillies 4, Montreal 1 (April 10, 1971).
First batter: Boots Day, Expos.
First hit: Larry Bowa, Phillies (single).
First run: Ron Hunt, Expos (6th inning).
First home run: Don Money, Phillies.
First winning pitcher: Jim Bunning, Phillies.
First-season attendance: 1,511,223.

Recreation Park (1883-86)
First game: Providence 4, Philadelphia 3 (May 1, 1883).

Huntington Street Grounds/Baker Bowl (1887-1938)
Capacity: 18,800.
First game: Phillies 19, New York 10 (April 30, 1887).

Shibe Park (1927, 1938-70)
Capacity: 33,608.
First game: St. Louis 2, Phillies 1 (May 16, 1927).
First-season attendance (1939): 277,973.

N.L. MVPs
Chuck Klein, OF, 1932
Jim Konstanty, P, 1950
Mike Schmidt, 3B, 1980
Mike Schmidt, 3B, 1981
Mike Schmidt, 3B, 1986

CY YOUNG WINNERS
Steve Carlton, LH, 1972
Steve Carlton, LH, 1977
Steve Carlton, LH, 1980
Steve Carlton, LH, 1982
John Denny, RH, 1983
Steve Bedrosian, RH, 1987

ROOKIES OF THE YEAR
Jack Sanford, P, 1957
Dick Allen, 3B, 1964
Scott Rolen, 3B, 1997

RETIRED UNIFORMS

No.	Name	Pos.
1	Richie Ashburn	OF
20	Mike Schmidt	3B
32	Steve Carlton	P
36	Robin Roberts	P

Chuck Klein (left) and Lefty O'Doul combined for 267 RBIs in a prolific 1929 season.

30-plus home runs

48—	Mike Schmidt	1980
45—	Mike Schmidt	1979
43—	Chuck Klein	1929
41—	Cy Williams	1923
40—	Chuck Klein	1930
	Richie Allen	1966
	Mike Schmidt	1983
39—	Greg Luzinski	1977
38—	Chuck Klein	1932
	Mike Schmidt	1975, 1976, 1977
37—	Mike Schmidt	1986
36—	Mike Schmidt	1974, 1984
35—	Greg Luzinski	1978
	Mike Schmidt	1982, 1987
34—	Deron Johnson	1971
	Greg Luzinski	1975
33—	Richie Allen	1968
	Mike Schmidt	1985
32—	Lefty O'Doul	1929
	Stan Lopata	1956
	Johnny Callison	1965
	Richie Allen	1969
31—	Don Hurst	1929
	Chuck Klein	1931
	Del Ennis	1950
	Johnny Callison	1964
	Mike Schmidt	1981
	Scott Rolen	1998
	Mike Lieberthal	1999
30—	Cy Williams	1927
	Del Ennis	1948
	Willie Montanez	1971
	Benito Santiago	1996

100-plus RBIs

170—	Chuck Klein	1930
165—	Sam Thompson	1895
146—	Ed Delahanty	1893
145—	Chuck Klein	1929
143—	Don Hurst	1932
141—	Sam Thompson	1894
137—	Ed Delahanty	1899
	Chuck Klein	1932
131—	Ed Delahanty	1894
130—	Greg Luzinski	1977
128—	Gavvy Cravath	1913
127—	Nap Lajoie	1897, 1898
126—	Sam Thompson	1893
	Ed Delahanty	1896
	Del Ennis	1950
125—	Lave Cross	1894
	Don Hurst	1929
	Del Ennis	1953
124—	Pinky Whitney	1932
123—	Sherry Magee	1910
122—	Lefty O'Doul	1929
121—	Chuck Klein	1931
	Mike Schmidt	1980
120—	Chuck Klein	1933
	Del Ennis	1955
	Greg Luzinski	1975
119—	Del Ennis	1954
	Mike Schmidt	1986
117—	Pinky Whitney	1930
116—	Mike Schmidt	1974
115—	Gavvy Cravath	1915
	Pinky Whitney	1929
114—	Cy Williams	1923
	Mike Schmidt	1979
113—	Mike Schmidt	1987
111—	Sam Thompson	1889
110—	Elmer Flick	1900

Righthander Robin Roberts.

	Del Ennis	1949
	Richie Allen	1966
	Scott Rolen	1998
109—	Ed Delahanty	1900
	Mike Schmidt	1983
	Darren Daulton	1992
108—	Ed Delahanty	1901
107—	Del Ennis	1952
	Don Demeter	1962
	Mike Schmidt	1976
106—	Ed Delahanty	1895
	Mike Schmidt	1984
105—	Darren Daulton	1993
104—	Sam Thompson	1892
	Ron Northey	1944
	John Callison	1964
	Rico Brogna	1998
103—	Sherry Magee	1914
	Pinky Whitney	1928
	Bill White	1966
102—	Sam Thompson	1890
	Dolf Camilli	1936
	Rico Brogna	1999
101—	Lave Cross	1895
	John Callison	1965
	Mike Schmidt	1977
	Greg Luzinski	1978
100—	Sam Thompson	1896
	Gavvy Cravath	1914
	Juan Samuel	1987

20-plus victories

1884—	Charlie Ferguson	21-25
1885—	Charlie Ferguson	26-20
	Ed Daily	26-23
1886—	Charlie Ferguson	30-9
	Dan Casey	24-18
1887—	Dan Casey	28-13
	Charlie Ferguson	22-10
	Charlie Buffinton	21-17
1888—	Charlie Buffinton	28-17
1889—	Charlie Buffinton	28-16
1890—	Kid Gleason	38-17
	Tom Vickery	24-22
1891—	Kid Gleason	24-22
	Charles Esper	20-15
1892—	Gus Weyhing	32-21
1893—	Gus Weyhing	23-16
1894—	Jack Taylor	23-13
1895—	Jack Taylor	26-14
	Kid Carsey	24-16
1896—	Jack Taylor	20-21
1898—	Wiley Piatt	24-14
1899—	Wiley Piatt	23-15
	Red Donahue	21-8
	Charles Fraser	21-12
1901—	Al Orth	20-12
	Red Donahue	21-13
1905—	Charlie Pittinger	23-14
1907—	Frank Sparks	22-8
1908—	George McQuillan	23-17
1910—	Earl Moore	22-15
1911—	Grover Alexander	28-13
1913—	Tom Seaton	27-12
	Grover Alexander	22-8
1914—	Grover Alexander	27-15
	Erskine Mayer	21-19
1915—	Grover Alexander	31-10
	Erskine Mayer	21-15
1916—	Grover Alexander	33-12
	Eppa Rixey	22-10
1917—	Grover Alexander	30-13
1950—	Robin Roberts	20-11
1951—	Robin Roberts	21-15
1952—	Robin Roberts	28-7
1953—	Robin Roberts	23-16
1954—	Robin Roberts	23-15
1955—	Robin Roberts	23-14
1966—	Chris Short	20-10
1972—	Steve Carlton	27-10
1976—	Steve Carlton	20-7
1977—	Steve Carlton	23-10
1980—	Steve Carlton	24-9
1982—	Steve Carlton	23-11

N.L. home run champions

1876—	George Hall	5
1889—	Sam Thompson	20
1893—	Ed Delahanty	19
1895—	Sam Thompson	18
1896—	Ed Delahanty	*13
1897—	Nap Lajoie	10
1913—	Gavvy Cravath	19
1914—	Gavvy Cravath	19
1915—	Gavvy Cravath	24
1917—	Gavvy Cravath	*12
1918—	Gavvy Cravath	8
1919—	Gavvy Cravath	12
1920—	Cy Williams	15
1923—	Cy Williams	41
1927—	Cy Williams	*30

SEASON

Batting

At-bats	701		Juan Samuel	1984
Runs	196		Billy Hamilton	1894
Hits	254		Lefty O'Doul	1929
Singles	181		Lefty O'Doul	1929
			Richie Ashburn	1951
Doubles	59		Chuck Klein	1930
Triples	26		Sam Thompson	1894
Home runs	48		Mike Schmidt	1980
Home runs, rookie	30		Willie Montanez	1971
Grand slams	4		Vince DiMaggio	1945
Total bases	445		Chuck Klein	1930
RBIs	170		Chuck Klein	1930
Walks	129		Lenny Dykstra	1993
Most strikeouts	180		Mike Schmidt	1975
Fewest strikeouts	8		Emil Verban	1947
Batting average	.408		Ed Delahanty	1899
Slugging pct.	.687		Chuck Klein	1930
Stolen bases	115		Billy Hamilton	1891

Pitching (since 1900)

Games	90		Kent Tekulve	1987
Complete games	38		Grover Alexander	1916
Innings	388.2		Grover Alexander	1916
Wins	33		Grover Alexander	1916
Losses	24		Chick Fraser	1904
Winning pct.	.800 (28-7)		Robin Roberts	1952
	.800 (16-4)		Tommy Greene	1993
Walks	164		Earl Moore	1911
Strikeouts	319		Curt Schilling	1997
Shutouts	16		Grover Alexander	1916
Home runs allowed	46		Robin Roberts	1956
Lowest ERA	1.22		Grover Alexander	1915
Saves	43		Mitch Williams	1993

GAME

Batting

Runs	5	Last by Mariano Duncan	5-3-92
Hits	6	Connie Ryan	4-16-53
Doubles	4	Last by Willie Jones	4-20-49
Triples	3	Harry Wolverton	7-13-00
Home runs	4	Chuck Klein	7-10-36
		Mike Schmidt	4-17-76
RBIs	8	Last by Mike Schmidt	4-17-76
Total bases	17	Mike Schmidt	4-17-76
Stolen bases	4	Sherry Magee	7-12-06, 8-31-06.

1929—	Chuck Klein	43
1931—	Chuck Klein	31
1932—	Chuck Klein	*38
1933—	Chuck Klein	28
1974—	Mike Schmidt	36
1975—	Mike Schmidt	38
1976—	Mike Schmidt	38
1980—	Mike Schmidt	48
1981—	Mike Schmidt	31
1983—	Mike Schmidt	40
1984—	Mike Schmidt	*36
1986—	Mike Schmidt	37

* Tied for league lead

N.L. RBI champions

1907—	Sherry Magee	85
1910—	Sherry Magee	123
1913—	Gavvy Cravath	128
1914—	Sherry Magee	103
1915—	Gavvy Cravath	115
1931—	Chuck Klein	121
1932—	Don Hurst	143
1933—	Chuck Klein	120
1950—	Del Ennis	126
1975—	Greg Luzinski	120
1980—	Mike Schmidt	121
1981—	Mike Schmidt	91
1984—	Mike Schmidt	*106
1986—	Mike Schmidt	119
1992—	Darren Daulton	109

* Tied for league lead

N.L. batting champions

1891—	Billy Hamilton	.340
1899—	Ed Delahanty	.410
1910—	Sherry Magee	.331
1929—	Lefty O'Doul	.398
1933—	Chuck Klein	.368
1947—	Harry Walker	*.363
1955—	Richie Ashburn	.338
1958—	Richie Ashburn	.350

*10 games with Cardinals; 130 with Phillies.

N.L. ERA champions

1915—	Grover Alexander	1.22
1916—	Grover Alexander	1.55
1917—	Grover Alexander	1.83
1972—	Steve Carlton	1.97

N.L. strikeout champions

1910—	Earl Moore	185
1912—	Grover Alexander	195
1913—	Tom Seaton	168
1914—	Grover Alexander	214
1915—	Grover Alexander	241
1916—	Grover Alexander	167
1917—	Grover Alexander	201
1940—	Kirby Higbe	137
1953—	Robin Roberts	198
1954—	Robin Roberts	185
1957—	Jack Sanford	188
1967—	Jim Bunning	253
1972—	Steve Carlton	310
1974—	Steve Carlton	240
1980—	Steve Carlton	286
1982—	Steve Carlton	286
1983—	Steve Carlton	275
1997—	Curt Schilling	319
1998—	Curt Schilling	300

No-hit pitchers
(9 innings or more)

1885—	Charles Ferguson	1-0 vs. Providence
1898—	Red Donahue	5-0 vs. Boston
1903—	Charles Fraser	10-0 vs. Chicago
1906—	John Lush	6-0 vs. Brooklyn
1964—	Jim Bunning	6-0 vs. New York (Perfect)
1971—	Rick Wise	4-0 vs. Cincinnati
1990—	Terry Mulholland	6-0 vs. San Francisco
1991—	Tommy Greene	2-0 vs. Montreal

Longest hitting streaks

36—	Billy Hamilton	1894
31—	Ed Delahanty	1899
26—	Chuck Klein	1930 (twice)
24—	Willie Montanez	1974
23—	Goldie Rapp	1921
	Johnny Moore	1934
	Richie Ashburn	1948
	Pete Rose	1979
	Lonnie Smith	1981
	Lenny Dykstra	1990
22—	Chuck Klein	1931
	Chick Fullis	1933
21—	Ed Dalahanty	1897
	Irish Meusel	1920
	Danny Litwhiler	1940
	Pete Rose	1982
20—	Nap Lajoie	1897
	Chuck Klein	1932
	Richie Ashburn	1951
	Pancho Herrera	1960
	Garry Maddox	1978

BATTING

Games

Mike Schmidt	2,404
Richie Ashburn	1,794
Larry Bowa	1,739
Tony Taylor	1,669
Del Ennis	1,630
Ed Delahanty	1,555
Sherry Magee	1,521
Willie Jones	1,520
Granny Hamner	1,501
Cy Williams	1,463

At-bats

Mike Schmidt	8,352
Richie Ashburn	7,122
Larry Bowa	6,815
Ed Delahanty	6,359
Del Ennis	6,327
Tony Taylor	5,799
Granny Hamner	5,772
Sherry Magee	5,505
Willie Jones	5,419
Johnny Callison	5,306

Runs

Mike Schmidt	1,506
Ed Delahanty	1,367
Richie Ashburn	1,114
Chuck Klein	963
Sam Thompson	924
Roy Thomas	923
Sherry Magee	898
Del Ennis	891
Billy Hamilton	874
Cy Williams	825

Hits

Mike Schmidt	2,234
Richie Ashburn	2,217
Ed Delahanty	2,213
Del Ennis	1,812
Larry Bowa	1,798
Chuck Klein	1,705
Sherry Magee	1,647
Cy Williams	1,553
Granny Hamner	1,518
Tony Taylor	1,511

Doubles

Ed Delahanty	442
Mike Schmidt	408
Sherry Magee	337
Chuck Klein	336
Del Ennis	310
Richie Ashburn	287
Sam Thompson	272
Granny Hamner	271
Johnny Callison	265
Greg Luzinski	253

Triples

Ed Delahanty	157
Sherry Magee	127
Sam Thompson	106
Richie Ashburn	97
Johnny Callison	84
Larry Bowa	81
Gavvy Cravath	72
Juan Samuel	71
Del Ennis	65
Dick Allen	64
Chuck Klein	64
John Titus	64

Home runs

Mike Schmidt	548
Del Ennis	259
Chuck Klein	243
Greg Luzinski	223
Cy Williams	217
Dick Allen	204
Johnny Callison	185
Willie Jones	180
Darren Daulton	134
Von Hayes	124

Total bases

Mike Schmidt	4,404
Ed Delahanty	3,230
Del Ennis	3,029
Chuck Klein	2,898
Richie Ashburn	2,764
Cy Williams	2,539
Sherry Magee	2,463
Johnny Callison	2,426
Greg Luzinski	2,263
Sam Thompson	2,238

Runs batted in

Mike Schmidt	1,595
Ed Delahanty	1,286

Del Ennis	1,124
Chuck Klein	983
Sam Thompson	957
Sherry Magee	886
Greg Luzinski	811
Cy Williams	795
Willie Jones	753
Pinky Whitney	734

Extra-base hits

Mike Schmidt	1,015
Ed Delahanty	686
Chuck Klein	643
Del Ennis	634
Sherry Magee	539
Johnny Callison	534
Cy Williams	503
Greg Luzinski	497
Sam Thompson	473
Dick Allen	472

Batting average
(Minimum 500 games)

Billy Hamilton	.361
Ed Delahanty	.348
Elmer Flick	.338
Sam Thompson	.333
Chuck Klein	.326
Spud Davis	.321
Fred Leach	.312
Richie Ashburn	.311
John Kruk	.309
Pinky Whitney	.308

Stolen bases

Billy Hamilton	508
Ed Delahanty	411
Sherry Magee	387
Jim Fogarty	289
Larry Bowa	288
Juan Samuel	249
Roy Thomas	228
Von Hayes	202
Richie Ashburn	199
Garry Maddox	189
Sam Thompson	189

PITCHING

Earned-run average
(Minimum 1,000 innings)

Grover Alexander	2.18
Tully Sparks	2.48
Earl Moore	2.63
Charlie Ferguson	2.67
Erskine Mayer	2.81
Eppa Rixey	2.83
Charlie Buffinton	2.89
Dan Casey	2.91
Jim Bunning	2.93
Steve Carlton	3.09

Wins

Steve Carlton	241
Robin Roberts	234
Grover Alexander	190
Chris Short	132
Curt Simmons	115
Al Orth	100
Charlie Ferguson	99
Jack Taylor	96
Curt Schilling	95
Tully Sparks	95

Losses

Robin Roberts	199
Steve Carlton	161
Chris Short	127
Curt Simmons	110
Eppa Rixey	103
Bill Duggleby	99
Jimmy Ring	98
Tully Sparks	95
Grover Alexander	91
Hugh Mulcahy	89

Innings pitched

Robin Roberts	3,739.1
Steve Carlton	3,697.1
Grover Alexander	2,513.2
Chris Short	2,253.0
Curt Simmons	1,939.2
Tully Sparks	1,698.0
Bill Duggleby	1,684.0
Eppa Rixey	1,604.0
Curt Schilling	1,546.2
Jim Bunning	1,520.2

Strikeouts

Steve Carlton	3,031
Robin Roberts	1,871
Chris Short	1,585
Curt Schilling	1,458
Grover Alexander	1,409
Jim Bunning	1,197

Curt Simmons	1,052
Larry Christenson	781
Charlie Ferguson	728
Kevin Gross	727

Bases on balls

Steve Carlton	1,252
Chris Short	762
Robin Roberts	718
Curt Simmons	718
Jimmy Ring	636
Grover Alexander	561
Kid Carsey	536
Earl Moore	518
Kid Gleason	482
Hugh Mulcahy	480

Games

Robin Roberts	529
Steve Carlton	499
Tug McGraw	463
Chris Short	459
Ron Reed	458
Turk Farrell	359
Grover Alexander	338
Jack Baldschun	333
Curt Simmons	325
Jim Konstanty	314

Shutouts

Grover Alexander	61
Steve Carlton	39
Robin Roberts	35
Chris Short	24
Jim Bunning	23
Curt Simmons	18
Tully Sparks	18
George McQuillan	17
Earl Moore	17
Bill Duggleby	16

Saves

Steve Bedrosian	103
Mitch Williams	102
Tug McGraw	94
Ron Reed	90
Ricky Bottalico	75
Turk Farrell	65
Jack Baldschun	59
Al Holland	55
Jim Konstanty	54
Gene Garber	51

SEASON

Batting

Most at-bats	5,685	1993
Most runs	944	1930
Fewest runs	394	1942
Most hits	1,783	1930
Most singles	1,338	1894
Most doubles	345	1930
Most triples	148	1894
Most home runs	186	1977
Fewest home runs	11	1908
Most grand slams	8	1993
Most pinch-hit home runs	11	1958
Most total bases	2,594	1930
Most stolen bases	200	1908
Highest batting average	.343	1894
Lowest batting average	.232	1942
Highest slugging pct.	.467	1929

Pitching

Lowest ERA	2.10	1908
Highest ERA	6.71	1930
Most complete games	131	1904
Most shutouts	24	1916
Most saves	48	1987
Most walks	682	1974
Most strikeouts	1,117	1993

Fielding

Most errors	403	1904
Fewest errors	104	1978
Most double plays	179	1961, 1973
Highest fielding average	.983	1978, 1979

General

Most games won	101	1976, 1977
Most games lost	111	1941
Highest win pct	.623	1886, 1976, 1977
Lowest win pct	.173	1883

GAME, INNING

Batting

Most runs, game	29	8-17-1894
Most runs, inning	12	10-2-1897, 7-21-23
Most hits, game	36	8-17-1894
Most home runs, game	7	9-8-98
Most total bases, game	49	8-17-1894

Hard-throwing lefthander Steve Carlton won 241 of his 329 games in 14-plus seasons with the Phillies.

PHILLIES YEAR-BY-YEAR

Year	W	L	Place	Games Back	Manager	Batting avg.	Hits	Home runs	RBIs	Wins	ERA
1901	83	57	2nd	7½	Shettsline	Delahanty, .354	Delahanty, 192	Delahanty, Flick, 8	Delahanty, 108	Donahue, 21	Orth, 2.27
1902	56	81	7th	46	Shettsline	S. Barry, .287	S. Barry, 156	S. Barry, 3	S. Barry, 58	White, 16	White, 2.53
1903	49	86	7th	39½	Zimmer	Thomas, .327	Thomas, 156	Keister, 3	Keister, 63	Duggleby, 13	Sparks, 2.72
1904	52	100	8th	53½	Duffy	Titus, .294	Gleason, 161	Dooin, 6	Magee, 57	Fraser, 14	Corridon, 2.19
1905	83	69	4th	21½	Duffy	Thomas, .317	Magee, 180	Magee, 5	Magee, 98	Pittinger, 23	Sparks, 2.18
1906	71	82	4th	45½	Duffy	Magee, .282	Magee, 159	Magee, 6	Magee, 67	Sparks, 19	Sparks, 2.16
1907	83	64	3rd	21½	Murray	Magee, .328	Magee, 165	Magee, 4	Magee, 85	Sparks, 22	Richie, 1.77
1908	83	71	4th	16	Murray	Bransfield, .304	Bransfield, 160	Bransfield, 3	Bransfield, 71	McQuillan, 23	McQuillan, 1.53
1909	74	79	5th	36½	Murray	Bransfield, .292	Grant, 170	Titus, 3	Magee, 66	Moore, 18	Moore, 2.10
1910	78	75	4th	25½	Dooin	Magee, .331	Magee, 172	Magee, 6	Magee, 123	Moore, 22	McQuillan, 1.60
1911	79	73	4th	19½	Dooin	Luderus, .301	Luderus, 166	Luderus, 16	Luderus, 99	Alexander, 28	Alexander, 2.57
1912	73	79	5th	30½	Dooin	Paskert, .315	Paskert, 170	Cravath, 11	Magee, 72	Alexander, 19	Rixey, 2.50
1913	88	63	2nd	12½	Dooin	Cravath, .341	Cravath, 179	Cravath, 19	Cravath, 128	Seaton, 27	Brennan, 2.39
1914	74	80	6th	20½	Dooin	Becker, .325	Magee, 171	Cravath, 19	Magee, 103	Alexander, 27	Alexander, 2.38
1915	90	62	1st	+7	Moran	Luderus, .315	Luderus, 157	Cravath, 24	Cravath, 115	Alexander, 31	Alexander, 1.22
1916	91	62	2nd	2½	Moran	Cravath, .283	Paskert, 155	Cravath, 11	Cravath, 70	Alexander, 33	Alexander, 1.55
1917	87	65	2nd	10	Moran	Cravath, Whitted, .280	Whitted, 155	Cravath, 12	Cravath, 83	Alexander, 30	Bender, 1.67
1918	55	68	6th	26	Moran	Luderus, .288	Luderus, 135	Cravath, 8	Luderus, 67	Hogg, Pendergast, 13	Jacobs, 2.41
1919	47	90	8th	47½	Coombs, Cravath	I. Meusel, .305	I. Meusel, 159	Cravath, 12	I. Meusel, 59	Meadows, 8	Meadows, 2.33
1920	62	91	8th	30½	Cravath	Williams, .325	Williams, 192	Williams, 15	Williams, 72	Meadows, 16	Meadows, 2.84
1921	51	103	8th	43½	Donovan, Wilhelm	Williams, .320	Williams, 180	Williams, 18	Williams, 75	Meadows, 11	Winters, 3.63
1922	57	96	7th	35½	Wilhelm	Walker, .337	Walker, 196	Williams, 26	Williams, 92	Meadows, Ring, 12	Weinert, 3.40
1923	50	104	8th	45½	Fletcher	Lee, .321	Holke, 175	Williams, 41	Williams, 114	Ring, 18	Ring, 3.87
1924	55	96	7th	37	Fletcher	Williams, .328	Williams, 183	Williams, 24	Williams, 93	Hubbell, Ring, 10	Ring, 3.97
1925	68	85	*6th	27	Fletcher	Harper, .349	Harper, 173	Harper, 18	Harper, 97	Ring, 14	Carlson, 4.23
1926	58	93	8th	29½	Fletcher	Leach, .329	Leach, 162	Williams, 18	Leach, 71	Carlson, 17	Carlson, 3.23
1927	51	103	8th	43	McInnis	Leach, Wrightstone, .306	Thompson, 181	Williams, 30	Williams, 98	Scott, 9	Ulrich, 3.17
1928	43	109	8th	51	Shotton	Leach, .304	Thompson, 182	Hurst, 19	Whitney, 103	Benge, 8	Benge, 4.55
1929	71	82	5th	27½	Shotton	O'Doul, .398	O'Doul, 254	Klein, 43	Klein, 145	Willoughby, 15	Willoughby, 4.99
1930	52	102	8th	40	Shotton	Klein, .386	Klein, 250	Klein, 40	Klein, 170	Collins, 16	Collins, 4.78
1931	66	88	6th	35	Shotton	Klein, .337	Klein, 200	Klein, 31	Klein, 121	J. Elliott, 19	Benge, 3.17
1932	78	76	4th	12	Shotton	Klein, .348	Klein, 226	Klein, 38	Hurst, 143	Collins, 14	Hansen, 3.72
1933	60	92	7th	31	Shotton	Klein, .368	Klein, 223	Klein, 28	Klein, 120	Holley, 13	Holley, 3.53
1934	56	93	7th	37	Wilson	Moore, .343	Allen, 192	Camilli, 12	Moore, 93	C. Davis, 19	C. Davis, 2.95
1935	64	89	7th	35½	Wilson	Moore, .323	Allen, 198	Camilli, 25	Camilli, 102	C. Davis, 16	S. Johnson, 3.56
1936	54	100	8th	38	Wilson	Moore, .328	Chiozza, 170	Camilli, 28	Camilli, 102	Passeau, Walters, 11	Passeau, 3.48
1937	61	92	7th	34½	Wilson	Whitney, .341	Whitney, 166	Camilli, 27	Camilli, 80	LeMaster, 15	Passeau, 4.34
1938	45	105	8th	43	Wilson, Lobert	Weintraub, .311	Martin, 139	Klein, 8	Arnovich, 72	Passeau, 11	Butcher, 2.93
1939	45	106	8th	50½	Prothro	Arnovich, .324	Arnovich, 159	Marty, Mueller, 9	Arnovich, 67	Higbe, 10	S. Johnson, 3.81
1940	50	103	8th	50	Prothro	May, .293	May, 147	Rizzo, 20	Rizzo, 53	Higbe, 14	Mulcahy, 3.60
1941	43	111	8th	57	Prothro	Etten, .311	Litwhiler, 180	Litwhiler, 18	Etten, 79	Hughes, Podgajny, 9	Pearson, 3.57
1942	42	109	8th	62½	Lobert	Litwhiler, .271	Litwhiler, 160	Litwhiler, 9	Litwhiler, 56	Hughes, 12	Hughes, 3.06
1943	64	90	7th	41	Harris, Fitzsimmons	Dahlgren, .287	Northey, 163	Northey, 16	Northey, 68	Rowe, 14	Barrett, 2.39
1944	61	92	8th	43½	Fitzsimmons	Northey, .288	Lupien, 169	Northey, 22	Northey, 104	Raffensberger, Schanz, 13	Raffensberger, 3.06
1945	46	108	8th	52	Fitzsimmons, Chapman	Wasdell, .300	Wasdell, 150	V. DiMaggio, 19	V. DiMaggio, 84	Karl, 9	Karl, 2.99
1946	69	85	5th	28	Chapman	Ennis, .313	Ennis, 169	Ennis, 17	Ennis, 73	Judd, Rowe, 11	Rowe, 2.12
1947	62	92	*7th	32	Chapman	Walker, .371	Walker, 181	Seminick, 13	Ennis, 81	Leonard, 17	Leonard, 2.68
1948	66	88	6th	25½	Chapman, Cooke, Sawyer	Ashburn, .333	Ennis, 171	Ennis, 30	Ennis, 95	Leonard, 12	Leonard, 2.51
1949	81	73	3rd	16	Sawyer	Ennis, .302	Ashburn, 188	Ennis, 25	Ennis, 110	Heintzelman, Meyer, 17	Heintzelman, 3.02
1950	91	63	1st	+2	Sawyer	Ennis, .311	Ennis, 180	Ennis, 31	Ennis, 126	Roberts, 20	Konstanty, 2.66
1951	73	81	5th	23½	Sawyer	Ashburn, .344	Ashburn, 221	W. Jones, 22	W. Jones, 81	Roberts, 21	Roberts, 3.03
1952	87	67	4th	9½	Sawyer, O'Neill	Burgess, .296	Ashburn, 173	Ennis, 20	Ennis, 107	Roberts, 28	Roberts, 2.59
1953	83	71	*3rd	22	O'Neill	Ashburn, .330	Ashburn, 205	Ennis, 29	Ennis, 125	Roberts, 23	Roberts, 2.75
1954	75	79	4th	22	O'Neill, Moore	Ashburn, .313	Hamner, 178	Ennis, 25	Ennis, 119	Roberts, 23	Simmons, 2.81
1955	77	77	4th	21½	Smith	Ashburn, .338	Ashburn, 180	Ennis, 29	Ennis, 120	Roberts, 23	B. Miller, 2.41
1956	71	83	5th	22	Smith	Ashburn, .303	Ashburn, 190	Lopata, 32	Ennis, Lopata, 95	Roberts, 19	B. Miller, 3.24
1957	77	77	5th	19	Smith	Ashburn, .297	Ashburn, 186	Repulski, 20	Bouchee, 76	Sanford, 19	Sanford, 3.08
1958	69	85	8th	23	Smith, Sawyer	Ashburn, .350	Ashburn, 215	H. Anderson, 23	H. Anderson, 97	Roberts, 17	Roberts, 3.24
1959	64	90	8th	23	Sawyer	Bouchee, .285	Ashburn, 150	Freese, 23	Post, 94	Roberts, 15	Conley, 3.00
1960	59	95	8th	36	Sawyer, Cohen, Mauch	Taylor, .287	Taylor, 145	Herrera, 17	Herrera, 71	Roberts, 12	Mahaffey, 3.31
1961	47	107	8th	46	Mauch	Gonzalez, .277	Callison, 121	Demeter, 20	Demeter, 68	Mahaffey, 11	Ferrarese, 2.76
1962	81	80	7th	20	Mauch	Demeter, .307	Callison, 181	Demeter, 29	Demeter, 107	Mahaffey, 19	Baldschun, 2.96
1963	87	75	4th	12	Mauch	Gonzalez, .306	Taylor, 180	Callison, 26	Demeter, 83	Culp, 14	Klippstein, 1.93
1964	92	70	*2nd	1	Mauch	Allen, .318	Allen, 201	Callison, 31	Callison, 104	Bunning, 19	Short, 2.20
1965	85	76	6th	11½	Mauch	Rojas, .303	Allen, 187	Callison, 32	Callison, 101	Bunning, 19	Bunning, 2.60
1966	87	75	4th	8	Mauch	Allen, .317	Callison, 169	Allen, 40	Allen, 110	Short, 20	Bunning, 2.41
1967	82	80	5th	19½	Mauch	Gonzalez, .339	Gonzalez, 172	Allen, 23	Allen, 77	Bunning, 17	Farrell, 2.05
1968	76	86	*7th	21	Mauch, Myatt, Skinner	Gonzalez, .264	Rojas, 144	Allen, 33	Allen, 90	Short, 19	L. Jackson, 2.77
							EAST DIVISION				
1969	63	99	5th	37	Skinner, Myatt	Allen, .288	Taylor, 146	Allen, 32	Allen, 89	Wise, 15	Wise, 3.23
1970	73	88	5th	15½	Lucchesi	Taylor, .301	D. Johnson, 147	D. Johnson, 27	D. Johnson, 93	Wise, 13	Selma, 2.75
1971	67	95	6th	30	Lucchesi	McCarver, .278	Bowa, 162	D. Johnson, 34	Montanez, 99	Wise, 17	Wise, 2.88
1972	59	97	6th	37½	Lucchesi, Owens	Luzinski, .281	Luzinski, 158	Luzinski, 18	Luzinski, 68	Carlton, 27	Carlton, 1.97
1973	71	91	6th	11½	Ozark	Unser, .289	Luzinski, 174	Luzinski, 29	Luzinski, 97	Brett, Carlton, Lonborg, Twitchell, 13	Twitchell, 2.50
1974	80	82	3rd	8	Ozark	Montanez, .304	Cash, 206	Schmidt, 36	Schmidt, 116	Lonborg, 17	Lonborg, 3.21
1975	86	76	2nd	6½	Ozark	Johnstone, .329	Cash, 213	Schmidt, 38	Luzinski, 120	Carlton, 15	Hilgendorf, 2.14
1976	101	61	†1st	+9	Ozark	Maddox, .330	Cash, 189	Schmidt, 38	Schmidt, 107	Carlton, 20	McGraw, 2.50
1977	101	61	†1st	+5	Ozark	Luzinski, .309	Bowa, 175	Luzinski, 39	Luzinski, 130	Carlton, 23	Garber, 2.35
1978	90	72	†1st	+1½	Ozark	Bowa, .294	Bowa, 192	Luzinski, 35	Luzinski, 101	Carlton, 16	Reed, 2.24
1979	84	78	4th	14	Ozark, Green	Rose, .331	Rose, 208	Schmidt, 45	Schmidt, 114	Carlton, 18	Carlton, 3.62
1980	91	71	‡1st	+1	Green	McBride, .309	Rose, 185	Schmidt, 48	Schmidt, 121	Carlton, 24	McGraw, 1.46
1981	59	48	§1st/3rd	—	Green	Rose, .325	Rose, 140	Schmidt, 31	Schmidt, 91	Carlton, 13	Carlton, 2.42
1982	89	73	2nd	3	Corrales	Diaz, .288	Matthews, 173	Schmidt, 35	Schmidt, 87	Carlton, 23	Reed, 2.66
1983	90	72	‡1st	+6	Corrales, Owens	Hayes, .265	Schmidt, 136	Schmidt, 40	Schmidt, 109	Denny, 19	Holland, 2.26
1984	81	81	4th	15½	Owens	V. Hayes, .292	Samuel, 191	Schmidt, 36	Schmidt, 106	Koosman, 14	Andersen, 2.38
1985	75	87	5th	26	Felske	Schmidt, .277	Samuel, 175	Schmidt, 33	Wilson, 102	Gross, 15	Rawley, 3.31
1986	86	75	2nd	21½	Felske	V. Hayes, .305	V. Hayes, 187	Schmidt, 37	Schmidt, 119	Gross, 12	Ruffin, 2.46
1987	80	82	*4th	15	Felske, Elia	M. Thompson, .302	Samuel, 178	Schmidt, 35	Schmidt, 113	Rawley, 17	Tekulve, 3.09
1988	65	96	6th	35½	Elia, Vukovich	M. Thompson, .288	Samuel, 153	James, 19	Samuel, 67	Gross, 12	G. Harris, 2.36
1989	67	95	6th	26	Leyva	Herr, .287	Herr, 161	V. Hayes, 26	V. Hayes, 78	Howell, Parrett, 12	Parrett, 2.98
1990	77	85	*4th	18	Leyva	Dykstra, .325	Dykstra, 192	V. Hayes, 17	V. Hayes, 73	Combs, 10	Mulholland, 3.34
1991	78	84	3rd	20	Leyva, Fregosi	Kruk, .294	Kruk, 158	Kruk, 21	Kruk, 92	Mulholland, 16	Greene, 3.38
1992	70	92	6th	26	Fregosi	Kruk, .323	Kruk, 164	Daulton, Hollins, 27	Daulton, 109	Schilling, 14	Schilling, 2.35
1993	97	65	‡1st	+3	Fregosi	Eisenreich, .318	Dykstra, 194	Daulton, Incaviglia, 24	Daulton, 105	Greene, Schilling, 16	Mulholland, 3.25
1994	54	61	4th	20½	Fregosi	Kruk, .302	Duncan, 93	Daulton, 15	Daulton, 56	D. Jackson, 14	Munoz, 2.67
1995	69	75	*2nd	21	Fregosi	Eisenreich, .316	Jefferies, 147	Hayes, Jefferies, Whiten, 11	Hayes, 85	Quantrill, 11	Schilling, 3.57
1996	67	95	5th	29	Fregosi	Jefferies, .292	Morandini, 135	Santiago, 30	Santiago, 85	Schilling, 9	Schilling, 3.19
1997	68	94	5th	33	Francona	Morandini, .295	Morandini, 163	Rolen, 21	Rolen, 92	Schilling, 17	Schilling, 2.97
1998	75	87	3rd	31	Francona	Abreu, .312	Glanville, 189	Rolen, 31	Rolen, 110	Schilling, 15	Schilling, 3.25
1999	77	85	3rd	26	Francona	Abreu, .335	Glanville, 204	Lieberthal, 31	Brogna, 102	Schilling, Byrd, 15	Schilling, 3.54

* Tied for position. † Lost Championship Series. ‡ Won Championship Series. § First half 34-21; second half 25-27.

Note: Batting average minimum 350 at-bats; ERA minimum 90 innings pitched.

PITTSBURGH PIRATES

FRANCHISE CHRONOLOGY

First season: 1882, as a member of the American Association. The Allegheny club finished its first Pittsburgh season 39-39, good for fourth place in the seven-team field.

1883-1900: The Pirates played five A.A. seasons before jumping to the National League in 1887. In their first 14 N.L. seasons, they never finished first. But they did rise to second place in 1900, setting the stage for three consecutive pennants.

1901-present: The Pirates, with the arrival of manager Fred Clarke and shortstop Honus Wagner, became a consistent member of the N.L.'s first-division fraternity—a membership they would keep through most of the century. But strong teams did not translate into many pennants. After losing the first World Series in 1903, the Pirates captured their first championship in 1909 and their second 15 years later. There would be only three more—a memorable 1960 Series victory that ended on Bill Mazeroski's immortal home run and triumphs in 1971 and '79. The Pirates' most successful run came in the 1970s when they won six division titles and finished second three times. Consecutive division titles in 1990, '91 and '92 all resulted in Championship Series losses. Pittsburgh was one of five teams placed in the Central Division when the N.L. adopted its three-division format in 1994.

Shortstop Honus Wagner.

PIRATES VS. OPPONENTS BY DECADE

	Braves	Cardinals	Cubs	Dodgers	Giants	Phillies	Reds	Astros	Mets	Expos	Padres	Marlins	Rockies	Brewers	D'backs	Interleague	Decade Record
1900-09	153-58	158-53	112-99	132-76	115-96	137-75	131-81										938-538
1910-19	109-104	127-83	95-118	105-110	86-123	105-107	109-102										736-751
1920-29	141-77	117-102	125-95	122-97	106-113	148-71	118-101										877-656
1930-39	125-92	121-99	100-120	105-113	95-125	126-90	140-79										812-718
1940-49	112-105	98-122	116-104	96-124	109-111	121-95	104-115										756-776
1950-59	81-139	87-132	106-114	79-141	89-131	88-132	86-134										616-923
1960-69	94-88	81-107	110-78	82-100	82-100	98-89	92-90	93-45	93-51	13-5	10-2						848-755
1970-79	77-43	101-79	111-66	55-65	58-62	101-79	54-65	75-44	98-78	107-73	79-41						916-695
1980-89	53-58	75-98	95-81	53-61	55-63	83-91	50-64	51-63	69-102	86-88	62-56						732-825
1990-99	45-62	76-62	76-63	50-61	55-52	66-58	59-64	54-67	67-58	61-65	55-53	42-30	34-36	9-14	5-11	20-23	774-779
Totals	990-826	1041-937	1046-938	879-948	850-980	1073-887	943-895	273-219	327-289	267-231	206-152	42-30	34-36	9-14	5-11	20-23	8005-7416

Interleague results: 4-4 vs. White Sox; 5-4 vs. Indians; 4-4 vs. Royals; 1-2 vs. Brewers; 4-5 vs. Twins; 2-4 vs. Tigers.

MANAGERS

Name	Years	Record
Al Pratt	1882-83	51-59
Ormond Butler	1883	17-36
Joe Battin	1883, 1884	8-18
Denny McKnight	1884	4-8
Bob Ferguson	1884	11-31
George Creamer	1884	0-8
Horace Phillips	1884-89	294-316
Fred Dunlap	1889	7-10
Ned Hanlon	1889, 1891	57-65
Guy Hecker	1890	23-113
Bill McGunnigle	1891	24-33
Tom Burns	1892	27-32
Al Buckenberger	1892-94	187-144
Connie Mack	1894-96	149-134
Patsy Donovan	1897, 1899	129-129
Bill Watkins	1898-99	79-91
Fred Clarke	1900-15	1422-969
Jimmy Callahan	1916-17	85-129
Honus Wagner	1917	1-4
Hugo Bezdek	1917-19	166-187
George Gibson	1920-22, 1932-34	401-330
Bill McKechnie	1922-26	409-293
Donie Bush	1927-29	246-178
Jewel Ens	1929-31	176-167

MANAGERS—cont'd.

Name	Years	Record
Pie Traynor	1934-39	457-406
Frank Frisch	1940-46	539-528
Spud Davis	1946	1-2
Billy Herman	1947	61-92
Bill Burwell	1947	1-0
Billy Meyer	1948-52	317-452
Fred Haney	1953-55	163-299
Bobby Bragan	1956-57	102-155
Danny Murtaugh	1957-64, 1967, 1970-71, 1973-76	1115-950
Harry Walker	1965-67	224-184
Larry Shepard	1968-69	164-155
Alex Grammas	1969	4-1
Bill Virdon	1972-73	163-128
Chuck Tanner	1977-85	711-685
Jim Leyland	1986-96	851-863
Gene Lamont	1997-99	226-259

WORLD SERIES CHAMPIONS

Year	Loser	Length	MVP
1909	Detroit	7 games	None
1925	Washington	7 games	None
1960	N.Y. Yankees	7 games	Richardson
1971	Baltimore	7 games	Clemente
1979	Baltimore	7 games	Stargell

N.L. PENNANT WINNERS

Year	Record	Manager	Series Result
1901	90-49	Clarke	None
1902	103-36	Clarke	None
1903	91-49	Clarke	Lost to Red Sox
1909	110-42	Clarke	Defeated Tigers
1925	95-58	McKechnie	Defeated Senators
1927	94-60	Bush	Lost to Yankees
1960	95-59	Murtaugh	Defeated Yankees
1971	97-65	Murtaugh	Defeated Orioles
1979	98-64	Tanner	Defeated Orioles

EAST DIVISION CHAMPIONS

Year	Record	Manager	NLCS Result
1970	89-73	Murtaugh	Lost to Reds
1971	97-65	Murtaugh	Defeated Giants
1972	96-59	Virdon	Lost to Reds
1974	88-74	Murtaugh	Lost to Dodgers
1975	92-69	Murtaugh	Lost to Reds
1979	98-64	Tanner	Defeated Reds
1990	95-67	Leyland	Lost to Reds
1991	98-64	Leyland	Lost to Braves
1992	96-66	Leyland	Lost to Braves

ATTENDANCE HIGHS

Total	Season	Park
2,065,302	1991	Three Rivers Stadium
2,049,908	1990	Three Rivers Stadium
1,866,713	1988	Three Rivers Stadium
1,829,395	1992	Three Rivers Stadium
1,705,828	1960	Forbes Field

BALLPARK CHRONOLOGY

Three Rivers Stadium (1970-present)

Capacity: 47,972.
First game: Cincinnati 3, Pirates 2 (July 16, 1970).
First batter: Ty Cline, Reds.
First hit: Richie Hebner, Pirates (single).
First run: Richie Hebner, Pirates (1st inning).
First home run: Tony Perez, Reds.
First winning pitcher: Clay Carroll, Reds.
First-season attendance: 1,341,947.

Exposition Park (1882-84)

Recreation Park (1887-90)

Exposition Park III (1891-1909)

Capacity: 16,000.
First game: Chicago 7, Pittsburgh 6, 10 innings (April 22, 1891).

Forbes Field (1909-70)

Capacity: 35,000.
First game: Chicago 3, Pirates 2 (June 30, 1909).
First-season attendance (1910): 436,586.

N.L. MVPs

Dick Groat, SS, 1960
Roberto Clemente, OF, 1966
Dave Parker, OF, 1978
*Willie Stargell, 1B, 1979
Barry Bonds, OF, 1990
Barry Bonds, OF, 1992

  * Co-winner.

CY YOUNG WINNERS

Vernon Law, RH, 1960
Doug Drabek, RH, 1990

MANAGERS OF THE YEAR

Jim Leyland, 1990
Jim Leyland, 1992

RETIRED UNIFORMS

No.	Name	Pos.
1	Billy Meyer	Man.
4	Ralph Kiner	OF
8	Willie Stargell	1B
9	Bill Mazeroski	2B
20	Pie Traynor	3B
21	Roberto Clemente	OF
33	Honus Wagner	SS
40	Danny Murtaugh	Man.

HISTORY

Roberto Clemente ranked among the game's elite for 18 outstanding Pittsburgh seasons.

MILESTONE PERFORMANCES

30-plus home runs

54— Ralph Kiner	1949
51— Ralph Kiner	1947
48— Willie Stargell	1971
47— Ralph Kiner	1950
44— Willie Stargell	1973
42— Ralph Kiner	1951
40— Ralph Kiner	1948
39— Brian Giles	1999
37— Ralph Kiner	1952
35— Frank Thomas	1958
Dick Stuart	1961
34— Barry Bonds	1992
33— Willie Stargell	1966, 1972
Barry Bonds	1990
32— Willie Stargell	1979
Bobby Bonilla	1990
31— Willie Stargell	1970
Jason Thompson	1982
30— Frank Thomas	1953
Dave Parker	1978
Jeff King	1996

100-plus RBIs

131— Paul Waner	1927
127— Ralph Kiner	1947, 1949
126— Honus Wagner	1901
125— Willie Stargell	1971
124— Pie Traynor	1928
123— Ralph Kiner	1948
121— Glenn Wright	1925
120— Bobby Bonilla	1990
119— Adam Comorosky	1930
Pie Traynor	1930
Roberto Clemente	1966
Willie Stargell	1973
118— Gus Suhr	1936
Ralph Kiner	1950
117— Dick Stuart	1961
Dave Parker	1978
116— Maurice Van Robays	1940
Barry Bonds	1991
115— Brian Giles	1999
114— Clyde Barnhart	1925
Barry Bonds	1990
112— Willie Stargell	1972
111— Glenn Wright	1924
Johnny Rizzo	1938
Jeff King	1996
110— Roberto Clemente	1967
109— Honus Wagner	1908
Ralph Kiner	1951
Frank Thomas	1958
108— Pie Traynor	1929
Bob Elliott	1944
Bob Elliott	1945
Kevin Young	1998
107— Lou Bierbauer	1894
Owen Wilson	1911
Gus Suhr	1930
Willie Stargell	1965
106— Pie Traynor	1925, 1927
Kevin Young	1999
105— Glenn Wright	1927
104— Elbie Fletcher	1940
Wally Westlake	1949
Bill Robinson	1977
103— Pie Traynor	1931

Gus Suhr	1934
Barry Bonds	1992
102— Honus Wagner	1912
Kiki Cuyler	1925
Bill Brubaker	1936
Frank Thomas	1953
Willie Stargell	1966
101— Honus Wagner	1903, 1905
Pie Traynor	1923
Bob Elliott	1943
Babe Dahlgren	1944
Dave Parker	1975
Jason Thompson	1982
100— Honus Wagner	1900, 1909
Paul Waner	1929
Vince DiMaggio	1941
Richie Zisk	1974
Bobby Bonilla	1988, 1991
Andy Van Slyke	1988

20-plus victories

1887— Pud Galvin	28-21
1888— Ed Morris	29-23
Pud Galvin	23-25
1889— Pud Galvin	23-16
Harry Staley	21-26
1891— Mark Baldwin	22-28
1892— Mark Baldwin	26-27
1893— Frank Killen	36-14
1895— Pink Hawley	31-22
1896— Frank Killen	30-18
Pink Hawley	22-21
1898— Jesse Tannehill	25-13
1899— Jesse Tannehill	24-14
Sam Leever	21-23
1900— Jesse Tannehill	20-6
Deacon Phillippe	20-13
1901— Deacon Phillippe	22-12
Jack Chesbro	21-10
1902— Jack Chesbro	28-6
Jesse Tannehill	20-6
Deacon Phillippe	20-9
1903— Sam Leever	25-7
Deacon Phillippe	25-9
1905— Sam Leever	20-5
Deacon Phillippe	20-13
1906— Vic Willis	23-13
Sam Leever	22-7
1907— Vic Willis	21-11
Al Leifield	20-16
1908— Nick Maddox	23-8
Vic Willis	23-11
1909— Howard Camnitz	25-6
Vic Willis	22-11
1911— Babe Adams	22-12
Howard Camnitz	20-15
1912— Claude Hendrix	24-9
Howard Camnitz	22-12
1913— Babe Adams	21-10
1915— Al Mamaux	21-8
1916— Al Mamaux	21-15
1920— Wilbur Cooper	24-15
1921— Wilbur Cooper	22-14
1922— Wilbur Cooper	23-14
1923— John Morrison	25-13
1924— Wilbur Cooper	20-14
1926— Remy Kremer	20-6
Lee Meadows	20-9

Hank Greenberg (left) and Ralph Kiner, two of the game's premier sluggers, joined forces for one Pittsburgh season in 1947.

INDIVIDUAL SEASON, GAME RECORDS

SEASON

Batting

At-bats	698	Matty Alou	1969
Runs	148	Jake Stenzel	1894
Hits	237	Paul Waner	1927
Singles	198	Lloyd Waner	1927
Doubles	62	Paul Waner	1932
Triples	36	Chief Wilson	1912
Home runs	54	Ralph Kiner	1949
Home runs, rookie	23	Johnny Rizzo	1938
		Ralph Kiner	1946
Grand slams	4	Ralph Kiner	1949
Total bases	366	Kiki Cuyler	1925
RBIs	131	Paul Waner	1927
Walks	137	Ralph Kiner	1951
Most strikeouts	163	Donn Clendenon	1969
Fewest strikeouts	7	Pie Traynor	1929
Batting average	.385	Arky Vaughan	1935
Slugging pct.	.658	Ralph Kiner	1949
Stolen bases	96	Omar Moreno	1980

Pitching

Games	94	Kent Tekulve	1979
Complete games	54	Ed Morris	1888
Innings	330.2	Burleigh Grimes	1928
Wins	34	Frank Killen	1893
Losses	21	Murry Dickson	1952
Winning pct.	.947 (18-1)	Elroy Face	1959
Walks	159	Marty O'Toole	1912
Strikeouts	276	Bob Veale	1965
Shutouts	12	Ed Morris	1886
Home runs allowed	32	Murry Dickson	1951
Lowest ERA	1.56	Howie Camnitz	1908
Saves	34	Jim Gott	1988

GAME

Batting

Runs	6	Ginger Beaumont	7-22-1899
Hits	7	Rennie Stennett	9-16-75
Doubles	4	Paul Waner	5-20-32
Triples	3	Last by Roberto Clemente	9-8-58
Home runs	3	Last by Darnell Coles	9-30-87
RBIs	9	Johnny Rizzo	5-30-39
Total bases	15	Willie Stargell	5-22-68
Stolen bases	4	Last by Tony Womack	9-6-97

1927— Carmen Hill	22-11
1928— Burleigh Grimes	25-14
1930— Remy Kremer	20-12
1943— Rip Sewell	21-9
1944— Rip Sewell	21-12
1951— Murry Dickson	20-16
1958— Bob Friend	22-14
1960— Vernon Law	20-9
1977— John Candelaria	20-5
1990— Doug Drabek	22-6
1991— John Smiley	20-8

N.L. home run champions

1902— Tommy Leach	6
1946— Ralph Kiner	23
1947— Ralph Kiner	*51
1948— Ralph Kiner	*40
1949— Ralph Kiner	54
1950— Ralph Kiner	47
1951— Ralph Kiner	42
1952— Ralph Kiner	*37
1971— Willie Stargell	48
1973— Willie Stargell	44

* Tied for league lead

N.L. RBI champions

1901— Honus Wagner	126
1902— Honus Wagner	91
1906— Jim Nealon	83
1908— Honus Wagner	109
1909— Honus Wagner	100
1911— Owen Wilson	107
1912— Honus Wagner	102
1927— Paul Waner	131
1949— Ralph Kiner	127
1973— Willie Stargell	119

N.L. batting champions

1900— Honus Wagner	.381
1902— Clarence Beaumont	.357
1903— Honus Wagner	.355
1904— Honus Wagner	.349
1906— Honus Wagner	.339
1907— Honus Wagner	.350
1908— Honus Wagner	.354
1909— Honus Wagner	.339
1911— Honus Wagner	.334
1927— Paul Waner	.380
1934— Paul Waner	.362
1935— Arky Vaughan	.385
1936— Paul Waner	.373
1940— Debs Garms	.355
1960— Dick Groat	.325
1961— Roberto Clemente	.351

1964— Roberto Clemente	.339
1965— Roberto Clemente	.329
1966— Mateo Alou	.342
1967— Roberto Clemente	.357
1977— Dave Parker	.338
1978— Dave Parker	.334
1981— Bill Madlock	.341
1983— Bill Madlock	.323

N.L. ERA champions

1900— Rube Waddell	2.37
1901— Jesse Tannehill	2.18
1903— Sam Leever	2.06
1926— Ray Kremer	2.61
1927— Ray Kremer	2.47
1935— Cy Blanton	2.59
1955— Bob Friend	2.84
1977— John Candelaria	2.34

N.L. strikeout champions

1900— Rube Waddell	130
1945— Preacher Roe	148
1964— Bob Veale	250

No-hit pitchers

(9 innings or more)

1907— Nick Maddox	2-1 vs. Brooklyn
1951— Cliff Chambers	3-0 vs. Boston
1969— Bob Moose	4-0 vs. New York
1970— Dock Ellis	2-0 vs. San Diego
1976— John Candelaria	2-0 vs. Los Angeles
1997— Francisco Cordova-Ricardo Rincon	3-0 vs. Houston (10 innings)

Longest hitting streaks

27— Jimmy Williams		1899
26— Jimmy Williams		1899
	Danny O'Connell	1953
25— Charlie Grimm		1923
	Fred Lindstrom	1933
24— Maury Wills		1968
23— Danny Murtaugh		1948
	Al Oliver	1974
22— Dave Parker		1977 (twice)
	Jay Bell	1992
21— Frank Gustine		1947
	Gene Alley	1969
	Richie Zisk	1974
	Al Oliver	1974
	Carlos Garcia	1995
20— Roberto Clemente		1965
	Rennie Stennett	1977
	Al Martin	1999

HISTORY

BATTING

Games

Roberto Clemente	2,433
Honus Wagner	2,433
Willie Stargell	2,360
Max Carey	2,178
Bill Mazeroski	2,163
Paul Waner	2,154
Pie Traynor	1,941
Lloyd Waner	1,803
Tommy Leach	1,574
Fred Clarke	1,479

At-bats

Roberto Clemente	9,454
Honus Wagner	9,034
Paul Waner	8,429
Max Carey	8,406
Willie Stargell	7,927
Bill Mazeroski	7,755
Pie Traynor	7,559
Lloyd Waner	7,256
Tommy Leach	5,910
Fred Clarke	5,472

Runs

Honus Wagner	1,521
Paul Waner	1,493
Roberto Clemente	1,416
Max Carey	1,414
Willie Stargell	1,195
Pie Traynor	1,183
Lloyd Waner	1,151
Fred Clarke	1,015
Tommy Leach	1,009
Arky Vaughan	936

Hits

Roberto Clemente	3,000
Honus Wagner	2,967
Paul Waner	2,868
Max Carey	2,416
Pie Traynor	2,416
Lloyd Waner	2,317
Willie Stargell	2,232
Bill Mazeroski	2,016
Arky Vaughan	1,709
Fred Clarke	1,638

Doubles

Paul Waner	558
Honus Wagner	551
Roberto Clemente	440
Willie Stargell	423
Max Carey	375
Pie Traynor	371
Dave Parker	296
Bill Mazeroski	294
Arky Vaughan	291
Al Oliver	276
Gus Suhr	276

Triples

Honus Wagner	232
Paul Waner	187
Roberto Clemente	166
Pie Traynor	164
Fred Clarke	156
Max Carey	148
Tommy Leach	139
Arky Vaughan	116
Lloyd Waner	114
Jake Beckley	112
Gus Suhr	112

Home runs

Willie Stargell	475
Ralph Kiner	301
Roberto Clemente	240
Barry Bonds	176
Dave Parker	166
Frank Thomas	163
Bill Mazeroski	138
Al Oliver	135
Richie Hebner	128
Dick Stuart	117
Andy Van Slyke	117

Total bases

Roberto Clemente	4,492
Honus Wagner	4,228
Willie Stargell	4,190
Paul Waner	4,127
Pie Traynor	3,289
Max Carey	3,288
Lloyd Waner	2,895
Bill Mazeroski	2,848
Arky Vaughan	2,484
Dave Parker	2,397

SEASON

Batting

Most at-bats	5,724	1967
Most runs	912	1925
Fewest runs	464	1917
Most hits	1,698	1922
Most singles	1,297	1922
Most doubles	319	1996
Most triples	129	1912
Most home runs	171	1999
Fewest home runs	9	1917
Most grand slams	7	1978, 1996
Most pinch-hit home runs	10	1996
Most total bases	2,430	1966
Most stolen bases	264	1907
Highest batting average	.309	1928
Lowest batting average	.231	1952
Highest slugging pct	.449	1930

Pitching

Lowest ERA	2.48	1918
Highest ERA	5.24	1930
Most complete games	133	1904
Most shutouts	26	1906
Most saves	52	1979
Most walks	633	1999
Most strikeouts	1,124	1969

Fielding

Most errors	295	1903
Fewest errors	105	1993
Most double plays	215	1966
Highest fielding average	.984	1992

General

Most games won	110	1909
Most games lost	113	1890
Highest win pct	.741	1902
Lowest win pct	.169	1890

GAME, INNING

Batting

Most runs, game	27	6-6-1894
Most runs, inning	12	4-22-1892, 6-6-1894
Most hits, game	27	8-8-22
Most home runs, game	7	6-8-1894, 8-16-47
Most total bases, game	47	8-1-70

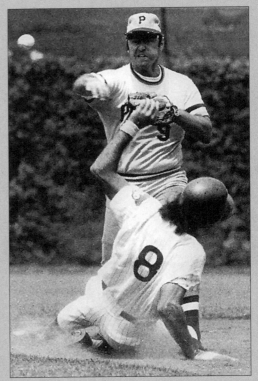

Second baseman Bill Mazeroski will always be remembered for his 1960 World Series home run.

Runs batted in

Willie Stargell	1,540
Honus Wagner	1,475
Roberto Clemente	1,305
Pie Traynor	1,273
Paul Waner	1,177
Bill Mazeroski	853
Ralph Kiner	801
Gus Suhr	789
Arky Vaughan	764
Dave Parker	758

Extra-base hits

Willie Stargell	953
Honus Wagner	865
Paul Waner	854
Roberto Clemente	846
Pie Traynor	593
Max Carey	590
Dave Parker	524
Bill Mazeroski	494
Arky Vaughan	491
Ralph Kiner	486

Batting average
(Minimum 500 games)

Paul Waner	.340
Kiki Cuyler	.336
Honus Wagner	.328
Matty Alou	.327
Arky Vaughan	.324
Elmer Smith	.324
Clarence Beaumont	.321
Pie Traynor	.320
Lloyd Waner	.319
Roberto Clemente	.317

Stolen bases

Max Carey	688
Honus Wagner	639
Omar Moreno	412
Patsy Donovan	312
Tommy Leach	271
Fred Clarke	261
Barry Bonds	251
Frank Taveras	206
Ginger Beaumont	200
Jake Stenzel	188

PITCHING

Earned-run average
(Minimum 1,000 innings)

Vic Willis	2.08
Lefty Leifield	2.38
Sam Leever	2.47
Deacon Phillippe	2.50
Howie Camnitz	2.63
Kent Tekulve	2.68
Jesse Tannehill	2.73
Wilbur Cooper	2.74
Babe Adams	2.74
Doug Drabek	3.02

Wins

Wilbur Cooper	202
Babe Adams	194
Sam Leever	194
Bob Friend	191
Deacon Phillippe	168
Vern Law	162
Ray Kremer	143
Rip Sewell	143
John Candelaria	124
Howie Camnitz	116
Jesse Tannehill	116
Bob Veale	116

Losses

Bob Friend	218
Wilbur Cooper	159
Vern Law	147
Babe Adams	139
Sam Leever	100
Rip Sewell	97
Roy Face	93
Deacon Phillippe	92
Ron Kline	91
Bob Veale	91

Innings pitched

Bob Friend	3,480.1
Wilbur Cooper	3,199.0
Babe Adams	2,991.1
Vern Law	2,672.0
Sam Leever	2,660.2
Deacon Phillippe	2,286.0
Rip Sewell	2,108.2
Ray Kremer	1,954.2
John Candelaria	1,873.0
Bob Veale	1,868.2

Strikeouts

Bob Friend	1,682
Bob Veale	1,652
Wilbur Cooper	1,191
John Candelaria	1,159
Vern Law	1,092
Babe Adams	1,036
Steve Blass	896
Dock Ellis	869
Deacon Phillippe	861
Rick Rhoden	852

Bases on balls

Bob Friend	869
Bob Veale	839
Wilbur Cooper	762
Rip Sewell	740
Steve Blass	597
Vern Law	597
Sam Leever	587
Howie Camnitz	532
Frank Killen	519
Ray Kremer	483

Games

Roy Face	802
Kent Tekulve	722
Bob Friend	568
Vern Law	483
Babe Adams	481
Wilbur Cooper	469
Dave Giusti	410
Sam Leever	388
Rip Sewell	385
Al McBean	376

Shutouts

Babe Adams	44
Sam Leever	39
Bob Friend	35
Wilbur Cooper	33
Vern Law	28
Lefty Leifield	28
Deacon Phillippe	25
Vic Willis	23
Rip Sewell	20
Bob Veale	20

Saves

Roy Face	188
Kent Tekulve	158
Dave Giusti	133
Stan Belinda	61
Al McBean	59
Bill Landrum	56
Jim Gott	50
Rich Loiselle	48
Don Robinson	43
Ramon Hernandez	39

PIRATES YEAR-BY-YEAR

				Games		Leaders					
Year	W	L	Place	Back	Manager	Batting avg.	Hits	Home runs	RBIs	Wins	ERA
1901	90	49	1st	+7½	Clarke	Wagner, .353	Wagner, 194	Beaumont, 8	Wagner, 126	Phillippe, 22	Tannehill, 2.18
1902	103	36	1st	+27½	Clarke	Beaumont, .357	Beaumont, 193	Leach, 6	Wagner, 91	Chesbro, 28	Tannehill, 1.95
1903	91	49	1st	+6½	Clarke	Wagner, .355	Beaumont, 209	Beaumont, Leach, 7	Wagner, 101	Leever, 25	Leever, 2.06
1904	87	66	4th	19	Clarke	Wagner, .349	Beaumont, 185	Wagner, 4	Wagner, 75	Flaherty, 19	Flaherty, 2.05
1905	96	57	2nd	9	Clarke	Wagner, .363	Wagner, 199	Wagner, 6	Wagner, 101	Leever, Phillippe, 20	Phillippe, 2.19
1906	93	60	3rd	23½	Clarke	Wagner, .339	Wagner, 175	Nealon, 3	Nealon, 83	Willis, 23	Willis, 1.73
1907	91	63	2nd	17	Clarke	Wagner, .350	Wagner, 180	Wagner, 6	Abbaticchio, Wagner, 82	Willis, 21	Leever, 1.66
1908	98	56	*2nd	1	Clarke	Wagner, .354	Wagner, 201	Wagner, 10	Wagner, 109	Maddox, Willis, 23	Camnitz, 1.56
1909	110	42	1st	+6½	Clarke	Wagner, .339	Wagner, 168	Leach, 6	Wagner, 100	Camnitz, 25	Adams, 1.11
1910	86	67	3rd	17½	Clarke	Wagner, .320	Byrne, 178	Flynn, 6	Wagner, 81	Adams, 18	Adams, 2.24
1911	85	69	3rd	14½	Clarke	Wagner, .334	Wilson, 163	Wilson, 12	Wilson, 107	Adams, 22	Adams, 2.33
1912	93	58	2nd	10	Clarke	Wagner, .324	Wagner, 181	Wilson, 11	Wagner, 102	Hendrix, 24	Robinson, 2.26
1913	78	71	4th	21½	Clarke	Viox, .317	Carey, 172	Wilson, 10	D. Miller, 90	Adams, 21	Adams, 2.15
1914	69	85	7th	25½	Clarke	Viox, .265	Carey, 144	Konetchy, 4	Viox, 57	Cooper, 16	Cooper, 2.13
1915	73	81	5th	18	Clarke	Hinchman, .307	Hinchman, 177	Wagner, 6	Wagner, 78	Mamaux, 21	Mamaux, 2.04
1916	65	89	6th	29	Callahan	Hinchman, .315	Hinchman, 175	Carey, 7	Hinchman, 76	Mamaux, 21	Cooper, 1.87
1917	51	103	8th	47	Callahan, Wagner, Bezdek	Carey, .296	Carey, 174	Fischer, 3	Carey, 51	Cooper, 17	Cooper, 2.36
1918	65	60	4th	17	Bezdek	Cutshaw, .285	Cutshaw, 132	Cutchaw, 5	Cutshaw, 68	Cooper, 19	Cooper, 2.11
1919	71	68	4th	24½	Bezdek	Southworth, .280	Bigbee, 132	Stengel, 4	Southworth, 61	Cooper, 19	Adams, 1.98
1920	79	75	4th	14	Gibson	Carey, .289	Southworth, 155	Bigbee, Nicholson, 4	Whitted, 74	Cooper, 24	Adams, 2.16
1921	90	63	2nd	4	Gibson	Cutshaw, .340	Bigbee, 204	Carey, Grimm, Whitted, 7	Grimm, 71	Cooper, 22	Adams, 2.64
1922	85	69	*3rd	8	Gibson, McKechnie	Bigbee, .350	Bigbee, 215	Russell, 12	Bigbee, 99	Cooper, 23	Cooper, 3.18
1923	87	67	3rd	8½	McKechnie	Grimm, .345	Traynor, 208	Traynor, 12	Traynor, 101	Morrison, 25	Meadows, 3.01
1924	90	63	3rd	3	McKechnie	Cuyler, .354	Carey, 178	Cuyler, 9	Wright, 111	Cooper, 20	Yde, 2.83
1925	95	58	1st	+8½	McKechnie	Cuyler, .357	Cuyler, 220	Cuyler, Wright, 18	Wright, 121	Meadows, 19	Aldridge, 3.63
1926	84	69	3rd	4½	McKechnie	P. Waner, .336	Cuyler, 197	Cuyler, Grantham, P. Waner, Wright, 8	Cuyler, Traynor, 92	Kremer, Meadows, 20	Kremer, 2.61
1927	94	60	1st	+1½	Bush	P. Waner, .380	P. Waner, 237	P. Waner, Wright, 9	P. Waner, 131	Hill, 22	Kremer, 2.47
1928	85	67	4th	9	Bush	P. Waner, .370	P. Waner, 223	Grantham, 10	Traynor, 124	Grimes, 25	Grimes, 2.99
1929	88	65	2nd	10½	Bush, Ens	Traynor, .356	L. Waner, 234	P. Waner, 15	Traynor, 108	Kremer, 18	Grimes, 3.13
1930	80	74	5th	12	Ens	P. Waner, .368	P. Waner, 217	Grantham, 18	Comorosky, Traynor, 119	Kremer, 20	French, 4.36
1931	75	79	5th	26	Ens	P. Waner, .322	L. Waner, 214	Grantham, 10	Traynor, 103	Meine, 19	Meine, 2.98
1932	86	68	2nd	4	Gibson	P. Waner, .341	P. Waner, 215	Grace, P. Waner, 8	Piet, 85	French, 18	Swetonic, 2.82
1933	87	67	2nd	5	Gibson	Piet, .323	P. Waner, 191	Suhr, 10	Vaughan, 97	French, 18	French, 2.72
1934	74	76	5th	19½	Gibson, Traynor	P. Waner, .362	P. Waner, 217	P. Waner, 14	Suhr, 103	Hoyt, 15	Hoyt, 2.93
1935	86	67	4th	13½	Traynor	Vaughan, .385	Jensen, 203	Vaughan, 19	Vaughan, 99	Blanton, 18	Blanton, 2.58
1936	84	70	4th	8	Traynor	P. Waner, .373	P. Waner, 218	Suhr, 11	Suhr, 118	Swift, 16	Hoyt, 2.70
1937	86	68	3rd	10	Traynor	P. Waner, .354	P. Waner, 219	Young, 9	Suhr, 97	Blanton, 14	Bauers, 2.88
1938	86	64	2nd	2	Traynor	Vaughan, .322	L. Waner, 194	Rizzo, 23	Rizzo, 111	Brown, 15	Klinger, 2.99
1939	68	85	6th	28½	Traynor	P. Waner, .328	Vaughan, 182	Fletcher, 12	Fletcher, 71	Klinger, 14	Brown, 3.37
1940	78	76	4th	22½	Frisch	Garms, .355	Vaughan, 178	V. DiMaggio, 19	Van Robays, 116	Sewell, 16	Sewell, 2.80
1941	81	73	4th	19	Frisch	Vaughan, .316	Fletcher, 150	V. DiMaggio, 21	V. DiMaggio, 100	Butcher, 17	Dietz, 2.33
1942	66	81	5th	36½	Frisch	Elliott, .296	Elliott, 166	V. DiMaggio, 15	Elliott, 89	Sewell, 17	Gornicki, 2.57
1943	80	74	4th	25	Frisch	Elliott, .315	Elliott, 183	V. DiMaggio, 15	Elliott, 101	Sewell, 21	Sewell, 2.54
1944	90	63	2nd	14½	Frisch	Russell, .312	Russell, 181	Dahlgren, 12	Elliott, 108	Sewell, 21	Ostermueller, 2.73
1945	82	72	4th	16	Frisch	Elliott, .290	Elliott, 157	Barrett, Salkeld, 15	Elliott, 108	Strincevich, 16	Roe, 2.87
1946	63	91	7th	34	Frisch, S. Davis	Cox, .290	Russell, 143	Kiner, 23	Kiner, 81	Ostermueller, 13	Bahr, 2.63
1947	62	92	*7th	32	Herman, Burwell	Kiner, .313	Gustine, 183	Kiner, 51	Kiner, 127	Ostermueller, 12	Sewell, 3.57
1948	83	71	4th	8½	Meyer	Walker, .316	Rojek, 186	Kiner, 40	Kiner, 123	Chesnes, 14	Higbe, 3.36
1949	71	83	6th	26	Meyer	Hopp, .318	Kiner, 170	Kiner, 54	Kiner, 127	Chambers, 13	Dickson, 3.29
1950	57	96	8th	33½	Meyer	Murtaugh, .294	Kiner, 149	Kiner, 47	Kiner, 118	Chambers, 12	Dickson, 3.80
1951	64	90	7th	32½	Meyer	Kiner, .309	Bell, 167	Kiner, 42	Kiner, 109	Dickson, 20	Dickson, 4.02
1952	42	112	8th	54½	Meyer	Groat, .284	Kiner, 126	Kiner, 37	Kiner, 87	Dickson, 14	Dickson, 3.57
1953	50	104	8th	55	Haney	O'Connell, .294	O'Connell, 173	Thomas, 30	Thomas, 102	Dickson, 10	Hetki, 3.95
1954	53	101	8th	44	Haney	Gordon, .306	Thomas, 172	Thomas, 23	Thomas, 94	Littlefield, 10	Littlefield, 3.60
1955	60	94	8th	38½	Haney	Long, .291	Groat, 139	Thomas, 25	Long, 79	Friend, 14	Friend, 2.83
1956	66	88	7th	27	Bragan	Virdon, .334	Virdon, 170	Long, 27	Long, 91	Friend, 17	Kline, 3.38
1957	62	92	*7th	33	Bragan, Murtaugh	Groat, .315	Thomas, 172	Thomas, 23	Thomas, 89	Friend, 14	Law, 2.87
1958	84	70	2nd	8	Murtaugh	Skinner, .321	Groat, 175	Thomas, 35	Thomas, 109	Friend, 22	Witt, 1.61
1959	78	76	4th	9	Murtaugh	Burgess, Stuart, .297	Hoak, 166	Stuart, 27	Stuart, 78	Face, Law, 18	Face, 2.70
1960	95	59	1st	+7	Murtaugh	Groat, .325	Groat, 186	Stuart, 23	Clemente, 94	Law, 20	Face, 2.90
1961	75	79	6th	18	Murtaugh	Clemente, .351	Clemente, 201	Stuart, 35	Stuart, 117	Friend, 14	Gibbon, 3.32
1962	93	68	4th	8	Murtaugh	Burgess, .328	Groat, 199	Skinner, 20	Mazeroski, 81	Friend, 18	Face, 1.88
1963	74	88	8th	25	Murtaugh	Clemente, .320	Clemente, 192	Clemente, 17	Clemente, 76	Friend, 17	Friend, 2.34
1964	80	82	*6th	13	Murtaugh	Clemente, .339	Clemente, 211	Stargell, 21	Clemente, 87	Veale, 18	McBean, 1.91
1965	90	72	3rd	7	Walker	Clemente, .329	Clemente, 194	Stargell, 27	Stargell, 107	Law, Veale, 17	Law, 2.15
1966	92	70	3rd	3	Walker	M. Alou, .342	Clemente, 202	Stargell, 33	Clemente, 119	Veale, 16	Veale, 3.02
1967	81	81	6th	20½	Walker, Murtaugh	Clemente, .357	Clemente, 209	Clemente, 23	Clemente, 110	Veale, 16	McBean, 2.54
1968	80	82	6th	17	Shepard	M. Alou, .332	M. Alou, 185	Stargell, 24	Clendenon, 87	Blass, 18	Kline, 1.68
							—EAST DIVISION—				
1969	88	74	3rd	12	Shepard, Grammas	Clemente, .345	M. Alou, 231	Stargell, 29	Stargell, 92	Blass, 16	Moose, 2.91
1970	89	73	†1st	+5	Murtaugh	Clemente, .352	M. Alou, 201	Stargell, 31	Stargell, 85	Walker, 15	Walker, 3.04
1971	97	65	‡1st	+7	Murtaugh	Clemente, .341	Clemente, 178	Stargell, 48	Stargell, 125	Ellis, 19	Blass, 2.85
1972	96	59	†1st	+11	Virdon	Davalillo, .318	Oliver, 176	Stargell, 33	Stargell, 112	Blass, 19	Blass, 2.49
1973	80	82	3rd	2½	Virdon, Murtaugh	Stargell, .299	Oliver, 191	Stargell, 44	Stargell, 119	Briles, 14	Giusti, 2.37
1974	88	74	†1st	+1½	Murtaugh	Oliver, .321	Oliver, 198	Stargell, 25	Zisk, 100	Reuss, 16	Rooker, 2.78
1975	92	69	†1st	+6½	Murtaugh	Sanguillen, .328	Oliver, Stennett, 176	Parker, 25	Parker, 101	Reuss, 18	Reuss, 2.54
1976	92	70	2nd	9	Murtaugh	Oliver, .323	Cash, 189	B. Robinson, Zisk, 21	Parker, 90	Candelaria, 16	Tekulve, 2.45
1977	96	66	2nd	5	Tanner	Parker, .338	Parker, 215	B. Robinson, 26	B. Robinson, 104	Candelaria, 20	Gossage, 1.62
1978	88	73	2nd	1½	Tanner	Parker, .334	Parker, 194	Parker, 30	Parker, 117	Blyleven, D. Robinson, 14	Tekulve, 2.33
1979	98	64	‡1st	+2	Tanner	Parker, .310	Moreno, 196	Stargell, 32	Parker, 94	Candelaria, 14	Tekulve, 2.75
1980	83	79	3rd	8	Tanner	Easler, .338	Moreno, 168	Easler, 21	Parker, 79	Bibby, 19	Solomon, 2.69
1981	46	56	§4th/6th	—	Tanner	Madlock, .341	Moreno, 120	Thompson, 15	Parker, 48	Rhoden, 9	Tekulve, 2.49
1982	84	78	4th	8	Tanner	Madlock, .319	Ray, 182	Thompson, 31	Thompson, 101	D. Robinson, 15	Scurry, 1.74
1983	84	78	2nd	6	Tanner	Madlock, .323	Pena, Ray, 163	Thompson, 18	Thompson, 76	Candelaria, McWilliams, 15	Tekulve, 1.64
1984	75	87	6th	21½	Tanner	Lacy, .321	Wynne, 174	Thompson, 17	Pena, 78	Rhoden, 14	Candelaria, Rhoden, 2.72
1985	57	104	6th	43½	Tanner	Orsulak, .300	Ray, 163	Thompson, 12	Ray, 70	Reuschel, 14	Reuschel, 2.27
1986	64	98	6th	44	Leyland	Ray, .301	Ray, 174	Morrison, 23	Morrison, 88	Rhoden, 15	Rhoden, 2.84
1987	80	82	*4th	15	Leyland	Bonilla, .300	Van Slyke, 165	Bonds, 25	Van Slyke, 82	Dunne, 13	Reuschel, 2.75
1988	85	75	2nd	15	Leyland	Van Slyke, .288	Van Slyke, 169	Van Slyke, 25	Bonilla, Van Slyke, 100	Drabek, 15	Walk, 2.71
1989	74	88	5th	19	Leyland	Bonilla, .281	Bonilla, 173	Bonilla, 24	Bonilla, 26	Drabek, 14	Drabek, 2.80
1990	95	67	†1st	+4	Leyland	Bonds, .301	Bonilla, 175	Bonds, 33	Bonilla, 120	Drabek, 22	Drabek, 2.76
1991	98	64	†1st	+14	Leyland	Bonilla, .302	Bonilla, 174	Bonds, 25	Bonds, 116	Smiley, 20	Tomlin, 2.98
1992	96	66	†1st	+9	Leyland	Van Slyke, .324	Van Slyke, 199	Bonds, 34	Bonds, 103	Drabek, 15	Wakefield, 2.15
1993	75	87	5th	22	Leyland	Merced, .313	Bell, 187	Martin, 18	King, 98	Walk, 13	Cooke, 3.89
							—CENTRAL DIVISION—				
1994	53	61	*3rd	13	Leyland	Garcia, .277	Bell, 117	Clark, 10	Merced, 51	Z. Smith, 10	Z. Smith, 3.27
1995	58	86	5th	27	Leyland	Merced, .300	Merced, 146	King, 18	King, 87	Neagle, 13	Neagle, 3.43
1996	73	89	5th	15	Leyland	Martin, .300	Martin, 189	King, 30	King, 111	Lieber, 9	Lieber, 3.99
1997	79	83	2nd	5	Lamont	Randa, .302	Womack, 178	Young, 18	Young, 74	Cordova, Lieber, Loaiza, 11	Cordova, 3.63
1998	69	93	6th	33	Lamont	Kendall, .327	Womack, 185	Young, 27	Young, 108	Cordova, 13	Cordova, 3.31
1999	78	83	3rd	18½	Lamont	Giles, .315	Young, 174	Giles, 39	Giles, 115	Ritchie, 15	Ritchie, 3.49

* Tied for position. † Lost Championship Series. ‡ Won Championship Series. § First half 25-23; second half 21-33.

Note: Batting average minimum 350 at-bats; ERA minimum 90 innings pitched.

HISTORY

ST. LOUIS CARDINALS

FRANCHISE CHRONOLOGY

First season: 1882, as a member of the new American Association. The "Browns" struggled to a 37-43 first-year record and finished fifth in the six-team field.

1883-1900: The Browns captured four consecutive A.A pennants from 1885 through 1888, but their success ended there. When the A.A. folded after the 1891 season, they joined the National League and sank quietly into the second division.

1901-present: The Cardinals trail only the Yankees in World Series championships and only the Yankees and Dodgers in pennants. And all of their success was achieved after 1926, when they captured their first N.L. flag and World Series. The history of Cardinals baseball has been colorful and consistent, spiced by some of the sport's most memorable moments. St. Louis won two pennants in the 1920s, three in the 1930s, four in the 1940s, three in the 1960s and three in the 1980s. Nine of the pennants led to championships, including the Gas House Gang's 1934 fall classic romp past Detroit and Enos Slaughter's 1946 Series-ending Mad Dash. The Cardinals have finished first only four times since division play began in 1969, but three of them resulted in World Series appearances (a 1982 victory, 1985 and '87 losses). The Cardinals, who lost in the seventh game of the 1996 N.L. Championship Series, were placed in the Central Division when the N.L. adopted the three-division format in 1994.

Outfielder Stan Musial.

CARDINALS VS. OPPONENTS BY DECADE

	Braves	Cubs	Dodgers	Giants	Phillies	Pirates	Reds	Astros	Mets	Expos	Padres	Marlins	Rockies	Brewers	D'backs	Interleague	Decade Record
1900-09	111-98	64-144	93-115	78-133	90-121	53-158	91-119										580-888
1910-19	100-110	78-136	104-105	81-131	98-112	83-127	108-109										652-830
1920-29	135-85	105-112	119-101	95-123	151-69	102-117	115-105										822-712
1930-39	121-98	109-111	127-91	107-110	159-61	99-121	147-73										869-665
1940-49	144-76	138-82	132-90	141-77	150-70	122-98	133-87										960-580
1950-59	101-119	113-107	85-135	108-112	113-107	132-87	124-96										776-763
1960-69	94-88	114-73	91-91	92-90	108-79	107-81	90-92	79-59	90-54	11-7	8-4						884-718
1970-79	69-51	87-93	53-67	60-60	86-91	79-101	46-74	64-56	93-85	93-85	70-50						800-813
1980-89	68-47	89-81	56-62	60-53	95-80	98-75	63-50	58-56	86-87	82-95	70-48						825-734
1990-99	43-71	67-71	55-52	58-54	67-57	62-76	51-62	62-60	55-67	61-64	56-51	40-29	37-40	14-10	11-6	19-24	758-794
Totals	986-843	964-1010	915-909	880-943	1117-847	937-1041	968-867	263-231	324-293	247-251	204-153	40-29	37-40	14-10	11-6	19-24	7926-7497

Interleague results: 5-4 vs. White Sox; 1-4 vs. Indians; 4-5 vs. Royals; 0-3 vs. Brewers; 5-4 vs. Twins; 4-4 vs. Tigers.

MANAGERS

Name	Years	Record
Ned Cuthbert	1882	37-43
Ted Sullivan	1883	53-26
Charlie Comiskey	1883, 1884-89, 1891	561-273
Tommy McCarthy	1890	15-12
John Kerins	1890	9-8
Chief Roseman	1890	7-8
Count Campau	1890	27-14
Joe Gerhardt	1890	20-16
Jack Glasscock	1892	1-3
John Stricker	1892	6-17
John Crooks	1892	27-33
George Gore	1892	6-9
Bob Caruthers	1892	16-32
Bill Watkins	1893	57-75
George Miller	1894	56-76
Al Buckenberger	1895	16-34
Chris Von Der Ahe	1895, 1896, 1897	3-14
Joe Quinn	1895	11-28
Lew Phelan	1895	11-30
Harry Diddlebock	1896	7-10
Arlie Latham	1896	0-3
Roger Connor	1896	8-37
Tom Dowd	1896-97	31-60
Hugh Nicol	1897	8-32
Bill Hallman	1897	13-36
Tim Hurst	1898	39-111
Patsy Tebeau	1899-1900	126-117
Patsy Donovan	1901-03	175-236
Kid Nichols	1904-05	80-88
Jimmy Burke	1905	34-56
Stanley Robison	1905	19-31
John McCloskey	1906-08	153-304
Roger Bresnahan	1909-12	255-352
Miller Huggins	1913-17	346-415
Jack Hendricks	1918	51-78
Branch Rickey	1919-25	458-485
Rogers Hornsby	1925-26	153-116
Bob O'Farrell	1927	92-61
Bill McKechnie	1928-29	129-88
Billy Southworth	1929, 1940-45	620-346
Gabby Street	1929, 1930-33	312-242
Frank Frisch	1933-38	458-354
Mike Gonzalez	1938, 1940	9-13
Ray Blades	1939-40	106-85
Eddie Dyer	1946-50	446-325
Marty Marion	1951	81-73
Eddie Stanky	1952-55	260-238
Harry Walker	1955	51-67
Fred Hutchinson	1956-58	232-220
Stan Hack	1958	3-7
Solly Hemus	1959-61	190-192
Johnny Keane	1961-64	317-249
Red Schoendienst	1965-76, 1980, 1990	1041-955
Vern Rapp	1977-78	89-90
Ken Boyer	1978-80	166-190
Whitey Herzog	1980, 1981-90	822-728
Joe Torre	1990-95	351-354
Mike Jorgensen	1995	42-54
Tony La Russa	1996-99	319-328

WORLD SERIES CHAMPIONS

Year	Loser	Length	MVP
1926	N.Y. Yankees	7 games	None
1931	Philadelphia	7 games	None
1934	Detroit	7 games	None
1942	N.Y. Yankees	5 games	None
1944	St.L. Browns	6 games	None
1946	Boston	7 games	None
1964	N.Y. Yankees	7 games	Gibson
1967	Boston	7 games	Gibson
1982	Milwaukee	7 games	Porter

A.A. PENNANT WINNERS

Year	Record	Manager	Series Result
1885	79-33	Comiskey	None
1886	93-46	Comiskey	None
1887	95-40	Comiskey	None
1888	92-43	Comiskey	None

N.L. PENNANT WINNERS

Year	Record	Manager	Series Result
1926	89-65	Hornsby	Defeated Yankees
1928	95-59	McKechnie	Lost to Yankees
1930	92-62	Street	Lost to A's
1931	101-53	Street	Defeated A's
1934	95-58	Frisch	Defeated Tigers
1942	106-48	Southworth	Defeated Yankees
1943	105-49	Southworth	Lost to Yankees
1944	105-49	Southworth	Defeated Browns
1946	98-58	Dyer	Defeated Red Sox
1964	93-69	Keane	Defeated Yankees
1967	101-60	Schoendienst	Defeated Red Sox
1968	97-65	Schoendiesnt	Lost to Tigers
1982	92-70	Herzog	Defeated Brewers
1985	101-61	Herzog	Lost to Royals
1987	95-67	Herzog	Lost to Twins

EAST DIVISION CHAMPIONS

Year	Record	Manager	NLCS Result
1982	92-70	Herzog	Defeated Braves
1985	101-61	Herzog	Defeated Dodgers
1987	95-67	Herzog	Defeated Giants

CENTRAL DIVISION CHAMPIONS

Year	Record	Manager	Div. Series Result	NLCS Result
1996	88-74	La Russa	Defeated Padres	Lost to Braves

ATTENDANCE HIGHS

Total	Season	Park
3,236,103	1999	Busch Stadium
3,195,021	1998	Busch Stadium
3,080,980	1989	Busch Stadium
3,072,121	1987	Busch Stadium
2,892,629	1988	Busch Stadium

BALLPARK CHRONOLOGY

Busch Memorial Stadium (1966-present)
Capacity: 50,297.
First game: Cardinals 4, Atlanta 3, 12 innings (May 12, 1966).
First batter: Felipe Alou, Braves.
First hit: Gary Geiger, Braves (single).
First run: Jerry Buchek, Cardinals (3rd inning).
First home run: Felipe Alou, Braves.
First winning pitcher: Don Dennis, Cardinals.
First-season attendance: 1,712,980.

Sportsman's Park I (1882-91)
Capacity: 6,000.
First game: St. Louis 9, Louisville 7 (May 2, 1882).

Union Park (1892-97)

League Park (1898)

Robison Field (1899-1920)
Capacity: 14,500.

Sportsman's Park II (1920-66)
Capacity: 30,500.
First game: Pittsburgh 6, St. Louis 2, 10 innings (July 1, 1920).
First full-season attendance: 384,773 (1921).

Note: Sportsman's Park was renamed Busch Stadium in 1953.

N.L. MVPs

Frank Frisch, 2B, 1931
Dizzy Dean, P, 1934
Joe Medwick, OF, 1937
Mort Cooper, P, 1942
Stan Musial, OF, 1943
Marty Marion, SS, 1944
Stan Musial, 1B, 1946

Stan Musial OF, 1948
Ken Boyer, 3B, 1964
Orlando Cepeda, 1B, 1967
Bob Gibson, P, 1968
Joe Torre, 3B, 1971
*Keith Hernandez, 1B, 1979
Willie McGee, OF, 1985
* Co-winner.

CY YOUNG WINNERS

Bob Gibson, RH, 1968
Bob Gibson, RH, 1970

ROOKIES OF THE YEAR

Wally Moon, OF, 1954
Bill Virdon, OF, 1955
Bake McBride, OF, 1974

Vince Coleman, OF, 1985
Todd Worrell, P, 1986

MANAGER OF THE YEAR

Whitey Herzog, 1985

RETIRED UNIFORMS

No.	Name	Pos.
1	Ozzie Smith	SS
2	Red Schoendienst	2B
6	Stan Musial	OF, 1B
9	Enos Slaughter	OF
14	Ken Boyer	3B
17	Dizzy Dean	P
20	Lou Brock	OF
45	Bob Gibson	P

MILESTONE PERFORMANCES

30-plus home runs
70— Mark McGwire ...1998
65— Mark McGwire ...1999
43— Johnny Mize ...1940
42— Rogers Hornsby ...1922
39— Rogers Hornsby ...1925
　　Stan Musial...1948
36— Stan Musial...1949
35— Rip Collins ...1934
　　Stan Musial...1954
　　Jack Clark ...1987
34— Dick Allen ...1970
　　Fernando Tatis ...1999
33— Stan Musial...1955
32— Stan Musial...1951
　　Ken Boyer...1960
31— Jim Bottomley ...1928
　　Joe Medwick...1937
　　Ray Lankford ...1997, 1998
30— Stan Musial...1953
　　Ron Gant ...1996

100-plus RBIs
154— Joe Medwick...1937
152— Rogers Hornsby ...1922
147— Mark McGwire ...1998
　　 Mark McGwire ...1999
143— Rogers Hornsby ...1925
138— Joe Medwick...1936
137— Jim Bottomley ...1929
　　 Johnny Mize ...1940
　　 Joe Torre ...1971
136— Jim Bottomley ...1928
131— Stan Musial...1948
130— Enos Slaughter ...1946
128— Jim Bottomley ...1925
　　 Rip Collins ...1934
126— Rogers Hornsby ...1921
　　 Joe Medwick...1935
　　 Stan Musial...1954
125— Chick Hafey ...1929
124— Jim Bottomley ...1927
123— Stan Musial...1949
122— Rip Collins ...1935
　　 Joe Medwick...1938
120— Jim Bottomley ...1926
119— Ken Boyer...1964
117— Joe Medwick...1939
　　 Pedro Guerrero ...1989
114— Frank Frisch ...1930
113— Johnny Mize ...1937
　　 Stan Musial...1953
112— Ray Jablonski ...1953
111— Jim Bottomley ...1924
　　 Chick Hafey ...1928
　　 Ken Boyer...1963
　　 Orlando Cepeda ...1967
110— Tom Herr ...1985
109— Buster Adams ...*1945
　　 Stan Musial...1950, 1956
　　 Bill White ...1963
　　 George Hendrick ...1980
108— Johnny Mize ...1939
　　 Stan Musial...1951, 1955
107— Chick Hafey ...1930
　　 Fernando Tatis ...1999
106— Joe Medwick...1934
　　 Jack Clark ...1987
105— Del Ennis ...1957
　　 Keith Hernandez ...1979
　　 Willie McGee ...1987
　　 Ray Lankford ...1998
104— Whitey Kurowski...1947
　　 Ray Jablonski ...1954
　　 George Hendrick ...1982
　　 Brian Jordan ...1996
103— Stan Musial...1946
　　 Ted Simmons ...1974

Todd Zeile ...1993
102— Austin McHenry ...1921
　　 Johnny Mize ...1938
　　 Ray Sanders ...1944
　　 Whitey Kurowski ...1945
　　 Stan Musial...1957
　　 Bill White ...1962, 1964
101— Enos Slaughter ...1950, 1952
　　 Joe Torre ...1969
　　 Dick Allen ...1970
100— Les Bell ...1926
　　 Johnny Mize ...1941
　　 Joe Torre ...1970
　　 Reggie Smith ...1974
　　 Ted Simmons ...1975

*8 with Phillies; 101 with Cardinals.

20-plus victories
1892— Kid Gleason ...20-24
1893— Kid Gleason ...21-22
1894— Ted Breitenstein ...27-23
1899— Cy Young ...26-16
　　　 Jack Powell ...23-19
1901— Jack Harper ...23-13
1904— Kid Nichols ...21-13
　　　 Jack Taylor ...20-19
1911— Bob Harmon ...23-16
1920— Bill Doak ...20-12
1923— Jesse Haines ...20-13
1926— Flint Rhem ...20-7
1927— Jesse Haines ...24-10
　　　 Grover Alexander ...21-10
1928— Bill Sherdel ...21-10
　　　 Jesse Haines ...20-8
1933— Dizzy Dean ...20-18
1934— Dizzy Dean ...30-7
1935— Dizzy Dean ...28-12
1936— Dizzy Dean ...24-13
1939— Curt Davis ...22-16
1942— Mort Cooper ...22-7
　　　 Johnny Beazley ...21-6
1943— Mort Cooper ...21-8
1944— Mort Cooper ...22-7
1945— Red Barrett ...*23-12
1946— Howie Pollet ...21-10
1948— Harry Brecheen ...20-7
1949— Howie Pollet ...20-9
1953— Harvey Haddix ...20-9
1960— Ernie Broglio ...21-9
1964— Ray Sadecki ...20-11
1965— Bob Gibson ...20-12
1966— Bob Gibson ...21-12
1968— Bob Gibson ...22-9
1969— Bob Gibson ...20-13
1970— Bob Gibson ...23-7
1971— Steve Carlton ...20-9
1977— Bob Forsch ...20-7
1984— Joaquin Andujar ...20-14
1985— Joaquin Andujar ...21-12
　　　 John Tudor ...21-8

*2-3 with Braves; 21-9 with Cardinals.

N.L. home run champions
1922— Rogers Hornsby ...42
1925— Rogers Hornsby ...39
1928— Jim Bottomley ...*31
1934— Rip Collins ...*35
1937— Joe Medwick...*31
1939— Johnny Mize ...28
1940— Johnny Mize ...43
1998— Mark McGwire ...70
1999— Mark McGwire ...65

*Tied for league lead.

N.L. RBI champions
1920— Rogers Hornsby ...*94
1921— Rogers Hornsby ...126
1922— Rogers Hornsby ...152

1925— Rogers Hornsby ...143
1926— Jim Bottomley ...120
1928— Jim Bottomley ...136
1936— Joe Medwick...138
1937— Joe Medwick...154
1938— Joe Medwick...122
1940— Johnny Mize ...137
1946— Enos Slaughter ...130
1948— Stan Musial...131
1956— Stan Musial...109
1964— Ken Boyer...119
1967— Orlando Cepeda ...111
1971— Joe Torre ...137
1999— Mark McGwire ...147

* Tied for league lead

N.L. batting champions
1901— Jesse Burkett ...376
1920— Rogers Hornsby ...370
1921— Rogers Hornsby ...397
1922— Rogers Hornsby ...401
1923— Rogers Hornsby ...384
1924— Rogers Hornsby ...424
1925— Rogers Hornsby ...403
1931— Chick Hafey ...349
1937— Joe Medwick...374
1939— Johnny Mize ...349
1943— Stan Musial...357
1946— Stan Musial...365
1948— Stan Musial...376
1950— Stan Musial...346
1951— Stan Musial...355
1952— Stan Musial...336
1957— Stan Musial...351
1971— Joe Torre ...363
1979— Keith Hernandez ...344
1985— Willie McGee ...353
1990— Willie McGee ...335

N.L. ERA champions
1914— Bill Doak ...1.72
1921— Bill Doak ...2.59
1942— Mort Cooper ...1.78
1943— Howie Pollet ...1.75
1946— Howie Pollet ...2.10
1948— Harry Brecheen ...2.24
1968— Bob Gibson ...1.12
1976— John Denny ...2.52
1988— Joe Magrane ...2.18

N.L. strikeout champions
1906— Fred Beebe ...171
1930— Bill Hallahan ...177
1931— Bill Hallahan ...159
1932— Dizzy Dean ...191
1933— Dizzy Dean ...199
1934— Dizzy Dean ...195
1935— Dizzy Dean ...182
1948— Harry Brecheen ...149
1958— Sam Jones ...225
1966— Bob Gibson ...268
1989— Jose DeLeon ...201

No-hit pitchers
(9 innings or more)
1924— Jesse Haines ...5-0 vs. Boston
1934— Paul Dean ...3-0 vs. Brooklyn
1941— Lon Warneke ...2-0 vs. Cincinnati
1968— Ray Washburn ...2-0 vs. San Francisco
1971— Bob Gibson ...11-0 vs. Pittsburgh
1978— Bob Forsch ...5-0 vs. Philadelphia
1983— Bob Forsch ...3-0 vs. Montreal
1999— Jose Jimenez ...1-0 vs. Arizona

Longest hitting streaks
33— Rogers Hornsby ...1922
30— Stan Musial...1950
29— Harry Walker ...1943
　　Ken Boyer...1959
28— Joe Medwick...1935
　　Red Schoendienst...1954
26— Lou Brock ...1971
25— Joe McEwing ...1999
24— Pepper Martin ...1935
　　Stan Musial...1952
　　Wally Moon ...1957
23— Pepper Martin ...1935
　　Jose Oquendo ...1989
22— Taylor Douthit ...1930
　　Johnny Mize ...1936
　　Harry Walker ...1943
　　Stan Musial...1943
　　Whitey Kurowski ...1943
　　Vada Pinson ...1969
　　Joe Torre ...1971
　　Willie McGee ...1990
21— Les Bell ...1926
　　Ernie Orsatti ...1932
　　Joe Medwick...1932
　　Enos Slaughter ...1940
　　Lou Klein ...1943
20— Ed Konetchy ...1910
　　Terry Moore ...1942
　　Stan Musial...1957
　　Wally Moon ...1957
　　Bill White ...1964
　　Lou Brock ...1967
　　John Mabry ...1997

INDIVIDUAL SEASON, GAME RECORDS

SEASON

Batting

At-bats	689	Lou Brock	1967
Runs	141	Rogers Hornsby	1922
Hits	250	Rogers Hornsby	1922
Singles	181	Jesse Burkett	1901
Doubles	64	Joe Medwick	1936
Triples	33	Perry Werden	1893
Home runs	70	Mark McGwire	1998
Home runs, rookie	21	Ray Jablonski	1953
Grand slams	3	3 times	
		Last by Fernando Tatis	1999
Total bases	450	Rogers Hornsby	1922
RBIs	154	Joe Medwick	1937
Walks	162	Mark McGwire	1998
Most strikeouts	162	Ron Gant	1997
Fewest strikeouts	10	Frank Frisch	1927
Batting average	.424	Rogers Hornsby	1924
Slugging pct.	.756	Rogers Hornsby	1922
Stolen bases	118	Lou Brock	1974

Pitching (since 1900)

Games	77	Mike Perez	1992
Complete games	39	Jack Taylor	1904
Innings	352.1	Stoney McGlynn	1907
Wins	30	Dizzy Dean	1934
Losses	25	Stoney McGlynn	1907
		Art Raymond	1908
Winning pct.	.833 (10-2)	John Tudor	1987
Walks	181	Bob Harmon	1911
Strikeouts	274	Bob Gibson	1970
Shutouts	13	Bob Gibson	1968
Home runs allowed	39	Murry Dickson	1948
Lowest ERA	1.12	Bob Gibson	1968
Saves	47	Lee Smith	1991

GAME

Batting

Runs	5	Last by J.D. Drew	5-1-99
Hits	6	Last by Terry Moore	9-5-35
Doubles	4	Joe Medwick	8-4-37
Triples	3	Last by Jim Bottomley	6-21-27
Home runs	4	Mark Whiten	9-7-93
RBIs	12	Jim Bottomley	9-16-24
		Mark Whiten	9-7-93
Total bases	16	Mark Whiten	9-7-93
Stolen bases	5	Lonnie Smith	9-4-82

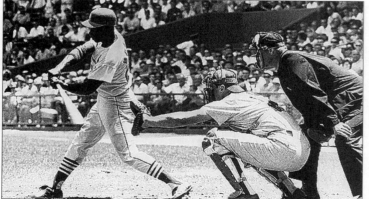

Outfielder Lou Brock, one of the great all-time basestealers, also wielded a lethal bat during his Hall of Fame career.

BATTING

Games
Stan Musial	3,026
Lou Brock	2,289
Ozzie Smith	1,990
Enos Slaughter	1,820
Red Schoendienst	1,795
Curt Flood	1,738
Ken Boyer	1,667
Willie McGee	1,661
Rogers Hornsby	1,580
Julian Javier	1,578

At-bats
Stan Musial	10,972
Lou Brock	9,125
Ozzie Smith	7,160
Red Schoendienst	6,841
Enos Slaughter	6,775
Ken Boyer	6,334
Curt Flood	6,318
Rogers Hornsby	5,881
Willie McGee	5,734
Ted Simmons	5,725

Runs
Stan Musial	1,949
Lou Brock	1,427
Rogers Hornsby	1,089
Enos Slaughter	1,071
Red Schoendienst	1,025
Ozzie Smith	991
Ken Boyer	988
Jim Bottomley	921
Curt Flood	845
Frankie Frisch	831

Hits
Stan Musial	3,630
Lou Brock	2,713
Rogers Hornsby	2,110
Enos Slaughter	2,064
Red Schoendienst	1,980
Ozzie Smith	1,944
Ken Boyer	1,855
Curt Flood	1,853
Jim Bottomley	1,727
Ted Simmons	1,704

Doubles
Stan Musial	725
Lou Brock	434
Joe Medwick	377
Rogers Hornsby	367
Enos Slaughter	366
Red Schoendienst	352
Jim Bottomley	344
Ozzie Smith	338
Ted Simmons	332
Ray Lankford	291

Triples
Stan Musial	177
Rogers Hornsby	143
Enos Slaughter	135
Lou Brock	121
Jim Bottomley	119
Ed Konetchy	94
Willie McGee	83
Joe Medwick	81
Pepper Martin	75
Garry Templeton	69

Home runs
Stan Musial	475
Ken Boyer	255
Rogers Hornsby	193
Jim Bottomley	181
Ray Lankford	181
Ted Simmons	172
Mark McGwire	159
Johnny Mize	158
Joe Medwick	152
Enos Slaughter	146

Total bases
Stan Musial	6,134
Lou Brock	3,776
Rogers Hornsby	3,342
Enos Slaughter	3,138
Ken Boyer	3,011
Jim Bottomley	2,852
Red Schoendienst	2,657
Ted Simmons	2,626
Joe Medwick	2,585
Curt Flood	2,464

Runs batted in
Stan Musial	1,951
Enos Slaughter	1,148

SEASON

Batting
Most at-bats	5,734	1979
Most runs	1,004	1930
Fewest runs	372	1908
Most hits	1,732	1930
Most singles	1,223	1920
Most doubles	373	1939
Most triples	96	1920
Most home runs	223	1998
Fewest home runs	10	1906
Most grand slams	7	1961
Most pinch-hit home runs	10	1998
Most total bases	2,595	1930
Most stolen bases	314	1985
Highest batting average	.314	1930
Lowest batting average	.223	1908
Highest slugging pct	.471	1930

Pitching
Lowest ERA	2.38	1914
Highest ERA	6.21	1897
Most complete games	146	1904
Most shutouts	30	1968
Most saves	54	1993
Most walks	701	1911
Most strikeouts	1,130	1997

Fielding
Most errors	354	1903
Fewest errors	94	1992
Most double plays	192	1974
Highest fielding average	.985	1992

General
Most games won	106	1942
Most games lost	111	1898
Highest win pct	.703	1876
Lowest win pct	.221	1897

GAME, INNING

Batting
Most runs, game	28	7-6-29
Most runs, inning	12	9-16-26
Most hits, game	30	6-1-1895
Most home runs, game	7	5-7-40, 7-12-96
Most total bases, game	49	5-7-40

Intimidating Bob Gibson powered his way to 251 victories and 3,117 strikeouts with the Cardinals.

Jim Bottomley	1,105
Rogers Hornsby	1,072
Ken Boyer	1,001
Ted Simmons	929
Joe Medwick	923
Lou Brock	814
Frankie Frisch	720
Ray Lankford	703

Extra-base hits
Stan Musial	1,377
Rogers Hornsby	703
Lou Brock	684
Enos Slaughter	647
Jim Bottomley	644
Joe Medwick	610
Ken Boyer	585
Ted Simmons	541
Ray Lankford	517
Red Schoendienst	482

Batting average
(Minimum 500 games)
Rogers Hornsby	.359
Johnny Mize	.336
Joe Medwick	.335
Stan Musial	.331
Chick Hafey	.326
Jim Bottomley	.325
Frankie Frisch	.312
George Watkins	.309
Joe Torre	.308
Rip Collins	.307

Stolen bases
Lou Brock	888
Vince Coleman	549
Ozzie Smith	433
Willie McGee	301
Ray Lankford	239
Jack Smith	203
Frankie Frisch	195
Tommy Dowd	187
Miller Huggins	174
Lonnie Smith	173

PITCHING

Earned-run average
(Minimum 1,000 innings)
Slim Sallee	2.67
Mort Cooper	2.77
Max Lanier	2.84

Harry Brecheen	2.91
Bob Gibson	2.91
Bill Doak	2.93
Dizzy Dean	2.99
Lee Meadows	3.00
Howie Pollet	3.06
Steve Carlton	3.10

Wins
Bob Gibson	251
Jesse Haines	210
Bob Forsch	163
Bill Sherdel	153
Bill Doak	144
Dizzy Dean	134
Harry Brecheen	128
Slim Sallee	106
Mort Cooper	105
Larry Jackson	101
Max Lanier	101

Losses
Bob Gibson	174
Jesse Haines	158
Bill Doak	136
Bill Sherdel	131
Bob Forsch	127
Ted Breitenstein	125
Slim Sallee	107
Larry Jackson	86
Bob Harmon	81
Harry Brecheen	79

Innings pitched
Bob Gibson	3,884.1
Jesse Haines	3,203.2
Bob Forsch	2,658.2
Bill Sherdel	2,450.2
Bill Doak	2,387.0
Slim Sallee	1,905.1
Ted Breitenstein	1,896.2
Harry Brecheen	1,790.1
Dizzy Dean	1,737.1
Larry Jackson	1,672.1

Strikeouts
Bob Gibson	3,117
Dizzy Dean	1,095
Bob Forsch	1,079
Jesse Haines	979
Steve Carlton	951
Bill Doak	938
Larry Jackson	899

Harry Brecheen	857
Vinegar Bemizell	789
Bill Hallahan	784

Bases on balls
Bob Gibson	1,336
Jesse Haines	870
Ted Breitenstein	825
Bob Forsch	780
Bill Doak	740
Bill Hallahan	648
Bill Sherdel	595
Bob Harmon	594
Vinegar Bend Mizell	568
Max Lanier	524

Games
Jesse Haines	554
Bob Gibson	528
Bill Sherdel	465
Bob Forsch	455
Al Brazle	441
Bill Doak	376
Todd Worrell	348
Lindy McDaniel	336
Larry Jackson	330
Al Hrabosky	329

Shutouts
Bob Gibson	56
Bill Doak	30
Mort Cooper	28
Harry Brecheen	25
Jesse Haines	24
Dizzy Dean	23
Max Lanier	20
Howie Pollet	20
Bob Forsch	19
Ernie Broglio	18

Saves
Lee Smith	160
Todd Worrell	129
Bruce Sutter	127
Dennis Eckersley	66
Lindy McDaniel	64
Al Brazle	60
Joe Hoerner	60
Al Hrabosky	59
Ken Dayley	39
Tom Henke	36

HISTORY

CARDINALS YEAR-BY-YEAR

Year	W	L	Place	Games Back	Manager	Leaders: Batting avg.	Hits	Home runs	RBIs	Wins	ERA
1901	76	64	4th	14½	Donovan	Burkett, .376	Burkett, 228	Burkett, 10	Wallace, 91	Harper, 23	Sudhoff, 3.52
1902	56	78	6th	44½	Donovan	Donovan, .315	Barclay, 163	Barclay, Smoot, 3	Barclay, 53	O'Neill, 17	Currie, 2.60
1903	43	94	8th	46½	Donovan	Donovan, .327	Smoot, 148	Smoot, 4	Brain, 60	M. Brown, McFarland, 9	M. Brown, 2.60
1904	75	79	5th	31½	Nichols	Beckley, .325	Beckley, 179	Brain, 7	Brain, 72	Nichols, Taylor, 21	Nichols, 2.02
1905	58	96	6th	47½	Nichols, Burke, Robison	Smoot, .311	Smoot, 166	Grady, 4	Smoot, 58	Taylor, Thielman, 15	B. Brown, 2.97
1906	52	98	7th	63	McCloskey	Bennett, .262	Bennett, 156	Grady, 3	Beckley, 44	Beebe, 9	Taylor, 2.15
1907	52	101	8th	55½	McCloskey	Murray, .262	Byrne, 143	Murray, 7	Murray, 46	Karger, 15	Karger, 2.04
1908	49	105	8th	50	McCloskey	Murray, .282	Murray, 167	Murray, 7	Murray, 62	Raymond, 14	Raymond, 2.03
1909	54	98	7th	56	Bresnahan	Konetchy, .286	Konetchy, 165	Konetchy, 4	Konetchy, 80	Beebe, 15	Sallee, 2.42
1910	63	90	7th	40½	Bresnahan	Konetchy, .302	Konetchy, 157	Ellis, 4	Konetchy, 78	Lush, 14	Sallee, 2.97
1911	75	74	5th	22	Bresnahan	Evans, .294	Konetchy, 165	Konetchy, 6	Konetchy, 88	Harmon, 23	Sallee, 2.76
1912	63	90	6th	41	Bresnahan	Konetchy, .314	Konetchy, 169	Konetchy, 8	Konetchy, 82	Harmon, 18	Sallee, 2.60
1913	51	99	8th	49	Huggins	Oakes, .291	Oakes, 156	Konetchy, 7	Konetchy, 68	Sallee, 18	Sallee, 2.71
1914	81	72	3rd	13	Huggins	D. Miller, .290	D. Miller, 166	Wilson, 9	D. Miller, 88	Doak, 20	Doak, 1.72
1915	72	81	6th	18½	Huggins	Snyder, .298	Long, 149	Bescher, 4	D. Miller, 72	Doak, 16	Doak, 2.64
1916	60	93	*7th	33½	Huggins	Hornsby, .313	Hornsby, 155	Bescher, Hornsby, J. Smith, 6	Hornsby, 65	Doak, Meadows, 12	Meadows, 2.58
1917	82	70	3rd	15	Huggins	Hornsby, .327	Hornsby, 171	Hornsby, 8	Hornsby, 66	Doak, 16	Packard, 2.47
1918	51	78	8th	33	Hendricks	Fisher, .317	Paulette, 126	Cruise, 6	Hornsby, 60	Packard, 12	Ames, 2.31
1919	54	83	7th	40½	Rickey	Hornsby, .318	Hornsby, 163	Hornsby, 8	Hornsby, 71	Doak, 13	Goodwin, 2.51
1920	75	79	*5th	18	Rickey	Hornsby, .370	Hornsby, 218	McHenry, 10	Hornsby, 94	Doak, 20	Doak, 2.53
1921	87	66	3rd	7	Rickey	Hornsby, .397	Hornsby, 235	Hornsby, 21	Hornsby, 126	Haines, 18	Doak, 2.59
1922	85	69	*3rd	8	Rickey	Hornsby, .401	Hornsby, 250	Hornsby, 42	Hornsby, 152	Pfeffer, 19	Pfeffer, 3.58
1923	79	74	5th	16	Rickey	Hornsby, .384	Bottomley, 194	Hornsby, 17	Stock, 96	Haines, 20	Haines, 3.11
1924	65	89	6th	28½	Rickey	Hornsby, .424	Hornsby, 227	Hornsby, 25	Bottomley, 111	Sothoron, 10	Dickerman, 2.41
1925	77	76	4th	18	Rickey, Hornsby	Hornsby, .403	Bottomley, 227	Hornsby, 39	Hornsby, 143	Sherdel, 15	Reinhart, 3.05
1926	89	65	1st	+2	Hornsby	Bell, .325	Bell, 189	Bottomley, 19	Bottomley, 120	Rhem, 20	Alexander, 2.91
1927	92	61	2nd	1½	O'Farrell	Frisch, .337	Frisch, 208	Bottomley, 19	Bottomley, 124	Haines, 24	Alexander, 2.52
1928	95	59	1st	+2	McKechnie	Hafey, .337	Douthit, 181	Bottomley, 31	Bottomley, 136	Sherdel, 21	Sherdel, 2.86
1929	78	74	4th	20	McKechnie, Southworth, Street	Hafey, .338	Douthit, 206	Bottomley, Hafey, 29	Bottomley, 137	Haines, Johnson, 13	Johnson, 3.60
1930	92	62	1st	+2	Street	Watkins, .373	Douthit, 201	Hafey, 26	Frisch, 114	Halahan, 15	Grimes, 3.01
1931	101	53	1st	+13	Street	Hafey, .349	Adams, 178	Hafey, 16	Hafey, 95	Hallahan, 19	Johnson, 3.00
1932	72	82	*6th	18	Street	Orsatti, .336	Collins, 153	Collins, 21	Collins, 91	D. Dean, 18	Hallahan, 3.11
1933	82	71	5th	9½	Street, Frisch	Martin, .316	Martin, 189	Medwick, 18	Medwick, 98	D. Dean, 20	Haines, 2.50
1934	95	58	1st	+2	Frisch	Collins, .333	Collins, 200	Collins, 35	Collins, 116	D. Dean, 30	D. Dean, 2.66
1935	96	58	2nd	4	Frisch	Medwick, .353	Medwick, 224	Collins, Medwick, 23	Medwick, 126	D. Dean, 28	Heusser, 2.92
1936	87	67	*2nd	5	Frisch	Medwick, .351	Medwick, 233	Mize, 19	Medwick, 138	D. Dean, 24	D. Dean, 3.17
1937	81	73	4th	15	Frisch	Medwick, .374	Medwick, 237	Medwick, 31	Medwick, 154	Warneke, 18	D. Dean, 2.69
1938	71	80	6th	17½	Frisch, Gonzalez	Mize, .337	Medwick, 190	Mize, 27	Medwick, 122	Weiland, 16	McGee, 3.21
1939	92	61	2nd	4½	Blades	Mize, .349	Medwick, 201	Mize, 28	Medwick, 117	Davis, 22	Bowman, 2.60
1940	84	69	3rd	16	Blades, Gonzalez, Southworth	Mize, .314	Mize, 182	Mize, 43	Mize, 137	McGee, Warneke, 16	Warneke, 3.14
1941	97	56	2nd	2½	Southworth	Mize, .317	J. Brown, 168	Mize, 16	Mize, 100	Warneke, White, 17	White, 2.40
1942	106	48	1st	+2	Southworth	Slaughter, .318	Slaughter, 188	Slaughter, 13	Slaughter, 98	M. Cooper, 22	M. Cooper, 1.78
1943	105	49	1st	+18	Southworth	Musial, .357	Musial, 220	Kurowski, Musial, 13	W. Cooper, Musial, 81	M. Cooper, 21	Pollet, 1.75
1944	105	49	1st	+14½	Southworth	Musial, .347	Musial, 197	Kurowski, 20	Sanders, 102	M. Cooper, 22	Munger, 1.34
1945	95	59	2nd	3	Southworth	Kurowski, .323	Adams, 169	Kurowski, 27	Kurowski, 102	Barrett, 21	Brecheen, 2.52
1946	98	58	†1st	+2	Dyer	Musial, .365	Musial, 228	Slaughter, 18	Slaughter, 130	Pollet, 21	Pollet, 2.10
1947	89	65	2nd	5	Dyer	Musial, .312	Musial, 183	Kurowski, 27	Kurowski, 104	Brecheen, Munger, 16	Brazle, 2.84
1948	85	69	2nd	6½	Dyer	Musial, .376	Musial, 230	Musial, 39	Musial, 131	Brecheen, 20	Brecheen, 2.24
1949	96	58	2nd	1	Dyer	Musial, .338	Musial, 207	Musial, 36	Musial, 123	Pollet, 20	Staley, 2.73
1950	78	75	5th	12½	Dyer	Musial, .346	Musial, 192	Musial, 28	Musial, 109	Pollet, 14	Lanier, 3.13
1951	81	73	3rd	15½	Marion	Musial, .355	Musial, 205	Musial, 32	Musial, 108	Staley, 19	Brazle, 3.09
1952	88	66	3rd	8½	Stanky	Musial, .336	Musial, 194	Musial, 21	Slaughter, 101	Staley, 17	Staley, 3.27
1953	83	71	*3rd	22	Stanky	Schoendienst, .342	Musial, 200	Musial, 30	Musial, 113	Haddix, 20	Haddix, 3.06
1954	72	82	6th	25	Stanky	Musial, .330	Musial, 195	Musial, 35	Musial, 126	Haddix, 18	Poholsky, 3.06
1955	68	86	7th	30½	Stanky, Walker	Musial, .319	Musial, 179	Musial, 33	Musial, 108	Haddix, 12	LaPalme, 2.75
1956	76	78	4th	17	Hutchinson	Musial, .310	Musial, 184	Musial, 27	Musial, 109	Mizell, 14	Dickson, 3.07
1957	87	67	2nd	8	Hutchinson	Musial, .351	Blasingame, Musial, 176	Musial, 29	Ennis, 105	Jackson, McDaniel, 15	Jackson, 3.47
1958	72	82	*5th	20	Hutchinson, Hack	Musial, .337	Boyer, 175	Boyer, 23	Boyer, 90	S. Jones, 14	S. Jones, 2.88
1959	71	83	7th	16	Hemus	Cunningham, .345	Blasingame, 178	Boyer, 28	Boyer, 94	Jackson, McDaniel, 14	Jackson, 3.30
1960	86	68	3rd	9	Hemus	Boyer, .304	Boyer, 168	Boyer, 32	Boyer, 97	Broglio, 21	McDaniel, 2.09
1961	80	74	5th	13	Hemus, Keane	Boyer, .329	Boyer, 194	Boyer, 24	Boyer, 95	Jackson, Sadecki, 14	C. Simmons, 3.13
1962	84	78	6th	17½	Keane	Musial, .330	White, 199	Boyer, 24	White, 102	Jackson, 16	Gibson, 2.85
1963	93	69	2nd	6	Keane	Groat, .319	Groat, 201	White, 27	Boyer, 111	Broglio, Gibson, 18	C. Simmons, 2.48
1964	93	69	1st	+1	Keane	Brock, .348	Flood, 211	Boyer, 24	Boyer, 119	Sadecki, 20	Gibson, 3.01
1965	80	81	7th	16½	Schoendienst	Flood, .310	Flood, 191	White, 24	Flood, 83	Gibson, 20	Gibson, 3.07
1966	83	79	6th	12	Schoendienst	Cepeda, .303	Brock, 183	Cepeda, 17	Flood, 78	Gibson, 21	Gibson, 2.44
1967	101	60	1st	+10½	Schoendienst	Flood, .335	Brock, 206	Cepeda, 25	Cepeda, 111	Hughes, 16	Briles, 2.43
1968	97	65	1st	+9	Schoendienst	Flood, .301	Flood, 186	Cepeda, 16	Shannon, 79	Gibson, 22	Gibson, 1.12
								EAST DIVISION			
1969	87	75	4th	13	Schoendienst	Brock, .298	Brock, 195	Torre, 18	Torre, 101	Gibson, 20	Carlton, 2.17
1970	76	86	4th	13	Schoendienst	Torre, .325	Torre, 203	Allen, 34	Allen, 101	Gibson, 23	Taylor, 3.11
1971	90	72	2nd	7	Schoendienst	Torre, .363	Torre, 230	Torre, 24	Torre, 137	Carlton, 20	Gibson, 3.04
1972	75	81	4th	21½	Schoendienst	M. Alou, .314	Brock, 193	T. Simmons, 16	T. Simmons, 96	Gibson, 19	Gibson, 2.46
1973	81	81	2nd	1½	Schoendienst	T. Simmons, .310	Brock, 193	T. Simmons, Torre, 13	T. Simmons, 91	Wise, 16	Gibson, 2.77
1974	86	75	2nd	1½	Schoendienst	McBride, R. Smith, .309	Brock, 194	R. Smith, 23	T. Simmons, 103	McGlothen, 16	McGlothen, 2.70
1975	82	80	*3rd	10½	Schoendienst	T. Simmons, .332	T. Simmons, 193	R. Smith, 19	T. Simmons, 100	Forsch, McGlothen, 15	Hrabosky, 1.66
1976	72	90	5th	29	Schoendienst	Crawford, .304	T. Simmons, 159	Cruz, 13	T. Simmons, 75	McGlothen, 13	Denny, 2.52
1977	83	79	3rd	18	Rapp	Templeton, .322	Templeton, 200	T. Simmons, 21	T. Simmons, 95	Forsch, 20	Carroll, 2.50
1978	69	93	5th	21	Rapp. Krol. Boyer	Hendrick, .288	Templeton, 181	T. Simmons, 22	T. Simmons, 80	Denny, 14	Vuckovich, 2.55
1979	86	76	3rd	12	Boyer	Hernandez, .344	Templeton, 211	T. Simmons, 26	Hernandez, 105	S. Martinez, Vuckovich, 15	Fulgham, 2.53
1980	74	88	4th	17	Boyer, Krol, Herzog, Schoendienst	Hernandez, .321	Hernandez, 191	Hendrick, 25	Hendrick, 109	Vuckovich, 12	Vuckovich, 3.41
1981	59	43	‡2nd/2nd	—	Herzog	Hernandez, .306	Hernandez, 115	Hendrick, 18	Hendrick, 61	Forsch, 10	Forsch, 3.19
1982	92	70	§1st	+3	Herzog	L. Smith, .307	L. Smith, 182	Hendrick, 19	Hendrick, 104	Andujar, Forsch, 15	Andujar, 2.47
1983	79	83	4th	11	Herzog	L. Smith, .321	McGee, 172	Hendrick 18	Hendrick, 97	LaPoint, Stuper, 12	Stuper, 3.68
1984	84	78	3rd	12½	Herzog	McGee, .291	McGee, 166	Green, 15	Hendrick, 69	Andujar, 20	Sutter, 1.54
1985	101	61	§1st	+3	Herzog	McGee, .353	McGee, 216	Clark, 22	Herr, 110	Andujar, Tudor, 21	Tudor, 1.93
1986	79	82	3rd	28½	Herzog	O. Smith, .280	O. Smith, 144	Van Slyke, 13	Herr, Van Slyke, 61	Forsch, 14	Worrell, 2.08
1987	95	67	§1st	+3	Herzog	O. Smith, .303	O. Smith, 182	Clark, 35	Clark, 106	Cox, Forsch, Mathews, 11	Worrell, 2.66
1988	76	86	5th	25	Herzog	McGee, .292	McGee, 164	Brunansky, 22	Brunansky, 79	DeLeon, 13	Magrane, 2.18
1989	86	76	3rd	7	Herzog	Guerrero, .311	Guerrero, 177	Brunansky, 20	Guerrero, 117	Magrane, 18	Magrane, 2.91
1990	70	92	6th	25	Herzog, Schoendienst, Torre	McGee, .335	McGee, 168	Zeile, 15	Guerrero, 80	Tudor, 12	Tudor, 2.40
1991	84	78	2nd	14	Torre	Jose, .305	Jose, 173	Zeile, 11	Zeile, 81	B. Smith, 12	DeLeon, 2.71
1992	83	79	3rd	13	Torre	Gilkey, .302	Lankford, 175	Lankford, 20	Lankford, 86	Tewksbury, 16	Perez, 1.84
1993	87	75	3rd	10	Torre	Jefferies, .342	Jefferies, 186	Whiten, 25	Zeile, 103	Tewksbury, 17	Osborne, 3.76
								CENTRAL DIVISION			
1994	53	61	*4th	13	Torre	Jefferies, .325	Jefferies, 129	Lankford, Zeile, 19	Zeile, 75	Tewksbury, 12	Palacios, 4.44
1995	62	81	4th	22½	Torre, Jorgensen	Mabry, .307	Jordan, 145	Lankford, 25	Lankford, 82	DeLucia, 8	Morgan, 3.56
1996	88	74	∞▲1st	+6	La Russa	Jordan, .310	Mabry, 161	Gant, 30	Jordan, 104	An. Benes, 18	Osborne, 3.53
1997	73	89	4th	11	La Russa	DeShields, .295	DeShields, 169	Lankford, 31	Lankford, 98	Morris, Stottlemyre, 12	Al. Benes, 2.89
1998	83	79	3rd	19	La Russa	Jordan, .316	Jordan, 178	McGwire, 70	McGwire, 147	Mercker, 11	Morris, 2.53
1999	75	86	4th	21½	La Russa	Lankford, .306	Renteria, 161	McGwire, 65	McGwire, 147	Bottenfield, 18	Bottenfield, 3.97

*Tied for position. † Won pennant playoff. ‡First half 30-20; second half 29-23. § Won Championship Series. ∞ Won Division Series. ▲ Lost Championship Series.

Note: Batting average minimum 350 at-bats; ERA minimum 90 innings pitched.

HISTORY

SAN DIEGO PADRES

FRANCHISE CHRONOLOGY

First season: 1969, as part of a two-team expansion that increased the National League field to 12. The Padres defeated Houston, 2-1, in their Major League debut but finished their first season mired deep in the N.L. West Division basement with a 52-110 record—41 games behind first-place Atlanta and 29 behind the fifth-place Houston Astros.

1970-present: The Padres finished last in each of their first six seasons, losing 100 or more games in four of them and at least 95 in the other two. Even when the Padres recorded their first winning record in 1978, their 10th season, they finished fourth, 11 games behind first-place Los Angeles. They have finished higher than third only four times, but they do have three division titles and two N.L. pennants to show for their 29-year existence. Their first excursion into the fall classic came in 1984 after an exciting come-from-behind five-game N.L. Championship Series victory over Chicago. Their second came in 1998, after an equally surprising NLCS victory over Atlanta. Both ended in losses—in '84 to the Detroit Tigers and in '98 to the New York Yankees.

Outfielder Tony Gwynn.

PADRES VS. OPPONENTS BY DECADE

	Braves	Cardinals	Cubs	Dodgers	Giants	Phillies	Pirates	Reds	Astros	Mets	Expos	Marlins	Rockies	Brewers	D'backs	Interleague	Decade Record
1969	5-13	4-8	1-11	6-12	6-12	4-8	2-10	7-11	8-10	1-11	8-4						52-110
1970-79	82-97	50-70	46-74	71-109	72-104	46-74	41-79	74-105	70-106	56-64	59-60						667-942
1980-89	89-88	48-70	53-61	95-78	91-84	57-56	56-62	78-96	87-89	57-58	51-63						762-805
1990-99	44-79	51-56	51-59	71-68	71-65	60-53	53-55	61-69	67-62	63-52	40-71	34-30	45-41	11-6	11-14	25-19	758-799
Totals	220-277	153-204	151-205	243-267	240-265	167-191	152-206	220-281	232-267	177-185	158-198	34-30	45-41	11-6	11-14	25-19	2239-2656

Interleague results: 7-3 vs. Angels; 4-6 vs. Athletics; 9-5 vs. Mariners; 5-5 vs. Rangers.

MANAGERS

Name	Years	Record
Preston Gomez	1969-72	180-316
Don Zimmer	1972-73	114-190
John McNamara	1974-77	224-310
Bob Skinner	1977	1-0
Alvin Dark	1977	48-65
Roger Craig	1978-79	152-171
Jerry Coleman	1980	73-89
Frank Howard	1981	41-69
Dick Williams	1982-85	337-311
Steve Boros	1986	74-88
Larry Bowa	1987-88	81-127
Jack McKeon	1988-90	193-164
Greg Riddoch	1990-92	200-194
Jim Riggleman	1992-94	112-179
Bruce Bochy	1995-99	409-383

N.L. PENNANT WINNER

Year	Record	Manager	Series Result
1984	92-70	Williams	Lost to Tigers
1998	98-64	Bochy	Lost to Yankees

WEST DIVISION CHAMPIONS

Year	Record	Manager	NLCS Result
1984	92-70	Williams	Defeated Cubs
1996	91-71	Bochy	Lost in Division Series
1998	98-64	Bochy	Defeated Braves

ALL-TIME RECORD OF EXPANSION TEAMS

Team	W	L	Pct.	DT	P	WS
Arizona	165	159	.509	1	0	0
Kansas City	2,471	2,412	.506	6	2	1
Toronto	1,784	1,818	.495	5	2	2
Houston	2,980	3,048	.494	6	0	0
Montreal	2,387	2,501	.488	2	0	0
Anaheim	2,987	3,201	.483	3	0	0
Milwaukee	2,348	2,542	.480	2	1	0
Colorado	512	559	.478	0	0	0
New York	2,840	3,178	.472	4	3	2
Texas	2,881	3,290	.467	4	0	0
San Diego	2,239	2,656	.457	3	2	0
Seattle	1,624	1,977	.451	2	0	0
Florida	472	596	.442	0	1	1
Tampa Bay	132	192	.407	0	0	0

Division Titles. P—Pennants won. WS—World Series won.

BALLPARK CHRONOLOGY

Qualcomm Stadium, formerly San Diego Jack Murphy Stadium (1969-present)

Capacity: 56,133.
First game: Padres 2, Houston 1 (April 8, 1969).
First batter: Jesus Alou, Astros.
First hit: Jesus Alou, Astros (single).
First run: Jesus Alou, Astros (1st inning).
First home run: Ed Spezio, Padres.
First winning pitcher: Dick Selma, Padres.
First-season attendance: 512,970.

ATTENDANCE HIGHS

Total	Season	Park
2,555,901	1998	Qualcomm Stadium
2,523,538	1999	Qualcomm Stadium
2,210,352	1985	Jack Murphy Stadium
2,187,886	1996	Jack Murphy Stadium
2,089,336	1997	Jack Murphy Stadium

N.L. MVP
Ken Caminiti, 3B, 1996

CY YOUNG WINNERS
Randy Jones, LH, 1976
Gaylord Perry, RH, 1978
Mark Davis, LH, 1989

ROOKIES OF THE YEAR
*Butch Metzger, P, 1976
Benito Santiago, C, 1987
   * Co-winner.

MANAGER OF THE YEAR
Bruce Bochy, 1996

RETIRED UNIFORM

No.	Name	Pos.
6	Steve Garvey	1B
35	Randy Jones	P

Outfielder Cito Gaston (left) and first baseman Nate Colbert were original Padres.

25-plus home runs
50— Greg Vaughn 1998
40— Ken Caminiti 1996
38— Nate Colbert 1970, 1972
35— Fred McGriff 1992
34— Dave Winfield 1979
    Phil Plantier 1993
33— Gary Sheffield 1992
31— Fred McGriff 1991
30— Steve Finley 1996
29— Ken Caminiti 1998
28— Steve Finley 1997
27— Nate Colbert 1971
26— Kevin McReynolds 1986
    Jack Clark 1989
    Ken Caminiti 1995, 1997
    Reggie Sanders 1999
25— Dave Winfield 1977
    Jack Clark 1989

100-plus RBIs
130— Ken Caminiti 1996
119— Tony Gwynn 1997
     Greg Vaughn 1998
118— Dave Winfield 1979
115— Joe Carter 1990
111— Nate Colbert 1972
106— Fred McGriff 1991
104— Fred McGriff 1992
100— Gary Sheffield 1992
     Phil Plantier 1993

20-plus victories
1975— Randy Jones 20-12
1976— Randy Jones 22-14
1978— Gaylord Perry 21-6

N.L. home run champions
1992— Fred McGriff 35

N.L. RBI champions
1979— Dave Winfield 118

N.L. batting champions
1984— Tony Gwynn .... .351
1987— Tony Gwynn .... .370
1988— Tony Gwynn .... .313
1989— Tony Gwynn .... .336
1992— Gary Sheffield .... .330
1994— Tony Gwynn .... .394
1995— Tony Gwynn .... .368
1996— Tony Gwynn .... .353
1997— Tony Gwynn .... .372

N.L. ERA champions
1975— Randy Jones 2.24

N.L. strikeout champions
1994— Andy Benes...................................189

No-hit pitchers
(9 innings or more)
None

Longest hitting streaks
34— Benito Santiago 1987
27— John Flaherty 1996
25— Tony Gwynn 1983
23— Bip Roberts 1994
21— Bobby Brown 1983
    Steve Finley 1996
20— Tony Gwynn 1997
19— Tony Fernandez...............................1992
    Tony Gwynn 1997
18— Tony Gwynn 1988
    Chris James 1989
    Gary Sheffield 1992
    Eric Owens 1999
17— Steve Garvey.....................................1984
    Roberto Alomar 1989
16— Dave Winfield 1977
    Tony Gwynn 1999
15— Ivan Murrell 1969
    Cito Gaston 1972
    Nate Colbert 1972
    Bobby Tolan 1984
    Jerry Mumphrey 1980
    Broderick Perkins 1981
    Tony Gwynn 1982
    Kevin McReynolds 1985
    Tony Gwynn 1986
    Tony Gwynn 1991
    Jeff Gardner 1993
    Tony Gwynn 1995

Switch-hitting shortstop Garry Templeton came to San Diego in the trade that sent Ozzie Smith to St. Louis.

SEASON

Batting

At-bats	655	Steve Finley	1996
Runs	126	Steve Finley	1996
Hits	220	Tony Gwynn	1997
Singles	177	Tony Gwynn	1984
Doubles	49	Tony Gwynn	1997
Triples	13	Tony Gwynn	1987
Home runs	50	Greg Vaughn	1998
Home runs, rookie	18	Benito Santiago	1987
Grand slams	2	Last by Steve Finley	1997
Total bases	348	Steve Finley	1996
RBIs	130	Ken Caminiti	1996
Walks	132	Jack Clark	1989
Most strikeouts	150	Nate Colbert	1970
Fewest strikeouts	16	Tony Gwynn	1992
Batting average	.394	Tony Gwynn	1994
Slugging pct.	.621	Ken Caminiti	1996
Stolen bases	70	Alan Wiggins	1984

Pitching

Games	83	Craig Lefferts	1986
Complete games	25	Randy Jones	1976
Innings	315.1	Randy Jones	1976
Wins	22	Randy Jones	1976
Losses	22	Randy Jones	1974
Winning pct.	.778 (21-6)	Gaylord Perry	1978
Walks	122	Steve Arlin	1972
Strikeouts	257	Kevin Brown	1998
Shutouts	6	Fred Norman	1972
		Randy Jones	1975
Home runs allowed	36	Ed Whitson	1987
Lowest ERA	2.10	David Roberts	1971
Saves	53	Trevor Hoffman	1998

GAME

Batting

Runs	4	Last by Quilvio Veras	8-6-99
Hits	5	Last by Tony Gwynn	4-28-98
Doubles	3	Last by Dave Magadan	5-19-99
Triples	2	Last by Mark Sweeney	8-27-98
Home runs	3	Last by Ken Caminiti	7-12-98
RBIs	8	Nate Colbert	8-1-72
		Ken Caminiti	9-19-95
Total bases	13	Steve Finley	6-23-97
Stolen bases	5	Last by Damian Jackson	6-28-99

Lefthander Randy Jones, the franchise's first Cy Young winner, recorded two of the Padres' three 20-victory seasons.

BATTING

Games
Tony Gwynn	2,333
Garry Templeton	1,286
Dave Winfield	1,117
Tim Flannery	972
Gene Richards	939
Nate Colbert	866
Terry Kennedy	835
Benito Santiago	789
Carmelo Martinez	783
Cito Gaston	766

At-bats
Tony Gwynn	9,059
Garry Templeton	4,512
Dave Winfield	3,997
Gene Richards	3,414
Nate Colbert	3,080
Terry Kennedy	2,987
Benito Santiago	2,872
Cito Gaston	2,615
Tim Flannery	2,473
Steve Finley	2,396

Runs
Tony Gwynn	1,361
Dave Winfield	599
Gene Richards	484
Nate Colbert	442
Garry Templeton	430
Steve Finley	423
Bip Roberts	378
Ken Caminiti	362
Benito Santiago	312
Terry Kennedy	308

Hits
Tony Gwynn	3,067
Garry Templeton	1,135
Dave Winfield	1,134
Gene Richards	994
Terry Kennedy	817
Nate Colbert	780
Benito Santiago	758
Bip Roberts	673
Cito Gaston	672
Steve Finley	662

Doubles
Tony Gwynn	522
Garry Templeton	195
Dave Winfield	179
Terry Kennedy	158
Steve Finley	134
Nate Colbert	130
Ken Caminiti	127
Benito Santiago	124
Gene Richards	123
Carmelo Martinez	111

Triples
Tony Gwynn	84
Gene Richards	63
Dave Winfield	39
Garry Templeton	36
Cito Gaston	29
Steve Finley	28
Tim Flannery	25
Luis Salazar	24
Nate Colbert	22
Bip Roberts	21

Home runs
Nate Colbert	163
Dave Winfield	154
Tony Gwynn	133
Ken Caminiti	121
Benito Santiago	85
Fred McGriff	84
Steve Finley	82
Carmelo Martinez	82
Greg Vaughn	78
Cito Gaston	77

Total bases
Tony Gwynn	4,156
Dave Winfield	1,853
Garry Templeton	1,531
Nate Colbert	1,443
Gene Richards	1,321
Terry Kennedy	1,217
Benito Santiago	1,167
Steve Finley	1,098
Ken Caminiti	1,086
Cito Gaston	1,054

Runs batted in
Tony Gwynn	1,104
Dave Winfield	626
Nate Colbert	481
Garry Templeton	427

SEASON

Batting
Most at-bats	5,655	1996
Most runs	795	1997
Fewest runs	468	1969
Most hits	1,519	1997
Most singles	1,105	1980
Most doubles	295	1998
Most triples	53	1979
Most home runs	172	1970
Fewest home runs	64	1976
Most grand slams	9	1995
Most pinch-hit home runs	10	1995
Most total bases	2,282	1997
Most stolen bases	239	1980
Highest batting average	.275	1994
Lowest batting average	.225	1969
Highest slugging pct	.409	1998

Pitching
Lowest ERA	3.22	1971
Highest ERA	4.98	1997
Most complete games	47	1971,1976
Most shutouts	19	1985
Most saves	55	1978, 1998
Most walks	715	1974
Most strikeouts	1,194	1996

Fielding
Most errors	189	1977
Fewest errors	104	1998
Most double plays	171	1978
Highest fielding average	.983	1998

General
Most games won	98	1998
Most games lost	110	1969
Highest win pct	.605	1998
Lowest win pct	.321	1969

GAME, INNING

Batting
Most runs, game	20	Last 7-27-96
Most runs, inning	13	8-24-93, 5-31-94
Most hits, game	24	4-19-82
Most home runs, game	6	Last 6-17-98
Most total bases, game	39	5-23-70

Former Dodger Steve Garvey led the Padres to their first World Series appearance in 1984.

Terry Kennedy	424
Ken Caminiti	396
Benito Santiago	375
Carmelo Martinez	337
Steve Garvey	316
Cito Gaston	316

Extra-base hits
Tony Gwynn	739
Dave Winfield	372
Nate Colbert	315
Garry Templeton	274
Ken Caminiti	250
Steve Finley	244
Terry Kennedy	241
Benito Santiago	224
Gene Richards	212
Carmelo Martinez	200

Batting average
(Minimum 500 games)
Tony Gwynn	.339
Bip Roberts	.298
Ken Caminiti	.295
Gene Richards	.291
Johnny Grubb	.286
Dave Winfield	.284
Steve Finley	.276
Steve Garvey	.275
Terry Kennedy	.274
Luis Salazar	.267

Stolen bases
Tony Gwynn	318
Gene Richards	242
Alan Wiggins	171
Bip Roberts	148
Ozzie Smith	147
Dave Winfield	133
Enzo Hernandez	129
Garry Templeton	101
Luis Salazar	93
Roberto Alomar	90

PITCHING

Earned-run average
(Minimum 500 innings)
Greg Harris	2.95
Dave Roberts	2.99
Dave Dravecky	3.12

Craig Lefferts	3.24
Bruce Hurst	3.27
Randy Jones	3.30
Andy Benes	3.57
Bob Shirley	3.58
Eric Show	3.59
Andy Ashby	3.60

Wins
Eric Show	100
Randy Jones	92
Ed Whitson	77
Andy Ashby	70
Andy Benes	69
Andy Hawkins	60
Joey Hamilton	55
Bruce Hurst	55
Dave Dravecky	53
Clay Kirby	52

Losses
Randy Jones	105
Eric Show	87
Clay Kirby	81
Andy Benes	75
Ed Whitson	72
Steve Arlin	62
Andy Ashby	62
Bill Greif	61
Andy Hawkins	58
Bob Shirley	57

Innings pitched
Randy Jones	1,766.0
Eric Show	1,603.1
Ed Whitson	1,354.1
Andy Benes	1,235.0
Andy Ashby	1,210.0
Clay Kirby	1,128.0
Andy Hawkins	1,102.2
Joey Hamilton	934.2
Bruce Hurst	911.2
Dave Dravecky	900.1

Strikeouts
Andy Benes	1,036
Eric Show	951
Andy Ashby	827
Clay Kirby	802
Ed Whitson	767
Randy Jones	677
Joey Hamilton	639
Bruce Hurst	616

Trevor Hoffman	554
Andy Hawkins	489

Bases on balls
Eric Show	593
Clay Kirby	505
Randy Jones	414
Andy Hawkins	412
Andy Benes	402
Steve Arlin	351
Ed Whitson	350
Dave Freisleben	346
Joey Hamilton	343
Tim Lollar	328

Games
Trevor Hoffman	411
Craig Lefferts	375
Eric Show	309
Rollie Fingers	265
Randy Jones	264
Dave Tomlin	239
Mark Davis	230
Gary Lucas	230
Lance McCullers	229
Ed Whitson	227

Shutouts
Randy Jones	18
Steve Arlin	11
Eric Show	11
Bruce Hurst	10
Andy Benes	8
Andy Hawkins	7
Clay Kirby	7
Dave Dravecky	6
Dave Freisleben	6
Fred Norman	6
Ed Whitson	6

Saves
Trevor Hoffman	226
Rollie Fingers	108
Rich Gossage	83
Mark Davis	78
Craig Lefferts	64
Gary Lucas	49
Randy Myers	38
Lance McCullers	36
Luis DeLeon	31
Gene Harris	23

Year	W	L	Place	Games Back	Manager	Batting avg.	Hits	Home runs	RBIs	Wins	ERA
								WEST DIVISION			
1969	52	110	6th	41	Gomez	O. Brown, .264	O. Brown, 150	Colbert, 24	Colbert, 66	J. Niekro, Santorini, 8	Kelley, 3.57
1970	63	99	6th	39	Gomez	Gaston, .318	Gaston, 186	Colbert, 38	Gaston, 93	Dobson, 12	Coombs, 3.30
1971	61	100	6th	28½	Gomez	O. Brown, .273	Colbert, 149	Colbert, 27	Colbert, 84	Kirby, 15	Roberts, 2.10
1972	58	95	6th	36½	Gomez, Zimmer	Lee, .300	Colbert, 141	Colbert, 38	Colbert, 111	Kirby, 12	Ross, 2.45
1973	60	102	6th	39	Zimmer	Grubb, .311	Colbert, Kendall, 143	Colbert, 22	Colbert, 80	Arlin, 11	R. Jones, 3.16
1974	60	102	6th	42	McNamara	Grubb, .286	Winfield, 132	McCovey, 22	Winfield, 75	Freisleben, Greif, Hardy, Spillner, 9	Freisleben, 3.65
1975	71	91	4th	37	McNamara	Fuentes, .280	Fuentes, 158	McCovey, 23	Winfield, 76	R. Jones, 20	R. Jones, 2.24
1976	73	89	5th	29	McNamara	Ivie, .291	Winfield, 139	Winfield, 13	Ivie, 70	R. Jones, 22	R. Jones, 2.74
1977	69	93	5th	29	McNamara, Skinner, Dark	Hendrick, .311	Winfield, 169	Winfield, 25	Winfield, 92	Shirley, 12	Fingers, 2.99
1978	84	78	4th	11	Craig	Winfield, Richards, .308	Winfield, 181	Winfield, 24	Winfield, 97	G. Perry, 21	D'Acquisto, 2.13
1979	68	93	5th	22	Craig	Winfield, .308	Winfield, 184	Winfield, 34	Winfield, 118	G. Perry, 12	G. Perry, 3.05
1980	73	89	6th	19½	Coleman	Richards, .301	Richards, 193	Winfield, 20	Winfield, 87	Fingers, Shirley, 11	Fingers, 2.80
1981	41	69	*6th/6th	—	Howard	Salazar, .303	Salazar, 121	Lefebvre, 8	Richards, 42	Eichelberger, 8	Lucas, 2.00
1982	81	81	4th	8	Williams	Kennedy, .295	Kennedy, 166	Kennedy, 21	Kennedy, 97	Lollar, 16	DeLeon, 2.03
1983	81	81	4th	10	Williams	Garvey, .294	Kennedy, 156	Kennedy, 17	Kennedy, 98	Show, 15	Thurmond, 2.65
1984	92	70	†1st	+12	Williams	Gwynn, .351	Gwynn, 213	McReynolds, Nettles, 20	Garvey, 86	Show, 15	Lefferts, 2.13
1985	83	79	‡3rd	12	Williams	Gwynn, .317	Gwynn, 197	C. Martinez, 21	Garvey, 81	Hawkins, 18	Dravecky, 2.93
1986	74	88	4th	22	Boros	Gwynn, .329	Gwynn, 211	McReynolds, 26	McReynolds, 96	Hawkins, McCullers, 10	McCullers, 2.78
1987	65	97	6th	25	Bowa	Gwynn, .370	Gwynn, 218	Kruk, 20	Kruk, 91	Whitson, 10	McCullers, 3.72
1988	83	78	3rd	11	Bowa, McKeon	Gwynn, .313	Gwynn, 163	C. Martinez, 18	Gwynn, 70	Show, 16	M. Davis, 2.01
1989	89	73	2nd	3	McKeon	Gwynn, .336	Gwynn, 203	J. Clark, 26	J. Clark, 94	Whitson, 16	M. Davis, 1.85
1990	75	87	‡4th	16	McKeon, Riddoch	Gwynn, B. Roberts, .309	Gwynn, 177	J. Clark, 25	Carter, 115	Whitson, 14	Harris, 2.30
1991	84	78	3rd	10	Riddoch	Gwynn, .317	Gwynn, 168	McGriff, 31	McGriff, 106	Benes, Hurst, 15	Harris, 2.23
1992	82	80	3rd	16	Riddoch, Riggleman	Sheffield, .330	Sheffield, 184	McGriff, 35	McGriff, 104	Hurst, 14	Rodriguez, 2.37
1993	61	101	7th	43	Riggleman	Gwynn, .358	Gwynn, 175	Plantier, 34	Plantier, 100	Benes, 15	Harris, 3.67
1994	47	70	4th	12½	Riggleman	Gwynn, .394	Gwynn, 165	Plantier, 18	Gwynn, 64	Hamilton, 9	Hamilton, 2.98
1995	70	74	3rd	8	Bochy	Gwynn, .368	Gwynn, 197	Caminiti, 26	Caminiti, 94	Ashby, 12	Ashby, 2.94
1996	91	71	∞1st	+1	Bochy	Gwynn, .353	Finley, 195	Caminiti, 40	Caminiti, 130	Hamilton, 15	Worrell, 3.05
1997	76	86	4th	14	Bochy	Gwynn, .372	Gwynn, 220	Finley, 28	Gwynn, 119	Hamilton, 12	Ashby, 4.13
1998	98	64	▲◆1st	+9½	Bochy	Gwynn, .321	Vaughn, 156	Vaughn, 50	Vaughn, 119	Brown, 18	Ashby, 3.24
1999	74	88	4th	26	Bochy	Gwynn, .338	Gwynn, 139	Sanders, 26	Nevin, 85	Ashby, 14	Boehringer, 3.24

* First half 23-33; second half 18-36. † Won Championship Series. ‡ Tied for position. ∞ Lost Division Series. ▲ Won Division Series. ◆ Won Championship Series.   Note: Batting average minimum 350 at-bats; ERA minimum 90 innings pitched.

Ollie Brown

ANSWERING the American League's decision to expand in the 1969 season, the National League approved franchises for San Diego and Montreal, bringing its roster to 12 teams. The "Padres" began operation as the N.L.'s third West Coast team and first since the move of the Dodgers and Giants to Los Angeles and San Francisco.

The Padres began their player-procurement efforts in the October 14, 1968, expansion draft by selecting outfielder Ollie Brown with their first pick and 30 players total. The team opened play April 8, 1969, with a 2-1 victory over Houston at San Diego Stadium.

Expansion draft (October 14, 1968)

Players

Jose Arcia	Chicago	infield
*Ollie Brown	San Francisco	outfield
Nate Colbert	Houston	first base
Jerry DaVannon	St. Louis	infield
Al Ferrara	Los Angeles	outfield
Tony Gonzalez	Philadelphia	outfield
Clarence Gaston	Atlanta	outfield
Fred Kendall	Cincinnati	catcher
Jerry Morales	New York	outfield
Ivan Murrell	Houston	outfield
Roberto Pena	Philadelphia	second base
Rafael Robles	San Francisco	shortstop
Ron Slocum	Pittsburgh	catcher/infield
Larry Stahl	New York	outfield
Zoilo Versalles	Los Angeles	shortstop
Jim Williams	Los Angeles	outfield

Pitchers

Steve Arlin	Philadelphia	righthanded
Mike Corkins	San Francisco	righthanded
Tom Dukes	Houston	righthanded
Dave Giusti	St. Louis	righthanded
Dick James	Chicago	righthanded
Fred Katawczik	Cincinnati	lefthanded
Dick Kelley	Atlanta	lefthanded
Clay Kirby	St. Louis	righthanded
Al McBean	Pittsburgh	righthanded
Billy McCool	Cincinnati	lefthanded
Frank Reberger	Chicago	righthanded
Dave Roberts	Pittsburgh	lefthanded
Al Santorini	Atlanta	righthanded
Dick Selma	New York	righthanded

*First pick

Opening day lineup

April 8, 1969

Rafael Robles, shortstop
Roberto Pena, second base
Tony Gonzalez, center field
Ollie Brown, right field
Bill Davis, first base
Larry Stahl, left field
Ed Spiezio, third base
Chris Cannizzaro, catcher
Dick Selma, pitcher

Ed Spiezio

Padres firsts

First hit: Ed Spiezio, April 8, 1969, vs. Houston (home run)

First home run: Ed Spiezio, April 8, 1969, vs. Houston

First RBI: Ed Spiezio, April 8, 1969, vs. Houston

First win: Dick Selma, April 8, 1969, vs. Houston

First shutout: Johnny Podres (7 innings), Tommie Sisk (2), April 9, 1969, 2-0 vs. Houston

First CG shutout: Joe Niekro, June 27, 1969, 5-0 vs. Los Angeles

HISTORY

SAN FRANCISCO GIANTS

Center fielder Willie Mays.

FRANCHISE CHRONOLOGY

First season: 1883, in New York, as a member of the National League. The "Gothams" defeated Boston, 7-5, in their debut and completed a respectable first-year showing with a 46-50 record.

1884-1900: The Giants captured consecutive pennants in 1888 and '89, but they would not taste success again until the turn of the century, when John McGraw began his 30-year managerial run.

1901-57: Under McGraw's direction, the Giants ruled the National League for three decades. His teams won 10 pennants, finished second 11 times and captured three World Series, a record unmatched over the period. And when McGraw retired during the 1932 season, first baseman Bill Terry took over and led the Giants to three more pennants and another championship in a 10-year reign. But spoiled Giants fans would enjoy only one more Series winner over the team's final 16 seasons in New York. That startling victory came in 1954, when the Giants swept the powerful Cleveland Indians in the fall classic.

1958-present: It's hard to believe the once-proud Giants have not won a World Series in their 40-year San Francisco stay. They came excruciatingly close in 1962 when they lost a seven-game battle to the Yankees, but West Division titles in 1971 and 1987 were followed by N.L. Championship Series losses and another in 1997 was followed by a Division Series loss. The Giants did return to the Series in 1989, but they were swept by Bay Area-rival Oakland in a classic memorable only because it was interrupted by a devastating earthquake.

GIANTS VS. OPPONENTS BY DECADE

	Braves	Cardinals	Cubs	Dodgers	Phillies	Pirates	Reds	Astros	Mets	Expos	Padres	Marlins	Rockies	Brewers	D'backs	Interleague	Decade Record
1900-09	125-83	133-78	97-115	128-80	121-87	96-115	123-87										823-645
1910-19	137-73	131-81	116-99	125-88	124-85	127-86	129-85										889-597
1920-29	137-82	123-95	121-99	113-106	149-65	113-106	134-86										890-639
1930-39	127-89	110-107	102-117	120-98	145-72	125-95	139-79										868-657
1940-49	116-100	77-141	109-110	82-137	129-91	111-109	100-120										724-808
1950-59	94-126	112-108	130-90	106-117	121-99	131-89	128-92										822-721
1960-69	91-97	90-92	106-76	108-83	105-77	100-82	103-84	89-55	87-51	11-1	12-6						902-704
1970-79	95-84	60-60	61-59	72-108	53-67	62-58	78-99	90-90	58-62	61-59	104-72						794-818
1980-89	94-79	53-60	61-57	79-95	54-61	63-55	85-91	79-98	65-49	56-59	84-91						773-795
1990-99	53-69	54-58	53-57	70-70	67-44	52-55	66-58	57-69	56-58	59-56	65-71	42-25	52-34	9-9	10-14	25-19	790-766
Totals	1069-882	943-880	956-879	1003-982	1068-748	980-850	1085-881	315-312	266-220	187-175	265-240	42-25	52-34	9-9	10-14	25-19	8275-7150

Interleague results: 7-3 vs. Angels; 7-7 vs. Athletics; 7-3 vs. Mariners; 4-6 vs. Rangers.

MANAGERS

(New York Giants, 1883-1957)

Name	Years	Record
John Clapp	1883	46-50
Jim Price	1884	56-42
Monte Ward	1884, 1893-94	162-116
Jim Mutrie	1885-91	529-345
Pat Powers	1892	71-80
George Davis	1895, 1900-01	107-139
Jack Doyle	1895	32-31
Harvey Watkins	1895	18-17
Arthur Irwin	1896	36-53
Bill Joyce	1896-98	179-122
Cap Anson	1898	9-13
John Day	1899	29-35
Fred Hoey	1899	31-55
Buck Ewing	1900	21-41
Horace Fogel	1902	18-23
Heinie Smith	1902	5-27
John McGraw	1902-32	2604-1801
Bill Terry	1932-41	823-661
Mel Ott	1942-48	464-530
Leo Durocher	1948-55	637-523
Bill Rigney	1956-60, 1976	406-430
Tom Sheehan	1960	46-50
Alvin Dark	1961-64	366-277
Herman Franks	1965-68	367-280
Clyde King	1969-70	109-95
Charlie Fox	1970-74	348-327
Wes Westrum	1974-75	118-129
Joe Altobelli	1977-79	225-239
Dave Bristol	1979-80	85-98
Frank Robinson	1981-84	264-277
Danny Ozark	1984	24-32
Jim Davenport	1985	56-88
Roger Craig	1985-92	586-566
Dusty Baker	1993-99	558-512

WORLD SERIES CHAMPIONS

Year	Loser	Length	MVP
1905	Philadelphia	5 games	None
1921	N.Y. Yankees	8 games	None
1922	N.Y. Yankees	5 games	None
1933	Washington	5 games	None
1954	Cleveland	4 games	None

N.L. PENNANT WINNERS

Year	Record	Manager	Series Result
1888	84-47	Mutrie	None
1889	83-43	Mutrie	None
1904	106-47	McGraw	None
1905	105-48	McGraw	Defeated A's
1911	99-54	McGraw	Lost to A's
1912	103-48	McGraw	Lost to Red Sox
1913	101-51	McGraw	Lost to A's
1917	98-56	McGraw	Lost to White Sox
1921	94-59	McGraw	Defeated Yankees

N.L. PENNANT WINNERS—cont'd.

Year	Record	Manager	Series Result
1922	93-61	McGraw	Defeated Yankees
1923	95-58	McGraw	Lost to Yankees
1924	93-60	McGraw	Lost to Senators
1933	91-61	Terry	Defeated Senators
1936	92-62	Terry	Lost to Yankees
1937	95-57	Terry	Lost to Yankees
1951	98-59	Durocher	Lost to Yankees
1954	97-57	Durocher	Defeated Indians
1962	103-62	Dark	Lost to Yankees
1989	92-70	Craig	Lost to A's

WEST DIVISION CHAMPIONS

Year	Record	Manager	NLCS Result
1971	90-72	Fox	Lost to Pirates
1987	90-72	Craig	Lost to Cardinals
1989	92-70	Craig	Defeated Cubs
1997	90-72	Baker	Lost Division Series

ATTENDANCE HIGHS

Total	Season	Park
2,606,354	1993	Candlestick Park
2,078,095	1999	3Com Park
2,059,829	1989	Candlestick Park
1,975,571	1990	Candlestick Park
1,925,634	1998	3Com Park

BALLPARK CHRONOLOGY

3Com Park, formerly Candlestick Park (1960-present)
Capacity: 63,000.
First game: Giants 3, St. Louis 1 (April 12, 1960).
First batter: Joe Cunningham, Cardinals.
First hit: Bill White, Cardinals (single).
First run: Don Blasingame, Giants (1st inning).
First home run: Leon Wagner, Cardinals.
First winning pitcher: Sam Jones, Giants.
First-season attendance: 1,795,356.

Polo Grounds I, New York (1883-88)
First game: Giants 7, Boston 5 (May 1, 1883).

Oakland Park, New York (2 games 1889)
First game: Boston 8, Giants 7 (April 24, 1889).

St. George Grounds, New York (25 games 1889)
First game: Giants 4, Washington 2 (April 29, 1889).

Polo Grounds II, New York (1889-90)
First game: Giants 7, Pittsburgh 5 (July 8, 1889).

Polo Grounds III, New York (1891-1957)
Capacity: 55,987.
First game: Boston 4, Giants 3 (April 22, 1891).

Seals Stadium, San Francisco (1958-59)
Capacity: 22,900.
First game: Giants 8, Los Angeles 0 (April 15, 1958).
First-season attendance: 1,272,625.

N.L. MVPs

Carl Hubbell, P, 1933
Carl Hubbell, P, 1936
Willie Mays, OF, 1954
Willie Mays, OF, 1965
Willie McCovey, 1B, 1969
Kevin Mitchell, OF, 1989
Barry Bonds, OF, 1993

CY YOUNG WINNER

Mike McCormick, LH, 1967

ROOKIES OF THE YEAR

Willie Mays, OF, 1951
Orlando Cepeda, 1B, 1958
Willie McCovey, 1B, 1959
Gary Matthews, OF, 1973
John Montefusco, P, 1975

MANAGER OF THE YEAR

Dusty Baker, 1993
Dusty Baker, 1997

RETIRED UNIFORMS

No.	Name	Pos.
	Christy Mathewson	P
	John McGraw	Man.
3	Bill Terry	1B
4	Mel Ott	OF
11	Carl Hubbell	P
24	Willie Mays	OF
27	Juan Marichal	P
30	Orlando Cepeda	1B
44	Willie McCovey	1B

Longest hitting streaks

33—	George Davis	1893
27—	Charles Hickman	1900
26—	Jack Clark	1978
24—	Mike Donlin	1908
	Fred Lindstrom	1930
	Don Mueller	1955
	Willie McCovey	1963
23—	Joe Moore	1934
22—	Alvin Dark	1952
	Willie McCovey	1959
21—	Mel Ott	1937
	Willie Mays	1954, 1957
	Don Mueller	1954
	Robby Thompson	1993
20—	Mike Tiernan	1891
	Joe Moore	1932
	Willie Mays	1964

MILESTONE PERFORMANCES

30-plus home runs
52— Willie Mays 1965
51— Johnny Mize 1947
Willie Mays 1955
49— Willie Mays 1962
47— Willie Mays 1964
Kevin Mitchell 1989
46— Orlando Cepeda 1961
Barry Bonds 1993
45— Willie McCovey 1969
44— Willie McCovey 1963
43— Matt Williams 1994
42— Mel Ott 1929
Barry Bonds 1996
41— Willie Mays 1954
40— Johnny Mize 1948
Willie Mays 1961
Barry Bonds 1997
39— Willie McCovey 1965, 1970
Bobby Bonds 1973
38— Mel Ott 1932
Willie Mays 1963
Matt Williams 1993
37— Willie Mays 1966
Barry Bonds 1994, 1998
36— Willard Marshall 1947
Willie Mays 1956
Willie McCovey 1966, 1968
35— Mel Ott 1934
Walker Cooper 1947
Willie Mays 1957
Orlando Cepeda 1962
Will Clark 1987
Kevin Mitchell 1990
34— Willie Mays 1959
Orlando Cepeda 1963
Matt Williams 1991
Barry Bonds 1999
33— Mel Ott 1936
Jim Hart 1966
Bobby Bonds 1971
Matt Williams 1990
Barry Bonds 1995
32— Bobby Thomson 1951
Bobby Bonds 1969
31— Mel Ott 1935, 1937
Orlando Cepeda 1964
Jim Hart 1964
Willie McCovey 1967
Jeff Kent 1998
Ellis Burks 1999
30— Sid Gordon 1948
Darrell Evans 1983

100-plus RBIs
151— Mel Ott 1929
142— Orlando Cepeda 1961
141— Willie Mays 1962
138— Johnny Mize 1947
136— George Kelly 1924
135— Mel Ott 1934, 1936
132— Irish Meusel 1922
129— Bill Terry 1930
Barry Bonds 1996
128— Jeff Kent 1998
127— Willie Mays 1955
126— Willie McCovey 1969, 1970
125— Irish Meusel 1923
Rogers Hornsby 1927
Johnny Mize 1948
Kevin Mitchell 1989
123— Mel Ott 1932
Willie Mays 1961
Barry Bonds 1993
122— George Kelly 1921
Walker Cooper 1947
Matt Williams 1990
122— Barry Bonds 1998
121— Monte Irvin 1951
Bill Terry 1927
Jeff Kent 1997
119— Mel Ott 1930
117— Bill Terry 1929, 1932
116— Mel Ott 1938
Will Clark 1991
115— Mel Ott 1931
114— Mel Ott 1935
Orlando Cepeda 1962
112— Bill Terry 1931
Willie Mays 1965
111— Irish Meusel 1925
Frankie Frisch 1929
Willie Mays 1964
Will Clark 1989
110— Johnny Mize 1942
Willie Mays 1954
Matt Williams 1993
109— Bobby Thomson 1949
Will Clark 1988
108— Sam Mertes 1905
Bobby Thomson 1952
107— George Kelly 1922
Fred Lindstrom 1928
Hank Leiber 1935
Willard Marshall 1947
Sid Gordon 1948
Dick Dietz 1970
106— Mike Donlin 1908
Fred Lindstrom 1930
Bobby Thomson 1953
105— Orlando Cepeda 1959
Willie McCovey 1968
104— Sam Mertes 1903
Norm Young 1941
Willie Mays 1959
Barry Bonds 1995
J.T. Snow 1997
103— George Kelly 1923
Mel Ott 1933
Willie Mays 1960, 1963, 1966
Jack Clark 1982
102— Henry Zimmerman 1917
Ross Youngs 1921
Irish Meusel 1924
Bobby Bonds 1971
Willie McCovey 1963
101— Bill Terry 1928
Travis Jackson 1934
Norm Young 1940
Bobby Thomson 1951
Barry Bonds 1997
Jeff Kent 1999
100— Frankie Frisch 1921

20-plus victories
1883— Mickey Welch 39-21
1884— Mickey Welch 39-21
1885— Mickey Welch 44-11
Tim Keefe 32-13
1886— Tim Keefe 42-20
Mickey Welch 33-22
1887— Tim Keefe 35-19
Mickey Welch 22-15
1888— Tim Keefe 35-12
1889— Tim Keefe 28-13
Mickey Welch 27-12
1890— Amos Rusie 29-34
1891— Amos Rusie 33-20
John Ewing 21-8
1892— Amos Rusie 31-31
Silver King 23-24
1893— Amos Rusie 33-21
1894— Amos Rusie 36-13
Jouett Meekin 33-9
1895— Amos Rusie 23-23
1896— Jouett Meekin 26-14
1897— Amos Rusie 28-10
Jouett Meekin 20-11
Cy Seymour 20-14
1898— Cy Seymour 25-19
Amos Rusie 20-11
1901— Christy Mathewson 20-17
1903— Joe McGinnity 31-20
Christy Mathewson 30-13
1904— Joe McGinnity 35-8
Christy Mathewson 33-12
Luther Taylor 21-15
1905— Christy Mathewson 31-9
Leon Ames 22-8
Joe McGinnity 21-15
1906— Joe McGinnity 27-12
Christy Mathewson 22-12
1907— Christy Mathewson 24-12
1908— Christy Mathewson 37-11
George Wiltse 23-14
1909— Christy Mathewson 25-6
George Wiltse 20-11
1910— Christy Mathewson 27-9
1911— Christy Mathewson 26-13
Rube Marquard 24-7
1912— Rube Marquard 26-11
Christy Mathewson 23-12
1913— Christy Mathewson 25-11
Rube Marquard 23-10
Jeff Tesreau 22-13
1914— Jeff Tesreau 26-10
Christy Mathewson 24-13
1917— Ferdie Schupp 21-7
1919— Jess Barnes 25-9
1920— Fred Toney 21-11
Art Nehf 21-12
Jess Barnes 20-15
1921— Art Nehf 20-10
1928— Larry Benton 25-9
Fred Fitzsimmons 20-9
1933— Carl Hubbell 23-12
1934— Hal Schumacher 23-10
Carl Hubbell 21-12
1935— Carl Hubbell 23-12
1936— Carl Hubbell 26-6
1937— Carl Hubbell 22-8
Cliff Melton 20-9
1944— Bill Voiselle 21-16
1947— Larry Jansen 21-5
1951— Sal Maglie 23-6
Larry Jansen 23-11
1954— Johnny Antonelli 21-7
1956— Johnny Antonelli 20-13
1959— Sam Jones 21-15
1962— Jack Sanford 24-7
1963— Juan Marichal 25-8
1964— Juan Marichal 21-8
1965— Juan Marichal 22-13
1966— Juan Marichal 25-6
Gaylord Perry 21-8
1967— Mike McCormick 22-10
1968— Juan Marichal 26-9
1969— Juan Marichal 21-11
1970— Gaylord Perry 23-13
1973— Ron Bryant 24-12
1986— Mike Krukow 20-9
1993— John Burkett 22-7
Bill Swift 21-8

INDIVIDUAL SEASON, GAME RECORDS

SEASON

Batting

At-bats	681	Joe Moore	1935
Runs	146	Mike Tiernan	1893
Hits	254	Bill Terry	1930
Singles	177	Bill Terry	1930
Doubles	46	Jack Clark	1978
Triples	26	George Davis	1893
Home runs	52	Willie Mays	1965
Home runs, rookie	31	Jim Hart	1964
Grand slams	3	3 times	
		Last by Jeff Kent	1997
Total bases	392	Bill Terry	1930
RBIs	151	Mel Ott	1929
Walks	151	Barry Bonds	1996
Most strikeouts	189	Bobby Bonds	1970
Fewest strikeouts	12	Frankie Frisch	1923
Batting average	.401	Bill Terry	1930
Slugging pct.	.677	Barry Bonds	1993
Stolen bases	111	John Ward	1883

Pitching

Games	89	Julian Tavarez	1997
Complete games	44	Joe McGinnity	1903
Innings	434	Joe McGinnity	1903
Wins	37	Christy Mathewson	1908
Losses	27	Luther Taylor	1901
Winning pct.	.833 (15-3)	Hoyt Wilhelm	1952
Walks	128	Jeff Tesreau	1914
Strikeouts	267	Christy Mathewson	1903
Shutouts	12	Christy Mathewson	1908
Home runs allowed	36	Larry Jansen	1949
Lowest ERA	1.14	Christy Mathewson	1909
Saves	48	Rod Beck	1993

GAME

Batting

Runs	6	Last by Mel Ott	4-30-44
Hits	6	Last by Mike Benjamin	6-14-95
Doubles	3	Last by Jeff Kent	9-18-98
Triples	4	Bill Joyce	5-18-1897
Home runs	4	Willie Mays	4-30-61
RBIs	11	Phil Weintraub	4-30-44
Total bases	16	Willie Mays	4-30-61
Stolen bases	5	Dan McGann	5-27-04

N.L. home run champions
1883— Buck Ewing 10
1890— Mark Tiernan *13
1891— Mark Tiernan *16
1909— Red Murray 7
1916— Dave Robertson *12
1917— Dave Robertson *12
1921— George Kelly 23
1932— Mel Ott *38
1934— Mel Ott *35
1936— Mel Ott 33
1937— Mel Ott *31
1938— Mel Ott 36
1942— Mel Ott 30
1947— Johnny Mize *51
1948— Johnny Mize *40
1955— Willie Mays 51
1961— Orlando Cepeda 46
1962— Willie Mays 49
1963— Willie McCovey *44
1964— Willie Mays 47
1965— Willie Mays 52
1968— Willie McCovey 36
1969— Willie McCovey 45
1989— Kevin Mitchell 47
1993— Barry Bonds 46
1994— Matt Williams 43

* Tied for league lead

N.L. RBI champions
1903— Sam Mertes 104
1904— Bill Dahlen 80
1917— Heinie Zimmerman 102
1920— George Kelly *94
1923— Irish Meusel 125
1924— George Kelly 136
1934— Mel Ott 135
1942— Johnny Mize 110
1947— Johnny Mize 138
1951— Monte Irvin 121
1961— Orlando Cepeda 142
1968— Willie McCovey 105
1969— Willie McCovey 126
1988— Will Clark 109
1989— Kevin Mitchell 125
1990— Matt Williams 122
1993— Barry Bonds 123

* Tied for league lead

N.L. batting champions
1885— Roger Connor .371
1890— Jack Glasscock .336
1915— Larry Doyle .320
1930— Bill Terry .401
1954— Willie Mays .345

N.L. ERA champions
1904— Joe McGinnity 1.61
1905— Christy Mathewson 1.28
1908— Christy Mathewson 1.43
1909— Christy Mathewson 1.14
1911— Christy Mathewson 1.99
1912— Jeff Tesreau 1.96
1913— Christy Mathewson 2.06
1917— Fred Anderson 1.44
1922— Phil Douglas 2.63
1929— Bill Walker 3.09
1931— Bill Walker 2.26
1933— Carl Hubbell 1.66
1934— Carl Hubbell 2.30
1936— Carl Hubbell 2.31
1949— Dave Koslo 2.50
1950— Sal Maglie 2.71
1952— Hoyt Wilhelm 2.43
1954— Johnny Antonelli 2.30
1958— Stu Miller 2.47
1959— Sam Jones 2.83
1960— Mike McCormick 2.70
1969— Juan Marichal 2.10
1983— Atlee Hammaker 2.25
1989— Scott Garrelts 2.28
1992— Bill Swift 2.08

N.L. strikeout champions
1888— Tim Keefe 335
1890— Amos Rusie 341
1891— Amos Rusie 337
1893— Amos Rusie 208
1894— Amos Rusie 195
1895— Amos Rusie 201
1898— Cy Seymour 239
1903— Christy Mathewson 267
1904— Christy Mathewson 212
1905— Christy Mathewson 206
1907— Christy Mathewson 178
1908— Christy Mathewson 259
1911— Rube Marquard 237
1937— Carl Hubbell 159
1944— Bill Voiselle 161

No-hit pitchers
(9 innings or more)
1891— Amos Rusie 6-0 vs. Brooklyn
1901— Christy Mathewson 5-0 vs. St. Louis
1905— Christy Mathewson 1-0 vs. Chicago
1908— George Wiltse 1-0 vs. Philadelphia
1912— Jeff Tesreau 3-0 vs. Philadelphia
1915— Rube Marquard 2-0 vs. Brooklyn
1922— Jesse Barnes 6-0 vs. Philadelphia
1929— Carl Hubbell 11-0 vs. Pittsburgh
1963— Juan Marichal 1-0 vs. Houston
1968— Gaylord Perry 1-0 vs. St. Louis
1975— Ed Halicki 6-0 vs. New York
1976— John Montefusco 9-0 vs. Atlanta

HISTORY

BATTING

Games
Willie Mays	2,857
Mel Ott	2,730
Willie McCovey	2,256
Bill Terry	1,721
Travis Jackson	1,656
Larry Doyle	1,622
Jim Davenport	1,501
Whitey Lockman	1,485
Mike Tiernan	1,476
George Burns	1,362

At-bats
Willie Mays	10,477
Mel Ott	9,456
Willie McCovey	7,214
Bill Terry	6,428
Travis Jackson	6,086
Larry Doyle	5,995
Mike Tiernan	5,906
Whitey Lockman	5,584
Jo Jo Moore	5,427
George Burns	5,311

Runs
Willie Mays	2,011
Mel Ott	1,859
Mike Tiernan	1,313
Bill Terry	1,120
Willie McCovey	1,113
George Van Haltren	973
Roger Connor	946
Larry Doyle	906
George Burns	877
George S. Davis	838

Hits
Willie Mays	3,187
Mel Ott	2,876
Bill Terry	2,193
Willie McCovey	1,974
Mike Tiernan	1,834
Travis Jackson	1,768
Larry Doyle	1,751
Joe Moore	1,615
George Van Haltren	1,575
Whitey Lockman	1,571

Doubles
Willie Mays	504
Mel Ott	488
Bill Terry	373
Willie McCovey	308
Travis Jackson	291
Larry Doyle	275
George Burns	267
Joe Moore	258
Mike Tiernan	256
Will Clark	249

Triples
Mike Tiernan	162
Willie Mays	139
Roger Connor	131
Larry Doyle	117
Bill Terry	112
Buck Ewing	109
George S. Davis	98
Ross Youngs	93
George Van Haltren	88
Travis Jackson	86

Home runs
Willie Mays	646
Mel Ott	511
Willie McCovey	469
Barry Bonds	269
Matt Williams	247
Orlando Cepeda	226
Bobby Thomson	189
Bobby Bonds	186
Will Clark	176
Jack Clark	163

Total bases
Willie Mays	5,907
Mel Ott	5,041
Willie McCovey	3,779
Bill Terry	3,252
Mike Tiernan	2,732
Travis Jackson	2,636
Larry Doyle	2,461
Orlando Cepeda	2,234
Whitey Lockman	2,216
Joe Moore	2,216

Runs batted in
Mel Ott	1,860
Willie Mays	1,859

SEASON

Batting
Most at-bats	5,650	1984
Most runs	959	1930
Fewest runs	540	1956
Most hits	1,769	1930
Most singles	1,279	1930
Most doubles	307	1999
Most triples	105	1911
Most home runs	221	1947
Fewest home runs	15	1906
Most grand slams	7	1951, 1954, 1970, 1998
Most pinch-hit home runs	11	1977, 1987
Most total bases	2,628	1930
Most stolen bases	347	1911
Highest batting average	.319	1930
Lowest batting average	.233	1985
Highest slugging pct.	.473	1930

Pitching
Lowest ERA	2.14	1908
Highest ERA	4.86	1995
Most complete games	127	1904
Most shutouts	25	1908
Most saves	50	1993
Most walks	660	1946
Most strikeouts	1,086	1998

Fielding
Most errors	348	1901
Fewest errors	101	1993, 1998
Most double plays	183	1987
Highest fielding average	.984	1993, 1998

General
Most games won	106	1904
Most games lost	100	1985
Highest win pct	.759	1885
Lowest win pct	.353	1902

GAME, INNING

Batting
Most runs, game	29	6-15-1887
Most runs, inning	13	Last 7-15-97
Most hits, game	31	6-9-01
Most home runs, game	8	4-30-61
Most total bases, game	50	5-13-58

Lefthander Carl Hubbell used his outstanding screwball to post 253 victories for the Giants.

Willie McCovey	1,388
Bill Terry	1,078
Travis Jackson	929
Mike Tiernan	851
George S. Davis	816
Roger Connor	786
Orlando Cepeda	767
George Kelly	762

Extra-base hits
Willie Mays	1,289
Mel Ott	1,071
Willie McCovey	822
Bill Terry	639
Mike Tiernan	524
Travis Jackson	512
Barry Bonds	501
Orlando Cepeda	474
Will Clark	462
Larry Doyle	459

Batting average
(Minimum 500 games)
Bill Terry	.341
George S. Davis	.332
Ross Youngs	.322
Frankie Frisch	.322
George Van Haltren	.321
Roger Connor	.319
Fred Lindstrom	.318
Emil Meusel	.314
Shanty Hogan	.311
Mike Tiernan	.311

Stolen bases
Mike Tiernan	428
George S. Davis	354
Willie Mays	336
George Burns	334
John Ward	332
George Van Haltren	320
Larry Doyle	291
Art Devlin	266
Bobby Bonds	263
Jack Doyle	254

PITCHING

Earned-run average
(Minimum 1,000 innings)
Christy Mathewson	2.12
Joe McGinnity	2.38

Jeff Tesreau	2.43
Red Ames	2.45
Hooks Wiltse	2.48
Tim Keefe	2.53
Mickey Welch	2.69
Dummy Taylor	2.77
Rube Benton	2.79
Juan Marichal	2.84

Wins
Christy Mathewson	372
Carl Hubbell	253
Juan Marichal	238
Mickey Welch	238
Amos Rusie	234
Tim Keefe	174
Freddie Fitzsimmons	170
Hal Schumacher	158
Joe McGinnity	151
Hooks Wiltse	136

Losses
Christy Mathewson	188
Amos Rusie	163
Carl Hubbell	154
Mickey Welch	146
Juan Marichal	140
Hal Schumacher	121
Freddie Fitzsimmons	114
Gaylord Perry	109
Dave Koslo	104
Dummy Taylor	103

Innings pitched
Christy Mathewson	4,771.2
Carl Hubbell	3,590.1
Mickey Welch	3,579.0
Amos Rusie	3,531.2
Juan Marichal	3,444.0
Freddie Fitzsimmons	2,514.1
Hal Schumacher	2,482.1
Gaylord Perry	2,294.2
Tim Keefe	2,265.0
Joe McGinnity	2,151.1

Strikeouts
Christy Mathewson	2,499
Juan Marichal	2,281
Amos Rusie	1,835
Carl Hubbell	1,677
Gaylord Perry	1,606
Mickey Welch	1,570

Tim Keefe	1,303
Red Ames	1,169
Mike McCormick	1,030
Bobby Bolin	977

Bases on balls
Amos Rusie	1,588
Mickey Welch	1,077
Hal Schumacher	902
Christy Mathewson	843
Carl Hubbell	725
Juan Marichal	690
Freddie Fitzsimmons	670
Cy Seymour	652
Jouett Meekin	648
Red Ames	620

Games
Gary Lavelle	647
Christy Mathewson	634
Greg Minton	552
Carl Hubbell	535
Randy Moffitt	459
Juan Marichal	458
Amos Rusie	427
Mickey Welch	426
Rod Beck	416
Freddie Fitzsimmons	403

Shutouts
Christy Mathewson	79
Juan Marichal	52
Carl Hubbell	36
Amos Rusie	29
Mickey Welch	28
Hal Schumacher	27
Jeff Tesreau	27
Hooks Wiltse	27
Joe McGinnity	26
Tim Keefe	22

Saves
Rod Beck	199
Gary Lavelle	127
Greg Minton	125
Randy Moffitt	83
Frank Linzy	78
Robb Nen	77
Marv Grissom	58
Ace Adams	49
Scott Garrelts	48
Stu Miller	47

GIANTS YEAR-BY-YEAR

Year	W	L	Place	Games Back	Manager	Leaders: Batting avg.	Hits	Home runs	RBIs	Wins	ERA
						NEW YORK GIANTS					
1901	52	85	7th	37	G. Davis	Van Haltren, .335	Van Haltren, 182	G. Davis, 7	Ganzel, 66	Mathewson, 20	Mathewson, 2.41
1902	48	88	8th	53½	Fogel, H. Smith, McGraw	Brodie, .281	H. Smith, 129	Brodie, 3	Lauder, 44	Mathewson, 14	McGinnity, 2.06
1903	84	55	2nd	6½	McGraw	Bresnahan, .350	Browne, 185	Mertes, 7	Mertes, 104	McGinnity, 31	Mathewson, 2.26
1904	106	47	1st	+13	McGraw	McGann, .286	Browne, 169	McGann, 6	Dahlen, 80	McGinnity, 35	McGinnity, 1.61
1905	105	48	1st	+9	McGraw	Donlin, .356	Donlin, 216	Dahlen, Donlin, 7	Mertes, 108	Mathewson, 31	Mathewson, 1.27
1906	96	56	2nd	20	McGraw	Devlin, .299	Devlin, 149	Seymour, Strang, 4	Devlin, 65	McGinnity, 27	Taylor, 2.20
1907	82	71	4th	25½	McGraw	Seymour, .294	Shannon, 155	Browne, 5	Seymour, 75	Mathewson, 24	Mathewson, 2.00
1908	98	56	*2nd	1	McGraw	Donlin, .334	Donlin, 198	Donlin, 6	Donlin, 106	Mathewson, 37	Mathewson, 1.43
1909	92	61	3rd	18½	McGraw	Doyle, .302	Doyle, 172	Murray, 7	Murray, 91	Mathewson, 25	Mathewson, 1.14
1910	91	63	2nd	13	McGraw	Snodgrass, .321	Doyle, 164	Doyle, 8	Murray, 87	Mathewson, 27	Mathewson, 1.89
1911	99	54	1st	+7½	McGraw	Meyers, .332	Doyle, 163	Doyle, 13	Merkle, 84	Mathewson, 26	Mathewson, 1.99
1912	103	48	1st	+10	McGraw	Meyers, .358	Doyle, 184	Merkle, 11	Murray, 92	Marquard, 26	Tesreau, 1.96
1913	101	51	1st	+12½	McGraw	Meyers, .312	Burns, 173	Doyle, Shafer, 5	Doyle, 73	Mathewson, 25	Mathewson, 2.06
1914	84	70	2nd	10½	McGraw	Burns, .303	Burns, 170	Merkle, 7	Fletcher, 79	Tesreau, 26	Tesreau, 2.37
1915	69	83	8th	21	McGraw	Doyle, .320	Doyle, 189	Doyle, Merkle, 4	Fletcher, 74	Tesreau, 19	Tesreau, 2.29
1916	86	66	4th	7	McGraw	Robertson, .307	Robertson, 180	Robertson, 12	Kauff, 74	Perritt, 18	Schupp, 0.90
1917	98	56	1st	+10	McGraw	Kauff, .308	Burns, 180	Robertson, 12	Zimmerman, 102	Schupp, 21	F. Anderson, 1.44
1918	71	53	2nd	10½	McGraw	Youngs, .302	Youngs, 143	Burns, 4	Zimmerman, 56	Perritt, 18	Sallee, 2.25
1919	87	53	2nd	9	McGraw	Youngs, .311	Burns, 162	Kauff, 10	Kauff, 67	J. Barnes, 25	Nehf, 1.50
1920	86	68	2nd	7	McGraw	Youngs, .351	Youngs, 204	Kelly, 11	Kelly, 94	Nehf, Toney, 21	Barnes, 2.64
1921	94	59	1st	+4	McGraw	Frisch, .341	Frisch, 211	Kelly, 23	Kelly, 122	Nehf, 20	J. Barnes, 3.10
1922	93	61	1st	+7	McGraw	Meusel, Youngs, .331	Bancroft, 209	Kelly, 17	I. Meusel, 132	Nehf, 19	Douglas, 2.63
1923	95	58	1st	+4½	McGraw	Frisch, .348	Frisch, 223	I. Meusel, 19	I. Meusel, 125	Ryan, Scott, 16	Jonnard, 3.28
1924	93	60	1st	+1½	McGraw	Youngs, .356	Frisch, 198	Kelly, 21	Kelly, 136	V. Barnes, Bentley, 16	McQuillan, 2.69
1925	86	66	2nd	8½	McGraw	Frisch, .331	Kelly, 181	I. Meusel, 21	I. Meusel, 111	V. Barnes, 15	Scott, 3.15
1926	74	77	5th	13½	McGraw	Jackson, .327	Frisch, 171	Kelly, 13	Kelly, 80	Fitzsimmons, 14	V. Barnes, 2.87
1927	92	62	3rd	2	McGraw	Hornsby, .361	Hornsby, 205	Hornsby, 26	Hornsby, 125	Grimes, 19	Grimes, 3.54
1928	93	61	2nd	2	McGraw	Lindstrom, .358	Lindstrom, 231	Ott, 18	Lindstrom, 107	Benton, 25	Benton, 2.73
1929	84	67	3rd	13½	McGraw	Terry, .372	Terry, 226	Ott, 42	Ott, 151	Hubbell, 18	Walker, 3.09
1930	87	67	3rd	5	McGraw	Terry, .401	Terry, 254	Ott, 25	Terry, 129	Fitzsimmons, 19	J. Brown, 1.80
1931	87	65	2nd	13	McGraw	Terry, .349	Terry, 213	Ott, 29	Ott, 115	Fitzsimmons, 18	Walker, 2.26
1932	72	82	*6th	18	McGraw, Terry	Terry, .350	Terry, 225	Ott, 38	Ott, 123	Hubbell, 18	Hubbell, 2.50
1933	91	61	1st	+5	Terry	Terry, .322	Ott, 164	Ott, 23	Ott, 103	Hubbell, 23	Hubbell, 1.66
1934	93	60	2nd	2	Terry	Terry, .354	Terry, 213	Ott, 35	Ott, 135	Schumacher, 23	Hubbell, 2.30
1935	91	62	3rd	8½	Terry	Terry, .341	Leiber, Terry, 203	Ott, 31	Ott, 114	Hubbell, 23	Schumacher, 2.89
1936	92	62	1st	+5	Terry	Ott, .328	Moore, 205	Ott, 33	Ott, 135	Hubbell, 26	Hubbell, 2.31
1937	95	57	1st	+3	Terry	Ripple, .317	Moore, 180	Ott, 31	Ott, 95	Hubbell, 22	Melton, 2.61
1938	83	67	3rd	5	Terry	Ott, .311	Ott, 164	Ott, 36	Ott, 116	Gumbert, 15	Hubbell, 3.07
1939	77	74	5th	18½	Terry	Bonura, .321	Demaree, 170	Ott, 27	Bonura, 85	Gumbert, 18	Hubbell, 2.75
1940	72	80	6th	27½	Terry	Demaree, .302	Whitehead, 160	Ott, 19	Young, 101	Schumacher, 13	Schumacher, 3.25
1941	74	79	5th	25½	Terry	Bartell, .303	Rucker, 179	Ott, 27	Young, 104	Schumacher, 12	Melton, 3.01
1942	85	67	3rd	20	Ott	Mize, .305	Mize, 165	Ott, 30	Mize, 110	Lohman, 13	Lohrman, 2.56
1943	55	98	8th	49½	Ott	Witek, .314	Witek, 195	Ott, 18	Gordon, 63	Adams, 11	Adams, 2.82
1944	67	87	5th	38	Ott	Medwick, .337	Medwick, 165	Ott, 26	Medwick, 85	Voiselle, 21	Voiselle, 3.02
1945	78	74	5th	19	Ott	Ott, .308	Hausmann, 174	Ott, 21	Ott, 79	Mungo, Voiselle, 14	Mungo, 3.20
1946	61	93	8th	36	Ott	Mize, .337	Marshall, 144	Mize, 22	Mize, 70	Koslo, 14	Kennedy, 3.42
1947	81	73	4th	13	Ott	Cooper, .305	Mize, 177	Mize, 51	Mize, 138	Jansen, 21	Jansen, 3.16
1948	78	76	5th	13½	Ott, Durocher	Gordon, .299	Lockman, 167	Mize, 40	Mize, 125	Jansen, 18	Hansen, 2.97
1949	73	81	5th	24	Durocher	Thomson, .309	Thomson, 198	Thomson, 27	Thomson, 109	Jansen, Jones, 15	Koslo, 2.50
1950	86	68	3rd	5	Durocher	Stanky, .300	Dark, 164	Thomson, 25	H. Thompson, 91	Jansen, 19	Hearn, 1.94
1951	98	59	†1st	+1	Durocher	Irvin, .312	Dark, 196	Thomson, 32	Irvin, 121	Jansen, Maglie, 23	Maglie, 2.93
1952	92	62	2nd	4½	Durocher	Dark, .301	Dark, 177	Thomson, 24	Thomson, 108	Maglie, 18	Wilhelm, 2.43
1953	70	84	5th	35	Durocher	Mueller, .333	Dark, 194	Thomson, 26	Thomson, 106	Gomez, 13	Wilhelm, 3.04
1954	97	57	1st	+5	Durocher	Mays, .345	Mueller, 212	Mays, 41	Mays, 110	Antonelli, 21	Wilhelm, 2.10
1955	80	74	3rd	18½	Durocher	Mays, .319	Mays, Mueller, 185	Mays, 51	Mays, 127	Antonelli, Hearn, 14	Antonelli, 3.33
1956	67	87	6th	26	Rigney	Brandt, .299	Mays, 171	Mays, 36	Mays, 84	Antonelli, 20	Antonelli, 2.86
1957	69	85	6th	26	Rigney	Mays, .333	Mays, 195	Mays, 35	Mays, 97	Gomez, 15	Barclay, 3.44
						SAN FRANCISCO GIANTS					
1958	80	74	3rd	12	Rigney	Mays, .347	Mays, 208	Mays, 29	Cepeda, Mays, 96	Antonelli, 13	Miller, 2.47
1959	83	71	3rd	4	Rigney	Cepeda, .317	Cepeda, 192	Mays, 34	Cepeda, 105	S. Jones, 21	S. Jones, 2.83
1960	79	75	5th	16	Rigney, Sheehan	Mays, .319	Mays, 199	Mays, 29	Mays, 103	S. Jones, 18	McCormick, 2.70
1961	85	69	3rd	8	Dark	Cepeda, .311	Cepeda, 182	Cepeda, 46	Cepeda, 142	Miller, 14	McCormick, 3.20
1962	103	62	†1st	+1	Dark	F. Alou, .316	Cepeda, 191	Mays, 49	Mays, 141	Sanford, 24	Marichal, 3.36
1963	88	74	3rd	11	Dark	Cepeda, .316	Mays, 187	McCovey, 44	Mays, 103	Marichal, 25	Marichal, 2.41
1964	90	72	4th	3	Dark	Cepeda, .304	Mays, 171	Mays, 47	Mays, 111	Marichal, 21	Marichal, 2.48
1965	95	67	2nd	2	Franks	Mays, .317	Hart, Mays, 177	Mays, 52	Mays, 112	Marichal, 22	Marichal, 2.13
1966	93	68	2nd	1½	Franks	McCovey, .295	Hart, 165	Mays, 37	Mays, 103	Marichal, 25	Marichal, 2.23
1967	91	71	2nd	10½	Franks	J. Alou, .292	Hart, 167	McCovey, 31	Hart, 99	McCormick, 22	Linzy, 1.51
1968	88	74	2nd	9	Franks	McCovey, .293	McCovey, 153	McCovey, 36	McCovey, 105	Marichal, 26	Bolin, 1.99
						WEST DIVISION					
1969	90	72	2nd	3	King	McCovey, .320	Bo. Bonds, 161	McCovey, 45	McCovey, 126	Marichal, 21	Marichal, 2.10
1970	86	76	3rd	16	King, Fox	Bo. Bonds, .302	Bo. Bonds, 200	McCovey, 39	McCovey, 126	Perry, 23	McMahon, 2.96
1971	90	72	‡1st	+1	Fox	Bo. Bonds, .288	Bo. Bonds, 178	Bo. Bonds, 33	Bo. Bonds, 102	Marichal, 18	Perry, 2.76
1972	69	86	5th	26½	Fox	Speier, .269	Bo. Bonds, 162	Kingman, 29	Kingman, 83	Bryant, 14	Barr, 2.87
1973	88	74	3rd	11	Fox	Maddox, .319	Maddox, 187	Bo. Bonds, 39	Bo. Bonds, 96	Bryant, 24	Moffitt, 2.42
1974	72	90	5th	30	Fox, Westrum	Matthews, .287	Matthews, 161	Bo. Bonds, 21	Matthews, 82	Caldwell, 14	Barr, 2.74
1975	80	81	3rd	27½	Westrum	Joshua, .318	Joshua, 161	Matthews, 12	Murcer, 91	Montefusco, 15	Montefusco, 2.88
1976	74	88	4th	28	Rigney	Matthews, .279	Matthews, 164	Murcer, 23	Murcer, 90	Montefusco, 16	Moffitt, 2.27
1977	75	87	4th	23	Altobelli	Madlock, .302	Madlock, 161	McCovey, 28	McCovey, 86	Halicki, 16	Lavelle, 2.05
1978	89	73	3rd	6	Altobelli	Madlock, .309	J. Clark, 181	J. Clark, 25	J. Clark, 98	Blue, 18	Knepper, 2.63
1979	71	91	4th	19½	Altobelli, Bristol	Whitfield, .287	J. Clark, 144	Ivie, 27	Ivie, 89	Blue, 14	Lavelle, 2.51
1980	75	86	5th	17	Bristol	J. Clark, .284	Evans, 147	J. Clark, 22	J. Clark, 82	Blue 14	Minton, 2.46
1981	56	55	§5th/3rd	—	Robinson	Herndon, .288	Herndon, 105	J. Clark, 17	J. Clark, 53	Alexander, 11	Holland, 2.41
1982	87	75	3rd	2	Robinson	Morgan, .289	C. Davis, 167	J. Clark, 27	J. Clark, 103	Laskey, 13	Minton, 1.83
1983	79	83	5th	12	Robinson	Youngblood, .292	Evans, 154	Evans, 30	Leonard, 87	Laskey, 13	Hammaker, 2.25
1984	66	96	6th	26	Robinson, Ozark	C. Davis, .315	C. Davis, 157	C. Davis, Leonard, 21	Leonard, 86	Krukow, 11	Lavelle, 2.76
1985	62	100	6th	33	Davenport, Craig	C. Brown, .271	C. Davis, 130	Brenly, 19	Leonard, 62	Garrelts, 9	Garrelts, 2.30
1986	83	79	3rd	13	Craig	C. Brown, .317	Thompson, 149	Maldonado, 18	Maldonado, 85	Krukow, 20	Krukow, 2.94
1987	90	72	‡1st	+6	Craig	Aldrete, .325	W. Clark, 163	W. Clark, 35	W. Clark, 91	LaCoss, 13	J.Robinson, 2.79
1988	83	79	4th	11½	Craig	Butler, .287	Butler, 163	W. Clark, 29	W. Clark, 109	Reuschel, 19	D. Robinson, 2.45
1989	92	70	∞1st	+3	Craig	W. Clark, .333	W. Clark, 194	Mitchell, 47	Mitchell, 127	Reuschel, 17	Garrelts, 2.28
1990	85	77	3rd	6	Craig	Butler, .309	Butler, 192	Mitchell, 35	M. Williams, 122	Burkett, 14	Burkett, 3.79
1991	75	87	4th	19	Craig	McGee, .312	W. Clark, 170	M. Williams, 34	W. Clark, 116	Wilson, 13	Brantley, 2.45
1992	72	90	5th	26	Craig	W. Clark, .300	W. Clark, 154	M. Williams, 20	W. Clark, 73	Burkett, 13	Beck, 1.76
1993	103	59	2nd	1	Baker	Ba. Bonds, .336	Ba. Bonds, 181	Ba. Bonds, 46	Ba. Bonds, 123	Burkett, 22	Swift, 2.82
1994	55	60	2nd	3½	Baker	Ba. Bonds, .312	Ba. Bonds, 122	M. Williams, 43	M. Williams, 96	Portugal, 10	Swift, 3.38
1995	67	77	4th	11	Baker	Carreon, .301	Ba. Bonds, 149	Ba. Bonds, 33	Ba. Bonds, 104	Leiter, 10	VanLandingham, 3.67
1996	68	94	4th	23	Baker	Ba. Bonds, .308	Ba. Bonds, 159	Ba. Bonds, 42	Ba. Bonds, 129	Gardner, 12	Rueter, 3.97
1997	90	72	▲1st	+2	Baker	Mueller, .292	Ba. Bonds, 155	Ba. Bonds, 40	Kent, 121	Estes, 19	Estes, 3.18
1998	89	74	◆2nd	9½	Baker	Ba. Bonds, .305	Ba. Bonds, 167	Ba. Bonds, 37	Kent, 127	Rueter, 16	Gardner, 4.27
1999	86	76	2nd	14	Baker	Benard, .290	Benard, 163	Ba. Bonds, 34	Kent, 101	Ortiz, 18	Ortiz, 3.81

* Tied for position. † Won pennant playoff. ‡ Lost Championship Series. § First half 27-32, second half 29-23. ∞ Won Championship Series. ▲ Lost Division Series. ◆ Lost wild-card playoff.
Note: Batting average minimum 350 at-bats, ERA minimum 90 innings pitched.

HISTORY

For the Record

The record-setting 1927 New York Yankees featured (from left) Babe Ruth, diminutive manager Miller Huggins and Lou Gehrig.

FOR THE RECORD

INTRODUCTION

IT DIDN'T EQUAL '98, BUT HOW COULD IT?

The 1999 season was no 1998, that's for sure. At least not in terms of a riveting assault on one of the game's storied records.

No, the nation wasn't caught up in anything resembling the record-shattering, feel-good exploits of home run king Mark McGwire. But when it came to rewriting the record book and reaching career milestones, baseball's finest players did have their moments in '99. Chronologically, it went like this:

■ April 14. John Franco became the second relief pitcher in major league history to record 400 saves. At season's end, he had 416—62 behind Lee Smith's record total.

■ April 23. Cardinals third baseman Fernando Tatis became the first player to hit two grand slams in one inning, doing it against the Dodgers.

■ April 30. Seattle's Ken Griffey Jr. hit a grand slam in his second consecutive game, equaling a major league record.

■ May 5. The Rockies tied a big-league record by scoring in every inning of a 13-6 rout of the Cubs.

■ May 10. Nomar Garciaparra became the 11th major leaguer to hit two grand slams in one game. The Boston shortstop turned the trick against Seattle in a game in which he drove in 10 runs.

■ May 20. Mets third baseman Robin Ventura slugged a grand slam in each game of a doubleheader, an unprecedented feat. He also became the only player in history to hit two bases-loaded homers in one day twice, having had two grand slams in one game while playing for the White Sox in 1995.

■ May 22. Yankees righthander Roger Clemens set an American League record with his 18th consecutive victory, beating the White Sox. His streak, established over two seasons, reached 20 before it was snapped by the Mets on June 6.

■ May 31. Red Sox reliever Tom Gordon extended his consecutive-saves record to 54. On June 5, the streak ended.

■ July 4. The Royals' Mike Sweeney tied a 58-year-old A.L. record by collecting an RBI in his 13th consecutive game. He was stopped in his next game.

■ July 18. The Yankees' David Cone pitched the 15th regular-season perfect game in history, shutting down the Expos.

■ August 2. Jeff Zimmerman matched the A.L. record for consecutive victories to start a career, improving his record to 9-0 with a win against Minnesota. The Texas rookie finally lost four days later.

■ August 5. McGwire became the 16th player to hit 500 career home runs—and the fastest to do so (in his 5,487th at-bat). The milestone came against San Diego.

■ August 6. The Padres' Tony Gwynn collected his 3,000th career hit in a game against Montreal.

■ August 7. Capping an extraordinary three-night run of baseball history-making, Tampa Bay's Wade Boggs became the 23rd player to reach 3,000 hits. And Boggs did it in a way no one ever had—with a home run (off Cleveland's Chris Haney).

■ August 9. A record five grand slams were hit in the majors in one day. Connecting were: St. Louis' Tatis, Montreal's Jose Vidro, Florida's Mike Lowell, the Yankees' Bernie Williams and Seattle's Jay Buhner.

■ August 17. Orioles reliever Jesse Orosco appeared in his 1,072nd major league game, breaking Dennis Eckersley's career mark.

■ August 22. Hitting two homers against the Mets, the Cards' McGwire reached 50 for a record fourth consecutive season.

■ August 26. Arizona's Randy Johnson got to 300 strikeouts in a season quicker than anyone in history—in his 29th start.

■ September 4. The Reds hit a National League-record nine home runs in a game against the Phillies.

■ September 14. Kansas City's Mark Quinn became the fourth player in history to hit two home runs in his first big-league game, accomplishing the feat against Anaheim.

■ September 18. The Cubs' Sammy Sosa became the first major leaguer to hit 60 homers in two seasons.

■ September 21. Chipper Jones of the Braves hit his 42nd and 43rd homers, breaking Todd Hundley's N.L. record (41) for a switch hitter. He finished the season with 45.

■ September 26. Atlanta clinched its eighth consecutive division title, a major league record.

■ October 3. McGwire hit his 65th homer of the year in a season-ending game in which Chicago's Sosa belted No. 63. The figures ranked third and fourth on the all-time list, behind the 70 that McGwire hit in '98 and the 66 that Sosa attained in the same season.

Though their amazing follow-up seasons lacked the drama of what unfolded a year earlier, McGwire and Sosa proved conclusively they were a special pair of sluggers—and that fans everywhere still loved the long ball.

FIRST, IT WAS GEORGE HALL

Of course, fascination with the long ball has existed as long as the game itself, and home run records have always been among the game's most-cherished marks. Philadelphia's George Hall was the majors' first home run king, hitting an N.L.-high five in 1876. His single-season record lasted for three years. By 1884, the big-league mark had risen to 27, a figure achieved by Ned Williamson of Chicago's N.L. club. Williamson's record lasted 35 years—until George Herman Ruth hit 29 for the Red Sox in 1919. The Babe made short shrift of his own record the next year when he slugged 54 for the Yankees. Ruth topped that mark with 59 in 1921, then reached his storied total of 60 in 1927. Ruth's figure ranked as the single-season high for 34 years. It was surpassed by another Yankee, Roger Maris, whose 61-homer performance in 1961 stood as the record for 37 years (until McGwire shattered it). ... Ruth became the modern career home run leader (Roger Connor had hit 138 homers while playing exclusively before the turn of the century) when he cracked No. 120 in June 1921, breaking the post-1900 record of 119 set by Gavvy Cravath, an outfielder who played most of his career with the Phillies. Ruth, who went on to hit 594 more homers and surpassed Connor later in the 1921 season, remained the all-time leader for 53 years—until Hank Aaron surpassed his total of 714. Aaron, of course, wound up with 755. ... The Cubs' Hack Wilson holds the majors' RBI record with a recently revised figure of 191, a mark set in baseball's offense-dominated season of 1930. Lou Gehrig, who had driven in 174 runs for the Yankees in '30, established the A.L. record the next year with 184. ... Hitting prowess, though, is much more than the ability to hit a baseball to faraway places. Ty Cobb proved that by compiling the best lifetime batting average in history, a .366 mark. He won the A.L.

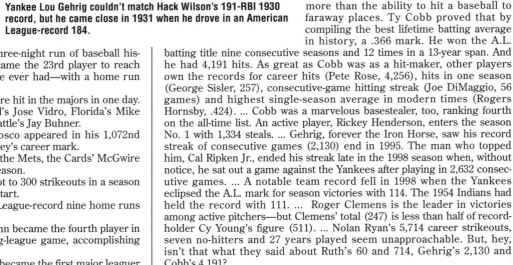

Yankee Lou Gehrig couldn't match Hack Wilson's 191-RBI 1930 record, but he came close in 1931 when he drove in an American League-record 184.

batting title nine consecutive seasons and 12 times in a 13-year span. And he had 4,191 hits. As great as Cobb was as a hit-maker, other players own the records for career hits (Pete Rose, 4,256), hits in one season (George Sisler, 257), consecutive-game hitting streak (Joe DiMaggio, 56 games) and highest single-season average in modern times (Rogers Hornsby, .424). ... Cobb was a marvelous basestealer, too, ranking fourth on the all-time list. An active player, Rickey Henderson, enters the season No. 1 with 1,334 steals. ... Gehrig, forever the Iron Horse, saw his record streak of consecutive games (2,130) end in 1995. The man who topped him, Cal Ripken Jr., ended his streak late in the 1998 season when, without notice, he sat out a game against the Yankees after playing in 2,632 consecutive games. ... A notable team record fell in 1998 when the Yankees eclipsed the A.L. mark for season victories with 114. The 1954 Indians had held the record with 111. ... Roger Clemens is the leader in victories among active pitchers—but Clemens' total (247) is less than half of record-holder Cy Young's figure (511). ... Nolan Ryan's 5,714 career strikeouts, seven no-hitters and 27 years played seem unapproachable. But, hey, isn't that what they said about Ruth's 60 and 714, Gehrig's 2,130 and Cobb's 4,191?

—JOE HOPPEL

Career

REGULAR SEASON

SERVICE

YEARS PLAYED

1.	Deacon McGuire	26
2.	Eddie Collins	25
	Bobby Wallace	25
4.	Ty Cobb	24
	Rick Dempsey	24
	Carlton Fisk	24
	Pete Rose	24
8.	Hank Aaron	23
	Rogers Hornsby	23
	Rabbit Maranville	23
	Tony Perez	23
	Brooks Robinson	23
	Rusty Staub	23
	Carl Yastrzemski	23
15.	17 tied with 22	

YEARS ONE CLUB

1.	Brooks Robinson, Orioles	23
	Carl Yastrzemski, Red Sox	23
3.	Cap Anson, Cubs	22
	Ty Cobb, Tigers	22
	Al Kaline, Tigers	22
	Stan Musial, Cardinals	22
	Mel Ott, Giants	22
8.	Hank Aaron, Braves	21
	George Brett, Royals	21
	Harmon Killebrew, Senators/Twins	21
	Willie Mays, Giants	21
	Willie Stargell, Pirates	21
13.	Luke Appling, White Sox	20
	Phil Cavarretta, Cubs	20
	Alan Trammell, Tigers	20
	Robin Yount, Brewers	20
17.	11 tied with 19	

YEARS PITCHED

1.	Nolan Ryan	27
2.	Tommy John	26
3.	Charlie Hough	25
	Jim Kaat	25
5.	Steve Carlton	24
	Dennis Eckersley	24
	Phil Niekro	24
8.	Dennis Martinez	23
	Jack Quinn	23
	Don Sutton	23
	Early Wynn	23
12.	Bert Blyleven	22
	Rich Gossage	22
	Sam Jones	22
	Joe Niekro	22
	Herb Pennock	22
	Gaylord Perry	22
	Jerry Reuss	22
	Red Ruffing	22
	Cy Young	22

YEARS PITCHED ONE CLUB

1.	Walter Johnson, Senators	21
	Ted Lyons, White Sox	21
	Phil Niekro, Braves	21
4.	Red Faber, White Sox	20
	Mel Harder, Indians	20
	Warren Spahn, Braves	20
7.	Jim Palmer, Orioles	19
8.	Babe Adams, Pirates	18
	Bob Feller, Indians	18
	Jesse Haines, Cardinals	18
11.	Bob Gibson, Cardinals	17
	Christy Mathewson, Giants	17
13.	Tommy Bridges, Tigers	16
	Whitey Ford, Yankees	16
	Carl Hubbell, Giants	16
	Vern Law, Pirates	16
	Charlie Root, Cubs	16
	Don Sutton, Dodgers	16
19.	16 tied with 15	

BATTING

GAMES

1.	Pete Rose	3,562
2.	Carl Yastrzemski	3,308
3.	Hank Aaron	3,298
4.	Ty Cobb	3,035
5.	Eddie Murray	3,026
	Stan Musial	3,026
7.	Willie Mays	2,992
8.	Dave Winfield	2,973
9.	Rusty Staub	2,951
10.	Brooks Robinson	2,896
11.	Robin Yount	2,856
12.	Al Kaline	2,834
13.	Eddie Collins	2,826
14.	Reggie Jackson	2,820
15.	Frank Robinson	2,808
16.	Honus Wagner	2,792
17.	Cal Ripken	2,790
18.	Tris Speaker	2,789
19.	Tony Perez	2,777
20.	Rickey Henderson	2,733

CONSECUTIVE GAMES PLAYED

1.	Cal Ripken	2,632
2.	Lou Gehrig	2,130
3.	Everett Scott	1,307
4.	Steve Garvey	1,207
5.	Billy Williams	1,117
6.	Joe Sewell	1,103
7.	Stan Musial	895
8.	Eddie Yost	829
9.	Gus Suhr	822
10.	Nellie Fox	798
11.	Pete Rose	745
12.	Dale Murphy	740
13.	Richie Ashburn	730
14.	Ernie Banks	717
15.	Pete Rose	678
16.	Earl Averill	673
17.	Frank McCormick	652
18.	Sandy Alomar Sr.	648
19.	Eddie Brown	618
20.	Roy McMillan	585

HIGHEST AVERAGE
(Minimum 1,500 hits)

1.	Ty Cobb	.366
2.	Rogers Hornsby	.358
3.	Joe Jackson	.356
4.	Ed Delahanty	.346
5.	Tris Speaker	.345
6.	Ted Williams	.344
	Billy Hamilton	.344
8.	Dan Brouthers	.342
	Babe Ruth	.342
	Harry Heilmann	.342
11.	Pete Browning	.341
	Willie Keeler	.341
	Bill Terry	.341
14.	George Sisler	.340
	Lou Gehrig	.340
16.	Tony Gwynn	.339
17.	Jesse Burkett	.338
	Nap Lajoie	.338
19.	Riggs Stephenson	.336
20.	Al Simmons	.334

YEARS LEADING LEAGUE IN AVERAGE

1.	Ty Cobb	12
2.	Tony Gwynn	8
	Honus Wagner	8
4.	Rod Carew	7
	Rogers Hornsby	7
	Stan Musial	7
7.	Ted Williams	6
8.	Wade Boggs	5
	Dan Brouthers	5
10.	Cap Anson	4
	Roberto Clemente	4
	Harry Heilmann	4
	Bill Madlock	4
14.	George Brett	3
	Pete Browning	3
	Jesse Burkett	3
	Nap Lajoie	3
	Tony Oliva	3
	Pete Rose	3
	Paul Waner	3
	Carl Yastrzemski	3

YEARS TOPPING .300

1.	Ty Cobb	23
2.	Cap Anson	19
3.	Tris Speaker	18
4.	Eddie Collins	17
	Tony Gwynn	17
	Stan Musial	17
7.	Babe Ruth	16
	Honus Wagner	16
	Ted Williams	16
10.	Wade Boggs	15
	Dan Brouthers	15
	Rod Carew	15

In the early 1960s, Pete Rose was a young player looking for recognition. By the time he retired, he was baseball's all-time career hit leader.

	Rogers Hornsby	15
	Nap Lajoie	15
	Pete Rose	15
16.	Hank Aaron	14
	Luke Appling	14
	Paul Waner	14
19.	9 tied with 13	

CONSECUTIVE .300 SEASONS

1.	Ty Cobb	23
2.	Tony Gwynn	17
3.	Stan Musial	16
4.	Cap Anson	15
	Rod Carew	15
	Honus Wagner	15
7.	Dan Brouthers	14
8.	Willie Keeler	13
9.	Lou Gehrig	12
	Billy Hamilton	12
	Harry Heilmann	12
	Paul Waner	12
13.	Ed Delahanty	11
	Frank Frisch	11
	Rogers Hornsby	11
	Joe Kelley	11
	Al Simmons	11
18.	Wade Boggs	10
	Jesse Burkett	10
	Nap Lajoie	10
	Joe Medwick	10
	Tris Speaker	10
	Bill Terry	10
	Arky Vaughan	10
	Ted Williams	10

AT-BATS

1.	Pete Rose	14,053
2.	Hank Aaron	12,364
3.	Carl Yastrzemski	11,988
4.	Ty Cobb	11,434
5.	Eddie Murray	11,336
6.	Robin Yount	11,008
7.	Dave Winfield	11,003
8.	Stan Musial	10,972
9.	Willie Mays	10,881
10.	Paul Molitor	10,835
11.	Cal Ripken	10,765
12.	Brooks Robinson	10,654
13.	Honus Wagner	10,430
14.	George Brett	10,349
15.	Lou Brock	10,332
16.	Luis Aparicio	10,230
17.	Tris Speaker	10,195
18.	Al Kaline	10,116
19.	Rabbit Maranville	10,078
20.	Frank Robinson	10,006

RUNS SCORED

1.	Ty Cobb	2,246
2.	Hank Aaron	2,174
	Babe Ruth	2,174
4.	Pete Rose	2,165
5.	Rickey Henderson	2,103
6.	Willie Mays	2,062
7.	Stan Musial	1,949
8.	Lou Gehrig	1,888
9.	Tris Speaker	1,882
10.	Mel Ott	1,859
11.	Frank Robinson	1,829
12.	Eddie Collins	1,821
13.	Carl Yastrzemski	1,816
14.	Ted Williams	1,798
15.	Paul Molitor	1,782
16.	Charley Gehringer	1,774
17.	Jimmie Foxx	1,751
18.	Honus Wagner	1,736
19.	Jesse Burkett	1,720
20.	Cap Anson	1,719
	Willie Keeler	1,719

YEARS LEADING LEAGUE IN RUNS

1.	Babe Ruth	8
2.	Mickey Mantle	6
	Ted Williams	6
4.	George Burns	5
	Ty Cobb	5
	Rickey Henderson	5
	Rogers Hornsby	5
	Stan Musial	5
9.	Lou Gehrig	4
	Billy Hamilton	4
	Pete Rose	4
	Harry Stovey	4
13.	Hank Aaron	3
	Eddie Collins	3
	King Kelly	3
	Chuck Klein	3
	Paul Molitor	3
	Frank Robinson	3
	Ryne Sandberg	3
	Duke Snider	3
	Arky Vaughan	3
	Carl Yastrzemski	3

100-RUN SEASONS

1.	Hank Aaron	15
2.	Lou Gehrig	13
	Rickey Henderson	13
4.	Charley Gehringer	12
	Willie Mays	12
	Babe Ruth	12
7.	Ty Cobb	11
	Jimmie Foxx	11
	Billy Hamilton	11
	Stan Musial	11
	George Van Haltren	11
12.	Ed Delahanty	10
	Mike Griffin	10
	Bid McPhee	10
	Pete Rose	10
	Sam Thompson	10
17.	10 tied with 9	

HITS

1.	Pete Rose	4,256
2.	Ty Cobb	4,189
3.	Hank Aaron	3,771
4.	Stan Musial	3,630
5.	Tris Speaker	3,514
6.	Carl Yastrzemski	3,419
7.	Honus Wagner	3,415
8.	Paul Molitor	3,319
9.	Eddie Collins	3,315
10.	Willie Mays	3,283
11.	Eddie Murray	3,255
12.	Nap Lajoie	3,242
13.	George Brett	3,154
14.	Paul Waner	3,152
15.	Robin Yount	3,142
16.	Dave Winfield	3,110
17.	Tony Gwynn	3,067
18.	Cap Anson	3,041
19.	Rod Carew	3,053
20.	Lou Brock	3,023

YEARS LEADING LEAGUE IN HITS

1.	Ty Cobb	8
2.	Tony Gwynn	7
	Pete Rose	7
4.	Stan Musial	6
5.	Tony Oliva	5
6.	Ginger Beaumont	4
	Nellie Fox	4
	Rogers Hornsby	4
	Harvey Kuenn	4
	Nap Lajoie	4
	Kirby Puckett	4
12.	Richie Ashburn	3
	George Brett	3
	Dan Brouthers	3
	Jesse Burkett	3
	Rod Carew	3
	Willie Keeler	3
	Frank McCormick	3
	Paul Molitor	3
	Johnny Pesky	3
	Sam Thompson	3

200-HIT SEASONS

1.	Pete Rose	10
2.	Ty Cobb	9
3.	Lou Gehrig	8
	Willie Keeler	8
	Paul Waner	8
6.	Wade Boggs	7
	Charley Gehringer	7
	Rogers Hornsby	7
9.	Jesse Burkett	6
	Steve Garvey	6
	Stan Musial	6
	Sam Rice	6
	Al Simmons	6
	George Sisler	6
	Bill Terry	6
16.	Tony Gwynn	5
	Chuck Klein	5
	Kirby Puckett	5
19.	14 tied with 4	

PINCH HITS

1.	Manny Mota	150
2.	Smoky Burgess	145
3.	Greg Gross	143
4.	Jose Morales	123
5.	Jerry Lynch	116
6.	Lenny Harris	115
7.	Red Lucas	114
8.	Steve Braun	113
9.	Terry Crowley	108
	John Vander Wal	108
	Denny Walling	108
12.	Gates Brown	107
13.	Mike Lum	103
14.	Jim Dwyer	102
15.	Rusty Staub	100
16.	Dave Clark	96
17.	Larry Biittner	95
	Vic Davalillo	95
	Gerald Perry	95
20.	Jerry Hairston	94

SINGLES

1.	Pete Rose	3,215
2.	Ty Cobb	3,053
3.	Eddie Collins	2,643
4.	Willie Keeler	2,513
5.	Honus Wagner	2,422
6.	Rod Carew	2,404
7.	Tris Speaker	2,383
8.	Paul Molitor	2,366
9.	Nap Lajoie	2,340
10.	Tony Gwynn	2,328
11.	Hank Aaron	2,294
12.	Jesse Burkett	2,273
13.	Sam Rice	2,271
14.	Carl Yastrzemski	2,262
15.	Wade Boggs	2,253
	Stan Musial	2,253
17.	Lou Brock	2,247
18.	Cap Anson	2,246
19.	Paul Waner	2,243
20.	Robin Yount	2,182

DOUBLES

1.	Tris Speaker	792
2.	Pete Rose	746
3.	Stan Musial	725
4.	Ty Cobb	724
5.	George Brett	665
6.	Nap Lajoie	657
7.	Carl Yastrzemski	646
8.	Honus Wagner	640
9.	Hank Aaron	624
10.	Paul Molitor	605
	Paul Waner	605
12.	Robin Yount	583
13.	Wade Boggs	578
14.	Charley Gehringer	574
15.	Cal Ripken	571
16.	Eddie Murray	560
17.	Harry Heilmann	542
18.	Rogers Hornsby	541
19.	Joe Medwick	540
	Dave Winfield	540

TRIPLES

1.	Sam Crawford	309
2.	Ty Cobb	295
3.	Honus Wagner	252
4.	Jake Beckley	243
5.	Roger Connor	233
6.	Tris Speaker	222
7.	Fred Clarke	220
8.	Dan Brouthers	205
9.	Joe Kelley	194
10.	Paul Waner	191
11.	Bid McPhee	188
12.	Eddie Collins	187
13.	Ed Delahanty	185
14.	Sam Rice	184
15.	Jesse Burkett	182
	Ed Konetchy	182
	Edd Roush	182
18.	Buck Ewing	178
19.	Rabbit Maranville	177
	Stan Musial	177

HOME RUNS

1.	Hank Aaron	755
2.	Babe Ruth	714
3.	Willie Mays	660
4.	Frank Robinson	586
5.	Harmon Killebrew	573
6.	Reggie Jackson	563
7.	Mike Schmidt	548
8.	Mickey Mantle	536
9.	Jimmie Foxx	534
10.	Mark McGwire	522
11.	Willie McCovey	521
	Ted Williams	521
13.	Ernie Banks	512
	Eddie Mathews	512
15.	Mel Ott	511
16.	Eddie Murray	504
17.	Lou Gehrig	493
18.	Stan Musial	475
	Willie Stargell	475
20.	Dave Winfield	465

HOME RUNS, A.L.

1.	Babe Ruth	708
2.	Harmon Killebrew	573
3.	Reggie Jackson	563
4.	Mickey Mantle	536
5.	Jimmie Foxx	524
6.	Ted Williams	521
7.	Lou Gehrig	493
8.	Carl Yastrzemski	452
9.	Jose Canseco	431
10.	Cal Ripken	402
11.	Al Kaline	399
12.	Ken Griffey Jr.	398
13.	Eddie Murray	396
14.	Dwight Evans	385
15.	Jim Rice	382
16.	Norm Cash	377
17.	Carlton Fisk	376
18.	Harold Baines	373
19.	Rocky Colavito	371
20.	Joe Carter	365

HOME RUNS, N.L.

1.	Hank Aaron	733
2.	Willie Mays	660
3.	Mike Schmidt	548
4.	Willie McCovey	521
5.	Ernie Banks	512
6.	Mel Ott	511
7.	Eddie Mathews	503
8.	Stan Musial	475
	Willie Stargell	475
10.	Barry Bonds	445
11.	Andre Dawson	409
12.	Duke Snider	407
13.	Dale Murphy	398
14.	Billy Williams	392
15.	Johnny Bench	389
16.	Gil Hodges	370
17.	Orlando Cepeda	358
18.	Ralph Kiner	351
19.	George Foster	347
20.	Frank Robinson	343

HOME RUNS, ONE CLUB

1.	Hank Aaron, Braves	733
2.	Babe Ruth, Yankees	659
3.	Willie Mays, Giants	646
4.	Harmon Killebrew, Senators/Twins	559
5.	Mike Schmidt, Phillies	548
6.	Mickey Mantle, Yankees	536
7.	Ted Williams, Red Sox	521
8.	Ernie Banks, Cubs	512
9.	Mel Ott, Giants	511
10.	Lou Gehrig, Yankees	493
	Eddie Mathews, Braves	493
12.	Stan Musial, Cardinals	475
	Willie Stargell, Pirates	475
14.	Willie McCovey, Giants	469
15.	Carl Yastrzemski, Red Sox	452
16.	Cal Ripken	402
17.	Al Kaline, Tigers	399
18.	Ken Griffey Jr.	398
19.	Billy Williams, Cubs	392
20.	Johnny Bench, Reds	389
	Duke Snider, Dodgers	389

HOME RUNS, RIGHTHANDER

1.	Hank Aaron	755
2.	Willie Mays	660
3.	Frank Robinson	586
4.	Harmon Killebrew	573
5.	Mike Schmidt	548
6.	Jimmie Foxx	534
7.	Mark McGwire	522
8.	Ernie Banks	512
9.	Dave Winfield	465
10.	Dave Kingman	442
11.	Andre Dawson	438
12.	Jose Canseco	431
13.	Cal Ripken	402
14.	Al Kaline	399
15.	Dale Murphy	398
16.	Joe Carter	396
17.	Johnny Bench	389
18.	Dwight Evans	385
19.	Frank Howard	382
	Jim Rice	382

HOME RUNS, LEFTHANDER

1.	Babe Ruth	714
2.	Reggie Jackson	563
3.	Willie McCovey	521
	Ted Williams	521
5.	Eddie Mathews	512
6.	Mel Ott	511
7.	Lou Gehrig	493
8.	Stan Musial	475
	Willie Stargell	475
10.	Carl Yastrzemski	452
11.	Barry Bonds	445
12.	Billy Williams	426
13.	Darrell Evans	414
14.	Duke Snider	407
15.	Ken Griffey Jr.	398
16.	Fred McGriff	390
	Graig Nettles	390
18.	Norm Cash	377
19.	Harold Baines	373
20.	Rafael Palmeiro	361

HOME RUNS, SWITCH HITTER

1.	Mickey Mantle	536
2.	Eddie Murray	504
3.	Chili Davis	350
4.	Reggie Smith	314
5.	Bobby Bonilla	277
6.	Ted Simmons	248
7.	Ken Singleton	246
8.	Mickey Tettleton	245
9.	Ruben Sierra	239
10.	Howard Johnson	228
11.	Ken Caminiti	209
12.	Devon White	190
13.	Tim Raines	168
14.	Roy Smalley	163
15.	Tony Phillips	160
	Pete Rose	160
	Roy White	160
18.	Chipper Jones	153
	Tom Tresh	153
20.	Roberto Alomar	151
	Bernie Williams	151

HOME RUNS, FIRST BASEMAN

1.	Mark McGwire	507
2.	Lou Gehrig	493
3.	Jimmie Foxx	480
4.	Willie McCovey	439
5.	Eddie Murray	409
6.	Norm Cash	367
7.	Johnny Mize	350
8.	Fred McGriff	344
9.	Gil Hodges	335
10.	Andres Galarraga	331

HOME RUNS, SECOND BASEMAN

1.	Ryne Sandberg	275
2.	Joe Morgan	266
3.	Rogers Hornsby	264
4.	Joe Gordon	246
5.	Lou Whitaker	239
6.	Bobby Doerr	223
7.	Bobby Grich	196
8.	Charley Gehringer	181
9.	Frank White	156
10.	Tony Lazzeri	149

HOME RUNS, THIRD BASEMAN

1.	Mike Schmidt	509
2.	Eddie Mathews	486
3.	Graig Nettles	368
4.	Ron Santo	337
5.	Gary Gaetti	333
6.	Matt Williams	315
7.	Ron Cey	312
8.	Brooks Robinson	266
9.	Ken Boyer	260
10.	Tim Wallach	249

HOME RUNS, SHORTSTOP

1.	Cal Ripken	345
2.	Ernie Banks	277
3.	Vern Stephens	213
4.	Alan Trammell	177
5.	Barry Larkin	166
6.	Joe Cronin	155
7.	Alex Rodriguez	148
8.	Eddie Joost	129
9.	Rico Petrocelli	127
10.	Pee Wee Reese	122
	Robin Yount	122

HOME RUNS, OUTFIELDER

1.	Babe Ruth	692
2.	Hank Aaron	661
3.	Willie Mays	642
4.	Ted Williams	514
5.	Mickey Mantle	490
6.	Frank Robinson	463
7.	Reggie Jackson	458
8.	Mel Ott	457
9.	Barry Bonds	442
10.	Andre Dawson	404

HOME RUNS, CATCHER

1.	Carlton Fisk	351
2.	Johnny Bench	327
3.	Yogi Berra	306
4.	Gary Carter	298
5.	Lance Parrish	295
6.	Roy Campanella	239
7.	Mike Piazza	237
8.	Gabby Hartnett	232
9.	Bill Dickey	200
10.	Ted Simmons	195

HOME RUNS, PITCHER

1.	Wes Ferrell	37
2.	Bob Lemon	35
	Warren Spahn	35
4.	Red Ruffing	34
5.	Earl Wilson	33
6.	Don Drysdale	29
7.	John Clarkson	24
	Bob Gibson	24
9.	Walter Johnson	23
10.	Jack Stivetts	20
	Dizzy Trout	20

HOME RUNS, DESIGNATED HITTER

1.	Don Baylor	219
2.	Harold Baines	203
3.	Chili Davis	200
4.	Jose Canseco	179
5.	Hal McRae	145

LEADOFF HOMERS

1.	Rickey Henderson	75
2.	Brady Anderson	36
3.	Bobby Bonds	35
4.	Paul Molitor	33
5.	Devon White	31
6.	Tony Phillips	30
7.	Davey Lopes	28
	Eddie Yost	28
9.	Chuck Knoblauch	27
10.	Brian Downing	25
11.	Lou Brock	24
12.	Tommy Harper	23
	Lou Whitaker	23
14.	Jimmy Ryan	22
15.	Craig Biggio	21
16.	Felipe Alou	20
	Barry Bonds	20
	Lenny Dykstra	20
19.	Eddie Joost	19
	Dick McAuliffe	19

20-HOME RUN SEASONS

1.	Hank Aaron	20
2.	Willie Mays	17
	Frank Robinson	17
4.	Reggie Jackson	16
	Eddie Murray	16
	Babe Ruth	16
	Ted Williams	16
8.	Mel Ott	15
	Willie Stargell	15
	Dave Winfield	15
11.	Mickey Mantle	14
	Eddie Mathews	14
	Mike Schmidt	14
	Billy Williams	14
15.	Ernie Banks	13
	Andre Dawson	13
	Lou Gehrig	13
	Harmon Killebrew	13
19.	10 tied with 12	

30-HOME RUN SEASONS

1.	Hank Aaron	15
2.	Babe Ruth	13
	Mike Schmidt	13
4.	Jimmie Foxx	12
5.	Willie Mays	11
	Frank Robinson	11
7.	Lou Gehrig	10
	Harmon Killebrew	10
	Eddie Mathews	10
	Mark McGwire	10
11.	Barry Bonds	9
	Mickey Mantle	9
13.	Albert Belle	8
	Jose Canseco	8
	Fred McGriff	8
	Mel Ott	8
	Ted Williams	8
18.	Ernie Banks	7
	Rocky Colavito	7
	Joe DiMaggio	7
	Reggie Jackson	7
	Ralph Kiner	7
	Dave Kingman	7
	Willie McCovey	7

BALLPARKS HITTING HOME RUNS

1.	Fred McGriff	36
2.	Ellis Burks	34

	Gary Gaetti	34
	Mark McGwire	34
5.	Devon White	33
6.	Joe Carter	32
	Roger Connor	32
	Chili Davis	32
	Eddie Murray	32
	Frank Robinson	32
	Rusty Staub	32
	Harry Stovey	32
	Dave Winfield	32
14.	Hank Aaron	31
15.	Ron Fairly	30
	Kirk Gibson	30
	Pete Incaviglia	30
	Al Oliver	30
	Paul O'Neill	30
	Gary Sheffield	30

PINCH-HIT HOME RUNS

1.	Cliff Johnson	20
2.	Jerry Lynch	18
3.	Gates Brown	16
	Smoky Burgess	16
	Willie McCovey	16
6.	George Crowe	14
7.	John Vander Wal	13
8.	Joe Adcock	12
	Bob Cerv	12
	Jose Morales	12
	Graig Nettles	12
12.	Jeff Burroughs	11
	Jay Johnstone	11
	Candy Maldonado	11
	Fred Whitfield	11
	Cy Williams	11
17.	11 tied with 10	

GRAND SLAMS

1.	Lou Gehrig	23
2.	Eddie Murray	19
3.	Willie McCovey	18
4.	Jimmie Foxx	17
	Ted Williams	17
6.	Hank Aaron	16
	Dave Kingman	16
	Babe Ruth	16
9.	Gil Hodges	14
10.	Harold Baines	13
	Joe DiMaggio	13
	George Foster	13
	Ralph Kiner	13
	Mark McGwire	13
	Robin Ventura	13
16.	Ernie Banks	12
	Don Baylor	12
	Ken Griffey Jr.	12
	Rogers Hornsby	12
	Joe Rudi	12
	Rudy York	12

MULTIPLE-HOME RUN GAMES

1.	Babe Ruth	72
2.	Willie Mays	63
3.	Hank Aaron	62
	Mark McGwire	62
5.	Jimmie Foxx	55
6.	Frank Robinson	54
7.	Eddie Mathews	49
	Mel Ott	49
9.	Harmon Killebrew	46
	Mickey Mantle	46
11.	Willie McCovey	44
	Mike Schmidt	44
13.	Dave Kingman	43
14.	Ernie Banks	42
	Barry Bonds	42
	Lou Gehrig	42
	Reggie Jackson	42
18.	Ken Griffey Jr.	40
	Ralph Kiner	40
20.	Andre Dawson	39
	Sammy Sosa	39

MOST HOMERS PER AT-BAT

1.	Mark McGwire	.092
2.	Babe Ruth	.085
3.	Ralph Kiner	.071
4.	Juan Gonzalez	.070
	Harmon Killebrew	.070
6.	Ken Griffey Jr.	.068
	Albert Belle	.068
	Ted Williams	.068
9.	Jose Canseco	.067
10.	Dave Kingman	.066
	Mickey Mantle	.066
	Mike Piazza	.066
	Jimmie Foxx	.066
	Mike Schmidt	.066
15.	Barry Bonds	.064
	Hank Greenberg	.064
	Willie McCovey	.064
	Sammy Sosa	.064
19.	Cecil Fielder	.062
	Darryl Strawberry	.062

TOTAL BASES

1.	Hank Aaron	6,856
2.	Stan Musial	6,134
3.	Willie Mays	6,066
4.	Ty Cobb	5,854
5.	Babe Ruth	5,793
6.	Pete Rose	5,752
7.	Carl Yastrzemski	5,539
8.	Eddie Murray	5,397
9.	Frank Robinson	5,373
10.	Dave Winfield	5,221
11.	Tris Speaker	5,101
12.	Lou Gehrig	5,060
13.	George Brett	5,044
14.	Mel Ott	5,041
15.	Jimmie Foxx	4,956
16.	Ted Williams	4,884
17.	Honus Wagner	4,862
18.	Cal Ripken	4,856
19.	Paul Molitor	4,854
20.	Al Kaline	4,852

300-TOTAL BASE SEASONS

1.	Hank Aaron	15
2.	Lou Gehrig	13
	Willie Mays	13
	Stan Musial	13
5.	Babe Ruth	11
6.	Jimmie Foxx	10
7.	Joe DiMaggio	9
	Billy Williams	9
	Ted Williams	9
10.	Rogers Hornsby	8
	Frank Robinson	8
12.	Hank Greenberg	7
	Mel Ott	7
	Paul Waner	7
15.	19 tied with 6	

SLUGGING PERCENTAGE
(Minimum 2,000 total bases)

1.	Babe Ruth	.690
2.	Ted Williams	.634
3.	Lou Gehrig	.632
4.	Jimmie Foxx	.609
5.	Hank Greenberg	.605
6.	Mark McGwire	.587
7.	Joe DiMaggio	.579
8.	Rogers Hornsby	.577
9.	Mike Piazza	.575
10.	Albert Belle	.573
	Frank Thomas	.573
12.	Juan Gonzalez	.572
13.	Ken Griffey Jr.	.569
14.	Larry Walker	.567
15.	Johnny Mize	.562
16.	Barry Bonds	.559
	Stan Musial	.559
18.	Willie Mays	.557
	Mickey Mantle	.557
20.	Hank Aaron	.555

EXTRA-BASE HITS

1.	Hank Aaron	1,477
2.	Stan Musial	1,377
3.	Babe Ruth	1,356
4.	Willie Mays	1,323
5.	Lou Gehrig	1,190
6.	Frank Robinson	1,186
7.	Carl Yastrzemski	1,157
8.	Ty Cobb	1,136
9.	Tris Speaker	1,131
10.	George Brett	1,119
11.	Jimmie Foxx	1,117
	Ted Williams	1,117
13.	Eddie Murray	1,099
14.	Dave Winfield	1,093
15.	Reggie Jackson	1,075
16.	Mel Ott	1,071
17.	Pete Rose	1,041
18.	Andre Dawson	1,039
19.	Cal Ripken	1,017
20.	Mike Schmidt	1,015

RUNS BATTED IN

1.	Hank Aaron	2,297
2.	Babe Ruth	2,213
3.	Lou Gehrig	1,995
4.	Stan Musial	1,951
5.	Ty Cobb	1,938
6.	Jimmie Foxx	1,922
7.	Eddie Murray	1,917
8.	Willie Mays	1,903
9.	Cap Anson	1,879
10.	Mel Ott	1,860
11.	Carl Yastrzemski	1,844
12.	Ted Williams	1,839
13.	Dave Winfield	1,833
14.	Al Simmons	1,827
15.	Frank Robinson	1,812
16.	Honus Wagner	1,732
17.	Reggie Jackson	1,702
18.	Tony Perez	1,652
19.	Ernie Banks	1,636
20.	Goose Goslin	1,609

RBIs, RIGHTHANDER

1.	Hank Aaron	2,297
2.	Jimmie Foxx	1,922
3.	Willie Mays	1,903
4.	Cap Anson	1,879
5.	Dave Winfield	1,833
6.	Al Simmons	1,827
7.	Frank Robinson	1,812
8.	Honus Wagner	1,732
9.	Tony Perez	1,652
10.	Ernie Banks	1,636
11.	Nap Lajoie	1,599
12.	Mike Schmidt	1,595
13.	Andre Dawson	1,591
14.	Rogers Hornsby	1,584
	Harmon Killebrew	1,584
16.	Al Kaline	1,583
17.	Cal Ripken	1,571
18.	Harry Heilmann	1,539
19.	Joe DiMaggio	1,537
20.	Ed Delahanty	1,464

RBIs, LEFTHANDER

1.	Babe Ruth	2,213
2.	Lou Gehrig	1,995
3.	Stan Musial	1,951
4.	Ty Cobb	1,938
5.	Mel Ott	1,860
6.	Carl Yastrzemski	1,844
7.	Ted Williams	1,839
8.	Reggie Jackson	1,702
9.	Goose Goslin	1,609
10.	George Brett	1,595
11.	Harold Baines	1,583
12.	Jake Beckley	1,575
13.	Willie McCovey	1,555
14.	Willie Stargell	1,540
15.	Tris Speaker	1,529
16.	Sam Crawford	1,525
17.	Dave Parker	1,493
18.	Billy Williams	1,475
19.	Rusty Staub	1,466
20.	Eddie Mathews	1,453

RBIs, SWITCH HITTER

1.	Eddie Murray	1,917
2.	Mickey Mantle	1,509
3.	George Davis	1,437
4.	Ted Simmons	1,389
5.	Chili Davis	1,372
6.	Pete Rose	1,314
7.	Frankie Frisch	1,244
8.	Bobby Bonilla	1,124
9.	Reggie Smith	1,092
10.	Ken Singleton	1,065
11.	Ruben Sierra	1,047
12.	John Anderson	976
13.	Tim Raines	964
14.	Terry Pendleton	946
15.	Tommy Tucker	932
14.	Terry Pendleton	917
16.	Duke Farrell	912
17.	Ken Caminiti	897
18.	Willie McGee	856
19.	Augie Galan	830
20.	Roberto Alomar	829
	Tony Fernandez	829

100-RBI SEASONS

1.	Jimmie Foxx	13
	Lou Gehrig	13
	Babe Ruth	13
4.	Al Simmons	12
5.	Hank Aaron	11
	Goose Goslin	11
7.	Joe Carter	10
	Willie Mays	10
	Stan Musial	10
10.	Joe DiMaggio	9
	Harmon Killebrew	9
	Mel Ott	9
	Mike Schmidt	9
	Honus Wagner	9
	Ted Williams	9
16.	12 tied with 8	

WALKS

1.	Babe Ruth	2,056
2.	Ted Williams	2,019
3.	Rickey Henderson	1,972
4.	Joe Morgan	1,865
5.	Carl Yastrzemski	1,845
6.	Mickey Mantle	1,733
7.	Mel Ott	1,708
8.	Eddie Yost	1,614
9.	Darrell Evans	1,605
10.	Stan Musial	1,599
11.	Pete Rose	1,566
12.	Harmon Killebrew	1,559
13.	Lou Gehrig	1,508
14.	Mike Schmidt	1,507

The majority of outfielder Rickey Henderson's 1,334 career stolen bases came during his four stints with the Oakland A's.

15.	Eddie Collins	1,499
16.	Willie Mays	1,464
17.	Jimmie Foxx	1,452
18.	Eddie Mathews	1,444
19.	Barry Bonds	1,430
20.	Frank Robinson	1,420

100-WALK SEASONS

1.	Babe Ruth	13
2.	Lou Gehrig	11
	Ted Williams	11
4.	Mickey Mantle	10
	Mel Ott	10
6.	Joe Morgan	8
	Frank Thomas	8
	Eddie Yost	8
9.	Max Bishop	7
	Barry Bonds	7
	Jimmie Foxx	7
	Rickey Henderson	7
	Harmon Killebrew	7
	Mike Schmidt	7
	Roy Thomas	7
16.	Harland Clift	6
	Eddie Joost	6
	Ralph Kiner	6
	Eddie Stanky	6
	Gene Tenace	6
	Jimmy Wynn	6
	Carl Yastrzemski	6

INTENTIONAL WALKS

1.	Barry Bonds	298
2.	Hank Aaron	293
3.	Willie McCovey	260
4.	George Brett	229
5.	Willie Stargell	227
6.	Eddie Murray	222
7.	Frank Robinson	218
8.	Mike Schmidt	201
9.	Tony Gwynn	200
10.	Ernie Banks	198
11.	Rusty Staub	193
12.	Willie Mays	192
13.	Carl Yastrzemski	190
14.	Chili Davis	188
	Ted Simmons	188
16.	Billy Williams	182
17.	Harold Baines	180
	Wade Boggs	180
19.	Dave Winfield	172
20.	Ken Griffey Jr.	170
	Dave Parker	170

STRIKEOUTS

1.	Reggie Jackson	2,597
2.	Willie Stargell	1,936
3.	Mike Schmidt	1,883
4.	Tony Perez	1,867
5.	Dave Kingman	1,816
6.	Jose Canseco	1,765
7.	Bobby Bonds	1,757
8.	Dale Murphy	1,748
9.	Lou Brock	1,730
10.	Mickey Mantle	1,710
11.	Harmon Killebrew	1,699
12.	Chili Davis	1,698
13.	Dwight Evans	1,697
14.	Dave Winfield	1,686
15.	Andres Galarraga	1,615
16.	Gary Gaetti	1,599
17.	Lee May	1,570
18.	Dick Allen	1,556
19.	Willie McCovey	1,550
20.	Dave Parker	1,537

100-STRIKEOUT SEASONS

1.	Reggie Jackson	18
2.	Dave Kingman	13
	Willie Stargell	13
4.	Mike Schmidt	12
5.	Fred McGriff	11
	Dale Murphy	11
7.	Dick Allen	10
	Bobby Bonds	10
	Jose Canseco	10
	Frank Howard	10
	Greg Luzinski	10
	Lee May	10
	Tony Perez	10
14.	Lou Brock	9
	Ray Lankford	9
	Mark McGwire	9
	Danny Tartabull	9
18.	13 tied with 8	

HIT BY PITCH

1.	Hughie Jennings	287
2.	Tommy Tucker	272
3.	Don Baylor	267
4.	Ron Hunt	243
5.	Dan McGann	230
6.	Frank Robinson	198
7.	Minnie Minoso	192
8.	Jake Beckley	183
9.	Curt Welch	173
10.	Kid Elberfeld	165
11.	Craig Biggio	153
	Fred Clarke	153

13.	Chet Lemon	151
14.	Carlton Fisk	143
15.	Nellie Fox	142
16.	Art Fletcher	141
17.	Bill Dahlen	140
18.	Frank Chance	137
	Andres Galarraga	137
20.	Brady Anderson	136

STOLEN BASES

1.	Rickey Henderson	1,334
2.	Lou Brock	938
3.	Billy Hamilton	912
4.	Ty Cobb	892
5.	Tim Raines	807
6.	Vince Coleman	752
7.	Eddie Collins	745
8.	Arlie Latham	739
9.	Max Carey	738
10.	Honus Wagner	722
11.	Joe Morgan	689
12.	Willie Wilson	668
13.	Tom Brown	657
14.	Bert Campaneris	649
15.	Otis Nixon	620
16.	George Davis	616
17.	Dummy Hoy	594
18.	Maury Wills	586
19.	George Van Haltren	583
20.	Ozzie Smith	580

CAUGHT STEALING

1.	Rickey Henderson	315
2.	Lou Brock	307
3.	Brett Butler	257
4.	Maury Wills	208
5.	Bert Campaneris	199
6.	Rod Carew	187
7.	Otis Nixon	186
8.	Omar Moreno	182
9.	Cesar Cedeno	179
10.	Ty Cobb	178
	Steve Sax	178
12.	Vince Coleman	177
13.	Eddie Collins	173
14.	Bobby Bonds	169
15.	Joe Morgan	162
	Billy North	162
17.	Pete Rose	149
18.	Ozzie Smith	148
19.	Tim Raines	146
20.	Sam Rice	143
	Juan Samuel	143

STEAL PERCENTAGE

1.	Tim Raines	84.68
2.	Eric Davis	84.43
3.	Barry Larkin	84.15
4.	Willie Wilson	83.29
5.	Stan Javier	83.09
6.	Davey Lopes	83.01
7.	Julio Cruz	81.47
8.	Joe Morgan	80.96
9.	Vince Coleman	80.95
10.	Rickey Henderson	80.90
11.	Andy Van Slyke	80.59
12.	Kenny Lofton	80.19
13.	Marquis Grissom	80.08
14.	Brian L. Hunter	80.07
15.	Lenny Dykstra	79.83
16.	Roberto Alomar	79.70
17.	Ozzie Smith	79.67
18.	Gary Redus	79.51
19.	Paul Molitor	79.37
20.	Luis Aparicio	78.82

50-STEAL SEASONS

1.	Rickey Henderson	13
2.	Lou Brock	12
3.	Billy Hamilton	9
	Arlie Latham	9
5.	Ty Cobb	8
	Tim Raines	8
7.	Bert Campaneris	7
	Vince Coleman	7
9.	Tom Brown	6
	Max Carey	6
	Cesar Cedeno	6
	Eddie Collins	6
	Kenny Lofton	6
	Harry Stovey	6
	Curt Welch	6
16.	Ned Hanlon	5
	Dummy Hoy	5
	King Kelly	5
	Omar Moreno	5
	Joe Morgan	5
	Otis Nixon	5
	Honus Wagner	5
	John Ward	5
	Maury Wills	5

STEALS OF HOME

1.	Ty Cobb	50
2.	Max Carey	33
3.	George J. Burns	28
4.	Honus Wagner	27
5.	Sherry Magee	23
	Frank Schulte	23
7.	Johnny Evers	21
8.	George Sisler	20
9.	Frankie Frisch	19
	Jackie Robinson	19
11.	Jimmy Sheckard	18
	Tris Speaker	18
	Joe Tinker	18
14.	Rod Carew	17
	Eddie Collins	17
	Larry Doyle	17
17.	Tommy Leach	16
18.	Ben Chapman	15
	Fred Clarke	15
	Lou Gehrig	15

PITCHING

GAMES

1.	Jesse Orosco	1,090
2.	Dennis Eckersley	1,071
3.	Hoyt Wilhelm	1,070
4.	Kent Tekulve	1,050
5.	Lee Smith	1,022
6.	Rich Gossage	1,002
7.	Lindy McDaniel	987
8.	Rollie Fingers	944
9.	Gene Garber	931
10.	Cy Young	906
11.	Sparky Lyle	899
12.	Jim Kaat	898
13.	Paul Assenmacher	884
14.	Jeff Reardon	880
15.	John Franco	878
16.	Don McMahon	874
17.	Phil Niekro	864
18.	Charlie Hough	858
19.	Roy Face	848
20.	Mike Jackson	835

GAMES STARTED

1.	Cy Young	815
2.	Nolan Ryan	773
3.	Don Sutton	756
4.	Phil Niekro	716
5.	Steve Carlton	709
6.	Tommy John	700
7.	Gaylord Perry	690
8.	Bert Blyleven	685
9.	Pud Galvin	681
10.	Walter Johnson	666
11.	Warren Spahn	665
12.	Tom Seaver	647
13.	Jim Kaat	625
14.	Frank Tanana	616
15.	Early Wynn	612
16.	Robin Roberts	609
17.	Grover Alexander	600
18.	Fergie Jenkins	594
	Tim Keefe	594
20.	Dennis Martinez	562

COMPLETE GAMES

1.	Cy Young	749
2.	Pud Galvin	639
3.	Tim Keefe	554
4.	Walter Johnson	531
	Kid Nichols	531
6.	Mickey Welch	525
7.	Charles Radbourn	489
8.	John Clarkson	485
9.	Tony Mullane	468
10.	Jim McCormick	466
11.	Gus Weyhing	448
12.	Grover Alexander	437
13.	Christy Mathewson	434
14.	Jack Powell	422
15.	Eddie Plank	410
16.	Will White	394
17.	Amos Rusie	393
18.	Vic Willis	388
19.	Warren Spahn	382
20.	Jim Whitney	377

OPENING DAY STARTS

1.	Tom Seaver	16
2.	Steve Carlton	14
	Walter Johnson	14
	Jack Morris	14
5.	Robin Roberts	13
	Cy Young	13
7.	Grover Alexander	12
	Bert Blyleven	12
9.	Fergie Jenkins	11
	Dennis Martinez	11
11.	Roger Clemens	10

	Bob Gibson	10
	Juan Marichal	10
	George Mullin	10
	Warren Spahn	10
16.	Phil Niekro	9
	Gaylord Perry	9
	Steve Rogers	9
	Nolan Ryan	9
	Rick Sutcliffe	9
	Don Sutton	9

INNINGS PITCHED

1.	Cy Young	7,356.0
2.	Pud Galvin	5,941.1
3.	Walter Johnson	5,914.2
4.	Phil Niekro	5,404.1
5.	Nolan Ryan	5,386.0
6.	Gaylord Perry	5,350.1
7.	Don Sutton	5,282.1
8.	Warren Spahn	5,243.2
9.	Steve Carlton	5,217.1
10.	Grover Alexander	5,190.0
11.	Kid Nichols	5,056.1
12.	Tim Keefe	5,049.2
13.	Bert Blyleven	4,970.0
14.	Mickey Welch	4,802.0
15.	Tom Seaver	4,782.2
16.	Christy Mathewson	4,780.2
17.	Tommy John	4,710.1
18.	Robin Roberts	4,688.2
19.	Early Wynn	4,564.0
20.	John Clarkson	4,536.1

INNINGS PITCHED, STARTER

1.	Cy Young	7,034.2
2.	Pud Galvin	5,872.2
3.	Walter Johnson	5,550.1
4.	Nolan Ryan	5,326.0
5.	Don Sutton	5,248.1
6.	Steve Carlton	5,165.0
7.	Gaylord Perry	5,161.2
8.	Phil Niekro	5,149.1
9.	Warren Spahn	5,106.2
10.	Tim Keefe	5,021.1
11.	Grover Alexander	4,983.1
12.	Bert Blyleven	4,957.1
13.	Kid Nichols	4,881.1
14.	Tom Seaver	4,776.0
15.	Mickey Welch	4,749.0
16.	Christy Mathewson	4,745.1
17.	Tommy John	4,622.0
18.	Robin Roberts	4,567.1
19.	John Clarkson	4,491.1
20.	Charles Radbourn	4,427.0

INNINGS PITCHED, RELIEVER

1.	Hoyt Wilhelm	1,871.0
2.	Lindy McDaniel	1,694.0
3.	Rich Gossage	1,556.2
4.	Rollie Fingers	1,500.1
5.	Gene Garber	1,452.2
6.	Kent Tekulve	1,436.1
7.	Sparky Lyle	1,390.1
8.	Tug McGraw	1,301.1
9.	Don McMahon	1,297.0
10.	Mike Marshall	1,259.1
11.	Lee Smith	1,252.1
12.	Tom Burgmeier	1,248.2
13.	Roy Face	1,212.1
14.	Clay Carroll	1,204.2
15.	Jesse Orosco	1,197.2
16.	Eddie Fisher	1,186.0
17.	Bill Campbell	1,177.1
18.	Ron Perranoski	1,170.2
19.	Bob Stanley	1,157.0
20.	Jeff Reardon	1,132.1

200-INNING SEASONS

1.	Don Sutton	20
2.	Phil Niekro	19
	Cy Young	19
4.	Walter Johnson	18
5.	Gaylord Perry	17
	Warren Spahn	17
7.	Grover Alexander	16
	Bert Blyleven	16
	Steve Carlton	16
	Tom Seaver	16
11.	Eddie Plank	15
	Jack Powell	15
13.	Jim Kaat	14
	Christy Mathewson	14
	Robin Roberts	14
	Red Ruffing	14
	Nolan Ryan	14
	Early Wynn	14
19.	9 tied with 13	

300-INNING SEASONS

1.	Cy Young	16
2.	Kid Nichols	12
3.	Pud Galvin	11
	Christy Mathewson	11
5.	Tim Keefe	10
6.	Grover Alexander	9
	Walter Johnson	9
	Joe McGinnity	9

Giants manager John McGraw (left) and pitching ace Christy Mathewson, who posted 373 career victories.

	Mickey Welch	9
	Gus Weyhing	9
11.	John Clarkson	8
	Jim McCormick	8
	Tony Mullane	8
	Charles Radbourn	8
	Amos Rusie	8
	Jim Whitney	8
	Vic Willis	8
18.	Charlie Buffinton	7
19.	12 tied with 6	

LOWEST ERA

(Minimum 1,500 innings)

1.	Ed Walsh	1.82
2.	Addie Joss	1.89
3.	Mordecai Brown	2.06
4.	John Ward	2.10
5.	Christy Mathewson	2.13
6.	Rube Waddell	2.16
7.	Walter Johnson	2.17
8.	Orval Overall	2.23
9.	Tommy Bond	2.25
10.	Will White	2.28
	Ed Reulbach	2.28
12.	Jim Scott	2.30
13.	Eddie Plank	2.35
14.	Larry Corcoran	2.36
15.	George McQuillan	2.38
	Ed Killian	2.38
	Eddie Cicotte	2.38
18.	Doc White	2.39
19.	Nap Rucker	2.42
20.	Jeff Tesreau	2.43

VICTORIES

1.	Cy Young	511
2.	Walter Johnson	417
3.	Grover Alexander	373
	Christy Mathewson	373
5.	Warren Spahn	363
6.	Kid Nichols	361
7.	Pud Galvin	360
8.	Tim Keefe	342
9.	Steve Carlton	329
10.	John Clarkson	328
11.	Eddie Plank	326
12.	Nolan Ryan	324
	Don Sutton	324
14.	Phil Niekro	318
15.	Gaylord Perry	314

16.	Tom Seaver	311
17.	Charles Radbourn	309
18.	Mickey Welch	307
19.	Lefty Grove	300
	Early Wynn	300

VICTORIES, RIGHTHANDER

1.	Cy Young	511
2.	Walter Johnson	417
3.	Grover Alexander	373
	Christy Mathewson	373
5.	Kid Nichols	361
6.	Pud Galvin	360
7.	Tim Keefe	342
8.	John Clarkson	328
9.	Nolan Ryan	324
	Don Sutton	324
11.	Phil Niekro	318
12.	Gaylord Perry	314
13.	Tom Seaver	311
14.	Charles Radbourn	309
15.	Mickey Welch	307
16.	Early Wynn	300
17.	Bert Blyleven	287
18.	Robin Roberts	286
19.	Fergie Jenkins	284
	Tony Mullane	284

VICTORIES, LEFTHANDER

1.	Warren Spahn	363
2.	Steve Carlton	329
3.	Eddie Plank	326
4.	Lefty Grove	300
5.	Tommy John	288
6.	Jim Kaat	283
7.	Eppa Rixey	266
8.	Carl Hubbell	253
9.	Herb Pennock	241
10.	Frank Tanana	240
11.	Whitey Ford	236
12.	Jerry Koosman	222
13.	Jerry Reuss	220
14.	Earl Whitehill	218
15.	Mickey Lolich	217
16.	Wilbur Cooper	216
17.	Billy Pierce	211
18.	Vida Blue	209
19.	Hal Newhouser	207
20.	Rube Marquard	201

VICTORIES, RELIEVER

1.	Hoyt Wilhelm	124
2.	Lindy McDaniel	119
3.	Rich Gossage	115
4.	Rollie Fingers	107
5.	Sparky Lyle	99
6.	Roy Face	96
7.	Gene Garber	94
	Kent Tekulve	94
9.	Mike Marshall	92
10.	Don McMahon	90
11.	Tug McGraw	89
12.	Clay Carroll	88
13.	Bob Stanley	85
14.	Jesse Orosco	84
15.	Bill Campbell	80
	Gary Lavelle	80
17.	Tom Burgmeier	79
	Stu Miller	79
	Ron Perranoski	79
20.	John Franco	77

OPENING DAY VICTORIES

1.	Walter Johnson	9
2.	Grover Alexander	8
	Jack Morris	8
4.	Jimmy Key	7
	Tom Seaver	7
6.	John Clarkson	6
	Wes Ferrell	6
	Dwight Gooden	6
	Mickey Lolich	6
	Juan Marichal	6
	Kid Nichols	6
12.	Don Drysdale	5
	Greg Maddux	5
	George Mullin	5
	Jim Palmer	5
	Robin Roberts	5
	Nolan Ryan	5
	Rick Sutcliffe	5
	Lon Warneke	5
	Cy Young	5

20-VICTORY SEASONS

1.	Cy Young	15
2.	Christy Mathewson	13
	Warren Spahn	13

4. Walter Johnson	12
5. Kid Nichols	11
6. Pud Galvin	10
7. Grover Alexander	9
Charles Radbourn	9
Mickey Welch	9
10. John Clarkson	8
Lefty Grove	8
Jim McCormick	8
Joe McGinnity	8
Tony Mullane	8
Jim Palmer	8
Eddie Plank	8
Amos Rusie	8
Vic Willis	8
19. 6 tied with 7	

20 VICTORIES, RIGHTHANDER

1. Cy Young	15
2. Christy Mathewson	13
3. Walter Johnson	12
4. Kid Nichols	11
5. Pud Galvin	10
6. Grover Alexander	9
Charles Radbourn	9
Mickey Welch	9
9. John Clarkson	8
Jim McCormick	8
Joe McGinnity	8
Tony Mullane	8
Jim Palmer	8
Amos Rusie	8
Vic Willis	8
16. Charlie Buffinton	7
Clark Griffith	7
Fergie Jenkins	7
Tim Keefe	7
Bob Lemon	7
Gus Weyhing	7

20 VICTORIES, LEFTHANDER

1. Warren Spahn	13
2. Lefty Grove	8
Eddie Plank	8
4. Steve Carlton	6
Jesse Tannehill	6
6. Carl Hubbell	5
Hippo Vaughn	5
8. Wilbur Cooper	4
Mike Cuellar	4
Tom Glavine	4
Lefty Gomez	4
Noodles Hahn	4
Dave McNally	4
Ed Morris	4
Hal Newhouser	4
Eppa Rixey	4
Rube Waddell	4
Wilbur Wood	4
19. 13 tied with 3	

CONSECUTIVE 20-VICTORY SEASONS

1. Christy Mathewson	12
2. Walter Johnson	10
Kid Nichols	10
4. Cy Young	9
5. John Clarkson	8
Jim McCormick	8
Joe McGinnity	8
Amos Rusie	8
9. Lefty Grove	7
Tim Keefe	7
Charles Radbourn	7
Mickey Welch	7
Gus Weyhing	7
14. Mordecai Brown	6
Bob Caruthers	6
Pud Galvin	6
Clark Griffith	6
Fergie Jenkins	6
Tony Mullane	6
Robin Roberts	6
Warren Spahn	6

30-VICTORY SEASONS

1. Kid Nichols	7
2. John Clarkson	6
Tim Keefe	6
4. Tony Mullane	5
Will White	5
Cy Young	5
7. Tommy Bond	4
Larry Corcoran	4
Silver King	4
Christy Mathewson	4
Jim McCormick	4
Amos Rusie	4
Mickey Welch	4
Gus Weyhing	4
15. Grover Alexander	3
Bob Caruthers	3
Pud Galvin	3
Bill Hutchison	3
Bobby Mathews	3

Ed Morris	3
Charles Radbourn	3

WINNING PERCENTAGE
(Minimum 75 victories)

1. Spud Chandler	.717
2. Dave Foutz	.690
Whitey Ford	.690
4. Bob Caruthers	.688
5. Don Gullett	.686
6. Pedro Martinez	.682
7. Lefty Grove	.680
8. Jay Hughes	.675
9. Mike Mussina	.673
10. Joe Wood	.672
11. Babe Ruth	.671
12. Bill Hoffer	.667
Vic Raschi	.667
14. Larry Corcoran	.665
Christy Mathewson	.665
16. Sam Leever	.660
17. Sal Maglie	.657
18. Sandy Koufax	.655
19. Johnny Allen	.654
20. Ron Guidry	.651

CONSECUTIVE VICTORIES

1. Carl Hubbell	24
2. Roy Face	22
3. Rube Marquard	20
Roger Clemens	20
5. Tim Keefe	19
6. Charles Radbourn	18
Pat Luby	18
8. Mickey Welch	17
Johnny Allen	17
Dave McNally	17
11. Jim McCormick	16
Bill Donovan	16
Walter Johnson	16
Joe Wood	16
Lefty Grove	16
Alvin Crowder	16
Schoolboy Rowe	16
Ewell Blackwell	16
Jack Sanford	16
Tom Seaver	16
Rick Sutcliffe	16
Randy Johnson	16

LOSSES

1. Cy Young	316
2. Pud Galvin	308
3. Nolan Ryan	292
4. Walter Johnson	279
5. Phil Niekro	274
6. Gaylord Perry	265
7. Don Sutton	256
8. Jack Powell	254
9. Eppa Rixey	251
10. Bert Blyleven	250
11. Robin Roberts	245
Warren Spahn	245
13. Steve Carlton	244
Early Wynn	244
15. Jim Kaat	237
16. Frank Tanana	236
17. Gus Weyhing	232
18. Tommy John	231
19. Bob Friend	230
Ted Lyons	230

LOSSES, RIGHTHANDER

1. Cy Young	316
2. Pud Galvin	308
3. Nolan Ryan	292
4. Walter Johnson	279
5. Phil Niekro	274
6. Gaylord Perry	265
7. Don Sutton	256
8. Jack Powell	254
9. Bert Blyleven	250
10. Robin Roberts	245
11. Early Wynn	244
12. Gus Weyhing	232
13. Bob Friend	230
Ted Lyons	230
15. Fergie Jenkins	226
16. Tim Keefe	225
Red Ruffing	225
18. Bobo Newsom	222
19. Tony Mullane	220
20. Jack Quinn	218

LOSSES, LEFTHANDER

1. Eppa Rixey	251
2. Warren Spahn	245
3. Steve Carlton	244
4. Jim Kaat	237
5. Frank Tanana	236
6. Tommy John	231
7. Jerry Koosman	209
8. Claude Osteen	195
9. Eddie Plank	194

10. Mickey Lolich	191
Jerry Reuss	191
Tom Zachary	191
13. Earl Whitehill	185
14. Curt Simmons	183
15. Wilbur Cooper	178
16. Rube Marquard	177
17. Larry French	171
18. Ted Breitenstein	170
19. Billy Pierce	169
20. Herb Pennock	162

SAVES

1. Lee Smith	478
2. John Franco	416
3. Dennis Eckersley	390
4. Jeff Reardon	367
5. Randy Myers	347
6. Rollie Fingers	341
7. Tom Henke	311
8. Rich Gossage	310
9. Jeff Montgomery	304
10. Doug Jones	301
11. Bruce Sutter	300
12. John Wetteland	296
13. Rick Aguilera	289
14. Rod Beck	260
15. Todd Worrell	256
16. Dave Righetti	252
17. Dan Quisenberry	244
18. Sparky Lyle	238
19. Roberto Hernandez	234
20. Trevor Hoffman	228

SHUTOUTS

1. Walter Johnson	110
2. Grover Alexander	90
3. Christy Mathewson	79
4. Cy Young	76
5. Eddie Plank	69
6. Warren Spahn	63
7. Nolan Ryan	61
Tom Seaver	61
9. Bert Blyleven	60
10. Don Sutton	58
11. Pud Galvin	57
Ed Walsh	57
13. Bob Gibson	56
14. Mordecai Brown	55
Steve Carlton	55
16. Jim Palmer	53
Gaylord Perry	53
18. Juan Marichal	52
19. Rube Waddell	50
Vic Willis	50

SHUTOUTS, RIGHTHANDER

1. Walter Johnson	110
2. Grover Alexander	90
3. Christy Mathewson	79
4. Cy Young	76
5. Nolan Ryan	61
Tom Seaver	61
7. Bert Blyleven	60
8. Don Sutton	58
9. Pud Galvin	57
Ed Walsh	57
11. Bob Gibson	56
12. Mordecai Brown	55
13. Jim Palmer	53
Gaylord Perry	53
15. Juan Marichal	52
16. Vic Willis	50
17. Don Drysdale	49
Fergie Jenkins	49
Luis Tiant	49
Early Wynn	49

SHUTOUTS, LEFTHANDER

1. Eddie Plank	69
2. Warren Spahn	63
3. Steve Carlton	55
4. Rube Waddell	50
5. Tommy John	46
6. Whitey Ford	45
Doc White	45
8. Mickey Lolich	41
Hippo Vaughn	41
10. Larry French	40
Sandy Koufax	40
Claude Osteen	40
13. Jerry Reuss	39
14. Billy Pierce	38
Nap Rucker	38
16. Vida Blue	37
Eppa Rixey	37
18. Mike Cuellar	36
Carl Hubbell	36
Curt Simmons	36

1-0 VICTORIES

1. Walter Johnson	38
2. Grover Alexander	17
3. Bert Blyleven	15
4. Christy Mathewson	14
5. Dean Chance	13

Eddie Plank	13
Ed Walsh	13
Doc White	13
Cy Young	13
10. Steve Carlton	12
Stan Coveleski	12
Gaylord Perry	12
13. Fergie Jenkins	11
Kid Nichols	11
Nap Rucker	11
Nolan Ryan	11
17. 9 tied with 10	

NO-HIT GAMES

1. Nolan Ryan	7
2. Sandy Koufax	4
3. Larry Corcoran	3
Bob Feller	3
Cy Young	3
6. Al Atkinson	2
Ted Breitenstein	2
Jim Bunning	2
Steve Busby	2
Carl Erskine	2
Bob Forsch	2
Jim Galvin	2
Ken Holtzman	2
Tom L. Hughes	2
Addie Joss	2
Dutch Leonard	2
Jim Maloney	2
Christy Mathewson	2
Allie Reynolds	2
Frank Smith	2
Warren Spahn	2
Bill Stoneman	2
Adonis Terry	2
Virgil Trucks	2
Johnny Vander Meer	2
Don Wilson	2

1-HIT GAMES
(No-hit games in parentheses)

1. Nolan Ryan (7)	12
Bob Feller (3)	12
3. Walter Johnson (1)	7
Addie Joss (1)	7
Charles Radbourn (1)	7
6. Mordecai Brown	6
Steve Carlton	6
8. Bert Blyleven (1)	5
Jim Maloney (2)	5
Jim Palmer (1)	5
Tom Seaver (1)	5
Dave Stieb (1)	5
Ed Walsh (1)	5
Grover Alexander	5
Tim Keefe	5
Don Sutton	5
Doc White	5

RUNS ALLOWED

1. Pud Galvin	3,315
2. Cy Young	3,167
3. Gus Weyhing	2,788
4. Mickey Welch	2,556
5. Tony Mullane	2,523
6. Kid Nichols	2,475
7. Tim Keefe	2,469
8. John Clarkson	2,384
9. Phil Niekro	2,337
10. Adonis Terry	2,298
11. Charles Radbourn	2,275
12. Nolan Ryan	2,178
13. Steve Carlton	2,130
14. Gaylord Perry	2,128
15. Red Ruffing	2,115
16. Don Sutton	2,104
17. Jim McCormick	2,095
18. Amos Rusie	2,068
19. Ted Lyons	2,056
20. Burleigh Grimes	2,050

HITS ALLOWED

1. Cy Young	7,092
2. Pud Galvin	6,352
3. Phil Niekro	5,044
4. Gaylord Perry	4,938
5. Walter Johnson	4,913
6. Kid Nichols	4,912
7. Grover Alexander	4,868
8. Warren Spahn	4,830
9. Tommy John	4,783
10. Don Sutton	4,692
11. Steve Carlton	4,672
12. Eppa Rixey	4,633
13. Bert Blyleven	4,632
14. Jim Kaat	4,620
15. Mickey Welch	4,588
16. Robin Roberts	4,582
17. Gus Weyhing	4,562
18. Ted Lyons	4,489
19. Tim Keefe	4,432
20. Burleigh Grimes	4,412

HOME RUNS ALLOWED

1.	Robin Roberts	505
2.	Fergie Jenkins	484
3.	Phil Niekro	482
4.	Don Sutton	472
5.	Frank Tanana	448
6.	Warren Spahn	434
7.	Bert Blyleven	430
8.	Steve Carlton	414
9.	Gaylord Perry	399
10.	Jim Kaat	395
11.	Jack Morris	389
12.	Charlie Hough	383
13.	Tom Seaver	380
14.	Catfish Hunter	374
	Jim Bunning	372
	Dennis Martinez	372
17.	Dennis Eckersley	347
	Mickey Lolich	347
19.	Luis Tiant	346
20.	Early Wynn	338

GRAND SLAMS ALLOWED

1.	Nolan Ryan	10
2.	Ned Garver	9
	Milt Pappas	9
	Jerry Reuss	9
	Lee Smith	9
	Frank Viola	9
7.	Bert Blyleven	8
	Jim Brewer	8
	Roy Face	8
	Bob Feller	8
	Alex Fernandez	8
	Mike Jackson	8
	Jim Kaat	8
	Johnny Klippstein	8
	Lindy McDaniel	8
	Tug McGraw	8
	Gaylord Perry	8
	Frank Tanana	8
	Early Wynn	8
20.	15 tied with 7	

STRIKEOUTS

1.	Nolan Ryan	5,714
2.	Steve Carlton	4,136
3.	Bert Blyleven	3,701
4.	Tom Seaver	3,640
5.	Don Sutton	3,574
6.	Gaylord Perry	3,534
7.	Walter Johnson	3,509
8.	Phil Niekro	3,342
9.	Roger Clemens	3,316
10.	Fergie Jenkins	3,192
11.	Bob Gibson	3,117
12.	Jim Bunning	2,855
13.	Mickey Lolich	2,832
14.	Cy Young	2,803
15.	Frank Tanana	2,773
16.	Randy Johnson	2,693
17.	Warren Spahn	2,583
18.	Bob Feller	2,581
19.	Tim Keefe	2,560
20.	Jerry Koosman	2,556

STRIKEOUTS, RIGHTHANDER

1.	Nolan Ryan	5,714
2.	Bert Blyleven	3,701
3.	Tom Seaver	3,640
4.	Don Sutton	3,574
5.	Gaylord Perry	3,534
6.	Walter Johnson	3,509
7.	Phil Niekro	3,342
8.	Roger Clemens	3,316
9.	Fergie Jenkins	3,192
10.	Bob Gibson	3,117
11.	Jim Bunning	2,855
12.	Cy Young	2,803
13.	Bob Feller	2,581
14.	Tim Keefe	2,560
15.	Christy Mathewson	2,502
16.	Don Drysdale	2,486
17.	Jack Morris	2,478
18.	David Cone	2,420
19.	Luis Tiant	2,416
20.	Dennis Eckersley	2,401

STRIKEOUTS, LEFTHANDER

1.	Steve Carlton	4,136
2.	Mickey Lolich	2,832
3.	Frank Tanana	2,773
4.	Randy Johnson	2,693
5.	Warren Spahn	2,583
6.	Jerry Koosman	2,556
7.	Mark Langston	2,464
8.	Jim Kaat	2,461
9.	Sam McDowell	2,453
10.	Sandy Koufax	2,396
11.	Rube Waddell	2,316
12.	Lefty Grove	2,266
13.	Eddie Plank	2,246
14.	Tommy John	2,245

15.	Vida Blue	2,175
16.	Fernando Valenzuela	2,074
17.	Billy Pierce	1,999
18.	Whitey Ford	1,956
19.	Chuck Finley	1,951
20.	Jerry Reuss	1,907

WALKS

1.	Nolan Ryan	2,795
2.	Steve Carlton	1,833
3.	Phil Niekro	1,809
4.	Early Wynn	1,775
5.	Bob Feller	1,764
6.	Bobo Newsom	1,732
7.	Amos Rusie	1,707
8.	Charlie Hough	1,665
9.	Gus Weyhing	1,566
10.	Red Ruffing	1,541
11.	Bump Hadley	1,442
12.	Warren Spahn	1,434
13.	Earl Whitehill	1,431
14.	Tony Mullane	1,408
15.	Sam Jones	1,396
16.	Jack Morris	1,390
	Tom Seaver	1,390
18.	Gaylord Perry	1,379
19.	Mike Torrez	1,371
20.	Walter Johnson	1,363

HIT BATSMEN

1.	Gus Weyhing	277
2.	Chick Fraser	219
3.	Pink Hawley	210
4.	Walter Johnson	205
5.	Eddie Plank	190
6.	Tony Mullane	185
7.	Joe McGinnity	179
8.	Charlie Hough	174
9.	Clark Griffith	171
10.	Cy Young	163
11.	Jim Bunning	160
12.	Nolan Ryan	158
13.	Vic Willis	156
14.	Bert Blyleven	155
15.	Don Drysdale	154
16.	Adonis Terry	148
17.	Bert Cunningham	147
18.	Silver King	146
19.	Win Mercer	144
20.	Frank Foreman	142

WILD PITCHES

1.	Tony Mullane	343
2.	Nolan Ryan	277
3.	Mickey Welch	274
4.	Tim Keefe	240
	Gus Weyhing	240
6.	Phil Niekro	226
7.	Mark Baldwin	221
	Will White	221
9.	Pud Galvin	220
10.	Charles Radbourn	214
	Jim Whitney	214
12.	Jack Morris	206
	Adonis Terry	206
14.	Matt Kilroy	203
15.	Tommy John	187
16.	Steve Carlton	183
17.	John Clarkson	182
18.	Charlie Hough	179
	Toad Ramsey	179
20.	Hardie Henderson	178

FIELDING

GOLD GLOVES, PITCHER

1.	Jim Kaat	16
2.	Greg Maddux	10
3.	Bob Gibson	9
4.	Bobby Shantz	8
5.	Mark Langston	7
6.	Phil Niekro	5
	Ron Guidry	5
8.	Mike Mussina	4
	Jim Palmer	4
10.	Harvey Haddix	3

GOLD GLOVES, CATCHER

1.	Johnny Bench	10
2.	Ivan Rodriguez	8
3.	Bob Boone	7
4.	Jim Sundberg	6
5.	Bill Freehan	5
6.	Del Crandall	4
	Charles Johnson	4
	Tony Pena	4
9.	Earl Battey	3
	Gary Carter	3
	Sherm Lollar	3
	Thurman Munson	3
	Tom Pagnozzi	3
	Lance Parrish	3
	Benito Santiago	3

GOLD GLOVES, FIRST BASE

1.	Keith Hernandez	11
2.	Don Mattingly	9
3.	George Scott	8
4.	Vic Power	7
	Bill White	7
6.	Wes Parker	6
7.	J.T. Snow	5
8.	Steve Garvey	4
	Mark Grace	4
10.	Gil Hodges	3
	Eddie Murray	3
	Rafael Palmeiro	3
	Joe Pepitone	3

GOLD GLOVES, SECOND BASE

1.	Ryne Sandberg	9
2.	Roberto Alomar	8
	Bill Mazeroski	8
	Frank White	8
5.	Joe Morgan	5
	Bobby Richardson	5
7.	Craig Biggio	4
	Bobby Grich	4
9.	Nellie Fox	3
	Davey Johnson	3
	Bobby Knoop	3
	Harold Reynolds	3
	Manny Trillo	3
	Lou Whitaker	3

GOLD GLOVES, THIRD BASE

1.	Brooks Robinson	16
2.	Mike Schmidt	10
3.	Buddy Bell	6
	Robin Ventura	6
5.	Ken Boyer	5
	Doug Rader	5
	Ron Santo	5
8.	Gary Gaetti	4
	Matt Williams	4
10.	Ken Caminiti	3
	Frank Malzone	3
	Terry Pendleton	3
	Tim Wallach	3

GOLD GLOVES, SHORTSTOP

1.	Ozzie Smith	13
2.	Luis Aparicio	9
3.	Mark Belanger	8
4.	Omar Vizquel	7
5.	Dave Concepcion	5
6.	Tony Fernandez	4
	Alan Trammell	4
8.	Barry Larkin	3
	Roy McMillan	3
	Rey Ordonez	3

GOLD GLOVES, OUTFIELD

1.	Roberto Clemente	12
	Willie Mays	12
3.	Ken Griffey Jr.	10
	Al Kaline	10
5.	Paul Blair	8
	Barry Bonds	8
	Andre Dawson	8
	Dwight Evans	8
	Garry Maddox	8
10.	Curt Flood	7
	Devon White	7
	Dave Winfield	7
	Carl Yastrzemski	7

UNASSISTED TRIPLE PLAYS

Neal Ball, SS, Indians	7-19-09
*Bill Wambganss, 2B, Indians	10-10-20
George Burns, 1B, Red Sox	9-14-23
Ernie Padgett, SS, Braves	10-6-23
Glenn Wright, SS, Pirates	5-7-25
Jimmy Cooney, SS, Cubs	5-30-27
Johnny Neun, 1B, Tigers	5-31-27
Ron Hansen, SS, Senators	7-30-68
Mickey Morandini, 2B, Phillies	9-20-92
John Valentin, SS, Red Sox	7-8-94

*World Series game

MANAGERIAL

YEARS AS MANAGER

1.	Connie Mack	53
2.	John McGraw	33
3.	Bucky Harris	29
4.	Sparky Anderson	26
	Gene Mauch	26
6.	Bill McKechnie	25
	Casey Stengel	25
8.	Leo Durocher	24
	Joe McCarthy	24
10.	Walter Alston	23
11.	Jimmy Dykes	21

	Tony La Russa	21
	Tom Lasorda	21
	Dick Williams	21
15.	Cap Anson	20
	Clark Griffith	20
	Ralph Houk	20
18.	Fred Clarke	19
	Charlie Grimm	19
	Ned Hanlon	19
	John McNamara	19
	Wilbert Robinson	19
	Chuck Tanner	19

VICTORIES, MANAGER

1.	Connie Mack	3,731
2.	John McGraw	2,763
3.	Sparky Anderson	2,194
4.	Bucky Harris	2,157
5.	Joe McCarthy	2,125
6.	Walter Alston	2,040
7.	Leo Durocher	2,008
8.	Casey Stengel	1,905
9.	Gene Mauch	1,902
10.	Bill McKechnie	1,896
11.	Tony La Russa	1,639
12.	Ralph Houk	1,619
13.	Fred Clarke	1,602
14.	Tom Lasorda	1,599
15.	Dick Williams	1,571
16.	Bobby Cox	1,521
17.	Clark Griffith	1,491
18.	Earl Weaver	1,480
19.	Miller Huggins	1,413
20.	Al Lopez	1,410

TEAMS MANAGED

1.	Frank Bancroft	7
2.	Jack Chapman	6
	Jimmy Dykes	6
	Bob Ferguson	6
	Rogers Hornsby	6
	Tom Loftus	6
	John McNamara	6
	Dick Williams	6
9.	John Clapp	5
	Patsy Donovan	5
	Chuck Dressen	5
	Ned Hanlon	5
	Bucky Harris	5
	Billy Martin	5
	Bill McKechnie	5
	Gus Schmelz	5
	Bill Watkins	5
	Don Zimmer	5

PENNANTS WON, MANAGER

1.	John McGraw	10
	Casey Stengel	10
3.	Connie Mack	9
	Joe McCarthy	9
5.	Walter Alston	7
6.	Miller Huggins	6
7.	Sparky Anderson	5
	Cap Anson	5
	Fred Clarke	5
	Bobby Cox	5
	Ned Hanlon	5
	Frank Selee	5
13.	Frank Chance	4
	Charlie Comiskey	4
	Bobby Cox	4
	Tom Lasorda	4
	Bill McKechnie	4
	Billy Southworth	4
	Earl Weaver	4
	Dick Williams	4
20.	10 tied with 3	

WORLD SERIES WON, MANAGER

1.	Joe McCarthy	7
	Casey Stengel	7
3.	Connie Mack	5
4.	Walter Alston	4
5.	Sparky Anderson	3
	Miller Huggins	3
	John McGraw	3
	Joe Torre	3
9.	Bill Carrigan	2
	Frank Chance	2
	Cito Gaston	2
	Bucky Harris	2
	Ralph Houk	2
	Tom Kelly	2
	Tom Lasorda	2
	Bill McKechnie	2
	Danny Murtaugh	2
	Billy Southworth	2
	Joe Torre	2
	Dick Williams	2

SERVICE

SERIES PLAYED

1.	Reggie Jackson	11
2.	Tom Glavine	8
	Richie Hebner	8
	Hal McRae	8
	John Smoltz	8
	Bob Welch	8
7.	Don Baylor	7
	Paul Blair	7
	Rick Honeycutt	7
	Greg Maddux	7
	Joe Morgan	7
	Graig Nettles	7
	Jim Palmer	7
	Pete Rose	7
15.	26 tied with 6	

SERIES PITCHED

1.	Bob Welch	8
	Tom Glavine	8
	John Smoltz	8
4.	Rick Honeycutt	7
	Greg Maddux	7
6.	Dennis Eckersley	6
	Don Gullett	6
	Catfish Hunter	6
	Jimmy Key	6
	Tug McGraw	6
	Jim Palmer	6
	Ron Reed	6
	Mark Wohlers	6
14.	23 tied with 5	

BATTING

GAMES

1.	Reggie Jackson	45
2.	Terry Pendleton	38
3.	David Justice	35
4.	Ron Gant	31
	Mark Lemke	31
6.	Rickey Henderson	30
7.	Jeff Blauser	29
	Chipper Jones	29
9.	Roberto Alomar	28
	Don Baylor	28
	Fred McGriff	28
	Hal McRae	28
	Pete Rose	28
14.	Bobby Bonilla	27
	Bob Boone	27
	George Brett	27
	Richie Hebner	27
	Joe Morgan	27
	Devon White	27
20.	Lonnie Smith	26
	Frank White	26

HIGHEST AVERAGE
(Minimum 50 at-bats)

1.	Mickey Rivers	.386
2.	Pete Rose	.381
3.	Dusty Baker	.371
4.	Bernie Williams	.367
5.	Steve Garvey	.356
6.	Brooks Robinson	.348
7.	Devon White	.347
8.	George Brett	.340
9.	Thurman Munson	.339
10.	Tony Fernandez	.338
11.	Bill Russell	.337
12.	Harold Baines	.333
13.	Javy Lopez	.329
14.	Cal Ripken	.328
15.	Paul O'Neill	.324
	Chipper Jones	.324
17.	Lenny Dykstra	.323
18.	Derek Jeter	.319
19.	Darrell Porter	.317
20.	Carney Lansford	.316

AT-BATS

1.	Reggie Jackson	163
2.	Terry Pendleton	135
3.	David Justice	122
4.	Pete Rose	118
5.	Ron Gant	117
6.	Roberto Alomar	114
	Rickey Henderson	114
8.	Mark Lemke	110
9.	Fred McGriff	109
10.	Chipper Jones	108
11.	George Brett	103
12.	Don Baylor	96
	Joe Morgan	96

14.	Devon White	95
15.	Jeff Blauser	92
	John Olerud	92
17.	Bobby Bonilla	90
	Steve Garvey	90
19.	Willie McGee	89
	Andy Van Slyke	89

RUNS SCORED

1.	George Brett	22
2.	Rickey Henderson	20
3.	Chipper Jones	19
4.	Jeff Blauser	18
	Fred McGriff	18
6.	Ron Gant	17
	David Justice	17
	Pete Rose	17
9.	Reggie Jackson	16
	Devon White	16
11.	Steve Garvey	15
	Willie McGee	15
13.	Roberto Alomar	14
	Ron Cey	14
	Lenny Dykstra	14
	John Olerud	14
	Darryl Strawberry	14
18.	Don Baylor	13
	Bernie Williams	13
20.	Dusty Baker	12
	Chuck Knoblauch	12
	Javy Lopez	12
	Joe Morgan	12
	Terry Pendleton	12

HITS

1.	Pete Rose	45
2.	Reggie Jackson	37
3.	Roberto Alomar	36
4.	George Brett	35
	Chipper Jones	35
6.	Fred McGriff	34
7.	Devon White	33
8.	Steve Garvey	32
9.	Mark Lemke	31
10.	Terry Pendleton	30
11.	Rickey Henderson	28
	David Justice	28
	Bill Russell	28
14.	Tony Fernandez	27
	John Olerud	27
16.	Don Baylor	26
	Bob Boone	26
	Willie McGee	26
19.	Ron Gant	25
	Richie Hebner	25
	Carney Lansford	25
	Javy Lopez	25

SINGLES

1.	Pete Rose	34
2.	Roberto Alomar	29
3.	Chipper Jones	26
	Devon White	26
5.	Bill Russell	25
6.	Bob Boone	24
	Reggie Jackson	24
	Mark Lemke	24
9.	Fred McGriff	23
10.	Carney Lansford	22
	Terry Pendleton	22
12.	John Olerud	21
13.	Tony Fernandez	20
	Steve Garvey	20
	David Justice	20
16.	Harold Baines	19
	Willie McGee	19
	Mickey Rivers	19
19.	Don Baylor	18
	Rickey Henderson	18
	Frank White	18

DOUBLES

1.	Ron Cey	7
	Richie Hebner	7
	Reggie Jackson	7
	Javy Lopez	7
	Fred McGriff	7
	Hal McRae	7
	Pete Rose	7
	Mike Schmidt	7
9.	Doug DeCinces	6
	Tony Fernandez	6
	Rickey Henderson	6
	Chipper Jones	6
	Mark Lemke	6
	Greg Luzinski	6
	Tim Raines	6
	Brooks Robinson	6
-	Andy Van Slyke	6
	Roy White	6
19.	20 tied with 5	

Royals third baseman George Brett, always in top form during the postseason, holds career LCS records for homers, runs scored and triples.

TRIPLES

1.	George Brett	4
2.	Mariano Duncan	3
	Keith Lockhart	3
	Kenny Lofton	3
	Willie McGee	3
6.	Johnny Bench	2
	Jeff Blauser	2
	Rickey Henderson	2
	Jose Lind	2
	Davey Lopes	2
	Terry Pendleton	2
	Luis Salazar	2
	Ozzie Smith	2
	Andy Van Slyke	2
15.	69 tied with 1	

HOME RUNS

1.	George Brett	9
2.	Steve Garvey	8
3.	Darryl Strawberry	7
4.	Reggie Jackson	6
	Manny Ramirez	6
	Jim Thome	6
7.	Sal Bando	5
	Johnny Bench	5
	Ron Gant	5
	Greg Luzinski	5
	Gary Matthews	5
	Graig Nettles	5
13.	Jeff Blauser	4
	Jose Canseco	4
	Ron Cey	4
	Lenny Dykstra	4
	Kirk Gibson	4
	David Justice	4
	Ryan Klesko	4
	Jeffrey Leonard	4
	Javy Lopez	4
	Bill Madlock	4
	Eddie Murray	4
	Boog Powell	4
	Bob Robertson	4
	Willie Stargell	4

TOTAL BASES

1.	George Brett	75
2.	Pete Rose	63
3.	Reggie Jackson	62
4.	Steve Garvey	61
5.	Fred McGriff	52
6.	Chipper Jones	50
7.	Roberto Alomar	49
8.	Ron Gant	45
	Darryl Strawberry	45
10.	Johnny Bench	44
	Rickey Henderson	44
	David Justice	44
	Javy Lopez	44
14.	Greg Luzinski	43
	Devon White	43
16.	Graig Nettles	42
	Terry Pendleton	42
18.	Don Baylor	41
	Ron Cey	41
	Richie Hebner	41

SLUGGING PERCENTAGE
(Minimum 50 at-bats)

1.	George Brett	.728
2.	Steve Garvey	.678
3.	Darryl Strawberry	.643
4.	Lenny Dykstra	.629
5.	Manny Ramirez	.619
6.	Bernie Williams	.600
7.	Dusty Baker	.597
8.	Greg Luzinski	.589
9.	Javy Lopez	.579
10.	Jim Thome	.577
11.	Pete Rose	.534
12.	Johnny Bench	.530
13.	Sal Bando	.527
14.	Brooks Robinson	.522
15.	Dave Henderson	.520
16.	Paul O'Neill	.514
17.	Ron Cey	.500
	Thurman Munson	.500
19.	Graig Nettles	.494
20.	Derek Jeter	.493

EXTRA-BASE HITS

1.	George Brett	18
2.	Reggie Jackson	13
3.	Steve Garvey	12
	Greg Luzinski	12
5.	Johnny Bench	11
	Ron Cey	11
	Javy Lopez	11
	Fred McGriff	11
	Pete Rose	11
10.	Lenny Dykstra	10
	Ron Gant	10
	Richie Hebner	10
	Rickey Henderson	10
	Darryl Strawberry	10
15.	Sal Bando	9
	Will Clark	9
	Chipper Jones	9
	Hal McRae	9
	Graig Nettles	9
	Willie Stargell	9
	Andy Van Slyke	9

RUNS BATTED IN

1.	Steve Garvey	21
2.	Reggie Jackson	20
3.	George Brett	19
	Graig Nettles	19
5.	Fred McGriff	18
6.	Don Baylor	17
	Ron Gant	17
	Darryl Strawberry	17
9.	John Olerud	16
10.	Roberto Alomar	15
	David Justice	15
	Al Oliver	15
13.	Ron Cey	14
	Terry Pendleton	14
15.	Dusty Baker	13
	Chipper Jones	13
	Mark Lemke	13
	Gary Matthews	13
	Eddie Murray	13

	Tony Perez	13
	Jim Thome	13
	Bernie Williams	13

WALKS

1.	Joe Morgan	23
2.	Chipper Jones	21
3.	David Justice	19
4.	Rickey Henderson	17
	Reggie Jackson	17
6.	Darrell Porter	16
7.	Roberto Alomar	15
	Jeff Blauser	15
	Ryan Klesko	15
	Mark Lemke	15
11.	Barry Bonds	14
	Bernie Williams	14
13.	Ron Cey	13
	Gene Tenace	13
15.	Fred McGriff	12
	Eddie Murray	12
17.	Don Baylor	11
	Bobby Bonilla	11
	George Brett	11
	Chili Davis	11
	Lenny Dykstra	11
	Keith Hernandez	11
	Tino Martinez	11
	John Olerud	11
	Manny Ramirez	11

STRIKEOUTS

1.	Reggie Jackson	41
2.	Ron Gant	26
3.	Cesar Geronimo	24
4.	Jeff Blauser	23
	Fred McGriff	23
6.	Bobby Grich	22
	Devon White	22
8.	Marquis Grissom	21
	Tino Martinez	21
	Willie McGee	21
	Darryl Strawberry	21
12.	Mariano Duncan	20
	David Justice	20
	Kenny Lofton	20
	Greg Luzinski	20
16.	Chili Davis	19
	Terry Pendleton	19
	Manny Ramirez	19
	Willie Stargell	19
20.	Rickey Henderson	18
	Mike Marshall	18
	Hal McRae	18
	Andy Van Slyke	18

STOLEN BASES

1.	Rickey Henderson	17
2.	Roberto Alomar	11
3.	Davey Lopes	9
4.	Ron Gant	8
	Joe Morgan	8
	Amos Otis	8
	Willie Wilson	8
8.	Kenny Lofton	7
	Omar Vizquel	7
10.	Barry Bonds	6
	Bert Campaneris	6
	Vince Coleman	6
	Kirk Gibson	6
	Steve Sax	6
	Walt Weiss	6
16.	Tony Fernandez	5
	Ken Griffey	5
	Marquis Grissom	5
	Derek Jeter	5
	Chipper Jones	5
	Otis Nixon	5

PITCHING

GAMES

1.	Rick Honeycutt	20
2.	Dennis Eckersley	18
	Randy Myers	18
	Mark Wohlers	18
5.	Tug McGraw	15
	John Smoltz	15
	Mike Stanton	15
8.	Jesse Orosco	14
9.	Paul Assenmacher	13
	Dave Giusti	13
	Tom Glavine	13
	Greg Maddux	13
	Alejandro Pena	13
	Ron Reed	13
15.	Armando Benitez	12
	Tom Henke	12
	John Rocker	12
18.	Steve Avery	11
	Rollie Fingers	11
	Orel Hershiser	11
	Duane Ward	11

GAMES STARTED

1.	Tom Glavine	13
	John Smoltz	13
3.	Greg Maddux	12
4.	Catfish Hunter	10
	Dave Stewart	10
6.	Steve Carlton	8
	David Cone	8
	Orel Hershiser	8
9.	Steve Avery	7
	Roger Clemens	7
	Doug Drabek	7
	Tommy John	7
	Jim Palmer	7
	Jerry Reuss	7
15.	Mike Cuellar	6
	Don Gullett	6
	Jimmy Key	6
	Dennis Leonard	6
	Jack Morris	6
	Don Sutton	6
	Bob Welch	6

GAMES RELIEVED

1.	Rick Honeycutt	20
2.	Randy Myers	18
	Mark Wohlers	18
4.	Dennis Eckersley	17
5.	Tug McGraw	15
	Mike Stanton	15
7.	Jesse Orosco	14
8.	Paul Assenmacher	13
	Dave Giusti	13
	Alejandro Pena	13
11.	Armando Benitez	12
	Tom Henke	12
	Ron Reed	12
	John Rocker	12
15.	Rollie Fingers	11
	Duane Ward	11
17.	Pedro Borbon	10
	Warren Brusstar	10
	Greg McMichael	10
	Jeff Nelson	10

COMPLETE GAMES

1.	Jim Palmer	5
2.	Catfish Hunter	3
	Tommy John	3
4.	Mike Boddicker	2
	Kevin Brown	2
	Danny Cox	2
	Mike Cuellar	2
	Doug Drabek	2
	Orel Hershiser	2
	Ken Holtzman	2
	Bruce Hurst	2
	Dennis Leonard	2
	Dave McNally	2
	Jack Morris	2
	Mike Scott	2
	Don Sutton	2
	Tim Wakefield	2
18.	39 tied with 1	

INNINGS PITCHED

1.	John Smoltz	92.1
2.	Tom Glavine	80.1
3.	Greg Maddux	75.1
	Dave Stewart	75.1
5.	Catfish Hunter	69.1
6.	Orel Hershiser	65.1
7.	Jim Palmer	59.2
8.	Steve Carlton	53.2
9.	David Cone	50.0
10.	Don Sutton	49.0
11.	Doug Drabek	48.1
12.	Tommy John	47.2
13.	Steve Avery	45.1
14.	Mike Cuellar	44.0
15.	Nolan Ryan	41.1
16.	Don Gullett	40.2
	Jack Morris	40.2
18.	Dave McNally	40.1
19.	Dwight Gooden	40.0
20.	Roger Clemens	39.1

LOWEST ERA

(Minimum 30 innings)

1.	Orel Hershiser	1.52
2.	Fernando Valenzuela	1.95
3.	Jim Palmer	1.96
4.	Don Sutton	2.02
5.	Dave Stewart	2.03
6.	Doug Drabek	2.05
7.	Ken Holtzman	2.06
8.	Tommy John	2.08
9.	Juan Guzman	2.27
10.	Steve Avery	2.38
11.	Dwight Gooden	2.47
12.	Charles Nagy	2.64
13.	Paul Splittorff	2.68
	Dave McNally	2.68
15.	Tom Seaver	2.84
16.	John Smoltz	2.92
17.	Danny Jackson	2.94
18.	John Tudor	3.00
19.	Mike Cuellar	3.07
20.	Charlie Leibrandt	3.09

VICTORIES

1.	Dave Stewart	8
2.	John Smoltz	6
3.	Juan Guzman	5
4.	Steve Avery	4
	Steve Carlton	4
	David Cone	4
	Tom Glavine	4
	Orel Hershiser	4
	Catfish Hunter	4
	Tommy John	4
	Bruce Kison	4
	Greg Maddux	4
	Jim Palmer	4
	Don Sutton	4
15.	10 tied with 3	3

LOSSES

1.	Tom Glavine	8
2.	Jerry Reuss	7
3.	Greg Maddux	6
4.	Doug Drabek	5
5.	Doyle Alexander	4
	Todd Stottlemyre	4
7.	Roger Clemens	3
	Alex Fernandez	3
	Gene Garber	3
	Don Gullett	3
	Ken Holtzman	3
	Catfish Hunter	3
	Charlie Leibrandt	3
	Dennis Leonard	3
	Chad Ogea	3
	Zane Smith	3
	Dave Stieb	3
18.	41 tied with 2	

SAVES

1.	Dennis Eckersley	11
2.	Tug McGraw	5
3.	Ken Dayley	4
	Dave Giusti	4
	Randy Myers	4
	Alejandro Pena	4
7.	Rick Aguilera	3
	Steve Bedrosian	3
	Pedro Borbon	3
	Rich Gossage	3
	Tom Henke	3
	Jose Mesa	3
	Jeff Reardon	3
	Mariano Rivera	3
	Duane Ward	3
16.	10 tied with 2	

RUNS ALLOWED

1.	Greg Maddux	42
2.	Tom Glavine	36
3.	John Smoltz	33
4.	Catfish Hunter	25
	Jerry Reuss	25
	Todd Stottlemyre	25
7.	Doyle Alexander	23
	Roger Clemens	23
	David Cone	23
10.	Steve Carlton	22
	Jack Morris	22
12.	Nolan Ryan	19
13.	Scott Erickson	18
	Don Gullett	18
	Bob Welch	18
16.	Ed Figueroa	17
	Tommy John	17
	Dave Stewart	17
19.	7 tied with 16	

HITS ALLOWED

1.	Tom Glavine	81
	John Smoltz	81
3.	Greg Maddux	72
4.	Catfish Hunter	57
5.	Steve Carlton	53
6.	Dave Stewart	52
7.	Orel Hershiser	49
8.	Jim Palmer	46
9.	David Cone	45
10.	Larry Gura	43
11.	Roger Clemens	41
12.	Doug Drabek	40
	Tommy John	40
14.	Jack Morris	39
15.	Danny Jackson	38
	Todd Stottlemyre	38
17.	Jimmy Key	37
	Jerry Reuss	37
	Don Sutton	37
20.	Bob Welch	36

HOME RUNS ALLOWED

1.	Catfish Hunter	12
2.	Andy Pettitte	8
	John Smoltz	8
4.	Tom Glavine	7
	Dave McNally	7
	Dave Stewart	7
7.	Doyle Alexander	6
	Steve Blass	6
	Scott Erickson	6
	Greg Maddux	6
	Jim Perry	6
12.	Andy Benes	5
	Steve Carlton	5
	David Cone	5
	Bruce Hurst	5
	Jim Palmer	5
	Tom Seaver	5
	Eric Show	5
	Todd Stottlemyre	5
	Don Sutton	5
	John Tudor	5

TOTAL BASES ALLOWED

1.	Tom Glavine	129
2.	John Smoltz	125
3.	Catfish Hunter	112
4.	Greg Maddux	108
5.	Steve Carlton	85
6.	Dave Stewart	80
7.	Jim Palmer	75
8.	David Cone	69
9.	Doyle Alexander	63
	Larry Gura	63
	Todd Stottlemyre	63
12.	Orel Hershiser	60
	Jack Morris	60
14.	Dave McNally	59
	Don Sutton	59
16.	Roger Clemens	58
	Bob Welch	58
18.	Scott Erickson	57
	Jimmy Key	57
	Dennis Leonard	57

STRIKEOUTS

1.	John Smoltz	88
2.	Tom Glavine	57
	Greg Maddux	57
4.	Orel Hershiser	47
5.	Jim Palmer	46
	Nolan Ryan	46
7.	David Cone	45
8.	Steve Carlton	39
	Dave Stewart	39
10.	Steve Avery	37
	Catfish Hunter	37
	David Wells	37
13.	Doug Drabek	33
14.	Dwight Gooden	32
15.	Roger Clemens	31
	Mike Mussina	31
17.	Dave McNally	30
	Don Sutton	30
19.	Mike Cuellar	28
	Dave Stieb	28
	Fernando Valenzuela	28

WALKS

1.	John Smoltz	34
2.	Tom Glavine	32
3.	Steve Carlton	28
4.	Dave Stewart	25
5.	David Cone	24
6.	Greg Maddux	23
7.	Orel Hershiser	20
8.	Mike Cuellar	19
	Jim Palmer	19
	Fernando Valenzuela	19
11.	Juan Guzman	18
	Catfish Hunter	18
13.	Steve Avery	17
	Jerry Reuss	17
15.	Dwight Gooden	16
	Tug McGraw	16
	Dave Stieb	16
18.	Danny Jackson	15
	Tommy John	15
	Dave McNally	15
	Bob Welch	15

WORLD SERIES

SERVICE

SERIES PLAYED

1.	Yogi Berra	14
2.	Mickey Mantle	12
3.	Whitey Ford	11
4.	Joe DiMaggio	10
	Elston Howard	10
	Babe Ruth	10
7.	Hank Bauer	9
	Phil Rizzuto	9
9.	Bill Dickey	8
	Frankie Frisch	8
	Gil McDougald	8
	Bill Skowron	8
13.	Joe Collins	7
	Frankie Crosetti	7
	Carl Furillo	7
	Lou Gehrig	7
	Jim Gilliam	7
	Gil Hodges	7
	Waite Hoyt	7
	Tony Lazzeri	7
	Roger Maris	7
	Pee Wee Reese	7
	Bobby Richardson	7
	Red Ruffing	7

SERIES PITCHED

1.	Whitey Ford	11
2.	Waite Hoyt	7
	Red Ruffing	7
4.	Catfish Hunter	6
	Johnny Murphy	6
	Jim Palmer	6
	Vic Raschi	6
	Allie Reynolds	6
9.	Chief Bender	5
	Joe Bush	5
	Don Drysdale	5
	Carl Erskine	5
	Lefty Gomez	5
	Don Gullett	5
	Clem Labine	5
	Don Larsen	5
	Ed Lopat	5
	Rube Marquard	5
	Art Nehf	5
	Herb Pennock	5
	Bob Shawkey	5
	Dave Stewart	5
	Ralph Terry	5
	Bob Turley	5

BATTING

GAMES

1.	Yogi Berra	75
2.	Mickey Mantle	65
3.	Elston Howard	54
4.	Hank Bauer	53
	Gil McDougald	53
6.	Phil Rizzuto	52
7.	Joe DiMaggio	51
8.	Frankie Frisch	50
9.	Pee Wee Reese	44
10.	Roger Maris	41
	Babe Ruth	41
12.	Carl Furillo	40
13.	Jim Gilliam	39
	Gil Hodges	39
	Bill Skowron	39
16.	Bill Dickey	38
	Jackie Robinson	38
18.	Tony Kubek	37
19.	Joe Collins	36
	Bobby Richardson	36
	Duke Snider	36

HIGHEST AVERAGE

(Minimum 50 at-bats)

1.	Pepper Martin	.418
	Paul Molitor	.418
3.	Lou Brock	.391
4.	Marquis Grissom	.390
5.	Thurman Munson	.373
	George Brett	.373
7.	Hank Aaron	.364
8.	Frank Baker	.363
9.	Roberto Clemente	.362
10.	Lou Gehrig	.361
11.	Reggie Jackson	.357
12.	Carl Yastrzemski	.352
13.	Earle Combs	.350
14.	Stan Hack	.348
15.	Joe Jackson	.345
16.	Jimmie Foxx	.344
17.	Rickey Henderson	.339
18.	Julian Javier	.333
	Billy Martin	.333
20.	Al Simmons	.329

AT-BATS

1.	Yogi Berra	259
2.	Mickey Mantle	230
3.	Joe DiMaggio	199
4.	Frankie Frisch	197
5.	Gil McDougald	190
6.	Hank Bauer	188
7.	Phil Rizzuto	183
8.	Elston Howard	171
9.	Pee Wee Reese	169
10.	Roger Maris	152
11.	Jim Gilliam	147
12.	Tony Kubek	146
13.	Bill Dickey	145
14.	Jackie Robinson	137
15.	Bill Skowron	133
	Duke Snider	133
17.	Gil Hodges	131
	Bobby Richardson	131
19.	Pete Rose	130
20.	Goose Goslin	129
	Bob Meusel	129
	Babe Ruth	129

RUNS SCORED

1.	Mickey Mantle	42
2.	Yogi Berra	41
3.	Babe Ruth	37
4.	Lou Gehrig	30
5.	Joe DiMaggio	27
6.	Roger Maris	26
7.	Elston Howard	25
8.	Gil McDougald	23
9.	Jackie Robinson	22
10.	Hank Bauer	21
	Reggie Jackson	21
	Phil Rizzuto	21
	Duke Snider	21
	Gene Woodling	21
15.	Eddie Collins	20
	Pee Wee Reese	20
17.	Bill Dickey	19
	Frank Robinson	19
	Bill Skowron	19
20.	Charlie Keller	18
	Davey Lopes	18
	Lonnie Smith	18

HITS

1.	Yogi Berra	71
2.	Mickey Mantle	59
3.	Frankie Frisch	58
4.	Joe DiMaggio	54
5.	Hank Bauer	46
	Pee Wee Reese	46
7.	Gil McDougald	45
	Phil Rizzuto	45
9.	Lou Gehrig	43
10.	Eddie Collins	42
	Elston Howard	42
	Babe Ruth	42
13.	Bobby Richardson	40
14.	Bill Skowron	39
15.	Duke Snider	38
16.	Bill Dickey	37
	Goose Goslin	37
18.	Steve Garvey	36
19.	Gil Hodges	35
	Reggie Jackson	35
	Tony Kubek	35
	Pete Rose	35

SINGLES

1.	Yogi Berra	49
2.	Frankie Frisch	45
3.	Joe DiMaggio	40
	Phil Rizzuto	40
5.	Pee Wee Reese	39
6.	Hank Bauer	34
7.	Eddie Collins	33
	Mickey Mantle	33
	Gil McDougald	33
10.	Tony Kubek	31
	Bobby Richardson	31
12.	Bill Dickey	30
13.	Steve Garvey	29
	Elston Howard	29
15.	Red Rolfe	28
16.	Gil Hodges	27
	Pete Rose	27
18.	Bill Skowron	26
19.	Goose Goslin	25
	Marquis Grissom	25

DOUBLES

1.	Yogi Berra	10
	Frankie Frisch	10
3.	Jack Barry	9
	Pete Fox	9
	Carl Furillo	9
6.	Lou Gehrig	8
	Lonnie Smith	8
	Duke Snider	8
9.	Frank Baker	7
	Lou Brock	7
	Eddie Collins	7
	Rick Dempsey	7
	Hank Greenberg	7
	Chick Hafey	7
	Elston Howard	7
	Reggie Jackson	7
	Marty Marion	7
	Pepper Martin	7
	Danny Murphy	7
	Stan Musial	7
	Terry Pendleton	7
	Jackie Robinson	7
	Devon White	7

TRIPLES

1.	Billy Johnson	4
	Tommy Leach	4
	Tris Speaker	4
4.	Hank Bauer	3
	Bobby Brown	3
	Dave Concepcion	3
	Buck Freeman	3
	Frankie Frisch	3
	Lou Gehrig	3
	Dan Gladden	3
	Mark Lemke	3
	Billy Martin	3
	Tim McCarver	3
	Bob Meusel	3
	Freddy Parent	3
	Chick Stahl	3
	Devon White	3
18.	34 tied with 2	

HOME RUNS

1.	Mickey Mantle	18
2.	Babe Ruth	15
3.	Yogi Berra	12
4.	Duke Snider	11
5.	Lou Gehrig	10
	Reggie Jackson	10
7.	Joe DiMaggio	8
	Frank Robinson	8
	Bill Skowron	8
10.	Hank Bauer	7
	Goose Goslin	7
	Gil McDougald	7
13.	Lenny Dykstra	6
	Roger Maris	6
	Al Simmons	6
	Reggie Smith	6
17.	Johnny Bench	5
	Bill Dickey	5
	Hank Greenberg	5
	Gil Hodges	5
	Elston Howard	5
	Charlie Keller	5
	Billy Martin	5

TOTAL BASES

1.	Mickey Mantle	123
2.	Yogi Berra	117
3.	Babe Ruth	96
4.	Lou Gehrig	87
5.	Joe DiMaggio	84
6.	Duke Snider	79
7.	Hank Bauer	75
8.	Frankie Frisch	74
	Reggie Jackson	74
10.	Gil McDougald	72
11.	Bill Skowron	69
12.	Elston Howard	66
13.	Goose Goslin	63
14.	Pee Wee Reese	59
15.	Lou Brock	57
16.	Roger Maris	56
	Billy Martin	56
18.	Bill Dickey	55
19.	Gil Hodges	54
	Phil Rizzuto	54

SLUGGING PERCENTAGE

(Minimum 50 at-bats)

1.	Reggie Jackson	.755
2.	Babe Ruth	.744
3.	Lou Gehrig	.731
4.	Lenny Dykstra	.700
5.	Al Simmons	.658
6.	Lou Brock	.655
7.	Pepper Martin	.636
	Paul Molitor	.636
9.	Hank Greenberg	.624
10.	Charlie Keller	.611
11.	Jimmie Foxx	.609
12.	Rickey Henderson	.607
13.	Dave Henderson	.606
14.	Hank Aaron	.600
15.	Duke Snider	.594
16.	Dwight Evans	.580
17.	Steve Yeager	.579
18.	Willie Stargell	.574
19.	Billy Martin	.566
20.	Carl Yastrzemski	.556

EXTRA-BASE HITS

1.	Mickey Mantle	26
2.	Yogi Berra	22
	Babe Ruth	22
4.	Lou Gehrig	21
5.	Duke Snider	19
6.	Reggie Jackson	18
7.	Joe DiMaggio	14
	Hank Greenberg	14
9.	Lou Brock	13
	Frankie Frisch	13
	Elston Howard	13
	Bill Skowron	13
	Lonnie Smith	13
14.	Hank Bauer	12
	Goose Goslin	12
	Gil McDougald	12
	Al Simmons	12
18.	Carl Furillo	11
	Dave Henderson	11
	Roger Maris	11
	Frank Robinson	11
	Devon White	11

RUNS BATTED IN

1.	Mickey Mantle	40
2.	Yogi Berra	39
3.	Lou Gehrig	35
4.	Babe Ruth	33
5.	Joe DiMaggio	30
6.	Bill Skowron	29
7.	Duke Snider	26
8.	Hank Bauer	24
	Bill Dickey	24
	Reggie Jackson	24
	Gil McDougald	24
12.	Hank Greenberg	22
13.	Gil Hodges	21
14.	Goose Goslin	19
	Elston Howard	19
	Tony Lazzeri	19
	Billy Martin	19
18.	Frank Baker	18
	David Justice	18
	Charlie Keller	18
	Roger Maris	18

WALKS

1.	Mickey Mantle	43
2.	Babe Ruth	33
3.	Yogi Berra	32
4.	Phil Rizzuto	30
5.	Lou Gehrig	26
6.	Mickey Cochrane	25
7.	Jim Gilliam	23
8.	David Justice	22
9.	Jackie Robinson	21
10.	Gil McDougald	20
11.	Joe DiMaggio	19
	Gene Woodling	19
13.	Roger Maris	18
	Pee Wee Reese	18
15.	Gil Hodges	17
	Gene Tenace	17
	Ross Youngs	17
18	Pete Rose	16
19.	Bill Dickey	15
	Reggie Jackson	15
	Eddie Mathews	15
	Joe Morgan	15
	Enos Slaughter	15

STRIKEOUTS

1.	Mickey Mantle	54
2.	Elston Howard	37
3.	Duke Snider	33
4.	Babe Ruth	30
5.	Gil McDougald	29
6.	Bill Skowron	26
7.	Hank Bauer	25
8.	Reggie Jackson	24
	Bob Meusel	24
10.	Joe DiMaggio	23
	George Kelly	23
	Tony Kubek	23
	Frank Robinson	23
	Devon White	23

New York Yankees lefthander Whitey Ford pitched more innings and won more games than any other pitcher in World Series history.

15.	Jim Bottomley	22
	Joe Collins	22
	Gil Hodges	22
	Lonnie Smith	22
19.	Steve Garvey	21
	Roger Maris	21
	Tony Perez	21

STOLEN BASES

1.	Lou Brock	14
	Eddie Collins	14
3.	Frank Chance	10
	Davey Lopes	10
	Phil Rizzuto	10
6.	Frankie Frisch	9
	Honus Wagner	9
8.	Johnny Evers	8
9.	Roberto Alomar	7
	Rickey Henderson	7
	Pepper Martin	7
	Joe Morgan	7
	Joe Tinker	7
14.	Vince Coleman	6
	Chuck Knoblauch	6
	Kenny Lofton	6
	Jackie Robinson	6
	Jimmy Slagle	6
	Bobby Tolan	6
	Omar Vizquel	6
	Maury Wills	6

PITCHING

GAMES

1.	Whitey Ford	22
2.	Rollie Fingers	16
3.	Allie Reynolds	15
	Bob Turley	15
5.	Clay Carroll	14
6.	Clem Labine	13
	Mark Wohlers	13
8.	Waite Hoyt	12
	Catfish Hunter	12
	Art Nehf	12
11.	Paul Derringer	11
	Carl Erskine	11
	Rube Marquard	11
	Christy Mathewson	11
	Vic Raschi	11
	Mike Stanton	11
17.	Chief Bender	10
	Pedro Borbon	10
	Don Gullett	10
	Don Larsen	10
	Herb Pennock	10
	Dan Quisenberry	10
	Red Ruffing	10
	Dave Stewart	10

GAMES STARTED

1.	Whitey Ford	22
2.	Waite Hoyt	11
	Christy Mathewson	11
4.	Chief Bender	10
	Red Ruffing	10
6.	Bob Gibson	9
	Catfish Hunter	9
	Art Nehf	9
	Allie Reynolds	9
10.	George Earnshaw	8

	Tom Glavine	8
	Rube Marquard	8
	Jim Palmer	8
	Vic Raschi	8
	John Smoltz	8
	Dave Stewart	8
	Don Sutton	8
	Bob Turley	8
17.	13 tied with 7	

GAMES RELIEVED

1.	Rollie Fingers	16
2.	Clay Carroll	14
3.	Mark Wohlers	13
4.	Clem Labine	12
5.	Mike Stanton	10
6.	Pedro Borbon	10
	Dan Quisenberry	10
	Mariano Rivera	10
9.	Paul Assenmacher	9
	Hugh Casey	9
	Tug McGraw	9
12.	Ken Dayley	8
	Rich Gossage	8
	Don McMahon	8
	Johnny Murphy	8
	Duane Ward	8
17.	11 tied with 7	

COMPLETE GAMES

1.	Christy Mathewson	10
2.	Chief Bender	9
3.	Bob Gibson	8
	Red Ruffing	8
5.	Whitey Ford	7
6.	Waite Hoyt	6
	George Mullin	6
	Art Nehf	6
	Eddie Plank	6
10.	Mordecai Brown	5
	Joe Bush	5
	Bill Donovan	5
	George Earnshaw	5
	Walter Johnson	5
	Carl Mays	5
	Deacon Phillippe	5
	Allie Reynolds	5
18.	15 tied with 4	

INNINGS PITCHED

1.	Whitey Ford	146.0
2.	Christy Mathewson	101.2
3.	Red Ruffing	85.2
4.	Chief Bender	85.0
5.	Waite Hoyt	83.2
6.	Bob Gibson	81.0
7.	Art Nehf	79.0
8.	Allie Reynolds	77.1
9.	Jim Palmer	64.2
10.	Catfish Hunter	63.0
11.	George Earnshaw	62.2
12.	Joe Bush	60.2
13.	Vic Raschi	60.1
14.	Rube Marquard	58.2
15.	Tom Glavine	58.1
16.	George Mullin	58.0
17.	Mordecai Brown	57.2
18.	Carl Mays	57.1
19.	Sandy Koufax	57.0
	Dave Stewart	57.0

LOWEST ERA

(Minimum 30 innings)

1.	Harry Brecheen	0.83
2.	Babe Ruth	0.87
3.	Sherry Smith	0.89
4.	Sandy Koufax	0.95
5.	Monte Pearson	1.01
6.	Christy Mathewson	1.06
7.	Eddie Plank	1.32
8.	Rollie Fingers	1.35
9.	Bill Hallahan	1.36
10.	George Earnshaw	1.58
11.	Spud Chandler	1.62
12.	Jesse Haines	1.67
13.	Ron Guidry	1.69
14.	Max Lanier	1.71
15.	Stan Coveleski	1.74
16.	Tom Glavine	1.75
	Lefty Grove	1.75
	Orval Overall	1.75
19.	Carl Hubbell	1.79
20.	Ernie Shore	1.82

VICTORIES

1.	Whitey Ford	10
2.	Bob Gibson	7
	Allie Reynolds	7
	Red Ruffing	7
5.	Chief Bender	6
	Lefty Gomez	6
	Waite Hoyt	6
8.	Mordecai Brown	5
	Jack Coombs	5
	Catfish Hunter	5
	Christy Mathewson	5
	Herb Pennock	5
	Vic Raschi	5
14.	19 tied with 4	

LOSSES

1.	Whitey Ford	8
2.	Joe Bush	5
	Rube Marquard	5
	Christy Mathewson	5
	Eddie Plank	5
	Schoolboy Rowe	5
7.	Chief Bender	4
	Mordecai Brown	4
	Paul Derringer	4
	Bill Donovan	4
	Burleigh Grimes	4
	Waite Hoyt	4
	Charlie Leibrandt	4
	Carl Mays	4
	Art Nehf	4
	Don Newcombe	4
	Bill Sherdel	4
	Dave Stewart	4
	Ed Summers	4
	Ralph Terry	4

SAVES

1.	Rollie Fingers	6
2.	Mariano Rivera	5
3.	Johnny Murphy	4
	Allie Reynolds	4
	John Wetteland	4
6.	Roy Face	3
	Firpo Marberry	3
	Will McEnaney	3
	Tug McGraw	3
	Herb Pennock	3
	Kent Tekulve	3
	Todd Worrell	3
13.	20 tied with 2	

RUNS ALLOWED

1.	Whitey Ford	51
2.	Red Ruffing	32
	Don Sutton	32
4.	Chief Bender	28
	Carl Erskine	28
	Burleigh Grimes	28
	Waite Hoyt	28
	Rube Marquard	28
9.	Mordecai Brown	26
	Paul Derringer	26
11.	Allie Reynolds	25
	Bob Shawkey	25
	Dave Stewart	25
14.	Catfish Hunter	24
15.	Don Gullett	23
	Art Nehf	23
	Jim Palmer	23
	Schoolboy Rowe	23
19.	Tommy Bridges	22
	Christy Mathewson	22
	George Mullin	22

HITS ALLOWED

1.	Whitey Ford	132
2.	Waite Hoyt	81

3.	Christy Mathewson	76
4.	Red Ruffing	74
5.	Chief Bender	64
6.	Allie Reynolds	61
7.	Catfish Hunter	57
8.	Walter Johnson	56
9.	Bob Gibson	55
	Jim Palmer	55
	Don Sutton	55
12.	Tommy Bridges	52
	Rube Marquard	52
	Vic Raschi	52
15.	Lefty Gomez	51
	Ed Lopat	51
17.	Mordecai Brown	50
	Art Nehf	50
	Schoolboy Rowe	50
20.	Joe Bush	49
	Burleigh Grimes	49

HOME RUNS ALLOWED

1.	Catfish Hunter	9
2.	Don Drysdale	8
	Whitey Ford	8
	Burleigh Grimes	8
	Don Newcombe	8
	Gary Nolan	8
	Allie Reynolds	8
	Charlie Root	8
9.	Don Sutton	7
10.	Lew Burdette	6
	Roger Craig	6
	Bob Gibson	6
	Bob Turley	6
14.	15 tied with 5	

TOTAL BASES ALLOWED

1.	Whitey Ford	184
2.	Christy Mathewson	105
	Allie Reynolds	105
4.	Red Ruffing	104
5.	Waite Hoyt	102
6.	Catfish Hunter	94
7.	Chief Bender	91
8.	Don Sutton	88
9.	Burleigh Grimes	87
10.	Bob Gibson	86
	Rube Marquard	86
12.	Walter Johnson	85
13.	Jim Palmer	82
14.	Vic Raschi	79
15.	Tommy Bridges	78
16.	Schoolboy Rowe	73
	Warren Spahn	73
18.	Jack Morris	70
19.	Ralph Terry	69
20.	4 tied with 68	

STRIKEOUTS

1.	Whitey Ford	94
2.	Bob Gibson	92
3.	Allie Reynolds	62
4.	Sandy Koufax	61
	Red Ruffing	61
6.	Chief Bender	59
7.	George Earnshaw	56
8.	John Smoltz	52
9.	Waite Hoyt	49
10.	Christy Mathewson	48
11.	Bob Turley	46
12.	Jim Palmer	44
13.	Vic Raschi	43
14.	Jack Morris	40
15.	Don Gullett	37
16.	Don Drysdale	36
	Lefty Grove	36
	George Mullin	36
19.	8 tied with 35	

WALKS

1.	Whitey Ford	34
2.	Art Nehf	32
	Allie Reynolds	32
4.	Jim Palmer	31
5.	Bob Turley	29
6.	Paul Derringer	27
	Red Ruffing	27
8.	Burleigh Grimes	26
	Don Gullett	26
10.	Vic Raschi	25
11.	Carl Erskine	24
12.	Bill Hallahan	23
	Dave Stewart	23
14.	Waite Hoyt	22
15.	Chief Bender	21
	Jack Coombs	21
	John Smoltz	21
18.	Joe Bush	20
	Tom Glavine	20
20.	Don Larsen	19
	Dave McNally	19
	Hal Schumacher	19

SERVICE

GAMES SELECTED, PLAYER

1.	Hank Aaron	25
2.	Willie Mays	24
	Stan Musial	24
4.	Mickey Mantle	20
5.	Ted Williams	19
6.	Yogi Berra	18
	Rod Carew	18
	Al Kaline	18
	Brooks Robinson	18
	Carl Yastrzemski	18
11.	Cal Ripken	17
	Pete Rose	17
	Warren Spahn	17
14.	Roberto Clemente	15
	Nellie Fox	15
	Tony Gwynn	15
	Ozzie Smith	15
18.	Ernie Banks	14
	Johnny Bench	14
	Reggie Jackson	14
	Frank Robinson	14

GAMES SELECTED, PITCHER

1.	Warren Spahn	17
2.	Tom Seaver	12
3.	Steve Carlton	10
	Don Drysdale	10
	Whitey Ford	10
	Juan Marichal	10
7.	Jim Bunning	9
	Bob Gibson	9
	Rich Gossage	9
	Carl Hubbell	9
	Early Wynn	9
12.	Bob Feller	8
	Catfish Hunter	8
	Sandy Koufax	8
	Nolan Ryan	8
	Hoyt Wilhelm	8
17.	11 tied with 7	

BATTING

GAMES

1.	Hank Aaron	24
	Willie Mays	24
	Stan Musial	24
4.	Brooks Robinson	18
	Ted Williams	18
6.	Cal Ripken	17
7.	Al Kaline	16
	Mickey Mantle	16
	Pete Rose	16
10.	Yogi Berra	15
	Rod Carew	15
12.	Roberto Clemente	14
	Ozzie Smith	14
	Carl Yastrzemski	14
15.	Ernie Banks	13
	Nellie Fox	13
	Tony Gwynn	13
18.	Johnny Bench	12
	Wade Boggs	12
	Reggie Jackson	12
	Dave Winfield	12

HIGHEST AVERAGE

(Minimum 10 at-bats)

1.	Richie Ashburn	.600
2.	Charley Gehringer	.500
	Ted Kluszewski	.500
4.	Al Simmons	.462
5.	Joe Carter	.455
	Leon Wagner	.455
7.	Ken Griffey Jr.	.435
8.	Billy Herman	.433
9.	Bill Skowron	.429
10.	Sandy Alomar Jr.	.417
11.	Stan Hack	.400
	Andy Pafko	.400
	Bill Terry	.400
14.	Steve Garvey	.393
15.	Bobby Bonilla	.385
	Will Clark	.385
	Ernie Lombardi	.385
18.	Enos Slaughter	.381
19.	Nellie Fox	.368
20.	Kenny Lofton	.364
	Arky Vaughan	.364

AT-BATS

1.	Willie Mays	75
2.	Hank Aaron	67
3.	Stan Musial	63
4.	Cal Ripken	47
5.	Ted Williams	46
6.	Brooks Robinson	45
7.	Mickey Mantle	43
8.	Yogi Berra	41
	Rod Carew	41
10.	Joe DiMaggio	40
11.	Nellie Fox	38
12.	Al Kaline	37
13.	Dave Winfield	36
14.	Carl Yastrzemski	34
15.	Ernie Banks	33
	Pete Rose	33
17.	Roberto Clemente	31
18.	Billy Herman	30
19.	Tony Gwynn	29
20.	4 tied with 28	

RUNS SCORED

1.	Willie Mays	20
2.	Stan Musial	11
3.	Ted Williams	10
4.	Rod Carew	8
5.	Hank Aaron	7
	Joe DiMaggio	7
	Nellie Fox	7
	Steve Garvey	7
	Al Kaline	7
	Joe Morgan	7
	Jackie Robinson	7
12.	Dave Winfield	6
13.	Roberto Alomar	5
	Johnny Bench	5
	Yogi Berra	5
	George Brett	5
	Fred Lynn	5
	Mickey Mantle	5
	Brooks Robinson	5
	Arky Vaughan	5

HITS

1.	Willie Mays	23
2.	Stan Musial	20
3.	Nellie Fox	14
	Ted Williams	14
5.	Hank Aaron	13
	Billy Herman	13
	Brooks Robinson	13
	Dave Winfield	13
9.	Al Kaline	12
	Cal Ripken	12
11.	Steve Garvey	11
12.	Ernie Banks	10
	Johnny Bench	10
	Rod Carew	10
	Roberto Clemente	10
	Charley Gehringer	10
	Ken Griffey Jr.	10
	Mickey Mantle	10
	Carl Yastrzemski	10
20.	Wade Boggs	9
	Joe DiMaggio	9

SINGLES

1.	Willie Mays	15
2.	Nellie Fox	14
3.	Stan Musial	12
4.	Hank Aaron	11
	Billy Herman	11
6.	Al Kaline	9
	Brooks Robinson	9
8.	Wade Boggs	8
	Charley Gehringer	8
	Mickey Mantle	8
	Cal Ripken	8
12.	Johnny Bench	7
	Yogi Berra	7
	Rod Carew	7
	Ken Griffey Jr.	7
	Rickey Henderson	7
	Ted Williams	7
	Carl Yastrzemski	7
19.	7 tied with 6	

DOUBLES

1.	Dave Winfield	7
2.	Ernie Banks	3
	Barry Bonds	3
	Joe Cronin	3
	Joe Gordon	3
	Ted Kluszewski	3
	Tony Oliva	3
	Al Oliver	3
	Cal Ripken	3
	Al Simmons	3
11.	21 tied with 2	

TRIPLES

1.	Willie Mays	3
	Brooks Robinson	3
3.	Rod Carew	2
	Steve Garvey	2
5.	26 tied with 1	

HOME RUNS

1.	Stan Musial	6
2.	Fred Lynn	4
	Ted Williams	4
4.	Johnny Bench	3
	Gary Carter	3
	Rocky Colavito	3
	Harmon Killebrew	3
	Ralph Kiner	3
	Willie Mays	3
10.	Hank Aaron	2
	Roberto Alomar	2
	Ken Boyer	2
	Frankie Frisch	2
	Steve Garvey	2
	Lou Gehrig	2
	Al Kaline	2
	Mickey Mantle	2
	Eddie Mathews	2
	Willie McCovey	2
	Mike Piazza	2
	Frank Robinson	2
	Al Rosen	2
	Arky Vaughan	2

TOTAL BASES

1.	Willie Mays	40
	Stan Musial	40
3.	Ted Williams	30
4.	Steve Garvey	23
5.	Brooks Robinson	22
6.	Dave Winfield	20
7.	Hank Aaron	19
	Johnny Bench	19
	Al Kaline	19
10.	Ernie Banks	18
	Fred Lynn	18
	Cal Ripken	18
13.	Roberto Clemente	17
	Harmon Killebrew	17
15.	Rocky Colavito	16
	Mickey Mantle	16
17.	Rod Carew	15
	Gary Carter	15
	Ken Griffey Jr.	15
	Billy Herman	15
	Arky Vaughan	15
	Carl Yastrzemski	15

SLUGGING PERCENTAGE

(Minimum 10 at-bats)

1.	Ralph Kiner	.933
2.	Ted Kluszewski	.929
3.	Fred Lynn	.900
4.	Steve Garvey	.821
5.	Al Rosen	.818
6.	Gary Carter	.750
7.	George Foster	.727
	Leon Wagner	.727
9.	Mike Piazza	.706
10.	Richie Ashburn	.700
	Larry Doby	.700
12.	Al Simmons	.692
13.	Arky Vaughan	.682
14.	Johnny Bench	.679
15.	Sandy Alomar Jr.	.667
	Mike Schmidt	.667
17.	Harmon Killebrew	.654
18.	Ken Griffey Jr.	.652
	Ted Williams	.652
20.	Rocky Colavito	.640

EXTRA-BASE HITS

1.	Willie Mays	8
	Stan Musial	8
3.	Ted Williams	7
	Dave Winfield	7
5.	Steve Garvey	6
6.	Ernie Banks	5
7.	Barry Bonds	4
	George Brett	4
	Roberto Clemente	4
	Rocky Colavito	4
	Ralph Kiner	4
	Ted Kluszewski	4
	Fred Lynn	4
	Cal Ripken	4
	Brooks Robinson	4
	Mike Schmidt	4
17.	21 tied with 3	

RUNS BATTED IN

1.	Ted Williams	12
2.	Fred Lynn	10
	Stan Musial	10
4.	Willie Mays	9
5.	Hank Aaron	8
	Rocky Colavito	8
7.	Steve Garvey	7
	Cal Ripken	7
9.	Johnny Bench	6
	Joe DiMaggio	6
	Al Kaline	6
	Harmon Killebrew	6
	Joe Medwick	6
14.	Barry Bonds	5
	George Brett	5
	Gary Carter	5
	George Foster	5
	Nellie Fox	5
	Lou Gehrig	5
	Ken Griffey Jr.	5
	Dick Groat	5
	Brooks Robinson	5
	Al Rosen	5
	Dave Winfield	5
	Carl Yastrzemski	5

Yankees All-Star Lefty Gomez.

WALKS

1.	Ted Williams	11
2.	Charley Gehringer	9
	Mickey Mantle	9
4.	Rod Carew	7
	Willie Mays	7
	Stan Musial	7
7.	Lou Gehrig	6
8.	Ron Santo	5
9.	Wade Boggs	4
	George Brett	4
	Bill Dickey	4
	Reggie Jackson	4
	Joe Morgan	4
	Enos Slaughter	4
	Carl Yastrzemski	4
16.	21 tied with 3	

STRIKEOUTS

1.	Mickey Mantle	17
2.	Willie Mays	14
3.	Ted Williams	10
4.	Roberto Clemente	9
	Reggie Jackson	9
	Mark McGwire	9
	Ryne Sandberg	9
8.	Hank Aaron	8
	Ernie Banks	8
	Joe Gordon	8
	Jim Rice	8
	Carl Yastrzemski	8
13.	Dick Allen	7
	Carlton Fisk	7
	Jimmie Foxx	7
	Elston Howard	7
	Stan Musial	7
	Frank Robinson	7
19.	11 tied with 6	

STOLEN BASES

1.	Willie Mays	6
2.	Roberto Alomar	5
	Kenny Lofton	5
4.	Rod Carew	3
	Steve Sax	3
6.	Hank Aaron	2
	Lou Brock	2
	Charley Gehringer	2
	Kelly Gruber	2
	Rickey Henderson	2
	Tim Raines	2
	Ozzie Smith	2
	Darryl Strawberry	2
14.	51 tied with 1	

PITCHING

GAMES

1.	Jim Bunning	8
	Don Drysdale	8
	Juan Marichal	8
	Tom Seaver	8
5.	Warren Spahn	7
	Dave Stieb	7
	Early Wynn	7
8.	Ewell Blackwell	6
	Roger Clemens	6
	Dennis Eckersley	6
	Whitey Ford	6
	Bob Gibson	6
	Rich Gossage	6
	Catfish Hunter	6
15.	14 tied with 5	

GAMES STARTED

1.	Don Drysdale	5
	Lefty Gomez	5
	Robin Roberts	5
4.	Jim Palmer	4
5.	Vida Blue	3
	Jim Bunning	3
	Whitey Ford	3
	Greg Maddux	3
	Jack Morris	3
	Billy Pierce	3
	Warren Spahn	3
12.	Steve Carlton	2
	Dean Chance	2
	Mort Cooper	2
	Dizzy Dean	2
	Paul Derringer	2
	Bob Feller	2
	Bob Friend	2
	Tom Glavine	2
	Dwight Gooden	2
	Randy Johnson	2
	Juan Marichal	2
	Vic Raschi	2
	Red Ruffing	2
	Curt Simmons	2
	Dave Stieb	2

GAMES RELIEVED

1.	Tom Seaver	7
2.	Rich Gossage	6
	Juan Marichal	6
	Early Wynn	6
5.	Ewell Blackwell	5
	Jim Bunning	5
	Roger Clemens	5
	David Cone	5
	Dennis Eckersley	5
	Rollie Fingers	5
	Bob Gibson	5
	Catfish Hunter	5
	Dave Stieb	5
14.	17 tied with 4	

INNINGS PITCHED

1.	Don Drysdale	19.1
2.	Jim Bunning	18.0
	Lefty Gomez	18.0
	Juan Marichal	18.0
5.	Robin Roberts	14.0
	Warren Spahn	14.0
7.	Ewell Blackwell	13.2
8.	Mel Harder	13.0
	Tom Seaver	13.0
10.	Catfish Hunter	12.2
	Jim Palmer	12.2
12.	Bob Feller	12.1
	Early Wynn	12.1
14.	Whitey Ford	12.0
15.	Dave Stieb	11.2
16.	Bob Gibson	11.0
	Vic Raschi	11.0
18.	Jack Morris	10.2
	Hal Newhouser	10.2
	Billy Pierce	10.2

1941 All-Star Game hero Ted Williams (left) gets a victory hug from American League manager Del Baker.

LOWEST ERA
(Minimum 9 innings)

1.	Juan Marichal	0.50
2.	Mel Harder	0.69
3.	Bob Feller	0.73
4.	Dave Stieb	0.77
5.	Jim Bunning	1.00
6.	Ewell Blackwell	1.32
7.	Don Drysdale	1.40
8.	Hal Newhouser	1.69
9.	Bucky Walters	2.00
10.	Vic Raschi	2.45
11.	Lefty Gomez	2.50
12.	Jack Morris	2.53
13.	Dizzy Dean	2.70
14.	Carl Hubbell	2.79
15.	Early Wynn	2.92
16.	Warren Spahn	3.21
17.	Bob Gibson	3.27
18.	Billy Pierce	3.38
19.	Nolan Ryan	4.50
20.	Tom Seaver	4.85

VICTORIES

1.	Lefty Gomez	3
2.	Vida Blue	2
	Don Drysdale	2
	Bob Friend	2
	Juan Marichal	2
	Bruce Sutter	2
7.	56 tied with 1	

LOSSES

1.	Mort Cooper	2
	Whitey Ford	2
	Dwight Gooden	2
	Catfish Hunter	2
	Claude Passeau	2
	Luis Tiant	2
7.	57 tied with 1	

SAVES

1.	Dennis Eckersley	3
2.	Mel Harder	2
3.	35 tied with 1	

RUNS ALLOWED

1.	Whitey Ford	13
2.	Robin Roberts	10
	Warren Spahn	10
4.	Tom Glavine	9
	Catfish Hunter	9
6.	Vida Blue	8
	Jim Palmer	8
	Tom Seaver	8
9.	Mort Cooper	7
	Rich Gossage	7
	Atlee Hammaker	7
	Claude Passeau	7
13.	Roy Face	6
	Lefty Gomez	6
	Tex Hughson	6
	Van Mungo	6
	Gaylord Perry	6
	Red Ruffing	6
19.	8 tied with 5	

HITS ALLOWED

1.	Whitey Ford	19
2.	Robin Roberts	17
	Warren Spahn	17
4.	Tom Glavine	15
	Catfish Hunter	15
6.	Jack Morris	14
	Gaylord Perry	14
	Tom Seaver	14
9.	Red Ruffing	13
10.	Vida Blue	12
11.	Bob Gibson	11
	Lefty Gomez	11
	Jim Palmer	11
14.	Dizzy Dean	10
	Don Drysdale	10
	Lefty Grove	10
	Tex Hughson	10
	Nolan Ryan	10
	Bucky Walters	10
	Lon Warneke	10

HOME RUNS ALLOWED

1.	Vida Blue	4
	Catfish Hunter	4

3.	Steve Carlton	3
	Mort Cooper	3
	Whitey Ford	3
	Jim Palmer	3
	Milt Pappas	3
	Robin Roberts	3
	Tom Seaver	3
10.	20 tied with 2	

STRIKEOUTS

1.	Don Drysdale	19
2.	Tom Seaver	16
3.	Jim Palmer	14
4.	Jim Bunning	13
	Bob Feller	13
	Catfish Hunter	13
7.	Ewell Blackwell	12
	Juan Marichal	12
	Sam McDowell	12
	Billy Pierce	12
11.	Carl Hubbell	11
	Johnny Vander Meer	11
13.	Dizzy Dean	10
	Bob Gibson	10
	Dick Radatz	10
	Nolan Ryan	10
	Warren Spahn	10
	Dave Stieb	10
19.	4 tied with 9	

WALKS

1.	Jim Palmer	7
2.	Carl Hubbell	6
	Robin Roberts	6
	Dave Stieb	6
	Lon Warneke	6
6.	Ewell Blackwell	5
	Steve Carlton	5
	Dizzy Dean	5
	Bob Gibson	5
	Bill Hallahan	5
	Nolan Ryan	5
	Warren Spahn	5
13.	16 tied with 4	

FOR THE RECORD

SINGLE SEASON

REGULAR SEASON (1876-1900)

BATTING

*HIGHEST AVERAGE

1.	Hugh Duffy, Boston N.L., 1894	.440
2.	Tip O'Neill, St. Louis A.A., 1887	.435
3.	Ross Barnes, Chicago N.L., 1876	.429
4.	Willie Keeler, Baltimore N.L., 1897	.424
5.	Fred Dunlap, St. Louis U.A., 1884	.412
6.	Ed Delahanty, Philadelphia N.L., 1899	.410
	Jesse Burkett, Cleveland N.L., 1896	.410
8.	Jesse Burkett, Cleveland N.L., 1895	.409
9.	Sam Thompson, Philadelphia N.L., 1894	.407
	Ed Delahanty, Philadelphia N.L., 1894	.407
11.	Billy Hamilton, Philadelphia N.L., 1894	.404
	Ed Delahanty, Philadelphia N.L., 1895	.404
13.	Pete Browning, Louisville A.A., 1887	.402
14.	Hughie Jennings, Baltimore N.L., 1896	.401
15.	Cap Anson, Chicago N.L., 1881	.399
16.	Ed Delahanty, Philadelphia N.L., 1896	.397
17.	Jesse Burkett, St. Louis N.L., 1899	.396
18.	Joe Kelley, Baltimore N.L., 1894	.393
19.	Sam Thompson, Philadelphia N.L., 1895	.392
20.	John McGraw, Baltimore N.L., 1899	.391

*Based on players averaging at least 3.1 at-bats for every game played by their teams.

RUNS SCORED

1.	Billy Hamilton, Philadelphia N.L., 1894	192
2.	Tom Brown, Boston A.A., 1891	177
3.	Tip O'Neill, St. Louis A.A., 1887	167
4.	Billy Hamilton, Philadelphia N.L., 1895	166
5.	Willie Keeler, Baltimore N.L., 1894	165
	Joe Kelley, Baltimore N.L., 1894	165
7.	Arlie Latham, St. Louis A.A., 1887	163
8.	Willie Keeler, Baltimore N.L., 1895	162
9.	Hugh Duffy, Chicago P.L., 1890	161
10.	Jesse Burkett, Cleveland N.L., 1896	160
	Hugh Duffy, Boston N.L., 1894	160
	Fred Dunlap, St. Louis U.A., 1884	160
13.	Hughie Jennings, Baltimore N.L., 1895	159
14.	Bobby Lowe, Boston N.L., 1894	158
15.	John McGraw, Baltimore N.L., 1894	156
16.	King Kelly, Chicago N.L., 1886	155
17.	Dan Brouthers, Detroit N.L., 1887	153
	Jesse Burkett, Cleveland N.L., 1895	153
	Billy Hamilton, Boston N.L., 1896	153
	Willie Keeler, Baltimore N.L., 1896	153

HITS

1.	Jesse Burkett, Cleveland N.L., 1896	240
2.	Willie Keeler, Baltimore N.L., 1897	239
3.	Ed Delahanty, Philadelphia N.L., 1899	238
4.	Hugh Duffy, Boston N.L., 1894	237
5.	Jesse Burkett, Cleveland N.L., 1895	225
	Tip O'Neill, St. Louis A.A., 1887	225
7.	Sam Thompson, Philadelphia N.L., 1893	222
8.	Jesse Burkett, St. Louis N.L., 1899	221
9.	Pete Browning, Louisville A.A., 1887	220
	Billy Hamilton, Philadelphia N.L., 1894	220
11.	Ed Delahanty, Philadelphia N.L., 1893	219
	Willie Keeler, Baltimore N.L., 1894	219
	Jimmy Williams, Pittsburgh N.L., 1899	219
14.	Willie Keeler, Baltimore N.L., 1898	216
	Willie Keeler, Brooklyn N.L., 1899	216
16.	Jesse Burkett, Cleveland N.L., 1898	213
	Willie Keeler, Baltimore N.L., 1895	213
18.	Bobby Lowe, Boston N.L., 1894	212
19.	Sam Thompson, Philadelphia N.L., 1895	211
20.	Steve Brodie, Baltimore N.L., 1894	210
	Willie Keeler, Baltimore N.L., 1896	210

HOME RUNS

1.	Ned Williamson, Chicago N.L., 1884	27
2.	Buck Freeman, Washington N.L., 1899	25
	Fred Pfeffer, Chicago N.L., 1884	25
4.	Abner Dalrymple, Chicago N.L., 1884	22
5.	Cap Anson, Chicago N.L., 1884	21
6.	Sam Thompson, Philadelphia N.L., 1889	20
7.	Ed Delahanty, Philadelphia N.L., 1893	19
	Bug Holliday, Cincinnati A.A., 1889	19
	Billy O'Brien, Washington N.L., 1887	19
	Harry Stovey, Philadelphia A.A., 1889	19
11.	Jerry Denny, Indianapolis N.L., 1889	18
	Hugh Duffy, Boston N.L., 1894	18
	Sam Thompson, Philadelphia N.L., 1895	18
14.	Jack Clements, Philadelphia N.L., 1893	17
	Roger Connor, New York N.L., 1887	17
	Bill Joyce, Washington N.L., 1894	17
	Bill Joyce, Washington N.L., 1895	17
	Bobby Lowe, Boston N.L., 1894	17
	Jimmy Ryan, Chicago N.L., 1889	17
20.	5 tied with 16	

TOTAL BASES

1.	Hugh Duffy, Boston N.L., 1894	374
2.	Tip O'Neill, St. Louis A.A., 1887	357
3.	Sam Thompson, Philadelphia N.L., 1895	352
4.	Ed Delahanty, Philadelphia N.L., 1893	347
5.	Ed Delahanty, Philadelphia N.L., 1899	338
6.	Buck Freeman, Washington N.L., 1899	331
7.	Jimmy Williams, Pittsburgh N.L., 1899	328
8.	Bobby Lowe, Boston N.L., 1894	319
9.	Sam Thompson, Philadelphia N.L., 1893	318
10.	Jesse Burkett, Cleveland N.L., 1896	317
11.	Ed Delahanty, Philadelphia N.L., 1896	315
12.	Sam Thompson, Detroit N.L., 1887	311
13.	Nap Lajoie, Philadelphia N.L., 1897	310
14.	Willie Keeler, Baltimore N.L., 1894	305
	Joe Kelley, Baltimore N.L., 1894	305
16.	George Davis, New York N.L., 1893	304
	Willie Keeler, Baltimore N.L., 1897	304
18.	Jake Stenzel, Pittsburgh N.L., 1894	303
19.	Honus Wagner, Pittsburgh N.L., 1900	302
20.	Dave Orr, New York A.A., 1886	301

EXTRA-BASE HITS

1.	Hugh Duffy, Boston N.L., 1894	85
	Tip O'Neill, St. Louis A.A., 1887	85
3.	Sam Thompson, Philadelphia N.L., 1895	84
4.	Ed Delahanty, Philadelphia N.L., 1896	74
	Joe Kelley, Baltimore N.L., 1894	74
6.	Ed Delahanty, Philadelphia N.L., 1899	73
7.	Ed Delahanty, Philadelphia N.L., 1893	72
	Nap Lajoie, Philadelphia N.L., 1897	72
	Jake Stenzel, Pittsburgh N.L., 1894	72
10.	Dan Brouthers, Baltimore N.L., 1894	71
	Honus Wagner, Pittsburgh N.L., 1900	71
12.	Ed Delahanty, Philadelphia N.L., 1895	70
	Harry Stovey, Philadelphia A.A., 1889	70
14.	Jake Beckley, Pittsburgh P.L., 1890	69
	Buck Freeman, Washington N.L., 1899	69
	Sam Thompson, Philadelphia N.L., 1894	69
17.	Dan Brouthers, Detroit N.L., 1887	68
	Roger Connor, New York-St. Louis N.L., 1894	68
19.	Harry Stovey, Boston N.L., 1891	67
20.	Dan Brouthers, Detroit N.L., 1886	66

RUNS BATTED IN

1.	Sam Thompson, Detroit N.L., 1887	166
2.	Sam Thompson, Philadelphia N.L., 1895	165
3.	Cap Anson, Chicago N.L., 1886	147
4.	Ed Delahanty, Philadelphia N.L., 1893	146
	Hardy Richardson, Boston P.L., 1890	146
6.	Hugh Duffy, Boston N.L., 1894	145
7.	Sam Thompson, Philadelphia N.L., 1894	141
8.	Ed Delahanty, Philadelphia N.L., 1899	137
9.	George Davis, New York N.L., 1897	136
10.	Steve Brodie, Baltimore N.L., 1895	134
	Joe Kelley, Baltimore N.L., 1895	134
12.	Ed McKean, Cleveland N.L., 1893	133
13.	Jimmy Collins, Boston N.L., 1897	132
14.	Ed Delahanty, Philadelphia N.L., 1894	131
15.	Roger Connor, New York N.L., 1889	130
	Walt Wilmot, Chicago N.L., 1894	130
17.	Hugh Duffy, Boston N.L., 1897	129
18.	Dan Brouthers, Baltimore N.L., 1894	128
	Oyster Burns, Brooklyn N.L., 1890	128
	Ed McKean, Cleveland N.L., 1894	128

STOLEN BASES

1.	Hugh Nicol, Cincinnati A.A., 1887	138
2.	Arlie Latham, St. Louis A.A., 1887	129
3.	Charlie Comiskey, St. Louis A.A., 1887	117
4.	Billy Hamilton, Kansas City A.A., 1889	111
	Billy Hamilton, Philadelphia N.L., 1891	111
	John Ward, New York N.L., 1887	111
7.	Arlie Latham, St. Louis A.A., 1888	109
8.	Tom Brown, Boston A.A., 1891	106
9.	Pete Browning, Louisville A.A., 1887	103
	Hugh Nicol, Cincinnati A.A., 1888	103
11.	Jim Fogarty, Philadelphia N.L., 1887	102
	Billy Hamilton, Philadelphia N.L., 1890	102
13.	Jim Fogarty, Philadelphia N.L., 1889	99
14.	Billy Hamilton, Philadelphia N.L., 1894	98
15.	Billy Hamilton, Philadelphia N.L., 1895	97
	Harry Stovey, Boston P.L., 1890	97
17.	Bid McPhee, Cincinnati A.A., 1887	95
	Curt Welch, Philadelphia A.A., 1888	95
19.	Mike Griffin, Baltimore A.A., 1887	94
20.	Tommy McCarthy, St. Louis A.A., 1888	93

PITCHING

COMPLETE GAMES

1.	Will White, Cincinnati N.L., 1879	75
2.	Charley Radbourn, Providence N.L., 1884	73
3.	Pud Galvin, Buffalo N.L., 1883	72
	Guy Hecker, Louisville A.A., 1884	72
	Jim McCormick, Cleveland N.L., 1880	72
6.	Pud Galvin, Buffalo N.L., 1884	71
7.	John Clarkson, Chicago N.L., 1885	68
	John Clarkson, Boston N.L., 1889	68
	Tim Keefe, New York A.A., 1883	68
10.	Bill Hutchison, Chicago N.L., 1892	67
11.	Jim Devlin, Louisville N.L., 1876	66
	Matt Kilroy, Baltimore A.A., 1886	66
	Matt Kilroy, Baltimore A.A., 1887	66
	Charles Radbourn, Providence N.L., 1883	66
	Toad Ramsey, Louisville A.A., 1886	66
16.	Pud Galvin, Buffalo N.L., 1879	65
	Bill Hutchison, Chicago N.L., 1890	65
	Jim McCormick, Cleveland N.L., 1882	65
19.	Silver King, St. Louis A.A., 1888	64
	Tony Mullane, Toledo A.A., 1884	64
	Mickey Welch, Troy N.L., 1880	64
	Will White, Cincinnati A.A., 1883	64

INNINGS PITCHED

1.	Will White, Cincinnati N.L., 1879	680.0
2.	Charles Radbourn, Providence N.L., 1884	678.2
3.	Guy Hecker, Louisville A.A., 1884	670.2
4.	Jim McCormick, Cleveland N.L., 1880	657.2
5.	Pud Galvin, Buffalo N.L., 1883	656.1
6.	Pud Galvin, Buffalo N.L., 1884	636.1
7.	Charley Radbourn, Providence N.L., 1883	632.1
8.	John Clarkson, Chicago N.L., 1885	623.0
9.	Jim Devlin, Louisville N.L., 1876	622.0
	Bill Hutchison, Chicago N.L., 1892	622.0
11.	John Clarkson, Boston N.L., 1889	620.0
12.	Tim Keefe, New York A.A., 1883	619.0
13.	Bill Hutchison, Chicago N.L., 1890	603.0
14.	Jim McCormick, Cleveland N.L., 1882	595.2
	John Ward, Providence N.L., 1880	595.0
16.	Pud Galvin, Buffalo N.L., 1879	593.0
17.	Lee Richmond, Worchester N.L., 1880	590.2
18.	Matt Kilroy, Baltimore A.A., 1887	589.1
19.	Toad Ramsey, Louisville A.A., 1886	588.2
20.	Charlie Buffinton, Boston N.L., 1884	587.0
	John Ward, Providence N.L., 1879	587.0

*LOWEST ERA

1.	Tim Keefe, Troy N.L., 1880	0.86
2.	Denny Driscoll, Pittsburgh A.A., 1882	1.21
3.	George Bradley, St. Louis N.L., 1876	1.23
4.	Guy Hecker, Louisville A.A., 1882	1.30
5.	George Bradley, Providence N.L., 1880	1.38
	Charles Radbourn, Providence N.L., 1884	1.38
7.	John Ward, Providence N.L., 1878	1.51
8.	Harry McCormick, Cincinnati A.A., 1882	1.52
9.	Will White, Cincinnati A.A., 1882	1.54
10.	Jim Devlin, Louisville N.L., 1876	1.56
11.	Tim Keefe, New York N.L., 1885	1.58
12.	Silver King, St. Louis A.A., 1888	1.64
13.	Mickey Welch, New York N.L., 1885	1.66
14.	Candy Cummings, Hartford N.L., 1876	1.67
15.	Tommy Bond, Hartford N.L., 1876	1.68
16.	Jim McCormick, Indianapolis N.L., 1878	1.69
17.	Charlie Sweeney, Prov. N.L.-St.L. U.A., 1884	1.70
18.	John Ward, Providence N.L., 1880	1.74
	Henry Boyle, St. Louis U.A., 1884	1.74
	Tim Keefe, New York N.L., 1888	1.74

*Leaders based on pitchers whose total innings equal or surpass total games played by their teams.

VICTORIES

1.	Charley Radbourn, Providence N.L., 1884	59
2.	John Clarkson, Chicago N.L., 1885	53
3.	Guy Hecker, Louisville A.A., 1884	52
4.	John Clarkson, Boston N.L., 1889	49
5.	Charlie Buffinton, Boston N.L., 1884	48
	Charles Radbourn, Providence N.L., 1883	48
7.	Al Spalding, Chicago N.L., 1876	47
	John Ward, Providence N.L., 1879	47
9.	Pud Galvin, Buffalo N.L., 1883	46
	Pud Galvin, Buffalo N.L., 1884	46
	Matt Kilroy, Baltimore A.A., 1887	46
12.	George Bradley, St. Louis N.L., 1876	45
	Silver King, St. Louis A.A., 1888	45
	Jim McCormick, Cleveland N.L., 1880	45
15.	Bill Hutchison, Chicago N.L., 1891	44
	Mickey Welch, New York N.L., 1885	44
17.	5 tied with 43	

LOSSES

1.	John Coleman, Philadelphia N.L., 1883	48
2.	Will White, Cincinnati N.L., 1880	42
3.	Larry McKeon, Indianapolis A.A., 1884	41
4.	George Bradley, Troy N.L., 1879	40
	Jim McCormick, Cleveland N.L., 1879	40
6.	Kid Carsey, Washington A.A., 1891	37
	George Cobb, Baltimore N.L., 1892	37
	Henry Porter, Kansas City A.A., 1888	37
9.	Bill Hutchison, Chicago N.L., 1892	36
	Stump Wiedman, Kansas City N.L., 1886	36
11.	Jim Devlin, Louisville N.L., 1876	35

Red Donahue, St. Louis N.L., 1897		35
Pud Galvin, Buffalo N.L., 1880		35
Hardie Henderson, Baltimore A.A., 1885		35
Fleury Sullivan, Pittsburgh A.A., 1884		35
Adonis Terry, Brooklyn A.A., 1884		35
17. Mark Baldwin, Colorado A.A., 1889		34
Bob Barr, Wash.-Ind. A.A., 1884		34
Matt Kilroy, Baltimore A.A., 1886		34
Bobby Mathews, New York N.L., 1876		34
Al Mays, New York A.A., 1887		34
Amos Rusie, New York N.L., 1890		34

SHUTOUTS

1. George Bradley, St. Louis N.L., 1876 ... 16
2. Pud Galvin, Buffalo N.L., 1884 ... 12
   Ed Morris, Pittsburgh A.A., 1886 ... 12
4. Tommy Bond, Boston N.L., 1879 ... 11
   Dave Foutz, St. Louis A.A., 1886 ... 11

Charles Radbourn, Providence N.L., 1884 ... 11
7. John Clarkson, Chicago N.L., 1885 ... 10
   Jim McCormick, Cle. N.L.-Cin. U.A., 1884 ... 10
9. Tommy Bond, Boston N.L., 1878 ... 9
   George Derby, Detroit N.L., 1881 ... 9
   Cy Young, Cleveland N.L., 1892 ... 9
12. Charlie Buffinton, Boston N.L., 1884 ... 8
    John Clarkson, Boston N.L., 1889 ... 8
    Tim Keefe, New York N.L., 1888 ... 8
    Ben Sanders, Philadelphia N.L., 1888 ... 8
    Al Spalding, Chicago N.L., 1876 ... 8
    John Ward, Providence N.L., 1880 ... 8
    Will White, Cincinnati A.A., 1882 ... 8
19. 10 tied with 7

STRIKEOUTS

1. Matt Kilroy, Baltimore A.A., 1886 ... 513
2. Toad Ramsey, Louisville A.A., 1886 ... 499

3. Hugh Daily, Chi.-Pit.-Wash. U.A., 1884 ... 483
4. Dupee Shaw, Detroit N.L.-Boston U.A., 1884 ... 451
5. Charles Radbourn, Providence N.L., 1884 ... 441
6. Charlie Buffinton, Boston N.L., 1884 ... 417
7. Guy Hecker, Louisville A.A., 1884 ... 385
8. Bill Sweeney, Baltimore U.A., 1884 ... 374
9. Pud Galvin, Buffalo N.L., 1884 ... 369
10. Mark Baldwin, Colorado A.A., 1889 ... 368
11. Tim Keefe, New York A.A., 1883 ... 359
12. Toad Ramsey, Louisville A.A., 1887 ... 355
13. Hardie Henderson, Baltimore A.A., 1884 ... 346
14. Mickey Welch, New York N.L., 1884 ... 345
    Jim Whitney, Boston N.L., 1883 ... 345
16. Jim McCormick, Cle. N.L.-Cin. U.A., 1884 ... 343
17. Amos Rusie, New York N.L., 1890 ... 341
18. Amos Rusie, New York N.L., 1891 ... 337
    Charlie Sweeney, Prov. N.L.-St.L. U.A., 1884 ... 337
20. Tim Keefe, New York N.L., 1888 ... 335

REGULAR SEASON (1901-1999)

BATTING

TRIPLE CROWN WINNERS

Nap Lajoie, A's	1901
Ty Cobb, Tigers	1909
Rogers Hornsby, Cardinals	1922
Rogers Hornsby, Cardinals	1925
Jimmie Foxx, A's	1933
Chuck Klein, Phillies	1933
Lou Gehrig, Yankees	1934
Joe Medwick, Cardinals	1937
Ted Williams, Red Sox	1942
Ted Williams, Red Sox	1947
Mickey Mantle, Yankees	1956
Frank Robinson, Orioles	1966
Carl Yastrzemski, Red Sox	1967

*HIGHEST AVERAGE

1. Nap Lajoie, A's, 1901 ... .426
2. Rogers Hornsby, Cardinals, 1924 ... .424
3. George Sisler, Browns, 1922 ... .420
   Ty Cobb, Tigers, 1911 ... .420
5. Ty Cobb, Tigers, 1912 ... .409
6. Joe Jackson, Indians, 1911 ... .408
7. George Sisler, Browns, 1920 ... .407
8. Ted Williams, Red Sox, 1941 ... .406
9. Rogers Hornsby, Cardinals, 1925 ... .403
   Harry Heilmann, Tigers, 1923 ... .403
11. Rogers Hornsby, Cardinals, 1922 ... .401
    Bill Terry, Giants, 1930 ... .401
    Ty Cobb, Tigers, 1922 ... .401
14. Lefty O'Doul, Phillies, 1929 ... .398
    Harry Heilmann, Tigers, 1927 ... .398
16. Rogers Hornsby, Cardinals, 1921 ... .397
17. Joe Jackson, Indians, 1912 ... .395
18. Tony Gwynn, Padres, 1994 ... .394
    Harry Heilmann, Tigers, 1921 ... .394
20. Babe Ruth, Yankees, 1923 ... .393

*Based on players averaging at least 3.1 at-bats for every game played by their teams.

HIGHEST AVERAGE, ROOKIE

1. Benny Kauff, Indianapolis F.L., 1914 ... .370
2. Lloyd Waner, Pirates, 1927 ... .355
3. Kiki Cuyler, Pirates, 1924 ... .354
4. Hack Miller, Cubs, 1922 ... .352
5. Dale Alexander, Tigers, 1929 ... .343
   Ralph Garr, Braves, 1971 ... .343
7. Patsy Dougherty, Red Sox, 1902 ... .342
   Earle Combs, Yankees, 1925 ... .342
9. Ike Boone, Red Sox, 1924 ... .337
10. Paul Waner, Pirates, 1926 ... .336
11. Charlie Keller, Yankees, 1939 ... .334
    Socks Seybold, A's, 1901 ... .334
13. Richie Ashburn, Phillies, 1948 ... .333
14. Earl Averill, Indians, 1929 ... .332
15. Fred Lynn, Red Sox, 1975 ... .331
    Johnny Pesky, Red Sox, 1942 ... .331
17. Rico Carty, Braves, 1964 ... .330
    Hal Trosky, Indians, 1934 ... .330
19. Bob Meusel, Yankees, 1920 ... .328
    Johnny Frederick, Dodgers, 1929 ... .328

RUNS SCORED

1. Babe Ruth, Yankees, 1921 ... 177
2. Lou Gehrig, Yankees, 1936 ... 167
3. Lou Gehrig, Yankees, 1931 ... 163
   Babe Ruth, Yankees, 1928 ... 163
5. Chuck Klein, Phillies, 1930 ... 158
   Babe Ruth, Yankees, 1920 ... 158
   Babe Ruth, Yankees, 1927 ... 158
8. Rogers Hornsby, Cubs, 1929 ... 156
9. Kiki Cuyler, Cubs, 1930 ... 155
10. Woody English, Cubs, 1930 ... 152
    Chuck Klein, Phillies, 1932 ... 152
    Lefty O'Doul, Phillies, 1929 ... 152

Al Simmons, A's, 1930 ... 152
14. Joe DiMaggio, Yankees, 1937 ... 151
    Jimmie Foxx, A's, 1932 ... 151
    Babe Ruth, Yankees, 1923 ... 151
17. Babe Ruth, Yankees, 1930 ... 150
    Ted Williams, Red Sox, 1949 ... 150
19. Lou Gehrig, Yankees, 1927 ... 149
    Babe Ruth, Yankees, 1931 ... 149

HITS

1. George Sisler, Browns, 1920 ... 257
2. Lefty O'Doul, Phillies, 1929 ... 254
   Bill Terry, Giants, 1930 ... 254
4. Al Simmons, A's, 1925 ... 253
5. Rogers Hornsby, Cardinals, 1922 ... 250
   Chuck Klein, Phillies, 1930 ... 250
7. Ty Cobb, Tigers, 1911 ... 248
8. George Sisler, Browns, 1922 ... 246
9. Babe Herman, Dodgers, 1930 ... 241
   Heinie Manush, Browns, 1928 ... 241
11. Wade Boggs, Red Sox, 1985 ... 240
12. Rod Carew, Twins, 1977 ... 239
13. Don Mattingly, Yankees, 1986 ... 238
14. Harry Heilmann, Tigers, 1921 ... 237
    Joe Medwick, Cardinals, 1937 ... 237
    Paul Waner, Pirates, 1927 ... 237
17. Jack Tobin, Browns, 1921 ... 236
18. Rogers Hornsby, Cardinals, 1921 ... 235
19. Kirby Puckett, Twins, 1988 ... 234
    Lloyd Waner, Pirates, 1929 ... 234

HITS, ROOKIE

1. Lloyd Waner, Pirates, 1927 ... 223
2. Ralph Garr, Braves, 1971 ... 219
3. Tony Oliva, Twins, 1964 ... 217
4. Dale Alexander, Tigers, 1929 ... 215
5. Benny Kauff, Indianapolis F.L., 1914 ... 211
6. Nomar Garciaparra, Red Sox, 1997 ... 209
   Harvey Kuenn, Tigers, 1953 ... 209
8. Kevin Seitzer, Royals, 1987 ... 207
9. Joe DiMaggio, Yankees, 1936 ... 206
   Johnny Frederick, Dodgers, 1929 ... 206
   Hal Trosky, Indians, 1934 ... 206
12. Johnny Pesky, Red Sox, 1942 ... 205

13. Earle Combs, Yankees, 1925 ... 203
14. Dick Allen, Phillies, 1964 ... 201
    Roy Johnson, Tigers, 1929 ... 201
16. Dick Wakefield, Tigers, 1943 ... 200
17. Earl Averill, Indians, 1929 ... 198
18. Buddy Hassett, Dodgers, 1936 ... 197
19. Carlos Beltran, Royals, 1999 ... 194
20. Smead Jolley, White Sox, 1930 ... 193
    Wally Moon, Cardinals, 1954 ... 193

LONGEST HITTING STREAKS

1. Joe DiMaggio, Yankees, 1941 ... 56
2. Pete Rose, Reds, 1978 ... 44
3. George Sisler, Browns, 1922 ... 41
4. Ty Cobb, Tigers, 1911 ... 40
5. Paul Molitor, Brewers, 1987 ... 39
6. Tommy Holmes, Braves, 1945 ... 37
7. Ty Cobb, Tigers, 1917 ... 35
8. George Sisler, Browns, 1925 ... 34
   George McQuinn, Browns, 1938 ... 34
   Dom DiMaggio, Red Sox, 1949 ... 34
   Benito Santiago, Padres, 1987 ... 34
12. Hal Chase, Yankees, 1907 ... 33
    Rogers Hornsby, Cardinals, 1922 ... 33
    Heinie Manush, Senators, 1933 ... 33
15. Nap Lajoie, Indians, 1906 ... 31
    Sam Rice, Senators, 1924 ... 31
    Willie Davis, Dodgers, 1969 ... 31
    Rico Carty, Braves, 1970 ... 31
    Ken Landreaux, Twins, 1980 ... 31
    Vladimir Guerrero, Expos, 1999 ... 31

LONGEST HITTING STREAKS, ROOKIE

1. Benito Santiago, Padres, 1987 ... 34
2. Jerome Walton, Cubs, 1989 ... 30
   Nomar Garciaparra, Red Sox, 1997 ... 30
4. Jimmy Williams, 1899 ... 27
5. Guy Curtright, White Sox, 1943 ... 26
6. Joe McEwing, Cardinals, 1999 ... 25
7. Chico Carrasquel, White Sox, 1950 ... 24
8. Richie Ashburn, Phillies, 1948 ... 23
   Al Dark, Braves, 1948 ... 23
   Kent Hrbek, Twins, 1982 ... 23
   Goldie Rapp, Phillies, 1921 ... 23

Pittsburgh's Waner brothers, Lloyd (left) and Paul, rank high among single-season rookie hitters.

	Mike Vail, Mets, 1975	23
13.	Ralph Garr, Braves, 1971	22
	Willie McCovey, Giants, 1959	22
	Dale Mitchell, Indians, 1947	22
	Johnny Mize, Cardinals, 1936	22
	Edgar Renteria, Marlins, 1996	22
18.	Lou Klein, Cardinals, 1943	21
	Danny Litwhiler, Phillies, 1940	21
	Jackie Robinson, Dodgers, 1947	21
	Dick Wakefield, Tigers, 1943	21
	Taffy Wright, Senators, 1938	21

CONSECUTIVE HITS

1.	Pinky Higgins, Red Sox, 1938	12
	Walt Dropo, Tigers, 1952	12
3.	Tris Speaker, Indians, 1920	11
	Johnny Pesky, Red Sox, 1946	11
5.	Ed Delahanty, Phillies, 1897	10
	Jake Gettman, Senators, 1897	10
	Ed Konetchy, Dodgers, 1919	10
	George Sisler, Browns, 1921	10
	Harry Heilmann, Tigers, 1922	10
	Kiki Cuyler, Pirates, 1925	10
	Harry McCurdy, White Sox, 1926	10
	Chick Hafey, Cardinals, 1929	10
	Joe Medwick, Cardinals, 1936	10
	Rip Radcliff, White Sox, 1938	10
	Buddy Hassett, Braves, 1940	10
	Woody Williams, Reds, 1943	10
	Ken Singleton, Orioles, 1981	10
	Bip Roberts, Reds, 1992	10
	Frank Thomas, White Sox, 1997	10
	Joe Randa, Royals, 1999	10

PINCH HITS

1.	John Vander Wal, Rockies, 1995	28
2.	Lenny Harris, Rockies-Diamondbacks, 1999	26
3.	Jose Morales, Expos, 1976	25
4.	Dave Philley, Orioles, 1961	24
	Vic Davalillo, Cardinals, 1970	24
	Rusty Staub, Mets, 1983	24
	Gerald Perry, Cardinals, 1993	24
8.	Sam Leslie, Giants, 1932	22
	Peanuts Lowrey, Cardinals, 1953	22
	Red Schoendienst, Cardinals, 1962	22
	Wallace Johnson, Expos, 1988	22
	Mark Sweeney, Cardinals-Padres, 1997	22
13.	Doc Miller, Phillies, 1913	21
	Smoky Burgess, White Sox, 1966	21
	Merv Rettenmund, Padres, 1977	21
16.	Ed Coleman, Browns, 1936	20
	Frenchy Bordagaray, Cardinals, 1938	20
	Joe Frazier, Cardinals, 1954	20
	Smoky Burgess, White Sox, 1965	20
	Ken Boswell, Astros, 1976	20
	Jerry Turner, Padres, 1978	20
	Thad Bosley, Cubs, 1985	20
	Chris Chambliss, Braves, 1986	20
	Dave Clark, Cubs, 1997	20

SINGLES

1.	Lloyd Waner, Pirates, 1927	198
2.	Wade Boggs, Red Sox, 1985	187
3.	Willie Wilson, Royals, 1980	184
4.	Matty Alou, Pirates, 1969	183
5.	Sam Rice, Senators, 1925	182
6.	Richie Ashburn, Phillies, 1951	181
	Jesse Burkett, Cardinals, 1901	181
	Lefty O'Doul, Phillies, 1929	181
	Pete Rose, Reds, 1973	181
	Lloyd Waner, Pirates, 1929	181
11.	Rod Carew, Twins, 1974	180
	Ralph Garr, Braves, 1971	180
	Lloyd Waner, Pirates, 1928	180
14.	Jack Tobin, Browns, 1921	179
	Maury Wills, Dodgers, 1962	179
16.	Curt Flood, Cardinals, 1964	178
	George Sisler, Browns, 1922	178
	Paul Waner, Pirates, 1937	178
19.	Tony Gwynn, Padres, 1984	177
	Bill Terry, Giants, 1930	177

DOUBLES

1.	Earl Webb, Red Sox, 1931	67
2.	George Burns, Indians, 1926	64
	Joe Medwick, Cardinals, 1936	64
4.	Hank Greenberg, Tigers, 1934	63
5.	Paul Waner, Pirates, 1932	62
6.	Charley Gehringer, Tigers, 1936	60
7.	Chuck Klein, Phillies, 1930	59
	Tris Speaker, Indians, 1923	59
9.	Billy Herman, Cubs, 1935	57
	Billy Herman, Cubs, 1936	57
11.	Craig Biggio, Astros, 1999	56
	George Kell, Tigers, 1950	56
	Joe Medwick, Cardinals, 1937	56
14.	Gee Walker, Tigers, 1936	55
15.	Mark Grudzielanek, Expos, 1997	54
	Hal McRae, Royals, 1977	54
	John Olerud, Blue Jays, 1993	54
	Alex Rodriguez, Mariners, 1996	54
19.	Don Mattingly, Yankees, 1986	53
	Stan Musial, Cardinals, 1953	53
	Al Simmons, A's, 1926	53
	Tris Speaker, Red Sox, 1912	53
	Paul Waner, Pirates, 1936	53

TRIPLES

1.	Chief Wilson, Pirates, 1912	36
2.	Sam Crawford, Tigers, 1914	26
	Kiki Cuyler, Pirates, 1925	26
	Joe Jackson, Indians, 1912	26
5.	Sam Crawford, Tigers, 1903	25
	Larry Doyle, Giants, 1911	25
	Tom Long, Cardinals, 1915	25
8.	Ty Cobb, Tigers, 1911	24
	Ty Cobb, Tigers, 1917	24
10.	Ty Cobb, Tigers, 1912	23
	Earle Combs, Yankees, 1927	23
	Adam Comorosky, Pirates, 1930	23
	Sam Crawford, Tigers, 1913	23
	Dale Mitchell, Indians, 1949	23
15.	12 tied with 22	

HOME RUNS

1.	Mark McGwire, Cardinals, 1998	70
2.	Sammy Sosa, Cubs, 1998	66
3.	Mark McGwire, Cardinals, 1999	65
4.	Sammy Sosa, Cubs, 1999	63
5.	Roger Maris, Yankees, 1961	61
6.	Babe Ruth, Yankees, 1927	60
7.	Babe Ruth, Yankees, 1921	59
8.	Jimmie Foxx, A's, 1932	58
	Hank Greenberg, Tigers, 1938	58
	Mark McGwire, A's-Cardinals, 1997	58
11.	Ken Griffey Jr., Mariners, 1997	56
	Ken Griffey Jr., Mariners, 1998	56
	Hack Wilson, Cubs, 1930	56
14.	Ralph Kiner, Pirates, 1949	54
	Mickey Mantle, Yankees, 1961	54
	Babe Ruth, Yankees, 1920	54
	Babe Ruth, Yankees, 1928	54
18.	George Foster, Reds, 1977	52
	Mickey Mantle, Yankees, 1956	52
	Willie Mays, Giants, 1965	52
	Mark McGwire, A's, 1996	52

HOME RUNS, RIGHTHANDER

1.	Mark McGwire, Cardinals, 1998	70
2.	Sammy Sosa, Cubs, 1998	66
3.	Mark McGwire, Cardinals, 1999	65
4.	Sammy Sosa, Cubs, 1999	63
5.	Jimmie Foxx, A's, 1932	58
	Hank Greenberg, Tigers, 1938	58
	Mark McGwire, A's-Cardinals	58
8.	Hack Wilson, Cubs, 1930	56
9.	Ralph Kiner, Pirates, 1949	54
10.	George Foster, Reds, 1977	52
	Willie Mays, Giants, 1965	52
	Mark McGwire, A's, 1996	52
13.	Cecil Fielder, Tigers, 1990	51
	Ralph Kiner, Pirates, 1947	51
	Willie Mays, Giants, 1955	51
16.	Albert Belle, Indians, 1995	50
	Jimmie Foxx, Red Sox, 1938	50
	Greg Vaughn, Padres, 1998	50
19.	Albert Belle, White Sox, 1998	49
	Andre Dawson, Cubs, 1987	49
	Harmon Killebrew, Twins, 1964	49
	Harmon Killebrew, Twins, 1969	49
	Willie Mays, Giants, 1962	49
	Mark McGwire, A's, 1987	49
	Frank Robinson, Orioles, 1966	49

HOME RUNS, LEFTHANDER

1.	Roger Maris, Yankees, 1961	61
2.	Babe Ruth, Yankees, 1927	60
3.	Babe Ruth, Yankees, 1921	59
4.	Ken Griffey Jr., Mariners, 1997	56
	Ken Griffey Jr., Mariners, 1998	56
6.	Babe Ruth, Yankees, 1920	54
	Babe Ruth, Yankees, 1928	54
8.	Johnny Mize, Giants, 1947	51
9.	Brady Anderson, Orioles, 1996	50
10.	Lou Gehrig, Yankees, 1934	49
	Lou Gehrig, Yankees, 1936	49
	Ken Griffey, Jr., Mariners, 1996	49
	Ted Kluszewski, Reds, 1954	49
	Babe Ruth, Yankees, 1930	49
	Larry Walker, Rockies, 1997	49
16.	Ken Griffey Jr., Mariners, 1999	48
	Willie Stargell, Pirates, 1971	48
18.	Lou Gehrig, Yankees, 1927	47
	Reggie Jackson, A's, 1969	47
	Ted Kluszewski, Reds, 1955	47
	Eddie Mathews, Braves, 1953	47
	Babe Ruth, Yankees, 1926	47

HOME RUNS, SWITCH HITTER

1.	Mickey Mantle, Yankees, 1961	54
2.	Mickey Mantle, Yankees, 1956	52
3.	Chipper Jones, Braves, 1999	45
4.	Mickey Mantle, Yankees, 1958	42
5.	Todd Hundley, Mets, 1996	41
6.	Ken Caminiti, Padres, 1996	40
	Mickey Mantle, Yankees, 1960	40
8.	Howard Johnson, Mets, 1991	38
9.	Mickey Mantle, Yankees, 1955	37
10.	Howard Johnson, Mets, 1987	36
	Howard Johnson, Mets, 1989	36
12.	Ripper Collins, Cardinals, 1934	35
	Mickey Mantle, Yankees, 1964	35
	Ken Singleton, Orioles, 1979	35
15.	Bobby Bonilla, Mets, 1993	34
	Tony Clark, Tigers, 1998	34
	Chipper Jones, Braves, 1998	34
	Mickey Mantle, Yankees, 1957	34
19.	Eddie Murray, Orioles, 1983	33
20.	8 tied with 32	

HOME RUNS, FIRST BASEMAN

1.	Mark McGwire, Cardinals, 1998	69
2.	Mark McGwire, Cardinals, 1999	65
3.	Hank Greenberg, Tigers, 1938	58
4.	Mark McGwire, A's-Cardinals, 1997	57
5.	Jimmie Foxx, A's, 1932	51
	Johnny Mize, Giants, 1947	51
7.	Jimmie Foxx, Red Sox, 1938	50
8.	Lou Gehrig, Yankees, 1934	49
	Lou Gehrig, Yankees, 1936	49
	Ted Kluszewski, Reds, 1954	49

HOME RUNS, SECOND BASEMAN

1.	Rogers Hornsby, Cardinals, 1922	42
	Davey Johnson, Braves, 1973	42
3.	Ryne Sandberg, Cubs, 1990	40
4.	Rogers Hornsby, Cardinals, 1925	39
	Rogers Hornsby, Cubs, 1929	39
6.	Jay Bell, Diamondbacks, 1999	38
7.	Joe Gordon, Indians, 1948	32
8.	Jeff Kent, Giants, 1998	31
9.	Joe Gordon, Yankees, 1940	30
	Bobby Grich, Angels, 1979	30
	Ryne Sandberg, Cubs, 1989	30

HOME RUNS, THIRD BASEMAN

1.	Mike Schmidt, Phillies, 1980	48
2.	Eddie Mathews, Braves, 1953	47
3.	Eddie Mathews, Braves, 1959	46
	Vinny Castilla, Rockies, 1998	46
5.	Mike Schmidt, Phillies, 1979	45
	Chipper Jones, 1999	45
7.	Al Rosen, Indians, 1953	43
	Matt Williams, Giants, 1994	43
9.	Harmon Killebrew, Senators, 1959	42
10.	Eddie Mathews, Braves, 1955	40
	Mike Schmidt, Phillies, 1983	40
	Ken Caminiti, Padres, 1996	40
	Vinny Castilla, Rockies, 1996	40
	Vinny Castilla, Rockies, 1997	40

HOME RUNS, SHORTSTOP

1.	Ernie Banks, Cubs, 1958	47
2.	Ernie Banks, Cubs, 1959	45
3.	Ernie Banks, Cubs, 1955	44
4.	Alex Rodriguez, Mariners, 1998	42
	Alex Rodriguez, Mariners, 1999	42
6.	Ernie Banks, Cubs, 1960	41
7.	Rico Petrocelli, Red Sox, 1969	40
8.	Vern Stephens, Red Sox, 1949	39
9.	Alex Rodriguez, Mariners, 1996	36
10.	Nomar Garciaparra, Red Sox, 1998	35

HOME RUNS, OUTFIELDER

1.	Sammy Sosa, Cubs, 1998	66
2.	Sammy Sosa, Cubs, 1999	63
3.	Roger Maris, Yankees, 1961	61
4.	Babe Ruth, Yankees, 1927	60
5.	Babe Ruth, Yankees, 1921	58
6.	Hack Wilson, Cubs, 1930	56
	Ken Griffey Jr., Mariners, 1998	56
8.	Babe Ruth, Yankees, 1920	54
	Babe Ruth, Yankees, 1928	54
	Ralph Kiner, Pirates, 1949	54
	Mickey Mantle, Yankees, 1961	54
	Ken Griffey Jr., Mariners, 1997	54
13.	Mickey Mantle, Yankees, 1956	52
	Willie Mays, Giants, 1965	52
	George Foster, Reds, 1977	52
16.	Ralph Kiner, Pirates, 1947	51
	Willie Mays, Giants, 1962	51
18.	Albert Belle, Indians, 1995	50
	Brady Anderson, Orioles, 1996	50
20.	Babe Ruth, Yankees, 1930	49
	Willie Mays, Giants, 1962	49
	Harmon Killebrew, Twins, 1964	49
	Frank Robinson, Orioles, 1966	49
	Andre Dawson, Cubs, 1987	49

HOME RUNS, CATCHER

1.	Todd Hundley, Mets, 1996	41
2.	Roy Campanella, Dodgers, 1953	40
	Mike Piazza, Dodgers, 1997	40
	Mike Piazza, Mets, 1999	40
5.	Johnny Bench, Reds, 1970	38
6.	Gabby Hartnett, Cubs, 1930	36
	Mike Piazza, Dodgers, 1996	36
8.	Walker Cooper, Giants, 1947	35
	Mike Piazza, Dodgers, 1993	35
10.	Johnny Bench, Reds, 1972	34
	Terry Steinbach, A's, 1996	34
	Javy Lopez, Braves, 1998	34

HOME RUNS, PITCHER

1. Wes Ferrell, Indians, 1931 9
2. Wes Ferrell, Indians, 1933 7
   Bob Lemon, Indians, 1949 7
   Don Newcombe, Dodgers, 1955 7
   Don Drysdale, Dodgers, 1958 7
   Don Drysdale, Dodgers, 1965 7
   Earl Wilson, Tigers, 1968 7

HOME RUNS, DESIGNATED HITTER

1. Rafael Palmeiro, Rangers, 1999 37
2. Dave Kingman, A's, 1984 35
   Dave Kingman, A's, 1986 35
   John Jaha, A's, 1999 35
5. Greg Luzinski, White Sox, 1983 32
   Gorman Thomas, Mariners, 1985 32
   Jose Canseco, Devil Rays, 1999 32
8. Jim Rice, Red Sox, 1977 31
   Rico Carty, Blue Jays-A's, 1978 31
   Andre Thornton, Indians, 1982 31
   Jose Canseco, Rangers, 1994 31

HOME RUNS, ROOKIE

1. Mark McGwire, A's, 1987 49
2. Wally Berger, Braves, 1930 38
   Frank Robinson, Reds, 1956 38
4. Al Rosen, Indians, 1950 37
5. Ron Kittle, White Sox, 1983 35
   Mike Piazza, Dodgers, 1993 35
   Hal Trosky, Indians, 1934 35
8. Walt Dropo, Red Sox, 1950 34
9. Jose Canseco, A's, 1986 33
   Jimmie Hall, Twins, 1963 33
   Earl Williams, Braves, 1971 33
12. Matt Nokes, Tigers, 1987 32
    Tony Oliva, Twins, 1964 32
14. Jim Ray Hart, Giants, 1964 31
    Tim Salmon, Angels, 1993 31
    Ted Williams, Red Sox, 1939 31
17. Bob Allison, Senators, 1959 30
    Nomar Garciaparra, Red Sox, 1997 30
    Pete Incaviglia, Rangers, 1986 30
    Willie Montanez, Phillies, 1971 30

CONSECUTIVE GAMES WITH HOME RUN

1. Don Mattingly, Yankees, 1987 (10) 8
   Dale Long, Pirates, 1956 (8) 8
   Ken Griffey Jr., Mariners, 1993 (8) 8
4. Frank Howard, Senators, 1968 (10) 6
   George Kelly, Giants, 1924 (7) 6
   Walker Cooper, Giants, 1947 (7) 6
   Willie Mays, Giants, 1955 (7) 6
   Roger Maris, Yankees, 1961 (7) 6
   Graig Nettles, Padres, 1984 (7) 6
   Ken Williams, Browns, 1922 (6) 6
   Lou Gehrig, Yankees, 1931 (6) 6
   Roy Sievers, Senators, 1957 (6) 6
   Reggie Jackson, Orioles, 1976 (6) 6
14. Jim Bottomley, Cardinals, 1929 5
    Babe Ruth, Yankees, 1921 5
    Vic Wertz, Tigers, 1950 5
    Johnny Bench, Reds, 1972 5
    Mike Schmidt, Phillies, 1979 5
    Note: Number in ( ) is homer total during streak.

MOST HOMERS PER AT-BAT

1. Mark McGwire, Cardinals, 1998 .... .138
2. Mark McGwire, Cardinals, 1999 .... .125
3. Mark McGwire, Cardinals, 1996 .... .123
4. Babe Ruth, Yankees, 1920 .... .118
5. Babe Ruth, Yankees, 1927 .... .111
6. Babe Ruth, Yankees, 1921 .... .109
7. Mark McGwire, A's-Cardinals, 1997 .... .107
8. Mickey Mantle, Yankees, 1961 .... .105
9. Hank Greenberg, Tigers, 1938 .... .104
10. Roger Maris, Yankees, 1961 .... .103
    Sammy Sosa, Cubs, 1998 .... .103
12. Sammy Sosa, Cubs, 1999 .... .101
    Babe Ruth, Yankees, 1928 .... .101
14. Jimmie Foxx, A's, 1932 .... .099
15. Ralph Kiner, Pirates, 1949 .... .098
    Mickey Mantle, Yankees, 1956 .... .098
17. Jeff Bagwell, Astros, 1994 .... .097
    Kevin Mitchell, Reds, 1994 .... .097
    Matt Williams, Giants, 1994 .... .097
20. Hack Wilson, Cubs, 1930 .... .096

PINCH-HIT HOME RUNS

1. Johnny Frederick, Dodgers, 1932 6
2. Joe Cronin, Red Sox, 1943 5
   Butch Nieman, Braves, 1945 5
   Gene Freese, Phillies, 1959 5
   Jerry Lynch, Reds, 1961 5
   Cliff Johnson, Astros, 1974 5
   Lee Lacy, Dodgers, 1978 5
   Jerry Turner, Padres, 1978 5
   Billy Ashley, Dodgers, 1996 5
10. 26 tied with 4

GRAND SLAMS

1. Don Mattingly, Yankees, 1987 6
2. Ernie Banks, Cubs, 1955 5
   Jim Gentile, Orioles, 1961 5
4. Frank Schulte, Cubs, 1911 4
   Babe Ruth, Red Sox, 1919 4

Roger Maris (left), Ted Williams (center) and Mickey Mantle rate high on baseball's all-time slugging charts.

Lou Gehrig, Yankees, 1934 4
Rudy York, Tigers, 1938 4
Vince DiMaggio, Phillies, 1945 4
Tommy Henrich, Yankees, 1948 4
Ralph Kiner, Pirates, 1949 4
Sid Gordon, Braves, 1950 4
Al Rosen, Indians, 1951 4
Ray Boone, Indians-Tigers, 1953 4
Jim Northrup, Tigers, 1968 4
Albert Belle, White Sox, 1997 4

TOTAL BASES

1. Babe Ruth, Yankees, 1921 457
2. Rogers Hornsby, Cardinals, 1922 450
3. Lou Gehrig, Yankees, 1927 447
4. Chuck Klein, Phillies, 1930 445
5. Jimmie Foxx, A's, 1932 438
6. Stan Musial, Cardinals, 1948 429
7. Hack Wilson, Cubs, 1930 423
8. Chuck Klein, Phillies, 1932 420
9. Lou Gehrig, Yankees, 1930 419
10. Joe DiMaggio, Yankees, 1937 418
11. Babe Ruth, Yankees, 1927 417
12. Babe Herman, Dodgers, 1930 416
    Sammy Sosa, Cubs, 1998 416
14. Lou Gehrig, Yankees, 1931 410
15. Lou Gehrig, Yankees, 1934 409
    Rogers Hornsby, Cubs, 1929 409
    Larry Walker, Rockies, 1997 409
18. Joe Medwick, Cardinals, 1937 406
    Jim Rice, Red Sox, 1978 406
20. Chuck Klein, Phillies, 1929 405
    Hal Trosky, Indians, 1936 405

*SLUGGING PERCENTAGE

1. Babe Ruth, Yankees, 1920 .... .847
2. Babe Ruth, Yankees, 1921 .... .846
3. Babe Ruth, Yankees, 1927 .... .772
4. Lou Gehrig, Yankees, 1927 .... .765
5. Babe Ruth, Yankees, 1923 .... .764
6. Rogers Hornsby, Cardinals, 1925 .... .756
7. Mark McGwire, Cardinals, 1998 .... .752
8. Jeff Bagwell, Astros, 1994 .... .750
9. Jimmie Foxx, A's, 1932 .... .749
10. Babe Ruth, Yankees, 1924 .... .739
11. Babe Ruth, Yankees, 1926 .... .737
12. Ted Williams, Red Sox, 1941 .... .735
13. Babe Ruth, Yankees, 1930 .... .732
14. Ted Williams, Red Sox, 1957 .... .731
15. Mark McGwire, A's, 1996 .... .730
16. Frank Thomas, White Sox, 1994 .... .729
17. Hack Wilson, Cubs, 1930 .... .723
18. Rogers Hornsby, Cardinals, 1922 .... .722
19. Lou Gehrig, Yankees, 1930 .... .721
20. Larry Walker, Rockies, 1997 .... .720

*Based on players averaging at least 3.1 at-bats for every game played by their teams.

EXTRA-BASE HITS

1. Babe Ruth, Yankees, 1921 119
2. Lou Gehrig, Yankees, 1927 117

3. Chuck Klein, Phillies, 1930 107
4. Albert Belle, Indians, 1995 103
   Hank Greenberg, Tigers, 1937 103
   Chuck Klein, Phillies, 1932 103
   Stan Musial, Cardinals, 1948 103
8. Rogers Hornsby, Cardinals, 1922 102
9. Jimmie Foxx, A's, 1932 100
   Lou Gehrig, Yankees, 1930 100
11. Albert Belle, White Sox, 1998 99
    Hank Greenberg, Tigers, 1940 99
    Babe Ruth, Yankees, 1920 99
    Babe Ruth, Yankees, 1923 99
    Larry Walker, Rockies, 1997 99
16. Hank Greenberg, Tigers, 1935 98
17. Juan Gonzalez, Rangers, 1998 97
    Joe Medwick, Cardinals, 1937 97
    Babe Ruth, Yankees, 1927 97
    Hack Wilson, Cubs, 1930 97

RUNS BATTED IN

1. Hack Wilson, Cubs, 1930 191
2. Lou Gehrig, Yankees, 1931 184
3. Hank Greenberg, Tigers, 1937 183
4. Jimmie Foxx, Red Sox, 1938 175
   Lou Gehrig, Yankees, 1927 175
6. Lou Gehrig, Yankees, 1930 174
7. Babe Ruth, Yankees, 1921 171
8. Hank Greenberg, Tigers, 1935 170
   Chuck Klein, Phillies, 1930 170
10. Jimmie Foxx, A's, 1932 169
11. Joe DiMaggio, Yankees, 1937 167
12. Lou Gehrig, Yankees, 1934 165
    Manny Ramirez, Indians, 1999 165
    Al Simmons, A's, 1930 165
15. Babe Ruth, Yankees, 1927 164
16. Jimmie Foxx, A's, 1933 163
    Babe Ruth, Yankees, 1931 163
18. Hal Trosky, Indians, 1936 162
19. Lou Gehrig, Yankees, 1937 159
    Vern Stephens, Red Sox, 1949 159
    Ted Williams, Red Sox, 1949 159
    Hack Wilson, Cubs, 1929 159

RBIs, RIGHTHANDER

1. Hack Wilson, Cubs, 1930 190
2. Hank Greenberg, Tigers, 1937 183
3. Jimmie Foxx, Red Sox, 1938 175
4. Hank Greenberg, Tigers, 1935 170
5. Jimmie Foxx, A's, 1932 169
6. Joe DiMaggio, Yankees, 1937 167
7. Manny Ramirez, Indians, 1999 165
   Al Simmons, A's, 1930 165
9. Jimmie Foxx, A's, 1933 163
10. Vern Stephens, Red Sox, 1949 159
    Hack Wilson, Cubs, 1929 159
12. Sammy Sosa, Cubs, 1998 158
13. Juan Gonzalez, Rangers, 1998 157

Al Simmons, A's, 1929	157
15. Jimmie Foxx, A's, 1930	156
16. Joe DiMaggio, Yankees, 1948	155
17. Joe Medwick, Cardinals, 1937	154
18. Tommy Davis, Dodgers, 1962	153
19. Albert Belle, White Sox, 1998	152
Rogers Hornsby, Cardinals, 1922	152

RBIs, LEFTHANDER

1. Lou Gehrig, Yankees, 1931	184
2. Lou Gehrig, Yankees, 1927	175
3. Lou Gehrig, Yankees, 1930	174
4. Babe Ruth, Yankees, 1921	171
5. Chuck Klein, Phillies, 1930	170
6. Lou Gehrig, Yankees, 1934	165
7. Babe Ruth, Yankees, 1927	164
8. Babe Ruth, Yankees, 1931	163
9. Hal Trosky, Indians, 1936	162
10. Lou Gehrig, Yankees, 1937	159
Ted Williams, Red Sox, 1949	159
12. Ken Williams, Browns, 1922	155
13. Babe Ruth, Yankees, 1929	154
14. Babe Ruth, Yankees, 1930	153
15. Lou Gehrig, Yankees, 1936	152
16. Lou Gehrig, Yankees, 1932	151
Mel Ott, Giants, 1929	151
18. Rafael Palmeiro, Rangers, 1999	148
19. Ken Griffey Jr., Mariners, 1997	147
20. Ken Griffey Jr., Mariners, 1998	146
Babe Ruth, Yankees, 1926	146

RBIs, SWITCH HITTER

1. Ken Caminiti, Padres, 1996	130
Mickey Mantle, Yankees, 1956	130
3. Ripper Collins, Cardinals, 1934	128
Mickey Mantle, Yankees, 1961	128
5. Eddie Murray, Orioles, 1985	124
6. Ripper Collins, Cardinals, 1935	122
7. Roberto Alomar, Indians, 1999	120
Bobby Bonilla, Pirates, 1990	120
9. Ruben Sierra, Rangers, 1989	119
10. Tony Clark, Tigers, 1997	117
Howard Johnson, Mets, 1991	117
12. Bobby Bonilla, Orioles, 1996	116
Eddie Murray, Orioles, 1980	116
Ruben Sierra, Rangers, 1991	116
15. Bernie Williams, Yankees, 1999	115
16. Carlos Baerga, Indians, 1993	114
Frankie Frisch, Cardinals, 1930	114
18. Chili Davis, Angels, 1993	112
Todd Hundley, Mets, 1996	112
20. 6 tied with 111	

RBIs, ROOKIE

1. Ted Williams, Red Sox, 1939	145
2. Walt Dropo, Red Sox, 1950	144
3. Hal Trosky, Indians, 1934	142
4. Dale Alexander, Tigers, 1929	137
5. Joe DiMaggio, Yankees, 1936	125
6. Wally Berger, Braves, 1930	119
7. Mark McGwire, A's, 1987	118
8. Jose Canseco, A's, 1986	117
Joe Vosmik, Indians, 1931	117
10. Alvin Davis, Mariners, 1984	116
Al Rosen, Indians, 1950	116
12. Smead Jolley, White Sox, 1930	114
Tony Lazzeri, Yankees, 1926	114
14. Ken Keltner, Indians, 1938	113
15. Ray Jablonski, Cardinals, 1953	112
Mike Piazza, Dodgers, 1993	112
17. Johnny Rizzo, Pirates, 1938	111
Glenn Wright, Pirates, 1924	111
19. Zeke Bonura, White Sox, 1934	110
20. Carlos Beltran, Royals, 1999	108

WALKS

1. Babe Ruth, Yankees, 1923	170
2. Mark McGwire, Cardinals, 1998	162
Ted Williams, Red Sox, 1947	162
Ted Williams, Red Sox, 1949	162
5. Ted Williams, Red Sox, 1946	156
6. Barry Bonds, Giants, 1996	151
Eddie Yost, Senators, 1956	151
8. Jeff Bagwell, Astros, 1999	149
Eddie Joost, A's, 1949	149
10. Babe Ruth, Yankees, 1920	148
Eddie Stanky, Dodgers, 1945	148
Jimmy Wynn, Astros, 1969	148
13. Jimmy Sheckard, Cubs, 1911	147
14. Mickey Mantle, Yankees, 1957	146
15. Barry Bonds, Giants, 1997	145
Harmon Killebrew, Twins, 1969	145
Ted Williams, Red Sox, 1941	145
Ted Williams, Red Sox, 1942	145
19. Babe Ruth, Yankees, 1921	144
Babe Ruth, Yankees, 1926	144
Eddie Stanky, Giants, 1950	144
Ted Williams, Red Sox, 1951	144

INTENTIONAL WALKS

1. Willie McCovey, Giants, 1969	45
2. Barry Bonds, Giants, 1993	43
3. Willie McCovey, Giants, 1970	40
4. Barry Bonds, Giants, 1997	34
5. John Olerud, Blue Jays, 1993	33

Ted Williams, Red Sox, 1957	33
7. Barry Bonds, Pirates, 1992	32
Kevin Mitchell, Giants, 1989	32
9. George Brett, Royals, 1985	31
10. Barry Bonds, Giants, 1996	30
11. Barry Bonds, Giants, 1998	29
Frank Howard, Senators, 1970	29
Dale Murphy, Braves, 1987	29
Adolfo Phillips, Cubs, 1967	29
Frank Thomas, White Sox, 1995	29
16. Ernie Banks, Cubs, 1960	28
Mark McGwire, Cardinals, 1998	28
18. Jeff Bagwell, Astros, 1997	27
Will Clark, Giants, 1988	27
Roberto Clemente, Pirates, 1968	27

STRIKEOUTS

1. Bobby Bonds, Giants, 1970	189
2. Bobby Bonds, Giants, 1969	187
3. Rob Deer, Brewers, 1987	186
4. Pete Incaviglia, Rangers, 1986	185
5. Cecil Fielder, Tigers, 1990	182
6. Mike Schmidt, Phillies, 1975	180
7. Rob Deer, Brewers, 1986	179
8. Jay Buhner, Mariners, 1997	175
Jose Canseco, A's, 1986	175
Rob Deer, Tigers, 1991	175
Dave Nicholson, White Sox, 1963	175
Gorman Thomas, Brewers, 1979	175
13. Sammy Sosa, Cubs, 1997	174
14. Bo Jackson, Royals, 1989	172
Jim Presley, Mariners, 1986	172
16. Reggie Jackson, A's, 1968	171
Sammy Sosa, Cubs, 1998	171
Sammy Sosa, Cubs, 1999	171
Jim Thome, Indians, 1999	171
20. Gorman Thomas, Brewers, 1980	170

STOLEN BASES

1. Rickey Henderson, A's, 1982	130
2. Lou Brock, Cardinals, 1974	118
3. Vince Coleman, Cardinals, 1985	110
4. Vince Coleman, Cardinals, 1987	109
5. Rickey Henderson, A's, 1983	108
6. Vince Coleman, Cardinals, 1986	107
7. Maury Wills, Dodgers, 1962	104
8. Rickey Henderson, A's, 1980	100
9. Ron LeFlore, Expos, 1980	97
10. Ty Cobb, Tigers, 1915	96
Omar Moreno, Pirates, 1980	96
12. Maury Wills, Dodgers, 1965	94
13. Rickey Henderson, Yankees, 1988	93
14. Tim Raines, Expos, 1983	90
15. Clyde Milan, Senators, 1912	88
16. Rickey Henderson, Yankees, 1986	87
17. Ty Cobb, Tigers, 1911	83
Willie Wilson, Royals, 1979	83
19. Bob Bescher, Reds, 1911	81
Vince Coleman, Cardinals, 1988	81
Eddie Collins, A's, 1910	81

PITCHING

GAMES

1. Mike Marshall, Dodgers, 1974	106
2. Kent Tekulve, Pirates, 1979	94
3. Mike Marshall, Expos, 1973	92
4. Kent Tekulve, Pirates, 1978	91
5. Wayne Granger, Reds, 1969	90
Mike Marshall, Twins, 1979	90
Kent Tekulve, Phillies, 1987	90
8. Mark Eichhorn, Blue Jays, 1987	89
Julian Tavarez, Giants, 1997	89
10. Mike Myers, Tigers, 1997	88
Sean Runyan, Tigers, 1998	88
Wilbur Wood, White Sox, 1968	88
13. Rob Murphy, Reds, 1987	87
14. Kent Tekulve, Pirates, 1982	85
Frank Williams, Reds, 1987	85
Mitch Williams, Rangers, 1987	85
17. Ted Abernathy, Cubs, 1965	84
Stan Belinda, Reds, 1997	84
Dan Quisenberry, Royals, 1985	84
Enrique Romo, Pirates, 1979	84
Dick Tidrow, Cubs, 1980	84

GAMES STARTED

1. Jack Chesbro, Yankees, 1904	51
2. Ed Walsh, White Sox, 1908	49
Wilbur Wood, White Sox, 1972	49
4. Joe McGinnity, Giants, 1903	48
Wilbur Wood, White Sox, 1973	48
6. Dave Davenport, St. Louis F.L., 1915	46
Christy Mathewson, Giants, 1904	46
Rube Waddell, A's, 1904	46
Ed Walsh, White Sox, 1907	46
Vic Willis, Braves, 1902	46
11. Grover Alexander, Phillies, 1916	45
Mickey Lolich, Tigers, 1971	45
Jack Powell, Yankees, 1904	45
14. Grover Alexander, Phillies, 1917	44
Christy Mathewson, Giants, 1908	44
Joe McGinnity, Giants, 1904	44

George Mullin, Tigers, 1904	44
Phil Niekro, Braves, 1979	44
George Uhle, Indians, 1923	44
20. 9 tied with 43	

COMPLETE GAMES

1. Jack Chesbro, Yankees, 1904	48
2. Vic Willis, Braves, 1902	45
3. Joe McGinnity, Giants, 1903	44
4. George Mullin, Tigers, 1904	42
Ed Walsh, White Sox, 1908	42
6. Noodles Hahn, Reds, 1901	41
Cy Young, Red Sox, 1902	41
Irv Young, Braves, 1905	41
9. Cy Young, Red Sox, 1904	40
10. Bill Dinneen, Red Sox, 1902	39
Joe McGinnity, Orioles, 1901	39
Jack Taylor, Cardinals, 1904	39
Rube Waddell, A's, 1904	39
Vic Willis, Braves, 1904	39
15. Grover Alexander, Phillies, 1916	38
Walter Johnson, Senators, 1910	38
Oscar Jones, Dodgers, 1904	38
Joe McGinnity, Giants, 1904	38
Jack Powell, Yankees, 1904	38
Cy Young, Red Sox, 1901	38

INNINGS PITCHED

1. Ed Walsh, White Sox, 1908	464.0
2. Jack Chesbro, Yankees, 1904	454.2
3. Joe McGinnity, Giants, 1903	434.0
4. Ed Walsh, White Sox, 1907	422.1
5. Vic Willis, Braves, 1902	410.0
6. Joe McGinnity, Giants, 1904	408.0
7. Ed Walsh, White Sox, 1912	393.0
8. Dave Davenport, St. Louis F.L., 1915	392.2
9. Christy Mathewson, Giants, 1908	390.2
10. Jack Powell, Yankees, 1904	390.1
11. Togie Pittinger, Braves, 1902	389.1
12. Grover Alexander, Phillies, 1916	389.0
13. Grover Alexander, Phillies, 1917	388.0
14. Cy Young, Red Sox, 1902	384.2
15. Rube Waddell, A's, 1904	383.0
16. George Mullin, Tigers, 1904	382.1
17. Joe McGinnity, Orioles, 1901	382.0
18. Cy Young, Red Sox, 1904	380.0
19. Irv Young, Braves, 1905	378.0
20. Cy Falkenberg, Indianapolis F.L., 1914	377.1

CONSECUTIVE SCORELESS INNINGS

1. Orel Hershiser, Dodgers, 1988	59
2. Don Drysdale, Dodgers, 1968	58
3. Walter Johnson, Senators, 1913	55.2
4. Jack Coombs, A's, 1910	53
5. Ed Reulbach, Cubs, 1908	*50
6. Bob Gibson, Cardinals, 1968	47
7. Carl Hubbell, Giants, 1933	45.1
8. Cy Young, Red Sox, 1904	45
Doc White, White Sox, 1904	45
Sal Maglie, Giants, 1950	45
11. Rube Waddell, A's, 1905	43.2
12. Rube Foster, Red Sox, 1914	42
13. Jack Chesbro, Pirates, 1902	41
Grover Alexander, Phillies, 1911	41
Art Nehf, Braves, 1917	41
Luis Tiant, Indians, 1968	41
17. Walter Johnson, Senators, 1918	40
Gaylord Perry, Giants, 1967	40
Luis Tiant, Red Sox, 1972	40
20. Mordecai Brown, Cubs, 1908	39.2
Billy Pierce, White Sox, 1953	39.2

*44 in 1908; 6 in 1909.

*LOWEST ERA

1. Dutch Leonard, Red Sox, 1914	0.96
2. Mordecai Brown, Cubs, 1906	1.04
3. Bob Gibson, Cardinals, 1968	1.12
4. Christy Mathewson, Giants, 1909	1.14
Walter Johnson, Senators, 1913	1.14
6. Jack Pfiester, Cubs, 1907	1.15
7. Addie Joss, Indians, 1908	1.16
8. Carl Lundgren, Cubs, 1907	1.17
9. Grover Alexander, Phillies, 1915	1.22
10. Cy Young, Red Sox, 1908	1.26
11. Ed Walsh, White Sox, 1910	1.27
Walter Johnson, Senators, 1918	1.27
13. Christy Mathewson, Giants, 1905	1.28
14. Jack Coombs, A's, 1910	1.30
15. Mordecai Brown, Cubs, 1909	1.31
16. Jack Taylor, Cubs, 1902	1.33
17. Walter Johnson, Senators, 1910	1.36
18. Walter Johnson, Senators, 1912	1.39
Mordecai Brown, Cubs, 1907	1.39
Harry Krause, A's, 1909	1.39

*Leaders based on pitchers whose total innings equal total games played by their teams.

VICTORIES

1. Jack Chesbro, Yankees, 1904	41
2. Ed Walsh, White Sox, 1908	40
3. Christy Mathewson, Giants, 1908	37
4. Walter Johnson, Senators, 1913	36
5. Joe McGinnity, Giants, 1904	35

Grover Alexander, a career 373-game winner, posted a record 16 shutouts in 1916.

6. Joe Wood, Red Sox, 1912	34
7. Grover Alexander, Phillies, 1916	33
Walter Johnson, Senators, 1912	33
Christy Mathewson, Giants, 1904	33
Cy Young, Red Sox, 1901	33
11. Cy Young, Red Sox, 1902	32
12. Grover Alexander, Phillies, 1915	31
Jim Bagby, Indians, 1920	31
Jack Coombs, A's, 1910	31
Lefty Grove, A's, 1931	31
Christy Mathewson, Giants, 1905	31
Joe McGinnity, Giants, 1903	31
Denny McLain, Tigers, 1968	31
19. Grover Alexander, Phillies, 1917	30
Dizzy Dean, Cardinals, 1934	30
Christy Mathewson, Giants, 1903	30

WINNING PERCENTAGE
(Minimum 15 victories)

1. Roy Face, Pirates, 1959	.947
2. Johnny Allen, Indians, 1937	.938
3. Greg Maddux, Braves, 1995	.905
4. Randy Johnson, Mariners, 1995	.900
5. Ron Guidry, Yankees, 1978	.893
6. Freddie Fitzsimmons, Dodgers, 1940	.889
7. Lefty Grove, A's, 1931	.886
8. Bob Stanley, Red Sox, 1978	.882
9. Preacher Roe, Dodgers, 1951	.880
10. Joe Wood, Red Sox, 1912	.872
11. David Cone, Mets, 1988	.870
12. Orel Hershiser, Dodgers, 1985	.864
13. Bill Donovan, Tigers, 1907	.862
Whitey Ford, Yankees, 1961	.862
15. Roger Clemens, Red Sox, 1986	.857
Dwight Gooden, Mets, 1985	.857
17. Pedro Martinez, Red Sox, 1999	.852
18. Chief Bender, A's, 1914	.850
John Smoltz, Braves, 1998	.850
20. Lefty Grove, A's, 1930	.848

CONSECUTIVE VICTORIES

1. Rube Marquard, Giants, 1912	19
2. Roy Face, Pirates, 1959	17
3. Walter Johnson, Senators, 1912	16
Joe Wood, Red Sox, 1912	16
Lefty Grove, A's, 1931	16
Schoolboy Rowe, Tigers, 1934	16
Carl Hubbell, Giants, 1936	16
Ewell Blackwell, Reds, 1947	16
Jack Sanford, Giants, 1962	16
10. Dazzy Vance, Dodgers, 1924	15
Alvin Crowder, Senators, 1932	15
Johnny Allen, Indians, 1937	15
Bob Gibson, Cardinals, 1968	15
Dave McNally, Orioles, 1969	15
Steve Carlton, Phillies, 1972	15
Gaylord Perry, Indians, 1974	15
Roger Clemens, Blue Jays, 1998	15
18. 12 tied with 14	

LOSSES

1. Vic Willis, Braves, 1905	29
2. George Bell, Dodgers, 1910	27
Paul Derringer, Cardinals-Reds, 1933	27
Dummy Taylor, Giants, 1901	27
5. Gus Dorner, Reds-Braves, 1906	26
Pete Dowling, Brewers-Indians, 1901	26
Bob Groom, Senators, 1909	26
Happy Townsend, Senators, 1904	26
9. Ben Cantwell, Braves, 1935	25
Patsy Flaherty, White Sox, 1903	25
Fred Glade, Browns, 1905	25
Walter Johnson, Senators, 1909	25
Oscar Jones, Dodgers, 1904	25
Stoney McGlynn, Cardinals, 1907	25
Harry McIntire, Dodgers, 1905	25
Scott Perry, A's, 1920	25
Bugs Raymond, Cardinals, 1908	25
Red Ruffing, Red Sox, 1928	25
Vic Willis, Braves, 1904	25
Irv Young, Braves, 1906	25

SAVES

1. Bobby Thigpen, White Sox, 1990	57
2. Trevor Hoffman, Padres, 1998	53
Randy Myers, Cubs, 1993	53
4. Rod Beck, Cubs, 1998	51
Dennis Eckersley, A's, 1992	51
6. Rod Beck, Giants, 1993	48
Dennis Eckersley, A's, 1990	48
Jeff Shaw, Reds-Dodgers, 1998	48
9. Lee Smith, Cardinals, 1991	47
10. Tom Gordon, Red Sox, 1998	46
Bryan Harvey, Angels, 1991	46
Jose Mesa, Indians, 1995	46
Dave Righetti, Yankees, 1986	46
Lee Smith, Cardinals-Yankees, 1993	46
15. Dennis Eckersley, A's, 1988	45
Bryan Harvey, Marlins, 1993	45
Jeff Montgomery, Royals, 1993	45
Randy Myers, Orioles, 1997	45
Dan Quisenberry, Royals, 1983	45
Mariano Rivera, Yankees, 1999	45
Bruce Sutter, Cardinals, 1984	45
Duane Ward, Blue Jays, 1993	45

SHUTOUTS

1. Grover Alexander, Phillies, 1916	16
2. Jack Coombs, A's, 1910	13
Bob Gibson, Cardinals, 1968	13
4. Grover Alexander, Phillies, 1915	12
5. Dean Chance, Angels, 1964	11
Walter Johnson, Senators, 1913	11
Sandy Koufax, Dodgers, 1963	11
Christy Mathewson, Giants, 1908	11
Ed Walsh, White Sox, 1908	11
10. Mort Cooper, Cardinals, 1942	10
Dave Davenport, St. Louis F.L., 1915	10
Bob Feller, Indians, 1946	10
Carl Hubbell, Giants, 1933	10
Bob Lemon, Indians, 1948	10
Juan Marichal, Giants, 1965	10
Jim Palmer, Orioles, 1975	10
John Tudor, Cardinals, 1985	10
Ed Walsh, White Sox, 1906	10
Joe Wood, Red Sox, 1912	10
Cy Young, Red Sox, 1904	10

RUNS ALLOWED

1. Snake Wiltse, A's-Orioles, 1902	226
2. Joe McGinnity, Orioles, 1901	219
3. Chick Fraser, A's, 1901	210
4. Pete Dowling, Brewers-Indians, 1901	209
5. Bobo Newsom, Browns, 1938	205
Togie Pittinger, Braves, 1903	205
7. Bill Carrick, Senators, 1901	198
8. Bill Phillips, Reds, 1901	196
9. Bill Carrick, Senators, 1902	194
10. Dummy Taylor, Giants, 1901	193
11. Harry Howell, Orioles, 1901	188
Harry McIntire, Dodgers, 1905	188
13. Sam Gray, Browns, 1931	187
14. Case Patten, Senators, 1902	186
15. Watty Lee, Senators, 1901	184
16. Bill Reidy, Brewers, 1901	183
17. Dickie Kerr, White Sox, 1921	182
18. Ray Kremer, Pirates, 1930	181
Al Orth, Senators, 1902	181
20. Ray Benge, Phillies, 1930	178

HITS ALLOWED

1. Joe McGinnity, Orioles, 1901	412
2. Snake Wiltse, A's-Orioles, 1902	397
3. Togie Pittinger, Braves, 1903	396
4. Joe McGinnity, Giants, 1903	391
5. Oscar Jones, Dodgers, 1904	387
6. Wilbur Wood, White Sox, 1973	381
7. George Uhle, Indians, 1923	378
8. Dummy Taylor, Giants, 1901	377
9. Vic Willis, Braves, 1902	372
10. Noodles Hahn, Reds, 1901	370
11. Bill Carrick, Senators, 1901	367

Al Orth, Senators, 1902	367
Case Patten, Senators, 1904	367
14. Ray Kremer, Pirates, 1930	366
15. Urban Shocker, Browns, 1922	365
16. Bill Phillips, Reds, 1901	364
Bill Reidy, Brewers, 1901	364
18. Jack Coombs, A's, 1911	360
Togie Pittinger, Braves, 1902	360
20. Dickie Kerr, White Sox, 1921	357
Vic Willis, Braves, 1904	357

STRIKEOUTS

1. Nolan Ryan, Angels, 1973	383
2. Sandy Koufax, Dodgers, 1965	382
3. Nolan Ryan, Angels, 1974	367
4. Randy Johnson, Diamondbacks, 1999	364
5. Rube Waddell, A's, 1904	349
6. Bob Feller, Indians, 1946	348
7. Nolan Ryan, Angels, 1977	341
8. Randy Johnson, Mariners-Astros, 1998	329
Nolan Ryan, Angels, 1972	329
10. Nolan Ryan, Angels, 1976	327
11. Sam McDowell, Indians, 1965	325
12. Curt Schilling, Phillies, 1997	319
13. Sandy Koufax, Dodgers, 1966	317
14. Walter Johnson, Senators, 1910	313
Pedro Martinez, Red Sox, 1999	313
J.R. Richard, Astros, 1979	313
17. Steve Carlton, Phillies, 1972	310
18. Randy Johnson, Mariners, 1993	308
Mickey Lolich, Tigers, 1971	308
20. Sandy Koufax, Dodgers, 1963	306
Mike Scott, Astros, 1986	306

WALKS

1. Bob Feller, Indians, 1938	208
2. Nolan Ryan, Angels, 1977	204
3. Nolan Ryan, Angels, 1974	202
4. Bob Feller, Indians, 1941	194
5. Bobo Newsom, Browns, 1938	192
6. Sam Jones, Cubs, 1955	185
7. Nolan Ryan, Angels, 1976	183
8. Bob Harmon, Cardinals, 1911	181
Bob Turley, Orioles, 1954	181
10. Tommy Byrne, Yankees, 1949	179
11. Bob Turley, Yankees, 1955	177
12. Bump Hadley, White Sox-Browns, 1932	171
13. Elmer Myers, A's, 1916	168
14. Bobo Newsom, Senators-Red Sox, 1937	167
15. Weldon Wyckoff, A's, 1915	165
16. Earl Moore, Phillies, 1911	164
Phil Niekro, Braves, 1977	164
18. Nolan Ryan, Angels, 1973	162
Johnny Vander Meer, Reds, 1943	162
20. Tommy Byrne, Yankees, 1950	160

HIT BATSMEN

1. Chick Fraser, A's, 1901	32
2. Jack Warhop, Yankees, 1909	26
3. Chief Bender, A's, 1903	25
4. Otto Hess, Indians, 1906	24
Eddie Plank, A's, 1905	24
6. Howard Ehmke, Tigers, 1922	23
Eddie Plank, A's, 1903	23
Jake Weimer, Reds, 1907	23
9. Cy Morgan, Red Sox-A's, 1909	22
10. Jack Chesbro, Pirates, 1902	21
Joe McGinnity, Orioles, 1901	21
Harry McIntire, Dodgers, 1909	21
Cy Morgan, A's, 1911	21
Tom Murphy, Angels, 1969	21
Doc Newton, Reds-Dodgers, 1901	21
Henry Schmidt, Dodgers, 1903	21
17. 10 tied with 20	

WILD PITCHES

1. Red Ames, Giants, 1905	30
2. Tony Cloninger, Braves, 1966	27
3. Larry Cheney, Cubs, 1914	26
Juan Guzman, Blue Jays, 1993	26
5. Jack Morris, Tigers, 1987	24
6. Tim Leary, Yankees, 1990	23
Christy Mathewson, Giants, 1901	23
8. Tony Cloninger, Braves, 1965	22
Jack Hamilton, Phillies, 1962	22
Mike Moore, A's, 1992	22
Bobby Witt, Rangers, 1986	22
12. Ken Howell, Phillies, 1989	21
Walter Johnson, Senators, 1910	21
Joe Niekro, Astros-Yankees, 1985	21
Nolan Ryan, Angels, 1977	21
Earl Wilson, Red Sox, 1963	21
17. Red Ames, Giants, 1907	20
Larry Dierker, Astros, 1968	20
Dave Lemanczyk, Blue Jays, 1977	20
Denny Lemaster, Braves, 1964	20
J.R. Richard, Astros, 1975	20
John Smoltz, Braves, 1991	20

FOR THE RECORD

BATTING

3-GAME SERIES

HIGHEST AVERAGE
(Minimum 9 at-bats)

1.	Jay Johnstone, Phillies, 1976	.778
2.	Brooks Robinson, Orioles, 1970	.583
3.	Darrell Porter, Cardinals, 1982	.556
	Ozzie Smith, Cardinals, 1982	.556
5.	Frank White, Royals, 1980	.545
6.	Art Shamsky, Mets, 1969	.538
7.	Sal Bando, A's, 1975	.500
	Jerry Mumphrey, Yankees, 1981	.500
	Graig Nettles, Yankees, 1981	.500
	Tony Oliva, Twins, 1970	.500
	Brooks Robinson, Orioles, 1969	.500
	Willie Stargell, Pirates, 1970	.500
	Bob Watson, Yankees, 1980	.500
	Richie Zisk, Pirates, 1975	.500

RUNS

1.	Mark Belanger, Orioles, 1970	5
2.	Tommie Agee, Mets, 1969	4
	Mark Belanger, Orioles, 1969	4
	Ken Boswell, Mets, 1969	4
	Rico Carty, Braves, 1969	4
	Dave Concepcion, Reds, 1976	4
	Carlton Fisk, Red Sox, 1975	4
	Phil Garner, Pirates, 1979	4
	Tony Gonzalez, Braves, 1969	4
	Davey Johnson, Orioles, 1970	4
	Cleon Jones, Mets, 1969	4
	Willie McGee, Cardinals, 1982	4
	Larry Milbourne, Yankees, 1981	4
	Boog Powell, Orioles, 1971	4
	Carl Yastrzemski, Red Sox, 1975	4

HITS

1.	Jay Johnstone, Phillies, 1976	7
	Brooks Robinson, Orioles, 1969	7
	Brooks Robinson, Orioles, 1970	7
	Art Shamsky, Mets, 1969	7
5.	Sal Bando, A's, 1975	6
	Paul Blair, Orioles, 1969	6
	Dave Concepcion, Reds, 1979	6
	Cleon Jones, Mets, 1969	6
	Larry Milbourne, Yankees, 1981	6
	Jerry Mumphrey, Yankees, 1981	6
	Graig Nettles, Yankees, 1981	6
	Tony Oliva, Twins, 1970	6
	Boog Powell, Orioles, 1970	6
	Pete Rose, Reds, 1976	6
	Willie Stargell, Pirates, 1970	6
	Bob Watson, Yankees, 1980	6
	Frank White, Royals, 1980	6

HOME RUNS

1.	Hank Aaron, Braves, 1969	3
2.	Tommie Agee, Mets, 1969	2
	Ken Boswell, Mets, 1969	2
	George Brett, Royals, 1980	2
	George Foster, Reds, 1976	2
	Reggie Jackson, A's, 1971	2
	Davey Johnson, Orioles, 1970	2
	Harmon Killebrew, Twins, 1970	2
	Boog Powell, Orioles, 1971	2
	Willie Stargell, Pirates, 1979	2

TOTAL BASES

1.	Hank Aaron, Braves, 1969	16
2.	Willie Stargell, Pirates, 1979	13
3.	Tommie Agee, Mets, 1969	12
4.	Paul Blair, Orioles, 1969	11
	Reggie Jackson, A's, 1971	11
	Cleon Jones, Mets, 1969	11
	Willie McGee, Cardinals, 1982	11
	Graig Nettles, Yankees, 1981	11
	Tony Oliva, Twins, 1970	11
	Boog Powell, Orioles, 1970	11
	Bob Watson, Yankees, 1980	11

RUNS BATTED IN

1.	Graig Nettles, Yankees, 1981	9
2.	Hank Aaron, Braves, 1969	7
3.	Paul Blair, Orioles, 1969	6
	Boog Powell, Orioles, 1970	6
	Willie Stargell, Pirates, 1979	6
6.	Ken Boswell, Mets, 1969	5
	Willie McGee, Cardinals, 1982	5
8.	Tommie Agee, Mets, 1969	4
	George Brett, Royals, 1980	4
	Mike Cuellar, Orioles, 1970	4
	George Foster, Reds, 1976	4
	Ken Griffey, Reds, 1975	4
	Davey Johnson, Orioles, 1970	4
	Cleon Jones, Mets, 1969	4
	Harmon Killebrew, Twins, 1970	4

	Tony Perez, Reds, 1975	4
	Willie Wilson, Royals, 1980	4

STOLEN BASES

1.	Joe Morgan, Reds, 1975	4
2.	Ken Griffey, Reds, 1975	3
3.	Tommie Agee, Mets, 1969	2
	Juan Beniquez, Red Sox, 1975	2
	Dave Collins, Reds, 1979	2
	Dave Concepcion, Reds, 1975	2
	Ken Griffey, Reds, 1976	2
	Rickey Henderson, A's, 1981	2
	Cleon Jones, Mets, 1969	2
	Bill Madlock, Pirates, 1979	2
	Joe Morgan, Reds, 1976	2
	Amos Otis, Royals, 1980	2

4-GAME SERIES

HIGHEST AVERAGE
(Minimum 12 at-bats)

1.	Dusty Baker, Dodgers, 1978	.467
	Mike Schmidt, Phillies, 1983	.467
3.	Reggie Jackson, Yankees, 1978	.462
4.	Wade Boggs, Red Sox, 1990	.438
	Chipper Jones, Braves, 1995	.438
	Carney Lansford, A's, 1990	.438
	Fred McGriff, Braves, 1995	.438
	Bob Robertson, Pirates, 1971	.438
9.	Gary Matthews, Phillies, 1983	.429
	Willie McCovey, Giants, 1971	.429
	Amos Otis, Royals, 1978	.429

RUNS

1.	George Brett, Royals, 1978	7
2.	Steve Garvey, Dodgers, 1978	6
3.	Al Bumbry, Orioles, 1979	5
	Dave Cash, Pirates, 1971	5
	Reggie Jackson, Yankees, 1978	5
	Fred McGriff, Braves, 1995	5
	Eddie Murray, Orioles, 1983	5
	Cal Ripken, Orioles, 1983	5
	Bob Robertson, Pirates, 1971	5
	Mike Schmidt, Phillies, 1983	5
	Roy White, Yankees, 1978	5

HITS

1.	Dave Cash, Pirates, 1971	8
2.	Dusty Baker, Dodgers, 1978	7
	Wade Boggs, Red Sox, 1990	7
	George Brett, Royals, 1978	7
	Rod Carew, Angels, 1979	7
	Steve Garvey, Dodgers, 1974	7
	Steve Garvey, Dodgers, 1978	7
	Chipper Jones, Braves, 1995	7
	Carney Lansford, A's, 1990	7
	Barry Larkin, Reds, 1995	7
	Rudy Law, White Sox, 1983	7
	Davey Lopes, Dodgers, 1978	7
	Fred McGriff, Braves, 1995	7
	Bob Robertson, Pirates, 1971	7
	Bill Russell, Dodgers, 1974	7
	Bill Russell, Dodgers, 1978	7
	Mike Schmidt, Phillies, 1983	7

HOME RUNS

1.	Steve Garvey, Dodgers, 1978	4
	Bob Robertson, Pirates, 1971	4
3.	George Brett, Royals, 1978	3
	Jose Canseco, A's, 1988	3
	Gary Matthews, Phillies, 1983	3
6.	Dusty Baker, Dodgers, 1977	2
	Sal Bando, A's, 1974	2
	Dan Ford, Angels, 1979	2
	Steve Garvey, Dodgers, 1974	2
	Richie Hebner, Pirates, 1971	2
	Reggie Jackson, Yankees, 1978	2
	Davey Lopes, Dodgers, 1978	2
	Greg Luzinski, Phillies, 1978	2
	Willie McCovey, Giants, 1971	2
	Willie Stargell, Pirates, 1974	2

TOTAL BASES

1.	Steve Garvey, Dodgers, 1978	22
2.	Bob Robertson, Pirates, 1971	20
3.	George Brett, Royals, 1978	19
4.	Davey Lopes, Dodgers, 1978	16
5.	Jose Canseco, A's, 1988	15
	Gary Matthews, Phillies, 1983	15
7.	Steve Garvey, Dodgers, 1974	14
	Greg Luzinski, Phillies, 1978	14
9.	Reggie Jackson, Yankees, 1978	13
10.	Dusty Baker, Dodgers, 1977	12
	Dan Ford, Angels, 1979	12
	Richie Hebner, Pirates, 1971	12
	Willie McCovey, Giants, 1971	12
	Mike Schmidt, Phillies, 1983	12
	Willie Stargell, Pirates, 1974	12

RUNS BATTED IN

1.	Dusty Baker, Dodgers, 1977	8
	Gary Matthews, Phillies, 1983	8
3.	Steve Garvey, Dodgers, 1978	7
4.	Reggie Jackson, Yankees, 1978	6
	Willie McCovey, Giants, 1971	6
	Bob Robertson, Pirates, 1971	6
7.	Mike Devereaux, Braves, 1995	5
	Steve Garvey, Dodgers, 1974	5
	Davey Lopes, Dodgers, 1978	5
	Eddie Murray, Orioles, 1979	5
	Al Oliver, Pirates, 1971	5

STOLEN BASES

1.	Amos Otis, Royals, 1978	4
2.	Davey Lopes, Dodgers, 1974	3
3.	Al Bumbry, Orioles, 1979	2
	Jose Canseco, A's, 1990	2
	Julio Cruz, White Sox, 1983	2
	Rickey Henderson, A's, 1990	2
	Pat Kelly, Orioles, 1979	2
	Rudy Law, White Sox, 1983	2
	Willie McGee, A's, 1990	2
10.	39 tied with 1	

5-GAME SERIES

HIGHEST AVERAGE
(Minimum 15 at-bats)

1.	Will Clark, Giants, 1989	.650
2.	Mark Grace, Cubs, 1989	.647
3.	Fred Lynn, Angels, 1982	.611
4.	Terry Puhl, Astros, 1980	.526
5.	Chris Chambliss, Yankees, 1976	.524
6.	Roberto Alomar, Blue Jays, 1991	.474
	Bernie Williams, Yankees, 1996	.474
8.	Jose Offerman, Red Sox, 1999	.458
9.	Pete Rose, Reds, 1972	.450
10.	George Brett, Royals, 1976	.444
	Hal McRae, Royals, 1977	.444

RUNS

1.	Will Clark, Giants, 1989	8
	Rickey Henderson, A's, 1989	8
3.	Brett Butler, Giants, 1989	6
	Tony Fernandez, Blue Jays, 1989	6
	Tony Gwynn, Padres, 1984	6
	Hal McRae, Royals, 1977	6
	Ryne Sandberg, Cubs, 1989	6
	Bernie Williams, Yankees, 1996	6
9.	Brady Anderson, Orioles, 1996	5
	Tom Brunansky, Twins, 1987	5
	Chris Chambliss, Yankees, 1976	5
	Doug DeCinces, Angels, 1982	5
	Bob Dernier, Cubs, 1984	5
	Gary Gaetti, Twins, 1987	5
	Greg Gagne, Twins, 1987	5
	Dan Gladden, Twins, 1987	5
	Derek Jeter, Yankees, 1996	5
	Chuck Knoblauch, Twins, 1991	5
	Felix Millan, Mets, 1973	5
	Kevin Mitchell, Giants, 1989	5
	Joe Morgan, Reds, 1972	5
	Mickey Rivers, Yankees, 1976	5
	Mickey Rivers, Yankees, 1977	5
	Robby Thompson, Giants, 1989	5
	Devon White, Blue Jays, 1991	5

HITS

1.	Will Clark, Giants, 1989	13
2.	Chris Chambliss, Yankees, 1976	11
	Mark Grace, Cubs, 1989	11
	Fred Lynn, Angels, 1982	11
	Jose Offerman, Red Sox, 1999	11
6.	Derek Jeter, Yankees, 1996	10
	Thurman Munson, Yankees, 1976	10
	Terry Puhl, Astros, 1980	10
9.	Roberto Alomar, Blue Jays, 1991	9
	Kirby Puckett, Twins, 1991	9
	Mickey Rivers, Yankees, 1977	9
	Pete Rose, Reds, 1972	9
	Bernie Williams, Yankees, 1996	9

HOME RUNS

1.	Rusty Staub, Mets, 1973	3
	Darryl Strawberry, Yankees, 1996	3
	Todd Zeile, Orioles, 1996	3
4.	Sal Bando, A's, 1973	2
	Scott Brosius, A's, 1999	2
	Tom Brunansky, Twins, 1987	2
	Bert Campaneris, A's, 1973	2
	Chris Chambliss, Yankees, 1976	2
	Will Clark, Giants, 1989	2
	Jody Davis, Cubs, 1984	2
	Leon Durham, Cubs, 1984	2
	Cecil Fielder, Yankees, 1996	2
	Gary Gaetti, Twins, 1987	2
	Greg Gagne, Twins, 1987	2

Nomar Garciaparra, Red Sox, 1999	2
Rickey Henderson, A's, 1989	2
Chet Lemon, Tigers, 1987	2
Gary Matthews, Cubs, 1984	2
Kevin Mitchell, Giants, 1989	2
Paul Molitor, Brewers, 1982	2
Joe Morgan, Reds, 1972	2
Graig Nettles, Yankees, 1976	2
Rafael Palmeiro, Orioles, 1996	2
Dave Parker, A's, 1989	2
Kirby Puckett, Twins, 1991	2
Pete Rose, Reds, 1973	2
Robby Thompson, Giants, 1989	2
Bernie Williams, Yankees, 1996	2
Matt Williams, Giants, 1989	2

TOTAL BASES

1.	Will Clark, Giants, 1989	24
2.	Chris Chambliss, Yankees, 1976	20
3.	Mark Grace, Cubs, 1989	19
4.	Bernie Williams, Yankees, 1996	18
5.	Tom Brunansky, Twins, 1987	17
	Todd Zeile, Orioles, 1996	17
7.	Nomar Garciaparra, Red Sox, 1999	16
	Fred Lynn, Angels, 1982	16
	Kirby Puckett, Twins, 1991	16
	Ryne Sandberg, Cubs, 1989	16

RUNS BATTED IN

1.	Don Baylor, Angels, 1982	10
2.	Tom Brunansky, Twins, 1987	9
	Matt Williams, Giants, 1989	9
4.	Chris Chambliss, Yankees, 1976	8
	Will Clark, Giants, 1989	8
	Cecil Fielder, Yankees, 1996	8
	Mark Grace, Cubs, 1989	8
8.	Steve Garvey, Padres, 1984	7
	Kevin Mitchell, Giants, 1989	7
10.	Jody Davis, Cubs, 1984	6
	Kirby Puckett, Twins, 1991	6
	Bernie Williams, Yankees, 1996	6

STOLEN BASES

1.	Rickey Henderson, A's, 1989	8
2.	Tony Fernandez, Blue Jays, 1989	5
	Davey Lopes, Dodgers, 1981	5
4.	Randy Bush, Twins, 1987	3
	Bert Campaneris, A's, 1973	3
	Kirk Gibson, Tigers, 1987	3
	Dan Gladden, Twins, 1991	3
	Nelson Liriano, Blue Jays, 1989	3
	Ryne Sandberg, Cubs, 1984	3
	Devon White, Blue Jays, 1991	3

6-GAME SERIES

HIGHEST AVERAGE
(Minimum 18 at-bats)

1.	Eddie Perez, Braves, 1999	.500
2.	Kenny Lofton, Indians, 1995	.458
3.	Tim Raines, White Sox, 1993	.444
	Devon White, Blue Jays, 1993	.444
5.	Harold Baines, A's, 1992	.440
	Omar Vizquel, Indians, 1998	.440
7.	Fred McGriff, Braves, 1993	.435
	Ozzie Smith, Cardinals, 1985	.435
9.	Roberto Alomar, Blue Jays, 1992	.423
10.	Carlos Baerga, Indians, 1995	.400

RUNS

1.	Paul Molitor, Blue Jays, 1993	7
	Dave Winfield, Blue Jays, 1992	7
3.	Harold Baines, A's, 1992	6
	Willie McGee, Cardinals, 1985	6
	Fred McGriff, Braves, 1993	6
	Paul O'Neill, Yankees, 1998	6
	Gary Sheffield, Marlins, 1997	6
8.	Brady Anderson, Orioles, 1997	5
	Wally Backman, Mets, 1986	5
	Jeff Blauser, Braves, 1993	5
	Jeff Blauser, Braves, 1997	5
	Jay Buhner, Mariners, 1995	5
	Lenny Dykstra, Phillies, 1993	5
	Rickey Henderson, A's, 1992	5
	Andruw Jones, Braves, 1999	5
	Chipper Jones, Braves, 1997	5
	Barry Larkin, Reds, 1990	5
	Bill Madlock, Dodgers, 1985	5
	John Olerud, Blue Jays, 1993	5
	Tim Raines, White Sox, 1993	5

HITS

1.	Tim Raines, White Sox, 1993	12
	Devon White, Blue Jays, 1993	12
3.	Roberto Alomar, Blue Jays, 1992	11
	Harold Baines, A's, 1992	11
	Kenny Lofton, Indians, 1995	11
	Omar Vizquel, Indians, 1998	11
7.	Carlos Baerga, Indians, 1995	10
	Fred McGriff, Braves, 1993	10
	Eddie Perez, Braves, 1999	10
	Ozzie Smith, Cardinals, 1985	10

HOME RUNS

1.	Jim Thome, Indians, 1998	4
2.	Jay Buhner, Mariners, 1995	3
	Bill Madlock, Dodgers, 1985	3
4.	Roberto Alomar, Blue Jays, 1992	2
	Brady Anderson, Orioles, 1997	2
	Jeff Blauser, Braves, 1993	2
	Ken Caminiti, Padres, 1998	2
	Lenny Dykstra, Phillies, 1993	2
	Dave Hollins, Phillies, 1993	2
	Chipper Jones, Braves, 1997	2
	Brian Jordan, Braves, 1999	2
	Ryan Klesko, Braves, 1997	2
	Candy Maldonado, Blue Jays, 1992	2
	John Olerud, Mets, 1999	2
	Eddie Perez, Braves, 1999	2
	Manny Ramirez, Indians, 1995	2
	Manny Ramirez, Indians, 1997	2
	Manny Ramirez, Indians, 1998	2
	Darryl Strawberry, Mets, 1986	2
	Jim Thome, Indians, 1995	2
	Dave Winfield, Blue Jays, 1992	2

TOTAL BASES

1.	Jim Thome, Indians, 1998	19
2.	Roberto Alomar, Blue Jays, 1992	18
	Jay Buhner, Mariners, 1995	18
	Bill Madlock, Dodgers, 1985	18
	Eddie Perez, Braves, 1999	18
	Devon White, Blue Jays, 1993	18
7.	Brady Anderson, Orioles, 1997	17
8.	Harold Baines, A's, 1992	16
	Paul Molitor, Blue Jays, 1993	16
	Ozzie Smith, Cardinals, 1985	16

RUNS BATTED IN

1.	Jim Thome, Indians, 1998	8
2.	Bill Madlock, Dodgers, 1985	7
	Ruben Sierra, A's, 1992	7
4.	Scott Brosius, Yankees, 1998	6
	Tom Herr, Cardinals, 1985	6
	Lance Johnson, White Sox, 1993	6
	Candy Maldonado, Blue Jays, 1992	6
	John Olerud, Mets, 1999	6
9.	Moises Alou, Marlins, 1997	5
	Jay Buhner, Mariners, 1995	5
	Chili Davis, Yankees, 1998	5
	Charles Johnson, Marlins, 1997	5
	Brian Jordan, Braves, 1999	5
	John Kruk, Phillies, 1993	5
	Paul Molitor, Blue Jays, 1993	5
	Terry Pendleton, Braves, 1993	5
	Eddie Perez, Braves, 1999	5
	Terry Steinbach, A's, 1992	5
	Darryl Strawberry, Mets, 1986	5
	Jim Thome, Indians, 1995	5
	Michael Tucker, Braves, 1998	5
	Robin Ventura, White Sox, 1993	5
	Bernie Williams, Yankees, 1998	5

STOLEN BASES

1.	Willie Wilson, A's, 1992	7
2.	Roberto Alomar, Blue Jays, 1992	5
	Kenny Lofton, Indians, 1995	5
4.	Roberto Alomar, Blue Jays, 1993	4
	Vince Coleman, Mariners, 1995	4
	Omar Vizquel, Indians, 1998	4
7.	Marquis Grissom, Indians, 1997	3
	Billy Hatcher, Astros, 1986	3
	Derek Jeter, Yankees, 1998	3
	Chipper Jones, Braves, 1999	3
	Barry Larkin, Reds, 1990	3
	Omar Vizquel, Indians, 1995	3
	Gerald Williams, Braves, 1999	3

7-GAME SERIES

HIGHEST AVERAGE
(Minimum 21 at-bats)

1.	Javy Lopez, Braves, 1996	.542
2.	Bob Boone, Angels, 1986	.455
3.	Mark Lemke, Braves, 1996	.444
4.	Chipper Jones, Braves, 1996	.440
5.	Spike Owen, Red Sox, 1986	.429
6.	Jeffrey Leonard, Giants, 1987	.417
7.	Jay Bell, Pirates, 1991	.414
8.	Tony Pena, Cardinals, 1987	.381
9.	Marty Barrett, Red Sox, 1986	.367
10.	Mike Scioscia, Dodgers, 1988	.364

RUNS

1.	Javy Lopez, Braves, 1996	8
	Jim Rice, Red Sox, 1986	8
3.	Marquis Grissom, Braves, 1996	7
	Steve Sax, Dodgers, 1988	7
5.	Don Baylor, Red Sox, 1986	6
	George Brett, Royals, 1985	6
	Lenny Dykstra, Mets, 1988	6
	Chipper Jones, Braves, 1996	6
	Fred McGriff, Braves, 1996	6
10.	14 players tied with 5	

HITS

1.	Javy Lopez, Braves, 1996	13
2.	Jay Bell, Pirates, 1991	12

Will Clark was prolific in the five-game 1989 NLCS when he played for the Giants.

	Mark Lemke, Braves, 1996	12
4.	Marty Barrett, Red Sox, 1986	11
	Chipper Jones, Braves, 1996	11
6.	Bob Boone, Angels, 1986	10
	Rich Gedman, Red Sox, 1986	10
	Marquis Grissom, Braves, 1996	10
	Jeffrey Leonard, Giants, 1987	10
10.	Don Baylor, Red Sox, 1986	9
	George Bell, Blue Jays, 1985	9
	Will Clark, Giants, 1987	9
	Doug DeCinces, Angels, 1986	9
	Gregg Jefferies, Mets, 1988	9
	Spike Owen, Red Sox, 1986	9
	Gary Pettis, Angels, 1986	9
	Dick Schofield, Angeles, 1986	9
	Darryl Strawberry, Mets, 1988	9
	Willie Wilson, Royals, 1985	9

HOME RUNS

1.	Jeffrey Leonard, Giants, 1987	4
2.	George Brett, Royals, 1985	3
3.	Ron Gant, Braves, 1992	2
	Ron Gant, Cardinals, 1996	2
	Kirk Gibson, Dodgers, 1988	2
	David Justice, Braves, 1992	2
	Javy Lopez, Braves, 1996	2
	Fred McGriff, Braves, 1996	2
	Kevin McReynolds, Mets, 1988	2
	Jim Rice, Red Sox, 1986	2
	Pat Sheridan, Royals, 1985	2

TOTAL BASES

1.	Javy Lopez, Braves, 1996	24
2.	Jeffrey Leonard, Giants, 1987	22
3.	George Brett, Royals, 1985	19
4.	Jay Bell, Pirates, 1991	17
	Mark Lemke, Braves, 1996	17
6.	Don Baylor, Red Sox, 1986	15
	Doug DeCinces, Angels, 1986	15
	Fred McGriff, Braves, 1996	15
	Kevin McReynolds, Mets, 1988	15
10.	Will Clark, Giants, 1987	14
	Rich Gedman, Red Sox, 1986	14
	Marquis Grissom, Braves, 1996	14
	David Justice, Braves, 1992	14
	Darryl Strawberry, Mets, 1988	14

RUNS BATTED IN

1.	Brian Downing, Angels, 1986	7
	Fred McGriff, Braves, 1996	7
3.	Ron Gant, Braves, 1992	6
	Rich Gedman, Red Sox, 1986	6
	Kirk Gibson, Dodgers, 1988	6
	David Justice, Braves, 1992	6
	Javy Lopez, Braves, 1996	6
	Jim Rice, Red Sox, 1986	6
	Darryl Strawberry, Mets, 1988	6
	Jim Sundberg, Royals, 1985	6

STOLEN BASES

1.	Ron Gant, Braves, 1991	7
2.	Steve Sax, Dodgers, 1988	5
3.	Barry Bonds, Pirates, 1991	3
	Otis Nixon, Braves, 1992	3
5.	Kirk Gibson, Dodgers, 1988	2
	Marquis Grissom, Braves, 1996	2
	Kevin McReynolds, Mets, 1988	2
	Gary Redus, Pirates, 1991	2
	John Shelby, Dodgers, 1988	2
	Robby Thompson, Giants, 1987	2

FOR THE RECORD

PITCHING

3-GAME SERIES

INNINGS PITCHED

1.	Ken Holtzman, A's, 1975	11.0
	Dave McNally, Orioles, 1969	11.0
3.	Dave Boswell, Twins, 1969	10.2
4.	Dock Ellis, Pirates, 1970	9.2
5.	Bert Blyleven, Pirates, 1979	9.0
	Mike Cuellar, Orioles, 1971	9.0
	Bob Forsch, Cardinals, 1982	9.0
	Don Gullett, Reds, 1975	9.0
	Larry Gura, Royals, 1980	9.0
	Dave McNally, Orioles, 1970	9.0
	Gary Nolan, Reds, 1970	9.0
	Jim Palmer, Orioles, 1969	9.0
	Jim Palmer, Orioles, 1970	9.0
	Jim Palmer, Orioles, 1971	9.0
	Luis Tiant, Red Sox, 1975	9.0

LOWEST ERA
(Minimum 9 innings)

1.	Bob Forsch, Cardinals, 1982	0.00
	Dave McNally, Orioles, 1969	0.00
	Gary Nolan, Reds, 1970	0.00
	Luis Tiant, Red Sox, 1975	0.00
5.	Dave Boswell, Twins, 1969	0.84
6.	Bert Blyleven, Pirates, 1979	1.00
	Mike Cuellar, Orioles, 1971	1.00
	Jim Palmer, Orioles, 1970	1.00
9.	Larry Gura, Royals, 1980	2.00
	Jim Palmer, Orioles, 1969	2.00

VICTORIES

1.	Joaquin Andujar, Cardinals, 1982	1
	Bert Blyleven, Pirates, 1979	1
	Mike Cuellar, Orioles, 1971	1
	Rawly Eastwick, Reds, 1975	1
	Rawly Eastwick, Reds, 1976	1
	Bob Forsch, Cardinals, 1982	1
	George Frazier, Yankees, 1981	1
	Don Gullett, Reds, 1975	1
	Don Gullett, Reds, 1976	1
	Larry Gura, Royals, 1980	1
	Dick Hall, Orioles, 1969	1
	Dick Hall, Orioles, 1970	1
	Grant Jackson, Pirates, 1979	1
	Tommy John, Yankees, 1981	1
	Dennis Leonard, Royals, 1980	1
	Aurelio Lopez, Tigers, 1984	1
	Dave McNally, Orioles, 1969	1
	Dave McNally, Orioles, 1970	1
	Dave McNally, Orioles, 1971	1
	Jim Merritt, Reds, 1970	1
	Roger Moret, Red Sox, 1975	1
	Jack Morris, Tigers, 1984	1
	Gary Nolan, Reds, 1970	1
	Fred Norman, Reds, 1970	1
	Jim Palmer, Orioles, 1969	1
	Jim Palmer, Orioles, 1970	1
	Jim Palmer, Orioles, 1971	1
	Dan Quisenberry, Royals, 1980	1
	Dave Righetti, Yankees, 1981	1
	Don Robinson, Pirates, 1979	1
	Nolan Ryan, Mets, 1969	1
	Tom Seaver, Mets, 1969	1
	Bruce Sutter, Cardinals, 1982	1
	Ron Taylor, Mets, 1969	1
	Luis Tiant, Red Sox, 1975	1
	Milt Wilcox, Reds, 1970	1
	Milt Wilcox, Tigers, 1984	1
	Rick Wise, Red Sox, 1975	1
	Pat Zachry, Reds, 1976	1

SAVES

1.	Dick Drago, Red Sox, 1975	2
	Don Gullett, Reds, 1970	2
3.	Pedro Borbon, Reds, 1975	1
	Pedro Borbon, Reds, 1976	1
	Clay Carroll, Reds, 1970	1
	Rawly Eastwick, Reds, 1975	1
	Rich Gossage, Yankees, 1981	1
	Willie Hernandez, Tigers, 1984	1
	Tug McGraw, Mets, 1969	1
	Dan Quisenberry, Royals, 1980	1
	Don Robinson, Pirates, 1979	1
	Bruce Sutter, Cardinals, 1982	1
	Ron Taylor, Mets, 1969	1
	Eddie Watt, Orioles, 1971	1

4-GAME SERIES

INNINGS PITCHED

1.	Don Sutton, Dodgers, 1974	17.0
2.	Dave Stewart, A's, 1990	16.0
3.	Gaylord Perry, Giants, 1971	14.2
4.	Pete Schourek, Reds, 1995	14.1
5.	Steve Carlton, Phillies, 1983	13.2

	Tommy John, Dodgers, 1977	13.2
7.	Dave Stewart, A's, 1988	13.1
8.	Bruce Hurst, Red Sox, 1988	13.0
9.	Mike Cuellar, Orioles, 1974	12.2
10.	Dennis Leonard, Royals, 1978	12.0
	Jerry Reuss, Dodgers, 1983	12.0

LOWEST ERA
(Minimum 9 innings)

1.	Vida Blue, A's, 1974	0.00
	Mike Boddicker, Orioles, 1983	0.00
	Ken Holtzman, A's, 1974	0.00
	Tommy John, Dodgers, 1978	0.00
	Scott McGregor, Orioles, 1979	0.00
6.	Don Sutton, Dodgers, 1974	0.53
7.	Steve Carlton, Phillies, 1983	0.66
	Tommy John, Dodgers, 1977	0.66
9.	Britt Burns, White Sox, 1983	0.96
10.	La Marr Hoyt, White Sox, 1983	1.00
	Jim Palmer, Orioles, 1974	1.00
	Don Sutton, Dodgers, 1977	1.00

VICTORIES

1.	Steve Carlton, Phillies, 1983	2
	Gene Nelson, A's, 1988	2
	Dave Stewart, A's, 1990	2
	Don Sutton, Dodgers, 1974	2
5.	40 tied with 1	

SAVES

1.	Dennis Eckersley, A's, 1988	4
2.	Dave Giusti, Pirates, 1971	3
3.	Dennis Eckersley, A's, 1990	2
4.	Ken Clay, Yankees, 1978	1
	Rollie Fingers, A's, 1974	1
	Mike Garman, Dodgers, 1977	1
	Rich Gossage, Yankees, 1978	1
	Al Holland, Phillies, 1983	1
	Rick Honeycutt, A's, 1990	1
	Tug McGraw, Phillies, 1977	1
	Greg McMichael, Braves, 1995	1
	Tom Niedenfuer, Dodgers, 1983	1
	Sammy Stewart, Orioles, 1983	1

5-GAME SERIES

INNINGS PITCHED

1.	Mickey Lolich, Tigers, 1972	19.0
2.	Ray Burris, Expos, 1981	17.0
3.	Tom Seaver, Mets, 1973	16.2
4.	Catfish Hunter, A's, 1973	16.1
5.	Dave Stewart, A's, 1989	16.0
6.	Steve Blass, Pirates, 1972	15.2
7.	Catfish Hunter, A's, 1972	15.1
8.	Orlando Hernandez, Yankees, 1999	15.0
	Andy Pettitte, Yankees, 1996	15.0
	Paul Splittorff, Royals, 1977	15.0

LOWEST ERA
(Minimum 9 innings)

1.	Joe Coleman, Tigers, 1972	0.00
	Burt Hooton, Dodgers, 1981	0.00
	Jon Matlack, Mets, 1973	0.00
	Joe Niekro, Astros, 1980	0.00
	Blue Moon Odom, A's, 1972	0.00
6.	Ray Burris, Expos, 1981	0.53
7.	Ken Holtzman, A's, 1973	0.82
8.	Sparky Lyle, Yankees, 1977	0.96
9.	Ross Grimsley, Reds, 1972	1.00
10.	Catfish Hunter, A's, 1972	1.17

VICTORIES

1.	Bert Blyleven, Twins, 1987	2
	Burt Hooton, Dodgers, 1981	2
	Catfish Hunter, A's, 1973	2
	Craig Lefferts, Padres, 1984	2
	Sparky Lyle, Yankees, 1977	2
	Jack Morris, Twins, 1991	2
	Blue Moon Odom, A's, 1972	2
	Dave Stewart, A's, 1989	2
9.	64 tied with 1	

SAVES

1.	Rick Aguilera, Twins, 1991	3
	Steve Bedrosian, Giants, 1989	3
	Dennis Eckersley, A's, 1989	3
4.	Pete Ladd, Brewers, 1982	2
	Tug McGraw, Phillies, 1980	2
	Jeff Reardon, Twins, 1987	2
	Mariano Rivera, Yankees, 1999	2
8.	18 tied with 1	

6-GAME SERIES

INNINGS PITCHED

1.	Mike Scott, Astros, 1986	18.0
2.	Dwight Gooden, Mets, 1986	17.0
3.	Dave Stewart, A's, 1992	16.2
4.	Doug Drabek, Pirates, 1990	16.1
5.	Curt Schilling, Phillies, 1993	16.0

6.	David Wells, Yankees, 1998	15.2
7.	Orel Hershiser, Dodgers, 1985	15.1
	Randy Johnson, Mariners, 1995	15.1
	Bob Knepper, Astros, 1986	15.1
10.	Kevin Brown, Marlins, 1997	15.0
	Alex Fernandez, White Sox, 1993	15.0
	Mike Mussina, Orioles, 1997	15.0

LOWEST ERA
(Minimum 9 innings)

1.	Denny Neagle, Braves, 1997	0.00
2.	Mike Scott, Astros, 1986	0.50
3.	Mike Mussina, Orioles, 1997	0.60
4.	Livan Hernandez, Marlins, 1997	0.84
5.	Sterling Hitchcock, Padres, 1998	0.90
6.	Wilson Alvarez, White Sox, 1993	1.00
	Bartolo Colon, Indians, 1998	1.00
8.	Dwight Gooden, Mets, 1986	1.06
9.	Orel Hershiser, Indians, 1995	1.29
10.	Greg Maddux, Braves, 1997	1.38

VICTORIES

1.	Jesse Orosco, Mets, 1986	3
2.	Kevin Brown, Marlins, 1997	2
	Juan Guzman, Blue Jays, 1992	2
	Juan Guzman, Blue Jays, 1993	2
	Livan Hernandez, Marlins, 1997	2
	Orel Hershiser, Indians, 1995	2
	Sterling Hitchcock, Padres, 1998	2
	Mike Scott, Astros, 1986	2
	Dave Stewart, Blue Jays, 1993	2
	David Wells, Yankees, 1998	2
	Mitch Williams, Phillies, 1993	2

SAVES

1.	Tom Henke, Blue Jays, 1992	3
	Randy Myers, Reds, 1990	3
3.	Ken Dayley, Cardinals, 1985	2
	Jose Mesa, Indians, 1997	2
	Robb Nen, Marlins, 1997	2
	Duane Ward, Blue Jays, 1993	2
	Mitch Williams, Phillies, 1993	2
8.	17 tied with 1	

7-GAME SERIES

INNINGS PITCHED

1.	Orel Hershiser, Dodgers, 1988	24.2
2.	Roger Clemens, Red Sox, 1986	22.2
3.	John Smoltz, Braves, 1992	20.1
	Dave Stieb, Blue Jays, 1985	20.1
5.	Dwight Gooden, Mets, 1988	18.1
6.	Tim Wakefield, Pirates, 1992	18.0
7.	Mike Witt, Angels, 1986	17.2
8.	Danny Cox, Cardinals, 1987	17.0
	Doug Drabek, Pirates, 1992	17.0
10.	Steve Avery, Braves, 1991	16.1

LOWEST ERA
(Minimum 9 innings)

1.	Steve Avery, Braves, 1991	0.00
	Danny Jackson, Royals, 1985	0.00
	Dennis Lamp, Blue Jays, 1985	0.00
4.	Doug Drabek, Pirates, 1991	0.60
	Dave Dravecky, Giants, 1987	0.60
6.	Zane Smith, Pirates, 1991	0.61
7.	John Candelaria, Angels, 1986	0.84
8.	Orel Hershiser, Dodgers, 1988	1.09
9.	John Smoltz, Braves, 1996	1.20
10.	Bud Black, Royals, 1985	1.69

VICTORIES

1.	Steve Avery, Braves, 1991	2
	Tim Belcher, Dodgers, 1988	2
	Tom Henke, Blue Jays, 1985	2
	Randy Myers, Mets, 1988	2
	John Smoltz, Braves, 1991	2
	John Smoltz, Braves, 1992	2
	John Smoltz, Braves, 1996	2
	Tim Wakefield, Pirates, 1992	2
9.	33 tied with 1	

SAVES

1.	Alejandro Pena, Braves, 1991	3
2.	Ken Dayley, Cardinals, 1987	2
	Mark Wohlers, Braves, 1996	2
4.	Dennis Eckersley, Cardinals, 1996	1
	Orel Hershiser, Dodgers, 1988	1
	Brian Holton, Dodgers, 1988	1
	Roger Mason, Pirates, 1991	1
	Donnie Moore, Angels, 1986	1
	Alejandro Pena, Dodgers, 1988	1
	Dan Quisenberry, Royals, 1985	1
	Jeff Reardon, Braves, 1992	1
	Calvin Schiraldi, Red Sox, 1986	1
	Bob Walk, Pirates, 1991	1
	Todd Worrell, Cardinals, 1987	1

BATTING

4-GAME SERIES

HIGHEST AVERAGE

(Minimum 12 at-bats)

1.	Billy Hatcher, Reds, 1990	.750
2.	Babe Ruth, Yankees, 1928	.625
3.	Chris Sabo, Reds, 1990	.563
4.	Bret Boone, Braves, 1999	.538
5.	Johnny Bench, Reds, 1976	.533
6.	Lou Gehrig, Yankees, 1932	.529
	Thurman Munson, Yankees, 1976	.529
8.	Tony Gwynn, Padres, 1998	.500
	Mark Koenig, Yankees, 1927	.500
	Joe Marty, Cubs, 1938	.500
	Vic Wertz, Indians, 1954	.500

RUNS

1.	Lou Gehrig, Yankees, 1932	9
	Babe Ruth, Yankees, 1928	9
3.	Earle Combs, Yankees, 1932	8
	Charlie Keller, Yankees, 1939	8
5.	Earle Combs, Yankees, 1927	6
	Billy Hatcher, Reds, 1990	6
	Dave Henderson, A's, 1989	6
	Babe Ruth, Yankees, 1932	6
	Hank Thompson, Giants, 1954	6
10.	8 tied with 5	

HITS

1.	Babe Ruth, Yankees, 1928	10
2.	Lou Gehrig, Yankees, 1932	9
	Billy Hatcher, Reds, 1990	9
	Rickey Henderson, A's, 1989	9
	Mark Koenig, Yankees, 1927	9
	Thurman Munson, Yankees, 1976	9
	Chris Sabo, Reds, 1990	9
8.	Johnny Bench, Reds, 1976	8
	Scott Brosius, Yankees, 1998	8
	Tony Gwynn, Padres, 1998	8
	Stan Hack, Cubs, 1938	8
	Riggs Stephenson, Cubs, 1932	8
	Vic Wertz, Indians, 1954	8

HOME RUNS

1.	Lou Gehrig, Yankees, 1928	4
2.	Lou Gehrig, Yankees, 1932	3
	Charlie Keller, Yankees, 1939	3
	Babe Ruth, Yankees, 1928	3
5.	Johnny Bench, Reds, 1976	2
	Scott Brosius, Yankees, 1998	2
	Bill Dickey, Yankees, 1939	2
	Dave Henderson, A's, 1989	2
	Tony Lazzeri, Yankees, 1932	2
	Dusty Rhodes, Giants, 1954	2
	Frank Robinson, Orioles, 1966	2
	Babe Ruth, Yankees, 1927	2
	Babe Ruth, Yankees, 1932	2
	Chris Sabo, Reds, 1990	2
	Greg Vaughn, Padres, 1998	2

TOTAL BASES

1.	Babe Ruth, Yankees, 1928	22
2.	Lou Gehrig, Yankees, 1928	19
	Lou Gehrig, Yankees, 1932	19
	Charlie Keller, Yankees, 1939	19
5.	Johnny Bench, Reds, 1976	17
	Rickey Henderson, A's, 1989	17
7.	Chris Sabo, Reds, 1990	16
8.	Billy Hatcher, Reds, 1990	15
	Vic Wertz, Indians, 1954	15
10.	Scott Brosius, Yankees, 1998	14
	Hank Gowdy, Braves, 1914	14

RUNS BATTED IN

1.	Lou Gehrig, Yankees, 1928	9
2.	Lou Gehrig, Yankees, 1932	8
3.	Dusty Rhodes, Giants, 1954	7
	Babe Ruth, Yankees, 1927	7
	Terry Steinbach, A's, 1989	7
6.	Johnny Bench, Reds, 1976	6
	Scott Brosius, Yankees, 1998	6
	Ben Chapman, Yankees, 1932	6
	Frankie Crosetti, Yankees, 1938	6
	Joe Gordon, Yankees, 1938	6
	Charlie Keller, Yankees, 1939	6
	Babe Ruth, Yankees, 1932	6

STOLEN BASES

1.	Rickey Henderson, A's, 1989	3
	Rickey Henderson, A's, 1990	3
	Derek Jeter, Yankees, 1999	3
4.	Brett Butler, Giants, 1989	2
	Charlie Deal, Braves, 1914	2
	Frankie Frisch, Cardinals, 1928	2
	Cesar Geronimo, Reds, 1976	2
	Billy Jurges, Cubs, 1932	2
	Tony Lazzeri, Yankees, 1928	2
	Rabbit Maranville, Braves, 1914	2
	Bob Meusel, Yankees, 1928	2
	Joe Morgan, Reds, 1976	2

5-GAME SERIES

HIGHEST AVERAGE

(Minimum 15 at-bats)

1.	Paul Blair, Orioles, 1970	.474
	Heinie Groh, Giants, 1922	.474
3.	Frankie Frisch, Giants, 1922	.471
	Harry Steinfeldt, Cubs, 1907	.471
	Hack Wilson, Cubs, 1929	.471
6.	Frank Baker, A's, 1913	.450
	Alan Trammell, Tigers, 1984	.450
8.	Duffy Lewis, Red Sox, 1915	.444
9.	Fred Luderus, Phillies, 1915	.438
10.	Eddie Collins, A's, 1910	.429
	Brooks Robinson, Orioles, 1970	.429

RUNS

1.	Frank Baker, A's, 1910	6
	Harry Hooper, Red Sox, 1916	6
	Lee May, Reds, 1970	6
	Danny Murphy, A's, 1910	6
	Boog Powell, Orioles, 1970	6
	Al Simmons, A's, 1929	6
	Lou Whitaker, Tigers, 1984	6
8.	18 tied with 5	

HITS

1.	Frank Baker, A's, 1910	9
	Frank Baker, A's, 1913	9
	Paul Blair, Orioles, 1970	9
	Eddie Collins, A's, 1910	9
	Heinie Groh, Giants, 1922	9
	Jo-Jo Moore, Giants, 1937	9
	Bobby Richardson, Yankees, 1961	9
	Brooks Robinson, Orioles, 1970	9
	Alan Trammell, Tigers, 1984	9
10.	11 tied with 8	

HOME RUNS

1.	Donn Clendenon, Mets, 1969	3
2.	Kurt Bevacqua, Padres, 1984	2
	Johnny Blanchard, Yankees, 1961	2
	Jimmie Foxx, A's, 1929	2
	Larry Gardner, Red Sox, 1916	2
	Kirk Gibson, Tigers, 1984	2
	Mule Haas, A's, 1929	2
	Mickey Hatcher, Dodgers, 1988	2
	Harry Hooper, Red Sox, 1915	2
	Charlie Keller, Yankees, 1942	2
	Lee May, Reds, 1970	2
	Joe Morgan, Phillies, 1983	2
	Eddie Murray, Orioles, 1983	2
	Mel Ott, Giants, 1933	2
	Boog Powell, Orioles, 1970	2
	Brooks Robinson, Orioles, 1970	2
	Frank Robinson, Orioles, 1970	2
	Al Simmons, A's, 1929	2
	Alan Trammell, Tigers, 1984	2
	Aaron Ward, Yankees, 1922	2

TOTAL BASES

1.	Brooks Robinson, Orioles, 1970	17
2.	Alan Trammell, Tigers, 1984	16
3.	Kurt Bevacqua, Padres, 1984	15
	Donn Clendenon, Mets, 1969	15
	Lee May, Reds, 1970	15
6.	Jimmie Foxx, A's, 1929	14
	Mickey Hatcher, Dodgers, 1988	14
8.	7 tied with 13	

RUNS BATTED IN

1.	Danny Murphy, A's, 1910	9
2.	Lee May, Reds, 1970	8
3.	Frank Baker, A's, 1913	7
	Kirk Gibson, Tigers, 1984	7
	Hector Lopez, Yankees, 1961	7
	Irish Meusel, Giants, 1922	7
	Wally Schang, A's, 1913	7
8.	Larry Gardner, Red Sox, 1916	6
	Mule Haas, A's, 1929	6
	Fred Luderus, Phillies, 1915	6
	Brooks Robinson, Orioles, 1970	6
	George Selkirk, Yankees, 1937	6
	Alan Trammell, Tigers, 1984	6

STOLEN BASES

1.	Jimmy Slagle, Cubs, 1907	6
2.	Frank Chance, Cubs, 1908	5
3.	Eddie Collins, A's, 1910	4
4.	Frank Chance, Cubs, 1907	3
	Eddie Collins, A's, 1913	3
	Bill Dahlen, Giants, 1905	3
	Art Devlin, Giants, 1905	3
	Johnny Evers, Cubs, 1907	3
	Kirk Gibson, Tigers, 1984	3
	Davy Jones, Tigers, 1907	3

6-GAME SERIES

HIGHEST AVERAGE

(Minimum 18 at-bats)

1.	Billy Martin, Yankees, 1953	.500
	Paul Molitor, Blue Jays, 1993	.500
	Dave Robertson, Giants, 1917	.500
4.	Roberto Alomar, Blue Jays, 1993	.480
5.	Amos Otis, Royals, 1980	.478
6.	Monte Irvin, Giants, 1951	.458
7.	Jake Powell, Yankees, 1936	.455
8.	Pat Borders, Blue Jays, 1992	.450
	Reggie Jackson, Yankees, 1977	.450
10.	Marquis Grissom, Braves, 1996	.444

RUNS

1.	Reggie Jackson, Yankees, 1977	10
	Paul Molitor, Blue Jays, 1993	10
3.	Lenny Dykstra, Phillies, 1993	9
	Roy White, Yankees, 1978	9
5.	Jake Powell, Yankees, 1936	8
	Babe Ruth, Yankees, 1923	8
	Devon White, Blue Jays, 1993	8
8.	Frank Baker, A's, 1911	7
	Davey Lopes, Dodgers, 1978	7
	Reggie Smith, Dodgers, 1977	7

HITS

1.	Roberto Alomar, Blue Jays, 1993	12
	Marquis Grissom, Braves, 1996	12
	Billy Martin, Yankees, 1953	12
	Paul Molitor, Blue Jays, 1993	12
5.	Monte Irvin, Giants, 1951	11
	Amos Otis, Royals, 1980	11
	Dave Robertson, Giants, 1917	11
	Bill Russell, Dodgers, 1978	11
9.	10 tied with 10	

HOME RUNS

1.	Reggie Jackson, Yankees, 1977	5
2.	Willie Aikens, Royals, 1980	4
	Lenny Dykstra, Phillies, 1993	4
4.	Ryan Klesko, Braves, 1995	3
	Ted Kluszewski, White Sox, 1959	3
	Davey Lopes, Dodgers, 1978	3
	Amos Otis, Royals, 1980	3
	Babe Ruth, Yankees, 1923	3
	Reggie Smith, Dodgers, 1977	3
10.	29 tied with 2	

TOTAL BASES

1.	Reggie Jackson, Yankees, 1977	25
2.	Paul Molitor, Blue Jays, 1993	24
3.	Billy Martin, Yankees, 1953	23
4.	Willie Aikens, Royals, 1980	22
	Amos Otis, Royals, 1980	22
6.	Lenny Dykstra, Phillies, 1993	21
7.	Ted Kluszewski, White Sox, 1959	19
	Babe Ruth, Yankees, 1923	19
9.	Charlie Neal, Dodgers, 1959	18
10.	Frank Baker, A's, 1911	17
	Jim Gilliam, Dodgers, 1953	17
	Davey Lopes, Dodgers, 1978	17
	Devon White, Blue Jays, 1993	17

RUNS BATTED IN

1.	Ted Kluszewski, White Sox, 1959	10
2.	Tony Fernandez, Blue Jays, 1993	9
3.	Willie Aikens, Royals, 1980	8
	Joe Carter, Blue Jays, 1993	8
	Lenny Dykstra, Phillies, 1993	8
	Reggie Jackson, Yankees, 1977	8
	Reggie Jackson, Yankees, 1978	8
	Billy Martin, Yankees, 1953	8
	Bob Meusel, Yankees, 1923	8
	Paul Molitor, Blue Jays, 1993	8

STOLEN BASES

1.	Kenny Lofton, Indians, 1995	6
2.	Otis Nixon, Braves, 1992	5
	Deion Sanders, Braves, 1992	5
4.	Roberto Alomar, Blue Jays, 1993	4
	Lenny Dykstra, Phillies, 1993	4
	Davey Lopes, Dodgers, 1981	4
7.	Roberto Alomar, 1992	3
	Larry Bowa, Phillies, 1980	3
	Eddie Collins, White Sox, 1917	3
	Mariano Duncan, Phillies, 1993	3
	Marquis Grissom, Braves, 1995	3
	Joe Tinker, Cubs, 1906	3

7-Game Series

HIGHEST AVERAGE
(Minimum 21 at-bats)

1.	Phil Garner, Pirates, 1979	.500
	Pepper Martin, Cardinals, 1931	.500
3.	Tim McCarver, Cardinals, 1964	.478
4.	Lou Brock, Cardinals, 1968	.464
5.	Max Carey, Pirates, 1925	.458
6.	Joe Harris, Senators, 1925	.440
7.	Tony Perez, Reds, 1972	.435
8.	Marty Barrett, Red Sox, 1986	.433
9.	Phil Cavarretta, Cubs, 1945	.423
	Rusty Staub, Mets, 1973	.423

RUNS

1.	Lou Brock, Cardinals, 1967	8
	Billy Johnson, Yankees, 1947	8
	Tommy Leach, Pirates, 1909	8
	Mickey Mantle, Yankees, 1960	8
	Mickey Mantle, Yankees, 1964	8
	Pepper Martin, Cardinals, 1934	8
	Freddy Parent, Red Sox, 1903	8
	Bobby Richardson, Yankees, 1960	8
	Jim Thome, Indians, 1997	8
	Matt Williams, Indians, 1997	8

HITS

1.	Marty Barrett, Red Sox, 1986	13
	Lou Brock, Cardinals, 1968	13
	Bobby Richardson, Yankees, 1964	13
4.	Lou Brock, Cardinals, 1967	12
	Roberto Clemente, Pirates, 1971	12
	Phil Garner, Pirates, 1979	12
	Buck Herzog, Giants, 1912	12
	Joe Jackson, White Sox, 1919	12
	Pepper Martin, Cardinals, 1931	12
	Sam Rice, Senators, 1925	12
	Bill Skowron, Yankees, 1960	12
	Willie Stargell, Pirates, 1979	12
	Robin Yount, Brewers, 1982	12

HOME RUNS

1.	Hank Bauer, Yankees, 1958	4
	Babe Ruth, Yankees, 1926	4
	Duke Snider, Dodgers, 1952	4
	Duke Snider, Dodgers, 1955	4
	Gene Tenace, A's, 1972	4
6.	14 tied with 3	

TOTAL BASES

1.	Willie Stargell, Pirates, 1979	25
2.	Lou Brock, Cardinals, 1968	24
	Duke Snider, Dodgers, 1952	24
4.	Hank Aaron, Braves, 1957	22
	Hank Bauer, Yankees, 1958	22
	Roberto Clemente, Pirates, 1971	22
	Joe Harris, Senators, 1925	22
8.	Goose Goslin, Senators, 1924	21
	Duke Snider, Dodgers, 1955	21
	Gene Tenace, A's, 1972	21
	Carl Yastrzemski, Red Sox, 1967	21

RUNS BATTED IN

1.	Bobby Richardson, Yankees, 1960	12
2.	Mickey Mantle, Yankees, 1960	11
3.	Sandy Alomar, Indians, 1997	10
	Yogi Berra, Yankees, 1956	10
5.	Moises Alou, Marlins, 1997	9
	Gary Carter, Mets, 1986	9
	Dwight Evans, Red Sox, 1986	9
	Gene Tenace, A's, 1972	9
9.	11 tied with 8	

STOLEN BASES

1.	Lou Brock, Cardinals, 1967	7
	Lou Brock, Cardinals, 1968	7
3.	Vince Coleman, Cardinals, 1987	6
	Honus Wagner, Pirates, 1909	6
5.	Pepper Martin, Cardinals, 1931	5
	Bobby Tolan, Reds, 1972	5
	Omar Vizquel, Indians, 1997	5
8.	Josh Devore, Giants, 1912	4
	Chuck Knoblauch, Twins, 1991	4
10.	15 tied with 3	

PITCHING

4-Game Series

INNINGS PITCHED

1.	Waite Hoyt, Yankees, 1928	18.0
	Sandy Koufax, Dodgers, 1963	18.0
	Dick Rudolph, Braves, 1914	18.0
	Red Ruffing, Yankees, 1938	18.0
5.	Dave Stewart, A's, 1989	16.0
6.	Paul Derringer, Reds, 1939	15.1
	Jose Rijo, Reds, 1990	15.1
8.	Jim Konstanty, Phillies, 1950	15.0
9.	Kevin Brown, Padres, 1998	14.1
10.	Bob Lemon, Indians, 1954	13.1
	Bill Sherdel, Cardinals, 1928	13.1

LOWEST ERA
(Minimum 9 innings)

1.	Wally Bunker, Orioles, 1966	0.00
	Don Drysdale, Dodgers, 1963	0.00
	Bill James, Braves, 1914	0.00
	Jim Palmer, Orioles, 1966	0.00
	Monte Pearson, Yankees, 1939	0.00
	Vic Raschi, Yankees, 1950	0.00
7.	Dick Rudolph, Braves, 1914	0.50
8.	Jose Rijo, Reds, 1990	0.59
9.	Johnny Antonelli, Giants, 1954	0.84
	Wilcy Moore, Yankees, 1927	0.84

VICTORIES

1.	Waite Hoyt, Yankees, 1928	2
	Bill James, Braves, 1914	2
	Sandy Koufax, Dodgers, 1963	2
	Mike Moore, A's, 1989	2
	Jose Rijo, Reds, 1990	2
	Dick Rudolph, Braves, 1914	2
	Red Ruffing, Yankees, 1938	2
	Dave Stewart, A's, 1989	2
9.	44 tied with 1	

SAVES

1.	Mariano Rivera, Yankees, 1998	3
2.	Will McEnaney, Reds, 1976	2
	Herb Pennock, Yankees, 1932	2
	Mariano Rivera, Yankees, 1999	2
5.	Johnny Antonelli, Giants, 1954	1
	Dennis Eckersley, A's, 1989	1
	Wilcy Moore, Yankees, 1927	1
	Johnny Murphy, Yankees, 1938	1
	Randy Myers, Reds, 1990	1
	Ron Perranoski, Dodgers, 1963	1
	Allie Reynolds, Yankees, 1950	1
	Hoyt Wilhelm, Giants, 1954	1

5-Game Series

INNINGS PITCHED

1.	Jack Coombs, A's, 1910	27.0
	Christy Mathewson, Giants, 1905	27.0
3.	Bill Donovan, Tigers, 1907	21.0
4.	Carl Hubbell, Giants, 1933	20.0
5.	Christy Mathewson, Giants, 1913	19.0
	Eddie Plank, A's, 1913	19.0
7.	Chief Bender, A's, 1910	18.2
8.	Orval Overall, Cubs, 1908	18.1
9.	10 tied with 18.0	

LOWEST ERA
(Minimum 9 innings)

1.	Mike Boddicker, Orioles, 1983	0.00
	Mordecai Brown, Cubs, 1907	0.00
	Mordecai Brown, Cubs, 1908	0.00
	Clay Carroll, Reds, 1970	0.00
	Whitey Ford, Yankees, 1961	0.00
	Carl Hubbell, Giants, 1933	0.00
	Christy Mathewson, Giants, 1905	0.00
	Joe McGinnity, Giants, 1905	0.00
	George Mullin, Tigers, 1908	0.00
	Allie Reynolds, Yankees, 1949	0.00
	Preacher Roe, Dodgers, 1949	0.00
	Marius Russo, Yankees, 1943	0.00
	Jack Scott, Giants, 1922	0.00
	Ernie White, Cardinals, 1942	0.00
	Earl Whitehill, Senators, 1933	0.00

VICTORIES

1.	Jack Coombs, A's, 1910	3
	Christy Mathewson, Giants, 1905	3
3.	Johnny Beazley, Cardinals, 1942	2
	Chief Bender, A's, 1913	2
	Mordecai Brown, Cubs, 1908	2
	Spud Chandler, Yankees, 1943	2
	Whitey Ford, Yankees, 1961	2
	Rube Foster, Red Sox, 1915	2
	Lefty Gomez, Yankees, 1937	2
	Orel Hershiser, Dodgers, 1988	2
	Carl Hubbell, Giants, 1933	2
	Jerry Koosman, Mets, 1969	2
	Jack Morris, Tigers, 1984	2
	Orval Overall, Cubs, 1908	2
	Ernie Shore, Red Sox, 1916	2

SAVES

1.	Rollie Fingers, A's, 1974	2
	Lefty Grove, A's, 1929	2
	Willie Hernandez, Tigers, 1984	2
	Tippy Martinez, Orioles, 1983	2
5.	17 tied with 1	

6-Game Series

INNINGS PITCHED

1.	Red Faber, White Sox, 1917	27.0
	Christy Mathewson, Giants, 1911	27.0
	Hippo Vaughn, Cubs, 1918	27.0
4.	Chief Bender, A's, 1911	26.0
5.	George Earnshaw, A's, 1930	25.0
6.	Eddie Cicotte, White Sox, 1917	23.0

	Lefty Tyler, Cubs, 1918	23.0
8.	Schoolboy Rowe, Tigers, 1935	21.0
9.	Jack Coombs, A's, 1911	20.0
10.	Mordecai Brown, Cubs, 1906	19.2

LOWEST ERA
(Minimum 9 innings)

1.	Gene Bearden, Indians, 1948	0.00
	Rube Benton, Giants, 1917	0.00
	Jack Kramer, Browns, 1944	0.00
4.	Ed Lopat, Yankees, 1951	0.50
5.	Lon Warneke, Cubs, 1935	0.54
6.	John Smoltz, Braves, 1996	0.64
7.	Tommy John, Yankees, 1981	0.69
8.	Larry Sherry, Dodgers, 1959	0.71
9.	George Earnshaw, A's, 1930	0.72
10.	Vic Raschi, Yankees, 1951	0.87

VICTORIES

1.	Red Faber, White Sox, 1917	3
2.	Chief Bender, A's, 1911	2
	Tommy Bridges, Tigers, 1935	2
	Steve Carlton, Phillies, 1980	2
	George Earnshaw, A's, 1930	2
	Tom Glavine, Braves, 1995	2
	Lefty Gomez, Yankees, 1936	2
	Lefty Grove, A's, 1930	2
	Jimmy Key, Blue Jays, 1992	2
	Bob Lemon, Indians, 1948	2
	Ed Lopat, Yankees, 1951	2
	Carl Mays, Red Sox, 1918	2
	Herb Pennock, Yankees, 1923	2
	Babe Ruth, Red Sox, 1918	2
	Larry Sherry, Dodgers, 1959	2
	Mike Torrez, Yankees, 1977	2
	Ed Walsh, White Sox, 1906	2
	Duane Ward, Blue Jays, 1992	2
	Lon Warneke, Cubs, 1935	2

SAVES

1.	John Wetteland, Yankees, 1996	4
2.	Rich Gossage, Yankees, 1981	2
	Tom Henke, Blue Jays, 1992	2
	Tug McGraw, Phillies, 1980	2
	Larry Sherry, Dodgers, 1959	2
	Duane Ward, Blue Jays, 1993	2
	Mark Wohlers, Braves, 1995	2
8.	24 tied with 1	

7-Game Series

INNINGS PITCHED

1.	Deacon Phillippe, Pirates, 1903	44.0
2.	Bill Dinneen, Red Sox, 1903	35.0
3.	Cy Young, Red Sox, 1903	34.0
4.	George Mullin, Tigers, 1909	32.0
5.	Christy Mathewson, Giants, 1912	28.2
	Warren Spahn, Braves, 1958	28.2
7.	Babe Adams, Pirates, 1909	27.0
	Lew Burdette, Braves, 1957	27.0
	Stan Coveleski, Indians, 1920	27.0
	Bob Gibson, Cardinals, 1964	27.0
	Bob Gibson, Cardinals, 1967	27.0
	Bob Gibson, Cardinals, 1968	27.0
	Waite Hoyt, Yankees, 1921	27.0
	Mickey Lolich, Tigers, 1968	27.0

LOWEST ERA
(Minimum 9 innings)

1.	Jack Billingham, Reds, 1972	0.00
	Nelson Briles, Pirates, 1971	0.00
	Joe Dobson, Red Sox, 1946	0.00
	Whitey Ford, Yankees, 1960	0.00
	Waite Hoyt, Yankees, 1921	0.00
	Clem Labine, Dodgers, 1956	0.00
	Don Larsen, Yankees, 1956	0.00
	Duster Mails, Indians, 1920	0.00
9.	Sandy Koufax, Dodgers, 1965	0.38
10.	Harry Brecheen, Cardinals, 1946	0.45

VICTORIES

1.	Babe Adams, Pirates, 1909	3
	Harry Brecheen, Cardinals, 1946	3
	Lew Burdette, Braves, 1957	3
	Stan Coveleski, Indians, 1920	3
	Bill Dinneen, Red Sox, 1903	3
	Bob Gibson, Cardinals, 1967	3
	Mickey Lolich, Tigers, 1968	3
	Deacon Phillippe, Pirates, 1903	3
	Joe Wood, Red Sox, 1912	3
10.	59 tied with 2	

SAVES

1.	Roy Face, Pirates, 1960	3
	Kent Tekulve, Pirates, 1979	3
3.	Rick Aguilera, Twins, 1991	2
	Rollie Fingers, A's, 1972	2
	Rollie Fingers, A's, 1973	2
	Darold Knowles, A's, 1973	2
	Firpo Marberry, Senators, 1924	2
	Bob McClure, Brewers, 1982	2
	Robb Nen, Marlins, 1997	2
	Jesse Orosco, Mets, 1986	2
	Bruce Sutter, Cardinals, 1982	2
	Todd Worrell, Cardinals, 1987	2

SINGLE GAME

REGULAR SEASON (1901-1999)

BATTING

FOUR-HOMER GAMES

1. Lou Gehrig, Yankees, June 3, 1932	1
Chuck Klein, Phillies, July 10, 1936 (10 inn.)	1
Pat Seerey, White Sox, July 18, 1948 (11 inn.)	1
Gil Hodges, Dodgers, Aug. 31, 1950	1
Joe Adcock, Braves, July 31, 1954	1
Rocky Colavito, Indians, June 10, 1959	1
Willie Mays, Giants, April 30, 1961	1
Mike Schmidt, Phillies, April 17, 1976 (10 inn.)	1
Bob Horner, Braves, July 6, 1986	1
Mark Whiten, Cardinals, Sept. 7, 1993	1

HITS, A.L.

1. Johnny Burnett, Indians, July 10, 1932 (18 inn.)	9
2. Rocky Colavito, Tigers, June 24, 1962 (22 inn.)	7
Cesar Gutierrez, Tigers, June 21, 1970 (12 inn.)	7
4. Mike Donlin, Orioles, June 24, 1901	6
Doc Nance, Tigers, July 13, 1901	6
Ervin Harvey, Indians, April 25, 1902	6
Danny Murphy, A's, July 8, 1902	6
Jimmy Williams, Orioles, Aug. 25, 1902	6
Bobby Veach, Tigers, Sept. 17, 1920 (12 inn.)	6
George Sisler, Browns, Aug. 9, 1921 (19 inn.)	6
Frank Brower, Indians, Aug. 7, 1923	6
George H. Burns, Indians., June 19, 1924	6
Ty Cobb, Tigers, May 5, 1925	6
Jimmie Foxx, A's, May 30, 1930 (13 inn.)	6
Doc Cramer, A's, June 20, 1932	6
Jimmie Foxx, A's, July 10, 1932 (18 inn.)	6
Sam West, Browns, April 13, 1933 (11 inn.)	6
Myril Hoag, Yankees, June 6, 1934	6
Bob Johnson, A's, June 16, 1934 (11 inn.)	6
Doc Cramer, A's, July 13, 1935	6
Bruce Campbell, Indians, July 2, 1936	6
Rip Radcliff, White Sox, July 18, 1936	6
Hank Steinbacher, White Sox, June 22, 1938	6
George Myatt, Senators, May 1, 1944	6
Stan Spence, Senators, June 1, 1944	6
George Kell, Tigers, Sept. 20, 1946	6
Jim Fridley, Indians, April 29, 1952	6
Jimmy Piersall, Red Sox, June 10, 1953	6
Joe DeMaestri, A's, July 8, 1955	6
Pete Runnels, Red Sox, Aug. 30, 1960 (15 inn.)	6
Floyd Robinson, White Sox, July 22, 1962	6
Bob Oliver, Royals, May 4, 1969	6
Jim Northrup, Tigers, Aug. 28, 1969 (13 inn.)	6
John Briggs, Brewers, Aug. 4, 1973	6
Jorge Orta, Indians, June 15, 1980	6
Jerry Remy, Red Sox, Sept. 3, 1981 (20 inn.)	6
Kevin Seitzer, Royals, Aug. 2, 1987	6
Kirby Puckett, Twins, Aug. 30, 1987	6
Kirby Puckett, Twins, May 23, 1991 (11 inn.)	6
Carlos Baerga, Indians, April 11, 1992 (18 inn.)	6
Kevin Reimer, Brewers, Aug. 24, 1993 (13 inn.)	6
Lance Johnson, White Sox, Sept. 23, 1995	6
Gerald Williams, Yankees, May 1, 1996 (15 inn.)	6
Garret Anderson, Angels, Sept. 27, 1996 (15 inn.)	6

HITS, N.L.

1. Rennie Stennett, Pirates, Sept. 16, 1975	7
2. Kip Selbach, Giants, June 9, 1901	6
George Cutshaw, Dodgers, Aug. 9, 1915	6
Carson Bigbee, Pirates, Aug. 22, 1917 (22 inn.)	6
Dave Bancroft, Giants, June 28, 1920	6
Johnny Gooch, Pirates, July 7, 1922 (18 inn.)	6
Max Carey, Pirates, July 7, 1922 (18 inn.)	6
Jack Fournier, Dodgers, June 29, 1923	6
Kiki Cuyler, Pirates, Aug. 9, 1924	6
Frankie Frisch, Giants, Sept. 10, 1924	6
Jim Bottomley, Cardinals, Sept. 16, 1924	6
Paul Waner, Pirates, Aug. 26, 1926	6
Lloyd Waner, Pirates, June 15, 1929 (14 inn.)	6
Hank DeBerry, Dodgers, June 23, 1929 (14 inn.)	6
Wally Gilbert, Dodgers, May 30, 1931	6
Jim Bottomley, Cardinals, Aug. 5, 1931	6
Tony Cuccinello, Reds, Aug. 13, 1931	6
Terry Moore, Cardinals, Sept. 5, 1935	6
Ernie Lombardi, Reds, May 9, 1937	6
Frank Demaree, Cubs, July 5, 1937 (14 inn.)	6
Cookie Lavagetto, Dodgers, Sept. 23, 1939	6
Walker Cooper, Reds, July 6, 1949	6
Johnny Hopp, Pirates, May 14, 1950	6
Connie Ryan, Phillies, April 16, 1953	6
Dick Groat, Pirates, May 13, 1960	6
Jesus Alou, Giants, July 10, 1964	6
Joe Morgan, Astros, July 8, 1965 (12 inn.)	6
Felix Millan, Braves, July 6, 1970	6
Don Kessinger, Cubs, July 17, 1971 (10 inn.)	6
Willie Davis, Dodgers, May 24, 1973 (19 inn.)	6
Bill Madlock, Cubs, July 26, 1975 (10 inn.)	6
Jose Cardenal, Cubs, May 2, 1976 (14 inn.)	6
Gene Richards, Padres, July 26, 1977 (15 inn.)	6
Jim Lefebvre, Padres, Sept. 13, 1982 (16 inn.)	6
Wally Backman, Pirates, April 27, 1990	6
Sammy Sosa, Cubs, July 2, 1993	6
Tony Gwynn, Padres, Aug. 4, 1993 (12 inn.)	6
Rondell White, Expos, June 11, 1995 (13 inn.)	6
Mike Benjamin, Giants, June 14, 1995 (13 inn.)	6
Andres Galarraga, Rockies, July 3, 1995	6
Edgardo Alfonzo, Mets, August 30, 1999	6

RUNS

1. Mel Ott, Giants, Aug. 4, 1934	6
Mel Ott, Giants, April 30, 1944	6
Johnny Pesky, Red Sox, May 8, 1946	6
Frank Torre, Braves, Sept. 2, 1957	6
Spike Owen, Red Sox, Aug. 21, 1986	6
Edgardo Alfonzo, August 30, 1999	6
7. Many tied with 5	

DOUBLES

1. Pop Dillon, Tigers, April 25, 1901	4
Gavvy Cravath, Phillies, Aug. 8, 1915	4
Denny Sothern, Phillies, June 6, 1930	4
Paul Waner, Pirates, May 20, 1932	4
Dick Bartell, Phillies, April 15, 1933	4
Ernie Lombardi, Reds, May 8, 1935	4
Billy Werber, Red Sox, July 17, 1935	4
Frankie Hayes, A's, July 25, 1936	4
Mike Kreevich, White Sox, Sept. 4, 1937	4
Joe Medwick, Cardinals, Aug. 4, 1937	4
Marv Owen, White Sox, April 23, 1939	4
Billy Werber, Reds, May 13, 1940 (14 inn.)	4
Johnny Lindell, Yankees, Aug. 17, 1944	4
Lou Boudreau, Indians, July 14, 1946	4
Willie Jones, Phillies, April 20, 1949	4
Al Zarilla, Red Sox, June 8, 1950	4
Jim Greengrass, Reds, April 13, 1954	4
Vic Wertz, Indians, Sept. 26, 1956	4
Charlie Lau, Orioles, July 13, 1962	4
Billy Bruton, Tigers, May 19, 1963	4
Billy Williams, Cubs, April 9, 1969	4
Orlando Cepeda, Red Sox, Aug. 8, 1973	4
Jim Mason, Yankees, July 8, 1974	4
Dave Duncan, Orioles, June 30, 1975	4
Rick Miller, Red Sox, May 11, 1981	4
Rafael Ramirez, Braves, May 21, 1986 (13 inn.)	4
Damaso Garcia, Blue Jays, June 27, 1986	4
Kirby Puckett, Twins, May 13, 1989	4
Billy Hatcher, Reds, Aug. 21, 1990	4
Jeff Bagwell, Astros, June 14, 1996	4
Sandy Alomar Jr., Indians, June 6, 1997	4
Albert Belle, Orioles, August 29, 1999	4
Albert Belle, Orioles, September 23, 1999	4

3-HOME RUN GAMES

1. Johnny Mize, Cardinals, 1938	2
Johnny Mize, Cardinals, 1939	2
Ralph Kiner, Pirates, 1947	2
Ted Williams, Red Sox, 1957	2
Willie Mays, Giants., 1961	2
Willie Stargell, Pirates, 1971	2
Dave Kingman, Cubs, 1979	2
Doug DeCinces, Angels, 1982	2
Joe Carter, Indians, 1989	2
Cecil Fielder, Tigers, 1990	2
German Berroa, A's, 1996	2
Steve Finley, Padres, 1997	2
Mark McGwire, Cardinals, 1998	2

2-HOME RUN GAMES

1. Hank Greenberg, Tigers, 1938	11
Sammy Sosa, Cubs, 1998	11
3. Jimmie Foxx, Red Sox, 1938	10
Ralph Kiner, Pirates, 1947	10
Mark McGwire, Cardinals, 1998	10
6. Willie Mays, Giants, 1955	9
George Bell, Blue Jays, 1987	9
Mark McGwire, Cardinals, 1999	9
9. Babe Ruth, Yankees, 1927	8
Hack Wilson, Cubs, 1930	8
Mickey Mantle, Yankees, 1961	8
Willie Mays, Giants, 1964	8
Reggie Jackson, A's, 1969	8
George Foster, Reds, 1977	8
Andre Dawson, Cubs, 1987	8
Albert Belle, Indians, 1995	8
Andres Galarraga, Rockies, 1996	8
Ken Griffey Jr., Mariners, 1997	8
Larry Walker, Rockies, 1997	8

HOME RUNS FIRST AT-BAT, A.L.

Luke Stuart, Browns	Aug. 8, 1921
Earl Averill, Indians	April 16, 1929
Ace Parker, A's	April 30, 1937
Gene Hasson, A's	Sept. 9, 1937

Yankees slugger Tony Lazzeri was the first player to hit two grand slams in a game.

Bill Lefebvre, Red Sox	June 10, 1938
Hack Miller, Tigers	April 23, 1944
Eddie Pellagrini, Red Sox	April 22, 1946
George Vico, Tigers	April 20, 1948
Bob Nieman, Browns	Sept. 14, 1951
Bob Tillman, Red Sox	May 19, 1962
John Kennedy, Senators	Sept. 5, 1962
Buster Narum, Orioles	May 3, 1963
Gates Brown, Tigers	June 19, 1963
Bert Campaneris, A's	July 23, 1964
Bill Roman, Tigers	Sept. 30, 1964
Brant Alyea, Senators	Sept. 12, 1965
John Miller, Yankees	Sept. 11, 1966
Rick Renick, Twins	July 11, 1968
Joe Keough, A's	Aug. 7, 1968
Gene Lamont, Tigers	Sept. 2, 1970
Don Rose, Angels	May 24, 1972
Reggie J. Sanders, Tigers	Sept. 1, 1974
Dave McKay, Twins	Aug. 22, 1975
Al Woods, Blue Jays	April 7, 1977
Dave Machemer, Angels	June 21, 1978
Gary Gaetti, Twins	Sept. 20, 1981
Andre David, Twins	June 29, 1984
Terry Steinbach, A's	Sept. 12, 1986
Jay Bell, Indians	Sept. 29, 1986
Junior Felix, Blue Jays	May 4, 1989
Jon Nunnally, Royals	April 29, 1995
Carlos Lee, White Sox	May 7, 1999
Russ Branyan, Indians	July 23, 1999

HOME RUNS FIRST AT-BAT, N.L.

Johnny Bates, Braves	April 12, 1906
Walter Mueller, Pirates	May 7, 1922
Clise Dudley, Dodgers	April 27, 1929
Gordon Slade, Dodgers	May 24, 1930
Eddie Morgan, Cardinals	April 14, 1936
Ernie Koy, Dodgers	April 19, 1938
Emmett Mueller, Phillies	April 19, 1938
Clyde Vollmer, Reds	May 31, 1942
Paul Gillespie, Cubs	Sept. 11, 1942
Buddy Kerr, Giants	Sept. 8, 1943
Whitey Lockman, Giants	July 5, 1945
Dan Bankhead, Dodgers	Aug. 26, 1947
Les Layton, Giants	May 21, 1948
Ed Sanicki, Phillies	Sept. 14, 1949
Ted Tappe, Reds	Sept. 14, 1950
Hoyt Wilhelm, Giants	April 23, 1952
Wally Moon, Cardinals	April 13, 1954
Chuck Tanner, Braves	April 12, 1955
Bill White, Giants	May 7, 1956
Frank Ernaga, Cubs	May 24, 1957
Don Leppert, Pirates	June 18, 1961
Cuno Barragan, Cubs	Sept. 1, 1961
Benny Ayala, Mets	Aug. 27, 1974
John Montefusco, Giants	Sept. 3, 1974
Jose Sosa, Astros	July 30, 1975
Johnnie Lemaster, Giants	Sept. 2, 1975
Tim Wallach, Expos	Sept. 6, 1980
Carmelo Martinez, Cubs	Aug. 22, 1983
Mike Fitzgerald, Mets	Sept. 13, 1983
Will Clark, Giants	April 8, 1986
Ricky Jordan, Phillies	July 17, 1988

Jose Offerman, Dodgers	Aug. 19, 1990
Dave Eiland, Padres	April 10, 1992
Jim Bullinger, Cubs	June 8, 1992
Jay Gainer, Rockies	May 14, 1993
Mitch Lyden, Marlins	June 16, 1993
Garey Ingram, Dodgers	May 19, 1994
Jermaine Dye, Braves	May 17, 1996
Dustin Hermanson, Expos	April 16, 1997
Brad Fullmer, Expos	Sept. 2, 1997
Marlon Anderson, Phillies	Sept. 8, 1998

GRAND SLAMS

1. Tony Lazzeri, Yankees, May 24, 1936 — 2
   Jim Tabor, Red Sox, July 4, 1939 — 2
   Rudy York, Red Sox, July 27, 1946 — 2
   Jim Gentile, Orioles, May 9, 1961 — 2
   Tony Cloninger, Braves, July 3, 1966 — 2
   Jim Northrup, Tigers, June 24, 1968 — 2
   Frank Robinson, Orioles, June 26, 1970 — 2
   Robin Ventura, White Sox, Sept. 4, 1995 — 2
   Chris Hoiles, Orioles, August 14, 1998 — 2
   Fernando Tatis, Cardinals, April 23, 1999 — 2

TOTAL BASES

1. Joe Adcock, Braves, July 31, 1954 — 18
2. Gil Hodges, Dodgers, Aug. 31, 1950 — 17
   Mike Schmidt, Phillies, April 17, 1976 (10 inn.) — 17
4. Ty Cobb, Tigers, May 5, 1925 — 16
   Lou Gehrig, Yankees, June 3, 1932 — 16
   Jimmie Foxx, A's, July 10, 1932 (18 inn.) — 16
   Chuck Klein, Phillies, July 10, 1936 (10 inn.) — 16
   Pat Seerey, White Sox, July 18, 1948 (11 inn.) — 16
   Rocky Colavito, Indians, June 10, 1959 — 16
   Willie Mays, Giants, April 30, 1961 — 16
   Fred Lynn, Red Sox, June 18, 1975 — 16
   Bob Horner, Braves, July 6, 1986 — 16
   Mark Whiten, Cardinals, Sept. 7, 1993 — 16
   Edgardo Alfonzo, Mets, August 30, 1999 — 16

RUNS BATTED IN

1. Jim Bottomley, Cardinals, Sept. 16, 1924 — 12
   Mark Whiten, Cardinals, Sept. 7, 1993 — 12
3. Tony Lazzeri, Yankees, May 24, 1936 — 11
   Phil Weintraub, Giants, April 30, 1944 — 11
5. Rudy York, Red Sox, May 27, 1946 — 10
   Walker Cooper, Reds, July 6, 1949 — 10
   Norm Zauchin, Red Sox, May 27, 1955 — 10
   Reggie Jackson, A's, June 14, 1969 — 10
   Fred Lynn, Red Sox, June 18, 1975 — 10
   Nomar Garciaparra, Red Sox, May 10, 1999 — 10

STOLEN BASES

1. Eddie Collins, A's, Sept. 11, 1912 — 6
   Eddie Collins, A's, Sept. 22, 1912 — 6
   Otis Nixon, Braves, June 16, 1991 — 6
   Eric Young, Rockies, June 30, 1996 — 6
5. Dan McGann, Giants, May 27, 1904 — 5
   Clyde Milan, Senators, June 14, 1912 — 5
   Johnny Neun, Tigers, July 9, 1927 — 5
   Amos Otis, Royals, Sept. 7, 1971 — 5
   Davey Lopes, Dodgers, Aug. 24, 1974 — 5
   Bert Campaneris, A's, April 24, 1976 — 5
   Lonnie Smith, Cardinals, Sept. 4, 1982 — 5
   Alan Wiggins, Padres, May 17, 1984 — 5
   Tony Gwynn, Padres, Sept. 20, 1986 — 5
   Alex Cole, Indians, May 3, 1992 — 5
   Damian Jackson, Padres, June 28, 1999 — 5

STEALING HOME

1. Honus Wagner, Pirates, June 20, 1901 — 2
   Ed Konetchy, Cardinals, Sept. 30, 1907 — 2
   Joe Tinker, Cubs, June 28, 1910 — 2
   Larry Doyle, Giants, Sept. 18, 1911 — 2
   Sherry Magee, Phillies, July 20, 1912 — 2
   Joe Jackson, Indians, Aug. 11, 1912 — 2
   Guy Zinn, Yankees, Aug. 15, 1912 — 2
   Eddie Collins, A's, Sept. 6, 1913 — 2
   Bill Barrett, White Sox, May 1, 1924 — 2
   Doc Gautreau, Braves, Sept. 3, 1927 — 2
   Vic Power, Indians, Aug. 14, 1958 (10 inn.) — 2

PITCHING

WALKS

1. Bruno Haas, A's, June 23, 1915 — 16
   Tommy Byrne, Yankees, Aug. 22, 1951 (13 inn.) — 16
3. Carroll Brown, A's, July 12, 1913 — 15
4. Henry Mathewson, Giants, Oct. 5, 1906 — 14
   Skipper Friday, Senators, June 17, 1923 — 14
6. Mal Eason, Braves, Sept. 3, 1902 — 13
   Pete Schneider, Reds, July 6, 1918 — 13
   George Turbeville, A's, Aug. 24, 1935 (15 inn.) — 13
   Tommy Byrne, Yankees, June 8, 1949 — 13
   Dick Weik, Senators, Sept. 1, 1949 — 13
   Bud Podbielan, Reds, May 18, 1953 (11 inn.) — 13

STRIKEOUTS

1. Tom Cheney, Senators, Sept. 12, 1962 (16 inn.) — 21
2. Roger Clemens, Red Sox, April 29, 1986 — 20
   Roger Clemens, Red Sox, Sept. 18, 1996 — 20
   Kerry Wood, Cubs, May 6, 1998 — 20
5. Luis Tiant, Indians, July 3, 1968 (10 inn.) — 19
   Steve Carlton, Cardinals, Sept. 15, 1969 — 19
   Tom Seaver, Mets, April 22, 1970 — 19
   Nolan Ryan, Angels, June 14, 1974 (12 inn.) — 19
   Nolan Ryan, Angels, Aug. 12, 1974 — 19
   Nolan Ryan, Angels, Aug. 20, 1974 (11 inn.) — 19
   Nolan Ryan, Angels, Aug. 7, 1977 (10 inn.) — 19
   David Cone, Mets, Oct. 6, 1991 — 19
   Randy Johnson, Mariners, June 24, 1997 — 19
   Randy Johnson, Mariners, Aug. 8, 1997 — 19

LEAGUE CHAMPIONSHIP SERIES

BATTING

RUNS

1. Bob Robertson, Pirates, Oct. 3, 1971 — 4
   Steve Garvey, Dodgers, Oct. 9, 1974 — 4
   Mark Brouhard, Brewers, Oct. 9, 1982 — 4
   Eddie Murray, Orioles, Oct. 7, 1983 — 4
   George Brett, Royals, Oct. 11, 1985 — 4
   Will Clark, Giants, Oct. 4, 1989 — 4
   Fred McGriff, Braves, Oct. 17, 1996 — 4
   Javy Lopez, Braves, Oct. 14, 1996 — 4
9. 29 tied with 3

HITS

1. Paul Blair, Orioles, Oct. 6, 1969 — 5
2. Brooks Robinson, Orioles, Oct. 4, 1969 — 4
   Don Buford, Orioles, Oct. 6, 1969 — 4
   Bob Robertson, Pirates, Oct. 3, 1971 — 4
   Ron Cey, Dodgers, Oct. 6, 1974 — 4
   Steve Garvey, Dodgers, Oct. 9, 1974 — 4
   Sal Bando, A's, Oct. 5, 1975 — 4
   Mickey Rivers, Yankees, Oct. 14, 1976 — 4
   Mickey Rivers, Yankees, Oct. 8, 1977 — 4
   Chris Chambliss, Yankees, Oct. 4, 1978 — 4
   Dusty Baker, Dodgers, Oct. 7, 1978 (10 inn.) — 4
   Terry Puhl, Astros, Oct. 12, 1980 (10 inn.) — 4
   Jerry Mumphrey, Yankees, Oct. 14, 1981 — 4
   Graig Nettles, Yankees, Oct. 14, 1981 — 4
   Steve Garvey, Padres, Oct. 6, 1984 — 4
   George Brett, Royals, Oct. 11, 1985 — 4
   Tito Landrum, Cardinals, Oct. 13, 1985 — 4
   Rich Gedman, Red Sox, Oct. 12, 1986 (11 inn.) — 4
   Spike Owen, Red Sox, Oct. 14, 1986 — 4
   Kevin McReynolds, Mets, Oct. 11, 1988 — 4
   Will Clark, Giants, Oct. 4, 1989 — 4
   Kelly Gruber, Blue Jays, Oct. 7, 1989 — 4
   Otis Nixon, Braves, Oct. 10, 1992 — 4
   Roberto Alomar, Blue Jays, Oct. 11, 1992 — 4
   John Olerud, Blue Jays, Oct. 11, 1992 (11 inn.) — 4
   Jerry Browne, A's, Oct. 12, 1992 — 4
   Paul Molitor, Blue Jays, Oct. 5, 1993 — 4
   Ed Sprague, Blue Jays, Oct. 5, 1993 — 4
   Tim Raines, White Sox, Oct. 8, 1993 — 4
   Manny Ramirez, Indians, Oct. 11, 1995 — 4
   Derek Jeter, Yankees, Oct. 9, 1996 — 4
   Chipper Jones, Braves, Oct. 9, 1996 — 4
   Mark Lemke, Braves, Oct. 14, 1996 — 4
   Javy Lopez, Braves, Oct. 14, 1996 — 4
   Keith Lockhart, Braves, Oct. 14, 1997 — 4
   Nomar Garciaparra, Red Sox, Oct. 16, 1999 — 4

HOME RUNS

1. Bob Robertson, Pirates, Oct. 3, 1971 — 3
   George Brett, Royals, Oct. 6, 1978 — 3
3. Boog Powell, Orioles, Oct. 4, 1971 — 2
   Reggie Jackson, A's, Oct. 5, 1971 — 2
   Sal Bando, A's, Oct. 7, 1973 — 2
   Rusty Staub, Mets, Oct. 8, 1973 — 2
   Steve Garvey, Dodgers, Oct. 9, 1974 — 2
   Graig Nettles, Yankees, Oct. 13, 1976 — 2
   Steve Garvey, Dodgers, Oct. 4, 1978 — 2
   Gary Matthews, Cubs, Oct. 2, 1984 — 2
   George Brett, Royals, Oct. 11, 1985 — 2
   Gary Gaetti, Twins, Oct. 7, 1987 — 2
   Rickey Henderson, A's, Oct. 7, 1989 — 2
   Will Clark, Giants, Oct. 4, 1989 — 2
   David Justice, Braves, Oct. 13, 1992 — 2
   Manny Ramirez, Indians, Oct. 11, 1995 — 2
   Jay Buhner, Mariners, Oct. 13, 1995 — 2
   Ron Gant, Cardinals, Oct. 12, 1996 — 2
   Darryl Strawberry, Yankees, Oct. 12, 1996 — 2
   Jim Thome, Indians, Oct. 9, 1998 — 2

RUNS BATTED IN

1. Will Clark, Giants, Oct. 4, 1989 — 6
2. Paul Blair, Orioles, Oct. 6, 1969 — 5
   Bob Robertson, Pirates, Oct. 3, 1971 — 5
   Don Baylor, Angels, Oct. 5, 1982 — 5
   Steve Garvey, Padres, Oct. 6, 1984 — 5
   Michael Tucker, Braves, Oct. 12, 1998 — 5
   John Valentin, Red Sox, Oct. 16, 1999 — 5
8. 27 tied with 4

TOTAL BASES

1. Bob Robertson, Pirates, Oct. 3, 1971 — 14
2. George Brett, Royals, Oct. 11, 1985 — 12
3. Steve Garvey, Dodgers, Oct. 4, 1978 — 11
   George Brett, Royals, Oct. 11, 1985 — 11
   Will Clark, Giants, Oct. 4, 1989 — 11
6. Paul Blair, Orioles, Oct. 6, 1969 — 10
   Steve Garvey, Dodgers, Oct. 9, 1974 — 10
   Manny Ramirez, Indians, Oct. 11, 1995 — 10
9. Reggie Jackson, A's, Oct. 5, 1971 — 9
   Ron Cey, Dodgers, Oct. 6, 1974 — 9
   David Justice, Braves, Oct. 13, 1992 — 9
   Darryl Strawberry, Yankees, Oct. 12, 1996 — 9
   Javy Lopez, Braves, Oct. 14, 1996 — 9

STOLEN BASES

1. Rickey Henderson, A's, Oct. 4, 1989 — 4
2. Joe Morgan, Reds, Oct. 4, 1975 — 3
   Ken Griffey Sr., Reds, Oct. 5, 1975 — 3
   Steve Sax, Dodgers, Oct. 9, 1988 (12 inn.) — 3
   Ron Gant, Braves, Oct. 10, 1991 — 3
   Willie Wilson, A's, Oct. 8, 1992 — 3
   Roberto Alomar, Blue Jays, Oct. 10, 1993 — 3

PITCHING

RUNS ALLOWED

1. Phil Niekro, Braves, Oct. 4, 1969 — 9
2. Jim Perry, Twins, Oct. 3, 1970 — 8
   Roger Clemens, Red Sox, Oct. 7, 1986 — 8
   Greg A. Harris, Padres, Oct. 2, 1984 — 8
   Greg Maddux, Cubs, Oct. 4, 1989 — 8
   Tom Glavine, Braves, Oct. 13, 1992 — 8
   Greg Maddux, Braves, Oct. 10, 1996 — 8
   Hideki Irabu, Yankees, Oct. 16, 1999 — 8
9. 11 tied with 7

HITS ALLOWED

1. Jack McDowell, White Sox, Oct. 5, 1993 — 13
   Hideki Irabu, Yankees, Oct. 16, 1999 — 13
3. Larry Gura, Royals, Oct. 9, 1986 — 12
4. Bruce Hurst, Red Sox, Oct. 8, 1986 — 11
   Roger Erickson, Orioles, Oct. 12, 1997 — 11
   Kevin Brown, Marlins, Oct. 14, 1997 — 11
7. Pat Jarvis, Braves, Oct. 6, 1969 — 10
   Jim Palmer, Orioles, Oct. 6, 1969 — 10
   Mike Cuellar, Orioles, Oct. 3, 1970 — 10
   Gaylord Perry, Giants, Oct. 6, 1971 — 10
   Burt Hooton, Dodgers, Oct. 4, 1978 — 10
   Larry Gura, Royals, Oct. 8, 1980 — 10
   Roger Clemens, Red Sox, Oct. 7, 1986 — 10
   Kirk McCaskill, Angels, Oct. 8, 1986 — 10
   Bob Ojeda, Mets, Oct. 9, 1986 — 10
   John Tudor, Cardinals, Oct. 7, 1987 — 10
   Al Leiter, Marlins, Oct. 11, 1997 — 10
   Tom Glavine, Braves, Oct. 14, 1997 — 10

STRIKEOUTS

1. Mike Mussina, Orioles, Oct. 11, 1997 — 15
   Livan Hernandez, Marlins, Oct. 12, 1997 — 15
3. Joe Coleman, Tigers, Oct. 10, 1972 — 14
   John Candelaria, Pirates, Oct. 7, 1975 — 14
   Mike Boddicker, Orioles, Oct. 6, 1983 — 14
   Mike Scott, Astros, Oct. 8, 1986 — 14
7. Tom Seaver, Mets, Oct. 6, 1973 — 13
8. Jim Palmer, Orioles, Oct. 5, 1970 — 12
   Jim Palmer, Orioles, Oct. 6, 1973 — 12
   Nolan Ryan, Astros, Oct. 14, 1986 — 12
   Pedro Martinez, Red Sox, Oct. 16, 1999 — 12

WALKS

1. Mike Cuellar, Orioles, Oct. 9, 1974 — 9
2. Fernando Valenzuela, Dodgers, Oct. 14, 1985 — 8
   Juan Guzman, Blue Jays, Oct. 5, 1993 — 8
4. Dave Boswell, Twins, Oct. 5, 1969 — 7
   Dave Stieb, Blue Jays, Oct. 12, 1985 — 7
   Tom Glavine, Braves, Oct. 14, 1997 — 7
7. Diego Segui, A's, Oct. 5, 1971 — 6
   Bruce Kison, Pirates, Oct. 8, 1974 — 6
   Matt Keough, A's, Oct. 15, 1981 — 6
   Bob Welch, Dodgers, Oct. 12, 1985 — 6
   Tom Glavine, Braves, Oct. 8, 1998 — 6

BATTING

RUNS

1. Babe Ruth, Yankees, Oct. 6, 1926	4
Earle Combs, Yankees, Oct. 2, 1932	4
Frankie Crosetti, Yankees, Oct. 2, 1936	4
Enos Slaughter, Cardinals, Oct. 10, 1946	4
Reggie Jackson, Yankees, Oct. 18, 1977	4
Kirby Puckett, Twins, Oct. 24, 1987	4
Carney Lansford, A's, Oct. 17, 1989	4
Lenny Dykstra, Phillies, Oct. 20, 1993	4

HITS

1. Paul Molitor, Brewers, Oct. 12, 1982	5
2. Tommy Leach, Pirates, Oct. 1, 1903	4
Ginger Beaumont, Pirates, Oct. 8, 1903	4
Frank Isbell, White Sox, Oct. 13, 1906	4
Ed Hahn, White Sox, Oct. 14, 1906	4
Ty Cobb, Tigers, Oct. 12, 1908	4
Larry Doyle, Giants, Oct. 25, 1911	4
Danny Murphy, A's, Oct. 26, 1911	4
Frankie Frisch, Giants, Oct. 5, 1921	4
George J. Burns, Giants, Oct. 7, 1921	4
Frank Snyder, Giants, Oct. 7, 1921	4
Ross Youngs, Giants, Oct. 13, 1923	4
Joe Dugan, Yankees, Oct. 14, 1923	4
Goose Goslin, Senators, Oct. 7, 1924	4
Fred Lindstrom, Giants, Oct. 8, 1924	4
Max Carey, Pirates, Oct. 15, 1925	4
Mel Ott, Giants, Oct. 3, 1933	4
Joe Medwick, Cardinals, Oct. 3, 1934	4
Hank Greenberg, Tigers, Oct. 6, 1934	4
Ripper Collins, Cardinals, Oct. 9, 1934	4
Bill Dickey, Yankees, Oct. 5, 1938	4
Charlie Keller, Yankees, Oct. 5, 1941	4
Stan Hack, Cubs, Oct. 8, 1945	4
Joe Garagiola, Cardinals, Oct. 10, 1946	4
Whitey Kurowski, Cardinals, Oct. 10, 1946	4
Wally Moses, Red Sox, Oct. 10, 1946	4
Enos Slaughter, Cardinals, Oct. 10, 1946	4
Monte Irvin, Giants, Oct. 4, 1951	4
Vic Wertz, Indians, Sept. 29, 1954	4
Jim Gilliam, Dodgers, Oct. 6, 1959	4
Mickey Mantle, Yankees, Oct. 8, 1960	4
Maury Wills, Dodgers, Oct. 11, 1965	4
Lou Brock, Cardinals, Oct. 4, 1967	4
Brooks Robinson, Orioles, Oct. 14, 1970	4
Reggie Jackson, A's, Oct. 14, 1973 (12 inn.)	4
Rusty Staub, Mets, Oct. 17, 1973	4
Thurman Munson, Yankees, Oct. 21, 1976	4
Dave Parker, Pirates, Oct. 10, 1979	4
Kiko Garcia, Orioles, Oct. 12, 1979	4
Bill Madlock, Pirates, Oct. 14, 1979	4
Willie Stargell, Pirates, Oct. 17, 1979	4
Robin Yount, Brewers, Oct. 12, 1982	4
Robin Yount, Brewers, Oct. 17, 1982	4
George Brett, Royals, Oct. 27, 1985	4
Lenny Dykstra, Mets, Oct. 21, 1986	4
Kirby Puckett, Twins, Oct. 24, 1987	4
Dave Henderson, A's, Oct. 19, 1988	4
Billy Hatcher, Reds, Oct. 17, 1990 (10 inn.)	4
Terry Pendleton, Braves, Oct. 26, 1991 (11 inn.)	4
Roberto Alomar, Blue Jays, Oct. 19, 1993	4
Bret Boone, Braves, Oct. 26, 1999	4

HOME RUNS

1. Babe Ruth, Yankees, Oct. 6, 1926	3
Babe Ruth, Yankees, Oct. 9, 1928	3
Reggie Jackson, Yankees, Oct. 18, 1977	3
4. Patsy Dougherty, Red Sox, Oct. 2, 1903	2
Harry Hooper, Red Sox, Oct. 13, 1915	2
Benny Kauff, Giants, Oct. 11, 1917	2
Babe Ruth, Yankees, Oct. 11, 1923	2
Lou Gehrig, Yankees, Oct. 7, 1928	2
Lou Gehrig, Yankees, Oct. 1, 1932	2
Babe Ruth, Yankees, Oct. 1, 1932	2
Tony Lazzeri, Yankees, Oct. 2, 1932	2
Charlie Keller, Yankees, Oct. 7, 1939	2
Bob Elliott, Braves, Oct. 10, 1948	2
Duke Snider, Dodgers, Oct. 6, 1952	2
Joe Collins, Yankees, Sept. 28, 1955	2
Duke Snider, Dodgers, Oct. 2, 1955	2
Yogi Berra, Yankees, Oct. 10, 1956	2
Tony Kubek, Yankees, Oct. 5, 1957	2
Mickey Mantle, Yankees, Oct. 2, 1958	2
Ted Kluszewski, White Sox, Oct. 1, 1959	2
Charlie Neal, Dodgers, Oct. 2, 1959	2
Mickey Mantle, Yankees, Oct. 6, 1960	2
Carl Yastrzemski, Red Sox, Oct. 5, 1967	2
Rico Petrocelli, Red Sox, Oct. 11, 1967	2
Gene Tenace, A's, Oct. 14, 1972	2
Tony Perez, Reds, Oct. 16, 1975	2
Johnny Bench, Reds, Oct. 21, 1976	2
Davey Lopes, Dodgers, Oct. 10, 1978	2

(continued top of next column)

Willie Aikens, Royals, Oct. 14, 1980	2
Willie Aikens, Royals, Oct. 18, 1980	2
Willie McGee, Cardinals, Oct. 15. 1982	2
Eddie Murray, Orioles, Oct. 16, 1983	2
Alan Trammell, Tigers, Oct. 13, 1984	2
Kirk Gibson, Tigers, Oct. 14, 1984	2
Gary Carter, Mets, Oct. 22, 1986	2
Dave Henderson, A's, Oct. 27, 1989	2
Chris Sabo, Reds, Oct. 19, 1990	2
Andruw Jones, Braves, Oct. 20, 1996	2
Greg Vaughn, Padres, Oct. 17, 1998	2
Scott Brosius, Yankees, Oct. 20, 1998	2
Chad Curtis, Yankees, Oct. 26, 1999	2

TOTAL BASES

1. Babe Ruth, Yankees, Oct. 6, 1926	12
Babe Ruth, Yankees, Oct. 9, 1928	12
Reggie Jackson, Yankees, Oct. 18, 1977	12
4. Duke Snider, Dodgers, Oct. 2, 1955	10
Gary Carter, Mets, Oct. 22, 1986	10
Dave Henderson, A's, Oct. 27, 1989	10
Lenny Dykstra, Phillies, Oct. 20, 1993	10
8. 12 tied with 9	

RUNS BATTED IN

1. Bobby Richardson, Yankees, Oct. 8, 1960	6
2. Bill Dickey, Yankees, Oct. 2, 1936	5
Tony Lazzeri, Yankees, Oct. 2, 1936	5
Ted Kluszewski, White Sox, Oct. 1, 1959	5
Mickey Mantle, Yankees, Oct. 6, 1960	5
Hector Lopez, Yankees, Oct. 9, 1961	5
Rusty Staub, Mets, Oct. 17, 1973	5
Johnny Bench, Reds, Oct. 21, 1976	5
Reggie Jackson, Yankees, Oct. 18, 1977	5
Davey Lopes, Dodgers, Oct. 10, 1978	5
Thurman Munson, Yankees, Oct. 15, 1978	5
Pedro Guerrero, Dodgers, Oct. 28, 1981	5
Kirk Gibson, Tigers, Oct. 14, 1984	5
Dan Gladden, Twins, Oct. 17, 1987	5
David Justice, Braves, Oct. 24, 1991	5
Milt Thompson, Phillies, Oct. 20, 1993	5
Tony Fernandez, Blue Jays, Oct. 20, 1993	5
Andruw Jones, Braves, Oct. 20, 1996	5
Gary Sheffield, Marlins, Oct. 12, 1997	5

STOLEN BASES

1. Honus Wagner, Pirates, Oct. 11, 1909	3
Willie Davis, Dodgers, Oct. 11, 1965	3
Lou Brock, Cardinals, Oct. 12, 1967	3
Lou Brock, Cardinals, Oct. 5, 1968	3

PITCHING

RUNS ALLOWED

1. Bill Kennedy, Pirates, Oct. 7, 1903	10
2. Andy Coakley, A's, Oct. 12, 1905	9
Mordecai Brown, Cubs, Oct. 18, 1910	9
Walter Johnson, Senators, Oct. 15, 1925	9
5. Jack Pfiester, Cubs, Oct. 12, 1908	8
Ed Summers, Tigers, Oct. 13, 1909	8
Hooks Wiltse, Giants, Oct. 26, 1911	8
Slim Sallee, Giants, Oct. 13, 1917	8
Grover Alexander, Cardinals, Oct. 5, 1928	8
Guy Bush, Cubs, Sept. 28, 1932	8

HITS ALLOWED

1. Walter Johnson, Senators, Oct. 15, 1925	15
2. Walter Johnson, Senators, Oct. 4, 1924	14
Waite Hoyt, Yankees, Oct. 6, 1926	14
Mike Caldwell, Brewers, Oct. 17, 1982	14
5. Mordecai Brown, Cubs, Oct. 18, 1910	13
Slim Sallee, Giants, Oct. 13, 1917	13
Jim Bagby Sr., Indians, Oct. 10, 1920	13
Walter Johnson, Senators, Oct. 8, 1924	13
Bob Turley, Yankees, Oct. 6, 1960	13
10. 7 tied with 12	

STRIKEOUTS

1. Bob Gibson, Cardinals, Oct. 2, 1968	17
2. Sandy Koufax, Dodgers, Oct. 2, 1963	15
3. Carl Erskine, Dodgers, Oct. 2, 1953	14
4. Howard Ehmke, A's, Oct. 8, 1929	13
Bob Gibson, Cardinals, Oct. 12, 1964 (10 inn.)	13
6. Ed Walsh, White Sox, Oct. 11, 1906	12
Bill Donovan, Tigers, Oct. 8, 1907 (12 inn.)	12
Walter Johnson, Senators, Oct. 24, 1924 (12 inn.)	12
Mort Cooper, Cardinals, Oct. 8, 1944	12
Tom Seaver, Mets, Oct. 16, 1973	12

WALKS

1. Bill Bevens, Yankees, Oct. 3, 1947	10
2. Jack Coombs, A's, Oct. 18, 1910	9
Rex Barney, Dodgers, Oct. 4, 1947	9
4. Jim Hearn, Giants, Oct. 6, 1951	8
Bob Turley, Yankees, Oct. 9, 1956 (10 inn.)	8
Jim Palmer, Orioles, Oct. 11, 1971	8
7. Art Nehf, Giants, Oct. 6, 1921	7
Tex Carleton, Cubs, Oct. 5, 1935	7
Lefty Gomez, Yankees, Oct. 2, 1936	7
Allie Reynolds, Yankees, Oct. 4, 1951	7
Ron Guidry, Yankees, Oct. 13, 1978	7
Fernando Valenzuela, Dodgers, Oct. 23, 1981	7

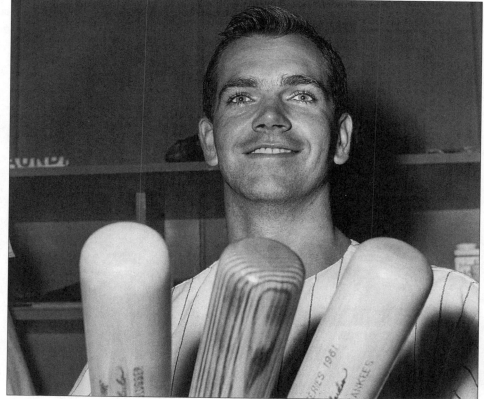

Yankees second baseman Bobby Richardson had six RBIs in a 1960 Series game against Pittsburgh.

HIGHEST AVERAGE
(Minimum 4 at-bats)
1. Ted Williams, Red Sox, 1946	1.000
2. Joe Medwick, Cardinals, 1937	.800
3. Roberto Alomar, Orioles, 1998	.750
Rickey Henderson, A's, 1982	.750
Lance Johnson, Mets, 1996	.750
Harmon Killebrew, Twins, 1964	.750
Willie Mays, Giants, 1960 (1st game)	.750
Willie Mays, Giants, 1960 (2nd game)	.750
Stan Musial, Cardinals, 1949	.750
Brooks Robinson, Orioles, 1966	.750
Ivan Rodriguez, Rangers, 1998	.750
Al Rosen, Indians, 1954	.750
Duke Snider, Dodgers, 1954	.750
Arky Vaughan, Pirates, 1941	.750
Leon Wagner, Angels, 1962 (2nd game)	.750
Carl Yastrzemski, Red Sox, 1967	.750

RUNS
1. Ted Williams, Red Sox, 1946	4
2. Joe DiMaggio, Yankees, 1941	3
Frankie Frisch, Cardinals, 1934	3
Jackie Robinson, Dodgers, 1949	3
Al Simmons, White Sox, 1934	3
6. 51 tied with 2	

HITS
1. Joe Medwick, Cardinals, 1937	4
Ted Williams, Red Sox, 1946	4
Carl Yastrzemski, Red Sox, 1970	4
4. 28 tied with 3	

DOUBLES
1. Ernie Banks, Cubs, 1959 (1st game)	2
Barry Bonds, Giants, 1993	2
Ted Kluszewski, Reds, 1956	2
Joe Medwick, Cardinals, 1937	2
Al Simmons, White Sox, 1934	2
6. 166 tied with 1	

HOME RUNS
1. Gary Carter, Expos, 1981	2
Willie McCovey, Giants, 1969	2
Al Rosen, Indians, 1954	2
Arky Vaughan, Pirates, 1941	2
Ted Williams, Red Sox, 1946	2
6. 140 tied with 1	

HOME RUN, FIRST AT-BAT
Max West, Braves, 1940
Hoot Evers, Tigers, 1948
Jim Gilliam, Dodgers, 1959 (2nd game)
George Altman, Cubs, 1961 (1st game)
Johnny Bench, Reds, 1969
Dick Dietz, Giants, 1970
Lee Mazzilli, Mets, 1979
Terry Steinbach, A's, 1988
Bo Jackson, Royals, 1989
Jeff Conine, Marlins, 1995
Javy Lopez, Braves, 1997

TOTAL BASES
1. Ted Williams, Red Sox, 1946	10
2. Al Rosen, Indians, 1954	9
Arky Vaughan, Pirates, 1941	9
4. Gary Carter, Expos, 1981	8
Vince DiMaggio, Pirates, 1943	8
Willie McCovey, Giants, 1969	8
7. Ken Griffey Jr., Mariners, 1992	7
8. 15 tied with 6	

RUNS BATTED IN
1. Al Rosen, Indians, 1954	5
Ted Williams, Red Sox, 1946	5
3. Rocky Colavito, Tigers, 1962 (2nd game)	4
Lou Gehrig, Yankees, 1937	4
Fred Lynn, Angels, 1983	4
Arky Vaughan, Pirates, 1941	4
Ted Williams, Red Sox, 1941	4
8. 15 tied with 3	

STOLEN BASES
1. Roberto Alomar, Blue Jays, 1992	2
Kelly Gruber, Blue Jays, 1990	2
Kenny Lofton, Indians, 1996	2
Willie Mays, Giants, 1963	2
5. 80 tied with 1	

PITCHING

RUNS ALLOWED
1. Atlee Hammaker, Giants, 1983	7
2. Sandy Consuegra, White Sox, 1954	5
Whitey Ford, Yankees, 1955	5
Tom Glavine, Braves, 1992	5
Jim Maloney, Reds, 1965	5
Blue Moon Odom, A's, 1969	5
Jim Palmer, Orioles, 1977	5
Claude Passeau, Cubs, 1941	5
9. 16 tied with 4	

Giants All-Stars: Two-homer man Willie McCovey (above) and six-strikeout man Larry Jansen (below).

HITS ALLOWED
1. Tom Glavine, Braves, 1992	9
2. Tommy Bridges, Tigers, 1937	7
3. Atlee Hammaker, Giants, 1983	6
Claude Passeau, Cubs, 1941	6
Lon Warneke, Cubs, 1933	6
6. 29 tied with 5	

STRIKEOUTS
1. Carl Hubbell, Giants, 1934	6
Larry Jansen, Giants, 1950	6
Fergie Jenkins, Cubs, 1967	6
Johnny Vander Meer, Reds, 1943	6
5. Don Drysdale, Dodgers, 1959 (2nd game)	5
Pedro Martinez, Red Sox, 1999	5
Stu Miller, Giants, 1961 (2nd game)	5
Joe Nuxhall, Reds, 1955	5
Billy Pierce, White Sox, 1956	5
Dick Radatz, Red Sox, 1963	5
Dick Radatz, Red Sox, 1964	5
Robin Roberts, Phillies, 1954	5
Hal Schumacher, Giants, 1935	5
Tom Seaver, Mets, 1968	5
Fernando Valenzuela, Dodgers, 1986	5

WALKS
1. Bill Hallahan, Cardinals, 1933	5
2. Jim Palmer, Orioles, 1978	4
3. Ewell Blackwell, Reds, 1948	3
Ralph Branca, Dodgers, 1948	3
Don Drysdale, Dodgers, 1959 (2nd game)	3
Jim Kern, Rangers, 1979	3
Bill Lee, Cubs, 1939	3
Mike McCormick, Giants, 1960 (1st game)	3
Sam McDowell, Indians, 1970	3
Andy Messersmith, Dodgers, 1974	3
Joe Nuxhall, Reds, 1955	3
Dan Petry, Tigers, 1985	3
Johnny Podres, Dodgers, 1960 (2nd game)	3
Vic Raschi, Yankees, 1949	3
Lon Warneke, Cubs, 1934	3
Lon Warneke, Cubs, 1936	3
Early Wynn, White Sox, 1959 (2nd game)	3

HIGHS AND LOWS (1901-1999)

PENNANTS, A.L.

1.	Yankees	36
2.	Athletics	15
3.	Red Sox	10
4.	Tigers	9
5.	Orioles/Browns	7
6.	Twins/Senators	6
7.	White Sox	5
	Indians	5
9.	Royals	2
	Blue Jays	2

PENNANTS, N.L.

1.	Dodgers	18
2.	Giants	17
3.	Cardinals	15
4.	Cubs	10
5.	Pirates	9
	Reds	9
	Braves	9
8.	Phillies	5
9.	Mets	3
10.	Padres	2

LCS WINNERS, A.L.

1.	Yankees	7
2.	Athletics	6
3.	Orioles	5
4.	Royals	2
	Red Sox	2
	Twins	2
	Blue Jays	2
	Indians	2
9.	Brewers	1
	Tigers	1

LCS WINNERS, N.L.

1.	Dodgers	5
	Reds	5
	Braves	5
4.	Phillies	3
	Cardinals	3
	Mets	3
7.	Pirates	2
	Padres	2
9.	Giants	1
	Marlins	1

WORLD SERIES WINNERS

1.	Yankees	25
2.	Cardinals	9
	Athletics	9
4.	Dodgers	6
5.	Giants	5
	Pirates	5
	Reds	5
	Red Sox	5
9.	Tigers	4
10.	Braves	3
	Orioles	3
	Twins	3

ALL-STAR GAME WINNERS

1.	National League	40
2.	American League	29
3.	games tied	1

VICTORIES, SEASON

1.	Cubs, 1906	116
2.	Yankees, 1998	114
3.	Indians, 1954	111
4.	Pirates, 1909	110
	Yankees, 1927	110
6.	Yankees, 1961	109
	Orioles, 1969	109
7.	Orioles, 1970	108
	Reds, 1975	108
	Mets, 1986	108

LOSSES, SEASON

1.	Mets, 1962	120
2.	Athletics, 1916	117
3.	Braves, 1935	115
4.	Senators, 1904	113
5.	Pirates, 1952	112
	Mets, 1965	112
7.	Red Sox, 1932	111
	Browns, 1939	111
	Phillies, 1941	111
	Mets, 1963	111

LARGEST 1ST/2ND-PLACE MARGIN

1.	Indians, 1995	30.0

2.	Pirates, 1902	27.5
3.	Yankees, 1998	22.0
4.	Mets, 1986	21.5
	Indians, 1999	21.5
6.	Braves, 1995	21.0
7.	Cubs, 1906	20.0
	Reds, 1975	20.0
	White Sox, 1983	20.0
10.	Yankees, 1936	19.5

LARGEST 1ST/LAST-PLACE MARGIN

1.	Cubs, 1906	66.5
2.	Pirates, 1909	65.5
3.	Yankees, 1939	64.5
4.	Yankees, 1932	64.0
5.	Cardinals, 1942	62.5
6.	Cubs, 1935	61.5
7.	Giants, 1962	60.5
8.	Indians, 1954	60.0
9.	Yankees, 1927	59.0
10.	Red Sox, 1915	58.5

MOST DAYS IN 1ST PLACE

1.	Orioles, 1997 (182)	182
2.	Tigers, 1984 (182)	181
	Phillies, 1993 (182)	181
	Indians, 1998 (181)	181
5.	Indians, 1999 (182)	179
6.	Reds, 1970 (179)	178
	Reds, 1990 (178)	178
	Rangers, 1999 (182)	178
9.	Dodgers, 1974 (181)	177
	Athletics, 1988 (182)	177
	Rangers, 1996 (183)	177

LONGEST WINNING STREAKS

1.	Giants, 1916	26
2.	Cubs, 1935	21
3.	White Sox, 1906	19
	Yankees, 1947	19
5.	Giants, 1904	18
	Yankees, 1953	18
7.	Giants, 1907	17
	Giants, 1916	17
	Senators, 1912	17
	Athletics, 1931	17

LONGEST LOSING STREAKS

1.	Phillies, 1961	23
2.	Orioles, 1988	21
3.	Red Sox, 1906	20
	Athletics, 1916	20
	Athletics, 1943	20
	Expos, 1969	20
7.	Braves, 1906	19
	Reds, 1914	19
	Tigers, 1975	19
10.	Athletics, 1920	18

	Senators, 1948	18
	Senators, 1959	18

HIGHEST TEAM AVERAGE

1.	Giants, 1930	.319
2.	Tigers, 1921	.316
3.	Phillies, 1930	.315
4.	Cardinals, 1930	.314
5.	Browns, 1922	.313
6.	Yankees, 1930	.309
	Pirates, 1928	.309
	Phillies, 1929	.309
	Cubs, 1930	.309
10.	Browns, 1920	.308

RUNS SCORED, SEASON

1.	Yankees, 1931	1,067
2.	Yankees, 1936	1,065
3.	Yankees, 1930	1,062
4.	Red Sox, 1950	1,027
5.	Indians, 1999	1,009
6.	Cardinals, 1930	1,004
7.	Yankees, 1932	1,002
8.	Cubs, 1930	998
9.	Mariners, 1996	993
10.	Cubs, 1929	982

FEWEST RUNS, SEASON

(Minimum 140 games)

1.	Cardinals, 1908	371
2.	Dodgers, 1908	377
3.	Senators, 1909	380
4.	Phillies, 1942	394
5.	Braves, 1906	408
6.	Cardinals, 1907	419
7.	Braves, 1909	435
8.	Senators, 1903	437
	Senators, 1904	437
10.	Browns, 1909	441

HOME RUNS, GAME

1.	Blue Jays, Sept. 14, 1987	10
2.	Reds, Sept. 4, 1999	9
3.	Yankees, June 28, 1939	8
	Braves, Aug. 30, 1953	8
	Reds, Aug. 18, 1956	8
	Giants, April 30, 1961	8
	Twins, Aug. 29, 1963	8
	Red Sox, July 4, 1977	8
	Expos, July 30, 1978	8
	Athletics, June 27, 1996	8
	Indians, April 25, 1997	8

HOME RUNS, SEASON

1.	Mariners, 1997	264
2.	Orioles, 1996	257
3.	Mariners, 1996	245
4.	Mariners, 1999	244

5.	Athletics, 1996	243
6.	Yankees, 1961	240
7.	Rockies, 1997	239
8.	Athletics, 1999	235
9.	Mariners, 1998	234
10.	Rangers, 1999	230

FEWEST HOME RUNS, SEASON

(Minimum 140 games)

1.	White Sox, 1908	3
2.	White Sox, 1909	4
	Senators, 1917	4
	Senators, 1918	4
5.	Phillies, 1902	5
	White Sox, 1907	5
	Cardinals, 1918	5
8.	Cubs, 1902	6
	Giants, 1902	6
10.	White Sox, 1906	7
	White Sox, 1910	7

STOLEN BASES, SEASON

1.	Giants, 1911	347
2.	A's, 1976	341
3.	Giants, 1912	319
4.	Cardinals, 1985	314
5.	Reds, 1910	310
6.	Giants, 1913	296
7.	Giants, 1905	291
8.	Reds, 1911	289
9.	Giants, 1906	288
	Yankees, 1910	288

LOWEST ERA, SEASON

1.	Cubs, 1907	1.73
2.	Cubs, 1909	1.75
	Cubs, 1906	1.75
4.	A's, 1910	1.79
5.	A's, 1909	1.93
6.	White Sox, 1905	1.99
7.	Indians, 1908	2.02
8.	White Sox, 1910	2.03
9.	Cubs, 1905	2.04
10.	White Sox, 1905	2.05

HIGHEST ERA, SEASON

1.	Phillies, 1930	6.72
2.	Tigers, 1996	6.38
3.	Browns, 1936	6.24
4.	Phillies, 1929	6.13
5.	Athletics, 1936	6.08
6.	Rockies, 1999	6.01
	Browns, 1939	6.01
8.	Browns, 1937	6.00
9.	Browns, 1938	5.81
10.	Athletics, 1939	5.79

FRANCHISE RECORDS

Franchise	Years	Games	Won	Lost	Pct.
Yankees/Orioles	1901 - 1999	15,253	8,610	6,643	.564
Giants	1901 - 1999	15,425	8,275	7,150	.536
Dodgers	1901 - 1999	15,422	8,061	7,361	.523
Pirates	1901 - 1999	15,421	8,005	7,416	.519
Cardinals	1901 - 1999	15,423	7,926	7,497	.514
Tigers	1901 - 1999	15,300	7,835	7,465	.512
Red Sox	1901 - 1999	15,271	7,810	7,461	.511
Indians	1901 - 1999	15,276	7,806	7,470	.511
Diamondbacks	1998 - 1999	324	165	159	.509
Royals	1969 - 1999	4,883	2,471	2,412	.506
Cubs	1901 - 1999	15,434	7,803	7,631	.506
Reds	1901 - 1999	15,439	7,795	7,644	.505
White Sox	1901 - 1999	15,258	7,683	7,575	.504
Blue Jays	1977 - 1999	3,602	1,784	1,818	.495
Astros/Colt .45s	1962 - 1999	6,028	2,980	3,048	.494
Expos	1969 - 1999	4,888	2,387	2,501	.488
Angels	1961 - 1999	6,188	2,987	3,201	.483
Brewers/Pilots	1969 - 1999	4,890	2,348	2,542	.480
Orioles/Browns	1901 - 1999	15,258	7,315	7,943	.479
Athletics	1901 - 1999	15,242	7,299	7,943	.479
Rockies	1993 - 1999	1,071	512	559	.478
Braves	1901 - 1999	15,396	7,342	8,054	.477
Twins/Senators	1901 - 1999	15,265	7,275	7,990	.477
Mets	1962 - 1999	6,018	2,840	3,178	.472
Rangers/Senators	1961 - 1999	6,171	2,881	3,290	.467
Phillies	1901 - 1999	15,400	7,055	8,345	.458
Padres	1969 - 1999	4,895	2,239	2,656	.457
Mariners	1977 - 1999	3,601	1,624	1,977	.451
Marlins	1993 - 1999	1,068	472	596	.442
Devil Rays	1998 - 1999	324	132	192	.407

LONGEST GAMES, INNINGS

1.	Dodgers 1 at Braves 1, May 1, 1920	26
2.	Cardinals 4 at Mets 3, Sept. 11, 1974	25
	White Sox 7 vs. Brewers 6, May 8, 1984	25
4.	A's 4 at Red Sox 1, Sept. 1, 1906	24
	Tigers 1 at Athletics 1, July 21, 1945	24
	Astros 1 vs. Mets 0, April 25, 1968	24
7.	Dodgers 2 at Braves 2, June 27, 1939	23
	Giants 8 at Mets 6, May 31, 1964	23
9.	8 tied at 22	

RUNS SCORED, GAME

1.	Red Sox vs. Browns, June 8, 1950	29
	White Sox vs. A's, April 23, 1955	29
3.	Cardinals vs. Phillies, July 6, 1929	28
4.	Indians vs. Red Sox, July 7, 1923	27
5.	Cubs vs. Phillies, Aug. 25, 1922	26
	Giants vs. Dodgers, April 30, 1944	26
	Indians vs. Browns, Aug. 12, 1948	26
	Phillies vs. Mets, April 11, 1985	26
	Cubs vs. Rockies, Aug. 18, 1995	26
	Rangers vs. Orioles, April 19, 1996	26

RUNS SCORED, INNING

1.	Red Sox vs. Tigers, June 18, 1953 (7th)	17
2.	Rangers vs. Orioles, April 19, 1996 (8th)	16
3.	Dodgers vs. Reds, May 21, 1952 (1st)	15
4.	Yankees vs. Senators, July 6, 1920 (5th)	14
	Cubs vs. Phillies, Aug. 25, 1922 (4th)	14
	Indians vs. A's, June 18, 1950 (1st)	14
	Reds vs. Astros, Aug. 3, 1989 (1st)	14
8.	19 tied with 13	

BASEBALL CLASSICS
MEMORABLE MOMENTS

MERKLE'S BONER

September 23, 1908,
at the Polo Grounds

New York Giants first baseman Fred Merkle claimed status as baseball's biggest goat when he failed to touch second base on an apparent game-ending hit against the Chicago Cubs, a mistake that would cost his team a pennant. With two out and runners on first and third in the bottom of the ninth of a 1-1 tie, Al Bridwell singled to center and Moose McCormick scored the winning run. But when Merkle failed to touch second, Cubs second baseman Johnny Evers appealed for the forceout and umpire Hank O'Day concurred, disallowing the run. League officials later declared the game a tie and the teams went on to finish the season with identical records. The Cubs won a makeup game—and the pennant.

Chicago	AB	R	H	PO	A	E
Hayden,rf	4	0	0	1	0	0
Evers,2b	4	0	1	3	7	0
Schulte,lf	4	0	0	1	0	0
Chance,1b	4	0	1	11	1	0
Steinfeldt,3b	2	0	0	0	1	1
Hofman,cf	3	0	1	2	0	0
Tinker,ss	3	1	1	8	6	2
Kling,c	3	0	1	0	1	0
Pfiester,p	3	0	0	1	0	0
Totals	30	1	5	27	16	3

New York	AB	R	H	PO	A	E
Herzog,2b	3	1	1	1	1	0
Bresnahan,c	3	0	0	10	0	0
Donlin,rf	4	0	1	2	0	0
Seymour,cf	4	0	1	1	0	0
Devlin,3b	4	0	2	0	2	0
McCormick,lf	3	0	0	1	0	0
Merkle,1b	3	0	1	10	1	0
Bridwell,ss	4	0	0	2	8	0
Mathewson,p	3	0	0	0	2	0
Totals	31	1	6	27	14	0

New York Giants first baseman Fred Merkle is usually blamed for his team's failure to win the 1908 National League pennant.

Chicago ....000 100 000— 1
New York ....000 010 000— 1

Runs batted in: Tinker, Donlin.
Home run: Tinker.
Sacrifice hits: Steinfeldt, Bresnahan.
Double plays: Tinker and Chance 2; Evers and Chance.
Left on bases: Chicago 3, New York 7.

Chicago	IP	H	R	ER	BB	SO
Pfiester	9	6	1	0	2	0

New York	IP	H	R	ER	BB	SO
Mathewson	9	5	1	1	0	9

Hit by pitcher: McCormick (by Pfiester).
Umpires: O'Day, Emslie.
Time: 1:30. **Attendance:** 20,000.

A GIANT MISPLAY

October 16, 1912, at Fenway Park

The Boston Red Sox, given life by New York Giants center fielder Fred Snodgrass' 10th-inning error, scored two runs and claimed a 3-2 victory in the decisive eighth game of the World Series. After Snodgrass dropped a routine fly ball to open the inning, the Giants also failed to catch a foul pop by Tris Speaker, who then singled home the tying run. Larry Gardner produced the winner with a sacrifice fly.

New York	AB	R	H	PO	A	E
Devore,rf	3	1	1	3	1	0
Doyle,2b	5	0	0	1	5	1
Snodgrass,cf	4	0	1	4	1	1
Murray,lf	5	1	2	3	0	0
Merkle,1b	5	0	1	10	0	0
Herzog,3b	5	0	2	2	1	0
Meyers,c	3	0	0	4	1	0
Fletcher,ss	3	0	1	2	3	0
bMcCormick	1	0	0	0	0	0
Shafer,ss	0	0	0	0	0	0
Mathewson,p	4	0	1	0	3	0
Totals	38	2	9	29	15	2

Boston	AB	R	H	PO	A	E
Hooper,rf	5	0	0	3	0	0
Yerkes,2b	4	1	1	0	3	0
Speaker,cf	4	0	2	2	0	1
Lewis,lf	4	0	1	0	0	0
Gardner,3b	3	0	1	1	4	2
Stahl,1b	4	1	2	15	0	0
Wagner,ss	3	0	1	3	5	1
Cady,c	4	0	0	5	3	0
Bedient,p	2	0	0	0	1	0
aHenriksen	1	0	1	0	0	0
Wood,p	0	0	0	0	2	0
cEngle	1	1	0	0	0	0
Totals	35	3	8	30	18	5

New York ....001 000 000 1—2
Boston ....000 000 100 2—3

a Doubled for Bedient in seventh.
b Flied out for Fletcher in ninth.
c Reached second on Snodgrass' error in 10th.
d Two out when winning run scored.

Runs batted in: Murray, Merkle, Speaker, Gardner, Henriksen.
Doubles: Murray 2, Herzog, Gardner, Stahl, Henriksen.
Sacrifice hit: Meyers.
Sacrifice fly: Gardner.
Stolen bases: Devore.
Left on bases: New York 11, Boston 9.

New York	IP	H	R	ER	BB	SO
Mathewson (L)	9⅔	8	3	2	5	4

Boston	IP	H	R	ER	BB	SO
Bedient	7	6	1	1	3	2
Wood (W)	3	3	1	1	1	2

Umpires: O'Loughlin, Rigler, Klem, Evans.
Time: 2:39. **Attendance:** 17,034.

A DOUBLE NO-NO

May 2, 1917, at Wrigley Field

Cincinnati lefthander Fred Toney and Chicago righthander Hippo Vaughn hooked up in the most efficient pitching duel in baseball history—the game's only double nine-inning no-hitter. Vaughn allowed two 10th-inning hits and the Cubs broke through for an unearned run that Toney made stand up in the bottom of the inning, completing his no-hit gem. Vaughn had to settle for a tough-luck loss.

Cincinnati	AB	R	H	PO	A	E
Groh,3b	1	0	0	2	2	0
Getz,3b	1	0	0	2	1	0
Kopf,ss	4	1	1	1	4	0
Neale,cf	4	0	0	1	0	0
Chase,1b	4	0	0	12	0	0
Thorpe,rf	4	0	1	1	0	0
Shean,2b	3	0	0	3	2	0
Cueto,lf	3	0	0	5	0	0
Huhn,c	3	0	0	3	0	0
Toney,p	3	0	0	0	1	0
Totals	30	1	2	30	10	0

Chicago	AB	R	H	PO	A	E
Zeider,ss	4	0	0	1	0	0
Wolter,rf	4	0	0	0	0	0
Doyle,2b	4	0	0	5	4	0
Merkle,1b	4	0	0	7	1	0
Williams,cf	2	0	0	2	0	1
Mann,lf	3	0	0	0	0	0
Wilson,c	3	0	0	14	1	0
Deal,3b	3	0	0	1	0	0
Vaughn,p	3	0	0	0	3	0
Totals	30	0	0	30	9	1

Cincinnati ....000 000 000 1—1
Chicago ....000 000 000 0—0

Runs batted in: Thorpe.
Stolen bases: Chase.
Double plays: Doyle, Merkle and Zeider; Doyle and Merkle.
Left on bases: Cincinnati 1, Chicago 2.

Cincinnati	IP	H	R	ER	BB	SO
Toney (W)	10	0	0	0	2	3

Chicago	IP	H	R	ER	BB	SO
Vaughn (L)	10	2	1	0	2	10

Umpires: Orth, Rigler.
Time: 1:50. **Attendance:** 3,500.

A 26-INNING STANDOFF

May 1, 1920, at Braves Field

Brooklyn's Leon Cadore and Boston's Joe Oeschger matched zeroes in the longest pitching duel in baseball history—a 26-inning, 1-1 marathon that was called because of darkness. Cadore allowed 15 hits and Oeschger nine, but neither pitcher surrendered a run over the last 20 innings. Brooklyn scored in the fifth and Boston tied the game an inning later.

Brooklyn	AB	R	H	PO	A	E
Olson,2b	10	0	1	6	9	1
Neis,rf	10	0	1	9	0	0
Johnston,3b	10	0	2	2	1	0
Wheat,lf	9	0	2	3	0	0
Myers,cf	2	0	1	2	0	0
Hood,cf	6	0	1	8	1	0
Konetchy,1b	9	0	1	30	1	0
Ward,ss	10	0	0	6	3	1
Krueger,c	2	1	0	4	3	0
Elliott,c	7	0	0	7	3	0
Cadore,p	10	0	1	0	12	0
Totals	85	1	9	78	33	2

Boston	AB	R	H	PO	A	E
Powell,cf	8	0	1	8	0	0
Pick,2b	11	0	0	5	10	2
Mann,lf	10	0	2	6	0	0
Cruise,rf	9	1	1	4	0	0
Holke,1b	10	0	2	43	1	0
Boeckel,3b	11	0	3	1	7	0
Maranville,ss	10	0	3	1	9	0
O'Neil,c	2	0	0	4	3	0
aChristenbury	1	0	1	0	0	0
Gowdy,c	6	0	1	6	0	0
Oeschger,p	9	0	1	0	11	0
Totals	87	1	15	78	41	2

a Singled for O'Neil in ninth.

Brk. 000 010 000 000 000
Bos...........000 001 000 000 000

Brk. ....000 000 000 00—1
Bos. ....000 000 000 00—1

Runs batted in: Olson, Boeckel.
Doubles: Oeschger, Maranville.
Triple: Cruise.
Sacrifice hits: Powell, O'Neil, Cruise, Hood, Holke.
Stolen bases: Myers, Hood.
Double plays: Olson and Konetchy; Oeschger, Gowdy, Holke and Gowdy.
Left on bases: Brooklyn 11, Boston 17.

Brooklyn	IP	H	R	ER	BB	SO
Cadore	26	15	1	1	5	7

Boston	IP	H	R	ER	BB	SO
Oeschger	26	9	1	1	4	7

Wild pitch: Oeschger.

Umpires: McCormick, Hart.
Time: 3:50. **Attendance:** 2,500.

SENATORIAL SPLENDOR

October 10, 1924, at Griffith Stadium

The Washington Senators, long the doormat of the American League, captured their first World Series when two routine Game 7 ground balls inexplicably hopped over the head of New York Giants third baseman Fred Lindstrom, producing three runs. The Senators tied the game, 3-3, on manager Bucky Harris' two-run, bad-hop single in the eighth inning and won in the 12th, 4-3, on Earl McNeely's bad-hop bouncer.

New York	AB	R	H	PO	A	E
Lindstrom,3b	5	0	1	0	3	0
Frisch,2b	5	0	2	3	4	0
Youngs,rf-lf	2	1	0	2	0	0
Kelly,cf-1b	6	1	1	8	1	0
Terry,1b	2	0	0	6	1	0
aMeusel,lf-rf	3	0	1	1	0	0
Wilson,lf-cf	5	1	1	4	0	0
Jackson,ss	6	0	1	4	2	2
Gowdy,c	6	0	1	8	0	0
Barnes,p	4	0	0	1	2	0
Nehf,p	0	0	0	0	0	0
McQuillan,p	0	0	0	0	0	0
eGroh	1	0	1	0	0	0
fSouthworth	0	0	0	0	0	0
Bentley,p	0	0	0	0	0	0
Totals	45	3	8	34	15	3

Washington	AB	R	H	PO	A	E
McNeely,cf	6	0	1	0	0	0
Harris,2b	5	1	3	4	1	0
Rice,rf	5	0	0	2	0	0
Goslin,lf	5	0	2	3	0	0
Judge,1b	4	0	1	11	1	1
Bluege,ss	5	0	0	1	7	2
Taylor,3b	2	0	0	0	3	1
bLeibold	1	1	1	0	0	0
Miller,3b	2	0	0	1	1	0
Ruel,c	5	2	2	13	0	0
Odgen,p	0	0	0	0	0	0
Mogridge,p	1	0	0	0	0	0
Marberry,p	1	0	0	1	0	0
cTate	0	0	0	0	0	0
dShirley	0	0	0	0	0	0
Johnson,p	2	0	0	0	1	0
Totals	44	4	10	36	14	4

New York..........0 0 0 0 0 3 0 0 0 0 0 0—3
Washington......0 0 0 1 0 0 0 2 0 0 0 1—4

a Flied out for Terry in sixth.
b Doubled for Taylor in eighth.
c Walked for Marberry in eighth.
d Ran for Tate in eighth.
e Singled for McQuillan in 11th.
f Ran for Groh in 11th.
g One out when winning run scored.

Runs batted in: Harris 3, McNeely, Meusel.
Doubles: Lindstrom, Leibold, Ruel, Goslin, McNeely.
Triple: Frisch.
Home run: Harris.
Sacrifice hit: Lindstrom.
Sacrifice fly: Meusel.
Stolen bases: Youngs.
Double plays: Kelly and Jackson; Jackson, Frisch and Kelly; Johnson, Bluege and Judge.
Left on bases: New York 14, Washington 8.

New York	IP	H	R	ER	BB	SO
Barnes	7⅔	6	3	3	1	6
Nehf	⅔	1	0	0	0	0
McQuillan	1⅔	0	0	0	0	1
Bentley (L)	1⅓	3	1	1	1	0

Washington	IP	H	R	ER	BB	SO
Odgen	⅓	0	0	0	1	1
Mogridge	4⅔	4	2	1	1	3
Marberry	3	1	1	0	1	3
Johnson (W)	4	3	0	0	3	5

Mogridge pitched to two batters in sixth.

Umpires: Dinneen, Quigley, Connolly, Klem.
Time: 3:00. **Attendance:** 31,667.

A'S VAULT PAST CUBS

October 12, 1929, at Shibe Park

Down 8-0 after six innings of World Series Game 4, the Philadelphia Athletics rocked the Chicago Cubs with a 10-run seventh-inning explosion that produced a 10-8 victory and a three-games-to-one advantage in the fall classic. The key blow in the biggest inning in Series history was a three-run, inside-the-park home run by Philadelphia's Mule Haas.

Chicago	AB	R	H	PO	A	E
McMillan,3b	4	0	0	1	3	0
English,ss	4	0	0	2	1	0
Hornsby,2b	5	2	2	1	1	0
Wilson,cf	3	1	2	3	0	1
Cuyler,rf	4	2	3	0	0	1
Stephenson,lf	4	1	1	2	1	0
Grimm,1b	4	2	2	7	0	0
Taylor,c	3	0	0	8	1	0
Root,p	3	0	0	0	0	0
Nehf,p	0	0	0	0	0	0
Blake,p	0	0	0	0	0	0
Malone,p	0	0	0	0	0	0
bHartnett	1	0	0	0	0	0
Carlson,p	0	0	0	0	1	0
Totals	35	8	10	24	8	2

Philadelphia	AB	R	H	PO	A	E
Bishop,2b	5	1	2	2	3	0
Haas,cf	4	1	1	2	0	0
Cochrane,c	4	1	2	9	0	0
Simmons,lf	5	2	2	0	0	0
Foxx,1b	4	2	2	10	0	0
Miller,rf	3	1	2	3	0	1
Dykes,3b	4	1	3	0	2	0
Boley,ss	3	1	1	1	5	0
Quinn,p	2	0	0	0	0	0
Walberg,p	0	0	0	0	0	1
Rommel,p	0	0	0	0	0	0
aBurns	2	0	0	0	0	0
Grove,p	0	0	0	0	0	0
Totals	36	10	15	27	10	2

Chicago ....0 0 0 2 0 5 1 0 0—8
Philadelphia ....0 0 0 0 0 0 1 0 0 x—10

a Popped out and struck out for Rommel in seventh.
b Struck out for Malone in eighth.

Runs batted in: Cuyler 2, Stephenson, Grimm 2, Taylor, Bishop, Haas 3, Simmons, Foxx, Dykes 3, Boley.
Doubles: Cochrane, Dykes.
Triple: Hornsby.
Home runs: Grimm, Haas, Simmons.
Sacrifice hits: Taylor, Haas, Boley.
Double play: Dykes, Bishop and Foxx.
Left on bases: Philadelphia 10, Chicago 6.

Chicago	IP	H	R	ER	BB	SO
Root	6⅓	9	6	6	0	3
Nehf	0	1	2	2	1	0
Blake (L)	0	2	2	2	0	0
Malone	⅔	1	0	0	0	2
Carlson	1	2	0	0	0	1

Philadelphia	IP	H	R	ER	BB	SO
Quinn	5	7	6	5	2	2
Walberg	1	1	1	0	0	2
Rommel (W)	1	2	1	1	1	0
Grove (S)	2	0	0	0	0	4

Nehf pitched to two batters in seventh.
Blake pitched to two batters in seventh.
Quinn pitched to four batters in sixth.
Hit by pitcher: Miller (by Malone).

Umpires: Van Graflan, Klem, Dinneen, Moran.
Time: 2:12. **Attendance:** 29,921.

RUTH'S CALLED SHOT

October 1, 1932, at Wrigley Field

New York slugger Babe Ruth, ever the showman, livened up Game 3 of the World Series with his dramatic called-shot home run, breaking a 4-4 tie and sparking the Yankees to a 7-5 victory. Responding to the taunting of Cubs players and fans, Ruth made a sweeping gesture toward the center-field stands and then deposited Charlie Root's 2-2 pitch precisely where he had pointed. The home run, his second of the game, helped the Yankees to a Series-controlling 3-0 lead.

New York	AB	R	H	PO	A	E
Combs,cf	5	1	0	1	0	0
Sewell,3b	2	1	0	2	2	0
Ruth,lf	4	2	2	2	0	0
Gehrig,1b	5	2	2	13	1	0
Lazzeri,2b	4	1	0	3	4	1
Dickey,c	4	0	1	2	1	0
Chapman,rf	4	0	2	0	0	0
Crosetti,ss	4	0	1	4	4	0
Pipgras,p	5	0	0	0	0	0
Pennock,p	0	0	0	0	1	0
Totals	37	7	8	27	13	1

Chicago	AB	R	H	PO	A	E
Herman,2b	4	1	0	1	2	1
English,3b	4	0	0	0	3	0
Cuyler,rf	4	1	3	1	0	0
Stephenson,lf	4	0	1	1	0	0
Moore,cf	3	1	0	3	0	0
Grimm,1b	4	0	1	8	0	0
Hartnett,c	4	1	1	10	1	1
Jurges,ss	4	1	3	3	3	2
Root,p	2	0	0	0	0	0
Malone,p	0	0	0	0	0	0
aGudat	1	0	0	0	0	0
May,p	0	0	0	0	0	0
Tinning,p	0	0	0	0	0	0
bKoenig	0	0	0	0	0	0
cHemlsey	1	0	0	0	0	0
Totals	35	5	9	27	9	4

New York ....3 0 1 0 2 0 0 0 1—7
Chicago ....1 0 2 1 0 0 0 0 1—5

a Popped out for Malone in seventh.
b Announced for Tinning in ninth.
c Struck out for Koenig in ninth.

Runs batted in: Ruth 4, Gehrig 2, Cuyler 2, Grimm, Chapman, Hartnett.
Doubles: Chapman, Cuyler, Jurges, Grimm.
Home runs: Ruth 2, Gehrig 2, Hartnett.
Stolen bases: Jurges.
Double plays: Sewell, Lazzeri and Gehrig; Herman, Jurges and Grimm.
Left on bases: New York 11, Chicago 6.

New York	IP	H	R	ER	BB	SO
Pipgras (W)	8	9	5	4	3	1
Pennock (S)	1	0	0	0	0	1

Chicago	IP	H	R	ER	BB	SO
Root (L)	4⅓	6	6	5	3	4
Malone	2⅔	1	0	0	4	4
May	1⅓	1	1	0	0	1
Tinning	⅔	0	0	0	0	1

Pipgras pitched to two batters in ninth.
Hit by pitcher: Sewell (by May).

Umpires: Van Graflan, Magerkurth, Dinneen, Klem.
Time: 2:11. **Attendance:** 49,986.

VANDER MEER'S DOUBLE

June 15, 1938, at Ebbets Field

Cincinnati lefthander Johnny Vander Meer pitched an historic 6-0 no-hitter against the Brooklyn Dodgers—his unprecedented second straight hitless game and the first night contest at Brooklyn's Ebbets Field. Vander Meer's victory came four days after he had no-hit Boston, 3-0.

Cincinnati	AB	R	H	PO	A	E
Frey,2b	5	0	1	2	2	0
Berger,lf	5	1	3	1	0	0
Goodman,rf	3	2	1	3	0	0
McCormick,1b	5	1	1	9	1	0
Lombardi,c	3	1	0	9	0	0
Craft,cf	5	0	3	1	0	0
Riggs,3b	4	0	1	0	3	0
Myers,ss	4	0	0	0	1	0
Vander Meer,p	4	1	1	2	4	0
Totals	38	6	11	27	11	0

Brooklyn	AB	R	H	PO	A	E
Cuyler,rf	2	0	0	1	0	0
Coscarart,2b	2	0	0	1	2	0
aBrack	1	0	0	0	0	0
Hudson,2b	1	0	0	1	0	0
Hassett,lf	4	0	0	3	0	0
Phelps,c	3	0	0	9	0	0
cRosen	0	0	0	0	0	0
Lavagetto,3b	2	0	0	0	2	2
Camilli,1b	1	0	0	7	0	0
Koy,cf	4	0	0	4	0	0
Durocher,ss	4	0	0	1	2	0
Butcher,p	0	0	0	0	1	0
Presnell,p	2	0	0	0	0	0
Hamlin,p	0	0	0	0	1	0
bEnglish	1	0	0	0	0	0
Tamulis,p	0	0	0	0	0	0
Totals	27	0	0	27	8	2

Cincinnati ....0 0 4 0 0 0 1 1 0—6
Brooklyn....................0 0 0 0 0 0 0 0 0—0

a Batted for Coscarart in sixth.
b Struck out for Hamlin in eighth.
c Ran for Phelps in ninth.

Runs batted in: McCormick 3, Riggs, Craft, Berger.
Double: Berger.
Triple: Berger.
Home run: McCormick.
Stolen bases: Goodman.
Left on bases: Cincinnati 9, Brooklyn 8.

Cincinnati	IP	H	R	ER	BB	SO
Vander Meer (W)	9	0	0	0	8	7

Brooklyn	IP	H	R	ER	BB	SO
Butcher (L)	2⅔	5	4	4	3	1
Pressnell	3⅔	4	1	1	0	3
Hamlin	1⅔	2	1	1	1	3
Tamulis	1	0	0	0	0	0

Umpires: Stewart, Stark, Barr.
Time: 2:22. **Attendance:** 38,748.

WILLIAMS' STAR RISES

July 8, 1941, at Briggs Stadium

Young Boston slugger Ted Williams carved his first niche in baseball lore with a two-out, three-run, ninth-inning homer that gave the American League a dramatic 7-5 victory over the National League in baseball's ninth All-Star Game. Williams capped the four-run A.L. ninth with a monster drive off Chicago's Claude Passeau that bounced off the upper right-field parapet of Detroit's Briggs Stadium.

National League	AB	R	H	PO	A	E
Hack,3b	2	0	1	3	0	0
fLavagetto,3b	1	0	0	0	0	0
Moore,lf	5	0	0	0	0	0
Reiser,cf	4	0	0	6	0	2
Mize,1b	4	1	1	5	0	0
McCormick,1b	0	0	0	0	0	0
Nicholson,rf	1	0	0	1	0	0
Elliott,rf	1	0	0	0	0	0
Slaughter,rf	2	1	1	0	0	0
Vaughan,ss	4	2	3	1	2	0
Miller,ss	0	0	0	0	1	0
Frey,3b	1	0	1	1	3	0
cHerman,2b	3	0	2	3	0	0
Owen,c	1	0	0	0	0	0
Lopez,c	1	0	0	3	0	0
Danning,c	1	0	0	3	0	0
Wyatt,p	0	0	0	0	0	0
aOtt	1	0	0	0	0	0
Derringer,p	0	0	0	0	1	0
Walters,p	1	1	1	0	0	0
dMedwick	1	0	0	0	0	0
Passeau,p	1	0	0	0	0	0
Totals	35	5	10	26	7	2

American League	AB	R	H	PO	A	E
Doerr,2b	3	0	0	0	0	0
Gordon,2b	2	1	1	2	0	0
Travis,3b	4	1	1	1	2	0
J.DiMaggio,cf	4	3	1	1	0	0
Williams,lf	4	1	2	3	0	1
Heath,rf	2	0	0	1	0	1
D.DiMaggio,rf	1	0	1	1	0	0
Cronin,ss	2	0	0	3	0	0
Boudreau,ss	2	0	2	0	1	0
York,1b	3	0	1	6	2	0
Foxx,1b	1	0	0	2	2	0
Dickey,c	3	0	1	4	2	0
Hayes,c	1	0	0	2	0	0
Feller,p	0	0	0	0	1	0
bCullenbine	1	0	0	0	0	0
Lee,p	1	0	0	0	1	0
Hudson,p	0	0	0	0	0	0
eKeller	1	0	0	0	0	0
Smith,p	0	0	0	1	0	1
gKeltner	1	1	1	0	0	0
Totals	36	7	11	27	11	3

National League ....0 0 0 0 0 1 2 2 0—5
American League ......0 0 0 1 0 1 0 1 4—7

a Struck out for Wyatt in third.
b Grounded out for Feller in third.
c Singled for Frey in fifth.
d Grounded out for Walters in seventh.
e Struck out for Hudson in seventh.
f Grounded out for Hack in ninth.
g Singled for Smith in ninth.
h Two out when winning run scored.

Runs batted in: Williams 4, Moore, Boudreau, Vaughan 4, D.DiMaggio, J.DiMaggio.
Doubles: Travis, Williams, Walters, Herman, Mize, J.DiMaggio.
Home runs: Vaughan 2, Williams.
Sacrifice hits: Hack, Lopez.
Double plays: Frey, Vaughan and Mize; York and Cronin.
Left on bases: National League 6, American League 7.

National League	IP	H	R	ER	BB	SO
Wyatt	2	0	0	0	1	0
Derringer	2	2	1	1	0	1
Walters	2	3	1	1	2	2
Passeau (L)	2⅔	6	5	5	1	3

American League	IP	H	R	ER	BB	SO
Feller	3	1	0	0	0	4
Lee	3	4	1	1	0	0
Hudson	1	3	2	2	1	1
Smith (W)	2	2	2	2	0	2

Umpires: Summers, Grieve, Jorda, Pinelli.
Time: 2:23. **Attendance:** 54,674.

DiMAGGIO'S STREAK ENDS

July 17, 1941, at Municipal Stadium

Cleveland pitchers Al Smith and Jim Bagby Jr. retired New York's Joe DiMaggio three times and ended the Yankees center fielder's record hitting streak at 56 games. DiMaggio, who had not gone hitless in more than two months, grounded out to third base twice, walked and bounced into an eighth-inning double play during the Yankees' 4-3 victory.

New York	AB	R	H	PO	A	E
Sturm,1b	4	0	1	10	2	0
Rolfe,3b	4	1	2	2	3	0
Henrich,rf	3	0	1	4	0	0
DiMaggio,cf	3	0	0	2	0	0
Gordon,2b	4	1	2	0	1	0
Rosar,c	4	0	0	5	1	0
Keller,lf	3	1	1	0	0	0
Rizzuto,ss	4	0	0	2	1	0
Gomez,p	4	1	1	2	1	0
Murphy,p	0	0	0	0	1	0
Totals	33	4	8	27	10	0

Cleveland	AB	R	H	PO	A	E
Weatherly,cf	5	0	1	4	0	0
Keltner,3b	3	0	1	1	4	0
Boudreau,ss	3	0	0	0	2	0
Heath,rf	4	0	0	0	0	0
Walker,lf	3	2	2	1	0	0
Grimes,1b	3	1	1	12	0	0
Mack,2b	3	0	0	4	7	0
aRosenthal	1	0	1	0	0	0
Hemsley,c	3	0	1	5	1	0
bTrosky	1	0	0	0	0	0
Smith,p	3	0	0	0	0	0
Bagby,p	0	0	0	0	0	0
cCampbell	1	0	0	0	0	0
Totals	33	3	7	27	14	0

New York ....1 0 0 0 0 0 1 2 0—4
Cleveland ....0 0 0 1 0 0 0 0 2—3

a Tripled for Mack in ninth.
b Grounded out for Hemsley in ninth.
c Hit into fielders choice for Bagby in ninth.

Runs batted in: Henrich, Walker, Gomez, Gordon, Rolfe, Rosenthal 2.
Doubles: Henrich, Rolfe.
Triples: Keller, Rosenthal.
Home runs: Walker, Gordon.
Sacrifice hit: Boudreau.
Double play: Boudreau, Mack and Grimes.
Passed ball: Hemsley.
Left on bases: New York 5, Cleveland 7.

New York	IP	H	R	ER	BB	SO
Gomez (W)	8	6	3	3	3	5
Murphy (S)	1	1	0	0	0	0

Cleveland	IP	H	R	ER	BB	SO
Smith (L)	7⅓	7	4	4	2	4
Bagby	1⅔	1	0	0	1	1

Gomez pitched to two batters in ninth.

Umpires: Summers, Rue, Stewart.
Time: 2:03. Attendance: 67,468.

OWEN'S PASSED BALL

October 5, 1941, at Ebbets Field
With his Dodgers leading the New York Yankees, 4-3, and one out away from evening the World Series at two games apiece, Brooklyn catcher Mickey Owen missed connections on a third strike, allowing Tommy Henrich to reach first base. Given new life, the Yankees exploded for four ninth-inning runs, recorded a 7-4 victory and set the stage for a Series-clinching victory the next day.

New York	AB	R	H	PO	A	E
Sturm,1b	5	0	2	9	1	0
Rolfe,3b	5	1	2	0	2	0
Henrich,rf	4	1	0	3	0	0
DiMaggio,cf	4	1	2	0	0	0
Keller,lf	5	1	4	1	0	0
Dickey,c	2	0	2	7	0	0
Gordon,2b	5	1	2	2	3	0
Rizzuto,ss	4	0	0	2	3	0
Donald,p	2	0	0	0	1	0
Breuer,p	1	0	0	0	1	0
bSelkirk	1	0	0	0	0	0
Murphy,p	1	0	0	0	0	0
Totals	39	7	12	27	11	0

Brooklyn	AB	R	H	PO	A	E
Reese,ss	5	0	0	2	4	0
Walker,rf	5	1	2	5	0	0
Reiser,cf	5	1	2	1	0	0
Camilli,1b	4	0	2	10	1	0
Riggs,3b	3	0	0	0	2	0
Medwick,lf	2	0	0	0	0	0
Allen,p	0	0	0	0	0	0
Casey,p	2	0	1	0	3	0
Owen,c	2	1	0	2	1	1
Coscarart,2b	3	1	0	4	2	0
Higbe,p	1	0	0	1	0	0
French,p	0	0	0	0	0	0
aWasdell,lf	3	0	1	2	0	0
Totals	35	4	9	27	14	1

New York .... 100 200 004—7
Brooklyn .... 000 220 000—4

a Doubled for French in fourth.
b Grounded out for Breuer in eighth.

Runs batted in: Keller 3, Sturm 2, Gordon 2, Wasdell 2, Reiser 2.
Doubles: Keller 2, Walker, Camilli, Wasdell, Gordon.
Home run: Reiser.
Double play: Gordon, Rizzuto and Sturm.
Left on bases: New York 11, Brooklyn 8.

New York	IP	H	R	ER	BB	SO
Donald	4	6	4	4	3	2
Breuer	3	3	0	0	1	2
Murphy (W)	2	0	0	0	0	1

Brooklyn	IP	H	R	ER	BB	SO
Higbe	3⅔	6	3	3	2	1
French	⅓	0	0	0	0	0
Allen	⅔	1	0	0	1	0
Casey (L)	4⅓	5	4	0	2	1

Donald pitched to two batters in fifth.
Hit by pitch: Henrich (by Allen).

Umpires: Goetz, McGowan, Pinelli, Grieve.
Time: 2:54. Attendance: 33,813.

SLAUGHTER'S MAD DASH

October 15, 1946, at Sportsman's Park
St. Louis Cardinals outfielder Enos Slaughter decided the World Series with his daring Game 7 dash around the bases on a hit to left-center field by Harry Walker. Slaughter's eighth-inning heroics were successful because Boston shortstop Johnny Pesky, obviously surprised that Slaughter didn't stop at third, hesitated before making a weak relay throw to the plate.

Boston	AB	R	H	PO	A	E
Moses,rf	4	1	1	1	0	0
Pesky,ss	4	0	1	2	1	0
DiMaggio,cf	3	0	1	0	0	0
cCulberson,cf	0	0	0	0	0	0
Williams,lf	4	0	0	3	1	0
York,1b	4	0	1	10	1	0
dCampbell	0	0	0	0	0	0
Doerr,2b	4	0	2	3	7	0
Higgins,3b	4	0	0	0	1	0
H.Wagner,c	2	0	0	4	0	0
aRussell	1	1	1	0	0	0
Partee,c	1	0	0	1	0	0
Ferriss,p	2	0	0	0	0	0
Dobson,p	0	0	0	0	1	0
bMetkovich	1	1	1	0	0	0
Klinger,p	0	0	0	0	1	0
Johnson,p	0	0	0	0	0	0
eMcBride	1	0	0	0	0	0
Totals	35	3	8	24	12	0

St. Louis	AB	R	H	PO	A	E
Schoendienst,2b	4	0	2	2	3	0
Moore,cf	4	0	1	3	0	0
Musial,1b	3	0	1	6	0	0
Slaughter,rf	3	1	1	4	0	0
Kurowski,3b	4	1	1	3	1	1
Garigiola,c	3	0	0	4	0	0
Rice,c	1	0	0	0	0	0
Walker,lf	3	1	2	3	0	0
Marion,ss	2	0	0	2	1	0
Dickson,p	3	1	1	0	1	0
Brecheen,p	1	0	0	0	0	0
Totals	31	4	9	27	6	1

Boston .... 100 000 020—3
St. Louis .... 010 020 01x—4

a Singled for H.Wagner in eighth.
b Doubled for Dobson in eighth.
c Ran for DiMaggio in eighth.
d Ran for York in ninth.
e Rolled out for Johnson in ninth.

Runs batted in: DiMaggio 3, Walker 2, Dickson, Schoendienst.
Doubles: Musial, Kurowski, Dickson, DiMaggio, Metkovich, Walker.
Sacrifice hit: Marion.
Left on bases: Boston 6, St. Louis 8.

Boston	IP	H	R	ER	BB	SO
Ferris	4⅓	7	3	3	1	1
Dobson	2⅔	0	0	0	2	2
Klinger (L)	⅔	2	1	1	1	0
Johnson	⅓	0	0	0	0	0

St. Louis	IP	H	R	ER	BB	SO
Dickson	7	5	3	3	1	3
Brecheen (W)	2	3	0	0	0	1

Dickson pitched to two batters in eighth.

Umpires: Barlick, Berry, Ballanfant, Hubbard.
Time: 2:17. Attendance: 36,143.

ROBINSON BREAKS BARRIER

April 15, 1947, at Ebbets Field
Jackie Robinson made his long-awaited debut as baseball's first black Major League player in more than six decades when he started at first base in Brooklyn's season-opening 5-3 victory over Boston. The 28-year-old Robinson, a former college football and track star, went 0-for-3 but reached base on a seventh-inning error and came around to score the winning run.

Boston	AB	R	H	PO	A	E
Culler,ss	3	0	0	0	2	0
eHolmes	1	0	0	0	0	0
Sisti,ss	0	0	0	0	0	0
Hopp,cf	5	0	1	2	0	0
McCormick,rf	4	0	3	2	0	0
Elliott,3b	2	0	1	0	2	0
Litwhiler,lf	3	1	0	1	0	0
Rowell,lf	1	0	0	0	0	0
Torgeson,1b	4	1	0	10	1	1
Masi,c	3	0	0	4	0	0
Ryan,2b	4	1	3	4	7	0
Sain,p	1	0	0	0	1	0
Cooper,p	0	0	0	0	0	0
dNeill	0	0	0	0	0	0
Lanfranconi,p	0	0	0	0	0	0
Totals	31	3	8	24	13	1

Brooklyn	AB	R	H	PO	A	E
Stanky,2b	3	1	0	0	3	0
Robinson,1b	3	1	0	11	0	0
Schultz,1b	0	0	0	1	0	0
Reiser,cf	2	3	2	2	0	0
Walker,rf	3	0	1	0	0	0
Tatum,rf	0	0	0	0	0	0
cVaughan	1	0	0	0	0	0
Furillo,rf	0	0	0	0	0	0
Hermanski,lf	4	0	1	3	0	0
Edwards,c	2	0	0	0	2	0
aRackley	0	0	0	0	0	0
Bragan,c	1	0	0	3	0	0
Jorgensen,3b	3	0	0	0	4	0
Reese,ss	3	0	1	3	2	0
Hatten,p	2	0	1	1	1	0
bStevens	1	0	0	0	0	0
Gregg,p	1	0	0	0	1	0
Casey,p	0	0	0	0	0	0
Totals	29	5	6	27	10	1

Boston .... 000 012 000—3
Brooklyn .... 000 101 30x—5

a Ran for Edwards in sixth.
b Struck out for Hatten in sixth.
c Grounded out for Tatum in seventh.
d Hit by pitch for Cooper in eighth.
e Flied out for Culler in eighth.

Runs batted in: Edwards, Hopp, Ryan 2, Jorgensen, Reiser 2, Hermanski.
Doubles: Reese, Reiser.
Sacrifice hits: Masi, Culler, Sain 2, Robinson.

Double plays: Stanky, Reese and Robinson; Culler, Ryan and Torgeson.
Left on bases: Boston 12, Brooklyn 7.

Boston	IP	H	R	ER	BB	SO
Sain (L)	6	6	5	4	5	1
Cooper	1	0	0	0	0	0
Lanfranconi	1	0	0	0	0	2

Brooklyn	IP	H	R	ER	BB	SO
Hatten	6	6	3	2	3	2
Gregg (W)	2⅓	2	0	0	2	2
Casey (S)	⅔	0	0	0	0	0

Sain pitched to three batters in seventh.
Hit by pitcher: Litwhiler (by Hatten), Edwards (by Sain), Neill (by Gregg).
Wild pitch: Hatten.

Umpires: Pinelli, Barlick, Gore.
Time: 2:26. Attendance: 25,623.

BEVENS' NEAR-MISS

October 3, 1947, at Ebbets Field
New York Yankees pitcher Bill Bevens, one out away from the first no-hitter in World Series history, surrendered a two-run double to Brooklyn pinch hitter Cookie Lavagetto and dropped a heart-breaking 3-2 decision to the Dodgers. After Bevens walked two Dodgers in the ninth inning of the Game 4 classic, his ninth and 10th free passes, Lavagetto lined an opposite-field drive off the right-field wall, allowing Brooklyn to tie the Series at two games apiece.

New York	AB	R	H	PO	A	E
Stirnweiss,2b	4	1	2	2	1	0
Henrich,rf	5	0	1	2	0	0
Berra,c	4	0	0	6	1	1
DiMaggio,cf	2	0	0	2	0	0
McQuinn,1b	4	0	1	7	0	0
Johnson,3b	4	1	1	3	2	0
Lindell,lf	3	0	2	3	0	0
Rizzuto,ss	4	0	1	1	2	0
Bevens,p	3	0	0	0	1	0
Totals	33	2	8	26	7	1

Brooklyn	AB	R	H	PO	A	E
Stanky,2b	1	0	0	2	3	0
aLavagetto	1	0	1	0	0	0
Reese,ss	4	0	0	3	5	1
Robinson,1b	4	0	0	11	1	0
Walker,rf	2	0	0	0	1	0
Hermanski,lf	4	0	0	2	0	0
Edwards,c	4	0	0	7	1	1
Furillo,cf	3	0	0	2	0	0
bGionfriddo	0	1	0	0	0	0
Jorgensen,3b	2	1	0	0	1	1
Taylor,p	0	0	0	0	0	0
Gregg,p	1	0	0	0	1	0
aVaughan	1	0	0	0	0	0
Behrman,p	0	0	0	0	1	0
Casey,p	0	0	0	0	0	0
cReiser	0	0	0	0	0	0
dMiksis	0	1	0	0	0	0
Totals	26	3	1	27	15	3

New York .... 100 100 000—2
Brooklyn .... 000 010 002—3

a Walked for Gregg in seventh.
b Ran for Furillo in ninth.
c Walked for Casey in ninth.
d Ran for Reiser in ninth.
e Doubled for Stanky in ninth.
f Two out when winning run scored.

Runs batted in: DiMaggio, Lindell, Reese, Lavagetto 2.
Doubles: Lindell, Lavagetto.
Triple: Johnson.
Sacrifice hits: Stanky, Bevens.
Stolen bases: Rizzuto, Reese, Gionfriddo.
Double plays: Reese, Stanky and Robinson; Gregg, Reese and Robinson; Edwards and Robinson.
Left on bases: New York 9, Brooklyn 8.

New York	IP	H	R	ER	BB	SO
Bevens (L)	8⅔	1	3	3	10	5

Brooklyn	IP	H	R	ER	BB	SO
Taylor	0	2	1	0	1	0
Gregg	7	4	1	1	3	5
Behrman	1⅓	2	0	0	0	0
Casey (W)	⅔	0	0	0	0	0

Taylor pitched to four batters in first.
Wild pitch: Bevens.

Umpires: Goetz, McGowan, Pinelli, Rommel, Boyer, Magerkurth.
Time: 2:20. Attendance: 33,443.

Brooklyn's Cookie Lavagetto (right) is mobbed after his Game 4-winning hit in the 1947 World Series ended Bill Bevens' hope for a no-hitter.

GIONFRIDDO SAVES THE DAY

October 5, 1947, at Yankee Stadium
Defensive replacement Al Gionfriddo jumped into the World Series spotlight when he made a spectacular sixth-inning catch of Yankees slugger Joe DiMaggio's bid for a home run, preserving an 8-6 victory that forced a decisive seventh game. With the Dodgers leading 8-5 and two New York runners on base, DiMaggio hit a monster drive that a twisting Gionfriddo speared at the 415-foot sign, just as it appeared the ball would drop into the bullpen for a game-tying homer. The Yankees rebounded to win the Series the next day.

Brooklyn	AB	R	H	PO	A	E
Stanky,2b	5	2	2	4	2	0
Reese,ss	4	2	3	2	1	0
J.Robinson,1b	5	1	2	7	1	0
Walker,rf	5	0	1	3	0	0
Hermanski,lf	1	0	0	0	0	0
bMiksis,lf	1	0	0	0	0	0
Gionfriddo,lf	2	0	0	0	0	0
Edwards,c	4	1	1	5	0	0
Furillo,cf	4	1	2	4	1	0
Jorgensen,3b	2	0	0	1	1	1
cLavagetto,3b	2	0	0	0	1	0
Lombardi,p	1	0	0	0	0	0
Branca,p	1	0	0	0	1	0
dBragan	1	0	0	0	0	0
eBankhead	0	1	0	0	0	0
Hatten,p	1	0	0	0	0	0
Casey,p	0	0	0	0	1	0
Totals	39	8	12	27	9	1

New York	AB	R	H	PO	A	E
Stirnweiss,2b	5	0	0	1	6	0
Henrich,rf-lf	5	1	2	1	0	0
Lindell,lf	2	1	2	0	0	0
Berra,rf	3	0	2	1	0	0
DiMaggio,cf	5	1	1	5	0	0
Johnson,3b	5	1	2	1	5	0
Phillips,1b	1	0	0	4	0	0
aBrown	1	0	1	0	0	0
McQuinn,1b	1	0	0	6	0	1
Rizzuto,ss	4	0	1	6	1	0
Lollar,c	1	1	1	0	0	0
A.Robinson,c	4	1	2	2	0	1
Reynolds,p	0	0	0	0	0	0
Drews,p	2	0	0	0	1	0
Page,p	0	0	0	0	0	0
Newsom,p	0	0	0	0	0	0
fClark	1	0	0	0	0	0
Raschi,p	0	0	0	0	0	0
gHouk	1	0	1	0	0	0
Wensloff,p	0	0	0	0	1	0
hFrey	1	0	0	0	0	0
Totals	42	6	15	27	14	2

Brooklyn ....2 0 2 0 0 4 0 0 0— 8
New York ....0 0 4 1 0 0 0 0 1— 6

a Singled for Phillips in third.
b Popped out for Hermanski in fifth.
c Flied out for Jorgensen in sixth.
d Doubled for Branca in sixth.
e Ran for Bragan in sixth.
f Lined out for Newsom in sixth.
g Singled for Raschi in seventh.
h Forced A.Robinson for Wensloff in ninth.

Runs batted in: J.Robinson, Walker, Stirnweiss, Lindell, Johnson, Brown, Berra, Lavagetto, Reese 2, Frey, Bragan.
Doubles: Reese, J.Robinson, Walker, Lollar, Furillo, Bragan.
Double play: Rizzuto and Phillips.
Passed ball: Lollar.
Left on bases: New York 13, Brooklyn 6.

Brooklyn	IP	H	R	ER	BB	SO
Lombardi	2⅔	5	4	4	0	2
Branca (W)	2⅓	6	1	1	0	2
Hatten	3	3	1	1	4	0
Casey (S)	1	1	0	0	0	0

New York	IP	H	R	ER	BB	SO
Reynolds	2⅓	6	4	3	1	0
Drews	2	1	0	0	1	0
Page (L)	1	4	4	4	0	1
Newsom	⅔	1	0	0	0	0
Raschi	1	0	0	0	0	1
Wensloff	2	0	0	0	0	0

Hatten pitched to two batters in ninth.
Wild pitch: Lombardi.

Umpires: Pinelli, Rommel, Goetz, McGowman, Boyer, Magerkurth.
Time: 3:19. **Attendance:** 74,065.

THE SHOT HEARD 'ROUND THE WORLD

October 3, 1951, at the Polo Grounds
Bobby Thomson's three-run, ninth-inning

Bobby Thomson poses with Giants owner Horace Stoneham (left) and manager Leo Durocher after his pennant-deciding homer.

home run, considered by many historians the most dramatic in baseball history, gave the New York Giants a 5-4 victory over Brooklyn and settled a wild N.L. pennant race. Thomson connected off Dodgers righthander Ralph Branca with two out and the Giants trailing, 4-2, in Game 3 of a pennant playoff series. Thomson's dramatics were preceded by Al Dark and Don Mueller singles and Whitey Lockman's run-scoring double.

Brooklyn	AB	R	H	PO	A	E
Furillo,rf	5	0	0	0	0	0
Reese,ss	4	2	1	2	5	0
Snider,cf	3	1	2	1	0	0
Robinson,2b	2	1	1	3	2	0
Pafko,lf	4	0	1	4	1	0
Hodges,1b	4	0	0	11	1	0
Cox,3b	4	0	2	1	3	0
Walker,c	4	0	1	2	0	0
Newcombe,p	4	0	1	1	1	0
Branca,p	0	0	0	0	0	0
Totals	34	4	8	25	13	0

New York	AB	R	H	PO	A	E
Stanky,2b	4	0	0	0	4	0
Dark,ss	4	1	1	2	2	0
Mueller,rf	4	0	1	0	0	0
cHartung	0	1	0	0	0	0
Irvin,lf	4	1	1	1	0	0
Lockman,1b	3	1	2	11	1	0
Thomson,3b	4	1	3	4	1	0
Mays,cf	3	0	0	1	0	0
Westrum,c	0	0	0	7	1	0
aRigney	1	0	0	0	0	0
Noble,c	0	0	0	0	0	0
Maglie,p	2	0	0	1	2	0
bThompson	1	0	0	0	0	0
Jansen,p	0	0	0	0	0	0
Totals	30	5	8	27	11	0

Brooklyn ....1 0 0 0 0 0 0 3 0— 4
New York ....0 0 0 0 0 0 1 0 4— 5

a Struck out for Westrum in eighth.
b Grounded out for Maglie in eighth.
c Ran for Mueller in ninth.
d One out when winning run scored.

Runs batted in: Robinson, Thomson 4, Pafko, Cox, Lockman.
Doubles: Thomson, Irvin, Lockman.
Home run: Thomson.
Sacrifice hit: Lockman.
Double plays: Cox, Robinson and Hodges; Reese, Robinson and Hodges.
Left on bases: Brooklyn 7, New York 3.

Brooklyn	IP	H	R	ER	BB	SO
Newcombe	8⅓	7	4	4	2	2
Branca (L)	0	1	1	1	0	0

New York	IP	H	R	ER	BB	SO
Maglie	8	8	4	4	4	6
Jansen (W)	1	0	0	0	0	2

Branca pitched to one batter in ninth.
Wild pitch: Maglie.

Umpires: Jorda, Conlan, Stewart, Goetz.
Time: 2:28. **Attendance:** 34,320.

MAYS STUNS INDIANS

September 29, 1954, at the Polo Grounds
Willie Mays took his place in baseball lore when he made a dramatic eighth-inning, over-the-shoulder catch on a 460-foot drive by Cleveland's Vic Wertz, saving the New York Giants in Game 1 of the World Series. Mays made his remarkable catch with the score tied 2-2 and Indians positioned on first and second base. The Giants went on to win the Series opener, 5-2, on Dusty Rhodes' 10th-inning homer, keying a stunning fall classic sweep.

Cleveland	AB	R	H	PO	A	E
Smith,lf	4	1	1	1	0	0
Avila,2b	5	1	1	2	3	0
Doby,cf	3	0	1	3	0	0
Rosen,3b	5	0	1	1	3	0
Wertz,1b	5	0	4	11	1	0
dRegalado	0	0	0	0	0	0
Grasso,c	0	0	0	1	0	0
Philley,rf	3	0	0	0	0	0
aMajeski	1	0	0	0	0	0
bMitchell	0	0	0	0	0	0
Dente,ss	0	0	0	0	0	0
Strickland,ss	3	0	0	2	3	0
cPope,rf	1	0	0	0	0	0
Hegan,c	4	0	0	6	1	0
eGlynn,1b	1	0	0	0	0	0
Lemon,p	4	0	0	1	0	0
Totals	38	2	8	28	12	0

New York	AB	R	H	PO	A	E
Lockman,1b	5	1	1	9	0	0
Dark,ss	4	0	2	3	2	0
Mueller,rf	5	1	2	2	0	2
Mays,cf	3	1	0	2	0	0
Thompson,3b	3	1	1	3	3	0
Irvin,lf	3	0	1	5	0	1
fRhodes	1	1	1	0	0	0
Williams,2b	4	0	0	1	1	0
Westrum,c	4	0	2	5	0	0
Maglie,p	3	0	0	0	2	0
Liddle,p	0	0	0	0	0	0
Grissom,p	1	0	0	0	0	0
Totals	36	5	9	30	8	3

Cleveland ....2 0 0 0 0 0 0 0 0— 2
New York ....0 0 2 0 0 0 0 0 3— 5

a Announced for Philley in eighth.
b Walked for Majeski in eighth.
c Called out on strikes for Strickland in eighth.
d Ran for Wertz in 10th.
e Struck out for Hegan in 10th.
f Hit home run for Irvin in 10th.
i One out when winning run scored.

Runs batted in: Wertz 2, Mueller, Thompson, Rhodes 3.
Double: Wertz.
Triple: Wertz.
Home run: Rhodes.
Sacrifice hits: Irvin, Dente.
Stolen bases: Mays.
Left on bases: Cleveland 13, New York 9.

Cleveland	IP	H	R	ER	BB	SO
Lemon (L)	9⅓	9	5	5	5	6

New York	IP	H	R	ER	BB	SO
Maglie	7	7	2	2	2	2
Liddle	⅓	0	0	0	0	0
Grissom (W)	2⅔	1	0	0	3	2

Maglie pitched to two batters in eighth.
Hit by pitcher: Smith (by Maglie).
Wild pitch: Lemon.

Umpires: Barlick, Berry, Conlan, Stevens, Warneke, Napp.
Time: 3:11. **Attendance:** 52,751.

AMOROS TO THE RESCUE

October 4, 1955, at Yankee Stadium
With his team leading 2-0 in the sixth inning of World Series Game 7, Brooklyn left fielder Sandy Amoros streaked into the left-field corner and made a spectacular, Series-saving catch of Yogi Berra's line drive. Amoros made the dramatic play with two Yankees on base, wheeled around and doubled Gil McDougald off first, securing Johnny Podres' shutout.

Brooklyn	AB	R	H	PO	A	E
Gilliam,lf-2b	4	0	1	2	0	0
Reese,ss	4	1	1	2	6	0
Snider,cf	3	0	0	2	0	0
Campanella,c	3	1	1	5	0	0
Furillo,rf	3	0	0	3	0	0
Hodges,1b	2	0	1	10	0	0
Hoak,3b	3	0	1	1	1	0
Zimmer,2b	2	0	0	2	2	0
aShuba	1	0	0	0	0	0
Amoros,lf	0	0	0	2	1	0
Podres,p	4	0	0	1	1	0
Totals	29	2	5	27	11	0

New York	AB	R	H	PO	A	E
Rizzuto,ss	3	0	1	1	3	0
Martin,2b	3	0	1	1	6	0
McDougald,3b	4	0	3	1	1	0
Berra,c	4	0	1	4	1	0
Bauer,rf	4	0	0	1	0	0
Skowron,1b	4	0	1	11	1	1
Cerv,cf	4	0	0	5	0	0
Howard,lf	4	0	1	2	0	0
Byrne,p	2	0	0	0	2	0
Grim,p	0	0	0	0	1	0
bMantle	1	0	0	0	0	0
Turley,p	0	0	0	0	0	0
Totals	33	0	8	27	14	1

—501—

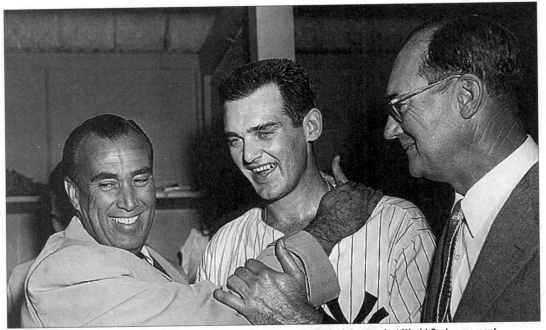

Don Larsen celebrates with Yankees owners Dan Topping (left) and Dell Webb in a perfect World Series moment.

Brooklyn...................000 101 000—2
New York ....000 000 000—0

a Grounded out for Zimmer in sixth.
b Popped out for Grim in seventh.

Runs batted in: Hodges 2.
Doubles: Skowron, Campanella, Berra.
Sacrifice hits: Snider, Campanella.
Sacrifice fly: Hodges.
Double play: Amoros, Reese and Hodges.
Left on bases: Brooklyn 8, New York 8.

Brooklyn	IP	H	R	ER	BB	SO
Podres (W)	9	8	0	0	2	4

New York	IP	H	R	ER	BB	SO
Byrne (L)	5⅓	3	2	1	3	2
Grim	1⅔	1	0	0	1	1
Turley	2	1	0	0	1	1

Wild pitch: Grim.

Umpires: Honochick, Dascoli, Summers, Ballanfant, Flaherty, Donatelli.
Time: 2:44. **Attendance:** 62,465.

WORLD SERIES PERFECTION

October 8, 1956, at Yankee Stadium
Yankees righthander Don Larsen retired all 27 Brooklyn Dodgers he faced in a perfect 2-0 World Series victory—the only no-hitter ever pitched in postseason play. Larsen, who went to ball three on only one batter, outdueled Dodgers starter Sal Maglie in the Game 5 classic and received all the run support he needed on Mickey Mantle's fourth-inning homer.

Brooklyn	AB	R	H	PO	A	E
Gilliam,2b	3	0	0	2	0	0
Reese,ss	3	0	0	4	2	0
Snider,cf	3	0	0	1	0	0
Robinson,3b	3	0	0	2	4	0
Hodges,1b	3	0	0	5	1	0
Amoros,lf	3	0	0	3	0	0
Furillo,rf	3	0	0	0	0	0
Campanella,c	3	0	0	7	2	0
Maglie,p	2	0	0	0	1	0
aMitchell	1	0	0	0	0	0
Totals	27	0	0	24	10	0

New York	AB	R	H	PO	A	E
Bauer,rf	4	0	1	4	0	0
Collins,1b	4	0	1	7	0	0
Mantle,cf	3	1	1	4	0	0
Berra,c	3	0	0	7	0	0
Slaughter,lf	2	0	0	1	0	0
Martin,2b	3	0	1	3	4	0
McDougald,ss	2	0	0	2	0	0
Carey,3b	3	1	1	1	1	0
Larsen,p	2	0	0	0	1	0
Totals	26	2	5	27	8	0

Brooklyn...................000 000 000—0
New York ....000 101 00x—2

a Called out on strikes for Maglie in ninth.

Runs batted in: Mantle, Bauer.
Home run: Mantle.
Sacrifice hit: Larsen.
Double plays: Reese and Hodges; Hodges, Campanella, Robinson, Campanella and Robinson.
Left on bases: Brooklyn 0, New York 3.

Brooklyn	IP	H	R	ER	BB	SO
Maglie (L)	8	5	2	2	2	5

New York	IP	H	R	ER	BB	SO
Larsen (W)	9	0	0	0	0	7

Umpires: Pinelli, Soar, Boggess, Napp, Gorman, Runge.
Time: 2:06. **Attendance:** 64,519.

AN IMPERFECT ENDING

May 26, 1959, at County Stadium
Pittsburgh lefthander Harvey Haddix retired 36 consecutive Milwaukee batters over 12 perfect innings, but he ended up losing the game on a 13th-inning error, walk and double. Milwaukee starter Lew Burdette shut out the Pirates on 12 hits and Joe Adcock broke Haddix's hitless string with his one-out blow—an apparent home run that was ruled a double because Adcock passed teammate Hank Aaron while circling the bases.

Pittsburgh	AB	R	H	PO	A	E
Schofield,ss	6	0	3	2	4	0
Virdon,cf	6	0	1	8	0	0
Burgess,c	5	0	0	8	0	0
Nelson,1b	5	0	2	14	0	0
Skinner,lf	5	0	1	4	0	0
Mazeroski,2b	5	0	1	1	1	0
Hoak,3b	5	0	2	0	6	1
Mejias,rf	3	0	1	1	0	0
aStuart	1	0	0	0	0	0
Christopher,rf	1	0	0	0	0	0
Haddix,p	5	0	1	0	2	0
Totals	47	0	12	38	13	1

Milwaukee	AB	R	H	PO	A	E
O'Brien,2b	3	0	0	2	5	0
bRice	1	0	0	0	0	0
Mantilla,2b	1	1	0	1	2	0
Mathews,3b	4	0	0	2	3	0
Aaron,rf	4	0	0	1	0	0
Adcock,1b	5	0	1	17	3	0
Covington,lf	4	0	0	4	0	0
Crandall,c	4	0	0	2	1	0
Pafko,cf	4	0	0	6	0	0
Logan,ss	4	0	0	3	5	0
Burdette,p	4	0	0	1	3	0
Totals	38	1	1	39	22	0

Pittsburgh ....000 000 000 000 0—0
Milwaukee ....000 000 000 000 1—1

a Flied out for Mejias in 10th.
b Flied out for O'Brien in 10th.
c Two out when winning run scored.

Run batted in: Adcock.

Double: Adcock.
Sacrifice hit: Mathews.
Double plays: Logan and Adcock; Mathews, O'Brien and Adcock; Adcock and Logan.
Left on bases: Pittsburgh 8, Milwaukee 1.

Pittsburgh	IP	H	R	ER	BB	SO
Haddix (L)	12⅔	1	1	1	1	8

Milwaukee	IP	H	R	ER	BB	SO
Burdette (W)	13	12	0	0	0	2

Umpires: Smith, Dascoli, Secory, Dixon.
Time: 2:54. **Attendance:** 19,194.

MAZEROSKI STUNS YANKEES

October 13, 1960, at Forbes Field
Second baseman Bill Mazeroski ended Pittsburgh's 35-year title drought when he hammered a stunning bottom-of-the-ninth-inning home run over the left-field fence against the New York Yankees, breaking a 9-9 tie in Game 7 of the World Series. Mazeroski, leading off the ninth after the Yankees had rallied for two runs in the top of the inning, became the first player to end a Series with a home run.

New York	AB	R	H	PO	A	E
Richardson,2b	5	2	2	2	5	0
Kubek,ss	3	1	0	3	2	0
DeMaestri,ss	0	0	0	0	0	0
dLong	1	0	1	0	0	0
eMcDougald,3b	0	1	0	0	0	0
Maris,rf	5	0	0	2	0	1
Mantle,cf	5	1	3	0	0	0
Berra,lf	4	2	1	3	0	0
Skowron,1b	5	2	2	10	2	0
Blanchard,c	4	0	1	1	1	0
Boyer,3b-ss	4	0	1	0	3	0
Turley,p	0	0	0	0	0	0
Stafford,p	0	0	0	0	1	0
aLopez	1	0	0	0	0	0
Shantz,p	3	0	1	3	1	0
Coates,p	0	0	0	0	0	0
Terry,p	0	0	0	0	0	0
Totals	40	9	13	24	15	1

Pittsburgh	AB	R	H	PO	A	E
Virdon,cf	4	1	2	3	0	0
Groat,ss	4	1	1	3	2	0
Skinner,lf	2	1	0	1	0	0
Nelson,1b	3	1	1	7	0	0
Clemente,rf	4	1	1	4	0	0
Burgess,c	3	0	2	0	0	0
bChristopher	0	0	0	0	0	0
Smith,c	1	1	1	1	0	0
Hoak,3b	3	1	0	3	2	0
Mazeroski,2b	4	2	2	5	0	0
Law,p	2	0	0	0	1	0
Face,p	0	0	0	0	1	0
cCimoli	1	1	0	0	0	0
Friend,p	0	0	0	0	0	0
Haddix,p	0	0	0	0	0	0
Totals	31	10	11	27	6	0

New York ....000 014 022—9
Pittsburgh ....220 000 051—10

a Singled for Stafford in third.
b Ran for Burgess in seventh.
c Singled for Face in eighth.
d Singled for DeMaestri in ninth.
e Ran for Long in ninth.
f None out when winning run scored.

Runs batted in: Mantle 2, Berra 4, Skowron, Blanchard, Boyer, Virdon 2, Groat, Nelson 2, Clemente, Smith 3, Mazeroski.
Double: Boyer.
Home runs: Nelson, Skowron, Berra, Smith, Mazeroski.
Sacrifice hit: Skinner.
Double plays: Stafford, Blanchard and Skowron; Richardson, Kubek and Skowron; Kubek, Richardson and Skowron.
Left on bases: New York 6, Pittsburgh 1.

New York	IP	H	R	ER	BB	SO
Turley	1	2	3	1	0	0
Stafford	1	2	1	1	1	0
Shantz	5	4	3	3	1	0
Coates	⅔	2	2	2	0	0
Terry (L)	⅓	1	1	1	0	0

Pittsburgh	IP	H	R	ER	BB	SO
Law	5	4	3	3	1	0
Face	3	6	4	4	1	0
Friend	0	2	2	2	0	0
Haddix (W)	1	1	0	0	0	0

Turley pitched to one batter in second.
Shantz pitched to three batters in eighth.
Terry pitched to one batter in ninth.
Law pitched to two batters in sixth.
Friend pitched to two batters in ninth.

Umpires: Jackowski, Chylak, Boggess, Stevens, Landes, Honochick.
Time: 2:36. **Attendance:** 36,683.

MARIS HITS 61ST

October 1, 1961, at Yankee Stadium
New York outfielder Roger Maris claimed baseball's single-season home run record when he drove a fourth-inning pitch from Boston righthander Tracy Stallard into the right-field seats on the final day of the regular season. Maris' 61st home run broke the 1927 record of Yankee predecessor Babe Ruth and provided the only run in a 1-0 victory.

Boston	AB	R	H	PO	A	E
Schilling,2b	4	0	1	3	2	0
Geiger,cf	4	0	0	1	0	0
Yastrzemski,lf	4	0	1	1	0	0
Malzone,3b	4	0	0	0	0	0
Clinton,rf	4	0	0	4	0	0
Runnels,1b	3	0	0	7	0	0
Gile,1b	0	0	0	0	0	0
Nixon,c	3	0	2	5	0	0
Green,ss	2	0	0	1	2	0
Stallard,p	1	0	0	0	1	0
bJensen	1	0	0	0	0	0
Nichols,p	0	0	0	0	1	0
Totals	30	0	4	24	5	0

New York	AB	R	H	PO	A	E
Richardson,2b	4	0	0	1	1	0
Kubek,ss	4	0	2	3	4	0
Maris,cf	4	1	1	3	0	0
Berra,lf	2	0	0	1	0	0
Lopez,lf-rf	1	0	0	2	0	0
Blanchard,rf-c	3	0	0	3	0	0
Howard,c	2	0	0	7	2	0
Reed,lf	1	0	1	1	0	0
Skowron,1b	2	0	0	4	0	0
Hale,1b	1	0	1	2	1	0
Boyer,3b	2	0	0	1	1	0
Stafford,p	2	0	0	0	0	0
Reniff,p	0	0	0	0	0	0
aTresh	1	0	0	0	0	0
Arroyo,p	0	0	0	0	0	0
Totals	29	1	5	27	8	0

Boston ....000 000 000—0
New York ....000 100 00x—1

a Popped out for Reniff in seventh.
b Popped out for Stallard in eighth.

Run batted in: Maris.
Triple: Nixon.
Home run: Maris.
Sacrifice hit: Stallard.
Stolen bases: Geiger.
Passed ball: Nixon.
Left on bases: Boston 5, New York 5.

Boston	IP	H	R	ER	BB	SO
Stallard (L)	7	5	1	1	1	5
Nichols	1	0	0	0	0	0

New York	IP	H	R	ER	BB	SO
Stafford (W)	6	3	0	0	1	7
Reniff	1	0	0	0	0	0
Arroyo (S)	2	1	0	0	0	1

Wild pitch: Stallard.

Umpires: Kinnamon, Flaherty, Honochick, Salerno.
Time: 1:57. **Attendance:** 23,154.

McLAIN WINS 30TH

September 14, 1968, at Tiger Stadium

Denny McLain became the first 30-game winner in 34 years when Detroit rallied for two ninth-inning runs and a 5-4 victory over Oakland. McLain, who struck out 10 and yielded two home runs to Reggie Jackson, joined a select circle when Willie Horton's single drove in Mickey Stanley with the winner. McLain became the first 30-win man since St. Louis star Dizzy Dean in 1934.

Oakland	AB	R	H	PO	A	E
Campaneris,ss	4	0	1	2	1	0
Monday,cf	4	0	1	2	0	0
Cater,1b	4	1	2	6	3	1
Bando,3b	3	0	0	1	0	1
Jackson,rf	4	2	2	3	1	0
Green,2b	4	0	0	2	1	0
Keough,lf	3	0	0	0	0	0
Gosger,lf	0	0	0	0	0	0
Duncan,c	2	1	0	7	0	0
Dobson,p	1	0	0	0	0	0
Aker,p	0	0	0	0	0	0
Lindblad,p	0	0	0	0	0	0
aDonaldson	0	0	0	0	0	0
Segui,p	1	0	0	2	1	0
Totals	30	4	6	25	7	2

Detroit	AB	R	H	PO	A	E
McAuliffe,2b	5	0	1	2	1	0
Stanley,cf	5	1	2	1	0	0
Northrup,rf	4	1	0	4	1	0
Horton,lf	5	1	2	0	0	0
Cash,1b	4	1	2	6	0	0
Freehan,c	3	0	1	10	2	0
Matchick,ss	4	0	1	2	0	1
Wert,3b	2	0	0	1	1	0
bBrown	1	0	0	0	0	0
Tracewski,3b	0	0	0	0	1	0
McLain,p	1	0	0	0	0	0
cKaline	0	1	0	0	0	0
Totals	34	5	9	27	6	1

Oakland ....000 211 000—4
Detroit ....000 300 002—5

a Sacrificed for Lindblad in fifth.
b Grounded out for Wert in eighth.
c Walked for McLain in ninth.
d One out when winning run scored.
Runs batted in: Campaneris, Jackson 3, Horton, Cash 3.
Home runs: Jackson 2, Cash.
Double plays: Northrup and Cash.
Sacrifice hits: Bando, Donaldson, McLain.
Left on bases: Oakland 2, Detroit 10.

Oakland	IP	H	R	ER	BB	SO
Dobson	3⅔	4	3	3	2	4
Aker	0	0	0	0	0	1
Lindblad	⅓	0	0	0	0	1
Segui (L)	4⅓	5	2	1	2	1

Detroit	IP	H	R	ER	BB	SO
McLain (W)	9	6	4	4	1	10

Aker pitched to one batter in fourth.
Wild pitch: Aker.
Umpires: Napp, Umont, Haller, Neudecker.
Time: 3:00. **Attendance:** 33,688.

AARON HITS 715TH

April 8, 1974, at Atlanta Stadium

Braves outfielder Hank Aaron unseated all-time home run king Babe Ruth when he connected for career home run No. 715 in the fourth inning of a game against Los Angeles. The three-run blast off Dodgers lefthander Al Downing helped the Braves secure a 7-4 victory.

Los Angeles	AB	R	H	PO	A	E
Lopes,2b	2	1	0	2	2	1
cLacy,2b	1	0	0	0	0	0
Buckner,lf	3	0	1	1	1	1
Wynn,cf	4	0	1	2	0	0
Ferguson,c	4	0	0	4	0	1
Crawford,rf	4	1	1	1	0	0
Cey,3b	4	0	1	2	3	1
Garvey,1b	4	1	1	11	0	0
Russell,ss	4	0	1	1	4	2
Downing,p	1	1	1	0	3	0
dJoshua	1	0	0	0	0	0
Hough,p	0	0	0	1	0	0
eMota	1	0	0	0	0	0
Totals	34	4	7	24	15	6

Atlanta	AB	R	H	PO	A	E
Garr,rf-lf	3	0	0	0	0	0
Lum,1b	5	0	1	10	0	0
Evans,3b	4	1	0	1	4	0
Aaron,lf	3	2	1	0	0	0
Office,cf	0	0	0	0	0	0
Baker,cf-rf	2	1	1	2	0	0
Johnson,2b	3	1	1	2	2	0
Foster,2b	0	0	0	0	0	0
Correll,c	4	1	0	11	0	0
Robinson,ss	0	0	0	0	1	0
aTepedino	1	0	0	0	0	0
Perez,ss	2	1	1	1	2	0
Reed,p	2	0	0	0	1	0
bOates	1	0	0	0	0	0
Capra,p	0	0	0	0	0	0
Totals	29	7	4	27	10	0

Los Angeles ....003 001 000—4
Atlanta ....010 402 00x—7

a Walked for Robinson in fourth.
b Reached on fielder's choice for Reed in sixth.
c Struck out for Lopes in seventh.
d Struck out for Marshall in seventh.
e Lined out for Hough in ninth.
Runs batted in: Wynn 2, Cey, Downing, Garr, Lum, Aaron 2, Tepedino, Oates.
Doubles: Baker, Russell, Wynn.
Home run: Aaron.
Sacrifice hit: Garr.
Sacrifice fly: Garr.
Passed ball: Ferguson.
Left on bases: Los Angeles 5, Atlanta 7.

Los Angeles	IP	H	R	ER	BB	SO
Downing (L)	3	2	5	2	4	2
Marshall	3	2	2	1	1	1
Hough	2	0	0	0	2	1

Atlanta	IP	H	R	ER	BB	SO
Reed (W)	6	7	4	4	1	4
Capra (S)	3	0	0	0	1	6

Downing pitched to four batters in fourth.
Wild pitch: Reed.
Umpires: Sudol, Weyer, Pulli, Davidson.
Time: 2:27. **Attendance:** 53,775.

FISK'S INSTANT WINNER

October 21, 1975, at Fenway Park

Boston catcher Carlton Fisk, leading off the bottom of the 12th inning of World Series Game 6, hit a high drive off the left-field foul pole at Fenway Park, giving the Red Sox a 7-6 victory over Cincinnati in one of the most dramatic games in fall classic history. Fisk's blast ended a see-saw battle and forced a decisive seventh game.

Cincinnati	AB	R	H	PO	A	E
Rose,3b	5	1	2	0	2	0
Griffey,rf	5	2	2	0	0	0
Morgan,2b	6	1	1	4	4	0
Bench,c	6	0	1	8	0	0
Perez,1b	6	0	2	11	2	0
Foster,lf	6	0	2	4	1	0
Concepcion,ss	6	0	1	3	4	0
Geronimo,cf	6	1	2	2	0	0
Nolan,p	0	0	0	0	1	0
aChaney	1	0	0	0	0	0
Norman,p	0	0	0	0	0	0
Billingham,p	0	0	0	0	0	0
bArmbrister	0	1	0	0	0	0
Carroll,p	0	0	0	0	0	0
cCrowley	1	0	1	0	0	0
Borbon,p	0	0	0	0	0	0
Eastwick,p	0	0	0	0	0	0
McEnaney,p	0	0	0	0	1	0
eDriessen	1	0	0	0	0	0
Darcy,p	0	0	0	0	1	0
Totals	50	6	14	33	14	0

Boston	AB	R	H	PO	A	E
Cooper,1b	5	0	0	8	0	0
Drago,p	0	0	0	0	0	0
fMiller	1	0	0	0	0	0
Wise,p	0	0	0	0	0	0
Doyle,2b	5	0	1	0	2	0
Yastrzemski,lf-1b	6	1	3	7	1	0
Fisk,c	4	2	2	9	1	0
Lynn,cf	4	2	2	2	0	0
Petrocelli,3b	4	1	0	1	1	0
Evans,rf	5	0	1	5	1	0
Burleson,ss	3	0	0	3	2	1
Tiant,p	2	0	0	0	2	0
Moret,p	0	0	0	0	0	0
dCarbo,lf	2	1	1	1	0	0
Totals	41	7	10	36	11	1

Cincinnati ......000 030 210 000—6
Boston ....300 000 030 001—7

a Flied out for Nolan in third.
b Walked for Billingham in fifth.
c Singled for Carroll in sixth.
d Homered for Moret in eighth.
e Flied out for McEnaney in 10th.
f Flied out for Drago in 11th.
Runs batted in: Griffey 2, Bench, Foster 2, Geronimo, Lynn 3, Carbo 3, Fisk.
Doubles: Doyle, Evans, Foster.
Triple: Griffey.
Home runs: Lynn, Geronimo, Carbo, Fisk.
Stolen bases: Concepcion.
Sacrifice hit: Tiant.
Double plays: Foster and Bench; Evans, Yastrzemski and Burleson.
Left on bases: Boston 11, Boston 9.

Cincinnati	IP	H	R	ER	BB	SO
Nolan	2	3	3	3	0	2
Norman	⅔	1	0	0	2	0
Billingham	1⅓	1	0	0	1	1
Carroll	1	1	0	0	1	1
Borbon	2	1	2	2	2	1
Eastwick	1	2	1	1	1	2
McEnaney	1	0	0	0	1	0
Darcy (L)	2	1	1	1	0	1

Boston	IP	H	R	ER	BB	SO
Tiant	7	11	6	6	2	5
Moret	1	0	0	0	0	0
Drago	3	1	0	0	0	1
Wise (W)	1	2	0	0	0	1

Borbon pitched to two batters in eighth.
Eastwick pitched to two batters in ninth.
Darcy pitched to one batter in 12th.
Tiant pitched to one batter in eighth.
Hit by pitcher: Rose (by Drago).
Umpires: Davidson, Frantz, Colosi, Barnett, Stello, Maloney.
Time: 4:01. **Attendance:** 35,205.

JACKSON SLUGS DODGERS

October 18, 1977, at Yankee Stadium

Reggie Jackson blasted the Los Angeles Dodgers into oblivion with three dramatic Game 6 home runs that gave the New York Yankees a World Series-clinching 8-4 victory and their first championship since 1962. Jackson hit two-run homers off Burt Hooton and Elias Sosa and a solo eighth-inning shot off Charlie Hough, capping the first five-homer Series in fall classic history.

Pirates 1960 World Series hero Bill Mazeroski heads for home after his championship-deciding home run.

FOR THE RECORD

Los Angeles	AB	R	H	PO	A	E
Lopes,2b	4	0	1	0	4	0
Russell,ss	3	0	0	1	4	0
Smith,rf	4	2	1	1	0	0
Cey,3b	3	1	1	0	1	0
Garvey,1b	4	1	2	13	0	0
Baker,lf	4	0	1	2	0	0
Monday,cf	4	0	1	3	0	0
Yeager,c	3	0	1	4	2	0
bDavalillo	1	0	1	0	0	0
Hooton,p	2	0	0	0	0	0
Sosa,p	0	0	0	0	0	0
Rau,p	0	0	0	0	0	0
aGoodson	1	0	0	0	0	0
Hough,p	0	0	0	0	0	0
cLacy	1	0	0	0	0	0
Totals	34	4	9	24	11	0

New York	AB	R	H	PO	A	E
Rivers,cf	4	0	2	1	0	0
Randolph,2b	4	1	0	2	3	0
Munson,c	4	1	1	6	0	0
Jackson,rf	3	4	3	5	0	0
Chambliss,1b	4	2	2	9	1	0
Nettles,3b	4	0	0	0	0	0
Piniella,lf	3	0	0	2	1	0
Dent,ss	2	0	0	1	4	1
Torrez,p	3	0	0	1	2	0
Totals	31	8	8	27	11	1

Los Angeles ....2 0 1 0 0 0 0 0 1—4
New York ....0 2 0 3 2 0 0 1 x—8

a Struck out for Rau in seventh.
b Bunted safely for Yeager in ninth.
c Popped out for Hough in ninth.

Runs batted in: Garvey 2, Smith, Davalillo, Chambliss 2, Jackson 5, Piniella.
Double: Chambliss.
Triple: Garvey.
Home runs: Chambliss, Smith, Jackson 3.
Sacrifice fly: Piniella.
Double plays: Dent, Randolph and Chambliss; Dent and Chambliss.
Passed ball: Munson.
Left on bases: New York 5, Los Angeles 2.

Los Angeles	IP	H	R	ER	BB	SO
Hooton (L)	3	3	4	4	1	1
Sosa	1⅔	3	3	3	1	0
Rau	1⅓	0	0	0	0	1
Hough	2	2	1	1	0	3

New York	IP	H	R	ER	BB	SO
Torrez (W)	9	9	4	2	2	6

Hooton pitched to three batters in fourth.

Umpires: McSherry, Chylak, Sudol, McCoy, Dale, Evans.
Time: 2:18. **Attendance:** 56,407.

ROSE PASSES COBB

September 11, 1985, at Riverfront Stadium

Pete Rose lined a 2-1 pitch from San Diego righthander Eric Show into left-center field for career hit No. 4,192, ending his long chase of Ty Cobb and securing his status as baseball's all-time top hit man. The first-inning drive touched off a wild celebration that included player congratulations, presentations and several long ovations before play resumed in the Reds' eventual 2-0 victory.

San Diego	AB	R	H	PO	A	E
Templeton,ss	4	0	0	3	3	0
Royster,2b	4	0	1	2	3	0
Gwynn,rf	4	0	1	2	0	0
Garvey,1b	4	0	0	6	0	0
Martinez,lf	3	0	0	4	0	0
McReynolds,cf	3	0	1	2	0	0
Bochy,c	3	0	1	3	1	0
Bevacqua,3b	3	0	1	2	1	0
Show,p	2	0	0	0	1	1
aDavis	1	0	0	0	0	0
Jackson,p	0	0	0	0	0	0
Walter,p	0	0	0	0	0	0
Totals	31	0	5	24	9	1

Cincinnati	AB	R	H	PO	A	E
Milner,cf	5	0	0	5	0	0
Rose,1b	3	2	2	6	1	0
Parker,rf	1	0	1	3	0	0
Esasky,lf	3	0	0	0	0	0
Venable,lf	0	0	0	0	0	0
Bell,3b	4	0	1	0	3	0
Concepcion,ss	4	0	1	1	2	0
Diaz,c	3	0	1	7	0	0
bRedus	0	0	0	0	0	0
Van Gorder,c	0	0	0	0	0	0
Oester,2b	3	0	1	4	3	0
Browning,p	4	0	1	0	0	0
Franco,p	0	0	0	0	0	0
Power,p	0	0	0	1	0	0
Totals	30	2	8	27	9	0

San Diego ....0 0 0 0 0 0 0 0 0—0
Cincinnati ....0 0 1 0 0 0 1 0 x—2

a Grounded into double play for Show in eighth.
b Ran for Diaz in eighth.

Runs batted in: Esasky 2.
Doubles: Browning, Diaz, Bell.
Triple: Rose.
Sacrifice fly: Esasky.
Stolen base: Gwynn.
Double plays: Templeton, Royster and Garvey; Concepcion, Oester and Rose.
Left on bases: San Diego 4, Cincinnati 11.

San Diego	IP	H	R	ER	BB	SO
Show (L)	7	7	2	2	5	1
Jackson	⅓	1	0	0	1	0
Walter	⅔	0	0	0	0	2

Cincinnati	IP	H	R	ER	BB	SO
Browning (W)	8⅓	5	0	0	0	6
Franco	⅓	0	0	0	0	0
Power (S)	⅓	0	0	0	0	0

Umpires: Weyer, Montague, Brocklander, Rennert.
Time: 2:17. **Attendance:** 47,237.

CLEMENS STRIKES OUT 20

April 29, 1986, at Fenway Park

Boston fireballer Roger Clemens claimed baseball's nine-inning strikeout record when he fanned 20 Seattle Mariners during a 3-1 victory. The Red Sox's "Rocket Man" struck out the side in three innings and fanned an A.L. record-tying eight straight batters from the fourth to the sixth. Clemens broke the record of 19 strikeouts shared by Steve Carlton, Tom Seaver and Nolan Ryan.

Seattle	AB	R	H	PO	A	E
Owen,ss	4	0	1	1	5	0
Bradley,lf	4	0	0	2	0	0
Phelps,1b	4	0	0	6	0	0
Thomas,dh	3	1	1	0	0	0
Presley,3b	3	0	0	1	1	0
Calderon,rf	3	0	0	1	1	0
Tartabull,2b	3	0	1	3	1	1
Henderson,cf	3	0	0	5	0	0
Yeager,c	2	0	0	4	2	0
bCowens	1	0	0	0	0	0
Kearney,c	0	0	0	1	0	0
Moore,p	0	0	0	0	0	0
Young,p	0	0	0	0	0	0
Best,p	0	0	0	0	0	0
Totals	30	1	3	24	10	1

Boston	AB	R	H	PO	A	E
Evans,rf	4	1	2	0	0	0
Boggs,3b	3	0	0	0	0	0
Buckner,dh	4	0	2	0	0	0
Rice,lf	4	0	1	1	0	0
Baylor,1b	3	0	1	1	1	1
Stapleton,1b	0	0	0	1	0	0
Gedman,c	4	0	1	20	0	0
Barrett,2b	3	0	0	0	1	0
Lyons,cf	3	1	1	3	0	0
Hoffman,ss	2	0	0	0	1	0
aRomero,ss	0	1	0	0	0	0
Clemens,p	0	0	0	1	0	0
Totals	30	3	8	27	3	1

Seattle ....0 0 0 0 0 0 1 0 0—1
Boston ....0 0 0 0 0 0 3 0 x—3

a Ran for Hoffman in seventh.
b Flied out for Yeager in eighth.

Runs batted in: Thomas, Evans 3.
Double: Buckner.
Home runs: Thomas, Evans.
Double play: Yeager and Tartabull.
Left on bases: Seattle 2, Boston 7.

Seattle	IP	H	R	ER	BB	SO
Moore (L)	7⅓	8	3	3	4	4
Young	⅓	0	0	0	0	0
Best	⅓	0	0	0	0	1

Boston	IP	H	R	ER	BB	SO
Clemens (W)	9	3	1	1	0	20

Umpires: Voltaggio, Welke, Phillips, McCoy.
Time: 2:39. **Attendance:** 13,414.

HERSHISER PASSES DRYSDALE

September 28, 1988, at Jack Murphy Stadium

Los Angeles ace Orel Hershiser completed the greatest run of pitching perfection in baseball history when he worked 10 shutout innings against San Diego on the final day of the regular season and extended his record scoreless-innings streak to 59. Hershiser, who recorded six straight shutouts, broke the 20-year-old scoreless-innings mark of former Dodger Don Drysdale, who ran off 58 in 1968.

Los Angeles	AB	R	H	PO	A	E
Sax,2b	5	0	0	3	7	0
Sharperson,2b	2	0	0	0	1	0
Stubbs,1b	5	0	0	21	0	1
gHatcher,1b	1	1	1	0	0	0
Gibson,lf	5	0	1	2	0	0
Orosco,p	0	0	0	0	0	0
Woodson,3b	2	0	1	1	1	0
Shelby,cf	5	0	1	2	0	0
C.Gwynn,lf	1	0	0	0	0	0
Mi.Davis,rf	4	0	0	4	0	0
Gonzalez,rf-lf-cf	3	0	0	2	0	0
Scioscia,c	4	0	0	2	0	0
Dempsey,c	3	0	0	5	2	0
Hamilton,3b	5	0	0	0	2	0
Crews,p	0	0	0	0	0	0
dHeep	1	0	0	0	0	0
K.Howell,p	0	0	0	0	0	0
Horton,p	0	0	0	0	0	0
Griffin,ss	5	0	1	4	5	0
Hershiser,p	3	0	1	0	5	0
Devereaux,rf	2	0	0	1	0	0
Totals	56	1	6	47	23	1

San Diego	AB	R	H	PO	A	E
R.Alomar,2b	7	0	1	0	5	0
Flannery,3b	4	0	1	1	0	0
bRoberts,3b	1	0	0	0	0	1
T.Gwynn,cf	5	0	0	10	0	0
Jefferson,cf	1	0	0	0	0	0
Martinez,1b	5	1	0	11	0	0
Wynne,rf	5	0	2	8	0	0
hParent	1	1	1	0	0	0
Santiago,c	5	0	0	13	0	0
Ready,lf	6	0	0	1	0	0
Templeton,ss	5	0	0	4	3	1
Hawkins,p	3	0	0	0	1	0
aMoreland	1	0	0	0	0	0
Ma.Davis,p	0	0	0	0	0	0
cNelson	1	0	0	0	0	0
McCullers,p	0	0	0	0	0	0
eBrown	0	0	0	0	0	0
fThon	0	0	0	0	0	0
Leiper,p	0	0	0	0	0	0
Totals	50	2	5	48	9	2

L.A. ....0 0 0 0 0 0 0 0 0 0 0 0 0 0 0 1—1
S Diego ..0 0 0 0 0 0 0 0 0 0 0 0 0 0 0 2—2

a Flied out for Hawkins in 10th.
b Ran for T.Gwynn in 11th.
c Struck out for Ma.Davis in 12th.
d Flied out for Crews in 14th.
e Walked for McCullers in 15th.
f Ran for Brown in 15th.
g Singled for Stubbs in 16th.
h Homered for Wynne in 16th.
i Two out when winning run scored.

Runs batted in: Parent 2.
Double: Griffin.
Triple: Woodson.
Home run: Parent.
Sacrifice hits: Hershiser, Santiago.
Stolen bases: T.Gwynn, Thon, Gonzalez.
Double play: Dempsey and Griffin.
Passed ball: Santiago.
Left on bases: Los Angeles 11, San Diego 10.

Los Angeles	IP	H	R	ER	BB	SO
Hershiser	10	4	0	0	1	3
Orosco	1	0	0	0	4	0
Crews	2	0	0	0	0	2
K.Howell	2⅔	0	1	1	3	3
Horton (L)	0	1	1	1	0	0

San Diego	IP	H	R	ER	BB	SO
Hawkins	10	4	0	0	2	6
Ma.Davis	2	0	0	0	0	4
McCullers	3	1	0	0	0	4
Leiper (W)	1	1	1	0	0	0

Horton pitched to one batter in 16th.
Hit by pitcher: Griffin (by Hawkins).

Umpires: West, Runge, Engel, Williams.
Time: 4:24. **Attendance:** 22,596.

GIBSON SHOCKS A'S

October 15, 1988, at Dodger Stadium

Los Angeles pinch hitter Kirk Gibson, limping badly on his injured leg and wincing with every painful swing, blasted a pitch from Oakland reliever ace Dennis Eckersley over the right-field fence with two out in the ninth inning, giving the Dodgers a 5-4 victory in a storybook conclusion to Game 1 of the World Series. With the Dodgers trailing 4-3 and a runner on base, Gibson looked overmatched as he worked the count to 3-2. That's when he connected for the first come-from-behind game-winning homer in Series history.

Oakland	AB	R	H	PO	A	E
Lansford,3b	4	1	0	2	2	0
Henderson,cf	5	0	2	4	0	0
Canseco,rf	4	1	1	3	0	0
Parker,lf	2	0	0	1	0	0
cJavier,lf	1	0	1	0	0	0
McGwire,1b	3	0	0	6	0	0
Steinbach,c	4	0	1	5	0	0
Hassey,c	0	0	0	1	0	0
Hubbard,2b	4	1	2	2	0	0
Weiss,ss	4	0	0	2	3	0
Stewart,p	3	1	0	0	0	0
Eckersley,p	0	0	0	0	0	0
Totals	34	4	7	26	5	0

Los Angeles	AB	R	H	PO	A	E
Sax,2b	3	1	1	3	1	0
Stubbs,1b	4	0	0	7	0	0
Hatcher,lf	3	1	1	1	0	0
Marshall,rf	4	1	1	2	0	0
Shelby,cf	4	0	1	3	0	0
Scioscia,c	4	0	1	9	0	0
Hamilton,3b	4	0	0	1	1	0
Griffin,ss	2	0	1	1	4	0
eM.Davis	0	1	0	0	0	0
Belcher,p	0	0	0	0	0	0
aHeep	1	0	0	0	0	0
Leary,p	0	0	0	0	1	0
bWoodson	1	0	0	0	0	0
Holton,p	0	0	0	0	1	0
dGonzalez	1	0	0	0	0	0
Pena,p	0	0	0	0	0	0
fGibson	1	1	1	0	0	0
Totals	32	5	7	27	8	0

Oakland ....0 4 0 0 0 0 0 0 0—4
Los Angeles ....2 0 0 0 0 1 0 0 2—5

a Grounded out for Belcher in second.
b Forced Griffin for Leary in fifth.
c Ran for Parker in seventh.
d Struck out for Holton in seventh.
e Walked for Griffin in ninth.
f Hit two run homer for Pena in ninth.

Runs batted in: Canseco 4, Hatcher 2, Scioscia, Gibson 2.
Double: Henderson.
Home runs: Hatcher, Canseco, Gibson.
Stolen bases: Canseco, Sax, M. Davis.
Double play: Lansford and McGwire.
Left on bases: Oakland 10, Los Angeles 5.

Oakland	IP	H	R	ER	BB	SO
Stewart	8	6	3	3	2	5
Eckersley (L)	⅔	1	2	2	1	1

Los Angeles	IP	H	R	ER	BB	SO
Belcher	2	3	4	4	4	3
Leary	3	3	0	0	1	3
Holton	2	0	0	0	1	0
Pena (W)	2	1	0	0	0	3

Hit by pitcher: Canseco (by Belcher), Sax (by Stewart).
Wild pitch: Stewart.
Balk: Stewart.

Umpires: Harvey, Merrill, Froemming, Cousins, Crawford, McCoy.
Time: 3:04. **Attendance:** 55,983.

CARTER'S HAPPY ENDING

October 23, 1993, at SkyDome

Toronto outfielder Joe Carter hit a three-run, ninth-inning home run off Philadelphia reliever Mitch Williams, giving the Blue Jays a dramatic 8-6 victory over Philadelphia and their second straight World Series championship. The see-saw Game 6 battle ended suddenly when Carter drove a one-out Williams pitch into the left-field seats at SkyDome and danced euphorically around the bases. It marked the first time a team trailing in the ninth had won a World Series on a home run.

Philadelphia	AB	R	H	PO	A	E
Dykstra,cf	3	1	1	5	0	0
Duncan,dh	5	1	1	0	0	0
Kruk,1b	3	0	0	6	0	0
Hollins,3b	5	1	1	0	1	0
Batiste,3b	0	0	0	0	0	0
Daulton,c	4	1	1	3	0	0
Eisenreich,rf	5	0	2	2	0	0
Thompson,lf	3	0	0	4	0	0
aIncaviglia,lf	0	0	0	3	0	0
Stocker,ss	3	1	0	0	1	0
Morandini,2b	4	1	1	2	0	0
Mulholland,p	0	0	0	0	1	0
Mason,p	0	0	0	0	0	0
West,p	0	0	0	0	0	0
Andersen,p	0	0	0	0	0	0
M.Williams,p	0	0	0	0	0	0
Totals	35	6	7	25	3	0

Toronto	AB	R	H	PO	A	E
Henderson,lf	4	1	0	2	0	0
White,cf	4	1	0	6	0	0
Molitor,dh	5	3	3	0	0	0
Carter,rf	4	1	1	3	0	0
Olerud,1b	3	1	1	6	0	0
bGriffin,3b	0	0	0	0	0	0
Alomar,2b	4	1	3	1	3	1
Fernandez,ss	3	0	0	1	0	0
Sprague,3b-1b	2	0	0	3	2	1
Borders,c	4	0	2	5	0	0
Stewart,p	0	0	0	0	1	0
Cox,p	0	0	0	0	0	0
Leiter,p	0	0	0	0	0	0
D.Ward,p	0	0	0	0	0	0
Totals	33	8	10	27	6	2

Philadelphia	000	100	500	—6
Toronto	300	110	003	—8

a Hit sacrifice fly for Thompson in seventh.
b Ran for Olerud in eighth.

Runs batted in: Dykstra 3, Hollins, Eisenreich, Incaviglia, Molitor 2, Carter 4, Alomar, Sprague.
Doubles: Daulton, Olerud, Alomar.
Triple: Molitor.
Home runs: Molitor, Dykstra, Carter.
Sacrifice flies: Incaviglia, Carter, Sprague.
Stolen bases: Dykstra, Duncan.
Left on bases: Philadelphia 9, Toronto 7.

Philadelphia	IP	H	R	ER	BB	SO
Mulholland	5	7	5	5	1	1
Mason	2⅓	1	0	0	0	2
West	0	0	0	0	1	0
Andersen	⅔	0	0	0	1	0
M.Williams (L)	⅓	2	3	3	1	0

Toronto	IP	H	R	ER	BB	SO
Stewart	6	4	4	4	4	2
Cox	⅓	3	2	2	1	1
Leiter	1⅔	0	0	0	1	2
D.Ward (W)	1	0	0	0	0	0

West pitched to one batter in eighth.
Stewart pitched to three batters in seventh.
Hit by pitcher: Fernandez (by Andersen).

Umpires: DeMuth, Phillips, Runge, Johnson, Williams, McClelland.
Time: 3:27. **Attendance:** 52,195.

RIPKEN PLAYS ON

September 6, 1995, at Camden Yards
Baltimore shortstop Cal Ripken played in his 2,131st consecutive game, passing Lou Gehrig on the all-time iron-man list. Ripken punctuated his record-setter with a fourth-inning home run and the celebration began an inning later when California batted to make the game official. After Ripken was honored in a memorable, nationally televised showcase, the Orioles went on to record a 4-2 victory.

California	AB	R	H	PO	A	E
Phillips,3b	4	0	0	0	3	1
Edmonds,cf	3	1	1	1	0	0
Salmon,rf	4	1	3	1	0	0
Davis,dh	3	0	0	0	0	0
Snow,1b	4	0	1	6	0	0
G.Anderson,lf	4	0	0	4	0	0
Hudler,2b	2	0	0	2	1	0
aOwen,2b	2	0	0	0	0	0
Fabregas,c	3	0	0	9	0	0
Easley,ss	2	0	1	1	0	0
bO.Palmeiro	1	0	0	0	0	0
Correia,ss	0	0	0	0	0	0
Boskie,p	0	0	0	0	0	0
Bielecki,p	0	0	0	0	0	0
Patterson,p	0	0	0	0	0	0
James,p	0	0	0	0	0	0
Totals	32	2	6	24	4	1

Baltimore	AB	R	H	PO	A	E
B.Anderson,cf	4	0	1	2	0	0
Alexander,2b	4	0	0	2	1	0
R.Palmeiro,1b	4	2	3	7	0	0
Bonilla,rf	4	1	1	1	0	0
J.Brown,rf	0	0	0	0	0	0
Ripken,ss	4	1	2	1	4	0
Baines,dh	4	0	1	0	0	0
Hoiles,c	4	0	1	8	1	0
Huson,3b	4	0	0	1	1	0
Smith,lf	2	0	0	5	0	0
Mussina,p	0	0	0	0	0	0
Clark,p	0	0	0	0	0	0
Orosco,p	0	0	0	0	0	0
Totals	34	4	9	27	7	0

California	100	000	010	—2
Baltimore	100	200	10x	—4

a Grounded out for Hudler in seventh.
b Grounded out for Easley in eighth.

Runs batted in: Salmon 2, R.Palmeiro 2, Bonilla, Ripken.
Doubles: Easley, Salmon, Baines.
Triple: Edmonds.
Home runs: Salmon, R.Palmeiro 2, Bonilla, Ripken.
Double play: Ripken and R.Palmeiro.
Left on bases: California 5, Baltimore 7.

California	IP	H	R	ER	BB	SO
Boskie (L)	5	6	3	3	1	4
Bielecki	1	1	0	0	0	2
Patterson	⅔	1	1	1	0	1
James	1⅓	1	0	0	0	1

Baltimore	IP	H	R	ER	BB	SO
Mussina (W)	7⅔	5	2	2	2	7
Clark	0	1	0	0	0	0
Orosco (S)	1⅓	0	0	0	0	2

Clark pitched to one batter in eighth.

Umpires: Barron, Kosc, Morrison, Clark.
Time: 3:35, **Attendance:** 46,272.

FOUR-HOMER GAMES

BOBBY LOWE

May 30, 1894, at Boston
Boston second baseman Lowe, baseball's first four-homer man, connected twice in the third inning of a 20-11 victory over Cincinnati.

Cincinnati	AB	R	H	PO	A	E
Hoy,cf	6	1	1	3	0	1
McCarthy,1b	5	2	2	9	1	0
Latham,3b	4	3	2	0	3	2
Holliday,lf	4	3	2	1	0	0
McPhee,2b	5	0	2	4	3	0
Vaughn,c	5	1	2	3	5	1
Canavan,rf	5	1	1	2	0	0
Smith,ss	5	0	1	1	5	1
Chamberlain,p	5	0	1	1	1	0
Totals	44	11	14	24	18	5

Boston	AB	R	H	PO	A	E
Lowe,2b	6	4	5	2	2	1
Long,ss	3	5	2	2	4	2
Duffy,cf	5	0	1	1	0	0
McCarthy,lf	6	2	3	3	0	0
Nash,3b	4	3	3	1	1	0
Tucker,1b	2	1	0	10	2	0
Bannon,rf	4	2	2	1	0	0
Ryan,c	5	2	2	5	0	0
Nichols,p	5	1	1	2	3	0
Totals	40	20	19	27	12	3

Cincinnati	200	040	005	—11
Boston	209	015	21x	—20

Runs batted in: Lowe 6, Nichols 4, Bannon 2, McCarthy 2, Ryan 2, Duffy, Long, Nash, Holliday 5, Vaughn 4, Canavan, Latham.
Doubles: Latham 2, Smith, Chamberlain, Long, McCarthy.
Home runs: Holliday 2, Vaughn, Canavan, Lowe 4, Long.
Stolen bases: Nash 2, Long, Duffy, Hoy, Latham.
Passed ball: Vaughn.
Left on bases: Cincinnati 7, Boston 10.

Cincinnati	IP	H	R	ER	BB	SO
Chamberlain (L)	8	19	20	18	8	3

Boston	IP	H	R	ER	BB	SO
Nichols (W)	9	14	11	11	2	3

Hit by pitcher: Long (by Chamberlain), Tucker (by Chamberlain).
Wild pitches: Chamberlain, Nichols.

Umpire: Swartwood.
Time: 2:15. **Attendance:** 8,000.

ED DELAHANTY

July 13, 1896, at Chicago
All four of Delahanty's homers were inside-the-park shots and the Philadelphia outfielder added a single for a record 17 total bases.

Philadelphia	AB	R	H	PO	A	E
Cooley,lf	3	1	1	1	0	0
Hulen,ss	4	1	1	1	4	0
Mertes,cf	5	1	0	1	0	0
Delahanty,1b	5	4	5	9	0	0
Thompson,rf	5	0	1	2	0	0
Hallman,2b	4	1	1	5	3	0
Clements,c	2	0	0	5	3	0
Nash,3b	4	0	0	0	3	1
Garvin,p	4	0	0	0	1	0
Totals	36	8	9	24	14	1

Chicago	AB	R	H	PO	A	E
Everitt,3b	3	1	2	1	3	0
Dahlen,ss	2	2	0	0	0	0
Lange,cf	4	2	2	4	0	0
Anson,1b	3	0	1	12	2	0
Ryan,rf	4	1	1	2	0	1
Decker,lf	4	1	1	0	0	1
Pfeffer,2b	4	0	2	1	4	0
Terry,p	4	1	2	2	3	0
Donohue,c	3	1	0	5	0	0
Totals	31	9	11	27	12	2

Philadelphia	120	030	101	—8
Chicago	104	010	03x	—9

Runs batted in: Delahanty 7, Garvin 1, Lange 5, Pfeffer 2, Anson.
Doubles: Thompson, Lange, Decker, Terry.
Triples: Lange, Pfeffer.
Home runs: Delahanty 4.
Double play: Hulen, Hallman and Delahanty.
Left on bases: Philadelphia 6, Chicago 4.

Philadelphia	IP	H	R	ER	BB	SO
Garvin (L)	8	11	9	8	4	4

Chicago	IP	H	R	ER	BB	SO
Terry (W)	9	9	8	7	3	4

Wild pitch: Garvin.

Umpire: Emslie.
Time: 2:15. **Attendance:** 1,100.

LOU GEHRIG

June 3, 1932, at Philadelphia
Yankees first baseman Gehrig became the first modern and A.L. player to hit four homers in a game and he narrowly missed a fifth in the ninth inning, when he flew out deep to center.

New York	AB	R	H	PO	A	E
Combs,cf	5	2	3	3	0	0
Saltzgaver,2b	4	1	1	3	2	0
Ruth,lf	5	2	2	3	0	1
Hoag,lf	0	1	0	1	0	0
Gehrig,1b	6	4	4	7	0	1
Chapman,rf	5	3	2	4	0	0
Dickey,c	4	2	2	5	0	0
Lazzeri,3b	6	3	5	0	1	0
Crosetti,ss	6	1	2	0	5	2
Allen,p	2	0	0	1	0	1
Rhodes,p	1	0	1	0	0	0
Brown,p	1	0	0	0	1	0
Gomez,p	1	1	1	0	0	0
Totals	46	20	23	27	9	5

Philadelphia	AB	R	H	PO	A	E
Bishop,2b	4	2	2	3	2	0
Cramer,cf	5	1	1	1	0	0
cRoettger	1	0	0	0	0	0
Miller,lf	0	0	0	0	0	0
Cochrane,c	5	1	1	10	2	0
dWilliams	1	0	0	0	0	0
Simmons,lf-cf	4	2	0	2	0	0
Foxx,1b	3	3	2	8	0	0
Coleman,rf	6	2	2	2	1	0
McNair,ss	5	1	3	1	2	0
Dykes,3b	4	1	1	0	1	0
Earnshaw,p	2	0	0	0	2	1
aHaas	1	0	1	0	0	0
Mahaffey,p	0	0	0	0	0	0
Walberg,p	0	0	0	0	0	0
Krausse,p	0	0	0	0	0	0
bMadjeski	1	0	0	0	0	0
Rommel,p	0	0	0	0	1	0
Totals	42	13	13	27	11	1

New York	200	232	326	—20
Philadelphia	200	602	021	—13

a Singled for Earnshaw in fifth.
b Reached on error for Krausse in eighth.
c Flied out for Cramer in eighth.
d Batted for Cochrane in ninth.

Runs batted in: Combs, Saltzgaver, Ruth, Gehrig 6, Chapman, Dickey, Lazzeri 6, Crosetti 2, Cramer 3, Cochrane 2, Foxx, Coleman 3, McNair 2.
Doubles: Ruth, Lazzeri, Coleman, McNair.
Triples: Chapman, Lazzeri, Bishop, Cramer, Foxx.
Home runs: Combs, Ruth, Gehrig 4, Lazzeri, Cochrane, Foxx.
Stolen bases: Lazzeri.
Double plays: Cochrane and McNair; Bishop and Foxx; Coleman and Cochrane.
Left on bases: New York 6, Philadelphia 11.

New York	IP	H	R	ER	BB	SO
Allen	3⅔	7	8	4	5	2
Rhodes	1⅓	1	2	2	2	0
Brown (W)	2	3	2	1	1	0
Gomez	2	2	1	1	0	1

Philadelphia	IP	H	R	ER	BB	SO
Earnshaw	5	8	7	6	2	8
Mahaffey (L)	1	6	4	4	0	0
Walberg	1	2	1	1	1	1
Krausse	1	4	2	2	0	0
Rommel	1	3	6	6	3	0

Wild pitch: Rhodes.

Umpires: Geisel, McGowan, Van Graflan.
Time: 2:55. **Attendance:** 7,300.

CHUCK KLEIN

July 10, 1936, at Pittsburgh
Philadelphia outfielder Klein needed a 10th inning to get his fourth homer and it proved to be the game-winner in a 9-6 Phillies victory over the Pirates.

Philadelphia	AB	R	H	PO	A	E
Sulik,cf	5	1	1	5	0	0
Moore,lf	5	1	1	1	0	0
Klein,rf	5	4	4	5	0	0
Camilli,1b	4	2	1	10	1	0
Atwood,c	4	0	1	2	0	0
Wilson,c	0	1	0	0	0	0
Chiozza,3b	5	0	2	1	1	0
Norris,ss	4	0	1	3	4	2
Gomez,2b	5	0	0	3	2	0
Passeau,p	4	0	1	0	0	0
Walters,p	0	0	0	0	1	0
Totals	41	9	12	30	9	2

Pittsburgh	AB	R	H	PO	A	E
Jensen,lf	4	1	1	3	0	0
L.Waner,cf	4	1	1	4	0	1
P.Waner,rf	4	2	2	1	0	0
Vaughan,ss	5	0	1	2	2	2
Suhr,1b	4	0	2	13	1	0
Brubaker,3b	5	0	0	1	1	0
Young,2b	3	0	1	1	5	0
Lavagetto,2b	1	1	0	1	1	1
Todd,c	2	0	0	3	0	0
Padden,c	2	1	0	1	0	0
Weaver,p	1	0	0	0	2	0
aLucas	1	0	0	0	0	0
Brown,p	1	0	0	0	2	0
bSchulte	1	0	1	0	0	0
cFinney	0	0	0	0	0	0
Swift,p	0	0	0	0	0	0
Totals	38	6	9	30	14	4

Philadelphia	400	010	100	3	—9
Pittsburgh	000	103	002	0	—6

a Batted for Weaver in fifth.
b Singled for Brown in ninth.
c Ran for Schulte in ninth.

Runs batted in: Klein 6, Chiozza, Norris 2, L.Waner, P.Waner, Vaughan, Suhr, Schulte.
Double: Camilli.
Triple: Suhr.
Home runs: Klein 4.
Double plays: Chiozza, Gomez and Camilli; Camilli, Norris and Camilli; Walters, Gomez and Camilli; Vaughan, Lavagetto and Suhr.
Left on bases: Philadelphia 5, Pittsburgh 7.

Philadelphia	IP	H	R	ER	BB	SO
Passeau	8⅔	8	6	4	2	1
Walters (W)	1⅓	1	0	0	2	0

Pittsburgh	IP	H	R	ER	BB	SO
Weaver	5	6	5	4	1	2
Brown	4	2	1	1	0	1
Swift (L)	1	4	3	2	0	0

Umpires: Sears, Klem, Ballanfant.
Time: 2:25. **Attendance:** 2,500.

PAT SEEREY

July 18, 1948, at Philadelphia
Seerey, like Klein, needed extra innings to tie the record and he also made his fourth homer a game-winner—an 11th-inning blast in Chicago's 12-11 victory over the Athletics.

Chicago	AB	R	H	PO	A	E
Kolloway,2b	7	2	5	5	2	0
Lupien,1b	7	1	1	8	2	0
Appling,3b	7	1	3	2	5	0
Seerey,lf	6	4	4	3	0	0
Robinson,c	6	0	3	4	1	0
Wright,rf	6	0	2	0	0	0
Philley,cf	6	1	2	5	0	0
Michaels,ss	6	3	4	6	3	1
Papish,p	0	0	0	0	1	0
Moulder,p	1	0	0	0	0	0
aHodgin	1	0	0	0	0	0
Caldwell,p	0	0	0	0	0	0
bBaker	1	0	0	0	0	0
Judson,p	3	0	0	0	0	0
Pieretti,p	0	0	0	0	0	0
Totals	57	12	24	33	14	1

Philadelphia	AB	R	H	PO	A	E
Joost,ss	7	4	4	1	2	0
McCosky,lf	2	2	1	3	1	0
White,cf	4	1	2	2	0	0
Brissie,p	0	0	0	0	0	0
dChapman	0	0	0	0	0	0
eDeMars	0	0	0	0	0	0
Fain,1b	5	0	0	13	0	0
Majeski,3b	5	0	1	0	3	0
Valo,rf	3	0	1	4	0	0
Rosar,c	3	0	0	5	0	0
Guerra,c	3	0	0	3	0	0
Suder,2b	5	2	1	2	1	0
Scheib,p	1	1	0	0	4	0
Savage,p	1	0	0	0	0	0
Harris,p	1	1	1	0	0	1
J.Coleman,p	0	0	0	0	0	0
cR.Coleman,cf	2	0	1	0	0	0
Totals	42	11	12	33	11	1

Chicago ....0 0 1 1 2 5 2 0 0 0 1—12
Philadelphia ......1 4 0 1 1 0 4 0 0 0 0—11

a Flied out for Moulder in fourth.
b Flied out for Caldwell in sixth.
c Grounded out for J.Coleman in ninth.
d Walked for Brissie in 11th.
e Ran for Chapman in 11th.

Runs batted in: Kolloway 3, Appling, Seerey 7, Baker, Joost 5, McCosky, Fain 2, Majeski.
Doubles: Robinson, Wright, Kolloway, Philley, Joost 2, Majeski.
Triple: Kolloway.
Home runs: Seerey 4, Joost.
Sacrifice hits: McCosky, White 2.
Stolen base: Appling.
Double plays: McCosky and Rosar; Kolloway, Michaels and Lupien.
Left on bases: Chicago 15, Philadelphia 14.

Chicago	IP	H	R	ER	BB	SO
Papish	1	3	5	4	4	0
Moulder	2	0	0	0	0	1
Caldwell	2	4	2	2	1	1
Judson (W)	5⅔	5	4	4	7	2
Pieretti (S)	⅓	0	0	0	0	0

Philadelphia	IP	H	R	ER	BB	SO
Scheib	4⅔	9	4	4	1	2
Savage	1	5	5	5	1	0
Harris	1⅔	4	2	1	0	0
J.Coleman	1⅔	2	0	0	1	1
Brissie (L)	2	4	1	1	0	1

Papish pitched to four batters in second.
Hit by pitcher: Valo (by Papish).
Wild pitches: Papish, Moulder, Savage.
Balk: Judson.

Umpires: Hurley, Berry, Grieve.
Time: 3:44. **Attendance:** 17,296.

GIL HODGES

August 31, 1950, at Brooklyn
Hodges, the Dodgers' big first baseman, connected off four different Boston pitchers and finished the game with nine RBIs.

Boston	AB	R	H	PO	A	E
Hartsfield,2b	5	0	1	4	1	3
Jethroe,cf	5	0	0	1	0	0
Torgeson,1b	4	1	1	7	0	0
Elliott,3b	3	0	1	1	4	0
Cooper,c	3	0	0	3	0	0
Crandall,c	1	1	0	2	0	1
Gordon,lf	4	1	3	4	0	0
Marshall,rf	4	0	2	1	0	0
Kerr,ss	3	0	0	1	4	0
Spahn,p	1	0	0	0	0	0
Roy,p	0	0	0	0	1	0
Haefner,p	0	0	0	0	0	0
aReiser	1	0	0	0	0	0
Hall,p	0	0	0	0	1	0
Antonelli,p	1	0	0	0	0	0
bHolmes	1	0	0	0	0	0
Totals	36	3	8	24	11	4

Brooklyn	AB	R	H	PO	A	E
Brown,lf	5	0	1	1	0	0
Reese,ss	5	1	2	1	4	1
Snider,cf	5	1	1	4	0	0
Robinson,2b	5	1	1	2	1	0
Morgan,3b	0	0	0	0	1	0
Furillo,rf	5	4	2	1	0	0
Hodges,1b	6	5	5	7	1	0
Campanella,c	4	2	2	4	0	0
Edwards,c	1	1	1	2	0	0
Cox,3b-2b	5	3	2	3	3	0
Erskine,p	5	1	4	2	0	0
Totals	46	19	21	27	10	1

Boston ....0 1 0 0 0 0 0 2 0—3
Brooklyn...................0 3 7 0 0 4 3 2 x—19

a Struck out for Haefner in fifth.

Chicago White Sox slugger Pat Seerey pays homage to the bat that cranked out four home runs in a game against the Athletics.

b Lined out for Antonelli in ninth.

Runs batted in: Hodges 9, Reese 3, Gordon 2, Snider 3, Brown 2, Marshall.
Doubles: Reese, Edwards, Marshall 2.
Home runs: Hodges 4, Gordon, Snider.
Sacrifice hit: Cox.
Left on bases: Boston 9, Brooklyn 12.

Boston	IP	H	R	ER	BB	SO
Spahn (L)	2	7	5	5	1	2
Roy	⅓	3	3	3	0	0
Haefner	1⅔	1	2	2	1	0
Hall	1⅔	6	4	4	3	1
Antonelli	2⅓	4	5	4	2	2

Brooklyn	IP	H	R	ER	BB	SO
Erskine (W)	9	8	3	3	2	6

Spahn pitched to two batters in third.
Hit by pitcher: Erskine (by Antonelli).

Umpires: Conlan, Gore, Stewart.
Time: 3:03. **Attendance:** 14,226.

JOE ADCOCK

July 31, 1954, at Brooklyn
Milwaukee first baseman Adcock homered off four different Dodgers pitchers and punctuated his big game with a double and a Major League-record 18 total bases.

Milwaukee	AB	R	H	PO	A	E
Bruton,cf	6	0	4	4	0	0
O'Connell,2b	5	0	0	4	4	0
Mathews,3b	4	3	2	3	2	0
Aaron,lf	5	2	2	0	0	0
Adcock,1b	5	5	5	11	0	0
Pafko,rf	4	2	3	0	0	0
Pendleton,rf	1	1	0	0	0	0
Logan,ss	2	1	1	1	1	0
Smalley,ss	2	1	1	0	1	0
Crandall,c	4	0	0	2	1	0
Calderone,c	1	0	1	2	0	0
Wilson,p	1	0	0	0	0	0
Burdette,p	3	0	0	0	4	0
Buhl,p	0	0	0	0	0	0
Jolly,p	1	0	0	0	0	0
Totals	44	15	19	27	13	0

Brooklyn	AB	R	H	PO	A	E
Gilliam,2b	4	1	4	3	1	0
Reese,ss	3	0	1	1	2	0
Zimmer,ss	1	0	0	1	1	0
Snider,cf	4	0	1	0	0	0
Shuba,lf	1	0	0	0	0	0
Hodges,1b	5	1	1	7	0	0
Amoros,lf-cf	5	2	3	6	0	0
Robinson,3b	0	0	0	0	0	0
Hoak,3b	2	1	1	0	1	1
Furillo,rf	5	1	2	3	0	0
Walker,c	5	1	1	6	1	0
Newcombe,p	0	0	0	0	0	0
Labine,p	0	0	0	0	0	0
aMoryn	1	0	0	0	0	0
Palica,p	0	0	0	0	0	0
Wojey,p	1	0	0	0	1	0
bPodres,p	2	0	2	0	1	0
Totals	39	7	16	27	8	1

Milwaukee ....1 3 2 0 3 0 3 0 3—15
Brooklyn...................1 0 0 0 0 1 0 4 1—7

a Grounded into double play for Labine in second.
b Singled for Wojey in seventh.

Runs batted in: Mathews 2, Snider, Adcock 7, Logan, Bruton, Pafko 2, Hoak 2, Hodges, Furillo, Walker 2.
Doubles: Gilliam, Pafko, Bruton 3, Amoros, Adcock, Aaron.
Triple: Amoros.
Home runs: Mathews 2, Adcock 4, Hoak, Pafko, Hodges, Walker.
Sacrifice hit: O'Connell.
Sacrifice fly: Hoak.
Double plays: Mathews, O'Connell and Adcock; O'Connell, Logan and Adcock; Zimmer, Gilliam and Hodges.
Left on bases: Milwaukee 5, Brooklyn 10.

Milwaukee	IP	H	R	ER	BB	SO
Wilson	1	5	1	1	0	0
Burdette (W)	6⅓	8	5	5	2	3
Buhl	0	2	0	0	0	0
Jolly	1⅔	1	1	1	1	1

Brooklyn	IP	H	R	ER	BB	SO
Newcombe (L)	1	4	4	4	0	0
Labine	1	1	0	0	0	0
Palica	2⅓	5	5	5	2	1
Wojey	2⅔	4	3	3	0	3
Podres	2	5	3	2	0	1

Hit by pitcher: Robinson (by Wilson).
Wild pitch: Podres.

Umpires: Boggess, Engeln, Stewart, Barlick.
Time: 2:53. **Attendance:** 12,263.

ROCKY COLAVITO

June 10, 1959, at Baltimore
Cleveland outfielder Colavito rocked the Orioles and joined Lowe and Gehrig as the only players to hit their four homers consecutively.

Cleveland	AB	R	H	PO	A	E
Held,ss	5	1	1	5	1	0
Power,1b	4	1	0	4	1	0
Francona,cf	5	2	2	2	0	0
Colavito,rf	4	5	4	3	0	0
Minoso,lf	5	1	3	1	0	0
Jones,3b	3	0	0	1	1	0
Strickland,3b	2	0	1	1	1	0
Brown,c	4	0	1	7	1	0
Martin,2b	3	1	1	3	0	0
aWebster,2b	1	0	0	0	0	0
Bell,p	3	0	0	0	1	0
Garcia,p	1	0	0	0	0	0
Totals	40	11	13	27	6	0

Baltimore	AB	R	H	PO	A	E
Pearson,cf	3	1	2	5	0	0
Pilarcik,rf	5	1	1	2	0	0
Woodling,lf	5	1	3	3	0	0
Triandos,c	2	0	1	5	0	0
Ginsberg,c	1	1	0	0	0	0
Hale,1b	3	0	0	4	0	0
Zuverink,p	0	0	0	0	0	0
bBoyd	1	0	0	0	0	0
Johnson,p	0	0	0	0	0	0
cNieman	1	1	1	0	0	0
Klaus,3b	5	0	2	0	1	0
Carrasquel,ss	5	0	0	2	3	0
Gardner,2b	4	1	1	1	5	0
Walker,p	1	1	1	0	0	0
Portocarrero,p	1	0	0	0	0	0
Lockman,1b	1	1	0	5	0	0
Totals	38	8	12	27	9	0

Cleveland ....3 1 2 0 1 3 0 0 1—11
Baltimore ....1 2 0 0 0 0 4 0 1—8

a Popped out for Martin in seventh.
b Flied out for Zuverink in seventh.
c Doubled for Johnson in ninth.

Runs batted in: Francona, Colavito 6, Minoso 3, Martin, Pilarcik 2, Woodling, Triandos, Klaus 4.
Doubles: Brown, Held, Francona, Klaus, Nieman.
Home runs: Minoso, Martin, Colavito 4.
Sacrifice fly: Triandos.
Stolen bases: Minoso.
Left on bases: Cleveland 0, Baltimore 8.

Cleveland	IP	H	R	ER	BB	SO
Bell (W)	6⅓	8	7	7	4	3
Garcia	2⅔	4	1	1	0	3

Baltimore	IP	H	R	ER	BB	SO
Walker (L)	2⅓	4	6	6	2	1
Portocarrero	3⅔	7	4	4	1	3
Zuverink	1⅓	0	0	0	0	0
Johnson	2	2	1	1	0	0

Umpires: Summers, McKinley, Soar, Chylak.
Time: 2:54. **Attendance:** 15,883.

WILLIE MAYS

April 30, 1961, at Milwaukee
New York Giants center fielder Mays connected in the first, third, sixth and eighth innings, driving in eight of his team's 14 runs against the Braves.

San Francisco	AB	R	H	PO	A	E
Hiller,2b	6	2	3	3	2	0
Davenport,3b	4	3	1	1	4	0
Mays,cf	5	4	4	3	0	0
McCovey,1b	3	0	0	5	0	0
Marshall,1b	0	0	0	3	0	0
Cepeda,lf	5	1	1	3	0	0
M.Alou,lf	0	0	0	1	0	0
F.Alou,rf	4	1	1	3	0	0
Bailey,c	4	0	0	3	0	0
Pagan,ss	5	3	4	2	1	0
Loes,p	3	0	0	0	2	0
Totals	39	14	14	27	9	0

Milwaukee	AB	R	H	PO	A	E
McMillan,ss	4	1	1	2	3	0
Bolling,2b	4	1	2	4	4	0
Mathews,3b	4	0	1	0	4	1
Aaron,cf	4	2	2	2	0	0
Roach,lf	4	0	1	2	0	0
Adcock,1b	4	0	0	13	1	0
Lau,c	3	0	1	2	0	0
McMahon,p	0	0	0	0	1	0
Brunet,p	0	0	0	0	1	0
cMaye	0	0	0	0	0	0
DeMerit,rf	4	0	0	0	0	0
Burdette,p	1	0	0	1	1	0
Willey,p	0	0	0	1	0	0
Drabowsky,p	0	0	0	0	0	0
aMartin	1	0	0	0	0	0
Morehead,p	0	0	0	0	0	0
MacKenzie,p	0	0	0	0	0	0
bLogan	1	0	0	0	0	0
Taylor,c	0	0	0	0	0	0
Totals	34	4	8	27	15	1

San Francisco............1 0 3 3 0 4 0 3 0—14
Milwaukee ....3 0 0 0 0 1 0 0 0— 4

a Flied out for Drabowsky in fifth.
b Struck out for MacKenzie in seventh.
c Walked for Brunet in ninth.

Runs batted in: Hiller, Davenport, Mays 8, Cepeda, F.Alou, Pagan 2, Aaron 4.
Doubles: Hiller 2.
Triple: Davenport.
Home runs: Mays 4, Pagan 2, Cepeda, F.Alou, Aaron 2.
Sacrifice hits: Loes 2.
Double plays: Davenport, Hiller and Marshall; Burdette, McMillan and Adcock; Bolling, McMillan and Adcock.
Left on bases: San Francisco 6, Milwaukee 4.

San Francisco	IP	H	R	ER	BB	SO
Loes (W)	9	8	4	4	1	3

Milwaukee	IP	H	R	ER	BB	SO
Burdette (L)	3	5	5	5	0	0
Willey	1	3	2	2	0	0
Drabowsky	1	0	0	0	1	0
Morehead	1	2	4	4	1	1
MacKenzie	1	0	0	0	0	1
McMahon	1	3	3	3	2	0
Brunet	1	1	0	0	0	0

Burdette pitched to one batter in fourth.
Hit by pitcher: Davenport (by Burdette), Bailey (by Mackenzie).

Umpires: Pelekoudas, Forman, Conlan, Donatelli, Burkhart.
Time: 2:40. **Attendance:** 13,114.

MIKE SCHMIDT

April 17, 1976, at Chicago

Philadelphia third baseman Schmidt hit a two-run shot in the 10th inning—his fourth consecutive homer in the Phillies' 18-16 victory.

Philadelphia	AB	R	H	PO	A	E
Cash,2b	6	1	2	4	3	0
Bowa,ss	6	3	3	2	0	0
Johnstone,rf	5	2	4	5	0	0
Luzinski,lf	5	0	1	0	0	0
Brown,lf	0	0	0	0	0	0
Allen,1b	5	2	1	5	0	0
Schmidt,3b	6	4	5	2	3	0
Maddox,rf	5	2	2	4	0	0
McGraw,p	0	0	0	0	0	0
eMcCarver	1	1	1	0	0	0
Underwood,p	0	0	0	0	0	0
Lonborg,p	0	0	0	0	0	0
Boone,c	6	1	3	8	0	0
Carlton,p	1	0	0	0	0	0
Schueler,p	0	0	0	0	0	0
Garber,p	0	0	0	0	0	0
aHutton	0	0	0	0	0	0
Reed,p	0	0	0	0	0	0
bMartin	1	0	0	0	0	0
Twitchell,p	0	0	0	0	0	0
cTolan,cf	3	2	2	0	0	0
Totals	50	18	24	30	6	0

Chicago	AB	R	H	PO	A	E
Monday,cf	6	3	4	4	0	0
Cardenal,lf	5	1	1	1	0	0
Summers,lf	0	0	0	3	0	0
dMitterwald	1	0	0	0	0	0
Wallis,lf	1	0	0	0	0	0
Madlock,3b	7	2	3	0	0	0
Morales,rf	5	2	1	1	0	0
Thornton,1b	4	3	1	10	1	0
Trillo,2b	5	0	2	2	3	0
Swisher,c	6	1	3	5	0	0
Rosello,ss	4	1	2	2	3	0
Kelleher,ss	2	0	1	1	1	0
R.Reuschel,p	1	2	0	1	3	0
Garman,p	0	0	0	0	0	0
Knowles,p	0	0	0	0	1	0
P.Reuschel,p	0	0	0	0	0	0
Schultz,p	0	0	0	0	2	0
fAdams	1	1	1	0	0	0
Totals	48	16	19	30	14	0

Atlanta third baseman Bob Horner became the first modern big-league player to hit four home runs in a game his team lost.

Philadelphia ....0 1 0 1 2 0 3 5 3 3—18
Chicago ....0 7 5 1 0 0 0 0 2 1—16

a Walked for Garber in fourth.
b Grounded out for Reed in sixth.
c Singled for Twitchell in eighth.
d Struck out for Summers in eighth.
e Singled for McGraw in 10th.
f Doubled for Schultz in 10th.

Runs batted in: Cash 2, Bowa, Johnstone 2, Luzinski, Allen 2, Schmidt 8, Maddox, Monday 4, Madlock 3, Thornton, Trillo 3, Swisher 4, Rosello.
Doubles: Cardenal, Madlock, Thornton, Boone, Adams.
Triples: Johnstone, Bowa.
Home runs: Maddox, Swisher, Monday 2, Schmidt 4, Boone.
Sacrifice hits: R.Reuschel, Johnstone.
Sacrifice flies: Luzinski, Cash.
Double plays: Trillo, Rosello and Thornton; Schmidt, Cash and Allen.
Left on bases: Philadelphia 8, Chicago 12.

Philadelphia	IP	H	R	ER	BB	SO
Carlton	1⅔	7	7	7	2	1
Schueler	⅔	3	3	3	0	0
Garber	⅔	2	2	2	1	1
Reed	2	1	1	1	1	1
Twitchell	2	0	0	0	1	1
McGraw (W)	2	4	2	2	1	2
Underwood	⅔	2	1	1	0	1
Lonborg (S)	⅓	0	0	0	0	0

Chicago	IP	H	R	ER	BB	SO
R.Reuschel	7	14	7	7	1	4
Garman	⅔	4	5	5	1	1
Knowles (L)	1⅓	3	4	4	1	0
P.Reuschel	0	3	2	2	0	0
Schultz	1	0	0	0	0	0

Knowles pitched to one batter in 10th.
P.Reuschel pitched to two batters in 10th.
Hit by pitcher: R. Reuschel (by Schueler), Thornton (by Garber), Monday (by Twitchell).
Balk: Schultz.

Umpires: Vargo, Olsen, Davidson, Rennert.
Time: 3:42. **Attendance:** 28,287.

BOB HORNER

July 6, 1986, at Atlanta

Atlanta first baseman Horner became the first four-homer man in 10 years and the first to accomplish the feat during a loss. The Expos defeated the Braves, 11-8.

Montreal	AB	R	H	PO	A	E
Webster,lf	6	2	5	1	0	0
Wright,cf	6	1	2	4	0	0
Dawson,rf	6	1	2	2	0	0
Brooks,ss	5	1	2	1	3	0
Wallach,3b	2	1	0	1	3	1
Galarraga,1b	2	0	0	4	1	0
Krenchicki,1b	1	0	1	3	0	0
Reardon,p	0	0	0	0	0	0
Fitzgerald,c	3	2	1	4	0	0
Newman,2b	4	3	2	5	3	0
McGaffigan,p	2	0	1	1	0	0
Burke,p	1	0	0	0	0	0
Law,1b	1	0	0	1	0	0
Totals	39	11	16	27	10	1

Atlanta	AB	R	H	PO	A	E
Moreno,rf	4	0	1	2	0	0
dSimmons,3b	1	0	0	0	0	0
Oberkfell,3b-2b	5	1	4	2	4	0
Murphy,cf	5	0	0	2	0	0
Horner,1b	5	4	4	8	1	1
Griffey,lf	5	0	2	0	0	0
Thomas,ss	4	0	1	0	4	0
Virgil,c	4	1	1	6	1	0
Hubbard,2b	3	1	1	6	2	0
bChambliss	0	0	0	0	0	0
Garber,p	0	0	0	0	0	0
Smith,p	1	0	0	0	1	0
Dedmon,p	0	1	0	0	0	0
aSample	1	0	0	0	0	0
Assenmacher,p	0	0	0	0	0	0
cRamirez,rf	1	0	0	1	0	0
Totals	39	8	14	27	13	1

Montreal....................0 0 1 3 6 0 1 0 0—11
Atlanta ....0 1 0 1 5 0 0 0 1— 8

a Grounded out for Dedmon in sixth.
b Walked for Hubbard in eighth.
c Struck out for Assenmacher in eighth.
d Grounded out for Moreno in eighth.

Runs batted in: Webster 3, Wright, Dawson 2, Fitzgerald 2, Newman 2, McGaffigan, Oberkfell, Horner 6, Hubbard.
Doubles: Dawson, Webster, Fitzgerald, Wright, Brooks, Virgil, Hubbard, Krenchicki.
Home runs: Horner 4, Newman, Webster, Dawson.
Sacrifice hits: McGaffigan, Dedmon, Krenchicki.
Stolen bases: Webster, Griffey.
Passed ball: Virgil.
Double plays: Brooks, Newman and Galarraga; Oberkfell and Horner; Wallach, Newman and Law.
Left on bases: Montreal 10, Atlanta 6.

Montreal	IP	H	R	ER	BB	SO
McGaffigan	4⅔	8	7	4	0	2
Burke (W)	2⅔	4	0	0	1	1
Reardon (S)	1⅔	2	1	1	0	1

Atlanta	IP	H	R	ER	BB	SO
Smith (L)	4	9	8	8	2	3
Dedmon	2	4	2	2	1	2
Assenmacher	2	2	1	1	2	1
Garber	1	1	0	0	0	0

Smith pitched to four batters in fifth.
Hit by pitcher: Galarraga (by Dedmon), Fitzgerald (by Dedmon).

Umpires: Poncino, Gregg, Davis, Harvey.
Time: 3:06. **Attendance:** 18,153.

MARK WHITEN

September 7, 1993, at Cincinnati

St. Louis outfielder Whiten doubled his pleasure by matching the Major League single-game records for homers and RBIs (12). His outburst came in the second game of a doubleheader after he had gone hitless in the opener.

St. Louis	AB	R	H	PO	A	E
Pena,2b	3	1	1	2	3	0
Maclin,lf	4	1	0	2	0	0
Gilkey,rf	5	1	1	3	0	0
Zeile,3b	2	3	1	0	0	1
Royer,3b	1	0	0	0	1	0
Perry,1b	4	4	3	8	0	0
Whiten,cf	5	4	4	5	0	0
Pagnozzi,c	5	0	1	4	0	1
Cromer,ss	5	0	0	2	4	0
Tewksbury,p	2	1	0	1	2	0
Totals	36	15	11	27	10	2

Cincinnati	AB	R	H	PO	A	E
Howard,lf	3	1	0	2	0	0
Dibble,p	0	0	0	0	0	0
Brumfield,cf	4	1	2	4	0	0
Morris,1b	2	0	1	5	0	0
Daugherty,rf	1	0	1	0	0	0
Sabo,3b	3	0	0	2	2	0
Varsho,lf	1	0	0	0	0	0
Costo,rf-3b	4	0	1	2	0	0
Samuel,2b	4	0	0	1	1	0
Wilson,c	4	0	0	10	1	0
Branson,ss	4	0	1	0	2	0
Luebbers,p	1	0	0	0	1	0
aTubbs	1	0	0	0	0	0
Anderson,p	0	0	0	0	0	0
Bushing,p	0	0	0	0	0	0
bDorsett,1b	2	0	1	1	0	0
Totals	34	2	7	27	7	0

St. Louis....................4 0 0 0 1 3 4 1 2—15
Cincinnati ....2 0 0 0 0 0 0 0 0— 2

a Grounded out for Luebbers in fifth.
b Singled for Bushing in seventh.

Runs batted in: Pena, Maclin, Perry, Whiten 12, Morris.
Double: Brumfield.
Home runs: Pena, Whiten 4.
Sacrifice hit: Pena.
Sacrifice flies: Maclin, Morris.
Stolen base: Maclin, Brumfield.
Left on bases: St. Louis 2, Cincinnati 7.

St. Louis	IP	H	R	ER	BB	SO
Tewksbury (W)	9	7	2	2	1	4

Cincinnati	IP	H	R	ER	BB	SO
Luebbers (L)	5	2	5	5	4	3
Anderson	1⅔	6	7	7	2	2
Bushing	⅓	0	0	0	0	0
Dibble	2	3	3	3	0	5

Wild pitch: Luebbers.

Umpires: Marsh, Kellog, Vanover, Wendelstedt.
Time: 2:17.

BABE RUTH'S 60 HOME RUNS—1927

HR No.	Team game No.	Date	Opposing pitcher, Club	Place	Inn.	On base
1.	4	April 15	Howard Ehmke (righthander), Philadelphia	H	1	0
2.	11	April 23	Rube Walberg (lefthander), Philadelphia	A	1	0
3.	12	April 24	Sloppy Thurston (righthander), Washington	A	6	0
4.	14	April 29	Slim Harriss (righthander), Boston	A	5	0
5.	16	May 1	Jack Quinn (righthander), Philadelphia	H	1	1
6.	16	May 1	Rube Walberg (lefthander), Philadelphia	H	8	0
7.	24	May 10	Milt Gaston (righthander), St. Louis	A	1	2
8.	25	May 11	Ernie Nevers (righthander), St. Louis	A	1	1
9.	29	May 17	Rip H. Collins (righthander), Detroit	A	8	0
10.	33	May 22	Benn Karr (righthander), Cleveland	A	6	1
11.	34	May 23	Sloppy Thurston (righthander), Washington	A	1	0
12.	37	May *28	Sloppy Thurston (righthander), Washington	H	7	2
13.	39	May 29	Danny MacFayden (righthander), Boston	H	8	0
14.	41	May ‡30	Rube Walberg (lefthander), Philadelphia	A	11	0
15.	42	May *31	Jack Quinn (righthander), Philadelphia	A	1	1
16.	43	May †31	Howard Ehmke (righthander), Philadelphia	A	5	1
17.	47	June 5	Earl Whitehill (lefthander), Detroit	H	6	0
18.	48	June 7	Tommy Thomas (righthander), Chicago	H	4	0
19.	52	June 11	Garland Buckeye (lefthander), Cleveland	H	3	1
20.	52	June 11	Garland Buckeye (lefthander), Cleveland	H	5	0
21.	53	June 12	George Uhle (righthander), Cleveland	H	7	0
22.	55	June 16	Tom Zachary (lefthander), St. Louis	H	1	1
23.	60	June *22	Hal Wiltse (lefthander), Boston	A	5	0
24.	60	June *22	Hal Wiltse (lefthander), Boston	A	7	1
25.	70	June 30	Slim Harriss (righthander), Boston	H	4	1
26.	73	July 3	Hod Lisenbee (righthander), Washington	A	1	0
27.	78	July †8	Don Hankins (righthander), Detroit	A	2	2
28.	79	July *9	Ken Holloway (righthander), Detroit	A	1	1
29.	79	July *9	Ken Holloway (righthander), Detroit	A	4	2
30.	83	July 12	Joe Shaute (lefthander), Cleveland	A	9	1
31.	94	July 24	Tommy Thomas (righthander), Chicago	A	3	0
32.	95	July *26	Milt Gaston (righthander), St. Louis	H	1	1
33.	95	July *26	Milt Gaston (righthander), St. Louis	H	6	0
34.	98	July 28	Lefty Stewart (lefthander), St. Louis	H	8	1
35.	106	Aug. 5	George S. Smith (righthander), Detroit	H	8	0
36.	110	Aug. 10	Tom Zachary (lefthander), Washington	A	3	2
37.	114	Aug. 16	Tommy Thomas (righthander), Chicago	A	5	0
38.	115	Aug. 17	Sarge Connally (righthander), Chicago	A	11	0
39.	118	Aug. 20	Jake Miller (lefthander), Cleveland	A	1	1
40.	120	Aug. 22	Joe Shaute (lefthander), Cleveland	A	6	0
41.	124	Aug. 27	Ernie Nevers (righthander), St. Louis	A	8	1
42.	125	Aug. 28	Ernie Wingard (lefthander), St. Louis	A	1	1
43.	127	Aug. 31	Tony Welzer (righthander), Boston	H	8	0
44.	128	Sept. 2	Rube Walberg (lefthander), Philadelphia	A	1	0
45.	132	Sept. *6	Tony Welzer (righthander), Boston	A	6	2
46.	132	Sept. *6	Tony Welzer (righthander), Boston	A	7	1
47.	133	Sept. †6	Jack Russell (righthander), Boston	A	9	0
48.	134	Sept. 7	Danny MacFayden (righthander), Boston	A	1	0
49.	134	Sept. 7	Slim Harriss (righthander), Boston	A	8	1
50.	138	Sept. 11	Milt Gaston (righthander), St. Louis	H	4	0
51.	139	Sept. *13	Willis Hudlin (righthander), Cleveland	H	7	1
52.	140	Sept. †13	Joe Shaute (lefthander), Cleveland	H	4	0
53.	143	Sept. 16	Ted Blankenship (righthander), Chicago	H	3	0
54.	147	Sept. †18	Ted Lyons (righthander), Chicago	H	5	1
55.	148	Sept. 21	Sam Gibson (righthander), Detroit	H	9	0
56.	149	Sept. 22	Ken Holloway (righthander), Detroit	H	9	1
57.	152	Sept. 27	Lefty Grove (lefthander), Philadelphia	H	6	3
58.	153	Sept. 29	Hod Lisenbee (righthander), Washington	H	1	0
59.	153	Sept. 29	Paul Hopkins (righthander), Washington	H	5	3
60.	154	Sept. 30	Tom Zachary (lefthander), Washington	H	8	1

*First game of doubleheader. †Second game of doubleheader. ‡Afternoon game of split doubleheader. New York A.L. played 155 games in 1927 (one tie on April 14), with Ruth participating in 151 games. (No home run for Ruth in game No. 155 on October 1.)

ROGER MARIS' 61 HOME RUNS—1961

HR No.	Team game No.	Date	Opposing pitcher, Club	Place	Inn.	On base
1.	11	April 26	Paul Foytack (righthander), Detroit	A	5	0
2.	17	May 3	Pedro Ramos (righthander), Minnesota	A	7	2
3.	20	May 6	Eli Grba (righthander), Los Angeles	A	5	0
4.	29	May 17	Pete Burnside (lefthander), Washington	H	8	1
5.	30	May 19	Jim Perry (righthander), Cleveland	A	1	1
6.	31	May 20	Gary Bell (righthander), Cleveland	A	3	0
7.	32	May *21	Chuck Estrada (righthander), Baltimore	H	1	0
8.	35	May 24	Gene Conley (righthander), Boston	H	4	1
9.	38	May *28	Cal McLish (righthander), Chicago	H	2	1
10.	40	May 30	Gene Conley (righthander), Boston	A	3	0
11.	40	May 30	Mike Fornieles (righthander), Boston	A	8	2
12.	41	May 31	Billy Muffett (righthander), Boston	A	3	0
13.	43	June 2	Cal McLish (righthander), Chicago	A	3	2
14.	44	June 3	Bob Shaw (righthander), Chicago	A	8	2
15.	45	June 4	Russ Kemmerer (righthander), Chicago	A	3	0
16.	48	June 6	Ed Palmquist (righthander), Minnesota	H	6	2
17.	49	June 7	Pedro Ramos (righthander), Minnesota	H	3	2
18.	52	June 9	Ray Herbert (righthander), Kansas City	H	7	1
19.	55	June †11	Eli Grba (righthander), Los Angeles	H	3	0
20.	55	June †11	Johnny James (righthander), Los Angeles	H	7	0
21.	57	June 13	Jim Perry (righthander), Cleveland	A	6	0
22.	58	June 14	Gary Bell (righthander), Cleveland	A	4	1
23.	61	June 17	Don Mossi (lefthander), Detroit	A	4	0
24.	62	June 18	Jerry Casale (righthander), Detroit	A	8	1
25.	63	June 19	Jim Archer (lefthander), Kansas City	A	9	0
26.	64	June 20	Joe Nuxhall (lefthander), Kansas City	A	1	0
27.	66	June 22	Norm Bass (righthander), Kansas City	A	2	1
28.	74	July 1	Dave Sisler (righthander), Washington	H	9	1
29.	75	July 2	Pete Burnside (lefthander), Washington	H	3	2
30.	75	July 2	Johnny Klippstein (righthander), Washington	H	7	1
31.	77	July †4	Frank Lary (righthander), Detroit	H	8	1
32.	78	July 5	Frank Funk (righthander), Cleveland	H	7	0
33.	82	July *9	Bill Monbouquette (righthander), Boston	H	7	0
34.	84	July 13	Early Wynn (righthander), Chicago	A	1	1
35.	86	July 15	Ray Herbert (righthander), Chicago	A	3	0
36.	92	July 21	Bill Monbouquette (righthander), Boston	A	1	0
37.	95	July *25	Frank Baumann (lefthander), Chicago	H	4	1
38.	95	July *25	Don Larsen (righthander), Chicago	H	8	0
39.	96	July †25	Russ Kemmerer (righthander), Chicago	H	4	0
40.	96	July †25	Warren Hacker (righthander), Chicago	H	6	2
41.	106	Aug. 4	Camilo Pascual (righthander), Minnesota	H	1	2
42.	114	Aug. 11	Pete Burnside (lefthander), Washington	A	5	0
43.	115	Aug. 12	Dick Donovan (righthander), Washington	A	4	0
44.	116	Aug. *13	Bennie Daniels (righthander), Washington	A	4	0
45.	117	Aug. †13	Marty Kutyna (righthander), Washington	A	1	1
46.	118	Aug. 15	Juan Pizarro (lefthander), Chicago	H	4	0
47.	119	Aug. 16	Billy Pierce (lefthander), Chicago	H	1	1
48.	119	Aug. 16	Billy Pierce (lefthander), Chicago	H	3	1
49.	124	Aug. *20	Jim Perry (righthander), Cleveland	A	3	1
50.	125	Aug. 22	Ken McBride (righthander), Los Angeles	A	6	1
51.	129	Aug. 26	Jerry Walker (righthander), Kansas City	A	6	0
52.	135	Sept. 2	Frank Lary (righthander), Detroit	H	6	0
53.	135	Sept. 2	Hank Aguirre (lefthander), Detroit	H	8	1
54.	140	Sept. 6	Tom Cheney (righthander), Washington	H	4	0
55.	141	Sept. 7	Dick Stigman (lefthander), Cleveland	H	3	0
56.	143	Sept. 9	Mudcat Grant (righthander), Cleveland	H	7	0
57.	151	Sept. 16	Frank Lary (righthander), Detroit	A	3	1
58.	152	Sept. 17	Terry Fox (righthander), Detroit	A	12	1
59.	155	Sept. 20	Milt Pappas (righthander), Baltimore	A	3	0
60.	159	Sept. 26	Jack Fisher (righthander), Baltimore	H	3	0
61.	163	Oct. 1	Tracy Stallard (righthander), Boston	H	4	0

*First game of doubleheader. †Second game of doubleheader. New York played 163 games in 1961 (one tie on April 22). Maris did not hit a home run in this game. Maris played in 161 games.

MARK McGWIRE'S 70 HOME RUNS—1998

HR No.	Team game No.	Date	Opposing pitcher, Club	Place	Inn.	On base
1.	1	March 31	Ramon Martinez (righthander), Los Angeles	H	5	3
2.	2	April 2	Frank Lankford (righthander), Los Angeles	H	12	2
3.	3	April 3	Mark Langston (righthander), San Diego	H	5	1
4.	4	April 4	Don Wengert (righthander), San Diego	H	6	2
5.	13	April 14	Jeff Suppan (righthander), Arizona	H	3	1
6.	13	April 14	Jeff Suppan (righthander), Arizona	H	5	0
7.	13	April 14	Barry Manuel (righthander), Arizona	H	8	1
8.	15	April 17	Matt Whiteside (righthander), Philadelphia	H	4	1
9.	19	April 21	Trey Moore (lefthander), Montreal	A	3	1
10.	23	April 25	Jerry Spradlin (righthander), Philadelphia	A	7	1
11.	27	April 30	Marc Pisciotta (righthander), Chicago	A	8	1
12.	28	May 1	Rod Beck (righthander), Chicago	A	9	1
13.	34	May 8	Rick Reed (righthander), New York	A	3	1
14.	36	May 12	Paul Wagner (righthander), Milwaukee	H	5	2
15.	38	May 14	Kevin Millwood (righthander), Atlanta	H	4	0
16.	40	May 16	Livan Hernandez (righthander), Florida	H	4	0
17.	42	May 18	Jesus Sanchez (lefthander), Florida	H	4	0
18.	43	May 19	Tyler Green (righthander), Philadelphia	A	3	1
19.	43	May 19	Tyler Green (righthander), Philadelphia	A	5	1
20.	43	May 19	Wayne Gomes (righthander), Philadelphia	A	8	1
21.	46	May 22	Mark Gardner (righthander), San Francisco	H	6	1
22.	47	May 23	Rich Rodriguez (lefthander), San Francisco	H	4	0
23.	47	May 23	John Johnstone (righthander), San Francisco	H	5	2
24.	48	May 24	Robb Nen (righthander), San Francisco	H	12	1
25.	49	May 25	John Thomson (righthander), Colorado	H	1	0
26.	52	May 29	Dan Miceli (righthander), San Diego	A	9	1
27.	53	May 30	Andy Ashby (righthander), San Diego	A	1	0
28.	59	June 5	Orel Hershiser (righthander), San Fran.	H	1	1
29.	62	June 8	Jason Bere (righthander), Chicago AL	A	4	1
30.	64	June 10	Jim Parque (lefthander), Chicago AL	A	3	2
31.	65	June 12	Andy Benes (righthander), Arizona	A	3	3
32.	69	June 17	Jose Lima (righthander), Houston	A	3	0
33.	70	June 18	Shane Reynolds (righthander), Houston	A	5	0
34.	76	June 24	Jaret Wright (righthander), Cleveland AL	A	4	0
35.	77	June 25	Dave Burba (righthander), Cleveland AL	A	1	0
36.	79	June 27	Mike Trombley (righthander), Minnesota AL	A	7	1
37.	81	June 30	Glendon Rusch (lefthander), Kansas City AL	A	7	0
38.	89	July 11	Billy Wagner (lefthander), Houston	H	11	1
39.	90	July 12	Sean Bergman (righthander), Houston	H	1	0
40.	90	July 12	Scott Elarton (righthander), Houston	H	7	0
41.	95	July 17	Brian Bohanon (lefthander), Los Angeles	H	1	0
42.	95	July 17	Antonio Osuna (righthander), Los Angeles	H	8	0
43.	98	July 20	Brian Boehringer (righthander), San Diego	A	5	1
44.	104	July 26	John Thomson (righthander), Colorado	A	4	0
45.	105	July 28	Mike Myers (lefthander), Milwaukee	H	8	0
46.	115	Aug. 8	Mark Clark (righthander), Chicago	H	4	0
47.	118	Aug. 11	Bobby Jones (righthander), New York	H	4	0
48.	124	Aug. 19	Matt Karchner (righthander), Chicago	A	8	0
49.	124	Aug. 19	Terry Mulholland (lefthander), Chicago	A	10	0
50.	125	Aug. *20	Willie Blair (righthander), New York	A	7	0

HR No.	Team game No.	Date		Opposing pitcher, Club	Place	Inn.	On base
51.	126	Aug.	†20	Rick Reed (righthander), New York	A	1	0
52.	129	Aug.	22	Francisco Cordova (righthander), Pitt.	A	1	0
53.	130	Aug.	23	Ricardo Rincon (lefthander), Pittsburgh	A	8	0
54.	133	Aug.	26	Justin Speier (righthander), Florida	H	8	1
55.	137	Aug.	30	Dennis Martinez (righthander), Atlanta	H	7	2
56.	139	Sept.	1	Livan Hernandez (righthander), Florida	A	7	0
57.	139	Sept.	1	Donn Pall (righthander), Florida	A	9	0
58.	140	Sept.	2	Brian Edmondson (righthander), Florida	A	7	1
59.	140	Sept.	2	Rob Stanifer (righthander), Florida	A	8	1
60.	142	Sept.	5	Dennis Reyes (lefthander), Cincinnati	H	1	1
61.	144	Sept.	7	Mike Morgan (righthander), Chicago	H	1	0
62.	145	Sept.	8	Steve Trachsel (righthander), Chicago	H	4	0
63.	152	Sept.	*15	Jason Christiansen (lefthander), Pitt.	H	9	0
64.	155	Sept.	18	Rafael Roque (lefthander), Milwaukee	A	4	1
65.	157	Sept.	20	Scott Karl (lefthander), Milwaukee	A	1	1
66.	161	Sept.	25	Shayne Bennett (righthander), Montreal	H	5	1
67.	162	Sept.	26	Dustin Hermanson (righthander), Montreal	H	4	0
68.	162	Sept.	26	Kirk Bullinger (righthander), Montreal	H	7	1
69.	163	Sept.	27	Mike Thurman (righthander), Montreal	H	3	0
70.	163	Sept.	27	Carl Pavano (righthander), Montreal	H	7	2

*First game of doubleheader. †Second game of doubleheader. St. Louis played 163 games in 1998 (one tie on Aug. 24). McGwire played in 155 games.

SAMMY SOSA'S 66 HOME RUNS—1998

HR No.	Team game No.	Date		Opposing pitcher, Club	Place	Inn.	On base
1.	5	April	4	Marc Valdes (righthander), Montreal	H	3	0
2.	11	April	11	Anthony Telford (righthander), Montreal	A	7	0
3.	14	April	15	Dennis Cook (lefthander), New York	A	8	0
4.	21	April	23	Dan Miceli (righthander), San Diego	H	9	0
5.	22	April	24	Ismael Valdes (righthander), Los Angeles	A	1	0
6.	25	April	27	Joe Hamilton (righthander), San Diego	A	1	1
7.	30	May	3	Cliff Politte (righthander), St. Louis	H	1	0
8.	42	May	16	Scott Sullivan (righthander), Cincinnati	A	3	2
9.	47	May	22	Greg Maddux (righthander), Atlanta	A	1	0
10.	50	May	25	Kevin Millwood (righthander), Atlanta	A	4	0
11.	50	May	25	Mike Cather (righthander), Atlanta	A	8	2
12.	51	May	27	Darrin Winston (lefthander), Phil.	H	8	0
13.	51	May	27	Wayne Gomes (righthander), Philadelphia	H	9	1
14.	56	June	1	Ryan Dempster (righthander), Florida	H	1	1
15.	56	June	1	Oscar Henriquez (righthander), Florida	H	8	2
16.	58	June	3	Livan Hernandez (righthander), Florida	H	5	1
17.	59	June	5	Jim Parque (lefthander), Chicago AL	H	5	1
18.	60	June	6	Carlos Castillo (righthander), Chi. AL	H	7	0
19.	61	June	7	James Baldwin (righthander), Chicago AL	H	5	2
20.	62	June	8	LaTroy Hawkins (righthander), Minn. AL	A	3	0
21.	66	June	13	Mark Portugal (righthander), Phil.	A	6	1
22.	68	June	15	Cal Eldred (righthander), Milwaukee	H	1	0
23.	68	June	15	Cal Eldred (righthander), Milwaukee	H	3	0
24.	68	June	15	Cal Eldred (righthander), Milwaukee	H	7	0
25.	70	June	17	Bronswell Patrick (righthander), Milw.	A	4	0
26.	72	June	19	Carlton Loewer (righthander), Phil.	H	1	0
27.	72	June	19	Carlton Loewer (righthander), Phil.	H	5	1
28.	73	June	20	Matt Beech (lefthander), Philadelphia	H	3	1
29.	73	June	20	Toby Borland (righthander), Philadelphia	H	6	2
30.	74	June	21	Tyler Green (righthander), Philadelphia	H	4	0
31.	77	June	24	Seth Greisinger (righthander), Det. AL	A	1	0
32.	78	June	25	Brian Moehler (righthander), Detroit AL	A	7	0
33.	82	June	30	Alan Embree (lefthander), Arizona	H	8	0
34.	88	July	9	Jeff Juden (righthander), Milwaukee	A	2	1
35.	89	July	10	Scott Karl (lefthander), Milwaukee	A	2	0
36.	95	July	17	Kirt Ojala (lefthander), Florida	A	6	1
37.	100	July	22	Miguel Batista (righthander), Montreal	H	8	2
38.	105	July	26	Rick Reed (righthander), New York	H	6	1
39.	106	July	27	Willie Blair (righthander), Arizona	A	6	1
40.	106	July	27	Alan Embree (lefthander), Arizona	A	8	3
41.	107	July	28	Bob Wolcott (righthander), Arizona	A	5	3
42.	110	July	31	Jamey Wright (righthander), Colorado	H	1	0
43.	115	Aug.	5	Andy Benes (righthander), Arizona	H	3	1
44.	117	Aug.	8	Rich Croushore (righthander), St. Louis	A	9	1
45.	119	Aug.	10	Russ Ortiz (righthander), San Francisco	A	5	0
46.	119	Aug.	10	Chris Brock (righthander), San Francisco	A	7	0
47.	124	Aug.	16	Sean Bergman (righthander), Houston	A	4	0
48.	126	Aug.	19	Kent Bottenfield (righthander), St.L.	H	5	1
49.	128	Aug.	21	Orel Hershiser (righthander), San Fran.	H	5	1
50.	130	Aug.	23	Jose Lima (righthander), Houston	H	5	0
51.	130	Aug.	23	Jose Lima (righthander), Houston	H	8	0
52.	133	Aug.	26	Brett Tomko (righthander), Cincinnati	A	3	0
53.	135	Aug.	28	John Thomson (righthander), Colorado	A	1	0
54.	137	Aug.	30	Darryl Kile (righthander), Colorado	A	1	1
55.	138	Aug.	31	Brett Tomko (righthander), Cincinnati	H	3	1
56.	140	Sept.	2	Jason Bere (righthander), Cincinnati	H	6	0
57.	141	Sept.	4	Jason Schmidt (righthander), Pittsburgh	A	1	0
58.	142	Sept.	5	Sean Lawrence (lefthander), Pittsburgh	A	6	0
59.	148	Sept.	11	Bill Pulphiser (lefthander), Milwaukee	H	5	0
60.	149	Sept.	12	Valerio de los Santos (lefthander), Mil.	H	7	2
61.	150	Sept.	13	Bronswell Patrick (righthander), Milw.	H	5	1
62.	150	Sept.	13	Eric Plunk (righthander), Milwaukee	H	9	0
63.	153	Sept.	16	Brian Boehringer (righthander), S.D.	A	8	3
64.	159	Sept.	23	Rafael Roque (lefthander), Milwaukee	A	5	0
65.	159	Sept.	23	Rod Henderson (righthander), Milwaukee	A	6	0
66.	160	Sept.	25	Jose Lima (righthander), Houston	A	4	0

*First game of doubleheader. †Second game of doubleheader. Chicago played 163 games in 1998 (playoff game on Sept. 28). Sosa played in 159 games.

HACK WILSON'S 191 RBIs, 56 HOME RUNS—1930

Date		Result	Site	AB	H	HR	RBI	HR Total	RBI Total
April	15	Cubs 9, Cardinals 8	A	4	1	0	1	0	1
	21	Cubs 9, Reds 1	A	5	1	1	3	1	4
	22	Cardinals 8, Cubs 3	H	4	1	1	3	2	7
	25*	Cubs 6, Reds 5	H	5	3	1	2	3	9
	28	Cubs 7, Pirates 4	H	2	1	0	1	3	10
	30	Cubs 5, Pirates 2	H	4	1	1	1	4	11
May	4	Cubs 8, Phillies 7	H	3	3	0	2	4	13
	6	Cubs 3, Dodgers 1	H	3	1	1	2	5	15
	7	Cubs 9, Dodgers 5	H	4	2	0	4	5	19
	8	Cubs 7, Dodgers 4	H	4	2	1	1	6	20
	9	Cubs 6, Giants 5	H	4	3	0	2	6	22
	10	Giants 9, Cubs 4	H	3	2	1	3	7	25
	12	Giants 14, Cubs 12	H	2	1	1	1	8	26
	13	Cubs 9, Braves 8	H	2	1	1	3	9	29
	15	Braves 10, Cubs 8	H	5	2	0	2	9	31
	18†	Cubs 9, Cardinals 6	A	3	2	2	3	11	34
	20	Cardinals 16, Cubs 3	A	4	1	1	1	12	35
	22	Cubs 12, Pirates 5	A	4	2	0	1	12	36
	24	Cubs 5, Pirates 3	A	4	1	0	1	12	37
	26	Reds 8, Cubs 2	H	4	1	1	2	13	39
	28	Cubs 6, Reds 5	H	3	1	0	2	13	41
	30‡	Cubs 9, Cardinals 8	H	3	1	1	1	14	42
	31	Cubs 6, Cardinals 5	H	5	1	0	2	14	44
June	1	Cubs 16, Pirates 4	H	5	4	2	5	16	49
	3	Cubs 15, Braves 2	A	4	1	0	1	16	50
	4	Cubs 18, Braves 10	A	5	2	0	1	16	51
	5	Cubs 10, Braves 7	A	6	2	1	1	17	52
	6	Cubs 13, Dodgers 0	A	5	2	0	1	17	53
	7	Dodgers 12, Cubs 9	A	4	1	1	2	18	55
	10	Phillies 6, Cubs 2	A	2	1	0	1	18	56
	12	Phillies 5, Cubs 3	A	2	1	0	2	18	58
	14	Cubs 8, Giants 5	A	3	1	0	2	18	60
	16	Cubs 8, Giants 5	A	4	1	0	1	18	61
	19	Cubs 10, Braves 4	H	4	1	1	3	19	64
	21*†	Cubs 5, Braves 4	H	5	3	1	2	20	66
	22	Braves 3, Cubs 2	H	4	1	1	1	21	67
	23	Cubs 21, Phillies 8	H	6	5	1	5	22	72
	24	Cubs 6, Phillies 1	H	5	2	0	1	22	73
July	1	Giants 7, Cubs 5	H	3	2	1	1	23	74
	2	Giants 9, Cubs 8	H	5	2	0	2	23	76
	4‡	Pirates 5, Cubs 1	A	3	0	0	1	23	77
	5	Cubs 12, Pirates 3	A	4	3	0	3	23	80
	6†	Reds 5, Cubs 4	A	3	2	1	1	24	81
	6‡	Reds 8, Cubs 7	A	4	2	0	1	24	82
	16†	Cubs 6, Dodgers 4	A	3	1	0	2	24	84
	18	Cubs 6, Dodgers 2	A	5	3	1	1	25	85
	19	Cubs 5, Dodgers 4	A	3	1	1	2	26	87
	20	Giants 13, Cubs 5	A	4	1	1	1	27	88
	21	Cubs 6, Giants 0	A	5	2	2	3	29	91
	24	Cubs 19, Phillies 15	A	5	2	0	1	29	92
	25	Cubs 9, Phillies 5	A	3	1	0	1	29	93
	26	Cubs 16, Phillies 2	A	5	3	3	5	32	98
	27	Reds 6, Cubs 5	A	2	1	0	1	32	99
	28†	Cubs 3, Reds 2	H	4	1	0	2	32	101
	28‡	Cubs 5, Reds 3	H	4	1	0	1	32	102
	29	Reds 4, Cubs 3	H	3	1	1	2	33	104
Aug.	1	Cubs 10, Pirates 7	H	3	1	0	2	33	106
	2	Pirates 14, Cubs 8	H	5	2	1	1	34	107
	3	Pirates 12, Cubs 8	H	4	2	1	2	35	109
	5	Cubs 5, Cardinals 4	A	3	1	1	2	36	112
	7	Cubs 6, Cardinals 5	A	3	2	0	3	36	114
	10†	Cubs 6, Braves 0	H	4	2	2	4	38	118
	10‡	Cubs 17, Braves 1	H	4	2	1	3	39	121
	13	Dodgers 15, Cubs 5	H	4	2	1	2	40	123
	14	Cubs 5, Dodgers 1	H	3	2	0	2	40	125
	15§	Cubs 4, Dodgers 3	H	4	1	0	1	40	126
	16†	Cubs 10, Phillies 9	H	5	2	1	3	41	129
	17	Cubs 5, Phillies 4	H	3	1	0	2	41	131
	18	Cubs 17, Phillies 3	H	5	4	1	4	42	135
	19†	Phillies 9, Cubs 8	H	4	3	1	1	43	136
	20	Phillies 10, Cubs 8	H	2	0	0	2	43	138
	21	Giants 13, Cubs 6	H	5	1	0	2	43	140
	22	Cubs 12, Giants 4	H	3	1	0	1	43	141
	23	Cubs 4, Giants 2	H	3	1	0	3	43	144
	26	Cubs 7, Pirates 5	H	3	2	1	4	44	148
	27	Pirates 10, Cubs 8	H	5	2	0	3	44	151
	30	Cubs 16, Cardinals 4	H	3	3	2	6	46	156
Sept.	3	Pirates 9, Cubs 6	A	5	3	0	1	46	158
	4§	Cubs 10, Pirates 7	A	5	2	0	1	46	159
	5	Pirates 8, Cubs 7	A	5	0	0	1	46	160
	6	Cubs 19, Pirates 14	A	6	3	1	4	47	164
	11	Dodgers 2, Cubs 1	A	4	1	1	1	48	165
	12	Cubs 17, Phillies 4	A	5	5	1	6	49	171
	15†	Phillies 12, Cubs 11	A	5	2	0	1	49	172
	15‡	Cubs 6, Phillies 4	A	3	1	1	1	50	173
	17	Cubs 5, Giants 2	A	4	3	2	4	52	177
	19	Cubs 5, Braves 4	A	4	1	0	1	52	178
	20	Braves 3, Cubs 2	A	3	1	0	1	52	179
	22	Cubs 6, Braves 2	A	4	2	1	3	53	182
	26	Cubs 7, Reds 5	H	4	2	1	3	54	185
	27	Cubs 13, Reds 8	H	4	2	2	4	56	189
	28	Cubs 13, Reds 11	H	3	2	0	2	56	191

* 12 innings. †First game of doubleheader. ‡ Second game of doubleheader. § 10 innings.

JOE DiMAGGIO'S 56-GAME HITTING STREAK—1941

Date		Opposing pitcher, Club	AB	R	H	2B	3B	HR	RBI
May	15	Eddie Smith, Chicago	4	0	1	0	0	0	1
	16	Thornton Lee, Chicago	4	2	2	0	1	1	1
	17	Johnny Rigney, Chicago	3	1	1	0	0	0	1
	18	Bob Harris (2), Johnny Niggeling (1), St. Louis	3	3	3	1	0	0	1
	19	Denny Galehouse, St. Louis	3	0	1	0	0	0	0
	20	Eldon Auker, St. Louis	5	1	1	0	0	0	1
	21	Schoolboy Rowe (1), Al Benton (1), Detroit	5	0	2	0	0	0	1
	22	Archie McKain, Detroit	4	0	1	0	0	0	1
	23	Dick Newsome, Boston	4	0	1	0	0	0	2
	24	Earl Johnson, Boston	4	2	1	0	0	0	2
	25	Lefty Grove, Boston	4	0	1	0	0	0	0
	27	Ken Chase (1), Red Anderson (2), Alex Carrasquel (1), Washington	5	3	4	0	0	1	3
	28	Sid Hudson, Washington	4	1	1	0	1	0	0
	29	Steve Sundra, Washington	3	1	1	0	0	0	0
	30	Earl Johnson, Boston	2	1	1	0	0	0	0
	30	Mickey Harris, Boston	3	0	1	0	0	0	0
June	1	Al Milnar, Cleveland	4	1	1	0	0	0	0
	1	Mel Harder, Cleveland	4	0	1	0	0	0	0
	2	Bob Feller, Cleveland	4	2	2	1	0	0	0
	3	Dizzy Trout, Detroit	4	1	1	0	1	0	1
	5	Hal Newhouser, Detroit	5	1	1	0	1	0	1
	7	Bob Muncrief (1), Johnny Allen (1), George Caster (1), St. Louis	5	2	3	0	0	0	1
	8	Eldon Auker, St. Louis	4	3	2	0	0	2	4
	8	George Caster (1), Jack Kramer (1), St. Louis	4	1	2	1	0	1	3
	10	Johnny Rigney, Chicago	5	1	1	0	0	0	0
	12	Thornton Lee, Chicago	4	1	2	0	0	1	1
	14	Bob Feller, Cleveland	2	0	1	1	0	0	1
	15	Jim Bagby, Cleveland	3	1	1	0	0	1	1
	16	Al Milnar, Cleveland	5	0	1	1	0	0	0
	17	Johnny Rigney, Chicago	4	1	1	0	0	0	0
	18	Thornton Lee, Chicago	3	0	1	0	0	0	0
	19	Eddie Smith (1), Buck Ross (2), Chicago	3	2	3	0	0	1	2
	20	Bobo Newsom (2), Archie McKain (2), Detroit	5	3	4	1	0	0	1
	21	Dizzy Trout, Detroit	4	0	1	0	0	0	0
	22	Hal Newhouser (1), Bobo Newsom (1), Detroit	5	1	2	1	0	1	2
	24	Bob Muncrief, St. Louis	4	1	1	0	0	0	0
	25	Denny Galehouse, St. Louis	4	1	1	0	1	3	
	26	Eldon Auker, St. Louis	4	0	1	1	0	0	1
	27	Chubby Dean, Philadelphia	3	1	2	0	0	1	2
	28	Johnny Babich (1), Lum Harris (1), Philadelphia	5	1	2	1	0	0	0
	29	Dutch E. Leonard, Washington	4	1	1	0	0	0	0
	29	Red Anderson, Washington	5	1	1	0	0	0	1
July	1	Mickey Harris (1), Mike Ryba (1), Boston	4	0	2	0	0	0	1
	1	Jack Wilson, Boston	3	1	1	0	0	0	1
	2	Dick Newsome, Boston	5	1	1	0	0	1	3
	5	Phil Marchildon, Philadelphia	5	2	1	0	0	1	2
	6	Johnny Babich (1), Bump Hadley (3), Phi.	5	2	4	1	0	0	2
	6	Jack Knott, Philadelphia	4	0	2	0	1	0	2
	10	Johnny Niggeling, St. Louis	2	0	1	0	0	0	0
	11	Bob Harris (3), Jack Kramer (1), St. Louis	5	1	4	0	0	1	2
	12	Eldon Auker (1), Bob Muncrief (1), St. Louis	5	1	2	1	0	0	1
	13	Ted Lyons (2), Jack Hallett (1), Chicago	4	2	3	0	0	0	0
	13	Thornton Lee, Chicago	4	0	1	0	0	0	0
	14	Johnny Rigney, Chicago	3	0	1	0	0	0	0
	15	Eddie Smith, Chicago	4	1	2	1	0	0	2
	16	Al Milnar (2), Joe Krakauskas (1), Cleveland	4	3	3	1	0	0	0
		Totals for 56 games	223	56	91	16	4	15	55

Note: Numbers in parentheses refer to hits off each pitcher. Streak stopped July 17 at Cleveland, New York won, 4-3. First inning, Al Smith pitching, thrown out by Ken Keltner; fourth inning, Smith pitching, received base on balls; seventh inning, Smith pitching, thrown out by Keltner; eighth inning, Jim Bagby Jr., pitching, grounded into double play.

RICKEY HENDERSON'S 130-STEAL SEASON—1982

SB No.	Team Game	Date	Opposing pitcher, Club	Base	Inning
1	3	April 8	Mike Witt, California	2	1
2	3	April 8	Luis Sanchez, California	2	14
3	4	April 9	Gaylord Perry, Seattle	2	7
4	5	April*11	Floyd Bannister, Seattle	2	5
5	5	April*11	Ed Vande Berg, Seattle	2	12
6	7	April 13	Terry Felton, Minnesota	2	8
7	8	April 14	Brad Havens, Minnesota	2	1
8	8	April 14	Terry Felton, Minnesota	3	4
9	9	April 15	Al Williams, Minnesota	2	4
10	10	April 16	Floyd Bannister, Seattle	2	1
11	11	April 17	Mike Moore, Seattle	2‡	2
12	11	April 17	Larry Andersen, Seattle	2	4
13	12	April 18	Ed Nunez, Seattle	2	6
14	14	April 20	Al Williams, Minnesota	2	5
15	15	April 21	Darrell Jackson, Minnesota	3	1
16	16	April 23	Ken Forsch, California	3	1
17	16	April 23	Ken Forsch, California	2	3
18	19	April*28	Mike Flanagan, Baltimore	3‡	2
19	20	April†28	Scott McGregor, Baltimore	3	3
20	21	April 29	Dennis Martinez, Baltimore	2	1
21	21	April 29	Dennis Martinez, Baltimore	2	2
22	22	April 30	John Denny, Cleveland	2	5
23	23	May 1	Ed Whitson, Cleveland	2	9
24	23	May 1	Ed Whitson, Cleveland	3	9
25	24	May 2	Rick Waits, Cleveland	2	1
26	25	May 3	Tommy John, New York	2	5
27	27	May 6	John Denny, Cleveland	2	1
28	27	May 6	John Denny, Cleveland	3	1
29	29	May 8	Len Barker, Cleveland	2	1
30	29	May 8	Len Barker, Cleveland	3	1
31	29	May 8	Dan Spillner, Cleveland	2	9

SB No.	Team Game	Date	Opposing pitcher, Club	Base	Inning
32	30	May 9	Lary Sorensen, Cleveland	2	9
33	31	May 10	Tim Stoddard, Baltimore	3	9
34	32	May 11	Scott McGregor, Baltimore	2	1
35	32	May 11	Scott McGregor, Baltimore	2	7
36	36	May 15	George Frazier, New York	3‡	1
37	37	May 16	George Frazier, New York	2	5
38	37	May 16	George Frazier, New York	3	5
39	39	May 19	Dan Petry, Detroit	2	1
40	42	May 22	Bob Ojeda, Boston	2	1
41	42	May 22	Bob Ojeda, Boston	3	1
42	43	May 23	Dennis Eckersley, Boston	2‡	3
43	45	May 26	Bob McClure, Milwaukee	2	7
44	45	May 26	Dwight Bernard, Milwaukee	2	9
45	45	May 26	Dwight Bernard, Milwaukee	3	9
46	49	May 30*	Pat Underwood, Detroit	2	1
47	49	May 30*	Pat Underwood, Detroit	3	1
48	49	May 30*	Pat Underwood, Detroit	2	3
49	49	May 30*	Pat Underwood, Detroit	3	3
50	51	June 1	Chuck Rainey, Boston	2	1
51	51	June 1	Chuck Rainey, Boston	2	3
52	53	June 4	Moose Haas, Milwaukee	2	1
53	55	June 6	Pete Vuckovich, Milwaukee	3	1
54	55	June 6	Pete Vuckovich, Milwaukee	2	3
55	57	June 8	Dennis Lamp, Chicago	2‡	5
56	57	June 8	Jerry Koosman, Chicago	2	7
57	57	June 8	Jerry Koosman, Chicago	3	7
58	58	June 9	LaMarr Hoyt, Chicago	2	3
59	61	June 13	Luis Leal, Toronto	2	2
60	61	June 13	Roy Jackson, Toronto	2	7
61	61	June 13	Roy Jackson, Toronto	3	7
62	61	June 13	Dale Murray, Toronto	2	8
63	62	June 14	Jerry Garvin, Toronto	2	7
64	63	June 15	LaMarr Hoyt, Chicago	2	1
65	66	June 18	Jerry Garvin, Toronto	2	1
66	66	June 18	Roy Jackson, Toronto	2	7
67	70	June 22	Dan Quisenberry, Kansas City	2	8
68	70	June 22	Dan Quisenberry, Kansas City	2	1
69	73	June 25	Frank Tanana, Texas	2	1
70	73	June 25	Frank Tanana, Texas	3	8
71	74	June 26	Steve Comer, Texas	3	5
72	77	June 29	Don Hood, Kansas City	2	1
73	78	June 30	Paul Splittorff, Kansas City	2	2
74	79	July 2	Charlie Hough, Texas	2	3
75	79	July 2	Charlie Hough, Texas	3	9
76	80	July 3	Rick Honeycutt, Texas	2	2
77	81	July 4	Doc Medich, Texas	2	1
78	83	July 6	Len Barker, Cleveland	2	1
79	83	July 6	Len Barker, Cleveland	2	5
80	85	July 8	Doyle Alexander, New York	2	1
81	85	July 8	Doyle Alexander, New York	3‡	1
82	86	July 9	Scott McGregor, Baltimore	3	1
83	87	July 10	Dennis Martinez, Baltimore	2	3
84	88	July 11	Storm Davis, Baltimore	2	3
85	89	July 15	Mike Morgan, New York	2	5
86	90	July 16	Roger Erickson, New York	2	1
87	93	July 19	Lary Sorensen, Cleveland	2	7
88	94	July 20	Ed Whitson, Cleveland	2	1
89	94	July 20	Ed Whitson, Cleveland	3‡	6
90	97	July 24	Scott McGregor, Baltimore	2	6
91	97	July 24	Scott McGregor, Baltimore	3	6
92	98	July 25	Dennis Martinez, Baltimore	2	1
93	99	July 26	Ken Forsch, California	2	1
94	99	July 26	Andy Hassler, California	H‡	8
95	100	July 27	Dave Goltz, California	2	1
96	102	July 29	Brad Havens, Minnesota	3‡	1
97	103	July 30	Al Williams, Minnesota	2	1
98	103	July 30	Al Williams, Minnesota	2	3
99	103	July 30	Ron Davis, Minnesota	2	8
100	106	Aug. 2	Mike Stanton, Seattle	2	7
101	108	Aug. 4†	Jim Beattie, Seattle	2	1
102	109	Aug. 4*	Rich Bordi, Seattle	2	1
103	109	Aug. 4*	Rich Bordi, Seattle	3	1
104	110	Aug. 6	Frank Viola, Minnesota	2	6
105	112	Aug. 8	Brad Havens, Minnesota	2	3
106	115	Aug. 11	Floyd Bannister, Seattle	2	5
107	115	Aug. 11	Floyd Bannister, Seattle	3	5
108	117	Aug. 14	Steve Renko, California	2	5
109	118	Aug. 15	Ken Forsch, California	3	2
110	120	Aug. 17	Moose Haas, Milwaukee	2	1
111	122	Aug. 19	Jim Slaton, Milwaukee	2	7
112	124	Aug. 21	Chuck Rainey, Boston	2	3
113	124	Aug. 21	Chuck Rainey, Boston	2	8
114	124	Aug. 21	Luis Aponte, Boston	2	8
115	126	Aug. 23	Dan Petry, Detroit	2	1
116	127	Aug. 24	Jerry Ujdur, Detroit	2	1
117	127	Aug. 24	Jerry Ujdur, Detroit	3‡	1
118	128	Aug. 26	Mike Caldwell, Milwaukee	2	3
119	129	Aug. 27	Doc Medich, Milwaukee	2	6
120	129	Aug. 27	Doc Medich, Milwaukee	2	8
121	129	Aug. 27	Doc Medich, Milwaukee	2	8
122	129	Aug. 27	Doc Medich, Milwaukee	3	8
123	132	Aug. 30	Mark Clear, Boston	3	8
124	135	Sept. 3	Jerry Ujdur, Detroit	2	1
125	154	Sept. 25	Dennis Leonard, Kansas City	2	4
126	158	Sept. 28	Jim Farr, Texas	2	6
127	161	Oct. 1	Bill Castro, Kansas City	2	3
128	162	Oct. 2	Vida Blue, Kansas City	2	2
129	162	Oct. 2	Vida Blue, Kansas City	2	4
130	162	Oct. 2	Vida Blue, Kansas City	3	4

*Second game of doubleheader. †First game of doubleheader. ‡Part of double steal.
Note: Oakland played 162 games and Henderson played in 149.

On the covers

Front (above)

Derek Jeter (Photo by John Dunn for The Sporting News).

Back

Clockwise from bottom left: The Astrodome (Robert Seale/The Sporting News); David Cone (Bob Leverone/The Sporting News); Candlestick Park (TSN Archives); Mark McGwire (Dilip Vishwanat/The Sporting News); Pedro Martinez (The Sporting News); and Tiger Stadium (Albert Dickson/The Sporting News).

Contributing Photographers

Major League Baseball Photos—Page 11L, R.

Bob Leverone/The Sporting News—Pages 9, 225, 227, 260, 265, 266.

Robert Seale/The Sporting News—Pages 73, 214, 215, 216, 229, 231, 257, 264, 345.

Dilip Vishwanat/The Sporting News—Pages 81T, 217, 218, 219, 261. 262.

Albert Dickson/The Sporting News—Pages 228, 230, 232, 263, 267, 331T.

Jason Wise for The Sporting News—Page 74.

Winslow Townson for The Sporting News—Pages 81, 226.

John Cordes for The Sporting News—Pages 82, 256.

John Dunn for The Sporting News—Page 258, 259.

David Durocher for The Sporting News—Page 265.

Jay Crihfield for The Sporting News—Page 268.

Steve Russell for The Sporting News—Page 349.

The Sporting News Archives—Pages 10, 80T, 233, 234, 235, 236, 239, 241, 242, 243, 244, 245, 246, 247, 248, 250, 251, 252, 253, 254, 255, 269, 271, 272, 282, 341B, 343, 347, 351, 352T, 352B, 353T, 353B, 354, 355T, 355B, 356T, 356B, 357, 358, 360T, 360B, 362, 364T, 364B, 365, 366, 368T, 368B, 370, 372T, 372B, 373, 374, 376T, 376B, 377T, 377B, 378, 379T, 379B, 380T, 380B, 381, 382, 384, 386, 388T, 388B, 389, 390, 392T, 392B, 393T, 393B, 394, 395T, 395B, 396T, 396B, 397, 398T, 398B, 399T, 399B, 400, 401T, 401B, 402T, 402B, 403T, 403B, 404, 405T, 405B, 406T, 406B, 407, 408, 409, 410, 412T, 412B, 413, 414, 416, 417, 418, 420T, 420B, 421, 422T, 422B, 423T, 423B, 424, 425T, 425B, 426T, 426B, 427T, 427B, 428, 429T, 429B, 430, 431, 432, 434T, 434B, 435T, 435B, 436, 437T, 437B, 438T, 438B, 439T, 439B, 440, 441T, 441B, 442T, 442B, 442T, 442B, 444, 445T, 445B, 446T, 446B, 447, 448, 450T, 450B, 451, 452, 454, 455, 456, 458T, 458B, 459T, 459B, 460, 461T, 461B, 462, 464, 467, 468, 469, 471, 472, 473, 474, 479, 480, 481, 483, 485, 487, 489, 493, 494, 495, 496T, 496B, 498, 500, 501, 502, 503, 506, 507.